preface

With this volume, THE AMERICANA ANNUAL completes its 50th year. The oldest encyclopedia yearbook in the United States in continuous publication, it has from its inception recorded those events, great and small, that have transformed the world of the 20th century beyond anyone's wildest imaginings.

It is customary in this space to summarize the year just past, but on the occasion of our golden anniversary it seems appropriate to take a backward glance at the year 1922 as detailed in the pages of the first edition. The world of that day was still recovering from the effects of World War I, and at various international conferences statesmen were wrestling with the issues of peacekeeping, disarmament, and reparations. Civil war raged in Ireland, and a visit to India by the Prince of Wales led to rioting there and the arrest of Gandhi. Cholera and typhus swept areas of Russia. In Italy, a young ex-journalist named Benito Mussolini became prime minister with broad powers.

The United States, still young in spirit and confident in its prestige and power, had entered the Roaring Twenties. President Harding in 1922 could point to a balanced budget and a reduction in the national debt, but he had to cope with widespread strikes of coal miners and railroad workers. The Republican President also signed into law the China Trade Act, offering tax incentives for U. S. companies engaged in trade with China.

The first edition of the Annual also reported nonpolitical developments. It noted, for example, the publication of Joyce's *Ulysses*—"a curious work that created much discussion." The baseball world was cheering the exploits of the Cardinals' Rogers Hornsby, who batted .401 that season. The recognition of women's athletics in the United States was seen as "highly significant." Radio broadcasting was only a healthy infant, but one author foresaw the day when the President could address a large part of the population by radio. Some interesting work was being done in color motion pictures, and sound movies were called a definite possibility. Brig. Gen. William Mitchell, flying an Army-Curtiss biplane, set a new world's record over a straightaway course with an average speed of 224.58 mph. Then, as now, the ANNUAL provided readers with information of a rather specialized nature: thus, we learn that in 1922 commercial watermelon acreage in the United States totaled 161,000, an increase of 47%.

The 50 volumes of THE AMERICANA ANNUAL stand as a chronicle—told in the words of men and women who witnessed the period unfold—of perhaps the most exciting time in human history. No one living in 1922 could have foreseen what the next 50 years would bring: the most devastating war ever fought; the dawning of the nuclear age; the advent of television, jet travel, wonder drugs, computers; the first men on the moon. And given the accelerating rate of change in the modern world, can anyone predict with confidence what mankind faces in the half-century ahead?

S. J. FODERARO, *Executive Editor*

UPI

British troops on patrol in Belfast as civil strife worsened in Northern Ireland.

CHRONOLOGY
1971

TWO VAST GALAXIES DISCOVERED

COLTS WIN SUPER BOWL

NEW YORK POLICE ON STRIKE

JANUARY						
S	M	T	W	T	F	S
					1	2
3	4	5	6	7	8	9
10	11	12	13	14	15	16
17	18	19	20	21	22	23
24	25	26	27	28	29	30
31						

JANUARY

1 Cuban Premier Fidel Castro informs nation it has few prospects of overcoming social and economic problems in 1971.

2 Crowd barrier collapses at soccer stadium in Glasgow, Scotland, killing 66 persons and injuring over 100.

4 Melvin H. Evans, a black physician, is installed as first elected governor of U. S. Virgin Islands.

8 French cruise liner Antilles burns in Caribbean as all 635 passengers and crew escape.

10 French couturier Gabrielle (Coco) Chanel dies in Paris at age 87. ● California astronomers announce discovery of two massive galaxies in "local group" that includes Milky Way.

12 Rev. Philip F. Berrigan and five others are indicted on charges of plotting to kidnap presidential adviser Henry A. Kissinger.

13 U. S. Postmaster General Winton M. Blount is named to head new Postal System.

16 Brazilian guerrillas free Swiss Ambassador Giovanni Enrico Bucher, held for 40 days, in exchange for asylum for 70 political prisoners.

17 Baltimore Colts defeat Dallas Cowboys, 16–13, to win National Football League's Super Bowl contest.

18 United States announces suspension of all arms aid to Ecuador following seizure of U. S. tuna boats.

19 New York City policemen end 6-day wildcat strike that involved at least 85 percent of force. ● President Nixon halts construction of Cross-Florida Barge Canal to prevent environmental damage.

20 Britain's 200,000 postal workers begin strike for pay increases.

21 Edward M. Kennedy (D.-Mass.) is ousted as majority whip in U. S. Senate by Robert C. Byrd (D.-W. Va.). ● Liner *Santa Rosa* arrives in New York City, completing last scheduled voyage of U. S.-flag ship serving East and Gulf ports.

22 Commonwealth meeting at Singapore ends after accord among members over British arms sales to South Africa.

25 Ugandan army ousts President Milton Obote; Maj. Gen. Idi Amin becomes chief of state.

29 Saudi Arabian oil begins flowing to Mediterranean as Syrian pipeline reopens after 9 months.

New York City patrolmen march in Manhattan during 6-day wildcat strike that ended January 19. Public criticized illegal action, but police won higher wages and fringe benefits.

THE NEW YORK TIMES

FEBRUARY

S	M	T	W	T	F	S
	1	2	3	4	5	6
7	8	9	10	11	12	13
14	15	16	17	18	19	20
21	22	23	24	25	26	27
28						

UAR EXTENDS TRUCE

QUAKE HITS LOS ANGELES

APOLLO 14 EXPLORES MOON

FEBRUARY

2 Episcopal Church in United States urges General Motors Corp. to cease manufacturing in South Africa.

3 United Arab Republic informs United States it will extend truce with Israel for one month.

4 Britain's Rolls-Royce, Ltd., maker of quality automobiles and jet engines, declares bankruptcy.

6 Earthquake strikes Tuscania, Italy, killing 20 persons and injuring 120 others. ● Britain flies 600 additional troops to Belfast, Northern Ireland, after night of rioting during which four persons die.

8 Thousands of South Vietnamese troops, aided by U. S. air and artillery support, strike at enemy supply lines in Laos.

9 Apollo 14 astronauts Alan B. Shepard, Jr., Edgar D. Mitchell, and Stuart A. Roosa splash down in Pacific after 9-day mission to lunar surface. ● Los Angeles, Calif., is shaken by severe earthquake killing 64 persons, injuring over 1,000, and damaging homes, hospitals, and freeways. ● European Economic Community agrees on concrete plan to unify member currencies over 10-year period.

11 United States, Soviet Union, and 61 other nations sign treaty barring nuclear weapons from ocean floor; pact will enter into force after ratification by 22 signatories.

14 USSR unveils new 5-year plan emphasizing consumer needs and standard of living. ● Twenty-three Western oil companies reach 5-year accord giving Persian Gulf oil states additional $10 billion.

19 Soviet official newspaper *Pravda* warns Soviet Jews against espousing Zionist beliefs or risk becoming "enemies of the Soviet people."

21 Pakistan and mainland China are linked by motor road as 380-mile (610-km) Karakoram highway is formally opened. ● Tornadoes sweep across Louisiana, Mississippi, and Tennessee, killing 93.

24 British government publishes plans designed to limit right of immigrants from Commonwealth to settle in country. ● Algeria takes over majority control of all local French oil interests.

26 France and United States sign accord on cooperation in police war against drug traffic.

28 Liechtenstein's all-male electorate rejects women's suffrage, leaving it the only country in the West to deny women the vote.

Rescue workers comfort patient pulled from wreckage of San Fernando Veterans Hospital after February 9 earthquake. Quake, centered about 40 miles north of Los Angeles, killed 64 persons.

THE NEW YORK TIMES

MARCH						
S	M	T	W	T	F	S
	1	2	3	4	5	6
7	8	9	10	11	12	13
14	15	16	17	18	19	20
21	22	23	24	25	26	27
28	29	30	31			

MARCH

1 Bomb explosion damages Senate wing of U.S. Capitol.

4 Canadian Prime Minister Pierre Elliott Trudeau, 51, weds 22-year-old Margaret Sinclair.

7 Mideast cease-fire, in effect since August 1970, ends, but fronts remain calm.

8 Boxing's heavyweight champion Joe Frazier retains his title in 15-round bout with challenger Muhammad Ali in New York City.

10 Australia's Liberal party ousts Prime Minister John Gorton and elects William McMahon, minister of foreign affairs, as his successor.

11 Indian Prime Minister Indira Gandhi wins huge majority, a personal triumph, in national elections. ● Whitney M. Young, Jr., executive director of National Urban League, dies in Nigeria.

14 Social Democrats suffer losses but retain majority in elections to West Berlin parliament.

16 Former New York State Gov. Thomas E. Dewey dies in Bal Harbour, Fla., at age 68.

17 Norwegian Labor party chairman Trygve Bratteli takes office as premier 15 days after Premier Per Borten resigned amid scandal over his releasing confidential report on Common Market talks.

19 Turkish constitutional crisis ends as President Sunay designates moderate Nihat Erim as premier one week after Suleyman Demirel is ousted.

22 North Vietnamese pursue over 2,000 South Vietnamese troops retreating from Laos as all available U.S. helicopters aid in rescue and evacuation.

23 Protestant moderate Brian Faulkner becomes Northern Ireland's sixth prime minister after resignation of James Chichester-Clark. ● U.S. Senate bars further funding for supersonic transport plane.

26 Lt. Gen. Alejandro Augustin Lanusse takes office as Argentine president three days after military junta ousts Roberto M. Levingston. ● Open rebellion breaks out in East Pakistan as Pakistani army moves to reimpose authority of West Pakistan.

29 Los Angeles, Calif., jury sentences "hippie" cult leader Charles Manson and three young women members of his "family" to gas chamber for Tate-LaBianca murders in August 1969.

31 U.S. Army jury sentences 1st Lt. William L. Calley, Jr., to life imprisonment for murder of at least 22 South Vietnamese civilians at My Lai in 1968.

UPI

Vietnam veterans protesting conviction on March 29 of 1st Lt. William L. Calley, Jr., picket outside military recruiting station in Trenton, N.J. Calley's conviction for murders at My Lai resulted in widespread appeals in United States for clemency.

APRIL						
S	M	T	W	T	F	S
				1	2	3
4	5	6	7	8	9	10
11	12	13	14	15	16	17
18	19	20	21	22	23	24
25	26	27	28	29	30	

STRAVINSKY DEAD AT 88

NEW YORK OPENS OFFTRACK BETTING

U.S. PING PONG TEAM IN CHINA

APRIL

4 Chilean President Allende's left-wing coalition wins 49.7 percent of votes in local elections.

6 Russian-born composer Igor Stravinsky dies in New York City at age 88.

7 Chicago's Mayor Richard J. Daley easily wins unprecedented fifth term in office.

8 First system of legal off-track wagering in United States begins in New York City.

9 Ceylon imposes 24-hour curfew as security forces battle insurgents led by leftist youths. ● Indiana becomes first state to ban most phosphate detergents.

11 North Vietnamese choose new 420-seat Assembly in first general elections since 1964.

14 Communist Chinese Premier Chou En-lai receives 15-member U.S. table tennis team, declaring the visit "opens a page in relations of Chinese and American people."

17 In Benghazi, Libya, leaders of Egypt, Libya, and Syria sign agreement on union with common stand of no compromise with Israel.

18 U.S. table tennis team leaves China after warm 7-day reception. ● Bitter 11-week teachers' strike ends in Newark, N.J.

19 Sierra Leone becomes republic; Justice C.O.E. Smith, acting governor general, becomes president.

20 U.S. Supreme Court upholds constitutionality of busing as means of eliminating dual school systems in South.

21 President François Duvalier of Haiti dies at age 64 in Port-au-Prince; he is succeeded by his 19-year-old son, Jean-Claude Duvalier.

24 About 200,000 persons rally in Washington, D.C., in protest against Vietnam War.

25 Austrian President Franz Jonas is reelected to second 6-year term.

26 U.S. Supreme Court upholds California law that permits a majority of voters in a community to block low-rent housing for poor.

27 South Korean national elections give President Chung Hee Park third 4-year term.

28 President Félix Houphouët-Boigny of Ivory Coast says black African nations should join in efforts for closer ties with South Africa.

NORMAN WEBSTER (C) THE GLOBE AND MAIL TORONTO

U.S. table tennis team rests along China's Great Wall in April. Visit, first to mainland by U.S. group since mid-1950's, signaled thaw in U.S.-Sino relations.

Horse players jam off-track betting office, which opened in early April in borough of Queens, New York City. New revenue plan was designed to aid city finances.

THE NEW YORK TIMES

MONEY CRISIS SHAKES WEST

12,000 SEIZED IN D.C. PROTESTS

BRITAIN CLEARED FOR MARKET

			MAY			
S	M	T	W	T	F	S
						1
2	3	4	5	6	7	8
9	10	11	12	13	14	15
16	17	18	19	20	21	22
23	24	25	26	27	28	29
30	31					

MAY

1 National Railroad Passenger Corporation (Amtrak) begins operation of U.S. intercity passenger railroad system. ● At Churchill Downs, Ky., the 97th consecutive Kentucky Derby is won by Canonero II. ● Premier Nihat Erim pledges to remove Turkish opium from illicit market by buying 1971 crop.

3 U.S. Supreme Court rules that juries can be empowered to impose death penalty. ● East German Communist party leader Walter Ulbricht resigns and is succeeded by Erich Honecker.

4 In Ceylon, 40 rebels are killed and more than 1,700 surrender during 4-day amnesty period. ● In St. Jeanne Vianney, Quebec, 31 persons die as huge landslide of mud and clay destroys 36 homes.

5 In deepening monetary crisis, central banks of West Germany, Switzerland, Belgium, the Netherlands, and Austria withdraw support for U.S. dollar and close their foreign exchange markets. ● Police in Washington, D.C., arrest more than 12,000 persons in three days of antiwar protests.

6 U.S. Food and Drug Administration advises public to stop eating swordfish because of excessive mercury content.

9 West Germany and the Netherlands allow their currency to float in relation to U.S. dollar as Switzerland and Austria revalue their currency upward.

14 Egyptian President Anwar el-Sadat installs new cabinet after declaring he foiled attempted coup.

18 U.S. Congress passes law requiring workers to end 2-day strike paralyzing nation's railroads.

19 In Moscow, Canadian Prime Minister Trudeau and Soviet Premier Kosygin sign agreement calling for greater amity between two countries.

20 Court in Leningrad, USSR, sentences nine Jews to prison camp for "anti-Soviet activity."

21 Britain and France reach agreements paving way for British entry into European Common Market.

22 Earthquake levels Bingol in eastern Turkey, killing about 1,000 persons.

23 Body of Israeli Consul General Efraim Elrom is found in Istanbul one week after his kidnapping.

25 In New Haven, Conn., charges against Bobby G. Seale and Mrs. Ericka Huggins for kidnapping and murder of Alex Rackley in May 1969 are dropped because of "massive publicity."

Thousands of anti–Vietnam War demonstrators arrested in early May in Washington, D. C., were bedded down in Washington Coliseum. Arrest procedures, defended by government, were denounced by civil rights groups.

UPI

JUNE

S	M	T	W	T	F	S
		1	2	3	4	5
6	7	8	9	10	11	12
13	14	15	16	17	18	19
20	21	22	23	24	25	26
27	28	29	30			

MT. ETNA ERUPTS IN SICILY

3 SOVIET SPACEMEN DEAD

COURT RELEASES PENTAGON PAPERS

JUNE

1 U. S. President Nixon pledges to undertake a "national offensive" against drug addiction. ● Protestant theologian Reinhold Niebuhr dies at age 78 in Stockbridge, Mass. ● Rumanian President Nicolae Ceauşescu begins state visit to mainland China.

2 In Yuba City, Calif., suspect Juan V. Corona pleads not guilty in death of transient laborers; a total of 25 bodies were found.

3 Metropolitan Pimen of Krutitsy and Kolomna is enthroned in Moscow as Russian Orthodox patriarch.

5 Tulsa, Okla., is linked to Gulf of Mexico as President Nixon dedicates vast $1.2 billion Arkansas River Navigation System.

6 DC-9 jetliner and Navy jet collide and crash northeast of Los Angeles, Calif., killing 50 persons.

8 World Health Organization announces that cholera is rampant on India-East Pakistan frontier. ● Sicilian volcano Mount Etna subsides after most menacing eruption in 43 years.

10 President Nixon ends 21-year U. S. embargo on trade with mainland China. ● At least nine students are dead and more than 130 wounded in rioting in Mexico City.

12 President Nixon's elder daughter Patricia, 25, is married to Edward Finch Cox, 24, in White House rose garden ceremony. ● In Sydney, Australia, a 29-year-old woman gives birth to nine babies in biggest human multiple birth on record; none of the infants survived.

17 United States and Japan sign treaty that will restore Okinawa to Japan in 1972.

21 International Court of Justice at The Hague rules that South Africa occupies South West Africa illegally and should end its administration of the territory.

28 U. S. Supreme Court forbids states to reimburse parochial schools for instruction in nonreligious subjects. ● Delaware bars heavy industry from its coastal area in landmark conservation law.

30 Three Soviet cosmonauts are found dead in their seats as spacecraft Soyuz 11 lands smoothly after record 24-day space mission. ● U. S. Supreme Court allows New York *Times* and Washington *Post* to resume publication of secret Pentagon Papers on Vietnam War despite government efforts at restraint. ● The 26th Amendment to the U. S. Constitution, lowering minimum voting age to 18, is ratified as Ohio becomes 38th state to approve.

Flames and lava from Mount Etna light up sky over Sicily. Most spectacular eruptions since 1928 drove many farmers from their homes and damaged an observatory.

UPI

U.S. LOWERS VOTING AGE

CHINESE REJOIN KOREAN TALKS

NIXON PLANS TO VISIT CHINA

JULY

S	M	T	W	T	F	S
				1	2	3
4	5	6	7	8	9	10
11	12	13	14	15	16	17
18	19	20	21	22	23	24
25	26	27	28	29	30	31

JULY

3 Indonesians vote in first national elections since 1955. ● At Wimbledon, England, Australia's John Newcombe defeats Stan Smith of United States in five sets to win All England tennis championship.

5 Premier Eisaku Sato of Japan appoints new cabinet to work out nation's domestic and external economic problems. ● President Nixon certifies 26th Amendment to U.S. Constitution, which lowers minimum voting age in all elections to 18.

6 Jazz trumpeter and singer Louis Armstrong dies in New York City at age 71.

7 U.S. government recalls products of Bon Vivant Soups, Inc., after some cans of vichyssoise are found to contain deadly botulinum toxin.

8 Connecticut enacts its first personal income tax law. ● Frank E. Fitzsimmons is unanimously elected president of International Brotherhood of Teamsters, succeeding James R. Hoffa.

9 Mainland Chinese delegation returns to Korean armistice talks after 5-year absence.

10 King Hassan II of Morocco is unharmed but 97 palace guests are dead during attempted coup.

12 USSR announces that death of three Soyuz 11 astronauts was due to rapid drop of air pressure within capsule just before landing. ● World Bank mission reports East Pakistan is so ravaged by military crackdown that new international development efforts would be pointless.

15 U.S. President Nixon announces that he will visit mainland China at the invitation of Premier Chou En-lai.

17 Britain cuts taxes by $564 million per year in effort to spur economy. ● Jordan announces government has rounded up 2,300 Arab commandos.

22 Sudanese leader Jaafar Mohammad al-Numeiry regains power in countercoup three days after overthrow by leftist military officers.

23 President William V. S. Tubman of Liberia dies in London at age 75.

28 About 100 persons die in flood and landslide in Hindu Kush mountains in Afghanistan.

29 Yugoslav Parliament unanimously reelects President Tito to 5-year term. ● Joe Kachingue of Malawi becomes first black ambassador to South Africa.

30 All Nippon Boeing 727 and Japanese jet fighter collide over northern Honshu, killing all 162 persons aboard jetliner, in history's worst air disaster.

New Communist Chinese delegate (left foreground) *joins armistice meetings at Panmunjom between North Korea and UN command in July. Chinese had not participated in deliberations for five years.*

UPI

AUGUST

S	M	T	W	T	F	S
1	2	3	4	5	6	7
8	9	10	11	12	13	14
15	16	17	18	19	20	21
22	23	24	25	26	27	28
29	30	31				

NEW RIOTING IN NORTHERN IRELAND

NIXON FREEZES WAGES, PRICES

INDONESIA WELCOMES DUTCH QUEEN

AUGUST

2 United States announces its support for seating mainland China in UN. ● U.S. Congress passes legislation to save Lockheed Aircraft Corporation from bankruptcy.

5 United States and Soviet Union present 14-point draft treaty banning germ warfare to UN Disarmament Conference. ● Britain enacts first comprehensive labor-relations law in its history in effort to cope with rash of wildcat strikes.

6 King Hassan II of Morocco names new government of 15 independents pledged to ridding country of corruption.

7 U.S. Apollo 15 astronauts David R. Scott, James B. Irwin, and Alfred M. Worden splash down safely in Pacific after 12-day moon-exploration mission; officials hail "epic scientific voyage."

9 Toll reaches 23 dead in third day of Northern Ireland rioting after government invokes emergency powers of preventive detention. ● New York City's Mayor John V. Lindsay switches party enrollment from Republican to Democratic. ● All 97 persons aboard Soviet TU 104 jetliner are dead in crash upon takeoff at Irkutsk.

12 Syria breaks diplomatic relations with Jordan and bans Jordanian planes from its airspace. ● Prime Minister William McMahon of Australia ousts predecessor John G. Gorton as head of defense.

15 U.S. President Nixon, in drastic new economic steps, severs link between dollar and gold, asks tax cuts, and orders 90-day wage-price freeze and 10% surcharge on imports. ● Persian Gulf state of Bahrain declares independence from Britain.

16 New York Stock Exchange has busiest day in its history as volume reaches 31.7 million shares and Dow-Jones industrial average climbs 32.93 points. ● Malawian President H. Kamuzu Banda begins 7-day state visit to South Africa.

17 Typhoon Rose strikes Hong Kong, killing over 100 persons and sinking or grounding 50 vessels.

22 At San Quentin, Calif., "Soledad Brother" George Jackson, two other prisoners, and three guards are killed during attempted prison break. ● Bolivian rebels oust left-wing Gen. Juan José Torres from presidency and install Col. Hugo Banzer Suarez.

26 Queen Juliana of the Netherlands receives tumultuous welcome from Indonesia as she begins 10-day state visit to former colony.

28 Japan announces yen will be allowed to float within limits against U.S. dollar.

UPI

Aged woman in Catholic area of Belfast apprehensively watches British soldier during August fighting.

Queen Juliana of Netherlands (left) sits with Mrs. Suharto, prime minister's wife, on Indonesian visit.

UPI

9

BIG FOUR IN BERLIN PACT

KENNEDY CENTER HAS PREMIERE

TROOPERS BREAK ATTICA SIEGE

SEPTEMBER

S	M	T	W	T	F	S
			1	2	3	4
5	6	7	8	9	10	11
12	13	14	15	16	17	18
19	20	21	22	23	24	25
26	27	28	29	30		

SEPTEMBER

2 Egyptian, Syrian, and Libyan voters overwhelmingly approve proposed federation of three nations.

3 Ambassadors of United States, Soviet Union, Britain, and France sign accord on future of West Berlin.

4 Jetliner crashes into mountain near Juneau, Alaska, killing all 109 persons on board. ● Anglo-French supersonic airliner Concorde 001 flies from Europe to South America in 4 hours 28 minutes.

8 In Washington, D. C., $70 million John F. Kennedy Center for the Performing Arts opens as glittering audience attends premiere of Bernstein's *Mass*.

9 In Uruguay, guerrillas release British Ambassador Geoffrey Jackson, held prisoner for 8 months.

11 Nikita S. Khrushchev, Soviet premier from 1953 to 1964, dies in Moscow at age 77.

13 Ten hostages and 30 convicts die as 1,000 state troopers storm state prison at Attica, N. Y., ending 4-day revolt by 1,200 prisoners. ● At least 10 persons die in pile-up of 200 cars in fog on superhighway between Manchester and Liverpool, England.

16 Cowles Communications, Inc., announces 34-year-old *Look* magazine will cease publication.

17 In New York City, RCA Corporation announces withdrawal from computer making.

18 Egypt and Israel exchange rocket fire across Suez Canal for first time in over 13 months.

21 The 26th UN General Assembly elects Adam Malik of Indonesia as its president and admits Bhutan, Bahrain, and Qatar to UN membership.

22 Italy adopts price controls in effort to curb swift rise in prices.

23 Associate Justice John M. Harlan, 72, retires from U. S. Supreme Court after 16 years of service.

24 Britain expels 105 Soviet representatives for espionage activities.

25 Hugo L. Black, champion of civil liberties for 34 years as U. S. Supreme Court Justice, dies at age 85 at Bethesda (Md.) Naval Hospital.

27 U. S. President Nixon greets Emperor Hirohito and Empress Nagako at Anchorage, Alaska, in historic first trip abroad by a reigning Japanese sovereign.

28 József Cardinal Mindszenty, primate of Hungary, accepts exile in Rome after self-confinement for 15 years in U. S. embassy in Budapest.

Leonard Bernstein embraces member of the cast following performance of his Mass *at opening of John F. Kennedy Center for the Performing Arts in Washington, D. C., on September 8.*

UPI

OCTOBER

S	M	T	W	T	F	S
					1	2
3	4	5	6	7	8	9
10	11	12	13	14	15	16
17	18	19	20	21	22	23
24	25	26	27	28	29	30
31						

THIEU WINS ONE-MAN RACE

SHAH HOSTS ANNIVERSARY FETE

UN SEATS COMMUNIST CHINA

OCTOBER

1 U. S. conductor Lorin Maazel, 41, is appointed director of the Cleveland Orchestra. ● Near Orlando, Fla., 100-acre, $400 million Walt Disney World opens.

2 All 63 persons aboard British Vanguard airliner are killed in crash near Ghent, Belgium.

3 South Vietnamese President Nguyen Van Thieu is reelected with 90% of vote after campaign marked by protests over his lack of opposition.

8 Chinese Chairman Mao Tse-tung appears in public for first time in two months as he greets Ethiopian Emperor Haile Selassie in Peking.

9 Two Argentine army units surrender after abortive coup against ruling military regime.

12 U. S. President Nixon discloses that he will visit Soviet leaders in Moscow in May 1972. ● Dean Acheson, former secretary of state and an architect of U. S. post-World War II policy, dies in Sandy Spring, Md., at age 78.

14 Shah Mohammed Reza Pahlavi of Iran commemorates 2,500th birthday of Persian Empire by entertaining 500 guests representing 70 nations at magnificent state dinner amid ruins of Persepolis.

15 Long textile dispute ends as Japan restricts textile flow to United States, and U. S. 10% surtax on textile imports is lifted.

17 Pittsburgh Pirates become baseball's World Series champions in dramatic upset of Baltimore Orioles, 2–1, in seventh game.

18 In Ottawa, Canada, visiting Soviet Premier Aleksei Kosygin escapes injury as police subdue assailant.

20 West German Chancellor Willy Brandt wins Nobel Peace Prize. ● Cambodian Premier Lon Nol declares emergency rule by "ordinance."

21 Chilean poet-diplomat Pablo Neruda is awarded 1971 Nobel Prize for literature.

22 U. S. President Nixon appoints Federal Judge George H. Boldt as chairman of Pay Board and C. Jackson Grayson, Jr., as chairman of Price Commission.

23 UN General Assembly votes, 76 to 35 with 17 abstentions, to seat Peking and expel Taipei as legitimate government of China; expulsion is diplomatic defeat for United States.

28 Britain's House of Commons votes, 356 to 244, for membership in European Common Market.

Prince Rainier and Princess Grace of Monaco stroll through Persepolis during October celebration of Iran's 2,500th anniversary.

PHOTOREPORTERS

11

NOVEMBER

S	M	T	W	T	F	S
	1	2	3	4	5	6
7	8	9	10	11	12	13
14	15	16	17	18	19	20
21	22	23	24	25	26	27
28	29	30				

NOVEMBER

1 Orissa state, India, is hit by cyclone and tidal wave leaving at least 10,000 persons dead. ● Anglican Dean Gonville A. ffrench-Beytagh of Johannesburg, South Africa, is sentenced to 5 years' imprisonment for violation of segregation laws.

2 In Vatican City, a synod of bishops reaffirms principle of celibacy for Roman Catholic priests.

4 Three official studies reveal U.S. population growth is turning rapidly and dramatically downward.

5 United States announces arrangements to sell $136 million in livestock feed grain to Soviet Union.

6 United States detonates powerful underground nuclear blast at Amchitka Island, Alaska, after Supreme Court decides against postponement.

10 Cuban Premier Fidel Castro is enthusiastically welcomed in Chile at beginning of 25-day official visit.

11 U.S. President Nixon accepts resignation of Secretary of Agriculture Clifford M. Hardin and nominates Earl L. Butz of Purdue University as his successor.

12 President Nixon announces planned withdrawal of 45,000 additional U.S. troops from Vietnam before Feb. 1, 1972, leaving 139,000 in country.

13 U.S. spacecraft Mariner 9 is placed in orbit around planet Mars.

14 Negotiators sign 3-year contract, ending 44-day strike by 100,000 U.S. soft-coal miners. ● Gov. Francis W. Sargent signs landmark bill easing Massachusetts narcotics laws.

17 Thai constitution is abolished and Parliament dissolved as Premier Thanom Kittikachorn seizes full power.

18 Federal court orders 23 companies in Birmingham, Ala., to halt production because of air pollution.

19 In Tokyo, six days of rioting over Okinawa treaty reach a climax with one person dead and 1,785 arrested.

22 India and Pakistan report a major military engagement between their troops in East Pakistan.

23 The Reading Company, parent of Reading Railroad, files bankruptcy petition.

24 Britain and Rhodesia sign agreement easing strained relations existent since Rhodesian declaration of independence in 1965.

25 Inmates at Rahway state prison in New Jersey end 24-hour rebellion after assurances of reform by Gov. William T. Cahill. ● On U.S. West Coast, hijacker of Northwest Airlines jetliner collects $200,000 ransom and escapes by parachute.

28 Uruguayan ruling Colorado party candidate Juan M. Bordaberry wins presidency in national elections. ● Jordanian Premier Wasfi al-Tal is assassinated while in Cairo, Egypt, for Arab League meeting.

Sen. Mike Gravel (center) picketed in Washington against November nuclear test. AEC Chairman Schlesinger cited safety measures and took daughters (right) to Amchitka Island for test.

UPI

UPI

DECEMBER

S	M	T	W	T	F	S
			1	2	3	4
5	6	7	8	9	10	11
12	13	14	15	16	17	18
19	20	21	22	23	24	25
26	27	28	29	30	31	

INDIA, PAKISTAN AT WAR

U.S. DEVALUES THE DOLLAR

SEOUL HOTEL FIRE KILLS 158

DECEMBER

2 Chile's President Salvadore Allende Gossens decrees a state of emergency after violence erupts in Santiago when 5,000 women protest food shortages and visit of Cuban Premier Fidel Castro. ● Major Cambodian military campaign north of Phnom Penh collapses in face of heavy North Vietnamese attacks. ● Six Persian Gulf sheikhdoms proclaim themselves the Union of Arab Emirates.

3 Full-scale war erupts between India and Pakistan; fighting is reported on eastern and western borders and in Kashmir.

6 United States brands India as the "main aggressor" in war with Pakistan and cuts off $87.6 million in development loans. ● India recognizes East Pakistan as independent nation of Bangladesh; Pakistan breaks diplomatic relations with India.

7 UN General Assembly approves resolution urging India and Pakistan to end fighting and pull back their troops. ● Ten members of NATO announce plans to increase their defense budgets in 1972 by more than $1 billion.

16 Pakistan's military command in East Pakistan surrenders unconditionally to India; India orders cease-fire with Pakistan on western front.

17 President Yahya Khan announces Pakistan's acceptance of cease-fire.

18 United States agrees to devalue the dollar by 8.57% as part of 10-national agreement on realignment of currency exchange rates.

20 Zulfikar Ali Bhutto is sworn in as president and martial-law administrator of Pakistan following resignation of Yahya Khan.

21 Kurt Waldheim, Austria's chief UN delegate, is chosen by Security Council to succeed U Thant as secretary general.

24 Giovanni Leone, a Christian Democrat, is named president of Italy on 16th day of voting by electoral college.

25 Hotel fire in Seoul, South Korea, kills 158 persons.

30 U.S. announces end of its intensified bombing of North Vietnam after five days of raids. ● Anglican and Roman Catholic churches announce they have reached agreement on the "essential" teachings about Holy Communion.

Hoping that mattress will break fall, guest plunges from Seoul, Korea, hotel in fire that took 158 lives.

PHOTOREPORTERS

Near victory, Bengali guerrilla captain pauses in East Pakistan during drive against Pakistani army.

UPI

Spotlight on

CHINA

Vibrant, busy Canton, a metropolis of about 3 million in the heart of the Canton Delta, is China's southern gateway. People, buses, carts, and bicycles jam the bridge over the Pearl River throughout the day. The river links the city, a major port, to the sea.

"Taking the long view, we simply cannot afford to leave China forever outside the family of nations, there to nurture its fantasies, cherish its hates and threaten its neighbors. There is no place on this small planet for a billion of its potentially most able people to live in angry isolation."

—Richard M. Nixon,
Foreign Affairs (October 1967)

BY HAROLD C. HINTON

The year 1971 saw an impressive growth in the diplomatic contacts and international influence of the People's Republic of China. Most striking were its arrangement with its adversary of two decades' standing, the United States, for President Richard M. Nixon to visit Peking in February 1972, and its admission to the United Nations.

THE NORMALIZATION CAMPAIGN

The trend toward normalizing China's external relations has existed since about the spring of 1969, shortly after the end of the period of internal upheaval known as the Cultural Revolution. Premier Chou En-lai, the main architect of China's foreign policy, has skillfully made the most of the latent good will of most nations toward China in order to accelerate the pace of normalization. His main single purpose has been

Harold C. Hinton, an American sinologist, is a specialist in the foreign policy of mainland China. Professor of political science at Georgetown University's Institute for Sino-Soviet Studies, he is the author of Communist China in World Affairs *(1966),* China's Turbulent Quest *(1970), and* The Bear at the Gate: Chinese Policy-Making Under Soviet Pressure *(1971).*

to help Peking cope with the threat posed by the buildup of Soviet forces just across the border to a level of about 40 divisions.

Diplomatic Initiatives. By late 1970, Peking had sent new ambassadors to nearly all the countries with which it had maintained diplomatic relations before the Cultural Revolution, the major exceptions being India, Indonesia, and the Mongolian People's Republic. And beginning with Canada in October 1970, Peking inaugurated diplomatic relations with about 20 countries, mainly in Africa, the Middle East, and western Europe. In no case did Peking allow the other country to continue a diplomatic relationship with the Republic of China (Nationalist China, on Taiwan). However, Peking did permit some latitude regarding the degree to which the other country recognized mainland China's sovereignty over Taiwan.

The People's Republic recently has tended to downgrade its support for armed revolutions—whether Communist or not—and to emphasize approaches and appeals likely to evoke support from the large number of small powers, especially among the unaligned nations of Asia, Africa, and Latin America known collectively as the Third World. Peking stresses its opposition to what it sees as the tendency of the two "superpowers"—the United States and the Soviet Union—to "collude" in order to dominate the world, while at the same time opposing each other on major issues.

UN Entry. One of the most conspicuous results of Peking's normalization campaign was its entry into the United Nations and its acquisition of China's permanent seat on the Security Council on Oct. 25, 1971. During the previous two years, Peking had grown increasingly interested in entering the United Nations, although not at the price of continued representation of the Republic of China. UN representation was desired not only as a badge of international status and a means of contact with foreign governments, but as a form of protection against possible Soviet pressures. Since its entry Peking has used the United Nations as a forum for its propaganda against the United States and the Soviet Union and in favor of its formula for disarmament—complete nuclear (not conventional) disarmament to be achieved through a summit conference of all states. On the other hand, Peking has not used, or threatened to use, its Security Council veto.

THE SINO-SOVIET DISPUTE

The massive buildup of Soviet forces near the Chinese border continued during 1971. Presumably the aims were to deter any possible threat from China, which is beginning to acquire deliverable nuclear weapons; to press China into signing a border agreement; and to compel Peking to moderate its political hostility toward the Soviet Union. This pressure has been unsuccessful in the last two respects and even counterproductive, as it has tended to drive Peking toward the United States and has contributed to the energy with which Peking has pursued its campaign to normalize relations with other countries around the world.

The Sino-Soviet border talks, which have been in progress since October 1969, remain essentially deadlocked. Peking refuses to enter into detailed negotiations while under military pressure and demands a prior cease-fire agreement and a mutual troop withdrawal from the border and from disputed areas. Peking also insists that any final agreement must include a Soviet recognition, in principle, that the original treaties under which tsarist Russia annexed much of Central Asia and the Far East from the Manchu Empire are "unequal," or, in other words, morally and legally invalid because they were extorted under duress. Nevertheless, Peking is not seriously demanding the return of the territories involved. Moscow apparently will not agree to these demands and wants to enter into detailed negotiations while keeping Peking under military pressure.

The Soviet Union has been interested in improving other aspects of the relations between the two states, and Peking has reciprocated to some extent. The last two months of 1970 saw an exchange of ambassadors, for the first time since 1966, and an agreement to increase Sino-Soviet trade. Peking has reduced its anti-Soviet propaganda since 1969, in view of the possible consequences of provoking the Soviet Union—something that has appeared especially risky since the invasion of Czechoslovakia. In the last few months of 1971, however, as Peking gained increased confidence through its contacts with the United States and its entry into the United Nations and as it felt outraged by Soviet support for India against China's ally Pakistan, Chinese anti-Soviet propaganda showed signs of picking up.

It is understood on both sides that, at least as long as Mao Tse-tung lives and as long as ideology remains an important preoccupation of some of the Soviet leaders, there will be no agreement on the issues that have separated them since Peking decided, about 1960, that the Soviet leadership was lapsing into unacceptable "revisionism," or moderate communism. Moscow for its part claims that, especially since the outbreak of Mao's Cultural Revolution in 1966, China has deviated from Leninism in the direction of nationalism and militarism. The two

'Journey for Peace'

Impressive cordiality marked the epic visit of President Nixon to China, in February 1972, on his proclaimed "journey for peace." Although initial greeting at Peking airport was restrained, the President's meeting with Communist party chairman Mao Tse-tung (right) came unexpectedly early in the visit. By the second day in Peking, gatherings were relaxed and informal. (Above) Touring the old Imperial Palace, President and Mrs. Nixon pause beside a bronze dragon. (Below) President Nixon attends ballet with, from left, Secretary of State Rogers; Chou En-lai; Chiang Ch'ing, Mao's wife; Mrs. Nixon; and Madame Chou.

sides exchanged occasional propaganda broadsides on ideological questions during 1971, and Peking boycotted the Soviet Communist party's 24th Congress, which was held on March 30–April 9.

OPENING TO THE UNITED STATES

China and the Soviet Union have been trying to improve their respective relations with the United States, in each case so as not to leave this vital field to the other. In this Peking has had the advantage, because the Nixon administration regards the Soviet Union as the greater threat to American interests.

Views and Goals. President Nixon and his advisers have perceived, since before coming into office, that Peking, too, has a serious Soviet problem and that this is not necessarily the only common interest between China and the United States. The administration has reasoned that an accommodation with Peking would improve its chances of reelection in 1972, not only by improving the general international atmosphere, but by facilitating the reduction of U. S. military involvement in Asia implicit in the Nixon Doctrine.

Washington hopes that its contacts with Peking will improve the prospects for a political settlement in Indochina, either by securing direct Chinese cooperation or, more probably, by putting indirect pressure on North Vietnam to be more cooperative in the Paris peace talks. The Nixon administration believes that the Chinese threat to Asia and to world peace has been overestimated, and that in fact Asian stability, world peace, and the cause of disarmament can prosper only if China is encouraged to play a constructive international role. Previous U. S. policy had attempted to isolate China from the rest of the world. Finally, Washington is interested in at least a modest level of trade and cultural exchange with China.

For its part, Peking has been interested in improving its relations with the United States primarily in order to put additional restraint, short of actual military deterrence, on the Soviet Union. Since it might be dangerous, or at least counterproductive, for Peking to discuss this objective publicly, it does not do so. Peking hopes to persuade the United States to reduce its military and political commitments to the Republic of China and so facilitate the achievement of one of Peking's major goals, the "liberation" of Taiwan. Mainly out of concern for its own security, Peking shares with Washington an interest in the withdrawal of U. S. forces from Indochina. China wants some sort of understanding with the United States so that Japan, which Peking sees as a rival and possible threat, will not fill whatever vacuum the United States may create by its disengagement from Asia and the Western Pacific under the Nixon Doctrine. Peking appears to be less interested than is the United States in matters of trade and cultural exchange.

Prelude to Nixon's Visit. Beginning in 1969, President Nixon conveyed privately to Peking, through intermediaries, the sincerity of his determination to "wind down" the war in Indochina and improve Sino-American relations. Peking was interested, but insisted on prior proof of the first of these before making any overt moves. Although shocked by the incursion of U. S. ground forces into Cambodia in the spring of 1970, Peking was evidently impressed by the absence of American troops when the South Vietnamese army briefly invaded southern Laos in February–March 1971. At about that time secret communication between Washington and Peking became more frequent and more positive, and these contacts were accompanied by overt gestures.

In April, Peking inaugurated a campaign of "ping-pong diplomacy" by inviting first an American table tennis team, and later selected American correspondents, to China, mainly in order to influence U. S. public opinion. On the other side, the spring of 1971 saw a series of measures removing all effective restrictions on travel by U. S. citizens to mainland China and greatly liberalizing restrictions on nonstrategic trade with China. Actually, few Americans have yet been granted visas, and Peking has as yet shown little interest in such trade.

By that time Peking probably was interested in a favorite project of President Nixon's, a visit on his part to Peking. After all, in Chinese tradition, it is the little man who goes to the big man. But a visit of such importance required careful planning. Accordingly, on July 9–11, President Nixon's adviser on foreign affairs, Henry A. Kissinger, paid a secret visit to Peking for this purpose. The news was announced on July 15, together with Peking's invitation to President Nixon to visit China by May 1972.

The Repercussions. The major power affected by this striking development in Sino-American relations was the Soviet Union. One of the signs of Moscow's concern was an outburst of diplomatic activity in Asia and Europe during the spring and autumn of 1971, some of it at least with a clearly anti-Chinese bent. A Soviet-Indian friendship treaty signed on August 9 was a source of particular concern to Peking. In addition, President Nixon was invited to visit Moscow.

Moscow held its propaganda fire on the developing Sino-American relationship until it became clear, from an important article published

Chinese UN delegation is led by Ch'iao Kuan-hua (left), shown during welcoming speech November 15.

CH'IAO KUAN-HUA, vice minister of foreign affairs of the People's Republic of China and head of the Communist Chinese UN delegation, was born to a bourgeois family in Yencheng, Kiangsu, in March 1914. After graduating from Tsinghua University in Peking in 1933, he entered the University of Tübingen in Germany, receiving his doctorate in philosophy in 1936. Returning to China when the Sino-Japanese War broke out in 1937, he worked as a journalist in Hong Kong and wrote for leftist publications. In 1942 he was appointed secretary to the Chinese Communist delegation at Chungking, where he became closely associated with Chou En-lai.

As an officer in the foreign affairs ministry, Ch'iao was frequently a member of Chinese foreign delegations. He served as Premier Chou En-lai's adviser at the Geneva Conference in 1954 and the Bandung Conference in 1955. In 1964 he was promoted and became a vice minister of foreign affairs. During the Cultural Revolution (1966–69), he was attacked by the radical Red Guards but survived with the support of Premier Chou. In 1969 he was given the important assignment of chief of the Chinese delegation for border talks with the Soviet Union at Peking. He became a world figure in 1971, when he headed the first Chinese Communist delegation to the United Nations.

In his maiden speech at the General Assembly, Ch'iao aligned China with the nations of the "third world." He attacked the hegemony of superpowers and accused them of bullying small nations. His speech was termed "intemperate" by the U. S. delegation, but others called it an eloquent restatement of known Chinese positions. In the debate on disarmament he charged the USSR with practicing "socialism in words, imperialism in deeds." Tall and slim, Ch'iao has an alert mind and an affable personality. A confidant of Chou En-lai, he is believed to have great influence in formulating Chinese foreign policy.

CHESTER C. TAN

in the Peking *People's Daily* on August 17, that Chou En-lai was trying, at least for domestic consumption, to rationalize his controversial opening to the United States as a move against Japanese "imperialism," while playing down its more significant anti-Soviet purpose. A series of strong articles in the Soviet press, beginning on August 20, showed that Moscow was not prepared to accept the anti-Japanese explanation; on September 6, Chou was explicitly accused of reaching an understanding with the United States, directed against the Soviet Union. A few days later, however, the articles were suspended; probably Moscow realized that a political crisis was in progress inside China at that time.

The crisis was mainly a reflection of domestic trends, but relations with the United States and the Soviet Union evidently played some part. Chou En-lai was probably determined to curb the political power of the army and of its senior figure, Defense Minister Lin Piao, who had bargained himself into the position of Mao Tse-

RECORD OF UN VOTING
ON ADMISSION OF COMMUNIST CHINA

Year	Membership	For	Against	Abstentions	Absent
1950	59	16	33	10	0
1951	60	11	37	4	no roll call
1952	60	7	42	11	0
1953	60	10	44	2	4
1954	60	11	43	6	0
1955	60	12	42	6	0
1956	79	24	47	8	0
1957	82	27	48	6	1
1958	81	28	44	9	0
1959	82	29	44	9	0
1960	98	34	42	22	0
1961	104	36	48	20	0
1962	110	42	56	12	0
1963	111	41	57	12	1
1964	no vote taken				
1965	117	47	47	20	3
1966	121	46	57	17	1
1967	122	45	58	17	2
1968	126	44	58	23	1
1969	126	48	56	21	1
1970	127	51	49	25	2
1971	131	76	35	17	3

tung's announced heir. Lin, however, was vulnerable in that he was opposed on ideological grounds to the opening to the United States and in that he was viewed with disfavor by Moscow for several reasons, including his alleged role in the Sino-Soviet border crisis of 1969. His elimination, therefore, would not only reduce the army's political influence but would facilitate the opening to the United States and remove an unnecessary irritant in Peking's delicate relationship with the Soviet Union. Accordingly, in mid-September, Lin and a number of his military supporters were purged, evidently at Chou's initiative.

After a period of uncertainty in Washington, it was announced on October 5 that Kissinger would make a scheduled second visit to Peking later in the month. The visit took place on October 20–26, by coincidence at the same time that Peking was voted into the United Nations. Meanwhile, on October 12, it had been announced that President Nixon would visit the Soviet Union in May 1972, a development that must have strengthened Peking's determination to continue cultivating its own contacts with Washington. On November 30, accordingly, Kissinger announced that the presidential visit to China would begin on Feb. 21, 1972. Making a gesture toward Peking's position that the Taiwan question is an internal Chinese matter, Kissinger stated his interest in seeing talks started between Peking and Taipei on the island's status.

THE RIVALRY IN EUROPE

Growing Soviet activity in Asia has been viewed by China as an irritant and even a political threat. Moscow has viewed Peking's increasing activity in Europe (especially Eastern Europe) in a similar light.

Eastern Europe. In Poland, East Germany, and Czechoslovakia, which are viewed in Moscow as exceptionally sensitive from the standpoint of Soviet security and influence and are receptive to Soviet direction, Peking's influence remains slight. Peking was slow in returning ambassadors to those countries, as well as to Bulgaria, presumably because of its resentment at their responsiveness to Soviet influence. In December 1970, at the time of the riots leading to the downfall of Polish First Secretary Gomułka, Peking denounced the new first secretary, Edward Gierek, as a "Soviet stooge" and an oppressor of the Polish workers.

The situation differs sharply in the more independent Communist countries of the Balkans. Here Peking is happy to play on anti-Soviet feelings to enhance its own influence. Chou En-lai took care, however, to remind a Yugoslav journalist in the summer of 1971 that "distant water cannot quench fire," meaning that China was in no position to give these countries effective protection should the Soviet Union threaten to do to them what it did to Czechoslovakia in 1968.

China has drawn closer to Rumania in common opposition to Soviet influence. Visiting China in June 1971, Rumania's President Nicolae Ceauşescu was apparently impressed with the tight social control there, which probably contributed to his subsequent crackdown on tendencies toward social spontaneity in his own country. Ceauşescu has been grateful for Chinese aid and support in countering Soviet pressure for closer integration of the Rumanian economy into the Soviet-dominated Council for Mutual Economic Assistance (Comecon). There is reason to believe that Ceauşescu brought a message to Peking from President Nixon that helped set the stage for the Kissinger talks and that he thus worsened Rumanian-Soviet relations.

Albania and Yugoslavia. Albania has received Chinese aid and support against Soviet and Yugoslavian pressures since 1960. In return, Albania has loudly supported Peking in its quarrel with the Soviet Union. In recent years, however, this friendship has cooled somewhat, even though China strongly declared its support of Albania when it provocatively withdrew from the Warsaw Pact after the invasion of Czechoslovakia. Albania, the symbol of anti-Soviet and pro-Chinese militancy, deplored Peking's tendency to downgrade its support for militant "Marxist-Leninist" movements in countries with whose governments it enjoys friendly relations and to establish contacts with "revisionist" Communist parties. Representatives of the Chinese Communist party were unprecedentedly absent from an Albanian party congress held in November 1971. Also, the Sino-Soviet border talks have evidently aroused some fear, in Albania as well as in Mongolia, of a possible Sino-Soviet deal involving Chinese abandonment of Albania in exchange for Soviet abandonment of the Mongolian People's Republic.

A common awareness of the enhanced threat from Moscow since the invasion of Czechoslovakia has contributed to a remarkable improvement in China's relations with Yugoslavia, which it had been denouncing as "revisionist" since 1958. Yugoslavia Foreign Minister Mirko Tepavac visited Peking in June. Apparently the budding relationship between China and Yugo-

(Continued on page 23)

Great Wall twists across rugged mountains for part of its 1,500-mile length. The largest defensive barrier ever built, its height ranges from 20 to 50 feet. Defenders could be moved quickly along the top of the wall.

THE LEADERS OF COMMUNIST CHINA

CAMERA PRESS

MARC RIBOUD FROM MAGNUM

MAO TSE-TUNG, chairman of the Chinese Communist party, was born to a peasant family in Hsiangtan, Hunan, on Dec. 26, 1893. After graduating from a Hunan provincial teachers' school in 1918, he went to Peking and came into contact with a group of radical students. He helped in the formation of the Chinese Communist party in 1921, and soon distinguished himself as a leader of guerrilla warfare and of the peasant movement. In 1935 he became party leader and 14 years later, when the Communists defeated the Nationalists, he was the ruler of mainland China.

Party opposition to him grew as a result of the failure of the Great Leap Forward in 1958, peasant discontent, and Peking's growing isolation from world affairs. In response Mao launched the Cultural Revolution in 1966 to eliminate opposition and to ensure the continuation of his policies. After three years of chaotic struggle, he had consolidated his power.

In 1971, Mao's major efforts were devoted to political stabilization. To blunt the rising influence of the military, Mao purged Defense Minister Lin Piao and elevated Chou En-lai to second place in the Communist hierarchy. In the economic field he resumed industrial development on the foundation of agriculture. In foreign relations he initiated a more flexible diplomacy. As early as December 1970 he had stated that he would welcome U. S. President Richard Nixon to China to discuss Sino-American problems. In spite of these conciliatory gestures, however, Mao was emphatic in his declaration of support for "national struggles against imperialism."

Mao looked fit and cheerful when he greeted Emperor Haile Selassie of Ethiopia in October 1971. At the age of 77, he remains the helmsman of China, making the final decisions on political action and strategy.

CHOU EN-LAI, premier of the People's Republic of China, was born in 1898 to a gentry family in Shaohing (Shaohsing), Chekiang. After graduating from Nankai Middle School in Tientsin in 1917, he studied first in Japan and then in France, where he joined the Chinese Communist party in 1922. Returning home in 1924, he quickly assumed a leading role in the party. In 1927 he was elected to the Politburo, a position he continued to hold despite stormy party leadership changes.

Chou became premier of the Communist government upon its establishment in 1949 and has displayed extraordinary administrative talents. Representing Communist China at the Geneva Conference in 1954 and the Bandung Conference in 1955, he won world fame as one of the most skillful negotiators in modern times. Chou signed the Sino-Soviet treaty of alliance in Moscow in 1950. He walked out of the Soviet Communist party conference in 1961 when Nikita Khrushchev attacked Albania.

During the Cultural Revolution (1966–69), Chou voted with the Maoists but at the same time attempted to curb the excessive militancy of the Red Guards. He emerged as a strong man toward the end of the Cultural Revolution, when China's return to political stability needed his moderation and flexibility. On Lin Piao's fall from influence in September 1971, Chou became the most powerful man in China after Mao Tse-tung.

In 1971, Chou helped normalize China's foreign relations. He captivated the U. S. table tennis team with his charm and diplomatic deftness. He was instrumental in inviting U. S. President Nixon to China and was to serve as the chief Chinese negotiator in the talks. Chou has insisted that U. S. forces be withdrawn from Taiwan and Vietnam, and has expressed concern over Japan's "rising militarism."

CHESTER C. TAN

(*Continued from page 20*)

slavia is less objectionable to Moscow than that between China and Rumania, because Yugoslavia is not a member of the Warsaw Pact.

Western Europe. In western Europe, Peking has been increasingly welcomed as a possible greater trading partner and as a counterweight to the Soviet Union, whose growing influence is widely feared. Peking, in turn, has expressed approval of the European Economic Community as a check on the two superpowers.

Peking continues to expand its trade with West Germany, a sensitive matter to Moscow, even though the West German government, since Chancellor Willy Brandt came to office in September 1969, has pursued its *Ostpolitik,* aimed at a détente with Eastern Europe. The agreement on West Berlin concluded by the Soviet Union with the United States, Britain, and France on Sept. 3, 1971, may have been inspired, in part, by a Soviet desire to compete with Peking in West Germany.

France, another country that tries to keep both the United States and the USSR at arm's length, continues to enjoy generally good relations with China. Since 1969, Peking's relations with Britain, which had deteriorated badly during the Cultural Revolution, have been improving. London stopped supporting the United States on the Chinese representation question at the UN in 1971 and is prepared to close its consulate on Taiwan. In return it expects to be allowed to upgrade its mission in Peking.

THE THIRD WORLD

The Middle East. Outside of Asia, Peking probably considers the Middle East the most important region of the Third World for its rivalry with the Soviet Union. It would probably like to play a role in any Middle Eastern settlement. It wants to improve its air communications via the Middle East with the Balkans and has already acquired landing rights in Turkey. Iran, Lebanon, and Turkey are among the Middle Eastern countries that have recognized Peking since 1970. The only remaining holdouts among the Arab countries are Saudi Arabia and Jordan.

After Nasser's death in September 1970, Peking saw reason to hope that Egyptian President Anwar el-Sadat would follow a line more independent of Moscow, and Sadat's coup of May 1971 against his leftist colleagues has strengthened this hope. Partly as a gesture to Cairo, Peking seems to have decreased its support for the Palestinian guerrillas, who in any case have not been doing well against the Jordanian and Israeli armies. On the other hand, Peking has continued its support for Arab guerrillas along the southern coast of the Arabian Peninsula. Peking has refused to have any overt contact with Israel, but there may be secret contacts.

Africa. In Africa, too, Peking has been pursuing its normalization campaign, with anti-Soviet overtones. Here as elsewhere in the Third World, China has been widely welcomed as a counterweight to the Soviet Union. In contrast

---

A SELECTION OF BOOKS ON CHINA

General Surveys

Elegant, Robert S., *The Center of the World* (Funk and Wagnalls 1968).

Liu, William T., ed., *Chinese Society under Communism* (John Wiley 1967).

MacFarquhar, Roderick, ed., *China under Mao* (MIT Press 1966).

Mancall, Mark, ed., *Formosa Today* (Praeger 1964).

Snow, Edgar, *Red China Today,* rev. ed. (Random House 1971).

For Specialized Study

Barnett, A. Doak, *Cadres, Bureaucracy, and Political Power in Communist China* (Columbia University Press 1967).

Bush, Richard C., Jr., *Religion in Communist China* (Abingdon Press 1970).

Chen, Nai-Ruenn, and Galenson, Walter, *The Chinese Economy under Communism* (Aldine Publishing Company 1969).

Cohen, Jerome A., ed., *Contemporary Chinese Law* (Harvard University Press 1970).

Dutt, Gargi, *Rural Communes in China* (Asia Publishing House 1967).

Eckstein, Alexander, and others, eds., *Economic Trends in Communist China* (Aldine Publishing Company 1968).

Fairbank, John K., *China: The People's Middle Kingdom and the U.S.A.* (Harvard University Press 1967).

Gittings, John, *Survey of the Sino-Soviet Dispute* (Oxford University Press 1968).

Goldman, Merle Dorothy, *Literary Dissent in Communist China* (Harvard University Press 1967).

Griffith, Samuel B., 2d, *The Chinese People's Liberation Army* (McGraw-Hill 1967).

Hinton, Harold C., *China's Turbulent Quest* (Macmillan 1970).

Hsu, Kai-yu, *Chou En-lai* (Doubleday 1968).

Huck, Arthur, *The Security of China* (Columbia University Press 1970).

Jacoby, Neil H., *U.S. Aid to Taiwan: A Study of Foreign Aid, Self-Help, and Development* (Praeger 1966).

Larkin, Bruce D., *China and Africa, 1949–1970* (University of California Press 1971).

Lindbeck, John M. H., *China: Management of a Revolutionary Society* (Univ. of Washington Press 1971).

Mendel, Douglas, *The Politics of Formosan Nationalism* (University of California Press 1970).

Ojha, Ishwer C., *Chinese Foreign Policy in an Age of Transition* (Beacon Press 1969).

Price, R. F., *Education in Communist China* (Praeger 1970).

Robinson, Thomas W., ed., *The Cultural Revolution in China* (University of California Press 1971).

Schram, Stuart, *Mao Tse-tung* (Simon & Schuster 1967).

Schurmann, Herbert Franz, *Ideology and Organization in Communist China* (University of California Press 1966).

Shen, T. H., *The Sino-American Joint Commission on Rural Reconstruction: Twenty Years of Cooperation for Agricultural Development* (Cornell University Press 1970).

Tan, Chester C., *Chinese Political Thought in the Twentieth Century* (Doubleday 1971).

Townsend, James R., *Political Participation in Communist China* (University of California Press).

—Compiled by Chester C. Tan

Premier Chou En-lai chats with Henry Kissinger (left), adviser to President Nixon, as presidential assistant Dwight L. Chapin listens in Peking on October 20. Kissinger, who had secretly visited China in July, returned to talk over details of Nixon's 1972 trip.

to its approach in the mid-1960's, Peking is currently stressing its relations with African governments and deemphasizing support for revolutionary organizations, except for those working against the white-dominated governments of the Portuguese possessions, Rhodesia, and South Africa. It appears, however, that Peking conducts some secret trade with South Africa.

China's influence is considerable in some of the French-speaking African nations, mainly Congo (Brazzaville), Guinea, and Mali, as well as in Equatorial Guinea and Tanzania, where Peking provides military training, arms, and substantial economic aid. It has contributed technical and financial support amounting to $400 million for the projected 1,000-mile (1,600-km) Tan-Zam (Tanzania-Zambia) Railway. Peking has been cultivating good relations with the government of the Sudan in spite of the anti-Communist purge of July 1971. Ethiopia recognized Peking early in 1971, and Emperor Haile Selassie, visiting China in October 1971, received a commitment of economic aid.

Latin America. In Latin America, Peking's obvious line is to stress common opposition to

the "colossus of the north," but here again it does so partly to gain support against its own northern neighbor. Peking has reduced its support for Latin pro-Chinese Communist and "Marxist-Leninist" parties and has concentrated on improving its relations with the more socialist and anti-American governments, notably those of Cuba, Ecuador, Peru, and Chile. In February 1971 the socialist government of Chile announced that it would sell China some much-needed copper.

Peking is giving Peru and Chile support in their claim to a 200-mile (322-km) limit on their territorial waters and seabed exploitation rights, not only to annoy the superpowers but to establish a possible precedent that would further Peking's growing interest in dominating its own continental shelf. China's relations with Cuba, which have been bad for several years because of Castro's essential dependence on Soviet aid and support, improved somewhat in 1971. Presumably, Peking hopes to compete with Moscow in Havana, or at least to be in a position to take advantage of any mistakes that Moscow may make there.

Asia Feels Impact of New Peking Policies

By Ishwer C. Ojha

Remarkable breakthroughs occurred in China's foreign policy during 1971. The Sino-American rapprochement, which had begun early in 1969, reached a peak with the announcement in July 1971 of President Richard Nixon's proposed visit to China. In October the People's Republic of China was admitted to the United Nations by an overwhelming majority. Throughout the year Peking moved to normalize relations with a large number of countries around the world. In expanding its contacts and commitments beyond Asia, China created a tremendous impact on the Asian international system, the full effects of which are yet to be determined.

While the Nixon Doctrine of a reduced U. S. presence in Asia provided the climate for the rapprochement with China, it was also interpreted in China as a revival of the Eisenhower Doctrine of having Asians fight Asians. China therefore set about to secure its position in Asia, primarily by outmaneuvering the Soviet Union in this sphere of influence.

THE OPENING TO THE WEST

Actually, Peking's ascent to new heights of diplomatic sophistication had begun several years earlier. By the middle of 1968 the impact of the Cultural Revolution on the Chinese foreign ministry had started to decline. Indicative of the inability of the radicals to influence foreign policy were the rapprochement with Yugoslavia in late 1968 and the greater tolerance of East European revisionism, as well as the decision to reopen the Sino-American talks in Warsaw early in 1970.

One of the specific reasons for Peking's rapid swing toward normalizing foreign relations was the Soviet invasion of Czechoslovakia in August 1968. The Czech incident had a more traumatic impact on Chinese foreign policy than did the Cultural Revolution at home, for it greatly increased Chinese insecurity. Following a period of mutual troop buildups, the Sino-Soviet border clashes in March 1969 were probably a Chinese test to determine how far the Soviets would go in extending to China the Brezhnev Doctrine of enforcing Soviet-style communism.

In the wake of the Soviet invasion of Czechoslovakia, China made definite and direct efforts to improve its foreign relations, especially with the United States. A Chinese offer to reopen the Sino-American talks in Warsaw was reciprocated by the United States' easing travel and trade restrictions with China. But hopes for a rapprochement were halted temporarily by the U. S. invasion of Cambodia in April 1970. Just as the Soviet invasion of Czechoslovakia sharply turned the Chinese toward easing relations with the United States, so did the U. S. invasion of Cambodia in the course of the Vietnam War move China in another direction.

Within a matter of days of the invasion, the Chinese had coordinated on behalf of the ousted Cambodian chief of state, Prince Norodom Sihanouk, a general united front of groups and parties in Laos, Cambodia, and Vietnam, all of which were already engaged in fighting the United States and its allies. More than any other event, the invasion of Cambodia swung the balance of power and the competition between Moscow and Peking for leadership in Southeast Asia in favor of the Chinese.

Yet China's desire to break through its containment was so strong that the Cambodian invasion delayed, but did not destroy, the budding Sino-American rapprochement. The invitation of an American table tennis team to China in early 1971 represented a bold, new initiative on the part of China for easing tensions with the United States.

CHINA AND JAPAN

Of all the Asian nations, Japan probably was most shaken by the Sino-American rapprochement. Since 1945, Japan has beeen unable to develop a foreign policy that does not depend exclusively on its relations with the United States.

Japan's China Policy. During the UN vote on China's admission in October 1971, Japan found itself the only major power to support the U. S. "two-Chinas" policy. In taking this stand, Japan sought to buy another year's time in which

Ishwer C. Ojha, chairman of the Department of Political Science at Boston University, has made contemporary China his area of special study. He is the author of Chinese Foreign Policy in an Age of Transition: The Diplomacy of Cultural Despair *(1969).*

either a premier less anti-Communist than Eisaku Sato would be installed, or Japan would, at least, redirect its own China policy. Thus, Japan insisted that it was not in favor of a permanent two-Chinas policy, but supported such an arrangement for a transitional period. Japan wistfully hoped that in the meantime China and Taiwan would solve the problem between themselves through negotiation.

In July 1971, when Nixon announced his forthcoming trip to China, Sato said that he, too, would go to China if necessary. Although domestic pressure had long been building up in Japan for normalization of relations with the People's Republic of China, Sato characteristically reacted only to Nixon's trip—not to pressures at home. Nevertheless such pressures, voiced strongly throughout 1971, would surely have an important effect on Japanese policy before long.

Significantly, the Dietmen's league for the normalization of Sino-Japanese relations, a new body within the Japanese parliament (Diet) formed in December 1970, drew legislators of all political persuasions, and by January 1971 represented more than 52% of the total membership of both houses. Japan's Socialist party went further in demanding that normalization of relations with China lead to the signing of a peace treaty as well as to diplomatic recognition of the Peking government.

China's Japan Policy. For its part, China continued to look upon Japan not as an independent actor, but as an ally of Nationalist Chinese President Chiang Kai-shek and particularly as an agent of the United States. Specific Chinese attacks have concentrated on U. S. support for Japanese rearmament and the use of these armaments to support the U. S. policy of military confrontation in Asia. China's policy, therefore, has been to isolate Japan and loosen it from its American moorings.

As late as April 1970, Chinese Premier Chou En-lai, while visiting North Korea, insisted that the U. S.-Japanese security treaty was a military alliance directed against China and North Korea. There is some reason to believe that this interpretation was not solely the result of Chinese paranoia. Chou's conviction can be traced back to the Nixon-Sato communiqué of 1969, which explicitly stated that "Japan's security is directly related to the security of South Korea and to the Taiwan Straits." Outsiders interpreted the communiqué as meaning that Sato was continuing to play a satellite security role as a price for the return of the U. S.-held island of Okinawa in 1972. When the U. S.-Japan Security Treaty was extended in June 1970, it was openly claimed that Japan was supposed to take over a part of the U. S. security tasks in the Pacific.

From these open admissions, Peking drew two conclusions: first, Japan had an important part in the Sino-U. S. confrontation; and second, the United States had assigned Japan an expanding, but still dependent, role, and Japan would continue to play it, with U. S. encouragement. It is these conclusions on which the Chinese fear of Japanese militarism is based. Chinese foreign policy aimed therefore at continuing to oppose a military alliance of the United States and Japan. In April 1970, a Japanese trade delegation in China agreed to sign a communiqué denouncing

Chinese and Indian soldiers confront each other in 1967 photo at border between Tibet and Indian-protected Sikkim.

UPI

Japanese "militarism" and claiming that the price for the return of Okinawa was to turn the whole of Japan into a U. S. military base.

Chinese concern with Japanese internal politics and the Japanese-U. S. alliance has been high and fairly constant, but only recently have the Chinese tried to sway Japanese foreign policy. In October 1971, the Chinese Communists spelled out in considerable detail the kind of relationship they would like to have with Japan. A Japanese parliamentary delegation agreed to a joint communiqué stating that diplomatic relations must be established between China and Japan at the earliest possible date and that such a relationship must be accompanied by Japan's severing diplomatic relations with Taiwan and abrogating the peace treaty that Japan had already signed with the Nationalists.

The two sides further agreed that a new peace treaty would be signed by Peking and Tokyo ending the state of war between them. Although the communiqué did say that both the Soviet Union and the United States must withdraw their armed forces stationed in foreign countries and hinted that China's foreign policy goal was a neutral Japan, it did not mention two things that the Chinese had emphasized in the past: first, Chinese leaders have always said that Japan owes China billions of dollars in reparations; that demand was not reiterated. Second, not a word was written of the U. S.-Japanese security defense treaty. The Chinese retreat on these polemical points is a clear indication that China is actively seeking to change Japanese policy by making concessions to potential supporters in the Japanese body politic.

Reaction in Japan. At least since the change in U. S. economic and China policies, the Japanese have begun to realize that their foreign policy has erred in the past by failing to use China and the United States as counterbalances. Additionally, there are growing indications that Japan may use the Soviet Union to strengthen its hand in dealing with Peking. Moscow by 1970 was trading with Japan on the same order of magnitude as China—a little over $800 million.

Russo-Japanese economic cooperation cannot get off the ground as long as the Soviet Union rejects Japanese demands for the return of some of the Kurile Islands. Nevertheless, the Peking *People's Daily* on June 19, 1970, stressed what it described as growing Soviet-Japanese collusion, particularly in the divided countries of Asia. The real possibility of increased Soviet-Japanese economic relations—which it is probable the Soviet Union will actively promote—has constantly worried Peking. In such an eventuality, Japan might well find itself, like the rest of Asia, internally divided between factions favoring China and those favoring the Soviet Union. Japan, then, would not be building bridges to the Asian mainland; but simply would be shifting its economic, military, and diplomatic dependence from the United States to the Soviet Union.

THE INDIAN SUBCONTINENT

A major Asian issue that confronted Chinese foreign policy during 1971 was the Indo-Pakistani conflict over the secessionist movement in East Pakistan. Fearing that China would support Pakistan in the event of a conflict arising out of this situation, India moved to bolster its position by signing a mutual aid treaty with the Soviet Union in August 1971.

Perhaps India's fears would have been lessened had it understood the growing indecision on the part of Chinese foreign-policymakers toward the situation in East Pakistan. Chinese foreign policy, even in its most revolutionary phases, has never supported a secessionist movement. By August 1971, the Chinese realized that they, like the Indians, had greatly underestimated the desperation of the Bengalis in East Pakistan and the strength of their rapidly growing guerrilla movement.

India, realizing that it could neither socially nor economically afford the burden of 10 million Pakistani refugees, decided to speed up the guerrilla warfare. Its policy was to encourage and assist the Bangladesh independence movement, with two specific ends in view: first, the refugees would return home; and second, with the creation of an independent Bangladesh, India would be the dominant power on the subcontinent. As these goals were being realized at year-end, India for the first time in over 20 years, was free to have a dynamic foreign policy and to take the initiative in seeking political accommodation or possible rapprochement with China.

China was noticeably restrained in its support of Pakistan throughout 1971 in contrast with its role in the 1965 conflict between India and Pakistan over Kashmir. Chinese foreign policy, both in and outside of the United Nations, provided only minimum verbal support to Pakistan and was generally much more cautious than that of the United States.

In Pakistan, the country's failure to receive concrete support from either of its major allies —China and the United States—not only has led to a serious realignment of political forces at home but also to a substantial reevaluation of national and foreign policy interests. It is quite possible that Pakistan will transfer its attention from the subcontinent and concentrate on its policy toward those nations of the Middle East not in the Soviet orbit of influence. Chinese activity in countries such as Iran could be aided

WELCOME TO CANADA'S CAPITAL

UPI

REPRODUCED BY PERMISSION OF PUNCH

(Left) *Chinese table tennis instructors are welcomed to Canada during a year when "Ping-Pong Diplomacy" became a catchphrase. Game was also linked with diplomacy in 1901 Punch cartoon about Boxer Rebellion negotiations with Britain.*

by a development of this kind, because Pakistan, fearful of creating a new enemy, no doubt will continue to maintain good relations with China.

OTHER ACTIVITY IN ASIA

Generally, throughout 1971, Asian countries went through a reassessment of their relations with China. The necessity of having to deal with China in regional organizations such as the UN Economic Committee for Asia and the Far East, along with the continuing U. S. withdrawal from Vietnam and the decision of the Nixon administration to build direct diplomatic and political bridges to China, ended the possibility of Asian countries avoiding all relations with China. Thailand, the Philippines, Indonesia, Burma, Malaysia, and Ceylon have all either normalized their relations with China or, at least, taken steps in that direction.

China's renewed dynamism in foreign policy has meant a new pattern of power not only in the international system but in Asia as well. The overall competition in Asia is now between the Soviet Union and China. It remains to be seen whether India and Japan will emerge to become independent economic and political counterweights. The Cold War days of military competition and confrontation appear to be over.

In the Middle East, China's foreign policy has slowly moved away from being solely an extension of its relations with Egypt. China has been actively normalizing its relations with both Arab and non-Arab states. During 1971, China was recognized by Kuwait, Lebanon, Turkey, and Iran. The largest Chinese embassy in the Middle East, which will probably be the focus of Chinese diplomatic activity in this region, will be located in Beirut, Lebanon. China's relations with Iran are crucial to the development of its international air routes. For the first time in 20 years, China has established diplomatic relations with all members of the Central Treaty Organization (CENTO).

Since the Israeli-Arab war of June 1967, China has supported the Palestine liberation movement. But Chinese policy has never condoned this movement's political aim of destroying Israel. Moreover, such support has not stopped China from normalizing relations with countries such as Lebanon, which hold guerrilla movements in disfavor. It seems that the Chinese are not satisfied with the political tactics and efficacy of the guerrilla organizations. Because of the developing strain between China and the Palestine Liberation Organization it is possible that the latter may lean toward the Soviet Union in the future.

Thus, 1971 has seen the expansion of China's diplomatic relations throughout Asia. China has followed a two-pronged strategy of normalizing relations with the United States and with its Asian allies, while competing with the Soviet Union for influence in Asia.

Inside China Today: Emerging from Chaos

BY CHESTER C. TAN

China's problems in 1971 were in large measure a legacy of the Cultural Revolution of 1966–69. The Cultural Revolution, which plunged China into chaos, was a political upheaval of immense consequence. It started as a struggle against "bourgeois thought" but soon developed into a brutal seizure of power. Through the organization of the Red Guards and the use of military force, Mao Tse-tung smashed the opposition, and with it the party organization. Since 1969, Peking's major task has been to restore political stability and to rebuild the party, which is ridden with factions. But the political forces set in motion by the Cultural Revolution were not easy to control, and the cleavages that had rent the nation foreshadowed further crises. Economic growth, which was halted by the Cultural Revolution, resumed in 1971 as China began its fourth 5-year plan. Ideologically, the nation appeared to be emerging from the confusion of the Cultural Revolution.

PARTY REORGANIZATION

To secure the support of the army for his struggle against his opponents, Mao Tse-tung had made Defense Minister Lin Piao his deputy and eventual successor. When the Chinese Communist party was reorganized in 1969, it fell under the dominance of military figures. Army men made up 45% of the Central Committee, and 6 of the 21 full members of the Politburo were close associates of Lin Piao. In the Standing Committee of the Politburo, the top echelon of party command, the radical Cultural Revolution group had firmer control, and Lin Piao was the only military representative.

During 1971 the ascendency of the military was particularly notable in the provinces. Of the 158 leaders in the newly reestablished provincial and regional party committees, 59.5% were army men, 34.8% were civilian cadres, and only 5.7% were "mass representatives," or radical elements.

The rise in the power of the military contrasted sharply with the decline of radical influence. Ch'en Po-ta, the head of the militant Cultural Revolutionary group who had risen to become a member of the Standing Committee of the Politburo and the fourth-ranking Communist in the party hierarchy, came under attack in August, following a long absence from the political scene. He was charged with being responsible for the excesses during the Cultural Revolution, including the occupation of the ministry of foreign affairs for a period by the Red Guards. Even Chiang Ch'ing, Mao Tse-tung's wife, mitigated the radical activity she had displayed so prominently during the Cultural Revolution.

Despite these developments, however, the leftists were not routed. In Shanghai, China's biggest city, Chang Ch'un-ch'iao, a militant Maoist who had helped start the Cultural Revolution, and Yao Wen-yuan, another prime mover of the radical movement, were elected as first and second secretaries respectively of the new party committee. Both were Politburo members and spent much of their time in Peking. They were outspoken against military domination and seemed to enjoy the confidence of Mao Tse-tung.

The Fall of Lin Piao. Until September the military were firmly in power. On Army Day, August 1, the ministry of national defense held a grand reception at which practically all high army men were present. Huang Yung-sheng, chief of the general staff, delivered the key speech. As late as September 1, Lin Piao, in his capacity as vice chairman of the Communist party, joined with Chairman Mao in sending a message of congratulations to North Vietnam on its 26th anniversary.

Then, suddenly, there was a series of mysterious events. On the night of September 12 a Chinese air force plane crashed deep in Mongolia, killing the nine persons aboard. Simultaneously, the air force was grounded. Around mid-September the traditional National Day parade in Peking was cancelled. Political and military leaders usually appear before the Gate of Heavenly Peace to review the National Day parade. The cancellation was therefore necessary if the absence of top leaders who had been purged was to be concealed.

The plane crash gave rise to wild speculations. One story maintains that Lin Piao was among the dead. According to this version, he had led attempts to assassinate Mao Tse-tung and then, when his involvement was found out, he and his wife and son had fled with the assistance of Wu Fa-hsien, the air force commander. Lin's

Chester C. Tan is professor of history at New York University. A graduate of Yenching University, China, he went to the United States on a State Department fellowship, and received his Ph.D. degree from Columbia University. He has published books and articles both in China and in the United States, including The Boxer Catastrophe (1967) *and* Chinese Political Thought in the Twentieth Century (1971).

Intricate terracing is characteristic of intense cultivation necessary to feed China's millions.

own daughter was supposed to have betrayed the escape plan, and the plane was pursued and shot down. Other accounts insist that Lin is alive.

Whether Lin is dead or alive, his political life is undoubtedly finished. His name has been dropped from public mention. The fall of Lin Piao was accompanied by a general decline of army influence as his military associates dropped out of sight. Among them were Huang Yung-sheng; Wu Fa-hsien; Li Tso-p'eng, the navy political commissioner; and Chiu Hui-tso, the director of general logistics—all members of the Politburo.

Causes of the Struggle. Though the fall of Lin Piao was shrouded in secrecy, it was believed that the conflict centered around the following issues. First, the predominence of the military worried Mao Tse-tung, who knew well the danger of the armed forces' falling outside party control. As Mao moved to reestablish party control over the army, Lin resisted, which resulted in his downfall. Second, Peking's new policy of trying to arrange a détente with the United States aroused the opposition of the army, which had long been indoctrinated to fight "U. S. imperialism." In an Army Day speech, Huang Yung-sheng condemned the United States for "pursuing expansion everywhere" and called upon the people of the world to carry through to the end the "great struggle against imperialism."

New Power Alignment. Lin Piao's fall has led to a new alignment of power in the Com-

munist leadership. While Mao Tse-tung remains the supreme leader, Premier Chou En-lai has risen to second place in the party hierarchy, although there is no indication that Chou has taken over Lin Piao's position as deputy leader. Chiang Ch'ing, Mao's wife, has advanced to the third position in the Politburo. After her is Yeh Chien-ying, an old associate of Chou En-lai's and a former chief of the general staff, who appears to have assumed some of the duties that had been handled by Lin Piao and Huang Yung-sheng.

Other Politburo members listed in order of importance in official announcements are: Chang Ch'un-ch'iao; Yao Wen-yuan; Li Hsien-nien, an economic expert and a trusted aide of Premier Chou; Tung Pi-wu, the 85-year-old deputy chief of state; and Ch'en Hsi-lien, commander of the armed forces in the Manchurian region.

Only these 9 of the 21 members of the Politburo are publicly active. Since Tung Pi-wu is too old to take any vigorous part and since Ch'en Hsi-lien seldom leaves his Manchurian base, only seven Politburo members, including Mao Tse-tung, are really involved in decision making. The rise of the leftist group led by Chiang Ch'ing is obvious, but a balance of power is maintained between the leftists and the moderate group led by Premier Chou. It seems that in the struggle against Lin Piao and his followers the astute Chou chose to cooperate with the radicals, which tipped the scales against the military group.

Political Outlook. The fall of Lin Piao is the second crisis since 1966, and it occurred only two years after Lin had been designated as Mao Tse-tung's deputy and political successor. Although the struggle was not carried out in the street this time, and in fact was barely noticed by the masses, its impact on political stability cannot be exaggerated. Not only has the rebuilding of the party been interrupted, but party unity is threatened anew. The vast influence that Lin Piao had built throughout the nation has to be eliminated, and it will be an enormous task to weed out his men who have infiltrated the party and government, from the central leadership down to local levels.

The attitude of the people toward the party has no doubt been affected by the frequent and sudden changes among party leaders. There was also some question whether the army would continue to be the focus of loyalty to Mao and an effective instrument of party unity. Mao's popularity and personality seem capable of holding the nation together as long as he lives, but his demise could leave the country wide open to fresh struggle and even upheaval. Apparently to avert this possibility, Communist China has stressed collective leadership since Lin's fall. A solid coalition has yet to develop, however, for the alliance between radicals and moderates is at best a marriage of convenience.

ECONOMY

Communist China has resumed its economic growth after interruptions caused by the Cultural Revolution. Reports from Peking indicate overall progress in 1971, the first year of its fourth 5-year plan. From January to August, the total output value of industry increased 18.7% over the same period in 1970. It is estimated that China's gross national product will register a 10% increase for 1971. China claims that its industry is supplying the country not only with consumer goods but also with capital equipment for industrial expansion.

Nevertheless, China still has, in general, a developing economy. As Premier Chou En-lai has admitted, China's industrial capacity is small compared with that of the United States, the Soviet Union, Japan, West Germany, and Britain. China has abandoned hopes, raised by optimism during the Great Leap Forward, of rapid industrial advance.

Industrial Decentralization. The fourth 5-year plan stresses industrial decentralization and local self-sufficiency. This policy was adopted not only to compensate for inadequate transportation and to absorb possible nuclear blows, but also to meet with China's specific conditions. It is based on the recognition that China has a vast territory with greatly varying economic and natural conditions. Economic development, Pe-

Propaganda slogans and portrait of Chairman Mao decorate facade of Peking Hospital. Only three small signs indicate that it is a major medical facility.

AUDREY TOPPING FROM RAPHO GUILLUMETTE

king holds, must not rely on the efforts of the central departments alone, for they are not in a position to tap fully the locally scattered mineral resources. Furthermore, people in different areas have different demands for manufactured goods. Only if local industry is developed can their needs be satisfactorily met and their initiative given full play.

A report from Peking in September claimed that more than half of the country's counties have set up their own small machinery, chemical fertilizer, and cement plants. Production of chemical fertilizer and cement by local plants accounted for 40% and 50% respectively of the national total in 1971. The revival of small local iron and steel plants, which were closed in 1961 when the Great Leap Forward proved to be a disaster, is also significant. Peking has not commented on the quality of these local products, but it is known that they have been used for the manufacture of farm and kitchen implements. Local industry is expected to play an important role in the mechanization of agriculture.

Agriculture. Since the Cultural Revolution, China has stressed agriculture as the foundation of the economy. "Industry must develop together with agriculture," said Mao Tse-tung, "for only thus can industry secure materials and a market, and only thus is it possible to accumulate fairly large funds for building a powerful industry."

According to Peking, China has achieved a self-sufficiency in grain and has even produced a surplus. If grain is still imported, Peking asserts, it is merely to increase varieties and "help other countries." China contracted to import 2.5 million tons of wheat from Canada in 1971; 5 million tons had been imported in 1970. The increase in grain production is attributable to large-scale water-conservation projects, greater use of chemical fertilizer, more intense cultivation, agricultural mechanization, and the extraordinary efforts of the peasants. The rise in cotton production places China in a better position to compete in Asian and African textile markets.

People's Communes. There have been changes in the communes, which have shifted back to some of the features originally advocated by Mao Tse-tung. The private plots allotted to each peasant family for growing vegetables and raising chickens had increased in size during the administration of Liu Shao-ch'i, who thought material incentives necessary in the face of peasant discontent with regimented communal life. Since Liu was purged during the Cultural Revolution, Peking has taken measures to cut back the size of the private lots. Free markets have been curbed, and the peasants are required to deal with the commune cooperatives. In line with industrial decentralization, backyard blast furnaces have risen again in the communes. In a county in Shansi province each of the 30 communes is said to have a small furnace, in addition to a machinery plant and a chemical fertilizer plant.

Living Standards. The Chinese people have enjoyed a steady improvement in their physical conditions, although the standard of living is still low in comparison with that of the advanced industrial countries. There are no more beggars, thieves, or starving poor. The distinction between the rich and the very poor has disappeared. Shanghai, once a glamorous city renowned for its pleasures and vices, has turned into a proletarian city where people are serious about their work and streets are kept clean. A stern orderliness has replaced noisy confusion. People in China look healthy and content. They are neatly dressed, both men and women, in simple blue cotton suits and cloth caps.

Factories have adopted a wage schedule with eight categories, ranging from 34 yuan (2.4 yuan = $1) to 108 yuan a month; apprentices earn 18 to 30 yuan. The wage level is set low, Peking says, in order to narrow the disparity in living conditions between urban and rural areas.

Wages in communes are based on the earnings of a peasant's production team. He is given work points for his daily labor. If his income is not enough to maintain his family, the commune will give him a subsidy, which is drawn from a welfare fund maintained by an annual deduction from the commune's earnings. Similarly, if an urban worker's earnings are below the minimum cost of living, the factory where he is employed will pay him a subsidy.

The low income of the Chinese worker or peasant is well compensated for by full employment, low rents, cheap prices, and the lack of a personal income tax. Monthly expenditures for food are about 10 yuan a person. A one-room apartment costs about 4 yuan a month. Medical treatment is practically free, and children are entitled to universal education through junior high school. Since wives usually work, it is common for a family to earn more than is needed for daily necessities. The extra money can be deposited in a bank at 4% interest or used to buy consumer goods.

Department stores in the cities are well stocked, but not with luxury items. While daily necessities are cheap, other items are expensive for an average wage earner. A simple cotton suit costs 13 yuan, but a wristwatch costs 120 yuan. People pay 30 yuan for a small transistor radio and 120 yuan for a better brand with shortwave reception.

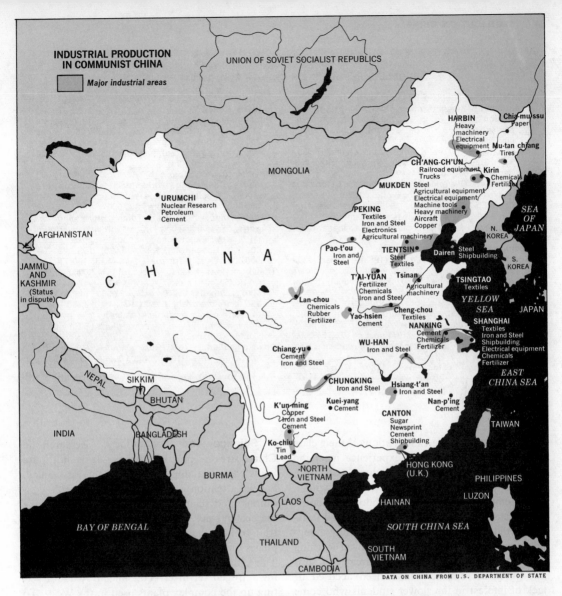

Primary products of the major industrial centers are shown under the cities' names.

Though new buildings have risen in big cities, many of the old ones are still in use. In the countryside new houses are badly needed, since numerous peasants still live in mud houses with thatched roofs. Motor vehicles are few. The bicycle is the popular means of urban transportation.

IDEOLOGY

Ideological struggle is the basis of political struggle in Communist China. It served as the spearhead for the Cultural Revolution, and it continues to be an essential part of Chinese Communism. Peking's slogan for 1971 was "Carry out education in ideology and politics." The Communist cadres are instructed to criticize revisionism and idealism and to oppose conceit and complacency. Thought reform is continually

enforced, the aim being to uphold the thought of Mao Tse-tung and to help attain ideological purity. The Maoists believe in unceasing class struggle and are not averse to intraparty struggle. The outward calm and relaxation seen by foreign reporters are largely deceptive. Tensions actually persist both in and outside the party.

Education. Chinese educational policy is summed up in Mao's directive: "The length of schooling should be shortened, education should be revolutionized, and the domination of schools and colleges by bourgeois intellectuals should not be tolerated any longer." The policy was first implemented in 1970 when Tsinghua University, China's foremost science and engineering institution, was organized to shorten the course of study from four to two or three years. Workers, peasants, and soldiers are now admitted to col-

PEOPLE'S REPUBLIC OF CHINA—A Statistical Profile

Official Name: People's Republic of China.

Area: 3,691,512 square miles (9,561,100 sq km).

Population (1971 est.): 800,000,000. *Density, 200 per square mile (77 per sq km). Annual rate of increase, 2.0%.*

Chief Cities (1971 est.): Peking, the capital, 7,000,-000; Shanghai, 10,000,000; Tientsin, 5,000,000; Canton, 3,000,000.

Government: *Chairman of the Chinese Communist party,* Mao Tse-tung (took office 1935). *Premier,* Chou En-lai (took office 1949). *Legislature*—National People's Congress (unicameral), 3,040 members. *Major political party*—Chinese Communist party.

Language: Mandarin Chinese (official).

Education: *School enrollment* (1959)—primary, 90,-000,000; secondary (1958), 9,990,000; technical/vocational (1958), 850,000; university/higher (1962), 820,000.

Finances (1960, last published budget): *Revenues,* $35,010,000,000; *expenditures,* $35,010,000,000; *monetary unit,* yuan (2.4 yuan = U.S.$1, 1971).

Gross National Product (1971 est.): $78,750,000,-000. *Average annual income per person* (1968 est.), $90.

Manufacturing (metric tons, 1969): Crude steel (1971 est.), 18,000,000; meat, 11,008,000; cement, 9,994,000.

Crops (metric tons, 1968 crop year): Total cereals (1971 est.), 215,000,000; rice, 91,000,000 (ranks 1st among world producers); wheat, 27,000,-000 (world rank, 3d); soybeans (1969), 10,920,-000 (world rank, 2d).

Minerals (metric tons, 1969): Coal, 330,000,000 (ranks 3d among world producers); iron ore (1968), 20,900,000; crude petroleum (1970), 20,-000,000; manganese ore, 300,000.

Foreign Trade (1971 est.): *Total exports and imports,* $4,500,000,000. *Chief trading partners* (1971 est., exports and imports)—Japan, $900,-000,000; Hong Kong, $550,000,000; USSR, $150,-000,000; West Germany (1969), $235,100,000.

Transportation: *Roads* (1971 est.), 125,000 miles (211,625 km); *motor vehicles* (1971 est.), 351,-000; *railroads* (1970 est.), 22,500 miles (36,-354 km); *merchant fleet* (1971), 1,022,000 gross registered tons; *national airline,* Civil Aviation Administration; *principal airports,* Shanghai, Canton, Peking.

Communications: *Television stations* (1968), 30; *television sets* (1969), 300,000; *radios* (1963), 8,000,000.

leges without entrance examinations if their class consciousness and political experience meet the requirements. A new curriculum has been adopted to combine labor and learning, with a strong emphasis on ideological indoctrination.

Because of free admission, workers and peasants without any previous schooling study alongside much younger students. The slower learning speed of the older students has created a serious problem. Teachers have been accused of lack of interest in the slower students who come from worker and peasant families. The government opposes any grading of students into separate groups and has called for methods to close the gap between old and young, even at the expense of the brighter students.

The purge of intellectuals and the disruption of training during the Cultural Revolution has resulted in a nationwide shortage of teachers in middle and primary schools. To meet the shortage, students and demobilized army men have been appointed teachers. Many of these, however, are poorly qualified, and it is imperative that their level of competence be raised as soon as possible. Aside from opening short-term training classes in the teachers colleges, the government has sent mobile groups to the rural areas to help improve teachers' qualifications. The Kwangtung Teachers College is reported to have sent 31 such groups, each 10-strong and consisting of teachers and party personnel, to 40 counties.

Science and Technology. Research in China stresses practical needs. It is not pure knowledge but applied science that is valued. Special attention is given to China's specific conditions, and scientists are told "not just to take the beaten track traversed by other countries and trail behind them at a snail's pace." The emphasis on ingenuity has led to some good results. The Chinese have developed a method for making nitrogen fertilizer economically without setting up the complex plants used in the West. To meet the shortage of physicians, farm workers are given short-term training at local hospitals, and these "barefoot doctors" are assigned to treat minor complaints in rural localities. Through extensive but simple programs China is rapidly eliminating alcoholism, venereal disease, and drug addiction and is bringing endemic and epidemic infections under control.

Of immense interest to the world medical profession is China's development of acupuncture, the traditional technique of using needles for surgical anesthetization. The practice of curing ailments and diseases by acupuncture began over 1,000 years ago, but the use of acupuncture for anesthesia is considered an important breakthrough in the attempt to explore traditional Chinese medicine and raise it to a higher level. Acupuncture is popular in China because it does not require complicated apparatus and is particularly suitable to rural and mountainous areas where modern facilities are lacking.

Taiwan: A Time for Reassessment

BY CHESTER C. TAN

The Republic of China (Nationalist China) endured its most troubled year in 1971. As a result of its expulsion from the United Nations in October, Nationalist China had to reassess its international relations, economic policies, and domestic political structure.

International Relations. Nationalist China suffered the greatest diplomatic setback in its history on October 25 when the UN General Assembly voted, 76 to 35, to admit Communist China and to expel the Nationalist government. A few moments before the final vote, when defeat appeared certain, Chou Shu-kai, the Nationalist minister of foreign affairs, led his delegation out of the assembly, thus ending Taiwan's 22-year participation in the United Nations.

The UN expulsion had a tremendous impact on the international position of Nationalist China. The overwhelming vote in favor of Peking reflected the increase in the number of nations recognizing Communist China. Even more important was the shifting position of the United States, hitherto the staunch supporter of Nationalist China and officially still its ally under a mutual-defense treaty.

The United States began its attempts at a détente with Peking in April and May when, in response to a softening in Peking's diplomatic position, reflected in the Communists' cordial reception of the U. S. table tennis team, Washington eased its restrictions on trade with Communist China. These efforts culminated in July when President Nixon announced his plan to visit Communist China before May 1972 to seek a normalization of relations between the two countries.

Taiwan objected vigorously to Nixon's plan, asserting that it would seriously injure the interests of Nationalist China. Although Washington declared repeatedly that it would not shirk its treaty obligations or abandon old friends, Taiwan was not sure how long the United States would honor its commitments, as Peking insisted on recovering Taiwan, which the Communists consider an integral part of their territory. Some U. S. military planners have already expressed the view that a U. S. withdrawal from Taiwan would entail little strategic loss for the United States.

The rapid changes in the international situation have compelled Taiwan to review its foreign policy. Recognizing the uncertainty of U. S.

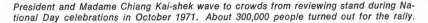

President and Madame Chiang Kai-shek wave to crowds from reviewing stand during National Day celebrations in October 1971. About 300,000 people turned out for the rally.

— NATIONALIST CHINA • Information Highlights —

Official Name: Republic of China.
Area: 13,885 square miles (35,961 sq km).
Population: 14,334,000 (1969 est.): Taipei, the capital, 1,712,108; Kaohsiung, 784,502; Tainan, 461,838.
Government: *President*—Chiang Kai-shek (reelected for 4th term March 21, 1966); *Premier*—Yeh Chia-kan (took office 1963). *Parliament*—Legislative Yüan, 493 members.
Language: Mandarin Chinese (official).
Education: *Literacy rate* (1970), over 80% of population. *Total school enrollment* (1968)—3,465,707 (primary, 2,-383,204; secondary, 770,102; teacher-training, 933; technical/vocational, 150,131; higher, 161,337).
Finance (1968 est.): *Revenues*, $622,000,000; *expenditures*, $729,000,000; *public debt*, $307,000,000; *monetary unit*, New Taiwan dollar (40.10 dollars equal U. S.$1, October 1971).
Gross National Product (1970): $5,427,000,000.
National Income (1969): $3,693,266,800; average annual income per person, $292.
Economic Indexes: Industrial production (1970), 312 (1963 = 100); *agricultural production* (1969), 134 (1963 = 100); *cost of living* (1969), 119 (1963 = 100).
Manufacturing (metric tons, 1969): Cement, 4,088,000; residual fuel oil, 2,247,000; sugar, 689,000; meat, 323,000; crude steel, 271,000.
Crops (metric tons, 1968–69 crop year): Sweet potatoes and yams, 3,445,000 (ranks 3d among world producers); rice (1969–70), 3,041,000; bananas, 645,000.
Minerals (metric tons, 1969): Coal, 4,645,000; salt, 383,000; crude petroleum, 82,000; natural gas, 893,000,000 cu meters.
Foreign Trade (1969): *Exports*, $1,049,000,000 (chief exports, 1967: sugar, $37,795,500; rice, $21,000,000; tea, $10,748,000; petroleum products, $501,000). *Imports*, $1,213,000,000 (chief imports, 1967: nonelectrical machinery, $138,745,600; transport equipment, $69,471,-000; iron and steel, $63,000,000). *Chief trading partners* (1968): Japan (took 18% of exports, supplied 41% of imports); United States (32%—31%).
Transportation: *Roads* (1969), 10,522 miles (16,933 km); *motor vehicles* (1969), 82,300 (automobiles, 39,600); *railways* (1969), 2,754 miles (4,400 km); *merchant vessels* (1970), 1,116,000 gross registered tons; *national airlines*, Civil Air Transport; Foshing Airlines; *principal airport*, Sungshan.
Communications: *Telephones* (1969), 280,192; *television stations* (1968), 4; *television sets* (1968), 193,000; *radios* (1969), 1,428,000; *newspapers* (1969), 37.

support, Taiwan has called for an independent policy that stresses self-reliance. Efforts are being made to strengthen relations with other nations, regardless of their political beliefs. The Nationalists are working under very unfavorable conditions, as several nations severed their ties with Taiwan in the months immediately before and after the UN vote. In November there were 65 governments recognizing Peking, while 56 still maintained diplomatic relations with Taiwan. Even Japan, which voted against Taiwan's expulsion, is seeking better relations with Communist China.

Economy. It is apparent that Taiwan's survival will depend greatly on the state of its economy. With $4 billion in U. S. aid between 1949 and 1960 and continued investment by foreign and overseas Chinese afterward, the Nationalists have succeeded in turning Taiwan's economy from an agricultural into a prosperous industrial one. It has registered an average annual economic growth of 10% since 1962. The gross national product was expected to surpass $6 billion in 1971, 13 times that of 1952. Taiwan's export trade has reached $2 billion, as great as that of the Chinese mainland.

Initial reports for 1971 are encouraging, with the gross national product expected to rise over 11% and industrial growth about 21%. The question, however, is whether Taiwan can continue its economic growth as Communist China applies diplomatic and economic pressure and as more nations break off relations with Nationalist China. Taiwan's industrial momentum and mon-

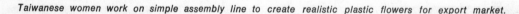

Taiwanese women work on simple assembly line to create realistic plastic flowers for export market.

etary stability are strong assets, but the picture could quickly change with an adverse turn in international relations.

In view of these difficult conditions, Taiwan took a number of economic measures in the aftermath of the UN defeat. To curb economic concentration of exports in the U.S. and Japanese markets, Taiwan decided to expand its trade with Southeast Asia, Africa, and Latin America. It is ready to develop trade relations with countries with which it maintains no diplomatic relations.

Taiwan is reshaping its industrial policy to place a strong emphasis on heavy and sophisticated industries, such as steel and precision machinery. In the agricultural sector, high priority is given to the mechanization of farming as a step toward agricultural industrialization. Efforts are also being made to increase the income of farmers and to lower agricultural production costs. With their usual courage and vitality, the Chinese in Taiwan are determined to ride out the diplomatic storm through continued economic development.

Domestic Politics. The independence movement in Taiwan remains a possible threat to Nationalist China's political stability. Many of the 13 million native-born Taiwanese, descendants of early settlers from the mainland, claim a separate identity from the 2,000,000 mainland Chinese who came to Taiwan in 1949 and have since dominated its politics. The independence movement has its headquarters in Japan and an active branch in the United States. There are defections from the leadership from time to time, but the movement continues. The expulsion of Nationalist China is viewed by some independence leaders as an improvement on their prospects, but Peking's insistence on recovering Taiwan as an integral part of Chinese territory should prove a formidable obstacle. The movement has no effective organization in Taiwan itself; its strength lies rather in the resentment harbored by the politically conscious against the Nationalist rule. While this feeling might explode over some controversial incident, the realization of independence would rely on strong international support, which is lacking.

The international reverses, however, have led to a reform movement on the part of younger people on the island. In a manifesto issued in October, the reformers demanded the simplification of the government structure, by broadening of representation in the legislative bodies, and wider participation of young men in government service. The government, conscious of the need for local support, is willing to go along with the reformers. People are freer now to criticize the government and to voice their demands.

UPI

Chiang Kai-shek (left) *walks with sons, Deputy Premier Chiang Ching-kuo and Chiang Wego.*

Chiang Kai-shek

Chiang Kai-shek, president of the Republic of China in Taiwan, was born in Chikou, Chekiang, China, on Oct. 31, 1887. After a traditional education, he attended a military school in Japan. He rose to prominence in the revolutionary Kuomintang party after Sun Yat-sen's death in 1925. Chiang led the Northern Expedition against the warlords in 1926. After capturing Shanghai and Nanking in March 1927, he purged the Communists, who had been cooperating with the Kuomintang. Chiang became chairman of the Nationalist government in 1928. From then until 1949 he was the supreme leader of China.

Chiang's control, however, was never complete. Many regional leaders were practically autonomous, and the Communists staged armed revolts. When the Sino-Japanese War erupted in 1937, Chiang's policy was to resist the Japanese on the one hand and to contain the Communists on the other. The subsequent eight years of war drained Chinese resources and sapped Nationalist morale, thus offering the Communists opportunities. When Japan surrendered in 1945, armed conflicts between the Nationalists and the Communists resumed. The Nationalist forces proved no match for the Communists, and Chiang was driven to Taiwan in 1949.

In Taiwan, Chiang initiated reforms that resulted in steady economic growth. But Nationalist China's international position deteriorated as more and more countries recognized Peking. The expulsion of the Nationalists from the United Nations in October 1971 was a crushing blow to Taiwan. As the United States moved toward reconciliation with Peking, Chiang called for an independent foreign policy based on self-reliance.

At the age of 84, Chiang appears in good health. He has, however, delegated some responsibilities to his son, Deputy Premier Chiang Ching-kuo, who is rising rapidly as a strong leader.

CHESTER C. TAN

Inmates at Attica prison gesture defiantly in D Yard on September 10. Rebellion's 43 deaths marked it as the most violent prison riot in U.S. history.

The Roots of Attica

Turmoil in the Prisons

"No one, literally no one, really understands what we ought to do with the delinquents and misfits of our society, but the real tragedy is that we are not applying what we do know by way of intensive educational training, of counseling, and of aid after release so that a former prison inmate can make the agonizing adjustments that must be made if the release is not to be followed by a return to criminal activity, as it is so often at the present time."
—Chief Justice Warren E. Burger

By Hans W. Mattick

Prisons are in the news again. The violent eruptions at Pendleton Reformatory in Indiana and at Soledad and San Quentin in California in 1969 and 1970 did not suffice to sound a general alarm about prison conditions. It took the bloody deaths at Attica, N. Y., in 1971 to bring prisons into the forefront of public consciousness.

To those who prefer simple analyses, the recent wave of prison disturbances is the work of a few evil conspirators, outside agitators, and revolutionary militants. Others, seeking simple answers, look to the specific grievances about the prisons affected. Everyone wants to know what it is about imprisonment that causes the inmates and their keepers to be so violent and mutually destructive. The roots of Attica run long and deep.

Yet, to the informed penologist, the only surprising aspect of prison disturbances is that the public should be surprised at the inevitable. The history of U. S. prisons has been a violent one. Usually the violence between guards and prisoners and among prisoners is contained internally. Occasionally confrontations and riots resound beyond the walls and are reported as "news" to a public that would rather forget those defined as criminals and that has maintained the prison system to put them out of sight and out of mind.

It is this invisibility, combined with a "hands off" attitude toward convicts on the part of the courts, that helps to explain the prison conditions that, in turn, lead to deprivation, alienation, and violence. So-called "correctional programs" are chronically underfinanced, are poorly planned and implemented, and rely most heavily on the fact of imprisonment itself, because the public is preoccupied with the apprehension and conviction of criminals—not with what happens to them afterward. Moreover, the prisoners are acutely aware that they have been temporarily banished, and will still be stigmatized as "ex-cons," even after being "treated" and released. This leads to a desperate need to call public attention to their situation and to justify themselves as human beings, and, in the absence of constructive intervention in their lives, a deepening embitterment and desire for revenge.

All of this is not to say that the general and specific conditions of prisons cannot be improved and ameliorated. But there will continue to be prison riots until today's prisons are abolished and a more rational way is found to deal with those who have offended society's laws.

Hans W. Mattick is the codirector of the Center for Studies in Criminal Justice, the Law School, the University of Chicago. He spent seven years in prison work—three as the sociologist at Stateville Penitentiary in Joliet, Ill., and four as assistant warden of the Cook County Jail in Chicago. He is also a past president of the Illinois Academy of Criminology. His books include Action on the Streets: A Handbook For Inner-City Youth Work *(1969) and* Illinois Jails: Challenge and Opportunity for the 1970's *(1970).*

HISTORY AND PHILOSOPHY OF U. S. IMPRISONMENT

In order to understand current prison problems, it is important to view imprisonment in historical perspective. The procedure of locking people up *after* they have been convicted of crime is relatively recent. Until the late 18th century, jails were used to hold people awaiting trial, debtors, and a few political or religious offenders. Facilities for confining the guilty did not exist, except in a few major cities. Rather, the guilty were punished physically or financially.

Early Prisons. Imprisonment of large numbers of offenders for long periods of time was a social invention of the United States, which was responding to new ideas about the futility and brutality of corporal punishment and execution. By 1840 most states had built prisons for serious offenders. Imprisonment was a lesser evil, not a carefully chosen method of dealing with offenders. Only later did penologists begin to seek seriously for positive goals to achieve with prisoners. Reform was buttressed by the religious belief that confinement and contemplation would lead to penitence—hence the name "penitentiary."

Another factor that encouraged imprisonment was the opportunity to profit from prison labor. Since imprisonment was considered humane, prison administrations were shielded from the public scrutiny that had led to criticism of corporal punishments. Brutal, corrupt, and exploitative practices were silently condoned from the very beginning, and it was no accident that economic, rather than human, values played a

major role in early U. S. penal reform. This preoccupation with money values has led to an understandable cynicism among inmates, who see themselves as neglected and exploited.

The second stage in U. S. prison history, from the early 19th century until about 1930, was largely dominated by exploitation. Wardenships were political plums. The labor of prisoners was leased to the highest bidder. Physical abuse, neglect of human decency, and great hardships were the inevitable outcome of this legally disguised form of slavery. Ironically, the major opposition to the system of prison contract labor was economic rather than humanitarian. The business and labor communities, which wanted to sell goods to states, resented convict competition, and the sale of prison-made goods was outlawed.

In this period, some progressive penal administrators, supported by scholars and social critics, began to think that imprisonment should be constructive. If the state was to be justified in depriving a man of his liberty, prison should offer a method of treatment, reform, and rehabilitation. Perhaps the finest early expression of these new sentiments was the famous Declaration of Principles issued in 1870 by the first American Prison Congress, which gave rise to the "New Penology," encouraged the reformatory movement and parole, and set forth ideals for U. S. prisons that they have, for the most part, not yet been able to attain. Unfortunately, the reformatory movement was limited to offenders under 30 and was badly compromised by most of the earlier assumptions, which were embodied in the old maximum-security architecture and still were believed by the staff. Nevertheless, the rehabilitative ideal, which was basic to the New Penology, represented a new direction.

After 1930. Since about 1930, the United States has been in a third stage of prison history. While prisoners are no longer exploited by private contractors, the pendulum has swung too far in the opposite direction. Inmates are often idle, engage in useless make-work, or are exploited by the state. One result of the ban on

SELECTED CHARACTERISTICS OF U. S. JAILS BY REGIONS, 1970[1]

Characteristic	United States	North-east	North Central	South	West
Jails, number	4,037	235	1,178	1,914	710
Percent overcrowded	5.1	13.6	3.4	4.8	5.8
Receiving juveniles	2,822	147	915	1,296	464
In cities (population 25,000 or more) and counties	3,319	226	1,028	1,574	491
Cells, total	97,891	26,365	22,922	34,702	13,902
Percent by age (in years):					
Under 50	74.9	63.7	67.0	82.3	90.5
50–100	19.6	24.1	27.2	15.3	9.5
100 and over	5.5	12.3	5.9	2.4	...[2]
Percent, without selected facilities:					
Educational	89.2	57.1	91.9	92.7	87.2
Recreational	86.4	49.6	91.3	90.5	80.0
Medical	49.0	22.6	46.3	57.3	40.3
Visiting	26.0	11.9	28.6	27.0	24.0

[1] Excludes federal and state prisons, state-operated jails in three states, and facilities that retain persons for less than 2 days.   [2] Represents zero. Source: U. S. Statistical Abstract 1971.

prison contract labor has been the encouragement it gave to "work release" programs, under which prisoners may engage in private employment but must return to prison during nonworking hours. Work release can have important rehabilitative advantages, and it lowers costs.

Rehabilitation is the dominant ideal of U. S. prisons, but it is still more rhetorical than real. Nowhere has it been fully implemented. Some prisons in the more progressive states make serious attempts at educational and vocational training. Experimental programs such as group therapy and machine-programed learning are under way. The prison systems, however, may have waited too long to admit social-science methods. There is a growing doubt, among both penologists and social scientists, of the efficacy of imprisonment as a *means* toward rehabilitation. Most evidence indicates that prisons serve mainly to maladjust men and confirm their criminal careers, rather than to prepare them for a free life; but the traditional prisons survive for lack of an alternative.

Most penologists still believe that minimum-security, community-based institutions can play a constructive role. Since nearly all prisoners must eventually return and adjust to society, only the most extreme cases should be removed from it. Current practice, however, is still to imprison too many offenders, and they are far too often kept in maximum-security prisons for too long.

PRISONS TODAY

Prisons, in the broadest sense, come in many organizational forms and sizes. The term "prison," however, is properly applied only to the large, walled state and federal facilities for adult offenders, usually those convicted of felonies and the more serious misdemeanors. Police lockups, local and juvenile facilities, and specialized institutions are not considered prisons. There are fewer than 500 state and federal prison facilities, while there are more than 700 juvenile institutions, nearly 5,000 local jails, and about 25,000 police and court lockups. Moreover, although (*Continued on page 44*)

Angry prison leaders at Attica debate status of Correction Commissioner Oswald (lower left). Some prisoners wanted to keep Oswald, who was negotiating with them, as a hostage.

WIDE WORLD

Prison Officials Are Frustrated By Neglect and Public Apathy

(Right) *Russell G. Oswald, New York State commissioner of correction, shows strain of events at Attica as he arrives in Albany shortly after uprising. (Opposite page) New Connecticut guards spend part of their training program in inmates' cells to sample life as a prisoner.*

UPI

BY E. PRESTON SHARP
and W. DONALD POINTER

Seldom have administrators in any field been confronted with the complex problems, sweeping changes, divisive issues, and social pressures that currently face those charged with managing U. S. correctional institutions. Prison administrators have suffered from a long legacy of neglect and a continuing lack of public support and understanding. They have therefore experienced persistent frustration in their efforts to plan and implement rehabilitation programs within the constraints imposed by facilities designed primarily for punishment and incapacitation.

The majority of U. S. institutions are monuments to public indifference, dangerously overcrowded, and remote from urban centers. Over half of the large state prisons now in operation were built before 1900, and many are designed to house several thousand inmates. Even effective custodial management of inmates in these massive institutions is difficult. The recruiting and keeping of personnel are severely handicapped by heavy work loads, low pay, and lack of adequate resources. The majority of institutions lack the financial resources to train personnel, who frequently have had little or no preparation for correctional work.

With inadequate funding and a consequent dearth of program resources and trained personnel, rehabilitation becomes an illusory goal. Most administrators are interested in and dedicated to improving rehabilitation programs. Many have pleaded unsuccessfully for years for funds to build smaller, more manageable, and more humane institutions and to staff them with qualified personnel who have the skills and training necessary to change the inmates' attitudes and behavior.

In spite of inadequate financial support, many administrators have been resourceful, inventive, and courageous in the search for new ways to reduce the negative impact of large institutions. They have tried to develop work-release programs, education and training furloughs, community correctional centers, expanded probation services, and other alternatives to incarceration for nondangerous offenders.

Although there have been limited achievements, meaningful and sustained progress in correctional programs cannot occur until there is a major change in public policy, and increased funding wins wide support. Studies by illustrious task forces and blue-ribbon commissions attesting to the crime-producing effects of neglected prisons have accomplished little in the way of increased budgetary and public support. Instead,

Dr. E. Preston Sharp, general secretary of the American Correctional Association since 1965, has held several supervisory positions in the corrections field. He was director of the Maryland Youth Commission (1948–52) and executive director of the Youth Study Center in Philadelphia (1952–65). W. Donald Pointer, associate general secretary of the American Correctional Association, has worked on experimental and demonstration projects to improve U. S. correctional procedures and programs and has been a probation officer.

prison administrators are constantly criticized by a divided and fickle public, one group decrying any effort at rehabilitation as coddling criminals, and another group charging mistreatment and abuse of inmates.

The spread of the radical movements from the ghettos and campuses into the prisons has added a new, explosive ingredient to growing inmate protests over prison conditions. Administrators recognize that revolutionary political ideas have spread among the inmates. Like so many social institutions, but to a much greater degree, the prisons merely reflect the many problems, generated by rapid change, in society at large. Racial tensions, political polarization, and other divisive elements are magnified by the prison environment. Growing militancy on the part of an inmate population that has been radicalized and is violence-prone, predominantly black, and younger and more politically aware than prisoners have heretofore been is a major problem facing administrators.

Most administrators admit that traditional approaches to management and control have been largely ineffective in dealing with inmates who consider themselves "political prisoners" oppressed by a racist society. The proportion of prisoners who are emotionally unstable activists, have been convicted of violent crimes, and have a history of drug use has increased. The older, more intelligent, and sophisticated among them are even more militant, paranoid, and intractable and tend to exert an undesirable influence on the other prisoners. Inmate militancy is further spurred by persons outside the prisons who foster this politicizing and radicalizing process. This buildup of pressures from both within and without has resulted in an unprecedented increase in violence among inmates and between inmates and the staff.

The rise in tension and in the level of violence in the deteriorating, overcrowded facilities, which are manned by undertrained personnel, has created a sense of near-desperation among prison administrators. The degree of this desperation has been intensified by the recent wave of disturbances across the United States. In addition, growing numbers of underpaid prison personnel are organizing to bargain for higher salaries and improved working conditions. A movement to establish prisoner unions to press for better prison conditions has also emerged.

Increasingly, the administrator is caught between formal collective staff pressure on the one hand and inmate pressure on the other. Making the task of the under-budgeted, beleaguered prison administrator even more difficult is the flood of litigation resulting from inmate class-action suits. Court appearances are making increasing demands on administrators, who are forced to meet court challenges without adequate legal support. Prison administrators, confronting a myriad of complicated problems, are struggling with limited support and inadequate resources to protect society and to rehabilitate offenders. Most acknowledge the limited efficiency of prisons as a means of integrating offenders into normal community roles. However, they also recognize that as long as people continue to be confined, society has no choice but to provide for their humane management and to make every reasonable effort to reclaim them.

(*Continued from page 41*)

prisons tend to be larger, some of them holding several thousand inmates, they receive and handle far fewer inmates. For example, at least 3 million people are annually committed to local jails, while state and federal prisons receive fewer than 80,000.

Thus, while this article's concern is with prisons in the sense of state and federal adult institutions, the greater importance of other penal facilities should not be forgotten, nor the fact that they share the same problems. These other facilities are usually far worse, especially the jails and lockups. Inmates are more transient, and there is more political interference in their management.

In general, there are relatively few federal prisons, and on the whole they tend to be better organized and administered than state prisons. There is some doubt whether most states are willing to invest enough to emulate even the modest federal improvements. Since state prisons have the most severe problems, the balance of this discussion will concentrate on them.

Organization of State Prisons. In terms of organization and structure, state prisons tend to be primitively divided by sex and age. Adult men, adult women, and youthful offenders are usually sentenced to separate facilities, as are minor offenders under state jurisdiction rather than local control. In the smaller, rural states, fewer separate facilities can be maintained.

Prisons tend also to be crudely graded as to their degree of security—maximum, medium, and minimum. In general, there are four prisons classified as medium and minimum for every maximum-security one. Moreover, since maximum-security institutions are so expensive to build, they tend to be used long after they are obsolete. Until they are razed, they will continue to exhibit the major problems that defeat rehabilitation: inflexibility, dehumanization, and demoralization.

Prisons also display a large variety of organizational forms, some of which imply specialized treatment. In a recent survey of 398 state penal institutions for adults, 170 were prisons, penitentiaries, or "major correctional institutions," that is, walled prisons, emphasizing

custody and security. Another 55 were reformatories, industrial schools, or vocational institutions with some emphasis on rehabilitation. Fully 148 had a rural orientation, despite the predominantly urban character of their inmates.

Of particular importance are the 170 major prisons, which confine the large majority of prisoners publicly stereotyped as convicts. These prisons are generally too old, too large, over-utilized, and too inflexible in their maximum-security construction to be useful. About 70 state prisons confine more than 1,000 inmates each, and 125 hold more than 500 each. There is general agreement that prisons are increasingly unsafe and unmanageable in direct proportion to their size; penologists have come to the conclusion that no institution should have more than 500 prisoners, and that the optimum size is about 300. It is in the context of the present inappropriate and unmanageable prisons, however, that the current, inadequate efforts at rehabilitation must be judged.

In recent years the population of the adult state and federal prisons has been less than 200,000, with about 80,000 new admissions and discharges a year. The inmates are overwhelmingly male, urban, and under 40. Minority groups are overrepresented, constituting at least one third of the total prison population and 70%–90% in prisons serving metropolitan areas. For this and other reasons, some observers have asserted that there is "a new breed of prisoners" in the prisons and that they are the source of recent disturbances. The fact is, however, that it is the old breed of prison guards and administrators, who have been shielded from social changes, who have to modernize their thinking. Prisoners' concern about civil and social rights is part of a wider movement for equality and justice. As long as prisons do not keep pace, every generation will seem to produce "a new breed of prisoners."

Personnel and Treatment. Prison personnel, even more than inmates or architecture, can influence the quality of penal practice. Of the 50,000 people who work in prisons, less than 10% are primarily concerned with treatment. Nearly two thirds are custodial personnel, and another 25%–30% are administrative or maintenance workers.

Since the ratio of inmates to treatment personnel is so high, only the most serious and obvious cases receive more than superficial attention. Only some of the treatment personnel have the required professional, educational, and character qualifications. The vast majority of security, administrative, and maintenance personnel have few minimum employment standards to meet, which maximizes the opportunity for po-

"Some observers have asserted that there is 'a new breed of prisoners' in the prisons and that they are the source of recent disturbances. The fact is, however, that it is the old breed of prison guards and administrators . . . who have to modernize their thinking."

Firemen extinguish blaze at New Jersey's Rahway State Prison in November. As at Attica, inmates took hostages, but rebellion ended peacefully when Governor Cahill intervened.

litical appointments. The standards for custodial workers are somewhat higher, but seldom exceed a high school education. Low salaries inhibit the recruitment of good personnel. In-service training, without which even the best-qualified personnel may lose touch with developments in penology, is still the exception.

An overview of the actual programs and treatment provided to inmates indicates the limitations of current penal practice. Most prisons make a serious effort to meet the basic needs of food, clothing, and shelter. Health and medical services are substandard but can meet emergencies. Academic and vocational instruction is frequently available but is insufficient to meet needs. Some recreation is usually available, but it is primarily indoor and passive. There is usually not enough work for the inmates, and much of it is useless make-work. Moreover, labor laws requiring that prison-made goods be sold only to nonprofit or tax-supported agencies limit both the amount and the rehabilitative value of prison industries. Finally, many states provide some kind of individual counseling, group therapy programs, or job placement service. But there is only one psychologist, social worker, or counselor for every 200 inmates, and some states do not meet even that ratio.

Prisoner Costs. In 1965 a survey of 398 state correctional units revealed that they cost $384,000,000 to operate, or about $2,000 per inmate per year, not counting capital expenditures. Over the past 50 years there has been a steady increase in the proportion of convicted persons placed on probation. Since a probation officer with a salary of $10,000 supervising 50 men can save a state about $90,000 a year, the economic motive is again contributing to penal reform. As more judges have become aware of the recidivism rate (rate of "repeating" criminals) in prisons, and as the public has become increasingly disillusioned with the efficacy of imprisonment, there has been a greater tolerance for community-based treatment. Unfortunately, the economic motive is more concerned with saving money than saving men. Probation officer case loads are often over 200, which makes probation supervision less effective and perpetuates the myth of imprisonment as the safer alternative.

The major U. S. prisons do not protect society from its criminals, do not deter criminals, do not reform, and do not rehabilitate. Rather, imprisonment serves two other functions. For the prisoners, it substitutes official neglect and abuse for private vulnerability and crime, and it confirms them in criminal careers. For society, it creates the illusion that rehabilitation is being accomplished. Although society and prisoners share an ardent desire for constructive action on prisons, nothing will be accomplished until the means are appropriate to the ends.

SOME PRISON REFORM MEASURES

Reforms that respond to immediate conditions, like the demands that tend to surface during prison riots, are useful but also superficial,

UPI

Oakland mourners give black power salute as casket of George Jackson passes under Black Panther banner. Jackson was shot on August 21 during attempted escape from San Quentin Prison.

for they are addressed to symptoms rather than causes. The first principle that must be established and realized is that criminal justice is a unified process. Every stage in the criminal justice process has important consequences for every other stage. A change in criminal law affects police activity and everything else in the criminal justice process. Unless officials fully realize the links within the criminal justice system, much that masquerades as reform will be mere tinkering, or the alleviation of obvious symptoms of limited importance.

Effective reform may involve measures that seem far removed from the prison gate, but that does not mean that they will not have a significant impact on prison problems. The traditional "solutions" are those announced by the New

Penology in 1870, calling for more and better staffs and facilities. For the most part, these recommendations are still relevant, but at worst they have been resisted by entrenched recalcitrance inside the criminal justice system, and at best have been neglected by a bored public. The more enlightened criminal justice officials and administrators have increasingly sought ways to resolve this dilemma of resistance to social change, while beginning to fashion substitute facilities, such as half-way houses.

Proposed Reforms. Without detracting from the importance of such reforms, it is clear that something more fundamental is required. A beginning must be made in criminal law reform. The range of human conduct defined as illegal has a direct relation to the number of prisoners.

There is hardly a maximum-security prison warden who does not agree that 50%–75% of the inmates do not require maximum security. Similar sentiments are expressed by superintendents of medium- and minimum-security institutions, who wonder why most of their inmates are not on probation or otherwise under supervision. Entirely too much human behavior that could be dealt with otherwise is defined as criminal. The criminal justice system is a poor instrument for dealing with the consequences of social and economic deficiencies.

The criminal justice system, including the police, the courts, and the prisons, is overloaded with the task of handling "crimes without victims." Human behavior that does not involve the use or threat of violence, or fraud, or attacks against property should, insofar as possible, be removed from criminal law. The "revolving-door drunk" is the classic example, but the gambler, the drug user, the sexual deviant, and the vagrant are other likely candidates. The criminal law has had these problems in its province for a very long time without much visible impact, and prisons actively contribute to these forms of social deviance. It is time to turn them over to health and social welfare agencies.

Such criminal law reform must be supplemented by procedural and administrative reforms designed to divert large numbers of persons at every stage of the criminal justice process. This is not simply a proposal to turn criminals loose on the community. It is a plea for more careful screening of cases to determine which persons can appropriately be released, consistent with public safety. Where these procedures have been tried, they have been found to be equal or superior to unnecessary custody. Beginning with a stricter application of the criteria for arrest to reduce some marginal input into the system, the overload in the pretrial stages can be reduced through (1) use of summons rather than arrest, (2) greater reliance on release on one's own recognizance, and (3) lowest possible bail.

At the posttrial level the overload may be reduced by (1) more use of suspended sentences, (2) greater resort to graded fines payable on the installment plan, (3) expanded use of more adequate probation, and (4) partial confinement in a community-based halfway house. Finally, even the impact of imprisonment can be moderated by sentences that permit work-release, incentive furloughs, and early parole. In every appropriate case, all forms of custody should be avoided.

Such a program of law and procedural reforms would go a long way toward reducing the overload of the criminal justice system. It would also enable the prisons to deal more rationally with the reduced prison population. Clearly, such reforms would require a redistribution of personnel and more adequate allocations for the health, education, and welfare agencies that would take on an increased work load. To be really effective, the reforms should include the systematic physical destruction of the older prisons. As long as prisons resemble zoos, they will continue to produce animals.

"On the line," Texas prisoners work in hot sun under watchful eyes of mounted guards. Many penologists criticize such programs because they have no rehabilitative value and create resentment among inmates, who feel that they are being exploited.

PHOTOGRAPH BY DANNY LYONS © 1968 MAGNUM PHOTOS

An Eyewitness Report On Five Terrible Days at

ATTICA

N. Y. State Senator Dunne pauses outside Attica after he was denied permission to speak to prisoners following rebellion.

THE NEW YORK TIMES

BY JOHN R. DUNNE

The long-neglected issue of penal reform was unexpectedly thrust upon the consciousness of the American public when 43 people lost their lives in a 5-day insurrection at Attica prison, in upstate New York, in September 1971.

The tragic ending to the worst prison revolt in U. S. history came early in the morning on Monday, September 13. Under cover of potent riot gas, state troopers rushed into the prison and opened fire on a group of inmates who had been holding 38 hostages at knifepoint for four days in the now-infamous D Yard of the maximum-security prison. As a result of the assault, 10 hostages and 29 inmates died. Three inmates and one guard had died earlier at the hands of inmates during the uprising.

In the heated public debate that followed the incident, some argued that the troopers should have been sent in sooner to put down the unlawful insurrection. Others argued that it was senseless for the troopers to go in at all, at least in the absence of proof that hostages were being massacred. Still others insisted that an appearance at the prison by New York Gov. Nelson Rockefeller might have resulted in a peaceful surrender by the inmates.

But no matter what their point of view, outraged citizens, many for the first time, began to ponder the social consequences of a poor penal system. They demanded explanations as to why the system, not only in New York but throughout the country, was in such a sad state of disrepair. Some of their questions were to be answered by

John R. Dunne, a New York state senator from Garden City, Long Island, was a member of the observers' committee during the Attica uprising. He has been in the forefront of the prison reform movement in New York and has introduced legislation calling for a more efficient criminal justice system. Senator Dunne is chairman of the New York State Senate Committee on Crime and Correction.

two investigations of the Attica incident, one by a congressional subcommittee and the other by a special committee selected by Chief Judge Stanley Fuld of the New York Court of Appeals. In addition, a New York State Select Committee, appointed by Governor Rockefeller, was charged with recommending specific prison reforms to the 1972 Legislature.

The Riot. The incident that gave rise to the public outcry began after several weeks of increasing tensions between correction officers and inmates, many of whom had been transferred to Attica following their participation in the New York City riots in 1970. On Thursday, September 9, a group being marched from breakfast back to their cells in A Block suddenly turned upon the correction officer escorting them. The prison alarm was then sounded, touching off rioting throughout the institution.

During the next half hour, rampaging inmates gained control of virtually the entire prison, seizing 38 hostages, including some civilian employees. In the process, they set fire to parts of the prison, broke through locked gates, using radiators as battering rams, and fatally injured William Quinn, a

48

generally popular correction officer. Quinn, who was beaten severely, was released by the prisoners to correction officials but died in the hospital two days later.

Aided by reinforcements who had responded to the alarm, correction officers brandishing tear gas canisters quickly regained possession of most of the prison, forcing the remaining 1,200 rebels—about half the Attica population—into D Yard with their blindfolded hostages.

New York State Commissioner of Correction Russell Oswald—who less than two months earlier has urged dissident inmate leaders at the prison to give him time to implement changes—went into the yard Thursday, but was unsuccessful in persuading them to give up their hostages.

On Friday, Saturday, and Sunday, a series of meetings to discuss inmate demands was held between the rebels and a committee of "observers" whose presence was requested by either the inmates or state officials. In addition to this author, the committee included, among others: Tom Wicker, columnist for *The New York Times;* Congressman Herman Badillo; Sen. Robert Garcia and Assemblyman Arthur Eve, members of the New York State Legislature; radical lawyer William Kunstler; and Clarence Jones, publisher of the *Amsterdam News.*

All but two of the inmates' demands—which included better medical care, more religious and political freedom, and better food—were acceptable to Commissioner Oswald. But he could not agree to the demands for amnesty and for the removal of the Attica superintendent, Vincent Mancusi. It had been hoped that the appearance by Black Panther leader Bobby Seale at the prison on

Saturday night would help resolve the conflict, but the rebellious inmates held out for their last two demands.

By Sunday, the mood had become uglier in the yard, and there were threats against the lives of the hostages, each guarded by an inmate whose announced intention was to slash his victim's throat at the first sign of reprisal by officials. In the last 20 hours of the insurrection, two desperate attempts were made to try to avoid the inevitable result. On Sunday afternoon, four observers pleaded in vain with Governor Rockefeller to come to the prison to talk with observers. And on Monday morning, Commissioner Oswald made a final written plea to the inmates. "Negative," came the reply from D Yard.

A few minutes later, the assault began.

Conclusions. The real test of Attica will be whether current public concern for penal reform is translated into meaningful change. Penal reform advocates have been arguing for several generations that society is the only loser if a prison system fails to rehabilitate its inmates, because an unrehabilitated inmate, upon release from prison, will often commit another, more vicious, crime against society.

President Nixon, long before the Attica incident, had instructed Attorney General Mitchell to convene the country's leading penal experts at a National Conference on Corrections in Williamsburg, Va., in December 1971. The conference produced many forward-looking ideas that, it is hoped, will be implemented. The President's decision to call such a conference is one good sign that penal reform will be taken more seriously in years to come.

Radical lawyer William Kunstler of observers' committee speaks to Attica inmates on September 11. Observers failed to reconcile differences between state officials and convicts.

UPI

New Funding, Legal Reform Offer Hope

By ARTHUR NIEDERHOFFER

The U. S. prison system, itself a prisoner of archaic facilities and rigid traditions, is striving to break free from the dead hand of the past. For centuries the prison has been a place of grief and degradation. Currently, there are two significant developments that offer hope of improvements: adequate financial support and sweeping judicial reform.

The infusion of millions of dollars into the correctional system for research, demonstration, and training projects is guaranteed nationally by the Law Enforcement Assistance Administration (LEAA), established in 1968. At state and local levels this program is administered by the state criminal justice planning agencies.

On the legal front, a radically new policy has emerged to permit court review of correctional administration. In 1971, a federal appeals court decision declared that a prisoner was not completely stripped of his rights and that he could legally challenge a warden's action. The prisoner, an inmate of a New York prison, was awarded damages because the warden wrongfully placed him in solitary confinement for over a year. In the past, there had been little precedent for such intervention since the courts considered the warden's decisions a legitimate exercise of administrative discretion. Moreover, imprisoned felons, deprived of most of their civil and constitutional rights, were almost automatically denied the legal standing necessary to become a court complainant.

The major new programs that are making an impact upon corrections can be divided into three main categories: (1) Programs to improve the physical structure and the organization of prisons; (2) Programs to give the staff professional training and rehabilitate the inmates; (3) Programs using innovative methods and theories.

PRISON STRUCTURE

The increase in the number of prisoners and the deterioration of ancient institutions have made it necessary to build new prisons. Prisons at Leesburg, N. J., and Lucasville, Ohio, reflect the contemporary idea that prisons ought not to obliterate human dignity. It is a sad commentary on the U. S. penal system that these two are possibly the only U. S. prisons that conform to the moderate standards for correctional institutions set in 1966 by the American Correctional Association. The recent establishment of a national clearinghouse for criminal-justice architecture at the University of Illinois may help to improve this bleak record.

Halfway Houses. Because of the dismal failure of large institutions, forward-looking administrators have grasped at the promise of the halfway house. In these smaller units prisoners and probationers reside in the community under supervision. Although halfway houses are predominantly occupied by juveniles, about 300 of them serve some 4,500 adult convicts. Enthusiastic supporters of the halfway-house experience claim high rates of successful rehabilitation.

A more penetrating appraisal, however, discloses certain built-in flaws. Typically, older buildings are bought or leased for these houses, and are ill adapted for correctional requirements. Well-qualified staff are difficult to recruit, which

Arthur Niederhoffer, a former police lieutenant in New York City and an attorney, is a professor of sociology at the John Jay College of Criminal Justice, City University of New York. He is the author of Behind the Shield *(1967), a study of police in urban society, and coauthor of* The Ambivalent Force *(1970) and* The Gang *(1958).*

NUMBER AND PERCENT OF U. S. JAIL INMATES NOT CONVICTED, BY AGE AND REGION[1]

(Data for March 1970)

Region	Total	Adult inmates			Juvenile inmates		
		Total	Not convicted[2]	Percent not convicted	Total	Not convicted[2]	Percent not convicted
Total, U. S.	160,863	153,063	77,921	50.9	7,800	5,158	66.1
Northeast	31,458	26,526	13,648	51.5	4,932	2,684	54.4
North Central	29,209	28,226	14,654	51.9	983	816	83.0
South	61,655	60,330	31,797	52.7	1,325	1,152	86.9
West	38,541	37,981	17,822	46.9	560	506	90.4

[1] Excludes federal and state prisons, state-operated jails in three states, and facilities that retain persons for less than 2 days. [2] Not-convicted inmates include persons held for other authorities, those not yet arraigned, and those arraigned and awaiting trial. Source: U. S. Dept. of Justice, 1970 National Jail Census.

Model facility at Leesburg, N.J., is a medium-security prison that has been praised for its modern design and relative openness. Glass-walled dining area links housing units and is raised for view of landscape. Prisoners' cells (right) are comfortable, but still secure—window louvers do not permit a head to pass through.

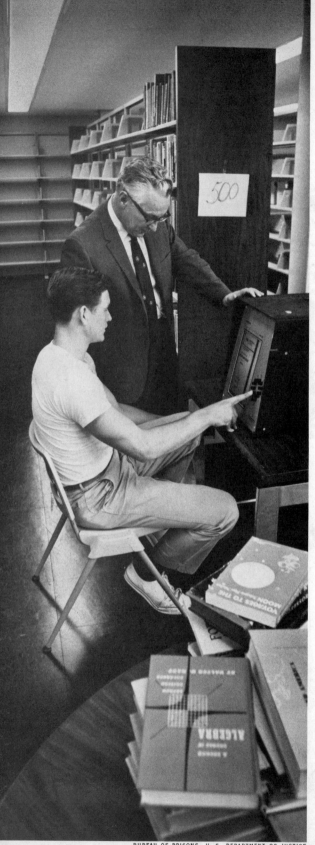

Federal youth center in Morgantown, W. Va., uses innovative materials, such as teaching machines (above), *to rehabilitate offenders.*

exacerbates morale and custody problems. These strains, often complicated by community antagonism, do not encourage a favorable prognosis.

The Therapeutic Community. Corrections has borrowed from the psychiatric hospital the concept of the therapeutic community, whose premise is that development of a sense of community through staff-inmate cooperation is the best preparation for outside life. Along with this goes a program of gradually increasing inmate responsibility and frequent group therapy. Since a prison is not a hospital, however, a prisoner does not react to treatment like a psychiatric patient. The California Youth Authority is in the vanguard of those using this approach. Other agencies have been reluctant to try it because its results have not been demonstrably superior.

Self-Government. The system of self-government used in the penitentiary at Walla Walla Wash., is an interesting and controversial variation of the therapeutic community idea. With administrative cooperation, the prisoners have adopted a constitution and have elected a council that has real responsibility in governing the institution. In addition, a furlough program permits inmates to visit their families who live near the prison.

It is axiomatic that any program that may contribute to the inmates' sense of their own dignity and encourage peaceful cooperation by them is desirable. Predictably, the presence of families and the right of conjugal visits will reduce sexual tension and lower the threat of homosexual assault. But it is unrealistic to expect that a period of self-government in the artificial prison environment will adequately rehabilitate people for life outside prison.

PEOPLE-ORIENTED PROGRAMS

Staff-training programs have rapidly multiplied across the country, with the aim of giving correctional personnel professional training. Several universities offer undergraduate and advanced degrees in correctional administration. However, correctional personnel often resist training programs because they are fragmented, poorly taught, and almost irrelevant to corrections officers' actual experience and needs. A hopeful new development to overcome these justified objections is the proposed National Corrections Academy, a center for correctional training, research, and policy development that will be under the Federal Bureau of Prisons.

Group Therapy. Disappointed by traditional treatments, correctional authorities have turned to group therapy and some of its popular variations. Group pressures do affect individual participants powerfully, although the dynamics are not completely understood. Unfortunately, the lack of trained leaders, the members' cynicism, and the prison milieu greatly lessen the probabilities of desirable character or personality changes.

Education and Training. A constant theme in corrections is academic and vocational education. For the most part academic education is a mockery, and vocational training is no better— few institutions even pretend to give inmates realistic preparation for outside jobs. Nonetheless, the economic gain and the possible rehabilitative effect have made prisoner work one of the most popular correction and rehabilitation theories.

The strategy of releasing prisoners for work outside and having them return to the prison afterward was utilized as far back as the era of chain gangs. It was only a brief step to the work-release programs, now authorized in two thirds of the states. Sensible and attractive in principle, the plan has been disappointing in practice. In institutions permitting work release, only 3% of the prisoners participate. The overriding obstacle is the refusal of the business world to hire prisoners, and it will require a forceful campaign to convince employers to change this policy.

The correctional system itself has been obliged to use prisoners as workers in many capacities, ranging from menial tasks to para-professional work in conducting group therapy. Ex-prisoners assist probation and parole officers in supervising their charges. These ex-convicts have a rapport and empathy with other former prisoners, and hence, it seems, are able to exert a beneficial influence on them. Behind this apparent reversal of tradition lie the difficulty of recruiting well-qualified professionals and the austere budgets that limit salaries at a level where they are unattractive.

The released prisoner, unemployed and desperate, often tries to find a solution to his problems by committing a new crime. In many large cities ex-offenders have organized to provide support for each other. In New York City, the Fortune Society provides counseling, job training, and a temporary "security" base to men just out of prison.

INNOVATIVE METHODS AND THEORIES

Early diversion, sometimes called community-based corrections, has become a favorite theory of the experts. In essence, it means keeping convicted defendants out of prison as much as possible and permitting them to function within their communities under supervision. It requires, in addition to increased probation and parole services, a variety of facilities such as halfway houses, residential treatment centers, and drug

THE NEW YORK TIMES

Women prisoners in New York City exercise in dance class that is part of school curriculum offered to inmates.

clinics. Evaluation studies of these projects have in the main been favorable.

One source of strength has been the increased cooperation between correctional institutions and the academic community. Intern programs at prisons are common and particularly favored by the behavioral sciences, and a number of psychological and sociological theories have been applied to corrections.

Differential Treatment. For some time, the best correctional systems have relied on central reception centers to diagnose and classify new prisoners. Unfortunately, the lack of resources prevents individual courses of treatment, except in a few institutions. Individual treatment is available in California, which tests, classifies, and assigns young prisoners to a special regime designed for each of the nine types suggested by the Grant Interpersonal Maturity Scale. At the Robert F. Kennedy youth center in West Virginia prisoners are divided into four groups on the basis of the Quay Typology, and cottages are designated for each group.

Conclusion. Obviously, these new programs are designed to achieve important goals—to care for the physical and mental health of the prisoners, to permit the individual to retain a sense of dignity, and to provide educational and vocational opportunities. But what about rehabilitation? Can the best correctional institution, once it releases a prisoner, prevail against the personal, cultural, and social forces that produce crime and criminals? That is the persistent problem facing the prison system.

everybody's going

Camping

Spurred by increased leisure time and the availability of a variety of handsome recreational vehicles, some 32 million Americans went camping in 1971. The new breed of campers toted along a vast assortment of equipment that provided them with most of the comforts of home . . . but in the National Parks, the swarm of visitors has created some familiar problems—traffic jams and pollution.

KOREN

By NORMAN STRUNG

Economics and the great outdoors make strange bedfellows, but by all accounts it is the changing economic patterns in the United States that seem in large part responsible for the sudden boom in the popularity of camping across the country. In the mid-1960's the trend toward automation and greater production efficiency created more leisure time for the average American workers. This increased spare time, combined with the attraction of inexpensive, mobile living and the sudden national awakening to the word "environment," provides a partial explanation of the camping boom in 1971, when an estimated 32 million men, women, and children took their places at campfires throughout the nation.

The impact of this unprecedented interest in camping has been staggering. On summer weekends campgrounds near all the great U. S. cities are jammed to capacity by Friday evening. At the height of the tourist season, roads in the underpopulated West stream with camping vehicles that have journeyed from thousands of miles away. Road signs on superhighways inform the

traveler not only of the availability of gas, food, and lodging but of campgrounds as well.

Campsites are springing up all over the countryside. The Woodall Publishing Company, publishers of a digest of campgrounds, lists more than 17,000 public and private campgrounds in the United States. These campgrounds contain nearly 710,000 campsites. And the Woodall list, which includes only those campgrounds meeting special requirements, might well double in length if the so-called "unimproved" campsites on public and private grounds were included.

Camping in the 1970's has come a long way from the bough beds, canvas lean-tos, and prim-

Norman Strung, a veteran outdoorsman, is the author of several books on modern camping and the pleasures of life in the wilderness. Educated at Montana State University where he has since taught literature and writing, Mr. Strung presently runs a Montana guiding service called "High Country." His latest book, Camping in Comfort: A Guide to Modern Outdoor Vacations (1971), was coauthored by his wife, Priscilla.

itive living conditions endured by outdoorsmen of earlier generations. Modern camping features comfort as its keynote.

The latest camping equipment incorporates the ultimate in outdoor ease and convenience. It includes easy chairs that can be blown up and then deflated into fist-sized packages; portable camp kitchens that contain a stove, a refrigerator, lights, and a space heater, all powered by a single propane tank; tents that pitch themselves, using a series of spring rods activated by a touch of the camper's hand; small portable generators to provide electricity in the wilderness; disposable sleeping bags; and sleeping bags designed to maintain preselected temperatures.

While much of camping's appeal lies in its economy—a family of four can purchase the basic equipment for less than $200—the big trend is toward bigger and better accommodations and more luxurious equipment. A tent camp, complete with a fair sampling of modern appurtenances for four, can cost as much as $1,000. Motor homes, the ultimate in recreational vehicles, can run as high as $20,000. But modern campers are willing to pay the price. It is estimated that in 1971 the new breed of vacationers spent over $1 billion in pursuit of comfortable living in the great outdoors.

Many Americans who are unaccustomed to the hardships of the backwoods are now hitting the road. The old concept of camping as a purely rigorous, outdoor pastime has undergone some radical revision. While a campfire was once the exclusive partner of the hunter, fisherman, and explorer, it now casts its flickering glow on the faces of retired senior citizens, touring vacationers, and young families on a weekend outing.

This broadening market, with its demands for "all the comforts of home," has created a variety of new industries bent on catering to the camper and coddling him. In terms of sales, the recreational vehicle is the basic unit of the fastest-growing of the new enterprises.

HOMES ON THE ROAD

Recreational vehicles, known as "recvees," have been in use since the 1930's, but in the period 1961–71 saw a phenomenal growth in their manufacture and use. In 1961 the total output of all classes of recvees reached 83,550 units. By 1971 an estimated 513,800 units were produced, and retail sales were well over $1 billion. It is further estimated that more than 3 million recvees are in use on U. S. highways today.

The recreational vehicle is an apt symbol of the new type of camping. It is compact, comfortable, mobile, and relatively expensive. The vehicles fall into five broad categories, each suited to a particular taste and situation.

Truck Caps. The truck cap is merely a wood and aluminum shelter mounted on the bed of a pickup truck. The most mobile of all the recvees, it offers a place to get in out of the weather and eliminates the need of pitching a tent at every stop. Since it adds very little weight and bulk to a truck, it is popular with hunters, fishermen, and others who get far off the beaten path. About 80,000 were sold in 1971.

The investment required for a truck cap is not great. The average price was estimated at about $325 in 1971, but this is somewhat misleading, since the buyer must first have a truck to carry the cap. Prices on suitable carriers run from $3,000 to $4,500.

Camping Trailers. The camping trailer is essentially a collapsible home on wheels. On the road it is towed behind a truck or car and resembles a wide, flat box. To set it up, one turns a crank, raising the roof. On the inexpensive models, canvas walls blossom out in the manner of a tent. The higher-priced units incorporate solid telescoping walls, usually made of plastic.

Camping trailers boast a wide range of accommodations. The least expensive units, selling for as low as $500, offer little more than beds for four persons and a table. Trailers in the $3,000 price range have beds for as many as six, a complete kitchen, thermostat-controlled heat, and a self-contained toilet.

Because the camping trailer is relatively light, it tows easily and can negotiate rough, back-country roads with ease. These qualities and its low cost make it popular with sportsmen and young families on a limited budget. Total sales in 1971 were estimated at 97,500 units.

Truck Campers. The truck camper is available in two designs. One type slides into the bed of a pickup truck, the other is bolted directly to the truck frame. The slide-in camper is far more popular since it can be removed from the truck with little effort, thereby affording the owner the use of a second vehicle around town.

Truck campers are the second most popular class of recvees, with sales reaching about 105,000 units in 1971. Both truck and living accommodations ride on the same wheels so that the owner can travel through rough country and tote a trailered boat. Minimum-convenience truck campers sell for as little as $1,000. Average prices in 1971 approached $2,000.

Accommodations in truck campers usually include beds for as many as six, controlled heating, a complete kitchen, and plenty of storage space. A self-contained unit of a toilet, shower, and holding tanks for sewage is usually optional. The increasing demand for the self-containment feature underlines the trend toward total camping comfort.

COLEMAN CO., INC.

Light, compact equipment has spurred camping boom. Portable stoves, unbreakable utensils, and comfortable tents have made "roughing it" a lot easier.

Travel Trailers. The travel trailer is the most popular of all the recvees. Approximately 180,000 units were sold in 1971. Towed by a car or truck, it is a solid-walled vehicle. Modest 16-foot models accommodate beds, heater, table, and cooking facilities. Such amenities as a bathtub, stereo tape system, and complete living room are commonly found in the big 28- to 30-foot luxury models.

Most travel trailers are self-contained, boasting a shower, toilet, holding tank, and hot and cold running water. This feature, combined with easy removal from the towing unit for trailer-free wandering, partially explains the immense popularity of the vehicles—especially with older campers and retired citizens. Prices on travel trailers start at about $1,600 and may reach $17,-000 for large, luxury models. The average retail price is slightly below $3,500.

Motor Homes. The motor home, a solid-walled shelter built onto a truck or bus chassis, is the ultimate in modern camping. It differs from the truck camper and travel trailer in that the driver is under the same roof as his passengers. Motor homes boast the plushest appointments of all. They offer self-contained plumbing,

their own electrical generators, and even food freezers and dishwashers as optional equipment.

Motor homes are the most expensive of the recvees, with average prices exceeding $10,000. Although they had the lowest estimated volume of sales for 1971 (50,600 units), sales of these vehicles showed the greatest gain of all recvees in 1970, with an increase of 31.2% over 1969.

Also included in the category of motor homes are the small *motor vans*. These are less expensive than the large motor homes. They also easily convert back to everyday use, since the appliances can be unbolted and removed.

COMMERCIAL CAMPGROUNDS

Although the manufacture of recreational vehicles is the largest industry geared to the new breed of camper, it is not the only business attempting to meet the outdoor tourist's demands for comfort and convenience. The commercial campground is a new feature on the scene.

Facilities. Unlike campgrounds maintained by state or federal agencies or campgrounds on private lands, the commercial campgrounds are privately owned businesses. Travelers can pull

(*Continued on page 60*)

Wide Range Of 'Recvees' Spark Boom In Camping

TRAVEL TRAILER

Most popular recreational vehicle, or "recvee," the travel trailer can be hauled by car or truck. Most are self-contained, with cooking, washing, and toilet facilities.

TRUCK CAP

Inexpensive and simple, truck caps provide basic shelter. The wood or aluminum frame is mounted on the bed of a pickup truck. They are popular with hunters and fishermen.

MOTOR HOME

Luxurious motor homes are built on a truck or bus chassis. Driving area leads directly into living quarters, which can be as comfortable as in a house.

INTERNATIONAL HARVESTER

TRUCK CAMPER

Camper units either slide on truck bed or are bolted to its frame. They offer sleeping accommodations, kitchens, and ample storage.

MOTOR VAN

Pop-up tops give some vans greater head-room. Since accessories are easily removed, these vehicles can be quickly converted back to everyday use.

VOLKSWAGEN OF AMERICA

CAMPING TRAILER

When being towed, relatively inexpensive camping trailers look like a flat, wide box. At a campsite, however, their expandable roof and sides make them into a roomy home.

COLEMAN CO., INC.

(*Continued from page 57*)

into these "camping motels" and hook up to a system of central sewage, water, and electricity. Virtually all commercial campgrounds provide laundry and recreational facilities, and the better sites offer swimming, riding, golfing, and fishing in stocked ponds. Some luxury sites have restaurants and entertainment.

Campground Chains. Chains of these commercial ventures now stretch from coast to coast. Campers can call ahead to their next stop before they leave their current campsite. At the height of the vacation season, the best campgrounds are often filled to capacity by 1 P.M., and a camper without a reservation might have to suffer the ultimate inconvenience of spending a night in the woods. Nightly fees at the campgrounds range from $1.50 to $7.00 for a family of four.

CAMPING ABROAD

Camping in foreign lands has become a popular extension of the new American pastime, and tourists from the United States are flocking to Canadian, Mexican, and European campgrounds in record numbers. Realizing the profits to be made from the boom, foreign countries are seeking to attract the modern-day gypsies.

Canada. Canadian campgrounds multiplied tenfold between 1966 and 1971. The number of parks now totals 2,766, and campsites 153,418. In addition, U.S. commercial chains have established themselves across the border. As a special convenience, Canadian public campgrounds (called provincial campgrounds) include a sheltered cooking compound so that travelers do not have to break out their camp kitchen.

Mexico. Mexico is slightly behind Canada in the development of its public facilities, but several U.S. chains are establishing a network of commercial campgrounds between the border and the Mexican interior at intervals of about 200 miles. Currently, private campgrounds number about 155, and campsites more than 5,000.

Mexico has begun a unique service to woo the camper from across the border. Two-man teams of mechanics called "green angels" drive in green trucks in search of campers who need directions, gas, or even free mechanical aid.

Europe. Camping in Europe has long been more than a leisure pastime—it's a way of life. As a result, campers from the United States are discovering a pleasant and inexpensive way to tour the Continent at approximately half the cost of the standard hotel-restaurant tour.

However, the American abroad has some adapting to do. Conveniences like trailer hookups are not common and, in general, facilities are not quite so comfortable as those back at home. Perhaps the greatest cultural shock of all occurs when the typical Yankee looks for a fireplace. Europeans are not nearly as endeared to the crackle of a campfire as their American cousins, and many campgrounds ban fires outright. Another difficult compromise for the American camper abroad concerns his beloved recvee. In some countries the size of a trailer is severely limited. Most European roads are too narrow and winding for the average camper or trailer, so the tourist must make do with the more conventional tent and the minibus, the most popular European recvee.

But the American campers have proved themselves adaptable. Several European car manufacturers are offering the vacationers attractive benefits if they buy their camping transportation from them. Benefits include credit for a used vehicle sold through their U.S. dealers and free transportation for the vehicle back home.

Commercial campgrounds in Europe charge from 80 cents to $3.00 per night. Tourists need a camper's *carnet* in order to be admitted to most of the campgrounds. The *carnet*, a card that functions as a credit card and a passport, is available at those campgrounds where they are required and, in the United States, through the American Automobile Association (AAA).

'The idea that flowered at
Yellowstone'

By George B. Hartzog, Jr.

In 1972, the 100th anniversary of the establishment of Yellowstone National Park, the United States and the world will observe the centennial of the national park idea.

Yellowstone became the world's first national park on March 1, 1872, when President Ulysses S. Grant signed the bill into law. When Congress approved this legislation, it did more than create a park. The action represented the beginning of an entirely new policy of public-land use, a policy that incorporated the concept that certain outstanding natural resources should be protected from private exploitation and set aside in perpetuity "as a pleasuring ground for the enjoyment and benefit of the people."

Since the founding of Yellowstone, the national park movement has spread around the world. In 1971 more than 1,200 national parks or equivalent reserves existed in some 93 countries, while the National Park System of the United States had 284 units comprising more than 30 million acres devoted to the nation's natural, historical, and cultural heritage, and to recreation.

NATIONAL PARK CENTENNIAL

To ensure that the 100th anniversary of the establishment of Yellowstone would be observed in an appropriate fashion, Congress established a 15-member National Parks Centennial Commission to provide planning leadership.

Looking to the Future. The commission decided at the outset to emphasize the second century of the parks idea rather than oversee a traditional birthday party focusing on the past. Thus, one of the major features of the centennial will be a National Parks Symposium conducted by the Conservation Foundation of Washington, D. C. The symposium, whose participants will be drawn from a broad spectrum of the American public, will concern itself with developing a basic statement of park philosophy for the coming century as well as pinpointing problems connected with the parks and suggesting solutions.

The Second World Conference on National Parks is another major event planned for the centennial. It is to be held at Yellowstone and Grand Teton national parks on September 18–26 and will have some 500 delegates from around the world in attendance.

PROBLEMS IN THE PARKS

As the first century of the national parks came to a close, the National Parks Service was grappling with problems undreamed of when Yellowstone was established. Attendance continued to rise, and over 200 million visitors jammed into the parks in 1971. This figure represented an increase of 100% over the past decade. It is estimated that by 1980 visits to the National Park System will approach 300 million. While this national enthusiasm for the parks is gratifying, the record-breaking attendance presents many new problems that must be solved if quality park experience is to be available in the years to come.

Not only are the parks becoming crowded, but the nature of the typical park visitor is changing as well. Generally he comes from urban areas and is unfamiliar with either the opportunities or the potential dangers of the natural environment of the parks.

Traffic and Pollution. Perhaps Yosemite National Park in California presents the best picture of the problems faced by the National Park Service and the steps it is taking to solve them. More than 2.5 million tourists visit Yosemite each year, and most of them are crammed into the 7 square miles (18 sq km) of Yosemite Valley. On the busiest summer weekends, as many as 55,000 persons may visit the valley. As a result the valley roads are frequent-

(*Continued on page 63*)

George Benjamin Hartzog, Jr., has been the director of the National Park Service of the U. S. Department of the Interior since 1964. He was educated at Wofford College in Spartanburg, S. C., and American University in Washington, D. C., and served with the Department of the Interior for almost 20 years before becoming associate director of the National Park Service in 1963. As director of the Service, he has endeavored to accommodate the growing number of visitors to the parks without harming the natural environment.

NATIONAL PARKS OF THE UNITED STATES

(Date of establishment as national park is given in parentheses.)

Acadia, Me. (1919). Rugged coastal area on Mount Desert Island (highest elevation on Eastern seaboard), picturesque Schoodic Peninsula on mainland, and half of Isle au Haut, exhibiting spectacular cliffs; 41,642 acres.

Arches, Utah (1971). Extraordinary products of erosion in the form of giant arches, windows, pinnacles, and pedestals; 82,953 acres.

Big Bend, Texas (1944). Spectacular mountain and desert scenery enclosed in the great bend of the Rio Grande; variety of unusual geological structures; 708,221 acres.

Bryce Canyon, Utah (1928). Amphitheaters filled with a countless array of fantastically eroded pinnacles of vivid coloring; 36,010 acres.

Canyonlands, Utah (1964). Geological wonderland of rocks, spires, and mesas, rising more than 7,800 feet; extensive petroglyphs made by Indians about 1,000 years ago; 337,258 acres.

Carlsbad Caverns, N. Mex. (1930). Largest underground chambers yet discovered; a series of connected caverns with countless magnificent and curious formations; 46,753 acres.

Crater Lake, Oreg. (1902). Lake of unique blue in heart of once-active volcano; surrounding multicolored lava walls are 500 to 2,000 feet high; 160,290 acres.

Everglades, Fla. (1947). Largest remaining subtropical wilderness in conterminous United States; extensive fresh- and saltwater areas, open Everglades prairies, mangrove forests; abundant wildlife including rare and colorful birds; 1,400,533 acres.

Glacier, Mont. (1910). Superb Rocky Mountain scenery, with numerous glaciers and lakes among the highest peaks; forms part of Waterton-Glacier International Peace Park; 1,013,101 acres.

Grand Canyon, Ariz. (1919). Most spectacular part of the 217-mile-long Grand Canyon of the Colorado River, deepest of the river's canyons; 673,575 acres.

Grand Teton, Wyo. (1929). Series of peaks constituting the most impressive part of the Teton range; includes part of Jackson Hole; winter feeding ground of largest American elk (wapiti) herd; 310,442 acres.

Great Smoky Mountains, N.C.–Tenn. (1934). Loftiest range east of the Black Hills and one of the oldest uplands on earth; diversified and luxuriant plant life, often of extraordinary size; 516,626 acres.

Guadalupe Mountains, Texas (authorized 1966). Mountain range of Trans-Pecos Texas, including highest peaks in the state; features tremendous earth fault and lofty peaks; not yet open to the public; 81,077 acres.

Haleakala, Hawaii (1961). Dormant volcano, with large and colorful crater in which grows a species of the rare silversword; interesting birdlife; 27,283 acres.

Hawaii Volcanoes, Hawaii (1916). Impressive, active volcanic areas on the island of Hawaii; luxuriant vegetation at lower elevations; rare plants and animals; 229,616 acres.

Hot Springs, Ark. (1921). Forty-seven hot mineral-water springs, used in the treatment of certain ailments; 3,535 acres.

Isle Royale, Mich. (1940). Forested island, largest in Lake Superior, and surrounding islets; distinguished for its wilderness; timber wolves and moose herd; pre-Columbian copper mines; 539,341 acres.

Kings Canyon, Calif. (1940). Mountain wilderness dominated by two enormous canyons of the Kings River and by the summit peaks of the High Sierra; 460,330 acres.

Lassen Volcanic, Calif. (1916). Unusual exhibits of volcanic activity; principal theater of Modoc Indian War, 1872–73; 106,934 acres.

Mammoth Cave, Ky. (1941). Interesting caverns, including spectacular cave onyx formations and river 360 feet below surface; 51,354 acres.

Mesa Verde, Colo. (1906). Most notable and best-preserved prehistoric cliff dwellings in the United States; 52,074 acres.

Mount McKinley, Alaska (1917). Mt. McKinley, highest mountain in North America; large glaciers of the Alaska Range; caribou, Dall sheep, moose, grizzly bears, and other wildlife; 1,939,493 acres.

Mount Rainier, Wash. (1899). Mt. Rainier, with the greatest glacial system of any peak in the United States; dense forests and flowered meadows; 241,992 acres.

North Cascades, Wash. (1968). Wild alpine region of jagged peaks, mountain lakes, glaciers, plant and animal communities; 505,000 acres.

Olympic, Wash. (1938). Mountain wilderness containing finest remnant of Pacific Northwest rain forest; active glaciers; Pacific shore; 896,599 acres.

Petrified Forest, Ariz. (1962). Extensive natural exhibit of petrified wood; Indian ruins and petroglyphs; portion of colorful Painted Desert; 94,189 acres.

Platt, Okla. (1906). Numerous mineral- and fresh-water springs, including bromide waters; showy foliage in spring and fall; 912 acres.

Redwood, Calif. (1968). Coast redwood forests containing virgin groves of ancient trees; 40 miles of scenic Pacific coastline; 56,201 acres.

Rocky Mountain, Colo. (1915). Includes Trail Ridge Road, giving views of the Continental Divide; 107 named peaks over 11,000 feet high; wildlife, camping, and 410 square miles of the Rockies' Front Range; 262,191 acres.

Sequoia, Calif. (1890). Great groves of giant sequoias, among the world's oldest living things; magnificent High Sierra scenery, including Mt. Whitney, highest mountain in conterminous United States; 386,863 acres.

Shenandoah, Va. (1935). Outstanding portion of Blue Ridge Mountains with Skyline Drive on crest; vistas of historic Shenandoah Valley; 193,537 acres

Virgin Islands, Virgin Islands (1956). Tropical island area rich in plant and animal life; prehistoric Carib Indian relics; 14,419 acres.

Voyageurs, Minn. (authorized 1971). Beautiful northern lakes and forests; interesting geology and history; 219,431 acres.

Wind Cave, S. Dak. (1903). Limestone caverns in scenic Black Hills, decorated with peculiar boxwork and calcite crystal formations; 28,059 acres.

Yellowstone, Wyo.-Mont.-Idaho (1872). World's greatest geyser area, with about 3,000 geysers and hot springs; spectacular falls; canyons of the Yellowstone River; first and largest national park; 2,221,773 acres.

Yosemite, Calif. (1890). Mountainous regions of unusual beauty; contains Yosemite Valley, nation's highest waterfall, and three groves of giant sequoias; 761,320 acres.

Zion, Utah (1919). Colorful canyon and mesa scenery; phenomenal shapes and landscapes created by erosion and faulting; 147,035 acres.

(Continued from page 61)

ly choked with cars whose presence in the park contributes to a worsening smog problem and denies the visitor a true wilderness experience.

To eliminate the unseemly congestion, the Park Service has taken steps to separate the visitor from his car. In 1971, traffic control was initiated in the park for the first time. Private vehicles are now barred from the Mariposa Grove and from the eastern end of the valley. Today, a free tram service provides visitors with a quiet, guided tour of the Mariposa Grove. In the eastern end of the valley, the visitor must leave his car in a parking lot. He may then tour the beautiful area in a free shuttle bus. Or he may walk, ride a horse, or travel by bus. The remainder of the valley road system has been converted to one-way traffic, allowing the visitor to enjoy the scenery without worrying about on-coming traffic.

The Generation Gap. It was at Yosemite that the parks' problems with the "generation gap" were exposed during the well-publicized confrontation in Stoneman Meadow on the Fourth of July weekend of 1970. For some time the park had experienced an influx of large numbers of young people whose values and life-styles contrasted radically with those of the more "straight" older visitors. Among these youths were some militants who deliberately provoked trouble.

In the Yosemite confrontation, park rangers fought more than 400 young people in the eastern end of the valley. The Rangers, who were not trained to handle civil protest tactics, found that new techniques of law enforcement had to be learned.

The ranger staff has since been given special training in riot control. A U. S. park policeman has been added to the Yosemite staff to provide professional advice, and extra rangers and park policemen are detailed to the park on holiday weekends. Park regulations are strictly enforced. As a result, Yosemite is now peaceful, and no further major disturbances have occurred.

An emphasis on law enforcement, however, is not sufficient to solve the problem of the generations. In the summer of 1971, officials of the National Park Service visited the park and found that there was a communications gap between them and the youthful visitors. As a first step to bridge the gap, Yosemite's interpretative program was strengthened. Fifteen young park interpreters, skilled in dealing with urban populations, were added to the staff.

Today many innovative new programs are aimed at visitors between the ages of 18 and 25, and the Park Service has sought to involve this group in its planning. Young people helped plan and build a new campground for those visitors

S. J. FODERARO

Young visitors enjoy an idle moment on the shore of String Lake, set amid the peaks of Grand Teton National Park, Wyoming. Park offers wide range of facilities.

who lacked cars or could not afford the regular $4 camping fee but were quite willing to pay 25 cents for a walk-in campsite.

Campfire talk programs, broadened to include multimedia shows and no-holds-barred "rap" sessions with rangers, have been increased. Other innovations include float trips down the Merced River and a series of Indian cultural demonstrations.

CULTURAL DEVELOPMENT

The 100th year of the national parks saw increased emphasis on cultural activities throughout the National Park System.

Cultural Parks. The new concept of a national cultural park became a reality on July 1, 1971, with the opening of Wolf Trap Farm Park for the Performing Arts near Vienna, Va., outside Washington, D. C. The park and its beautiful new Filene Center amphitheater drew more than 330,000 persons to an initial season of opera, ballet, symphony, and jazz presentations.

The National Park Service signed cooperative agreements with the National Folk Festival Association and the American Crafts Council. In Washington, D. C., an Art Barn was opened in Rock Creek Park and an "Art on the Mall"

Park ranger pauses on his early morning rounds to chat with admiring children in Yosemite National Park. More than 2.5 million people visit Yosemite each year.

exhibit was held for local artists. The Service cosponsored a series of concerts by the National Symphony Orchestra in downtown Washington and outlying parks.

Environmental Education. During 1971, the Park Service placed new emphasis on its ongoing programs of environmental education, particularly for the nation's children. A grant from the National Park Foundation made possible the publication of elementary school materials for a National Environmental Education Development (NEED) program.

Another phase of the education effort provides National Environmental Study Areas (NESA's) where both school children and adults can learn more about the environment. At year-end, 81 NESA sites had been designated on National Park lands, and more than 50 other sites at other locations.

For the first time in 1971, sites with national landmark significance in environmental education were given formal recognition. Secretary of the Interior Rogers C. B. Morton designated 11 National Environmental Educational Landmarks (NEEL's) during the year.

NEW NATIONAL AREAS

The National Park System continued to expand in 1971, and efforts were made by the government to place parks in and near urban areas.

Parks. Congress authorized the Voyageurs National Park in Minnesota's north country. Arches National Park in Utah, formerly a national monument, gained park status. It thus became the 37th national park. Canyonlands

National Park in Utah was enlarged by nearly 80,000 acres.

Recreation Areas. The easiest, most economical, and most convenient way to travel to many of the national parks is by family car. But millions of Americans, living in the centers of large cities, do not have cars and cannot afford long-distance public transportation. These people, whose daily environment is brick, steel, and concrete, have a desperate need for the personal enrichment that comes with a visit to a national park.

To provide such an experience, the national administration has sought to bring parks to the people. It has proposed the creation of a Gateway National Recreation Area in New York Harbor that would preserve areas of unspoiled beaches and estuaries and provide a superb recreational resource for about 14 million city dwellers in the New York–New Jersey area. The Golden Gate National Recreation Area in California is in the planning stage. It would provide much-needed recreational facilities in the San Francisco area. The Gateway and Golden Gate projects are based largely on the availability of federally owned properties presently in use for military purposes.

The Future. The national parks of the United States, originally designed to preserve spectacular natural resources, have evolved during the past century in response to national needs. The "idea that flowered at Yellowstone" can and must adapt to meet the nation's requirements in the future. The ability to respond to change may prove to be its greatest strength.

Homeless Bengalis jam primitive refugee camp near Krishnagar, India. About 10 million people fled to India to escape the upheaval and strife in East Pakistan.

1971
REVIEW
OF THE YEAR

UPI

(Above) BIZARRE crash left motorcyclist pinned under truck wheel in Tampa, Fla., in October. (Below) Train derailment at 90 miles per hour near Salem, Ill., on June 10 killed 10 persons and caused injury to about 100.

UPI

ACCIDENTS AND DISASTERS

The passage of the Williams-Steiger Occupational Safety and Health Act of 1970, which became effective on April 28, 1971, was one of the most important events in the history of the safety movement and certainly the most significant law ever enacted to protect the employee in the workplace. The legislation will affect over 57 million employees in more than 4 million places of employment and is applicable to all industries affecting interstate commerce, except where a federal agency other than the Department of Labor exercises statutory authority.

The new occupational safety and health act is administered and enforced under the authority of the U. S. Department of Labor and the Occupational Safety and Health Review Commission, a quasi-judicial body appointed by the President. The secretary of labor has the authority to promulgate occupational standards for the avoidance of hazards known to be harmful to personal health and safety. Provisions of the act call for workplace inspections to determine compliance with the law.

Vehicle Safety. In 1970 there were more than 16 million motor vehicle accidents of all kinds, involving 27.7 million drivers and resulting in an estimated $4.7 billion in property damage. Efforts

U. S. ACCIDENT FATALITY TOLL

	1971	1970	1969
All accidents[1]	114,000	114,000	115,000
Motor vehicle	55,000	54,800	56,000
Public non-motor vehicle	21,500	22,000	22,000
Home	26,500	26,500	26,500
Work	14,200	14,200	14,200

[1] Duplications among motor vehicle, work, and home accidents are eliminated in total. Source: National Safety Council estimates.

have increased to improve highways, to tighten safety standards for automobiles, and to maintain programs of recalling vehicles that may have defective parts. The federal government continues to be heavily involved with the problem of reducing automobile accident fatalities and injuries. New standards require that automobiles manufactured after Aug. 15, 1975, have passive protection for all occupants of a car in case of a crash. In cars manufactured after Aug. 15, 1973, an ignition interlock system is required that will prevent the car from starting until the front seat occupants have buckled their safety belts.

Recreational Safety. Americans, with more and more free time, have been expanding their recreational activities and at the same time meeting with new hazards. Efforts have focused on snowmobile problems, and a growing number of states have passed legislation limiting their use.

Another important issue is water safety. The Federal Boating Act, designed to protect the estimated 40 million people who go boating every year, was signed into law in 1971. Between 1965 and 1970, some 7,000 Americans had been killed in boating accidents. The number of drownings, which had been accelerating, reached 7,300 in 1970.

Household Safety. Protection of the individual in his home as a consumer, one of the most important and most neglected aspects of safety, received long overdue attention in 1971. New safety standards were developed and existing ones upgraded for such household products as lawn mowers, flammable fabrics, and safety closure for the packaging of hazardous products. Standards are being developed for other products, including children's toys, infant furniture, and backyard equipment.

HOWARD PYLE
President, National Safety Council

MAJOR ACCIDENTS AND DISASTERS OF 1971

AVIATION

Jan. 18—Bulgarian airliner crashes in heavy fog near Zürich airport, Switzerland, killing 35 of the 37 persons aboard.

Jan. 20—All 31 persons aboard a Peruvian air force plane are killed as it crashes into a mountain near Lima.

April 15—Philippine airliner crashes soon after takeoff near Manila, killing 39 of 40 persons aboard.

May 23—Yugoslav jetliner crashes in northwestern Yugoslavia, killing 78 persons.

May 26—Three jets rehearsing for anniversary celebration of South Africa crash on Table Mountain at Capetown, killing 11 persons.

June 6—U. S. jetliner and Navy jet collide and crash near Los Angeles, Calif., killing 49 persons.

July 3—All 68 persons aboard a Japanese airliner are killed as plane crashes on Hokkaido Island.

July 30—Japanese commercial and air force jets collide over northern Honshu Island; all 162 persons aboard airliner are killed in history's worst air disaster.

Aug. 9—All 97 persons aboard a Soviet jetliner are killed as plane crashes and explodes on takeoff at Irkutsk Airport.

Aug. 18—U. S. helicopter crashes near Nuremberg, West Germany, killing 37 G. I.'s.

Sept. 4—Jetliner crashes into mountain near Juneau, Alaska, killing all 111 persons aboard.

Sept. 28—All 32 persons aboard a Brazilian airliner are killed as plane crashes in Amazon jungle.

Oct. 2—British airliner crashes near Ghent, Belgium, killing all 63 persons aboard.

Nov. 27—All 33 military personnel aboard U. S. helicopter are killed as it crashes off coast of South Vietnam.

Nov. 9—British air force plane crashes off the coast of Leghorn, Italy, killing all 52 persons aboard.

EARTHQUAKES

Feb. 6—Town of Tuscania, Italy, is virtually destroyed by earthquakes; an estimated 20 persons are killed and 5,000 are made homeless.

Feb. 9—Severe earthquake shakes Los Angeles, Calif., killing 65, injuring over 1,000, and causing an estimated $1 billion in property damage.

May 12—Earthquake in area of Burdur, southwestern Turkey, kills at least 100 persons.

May 22—Town of Bingöl in eastern Turkey is leveled by earthquake; about 1,000 persons are killed.

July 8—Earthquake hits Chile's central provinces, killing 90 persons and injuring over 400.

FLOODS, LANDSLIDES, AND AVALANCHES

Jan. 5–7—Flooding in Malaysia caused by torrential rains kills at least 33 persons and causes 114,000 to be evacuated.

Jan. 29—Floods devastate vast areas of northeastern Mozambique; hundreds of persons are feared dead.

Feb. 26—Flash flood sweeps through Rio de Janeiro, Brazil, killing about 100 persons.

March 19—Avalanche in the Andes mountains in Peru causes an estimated 400 to 600 deaths.

April 26–28—Flood waters engulf large sections of Salvador, Brazil, leaving 140 dead and 10,000 homeless.

July 28—Flood and landslide hit Hindu Kush mountains in Afghanistan, killing some 100 persons.

Sept. 9—At least 300 persons are killed as floods hit northern India.

LAND AND SEA TRANSPORTATION

Jan. 3—Truck crashes on bridge in Nigeria, killing 28 persons.

Jan. 11–12—Panamanian tanker collides with Peruvian ship and explodes in the English Channel; 8 crew members are killed as tanker splits in two and sinks. German freighter hits wreckage of tanker and sinks, killing at least 7 crew members.

Feb. 5—Bus crashes into deep gorge in western Iran, killing 30 persons.

Feb. 14—Yugoslav train catches fire inside tunnel, killing 34 persons.

May 10—Bus carrying 100 passengers—some 45 more than capacity—plunges into a reservoir near Kapyong, South Korea, killing 77 persons.

May 24—Commuter bus crashes through guardrail on bridge of the Panama Canal, killing 38 passengers.

May 27—Train carrying 100 children from an outing collides with freight train near Radevormwald, West Germany, killing 45 persons, 40 of them children.

Aug. 28—At least 25 persons are killed as Greek ferry burns off Brindisi, Italy.

Nov. 22—Philippine ferry sinks in choppy seas; 16 persons are killed and at least 90 are missing.

STORMS

Feb. 21—Tornadoes sweep across Louisiana, Mississippi, and Tennessee, killing 93 persons and causing property damage in excess of $10 million.

Aug. 17—Typhoon Rose hits Hong Kong, taking over 100 lives, damaging homes, and sinking or grounding 50 vessels.

Nov. 1—Cyclone and tidal wave strike Orissa state in India, killing at least 10,000 persons.

FIRES AND EXPLOSIONS

Feb. 3—At least 25 are killed and 100 injured in an explosion in a munitions building near Brunswick, Ga.

March 6—Fire in a psychiatric clinic in Zürich, Switzerland, kills 28 patients, all by suffocation.

May 22—Explosion and fire tear through crew's quarters of Norwegian liner *Meteor* of Vancouver, British Columbia, killing 32 crew members.

June 24—Explosion and fire kill 17 workmen drilling water tunnel below Sylmar, Calif.

Dec. 2—Coal mine explosion in Taiwan kills at least 41 miners.

Dec. 11—Gas explosion in a water tunnel being built under Lake Huron in Michigan kills 22 workers.

Dec. 25—Hotel fire in Seoul, South Korea, kills 158.

MISCELLANEOUS

Jan. 2—Crowd barrier collapses at soccer stadium in Glasgow, Scotland, killing 66 and injuring over 100.

Feb. 4—Government exhibit hall under construction in Belo Horizonte, Brazil, collapses, killing at least 63 workmen.

ACHESON, Dean Gooderham

U. S. Secretary of State: b. Middletown, Conn., April 11, 1893; d. Sandy Spring, Md., Oct. 12, 1971.

Dean Acheson was one of the towering world figures of the years immediately following World War II. As the principal architect of foreign policy during that period, he was responsible for a whole series of measures intended to bolster the non-Communist world and to guard against Soviet expansion. Later, some critics argued that these measures had been unnecessary, but Acheson never doubted that his vigorous policy had been right, as he showed in his detailed account of his State Department years, *Present at the Creation* (1969). The

WIDE WORLD

controversy over his postwar policies was only one of many in which he was involved. His self-confident manner, telling verbal style, and caustic wit all invited battle. Assailed by the left for his skepticism about Soviet good intentions, he was also attacked by the right and Sen. Joseph McCarthy for alleged softness on communism.

In the early 1960's he alienated Britons by a ruthless account of their country's diminished status, and in his last years he exasperated many by his condemnation of UN sanctions against Rhodesia.

Earlier Years. The son of the Episcopalian bishop of Connecticut, Acheson went to Groton, Yale, and Harvard Law School. In 1921, after two years as law secretary to Supreme Court Justice Louis Brandeis, he began a connection with an eminent law firm (now Covington and Burling) that lasted until his death.

In 1933, Acheson became undersecretary of the treasury, but he was dismissed after six months because of his expressed dislike of President Roosevelt's fiscal policies. He returned to government in 1941 and, as assistant secretary of state, led the U. S. delegation at the 1944 Bretton Woods Conference. From 1945 to 1947 he served as undersecretary of state and was directly involved in framing the Truman Doctrine and launching the Marshall Plan.

Secretary of State. In January 1949, Acheson began a four-year tenure as secretary of state under President Truman. Acheson's major achievements as secretary were the creation of the North Atlantic Treaty Organization (NATO), rearming West Germany, and handling the diplomacy of the Korean War.

The relationship of trust between Truman and Acheson was most clearly demonstrated when, in 1949, Acheson came under bitter attack from the right for the failure of U. S. policies to prevent the collapse of the Nationalist regime in mainland China. Acheson was firmly supported by Truman, who declared that "communism—not our country— would be served by losing Dean Acheson."

After his retirement from public office in 1953, Acheson frequently served as a presidential consultant. He died suddenly on Oct. 12, 1971.

ARTHUR CAMPBELL TURNER
University of California, Riverside

ADVERTISING

The year 1971 saw advertising grow a respectable 4.8% in dollar volume, despite a sluggish economy. It was also the year when the consumer movement made its presence felt in advertising. The tone of advertising changed, becoming more direct and informational and openly tackling a variety of social concerns.

In other developments, the nationwide nostalgia kick found its way into ads and commercials. Within the business, advertisers and agencies, attempting to trim costs and increase advertising effectiveness, experimented with flexible approaches to compensation and services.

Creative. Advertising in 1971 mirrored two trends in contemporary life. First was the movement toward more honest and informative copy. Faced by consumer pressures and an increasingly educated and skeptical audience, advertisers found fresh and more effective ways to communicate. Increasingly they dealt with controversial social issues —from population control to product quality. Many advertisers—notably in the automobile, appliance, and insurance fields—invited two-way communication with consumers.

The second trend was a flurry of nostalgic themes and executions reflecting a yearning, in the face of pressures and problems, for the remembered simplicity and charm of the "good old days."

Consumerism. Consumer advocates threatened advertising with regulation on the local, state, national, and even international levels. In Canada, for example, all cigarette advertising was banned beginning Jan. 1, 1972. The scrutiny culminated in the fall in extensive hearings by the U. S. Federal Trade Commission into "modern advertising practice," significant in terms of potential long-term influence on advertising.

The advertising industry, after 18 months of preparation, established the National Advertising Review Board, headed by Charles Yost, former U. S. ambassador to the United Nations, a promising effort at industry self-regulation. Meanwhile, the advertising community sought to educate the FTC about the intricacies of the advertising process and its self-regulation.

Advertising Practices. Flexibility in handling the advertising function was sought increasingly in 1971. Profit pressures led some advertisers and agencies to reassess relationships and compensation. Shifting from the traditional total marketing partnership relationships, a few full-service advertising agencies offered their services—from creative and media placement to research and sales promotion— in packages tailored to individual client needs and budgets.

Flexibility was the keynote in compensation, too. A few advertisers assumed responsibility for advertising with in-house capability; some tried to experiment with buying advertising services a la carte from independent suppliers, such as creative "boutiques" and media-buying companies. However, the proliferation of such services slowed significantly.

Media. Government action affected several media in 1971. The U. S. ban on broadcast cigarette advertising that began on Jan. 2, 1971, diverted more than $200 million from radio and TV. Magazines picked up the major portion, and newspapers, Sunday supplements, and outdoor advertising also benefited.

To encourage local TV programming, the FCC ruled that each network must turn over one-half hour of 7-to-11 P. M. prime time to local stations, with resultant loss of network revenue. However, since few local stations could afford to produce programs, most turned to reruns and syndicated shows and also ran more commercials. (For magazine problems, see PUBLISHING—*Magazines*.)

Expenditure. Despite uncertainty about the effects of anti-inflation programs on advertising volume, estimates placed outlays in all media at about $20,435,000,000 for 1971, up 4.8% from the $194,-910,000,000 spent in 1970. TV again led in share of national dollars, with network and spot revenues increasing 8.1% to $3,200,000,000.

Advertising expenditures in magazines rose 4.3% to $1,380,000,000 and in newspapers 8% to $1,095,000,000. National spending in radio remained at the 1970 level of $430,000,000, and spending in business papers held at $750,000,000. Expenditures in all other media—from posters to paperbacks—showed a 3.3% gain to $5,060,000,000. National volume totaled $11,915,000,000 for 1971, or 4.7% ahead of 1970. Local advertising grew 5% to $8,520,000,000. (The figures are Grey Advertising projections based on *Marketing/Communications* official statistics.)

EDWARD H. MEYER
President and Chief Executive Officer
Grey Advertising Inc.

Advertisers turned to nostalgia in 1971 in an attempt to attract customers. At bottom, Ann Miller celebrates Heinz soups in production reminiscent of Busby Berkeley musicals. Ford ad stresses its years of experience, while State Farm Insurance invoked childhood memories to underline continuing concern for its clients.

F-4 PHANTOM jets are assembled at a St. Louis plant. In 1971, West Germany placed an order for 175 of these highly rated fighter planes.

AEROSPACE INDUSTRY

The fortunes of the U. S. aerospace industry continued a 3-year decline in 1971. The nation's manufacturers of space systems, military hardware, and commercial jets felt the multiple impact of the national recession, a reordering of government priorities, the winding down of the Vietnam War, and the growing public challenge to many of its products and its ways of doing business.

The industry increasingly came under criticism for cost overruns, for failure to meet performance requirements of major defense contracts, and for turning out products with an adverse impact on the environment. Industry leaders warned that in cutting back on many advanced technology projects, such as the supersonic transport (SST), the nation was forfeiting its historic leadership in technology.

Sales. According to preliminary year-end estimates, U. S. aerospace industries had total sales of $24.5 billion in 1971, or 4% less than in 1971 and 17% below the industry's peak in 1968.

Employment. Declining sales were reflected in continuing heavy layoffs of aerospace workers. The Aerospace Industries Association said that total employment at the end of 1971 was 940,000—24% lower than the peak of 1,418,000 in 1968.

Engineers and scientists whose training and experience were limited to narrow aerospace specialties were hardest hit by the cutbacks. Congress appropriated $42 million to finance a retraining program for these people, but first reports indicated it had had limited success.

Setbacks. The aerospace industry was affected by several major setbacks. As Vietnam War hostilities lessened, the Pentagon bought fewer aircraft and less other war material. Pressure within Congress to cut defense spending restricted the awarding of contracts. Orders for jetliners almost came to a halt in 1971 because most airlines had ordered new planes in the late 1960's, and a slump in traffic caused by the recession had left them with more planes than they needed. The recession also crimped sales of light planes.

In addition, there were fewer orders for rockets and space satellites, as public enthusiasm for space exploration waned following the first landings of men on the moon in 1969.

SST Killed. Climaxing a bitter 3-year debate, Congress killed the federally subsidized project to develop a supersonic transport that could carry 300 passengers at 1,800 mph. Opposition was led by Sen. William F. Proxmire of Wisconsin and a group of environmentalists, who argued that the craft would disrupt the environment because of its noise and engine pollution in the stratosphere. The Boeing Company, which was building the SST, and General Electric Company, which was developing its engines, did not support subsequent efforts to revive the project, largely because the development costs, they said, would exceed what the government would give them. Two European SST's—the British-French Concorde and the Soviet Union's TU-144, which will cruise at 1,400 to 1,500 mph—continued flight trials and were scheduled to enter airline service in 1973.

Lockheed. The nation's largest defense contractor, Lockheed Aircraft Corporation, moved to the brink of bankruptcy before Congress came to its rescue. After agreeing to take a $200 million loss on the Air Force's troubled C-5A transport, the world's largest plane, Lockheed saw its problems compounded in February when Britain's Rolls-Royce went into receivership. The Rolls-Royce trouble stemmed from skyrocketing costs on its contract to build jet engines for Lockheed's L-1011 TriStar airbus. In a 49-to-48 vote, the Senate agreed to federal guarantees of $250 million in bank loans to Lockheed.

DC-10. The McDonnell Douglas DC-10, which carries up to 300 passengers, entered service in August, joining the Boeing 747 as a wide-body jet.

Space Shuttle. The National Aeronautics and Space Administration moved forward with planning of its space shuttle, which will take off and land like a conventional aircraft but will operate like a spacecraft when out of the atmosphere.

F-14. The Grumman Aerospace Company ran into difficulties in developing the Navy's new F-14 jet fighter. Original construction costs, estimated at $11 million per plane, jumped to $16 million. The Defense Department said that, in policing contracts in the future, it would lean more on a concept used in previous years. This calls for fabrication and testing of prototype planes and development of accurate estimates before production is authorized.

See also AIR TRANSPORTATION; DEFENSE; SPACE EXPLORATION.

ROBERT H. LINDSAY
Aviation Reporter, "The New York Times"

AFGHANISTAN

After three and a half years of relative serenity, Afghanistan gained a new cabinet in May 1971, and the tempo of political activity began to accelerate. Both right- and left-wing elements took to the streets, although there was little violence.

Political Developments. The government of Prime Minister Nur Ahmad Etemadi fell on May 6, following disputes over several constitutional issues. After 17 days of debate, the lower house approved a new 18-member cabinet with Dr. Abdul Zahir as prime minister. It was hoped that the indicated rapprochement between the executive and legislative branches might speed up political and economic development.

Among several positive steps, the Zahir government abolished prepublication censorship of the press and reshuffled top personnel at several ministries in an attempt to break bureaucratic deadlocks.

Guidelines for much-needed bureaucratic reforms were established by a new civil service law. Still to be acted upon late in 1971 were a political parties bill, a provincial councils law, and a municipal elections act. Several political demonstrations occurred during the year despite the fact that political parties were not officially recognized.

Economy. Levels of private and foreign investment rose, but the benefits of this spurt were diluted because of the lagging pace of government-sponsored economic reform. Parliamentary passage of a law authorizing creation of industrial development banks gave promise of a future boost to the economy. Meanwhile, tourism continued its rapid growth, with more than 100,000 visitors arriving in 1971. In August a cola and fruit juice bottling plant, with a daily production capacity of 96,000 bottles, began operations in the capital, Kabul.

Pakistan's withdrawal from circulation of its 500- and 100-rupee notes in June caused a major fiscal crisis in the bazaar, where cash transactions, though illegal, continued to make up a significant part of the Afghan-Pakistani import-export trade.

A second year of severe drought in some areas, plus unseasonal floods in others, caused a great drop in agricultural and livestock production. In the southwest, migratory birds threatened to minimize the experimental "Green Revolution."

International Affairs. In late 1970, a meeting in Kabul of the Council of Ministers for Asian Economic Cooperation and of associate members of the UN's Economic Commission for Asia and the Far East (ECAFE) produced the Kabul Declaration, which emphasized regional development within the framework of an Asian Clearing Union and an Asian Reserve Bank. In 1971, King Mohammed Zahir visited the USSR and the Mongolian People's Republic.

LOUIS and NANCY HATCH DUPREE
American Universities Field Staff

——— **AFGHANISTAN • Information Highlights** ———

Official Name: Kingdom of Afghanistan.
Area: 250,000 square miles (647,497 sq km).
Population (1970 est.): 17,120,000. *Density,* 67 per square mile (26 per sq km). *Annual rate of increase,* 2.3%.
Chief Cities (1970 est.): Kabul, the capital, 292,000; Kandahar, 112,000.
Government: *Head of state,* Mohammed Zahir Shah, King (acceded Nov. 8, 1933). *Head of government,* Abdul Zahir, Prime Minister (took office June 9, 1971). *Legislature*—Shura; House of Elders, 84 members; House of the People, 215 members.
Languages: Pushtu and Dari (Persian) (both official).
Education: *Literacy rate* (1970), 10% of population. *Expenditure on education* (1966), 13.2% of total public expenditure. *School enrollment* (1969)—primary, 500,665; secondary, 99,158; technical/vocational, 6,138; university/higher, 5,680.
Finances (1970 est.): *Revenues,* $81,500,000; *expenditures,* $88,800,000; *monetary unit,* afghani (87.8 equal U. S.$1, Aug. 1971).
National Income (1966): $1,040,000,000; *national income per person,* $69.
Manufacturing (metric tons, 1969): Cement, 180,000; meat, 150,000; sugar, 20,000; woven cotton fabrics, 49,000,000 meters; sawn wood, 715,000 cu. meters.
Crops (metric tons, 1969 crop year): Wheat, 2,401,000; corn, 785,000; rice, 407,000; barley, 365,000; sugar beets (1968), 60,000; cotton (lint), 29,000.
Minerals (metric tons, 1969): Coal, 136,000; salt, 37,000; natural gas, 2,029,000 cubic meters.
Foreign Trade (1969): *Exports,* $71,800,000 (chief exports, 1967, fruits and nuts, $25,780,000; karakul skins, $14,070,000; raw cotton, $7,840,000; carpets, $5,170,000). *Imports,* $124,400,000 (chief imports, 1967, wheatmeal and flour, $12,467,000; machinery and transport equipment, $7,026,000; petroleum products, $5,096,000). *Chief trading partners*—USSR (took 37% of exports, supplied 38.4% of imports); India (21.9%—9.2%); United States.
Transportation: *Roads* (1970), 10,700 miles (17,220 km); *motor vehicles* (1969), 49,000 (automobiles, 30,800); *principal airports,* Kabul, Kandahar.
Communications: *Telephones* (1969), 10,833; *radios* (1968), 375,000; *newspapers* (1967), 20 (daily circulation, 105,000).

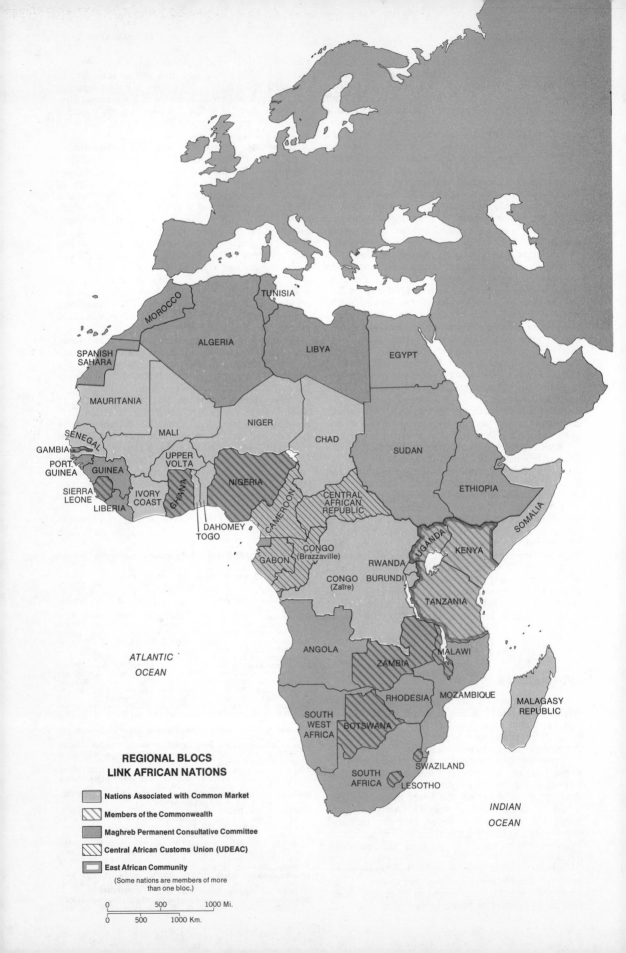

REGIONAL BLOCS
LINK AFRICAN NATIONS

- Nations Associated with Common Market
- Members of the Commonwealth
- Maghreb Permanent Consultative Committee
- Central African Customs Union (UDEAC)
- East African Community

(Some nations are members of more than one bloc.)

0   500   1000 Mi.

0   500   1000 Km.

MOROCCO
TUNISIA
SPANISH SAHARA
ALGERIA
LIBYA
EGYPT
MAURITANIA
NIGER
MALI
SENEGAL
GAMBIA
CHAD
SUDAN
PORT. GUINEA
GUINEA
UPPER VOLTA
SIERRA LEONE
IVORY COAST
GHANA
NIGERIA
DAHOMEY
TOGO
LIBERIA
CAMEROON
CENTRAL AFRICAN REPUBLIC
ETHIOPIA
SOMALIA
GABON
CONGO (Brazzaville)
CONGO (Zaïre)
RWANDA
BURUNDI
UGANDA
KENYA
TANZANIA
ATLANTIC OCEAN
ANGOLA
MALAWI
ZAMBIA
RHODESIA
MOZAMBIQUE
MALAGASY REPUBLIC
SOUTH WEST AFRICA
BOTSWANA
SWAZILAND
SOUTH AFRICA
LESOTHO
INDIAN OCEAN

AFRICA

Various conflicting trends made up the pattern of events in Africa in 1971. Most of these trends were not particularly novel but represented the continuation of tendencies inherited from previous years. There were a large number of coups or attempted coups, which testified to the continuing political instability that has plagued Africa. Some of these events affected relations between African states or with states outside Africa. Several "forgotten wars" dragged on. Here and there, in more fortunate areas, stability and prosperity appeared to be growing.

Some black African leaders, though still a minority, thought the time was ripe to try a policy of "dialogue" with the government of South Africa. The hitherto unproductive policy of encouraging insurrections in white-dominated countries continued, and, as before, there was more rhetoric than results. A major event in southern Africa was the agreement ending the 6-year-long split between Britain and Rhodesia.

POLITICAL TURMOIL

Significant instances of political turmoil occurred in perhaps a dozen countries. In most such states tribal loyalties accentuated political instability. But otherwise there was great variety among the incidents in terms of motivation, success or failure encountered, and policy implications.

Uganda. The government of President Milton Obote was overthrown on Jan. 25, 1971, while he was en route home from the Commonwealth prime ministers' conference in Singapore. A military government was set up under the army commander, Maj. Gen. Idi Amin. President Obote had been losing support for some time. He himself had gained the presidency by a coup in 1966, overthrowing the country's first president, Sir Edward Mutesa, kabaka (king) of the powerful province of Buganda. The kabaka had then fled to London, where he died in poverty in 1969. Obote's rule had been maintained by increasingly repressive measures, and had been marked by the corruption of the ruling elite, a policy of nationalizing all major economic activities, and the threat of a general forced labor program.

President Amin's sharply contrasting policy has been broadly conservative, pro-Western, and specifically pro-British. Nationalization was discontinued, political prisoners were released, and an attack was made on corrupt practices. The repatriated body of the late Kabaka Mutesa was buried with honor on April 4.

The deposed Obote found a haven in neighboring Tanzania. The new government of Uganda was denounced by President Julius Nyerere of Tanzania, President Kenneth Kaunda of Zambia, and other champions of "African socialism." There was confused, small-scale fighting on the Uganda-Tanzania border in July and August. Disputes imperiled the future of the East African Community, which controls a number of common services in Uganda, Kenya, and Tanzania, and led to a withdrawal of Zambia's application for membership.

Sudan. Sudan was the scene of a bizarre sequence of coup and countercoup in mid-1971. The government of Gen. Jaafar Mohammad al-Numeiry was overthrown in a palace coup by a small group of army officers on July 19. But on July 22 the rebellion was suppressed, and General Numeiry regained power. The crucial incident in the failure of the coup occurred on July 22, when Libya forced down the BOAC aircraft carrying the two leaders of the new government from London to Sudan; they and others were later executed by Numeiry. The 4-day rebel regime appeared to have been Communist.

Morocco. The Moroccan monarchy was shaken by a bloody attempt to overthrow it during a birthday party for King Hassan at the Skhirat summer palace on July 10. Although the attempt failed, popular disillusionment with the corrupt administration under Hassan has been growing. The loyalty of the army can no longer be depended on, and the future of the conservative, monarchical regime must be regarded as uncertain.

Sierra Leone and Guinea. Sierra Leone's prime minister, Siaka Stevens, who had declared a state of emergency and assumed extraordinary powers in September 1970, was the target in March 1971 of two attempts on his life and an abortive coup. Stevens has adopted a policy of inviting troops from neighboring Guinea to maintain him in power, and seems on the way to complete dependence on the goodwill of President Sékou Touré. On April 19, Sierra Leone became a republic within the Commonwealth of Nations, and two days later Stevens was sworn in as president. The country's economy grew weaker in 1971, largely as a result of uncertainty stemming from Stevens' policies.

In Guinea, Sékou Touré's regime showed an atmosphere of mounting hysteria and paranoia. The nature of the alleged invasion of Guinea in November 1970 had never been entirely clear. The United Nations had accepted Touré's charge that it was an abortive invasion mounted by the Portuguese and other foreigners. But the invasion was at least as likely to have been an attempt by Guinean exiles to overthrow Touré's dictatorship.

Treason trials, numerous executions, and so-called suicides were common in Guinea in January 1971. The Roman Catholic archbishop of Conakry was sentenced to life imprisonment on charges of aiding the invasion. Touré spoke of threats to his government from a conspiracy of such countries as West Germany, France, Portugal, and Lebanon. In August, he urgently requested UN assistance against an imminent invasion, which failed to occur.

Events in Guinea have obstructed the working of the Organization of Senegal River States, consisting of Guinea, Mali, Senegal, and Mauritania. A conference of the organization's members was held on January 18, but the meeting scheduled for April 20 was canceled because of Touré's failure to attend.

Instability in Other States. Intrigues, abortive coups, treason trials, and other symptoms of political unrest were also seen in many other states, including Chad, Tanzania, Kenya, Mali, and Somalia. The most obscure and curious of these incidents took place in the Malagasy Republic. The ailing President Philibert Tsiranana arrested André Resampa, the second vice president, on June 1 on charges of plotting to overthrow his government in collusion with an unnamed foreign power, supposedly the United States.

"Forgotten Wars." Another aspect of instability in some African states has been the existence of chronic regional insurrections. It has been incon-

THE NEW YORK TIMES

UPPER VOLTA'S Mogho Naba greets Walter Washington, mayor of Washington, D. C., in Ouagadougou. Mossi tribal king has lost power to the modern state.

venient or dangerous for television to cover these neglected conflicts, and therefore, in contemporary circumstances, they have remained invisible to world opinion. Yet they have continued, making settled life a nightmare over large areas, and causing several thousand casualties each year.

Wars of this character continued sporadically in 1971 in Chad, Sudan, and Ethiopia. In Chad it was a rebellion of the Arabs of the north against the dominant black Christian peoples of the south, supported by French troops. There was a lull in the struggle after November 1970, but further fighting followed in 1971. Chadian officials felt that order had been restored in the center and east of the country, but there was little reliable information about the status of the north. The rebels were said to be assisted by Libya, with which President François Tombalbaye broke off relations at the end of August. He had also taken measures in June to conciliate Muslim opinion, such as including Muslims in his cabinet.

In Sudan the situation was reversed. The black peoples of the south have long refused to be ruled by the Arab Muslim majority in the north. The Khartoum government's campaign met with considerable but not final success in 1971, aided by Egyptian and Soviet equipment and advisers. One of the more interesting features of the Sudan situation has been the refusal of the Organization of African Unity to consider the situation, despite several appeals from the rebel leaders.

In neighboring Ethiopia, Emperor Haile Selassie's government still had to cope with the resistance of the Eritrean Liberation Front in the Red Sea province.

Wars maintained by various nationalist groups in the Portuguese African territories might also be classed among these forgotten wars. They have tied down over 100,000 Portuguese troops and caused several hundred Portuguese casualties annually. The Portuguese claim to have killed several thousand rebels.

FRENCH-SPEAKING AFRICA

It would, of course, be incorrect to suppose that all is disorder and instability in contemporary Africa. A good many countries in 1971 showed continuing stability and economic advance. Among

these was the former Belgian Congo. This state, known in recent years as Congo (Kinshasa), renamed itself "Zaïre" in October 1971, after an ancient name for the great river whose basin the country occupies. Under President Joseph Mobutu's rule Congo, or Zaïre, has been relatively stable and has attracted foreign investment.

Probably the most successful group of black African states is that constituted by some of the former French colonies of West Africa. President Georges Pompidou of France visited five of these states— Mauritania, Senegal, Ivory Coast, Cameroon, and Gabon—from February 3 to 13 and was enthusiastically received. The connection between France and most of its former colonies in Africa has remained amazingly strong, and French prestige in these areas has remained very high. The maintenance of the connection has been welcomed by the African ruling elites, themselves testimony to the strength and attractiveness of French culture.

No comparable attitude toward the former imperial power is to be observed in the former British colonial areas in Africa. The contrast may be partly explained by the closer integration with the metropolitan country's political system that the French practiced; in fact, many present-day rulers of the Francophone countries have themselves served as members of French cabinets in Paris.

The Francophone African states have their own 15-member Afro-Malagasy and Mauritius Joint Organization (OCAMM). The 7th summit conference of the OCAMM was held in Fort-Lamy, Chad, on January 29–30, and an unusual number of differences of opinion appeared. These concerned both commercial matters (Senegal withdrew from the sugar agreement and Cameroon from the joint airline, Air Afrique) and the larger question of possibly entering into relations with South Africa.

The smaller group of Francophone states forming the Council of the Entente—Ivory Coast, Dahomey, Upper Volta, Niger, and Togo—also differed on the question of South Africa at their meeting at Ouagadougou, Upper Volta, on May 17. At the council meeting at Abidjan, Ivory Coast, on June 9 they were unanimous in opposing attempts to boycott the new government of Uganda.

THE OAU AND SOUTHERN AFRICA

The proceedings of the Organization of African Unity (OAU) in 1971 were dominated by the attitude to be adopted toward General Amin's government in Uganda and the question of opening a dialogue with South Africa. Both controversies revealed deep splits among the African states.

At the 16th session of the OAU Council of Foreign Ministers at Addis Ababa, Ethiopia, in late February–early March, the friends of the deposed Obote managed to prevent the seating of the delegation sent by General Amin. When the 16th session reconvened on June 11, Amin's Ugandan delegation was seated without opposition. But Uganda boycotted both the 17th council session, which began on June 15, and the heads of state meeting, which began on June 21, because the site of the latter meeting had been changed from Kampala, Uganda, to Addis Ababa.

The main cohesive force within the OAU—a skeptic might say the only cohesive force—has always been opposition to the remaining vestiges of colonialism, mainly found in southern Africa. The policy projected by President Félix Houphouët-

Boigny of Ivory Coast, which would open discussions with South African Prime Minister Johannes Vorster on the modification of apartheid, is therefore a peculiarly explosive one, ideally calculated to separate moderates from radicals in black Africa.

The proposal for a dialogue with South Africa led to a stormy debate at the June OAU foreign ministers' conference. On June 18 the Ivoirien and four other delegations walked out to protest the way in which the proposal was being handled by the conference. The same proposal was debated at the summit meeting. By a vote of 28 to 6, with 5 abstentions, the OAU opposed the opening of a dialogue with South Africa.

Guerrilla Activity. Activity by various guerrilla movements against colonial or quasi-colonial regimes met with mixed success in 1971. There was no progress in Rhodesia. Success was perhaps greatest in Portuguese Guinea, where indigenous forces have been supported by Cuban personnel and Nigerian weapons. In sparsely populated Angola the Portuguese situation was also serious. Angolan guerrillas have been able to operate from bases in Zambia or Congo (Brazzaville). In Zambia the guerrilla fighters have been trained by the Communist Chinese. Guerrillas enjoyed less success in Mozambique, despite efforts to hamper the building of the great Cabora Bassa hydroelectric project.

South Africa. At the Commonwealth conference held in Singapore in January, British Prime Minister Edward Heath adopted a more uncompromising attitude toward the non-white members of the Commonwealth than any British government had previously shown. Over the strenuous protests of President Kaunda of Zambia and others, Heath extorted from the conference an agreement that Britain would be free to use its own judgment in the matter of supplying arms to South Africa. France has all along been supplying South Africa with weapons and ships.

Rhodesia. The anomalous situation that had existed in regard to Rhodesia since its unilateral declaration of independence from Britain on Nov. 11, 1965, appeared about to be tidied up in 1971. An agreement was reached between the two countries on November 24, after a week of negotiations between Rhodesian Prime Minister Ian Smith and Sir Alex Douglas-Home, the British foreign secretary.

The agreement, which represented substantial concessions by both countries, envisaged a sequence of steps by which the black majority in Rhodesia will be able, over a period of many years, to achieve first political parity with the ruling white minority and then (possibly) superiority. The agreement, however, still awaited British and Rhodesian ratification, pending which, British sanctions against Rhodesia remained in force.

ARTHUR CAMPBELL TURNER
University of California, Riverside

AGNEW, Spiro T. See BIOGRAPHY.

SUDANESE army officer Lt. Col. Babakr al-Nur (*right*), leader of abortive coup in July, is questioned by Defense Minister Khaled Abbas before execution.

UPI

President Nixon chats with Nobel laureate Norman Borlaug (*left*) at White House salute to agriculture in May.

agriculture

How agriculture fared in 1971—production trends, scientific developments, and other news—is reviewed in this article. It consists of the following sections: (1) World Agriculture; (2) U. S. Agriculture; (3) U. S. Agricultural Research; (4) Dairy Products; (5) Livestock and Poultry; (6) Grains; (7) Fruits; and (8) Vegetables.

World Agriculture

World agricultural production in 1971 rose substantially from the previous year, but preliminary information available late in the year was so sketchy that it was not clear whether the increase matched the very large gain that was achieved in 1967.

"Calendar 1971 was a bountiful year, especially for grains," says a U. S. Department of Agriculture (USDA) expert charged with monitoring the international farm situation. "In general, good weather prevailed. There wasn't much increase in total planted acreages. So that means per-acre yields were up sharply."

There were exceptions, of course. Civil disorders hampered farm production in Pakistan. War disrupted Vietnam, Laos, and Cambodia. Drought plagued Iran, Iraq, and Afghanistan.

USDA monitors cautiously placed the world increase in 1971 at slightly above 3% over the previous year. If that usually conservative estimate turns out to be accurate, 1971 total world agriculture production would rise to an index number of 157 (1952–56 average = 100). This compares with 151 in 1970 and 121 a decade earlier, according to the United Nation's Food and Agriculture Organization (FAO). A rise of 6 points in this index in 1971 would just about match the 1967 increase that made so many headlines as the "green revolution."

Adding importantly to farm production increases were the agriculturally advanced countries of the West, most of which had cut back output in 1969 and 1970. In those years, world food and fiber production had risen sharply in the less-developed lands. But 1971 was markedly different. Perhaps most significant was the mammoth increase in U. S. crop production to an index number of 113 (1967 = 100), up from 100 in the previous year and above the previous record of 104 in 1969. Production of U. S. livestock products rose substantially, too.

Record grain crops were produced also in Britain and West Germany. Italy produced its largest rice crop. It was clear that world pork production in 1971 reached a record high. Clarence D. Palmby, U. S. assistant secretary of agriculture, said that in 1970 and 1971 production cycles in the United States, Canada, Europe, and other important areas all peaked at the same time.

Preliminary data indicated that Russia's key winter-sown grain crops were in good condition in midyear. China's output is especially difficult to assess, but farm output there appeared to be making rapid recovery from the disruptions of the Cultural Revolution of 1967 and 1968. With no major adverse weather or other bad growing conditions reported, it was assumed that farm output continued to benefit also from announced huge government inputs into agriculture, especially of chemical fertilizers, irrigation, machinery, and new seed varieties.

The FAO late in 1971 issued data showing that 1970 was the third successive year in which continued growth in farm output occurred in the developing countries, while production in the more-developed lands stayed about the same. The FAO's preliminary index of world agriculture production in 1970 was up 2%. Fishery output, growth of which had slowed in 1969, accelerated in 1970, but, since most of the increase was in fish not used for food, the direct impact on the nutritional situation was somewhat limited. Forest production was estimated to have continued to expand slowly.

The index of total world production of agricultural, fishery, and forest products in 1970 was placed at 150 (1952–56 average = 100), up from 147 in 1969 and from 119 a decade earlier. Since the population increase was assumed to be about 2% a year, per capita production did not increase worldwide, and it decreased in some developing lands, especially in Africa and the Near East.

1971 Developments. Although many researchers warned that the so-called green revolution still has not ended the threat of starvation of millions, there was more and more talk about production "adjustments" and the impact of recent farm plenty on exports, imports, and domestic prices. The green revolution refers to development and widening use of new higher-yielding wheat and rice varieties.

Dr. A. H. Boerma, director general of the FAO, said the problem of correcting the "completely unbalanced" state of world agriculture transcends national boundaries. He added that it "covers nearly all the other major problems—the surpluses and unprofitable situations of farmers in the developed countries, and the chances, not only for more trade, but also for increased agricultural production, employment, and purchasing power in the developing ones." The director general appealed to governments to make effective use of existing international organizations, including the United Nations, rather than depending on individual national policies.

The USDA's Palmby, in testimony before a U. S. Senate subcommittee on international trade, made it clear that an economically advanced land such as the United States could be threatened by surpluses, just as well as less-developed countries are so threatened. First, Palmby pointed out that the U. S. agriculture's export market now takes the produce of 70 million U. S. acres out of a total harvested acreage of about 290 million acres.

"It is a matter of very great concern to us that the developed countries of Europe, where we would expect to find our major markets as well as Japan, are following policies which restrict trade growth," Palmby said.

Restrictions, he continued, are most striking in the European Economic Community, made up of France, West Germany, Italy, Belgium, the Netherlands, and Luxembourg. Protectionism also threatens in such other commercially associated groups as the Caribbean Free Trade Area and the Latin America Free Trade area.

The bumper crops of 1971 intensify competition for what seems almost certain to be shrinking international markets. "Even some importing lands have surpluses as the result of 1971's enormous production," says a USDA trade expert.

Canada. Wheat is Canada's most important crop, and 1971 production was huge by any measure, far larger than the 1970 crop that was abbreviated by a drastic 50% reduction in plantings. That cutback stemmed from large surpluses produced in 1968 and 1969. The 1971 increase was permitted because world market demand and prices improved sharply. As a result, the larger wheat exports, along with oilseeds sales abroad, helped boost Canadian net farm income to $1.4 billion in 1971, up 14% over 1970's net.

Canadian poultry production continued to expand in 1971, depressing prices. Cattle slaughter rose, but hog marketings were below the 1970 record. Grain trade with Communist customers continued below the high levels of earlier years, but Canada expanded its wheat sales elsewhere.

Latin America. Increased agricultural production in 1971 helped many lands toward economic recovery. In Mexico, agriculture continued to recover from the 1969 drought, and in 1971 production returned to the 5% average gain of the 1960–68 period. Cotton plantings expanded, but Mexico's cattle supply and beef output continued to be held down because of heavy marketings in 1968 and 1969.

In the Caribbean area, favorable growing conditions produced increased 1971 yields for sugarcane, coffee, and cocoa. Rehabilitation of banana plantings boosted production of that fruit. And increased farm output helped the Central American countries recover from their slumps of the late 1960's.

In South America, Argentina's feed-grain output was at a record high in 1971, and wheat production rose from the low levels of 1970. Cattle production continues at a lower pace, following heavy cattle slaughter in 1969 and 1970 that stemmed from drought-caused feed shortages. Brazil's production of wheat leaped to a record high, but drought cut the corn and rice harvests. Coffee output rose.

Significant recovery of crop production occurred in Colombia. Farm output continued to improve in Ecuador and Peru after the severe droughts of 1968 and 1969. Output of wheat, corn, oilseeds, meat, and milk rose significantly in Uruguay and Venezuela. Farm output slowed slightly in Bolivia and Guyana in 1971, but Paraguay's production gained.

Europe and the Soviet Union. Wheat production recovered sharply in western Europe from the 1970 decline. Output of feed grains established a record high. Production of pork and poultry rose, but beef output remained about the same. With huge expenditures for export subsidies and other subsidized sales, western European lands sharply reduced surpluses of wheat and dairy products.

In eastern Europe, the 1971 production of farm goods was spotty. Only Bulgaria recorded a significant increase in output, and poor weather plagued the other countries in this region, especially East Germany. Plantings of wheat and rye were expanded sharply and good crops were harvested in Rumania, Bulgaria, Yugoslavia, and Hungary.

Livestock inventories in eastern Europe increased in 1971, and numbers of hogs and poultry rose sharply. Except for Poland, cattle and hog inventories rose in all these countries.

In the Soviet Union, meat production rose, especially for pork and poultry. Grain crops may have produced increases even above the record harvest of 1970. The sharp increase in agricultural production in 1970 was due mainly to better weather, and good growing conditions prevailed generally in 1971, too. But a series of continuing favorable government policy changes, in force since 1965, also are contributing to larger production. These changes include guaranteed wage scales and larger bonuses, higher state purchasing prices, and increased investment in fertilizers and machinery.

Africa and West Asia. The Republic of South Africa's wheat crop set a record in 1971. Two other major agricultural producers, Nigeria and Egypt, also showed gains. Millet, grain sorghums, and peanuts were produced in larger quantities in Nigeria.

POLYETHYLENE FILM insulates spring cabbages from unpredictable Russian weather. This Uzbekistan collective farm supplies vegetables to nearby Tashkent.

Cotton output rose in Egypt. A near-record corn crop was harvested in Rhodesia, but there was little change in Africa's major output of its leading export crops—coffee, cotton, and cocoa.

West Asia's major crops are wheat and cotton, and Turkey and Iran produce most of those commodities. Although drought plagued farm output in Iraq and Iran, Turkey's grain production was record high.

Asia and the Far East. Farm production rose substantially in most of the developing lands of the Far East, but government checkreins held down output in the more developed nations, Japan, Australia, and New Zealand. Japan reduced rice plantings by an additional 500,000 hectares in 1971, following a reduction of 350,000 hectares in 1970.

In China, reports revealed that adverse weather in 1971 had hurt farm output. The government there rarely has any farm production statistics. But with the official policy of putting larger investment in agriculture, it is assumed that farm production is robust, even though it was, in 1971, about average and below the record 1970 crop.

Outlook. Even though the new high-yielding varieties of wheat and rice are boosting production in some developing lands, world farm leaders are warning that the green revolution is far from finished and that agrarian reform is essential if social disruption is to be averted.

"Over the entire decade of the 1960's, the trend of food production per head showed virtually no increase in any of the developing regions, and actually fell somewhat in Africa," the UN's Dr. Boerma said in an FAO report in late 1971. An acceleration in food and fiber production is needed, he continued, adding: "Failure to achieve this acceleration in production will mean that large numbers of people will be condemned to continue on substandard diets, that agriculture will be a general drag on economic growth, and that the already acute social tensions in many developing countries will be aggravated."

JOE WESTERN
Kominus Agri-Info Associates

U. S. Agriculture

The enormous productivity of U. S. farmers was demonstrated in 1971 as perhaps never before. Despite another sizable drop in the population of working farmers, agricultural output leaped to record highs.

Production. U. S. farm production of crops and livestock reached an index number of 113 (1967 = 100), far above the previous year's index of 100, and up from the previous record of 104 in 1969.

The main reason for the sharp production increase was that new federal legislation, enacted in 1970, gave farmers more freedom to plant wheat, soybeans, and feed grains. Beef herds continued to expand in response to continued high prices and to consumer preference for beef over poultry and pork, even though the poultry and pork were less expensive. Pork output rose because farmers overproduced animals; as a result, prices fell and slaughter ensued as a means to cut losses.

U. S. farm production was so huge that political Washington was astir with concern that the staggering surpluses might again become an issue as it had been in the late 1950's and early 1960's. Of greatest concern was the mammoth 1971 corn crop of nearly 5.6 billion bushels, up from 4.1 billion bushels in the previous year—a fantastic 31% increase. That increase of 1.3 billion bushels was nearly as large as the entire U. S. wheat crop in some years. The previous record-large corn crop was nearly 4.8 billion bushels in 1967. Early planting, favorable growing weather, and unexpectedly small damage from the Southern corn leaf blight, which devastated part of the 1970 corn crop, accounted for the huge increase. Too, in trying to offset the feared damage from the blight, many farmers increased corn plantings. Corn yield per acre was 86.6 bushels, up from the blighted 71.7 bushels in 1970, and up from the previous record of 83.9 in 1969.

Total production of corn and the other three feed grains, oats, barley, sorghum grain—the four constitute the major raw materials for meat and milk production in the United States—totaled a record 202 million tons. This was 29% more than in 1970, and almost 18% above the previous record of nearly 175 million tons in 1969.

Record production occurred in many crops besides corn and feed grains. Wheat output of more than 1.6 billion bushels ran 18% more than in 1970 and 3% more than the previous record in 1968.

Output was record high also for soybeans and peanuts, pushing total oilseed production, which includes cottonseed and flaxseed, to a high of 42.5 million tons, 5% more than the previous record in 1970.

Hay production at 131.1 million tons set a record, up from the previous peak of 127.9 million tons in 1970.

The index for per-acre yield for 28 leading crops was calculated at 110, up from 102 in 1970, and up from the previous peak of 107 in 1969.

Crops planted in 1971 covered 303 million acres, the most since 1960 and 13 million acres more than in 1970. Feed-grain acreage rose almost 8 million acres, with most of the increase in corn. Plantings expanded also in wheat and rye.

Livestock and poultry production was placed at an index of 107, bettering the previous high of 106 in 1969. Most of the increase was in pork, with beef and chicken output about the same as in 1970 and lamb and veal production down from the previous year. Milk production was up about 1% above the 117.4 billion pounds of 1970. Egg output rose a bit over the previous year's total of 195.3 million cases. The 1971 turkey crop totaled nearly 118 million birds, about 2 million more than in 1970 but 8 million fewer than the 1967 record crop.

Production of red meat in 1971 was estimated at about 4% more than the 36.2 billion pounds in 1970. To produce that much meat in 1970 required the slaughter of 35.3 million cattle, 4.2 million calves, 87 million hogs, and 10.8 million sheep and lambs. Nearly 3 billion broilers and 116 million turkeys provided most of the country's poultry meat in 1970.

Consumption. An increase of nearly 1% in U. S. per capita food consumption occurred in 1971. This pushed the index 6% higher than in 1965. The index for 1971 was placed at 103.5 (1967 = 100).

Nearly all the increase over 1970 was attributed to food from animal sources, primarily meats. Pork consumption advanced the most. Large gains in per capita consumption of red meat and smaller increases for fruit, potatoes, eggs, cereal products, and vegetable oils outweighed decreases for poultry, vegetables, melons, coffee, fish, and animal fats. Poultry consumption, although down slightly, remained close to the level of the previous year, as slightly larger turkey supplies almost offset a dip in supplies of chicken.

Americans ate about 192.2 pounds of red meat in 1971, up from 186.3 pounds in the previous year. Of the total, 113.6 pounds were beef, down a bit from 113.7 pounds in 1970; and 72.7 pounds were pork, up sharply from 66.4 pounds in 1970.

Employment. The index of farm wage rates (1967 = 100) rose to a new high of about 133 in 1971, up from 127 in 1970. Wages averaged $1.50 an hour, a rise of about 8 cents from 1970. The farm labor force declined to about 4 million, a drop from 4.5 million a year earlier.

Assets and Land Values. The market value of farm real estate on March 1, 1971, totaled an estimated $214 billion, up $5.8 billion from a year earlier and $11 billion more than in 1969. The value of agricultural assets, as of Jan. 1, 1972, including crop and livestock inventories, was estimated at $332.8 billion, up from $318.4 billion the previous year. Liabilities were estimated at $66.3 billion, leaving $266.5 billion in equities.

Exports. For the fiscal year ending June 30, 1971, exports of U. S. farm commodities for cash, credit, and donations reached a record of about $7.8 billion, up from about $6.6 billion in the previous fiscal year and 14% more than the previous record in the fiscal year ending in mid-1967.

Most of the gain was for hard-cash sales to developed nations, led by western Europe, Japan, and Canada. Demand for U. S. food and fiber expanded in these lands in response to rising economic activity, reduced grain supplies, and a continued increase in livestock production.

Late in 1971, the Soviet Union agreed to buy about 3 million tons of U. S. grain, mainly corn but including barley and oats, worth about $135 million, by July 1972. It is the first such agreement by the USSR to buy U. S. grain in several years.

Income. Gross farm income increased to about $58.7 billion, up $2 billion from the 1970 total. Because prices that farmers paid for the means of production rose again, expenditures totaled about $43 billion. So farmers' realized net farm income may match the 1970 net of $15.7 billion.

This was below the 1969 net of nearly $16.8 billion and below the record high of $17.1 billion in 1947. But because the number of farms continued to decline, net income per farm rose to $5,400, up from $5,374 in 1970 but still below the record of $5,654 in 1969.

Cash receipts from livestock marketings topped the previous year's $29.6 billion. And receipts from crop marketings were 10% larger than in 1970. But government payments fell to about $3.2 billion from $3.7 billion in the previous year. The drop in these direct payments to farmers was attributed mainly to smaller outlays to feed-grain producers, many of whom ignored the government's offer to pay them to grow trees, grass, and other conserving crops instead of corn, wheat, and other grains.

The per capita personal income of the farm population from all sources set a record of about $3,000 in 1971, up from $2,832 in 1970. Income from nonfarm sources again rose faster than income from farm operations.

10-Year Comparison. Late in 1971, the U. S. Department of Agriculture reported on an analysis of the previous decade's farm income structure and found "significant" changes.

"For example," the report said, "in 1970, farms with sales of $40,000 or more made up 8% of all farms, yet accounted for over 52% of cash receipts from farming and over 36% of realized net income. In 1960, this same group of farms made up only 3% of all farms, had 33% of cash receipts, and 18% of net income."

The study noted that nonfarm income of farm operators exceeded farm-derived income by a substantial amount. Average net income from farming in 1970 was $5,374, compared with income from off-farm sources at $5,833. Put another way: nonfarm income provided farm operators with 52% of their total income. A decade earlier, farmers' net income from farming operations averaged $2,962, and from nonfarm sources, $2,140; in 1960, nonfarm income provided farmers with only about 42% of their total income.

JOE WESTERN
Kominus Agri-Info Associates

U. S. Agricultural Research

The Agricultural Research Service (ARS), principal research agency of the U. S. Department of Agriculture, directs research and regulatory and control programs responsive to the nation's needs. During 1971, ARS placed added emphasis on research affecting some of the critical issues of the day, such as devising ways to protect the environment from pollutants and developing more in-depth knowledge of foods and nutrition. ARS was also active in protecting animals and plants from disease, developing new consumer and industrial products, and overseeing humane treatment of animals.

Disease Research. A new kind of disease-producing particle, smaller than a virus, was isolated and identified by ARS scientists. Named a viroid, the infectious particle causes potato spindle tuber. It has taken over 50 years to find the causal agent of this disease. The discovery may have implications in the elusive nature of some human diseases, such as multiple sclerosis, infectious hepatitis, and some types of cancer. Many plant and animal diseases whose causes have eluded scientists may also be caused by viroids.

Waste Disposal. ARS scientists made progress in recycling agricultural wastes into useful products. They found that high pressure steam processing of wood chips made clean wood fibers for hardwood plus a liquor that could be concentrated for use as a molasses substitute in cattle feed. Also, since cattle use only 40%–60% of the energy in the feed they eat, barn wastes can be blended into rations to make further use of the remaining nutritive value.

As part of the general effort to make ruminant animals such as cattle more efficient users of materials that man cannot eat, ARS scientists found that newsprint and molasses could partially replace hay. Overall, newsprint did not appear to have any adverse effects on the steers studied, and it was discovered that about 8% of the animal's daily intake can serve as roughage.

Nutrition. Nutrition studies continued on trace elements which appear to be essential for good health in man. Nickel may soon join copper, iodine, iron, zinc, and others on the list of these nutrients. ARS scientists produced symptoms of nickel deficiency in chicks, indicating that this trace element may be essential to good health. Chromium may provide the solution to a frequent health hazard of old age—the body's failure to use carbohydrates efficiently. Small amounts of chromium added to the diet restored normal carbohydrate utilization in some diabetics, middle-aged and elderly people, and undernourished children—where chromium deficiency had existed.

Preliminary results of an ARS study evaluating current human nutrition research in the United States found that many of the health problems underlying the leading causes of death, such as heart and vasculatory diseases, could be modified by improvements in diet.

Two "new" foods were developed in 1971. Crisp, crunchy apple snacks can be made with explosion-puffed apple pieces, now that a way has been found to retain their crispness, and mushrooms can now be dried and stored, while still retaining their distinctive flavor and color. A near relative of collard and mustard greens, *Brassica carinata*, may one day become available as a tasty new leafy green vegetable for American tables. ARS scientists imported the plant from Ethiopia and are studying it for nutrient content, taste, and yield.

Disease Control. Venezuelan equine encephalomyelitis (VEE), a virus disease of horses and humans, crossed from Mexico into Texas in late June 1971. ARS officials estimated that at least 500 horses died and many hundreds of thousands were exposed to the disease. Transmitted by mosquitoes and possibly other biting insects, VEE can cause mortality as high as 90%. In humans, it usually produces a mild to severe respiratory illness.

A voluntary vaccination program was begun on June 25 in Texas with an experimental vaccine. The experimental label was later removed, and a massive free vaccination program was conducted in 18 additional states and the District of Columbia. For mosquito abatement, U. S. Air Force and commercial planes made ultra-low volume applications of insecticides.

Confirmed hog cholera cases totaled only 418 in fiscal 1971, the lowest year on record. All states were actively participating with ARS in the campaign to eradicate this disease. By mid-1971, 23 states were free from hog cholera.

Pest Control. Nonchemical methods of pest control continued to be explored by the ARS. Although costly—they require insect-by-insect study and a sizable research investment—these techniques meet all the standards of environmental safety. They leave no chemical residue and they pollute no streams. Among the innovations was the use of a parasitic wasp against the alfalfa weevil and the use of the bacterial pathogen *Bacillus thuringiensis* against several insects. Synthetic hormones that interrupt growth processes were also being studied.

Disparlure, a synthetic sex attractant for the gypsy moth, was developed by ARS scientists after nearly 30 years of research. Early tests showed that disparlure is more persistent and more powerful than the natural attractant. It has potential for controlling the gypsy moth by luring it into traps. This insect defoliated nearly 2 million acres (809,400 hectares) of woodlands in the northwestern United States during 1971, and was spreading southward along the Atlantic Coast.

ARS scientists also developed artificial insect eggs. These inexpensive eggs—less than $5 per pound—will help scientists rear large numbers of aphid lions, a predator of bollworms and tobacco budworms on cotton, for biological control experiments. Real insect eggs cost up to $300 per pound.

Pilot studies in North Carolina tobacco fields demonstrated the value of scouting as compared to applying pesticides by the calendar. Trained agricultural scouts evaluate insect populations—both beneficial and detrimental—and recommend pesticide application. ARS scientists believe the cost of scouting may be more than offset by the reduced costs in pesticide applications.

State government agencies and industry cooperated with ARS in 1971 to find if integrated control techniques can eliminate the boll weevil, the country's worst cotton pest. The project, which began in July and was planned to continue for two years in Mississippi and parts of Alabama and Louisiana, is the first large-scale coordinated test of all the biological and nonpersistent chemical suppression techniques developed during the last decade.

Animal Welfare. ARS authority in the field of humane treatment of animals was extended by two new acts of Congress. A new Animal Welfare Act, which went into effect in December 1971, provides for the licensing of wholesale dealers in pets and dealers in circus and zoo animals. The Horse Protection Act of 1970 was intended to stop the soring —injuring of the legs—of show horses to affect their gait.

ROBERT B. RATHBONE
U. S. Agricultural Research Service

Dairy Production

Dairy farmers in the United States produced about 118.6 billion pounds of milk in 1971, up from the previous year's 117.4 billion. It was the second year-to-year increase after output fell steadily to 116.3 billion pounds in 1969 from the record high of nearly 127 billion pounds in 1964.

Output per cow, which has been gaining annually since World War II, continued to increase in 1971 but at a smaller rate. The average was estimated at 9,570 pounds, up only about 2% from 1970—recent annual growth had averaged 3%. In 1961 the average was only 7,290 pounds. A good supply of herd replacements, an easing labor situation, and record-high milk prices in 1971 encouraged greater milk production. The higher total output occurred even though the number of cows continued to decline.

The downward trend in the number of milk cows on farms, begun in 1945, continued in 1971, when the number of cows averaged about 12.4 million, or about 1% less than the 1970 average. Milk–cow numbers are at their lowest level in the United States since the late 1800's.

Use of milk in commercial markets decreased slightly from 1970. Sales of cheese, low-fat fluid milk, cream, nonfat dry milk, and cottage cheese were up. Declines occurred in whole fluid milk, butter, canned milk, and mixtures of milk and cream. Per capita civilian consumption of milk in all forms was estimated at 557 pounds in 1971, down 1% from 1970.

Supplies of milk and dairy products in 1971 exceeded use by a larger amount than in 1970, resulting in more federal purchases to support milk prices. The Commodity Credit Corporation (CCC) bought products equal to about 7.4 billion pounds of milk in 1971, up from 5.8 billion pounds in 1970. Record CCC purchases were in 1962 when the total was 10.8 billion pounds.

Dairy products in commercial and government stocks at the end of 1971 totaled the equivalent of about 6 billion pounds, slightly above the amount at the end of 1970.

Imports of dairy products were down substantially, and final totals may place the decline at around 20% less than the 1.9 billion pounds in 1970. This was attributed to reduced import quotas, the West Coast dock strike, and a sharp drop in world supplies. Exports in 1971 were significantly above the low level of 1970's equivalent of 438 million pounds of milk.

World Production. Milk output in the 36 lands that usually produce 85% of the world's milk was down significantly to around 680 billion pounds from 715 billion in 1970. Drought and government production controls accounted for the drop.

JOE WESTERN
Kominus Agri-Info Associates

Livestock and Poultry

The total number of cattle in the United States rose in 1971, but the hog, sheep, and lamb populations declined. Broiler output was about the same as that of 1970. World populations of cattle, hogs, and sheep increased in 1971.

U. S. Livestock. The number of cattle in the United States increased substantially to about 118 million head on Jan. 1, 1972, up in one year from

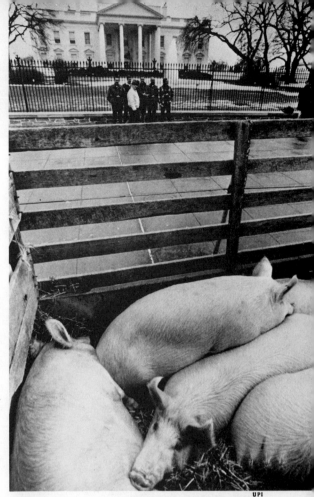

UPI
HOGS were taken to White House by National Farmers Organization in January to protest low pork prices.

114.6 million and in 10 years from 100.4 million. The number of hogs on farms on Dec. 1, 1971, totaled 63 million, down 7% in a year, whereas the number slaughtered commercially rose 10%, to 95 million. The pig crop was 98 million head, down 4% from the 1970 total of 102.3 million. The U. S. sheep population declined for the 12th year, dropping from 19.8 million in 1970 to 18.9 million in 1971. About 10.5 million sheep and lambs were slaughtered. The lamb crop declined by 5%.

World Livestock. Cattle and buffalo increased slightly in 1971, reaching a record high of about 1.2 billion head—a substantial rise over 1961–65 averages. Cattle numbers were down in western Europe, but up in the United States, Australia, New Zealand, USSR, and South America. Hogs increased for the seventh year to more than 560 million—nearly 8% above the 1970 total and far above the 1961–65 average. Numbers of hogs rose in many regions, especially in North America, all of Europe, and the USSR. The world total of sheep was about 1.5 billion, a slight increase over the 1970 total and a 6% increase over 1961–65.

U. S. Eggs and Poultry. U. S. egg production in 1971 was a record high at 2% above the 1970 output of 70.3 billion eggs. Broiler production was about the same as the record in 1970—about 3 billion birds. The 1971 turkey crop was about 118 million birds—about 2 million more than in 1970 but 8 million below the 1967 record crop.

World Eggs and Poultry. Rough estimates suggest that world poultry and egg production rose significantly, mainly because good grain crops helped hold feed costs low. U. S. Department of Agriculture estimates place world poultry population at about the same figure as the world's human population—about 3.706 billion at mid-1971.

JOE WESTERN
Kominus Agri-Info Associates

Grains

In 1971, the world produced more wheat, rye, corn, oats, and barley than a year earlier, but less rice. In the United States, production of food grains—wheat, rye, and rice—increased. Increases were also registered for three of the four feed grains—corn, barley, and sorghum.

Wheat. The United States produced a record 1,639,516,000 bushels of wheat in 1971. The crop was 20% larger than the 1970 crop and 12% larger than the 1969 crop. It was harvested from 48,453,000 acres, up 9% from 1970 and 2% from 1969. The average yield per acre was a record 33.8 bushels, up 2.8 bushels from 1970 and 3.1 bushels from 1969. Kansas led all the states by producing 312,605,000 bushels. North Dakota ranked second, followed by Washington, Montana, and Nebraska.

Winter-wheat production totaled 1,163,420,000 bushels, up 5% from 1970 and 1% from 1969. The acreage harvested totaled 33,049,000 acres, about 1% less than in 1970 and 10% less than in 1969. A record yield that averaged 35.2 bushels per acre more than offset the decline in acreage. The 1971 yield per acre was 1.9 bushels more than in 1970 and 4 bushels more than in 1969. Kansas led the states in winter-wheat production.

Production of spring wheat other than durum totaled 388,276,000 bushels, up about 85% from 1969 and 1970. Some 12,654,000 acres were harvested—a 43% increase over 1970 and 68% over 1969. The yield per acre averaged a record 30.7 bushels, up 7 bushels from 1970 and 3.2 bushels from 1969. North Dakota led the states in the production of spring wheat by harvesting 205,191,-000 bushels.

Durum-wheat production totaled 87,038,000 bushels in 1971, up 72% from 1970 but still 18% less than the record 1969 crop. The durum crop was harvested from 2,687,000 acres, up 33% from 1970 but still 19% smaller than the 1969 acreage. The yield per acre averaged a record 32.4 bushels, up 7.4 bushels from the 1970 crop and 0.5 of a bushel above 1969. North Dakota led the states in durum wheat, with a crop of 76,890,000 bushels.

The world produced a near-record 304,000,000 metric tons of wheat in 1971, up from 288,000,000 tons in 1970. The crop is second only to the record 308,000,000-ton crop of 1968. The world harvested about 521,838,000 acres of wheat, 3% more than in 1970 but 2% under the 1965–69 average. The yield per acre averaged 21.4 bushels, up 0.5 of a bushel from 1970.

Rice. Production of rice in the United States totaled 84,315,000 bags (of 100 pounds each), up 1% from 1970 but 7% under 1969. The yield averaged a record 4,638 pounds per acre, up 23 pounds from 1970 and 370 pounds from 1969. About 1,818,000 acres were harvested—the same areas as in 1970 but 15% less than in 1969. Texas led the states by harvesting 22,932,000 bags.

Rye. Rye production in the United States totaled 50,935,000 bushels in 1971, up 31% from 1970 and 66% from 1969. The yield per acre averaged a record 28 bushels, up 2 bushels from 1970 and 4.5 bushels from 1969. South Dakota led the states in rye production.

World rye production totaled 29,700,000 metric tons in 1971, up 11% from 1970 but 3% under the 1965–69 average. The yield per acre averaged a record 24.3 bushels, up 22.9 bushels in 1970.

Corn. The U. S. corn crop totaled a record 5,540,253,000 bushels in 1971. The crop was 35% greater than the 1970 crop, which was damaged by blight, and 21% greater than the 1969 crop. Yields

WORLD PRODUCTION OF GRAINS BY LEADING COUNTRIES
(In metric tons)

	Average 1965–69	1970	1971
Wheat			
USSR	66,900,000	80,000,000	70,000,000
United States	38,475,000	37,516,000	44,235,000
China, Mainland	21,920,000	24,500,000	
India	13,860,000	20,093,000	23,247,000
France	13,886,000	12,922,000	14,566,000
Canada	18,527,000	9,023,000	13,811,000
Turkey	8,266,000	8,000,000	10,000,000
Italy	9,580,000	9,631,000	9,852,000
Australia	10,590,000	7,987,000	...
Pakistan	5,170,000	7,399,000	6,808,000
Rye			
USSR	12,200,000	12,000,000	11,000,000
Poland	8,022,000	5,460,000	8,100,000
West Germany	2,952,000	2,665,000	3,000,000
East Germany	1,782,000	1,483,000	1,500,000
United States	712,000	979,000	1,329,000
Turkey	771,000	680,000	760,000
Canada	383,000	570,000	625,000
Czechoslovakia	751,000	450,000	550,000
Austria	382,000	363,000	396,000
Spain	350,000	206,000	360,000
Barley			
USSR	23,020,000	29,500,000	27,000,000
Canada	6,395,000	9,051,000	13,993,000
United States	8,702,000	8,936,000	10,230,000
France	8,604,000	8,009,000	8,601,000
United Kingdom	8,699,000	7,496,000	7,950,000
West Germany	4,414,000	4,754,000	5,700,000
Denmark	4,954,000	4,813,000	5,500,000
Spain	2,830,000	3,092,000	4,400,000
Turkey	3,520,000	3,300,000	4,000,000
India	2,635,000	2,716,000	2,865,000
Oats			
United States	12,792,000	13,201,000	12,841,000
USSR	8,420,000	10,500,000	12,000,000
Canada	5,637,000	5,673,000	5,567,000
West Germany	2,596,000	2,484,000	2,930,000
Poland	2,769,000	3,214,000	2,800,000
France	2,537,000	2,070,000	2,146,000
Sweden	1,308,000	1,685,000	1,938,000
Finland	1,010,000	1,395,000	1,425,000
United Kingdom	1,275,000	1,233,000	1,200,000
Czechoslovakia	836,000	940,000	900,000
Corn			
United States	111,448,000	104,393,000	141,020,000
Mexico	8,160,000	9,200,000	9,500,000
USSR	7,740,000	7,500,000	9,500,000
Rumania	7,108,000	6,395,000	9,000,000
France	4,593,000	7,420,000	8,517,000
Yugoslavia	7,146,000	6,933,000	7,179,000
India	5,460,000	7,413,000	6,500,000
Hungary	3,902,000	4,072,000	5,000,000
Italy	3,837,000	4,729,000	4,450,000
Bulgaria	1,911,000	2,411,000	3,000,000
Rice			
China, Mainland	91,190,000	97,540,000	94,000,000
India	52,925,000	63,736,000	66,066,000
Indonesia	15,552,000	23,064,000	24,454,000
Pakistan	18,911,000	20,034,000	18,994,000
Japan	17,019,000	15,861,000	13,570,000
Thailand	11,935,000	13,270,000	13,400,000
Burma	7,694,000	8,128,000	8,250,000
Korea, South	4,988,000	5,571,000	5,800,000
Vietnam, South	4,665,000	5,700,000	5,800,000
Philippines	4,494,000	5,343,000	5,180,000

Source: Foreign Agricultural Service, U. S. Department of Agriculture.

of corn were a record 86.8 bushels per acre, up 15.2 bushels from 1970 and 2.9 bushels from the previous record of 1969. The acreage harvested totaled 63,819,000 acres, up 12% from 1970 and 17% from 1969. Iowa led the states in corn production by harvesting 1,180,140,000 bushels. Illinois, which also produced more than a billion bushels, ranked second.

Barley. The United States produced 462,484,000 bushels of barley in 1971, up 13% from 1970 and 11% from 1969. The yield per acre averaged a record 45.6 bushels, up 3 bushels from 1970 and 1.2 bushels from 1969. North Dakota led the states in barley production.

The world produced 127,418,000 metric tons of barley in 1971, up 10% from 1970 and 21% from the 1965–69 average.

Oats. Oat production totaled 875,775,000 bushels in the United States in 1971, a drop of 4% from 1970 and 8% less than in 1969. The average yield per acre was 55.7 bushels, up 6.6 bushels from 1970 and 2.7 bushels from 1969. Minnesota led the states in oat production.

World oat production totaled 52,279,000 metric tons in 1971, up 4% from 1970 and 9% from the 1965–69 average.

Sorghum Grain. Production of sorghum grain totaled a record 895,349,000 bushels in 1971, up 29% from 1970 and 19% from 1969. The crop yielded an average 53.9 bushels per acre, up 3.2 bushels from 1970 but 1.4 bushels less than the 1969 crop. Texas led the states in sorghum grain production.

NICHOLAS KOMINUS
Kominus Agri-Info Associates

Fruits

The United States produced another record citrus crop in 1971–72, with production up slightly from the 12-million-ton total of the preceding year and up 6% from 1969–70. Deciduous fruit production totaled 10.4 million tons in 1971, up 7% from 1970, but down 6% from 1969.

Citrus. During the nation's second straight record-breaking year of citrus fruit production, increases in the crops of grapefruit, lemons, tangelos, and temples offset decreases in orange and tangerine production. Of the total crop, 68% was oranges, 21% grapefruit, 6% lemons, and 5% other citrus. Florida accounted for 72% of the citrus crop, California for 20%, and Arizona and Texas for nearly all of the remaining.

Orange production totaled 189.6 million boxes, 1% less than that of the preceding crop year, but up 2% from 1969–70. Production was up in California but down in Florida. Florida produced 136 million boxes of oranges, down 4% from the preceding year and 1% from 1969–70. California produced 44 million boxes of oranges, up 14% from 1970–71. Arizona produced fewer oranges, and Texas production remained unchanged.

The nation produced 61.1 million boxes of grapefruit, up 1% from the preceding year, and 13% above the 1969–70 crop. Florida produced 44 million boxes, up 3% from 1970–71. Production increased in California but declined in Texas and Arizona. Lemon production totaled 17.5 million boxes nationally, up 6% from 1970–71. The tangelo crop totaled 3.3 million boxes, up 22%; tangerine, 4.5 million boxes, a drop of 8%; and temple, 6 million boxes, up 20%.

Apples. The nation's apple crop totaled 6,127 million pounds in 1971, 3% less than 1970 production, and 9% less than that of 1969. The crop was up 8% from the preceding year in the Eastern states and up 5% in the Central states, but down 17% in the Western states. The Eastern states accounted for 51% of the crop, the Central states for 21%, and the Western states for 28%.

Six varieties—Delicious, Golden Delicious, McIntosh, Rome Beauty, Jonathan, and York Imperial—accounted for 73% of the total. Delicious, the leading variety, accounted for 29% of the crop, and second-ranked Golden Delicious accounted for 12%.

U. S. PRODUCTION OF APPLES, PEACHES, AND PEARS, BY LEADING STATES
(In pounds)

	1969	1970	1971
Apples[1]			
New York	855,000,000	945,000,000	1,050,000,000
Washington	1,675,000,000	1,320,000,000	1,000,000,000
Michigan	720,000,000	710,000,000	720,000,000
Pennsylvania	525,000,000	510,000,000	540,000,000
Virginia	472,000,000	463,000,000	510,000,000
California	540,000,000	500,000,000	420,000,000
West Virginia	260,000,000	242,000,000	275,000,000
North Carolina	204,000,000	223,000,000	172,000,000
Ohio	147,000,000	135,000,000	160,000,000
New Jersey	119,700,000	99,000,000	130,000,000
Total U. S.	6,751,800,000	6,222,500,000	6,152,900,000
Peaches			
California	2,280,000,000	1,842,000,000	1,640,000,000
South Carolina	338,000,000	270,000,000	235,000,000
Georgia	175,200,000	160,000,000	125,000,000
New Jersey	104,500,000	86,400,000	115,000,000
Pennsylvania	120,000,000	84,000,000	106,000,000
Michigan	97,000,000	75,000,000	100,000,000
Arkansas	42,000,000	40,000,000	42,000,000
Virginia	44,700,000	42,500,000	42,000,000
Washington	40,800,000	40,000,000	36,000,000
North Carolina	56,000,000	42,000,000	32,000,000
Total U. S.	3,665,400,000	3,011,400,000	2,813,800,000

Pears	(In tons)		
California	351,000	258,000	333,000
Oregon	191,000	90,000	172,000
Washington	107,900	144,500	167,000
Michigan	23,000	16,000	24,000
New York	18,000	13,500	19,000
Colorado	7,800	4,530	6,000
Utah	5,500	4,300	5,600
Pennsylvania	3,200	3,400	2,600
Idaho	2,100	1,200	2,300
Connecticut	2,150	1,650	1,630
Total U. S.	711,650	537,080	733,130

[1] In orchards of 100 or more bearing-age trees.   Source: Crop Reporting Board, U. S. Department of Agriculture.

U. S. CITRUS PRODUCTION BY LEADING STATES[1]
(In number of boxes)[2]

	1969–70	1970–71	1971–72
Oranges			
Florida	137,700,000	142,300,000	136,000,000
California	39,000,000	38,600,000	44,000,000
Texas	4,200,000	6,200,000	6,200,000
Arizona	4,630,000	3,560,000	3,350,000
Total	185,530,000	190,660,000	189,550,000
Grapefruit			
Florida	37,400,000	42,900,000	44,000,000
Texas	8,100,000	10,100,000	9,700,000
California	5,250,000	5,160,000	5,200,000
Arizona	3,160,000	2,520,000	2,200,000
Total	53,910,000	60,680,000	61,100,000
Lemons			
California	12,300,000	13,300,000	14,500,000
Arizona	2,820,000	3,150,000	3,000,000
Total	15,120,000	16,450,000	17,500,000
Tangerines			
Florida	3,000,000	3,700,000	3,500,000
California	760,000	800,000	700,000
Arizona	350,000	390,000	300,000
Total	4,110,000	4,890,000	4,500,000

[1] The crop year begins with the bloom of the first year shown and ends with completion of harvest the following year.   [2] Net content of box varies. Approximate averages are as follows: Oranges—California and Arizona, 75 pounds; Florida and other states, 90 pounds. Grapefruit—California Desert Valleys and Arizona, 64 pounds; other California areas, 67 pounds; Florida, 85 pounds; Texas, 80 pounds. Lemons—76 pounds. Tangerines—California and Arizona, 75 pounds; Florida, 95 pounds. Source: Crop Reporting Board, U. S. Department of Agriculture.

Peaches. The 1971 peach crop totaled 2,894 million pounds, down 4% from 1970 and 21% from 1969. Most of the drop was due to a decline in California Clingstone production, which totaled 1,260 million pounds, as compared to 1,442 million pounds in 1970. California Clingstone peaches, which are used primarily for canning, account for around 45% of total peach production. Production of other peaches totaled 1,554 million pounds, a drop of 1% from 1970.

Pears. The nation's pear crop totaled 687,970 tons in 1971, up 28% from 1970, but down 3% from 1969. The Pacific Coast Bartlett pear crop totaled 520,000 tons, up 35% from 1970. Three states—California, Washington, and Oregon—accounted for 92% of the pear crop.

Cherries. The 1971 sweet cherry crop totaled 139,440 tons, 15% above 1970 production and 10% more than that of 1969. Washington, Oregon, and California accounted for 70% of the crop. Oregon was the leading producer of sweet cherries. Production of tart cherries totaled 139,260 tons in 1971, an increase of 17% from 1970, but a decrease of 8% from 1969. Michigan, New York, Pennsylvania, Ohio, and Wisconsin produced 90% of the tart cherry crop.

Grapes. The United States produced 4 million tons of grapes in 1971, up 27% from 1970. California led the states in grape production with 3,475,000 tons, or 89% of the total crop, and New York ranked second with 180,000 tons. Raisin varieties accounted for 68% of the California crop, wine varieties for 20%, and table varieties for 12%.

Apricots. The apricot crop totaled 149,100 tons, a drop of 15% from 1970 and 35% from the 1969 production total. California accounted for 96% of the crop.

Plums and Prunes. Production of plums and prunes in Michigan, Idaho, Washington, and Oregon totaled 60,300 tons, up 29% from the small 1970 crop. Production was up in all of these states. The 1971 California prune crop totaled 131,000 tons, a drop of 34% from 1970 but up slightly from 1969.

Cranberries. The 1971 cranberry crop totaled a record 2,204,000 barrels, up 8% from 1970 and 21% from 1969. Massachusetts, the leading state, accounted for nearly half of the crop.

Avocadoes. California's production of avocadoes in 1971 totaled 64,600 tons, nearly twice the 1970 crop. Florida grew 18,800 tons of avocadoes in 1971, upping its production by 34%.

NICHOLAS KOMINUS
Kominus Agri-Info Associates

Vegetables

The United States produced more vegetables for processing and more strawberries in 1971 than a year earlier, but there were fewer vegetables for the fresh market, melons, potatoes, and sweet potatoes.

Vegetables for Processing. Production of the 10 principal crops grown for commercial totaled 10,035,400 tons in 1971—7% more than in both 1970 and 1969. Production of 7 of the 10 crops increased. Increases were as follows: asparagus, up 1%; green lima beans, up 1%; snap beans, up 5%; sweet corn, up 9%; green peas, up 9%; spinach, up 7%; and tomatoes, up 10%. Decreases in production were: beets, down 8%; cabbage for kraut, down 11%; and cucumbers for pickles, down 4%.

Average yields per acre in 1971 were above or the same for all crops except snap beans, which was down slightly from 1970. The total value of the 10 crops was $480,000,000 in 1971, up 8% from 1970. California accounted for 35% of the value of the crops. It also produced 42% of the crop tonnage.

Vegetables and Melons. Production of the 19 principal vegetable crops and 3 melon crops for the fresh market in 1971 totaled 223,895,000 hundredweight, a decline of 1% from a year earlier. For the major vegetable crops, decreases from 1970 for tomatoes, onions, and sweet corn more than offset increases for carrots, celery, cabbage, and lettuce. Production of all three melon crops declined.

The 22 vegetable and melon crops had a value of $1,359,000,000—13% more than in 1970. Leading crops in value were lettuce, tomatoes, and onions. The combined value of those three crops accounted for 46% of the total value of all vegetable and melon crops. The crops were harvested from 1,535,910 acres, 67,730 fewer than in 1970.

The leading states in production for the fresh market were California, Florida, Texas, Arizona, and New York. These states accounted for 63% of the harvested acreage, 74% of the production, and 77% of the value of these crops. California accounted for 40% of the production and 42% of the total value of the crops.

Potatoes. The 1971 potato crop totaled 316,083,-000 hundredweight, a decline of 3% from the record 1970 crop. The yield of potatoes per acre averaged 229 hundredweight, matching the record yield of 1970. The crop was harvested from 1,380,300 acres, a decline of 2% from 1970. Idaho led by producing 75,850,000 hundredweight.

The only increase in production was registered by the late spring crop. All other seasonal groups —winter, early spring, early and late summer, and fall—declined.

The fall crop, which accounted for 79% of the total potato crop, yielded 249,895,000 hundredweight of potatoes, a drop of 1% from 1970. Idaho led in fall production. Winter production, divided about equally between Florida and California, totaled 3,088,000 hundredweight. The early spring crop totaled 3,735,000 hundredweight. Florida led in early spring production. The late spring crop totaled 19,899,000 hundredweight, down slightly from 1970. California was the leading state. Early summer production totaled 11,845,000 hundredweight. Virginia led in early summer production. Washington led in late summer production, which totaled 27,621,000 hundredweight.

Sweet Potatoes. The nation produced 11,888,-000, hundredweight of sweet potatoes in 1971, a drop of 14% from 1970. The crop was harvested from 115,300 acres, 12% less than a year earlier. The yield per acre averaged 103 hundredweight, equal to the record yield of 1970. North Carolina led in sweet potato production, followed by Louisiana. North Carolina also led in yields.

Strawberries. The 1971 strawberry crop totaled 5,171,000 hundredweight, up 5% from 1970 and up 6% from 1969. Production for the fresh market accounted for 65% of the strawberry crop, and processing accounted for the remainder. California led in strawberry production.

NICHOLAS KOMINUS
Kominus Agri-Info Associates

AIR FORCE. See DEFENSE FORCES.

U. S. PRODUCTION OF VEGETABLES AND MELONS FOR THE FRESH MARKET
(Hundredweight)

	1969	1970	1971
Vegetables			
Artichokes	657,000	671,000	792,000
Asparagus	850,000	952,000	904,000
Beans, snap	3,328,000	3,149,000	3,090,000
Broccoli	2,509,000	3,104,000	3,224,000
Brussels sprouts	579,000	587,000	628,000
Cabbage	18,439,000	18,551,000	19,155,000
Carrots	18,732,000	18,498,000	18,561,000
Cauliflower	2,440,000	2,279,000	2,514,000
Celery	15,509,000	15,272,000	16,073,000
Corn, sweet	12,562,000	12,890,000	12,242,000
Cucumbers	4,424,000	4,610,000	4,278,000
Eggplant	514,000	501,000	485,000
Escarole	1,102,000	1,101,000	1,145,000
Garlic	876,000	728,000	518,000
Lettuce	44,551,000	46,163,000	46,258,000
Onions	28,317,000	30,578,000	29,854,000
Peppers, green	4,368,000	3,876,000	4,115,000
Spinach	704,000	620,000	677,000
Tomatoes	19,409,000	18,416,000	17,706,000
Total	179,870,000	182,546,000	182,219,000
Melons			
Cantaloupes	13,759,000	13,367,000	12,450,000
Honeydew melons	1,969,000	1,931,000	1,958,000
Watermelons	26,308,000	27,528,000	27,268,000
Total	42,036,000	42,826,000	41,676,000

Source: Crop Reporting Board, U. S. Department of Agriculture.

U. S. PRODUCTION OF VEGETABLES FOR PROCESSING
(Tons)

	1969	1970	1971
Asparagus	103,400	91,450	92,550
Beans, lima, shelled	98,700	78,750	79,250
Beans, snap	568,450	570,150	596,550
Beets, for canning	219,550	205,650	189,100
Cabbage, for kraut	224,150	266,500	236,200
Corn, sweet, in husk	2,109,350	1,879,050	2,046,100
Cucumbers, for pickles	503,100	589,250	562,850
Peas, green, shelled	524,400	476,250	520,350
Spinach	133,600	150,350	160,350
Tomatoes	4,897,700	5,058,950	5,552,100
Total	9,382,400	9,366,350	10,035,400

Source: Crop Reporting Board, U. S. Department of Agriculture.

U. S. PRODUCTION OF FROZEN VEGETABLES
(Pounds)

	1969	1970
Asparagus	23,033,000	25,925,000
Beans, green, regular cut	117,800,000	119,099,000
Beans, green, French cut	61,953,000	75,817,000
Beans, green, whole	5,013,000	4,287,000
Beans, green, Italian	7,618,000	6,983,000
Beans, wax	5,415,000	6,176,000
Broccoli	153,784,000	185,157,000
Brussels sprouts	40,083,000	42,663,000
Butter beans, speckled	7,847,000	14,674,000
Carrots, diced	100,700,000	105,267,000
Carrots, sliced, and crinkle cut	24,308,000	47,058,000
Carrots, chips, chunks, and julienne	25,937,000	20,729,000
Cauliflower	69,744,000	59,782,000
Celery	3,415,000	7,210,000
Collards	18,408,000	19,818,000
Corn, cut	289,268,000	216,097,000
Corn-on-cob	73,914,000	80,889,000
Kale	4,762,000	6,488,000
Lima beans, baby	82,562,000	73,012,000
Lima beans, emerald	4,221,000	3,538,000
Lima beans, fordhook	55,792,000	36,844,000
Mustard greens	10,351,000	15,597,000
Okra	38,250,000	44,168,000
Onions	37,881,000	52,205,000
Peas, blackeye	20,647,000	30,084,000
Peas, green	367,323,000	344,520,000
Potatoes	2,048,408,000	2,404,389,000
Pumpkin and cooked squash	26,091,000	27,241,000
Rhubarb	7,599,000	7,950,000
Spinach	107,182,000	145,694,000
Squash, summer	17,318,000	18,953,000
Sweet potatoes and yams	12,854,000	10,913,000
Turnip greens	19,873,000	18,943,000
Turnips, turnip greens with turnips	10,520,000	23,415,000
Miscellaneous vegetables	15,357,000	15,146,000
Total	3,915,231,000	4,316,731,000

Source: American Frozen Food Institute.

Dart-shaped Concorde, the Anglo-French supersonic airliner, went through further tests in 1971. The 1,400-mile-an-hour craft is scheduled to enter service in 1974.

air transportation

In terms of miles flown, passengers carried, routes served, and numbers of aircraft in service, the world's air transportation system continued to grow in 1971. But rising costs, due to inflation, and a slump in travel over some routes, due largely to the U. S. recession, created severe economic headwinds that resulted in heavy losses for many of the airlines.

As the year ended there were signs of an upturn for some lines, but others were still searching for a solution to their difficulties. The economic problems brought a flurry of proposed mergers, efforts to reduce excess capacity, and the threat of an international price war on air fares.

A number of crashes marred air travel's safety record, which had improved dramatically in 1969 and 1970. Nevertheless, on a statistical basis, air travel was far safer in 1971 than it had been a decade earlier.

Traffic. Preliminary estimates indicated that major U. S. airlines logged an increase of about 1.5% in passenger traffic for the year—to about 133 billion passenger miles. On a worldwide basis, scheduled airline traffic increased about 5%. In the continuation of a 5-year trend, traffic increased much faster on nonscheduled air services than on scheduled flights. This reflected the growing popularity of low-cost charter flights between the United States and Europe and between northern Europe and tourist spas in southern Europe.

Financial Picture. The Air Transport Association, a trade organization of scheduled airlines, reported that U. S. carriers suffered a net loss of $132.4 million during the first six months of 1971, compared with a loss of $58.1 million during the same period of 1970.

In the late summer and fall, the airlines' economic picture improved somewhat as traffic on some routes began to pick up. As a result, some airline economists predicted the industry would soon be in the profit column again. The agency that regulates domestic airlines, the Civil Aeronautics Board, credited cost-cutting programs with helping to speed the airlines' recovery. But the CAB said that it remained concerned about the economic survivability of several airlines, particularly Pan American World Airways, which suffered heavy losses during the year.

Mergers. As during past periods when economic hardships bedeviled the airlines, many lines discussed possible mergers. Virtually every U. S. carrier conducted at least some preliminary merger discussions. Tentative merger agreements were made by Northwest and National; Delta and Northeast; Allegheny and Mohawk; and American and Western. All are subject to government approval.

Pan American and Trans World Airlines held lengthy negotiations aimed at creating a single major U. S. international flag airline. But, because of expected Justice Department opposition and policy differences in consummating the proposed merger, the discussions were called off.

New Aircraft. The Boeing 707, DC-8, and other jets that dominated air transportation in the 1960's have cabins about 13 feet wide. In 1971, the "wide-body look"—a new era of in-the-air spaciousness where the cabins measure up to 20 feet across—began to take over much of the global air transportation system.

The Boeing 747, introduced early in 1970, was the first of the wide bodies. By the end of 1971, there were more than 150 in service, each carrying from 300 to 490 persons. In the summer of 1971, passengers got a look at the second jumbo jet—the McDonnell Douglas DC-10. It carries up to 300 persons, and brought the wide-body look to shorter (500- to 1,500-mile) routes than covered by the transoceanic 747.

That travelers would see a third wide-body—Lockheed's L-1011 TriStar—in 1972 was assured when Congress voted to back $250 million in bank loans for Lockheed. The TriStar's future had hung in doubt much of the year after Britain's Rolls-Royce Ltd. went into receivership because of heavy losses experienced in developing the TriStar's engines. The loan guarantees in the United States and emergency assistance to Rolls-Royce by the British government kept the project alive.

Congress voted to end federal support of the U. S. project to develop an 1,800-mile-an-hour supersonic transport, largely because of opposition from the environmental lobby. Development continued on two other SST's—the British-French Concorde and Russia's TU-144.

Capacity Control. The growing utilization of the high-capacity jumbo jets aggravated the problems that airlines faced in dealing with excess seating capacity at a time of economic recession. In one effort to reduce the surplus of seats, the Civil Aeronautics Board authorized American Airlines, United Air Lines, and Trans World Airlines to negotiate an agreement to jointly reduce their flights an average of 28% on four routes where their load factors (percentage of seats occupied) averaged less than 36%. The affected routes were between New

York and Los Angeles; New York and San Francisco; Washington and Los Angeles; and Chicago and San Francisco.

Fares. The price of tickets on most international routes increased an average of 5% during the year. On domestic routes, the CAB permitted fares to increase 6%. An additional 3% hike was in the offing before the Nixon administration imposed wage-price controls in August.

At year-end, some air fares began to slice downward. Domestic lines introduced a series of discount fares aimed at encouraging vacation travel by air. One example of the new fares was the lowest-priced transcontinental round-trip fare ever offered—$99, for wives traveling with their husbands between New York and California on business trips lasting no more than four days.

Members of the International Air Transport Association, meeting in Montreal during the summer, drafted proposed fares for transatlantic travel beginning April 1, 1972. The new rates included several new discount fares much cheaper than any previously available. But one carrier, Lufthansa of West Germany, vetoed the agreement, saying that some of the new special fares would be unprofitable and that they would not enable the scheduled airlines to compete with low-cost nonscheduled charter airlines. Lufthansa decided to offer its own discount fares effective Feb. 1, 1972, that undercut those agreed to in Montreal. Other airlines soon announced comparable cuts to meet Lufthansa's rates. Many airline officials forecast that the developing price war would result in huge losses for all lines. In a last-ditch effort to avoid the rate war, airline executives convened in Honolulu in November and reached a compromise agreement. It will result in sharply lower transatlantic fares in 1972—but not as low as those proposed by Lufthansa.

Environmental Problems. From Tokyo to New York and London, the mounting opposition to airport construction and jet aircraft noise presented significant problems. Environmental groups forced government planners to select a new airport site more than 56 miles from London. In Tokyo, farmers opposing use of their land for a new airport met

LOCKHEED experienced difficulties with its wide-bodied TriStar in 1971 when craft's engine maker went bankrupt, but plane is scheduled to begin service in 1972.

LOCKHEED AIRCRAFT CORP.

the police in pitched battles that resulted in several deaths. Environmentalists' opposition killed plans to expand congested Kennedy International Airport at New York and blocked construction of new jetports in Los Angeles, Boston, Atlanta, Portland, Oreg., and elsewhere. In Los Angeles, community protests over noise were so severe that the city decided to spend more than $200 million to purchase and destroy 2,000 homes adjacent to the airport.

Warning that the growing resistance to jetports could seriously hamper the nation's economic growth, government aviation leaders sought ways to make jetports more acceptable. The Federal Aviation Administration said it would require modifications to 1,100 two- and three-engine jets—Boeing 727 and 737 and DC-9—to make them quieter. The government officials pointed out that the 747, DC-10, and L-1011 have engines inherently quieter than those of earlier jets and that the growing use of these craft would progressively reduce noise.

Air Safety. Several serious accidents marred the safety record of U.S. airlines, which had improved during the preceding two years. Fifty persons died on June 6 when an Air West DC-9 airliner collided with a Navy fighter near Los Angeles. Thirty-four persons were injured, none seriously, on June 10 when a Pan American 747 with 212 persons aboard clipped a runway approach light at San Francisco during take-off. And, in the worst accident ever involving a single U.S. commercial airliner, 111 persons were killed on September 4 when an Alaska Airlines Boeing 727 crashed at Juneau, Alaska.

There were also serious crashes in Germany, Belgium, Brazil, Denmark, and the Soviet Union. In Japan, a military plane flown by a student pilot collided with a commercial airliner on July 30; 161 persons died, the largest toll in history in a plane accident.

To reduce the risk of midair collisions, the FAA began implementing a program requiring all planes flying near major U.S. jetports to be under "positive control" of radar controllers. Any planes operating near the airports must have radios and navigation aids. Student pilots were banned from the safety zones, called "terminal control areas."

Hijacking. The problem of aerial hijackings, which exploded into a perilous tactic of extortion by Arab guerrillas in 1970, ebbed slightly in 1971. But the aviation world and world governments still had not learned how to stop hijacking.

The increasing use of weapon detectors at airports, searches of suspicious passengers, use of armed guards on selected flights, and generally tightened security provisions introduced after the wave of guerrilla hijackings in the Middle East in 1970 all contributed to a general decrease in the number of hijacking attempts. Three would-be hijackers were killed in the U.S. by authorities during the year. As a result of airport surveillance, more than 1,000 persons were arrested on charges that included possession of dangerous weapons and possession of drugs.

Commuter Airlines. One of the most significant trends in the U.S. transportation system was the vigorous growth of commuter airlines. These are scheduled airlines that fly small planes—usually 5 to 15 passengers—in relatively short hops of up to 200 miles or so. They link many small towns formerly served by conventional airlines that say they cannot do so now because it is not practical to fly jets to small towns. There are 105 scheduled commuter lines, but about 50 account for 90% of the traffic. The largest are Executive Airlines, Puerto Rico International Airlines, Shawnee Airlines, Air Wisconsin, and Golden West Airlines.

The Future. U.S. Government and airline economists predicted the nation's air transportation system would have a strong future in spite of the problems that bedeviled it in 1970 and 1971. However, few expected a resumption of the annual growth rate in passenger traffic that had averaged from 12% to 18% in the 1960's.

The FAA estimated that the number of passengers carried on scheduled carriers would increase from 173 million in the 1971 fiscal year to 198 million in the 1972 fiscal year, and that the number would continue to grow at about 10% annually through the 1970's.

ROBERT H. LINDSEY
Aviation Reporter, "The New York Times"

DC-10, which entered service in 1971, is designed for use over medium-length and long-haul passenger routes.

MCDONNELL-DOUGLAS CORPORATION

ALABAMA

The Legislature met in both regular and special sessions during 1971, with the result that many of the significant developments occurring in Alabama related to that branch of the state government.

Legislative Developments. Gov. George C. Wallace called the Legislature into special session in March and April to consider a multimillion-dollar bond program proposed by the administration. This special session marked the emergence of a group of legislators, primarily in the Senate, who challenged the strong control traditionally exercised over the Legislature by the executive in Alabama.

During the session, legislation was enacted to authorize bond issues for medical education facilities, mental health centers, and improvements at the state docks. Also approved was a measure regulating budgeting and expenditure processes in the state highway department.

The group of independent legislators centered their opposition on a proposed bond issue for state highways. The Legislature failed to pass the highway bond issue, as well as a bond issue for state parks also requested by Governor Wallace.

However, a reduced highway bond issue was introduced and subsequently passed in the regular session, which convened in May. A relatively large number of legislators continued to assert their independence from executive control during the regular session.

Noteworthy legislation passed during the regular session included: more stringent air and water pollution control measures; a measure permitting students to vote by absentee ballot; a somewhat controversial measure regulating consumer credit; a proposed constitutional amendment providing for annual sessions of the Legislature; and an antibusing law requested by Governor Wallace. Funding of mental health programs proved to be the most controversial issue during the regular session. The focal point of the controversy involved administration proposals to divert education funds to provide additional financing for the state mental health program.

As a result of the controversy over mental health funding, the Legislature adjourned its regular session without passing appropriation acts for the operation of the government during the forthcoming biennium. The Legislature also failed to deal with such programs as property tax reform, legislative reapportionment, and congressional redistricting. Redistricting became necessary because of the projected loss of one U. S. representative as a result of the 1970 census.

Although the attorney general of Alabama ruled that the state government could not function without legislative appropriations of funds, Governor Wallace did not call an immediate special session to deal with the problem. Instead, he arranged with several banks within the state to make interest-free loans to state employees as a means of meeting the state payroll. Eventually the governor called the Legislature into a special appropriations session beginning on November 15 and announced plans for future sessions on other subjects.

School Desegregation. As the 1971 school year opened, new desegregation plans precipitated another confrontation between Governor Wallace and the federal courts. The new plans calling for closing some schools and mandatory busing were met by Wallace's executive orders directing local school authorities to ignore portions of the desegregation plans. Although one federal district judge characterized Wallace's efforts as legally meaningless, and the plans were generally carried out, the governor continued to voice his opposition to the plans and to insist on the enforcement of the new antibusing statute.

Judicial Developments. In May, President Nixon visited Birmingham and Mobile and, while in Mobile, officiated at the beginning of construction on the proposed Tennessee-Tombigbee Waterway. Construction on the project was later enjoined, however, by a federal district court in Washington, D. C. The injunction was based on the charge that the requirement for an environmental impact study had not been adequately met.

The state's most interesting legal case in 1971 was filed in the federal district court for the Middle District of Alabama and was designed to improve the treatment of patients confined in the state mental hospitals. The suit charged that patients in Alabama's mental institutions were deprived of their liberty without due process of law since they did not receive adequate treatment. In effect, the court ordered the state mental health department to implement an adequate treatment program.

JAMES D. THOMAS
University of Alabama

——— **ALABAMA • Information Highlights** ———

Area: 51,609 square miles (133,667 sq km).
Population (1970 census): 3,444,165. *Density:* 69 per sq mi.
Chief Cities (1970 census): Montgomery, the capital, 133,-386; Birmingham, 300,910; Mobile, 190,026; Huntsville, 137,802; Tuscaloosa, 65,773; Gadsden, 53,928; Prichard, 41,578.
Government (1971): *Chief Officers*—governor, George C. Wallace (D); lt. gov., Jere Beasley (D); secy. of state, Mrs. Mabel Amos (D); atty. gen., William J. Baxley (D); treas., Mrs. Agnes Baggett (D); supt. of education, LeRoy Brown; chief justice, Howell T. Heflin (D). *Legislature*—Senate, 35 members (35 Democrats, 0 Republicans); House of Representatives, 106 members (103 D, 2 R, 1 other).
Education (1970–71): *Enrollment*—public elementary schools, 424,511 pupils; 16,145 teachers; public secondary, 378,-996 pupils; 16,881 teachers; nonpublic schools (1968–69) 28,900 pupils; 1,450 teachers; college and university (fall 1968), 94,850 students. *Public school expenditures* (1970–71), $369,773,000 ($489 per pupil). *Average teacher's salary,* $7,376.
State Finances (fiscal year 1970): *Revenues,* $1,351,141,000 (4% general sales tax and gross receipts taxes, $212,-383,000; motor fuel tax, $116,760,000; federal funds $409,-266,000). *Expenditures,* $1,369,773,000 (education, $582,-796,000; health, welfare, and safety, $216,694,000; highways, $185,966,000). *State debt,* $742,871,000.
Personal Income (1970): $9,882,000,000; per capita, $3,828.
Public Assistance (1970): $206,414,000; *Average monthly payments* (Dec. 1970)—old-age assistance, $70.70; aid to families with dependent children, $59.95.
Labor Force: *Nonagricultural wage and salary earners* (June 1971), 1,016,600. *Average annual employment* (1969)—manufacturing, 324,000; trade, 185,000; government, 205,-000; services, 127,000. *Insured unemployed* (Oct. 1971)—22,800 (3.2%).
Manufacturing (1967): *Value added by manufacture,* $3,525,-500,000; primary metals, $638,600,000; chemicals and allied products, $418,200,000; paper and allied products, $323,200,000; textile mill products, $322,100,000.
Agriculture (1970): *Cash farm income,* $821,069,000 (livestock, $534,547,000; crops, $207,059,000; government payments, $79,463,000). *Chief crops* (1970)—Peanuts, 313,740,000 pounds (ranks 4th among the states); soybeans, 14,312,-000 bushels; corn, 12,535,000 bushels; cotton lint, 510,000 bales.
Mining (1969 est.): *Production value,* $280,382,000 (ranks 22d among the states). Chief minerals (tons)—Stone, 19,208,-000; coal, 16,990,000; cement, 8,408,000; petroleum, 7,-720,000 barrels.
Fisheries (1970): *Commercial catch,* 32,700,000 pounds ($10,-800,000). *Leading species by value* (1967), shrimp, $6,048,-511; red snapper, $659,167; blue, hard crabs, $187,576; black mullet, $156,060.
Transportation: *Roads* (1969), 78,080 miles (125,654 km); *motor vehicles* (1969), 1,857,000; *railroads* (1968), 4,577 miles (7,366 km); *airports* (1969), 83.
Communications: *Telephones* (1971), 1,562,800; *television stations* (1969), 15; *radio stations* (1969), 178; *newspapers* (1969), 20 (daily circulation, 703,000).

NUCLEAR TEST in Alaska's Aleutian Islands on November 6 created widespread controversy in United States. Many groups feared that 5-megaton warhead, most powerful U. S. device to be tested underground, might release dangerous radiation or cause an earthquake. In pretest news conference (*above*), Atomic Energy Commission Chairman James Schlesinger points out blast site on Amchitka Island. (*Left*) To demonstrate absence of danger after test, Schlesinger (*foreground*) visited Amchitka with atomic energy officials on November 7.

ALASKA

In 1971 attention in Alaska was focused on native land claims, a delay in laying a pipeline to carry oil from the North Slope fields, and an underground nuclear test in the Aleutian Islands.

Native Land Claims. The Native Land Claims bill was passed by the U. S. Congress on Dec. 14, 1971. Alaska's three congressional delegates had combined their efforts to get the bill enacted despite pressures from conservationists. The measure, which was a compromise bill worked out by a Senate-House conference committee, grants to Eskimos, Indians, and Aleuts full title to 40 million acres of land and $962.5 million in cash—$462.5 million to come from the federal government over an 11-year period and the remainder to come from mineral revenues. The cash will be handled by 12 regional corporations and the land will be divided among some 220 villages and the 12 corporations. The bill also ends the freeze that the U. S. Department of the Interior had placed on the further distribution of federal lands pending settlement of the claims.

The bill was in answer to native claims to Alaskan lands. The claimants said that the land, on which they had lived for as long as anyone could remember, had been illegally taken from them by the federal government, which, in the 1959 Statehood Act, gave the state the right to select 103 million acres of land. The state then selected and later leased the North Slope lands to oil companies.

Transportation. The Alyeska Pipeline Service Co. was unable to obtain a permit in 1971 to lay an oil pipeline from the Yukon River to the North Slope. The main obstacle to obtaining the permit was the uncertainty, until mid-December, about the settlement of the land claims. However, the company tentatively agreed that it would, upon receiving a permit, build a 300-mile pipeline haul road to state secondary-highway standards at no cost to the state. Meanwhile, the 48-inch pipe from Japan was stored at Valdez, Fairbanks, and Prudhoe Bay.

Alaska's two largest centers of population, Anchorage and Fairbanks, were brought 90 miles closer together by the completion of a 353-mile, $2.7 million highway skirting Mt. McKinley National Park. U. S. Air transportation suffered its heaviest toll in history when an Alaska Airlines jetliner crashed in heavy fog and rain near Juneau, killing 111.

The Legislature. Alaska's lawmakers in their second-longest session in history adopted a $292 million budget for fiscal 1972, up 12% from that of 1971. The Legislature established a committee to study economic, ecological, and transportation problems involved with the North Slope pipeline. It also created a state department of environmental affairs and provided money for flood control, hospitals, and a 5% pay raise for state employees.

The Legislature provided $892,000 in state funds to Alaska Methodist University and to Sheldon Jackson College for contractual education services. This will save the two private schools from closing.

Area: 586,412 square miles (1,518,807 sq km).
Population (1970 census): 302,173. *Density,* 0.5 per sq mi.
Chief Cities (1970 census): Juneau, the capital, 6,050; Anchorage, 48,081; Fairbanks, 14,771; Ketchikan, 6,994.
Government (1971): *Chief Officers*—governor, William A. Egan (D); lt. gov., H. A. Boucher (D); atty. gen., John E. Havelock (D); treas., Eric E. Wohlforth; commissioner, Dept. of Education, Marshall L. Lind; chief justice, George F. Boney. *Legislature*—Senate, 20 members (10 Democrats, 10 Republicans); House of Representatives, 40 members (31 D, 9 R).
Education (1970–71): *Enrollment*—public elementary schools, 59,783 pupils, 2,349 teachers; public secondary, 18,831 pupils, 1,472 teachers; nonpublic schools (fall 1968), 2,-300 pupils, 170 teachers; college and university (fall 1968), 7,193 students. *Public school expenditures* (1970–71), $105,744,000 ($1,330 per pupil). *Average teacher's salary* (1970–71), $13,570.
State Finances (fiscal year 1970): *Revenues,* $1,211,648,000 (total sales and gross receipts taxes, $20,408,000; motor fuel tax, $10,372,000; federal funds, $103,453,000). *Expenditures,* $354,128,000 (education, $120,066,000; health, welfare, and safety, $21,887,000; highways, $68,894,000). *State debt,* $222,255,000 (June 30, 1970).
Personal Income (1970): $1,452,000,000; per capita, $4,676.
Public Assistance (1970): $12,387,000. *Average monthly payments* (Dec. 1970)—old-age assistance, $138.05; aid to families with dependent children, $226.35.
Labor Force: *Nonagricultural wage and salary earners* (June 1971), 100,600. *Average annual employment* (1969)—manufacturing, 7,000; trade, 14,000; government, 33,000; services, 11,000. *Insured unemployed* (Oct. 1971)—3,000.
Manufacturing (1967): *Value added by manufacture,* $130,400,-000; Food and allied products, $52,600,000; lumber and wood products, $24,600,000.
Agriculture (1970): *Cash farm income,* $4,360,000 (livestock, $3,108,000; crops, $1,168,000; government payments, $84,000).
Mining (1970): *Production value,* $299,372,000 (ranks 25th among the states). Chief minerals (tons)—Sand and gravel, 20,365,000; gold, 38,400 troy ounces; natural gas, 59,-185,000,000 cubic feet; petroleum, 82,250,000 barrels.
Fisheries (1970): *Commercial catch,* 526,600,000 pounds ($89,700,000). *Leading species* by value (1967), salmon, $24,631,235; king crabs, $14,969,768.
Transportation: *Roads* (1969), 7,123 miles (11,463 km); *motor vehicles* (1969), 131,000; *railroads* (1968), 552 miles (890 km); *airports* (1969), 495.
Communications: *Telephones* (1970), 85,300; *television stations* (1969), 7; *radio stations* (1969), 21; *newspapers* (1969), 6 (daily circulation, 68,000).

The Economy. In the absence of a permit to build its pipeline across federal lands, the oil industry's operations on the North Slope came almost to a standstill. However, some activity continued to the south in the Gulf of Alaska. Employment in the oil industry dropped 60% in 1970 from the previous year. Expenditures for oil operations in 1970 fell more than $90 million.

The West Coast longshoremen's strike created materials shortages in the building industry and hampered fishermen in marketing their product. Consumer prices for 1971 were up 3.8%–4.3% in major centers, with housing costs rising the most.

Canniken. In November the Atomic Energy Commission conducted project Canniken, a 5-megaton nuclear explosion beneath the Aleutian island of Amchitka. The commission proceeded with the test—the largest such ever made—despite protests from Alaska's governor and congressional representatives and from other Americans, as well as from the Canadian and Japanese governments. Court suits to stop the blast went all the way up to the U. S. Supreme Court, but without success. Fears of earthquakes (the test site was on the San Andreas fault), tidal waves, and radiation leaks were voiced, but no immediate harmful effects were noted.

Imperial Visit. Alaska was host to a historic meeting in September 1971, when President Nixon greeted Emperor Hirohito of Japan, who was en route to Europe. It was the first time a reigning Japanese monarch had ever set foot on foreign soil. Millions in Japan watched on television.

RONALD E. CHINN
University of Alaska

ALBANIA

The year 1971 marked the 25th anniversary of the establishment of the People's Republic of Albania and the 30th anniversary of the founding of the ruling Albanian Party of Labor (APL).

Sixth Congress of the APL. The 6th Congress of the APL met on November 1–7 in Tiranë. Enver Hoxha, first secretary of the party since 1941, was reelected to that position. The APL leadership indicated that the Ideological and Cultural Revolution would continue to be the major feature of the regime's domestic program and that there would be no significant changes in the area of foreign policy.

The official results of the fourth 5-year plan (1966–70) were announced at the congress: agricultural output had increased by only 33%, less than half the planned goal of 71%–76%; industrial production, on the other hand, had risen by 83%, greatly exceeding the projected target of 50%–54%. Acknowledging that the resolution of the agricultural problem remains one of the country's most pressing economic tasks, the fifth 5-year plan (1971–75) retains the development priorities of the previous plan. It projects a 61%–66% increase in industrial production and a 65%–69% rise in agricultural output during the plan period.

Domestic Affairs. During 1971 a new theme in the Ideological and Cultural Revolution was developed. It emphasized the need to transform the Albanian people into a "voluntary self-defense force," capable of fighting beside the armed forces to preserve the nation's "Marxist-Leninist" system.

Although the country's television industry was still in its infancy in 1971, the leadership expressed concern about the potential impact on the young of telecasts emanating from neighboring states.

In accordance with the new principle of "socialist humanism," the regime embarked on programs to upgrade health and social services.

Official Name: People's Republic of Albania.
Area: 11,000 square miles (28,748 sq km).
Population (1970 est.): 2,100,000. *Density,* 189 per square mile (72 per sq km). *Annual rate of increase,* 3.0%
Chief Cities (1968 est.): Tiranë, the capital, 170,000; Durrës (1967 est.), 53,000; Shkodër (1967 est.), 50,000.
Government: *Head of state,* Haxhi Lieshi, president of the presidium (took office in 1953). *Head of government,* Maj. Gen. Mehmet Shehu, premier (took office in 1954). *First secretary of the Albanian Party of Labor,* Gen. Enver Hoxha (took office in 1946). *Legislature*—People's Assembly (unicameral), 240 members (all members of the Albanian Party of Labor.
Languages: Albanian (official).
Education: *Literacy rate* (1969), 75% of population. *School enrollment* (1968)—primary, 473,687; secondary, 52,695; technical/vocational, 29,822; university/higher, 16,649.
Finances (1968 est.): *Revenues,* $805,000,000; *expenditures,* $795,000,000; *monetary unit,* lek (5 leks equal U. S.$1, 1971).
Gross National Product (1970 est.): $900,000,000.
Manufacturing (metric tons, 1969): Cement, 220,000; meat, 48,000; nitrogenous fertilizer, 29,000; sugar, 17,000; cigarettes, 4,850,000,000 units.
Crops (metric tons, 1968 crop year): Maize, 220,000; sugar beets (1968/69), 208,000; wheat, 180,000.
Minerals (metric tons, 1969): Crude petroleum, 1,147,000; chromium ore, 172,000; copper ore, 6,000.
Foreign Trade (1964): *Exports,* $60,000,000 (chief export—fuels, minerals and metals, $32,500,000). *Imports,* $98,-000,000 (chief imports—machinery and equipment, $48,-680,000; fuels, minerals and metals, $14,680,000). *Chief trading partners* (1964)—People's Republic of China (took 40% of exports, supplied 63% of imports); Czechoslovakia.
Transportation: *Roads* (1960), 1,926 miles (3,100 km); *motor vehicles* (1966), 9,900 (automobiles, 2,500); *railroads* (1965), 65 miles (105 km); *principal airport,* Tirane.
Communications: *Telephones* (1969), 4,813; *television stations* (1968), 1; *television sets* (1969), 2,500; *radios* (1969), 160,000; *newspapers* (1969), 2.

ALBANIA successfully sponsored Communist China for admission to United Nations in 1971. Here, Deputy Foreign Minister Malile (*right*) and other delegation members arrive for General Assembly meeting in October.

Foreign Relations. In February, Albania and Yugoslavia agreed to conduct their diplomatic relations on the ambassadorial level, and in May, Albania and Greece reestablished diplomatic relations. Albanian-Rumanian relations continued to improve, especially in the cultural realm. Thus, by the end of 1971, Albania maintained normal relations with all the Balkan states except pro-Soviet Bulgaria. During the year, Albania also established diplomatic relations with Norway, Iran, and Chile and raised its diplomatic representation with Ethiopia to the ambassadorial level.

Albanian-Soviet relations remained cool. Albania did not send a delegation to the 24th Congress of the USSR Communist party.

Although it was clear that the Albanians did not intend to follow Communist China in their policy toward the United States, the Sino-Albanian alliance appeared to be as firm as ever. Albania was one of the leaders in the successful move to secure recognition of Communist China as the sole representative of China in the United Nations.

NICHOLAS C. PANO
Western Illinois University

ALBERTA

Amid continuing prosperity, voters in the resource-rich Canadian province of Alberta elected a Conservative legislature in 1971, ousting a Social Credit government that had held power continuously since the elections of 1935.

Election. With the slogan "36 years is enough," the Conservative party, led by 41-year-old Peter Lougheed, captured 49 of the 75 seats in the Legislative Assembly in the election of August 30. The subsequent municipal elections provided few surprises: most incumbents were returned to office.

Industry. The 10% import surtax announced by the United States government in August posed little threat to Alberta, since its exports—oil, gas, and agricultural products—were among the products exempted. Unemployment in the province remained substantially below the national average. A new extractive plant was to be constructed in the Athabasca oil sands area, although the existing plant continued to be plagued by technical difficulties.

Unlike many other North American cities, Edmonton and Calgary were avoiding downtown decay. Construction was continuing apace in both cities: among the projects were a department store, a bank, and an oil refinery soon to be built in Edmonton.

Ecology and Agriculture. A heavy June rainfall provided adequate moisture for cereal crops and reduced forest fires. Strip coal mining near Banff was causing concern among ecologists.

Education. Postsecondary educational institutions again fell below the enrollments forecast, causing financial difficulties, but school construction continued at high levels. A new provincial institution, the Grant MacEwan Community College, opened in leased quarters in Edmonton.

JOHN W. CHALMERS, *University of Alberta*

ALBERTA • Information Highlights

Area: 255,285 square miles (661,189 sq km).

Population: 1,628,000 (April 1971 est.)

Chief Cities (1969 est.): Edmonton, the capital (410,105); Calgary (369,025); Lethbridge (38,749); Red Deer (26,924); Medicine Hat (25,713).

Government: *Chief Officers*—lt. gov., J. W. Grant MacEwan; premier, Peter Lougheed (Progressive Conservative); atty. gen., Mervin Leitch (P. C.); prov. treas., Gordon Miniely (P. C.); min. of educ., Lou Hyndman (P. C.); min. of advanced educ., James Foster (P. C.); chief justice, Sidney Bruce Smith. *Legislature*—Legislative Assembly (convened Sept. 3, 1971); 75 members (49 Progressive Conservative, 25 Social Credit, 1 New Democratic Party).

Education: *School enrollment* (1968–69 est.)—public elementary and secondary, 385,972 pupils (17,492 teachers); private schools, 5,614 pupils (313 teachers); Indian (federal) schools, 3,668 pupils (179 teachers); college and university, 19,688 students. *Public school expenditures* (1971 est.), $202,270,000; *average teacher's salary* (1968–69 est.), $7,600.

Public Finance (fiscal year 1971 est.): *Revenues,* $1,020,-380,000 (sales tax, $93,600,000; income tax, $219,269,000; federal funds, $239,455,000). *Expenditures,* $142,621,000 (education, $366,430,000; health and social welfare, $400,-810,000; transport and communications, $102,280,000).

Personal Income (1969 est.): $4,550,000,000.

Social Welfare (fiscal year 1971 est.): $80,790,000 (aged and blind, $3,240,000; dependents and unemployed, $55,800,-000).

Manufacturing (1968): *Value added by manufacture,* $604,-529,000 (food and beverages, $155,712,000; fabricated metals, $55,670,000; primary metals, $41,025,000; transportation equipment, $16,258,000; nonelectrical machinery, $12,667,000; electrical machinery, $10,105,000).

Agriculture (1969 est.): *Cash farm income* (exclusive of govt. payments), $729,559,000 (livestock, $671,099,000; crops (1968 est.), $371,474,000). *Chief crops* (cash receipts)—Wheat, $155,941,000 (ranks 2d among the provinces); barley, $48,153,000 (ranks 1st); rapeseed, $15,232,000 (ranks 1st); sugarbeets, $7,024,000 (ranks 1st); oats, $6,340,000 (ranks 2d).

Mining (1969 est.): *Production value,* $1,193,279,800. *Chief minerals*—crude petroleum, 284,241,338 bbl (ranks 1st); natural gas, 1,609,325,945,000 cubic feet (ranks 1st); sulphur, 2,894,200 tons (ranks 1st among the provinces).

Transportation: *Roads* (1968) 97,151 miles (156,315 km); *motor vehicles* (1969), 735,729; *railroads* (1969), 5,950 track miles (9,576 km); *licensed airports* (1970), 56.

Communications: *Telephones* (1969), 696,098; *television stations* (1970), 8; *radio stations* (1967), 21; *newspapers* (1970), 7 (daily circulation, 332,832).

All figures given in Canadian dollars.

ALGERIA

Disputes over French oil concessions highlighted economic events during 1971. Continued Arabicization in the schools and courts reflected Algeria's determination to reject its French colonial past.

Economy. Algeria's current 4-year economic development plan, which places extraordinary emphasis on industry, entered its second year in 1971. About 45% of the plan's budget is earmarked for industry. Important new projects begun during the year included a contract signed with a U. S. firm to build a vast gas liquefaction plant at Arzew and an agreement with the Soviet Union to undertake a joint comprehensive survey of Algeria's mineral resources. After a visit in October by Soviet Premier Kosygin, who received a warm welcome, it appeared that Algeria's slight trade with the USSR might increase.

After industry the principal areas of investment were education and infrastructure. Agriculture continued to appear as the "poor cousin" of the economic planners, being earmarked for only 15% of capital investment. Long-promised agricultural reforms had not been put into effect by the end of the year. Complaints of inefficiency and declining productivity in agriculture were widespread.

Some of the difficulties encountered by the development program stemmed from the fact that about 60% of the population is 20 years old or younger and therefore, in economic terms, more of a liability than an asset. It appeared that while the percentage of unemployed was declining, unemployment in absolute numbers was increasing.

In addition, the government had severe difficulty accumulating sufficient foreign currency for necessary capital investment. Early in the year, 60% of foreign earnings were projected to come from exports of petroleum and its derivatives, but declines in sales followed disputes with French oil companies after February. Stringent regulations were placed on imports, and by autumn many consumer goods had disappeared or were in short supply. Algerians were clearly being asked to defer present consumption in order to help finance the growth of a more impressive industrial plant from which benefits could be reaped in the future.

The most dramatic event in 1971 involved Algeria's conflict with France and the French oil companies over the latter's large investment in the Saharan petroleum complex. Disagreements over crude oil prices had simmered since 1969, and Franco-Algerian relations had been further strained by France's decision in 1970 to halt its imports of Algerian wine. The dispute led by February 24 to the nationalization of 51% of the French companies' stock and by April 12 to total nationalization.

When the Algerian authorities demanded advance payments for further oil shipments, the companies stopped loading their ships and warned potential buyers of lawsuits if they agreed to purchase from the Algerian state company, Sonatrach, oil the French corporations considered their property. During the dispute President Pompidou of France declared that the special relationship that had existed between the two countries was terminated. On June 30, one French company reached an agreement with Sonatrach for a minority partnership relationship. In September a similar accord was reached with a second French group. By mid-autumn the chill in Franco-Algerian relations was beginning to dissipate.

Domestic Issues. The regime of President Houari Boumedienne continued to be one of the most stable in the Arab world. Most visible opposition stemmed from an illegal socialist party, a descendant of the outlawed Communist party. Communal elections in February had a 76% turnout and were heralded in official circles as one step toward eventual election of a national assembly.

During January and February students said to belong to the socialist party spearheaded disorders at the University of Algiers. The school was returned to normal only after guards were placed on the campus and the Algerian National Students' Union was dissolved.

Arabicization. The process of Arabicizing the cultural and administrative life of the country continued during 1971. The first two years of primary schools were totally Arabicized, while two thirds of the curriculum in succeeding years continued in French. Although 22 secondary schools were Arabicized completely, the majority continued to be dominated by French. The same was true at the universities, where half the professors were French.

A major step toward the official use of Arabic was taken on October 1, when all law courts were required to function in Arabic, providing French translations of conclusions and decisions. In addition, a national commission was created to discuss new legal codes to replace the legal system largely inherited from colonial times. President Boumedienne specified that the new codes should be based in Islamic sources.

JOHN D. RUEDY
Georgetown University

——————— **ALGERIA • Information Highlights** ———————

Official Name: Democratic and Popular Republic of Algeria.
Area: 919,593 square miles (2,381,741 sq km).
Population (1970 est.): 14,000,000. *Density,* 15 per square mile (6 per sq km). *Annual rate of increase,* 3.2%.
Chief Cities (1966 census): Algiers, the capital, 943,142; Oran, 328,257; Constantine, 253,649; Annaba, 168,790.
Government: *Head of state,* Houari Boumedienne, president (took office June 19, 1965). *Head of government,* Houari Boumedienne.
Languages: Arabic (official), French.
Education: *Literacy rate* (1970), 20–25% of population. *Expenditure on education* (1968), 17.6% of total public expenditure. *School enrollment* (1968)—primary, 1,585,-682; secondary, 177,382; technical/vocational, 40,684; university/higher, 10,681.
Finances (1970): Revenues, $1,311,000,000; *expenditures,* $2,123,500,000; *monetary unit,* dinar (4.937 dinars equal U. S.$1, Sept. 1971).
Gross National Product (1969): $4,015,000,000.
National Income (1965 est.): $2,259,000,000; *national income per person,* $193.
Economic Indexes: *Mining production* (1969), 131 (1963= 100); *consumer price index* (1967), 104 (1963=100).
Manufacturing (metric tons, 1969): Cement, 949,000; natural gas products, 930,000; wheat flour (1968), 515,000; meat, 76,000; wine (1968), 9,951,000 hectoliters.
Crops (metric tons, 1968 crop year): Wheat, 1,534,000; grapes for wine, 1,264,000; oranges and tangerines, 381,000.
Minerals (metric tons, 1969): Crude petroleum, 43,841,000; iron ore, 1,599,000; phosphate rock, 420,000; natural gas, 2,985,000,000 cubic meters.
Foreign Trade (1968): Exports (1969), $934,000,000 (chief exports—petroleum, $579,000,000; alcoholic beverages, $78,800,000; liquefied natural gas, $29,900,000; fruit and nuts, $28,100,000). *Imports* (1969) $1,009,000,000 (chief imports—nonelectrical machinery, $162,000,000; iron and steel, $82,100,000; transport equipment, $67,100,000; cereals, $51,700,000). *Chief trading partners* (1968)—France (took 55% of exports, supplied 50% of imports); West Germany (13%—5%); Italy (6%—5%).
Transportation: *Roads* (1966), 55,000 miles (88,945 km); *motor vehicles* (1969), 192,000 (automobiles, 121,200); *railroads* (1970), 2,218 miles (3,569 km); *national airlines,* Air Algeria; *principal airports,* Algiers, Oran, Annaba, Constantine.
Communications: *Telephones* (1970), 169,180; *television stations* (1968), 9; *television sets* (1969), 100,000; *radios* (1969), 700,000; *newspapers* (1968), 4 (daily circulation, 185,000).

BIG FOUR ambassadors reached agreement on status of West Berlin on August 23. From left, ambassadors Abrasimov of USSR, Rush of United States, Jackling of Britain, and Sauvagnargues of France leave Berlin conference.

AMBASSADORS AND ENVOYS

The most spectacular incident in diplomatic circles in 1971 was the British expulsion of a large number of Soviet diplomatic and commercial personnel on charges of espionage. In March, the Mexican government informed the USSR that the five Soviet diplomats in Mexico were personae non gratae after discovering a connection between the Revolutionary Action Movement (MAR) and the Patrice Lumumba University in Moscow. The Mexican government charged that the MAR intended to use force to set up a Communist regime in Mexico.

The threat of terrorist kidnapping continued to worry diplomats in Latin America and other areas, and the Organization of American States condemned the practice, regardless of the political motives of the kidnappers.

The emerging nations continued their role in world diplomacy during 1971. The ambassador of newly independent Fiji presented his credentials in Washington, and Bhutan, Bahrain, and Qatar were admitted to the United Nations. In Africa, Malawi appointed Joe Kachingue as its ambassador to South Africa. He was the first black diplomat to have been accredited to that country.

In the following list of ambassadors and envoys from and to the United States as of Dec. 31, 1971, A designates ambassador extraordinary and plenipotentiary; CA, chargé d'affaires.

LIST OF AMBASSADORS AND ENVOYS

Country	From U.S.	To U.S.
Afghanistan	Robert G. Neumann (A)	Abdullah Malikyar (A)
Argentina	John Davis Lodge (A)	Carlos Manuel Muñiz (A)
Australia	Walter L. Rice (A)	Sir James Plimsoll (A)
Austria	John P. Humes (A)	Karl Gruber (A)
Barbados	Eileen R. Donovan (A)	Valerie Theodore McComie (A)
Belgium		Walter Loridan (A)
Bolivia	Ernest V. Siracusa (A)	Edmundo Valencia-Ibáñez (A)

Country	From U.S.	To U.S.
Botswana	Charles J. Nelson (A)	Linchwe II Molefi Kgafela (A)
Brazil	William M. Rountree (A)	João Augusto de Araujo Castro (A)
Bulgaria	Horace G. Torbert, Jr. (A)	Luben Guerassimov (A)
Burma	Edwin W. Martin (A)	U San Maung (A)
Burundi	Thomas Patrick Melady (A)	Nsanze Terence (A)
Cambodia	Emory C. Swank (A)	Sonn Voeunsai (A)
Cameroon	Lewis Hoffacker (A)	François-Xavier Tchoungui (A)
Canada	Adolph W. Schmidt (A)	Marcel Cadieux (A)
Central Afr. Rep.	Melvin L. Manfull (A)	Christophe Maidou (A)
Ceylon	Robert Strausz-Hupé (A)	Neville Kanakaratne (A)
Chad	Terence A. Todman (A)	Lazare Massibe (A)
Chile	Nathaniel Davis (A)	Orlando Letelier (A)
China (Taiwan)	Walter P. McConaughy (A)	James C. H. Shen (A)
Colombia	Leonard J. Saccio (A)	Douglas Botero-Bashell (A)
Costa Rica	Walter C. Ploeser (A)	Rafael Alberto Zuñiga (A)
Cyprus	David H. Popper (A)	Zenon Rossides (A)
Czechoslovakia		Jaroslav Zantovský (CA)
Dahomey	Matthew J. Looram, Jr. (A)	Wilfrid De Souza (A)
Denmark	Guilford Dudley, Jr. (A)	Eyvind Bartels (A)
Dominican Republic	Francis E. Meloy, Jr. (A)	S. Salvador Ortiz (A)
Ecuador	Findley Burns, Jr. (A)	Carlos Mantilla-Ortega (A)
El Salvador	Henry E. Catta, Jr. (A)	Col. Julio A. Rivera (A)
Equatorial Guinea	Lewis Hoffacker (A)	
Ethiopia	E. Ross Adair (A)	Ghebeyehou Mekbib (CA)
Fiji		S. A. Sikivou
Finland	Val Peterson (A)	Olavi Munkki (A)
France	Arthur K. Watson (A)	Charles Lucet (A)
Gabon	John A. McKesson (A)	Gaston R. Bouckat-Bou-Nziengui (A)
Gambia	G. Edward Clark (A)	
Germany	Kenneth Rush (A)	Rolf Pauls (A)
Ghana	Fred L. Hadsel (A)	Ebenezer Moses Debrah (A)
Great Britain	Walter H. Annenberg (A)	The Earl of Cromer (A)
Greece	Henry J. Tasca (A)	Basil George Vitsaxis (A)

LIST OF AMBASSADORS AND ENVOYS (continued)

Country	From U.S.	To U.S.
Guatemala	William G. Bowdler (A)	Julio Asensio-Wunderlich (A)
Guinea	Albert W. Sherer, Jr. (A)	Elhadj Mory Keita (A)
Guyana	Spencer M. King (A)	Rahman B. Gajraj (A)
Haiti	Clinton E. Knox (A)	René Chalmers (A)
Honduras	Hewson A. Ryan (A)	Roberto Gálvez-Barnes (A)
Hungary	Alfred Puhan (A)	Károly Szabó (A)
Iceland	Luther I. Replogle (A)	Guðmundur Í. Guðmundsson (A)
India	Kenneth B. Keating (A)	Lakshmi Kant Jha (A)
Indonesia	Francis J. Galbraith (A)	Sjarif Thajeb (A)
Iran	Douglas MacArthur II (A)	Amir-Aslan Afshar (A)
Ireland	John D. J. Moore (A)	William Warnock (A)
Israel	Walworth Barbour (A)	Lt. Gen. Yitzhak Rabin (A)
Italy	Graham A. Martin (A)	Egidio Ortona (A)
Ivory Coast	John F. Root (A)	Timothée N'Guetta Ahoua (A)
Jamaica	Vincent de Roulet (A)	Sir Egerton R. Richardson (A)
Japan	Armin H. Meyer (A)	Nobuhiko Ushiba (A)
Jordan	L. Dean Brown (A)	Abdul Hamid Sharaf (A)
Kenya	Robinson McIlvaine (A)	Leonard Oliver Kibinge (A)
Korea	Philip C. Habib (A)	Dong Jo Kim (A)
Kuwait	John Patrick Walsh (A)	Salem S. al-Sabah (A)
Laos	G. McMurtrie Godley (A)	Prince Khammao (A)
Lebanon	William B. Buffum (A)	Najati Kabbani (A)
Lesotho	Charles J. Nelson (A)	Mothusi T. Mashologu (A)
Liberia	Samuel Z. Westerfield, Jr. (A)	S. Edward Peal (A)
Libya	Joseph Palmer 2d (A)	Abdalla Suwesi (A)
Luxembourg	Kingdon Gould, Jr. (A)	Jean Wagner (A)
Malagasy Republic	Anthony D. Marshall (A)	Jules A. Razafim-bahiny (A)
Malawi	William C. Burdett (A)	Nyemba Wales Mbekeani (A)
Malaysia	Jack W. Lydman (A)	Tan Sri Yoke Lin Ong (A)
Maldives	Robert Strausz-Hupé (A)	
Mali	Robert O. Blake (A)	Seydou Traoré (A)
Malta	John C. Pritzlaff, Jr. (A)	Joseph Attard-Kingswell (A)
Mauritania	Richard W. Murphy (A)	M'Bareck Ould Bouna (CA)
Mauritius	William D. Brewer (A)	Pierre Guy Girald Balancy (A)
Mexico	Robert H. McBride (A)	José Juan de Olloquí (A)
Morocco	Stuart W. Rockwell (A)	Badreddine Senoussi (A)
Nepal	Carol C. Laise (A)	Kul Shekhar Sharma (A)
Netherlands	J. William Middendorf II (A)	Baron Rijnhard B. van Lynden (A)
New Zealand	Kenneth Franzheim II (A)	Frank Corner (A)
Nicaragua	Turner B. Shelton (A)	Guillermo Sevilla-Sacasa (A)
Niger	Roswell D. McClelland (A)	Georges M. Condat (A)
Nigeria	John E. Reinhardt (A)	Joe Iyalla (A)
Norway	Philip K. Crowe (A)	Arne Gunneng (A)
Pakistan	Joseph S. Farland (A)	Nawabzada Agha Mohammad Raza (A)
Panama	Robert M. Sayre (A)	José Antonio de la Ossa (A)
Paraguay	J. Raymond Ylitalo (A)	Roque J. Ávila (A)
Peru	Taylor G. Belcher (A)	Fernando Berckemeyer (A)
Philippines	Henry A. Byroade (A)	Eduardo Z. Romualdez (A)
Poland	Walter J. Stoessel, Jr. (A)	Ryszard Frackiewicz (CA)
Portugal	Ridgway B. Knight (A)	Antonio Cabrita Matias (CA)
Rumania	Leonard C. Meeker (A)	Corneliu Bogdan (A)

Country	From U.S.	To U.S.
Rwanda		Fidèle Nkundabagenzi (A)
Saudi Arabia	Nicholas G. Thacher (A)	Ibrahim A Sowayel (A)
Senegal	G. Edward Clark (A)	André Coulbary (A)
Sierra Leone	Howard P. Mace (A)	Jacob A. C. Davies (A)
Singapore	Charles T. Cross (A)	Ernest Steven Monteiro (A)
Somali		Abdullahi Addou (A)
South Africa	John G. Hurd (A)	Johan S. F. Botha (A)
Spain	Robert C. Hill (A)	Jaime Arguelles (A)
Swaziland	Charles J. Nelson (A)	S. T. Msindazwe Sukati (A)
Sweden	Jerome H. Holland (A)	Hubert de Besche (A)
Switzerland	Shelby Davis (A)	Felix Schnyder (A)
Tanzania	Claude G. Ross (A)	Gosbert Marcell Rutabanzibwa (A)
Thailand	Leonard Unger (A)	Sunthorn Hongladarom (A)
Togo	Dwight Dickinson (A)	Epiphine Ayi Mawussi (A)
Trinidad and Tobago	J. Fife Symington, Jr. (A)	Ellis Emmanuel Innocent Clarke (A)
Tunisia	John A. Calhoun (A)	Slaheddine El Goulli (A)
Turkey	William J. Handley (A)	Melih Esenbel (A)
Uganda	Clarence Clyde Ferguson, Jr. (A)	Mustapha Ramathan (A)
USSR	Jacob D. Beam (A)	Anatoliy F. Dobrynin (A)
Upper Volta	Donald B. Easum (A)	Paul Rouamba (A)
Uruguay	Charles W. Adair, Jr. (A)	Hector Luisi (A)
Venezuela	Robert McClintock (A)	Julio Sosa-Rodríguez (A)
Vietnam	Ellsworth Bunker (A)	Bui Diem (A)
Yugoslavia	Malcolm Toon (A)	Toma Granfil (A)
Zaïre	Sheldon B. Vance (A)	Pierre Ileka (A)
Zambia	Oliver L. Troxel, Jr. (A)	Unia G. Mwila (A)

AMERICAN INDIANS. See INDIANS, AMERICAN.
AMERICAN LITERATURE. See LITERATURE.

HUANG HUA, first Communist Chinese ambassador to Canada, enters Government House in Ottawa in July. He later became deputy head of China's UN delegation.

ANGOLA

The war between the Angolan nationalists and Portuguese forces entered its 11th year in 1971. In June the Portuguese National Assembly approved a bill authorizing greater autonomy for the overseas territories. The bill, applying particularly to Angola and Mozambique, authorized local legislation to organize provincial administration and to raise revenue in accordance with budgets drafted and approved by local assemblies. The Portuguese government, however, retained control of territorial defense and foreign policy.

The War. The Portuguese government remained determined to hold its African territories. In March, three French-manufactured SA-330 helicopters were delivered to government troops in Angola. The helicopters are capable of carrying 24 soldiers each and will be used by Portuguese patrols to "disrupt" guerrilla supply lines.

On March 30, a Portuguese court sentenced a Catholic priest, Joaquim Pinto de Andrade, to three years' imprisonment and the loss of his political rights for 15 years on charges of supporting the Popular Movement for the Liberation of Angola. Eight other persons were given shorter prison terms on the same charge.

Foreign Relations. A report to the UN Commission on Human Rights in February charged that "elements of genocide" existed in Angola, where "Portugal had carried out mass executions of civilians and of persons suspected of opposing the regime and had carried out collective punishment against the civilian population."

In May, Portuguese Foreign Minister Rui Patricio announced that Portugal was withdrawing from UNESCO. He also invited the UN Committee on Colonization to visit Angola to investigate the validity of charges of dereliction in administration.

Angola's trade with South Africa increased threefold between 1968 and 1971, and Rhodesian businessmen have tried to improve trade and investments in Angola. But in spite of increased economic independence, Angola still relies on Portugal for military expenditures.

Epidemic. On April 3 an epidemic of yellow fever was reported in Luanda, where 80 persons had died of the disease. It was the first such crisis since 1900.

RHEA MARSH SMITH, *Rollins College*

ANGOLA • Information Highlights ---

Official Name: Overseas Province of Angola.
Area: 481,351 square miles (1,246,700 sq km).
Population (1969 est.): 5,430,000. *Density,* 11 per square mile (4 per sq km). *Annual rate of increase,* 1.3%.
Chief City (1966 est.): Luanda, the capital, 250,000.
Government: Local administration is headed by the governor general, appointed by the Portuguese government.
Languages: Portuguese (official), Bantu languages.
Education: *Literacy rate* (1970), 10% of population. *Expenditure on education* (1966), 4% of total public expenditure. *School enrollment* (1967)—primary, 296,269; secondary, 41,292; technical/vocational, 18,797; university/higher, 989.
Finances (1969 est.): *Revenues,* $227,900,000; *expenditures,* $227,900,000; *monetary unit,* escudo (27.66 escudos equal U.S.$1, Sept. 1971).
Gross National Product (1967 est.): $997,000,000.
National Income (1963): $321,000,000; *national income per person,* $64.
Manufacturing (metric tons, 1969): Residual fuel oil, 389,000; cement, 383,000; fishmeals, 98,900; wheat flour, 61,000; sawnwood, 281,000 cubic meters.
Crops (metric tons, 1969 crop year): Fish, 417,500; maize (1968), 400,000; coffee, 204,000; cotton lint, 21,000.
Minerals (metric tons, 1969): Iron ore, 3,396,000; crude petroleum, 2,458,000; diamonds, 2,022,000 metric carats.
Foreign Trade: *Exports* (1970), $423,000,000. *Imports* (1970), $369,000,000. *Chief trading partner* (1968)—Portugal (took 34% of exports, supplied 36% of imports).

ANTARCTICA

Several research programs, including studies of man's pollution of the polar environment, were carried out in Antarctica by nearly 150 investigators in the summer of 1970–71. President Nixon reaffirmed U. S. interest in scientific work undertaken in cooperation with the Special Committee on Antarctic Research, which coordinates exchanges of information between scientists of the 12 nations that signed the 1959 Antarctic Treaty.

Pollution Problems. Since 1965, when DDT was first found in fatty tissues of Antarctic animals, measurements have been made on the growing amounts of radioactive fallout as well as chlorinated hydrocarbons in that region. The results, together with local pollution problems, have increased man's awareness of the need for corrective measures. The use of the surrounding ocean for waste disposal has already upset the Antarctic marine ecosystem to a degree that could easily require more than a century for recovery. Studies are being made of the technology that will be needed to deal with these problems. Immediate measures include local cleanup campaigns, installation of a sewage treatment plant and an incinerator at McMurdo Station, coordination and implementation of agreed-upon measures for protecting plant and animal life cycles by selection of protected areas, and limitation of the use of radioisotopes in scientific work.

Biological Studies. Studies continued of the lives of seals, penguins, skuas, and fish in the areas of McMurdo and Palmer Stations and Capes Hallett and Crozier, as did biological research in Antarctica's dry valleys. Bacterias, yeasts, lichens, and algae were found in new locations near the South Pole—the most southerly thus far.

The U. S. research ship *Eltanin* conducted year-round activities in Antarctic seas, while the *Hero* observed the structure and tectonic history of the Scotia Ridge off the Antarctic Peninsula. The two ships were augmented by vessels of the Scripps Institute of Oceanography: the *Thomas Washington,* which operated north of the Ross Sea; and the *Alpha Helix,* which performed animal physiology studies near Palmer Station. Of particular interest were those on Chaenichthyids, or "icefish," the only adult vertebrates known to lack hemoglobin.

A party of 15 scientists, under the supervision of David H. Elliot of Ohio State University, continued investigations in the Transantarctic Mountains. Their first day was rewarded by the finding of a 200 million-year-old fossil of a cynodont, a carnivorous reptile with doglike teeth. Other important finds included fossils of amphibians and mammal-like reptiles closely related to forms in South Africa and India. These animals could have migrated to Antarctica only across extensive dry-land connections in the past.

Further Evidence for Continental Drift. The fossil discoveries, together with information from sources such as the rubidium-strontium dating of the Antarctic crust, give further support to the theory of continental drift—the concept that a former supercontinent, Gondwanaland, fragmented about 150 to 200 million years ago and that the fragments drifted to their present locations and are continuing to drift. Data from cores drilled at Byrd Station confirm the belief that, beneath its ice, Antarctica consists of three geological units: East Antarctica, which probably drifted from the Indian

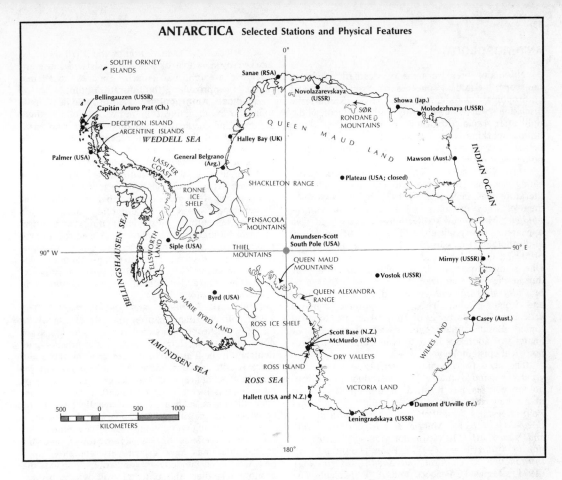

Ocean; the Antarctic Peninsula, a continuation of the Andes Mountains; and West Antarctica, a crustal block that separated from Gondwanaland by sea-floor spreading.

Glaciological studies in Marie Byrd Land indicate that Antarctica has been covered by its ice cap for as long as the continent has occupied its polar position. Additional investigations substantiate the theory that ice ages were caused by surges of vast quantities of Antarctic ice into the ocean every 100,000 years or so.

Geophysical Research. Eight scientists from Argentina, Chile, Britain, the Soviet Union, and the United States studied the changes on Deception Island that followed the most recent and violent eruption, on Aug. 12, 1970, of Antarctica's only active volcano. Another party of eight scientists carried out the second year of a geological mapping and geodetic survey of the Lassiter Coast area. A six-man Norwegian party was landed in the Sverdrup Mountains by U. S. planes to conduct a wide range of studies, while at the same time a four-man British geological survey party was flown to Shackleton Range to continue work there. The National Science Foundation also continued its long-range flights using radio echo soundings to measure ice thickness along preselected routes.

Each month the observatory in year-round operation at McMurdo obtains data from about 1,000 satellite passes. Byrd substation, where two women from the United States and New Zealand operated a radio research program during the past season, will be replaced by strategically located Siple Station as the major U. S. year-round site for research into ionospheric and magnetospheric physics.

Soviet Activities. At present the Soviet Union maintains six wintering stations, and it plans to build a seventh at Cape Dart. The most recently established one, Leningradskaya, opened on Feb. 27, 1971. Thus the Soviet Union will have at least one station in each quadrant of the continent, as well as Vostok Station near the geomagnetic pole. Vostok, at an altitude of about 12,000 feet (nearly 3,500 meters), is the coldest place on earth to be inhabited by man; on Aug. 27, 1960, the temperature there dropped to $-127°$ F ($-88.5°$ C). In addition, the Soviet resupply ships *Professor Vize* and *Professor Zubov*—both built in 1967—carry out oceanographic and meteorological research.

Personnel and Other News. The opening day of the season, Oct. 7, 1970, was marred by a crash landing at McMurdo Station. Five of the 80 Navy personnel aboard were injured, and the Super Constellation was completely wrecked. On Feb. 15, 1971, an LC-130F Hercules caught fire at McMurdo while taxiing for take-off, but no one was injured. And when U. S. coast guard cutter *Staten Island* struck an uncharted pinnacle near Australia's Mawson Station, a crack in the hull forced the ship to withdraw from Antarctica. On the positive side, a U. S. Air Force C-133 Cargo Master—the largest plane ever to land on the continent—safely carried three helicopters to McMurdo, and a two-story administration building was completed at the station.

Soviet ionospheric physicist Aleksandr Shirochkov spent the winter at Byrd Station, and American radio electronics engineer Dale Vance spent the year at Vostok. Since 1958, 12 Americans have spent the winter at Soviet stations.

EDITH M. RONNE, *Antarctic Specialist*

ANTHROPOLOGY

No major breakthroughs or dramatic shifts in the scope, theoretical concerns, or basic structure of anthropology were apparent in 1971. Rather, the discipline seems to be entering a phase of consolidation after rapid expansion in the 1960's. Some trends marking this consolidation are discussed below, as are some subfields of sociocultural anthropology that seem most active at present.

New Publications. The problem of communicating the vast amount of current anthropological literature was facilitated in 1971 by the establishment of a new quarterly called *Abstracts in Anthropology.* Many new collections of readings also appeared, and publishing firms are bringing out anthropological classics that have long been out of print and unavailable except in specialized libraries. One significant synthesizing publication to appear during the last year was *A Handbook of Method in Cultural Anthropology*, edited by Raoul Naroll and Ronald Cohn. This useful volume contains articles on a wide range of cultural anthropological topics. Besides focusing on specific techniques of analysis, it addresses itself to issues of basic anthropological epistemology.

The need for teaching materials to service the greatly expanded market for introductory anthropology courses has resulted in the appearance of many new textbooks. These include Roger and Felix Keesing's *New Perspectives in Cultural Anthropology* (1971), Marvin Harris' *Culture, Man, and Nature* (1971), Victor Barnouw's *An Introduction to Anthropology* (1971), Peter Hammond's *An Introduction to Cultural and Social Anthropology* (1971), James L. Peacock and A. T. Kirsch's *The Human Direction* (1970), and Ralph L. Beals and J. Hoijer's *An Introduction to Anthropology*, 3d ed. (1970).

Kinship Studies. Studies of kinship and social organization continue to account for many journal articles and technical monographs. *Kinship and Culture* (1971), a collection of original papers edited by F. L. K. Hsu, represents a somewhat new departure. Hsu's central thesis is that the dominant dyads, or pairs, in a given kinship system tend to determine the attitudes and action patterns that the individual develops toward other relationships both within and outside that system. This hypothesis is examined in Hsu's book by 18 authors representing different disciplines and sources of comparative data —an approach that may help to offset the heavy emphasis on mathematical and linguistic approaches in recent years.

Myth, Ritual, and Art. Structural and symbolic analysis of myth and ritual, pioneered by Claude Lévi-Strauss, Edmund R. Leach, Victor W. Turner, Clifford Geertz, and others, continues to stimulate further research as well as reanalysis of previously gathered data. In *Claude Lévi-Strauss* (1970), Leach has provided a concise and thoughtful introduction to the contributions of the French master. Another work that will help guide the neophyte through the maze of structuralist thinking in anthropology and related fields is *Structuralism: A Reader* (1970), edited by Michael Lane.

There also appears to be a resurgence of interest in the subject of primitive art. Two valuable anthologies have been published: *Art and Aesthetics in Primitive Societies* (1970), edited by Carol F. Jopling; and *Anthropology and Art* (1970), edited by Charlotte M. Otten. Perhaps the 1970's will be marked by a return of anthropologists to museum-oriented research, particularly since the academic market is approaching the saturation point.

Medical Anthropology. Anthropologists have long shown an interest in native or folk medical systems, and medical anthropology is emerging as a specialized subdiscipline. In recent work, linguistic models are being employed to formalize the categories of disease, diagnosis, and treatment procedure that are used in various indigenous settings. This work has practical implications in that it helps in introducing modern medicine to tribal groups and underdeveloped areas by highlighting those points where cross-cultural misunderstandings may arise. A more biologically based focus of medical anthropology is the approach that views human behavior, in relation to disease, in terms of an ongoing evolutionary process. This approach is systematically explored by Alexander Alland, Jr., in *Adaptation in Cultural Evolution* (1969).

Fieldwork Problems and Developments. The world political situation often directly affects where and how anthropologists can work. Some areas are now closed to Western scientists, while others—particularly in the Third World—are growing more and more sensitive about endorsing anthropological research. The concept of knowledge for the sake of knowledge is increasingly being called into question, and officials in such areas now usually have to be convinced of the direct "relevance" of the research. The anthropologist is being held accountable for the possible effects of his investigations, and his ethical dilemmas have grown very complex, since he owes a certain loyalty and obligation to the group he studies, the political unit where his research is conducted, his funding agency, the academic community and general public, and his own intellectual and moral integrity. One encouraging development is the emergence of an increasing number of trained native anthropologists. As this trend continues, the quality of ethnographic reporting should improve and sensitivity to local problems grow more acute. Anthropology will become less a stepchild of former colonial powers and gain a more universal perspective.

In the United States, much recent fieldwork has reflected the growing popularity of urban anthropology and the study of ethnic groups as distinctive subcultures. Along with increased interest in Afro-American and Mexican-American cultures has come a revitalized interest in American Indians —their traditional societies, existence on modern reservations, and adjustment to urban situations. Modern Indian political movements are being seen in terms of efforts toward self-determination, redress of long-standing grievances, and attainment of positive ego-identity.

Academic Outlook. In the U. S. academic world, economic conditions have severely cut into sources of funds for government, foundation, and university-sponsored research and training programs in anthropology. Enrollment in this field in graduate schools has leveled off. It is hoped that the next several years will witness the discovery of new areas to which anthropological skills and knowledge can be applied usefully, and professors of anthropology will be training students for other than academic careers.

(See also ARCHAEOLOGY.)

RAYMOND D. FOGELSON
University of Chicago

ARCHAEOLOGY

Some major archaeological finds were made in 1971. Discovery of a jaw fragment in Africa increased the known age of the earliest form of man to 5 million years. A 200,000-year-old skull found in France may become a key in reconstructing man's history. Also, certain stone artifacts can now be dated and interpreted by means of thermoluminescent testing.

EASTERN HEMISPHERE

New techniques and discoveries advanced archaeological knowledge in 1971, though there were curtailments in funds and work permits.

Direct Dating of Stone Tools. A method for direct dating and interpretation of certain stone artifacts has been worked out by a trio of Midwestern scientists. Their method is based on the thermoluminescence of a material—that is, the emission of light from the material when it is heated. The method can be used to date and interpret any flint or other stone artifacts that were intentionally heated prior to chipping or were incidentally heated, such as by having been dropped in a fireplace. Dating and interpretation of such artifacts are accomplished by reheating them over a range of temperatures and measuring their output of light.

Thermoluminescence is used in archaeology mainly for interpreting the technique of manufacture and the use of an artifact. For instance, it recently was verified that some flints were intentionally heated prior to chipping. Thermoluminescent testing also serves as the only reliable technique for dating archaeological sites older than 50,000 years (beyond the range of radiocarbon dating) or younger than 500,000 years (too recent for potassium-argon dating). The 50,000- to 500,000-year time-span includes 90% of the time that man has lived outside of Africa. Another use of thermoluminescent testing is for the detection of faked artifacts.

Oldest Human. The known antiquity of the earliest form of man, Australopithecus, was increased by one million years in 1971. In the fossil-rich region of northern Kenya near Lake Rudolf, scientists found a jaw fragment of an Australopithecine who lived five million years ago, as determined by radioactive dating techniques. Apparently, the earliest Australopithecines did not make stone tools.

Old Stone Age Cultures. Upper Acheulean hand axes from the Riss glaciation (which began about 200,000 years ago) are remarkably long, thin, and finely chipped implements often made of attractively colored stone. The hand-ax makers also made a fairly varied series of flaked stone tools. Until 1971 the people who made these tools were unrepresented among the discovered fossil men, except for two broken forehead fragments of females.

In 1971 archaeologists excavated a nearly complete male skull (lacking only the lower jaw) from a cave near the village of Tautavel in the French Pyrenees. The skull has large eye sockets, large eyebrow ridges, a retreating forehead, and a small braincase. These features suggest that it is intermediate between *Homo erectus,* such as Java man, and Neanderthal man. The skull was found in a layer filled with Upper Acheulean tools.

A new Upper Palaeolithic culture, the Changpinian, was identified from finds at the "Eight Fairy Caves" in the conglomerate cliffs on the Pacific

JADE SHROUDS, discovered in China in 1968, were revealed for first time in 1971. An extraordinary example of Han dynasty art, they were made about 2,000 years ago for Prince Liu Sheng (*above*) and his wife. Jade squares are stitched together with gold thread.

coast of Taiwan. The early Changpinians were hunters and fishers, who made bone implements and used many unifacial flakes and chopping tools. The Changpinian culture existed as early as 13,000 B.C., as determined by radiocarbon dating, and it continued into the post-Pleistocene period, which began about 10,000 years ago. The later culture resembled the Hoabhinian culture of Southeast Asia, which developed an early form of agriculture.

Early Civilizations. Imhotep was a versatile Egyptian genius who designed the first pyramid, called the Step Pyramid. In 1971 the English archaeologist Walter Emery, who was searching for Imhotep's grave, collapsed at the entrance to a passageway near the pyramid and later died. He had found immense subterranean galleries containing thousands of mummified ibises, a species of bird sacred to Imhotep. Another gallery contained hundreds of mummified baboons, a symbol of sagacity. In a chamber containing mummified falcons, sacred to Horus, was a small stone plaque inscribed with a direct reference to "Imhotep the Great."

A Mycenaean-period cemetery with trench graves refilled with red sand was found near 'Akko (formerly Acre or Accho), Israel. Pottery at the site included Mycenaean amphorae, Cypriot milk bowls, and Syrian flasks. There were also Egyptian seals and rings, with one having the cartouche of Amenophis III (c. 1350 B.C.). A man buried at right angles beneath a woman was equipped with a springy bronze trident; the woman held a bronze mirror. A chariot was found in a nearby grave.

PREHISTORIC frescoes, buried in volcanic ash for 3,500 years, were found on Thera. One has unusual stylized antelopes, the other depicts a boxing match.

For years archaeologists had wondered about the cultural and chronological contexts of great numbers of ornamented bronze and iron tools and weapons that appeared on the clandestine antiquities market from Luristan, Iran. Belgian archaeologists in Luristan succeeded in excavating and analyzing a number of graves that contained just such bronzes, and a basic chronology was established for dating them (c. 1100–700 B.C.). The bronzes are highly aesthetic and tell much about the people who used them.

Indian Metallurgists. Indian archaeologists have unearthed stratified remains of the Malwa and Jorwe cultures in central India. The Malwa, who occupied the region about 2000 B.C., fashioned a distinctive black-painted pink pottery. They mostly had stone tools but used some copper ones. The later Jorwe culture had a bronze technology. Both the Malwa and the Jorwe peoples lived in round houses and subsisted by self-sufficient agriculture.

Iron-Age Tribes. Excavations in an area 300 miles northeast of Johannesburg, South Africa, have uncovered dwellings and forges of iron-using agricultural peoples. These people made sand-tempered globular pottery and copper artifacts as well. Their earlier settlements, radiocarbon dated to about 1000 A.D., were in the lowlands. The later people, either because of disease or warfare, turned to the small hills to emplace their round houses. Some of the first Iron Age burials found in South Africa were discovered under the floors of these houses.

Roman City. The imperial Roman city of Sirmium, lost since the fall of the Roman Empire, was discovered under the modern Yugoslav town of Sremska Mitrovica. An international team cleared the first hippodrome (scene of Roman chariot races) found in Yugoslavia. Distinctive styles in jewelry and fresco painting show the innovative importance of the city before it was sacked in 583 A.D.

Han Dynasty Relics. On mainland China the Red Guard movement has halted archaeological research since 1966, but discoveries still continue. While searching near Peking for caves that would be useful as bomb shelters, soldiers came upon a remarkable tomb of a Han dynasty prince and his wife. The royal couple, who died about 113 B.C., had been covered from head to toe by form-fitting mosaic shrouds made of thousands of jade squares sewn together with thread of gold. These bodies, with outlays of ornaments and implements, have become a tourist attraction.

Anatolian Underground Cities. Two underground cities, Kaymakli and Derinkuyu, have been found southeast of Ankara on the Anatolian Plateau. Kaymakli consists of seven levels descending 70 feet into the earth. The city is an enormous mazelike construction, and its fullest extent has not yet been found. It is estimated that the city structures furnished living quarters for about 50,000 persons. Both cities contain residences, churches, oil and wine presses, air shafts, and deep wells. They provided hideouts for Christians during the Muslim conquest in the first half of the 7th century.

RALPH M. ROWLETT
University of Missouri

WESTERN HEMISPHERE

Archaeologists continued to work in 1971 at a number of ancient urban sites in the Western Hemisphere. Recent studies of the processes by which such sites developed have suggested that many of the processes were largely analogous with patterns of urban growth today.

Peru. Harvard University archaeologists in the Moche Valley of northern Peru pursued their studies of the urban-rural relationships that allowed the ancient Chimu capital to grow and prosper between 1200 and 1400 A.D. The site covers at least 7.7 square miles (20 sq km) and contains many preserved architectural features. Excavations thus far have succeeded in defining the city as a densely populated urban center, rigidly planned and economically sustained by a network of rural settlements throughout the Moche Valley.

Constructed of adobe brick and field stone, the city of Chan-Chan seems to have been socially stratified much as are modern urban centers. The bulk of the population apparently was quartered in small structures peripheral to more spacious residences, religious monuments, and civic structures.

Of particular interest is the discovery of "sunken gardens" designed so that the plants could reach the underlying water table.

Mexico. A milestone was reached in the study of Mexican prehistory with the reported completion of the mapping of Teotihuacán, the largest prehistoric urban site in the Western Hemisphere. Population estimates for Teotihuacán range from 75,000 to more than 200,000. The city apparently flourished from about 200 to 800 A. D. as a hub for commerce in the Valley of Mexico and adjacent regions, and as the center for the state's civic administration and religion.

Intensive investigations of the thousands of structures within the geometrically arranged quadrants of the city have enabled archaeologists to locate at least 500 shop areas specializing in a variety of exports, such as obsidian implements, ceramics, figurines, and sculptures. In all, more than 2,600 room complexes and temple structures are now completely mapped to scale, and it is obvious that from Teotihuacán's beginnings the city was a systematically planned and thoroughly organized prehistoric urban community.

Labrador. In studies sponsored by the National Science Foundation, archaeologists from several universities have located, on Rose Island, the most northerly archaeological site from the Archaic Period. Dated by carbon-14 at 2580 B. C., the culture thus located is distinct in type from the more recent Eskimo populations usually associated with arctic regions. Future work in the area may be able to pinpoint the cause of the disappearance of this archaic population, which is believed to have possessed a relatively sophisticated society featuring ritual burial, intricate tools, and a seasonal economy.

Virginia. In the Shenandoah Valley of Virginia, considerable attention has been focused on a site believed to date from the Paleo-Indian Period of 9,000 to 12,000 years ago. Archaeologists have uncovered a habitation area apparently situated near a jasper quarry, a source for tool materials. Discovery of this important site was credited to members of the Shenandoah Valley chapter of the Virginia Archaeological Society.

Illinois. Work continues on the mound complex at Cahokia, Ill., that dates from the Mississippian Period of about 750 to 1200 A. D. Archaeologists from three major universities are now prepared to describe this extensive complex as the largest settlement of American Indians north of Mexico. Contrary to earlier identifications with South and Central American prehistoric cultures, current workers at the site feel that the origin of Cahokia is purely North American.

The major growth of the Cahokia complex did not occur until about 850 A. D., when—as archaeologists theorize—the flint spade was introduced. The tool enabled people to dig into the dense prairie turf, so that vast acreages could be cultivated. A striking characteristic of some of the burial mounds is that of sacrificial burial, with possibly as many as 200 skeletons being associated with a single grave, probably that of a ruler. The largest temple mound at Cahokia stands 100 feet (30 meters) high, and the entire complex apparently was enclosed by a palisade that may have used as many as 14,000 20-foot (6-meter) logs. At least five satellite towns within 20 miles (30 km) have been identified, and an additional 100 villages are closely related.

Cahokia was also a great commercial center, receiving and distributing goods from Florida, the Great Lakes, and the Appalachian area.

Missouri. In eastern Missouri, archaeological researchers under the direction of the University of Missouri have been focusing their attention on a large town and mound complex that was occupied from about 900 to 1400 A. D. Of considerable significance was the discovery of a macelike flint implement about 16 inches (40 cm) long, since similar artifacts normally have been associated only with mound complexes east of the Mississippi River.

Kansas. Near Lyons, Kans., a Smithsonian Institution field party reported the discovery of fragments of chain mail armor, possibly introduced by Spanish conquistadores in an expedition into south central Kansas in 1541. Additional excavations of some 30 outside storage pits produced evidence of further contact with the southwest, such as Pueblo sherds, torquoise beads, and the incisor of a horse.

Oregon. Smithsonian excavators on the northern Oregon coast have reported the discovery of whalebone spear-throwing boards, or *atlatls,* associated with a prehistoric maritime culture at least 2,000 years old. This discovery is rare in the Western Hemisphere, since *atlatls* usually were made of wood and hence were extremely perishable.

Washington and Idaho. Near Vancouver, Wash., archaeologists from the University of Washington located a substantial lower Chinookan occupation site as they worked in advance of highway construction. More than a thousand artifacts have thus far been recovered from the site, which is believed to be 1,000 to 2,000 years old. Meanwhile, in eastern Washington and Idaho, archaeologists from several universities expressed serious concern over grave robbing in the vicinity of the Snake and Clearwater rivers. Construction of new dams in the area required relocation of 19th century Indian graves that were there, but this was unfortunately prevented by the robbing of the graves.

GEORGE E. PHEBUS, JR.
Smithsonian Institution

EXPLORER Fred Dickson, Jr., with student, holds wood he believes is from *Santa Maria,* Columbus' flagship. He is searching for ship, which sank off Haiti in 1492.

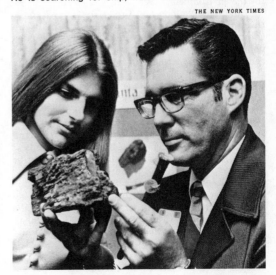

architecture

MUMMERS THEATER, Oklahoma City, Okla., was designed by John Johansen. Units are blocks of concrete connected by tubes and catwalks.

Although some monumental buildings were produced in 1971, there was an increasing trend toward pragmatic structures, frequently characterized by lightweight materials, new techniques, and respect for the environment.

Cultural Buildings and Urban Design—*Pragmatism*. Standardized prefabricated metal buildings or components of minimal cost, arranged with great imagination, distinguished two community services centers by Hardy, Holtzman & Pfeiffer at Shaw University, Raleigh, N. C., and in eastern New York state. The use of metal combined with functional flexibility characterized John Johansen's Mummers Theater in Oklahoma City, opened in December 1970. This extraordinary assemblage of raw concrete boxes connected by air-conditioning ducts and brightly painted, corrugated steel-clad "people tubes" comprises a large and a small theater, which can be rearranged internally to meet a variety of needs.

Metal construction and adaptibility to changing functions were features of the winning entry in an international competition for an art center on the former site of Les Halles in Paris. The Italian Renzo Piano and the English architects Richard and Sue Rodgers proposed fully movable floors and walls in a steel framework to house shifting displays. Fire escapes, elevators, and escalators can be clipped on

the framework as needed through the use of roof cranes.

Particularly well suited to its function was Richard Meier's plan for an elegant, steel-framed, enamel-clad gymnasium complex for the New York State University College at Fredonia. By contrast, a ponderous, overstated, concrete gymnasium with exposed tubular steel trusses by Kallman and McKinnell for Philips Exeter Academy, Exeter, N. H., did not effectively serve its purpose.

Many new buildings showed due regard for both function and the man-made or natural environment. Marcel Breuer's extension to the neoclassical Cleveland Museum of Art is a successful addition of new to old. His lively design provides lecture halls, classrooms, and generous gallery space behind a facade of concrete panels faced with granite in alternating horizontal bands of light and dark gray.

The Cleo Rodgers Memorial Library, designed by I. M. Pei and completed in the latter part of 1970, is an urbane, brick-clad structure of two stories opposite Eliel Saarinen's First Christian Church, which creates the first civic space in downtown Columbus, Ind. Pei's plan for the East Building of the National Gallery in Washington, D. C., not only provides small gallery units for advanced study of the visual arts and large areas for tourists. It also fits a trapezoidal plot and connects through a plaza to the neoclassical National Gallery.

Adapting to the man-made environment by the skillful reuse of a viable, already existing building, James Stewart Polshek converted the 7th District Police Court Building in Manhattan into the Clinton Youth and Family Center.

In Toronto, Craig, Zeidler, and Strong adjusted to the natural environment by setting the six spare, square, white-enameled metal exhibition pavilions of the new Ontario Fair and Pleasure Grounds in the middle of a lake. Interconnected and suspended above the water from four tall, pipelike columns, they resemble a pier or an oil rig.

McCormick Place, Chicago's lakeside exhibition center, which was destroyed by fire in 1967, was replaced by an $83 million development by C. F. Murphy Associates. Its 20-acre (8-hectare) area, including two buildings for a large exhibition hall and the 4,350-seat Aire Crown Theatre, is covered by an exposed steel space frame with 75-foot (23-meter) cantilevers around the perimeter. The parking lot is underground as a result of petitions from conservation and community groups.

Monumentality. Two new cultural buildings put monumentality first. The $18 million Lyndon Baines Johnson Library in Austin, Texas, by Skidmore, Owings & Merrill, is nothing if not ostentatious. The largest presidential library in the United States, it is an 8-story windowless box 65 feet (20 meters) high set on its own plaza, dominating the University of Texas campus. The 90-foot (28-meter) facade is recessed between two side walls 200 feet (62 meters) long that curve from top to bottom. The walls, covered with cream travertine, are topped by a cantilevered upper story, which houses administrative offices. Inside, overlooking the huge Great Stair Hall and displayed row on row, are 4,200 red buckram boxes containing the presidential papers.

Completed more than 10 years after its inception, the $70 million John F. Kennedy Center for the Performing Arts in Washington, D. C., provides a much-needed theater, concert hall, and opera house. The massive, white marble-clad box designed by Edward Durell Stone was lambasted by some critics for its uninspired design.

Commercial Building. Among noteworthy commercial buildings is I. M. Pei's National Airlines terminal at Kennedy Airport, New York City. Enclosed in glass walls supported by glass mullions, it

has two adjoining boarding pavilions and a steel-framed roof resting on 16 cast-in-place concrete columns. In Tampa, Fla., the Landside/Airside Terminal, by Reynolds, Smith, and Mills, has at its center a complex transportation interchange in which a traveler is shuttled by an automated vehicle from his car to one of four boarding pavilions.

The Olivetti typewriter and computer plant in Harrisburg, Pa., by Louis I. Kahn, has production, office, and cafeteria space under a long-span concrete roof of cast-in-place inverted "umbrellas" and 20-foot-square (6-meter) reinforced plastic skylights by Renzo Piano. Inside, stainless-steel air ducts assume a sculptural quality.

The American Can headquarters in Greenwich, Conn., by Skidmore, Owings & Merrill, carefully

THE NEW YORK TIMES

THE JOHN F. KENNEDY CENTER for the Performing Arts, Washington, D. C., had its official opening on Sept. 8, 1971. The center's architect was Edward Durell Stone. Grand foyer of the Center (*above*) has a head of President Kennedy by Robert Berks. The striking crystal chandeliers were a gift from Sweden.

UPI

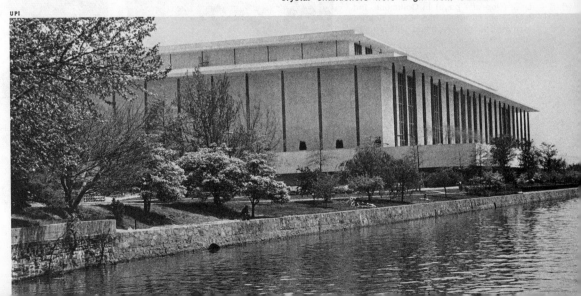

GEORGE CSERNA

HARMONY with adjacent structures was the designer's intent in these three new buildings. (*Above*) In Albany, the headquarters of the New York State Bar Association, designed by James Stewart Polshek and Associates, involved joining a new building to three 19th century townhouses. (*Right*) The architectural firm of Hartman-Cox repeated the red-brick-and-slate motif used in surrounding older buildings for the new Mount Vernon College chapel in Washington, D.C. (*Opposite page*) In Columbus, Ind., I. M. Pei designed the Cleo Rodgers Memorial Library to blend with an Eliel Saarinen church.

R. LAUTMAN

preserves its heavily wooded estate site. The main building is constructed across a ravine, which hides six lower stories for parking and other uses, thus ensuring minimum interruption of the landscape. The three upper stories of offices form a block around a central landscaped court. The block is made of cast-in-place concrete walls and girders spanning bays 60 feet (18 meters) wide. Executive offices are accommodated in a smaller adjoining square building of one story, which also sits over its own parking area.

Governmental Buildings. In Columbus, Ind., a new privately funded post office by Kevin Roche, John Dinkeloo and Associates adds to that city's distinguished collection of modern buildings. The silotile and steel structure fills one city block and accommodates a pedestrian arcade.

In California the Hall of Justice completes Frank Lloyd Wright's civic center for Marin county. The arcaded facade of the complex, nearly one-quarter mile (409 meters) long, adjusts to irregularities on the site, which is in the low hills north of San Rafael, and in doing so somewhat resembles them. The Orange County Government Center in Goshen, N.Y., designed by Paul Rudolph, continues his exuberant style in an intensely articulated display of shifting planes of concrete block that leaves the spectator breathless if not exasperated.

George White replaced J. George Stewart as Architect to the Capitol, the first time since 1865 that a practicing architect has held that post. White released a report by Prager, Kavanagh, and Waterbury, which proposed only a $15 million restoration instead of the $45 million revamping of the walls recommended by Stewart.

Churches. The Roman Catholic cathedral of San Francisco, burned in 1962, was rebuilt by the two little-known firms of McSweeney and of Ryan and Lee in collaboration with the renowned American architect Pietro Belluschi and the Italian engineer Pier Luigi Nervi. They have produced a 2,500-seat, square building with four massive columns at the corners supporting 140-foot-wide (43-meter) arches, which in turn hold up a cupola consisting of four hyperbolic concrete shells. The thin rectangular spaces between the shells are filled with stained glass by Gyorgy Kepes of M. I. T., while a shimmering baldachino by Richard Lippold covers the altar.

In Washington, D. C., Hartman-Cox built a simple chapel for Mount Vernon College ingeniously sited against the slope of a ravine. The red-brick walls and slate roof match the surrounding buildings, and the interior is subtly lit from louvered windows.

Housing. Public housing projects were generally disappointing. Operation Breakthrough, a federal experiment in prefabricated housing, has not yet been able to bring the high cost of prefabrication for pilot projects into competition with traditional construction methods.

Some developments, however, were encouraging. Stanley Tigerman in Woodlawn Gardens, Chicago, achieved a distinguished "non-project" look by arranging three-story, brick-faced buildings to give each housing block its own open space. A 1963 design by Hodne/Stageberg & Partners for 1,600 family units on the East River in New York City finally found a sponsor. The units make up four 14-story, stepped and U-shaped blocks staggered to take advantage of the river view.

Awards. The American Institute of Architects (AIA) Gold Medal for 1971 was awarded to Louis I. Kahn, an American architect who has had unusually great influence on younger architects and students. Among his American buildings are the Richards Laboratories at the University of Pennsylvania and the Dr. Jonas Salk Institute in San Diego, Calif. A major work abroad is the capital complex in Dacca, East Pakistan (Bangladesh).

The AIA critics award was given posthumously to the selfless critic and educator Sibyl Moholy-Nagy, wife of the Hungarian-born painter and designer László Moholy-Nagy. The Bard Award for excellence in architecture and public design went to the Graduate Center Mall of the City University of New York by Carl J. Petrilli and to the Technology Building II for New York University in the Bronx by Breuer and Hamilton Smith.

JOHN FOWLER
Architect

BALTHAZAR KORAB

ARCTIC REGIONS

Events of 1971 emphasized that the Arctic regions are no longer the isolated areas they were in the past. Modern transportation and communications tie the future of the Arctic closely to that of the rest of the globe. Consequently, the Arctic has taken on some of the problems of the rest of the world, including the rights of native peoples, damage to the environment, and global climate.

Alaska's North Slope. Alaskan Eskimos filed a suit claiming the entire North Slope of Alaska. They based the claim on their occupation and use of the land for as long as anyone could remember. The Eskimos say that the land was illegally taken from them by the federal government and given to the state, which in turn leased 413,000 acres (167,000 hectares) of it to oil companies after vast oil deposits were discovered at Prudhoe Bay in 1968. On October 20, the U. S. House of Representatives voted 343 to 63 to give to the Eskimos, Indians, and Aleuts a total of $925 million in cash and 40 million acres (16 million hectares) of land. For details of the bill as finally approved, see ALASKA.

Plans for an 800-mile (1,300-km) pipeline to carry oil from Prudhoe Bay to Valdez, Alaska, remained stalled in 1971 because of serious opposition from conservationists who claimed that the pipeline might endanger the delicate balance of the tundra. The conservationists feared oil spillage from a rupture in the line and also that it would be a barrier which would disrupt the migration of caribou.

World Climate. Concern over world climate led to the development of a new scientific research program on the Arctic ice pack—the Arctic Ice Dynamics Joint Experiment (AIDJEX). The central Arctic Ocean is covered throughout the year with sea ice about 10 feet (3 meters) thick. This ice pack, with its countless floes, is in constant motion, but its complex behavior is known principally from studies with a single ice station, which gives only a limited view of one small area.

A fuller understanding of the Arctic pack ice is important, since it is believed to be a crucial influence on world climate. Some theories postulate that the presence or absence of the ice—which could presumably be destroyed by natural or artificial means—is a key factor in triggering ice ages. The ice pack is a good reflector of the sun's energy. The open sea that would result from its loss is a good absorber of solar energy. Thus the change in global climate attendant upon such a drastic change in reflectivity might be profound. AIDJEX will study ice pack behavior in the hope of developing a model for predicting ice behavior and assessing its influence on global climate.

A pilot program designed to test concepts and equipment was jointly sponsored by the United States and Canada in 1971. A second pilot program was planned for 1972, and the main experiment with four manned ice stations was planned for 1974.

Polar Visits. In 1971 the North Pole was reached by two groups, whose modes of transportation contrasted sharply. The British nuclear submarine *Dreadnought* surfaced at the pole in March. A dogsled under the leadership of Guido Monzino, an Italian, reached the pole on May 19, after having retraced Robert Edwin Peary's route of 1909.

KENNETH L. HUNKINS
*Lamont-Doherty Geological Observatory
of Columbia University*

ARGENTINA

Argentina experienced another coup d'etat in March 1971. Gen. Alejandro Lanusse, the leader of the 3-man military junta that had deposed President Juan Carlos Onganía in June 1970, dismissed Ongania's replacement, Roberto M. Levingston and assumed the presidency himself. This occurred against a background of economic troubles.

Cordobazo II. The provincial industrial center of Córdoba could claim, after March 1971, that it had played the leading role in ending the terms of the nation's two most recent presidents. The serious civil disturbance in that city in May 1969, which became known as the *Cordobazo,* had begun the erosion of Onganía's authority that led to his ouster more than a year later. Levingston's brief presidency ended almost immediately after another outbreak of rioting and destruction had run its course in Córdoba on March 13–18, 1971.

As the month began, the city, threatened with a strike by public employees, saw the appointment of a new, hard-line provincial governor, José Camilo Uriburu, who entered office with a vow to "cut off the serpent's head"—a reference to the Córdoba General Confederation of Labor (CGT). Labor called a general strike and mounted demonstrations that gained broad support among students, government workers, and small shopowners. The local police were ordered to refrain from violence in the defense of property, and the army refused to intervene until long after the need for action had passed. As a result, much property was destroyed, although only two persons were killed, whereas the death toll during *Cordobazo I* had been more than 20. Uriburu resigned on March 16, and the city, which

----

ARGENTINA · Information Highlights

Official Name: Argentine Republic.
Area: 1,072,158 square miles (2,776,889 sq km).
Population (1970 est.): 24,350,000. *Density,* 23 per square mile (9 per sq km). *Annual rate of increase,* 1.5%.
Chief Cities (1960 census): Buenos Aires, the capital (1969 est.), 3,549,000; Rosario, 591,428; Córdoba, 586,015.
Government: *Head of state,* Alejandro Lanusse, president (took office March 25, 1971). *Head of government,* Alejandro Lanusse. *Legislature*—National Congress (suspended, June 1966).
Languages: Spanish (official).
Education: *Literacy rate* (1971), 90% of population. *Expenditure on education* (1968), 21% of total public expenditure. *School enrollment* (1968)—primary, 3,238,936; secondary, 887,236; technical/vocational, 485,724; university/ higher, 19,137.
Finances (1969): *Revenues,* $2,792,000,000; *expenditures,* $2,916,000,000; *monetary unit,* peso (5 pesos equal U. S. $1, Sept. 1971).
Gross National Product (1969): $19,860,000,000.
National Income (1969): $16,366,000,000; *national income per person,* $682.
Manufacturing (metric tons, 1969): Residual fuel oil, 7,825,000; cement, 4,347,000; meat, 2,233,000; wheat flour, 2,190,000; crude steel, 1,697,000.
Crops (metric tons, 1969 crop year): Wheat, 7,020,000; maize, 6,900,000; grapes (1968), 2,540,000; cattle, 51,200,000 head.
Minerals (metric tons, 1969): Crude petroleum, 18,096,000; salt, 750,000; coal, 522,000; natural gas, 5,366,000,000 cubic meters.
Foreign Trade (1970): *Exports,* $1,773,000,000 (chief exports—meat, $438,100,000; corn, $265,000,000; wheat, $126,000,000; hides and skins, $96,600,000). *Imports,* $1,685,000,000 (chief imports, 1968—nonelectrical machinery, $222,000,000; chemicals, $167,900,000; iron and steel, $123,700,000. *Chief trading partners* (1968)—Italy (took 14% of exports, supplied 6% of imports); United States (12%–23%); Brazil (9%–12%); West Germany.
Transportation: *Roads* (1969), 124,900 miles (201,002 km); *motor vehicles* (1968), 1,859,100 (automobiles, 1,184,500); *railroads* (1965), 27,169 miles (43,470 km); *merchant fleet* (1971), 1,312,000 gross registered tons; *national airline,* Aerolineas Argentinas; *principal airport,* Buenos Aires.
Communications: *Telephones* (1970), 1,668,426; *television stations* (1969), 29; *television sets* (1969), 3,100,000; *radios* (1968), 9,000,000; *newspapers* (1966), 178.

had become the focal point of radical politics in Argentina, returned to calm, if not peace.

Change of Government. General Lanusse, who had been largely responsible for the compromise that had elevated Levingston to the presidency in 1970, assumed the office himself on March 25. The coup was, in an important sense, an admission of the military's failure to solve the continuing crisis that it had reacted to in 1966 by seizing power. The same old problems persisted. They included a stagnant economy, an accelerating rate of inflation, decreasing wheat and beef production, dissatisfied workers and officials, foreign domination of the economy, increasing regional awareness, daily acts of political terror, and *Peronismo,* the powerful movement led by admirers of Juan Perón, the former dictator who remained in exile in Spain.

Lanusse had outlined what he considered a rational political program in a speech of March 2, on becoming head of the military joint chiefs. He had called for a "great national agreement," the key goals of which would be to bring the Peronistas back into national political life, accelerate economic growth in order to calm the social conflict caused by a "distorted economy," increase national—not state—participation in the economy, and distribute the wealth more equitably.

Despite this clear signal of his intentions, Lanusse's early moves as president astounded nearly everybody. He opened direct negotiations with Perón, declared political party activities legal (early in April), lifted all ceilings on wage increases, and made it clear that he expected to return the military to its barracks as soon as possible. An even more dramatic development was the return of the body of Perón's late wife, Eva, to Madrid in September. Late in the year, it was announced that elections had been scheduled for March 25, 1973. These actions appeared to indicate that Lanusse intended to oppose important elements within the military establishment, compromise with the inevitable, and return the nation to a civilian and, very possibly, a Peronist government.

To many Argentines, such a reversal was intolerable. Anti-Peronists, both in and out of the armed forces, had not forgotten their tribulations during the Perón era (from 1946 to 1955). In mid-April, by Lanusse's order, the powerful Gen. Juan Enrique Guglialmelli, who had criticized the decision to lift the ban on political parties, was confined to barracks. The first week of May brought an attempted coup in Tucumán by several army units and a few civilian politicians who opposed a return to electoral politics. Another unsuccessful revolt occurred within the armed forces on October 8–9, apparently also aimed at preventing future elections. Guglialmelli, former President Levingston, and other high-ranking officers were arrested.

The Unity Movement. Seeking civilian support for his regime while easing the military out of politics, Lanusse encouraged a broad coalition of parties, *La Hora del Pueblo.* From Madrid, Perón ordered his Justicialist Movement to enter the coalition. The UCRP, Argentina's major middle-class party, was already included. Lanusse seemed to regard *La Hora* as the strongest possible barrier to either total Peronist domination or revolution from the left.

Almost the only force that held this coalition together, however, was a common dislike of the military. The CGT, Argentina's huge labor confedera-

tion, was very much divided as to the nature of an ideal political solution, beyond agreement that the new government should be civilian and pro-labor. The UCRP, never completely unified, was further split when Lanusse appointed one of its leaders, Arturo Mor Roig, to the post of minister of the interior. Some UCRP members felt that this was too much of a concession to the military government, while others feared that Mor Roig would be forced to preside over an eventual Peronist victory. Relations between the Radicals and the Peronists (who were themselves divided) were strained, as usual, and the left continued to be divided.

Terrorism. Argentina was plagued in 1971 by increasing terrorist activity. There were at least five distinct groups operating in both rural and urban areas. Ideologically, they ranged from Fascist to Maoist and included some revolutionary Peronists. On May 23, terrorists kidnapped the British consul in Rosario. Seven days later he was released, unharmed, for a ransom of money and beef, which his captors immediately distributed to the poor of a Rosario slum. During the first seven months of 1971, armed robberies were up 50% over the same period in 1970. The military was becoming increasingly involved in aggressive anti-terrorist activity.

Economic Affairs. For the Argentine economy, 1971 was a grim year. Levingston's minister of economy, Aldo Ferrer, followed a policy designed to stimulate rapid development. He permitted substantial wage increases, eased credit, placed some restrictions on foreign investors, and, when necessary, controlled prices. This policy, together with a serious beef shortage, led to a sharp rise in the rate of inflation and a loss of confidence in the government by business. Nor did it bring much popular support. Surprisingly, Lanusse retained Ferrer, but in late May, confronted by the obvious failure of his policies, the minister resigned.

This led to a reorganization of the cabinet, but the battle over economic policy raged on as Lanusse remained trapped between popular demands and the needs of business. A succession of appointments to and resignations from critical jobs in the government indicated the intractability of the problems.

In other economic news, the trade deficit preoccupied many observers. Nationalists were particularly upset when it was revealed in August that the deficit in trade with Brazil would approximate some $80 million, a rise of $30 million over the 1970 total. The rise was attributed to poor wheat production and low prices for Argentine goods.

The peso lost value steadily, reaching a level of about 8.6 to the U. S. dollar by early December. It was estimated that inflation would be 50% greater in 1971 than in 1970, while real wages would remain stable, at best. The cost of living during the period January to September 1971 rose 21.3%, whereas the rise during the same months of 1970 was 11.9%.

International Developments. In foreign relations, the advent of Lanusse brought increased diplomatic activity. The chief executive met twice with Chile's Marxist president, Salvador Allende—once in Argentina and once in Chile. During the second meeting, Lanusse was quoted as saying that his own government was one of the "center-left."

The Lanusse administration supported the admission of the People's Republic of China to the United Nations. On the U. S.-sponsored resolution to main-

FUMES that pollute Arizona's clear desert air have caused serious concern. New laws will force plants such as this copper smelter to reduce emissions.

tain Taiwan's UN seat, the Argentine delegation abstained from voting. Argentina led Latin American resistance to the U. S. import surcharge imposed by President Nixon in mid-August. Other subjects of Argentine concern in 1971 included the political turmoil in neighboring Uruguay and the threat posed by the continued growth of Brazil's economic and political power in South America.

JAMES R. LEVY
Pomona College

ARIZONA

Important local elections and controversies over air pollution and legislative apportionment shared Arizona headlines in 1971.

Pollution. New and stricter air pollution standards enacted by the Legislature in 1970 went into effect but were strongly attacked by mining interests, who argued that the new standards would make some of the copper mining and smelting operations economically unsound. They predicted that unless some relaxation of controls was permitted, important installations inevitably would be closed down with major losses to the economy of the state, which is the leading copper producer in the United States.

Much of the controversy centered on the expensive and difficult task of removing sulfur dioxide contaminants from the emissions of copper smelters.

The mining interests pointed out that Arizona's standards are much more severe than those prescribed by the U. S. Environmental Pollution Agency, and they petitioned the state board of health to relax Arizona standards to federal levels. In November the board agreed to begin a review of all control standards on December 30.

In the pollution controversy, the small mining communities sided with the industries that sustain them and against the metropolitan cities, where most of Arizona's population growth has occurred and where political power has increasingly centered since the reapportionment decisions of the U. S. Supreme Court in the early 1960's.

Reapportionment. In a special session, the Arizona Legislature reapportioned itself and also made provision for a new fourth congressional district, to which the state became entitled as a result of the 1970 census. Both the legislative reapportionment and the new congressional districting seem likely to solidify the new political power of the Phoenix area, which contains well over half the entire state population.

The reapportionment created by the Republican-controlled Legislature established new districts remarkably even in population, but Democrats charged that the Republicans had gerrymandered the districts in favor of Republican incumbents. The Democrats asked the federal courts to refuse to allow the use of the new districts in the 1972 elections.

─────── ARIZONA · Information Highlights ───────

Area: 113,909 square miles (295,024 sq km).
Population (1970 census): 1,772,482. *Density:* 15 per sq.mi.
Chief Cities (1970 census): Phoenix, the capital, 581,562; Tucson, 262,933; Scottsdale, 67,823; Tempe, 63,550; Mesa, 62,853; Glendale, 36,228; Yuma, 29,007.
Government (1971): *Chief Officers*—governor, Jack Williams (R); secy. of state, Wesley Bolin (D); atty. gen., Gary K. Nelson (R); treas., Ernest Garfield (R); supt. of public instruction, Weldon P. Shofstall (R); chief justice, Fred C. Stockmeyer, Jr. *Legislature*—Senate, 30 members (18 Republicans, 12 Democrats); House of Representatives, 60 members (34 R, 26 D).
Education (1970–71): *Enrollment*—public elementary schools, 305,000 pupils, 13,545 teachers; public secondary, 133,000 pupils, 5,778 teachers; nonpublic schools (1968–69), 32,900 pupils, 1,450 teachers; college and university (fall 1970), 110,000 students. *Public school expenditures* (1970–71), $333,245,000 ($825 per pupil). *Average teacher's salary*, $8,270.
State Finances (fiscal year 1970): *Revenues*, $875,902,000 (3% general sales tax and gross receipts taxes, $173,739,000; motor fuel tax, $64,974,000; federal funds, $187,748,000). *Expenditures*, $779,322,000 (education, $374,768,000; health, welfare, and safety, $56,995,000; highways, $111,122,000). *State debt*, $90,929,000 (June 30, 1970).
Personal Income (1970): $6,510,000,000; per capita, $3,542.
Public Assistance (1970): $43,562,000. *Average monthly payments* (Dec. 1970)—old-age assistance, $70.90; aid to families with dependent children, $125.35.
Labor Force: *Nonagricultural wage and salary earners* (June 1971), 558,500. *Average annual employment* (1969)—manufacturing, 93,000; trade, 117,000; government, 113,000; services, 85,000. *Insured unemployed* (Oct. 1971)—8,800 (2.2%).
Manufacturing (1967): *Value added by manufacture*, $773,300,000; Electrical equipment and supplies, $224,300,000; nonelectrical machinery, $192,400,000; food and kindred products, $65,600,000; fabricated metal products, $33,500,000.
Agriculture (1970): *Cash farm income*, $699,294,000 (livestock, $373,227,000; crops, $274,117,000; government payments, $51,950,000). *Chief crops* (1970)—Sorghum grain, 12,670,000 bushels; barley, 10,640,000 bushels; hay, 1,318,000 tons; cotton lint, 489,000 bales.
Mining (1970): *Production value*, $1,159,863 (ranks 10th among the states). *Chief minerals* (tons)—Sand and gravel 15,700,000; copper, 910,000; molybdenum, 14,008,000 pounds; silver, 6,191,000 troy ounces; gold, 111,000 troy ounces.
Transportation: *Roads* (1969), 41,773 miles (67,225 km); *motor vehicles* (1969), 1,024,000; *railroads* (1968), 2,052 miles (3,302 km); *airports* (1969), 100.
Communications: *Telephones* (1971), 953,700; *television stations* (1969), 11; *radio stations* (1969), 72; *newspapers* (1969), 13; (daily circulation, 424,000).

The Legislature drew congressional district lines that seem likely to ensure the reelection of the three incumbents, two of whom are Republicans. Most political observers agree that the new fourth district will probably also go Republican, although Democrats are conceded a chance if they are able to produce a strong candidate. Critics of the congressional redistricting allege that three of the four districts will be controlled by the Phoenix metropolitan area.

Elections. Important municipal elections were held in Phoenix and Tucson. In Phoenix, the Charter Committee continued its long dominance of the nonpartisan city elections, winning a clean sweep in the mayoral and city council elections. Phoenix voters also approved a number of amendments to the city charter but defeated proposals to increase the term of office of the mayor and council from two to four years and to increase the salaries of city officials.

In Tucson, which has partisan city elections, Democratic Mayor James Corbett was unseated by Republican Herbert Williams, whose party retained the control of the council.

JOHN P. WHITE
Arizona State University

ARKANSAS

With a popular Democrat, Dale L. Bumpers, as governor, a more productive atmosphere prevailed in Arkansas government in 1971 than during the previous four years, when the legislature was Democratic and the governor was Republican. This cooperative spirit between the two branches resulted in the adoption of many reform measures, even some recommended by former Gov. Winthrop Rockefeller.

Legislature. The General Assembly passed a record 829 bills, including about 85% of those backed by Governor Bumpers. Among the measures enacted were a major reorganization of state administration that placed about 60 agencies under the management control of the governor, a $26 million tax increase program, and the first change in the personal income tax rate since 1929. In addition, legal recognition of the American Independent party, which had won the 1968 presidential election in Arkansas for George C. Wallace and polled about 6% of the gubernatorial vote in 1970, was withdrawn by requiring that a party's gubernatorial candidate receive at least 7% of the votes cast if the party was to be placed on the next election ballot.

Reapportionment. The board of apportionment —consisting of the governor, secretary of state, and attorney general, all Democrats—redrew legislative district lines so that all state senators and most representatives would be elected from single-member districts. As had been expected, there was dissatisfaction with the reapportionment. District boundaries cut across county lines for the first time, Ft. Smith Republicans charged gerrymandering, and a suit was filed against the plan. However, this major reform improved the likelihood of a black being elected to the state legislature for the first time since Reconstruction.

State Finances. Need for more revenue was a major state problem. The governor froze purchasing and hiring for several months. Medical facilities and higher education institutions experienced severe financial problems. The legislature created a department of higher education with planning and

---

ARKANSAS • Information Highlights

Area: 53,104 square miles (137,539 sq km).
Population (1970 census): 1,923,295. *Density:* 38 per sq mi.
Chief Cities (1970 census): Little Rock, the capital, 132,483; Fort Smith, 62,802; North Little Rock, 60,040; Pine Bluff, 57,389; Hot Springs, 35,631; Fayetteville, 30,729.
Government (1971): *Chief Officers*—governor, Dale Bumpers (D); lt. gov., Robert C. Riley (D); secy. of state, Kelly Bryant (D); atty. gen., Ray Thornton (D); treas., Nancy J. Hall (D); comm., Dept. of Education, A. W. Ford; chief justice, Carleton Harris. *General Assembly*—Senate, 35 members (34 Democrats, 1 Republican); House of Representatives, 100 members (98 D, 2 R).
Education (1970–71): *Enrollment*—public elementary schools, 252,046 pupils, 9,638 teachers; public secondary, 211,272 pupils, 10,033 teachers; nonpublic schools (1968–69), 12,700 pupils, 600 teachers; college and university (fall 1970), 51,000 students. *Public school expenditures* (1970–71), $239,832,000 ($578 per pupil). *Average teacher's salary,* $6,668.
State Finances (fiscal year 1970): *Revenues,* $656,703,000 (3% general sales tax and gross receipts taxes, $108,719,000; motor fuel tax, $74,897,000; federal funds, $207,268,000). *Expenditures,* $619,211,000 (education, $245,731,000; health, welfare, and safety, $100,881,000; highways, $104,740,000). *State debt,* $100,810,000 (June 30, 1970).
Personal Income (1970): $5,338,000,000; per capita, $2,742.
Public Assistance (1970): $96,051,000. *Average monthly payments* (Dec. 1970)—old-age assistance, $64.75; aid to families with dependent children, $93.75.
Labor Force: *Nonagricultural wage and salary earners* (June 1971), 546,200. *Average annual employment* (1969)—manufacturing, 168,000; trade, 105,000; government, 101,000; services, 72,000. *Insured unemployed* (Oct. 1971)—12,300 (3.1%).
Manufacturing (1967): *Value added by manufacture,* $1,557,700,000; Food and kindred products, $262,800,000; electrical equipment and supplies, $150,700,000; paper and allied products. $150,200,000.
Agriculture (1970): *Cash farm income,* $1,161,182,000 (livestock, $566,281,000; crops, $507,154,000; government payments, $87,747,000). *Chief crops* (1970)—Soybeans, 97.043,000 bushels (ranks 4th among the states); rice, 21,024,000 cwt. (ranks 3d); hay, 1,348,000 tons.
Mining (1970): *Production value,* $217,506,000 (ranks 28th among the states). *Chief minerals* (tons)—Stone, 13,994,000; bauxite, 1,785,000; natural gas, 185,120,000,000 cubic meters; petroleum. 17,940,000 barrels.
Transportation: *Roads* (1969), 78,861 miles (126,911 km); *motor vehicles* (1969). 951,000; *railroads* (1968), 3,605 miles (5,802 km): *airports* (1969). 67.
Communications: *Telephones* (1971), 858,900; *television stations* (1969). 6; *radio stations* (1969), 111; *newspapers* (1969), 35 (daily circulation, 427,000).

---

review powers over fiscal and curricular matters. It also added to the growing University of Arkansas system two financially troubled state colleges, Arkansas A & M College and predominantly black Arkansas AM & N College.

Appointments. Patronage was a perplexing problem as Democrats sought state jobs. While most administrators appointed by Rockefeller were replaced, Dr. Max Milum, department of administration director and a major architect of the reorganization plan, remained. The legislature forced the outspoken, reform-minded corrections commissioner, C. Robert Sarver, out of office. Prison reform, however, remained a goal of the new commissioner, Terrell Don Hutto, the governor, and the legislature.

Civil Rights. Open conflict between blacks and whites took place in Marianna and other eastern towns. Federal court-ordered busing to achieve racial balance in schools was bitterly resented in some cities. Governor Rockefeller commuted the death sentence of all 15 prisoners on death row.

Natural Gas Shortage. Two powerful utilities, Arkansas-Louisiana Gas Company and Arkansas Power and Light Company, clashed when the gas company moved to raise rates and to curtail deliveries because of dwindling gas reserves. Other industries also opposed the gas company's plans.

WILLIAM C. NOLAN
Southern State College

ARMS CONTROL. See DISARMAMENT.
ARMY, U. S. See DEFENSE FORCES.

"If anybody was Mr. Jazz it was Louis Armstrong. He was the epitome of jazz and always will be."

—*Duke Ellington*

ARMSTRONG, Louis

American jazz trumpeter and singer; b. New Orleans, La., July 4, 1900; d. New York City, July 6, 1971.

Louis Armstrong was the keystone in the development of American jazz from a relatively limited urban folk music to an art form that has become an accepted part of the global culture. His virtuosity and creative brilliance as an improvising soloist on cornet and trumpet changed the basis of jazz from ensemble improvisation to solo-oriented music for small groups. At the same time, he provided a vital spark that enabled big band jazz—played by groups of 12 to 20 musicians—to take viable shape.

In addition to his creative genius as a musician, "Satchmo," as Armstrong was popularly known, was also a superb entertainer and show business personality. With this extra-musical talent he was able to win to jazz a worldwide audience that might otherwise have been less inclined to listen to the music. By the same means he prolonged his career long after he had passed his peak as an innovator and as a trumpet virtuoso.

Early Life. Louis Armstrong and jazz virtually arrived simultaneously in New Orleans. The mixture of musical elements that formed the basis for jazz were coalescing there when Armstrong was born on the Fourth of July, 1900.

Young Louis grew up in a Negro section called Back o' Town in a world of poverty and prostitutes. He was briefly removed from this when, to celebrate New Year's Eve on Dec. 31, 1913, he rushed into the street firing a revolver. The 13-year-old boy was arrested and sent to the Colored Waifs Home for Boys, where he remained for a year and a half. At the home, he was taught to play the bugle and the cornet by Peter Davis, one of the instructors. This was the only formal musical education Armstrong had. By the time he was released, he had become an outstanding member of the home's brass band.

During the next three years, young Louis became the protégé of Joseph "King" Oliver, considered the best cornetist in New Orleans. When Oliver moved to Chicago in 1918, Armstrong took his place in Kid Ory's band. At the same time, he was marching in street parades, playing on advertising wagons and at dances and picnics, and working on Mississippi River steamboats in Fate Marable's band. During one trip up the Mississippi, Armstrong was taught to read music by Dave Jones, a mellophone player.

Innovator. In 1922, King Oliver, whose Creole Jazz Band had become a sensation in Chicago, sent for his onetime protégé. They formed an unprecedented two-cornet team, celebrated for unique "breaks"—brief pauses in the rhythm when, normally, one instrument improvises unaccompanied, but done as duets by Oliver and Armstrong. Armstrong made his first recordings in 1923 with Oliver.

Armstrong's marriage in 1924 to Lil Hardin, Oliver's pianist, brought an influential guiding hand to his career. Mrs. Armstrong (who died on Aug. 27, 1971) encouraged her husband to get away from the pervasive shadow of Oliver. So he left Oliver's band in that year, played briefly at the Dreamland Cafe, and then went to New York City to join Fletcher Henderson's orchestra. Organized the year before, Henderson's ensemble was attempting to transfer the traditional jazz qualities of a 5- or 6-piece group to a band of 10 to 12 musicians. Henderson's men, most of them well-schooled Easterners and Midwesterners with little jazz experience, were rarely able to project a jazz quality until Armstrong's arrival gave them their first contact with the New Orleans roots of jazz. Through his forceful musical personality, he helped to make this the first successful "big" jazz band and to guide such sidemen as Coleman Hawkins, the tenor saxophonist.

After a year with Henderson, Armstrong returned to Chicago, where he played with various small groups and with Erskine Tate's theater orchestra. His most important activity, however, was a series of recordings begun in November 1925 and continuing through 1929, on which he led groups usually identified as his Hot Five or Hot Seven. On these recordings, Armstrong's solo virtuosity became more and more dominant, changing the emphasis from the ensemble playing that had typified jazz until that time. With this emergence of the soloist in jazz, personal style and individuality became possible to an extent never approached by ensemble groups. These are the characteristics that have been consistently in the forefront of developments in jazz since Armstrong's ground-breaking recordings.

Entertainer. By 1930, Armstrong's influence as a creative force in jazz had run its course. For the next 40 years he worked primarily as an entertainer. Along with a 6-man group, his All-Stars, he toured the world for almost 25 years, welcomed everywhere as an "Ambassador of Good Will."

JOHN S. WILSON
"The New York Times"
and "High Fidelity" Magazine

art

In 1971 the art world seemed lacking in direction. There were, rather, protests and failures.

CURRENT DEVELOPMENTS

Protest. Social protest led to growing tension between artists and art institutions. Artists boycotted the Guggenheim Museum (New York) when it cancelled an exhibition documenting New York slum ownership. Fifteen artists withdrew from the Contemporary Black Artists in America exhibition at the Whitney Museum (New York) to protest the absence of a black curator.

Social protest was especially evident in the area of Women's Liberation. Art critic Lucy Lippard led demonstrations at the Whitney, many articles on women's art were published, and feminist art programs were set up "by women, for women, and about women." The Whitney showed the work of 50 women from its permanent collection, and the Aldrich Museum (Ridgefield, Conn.) presented the art of 26 young women. The Brooklyn Museum's display of 150 prints titled Pride and Prejudice: A Women's Exhibition drew protest because the works were by men. Social injustice inspired the Artist as Adversary (Museum of Modern Art, New York) and Some Elements in American History, dealing with slavery (Houston Museum of Fine Arts).

Failures. Some highly publicized and expensive art "events" were dismal failures. The appeal of anti-object, process, and conceptual art was dimmed by Michael Heizer's attempt to haul a huge granite block across the lawn of the Detroit Institute of Arts and Robert Morris' attempt to drag a five-ton steel plate through wet concrete in Boston. No more inspiring was the display of this kind of art at the Guggenheim International Exhibition or at Projects Pier 18 at the Museum of Modern Art.

The Art and Technology show at the Los Angeles County Museum of Art raised suspicions that the effort to encourage cooperation between artists and industry was losing impetus. Out of 80 artists approached, only 16 produced entries. They showed no radical departure from established visual forms, although Claes Oldenburg's dancing *Giant Icebag* and Robert Rauschenburg's bubbling vat of mud, *Mud Muse,* were visually effective. The Jewish Museum (New York) announced that it would give up its policy of supporting technologically sophisticated art to deal only with art of Jewish content.

Official portraits of President John F. Kennedy and widow, now Mrs. Jacqueline Onassis, were added to White House Collection in February. Painted by Aaron Shikler, portraits have a muted, pensive air.

THE WHITE HOUSE COLLECTION

THE WHITE HOUSE COLLECTION

Dürer-Jahr 1971 Nürnberg
Dürer-Year 1971 Nürnberg
Année Dürer 1971 Nürnberg

Outdoor Art. There was some encouragement, however, in the increasing popularity of "street," or "wall," art and in giant outdoor sculpture. Outdoor mural art, ranging from provocative political statements to non-objective decoration, has covered scores of walls in Chicago, New York, and Detroit. Particularly effective was a 20 x 69-foot (6 x 21-meter) magic-realist painting in Venice, Calif., of that snowless town, called *Venice in the Snow*.

A growing number of sculptors created large projects for display along highways or in urban settings. In New York, Hammarskjöld Plaza was adorned with the giant constructions of Alexander Liberman and nine sheet-aluminum figures by William King. A Louise Nevelson welded steel construction rose before the Seagram Building, and Richard Serra's *Base Plate Hexagram* was imbedded in the middle of 183d Street in the Bronx.

Anti-object, Environmental, Process, and Conceptual Art. Robert Morris, a leading exponent of anti-object, environmental, process, and conceptual art, emphasized that significant art is still moving away from portable, saleable art objects. Such art, he claimed, is essentially physically or intellectually oriented activity intended to deepen sensibilities or heighten awareness. Sometimes, however, the activity can get out of hand, as happened when overly enthusiastic art lovers wrecked so many works in Morris' activity exhibition at the Tate Gallery, London, that it had to be closed. Also, many examples of this kind of art remain saleable, for the art object is often replaced by purchasable documentation—films, slides, articles, photographs, and tape recordings.

The most spectacular exhibition of anti-object art was Earth, Air, Fire, Water: Elements of Art at the Boston Museum of Fine Arts. It presented 50 artists, who created burning fires, falling water, and moving air.

New Realism. At the opposite extreme from anti-object art was new realism. Young painters and sculptors revealed increased interest in representational work, especially with photographically or magically realistic effects. The most ambitious painting was Walter Midgette's actual-size *Studio* (Frumkin, New York), which created virtually a total environment of mysterious and confusing illusions. Sculptors worked in a variety of media—Howard Kalish in painted terra cotta, Thyra Davidson in wood, David Klass in bronze, and Richard Miller in wax.

Among outstanding exhibitions of new realism were a survey at the Danenburg Gallery (New York), Paul Staiger's Houses of Movie Stars (San Francisco Museum of Art), paintings by David Levine and Aaron Shikler (Brooklyn Museum), and works by David Legare and Robert Sarsony (A. C. A., New York).

Non-representational Sculpture. Many sculptors continued a non-representational approach. Some used relatively traditional materials, such as wood and metal, as for example, in New York, Tony Smith's primary structures of welded metal (Knoedler) and Carl André's metal floor sculpture

(Dwan). Louise Nevelson's welded metal sculptures (Pace) were a departure from the wall-filling compartmented boxes of painted wood shown at the Whitney in late 1970.

Other non-representational sculptors used once new, now familiar materials and techniques, such as light, sound, motion, and plastics. Working with neon light were Dan Flavin (Castelli), Neil Jenny (Whitney), Laddie John Dill (Sonnabend), and Stephen Antonakos (Fischbach), all in New York. Sonic works were produced by Howard Jones (Wise; New York). Glass or different plastics were chosen by Ivor Abrahams (Feigen), Peter Alexander (Elkon), Robert Graham (Sonnabend), John Chamberlain (Castelli), Gio Pomodoro (Jackson), David Weinrib (Marks), and Lee Bontecu (Castelli), all in New York. Of note were Larry Bell's environmental mirrored glasses (Pace). The Belgian Pol Bury's eerie kinetic works received special attention in three New York showings (Guggenheim; Lefebre; Weintraub).

RETROSPECTIVES AND OTHER EXHIBITIONS

Old Masters. There were various exhibitions of Old Masters, many of them, as in previous years, outside New York. The 500th anniversary of the birth of Dürer was celebrated by large exhibitions of his paintings and prints around the world, most notably in his native city of Nuremberg. In the United States his work was shown in Washington, Boston, Birmingham, New York, Princeton, Ann Arbor, and Portland, Oreg. Caravaggio and his followers were seen at the Cleveland Museum of Art, and Callot's etchings at the Association of American Artists (New York). The 18th century was represented by Dutch masters at the Minneapolis Institute of Arts, Italian masters at the Toledo Museum of Art, and Italian drawings at the Metropolitan Museum of Art (New York).

The 19th century was represented by 150 drawings of Rome by Ingres (National Gallery, Washington; New York, Philadelphia, and Kansas City) and by the first major Géricault exhibit (Los Angeles County Museum, Detroit, and Philadelphia). An important collection of Monet's works, given by his son, were displayed at the Marmottan Museum, Paris. There was a Cézanne retrospective (Art Institute of Chicago, then Boston) and an exhibition of Vuillard (Art Gallery of Toronto, San Francisco, and Chicago). A Van Gogh collection, given by his family, was hung at the Brooklyn Museum before being installed in permanent quarters by the Dutch government.

European Moderns. Modern painters who received much attention included Matisse in drawings and cutouts (Baltimore Museum of Art, then San Francisco) and Picasso in several exhibitions in honor of his 90th birthday (Louvre, Paris; Saidenberg, Marlborough, New York). Max Ernst's 80th birthday was marked by a restrospective (L'Orangerie, Paris). Other European moderns honored in New York included Piet Mondrian (Guggenheim), Paul Delvaux (Staempfli), Kathe Köllwitz (St. Étienne), Alfred Kubin (Sabarsky, Wilfredo Lam (Gimpel), George Grosz (Cohn), and Oskar Kokoschka (Sabarsky).

Important group exhibitions of the modern period were the Cubist Epoch (Los Angeles County Museum, Metropolitan), the Collections of Gertrude, Leo, Michael, and Sarah Stein, and Ways of Looking (both Museum of Modern Art).

WORLDWIDE celebration of Albrecht Dürer's 500th birthday in 1971 included large and elaborate exhibition in Nuremberg, his birthplace. Official poster (left) for Dürer year has composite of strong faces that marked his art.

American Painters. Older masters of American art shown included Whistler (Wildenstein, New York) and the realists John Sloan (National Gallery), Everett Shinn (New Jersey State Museum, Trenton), George Bellows (Hirschl & Adler, New York), and Edward Hopper (Whitney). Retrospectives were given to the watercolorist John Marin (National Gallery and Los Angeles County Museum) and the great abstractionists Josef Albers (Princeton University Art Museum and the Metropolitan) and Barnett Newman (Museum of Modern Art). Other 20th century painters shown in New York included Charles Burchfield (Rehn), Ralston Crawford (Nordness, Zabriskie), and Max Weber (Danenberg).

Among younger American painters shown in New York were Andy Warhol (Whitney) and Gene Davis (Fischbach) in retrospectives and, in one-man shows, David Hockney (Emmerich), Richard Anuszkiewicz (Janis), Ron Davis (Castelli), and James Brooks (Jackson).

Afro-American Art. Important exhibitions of Afro-American art were Contemporary Black Artists in America (Whitney) and the collages of Romare Bearden and the welded metal sculpture of Richard Hunt (Museum of Modern Art). The Rath Museum in Geneva, Switzerland, displayed the painting and sculpture of Eight Afro-American Artists. Early 19th century primitive portraits by Joshua Johnston, probably the first professional Negro artist in America, were shown at the Peridot Gallery, New York. African art from the Mr. and Mrs. Gaston de Havenon collection was presented at the opening of a new wing of the Museum of African Art in Washington.

EMPLOYEES of New York's Museum of Modern Art struck in August to protest staff dismissals. Picket in foreground carries reproduction of Andrew Wyeth's *Christina's World*, to which "strike" was added.

Non-Western Art. Drawing on its own holdings, the Metropolitan displayed bronze sculpture, painted scrolls, and jeweled objects from the Roof Tops of Asia—Tibet, Nepal, and Kashmir. Also presented were Ancient Egyptian Writing (Metropolitan) and a major exhibition of Chinese calligraphy (Philadelphia Museum of Art). New Yorkers were offered the Ben Heller collection of African and Asian sculpture (Saidenberg), splendid Japanese screens (Asia House), and scrolls, screens, and lacquer of the Rimpa school (Japan House). The Indonesian government lent Buddhist stone and metal sculpture for Ancient Indonesian Art (Asia House, Los Angeles, Kansas City, San Francisco).

MUSEUMS AND COLLECTIONS

New Museums and Additions. Although the economic recession was partially responsible for some museums' closing galleries and charging admission, it did not prevent new building. The National Gallery made public plans by I. M. Pei for a $45 million marble extension, to be completed in 1975. Denver opened a $6 million art museum, and Minneapolis added a new $5.5 million building to the Walker Art Center. At Chadds Ford, Pa., an old grist mill was converted into the Brandywine River Museum, containing the work of three generations of Wyeths—N. C., Andrew, and James.

Appointments. President Nixon named trustees for the uncompleted Hirshhorn Museum in Washington: H. H. Arnason, Elizabeth Houghton, Taft B. Schreiber, Hal B. Wallis, Leigh B. Block, Theodor E. Cummings, George Hamilton, and Daniel Moynihan. Block was also elected president of the Art Institute of Chicago. Other new directors included Stephen Prokopoff, Chicago Museum of Contemporary Art; Harold Stern, Freer Gallery (Washington); and Daniel Robbins, Fogg Museum (Cambridge).

Grants. The National Endowment for the Arts gave matching grants of $10,000 each to museums in Baltimore, Santa Barbara, Indianapolis, Brooklyn, Berkeley, Oklahoma City, Salt Lake City, and Honolulu to buy works of contemporary Americans. The Endowment also awarded museums 103 grants totaling $990,000 for pilot programs in the areas of special exhibitions, conservation, and museum training.

Acquisitions. The Guggenheim received 250 works of modern art from the collection of Baroness Hilda Rebay, a former director. The Whitney was given 1,500 works from the estate of Edward Hopper, many of which will gradually be sold. Picasso gave to the Museum of Modern Art his important cubist construction *Guitar* (1912). The Metropolitan revealed that it was the purchaser of the Velázquez portrait of *Juan de Pareja,* auctioned in 1970.

Thefts. Italy was plagued by an unprecedented looting of masterpieces from churches, many of which have not been recovered. Belgium, more fortunate, recovered 11 paintings stolen from English loan collections and found in a matter of days Vermeer's priceless *Love Letter,* which had been stolen and held for ransom to benefit East Pakistani refugees. In the United States an El Greco stolen in Spain during the Civil War was recovered by the F. B. I. The U. S. Customs Bureau seized from the Boston Museum of Fine Arts another masterpiece, thought to be a Raphael portrait, which had been allegedly smuggled out of Italy.

BRANDYWINE RIVER MUSEUM unites a century-old grist mill with modern galleries in rolling countryside in Chadds Ford, Pa. Opened in June, the museum has permanent displays of the work of Andrew and Jamie Wyeth and other artists of the Brandywine school. At right is *Siri*, a 1970 tempera portrait by Andrew Wyeth that was shown at the opening exhibition.

Forgeries and Authentications. British experts warned collectors and museums that many examples of rare Neolithic pottery and figurines from Anatolia now in museums are fakes. A portrait bought by Ira Spanierman in 1968 was authenticated as a portrait of Lorenzo, Duke of Urbino, by Raphael.

Auctions. Records were set in auctions—for sculpture, Degas' *Petite Danseuse* in bronze, $380,-000; for prints, Rembrandt's *Christ Presented to the People,* $83,000; for American painting, Thomas Eakins' *Cowboys in the Badlands,* $210,000; and for non-objective painting, Kandinsky's *Picture with Three Spots,* $300,000. The highest totals reached by an art auction were, in the United States, $6,506,300 for the Norton Simon collection at Parke-Bernet and, in Britain, $8,735,580 at Christie's. The Christie's sale included $4,032,000 for Titian's *Death of Actaeon,* sold to the J. Paul Getty Museum (Malibu, Calif.).

AWARDS, HONORS, AND GRANTS

Guggenheim fellowships went to artists Ben Berns, Rosemarie Castoro, Vincent Longo, Philip Pearlstein, Edward Ruscha, Richard Serra, and Doug Wheeler, among others. The National Institute of Arts and Letters awarded $3,000 each to painters Ilya Bolotowsky, Robert Goodnough, Alfred Leslie, Norman Lewis, Ludwig Sander, and Hedda Sterne and to sculptor Harold Tovish. The National Endowment for the Humanities and the Arts gave grants to art scholars Peter Selz, H. H. Arnason, Bruce Cole, David Rosand, Fuad Bahov, and Margaret Bieber. A. Hyatt Mayor, curator of prints emeritus at the Metropolitan, received the first Boston Museum of Fine Arts award.

OBITUARIES

Among notables in the art world who died in 1971 were Marcel Gromaire (78), French expressionist painter; Alberto Magnelli (83), pioneer Italian abstractionist; and Edgar Wind (71), German-born Renaissance art historian. American notables included Rockwell Kent (89), painter and illustrator; Oliver Larkin (74), historian of American art; Sibyl Moholy-Nagy (68), architectural critic; and I. Rice Pereira (64), geometrical abstractionist.

VICTOR H. MIESEL, *University of Michigan*

ASIA

For Asia, 1971 was an epochal year. A revolution in Sino-American relations that led to the admission of the People's Republic of China into the United Nations and the consequences of war in South Asia dominated world affairs. For the first time in a decade Indochina did not overshadow other Asian events, despite the spreading of war in Laos and Cambodia.

By year's end Asian governments were faced with a greatly changed international landscape. Persisting internal crises were critical for most of them. In short, few Asian nations enjoyed tranquility. Japan's Premier Eisaku Sato was not alone in his January misprophecy that 1971 would be a year of "quiet development." He and most other Asian leaders were to be quickly thrown on the defensive by the course of events.

A NEW ERA IN INTERNATIONAL RELATIONS

The ramifications of Communist China's new international role were global, but they had particular importance for other Asians. Relaxed hostility between Peking and Washington foreshadowed incal-

culable changes in big-power relations. For Asians, the simple alternatives of alliance or nonalignment with one of the cold war blocs became less attractive or workable. The rift between the USSR and the Chinese Communists had earlier complicated cold war diplomacy in Asia. The Chinese People's Republic stood forth as a universally recognized world power. In addition to its enormous size, expanding economy, and nuclear capability, it now had a seat in the United Nations. An era of at least three-sided great-power rivalry in Asia had begun.

In these new circumstances middle- and small-strength Asian governments contended with new uncertainties over the largely unshaped relationships between the Russians, the Chinese, and the Americans. The adjustment proved especially difficult for the governments most dependent on the major powers. North Vietnamese and North Korean anxiety over the changing diplomacy of their Chinese and Russian allies paralleled the discomfiture of their southern counterparts, but it was more than matched by the anguish of the Chinese on Taiwan. Thailand, the Philippines, and Malaysia were reex-

DRAMATIC UPHEAVALS on Indian subcontinent created millions of refugees in 1971. Here, Bengalis at frontier station of Taki board trains without knowing their final destination.

amining their anti-Communist foreign policies. For them, questions of trade meshed with threats to political security. The need to disentangle these issues was particularly urgent in the case of Japan.

Pressures for responding to the new big-power relations were not as strong for Asian governments that had maintained neutral foreign policies. Yet as a new Asian international system emerges, such established neutrals as Indonesia, Ceylon, Nepal, Burma, and Afghanistan may find it necessary to remold their foreign policies.

THE NEW ROLE OF THE CHINESE PEOPLE'S REPUBLIC

The flexibility in foreign policy displayed by Communist China in 1970 produced startling results in 1971. In quick succession quiet probings toward accommodation between Peking and Washington bore fruit. American willingness to improve relations was hinted in February when President Nixon, in a foreign policy report to Congress, referred to the Peking government as "the People's Republic of China." In April the Chinese played host to a U. S. table-tennis team. This "ping-pong diplomacy" pro-

vided public notice that a fundamental change was imminent. Throughout spring and early summer American and western European visitors, many of them scientists, journalists, or former diplomats or missionaries, were given considerable freedom of contact both with ordinary Chinese and high-level officials, including Premier Chou En-lai. In mid-July came an announcement that President Nixon would visit China in 1972. This was accompanied by the U. S. easing of trade barriers between the two countries.

In their discussions with visiting journalists the Chinese made clear their intention to widen their diplomatic influence, a resource that Peking had almost totally abandoned during the Cultural Revolution. Among their most immediate objectives were admittance into the United Nations and the establishment of a wider basis for foreign trade. With regard to long-term developments, the Chinese showed concern that a possible U. S. withdrawal from Asia would produce a vacuum that the Russians and the Japanese might fill. China's diplomatic isolation had become increasingly dangerous.

The People's Republic of China entered the United Nations in October with U. S. support. American hopes to salvage UN membership for the Taiwan government—the "two Chinas" policy—were dashed when many U. S. allies joined a large General Assembly majority in ousting Taiwan's delegation.

Peking also made some attempt to improve relations with the USSR. One instance was the relaxation of their unresolved border dispute. However, the two Communist governments remained widely separated by ideological and geopolitical irritants. Sino-Japanese relations were also clouded by suspicion and were still embittered by Chinese memories of Japanese militarism. In addition Japan's close economic and diplomatic ties with Taiwan obviously disturbed Peking.

Thus behind Communist China's new diplomacy was a growing uneasiness over developments in Asia and its ability to influence them. And in December the Chinese (and the Americans) were given a graphic demonstration of the limits of their control over events when they could not prevent Pakistan's military and political disaster. (See also special report on China beginning on page 14.)

WAR IN SOUTH ASIA

By March, Pakistan had become engulfed in a political and human tragedy. Of the country's two widely separated regions, East Pakistan (East Bengal), although the more populous and the earner of more than half of the nation's foreign exchange, had been dominated by West Pakistan. Ironically, an attempt to formulate a new constitution that would give Pakistan's Bengalis their due share of political power led to civil war and the independence of East Pakistan as the republic of Bangladesh.

Pakistan's first direct national election, in December 1970, had been won by the Awami League of East Pakistan. Under the leadership of Sheikh Mujibur (Mujib) Rahman, the League had campaigned for internal autonomy. It had gained a majority in the National Assembly, which was to draft the constitution. Between December and March, Sheikh Mujib, President Yahya Khan, and Zulfikar Ali Bhutto, leader of the major party in West Pakistan, tried to establish a formula that would encompass both autonomy for the East and effective national unity. Protesting delays in convening the Assembly, the Awami League took virtual control of East Pakistan in early March. Yahya Khan responded by sending in more West Pakistani troops. After a hectic round of conferences, on March 25 he ordered the army to restore the central government's control. Sheikh Mujib was imprisoned in West Pakistan, and the army began a bloody repression of Bengali resistance. Rebel leaders then proclaimed the independence of Bangladesh. In the following months guerrilla units, with Indian assistance, extended their hold over the countryside. As the civil war spread, eventually 10 million East Pakistani refugees fled to India.

Largely in response to the internal political and economic pressures caused by warfare in East Pakistan, the Indian government in July signed a friendship treaty with the USSR. The Russians pledged diplomatic, economic, and military support but did not guarantee direct military intervention. Indian Prime Minister Indira Gandhi denied that the pact meant an end to India's long-standing policy of cold war nonalignment.

Indo-Pakistani hostility reached a flash point in October. In Bengal—divided between Pakistan and India—there were constant clashes between border patrols and frequent use of artillery against cross-border targets. Mrs. Gandhi visited West European capitals and Washington to obtain support for refugee relief and to mobilize pressure on the Pakistan government to accept a political settlement with the Bengalis. The results of the tour were disappointing to India, and by late November, Indian units were probing several miles into East Pakistan with the declared purpose of destroying artillery positions. Full-scale war became inevitable when Pakistan launched air attacks on airfields in western India. Outnumbered, cut off from outside support, and harassed by Bengali guerrillas, the West Pakistani forces in Bengal surrendered to India on December 16. The next day a cease-fire came into effect on the western front in Punjab and Kashmir.

The consequences of the war were momentous for South Asia. Great-power alignments and the United Nations were also severely shaken. Yahya Khan was forced to resign. The provisional government of Bangladesh, led by lieutenants of Sheikh Mujib, was installed in Dacca, the capital of former East Pakistan. India had exchanged the burden of supporting the refugees for the problems of coming to terms with the surviving segment of Pakistan and coping with an economically and politically dependent Bangladesh. Bengali nationalism could also have a political impact on Indian West Bengal.

The Soviet Union's support of India and Bangladesh brought a great immediate increase in Russian influence in South Asia. The Chinese Communists and the Americans found themselves backing a truncated Pakistan that could no longer counterbalance India. While maintaining official neutrality, Washington criticized India's intervention in East Bengal and suspended economic aid. Military aid to both combatants had been cut off earlier. Indo-American relations quickly soured as a result. Peking unequivocally took the side of the Pakistan government, but its support did not extend beyond moving the censure of India in the UN Security Council and supplying some military assistance. (See also INDIA-PAKISTAN WAR.)

THE INDOCHINA WAR

Warfare in Indochina continued in an often baffling and conflicting pattern. U. S. troop levels were cut to less than 160,000 by the end of the year. Few combat units were left, and by autumn U. S. battle deaths had averaged less than 10 a week. The withdrawal was accompanied by reduced fighting throughout most of South Vietnam. Yet it was not clear whether this was the result of a lowered capacity of the Vietcong and North Vietnamese to continue the war in the south.

To a large degree fighting shifted from Vietnam into Cambodia and Laos, where North Vietnamese forces achieved notable successes. They repulsed a U. S.-supported South Vietnamese attack on the Ho Chi Minh trail in southeastern Laos in February and March. And they gained control of more territory in both Laos and Cambodia, badly mauling those countries' armies. The likelihood grew that without a political settlement in Indochina, the survival of the Vientiane and Phnom Penh governments would require prolonged U. S. military assistance and air support. South Vietnamese forces also were increasingly committed to Cambodia's defense.

It remained uncertain what impact the revolution in Asian diplomatic relations would have on the war. Peking-Washington negotiations largely avoided discussing the U. S. and Chinese roles in Indochina. The North Vietnamese government appeared to be anxious about China's reducing or withdrawing support for it but seemed to have been reassured by Peking. Even before the Chinese-U. S. contacts were made public the Thai government had begun to shift toward friendlier relations with both the USSR and China.

Late in the year Nguyen Van Thieu was reconfirmed as South Vietnam's president in an uncontested election that met with obvious U. S. displeasure. Afterward the Saigon government displayed greater independence in foreign policy. Thus, while 1971 brought no end to a generation of war in Indochina, the shuffling of alignments within and outside the region may have provided new avenues to political settlement. (See also INDOCHINA WAR.)

INTERNAL POLITICAL AND ECONOMIC DEVELOPMENTS

Although the Chinese People's Republic, India, and Indonesia strengthened their political systems during 1971, many of Asia's smaller nations faced serious internal crises.

Understanding of the trends of internal Chinese affairs remained difficult, but it became increasingly apparent that moderate pragmatists had gotten the upper hand. High domestic priority was given the reconstruction of party and government institutions and the further expansion of the economy. By summer all of the provincial revolutionary committees formed during the Cultural Revolution had been brought under the combined control of professional military officers and moderate Communist party officials. The direction of events at the highest level was evident in Chou En-lai's apparent command of foreign policy and by the mysterious fall of Lin Piao, Chairman Mao's designated successor and the commander of the army. The exact status of the internal struggle remained unknown, but apparently such champions of the Cultural Revolution as Lin and Chen Po-ta had been silenced or eliminated.

Though softened in impact by war in Bengal, the sweeping victory of Indira Gandhi in India's fifth national election was one of the greatest triumphs achieved within Asian democracy. On a platform of reinvigorating economic development and renewing socioeconomic reform, Mrs. Gandhi's segment of the Congress party won more than two thirds of the seats in the governing house of India's Parliament. This majority enabled her to abolish by constitutional amendment the special status held by India's former ruling princes. Yet the war denied her government an opportunity to initiate new economic and social programs, and the cost of refugee relief crippled efforts to spur economic development.

The domestic scene in Indonesia bore little resemblance to the turbulence elsewhere in Asia. For the first time since 1955 an Indonesian government felt secure enough to hold a national election. Although the campaign was carefully restricted to ensure the victory of the Sekber Golkar, the semigovernmental party, the competition was open enough to demonstrate the general popularity of President Suharto's regime. The Sekber Golkar won 63% of the popular vote and 66% of the elective seats in the House of Representatives. The government's stability enabled it to initiate closer contacts with Peking and Moscow, although it continued to depend primarily upon U. S. military assistance and Western and Japanese support in the task of economic revival.

Other Asian governments were often on the defensive. President Ferdinand E. Marcos of the Philippines had a public quarrel with his vice president and was harassed by continual and often violent demonstrations of students demanding economic and social reform. He suffered a serious defeat in a congressional election after all eight opposition Liberal party senatorial candidates had been injured in an assassination attempt.

Ceylon experienced even greater disruption. An extreme left-wing Marxist youth revolt caught the government of Prime Minister Sirimavo Bandaranaike without adequate police resources. The rebels were crushed only after two months of fighting.

Political opposition was more peaceful in South Korea, but in the April presidential election President Park Chung Hee was seriously challenged by Kim Dae Jung of the New Democratic party. The New Democrats won 89 of the 204 seats in the National Assembly in May. Such progress toward representative government was jeopardized in December when Park declared a national emergency, alleging danger of immediate attack by North Korea.

Other Asian leaders silenced opposition more abruptly. The powerless national assemblies of Thailand and Cambodia were abolished, and while there was some attempt to enlist native Taiwanese support for Chiang Kai-shek's government, prominent intellectuals identified with Taiwanese self-rule were jailed. The Burmese government of Ne Win held its own against continued rebellions.

JAPAN'S AMBIVALENT ROLE

Amidst the currents of change throughout Asia, Japan continued to remain a society apart. International realignments exerted increasing pressure against the Japanese posture of active trade and passive diplomacy under U. S. tutelage. American withdrawal from Asia under the "Nixon doctrine" and the new U. S. contacts with China undermined Tokyo's foreign policy. Even Japan's remarkable economic progress was threatened. While its gross national product had climbed past $200 billion in fiscal 1970, the pace of annual growth had slowed to less than 5%, below half that of the 1960's. Japan's highly favorable balance of trade with the United States was endangered in 1971 by a temporary American import surcharge and a revised monetary policy. Suddenly, the Japanese had to adjust to restricted foreign market opportunities.

Foreign relations and military policy required new responses. While the Americans pushed the Japanese to assume greater defense responsibilities, the Chinese Communists voiced alarm, envisaging the possibility of renewed Japanese militarism. Japan's long-sought opportunity for greater trade with the Chinese mainland remained blocked by Peking's insistence that closer trade and diplomatic relations required a complete break with Taiwan, one of Japan's most valuable trading partners. Thus, the era of nearly exclusive attention to economic growth was ending for Japan. Its evolving relations with the United States, Communist China, and the USSR suggested that Tokyo might soon be forced to play the role of a fourth great power in Asia. (See also MIDDLE EAST and articles on Asian countries.)

RICHARD S. NEWELL
University of Northern Iowa

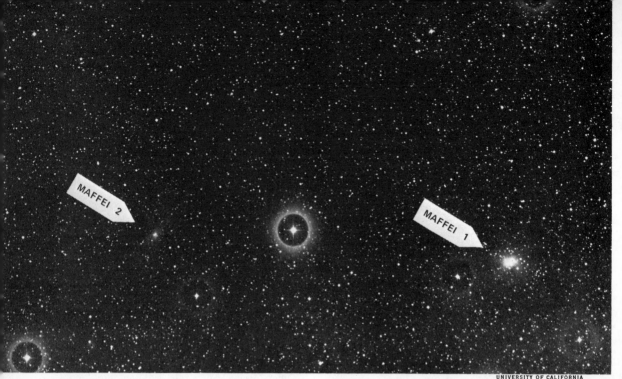

MAFFEI 2

MAFFEI 1

UNIVERSITY OF CALIFORNIA

Two new galaxies were identified as members of our local cluster of galaxies by a team of scientists at the University of California, including (*at right*) Hyron Spinrad, Ivan King, and Nannielou Dieter. The galaxies are named after Italian astronomer Paolo Maffei, who sighted the objects through thick clouds of cosmic dust.

astronomy

$$M/L = \frac{C\sigma^2}{I_0 r_c d}$$

UPI

The year 1971 was important in the exploration of Mars. Also, theories on star formation were further developed, and the possibility of life on other worlds was enhanced by the discovery of new kinds of organic molecules in space.

Mars Probes. Mars passed closer to earth in 1971 than at any time since 1924, and so the United States launched one and the Soviet Union two successful probes toward the planet. The U.S. craft, Mariner 9, entered Martian orbit in mid-November, while Mars 2 and 3 arrived within the following month. The probes were to map the planet's surface, but a severe dust storm that sprang up about September 22 obscured the surface and began to subside only toward the end of November. However, Mariner 9 completed some of its mission and photographed the two tiny Martian satellites, Deimos and Phobos. Mars 2 ejected a noninstrumented and Mars 3 an instrumented capsule that landed on Mars, the latter briefly relaying back data.

Star Formation and Density Waves. A newly observed phenomenon closely associated with our galaxy's spiral structure has been suggested as a source for the formation of protostars. The density-wave theory of U.S. scientists C. C. Lin and F. K. Shu is generally accepted as the explanation for the production and maintenance of large-scale spiral structures, holding that a gravitational potential field of spiral shape rotates within the central plane of a spiral galaxy and produces rather dense concentrations of gas and cosmic dust that become visible as spiral arms. In the past year W. W. Roberts of the University of Virginia has shown that high-pressure shock waves are associated with this phenomenon. The waves must produce zones of very high density in the spiral arms while moving through interstellar gas, the conditions for the piling up of gas and cosmic dust being most favorable along the insides of the arms. Eventually these concentrations condense into small gaseous clouds and then into stars and star clusters, all of this taking place within cosmically short time periods on the order of one to ten million years.

Young stars may be expected to occur along the central line of a spiral arm. Most of them should be blue-white supergiants rich in ultraviolet radiation and capable of producing beautiful, bright nebulae. Since there would be density fluctuations along the wave front, star formation may occur only in regions of more than average density, causing the stars to appear like beads along the string of the passing shock wave. Astrophysicists are generally agreed that this picture of star formation has very strong observational backing.

Star Formation and Dark Nebulae. Unit dark nebulae—cosmic dust clouds that often look like dark holes against a rich stellar background—also may be sites of large-scale star formation. There are three basic varieties of dark nebulae. The largest have diameters of about 25 light-years and masses probably on the order of 2,000 solar masses. Next come the large globules, about three light-years wide and with masses probably on the order of 30 solar masses. Finally there are small globules, with diameters of about 0.1 light-year and masses ranging from about 0.1 to 1 solar mass.

All of the unit dark nebulae are almost certain to condense gradually into protostars or clusters of protostars. The larger ones will probably do so through gravitational collapse, while the smallest may be pushed together by pressure waves from bright nebulae. It is increasingly evident that many of the small dark nebulae possess all of the necessary properties to become protostars. A variety of variable stars known as T-Tauri, among the youngest in our galaxy, are found almost exclusively near the edges of complexes of dark nebulae.

Star Formation and Supernovae. It has also been suggested that stars may form in the region of nebulae associated with the remnants of supernova explosions. In 1971 particular attention was drawn to the Gum Nebula, which is related to a supernova-pulsar located about 1,400 light-years away in the constellation Vela. The explosion, which occurred about 12,000 years ago, added large amounts of gas enriched with heavy elements to the surrounding interstellar medium, and transmitted tremendous amounts of energy to the medium in the form of explosive shock waves. Indeed, one of the most striking features of the nebula is its filamentary structure, a feature that would be expected from the passage of energetic shock waves through the interstellar medium. The filaments must represent highly condensed gas, and it would not be surprising if some were to break up into strings of stars.

However, it is a bit uncomfortable to those who support the supernova theory of star formation that no massive stellar production is in fact being observed at such sites. Recent radio observations have also uncovered unfavorable evidence. The Australian radio astronomer D. S. Mathewson and his Dutch colleagues P. C. van der Kruit and W. N. Brouw have prepared a radio map of the spiral galaxy Messier 51, the so-called Whirlpool Nebula, using the array of 12 interconnected radio telescopes located at Westerbork in the Netherlands. The map shows that the radio and dust arms of the galaxy lie at the insides of its bright optical arms—a result expected on the basis of the shock-wave theory of star formation but arguing against the supernova theory.

Puzzling New Data on Quasars. Radio interferometer observations are providing fundamental new data on quasars, yielding information on structures no larger than 0.001 second of arc. One of the best-known quasars, 3C 279, has been found to be a double source, with the two parts flying away from each other at a tremendous rate. If it is assumed that the quasar lies at the "cosmological" distance indicated by its redshift, the two blobs would be separating at a velocity ten times the speed of light—a state of affairs not tolerated by conventional relativistic physics. The obvious conclusion is that 3C 279 is not as far away as its redshift suggests.

The past year has produced more evidence to this effect. Pairs and small groups of galaxies are being discovered that are clearly interconnected and yet appear to have very different redshifts. Theorists cannot help but suspect that the observed redshifts may be a mixture of the known effect and some other phenomenon not yet understood. To complicate matters further, a galaxy has been found whose spectrum has eight different groups of spectral lines each having its own redshift value. It is hoped that further work will provide some clarification of this confusing state of affairs.

New Clues Hint at Life Elsewhere in the Universe

During 1971 the number of kinds of molecules detected in space increased from 10 to more than 25. Some of the molecules are complex organic species, and they seem to exist in many parts of our galaxy.

The key to the existence of such molecules appears to be a reasonable absence of ultraviolet radiation. This is especially apparent in the densest, darkest central regions of the dark nebulae, which radio studies in 1971 have shown to be at about 3° Kelvin or even cooler. Cosmic dust particles serve to filter ultraviolet radiation from light rays entering the cloud, radiation that would tend to destroy organic molecules that formed there. Thus formaldehyde molecules are common in the centers of dark nebulae, along with carbon monoxide and hydroxyl (OH) molecules, whereas the more stable carbon monoxide molecules can also be traced out almost to the rims of the clouds.

Small and very cold particles appear to serve as "cold fingers" that capture interstellar atoms, holding them temporarily. The atoms can take their time, waiting for other atoms to come along and form molecules. These molecules ultimately can be expelled back into the dark clouds.

From laboratory experiments involving electrical discharges and ultraviolet radiation, scientists are beginning to understand the processes by which complex molecules can be produced from simple ones. Amino acids and other complex compounds have been produced in such experiments, and it seems likely that the kinds of molecules that biologists associate with actual life would eventually be formed. The laboratory conditions bear resemblances to conditions on earth and in its atmosphere, and presumably to those in the atmospheres of giant planets such as Jupiter. Studies of ancient meteorites have revealed that many basic components of the molecules associated with lifelike phenomena have also been found in these bodies dating from the earliest days of the solar system.

What do all these findings mean for the possibility of life in the universe? They show that simple organic chemistry can take place under a wide variety of conditions, provided that temperature is kept relatively low and ultraviolet radiation is essentially excluded. This does not imply that lifelike phenomena could occur under the extreme conditions of interstellar space. To produce lifelike molecules requires the special conditions present only in planetlike bodies. However, it does not seem unlikely that many stars possess planetary systems, nor that in these systems conditions favorable to the development of life will arise.

B. J. B.

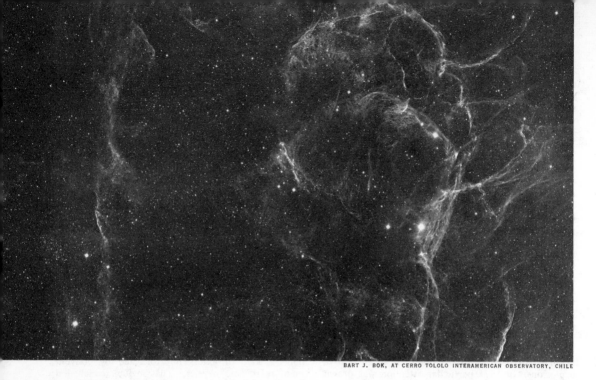

GUM NEBULA in Vela was photographed in Chile by Bart J. Bok. This particular section marks the direction in which radio astronomers have located the Vela short-period pulsar. The threadlike structure of the portion of the nebula shown here is probably produced by the advancement of shock waves emitted by the pulsar into the interstellar medium.

A "BLACK HOLE," in theory, is a collapsed star so dense that radiation and particles cannot escape the star's extremely intense gravitational field. In this interpretation by an artist, a "black hole" has drawn a passing ray of light into its field.

Satellite Research. The Uhuru X-ray satellite, launched in 1970 by Italian engineers, is performing well. Now known to be in or associated with our galaxy are 29 X-ray sources. One in Cygnus exhibits marked variations in intensity at irregular intervals of about half a minute. In a way, another Cygnus source—Cygnus X-1—is the most puzzling of all. It is not associated with any radio or optical source and may instead represent a "black hole"—a collapsed star so dense that almost all of its radiation is held captive by its own gravitational field. Uhuru also confirmed the discovery, made in March by a U. S. Naval Research Laboratory rocket, of an extragalactic X-ray source that is apparently a Seyfert galaxy, a sort of missing link between normal galaxies and quasars.

OAO 2, the U. S. orbiting astronomical observatory launched in 1968, is observing ultraviolet radiation from stars, planets, comets, and interstellar matter. Its far ultraviolet studies made possible the detection of molecular hydrogen, the most elusive although probably the most common interstellar molecule. OAO data also indicate that neutral atomic hydrogen is about 100 times as dense as cosmic dust in interstellar space, and that cosmic dust particles are very complex.

Hidden Galaxies. Red and infrared photography reveals objects hidden from direct view or obscured by intervening dust. An Italian astronomer, Paolo Maffei, first drew attention to two such hidden galaxies in Casseiopia. The first, Maffei 1, was identified in 1971 as a giant elliptical galaxy perhaps three to four million light-years away. The second, Maffei 2, seems to be a more distant spiral galaxy. Infrared surveys in the direction of our own galaxy's center have revealed an interesting object that is most likely a globular cluster but may possibly be a neighboring dwarf galaxy.

Coming Solar Eclipse. On July 10, 1972, there will be a total eclipse of the sun with a maximum duration of 156 seconds. The path of totality will extend across the Bering Strait, Alaska, Canada, and Nova Scotia, ending in the North Atlantic Ocean.

BART J. BOK, *University of Arizona*

ATLANTA

In 1971, Atlanta began to feel the effects of a power shift away from an elite group of white businessmen, as Mayor Sam Massell, a white liberal, and Vice Mayor Maynard Jackson, a black, took steps to move government closer to the people.

For years, the group of white businessmen who dominated Atlanta had projected the image of a progressive city "too busy to hate," in the words of a long-time mayor, William B. Hartsfield. On February 22, however, Hartsfield, mayor from 1936 to 1962, except for one year in World War II, died at the age of 80. By the end of 1971 some others in the group had either left Atlanta or were taking a less active role in civic affairs.

When the official 1970 census was released in mid-1971, it was found that the central city's population was 51.3% black, a jump from 38.3% in 1960. The total population of the central city (496,973) was about the same as in 1960, but the population of the metropolitan area increased by 35% (to 1,390,164), reflecting a 65% population growth in outlying areas.

Massell, elected with heavy black support, enraged some black leaders when he charged in October that it is "political blindness for blacks not to get alarmed when the city's resources begin to diminish while the governmental needs of its citizens grow at an accelerated pace." Noting that the median income for white families in Atlanta is $13,400, compared with $8,900 for blacks, Massell said that the influx of the poor into the central city and the out-migration of the affluent is "a deadly trap."

Transit and Schools. On November 9, Atlanta area voters went to the polls and narrowly approved construction of a $1.4 billion, 70-mile rapid transit system for the metropolitan area. Two outlying counties, by voting against construction, opted not to be included in the system. The first lines of the rail system should be in operation by mid-1976,

with a 15-cent fare. The federal government will bear two thirds of the cost, with the other third funded through a sales tax increase in the areas served by the line. The proposal also included city ownership of the bus lines and a fare reduction from 40 cents to 15 cents.

On July 28 the U. S. District Court declared that Atlanta had finally established a unitary school system. But on October 21, the 5th Circuit Court of Appeals in New Orleans reopened the Atlanta school integration case, declaring that the court had to hear an alternate integration plan—requiring massive busing—proposed by the NAACP.

Housing. Atlanta area growth continued at a phenomenal rate. It had the most booming housing market in the nation, with 22 housing permits per 1,000 population. The national average is 6.5.

Housing and zoning were of great concern to officials. A study made by the Urban Observatory at Georgia State University showed that zoning was done haphazardly by politicians, instead of zoning experts, and that the city was in danger of making the environmental and demographic mistakes that are causing decay in northern cities.

A National Urban League study found, however, that Atlanta was a national symbol of achievement in fighting the "crisis ghetto pattern" that has nearly ruined much inner city housing. It said that Atlanta had avoided the pitfalls because of progressive banks, strict housing code enforcement, and a generally healthy economy.

On August 22 ground was broken for the first Model Cities housing in Atlanta. Model Cities director Johnny Johnson said 6,000 units are needed. Some 530 units were under construction by the end of 1971, with an additional 500 scheduled for 1972 and 750 for 1973.

GENE STEPHENS
The Atlanta "Constitution"

ATOMIC ENERGY. See NUCLEAR ENERGY.

In Atlanta to honor late U. S. Senator Russell, the Nixons are greeted by Georgia Governor and Mrs. Carter.

UPI

UPI

Sydney, the capital of New South Wales, and Australia's biggest city, as seen from the air in photo taken on Nov. 25, 1971. Founded in 1788 as a penal settlement, Sydney experienced rapid development in the 1960's, when skyscrapers replaced many older buildings.

AUSTRALIA

In 1971, Australia acquired a new prime minister, decided to withdraw all of its troops from Vietnam, and took anti-inflationary action.

Government Changes. On March 10, Prime Minister John G. Gorton lost a vote of confidence by members of the Liberal party and thereby lost his positions as leader of the party and prime minister. William McMahon, the foreign minister, was elected to take his place. Gorton had been charged with dictatorial tendencies and disregard of the claims of the six states on matters such as offshore mineral rights and distribution of tax revenue.

The vote against Gorton was precipitated by the resignation of Defense Minister Malcolm Fraser, who charged that Gorton was unfit "to hold the great office of prime minister." Following the vote of no confidence, in which Gorton voted against himself to break a tie, the former prime minister was elected deputy leader of the Liberal party and

appointed defense minister. Labour opposition leader Gough Whitlam called for an immediate general election.

On February 2, J. Douglas Anthony was unanimously elected to succeed the retiring Sir John McEwen as head of the Country party. Subsequent ministerial changes included the selection of Anthony as deputy prime minister and as minister of trade and industry. Ian Sinclair became deputy leader of the Country party and minister for primary industry. Peter Nixon became minister for shipping and transport, and Ralph Hunt was appointed minister for the interior.

On August 1, Leslie H. E. Bury was replaced as minister for foreign affairs by Nigel Bowen, former attorney general Sen. Ivor J. Greenwood replaced Bowen as attorney general, and Sen. Sir Kenneth Anderson took over Senator Greenwood's portfolio as minister of health. R. V. Garland filled Ander-

──────── **AUSTRALIA · Information Highlights** ────────

Official Name: Commonwealth of Australia.
Area: 2,967,910 square miles (7,686,810 sq km).
Population (1970 est.): 12,550,000. *Density,* 5 per square mile (2 per sq km). *Annual rate of increase,* 2.0%.
Chief Cities (1968 est.): Canberra, the capital, 124,500; Sydney (metropolitan area), 2,646,800; Melbourne (metropolitan area), 2,319,700; Brisbane, 813,300; Adelaide, 794,300.
Government: *Head of state,* Elizabeth II, queen (acceded Feb. 6, 1952); represented by Governor General Sir Paul B. Hasluck (took office April 30, 1969). *Head of government,* William McMahon, prime minister (took office March 10, 1971). *Legislature*—Parliament: Senate, 60 members; House of Representatives, 125 members. *Major political parties*—Liberal party, Country party; Labour party, Democratic Labour party.
Languages: English (official).
Education: *Literacy rate* (1970), 99% of population (excluding aborigines). *Expenditure on education* (1967), 11.9% of total public expenditure. *School enrollment* (1968)—primary, 1,768,060; secondary, 1,080,524; technical/vocational, 189,985; university/higher, 164,528.
Finances (1970): *Revenues,* $7,890,000,000; *expenditures,* $7,898,000,000; *monetary unit,* Australian dollar (0.8224 Australian dollar equals U.S.$1, Dec. 30, 1971).
Gross National Product (1970): $33,000,000,000.
National Income (1970): $26,462,000,000; *national income per person,* $2,108.
Economic Indexes: *Industrial production* (1970), 140 (1963=100); *agricultural production* (1969), 120 (1963=100); *consumer price index* (1970), 124 (1963=100).
Manufacturing (metric tons, 1969): Residual fuel oil, 8,609,000; crude steel, 7,016,000; gasoline, 6,934,000; cement, 4,042,000; sugar, 2,269,000; meat, 1,979,000.
Crops (metric tons, 1969 crop year): Cow milk, 7,807,000; barley, 1,789,000; oats, 1,677,000; wool, 927,000 (ranks 1st among world producers); sheep, 174,602,000 head.
Minerals (metric tons, 1969): Coal, 42,493,000; iron ore, 24,861,000; lignite, 23,279,000; crude petroleum, 18,096,000; bauxite, 7,924,000 (ranks 2d among world producers); lead ore, 451,200 (world rank 3d).
Foreign Trade: *Exports* (1970), $4,621,000,000 (chief exports—wool, $728,600,000; wheat, $433,200,000). *Imports* (1970), $4,480,000,000 (chief imports, 1968—nonelectrical machinery, $681,000,000; transport equipment, $594,000,000; chemicals, $376,100,000; textiles, $289,300,000). *Chief trading partners* (1968)—United States (took 14% of exports, supplied 26% of imports); United Kingdom (14%—22%); Japan (21%—10%).
Tourism: *Receipts* (1970), $105,000,000.
Transportation: *Roads* (1969), 570,000 miles (917,301 km); *motor vehicles* (1969), 4,626,900 (automobiles, 3,677,000); *railroads* (1969), 25,000 miles (40,233 km); *merchant fleet* (1971), 1,105,000 gross registered tons; *national airline,* Qantas Airways, Ltd.; *principal airport,* Sydney.
Communications: *Telephones* (1969), 3,598,692; *television stations* (1967), 79; *television sets* (1969), 2,649,000; *radios* (1968), 2,650,000; *newspapers* (1968), 61 (daily circulation, 4,732,000).

There was little public reaction in Australia to the new economic policies adopted by the United States in August, though the chairman of the Australian wool board indicated that the 10% surcharge on U.S. imports would hurt the Australian wool industry. Treasurer Snedden said that the United States apparently did not intend to interfere with exports of U.S. capital to Australia. He stated in September that the Australian dollar had appreciated by 2%–3% during the currency upheaval caused by the de facto devaluation of the U.S. dollar.

Prime Minister McMahon, on May 5, said that immense benefits would come from the increasing trade between Australia and Japan. He indicated that Japan now takes about 25% of Australia's exports. Later in the year, Minister of Trade and Industry Anthony expressed the government's "disillusionment" with the British negotiations to enter the European Economic Community. He suggested that Australia, the United States, Canada, and Japan would soon have to work out mutually beneficial trade arrangements.

On March 15, J. Douglas Anthony, minister for trade and industry, said that Australian meat exports to the United States in 1971 would amount to $266 million, somewhat more than in the previous year.

Australia's trade was disrupted in June, when 4,000 waterfront workers went on strike in support of longshoremen who had refused to handle South African cargo from a Dutch freighter. The longshoremen were protesting South Africa's apartheid policy, particularly as related to the Australian tour of the Springboks, an all-white rugby team.

Budget. In August, Snedden stated that it was essential that government expenditures be high enough to achieve full employment but not so high

AUSTRALIA'S NEW PRIME MINISTER, William McMahon, and his wife. They were photographed in Canberra after McMahon assumed office in March 1971.

son's place as minister for supply. Bury said that he had been "sacked" by McMahon but gave no reason.

On August 12, Gorton was fired from the cabinet after the publication in a newspaper of articles in which he charged that other cabinet members had leaked government information. Gorton was replaced as minister of defense by David M. Fairbairn, and the Liberal party elected Treasurer Billy M. Snedden as deputy leader.

Economy. In August, Treasurer Snedden said that Australia was in the grip of inflationary forces. He described the fast rate of increase in costs and prices as "serious." During 1971 average weekly earnings rose by more than 10%, and the consumer price index rose by 4.8%. On the other hand, employment rose by 3.7%, and the external payments and reserves position improved. Snedden said that this improvement occurred despite a decline in the position of rural industries, including a severe slump in the case of wool.

Minister for National Development Reginald W. C. Swartz announced in February that Australia would end restrictions on the export of uranium because of recent discoveries of large deposits in the Northern Territory.

During the year the world's largest bauxite refinery went into operation in Queensland. It produces over 1.25 million tons of alumina a year.

SURGERY for removal of an abdominal tumor is performed on Tara, a 2-ton elephant, by a team of 10 veterinarians from the University of Sydney. The operation was successful.

as to encourage further cost and price increases. Though the budget provided increased appropriations to meet high-priority needs in social welfare, the rural sector, and defense, he indicated that the government had been "ruthless" in pruning expenditures. The budget surplus would be $706 million.

Taxes on income, cigarettes, and gasoline were raised, as were charges for postage and telephones, and higher charges for radio and television licenses were introduced. Defense expenditures were increased by 10.3%, and the government introduced a plan to subsidize wool at a price of 40 cents per pound. Various types of pensions were increased by $1.40 per week. Child allowances went up by 50 cents per week for every child in excess of two per family. Pensions for veterans were increased. The level of financial grants to the states, both to support housing construction and for other purposes, was also raised.

Labour opposition leader Gough Whitlam introduced a motion in Parliament criticizing the budget on the grounds that it did not include a complete review of social services; that it did not balance the finances of the national government, the states, and localities; and that it produced no "high national objectives" for social welfare, economic strength, and national security.

Foreign Affairs. In March, Foreign Minister McMahon applauded U. S. President Nixon's statement looking toward a two-China policy. After he became prime minister, McMahon stated that Australia favored Taiwan remaining a member of the United Nations should mainland China be admitted. He said that Australia was in many ways ahead of the United States in its attitude toward mainland China, adding that Australia placed no obstacles in the way of individuals visiting there and that Australian ships could freely use Chinese ports. An Australian table-tennis team visited China in April.

In May the prime minister announced a plan to improve Australian contacts with mainland China and the Soviet Union. He said there would be a diplomatic initiative aimed at opening a dialogue with Peking. He added that Australia had agreed to Soviet requests to establish a commercial office and appoint a shipping representative in Sydney and an agricultural attaché to the Soviet embassy. McMahon's statement immediately followed an announcement by the Labour party that it had been invited to send a delegation to China to meet Chou-En-lai. After the visit, which took place in July, Labour leader Gough Whitlam reported that Chou had expressed Chinese willingness to participate in a renewed Geneva Convention to end the war in Vietnam. The Labour party has long advocated recognition of Communist China and immediate withdrawal of U. S. troops from Vietnam.

In July, Prime Minister McMahon stated that he welcomed U. S. President Nixon's proposed visit to China, though the government was apparently annoyed that it had not been consulted in advance. After the expulsion of Taiwan from the United Nations in October, Foreign Minister Bowen expressed regret but reiterated the government's intention of achieving "progressive normalization" of relations with mainland China.

Early in the year the government announced that 1,000 troops would be withdrawn from Vietnam over a six-month period beginning in May. On August 18 the prime minister reported a change in this policy: all Australian troops were to be withdrawn within six months.

Elections. In the state elections in February, the Liberal-Country party coalition was reelected in New South Wales, and the Labour party won control of the government in Western Australia for the first time in 12 years. In June the Queensland Parliament elected an aborigine to the national Senate, the first time that an aborigine had been chosen a member of Parliament.

RUSSELL H. BARRETT
University of Mississippi

AUSTRIA

Politics held the spotlight in 1971, as both presidential and parliamentary elections were held. The year also brought an upward revaluation of the schilling, diplomatic recognition of Communist China, and further agreement with Italy on South Tyrol.

Presidential Election. Austria elected a president for a 6-year term on April 25. The 71-year-old incumbent, Franz Jonas, a Socialist, received 2,488,-372 votes, or 52.79% of the total, defeating the candidate of the more conservative People's party, Kurt Waldheim. Waldheim, a former foreign minister and, at that time, the Austrian ambassador to the UN (he became UN secretary-general on Jan. 1, 1972), received 2,225,368 votes.

President Jonas' majority of 263,004 votes was a considerable improvement over his 63,482-vote majority in 1965, when he had defeated Alfons Gorbach. The election result was generally hailed as an endorsement of the policies of Chancellor Bruno Kreisky, whom the president had entrusted with the formation of a minority government in April 1970.

People's Party Reorganization. After the election, Karl Schleinzer was chosen chairman of the People's party at a special party congress on June 4. He succeeded Hermann Withalm. Hermann Kohlmaier, a member of the Federal Assembly and an expert on social services, took over Schleinzer's previous post as secretary general of the party. The new leader was immediately faced with a general election, as the parliament voted for dissolution on July 14.

Parliamentary Election. The Socialist minority government of Bruno Kreisky, with 81 seats in the 165-member National Council, Austria's lower house, had been able to govern only with the support of the right-wing Freedom party, which held 6 seats. The major opposition party, the People's party, had commanded 78 seats. Chancellor Kreisky decided in July to risk an early election in hopes of establishing a more stable parliamentary position.

A change in the election law had redefined electoral boundaries and increased the membership of the National Council to 183. The elections were held on October 10 and, for the first time since World War I, one party emerged with a clear majority of seats. The Socialists elected 93 members, or one more than would have constituted a simple majority. The People's party captured 80 seats, and the Freedom party, 10. As in the preceding general election, the showing of the Communists was weak.

If the June results were interpreted as a tribute to the chancellor, the October vote was regarded as major personal triumph. Kreisky's generally moderate stand on the issues and his liberal but businesslike approach to government had done much to dispel the fears of many non-Socialist voters about casting their ballots for a party of the left.

Economic Developments. In 1970, the Austrian economy had experienced its fastest growth in 10 years, registering a 7.1% increase in the gross national product (GNP). This expansion had been a balanced one, with all economic sectors gaining.

Expansion slowed somewhat in 1971. The first quarter of the year showed a GNP growth rate of 6.3%, whereas in the first quarter of 1970 it had been 7.0%. On May 10, the schilling was revalued as a result of the unstable international monetary

---

———— AUSTRIA · Information Highlights ————

Official Name: Republic of Austria.
Area: 32,374 square miles (83,849 sq km).
Population (1971 census): 7,443,809. *Density,* 226 per square mile (88 per sq km). *Annual rate of increase,* 0.5%.
Chief Cities (1968 est.): Vienna (1969 est.), the capital, 1,700,000; Graz, 253,000; Linz, 205,700; Salzburg, 120,000.
Government: *Head of state,* Franz Jonas, president (took office June 9, 1965). *Head of government,* Bruno Kreisky, chancellor (took office April 21, 1970). *Legislature*—Federal Assembly: Federal Council, 54 members; National Council, 183 members. *Major political parties*—Socialist party, People's party, Freedom party.
Languages: German (official).
Education: *Literacy rate* (1970), 99% of population. *Expenditure on education* (1968), 7.6% of total public expenditure. *School enrollment* (1968)—primary, 862,193; secondary, 377,749; vocational, 226,505; university/higher, 52,527.
Finances (1970 est.): *Revenues,* $3,551,000,000; *expenditures,* $3,896,000,000; *monetary unit,* schilling (23.30 schillings equal U. S.$1, Dec. 30, 1971).
Gross National Product (1970): $14,382,000,000.
National Income (1970): $10,798,000,000; *national income per person,* $1,479.
Economic Indexes: *Industrial production* (1970), 153 (1963=100); *agricultural production* (1969), 107 (1963=100); *consumer price index* (1970), 128 (1963=100).
Manufacturing (metric tons, 1969): Cement, 4,558,000; crude steel, 3,926,000; meat, 472,000; beer, 7,365,000 hectoliters; wine, 2,263,000 hectoliters.
Crops (metric tons, 1969 crop year): Potatoes, 2,941,000; sugar beets (1968–69) 1,936,000; wheat, 950,000; barley, 934,000; oats, 288,000.
Minerals (metric tons, 1969): Lignite, 3,841,000; crude petroleum, 2,758,000; magnesite, 1,608,400.
Foreign Trade (1968): *Exports* (1970) $2,857,000,000 (chief exports—iron and steel, $241,800,000; nonelectrical machinery, $226,700,000; textile yarn, fabrics, $168,700,000; wood, lumber and cork, $133,300,000). *Imports* (1970), $3,549,000,000 (chief imports—nonelectrical vehicles, $220,000,000; textile yarn, fabrics, $199,700,000; electrical machinery and appliances, $175,600,000). *Chief trading partners* (1968)—West Germany (took 23% of exports, supplied 41% of imports); Italy (10%—7%); Switzerland.
Tourism: *Receipts* (1970) $998,800,000.
Transportation: *Roads* (1969) 20,000 miles (32,200 km); *motor vehicles* (1969), 1,512,900 (automobiles, 1,124,200); *railroads* (1965), 4,094 miles (6,587 km).

---

situation, its value in terms of the U. S. dollar being increased by 5.05%.

Links with China. On March 4 the Federal Assembly unanimously authorized negotiations for the establishment of diplomatic relations with Communist China. These negotiations were soon taking place in Bucharest, Rumania. On May 27 a statement announcing mutual recognition and a forthcoming exchange of ambassadors was published in Vienna and Peking. China recognized Austria's special status of neutrality, while the Austrians recognized Peking as China's sole legal government.

Agreement With Italy. On July 17, Italy and Austria signed a treaty under which they agreed to refer to the International Court of Justice at The Hague any future disputes arising out of their 1969 accord on South Tyrol (Alto Adige). In November, President Jonas was in Rome on the first state visit to Italy by an Austrian head of state since 1875.

Austria and the Common Market. As a result of the new treaty, Italy finally pledged to support Austria's bid for a special associate membership in the European Economic Community (EEC) under terms that would harmonize with Austria's status of neutrality. A series of discussions of this topic had begun in November 1970, and had been resumed in January and March 1971. The talks were devoted principally to the size and implementation of tariff reductions, quantitative import restrictions on the part of EEC, agricultural problems, and EEC's reservations about the treatment accorded Austrian steels and paper.

ERNST C. HELMREICH
Bowdoin College

AUTOMATION. See COMPUTERS.

automobiles

Imported economy cars, such as these Toyotas that were shipped to Boston, gained a large share of the U. S. market during 1971.

For the second time in a row, U. S. automobile manufacturers produced fewer cars in the 1971 model year than in the previous 12-month period. An 8-week strike against General Motors Corporation, the world's largest car builder, and record-breaking sales of imported vehicles combined to pull 1971-model production 5.4% below the total for 1970 models. The final production figures read: 7,203,767 cars for 1971 and 7,595,790 for 1970.

The decline, however, was substantially smaller than that from 1969 to 1970. In 1969, output of 8,652,136 cars had established the all-time record for U. S. domestic car production.

Consumer interest during the 1971-model year swung even further away from the so-called standard-sized cars that had dominated the U. S. market in the 1950's and 1960's. American-made compacts and subcompacts vied with imported economy cars for a steadily growing share of the U. S. market. Sporty cars and convertibles gave ground to the lowest-priced models. Only the highest-priority "luxury" makes were holding their own as the model year closed.

1971 MODEL PRODUCTION

Idled for nearly two months by a United Automobile Workers strike in the fall of 1970, General Motors built slightly less than half of the 7.2 million cars produced as 1971 models. This compared with 53.3% of the 1970 models. The GM total of 1971 models was 3,556,263, off from 4,049,186. Ford Motor Company's total rose from 1,997,441 to 2,141,-837, while that of Chrysler Corporation declined from 1,301,412 to 1,256,259. American Motors showed a small gain—from 242,664 to 244,758.

The GM strike allowed Ford Division to outproduce Chevrolet Division in 1971 by a slender margin —1,748,138 to 1,720,065. However, in the new subcompact segment, Chevrolet's Vega exceeded Ford's Pinto, 269,928 to 255,394, because of a lengthy strike at Ford of England, source of Pinto engines. The third entry in the U. S. subcompact field, AMC's Gremlin, showed a model-year output gain to 53,480 from 25,300. The standard-sized Ford series outproduced the standard-sized Chevrolet by a wide margin in the latest model year—814,421 to 676,569.

Four makers built more than 500,000 cars each in a close contest for the industry's No. 3 spot. Plymouth led with 625,812, enjoying industry leadership in the compact field with its Valiant model. Oldsmobile finished with 560,426, Buick with 551,-118, and Pontiac with 536,047. Pontiac added a compact of its own during the 1971 model year— the Ventura II—and Oldsmobile announced plans to introduce a 1973-model compact.

Plymouth's leadership in production of compacts was achieved on a 231,559 total for Valiant. The Valiant had finished ahead of Ford's Maverick and behind Chevrolet's Nova in the 1970 model year, but in 1971 it benefited not only from the GM strike but also from a Chrysler Corporation decision not to produce a domestic subcompact. Maverick

1970 MOTOR VEHICLE DATA

Country	1970 cars produced	1970 trucks and buses produced	1970 vehicle registrations
United States	6,550,128	1,733,821	105,403,557[1]
Canada	937,219	250,211	7,952,000
Argentina	168,044	51,555	2,000,000
Australia	447,266	26,524	4,700,000
Austria	...	996	1,243,755
Belgium	252,729	19,704	2,117,106
Brazil	249,920	166,127	3,202,000
Czechoslovakia	142,856	27,064	991,938
Finland	...	983	748,151
France	2,458,038	292,048	13,770,000
Germany, East	115,000	25,000	1,449,975
Germany, West	3,129,112	713,135	13,694,723
Hungary	...	9,200	262,300
India	35,203	37,893	1,028,500
Italy	1,719,715	134,537	9,854,205
Japan	3,178,708	2,110,449	15,145,611
Mexico	136,712	56,129	1,636,733
Netherlands	67,262	11,597	2,585,000
Poland	64,152	48,935	732,686
Portugal	...	190	599,140
Rumania	7,500	26,000	43,885
Spain	450,426	85,600	2,681,800
Sweden	278,971	31,916	2,349,815
Switzerland	...	944	1,389,319
United Kingdom	1,640,966	457,532	13,084,320
USSR	352,000	570,000	5,400,000
Yugoslavia	111,159	19,000	671,090
World total	22,493,086	6,907,450	231,472,802[2]

[1] Excludes Puerto Rico, 478,000; Virgin Islands, 20,072; and Canal Zone, 20,048. [2] Includes all countries, of which others with more than 1,000,000 registrations are: Denmark, 1,285,822; New Zealand, 1,031,854; and South Africa, 1,928,000, a motor vehicle producer whose output totals are not available. Sources: Automobile Manufacturers Association and "Automotive News."

wound up the 1971 model run with 145,371 cars, a drop from 210,885, while Nova was cut by the strike from 316,621 to 197,361. Another Chrysler Corporation compact, the Dodge Dart, rose to 136,658 from 37,090. Two new compacts, the Mercury Comet and Pontiac Ventura II, had 83,000 and 48,484, respectively. The AMC Hornet rose from 73,572 to 74,685.

Inroads on personal sports cars were widespread during the 1971 model year. Ford's Mustang, which once sold half a million units in a model year, slid to 149,678 from 190,727. Chevrolet's Camaro declined less steeply, from 124,899 to 114,643. The Mercury Cougar, Ford Thunderbird, Buick Riviera, AMC Javelin-AMX, and Chrysler Corporation's Barracuda and Challenger all suffered substantial declines. The only sports cars on the plus side from 1970 to 1971 were the Cadillac Eldorado, Oldsmobile Toronado, and Pontiac Firebird.

THE 1972 MODELS

U. S. producers held styling changes to a minimum for 1972. Research and development efforts were being concentrated on a host of safety and emissions standards being required by federal and some state administrative agencies for 1973 through 1976 models. As a result, and with the GM strike a factor in that corporation's new-model styling decisions, only four volume series were changed appreciably in appearance for 1972. These were the Dodge Polara and Plymouth Fury, both of standard size, and the Ford Fairlane and Mercury Montego, both intermediates. The Ford Thunderbird and Lincoln Mark IV also were revamped.

GM incorporated a major safety change by offering stronger, more-resilient front bumpers on all of its five standard-size series—Buick, Chevrolet, Cadillac, Pontiac, and Oldsmobile. The National Highway Traffic Safety Administration will require that bumpers on all 1973 models resist impacts of up to 5 miles per hour without damage to any car body components. GM's 1972-model bumpers still do not meet the minimum requirement.

In a continuing tightening of model selections, the U. S. auto industry dispensed with 45 models for 1972 and started the year with 296 separate offerings, the lowest total since 1962. A total of 375 models had been offered in 1970—the postwar high —which in turn had been reduced to 341 by the end of the 1971 model year.

BETTER BUMPERS will be required on 1974 model U. S. cars. A firm under federal contract is developing a test car (model, below) with an energy-absorbing bumper. An insurer pledges (right) lower rates for sturdier cars.

REPUBLIC AVIATION DIVISION, FAIRCHILD HILLER

Chrysler Corporation dispensed with 20 models for 1972; Ford Motor, 10; GM, 9; and AMC, 6. The corporate totals as the 1972 model year began were: GM, 125; Chrysler, 81; Ford Motor, 75, and AMC, 15. Four-door sedans were reduced from 68 to 61; 2-door coupes from 37 to 28; 4-door hardtops from 44 to 38; 2-door hardtops from 105 to 87, and convertibles from 23 to 17 (with none offered by either Chrysler or AMC). Only station wagons gained, adding one to 65.

In keeping with the standpat trend on styling, the domestic makes held steady on model names for 1972. The only "newcomers" in name were in the import field. No new domestic entry was to become available until the Oldsmobile compact for 1973.

Styling. The most distinctive U. S.-made cars for 1972 were those at the two extreme ends of the price spectrum. Opera windows highlighted the Cadillac Eldorado and Lincoln Mark IV. The Lincoln silhouette was adapted for the restyled intermediate Mercury Montego; earlier, it had been used on the standard-sized Mercury Marquis. During the model year the subcompact Ford Pinto added a "hatchback" model, as already offered by the Chevrolet Vega.

The ventless window theme spread to the new Plymouth Fury, Dodge Polara, Ford Fairlane, and Mercury Montego models.

Safety. From Jan. 1, 1972, all cars sold in the United States were required by the National Highway Traffic Safety Administration to offer as standard equipment a buzzer-and-light combination that is actuated if front-seat belts are not fastened. The NHTSA postponed until 1976 a requirement for air bags in front seats, but it ordered that, beginning with 1974 models, provision be made that unfast-

Company and make	1970 models	1971 models
AMERICAN MOTORS CORPORATION		
Ambassador	59,941	41,674
Hornet	73,572	74,685
Gremlin	25,300	53,480
Matador-Rebel	49,701	45,789
Javelin-AMX	34,150	29,130
Total AMC	242,664	244,758
CHRYSLER CORPORATION		
Valiant	241,557	231,559
Barracuda	55,499	18,690
Satellite-Belvedere	160,736	102,976
Fury	267,797	272,587
Subtotal Plymouth Division	725,589	625,812
Chrysler	180,777	174,291
Imperial	11,816	11,432
Dart	37,090	136,658
Coronet-Charger	171,284	165,387
Challenger	83,032	29,883
Polara	91,284	112,796
Subtotal Dodge Division	382,230	444,724
Total Chrysler Corporation	1,301,412	1,256,259
FORD MOTOR COMPANY		
Club Wagon	44,984	21,056
Torino-Fairlane	328,710	326,463
Ford	807,328	814,421
Mustang	190,727	149,678
Thunderbird	50,364	36,055
Maverick	210,885	145,371
Pinto	...	255,394
Subtotal Ford Division	1,632,998	1,748,138
Lincoln	37,695	35,551
Mark III	21,432	27,091
Montego	103,873	57,094
Mercury	129,080	128,099
Cougar	72,363	62,864
Comet	...	83,000
Subtotal Mercury Division	305,316	331,057
Total Ford Motor Company	1,997,441	2,141,837
GENERAL MOTORS CORPORATION		
Buick	402,744	333,803
Riviera	37,336	33,810
Skylark	226,421	184,075
Subtotal Buick Division	666,501	551,188
Cadillac	214,903	161,169
Eldorado	23,842	27,368
Subtotal Cadillac Division	238,745	188,537
Chevelle	394,317	327,159
Corvette	17,316	21,806
Chevrolet	891,135	676,569
Nova	316,621	197,361
Monte Carlo	145,975	112,599
Camaro	124,899	114,643
Vega	...	269,928
Subtotal Chevrolet Division	1,890,263	1,720,065
F-85	310,273	264,091
Oldsmobile	299,725	267,070
Toronado	25,475	29,265
Subtotal Oldsmobile Division	635,473	560,426
Pontiac	290,476	210,476
LeMans-Tempest	213,239	165,638
Firebird	48,739	53,124
Grand Prix	65,750	58,325
Ventura II	...	48,484
Subtotal Pontiac Division	618,204	536,047
Total General Motors Corporation	4,049,186	3,556,263
CHECKER MOTORS	5,267	4,650
Total U. S. production	7,595,970	7,203,767

Source: "Automotive News."

ened front-seat belts would prevent ignitions from being operated.

Prices. The Big Three auto manufacturers announced plans for 1972-model price increases of up to 4.5%, only to rescind these plans when President Nixon announced a 90-day wage-price freeze on Aug. 15, 1971. Several rounds of price increases had been posted on 1971 models to offset higher costs for materials and labor. Repeal of the 7% auto excise tax on all cars, retroactive to August 15, was approved by Congress.

Imports. A total of 7,049,348 foreign-built cars was in operation on U. S. roads on Jan. 1, 1971, compared with 6,209,000 a year earlier. About 1,109,000 imported cars were sold in the United States in the first nine months of 1971, compared with 890,000 for the same period of 1970. Volkswagen led in 1971 sales, followed by Toyota and Datsun.

Registrations. U. S. passenger-car registrations reached 92,082,000 by the end of 1971, up 3.1% from 1970, and trucks and buses 19,928,000, up 4.2%.

MAYNARD M. GORDON
Editor, "Motor News Analysis"
and "The Imported Car Reports"

AVIATION. See AIR TRANSPORTATION; DEFENSE FORCES.
AWARDS. See PRIZES AND AWARDS.
BALLET. See DANCE.

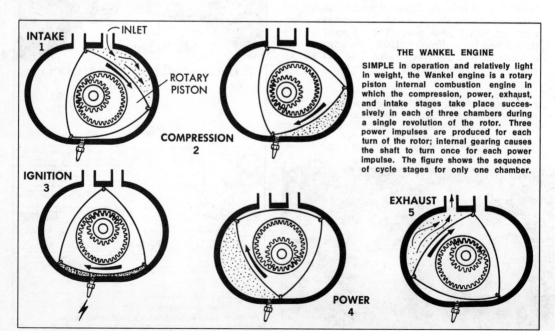

THE WANKEL ENGINE

SIMPLE in operation and relatively light in weight, the Wankel engine is a rotary piston internal combustion engine in which the compression, power, exhaust, and intake stages take place successively in each of three chambers during a single revolution of the rotor. Three power impulses are produced for each turn of the rotor; internal gearing causes the shaft to turn once for each power impulse. The figure shows the sequence of cycle stages for only one chamber.

BALTIMORE

Baltimore voters elected Democrat William Donald Schaefer mayor in November 1971. Schaefer, former City Council president, easily defeated Republican Ross Z. Pierpont. He succeeded retiring mayor Thomas D'Alesandro III.

It was a good year for the city's professional sports teams. The Colts (football) won the 1971 Super Bowl by beating Dallas. The Bullets finished second in the National Basketball Association, behind Milwaukee. The Orioles (baseball) won the American League pennant for the third straight year, but lost the World Series to Pittsburgh.

Public Finance. The City Council approved another increase in the property tax for the fiscal year 1971–72, up 31 cents to $5.65 on each $100 of appraised value. The city also won an increase in its share of the state amusement tax. To help the city financially, the state assumed responsibility for milk processing and production inspections in the city, took over operation of the central library, and promised a $7 million grant to improve Memorial Stadium. Most important, the state assumed the full cost of construction of city schools, representing fiscal relief in excess of $100 million.

Labor. In July, for the first time, the city unemployment rate was counted separately from that of the metropolitan area. By midyear it had reached 7.5%, which reflected the chronic joblessness of the inner city. Metropolitan area unemployment was 5.6% in July, the highest since 1962.

The area's biggest employment losses were in manufacturing. Some 13,000 jobs disappeared in such industries as metals and electrical equipment.

City employees won a 2.5% salary increase for fiscal 1971-72, but Mayor D'Alesandro ordered the fall increases withheld in compliance with President Nixon's wage and price freeze. Fire fighters engaged in a partial work stoppage to demonstrate dissatisfaction with the city's wage offer.

Transport. Lawsuits and neighborhood opposition stalled progress on a network of highways through Baltimore. The roads, first proposed in 1956, include the City Boulevard, a planned 33-block, six-lane highway through the center of town; the Interstate 70 spur through west Baltimore; and the East-West Expressway through historic Fells Point. The municipal elections increased the number of expressway opponents in the City Council.

Education. Pressed by rising education costs, Mayor D'Alesandro brought suit in an attempt to force the state to assume the full cost of education in the city. He was prompted by a California supreme court decision that declared the property tax unconstitutional for financing education.

Baltimore hired a new school superintendent. Dr. Roland Patterson, a black man from Seattle, was chosen for the $50,000 post.

Race Relations. The year's most serious incident of racial conflict occurred in April, when black youths disrupted the 1971 Flower Mart.

The Baltimore City Fair, held in September, proved an unquestionable success, with virtually every black and white neighborhood participating. It was the second successful year for the event.

RICHARD O'MARA
"The Evening Sun," Baltimore

BANGLADESH. See INDIA; INDIA-PAKISTAN WAR; PAKISTAN.

BANKING

Economic expansion characterized the first three quarters of 1971, even though the rate of growth in U. S. real output declined. Real growth fell from an annual rate of more than 10% in the first quarter (following settlement of the protracted General Motors strike in December 1970) to only 3% in the third quarter. Nevertheless, the increase in activity was sufficient to lower the unemployment rate slightly.

Price inflation persisted (although it tapered off late in the year), and the U. S. balance of international payments continued to deteriorate. A trade deficit—an excess of imports over exports—that began in April led to speculation that the United States, for the first time since 1893, might end the year with an unfavorable balance of trade. International concern over this possibility, and the continued domestic price inflation, produced increasing pressure for devaluation of the dollar.

On August 15, President Nixon announced a new economic policy aimed at stimulating domestic demand, reducing inflation, and eliminating balance-of-payments deficits. Phase I included a 90-day wage-price freeze, a 10% surcharge on U. S. imports, and the "floating" of the dollar in relation to other currencies. In Phase II beginning in November, the wage-price freeze was replaced by "guidelines." On December 18 the 10 leading non-Communist industrial nations agreed to a new pattern of currency exchange rates, including devaluation of the dollar as the price of gold was raised. Nixon removed the surcharge two days later. (For details of the economic climate in which banks operated, see also ECONOMY OF THE U. S.; INTERNATIONAL FINANCE; INTERNATIONAL TRADE.)

Monetary Policy. The Federal Reserve System, the central bank of the United States, attempted to encourage domestic output and employment expansion during the first half of 1971 by continuing the conditions of relative monetary ease it had maintained throughout 1970. The discount rate—at which Federal Reserve banks lend reserves to commercial banks—was lowered twice in January and once in February, to a new level of 4¾%.

By midyear, the monetary authorities had apparently concluded that conditions were easy enough, and indeed that somewhat less ease was beginning to be desirable to prevent "sloppiness" in financial markets and also to minimize continuing inflationary pressures on prices. Thus the discount rate was raised back to 5% in July, and the thrust of Federal Reserve open-market operations—purchases and sales of U. S. government securities—shifted markedly in the latter half of the year. From August on, in fact, the Federal Reserve was seemingly much concerned with having its actions conform to the anti-inflationary aspects of the Nixon administration's new economic policy.

Bank Reserves and Money Supply. The principal monetary aggregates—bank deposits and reserves, and the money supply—grew rapidly during the first half of the year. Average money stock increased at annual rates of 8.9% in the first quarter and 11% in the second; in contrast, the annual rate for all of 1970 had been only 6%.

Federal Reserve authorities viewed these money supply increases as excessive and concluded by midyear that the system should pursue its expansionary open-market operations less aggressively by purchasing U. S. government securities in smaller volume than in previous months. This policy of moderating further growth in the monetary aggregates was actively pursued for the remainder of the year.

Its results became evident rather quickly. Net borrowed reserves of the banking system, which hovered around $300 million per month from January through July, rose above $800 million in July and August. Although they receded from this peak in the remaining months of 1971, bank borrowings of reserves remained well above earlier levels. Also, and in response, the money supply's rate of increase fell sharply and became negative—that is, the money supply was decreasing slightly—by November.

Interest Rates, Loans, and Investments. Short-term interest rates declined sharply in the first quarter as deposits—and especially time deposits—increased substantially at the nation's banks. Despite increased availability of funds at lower rates, however, business-loan demand remained sluggish. Many large corporate borrowers had substantially replenished their liquidity by tapping the capital markets—by way of new issues of stock and, especially, bonds—in 1970. Net loans of banks did increase somewhat in the first quarter, but the bulk of the banks' new funds were used to purchase government securities.

The decline in short-term rates reversed itself in the second quarter. Still, deposits continued to grow more rapidly than business lending, which expanded at an annual rate of only about 3%. Many large firms continued the process of balance-sheet "restructuring," floating large new issues of long-term debt and equity in the capital markets. In substantial measure, proceeds of these open-market financings were used to repay short-term debt to banks and also to satisfy current funds requirements that otherwise would have been met with bank loans.

Overall, loan demand increased in the second half of 1971, moving up to an annual rate of about 10% in September, for example. In spite of this encouraging development, however, the whole term structure of interest rates—long and short alike—generally drifted downward from August through October. By November, this downward trend in interest rates appeared to be bottoming out, and some began to move upward, suggesting that the Federal Reserve's policy of moderating monetary growth was becoming effective.

The banks' prime loan rate—applicable to their biggest and best corporate borrowers—began the year at 6¾% and closed at 5¼ to 5½%. During the year, the First National City Bank and the Irving Trust Company, both of New York, introduced the floating prime rate, pegged to rates in the dealer market for commercial paper.

Banking Structure. In early 1971, Congress extended the Bank Holding Company Act of 1956 to cover one-bank holding companies, designating the Federal Reserve Board of Governors as regulator of these financial congenerics. Their number had increased rapidly, to about 1,200, in the 1968–70 period, before uncertainty about congressional intent slowed their growth. With the legislative ground rules governing their operations now established, their numbers were expected to begin again to increase, although at a more moderate rate than in the previous several years.

CLIFTON H. KREPS, JR.
University of North Carolina at Chapel Hill

BARBADOS

Politics monopolized public attention in Barbados in 1971. On September 9, the island held its first election since becoming an independent state in the Commonwealth of Nations in 1966. Prime Minister Errol Barrow improved his position as his Democratic Labour party captured three fourths of the seats in the House of Assembly.

The Election. Voting was conducted under terms of a new electoral law which reapportioned the Assembly. Whereas each parish had previously commanded two Assembly seats, one seat was now allotted to each of 24 constituencies, with the number of constituencies per parish ranging from one to as many as eight, depending on population.

The prime minister's party and the Barbados Labour party, led by Bernard St. John, waged an intensive campaign among the island's quarter of a million citizens. Both appealed mainly to the working population and vied to project the more radical image. Each approved the government's greatly expanded role in maintaining prosperity.

Prime Minister Barrow, a former RAF pilot, covered the island by private plane and car and visited some areas on horseback or on foot as he sought to explain the achievements of his government since independence. Though a close election was anticipated, the result proved to be one-sided. The majority party increased its representation in the 24-member House of Assembly from 14 seats to 18 seats.

The Economy. The success of the party in power was attributed to the relative prosperity achieved in the previous five years. In spite of a decline in sugar production, the economy continued to grow, bolstered by a successful industrialization program and a booming tourist industry. More than 150,000 visitors had come to the island in 1970, a 17% increase over the preceding year. The rate of economic growth from 1969 through 1971 was estimated to average 8% a year, almost double the UN target rate for developing countries.

In July the government announced tax reforms designed to remove the tax burden from about 10,000 persons in the lower income brackets.

THOMAS G. MATHEWS
University of Puerto Rico

--------- **BARBADOS · Information Highlights** ---------

Official Name: Barbados.
Area: 166 square miles (430 sq km).
Population (1970 estimate): 270,000. *Density,* 1,525 per square mile (590 per sq km). *Annual rate of increase,* 1.1%.
Chief City (1960 census): Bridgetown, the capital, 11,452.
Government: *Head of state,* Sir Winston Scott, governor-general (appointed May 1966). *Head of government,* Errol Walton Barrow, prime minister (took office for 3d 5-year term, Nov. 1971). *Legislature*—Parliament; Senate (appointed), 21 members; House of Assembly (elected), 24 members. *Major political parties*—Democratic Labour party; Barbados Labour party.
Education: Literacy rate (1969), 98% of population, 15 and over. *School enrollment* (1966)—primary, 40,712; secondary, 27,798; technical/vocational, 2,362; university/higher, 373.
Finances (1970 estimate): *Revenues,* $38,400,000; *expenditures,* $44,750,000; *monetary unit,* East Caribbean dollar (2 ECD equal U. S.$1, August 1971).
Gross National Product (1968): $108,300,000.
National Income (1967): $102,000,000; *per person,* $409.
Crops (metric tons, 1968–69 crop year): Sugarcane, 1,200,000.
Foreign Trade (1969): *Exports,* $37,127,000 (chief 1968 exports—sugar, $14,750,000; fresh fish, $3,614,000). *Imports,* $97,-275,000.
Transportation: *Roads* (1970), 800 miles (1,287 km); *motor vehicles* (1969), 22,400 (automobiles, 17,400).
Communications: *Telephones* (1969), 26,078; *television stations* (1968), 1; *television sets* (1969), 15,000; *radios* (1969), 57,000; *newspapers* (1967), 2 (daily circulation, 69,000).

BELGIUM

In Belgium the year 1971 was marked by rapid inflation and continuation of the long-standing linguistic dispute between the Walloons and Flemish.

The Economy. It became apparent in 1971 that the favorable combination of rapid economic expansion and a relatively moderate rate of price increases had ended and that inflation had become the major problem. The consumer price index rose from 130.1 to 134.5 during the first six months of 1971. Wage increases in 1970 were more rapid than gains in productivity.

In accordance with a 1967 directive of the European Economic Community (EEC), Belgium put into effect the value-added tax on January 1. However, this levy, while it tended to equalize competitive conditions within the EEC, exerted an inflationary pressure within the country. A number of measures were taken to control inflation. To restrict the inflow of capital the National Bank lowered the discount rate several times: from 7.5% on Oct. 22, 1970, to 6% on March 25, 1971.

The change in economic conditions was accompanied by social strains. Merchants staged a general strike on February 18 to protest against the value-added tax. Teachers engaged in wildcat strikes on March 22–24 and again on March 29 for higher salaries, better working conditions, and a voice in the reform of the educational system. The police also struck in March. However, on April 6 employers and trade unions reached a collective agreement for 1971–72. The accord provided for a reduced workweek and increased pensions.

Politics. Cabinet changes were made necessary by the death on February 15 of Freddy Terwagne, Walloon minister for relations between the Flemish and Walloon communities, and the resignation of Edmond Leburton, minister of economic affairs, to become president of the Socialist party. Terwagne was succeeded by Sen. Fernand De Housse and Leburton by André Cools. Maurice Denis was made minister of the budget. The new ministers, like their predecessors, are Walloon Socialists.

Friction between the two coalition members, the Social Christian and the Socialist parties, was caused by the latter's demand for strict price controls. This threat to the coalition was resolved on April 23 by a compromise agreement on an economic program that called for price controls but with recourse to the courts in controversial cases.

Constitutional Reforms. At midyear it seemed as if Premier Gaston Eyskens' coalition ministry had solved the linguistic conflict between the Dutch-speaking Flemish and the French-speaking Walloons that has plagued Belgium for decades. The Chamber of Deputies on July 16 and the Senate on July 19 approved two bills that granted autonomy in cultural affairs to the two principal language groups and determined the bilingual and administrative status of Brussels. The reform imposed fixed boundary lines on the capital city and regulated the lingual rights of its Dutch-speaking and French-speaking residents. As a concession to the Walloons, the law making the language of a child's origin the medium of his instruction was repealed, and the father was given the right to choose the language in which the child was to be instructed. The reform also made a German-speaking area on the eastern border a special district under the direct administration of the minister of interior.

Since legislation for the reform of the constitution requires a two-thirds majority in both houses of Parliament, the government had to obtain the support of the main opposition party, the Party of Freedom and Progress (Liberal). This was achieved by promising guaranties of minority rights.

Election. The passage of the reform bills did not, however, resolve the tension between the two coalition parties. The Socialists were unhappy about the grant of cultural autonomy to the linguistic communities. On September 24, Eyskens announced that King Baudouin had granted his request that Parliament be dissolved, and the general election, which normally would have been held in May 1972, was advanced to November 7. The election results indicated that the constitutional compromise had not settled the linguistic-cultural problem. The extremist French-speaking Democratic Front in Brussels doubled its vote, as did also the allied Union Party in Wallonia. The Social Christian-Socialist coalition continues in power but with so slim a majority that it may be unable to implement the reforms.

Foreign Relations. The Benelux countries—Belgium, the Netherlands, and Luxembourg—signed a trade treaty with the USSR on July 14. This was the first time that the USSR had made an agreement with a multinational economic unit. The treaty will expire before 1975, when presumably it will be replaced by an agreement with the EEC.

King Baudouin and Queen Fabiola made a 4-day visit to West Germany in April—the first state visit of a Belgian monarch to Germany in 60 years. Foreign Minister Pierre Harmel visited Madrid in June. This was the first visit by a Belgian cabinet member to Spain since the Spanish Civil War.

AMRY VANDENBOSCH
University of Kentucky

BELGIUM • Information Highlights

Official Name: Kingdom of Belgium.
Area: 11,781 square miles (30,513 sq km).
Population (1970 est.): 9,680,000. *Density,* 820 per square mile (316 per sq km). *Annual rate of increase,* 3.3%.
Chief Cities (1968 est.): Brussels, the capital, 166,920; Antwerp, 234,100; Liège, 150,200.
Government: *Head of state,* Baudouin I, king (acceded July 17, 1951). *Head of government,* Gaston Eyskens, prime minister (took office June 17, 1968). *Legislature*—Parliament: Senate, 178 members; Chamber of Deputies, 212 members. *Major political parties*—Social Christian party; Socialist party; Party of Freedom and Progress; Democratic Front; Walloon Union; Flemish People's Union; Communist party.
Languages: French (official), Flemish (official).
Education: *Literacy rate* (1970), 98% of population. *Expenditure on education* (1968), 5% of gross domestic product. *School enrollment* (1967)—primary, 1,015,563; secondary, 812,837; technical/vocational, 487,889; higher, 59,172.
Finances (1970): *Revenues,* $6,041,000,000; *expenditures,* $6,520,000,000; *monetary unit,* franc (44.826 francs equal U. S.$1, Dec. 30, 1971).
Gross National Product (1970 est.): $24,900,000,000.
National Income (1969): $18,068,000,000; *national income per person,* $1,873.
Manufacturing (metric tons, 1969): Crude steel, 12,837,000; pig iron and ferroalloys, 11,211,000; cement, 6,269,000.
Crops (metric tons, 1969 crop year): Sugar beets (1968–69), 4,108,000; potatoes, 1,478,000; wheat, 779,000.
Foreign Trade including Luxembourg (1968): *Exports* (1970), $11,609,000 (chief exports—iron and steel, $1,311,300,000; transport equipment, $772,100,000; nonferrous metals, $738,900,000). *Imports* (1970), $11,344,000,000 (chief imports—nonelectrical machinery, $738,850,000; nonferrous metals, $661,400,000). *Chief trading partners* (1968)—Netherlands; West Germany; France.
Tourism including Luxembourg: *Receipts* (1970), $348,000,000.
Transportation: *Roads* (1964), 58,036 miles (93,397 km); *motor vehicles* (1969), 2,279,900 (automobiles 1,920,600); *railroads* (1968), 2,661 miles (4,282 km); *merchant fleet* (1971), 1,183,000 gross registered tons; *national airline,* Sabena; *principal airports,* Antwerp, Zaventem, Ostend, Middelkerke, Gosselies.
Communications: *Telephones* (1970), 1,936,814; *television stations* (1968), 5; *television sets* (1969), 2,000,000; *radios* (1969), 3,303,000; *newspapers* (1968), 33.

BERMUDA

In common with North America and many of the Caribbean islands, Bermuda faced problems of inflation in 1971. Income from tourism was on the increase, however, and racial friction declined.

Political Affairs. There was no recurrence of the widespread race riots that preceded the 1968 general election. Even the more modest outbreaks that marred the year 1970 were not repeated in 1971. Commanding 30 of the 40 seats in the House of Assembly, Prime Minister Sir Henry Tucker's multiracial, moderately conservative United Bermuda party pursued its established integrationist policies, seeking to improve the economic lot and educational standards of the black majority.

About 20% of Bermuda's tax revenue was being spent on education. Free secondary schooling had been introduced in 1965, and a government school integration plan took effect in September 1971.

Economy. A boom in hotel building, as well as the decrease in racial strife, was largely responsible for a rise in tourist business. Nearly 400,000 visitors —about 90% of them from North America—went to Bermuda in 1970, more than double the number of arrivals in 1964.

The government derives much of its income from an excise tax, but there is no income tax, estate duty, or capital gains tax. Between 1956—when a free port was established on Ireland Island—and early 1971, Bermuda had acquired 90 new industries with total annual production of $25 million.

RICHARD E. WEBB
Former Director, Reference and Library Division
British Information Services, New York

BERNSTEIN, Leonard. See BIOGRAPHY.

BHUTAN

Bhutan took a significant step into the international community on Sept. 21, 1971, when it became a member of the United Nations. Bhutan had ended its policy of isolation in 1949, when it signed a treaty of friendship with India. In 1959 it had agreed to allow India to build road and air links between the two countries. Under Indian sponsorship, Bhutan had become a member of the Colombo Plan in 1963 and a member of the International Postal Union in 1966.

Between 1949 and 1971, Bhutan was only nominally independent. The Bhutanese king, Jigme Dorji Wangchuk, controlled domestic policy, while the Indian government determined Bhutan's foreign affairs. Basically, India's policy was to build a system of defenses against China along the Bhutan-Tibet border. Although Bhutan will maintain its special relationship with India because of its strategic position between India and Chinese-controlled Tibet, UN membership will help Bhutan cast off its protectorate image.

Government. Bhutan's king rules with an advisory council of nine appointees, and he is also assisted by a National Assembly of 130 representatives. Political parties are banned.

Economy. Bhutan began its third 5-year plan in 1971. The plan will cost an estimated $46.7 million, and it will be financed almost entirely by India. Its major goals are to increase agricultural production; to extend communications and improve transportation services; to extend primary and secondary

NEWLY SEATED Bhutan delegation listens to speeches in UN General Assembly. The small kingdom in the Himalaya was admitted to the United Nations in September 1971.

————— **BHUTAN** • **Information Highlights** —————

Official Name: Kingdom of Bhutan.
Area: 18,147 square miles (47,000 sq km).
Population (1969 est.): 770,000. *Density,* 41 per square mile (16 per sq km).
Chief City (1970): Thimbu, the capital, 11,000.
Government: *Head of state,* Jigme Dorji Wangchuk, King (acceded Oct. 27, 1952). *Head of government,* Jigme Dorji Wangchuk. *Legislature*—National Assembly, 130 members.
Languages: Bhutanese (Druk-Ke) (official), Hindi, Nepali.
Education: *Literacy rate* (1969), less than 5% of population. *Total school enrollment* (1968)—15,528.
Monetary Unit: Rupee (7.499 rupees equal U.S.$1, Sept. 1971).
Gross National Product (1967): $48,000,000.
Manufacturing: Weaving.
Crops: Rice, wheat, barley.
Minerals: Coal.
Foreign Trade: *Exports,* timber, fruit. *Imports,* textiles. *Chief trading partner,* India.

education; and to survey forest and mineral resources for industrial development.

Nepali Influx. The Bhutanese government continues to feel threatened by the influx of agricultural migrants from Nepal. Nepali-speaking people represent an estimated 50% of the population. The government has restricted them to the southern, less mountainous, part of the country, where they have gradually gained control of the best farmland.

FREDERICK H. GAIGE
Davidson College

BIOCHEMISTRY

The year 1971 was a productive and exciting year for scientists in the field of biochemistry, with interest centered on DNA and RNA, vitamin C, the human growth hormone, aspirin, and interferon.

DNA and RNA. Many laboratories feverishly pursued the finding of the so-called reverse transcriptase, the enzyme that permits viruses whose genetic information is coded in RNA to use the RNA as a template to make DNA. Since only viruses are known to code their genetic information in RNA, the presence of reverse transcriptase is already being used to determine if virus is present in suspected human tumor tissues. Following a report that virus particles resembling those that cause breast cancer in mice were found in human milk, three biochemists—J. Schlom, Sol Spiegelman, and D. Moore—assayed human milk for reverse transcriptase activity and virus particles. Of 13 milk samples, 4 had both virus particles and enzyme. This work is on the road to demonstrating virus as a cause of human breast cancer and supports the hope that reverse transcriptase will be a useful tool.

Other work involving DNA has led to the successful alteration of a cell's genetic makeup. Two biochemists—M. Hill and J. Hillova—incubated chicken cells in tissue culture with DNA extracted from mice and previously labeled with the radioactive isotope tritium. Also included in the incubation medium was carbon-14-labeled bromodeoxyuridine, a chemical similar to one of the base constituents of DNA. Hill and Hillova reasoned that any strands of DNA synthesized during the incubation period should contain some of the tritium label and some bromodeoxyuridine since the mouse DNA would be degraded, or broken down, during the incubation and the new base would be incorporated into the newly synthesized DNA. The experimental results showed that a small percentage of the newly synthesized DNA in the chicken cells contained intact segments of mouse DNA.

In a report appearing in *Nature,* three molecular biologists—Carl R. Merril, Mark R. Geier, and John C. Petricciani—described a series of experiments in which human cells took up and used genetic material native to bacteria. The cells were taken from a person with galactosemia, a disease caused by a genetic defect that makes the person incapable of handling the simple sugar galactose. The cells were exposed to a virus that had previously been infected with the genetic information necessary for the production of the enzyme that breaks down galactose. Through radioactive labeling the three scientists were able to determine that the human cells took up and were able to use the alien genetic information—that is, they became capable of producing the galactose enzyme. This reported alteration of the genetic makeup of human cells could open the way to the correction of genetic defects in humans.

Vitamin C. The controversy over Dr. Linus Pauling's suggestion that large doses of vitamin C can protect against the common cold continued in 1971. Vitamin C is important in many metabolic activities of the body, including the synthesis of almost all proteins and the adrenal gland hormones. It remains to be seen if increased doses of vitamin C lead to increased levels of these substances. Certainly the increased feeling of well-being that is experienced by many people taking vitamin C might be explained by this relationship. However, several questions remain, including one concerning the possible effect of increased doses of vitamin C on the production of adrenal hormones, and some biochemists are recommending caution in following Pauling's advice.

Human Growth Hormone. In January 1971 a flurry of excitement was created by the announcement from the laboratory of Dr. Choh Hao Li at the University of California in San Francisco of the synthesis of the human growth hormone. The yield of product was very low and its biological activity only a fraction of that of the naturally occurring molecule. It now appears, however, that the correct molecule of human growth hormone was not synthesized. The biochemist H. D. Niall and others have shown that the amino acid sequence followed was incorrect, and Li and his colleagues J. S. Dixon and D. Chung have recently published data recognizing their original error and now in substantial agreement with Niall and others. However, some interesting questions remain. If indeed the molecule synthesized by Li was biologically active, then the possibility that the activity of the human growth hormone may reside in only a small portion of the molecule—in the part Li correctly synthesized—is strengthened, and the realization of an active human growth hormone is brought closer to reality.

Aspirin and the Prostaglandins. Several reports suggesting that aspirin acts by inhibiting the synthesis of prostaglandins appeared during the year. This may provide a possible answer to the long puzzling question of how aspirin works in the human body.

Interferon. Jacqueline and Edouard de Maeyer reported that by interfering with the function of lymphocytes, either by radioactivity or antilymphatic serum, they reduced markedly the production of interferon in response to the virus associated with Newcastle disease. This suggests that lymphocytes may be a primary source of interferon.

STEPHEN N. KREITZMAN
Emory University

Biography

A selection of biographical sketches of persons prominent in the news during 1971 appears on this and the following pages. The subjects include men and women from many parts of the world, and representing a wide variety of pursuits. The list is confined to living persons; for biographical data on prominent people who died during the year, see Necrology (beginning on page 761). For biographies of Chinese leaders see special report on China, beginning on page 14, and for U.S. presidential contenders see Political Parties, beginning on page 546.

AGNEW, Spiro T.

U. S. Vice President Spiro T. Agnew continued in 1971 to speak out vigorously against dissenting voices in the country while endeavoring to appeal to "middle America." He denounced the "masochism" of those who emphasized the negative aspects of U. S. foreign and domestic policies and defended the national economy under the Nixon administration against what he called purveyors of "pallbearer polemics."

In line with his earlier attacks on the liberal news media, Agnew lashed out against the CBS television network for its documentary *The Selling of the Pentagon* and criticized a *Newsweek* article about his image. He also accused the American Medical Association of engaging in "scare rhetoric" in its warnings about pollution-related diseases, and he condemned UN delegates who applauded the expulsion of Nationalist China. As Nixon's "emissary to the right," Agnew tried in December to block an insurgent movement by right-wing Republicans opposed to the President's economic policies and planned visit to Peking.

The vice president also continued to provoke controversy in his role as diplomat. During his 32-day goodwill tour of 10 Asian, African, and European nations in June and July he provoked the wrath of black

VICE PRESIDENT Spiro Agnew, whose shots have hit golf spectators, laughs as he receives bag with red cross.

communities in the United States by comparing American black leaders unfavorably with the heads of African states. Following a visit to Greece in October, he charged U. S. liberals with making the Greek military regime their "favorite whipping boy." With reference to his original misgivings about improved U. S.–Chinese relations, Agnew later explained: "My objection was not to the policy, only to the euphoria induced by certain news reports."

By the fall of 1971, polls seemed to indicate that Agnew's popularity among the general electorate had waned, giving rise to speculation that Nixon might "dump" him as a running mate in 1972. Some analysts, noting that the vice president did not relish the role of "battering ram" of the Republican party that had been given to him, suggested that Agnew might voluntarily retire at the end of his term. Nixon, however, in an interview in early January 1972, expressed full confidence in his vice president.

The son of a Greek immigrant, Spiro Theodore Agnew was born in Baltimore, Md., on Nov. 9, 1918. After combat service as a company commander in the army during World War II, he graduated from Baltimore Law School in 1947 and entered private law practice. Originally a Democrat, Agnew later switched to the Republican party, and was elected chief executive of Baltimore county in 1962. In 1966 he was elected governor of Maryland, and during his first year in office he compiled a fairly liberal and reformist record, although he later shifted to a more conservative position. He was nominated as Nixon's running mate at the 1968 Republican convention.

HENRY S. SLOAN

BERNSTEIN, Leonard

The opening ceremonies of the new John F. Kennedy Center for the Performing Arts in Washington, D. C. on Sept. 8, 1971, were highlighted by the premier performance of Leonard Bernstein's *Mass* (subtitled *A Theater Piece for Singers, Players and Dancers*), conducted by the composer. Bernstein, the former conductor of the New York Philharmonic Orchestra and one of the most versatile figures in the world of music, composed the *Mass* at the request of the late President Kennedy's widow, Mrs. Jacqueline Onassis. Using the liturgy of the Roman Catholic Mass as a framework, the 100-minute work incorporates virtually every musical style, including opera, gospel, jazz, rock, and 12-tone. It requires a cast of more than 200. Reactions from the critics were widely divergent, but the composer himself called it "the most rewarding thing of my life."

The son of Russian Jewish immigrants, Bernstein was born on Aug. 25, 1918, in Lawrence, Mass. He began to play the piano at the age of 10. After graduating from Harvard in 1939, he studied for two years under Fritz Reiner at the Curtis Institute of Music in Philadel-

LEONARD BERNSTEIN, whose *Mass* opened John F. Kennedy Center for the Performing Arts, accepts dedicatory medal from Mrs. Rose Kennedy and Sen. Edward M. Kennedy.

phia. His first major composition, the Jeremiah Symphony (1942), won a New York Music Critics Circle Award. In November 1943, as assistant conductor of the New York Philharmonic, he scored a major triumph when he substituted for the ailing Bruno Walter, becoming the first U. S.-born and U. S.-trained conductor of a major American orchestra. His talent and showmanship earned him a reputation as one of the world's foremost conductors and a leading interpreter of contemporary music. He was musical director of the New York Philharmonic from 1958 to 1969, during which period he also directed the Philharmonic's Young People's Concerts on television.

Bernstein's major compositions include the musicals *On the Town* (1944), *Wonderful Town* (1953), *Candide* (1956), and *West Side Story* (1957); the symphonies *Age of Anxiety* (1949) and *Kaddish* (1963); *Serenade for Violin, Strings and Percussion* (1954); and *Chichester Psalms* for chorus and orchestra (1965). Bernstein is a strong supporter of Israel, and he devotes much energy to peace and civil rights activities.

HENRY S. SLOAN

BHUTTO, Zulfikar Ali

On Dec. 20, 1971, after Indian troops had occupied much of East Pakistan and the Indian-Pakistani war had been suspended by a cease-fire, President Agha Mohammed Yahya Khan of Pakistan resigned under pressure from his country's military leaders. He was replaced by Pakistan's foreign minister and deputy prime minister, Zulfikar Ali Bhutto, who had been pleading his nation's cause at a meeting of the UN General Assembly in New York.

As he embarked for Islamabad to form a new government, Bhutto, the leader of Pakistan's People's party, refused to recognize the independence of Bangladesh, or Bengal Nation, the country's secessionist east wing. Soon after his arrival in the capital, however, he announced his willingness to accept a looser federation of East and West Pakistan, though he continued to assert that Pakistan would remain a "single, united nation." On December 21 he appointed a Bengali as vice president of Pakistan, and a week later he began a series of talks with Sheikh Mujibur Rahman, the captive Bengali leader who had been named, in absentia, as president of the independent Bangladesh regime recognized by India. Soon after, Bhutto permitted Sheikh Muhjib to leave. Also within a few days of taking office, Bhutto nationalized West Pakistan's industries and removed several high-ranking military officers.

Zulfikar Ali Bhutto was born on Jan. 5, 1928, in Larkana, within the borders of what is now West Pakistan. A member of the landed aristocracy, he received his education in Bombay, India; the University of California at Berkeley (A. B. 1950); and Oxford University

(M. A. in law, 1952). In 1958, when the military strongman Mohammed Ayub Khan assumed the presidency of Pakistan, Bhutto, though only 30, joined his cabinet as minister of commerce. In 1963 he became foreign minister, but resigned three years later after a rift had developed between himself and President Ayub. Late in 1968 he was placed under house arrest and was released only after Ayub Khan was ousted from power in March 1969.

In the national elections of December 1970, Bhutto led his People's party to victory in West Pakistan, but the elections were voided when the new president, Yayha Khan, refused to accept the results in East Pakistan, where the winners were proponents of autonomy for that region. The president then appointed Bhutto to the offices that he held at the time of his own assumption of the presidency.

BLOUNT, Winton M.

In October 1971, Winton M. Blount resigned as postmaster general. During his term of office, he had presided over significant events in American postal history.

Blount came to Washington with the original Nixon cabinet in January 1969, after having headed a construction company in Alabama. The Post Office Department was troubled by inefficiency and labor disputes. Blount attacked these problems by recommending that the postal system be transformed into an independent government agency. These recommendations were approved and, in January 1971, Blount was named head of the new United States Postal Service. He became, as a result, the last postmaster general to serve in the presidential cabinet.

The new postal service was formally inaugurated on July 1, 1971. Before that time postal rates had been increased in many categories, first class costs rising from 6 to 8 cents per ounce. Blount had also consolidated the 15 existing postal regions into five. He moved to automate and rationalize a variety of postal activities. In July the Postal Service signed a collective bargaining agreement affecting 650,000 workers and seven postal unions.

At first-day ceremonies in Dallas for the new "Fight Drug Abuse" stamp, Blount charged several friendly foreign countries with failure to support U. S. efforts to stem the illegal drug traffic.

According to reports, Blount planned to enter elective politics in Alabama, probably to challenge John Sparkman for the U. S. Senate seat open in 1972.

Winton Malcolm Blount was born in Union Springs, Ala., on Feb. 1, 1921. He attended the University of Alabama and served in the Air Force during World War II. He was active in business in Montgomery, Ala., before going to Washington.

WALTER DARNELL JACOBS

BOK, Derek Curtis

Derek Bok, dean of the Harvard Law School, was named the 25th president of Harvard University on Jan. 11, 1971. His appointment ended an 11-month search for a successor to the retiring president, Nathan M. Pusey. Bok is an authority on labor and antitrust law and an expert on collective bargaining. He established a reputation as a skillful mediator during the period of campus turmoil in the late 1960's, when he played a key role in conciliating differences between students and faculty.

After taking office as president on July 1, Bok created a more harmonious atmosphere on campus by establishing closer communications with students. He revamped the antiquated administration by appointing a group of nonacademic professional managers to top positions. Convinced that sound teaching and scholarship are the primary responsibilities of the university, Bok has placed improvement of undergraduate education at the top of his priorities.

A member of a prominent Philadelphia family and the son of a Pennsylvania supreme court justice, Derek Bok was born at Bryn Mawr, Pa., on March 22, 1930. He spent most of his early years in California and graduated from Stanford University with a B. A. degree in political science in 1951. After obtaining his LL. B. degree magna cum laude from Harvard Law School in 1954, he spent a year at the University of Paris on a Fulbright scholarship and then three years in the U. S. Army on the staff of the judge advocate general. Bok joined the Harvard Law School faculty as an assistant professor in 1958, became a professor in 1961, and succeeded Erwin N. Griswold as dean in 1968. Among the reforms he instituted at the law school were a liberalized grading system, stepped-up recruitment of blacks and women, and the introduction of new courses on criminal law, poverty, and the environment. He is coauthor, with John Dunlop, of *Labor and the American Community* (1970).

HENRY S. SLOAN

BRANDT, Willy

In October 1971, Willy Brandt, West German chancellor and chairman of the German Social Democratic party (SPD), won the Nobel Peace Prize. The award was given to him in recognition of his efforts to help relax tensions between East and West. Specifically, the award committee cited Brandt's signing of the treaty preventing the spread of nuclear weapons, his conclusion of nonaggression pacts with the Soviet Union and Poland, and his endeavors on behalf of the freedom and security of West Berlin. It added that he had also taken important initiatives in furthering political and economic cooperation in western Europe as part of a peace plan for all of Europe.

"Ostpolitik." Brandt was chosen for the Nobel Peace Prize just after his *Ostpolitik* ("Eastern policy"), aiming at a rapprochement with eastern Europe, received a significant boost. Early in September the United States, the Soviet Union, Britain, and France, as supervisory powers, signed an agreement giving West Berlin improved access to East and West Germany and delineating more clearly the city's relationship with West Germany. The agreement also strengthened Brandt's domestic position. After almost two years of electoral setbacks, the SPD scored its first advance at the polls in the state elections in Bremen in early October.

Brandt's *Ostpolitik* did not imply, however, a weakening of ties with the West. The chancellor worked hard for Britain's admission to the Common Market, and twice during the year he conferred with President Nixon about the coordination of U. S. and West German policies toward the East.

Economic Problems. Throughout 1971, Brandt was faced with mounting economic difficulties. Inflation in West Germany, driving up prices by an average 6% annually, was turning into "stagflation." Little schooled in economic affairs, Brandt let Karl Schiller, his economics and finance minister, take the limelight on all matters of economic concern. On Schiller's advice, he postponed long-pledged social reforms, and despite all earlier promises to the contrary he also proposed a substantial tax increase.

Given the small majority his government has in the Bundestag (six votes), Brandt's ability to survive opposition efforts to unseat him attests to his political skill. The chancellor also owes his political effectiveness to his personal integrity, which impresses even bitter opponents.

Background. Willy Brandt was born in Lübeck on Dec. 18, 1913. He joined the SPD in 1930 at the age of 16, but soon switched to the more militant Socialist Workers party. Spending the Nazi era in exile in Norway and Sweden, he resumed his German citizenship in 1948 and rejoined the SPD.

Brandt was elected a member and later president of West Berlin's parliament and, in 1957, became mayor of West Berlin. After having bid unsuccessfully for the West German chancellorship in 1961 and 1965, he became foreign minister in a coalition government formed by the Christian Democratic Union and the SPD in 1966. When the coalition broke up after the 1969 elections, Brandt became chancellor of a government resting on a coalition of the SPD and the small Free Democratic party.

ANDREAS DORPALEN

BREZHNEV, Leonid Ilich

Leonid Brezhnev, secretary-general of the Soviet Communist party, chairman of the party Politburo, and member of the Presidium of the Supreme Soviet, received more publicity in 1971 than any other Soviet leader but was still unable to establish unchallenged authority. As the year began, some Soviet official calendars shifted his birthday from December 19 to January 1, the greatest Soviet winter holiday. This crude attempt at greater glory was quickly blocked by other Soviet leaders, and most calendars reverted to accuracy. Brezhnev, however, managed to break precedent by addressing the nation on radio and television on January 1. His speech replaced the usual New Year's greeting from top Soviet governmental and party organizations.

In his keynote speech on March 30 at the Communist party congress, Brezhnev stressed his interest in more consumer goods for the people and a desire for international arms reductions. He repeated both themes in later speeches elsewhere.

During the year he traveled widely in East Europe, visiting Bulgaria, Czechoslovakia, East Germany, Hungary, Poland, and Yugoslavia. In Prague he reaffirmed the so-called Brezhnev doctrine, stating the right of the USSR to intervene in the internal affairs of other Communist nations, but in Belgrade he wooed Yugoslavia by declaring that all Communist countries are sovereign and equally independent. His most important journey was to France, where he concluded a Franco-Soviet economic, technical, and industrial cooperation treaty in October. This pact was his first major diplomatic negotiation with any Western power.

Background. Brezhnev was born in Dneprodzerzhinsk, the Ukraine, on Dec. 19, 1906. He is a man of varied experience and has worked as a surveyor, agricultural administrator, metallurgical engineer, regional Communist party chief, high-ranking army political officer, and secretary of the party's central apparatus. From 1960 to 1964 he served as president of the USSR, a post he relinquished shortly before helping to oust Nikita Khrushchev from power.

ELLSWORTH RAYMOND

BURGER, Warren E.

The court opinions of Warren E. Burger, chief justice of the United States, continued in 1971 to reflect his policy of judicial restraint and "strict constructionism."

He generally upheld the Nixon administration's views, notably by his dissention from the court's decision, in June, to allow resumption of publication of the Pentagon Papers, and in his support of the majority opinion rejecting environmentalists' pleas to delay underground nuclear tests on Amchitka Island in November. But he differed with the President on the key issue of the busing of schoolchildren to achieve desegregation of Southern schools. He pointed out, however, that the court's decision in favor of busing was merely a remedy for constitutional wrongs and was not to be construed as mandating a fixed racial balance.

In the area of criminal justice, the court under Burger's leadership modified the rights of defendants in several instances; for example, it ruled that confessions of a kind that the 1966 Miranda decision had declared inadmissible in a trial might be used in refuting a defendant's testimony. Burger has also called on the legal profession to impose more stringent discipline on unruly or unethical lawyers to avert the imposition of legal ethical standards by outside forces. To ease the heavy work load borne by the federal courts, he has said that state courts should exercise original jurisdiction over cases involving state law.

Of Swiss-German ancestry, Warren Earl Burger was born in St. Paul, Minn., on Sept. 17, 1907. He studied at the University of Minnesota and at St. Paul College of Law, which awarded him his LL. B. degree, magna cum laude, in 1931. He then practiced law in St. Paul, serving concurrently on the faculty of St. Paul College. An active Republican, he helped Dwight D. Eisenhower obtain the presidential nomination at the 1952 Republican National Convention. Burger served as assistant attorney general in charge of the civil division of the U. S. Justice Department from 1953 until 1956, when he was appointed judge of the court of appeals for the District of Columbia.

As appeals court judge, Burger acquired a reputation as an "enlightened law-and-order man." He took a conservative position in the application of criminal law, criticized Supreme Court decisions that, he held, weakened the processes of law enforcement, and urged jurists not to overstep the bounds of their authority. On the other hand, he advocated a number of judicial reforms and compiled a moderately liberal record on civil rights. Appointed by President Nixon to succeed retiring Chief Justice Earl Warren, Burger was sworn in on June 24, 1969, as the 15th U. S. chief justice.

HENRY S. SLOAN

BURNS, Arthur F.

During his second year as chairman of the U. S. Federal Reserve Board, Arthur F. Burns continued to fight inflation while warning of a recession if governmental intervention in the economy became too restrictive.

In January 1971, the Board cut the interest rate at which it loans money to member banks to the lowest level since 1968. Burns later said that little success had been attained in checking inflation. He added that inflation remained a "very grave obstacle" to economic recovery.

On the basis of such considerations, Burns joined Secretary of the Treasury John Connally and other administration advisers in supporting the new economic policies announced by President Nixon in August 1971. The wage-price freeze of three months was followed by a Phase II, of modified controls, under a Cost of Living Council. These presidential initiatives resulted largely from advice given him by Connally and Burns. In Phase II, Burns served as chairman of the Committee on Interest and Dividends, which reports to the Cost of Living Council.

Burns has continued to maintain that inflation must be halted without creating a system of rigid governmental controls. He has opposed increased governmental spending. He has argued that wage gains have exceeded productivity gains and that the two must be brought into some rational relationship.

Background. Arthur Frank Burns was born in Stanislau, Austria, on April 24, 1904. He went to the United States and worked his way through Columbia University, where he received his Ph. D. in economics. After teaching at Rutgers University, Burns returned to Columbia in 1944 to teach economics. He was an adviser to President Eisenhower and served President Nixon as a counselor, with cabinet rank, until appointed chairman of the Federal Reserve Board in 1970.

WALTER DARNELL JACOBS

BUTZ, Earl L.

On Nov. 11, 1971, President Nixon nominated Dr. Earl L. Butz, a dean of Purdue University and former official in the U. S. Department of Agriculture, to succeed Clifford M. Hardin as secretary of agriculture. At the same time, apparently bowing to pressure from farm leaders and members of Congress, the President announced that he was abandoning his plan to merge the functions of the Department of Agriculture with other agencies. The President's nominee was described by one official as "realistically market-oriented," but was denounced by some critics as "an agent of giant agribusiness corporations dedicated to driving farmers off the land." At hearings called by the agriculture committee of the U. S. Senate to consider his nomination, Butz affirmed that family farms "must be preserved." He endorsed existing farm support programs, asserting that measures must be taken to increase depressed grain prices. Despite opposition by farm organizations and key Democratic senators, Butz was confirmed by a Senate vote of 51 to 44.

Earl Lauer Butz was born at Albion, Ind., on July 3, 1909, and grew up on a nearby farm. He studied at Purdue University and, after obtaining his Ph. D. degree there in 1937, joined the school's faculty. He became head of the agricultural economics department in 1946. From 1954 to 1957 he was assistant secretary for marketing and foreign agriculture under President Eisenhower's secretary of agriculture, Ezra Taft Benson. During that period he also headed the U. S. delegation to the UN Food and Agriculture Organization. Butz returned to Purdue in 1957 as dean of agriculture and was named dean of continuing education in 1968. He is the author of *The Production Credit System for Farmers* (1944).

HENRY S. SLOAN

CASALS, Pablo

Pablo Casals, the undisputed master of the cello and one of the most venerated personalities of the musical world, continued in 1971 to speak out in behalf of world peace and human brotherhood. At the age of 95, his creative powers seemed undiminished. On Oct. 24, 1971, at the annual United Nations Day Concert, he conducted two Bach concertos and performed a cello solo of the Catalan *Song of the Birds*. The concert was highlighted by the premiere performance of Casals' stirring *Hymn to the United Nations*, which he composed for a poem written by W. H. Auden at the request of retiring UN Secretary General U Thant. Presenting Casals with the UN Peace Medal, U Thant cited him for a life devoted "to truth, to beauty, to peace." Casals, who considers himself "a man first, an artist second," has said: "As a man, my first obligation is to the welfare of my fellowmen."

Pau Carlos Salvador Defilló de Casals, one of 11 children of a church organist, was born in the Catalonian village of Vendrell, Spain, on Dec. 29, 1876 ("Pau" is the Catalan form of the name "Paul," or in Spanish, "Pablo"). He learned to play the violin, piano, and organ as a child. At 11 he began to study the cello at the Municipal School of Music in Barcelona, and later studied at the Royal Conservatory in Madrid. He made his concert debut in Paris in 1899, and during the next two decades he became renowned for his cello performances throughout Europe and the

Americas. In 1920 he founded the Pau Casals Orchestra in Barcelona. A few years later, also in Barcelona, he established the Workingmen's Concert Association.

A foe of totalitarianism, Casals exiled himself from his native Spain when Franco came to power in 1939, and settled in the town of Prades in southern France. For many years he refused to play or conduct in any country that recognized the Franco regime, but in 1950 he was persuaded to inaugurate the annual Prades music festivals. He moved to Puerto Rico, his mother's birthplace, in 1956, and the next year he established the annual Casals Festival there. He founded the Puerto Rico Symphony Orchestra in 1958.

More than any other individual, Casals is responsible for developing the modern playing techniques for the cello. His compositions include symphonies, oratorios, masses, choral works, and string quartets. Among the many honors and decorations he has received is the U. S. Presidential Medal of Freedom, presented to him by President John Kennedy in 1963.

HENRY S. SLOAN

CLEMENTE, Roberto

When Roberto Clemente appeared at the microphone in the dressing room after Pittsburgh had won the World Series, he asked if he might say a few words to his parents. Then, speaking in Spanish over a worldwide hookup, the Puerto Rican right fielder, who had been acclaimed the outstanding player in the series, humbly asked his parents for their blessing.

Clemente, 37, had been the chief scourge of Baltimore in the Series with his hitting, fielding, and accurate throwing. He hit a home run in the fourth inning of the final game that put the Pirates ahead by a run, their winning margin. It was his second homer and 12th hit, as he batted .414. When the Pirates beat the Yankees in the 1960 Series, Clemente batted .310 with 9 hits. For the two series, in which he hit safely in all 14 games, he collected 21 hits.

Roberto Walker Clemente was born in Carolina, Puerto Rico, on Aug. 18, 1934. Pittsburgh bought his contract from Montreal in 1955. In 1971, in his 17th season with the club, he hit .341, for a lifetime average of .318. In the two preceding seasons he batted .345 and .352, but he failed to win the National League batting title as he had done in 1961, 1964, 1965, and 1967. Clemente was named the NL's most valuable player in 1966, and he has played in 14 All-Star games. In 1967 he set a major league record for the most years leading in assists by an outfielder (5), and in 1970 he stroked a total of 10 hits in two consecutive games for another record.

One thing that Clemente hopes to see accomplished soon is the building of a sports complex for children in Puerto Rico. He is working with groups in New York and San Juan to obtain funds for a project that he considers vital to every nation.

BILL BRADDOCK

COLOMBO, Emilio

Italian Premier Emilio Colombo's center-left coalition government was confronted with serious problems in 1971, including a growing economic crisis, continued labor unrest, controversy over Italy's new divorce law, and increasing political instability. The resignation in February of the minister of justice removed Republican representation from the government, which became a 3-party coalition of Christian Democrats, Social Democrats, and Socialists. Although Colombo won parliamentary votes of confidence in early March, the discovery that month of evidence that seemed to indicate a plot by ultra-rightist elements led to criticism of him for not proceeding more vigorously against the extreme right. The premier suffered a setback in June, when neo-Fascists scored gains in local elections at the expense of Christian Democrats.

Colombo announced an economic expansion program in July, and engineered Parliament's adoption of important tax and housing bills in August, threatening to resign if they failed to pass. He affirmed Italy's solidarity with the West during visits to France in January and to the United States in February, and he was host to President Tito of Yugoslavia in March. A 16-day deadlock in the electoral college because of the failure of Christian Democrats and Socialists to agree on a presidential candidate ended when Giovanni Leone, a Christian Democrat, was finally chosen on December 24. Leone asked Colombo's cabinet to remain in office, but a government crisis was considered likely early in 1972.

Emilio Colombo was born in Potenza, in southern Italy, on April 11, 1920. His involvement in politics began as a teen-ager, when he became an officer of a Catholic Action youth group. He was elected to Italy's Constituent Assembly in 1946 and became a deputy in Parliament in 1948. Colombo helped draft important post-war economic reforms, and had a key role in the creation of the European Economic Community in 1958. As minister of the treasury from 1963 to 1970 he helped revive the country's economy by instituting unpopular austerity measures and tax increases. He became premier of Italy's 32d post-Fascist government on Aug. 6, 1970.

HENRY S. SLOAN

CONNALLY, John B.

Described by President Nixon as "my chief economic spokesman," Secretary of the Treasury John B. Connally emerged as a major and dynamic figure on the national scene in 1971.

As the U. S. ground combat role in Vietnam neared an end, the national economy became the center of administration activity. Connally figured prominently in the President's new economic policies, announced on August 15, and in Phase II, which followed in November. These moves were designed to reduce the rate of inflation and to give an impetus to economic recovery. Connally served as presidential spokesman for the new policies and as coordinator for Phase II, and he became chairman of the Cost of Living Council. The council was supported by a Pay Board and a Price Commission designed to supervise wage and price regulation. Also reporting to Connally was a Service and Compliance Administration as well as committees on interest and dividends, the health services industry, state and local government cooperation, and productivity.

Connally was also active in matters of international economic relations. In September he discussed the dollar crisis with the Group of Ten finance ministers in London and challenged them to find ways to improve the U. S. balance of payments. He was quoted as saying, "All I want is a fair advantage." Later, at a meeting of the International Monetary Fund's 118-member nations, Connally hinted that the 10% surcharge on imports might be removed if other countries compromised on currency exchange rates and if they made progress toward "dismantling specific barriers to trade." His efforts culminated in the broad currency realignments announced at a Group of Ten meeting in Washington, D.C., on December 18. (See INTERNATIONAL FINANCE.)

Connally represented the president at the inauguration of President Thieu in Vietnam. Earlier, he had supported a government loan guarantee of $250 million to the Lockheed Corporation. He had also reported that a deficit of $23.2 billion, the largest since 1945, would accrue in fiscal year 1971.

Connally's national prominence stirred speculation about his political future, and some observers saw him replacing Spiro T. Agnew as the Republican vice presidential candidate in 1972.

Early Career. John Bowden Connally, Jr., was born in Floresville, Texas, on Feb. 27, 1917. He earned an LL. B. at the University of Texas before joining the staff

(*Top left*) PABLO CASALS plays Catalonian folk song on his 95th birthday. (*Above*) ROBERTO CLEMENTE of the Pirates, with his wife, accepts keys to new car presented at "Clemente Night" in New York. (*Right*) RICHARD J. DALEY won reelection as mayor of Chicago.

of Congressman Lyndon B. Johnson. Connally returned to Texas in 1952 to practice law. He continued a close association with Johnson and became President Kennedy's secretary of the Navy in 1961. He ran for governor of Texas in 1962, and was elected to three terms. Connally was wounded while riding in the car in which President Kennedy was assassinated. He recovered and remained active in Texas politics, supporting the conservative faction in Democratic party affairs.

WALTER DARNELL JACOBS

DALEY, Richard J.

On April 6, 1971, Richard J. Daley was elected to an unprecedented fifth term as mayor of Chicago. He defeated Richard E. Friedman, an independent Democrat running as a Republican, by a vote of 735,787 to 318,-059. During the campaign, Friedman attacked what he considered Chicago's inadequate standards of education and public health and insufficient public housing, while Daley claimed to have compiled a record of sound municipal government.

As chairman of the Cook county Democratic organization, Daley is the boss of one of the nation's most powerful political machines, and he is considered a master of political strategy. His influence has often been decisive in national as well as state and local elections. A month before his reelection, Daley, in a bid for white-middle class and blue-collar votes, denounced a federally mandated plan to construct low-income public housing in middle-class neighborhoods. On the other hand, he acceded to demands of black community leaders and liberals when he withdrew organization support from state's attorney Edward V. Hanrahan, who was under indictment for conspiracy to obstruct justice in connection with a 1969 raid in which two Black Panther leaders were killed.

Richard Joseph Daley was born in Chicago, Ill., on May 15, 1902. He worked his way through De Paul University law school and was admitted to the bar in 1933. He was a member of the Illinois House of Representatives (1936–38) and of the state Senate (1939–46), and later served as state director of revenue from 1948 to 1950 and as Cook county clerk from 1950 until his election as mayor in 1955. Daley was widely criticized after a ghetto riot in the spring of 1968 for his statement that police should shoot arsonists and looters. During the 1968 Democratic National Convention in Chicago, he became the object of nationwide controversy because of the force with which police, acting under his orders, subdued demonstrators protesting convention proceedings.

HENRY S. SLOAN

ELLSBERG, Daniel

A former U. S. military strategist, Daniel Ellsberg was indicted on Dec. 30, 1971, by a federal grand jury in Los Angeles on 12 criminal charges of having appropriated the Pentagon Papers—a classified docu-

141

mentary study of U.S. involvement in Indochina from World War II to 1967—from the Rand Corporation, where he had been employed, and releasing them to the news media. Ellsberg had first been indicted in June, on lesser charges, after installments of the 47-volume Pentagon study, which he had helped to prepare in 1968, had appeared in the New York *Times* and other newspapers. The documents were subsequently declassified after the U.S. Supreme Court ruled that their publication could be resumed.

DANIEL ELLSBERG made headlines in 1971 by releasing Pentagon Papers, which revealed U.S. role in Indochina conflict.

UPI

Declaring that he had released the papers on his own initiative, Ellsberg insisted that he violated no laws and acted in the nation's best interests. Originally an ardent supporter of the Vietnam War, Ellsberg became increasingly disillusioned with U.S. involvement in it. Since leaving the Rand Corporation in 1970 he has been a senior research associate with the Center for International Studies at the Massachusetts Institute of Technology.

Ellsberg was born in Chicago on April 7, 1931, the son of an engineer, and grew up in Detroit, where he attended private schools. After receiving his B.A. degree in economics in 1952 from Harvard University, he studied for a year at Cambridge, England. From 1954 to 1957, Ellsberg served in the U.S. Marine Corps, rising to the rank of first lieutenant. In 1959, after obtaining his Ph.D. degree from Harvard University, he joined the Rand Corporation, where he specialized in nuclear war strategy.

In 1964, Ellsberg began to work on Vietnam War strategy as a special assistant to the assistant secretary of defense for international security affairs, and the following year he was sent to Vietnam by the State Department to work in the pacification program. Although he had begun to express skepticism about U.S. involvement in Indochina, he continued to work on Vietnam planning after his return to the Rand Corporation in 1967. In the spring of 1969 he served briefly as a consultant to presidential adviser Henry A. Kissinger. (See also CENSORSHIP.)

HENRY S. SLOAN

FISCHER, Bobby

On Oct. 26, 1971, U.S. chess grand master Bobby Fischer became the first American to reach the final step in competition for the world chess championship. On that day he defeated the Soviet grand master, Tigran Petrosian, a former world champion, in the ninth game of a scheduled 12-game elimination series at Buenos Aires, winning by a score of 6½ to 2½. He had previously beaten Petrosian 3–1 in a 4-game match in March 1970. His 1971 victory made him eligible to challenge the world champion, Boris Spassky of the USSR, in the spring of 1972.

An 8-time winner of the U.S. championship, the 28-year-old Fischer, once known as the *enfant terrible* of chess, is noted for his keenly analytical mind, his cool,

rational approach, and his total dedication to the game. Once quoted as saying that he liked to "see his opponents squirm," Fischer is said to strike terror into the hearts of some of his opponents.

The son of a biophysicist, Robert James Fischer was born in Chicago, Ill., on March 9, 1943. His parents were divorced when he was two. Brought to Brooklyn, N.Y., in 1948 by his mother, a teacher and nurse, he began to play chess at the age of 6, and, by the time he was 12, was holding his own among some of the best U.S. players at chess clubs in the New York area. At 13 he was the youngest player ever to win the national junior championship. When not yet 15, he became the U.S. champion on Jan. 7, 1958, defeating Arthur B. Bisguier at the Manhattan Chess Club. Named an international grand master in September 1958, the youngest in the history of chess, he dropped out of high school at 16 to devote his full time to the game.

Fischer was a persistent critic of the international "chess establishment," the Fédération Internationale des Échecs (FIDE), under whose standards, he claimed, Soviet players were at a clear advantage. Largely as a result of his efforts, the FIDE revised some of its rules. He was also credited with having successfully fought for improved playing conditions and higher purses for chess players.

HENRY S. SLOAN

FRANKLIN, Aretha

Popular singer Aretha Franklin received the National Academy of Recording Arts and Sciences Grammy award in March 1971 as the best female rhythm and blues vocal performer for her 1969 recording of *Don't Play That Song*. Miss Franklin, the undisputed "queen of soul," was among the featured performers at the Rev. Jesse Jackson's Black Expo, which opened in Chicago on Sept. 29, 1971, and she was enthusiastically received at her concert at New York's Madison Square Garden in October. Among her 1971 releases was the recording *Spirit in the Dark*.

The daughter of a well-known Baptist minister, Aretha Franklin was born in Memphis, Tenn., on March

BOBBY FISCHER, shown in series with Tigran Petrosian, won right to play for world chess championship.

THE NEW YORK TIMES

25, 1942, and grew up in Detroit. Among the regular visitors to her childhood home were such notables in the music world as Mahalia Jackson, Dinah Washington, and B. B. King. At an early age Miss Franklin began to sing gospel songs at local churches and was a member of her father's church choir. Determined to become established as a rhythm and blues performer, she moved to New York in 1960 but had only moderate success over the next few years as a recording artist for Columbia Records and as a nightclub singer.

Miss Franklin finally attained status as a top performer in 1967, when the sales of several of her recordings for Atlantic Records topped the 1 million mark, and she scored triumphs with her first European tour and her appearance at New York's Philharmonic Hall. *Billboard* and other trade magazines in the music field named her the best female performer, and over the next few years she won several Grammy awards. A leader in the movement to foster black consciousness and identity, Miss Franklin received a special citation from the Southern Christian Leadership Conference in 1967. Her award-winning recording of *Respect* has been described as a "Negro national anthem." Her best-selling albums include *I Never Loved a Man, Aretha Arrives, Lady Soul, Aretha Now,* and *Aretha in Paris.*

HENRY S. SLOAN

GANDHI, Indira

Prime Minister Indira Gandhi of India was named "the most admired person in the world" in a Gallup poll of leaders representing 70 countries that was published in May 1971. Mrs. Gandhi won a major political victory in early March, when in bitterly fought national elections her New Congress party won a two-thirds majority in the Lok Sabha, the lower house of Parliament, enough to enable it to pass constitutional amendments. The result was seen as a vote of confidence for her program of democratic socialism.

During most of 1971, Mrs. Gandhi was faced with a major crisis in India's long-standing conflict with Pakistan. The crisis erupted in late March, when the military government of Pakistan used force to try to suppress a Bengali separatist movement in East Pakistan. Ten million Bengali refugees fled into neighboring India, which supported the rebels. The influx of refugees into India, already plagued by perennial poverty and overpopulation, subjected the country to unbearable pressures.

To strengthen India's hand against Pakistan, which had the support of Communist China, Mrs. Gandhi concluded a 20-year treaty of friendship with the USSR in August. In November, she embarked on a tour of Western nations to persuade President Nixon and other government leaders to press Pakistan to seek a political settlement with East Pakistan. Mounting tensions led to the outbreak of full-scale war between India and Pakistan early in December, and India officially recognized the East Pakistani rebel nation of Bangladesh on December 6. Hostilities ended when Pakistani forces surrendered to advancing Indian troops in East Pakistan on December 16, and Pakistan accepted a cease-fire on the western border on December 17. Mrs. Gandhi was acclaimed by a resolution in Parliament as the "chosen instrument of national destiny," who managed to "raise the honor of India to new heights."

Background. Indira Gandhi, the daughter of the late Prime Minister Jawaharlal Nehru, was born in Allahabad on Nov. 19, 1917. She was educated in India and at Oxford, and after joining the Indian National Congress party in 1938, she became increasingly active in the independence movement. She was imprisoned by the British in 1942 for her participation in the "Quit India" movement.

When her father became the first prime minister of the Republic of India in 1947, Mrs. Gandhi became his official hostess. She acted as president of the Congress party in 1959–60, and served as minister of information and broadcasting in the cabinet of Prime Min-

ister Lal Bahadur Shastri from 1964 to 1966. After Shastri's death she became India's third prime minister, on Jan. 24, 1966. Ideological differences between Mrs. Gandhi and the right-wing old guard led to a split in the Congress party. To obtain a parliamentary majority for her New Congress party, she dissolved Parliament in December 1970 and called for new elections in 1971, a year ahead of schedule.

HENRY S. SLOAN

GENTELE, Goeran

Goeran Gentele, the former general manager of the Swedish Royal Opera in Stockholm, moved into offices at the Metropolitan Opera in New York in June 1971 to begin a year's preparation for his duties as its general manager, a post he is scheduled to assume at the opening of the 1972–73 season. His appointment in December 1970 had ended a 3-year search for a successor to Rudolf Bing.

Gentele is noted for his artistic sense, his financial expertise, his flair for public relations, and his skill in handling labor-management problems—qualities that will be of value to him as head of the Metropolitan Opera, which, unlike the largely government-subsidized Stockholm Opera, has been plagued by financial crises and strikes. In contrast with Bing, who is primarily an administrator, Gentele expects to take an active part in the staging of operas. He plans to make opera, which he views as a "folk art," more attractive to young people by creating a more informal atmosphere and by adding more modern and experimental works to the company's repertoire.

The son of an officer in the Swedish army, Claes-Goeran Herman Arvid Gentele was born in Stockholm on Sept. 20, 1917. After studying at the Sorbonne and the University of Stockholm, he decided on a theatrical career and enrolled in the Royal Dramatic Acting School. He joined the Royal Dramatic Theater in Stockholm as an actor in 1940, but gradually concentrated on directing, eventually becoming successful as a director of plays and motion pictures. He appeared as a guest director at the Swedish Royal Opera in 1951 and was appointed a staff director in 1952. Gentele was named general manager when that post became vacant in 1963. Under his direction, the Royal Opera's administration was modernized and the artistic quality of its productions was considerably improved.

HENRY S. SLOAN

HARRIS, Patricia Roberts

Mrs. Patricia Roberts Harris, a Washington attorney, was elected on Oct. 13, 1971, temporary chairman of the important Credentials Committee for the 1972 Democratic National Convention. The candidate of the party "regulars" and of organized labor, Mrs. Harris, who is black, was chosen by the Democratic National Committee by a vote of 72 to 31 over the "reform" candidate, Sen. Harold E. Hughes of Iowa. Despite her identification with the party's Old Guard, Mrs. Harris is committed to reform and has indicated that she is not beholden to the National Committee's leadership. "Reform is not a mystical word for me," she has said. "It means very simply that we are not going to have the political bosses telling us who is going to the Convention. And we're going to let the public know that now *they* can choose the delegates."

The daughter of a railroad waiter, Patricia Roberts was born on May 31, 1924, at Mattoon, Ill., and grew up in the Chicago area. She graduated summa cum laude from Howard University in 1945 and then served as program director of the Chicago YWCA and as assistant director of the American Council on Human Rights. In 1955 she married William Beasley Harris, a law professor.

In 1960 Mrs. Harris graduated at the head of her class from George Washington Law School. She was a lawyer with the Justice Department for a year before joining the law faculty of Howard University. She

Mrs. Patricia Harris

UPI

served briefly as associate dean of the law school in 1963 before she resigned, refusing to yield to militant student demands.

An active Democrat since 1948, Mrs. Harris gave one of the seconding speeches for Lyndon Johnson's presidential nomination at the 1964 convention. She became the first American black women to hold ambassadorial rank in 1965, when President Johnson appointed her ambassador to Luxembourg, a post she held for two years. She was an alternate delegate to the UN General Assembly in 1966. Mrs. Harris is a member of the prestigious Washington law firm of Fried, Frank, Harris, Shriver, & Kampelman, and she serves on the boards of directors of the IBM Corporation, Scott Paper Company, Chase Manhattan Bank, and the NAACP Legal Defense Fund.

HENRY S. SLOAN

HEATH, Edward

The signing of the Treaty of Accession to the European Economic Community (EEC or Common Market) in Brussels, on Jan. 22, 1972, represented the crowning achievement in the career of Edward Heath, Conservative prime minister of Britain. It marked the culmination of 10 years effort in Britain's pursuit of membership in the Common Market, part of a Heath policy of "Europeanism." In 1961–62, as lord privy seal in the government of Prime Minister Harold Macmillan, Heath had been in charge of the first unsuccessful bid for entry.

Talks between Heath and French Premier Georges Pompidou in Paris, May 20–21, 1971, preceded the announcement on June 23 that Britain and the EEC Council had reached substantial agreement on terms for membership. Negotiations on the outstanding issue of fisheries policy were concluded in December. In October, Parliament had voted to support entry into EEC in principle, despite Labour opposition to the terms worked out by the Heath government. Ratification proceedings were to follow the treaty signing. For his services to Europe, Heath was awarded a prize of £36,000 by the Institute for European Unity.

The Heath government in 1971 also succeeded in producing a proposal to end the deadlock over terms for accepting the independence of Rhodesia. The settlement, negotiated in Rhodesia in late November by Foreign Secretary Sir Alec Douglas-Home, represented the culmination of Prime Minister Heath's efforts to reach a compromise between immediate African majority rule and the present all-white Rhodesia government system. Approved by the British House of Commons, the agreement was conditioned upon the assessment of African opinion by an independent commission.

The strife in Northern Ireland continued to bedevil British politics in 1971. Heath met with Irish representatives several times during the year and paid a surprise visit to the British troops stationed in Ulster in December. He warned Prime Minister John Lynch of Ireland (Eire) not to interfere in affairs of the United Kingdom. As the death toll in Northern Ireland rose, internment was introduced. Heath reaffirmed his policy of maintaining law and order while pressing forward with political and social reforms.

Heath's reputation for consistency was displayed by the near-absence of cabinet changes during 1971. The prime minister did waver somewhat on his economic policy, introducing expansionary measures into the sagging economy to counter widespread unemployment. Conservative party prestige went down with the economy; so, to a lesser extent, did Heath's personal popularity.

Commonwealth and Common Market diplomacy took Heath to Cyprus, Pakistan, India, Malaysia, Singapore, Paris, Ottawa, and Bermuda, where he conferred with U. S. President Richard Nixon. He also found time to conduct the London Symphony Orchestra and to lead his team to victory in the Admiral's Yachting Cup race.

Background. Edward Richard George Heath was born in Broadstairs Kent, on July 9, 1916, and was educated at Balliol College, Oxford. After military service during World War II, he entered the civil service as an administrator of civil aviation. Since 1950 he has represented Bexley, a London suburb, as a Conservative in Parliament. Successively party whip, minister of labor, and lord privy seal, he was elected Conservative party leader in 1965 and became prime minister after the Conservative victory in the 1970 election.

A. J. BEATTIE

HIROHITO

Emperor Hirohito, the 124th ruler of Japan, celebrated his 70th birthday in 1971 and, with Empress Nagako, visited several European countries in September and October. The journey, his first since he visited Europe as crown prince in 1921, was the first trip abroad by a reigning Japanese monarch. During a stopover in Anchorage, Alaska, on September 26, Hirohito met with President Richard Nixon in the first encounter between a Japanese emperor and a U. S. president. The meeting was considered a symbolic effort to alleviate recent tensions between the two countries, especially in the area of trade.

Hirohito is the subject of the book *Japan's Imperial Conspiracy* by U. S. journalist David Bergamini, published in 1971, which contends that the emperor had a major role in Japanese military planning in the 1930's and 1940's. In November, at his first public meeting with foreign journalists, Hirohito denied that he had played an active part in the conduct of World War II, asserting that his powers had been constitutionally limited.

Hirohito, the son of Emperor Yoshihito and grandson of Emperor Meiji, was born in Tokyo on April 29, 1901. According to tradition, Hirohito is a direct descendant of the Sun Goddess and of Jimmu, who is said to have founded the Japanese Empire in the 7th century B. C. Hirohito was educated at the Peers' School and at an institute headed by Admiral Heihachiro Togo. He was designated heir apparent in 1912 and was named regent for his ailing father in 1921, after his return from his first visit to Europe. Hirohito ascended the throne on Dec. 25, 1926, and was formally enthroned in 1928.

As emperor, Hirohito was considered divine in the Shinto religion. He ruled as a constitutional monarch, but in August 1945 he overruled die-hard militarists and announced Japan's surrender in World War II. Renouncing his status as a divinity, Hirohito was designated a "symbol of the state and the unity of the people" in the constitution of 1947. His functions in postwar years have been largely ceremonial. He is a specialist in marine biology, on which he has published several books.

HENRY S. SLOAN

HONECKER, Erich

On May 3, 1971, Erich Honecker was named first secretary of the Socialist Unity (Communist) party of the German Democratic Republic (East Germany), succeeding Walter Ulbricht, who announced his retirement. Although Honecker, a hard-line party functionary, is a protégé and long-time associate of Ulbricht, he is apparently more pragmatic and less ideological than his predecessor. He is therefore considered more suitable by the USSR to occupy East Germany's top position of power at a time of détente between East and West.

Addressing the eighth Socialist Unity party congress in June, Honecker stressed East Germany's "ties of socialist brotherhood" with the USSR, whose preeminence in the Communist world he recognized; called for the establishment of "normal relations" with West Germany and recognition of a "special political status" for West Berlin; endorsed West Germany's recently concluded nonaggression treaties with the USSR and Poland; and called for increased industrial production. In June he was also named to succeed Ulbricht as chairman of the National Defense Council. In talks with Soviet leaders in late October, Honecker pledged East German cooperation in seeking an agreement with the West German government to implement a recent 4-power accord on Berlin. A final agreement on Berlin was concluded between East and West German representatives in December.

Honecker was born in the city of Neunkirchen on Aug. 25, 1912. He became active in a Communist youth group at the age of 10, and joined the German Communist party in 1929. He went to Moscow for training in 1930 and the following year became a functionary in the German Communist youth movement. Arrested by the Nazis for underground activities in 1935, he spent most of the next 10 years in solitary confinement. He was freed by Soviet troops at the end of World War II, and served as chairman of the militant Free German Youth from 1946 until 1955, when he went to Moscow for more training. Since 1958 he had been a member of the secretariat of the Socialist Unity party's Central Committee, with special responsibility for security matters.

HENRY S. SLOAN

HOOVER, J. Edgar

J. Edgar Hoover, director of the U. S. Federal Bureau of Investigation for 47 years, came increasingly under fire from various sources during 1971, despite the consistently high praise accorded him by President Nixon. Criticisms of Hoover centered around his virtually absolute authority; his agency's use of methods of surveillance of questionable constitutional legality; his persistence in remaining in office far beyond the normal age of retirement; and what some consider his personal vendettas against student activists, antiwar demonstrators, and militant spokesmen for racial minorities.

Former Attorney General Ramsey Clark, a member of the recently established Committee for Public Justice, has said that the FBI under Hoover suffered from "a lack of objectivity in pursuing facts and an intolerance of internal criticism," and Sen. Edmund S. Muskie, in the spring of 1971, presented evidence of FBI surveillance of Earth Day activities in 1970.

The bureau's methods of gathering and issuing statistical data were among the objects of criticism in a report submitted to the President in December by the Commission on Federal Statistics, which recommended that the task of compiling data on crime be transferred from the FBI to an independent agency. Despite growing pressure for his removal, Hoover appeared to be firmly entrenched as the chief U. S. police official at the end of the year.

The son of a government employee, John Edgar Hoover was born in Washington, D. C., on New Year's Day, 1895. He studied at night at George Washington University law school (LL. B., 1916; LL. M., 1917) and began his career in 1919 as a special assistant to Attorney General A. Mitchell Palmer. Appointed assistant director of the FBI in 1921, he became director in 1924. During the 1930's the FBI under Hoover played a leading role in the war against organized crime, and during World War II it dealt with espionage, sabotage, and the rounding up of enemy aliens. Its anti-Communist emphasis of the postwar years is reflected in Hoover's books *Masters of Deceit* (1958) and *A Study in Communism* (1962).

HENRY S. SLOAN

HOUPHOUËT-BOIGNY, Félix

President Félix Houphouët-Boigny of the Ivory Coast stirred considerable controversy in 1971 when he repeated his 1970 appeal calling on Black African nations to establish a diplomatic "dialogue" with South Africa. Referring to South African Prime Minister Balthazar J. Vorster's declaration that he intended to invite black African leaders for talks, Houphouët-Boigny said that acceptance of the invitation would not imply approval of South African policies. While conceding that "the revolting system of apartheid outrages us all," he asserted that it was a "matter within the domestic jurisdiction" of South Africa. "What must be decided," he declared, "is whether bellicose verbalism ... or a carefully thought out approach ... would serve more faithfully the dignity, the pride, and the best interests of our continent." In a reorganization of his government in June, Houphouët-Boigny assumed the portfolio of national education in order to cope with student unrest that a few months earlier had forced the closing of the University of Abidjan.

The son of a tribal chief who owned large coffee and cacao plantations, Houphouët-Boigny was born in the village of Yamoussoukro on Oct. 18, 1905. After completing his studies at the École de Médecine in Dakar, Senegal, in 1925, he worked as a public health official for 15 years. He then returned to his father's plantations and in 1944 founded the African Farmers Union, which sought to improve workers' living standards. The Rassemblement Démocratique Africain, which he founded in 1946, later became the governing party of the Ivory Coast.

J. EDGAR HOOVER, in rare social appearance, seats Martha Mitchell, attorney general's wife, at dinner.

UPI

MARC & EVELYNE BERNHEIM
FROM RAPHO GUILLUMETTE
Félix Houphouët-Boigny

WIDE WORLD

JESSE JACKSON (*left*) welcomes Cleveland's Mayor Stokes to Chicago.

After World War II, Houphouët-Boigny served as a deputy from the Ivory Coast in the French National Assembly. He held several ministries in the French cabinet between 1956 and 1960, and in 1957–58 he also served as president of French West Africa's federal grand council. He was elected president of the newly independent Republic of Ivory Coast in 1960 and was re-elected, without opposition, in 1965 and 1970. His encouragement of foreign investments and cooperation with the West has brought his country considerable prosperity.

HENRY S. SLOAN

JACKSON, Jesse L.

The Rev. Jesse·L. Jackson, one of the most popular and influential of the younger generation of black civil rights leaders, resigned as national director of Operation Breadbasket, the Chicago-based economic arm of the Southern Christian Leadership Conference (SCLC), on Dec. 11, 1971. His resignation was the final step in a growing rift between Jackson and the older, Southern-oriented leadership of the SCLC, an organization that was founded by the late Martin Luther King, Jr.

Jackson, who earlier in the year had unsuccessfully challenged Chicago's Mayor Richard J. Daly in his bid for reelection, was the chief organizer of Operation Breadbasket's third annual Black Business and Cultural Exposition—or Black Expo—a 5-day fair emphasizing black achievement, that opened in Chicago on Sept. 29, 1971. In his keynote address, Jackson called on the U. S. government to help black communities develop their resources by means of a domestic "Marshall Plan." On December 3, he was suspended for 60 days by the SCLC, which charged that he had violated its regulations by creating two corporations to operate Black Expo without consulting the parent organization. Jackson resigned a week later and announced that Operation Breadbasket would be replaced by the more militant Operation Push (People United to Save Humanity), to be launched on Christmas day.

Jesse Louis Jackson was born on Oct. 8, 1941, in Greenville, S. C., where he grew up amid poverty. He attended the University of Illinois on a football scholarship and graduated with honors from North Carolina Agricultural and Technical College in 1964. While attending the Chicago Theological Seminary in 1965 he became associated with the Rev. Martin Luther King, Jr., whom he helped to launch Operation Breadbasket. He became director of its Chicago office in 1966. As its national director from August 1967, Jackson, an ordained Baptist minister, worked closely with black clergymen, businessmen, and intellectuals to uplift the black communities. Through the strategic use of the economic boycott, Operation Breadbasket obtained jobs for thousands of ghetto dwellers and successfully promoted the marketing of goods and services offered by black-owned concerns.

HENRY S. SLOAN

JORDAN, Vernon Eulion, Jr.

Vernon Eulion Jordan, Jr., the head of the United Negro College Fund, was appointed on June 15, 1971, to succeed the late Whitney M. Young, Jr., as executive director of the National Urban League, one of the most influential and respected black civil rights organizations in the United States (see YOUNG, WHITNEY). A veteran of civil rights struggles, Jordan is noted for his tenacity, persuasive power, talent for fund raising, and ability to deal with the white establishment. Addressing the National Urban League's 61st annual conference at Detroit in July, he charged the Nixon administration with compiling a "record of ambiguity" toward black Americans. Jordan decided to remain with the United Negro College Fund for the remainder of 1971 to allow himself time to complete the year's fund-raising drive and to study the operations of the National Urban League. He was to assume his new post in January 1972.

Jordan was born in Atlanta, Ga., on Aug. 15, 1935. His father was a post office supervisor and his mother conducted a food-catering business. He graduated from DePauw University in 1957 and earned his law degree from Howard University in 1960. In the early 1960's, Jordan was associated with the late Rev. Martin Luther King, Jr., in civil rights activities in the South. He took part in the struggle to integrate the University of Georgia in 1961, and as field secretary of the Georgia branch of the NAACP in 1962 he led a boycott of Augusta stores practicing discrimination in hiring. During the Johnson administration he served on the National Advisory Commission on Selective Service and was director of the Southern Regional Council's voter education project in the late 1960's. Appointed executive director of the United Negro College Fund in January 1970, he raised a record $7 million for 36 colleges during his first year in that office.

HENRY S. SLOAN

KISSINGER, Henry A.

For Henry Kissinger, President Nixon's assistant for national security affairs since 1969, the year 1972 was one of surreptitious globe-trotting. On July 15, 1971, the President, while announcing his plan to visit Peking, revealed that Kissinger had flown to the Chinese capital and made arrangements for the presidential trip in conferences with Chou En-lai on July 9–11. On Jan. 15, 1972, the President announced that during the preceding months his 48-year-old adviser had made 12 clandestine trips to Paris to discuss a secret presidential peace proposal at the Paris Conference.

While these dramatic assignments gained the former Harvard professor some fresh notoriety as President Nixon's "secret agent," they could hardly add to the reputation of an individual already considered by many to be the second most powerful man in Washington. Conferring almost daily with the President, leading the meetings of the National Security Council, and chairing many of its committees, Kissinger had assumed many prerogatives exercised by secretaries of state. His energy, expertise, and administrative ability made him an ideal servant of the President, who preferred to keep Washington's various bureaucracies at arm's length and function through a handful of close personal aides.

Background. Henry Alfred Kissinger was born in Fürth, Germany, on May 27, 1923. He went to New York City with his German-Jewish parents in 1938, when the family fled from Hitler's Reich. After serving as an enlisted man in the U. S. Army during World War II, Kissinger entered Harvard, graduating *summa cum laude* in 1950. In 1951 he became executive director of the university's International Seminar, and in 1957, three years after earning his Ph. D. degree, published *Nuclear Weapons and Foreign Policy*, a book that immediately established him as a major theorist in the fields of foreign affairs and defense.

A full professor at Harvard's Center for International Affairs from 1962 to 1969, he was also consultant to the National Security Council (1961–62) and the U. S. Arms Control and Disarmament Agency (1961–67). Kissinger was Gov. Nelson A. Rockefeller's principal foreign affairs adviser in the 1960's, becoming acquainted with Richard Nixon only after Rockefeller's bid for the Republican presidential nomination had been thwarted in 1968.

WILLIAM B. CUMMINGS

KLASSEN, Elmer Theodore

On Dec. 7, 1971, the board of governors of the new U. S. Postal Service, an independent government agency since August 1970, named one of its members, Elmer T. Klassen, as the new postmaster general of the United States. He succeeded Winton M. Blount, the first executive chief of the new system. The 63-year-old Klassen had served for two years as deputy postmaster general and in that capacity had functioned as the principal negotiator with the postal unions.

Born in Hillsboro, Kans., on Nov. 6, 1908, Klassen attended public schools in California and joined the American Can Company as a messenger in 1925. Despite his lack of a college education, he rose steadily through company ranks. After studying business management at Harvard in the mid-1950's, he advanced to a divisional vice presidency and, in 1964, to the post of executive vice president for corporate operations. He was named president of American Can in April 1965. In May 1968 he resigned, ending a 43-year career with a company that he had helped to build into a corporate giant.

On joining what was then the U. S. Post Office Department in 1969 as its second-ranking executive, Klassen proposed and supervised a thorough review and reorganization of operating procedures in each department. Although he failed to prevent a walkout of postal employees in March–April 1970, his patient handling of negotiations with the leaders of seven unions was thought to have delayed the strike and mitigated its severity.

KOSYGIN, Aleksei Nikolayevich

Soviet Premier Kosygin, despite some Western predictions that he might retire in 1971, was very active during the year as head of the government of the USSR. He continued to hold the second-highest rank in the Soviet hierarchy, yielding in prestige and publicity only to Leonid Brezhnev, secretary-general of the Communist party. At the party congress in March–April, Kosygin introduced the new 5-year economic plan for 1971–75 and managed to install more than a dozen of his subordinates as full members of the party's Central Committee. As a result of these promotions, almost one third of the full members were government executives directly or indirectly subordinate to Kosygin.

Traveling widely during the year, Kosygin in July visited Mongolia, where he concluded a 10-year treaty of Soviet-Mongol cultural and scientific cooperation. In July he was also in Rumania to help draft a 20-

year program for the Council of Mutual Economic Assistance (CMEA, or Comecon, the Communist counterpart of the Common Market). In October he was in Algeria and Morocco, concluding a new Soviet technical aid pact with the latter. In late October he toured Canada, where the visit was marred by many anti-Soviet demonstrations. On the way back from Canada he made a brief stopover in Cuba, and in December he visited Denmark and Norway. On all these trips Kosygin was very friendly to his foreign hosts.

Background. Kosygin was born in St. Petersburg (now Leningrad) on Feb. 20, 1904. He is an experienced economist and since 1939 has held such high posts as chairman of the State Planning Committee, deputy premier of the USSR, premier of the Russian republic, and head of the ministries for the textile industry, light industry, the consumer goods industry, and finance. He was a Politburo member from 1946 to 1952 and again after 1957. Following the ouster of Nikita Khrushchev as premier in 1964, Kosygin succeeded him. He is one of the more popular Soviet leaders and is considered a skilled industrial administrator and an astute diplomat.

ELLSWORTH RAYMOND

KUZNETS, Simon

U. S. economist and statistician Simon Kuznets was awarded the third annual Alfred Nobel Memorial Prize in Economic Science on Oct. 15, 1971, for his "empirically founded interpretation of economic growth which has led to new and deepened insight into the economic and social structure and process of development." Kuznets is credited with having developed the concept of gross national product—the total of a nation's goods and services—which was adopted as the official measure of the U. S. economy and is used by many countries as a gauge of economic activity.

Kuznets developed his ideas independently of textbooks or established theories, working from statistical data and taking into consideration such noneconomic factors as population change, technological development, and industrial structure. Since World War II he has been engaged in research on the quantitative aspects of long-term economic growth of developed and developing countries. He retired from his professorship at Harvard University on July 1, 1971, becoming professor emeritus.

Kuznets was born in Kharkov, the Ukraine, on April 30, 1901. As a secondary school student he became convinced that economics was "the basis of all social problems." After moving to the United States in 1922, he studied at Columbia University (B. A., 1923; M. A., 1924; Ph. D., 1926). He was a fellow of the Social Science Research Council from 1925 until 1927. He then joined the National Bureau of Economics, where he began his studies of business cycles and developed the foundations of national incomes accounting that contributed to the theories of British economist John Maynard Keynes. Kuznets taught at the University of

SIMON KUZNETS, Harvard University economist who developed concept of gross national product, won 1971 Nobel Prize for economics.

UPI

Pennsylvania and at Johns Hopkins University before joining the Harvard faculty in 1960. In 1942–44 he was associate director of the Bureau of Planning and Statistics of the War Production Board. His publications include his monumental study *National Income and its Composition, 1919 to 1938* (2 vols., 1941), *Modern Economic Growth* (1966), and *Economic Growth of Nation* (1971).

HENRY S. SLOAN

LAIRD, Melvin R.

National security problems facing Secretary of Defense Melvin R. Laird changed sharply during 1971. No longer was the counterinsurgency action in Vietnam the central issue. A rapid rise in Soviet strategic power dominated the picture, and the military power of the United States did not appear so impressive as it had previously.

The Vietnamization program proceeded according to schedule, with U. S. troop strength reduced to less than 184,000 on December 1. American casualties declined to a low level. Laird made an inspection trip to Vietnam in November.

The strategic situation was complicated by Soviet deployments of new missiles and new submarines capable of firing nuclear payloads. In October, Laird reported that the USSR had exceeded intelligence predictions by deploying 1,500 intercontinental ballistic missiles and by improving its Y-class submarine production so that the Soviet submarine-launched missile capability would equal that of the United States by 1973, a year earlier than had been expected. The Soviet Union also continued to expand its naval and other forces and to extend its global operational capabilities. Laird main-

tained that the strategy of realistic deterrence, which he outlined in his annual defense report, was still effective, but that the rate of Soviet rearmament might raise new questions if present trends continued.

Personnel problems in the armed forces were connected with the rapid demobilization of men returning from Vietnam and with the attempt to create an all-volunteer force. Discipline was affected by incidents of racial disorder, drug abuse, and incidents of refusal to obey orders.

Laird did not recommend major expenditures for new military equipment. He reiterated his hopes for the Strategic Arms Limitation Talks, mutually balanced force reductions, and the success of the Nixon Doctrine which places more responsibility on other countries for their own defense.

Background. Melvin Robert Laird was born in Omaha, Nebr., on Sept. 1, 1922, and grew up in Marshfield, Wis. He graduated from Carleton College and served in the Navy during World War II. In 1952 he was elected to the U. S. House of Representatives, where he served as chairman of the House Republican Conference.

WALTER DARNELL JACOBS

McMAHON, William

William McMahon became Australia's 20th prime minister on March 10, 1971, following his election as Liberal party leader. He succeeded John G. Gorton, who resigned after losing a vote of confidence among members of his own party. McMahon, who had been minister of foreign affairs in the Gorton cabinet, took steps soon after assuming office to rebuild the weakened Liberal-Country party coalition, which has governed Australia for 22 years, and ordered a review of the economy to deal with mounting inflation and other problems. Although he had established a reputation as a strong anti-Communist, he explored the prospects of closer relations with Communist countries, including China, in view of eased cold war tensions, and he continued his predecessor's policy of gradually disengaging Australian military forces from Indochina.

In August, McMahon dismissed Gorton, who had been appointed defense minister, claiming that he had violated cabinet solidarity. Later that month McMahon survived a motion of no confidence introduced by the opposition Labor party, charging that he was subservient to foreign interests. During his visit to the United States in November, he discussed economic and security matters with President Nixon.

A member of a wealthy and socially prominent family, McMahon was born in Sydney on Feb. 23, 1908. He received a law degree, and, later, a degree in economics, from the University of Sydney, and worked for a time as a solicitor for a Sydney law firm. During World War II he served with the Australian Army, rising to the rank of major. In 1949 he was elected to the national House of Representatives, and after entering the government in 1951 he served successively as minister for navy and air, minister for social services, minister for primary industry, and minister for labor and national service. He distinguished himself as treasurer, Australia's key economic post, from 1966 to 1969, continuing in that office in the Gorton cabinet after making an unsuccessful bid to become prime minister in 1968. Appointed minister for external affairs in 1969, he reorganized his department to obtain greater efficiency, and changed his title to minister of foreign affairs. He strongly supported U. S. military involvement in Vietnam, and promoted friendly relations with neighboring countries.

HENRY S. SLOAN

UPI

(Above) WILLIAM McMAHON, prime minister of Australia, and his family. *(Left)* GEORGE MEANY, president of AFL-CIO.

WIDE WORLD

MEANY, George

George Meany, president of the 13.6 million-member AFL-CIO, emerged in 1971 as one of the chief domestic adversaries of President Nixon. Meany had originally assumed a "wait-and-see" attitude when Nixon took office in 1969, but he soon became increasingly critical of administration policies that he considered biased against labor. Although Meany had generally supported Nixon on the Vietnam War and on other foreign policy issues, he denounced the President's announcement in July 1971 that he would visit Communist China early in 1972.

When President Nixon, without consulting labor, announced the 90-day wage-price freeze in August as the first phase of his new economic program, Meany at first threatened noncooperation. He decided to go along with the program after being assured that the Pay Board to be set up under Phase II would have real authority, and he agreed to serve as one of its labor members.

The dispute between Meany and the President reached a climax at the AFL-CIO convention at Miami Beach in November. Denouncing the Pay Board's decision not to grant retroactive payment of wage increases cancelled during the freeze, Meany charged that the government sought to destroy the concept of collective bargaining. The coolness with which President Nixon's address to the convention was received by Meany and the delegates was seen as tantamount to a break in relations between labor and the administration. The convention delegates reelected Meany by acclamation and, in apparent defiance of the administration, voted to increase his salary from $70,000 to $90,000 a year.

William George Meany was born in New York City on Aug. 16, 1894. He dropped out of school at 16 to become an apprentice plumber and received his journeyman's certificate in 1915. By 1922 he was business agent of his union local, and in 1934 he was elected president of the New York State Federation of Labor. He became secretary-treasurer of the American Federation of Labor in 1939, and during World War II he served on the War Labor Board. After the war he was a prime mover in the massive expansion of organized labor and in the drive against communism and corruption in the union movement. He became president of the AFL in 1952 and was unanimously elected president of the newly merged AFL-CIO in 1955.

HENRY S. SLOAN

MEIR, Golda

Israeli Premier Golda Meir continued in 1971 to seek support for her country in its conflict with Egypt. She reaffirmed Israel's willingness to withdraw to "secure, recognized, and agreed boundaries" as part of a general peace settlement arrived at through direct negotiations with Arab countries. But she rejected proposals made by UN negotiator Gunnar Jarring that Israel commit itself to withdrawal to pre–1967 armistice lines. On the domestic scene, her coalition government was faced with problems of labor unrest, poverty, communal strife, crime, and tensions between the religious and secular communities.

Mrs. Meir asserted that the existing cease-fire between Israel and Egypt could be maintained only if Soviet aid to Egypt was balanced by a continued flow of arms from the United States to Israel. During the year some friction developed between the United States and Israel over U. S. reluctance to continue to supply Israel with Phantom jets. Mrs. Meir was also troubled by what she considered Secretary of State William Rogers' partiality to Egypt in his effort to negotiate an interim settlement for the reopening of the Suez Canal. On November 30, she made an extended visit to the United States to establish a more solid relationship between the two governments and to make U. S. officials aware of Israel's needs. In discussions with President Nixon, Mrs. Meir received assurances that the United States would not permit the balance of power in the Middle East to shift against Israel, and she expressed willingness to resume the stalled negotiations for an interim settlement, provided she could do so without preconditions.

JÓZSEF CARDINAL MINDSZENTY (*left*), Hungarian primate, receives Pope Paul's Vatican Council ring during emotional reunion at Vatican in September.

UPI

Mrs. Meir was born Golda Mabovitch in Kiev, Russia, on May 3, 1898. She went to the United States in 1906 and grew up in Milwaukee, Wis., where she attended a teachers' training college and became active in Socialist and Zionist movements. In 1917 she married Morris Meyerson, with whom she immigrated to Palestine in 1921. After working on a kibbutz she became associated with Histadruth, the labor confederation, and played an active role in organizations engaged in the building of a Jewish state. She was one of the signers of Israel's proclamation of independence in May 1948, and in 1948–49 she was Israel's first minister to the Soviet Union. She also served as minister of labor (1949–56), foreign minister (1956–66), and secretary general of the Mapai party (1966–68). She was sworn in as Israel's fourth premier on March 17, 1969.

HENRY S. SLOAN

MINDSZENTY, József Cardinal

József Cardinal Mindszenty, Roman Catholic primate of Hungary, ended nearly 15 years of self-imposed asylum on Sept. 28, 1971, when he left the sanctuary of the U. S. embassy in Budapest and flew to the Vatican. An outspoken opponent of communism, Mindszenty had become an international symbol of eastern European church-state struggles of the cold war when he was sentenced to life imprisonment by the Hungarian Communist government in 1949. The cardinal had consistently rejected any arrangement for his freedom that failed to provide for his rehabilitation by the government. But he finally agreed to accept what he called "the heaviest cross of my life" and leave his native country permanently at the request of Pope Paul VI, who had been seeking improved relations with Communist governments and was concerned about Mindszenty's health. His departure was arranged by an agreement between the Vatican and the Hungarian government, by which the latter indirectly rescinded the 1949 conviction by its tacit acknowledgment of the cardinal's position. On October 23, Cardinal Mindszenty left the Vatican for Vienna, where he was expected to live permanently.

József Mindszenty, whose original surname was Pehm, was born on March 29, 1892, in the village of Csehimindszent, where his father had served as mayor. He was educated at a seminary in Szombathely and was ordained a priest in 1915. During Hungary's brief period of Communist rule in 1919, Mindszenty was arrested as an opponent of the regime. He served as a parish priest after World War I, and during the 1930's he published a newspaper that denounced the growing influence of nazism. He was arrested after the German occupation of Hungary in 1944, the year he was named bishop of Veszprém, but was freed the following year when Soviet troops captured Budapest.

With his appointment as archbishop of Esztergom in 1945, Mindszenty became prince primate of Hungary, and he was elevated to the Sacred College of Cardinals in 1946. His opposition to the Communist regime led to his arrest in 1948 on charges of treason and currency violations, and in 1949 he was sentenced to life imprisonment. He was briefly freed during the Hungarian revolt in 1956, but after it was suppressed by Soviet forces he fled to the asylum of the U. S. embassy.

HENRY S. SLOAN

MITCHELL, John Newton

Amid reports that he would soon be leaving the cabinet to manage Richard M. Nixon's 1972 campaign, Attorney General John N. Mitchell continued to administer Department of Justice affairs competently and to maintain close personal relations with the President.

The sharp social fissures that had developed in the country seemed to ease somewhat in 1971, but disputes over student busing, the illegal drug traffic, internal surveillance methods, and voting rights continued.

Mitchell cooperated with the President's directive that busing be held to a minimum. He worked out a voluntary quota by drug manufacturers on the production of amphetamines and methamphetamines. In May, he issued guidelines on voting in seven Southern states. He supported the mass arrests carried out by the District of Columbia police during the May antiwar demonstrations. In a midyear report, he noted that violent crimes in the nation had increased by 11% and serious crimes of all sorts by 7%.

When critics in Congress and elsewhere called for the dismissal of FBI Director J. Edgar Hoover, Mitchell issued a strong statement of support for Hoover, his nominal subordinate.

Mitchell sought indictments of persons involved in the removal of the "Pentagon Papers" from their security cover, but he failed in the attempt to restrain their publication by the New York *Times* and other large newspapers.

Mitchell announced that the American Bar Association would no longer screen prospective nominees to the U. S. Supreme Court. Mitchell had been angered when ABA committee opposition to two prospective nominees became public. Later, William H. Rehnquist, an assistant to Mitchell, and Lewis F. Powell, Jr., both recommended by the attorney general but not screened by the ABA, were confirmed by the Senate.

Career. Mitchell was born in Detroit, Mich., on Sept. 5, 1913. He practiced law in New York and, after serving in the Navy in World War II, met Nixon when their law firms merged in 1967. A close friendship developed between Mitchell and Nixon, and he managed Nixon's 1968 campaign for President. He was sworn in as attorney general on Jan. 22, 1969. Mitchell's wife, Martha, continued to attract the attention of the media in 1971 for her outspoken and lively comments on public issues.

WALTER DARNELL JACOBS

MORTON, Rogers C. B.

Former congressman and Republican party chairman Rogers C. B. Morton succeeded Walter J. Hickel as the Nixon administration's secretary of the interior on Jan. 29, 1971. He focused his attention during the year on the problem of balancing the growing demands of industrial society with conservationists' concern for preserving national resources. He won the approval of environmentalists by delaying indefinitely the construction of the controversial trans-Alaska oil pipeline and by declaring that no offshore oil drilling would be sanctioned without full consideration of possible effects on the environment. Taking what he calls a "common sense" approach to conservation, he told a group of conservationists in New Jersey in September that they would have to live with more power plants, offshore oil wells, bridges, and highways, but he also stressed the need for preserving parklands and wilderness areas. In response to demands by militant American Indian civil rights groups, Morton pledged in October that the Bureau of Indian Affairs would be subjected to thoroughgoing reform, with increased emphasis on self-determination for Indians.

A member of a socially prominent Kentucky family, Rogers Clark Ballard Morton was born in Louisville on Sept. 19, 1914. He graduated from Yale University in 1937, and served as a captain in the field artillery during World War II. He then helped his brother Thruston B. Morton in his political campaigns. He was president of the family flour-milling firm, Ballard and Ballard, from 1947 until 1951, when it merged with the Pillsbury Company. In the 1950's he raised cattle and ran a feed business in eastern Maryland.

Morton was elected to the U. S. House of Representatives as a Republican from Maryland in 1962, and served for four consecutive terms. He compiled a generally conservative voting record, while taking a moderately liberal stand on such issues as civil rights and promoting measures to protect the environment. He was unanimously elected chairman of the Republican National Committee in 1969.

HENRY S. SLOAN

MUJIB, Sheikh

Mujibur Rahman, known to his people as Sheikh Mujib, assumed the post of prime minister of the newly proclaimed independent nation of Bangladesh (formerly East Pakistan) on Jan. 13, 1972. He had survived several months of imprisonment in West Pakistan in 1971, narrowly escaping execution at the hands of Pakistani President Agha Mohammed Yahya Khan while the India-Pakistan war was raging in East Pakistan in December.

Sheikh Mujib established himself as the undisputed leader of East Pakistan's Bengali majority in 1970. In that year, his political party, the Awami League, waged a year-long campaign to elect members to a national assembly that was to draft a new civilian constitution for Pakistan, whose government had long been dominated by Punjabi military elements in the less populated western region of the country. In the December 1970 election, Mujib's party, which favored the virtual independence of East Bengal (East Pakistan), won an assembly majority by capturing nearly all of the East Pakistani seats.

Early in 1971, President Yahya Khan cancelled the election result, arrested Mujib, and ordered the suppression of the Bengalis, but Yahya was forced to resign in December after his army had been defeated in East Bengal. His successor, Zulfikar Ali Bhutto, ordered Mujib's release from prison and sought to persuade him to work for the retention of some link between Pakistan's eastern and western wings. Early in January, he allowed Mujib to return to Dacca to assume the presidency of Bangladesh—already recognized as an independent state by India. Decreeing on January 11 that the new nation would have a parliamentary system of government, Mujib surrendered the presidency and assumed the premiership.

The son of a middle-class landowner, Mujibur Rahman was born in Tongipara in East Bengal (then a part of India) on March 17, 1920. As a student at Islamia College in Calcutta and at Dacca University, he engaged in agitation against British rule and suffered the first of several prison terms for political insurgency. A spellbinding orator, Mujib emerged as a leading champion of autonomy for East Pakistan in the mid-1960's. In 1968 his trial with 34 others on charges of conspiring to divide the nation caused widespread protests and hastened the end of the 11-year dictatorship of Ayub Khan.

NADER, Ralph

Known as a "watchdog for the public," consumer advocate Ralph Nader continued to work in 1971 to protect the average citizen from the hazards of an increasingly complex technological and bureaucratic society. Nader, who calls himself a "public interest lawyer," heads the Public Interest Research Group and the Center for the Study of Responsive Law.

Aided by a staff of lawyers and a group of enthusiastic young volunteers, popularly known as "Nader's Raiders," Nader has conducted extensive investigations of corporations, government agencies, and public institutions. He has testified before congressional committees, instituted federal lawsuits in behalf of the public, and lectured extensively throughout the country. Through his recently launched fund-raising organization, Public Citizen, Inc., Nader hopes to promote "an effective citizen's campaign to make government agencies and industry management sensitive and responsive to the needs of the people."

Nader charged on several occasions in 1971 that government and business were collaborating to defraud the public. His charges included assertions that General Motors Corporation had advance knowledge of President Nixon's wage-price freeze, that thousands of workers were killed and disabled annually because of inadequate enforcement of federal health and safety standards, and that Congress had virtually abdicated its role as protector of the public interest. Although Nader has been mentioned as a possible candidate for president, he has steadfastly denied any ambition to seek public office.

The son of Lebanese immigrants, Ralph Nader was born in Winsted, Conn., on Feb. 27, 1934. He graduated with honors from Princeton in 1955, and after receiving his law degree from Harvard in 1958 he entered private law practice. From 1961 to 1963 he lectured on government and history at the University of Hartford. In 1964–65 he was a consultant on auto safety to U. S. Assistant Secretary of Labor Daniel P. Moynihan. Nader's book *Unsafe at Any Speed* (1965) provided the impetus for enactment of the 1966 National Traffic and Motor Vehicle Safety Act. He has successfully lobbied for legislation in such areas as coal mine and gas pipeline safety and the inspection of meat and other consumer products, and he has launched intensive investigations of federal regulatory agencies.

HENRY S. SLOAN

NERUDA, Pablo

Chilean poet and diplomat Pablo Neruda was awarded the 1971 Nobel Prize in Literature "for poetry that, with the action of an elemental force, brings alive a continent's destiny and dreams." He is a member of the central committee of Chile's Communist party and a recipient of the Soviet Union's Lenin and Stalin prizes. Considered by many as Latin America's greatest contemporary poet, Neruda had been nominated for a Nobel Prize on several occasions. In announcing the Nobel award, Karl-Ragnar Gierow, the secretary of the Swedish Academy, noted that Neruda had become "the poet of violated human dignity." In January 1971, Neruda was appointed Chilean ambassador to France.

Neruda, the son of a railroad worker, was born Neftalí Ricardo Reyes Basualto on July 12, 1904, in Parral, southern Chile. He grew up in Temuco and was educated at a teachers college in Santiago. He began to write poetry as a child. At the age of 17 he published his first poems, taking the surname of the Czech writer Jan Neruda as his pen name. He soon developed a highly individual style and became well established with his *Veinte poemas de amor y una canción desesperada* (1924). Appointed to the Chilean consular service in 1927, he served in diplomatic posts in Asia and later in Argentina, Spain, and Mexico. His *Residencia en la tierra* (3 vols., 1933–47), written in a surrealistic vein, earned him recognition as one of the foremost literary figures of the Spanish-speaking world.

Neruda's experiences during the Spanish Civil War aroused his political and social consciousness and ultimately led him to the Communist party. He was elected to the Chilean Senate in 1944. During a period of exile in Mexico he completed his masterpiece, *Canto general* (1950), a Marxist epic of Chile and the South American continent. Among his other major works is his five-volume autobiography in verse *Memorial de Isla Negra* (1964). Neruda was the Communist party's nominee for president of Chile in 1970, but he stepped aside in favor of Salvador Allende, the Socialist candidate of the united left.

HENRY S. SLOAN

NICHOLSON, Jack

Film actor Jack Nicholson typifies the "nonheroic" hero who cannot quite find his place in contemporary society. He attained instant popularity with his sympathetic portrayal of the alcoholic lawyer who befriends Peter Fonda and Dennis Hopper in *Easy Rider* (1969), a portrayal that earned him an Oscar nomination and a New York Film Critics Award as best supporting actor. He received his second Oscar nomination for his starring performance in *Five Easy Pieces* (1970) as a musical prodigy who rejects his aristocratic family background to take up the life of an oil-field laborer. His first venture as a film director, *Drive, He Said*, centering on a college basketball star and a campus radical, caused a stir at the 1971 Cannes film festival because of its candid and unglamorous treatment of sex, but he received some favorable reviews in the United States. In 1971, Nicholson appeared in *Carnal Knowledge*, directed by Mike Nichols and based on a screenplay by Jules Feiffer, tracing the amorous adventures of two college friends from youth to middle age; and *A Safe Place*, co-starring Tuesday Weld and Orson Welles.

Jack Nicholson was born in Neptune, N. J., on April 22, 1937. He began acting in school, where he was known as the "class clown." After graduating from high school he went to California and took a job in the cartoon department of a major studio, studying at the Players Ring Theater in his free time. He gradually drifted into acting, obtaining his first film role, in *Cry Baby Killer*, in 1958. Over the next 10 years he appeared in television soap operas, Westerns, motorcycle films, and horror movies, most of them of minor importance, and he also began to show some promise as a writer and producer. As a result of his contacts as a producer, he was chosen for the role in *Easy Rider*. His next role, as a hippie in *On a Clear Day You Can See Forever* (1970), starring Barbra Streisand, failed to evoke enthusiasm from critics.

HENRY S. SLOAN

JACK NICHOLSON as a glib collegian in *Carnal Knowledge*. Movie also starred Candace Bergen.

PRESIDENT Richard M. Nixon answers questions during visit to a school in San Clemente, Calif.

NIXON, Richard Milhous

The third year of the presidency of Richard Nixon was dominated by a series of dramatic initiatives in foreign policy that confounded his critics and laid the groundwork for his 1972 reelection effort. The President in 1971 characteristically steered a middle course between those on the left who accused him of doing too little and those on the right who threatened to desert him for doing too much.

Foreign Affairs. The war in Vietnam showed signs in 1971 of responding to President Nixon's de-escalation moves. By the end of the year he had announced the planned withdrawal of all but 139,000 of the 543,000 U. S. troops that had been in Vietnam when he took office. Combat involvement of U. S. ground troops had almost come to an end, although air strikes continued unabated.

President Nixon's efforts to improve relations with the People's Republic of China were capped by his announcement of plans to visit Peking and by the reversal of the long-standing U. S. policy on the admission of Communist China to the United Nations. In October the Communist Chinese were admitted to the world body, and the Nationalist regime on Taiwan was ousted over the objections of the United States, which supported a "two-China policy" designed to permit UN membership for both Chinese governments.

Presidential adviser Henry Kissinger made two trips to Peking to complete arrangements for the President's announced visit in February 1972. Late in 1971 plans for a presidential trip to Moscow in 1972 were announced, and Nixon began several preliminary visits with the heads of government of major U. S. allies.

Relations with Congress. President Nixon's 1971 State of the Union message enumerated six goals of his administration: revenue sharing, welfare reform, additional environmental initiatives, health insurance reform, governmental reorganization, and full employment. By the end of the year none of his proposals had been accomplished. Administration spokesmen blamed the Democratic-controlled Congress, while the Democrats blamed the administration for its lack of initiative.

Economic Policy. Efforts to curb inflation and unemployment had eluded President Nixon during the first three years of his administration. But in a dramatic television announcement on August 15, the President froze wages, prices, and rents for 90 days and set up temporary administrative mechanisms to administer the freeze. He asked Congress for new legislation to grant investment tax credits on an accelerated schedule, to

remove the excise tax on automobiles, and to speed up scheduled increases in personal tax exemptions. The program also included a 10% surtax on imports and suspension of the $35-per-ounce fixed price for gold on the international market. On December 18 the President announced that as part of a 10-nation monetary agreement the U. S. dollar would be devalued 8.57%. He also announced that the 10% import surtax would be lifted.

After the first two months of the freeze, Nixon established much of the Phase II program by executive order, establishing a Pay Board with five representatives each from the public, organized labor, and management, and a seven-member Price Commission. Politically, the moves appeared to be popular with the general public but angered organized labor and caused a major rift between the AFL-CIO leadership and the White House.

Nominations. The resignations of Supreme Court Associate Justices Hugo Black and John Harlan presented the President with his third and fourth high court vacancies. After several weeks of public speculation President Nixon nominated Lewis F. Powell, a highly respected former president of the American Bar Association, and William H. Rehnquist, an assistant attorney general. The nomination of Powell was generally well received, and the Senate promptly confirmed him with only one dissenting vote. The Rehnquist nomination was challenged by a number of senators concerned with his activist conservative legal philosophy. But he was confirmed by a vote of 68 to 26.

The President became involved in another political controversy over his nomination of Earl Butz to succeed Clifford Hardin as secretary of agriculture. Butz was charged with a lack of sympathy for or understanding of the small farmer but was confirmed by the Senate in a close vote.

Background. Richard M. Nixon was born in Yorba Linda, Calif., on Jan. 9, 1913. After service in the Navy during World War II he was elected to the House from California in 1946 and to the Senate in 1950. He served as vice president during both terms of President Eisenhower and received the Republican nomination for president in 1960. After being narrowly defeated by John F. Kennedy, he returned to California, where he ran for governor and lost in 1962. He then joined a Wall Street law firm in New York City, but maintained his interest in Republican party affairs. He was nominated and elected president in 1968 after one of the most striking comebacks in U. S. political history.

ROBERT J. HUCKSHORN

PAUL VI, Pope

Much of Pope Paul's energy during 1971 was occupied by the World Synod of Bishops, which met in Rome in October. It supported him in his insistence on clerical celibacy (see RELIGION—*Roman Catholicism*). The pope also devoted much time to working for world peace. Although his pleas to both India and Pakistan to end their strife went largely unheeded, his voice continued to be raised in the cause of peace.

The pope's special concern with social justice, particularly in the Third World, was expressed in an apostolic letter dated May 14, the 80th anniversary of Leo XIII's great encyclical of social reform, *Rerum novarum*. In the letter, Paul reiterated his earlier statement: "Today the principal fact that we must all recognize is that the social question has become worldwide." In addition, he stressed the rights of women, the right of people to emigrate, and the new social needs brought about by massive urbanization and changes in the environment. Some observers noted that this lengthy, 12,000-word document hardly mentioned the pressing problems of increasing world population and birth control.

Illustrating the pope's concern for both peace and the poor was the establishment of a new award, the Pope John XXIII Peace Prize. Paul presented the $25,000 prize, on the feast of the Epiphany to Mother Teresa, an Albanian-born nun, who had founded the Missionaries of Charity in India. The choice of Mother Teresa, whose lifework has been carried out among the very poorest of Calcutta, was widely praised.

Also concerned with ecumenism, the pope, with the archbishop of Canterbury, approved a joint Anglican-Roman Catholic document stating common beliefs about the Eucharist. On October 25 the pope met in Rome with Ignatius Jacob III, patriarch of Antioch of the Syrian Orthodox, or Jacobite, Church. It was the first such meeting since the Jacobite Church broke relations with the rest of the Christian church 1,520 years ago for what was considered its heretical monophysite doctrine about the nature of Christ. The pope and the patriarch issued a declaration of their common heritage and intentions of future cooperation.

In the area of theology the pope remained outside a discussion over what has historically been one of the most disputed attributes of his office, that of infallibility. *Infallible? An Inquiry* (1970; trans. 1971) by Hans Küng, a theologian at Tübingen University, challenges traditional Catholic teaching that the pope is infallible. The book, which was widely read in 1971, provoked controversy, notably between Küng and his former teacher, the liberal theologian Karl Rahner, who held that Küng's position was extreme. The German bishops issued a statement on the book that defended the position of the Roman Catholic Church. Italian bishops later produced a similar statement.

The pope ended the year with a typically cautionary address to members of the Curia warning of dangers facing the church. He also, however, noted "a growth in self-awareness within [the] ranks of the Roman Catholic Church" as a major accomplishment of 1971 and indeed of the years since Vatican Council II. The pope made no mention of his possible resignation from office in 1972, when he will reach 75, the age he has recommended for the retirement of other bishops. Speculation continues as to whether he will take the almost unprecedented step of retiring.

C. J. MCNASPY, S. J.

PICASSO, Pablo

Pablo Picasso, one of the great creative geniuses in the world of art, was honored on his 90th birthday in 1971 throughout the civilized world. In France, where he has made his home for many years, he was acclaimed by the government, and the Riviera town of Vallauris, near Mougins, where he lives in seclusion with his wife, Jacqueline, staged an international festival in his honor. In New York, celebrations of the event were highlighted by a retrospective exhibition, "Hommage à Picasso," at the Saidenberg Gallery. An avowed enemy of the Franco regime, Picasso received no official recognition on the occasion from the government of his native Spain. However, the influential Spanish news magazine *Mundo* proclaimed him "Spaniard of the Year" for 1971.

Picasso's longevity appears to have brought no slackening of his creative powers, and he has continued to produce an abundance of paintings, drawings, etchings, ceramics, and sculptures. His play *The Four Little Girls*, a surrealist evocation of scenes of childhood, had its premiere in London in December 1971.

Background. Picasso, who was born in Málaga, Spain, on Oct. 25, 1881, learned the rudiments of art during childhood from his father, a Basque drawing teacher, and studied at the School of Fine Arts in Barcelona. Influenced by French impressionist and post-impressionist painters, he embarked on his "blue period" about 1902, depicting the seamy side of life in Barcelona, and in Paris, where he settled in 1904. His "rose period" of 1905–6, reflecting a more positive outlook, is represented by such paintings as his *Boy Leading a Horse,* and his portrait of Gertrude Stein. With his *Demoiselles d'Avignon* (1907), influenced by the distortions he found in African sculptures, he heralded the worldwide movement of cubism, which separates components of natural objects into geometric forms and reassembles them according to the artist's subjective vision.

About 1915, Picasso returned to naturalism, and his work during the next few years included the design of costumes and scenery for Diaghilev's ballets in Rome. In the late 1920's he began to experiment with surrealism. A champion of the Loyalist cause in the Span-

PABLO PICASSO, foremost painter of the 20th century, celebrated his 90th birthday in October.

WIDE WORLD   UPI

LEWIS F. POWELL, JR. (*left*) and WILLIAM REHNQUIST were seated on Supreme Court in 1971. They brought total of Nixon's high court appointees to four.

ish Civil War, Picasso expressed his rage at the Fascist bombing of an undefended Basque town in his gigantic surrealist painting *Guernica* (1937), which is considered his masterpiece. His works of recent years, including landscapes, portraits, scenes from classical mythology, and reinterpretation of some of his earlier paintings, reflect a partial return to naturalism. A member of the French Communist party since 1944, Picasso was twice awarded the Lenin Peace Prize. His lithograph *Peace Dove* (1949) became the symbol of the World Peace Congress. "I've never believed in doing painting for the 'happy few' . . . ," Picasso once said. "I want to provide something for every level of thinking."

HENRY S. SLOAN

POMPIDOU, Georges

The year 1971 confirmed previous impressions that President Pompidou intended to be a strong though not inflexible chief of state. His statements reflected the orthodox Gaullist line, but his approach to domestic and international problems was entirely independent.

Politically, he insisted on retaining personal control of the Union of Democrats for the Republic (UDR) and beat back an attempt to have it elect a party president. As inheritor of de Gaulle's mantle, he refused to permit this party to be called a party, insisting that it was "a movement" unlike other political organizations. Yet he seemed unable or unwilling to prevent cabinet ministers from displaying the rifts developing among the Gaullists. Accused by his critics of being a latter-day Louis Philippe, he was, nevertheless, backed by a substantial majority in the National Assembly and presided without serious challenge over a prosperous but not untroubled nation.

Leaving routine domestic chores to the premier, Pompidou played the cautious role of a chief of state, aware of the limited options open to him in international relations. Though irked by the evident prestige and independence of West German Chancellor Willy Brandt, he refused to outbid him in dealing with the Soviet Union. At the same time, he decided to drop France's veto against British membership in the Common Market. The initiatives he permitted his foreign minister to take indicated an eclectic policy, based on the maximization of limited resources and the goal of damping down international conflicts.

One of Pompidou's major achievements on the international scene in 1971 came with the currency realignments announced in December. His talks with U. S. President Nixon in the Azores that month produced an agreement on the part of the United States to devalue the dollar, a move that Pompidou had insisted upon during the long currency crisis. Meanwhile, France maintained the par value of the franc.

Background. Pompidou was born in Montboudif on July 5, 1911. He was a brilliant teacher before joining de Gaulle's staff in 1944. Having served the general discreetly, he went over to banking with the Rothschilds in 1951. De Gaulle, returning to power in 1958, "borrowed" him for six months, offered him a ministry the next year, but permitted him to return to banking as director-general of the Rothschild house.

In April 1962, Pompidou was named premier. His partnership with de Gaulle lasted through the momentous strikes and disorders of 1968, with Pompidou rescuing the president from the consequences of his misunderstandings and miscalculations, only to be discharged for his success and evident ambition. Following de Gaulle's resignation in the spring of 1969, Pompidou stepped forward to seek the presidency and was elected by 58% of the vote.

JOHN C. CAIRNS

POWELL, Lewis F., Jr.

The distinguished Virginia lawyer Lewis F. Powell, Jr., was nominated by President Nixon on Oct. 21, 1971, as associate justice of the U. S. Supreme Court, to fill the seat formerly occupied by the late Hugo L. Black. Powell, whose appointment was generally seen as meeting the President's aim of placing a Southern conservative on the nation's highest tribunal, describes himself as "a lawyer who believes in the judicial . . . and constitutional system" but rejects such labels as "strict constructionist," although he is expected to align himself with the high court's conservative bloc, led by Chief Justice Warren E. Burger.

In recent articles and speeches Powell dismissed the charge that the U. S. is a repressive society as "standard leftist propaganda" and condemned demonstrators who go beyond their constitutional rights by "occupying buildings and tying up traffic." He also defended government use of wiretapping in serious criminal and national security cases. On the other hand, he has a reputation as a liberal on racial matters and a champion of equal justice for the poor, and for his critical of police and prosecutors who are "overzealous" in trying to obtain criminal convictions. Unanimously endorsed by the Senate judiciary committee, Powell was confirmed by a Senate vote of 89 to 1 on December 6. He was sworn in as associate justice on Jan. 7, 1972.

A member of a prominent Southern family, Lewis Franklin Powell, Jr., was born in Suffolk, in southeastern Virginia, on Sept. 19, 1907. He graduated *magna cum laude* from Washington and Lee University in 1929 and obtained his LL. B. degree there in 1931. After qualifying for the LL. M. degree at Harvard Law School in 1932 he practiced law in Richmond, becoming a partner in the illustrious law firm of Hunton, Williams, Gay, Powell & Gibson in 1938. During World War II he was a combat and intelligence officer in the Army Air Force and rose to the rank of colonel.

As chairman of the Richmond public school board from 1952 to 1961, Powell supervised the smooth racial integration of the city's public schools, and after a trip to the USSR in 1958 he introduced a course on life under communism and classes in the Russian language in the Richmond school system. During the Johnson administration, Powell, who is a Democrat, served on the president's Commission on Law Enforcement and Administration of Justice. He was president of the American Bar Association in 1964–65 and of the American College of Trial Lawyers in 1969–70, and was chosen president of the American Bar Foundation in 1969.

HENRY S. SLOAN

REHNQUIST, William H.

Assistant Attorney General William H. Rehnquist was nominated by President Nixon on Oct. 21, 1971, to occupy the U. S. Supreme Court seat vacated by the retirement of Associate Justice John Marshall Harlan. Rehnquist, who is a protégé of Deputy Attorney General Richard Kleindienst, has headed the Justice Department's Office of Legal Counsel since joining the Nixon administration in early 1969. Described as the "President's lawyer's lawyer," he has been "chief interpreter for the whole administration of the Constitution and the statutes," according to Nixon, who said that Rehnquist has "one of the finest legal minds" in the country and "rates at the very top as a constitutional lawyer."

In the weeks that followed the nomination, controversy built up around the choice of Rehnquist. His critics charged that he had been an activist for right-wing causes and had consistently opposed civil rights measures. He was also denounced by some as the Nixon administration's chief defender of the use of wiretapping and other means of surveillance against those suspected of subversive activities. Despite the objections of spokesmen for labor, civil rights, and liberal organizations, Rehnquist's appointment was approved on December 10 by a Senate vote of 68 to 26, and he took his seat on the Supreme Court in January 1972.

William Hubbs Rehnquist was born in Milwaukee, Wis., on Oct. 1, 1924. He served in the Army Air Force in World War II, graduated from Stanford University "with great distinction" in 1948, obtained a master's degree from Harvard in 1950, and ranked first in his class when he received his law degree from Stanford in 1952. After serving as law clerk to the late Supreme Court Justice Robert H. Jackson in 1952–53, Rehnquist settled in Phoenix, Ariz., where he entered private law practice and became active in community affairs and Republican politics. In 1964 he was a strong supporter of the presidential campaign of Sen. Barry Goldwater.

HENRY S. SLOAN

ROGERS, William P.

War on the Asian subcontinent and a threat of war in the Middle East dominated an active year for Secretary of State William P. Rogers in 1971. The year also saw a sweeping change in U.S. policy toward China and continued U.S. attempts to improve relations with the Soviet Union.

In the Middle East, Rogers and his assistant, Joseph J. Sisco, searched for a formula for a peace agreement between Israel and Egypt. With the USSR providing supplies and advisers to Egypt and the United States providing some supplies to Israel, the situation remained critical, and a renewal of hostilities in the area was feared. On the subcontinent, war broke out between India and Pakistan in spite of attempts by Rogers to cool tempers. In this area, the USSR gave aid to India, while mainland China appeared to be supporting Pakistan.

Rogers kept in close touch with Moscow and participated in the signing of agreements to reduce the risk of nuclear war. He also oversaw U.S. participation in the Strategic Arms Limitation Talks and responded to Soviet initiatives for talks on mutually balanced force reductions in Europe.

The U.S. attitude toward China was declared by Rogers to be one of support for membership of Peking in the United Nations while maintaining a UN seat for Taiwan. The General Assembly, however, voted to oust the Taiwan representative. Rogers expressed his disappointment at this action. As presidential adviser Henry A. Kissinger made two trips to Peking and seemed to be more prominent in Chinese affairs than Rogers, the question of relations between the two men was again raised. A State Department spokesman said that Rogers "has played and continues to play a decisive role in foreign policy decisions."

Background. William Pierce Rogers was born in Norfolk, N.Y., on June 23, 1913. He obtained a B.A. from Colgate University and an LL.B. from Cornell Law School. After serving as assistant district attorney to Thomas E. Dewey he served in the Navy in World War II. He met Richard Nixon after the war while acting as counsel to U.S. Senate committees dealing with government expenditures. He was deputy attorney general (1953–57) and attorney general (1957–61). He practiced law until he became secretary of state in Nixon's cabinet in 1969.

WALTER DARNELL JACOBS

RUCKELSHAUS, William D.

The Nixon administration undertook a campaign during 1971 for the protection of the quality of air, water, and other natural resources through its Environmental Protection Agency, launched in December 1970 under the direction of William D. Ruckelshaus. Convinced that the environmental crisis necessitates a drastic change in the attitudes of those in responsible positions, Ruckelshaus has said: "We are the victims of a point of view which has long been obsolete, ... that man can conquer nature. We have clung to this vision with such tenacity that we now inherit the spoils of a 300-year war against nature."

During 1971, Ruckelshaus initiated legal actions against several industrial firms charged with polluting waterways, took steps to force cities to bring sewage treatment plants up to federal standards, and applied pressure on the automobile industry to reduce the carbon monoxide emission of its engines in accordance with the 1970 Clean Air Act. Conservationists approved Ruckelshaus' action of requesting the Interior Department in March to delay construction of a controversial oil pipeline through Alaska, but criticized his refusal to enforce a total ban on such substances as DDT, pending further study.

A member of a family long active in law and Republican politics, William Doyle Ruckelshaus was born in Indianapolis, Ind., on July 24, 1932. He graduated from Princeton *cum laude* in 1957 and received his doctorate in law from Harvard in 1960. He then practiced as an attorney with his family's Indianapolis law firm, while serving as a deputy, and then as chief counsel, in the state attorney general's office. He was elected to the Indiana House of Representatives in 1966, and made an unsuccessful bid for the U.S. Senate seat held by Birch Bayh in 1968. In 1969 he was appointed assistant attorney general in the civil division of the Justice Department. Given the task of negotiating with militant student antiwar demonstrators in Washington in the spring of 1970, he was credited with having averted a violent confrontation through his conciliatory attitude.

HENRY S. SLOAN

SADAT, Anwar el-

Anwar el-Sadat became president of Egypt after the death of Nasser in September 1970. His first weeks in office were uncertain ones, but in the course of 1971 he steadily increased his power and prestige. He no longer rules Egypt as the successor to Nasser but rather in his own right.

Sadat consolidated his position most notably in May 1971, when he removed from his cabinet a number of rivals who, he alleged, had attempted a coup against him. Among those ousted were the ministers of war and the interior as well as Aly Sabry, vice president and one of the original officers who led the coup against King Farouk in 1952. Sadat also purged several hundred military officers and other officials.

In July, Sadat presented a new 10-year plan for social and economic development. He also introduced a new, more liberal constitution, which was approved by referendum in September. Other popular measures announced during the year included the end of telephone tapping and the return of some properties confiscated by the government during the Nasser years.

Sadat's principal achievement in foreign affairs was the establishment of the Federation of Arab Republics,

a union of Egypt, Libya, and Syria, which was agreed upon in April. A 15-year Soviet-Egyptian treaty was signed in May, and Sadat visited Moscow in October, although he had been sharply critical of communism in previous weeks. He also met repeatedly with U. S. officials during the year with the aim of developing some plan to alleviate the critical Egyptian-Israeli situation.

The Arab-Israeli conflict continued, however. In July, Sadat vowed that he would do something before year-end to drive Israel out of Arab territory, and in November he declared his intention of going to war. However, there was no resumption of fighting by the end of the year.

Background. Anwar el-Sadat was born on Dec. 25, 1918, in the village of Talah Monufiya in the Nile delta. In 1936 he entered the Abbassia Military Academy where he met Gamal Abdel Nasser. The two became close friends. In 1938, Nasser and Sadat formed a secret group with 10 other army officers to work for the liberation of Egypt from its feudal monarchy and from British influence. This group formed the nucleus of the Free Officers' Committee that overthrew King Farouk in 1952.

Though influential, Sadat did not hold prominent office in Nasser's government until 1969, when he was appointed vice president. In this capacity, he succeeded automatically to the presidency when Nasser died on Sept. 28, 1970. He was elected president in his own right on Oct. 15, 1970, and within a year had shown himself to be a shrewd, competent, and resourceful leader.

CARL LEIDEN

SATO, Eisaku

Eisaku Sato, Japan's 62d prime minister, formed his fourth cabinet in July 1971. His reelection in October 1970 as president of the Liberal Democratic party (LDP) made him the first person to be chosen for that post four times in succession. By 1971 he had surpassed the record (6 years, 2 months) for holding the premiership, previously established by his mentor, the late Shigeru Yoshida.

The prime minister is so cautious that associates say "he would tap his way across a stone bridge." He is one of a succession of post-world War II bureaucrat-politicians including Premiers Yoshida, Nobusuke Kishi, and Hayato Ikeda. Ikeda nominated Sato as his successor, and Sato was first elected prime minister by the Diet on Nov. 9, 1964. His party won the first general election under his leadership on Jan. 29, 1967. Reelected prime minister on February 17, Sato formed his second cabinet. Reelected president of the majority LDP in 1968, he won a resounding victory in his second general election on Dec. 27, 1969. He formed his third cabinet in January 1970.

Policy. In his policy speech to the Diet on July 17, 1971, Sato said that Japan's aim during the 1970's would be "to bring about a new harmony between man and nature and between man and his environment." He stressed the utmost importance of maintaining good relations with the United States. Also, while continuing recognition of the Republic of China (Taiwan), Sato promised that he would promote interchange with the People's Republic of China (mainland China).

Doubtless the capstone of Sato's career was the signature, on June 17, 1971, of a treaty with the United States providing for the return of Okinawa to Japan. Approval by the U. S. Senate and by Japan's House of Representatives in November 1971 seemed to assure the island's return in 1972.

Late in 1971, however, Sato's faction in the ruling LDP was under heavy pressure following major changes in U. S. foreign and economic policies. The Japanese were concerned over the abrupt shift of the U. S. policy toward China, worried about implications of the U. S. dollar defense plan, and angered over Sato's submission to U. S. President Richard Nixon's ultimatum concerning textile trade. Newsmen predicted that the

prime minister's long career would end after the restoration of Okinawa in 1972.

Early Career. Eisaku Sato was born on March 27, 1901, in Yamaguchi prefecture. After graduation from Tokyo (Imperial) University in 1924, he entered the ministry of railways. After World War II, he was chosen by Premier Yoshida to be chief cabinet secretary. Later he served as minister of finance and as state minister for the Olympic Games held in Tokyo in 1964. Sato and his wife, Hiroko, were married in 1926. Their two sons are in business. His brother is the former premier Nobusuke Kishi, whose name was changed upon adoption by an uncle.

ARDATH W. BURKS

STAUBACH, Roger

Players at the Dallas Cowboys' 1968 training camp were surprised to find a 26-year-old Navy lieutenant on leave working out with them. Like many fans, they had forgotten Roger Staubach, the quarterback who had won the Heisman Trophy in his junior year at the Naval Academy. Staubach, however, was still of a mind to play pro football, and he had a contract with the Cowboys. It had been drawn up rather casually after Dallas had picked him 10th in the draft five years previously.

After graduating from the Naval Academy, Staubach had four years to serve in the Navy. He kept in shape even while serving as the head of a dock unit for a year in Vietnam. Then he was assigned to the Pensacola (Fla.) Naval Station and played quarterback on its football team.

Staubach first played football at Purcell High in Cincinnati, where he was born on Feb. 5, 1942. After a year at New Mexico Military Institute, he was appointed to Annapolis. He set academy records by gaining 4,235 yards passing and running, and he completed 63.6% of his passes. He won the Heisman Trophy as the best college player of 1963 and was picked as the outstanding player in two wire-service polls.

After reporting as a 27-year-old rookie to the Cowboys in 1969, Staubach remained tenacious in his desire and finally became starting quarterback midway through the 1971 season. His ability to run with the ball and to scramble in evasion of a pass rush had much to do with his success.

On being selected the outstanding player in the 1972 Super Bowl game, the modest-living Staubach characteristically asked that his prize be a station wagon instead of the usual sports car. He revealed that religion was a strong influence in his life. He had been an altar boy and has continued to live by the tenets of his faith. Staubach and his wife, Marianne, have three daughters.

BILL BRADDOCK

STEIN, Herbert

Herbert Stein, chairman of the U. S. Council of Economic Advisers, and the chief architect of Phase II of the Nixon administration's New Economic Policy, was appointed by the President on Nov. 24, 1971, to succeed Paul W. McCracken as chairman of the 3-member council effective Jan. 1, 1972. Stein, who belongs to the University of Chicago group of economists, is a fiscal conservative and a strong believer in a free-market economy.

Although Stein had long been opposed to government intervention in private wage and price decisions, he became convinced in 1971 that "radical surgery" was needed to cope with mounting inflation. He was one of a small group of economists present at Camp David in August, when Nixon decided on his new economic program, including an immediate 90-day freeze on wages and prices. Stein headed the task force that did the preliminary planning for Phase II of the program —the first effort to impose peacetime wage and price controls in U. S. history—which went into effect after the freeze, on November 14, and established guidelines for wages, prices, and dividends. He is also responsible for overseeing its effectiveness and proposing remedies where needed.

Stein has warned business executives not to expect the stabilization policy to be "designed or executed in the image of the business community." He regards Phase II as a temporary expedient, reflecting "realities of life" and the existing "balance of power," and he has suggested that it "bears about the same relation to the freeze as an occupation bears to a war." In his view, Phase II, which he expects to end in 1973, will go a long way toward curbing inflation, as well as reducing unemployment.

The son of a machinist, Stein was born in Detroit, Mich., on Aug. 27, 1916. Influenced by the Depression in becoming an economist, he graduated from Williams College in 1935 and received his Ph. D. from the University of Chicago. He began his government career in 1938 with the Federal Deposit Insurance Corporation. During World War II he worked successively for the National Defense Advisory Commission, the Wage-Price Board, and the Office of War Mobilization, and he served for a time in the naval reserves. After 22 years on the staff of the privately supported Committee for Economic Development, he became a senior fellow with the Brookings Institution. After Nixon was elected president in 1968, he appointed Stein to the Council of Economic Advisers. Stein is the author of *The Fiscal Revolution in America* (1969).

HENRY S. SLOAN

SUHARTO

President Suharto of Indonesia took his country an important step forward on the road to democracy in 1971. Under his leadership, Indonesia in July held its first national elections since 1955. Although voters apparently were subjected to some pressure by government officials and the army, the elections took place peacefully. The government party, Sekber Golkar, won about two thirds of the elective seats in the House of Representatives.

Background. Suharto was born on June 8, 1921, near Djokjakarta, in central Java. His military career began with service in the Netherlands Indies army before World War II. He served in the local defense corps during the Japanese occupation, and after the war he took part in the struggle for independence from the Netherlands. An alert, efficient officer, he rose steadily in the ranks of the army of the Republic of Indonesia, and he was a lieutenant general at the time of the abortive Communist coup in Indonesia in 1965.

The coup precipitated a national crisis, and, although shy and modest, General Suharto took command and crushed the revolt. Soon after he was named army chief of staff, and on Feb. 1, 1966, he became defense minister.

President Sukarno's foreign and domestic policies had brought economic and political chaos to Indonesia. It became increasingly clear that the president had almost certainly been involved in the attempted coup. Still, Suharto did not proceed directly against him, since Sukarno had considerable popular support. Shrewdly, Suharto maneuvered the flamboyant president into issuing in his own name decrees that gradually stripped him of his powers. Threatened by continued disorders and hostile demonstrations, Sukarno agreed to transfer executive power to Suharto on March 12, 1966. In June the People's Consultative Congress confirmed Suharto as head of the government, made him acting president on March 12, 1967, and a year later unanimously elected him president for a 5-year term.

Suharto's austere economic measures and his reversal of Sukarno's domestic and foreign policies gradually brought order to Indonesia. President Suharto has been characterized as a rock with flexibility.

AMRY VANDENBOSCH

THANT, U

The Burmese statesman U Thant completed his 10th year as secretary-general of the United Nations in 1971 and retired on December 31. He was succeeded by Kurt Waldheim of Austria. Thant had been reluctant to accept a second 5-year term in 1966, and on several occasions in 1971 he repeated that he would not continue in the office, because of its strenuous pressures.

On December 22, in his last formal statement to the General Assembly, Thant urged that a deputy secretary-general be appointed for the sake of good management and of his successor's health. He said he was leaving with feelings of sadness as well as "great relief, bordering on liberation."

The frustrations of the secretary-generalship, whose holder must deal with crises and potential crises while walking a tightrope of neutrality among the major powers, were amply illustrated in 1971. Thant tried repeatedly to assist in developing stability in the Middle East and in improving the lot of the Palestinian refugees. He showed leadership in trying, through the United Nations, to mobilize the international community to solve environmental problems and—unsuccessfully —to make meaningful attempts to limit the arms race. He spoke out for patience in Northern Ireland, for tolerance in racial conflicts, and for the seating of Communist China in the United Nations.

When the United Nations failed to react to the problems developing in East Pakistan, his voice was one of the few warning of the inherent dangers of the situation. When it became apparent that the interests of the major powers would preclude UN intervention in East Pakistan, Thant wrote President Yahya Khan of Pakistan on April 22 and offered, "on purely humanitarian grounds," UN assistance in helping to relieve the desperate condition of the East Pakistanis.

In April, Thant visited Nicaragua and Costa Rica and spoke before the Organization of American States. He had planned extensive trips to Africa and Europe for August and September, but they were canceled when he was taken ill on June 19. The physical demands of his office led to further illness in November, and he was hospitalized for most of the month.

Background. Born in Pantanaw, Burma, on Jan. 22, 1909, U Thant was educated at the University College in Rangoon and taught English and modern history. He later served as headmaster of the National School in Pantanaw. When Burma became independent in 1948, Thant became the principal adviser to U Nu, Burma's first prime minister. In 1949, Thant was made the country's minister of information and broadcasting.

He served on Burma's UN delegation in 1952 and 1953 and became Burma's permanent UN representative in 1957. He was elected acting UN secretary-general on Nov. 3, 1961, following the death in an airplane crash of Dag Hammarskjöld. Thant was confirmed as secretary-general on Nov. 3, 1962, and was reelected for a second 5-year term on Dec. 2, 1966.

THOMAS HOVET, JR.

THIEU, Nguyen Van

On Oct. 31, 1971, Nguyen Van Thieu was inaugurated for a second 4-year term as president of South Vietnam amid security precautions that included the mobilization of 40,000 troops. He had been reelected unopposed on October 3 with 91.5% of the vote after announcing that he would consider the election a popular referendum. Two other candidates, Gen. Duong Van "Big" Minh and outgoing Vice President Nguyen Cao Ky, had withdrawn from the race in August, charging that Thieu was planning to rig the election.

During the year, Thieu sought to consolidate his position by shakeups in local officialdom and the military and by taking steps to gain firm control of the legislature. Thieu continued the struggle against Communist forces and persisted in rejecting neutralism or a coalition government, but he offered amnesty to defecting members of the National Liberation Front.

(*Left*) PIERRE TRUDEAU, prime minister of Canada, was married to Margaret Sinclair in March. (*Above*) LEE TREVINO hoists British Open golf trophy in July.

On November 15, Thieu announced a series of economic reforms. These included devaluing the currency, establishing a loan fund for the development of industry, increasing the pay of civil servants and the military, and overhauling the fiscal and commercial structure. On December 4 he declared that "the big powers do not have any authority to impose any solution on our people" and that "any solution to the Vietnam problem . . . must come from me, President Nguyen Van Thieu."

The son of a small landholder and fisherman, Thieu was born in the village of Trithuy, in Amman, French Indochina, on April 5, 1923, and was educated in a Roman Catholic school. He fought briefly with Ho Chi Minh's Vietminh forces after World War II and then attended a merchant marine school before entering a French military academy at Dalat.

After the establishment of the Republic of Vietnam in 1954, Thieu rose rapidly through the military ranks. He took part in the coup that overthrew Ngo Dinh Diem in 1963 and became nominal chief of state when Nguyen Cao Ky assumed power as premier in 1965. In the first national election under a new constitution, Thieu, with Ky as his running mate, defeated 10 other candidates with a plurality of 34.8%, and was sworn in as president on Oct. 31, 1967.

HENRY S. SLOAN

TITO (Josip Broz)

President Tito of Yugoslavia was elected on July 29, 1971, as chairman of a new collective presidency that had recently been established to eventually succeed him. As a leader of the nonaligned world he traveled extensively during the year. In February he conferred with Egyptian President Anwar el-Sadat in Cairo, and in March he met with Italian leaders in Rome, where he was received by Pope Paul VI, becoming the first Communist head of state to pay an official visit to the Vatican. Following a meeting between Tito and Soviet Communist party chief Leonid I. Brezhnev in September, the two leaders issued a statement affirming Yugoslavia's unaligned status within the Communist bloc. In October, Tito made his first state visit to the United States, where he discussed a wide range of issues with President Nixon, who called him "a world statesman of the first rank."

Although Tito had prided himself on his ability to forge harmony among Yugoslavia's various ethnic groups, national unity was threatened late in the year by demonstrations of Croatian nationalism, including student riots. After forcing the resignations of "nationalist" and "chauvinist" leaders of the Croatian Communist party, Tito assured Yugoslavs that "we are capable of safeguarding our unity and independence."

Tito, whose real name is Josip Broz, was born in the Croatian village of Kumrovec on May 25, 1892. After being drafted into the Austro-Hungarian army, he was captured by the Russians in 1915 and imprisoned until his liberation by Bolshevik forces in 1917. Returning to Yugoslavia in 1920, he became a leader in the labor union movement and the outlawed Communist party, and spent several years in prison. He became secretary general of the Yugoslavian Communist party in 1937. As leader of an anti-Fascist Partisan guerrilla force during World War II, Tito was a legendary figure. He became premier of Yugoslavia's postwar Communist regime in 1945 and has served as president since 1953. In 1948 he led Yugoslavia away from the rigid control of the Soviet Union, and he soon won international recognition for his independent form of national communism.

HENRY S. SLOAN

TREVINO, Lee

On arriving in England after winning the U. S. Open golf championship for the second time and the Canadian title, Lee Trevino could not contain his enthusiasm over playing in the British Open. "I want this one, very, very bad. I'm having the best season of my life, but I would gladly trade one of my United States titles for this British crown."

Since swapping was out, he took the British crown the hard way, by carding a 278 for the 72 holes and posting a one-stroke triumph. In celebration and humility, he donated $4,800 of his $13,200 winnings to an English orphanage.

The son of a Mexican-American laborer, Trevino was born in Dallas, Texas, on Dec. 1, 1939. He knew poverty before his golf earnings brought him luxuries. As a caddie he learned to play the game so well that he even used a soft-drink bottle as his only club in winning wagers. He broke in on the Professional Golfers' Association tour in 1966, earning $600 his first year.

His first tour victory came in the U. S. Open at Rochester, N. Y., in 1968 when he beat Jack Nicklaus by four strokes. In the process he delighted the gallery and his interviewers with his banter. "I love to see people laugh because it makes me feel good. Being on the tour is real fun for me, and I hope I can pass on some of the enjoyment to the people who come out and watch us," he said. By the end of 1971 he had moved up to ninth place in the all-time money-winning list with $644,617 and had thousands of admirers. He was named Golfer of the Year and Male Athlete of the Year in 1971.

Trevino, who lives in El Paso, Texas, with his wife, Claudia, and three children, donated a $2,000 purse to a scholarship fund for caddies in Singapore and $10,000 to a trust fund for the son of Ted Makalena, a Hawaiian pro who was killed in an accident. "Golf has changed my life," Trevino said. "I don't want to take everything out of this game. I'd like to put something back."

BILL BRADDOCK

TRUDEAU, Pierre Elliott

Canadian Prime Minister Pierre Trudeau jealously guards his privacy, but that did not prevent him from visiting Canada coast to coast and making extensive trips abroad in 1971. His office revealed in September that in the year ending August 15, he had been away from Ottawa for 107 days, 36 of them outside the country. His domestic activities, ranging from casual talks with lobster fishermen in the east to federal-provincial conferences in the west, were a reflection of his belief that the times required him to seek direct contact with the largest possible number of citizens.

Activities in 1971. Inevitably, Trudeau's extensive travels sharpened the criticisms of those who felt that the prime minister was neglecting Parliament, and in the House of Commons his every gesture was likely to become a news item. In a celebrated incident on February 16, Trudeau was accused of silently mouthing an obscenity at an opponent; he said the only words mouthed were "fuddle-duddle." Shortly, lapel buttons, T-shirts, and a magazine appeared, all labeled with those words.

Trudeau's staff is the largest a Canadian prime minister has ever had, and so is his cabinet. The growth of the executive staff, which led to the planned displacement of members of Parliament from offices on Parliament Hill, brought complaints from some of Trudeau's Liberal supporters. The liaison between the party leadership and the rank and file, in keeping with Trudeau's views on participatory democracy, was the subject of a 2-day "retreat" held in July. Despite such efforts, opinion polls indicated that Trudeau's popularity dropped markedly during 1971 and that of his party even more.

But both remained well ahead of their rivals, and on March 4 the prime minister enhanced his public image by marrying Margaret Sinclair, the 22-year-old daughter of a former Liberal minister. He was the first prime minister to marry in office, and the son born to the Trudeaus on December 25 was the first prime-ministerial baby since 1869.

Trudeau played a major role as a mediator between white and nonwhite members of the British Commonwealth at a difficult meeting in Singapore in January. He played a similar part in relations between Canada and the USSR, visiting Russia in May and receiving Premier Aleksei N. Kosygin in Canada in October. Within Canada, Trudeau's status as a bilingual Canadian of mixed French and British ancestry continued to be a significant factor in his management of domestic issues, particularly concerning Ottawa's relations with Quebec.

Background. Trudeau, prime minister since 1968, was a leading Quebec scholar, writer, and lawyer before his entry into federal politics in 1965. Born in Montreal on Oct. 18, 1919, a member of a wealthy family, he studied at the University of Montreal and abroad before taking up a career as a social critic and teacher.

NORMAN WARD

WALDHEIM, Kurt

Kurt Waldheim, Austria's permanent representative to the United Nations, was elected UN secretary-general on December 22 by the General Assembly. His 5-year term began on Jan. 1, 1972. The Security Council had recommended his appointment on December 21, after three ballots. His selection was made possible when Communist China, which had previously opposed him, abstained on the third ballot. The General Assembly, departing from its tradition of secret voting, ratified the nomination by acclamation. The Austrian diplomat, a former foreign minister, had been the unsuccessful People's party candidate in Austria's presidential election in April.

In his acceptance speech to the General Assembly, Waldheim asked for the "full support of all member states" and the "loyal collaboration of all members of the Secretariat." He indicated that he agreed with the policies of U Thant and said that he would "endeavor to be as imaginative and realistic as he [Thant] was in devising new approaches to the common objectives which unite us in this organization." Waldheim warned that the future of the United Nations depended on a solution of its financial problems. He also urged the delegates to recognize the fact that the organization's prestige had been damaged by its inability to halt the India-Pakistan war and other conflicts.

Background. The son of a government official, Kurt Waldheim was born in Sankt Andrä-Wördern, near Vienna, on Dec. 12, 1918. He was educated at the Consular Academy of Vienna and took a law degree from the University of Vienna in 1944.

Entering the foreign service in 1945, Waldheim served in Paris (1945–51), headed the personnel division of the foreign ministry (1951–55), and then led the Austrian observer mission to the UN (1955–56), in the period before Austria's admission. He represented Austria in Canada from 1956 through 1960, first as minister and from 1958 as ambassador. In 1958 he led Austria's first delegation to the UN General Assembly. From 1960 to 1964 he served as director general for political affairs in the foreign ministry, and from 1964 to 1968 he was Austria's permanent representative to the United Nations. During this period he was named chairman of the UN Committee on Outer Space. He served as Austria's minister for foreign affairs from 1968 to 1970, when he again became permanent representative to the United Nations.

THOMAS HOVET, JR.

BIOLOGY. See BIOCHEMISTRY; BOTANY; GENETICS; MARINE BIOLOGY; MEDICINE; ZOOLOGY.

BIRTHRATES. See POPULATION; VITAL STATISTICS.

THE NEW YORK TIMES

KURT WALDHEIM, secretary-general of the United Nations.

WIDE WORLD

HUGO L. BLACK (1886–1971)

"I believe that our Constitution, with its absolute guarantee of individual rights, is the best hope for the aspirations of freedom which men share everywhere."

BLACK, Hugo LaFayette

Associate Justice of the U. S. Supreme Court: b. Harlan, Clay County, Ala., Feb. 27, 1886; d. Bethesda, Md., Sept. 25, 1971.

An outstanding defender of individual rights and civil liberties, Black had a powerful mind and a coherent judicial philosophy grounded in the Bill of Rights. His opinions were models of prose style. His impact on American constitutional doctrine exceeded that of any other Supreme Court justice in the 20th century, and he was recognized as one of the outstanding justices in American history.

Black died on Sept. 25, 1971, at the age of 85. He had resigned on September 17 because of illness, having served on the court for 34 years, a tenure exceeded by only two other justices.

Early Years. Hugo Black was born in Harlan, Clay County, Alabama, on Feb. 27, 1886, the eighth child of a storekeeper and farmer. With little more than a high school education, Black entered the University of Alabama Law School and graduated with honors at the age of 20. He began law practice in Ashland, Ala., but soon moved to Birmingham.

In 1914, Black was elected county prosecutor. He volunteered for the army in 1917, and after discharge resumed his law practice. He specialized in labor and industrial injury cases, developing an unusual skill in winning jury verdicts. He was elected to the U. S. Senate in 1926 after a vigorous primary contest against four better-known Democrats.

New Deal. Reelected in 1932, Black became a prominent and controversial figure in New Deal politics. He sponsored wage and hour legislation that eventually became the Fair Labor Standards Act, and he conducted a series of major investigations into lobbying activities, airline subsidies, and public utility holding companies.

Supreme Court. During President Franklin Roosevelt's first term the Supreme Court, dominated by conservatives, had struck down major New Deal measures. After reelection Roosevelt undertook to reform the court by legislation adding six new members, which Black supported. Though the court-packing plan was defeated, retirement of Justice Willis Van Devanter in the summer of 1937 gave the President his first court vacancy. Roosevelt's surprise appointment of Black to the post of associate justice was widely regarded as presidential revenge on the conservatives who had defeated the court plan. However, the nomination was confirmed by a vote of 63 to 16. Before the fall term of the court began, a newspaper revealed Black's brief membership in the Ku Klux Klan in the 1920's. A storm of opposition blew up. However, Black pointed to his subsequent record as refuting any implication of racial or religious intolerance.

Black was soon joined on the court by other Roosevelt appointees, including Harvard law professor Felix Frankfurter. All were economic liberals, so the disputes about regulation of the economy that had caused the New Deal court fight disappeared. However, other issues soon arose to divide the court. Black believed in the use of judicial power to achieve libertarian policy goals, while Frankfurter thought self-restraint was the more proper judicial role. During the 1940's and 1950's Black, usually joined by Justice William O. Douglas, was occasionally able to win approval of a court majority for his activist defense of the Bill of Rights, but more often he was in dissent. On the Warren Court of the 1960's, however, Black saw much of his basic constitutional philosophy adopted.

Principles. Black was an absolutist in his interpretation of the First Amendment. He took literally the prohibition that Congress "shall make no law" abridging the protected freedoms of speech, press, and religion. He insisted on strict separation of church and state. He denied the validity of laws punishing libel or obscenity. His dissenting opinion in *Dennis* v. *United States* (1951) defied McCarthyism by holding the anti-Communist Smith Act invalid. He objected to all prior restraints on speech or press, and his last opinion was a ringing defense of freedom of the press in the Pentagon Papers case. (See CENSORSHIP.)

Black was equally concerned with enforcing constitutional standards in administering criminal justice. He believed the Fourteenth Amendment had "incorporated" the procedural protections of the Bill of Rights and made them applicable to state prosecutions. Defeated on this issue in 1947, he eventually won an almost complete victory. He wrote the famous *Gideon* v. *Wainwright* decision in 1963, requiring counsel for defendants in all criminal cases. He was one of the Warren Court majority in *Escobedo* v. *Illinois* (1964) and *Miranda* v. *Arizona* (1966), extending the counsel requirement.

Black was a major force in the adoption of the "one man, one vote" doctrine by the Warren Court. In *Colegrove* v. *Green* (1946) he had argued unsuccessfully with Frankfurter that unequal population in legislative electoral districts denied equal protection of the laws; but in 1962, in *Baker* v. *Carr,* the court had come around to his view.

C. HERMAN PRITCHETT
University of California, Santa Barbara

BLOUNT, Winton. See BIOGRAPHY.

BOATING

A milestone in boating in 1971 was passage of the Boating Safety Act. In other developments, yachtsmen rescued 635 persons from a burning cruise ship in the Caribbean; the Hennessy Grand Prix was won by Bob Magoon; and the Annapolis-Newport Race went to James Baldwin.

Safety. After four years of legislative struggle, the Boating Safety Act of 1971 became law in July. Widely hailed as the most significant boating legislation in years, the act was endorsed by the Boating Industry Association, federal agencies, and organized boating consumer groups. Key provisions include: (1) federal construction and performance standards for all boats, to be set and enforced by the U. S. Coast Guard; (2) notification by the manufacturer of any defects in boat design or construction, both to the dealer and buyer; (3) mandatory registration of all boats regardless of size or horsepower; and (4) federal-aid appropriations of $7 million annually for five years to augment state boating programs.

The act drastically increases the powers of the U. S. Coast Guard. Formerly, the Coast Guard had to wait until a boat got into trouble before taking action. The "Termination of Unsafe Use" clause now empowers Coast Guardsmen to take whatever steps they deem necessary for the safety of those aboard any boat, including ordering the boat back to its mooring or to safer waters.

The Coast Guard began making studies to establish performance and construction standards. The initial concern was for safe loading and powering of all boats, proper amounts and locations of flotation material in case of capsizing or swamping, and prevention of fire and explosion.

With most observers crediting local boating-safety programs as the cause, boating accidents continued to decline. The Coast Guard listed 3,803 accidents for 1970, down from 4,067 in 1969. Fatalities edged higher, from 1,350 to 1,418. The record was more significant when viewed against boating growth. The Boating Industry Association estimated that in 1970 more than 44 million people used about 8,814,000 recreational boats and spent some $3,440,000,000 on boating, up $148 million from 1969.

Amateur Rescue. A vacation cruise ship that ran aground in the Caribbean and caught fire triggered one of the greatest amateur sea rescues in history. The French ship *Antilles* struck bottom off an islet in the Grenadine chain, Jan. 8, 1971, about 4:30 P. M. At first, offers of assistance were spurned. Two hours later, fire broke out, the liner's lights went dark, and immediate rescue was required for the hundreds of persons aboard. An estimated 15 privately owned yachts converged on the stricken ship and towed her overloaded lifeboats through treacherous currents to nearby islands. Operating on a hastily organized pattern, search and rescue missions continued through the night. At daylight it was found that all 635 persons aboard had been saved without even a minor injury.

Power Racing. What has come to be ocean racing's most outstanding spectacle, the Hennessy Grand Prix, was won in 1971 by a Miami surgeon, Dr. Bob Magoon, who became the only man to win the furiously contested 206-mile (331-meter) race twice in a row. His boat averaged 70.2 mph (113 kms/hr) in heavy seas. The race, started and finished in the waters off Manasquan, N. J., attracts an estimated 200,000 persons on shore and a spectator fleet estimated at 1,200 boats. The famous Italian racer Vincenzo Balestrieri was second, finishing 3 minutes 43 seconds behind Magoon.

Sail Racing. With the windjammers, the 61-foot (18.6-meter) sloop *Sorcery,* designed by Cuthbertson & Cassian and owned by James Baldwin of Oyster Bay, N. Y., won the Annapolis-Newport classic, which is sailed alternately with the Bermuda race. A converted 12-meter yacht, *American Eagle,* owned by Ted Turner, was second. Third was David Steere's *Yankee Girl.* Although the previous Annapolis-Newport had been sailed in hard gales that sent many contestants scurrying to safety, light air and fog plagued the 86-boat fleet in 1971.

ZACK TAYLOR, *Boating Editor, "Sports Afield"*

BOK, Derek C. See BIOGRAPHY.

BOLIVIA

On Aug. 22, 1971, Gen. Juan José Torres, leftist president of Bolivia since October 1970, was deposed by a right-wing military faction. Col. Hugo Banzer Suárez, heading a three-man junta, assumed the presidency. It was Bolivia's 187th revolution in the 146 years since its independence.

Ouster of Torres. General Torres had sat uneasily in the presidential chair since he had forcibly deposed Gen. Alfredo Ovando Candia late in 1970. He was backed by an uncertain coalition of university students, tin miners, and organized peasant groups, but his control was slowly eroded as conflicts between his supporters grew and the opposition of business, professional, and right-wing mili-

---
BOLIVIA • Information Highlights

Official Name: Republic of Bolivia.
Area: 424,163 square miles (1,098,581 sq km).
Population (1970 est.): 4,930,000. *Density,* 10 per square mile (4 per sq km). Annual rate of increase, 2.5%.
Chief Cities: Sucre (1965 est.), the capital, 58,400; La Paz (1970 census), 562,000; Cochabamba (1969 est.), 157,000.
Government: *Head of state,* Hugo Banzer Suarez, president (took office Aug. 22, 1971). *Head of government,* Hugo Banzer Suarez. *Legislature*—Congress (suspended Sept. 1969); Senate, 27 members; Chamber of Deputies, 102 members.
Languages: Spanish (official), Quechua, Aymará.
Education: *Literacy rate* (1970), 20% of population. *Expenditure on education* (1967), 28.9% of total public expenditure. School enrollment (1968)—primary, 612,629; secondary, 132,858; technical/vocational, 10,684; university/higher (1966), 13,312.
Finances (1967): *Revenues,* $64,933,000; *expenditures,* $101,852,000; monetary unit, peso (11.88 pesos equal U. S.$1, Sept. 1971).
Gross National Product (1969): $911,000,000.
National Income (1969): $800,000,000; *national income per person,* $167.
Economic Indexes: *Manufacturing production* (1966), 139 (1963=100); *agricultural production* (1969), 112 (1963=100); *consumer price index* (1970), 151 (1963=100).
Manufacturing (metric tons, 1969): Gasoline, 217,000; sugar, 113,000; cement, 80,000.
Crops (metric tons, 1969 crop year): Potatoes (1968), 660,000; maize, 228,000; cassava (1968), 160,000; barley, 55,000; wheat, 47,000.
Minerals (metric tons, 1969): Crude petroleum, 1,873,000; tin concentrates, 30,073 (ranks 2d among world producers); antimony, 13,111 (world rank 2d); gold, 2,123 kilograms.
Foreign Trade (1968): *Exports* (1969), $182,000,000 (chief exports—tin ore, $72,500,000; crude petroleum, $24,260,000; silver, $11,200,000). *Imports* (1970), $155,000,000 (chief imports—wheat flour, $10,120,000; commercial motor vehicles, $7,590,000; iron tubes and pipes, $5,070,000; mining machinery, $4,120,000). *Chief trading partners* (1968) —United Kingdom (took 43% of exports, supplied 5% of imports); United States (35%—40%).
Transportation: *Roads* (1970), 20,000 miles (32,200 km); *motor vehicles* (1969), 41,400 (automobiles, 17,700); *railroads* (1965), 1,734 miles (2,790 km); *national airline,* Lloyd Aero Boliviano; *principal airport,* La Paz.
Communications: *Telephones* (1970), 37,551; *radios* (1968), 1,350,000; *newspapers* (1969), 17.

tary elements increased. Unrealistic promises to peasants and mining unions had remained unfulfilled, and Torres had failed to halt a decline in agricultural production. He was also accused of having "frightened away" much-needed foreign capital.

The Banzer coup began in the city of Oruro on Aug. 19, 1971. Right-wing military units, supported by civilians, marched against local government troops, who capitulated after a spirited but brief skirmish. On the next day the uprising spread to Santa Cruz, Cochabamba, and finally to La Paz. Heavy fighting took place in Santa Cruz and Cochabamba, where the rebels were again successful. Shortly thereafter the commander of the Bolivian Army asserted his support of Banzer and called on all men under arms to "oust Torres for the political and economic good of the nation." Torres fled from the presidential palace on August 21.

The Banzer Government. In a statement to the press, Colonel Banzer described himself as a liberal-conservative, who intended to carry out the reform policies of the National Revolutionary Movement (MNR) that had come to power in 1952. He was, in fact, aligned politically with the conservative wing of the MNR and with the Bolivian Socialist Falange (FSB), a militantly rightist party that advocated a strong government on the model of the regime of Francisco Franco in Spain. FSB stalwarts were well represented in the new cabinet. The vice chairman of the three-man Banzer junta was Col. Andrés Selich, the commander of the forces that had run down Che Guevara's guerrillas in 1967.

One of Banzer's first moves was to outlaw the People's Council, presided over by a Marxist, Juan Lechín. The council had been appointed by Torres to replace the elected Congress.

In another significant move, the new government invited Víctor Paz Estenssoro to return to La Paz after seven years' exile in Peru. The 71-year-old Paz was renowned as a founder and the principal architect of the MNR. As president, he had nationalized the rich tin mines and had broken up Bolivia's monopolistic land system.

International Affairs. Under Torres, economic ties with the Communist nations had been strengthened. With the accession of Banzer, other Latin heads of state began to watch closely for signs of an abrupt swing to the right. Of special concern was Bolivia's policy toward the Andean Group, a modified common market in which Bolivia and four other nations participated. Banzer gave no early indication of repudiating the organization's code, which included a controversial "fade-out" clause that would require foreign corporations gradually to dispose of majority ownership in their operations to local private or state interests.

Economic Affairs. The Bolivian economy remained fairly stable in 1971. The gross national product was growing at a rate of 4% for the year, down from 4.7% in 1970. Relatively high prices for tin in world markets and the resumption of some exports of petroleum made up for deficits in other sectors, including agriculture. Despite further shifts from handicrafts to machine production, however, there was no evidence of real improvement in the lot of Bolivia's destitute majority.

OLEN E. LEONARD
University of Arizona

BONDS. See STOCKS AND BONDS.
BOOK PUBLISHING. See PUBLISHING.

BOSTON

Boston has been called two cities. There is the active, cosmopolitan Boston—a city of colleges and universities, new high-rise buildings, culture, and history. And there is the Boston of neighborhoods that are Irish, Italian, or black—a city that is locally oriented and occasionally cantankerous.

During 1971 these two Bostons met head-on in municipal elections. Kevin H. White, 42, easily won a second 4-year term as mayor, and the balloting produced little change in the composition of the city council and the school committee.

Many observers called the elections dull and uneventful, and it was true that the final weeks before the balloting were remarkably calm for Boston politics. But the elections colored local politics all through the year, and there were significant issues.

Halt in Airport Expansion. Typical of the long-standing problems that reached a turning point in an election year was the issue of runway expansion at Logan International Airport. The airport, the eighth-busiest in the world, has been developing rapidly in recent years, growing ever closer to East Boston, a predominantly Italian district. Opposition to the continuing expansion of the airport had become especially active since 1968. The protests of East Boston residents finally paid off late in the summer of 1971, when Mayor White and other community leaders persuaded Gov. Francis W. Sargent to order the Massachusetts Port Authority, the operator of the airport, to halt all construction pending further studies.

Worries. The pattern of local protest was similar elsewhere. In Roxbury, a black area, housing, unemployment, crime, and welfare were major issues. Boston's black population has increased from 9.1% to 16.3% in the 10 years ending in 1970.

In Jamaica Plain, a largely white residential area south of the city's center, a primary concern was the construction of Interstate 95, a superhighway that is scheduled to cut a swath through the district.

In Boston's Back Bay, the construction of yet another skyscraper, the new John Hancock Life Insurance Co. building, caused worries over the added congestion and over the aesthetic effect of juxtaposing this latest manifestation of the "new Boston" with the architecture of an earlier era.

Almost every area of the city felt the effects of unrest in the public high schools. A series of disturbances, at least partially racial in nature, forced several high schools to close for short periods. Of citywide concern, too, were growing crime and drug problems.

Elections. In a field of six candidates in the September primary for the mayor's seat, White came in first, and U. S. Rep. Louise Day Hicks placed second, opening the way for a confrontation between them in the November 2 general election. Four years previously, White had defeated Mrs. Hicks for the office in an atmosphere charged with racial tensions. Now Mrs. Hicks was running for mayor while serving her first term in Congress, where she occupies the seat vacated by House Speaker John McCormack. The racial element proved to be of decidedly minor importance in the 1971 general election. White received 113,137 votes to Mrs. Hicks' 70,331.

HARVEY BOULAY
Boston University

BOTANY

Botanical research in 1971 showed an increase in interdisciplinary studies, with studies centered on the causes of changes within cells and differentiating tissues and on plant-insect relationships. An electronic data bank is being organized to provide information about the plants of North America, and there is a search for data to explain the origin and evolution of plants.

Growth and Development. One of the most important problems in biology involves the differentiation of apparently similar young cells into different types of specialized mature cells. J. G. Torrey, D. E. Fosket, and P. K. Hepler have traced the development of xylem, the water-conducting tissue, from genesis to death. They report that xylem differentiation is a highly ordered sequence of events, and once the development of xylem is initiated, the process goes to completion. Partial differentiation does not occur. Such data indicate that the past tendency to treat each event of development as a separate phenomenon, associating specific hormones with each step, caused misunderstanding of the differentiation process.

Studies of plants have been used to provide most of the available information on polyploidy—an increase of chromosome number in a cell. In recent studies, A. E. DeMaggio has used ferns to investigate problems relating to polyploidy and gene dosage during development. He has demonstrated that cell and nuclear size increase with an increase in chromosome number and that these size increases are proportional to the increases in the amount of nuclear DNA. He also reported that respiration and photosynthesis rates do not increase with chromosome number and that there is no direct relationship between chromosome number and protein content.

Plant-Insect Relationships. The development of varieties or strains of plants that are resistant to insect attack would be an excellent method of preventing insect damage without the use of dangerous chemicals. C. P. DaCosta and C. M. Jones have demonstrated that certain cucumbers produce a terpenoid substance that acts as a specific feeding attractant for cucumber beetles. The production of the terpenoid is controlled by a gene. Plants lacking this gene do not produce the terpenoid and thus do not attract beetles. However, they do attract mites, which destroy them. This is an example of plant-insect coevolution associated with a one-gene inheritance of a chemical substance.

Electronic Data Banks. The Flora North America Project (FNA) is the first attempt to create a comprehensive data bank concerned with storing data about the kinds of higher plants found on a continent. It is a new type of computer venture in botany and has far-reaching implications for taxonomists, ecologists, and environmental biologists.

Insectivorous Plants. Botanists have studied insectivorous plants since the late 1700's. The best known of these insect-eating plants is the Venus' flytrap (*Dionaea muscipula*). The leaves of these plants fold quickly when sensitive hairs on their surface are touched. M. E. Williams and H. N. Mozirgo have studied the fine structure of the trigger hairs on the leaves and have discovered that each active zone of a hair contains protein bodies, mitochondria, vacuoles, endoplasmic reticulum, and protoplasmic strands interconnecting with other cells. Touching the trigger hairs produces an action potential in the sensitive cells of the hairs. The action potential propagates rapidly to the leaf surface, causing the leaves to fold and form a trap.

Evolution and Classification. Higher plants have specialized organelles, such as chloroplasts (plastids) and mitochondria, enclosed within the cell. Several recent biologists have suggested that these essential organelles were once independent organisms. Lynn Margulis endeavored to demonstrate a connection between symbiosis and evolution. Data indicate that mitochondria were probably once free-living bacteria that established symbiotic relationships and ultimately evolved into a life within plant and animal cells. A similar symbiotic history holds true for plastids, which probably were once free-living algae. A third group of organelles—flagella and cilia—became associated with certain cells and formed another type of symbiotic association. This theory of the symbiotic origin of some cell organelles provides a unified framework upon which to evaluate both the rapid influx of fossil data and contemporary genetic and organelle research. These hypotheses have led to the development of a new classification of organisms into five kingdoms—Monera, Protista, Plant, Animal, and Fungi—to replace the conventional two kingdoms —Plant and Animal.

DAVID E. FAIRBROTHERS, *Rutgers University*

BOTSWANA

Rising income from mining and the completion of plans for a road link with Zambia made 1971 an encouraging year for Botswana. The United States recognized Botswana's growing significance by appointing its first ambassador to the young nation.

Warning Against Racism. On May 22, Vice President Quett K. Masire warned a white audience in Francistown, in northeastern Botswana near Rhodesia, that white shopkeepers who did not observe Botswana's "policy of nonracialism" by treating all customers equally would be asked "if they might

--- BOTSWANA · Information Highlights ---

Official Name: Republic of Botswana.
Area: 231,804 square miles (600,372 sq km).
Population (1970): 650,000. *Density*, 2.6 per square mile (1 per sq km). *Annual rate of increase*, 3.0%.
Chief Cities (1970 est.): Gaborone, the capital, 20,000; Francistown (1969), 39,020; Serowe, 35,000; Kanye, 35,000.
Government: *Head of state*, Sir Seretse Khama, president (took office Sept. 30, 1966). *Head of government*, Sir Seretse Khama. *Legislature*—Parliament; National Assembly, 36 members; House of Chiefs (a consultative body), 15 members. *Major political parties*—Democratic party; People's party; National Front.
Languages: English (official), Tswana.
Education: *Literacy rate* (1970), 25% of population. *Expenditure on education* (1966), 13.3% of total public expenditure. *School enrollment* (1968)—primary, 78,963; secondary, 3,213; technical/vocational, 592.
Finances (1970–71 estimate): *Revenues*, $18,000,000; *expenditures*, $22,000,000; *monetary unit*, rand (0.7134 rand equal U.S.$1, Aug. 1971).
Gross National Product (1967 estimate): $58,000,000.
National Income (1966): $49,000,000; *national income per person*, $86.
Manufacturing: beef and veal, clothing, soap, tannery products.
Crops: corn, sorghum, millet, cotton, peanuts.
Minerals: manganese ore, diamonds, nickel, copper.
Foreign Trade (1969): *Exports*, $18,675,000 (chief exports— livestock, hides and skins, canned meats, manganese). *Imports*, $44,092,000 (chief imports—cereals, textiles, petroleum products, sugar). *Chief trading partners* (1969), South Africa, Rhodesia.
Transportation: *Roads* (1968), 5,016 miles (8,071 km); *motor vehicles* (1969), 4,800 (automobiles, 2,300); *railroads* (1969), 394 miles (634 km); *national airline*, Botswana Airways Corp.; *principal airports*, Gaborone, Maun, Francistown, Ghanzi.
Communications: *Telephones* (1969), 3,536; *radios* (1969), 6,500.

not be happier somewhere else." Local white organizations that continued to exclude blacks would be closed, Masire declared. Francistown's 1,000 or so white residents, mostly from South Africa and Rhodesia, have traditionally kept apart from the black community. Less than 1% of the nation's total population is white.

United States Recognition. On May 28 the White House announced that the United States was raising the status of its diplomatic relations with Botswana, Lesotho, and Swaziland to full embassy level. President Nixon nominated Charles J. Nelson as the U. S. ambassador to the three countries. Nelson, a black foreign-service officer and former Peace Corpsman, had been director of the U. S. economic mission in Tanzania since 1968.

Mineral Production and Income. Diamond production at Orapa was approaching peak capacity in 1971, while copper and nickel mines at Selebe-Pikwe were expected to attain full production in 1973. Anticipated increases in tax revenues from these and other projects caused the government to look forward to a balanced budget by fiscal 1972–73 and to an end of reliance on British grants.

Road Link with Zambia. A 190-mile (305-km) road from Nata to Kazungula, with a connecting ferry crossing on the Zambesi River, was expected to be built by 1974, facilitating trade with Zambia and other African countries to the north. The United States committed itself to more than $6 million in aid toward construction costs, and the Republic of South Africa was expected to drop its legal opposition to the project.

FRANKLIN PARKER, *West Virginia University*

BRANDT, Willy. See BIOGRAPHY.

BRAZIL

Long called "the land of the future," Brazil was beginning to see itself in 1971 as "the land of today," at least on the economic front. Statistics for the year indicated a continuing growth that some economists have described as "stunning." Yet such progress was benefiting few among the majority of Brazilians who live in destitution, and it was taking place in a political climate that was anything but democratic.

Political Repression. In a speech to Congress on March 31, 1971—the seventh anniversary of the advent of military rule—President Emilio Garrastazú Médici announced his satisfaction with the current "democratic order" and made no promise that his administration would change its policies.

A major feature of these policies was political repression. There was no letup in the government's harassment of "subversives," a term applied indiscriminately to opponents of the regime. Many individuals had suffered arrest, and some had experienced prolonged detention and brutal interrogation. It was also estimated that, since 1964, more than 1,300 Brazilians had been victims of presidential decrees denying them political rights for 10 years. Among these political "nonpersons," forbidden to participate in elections or stand for political office, were former presidents of the republic, members of the Congress, governors, mayors, and judges.

Extremists within the ranks of "subversives" continued to engage in acts of violence ranging from sabotage and armed robbery to kidnapping, bombing, and murder. A prominent businessman in São Paulo, Henning Albert Boilesen, was assassinated, apparently in reprisal for his support of government measures against subversive activities. In order to secure the release of the kidnapped Swiss ambassador, Giovanni Erico Bucher, the government on Jan. 14, 1971, freed 70 prisoners and allowed them to go to Chile. It then announced that it would ransom no more foreign diplomats.

Prominent Roman Catholic clerics continued to embarrass the government by publicly calling into question its tactics against the subversives and condemning police brutality. The most extreme of the critics was Hélder Câmara, the leftist archbishop of Olinda and Recife, who characterized the terrorists as patriotic revolutionaries whose acts of violence were legitimate forms of protest. A bishops' conference in Belo Horizonte issued a letter supporting Bishop Valdir Calheiros of Volta Redonda, who had been accused of subversive activities. The letter declared that "torture unfortunately exists in our country and in some circumstances in an atrocious manner."

Congressional Elections. In November 1970, the first general elections in four years were held. The government's National Renewal party (ARENA) increased its already substantial majority over the only legally recognized opposition party, the Brazilian Democratic Movement (MDB). About 30 million Brazilians cast ballots for 46 senators, 310 deputies, and 701 members of state assemblies and municipal councils.

International Relations. Brazil is one of nine Latin American nations that have claimed sovereignty over the seas adjacent to their countries to a distance of 200 miles (320 km) from shore. On June 1, 1971, it gave notice of its intention to begin naval and air patrols in the extended area. This action seemed destined to contribute to diplomatic friction with a number of countries whose nationals were accustomed to fish in Brazilian waters. While some countries, such as France, Trinidad and Tobago, and Surinam, appeared willing to negotiate, others—specifically, the United States and Japan—announced that they did not recognize Brazil's claims. Under Brazilian law, foreign vessels were required to purchase a Brazilian license to fish within the 200-mile zone. The U. S. State Department told American fishermen that they were not obligated under international law to purchase licenses.

An unexpected repercussion of Brazil's maritime claims was U. S. retaliation on the coffee issue. In the U. S. Congress, the House Ways and Means Committee, in an effort to force Brazil to modify its policies on fishing, decided to postpone action on a bill extending U. S. membership in the International Coffee Agreement. U. S. nonparticipation in the agreement threatened to throw the world coffee market into chaos, but it remained doubtful that Brazil would bend to U. S. pressure.

In March, a 5-year controversy over soluble coffee exports to the United States was resolved. Brazil agreed to limit its sales of instant coffee to the United States, and to ship to the United States, on a tax-free basis, a given amount of green coffee to be prorated among the instant-coffee processors.

In July, President Médici paid an official visit to Paraguay, where he and President Alfredo Stroessner discussed joint Brazilian-Paraguayan efforts to harness the Paraná River. Later, Médici visited Colombia, and in December he paid a three-day state visit to the United States.

The Beleaguered Diplomats. Aloysio Dias Gomide, the Brazilian consul at Montevideo, Uruguay, who had been kidnapped by that country's leftist Tupamaro organization in July 1970, was finally released in February 1971, presumably after payment of a ransom supplied by private sources. Diplomatic kidnappings forced Brazil and other Latin American nations to adopt restrictive security measures to protect diplomatic personnel.

The problem of the kidnappings of diplomats was so serious that the Council of the Organization of American States (OAS) called an extraordinary session in Washington in January 1971 to consider what could be done about it. The demands of Brazil and five other nations that the community of OAS states deal firmly with the problem were frustrated, however, because some nations were extremely sensitive to any implied threat to national sovereignty.

Also contributing to a decline in morale at the foreign embassies in Brazil was the unwelcome prospect of moving to Brasília. The Brazilian Foreign Office ordered that foreign embassies be transferred to the new inland capital by October 1972. In contrast with glamorous Rio de Janeiro, Brasília was regarded by embassy personnel as a hardship post.

End of U. S. Police-Training Program. The United States discontinued the Brazilian phase of its police-training program, called "public safety assistance," which it had been supplying to 15 Latin American countries. It maintained that the program had served its purpose. The decision was probably hastened, however, by congressional probing of U. S. involvement in Brazilian police repression.

Economic Affairs. In 1971, Brazil continued its rapid economic expansion for the fourth consecutive year, showing a 9% rate of economic growth. Meanwhile, inflation was held at its lowest rate in a decade. A strong balance of payments resulted from a large rise in exports and a sizable inflow of investment capital. The continuing growth in the export of manufactured goods was decreasing Brazil's reliance on coffee sales abroad, which have come now to represent only one third of Brazil's export income. As a result of the government's program to diversify farm products, coffee acreage had declined by over 30% between 1960 and 1971. A less welcome cause of the reduction of the coffee crop was a fungus blight, coffee rust, which had spread to São Paulo state, with no solution in sight.

Brazil has initiated a 10-year steel expansion program to make the country self-sufficient in steel products. In 1970, steel production was 5.2 million tons. It was hoped that by 1980 it would reach 20 million tons. A petroleum deficit was a debit in the economy. In 1971, Brazil's production met only about 40% of its national needs in crude oil. Since known reserves were scanty, Petrobras, the national oil agency, was spending one third of its budget prospecting for new wells, both inland and offshore. Oil production is a federal monopoly.

Because of the economic boom and the favorable attitude of the Brazilian government toward foreign investments, Brazil was regarded as South America's best option for foreign investors. Of the total foreign investments of about $4 billion in 1971, U. S. private investors held an estimated stake of $1.7 billion. Possibly because their profits were subject to a 25% remittance tax, U. S. entrepreneurs were remitting only about a third of their profits and plowing the other two thirds back into new Brazilian ventures.

──────── BRAZIL · Information Highlights ────────

Official Name: Federative Republic of Brazil.
Area: 3,286,478 square miles (8,511,965 sq km).
Population (1970 census): 93,200,000. *Density,* 31 per square mile (12 per sq km). *Annual rate of increase,* 2.7%.
Chief Cities (1970 est.): Brasília, the capital, 500,000; São Paulo, 6,000,000; Rio de Janeiro, 4,500,000; Belo Horizonte, 1,200,000.
Government: *Head of state,* Emilio Garrastazú Médici, president (took office Oct. 30, 1969). *Head of government,* Emilio Garrastazú Médici. *Legislature*—National Congress: Chamber of Deputies, 310 members; Federal Senate, 66 members. *Major political parties*—Aliança Renovadora Nacional (ARENA), Movimento Democrático Brasiliero (MDB).
Languages: Portuguese (official).
Education: *Literacy rate* (1970), 61% of population. *Expenditure on education* (1970), 7% of total public expenditure. *School enrollment* (1968)—primary, 11,943,506; secondary, 3,205,689; technical/vocational, 542,418; university/higher, 282,653.
Finances (1969): *Revenues,* $3,210,000,000; *expenditures,* $3,383,000,000; *monetary unit,* new cruzeiro (5.405 equal U. S.$1, Aug. 1971).
Gross National Product (1969 est.): $32,300,000,000.
National Income (1967): $23,220,000,000; *national income per person,* $271.
Economic Indexes: *Industrial production* (1967), 117 (1963=100); *agricultural production* (1969), 122 (1963=100); *consumer price index* (1969), 151 (1963=100).
Manufacturing (metric tons, 1969): Residual fuel oil, 8,478,-000; cement, 7,819,000; crude steel, 4,925,000; pig iron, 3,717,000; meat, 2,485,000; cotton fabrics, 1,170,000,000 meters.
Crops (metric tons, 1968 crop year): Sugarcane, 76,611,000; cassava, 29,203,000; maize, 12,683,000 (world rank 2d); rice, 6,652,000; bananas, 5,484,000 (world rank 1st); coffee, 1,057,500 (world rank 1st).
Minerals (metric tons, 1968): Iron ore, 17,084,000; crude petroleum, 8,360,000; coal (1969), 2,437,000; salt, 1,630,-000; manganese ore, 922,500; natural gas (1969), 1,248,-000,000 cu. meters; gold, 5,290 kilograms.
Foreign Trade: *Exports* (1970), $2,738,000,000 (chief exports—coffee, $943,000,000; iron ore, $208,000,000; cotton, $156,-000,000; cacao, $78,000,000). *Imports* (1970), $2,849,000,-000 (chief imports, 1968—machinery and transport equipment, $659,400,000; chemicals. $342,020,000; cereals and cereal preparations, $207,780,000; petroleum, crude and partly refined, $199,480,000). *Chief trading partners* (1968)—United States (took 33% of exports, supplied 32% of imports); West Germany (8%—11%); Argentina (6%—7%).
Transportation: *Roads* (1965), 497,902 miles (801,124 km); *motor vehicles* (1965), 2,750,000 (automobiles, 1,650,000); *railroads* (1965). 20,806 miles (33,477 km); *merchant fleet* (1970), 1,722,000 gross registered tons; *national airline,* Varig (VASP); *principal airports,* Brasília, Rio de Janeiro, São Paulo.
Communications: *Telephones* (1969), 1,787,000; *television stations* (1967), 38; *television sets* (1969), 6,500,000; *radios* (1969), 5,575,000; *newspapers* (1968), 250 (daily circulation, 3,250,000).

Social Lag. Despite Brazil's economic expansion, the gains are unevenly distributed among the people. President Médici himself said that "the economy may be doing fine, but the majority of the people are still doing badly."

Of Brazil's more than 90 million inhabitants, some 50 million are regarded as impoverished. In the drought-stricken northeast, where the population is about 25 million, the per capita income in 1971 was only $100, and life expectancy was 34 years. One of the objectives of the construction of the Trans-Amazon Highway, which was to extend from Recife to the Peruvian border, was to draw some of the underprivileged population of the northeast into the undeveloped interior. In the meantime, major relief projects were maintained in the stricken area.

Even in the big cities, the nation's poor seemed to be getting poorer. In the booming São Paulo industrial area, unemployment was pronounced. Also, health standards were unbelievably low. Half of all Brazilians were without minimal sanitary facilities. A major government effort was being made in the field of housing, but all such programs were being canceled out by an enormous rate of population growth. There was no official birth-control program because of religious and nationalistic taboos. And one out of every three Brazilians was illiterate,

EXPLOSIVES topple center section of old bridge across Hudson River between Albany and Rensselaer, N. Y. Bridge has been superseded by new span in background.

despite the fact that education was getting the largest share (nearly 13%) of the national budget.

Vanishing Indians. A three-man group of experts, sent to Brazil by the International Red Cross to investigate charges that genocide was being practiced against the Indians, found no evidence of killings or any indication of physical mistreatment of these peoples. Nevertheless, the penetration of highways into the jungles and the rapid expansion of the frontiers were creating conditions that threatened not only the land rights but even the survival of the indigenous population.

J. LLOYD MECHAM
University of Texas

BREZHNEV, Leonid Illich. See BIOGRAPHY.

BRIDGES

Bridge building progressed throughout the United States in 1971 to serve a variety of needs. Most of the new structures were vehicular spans over rivers, but there was a surprising amount of activity in building bridges to carry railroads—despite the phasing out of much passenger-train service in recent years.

Piscataqua River Bridge. Many of the vehicular bridges will carry federal interstate highways. The largest bridge ever undertaken in either Maine or New Hampshire will connect the two states with a crossing at the Piscataqua River. It will carry Interstate 95, in six lanes plus full shoulders, between Portsmouth, N. H., and Kittery, Me.

Construction started in the spring of 1968 and is scheduled for completion by the end of 1972. The bridge has a 1,344-foot (410-meter) three-span continuous tied-arch truss. Measuring 108 feet (33 meters) wide, center to center of trusses, the structure has a minimum clearance over water of 135 feet (41 meters), with the highest steel 250 feet (76 meters) above the river. The center span measures 756 feet (230 meters) between its supporting piers. At either end are the anchor spans, each 294 feet (90 meters) long. With approaches, the bridge is 4,498 feet (1,371 meters) long.

Costing $21 million and containing 10,000 tons of steelwork for the main river structure, the new bridge replaces a heavily congested three-lane vertical lift bridge about a half-mile downstream.

North Philadelphia-Pennsauken Bridge. Spanning the Delaware River between Pennsylvania and southern New Jersey can be a costly construction project. In that area the land is flat, and it is expensive to raise structures high enough to bridge the considerable width of river while maintaining clearance for the shipping channel. Height of piers for this 4,400-foot (1,341-meter) bridge between North Philadelphia, Pa., and Pennsauken Township, N. J., ranges from 63 feet (19 meters) to 166 feet (51 meters). The structure is 90 feet (27 meters) wide to carry eight lanes of traffic. On completion in 1972, it will clear high water by 135 feet (41 meters) with a 729-foot (222-meter) through-truss span over the channel.

Ohio River Bridge. Work got under way in 1971 on the new Interstate 279 bridge over the Ohio River at Neville Island near Pittsburgh, Pa. The bridge, 4,550 feet (1,387 meters) long and 110 feet (34 meters) wide, will include a 750-foot (229-meter) tied-arch span over the main channel, and two girder spans over the back channel. The $41 million project should be completed by mid-1976.

Mississippi River Bridge. The $50 million Interstate 40 bridge over the Mississippi River will carry six lanes of traffic between downtown Memphis, Tenn., and Arkansas. Its seven-span, 3,660-foot (1,116-meter) length includes two spans of tied-arch truss construction, each 900 feet (274 meters) long.

They will give the bridge a vertical clearance of between 60 feet (18 meters) and 90 feet (27 meters), depending on the water level. The roadbed, 84 feet (26 meters) wide, will be supported by structural strands suspended from the arches.

The superstructure also includes five continuous box-girder spans (two girders per span) ranging from 339 feet (103 meters) to 400 feet (122 meters) in length, and weighing from 366 to 422 tons per piece. They measure 16 feet (5 meters) high by 5.5 feet (1.7 meters) wide. Completion of the project is expected in 1972.

Milwaukee Harbor Bridge. Interstate 794 will cross the harbor mouth in Milwaukee, Wis., on a 1,140-foot (347-meter) tied-arch bridge. Construction on the $8.8 million structure started in 1971 and is scheduled for completion in 1974. The 600-foot-long (183-meter) main arch will soar more than 200 feet (61 meters) above the Milwaukee River. The deck will accommodate six lanes of traffic, with shoulder lanes for disabled cars.

Railroad Bridges. The Boston transit system is being improved with the building of a new $9 million bridge over the Mystic River. The new structure consists essentially of two different bridges about an inch apart but sharing the same piers. The 965-foot-long (294-meter), 64-foot-wide (20-meter) structure has a minimum river clearance of 30 feet (9 meters). The center span, at 125 feet (38 meters), is the longest. One of the 11-span bridges, of heavy box-girder construction, carries one track of the Boston & Maine Railroad. The other bridge, of plate-girder construction, carries three tracks of the rapid-transit system, which is being extended by way of the new bridge. It is expected to ease travel between the northern suburbs and downtown Boston. Work on the bridge started in 1969 and was scheduled for completion in 1972.

A dual-track, continuous-welded box-girder bridge is being built in Detroit for the Chesapeake and Ohio Railroad. The 630-foot (192-meter) structure will span 12 lanes of Interstate 96. It will replace the C&O's main-line tracks, now at grade. The $4 million project, scheduled for completion in 1973, is a four-span continuous structure with two lines of box girders 35 feet (11 meters) apart. Ver-

tical clearance for traffic, projected to reach 200,000 vehicles per day by 1990, will be 14.5 feet.

A 2,110-foot (643-meter) bridge was completed in 1971 over the Arkansas River in eastern Oklahoma for the Kansas City Southern Railway Co. The new nine-span, $4.5 million structure is a continuous-welded box-girder bridge with a main channel span of 330 feet (101 meters). In addition to a 52-foot (16-meter) vertical clearance, the structure provides a navigation clearance of 300 feet (91 meters) horizontally. It replaces a 24-span truss and plate-girder bridge, which, because of low clearance and many piers, restricted navigation.

Because of a line change between Spokane and Lyons, Wash., the Burlington Northern Railroad is building a 930-foot (283-meter) steel box-girder bridge across Indian Canyon.

Intracoastal Canal Bridge. New to the United States, but not to Europe, is the concept of utilizing precast concrete units erected in segments to form long-span bridges. The segments are joined together with prestressed steel cables. The Texas Highway Department is constructing such a bridge over the Intracoastal Canal near Corpus Christi.

Developed by the University of Texas, the structure will be 400 feet (122 meters) long, consisting of a 200-foot (61-meter) main span and 100-foot (30.5-meter) side spans. It will stand 72 feet (22 meters) out of the water. The 56-foot-wide (17-meter) bridge consists of two 27-foot-wide (8.3-meter) boxes, with a median strip that is cast in place between the boxes. Construction started late in 1971 from both sides of the canal at the top of each pier. Closure of the center span is achieved when the two 100-foot sections of trapezoidal boxes meet at the center to form a precast bridge joined with prestressed steel cables.

Japan Aqueduct Bridge. The longest aqueduct bridge in the Far East is being built across Sagami River in Japan. To be completed in 1973, the $2.3 million, 2,722-foot (830-meter) bridge will be 11 feet (3 meters) wide, 12.5 feet (4 meters) high, and have 15 spans. The five longest will be steel arches; the others will be plate girders.

WILLIAM H. QUIRK
"Contractors & Engineers" Magazine

Crane lowers girder to close gap in new Piscataqua River bridge between Portsmouth, N. H., and Kittery, Me.

BRITISH COLUMBIA

Economic progress continued during 1971, the centenary year of British Columbia's confederation into Canada. In May the province was honored by a visit from the British royal family. In October it was host to USSR Premier Aleksei N. Kosygin.

Visitors. Queen Elizabeth II, together with the Duke of Edinburgh and Princess Anne, toured British Columbia for 10 days in May 1971. The royal party was accompanied by the Canadian prime minister, Pierre Trudeau.

The visit of Soviet Premier Kosygin in October was notable for the friendly reception that he received from an audience at a professional hockey match in Vancouver.

Government Activity. William A. C. Bennett, the provincial premier and leader of the dominant Social Credit party, announced the appointment of a minister for the department of labor, awarding the new portfolio to James R. Chabot.

Legislative action included the establishment of a $25 million perpetual fund to combat drug, alcohol, and tobacco abuse. All liquor and tobacco advertising was banned from Sept. 1, 1971.

Economic Developments. A high level of investment continued to sustain rapid growth: capital and repair spending was estimated to total nearly $3.7 billion in 1971. Production began at new mines near Port Hardy and Elkford. Three pulp-mill projects, valued at over $250 million, were scheduled for completion in 1972, and four major metal-mining and -milling operations, worth some $325 million,

——— BRITISH COLUMBIA • Information Highlights ———

Area: 366,255 square miles (948,597 sq km).
Population (1971 est.): 2,196,000.
Chief Cities (1970 est.): Metro Victoria, the capital (189,000); Metro Vancouver (1,012,000).
Government: Chief Officers—lt. gov., John Robert Nicholson; premier, William A. C. Bennett (Social Credit party); prov. secy., Wesley Drewett Black (SC); atty. gen., Leslie R. Peterson (SC); min. of educ., Donald L. Brothers (SC); min. of labor, James R. Chabot (SC); chief justice, Herbert W. Davey (SC). Legislature: Legislative Assembly (convened Jan. 21, 1971); 55 members (37 SC, 12 New Democrat, 5 Liberal, 1 Independent).
Education: School enrollment (June 1971)—public elementary and secondary, 527,106 pupils; private schools, 22,359 pupils; Indian (federal) schools, 3,491 pupils; college and university (fall 1970), 37,461 students. Public school expenditures (1970–71), $358,912,000; median teacher's salary (1970–71), $9,252.
Public Finance (fiscal year 1971–72 est.): Revenues, $1,301,-232,000 (sales and fuel taxes, $328,000,000; income and inheritance taxes, $338,000,000; natural resources taxes, $205,700,000). Expenditures, $1,300,693,000 (education, $403,960,000; health and social services, $495,373,000).
Personal Income (1970 est.): $7,037,000,000; average annual income per person, $3,293.
Public Assistance (fiscal year 1971–72 est.): $136,615,000 (social allowances and supplements, $125,000,000).
Manufacturing (1970): $3,688,000,000 (wood industries, $1,-050,000,000; paper and allied products, $680,000,000; food and beverages, $650,300,000).
Agriculture (1970): Total cash receipts, $205,868,000; (livestock, $138,127,000; crops, $65,059,000). Chief crops (cash receipts): dairy products, $50,665,000 (ranks 3d among the provinces); cattle and calves, $34,683,000 (ranks 6th); fruit, $26,895,000 (ranks 2d); eggs, $22,602,000 (ranks 3d).
Mining (1970): Production value, $485,234,000. Chief minerals (lbs): copper, 206,735,000 (ranks 3d among the provinces); zinc, 275,591,000 (ranks 5th); lead, 214,838,000 (ranks 2d); molybdenum, 31,276,000 (ranks 1st).
Forest Products (1970): Lumber, 7,697,500,000 board feet; pulp, 4,521,000 tons; paper, 1,810,000 tons.
Fisheries (1970): Total fish landings, 238,501,000 pounds ($60,-255,000). Leading species: salmon, 154,486,000 pounds ($45,076,000).
Transportation: Roads (1970), 27,686 miles; motor vehicles (1970), 1,019,000; railroads (1970), 4,540 miles of 1st main track (7,300 km).
Communications: Telephones (1970), 1,038,000; television stations (1970), 9; radio stations (1970), 60; daily newspapers (1970), 18.
(All monetary figures given in Canadian dollars.)

were to begin shipments in that year. The provincially owned Pacific Great Eastern Railway was extended about 250 miles (400 km) to Fort Nelson, near the border of the Yukon Territory.

A major program by the Westcoast Transmission Company to extend natural gas pipelines was budgeted at about $200 million for 1971–72. In addition, the provincial government called for bids on a $100 million natural-gas pipeline connection with Vancouver Island. Equipment contracts for new electrical generating plants were awarded as part of a planned $950 million, 5-year power-expansion program by the British Columbia Hydro and Power Authority.

Fair. Impo-Expo 71, the fourth international trade fair sponsored by the provincial government, was held in Vancouver on June 2–12. There were 420 exhibitors, and the displays of 18 countries, about a third of them new participants, were highlighted.

J. R. MEREDITH
Director, B. C. Bureau of Economics and Statistics

BUDDHISM. See RELIGION—*Oriental Religions.*
BUILDING AND CONSTRUCTION. See ECONOMY; HOUSING.

BULGARIA

Bulgaria's strong ties with the Soviet Union were reaffirmed during 1971, a year in which the Communist party held its 10th congress. A new 5-year plan and a new constitution were adopted at the congress. In foreign affairs, Bulgaria moved to improve its relations with other Balkan states.

Domestic Politics. The government continued its policies of strengthening the "socialist structure" of the country, of recognizing the Soviet Union as a "model," and of opposing economic as well as cultural liberalization.

In April the 10th congress of Bulgaria's Communist party met in Sofia. Todor Zhivkov, head of the party for over 17 years, was reelected as first secretary for another 5-year term. All 11 members of the Politburo were reelected except the foreign trade minister, Lachezar Avramov. Leonid Brezhnev, Soviet Communist party leader, attended the congress as a representative of the USSR. He warmly praised the achievements of Bulgaria's leadership and called for still closer Bulgarian-Soviet relations.

Economy. According to the data and resolutions of the party congress, Bulgaria has entered the "developed state of socialism." The congress called on the government to strengthen the "socialist structure" and to eradicate any tendencies toward "bourgeois-capitalist individualism." The country has become a semi-industrial state, with agriculture representing less than 25% of the national product. In the past five years production of electric power, plastics, cement, and fertilizers has doubled, while steel output has tripled.

The party recommendations were implemented in Bulgaria's sixth 5-year plan (1971–75). The economy is to operate under rigidly centralized government control and planning with a degree of nationalization and socialization comparable only to the USSR's. No small-scale private enterprises or limited-market mechanisms will be allowed.

The agro-industrial complexes, which began on an experimental basis in 1969, will continue to enjoy government support. The plans provide for 150

——————— BULGARIA · Information Highlights ———————

Official Name: People's Republic of Bulgaria.
Area: 42,823 square miles (110,912 sq km).
Population (1970 est.): 8,490,000. *Density,* 197 per square mile (76 per sq km). *Annual rate of increase,* 0.7%.
Chief City (1968 est.): Sofia, the capital, 840,113.
Government: *Head of state,* Georgi Traika, chairman of the Presidium (took office April 23, 1964). *Head of government,* Todor Zhivkov, first secretary of Communist party and president (took office Nov. 19, 1962). *Legislature*— National Assembly (unicameral), 416 members. (All members of the Fatherland Front.)
Language: Bulgarian (official).
Education: *Literacy rate* (1969), 95% of population. *Expenditure on education* (1968), 4.5% of net material product. *School enrollment* (1968)—primary, 1,079,251; secondary, 374,722; vocational, 266,540; university/higher, 90,024.
Finances (1970 est.): *Revenues,* $4,475,000,000; *expenditures,* $4,465,000,000; *monetary unit,* lev (1.17 leva equals U.S.$1, 1971).
Manufacturing (metric tons, 1969): Cement, 3,551,000; residual fuel oil, 2,244,000; wheat flour, 1,563,000; crude steel, 1,515,000; beer, 2,726,000 hectoliters.
Crops (metric tons, 1969 crop year): Wheat, 2,569,000; maize, 2,415,000; sugar beets (1968–69), 1,447,000.
Minerals (metric tons, 1969): Lignite, 28,632,000; iron ore, 881,000; coal, 370,000; zinc ore, 77,000.
Foreign Trade (1968): *Exports* (1970), $2,004,000,000 (chief exports—clothing, $103,800,000; raw tobacco, $100,342,-000; alcoholic beverages, $99,800,000). *Imports* (1970), $1,831,000,000 (chief imports—machinery and equipment, $800,000,000; fuels, minerals, and metals, $430,000,000). *Chief trading partners* (1968)—USSR (took 55% of exports, supplied 53% of imports); East Germany (7%–8%).
Tourism: *Receipts* (1970), $85,000,000.
Transportation: *Roads* (1968), 18,531 miles (29,821 km); *motor vehicles* (1966), 26,900 (automobiles, 10,400); *railroads* (1968), 3,681 miles (5,923 km); *merchant fleet* (1970), 686,000 gross registered tons; *national airline,* Balkan (Bulgarian Airlines); *principal airport,* Sofia.
Communications: *Telephones* (1970), 414,113; *television stations* (1968), 5; *television sets* (1969), 829,000; *radios* (1969), 2,271,000; *newspapers* (1969), 12.

complexes, each covering an area of some 50,000 to 125,000 acres. The new regulations issued by the council of ministers strengthened government control over their administration in order to make production more efficient.

Since collectivized farmers still continued to devote most of their energies to the "private lots" and not to the commonly owned land, special "educational programs in socialism" were to be established. According to the statistics, the "private lots, covering no more than 2%–4% of collectivized land, accounted for over 20% of agricultural production, for 25% of meat and wool production, and for over 30% of eggs.

Foreign Policy and Trade. The cult of the Soviet Union and Bulgarian-Soviet friendship continued to dominate all spheres of public life. The new constitution links Bulgaria's foreign policy to that of the Soviet Union. The 5-year development plan provides for further economic integration of both countries, and within the next five years the Soviet Union will give Bulgaria about $350 million in credits. The 5-year plan also called for increased integration of Bulgaria's economy with Comecon, the Communist equivalent of the Common Market. The Comecon countries' share in Bulgaria's exports and imports is to reach 82% and 87%, respectively, by 1975.

In September, Brezhnev visited Sofia for the second time in 1971. He was greeted by well-staged mass demonstrations. Zhivkov called the visitor his "senior comrade, friend, and brother" and pledged Bulgaria's allegiance to the Warsaw Pact "in work and war" against "imperialist forces."

In October, in an apparent effort to reduce friction with Yugoslavia, the government removed Boris Krumov, the editor of a highly political weekly, *Anteni.* In the past he and his paper had been accused by Belgrade of revanchism directed

against Yugoslavian Macedonia, an apple of discord between both countries for centuries.

In the same month, Turkey's Premier Süleyman Demirel paid an official visit to Sofia. While he was there, Bulgaria reached an agreement with Turkey that provided for intensification of long-range trade, cooperation in industry and technology, and promotion of cultural exchange. To facilitate cooperation, a new railroad connecting both countries directly, without passing through Greece, was constructed. As an indication of Bulgaria's good intentions toward Turkey, the Bulgarian press has often reminded Bulgarian citizens of Turkish descent that they are free to emigrate to Turkey.

Exchange of visits and official talks with Greek and Rumanian leaders further indicated Sofia's interest in promoting stability in the traditionally unstable Balkan peninsula.

In the middle of 1971 an important trade protocol with West Germany was signed by Foreign Trade Minister Luchezar Avramov and his German counterpart, Karl Schiller. West Germany had been Bulgaria's largest non-Communist trading partner until 1969, when economic exchanges between both countries began to slow down. The protocol provided for mutual reduction of tariffs, expansion of commodity exchanges, and industrial as well as technological cooperation.

In September the 27th International Fair opened in Plovdiv. Over 420 firms, representing 43 countries, displayed their products. Contracts reached at the fair increased 50% in value over those of the 1970 fair.

JAN KARSKI, *Georgetown University*

BURGER, Warren E. See BIOGRAPHY.

BURMA

Burma's strong-man ruler, Gen. Ne Win, although in ill health, took steps in both domestic and foreign affairs to strengthen his government's threatened political position in 1971. To lessen tensions along two of his country's troubled borders he visited China and was host to Thailand's deputy foreign minister. In September it was announced that a commission was to be formed to draft a new constitution; this was designed to broaden support of his regime at home.

Politics. Ne Win's persisting ill health was a factor in the government's consolidation moves. Returning from medical treatment in Britain in January, the Burmese leader cancelled a scheduled state visit to Nepal in February to return to London for further medical attention. On the return trip to Rangoon in April, he was forced to undergo hospitalization in India.

A speech read on Ne Win's behalf in Rangoon on May Day promised the country a new constitution (the old one had been discarded when Premier U Nu was overthrown in 1962). Following the first congress of the Burma Socialist Program party (the only officially allowed party) in late June and early July, a 30-man, all-civilian board was named to advise the ruling military Revolutionary Council.

Brigadier San Yu, who was in charge when Ne Win was out of the country, was officially designated deputy premier in September. He was also named head of a 97-member commission appointed to draw up a new constitution for presentation by August 1973.

Insurgencies. Former Premier Nu's insurgent coalition of Karen, Mon, and Shan minority elements conducted its first serious military probing actions in eastern and southeastern Burma in the spring. By August, Nu's supporters had stepped up their activities, and the government moved vigorously against them near the Thailand border.

Communist insurrectionary activity declined early in the year after Rangoon and Peking resumed diplomatic relations and again exchanged ambassadors. The government continued its mop-up of Communist insurgents in central Burma, destroying the headquarters of the pro-Communist rebel faction of the Karen minority and killing its leader. But insurgent activity in the north increased.

Foreign Affairs. Burma sought to improve relations with both China and Thailand, its neighbors to the north and east. Ne Win visited Peking in August and subsequently announced that Chinese aid, which had been discontinued in 1967 after a quarrel between the two countries over anti-Chinese rioting in Rangoon, would be resumed. China stopped its radio broadcasts attacking Ne Win, but permitted Burmese Communists to use a new transmitter on Chinese soil to broadcast more hours than Peking formerly did.

Thai Deputy Foreign Minister Sa-Nga Kittikachorn visited Rangoon in October, after incidents in which Burmese troops had crossed into Thailand and Burma had shot at and seized a Thai vessel.

A U. S. military sales program was allowed to lapse in June, and the remaining members of a U. S. military equipment delivery team left the country. In October, Soviet President Nikolai Podgorny visited Burma en route to North Vietnam.

Economy. The main report to the party congress admitted major economic shortcomings but predicted these would be overcome by a 1971–75 economic plan. The 1971–72 budget revealed deficit financing for Burma's modest development efforts. Foreign exchange reserves fell by mid-1971 to $50 million, the lowest level since independence. Inflation and rationing continued, with black-market prices 10 times higher than official ones.

RICHARD BUTWELL
State University of New York at Brockport

BURNS, Arthur F. See BIOGRAPHY.

──────── **BURUNDI** • Information Highlights ────────

Official Name: Republic of Burundi.
Area: 10,747 square miles (27,834 sq km).
Population (1970 est.): 3,600,000. *Density,* 324 per square mile (125 per sq km). *Annual rate of increase,* 2.0%.
Chief City (1970 est.): Bujumbura, the capital, 100,000.
Government: *Head of state,* Michel Micombero, president (took office Nov. 28, 1966). *Head of government,* Michel Micombero. *Legislature—Parliament* (dissolved in October 1965). *Major political party—*National Unity and Progress party (UPRONA).
Languages: Kirundi (official), French (official).
Education: *Literacy rate* (1967), 23% of population. *Expenditure on education* (1968), 25.6% of total public expenditure.
Finances (1968 est.): *Revenues,* $15,802,000; *expenditures,* $20,475,000; *monetary unit,* franc (87.50 francs equal U. S. $1, Sept. 1971).
Gross National Product (1967 est.): $174,000,000.
National Income (1965): $148,000,000; *national income per person,* $46.
Crops (metric tons, 1969 crop year): Coffee, 14,600; potatoes, 41,000; cotton lint, 3,000; rice, 3,000.
Foreign Trade: *Exports* (1970) $24,365,000 (chief export—coffee, $20,570,000). *Imports,* $22,355,000 (chief imports, 1967—food products; lubricants). *Chief trading partner* (1966)—United States.

BURUNDI

Burundi remained firmly under the control of President Michel Micombero in 1971. Ever since an attempted coup in 1969, he has been trying to institutionalize his regime's hold over the country. Under the provisions of a new constitution adopted at the end of 1970, the Parti de l'Unité et du Progrès National du Burundi (UPRONA) would officially become the country's only political party.

Internal Affairs. Military strength was not neglected, and it was learned in February that a group of 200 soldiers were undergoing paratrooper training in Congo (Zaïre). An earlier group of 150 paratroopers trained in the same fashion in 1968 had been instrumental in putting down the 1969 attempted coup against Micombero. But rifts apparently continued to exist within the military establishment. In July 1971, several officers and two cabinet ministers were arrested in connection with an alleged plot against the regime.

Foreign Relations. Burundi continued to maintain good relations with the two other states of former Belgian Africa, Congo (Zaïre) and Rwanda. Burundi is also interested in developing links with its East African neighbors and has applied for membership in the proposed East African Community. Burundi supported most African states in opposing a "dialogue" with South Africa.

Economy. Regional economic cooperation may improve the country's economic situation. Burundi, Rwanda, and Congo (Zaïre) formed a planning commission to study the joint exploitation of the hydraulic resources of the lakes forming their common borders. In June the UN Development Program announced plans to assist Burundi, Rwanda, and Tanzania in the development of the Kagera River basin.

EDOUARD BUSTIN
Boston University

──────── **BURMA** • Information Highlights────────

Official Name: Union of Burma.
Area: 261,789 square miles (678,033 sq km).
Population (1970 est.): 27,580,000. *Density,* 104 per square mile (40 per sq km). *Annual rate of increase,* 2.2%.
Chief City (1964 est.): Rangoon, the capital, 1,530,434.
Government: *Head of state,* Gen. Ne Win, chairman, Council of Ministers (took office March 2, 1962). *Head of government,* Gen. Ne Win, prime minister. *Legislature—*Parliament (dissolved on March 3, 1962).
Languages: Burmese (official), English (official).
Education: *Literacy rate* (1970), 70% of population. *Expenditure on education* (1967), 16.8% of total public expenditure. *School enrollment* (1966)—primary, 2,635,497; secondary (1965), 425,214; technical/vocational (1965), 3,455.
Finances (1970–71 est.): *Revenues,* $1,842,000,000; *expenditures,* $1,945,000,000; *monetary unit,* kyat (4.715 kyats equal U. S.$1, Aug. 1971).
Gross National Product (1970): $3,200,000,000.
National Income (1968): $1,763,000,000; *national income per person,* $67.
Manufacturing (metric tons, 1969): Distillate fuel oils, 253,-000; kerosene, 239,000; cement, 183,000.
Crops (metric tons, 1969 crop year): Rice, 7,996,000 (ranks 6th among world producers); sugarcane (1968-69), 1,700,-000; groundnuts, 460,000; sesame seeds (1968) 83,300.
Minerals (metric tons, 1969): Crude petroleum, 746,000; salt, 179,000; lead ore, 11,400; zinc ore, 4,700.
Foreign Trade (1970): *Exports,* $105,000,000 (chief exports—rice, $52,957,000; teak, $23,700,000; oil cakes, $7,372,000). *Imports* (1968), $150,000,000 (chief imports—textile yarn and fabrics, $32,615,000; nonelectrical machinery, $25,-287,000; transport equipment, $16,516,000; mineral fuels and lubricants, $11,265,000). *Chief trading partner* (1968)—India (took 23% of exports).
Transportation: *Roads* (1970), 16,000 miles (26,000 km); *motor vehicles* (1969), 59,400 (automobiles, 29,400); *railroads* (1970), 1,925 miles (3,097 km).
Communications: *Telephones* (1970), 24,654; *radios* (1969), 399,000; *newspapers* (1966), 27.

CABINET, U. S. See UNITED STATES.

CALIFORNIA

A long, costly dock strike, high unemployment, rancorous conflict between the governor and the Legislature, spectacular crimes and trials, and a serious earthquake marked 1971 in California.

The Economy. Throughout the year the percentage of jobless persons was higher in California than in the nation as a whole, although by November the gap had nearly closed (6.2% as compared with 6.0%). Much of the difficulty stemmed from cutbacks in the aerospace industry, where employment dropped to a year's low of 433,900 in July, a 30% cutback from December 1967.

Another cause of unemployment was the long dock strike that tied up all of the state's major ports —Los Angeles-Long Beach, San Diego, and San Francisco-Oakland—from July through mid-October, when dockworkers were enjoined under the Taft-Hartley act. Additional labor troubles in the state included a long strike by lettuce workers in the Salinas Valley, which resulted in the loss of almost the entire crop, and an effort by the Teamsters' Union to organize vineyard and produce workers, thus bringing it into conflict with Cesar Chavez' United Farm Workers' union.

Earthquake. An earthquake that measured 6.6 on the Richter scale struck in the northern end of the San Fernando Valley on February 9, resulting in many deaths and injuries, as well as much property damage. (See also Los ANGELES.)

The disaster spurred demands for greater safety standards in construction, but the California Legislature passed no important bills in this respect during the 1971 session. The state remains unnecessarily vulnerable to earthquake damage in many ways. For example, San Francisco and some other major cities do not have legislation outlawing unanchored overhanging trim on buildings. Under a state law requiring schools to be made "earthquake safe," existing buildings need not be brought into compliance before 1975. At the time of the 1971 quake, Los Angeles had 177 schools that did not meet the safety standards. Of these, 13 were badly damaged. No children were killed, but only because the event occurred before school hours.

The California earthquake problem stems from an unstable geologic system that encircles the Pacific Ocean. Dozens of "faults" along which quakes may occur are located in the state. The most important is the San Andreas fault, which moves inland from the Pacific Ocean just north of Point Arena, hugs the coast, passing just to the west of downtown San Francisco, then gradually moves inland. In Southern California it goes eastward along the San Gabriel and San Bernardino mountains, then southward along the San Jacintos into Mexico. In many areas buildings have been constructed directly over the fault. After a Veterans Administration hospital was destroyed by the February 9 earthquake, further controversy was created by proposals to replace the building with a new one near Loma Linda University in San Bernardino county —within a short distance of the main fault. Seismologists agreed that California was overdue for an even greater earthquake.

Education. The California campuses were quiet, at least in comparison with the previous several years. Austerity budgets were the rule, and state college and university faculty members were denied a cost-of-living allowance for the second consecu-

——————CALIFORNIA • Information Highlights——————

Area: 158,693 square miles (411,015 sq km).
Population (1970 census): 19,953,134. *Density:* 124 per sq mi.
Chief Cities (1970 census): Sacramento, the capital, 254,413; Los Angeles, 2,816,061; San Francisco, 715,674; San Diego, 696,769; San Jose, 445,779; Oakland, 361,561.
Government (1971): *Chief Officers*—governor, Ronald Reagan (R); lt. gov., Ed Reinecke (R); secy. of state, Edmund G. Brown, Jr. (D); atty. gen., Evelle J. Younger (R); supt. of public instruction, Wilson C. Riles (NP); chief justice, Donald R. Wright. *Legislature*—Senate, 40 members (20 Democrats, 19 Republicans); Assembly, 80 members (43 D, 37 R).
Education (1970–71): *Enrollment*—public elementary schools, 2,938,000 pupils; 112,000 teachers; public secondary, 1,-764,000 pupils; 72,000 teachers; nonpublic schools (1968-69), 429,000 pupils; 18,040 teachers; college and university (fall 1968), 1,103,594 students. *Public school expenditures* (1970–71), $3,742,000,000 ($799 per pupil). *Average teacher's salary*, $11,022.
State Finances (fiscal year 1970): Revenues, $11,397,038,000 (5% general sales tax and gross receipts taxes, $1,-756,935,000; motor fuel tax, $672,410,000; federal funds, $3,017,394,000). *Expenditures*, $10,760,359,000 (education, $2,840,178,000; health, welfare, and safety, $1,166,017,000; highways, $1,007,499,000). *State debt*, $5,334,537 (June 30, 1970).
Personal Income (1970): $91,510,000,000; per capita, $4,469.
Public Assistance (1970): $2,724,211,000. *Average monthly payments* (Dec. 1970)—old-age assistance, $116.95; aid to families with dependent children, $192.90.
Labor Force: *Nonagricultural wage and salary earners* (June 1971), 7,001,200. *Average annual employment* (1969)—manufacturing, 1,655,000; trade, 1,494,000; government, 1,387,000; services, 1,217,000. *Insured unemployed* (Oct. 1971)—226,800 (4.4%).
Manufacturing (1967): *Value added by manufacture*, $23,393,-600,000 (transportation equipment, $3,653,700,000; electrical equipment and machinery, $3,012,900,000; food and kindred products, $2,986,400,000).
Agriculture (1970): *Cash farm income*, $4,588,025,000 (livestock, $1,790,167,000; crops, $2,665,921,000; government payments, $131,937,000). *Chief crops* (1970)—Sugar beets, 7,856,000 tons (ranks 1st among the states); hay, 7,774,-000 tons (ranks 3d); grapes, 2,760,000 tons (ranks 1st).
Mining (1969): *Production value*, $1,880,000,000 (ranks 3d among the states). *Chief minerals* (tons)—Sand and gravel, 120,200,000; petroleum, 375,220,000 barrels.
Fisheries (1970): *Commercial catch*, 694,200,000 pounds ($84,-500,000). *Leading species by value* (1969), Yellowfin, $19,-404,938; skipjack, $11,243,779; jack mackerel, $1,447,132.
Transportation: *Roads* (1969), 162,223 miles (261,065 km); *motor vehicles* (1969), 11,602,000; *railroads* (1968), 7,483 miles (12,042 km); *airports* (1969), 253.
Communications: *Telephones* (1971), 13,305,500; *television stations* (1969), 49; *radio stations* (1969), 372; *newspapers* (1969), 134 (daily circulation, 5,814,000).

tive year. Auditors were instructed to seek every possible way to cut costs or generate revenue. A proposal that the university system sell its rare-book collection was rejected.

Crime. The spectacular murder trials of the members of Charles M. Manson's "family" ended in convictions and penalties of death or life imprisonment. In another dramatic criminal episode six persons died during an abortive escape attempt from San Quentin prison on August 21. Possibly the greatest mass murder ever allegedly committed by a single individual in American history was laid to a farm labor broker named Juan Corona of Yuba City, north of Sacramento, who was indicted on June 2 for the murders of 25 itinerant workers.

Government and Politics. Gov. Ronald Reagan began his second term of office by urging a number of governmental reforms. After a bitter struggle the Legislature approved Reagan's changes in the public welfare program. However, tax reform, supplemental taxes to balance the budget, and legislative reapportionment were areas in which the Democratic majority in the Legislature and the governor could not agree. The longest legislative session in California history ended in chaos on December 3. The Democrats refused to go along with the governor's tax proposals. A tax program to balance the state's budget was adopted at a special session of the legislature, Dec. 6–20, 1971.

Reapportionment. On December 11, Lt. Gov. Ed Reinecke, chairman of the state Reapportion-

FREEWAYS buckled when severe earthquake struck southern California. The tremor killed 64 persons and caused extensive damage.

ment Commission, said that seldom-used body would plan reapportionment, in view of the Legislature's failure. The special session on December 20 passed reapportionment bills designed to assure Democratic majorities in congressional, state Senate, and Assembly seats. Reagan's veto was expected, setting up a dispute as to whether the Reapportionment Commission or the state supreme court would reapportion the electorate. California was eligible for five more congressional seats because of population gains.

CHARLES R. ADRIAN
University of California, Riverside

CAMBODIA

Cambodia's war with the Vietnamese Communists, which had seemed to advance during the second half of 1971, took a turn for the worse in November—requiring stepped-up U. S. air cover and a new South Vietnamese ground-force intervention. A major stroke partly paralyzed the country's leader, Premier Lon Nol, in February, and his illness was followed by intense jockeying for political power. Such activity, however, did not interfere with military activity against Vietnamese and local Communists, who controlled no more of the country at the end of 1971 than they had at the start of the year despite the increased fighting in November–December.

Fighting. A standoff seemed to have developed between government and Communist forces by November. Fighting took place near Phnom Penh as late as June, but the government used the subsequent rainy season to advantage. With only minimal opposition, its forces occupied about one third of the territory previously held by the Vietnamese Communists and the Khmer Rouge insurgents. At the end of October, the Communists controlled only the thinly populated areas of the east and northeast that they had seized at the start of the war in 1970—which was, nonetheless, about half of the national territory. With the end of the annual monsoon, however, the fighting accelerated dramatically.

During the period from March–May 1970 to late 1971, the Cambodian armed forces had been expanded from 35,000 ill-trained personnel to a not ineffective fighting force of about 190,000. Not all of the troops, however, were by any means sufficiently trained or equipped. There were an estimated 60,000 Communist Vietnamese troops in the country in late 1971, while more than 25,000 South Vietnamese were helping the Cambodians.

The cost of the war was high. More than 5,000 Cambodians had died by November 1971, and one million persons had been displaced (in a population of 7 million) by the fighting and U. S. air strikes in support of Cambodian troops.

Leadership Crisis. The cerebral thrombosis suffered by the premier, Marshal Lon Nol, on February 8 set in motion a chain of events that culminated in the dissolution of the National Assembly as the country's legislature in mid-October.

The marshal underwent two months' treatment and recuperation in Honolulu and returned home in April to submit his resignation as prime minister.

An 18-day crisis ensued, during which Prince Sisowath Sirik Matak, co-leader with Lon Nol of the March 1970 coup that ousted Prince Norodom Sihanouk, was unable to maneuver himself into the leadership position occupied by Lon Nol.

The crisis seemed to be resolved in early May, when Lon Nol agreed to resume the premiership on an initially nominal basis, Sirik Matak became "premier-delegate" acting on his behalf, and the National Assembly endorsed this arrangement by a 50–6 vote. Lon Nol, in surprisingly good health following his near-fatal stroke, presided over his first cabinet meeting in August, but the political role of his confidant and co-leader, Sirik Matak, grew in the intervening months.

Government by Decree. On October 18, Lon Nol personally announced that the National Assembly would meet henceforth only as a constituent assembly to review the strong presidential constitution being drawn up by a previously appointed committee. Democracy, he said, was a "sterile game" in wartime, and anarchy was imminent as "certain groups" sought to "divide the country by sowing confusion." His reference was mainly to opponents of Sirik Matak, such as the recently deposed First Deputy Premier In Tam, the writer-intellectual Douc Rasy, and "anti-royalist" Buddhist monks, who continued their hostility to Sirik Matak even after he renounced his title of prince in 1970.

Premier Lon Nol also declared a state of emergency and appointed a new government composed of the same persons who were already helping him to run the country. They would rule by decree.

Economy. The Cambodian economy was almost completely disrupted by the war. While as recently as 1969 Cambodia had exported 186,000 tons of rice, by late 1971 the government was dipping into its rice stocks for current consumption purposes. Even more, it was expected that 100,000 to 200,000

——— **CAMBODIA • Information Highlights** ———

Official Name: Khmer Republic.
Area: 69,898 square miles (181,035 sq km).
Population (1969 est.): 6,700,000. *Density,* 103 per square mile (40 per sq km). *Annual rate of increase,* 2.2%.
Chief Cities (1962 census): Pnompenh, the capital, 393,995; Battambang, 38,846; Kompong Cham, 28,534.
Government: *Head of state,* Chen Heng, president (took office Oct. 9, 1970). *Head of government,* Lon Nol, premier (took office Aug. 13, 1969). *Legislature*—Parliament; Senate, 24 members; National Assembly, 82 members.
Languages: Cambodian (official), French.
Education: *Literacy rate* (1970), 58% of population. *Expenditure on education* (1967), 21.6% of total public expenditure. *School enrollment* (1967)—primary, 934,292; secondary, 105,361; technical/vocational, 5,787; university/higher, 8,929.
Finances (1969 budget est.): *Revenues,* $153,000,000; *expenditures,* $153,000,000; *monetary unit,* riel (55.54 riels equal U. S.$1, Sept. 1971).
Gross National Product (1970 est.): $910,000,000.
National Income (1966): $749,000,000; *national income per person,* $119.
Manufacturing (metric tons, 1969): Meat, 35,000; sawnwood, 223,000 cubic meters; cigarettes, 3,807,000,000 units.
Crops (metric tons, 1969 crop year): Rice, 2,503,000 bananas (1968), 189,000; maize, 118,000; natural rubber, 51,800.
Foreign Trade (1968): *Exports,* 1970 $40,000,000 (chief exports—rice, $41,743,000; natural rubber and rubberlike gums, $18,698,000; fruits and vegetables, $12,100,000). *Imports,* 1970 $48,000,000 (chief imports—chemicals, $18,900,000; transport equipment, $14,371,000; nonelectrical machinery, $11,920,000; textile yarn and fabrics, $10,450,000). *Chief trading partners* (1968)—France (took 8% of exports, supplied 30% of imports); Japan (4%—23%); Singapore (8%—8%).
Tourism: *Receipts* (1970), $1,350,000.
Transportation: *Roads* (1970), 3,200 miles (5,150 km); *motor vehicles* (1968), 33,800 (automobiles, 23,100); *railroads* (1970), 291 miles (468 km); *national airline,* Air Cambodge; *principal airports,* Pnompenh, Siem Reap, Kompong Som.
Communications: *Telephones* (1970), 8,024; *television stations* (1969), 1; *television sets* (1969), 50,000; *radios* (1968), 1,000,000; *newspapers* (1968), 26 (daily circulation, 145,-000).

DESPERATE Cambodian woman, with her child, implores South Vietnamese not to take her husband away. A suspected Communist, he was detained in August.

tons of rice would be imported in 1972. The low price the government paid farmers for their rice resulted in only one third of the available land in the west being planted in 1971. Communist control of eastern Cambodia in 1970 had halted the export of rubber, grown wholly in that part of the country.

Prices in Cambodia about doubled during the year. Prodded by the International Monetary Fund and the United States, the government in October effectively devalued its currency, the riel, by permitting it to float. The official rate had previously been 55 riels to U.S.$1, and the government's action was expected to result in a change in its value to about 140 riels to the dollar. New credit restrictions and import taxes were also announced, and a multination stabilization fund was expected to be established in early 1972.

Foreign Affairs. The Cambodian government tried to improve relations with its most important allies, the United States and South Vietnam, in 1971.

Premier Lon Nol made a 2-day trip to South Vietnam in January before his illness, and the two governments agreed to expand relations and reduce tensions. "Premier-Delegate" Sirik Matak traveled to the United States in August and returned to report that President Richard Nixon was sympathetic to his request for more aid. The U.S. Senate Foreign Relations Committee, however, was not in agreement with the President. In October it recommended a $250 million ceiling on military and economic aid to Cambodia, which was about what it had totaled between July 1970 and June 1971. The Nixon administration had sought $350 million for 1971–72.

RICHARD BUTWELL
State University of New York at Brockport

CAMEROON

In 1971 the Federal Republic of Cameroon celebrated the 10th anniversary of its formation. It had been created on Oct. 1, 1961.

Domestic Affairs. In January the verdicts were announced in the "rebellion" and conspiracy trials that had been held before a military court in Yaoundé late in 1970. In the "rebellion" trial, the vice president of the illegal Union des Populations du Cameroun, Ernest Ouandié, and 2 others were condemned to death, 10 were acquitted, and 17 were sentenced to prison terms. In the conspiracy trial, three of those accused of plotting to kill President Ahmadou Ahidjo, including Albert Ndongmo, the Roman Catholic bishop of Nkongsamba, were sentenced to death. Of the remaining defendants, 15 were acquitted, and 58 received prison terms.

Following pleas for clemency from many sources, including the Vatican, President Ahidjo commuted the death sentences of Bishop Ndongmo and his two co-conspirators to life imprisonment. But on January 15, Ouandié and the two rebels condemned to die in the first trial were executed by a firing squad.

Foreign Affairs. Cameroon was busy on both African and worldwide diplomatic fronts in 1971. French President Georges Pompidou visited Cameroon in February, and the Nigerian head of state, Gen. Yakubu Gowon, paid a 5-day visit in April. On April 2 it was announced that Cameroon and the People's Republic of China would establish diplomatic relations at the ambassadorial level.

During the year, Cameroon reiterated its opposition to the policy of a dialogue with South Africa. It also formally withdrew from participation in Air Afrique, the multinational West African airline, and set up its own national airline, Cameroon Airlines.

Economy. The general improvement of the country's economy noted in previous years was marred by the consequences of a severe drought that hit much of West Africa in 1970–71. There were serious shortages of peanuts, cotton, and cacao, and in April, Cameroon announced its first trade deficit since 1967.

Despite the economic reverses, the government announced its third 5-year plan (1971–75). The plan envisioned a gross national product of $1,380 million by 1975.

VICTOR T. LE VINE
Washington University, St. Louis

——— **CAMEROON · Information Highlights** ———

Official Name: Federal Republic of Cameroon.
Area: 183,569 square miles (475,442 sq km).
Population (1970 est.): 5,840,000.
Chief City (1965 est.): Yaoundé, the capital, 101,000.
Government: *Head of state,* Amadou Ahidjo, president (re-elected March 28, 1970). *Head of government,* Amadou Ahidjo. *Legislature*—Federal National Assembly.
Languages: French (official), English (official).
Education: *Literacy rate* (1970), 15% of population. *Expenditure on education* (1968), 18.6% of total public expenditure.
Finances (1970 est.): *Revenues,* $128,500,000; *expenditures,* $128,500,000; *monetary unit,* CFA franc (277.71 francs equal U.S.$1, Sept. 1971).
Gross National Product (1968): $936,000,000.
National Income (1968): $779,000,000; *national income per person,* $137.
Manufacturing (metric tons, 1969): Meat, 48,000; aluminum, 46,700; sawnwood (1968), 84,000 cubic meters.
Crops (metric tons, 1968 crop year): Maize, 319,000; sweet potatoes and yams, 300,000; cocoa beans (1969), 110,000.
Foreign Trade (1970): *Exports,* $226,000,000 (chief exports—cacao, $55,022,000; coffee, $53,077,000). *Imports,* $184,-000,000 (chief import, 1966—textile yarn and fabrics, $16,558.000). *Chief trading partner* (1968)—France.
Transportation: *Roads* (1967), 20,000 miles (32,186 km); *motor vehicles* (1969), 58,200 (automobiles, 28,200).

TASS FROM SOVFOTO

Prime Minister Trudeau (*above right*) inspects honor guard with Soviet Premier Kosygin at Moscow airport on May 17. Kosygin returned Trudeau's visit and toured Canada in October. Talks between the two covered topics of Canadian-Soviet concern. (*Right*) Kosygin chats with Prime Minister and Mrs. Trudeau at Moscow reception.

CANADIAN PRESS

CANADA

For Canada, the year 1971 included some major paradoxes. The economy appeared strong on all leading fronts; yet the number of unemployed continued to rise. The crisis caused by political kidnappings and murder in Quebec, which had led to proclamation of the War Measures Act in 1970, appeared to be over, and the Public Order (Temporary Measures) Act passed because of it was allowed to expire on April 30. Yet the disruption of trials and sporadic bombings continued, and in October the Canadian secretary of state said that, because of unemployment, the danger of a more broadly based public uprising in Quebec was potentially greater than ever. Canada's direct relations with mainland China and the Soviet Union grew in cordiality. But those with an old friend and chief trading partner, the United States, deteriorated unmistakably.

DOMESTIC AFFAIRS

Paul Rose and Francis Simard, members of the separatist Front for the Liberation of Quebec, were convicted of the October 1970 murder of Pierre Laporte, Quebec's minister of labor and immigration, and were sentenced in March and May, respectively, to life imprisonment. Trials of others continued during the year.

The chief domestic issues were economic and constitutional, with the economic paramount, especially after the United States announced on August 15 that a 10% surcharge would be imposed on all dutiable imports. (Subsequently, in late December, an international monetary accord resulted in removal of the surcharge.) U.S. investments in Canadian resources also continued to arouse those who believe that Canada should possess its own facilities. Although the fortunes of the Liberal party declined, Prime Minister Pierre Trudeau said in late July that he did not expect to recommend a federal election until 1972.

Federal-Provincial Relations. Canada's economic situation inevitably affects many negotiations between the federal government and the provinces, and of five top-level conferences held in 1971, three were specifically on economic issues. Apart from these conferences, federal-provincial relations were highlighted by a variety of discussions and negotiations. Notable among these were renewed discussions over offshore mineral rights, which were stimulated by an oil find on Sable Island—a small island some 100 miles (160 km) off the coast of Nova Scotia and claimed by that province. In the west, a prolonged argument revolved around a federal plan to stabilize grain farmers' incomes.

THE CANADIAN MINISTRY, 1971

(In order of precedence in the Privy Council)

Pierre Elliott Trudeau, Prime Minister

Paul Martin, Leader of the Government in the Senate

Mitchell Sharp, Secretary of State for External Affairs

Arthur Laing, Minister of Public Works

Allan J. MacEachen, President of the Queen's Privy Council for Canada

Charles Mills Drury, President of the Treasury Board

Edgar J. Benson, Minister of Finance

Jean-Luc Pepin, Minister of Industry, Trade and Commerce

Jean Marchand, Minister of Regional Economic Expansion

John J. Greene, Minister of Energy, Mines and Resources

Jean-Pierre Côté, Postmaster General

John N. Turner, Minister of Justice

Jean Chrétien, Minister of Indian Affairs and Northern Development

Bryce S. Mackasey, Minister of Labour

Donald S. Macdonald, Minister of National Defence

John C. Munro, Minister of National Health and Welfare

Gérard Pelletier, Secretary of State of Canada

Jack Davis, Minister of the Environment and Minister of Fisheries

Horace A. Olson, Minister of Agriculture

Jean-Eudes Dubé, Minister of Veterans Affairs

Stanley Ronald Basford, Minister of Consumer and Corporate Affairs

Donald C. Jamieson, Minister of Transport

Robert K. Andras, Minister of State for Urban Affairs

James A. Richardson, Minister of Supply and Services

Otto E. Lang, Minister of Manpower and Immigration

Herb Gray, Minister of National Revenue

Robert D. G. Stanbury, Minister of Communications

Jean-Pierre Goyer, Solicitor General of Canada

Alastair W. Gillespie, Minister of State for Science and Technology

Martin P. O'Connell, Minister of State

Economic Conferences. The first conference, held in Ottawa on July 12–13, was for ministers of finance, and the chief item on the agenda was the distribution of tax revenues between the two levels of government in the light of federal proposals for tax reform. Under a long-standing series of agreements, the federal government collects both federal and provincial income and corporation taxes (except for Quebec) and pays money back to the provinces according to a complex formula guaranteeing that even the poorest provinces receive a per capita revenue roughly equal to the national average. The existing agreements expire in 1972, and the federal government's original plan was to guarantee that the proposed tax reform would not cost any province a loss in revenue for the next three years.

Because the provinces expected rising costs in several of their most important activities and faced a federal decision to relinquish taxes on the estates of deceased persons (from which the provinces receive three fourths of the revenue), they wanted both a more generous agreement and a longer guarantee. The federal government remained adamant until the conference reconvened on November 1. It then accepted another 5-year agreement and conceded more liberal monetary terms.

Another economic conference, scheduled to start on December 6 but moved forward to November 15, was a summit meeting of the prime minister and the provincial premiers, held behind closed doors. Nonetheless, most of those attending made their positions clear in interviews. And Prime Minister Trudeau, anticipating criticism of his government's relations with the United States, released on November 14 a prepared television talk affirming his faith in the two countries' long friendship and dismissing as "completely ridiculous" the accusation that the U. S. surcharge was a retaliatory gesture toward Canada. The conference did discuss the surcharge, however, as well as problems created by foreign investment in Canada.

The efficacy of existing methods of financing health care was analyzed unfavorably by two federal ministers. Citing the fact that Canada devotes more of its gross national product to health (5.2%) than any other country, they argued that the nation was getting inadequate services. The premiers were a receptive audience, since health services consume about one third of their budgets.

The conference also examined the status of cities —several of which in Canada are more populous than most of the provinces. The possibility of a future federal-provincial conference involving municipalities in an active role undoubtedly moved closer. A noncommittal communiqué at the end of the conference suggested that the meeting had been a satisfactory one, in which winter plans for employment were reviewed.

Constitutional Conferences. The main federal-provincial conferences, and the least conclusive, were those on the constitution, held in Ottawa in February and in Victoria, B. C., in June. At the first meeting the western premiers were eager to study economic matters as well, but the major agreement was on a proposed formula for bringing the Canadian constitution—the British North America Act—home to Canada from Britain and providing for its amendment thereafter. The archaic act is still a statute of the United Kingdom.

The February meeting was adjourned until June, and in the interim the participants were to prepare their final positions on the formula, which included several immediate changes in the constitution. Fundamental rights, including English and French language rights, were to be entrenched. The Supreme Court was to be reconstituted under the constitution, instead of under the existing federal law through which the federal executive alone appoints all the judges. A conference of the prime minister and premiers was to be called every year unless a majority of those concerned decided against it.

The amending formula itself was a proposal of great significance in Canadian history. As finally approved at the Victoria meeting, in the so-called "Victoria Charter," it read:

"Amendments to the Constitution of Canada may from time to time be made by proclamation issued by the Governor-General under the Great Seal of Canada when so authorized by resolutions of the Senate and the House of Commons and of the legislative assemblies of at least a majority of the provinces. That includes: (1) Every province that at any time before the issue of such proclamation had, according to any previous general census, a population of at least 25 per cent of the population of Canada; (2) At least two of the Atlantic provinces; (3) At least two of the Western provinces that have, according to the then latest general census, combined populations of at least 50 per cent of the population of all the Western provinces."

For practical purposes, the formula meant that no amendment could be made without the consent of Ontario and Quebec, and British Columbia would have to be one of the two western provinces whose approval was needed if any other two were opposed. Another clause permitted the House of Commons, in effect, to overrule the Senate if the latter did not pass a desired amendment.

The Victoria conference adjourned on June 17, with the understanding that all provinces were to indicate by June 28 whether they accepted the charter. In most cases, approval would have to be executive. Few legislatures were in session, and Saskatchewan was in the midst of an election. The premier who was under grestest pressure was Robert Bourassa of Quebec. His province had long been pushing for wider constitutional powers, even in international affairs involving French-speaking educational and cultural conferences. Domestically, Quebec desired provincial rather than federal primacy in social security, the policies for which have developed largely through programs under both levels of government.

The other provinces appeared certain to approve the charter, although several premiers favored in principle a more decentralized federalism. To no one's surprise, Premier Bourassa cast a negative vote on June 23 because of uncertainty over the province's rights, particularly in regard to income security. Spokesmen in other provinces were critical of his decision. But provinces other than Quebec have delayed constitutional reform in the past, and Quebec's rejection was accepted as one more obstacle in a long, slow course dating back to the 1930's.

Politics and Elections. Although 1971 was a discouraging year for the federal Liberal party, it was not alone in encountering difficulties. Other parties also had to deal with lost elections, resignation of prominent members, and new political movements.

Liberal Party. In an unusually lively series of campaigns, provincial Liberal governments were defeated badly in Saskatchewan and narrowly in Newfoundland. In Ontario, the Liberals, as an opposition party, received a severe setback. And in Alberta, where they have been weak for decades, the Liberals again got nowhere when the Progressive Conservatives overturned a Social Credit government that had been in power since 1935.

If the Liberal party's fortunes had included only two provincial defeats, no one could have concluded that the results were necessarily bad news for the national leadership. But there were other developments. On April 29, Eric Kierans resigned as minister of communications in the Trudeau cabinet, asserting his disapproval of the government's economic policies, which he said were biased too heavily in favor of exporting raw materials and investing in machinery rather than creating jobs. Kierans had previously criticized the government on several occasions, most notably when he urged a Canadian withdrawal of military commitments to NATO and NORAD. His was the second departure from the Liberal cabinet.

Paul Hellyer, who had resigned as minister of defense in 1969, left the Liberal caucus altogether on May 21 to sit in the Commons as an Independent Liberal. A week later he announced the founding of a new movement, Action Canada, which held its first convention early in October. By that time the group had spent several weeks trying to attract support, generally from the right of center, and it claimed a membership of 4,800. The convention chose Hellyer as leader and adopted a platform calling for immediate tax cuts and mandatory wage and price guidelines. Although extremist elements were present, including the leader of the Canadian Nazi party, the initial activities of Action Canada reflected only moderately right-wing views.

UPI

QUEEN ELIZABETH II greets Indian children in Kamloops, British Columbia. With Prince Philip and Princess Anne, the queen toured British Columbia on May 3–12 to help the province celebrate its centennial.

On May 20, Philip Givens, a former mayor of Toronto, announced his resignation from the Commons to go into Ontario provincial politics. He was the second member from metropolitan Toronto, where the Liberals have been strong, to leave the federal caucus within eight months, Perry Ryan having defected to the Progressive Conservatives in September 1970. On top of that, the Liberals fared badly in federal by-elections. On May 31 they retained the Quebec seats of Chambly and Trois-Rivières but lost Brant, Ontario, to the New Democrats. On November 8 they lost Assiniboia, Saskatchewan, to the same party. The loss in Saskatchewan, which reduced to one the party's representation from the province, was widely interpreted as evidence of dissatisfaction with the Liberals' grain policies.

Other Parties. The Progressive Conservatives, apart from their unprecedented Alberta victory, retained Central Nova, Nova Scotia, in a federal by-election but lost by defection one Commons seat in Quebec, where the federal wing was in disarray. The party's provincial president resigned on April 29 in a disagreement with the party's line on Quebec and was later active in an abortive new nationalist party. In the west, the party appeared stronger, but in November a veteran member of Parliament from Saskatchewan, critical of Robert Stanfield's national party leadership, announced that he planned to sit as an Independent Conservative. Further evidence of dissatisfaction with both the Liberal and Progressive

MARGARET TRUDEAU, prime minister's wife, holds son, Justin, born on Christmas day. He was first son born to a prime minister in office since the 19th century.

Conservative parties was seen in the formation of the Western Canada party and in the growing strength of the New Democrats.

The Cabinet. Having surveyed the political scene, Prime Minister Trudeau substantially reorganized his cabinet to make it more responsive to contemporary needs, creating new ministries in science and technology, the environment, and urban affairs. He also obtained legislation to permit the creation of a new office, minister of state, in which incumbents would be given specific assignments rather than particular departments. Appointments connected with these moves brought Trudeau's cabinet back to 30 and also permitted him to balance his Montreal-Toronto representation at five ministers each. Provision was later made for the appointment of 30 parliamentary secretaries to ministers (an increase of 14), thus making 60 executive posts available to members of parliament.

The opposition parties generally regarded this number as too large. They tied their objections to the growing staff in the prime minister's office, which was approaching 100, and accused Trudeau of trying to become a president, as distinct from a prime minister responsible to Parliament.

Legislation. The cabinet introduced a great deal of housekeeping legislation, ranging from an increase in old-age assistance to sharp restrictions on police wiretapping and increased liberalization of labor laws. Its major successes included setting up the Federal Court of Canada, designed to lighten the work of the Supreme Court and also to sit in regional panels instead of being fixed at Ottawa, and the Canada Development Corporation, created with a $2 billion venture capital fund.

Some legislation nonetheless bogged down in Parliament, and the government not only found its timetable slowed but decided to abandon some bills, among them the Young Offenders Act and the Prairie Grain Stabilization Act. The latter had unusual interest because the government, anticipating its passage, had left unfulfilled its obligations under another law, and several ministers were sued by some Saskatchewan farmers for their failure to act. But the suit was dropped when the existing law was complied with.

The Economy. Inflation and unemployment were the major preoccupations of the federal government.

General Conditions. The year began with a record-breaking gross national product (GNP) of $84.5 billion for 1970. Virtually all relevant indexes of expansion continued to rise throughout 1971, with preliminary figures indicating a final GNP well in excess of $90 billion. Significant gains were enjoyed in agriculture, construction, and the services generally (including transportation), while mining and manufacturing held their own strongly. Retail sales rose sharply, the annual rate passing $30 billion in April.

Civilian wages and salaries, which had totaled somewhat more than $47 billion in 1970, seemed certain to pass $50 billion in 1971. The labor force continued to increase and by year-end was approaching 9 million, while the number of gainfully employed continued to rise. So did the cost of living. In August the consumer price index (1961 = 100) reached 135 for the first time. The number of unemployed also rose, hovering between 6% and 7%.

--------- CANADA • Information Highlights ---------

Official Name: Canada.
Area: 3,851,809 square miles (9,976,185 sq km).
Population (1970 est.): 21,410,000. *Density,* 5 per square mile (2 per sq km). *Annual rate of increase,* 1.8%.
Chief Cities (1968 est.): Ottawa, the capital, 290,741; Montreal, 1,222,255; Toronto, 664,584; Vancouver, 410,375.
Government: *Head of state,* Elizabeth II, queen; represented by Roland Michener, governor general (took office April 20, 1968). *Head of government,* Pierre Elliott Trudeau, prime minister (took office April 20, 1968). *Legislature—* Parliament: Senate, 102 members; House of Commons, 264 members. *Major political parties*—Liberal, Progressive Conservative, New Democratic, Ralliement Créditiste.
Languages: English (official), French (official).
Education: *Literacy rate* (1961), 98% of population aged 15 and over. *Expenditure on education* (1968), 8.3% of gross national product. *School enrollment* (1968)—primary, 3,832.309; secondary, 1,616,920; technical/vocational, 188,694: university/higher, 477,967.
Finances (1969–70): *Revenues,* $11,510,000,000; *expenditures,* $11,160,000,000; *monetary unit,* Canadian dollar (1.0034 C. dollar equal U. S.$1, Oct. 1971).
Gross National Product (1971 est.): $90,000,000,000.
National Income (1970): $63,140,000,000; *per person,* $2,949.
Economic Indexes: *Industrial production* (1970), 148 (1963 = 100); *agricultural production* (1969), 106 (1963 = 100); *consumer price index* (1970), 126 (1963 = 100).
Manufacturing (metric tons, 1969): Gasoline, 18,441,000; crude steel, 9,350,000; newsprint, 7,944,000.
Crops (metric tons, 1969 crop year): Wheat, 18,623,000; barley, 8,238,000; oats, 5,728,000 (ranks 2d among world producers); potatoes, 2,362,000.
Minerals (metric tons, 1969): iron ore, 22,318,000 (ranks 4th among world producers); asbestos, 1,448,300 (world rank 1st); zinc, 1,194,200 (world rank 4th).
Foreign Trade (1970): *Exports,* $16,187,000,000 (chief exports —manufactured goods, $6,784,000,000; newsprint, $1,099,-000,000). *Imports,* $13,349,000,000 (chief imports, 1968— transport equipment, $2,878,000,000; nonelectrical machinery, $2,082,300,000). *Chief trading partners* (1968)— United States (took 68% of exports, supplied 73% of imports); United Kingdom (9%—6%).
Tourism: Receipts (1970), $1,192,000,000.
Transportation: *Roads* (1968), 523,891 miles (843,098 km); *motor vehicles* (1969), 8,115,800 (automobiles, 6,433,300); *railroads* (1968). 44,030 miles (70,857 km).
Communications: *Telephones* (1970), 9,302,828; *television stations* (1969), 345; *television sets* (1968), 6,100,000; *radios* (1969), 14,740,000; *newspapers* (1968), 118 (daily circulation, 4,527,000).

Finance. The budget for 1971–72, presented to the House of Commons on June 18 by Minister of Finance Edgar J. Benson, was an unusually complicated one. Not only was it based on an expansionary approach that required several tax changes, but it was also intended to be the prelude to a reform of the tax system itself, which in previous years had been studied by one royal commission and two parliamentary committees. Forecasting expenditures of about $14.4 billion, the minister of finance allowed for a deficit of $750 million and proposed to raise the revenues needed through a tax system that included much lighter tax burdens on lower-income groups, a capital gains tax, and progressive reductions of corporation taxes. These changes, with others designed to assist small businesses and to help control the inflow of U. S. capital, were expected to encourage Canadians to invest in domestic enterprises. In late December, Parliament approved the new tax system, to become law on Jan. 1, 1972.

Further Unemployment Measures. The anticipated effects of the government's economic policies on unemployment were not realized as soon as expected. And on October 14, when a sharp rise in unemployment (in part clearly attributed by the government to the U. S. surcharge) was evident, the finance minister produced a "mini-budget" for slightly over $1 billion, which included retroactive reductions of personal income and corporation taxes and plans for creating jobs though financing provincial and municipal projects and other work-intensive operations suitable to the winter months. The last unemployment statistics for the year showed a rise, and by then a Senate committee had published a comprehensive report on poverty, urging the abandonment of most social welfare programs and the institution of a guaranteed annual income.

FOREIGN RELATIONS

Apart from a deterioration of relations with the United States, the year 1971 was an unusual one for Canada in the number of international exchanges made possible by the travels of Canada's highest-ranking officials and the reception in Canada of distinguished foreign visitors.

U. S. Relations. Canadians, at least, blamed U. S. actions for the deterioration of Canada–U. S. relations. The nuclear test in November at Amchitka Island, Alaska, was protested by the House of Commons, which asked the United States on October 4 to cancel the blast. Plans to bring oil south from Alaska aroused strong opposition—proposals for pipelines because of potential damage to the Canadian environment, and plans for using tankers because of possible spills off the coast of British Columbia. Agitation over U. S. investments in Canadian resources culminated in the publication in a Toronto magazine on November 12 of a confidential cabinet document on foreign ownership—and possible ways of offsetting its disadvantages while retaining the benefits.

None of the foregoing had the sustained impact of the 10% surcharge on U. S. imports. The immediate reaction of the Canadian government to this added burden in the country's largest market, affecting over $2.5 billion of Canadian exports, was to send a delegation of senior ministers to Washington, D. C., to request exemptions. They obtained a polite reception—and nothing more. Prime Minister Trudeau cut short a European holiday and returned to Canada to help cope with what he called "a very serious matter," and subsequently his government introduced legislation to make up for the loss of 90,000 jobs, which the U. S. action was expected to cost over the first year. The government also foresaw a possible exodus of manufacturing from Canada if the impost was not removed, and found such a move harder to counteract. Trading concessions that Canada might make were of course canvassed. But the most potentially significant of the concessions that seemed to interest the United States —the pact guaranteeing certain production of automobiles in Canada—was in an area where Canada itself needed strengthening.

The most obvious immediate result of the surcharge was a reexamination by Canadian journals of the famous undefended frontier between the two countries. The latter part of the year found major newspapers carrying stories under headings such as "Canada, U. S. on Collision Course," while Prime Minister Trudeau himself said in October, "If they

DISCOVERY in 1971 of oil on Sable Island, in Atlantic off Nova Scotia, may sharply increase Canadian reserves.

do not realize what they're doing and if it becomes apparent that they want us to be sellers of natural resources to them and buyers of their manufactured products . . . we will have to reassess fundamentally our relations with them."

The other side of Canadian opinion was expressed in mid-November by Premier William A. C. Bennett of British Columbia, who favored the creation of a North American common market. On the same day the Committee for an Independent Canada, a broadly based organization whose leadership includes well-known writers and publishers, released plans for its first annual conference.

On December 6–7, Prime Minister Trudeau conferred with President Richard Nixon in Washington and received what he described as a "fantastically new statement" by a U. S. president in regard to Canadian independence from U. S. economic domination. The Prime Minister made clear that President Nixon had not requested that Canada maintain an open-door policy toward private investment from abroad, including the United States.

Other Relations. Soviet Premier Aleksei N. Kosygin was in Canada in October, immediately after the most dramatic part of the cabinet's grain troubles. This opportunity for Premier Kosygin to observe an executive in difficulties was perhaps a demonstration of what Prime Minister Trudeau hoped to gain from international exchanges during 1971. Governor General Roland Michener was received abroad as a head of state, not solely as representative of the Queen.

In January the prime minister traveled to Singapore, where he played a conciliatory role at a complex Commonwealth conference dealing with the proposed sale of British arms to South Africa. In the negotiations, Canada was the only government with a white majority to side with African countries against the British plan. On this trip, Trudeau visited several countries. In May he went to the Soviet Union, where he signed a protocol on joint cooperation in economic, scientific, and cultural matters. In July, Trade Minister Jean-Luc Pepin headed an economic mission to mainland China, and the possibility of a Chinese trade mission to Canada was discussed. President Tito of Yugoslavia visited Canada in November.

The new liaisons with China and the Soviet Union—set against the government's reaction to U. S. economic policies and its refusal to accept U. S. attempts to seat both mainland China and Taiwan at the United Nations—aroused a good deal of criticism in Canada, even within the Liberal party. Prime Minister Trudeau insisted that other friendships for Canada need not be at the expense of relations with the United States, and he and other supporters emphasized that Canadian–U. S. cordiality was based on too deep and too long a connection to be adversely affected by the government's newer policies. Canada's continued support of NATO and NORAD, which the United States also supports, was cited as indicative of Canada's most important commitments.

But when Premier Kosygin was sharply critical of U. S. policies during his October visit, the government was inevitably accused of encouraging anti–U. S. sentiments in Canada, and it appeared to be increasingly sensitive to the charge as 1971 wore on. In a television talk on November 14, Prime Minister Trudeau stressed Canadian–U. S. friendship but spoke at greater length of the need for Canada to play a growing role in foreign affairs, in the interest of her own independence and prosperity and of world peace.

NORMAN WARD
University of Saskatchewan, Saskatoon

CANADIAN LITERATURE. See LITERATURE.

SOVIET PREMIER Kosygin strains as self-styled Hungarian "freedom fighter" attacks him in Ottawa on October 18, during state visit. The premier was unharmed. Prime Minister Trudeau is at right.

DOUG GRIFFIN, TORONTO STAR

CANALS

Legal actions in 1971 halted several canal projects in the United States. Among the canals that figured prominently in the court suits brought by environmentalists fighting potential ecological damage were the Cross-Florida Barge Canal, the Tennessee-Tombigbee ship canal, and parts of the California water project.

Cross-Florida Barge Canal. President Richard M. Nixon ordered a halt to further construction of the Cross-Florida Barge Canal, a 107-mile (172-km) waterway designed to link the Atlantic Ocean and the Gulf of Mexico. The President's decision, which was surprising since some $54 million had already been spent on the project, was based on recommendations of the Environmental Quality Control Council. In announcing the action, Nixon said that the effect on the environment must be taken into account in future projects.

The Environmental Defense Fund, Inc., in leading the court battle against the Corps of Engineers, charged that the project threatened to cut off the Florida Aquifer, a water-bearing limestone formation that the group said is the peninsula's primary source of potable groundwater. They further charged that the project was endangering fish and wildlife in the Florida swamps and destroying the Oklawaha River. Nixon's action was believed to be the first of its kind ever taken by a president—stopping for environmental reasons a construction project that was well under way.

Tennessee-Tombigbee Ship Canal. Citing potential hazards to the environment, a federal judge granted a preliminary injunction against construction of the Tennessee-Tombigbee ship canal, which would connect the central United States with the Gulf of Mexico via the Tennessee and Tombigbee rivers in Alabama and Mississippi. The suit, brought against the project by the Environmental Defense Fund, Inc., contended that the study submitted by the Corps of Engineers on the effect of the project on the environment was misleading and incomplete. It asked that a full study be made before work on the project began.

Among the points cited against the proposed 245-mile (394-km), $400-million canal were: (1) that it was no longer needed; (2) that unacceptable water pollution would result if the Tennessee River —which is heavily laden with industrial wastes and a dangerous mercury level—was allowed to flow into the Tombigbee; and (3) that it would damage the natural environment—particularly several historic, scenic, and scientific excavation sites.

California Water Project. The Sierra Club and the Friends of the Earth brought suit to delay or curtail construction and operation of the Peripheral Canal, the San Luis Drain, and the East Side Canal —parts of California's $3 billion state water project —until Congress authorizes them and the Corps of Engineers approves them. Such approvals would depend on studies and reports required by federal environmental laws. The California water project is a complicated series of reservoirs, canals, and pumping stations that would supply water from the state's wet northern areas to its drier southern parts. Construction had begun in 1960, and its first stage was near completion when suit was brought.

Elbe Seiten Canal. West Germany continued adding to its extensive canal system in 1971 with the construction of the 73-mile (118-km) Elbe Seiten Canal, which was scheduled for completion in 1976. It will serve the 1,200-year-old port city of Hamburg as an inland shipping connection to the German canal network, most of which fans out from the Mittelland Canal, Germany's east-west waterway. It will also funnel off into the Elbe River floodwaters from two small rivers crossing it and will provide water for cash crops growing close by. In its course from the Mittelland Canal to the Elbe, the Elbe Seiten Canal will drop some 200 feet (61 meters). The difference will be overcome by a 75-foot (23-meter) standard lift lock south of Uelzen, and a twin shiplock at Scharnebeck, whose 124-foot (38-meter) lift will be the highest single lift in the world.

Europa Canal. Land-locked farms in the heart of Europe will have a gateway to the ocean once the Europa (Rhine-Main-Danube) Canal is finished. This canal will tie together the Rhine and Danube rivers, thus providing a shipping lane from the North Sea to the Black Sea for 13 countries in between. In 1971 a 30-mile (48-km) section of the 105-mile (169-km) waterway was under construction. The first 20 miles (32 km) of the canal will rise 306 feet (93 meters) in three steps to the canal's highest point in the Franconian Jura Mountains. On the Danube side, the drop of about 300 feet (91 meters) in 60 miles (97 km) is to be made with four locks.

KENNETH E. TROMBLEY
Editor, "Professional Engineer"

CARIBBEAN

The economy of the Caribbean area was adversely affected in 1971 by a slight decline in the tourist trade, a result of the slowing of economic activity in the United States and Europe. Agricultural production continued to improve slightly, but industry was plagued by labor unrest, due in part to the fact that price rises were exceeding wage increases. On the political front, there were some important elections. Outbreaks of violence were few, although rumblings could still be heard from earlier disturbances in Trinidad and Curaçao. Steps intended to lead to regional unity or, at the very least, stronger regional institutions yielded generally disappointing results.

Agriculture. The Caribbean experienced a record number of tropical storms in 1971. Fortunately, the hurricanes' potentially destructive winds bypassed all important landmasses, and little damage resulted from the storms.

The rains were credited as the principal factor responsible for a favorable record in the production of sugar, the Caribbean's principal agricultural product. Sizable increases in the harvest were noted in Antigua, Guyana, and Jamaica, although declines occurred in Puerto Rico, Barbados, and Cuba. The drop in Cuban sugar production was to be expected after the major effort of 1970 to reach a 10-million-ton harvest. Puerto Rico's continuing decline in sugar output was the result of problems other than adverse weather conditions. The decline in Barbados was believed to be only temporary.

Industry and Labor. Serious labor troubles slowed industrial growth in Trinidad and Guyana and contributed to economic problems in Puerto Rico and the U. S. Virgin Islands. Efforts to set up a desulfurization plant for the petroleum industry on Trinidad were aborted when violent labor strife

FRENCH liner *Antilles* burns after hitting a sunken reef near the Caribbean island of St. Vincent, January 8. All 690 cruise passengers and crewmen were removed safely.

hit the refining area, forcing the staff of a key corporation in that industry to withdraw abruptly. In Guyana, labor troubles hampered the government's efforts to operate the country's major bauxite concern after its nationalization in July.

Prices were increasing more rapidly than wages in the Virgin Islands and Puerto Rico, prompting a number of strikes. As in earlier years, teachers in the Virgin Islands delayed the opening of school when the government failed to reach agreement with them over their contracts.

On Hispaniola, the industrial picture continued to improve for the Dominican Republic, while impoverished Haiti, for the first time in many years, was looking forward to better economic conditions, owing to a change in government.

A decline in income from the tourist trade was especially harmful to the smaller islands in the northeastern Caribbean, where tourism had been the only major industry. These islands were also hurt by the forced return of many of their citizens from the U. S. Virgin Islands. These returnees were workers who had temporarily emigrated to those three islands, where their services had been in constant demand during more prosperous times. With a decline in labor demand, the new Virgin Islands administration had decided to regulate this immigration. On repatriation to their home islands, many of these workers reentered labor markets that were far more restricted.

Elections. Major elections were held in Trinidad and Tobago, Barbados, and Montserrat, and an important change in government took place in Haiti as a result of the death of the Haitian chief of state, President-for-life François Duvalier. Minor but significant elections were held in Guadeloupe and Martinique, where, in two of the principal cities, Communist mayors were returned to office with impressive majorities.

In Trinidad and Tobago, Barbados, and St. Kitts, incumbent prime ministers easily won new terms over disorganized or inactive opposition. By contrast, on Antigua and Montserrat presumably secure political organizations were swept out of power. The defeat of William Bramble's party in Montserrat came at the hands of his son Austin, whose forces won all 7 of the contested seats in an 11-member legislature. In Antigua, George Walter brought down the Vere Bird political machine that had dominated the island for more than 20 years. On becoming prime minister, Walter promptly disbanded the army created by his predecessor.

Europe in the Caribbean. World attention was brought to focus in 1971 on some of the lesser-known English-speaking islands of the West Indies when a UN special committee on colonies criticized Britain for refusing to present to the United Nations any reports on the six associated states of the Commonwealth in the Caribbean. In addition to its influence in these states, Britain exercised even greater control over such islands as Montserrat, Anguilla, and the British Virgin Islands. Anguilla, which had defiantly separated itself from St. Kitts and Nevis, was admitted back to colonial status in 1971, at the request of its inhabitants. Elsewhere, however, popular sentiment tended to favor greater independence from Britain.

The call for further liquidation of colonial control was being voiced also in the southern Caribbean, where the influence of the Netherlands persisted. Both Surinam, on the South American mainland, and the Dutch-speaking Netherlands Antilles, off the continent's northeastern coast, are ostensibly equal partners with the European Netherlands in a tripartite nation known as the Kingdom of the Netherlands. Although this unique government structure allows complete local autonomy to the New World dominions, it hardly represents a union of equals. Talk about complete independence has increased since destructive riots shook Curaçao and Aruba, two of the islands of the Netherlands Antilles, in 1969.

In October 1971 a group of Dutch political leaders visited Paramaribo, in Surinam, and Willemstad, in Curaçao. In the course of their public statements, they made it clear that the Netherlands would be glad to honor at once any request for independence. In the Netherlands Antilles, these offers gave rise to sober second thoughts among all but the most radical politicians, since the islands rely heavily on external resources for their economic well-being. Even in Surinam, which could count on a rich reserve of mineral wealth, no one was hurrying to open the door that the Dutch had unlocked.

Moves Toward Unity. Progress toward Caribbean regional unity through the activities and programs of regional institutions was disappointingly slow in 1971. The Caribbean Development Bank, which at one period in its short history had vigorously encouraged an expansion in its membership, suddenly demonstrated a great reluctance to admit new members. After almost a full year's delay, Colombia's request for membership was granted under conditions that were far from attractive to the petitioner. Specifically it was clear that any new member would have to wait 5 years before becoming eligible for consideration for loans from the bank. It was feared that other nations would be reluctant to join under such terms.

Another disappointing development for those interested in greater regional unity was the lack of enthusiastic response to the long-awaited Declaration of Grenada, which was placed before the public on November 1. The declaration, which was prepared in July by representatives of several of the associated states of the Caribbean and the Cooperative Republic of Guyana, proclaimed the signatories' intention of exploring means of setting up some form of federated state within the Caribbean. The economic impetus behind the declaration came from the secretary general of the Caribbean Free Trade Association (CARIFTA), who argued that the association could not continue to operate effectively and grow in importance unless supported by some kind of federated government structure.

The original discussions in the summer did not include Barbados, which eventually rejected the declaration. Trinidad, which had sent a low-level minister to the summer meeting, declined to endorse the declaration, pleading that its citizens would have to be consulted on the matter and that such a consultation would have to wait because of more pressing national problems. Antigua, which had enthusiastically participated in the July meeting, refused to endorse the declaration, its new government having repudiated the position of the previous prime minister.

(See also separate articles on the Caribbean countries.)

THOMAS G. MATHEWS, *University of Puerto Rico*

CASALS, Pablo. See BIOGRAPHY.
CATHOLIC CHURCH. See RELIGION.

CENSORSHIP

The United States faced its first act of direct political censorship in 1971 as the federal government briefly succeeded in its efforts to halt publication of the Pentagon Papers, a collection of documents relating to the conduct of the war in Indochina (see special report on page 184). In a classic exercise of censorship the Public Broadcast Service ordered National Educational Television, program producer for the PBS network, to cut from a documentary a segment thought to reflect unfavorably on the Federal Bureau of Investigation. Importation of printed material from North Vietnam was prohibited by the government under the Foreign Assets Control Act. Such overt acts of censorship were rare, however, as the government preferred subtler means of controlling communications.

While no formal censorship system emerged in coverage of the war in Indochina, the Associated Press reported that "journalistic veterans of the war say they have never encountered a more concerted effort by ... authorities to restrict the flow of information." Other observers testified to the same effect. For example, information known only to the military was withheld from the press by the simple expedient of giving it a security classification. Under threat of loss of accreditation, correspondents were forced to withhold information over time periods specified by the military. The "embargoes" on news came under heavy attack during the Laotian campaign in early 1971.

In general the public was more disposed to censor books thought to be radical than those thought to be obscene. A spokesman for the Association of American Publishers noted that pressures from private groups to remove certain titles from public and school libraries had moved from sex education and the allegedly pornographic to books presenting two sides of the Vietnam War, certain aspects of the race problem, and the United States "as a country that's been right sometimes and wrong at others."

"Conspiracy" to Control the News Media. The contention that the executive branch of the federal government had embarked on a campaign of media intimidation through which it sought to stifle criticism of administration policies gained wide acceptance. A study sponsored by the American Civil Liberties Union concluded that "... attacks on the press by officers of government have become so widespread and all pervasive that they constitute a massive federal-level attempt to subvert the letter and the intent of the First Amendment...."

Whether part of a concerted action or not, the government increasingly used its subpoena power in attempts to force newsmen to divulge notes and film footage not previously published and to name sources

(Continued on page 185)

Army sergeant rolls boxes of Pentagon Papers, still marked top secret, into Senate on June 28.

The Pentagon Papers

"Through the use of the devices of secrecy, the government attains the power to 'manage' the news and use it to manipulate public opinion. Such governmental power is not consonant with a nation of free men and must be curtailed."

**—Sen. Sam J. Ervin, Jr. (Dem.-N.C.),
Chairman, Subcommittee on
Constitutional Rights**

On June 13, 1971, the New York *Times* commenced publication of a series of articles drawn from the classified 47-volume "History of U. S. Decision-Making Process on Vietnam Policy." The documents had been secretly taken from Defense Department files and clandestinely submitted to the *Times* and a few other metropolitan newspapers.

Popularly called the Pentagon Papers, they indicated that four successive administrations had frequently made military and political decisions without the knowledge of the public and Congress, and that governmental spokesmen not infrequently had issued public statements at variance with facts.

Acting on the contention of the Justice Department that publication of the material involved a great breach of security and that further publication would bring "irreparable injury to the national defense," a court on June 15 entered a temporary restraining order against further publication by the *Times.* It was the first direct act, however temporary, of political censorship since the founding of the nation.

Shortly, as other papers took up publication, other courts wrestled with the legal issues, with disparate results. Temporary restraints were placed on the St. Louis *Post-Dispatch* and Boston *Globe,* while the Washington *Post* was variously freed and restrained from publication in a series of decisions. No court acceded to the government application for a preliminary injunction. On June 25 the case was cleared for hearing by the U. S. Supreme Court.

On June 30, in a 6–3 decision, the court ruled against the government and thus allowed publication to resume. In a brief, unsigned opinion the court said, "Any system of prior restraints of expression comes to this court wearing a heavy presumption against its constitutional validity." It added that the government "carries a heavy burden of showing justification for the enforcement of such restraints" and said that in its arguments the government had failed to justify its action.

All nine justices filed separate opinions. Three (Black, Brennan, Douglas) were solidly opposed to the government's action on the basis of the First Amendment's prohibition of prior restraint of freedom of the press. Three favoring resumption of publication (Marshall, Stewart, White) indicated that under a different set of circumstances they might favor prior restraint. The three justices who dissented from the majority opinion (Burger, Blackmun, Harlan) said in effect that, under the doctrine of separation of powers, it was up to the executive branch, and not the judiciary, to decide on the basis of national security what information was to be disclosed and what was to be withheld.

Civil libertarians, noting the wide variance of opinion entertained by the justices, were inclined to count it a flawed victory for press freedom. They noted that, although ultimately the press was made free to publish, it had been silenced for 15 days by the government and that the First Amendment guarantees of freedom from government control had been suspended during that time.

This massive effort by the government to halt publication for political reasons threw the basic democratic dilemma into bold relief: how to square the occasional demands for secrecy in the name of national security with democratic belief in an open society; how to draw the line between the fullest flow of free information, enabling the citizen to cast an intelligent vote, and the abridging of that information when it is deemed contrary to the interests of national security.

Congress received a number of proposals intended to ameliorate, if not solve, the hydra-headed problem of maintaining a full flow of news without damage to national security. Several proposals concerned establishment of a citizens commission. Under one plan, the commission would constantly review the classification of documents, with power to make the documents public after two years and to forward relevant documents to appropriate congressional committees at any time. Under terms of another proposal, officials wishing to withhold information from Congress on the plea of executive privilege would be required to do so in person before the concerned committee and to obtain the President's written approval.

On September 27 the Defense Department issued a 12-volume version of the Pentagon Papers. Four of the original 47 volumes were totally withheld, as was some material published earlier by the press. The department said 95% of the material in the 43 volumes was in the declassified edition.

PAUL FISHER

(*Continued from page 183*)
of information. Attacks on the news media by high government officials were said to cause the media—especially broadcasting, where survival depends on licensing—to practice a high degree of self-censorship, steering clear of controversial issues.

Among those discerning no conspiracy was Sen. Sam J. Ervin, Jr. (Dem., N. C.), who observed that "a free press in a free society necessarily means there will be tension and sometimes hostility between the press and the government which attests to the vitality of the First Amendment." Nevertheless, Senator Ervin's Subcommittee on Constitutional Rights undertook a broad study of the state of press freedom in the United States to determine whether Congress should enact legislation that would strip the government of its power to force disclosure of information by reporters.

Proponents of such legislation claimed that this power in government must be calculated as exerting a censoring effect on communications. It was logical to assume, they felt, that people would not come forth with information for fear that courts might force their identities from reporters. Clarification of the issue was expected from the U. S. Supreme Court, which has agreed to hear, simultaneously, three cases in which newsmen plead the right to be silent under the First Amendment.

Censorship at the Source. Sparked by the Pentagon Papers affair, charges of excessive secrecy, of improperly concealing information, were leveled at the executive branch. In response, administration spokesmen argued that withholding information deemed by the President or his delegates not in the public interest was a proper exercise of executive privilege, a right intrinsic in the doctrine of separation of powers. Thus, for example, Congress was thwarted in its efforts to gain information on the Laotian campaign, the deployment of nuclear weapons abroad, and the gross budget of the Central Intelligence Agency. And President Nixon personally invoked executive privilege when he denied a request of Congress to inspect the Defense Department's five-year foreign military assistance plan.

One court reasoned that executive privilege was not an absolute right, at least not beyond judicial questioning. Petitioned by environmental groups to stop an underground nuclear test, the Court of Appeals, District of Columbia, ruled that executive privilege did not prevent the court from inspecting documents pertinent to the argument so long as these did not reflect diplomatic and military secrets.

Censorship and Morality. Efforts by the federal government to proscribe obscenity seemed to lose force during 1971. This was possibly a result of the 1970 findings of the Presidential Commission on Pornography and Obscenity, which tended to rate such publication as a limited threat to the social order. Still the Postal Service, under statutes prohibiting the sending of obscene materials across state lines, was said to be prosecuting 80 cases, in contrast with fewer than a dozen cases two years earlier. In New York the legislature empowered the police to seize assaultive obscenity—that is, materials one might see, willingly or not, displayed along public thoroughfares. Local efforts to stem the tide of "blue" movies or "skin flicks" flourished.

The Supreme Court paid scant attention to the problem. While upward of two dozen obscenity cases were on its docket, the court came up with only a split decision on the obscenity of the film *I*

Am Curious (*Yellow*), which, in effect, continued censorship of that film in Maryland. Legal observers noted a new tendency on the part of the court, wherever possible, to leave obscenity decisions to state courts, which generally have been more inclined to find materials obscene than has the high court. Noted also was the fact that the Supreme Court has been presenting the vaguely worded Roth case (*Roth* v. *United States,* 1957) as adequately stating its understanding of obscenity. If interpreted by an increasingly conservative court, this is expected to result in more restrictive opinions.

School Press Censorship. The school and underground press continued to test free-press guarantees. The sorest issue proved to be the advertising of abortion services, which, forbidden by statute in most states, resulted in dismissals and prosecutions of some editors. Midway through the school year the American College Press Service reported 25 "overt acts of censorship" of the college press. Of editors responding to a CPS questionnaire, 40% claimed that they had experienced some censorship or harassment.

A federal district court found Southern Colorado State College officials guilty of violating the 1st Amendment rights of the editor of the college newspaper, whose writing was censored before her suspension. The court ordered the editor reinstated with her independence guaranteed. The Second United States Court of Appeals upheld the right of Stamford, Conn., school officials to censor student publications, but called on them to indicate clearly what must be submitted for approval and the degree of disorder that must be tolerated before censorship would be justified.

Other Countries. Economic uncertainties, wars, changing regimes, and other tensions enforced censorship practices in a variety of countries. The International Press Institute entitled its annual review of press freedom "Under Siege From All Quarters," and reports from the Associated Press and the Inter-American Press Association agreed that, worldwide, censorship had increased. Amnesty International, an organization dedicated to the release of political prisoners, reported that 47 reporters, editors, and publishers were known to be imprisoned in 13 countries.

Press freedom was especially battered in Latin America. In Cuba and Haiti there was total government control, while Brazil, Bolivia, Panama, Peru, and Paraguay witnessed exceptional interference. Most Asian countries knew only a controlled press, Japan being a notable exception.

Highly repressive regimes controlled the press in Greece, Spain, and Portugal. In the Soviet Union a small but growing band of intellectuals openly challenged the state's control of communications, sometimes suffering imprisonment or commitment to mental institutions in consequence. *Samizdat* (self-publishing) gained momentum as unofficial publications were reproduced by hand and typewriter for underground circulation.

The IPI noted "a tender bloom" in Africa, where freedom of press seemed gradually to be taking root. However, the institute considered it likely that economics would dictate continued dependence on government supported and directed networks of news media for some time.

PAUL FISHER
Director, Freedom of Information Center
University of Missouri

186

CENTRAL AFRICAN REPUBLIC

Events in the Central African Republic (CAR) in 1971 continued to be dominated by the activities of President Jean Bedel Bokassa.

Domestic Affairs. President Bokassa reshuffled his cabinet five times during the year. In June, in honor of Mother's Day, he simultaneously ordered the release of all women in prison and the execution of all male prisoners sentenced to death for murdering their wives.

The president announced in July that the CAR French-supported air force was being disbanded until the country was able to support it by itself. At the time of its disbanding the air force had 100 men, two transport aircraft, and three helicopters.

On September 1, President Bokassa ordered the weekly journal *Jeune Afrique* (published in Paris) banned for three years. No reasons were given for the measure, but unofficial reports indicated that the president was angered by the magazine's handling of stories about himself.

Foreign Relations. In March, following Bokassa's visit to the Ivory Coast, the two countries announced the establishment of diplomatic relations at the ambassadorial level. The CAR government also indicated that it supported the proposal of President Houphouët-Boigny of the Ivory Coast for a dialogue with South Africa.

President Bokassa announced on August 13 that his government was suspending diplomatic relations with East Germany—which had been established in 1970—because East German aid had been "practically nonexistent." The CAR was one of 15 African states that voted in October against the admission of mainland China to the United Nations.

Economy. During the year the government signed a number of agreements for economic cooperation, notably with Libya, Chad, and Egypt. In August the CAR withdrew from Air Afrique, the multinational West African airline.

VICTOR T. LE VINE
Washington University, St. Louis

CENTRAL AFRICAN REPUBLIC · Information Highlights

Official Name: Central African Republic.
Area: 240,535 square miles (622,984 sq km).
Population (1970 est.): 1,520,000. *Density,* 5 per square mile (2 per sq km). *Annual rate of increase,* 2.4%.
Chief City (1968 est.): Bangui, the capital, 240,000.
Government: *Head of state,* Jean Bedel Bokassa, president (seized office Jan. 1, 1966, in a military coup). *Head of government,* Jean Bedel Bokassa. *Political party*—Mouvement pour l'Évolution Sociale de l'Afrique Noire.
Languages: French (official), Sango.
Education: *Literacy rate* (1971), 18% of population. *Expenditure on education* (1968), 16.3% of total public expenditure.
Finances (1970 budget): *Revenues,* $40,330,000; *expenditures,* $40,700,000; *monetary unit,* CFA franc (277.71 francs equal U. S.$1, Sept. 1971).
Gross National Product (1968): $200,000,000.
Average Annual Income Per Person (1968 est.): $136.
Manufacturing (metric tons, 1969): Meat, 12,000; woven cotton fabric, 5,000,000 meters; beer, 97,000 hectoliters.
Crops (metric tons, 1968 crop year): Cassava, 1,000,000; groundnuts, 208,000; sweet potatoes and yams, 42,000.
Minerals (1969): Diamonds, 646,000 metric carats.
Foreign Trade (1970): *Exports,* $31,000,000 (chief exports—diamonds, $12,481,000; cotton, $6,822,000; coffee, $6,-712,000). *Imports,* $34,000,000 (chief imports, 1968—transport equipment, $5,951,000; textile yarn and fabrics, $4,298,000; nonelectrical machinery, $3,893,000; chemicals, $3,346,000). *Chief trading partners* (1968)—France (took 38% of exports, supplied 55% of imports); United States.
Transportation: *Roads* (1970), 12,000 miles (19,312 km); *motor vehicles* (1969), 11,000 (automobiles, 5,000).
Communications: *Telephones* (1969), 2,800; *radios* (1967), 48,000; *newspapers* (1967), 2 (daily circulation, 800).

CENTRAL AMERICA. See LATIN AMERICA and the articles on Central American countries.

CEYLON

The year 1971 was a particularly difficult one for Ceylon. In April a group of young insurgents staged an armed uprising that threatened to topple the government of Prime Minister Sirimavo Bandaranaike. The rebellion was brought under control only after weeks of continuing insurgency. The economic situation, already grim, deteriorated further.

Rebellion. Even before the April uprising, discontent among educated, unemployed, middle-class youths had led to a growing insurgency movement, directed by the Marxist People's Liberation Front (Janatha Vimukthi Peramuna, or JVP). On March 6, JVP supporters attacked the U. S. embassy in Colombo. The armed forces were mobilized, and a state of emergency was proclaimed.

On April 5 the insurgents, called "Che Guevarists" by the government, launched a series of coordinated attacks on police stations, security patrols, and government buildings. Mrs. Bandaranaike later described the insurrection as "a carefully prepared plan to seize government power in a single day."

For a time the government seemed to be paralyzed, but then it acted vigorously. Mrs. Bandaranaike adjourned the legislature, imposed a dawn-to-dusk curfew throughout the country, and ordered the 11,000-man army and 13,000-man police force to crush the uprising. All educational institutions were closed. On April 6 the JVP was outlawed. Mrs. Bandaranaike appealed for foreign military equipment, which was promptly forthcoming from a number of states, including the United States, the USSR, Britain, India, Pakistan, and Egypt. Gradually the army and police gained the upper hand over the insurgents.

Economic Crisis. The April insurrection and its aftermath added to the already staggering economic

——— CEYLON · Information Highlights ———

Official Name: Ceylon.
Area: 25,332 square miles (65,610 sq km).
Population (1970 est.): 12,510,000. *Density,* 484 per square mile (187 per sq km). *Annual rate of increase,* 2.4%.
Chief City (1967 est.): Colombo, the capital, 551,200.
Government: *Head of state,* Elizabeth II, queen, represented by William Gopallawa, governor-general (took office May 29, 1970). *Head of government,* Mrs. Sirimavo Bandaranaike, prime minister (took office May 29, 1970). *Legislature*—House of Representatives (unicameral), 157 members. *Major political parties*—Sri Lanka Freedom party, Lanka Sama Samaj party, United National party, Communist party.
Languages: Sinhalese (official), Tamil (semiofficial), English.
Education: *Literacy rate* (1970), 81% of population. *Expenditure on education* (1967), 18.9% of total public expenditure. *School enrollment* (1967)—primary, 2,594,072; secondary, 5,570; university/higher, 16,098.
Finances (1970): *Revenues,* $452,800,000; *expenditures,* $605,-600,000; *monetary unit,* rupee (5.958 rupees equal U. S. $1, Sept. 1971).
Gross National Product (1970): $2,120,000,000.
National Income (1969): $1,676,000,000; *national income per person,* $137.
Economic Indexes: *Industrial production* (1966), 115 (1963 = 100); *agricultural production* (1969), 112 (1963 = 100).
Manufacturing (metric tons, 1969): Cement, 283,000; meat, 18,000; sugar, 10,000; cotton yarn, 2,300.
Crops (metric tons, 1969 crop year): Rice, 1,374,000; cassava (1968), 425,000; tea, 219,600 (ranks 2d among world producers); natural rubber, 150,800.
Minerals (metric tons, 1969): Salt, 118,000; ilmenite, graphite.
Foreign Trade (1970): *Exports,* $339,000,000 (chief exports—tea, $187,605,000; rubber, $73,702,000; coconut products, $39,698,000). *Imports,* $389,000,000 (chief imports—cereals and preparations, $101,692,000; chemicals, $36,170,-000; petroleum products, $32,247,000; textile yarn and fabric, $26,670,000). *Chief trading partners* (1968)—United Kingdom (took 25% of exports, supplied 15% of imports); Communist China (10%—12%); United States.
Tourism: *Receipts* (1970), $3,610,000.
Transportation: *Roads* (1969), 21,000 miles (33,800 km); *motor vehicles* (1969), 128,600 (automobiles, 86,500); *railroads* (1970), 935 miles (1,505 km).
Communications: *Telephones* (1970), 60,841; *radios* (1969), 500,000; *newspapers* (1969), 17.

CEYLON'S prime minister, Mrs. Sirimavo Bandaranaike (*right*), shovels at construction project in Colombo. She was performing *shramadana,* or voluntary labor, at site of conference hall named in memory of her husband.

burdens, causing economic dislocation, a decline in crop production, increased defense expenditures, and heavy budget deficits. In her address to the UN General Assembly on October 12, Mrs. Bandaranaike said: "The prices of our exports have continued to show a remorseless and sharp decline.... In contrast, there has been a sharp rise in the prices payable by us on our imports." She referred to "the rising level of unemployment" as "the most pressing problem that my government have to face." While in the United States, Mrs. Bandaranaike visited President Nixon.

In November the finance minister introduced new budget proposals, calling for higher taxes and various austerity measures, and Mrs. Bandaranaike announced a new $3.15 billion 5-year plan (1972–76).

New Constitution. On January 17 the draft of a proposed new constitution was made public. Ceylon would cease to be a dominion within the Commonwealth of Nations and would become "a free, sovereign and independent republic."

Foreign Relations. In mid-April the ambassador of North Korea and his staff were forced to leave Ceylon, presumably because of complicity in the insurrection. During the year Ceylon and the People's Republic of China signed agreements for interest-free loans to Ceylon totaling nearly $40 million. At the Commonwealth Prime Ministers' Conference in January and in her address to the UN General Assembly in October, Mrs. Bandaranaike presented her long-cherished proposal "that the Indian Ocean be declared a Zone of Peace."

NORMAN D. PALMER
University of Pennsylvania

CHAD · Information Highlights

Official Name: Republic of Chad.
Area: 495,754 square miles (1,284,000 sq km).
Population (1970 est.): 3,710,000.
Chief City (1967 est.): Fort-Lamy, the capital, 91,700.
Government: *Head of state,* François Tombalbaye, president (took office Aug. 12, 1960). *Head of government,* François Tombalbaye. *Legislature* (unicameral)—National Assembly.
Languages: French (official), Arabic, African languages.
Education: *Literacy rate* (1970), less than 10% of population. *Expenditure on education* (1966), 14.3% of total public expenditure. *Total school enrollment* (1968), 190,637.
Finances (1970 budget est.): *Revenues,* $48,600,000; *expenditures,* $48,600,000; *monetary unit,* CFA franc (277.71 francs equal U. S.$1, Sept. 1971).
Gross National Product (1968 est.): $220,000,000.
Crops (metric tons, 1969 crop year): Millet and sorghum (1968), 711,000; groundnuts, 115,000.
Foreign Trade (1970): *Exports,* $28,000,000 (chief export—cotton, $19,640,000). *Imports,* $52,000,000 (chief imports, 1968—petroleum products, $5,481,000; textile yarn and fabrics, $3,205,000; transport equipment, $3,172,000). *Chief trading partner* (1968)—France.
Transportation: *Roads* (1970), 20,000 miles (32,200 km); *motor vehicles* (1969), 8,300.

CHAD

Political life in Chad in 1971 continued to be dominated by the sporadic violence and military operations connected with the revolt that had broken out in northern areas in 1968.

The problem was still unresolved at the end of 1971, despite President François Tombalbaye's efforts to achieve a reconciliation. Over 3,000 French troops and military advisers remained in Chad, although French and Chadian authorities predicted that the troops would be withdrawn by March 1972.

Domestic Affairs. At the annual congress of the ruling Chadian Progressive party, which opened on March 30, President Tombalbaye announced a new policy of "national reconciliation and development." On April 18 he reported that political prisoners would be released, and on May 23 he revealed a new cabinet in which three of the new ministers were former political prisoners. The government announced in late August that it had foiled an attempted coup d'etat.

Foreign Relations. Relations with Libya worsened during the year. On August 27, Chad broke diplomatic relations with Libya, accusing it of complicity in the attempted coup. President Tombalbaye threatened to grant the Libyan opposition a base in Chad, and he also indicated that flights from Chad to Europe would avoid travel via Libya. In September, Libya recognized the Chad rebel organization, the Chad National Liberation Front (FROLINAT).

Relations with Sudan improved in 1971. The Sudanese government donated some 5,800 Arabic textbooks and offered up to 20 scholarships to Chadian students to allow them to study at the University of Khartoum.

In October, Chad voted against the admission of mainland China to the United Nations.

Economy. Chad's economy continued to deteriorate in the wake of the serious drought that affected most of West Africa in 1970–71 and the continued internal problems posed by the rebellion in the north. Agricultural production was down from previous levels, and external investment declined. Exports covered only 47% of the cost of imports in 1971, and French financial aid had to cover almost half the current operating budget.

VICTOR T. LE VINE
Washington University, St. Louis

CHANEL, Gabrielle. See FASHION.

CHEMISTRY

The year 1971 was characterized by increasing concern and controversy over the variety of chemicals that man is adding to his environment. There was a corresponding rise in "consumerism," or public reaction to such problems, and further efforts were made to bring about stricter governmental regulation of environmental quality standards.

Plastics. Plastics have been considered a problem in waste disposal because of their chemical inertness, or inability to be broken down readily into safely dispersible substances. However, it has been found that plastics may not be so stable after all. According to reports, the polyvinyl chloride bags that are used to store blood may release two plasticizers—chemicals added to increase the plastic's flexibility. The chemicals are suspected of contributing to the condition called "shock lung," sometimes found after blood transfusions, which is caused by tiny blood clots in lung tissue. In laboratory tests, the plasticizers were lethal to chick embryo heart cells. Lodged in the mitochondria of cells, they can alter membrane permeability and change metabolic processes.

Another indication that plasticizers can migrate out of plastics was discovered in the vinyl upholstery of automobiles. The plasticizers contribute to the film that may form on the inside of car windows, and they may also enter the body through inhalation or even through the skin. Use of vinyl plastics in spacecraft was discontinued because of this volatility of the plasticizers.

After long having searched for additives that can protect plastics from decomposition by ultraviolet light, chemists in 1971 searched instead for additives that would promote such reactions and aid in waste disposal. A biodegradable polystyrene was made commercially available with a degradation time that can be varied from a few hours to days or weeks by varying the amount of additives. Ultraviolet light reduces the plastic to a powder that can then be attacked by bacteria.

Lead. In the past few years new hazards have been discovered in the use of lead, as in glazes on pottery in which food is placed. A family became seriously ill after using over a period of time an earthenware pitcher to contain orange juice. Acid in the juice had dissolved the lead used in the glaze. Other pottery was found to contain hazardous amounts of both lead and cadmium. The U. S. Food and Drug Administration (FDA) established guidelines for such glazes, permitting 7 parts per million of lead and 0.5 part per million of cadmium. Most of the pottery with hazardous lead content was handcrafted; if glazes are properly processed, no danger from lead is involved.

Paint on some pencils has been found to contain more than the 1% of lead considered safe by the American Standards Association. Nearly one third of the 17 brands tested exceeded this limit, and one brand contained nearly 12%. Some authorities considered the principal ingredient, lead chromate, safe because it is insoluble, but others said that it becomes soluble when it is ingested and enters an acid medium. The FDA is gathering data on this. Lead in paint has also been named as the cause of the death of one leopard and the illness of other animals in the Staten Island Zoo. Coatings of paint containing up to 3% lead were found there, even though they had been marketed as lead-free.

A controversy arose over the levels of lead in the blood of city dwellers. Lead alkyls such as the tetraethyl lead used in gasoline are more toxic than inorganic lead compounds, and one authority stated that 50% of the lead the people breathe can be absorbed by the body, accumulating to toxic levels over a long period of time. The National Research Council reported that present levels of lead in city air might be dangerous for children, traffic policemen, and garage workers. Removal of lead from gasoline would reduce octane numbers, so that the possibility of adding aromatic hydrocarbons instead is being developed. However, these chemicals are more expensive for motorists and, furthermore, since the only use for tetraethyl lead is in gasoline, its producers have a multimillion dollar investment to protect. Liquid hydrogen has been proposed as a substitute for gasoline, since its sole combustion product is water and its cost about equals that of gasoline in terms of volume. One California group has already test-driven cars propelled with liquid hydrogen. The main drawbacks to the use of hydrogen are its very low boiling point and explosive flammability.

Detergents. When federal authorities advised consumers in 1970 to avoid using phosphate detergents, substitutes quickly appeared. Many were made by companies that were small or new to the business, and some were inadequately labeled. The substitutes included chemicals such as lye, sodium silicate and metasilicate, and sodium carbonate. Lye is extremely corrosive to the skin, and all the substitutes can be toxic if ingested; in fact, a 15-month-old child died in August after eating one such detergent. Shortly thereafter the FDA published a list of 39 harmful detergents, three of which could burn the skin. In contrast, no cases of phosphate poisoning have been reported, and so the surgeon general advised consumers to return to phosphate detergents.

This decision added fuel to the controversy over whether or not phosphates are a major contributor to the aging of lakes, with the case for the affirmative somewhat weakened. An experiment on marine coastal waters with samples enriched in both phosphates and nitrogen showed that nitrogen contributed more than the phosphates to algae growth. At any rate, the entire problem might become academic in 60 years. The Ecology Institute in Washington, D. C., reported that if current trends continue, the natural reserves of phosphates—estimated at 30 billion tons—would by then be exhausted.

Polychlorinated Biphenyls. Chemically and in physiological effects, polychlorinated biphenyls (PCB) are similar to DDT. They are used in sealants, rubber, paints, plastics, and industrial equipment such as heat-transfer mechanisms. Unusually stable, they can pass unchanged through processes such as incineration to enter the environment. In a North Carolina fish meal plant using PCB, a leak that began in April was not detected until 21½ months later. By that time 16,000 tons of meal had been distributed to more than 60 companies in 10 states, and the hatchability of eggs from hens that had been fed the meal decreased alarmingly. About 60,000 contaminated eggs were consumed in the Washington, D. C., area, while 75,000 others were seized by the FDA. Other countries also produce the chemicals, and PCB have been found throughout the world in the tissues of fish, birds, and people —in some, up to 250 parts per million.

Consumerism. Efforts by public groups and individuals to react to such problems as environmental pollution have come to be called consumerism. One main target of consumer groups was the addition of chemicals to food, both intentionally as preservatives and unintentionally as pesticides. In April, Sen. Abraham Ribicoff (D., Conn.) started a series of hearings dealing with a possible link between additives and birth defects, genetic damage, and cancer. A month earlier Rep. L. H. Fountain (D., N. C.) held similar hearings. In October, consumer groups asked a federal court in Washington, D. C., to ban the use of diethylstilbestrol for fattening livestock because residues were found in meats. The chemical is a female sex hormone that has caused cancer in laboratory mice and in daughters of some women given the chemical during pregnancy.

Meanwhile, the gap widened between consumers and farmers and producers of chemical pesticides. Several states enacted or proposed legislation to restrict pesticide use, although producers argue that they have to spend money on defensive research rather than on developing safer pesticides. At the same time the so-called "organic food" movement accelerated. Some 2,500 health food stores reported total sales of about $200 million in 1971.

Attacks on the drug industry were spearheaded by Sen. Gaylord Nelson (D., Wisc.) and Rep. Fountain, particularly on the issues of pricing, unnecessary prescribing, fraudulent advertising of so-called over-the-counter drugs, and combining of drugs in a single dose that is no more effective than when each drug is used alone. A woman who had been given Methotrexate for psoriasis won a malpractice suit against her dermatologist because she developed aplastic anemia, a malignant disease. The drug, an anticancer agent, had not been approved for treating psoriasis.

The public began to demand safer household chemicals, as well, with spray cans as an important point of attack. Spray-can dangers relate to active ingredients, propellants, pressure, or all three; the sprays can affect mouth, face, and eyes, and—with continued use—cause lung damage. Deaths of teenagers who deliberately sniffed some sprays have been reported. Producers of spray cans said that the answer does not lie in better labeling but in education of the public regarding potential dangers.

Oil from Animal Wastes. The U. S. Bureau of Mines has developed a process for converting animal waste into crude fuel oil. The manure or other cellulosic waste together with carbon monoxide is heated for 20 minutes at 716° F (380° C) and an initial pressure of 1,200 pounds per square inch (84,370 grams per sq cm). The yield is about 3 barrels per ton of dry manure. A spokesman for the Bureau said that about half the oil supply of the United States could be obtained in this way, but that refining would be more difficult than with natural oil.

Industrial Alcohol from Waste Paper. Alcohol is being produced in the laboratory by pulping paper-containing refuse and separating light and heavy materials by flotation. The light material is then fed to a centrifuge containing screens that filter out particles such as plastics and is converted to sugar by digesting it at 446° F (230° C) in a 0.4% solution of sulfuric acid. The sugars are then allowed to ferment. A plant in Britain claims that by processing 250 tons per day of refuse consisting of 60% paper, it could make an annual profit of $500,000.

Chemistry of the Primitive Earth. According to one scientific suggestion, the primordial earth was covered by an "oil slick" 3 to 30 feet (1 to 10 meters) deep before life evolved. The supposition is that the primitive atmosphere contained mostly nitrogen and methane, with lesser amounts of water vapor, hydrogen, carbon monoxide, and ammonia. Electrical discharges caused methane molecules to combine and form heavier hydrocarbons over a period of several million years, with solar ultraviolet radiation aiding the process, until finally the hydrocarbons settled at the earth's surface to form the slick. This study could have a bearing on chemical theories of the origin of life.

Another study indicated that the vitamins nicotinic acid and nicotinamide may have been formed on the primitive earth through the action of electrical discharges on mixtures of water, hydrocarbons, and ammonia or nitrogen. The presence of nicotinamide in the primitive ocean suggests that nicotinamide adenine dinucleotide—the carrier of hydrogen for the entire biological world—could have been synthesized there. Thus, chemical reactions similar to those occurring in modern life might have evolved very early in the history of the earth.

EUGENIA KELLER
Managing Editor, "Chemistry" Magazine

CHICAGO

The year 1971 in Chicago was marked by the reelection of Mayor Richard J. Daley; a major political controversy stirred up by the police raid on a Black Panther headquarters in 1969; a continuing financial and racial crisis in the city's schools; and a conflict between the medical staff and administration of Cook County Hospital. On October 8, Chicago observed the 100th anniversary of its great fire.

Politics. In municipal elections in February, Mayor Daley's local Democratic organization won a heavy majority of the city council's 50 seats, thus ensuring the organization's control of the city government for the next four years.

On April 6, Daley won an unprecedented fifth term as mayor of Chicago. He easily defeated Richard Friedman, an independent Democrat who ran as the Republican candidate; Daley won 70% of the vote and carried 48 of the city's 50 wards.

Chicago lost two congressional seats under the new reapportionment plan for Illinois approved by a federal court. The city's congressional delegation was thus reduced to seven.

The police raid on a Black Panther headquarters on Dec. 4, 1969, which resulted in the killing of two Black Panther leaders, had led to the appointment of a special prosecutor, Barnabas Sears, and an investigation of the affair by a special county grand jury. As a consequence of that investigation, State's Attorney Edward Hanrahan was indicted for conspiring to obstruct justice. In December the Democratic party, led by Mayor Daley, slated Hanrahan to run for another term but withdrew the endorsement after protests by liberal and black leaders. Hanrahan decided to fight the party action in the primary election.

Education. Chicago's teachers went on strike on January 12, closing the nation's second-largest school system. They returned to work on January 17 after accepting a new 2-year contract.

A continuing financial crisis plagued Chicago's schools in 1971. The board of education decided the city's schools would have to be closed for 12 days in December in order to balance the budget. But that action was postponed until June 1972, despite predictions that the 1972 school budget would be even more seriously unbalanced. The chancellor of the city's junior college system declared that to balance its 1972 budget it would be necessary either to discharge several hundred teachers or to cut the salaries of all teachers.

State Superintendent of Schools Michael Bakalis threatened to reduce state aid to Chicago's schools unless the board of education proceeded immediately with a busing plan to integrate all classrooms in proportion to the racial makeup of the pupils.

Cook County Hospital. A continuing conflict between the medical staff and the newly appointed director of Cook County Hospital led to an attempt to fire the leaders of the medical staff organization. After a threat of mass resignations by the medical personnel, a tentative compromise was reached between the hospital's governing commission and the medical staff over health policies and control of the hospital.

Other Events. The Rev. Jesse Jackson was suspended as director of the local Operation Breadbasket by the Southern Christian Leadership Conference (SCLC). Jackson then resigned to form his own organization, thus signifying a split between local black leadership and the SCLC.

The 1970 census figures showed a decrease in Chicago's population from 3,550,404 in 1960 to 3,366,957 in 1970. During the same period the city's black population increased from 812,637 to 1,102,-363.

MILTON RAKOVE
University of Illinois at Chicago Circle

CHILD WELFARE. See SOCIAL WELFARE.
CHILDREN'S LITERATURE. See LITERATURE.

CHILE

Affairs in Chile in 1971 revolved around President Salvador Allende's attempt to transform the country into his kind of "socialist" state. Debate raged as to whether this could be done without destroying Chile's democratic political institutions, and elections polarized the forces for and against Allende's program. In the meanwhile, the nation's economic problems multiplied.

Drive to Revolutionize Chile. By the end of Allende's first year in office (Nov. 4, 1971), Chile had either nationalized or bought control of all copper, coal, and steel installations, 60% of the country's private banks, many of its manufacturing concerns, and its largest publishing firm. About 1,400 farms were taken over under agrarian reform to be redistributed to farm workers. It was estimated that during 1971 the private sector's contribution to the gross national product dropped from about 70% to less than 60%.

Allende's most controversial proposals were his draft laws to reorganize the judicial and legislative systems. After submitting his judicial plan to Congress, he withdrew it because of the great opposition that it aroused. In November he announced that he would introduce a bill to abolish the bicameral Congress and substitute a unicameral body. He stated that if the legislature refused to enact the measure, he would submit it to a referendum, and let the people decide.

CHILE · Information Highlights

Official Name: Republic of Chile.
Area: 292,257 square miles (756,945 sq km).
Population (1970 est.): 9,780,000. *Density,* 34 per square mile (13 per sq km). *Annual rate of increase,* 2.4%.
Chief Cities (1968 est.): Santiago, the capital, 2,447,741; Valparaiso, 286,108.
Government: *Head of state,* Salvador Allende Gossens, president (took office Nov. 4, 1970). *Head of government,* Salvador Allende Gossens. *Legislature*—Congress: Senate, 50 members; Chamber of Deputies, 150 members. *Major political parties*—Christian Democratic party, Socialist party, National party, Communist party.
Language: Spanish (official).
Education: *Literacy rate* (1970), 80% of population aged 14 and over. *Expenditure on education* (1966), 9.0% of total public expenditure. *School enrollment* (1968)—primary, 1,934,478; secondary, 232,749; technical/vocational, 73,142; university/higher, 57,146.
Finances (1970 est.): *Revenues,* $1,428,000,000; *expenditures,* $1,410,000,000; *monetary unit,* escudo (12.23 escudos equal U. S.$1, Sept. 1971).
Gross National Product (1969): $5,830,000,000.
National Income (1969): $4,711,000,000; *national income per person,* $493.
Economic Indexes: *Manufacturing production* (1970), 121 (1963=100); *agricultural production* (1969), 105 (1963=100); *consumer price index* (1970), 598 (1963=100).
Manufacturing (metric tons, 1969): Cement, 1,436,000; residual fuel oils, 1,332,000; gasoline, 1,167,000; wheat flour, 802,000; crude steel, 601,000.
Crops (metric tons, 1969 crop year): Wheat, 1,214,000; sugar beets (1968–69), 1,143,000; potatoes, 602,000; maize, 154,000.
Minerals (metric tons, 1969): Iron ore, 7,161,000; potash, 2,854,000; coal, 1,558,000; copper ore, 669,100 (ranks 4th among world producers); gold, 1,827 kilograms.
Foreign Trade (1969): *Exports,* $1,068,000,000 (chief exports —Copper, $810,400.000; iron ore, $70,900,000; nitrates, $20,300,000). *Imports,* $907,000,000 (chief imports, 1968 —automobiles, trucks. $53,869,000; electrical machinery and apparatus, $52,818,000; chemical products, $29,192,-000). *Chief trading partners* (1968)—United States (took 22% of exports, supplied 38% of imports); United Kingdom (15%—6%); West Germany.
Transportation: *Roads* (1964), 36,425 miles (58,619 km); *motor vehicles* (1969), 268,300 (automobiles, 136,700); *railroads* (1970), 5,000 miles (8,047 km); *merchant fleet* (1970), 308,000 gross registered tons; *national airline,* Linea Aerea Nacional de Chile (LAN).
Communications: *Telephones* (1970), 348,258; *television stations* (1967), 4; *television sets* (1969), 400,000; *radios* (1969), 1,375,000; *newspapers* (1968), 122 (daily circulation, 818,000).

Elections. Chile's local elections on April 4 were widely regarded as an early referendum on Allende's attempts to transform the nation, but the vote proved inconclusive. The government coalition of parties increased its share of the total vote from 36.3% in the presidential election of 1970 to

SALVADOR ALLENDE, Chile's president, poses with his collie. His first year in office was tempestuous.

UPI

CHILE'S relations with United States became strained in 1971 after U. S. copper interests were nationalized in July. This smelter services giant El Teniente mine.

49.7%. The Christian Democrats, the leading opposition group, remained the country's largest party, with 25.6% of the vote, while Allende's Socialist party climbed to 22.4%. The opposition National party was third with 18.2%. The Communists, who supported Allende, received 17%.

In a July contest to fill one congressional seat, an opposition candidate narrowly defeated the nominee of Allende's Popular Unity coalition.

The Economy. Soon after taking office, Allende froze prices and rents and granted wage increases of from 40% to 60%. This caused a tremendous spurt in the purchase of consumer goods, which produced shortages, inflation, a black market, and, in time, a decline in production. Also upsetting to the economy was a slackening in industrial discipline, due largely to rising expectations fostered by constant talk of a socialist revolution. Strikes and worker absenteeism were growing problems.

The state reorganization of agriculture, frequent illegal seizures of farms by squatters, and Chile's harshest winter in 50 years all contributed to severe agricultural shortages and increases in food imports. Toward the end of the year, Chile's foreign exchange reserves had declined to such a low level that the government drastically restricted imports and briefly suspended all foreign exchange transactions.

State of Emergency. Food supply problems were a major factor provoking a "housewives' march" against the administration in Santiago on December 1, during the last days of a 25-day official visit to Chile by Cuban Premier Fidel Castro. Police used tear gas to quell the demonstration, and Allende imposed a state of emergency which lasted a week (December 2–9). On December 8, the president announced that as part of an "offensive against Fascist sedition," the government would assume control of national food distribution.

Throughout the year, ultra-leftist groups encouraged peasant farm takeovers and organized robberies and assassinations. The event that aroused the most passion was the murder by leftist gunmen of Edmundo Pérez Zukovic, a former minister of the interior.

International Relations. In 1971, Chile established diplomatic relations with mainland China, East Germany, and Libya and sent commercial missions to North Vietnam and North Korea. In April it ratified the new charter of the Organization of American States.

Relations with the United States were cool because of the nationalization, without compensation, of copper facilities owned by private U. S. concerns. In December, Allende cited an injudicious remark by a spokesman for the U. S. government as proof that the United States was willing to exploit Chile's economic difficulties.

Earthquake. On July 9 a severe earthquake in north-central Chile killed some 90 persons, injured about 500, left tens of thousands homeless, and caused hundreds of thousands of dollars of damage.

HARRY KANTOR
Marquette University

CHINA. See special feature beginning on page 14.

Employee demands contributed to the growing urban crisis in 1971. In June, New York City employees seeking higher pensions opened city's drawbridges in unprecedented action that caused massive traffic jams.

cities and urban affairs

Over the last three decades, the United States has become a highly urbanized nation. Nearly two thirds of the people live in urban communities. The domestic problems of the nation are, to a large extent, the problems of urbanization: welfare, health, crime, education, housing, employment, environmental control, and transportation. Lumped together, these problems are known as the urban crisis.

The urban crisis has been characterized by a number of events. Perhaps most dramatic and tragic were the race riots in the summers of 1965, 1966, and 1967. But the day-to-day quality of life in urban areas is the real measure of the crisis. And American cities generally are measuring up poorly. For example, in Newark, N. J.:

• One out of every three residents is receiving some form of public assistance.

• 14% of the labor force are unemployed, and another 25% are underemployed or underutilized.

• 20,000 of the 400,000 citizens are addicted to drugs; rehabilitation and treatment centers care for only 75% of those addicted.

• The crime rate and the per capita incidence of venereal disease and infant mortality are among the highest in the nation.

• 35% of the housing stock is substandard.

During 1971 the urban crisis was as severe as ever, as citizens and public officials struggled to curb and reverse it. Congress began to recognize that cities are in a financial bind. The administration sponsored a massive aid program, in the form of general revenue sharing, designed to "save the cities," but it was not enacted during the year. Some relief for unemployment was provided through the Emergency Employment Act of 1971. Progress was made in the solution of metropolitan problems. And the mayors of several cities banded together into the Legislative Action Committee to focus public attention on the urban crisis and to lobby for urban legislation in Congress. Long-range solutions have yet to emerge.

Financial Crisis. The capacity of cities to cope effectively with their problems is small and diminishing. U. S. cities are being squeezed in a financial vise, one jaw of which is the rapidly increasing urban service needs and costs, and the other is the inability of many cities to raise the revenues required to maintain even their present degree of services. In some cities the tax base is actually declining because of the flight of business and middle-class residents to the suburbs.

The heart of the fiscal crisis is the relation of the cities to their state government. Cities are not sovereign entities, but creatures of the states. They are allowed to impose only a few taxes, the predominant one being the property tax. Historically, this tax was considered appropriate because most municipal services rendered—police and fire protection, in particular—benefited the property owner. This reasoning, however, is no longer valid. Low-income people, concentrated in many central city neighborhoods, have created a skyrocketing demand for municipal services. Large numbers of nonresident daytime workers use many city services—such as transportation, police and fire protection, and water supply—without paying central-city property taxes. Furthermore, the property tax is regressive—that is, it does not relate to the taxpayer's ability to pay.

Because cities must depend on the property tax for revenues, their attempts to solve urban problems are often self-defeating. As Mayor Kenneth A. Gibson of Newark stated in his 1971 budget message:

"We must rely upon our local property tax for 65% of our revenues. In a city where we already have one of the highest and most confiscatory rates in the country, we were forced to raise the rate of taxation this year by almost 10%. This increase means that an owner of a $20,000 home will pay about $1,850 in annual property taxes. We have reached a point where our property tax has only hastened the flight of industry, commerce, and the remaining middle class homeowners out of Newark. The excessive rates we are forced to impose have actually been the cause of abandonment, deterioration, and a decline in our tax bases. The stark reality finds buildings being abandoned at the clip of one a day."

To fight the urban crisis, cities have sought and received aid from Congress. Unfortunately, federal grant programs largely miss the target. For the most part they have been restricted to new, enriched, or innovative programs and have made virtually no contribution to the basic public needs, such as education and police, fire, and sanitary services.

Revenue Sharing. In 1970 the National League of Cities, U. S. Conference of Mayors, National Association of Counties, National Governors' Conference, National Legislative Conference, and Inter-

national City Management Association formed a coalition to sponsor legislation to return a greater amount of federal revenues directly back to the state and local governments to be used for basic public services. The coalition developed a revenue-sharing plan, which President Nixon introduced in his 1971 State of the Union Message as a "General Revenue Sharing Program." This program provided $5 billion a year to state and local governments, with only a few federal controls.

The President also announced a "Special Revenue Sharing Program," which would consolidate some 130 existing categorical grants into six broad-purpose packages. This plan would provide $11 billion with few controls and no required matching to help states and localities finance education, law enforcement, manpower training, urban and rural community development, and transportation.

In June 1971 hearings were held in Congress on general revenue sharing. The response was not wholly favorable. Critics objected that it (1) did not distribute funds to local governments on the basis of their needs, (2) divorced the responsibility for raising revenues from the spending of funds, (3) added another uncontrollable expenditure to the federal budget, and (4) did not encourage state and local governments to help themselves out of financial difficulties.

Preoccupied with cutting government expenditures, President Nixon himself, in August, recommended a delay in implementing the revenue-sharing plan. Meanwhile, he announced a new plan to revitalize the model cities program enacted in 1966. Under the Nixon "planned variations," 20 cities were given new authority and almost $800 million in model city funds to be used for a variety of programs aimed at revitalizing urban life. Efforts will be made to coordinate and better implement the previously widely dispersed programs and funds.

While opposition to revenue sharing is substantial in Congress, a program circumventing congressional objections still may be enacted to aid state and local governments. The fate of revenue sharing

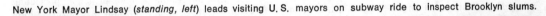

New York Mayor Lindsay (*standing, left*) leads visiting U. S. mayors on subway ride to inspect Brooklyn slums.

THE NEW YORK TIMES

or a similar program to assist cities rests with the 92d Congress in 1972.

Emergency Employment Act. A major problem plaguing cities in 1971 was unemployment. By September 1971, 64 of 150 major metropolitan areas had an unemployment rate of 6% or more. Unemployment brings added burdens to financially pressed cities because of the increased need for social services. More important, it is a cause of social unrest. Paradoxically, unemployment is a problem almost completely beyond city control. The federal government, through its fiscal and monetary program, controls the general level of unemployment.

On July 12, 1971, the Emergency Employment Act was signed into law by President Nixon. It authorized a $2.25 billion federally supported job program for two years. The jobs, to be provided by state, city, and county governments, are in areas such as health, transportation, and environmental quality. Thus this program aims at both reducing unemployment and providing improved public services.

Metropolitan Problems. Not only are cities in a financial squeeze and plagued by unemployment, but their organizational structure virtually prohibits them from solving metropolitan-wide problems. This is due largely to the astonishing proliferation of units that govern U. S. urban areas. In 1967 the nation's 230 metropolitan areas were served by 20,703 local governments, an average of 90 in each. The Chicago metropolitan area, for example, has 1,113 local governments; the Philadelphia area, 871; the Pittsburgh area, 704; and the New York area, 551.

In order to attack metropolitan problems, cities and counties in most metropolitan areas have joined together into regional councils. Advisory in nature, these councils lack the normal governmental powers of taxation, regulation, and operation of public facilities. They provide a forum for dialogue and joint decision-making between adjacent city and county jurisdictions, but must rely on the cities and counties to implement their decisions.

Regional council programs vary from one metropolitan area to another. Many include planning for physical development (land use, transportation, improving environmental quality) and economic development. Some provide human resources planning.

Legislative Action Committee. In 1971 the U. S. Conference of Mayors established the Legislative Action Committee. Composed of 17 mayors, representing every section of the country, and headed by Mayor John V. Lindsay of New York, the committee implements the policy of the Conference of Mayors. In 1971 it stressed three priority concerns: (1) the enactment of a revenue-sharing program; (2) the release by the federal government of $1.5 billion in urban funds appropriated by Congress but frozen by the administration; (3) the enactment of the Emergency Employment Act (which was achieved).

Committee spokesmen also testified before Congress on urban issues and visited several cities to dramatize the fact that urban problems are nationwide. They examined the housing problems in San Francisco, unemployment in Seattle, and the need for more urban mass transit funds in Atlanta. In New York the committee toured neighborhoods that one member said looked "like Dresden after the war."

RICHARD E. THOMPSON
Legislative Counsel, National League of Cities and U. S. Conference of Mayors

CIVIL LIBERTIES AND CIVIL RIGHTS

The year 1971 saw a reduction in the number and intensity of protests against allegedly unjust social conditions, and the Supreme Court sharply reduced the number of cases in which it upheld appeals, founded on the Bill of Rights, regarding government infringement of individual rights. The latter trend of the court, largely reflecting the views of Nixon appointees Chief Justice Warren Burger and Justice Harry Blackmun, is expected to continue and deepen with the change of Supreme Court membership caused by the loss of Justices Hugo Black and John Marshall Harlan and their replacement by Lewis Powell and William Rehnquist.

In this context, the activities of the Department of Justice during the year took on added importance. The department, hoping to reduce the high level of crime, to minimize the influence of what it regarded as disloyal citizens, and to mute critical coverage by the news media, lent its support to certain measures that resulted in a tense climate concerning civil liberties. These included preventive detention of certain suspects, wiretapping (including taps without court order in "national security" cases), limitations on federal habeas corpus, the subpoenaing of confidential notes of news reporters, the resurrection of the Subversive Activities Control Board, the use of loyalty oaths on passports, and what the department called "qualified martial law" in response to a large and sometimes unruly antiwar protest in Washington, D. C. Most of these efforts have yet to be tested by the courts.

Free Expression. The most important controversy of the year involving the Bill of Rights resulted from the attempt of the U. S. government to halt the publication of the classified documents known as the "Pentagon Papers" by the New York *Times* and the Washington *Post*. In a decision in which each justice rendered an opinion, the Supreme Court held that the government had failed to meet the heavy burden of justifying a "prior restraint"— that is, an injunction—on publication by the press.

In some quarters the Pentagon Papers case was viewed as establishing a new principle protecting freedom of expression. Certainly a contrary ruling would have been a heavy blow to the 1st Amendment. On the other hand, the controversy can also be viewed as a setback to free expression because of the government's unprecedented attempt to enjoin the press, because of the court's willingness to allow publication to be halted pending the outcome of the case, and, most important, because the court explicitly rejected the view that prior restraints of this kind are invariably unconstitutional. As the year ended, it appeared that the case would have a sequel because Daniel Ellsberg, who admitted making the Pentagon Papers available to the press, was indicted under the Espionage Act, and other individuals who may have cooperated with Ellsberg, including reporters for the *Times* and the *Post,* were under investigation by grand juries.

The Supreme Court dealt with several other important controversies involving free expression. In one set of cases it limited, but refused to prevent, states from questioning applicants for admission to the bar about membership in possibly subversive organizations. The court also ruled that an applicant could not be required to disclose whether he was a member of the Communist party or to list

(Continued on page 197)

Surveillance, American Style
BIG BROTHER IS WATCHING

'Americans today are scrutinized, measured, watched, counted, and questioned more than at any time in history.'

In 1971 there were significant disclosures about a new breed of surveillance activities that appear to be widely practiced. The result has been a growing sensitivity to the possibility that whenever a citizen files a tax return, applies for life insurance or a credit card, seeks government benefits, or interviews for a job, a dossier is opened on him and his information profile is sketched.

These revelations make it clear that Americans today are scrutinized, measured, watched, counted, and questioned more than at any time in their history. Modern wiretapping, eavesdropping, and optical technology are being used to make unprecedented inroads on traditional bastions of physical and informational privacy. In addition, federal agencies and private companies are using computers and microfilm technology to collect, store, and exchange information about millions of Americans. Coming to light in 1971, for example, were the existence of the Department of Housing and Urban Development's Adverse Information File, the National Science Foundation's data bank on scientists, the Customs Bureau's computerized data bank on "suspects," the Civil Service Commission's "investigative" and "security" files, the Secret Service's dossiers on "undesirables," and the surveillance activities of the U. S. Army.

Army Surveillance. The Army's domestic spying operations were a target of the Senate Subcommittee on Constitutional Rights, under the chairmanship of Sen. Sam J. Ervin, Jr., of North Carolina. Hearings in February and March of 1971 investigated charges that unauthorized and uncontrolled military surveillance of civilian groups and activities was endangering the constitutional rights of free speech, assembly, and petition.

Testimony before the subcommittee revealed that a vast number of dossiers were being developed by the Army, ostensibly for use as an aid in quelling civil disturbances. There also was evidence that organizations were being infiltrated and people attending a wide range of public activities were being photographed. Although there is some justification for the Army's collection of certain types of information directly related to its duties, critics charged that dossier-building on people pursuing lawful activities has little to do with the military's role during civil disorders.

Those under surveillance apparently included people who were not extremists or a threat to internal security as well as citizens who had written antiwar letters to congressmen, signed antiwar petitions, and marched in peace demonstrations. The list also included a wide spectrum of public figures. Intelligence reports on individual social activists and organizations went into the Army's files along with reports on those deemed "dangerous" to the nation. How the Army used this information and who had access to it are still unclear, but its reports did circulate through a teletype network to every major troop center in the United States.

After the initial public disclosure of these undercover activities, the Army announced it would not develop its proposed data bank. Closer inquiry in 1971 revealed, however, that only a centralized file at Fort Holabird in Baltimore had been "abandoned." Indeed, the Senate hearings disclosed that the data at Fort Holabird may not actually

Sen. Sam Ervin brandishes microfilm during hearings on computerized data collection and its effect on individuals.

ENGELHARDT IN THE ST. LOUIS POST-DISPATCH

"Back, I Say—Get Back"

have been destroyed, merely stored. The Army apparently continues to collect and distribute data to seven military intelligence group headquarters, although it may actually have ceased spying on civilians.

According to Senator Ervin, government spying and computer technology present a real danger of a "mass surveillance system unprecedented in our history." The possible abuse and intimidation inherent in the pooling of vast quantities of information—some factual, some trivial, some rumored—about large numbers of unsuspecting individuals who are under scrutiny for reasons ranging from suspected criminal conduct to merely applying for a passport seem to be legitimate causes for alarm as well as for continuous and close watching of the watchers.

Other Surveillance Systems. Revelations in 1971 concerning the development of information systems other than the Army's underscore the potential threat to personal privacy and the possible "chilling effect" on constitutional rights of information surveillance. For example, the Federal Bureau of Investigation's constantly expanding National Crime Information Center provides state and city police with immediate access to computerized files on many people. Although it currently contains only data on fugitives and stolen property, in the future it may store and circulate a wide range of intelligence information. State and local law-enforcement surveillance systems are also being expanded.

Unease concerning the ultimate use and power of surveillance systems expressed itself when a group publicized papers stolen from the FBI's Media, Pa., office. The contents of these docu-

ments revealed an effort to harass and frighten certain groups through systematic intelligence activities. Concern was heightened during the year by the federal government's claim that it has an inherent right to wiretap when it believes it to be in the interests of domestic security. The issue is before the Supreme Court and should be resolved in 1972.

Data-gathering and dossier-building also are prevalent in the private sector. The consumer-reporting industry is turning to computerization with an eye toward providing individualized information instantaneously anywhere in the country. The surveillance activities of certain companies have resulted in information misuse, gross inaccuracies, collection of highly personal data, preservation of unverified information, and failure to acknowledge the crippling potential of information or misinformation.

The first step toward eliminating the abuses of the unregulated buying and selling of personal information and the surveillance of individuals by large companies was the enactment of the Federal Fair Credit Reporting Act, which became effective in 1971. The act allows individuals to see their own files in consumer reporting agencies and to correct any errors. The subject also must be told who has had access to his dossier.

Threats to Privacy. The publication in 1971 of *The Assault on Privacy* by Arthur R. Miller made it clear that surveillance activities encompass more than the acquisition and preservation of personal information through snooping and electronic devices. For example, the computer is being used to analyze seemingly unrelated data on large numbers of people to determine whether a particular individual's activities bear any relation to the conduct of other investigation subjects or groups. This practice might be extended to the data gathered through computerized reservation services for hotels, car rental agencies, theaters, sports arenas, planes, and trains. Access to this information would permit inferences to be drawn about a person's activities, associations, and interests.

Perhaps the most significant threats to personal freedom are presented by the inevitable linking of computers to surveillance devices that can monitor people and their communications. By using a device like the optical scanner in conjunction with a computer, data in unprecedented quantities could automatically be recorded and forwarded to a computer for analysis, and the possible relationships among thousands of individuals and organizations could be analyzed.

A number of laws to protect personal privacy were proposed in 1971. One suggestion would require advising each individual when a noncriminal file is begun on him. The subject could then see that file, challenge the information he considers inaccurate, and be advised of the identity of those who have been given access to it.

But until legislation is enacted, citizens' privacy depends on the good judgment and self-regulation of the information-gathering and -using communities in both government and industry. In the long run, however, what is needed is a broad range of technical, administrative, and procedural protections that can be imposed on all information systems and surveillance activities.

ARTHUR R. MILLER
University of Michigan

(*Continued from page 194*)
all the organizations to which he had belonged since the age of 16. But it upheld New York's procedures that require an applicant to swear that he "believes in the form of government of the United States" and is loyal to that government and to disclose membership in any group advocating the violent overthrow of the government.

The Supreme Court extended the constitutional protection given publications against libel action in two cases by holding that a "public figure" could not sue if falsely charged with perjury even though this charge had nothing to do with his official duties, and by ruling that a private individual could not sue for a report that falsely involved the individual in an event of public interest.

Finally, in a series of important cases, the court narrowed considerably the role the federal courts would play when state statutes were alleged to be in violation of the 1st Amendment. In the future, the state courts will be given a broader opportunity to issue rulings on its own laws.

Obscenity. The Supreme Court upheld two federal antiobscenity statutes, one dealing with the importation of obscene matter and another barring the mail delivery of such matter even to adults who wish to receive it. On the other hand the court struck down certain sections of a law that gave the postmaster general power to halt the use of the mails, without a prior judicial hearing, by a person promoting the sale of obscene matter. In a related case the court held that the public display of an obscenity designed to influence public opinion was not a criminal offense.

Voting Rights. In a major constitutional ruling the Supreme Court held that a 1970 congressional statute that lowered the voting age to 18 was valid as to federal elections but invalid as to state elections. In the same litigation the court unanimously upheld a general ban on literacy tests and a ban on residence requirements for presidential elections. It also approved certain limitations on minority political parties by upholding a Georgia procedure that required independent candidates to file nominating petitions signed by 5% of those eligible to vote for the office in the last election.

Religion. The Supreme Court held, 8–1, that state laws granting substantial financial assistance to nonpublic elementary and high schools violated the no-establishment clause of the 1st Amendment. At the same time a 5–4 majority upheld the constitutionality of certain grants to church-related colleges under the 1963 Federal Education Act. Other state laws making such grants came under review in legislatures and courts.

The court rejected a claim that the 1st Amendment required the government to grant conscientious objector status to individuals who objected to military service in a particular war rather than in all wars. It also held that a Selective Service board acted properly in declining to consider a conscientious objector claim that was not raised until the individual received an induction date. Nevertheless, the court overturned the 1967 conviction of boxer Muhammad Ali (Cassius Clay) for refusal to submit to induction, ruling that the case had been flawed by procedural errors and was invalid.

Rights of Criminal Suspects. Reversing a recent trend, the Supreme Court in 1971 for the most part declined to extend protections for individual defendants. The court limited the landmark case of *Miranda* v. *Arizona* (1966) by ruling that the trial testimony of a defendant could be impeached by use of his own prior statements, which otherwise (under *Miranda*) would be inadmissable because they were taken by the police without the defendant being fully aware of his legal rights. The court also rejected two arguments against the death penalty: one, that death sentences were imposed by juries without instructions to guide them; and another, that the sentence should not be determined in the same proceeding that determined guilt. And the court refused to require a trial by jury in cases of minors involved in juvenile court proceedings.

Racial Discrimination. In proceedings affecting school desegregation, the Supreme Court strengthened the power of the federal courts to undo the effects of past segregation. It ruled that the courts may take race into consideration in framing corrective orders and that school busing was permissible to achieve integrated classrooms. The court also interpreted the federal fair employment law to bar employers from using tests for skills not related to the job; such tests had tended to exclude blacks. On the other hand the court held that the U. S. Constitution did not bar Jackson, Miss., from closing public swimming pools that had been ordered desegregated by a federal court. (See also EDUCATION.)

Rights of Women. The Equal Rights Amendment, which would ban all state and federal discrimination on the basis of sex, was passed in the House of Representatives but stalled in the Senate Judiciary Committee. On the judicial side, the Supreme Court ruled illegal, under the Civil Rights Act of 1964, an employer's refusal to hire women with preschool age children while it hired men with such children. The court also rendered its first constitutional decision prohibiting sex discrimination by invalidating an Idaho statute that mandated the appointment of males over females as administrators of estates of persons who die without a will. (See also WOMEN'S LIBERATION MOVEMENT.)

Discrimination Against the Poor. The Supreme Court extended the rights of the poor in two notable cases: it held that due process of law prohibits states from denying access to its courts to indigents seeking a divorce, and it ruled that a person fined for a traffic violation for which no jail sentence could be imposed might not be imprisoned because he could not pay the fine without affording him the opportunity to pay by installments or other means.

On the other hand the court upheld a California constitutional provision that gave local residents a veto, through referendum, over low-cost public housing; and it upheld a New York law that made payment of welfare stipends dependent upon the recipient allowing home visits by caseworkers.

Rights of Other Groups. The Supreme Court refused to apply an earlier ruling barring one type of discrimination against illegitimate children to invalidate a state law limiting their inheritance rights. The court also upheld a federal statute imposing residence requirements on the retention of U. S. citizenship of persons born abroad of one American parent. But it unanimously invalidated statutes denying welfare benefits to resident aliens.

(See also CENSORSHIP; CRIME; LAW.)

NORMAN DORSEN
New York University School of Law

CIVIL RIGHTS MOVEMENT. See RACE RELATIONS.
CLEMENTE, Roberto. See BIOGRAPHY.

CARL STOKES (*top*), who decided not to seek reelection as mayor of Cleveland, supported a black candidate in the November contest. But Ralph J. Perk (*bottom*), a Republican, scored an upset victory.

CLEVELAND

The largest city in Ohio and a principal Great Lakes port, Cleveland celebrated its 175th birthday on July 22, 1971. In 1971, Cleveland elected a Republican mayor for the first time in 32 years, held a birthday celebration, planned a new sports arena, and added buildings to its museums, university, and renewal area.

Election. In an upset, Ralph J. Perk, 57, defeated Arnold R. Pinkney, a black candidate backed by former Mayor Carl B. Stokes, and James A. Carney, a businessman who had won the Democratic primary. Pinkney, the president of the Cleveland board of education, ran as an independent Democrat. The vote: Perk 88,774; Pinkney, 72,785; and Carney 65,877.

Stokes, who as a black office-seeker attracted national attention by being elected for 2-year terms as mayor in 1969 (when he beat Perk) and 1967, startled Clevelanders on April 16 when he announced that he would not seek reelection. Instead, he said, he would try to influence minority groups toward greater political and social activity on a national scale. His administration had suffered two financial setbacks in 1970 and 1971, when voters had rejected his proposals to boost the 1% Cleveland municipal income tax, first to 1.8%, and then to 1.6%. The two defeats, added to declines in in-

dustrial employment, forced Stokes to lay off 1,740 city workers, including policemen. The city appeared headed for even further reductions in its force of 10,000 employees after Perk took his oath on November 8. The operating deficit for the city in 1971 was estimated at $2 million by Stokes, and at $27 million by Price, Waterhouse & Co. accountants.

Mayor Perk promised to increase police protection and to cooperate with the City Council—Stokes had attended no Council meetings in his last eight months in office. Perk, who lived in a Polish, Czech, Negro area of Cleveland's southeast side, had been a councilman from 1952 to 1962, when he became auditor of Cuyahoga county and the first Republican to be elected at the county level in 30 years.

Death. The colorful Thomas A. Burke, elected to four terms as mayor of Cleveland, 1945–53, died Dec. 5, 1971. He was U. S. Senator from Ohio, 1953–54.

Birthday. Cleveland's "Supersesquicentennial" in the second half of July paid tribute to Gen. Moses Cleaveland's founding of the city on July 22, 1796. There were parades, speeches, and special entertainment featuring former Clevelander Bob Hope.

Fire. A major tragedy struck downtown Cleveland on April 13, when a fire in the lower floors of the 500-room Carter Hotel killed seven persons, including the wives and two children of two members of the cast of *Hair,* which was playing nearby.

Arena. The management of the Cleveland professional hockey and basketball teams reported plans for a multimillion-dollar arena for both types of games in West Richfield, between Akron and Cleveland. It would replace the teams' home near downtown Cleveland.

Construction. A $10 million "education wing" of the Cleveland Museum of Art, designed by Marcel Breuer, was dedicated in February. The museum's May Show of the works of Cleveland artists was held in 1971. It had been canceled in 1970 because of the construction. Other civic dedications marked the completion of an extension of the Natural History Museum and of Cleveland State University's $33 million additions.

Extensive building of office and apartment structures along Superior Avenue N. E. between East 9th and 13th Streets continued as part of the Erieview renewal program.

Conductors. Lorin Maazel, associate principal conductor of the New Philharmonia of London, was named the Cleveland Orchestra's music director on October 1 under a 5-year contract. He succeeded the famed George Szell, who died in 1970.

JOHN F. HUTH, JR.
"The Plain Dealer," Cleveland

CLOTHING INDUSTRY

Dilution of fashion authority, profusion and confusion of style trends, and a rising tide of apparel imports, in addition to the slowdown in the economy, depressed a number of principal divisions of the clothing industry in 1970.

During the year none of the 11 sales categories of male and female wearing apparel advanced in both unit production and dollar volume, whereas three divisions had gone ahead on both counts in 1969. Losses in both unit and dollar sales were suffered by six types of garments—women's suits, unit-priced dresses, skirts and jackets, girls', child-

U. S. APPAREL SHIPMENTS AND PRODUCTION

	Output		Net value of shipments	
	1970	1969	1970	1969
		(in millions)		
Unit-priced dresses	159.08	166.49	$1,707.8	$1,791.8
Dozen-prized dresses	92.46	100.37	393.1	379.7
Coats	21.77	21.66	542.9	575.4
Suits	8.83	11.81	179.6	260.2
Blouses	208.38	214.07	676.4	641.1
Skirts & jackets	91.75	108.25	402.3	456.1
Girls', children's, and infants' outerwear	459.60	499.45	1,047.7	1,068.8
Men's suits	18.19	21.69	885.4	962.0
Men's overcoats and topcoats	4.40	4.06	109.3	118.0
Men's tailored dress and sport coats	15.22	17.68	389.3	445.7
Men's and boys' dress and sport trousers	247.29	248.64	1,181.2	1,121.3

ren's, and infants' outerwear, and men's suits and tailored dress coats and sports coats. Two categories —women's coats and men's overcoats and topcoats —showed improvement in output. Three groups— dozen-priced dresses, blouses, and men's trousers— increased in net value of shipments; units were down and dollars up, reflecting inflationary trends.

Fashion innovations continued to be inspired by younger people of moderate means. The search for individuality permeated all social and income levels, and a single look, one length, a few colors, no longer satisfied the female customer. Sportswear was dominant in both women's and men's wear. Blouses, pants, and pantsuits also achieved high popularity in women's fashion. The U. S. Census Bureau included pantsuits and jumpsuits in its report on women's wear for the first time in 1970.

Women's and children's wear production in the first eight months of 1971 decreased for four items and increased for two. Skirts declined 25.7%; dozen-priced dresses, 14.8%; blouses, 9.9%; and coats, 5.8%. Unit-priced dresses increased 7.5% and suits, 2.1%. The production of men's wear also witnessed declines in the first six months of 1971.

New York City retains its leadership among U. S. markets in manufacturers' sales of women's, men's, and children's wear. Other prominent markets for women's wear are Los Angeles, Philadelphia, Chicago, and Boston. In men's wear, Philadelphia, Los Angeles, and Chicago follow New York City.

The dollar volume for the sale of the 11 major women's, men's, and children's categories in 1970, according to the U. S. Census Bureau data, amounted to $7.515 billion, compared with $7.820 billion in 1969, a drop of 3.9%.

In Canada, the factory value of shipped clothing increased from $1.026 billion in 1968 to $1.089 billion in 1969.

(See also FASHION.)

SAMUEL FEINBERG, *"Women's Wear Daily"*

FAIR-TEX MILLS

(*Right*) WORKER adjusts double-knit fabric machine in plant in Allentown, Pa. Growing popularity of double-knits has led many companies to expand their mills.

(*Below*) LASER BEAM, part of computerized garment cutter in Fredericksburg, Va., plant, cuts fabric for suits. Beam severs cloth with intense light waves.

HUGHES AIRCRAFT COMPANY

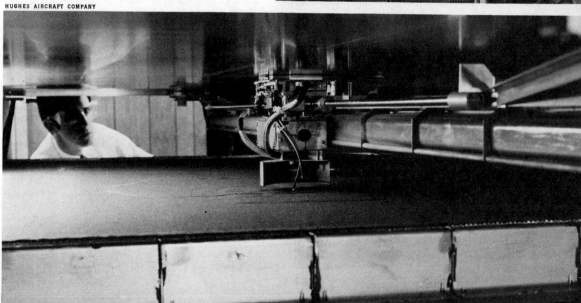

COAST GUARD

The U. S. Coast Guard, an agency of the Department of Transportation since 1967, continued in 1971 to promote maritime safety, enforce marine law, combat pollution, further oceanographic research, and assist the Navy in Vietnam.

Vietnam. Two of the Coast Guard's high-endurance cutters (311 feet, or 94.8 meters) were transferred to the South Vietnamese navy, continuing Coast Guard withdrawal under the Vietnamization program. The Coast Guard continued operating two cutters in South Vietnamese waters and operated a merchant marine detail in Saigon.

Search and Rescue. The Coast Guard responded to more than 50,000 calls for assistance—two thirds concerning recreational boats and the rest commercial vessels and civilian and military aircraft. Some 3,000 lives were saved, over 100,000 persons aided, and $900 million in property saved.

Law Enforcement. Coast Guardsmen inspected 958 foreign vessels, inspected 5,722 U. S. vessels for certification, conducted 4,900 drydock examinations, and reinspected 4,710 vessels. There were also 26,942 miscellaneous inspections. Other laws enforced concerned navigation, fishing rights, pollution, port security, and safety.

Aids to Navigation. The Coast Guard maintained 44,706 varied aids to navigation, including 202 operating lighthouses (to be reduced to 49), 7 lightships, 5 large navigational buoys (LNB) replacing lightships, and 64 loran stations.

Marine Science. Oceanic, ice, and weather research was continued by the Coast Guard's International Ice Patrol, 7 polar icebreakers, and 5 Atlantic and 2 Pacific ocean stations. The Coast Guard was building a 400-foot (121-meter), 60,000 hp icebreaker, to be the world's most powerful.

Boating Safety. More than 45 million people used more than 8 million boats in 1970. The Coast Guard sets boat construction standards and enforces boating safety laws. The Coast Guard Auxiliary's 30,000 volunteer members instructed 209,521 persons in safe boating and saved 527 lives.

Budget and Strength. The Coast Guard budget for fiscal 1971 was $653,400,000. There were 39,303 military and 6,463 civilian personnel. The Coast Guard had 308 floating units and 165 aircraft.

CHESTER R. BENDER, *Admiral, USCG*
Commandant, U. S. Coast Guard

COIN COLLECTING

In numismatics, 1971 was a busy year. Events included the announcement of the Eisenhower "silver" dollar; an error that made U. S. proof sets valuable; an unusual surplus of Kennedy half dollars; a proposal for a new $2 bill; a short-lived U. S. market in British gold coins; hedging with gold coins against inflation; the announcement of a Panamanian 20-balboa silver coin; and a rash of proof coins from small countries solely for sale to collectors.

Eisenhower Dollar. The most important news event for U. S. collectors was the announcement of the Eisenhower "silver" dollar—the first U. S.$1 coin to be issued since silver-dollar coinage was suspended in 1935. After the enabling legislation was signed by President Nixon on Dec. 31, 1970, the Denver and San Francisco mints prepared to strike the coins. The design, by Frank Gasparro, featured a portrait of President Dwight D. Eisenhower on the obverse and the symbolic landing of an American eagle on the moon on the reverse.

By means of direct mail, order forms distributed through the Post Office and the banking system, and other promotional methods, the public was encouraged to order the dollars. The dollars, whose silver content was 40%, were available in proof condition. The coins were struck at the San Francisco Mint, bore an S mintmark, and sold for $10 each. Over 4 million orders were received, and the first proofs were mailed on October 14. Uncirculated-grade 40% silver Eisenhower dollars, also with S mintmarks, were sold for $3 each. Several million were ordered. Eisenhower dollars with copper core and nickel surfaces and bearing D (for Denver) mintmarks were released into banking channels beginning November 1, at face value of $1 each.

U. S. Proof Sets. Orders for 1971 proof coin sets (containing the 1-, 5-, 10-, 25-, and 50-cent coins, all with S mintmarks) were accepted during 1970. The distribution of approximately 3 million sets commenced in February 1971.

Early in 1971 the Mint released the total proof-set mintage figures for 1970—2,632,810 sets, including about 2,200 sets erroneously made without the S mintmark on the dime. "S-less dime sets" of 1970 climbed in price to $300.

Kennedy Half Dollars. Kennedy half dollars, minted by the hundreds of millions since 1964, have rarely been seen in circulation because of hoarding. By mid-1971, however, the Treasury announced that for the first time there was a surplus.

$2 Bill Proposed. An effort to revive the $2 bill, a denomination not used for several years, was made in November when Republican Rep. Seymour Halpern of New York and 32 other members of Congress introduced legislation for a $2 bill bearing the portrait of Susan B. Anthony.

Gold Sovereign Market. In July the West Coast Commodity Exchange in Los Angeles introduced futures trading in bulk lots of British gold sovereigns—gold coins with an original face value of £1 sterling, but with an intrinsic, or gold, value of about $10. After three days of hectic trading the activity was halted by the Treasury Department.

Hard-Money Hedge. Many investors, fearful of a softening of the U. S. paper dollar, sought British gold sovereigns, Colombian 5-peso gold coins, and other gold coins as a "hard money" hedge against devaluation. Coin dealers reported record sales of both common and rare gold coins.

Panama Silver. Panama announced the production of a 20-balboa (convertible at par into U. S. $20) silver proof coin—the largest silver coin of modern times. The release was planned for 1972.

Nonmonetary Coinage. Many principalities, protectorates, sheikhdoms, and other small countries, known for their mass issues of commemorative postage stamps over the years, accelerated their numismatic activities. Proof coins, made at mints in Britain, West Germany, Italy, and at U. S. private mints, and never intended for use in the countries whose names the coins bear, were sold in large quantities in 1971. To aid sales, such popular subjects as Eisenhower, Kennedy, Martin Luther King, and others are featured on the coins.

Q. DAVID BOWERS
Author of "Coins and Collectors"
Columnist for "Coin World"

COLLEGES. See EDUCATION; UNIVERSITIES.

COLOMBIA

After several years of accelerated national development, the Colombian political and economic picture became more somber in 1971. A marked decline in the rate of economic growth, a resurgence of guerrilla activity and student unrest, and increased dissatisfaction within the armed forces were creating concern about the nation's future.

Political Affairs. Contributing to the general uneasiness was the lingering sense of uncertainty produced by the indecisive 1970 elections. Many observers saw in the elections a sign that the century-old dominance of the political scene by the Liberal and Conservative parties was coming to an end and that political forces would realign themselves ideologically, with divisive results. A 16-year National Front coalition agreement, under which Liberals and Conservatives had alternated in the presidential office according to a prearranged schedule, was to come to an end in 1974. There was speculation that the National Front might then emerge as a single party with an evolutionary political outlook, while ANAPO, the party of former dictator Gustavo Rojas Pinilla, would become the major opposition, offering a populist or radical alternative to the Front.

During 1971, the first full year of the Conservative government of President Misael Pastrana Borrero, the ruling coalition appeared to be obsessed by the threat posed to it by ANAPO, which had sprung from nowhere and nearly captured power in 1970. President Pastrana was forced to deal with a Congress in which ANAPO and a handful of dissident Liberals and Conservatives could combine to defeat any administration initiative. Though necessarily more given to political maneuvering and compromise than was his predecessor Carlos Lleras Restrepo, Pastrana pushed vigorously for passage of agrarian and urban reform bills, risking some defections among establishment supporters. In June, however, he brought into his cabinet new ministers of agriculture and finance, both of whom were popular in the business community. The administration earlier had increased sales taxes and stamp taxes and had ended a long-standing subsidy to petroleum users. Pastrana traveled to nearly every part of Colombia drumming up support both for his programs and for himself.

Economic Affairs. A poor performance by the economy in 1971 was a major cause of political problems during the year. The rate of growth, which had been at or above 6% in each of the three preceding years, slackened considerably. The heaviest rains of the century, as well as a tight money policy designed to combat inflation, contributed to the lower growth rate. The domestic price level was up 7.5% during the first six months of 1971, while gross reserves declined by $44 million during the first eight months. Average unemployment climbed from 11.6% in 1970 to 14% in 1971. A better year was generally being predicted for 1972, especially if coffee prices should firm as expected. The 10% import surcharge imposed by the United States in August, however, threatened the expected benefits.

International Developments. Colombia's dispute with Venezuela over ownership of the undersea platform extending northward from the Guajira Peninsula appeared somewhat closer to solution in 1971, in spite of an incident in June involving aircraft of the two countries.

COLOMBIA · Information Highlights

Official Name: Republic of Colombia.
Area: 439,736 square miles (1,138,914 sq km). *Density,* 48 per square mile (18 per sq km). *Annual rate of increase,* 3.2%.
Chief Cities (1970 est.): Bogotá, the capital, 2,500,000; Medellín, 1,400,000; Cali, 972,000; Barranquilla, 690,000.
Government: *Head of state,* Misael Pastrana Borrero, president (took office Aug. 7, 1970). *Head of government,* Misael Pastrana Borrero. *Legislature*—Congress: Senate, 118 members; House of Representatives, 210 members. *Major political parties*—Conservative party, Liberal party, National Popular Alliance (ANAPO).
Languages: Spanish (official).
Education: *Literacy rate* (1970), 75% of population. *Expenditure on education* (1966), 13.6% of total public expenditure. *School enrollment* (1967)—primary, 2,586,288; secondary, 577,417; technical/vocational, 137,274; university/higher, 58,417.
Finances (1969): *Revenues,* $533,217,000; *expenditures,* $580,285,000; *monetary unit,* peso (20.31 pesos equal U. S.$1, Aug. 1971).
Gross National Product (1969): $6,039,000,000.
National Income (1968): $5,927,000,000; *national income per person,* $299.
Economic Indexes: *Industrial production* (1969), 139 (1963=100); *agricultural production* (1969), 124 (1963=100); *consumer price index* (1970), 197 (1963=100).
Manufacturing (metric tons, 1969): Residual fuel oil, 2,430,000; cement, 2,393,000; sugar, 709,000; crude steel, 206,000; meat, 477,000.
Crops (metric tons, 1969 crop year): Potatoes, 1,000,000; maize, 796,000; bananas, 770,000; coffee, 486,000.
Minerals (metric tons, 1969): Crude petroleum, 10,689,000; coal, 3,317,000; salt, 637,000; gold, 6,808 kilograms.
Foreign Trade (1970): *Exports,* $674,000,000 (chief exports, 1968—nonelectrical machinery, $152,590,000; transport equipment, $101,350,000; iron and steel, $39,299,000. *Chief trading partners* (1968)—United States (took 42% of exports, supplied 50% of imports); West Germany (11%—9%); Spain (4%—6%).
Transportation: *Roads* (1970), 28,100 miles (45,221 km); *motor vehicles* (1968), 264,300 (automobiles, 1969, 150,500); *railroads* (1965), 2,164 miles (3,482 km); *merchant fleet* (1970), 235,000 gross registered tons; *national airline,* Avianca; *principal airport,* Bogotá.
Communications: *Telephones* (1970), 545,851; *television stations* (1966), 15; *television sets* (1969), 622,000; *radios* (1969), 2,214,000; *newspapers* (1967), 25.

Marxist President Salvador Allende of Chile visited Colombia in September, and was received cordially. Ties with the Andean Group (Colombia, Ecuador, Peru, Bolivia, Chile) were strengthened by this visit and by Colombian approval of the Andean Foreign Investment Statute, which placed limitations on the investment of foreign private capital. The U. S. import surcharge also served to bring the members of the Group together.

Pan American Games. The Pan American Games of 1971, held in Cali in August, resulted in the expected U. S. triumph, but the Cubans were a strong second, defeating U. S. teams in several key contests. The games proved to be an economic boon to the rapidly modernizing city of Cali.

Death of León Valencia. Guillermo León Valencia, a key Conservative leader in the National Front and Colombia's president in 1962–66, died on Nov. 4, 1971, while visiting New York City.

ERNEST A. DUFF
Randolph-Macon Woman's College

COLOMBO, Emilio. See BIOGRAPHY.

COLORADO

The Colorado legislature in 1971 approved the largest budget in the state's history, allocating increased funds for education and highway construction. Several important environmental protection bills were passed, and 18-year-olds were given the right to vote. The Denver Olympic Committee announced that plans for the 1976 Winter Olympic Games, to be held in Denver, were on schedule. Estes Park was the site of the White House Conference on Youth, held in April.

WHITE HOUSE Conference on Youth was held in Estes Park in April. About 1,500 delegates, representing diverse interests, attended discussions in the Rocky Mountains.

UPI

─────── **COLORADO • Information Highlights** ───────

Area: 104,247 square miles (270,000 sq km).
Population (1970 census): 2,207,259. *Density:* 20 per sq mi.
Chief Cities (1970 census): Denver, the capital, 514,678; Colorado Springs, 135,060; Pueblo, 97,453; Lakewood, 92,787; Aurora, 74,974; Boulder, 66,870; Fort Collins, 43,337; Greeley, 38,902; Englewood, 33,695; Wheat Ridge, 29,795; Northglenn, 27,937.
Government (1971): *Chief Officers*—governor, John A. Love (R); lt. gov., John D. Vanderhoof (R); secy. of state, Byron A. Anderson (R); atty. gen., Duke W. Dunbar (R); treas., Palmer Burch (R); supt. of public instruction, vacancy; chief justice, Edward E. Pringle. *General Assembly*—Senate, 35 members (21 Republicans, 14 Democrats); House of Representatives, 65 members (38 Republicans, 27 Democrats).
Education (1969–70): *Enrollment*—public elementary schools, 325,000 pupils; 12,400 teachers; public secondary, 240,-000 pupils; 11,000 teachers; nonpublic schools (1968–69), 43,100 pupils; 2,330 teachers; college and university (fall 1968), 102,822 students. *Public school expenditures* (1969–70), $348,000,000 ($695 per pupil). *Average teacher's salary,* $7,600.
State Finances (fiscal year 1970): *Revenues,* $956,014,000 (3% general sales tax and gross receipts taxes, $137,-768,000; motor fuel tax, $71,801,000; federal funds, $244,-505,000). *Expenditures,* $885,423,000 (education, $391,-339,000; health, welfare, and safety, $62,074,000; highways, $109,604,000). *State debt,* $124,532,000 (June 30, 1970).
Personal Income (1970): $8,402,000,000; per capita income, $3,751.
Public Assistance (1970): $143,446,000. *Average monthly payments* (Dec. 1970)—old-age assistance, $76.05; aid to families with dependent children, $184.05.
Labor Force: *Nonagricultural wage and salary earners* (June 1971), 762,800. *Average annual employment* (1969)—manufacturing, 114,000; trade, 168,000; government, 165,000; services, 123,000. *Insured unemployed* (Oct. 1971)—5,900 (1.1%).
Manufacturing (1967): *Value added by manufacture,* $1,509,-200,000; Food and kindred products, $310,700,000; non-electrical machinery, $254,100,000; transportation equipment, $134,500,000; primary metals, $109,500,000; electrical equipment, $105,700,000; printing and publishing, $97,900,000; rubber and plastic, $96,500,000.
Agriculture (1970): *Cash farm income,* $1,249,552,000 (livestock, $921,689,000; crops, $259,828,000; government payments, $68,035,000). *Chief crops* (1970)—Wheat, 68,944,-000 bushels; corn, 31,872,000 bushels; hay, 3,364,000 tons; sugar beets, 2,416,000 tons.
Mining (1969): *Production value,* $370,900,000 (ranks 16th among the states). *Chief minerals* (tons)—Coal, 5,350,000; molybdenum, 62,610,000 pounds; natural gas, 123,840,000,-000 cu. ft.; petroleum, 28,700,000 barrels.
Transportation: *Roads* (1969) 81,999 miles (131,961 km); *motor vehicles* (1969), 1,374,000; *railroads* (1968) 3,737 miles (6,014 km): *airports* (1969), 70.
Communications: *Telephones* (1971), 1,374,400; *television stations* (1969), 11; *radio stations* (1969), 90; *newspapers* (1969), 26 (daily circulation, 698,000).

Legislation. The long term of the 18th General Assembly convened on January 6 and closed on May 17. The legislators approved a $1.1 billion budget for the fiscal year 1971–72, including $177 million for elementary and secondary education and $299 million for higher education.

In the environmental field, 19 measures were approved. These included a bill setting up standards and procedures for abatement of noise pollution. Land use legislation was strengthened, and the state was given the power to prevent irreparable land damage if local officials fail to act. In addition to giving 18-year-olds the right to vote, the legislators created a uniform consumer credit code and revised the state's criminal code. A sweepstakes bill also was passed and will be placed on the November 1972 ballot for voter approval.

Economy and Tourism. The state division of commerce and development stated that in 1971 some 45 new industries announced plans to build in Colorado and 47 to expand. Manufacturing, Colorado's largest industry in addition to agriculture, showed a slight increase in employment.

The number of visitors to Colorado through September, some 8.4 million, represented a 7% increase over the same period last year. Their spending was estimated at $610 million. Visitors to nine federal park and recreation areas in the state totaled 4.8 million through September, an increase of 6.7%.

Olympics. The General Assembly created an 11-member Colorado Olympic Commission to oversee state spending and interests for the 1976 games and to persuade game organizers to make wise choices in site selection and land use. The total cost of staging the games was placed at $30 million, with $19.5 million to come from the federal government. Final site selection for Alpine and Nordic events is expected to be made by January 1972. The American Revolutionary Bicentennial Commission has indicated that it will participate in the games.

White House Conference on Youth. In a departure from the regular White House Conference on Children and Youth, held every decade since 1909, the conference on youth for the 1970's was scheduled separately from the conference on children. The latter was held in Washington, D. C., in December 1970. The White House Conference on Youth met at Estes Park on April 18–21, 1971.

Of the 1,400 delegates, about 900 were young people, age 14 to 25, representing working or unemployed youths, students, and members of the armed forces. The discussions and recommendations of the conference reflected less concern for problems of youth than for issues confronting the nation, especially war, racism, poverty, and ecology.

LOIS F. BARR
The Denver "Post"

COMMONWEALTH OF NATIONS

Britain's application for membership in the European Economic Community (EEC) remained one of the major subjects of Commonwealth concern in 1971. Also of great interest to Commonwealth members were the United Kingdom's policy of supplying arms to South Africa and its policy on immigration into Britain itself.

Constitutional Changes. Only minor constitutional changes took place within the Commonwealth during 1971. The parliament of Sierra Leone enacted a republican constitution by a vote of 53 to 10 on April 19, and Prime Minister Siaka Stevens was sworn in as president on April 21.

An Anguilla bill, which became law on July 27, empowered Queen Elizabeth II to make detailed provision for the administration of the island and to appoint a commissioner. Under terms of this law, if St. Kitts-Nevis-Anguilla were to decide to become independent, the queen was empowered to give Anguilla a separate constitution, thus allowing it to decide its own future.

Commonwealth Relations. British Prime Minister Edward Heath and Foreign and Commonwealth Secretary Sir Alec Douglas-Home attended the meeting of Commonwealth heads of government at Singapore from January 14 to 22. It was the first such meeting held in Asia. The meeting issued a Commonwealth declaration in an attempt to define Commonwealth objectives and the responsibilities of the members. There was prolonged discussion about Britain's supply of arms to South Africa, a British policy strongly opposed by most of the African and Asian members.

Also discussed in the Singapore meeting was Britain's proposed entry into the European Economic Community as well as various aspects of the world economic situation. A special group was formed to study the security of trade routes in the south Atlantic and Indian oceans. The group consisted of Australia, Britain, Canada, India, Jamaica, Kenya, Malaysia, and Nigeria.

Following the announcement on February 22 that Britain would supply Wasp helicopters to South Africa if requests for them were received, the Zambian high commissioner in London called on the British prime minister to clarify British policy. Meetings at the foreign and Commonwealth office between Sir Alec Douglas-Home and the high commissioners of Nigeria, India, Malaysia, Zambia, Ceylon, Kenya, and Gambia failed to satisfy the high commissioners. Nigeria, India, and Malaysia subsequently withdrew from the group studying Indian Ocean security.

The arrangements governing the future relationship of Commonwealth members with the EEC were published in a British white paper in July. In general, it was promised that all British dependent territories (except Hong Kong and Gibraltar, for which special arrangements were made) and all independent developing Commonwealth countries (except those in Asia) could become associated with the enlarged Community or conclude trade agreements with it. Special consideration was to be given to the problems of the Asian members, and special arrangements were to apply to New Zealand's exports of dairy produce and lamb. The more highly industrialized members of the Commonwealth, such as Canada and Australia, were to be subject to the common external tariff of the Community, applied gradually during a transition period.

An immigration bill, passed in July, defined the limited groups entitled to settle in Britain free from all control. All others, whether aliens or Commonwealth citizens, were to register with the police (a rule formerly applying only to aliens) and secure work permits that would have to be revalidated annually. Normally, after four years' residence, the limitations were to be removed.

As a result of discussions with the East African governments, Home Secretary Reginald Maudling announced on May 26 that the number of immigration vouchers for holders of British passports from East Africa would be doubled, from 1,500 to 3,000 a year, and that their dependents would be allowed entry. In addition, 1,500 extra vouchers would be issued to East Africans over a 6-month period, but the number of general employment vouchers issued would be reduced from 4,000 to 2,000.

Defense. A conference in London on April 15 and 16 to consider the external defense of Malaysia and Singapore resulted in an agreement that came into force on Nov. 1, 1971, after the expiration of the Anglo-Malaysian defense agreement. It set up an air defense council composed of five members, one for each of the participating countries (Australia, Britain, Malaysia, New Zealand, and Singapore). It also established a joint council for regular consultation on defense arrangements. An integrated air defense system for Malaysia and Singapore was put into operation on Sept. 1, 1971.

Pakistan. The British government's attitude toward the civil war in Pakistan was summarized by Sir Alec Douglas-Home on April 6, when he said that Britain did not plan to interfere, but was encouraging a peaceful settlement. The British were willing "to mitigate the suffering in East Pakistan should they be asked to do so." On January 9, Prime Minister Heath had announced that Britain was offering a further £ 2 million toward the reconstruction of devastated areas in East Pakistan. By that time, private British contributions to Pakistan relief already totalled £ 1,472,000.

Other Developments. Elections were held in Antigua on February 11, and the Progressive Labour Movement won 13 of 17 parliamentary seats; George Walter became prime minister. In elections in St. Kitts-Nevis-Anguilla on May 10, Prime Minister Robert Bradshaw's Labour party won all seven seats in St. Kitts, and lost the two in Nevis. Eric Williams' ruling People's National Movement won all 36 seats in Trinidad and Tobago on May 24 as opposition parties boycotted elections. British Honduras became the 12th member of the Caribbean Free Trade Association (CARIFTA) on May 1.

COMMONWEALTH OF NATIONS

Component	Area (sq mi)	Pop. (mid-1970)	Status
EUROPE			
Great Britain & islands of British seas[1]	94,522	55,711,000	Sovereign state
Gibraltar	2	26,000	Colony
Malta	122	322,000	Sovereign state
Total in Europe	94,646	56,059,000	
AFRICA			
Botswana	222,000	648,000	Sovereign state
Gambia	4,003	364,000	Sovereign state
Ghana	91,843	9,026,000	Sovereign state
Kenya	224,960	10,898,000	Sovereign state
Lesotho	11,716	1,043,000	Sovereign state
Malawi	46,066	4,530,000	Sovereign state
Mauritius	809	836,000	Sovereign state
Nigeria[2]	356,668	55,074,000	Sovereign state
Rhodesia[2]	150,333	5,270,000	Internally self-governing colony
St. Helena	47	5,000	Colony
Ascension	34	1,266	
Tristan da Cunha	81	275	
Seychelles	156	52,000	Colony
Sierra Leone	27,925	2,512,000	Sovereign state
Swaziland	6,704	408,000	Sovereign state
Tanzania	362,820	13,273,000	Sovereign state
Uganda	92,525	9,764,000	Sovereign state
Zambia	288,129	4,295,000	Sovereign state
Total in Africa	1,886,819	117,999,541	
AMERICA			
Antigua	171	60,000	Associated state
Bahamas	4,400	161,000	Internally self-governing colony
Barbados	166	256,000	Sovereign state
Bermuda	20	54,000	Colony
British Honduras	8,867	126,000	Internally self-governing colony
British Virgin Islands	59	11,000	Colony
Canada	3,851,802	21,406,000	Sovereign state
Cayman Islands	100	10,000	Colony
Dominica	305	74,000	Associated state
Falkland Islands[3]	4,618	2,000	Colony
Grenada	133	103,000	Associated state
Guyana	83,000	763,000	Sovereign state
Jamaica	4,232	1,196,000	Sovereign state
Montserrat	32	15,000	Colony
St. Kitts-Nevis-Anguilla	153	62,000	Associated state
St. Lucia	238	115,000	Associated state
St. Vincent	150	96,000	Associated state
Trinidad and Tobago	1,980	945,000	Sovereign state
Turks and Caicos	166	6,000	Colony
Total in America	3,960,592	25,471,000	
ASIA			
British Indian Ocean Territory[4]	30	2,000	Colony
Brunei	2,226	121,000	Internal self-governing sultanate
Ceylon	25,332	12,514,000	Sovereign state
Cyprus	3,572	633,000	Sovereign state
Hong Kong	398	4,089,000	Colony
India	1,176,150	550,376,000	Sovereign state
Jammu and Kashmir	86,023	3,729,000[5]	In dispute
Malaysia	128,430	10,986,000	Sovereign state
Pakistan	365,528	114,189,000	Sovereign state
Sikkim	2,744	194,000	Protected state
Singapore	224	2,050,000	Sovereign state
Total in Asia	1,790,657	698,883,000	
OCEANIA			
Australia	2,971,021	12,552,000	Sovereign state
Christmas Island	62	3,000	External territory
Cocos Islands	5	1,000	External territory
New Guinea, Terr.	92,996	1,752,000	Trusteeship
Norfolk Island	14	1,000	External territory
Papua	90,540	669,000	External territory
Fiji	7,055	520,000	Sovereign state
Nauru	8	7,000	Sovereign state
New Hebrides	5,700	84,000	Condominium
New Zealand	103,736	2,816,000	Sovereign state
Pitcairn Island	2	82	Colony
Tonga	269	87,000	Sovereign state
Western Pacific Islands: British Solomon Islands	11,500	163,000	Protectorate
Gilbert and Ellice Islands	349	56,000	Colony
Western Samoa	1,097	143,000	Sovereign state
Total in Oceania	3,284,354	18,854,082	
Grand total	11,017,068	917,266,623	

[1] Includes Northern Ireland, Channel Islands, and Isle of Man.
[2] Rhodesia declared its independence Nov. 11, 1965, but technically retains Commonwealth status. [3] Excludes dependencies. [4] Includes Chagos Archipelago and Aldabra, Farquhar, and Desroches islands; 1966 estimate. [5] 1964 estimate of India-held portion only.

In elections in Malta on June 13 and 14, the Labour party, led by Dom Mintoff, won 28 of the 55 parliamentary seats, and Mintoff was sworn in as prime minister on June 21. The British governor, Sir Maurice Dorman, resigned at the request of the Mintoff government on June 22, and Mintoff immediately put forward proposals for a revision of Malta's defense and assistance agreements with Britain. He also requested withdrawal of the NATO Mediterranean naval headquarters from the island.

Royal visits to Commonwealth countries during the year included those of Princess Anne and the Prince of Wales to Kenya on February 7, and the Duke of Edinburgh's tour of the Pacific islands and Australia from February 2 to April 4.

Aid to Commonwealth Territories. The 21st meeting of the consultative committee of the Colombo Plan for cooperative economic development in south and southeast Asia was held in Manila from February 16 to 25. Britain has contributed £736 million to the plan since its inception in 1951.

The Commonwealth Development Corporation, financed by the British government, had allocated capital outlays of £171.6 million by January 1, 1971. Money actually invested totalled £138.3 million, and the corporation showed an operating surplus of £9.4 million for 1970.

A policy of encouraging private investment in developing countries was announced in a British government white paper published on April 26. It included among its major points a provision for insurance against the risks involved in such investment, as well as increased tax relief.

Total British aid to the remaining dependencies in 1969–70 had amounted to £12.6 million, of which £11.6 million was in direct grants. Voluntary grants of overseas aid by Britain in 1970 totalled $45.6 million.

Major developments in aid to India in 1971 were the signing on March 18 of agreements for three interest-free loans totalling £16 million to finance Indian purchases of British capital goods; the announcement of a loan of £7 million in June toward the construction of a fertilizer complex in Gujerat (a U. S. loan of $20.6 million was announced at the same time); and, on June 21, a pledge of £54.5 million in general aid for 1971–72.

Ceylon received grants totalling £1 million in the first half of 1971 for the purchase of wheat and flour, as well as an interest-free loan of £2 million. On May 5, Gibraltar was promised £5.15 million in aid for a housing project. Grants or loans of less than £1 million each for various purposes were promised to Pakistan, Malaysia, St. Kitts, and the Seychelles.

An interest-free loan of £11 million to East Africa to buy locomotives was made on March 11, 1971. On March 17, an agreement with Kenya was signed providing £11.5 million in aid, of which £3.75 million was earmarked for the purchase of British-owned farms. On July 16 a loan of £10 million to Uganda over the period 1972–75 was announced.

(See also articles on GREAT BRITAIN and other member states of the Commonwealth.)

RICHARD E. WEBB
Former Director, Reference and Library Division, British Information Services, New York

COMMUNICATIONS. See POSTAL SERVICE; TELECOMMUNICATIONS; TELEVISION AND RADIO.

TOP Soviet officials Suslov, Podgorny, Brezhnev, and Kosygin (*left to right*) hold unusual meeting at Moscow airport on September 27. Upheaval in Communist Chinese hierarchy or Britain's expulsion of alleged Soviet spies may have prompted the conference.

COMMUNISM

The international Communist movement continued in disarray in 1971. The 13-year-old Sino-Soviet dispute presented Communist parties every-, where with the quandary of which side to support. More than two fifths of the world's approximately 90 Communist parties upheld the Soviet Union, while only five firmly backed Communist China. About one third of the Communist parties had split into pro-Soviet and pro-Chinese factions, many of these in turn becoming separate political organizations. Ten parties remained neutral in the controversy. Thus neither Communist China nor the USSR controlled the world Communist movement.

Some Communist parties and nations quarreled over other crucial issues. Rumania and Yugoslavia, for example, continued to oppose the "Brezhnev doctrine" (the USSR's asserted right to intervene in the domestic affairs of other Communist nations).

Despite all this dissension, world Communist party membership in 1971 increased by about 800,-000 persons to a total of 46.7 million, of which 94% resided in Communist-ruled countries. Most of the increase also occurred in the Communist countries, abetted by small gains in Asia and Latin America. In Africa and non-Communist Europe, party membership continued to decline.

USSR and China. The Soviet Union and Communist China continued to wage their war of words, each accusing the other of being un-Marxist, un-Leninist, imperialist, and fascist. The Soviet press charged that China encouraged blind adoration of Mao Tse-tung, used the Chinese army to oppress the Chinese people, and was making chauvinistic claims to Soviet territories, interfering in the internal affairs of India and Pakistan, and trying to split both the Soviet camp of nations and the world Communist movement. Another Soviet accusation was that China's new friendliness toward the United States aided the U. S. war effort in Vietnam.

China retorted that the USSR was using Soviet troops and police to suppress non-Russian minorities within the Soviet Union, was enslaving the peoples of East Europe and Mongolia by means of Soviet military occupation, and had abandoned the world Communist revolution and espoused the "fascist" theory that Moscow should dominate the world Communist parties. The Chinese repeated their allegation that the USSR and United States were in collusion to encircle China and to divide the world into two spheres of influence.

Neither China nor the USSR reported any skirmishes along their 2,000-mile (3,200-km) common border during 1971, but negotiations to delimit their frontier more precisely were bogged down in disagreement throughout the year. A Sino-Soviet trade pact was concluded in August, however, in an attempt to increase their tiny mutual trade.

Eastern Europe. The Communist countries of East Europe in 1971 remained divided in their positions on the Sino-Soviet dispute. Bulgaria, Czechoslovakia, East Germany, Hungary, and Poland supported the USSR, Albania backed Communist China, and Rumania and Yugoslavia stayed neutral. To improve relations with Yugoslavia, Soviet party leader Leonid Brezhnev in September issued a joint declaration with Yugoslav President Tito proclaiming that Communist countries could have differing types of socialism. In effect, this declaration was a Soviet renunciation of the Brezhnev doctrine.

Meanwhile, Rumania improved its relations with China by accepting Chinese munitions-making machinery on credit. During August, Rumania was visited by a high-level Chinese military delegation, headed by a candidate member of China's Politburo. Rumanian spokesmen approved the forthcoming visit of U. S. President Nixon to Communist China and stated that the world Communist movement needed no leading center (such as Moscow desires).

In 1971, Rumanian resistance continued to weaken CEMA, or Comecon (the Council for Mu-

TASS FROM SOVFOTO

PRESIDENT Tito of Yugoslavia (*right*) and Soviet party chief Brezhnev sign joint declaration in Belgrade on September 25. Document reasserted Yugoslavia's independence and called for stronger party links.

tual Economic Assistance, which is composed of Bulgaria, Czechoslovakia, East Germany, Hungary, Poland, Rumania, Mongolia, and the USSR). Therefore the new CEMA 20-year program, proclaimed on August 7, called for only limited coordination of national economic plans, more joint industrial and research projects, and eventually a single currency for use throughout the CEMA area. But the program qualified these goals by providing that any member country could refuse to participate in any CEMA project and that no CEMA supranational office could be created without the unanimous consent of all the member nations. Rumania, however, in January did join the CEMA international investment bank, which it had previously refused to join.

The USSR in 1971 kept two Soviet army divisions in Poland, four in Hungary, five in Czechoslovakia, and 20 in East Germany. Altogether these troops totaled 285,500 men equipped with more than 7,000 tanks, among other weapons.

From June through September, Soviet and allied troops conducted joint maneuvers at various times in Czechoslovakia, East Germany, Hungary, and Poland. During the summer, joint Soviet-Polish-East German naval exercises were held in the Baltic Sea, and joint Soviet-Bulgarian naval maneuvers took place in the Mediterranean. All these land and sea exercises were held under the terms of the Warsaw Pact military alliance (composed of Bulgaria, Czechoslovakia, East Germany, Hungary, Poland, Rumania, and the USSR). Rumania refused to permit Warsaw Pact joint maneuvers on its territory.

Czechoslovakia and East Germany. The two East European satellites in which the USSR maintains the most Soviet troops conducted purges in accordance with Soviet wishes. Between 1970 and 1971, Czechoslovak Communist party membership declined by 450,000 members, as that number were expelled for being too liberal for Moscow. In May, Walter Ulbricht was forced to resign as the head of the East German party, apparently because he op-

posed Soviet negotiations with Britain, France, and the United States to keep West Berlin out of East German control.

A 1971 CEMA statistical compendium presented previously unpublished data indicating that, in comparison with its East European allies, the USSR has the lowest grain yield per acre and uses the least amount of fertilizer per acre of cropland.

Western Europe. The total membership of the Communist parties of the non-Communist countries of Europe in 1971 was approximately 1.9 million. Of this total, three fourths belonged to the enormous Italian Communist party and one seventh to that of France. In comparison with 1970, slight gains in membership were registered by the Communist parties of Finland, Ireland, and Britain. Meanwhile, party membership declined in Denmark, Norway, Sweden, and Switzerland.

Almost half of the Communist parties of non-Communist Europe supported the USSR in the Sino-Soviet dispute. But the parties of Austria, Belgium, France, West Germany, Greece, Italy, Portugal, Spain, Sweden, and Switzerland were sharply divided on this issue, while the Dutch party continued neutral. Neither the Dutch nor the Icelandic party sent observers to the 1971 USSR Communist party Congress, which invited representatives from Communist parties throughout the world.

Despite many differences of opinion, Western European Communists of all varieties were united in demanding withdrawal of U. S. troops from Europe, dissolution of the North Atlantic Treaty Organization (NATO), disarmament of Western Europe, diplomatic recognition of East Germany, and the cessation of the attempts of Britain, Denmark, and Norway to join the European Common Market.

Asia and Oceania. Membership in the Communist parties of non-Communist Asia in 1971 totaled about 535,000, of whom more than half belonged to the large Japanese party and over one fourth to the Communist party of India. Membership of the Indian and Japanese parties increased over that of 1970, while that of the Australian and New Zealand parties declined.

In all Asia, Communist and non-Communist, about one third of the parties were badly split into pro-Soviet and pro-Chinese factions, and this was also true for the Communist parties of Australia and New Zealand. In the Sino-Soviet controversy the USSR was solidly supported by only six parties: those of Afghanistan, Iran, Jordan, Mongolia, the Philippines, and Turkey. The Communists of Japan, Laos, North Korea, and North Vietnam attempted to maintain good relations with both Communist China and the USSR. Only the parties of Malaysia, Singapore, and Thailand were completely pro-Chinese, mainly because a majority of Communists in those three countries are descendants of Chinese immigrants.

During 1971 the USSR increased its influence in satellite Mongolia by concluding Soviet-Mongol 1- and 5-year trade pacts, as well as a 10-year pact for scientific and cultural cooperation. Three Soviet army divisions (about 30,000 men) were in Mongolia to protect it from China. Another 27 Soviet divisions (270,000 men) were based in East Siberia close to China's Manchurian frontier.

In Indochina in 1971 the Communist-led troops and guerrillas of North Vietnam, the Vietcong, and Pathet Lao were still stalemated in their attempts to conquer all of Cambodia, Laos, and South Vietnam.

Despite material Chinese aid, the Communist-led guerrillas in northern and central Burma won only local successes over Burmese troops.

During 1971, Far Eastern Communist parties—pro-Soviet, pro-Chinese, and neutral—reiterated their demands for the withdrawal of U. S. troops from Japan, South Korea, Taiwan, Laos, South Vietnam, and Thailand. The Japanese party also continued in strong opposition to Japan's plan to rearm. Communists in the Middle East supported the Arab countries against Israel, condemned alleged Israeli expansionism and aggression, and opposed Western control over Middle Eastern oil fields. The Israeli Communist party was torn apart into pro-Arab and pro-Jewish factions.

Africa. In most African countries in 1971 there were no Communist parties as such, only individual Communists, whose Marxism was less popular than the widespread ideologies of African socialism and African nationalism. At the start of the year there were only about 9,500 Communists in all of Africa, and four fifths of these Marxists were in the large Sudanese Communist party. During July a left-wing group with Communist support briefly overthrew the Sudanese government, and the Soviet press approved of the coup. But the government quickly regained power, executed many leading Communists, and largely destroyed the Sudanese Communist party. Thus African Communism was dealt a heavy blow, and the number of Communists in Africa drastically declined. On August 2 at a meeting in the Soviet Crimea, the leaders of all the CEMA countries except Rumania issued a joint declaration deploring this slaughter of Communists in the Sudan.

Of the few African Communist parties, those of Algeria, Nigeria, South Africa, and Tunisia were pro-Moscow in the Sino-Soviet dispute, as the Sudanese party had also been before it was suppressed. Neutrality was maintained by the Communist parties of Morocco and Réunion.

African Communists propagandized mainly for African political, economic, and cultural independence from West European and U. S. influence. As they had in the past, they also opposed the white-dominated governments of South Africa and Rhodesia and supported the independence movement in Portugal's African colonies.

Latin America. The total number of Communist party members in Latin America in 1971 remained about 300,000, of whom more than two fifths resided in Cuba, about one fifth in Argentina, and over one sixth in Chile. In 1971, Communist party membership increased over the 1970 figures in Argentina, Bolivia, Costa Rica, Cuba, and the Dominican Republic, but declined in Brazil, Ecuador, El Salvador, Nicaragua, Panama, and Peru.

More than half of the Latin American Communist parties were Soviet-oriented, but those of Bolivia, Brazil, Colombia, the Dominican Republic, Ecuador, Honduras, Paraguay, Peru, and Venezuela were split into pro-Moscow and pro-Peking factions. Cuba remained neutral, although it received great material aid from the USSR and very little from Communist China. Cuban neutrality largely resulted from competition between Cuba and the USSR to control Latin American communism, Havana advocating violent guerrilla revolution and Moscow urging a peaceful Communist takeover of power. As 1971 ended, the legally elected Socialist-Communist coalition was consolidating its position in Chile.

WORLD COMMUNIST MEMBERSHIP, 1971

Country	Membership	Country	Membership
Africa		**Hungary**	662,400
Algeria*	400	Iceland	1,000
Morocco*	300	Ireland	200
Nigeria*	1,000	Italy	1,500,000
Réunion	500	Luxembourg	500
South Africa*	100	Malta	100
Sudan*	7,500	Netherlands	11,000
Tunisia*	100	Norway	2,000
Asia and Oceania		Poland	2,296,000
Afghanistan	400	Portugal*	2,000
Australia	3,900	Rumania	1,999,700
Ceylon	2,300	Spain*	5,000
China	17,000,000	Sweden	17,000
India	144,500	Switzerland	3,500
Iran*	500	United Kingdom	32,000
Iraq*	2,000	Yugoslavia	1,146,100
Israel	2,000	**North America**	
Japan	300,000	Canada	2,000
Jordan*	700	Costa Rica*	1,000
Korea, North	1,600,000	Cuba	125,000
Laos	13,000	Dominican Republic*	1,700
Lebanon	1,500	El Salvador*	100
Malaysia*	2,000	Guadeloupe	1,500
Mongolia	48,600	Guatemala*	750
Nepal*	9,000	Honduras*	300
New Zealand	300	Martinique	1,300
Pakistan*	1,450	Mexico	5,000
Philippines*	2,000	Nicaragua*	100
Singapore*	200	Panama*	125
Syria*	3,000	United States	15,000
Thailand*	1,000	**South America**	
Turkey*	1,250	Argentina*	60,000
Vietnam, North	1,100,000	Bolivia*	4,500
Europe		Brazil*	14,000
Albania	75,700	Chile	45,000
Austria	25,000	Colombia	9,000
Belgium	12,500	Ecuador*	1,250
Bulgaria	637,300	Guyana	100
Cyprus	13,000	Paraguay*	4,500
Czechoslovakia	1,200,000	Peru	3,200
Denmark	5,000	Uruguay	20,000
Finland	47,000	Venezuela	8,000
France	275,000	**USSR**	
Germany, East	1,900,000	USSR	14,455,000
Germany, West	28,500		
Greece*	28,000		

* Countries in which the Communist party is illegal. (Source: U.S. Department of State.)

Latin American Communists all united in advocating trade and diplomatic relations with Communist Cuba, and in protesting political and economic "domination" by the United States.

North America. The tiny Canadian Communist party, located mostly in the cities of the province of Ontario, had fewer members in 1971 than the year before. Canadian Communists continued to urge their country to withdraw from the North Atlantic Treaty Organization and to reduce U. S. influence over the Canadian economy. The party was pro-USSR in the Sino-Soviet dispute.

The small Communist party of the United States, located mostly in cities along the East and West coasts, propagandized for withdrawal of U. S. armed forces from Vietnam, reduction of U. S. armament, removal of the U. S. partial embargo on trade with Communist countries, and cessation of U. S. governmental financing of Radio Free Europe and Radio Liberty, both of which broadcast anti-Communist programs to populations behind the Iron Curtain.

The U. S. party supported the Arab countries in the Arab-Israeli dispute, was pro-Moscow in the Sino-Soviet dispute, and opposed U. S. President Nixon's planned visit to Communist China. On internal matters the U. S. Communists stood for Negro equality with whites, and interpreted President Nixon's wage and price freeze as detrimental to labor and favorable to big business.

(See also separate articles on the Communist countries.)

ELLSWORTH RAYMOND
New York University

COMPUTERS

The computer industry, after lusty growth throughout the 1960's, experienced its second straight disastrous year in 1971. Scores of computer firms failed during the year, following the pattern begun in 1970. Although 1971 was a poor year for celebrating the 25th anniversary of the invention of the electronic computer, there were some bright spots. In particular, the market for minicomputers continued to grow strongly, and the computer industry began to move rapidly into the medical field.

Company Failures. After a brief existence, bankruptcy hit the Viatron Computer Systems Corp. The embryonic firm had set the computer world astir when it announced its goal to mass market computers at extraordinarily low prices through the use of a new integrated circuit technology. On the basis of its potential, Viatron had raised $60 million from investors. By year-end, however, the firm was threatened with liquidation.

On Sept. 18, 1971, the giant RCA Corp. announced that it would no longer manufacture large-scale, general-purpose computers, even though it had spent $250 million to develop the business. The Univac Division of the Sperry Rand Corp. agreed to buy the bulk of RCA's defunct computer operations, making Univac the second-largest computer manufacturer in the United States (after IBM).

Minicomputers. In contrast to the overall gloomy picture, minicomputers continued their lofty sales climb by posting a 25% gain in 1971. The health of this segment of the computer business was exemplified by a licensing agreement between the Data General Corp. of Southboro, Mass., and the Nippon Mini-Computer Company, located in Japan. Under the agreement, the Japanese firm acquired the rights to manufacture and market a line of Data General minicomputers throughout Japan and the Far East.

IBM 3270 information display system enables executives to call for detailed breakdown of an item in a summary report through the touch of an electronic pen.

IBM

Computers in Medicine. While 1971 mainly was a shake-out and consolidation period for computer companies, new applications for sophisticated machines continued to flourish, particularly in the field of medicine. In fact, the medical profession has begun to embrace electronic data processing in the same way that the business community did in the early 1950's. According to one forecast, computer processing of medical data will become a $1 billion market by 1980, and its ultimate potential will be a $3.5 billion market—with every hospital bed in the United States linked to some computer.

In California, some hospitals are using computers to interpret electrocardiograms (EKG) through a technique called "heart-lines." The core of the system is a remotely located computer to which subscribing hospitals connect their EKG instruments by means of acoustic couplers and telephone lines. When an EKG is administered, the electrical output generated by the instrument is converted to coded digital signals, which are transmitted over telephone lines to the heart-line computer. The computer detects any abnormal signals, which may indicate heart trouble.

In still another pioneering application, IBM has introduced a computer program that helps doctors to examine as many as 15 patients simultaneously, using a number of television-like screens connected to a central computer. In this system, images of the body appear on each screen in a hospital or physician's office. Questions are flashed on the screen, and each patient answers by using an electronic implement called a light pen. In one case, for example, a human torso is shown, and the patient is requested to place the pen on the screen image location corresponding to where he feels pain in his body. Each patient also is given a test booklet of coded punch cards. The punch-card and light-pen replies are all processed by the computer.

Used Computers. As a result of the recession in 1971, the market for used computers was brisk. For example, the U. S. Department of Labor purchased a used IBM System/360 computer for $1.6 million—$250,000 less than the list price for a new machine.

Off-Track Betting System. Not all goes smoothly in the application of computers to men's affairs. The pioneering computer system installed by New York City for its off-track betting operation broke down repeatedly throughout 1971, forcing the city to rely on manual methods during the failures.

Anniversary. The 25th anniversary of the invention of the electronic computer was marked at a banquet held in Chicago on Aug. 3, 1971. Guests of honor were James W. Mauchley and J. Presper Eckert, coinventors of ENIAC (Electronic Numerical Integrator and Calculator), the first large electronic digital computer. This machine was formally dedicated on Feb. 15, 1946.

STANLEY KLEIN
Science Editor, WEVD Radio, New York, N. Y.

CONGO, Democratic Republic of (Zaïre)

Congo changed its name to "Zaïre Republic" on Oct. 27, 1971. The new name is taken from the name originally given by the Portuguese to the Congo River, based on an approximate rendition of the Kikongo word *nzadi* ("river"). The economic climate became uncertain as a result of the declining price of copper and signs of political discontent.

A.F.P. FROM PICTORIAL
PRESIDENT Joseph Mobutu of Congo (now Zaïre) confers with French President Georges Pompidou in Paris in March. The two leaders discussed economic and technical affairs.

Political Affairs. President Joseph Mobutu, who had been reelected in a one-man contest in November 1970, began his new term in office by offering a general amnesty for all acts committed against the government since independence. Thousands of refugees reportedly took advantage of this offer, including two ranking political exiles—Christopher Gbenye, onetime head of the Kisangani-based "People's Republic of Congo" and Nicolas Olenga, former commander of the "People's Liberation Army." Others, mindful of the fate of guerrilla leader Pierre Mulele, who had been executed in October 1968 after accepting a similar amnesty, preferred to remain abroad.

In August, Olenga and a handful of associates were sentenced to 10 years' imprisonment on charges of planning to overthrow the regime in favor of exiled leader Antoine Gizenga. Six weeks later, two of Congo's most durable political personages and longtime associates of Mobutu, Justin Bomboko and Victor Nendaka, as well as a senior officer, were also arrested and charged with subversive activities. Mobutu alleged that there had been foreign complicity in the plots, and in July some 30 eastern European diplomats were expelled.

Student disturbances during the spring were perhaps more embarrassing to the government. A series of minor incidents at the University of Kisangani in March were followed on June 4 by a violent confrontation on the Kinshasa campus of Lovanium University between a small party of soldiers and a group of students who were commemorating the 1969 incident in which several students had been shot and killed. President Mobutu promptly closed down the university and forcibly enrolled its student population (including girls) into the army.

Demonstrations of solidarity by other students throughout the country further reinforced the government's determination to tighten its control over the universities. The result was the merging of Congo's three universities—at Kinshasa, Lubumbashi, and Kisangani—into a single national university of the Congo with three campuses. Fifteen students were sentenced to life imprisonment for their part in the incidents, and by the fall normal instruction was resumed.

Foreign Affairs. Congo maintained an ostensibly nonaligned yet basically pro-Western attitude. Kinshasa was one of only four African capitals to welcome U. S. Vice President Spiro Agnew in June. Earlier in the year, President Mobutu had been given elaborate receptions during his official visits to France, Japan, and Taiwan.

On the African scene, Congo tried assiduously to be everyone's friend. During his visit to Sudan in February, Mobutu expressed his support for the UN Security Council resolution of Nov. 22, 1967, on the Middle East, two months after having ratified a comprehensive friendship treaty with Israel. Another delicate balancing act involved reconciling

─────── **CONGO (ZAÏRE)** • **Information Highlights** ───────

Official Name: Zaïre Republic.
Area: 905,565 square miles (2,345,409 sq km).
Population (1970 est.): 17,480,000. *Density,* 17 per square mile (7 per sq km). *Annual rate of increase,* 2.3%.
Chief City (1969 est.): Kinshasa, the capital, 1,200,000.
Government: *Head of state,* Joseph Désiré Mobutu, president (took office Nov. 25, 1965). *Head of government,* Joseph Désiré Mobutu. *Legislature*—National Assembly (unicameral). *Political party*—Popular Movement of the Revolution.
Languages: French (official), Kikongo and other Bantu languages.
Education: *Literacy rate* (1970), 58% of population. *Expenditure on education* (1967), 20.8% of total public expenditure. *School enrollment* (1967)—primary, 2,338,895; secondary, 173,124; technical/vocational, 34,704; university/ higher, 5,827.
Finances (1970 est.): *Revenues,* $430,000,000; *expenditures,* $600,000,000; *monetary unit,* zaire (0.50 zaïre equals U. S.$1, Sept. 1971).
Gross National Product (1968): $1,330,000,000.
National Income (1968): $875,000,000; *national income per person,* $52.
Manufacturing (metric tons, 1969): Cement, 322,000; sulfuric acid, 126,000; sugar, 40,000.
Crops (metric tons, 1969 crop year): Palm oil, 223,500; groundnuts (1968), 115,000; coffee, 66,000.
Minerals (metric tons, 1969): Copper ore, 356,900; manganese ore, 165,000; tin concentrates, 6,639; industrial diamonds, 11,621,000 metric carats (ranks 1st in world).
Foreign Trade (1969): *Exports,* $644,000,000 (chief exports— copper, $419,400,000; diamonds, $34,200,000; tin and cassiterite, $22,600,000; palm oil, $19,200,000). *Imports,* $410,000,000 (chief imports, 1967—transport equipment, $37,024,000; chemicals, $22,958,000; nonelectrical machinery, $21,944,000; cotton fabrics, $18,074,000). *Chief trading partners* (1967)—Belgium Luxembourg (took 30% of exports, supplied 32% of imports); Italy (12%—8%).
Transportation: *Roads* (1964), 90,430 miles (145,529 km); *motor vehicles* (1968), 72,300 (automobiles, 46,100); *railroads* (1970), 3,108 miles (5,002 km); *national airline,* Air Congo; *principal airport,* Kinshasa.
Communications: *Telephones* (1970), 22,092; *radios* (1964), 200,000; *newspapers* (1969), 7 (daily circulation, 25,000).

Kinshasa's fundamental sympathy toward the new military regime in Uganda with the preservation of normal relations with Tanzania and Zambia, which had strong reservations about Maj. Gen. Idi Amin's takeover of the government.

Relations with Congo (Brazzaville), which had returned to a relatively normal state in January, once again reverted to their more traditional pattern of mutual suspicion in August, when the Ngouabi regime was again accused of sympathy for anti-Mobutu subversives.

President Mobutu sided with the majority of OAU members in denouncing the idea of a "dialogue" with South Africa.

Economy. Economic developments were dominated by the decline in the price of copper, which accounts for 60% of Congo's exports and for 45% of its budgetary resources. The price of copper fell from $1,460 per metric ton in 1969 to $1,130 during the last quarter of 1970. As a result of increased production the trade balance maintained a comfortable surplus of $238 million. But uncertain prospects caused the government to base its 1971 revenue estimates on a moderate figure of $1,000 per metric ton of copper and to trim its projected expenditure by 5%.

Such temporary setbacks, however, did not significantly affect Congo's remarkable prospects, which have made it the most attractive investment site on the continent, after South Africa. Economic projects in various stages of development included the opening of new mineral deposits and the announcement by Gulf Oil in January that offshore oil deposits had been discovered; the development of the vast hydroelectric project at Inga; and the expansion of the transportation infrastructure by extending and modernizing the rail, road, and river systems. Loans totaling $150 million were secured during the year, mostly from Japan, the United States, and the Common Market.

Congo's rapid and largely uncontrolled development, combined with worldwide inflationary trends, resulted in a significant amount of domestic inflation. The government tried to counteract the inflation by two somewhat contradictory measures: a 30% wage increase for civil servants and a rather ineffectual price freeze.

EDOUARD BUSTIN, *Boston University*

CONGO, People's Republic of the (Brazzaville)

Congo continued its move to the left in 1971 with a cautious but systematic policy of nationalization. The leftward drift has been apparent in Brazzaville since the abortive coup of 1969, and led the country to change its name to "People's Republic of the Congo" in January 1970.

Nationalization. Land and air transportation had been nationalized early in 1970, and later in the year two major sugar firms, controlled by French interests, and a wood-processing plant at Point-Noire were nationalized. In February 1971, Congo announced the nationalization of 200,000 acres of timberland concessions in the Kouilou-Niari region. The government justified its decisions by charging the foreign management of these firms with a callous disregard for their African employees and for Congo's long-term interests. But the government took care to specify that these measures should not be construed as directed against France.

─── **CONGO** • **Information Highlights** ───

Official Name: People's Republic of the Congo.
Area: 132,047 square miles (342,000 sq km).
Population (1970 est.): 940,000. *Density,* 8 per square mile (3 per sq km). *Annual rate of increase,* 1.2%.
Chief City (1971 est.): Brazzaville, the capital, 160,000.
Government: *Head of state,* Marien Ngouabi, chairman of the Council of State (took office Jan. 2, 1969). *Head of government,* Marien Ngouabi. *Executive body,* Council of State. *Political Party*—Congolese Worker's party.
Language: French (official).
Education: *Literacy rate* (1971), 50% of population. *Expenditure on education* (1968), 21.7% of total public expenditure. *School enrollment* (1968)—primary, 212,259; secondary, 25,112; technical/vocational, 2,607; university/higher, 1,485.
Finances (1966 est.): *Revenues,* $33,400,000; *expenditures,* $33,400,000; *monetary unit,* CFA franc (277.71 francs equal U. S.$1, Sept. 1971).
Gross National Product (1968 est.): $203,000,000.
National Income Per Person (1968), $220.
Consumer Price Index (1970), 119 (1963=100).
Manufacturing (metric tons, 1969): Sugar, 95,000; sawnwood, 38,000; beer, 76,000 hectoliters.
Crops (metric tons, 1969 crop year): Groundnuts, 20,000; coffee, 1,800; cocoa beans, 1,400.
Minerals (metric tons, 1969): Crude petroleum, 24,000; tin concentrates, 6,639; lead ore, 2,200; diamonds (1968), 4,343,000 metric carats.
Foreign Trade (1968): *Exports* (1970), $31,000,000 (chief exports—wood, $20,093,000; diamonds, $15,532,000). *Imports* (1970), $57,000,000 (chief imports—nonelectrical machinery, $14,705,000). *Chief trading partners* (1968)—France (took 10% of exports, supplied 58% of imports); West Germany (22%—10%).
Transportation: *Roads* (1969), 6,737 miles (10,839 km); *motor vehicles* (1966), 11,400 (automobiles, 6,500); *railroads* (1969), 548 miles (822 km); *national airline,* Lina Congo.
Communications: *Telephones* (1970), 9,812; *television stations* (1968), 1; *television sets* (1969), 500; *radios* (1969), 62,000; *newspapers* (1966), 3.

Political Developments. Conspiratorial activities have been recurrent in Congo's domestic affairs, and 1971 was no exception. But none of the incidents during the year appeared to have raised a serious challenge to the regime of President Marien Ngouabi.

Foreign Relations. Brazzaville's increasingly radical posture has tended to isolate it from the basically "moderate" and pro-French countries of former French Equatorial Africa. But the economic and technical interconnections between these various states remained strong and made it unlikely that any formal break could occur in the near future.

The reconciliation with Congo (Zaïre), which had led to the resumption of full diplomatic relations by the end of 1970, was again jeopardized in August when the government of President Mobutu accused Brazzaville of being implicated in subversive activities in Kinshasa.

Brazzaville characterized the proposal by some African states to engage in a "dialogue" with South Africa as a form of complicity in a plan of neocolonial reconquest.

EDOUARD BUSTIN, *Boston University*

CONNALLY, John B. See BIOGRAPHY.

CONNECTICUT

The effects of inflation and the rising cost of government services caught up with Connecticut's residents and public servants in 1971. Through much of the year, interest focused on the struggle between the Republican governor and the Democratic legislature to provide an acceptable tax package.

Tax Controversy. In his inaugural message, Gov. Thomas J. Meskill, who had been elected in November 1970, called for drastic cuts in state spending and hiring, and for additional taxes, amounting to $800 million, to pay off the state deficit. He proposed a 7.5% sales tax. On the closing day of its regular session in June, the General Assembly put together a package of taxes on interest, dividends, and capital gains, which the governor promptly vetoed. Called back into special session, the General Assembly stunned the state by adopting Connecticut's first income tax. The governor allowed the measure to become law without his signature. The new tax was especially hard on middle-income persons, and after what some legislators described as "a 42-day life of hell," the Assembly called itself back into session and killed the income tax (August 12).

The substitute measure subsequently enacted included a sales tax of 6.5%, a 10¢-per-gallon gasoline tax, and a 21¢-per-pack cigarette tax, all of which were the highest such levies in any state. In addition, a $350 tuition charge was imposed at the University of Connecticut which had traditionally been free to. Connecticut residents. As the budget was still unbalanced, Governor Meskill announced spending cuts of $85 million, including a cut of $23 million from the grants to cities and towns for education and services.

Other Legislation. The General Assembly also passed laws that: created a new environmental protection department to coordinate programs of conservation and pollution control; instituted an ethics code for state officers, employees, and legislators; provided for unit pricing in large food stores; imposed a minimum wage of $1.85 per hour; and

GOVERNOR Thomas J. Meskill addresses legislature in June. Republican governor clashed with Democratic-controlled legislature over the state budget.

--------- CONNECTICUT • Information Highlights ---------

Area: 5,009 square miles (12,973 sq km).
Population (1970): 3,032,217. *Density:* 612 per sq mi.
Chief Cities (1970 census): Hartford, the capital, 158,017; Bridgeport, 156,542; New Haven, 137,707; Stamford, 108,-798; Waterbury, 108,033; New Britain, 83,441.
Government (1971): *Chief Officers*—governor, Thomas J. Meskill (R); lt. gov., T. Clark Hull (R); secy. of state, Mrs. Gloria Schaffer (D); atty. gen., Robert K. Killian (D); treas., Robert I. Berdon (R); commissioner, Dept. of Education, William J. Sanders; chief justice, Charles S. House. *General Assembly*—Senate, 36 members (19 Democrats, 17 Republicans); House of Representatives, 177 members (99 D, 78 R).
Education (1970–71): *Enrollment*—public elementary schools, 471,677 pupils; 18,700 teachers; public secondary, 174,454 pupils; 12,942 teachers; nonpublic schools (1968–69), 119,100 pupils; 6,010 teachers; college and university (fall 1968), 106,234 students. *Public school expenditures* (1970–71), $600,000,000 ($997 per pupil). *Average teacher's salary,* $9,600.
State Finances (fiscal 1970): *Revenues,* $1,236,950,000 (6.5% general sales and gross receipts taxes, $258,659,000; motor fuel tax, $99,191,000; federal funds, $215,672,000). *Expenditures,* $1,347,675,000 (education, $420,394,000; health, welfare, and safety, $208,795,000; highways, $169,-902,000). *State debt,* $1,919,455,000 (June 30, 1970).
Personal Income (1970): $14,871,000,000; per capita, $4,807.
Public Assistance (1970): $188,665,000. *Average monthly payments* (Dec. 1970)—old-age assistance, $100.70; aid to families with dependent children, $242.20.
Labor Force: *Nonagricultural wage and salary earners* (June 1971), 1,189,200. *Average annual employment* (1969)—manufacturing, 475,000; trade, 218,000; government, 148,-000; services, 175,000. *Insured unemployed* (Oct. 1971)—61,700 (6.1%).
Manufacturing (1967): *Value added by manufacture,* $6,389,-800,000. Transportation equipment, $1,444,300,000; non-electrical machinery, $974,200,000; electrical equipment and supplies, $639,000,000; fabricated metal products, $627,200,000.
Agriculture (1970): *Cash farm income,* $167,611,000 (livestock, $102,871,000; crops, $63,967,000; government payments, $773,000). *Chief crops* (1970)—Apples, 50,400,000 pounds; tobacco, 7,884,000 pounds; potatoes, 1,127,000 cwt.; hay, 203,000 tons.
Mining (1970): *Production value,* $28,381,000 (ranks 45th among the states). *Chief minerals* (tons)—Sand and gravel, 8,815,000; stone, 7,789,000; clays, 190,000.
Fisheries (1970): *Commercial catch,* 5,600,000 pounds ($2,-100,000). *Leading species by value* (1967): Blackback flounder, $70,609; cod, $3,346.
Transportation: *Roads* (1969), 18,251 miles (29,371 km); *motor vehicles* (1969), 1,677,000; *railroads* (1968), 695 miles (1,118 km); *airports* (1969), 13.
Communications: *Telephones* (1971), 2,061,200; *television stations* (1969), 5; *radio stations* (1969), 55; *newspapers* (1969), 28 (daily circulation, 951,000).

legalized lotteries and parimutuel and off-track betting. A law requiring one year of residence for public welfare applicants was declared unconstitutional, and hence a 15% cut in family welfare grants was made, but later halted by a temporary court injunction. The U. S. Supreme Court ruled that 1969 legislation granting $6 million in aid to parochial and private schools was unconstitutional.

Reapportionment. Attempts by the legislature to reapportion itself failed. In October a panel of superior court justices (two Republicans and one Democrat) reapportioned the state into 36 senatorial districts with average populations of 84,200. The House districts were reduced from 177 to 151, with populations averaging 20,000 each. This loss of 26 representatives, mostly from large-city, normally Democratic districts, led to a court challenge of the scheme by the Democrats.

Economic Conditions. Total personal income from all sources reached $14.6 billion in 1970, up 6.3% over 1969. For the seventh year, Connecticut's per capita income of $4,807 was the highest in the nation. However, unemployment rose to 9.4%.

Deaths. Thomas J. Dodd, a prosecutor at the Nuremberg trials and a former U. S. senator (1959–71) died on May 24, 1971, at Old Lyme.

In June, 28 persons died in the state's worst air disaster, as an Allegheny Airlines plane crashed in a fog at Tweed-New Haven airport.

Black Panthers. Connecticut's longest and costliest trial came to an end in New Haven when Judge Harold M. Mulvey dismissed charges against Black Panther leader Bobby Seale and Mrs. Ericka Huggins in the kidnapping and slaying of a fellow Panther, Alex Rackley, in May 1969.

Submarines. The Navy's 100th and 101st nuclear submarines, *Silversides* and *Batfish,* were launched at the Electric Boat Division of General Dynamics at Groton.

GEORGE ADAMS, *Connecticut State Library*

POISONED EAGLES are examined by Sen. Gale McGee of Wyoming (*left*) and government officials in June. Federal laws protect many eagles, some belonging to endangered species.

CONSERVATION

What is in effect a crusade for environmental quality conservation continued in the United States in 1971. There were significant advances in preserving parks, other outdoor recreation resources, and wildlife. (For the year's developments relating to pollution, see ENVIRONMENT.)

In a message to Congress on February 8, President Nixon declared that more national park lands should be acquired and reiterated a federal policy of encouraging the establishment of outdoor recreation areas accessible to urban areas.

"The job of filling out the national park system," the President said, "is not complete. Other unique areas must still be preserved. Despite all our wealth and scientific knowledge we cannot recreate these unspoiled areas once they are lost to the onrush of development. . . . We must bring parks to where the people are, so that everyone has access to nearby recreation areas."

National Park System. Pressure on the National Park System increased during the year as 171 million visitors crowded in, an increase of 4.9% over 1970. There was further concern about providing access to the parks without destroying the values for which they were established. Yosemite National Park initiated traffic control for the first time by closing the eastern end of the valley and providing free bus transportation for visitors. At Yellowstone serious consideration was given to providing a monorail mass transportation system and to limiting the number of visitors. Because of increasing problems, the U. S. Department of the Interior formed an interagency task force to investigate use of snowmobiles, dune buggies, motorbikes, and other motorized recreation vehicles on public land.

The Voyageurs National Park in Minnesota, with 139,000 acres of lake country, and the Gulf Islands National Seashore, covering parts of Florida and Mississippi, were added to the National Park System in 1971. Legislation was signed making the Chesapeake and Ohio Canal National Monument a national park, at the same time authorizing $17 million for acquisition to 20,000 acres and for restoring and rewatering this historic canal.

Four other areas were included in the National Park System late in 1970. They were the Apostle Islands National Lakeshore, Lake Superior; Sleeping Bear Dunes National Lakeshore, Michigan; Andersonville National Historic Site, Georgia; and Fort Point National Historic Site, California. The National Park System had 283 units by the end of 1971. (See special feature beginning on page 56.)

Taking Parks to the People. In pursuing the policy of locating parks in and near urban areas, the Department of the Interior announced plans in 1971 for acquiring land and developing 14 major public recreation areas. The parks and the cities served are:

Gateway National Recreation Area, New York City–Newark, N. J.
Connecticut River National Recreation Area, Hartford–Springfield.
Chesapeake and Ohio Canal National Historical Park, Washington, D. C.
Anacosta National Recreation Area, Washington, D. C.
Lake Michigan Beach National Lake Shore, Chicago–Milwaukee.
Lake Erie National Lakeshore, Detroit.
Upper Mississippi National Recreation Area, Minneapolis–St. Paul.
Meramec National Recreation Area, St. Louis.
Huck Finn National Recreation Area, Memphis.
Chattahoochee National Recreation Area, Atlanta.
Four Seasons National Recreation Area, Denver.
Buffalo–Bayou National Recreation Area, Houston.
Golden Gate National Recreation Area, San Francisco.
Santa Monica Mountains National Recreation Area, Los Angeles.

National Trails. Major consideration was given during 1971 to enlargement of the National Trails System, in which the Appalachian Trail and the Pacific Crest Trail are the officially designated national scenic trails. Studies were begun or were under way on other prospective national scenic trails: Continental Divide Trail; Potomac Heritage Trail; the Oregon Trail; Mormon Trail; Mormon Battalion Trail; and El Camino Real in Florida.

Island Resources. The Bureau of Outdoor Recreation completed a study of the recreational potentials of the nation's islands. It reported that there are 26,235 islands 10 acres or more in size. They cover 28.6 million acres, of which 21 million acres are in Alaska. The study concluded that high priority should be given to legislative action by Congress to conserve aesthetic and wildlife features of Kauai Island, Hawaii, and four island groups—Channel Islands, California; Cumberland Islands, Georgia; Ten Thousand Islands, Florida; and Virginia Barrier Islands, Virginia.

Surplus Property for Parks. Surplus federal properties may now be transferred to state and local political divisions for park and recreation purposes, and up to 100% of the costs may be waived. The transfers were made possible by legislation in late 1970 that amended the Federal Property and Administration Service Act of 1949. Under the new authority, a number of federal areas were made available in 1971. This included 1,033 acres of Fort Hancock, N.J.; 426 acres of Fort Lawton, in Seattle, Wash.; 372 acres at Border Field, Calif.; 210 acres at Fort Worth, Texas; 128 acres at Sands Point, N.Y.; and 93 acres of the Cleveland Army Center at Parma, Ohio.

Wildlife. Conservationists directed heavy criticism against the annual seal harvest in the Pribilof Islands off Alaska. Secretary of Commerce Maurice H. Stans, after visiting the area, said that the allegations that baby seals were being harvested and that the herds were being depleted "are totally unfounded." He pointed out that, under management, the number of seals has increased from about 200,000 in 1911 to 1.3 million. In Canada, however, a 6-man task force was appointed to study the seal harvest, and a significant reduction was forecast for the authorized harvest.

Secretary Stans ordered the termination of U.S. licensing for whale hunting, thus ending a historic marine industry in the nation.

The Senate environmental appropriations subcommittee heard testimony detailing the killings of hundreds of eagles and other wildlife by thallium poisoning and by airborne sharpshooters in Wyoming and Colorado. A witness attributed the killings to sheep ranchers. Court actions were taken to prevent further killings.

The American alligator received additional protection through an Endangered Species Act prohibiting interstate transfer of illegally obtained hides.

Canal Construction Halted. In January, President Nixon ordered work stopped on the Cross-Florida Barge Canal to protect the wild and scenic environment of the Oklawaha River in Florida. And in September, the Tennessee-Tombigbee Ship Canal, authorized to provide a route from the Gulf of Mexico to the Tennessee River, was halted by a temporary injunction. For details, see CANALS.

J. GRANVILLE JENSEN
Oregon State University

UPI

ENDANGERED SPECIES OF THE UNITED STATES
Official list, Bureau of Sports Fisheries and Wildlife, Interior Department

MAMMALS

Hawaiian hoary bat
Indiana bat
Delmarva Peninsula fox
    squirrel
Morro Bay kangaroo rat
Salt marsh harvest mouse
Eastern timber wolf
Red wolf
San Joaquin kit fox
Black-footed ferret
Florida panther
Florida manatee (sea cow)
Key deer
Columbian white-tailed deer
Sanoran pronghorn

BIRDS

Hawaiian dark-rumped petrel
California least tern
Hawaiian goose (nene)
Aleutian Canada goose
Laysan duck
Hawaiian duck (koloa)
Mexican duck
Brown pelican
California condor
Florida everglade kite
    (snail kite)
Hawaiian hawk (io)
Southern bald eagle
American peregrine falcon
Arctic peregrine falcon
Attwater's greater prairie
    chicken
Masked bobwhite
Whooping crane
Yuma clapper rail

California clapper rail
Light-footed clapper rail
Hawaiian gallinule
Hawaiian coot
Eskimo curlew
Hawaiian stilt
Puerto Rican plain pigeon
Puerto Rican parrot
Ivory-billed woodpecker
Red-cockaded woodpecker
Hawaiian crow (alala)
Small Kauai thrush (puaiohi)
Large Kauai thrush
Molokai thrush (Olomau)
Nilhoa millerbird
Kauai oo (oo aa)
Crested honeycreeper
    (akohekohe)
Hawaii akepa (akepa)
Maui akepa (akepuie)
Oahu creeper (alauwahio)
Molokai creeper (kakawahie)
Akiapolaau
Kauai akialoa
Kauai and Maui nukupuus
Laysan and Nihoa finches
Ou
Palila
Maui parrotbill
Bachman's warbler
Kirtland's warbler
Dusky seaside sparrow
Cape Sable sparrow

REPTILES AND AMPHIBIANS

American alligator
Blunt-nosed leopard lizard
San Francisco garter snake

Puerto Rican boa
Santa Cruz long-toed
    salamander
Texas blind salamander
Houston toad

FISHES

Shortnose sturgeon
Longjaw cisco
Lahontan cutthroat trout
Piute cutthroat trout
Greenback cutthroat trout
Gila trout
Arizona (Apache) trout
Humpback chub
Mohave chub
Pahranagat bonytail
Moapa dace
Woundfin
Colorado River squawfish
Kendall Warm Springs dace
Cui-ui
Devil's Hole pupfish
Comanche Springs pupfish
Tecopa pupfish
Warm Springs pupfish
Owens River pupfish
Pahrump killifish
Big Bend gambusia
Clear Creek gambusia
Pecos gambusia
Unarmored threespine
    stickleback
Gila topminnow
Fountain darter
Watercress darter
Maryland darter
Blue pike

Innocent-looking toys that can cause severe injury drew the ire of consumer groups in 1971. This child's top has a potentially lethal steel spike under the base's suction cup. Other toys can transmit electric shocks.

consumer affairs

The consumer movement continued to thrive in 1971. Both government and the business community responded to the increasingly effective voice of consumer advocates.

U. S. Government. In the nation's capital the Congress, as well as the executive branch of government, dealt with a number of important issues. Although no major new consumer legislation was enacted, the groundwork was laid for significant advances at the federal level.

Independent Consumer Agency. Perhaps the biggest consumer controversy in Congress during 1971 centered on a proposed new federal agency to represent the consumer interest. The militant "consumerists"—led by Ralph Nader, who heads the Center for Study of Responsive Law, in Washington, D. C.—worked feverishly for the creation of a strong independent agency, empowered to act as a watchdog over the federal government's entire consumer activities. Such an agency would become a participant in the day-to-day decisions of the government that affect consumers. The decision might be a Food and Drug Administration ruling on whether to allow a particular drug to be placed on the market. It might pertain to the granting of a television license by the Federal Communications Commission, or it might involve deliberations of the Federal Trade Commission on what is, or is not, a fraudulent selling device.

A bill to create an independent agency—but in a weaker form than that asked for by the leading consumer advocates—passed the House of Representatives in October. The bill would authorize the new agency to intervene in formal proceedings of federal regulatory agencies, maintain public files on consumer complaints, and carry out or sponsor tests and surveys. Consumer advocates pledged an all-out effort in the Senate in 1972 to strengthen the proposed new agency, especially by empowering it to intervene in informal proceedings of regulatory agencies and to participate in cases involving the imposition of fines and penalties.

Product Safety. In 1970 the National Commission on Product Safety, a presidentially appointed commission, issued a report on the subject of unsafe household products. After making the most comprehensive study ever undertaken on this subject, this bipartisan group recommended passage of a strong federal product-safety law. Both the House of Representatives and the Senate held hearings during 1971 on this recommendation, and prospects for passage of a new law looked favorable.

Strengthening the Federal Trade Commission. In November the Senate passed a bill to increase the authority of the Federal Trade Commission to issue and enforce rules against consumer deception. For example, one provision would allow the commission, as a follow-up on a cease-and-desist order issued against a company accused of deceiving consumers, to bring a lawsuit requiring the accused company not only to promise to discontinue the deceptive practice but also to compensate previously aggrieved consumers by giving them refunds.

Another provision would require that product warranties include a clear and simple statement of the guarantee, including its exact coverage and duration and the procedure to be followed by the customer in obtaining satisfaction. Warranties that fail to meet federal standards would have to be plainly labeled with a designation such as "partial." Although the bill was vigorously opposed by some members of the business community, prospects for final enactment in 1972 seem good.

Federal Agencies. Congress was not alone in responding to demands for greater consumer protection. A number of significant investigations and regulatory actions were taken by various federal agencies as well.

The Federal Trade Commission, only recently scored as ineffective by "Nader's Raiders" (the group of young lawyers and students assisting Ralph Nader), went through a metamorphosis of sorts and initiated some of the most innovative actions of 1971 in the consumer-protection field. The commission promulgated new trade rules requiring disclosure of octane ratings of gasoline and permanent-care labeling on most articles of clothing. It began to require manufacturers to substantiate claims made in advertisements and initiated experiments with "corrective ads"—a procedure whereby companies charged with having run deceptive advertisements are required to run corrections in subsequent advertisements.

The Food and Drug Administration took initial steps to get some unsafe toys off the market before the 1971 Christmas season (after having been sued by Consumers Union in 1970 for failing to enforce the law that year). The Federal National Mortgage Association produced standard mortgage forms and new credit guidelines to make home purchasing fairer for the buyer.

In addition, the National Highway Traffic Safety Administration prevailed on the General Motors Corporation to send notices to 786,000 owners of the Chevrolet Corvair warning of possible carbon monoxide leaks in the heating systems of their cars. That administration also issued a special consumer bulletin warning of a possible defect in the front engine mount of 1965–69 Chevrolet automobiles— a defect that could cause the accelerator to jam and the driver to lose control of the vehicle, totally or partially. Spokesmen for Chevrolet indicated that the company would cooperate in the investigation.

The States. Although the states were active in consumer protection, their legislatures passed fewer major new consumer laws in 1971 than in the two previous years. The trend toward enactment of broad consumer codes, with provisions for their enforcement, continued. Three states—Maryland, Connecticut, and Massachusetts—enacted unit pricing laws, and the question of automobile insurance reform was widely debated.

Four states—Delaware, Florida, Illinois, and Oregon—adopted "no fault" automobile insurance plans in 1971. Under such a system of insurance, the policyholder recovers his loss from his own insurance company without regard to who was at fault in an accident. Massachusetts had adopted "no fault" automobile insurance previously, and plans were under active consideration in more than 30 other state legislatures.

Congress, too, considered various proposals for a national "no fault" automobile insurance system. Some form of federal-state reform seemed imminent as 1971 drew to a close.

The Business Community. Members of the business community also responded to the new consumerism. A new Council of Better Business Bureaus, to replace the former National Better Business Bureau, came into being. The new council pledged itself to the task of upgrading the services of the 144 local Better Business Bureaus, including a major experimental program to arbitrate consumer complaints.

The Council of Better Business Bureaus also became a major sponsor of the National Advertising Review Board, a 50-member self-regulatory body established "to be more responsive to public concerns with advertising and provide a vehicle for continual improvement of advertising practices to better serve the public." The review board promised to respond to citizens' complaints about false and deceptive advertising and outlined its plans for attempting to persuade advertisers to change advertisements that the board considered to be misleading. If it failed, it would refer the matter to the appropriate government agency and would publicize its own findings. By the end of 1971, consumer groups were making plans to see how far self-regulation would go.

Robert Choate, a consumer advocate, received nationwide publicity when he charged at a congressional hearing in 1970 that dry breakfast cereals

TAINTED food, particularly soup, caused consumer alarm during the summer and led to demands for stricter federal inspections. A Food and Drug Administration biologist tests for presence of botulism, a deadly toxin.

were poor in nutrients. In 1971 he reported that by increasing the nutrient content, six companies had "drastically reformulated" 26 of the 40 cereals he had criticized.

Consumer leaders who have been seeking legislation at national, state, and local levels to establish unit pricing in supermarkets could count gains in 1971. Unit pricing—the posting of prices by the ounce, pint, pound, or other appropriate unit—is a device that allows the shopper to tell at a glance which brand or size of a product is most economical, regardless of the size of the package the merchandise comes in.

As has been noted, Maryland and Massachusetts enacted unit pricing laws in 1971. The Maryland law becomes effective in January 1972. The Massachusetts law is effective in stages, beginning in May 1971. New York City's unit pricing law, which is applicable to all food stores doing at least $2 million worth of business annually, went into effect in June 1971. Several other states, as well as 200 cities and counties, were considering adoption of such laws. In the meantime, hundreds of supermarkets all over the country have voluntarily established unit pricing systems.

Wage-Price Freeze. Most of all, however, 1971 will be remembered as the year in which the wage-price freeze was imposed. Acting to stop growing inflation, President Nixon imposed a 90-day freeze on wages and prices in August 1971. Three months later, plans for "Phase II" were announced, and an elaborate system of price and wage controls came into being.

Consumer advocates were generally supportive of the President's action to keep the lid on inflation. They wondered, however, whether there would be adequate consumer involvement in Phase II or adequate enforcement of the control system. In short, they wondered whether this latest attempt to keep prices down would gain and keep the confidence of the citizenry, for it was widely agreed that without confidence this latest effort at wage and price control would be doomed to failure.

DAVID A. SWANKIN
Director, Washington Office, Consumers Union

COSTA RICA

The first full year of the third administration of President José Figueres Ferrer brought no important alteration in the internal affairs of Costa Rica. However, it did produce a dramatic development in the field of international relations as Costa Rica reestablished diplomatic ties with the USSR.

Domestic Affairs. Probably the most significant trend in national politics in 1971 was the growing rapprochement between leading figures in the administration, including President Figueres himself, and their traditional political opponents, the National Republicans. This provoked considerable worry among some elements of the President's own National Liberation party. Many party members were also upset by what they felt was the administration's failure to put sufficient emphasis on reform.

The Economy. Economic development continued in 1971. The country received a number of international loans. Among them was one for $6.3 million from the Inter-American Development Bank for improving the water systems of Costa Rican cities, and another for $3.5 million for improving agricultural and vocational education.

COSTA RICA • Information Highlights

Official Name: Republic of Costa Rica.
Area: 19,575 square miles (50,700 sq km).
Population (1969 est.): 1,690,000. *Density,* 85 per square mile (33 per sq km). *Annual rate of increase,* 3.3%.
Chief Cities (1970 census): San José, the capital.
Government: *Head of state,* José Figueres Ferrer, president (took office May 8, 1970). *Head of government,* José Figueres Ferrer. *Legislature*—Legislative Assembly (unicameral), 57 members. *Major political parties*—Party of National Liberation; Party of National Unification; National Republican party.
Languages: Spanish (official).
Education: *Literacy rate* (1970), 85% of population. *Expenditure on education* (1968), 4.7% of gross national product. *School enrollment* (1968)—primary, 322,683; secondary, 62,256; technical/vocational, 6,524; higher, 11,449.
Finances (1970 est.): *Revenues,* $190,780,000; *expenditures,* $190,780,000; *monetary unit,* colon (662 colones equal U. S.$1, Sept. 1971).
Gross National Product (1970): $925,000,000.
National Income (1970): $765,250,000; *per person,* $453.
Manufacturing (metric tons, 1969): Cement, 160,000; sugar, 140,000; meat, 48,000.
Crops (metric tons, 1968 crop year): Sugarcane (1968–69), 1,900,000; bananas, 703,000; coffee, 91,200.
Foreign Trade (1970): *Exports,* $229,000,000 (chief exports—coffee, $72,840,000; bananas, $66,460,000). *Imports,* $317,000,000. *Chief trading partners* (1968)—United States (took 47% of exports, supplied 38% of imports).
Transportation: *Roads* (1970). 3,600 miles (5,793 km); *motor vehicles* (1969). 56,700 (automobiles, 36,100); *railroads* (1970). 661 miles (1,064 km); *national airline,* LACSA; *principal airport,* El Coco (San José).
Communications: *Telephones* (1970), 56,261; *television stations* (1968), 3; *television sets* (1969), 100,000; *radios* (1969), 106,000; *newspapers* (1967), 5.

One of the year's major economic problems was the country's balance of payments deficit. To slow the outflow of funds, the government on June 18 imposed an import surcharge. On July 14, however, as a result of protests from Costa Rica's partners in the Central American Common Market (CACM), all market members, as well as Panama, were exempted from the surcharge. Earlier, the threatened collapse of the CACM had been the subject of a meeting of Costa Rican and other Central American delegates in Antigua, Guatemala, where changes in the structure of the market were suggested to aid the less industrialized member-nations of the group.

International Affairs. A striking change occurred in Costa Rica's relations with the Soviet Union. At the beginning of the year, President Figueres announced that his government intended to reestablish diplomatic ties with the USSR. In June, after protracted negotiations, a Soviet embassy was established in San José. At the end of August, Foreign Minister Gonzalo Facio announced that the Soviet Union had expressed willingness to grant Costa Rica a credit of $200 million to strengthen trade relations. The credit was to be used to buy Soviet machinery, equipment, and manufactured goods. For its part, the USSR was to buy greater quantities of Costa Rican coffee and bananas.

It did not appear in 1971 that the forging of new ties with the USSR would diminish the traditionally friendly disposition of President Figueres towards the United States. This was demonstrated early in the year when potentially damaging newspaper allegations of anti-administration activities by the CIA in Costa Rica were dismissed by Figueres as baseless. In October, Costa Rica cosponsored the U. S.-backed resolution to admit the People's Republic of China to the United Nations while preserving the Assembly seat of Nationalist China.

In June, President Figueres announced that the long period of hostility between Costa Rica and neighboring Nicaragua should be considered at an end. In August, the president embarked on a brief state visit to Jamaica.

ROBERT J. ALEXANDER, *Rutgers University*

Patrick Murphy, New York City police commissioner, and Rep. John Murphy (*right*) show examples of "Saturday Night Specials," cheap handguns that figure prominently in violent crimes.

CRIME

Crime in the United States in 1971 continued to be a subject of intensive discussion with political overtones. Much of the debate centered on the issue: Is crime increasing dramatically in the country or have the "law and order" efforts of the Nixon administration succeeded in bringing the crime problem more nearly under control?

The answer to that question depends, apparently, on who is looking at the matter. Attorney General John N. Mitchell, examining the most recent crime statistics, found much that encouraged him. The crime figures, compiled by the Federal Bureau of Investigation in the *Uniform Crime Reports—1970,* showed an increase in the crime rate of 11% between 1969 and 1970. This rate, Mitchell pointed out, was less than the 12% for the previous year, and therefore indicated a slowing in the growth of crime. In addition, Mitchell was gratified by the fact that reported crimes in the large cities of the United States rose by only 6% in 1970, after having shown a 9% increase in 1969 and an 18% increase in 1968.

Opponents of the Nixon administration tended, however, to look at the crime figures from a different perspective. To them, the 11% rise in crime indicated an increasing deterioration of control efforts and a failure for the Nixon program. The decelerating pace of increase, they maintained, was a consequence of nothing more than the fact that crime totals are now so high that it would take a gigantic continuing rise to maintain the same percentage of increase. For them, the attorney general's interpretation was nothing more than a statistical artifice. Opponents of the Nixon administration noted that in 1970 there were 5,568,200 major crimes, an increase of more than one million such offenses over 1968, the last year of the Democratic administration.

The Public and Crime. The argument between the administration and its opponents over crime statistics indicated primarily that crime continues to be as much a political as a social issue. Public opinion polls show, however, that the grip of the "crime problem" on the nation's emotions is lessening, in part perhaps because it is often difficult for the public to remain continuously aroused over a specific problem. In 1971 a Gallup poll, reversing an earlier result, disclosed that economic issues and the Vietnam War were defined by adults as more pressing matters than crime. Among young people, a national magazine survey found that air and water pollution rated as the leading national problems in 1971; the war and drug abuse were listed second; and crime was third, ahead of both inflation and race relations.

Statistical Data. Most impressive among the national statistics issued by the FBI was the 17% rise in robberies from individual persons and the 29% increase in bank robberies. Because robberies are serious offenses, involving considerable potential danger to the victim, and because they tend to be regularly reported to the police, they are usually regarded as offenses that indicate with some accuracy important changes in the total crime picture.

The striking increase in bank robbery, a continuing phenomenon in the United States, is believed to be a result of the opening of numerous branch banks in the suburbs, where they are more vulnerable to attack than they are in central business districts. In contrast to earlier times, today's typical bank robber is not a professional, but rather a debt-pressed amateur who works by himself. To combat the growing tide of robberies, some banks now use "television tellers," that is, persons whose images can be seen only on screens by customers, and who conduct all business through an intercom system and by use of pneumatic tubes. It should be noted, however, that banks still lose more from employee embezzlement than they do from robbery. Robbers generally account now for about $10 million in bank losses annually, while embezzlers, many of whom remain undetected, are known to derive at least $17 million each year from their peculations.

SEARCHERS (*left*) unearthed 25 bodies near Yuba City, Calif., in the spring. Juan V. Corona (*above, left*) was accused of grisly murders.

Rape and Murder. Several major studies of specific kinds of crime were published during the year. Menachem Amir's *Patterns in Forcible Rape* (1971), disclosed that in 48% of the forcible rape cases reported to the police in Philadelphia, the victim and the offender were known to each other prior to the alleged criminal offense. In 21% of the cases, Amir reported, both the victim and the offender had been drinking prior to the reported criminal act. It was also learned that 19% of the victims of forcible rape had previous arrest records, 56% of these arrests having been for "some sort of sexual offense." The Amir study also discovered that 43% of the forcible rape cases in Philadelphia involved more than one offender against a lone victim.

A second study, *Homicide in Chicago, 1965–1970,* by Richard Block and Franklin E. Zimring of the University of Chicago Law School, indicated a doubling of the homicide rate in Chicago during the past five years. Homicide was found to be 90% intraracial (that is, involving offenders and victims of the same race). Guns had been used in homicides 50% of the time in 1965. By 1970, that figure had risen to 65%.

Correlates of Crime. Especially notable in the rise of crime figures has been the disproportionately rapid increase in serious crimes committed by women. Between 1960 and 1970, the national increase in the female crime rate was 202%, whereas the male crime rate increased 73%. At the end of 1971, four women were listed on the FBI roster of the ten most wanted criminals, three of them in connection with political activity. Such offenses, combined with growing female involvement in narcotics use, and the general loosening of the social restric-

tions that have previously inhibited female criminal activity, are believed to account for the sharp rise in crime by women. Such increases are just as pronounced in regard to youthful offenses. Between 1960 and 1970, the crime rate for girls under 18 rose 204.1% but for boys only 97.9%.

That crime rates, such as those for females in the United States, are a consequence of social conditions was particularly underlined with the release of 1970 crime statistics for the city of Tokyo. The Japanese capital, whose 11 million inhabitants make it the world's largest city, reported only 474 robberies, a figure that compares to the 74,102 robberies in New York City (population about 8 million) during the same period. Tokyo had only three persons killed with handguns during the year; New York had 438 such deaths. In Tokyo, there were about 500 victims of rape, in New York 2,141 such victims. The Japanese capital had 292 narcotics cases. In New York, the 1970 figure for narcotics arrests was 52,479.

Recidivism. Calculations made during the year regarding the previous criminal histories of persons arrested on federal charges indicated with some force the ineffectiveness of rehabilitation efforts in the United States. Of the 37,884 persons arrested on federal charges, 68% had previously been arrested for criminal offenses. From their first to their most recent arrest—an average period of about five and a half years—the 37,884 offenders had been arrested an average of four times each on criminal charges, making a grand total of 158,000 such charges among them.

"White-Collar Crime." Attempts to broaden the general understanding of the term "crime" so that it comes to include *all* violations of the criminal law were carried on throughout the year by Ralph Nader and a group of young lawyers working with him. In particular, Nader and his associates concentrated on lawbreaking by corporations and their executives, or what they labeled "crime in the suites," a catchier name for what is generally known as "white-collar crime." "If there are criminal penalties for the poor and deprived when they break the law," Nader told a Senate Commerce Committee hearing, "then there must be criminal penalties for the automobile industry when its executives knowingly violate standards designed to protect citizens from injuries and systematic fraud." Interrupted by a senator who insisted that the witness was not giving adequate credit to American industry for its many outstanding achievements, Nader was afforded an opportunity to drive his point deeper: "Do you give credit to a burglar," he asked, "because he doesn't burglarize 99 percent of the time?"

Similarly, Nader argued that the exhausts of air contaminants from motor vehicles "has taken on the proportions of a massive crime wave," though crime statistics continue to "pay attention to 'muggers' and to ignore 'smoggers.'" Nader was also quoted during the year as saying: "When you talk about violence, don't talk about the Black Panthers. Talk about General Motors." His views were reinforced by the publication in 1971 of *America, Inc.,* by Morton Mintz and Jerry S. Cohen. Among the themes in the book is one which charges that "large corporations commonly engage in criminal behavior, although sustained underreporting of this fact in communications media severely limits public appreciation of it."

Capital Punishment. For a time in 1971, it appeared that there might be a blood bath of executions of criminals in the United States. On May 4, in *McGautha* v. *California,* the Supreme Court by a 6–3 vote rejected the claim that juries must be provided with guidelines by federal or state legislatures for use in deciding which convicted offenders shall live and which shall die. At that time more than 600 persons were imprisoned in death rows around the nation, awaiting execution, which, depending on the state in which they were held, would be by electrocution, gassing, hanging, or shooting. However, the Supreme Court agreed to decide specifically in its next term on the constitutionality of capital punishment, and to determine whether its use violates the 8th Amendment provision against "cruel and unusual punishment."

The cases at issue involved two black men convicted of rape, one in Texas and the other in Georgia, and two other black men convicted of murder, one in California, the second in Georgia.

By year-end, the lives of about 650 persons, including six women, were dependent on the Supreme Court's decision.

It was found that the largest number of persons awaiting execution were in California and Florida. This indicates, perhaps, some correlation between crimes of violence and the moderate climate that encourages outdoor activity.

Crime in the News. The most sensational criminal event of the year was the discovery in June of 25 bodies in an orchard in Yuba City, Calif., 45 miles (72 km) north of Sacramento. The bodies were those of itinerant farm workers, vagrants, and homeless men who, the authorities believed, had been killed by Juan V. Corona, a 37-year-old farm labor contractor. The total number of victims exceeded that of the most notorious of recent mass murders in the United States: Charles J. Whitman, who had fatally shot 16 persons from atop a tower on the University of Texas campus in 1966, and Howard B. Unruh, a war veteran who in 1949 had silently walked through the streets of Camden, N. J., gunning down 13 persons. The Yuba City murders were also notable for having been committed in a calculated manner. In most mass murders, the offender tends to go on a berserk rampage.

On June 28, Joseph Colombo, Sr., 48, the founder of the Italian-American Civil Rights League and reputedly head of one of the five organized crime syndicate "families" in New York City, was shot down during a rally in midtown Manhattan. Colombo's alleged assailant, Jerome A. Johnson, 24, was immediately killed by a still-unidentified person, in a blood-soaked vignette reminiscent of the gangland slayings of the 1930's. At year-end, Colombo remained in grave condition.

George Jackson, well-known throughout the country as author of the book *Soledad Brother,* was killed in August during an attempted jail break from the California State Prison in San Quentin. Jackson had been facing charges of participating in a shoot-out in the Marin County Courthouse at San Rafael the year before.

GILBERT GEIS
Coauthor, "Man, Crime, and Society"

Bank robbery suspect with briefcase full of money screams at capture in Stamford, Conn., on March 30.

UPI

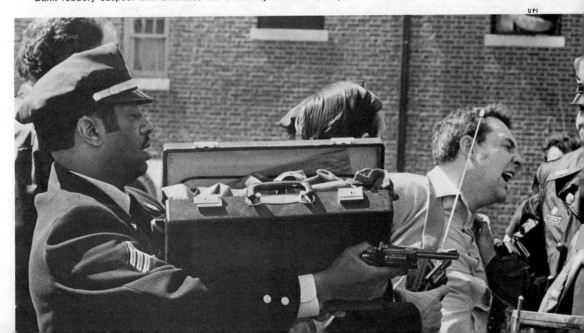

Fidel Castro, on his first Latin American trip in 11 years, parades in Santiago with Chile's President Allende (*right*).

CUBA

During 1971, officially designated "The Year of Productivity," the government of Premier Fidel Castro imposed tighter discipline on Cuban workers, cracked down on intellectual dissent, ordered an end to the air-lift of Cuban refugees to the United States, and strengthened ties with the Soviet Union. Late in the year Premier Castro visited Chile.

Sugar Harvest. Managerial inefficiency, absenteeism, and low labor productivity continued to plague Cuba's principal industry after the failure of the campaign to produce 10 million tons of sugar in 1970. The goal for 1971 was set more realistically at 7 million tons, but the harvest fell short of this figure by a million tons. A severe drought was in part responsible for the disappointing yield.

During the harvest season, laws were enacted requiring work by all men aged 17 to 60 and women aged 17 to 55 and specifying harsh punishment for "vagrants" and "parasites." At the same time, "moral incentives" were played down as Castro held out the promise of higher wages and the distribution of a few refrigerators and other consumer goods to exemplary workers. Greater government control over the work force was expected to result from a new identification system.

Suppression of Critics. While prison terms of up to 15 years were being meted out to an increasing number of Cubans convicted of black marketeering and other economic crimes, an international furor was raised by the detention for six weeks of Cuban poet Herberto Padilla. Following Padilla's arrest in March, the Paris newspaper *Le Monde* published an open letter to Castro, signed by some of the Western world's leading leftist intellectuals, including Jean-Paul Sartre and Susan Sontag, which expressed concern for the poet and deplored the "reappearance of sectarianism" in Cuba. Reacting to the letter and to the publication of books critical of Cuba by socialist writers K. S. Karol and René Dumont, Castro lashed out at "pseudo-revolutionary intellectuals" and "bourgeois intrigue-mongers."

In the meantime, Padilla was released after having publicly confessed to being a "counter-revolutionary" and a "vicious character." In a signed statement the poet disavowed his foreign defenders, expressed regret for his past attitudes, and declared that he had come to realize his errors after "discussions" with government security forces. The new head of the Cuban Institute of Culture, Luis Pavón Tamayo, appointed in May, was expected to keep a tight rein on the intellectuals.

End of Airlift. Until the summer of 1971 Cubans who found the Castro regime intolerable could hope to emigrate on one of the twice-daily flights between Cuba and the United States that the U. S. government had operated since 1965. But, after nearly 250,000 Cubans had taken this route to exile, Castro terminated the air-lift agreement, and regular flights ceased on September 1.

The emigration had contributed to the decline in Cuba's rate of population growth. The decline in growth was revealed when the results of the Cuban census of 1970, the first since 1953, were published in Janauary 1971. A significant drop in the birthrate was attributed to increased job opportunities

───── **CUBA • Information Highlights** ─────

Official Name: Republic of Cuba.
Area: 44,218 square miles (114,524 sq km).
Population (1970 census): 8,553,395. *Density,* 186 per square mile (72 per sq km). *Annual rate of increase,* 2.0%.
Chief Cities (1966 est.): Havana, the capital, 990,000; Santiago de Cuba, 249,600; Camagüey, 170,500.
Government: *Head of state,* Osvaldo Dorticos Torrado, president (took office July 18, 1959). *Head of government,* Fidel Castro Ruz, premier (took office Feb. 15, 1959).
Language: Spanish (official).
Education: *Literacy rate* (1968 est.), over 90% of population aged 15 and over. *Expenditure on education* (1966), 16.1% of total public expenditure. *School enrollment* (1968)—primary, 1,332,659; secondary, 261,598; technical/vocational, 46,962; university/higher, 30,311.
Finances (1965 est.): *Revenues,* $2,535,000,000; *expenditures,* $2,535,000,000; *monetary unit,* peso (1 peso equals U. S. $1, 1971).
Gross Domestic Product (1968): $3,100,000,000.
Average annual income per person (1968), $413.
Economic Indexes: *Industrial production* (1966), 116 (1963= 100); *agricultural production* (1969), 114 (1963=100).
Manufacturing (metric tons, 1969): Sugar, 5,534,000; residual fuel oils, 2,735,000; cement (1968), 780,000; cigarettes, 22,000,000 units.
Crops (metric tons, 1968 crop year): Sugarcane (1968–69), 39,000,000 (ranks 3d among world producers).
Minerals (metric tons, 1968): Salt, 99,000; crude petroleum (1969), 91,000; nickel, 37,321; manganese ore, 20,400.
Foreign Trade (1967): *Exports,* 1968, $650,000,000 (chief exports—Sugar, $600,780,000). *Imports,* 1968, $1,095,000,000 (chief imports—machinery and transport equipment, $161,-600,000; chemicals, $100,080,000; petroleum, crude and partly refined, $60,050,000). *Chief trading partners* (1967) —USSR (took 52% of exports, supplied 58% of imports).
Transportation: *Roads* (1969), 8,300 miles (13,357 km); *motor vehicles* (1965), 165,700 (automobiles, 162,000); *railroads* (1969), 3,714 miles (5,977 km).
Communications: *Telephones* (1970), 263,166; *television stations* (1963), 7; *television sets* (1970), 555,000; *radios* (1964), 1,345,000; *newspapers* (1961), 10.

and better education for women in Cuba's socialist society, but the Castro regime, already feeling the effects of a labor shortage, probably felt it could no longer afford the drain of workers by the airlift. The labor shortage of 1971 contrasted strikingly with the high unemployment rates of pre-Castro Cuba.

Cuban-Soviet Relations. Cuba's economic ties to the USSR were strengthened by a new trade agreement, signed in February 1971, which provided for a $100 million increase in Soviet exports to Cuba in 1971 over the 1970 total of about $500 million. Cuba's trade deficit with the USSR was not made public, but Castro acknowledged it to be very large.

Cuban-Soviet friendship was underscored in October when Premier Aleksei Kosygin visited the island. While Kosygin was in Havana the U. S. Department of Defense reported that five MIG fighter aircraft had been delivered to Cuba, the first Castro had received in more than four years. After Kosygin's departure, a "courtesy call" by a Soviet task force of five warships indicated the importance of Cuba to Moscow's increasingly influential naval strategists.

Soviet-Cuban cordiality did not prevent Castro from improving his relations with Peking. In 1971, for the first time in five years, a Chinese ambassador was in residence in Havana.

Inter-American Affairs. Castro strongly disclaimed any desire to reestablish diplomatic relations with the United States. Nor was Cuba eager to rejoin the Organization of American States, although Castro expressed interest in reestablishing diplomatic ties with Latin American neighbors on a bilateral basis. For the first time in more than a decade, the Cuban premier visited another Latin American country, spending 25 days (Nov. 10–Dec. 4, 1971) in Chile as a guest of that nation's Socialist president, Salvador Allende. Earlier in the year Chile and Cuba had entered into a trade agreement, whereby $12 to $15 million worth of Cuban sugar and tobacco was to be exchanged for Chilean industrial and farm goods.

Controversy with Spain. From the standpoint of trade, however, Chile was still far less important to Cuba than was Spain, whose barter trade with the island amounted to some $70 million in 1970. In 1971 diplomatic relations between Havana and Madrid were strained as the Spanish government accused Cuban diplomats of dispensing Communist propaganda in Spain. The Cuban embassy in Madrid was closed in July, although diplomatic relations between the two countries were not officially severed.

NEILL MACAULAY
University of Florida

CYPRUS

In 1971, Cyprus once again failed to find a formula for reconciling the Greek Cypriot majority with the Turkish Cypriot minority, or to establish a government that both could accept. UN forces remained stationed on the island as they had been since 1964 to keep the peace.

Unionist Issue. Tensions mounted with the resurgence among rightist Greek Cypriots of a desire for union (*enosis*) with Greece. The president, Archbishop Makarios, leader of the unionists before independence, now stood for the maintenance of a

— CYPRUS • Information Highlights —

Official Name: Republic of Cyprus.
Area: 3,572 square miles (9,251 sq km).
Population (1970 est.): 630,000. *Density,* 176 per square mile (68 per sq km). *Annual rate of increase,* 1.7%
Chief City (1970 est.): Nicosia, the capital, 110,000.
Government: *Head of state,* Archbishop Makarios III, president (reelected to a 5-year term, Feb. 25, 1968). *Head of government,* Archbishop Makarios. *Legislature*—House of Representatives (unicameral), 50 members. *Major political parties*—Greek Cypriots, Turkish Cypriots.
Languages: Greek, Turkish, English (official).
Education: *Literacy rate* (1970), 82% of population. *Expenditure on education* (1968), 16.5% of total public expenditure. *School enrollment* (1968)—primary, 71,745; secondary, 37,489; vocational, 4,355; higher, 446.
Finances (1969): *Revenues,* $85,743,000; *expenditures,* $66,915,000; *monetary unit,* pound (.4167 pound equals U. S. $1, Sept. 1971).
Gross National Product (1969): $503,760,000.
National Income (1969): $446,880,000; *national income per person,* $709.
Manufacturing (metric tons, 1969): Cement, 246,000; meat, 24,000; wine (1968), 436,000 hectoliters.
Crops (metric tons, 1968 crop year): Grapes, 169,000; citrus fruits, 20,000; olives, 15,000.
Minerals (metric tons, 1969): Sulfur, 464,000; asbestos, 21,700; copper, 19,200; chromium ore, 11,500.
Foreign Trade (1970): *Exports,* $109,000,000 (chief exports—copper, $22,824,000; citrus fruit, $17,256,000). *Imports,* $238,000,000 (chief imports (1968)—nonelectrical machinery, $18,295,000; chemicals, $16,541,000; textile yarn and fabrics, $15,293,000). *Chief trading partners* (1968)—United Kingdom (took 37% of exports, supplied 33% of imports); West Germany; Italy.
Transportation: *Roads* (1964), 24,820 miles (39,943 km); *motor vehicles* (1969), 62,900 (automobiles, 49,000); *merchant fleet* (1971), 1,498,000 gross registered tons; *national airline,* Cyprus Airways.
Communications: *Telephones* (1970), 42,261; *television stations* (1968), 2; *television sets* (1969), 42,000; *radios* (1969), 159,000; *newspapers* (1969), 10.

separate state, though his public utterances did not rule out eventual union with Greece.

The unionist cause found support from the Cyprus-born Greek general, George Grivas, a former commander of the Cyprus National Guard (1964–67). In September 1971, Grivas disappeared from Athens and traveled clandestinely to Cyprus.

Intercommunal Talks. Negotiations conducted by Glavkos Clerides, president of the House of Representatives, and Rauf Denktaş, president of the Turkish Cypriot Communal Chamber, entered their fourth year. They proved as unproductive as previously, since the Turkish Cypriots, some 18% of the population, held out for extensive autonomous rights while the Greek Cypriots, who constitute about 80%, were adamant against any solution that might lead to a permanent partition of the island into two administrative parts.

Foreign Affairs. In January, British Prime Minister Heath visited Cyprus and conferred with Archbishop Makarios and Dr. Fazıl Küçük, the Turkish Cypriot leader. That same month Makarios attended a conference of the heads of the Commonwealth of Nations at Singapore.

In March, Makarios went to Kenya where he met President Jomo Kenyatta and baptized approximately 5,000 Africans into the Greek Orthodox faith. In June the Cypriot president visited the Soviet Union to be present at the enthronement of the new Russian patriarch and to hold talks with President Nikolai Podgorny and other officials.

Discussions between Makarios and Premier George Papadopoulos of Greece in Athens in September resulted in a vague communiqué, which tended to support rumors that the archbishop and the Greek government were at odds over Cypriot policy. The Turkish government through the year emphasized its solidarity with the Turkish Cypriots.

GEORGE J. MARCOPOULOS, *Tufts University*

INSTRUCTION in machine operation is given North Vietnamese girl, one of trainee group in Czechoslovakia.

CZECHOSLOVAKIA

Two events dominated the political scene in Czechoslovakia in 1971, the 14th Congress of the Communist party and the elections for representatives at all levels, from the Federal Assembly down to the local councils. The year was also marked by the beginning of the fifth 5-year plan.

Communist Party Congress. Having completed, by the end of 1970, the purge of "revisionists" and "right-wing opportunists," the party leadership felt safe to convene the long-delayed 14th Communist party Congress. The congress was held on May 25–29 and was attended by almost 1,200 delegates. It was designed to mark the official conclusion of the period of "consolidation" that had begun with Gustav Husák's assumption of party leadership in April 1969. The entire proceeding of the congress, from Husák's report to the unanimous election of the new party functionaries, bore telling testimony to the party's return to Soviet-style orthodoxy.

There was a major reshuffle in the composition of the Central Committee: only 26 members elected at the previous congress were reelected to the 115-man Central Committee in 1971. On the other hand, the new 11-man Presidium of the Central Committee, which had already been purged of Alexander Dubček and his associates in the previous two years, registered only one change. Evžen Erban, a reconstructed onetime reformer, was replaced by Karel Hoffmann, a noted hardliner. Husák was reelected as head of the party, with a change in title from first secretary to secretary general. All the other secretaries of the Central Committee were also reelected.

The congress made several changes in the party rules. The congresses of the Czechoslovak and Slovak Communist parties are to be held every five years, instead of four, and regional and district party conferences every two to three years. The candidature, a probationary period preceding the granting of party membership, was restored and set at two years.

Elections. As the party congress was meant to be the concluding act in the "consolidation" of the party, so the November elections to the Federal Assembly and all the lower levels of representation were to symbolize the completion of the "normalization" of political life. Since the new electoral laws gave the Communist-controlled National Front the exclusive authority to place candidates on all the ballots and to control the electoral process, the outcome was a foregone conclusion. Fearful of the regime's reprisals if they failed to vote, 99.4% of the voters went to the polls and most delivered their votes for the regime-sponsored candidates.

Increased Centralization. The process of recentralization, begun in 1970, gathered momentum in 1971. Several constitutional provisions adopted on Dec. 20, 1970, gave the federal government exclusive authority in a number of major areas of economic activity, such as fuel and power, the foundry and engineering industries, transportation, and telecommunications. Several new federal ministries were set up to handle these matters, and corresponding state ministries were abolished.

Economy. Czechoslovakia entered the first year of its fifth 5-year plan for economic development in 1971. As approved by the party congress, the new plan calls for marked progress in numerous

—— CZECHOSLOVAKIA • Information Highlights ——

Official Name: Czechoslovak Socialist Republic.
Area: 49,370 square miles (127,869 sq km).
Population (1970 est.): 14,470,000. *Density,* 290 per square mile (113 per sq km). *Annual rate of increase,* 0.5%.
Chief Cities (1967 est.): Prague, the capital, 1,031,070; Brno, 333,831; Bratislava, 278,835; Ostrava, 271,905.
Government: *Head of state,* Ludvík Svoboda, president (took office March 30, 1968). *Head of government,* Lubomir Štrougal, premier (took office Jan. 28, 1970). *Communist party secretary general,* Gustav Husák (took office April 17, 1969). *Legislature*—Federal Assembly; Chamber of People, 200 members; Chamber of the Nations, 150 members.
Languages: Czech (official), Slovak (official), Hungarian, German.
Education: *Literacy rate* (1970), almost 100% of population. *Expenditure on education* (1968), 4.7% of net material product. *School enrollment* (1968)—primary, 2,052,526; secondary, 386,663; technical/vocational, 270,208; university/higher, 137,654.
Finances (1969): *Revenues,* $21,695,000,000; *expenditures,* $21,695,000,000; *monetary unit,* koruna (7.20 korun equal U.S.$1, 1971).
Net Material Product (1969): $41,139,000,000.
Average Annual Income Per Person, $2,262.
Economic Indexes: *Industrial production* (1970), 154 (1963 = 100); *consumer price index* (1970), 102 (1969 = 100).
Manufacturing (metric tons, 1969): Crude steel, 10,802,000; pig-iron and ferroalloys, 7,115,000; cement, 6,733,000; wheat flour, 1,245,000; beer, 20,817,000 hectoliters.
Crops (metric tons, 1969 crop year): Sugar beets (1968–69), 8,098,000; potatoes, 5,180,000; wheat, 3,257,000.
Minerals (metric tons, 1969): Lignite, 80,337,000 (ranks 4th among world producers); coal, 27,068,000; magnesite, 1,814,400; iron ore, 442,000.
Foreign Trade (1967): *Exports* (1970), $3,792,000,000 (chief exports—nonelectrical machinery, $776,670,000; transport equipment, $432,080,000; iron and steel, $242,640,000; electrical machinery and appliances, $174,860,000; chemicals, $140,695,000). *Imports* (1970), $3,698,000,000 (chief imports—nonelectrical machinery, $537,360,000; mineral fuels and lubricants, $239,860,000; chemicals, $165,140,000; textile fibers and waste, $156,805,000). *Chief trading partners* (1968)—USSR (took 34% of exports, supplied 33% of imports); East Germany (11%–13%); Poland.
Tourism: *Receipts* (1970), $46,100,000.
Transportation: *Roads* (1967), 45,398 miles (73,057 km); *motor vehicles* (1969), 846,000 (automobiles, 684,200); *railroads* (1967), 8,313 miles (13,376 km); *merchant fleet* (1970), 89,000 gross registered tons.
Communications: *Telephones* (1970), 1,895,229; *television stations* (1968), 23; *television sets* (1969), 2,996,000; *radios* (1968), 3,967,000; *newspapers* (1968), 27.

areas. National income is to rise 28%, of which at least 95% is to be achieved by increased labor productivity. Industrial production is scheduled to increase by 34%–36%, labor productivity in industry by 30%–32%, construction by 28%, and agricultural production by 14%. Capital investments are scheduled to rise by 35%–37%, foreign trade by 36%–38%, and retail trade by 28%–30%.

During the first six months of 1971 the plan's actual results were encouraging in relation to the corresponding period of 1970. Industrial production increased by 7.7%, labor productivity in industry by 7.5%, construction by 9.2%, and foreign trade by 10.1%. The 1971 harvest was reported to have been "the largest in the history of Czechoslovak agriculture."

Cultural and Political Repression. The offensive against the remnants of liberalism in culture and education continued unabated throughout 1971. The liquidation of the Czechoslovak writers' union in 1970 was followed in 1971 by the disbandment of the unions of composers, graphic and plastic artists, architects, and theatrical artists. A new, orthodox writers' union, consisting of some 90 lesser writers, was established, and a new socialist association for science, culture, and politics was created for the avowed purpose of fighting deviations from Marxist-Leninist orthodoxy in the ranks of the intelligentsia. In spite of Husák's assurances that no political trials would be held, several erstwhile reformers were tried and convicted for their activities in 1968–69.

Foreign Affairs. Czechoslovak actions and statements in the field of foreign relations continued to follow the Soviet line. Czechoslovakia's spokesmen kept pressing for the eviction of Radio Free Europe and Radio Liberty from Munich. They also expressed displeasure over Rumania's overtures toward Communist China, and they charged Austria with allowing espionage against Communist countries to be carried out on Austrian territory—which they termed "unneutral behavior." Negotiations were begun with West Germany in an endeavor to get the West German government to declare the 1938 Munich agreement, which had dismembered Czechoslovakia, invalid from its very inception.

EDWARD TABORSKY
University of Texas

DAHOMEY

Dahomey's three-man Presidential Commission maintained political stability during 1971, despite rivalries among its members that threatened its effectiveness. The Commission had been set up in May 1970 to mitigate long-standing regional conflicts. Its members are to alternate as president, with Hubert Maga of the north in the post until 1972, followed by Justin Ahomadegbe of the center in 1972–74 and Sourou Migan Apithy of the south in 1974–76.

Domestic Affairs. Rivalry within the Commission erupted over the location of the new Dahomean university. A UNESCO commission recommended Porto-Novo, the focus of Apithy's strength. But a site near Abomey, Ahomadegbe's focus of power, was selected, leading Apithy to walk out of a cabinet meeting. By the fall of 1971, departments or institutions of linguistics, literature, natural science, and regional development had opened. In addition, France agreed to construct buildings for a proposed medical school.

————— DAHOMEY • Information Highlights —————

Official Name: Republic of Dahomey.
Area: 43,483 square miles (112,622 sq km).
Population (1970 est.): 2,690,000. *Density,* 59 per square mile (23 per sq km). *Annual rate of increase,* 2.8%.
Chief City (1965 est.): Porto-Novo, the capital, 74,500.
Government: *Head of state,* Hubert Maga, president (took office May 12, 1970), head of 3-member Presidential Commission. *Head of government,* 3-member Presidential Commission.
Languages: French (official), numerous tribal languages.
Education: *Literacy rate* (1970), 5% of population. *Expenditure on education* (1967), 22.4% of total public expenditure. *School enrollment* (1967)—primary, 139,734; secondary, 14,210; technical/vocational, 727; higher, 115.
Finances (1970 est.): *Revenues,* $30,065,000; *expenditures,* $35,418,000; *monetary unit,* CFA franc (277.71 francs equal U. S.$1, Sept. 1971).
Gross National Product (1968): $182,000,000.
Average Annual Income Per Person (1968): $70.
Crops (metric tons, 1969 crop year): Cassava (1968), 1,142,-000; sweet potatoes and yams (1968), 500,000.
Foreign Trade (1966): *Exports* (1967), $15,191,000 (chief exports—palm and palm kernel oil, $4,236,000; oil seeds, nuts and kernels, $2,015,000; raw cotton, $1,101,000). *Imports* (1967), $43,526,000 (chief imports—woven cotton fabrics, $6,163,000; beverages and tobacco, $2,675,000; motor vehicles, $2,178,000; nonelectrical machinery, $2,-010,000). *Chief trading partner* (1967)—France.
Transportation: *Roads* (1968), 8,828 miles (14,207 km); *motor vehicles* (1969), 17,100 (automobiles, 10,600).
Communications: *Telephones* (1969), 5,639; *radios* (1968), 60,000; *newspapers* (1968), 1 (daily circulation, 1,000).

The general level of political activity remained low. Trade union members, traditionally the most militant, were mollified by the lifting of a special 20% tax that had been levied on all workers. Students at the technical *lycée* briefly boycotted classes in January to protest examination fees and regulations that prohibited meetings in school of the Dahomean students' union.

Dahomey's economic situation remained bleak. The annual deficit continued at nearly one seventh of the total budget—and, as usual, French assistance covered the gap of nearly $5 million. Major industrial changes during the year included the opening of a $4.5 million palm oil mill near Cotonou.

Foreign Affairs. Dahomey supported a controversial call by President Félix Houphouët-Boigny of the Ivory Coast for "dialogue" with South Africa.

CLAUDE E. WELCH, JR.
State University of New York at Buffalo

DAIRY PRODUCTS. See AGRICULTURE.
DALEY, Richard J. See BIOGRAPHY.

DALLAS

Dallas, with a population of 859,312, is the second-largest city in Texas and the eighth-largest in the United States. Serving as the wholesale, retail, and insurance center of the Southwest, Dallas continued to grow and prosper during 1971.

Construction. Dallas is the airline approach to the states of Texas, Oklahoma, and New Mexico. Construction of the Dallas–Fort Worth Regional Airport—which will be the world's largest international air facility, occupying a site of more than 18,000 acres—was ahead of schedule in 1971. Additions made to the Dallas central business district during the year included the new 40-story 2001 Building, a mirror-glass and steel structure; the 25-story Main Plaza Building; and an additional block of landscaped area surrounding the historic log cabin of Dallas' founder, John Neely Bryan.

Attesting to the rapid business growth of the city is the fact that office space occupancy in the core district remained at 84% in 1971. Nearing completion was the addition of 24 acres of floor space to the Dallas Memorial Auditorium–Convention Center, which will enhance the city's position as the fourth-largest convention site in the nation.

Mayoralty Election. Wes Wise, a former television sportscaster and one-term city councilman, was elected mayor of Dallas in a run-off election on April 20. Wise, who received 59% of the vote, was only 43 years old, making him the youngest mayor of Dallas since the city adopted the Council-Manager form of government in 1931.

All-America City. In March 1971, *Look* magazine and the National League of Cities named Dallas an All-America City in recognition of its wide range of "people services." In the previous two years the city had added four new libraries to its nationally acclaimed public library system. The city's parks department has over 16,000 acres in developed recreation areas, and continues acquisition—48% complete—of a green belt that will surround the central city and preserve the ecological balance. Located in the 52-mile-long "park" will be game preserves, fishing sites, shooting ranges, and recreation facilities. The parks department also sponsors seasonal concerts by the Dallas Symphony Orchestra.

The Crossroads Community Center began operation in September. The center, which functions as a multiservice agency, was created to assist residents in upgrading the quality of their daily lives. Crossroads is a complex of medical, welfare, recreational, and educational facilities, and has merged all social agencies—federal, state, county, city, and private—into one neighborhood location.

Education. Southern Methodist University, the largest private university in the southwestern United States, expanded its community outreach programs via its school of Continuing Education. More than 7,000 adult students registered for credit courses, special-interest seminars, training programs, and noncredit offerings in the 1970–71 academic year. Owning the state's second-largest library collection, the university extended on-site research materials by teletype connections with other colleges and universities in the area.

In its fifth year of operation, Dallas County Junior College System boasted an enrollment, for 1970–71, of more than 15,000 students at its one downtown and two suburban campuses. A fourth campus was scheduled to begin operation in 1972.

SALLY C. HARTLING
University of Texas at Arlington

DAMS

With a worldwide demand for electric power, water supply, flood control, irrigation, and navigable waterways, dam construction continued in 1971 in many parts of the world, including developed and developing nations. This work went on despite growing opposition by ecologists and conservationists, who objected to the appropriation of land for reservoirs and to what they considered to be interference with the flow of rivers.

The United States. The Army Corps of Engineers was occupied with construction of a number of dams in the United States during the year. Major projects were under way in Ohio, Indiana, Alabama, California, and Washington.

Near Hillsboro, Ohio, the Paint Creek Dam and Reservoir was being constructed as a flood control and conservation project. The earth and rockfill dam, scheduled for completion by mid-1973, will be 175 feet (53 meters) high and 870 feet (266 meters) long. Its cost was estimated at $23 million.

Newburgh Dam was being built on the Ohio River near Evansville, Ind. This $42 million project, scheduled for completion in early 1974, is part of a long-range modernization of the Ohio River navigation channel in which 19 new or improved locks and high-lift dam installations will eliminate 46 obsolete facilities. The Newburgh project includes a dam section that is 1,152 feet (351 meters) long and has 9 tainter gates (pivoted radial crest gates for regulating the flow of water) and a fixed weir 1,123 feet (342 meters) long that extends from the river end of the dam to the Kentucky bank.

The Alabama River was also being improved to provide barge navigation from Mobile, on the Gulf of Mexico, to Alabama's capital, Montgomery. Improvements will include three dams with navigation locks, two hydroelectric power installations, and a 9-foot (3-meter) navigation channel. Total cost of the projects will be approximately $146.2 million. The first unit—Millers Ferry Lock, Dam, and Powerhouse—was in operation in early 1971. It consists of a concrete dam 994 feet (303 meters) long with 17 tainter gates and with earth dikes at both wings, a navigational lock 600 feet (183 meters) long and 86 feet (26 meters) wide with a maximum lift of 48 feet (15 meters), and a powerhouse located 3,100 feet (945 meters) downstream from the main dam with three 25,000-kw generators. An upstream companion dam at Jones Bluff —15 miles (24 km) above Selma, Ala.—which will provide hydroelectric power, and a smaller downstream structure at Claiborne, which will help maintain channel depth, were expected to be operating in early 1972.

New Melonese Dam on the Stanislaus River, about 35 miles (56 km) east of Stockton, Calif., was in an early stage of construction in 1971. The plans are for a rockfill dam 600 feet (183 meters) high that will create a 2.4-million-acre-foot reservoir for flood control, irrigation, power, water quality control, and recreational development. The power plant will have a 300-megawatt capacity. The entire project was scheduled for completion in 1977.

Dominican Republic. In the Dominican Republic two major dams were under construction in 1971, the $41 million Tavera and the $22 million Valdesia. Tavera Dam on the Río Yaque del Norte is the nation's first major hydroelectric and irrigation project. Scheduled for completion in late 1972, the earthfill barrier will be 260 feet (79 meters) high and 1,100 feet (335 meters) long, requiring 2 million cubic yards (1.5 million cu meters) of embankment fill. It will create a reservoir that will be 5 miles (8 km) long, have a capacity of 138,000 acre feet, and irrigate more than 1 million acres (404,700 hectares) of farmland. Some 200,000 cubic yards (153,000 cu meters) of concrete will be used in building the six spillways, tunnels, and a power plant which will house two 40,000-kw generators.

Valdesia Dam on the Nizao River will be 1,000 feet (305 meters) long and 270 feet (82 meters) high, and will have two 25,000-kw generators. The reservoir formed by the dam will be 4 miles (7 km) long and 2 miles (3 km) wide. It will furnish potable water to several cities and irrigate some 80,000 acres (32,400 hectares) of farmland. It will be completed in 1973.

CONSTRUCTION at Libby Dam received help from (*left to right*) Sen. Mike Mansfield, Rep. Richard Shoup, and President Nixon in September. Project is in Kalispell, Mont.

West Germany. Obernau Dam, near Frankfurt am Main, was completed in 1971. It is a rockfill structure 197 feet (60 meters) high, and 984 feet (300 meters) long. Its base is 820 feet (250 meters) wide, narrowing to 33 feet (10 meters) at the crest. About 1.3 million cubic yards (1 million cu meters) of material makes up the embankment on the Obernau River to form a 213-acre (86-hectare) reservoir, which supplies the town of Siegen with potable water.

Saudi Arabia. In 1971, Saudi Arabia completed Wadi Jizen Dam, a $9 million project that will make arable some 30 square miles (48 sq km) of harsh wasteland. The concrete structure is 135 feet (41 meters) high and 1,027 feet (313 meters) long, and can store about 93 million cubic yards (71 million cu meters) of floodwater.

Africa. The Republic of South Africa started work in 1971 on the P. K. le Roux Dam on the Orange River about 62 miles (100 km) downstream of the existing Hendrik Verwoerd Dam. The new concrete arch structure, which will cost about $60 million, will be 344 feet (105 meters) high and contain about 1.7 million cubic yards (1.3 million cu meters) of concrete. The project, designed for irrigation and electric power, is due to be completed in 1977.

Work was progressing on the Kossou Dam astride the Bandama River in Ivory Coast. The rockfill barrier, scheduled for completion in 1972, will be 1 mile (1.6 km) long and 187 feet (57 meters) high, and will contain 7 million cubic yards (5.4 million cu meters) of material. The multipurpose project, costing $105 million, will provide hydroelectric power, water supply, irrigation, navigation, and recreation. When filled, the reservoir will store 24,000 acre feet of water.

Tasmania. Tasmania, the island state off the southeast coast of Australia, instituted a major program of dam building. In the southwest part of the island, construction began on three dams, one concrete and two rockfill, which will provide approximately 12 million acre feet of water to develop 750 megawatts of hydroelectric power. Gordon Dam on the Gordon River will be a double curvature arch 460 feet (140 meters) high and 600 feet (183 meters) long, involving 196,000 cubic yards (150,000 cu meters) of concrete. On the nearby Serpentine River, the Serpentine rockfill dam will create Lake Pedder, with an embankment that will be 130 feet (40 meters) high and will contain 170,000 cu yards (130,000 cu meters) of material. The third dam, Scotts Peak on the Huon River, will be 140 feet (43 meters) high and will contain 765,000 cubic yards (585,000 cu meters) of rockfill. The entire project is scheduled for completion sometime in 1976 at an estimated cost of $76 million.

In northern Tasmania, on the Mersey and Forth rivers, three other power stations were under construction in 1971. The major structure of the complex will be Cethana Dam, a 365-foot-high (111-meter) rockfill embankment faced with concrete.

Indochina. The Indochina War halted work on the Prek Thnot project, which was started in 1969 under a United Nations program to develop the Mekong River basin. The dam site is in Cambodia. Besides the dam, the project includes an 18-megawatt hydroelectric power plant and facilities to irrigate over 12,000 acres (5,000 hectares). It would benefit the people of Cambodia, Laos, Thailand, and Vietnam.

WILLIAM H. QUIRK
"Contractors & Engineers" Magazine

Erik Bruhn and Carla Fracci, two of the stars of the American Ballet Theatre, appear in a scene from *Giselle*.

dance

Often considered the orphan among the performing arts, the dance was accorded equal status in 1971 at the glittering official opening in September of the John F. Kennedy Center for the Performing Arts in Washington, D. C.

The opening-night work, Leonard Bernstein's *Mass*, commissioned for the occasion, featured members of the Alvin Ailey American Dance Theater as well as singers and instrumentalists. Later in the week, the American Ballet Theatre (ABT), the Kennedy Center's resident dance company, appeared in a program that brilliantly demonstrated ABT's wide range. It consisted of Antony Tudor's *Romeo and Juliet*, a dramatic ballet; Ailey's *The River*, a modern work set to a score by Duke Ellington; and Harald Lander's *Etudes*, a showpiece of classical ballet technique. Dance fans rejoiced that the ABT, one of the world's greatest companies, had at last found an official home.

Earlier in the year, in July, the New York City Center Joffrey Ballet performed in Vienna, Va., at the opening of the Filene Center at Wolf Trap Farm Park, the first national park for the performing arts. The stage at the Filene Center, which is partly open to the outdoors, was judged to be especially good for dancing.

American Ballet Companies. The most important new work to enter the repertoire of the New York City Ballet (NYCB) was Jerome Robbins' *Goldberg Variations* (Bach). Audiences generally found the ballet long, cold, and boring, but the critics loved it. Clive Barnes of the New York *Times* said of *Goldberg Variations:* "... this coldly augustan love poem to the artist's own discipline is an intricate architectural toy of perpetual delight." Critics and audiences liked Robbins' *The Concert,* a 1956 work that was revived in December.

Several young choreographers created new works for the NYCB repertoire. Among these new ballets, all slight works, were John Clifford's *Kodály Dances,* Lorca Massine's *Four Last Songs,* and Richard Tanner's *Concerto for Two Solo Pianos.* George Balanchine presented his *PAMTGG,* inspired by the airline commercial "Pan Am Makes the Going Great." A trivial piece in the style of the 1930's Broadway musicals, it was an artistic disaster.

In the past year or so, NYCB's Patricia McBride emerged as a great ballerina at the peak of her career. The company's male contingent was strengthened by the addition of Helgi Tomasson, who performed especially well in *Dances at a Gathering* and *Tchaikovsky Suite No. 3,* and of Jean-Pierre Bonnefous, who was seen to good advantage in *Symphony in C, Who Cares?,* and *In the Night.*

In 1971, the American Ballet Theatre, probably the world's most versatile company, danced especially well in the classics, including *Giselle, Swan Lake, Coppélia,* and *La Sylphide.* ABT's stars included the ballerinas Carla Fracci, Natalia Makarova, Lupe Serrano, and the young Cynthia Gregory and the *premiers danseurs* Erik Bruhn and Ivan Nagy. There were also excellent dancers in every category in the company.

Among ABT's new works of 1971 were Marius Petipa's *Paquita* (restaged by Rudolf Nureyev), Michael Smuin's *Schubertiade,* Dennis Nahat's *Mendelssohn Symphony,* and Ulf Gadd's *The Miraculous Mandarin* (Bartok). Antony Tudor's *Romeo and Juliet* was revived, and Auguste Bournonville's *La Sylphide* was revised by Erik Bruhn. The latter was not entirely satisfactory, but it was an improvement over ABT's previous version by Harald Lander.

The City Center Joffrey Ballet gave two 6-week seasons at its home theater in New York. Among the new works it introduced were Ailey's *Feast of Ashes* (Carlos Surinach); Gerald Arpino's *Reflections* (Tchaikovsky), *Valentine* (Jacob Druckman), and *Kettentanz* (Viennese waltzes); Margo Sappington's *Weewis* (Stanley Walden); and Balanchine's *Square Dance* (Corelli, Vivaldi). The company's first visit to London brought scathing reviews from most of the major British critics. Joffrey's principal choreographer, Arpino, came in for the worst critical drubbing, but the dancers also failed to please.

The National Ballet of Washington outdid itself in its most ambitious undertaking, a production of the full-length Petipa-Tchaikovsky *The Sleeping Beauty,* staged by the company's co-director Ben Stevenson. Margot Fonteyn, one of the leading exponents of the title role, danced in most of the performances.

Arthur Mitchell's Dance Theater of Harlem had a brief and successful Broadway debut, with such ballets as Robbins' *Afternoon of a Faun*, Balanchine's *Concerto Barocco*, John Taras' *Design for Strings*, and several works by Mitchell himself. Eliot Feld's American Ballet Company, at the Brooklyn Academy, disbanded after only 2½ years.

Modern Dance. Alvin Ailey's American Dance Theater was the most prominent modern U. S. company in 1971. Returning from triumphant engagements in the USSR and elsewhere in Europe, including London, the group had equal success on its home ground in New York in the City Center American dance series. Among Ailey's new works were a long solo for Judith Jamison, called *Cry* (Alice Coltrane, Laura Nyro, and the Voices of Harlem); *Flowers* (music by Big Brother and the Holding Company, Janis Joplin, and others), which featured Lynn Seymour of Britain's Royal Ballet as soloist; and *Choral Dances* (Benjamin Britten). All were widely hailed, but especially Miss Jamison, Dudley Williams, and Kelvin Rotardier.

The companies of Pearl Lang, Eleo Pomare, Erick Hawkins, Louis Falco, and Paul Taylor were among those that also performed in the City Center series during the year. Taylor's repertoire included the premier of *Big Bertha* (music from the St. Louis Melody Museum collection of band machines), an eerie work about a corrupting automaton, played to great effect by Bettie de Jong. It was interpreted by some critics as an allegory of the events at My Lai in Vietnam, by others as a comment on the conflict between man and machine.

In April, the Alwin Nikolais troupe embarked on a 16-week tour with 90 performances scheduled in 11 countries in Europe and the Middle East. The tour, which was sponsored by the U. S. Department of State, included appearances in Germany, Austria, Holland, Yugoslavia, Iran, and Tunisia.

Visiting Companies. The appearance of Maurice Béjart's Ballet of the 20th Century, from Belgium, which danced at the Brooklyn Academy in January and February and at the City Center in December, generated some controversy. Béjart is regarded as a choreographic innovator in Belgium, France, and other parts of Europe outside the mainstream of contemporary dance. To sophisticated American audiences, however, his outmoded expressionism, tedious gymnastics, and hokey Orientalism seemed dated, often pretentious, and sometimes ludicrous. The dancers in the company, including Suzanne Farrell, formerly of the New York City Ballet, fared better. Winthrop Sargeant, critic of the *New Yorker*, wrote: "... the Béjart company is a group of fifty splendid dancers in search of a choreographer."

The Bolshoi Ballet of Moscow, which was expected to appear in New York, canceled the engagement. Its place was filled by the Stuttgart Ballet with its repertoire of works by John Cranko. Cranko's new *Carmen*, superficial, trashy, and too short (75 minutes), was a serious failure. The Australian Ballet in its first American appearance made a favorable impression, though it was somewhat overshadowed by its guest star, Rudolf Nureyev. Other foreign companies that toured the United States were the Vienna State Opera Ballet, Inbal from Israel, Masowsze from Poland, Nederlands Dans Theater, and the Siberian Dancers and Singers of Omsk. The Ballet Nacional de Cuba, starring Alicia Alonso, toured Canada. This company is still not allowed to appear in the United States, although Russian companies are welcome.

Other Dance News. A nostalgic dance event in 1971 was the Broadway revival of the 1925 Vincent Youmans' musical *No, No Nanette*, with Ruby Keeler. The year also saw the release of the dance film *Peter Rabbit and Tales of Beatrix Potter*, with choreography by Frederick Ashton, and featuring Ashton and members of Britain's Royal Ballet.

WILLIAM LIVINGSTONE
Member of Reviewers Panel, "Ballet Review"
Managing Editor, "Stereo Review"

DEATH RATES. See VITAL STATISTICS.

George Balanchine, director of the New York City Ballet, and Arthur Mitchell, head of the Dance Theater of Harlem.

MARTHA SWOPE

Egyptian paratroopers file onto Russian-made AN-12 for desert maneuvers. Soldiers reportedly trained for raids against Israeli positions in Sinai.

DEFENSE FORCES

Arms spending generally increased around the world in 1971, partly occasioned by inflationary costs. There were both optimism and pessimism regarding possibilities of reducing arms competition.

For example, there were hopes that the Strategic Arms Limitation Talks (SALT) between the Soviet Union and the United States would result in a damper being placed on major weapons competition between the two superpowers, and that this would help to ease world tensions. On the other hand, fears were voiced with regard to SALT. The pessimistic view was that the USSR was using the negotiations and the U. S. desire for agreement as stalling measures to impede U. S. arming while Soviet missile and submarine deployment continued near capacity. (See also DISARMAMENT.)

The proliferation of nuclear weapons beyond the five nations possessing them (Britain, France, People's Republic of China, Soviet Union, and United States) was seen by many as an ominous possibility. A basic reason for such fears was the unfolding of the Nixon Doctrine involving further reduction of U. S. military presence overseas. This, it was said, might cause near-nuclear states to fear that the United States could no longer be counted on in an emergency, thus forcing them to develop their own nuclear weapons. The continued growth in Chinese nuclear strength was perceived as foreshadowing increased pressures on China's neighbors, India and Japan, to acquire nuclear weapons. Japan's economic and political squabbles with the United States may have increased Japanese doubts regarding the reliability of U. S. guarantees. Israel, nearly surrounded by hostile Arab states, was rumored to be near nuclear-weapon capability.

Optimism over military reductions in Europe was linked to the distant possibility of mutual U. S. and Soviet withdrawals from eastern and western Europe.

UNITED STATES

U. S. defense policy in 1971 constituted a compromise among several points of view. There were those who argued for a "reordering of national priorities," by which they meant the reduction of military spending coincident with substantial increases in expenditures for domestic programs.

Others justified their demand for increased U. S. military spending by citing both the Soviet military buildup and the U. S. neglect of strategic nuclear arms and other forces caused by the preemption of resources for the war in Southeast Asia. Many groups and individuals expressed reservations over current U. S. defense policy.

Southeast Asian Policy. By the end of 1971 it seemed clear that a substantial number of Americans, for widely varying reasons, supported the reduction of U. S. participation in the Vietnam War. On the one hand were those who thought the war was immoral or who believed the money spent in Vietnam could be better spent on pressing problems within the United States. Others wanted to "wind down" the war so as to be able to transfer funds from that effort to improving the U. S. strategic nuclear forces, modernizing the Navy, and improving U. S. ability to deter war in Europe. Still others favored withdrawal because they feared the U. S. Army, faced with a drug problem, resignations, arguments as to its role, and hostility from portions of the public, might become one of the major casualties of the war if U. S. participation continued at a high level.

Thus there was general acceptance of the government's withdrawal objective, if not the speed of its implementation. Regarding the phased withdrawal of U. S. troops, the Nixon administration claimed by the close of 1971 that the first phase of

Vietnamization had been successfully concluded. This involved turning over to the South Vietnamese forces primary responsibility for conducting the ground war. It was further claimed that the second phase of Vietnamization was proceeding satisfactorily. This phase involved the development within South Vietnam of air, naval, artillery, and logistic capabilities sufficient to maintain the nation's security. The third phase of Vietnamization remained to be accomplished. This will consist of reducing U. S. forces to a military advisory mission and small security forces to protect the mission. The U. S. government held forth the prospect that at some future date the South Vietnamese would be sufficiently strong that, as Secretary of Defense Melvin R. Laird put it, "no more U. S. military presence is required."

Although criticism of U. S. defense policy in Vietnam was muted by the Nixon withdrawal policy, doubts still were voiced about the continued U. S. presence in the area. In particular some expressed fears over U. S. involvement in Laos and Cambodia. Others criticized the stepped-up "protective reaction" air strikes into North Vietnam. These were air raids the government claimed were necessary to protect U. S. troops and equipment.

Strategic Nuclear Forces and Policy. During 1971 the continued growth in the quality and quantity of Soviet strategic nuclear forces intensified the debate within and beyond the Pentagon as to the proper U. S. response. The official context of the debate appeared to be set by statements that the USSR might be seeking a first-strike capability against U. S. strategic nuclear retaliatory forces. Achievement of such a capability might mean that many, if not most, U. S. land-based nuclear forces could be destroyed in a sneak attack. This possibility might be compounded by the development of either an effective antisubmarine-warfare capability against U. S. missile-carrying submarines, or an effective antiballistic-missile (ABM) capacity against incoming U. S. warheads, regardless of their origin, or both events. Such a combination was held by some to pose the greatest military peril to the United States of any time in the 25 years of the Cold War.

For those who saw sinister motives in the Soviet missile buildup the proper response seemed to be adopting actions designed to deprive the USSR of a first-strike capability, if indeed that was its goal. A number of ways to achieve such a goal were discussed. Some argued for the triad concept. This involved the maintenance of three types of strategic offensive forces, which it was claimed would force the Soviets to spread their limited resources so thin in an effort to defend against the U. S. forces that their efforts would be unsuccessful.

The U. S. triad consisted of land-based intercontinental ballistic missiles (ICBM), ocean-based intermediate-range missiles (IRBM) in submarines, and land-based bombers. Various modifications of the triad concept were examined. For its part the administration seemed to prefer a triad which deemphasized the role of manned bombers, and sought to enhance the survivability of the ICBM's by deployment of ABM's near the ICBM sites. The argument by the administration was that in this way the ICBM's could be protected from a Soviet missile strike.

Strong elements of opposition developed in Congress as to the size of the ABM deployment suggested by the White House. The opposition believed that the U. S. ABM deployment would stimulate the arms race.

Late in 1971 a Senate-House conference committee finally decided to support appropriations for only a limited ABM deployment, pending the outcome of the SALT negotiations wherein ABM controls were under discussion. Thus the administration was limited to funds for deployment of the Safeguard ABM system at two sites, and the advance preparation of two other sites.

An alternative to the triad seemed to be supported by the Navy, and many strategic planners believed altered conditions appeared to favor a strategic force featuring heavy reliance on naval retaliatory weapons. The Navy-emphasis argument rested on the increasing vulnerability of land-based forces, either missiles or bombers, to a Soviet first strike by missiles; the apparent invulnerability of U. S. missile-carrying submarines to any kind of Soviet attack; the vulnerability of U. S. bombers to Soviet air defenses; and the expectation that the SALT meetings would result in severe limitations being placed on ABM deployment.

Late in 1971 administrative support for a Navy-emphasis program appeared in the form of an announcement by Deputy Secretary of Defense David Packard. According to Packard, the United States would hedge against failure or partial failure of the SALT negotiations to limit nuclear arms acquisitions by preparing to develop a new ballistic missile for retrofitting aboard the 41 currently operating U. S. missile-carrying submarines.

The new missile, as yet unnamed, would have a range of 4,500 to 5,000 miles as compared with the

MUSHROOM CLOUD rises (*top*) from Vietnam jungle as 7½-ton blockbuster, largest non-nuclear U. S. bomb, explodes. Bomb can be used to clear helicopter landing zones (*bottom*) or against troop concentrations.

UPI

DIRECTORY OF MAJOR U. S. MISSILES

Missile	Status[1]	Service	Range[2] (nautical miles)	Propulsion
Surface-to-Surface				
Asroc[3]	O	Navy	...	Solid
Dragon[4]	O	Army	...	Solid
Lance	D	Army	...	Storable liquid
Honest John	O	Army	20	Solid
Minuteman I, II	O	AF	6300 and 7000	Solid
Minuteman III	O	AF		Solid
Pershing IA	O	Army	400	Solid
Polaris A-2, A-3[5]	O	Navy	1500 and 2500	Solid
Poseidon[5]	O	Navy	2500	Solid
Sergeant	O	Army		Solid
Shillelagh	O	Army	short	Solid
STAM[3]	S	Navy		...
Subroc[5]	O	Navy	10+	Solid
Titan II	O	AF	6300+	Storable liquid
Tow[4]	O	Army	...	Solid
ULMS and SLMS	D	Navy	5000+	Solid
Surface-to-Air				
APDMS	S	Navy		...
Bomarc B	O	AF	400	Solid or ramjet
Chaparral	O	Army	...	Solid
Hawk	O	Army	22	Solid
Improved Hawk	P	Army	...	Solid
Nike Hercules	O	Army	75	Solid
Redeye	O	Army	...	Solid
Sam-D	D	Army	...	Solid
Sea Sparrow	O	Navy	...	Solid
Sea Sparrow, NATO	D	Navy, NATO	...	Solid
Spartan	P	Army	Several hundred	Solid
Sprint	P	Army	25	Solid
Standard	O	Navy	10–30+	Solid
Talos	O	Navy	65+	Solid or ramjet
Tartar	O	Navy	10+	Solid
Terrier	O	Navy	20+	Solid
Air-to-Air				
Dogfight, AF	S	AF	...	...
Dogfight, Navy	S	Navy	...	...
Falcon	O	AF	2+	Solid
Genie	O	AF	6+	Solid
Phoenix	D	Navy	...	Solid
Sidewinder	O	AF–Navy	2+	Solid
Sparrow	O	AF–Navy	12	Solid
Sparrow (Advanced)	D	AF–Navy	...	Solid
Air-to-Surface				
Condor	D	Navy	...	Solid
Hound Dog	O	AF	600+	Turbojet
Maverick	P	AF	...	Solid
SCAD	S	AF	1000	Turbojet
Shrike	O	AF–Navy	...	Solid
SRAM	D	AF	50+	Solid
Standard ARM	O	AF–Navy	...	Solid
Walleye	O	AF–Navy	3–6	None
Zuni	O	Navy	5	Solid

[1] Status code: D, under development; O, operational; P, production; S, study. [2] One nautical mile equals 1.15 statute miles or 1.85 km. [3] Antisubmarine missile. [4] Antitank missile. [5] Subsurface to surface.

3,000-mile range of the newest operational Navy missile, Poseidon. Such a range extension would permit submarines carrying the new missile to operate farther out in the oceans from their targets in Eurasia, thus substantially increasing the difficulty faced by Soviet antisubmarine forces.

In support of the new missile the point was made that if time became a critical factor, it would be much quicker to fit a new missile into currently operating submarines than to develop both a new missile and a new submarine to carry it. If the latter is desired, the Navy has long had plans for the ULMS (Underseas Long-range Missile System) program, which includes a 6,000-mile missile and a new submarine to launch it.

Despite evidence that if the United States decided to build a new strategic nuclear system it would probably be ocean-based, the Air Force continued to receive funding for a new long-range bomber, the B-1 advanced manned strategic aircraft. Another hedge at the strategic nuclear level against the failure of SALT, or Soviet duplicity, was the continued procurement of MIRV's (multiple independently targeted reentry vehicles) for attachment to ICBM's and the submarine missiles. The administration held that the 3-to-10 warheads for each missile provided by the MIRV system would be an effective counter to possible Soviet ABM improvement.

The notion of hedging against Soviet duplicity or SALT failure was rejected by some in government, more in the Senate than in the Pentagon. Their argument was that procurement of the items for hedging would merely appear threatening to the USSR and thus stimulate increased Soviet arms acquisition, which would further stimulate U. S. arms acquisition, *ad infinitum*. Some of those holding such a view suggested then that it would be useful to allow the USSR to catch up with the United States in the strategic nuclear field so that the USSR could approach the conference table as an equal, relieved of the pressure to build ever more weapons.

In discussions concerning the Soviet strategic buildup and alternative U. S. responses, spokesmen for the Pentagon often pointed to two other fears in addition to the danger of a Soviet first strike on American strategic retaliatory forces. One such danger is the possibility that near-equality between the two superpowers in strategic nuclear weapons would mean a greater probability that any confrontations would be fought with non-nuclear weapons, a level where the United States was reducing its strength.

Second, it was noted that should the USSR dramatically surpass U. S. strength in strategic weapons, the USSR might expect to reap the psychological advantage of superiority in future confrontations with the United States, something the United States enjoyed during the Cuban missile crisis.

The answer suggested for the first danger by many in the Department of Defense was beefing up the non-nuclear forces. This was not done in 1971. The suggested answer to the second danger favored by the Pentagon, greater procurement of strategic weapons, was not done to the satisfaction of the Department of Defense either.

By the end of 1971 the strategic nuclear forces of the United States seemed adequate to some, more than adequate to the point of being provocative to the Soviets to others, and clearly inadequate to the point of placing the United States in jeopardy according to still others.

The numbers of U. S. strategic forces were: 1,000 Minuteman II and III and 54 Titan ICBM's; 656 Polaris and Poseidon submarine-launched missiles; 510 B-52 and B-111 bombers; 11 interceptor squadrons; and 21 antibomber missile batteries. The official purpose in maintaining these forces was to deter nuclear attack upon the United States and, in some instances, its allies, and to wage war successfully if deterrence failed and war came.

General Purpose Forces and Policy. It was the general purpose forces, whose mission is to deter or fight wars from just below the strategic nuclear level down to insurgency actions, that received the least emphasis during 1971. The government justified the de-emphasis on the basis that its allies were expected to do more, not that the enemy threat was less. For example, in deterring theater-wide conventional war Secretary Laird stated, "U. S. and allied forces share the responsibility." Regarding any small sub-theater or local war the secretary said, "The country or ally which is threatened bears the primary burden, particularly for providing manpower."

New Designs Beef Up U.S. Air Strength

OFFICIAL U. S. NAVY PHOTOGRAPH

NORTHROP CORPORATION

REPUBLIC AVIATION DIVISION, FAIRCHILD HILLER CORPORATION

McDONNELL DOUGLAS CORPORATION

NORTH AMERICAN ROCKWELL CORPORATION

U.S. airpower will be bolstered by a variety of new aircraft now in development. Navy's F-14A (top), a swing-wing, missile-firing jet, is scheduled for 1973 delivery. The Air Force will choose between A-9A (center left) and A-10A (center right) prototypes being developed by competing companies. Both are close-support, low-level bombers. The F-15 (above), a twin-engine fighter, is scheduled to make first flight in 1972. Air Force's newest heavy strategic bomber, the B-1 (right), has four engines and will be swing-winged.

The major exception to the decreased emphasis on general purpose forces was the beginning of efforts to modernize the Navy in response to the growth of the Soviet navy. Thus the Navy proposed an 11-year modernization program estimated to cost over $50 billion.

Administration. Melvin R. Laird continued as secretary of defense, but David Packard resigned as the deputy in December. Adm. Thomas H. Moorer remained chairman of the Joint Chiefs.

ROBERT W. LAWRENCE
Colorado State University

U. S. AIR FORCE

The primary mission of the Air Force—to deter a major war—remained unchanged in 1971. To fulfill that mission, the Air Force continued to shape a second-strike, retaliatory force.

Strategic Air Command. SAC has 450 B-52 manned bombers, is gradually increasing to a total of 70 FB-111 manned fighter-bombers, and has the B-1 bomber on the drawing board. All are for delivery of conventional or nuclear bombs.

The B-52, operational since 1955, flies at subsonic speeds at altitudes over 50,000 feet (15,240 meters). Later models can cruise 10,000 miles (16,090 km) unrefueled.

The FB-111, which began entering inventory in 1970, has variable-sweep wings. It flies at Mach 2 speeds and has advanced electronic equipment. About 40% of the bomber-tanker force can be airborne in minutes.

The B-1 was in the engineering development stage at the end of 1971, with three flight-test aircraft authorized for construction. If tests are satisfactory and Congress approves funds for production, the B-1 could replace the B-52 by the late 1970's.

SAC's missile force in late 1971 consisted of 54 Titan II liquid-fueled and 1,000 Minuteman solid-fueled ICBM's. The Minuteman was being updated; Minuteman II began entering inventory in 1965 and Minuteman III in 1970. Eventually, the force will have 550 Minuteman III missiles capable of carrying MIRV (multiple independently targeted reentry vehicles). SAC had about 161,000 men at the end of 1971.

Tactical Air Command. TAC has been concentrating for several years on improving its mobility and capability for quick response. The ability to use a "bare base," proved in exercise Harvest Bare in 1971, enables a tactical fighter squadron to use any of some 1,400 sites around the world, carrying with it everything needed to be combat ready. The "instant air base" can be repacked and brought home when the emergency ends.

In 1971, TAC continued its combat role in Southeast Asia, trained air crews, made worldwide relief missions, supported NATO, and furnished tactical airlift.

Aerospace Defense Command. ADC's mission is to defend the United States and North America from attack by air or from space. Its 400 aircraft and 44,000 personnel are the largest part of NORAD, the joint U. S.-Canadian North American Air Defense Command. Fighter-bombers are on constant alert against the manned-bomber threat.

ADC is developing the AWACS (airborne early warning and control system), a command, control, and surveillance aircraft for tactical or air defense operations. In conjunction with OTH (over the horizon) radars, AWACS will detect and track enemy aircraft at extreme range, and direct defensive weapons against them.

The growing possibility of a threat from SLBM's (sea-launched ballistic missiles) launched from peripheral waters is being met by radars especially modified to provide warning of such attacks. At the same time, ADC's sensors monitor all ballistic-missile launches around the world and keep continuous track of every man-made object in space to forestall any threat from orbiting vehicles.

An Air Force Titan 3 rocket on Nov. 2, 1971, lofted two communications satellites into orbit. One was to be placed in stationary orbit above the Atlantic, the other over the Pacific, to replace 26 smaller military communications satellites. The two stations were expected to link the Pentagon with military units and ships all over the world.

Budget and Personnel. The Air Force budget, in a decline, was just over $25 billion for fiscal 1968, and for fiscal 1972 the budget request was about $22.8 billion.

Air Force active-duty personnel strength, also in a decline, stood at 783,250 on June 30, 1970, and 755,300 a year later.

On July 16, 1971, Jeanne M. Holm, promoted to brigadier general, became the Air Force's first female general officer.

Capt. Susan Struck, an unwed nurse, became the first Air Force officer to give birth while on active duty. She had sued against the Air Force regulation requiring honorable discharge of pregnant women. A U. S. appeals court upheld the regulation.

HARRY M. ZUBKOFF
Office of the Secretary of the Air Force

U. S. ARMY

Manpower reductions continued in the Army with concomitant organizational and personnel problems. The racking racial problems of 1970 were neither as frequent nor as large in 1971. Combat operations in Vietnam involving U. S. personnel were practically at a standstill on the ground, but Army men were targets for terrorists.

It was reported that some 90% of U. S. ground forces had departed Vietnam. At the end of 1971 the American Division was returning home and was to be disbanded.

Forces. Total Army strength as of June 30, 1972, was limited by Congress in late 1971 to 892,000, compared with 1,107,000 on June 30, 1971. Army draft calls were less than 100,000 for 1971 as compared with 163,500 for 1970.

For the first time the Army recruited with paid advertising on radio and television. Preliminary results indicated moderate success—7,642 enlistees in combat arms in March, April, and May 1971, compared with 1,039 in the 1970 period—but the 13-week, $10.6 million program was stopped because it interfered with the recruiting of other services.

A reluctant Congress passed a long-delayed draft law in September 1971. Many believe such a law necessary to maintain a flow of enlistments. Substantial pay incentives were included in the draft law, as well as reenlistment bonuses, to a ceiling of $10,000. With these inducements the Army was moving toward "zero draft." Another inducement was the well-publicized Project VOLAR (Volunteer Army), a program to humanize Army training practices and eliminate obnoxious or demeaning chores.

About 43,000 draftees assigned to units in the continental United States were released as much as 120 days early. Many had served in Vietnam or Korea and could not be sent overseas again because their time was too short. In an experimental program, soldiers were released two months early if they would join the National Guard or Reserve.

The Army began the Qualitative Management Program in an effort to upgrade the quality of enlisted men. Some, denied reenlistment under the program, were released up to six months early. Another new program was Project Transition, part of a triservice job counseling and placement plan. To ferret out drug abuse, the Army began requiring urinalysis tests for all dangerous drugs.

Logistics. The Army's struggle to obtain a satisfactory main battle tank moved again to Congress. The Army testified that even an "austere" version of the controversial Main Battle Tank (MBT 70 XM-803) would be markedly superior to the M-60 tank. The Army was readying a dozen preproduction test models of the austere version, to cost $600,000 each, according to the *Armed Forces Journal.* This long-standing equipment dilemma includes basic questions as to how much improvement of former tank models is possible. The "K" version of the M-60, reported to cost about $400,000, approaches the characteristics of the MBT 70 except for the loader. In December, Congress ordered the Army to cease pursuit of the expensive Main Battle Tank being developed.

As the Army withdrew from Vietnam, supply deficiencies and equipment imbalances were so serious as possibly to reduce Army effectiveness.

Crime and Scandal. War crimes trials resulting from the My Lai massacre of over 100 civilian Vietnamese in 1968 led to a 20-year sentence for 1st Lt. William J. Calley, exoneration for Capt. Ernest L. Medina, disciplining of some officers for insufficient investigation of the slayings, and the dropping of murder charges against 26 enlisted men present at the massacre.

The Senate investigations subcommittee ended a 3-year probe of Army exchanges and noncommissioned officers' clubs with a 150,000-word report charging servicemen, Army administrators, and big businessmen with "corruption, criminality, and moral compromises." Many indictments and several proposals for regulatory laws resulted.

In Vietnam, the tough officer or sergeant who refused to "talk over" an unpopular order with his troops was in danger of being "fragged" by them: 78 have been killed and over 600 wounded, usually by a fragmentation hand grenade.

Army responsibility for control of major riots led Army intelligence to investigate 18,000 civilians by 1969. Under pressure from Congress and the public, the files were destroyed and a review board was appointed to prevent recurrence.

Command. On June 29, 1971, Stanley R. Resor resigned after six years as secretary of the Army and was replaced by Robert F. Froehlke.

Gen. William Westmoreland remained chief of staff and Gen. Creighton Abrams retained command in Vietnam. Brig. Gen. Elizabeth P. Hoisington was succeeded as director of the Women's Army Corps by Brig. Gen. Mildred S. Bailey. The National Guard named its first Negro general, Brig. Gen. Cunningham C. Bryant.

WILLIAM J. McCONNELL, *Colonel, USA, Retired*
Colorado State University

SAILORS try out U. S. Navy's new uniforms that will replace familiar bell bottoms, jumpers, and small white hats. Seamen's uniforms, which will be issued in 1973, are like those of officers and chief petty officers.

U. S. NAVY

For the U. S. Navy, 1971 was in many ways a year of contradiction and change. Global responsibilities on the seas were being further extended at a time when resources were being further reduced. The U. S. Fleet was cut to 714 ships, down from 886 two years earlier—an unlikely response to the increasing prominence of sleek, modern Soviet warships on the oceans. New-construction programs met heavy debate within the Navy as to the shape of the future fleet and in Congress as to its size.

Budget. Even though the Navy received the largest percentage of the 1972 defense budget since 1946, and almost half of the procurement and research and development funds, inflation and a shrinking slice to the armed services dropped the totals to the lowest since 1950 in actual buying power—far below the minimum of $50 billion required to rebuild a worn-out fleet within 10 years. Grave concern permeated senior ranks as the fleet headed for second place behind that of the USSR. Questioning of old naval theories was welcomed by many officers. Central to both groups was the aggressive and dynamic young chief of naval operations, Adm. Elmo R. Zumwalt, Jr., who became a national figure.

Mission. Admiral Zumwalt described the role of the rejuvenated Navy as a 4-part assignment: (1)

overseas presence; (2) projection of U. S. power abroad; (3) sea control; (4) strategic deterrence.

"Overseas presence" involves showing the flag, the historic role of gaining political ends by a visible display of power. The Navy sees "projection forces" as essential to the military role in national policy contained in the Nixon Doctrine, a blue-water strategy in support of commitments to allies, including use of U. S. firepower and limited short-term commitment of U. S. troops if necessary. The reduced Army and Air Force garrisons overseas under the existing goal of a diminished U. S. presence means that the Navy must provide most of the quick-reaction forces.

"Sea control" is vital to protect U. S. shipping and to protect troops, firepower, and logistic support abroad, Zumwalt said. He cited the aircraft carrier as "guarantor of open sea lanes and repository of strike aircraft which can go into battle far from American shores." The fourth mission, "strategic deterrence," places U. S. missile retaliatory forces underwater, away from the homeland and the danger of nuclear devastation of fixed land sites.

Procurement. To cope with growing Soviet power on the seas despite dwindling U. S. fleet strength, the Navy reoriented its priorities toward additional offensive forces. Missile submarines retained first priority. Second priority went to aircraft carriers, ships, and aircraft needed for sea control and preservation of sea lanes to deployed fleets and allied forces. Now in third place were amphibious and air-assault projection forces for penetrating enemy territory.

The primary needs are (1) better ways to cope with enemy submarines and antiship cruise missiles; and (2) to reverse the past practice of building costly, sophisticated, all-purpose weapons in favor of developing faster, cheaper, special-purpose ships with potent striking power such as the high-speed gas-turbine "patrol frigate." Zumwalt stated: "The heritage we must leave and plan for the future Navy is keyed to two prime issues—flexibility and mobility—to change dramatically our methods of conducting war at sea."

Personnel. John H. Chafee remained secretary of the Navy. Admiral Zumwalt's widely heralded improvements in Navy personnel's privileges and living conditions resulted in marked increases in re-enlistments. Although the encouraging results were partly attributable to lack of civilian jobs, morale did improve. Retention of skilled ratings continued to be a problem, however, and not enough submarine and aviation officers, even with additional pay and bonuses, were choosing service careers.

Manpower totals showed a reduction of over 10% to 622,500 from 692,435 a year earlier. Negroes increased to 35,000 or 5.6%. Capt. Samuel L. Gravely, Jr., became the Navy's first black rear admiral. Another historic action was abandonment of the bell-bottom trousers, jumper, and kerchief that sailors had worn for 130 years, in favor of a uniform and cap like those of chief petty officers.

Record Flight. A Navy P-3C Orion heavy turboprop aircraft, on Jan. 22, 1971, made a new long-distance record. It was flown without refueling from Atsugi, Japan, to Patuxent River, Md.—6,857 miles—breaking a Soviet IL-8 record of 4,761 miles. The P-3C broke seven more records in the next three weeks.

PAUL R. SCHRATZ, *Captain, USN, Retired*
University of Missouri

U. S. MARINE CORPS

The Vietnam War ended for the U. S. Marine Corps in 1971. From a peak strength of 84,000 in Vietnam in 1968, the reduction left only about 500 Marines—U. S. Embassy guards, men in various headquarters, and advisers to the Marine Corps of South Vietnam. No U. S. Marine combat units remained in Vietnam. More than 450,000 Marines had served in Southeast Asia, many for multiple tours. About three times as many Marines were killed in Vietnam as in the Korean War.

Strength. At the end of 1971 the Corps' strength was 206,000, a figure expected to be relatively permanent. It compares with 317,000 in 1968, but 206,000 is still the largest peacetime strength in the history of the Corps and will mean a return to the traditional posture of three Marine divisions and three aircraft wings, with an additional division and aircraft wing in reserve. This continues the Marines in their familiar role as the force-in-readiness of the United States. During 1972 emphasis was to be placed on readiness, as exemplified by the expected return of three fixed-wing squadrons to Navy carrier groups on a continuing basis.

Logistics. During the withdrawal from Vietnam the Marines substantially refitted themselves—regular and reserve, air and ground—with late-model equipment, much of which was new. Marine logistic procurement continued to improve.

The basic amphibious assault vehicle, LVTP-7, was in production and the first few were delivered. The AV-8A Harrier aircraft was being inspected and tested. This is a vertical or short takeoff and landing (V/STOL) aircraft which can use small, primitive landing fields. The Marines plan to use the Harrier for assault support.

The Marines also acquired the new twin-engine Cobra helicopter gunship and sought continued procurement of the UH-1N helicopter. This assortment of new materiel gave the Marines the unique task of reexamining tactical doctrine *after* procurement of inventory—a new order of events.

Command. Lt. Gen. Robert E. Cushman was nominated by President Nixon to be commandant on the retirement of Gen. Leonard F. Chapman, Jr., at the end of 1971. Gen. Raymond G. Davis became assistant commandant, replacing Gen. Lewis W. Walt, who retired. Gen. Keith B. McCutcheon, named to the post, had died.

Looking to the future, General Chapman enunciated a policy for the Corps, that of "maintaining it with high-quality personnel in an all-volunteer, no-draft environment." In an address to marines on duty in Brazil in 1971, General Chapman stated, "We have a national duty to provide America with a model military force."

WILLIAM J. MCCONNELL, *Colonel, USA, Retired*
Colorado State University

NORTH ATLANTIC TREATY ORGANIZATION

Ambiguous and conflicting pressures developed for the NATO nations regarding their future defense policies. This was particularly so for the three major European members—Britain, France, and West Germany. There appeared to be possibilities of a normalizing of relations with the USSR and its satellites, which would permit arms reduction. Optimism was bolstered by the success of West German Chancellor Willy Brandt in signing a treaty with the USSR and the later "Big Four" negotiations on the status of Berlin. Perhaps the most important matter on the NATO agenda was the suggestion that the armed forces in both eastern and western Europe be reduced, in what was called Mutual Balanced Force Reductions (MBFR).

Uncertainty concerning U. S. willingness to meet NATO obligations created fear among some Western Europeans that the United States might not remain a reliable partner. U. S. officials announced in November 1971, however, that the total U. S. force in Europe had been increased from 300,000 to 310,000, constituting 99.2% of war strength.

Reacting to U. S. criticism that European NATO members were not doing their share militarily, the 10 military members of NATO in late 1970 formed Eurogroup, consisting of the defense ministers of Britain, West Germany, Italy, the Netherlands, Belgium, Luxembourg, Norway, Denmark, Greece, and Turkey. Eurogroup announced on Dec. 7, 1971, that it planned to increase its share of the NATO defense budget by well over $1 billion in 1972.

Britain. Lord Carrington, defense minister of Britain, announced a 3-year, $260 million plan for strengthening British forces. The naval construction program was augmented to include two new guided-missile destroyers, four new frigates, and support ships and small craft. In Britain's army, strained by the crisis in Northern Ireland, four company-size units were to be expanded to battalions of about 800 men each. The Royal Air Force was to receive an additional squadron of Buccaneer strike aircraft. It was expected that other Eurogroup members would also begin strengthening their forces, or would at least announce plans to do so.

Hedging against an uncertain future, in 1971 the British operated four nuclear-powered subma-

rines, each carrying 16 U. S. Polaris A3 ballistic missiles with warheads made in Britain. The approximately 56 Vulcan jet bombers that formerly constituted the British strategic nuclear force were reassigned to a tactical role. In addition, the British had about 150 bombers to deliver tactical nuclear weapons. These planes were based in Britain, western Europe, and aboard the Royal Navy's two remaining operational aircraft carriers.

In November 1971, Britain gave up its great base at Singapore. Its only remaining military presence east of Suez consists of small infantry forces in Malaysia and Hong Kong, and RAF bases on the Persian Gulf and on the island of Gan in the Indian Ocean.

France. The first French nuclear-powered submarine, carrying 16 ballistic missiles, became operational in 1971. It is to be followed by three more, expected to enter service by 1977. In addition, the French nuclear-missile forces included nine land-based medium-range ballistic missiles, with nine more scheduled for readiness in 1972. The French air force had about 36 operational Mirage IV medium bombers. When equipped with nuclear weapons, these are considered a strategic force. Nearly 180 fighter-bombers, some carried aboard France's two aircraft carriers, constituted the bulk of the French tactical nuclear force.

During 1971 the French maintained their policy of refusing to integrate their forces with those of their NATO allies, despite continuing membership.

West Germany. Although the West Germans did not possess their own nuclear weapons, arrangements continued in effect by which U. S. tactical nuclear weapons could, under certain circumstances, be released to them. The West German army re-

British commando snow warfare specialists, attached to NATO, train with Hovercraft in rugged northern Norway.

Soviet guided missile cruiser sails in Hawaiian waters as U. S. Navy vessel (*background*) monitors its course.

mained at 12 divisions, the largest single ground component in NATO committed to Europe.

Greece. The problem with Greece intensified in 1971. The Greek government was considered by many in other NATO nations to be glaringly undemocratic and possibly not deserving of support and cooperation. The U. S. Senate went so far as to consider cutting off military aid to Greece as a rebuke to the authoritarian government. President Nixon could override such action by declaring this assistance of paramount importance to U. S. security. U. S. Vice President Spiro Agnew's week-long visit in October reassured the Greeks of continued U. S. support.

SOVIET UNION

In 1971 the USSR continued the general trend of expanding its military forces, although there was some evidence that the expansion in regard to intercontinental ballistic missiles might have slowed. A major exception in the increasing momentum of Soviet arms acquisition was perceived in regard to long-range bombers. A gradual decline in numbers of planes in operation was evident.

By the end of 1971 the Soviet Union possessed far more ICBM's than the United States. The exact figure was disputed, but it was around 1,500. These ICBM's were of several types. The missiles designated SS-11 and SS-13 were thought to be "city busters"—their destructive payloads and accuracy seemed designed for use against cities.

The SS-9, on the other hand, was viewed in the Pentagon as a potential first-strike weapon aimed at U. S. ICBM's. The supportive reasoning was that the improved accuracy of the SS-9 and its large multimegaton warhead (or in some instances three warheads) appeared to fit it for "digging out" the U. S. ICBM's buried in concrete silos in the ground under steel lids, or for attacking underground command centers.

Considerable debate was generated in Washington by what appeared to be a slowing of Soviet ICBM silo construction. Several schools of thought attempted to explain this development. The most hopeful view was that the USSR was reaching its planned force level for ICBM's and was ready to cease further construction and agree upon a SALT type of arms control treaty.

Less optimistic were views that the slowed silo construction meant either that the USSR was retrofitting the old silos with new and improved missiles, or that it had achieved the planned deployment of current missiles and was ready to begin deployment of new missiles requiring new silos.

Augmenting the Soviet ICBM force was a growing number of ballistic missiles aboard submarines. It was estimated that the USSR had some 400 such missiles. Of greater concern to the Pentagon was the fact that the USSR seemed to be producing seven to eight missile-carrying submarines each year. This rate of production meant that the Soviet undersea missile force would equal in size that of the United States by 1974 if the U. S. forces were not enlarged.

The Soviet submarine missiles were thought capable of only about half the range of the latest U. S. missiles—1,300 to 3,000 miles (2,400 to 5,600 km). The USSR was thought to be developing a new longer-range submarine missile, but the deployment schedule remained unknown in the West.

The USSR had encircled Moscow with an antiballistic-missile system several years earlier, and was continuing to maintain it. In addition, the Pentagon reported that research and development were proceeding upon what appeared to be a new ABM system. For air defense the Soviet air force had some 3,000 jet interceptors, and up to 10,000 surface-to-air missiles. Some defense experts feared that some of the Soviet air-defense missiles could be upgraded to perform an antiballistic-missile role.

One of the areas of greatest Soviet military growth was in its high-seas fleet. Secretary of Defense Melvin Laird said, "It is obvious that an open-ocean navy has been developed by the Soviet

Union." The USSR seemed to be concentrating upon acquisition of ships and submarines carrying guided missiles. The USSR had the largest submarine fleet in the world. In addition to its ballistic-missile-firing submarines, it had more than 230 attack submarines, and some 60 submarines equipped with antiship guided missiles. The Soviet navy had 215 major surface ships, one quarter of which fired missiles. Expectations were that within several years nearly half the Soviet fleet would be so equipped.

The Soviet Union maintained its ability to devastate western Europe and parts of China with tactical nuclear weapons. These could be delivered by medium-range jet bombers, of which there were some 700 in the air force, with an additional 400 in the naval air arm. Augmenting the bombers were numerous short-, medium-, and intermediate-range ballistic missiles.

The gradually decreasing Soviet long-range bomber force had approximately 180 planes, of which nearly 50 were tanker aircraft. Questions as to whether a new "swing-wing" jet bomber would appear in large numbers remained unanswered.

The Red Army had 160 divisions, in contrast to the 13⅓ divisions in the U. S. Army and the three Marine divisions. Many of the Soviet divisions, which are smaller in numbers of men than U. S. divisions, were located on the Soviet-Chinese border. In terms of overall manpower under arms, the Soviet Union had slightly over 3.3 million in contrast to the 2.6 million U. S. servicemen and women.

WARSAW PACT NATIONS

Originally consisting of Poland, East Germany, Czechoslovakia, Hungary, Rumania, Bulgaria, Albania, and the dominating USSR, the Warsaw Pact alliance was created in 1955 as a response to the formation of NATO. Albania ceased participation in 1961 after aligning with China in the Sino-Soviet dispute. Rumania has for several years refused to participate in Pact military maneuvers.

The predominant forces in the Warsaw Pact are those of the USSR. In addition to forces kept within the Soviet borders, some 30 Soviet divisions remain in eastern Europe. The other Communist nations adhering to the Pact contribute about 60 divisions, 3,000 aircraft of all types, and eight conventionally powered submarines. These non-Soviet forces are generally thought to be less than completely reliable, depending on the circumstances of their use. Evidence of their unreliability is the fact that the Soviet Union does not entrust nuclear weapons to other members of the alliance.

To strengthen its control over the Warsaw Pact nations, the USSR has bilateral treaties with: East Germany (1964), Poland (1965), Hungary and Bulgaria (1967), and Czechoslovakia (1970). Treaties of 1967 and 1970 broadened conditions under which military assistance would be required. The Soviet-Czech treaty also promised "to defend socialist gains"—a legal basis for possible Soviet intervention. The Warsaw Pact's political committee and high command, both in Moscow, coordinate foreign policy and control military action of members.

The Warsaw Pact's 20-year initial term expires in May 1974. For members who do not denounce the pact before then, it continues in force 10 years more. A Warsaw Pact statement in 1966, repeated by Leonid Brezhnev on March 30, 1971, proposed eliminating NATO and the Warsaw Pact and replacing them with "a system of European security."

Soviet bilateral treaties would remain, so the Soviet intent would seem to be removal of U. S. and Canadian influence and forces from western Europe to make way for Soviet domination of all Europe.

PEOPLE'S REPUBLIC OF CHINA

China's military chiefs appeared to be involved in the nation's internal struggle regarding the succession of political power. (See special report on China beginning on page 14.) But political events had little effect on the steady development during 1971 of China's military establishment.

Chinese military progress included the development of a twin-jet fighter-bomber, construction of one or possibly two nuclear submarines, and deployment of a dozen or so medium-range ballistic missiles carrying nuclear warheads. In addition, the Chinese were reported to be operating more than 40 conventionally powered attack submarines and an increasing number of guided-missile patrol boats.

The Chinese air force, including the fleet air arm, consisted of some 4,000 aircraft. Of these, approximately 300 were light jet bombers, and most of the remainder were jet fighters.

The Chinese army, which is not credited with much capability in areas considerably beyond its borders—particularly if it must operate under air attack on logistic lines—numbered 2.5 million men. Thus it is the largest ground force in the world. The bulk of the Chinese army is organized into infantry divisions.

Contrary to the expectations of some observers, the Chinese did not test an intercontinental ballistic missile in 1971. It was assumed, however, that such a test could come at any time, with the Chinese firing their new weapon into the Pacific Ocean or across Pakistan into the Indian Ocean. There were occasional reports of the construction of Chinese telemetry stations on the coast of East Africa.

It was believed in the Pentagon that the Chinese could have an operational ICBM capacity within three years after a successful test flight. Such forecasting was based in part on the successful orbiting of a 381-pound (173-kg) earth satellite by the Chinese in 1970.

When the country develops its ICBM, it is expected that the warhead will be a thermonuclear one in the multimegaton range. However, such a weapon is thought of as being primitive—that is, an ICBM without the sophisticated devices used by the Soviets and the Americans to penetrate enemy ABM systems, and lacking the accuracy of the weapons possessed by the superpowers. Hence it is often argued that both the Soviet and American ABM's would be competent to defend against the early Chinese ICBM threat.

Improvement in Chinese nuclear weapons was less readily discernible in 1971 than it had been previously. The reason was that the Chinese began to test their nuclear weapons underground, thus preventing the United States from obtaining samples of bomb residue, which had been used to analyze the Chinese advances.

In addition to providing for their own growing military forces, the mainland Chinese sent substantial amounts of military assistance to North Vietnam, Pakistan, and the East African nation of Tanzania. In addition, a lesser amount of Chinese military aid was extended to North Korea.

ROBERT M. LAWRENCE
Colorado State University

DELAWARE

Conservation legislation enacted in Delaware in 1971, protecting the state's coastline from industrial polluters, won acclaim as a landmark for the nation as well as for Delaware. In October, Gov. Russell W. Peterson received an award of merit from the World Wildlife Fund for his work in promoting clean air and water in Delaware.

Other major legislation provided for no-fault automobile insurance and enabled the state to continue its efforts to reorganize and integrate both its administrative agencies and its judiciary.

Legislation. In June, after a protracted fight in the General Assembly, Governor Peterson was successful in his efforts to obtain a coastal zoning act prohibiting further construction of heavy industry, including oil refineries, along the Delaware littoral in the Delaware river and bay and the Atlantic Ocean. The area protected varies in width from a mile on the northern part of the river to about 10 miles at the widest part of the bay. The seaward extension includes the three-mile territorial limit in the Atlantic. Wetlands on the western side of the area also were protected.

The compulsory no-fault automobile insurance enacted in May will become effective in January 1972. The discovery in June that anticipated state revenue for fiscal 1971–72 had been overestimated necessitated a revision of both operating and capital budgets at the state level. To make up the deficit, the assembly approved new taxes, including increases in income taxes and in taxes on gasoline, cigarettes,

and liquor. Efforts to reorganize the judiciary were concentrated on the family court structure. The three county family courts were merged into one state court, and a president judge was appointed to direct the work of the newly constituted court.

Other Judicial News. By 1971 the work of a citizens' committee appointed by the governor in 1970 to recommend candidates for the justice of the peace courts had resulted in improvement of the personnel and function of these courts. Coordination of their work had been advanced by the appointment of a deputy administrator responsible to the chief justice of the state supreme court. In July a new state correctional facility was opened in Smyrna, replacing the decrepit 19th century workhouse that had served as a local lockup as well as a penitentiary for nearly a century.

Economy. By September, unemployment in Delaware was well below the national average. Building was set back severely during the year by a sustained strike among construction workers, but the periodic strikes in the automotive industry did not seem to have had a serious effect on the state's economy.

Education. As of September 1971, public elementary school enrollment showed a slight increase over 1970, and enrollment at higher levels continued to rise. The University of Delaware's enrollment of more than 16,000 students represented the highest in its history. The state-maintained technical institutes, at Dover and Wilmington, became two-year community colleges at the beginning of the fall term.

PAUL DOLAN, *University of Delaware*

DEMOCRATIC PARTY. See ELECTIONS; POLITICAL PARTIES.

DENMARK

Unfavorable economic conditions persisted throughout 1971, and the public's dissatisfaction with the economic situation was reflected in the September elections, which resulted in the defeat of the bourgeois coalition headed by Hilmer Baunsgaard.

Elections. Voting on September 21 brought down Baunsgaard's coalition government and led to the formation of a minority cabinet headed by Social Democrats, on October 11. The Liberals and Conservatives of Baunsgaard's coalition lost seats in the Folketing, and the Social Democratic and Socialist Peoples' parties that formed the new ministry led by Jens Otto Krag gained seats. The Social Democratic-Socialist Peoples' group emerged with a one vote margin.

Results were so close, however, that the outcome of the election hinged on the "Atlantic vote" of the four delegates from Greenland and the Faeroes. The new ministry's slim margin ensures that the government's course will be full of pitfalls.

Prime Minister Krag's new ministry featured strong men in trade, commerce, budget, and finance and younger and newer faces in foreign affairs and defense. The cabinet's longevity will depend on both the votes of the Socialist Peoples' party and Danish attitudes toward European Economic Community (Common Market) membership, which will later be submitted to a plebiscite.

Economic Problems. To succeed, the new cabinet will have to continue economic controls and to achieve stability in the face of unemployment, falling exports (a result of U. S. import policies), im-

---

——— DELAWARE · Information Highlights ———

Area: 2,057 square miles (5,328 sq km).
Population (1970 census): 548,104. *Density:* 273 per sq mi.
Chief Cities (1970 census): Dover, the capital, 17,488; Wilmington, 80,386; Newark, 21,078; Elsmere, 8,415; Seaford, 5,537; Milford, 5,314; Smyrna, 4,243.
Government (1971): *Chief Officers*—governor, Russell W. Peterson (R); lt. gov., Eugene D. Bookhammer (R); secy. of state, Walton H. Simpson (R); atty. gen., W. Laird Stabler, Jr. (R); treas., Emily H. Womach (D); supt. of public instruction, Kenneth C. Madden; chief justice, Daniel F. Wolcott. *General Assembly*—Senate, 19 members (13 Republicans, 6 Democrats); House of Representatives, 39 members (25 R, 14 D).
Education (1970–71): *Enrollment*—public elementary schools, 73,887 pupils; 3,105 teachers; public secondary schools, 61,126 pupils, 3,210 teachers; nonpublic schools (1968–69) 19,600 pupils; 850 teachers; college and university (fall 1971), 18,836 students. *Public school expenditures* (1970–71), $91,850,000 ($680 per pupil). *Average teacher's salary* (1969–70), $8,900.
State Finances (fiscal year 1971): *Revenues,* $246,070,315 (total sales and gross receipts taxes (1970), $42,798,000; motor fuel tax, $19,462,955; federal funds (1970), $42,006,000). *Expenditures,* $257,055,657 (education, $85,613,375; health, welfare, and safety, $50,069,380; highways, $10,703,117). *State debt,* $335,595,000 (June 30, 1971).
Personal Income (1970): $2,450,081,696; per capita, $4,324.
Public Assistance (1970): $21,641,000. *Average monthly payments* (Dec. 1970)—old-age assistance, $73.50; aid to families with dependent children, $134.40:
Labor Force: *Nonagricultural wage and salary earners* (Aug. 1971), 232,800. *Average annual employment* (1969)—manufacturing, 73,000; trade, 43,000; government, 30,000; services, 29,000. *Insured unemployed* (Oct. 1971)—2,800 (1.7%).
Manufacturing (1967): *Value added by manufacture,* $958,400,000. Food and kindred products, $156,500,000; apparel, $44,600,000; rubber and plastics products, $42,600,000.
Agriculture (1970): *Cash farm income,* $148,949,000 (livestock, $98,440,000; crops, $48,857,000; government payments, $1,652,000). *Chief crops* (1970)—Corn, 13,690,000 bushels; soybeans, 3,402,000 bushels; potatoes, 1,512,000 cwts.
Mining (1970): *Production value,* $1,485,000 (ranks 50th among the states). *Chief minerals* (tons)—Sand and gravel, 1,467,000; clays, 11,000.
Fisheries (1970): *Commercial catch,* 3,500,000 pounds ($500,000).
Transportation: *Roads* (1970), 4,408 miles (7,094 km); *motor vehicles* (1970), 331,481; *railroads* (1970), 340 miles.
Communications: *Telephones* (1971), 379,600; *television stations* (1970), 1; *radio stations* (1970), 12; *newspapers* (1970), 3 (daily circulation, 156,000).

balances in foreign trade payments, and a shocking foreign debt. As a first step, Krag imposed a 10% surtax on imports on October 20, promising to announce a comprehensive program later.

The most pressing issues for the new cabinet were restoring economic stability and increasing Danish trade. The shipping, shipbuilding, electrical products, machines, and chemical industries felt the full effect of the shifts in U. S. economic policies. Public debt, deficits in trade balances, and unemployment all rose. Reserves in holdings of gold and foreign currencies were at an all-time low, despite an increase in foreign trade in the first half of 1971. Inflation resulted from March wage agreements that added some 12% to labor costs.

Agriculture seemed sound, with good harvests and increasing exports, and was the brightest area of the economy. The former cabinet had mandated a land reform that offers government assistance in merging small farms into more efficient larger units and inducements to younger people to take up farming as an occupation.

Foreign Affairs. Entry into the Common Market was the predominant problem in foreign policy. The question of preferential treatment for agricultural and fisheries products seemed, to some extent, to have been resolved by government supports to ease the transition to full competition. Denmark announced its withdrawal from the European Free Trade Association, effective in January 1973, as part of its determination to enter the Common Market. But its announcement of the 10% surtax raised angry criticism from Common Market ministers.

——————— DENMARK · Information Highlights ———————

Official Name: Kingdom of Denmark.
Area: 16,629 square miles (43,069 sq km).
Population (1970 est.): 4,920,000. *Density,* 297 per square mile (114 sq km). *Annual rate of increase,* 0.7%.
Chief Cities (1966 est.): Copenhagen (1970 est.), the capital, 875,000; Aarhus, 115,804.
Government: *Head of state,* Margrethe II, queen (acceded Jan. 14, 1972). *Head of government,* Jens Otto Krag, premier (took office Oct. 11, 1971). *Legislature*—Folketing (unicameral), 179 members. *Major political parties*—Social Democratic party, Conservative People's party, Liberal party; Radical Liberal party, Socialist People's party.
Language: Danish (official).
Education: *Literacy rate* (1970), 100% of population. *Expenditure on education* (1968), 18.0% of total public expenditure. *School enrollment* (1968)—primary, 506,131; secondary, 328,381; vocational, 133,552; higher, 69,425.
Finances (1970 est.): *Revenues,* $3,870,000,000; *expenditures,* $3,750,000,000; *monetary unit,* krone (7.285 kroner equal U. S.$1, Sept. 1971).
Gross National Product (1970): $16,000,000,000.
National Income (1969): $10,677,000,000; *national income per person,* $2,183.
Economic Indexes: *Manufacturing production* (1969), 152 (1969=100); *agricultural production* (1969), 106 (1963=100); *consumer price index* (1970), 145 (1964=100).
Manufacturing (metric tons, 1969): Beer, 6,523,000 hectoliters; residual fuel oil, 3,996,000; cement, 2,607,000.
Crops (metric tons, 1969 crop year): Barley, 5,255,000; sugar beets (1968–69), 2,339,000; oats, 765,000.
Minerals (metric tons, 1969): Lignite, 431,000; salt, 246,000; iron ore, 11,000; sulfur, 7,000.
Foreign Trade (1968): *Exports,* 1970, $3,356,000,000 (chief exports—nonelectrical machinery, $343,555,000; manufactured goods, $249,005,000; bacon, $220,425,000). *Imports,* 1970, $4,404,000,000 (chief imports—nonelectrical machinery, $355,430,000; transport equipment, $342,115,000; chemicals, $297,320,000; electrical machinery and appliances, $196,655,000). *Chief trading partners* (1968)—United Kingdom (took 21% of exports, supplied 14% of imports); Sweden (15%—15%); West Germany.
Tourism: *Receipts* (1970). $314,300,000.
Transportation: *Roads* (1969), 44,850 miles (72,177 km); *motor vehicles* (1969), 1,289,000 (automobiles, 1,023,100); *railroads* (1965), 2,476 miles (3,984 km); *merchant fleet* (1971), 3,520,000 gross registered tons; *national airline* (with Norway and Sweden), Scandanavian Airlines System; *principal airport,* Copenhagen.
Communications: *Telephones* (1970), 1,599,952; *television stations* (1968), 11; *television sets* (1969), 1,228,000; *radios* (1968), 1,566,000; *newspapers* (1969), 59.

Culture. The loss of the 222-year-old newspaper *Berlingske Aftenavis* coincided with the laying of the cornerstone of a new school of journalism to be opened in 1973. Thorkild Hansen, a Dane, received the Nordic literary prize for his work on the African slave trade and its modern parallels.

On April 21, Denmark formally delivered to Iceland the *Codex Regius* (containing most of the *Elder Edda*) and *Flateyjárbok,* medieval Icelandic manuscripts previously in Copenhagen. This gift started a flow to Iceland of medieval documents, a flow that will continue slowly after these precious papers have been cleaned and microfilmed at the Danish National Archives.

RAYMOND E. LINDGREN
California State College, Long Beach

DENTISTRY

The dental profession has been deeply concerned with ways to make dental health a realizable goal for all Americans. Pointing out that several national health insurance proposals introduced to Congress did not include dental care, the profession reemphasized that total health is impossible without dental health and that dental care is indispensable to the total well-being of the people.

Guidelines for Dentistry's Position in a National Health Program. After 18 months of study and consultation, a task force of experts on the role of dentistry in a national health program delivered an extensive report and list of recommendations to U. S. dentists. This report, a milestone in the history of American dentistry, was the basis for the profession's official statement, "Guidelines for Dentistry's Position in a National Health Program."

Fundamental principles of the guidelines are that dentistry should take an active part in the design and support of a program that includes dental service for all the people, and that public funds should not be used to provide health care for persons financially able to pay for this care themselves. Priority is asked for dental care for 2-, 3-, and 4-year-old children, with a 10-year phasing-in schedule for successive age groups until the entire population is included in the program. Emergency dental services are asked for all age groups from the initiation of the program.

Considerable emphasis is given to the prevention of dental disease through community measures such as fluoridation of drinking water supplies and an effective dental health education program that will motivate people to practice good personal oral hygiene and make full use of their dental care benefits. The guidelines also assert that consumers should play a key role at all levels of formulating dental health policy and of monitoring the results of a national program and that there should be no trace of racial discrimination.

Other important sections of the guidelines deal with the recruitment and education of sufficient numbers of dentists, dental auxiliaries, and dental technicians to provide service for all, and with continuing education programs for practicing dentists. Of particular concern is the recruitment of capable minority group students and the assignment of dental graduates to underserved areas of the country. Strongly urged is the expansion of clinical duties of dental auxiliaries so that more patients can receive treatment under the supervision of the available dentists.

Preventive Dentistry. In 1971 the National Institute of Dental Research launched a national caries (cavities) program with funds appropriated by Congress. It is designed to speed up development of preventive measures and to extend capabilities of the dentist, the hygienist, and others involved in public health to reduce the incidence of caries. The program will study alternate means of administering fluoride; development of long-lasting sealants; evaluation of sugar substitutes, dietary additives, and trace elements as caries inhibitors; development of more effective methods of mechanical cleansing; means of preventing adhesion of plaque-forming bacteria and of inhibiting growth of caries-inducing bacteria; and feasibility of immunization against cariogenic (cavity-causing) bacteria and their antigenic products.

Other oral disease prevention efforts included publication by the American Dental Association of an oral cancer prevention guide and a chart to aid dentists in the detection of early oral cancer. Research work in dental disease prevention included studies of the effectiveness of dextranase against plaque and the use of fluoride additives in restorative materials, dental cements, and pit and fissure sealants.

Efforts to expand dental health education included two new programs initiated by local dental societies. In California, a county dental society bought a school bus and converted it into a "Brushmobile" containing sinks, mirrors, and stereo equipment. Manned by volunteers and dental assistants, the traveling Brushmobile provides oral hygiene instruction at some 225 schools. In Detroit, as a result of action by the district dental society, the public school system has begun a dental care education program.

Dental Auxiliaries. Many studies have been in progress on how to increase the patient load that a dentist can effectively care for. At the Dental Manpower Development Center in Louisville, it was demonstrated that the use of auxiliaries specially trained to perform certain procedures traditionally done by dentists can more than double the volume of high-quality dental services. In a pedodontics auxiliary program at the University of Minnesota, experimental teams including specially trained auxiliaries performed 50% more dental procedures than teams including regular dental assistants.

Materials and Techniques. A new technique has been developed for ultraviolet illumination in oral diagnosis that allows a dentist to observe early caries before it can be diagnosed with the usual clinical procedures. It was reported that the use of mercury in dental amalgams poses no hazard to patients or to the environment, and that any hazard to dental personnel can be avoided by good office hygiene. Research continues in restorative materials that will bind chemically to the teeth, in local anesthetics, and in metal implants that can be placed in the jaw to hold prosthetic devices.

LELAND V. HENDERSHOT, D. D. S.
Editor-in-Chief, American Dental Association

DETROIT

A court decision on school desegregation overshadowed other events in Detroit during 1971, arousing controversy throughout the metropolitan area. A garbage strike and new police policies also made headlines.

School Desegregation. Federal District Judge Stephen J. Roth ruled on September 27 that Detroit public schools and the state of Michigan were guilty of "actions and inactions" resulting in school segregation. Since the segregation was the result of governmental policy, the ruling obligated public officials to take positive action to correct segregation. Judge Roth ordered both Detroit and state school officials to draw up plans to desegregate schools and to submit the plans for court appraisal. The decision opened the possibility of busing students across suburban school district boundaries to achieve integration and prompted the organization of numerous anti-busing groups.

On June 8, in a preliminary order, Judge Roth blocked Detroit schools from expanding school facilities pending final settlement of the desegregation lawsuit. The National Association for the Advancement of Colored People (NAACP) had filed a suit requesting the order to prevent construction. The NAACP argued that new construction might serve to perpetuate segregation.

Acting under an earlier, less sweeping federal court order of 1970, which also directed action to obtain greater school integration, the Detroit board of education put into effect in September 1971 a "magnet" plan involving 27 schools, including all 22 high schools. Each magnet school, in addition to offering regular courses, specialized in an area of learning, such as vocational training or performing arts. The plan was designed to induce interested students, both black and white, to transfer from their neighborhood school to the magnet school. Preliminary studies indicated the plan was only partially successful in furthering integration.

Detroit schools began operating on Jan. 1, 1971, under a new organization plan expected to decentralize school administration by allowing eight regional school boards partial control over neighborhood schools. The boards proved less successful than decentralization promoters had hoped, but school officials predicted eventual success.

Police Controversy. Police reported a slight decrease in crime during the first 10 months of 1971, compared with the 1970 period. Police Commissioner John F. Nichols credited the decrease to a new—and controversial—program in which officers, working in plain clothes, act as decoys in high-crime areas. By mid-November, 11 persons had been killed by officers in the program. One policeman in the program was also slain. Although overall crime decreased, the city's soaring murder rate prompted Mayor Roman Gribbs on September 11 to propose a state-wide ban on handguns.

Sixteen Detroit policemen, including an inspector, were among 151 persons arrested May 6 on federal warrants charging them with involvement in a $15 million-per-year illegal gambling operation.

Garbage Strike. Uncollected garbage threatened to become a health hazard during a five-day strike, July 1–5, by the city's 1,400 sanitation workers. The strike was settled when workers agreed to a three-year contract that provided for an immediate pay raise of 28½ cents per hour.

Construction. On November 24, Henry Ford II announced plans for a $500 million commercial and residential complex to revitalize downtown Detroit. Mayor Gribbs termed the effort "magnificent." The Institute of Arts completed a 10-year building program by opening its $7.5 million North Wing.

CHARLES W. THEISEN, *The Detroit "News"*

DEWEY, Thomas Edmund

Three-term governor of New York and twice Republican presidential nominee; b. Owosso, Mich., March 24, 1902; d. Bal Harbour, Fla., March 16, 1971.

Thomas Edmund Dewey was one of New York's ablest and most popular governors. He gave the state 12 years of business-like, efficient government; retained and elaborated upon the liberal reforms of his Democratic predecessors, Al Smith, Franklin D. Roosevelt, and Herbert H. Lehman; and made the Republican party the state's normal majority party. A power in national Republican politics from 1940 until his death, he ran for the presidency in 1944 and 1948, narrowly missing election on the second occasion. Dewey played a major role in keeping the national GOP from succumbing to a narrow-minded negativism and obstructionism that might have doomed his party to permanent minority status.

Early Life. Dewey was born on Mar. 24, 1902, in Owosso, Mich., the son of a local newspaper publisher. After receiving his A. B. from the University of Michigan in 1923, he went to New York City to study for a singing career. But he enrolled in Columbia Law School to have an alternative career to fall back upon and, after his graduation in 1925, took a job with a downtown law firm. He built a successful practice, was active in Republican affairs, and served as chief assistant U. S. attorney for the Southern District of New York (1931–33).

Political Career. The turning point in Dewey's career was his appointment in 1935 as special prosecutor to investigate crime in New York City. Two years later he was elected district attorney of New York County (Manhattan). Capitalizing on his reputation as a "racket buster," he ran for governor of New York in 1938. Although he lost to the Democratic incumbent, Herbert H. Lehman, he ran so strongly that he went to the 1940 Republican national conventions as the leading candidate for the GOP presidential nomination, only to lose out to Wendell Willkie. Two years later, he was elected governor, and in 1944 was named the GOP presidential standard bearer. But he could not match Franklin D. Roosevelt's tremendous personal following nor overcome the voters' reluctance to transfer executive power in the midst of World War II.

In 1946, however, Dewey was reelected governor by a record-breaking majority and, two years later, was renominated for the presidency. Most observers and opinion pollsters predicted that he would easily defeat F. D. R.'s successor, Harry S Truman. Truman's party was badly split, with its most conservative members backing J. Strom Thurmond on a states' rights ticket, and many left-wing Democrats defecting to Henry A. Wallace and his Progressive party. The resulting Republican overconfidence led Dewey to run a low-key campaign designed to avoid offending anyone. By contrast, Truman energetically stumped the country, taking full advantage of farmer and labor dissatisfaction by attacking what he called the "do-nothing" Republican 80th Congress. The result was a stunning upset victory for Truman.

Dewey was reelected governor for a third term in 1950. In 1952, he played a key role in winning the GOP presidential nomination for Gen. Dwight D. Eisenhower over the candidate of the party's Old Guard-isolationist wing, Sen. Robert A. Taft of Ohio. Although Dewey retired from public office in

THOMAS EDMUND DEWEY (1902–1971)

Although failing in two presidential bids, he was the "forerunner of middle-of-the-road Republicanism" that later triumphed.

1954 to reenter law practice in New York City, he remained influential in Republican councils. After the election of 1968, President Richard M. Nixon offered him the chief justiceship of the U. S. Supreme Court, but Dewey declined because of his age. Felled by a heart attack while vacationing in Florida, he died on March 16, 1971.

The Man and His Achievements. Though warm and gracious in private, Dewey maintained in public a stiffly formal and aloof manner that inspired jibes that he resembled "a groom on a wedding cake." Not a charismatic leader, he was nevertheless a skillful politician with a first-rate legal mind.

As governor, Dewey was responsible for placing New York State on a pay-as-you-go basis in capital construction, for increasing state aid to education, and for passage of the first state law prohibiting religious and racial discrimination in employment. He also revised New York's tax laws and reorganized state government along more efficient lines. He was sufficiently liberal to undercut the Democrats, while using his power of patronage to make himself the undisputed master of the state GOP.

In national politics, Dewey belonged to the liberal-internationalist wing of the Republican party. His acceptance of major New Deal reforms led to bitter complaints of "me-tooism" from the GOP Old Guard, while his support of foreign aid, American membership in the United Nations, and Truman's foreign policies brought him into conflict with his party's isolationist wing. But he was the forerunner of the middle-of-the-road Republicanism that triumphed with the elections of Eisenhower and Nixon.

Personal Life. Dewey married Frances Eileen Hutt of Sapulpa, Okla., on June 26, 1928. The couple had two sons, Thomas Edmund, Jr., and John Martin. Mrs. Dewey died in July 1970.

JOHN BRAEMAN
University of Nebraska—Lincoln

Historic treaty signed on February 11 barred nuclear weapons from the ocean floor. Secretary of State Rogers (*far left*) signed for United States in Washington ceremony attended (*from left*) by President Nixon and British and Soviet ambassadors.

Disarmament and Arms Control

Developments during 1971 can be seen in clearer perspective if the distinction between disarmament and arms control is understood. Generally, disarmament refers to the reduction in the level of military weapons by agreement between two or more states. Arms control, on the other hand, embraces a variety of measures including those designed to stabilize the military balance and thus make war less likely. The deterrence of war is the chief objective of arms control, while disarmament has the additional objective of decreasing the cost of arms.

No progress was made in 1971 in reducing the general level of nuclear or conventional weapons, but several significant steps were taken toward stabilizing the nuclear weapons balance.

The U. S. Arms Control and Disarmament Agency reported in May that worldwide military expenditures had reached $204 billion per year, about the same as the previous year in terms of constant dollars. The share of the world gross product going to military programs declined from a high of 7.3% in 1967 to 6.4% in 1970.

Balance of Power. Affecting the strategic balance between the two nuclear superpowers was a significant increase in the number of Soviet delivery vehicles compared with those of the United States. While exact comparisons of strategic capability are not possible, it is clear that America's lead of the mid-1960's had been greatly narrowed.

According to the International Institute for Strategic Studies in London, the Soviet Union, with an estimated 1,510 intercontinental ballistic missiles (ICBM's) had surpassed the U. S. force of 1,054. At the current Soviet rate of ballistic-missile submarine launchings—8 to 10 per year—Moscow could achieve numerical equality in missiles deployed with

the American fleet by 1974. In military manpower, U. S. forces had declined to approximately 2.5 million men from their 1968 peak, while the USSR maintained over 3 million men under arms. (See also DEFENSE FORCES.)

Strategic Arms Limitation Talks (SALT). Given the potential danger and present burden of nuclear arms, Moscow and Washington continued to seek agreements at the SALT negotiations, initiated Nov. 17, 1969, and carried on alternately in Vienna and Helsinki. Arms Control Director Gerard C. Smith headed the U. S. team and Deputy Foreign Minister Vladimir S. Semyonov, the Soviet delegation.

On May 20, President Nixon and the Soviet government simultaneously announced that a decision had been made at "the highest level of both governments" to concentrate on an agreement to limit the deployment of antiballistic missile systems (ABM's) and that along with such an agreement, the two powers would agree on certain measures to limit offensive weapons. The President declared that a deadlock of more than a year's duration had been broken.

Many observers expected an announced ABM-limitation agreement, possibly coupled with a constraint on offensive arms, before the end of 1971, but this did not happen, in spite of serious negotiation, primarily because significant differences persisted in the American and Soviet views of what constituted parity and sufficiency in both defensive and offensive systems. The press reported that the United States held that its Safeguard ABM system (not yet in operation) would eventually need more launchers than the small Russian ABM system around Moscow (already in operation), in part because the Soviet offensive force, particularly its large SS-9 ICBM's, was a greater threat to the U.S. land-based ICBM's than U.S. missiles were to the Soviet deterrent force.

On the question of offensive weapons, the Soviets continued to insist that U.S. tactical nuclear arms deployed in western Europe be considered in the strategic equation. There also was the problem of how to measure the Soviet lead in ICBM's against the present U.S. lead in submarine missiles.

There was some speculation that President Nixon's announced trips to Peking and Moscow early in 1972 may also have had the effect of postponing even a SALT agreement limited to ABM systems until the President had had the opportunity to discuss these vital matters with the leaders of the two Communist powers. Both Peking and Moscow were suspicious of each other and fearful that the other might make a deal with Washington at its expense.

Two Limited SALT Agreements. In spite of the continued stalemate over the major strategic arms control questions, SALT registered two small gains in the form of two pacts between Washington and Moscow to reduce the risk of nuclear war, both signed on September 30. One agreement sought to make nuclear war by accident less likely, and the other supplemented it by modernizing the Washington-Moscow Direct Communications Link, or "hot line." The first pact embraced a pledge by both sides to take steps to guard against the accidental or unauthorized use of nuclear weapons, arrangements for rapid communications should the danger of war arise from such nuclear accidents or from the detection of unidentified objects on early-warning systems, and a pledge to notify the other in advance of certain planned missile launches.

The supplementary "Hot Line" pact provided for the establishment of two satellite circuits, one by each party to the agreement, and multiple terminals to increase the capability and reliability of the communications link.

Geneva Disarmament Conference. Since 1962 the Conference of the Committee on Disarmament, meeting in Geneva, had been the principal forum for negotiating more limited multilateral arms control agreements. It had served as the focal point for the earlier partial test-ban, non-proliferation, and seabed arms control treaties. It continued in 1971 to grapple with a number of questions, including the banning of underground nuclear tests, which re-

mained unresolved primarily because of the Soviet refusal to agree to on-site inspection by independent observers.

Chemical and Biological Weapons. On Sept. 30, 1971, the Geneva Disarmament Conference forwarded to the UN General Assembly a U.S.-USSR draft convention banning biological weapons. The agreement was made possible when Moscow reversed itself and agreed with Washington and London that chemical agents should not be included in the prohibition. The treaty committed the parties "never in any circumstances to develop, produce, stockpile or otherwise acquire or retain": (1) microbial or other biological agents, or toxins, "whatever their origin or method of production," except for peaceful purposes; and (2) weapons, equipment, or means of delivery "designed to use such agents or toxins for hostile purposes or in armed conflict."

The treaty also required the destruction of existing stockpiles. In accordance with President Nixon's announcement of Nov. 25, 1969, the United States in July 1971 initiated a 14-month program for the complete destruction of its arsenal of biological weapons.

On December 7, the UN General Assembly commended the treaty for the signature of its member states by a vote of 104 to 2, with 2 abstentions.

This new treaty should not be confused with the similar but more general Geneva Protocol of 1925 against the use of chemical and biological weapons, which was before the U.S. Senate again in 1970. The United States was the only major power that had not ratified the treaty, though it had observed its provisions. Washington's delay was partly due to a controversy over whether the treaty should be interpreted to prohibit tear gas and defoliants.

Seabed Treaty. Negotiated at the Geneva Conference in 1970, the "Seabed Treaty" barred nuclear and other weapons of mass destruction from the ocean floor beyond the national 12-mile (19-km) limit. By the end of the year more than 80 states had signed the treaty and 23 had ratified it. It was to come into effect when the United States and the Soviet Union completed ratification.

Peripheral UN Role. Originally established to "save succeeding generations from the scourge of war," the United Nations has played only an occasional and largely ceremonial role in arms control

WIDE WORLD

UNITED STATES and Soviet Union agreed on September 30 to modernize Washington-Moscow "hot line" and to avoid accidental nuclear war. Secretary of State Rogers (*foreground*) and Soviet Foreign Minister Gromyko (*center*) signed. Seated in background is Soviet Ambassador Dobrynin.

agreements. The bilateral SALT negotiations and the Geneva Conference, of which the U. S. and USSR are permanent co-chairmen, have been the principal stages for efforts to limit arms.

In 1971 as in the past, the General Assembly exhorted the nuclear powers, but made no effort to curb conventional arms. On December 16 it adopted by large majorities three resolutions to end nuclear tests. One condemned all tests, another asked nuclear powers to desist from tests, and the third called on all states (meaning especially the non-signatories France and Communist China) to adhere to the existing partial test-ban treaty. Washington, Moscow, London, and Paris abstained on all three resolutions, and Communist China voted against them. The UN also passed (by 101 to 0 with 10 abstentions) a resolution urging a moratorium on the development, production, and stockpiling of chemical weapons.

In a speech before the Geneva Conference on Aug. 26, 1971, Ambassador James F. Leonard, the U. S. representative, pleaded for the Geneva Conference and the UN General Assembly to give more attention to the curbing of conventional arms, noting that this was not "a generally popular topic" among the non-nuclear states. He could have added that since Hiroshima all the local and regional wars in Asia, Africa, and Latin America had been fought with conventional weapons.

ERNEST W. LEFEVER, *The Brookings Institution*

DISASTERS. See ACCIDENTS AND DISASTERS.
DISTRICT OF COLUMBIA. See WASHINGTON, D. C.

DOMINICAN REPUBLIC

President Joaquín Balaguer continued in office in the Dominican Republic through 1971, weathering both a military plot to overthrow his regime and an onslaught of political terrorism that caused some to question whether he fully controlled his own administration.

Attempted Coup. An attempt at a military coup came to light on June 30. That evening, President Balaguer appeared on nationwide television, and, with Gen. Elías Wessin y Wessin standing beside him, announced that the general had organized an unsuccessful effort to oust him from the presidency.

General Wessin had been a pricipal figure on the conservative side of the civil war in 1965. Thereafter, he had spent several years in decorous exile as consul general in Miami, returning in time for an unsuccessful campaign for the presidency in 1970. Shortly after President Balaguer's announcement of the conspiracy, a court-martial ordered Wessin's exile to Spain.

Terrorist Activity. Virtually from the time that President Balaguer took office in 1966, the country had been in the grip of political violence perpetuated by underground organizations. Some of it could be traced to left-wing groups seeking vengeance for events of the 1965 civil war, but most of the terrorism was increasingly attributable to right-wing elements. Rightist assassins killed not only left-wing extremists but also members of the moderately leftist Dominican Revolutionary party, headed by former President Juan Bosch.

Anti-administration figures, including Bosch and members of the hierarchy of the Roman Catholic Church, had long charged that many of the terrorists were associated with the police and the military.

In August 1971, the New York *Times* printed several articles describing a major terrorist group called La Banda. They alleged that the group, consisting of about 400 members, was sponsored by Gen. Enrique Pérez y Pérez, commander of the armed forces, and that it had murdered at least 50 people.

Goaded, perhaps, by such criticism from abroad, President Balaguer, who had previously denied the existence of the group, on September 13 ordered the arrest of 250 members of La Banda. They were to be tried for "association to commit crimes." A few days later, however, 100 of those arrested were released for "lack of evidence."

The Nonviolent Opposition. In spite of the terrorists, the political opposition remained active. A 4-day general strike in the provincial city of San Francisco de Macorís in February was widely attributed to the influence of Bosch and his party. The strikers demanded the ouster of the local chief of police, Lt. Col. Eridio Pérez Naud, who was, in fact, replaced shortly after the strike had ended.

The extreme left was also busy. On February 25, two of its elements, the Popular Democratic Movement (MPD) and the so-called 24th of April Movement, signed an accord, pledging themselves to work for the unity of "all revolutionary organizations and progressive and anti-imperialist groups."

Economic Affairs. The Dominican economy's slow recovery from the disastrous 1965 civil war continued, with improvement recorded especially on the industrial and trade fronts. However, a review of the national economy by the Alliance for Progress pointed out that the country's per capita gross domestic product remained only $274 in 1970, compared with $282 in the prewar year of 1964.

ROBERT J. ALEXANDER, *Rutgers University*

--- **DOMINICAN REPUBLIC** • Information Highlights ---

Official Name: Dominican Republic.
Area: 18,816 square miles (48,734 sq km).
Population (1970 est.): 4,320,000. *Density,* 220 per square mile (86 per sq km). *Annual rate of increase,* 3.5%.
Chief Cities: Santo Domingo (1970 est.), the capital, 671,400; Santiago de los Caballeros (1969 est.), 103,861.
Government: *Head of state,* Joachín Balaguer, president (took office July 1, 1966). *Head of government,* Joachín Balaguer. *Legislature*—National Congress: Senate, 27 members; Chamber of Deputies, 74 members. *Major political parties*—Reformist party, Dominican Revolutionary party, Popular Democratic Movement.
Language: Spanish (official).
Education: *Literacy rate* (1970), less than 50% of population. *Expenditure on education* (1968), 14% of total public expenditure. *School enrollment* (1968)—primary, 685,562; secondary, 90,400; technical/vocational, 2,098; university/higher, 15,757.
Finances (1969 est.): *Revenues,* $186,700,000; *expenditures,* $230,400,000; *monetary unit,* peso (1 peso equals U. S.$1, Dec. 30, 1971).
Gross National Product (1969 est.): $1,251,000,000.
National Income (1969): $960,000,000; *average annual income per person* (1969 est.), $305.
Economic Indexes: *Manufacturing production* (1966), 103 (1963=100); *agricultural production* (1969), 109 (1963= 100); *consumer price index* (1970), 104 (1963=100).
Manufacturing (metric tons, 1969): Sugar, 886,000; cement, 390,000; wheat flour, 57,000; meat, 27,000.
Crops (metric tons, 1968 crop year): Sugarcane (1968–69), 6,800,000; bananas, 230,000; rice, 195,000.
Minerals (metric tons, 1969): Bauxite, 1,103,000.
Foreign Trade (1970): *Exports,* $214,000,000 (chief exports —sugar, $110,800,000; coffee, $28,900,000; cacao, $19,-600,000; bauxite, $15,100,000). *Imports,* $267,000,000 (chief imports—chemicals and pharmaceuticals, $16,850,000; non-electrical machinery, $16,080,000; electrical machinery, $9,030,000; gasoline, $6,190,000). *Chief trading partners* (1968)—United States (took 89% of exports, supplied 55% of imports); Japan (1%—6%); Netherlands (1%—3%).
Transportation: *Roads* (1970), 5,280 miles (8,497 km); *motor vehicles* (1969), 50,600 (automobiles, 32,900).
Communications: *Telephones* (1970), 40,174; *television stations* (1967), 4; *television sets* (1969), 100,000; *radios* (1969), 160,000; *newspapers* (1969), 6 (daily circulation, 133,000).

Rising drug abuse in South Vietnam, where drugs are plentiful and cheap, led U.S. military authorities to intensify their campaign against addiction in 1971. Several rehabilitation centers, such as the one above at Longbinh, were established at Vietnam bases.

DRUG ADDICTION AND ABUSE

Developments in the area of drug dependence during 1971 reflected swiftly changing patterns. If 1967 can be thought of as the peak of the LSD wave and 1969 as the year of the "speedfreak" (intravenous amphetamine user), then 1971 can be considered the year that heroin invaded new consumer markets. Recent trends also indicate that multiple drug use is becoming more prevalent, that the age of users is decreasing, and that the roles of "pusher" and user are tending to fuse.

Heroin. Heroin addiction increased markedly in 1971, and intense activity with related problems became evident. The appearance of large numbers of young, white, middle-class heroin addicts for the first time evoked a demand for improved control of contraband supplies and expanded treatment programs for opiate addicts. The issue was dramatized in June 1971 when President Nixon stated that narcotic addiction was the nation's number one health problem and appointed Dr. Jerome H. Jaffe as special presidential adviser on drug abuse prevention. Dr. Jaffe will coordinate and guide the multiple federal efforts in drug abuse treatment and prevention.

Control of narcotic supplies at the source is an ideal way to deal with the problem of addiction. Turkey, the world's largest grower of the Oriental poppy (*Papaver somniferum*), the source of opium and its derivatives, including morphine, codeine, and heroin, announced that it would discontinue its cultivation beginning with the 1972 crop. It has been estimated that the major share of the heroin smuggled into the United States is manufactured from Turkish opium, and Turkish farmers are being reimbursed for the loss of their cash crops with subsidies paid from a grant from the U. S. government. However, considerable opium is still cultivated in southeast Asia, Mexico, Afghanistan, and other countries, and portions of these harvests are subject to diversion into illicit channels.

A spectacular increase in heroin addiction among U. S. servicemen in Vietnam was uncovered during 1971. Drugs of all sorts are readily available in Saigon and other South Vietnamese cities, and heroin of 90% purity is relatively inexpensive. (Black market heroin in the United States, in contrast, averages 5 to 10% purity.) Congressional investigators returning from visits to South Vietnam estimated that from 10 to 20% of the U. S. servicemen may be involved in heroin use. Urine analyses of veterans returning to the United States revealed slightly more than 5% had been using heroin. The figures are, however, open to question. Special amnesty programs allow addicted persons to submit voluntarily to detoxification treatment, and Veterans Administration hospitals are setting up narcotic treatment centers to provide long-term care when needed.

DRUG ABUSE exhibition opened in Museum of City of New York in February. Different coffins in this exhibit symbolize point that addiction strikes all classes.

The treatment of heroin addiction through the use of methadone maintenance—the daily ingestion of sufficient methadone to suppress the craving for heroin and to block the effects of heroin if it is ingested—increased during 1971. More than 300 applications to establish methadone maintenance programs have been filed with the Food and Drug Administration. An estimated 30,000 addicts are active patients in these programs, and the number is expected to rise to 80,000 by the end of 1972.

Usually, about 50% of the heroin addicts in a community will come forward and involve themselves in treatment. Of these, half will do well over a period of years, the remainder relapsing to heroin or the use of other drugs. Methadone maintenance alone, however, is not enough to provide effective treatment. The addicts must adopt a whole new life style, and rehabilitation supports are required by most patients. Still, methadone maintenance constitutes a promising way to treat large numbers of addicts relatively inexpensively, the cost being $1,000 to $2,000 per addict per year, and the results surpass any other treatment method available.

Sedatives, Including Barbiturates, Tranquilizers, and Alcohol. The sedatives are a heterogeneous group of drugs that depress the central nervous system producing calming or sleep. The swallowing of sleeping pills—generally barbiturates—continues to increase among all age groups with "downers" now being "dropped," or taken, even by grade school youngsters in certain urban sections. In some respects, sleeping pill abuse can be more life endangering than narcotic dependence. The degree of incoordination, impaired judgment, and inability to perform ordinary acts is greater under the influence of barbiturates than with narcotics. Fatalities from overdose of barbiturates are not infrequent, and death can also be associated with the sudden discontinuance of barbiturate use. The combination of alcohol and barbiturates is particularly dangerous. Legal restrictions on the distribution of sleeping pills have been tightened.

A problem also exists with the excessive use by adults of certain tranquilizers, such as meprobromate (Miltown and Equanil). The massive problem of alcoholism—the largest drug abuse problem in North America—also belongs in this category.

Stimulants, Including Cocaine. Stimulants produce central nervous system excitation. The amphetamines are the most widely used and misused stimulants. The most bizarre type of abuse is the intravenous injection of high doses of methamphetamine, or "speed." The "speedfreak" is subject to unthinking, impulsive outbursts of hyperactivity during which he may harm himself or others. His thinking eventually becomes overly suspicious or paranoid, and hallucinations and delusions are consistently described. The amphetamine psychosis is a close mimicker of paranoid schizophrenia, and prolonged breakdowns are a real possibility. In addition, brain and liver damage can result from long-term use of large amounts of amphetamines, and recently an inflammatory disease of the artery walls has been described in speedfreaks. Considerable tightening of legal controls on the distribution of amphetamines has occurred, and they have been placed in the same category as narcotics for penalty purposes.

The reappearance of cocaine on the black market after an absence of half a century is noteworthy. Cocaine, an addictive drug made from the leaves of a South American shrub, is "snorted" or "mainlined." It stimulates the central nervous system, and its abuse causes complications similar to those that occur with the amphetamines.

Marihuana and Other Hallucinogens. Marihuana, *Cannabis sativa,* is now confidently classified as a hallucinogen. Work with its active ingredient, Δ^9-tetrahydrocannabinol (THC), has proved that classic hallucinogenic effects, such as delusions, hallucinations, perceptual distortions, feelings of unreality, and loss of ego integrity, can be induced. Marihuana ("pot") as smoked in the United States is of low potency, and sometimes its sedative or stimulant effects mask the early hallucinogenic symptoms.

Considerable research is under way to answer many questions about marihuana. It is now known that there are two varieties of *Cannabis sativa.* North American and West European plants are of the so-called fiber type, which is low in THC, while Nepalese, Mexican, Vietnamese, and other tropical specimens are of the so-called drug type, which is high in THC. Contrary to popular opinion, the male plant is as potent as the female plant. The stems, roots, and seeds contain little THC, while the flowers and bracts have the highest THC content and the leaves a lesser amount. Fiber-type marihuana has 0.05 to 0.2% THC; drug-type marihuana has 0.8 to 5% THC. A closely related drug —hashish, or charas—made from the resin of the tops of drug-type plants, has about 10% THC.

The consistent physiological changes noted in marihuana use are an increase in pulse rate and dilation of the blood vessels of the whites of the eyes. The often-reported dilation of the pupils does not occur. The psychological alterations that have been reported are impairments of immediate recall, complex reaction time, and time estimation. Short-term side effects are infrequently anxiety and psychotic reactions. Longer-term adverse effects among heavy users include confusional states and diminished drive. Studies on the possible long-term toxicity of marihuana smoke are under way, as are studies of the possible therapeutic potential of the constituents of marihuana.

Increased legal activity concerning marihuana was also evident during 1971. In general, the severity of punishments, particularly for possession, is being reduced. Efforts to legalize marihuana continue, and a U. S. Presidential Commission is studying this and other problems. In 1971 the Canadian Commission of Inquiry into the Nonmedical Use of Drugs recommended legalization of marihuana.

The use of other, generally stronger, hallucinogens—such as LSD, mescaline, psilocybin, STP, MDA, and THC, continued—although "acidheads," as habitual users are called, seem to be rarer than a few years ago. The street quality of these drugs remains questionable; for example, mescaline, psilocybin, or THC bought on the black market were found to contain no mescaline, psilocybin, or THC. LSD also varied considerably in dosage and purity. Strange adulterants also appeared from time to time. This lack of information about the nature of the material ingested makes emergency treatment of patients very precarious.

SIDNEY COHEN, M. D.
Consultant, National Institute of Mental Health

DUVALIER, François. See HAITI.

EARTHQUAKES

Earthquake activity in 1971 was somewhat greater than usual. Two earthquakes were recorded with a magnitude of 8.1 on the Richter scale, and there were many between magnitudes 7 and 8. For the most part, however, these large quakes occurred in uninhabited areas and did no damage.

Southern California. The earthquake of most interest to Americans took place on February 9 in southern California. It occurred at 6 A. M. Pacific Standard Time. Its location was 34.4°N, 118.4°W in the San Fernando region, and it centered in the San Gabriel Mountains near the San Gabriel fault. Its magnitude was 6.6 on the Richter scale. It took 64 lives and did property damage estimated at between a half billion and a billion dollars. Although some called it the most destructive earthquake in U. S. history, the San Francisco quake of 1906 was of magnitude 8.25, took 700 lives, and did $400 million damage. Taking into account the change in monetary values, this would exceed the property damage of the 1971 quake.

The main shock of the San Fernando quake was felt over approximately 80,000 square miles (207,-000 sq km), extending into Nevada and Arizona. Most of the casualties resulted from the collapse of two veterans' hospitals. In one near Sylmar, Calif., built in 1926, two buildings housing five wards crashed into rubble, giving patients, staff, and workers no chance to get out. Olive View Hospital, 1.5

miles (2.4 km) away, a building completed the previous October, was a total loss. New skyscrapers in downtown Los Angeles withstood the shock.

The dam at one side of the 3.6-billion-gallon Van Norman reservoir in San Fernando gave cause for worry for a time. The outside concrete facing gave way, but the earthen dam withstood the pressure. The Los Angeles department of water and power at once released the water at a rate of 250,-000 gallons per hour into the Los Angeles River, and danger was averted.

California's seismic history seems to indicate that it may expect a major quake about every 100 years. However, information about the causes of earthquakes is so inadequate that any statement that California is soon to have a much bigger quake than the San Francisco one of 1906 is based on hysteria rather than knowledge.

Other Earthquakes. The first major quake of 1971 occurred on January 3 in the South Atlantic Ridge. It was of magnitude 7.1 but did no damage except perhaps to fish. The two largest quakes of the year (each of magnitude 8.1) occurred on January 10 in New Guinea and July 14 at Bougainville, Solomon Islands. The first did no damage. In the second, only one casualty was reported, but a 7-foot (2-meter) tsunami (water wave) in Rabaul harbor did extensive damage and caused landslides. From July through October there were 10 severe quakes in the Solomons.

The first disastrous 1971 quake occurred near Tuscania, Italy, on February 6. Twenty persons died, and some 5,000 were made homeless. It was a small quake (magnitude 4.6), and damage was due to poor construction. On March 3 a quake of magnitude 5.1 occurred at 22.1°N, 59.2°E in the eastern Arabian Peninsula. It did no damage but was the first quake ever recorded from the Arabian Peninsula. On May 12, at 37.6°N, 29.8°E in Turkey, a quake of magnitude 6.3 killed 100 persons and did major damage in the Burdur area. Also in Turkey, on May 22 at 38.8°N, 40.5°E, a quake of magnitude 7 killed about 1,000 persons and was felt in 11 provinces of Anatolia.

On June 17 a quake of magnitude 7 occurred on the Chile-Argentina border about 200 miles (320 km) southeast of the city of Antofogasta. Only one casualty was reported. On July 8, at 32.5°S, 71.4°W near the coast of central Chile, a quake of magnitude 7.8 killed 90 persons and injured 447. On July 15 a quake of magnitude 5.2 struck northern Italy, killing two persons and doing damage in Parma. On July 27, at 2.7°S, 77.4°W on the Peru-Ecuador border, a quake of magnitude 7.5 killed one person and did extensive damage in southern Ecuador. On August 15 a quake of magnitude 4.6 occurred in the North Atlantic, 150 miles (240 km) east of Newfoundland—the first recorded from this region.

Nuclear Test. On November 6, on the island of Amchitka in the Aleutians, a seismic event occurred that, though not an earthquake, was a first cousin to one. The United States set off an underground nuclear explosion, equivalent to 5 million tons of TNT, a mile (1.6 km) below the surface. It registered magnitude 7 but did not trigger any earthquakes or other disasters as some had predicted.

J. JOSEPH LYNCH, S. J.
Director, Fordham University Seismic Observatory

EASTERN ORTHODOXY. See RELIGION.
ECOLOGY. See CONSERVATION; ENVIRONMENT.

Economy of the U.S.

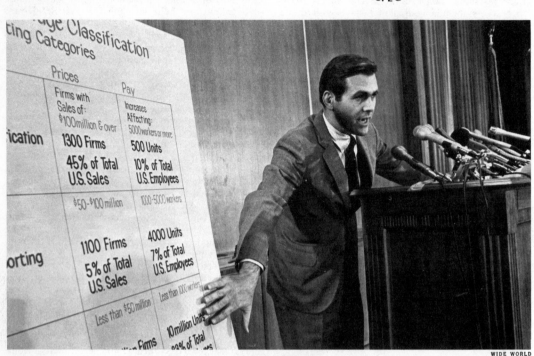

WIDE WORLD

Government attempts to halt inflation included voluntary efforts, symbolized by emblem (*top*), and wage and price controls. Donald Rumsfeld, Cost of Living Council director, explains Phase II controls at November 15 news conference.

Economic activities in the United States in 1971 are examined in this article under the following headings: (1) Economic Review; (2) National Income and Product; (3) Industrial Production; (4) Retail Sales; and (5) Wholesale Sales.

Other related developments are reviewed in AUTOMOBILES; BANKING; ELECTRICAL INDUSTRIES; HOUSING; INTERNATIONAL FINANCE; INTERNATIONAL TRADE; LABOR; MINING; STEEL; STOCKS AND BONDS; TAXATION; and UNITED STATES.

ECONOMIC REVIEW

During 1971 the U. S. economy made a slow recovery from the recession of 1970. However, inflation, unemployment, erratic industrial activity, and weakness of the dollar in international trade plagued the quest for greater and more rapid prosperity. In response, President Nixon made two dramatic moves—instituting his Phase I program on August 15 and his Phase II program on November 13. At year-end, the real output of the U. S. economy was rising, there were signs that the rate of inflation had slowed, and there seemed to be less pressure from abroad.

Phase I. In a dramatic shift in economic strategy, President Nixon established a wide-ranging program (later known as Phase I) aimed at creating more jobs, halting the rise in the cost of living,

and protecting the dollar from attacks by international money speculators. The highlights of this program were: (1) a 90-day freeze on wages, prices, and rents; (2) the establishment of a Cost of Living Council to administer the freeze and to recommend measures for a second stage of wage and price stabilization after the 90-day freeze; (3) a temporary 10% surcharge on most imports; (4) a suspension of the convertibility of foreign-held dollars into gold; (5) a variety of tax measures to stimulate the economy; and (6) a proposed reduction in federal expenditures. The immediate effect of Phase I was an increase in confidence.

Phase II. The Phase II program, which went into effect when the 90-day wage and price freeze expired on November 13, inaugurated an indefinite period of close governmental supervision of the economy in an effort to limit inflation to a rate of 2% to 3% per year—about half the rate prevailing before the freeze. President Nixon set up a number of new groups to govern wages and prices; in particular, a 15-member Pay Board and a 7-member Price Commission, both of which are organizationally under the cabinet-level Cost of Living Council. By year-end the Pay Board had set a 5.5% flexible ceiling on pay increases, and the Price Commission had set a 2.5% average ceiling on price increases.

International Trade Relations. On the international scene, the U. S. economy ran into problems that have been developing for a number of years. For the first time since 1893, the United States showed a trade deficit, with imports exceeding exports at an annual rate of about $1.7 billion. This deficit, along with monetary outflows for military spending and foreign aid, compounded the chronically unfavorable balance-of-payments deficit and resulted in monetary pressures. These pressures were made evident by an outflow of U. S. gold and intense currency speculation. The result was the August 15 announcement by the President and a later 8.57% devaluation of the U. S. dollar—increasing the official price of gold from $35 to $38 an ounce. This devaluation, the revaluation of major foreign currencies, and control of inflation were expected to improve the U. S. position in world trade.

Unemployment. The unemployment situation showed no improvement in 1971, underlining the lethargic nature of the recovery during the year. The civilian labor force continued to expand, topping a record 85 million late in 1971. However, the unemployment rate remained consistently around 6% throughout the year—it was 6.1% in December 1971. At this high plateau, unemployment was not as high as the peaks reached in three other postwar recessions—6.8% in the last half of 1949, 7.5% for a few months in 1958, and 7.0% for four months of 1961. However, the 14-month period from November 1970 to December 1971 showed the longest sustained high level of unemployment since the 1930's.

Performance of the Total Economy. The U.S. gross national product (GNP) was in excess of one trillion dollars for the first time in history in 1971, registering a gain of nearly 7.5% over 1970. This gain was better than the 4.9% gain in 1970 and was nearly equal to the increase in 1969. In real terms (eliminating the effect of price increases), the GNP was up 2.7% in 1971 as compared with a decline of 0.6% in 1970 and a gain of 2.5% in 1969. Overall, this is a picture of an inflation-ridden economy operating at a high level of stagnation. However, there were some cheerful signs. In the fourth quarter of 1971, the real GNP was up more than 6% on a seasonally adjusted annual rate basis, and the total gain in prices in the fourth quarter was a moderate 1.5% compared with 5.5% in the first quarter.

Industrial Sector. The sluggish nature of the recovery was evident in the dull performance of the industrial sector, which at no time got back to the record-high marks of 1969. In that year industrial output showed gains over the first three quarters of the year and for the year as a whole averaged 10.7% higher than in 1967. In 1971, however, the Federal Reserve Board's index of industrial production (1967 = 100) trailed corresponding months in 1970 until the last quarter, when it ran slightly over 3% ahead of the 1967 base. The course of industrial output during 1971 was affected by copper, railroad, and coal strikes; the aftermath of auto strikes; and inventory hedging in steel.

The steel industry was in a depressed state in 1971, first producing at above average levels to meet prestrike hedging, then drastically cutting back production as swollen inventories were worked off when an August 1 strike was averted by a contract settlement. In addition, steel imports again reached near-record levels, cutting sharply into demand for domestic steel. As a result, the industry's output for the year dropped to about 120 million tons, the poorest showing since 1963.

Automobile production also showed erratic movements during 1971. Following the strike of 1970, there was an initial surge in which the industry tried to catch up. Then, following a slowdown, there was a second surge in which domestic industry benefited from the 10% import surcharge and the proposed repeal (later enacted) of the 7% federal excise tax on autos. As a result, domestic production for 1971 totaled 8.6 million units, up sharply from the 6.5 million units in 1970 but still below the record 9.3 million units in 1965.

Business Sector. Some of the improvement in the economy was in the business sector. By the last half of 1971, corporate profits before taxes had risen to a level of $83.5 billion, well up from the $71.5 billion level of late 1970 but still below the $89 billion level of late 1968. The recovery in pretax profits might have been better by some $3.5 billion except for the liberalized depreciation rules instituted by the Treasury Department in June. Although this step lowered the pretax profit figure, to some extent it achieved the wider goal of increasing business spending for capital additions.

However, the weak level of capital expenditures by business did reflect the lack of zest in the recovery in 1971. For the full year total business spending for new plant and equipment was estimated at about $81.5 billion, up only 2.2% from 1970 as compared with gains of 5.5% in 1970 and 11.5% in 1969. Capital outlays, however, are conventional laggards in business cycles.

According to a late 1971 survey by the Department of Commerce and the Securities and Exchange Commission, business expects to increase capital outlays in the first half of 1972 to 9% above the level in the first half of 1971. As business gains confidence in an upturn, it usually raises its capital outlay expectations, and this eventually leads to improvements in employment and production.

Government Sector. Government purchases of goods and services rose only moderately during 1971, mostly in the area of state and local government outlays. Federal defense spending was down from the 1969 peak levels, and the cutback contributed to the slowdown in defense-related industries. In the third quarter of 1971, defense spending was at a $70.8 billion annual rate, compared with $79.8 billion in 1969. However, state and local government spending continued to rise; by the end of the year, it was nearly double the level of 1965. With the continued easing of money rates during the year, state and local governments stepped up their capital outlays. Also, new offerings of state and local bonds totaled $24.3 billion, up 37% over 1970. Future additions to government outlays may arise from deferred federal pay increases; restocking of defense inventories; and increased local attention to environmental protection, including waste disposal, sewage treatment, and air pollution control.

Consumer Sector. The high rate of unemployment and the continued inflation dampened consumer enthusiasm for some months, but there appeared to be some return of confidence toward the end of 1971. Personal consumption expenditures during 1971 were up about 8%. One deterrent to greater consumption was the 6.5% rise in personal income, the smallest percentage gain since 1963.

TREASURY SECRETARY Connally addresses International Monetary Fund and World Bank members in Washington, D. C., on September 30. Connally indicated conditions for removal of the import surtax.

Savings as a percentage of disposable personal income were at a high mark of more than 8% in the last half of 1970 and the first half of 1971, but the rate lessened toward the end of the year. From the end of 1970 to the last part of 1971, consumer installment credit rose to a seasonally adjusted annual rate of $10.25 billion. Thus, consumers seemed to be showing an increased willingness to cut their savings rate and to make greater use of their credit.

Housing has been a major source of strength in the U. S. economy in recent years, and there were further gains in 1971. Housing starts were estimated at a record 2,048,200 in 1971, up 43% over 1970 and 7% above the previous high in 1950. A large spurt in single-family dwellings, which are higher average-cost-per-unit structures than multiple-family dwellings, was aided by the availability of mortgage money. This money came from the support of federal agencies and the savings flows into savings associations and savings banks.

Outlook. Despite the confidence that inflation was being attacked realistically, consumer prices and wholesale prices were up in December 1971. The question was whether this was a temporary reaction to the first relaxation of the controls or whether it was the resumption of what had inspired the controls. There was a further uncertainty stemming from the continuing high rate of unemployment. How the unemployment problem could be attacked without upsetting the fight on inflation remained the most pressing matter in the U. S. economy.

JACKSON PHILLIPS
Vice President, Moody's Investors Service

NATIONAL INCOME AND PRODUCT

National income rose at a much faster pace in the United States during 1971 than in the previous year. The acceleration resulted from an increase in the volume of production that was not fully offset by a slowdown in the rate of increase of prices.

Real output increased 2.7% during 1971, in contrast with a decrease in 1970. Real output, including higher prices, rose 8.0% at seasonally adjusted annual rates in the opening quarter of 1971,

then increased 3.4% in the second quarter, 2.7% in the third, and 6.1% in the fourth quarter.

Prices rose 4.6% in the year—substantially less than the 5.5% price rise in 1970. In fact, 1971 was the first year since 1962 in which the implicit price deflator (the ratio of gross national product in current prices to GNP in constant terms) rose at a slower pace than it had during the prior year.

National Income. The national income of the United States totaled $850.8 billion in 1971, 6.9% more than in 1970. National income had increased only 4.2% in the previous year.

The acceleration in the growth of national income featured sharp swings from declines to increases in corporate profits and farm proprietors' income, and some upward movement in most other types of income. Corporate earnings of $80.7 billion were up 14% from 1970 as output accelerated and profit margins were expanded. In the earlier year profits had declined 9.9%. Farm proprietors' income rose 3.2% to a total of $16.3 billion in 1971. This was a marked turnaround from the 1970 experience, when farm proprietors' income had declined 5.6%.

Compensation of employees totaled $641.8 billion in 1971, up 6.6% from the previous year, compared with a gain of 6.4% in 1970. Nonfarm proprietors' income, at $52.1 billion in 1971, was up 2.2% from the previous year. In 1970 such income had fallen 5.6%. Rental income rose 4.3% to $24.3 billion in 1971. In the previous year such income had risen 3.1%. Net interest rose 7.6% in 1971 to a total of $35.6 billion. In 1970 it had risen 10.3%.

Personal Income. The acceleration in the growth of national income was not matched in personal income, which is current income received by persons from all sources, inclusive of transfers from government and business. Personal income, at $857 billion in 1971, was up 6.6% over 1970.

The rate of increase in personal income did not accelerate in 1971 as did national income because: (1) a major share of the acceleration in national income occurred in corporate profits, which is not a component of personal income; (2) there was a marked expansion in contributions for social insurance, which also is not a component of personal income; and (3) the expansion in government transfer payments to persons—which are included in personal income but not in national income—was at a moderately slower pace than in 1970. Government transfer payments to persons totaled $90.5 billion in 1971—19.6% more than in 1970.

Although personal income grew in 1971, personal tax payments fell 0.1% in the year. In 1970 they had fallen 0.3%. The drop in personal tax payments in the face of a growth in personal income reflected the fact that the income-tax surcharge did not affect 1971, while it had been in effect at a 5% rate for the first half of 1970, and substantial underwithholding in certain income brackets in 1971.

With taxes reduced as personal income rose, disposable personal income—the income of persons available for spending or saving—increased 7.6% in 1971 to a total of $741.2 billion, as contrasted with a gain of 8.3% in 1970.

The growth of disposable personal income somewhat exceeded the increase in personal outlay, so that personal savings grew. Personal savings totaled $60.4 billion in 1971, 11.6% more than in 1970. In

(*Continued on page 252*)

THE U.S. ECONOMY IN 1971 — A MUDDLED PICTURE

GROSS NATIONAL PRODUCT passes $1 trillion, but...

Billions of dollars
(Quarterly)

In constant (1958) dollars

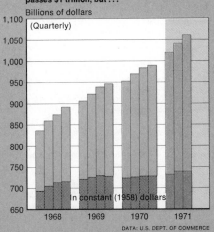

DATA: U.S. DEPT. OF COMMERCE

INDUSTRIAL PRODUCTION is sluggish...

1957-59 = 100
(Seasonally adjusted index)

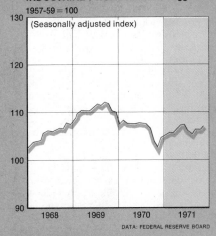

DATA: FEDERAL RESERVE BOARD

UNEMPLOYMENT RATE remains high...

Percent
(Monthly)

Total

Married men

DATA: U.S. DEPT. OF LABOR

INTEREST RATES move downward, and...

Percent

Treasury bills

Long-term government securities

Federal Reserve discount rate

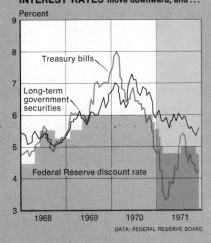

DATA: FEDERAL RESERVE BOARD

CONSUMER PRICES soar further...

1967 = 100
(Monthly index)

All services

All items

Food

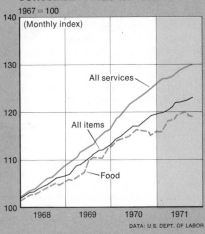

DATA: U.S. DEPT. OF LABOR

PERSONAL INCOME climbs.

Billions of dollars
(Seasonally adjusted at annual rates)

Total
(left scale)

Wages and salaries
(right scale)

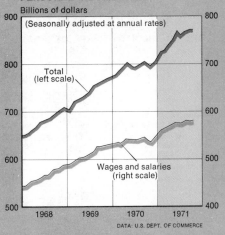

DATA: U.S. DEPT. OF COMMERCE

(*Continued from page 250*)
1970 savings had risen sharply—by 42.8%. This further growth in personal savings brought the saving rate up to 8.1% of disposable personal income in 1971 from the 7.9% recorded in 1970.

Gross National Product. The slowing in economic activity can be analyzed in terms of the gross national product, which is the market value of the output of goods and services produced by the nation's economy. The GNP rose 7.5% in 1971 to reach a total of $1,046.8 billion. In 1970 it had increased at a rate of 4.8%.

The acceleration in the growth of total GNP during the year reflected a marked increase in the volume of residential construction, as well as accelerations in the pace of increases in personal consumption expenditures, nonresidential fixed investment, and government purchases. Residential structures, at $40.6 billion, were up 33.6% for the year, in contrast with a decline of 4.4% in 1970.

Personal consumption expenditures rose 7.5% in 1971 to a total of $662.2 billion. In 1970 such outlays had increased 5.8%. Purchases of consumer durable goods led the acceleration in consumer spending as durables rose 13.3% in 1971, as compared with a drop of 1.5% in the previous year. Purchases of nondurable goods, at $278.8 billion in 1971, were up 4.6% from 1971. In the previous year the rate of increase had been 6.8%. Purchases of services rose at a slower rate—7.8%—in 1971 than 1970, when such outlays had increased 8.4%.

Federal government purchases of goods and services at $97.6 billion were up 0.4% in 1971, as contrasted with a drop of 1.9% in 1970. State and local government purchases of goods and services, at $135.4 billion, were up 10.8% in 1971, as against the previous year's gain of 10.5%. Business put $108.2 billion in nonresidential fixed investment in 1971, 6.0% more than in 1970. In the previous year business fixed investment had risen 3.5%.

Business inventory accumulation totaled $2.1 billion in 1971, off moderately from the pace a year earlier. In 1970 businesses had added $2.8 billion.

JOHN A. GORMAN
National Income and Wealth Division, Bureau of Economic Analysis, U. S. Department of Commerce

INDUSTRIAL PRODUCTION

U. S. industrial production declined for the second straight year in 1971. It drifted downward by

NATIONAL INCOME BY TYPE OF INCOME

(Billions of dollars)[1]

	1968	1969	1970	1971
National income	711.1	763.7	795.9	850.8
Compensation of employees	514.6	565.5	601.9	641.8
Wages and salaries	464.9	509.6	541.4	574.2
Private	369.2	405.5	426.6	450.3
Government	95.7	104.1	114.8	123.8
Supplements to wages and salaries	49.7	56.0	60.5	67.7
Proprietors' income	64.2	67.0	66.9	68.3
Business and professional	49.5	50.3	51.0	52.1
Farm	14.7	16.8	15.8	16.3
Rental income of persons	21.2	22.6	23.3	24.3
Corporate profits and inventory valuation adjustment	84.3	78.6	70.8	80.7
Profits before tax	87.6	84.2	75.4	85.2
Profits tax liability	39.9	39.7	34.1	37.7
Profits after tax	47.8	44.5	41.2	47.4
Inventory valuation adjustment	−3.3	−5.5	−4.5	−4.4
Net interest	26.9	29.9	33.0	35.6

[1] Detail may not add to total because of rounding. Source: Bureau of Economic Analysis, U. S. Department of Commerce.

GROSS NATIONAL PRODUCT OR EXPENDITURE

(Billions of dollars)[1]

	1968	1969	1970	1971
Gross national product	864.2	929.1	974.1	1,046.8
Personal consumption expenditures	536.2	579.6	615.8	662.2
Durable goods	84.0	89.9	88.6	100.4
Nondurable goods	230.8	247.6	264.7	278.8
Services	221.3	242.1	262.5	283.0
Gross private domestic investment	126.0	137.8	135.3	150.8
Fixed investment	118.9	130.4	132.5	148.7
Nonresidential	88.8	98.6	102.1	108.2
Structures	30.3	34.5	36.8	38.1
Producers' durable equipment	58.5	64.1	65.4	70.1
Residential structures	30.1	31.8	30.4	40.6
Change in business inventories	7.1	7.4	2.8	2.1
Net exports of goods and services	2.5	2.0	3.6	.7
Government purchases of goods and service	199.6	209.7	219.4	233.1
Federal	98.8	99.2	97.2	97.6
State and local	100.8	110.6	122.2	135.4

[1] Detail may not add to total because of rounding. Source: Bureau of Economic Analysis, U. S. Department of Commerce.

0.4% after having dropped almost 3.5% in recession-stunted 1970.

The industrial production index, prepared monthly by the Board of Governors of the Federal Reserve System, measures the physical volume of production by U. S. factories, mines, and utilities. It covers about two fifths of the nation's total output of goods and services and reflects current trends in the economy as a whole. In mid-1971, the index was revised—the first general revision in more than 10 years. The number of market and industry divisions in the index was changed to 227, and the comparison base (industrial index = 100) was changed from the 1957–59 period to the single year 1967.

Effects of Strikes and Strike Threats. Actual and threatened strikes considerably affected industrial output in 1971. Early in the year, an upswing in manufacturing reflected the boost in automobile production as General Motors made up for time lost by a strike in late 1970. At midyear, steel-using industries scrambled to build up inventories in anticipation of a strike in August. They made heavy purchases of domestic steel and sharply stepped up metal purchases from abroad, partly to avoid further supply complications arising from the longshoremen's strike. After the steel industry reached a labor settlement without a strike, steel users sharply curtailed purchases and began to draw on their heavy inventories. As a result, production of domestic steel slumped 40% from August to September. Despite improvement later in the year, steel production for all of 1971 showed a drop of 8%. Steel shipments totaled 53 million tons in the first half of the year but shrank to about 35 million tons in the second half.

Production of bituminous coal was severely affected by a 45-day labor stoppage that began on October 1. In the first month of the strike, soft-coal output sank to about one-fourth of what it had been in September. Despite a rapid poststrike recovery, the total output of the nation's mines—including coal, oil, gas, metals, stone, and other minerals—registered a drop of 2.5% in 1971, partly because of the coal strike and partly because of the generally lackluster industrial demand.

Effects of the New Economic Policy. The sluggish demand for the nation's industrial output in 1971 was a reflection of the relatively low level of business investment, the unwillingness of consumers to spend generously in the face of substantial unemployment and rising prices, the cutbacks in defense procurement, and the rising volume of imports. On August 15, President Nixon announced his New Economic Policy (NEP) to deal with the problems of inflation, the balance-of-payments deficits, and the sluggish economic recovery.

The effectiveness of the economic stabilization policy was evident in the prices of manufactured goods, which showed no appreciable change between October and November. However, prices of manufactured goods rose about 3% during the full year, as measured by the wholesale price index of the Bureau of Labor Statistics. Average weekly earnings of production workers in manufacturing were practically unchanged during the Phase I freeze of the NEP. However, average weekly earnings of factory workers were about $145 at year-end, up $10.

The most visible impact on the NEP was on automobile production. Lured by frozen prices and the repeal of the 7% excise tax on automobiles, consumers in record numbers swarmed to showrooms in September and October. Reflecting both the recovery from the 1970 General Motors strike and the NEP-stimulated consumer demand, domestic automobile production jumped some 30% in 1971, to 8.6 million units, making it the biggest year since 1968, when 8.8 million units were produced.

Survey of Manufacturing. The bright spots in industrial production in 1971 were consumer goods and utilities, each registering volume advances of

OSRIN IN THE CLEVELAND PLAIN DEALER

"Don't worry...we'll keep trying till we get it right."

U. S. INDUSTRIAL PRODUCTION INDEX
(1967 = 100)

	1970	1971[1]
Industrial production, total	106.7	106.3
Major industry groupings		
Manufacturing, durable and nondurable	105.2	104.8
Mining	109.7	107.1
Utilities	128.5	135.1
Major market groupings		
Consumer goods	110.3	115.3
Equipment, including defense	96.2	89.1
Materials	107.8	106.7

[1] Preliminary. Source: Board of Governors of the Federal Reserve System.

ANNUAL SURVEY OF MANUFACTURES, 1969

	Number of employees	Payroll (millions of dollars)	Value added by manufacture (millions of dollars)
All manufacturing establishments, including administrative and auxiliary units, total[1]	20,029,700	152,504	305,908
Operating manufacturing establishments	19,141,000	142,323	305,908
Nondurable goods			
Food and kindred products	1,656,200	11,136	30,120
Tobacco manufactures	72,100	410	2,385
Textile mill products	971,900	5,149	9,672
Apparel and other textile products	1,382,900	6,401	11,639
Paper and allied products	664,000	5,152	11,284
Printing and publishing	1,082,000	8,290	16,615
Chemicals and allied products	882,900	7,585	27,177
Petroleum and coal products	141,900	1,368	5,725
Rubber and plastics products	570,000	4,040	8,495
Leather and leather products	330,700	1,598	2,944
Durable goods			
Lumber and wood products	565,100	3,233	6,359
Furniture and fixtures	455,600	2,679	5,056
Stone, clay, and glass products	611,900	4,466	10,049
Primary metal industries	1,305,400	11,389	22,714
Fabricated metal products	1,402,800	10,792	20,841
Machinery, except electrical	1,937,700	16,382	31,983
Electrical equipment and supplies	1,915,900	14,792	28,275
Transportation equipment	1,912,300	17,602	35,068
Instruments and related products	414,400	3,271	7,589
Miscellaneous manufacturing industries	445,600	2,639	5,311
Ordnance and accessories	419,700	3,949	6,606

[1] Warehouses, power plants, repair shops and similar facilities that serve the manufacturing establishments of a company rather than the general public were reported separately. Source: U. S. Department of Commerce, Bureau of the Census.

about 5%. The output of consumer goods picked up at midyear and showed signs of continued strength into 1972. Record residential construction in 1971 and the prospect of an excellent housing performance in 1972 led to an upswing in the output of appliances, television sets, and furniture.

Production of business equipment, which had dropped sharply in 1970, declined by 8% in 1971. The output of business equipment slowed in response to the relatively low business expenditures for new plant and equipment.

Manufacturing industries produced a shade less in 1971 than in the year before. As measured by the industrial production index, manufacturing output reached only 104.8 (1967 = 100), compared with 105.2 in 1970. The utilization of manufacturing plant capacity continued to decline in 1971. About 25% of plant capacity was unused, the slackest performance in 13 years. Unused plant capacity amounted to about 22% in 1970.

According to the Annual Survey of Manufactures issued by the Census Bureau in May 1971, more than 20 million persons were employed in manufacturing in 1969, about 500,000 more than in 1968. Wages paid by manufacturing firms totaled $152.2 billion in 1969, $10 billion more than in the previous year. Value added by manufacture reached $305.9 billion in 1969, an increase of almost $16 billion over 1968. (Value added represents the difference between the value of products shipped by manufacturers and the value of the materials and supplies sent to manufacturers for use in production.) In terms of value added, the leading manufacturing groups include the producers of food, chemicals and allied products, nonelectrical machinery, electrical equipment and supplies, and transportation equipment.

AGO AMBRE
Current Business Analysis Division, Office of Business Economics, U. S. Department of Commerce

SALES OF RETAIL STORES, 1969-71
(millions of dollars)

	1970	1969	1971[1]	1970
	Full year		First six months	
All retail stores..............	364,571	351,633	186,258	173,598
Durable goods stores[2].........	109,694	112,779	59,856	54,388
Automotive group............	62,847	66,911	37,120	32,840
Furniture and appliance group....	16,817	16,719	8,064	7,913
Lumber, building, hardware group.	14,535	14,562	7,406	6,650
Nondurable goods stores[2]......	254,877	238,854	126,402	119,210
Apparel group.................	20,396	20,158	9,406	9,022
Drug and proprietary group......	12,750	11,863	6,393	6,048
Eating and drinking places......	27,872	25,849	13,668	13,267
Food group....................	81,466	75,866	41,574	39,597
Gasoline service stations........	26,504	25,116	13,283	12,944
General merchandise group, with nonstores...............	62,867	58,615	30,038	26,978
Department stores..............	38,558	36,411	18,299	16,431

[1] Preliminary. [2] Includes estimates for other kinds of business not shown separately. Source: U.S. Department of Commerce.

RETAIL SALES

Retail sales, which were quite weak in 1970, rose sharply in the first six months of 1971. Spurred by the cyclical recovery in the economy and a resurgence of auto sales as an aftermath of the late-1970 General Motors strike, retail sales for the first half of 1971 totaled $186.3 billion, up 7.3% from a year earlier.

The small rise in retail sales that did occur in 1970 was attributed entirely to inflationary prices rather than to higher physical volume; in the first half of 1971, however, the increase was divided about equally between price advance and physical volume.

In dollar terms, consumer buying failed to keep pace with rising incomes. Personal saving reached the unusually high rate of 8% of income in 1970, and it held that rate throughout the first half of 1971.

Inventories. Stocks at retail stores on June 30, 1971, had a book value of $47.5 billion, an addition of $2.7 billion from a year earlier. Durable and nondurable goods stores shared about equally in the increase. For retailers as a whole, the accumulation in inventory failed to keep pace with the sales advance, and as a result the stock-sales ratio fell from 1.47 months in June 1970 to 1.43 months in June 1971.

Sales Trends. Sales of durable goods stores totaled $59.9 billion in the first six months of 1971, a 10% rise from the corresponding period of 1970. Marketings by automotive dealers advanced 13% over this period, partly due to the making up of sales lost during the auto industry strike late in 1970. Sales by lumber, building, and hardware dealers also rose substantially: the 11% gain reflected the recovery in homebuilding. Sales by furniture and appliance stores, however, were sluggish in the first half of 1971, rising only 2% from a year earlier.

Sales of nondurable goods stores rose 6% from the first half of 1970 to the first half of 1971. Department stores and other general merchandise stores each reported sales gains of more than 11%. For food, apparel, and drug stores, sales gains ranged from 4% to 6%. Eating and drinking establishments and gasoline service stations registered 3% increases.

Total retail sales rose 8% from the first half of 1970 to the first half of 1971 in the North Central states, the South, and the West, but by only 4% in the Northeast.

WHOLESALE SALES

Sales by merchant wholesalers totaled $128.8 billion in the first six months of 1971, an advance of 7.5% from the corresponding months of 1970. About three fifths of this increase reflected a higher physical volume of goods passing through wholesale channels, and the rest resulted from a 3% rise in wholesale prices. Sales declines were confined to dealers in metals and metalwork and in scrap and waste materials.

Inventories. The book value of inventories held by merchant wholesalers totaled $27.4 billion on June 30, 1971, up $2.4 billion from mid-1970. This was a smaller increase than was experienced in sales over this period. As a consequence, the stock-sales ratio fell from 1.18 months in June 1970 to 1.15 months in June 1971.

Sales Trends. Sales by establishments dealing primarily in durable goods totaled a record $58.6 billion in the first half of 1971, up 7% from a year earlier. The sharp recovery in residential construction activity from its depressed level in early 1970 produced above-average sales advances in three segments: lumber and construction materials, up 13%; furniture and home furnishings, up 12%; and hardware, plumbing, heating equipment, and supplies, up 9%. Motor vehicles and automotive equipment advanced even more—by 19%.

Sales by nondurable goods wholesalers reached a record $70.1 billion for the first half of 1971, up almost 8%. Sales of farm products (raw materials) were particularly strong—up 15%. Dry goods and apparel sales rose 14%. Sales of beer, wine, and alcoholic beverages rose 9%, and sales of tobacco and tobacco products gained 8%. Sales increases were below average—about 4% each—for groceries and related products, paper and paper products, and drugs, chemicals, and allied products. Among food wholesalers, sales of grocery products were stronger than those of meats, poultry, fruits, and vegetables.

LAWRENCE BRIDGE
Office of Business Economics
U. S. Department of Commerce

MERCHANT WHOLESALERS' SALES, 1969-71
(millions of dollars)

	1970	1969	1971	1970
	Full year		First six months	
Merchant wholesalers, total...	246,643	236,708	128,749	119,782
Durable goods[1]	111,778	109,578	58,648	54,777
Motor vehicles, automotive equipment...............	20,202	18,493	11,736	9,871
Electrical goods.............	15,808	15,748	7,793	7,497
Furniture, home furnishings..	5,345	5,422	2,851	2,553
Hardware, plumbing, heating equipment, supplies.	10,634	10,748	5,587	5,133
Lumber, construction materials................	10,837	11,750	5,843	5,156
Machinery, equipment, supplies..................	28,516	28,093	15,040	14,100
Metals, metalwork (except scrap).............	12,626	11,794	6,301	6,396
Scrap waste material.........	5,985	5,542	2,656	3,238
Nondurable goods[1]........	134,865	127,130	70,101	65,005
Groceries and related products..................	50,431	47,771	25,894	24,843
Beer, wine, distilled alcoholic beverages........	12,860	11,913	6,420	5,879
Drugs, chemicals, allied products............	9,619	9,369	4,983	4,753
Tobacco, tobacco products....	6,117	5,752	3,152	2,914
Dry goods, apparel..........	10,390	10,157	5,564	4,891
Paper, paper products (excluding wallpaper)......	7,318	7,296	3,749	3,612
Farm products (raw materials)...........	14,336	13,449	7,821	6,798
Other nondurable goods.....	23,794	21,514	12,519	11,316

[1] Totals include data for some kinds of business not listed separately. Source: U.S. Department of Commerce.

ECUADOR

Political uncertainty continued to prevail in Ecuador in 1971. The nation's 78-year-old president, José María Velasco Ibarra, who had been elected to the presidency for the fifth time in 1968 and had seized dictatorial power in June 1970, ruled by decree throughout the year.

Political Developments. The 1970 coup had given the president an opportunity to tighten control of administrative and economic affairs in Ecuador. Investigation had proved that over 50% of the people and corporations with taxable incomes had evaded payment entirely. Vigorous collection procedures were instituted, and although they evoked sharp protests, they succeeded in reducing a projected budget deficit from 2.5 billion sucres ($100 million) to 29 million sucres. In August 1971 a 39% devaluation of the sucre began a process that was expected to treble the Central Bank's foreign exchange holdings by the end of the year.

Meanwhile, partisan political activity was sharply restricted, and many opposition leaders were jailed or expelled. Young and generally leftist army officers presumed to favor Velasco were given important posts, but the limits on the president's power became evident in April, when his nephew, Defense Minister Jorge Acosta Velasco, was forced to leave the country after seeking the removal of several conservative senior army officers.

Prospective Elections. In July it was announced that general elections were being scheduled for June of 1972. Velasco let it be known that he would support former President Camilo Ponce Enríquez, a Christian Democrat, for the presidential office. It appeared that Asaad Bucaram, a populist and leftist, would become the principal opposition candidate.

The voters were also to be asked to choose in 1972 between the 1946 and 1967 constitutions. The latter, which had been in force when Velasco won election in 1968, was decidedly parliamentary in character. Velasco favored the 1946 constitution, which, if adopted, would restore a strong presidency.

Economic Affairs. Economic developments remained generally favorable in 1971; the gross national product (GNP) was expected to rise at a rate approximating the more than 4.5% recorded in 1969 and 1970. Industry's share of the GNP, which had risen to 20% of the total in 1970, continued to grow.

Agricultural conditions were good, with exports of bananas, coffee, cacao, and sugar continuing to increase. Ecuador had led the world in banana exports in 1970. With the nation's total imports holding steady in the first half of 1971 while total exports rose, a 50% cut in the foreign trade deficit was being predicted for the year.

Ecuador's industrial growth was being aided by dynamic government and private financing policies and sizable international loans. As in other Latin American countries, however, the gains were hardly keeping pace with population expansion. Hopes for more spectacular development focused on the growth potential of the budding 5-nation common market called the Andean Group and, to an even greater degree, on an anticipated bonanza from oil.

Petroleum. Oil profits were expected to begin adding significantly to the GNP after 1972. Coastal drilling had proved the existence of large natural gas resources, while drilling northeast of the Andes had raised daily petroleum production capacity to more than 50,000 barrels by August 1971. The Texaco-Gulf consortium's pipeline over the mountains to the port of Esmeraldas was to have a capacity of 250,000 barrels per day and was scheduled for completion in late 1972, and Ecuador's oil exports were expected to reach one million barrels a day by 1978. Some 20 U. S. and British companies held petroleum concessions in the eastern region. On Jan. 28, 1971, the Ecuadorian State Petroleum Corporation (CEPE) was established to hold all state petroleum assets and to succeed to the titles of properties as private concessions expire.

Inter-American Affairs. Relations with the United States were tense during the 1970–71 tuna season, as Ecuador seized 18 California-based tuna boats for poaching in its "territorial waters." Ecuador claimed control of its offshore waters to a distance of 200 miles (320 km), while the United States recognized only a 12-mile (19-km) limit. Fines totaling nearly $1 million were levied against U. S. shipowners. The Council of the Organization of American States debated the matter in January 1971 and supported Ecuador. The United States briefly suspended military sales to Ecuador in retaliation. Bilateral negotiations failed to resolve the dispute.

Cooperative programs with neighboring Peru and Colombia were mounted for joint development of border regions. In August, Chile's leftist president, Salvador Allende, visited Ecuador during a goodwill tour of west-coast countries.

Ecuador seemed much more sympathetic to nationalist and leftist regimes in 1971, urging Cuba to return to the OAS and voting for the admission of the People's Republic of China to the United Nations in October.

PHILIP B. TAYLOR, JR.
University of Houston

ECUADOR • Information Highlights

Official Name: Republic of Ecuador.
Area: 109,483 square miles (283,561 sq km).
Population (1970 est.): 6,100,000. *Density,* 54 per square mile (21 per sq km). *Annual rate of increase,* 3.4%.
Chief Cities (1970 est.): Quito, the capital, 530,000; Guayaquil, 790,000.
Government: *Head of state,* José María Velasco Ibarra, president (took office Sept. 1, 1968). *Head of government,* José María Velasco Ibarra.
Languages: Spanish (official).
Education: *Literacy rate* (1971), 68% of population. *Expenditure on education* (1968), 21.8% of total public expenditure. *School enrollment* (1967)—primary, 897,539; secondary, 151,197; technical/vocational, 49,629; university/higher, 19,600.
Finances (1968): *Revenues,* $152,500,000; *expenditures,* $216,500,000; *monetary unit,* sucre (25.00 sucres equal U. S.$1, Sept. 1971).
Gross National Product (1969): $1,627,200,000.
National Income (1969): $1,391,750,000.
Economic Indexes: *Manufacturing production* (1968), 180 (1963=100); *agricultural production* (1969), 133 (1963=100); *consumer price index* (1969), 120 (1965=100).
Manufacturing (metric tons, 1969): Residual fuel oil, 352,000; sugar, 250,000; wheat flour, 92,000; meat, 85,000; beer, 589,000 hectoliters.
Crops (metric tons, 1968 crop year): Bananas, 2,693,000 (ranks 3d among world producers); rice (1969), 288,000; cassava, 280,000; maize (1969), 210,000.
Minerals (metric tons, 1969): Crude petroleum, 207,000; salt, 40,000; silver, 3.9.
Foreign Trade (1970): *Exports,* $218,000,000 (chief exports—bananas, $111,000,000; coffee, $50,500,000; cacao, $22,100,000). *Imports,* $247,000,000 (chief imports, 1968—mineral fuels and lubricants, $12,895,000; food, $12,690,000). *Chief trading partners* (1968)—United States (took 42% of exports, supplies 35% of imports); West Germany (11%–13%); Japan (10%–7%).
Transportation: *Roads* (1970), 7,077 miles (11,389 km); *motor vehicles* (1969), 59,500 (automobiles, 25,500); *railroads* (1970), 727 miles (1,170 km); *principal airports,* Quito, Guayaquil.
Communications: *Telephones* (1970), 94,300; *television stations* (1968), 7; *television sets* (1968), 71,000; *radios* (1969), 1,200,000; *newspapers* (1969), 25.

Surging admissions frequently force schools to set up temporary classrooms in all available space. City College of New York crammed six rooms into its Great Hall.

education

In 1971 public debate over issues related to education reached new levels of intensity. The busing of pupils from their residential areas to achieve racial balance in individual public schools became a matter of heated controversy, and certain groups advocated a constitutional amendment to prohibit the practice.

School integration became a way of life in the South, but segregated private academies continued to increase. Methods of school financing, the plight of parochial schools, direct federal aid to colleges and universities, and the legality of school prayer were among the problems that engaged the attention of large segments of the population and their elected representatives.

INTEGRATION

Progress in the South. In the 11-state South, the percentage of Negro students in schools having a majority of white students more than doubled between 1968–69 and 1970–71, rising from 18% to 39%, according to a detailed national survey made by the U.S. Office of Education. The greatest amount of integration appeared to have been achieved in the South. Nationally, the total of Negro students in majority-white schools rose only from 23% to 33%. By regions, the percentage in the 32 Northern and Western states remained un-

changed at 28%. In terms of numbers, 756,000 more Negro students were in majority-white schools in 1970 than in 1968. A total of 690,000 of these students were in the 11-state South, and only 66,-000 in 38 other states (Hawaii was not included).

Even more striking statistics were reported for all-Negro schools. Nationally, the percentage of Negroes in schools with a 100% nonwhite enrollment decreased from 40% to 14% in the 2-year period, or from 2,500,000 to 941,000. In the 11 Southern states, the decrease was even more marked, down from 68% to 14%, or in terms of numbers of students, from 2,000,000 to 443,000.

Data on the nation's 100 largest school systems were also obtained. In 17 of these systems, the majority of the pupils were black. The percentage of Negroes in the 100 largest cities who attended majority-white schools increased from 13% in 1968 to 16% in 1970. In many Northern cities racial isolation actually increased, as the percentage of blacks in white-majority schools dropped.

In January 1972, U.S. District Court Judge Robert R. Merhige, Jr., in a decision having far-ranging implications for metropolitan areas in both North and South, ordered the merger of the schools of two mostly black counties in Virginia with the schools of mostly white Richmond. The ruling was being appealed.

Segregated Private Schools. Private schools continued to spring up in the South. The Southern Regional Council estimated that between 450,000 and 500,000 students in 11 Southern states were attending private segregated schools in 1971. This equaled about 4% of the total public school enrollment of 11.7 million in these states.

The council asserted that these new academies tended to offer substandard, academically inferior education to a growing number of white students, while posing a great threat to public education in some areas, especially where funds are alloted on the basis of public school enrollment. In addition, there was a tendency to vote down bond issues for public schools in districts where many children are sent to private schools.

The greatest development of private segregated schools occurred in Mississippi, Alabama, Louisiana, and South Carolina, where there was a decline in public school enrollment.

During the year federal courts began an examination of the tax-exempt status of these schools.

SCHOOL PRAYER ISSUE

Outlawed by the U. S. Supreme Court in 1962 and again in 1963, organized prayers in public schools still have their staunch supporters. Scores of proposals for a constitutional amendment perished in the House Judiciary Committee. In 1971 advocates resorted to petition to compel action by the House. Under the leadership of Rep. Chalmers P. Wylie of Ohio, the necessary 218 members signed a petition to bring the amendment out of the Judiciary Committee to a vote by the House.

The amendment, as finally worded, read: "Nothing contained in this Constitution shall abridge the right of persons lawfully assembled, in any public building which is supported in whole or in part through expenditure of public funds, to participate in voluntary prayer or meditation."

A two-thirds majority was necessary for House approval. When the amendment came to a vote on Nov. 8, 1971, it failed by 28 votes to win this majority. The vote was 240 in favor and 162 opposed.

Sponsors of the amendment claimed that the majority of Americans wanted it. Opponents, including many leaders of major church organizations, called it an attack on the religious freedom guarantee in the Bill of Rights. They charged that the amendment would endanger religious freedom by involving the state in religion.

FINANCING EDUCATION

During the 1970–71 school year, a total of $28 billion was spent for higher education ($18.1 billion for public and $9.9 billion for private), while the cost of elementary and secondary education reached $49.6 billion ($44.6 billion for public and $5 billion for private).

Expenditures for 1971–72 were expected to rise to $31 billion for higher education and $54.1 billion for elementary and secondary education, according to U. S. Office of Education estimates.

Federal grants for education continued to grow. They rose from $3.4 billion in 1965 to $10.1 billion in 1971, and were expected to reach $11.4 billion in the fiscal year ending June 30, 1972.

In July 1971, President Nixon signed into law a $5.15 billion education appropriation bill that increased spending for the coming school year by $375 million above the President's request. When

such legislation exceeded his budget in 1969 and again in 1970, he vetoed the appropriation bills. In 1970 Congress overrode the veto. The 1971 bill was the largest appropriation in history for the U. S. Office of Education.

Support of Schools by Property Taxes. On Aug. 30, 1971, the California supreme court, in a precedent-shattering decision, ruled that the system of financing schools largely by local property taxes is unconstitutional, since its effect is to discriminate against the poor. Local property taxes produce greater revenues in the wealthier school districts, thus making possible a high-quality education for these children even though the tax rate itself may be lower than in the poorer districts.

Almost all of the states use this method of financing schools, and the system almost invariably produces wide disparities in revenue per school child between the rich districts and the poor districts. About 50% of the school funds raised nationally come from local school taxes. In California it is about 56%.

Government and school officials termed the ruling a landmark decision. If sustained by the U. S. Supreme Court—and an appeal was planned—it could revolutionize the financing of schools in the United States. Almost certainly, more of the burden of providing school revenue would be shifted to the state level, which now provides an average of 41% of education costs.

Parochial School Aid. On June 28, 1971, the U. S. Supreme Court declared unconstitutional the programs for aiding parochial schools through the use of public funds in Rhode Island and in Pennsylvania. Both plans involved paying part of the salaries of teachers of secular subjects. While the decision affected all church-related schools below college level, the Roman Catholic educational system felt the impact most keenly. Of the 6 million children

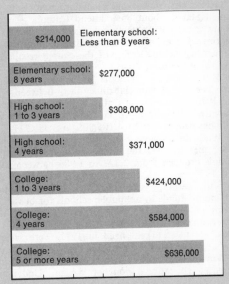

EFFECT OF EDUCATION ON EARNING POWER
(Lifetime income of men, by years of school completed.[1])

$214,000	Elementary school: Less than 8 years
Elementary school: 8 years	$277,000
High school: 1 to 3 years	$308,000
High school: 4 years	$371,000
College: 1 to 3 years	$424,000
College: 4 years	$584,000
College: 5 or more years	$636,000

[1]U.S. Data for 1968 from U.S. Bureau of Census; chart adapted from *American Education* magazine, U.S. Department of Health, Education, and Welfare.

WILLIAM J. COOK—NEWSWEEK

CHILDREN in Livermore, Calif., listen to tape-recorded lessons without direct supervision. Informal education, designed to put the joy back in learning, is becoming increasingly popular in U. S. schools.

in private elementary and secondary schools in the United States, about 85% attend Catholic schools. Rising costs of educational facilities, increasing salaries of teachers, and diminishing numbers of women in teaching orders of the church resulted in a growing financial crisis.

Many parochial schools have been forced to close because of financial difficulties. Between 1967 and 1970 the number of Catholic elementary schools decreased 10%, from 10,350 to 9,366, and the enrollment dropped from 4,105,805 to 3,359,311. While the secondary enrollment remained slightly over one million, the number of Catholic high schools dropped from 2,277 to 1,986 between 1967 and 1970.

Still operating were several programs that provide public funds to nonpublic schools for bus transportation, school lunches, secular textbooks, and driver training. Advocates of aid for teachers' salaries, the most urgent need in 1971, were seeking new approaches to the problem.

Voucher System. There is growing interest in a proposed educational voucher system. Under this plan, families would be issued vouchers that could be used to pay for the education of each school-age child at any school, public or private, he wished to attend. Such a plan provides aid to pupils rather than to schools. Public school administrators have opposed the plan.

Federal Aid to Higher Education. Many institutions of higher learning are experiencing financial difficulties. Costs for salaries and operation continue to rise. Tuition charges, already at an all-time high, have not kept pace with upward-spiralling costs.

In 1971 both the House and the Senate passed legislation to give general-purpose federal grants to every college and university. For years, federal funds were granted for special purposes, such as research, construction, or student aid; however, there had never been a program of direct assistance that would let the colleges use the federal funds as they wish.

Some form of direct federal assistance seemed certain. However, the House amended the higher education bill to include restrictions on federal action related to busing. Before a House-Senate conference could work out a compromise measure, the Senate had to combine its own two bills. On November 25, the Senate postponed further action until January 1972.

By a 5-to-4 decision the Supreme Court ruled that the federal government can use tax money to help church-affiliated colleges and universities build libraries, science laboratories, and gymnasiums. Over $240 million was allocated to private colleges, including church-related institutions, for such construction under the Federal Higher Education Facilities Act of 1963.

ENROLLMENT AND TEACHER SUPPLY

Enrollment Trends. For the 27th consecutive year the enrollment in the nation's public and private educational institutions increased, heading toward a predicted record of 60,200,000. At the same time, expenditures for public and private education at all levels of 1971–72 were expected to reach $85.1 billion, or 8% of the gross national product, according to the National Center for Educational Statistics, U. S. Office of Education.

The secondary school enrollment (grades 9–12) increased slightly from 14,840,000 in fall 1970 to 15,150,000 in fall 1971, according to estimates of the U. S. Office of Education. During the same period the elementary school enrollment dropped less than 1%, from 36,970,000 to 36,700,000, a result of the decline in births during the mid-1960's.

The high school graduating class of 1972 is expected to total a record 3.1 million. In 1971, 3 million persons received diplomas. Approximately 77.1% of all 18-year-olds were graduating from high school by 1971, and 60% of these graduates were going on to college.

The projected increase in higher education enrollment—6%—would be the highest ever recorded. The estimated fall 1971 enrollment of 8,400,000 represented an increase of 500,000 over the previous year. These figures did not include nearly 700,000 undergraduates in occupational or general studies programs not leading to a degree.

The most marked increase occurred in the public institutions, especially 2-year community colleges. Many small private colleges experienced losses in enrollment and faced financial difficulties.

Teaching Staff. The teaching staff for fall 1971 was estimated to total 2,360,000, an increase of about 20,000 over 1970. The number of college and university teachers was expected to total 617,000, an increase of 30,000 in one year.

The percentage of new teachers in public schools has been increasing. In 1970–71 they totaled 32.7% (13.7% of the elementary and 53.7% of the secondary). About 86% of the men and 77% of the women teachers were married.

The average annual salary of teachers continued its upward trend. It went from $8,250 in 1969–70 to an estimated $9,210 in 1970–71, according to the National Center for Educational Statistics. The average salary of all institutional personnel (including principals and supervisors) rose from $8,840 to $9,600 in the same period.

Oversupply of Teachers. The number of college graduates completing preparation for teaching reached a record level while the need for new teachers dropped to its lowest point in recent history. The National Education Association's annual survey revealed that the 1970 supply of beginning elementary teachers was 37,600 more than the number of positions to be filled. In secondary schools the 1970 supply exceeded the demand by 50,650, whereas the margin was 41,400 in the previous year.

The fields in which teachers were in short supply were mathematics, physical sciences, industrial arts, special education, and some vocational technical subjects. However, cutbacks in the space program provided a new source of teachers of mathematics and the physical sciences.

It is estimated that by 1980 there will be two teachers for every job opening. The reasons given for the oversupply are the sharp drop in the birthrate in the 1960's, with a corresponding leveling off of the increase in the number of children in the first grade; the large number of young people born during the baby boom following World War II who chose teaching as a career; and the reduction or lack of increase in teaching staff in large city school systems faced with budget difficulties.

Institutions preparing teachers are designing new curricula for other types of service careers, for example in human resources, health care, urban problems, and business.

TRENDS IN HIGHER EDUCATION

Degrees Conferred. Data published in 1971 showed that the number of bachelor's and advanced degrees conferred in the United States within a 12-month period had passed the one million mark. A survey by the U. S. Office of Education reported that during the year ending June 30, 1970, 1,072,-581 degrees were awarded by 1,617 institutions of higher learning. This was an increase of 50% over the 714,624 degrees conferred during the 12-month period that ended June 30, 1966.

There was a marked increase in the proportion of women earning degrees, although they continued to lag behind the men in the actual number conferred.

In the decade ending June 1970, more doctor's degrees were conferred than in all previous years combined. From the time the first Ph. D. degree in this country was conferred by Yale in 1861 through June 1960, only about 177,000 doctorates were awarded, according to the National Center for Educational Statistics. However, in the next 10 years, approximately 184,000 were awarded. The number of doctorates trebled between 1959–60, when 9,829 were awarded, and 1969–70, when 29,-866 were conferred. These statistics do not include first professional degrees, such as M. D., D. D. S., and D. V. M.

College Presidents in Demand. One result of unrest on college campuses has been the reluctance of educators to contend with the succession of problems and crises that chief administrative responsibility involves. By 1971 the average college president remained in office only about five years. The annual turnover had risen nearly 30% in three years.

Innovations in Higher Education. In an authoritative report entitled *Less Time, More Options: Education Beyond the High School*, the Carnegie Commission on Higher Education called for some basic and far-reaching changes in the traditional structure of higher education.

It reported that undergraduate education can be reduced in length by one fourth without reducing quality. It suggested that young people have the option of deferring college attendance, or of dropping out for a time for work or service experience. It proposed greater use of the new degrees of Master of Philosophy (M. Phil.) and Doctor of Arts (D. A.). It emphasized that higher education should be viewed as a lifetime process, a combination of work and study, rather than just a program for recent high school graduates. Such a mixture would reduce the isolation between students and workers or students

TEACHERS picket outside high school in Decatur, Ill., on August 25 as amused members of school's football team encourage them. Strike was one of the first in response to President Nixon's wage and price freeze.

UPI

and the more mature. Part-time study and return to study later in life should be encouraged. These reforms could result in a substantial reduction in operating expenses, the commission stated.

Meanwhile, many changes were occurring. Rigid requirements for the bachelor's degree were giving way to individually planned programs along the lines of the student's interests. Many colleges permit students to do up to one fourth of their work in independent study. Innovative procedures include permitting students who feel they already know the content of a required course to take a test and, if successful, to receive credit for the course.

In line with the Carnegie report, some colleges have established routine 3-year degree programs and also decelerated programs that permit time out for work or travel. Career counseling and guidance have become increasingly important. For the faculty, much more emphasis was placed on teaching and a great deal less on research.

Trend Toward Coeducation. In 1970–71 there were 2,573 colleges, universities, and professional schools in the United States and its outlying areas, an increase of 545 in a decade. During this period the number of coeducational institutions rose from 1,533 to 2,226; the number for men only dropped from 236 to 154; and the number for women only dropped from 259 to 193.

Only 16 of the single-sex institutions (11 for men and 5 for women) are publicly controlled. Two fifths of the privately controlled men's or women's colleges are church-affiliated.

Most of the institutions now attended exclusively by men or women are small; four fifths enroll fewer than 1,000 students. The entire group of 347 institutions enrolls only about 3% of all college students today.

Coeducational Fraternities and Dormitories. College fraternities are becoming coeducational, according to the Washington *Post*. The national office of Delta Psi, a fraternity known on many campuses as St. Anthony Hall, approved in 1971 the pledging of seven women students as members of the University of North Carolina Chapter, thus making Delta Psi the first national fraternity to accept women on the same basis as men. It was anticipated that plans to permit the women to reside in St. Anthony Hall would be approved.

At Stanford University, women members living in the Lambda Nu house occupy one wing of the building. Local fraternities have been electing and housing women students for the past three years.

Co-ed dormitories are operating successfully at such institutions as Oberlin, Stanford, Michigan State, the University of Michigan, and the University of Maryland. Most plans provide for an alternate-floor setup and restrict room visiting after certain hours. Oberlin permits the students to make their own residential rules. College administrators report that co-ed living does not lead to promiscuity.

Yale University announced the appointment of two women to the board of trustees, the first since its founding. One of them was the second black to serve on the Yale Corporation.

OTHER DEVELOPMENTS

Multi-ethnic Textbooks. In 1971 educators and publishers accelerated their efforts to depict blacks and other minorities more representatively and positively in textbooks. Reading texts now picture and describe the activities of black children in inner-city environments, as well as the familiar suburban characters. History books recount the contributions of blacks and other minority groups to the development of the nation.

Year-round Schools. The year-round operation of schools has long been advocated as a means of reducing school costs, more effectively utilizing both school plant and teaching and supervisory staff, providing a more flexible program of instruction, and avoiding an enforced idleness of teachers and students for a 3-month period. Family vacation patterns have changed, and summer employment opportunities for youth are more limited, so that the loss of summer breaks seems less objectionable.

In 1971, about 600 school systems in the United States were considering various plans for year-round operation, such as the 4-quarter and the 11-month systems. In Virginia, 15 school divisions were developing pilot programs. Prince William county, not far from Washington, was seeking to accommodate large increases in school enrollment by the year-round operation of selected schools. Pupils in these schools were divided into four groups, with each group going to school for nine weeks and then being off three weeks so that only three student clusters would be in school at the same time.

Environmental Education. A groundswell in favor of environmental improvement, sponsored especially by young people, has resulted in new educational measures on the state and national level. In July 1971, the Office of Education announced 74 grants totaling $1.7 million as the first awards under the Environmental Education Act of 1970.

Projects funded include community education plans, curriculum development, establishment of environmental education centers, personnel training, and dissemination of information. Environmental quality and ecological balance are the goals sought.

Performance Contracting. One new idea in education involves paying private firms to teach certain school subjects with the provision that the contractors' pay is determined solely by their success in improving the skill of the students. As tested experimentally by the Office of Economic Opportunity in 1970–71 through grants to 18 widely scattered school districts, the program was limited to teaching underachievers reading and mathematics. The level had to be improved at least 1.6 grades before the contractor would begin to make a profit.

In Virginia the experiment involved 2,400 children in seven school divisions, all of them at least two years behind in reading ability. The contractor lost heavily. Only about a fourth of the children registered the promised gain. One third of them made no gain at all, according to results reported to the state board of education.

In Gary, Ind., where, three years earlier, many black students were below the national average for their grade in reading, performance contracting, using specially trained teachers and individual workbook materials, enabled 73% of the children to reach or exceed national norms in reading and mathematics. However, the results were spotty. Only 40% of the sixth graders reached the average level in reading and 69% attained the average level in mathematics. As a result, the contracting firm had to refund $75,000 to the school system.

EDWARD ALVEY, JR.
Mary Washington College
of the University of Virginia

BATTLE OVER BUSING

Conflicts between Health, Education, and Welfare Department's desegregation guidelines and anti-busing statements by President Nixon caused confusion.

DON WRIGHT/THE MIAMI NEWS

When the public schools opened in the fall of 1971, hundreds of thousands of children were bused out of their home neighborhoods in an effort to create an equitable balance of black and white pupils in the classrooms. In many districts students and parents accepted busing, and schools functioned without serious disruptions. This transporting of students was done in compliance with orders of federal courts and policies of the federal Department of Health, Education, and Welfare (HEW). On the other hand, the White House expressed opposition to large-scale busing. Some white citizens tried threats and boycotts to stop busing. Congressmen introduced legislation to restrict busing for racial integration. In general, there was evidence of confusion in government policy and public attitudes.

In April 1971, the U. S. Supreme Court unanimously approved large-scale busing and limited racial balancing as means of assuring an integrated education for black children. Dismissing arguments against busing, the court ruled that "desegregated plans cannot be limited to the walk-in school." In a case involving Charlotte, N. C., the court approved an extensive bus plan to exchange pupils between city schools and schools in surrounding Mecklenburg county.

The ruling ran counter to a position the Nixon administration had already taken in opposition to massive busing and in support of the neighborhood school concept. In August, President Nixon, discussing a plan involving extensive busing drawn up by HEW for Austin, Texas, restated his opposition to busing "for the sake of busing." He ordered HEW to work with school districts "to hold busing to the minimum required by law."

When schools opened in September, at least 300,000 pupils were being transported in accordance with desegregation plans set up by courts or by HEW. This extensive busing was not new. In 1970–71 much of the progress toward racial balance in Southern schools was achieved by busing students from black neighborhoods to schools in white areas, many in the suburbs, and vice versa. The fall 1971 drive increased the numbers involved in an attempt to achieve racial balance in every school.

There was confusion over what the law really required—over how much busing and what extent of racial mixing was necessary. Chief Justice Warren Burger, in a 10-page decision, seemed to express some misgivings about the busing orders being handed down by lower courts to achieve racial balance in every school. "The constitutional command to desegregate schools," wrote Justice Burger, "does not mean that every school in every community must always reflect the racial composition of the school system as a whole."

Nevertheless, Chief Justice Burger said, quoting from the ruling in the Charlotte case, ". . . We find no basis for holding that the local school authorities may not be required to employ bus transportation as one tool of school desegregation." He stated that districts must weigh factors such as time or distance of travel and age of pupils in ordering bus transportation programs.

In most instances, court-ordered busing increased greatly the number of pupils transported. There was a shortage of school buses, and in some areas public bus companies did not have enough equipment to help out. In Richmond, Va., a court-ordered integration plan required the transportation of 18,000 of the city's 48,000 pupils, or 7,000 more than in the preceding year. Similar increases were ordered for other Virginia cities. In Norfolk, 24,000 pupils were being bused to improve racial balance in the schools. Norfolk lost 2,100 white students from public schools in 1970–71, the first year of the busing program.

In Richmond, Va., a suit was brought in the U. S. District Court to compel the merger of the schools of the city, two thirds black, with the schools of suburban Henrico and Chesterfield counties, 90% white. The plan would produce a racial balance of 7 whites to 3 blacks in each school, but long-distance busing would be required. Backers of the plan called it the only way to achieve racial balance. The flight of families to the suburbs did not leave enough white pupils to provide balance.

As court-ordered busing programs went into effect in hundreds of school districts, confusion and resentment were evident. In general, however, classes began on schedule in an atmosphere of relative calm. There were numerous small incidents in individual schools, but these were handled with firmness and dispatch by school authorities.

On the other hand, open defiance flared in spots. In Pontiac, Mich., an automobile manufacturing town of about 84,000 near Detroit, 8,700 of the 24,000 elementary and junior high school pupils were ordered bused. Eight days before school opened 10 school buses were blown up in the night. An ex-grand dragon of the Michigan Ku Klux Klan, along with four other men, was charged with the dynamiting. Meanwhile, white parents organized the National Action Group Against Busing. This group repudiated the violence of the bombers. However, Pontiac mothers tried to block the school buses from moving out on the first day of school, and protesters succeeded in shutting down the Fisher Body Works for a day.

In San Francisco the school board lost an appeal to block busing of 20,000 school children to mix Negroes, Chinese, and whites in class-rooms. Resentment against the plan was especially strong among the Chinese. They declared that they wanted their children to stay in neighborhood schools and preserve the traditions of Chinese culture. A city-wide boycott cut public elementary school attendance to 58.6% on opening day. While attendance later climbed to 72%, large numbers of Chinese kept their children out of public school. Four private elementary schools opened in Chinatown with an initial enrollment of about 1,000.

Perhaps the largest busing operation in the country faced the city of Los Angeles. A federal court ordered a busing program that would entail transporting 240,000 pupils a day for distances ranging up to 25 miles. The cost was estimated

at $180 million over an eight-year period. School authorities appealed to a higher court.

In addition to local protests, there was evidence that resistance to busing was growing across the nation. On October 26, 28 leaders of antibusing groups from 47 cities met in Washington to support a constitutional amendment to end com-pulsory busing to achieve racial balance in schools. The proposed amendment provides that "No public-school student shall, because of his race, creed, or color, be assigned to or required to attend a particular school." It was introduced by Rep. Norman F. Lent of New York, who declared that America's educational system had become completely color-conscious as a result of the busing program. By November more than 100 representatives had signed a discharge petition to move the measure out of the House Judiciary Committee to the floor for a vote. To do this, 218 signatures are required.

Leaders of a movement called United Con-cerned Citizens of America talked with members of Congress and picketed the Supreme Court building. They maintained that the right of a parent to send his child to his neighborhood school should be restored, even if a constitutional amendment proved necessary.

On October 26 the U. S. Supreme Court unani-mously refused, without comment, to review the order of a federal district court that required the busing of some 10,000 pupils to improve racial balance in the public schools of Pontiac, Mich. On October 27 the Michigan legislature formally recorded its opposition to such busing and urged amending the U. S. Constitution to prohibit it.

Results of a Gallup Poll released on Nov. 1, 1971, showed that 76% of the respondents op-posed the busing of Negro and white children from one school district to another. A majority of white parents who opposed busing said they would not mind sending their children to schools where the proportion of Negroes was as high as 50%.

The chief reasons cited for opposition to busing, according to the Gallup Poll, were the following: Opponents felt that children should go to school where they live. Objectors saw busing as an unneeded expense—the money could be better spent to improve the quality of education for all pupils. They considered the time spent on long bus trips enervating and wasteful.

The 18% reported as in favor of busing said that it would upgrade the quality of education for Negroes and, in time, improve race relations.

On November 5 the House approved President Nixon's request for $1.5 billion to help schools desegregate but added strong restrictions on the use of busing to accomplish the goal. One restric-tion banned the expenditure of any federal funds on busing; another prevented the federal govern-ment from requiring a state to use its own funds for busing; and a third delayed the effective date of court-ordered busing plans until all appeals have been exhausted.

The desegregation measure and the antibusing amendments were actually additions to a multi-billion-dollar higher education bill. The Senate had passed separate bills to aid higher education and desegregation without any busing restrictions. Attempts to combine the two bills were postponed until January 1972.

EDWARD ALVEY, JR.

PROTESTERS block school buses in Pontiac, Mich., at start of school year in September. Bitter opposition to court–ordered busing to achieve racial balance in schools led to bombing of 10 buses in city in August.

UPI

ASWAN High Dam, built with Soviet aid, was dedicated on January 15. President Sadat and Soviet President Podgorny (*left of center*) attended ceremonies opening vast power and irrigation project.

EGYPT

In 1971, following the establishment of a federation with Libya and Syria, Egypt formally changed its name from the United Arab Republic to the Arab Republic of Egypt. After overcoming a threatened coup in May, President Anwar el-Sadat seemed firmly in control of the country. The struggle with Israel continued in its unhappy course, and by the end of the year it appeared that the Egyptians were determined on war.

Domestic Affairs. President Sadat powerfully consolidated his position during the year. In May he alleged that a coup had been attempted against him by such highly placed figures as Aly Sabry, vice president and long-time associate of Nasser; Gen. Mohammed Fawzi, minister of war; and Sharawy Gomaa, minister of the interior. Sadat forced a number of prominent government officials to resign and then purged government and military ranks of several hundred individuals. Altogether some 91 defendants were tried for treason, 4 of them, including Sabry, were condemned to death, but Sadat commuted their sentences to life imprisonment.

Sadat had made other moves to establish an independent political base for himself. In late December 1970 he had banned most of the arbitrary seizures of property that had come to characterize the Nasser period, and shortly thereafter he ordered the return of some of this property to its original owners. In May he declared the necessity of building a new Egypt, in which all could be "free and secure." As if to symbolize this, he personally helped in the public burning of secret dossiers and tapes of telephone conversations taken from the ministry of the interior after Gomaa's downfall.

In July, Sadat introduced a new constitution, which was approved by referendum in September. The constitution strengthened civil rights and gave more power to the National Assembly, but the country's basically presidential government was retained. July also saw the reorganization of Egypt's only political party, the Arab Socialist Union, as a result of elections that were almost certainly intended to remove elements potentially hostile to Sadat. Inevitably the National Assembly was dissolved (September); the new one would be even more pro-Sadat.

The Impasse with Israel. At the end of 1971, President Sadat spelled out his attitude toward a settlement with Israel. He demanded that Israel return all the Arab territory seized in 1967, stating that in return Egypt would recognize Israel's right to exist and would accept Israeli right of passage through the Gulf of Aqaba. If the Palestinian refugee problem were settled as well, Israel could have transit rights through the Suez Canal. Sadat stressed, however, that there would never be normal diplomatic relations between Egypt and Israel.

In February the Egyptians agreed to a 30-day extension of the cease-fire along the Suez Canal. They also proposed that Israeli troops make a partial withdrawal from the canal, permitting that waterway to be cleared and reopened for traffic. During the remainder of the year, there were many more offers and counteroffers concerning the canal but no actual move to reopen it.

The cease-fire ran out in March, but neither side renewed hostilities. In July, Sadat promised the United States that he would not resume fighting until mid-August, thus in effect extending the original cease-fire again. However, this deadline

263

SOLDIERS maintained a high state of readiness during 1971 as Egyptian-Israeli tensions continued unabated. Here, an Egyptian anti-aircraft unit on maneuvers scans sky as observer reports to headquarters by telephone.

came and went, and there was still no war. In September rocket fire was exchanged along the canal, but it did not trigger a large-scale conflict.

As early as April, the influential editor of the Cairo newspaper *Al-Ahram,* Mohammed Hassenein Heykal, declared that unless Israel made some accommodation Egypt might have to resort to war again. In July, Sadat said that he was determined to act in one way or another by the end of the year, and on November 1, he moved to army headquarters, declaring that he had decided to go to war. At the end of the year, therefore, both sides were on a military alert.

Relations with the United States. The United States played an important role in the behind-the-scene negotiations over the cease-fire and its extensions, the proposed reopening of the canal, and a possible settlement of the main issues between Egypt and Israel. In September, Sadat accused the United States of "deception and procrastination" in attempts to settle the dispute, and in November he declared that the United States was exploiting his offer on the reopening of the canal by neglecting the broader aspects of a settlement.

Earlier in the year Egypt had made determined efforts to win U. S. support, almost certainly thinking that this was necessary in order to reach any agreement with the Israelis. The Egyptians agreed to begin repaying various debts to American agencies. But diplomatic relations, which had been broken during the 1967 Israeli-Arab war, were not restored.

Relations with the Soviet Union. Relations with the USSR remained close throughout the year, although there were occasional signs of friction. The Soviet Union continued to supply the Egyptians with arms, including giant helicopters, jet interceptors, and FROG-7 missiles. It was reported in August that additional squadrons of Russian-piloted jet fighters had been sent to Egypt, and in November,

Egypt received a number of Soviet bombers, equipped with air-to-ground missiles.

In May, President Nikolai Podgorny of the USSR visited Cairo and signed a 15-year treaty of cooperation with the Egyptians. Sadat returned the visit in October. Despite the fact that he had been somewhat critical of the Soviet Union in previous months, he was reported to have returned from Moscow with "long-range commitments" from the Soviets.

Relations with Other Arab Countries. Sadat's leadership generally met with sympathy among other Arab countries, partly because they expected less interference in their internal affairs than they had suffered during Nasser's regime. Egyptian newspapers condemned King Hassan of Morocco for his action against the abortive coup leaders in July, and in the same month Cairo supported the suppression of a left-wing coup in the Sudan. The assassination of the Jordanian premier, Wasifi al-Tal, in Cairo on November 28 created new tension between Egypt and Jordan.

In April, Egypt, Libya, and Syria agreed to form the Federation of Arab Republics, and in September their respective populations voted their approval of the union. The federation is not actually a political union, but it does call for a joint military command.

Economy. The Aswan High Dam was completed in late 1970 and dedicated in January 1971 by Sadat and President Podgorny of the USSR. The potential of the dam will not be fully felt for many years, though some advantages have already come from it. The Egyptian economy is still on a war footing and suffers from the continuing crisis with Israel.

CARL LEIDEN, *University of Texas*

EGYPT • Information Highlights

Official Name: Arab Republic of Egypt.
Area: 386,660 square miles (1,001,449 sq km).
Population (1971 est.): 34,000,000. *Density,* 88 per square mile (32 per sq km). *Annual rate of increase,* 3.0%.
Chief Cities (1966 census): Cairo, the capital, 4,219,853; Alexandria, 1,801,056; Giza, 571,249; Port Said, 282,977.
Government: *Head of state,* Anwar el-Sadat, president (took office Oct. 15, 1970). *Chief minister,* Mahmoud Fawzi, premier (took office Oct. 21, 1970). *Legislature*—National Assembly, 360 members. *Major political party*—Arab Socialist Union.
Languages: Arabic (official), English, French.
Education: *Literacy rate* (1969), 35% of population. *School enrollment* (1968)—primary, 3,550,462; secondary, 1,283,-892; technical/vocational, 202,585; university/higher, 174,614.
Finances (1969–70 est.): *Revenues,* $3,800,000,000; *expenditures,* $3,800,000,000; *monetary unit,* pound (0.4348 pound equals U. S.$1, Sept. 1971).
Gross National Product (1970 est.): $6,430,000,000.
National Income (1968): $5,147,000,000; *national income per person,* $162.
Economic Indexes: *Industrial production* (1969), 136 (1963 = 100); *agricultural production* (1969), 122 (1963 = 100); *consumer price index* (1969), 107 (1967 = 100).
Manufacturing (metric tons, 1969): Cement, 3,613,000; residual fuel oil, 1,428,000.
Crops (metric tons, 1969 crop year): Rice, 2,557,000; maize, 2,366,000; wheat, 1,269,000; cottonseed (1968), 785,000.
Minerals (metric tons, 1969): Crude petroleum, 12,963,000; phosphate rock, 660,000; iron ore, 230,000.
Foreign Trade: *Exports* (1970), $762,000,000 (chief exports, 1969—cotton, $300,610,000; rice, $127,190,000). *Imports* 1970, $770,000,000 (chief imports, 1968—Cereals and preparations, $144,509,000; chemicals, $76,130,000; non-electrical machinery, $66,792,000; transport equipment, $63,319,000). *Chief trading partner* (1968)—USSR (took 28% of exports, supplied 16% of imports).
Tourism: Receipts (1969), $65,600,000.
Transportation: *Roads* (1964), 26,627 miles (42,851 km); *motor vehicles* (1969), 149,900 (automobiles, 121,800); *railroads* (1970), 4,200 miles (6,759 km); *merchant fleet* (1970), 238,000 gross registered tons; *national airline,* United Arab Airlines; *principal airports,* Alexandria, Cairo, Luxor, Mersa Matruh, Aswan.
Communications: *Telephones* (1968), 365,000; *television stations* (1968), 28; *television sets* (1969), 550,000; *radios,* (1968), 4,275,000; *newspapers* (1967), 12 (daily circulation, 850,000).

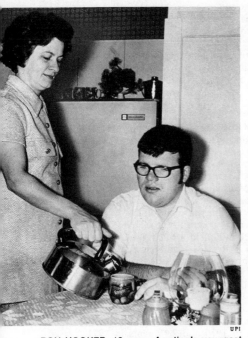

RON HOOKER, 19, one of nation's youngest mayors-elect, has breakfast at home after winning Newcomerstown, Ohio, race.

NORMAN MINETA, who won San Jose, Calif., mayoral election in November, plays ball with son. Mineta is first Japanese-American mayor of major U.S. city.

ELECTIONS

Scattered elections in 1971, few of them of national significance, gave no clear indication of political trends foreshadowing the presidential elections of 1972. (See POLITICAL PARTIES.)

Ratification of the 26th Amendment to the Constitution, lowering the voting age to 18 in all elections—national, state, and local—was a major development. Proposed by Congress on March 23, 1971, the amendment was approved by the necessary two thirds of the state legislatures in record time on June 30. Registration of some 11 million youths was delayed in some states by disputes over residence requirements, notably at colleges. A "youth caucus" was formed on Dec. 5, 1971, in Chicago, to get young people to vote, become convention delegates, and assert their power in 1972.

State Elections. By election of Lt. Gov. Wendell Ford as governor in Kentucky, on November 2, Democrats increased their control of governorships to 29. Ford, who stressed economic issues and attacked President Nixon, defeated Republican Thomas D. Emberton to succeed Republican Gov. Louie B. Nunn.

In Mississippi, also on November 2, Democrat William Waller was elected governor by 77% of the vote to 21% for Charles Evers, mayor of Fayette. Evers, an independent, was Mississippi's first black candidate for governor. Tom P. Brady, also on the ballot, had thrown his support to Waller. Evers' candidacy had attracted support from many liberals. Despite charges of some illegal exclusion of poll watchers and other irregularities, candidates agreed that the election dealt a heavy blow to racial discrimination in Mississippi voting. Of 284 black candidates for other state and local offices, 32 won.

Virginia voters on November 2 elected as lieutenant governor liberal populist Henry E. Howell, a Democratic state senator running as an independent in a test of strength for future control of the state. He received about 40% of the vote to about 38% for Democratic nominee George J. Kostel and 22% for Republican George P. Schafran, who was supported by Gov. Linwood Holton.

Democrats gained substantially in the legislatures of New Jersey, Virginia, and Kentucky.

In New York, Gov. Nelson A. Rockefeller, Mayor John V. Lindsay, and other leaders received a rebuff when voters on November 2 rejected a $2.5 billion transportation bond issue.

City Elections. Women, blacks, and young persons were elected to city offices in increasing numbers in 1971. On April 6, Mrs. Patience Latting was elected as the first woman mayor of Oklahoma City; Warren Widener was elected the first black mayor of Berkeley, Calif.; and James E. Williams the first black mayor of East St. Louis, Ill. Norman Y. Mineta, elected mayor of San Jose, Calif., on April 13, became the first Japanese-American to head a major city on the U. S. mainland.

Election of Ralph J. Perk as the first Republican mayor of Cleveland in 30 years was the most unexpected result on November 2. (See CLEVELAND.)

In Philadelphia, voters chose as mayor Democrat Frank L. Rizzo, law-and-order candidate and former police official, over Republican reformer W. Thacher Longstreth. Boston voters in a nonpartisan race reelected Mayor Kevin H. White, defeating conservative U. S. Rep. Louise Day Hicks in her second campaign. Mayor Joseph Alioto, a Democrat, handily won reelection in San Francisco's nonpartisan race, calling it a vote of confidence against a federal indictment. San Diego Republican Pete Wilson was elected mayor, and Sacramento Mayor Richard Marriott won a second term against the city's first black councilman. Houston reelected Mayor Louie Welch to a record fifth term.

Jersey City, N. J., elected Dr. Paul Jordan, reform candidate for mayor, breaking a long-standing Democratic-machine dominance. In Gary, Ind., Democrat Richard G. Hatcher, the city's first black mayor, was easily reelected. Indianapolis reelected Republican Mayor Richard G. Lugar. Baltimore, Md., in a light vote, elected all Democratic candidates, choosing William D. Schaefer mayor. Ohio Republicans retained mayoralties in Akron, Youngstown, and Canton. In Columbus, Republican Tom Moody, aided by youths, upset a 4-term Democrat, Mayor M. E. Sensenbrenner.

In an earlier election, April 6, Richard J. Daley, Democrat, was elected to a fifth term as mayor of Chicago, receiving 70% of the vote against Republican nominee Richard J. Friedman.

On November 2, Democrats replaced Republicans in 24 Connecticut communities, and in 13, Republicans overturned Democrats.

Congressional Elections. The District of Columbia on March 23 elected Democrat Walter E. Fauntroy, Baptist clergyman, to the newly created seat of nonvoting delegate in Congress, increasing the black caucus in the House to 13. Special elections to fill vacancies made no changes in party numbers in the House. Mendel J. Davis (Dem.-S. C.) was elected on April 27 to fill out the unexpired term of the late L. Mendel Rivers; William D. Mills (Rep.-Md.) was elected on May 25 to replace Rogers C. B. Morton, who was appointed secretary of the interior; H. J. Heinz, 3d (Rep.-Pa.) won election to succeed the late Robert J. Corbett; and William P. Curlin, Jr. (Dem.-Ky.) was elected to the seat of the late John C. Watts.

FRANKLIN L. BURDETTE, *University of Maryland*

ELECTRICAL INDUSTRIES

Record highs in generation of electricity, generating capacity, sales, and revenues were reached by the electrical utility industry in the United States in 1971. But because the demand for electric power continues to rise year after year, "there are some areas of the country in which reserve margins are less than desirable," conceded the Edison Electric Institute, a trade association.

In a related industry, the National Electrical Manufacturers Association estimated that its members shipped more electrical products than ever before—$47.5 billion worth in 1971, an increase of $2 billion over the 1970 total.

Power Supply. To keep pace with rising demand, the investor-owned companies spent a record $12 billion on new generating plant and equipment in 1971. This constituted 14.7% of the new construction expenditures by all U. S. industry.

Electric utilities are "thinking nuclear" in their expansion. They were operating 22 nuclear plants at the end of 1971 and had announced plans to build 24 more. The Edison Electric Institute expected nuclear steam turbine-generators to increase their share of total output of the nation's electricity from 1.4% in 1970 to 13.1% in 1976. (For a longer-range forecast on even greater gains in nuclear power, see NUCLEAR ENERGY.)

Production by electric utilities in 1971 was 1.618 trillion kw-hrs, an increase of 88 billion kw-hrs, or 5.8%, over the 1970 output. When railroads and industrial power plants producing for their own use are included, total generation of electric energy reached a new high of 1.721 trillion kw-hrs.

At year-end, the capability of all generating facilities was estimated at 389.4 million kw, a 9.1% increase over the 1970 total of 356.8 million kw. The investor-owned firms had 77.2% of this capacity, and government power agencies and rural electric cooperatives provided the rest. The annual margin of reserve was estimated at 21.2% above the estimated annual peak demand.

Sales. An estimated 1.466 trillion kw-hrs were sold in 1971, a 5.4% gain over the 1970 total of 1.391 trillion kw-hrs—and that, in turn, represented a 6.4% gain over the 1969 total. The average use of electric power in the American home rose during the year to a record 7,430 kw-hrs, up 364 kw-hrs over 1970.

By adding about 1.5 million new customers, the industry brought its total up to 74 million. More than 90% of the new customers were residential. Gross electric revenues of the investor-owned firms totaled $21 billion in 1971, an 11.5% annual gain.

Rates. For more than four decades, the utilities had been able each year to reduce the average price per kw-hr used in residential electric service. They whittled the rate from 7.23 cents in 1925 to 2.09 cents in 1969 in an unbroken string of annual reductions; but then inflationary pressures on fuel, wages, and other costs pushed the average up to 2.10 cents in 1970 and 2.19 cents in 1971.

Environment. A U. S. Court of Appeals decision handed down in Washington, D. C., on July 23 required the Atomic Energy Commission to review environmental aspects of nuclear power plants. New regulations then were adopted by the AEC. The Edison Electric Institute said that these regulations "hold the potential of delaying the completion of some nuclear power plants as much as one or even two years."

Seventy-nine electric utility companies have pledged $210 million toward a funding objective of $250 million over a 10-year period for the building of a liquid-metal fast-breeder reactor demonstration plant. President Nixon, in an energy message in June, called the fast-breeder reactor "our best hope today for meeting the nation's growing demand for economical, clean energy."

Electric Manufacturing. Power equipment led all electrical-product categories in growth in 1971, advancing by 10% over 1970 with estimated shipments of $5.3 billion. Industrial electronics and communications equipment led in total value of shipments, at $15.3 billion, up 5%.

Other categories and their 1971 shipments, as estimated by the National Association of Electrical Manufacturers, were: consumer products, $10.5 billion, up 5%; industrial equipment, $7 billion, unchanged; lighting equipment, $3.5 billion, up 5%; insulated wire and cable, $3.1 billion, unchanged; building equipment, $1.8 billion, up 7.5%; and insulating materials, $749 million, up 5%.

WILLIAM E. KENNEDY

ELECTRONICS

The electronics industry in the United States began to climb out of a two-year-long period of unsteady sales at the end of 1971. Because government buying continued at a weak pace, companies developed new products for such old but suddenly burgeoning markets as mass transportation, pollution monitoring, education, and alarm and security systems.

Sales and Sales Outlook. The Electronic Industries Association (EIA) decided against releasing its forecast of annual sales in the four major product categories—government, industrial, and consumer electronic products, and replacement components. However, EIA's marketing services department reported it is anticipating a 4.2% growth in overall industry sales for 1972.

Industry sources said they expected shipments of electronic products to reach $29 billion in 1972, up about $1 billion over shipments in 1971. In 1972, communications equipment was expected to contribute $4.1 billion, a 6% increase over 1971. Computing and accounting machine shipments should reach $5.23 billion in 1972, a 10% annual gain as compared with only a 5% increase in 1971.

A significant development in the computer industry has been the seemingly sudden emergence and success of minicomputers. They are somewhat larger and more sophisticated than electronic desktop calculators and are priced in the $5,000 to $25,000 range, in contrast to the $100,000 or more for larger and higher capacity computer systems. The number of minicomputers has grown from about 500 in 1965 to more than 15,000 in 1971. (See also COMPUTERS.)

Radio and TV receiver manufacturers recovered strongly in 1971 with total sales of $3.76 billion, a 13% increase over the previous year. A further 6% increase is expected in 1972.

Shipments of electronic components underwent an 11% decline in 1971. However, a 12% increase was forecast for 1972, with sales reaching $5.7 billion in shipments to original equipment manufacturers and the replacement market.

Sales to the government, particularly the Department of Defense and the National Aeronautics and Space Administration (NASA), continued to depress the electronics industry. A 10-year forecast of government markets was released by EIA late in 1971; with few exceptions, the forecast was filled with pessimism. The forecast—actually a consensus of 18 major electronic component and aerospace manufacturers—indicated that the Defense Department's research and development expenditures would increase from $7 billion in 1971 to $8 billion in 1977, to $9.7 billion in 1980, and to $10 billion in 1985. "Taking into account a 4 to 5% inflationary factor each year, however, Department of Defense procurement will not keep pace with inflation," noted Clifford A. Bean, chairman of the EIA studies and forecast subcommittee.

Also, the EIA forecasts expenditures for intelligence and communications systems will climb from $5.6 billion in 1972 to about $6.5 billion in fiscal 1980. Conversion from analog systems to more sophisticated digital systems was cited as one reason for this expected upswing.

The EIA forecast placed Department of Defense and NASA outlays for space programs at $3.6 billion in fiscal 1972 and at $4.9 billion by 1980, assuming the proposed space shuttle and the orbiting Skylab programs continue.

Data Communications. In 1970 the Federal Communications Commission (FCC) issued a landmark ruling allowing new communications firms to compete with existing common carriers—mainly the American Telephone & Telegraph Company and Western Union—for computer data communications and private-line service to large industrial and noncommercial customers.

UPI

BLIND student in Berkeley, Calif., "reads" notice with Optacon, electronic device developed at Stanford University. "Camera" in right hand scans notice and transmits letters to unit, which vibrates pins into letter shapes that she identifies with her left hand.

By the end of 1971 data communications was one of the fastest growing industries in the United States, showing gains in revenues averaging 50% annually. Moreover, the FCC decision is expected to widen the scope of the market for equipment and component suppliers to the point where data communications is likely to be a $5.8-billion business by the end of the 1970's.

The substantial growth in demand for telecommunications services is expected to benefit the existing carriers, but the largest relative growth is likely to occur among the newly emerging specialized carriers. Thirty-four aspiring carriers already have filed more than 1,900 applications with the FCC for microwave data communications stations in the United States.

Communications Satellites. The growth in satellite communications has been phenomenal, and it continues at a rapid pace. A total of 80 countries are now members of Intelsat, the international satellite consortium, and 56 of these are expected to have their own earth stations by the end of 1974.

Significantly, Intelsat's annual charge for the rental of a satellite channel has dropped from $32,000 in 1965 to $15,000 in 1971, and another 50% cut is expected by the mid-1970's. The eventual introduction of a domestic satellite communications system in the United States will mean drastically reduced rates for long-distance telephone calls. The charge for long-distance calls traditionally has been dependent on the distance of the call. With satellite communications, however, the signal will travel approximately the same distance between any two cities on the U. S. mainland. Eight applicants have filed with the FCC, asking permission to build a domestic satellite communications system, but their proposals were tied up by requests from the FCC for additional comments on technical and legal questions. (See also TELECOMMUNICATIONS.)

Medical Electronics. A Stanford Research Institute (SRI) study indicates the biomedical electronics market is on the verge of passing the $700 million mark and will nearly double to $1.28 billion by 1975. The report does not include X-ray equipment. "The highest growth rates lie in patient-monitoring, therapeutic, and data-processing equipment," the report stated. Overall, the SRI study indicated the biomedical electronics market will grow at a rate of 14% for the 1970–75 period.

Electronic Repair Shops. The New York State Joint Legislative Committee on Consumer Protection heard testimony in 1971 with regard to a bill to require all electronic repair shops to register with the state. According to witnesses in support of the bill, TV set repair is a "scandal." Under the bill, a repair shop, if found guilty of gross negligence, fraud, or deception, would face loss of registration and a fine up to $500. Under existing practices, any one can set up a repair shop.

RONALD A. SCHNEIDERMAN
"Electronic News"

EL SALVADOR

Major political developments in El Salvador in 1971 included the kidnapping and murder of a wealthy Salvadoran businessman, apparent factionalism within the ruling military elite, and preliminary maneuvering for advantage in the 1972 elections.

Regalado Dueñas Murder. On Feb. 11, 1971, Ernesto Regalado Dueñas, a 36-year-old business executive and a member of one of El Salvador's prominent families, was forcibly abducted near his home in San Salvador. The kidnappers demanded $1 million in ransom. While negotiations over the ransom were still in progress, Regalado's body was discovered on a dirt road in the northwestern part of the capital.

Two students, alleged to have leftist leanings, were immediately arrested by the government, but this prompt action failed to halt speculation over the motive for the kidnapping and assassination, since Regalado's family was known to oppose the land reform program of the government of President Fidel Sánchez Hernández. Gen. Fidel Torres, the defense minister, hinted that the purpose of the crime was to discredit the Sánchez Hernández regime.

Dissension at the Top. An apparent indication of disunity within El Salvador's ruling military clique was the arrest and imprisonment, on Dec. 4, 1970, of a powerful general, José Alberto Medrano, commander of the National Guard Police. Medrano was charged with the murder of a police officer assigned to protect his home. He denied the charge, but the government persisted in its allegation.

Political Maneuvering. The nation saw the beginning of preparations for the March 1972 elections, in which the presidency and vice presidency, all 52

EL SALVADOR • Information Highlights

Official Name: Republic of El Salvador.
Area: 8,260 square miles (21,393 sq km).
Population (1970 est.): 3,530,000. *Density,* 409 per square mile (158 per sq km). *Annual rate of increase,* 3.4%.
Chief Cities (1968 est.): San Salvador, the capital, 340,544; Santa Ana, 162,937; San Miguel, 104,233.
Government: *Head of state,* Fidel Sánchez Hernández, president (took office July 1, 1967). *Head of government,* Fidel Sánchez Hernández. *Legislature*—Legislative Assembly (unicameral), 52 members. *Major political parties*—Party of National Conciliation, Christian Democratic party.
Language: Spanish (official).
Education: *Literacy rate* (1971), 49% of population. *Expenditure on education* (1967), 25.4% of total public expenditure. *School enrollment* (1968)—primary, 471,622; secondary, 79,564; technical/vocational, 22,681; university/higher (1967), 6,748.
Finances: *Revenues* (1969 est.), $112,000,000; *expenditures* (1970 est.), $110,000,000; *monetary unit,* colon (2.50 colones equal U. S.$1, Sept. 1970).
Gross National Product (1970 est.): $1,000,000,000.
National Income (1970): $878,000,000; *national income per person,* $249.
Consumer Price Index (1970), 108 (1963=100).
Manufacturing (metric tons, 1969): Cement, 142,000; sugar, 109,000; gasoline, 68,000; beer, 153,000 hectoliters.
Crops (metric tons, 1969 crop year): Sugarcane (1968–69), 1,780,000; coffee, 150,000; cottonseed (1968), 73,000.
Foreign Trade (1970): *Exports,* $228,000,000 (chief exports—coffee, $113,760,000; cotton, $23,200,000). *Imports,* $214,-000,000 (chief imports—chemicals, $42,420,000; nonelectrical machinery, $18,296,000; textile yarn and fabrics, $16,012,000; base metals, $11,920,000). *Chief trading partners* (1968)—United States (took 20% of exports, supplied 29% of imports); Guatemala (15%–16%).
Transportation: *Roads* (1969), 7,077 miles (11,389 km); *motor vehicles* (1965), 50,500 (automobiles, 34,100).
Communications: *Telephones* (1970), 35,495; *television stations* (1966), 3; *television sets* (1969), 75,000; *radios* (1969), 400,000.

---

seats in the Legislative Assembly, and 261 municipal positions were to be at stake. The main opposition party, the Christian Democrats (PDC), appeared to be willing to alter its moderate political program in order to join the more radical Democratic National Union (UDN) and National Revolutionary Movement (MRN) in a united front against the National Conciliation party (CN) of President Sánchez Hernández. In the 1971 legislature, the PDC held only 15 seats, as against the 34 held by the dominant CN.

Honduras Dispute. Relations between Honduras and El Salvador remained strained. The migration of Salvadorans across the poorly defined border into Honduras—the major cause of the brief 1969 war between the two nations—continued in 1971 and led to several minor clashes.

The election of Ramón Ernesto Cruz to the Honduran presidency in March 1971 brought about renewed attempts to settle the dispute. On June 7 it was announced that telephone, telegraph, and postal links had been reestablished between the two countries. In August, prisoners were exchanged.

The Economy and the Common Market. El Salvador registered some economic gains in 1971, but it was clear that future progress was being jeopardized by the disputes plaguing the Central American Common Market (CAM)—some caused by the 1969 war, others having deeper roots. In late 1970, Honduras had suspended its participation in the market, claiming that El Salvador and Guatemala were using their superior industrial power to dominate the organization. In July 1971, the finance ministers of the four remaining member nations agreed to undertake major structural reforms in the market.

ROBERT L. PETERSON
University of Texas, El Paso

ELLSBURG, Daniel. See BIOGRAPHY.
ENGLISH LITERATURE. See LITERATURE.

Rotting piles of debris at Caven Point are typical of much of New York Harbor. Clean harbors are a concern of the Environmental Protection Agency, whose new emblem (*right*) symbolizes the total environment.

environment

Global efforts in 1971 to cope with problems of the human environment took on not only an increased urgency but an increased orderliness and sense of purpose. Among political leaders there was evidence of a widespread desire to learn more and do more about the gloomy scientific findings that if humanity continued to grow in numbers, to exploit the resources of the life-giving biosphere without inhibition, and to pollute and litter the planet, the already visible aesthetic degradation would turn to grave risk of human extinction or, at least, biological alteration.

Without necessarily accepting the cataclysmic premise, the nations of the world began preparations for the United Nations Conference on the Human Environment, to be held in Stockholm, June 5–16, 1972. The new ecological awareness was also underscored in reports of action in individual countries and in reports of international agreements and meetings.

PREPARATIONS FOR THE UN CONFERENCE

When Sweden's proposal for a conference on the human environment was approved by the General Assembly in 1968, the agreed underlying purpose was to sound a tocsin. At that time not enough people, particularly political leaders, understood the environmental peril. But by 1971, world opinion had been duly alerted. Preparations for the UN conference were geared more to action than to propaganda.

Organization for Action. Attention focused on the six items on the Stockholm agenda: (1) planning and management of human settlements for environmental quality; (2) environmental aspects of natural resources management—broadly defined to include animal, botanical, and mineral resources; (3) identification and control of pollutants and nuisances of broad international significance; (4) educational, informational, social, and cultural aspects of environment issues; (5) development and environment; and (6) international organizational implications of action proposals. An intergovernmental committee worked on a "Declaration of Stockholm," to serve as a standard of ethics and conduct and possibly as a basis for international legal action.

The emphasis on action was inherent in the method of work adopted by the secretary general of the conference, Maurice F. Strong, who at the time of his appointment was president of Canada's International Development Agency. He drew not only on the 27-member Preparatory Committee but on many unofficial organizations and individuals for counsel, research, and financial support. The Preparatory Committee held three meetings and various regional seminars and intergovernmental meetings.

Attempts to Identify Problems. Preparations for the world conference helped to define the "internationalism" of the various environmental threats cited by scientists and to bring out some of the attendant political, economic, and diplomatic problems that must be faced in dealing with them.

Political Aspects. Fundamental environmental dangers transcend political boundaries. For example, pesticides have been used throughout the world to facilitate agricultural production or to stamp out disease. Yet if most countries—but not all—halted their use, pesticides would still have global impact, because of their persistence and mobility, through the action of air, water, and living carriers. Similarly, air pollution has global consequences, especially pollution due to the burning of fossil fuels, which releases carbon dioxide and minute particles of matter. These substances tend to remain suspended in the atmosphere, covering geographical areas much wider than the country in which the fuels are used.

The dumping or spillage of oil at sea results not only in aesthetic damage of relatively narrow confines but also in widespread damage to marine life, thus affecting the fishing economies of the world. There is also the familiar problem of worldwide nuclear radiation. For the time being, the Nuclear Test-Ban Treaty of 1963 copes with this problem. But the treaty is still incomplete in regard to existing and potential possessors of nuclear energy devices.

Some international environment problems are more regional in nature. For example, the Rhine River serves as "sewer" for France and Germany, but it is the water supply for the Netherlands. And some environmental problems—such as excessive population growth, often combined with hunger and poverty—are rooted in mankind's deepest religious, cultural, and psychological behavior patterns.

Economic Implications. The international economic implications of environmental action also drew attention. As automobile-buying nations such

PICTORIAL PARADE

PARIS installed giant air filters (*left*) in October in pilot project aimed at reducing pollution hazards.

OIL SPILL followed January collision of Standard Oil tankers in San Francisco Bay. Demonstrators (*below*) hung bodies of oil-soaked gulls on the company's doors.

UPI

Girl at London environmental exhibition in June drinks from Swedish bioreactor, which purifies polluted water.

as the United States set new emission standards, these will be reflected in the type and price of both U. S. and foreign manufactures. As towns and villages set sulfur-emission standards for fossil fuels, the impact is felt in the fuel resource countries of origin. As standards become relatively intolerable in one country, industrial havens, such as shipping flags of convenience, may develop in other countries. Underscoring the internationalism of environmental concern and action, the World Bank took environmental impact into account in its assessment of potential projects.

These and similar considerations posed hard choices—"trade-offs"—between environmental protection and social goals. (In the less-developed countries of the world, an active smokestack was deemed a sign of progress.) But as preparations for the UN conference advanced, a consensus emerged that environmental protection and economic progress are not mutually exclusive, given wise management and rational priorities. In July a group of experts on economic development, meeting in Switzerland, expressed the view that "in a large measure the kind of environmental problems that are of importance to developing countries are those that can be overcome by development itself." In September, Secretary General Strong reported that the degree of participation by developing countries had increased significantly.

Diplomatic Considerations. The admission of mainland China to the UN in October and the ousting of Taiwan reinforced speculation that the Peking government might participate in the Stockholm Conference. Meanwhile, Taiwan had made elaborate plans to attend. A related problem was whether China would join the Soviet Union in insisting on the admission of East Germany.

The environment meeting of the UN Economic Commission for Europe, held in Prague in June, had to be downgraded to one of experts, rather than governments, because the Eastern Bloc insisted on full, coequal participation by East Germany. The Western Bloc (including the United States) stood by the standard UN meeting formula of expert-observer status for the East Germans.

Nevertheless, the Soviet Union's interest in global efforts to deal with environmental problems was manifested on several important occasions. At the 24th Soviet Communist Party Congress in April, Secretary General Leonid I. Brezhnev stressed the Soviet Union's readiness to participate with other states concerned with settling problems such as the conservation of the environment. In April, the Soviet Union's United Nations Association sent a delegation to the United States to discuss environmental issues with that country's United Nations Association. The Soviet delegation, headed by Fedor V. Konstantinov, a member of the Academy of Sciences of the USSR, included both scientists and government officials. The U. S. delegation—headed by Robert O. Anderson, cochairman of the International Institute for Environmental Affairs—included scientists, economists, and other experts. After meetings in New York, the Soviet group was flown to Colorado to visit the Aspen Institute for Humanistic Studies, at Aspen, and the National Center for Atmospheric Research, at Boulder. At a follow-up meeting in Moscow in September, agreement was reached on joint publication of papers dealing with environmental problems and on an effort to reach concurrence on priorities.

REPORTS FROM AROUND THE WORLD

Although concern and action focused on a variety of environmental perils, water pollution received major attention.

National Concern and Action—*Western Europe*. The British government, successful in earlier efforts to clean the Thames River, asserted in April legal authority to seize or sink any oil tanker, whether inside or outside its territorial waters, that threatened to pollute Britain's shores. This action followed a series of dangerous oil spills in the English Channel.

In Finland a running battle developed between the pulp and paper industry and the government over strict new antipollution policies. The government fined the owners of a pulp mill for failing to treat its sulfite waste. The owners chose to close the mill rather than pay. The Swedish government set aside some $10 million a year, to be spent over a period of five years, as a 30–50% contribution to private industry's efforts to carry out water purification measures.

EARTH WEEK observances in New York City in April closed some streets during lunch hours. Here, office workers along car-free Madison Avenue play Frisbee.

The Rhine River was reported in May to be again near the level of pollution that had caused the death in 1969 of almost all its fish life in the section from Bingen, West Germany, to the Netherlands border.

Along the Italian shore from Nice to Naples, the celebrated blue of the Tyrrhenian Sea was found to be changing to a dull gray. The Tiber River was found to be dangerously polluted for 25 miles from its mouth to near Rome, causing the death of virtually all the fish in the area. Exemplifying mounting concern, Italian authorities in May impounded two tanker terminals off the fishing harbor of Fiumicino, near the mouth of the Tiber, and closed pipelines linking the terminals with an inland oil refinery. They also ordered the director of Rome's international airport, at Fiumicino, to have its drainage system cleaned and overhauled as a measure against spillage of aircraft fuel into the estuary of the Tiber. The mayor of Civitavecchia, the port city of Rome, was arrested and imprisoned for 30 hours in late November when a magistrate found that sewage effluents had worsened the condition of the sea, despite a year of importunings.

An experiment in Paris that attracted widespread attention was the erection in October of two giant "vacuum cleaner" towers. The towers were designed to suck in the grimy air, filter it, and release it—clean, it was hoped.

Egypt and Other African Countries. Early in the year worldwide publicity developed over reported ecological side effects of the Aswan High Dam, on the Nile River in Egypt. The dam, one of the world's great engineering feats, regulated the flow of the Nile, doubled Egypt's electric power capacity, and added the equivalent of 2 million acres in cropland. But it caused increased erosion downstream, necessitating the construction of 10 new diversion dams at great cost. Salt water was found to be moving upstream in the delta, eroding farmlands and rendering them saline. There was a

sharp increase in schistosomiasis, a severe intestinal disease carried by snails that flourish in irrigation canals. The dam withheld rich silt from downstream farmlands and essential nutrients from a sardine fishery, with the result that the fishery was virtually ruined.

Similar ecological damage was reported to have accompanied superdams in other African countries —Ghana, Nigeria, Zambia, and the Ivory Coast— as well as in Asian countries, including Iran, India, and Pakistan. Worldwide protests developed over Uganda's plan to build a hydroelectric plant that would cut by 90% the flow through Murchison Falls, on the Upper Nile.

The USSR. The Soviet Union, no less than the capitalist and industrialized West, was concerned with its environmental problems—including, ironically, dam construction (the USSR assisted in the building of the Aswan High Dam). A sharp controversy was reported at the Soviet Communist Party Congress in April. Electric-power and farm interests argued whether fertile bottom lands of great river valleys should be flooded in the construction of dams and reservoirs intended for hydroelectric power.

In September a decree by the Central Committee ordered new deadlines for the installation of treatment devices to purify wastes discharged by pulp mills and other industries on the shore of Lake Baikal (in Siberia), the world's largest freshwater lake by volume. An earlier directive had been issued in February 1969. The lag disclosed the difficulties of Communist governments, no less than Western democracies, in bringing industrial interests into line.

The Far East. In Japan, where phenomenal industrial growth had brought acute pollution, 14 pollution-control bills were passed in an extraordinary session of the Diet (Parliament) at the end of 1969. These included a law against the production of any "substance injurious to human health," with a liability of up to 3 years in jail. By contrast, visitors to Singapore reported how well that city had progressed in its efforts to become "the cleanest city in Asia." Heavy fines for littering had their effect, but the results seemed to have been generated by popular determination.

United States. As the most industrialized country in the world, the United States was watched everywhere as a responsible pacesetter. In the preparations for the Stockholm conference, the U. S. government sought to take a clear lead. It participated in all the committee work and hinted that if any "world environmental fund" were created, it would make a sizable contribution.

President Richard Nixon—who had accorded Earth Day, in April 1970, no official recognition—proclaimed an Earth Week (April 18–24) in 1971. The President's Council on Environmental Quality, in its second report to Congress, pointedly noted that the cost of controlling pollution would be high but manageable.

Like many other countries, the United States moved vigorously on environmental matters. An activist, William D. Ruckelshaus, took office in December 1970 as head of the Environmental Protection Agency. And Congress, keyed to the general popular mood, headed toward a policy of strict, far-reaching water-pollution control in a bill (passed by the Senate in November 1971 by a vote of 86 to 0) to require permits for discharge of industrial waste and sewage into waterways.

The administration, however, overrode protests in the United States and abroad against a powerful underground nuclear test at Amchitka Island (in the Aleutians, Alaska) on Nov. 6, 1971. Environmentalists had warned that the explosion could

cause dangerous tidal waves or a series of earthquakes. These did not occur, but a large number of sea otters were reported killed.

The government also caused considerable confusion when, after several years of warnings against phosphate detergents, a spokesman said in September that phosphates were preferable to other detergents, notably caustic soda. Still unresolved at the end of the year was a controversial project to build a trans-Alaskan pipeline to carry oil from the North Slope to the Gulf of Alaska. Environmentalists had prevailed upon the administration to withhold the needed licenses.

International Agreements and Meetings. Notable among agreements was the United States–Canadian compact, signed in June, to eliminate water pollution in the Great Lakes by 1975. The plan for financing according to responsibility will require the United States to bear the major share of the estimated cost of $2 to $3 billion.

Scientific Meetings. Several major scientific meetings took place in 1971. The International Confederation of Scientific Unions held a special committee meeting at Canberra, Australia, in August. The committee called for (1) creation of national environmental councils by developing countries, (2) action by national councils and governments to establish trans-national environmental "networks," and (3) immediate steps by the UN to fund environmental research through appropriate agencies.

At a meeting in Stockholm in July, distinguished scientists from 14 countries rejected doomsday prophecies about global climatic conditions. They noted that man has changed the climate over large regions of the earth and confirmed some consternation-provoking evidence that the oceans are rising (nearly

DEPRADATIONS of strip mining in 1971 spurred efforts by conservationists to halt surface operations. This mine near Soda Springs, Idaho, impinges on forest land.

RECYCLING of containers and paper stirred consumer interest in 1971. Some manufacturers aided reclamation projects by helping with collection and paying for cans.

10 inches since 1890). But the rise, they said, is not due to man's pollution of the air. Neither is the Arctic icecap melting (and contributing to the rise), as had been feared. Although man is polluting the atmosphere, the scientists expressed the opinion that climate is affected more by nature's own volcanic eruptions.

At Brussels in September, the International Astronautical Congress wrestled with the means of developing a kind of distant early warning system that would identify disastrous ecological changes before they have passed the point of no return. The most practical and economical early warning system, it was said at the congress, would be a monitoring system of space satellites. The first in a series of earth satellites designed to perform such roles is scheduled to be launched by the United States in May 1972. They will be called Earth Resources Technology Satellites (ERTS). A center for processing data from these satellites is being established at Sioux Falls, S. Dak.

Other Meetings. The growing involvement of the world business community in environmental problems was reflected in a meeting of the International Chamber of Commerce in Vienna in April and the establishment by that organization in November of a staff-supported environmental committee. At another conference, called Pacem in Maribus II, which was held in Malta in July, more than 180 diplomats and scientists from 30 countries agreed on the urgency of multilateral legislation to save the Mediterranean from becoming a dead sea.

At an October meeting in Oslo, Norway, conferees of 11 nations belonging to the North Atlantic Fisheries Commission drafted a strong statement for "all possible steps" to prevent harmful ocean dumping.

The Aspen Institute for Humanistic Studies and the Institute on Man and Science (Rensselaerville, N. Y.) conducted an international conference in May to consider international organization and the human environment. The study of this subject was continued at a 7-week workshop, cosponsored by the Aspen Institute and the International Institute for Environmental Affairs and participated in by 55 specialists from around the world. The International Institute then prepared a Basic Paper for the Stockholm Conference Secretariat, recommending (1) a high-level center for environmental affairs at the UN, (2) an independent world environmental science center, (3) a network of regional science centers, and (4) a world fund for the environment.

JACK RAYMOND, *President, International Institute for Environmental Affairs*

EQUATORIAL GUINEA

The main developments in Equatorial Guinea in 1971 were a bizarre death in the two-man U. S. embassy and continued friendly relations with Peking.

U. S. Embassy Death. Confusing messages from its embassy in Santa Isabel prompted the U. S. State Department to dispatch U. S. Consul Leonard G. Shurtleff from nearby Cameroon to investigate. On August 30 he found the body of Donald J. Leahy, a foreign service staff officer, in the U. S. chancery code room. Later reports said that Leahy had been stabbed with scissors. Also found was Leahy's supervisor, Chargé d'Affaires Alfred J. Erdos, incapacitated and apparently suffering a nervous breakdown. Spanish sources reported that personal problems had existed between the two men, that a fight had occurred in the embassy, and that Erdos had sought refuge in the Nigerian embassy.

U. S. Ambassador Lewis Hoffacker, who is accredited to Equatorial Guinea and Cameroon, directed the investigation. Erdos was charged with murder when he returned to the United States.

Delegation to Peking. In mid-January a delegation of Equatorial Guinean cabinet officers went to China, where they were entertained at an elaborate banquet in Peking. At the banquet one of Equatorial Guinea's ministers said that the two countries pursued "the same objective: struggle against imperialism, colonialism, neocolonialism and racial discrimination."

FRANKLIN PARKER, *West Virginia University*

—— **EQUATORIAL GUINEA · Information Highlights** ——

Official Name: Republic of Equatorial Guinea.
Area: 10,831 square miles (28,051 sq km).
Population (1970 est.): 300,000. *Density,* 26 per square mile (10 per sq km). *Annual rate of increase,* 1.8%.
Chief City (1970 est.): Santa Isabel, the capital, 38,000.
Government: *Head of state,* Francisco Macias Nguema, president (took office Oct. 12, 1968). *Head of government,* Francisco Macias Nguema. *Legislature*—National Assembly (unicameral), 35 members.
Languages: Spanish (official), various African dialects.
Education: *Expenditure on education* (1964), 2.4% of total public expenditure.
Finances (1969–70): *Revenues,* $10,218,000; *expenditures,* $16,335,000; *monetary unit,* Guinea peseta (69.73 pesetas equal U. S.$1, 1970).
Crops (metric tons, 1969 crop year): Cocoa beans, 30,300; bananas (1968), 12,000; coffee, 7,200.
Foreign Trade (1966): *Exports,* $20,743,000 (chief export, 1965—Cacao). *Imports,* $24,071,000 (chief import, 1965—rice; oil products). *Chief trading partner* (1966)—Spain.

ETHIOPIA

In 1971, Ethiopia granted recognition to a number of states after having first recognized the People's Republic of China in late 1970. The Ethiopian government blunted the impact of the Eritrean Liberation Front in 1971, but student unrest continued. The country also maintained its policy of normalizing relations with neighboring states, and a large U. S. military grant was disclosed.

International Relations. On Dec. 2, 1970, Ethiopia recognized the People's Republic of China as the "sole legal government representing the entire Chinese people." In mid-1971 the accreditation of ambassadors took place. Ethiopia's recognition of China came at a time when numerous other nations were accepting the legitimacy of the Peking regime. In early October, Emperor Haile Selassie visited China, where he met with Chairman Mao Tse-tung and Premier Chou En-lai.

Nepal, Mongolia, and Sierra Leone all opened embassies in Addis Ababa during 1971, and a treaty of friendship was signed with Senegal. After meeting with U. S. Vice President Spiro T. Agnew, who was visiting Ethiopia, Haile Selassie announced that his nation's close relationship with the United States would continue. At a meeting of the heads of state of the member nations of the Organization of African Unity (OAU), the emperor opposed any dialogue with South Africa, claiming it would be "self-defeating and a waste of time." In mid-October, Haile Selassie flew to Persepolis, Iran, where he attended the 2,500th anniversary celebration of the Persian Empire.

Since the early 1960's, refugees from Sudan and Eritrea had been the cause of numerous border incidents. In 1971 the foreign minister of Ethiopia visited Sudan and later announced that both countries would take steps to prevent further border fighting. Ethiopia and Kenya announced a similar agreement.

Domestic Affairs. The Ethiopian military took stringent measures against the Eritrean Liberation Front (ELF), a Muslim separatist organization active since 1952. In January, Lt. Gen. Debebe Haile Mariam, commander of ground forces, was appointed governor-general of Eritrea. The emperor announced an amnesty for all rebels who would voluntarily hand over their weapons to the government. Although a U. S. Army soldier was shot and killed in Eritrea—reportedly by the ELF—and numerous Ethiopian soldiers were also killed, far fewer incidents occurred in 1971 than in 1970.

Trouble with high school students, endemic in Ethiopia, continued during the year. In May, 11 vocational and secondary schools were closed by the government as students protested rules limiting the authority of the student union. Student leaders were arrested in June after they refused to halt their protests despite government warnings.

Yilma Deressa, minister of commerce, industry, and tourism, and former minister of finance, was appointed crown counsellor in August. This was seen by many as a demotion for the once powerful cabinet minister. Minassie Haile replaced Ketema Yifru as foreign minister.

Three land reform bills proposed by the emperor in 1968 continued to languish in Parliament, where approval is necessary if the bills are to become law. Using delaying tactics to stifle the bills, which were concerned with the tax on unutilized land, registration of immovable property, and regulation of agricultural relationships, Parliament was seen as defending traditional Ethiopian norms.

In April, Haile Selassie confirmed the appointment of Archbishop Theophilos as the new patriarch of the Ethiopian Orthodox Church. The archbishop succeeded Patriarch Basilos, who had died in October 1970. Archbishop Theophilos had been acting patriarch during his predecessor's illness.

Foreign Assistance. It was disclosed by the U. S. Senate that the Nixon administration planned to grant to Ethiopia a total of $12,790,000 in military assistance during the 1971–72 fiscal year. Some senators felt that part of the money would go to support Ethiopian military operations against the ELF. They were clearly unhappy over this support, since they felt that the United States should not interfere in internal Ethiopian developments.

Sweden announced a decrease in its aid to Ethiopia, which normally is about $6 million a year. It was understood that the action was a result of the Swedish government's displeasure with the slow pace of land reform in Ethiopia.

The International Development Association (IDA) announced a $10 million loan to increase skilled manpower. Along with an allocation by Ethiopia of $4 million, the capital would be used to build a teacher-training and agricultural institute. New York University announced that it would send a team of doctors to aid in the training of Ethiopian doctors. An All-Africa leprosy hospital was opened in Addis Ababa in March 1971.

PETER SCHWAB
State University of New York at Purchase

--------- **ETHIOPIA • Information Highlights** ---------

Official Name: Empire of Ethiopia.
Area: 471,777 square miles (1,221,900 sq km).
Population (1970 est.): 25,050,000. *Density,* 52 per square mile (20 per sq km). *Annual rate of increase,* 2.1%.
Chief Cities (1967 census): Addis Ababa, the capital, 644,120; Asmara (1968 census), 190,500.
Government: *Head of state,* Haile Selassie I, emperor (proclaimed emperor April 2, 1930). *Head of government,* Tsafi Tizaz Akilu Habte-Wold, prime minister (took office April 17, 1961). *Legislature*—Parliament: Senate, 125 members (appointed); Chamber of Deputies, 250 members (elected).
Languages: Amharic (official), English.
Education: *Literary rate* (1969), 5% of population. *Expenditure on education* (1966), 10.0% of total public expenditure. *School enrollment* (1967)—primary, 452,457; secondary, 79,534; technical/vocational, 6,251; university/higher, 3,870.
Finances (1970 est.): *Revenues,* $210,600,000; *expenditures,* $200,560,000; *monetary unit,* Ethiopian dollar (2.5 Ethiopian dollars equal U. S.$1, Aug. 1971).
Gross National Product (1968 est.): $1,700,000,000.
National Income (1967): $1,344,000,000; *national income per person,* $57.
Economic Indexes: *Agricultural production* (1969), 116 (1963=100); *consumer price index* (1969), 130 (1963=100).
Manufacturing (metric tons, 1969): Meat, 335,000; residual fuel oil, 272,000; cement, 166,000; sugar, 70,000; cigarettes, 750,000,000 pieces.
Crops (metric tons, 1969 crop year): Millet and sorghum, 2,500,000; barley, 1,450,000; maize, 850,000; wheat, 760,000; coffee, 165,000; cattle and sheep, 38,500,000 head.
Minerals (metric tons): Salt (1969), 263,000; gold (1968), 1,119 kilograms.
Foreign Trade (1969): *Exports,* $119,400,000 (chief exports—Coffee, $69,560,000; hides and skins, $11,000,000; cereals, $9,600,000; oilseeds, $9,280,000). *Imports,* $155,320,000 (chief imports [1968]—Machinery and transport equipment, $70,834,000; chemicals, $16,383,000; iron and steel, $8,301,000; textiles, $7,663,000). *Chief trading partners* (1968 est.)—United States (took 43.4% of exports, supplied 14.5% of imports); West Germany (7.8%—11.6%); Japan (4.6%—10.0%).
Transportation: *Roads* (1970), 4,000 miles (6,436 km); *motor vehicles* (1969), 43,800 (automobiles, 33,000); *railroads* (1965), 423 miles (681 km); *national airline,* Ethiopian Airlines; *principal airports,* Addis Ababa, Asmara.
Communications: *Telephones* (1969), 41,106; *television stations* (1968), 1; *television sets* (1969), 8,000; *radios* (1969), 155,000; *newspapers* (1969), 8.

Relaxing in the Crimea, West German Chancellor Willy Brandt (*left*) and Soviet Communist party chief Leonid Brezhnev begin conference in September. Leaders discussed wide range of topics, including European armament reductions, during 3-day talks.

EUROPE

The year 1971 in Europe was distinguished by two landmark events, each of which definitively marked the end of one era and the beginning of another. One of these events affected East-West relations, while the other had profound implications for future relations among western European countries. The latter event was the achievement in June of agreement in the negotiations about Britain's application for membership in the European Economic Community (EEC, or Common Market). The other milestone was the conclusion of the four-power agreement on Berlin, whose status had troubled relations between the USSR and the Western allies since World War II.

These were both positive events, affording some ground for optimism about Europe's future, and there were other positive signs. The leaders of the three major western European states—France, West Germany, and Britain—were all comparatively new occupants of their offices, but all were showing that they had impressive capacities for statesmanship. As Edward Heath moved into his second year as British prime minister, and Georges Pompidou and Willy Brandt into their third years as president of France and chancellor of West Germany respectively, their policies were showing a greater degree of self-confidence and firmness than many expected when they first entered office.

Europe continued to enjoy prosperity and a rising standard of living, but the rate of improvement slackened. In contrast to 1969 and 1970, 1971 was not a boom year, and signs of strain were developing. The western European countries, as did much of the world, suffered from continuing inflation.

EAST-WEST RELATIONS

The most important new development in relations between the eastern and western halves of divided Europe—and presumably one of the most important events to occur in Europe since World War II—was the four-power Berlin agreement signed on September 3. The entire question of the status of Berlin and of access to it from West Germany has constituted one of the most troublesome legacies of the war. The Western allies had no guaranteed rights or routes of access to the city, deep in the Communist-controlled area of Germany. The necessity of such rights had been largely overlooked as World War II was ending. The ambiguities of the situation had been exploited by the Soviet Union and had led to the embargo on land access from the West in 1948–49 and the division of the city by East Germany's Berlin Wall in 1961. Through 1971, there was sporadic harassment of surface traffic to Berlin. Although the unsatisfactory status of Berliners was not completely resolved in 1971, a decisive step to alleviate tension was taken.

Berlin Agreement. On September 3 in West Berlin, the representatives of the United States, the Soviet Union, Britain, and France—the four powers responsible for Berlin—signed an overall agreement on the status of the city and traffic to it from the West. The agreement was the result of prolonged negotiations that had begun in March 1970.

The document had several main provisions. The Soviet Union declared that traffic across East German territory between West Germany and the western sectors of Berlin would be unimpeded and that the Soviet Union, not East Germany, should be ultimately responsible for this free access. West Berliners were to be able to visit East Berlin and East Germany under the same conditions as non-Berliners. The ties between West Berlin and West Germany were to be maintained, taking into account that West Berlin is not a constituent part of West Germany and is not to be governed by it. The agreement provided that details regarding access and other matters were to be worked out between representatives of West Germany and West Berlin and those of East Germany. However, these negotiations proved complicated, as the East German envoys immediately raised many technical difficulties. These obstacles seemed likely to delay the full implementation of the document. Walter Ulbricht, the long-term East German leader, resigned in May, but West Germany's relations with his successor, Erich Honecker, also proved difficult. However, on December 21 an agreement between East and West Germany was signed, giving West Berliners 30 visiting days a year in East Germany and also providing for arrangements on the West Berlin enclaves in East German territory.

Eastern Europe. The agreement on Berlin, strictly a four-power matter, did not signify that Chancellor Brandt's *Ostpolitik* (Eastern policy), launched in 1970, was progressing. On the contrary, it made very little headway. The Soviet-West German and Polish-West German treaties were not ratified by West Germany. The only concrete result was that German-speaking residents of Poland who wished to emigrate to West Germany began to do so in some numbers in 1971, as arranged by the Polish treaty.

In general terms there appeared to be a lessening of tension between the Soviet Union and its Communist satellite states on the one hand and western Europe on the other. One symbol of this was the successful visit paid by Soviet Communist party chief Leonid Brezhnev to France from October 25 to 30, which resulted in the signing of a 10-year Franco-Soviet economic cooperation agreement. The Soviet Union also continued to propose European security conference. The United States, under congressional pressure to reduce its troops in Europe, pushed for negotiations with the USSR on mutual reductions of forces in Europe. Some observers considered the attitudes of the Western countries unrealistic. They could point to the steady increase in Soviet ground forces in recent years, while U. S. forces were reduced; to a corresponding shift in air power; to the growing Soviet presence in the eastern Mediterranean; or to Britain's expulsion in September of 105 Soviet officials for espionage.

Problem Areas. The problem of Northern Ireland, which is part of Britain, continued to be severe. Conditions actually worsened in 1971 in a deepening spiral of violence that appeared to present the British government with an insoluble dilemma. The nation with the most disordered politics in western Europe was Italy, where weak parliamentary government combined with serious rioting and rising unemployment to discredit the institutions of the republic. The election in December of the able Giovanni Leone to a 7-year term as president took 23 ballots. In Belgium, new laws were passed in July in an effort to resolve disputes among the linguistic groups that divide the country, but there was no certainty of success.

In eastern Europe a somewhat similar problem, on a larger scale, threatened the multi-ethnic society of Yugoslavia with disintegration. Only the strenuous interventions of Marshal Tito damped down secessionist sentiment in Croatia, which feels that it is being exploited to benefit more backward Serbia. Internal trouble in Yugoslavia is good news for the Soviet Union, which appears to be actively fomenting the dissension.

EUROPEAN COMMUNITY

The structure of international organizations in Europe is in a phase of transition, and a new structure will presumably emerge. The one great factor in the change, which has widespread implications, is the virtual certainty that Britain will join the EEC. Since 1958, six western European nations—France, West Germany, Italy, Belgium, the Netherlands, and Luxembourg, called "the Six"—have been linked in three functional bodies. Known collectively as the European Community, they are the European Economic Community, the European Coal and Steel Community (ECSC), and the European Atomic Energy Community (Euratom). Another western European trading bloc, looser than the EEC, is the European Free Trade Association (EFTA), whose members are Austria, Denmark, Iceland, Norway, Portugal, Sweden, Switzerland, and Britain, with Finland an associate member. Three EFTA members, Britain, Denmark, and Norway, as well as Ireland, whose economy is indissolubly linked to that of Britain, have been accepted for full EEC membership. Three other EFTA members, Austria, Sweden, and Switzerland, have been holding exploratory talks on a possible future relationship with the EEC, the ECSC, and Euratom.

Britain and the EEC. Britain's admission to the EEC has been in the air since 1961, when Prime Minister Macmillan's government announced its decision to seek membership. Membership will mean great changes for the Common Market, as well as for Britain, which in a preliminary step decimalized its currency on February 15.

British membership was agreed on after a year of intensive negotiations in Britain's third bid for entry. Britain reached final agreement with the EEC on the remaining major obstacles to membership on June 23. Some important points had been cleared up earlier. On June 7, Britain and the EEC ministers agreed on the phasing-out of sterling as an international reserve currency. On June 3, in London, ministers from 14 sugar-producing nations of the Commonwealth of Nations accepted the terms on sugar offered by the EEC in connection with Britain's entry. Agreement on New Zealand's exports to Britain, and Britain's contributions to EEC finances, as well as on minor issues, was reached in Luxembourg on June 21–23.

The final agreement consisted of several points. The Common Market will guarantee outlets for 71% of New Zealand's dairy exports to Britain until the end of 1977. Britain's contribution to the EEC budget is to reach about 19% by 1977. The EEC agreed that special measures might be necessary to enable continued hill farming in Britain to be profitable. The EEC also assented to temporary restrictions on the other members' fishing in British waters. It was agreed that even before membership of the current applicants becomes effective, the EEC will consult them when making decisions.

Britain is to be given a period of 4½ years in which to abolish all tariffs with the Six and become a part of the industrial common market. There will be a 5-year period in which to adjust to the market's agricultural policy. Britain will enter the European Coal and Steel Community during a 5-year transition period and Euratom after one year.

The successful conclusion of the negotiations left a number of transitional problems for Britain before membership, provisionally scheduled for Jan. 1, 1973. One problem was the opposition to membership by Harold Wilson's Labour Party, which had actively pursued admittance while in office. The House of Commons approved membership in principle by a large majority on October 28, but much enabling legislation remained to be passed.

Other EEC Developments. In many respects it was not a happy year for the community. Among the Six there was international monetary uncertainty and continued domestic inflation combined with a business slowdown. The 1970 Werner Report, contemplating "full economic and monetary union within the decade," was formally accepted as a policy goal on Feb. 9, 1971. The international monetary crisis of 1971, however, not only disturbed the economies of member-states but led to the adoption of individual monetary policies. The failure to achieve a common policy was even more striking after the surprise announcement of new U. S. policies on August 15. (See also INTERNATIONAL FINANCE.)

On July 23, the EEC agreed to extend generalized preferences to developing countries. On November 8 a trade agreement was signed with Argentina, the first between the EEC and a Latin American country. On October 18, Aldo Mazio became head of the first permanent EEC delegation to the United States.

European Coal and Steel Community. A survey of coal and steel capacity and contemplated investments suggested that annual coal output would probably decline some 22 million tons between 1970 and 1974, reaching a level of 161 million tons. This would be an annual decline of 3%, as against the 5% decline of 1966–70. On the other hand, after declining for 10 years, coking capacity is expected to increase in 1970–74 at an annual average rate of some 3%. There is vigorous continuing investment in steelmaking capacity, which is expected to increase from 127 to 161 million tons in 1970–74. An even higher growth rate, amounting to 7% annually, is expected in pig iron.

European Atomic Energy Community. The joint commission of the three European communities appointed Pietro Caprioglio as director general of the Euratom joint research center on February 4. His selection followed the commission's decision to grant greater functional autonomy to the center and testified to a certain revival of interest in Euratom. On October 1 the commission proposed that $145 million be allocated over the next three years to Euratom research and development.

OTHER EUROPEAN ORGANIZATIONS

European Free Trade Association. Total trade of the EFTA countries rose by some 10% in 1971, but this was only about two thirds of the rate of increase of the year before. The rate of increase of trade among EFTA members was 13%.

Negotiations opened early in December between the EEC and the six EFTA members (Iceland, Sweden, Finland, Switzerland, Austria, and Portugal) that are not seeking full EEC membership. The negotiations aim at establishing a free trade area in western Europe, embracing both the EEC and EFTA, for industrial products.

Organization for Economic Cooperation and Development. The OECD is now more than a purely European organization. The annual ministerial meeting of the OECD council was held in Paris on June 6–8, with U. S. Secretary of State Rogers presiding. The council admitted Australia as its 23d member. The final communiqué called for closer international cooperation to combat inflation.

Council of Europe. The council, a quasiparliamentary body, held the normal three annual sessions of its Consultative Assembly in January, May, and September. The chief topic of debate was the proposed enlargement of the European community. The low level of public interest in the council is suggested by the fact that Malta and Cyprus did not send delegations in May.

Western European Union. WEU, which consists of the Six and Britain, is primarily concerned with defense. It met in Paris on June 15–18 and recommended that, when Britain joined EEC, the three other EEC applicants (Ireland, Norway, and Denmark) should be invited to join the WEU.

North Atlantic Treaty Organization. The NATO foreign ministers met in Lisbon on June 4–5. The final communiqué agreed conditionally with the Soviet proposal for a conference on security and cooperation in Europe. It welcomed, but sought further clarification of, the Soviet response to NATO's 1968 proposal on mutual and balanced force-reduction in Europe. It was also announced on June 4 that Dutch Foreign Minister Joseph Luns would become NATO secretary general. The December meeting at NATO headquarters in Brussels edged closer to the proposed security conference. But by December the USSR was making West German ratification of the Soviet-West German and Polish-West German treaties a precondition to such a conference, which would undoubtedly delay it. The chief news of the December meeting was a decision by the 10 West European members to spend $1 billion more for their common defense in 1972, a decision welcomed by the United States.

At the request of Dom Mintoff, who became prime minister of Malta in June, NATO withdrew from the strategic island in 1971. Mintoff demanded a much higher rent for the use of the island's facilities, and in August NATO naval headquarters were moved from Malta to Naples. In September, Britain and NATO agreed to double their annual payments to Malta to $23.6 million. In December, Mintoff upped his demands to $46 million, including an immediate down payment of $11 million. The British government then ordered the withdrawal of all its forces from the island. While Malta is no longer regarded as essential for NATO's use, its use by the Soviets would give them a long-sought foothold in the western Mediterranean. Developments in Malta accentuate the concern for the growing weakness on NATO's southern flank.

See also COMMUNISM and articles on individual countries in Europe.

ARTHUR CAMPBELL TURNER
University of California, Riverside

EYE DISEASES. See MEDICINE.

Fashion

MANING

"We're ready for some sensible clothes."

"A woman should look like a woman, not a joke."

The first quote came from an executive of a New York specialty store; the second from a fashion expert in Italy. In 1971, from both sides of the Atlantic, the reaction had set in and the cry went out against the gypsy, the tramp, and the goddess styles in fashion, which had been confusing women and slowing down business.

Classicism. The United States is in a particularly fortunate position in this circumstance, because it is able to fall back on classics and separates, indigenous clothes that are surefire. Its designers did just that in 1971, and most European designers followed suit. These basics looked new as well as timeless.

THE RUFFLED LOOK, a fashion favorite in 1971, was stimulated by Yves St. Laurent's Proustian evening dresses.

BLAZER JACKETS for men and women returned to the forefront of fashion in 1971. These couples are wearing matching pantsuits designed by Pierre Balmain.

surprising demand on the part of urban women for ankle-length skirts for daytime wear. Was this a fad, or a fashion to be continued? Only time would tell.

Trends. The Chinese influence, which sprang up on the heels of Communist China's growing internationalism, fit hand-in-glove with the separate look. American designers brought out coolie coats and pants, tunic jackets, quilted jackets, and mandarin collars galore in cottons, satins, and exotic prints. Chinese motifs—dragons, chrysanthemums, and pagodas—were used in prints and in jewelry.

The emphasis on classics did not mean that revolutionary, more extreme fashions had disappeared. Hot pants continued to be the rage. Actually, they were the short-shorts of the 1950's, but worn on city streets. "Protest clothes" included old army surplus fatigues, work clothes, and jeans that were more and more ragged, dirty, and beat-up. The no-bra look and see-through fabrics continued in both hippie and sophisticated circles.

Coats came in a variety of styles. In addition to the wrapped coat, styles included short-and-chunkies, big tents and little tents, slim and long cardigans, the soft coat with tucked top and flaring shirt, and the blouson shape. Perhaps most welcome of all was the return of the flattering fur-collared coats, because they have the look of luxury most women love.

First, there was the blazer jacket, going with skirts or pants in any season, for any age, making the old look young and the young look well-put-together. In 1971 the jacket came not only in velveteen and flannel, but in satin—especially red satin—in burlap, velvet, and prints. Along with blazers came the inevitable pleated skirt.

Pants reasserted themselves. It had been rumored that pants were merely the recourse of women who were in doubt about skirt lengths and that they might be going out of fashion, but this was not the case. Pants proved classic for American women, and never more so than in 1971. Pants included thousands of blue jeans for the "dungaree generation"; sharkskin, linen, tweed, and velvet for the more sophisticated. Trousers looked new in wide-legged sheer wools worn with chiffon blouses for evening, and in crisper daytime styles worn with long, sleeveless sweaters, peasant shirts, or smock tops.

The wrapped coat tied softly with a self-belt, which a few years ago belonged in every suburb and on every campus, came not only in the original camel color and in white, but in gray and in black. Sweaters were classic in name but not in appearance. Most were long and sleeveless, or bulky and boldly striped. Some, for resort and evening wear, were strapless, indicating a new trend. The little black dress came back again for day and night, but fitted and sexy, not in shapeless shifts.

Hems. Skirt lengths reverted to the timeless, Chanelish-length for day, hovering around knee length. Minis were still much in evidence. During the summer months, young women could be seen in ankle-length cotton dresses and skirts, and floppy hats, looking cool and assured in contrast to those in hotpants and minis. Late in the fall, there was a

PANTSUIT by Anne Klein features tweed pants and vest and blazer of tapestry fabric. The rust and cream outfit is worn with a cream-colored stock shirt in satin.

This was the year women could easily find a dress. The classic that Claire McCardell called the Monk's dress in the 1940's now became the "tent," bound around the bustline, Greek fashion, or flowing free. In contrast, the body dress hugged the bustline, then flared, often bias-cut, to the hem. Shirt dresses reverted to the classic with pleated skirts and waistlines. Jumpers were popular for all ages. Smocks provided a modified mini look. Dolman-sleeves produced another dress silhouette.

A great vogue for dress-up dresses included taffetas and ruffled black dresses, often with bare backs or camisole necklines with rhinestone shoulder straps. The "Proust dress," designed by Yves St. Laurent and widely copied, stimulated the "ruffled black" fashion. Mark Bohan of Christian Dior did his part with the thirty-yards of chiffon dress, as did Pierre Cardin with the theatrical American Beauty taffeta ballgown. American designers loved plaid taffeta and dark chiffons, and made sensations with sheer shimmery knits.

Suits appealed to many women. The Chanel collection instituted shorter jackets in black, pink, and gray, and featured a tweed jumper with its own matching jacket. St. Laurent called his 4-pocket Safari style "the quiet suit" but made it in green, white, and orange tweed, a big hit in the United States. Bill Blass showed a popular divided skirt in plaid wool with a matching topcoat and another best seller in black wool with its jacket outlined in red fox. Other best sellers were the classic pleated skirts and blazers.

Fabrics. America continued to turn out most of the world's knitwear. New wool jerseys were as washable as nylons. Patterns included stars, flowers, big arrows, new ribs and zigzag argyles, porous crochet knits, and Zodiac signs. There were new combinations of acetate and nylon, of polyester, nylon and flax, and many variations of cotton and dacron. Satins were made of nylon blends rather than the more expensive silk. Seersucker made a big comeback. A new denim seersucker had a denim weave and a seersucker crinkle. Quilting, from calico to satin fabrics, was popular, and taffeta enjoyed the biggest revival in years.

Colors. Black was emphatically "in" again, for day and night. Little black bras and black nylons were in demand. Red was a sure thing, whether in satin jackets or shoes, as were strong pinks and pure orange. Women who had never worn purple reached for it. Red, white, and navy were natural for the classics. Turquoise blue and enamel yellow grew out of the Chinese trend.

Accessories. Stretch pantyhose were so popular that women often found it difficult to locate regular nylon stockings, which often turned up in bins in discount stores. Body stockings, like ballet dancers' leotards, were an outgrowth of pantyhose. Textures and bright colors continued to play up legs. Higher heels, still in the blocky shapes popular in 1970, grew in acceptance. Wedges which made women taller were especially welcome after years of the flat-footed look. Nothing really new appeared on the hat horizon.

(Continued on page 284)

PANTS proved to be a fashion classic for women. Despite rumors that they were going out of favor, pants remained popular with all groups. This pantsuit is by Norman Norell.

GABRIELLE CHANEL (1883–1971)

CHANEL

'COCO'

On Jan. 11, 1971, the world lost one of its foremost fashion designers. Gabrielle Bonheur Chanel, nicknamed "Coco" ("Little Pet") by her father, died in her apartment at the Ritz Hotel in Paris at the age of 87. She had not been ill, and had worked up to the last day on her spring collection. Her own words are her best epitaph:

"There is time for work. And time for love. That leaves no other time."

The New York *Times* called her "the fashion spirit of the 20th century." *Women's Wear Daily* said, "She was probably the greatest fashion force who ever lived," and *Vogue* summarized her influence: "Her indomitable spirit, logic and foresight swept women out of the 18th century, straight into the 20th."

Early Life. Chanel was born on Aug. 19, 1883, near Issoire, in south central France. Her career began in 1911, selling hats in a tiny shop in Paris. In 1914, she opened a shop at 31 Rue Cambon, where her couture house is located today. By 1924, she dominated the Paris fashion world. During World War II she went into seclusion, but in 1954 she made her famous comeback, and the Chanel suit became the uniform of well-dressed women around the world. In 1969 the musical *Coco* was produced on Broadway.

Many of her fashion ideas grew out of her colorful personal life. In 1914, during one chilly day at the races, she borrowed a sweater from a jockey, and within a week sweaters were "in." In Venice, she wore trousers because they were comfortable in gondolas. In the 1920's she became sunburned, and suntans became the vogue.

Chanel's romances and friendships made public headlines. It was to Hugh Richard Arthur Grosvenor, 2d Duke of Westminster, after his proposal of marriage, that she made her noted remark "There are a lot of duchesses, but only one Coco Chanel." She supported Sergei Diaghilev's ballet when he was hard pressed, and she was a friend of Stravinsky, Picasso, and Balenciaga.

The Chanel Look. Chanel liberated women from stilted styles and constricted clothes and created the casual, young look usually associated with American fashion. Technically, she eliminated the bosom dart, made the armhole high, small and tight, and inserted a narrow strip of fabric at the side seams.

Asked for the secret of her universally wearable clothes, especially her suit, one of her close associates answered, "She knew the body, was a sculptor with her hands."

Her most popular style was the Chanel suit, usually in tweed, with an easy skirt and a collarless, patch-pocketed jacket. It was copied at more prices than any other single fashion ever designed. Jersey was used as a dress fabric; there were trousers for women, sweaters, trenchcoats, and pea jackets. Her signature included the bow-neckline blouse, bobbed hair, the "little black dress," the quilted bag with the chain handle, sling-back pumps, hairbows at the nape of the neck, berets and sailor hats, pearls and chain necklaces.

Chanel loved the youthful look, but despised "old little girls." She berated the entire mini fashion, calling it "an exhibition of meat." True to her own standards of taste and wearability, she consistently kept skirt lengths just below the knee.

Chanel was a Leo, with all the strong-willed qualities this sign of the Zodiac represented. Her favorite color was white, with beige next; her flower the gardenia; her jewel the ruby. She was superstitious: a fortune-teller once declared that her lucky number was 5—hence, the name of her perfume, "Chanel No. 5," introduced in 1922, which made her a millionaire. Chanel loved simplicity and elegance and detested the contrived and the pompous.

After Chanel. In April 1971, this reporter visited 31 Rue Cambon, was shown Mademoiselle's private quarters with the famous antique Coromandel screens, and saw her last collection. Chanel had left a wealth of ideas but no financial endowment for her house. Her associates simply took it for granted that she would want them to continue. A team of designers, coordinated by Gaston Berthelot, designed the fall 1971 collection, which was well received.

The beautiful tweeds were in pale apricot, violet and white, peach and brown, and beige and white. The lamé dinner suits were in pink and violet. A scarlet-red sweater suit was widely acclaimed; the little white suit was still there, along with the braid bindings, the chains and hairbows, the simple tweed coats, and the sling pumps. All was a tribute to Chanel, testifying to her influence on her staff. The Spring '72 collection was scheduled for January as usual.

RUTH MARY (PACKARD) DuBOIS

THE CHANEL LOOK, seen here in designs from her last collection, has a timeless quality. The classic Chanel suit was her most popular design, and throughout the mini-midi furore her skirt lengths never varied. The elegance associated with her clothes is evident in this romantic and feminine evening dress. Chanel also introduced one of the world's most popular fragrances—Chanel No. 5.

PHOTOS BY CHANEL

THE WRAPPED COAT was one of the year's big hits. Tied with a soft belt, it came in all colors and lengths. Among the favorite designs were (*left to right*) a vicuna-colored coat by Muriel Reade for the Joseph Stein Collection, a navy coat with brass buttons from Originala by Elie Wacs, Calvin Klein's grey flannel coat, and a polo coat by Jaeger.

(Continued from page 281)

Shawls continued colorful and wearable. Rhinestone jewelry, looking well with black, was another 1940's revival, and rhinestone pins and earrings, in various shapes including stars, chevrons, and animals, had infallible appeal. Quantities of long chains and quilted bags were part of the classic Chanel style. Wide bracelets and ethnic necklaces contributed an international flavor.

Makeup grew brighter. Bright red was seen again on lips and fingernails. No one hairdo dominated the scene, and wigs were everyday affairs.

Children's Fashions. Little girls loved long dresses. More nightgowns were sold to wear by day than by night. Little boys enjoyed work clothes, usually made of blue denim. Sweaters came with designs of apples, fairytale castles, and dolls that looked like paper cut-outs. Chinese pajamas, often with quilted tops, made good dress-up clothes for girls. Other popular dresses had long sleeves and

HOT PANTS were the rage of Summer '71. Really the short-shorts of the 1950's, they were jazzed-up and worn on city streets. Women had found a way to avoid the midi and still remain "fashionable."

were often in challis-type prints. Bright jumpers, often in quilted cotton, were worn with dark turtlenecks and matching tights.

Men's Fashions. If any one type of fabric could be called most typical of the contemporary era, the knitted blends would be top choice. Knits extended to the entire area of men's clothes in 1971. Business suits and daytime dress shirts in knitted fabrics were the big news.

Many suits were double-knits and stretch knits and came in wool blends and polyesters. Some of the fabrics were from London, still a prestige spot for men's fashions. Jacket and slacks coordinates were popular in knits, in varied weaves and colors.

Wide lapels were accepted fashion, as were wide ties, many in big florals like drapery fabrics. Striped shirts persisted, but perhaps were not as bold as in previous years. Color blends became fashionable; for example, a dusty rose shirt and maroon floral tie, worn with a gray or brown suit.

The casual trend grew. During the summer, highly colorful combinations were seen at country clubs and afternoon parties: pink and purple shirts with classic blazers. The tieless, open-at-the-neck shirt was customary for almost every occasion except strictly business. The over-shirt, worn outside the trousers, was more in evidence—not the "Key West floral" but more sophisticated two-piece coordinates. One example was the velveteen shirt and trouser for at-home wear.

The newest suede jacket was the four-pocket Safari style. An old favorite, the reindeer sweater, often in sleeveless styles, was revived in 1971. Sports shirts came in ecological prints, geometrics, Western patterns, and madras stripes and plaids.

Bluejeans were sold by the thousands. "Cheap jeans" were advertised as "made expensively and sold only at the finest stores." A winter-weight denim used in tailored suits, jackets, and coats countered the cheap-denim trend.

Men's shoes were more interesting than in previous years. Boot styles gained in importance. Two-color, two-fabric, or two-leather shoes were popular all year, another indication that men were seeking more variety and independence in their wardrobes than ever before.

RUTH MARY (PACKARD) DuBOIS
Fashion Institute of Technology, New York City

FEDERATION OF ARAB REPUBLICS

On Sept. 1, 1971, Syria, Libya, and Egypt officially formed a union called the Federation of Arab Republics. The federation was overwhelmingly approved by the voters of all three countries. Egypt, which had called itself "The United Arab Republic" since its merger with Syria in 1958 (although Syria had broken away again in 1961), assumed the name "Arab Republic of Egypt." See EGYPT; LIBYA; SYRIA.

FIJI

Economic expansion dominated activities in Fiji in 1971, its first year as an independent nation.

Government Plans. A 5-year development plan was initiated in 1971. It provides for increased borrowing to finance improvements in agriculture, fisheries, forestry, tourism, and social services. Specific projects include a new parliament building in Suva and a hospital at Lautoka.

In March the government announced a combined loan and grant to finance continued operations by the Emperor Gold Mining Company at Vatukoula. Industry will be developed on part of the company's land to provide work as mining declines. In April 1973 the government will take over all shares in the South Pacific Sugar Mills, Ltd., a subsidiary of the Australian-owned Colonial Sugar Company, which in 1970 gave notice of its intention to withdraw from all milling operations in Fiji.

New Industries. Factories to manufacture food products, clothing, and building supplies were being established on an industrial park between Suva and Nausori in 1971. Fiji's second brewery and an industrial alcohol distillery were to be built at Lautoka. The Fijian government approved construction of an American oil refinery on the northwest coast of Viti Levu.

University Plans. The University of the South Pacific at Suva began organizing a series of regional university centers in the Pacific Islands. One of the first will be on Tarawa in the Gilbert and Ellice Islands.

HOWARD J. CRITCHFIELD
Western Washington State College

--------- FIJI • Information Highlights ---------

Official Name: Fiji.
Area: 7,055 square miles (18,272 sq km).
Population (1970 est.): 520,000. *Density,* 60 per square mile (28 per sq km). *Annual rate of increase,* 2.5%.
Chief City (1970 est.): Suva, the capital, 55,000.
Government: *Head of state,* Elizabeth II, queen (represented by Sir Robert Foster, governor-general, took office 1970). *Head of government,* Ratu Sir Kamisese Kapaiwai Tumacilai Mara, prime minister (took office Oct. 10, 1970). *Legislature*—Parliament; Senate, 22 members; House of Representatives, 52 members.
Language: English (official).
Finances (1970): *Revenues,* $41,633,000; *expenditures,* $40,-307,000; *monetary unit,* Fiji dollar (.8849 F. dollar equals U. S.$1, 1971).

FINLAND

Domestic politics and foreign affairs were lively in Finland in 1971. The Communists were maneuvered out of the coalition government; the government fell in a price crisis; joint undertakings were set up with the USSR; and Finland raised the issue of normalizing relations with the two Germanys.

On January 20, Finland proposed Max Jakobson, its delegate to the United Nations, as a candidate for the UN secretary-general post.

--------- FINLAND • Information Highlights ---------

Official Name: Republic of Finland.
Area: 130,120 square miles (337,009 sq km).
Population (1970 est.).: 4,700,000. *Density,* 36 per square mile (14 per sq km). *Annual rate of increase,* 0.7%.
Chief Cities (1970 est.): Helsinki, the capital, 535,200; Tampere, 155,600; Turku, 154,700.
Government: *Head of state,* Urha Kaleva Kekkonen, president (took office March 1, 1968, for 3d 6-year term). *Prime Minister,* Teuvo Aura (took office Oct. 29, 1971). *Legislature* (unicameral)—Eduskunta, 200 members. *Major political parties*—Social Democratic party, National Coalition party, Center party, People's Democratic League (Communist), Swedish People's party, Liberal party, Christian party, Rural party.
Languages: Finnish (official), Swedish (official).
Education: *Literacy rate* (1971), 99% of population. *Expenditure on education* (1968), 23% of total public expenditure. *School enrollment* (1968)—primary, 407,245; secondary, 488,870; technical/vocational, 99,313; university/higher, 54,886.
Finances (1970): *Revenues,* $2,447,000,000; *expenditures,* $2,180,000,000; *monetary unit,* markka (4.20 markkaa equal U. S.$1, Aug. 1971).
Gross National Product (1970): $10,221,000,000.
National Income (1970): $8,022,800,000; *national income per person,* $1,706.
Economic Indexes: *Industrial production* (1970), 161 (1963 = 100); *agricultural production* (1969), 118 (1963 = 100); *consumer price index* (1970), 115 (1967 = 100).
Manufacturing (metric tons, 1969): Sawnwood, 6,648,000; residual fuel oil, 2,865,000; wood pulp, 1,834,000; cement, 1,759,000; newsprint, 1,240,000.
Crops (metric tons, 1969 crop year): Oats, 1,146,000; potatoes, 1,029,000; barley, 855,000.
Minerals (metric tons, 1969): Iron ore, 393,000; zinc ore, 77,300; nickel ore, 4,819; vanadium ore, 1,226.
Foreign Trade (1970): *Exports,* $2,306,000,000 (chief exports —paper, $630,000,000; wood, $365,000,000; wood pulp, $291,000,000). *Imports,* $2,636,000,000 (chief imports, 1968—nonelectrical machinery, $213,000,000; mineral fuels and lubricants, $207,000,000; chemicals, $186,000,000). *Chief trading partners* (1968)—United Kingdom (took 20% of exports, supplied 13% of imports); USSR (15%—16%); West Germany (10%—15%).
Transportation: *Roads* (1970), 44,149 miles (71,048 km); *motor vehicles* (1969), 748,000 (automobiles, 643,100); *railroads* (1969), 3,553 miles (5,717 km); *merchant fleet* (1971), 1,471,000 gross registered tons; *national airline,* Finnair; *principal airport,* Helsinki.
Communications: *Telephones* (1970), 1,089,700; *television stations* (1968), 35; *television sets* (1969), 987,000; *radios* (1969), 1,717,000; *newspapers* (1969), 68.

Cabinet Crises. Three Communist ministers—members of the People's Democratic League, or SKDL—in Prime Minister Ahti Karjalainen's 5-party coalition, which had been formed in June 1970, voted on March 16 against a government-backed price increase. Although Karjalainen won a 131-to-51 vote of confidence, he resigned the next day, and on March 26 he reconstituted his cabinet, replacing Communists with Socialists. Thus ended a 5-year "Finnish model" in which Communists took part in coalitions.

On October 29, after an unexpected crisis over farm prices caused the fall of the Karjalainen government, President Urho Kaleva Kekkonen named Teuvo Aura, the mayor of Helsinki, to head a caretaker cabinet, dissolved the parliament, and ordered new elections for early 1972.

Relations with the USSR. On his return in April from a visit to the USSR, Karjalainen said, "Our relations have not in any way been disturbed by recent domestic events." Additional comfort was found in Soviet leader Leonid Brezhnev's words, "Good neighborliness and cooperation with Finland have strengthened." In 1971 a new 5-year trade pact with the USSR came into force. Agreements were signed for large-scale deliveries of natural gas to Finland, for Finnish participation in building a Soviet forest products complex, and for purchase of a second Russian nuclear reactor. The first nuclear plant, at Loviisa, will be completed in 1976.

German Policies. The four-power Berlin agreement and other favorable European developments prompted the Finnish government to move in September toward more normal diplomatic relations with both German regimes. It was explained as "a logical continuation of Finland's German policies, within the framework of strict neutrality." East Germany's response was affirmative; West Germany was evasive; Washington complained that the timing was "unfortunate."

Conference Hopes. President Kekkonen's pet project—a European, U. S., and Canadian security conference—appeared more imminent at year's end. Foreign Minister Väinö Leskinen predicted a preliminary big-power meeting at Helsinki in 1972.

Economic Slowdown. Most economic indicators dipped in 1971. The slowdown was attributed to strikes in metals, building, and other sectors of industry, greater unemployment, reduced demand for Finnish exports—which account for 25% of total industrial production—and an alarming growth in imports. Gross national product rose by only 3%, in contrast to 7% in 1970. For the first eight months of the year, industrial production was down 2%. Living costs, meanwhile, rose by nearly 8%, and wages increased by more than 9%, partly because of a new national minimum wage law. Unemployment averaged more than 50,000, out of a work force of 2.4 million.

For the January-August period of 1971, imports rose 5% over the record 1970 level, while exports remained unchanged, resulting in a large trade deficit. About 60% of the exports to the United States were affected by the U. S. 10% surcharge imposed in August.

Agricultural production grew by 3% in 1971, as against a rise of only 0.4% in 1970. Some advances were made toward providing reasonable incomes for a dwindling rural work force.

Budgeted expenditures for 1972 showed an overall increase of 15% over the previous year.

Long-range favorable factors appeared ahead, however. They included a forthcoming reduction in the size of the wage-earning population; the ministry of labor's coordination of manpower with economic, educational, housing, and retraining policies; and a new Regional Development Fund that began its operations on May 1.

JOHN I. KOLEHMAINEN
Heidelberg College, Ohio

FIRES

Fires in the United States in 1971 killed 12,200 persons and caused $2.8 billion in property losses, according to preliminary estimates of the National Fire Protection Association (NFPA).

The nation continued to make headway against the fire problem, NFPA studies showed. During the 10-year period ending in 1970, the number of fire deaths per 1,000 population declined slightly and the number of fires per 1,000 population rose only 0.74% despite a great increase in the amount of property subject to burning. Substantially because of inflation, the per capita cost of fire continued to climb, rising from $8.61 in 1960 to $12.81 in 1970.

Worst Fires. The greatest loss of life from fire during the first half of 1971 occurred on June 7, when rapidly spreading flames followed the crash and explosion of an airliner in East Haven, Conn., killing 28 of the 31 persons aboard. In Brunswick, Ga., 24 lives were lost in the February 3d fire and explosion at a plant that manufactures military flares. In major residential disasters, 13 persons died

in an early morning apartment house fire in Seattle, Wash., on April 25, apparently caused by careless smoking, and 10 of the 94 residents of a home for senior citizens in Buechel, Ky., died—mainly of smoke inhalation—in a fire on January 14.

On June 24, fire aboard the ore carrier *Roger Blough*—which was nearing completion in the shipbuilding yards in Lorain, Ohio—resulted in losses of $10 million. A $9 million loss occurred on April 12 in Emporia, Va., where fire at a plywood manufacturing plant was set off by explosions in an electrical switch box. On February 26, at an automobile parts warehouse and distribution center in San Antonio, Texas, an electric motor on a floor sander sparked and ignited some solvent that had been used on the floor, resulting in fire losses of $8.1 million. An explosion costing $5.3 million occurred in a polystyrene foam manufacturing plant in Covington, Ga., on April 21.

1970 Losses. Final NFPA estimates for 1970 show that 2,549,550 fires claimed 12,200 lives and destroyed property valued at $2,630,400,000.

LARGE-LOSS FIRES IN THE UNITED STATES, 1970
(Individual loss of $250,000 or more)

Classification	Number	Loss
Industrial	110	$136,111,000
Storage and warehousing	106	85,044,000
Stores and offices	106	78,704,000
Schools and colleges	26	18,315,000
Churches	18	10,555,000
Restaurants and nightclubs	17	10,117,000
Hotels and motels	14	7,492,000
Apartments	14	6,421,000
Buildings under construction	13	12,183,000
Miscellaneous	80	119,853,000
Total	504	$484,795,000

Building fires numbered 992,000 (up 1.9%) and cost $2,209,200,000 (up 14.2%). There were 634,700 fires in homes and apartments, resulting in 6,550 deaths and $736 million in property losses.

Fires in places other than buildings involved farm, construction and transportation vehicles of all types (500,850 fires) and forests, farmland, grass, brush, and rubbish (1,056,700 fires). These 1,557,550 non-building fires were 7.3% more than in the previous year.

CHARLES S. MORGAN
National Fire Protection Association

FISCHER, Bobby. See BIOGRAPHY.

FISHERIES

The 1971 U. S. domestic catch was 4.94 billion pounds—slightly above the 4.88 billion pounds of 1970. An increase in menhaden catches more than offset lower landings of salmon, tuna, shrimp, and several other species. U. S. fishermen received about $584 million for their efforts in 1971—down slightly from $602 million received in 1970. Prices of most fish were higher in 1971, but lower quantities caught brought total earnings down, particularly for salmon and tuna.

The 1971 U. S. fishing fleet included about 13,000 vessels of 5 gross tons and over and some 68,000 smaller boats, and it was manned by about 130,000 fishermen. The vessels took about 75% of the catch and the boats about 25%. Over 90% of the U. S. catch is taken in coastal waters, and the remainder—primarily tuna—is taken off the coasts of other countries. The total annual catch has been relatively uniform for 35 years.

U. S. COAST GUARD launch off Cape Cod heads for conference aboard Soviet fishing trawler. Russian fishermen were accused in 1971 of cutting American lobstermen's lines.

Per capita consumption of edible commercial fishery products was about 11.2 pounds in 1971—off slightly from 11.4 pounds in 1970. Consumption has ranged between 10 and 11 pounds per capita for several decades.

Fish farms are a rapidly growing segment of U. S. fisheries. In 1970 about 148 million pounds were harvested from commercial farms in 39 states. This production resulted in an income of about $57 million with an estimated retail value of $121 million.

Tuna. Total landings of tuna in the continental United States and Hawaii were about 340 million pounds in 1971 and were valued at $74 million. Although the quantity was down by about 14% from 1970, the value of the catch was almost the same because of the higher prices paid to fishermen.

Salmon. The U. S. salmon catch in 1971 was about 268 million pounds, valued at $65 million. This catch was about one-third less than that of 1970. Alaska had 188 million pounds, and the combined catch in Washington, Oregon, and California was 80 million pounds.

Groundfish. Most fish in this category are sold as fillets or in fish-and-chips restaurants. The cod catch in 1971 was about 53 million pounds, or about the same as the year before. Haddock has been overfished, and stocks have been declining steadily for several years. The U. S. catch of haddock in 1971 was about 21 million pounds—the smallest in this century. Pollock catches rose for the third consecutive year in 1971 to nearly 12 million pounds. Atlantic ocean perch catches were a little above 1970 at about 60 million pounds. Whiting catches were a little less than 30 million pounds—the lowest in the past 20 years.

Shrimp. The U. S. catch of shrimp was a record 235 million pounds (heads-off weight) in 1971. More than half of the catch came from the Gulf of Mexico. Louisiana was the leading shrimp-producing state with 59 million pounds.

Menhaden. Nearly half of the United States fish catch is composed of menhaden. This is an industrial fish that is ground into a fish meal which becomes an important part of the feed of chickens. The U. S. catch of menhaden in 1971 was about 2.15 billion pounds, the largest since 1962 and one of the top four years in the history of this fishery.

Whaling. The Department of Commerce issued an order prohibiting commercial whaling by U. S. fishermen after Dec. 31, 1971. Importation of whale products after this date was prohibited by an Interior Department order issued under the Endangered Species Act.

World Catch. The world fish catch rose by more than 10% during 1970, the Food and Agriculture Organization reported. The total 1970 catch reached a new record of 69.3 million metric tons. In the previous year it had been 62.9 million metric tons. Peru remained the leading fishing nation in 1970, with a total of 12.6 million tons.

Centennial. The National Marine Fisheries Service (formerly the Bureau of Commercial Fisheries) observed its 100th anniversary in 1971. On Feb. 9, 1871, President Ulysses S. Grant signed into law a joint resolution for the protection and preservation of the food fishes off the coasts of the United States. Since its formation, the agency has made many notable contributions to the proper use and conservation of U. S. fishery resources.

DONALD R. WHITAKER
National Marine Fisheries Service

FLORIDA

The major issues in Florida in 1971 were economic growth, ecology, and tax reform.

Economic Growth. Although the nation's economy as a whole appeared to enter a period of stagnation in 1971, Florida's economy continued to expand rapidly, with new industries and other businesses attracted to the state, partly as a result of Florida's mild climate. The most dramatic growth potential stemmed from the opening of Walt Disney World, near Orlando, on October 1. A larger version of California's Disneyland, Walt Disney World, which had 400,000 visitors during the opening month, is expected to make central Florida the convention and vacation center of the East.

Natural resources continued to be developed apace. With the exploitation of significant petroleum deposits in northwest Florida in 1971, several major oil companies sought authorization to search for deposits in the central and southeastern areas of the state.

Ecology. While new residents and industries are a welcome source of prosperity, Floridians are increasingly aware of the problems that are in part a by-product of growth. Alarmed by the serious pollution of Escambia Bay, near Pensacola, which caused a major fish kill and destroyed valuable

--------- **FLORIDA • Information Highlights** ---------

Area: 58,560 square miles (151,670 sq km).
Population (1970 census): 6,789,443. *Density,* 117 per sq mi.
Chief Cities (1970 census): Tallahassee, the capital, 71,897; Jacksonville, 528,865; Miami, 334,859; Tampa, 277,767; Saint Petersburg, 216,232; Fort Lauderdale, 139,590.
Government (1971): *Chief Officers*—governor, Reubin O'D. Askew (D); lt. gov., Tom Adams (D); secy. of state, Richard B. Stone (D); atty. gen., Robert L. Shevin (D); treas., Thomas D. O'Malley (D); supt. of public instruction, Floyd T. Christian (D); chief justice, B. K. Roberts. *Legislature*—Senate, 48 members (30 Democrats, 15 Republicans); House of Representatives, 119 members (81 D, 38 R).
Education (1970–71): *Enrollment*—public elementary schools, 781,703 pupils; 32,418 teachers; public secondary, 646,193 pupils; 30,153 teachers; nonpublic schools (1968–69), 89,-500 pupils; 4,170 teachers; college and university (fall 1968), 201,914 students. *Public school expenditures* (1970–71), $1,040,381,000 ($765 per pupil). *Average teacher's salary,* $8,805.
State Finances (fiscal year 1970): *Revenues,* $2,226,037,000 (4% general sales tax and gross receipts taxes, $658,-197,000; motor fuel tax, $225,399,000; federal funds, $385,525,000). *Expenditures,* $2,116,316,000 (education, $1,075,701,000; health, welfare, and safety, $223,923,000; highways, $261,468,000). *State debt,* $891,039,000 (June 30, 1970).
Personal Income (1970): $25,397,000,000; per capita, $3,584.
Public Assistance (1970): $193,485,000. *Average monthly payments* (Dec. 1970)—old-age assistance, $56.45; aid to families with dependent children, $89.90.
Labor Force: *Nonagricultural wage and salary earners* (June 1971), 2,176,200. *Average annual employment* (1969)—manufacturing, 329,000; trade, 539,000; government, 379,-000; services, 387,000. *Insured unemployed* (Oct. 1971)—37,200 (2.4%).
Manufacturing (1967): *Value added by manufacture,* $3,682,-700,000. Food and kindred products, $627,200,000; chemicals, $466,100,000; ordnance and accessories, $407,700,-000; paper and allied products, $290,900,000.
Agriculture (1970): *Cash farm income,* $1,286,090,000 (livestock, $395,644,000; crops, $871,956,000; government payments, $18,490,000). *Chief crops* (1970)—Oranges, 6,197,-000 tons (ranks 1st among the states); sugarcane for sugar and seed, 5,997,000 tons (ranks 3d); grapefruit, 1,590,000 tons (ranks 1st); tobacco, 28,923,000 pounds.
Mining (1971): *Production value,* $318,682,000 (ranks 18th among the states). *Chief minerals* (tons)—Stone, 40,504,-000; sand and gravel, 12,975,000; clays, 962,000; petroleum, 5,260,000 barrels.
Fisheries (1970): *Commercial catch,* 187,700,000 pounds ($40,200,000). *Leading species by value* (1970)—Shrimp, $15,752,624; red snapper, $2,505,185; blue, hard crabs, $1,727,297; groupers, $1,433,043.
Transportation: *Roads* (1969), 87,654 miles (141,062 km); *motor vehicles* (1969), 3,895,000; *railroads* (1968), 4,348 miles (6,997 km); *airports* (1969), 113.
Communications: *Telephones* (1971), 4,141,600; *television stations* (1969), 24; *radio stations* (1969), 264.

oyster beds, as well as by growing pollution in major lakes, conservationists and interested citizens are calling for government on all levels to take concerted action to prevent further ecological disasters. The success registered in 1971 was due in no small degree to the leadership of Florida's new governor, Reubin Askew, and other state officials.

A signal victory for conservation came on January 19, when President Nixon issued an executive order halting construction of the controversial Florida Barge Canal. Canal opponents nationwide had warned that the economic and recreational value of the waterway was insufficient to justify the risk of damaging the porous underground limestone stratum that stores Florida's vital freshwater supply. Despite challenges by procanal forces in federal courts, Congress voted $665,000 to begin restoring the canal route to its original state. This action seemed to indicate the end of the canal, although some completed sections may be retained as recreational areas.

The canal victory resulted in part from warnings by geologists that if Florida's population continues its present rate of increase the state will face a shortage of fresh water by the end of the century, especially as a result of improper development of major river-basin ecosystems. Governor Askew convened a special water-management conference in Miami in September to discuss such problems as water pollution. He also recommended that the federal government assist Florida in acquiring vital aquifer areas, including parts of the Everglades and Big Cypress Swamp. By the summer, water-control boards reversed the policy of drainage and flood control and took measures to preserve and restore important freshwater basins. Also, in some areas zoning laws have been passed to prevent extensive development of such basins by realtors.

Tax Reform. Governor Askew, elected in 1970 on a platform of tax reform, began pushing through the Legislature a series of bills designed to ease the tax burden on individuals and increase taxes on corporations. The heart of his program was a constitutional amendment to permit a corporate profits tax, which was overwhelmingly approved in a referendum on November 3. The new tax will produce an estimated $100 million in new revenue, thus permitting the repeal or reduction of consumer taxes.

Other Legislation. The Florida Legislature failed to satisfy everyone, but it did achieve a remarkable record in 1971. Its actions included the state's first severance tax and provided new sources of revenue for cities through increased cigarette and gasoline taxes. It also liberalized divorce laws, created a no-fault automobile insurance system for the state, and ordered that a presidential preference primary be held on March 14 of presidential election years. These actions, plus reforms in the civil and criminal codes, marked the 1971 Legislature as one of Florida's most progressive.

Education. The tensions and disruptions caused by desegregation in 1970 subsided in 1971, and the emphasis in education was on improving the quality of the state system. In July, Governor Askew appointed a Citizens Commission on Education, which will submit recommendations for a complete revision of the system. The commission will cooperate with the Legislature's house education committee and has the support of the Florida Education Association.

J. LARRY DURRENCE, *Florida Southern College*

Italian farmers in Ferrara reacted to government's food price freeze by destroying fruit crop in September. Freeze was part of state's effort to combat recession.

food

The world production of food increased significantly in 1971 over 1970. Industrialized nations outstripped the less developed countries in production of both grain and meat. Larger harvests of grain would have enabled India to reach self-sufficiency in 1971, except for the disrupting presence of 10 million East Pakistani refugees. In the United States interest centered on food contamination and the problems of better labeling and measuring of packaged foods.

WORLD FOOD SUPPLY

World food production was significantly higher in 1971 than in 1970, with grain production increasing at least 7% and harvests of the major oilseeds —soybeans, peanuts, cottonseed, and copra—at least 4%. Meat production, which had been rising 3% per year in the 1960's, probably increased at an even higher rate in 1971 because of favorable pasture conditions, abundant supplies of feed in most industrialized countries, and strong consumer demand. Milk and sugar were the only important foods whose production did not keep up with population growth in 1971, but both showed gains in total output in industrialized countries and especially in Europe and the Soviet Union. A sharp drop in sugar production in the Caribbean area in early 1971 more than offset increases elsewhere in the less developed countries.

Increases in Grain Yields. The record-breaking grain production of 1971 resulted in part from exceptionally high yields, especially in the developed countries. Thus the combined average yield of all grains in western Europe was about 13% higher than in 1970 and at least 9% better than the previous record. Average yields of all grains in the United States were up by 17%.

In particular, record wheat yields were achieved in Austria, Belgium, Czechoslovakia, Egypt, Hungary, India, Portugal, Spain, the United States, West Germany, and Yugoslavia. New records for barley yields were set in Austria, Canada, India, Italy, Spain, Sweden, the United States, and West Germany.

However, the increase in average yield for the less developed countries from 1970 to 1971 was only half as large as for the developed countries. High-yielding varieties were planted on about 16% of the wheatland and 8% of the riceland in the less developed countries, a total of 52 million acres (21 million hectares). This total, while 9 million acres (3.6 million hectares) above 1970, was still only 6% of the total area planted with cereals. Little progress has been made in the development and use of higher yielding varieties of millet, sorghum, and corn, yet they account for 40% of the land devoted to cereals in India and Pakistan and even more in Africa and Latin America.

Farmers in industrialized countries continue to raise yields by adopting new varieties of grain, applying more fertilizer and pesticides, and changing their farming practices. The superiority of the developed countries in this respect is shown in the accompanying table, which is based on statistics from

AVERAGE YIELDS OF CEREALS

Region or country	Yield 1966–70 100 lbs/acre*	Percentage increase from 1961–65	1952–56	1948–52
Developed Countries				
Japan	44.9	18	44	53
United States	28.3	16	77	90
Europe	23.2	20	55	73
Canada	16.3	19	20	36
USSR	12.0	32	57	80
Australia, New Zealand, and South Africa	10.6	3	18	25
Average (weighted)	18.8	20	52	64
Less Developed Countries				
India and Pakistan	9.5	8	26	37
Other Far East areas (except Japan and Communist Asia)	15.7	7	21	27
Latin America	12.5	6	22	26
Near East	10.9	8	13	17
Africa (except Republic of South Africa)	7.5	5	25	31
Average (weighted)	10.8	7	23	32

* 100 lbs/acre equals 111 kg/hectare.

the Food and Agriculture Organization (FAO) of the United Nations.

Increase in Harvested Areas. An increase in area harvested accounted nearly as much for the big surge in grain production as did the increase in yields. Both the United States and Canada, after having cut acreages in 1970, raised them in 1971. In Canada barley acreage was raised almost 50%. U.S. farmers were encouraged to plant more wheat to rebuild depleted stocks, and more corn to offset a feared repetition of low yields caused by the Southern corn leaf blight. In Australia restraints on grain marketing were eased, and the total area for the 1971 grain crops rose almost 10%.

In all, the developed countries harvested 10% more grain from 5% more land in 1971 than in 1970, while the less developed countries reaped 5% more from 2% more land. These larger harvests enabled some grain-importing, less developed countries to reduce their imports. India would have achieved self-sufficiency but for the inflow of some 10 million refugees from East Pakistan (Bangladesh), a food-importing area in which food distribution was badly disrupted by aftereffects of the typhoon and flood of November 1970 and by the war in 1971.

Shortage in Animal Protein. The larger output of grain and other food crops enabled the majority of consumers in less developed countries to main-

PRODUCTION OF BEEF PER HEAD OF CATTLE

Region or country	1966–70 average (pounds per year)*	Percentage increase from 1961–65	1952–56	1948–52
Developed Countries				
United States	199	16	33	52
Canada	173	10	32	24
Europe	146	8	33	59
Japan	125	3	64	124
USSR	102	32	44	50
Australia, New Zealand, and Republic of South Africa	90	−3	12	21
Average (weighted)	145	13	30	40
Less Developed Countries				
Latin America	62	1	†	−2
Near East	37	0	†	22
Africa (except Republic of South Africa)	31	0	†	−3
Far East (except Japan)	7	6	†	10
Average (weighted)	30	4	†	6

* 1 pound = 0.45 kilogram.   † Comparable data not published.

tain or increase their carbohydrate intake, but there will be a continuing shortage of animal protein. According to FAO statistics, production of red meat—beef, mutton, and pork—averaged 105 pounds (47 kg) per person in the developed countries in the 1966–70 period, but only 21 pounds (9.4 kg) in the less developed countries. Moreover, some of the meat produced in the latter countries was exported to the richer lands.

Less developed countries have nearly twice as many cattle but get less than half as much beef from them, partly because few Indian cattle are slaughtered but largely because cattle there are not fed grain. The accompanying table shows the 1966–70 average yield of beef per head of cattle as 145 pounds (65 kg) per year in the developed countries, but only 30 pounds (13 kg) in the less developed countries. The table also shows that the former have made large gains since earlier periods, whereas the less developed lands have gained relatively little in the average yield of beef.

CHARLES A. GIBBONS
Economic Research Service
U. S. Department of Agriculture

U. S. FOOD INDUSTRY

The safety of foods continued to be a major concern of the food industry in 1971. In particular, several shipments of canned foods had to be recalled from the market because of the danger of botulism—a rare but deadly form of poisoning that can be caused by eating improperly prepared foods. In other developments, the National Academy of Sciences began studies to reappraise the safety of food additives, and the Food and Drug Administration (FDA) began to develop a quality assurance program for regulating the quality and safety of products made by food processors.

Contamination of Canned Foods. The entire line of canned foods manufactured by Bon Vivant, Inc., was recalled by the FDA early in July, soon after the FDA had determined that botulin—a bacterium-secreted toxin that causes botulism—was present in some cans of vichyssoise made by Bon Vivant. The recall, which included canned soups, sauces, and stews, was triggered by the death of a man who had eaten vichyssoise from one of the cans. Later, an investigation disclosed that the correct thermal sterilizing treatment had not been used in processing a batch of vichyssoise.

In August, the Campbell Soup Company recalled all of the chicken vegetable soup (about 4,600 cases) packed by its Paris, Texas, plant after discovering that at least one of the cans contained the botulin toxin. After an extensive investigation, William B. Murphy, Campbell's president, said the contamination was due to a combination of conditions. "These were above-average viscosity of the can contents, overfill of the can, and incomplete hydration of the dry ingredients, coupled with the Paris process used for the products that spoiled," he said.

On October 29, the FDA issued a warning that a quantity of Stokely-Van Camp canned green beans might be contaminated by the botulin toxin. However, it rescinded the warning a few days later after further testing showed that there was no botulin toxin in the cans.

On October 25, the nation's canners, through the National Canners Association, asked the FDA to institute more stringent regulations for canning operations. Their proposals included specific procedures for processing low-acid foods, for coding each lot processed, and for verifying the adequacy of the thermal process used. The FDA is expected to adopt these proposals and promulgate other provisions to ensure that canned foods are always processed safely.

Food Additives. Extensive studies of some 600 food additives that are on the FDA's Generally Recognized As Safe (GRAS) list were begun by the National Academy of Sciences for the FDA. After more refined testing, an independent scientific advisory body will determine whether previous judgment on these additives are still valid. The same appraisal was being applied to food coloring additives. As one result, the use of FDC Red 2 (amaranth), which is widely used in foods, will be disallowed in some foods and curtailed in others.

Quality Assurance Program. The incidents involving canned foods in 1971 focused attention on the need for improved federal controls to cope with the complexity of modern food processing. Many congressmen and consumer advocates called for more frequent inspections and more policing actions.

The 1971 FDA field staff could inspect each food plant only once every two years, on the average. However, the FDA is increasing the effectiveness of its inspection and policing action by establishing a quality assurance program in which factors critical to quality and safety are routinely monitored by the food processor. The significance of the program is that if the FDA inspects the quality control system and finds it satisfactory, it can have more confidence in what is happening in the plant on the days when its inspector is not there. This program, which the FDA has been developing with a small number of processors, eventually will be extended to the whole food processing industry.

Labeling. General Foods and Del Monte announced plans for listing all ingredients, including functional descriptions of additives, on the labels of their products, even though the FDA does not have the legal authority to require such labeling for foods having a standard of identity (most canned fruits and vegetables, preserves, jams, jellies, bread, cheese, ice cream, mayonnaise, salad dressing, peanut butter, etc.). Meanwhile, in partial response to a petition from one of Ralph Nader's consumer groups, the FDA said that all optional ingredients in foods having a standard of identity would have to be listed on the label.

THE NEW YORK TIMES

BOOM in popularity of health foods has been accelerated by increased concern for the environment. These organic vegetables in Burbank, Calif., market have been grown without use of synthetic fertilizers or pesticides.

Open dating, such as JAN 25 on a milk container, was another much-debated issue at several industry-government-consumer meetings. One major problem is that dates by themselves are not too meaningful since the quality of a food product is determined more by storage conditions than by age. Nevertheless, greater use of open dating appears inevitable; in fact, some food processors already have begun to replace coded dates with open dates.

Development of New Products. The development of distinctly new types of foods, often designated as engineered or fabricated foods, was stimulated by the school lunch program in 1971. The Department of Agriculture's overall objective for new fortified and extended foods was to cut costs or improve nutrition, using school lunches as a ready-made market. For example, a fortified baked product with cream filling can be used in school breakfasts as a replacement for fruit juice and bread and cereal. Also, meat extended with textured vegetable (soy) protein not only increases the nutritional value of the meat but also cuts costs. A meat hamburger patty extended with 30% soy protein cuts costs from 12 cents to 9 cents. Used in servings twice a week in the school lunch program, the annual savings are as much as $36 million for this one item alone.

HOWARD P. MILLEVILLE
Oregon State University

U. S. FOOD INDUSTRY

Group	Employees[1] 1968	Employees[1] 1969	Value added by manufacture (billions) 1968	Value added by manufacture (billions) 1969	Value of shipments (billions) 1968	Value of shipments (billions) 1969
Meat and poultry products........	308,000	311,000	$3.9	$4.1	$22.5	$24.9
Dairy products.....	219,000	213,000	3.5	3.5	13.2	13.4
Canned, preserved, frozen foods.....	268,000	271,000	3.8	4.1	10.0	10.7
Grain mill products........	110,000	112,000	3.0	3.3	9.8	10.4
Bakery products...	258,000	268,000	3.6	3.9	6.7	7.0
Sugar (raw and refined)........	31,000	31,000	0.7	0.7	2.4	2.5
Confectionery and related products..	83,000	83,000	1.3	1.4	2.9	3.1
Beverages, alcoholic and nonalcoholic.	221,000	227,000	5.2	5.7	10.0	11.1
Miscellaneous food products[2]........	135,000	139,000	3.1	3.5	9.9	10.5
Total[3]........	1,632,000	1,656,000	$28.2	$30.1	$87.3	$93.5

[1] Excludes employees at central administrative offices, distribution warehouses, and other auxiliary establishments. [2] Includes animal and vegetable oils and fats, roasted coffee, macaroni, potato chips, etc. [3] Details may not add to totals because of rounding. Source: Annual Survey of Manufacturers, U. S. Bureau of the Census.

NUTRITION

Nutritionists and consumer advocates in the United States addressed themselves in 1971 to the question of labeling foods for nutritional content beyond standards presently set by federal regulations. Discussion centered on what types of information would be most meaningful and how such information should be expressed. A basic issue was which foods should be labeled.

Labeling Nutritional Content. Consumer groups have proposed upgrading the nutritional status of processed foods—and perhaps unprocessed foods as well—by providing label information on the kinds and amounts of nutrients present. But which foods should be labeled? How should this be done? And would the cost be prohibitive?

Which Foods Should Be Labeled? Should all canned, frozen, and otherwise processed foods be included in such a program? And what about unprocessed foods? The U. S. Department of Agriculture data on the sale of food in the United States indicates that processed foods account for only about 25% of an individual's intake. The latest figures (for 1963) show that per capita consumption of food is a staggering 1,420 pounds a year, of which about 12% is commercially canned, 4.5% frozen (including ice cream and juice concentrates), and 10% cereals, grains, and baked foods. Even if all these foods were to be labeled for nutrient content, almost 75% of the food consumed in the United States would remain unlabeled.

Labeling unprocessed foods presents particular problems. Fresh fruits and vegetables throughout the country might well vary in nutrient content. The concentration of certain nutrients in some fresh produce depends on the weather just before harvesting. For example, the vitamin C content of tomatoes is related to the hours of sunshine the plant receives a day or so prior to picking. Furthermore, one plant might produce ripe tomatoes with varying vitamin C content, depending on the sunshine each tomato receives.

Federal Standards. Food and Drug Administration (FDA) regulations currently require that the label for processed foods state the name and address of the processor and the net weight of contents, and that it list the ingredients in decreasing order of concentration if there is no FDA standard of identity for the food. Standards of identity, specifying kinds and amounts of required and optional ingredients, have been established by the FDA for certain foods to prevent their adulteration and to facilitate their recognition by consumers. Such standardized foods include bread, rolls, enriched flour and other cereal products, canned fruit, evaporated milk with added vitamin D, and margarine with added vitamin A.

Enrichment. Since 1942, various processed foods have been supplemented with vitamins and/or minerals, the kinds and amounts of which are controlled by federal regulation. Such foods are labeled "enriched." Additional regulations affecting enrichment of foods provide that (1) the food should "make a significant contribution to the diet"; (2) the added nutrient should not unbalance the other nutrients in the foods; (3) no toxicity should result from normal usage of the enriched foods; (4) the nutrients should remain stable while the food is in storage and thus be available to the body.

Efforts have been made to provide the consumer with information about the added nutrients, but there are no guarantees that this will be of help. Vitamins added to a food as well as those naturally present may be destroyed by storage of the food under adverse conditions or during preparation. The important factor is the nutrient content of the food when it is eaten.

Units and Measures. The mechanics of displaying nutrient content on labels present special problems. For example, should the concentration of vitamin B_1 (thiamin) be given in units of weight—that is, milligrams per ounce—or as a percentage of the recommended dietary allowance? Initially, the latter course might appear more desirable—for example, 25% of the daily allowance for thiamin in a food. However, there are marked differences in thiamin allowances for growing children and adults, as listed in the Food and Nutrition Board's Recommended Dietary Allowances, and there is no constant relation between the nutrient requirements of different age groups. Thus it is difficult to select an age group as the standard of reference.

Another problem is selecting the unit of food for denoting nutrient content. An ounce may not be satisfactory for all foods, and the term "serving" is not precise. A can of peas may serve six persons in one family but only two in another.

Words describing the nutrients on a label may be misinterpreted. The sale of iodized salt decreased because some people believed the words "potassium iodide" represented a chemical additive, possibly toxic. Actually, for certain individuals iodized salt compensates for an iodide deficiency that might otherwise produce goiters. It is feared that some people may react similarly to other nutrients listed on a label and consume inadequate amounts of foods essential for good health.

Labeling Calorie Content. In the United States a nutrient that elicits much interest is the calorie, and a labeling program might well start with the caloric content of foods. Calories are recognized by a large segment of the public. The listed caloric content would be helpful in this period when so many new food products being introduced reportedly contain fewer calories than the products they are attempting to replace. The calorie is one of the more readily defined units and is not subject to many of the difficulties posed by citing other nutrients. The experience gained in resolving any problems associated with labeling this simple parameter should facilitate extending the labeling program to other nutrients.

Economics of Labeling. To ascertain the precise nutrient content of any food would require the application of analytical procedures to each batch of processed foods. If there is any marked deviation in the nutrient content, disruption and delays may result. The expense is sure to be high.

Some government agency would have to make certain that the statements on the label are accurate. The magnitude of the food industry is such that a tremendous effort would have to be made to monitor any nutrient labeling program. This could become a major and costly government operation.

If nutrient labeling were required for processed foods only, an economic advantage might accrue to unprocessed foods. The cost of nutritional labeling may increase the price of processed foods, and the increased sales of cheaper fresh products might reduce the efficacy of the program.

OLAF MICKELSEN and MODESTO G. YANG
Michigan State University

FOREIGN AID

In 1971 the world's richer nations made a generally unimpressive showing in supplying economic assistance to poorer nations, although recipients scored significant economic advances.

Overall Economic Aid Flow. In a worldwide review of economic aid in 1971, the Development Assistance Committee (DAC) noted that despite lagging contributions from richer nations, the average gross national product (GNP) of poorer states was increasing considerably faster than the 6% a year set by the United Nations as a minimum target for the 1970's. However, an annual population growth of nearly 2½% cut heavily into per capita gains. Also, much of the new wealth was concentrated in the hands of a few individuals rather than being widely distributed.

DAC Aid. Counting official and private sources, the 16 members of the DAC, who account for virtually all aid from non-Communist, industrialized states, provided $15.5 billion in net economic aid in 1970, an increase of 7% over 1969. The DAC review observed, however, that nearly half the rise was attributable to inflation. A 3% rise to $6.8 billion in the key category of government assistance was ascribed entirely to price increases.

Among DAC members, Japan's net economic aid in 1970 climbed to $1,824 million, an increase of 44% from 1969. Japan thus advanced from fourth place in amount of aid, behind France and Germany, to become second only to the United States. Japan's aid approached the 1% of GNP set as a target by the UN. Six DAC countries have achieved the target—Australia, Belgium, Britain, France, the Netherlands, and Portugal.

U. S. Aid. The United States raised its economic aid by some $700 million to $5.97 billion in 1970. It thus remained by far the world's largest donor, although in proportion of aid to GNP it ranked next to last among DAC nations.

Political developments in 1971 raised doubts about the future of U. S. foreign aid. In April, President Nixon submitted to Congress a sweeping plan to reorganize foreign aid based on the Peterson Report of 1970. He proposed splitting the traditional, single-package, annual military-and-economic aid measure into two, one dealing with economic and humanitarian aid and the other with security. The decade-old Agency for International Development (AID) would be replaced by two new institutions.

The House put off action on reform and on August 3 voted by a narrow margin of 200 to 192 to continue the present foreign aid program. On October 29 the Senate surprised and shocked the administration by voting 41 to 27 to kill the present program. Under strong pressure from the administration, Congress finally passed a temporary stopgap bill to continue the aid program.

Meanwhile, the administration was itself restricting foreign aid. The President ordered a 10% cut in U. S. outlays as part of his August 15 emergency economic program. Aid to India and Pakistan, two of the largest recipients, was curtailed and reviewed in light of the South Asian conflict.

Multilateral Aid. International non-Communist institutions continued to increase their economic aid. Contributions to multilateral agencies from the governments of DAC countries amounted to $1.1 billion in 1970, accounting for 16% of all official development assistance, compared with 6% in 1966. The World Bank group reported "good progress" in fiscal 1971 toward doubling its lending in the period 1969–73 over the preceding 5-year period. It listed its total development financing commitments in 1971 at $2.58 billion. The UN Development Program approved $130.9 million to aid 96 underdeveloped countries, who must themselves contribute $164.4 million. The EEC allocated $46 million to aid African countries.

Communist Aid. Economic aid from Communist states amounted to only a fraction of that from non-Communist sources. A 1971 Western intelligence survey estimated that pledged Communist economic aid climbed to $1.1 billion in 1970, an increase of about 25% from 1969. The largest figure in the total was about $700 million pledged by mainland China, a sum that nearly matched that nation's entire aid commitment in 1956–69 and marked its increased activity in international affairs. The major item in China's budget was more than $400 million for the Tan Zam railroad in East Africa. China was also said to have pledged $200 million to Pakistan.

Soviet economic aid pledged to non-Communist countries totaled about $200 million, the smallest amount since 1962. The balance of the Communists' $1.1 billion was made up of $185 million pledged by East European states for aid to less developed countries in Africa, Latin America, and the Middle East.

LEWIS GULICK
Diplomatic Affairs Reporter, Associated Press

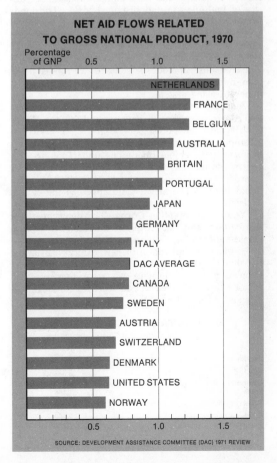

NET AID FLOWS RELATED TO GROSS NATIONAL PRODUCT, 1970

Percentage of GNP

- NETHERLANDS
- FRANCE
- BELGIUM
- AUSTRALIA
- BRITAIN
- PORTUGAL
- JAPAN
- GERMANY
- ITALY
- DAC AVERAGE
- CANADA
- SWEDEN
- AUSTRIA
- SWITZERLAND
- DENMARK
- UNITED STATES
- NORWAY

SOURCE: DEVELOPMENT ASSISTANCE COMMITTEE (DAC) 1971 REVIEW

FORESTRY AND LUMBERING

Continuing controversy over clear cutting in timber stands, legislative proposals for administration of the public lands, and litigation over the sale of federal timber in Alaska highlighted forestry and lumbering developments in the United States in 1971. A number of areas suffered losses from insect depredations.

Inquiry into Clear Cutting. The practice of clear cutting, or the complete removal of mature timber stands in given areas, continued to be criticized by the Sierra Club and other preservationist groups. Congressional committee hearings were held on the subject, and legislation was introduced to declare a moratorium on clear cutting on federal lands. Representatives of the U. S. Forest Service and the forest industries explained that the practice was necessary in the management of certain types of forest which can reproduce themselves only on open ground with full sunlight. The valuable Douglas fir in the Pacific Northwest is in this category.

Public Lands Administration. Legislative proposals were before Congress in 1971 to implement the recommendations of the Public Land Law Review Commission, which had completed a 5-year study of the vast hodge-podge of laws affecting the unreserved and unappropriated public domain. The public domain comprises some 484 million acres in the 48 contiguous states and Alaska, under administration of the Bureau of Land Management, Department of the Interior. The administration's proposals called for retention of most of this land in federal ownership and its administration under policies of multiple use and sustained yield. The lands would be known as "National Resource Lands."

Several bills introduced in the House and Senate called for repeal of the obsolete Mining Law of 1872, under which many claims were filed on public lands by unscrupulous persons for purposes other than mining. The bills proposed substitution of a mineral leasing system.

Alaska Timber Sale. The U. S. District Court for Alaska dismissed a suit entered by the Sierra Club against the Forest Service and U. S. Plywood-Champion Papers, Inc., under which the plaintiffs had sought to enjoin operations under a long-term contract to purchase 8.7 billion board feet of timber awarded to the company in Alaska's Tongass National Forest. The Sierra Club appealed the court's decision.

Youth Conservation Corps. The departments of Agriculture and the Interior operated 60 Youth Conservation Corps camps during the summer of 1971, under authorization of new federal legislation. In the program, about 2,200 young men and women, aged 15 through 18, were employed on various types of conservation work in national forests and other public areas.

Forest Management Program. An agreement for a cooperative federal-state program to provide technical advice and assistance on forest management to private landowners was signed by Gov. Jack Williams of Arizona and Secretary of Agriculture Clifford M. Hardin. Such programs were already operating in the other 49 states. In another of its phases, the cooperative program provides technical aid to operators of small wood-processing plants.

Timber Losses. Severe defoliation of trees by gypsy moth larvae was reported on one million acres in northeastern states in 1971. Tent caterpillars defoliated almost 2 million acres in Minnesota and substantial areas along the Ohio-West Virginia and Maryland-Pennsylvania borders. The gypsy moth, one of the world's worst forest pests, was introduced into the United States in 1869. It has since spread through most of New England, New York, New Jersey, and Pennsylvania, and was found in 1971 in Maryland and the District of Columbia.

In all, some 25 species of defoliators caused more than 7 million acres of defoliation during the year in the United States. In the West and South, bark beetles were the dominant marauders, causing the loss of several billion board feet of timber.

Favorable weather helped to hold forest-fire damage to moderate levels in the West during the first half of 1971, although serious situations developed in some areas later in the year.

Tree Planting. Area planted to trees for forest and wind-barrier purposes in 1970 totaled 1,599,819 acres, an increase of 142,349 acres over the preceding year. The 1970 total was the highest for any year since 1961, when 1,796,200 acres were planted. Of the 1970 plantings, federal agencies planted 317,782 acres; states and other non-federal public agencies planted 74,273 acres; and private landowners planted 1,185,190 acres. Forest industries accounted for 763,344 acres of the private plantings. Of the total plantings by all agencies, Oregon ranked first among the states with 162,375 acres; Florida second with 160,745; and Alabama third with 145,080 acres.

U. S. Forest Service. For the fiscal year 1972, the President's budget requested a total of $458,884,035 for the Forest Service, U. S. Department of Agriculture. This was an increase of $55 million over 1971 appropriations. The 1972 total included $225,118,000 for national forest management, $47,668,000 for forest research, $135,668,000 for forest roads and trails, and $24,067,000 for federal cooperation with states and private owners.

Lumber. Production of lumber in the United States in 1970 was estimated by the National Forest Products Association at 36,603,000,000 board feet, a drop of 1.35 billion from 1969. Lumber output in the first three months of 1971 was running at a seasonally adjusted rate that was about 2.6% above that recorded in 1970.

In Canada, lumber production in 1969 was 11,574,000,000 board feet, of which more than 95% was softwood. This was up about 4½% from 1968.

Estimated world production of sawnwood in 1969, according to the United Nations, was 408.5 million cubic meters, an increase of about 7.5 million cubic meters over the revised 1968 figure. (One cubic meter equals 424 board feet.) The increase was almost wholly in softwood production. The USSR ranked first in lumber production, followed by the United States, Japan, and Canada.

CHARLES E. RANDALL, *"Journal of Forestry"*

U. S. LUMBER PRODUCTION, 1969–70
(In million board feet)

Producing Regions	1969	1970
Southern pine region	7,645	7,700
Douglas-fir region	8,218	8,071
Western pine region	9,999	9,378
California redwood region	2,471	2,374
Other softwoods	1,148	1,116
Total softwoods	29,481	28,639
Southern hardwoods	3,986	3,936
Appalachian hardwoods	1,786	1,493
Other hardwoods	2,696	2,535
Total hardwoods	8,468	7,964

President Pompidou (*right*) confers with Britain's Prime Minister Heath on May 20. Leaders discussed unity of Europe and Britain's entry into Common Market.

FRANCE

The year 1971 was a relatively unexceptional one in France, marked by neither domestic nor foreign upsets. Nagging problems in politics, economics, and social policy remained unresolved. The overall national mood was subdued, though the country was somewhat unsettled by inflation, unemployment, restlessness among youth and farmers, and discontent among the middle-class supporters of the regime. There was also some preoccupation with the elections that must come by the spring of 1973. But the government tried to make light of its difficulties and failings. "Is an upward surge of prices, a difficult negotiation, or the disorderliness of a handful of fractious persons enough to disturb the French people and make them lose courage?" Premier Jacques Chaban-Delmas asked the National Assembly on April 20.

DOMESTIC AFFAIRS

Politics. The Gaullists of the Union of Democrats for the Republic (UDR) remained solidly in control of legislature, executive, and nation. Yet cracks widened in the structure of this party, which insisted it was "a movement" above parties. Jacques Vendroux, de Gaulle's brother-in-law, resigned in February, as did Christian Fouchet, many times a minister and a Gaullist from the first. Jean-Marcel Jeanneney, also a former minister, left in November. Some who remained, such as former premier

and longtime foreign minister Maurice Couve de Murville, expressed reservations about the policies of President Georges Pompidou. These included the making of overtures to de Gaulle's rebellious follower Jacques Soustelle, the acceptance of British application for Common Market (EEC) membership, and the blatant changing of the UDR into the instrument of the wealthier classes. Such dissidents held that in his last years General de Gaulle had been profoundly inclined to domestic change, including the restructuring of education and regional government, the strengthening of the Senate, and workers' participation in ownership and management. They concluded that all this was being jettisoned by the regime. Others, like Edgar Faure, tried to create resistance within the party, presiding over the "Left Gaullists." They hoped to retain the votes of the working class, bourgeois progressives, and certain intellectuals in danger of being lost by Pompidou in the 1973 elections.

By November the debate on the nature and structure of the UDR had reached serious proportions. Even cabinet ministers proclaimed opposing views. Before the Strasbourg congress on November 19–21, Pompidou tried to plaster over the cracks, but they remained. The UDR was in fact a "mass movement," embracing an absolutely independent right wing, the Independent Republicans, and four left-wing groups. It was supported by one

POMPIDOU waves to crowds in Yaoundé, Cameroon, during February tour of former French colonies in Africa. He also visited Mauritania, Senegal, Ivory Coast, and Gabon.

part of the political center but opposed by another. It denied that it was a party but had an electoral organization of flexibility and strength.

Indicative of this complex party situation was the attitude of Finance Minister Valéry Giscard d'Estaing, who was reelected president of the Independents on October 10. He stood for total support of Pompidou, a separate and strengthened identity of the Independents within the Gaullist majority, and the eventual establishment of a working majority by the Independents so that they would become the heirs of the Gaullist movement. The plan was that in 1973, the Independents would run their own candidates wherever the UDR men were not likely to win. In short, this party hoped (as "the only movement which shows strong signs of growth"), while flying Gaullist colors, to make off with the mass of votes now restlessly grouped under the sign of the UDR. With its intensely conservative image, it seemed unlikely it would achieve that goal.

Socialist and Communist Parties. Also competing for center votes, the Radical Socialist party continued to be shaken up by Jean Jacques Servan-Schreiber. Recovering from his 1970 error of tackling Premier Chaban-Delmas in his home constituency of Bordeaux, he now challenged Maurice Faure, president of the party, who had brought Servan-Schreiber into the Radicals as secretary-general to restore their declining fortunes. Servan-Schreiber easily won the presidency. He then approached groups to the left of the orthodox Gaullists. Intending to be the senior partner in any combination, he had little to offer the Communists, the Socialists (whose new leader, François Mitterrand, would not readily play second to the newcomer), or the left-wing Gaullist followers of Edgar Faure.

Within the Socialist party, disagreement continued to prevail. A right wing, led by Gaston Defferre, mayor of Marseille, supported accommodation with the centrist parties. But a majority variously distributed behind Alain Savary and Guy Mollet urged continued efforts to reach agreement with the Communists. More wary, Mitterrand emerged from the Épinay congress (June 11–13) as secretary-general and leader. Though faithful to his long record of seeking an opening to the left, he still refused binding union with the Communists.

The dilemma for the Socialists was that, while fearing the Communists would ultimately refuse to abide by the rules of the parliamentary game, they had no hope of forming a leftist government without Communist support. Under Mitterrand they slowed their approaches, kept open the possibility of a deal with the center, and sought to increase support for their own democratic socialism.

The Communist party, led by its deputy secretary-general Georges Marchais, persistently pursued the vision of a popular-front government. It could point to a poll showing that 60% of French voters were ready to accept Communist ministers in such a government, but it could not convince the reluctant Socialists of its democratic sentiments. Thus it could not hope to alter the discriminatory electoral law that undoubtedly minimized its representation. In its substantial program for "a democratic government of popular union," published in October, it even admitted the legitimacy of "an important private sector" in a socialized economy. But for the moment the gulf between it and the non-Communist left remained unbridgeable.

In the municipal elections of March 14–21, Communists and Socialists cooperated in the runoff ballot, thus polarizing the political struggle at the local level. The center parties were their chief victims. But nothing suggested extension of this tactic to the national scene. The Gaullists made slight gains, but the prevailing tendency was support of incumbent mayors of whatever stamp.

Senate. The triennial Senate elections of September 26, in which one third of the upper house was elected, similarly showed no big changes. Incumbents were generally returned for a 9-year term. The Senate retained the centrist and conservative charter on whose reform de Gaulle had, in part, disastrously staked his presidency in 1969.

Government Under Attack. Much greater concern was aroused by a series of scandals, some of which involved France's counterespionage forces, and some involved real-estate companies using legislators to abet their malpractices. The facts regarding drug trafficking and a treason scandal in the secret intelligence agency remained obscure, but they caused fresh quarrels in the UDR. The arrest and imprisonment of one real-estate promotor, Robert Frenkel, brought to light close connections between deputies—and even aides to Chaban-Delmas and Pompidou—and corrupt businessmen. Scandals involving murder and the miscarriage of justice were not new to the Fifth Republic. The regime had always managed to suppress inquiries leading to those in high places, however, and it seemed unlikely that opposition cries would much damage the government.

Nevertheless, press and parliamentary discussions were sufficiently embarrassing for Pompidou to give an account of his financial affairs at a press conference. This incident marked the distance the regime had come. Such charges against his predecessor would have been unthinkable.

At the end of November the National Assembly approved a government bill that would forbid a deputy to have business connections with companies receiving public subsidies or contracts, or with companies promoting real estate or building apartments. The bill resulted from charges brought against a Gaullist deputy from Paris, who allegedly had been involved in fraudulent real-estate operations and who was expelled from the UDR.

Further discredit to political parties resulted from the intemperate denunciation of judges by the new secretary-general of the UDR, René Tomasini, on February 16. A formidable organizer and lobbyist, he found the courts too soft on young agitators, the radio and television networks too much inclined to play up "the negative aspects of French society," and Chaban-Delmas weak for permitting this situation. The day after his outburst, hundreds of magistrates staged a massive silent demonstration against the charge of cowardice. The heads of the highest appeals court asked the president for action. It was announced that Tomasini had apologized.

Civil Unrest. Nonetheless, many Frenchmen agreed with Tomasini's views. Raymond Marcellin, minister of the interior, repeatedly manifested a very hard government line against the militant left. Many politicians, lawyers, and churchmen warned that freedom of expression was being threatened. Since the fall of 1970, the State Security Court had given special attention to Maoists, Trotskyites, and other extremists. Merely for selling the *Cause du Peuple,* organ of the imprisoned Alain Geismar's banned proletarian movement, young people from 18 to 24 lost their civic and family rights and were given sentences up to one year. The release of 18-

year-old Gilles Guiot on February 19, on appeal from a 6-month term for allegedly punching a policeman, was a setback to the arbitrary measures favored by Marcellin, however, and an encouragement to the troubled minister of justice, René Pleven, saddled with the task of separating justice from politics.

A blow for civil liberties was struck on July 17 by the Constitutional Council when it declared unconstitutional the recent law restricting the right of association. Rejection of this legislation, passed by the Assembly over Senate opposition, marked the first occasion that this highest legal authority, filled with Gaullists, had opposed the government on a fundamental point of law.

The Paris police force was also a focal point of discontent. Affronted by attacks upon them as "fascists" and "sadists," the police on March 4 handed out leaflets explaining their difficulties. At the same time, accused of repeatedly brutalizing the young and the journalists reporting street encounters, they were disciplined for an apparent demonstration against such charges when, on June 5, they had refused for two hours to respond to calls from shopkeepers whose premises were being damaged or looted. The police unions complained bitterly. They were still smarting from an incident on March 9, when thousands of leftists attacked a right-wing rally in Paris, and 73 policemen were reported injured. The police threatened to occupy government buildings unless certain wage and other demands were met. This in turn occasioned further dismissals and protests.

There were strikes in various parts of the labor force. Soon after a government settlement in January with the railwaymen, linking wages to the cost of living, the airlines were shut down by flight crews. The big Renault motor works was hit by a strike in May. Some 20,000 civil servants marched silently in Paris on June 4 to draw attention to their demands for larger wage increases. Notwithstanding the January settlement, the railways were disrupted in mid-June by nearly two weeks of wildcat strikes. A crippling subway strike turned the capital streets into chaos in October. Nevertheless, the year did not give rise to an unusual number of strikes and social unrest in a nation where public discontent with employers, state or private, had tended recently to a flouting of the constraints of official labor organizations.

Economy. The economy remained fairly healthy. The austerity measures introduced following the 1968 events had been effective. The franc had become a sound currency (backed by more than $5 billion in reserves, 80% of it in gold), the gross national product in 1970 had increased by 6.2%, while prices rose (so the government claimed) only 5.2%. Giscard d'Estaing predicted a 5.7% growth rate for the 1971 economy, a rate second only to Japan's. The optimistic target of the sixth 5-year plan was a 5.9% growth rate per year.

Still, there were half a million unemployed, and there was constant pressure from unions for reduction of one of the longest workweeks in Europe— from 50 to 40 hours—and for lowering retirement age from 65 to 60. Neither was envisaged in the new 5-year plan. Moreover, prices were rising steeply again. The $40 billion expenditure called for in the budget of September 15 revealed that in the face of the U. S. 10% surcharge on imports and strong pressure to revalue the franc upward, the government was determined to offset foreign revenue losses by substituting a domestic stimulus to production through tax cuts. Giscard told the Assembly that the "troika" of French expansion in 1972 would be exports, investments, and domestic consumption.

In general, some doubt, reinforced by the slackness of Western economies, hung over France. Many businessmen, wary of new investment, predicted world recession for 1972.

Defense. Pompidou still refused to adhere to the partial nuclear test-ban treaty or the nonproliferation pact. From June to August, thermonuclear devices were exploded at the test site in Polynesia. Protests from Japan, New Zealand, and Peru were ignored as before. It appeared that France was seeking a smaller version of the weapon supplied to the Mirage-4 bombers for use with the new Anglo-French Jaguar supersonic aircraft and the improved Mirage 3E fighter-bomber.

At the international level, France supported a two-stage European security conference: first, a meeting of the foreign ministers and special committees on security, trade, and exchange of ideas and people; then, if successful, a meeting of the heads of state. Foreign Minister Maurice Schumann told the Assembly on November 3 that France would back a disarmament conference if it embraced all five nuclear powers, which seemed unlikely.

─────── **FRANCE • Information Highlights** ───────

Official Name: French Republic.
Area: 211,207 square miles (547,026 sq km).
Population (1970 est.): 50,780,000. *Density,* 248 per square mile (92 per sq km). *Annual rate of Increase,* 0.9%.
Chief Cities (1968 census): Paris, the capital, 2,590,771; Marseille, 889,029; Lyon, 527,800.
Government: *Head of state,* Georges Pompidou, president (took office June 20, 1969). *Chief minister,* Jacques Chaban-Delmas, premier (took office June 24, 1969). *Legislature*—Parliament: National Assembly, 487 members; Senate, 283 members. *Major political parties*—Union of Democrats for the Republic; Independent Republican; Socialist; Communist; Center for Progress and Modern Democracy.
Languages: French (official).
Education: *Literacy rate* (1970), 100% of population. *Expenditure on education* (1968), 19.1% of total public expenditure. *School enrollment* (1968)—primary, 5,163,575; secondary, 3,870,333; technical/vocational, 962,670; university/higher, 622,405.
Finances (1970): *Revenues,* $30,777,000,000; *expenditures,* $30,107,000,000; *monetary unit,* franc (5,1157 francs equal U. S.$1, Dec. 30, 1971).
Gross National Product (1970 est.): $140,000,000,000.
National Income (1969): $105,964,000,000; *national income per person,* $2,106.
Economic Indexes: *Industrial production* (1970), 152 (1963=100); *agricultural production* (1969), 117 (1963=100); *consumer price index* (1970), 131 (1963=100).
Manufacturing (metric tons, 1969): Cement, 27,697,000; crude steel, 22,511,000; meat, 2,833,000; sugar (1968), 2,301,-000; wine, 51,290,000 hectoliters.
Crops (metric tons, 1969 crop year): Wheat, 14,535,000; grapes (1968), 9,929,000 (ranks 2d among world producers); barley, 9,347,000 (world rank 2d); potatoes, 8,-962,000; apples (1968), 2,316,000 (world rank 2d).
Minerals (metric tons, 1969): Coal, 40,583,000; iron ore, 18,013,000; salt, 4,916,000; bauxite, 2,773,000.
Foreign Trade (1968): *Exports* (1970), $17,742,000,000 (chief exports—nonelectrical machinery, $1,592,500,000; chemicals, $1,361,000,000; motor vehicles, $1,078,400,000; iron and steel, $1,013,300,000). *Imports* (1970), $18,780,000,-000 (chief imports—nonelectrical machinery, $1,847,000,-000; petroleum, $1,387,500,000). *Chief trading partners* (1968)—West Germany (took 19% of exports, supplied 21% of imports); Belgium-Luxembourg (10%—10%); Italy (9%—9%); United States (6%—9%).
Tourism: *Receipts* (1970). $1,191,500,000.
Transportation: *Roads* (1964), 888,559 miles (1,429,958 km); *motor vehicles* (1969), 14,650,800 (automobiles, 12,000,-000); *railroads* (1966), 24,000 miles (38,623 km); *merchant fleet* (1971), 7,011,000 gross registered tons; *national airline,* Air France.
Communications: *Telephones* (1970), 8,114,041; *television stations* (1968), 94; *television sets* (1969), 10,121,000; *radios* (1969), 15,796,000; *newspapers* (1968), 109 (daily circulation, 12,150,000).

FOREIGN AFFAIRS

The year was remarkable for a decisive alteration in France's European policy. Having no further hope of dominating West Germany, a fact that was apparent even before de Gaulle's resignation, Pompidou finally abandoned his predecessor's veto on Britain's entry into the Common Market, clearly welcoming the British as a potential counterweight to the Germans. On January 21, Pompidou stated that outstanding differences with Britain were "reconcilable," although he accused Britain of holding out for unrealistic terms. On May 10, Foreign Minister Schumann announced a "thaw" in the almost unyielding agricultural discussions. After secret talks in Paris on May 20, Prime Minister Edward Heath and Pompidou proclaimed their general agreement on the principle of British entry. Both German Chancellor Willy Brandt and Italian Premier Emilio Colombo had exerted direct pressure on Pompidou.

Relations with West Germany grew a little cooler, beset as they were by currency reform differences, Brandt's support of the British case in the Common Market negotiations, and the dramatic German initiative in seeking a direct understanding with the Soviet Union in the Yalta talks. Since he had not been consulted on the talks, Pompidou took them as an affront to France. The twice-yearly high-level Franco-German talks occurred as usual in January and July. Brandt asked for, and Pompidou extended, an invitation to a special meeting in Paris on December 3. But clearly Germany no longer recognized the special position in Europe that France had enjoyed under de Gaulle.

Differences with Italy followed from their varying conceptions of Europe. The Italians still held out for some movement toward a supranational organization. The French, however, insisted on a pragmatic approach that would preserve untrammeled national sovereignty.

Contacts with the Soviet Union were good. Leonid Brezhnev, secretary-general of the Soviet Communist party, received a head of state's reception in France on October 26–30. This extraordinary visit to the West was taken as a mark of the Soviet Union's regard for France's strong and independent policy, as well as a further step in the direction of an East-West détente. The Russians hoped to secure strong French support for a European security conference. Nevertheless, Pompidou refused the suggested Franco-Soviet treaty, and a mere "declaration of principles," signed the final day, was all Brezhnev took away. His visit to East Berlin en route home seemed to reflect a desire to underline Soviet pique with this French holdout by slightly downgrading the special nature of the journey to France.

North America. France disputed with the United States over whether the franc should be revalued upward or the dollar devalued. The U. S. import surtax, Pompidou told his press conference on September 23, "is a big stick that might possibly be transformed into a carrot if one were disposed to play the role of donkey, which is not our intention."

A breakthrough in the international currency crisis was achieved in a personal meeting between Pompidou and U. S. President Richard Nixon in December. The talks, held in the Azores on December 13–14, produced an announcement by the United States that it would devalue the dollar as part

UPI
DEMOLITION of Les Halles, Paris' famed central market, left jumble of 19th century ironwork. Newer facilities on outskirts of capital are more efficient but have less charm.

of a broad agreement involving currencies of the other leading non-Communist nations. Such an accord was reached in Washington a few days later. (See INTERNATIONAL FINANCE.)

The old quarrel about control of the drug traffic continued on past the February 6 agreement for police cooperation in stopping the flow of drugs to the United States. Matters were not made more amicable by the labyrinthine scandal concerning drugs and the French counterespionage service, some of whose officers were accused in the United States of complicity in smuggling. French Defense Minister Michel Debré, an old hand at denying unpleasant home truths about the Gaullist regime, branded all this "a fairy tale worthy of a concierge."

The thaw in Franco-Canadian relations continued, helped by a brief visit to Ottawa on October 1 of the agreeable French foreign minister, Maurice Schumann. "There are all the reasons in the world," he noted, "why there should be no bone of contention between our two countries." The Pompidou government was ready to bury an unhappy quarrel inherited from de Gaulle. Significantly, the second general conference of the multinational Agence de Coopération Culturelle et Technique was held in Ottawa and Quebec City on October 11-15.

Middle East, Africa, and Asia. In North Africa and the Middle East no great policy changes occurred. But France eased its relations with Israel with the assurance that the 50 Mirage fighters blocked by de Gaulle in 1967 would be absorbed by the French Air Force and not find their way to Libya, and by ratifying on November 14, after an 11-year delay, the 1958 extradition treaty. France continued the dispute with the Algerians over the nationalization of French oil holdings. A 5-month crisis was resolved on June 30, when France abandoned its embargo on Algerian oil imports and its efforts to prevent others from buying Algerian oil.

With the sub-Saharan nations France sought to reaffirm close ties, sending Pompidou on a visit to Mauritania, Senegal, the Ivory Coast, Gabon, and Cameroon between February 3 and February 13. At enormous cost to the French taxpayer, nearly the whole of what had once been French Equatorial and French West Africa remained financed by and tightly bound economically and culturally to France. Nationalist denunciations of this special relationship were heard in Africa, and there were protests in France against its expense. But there was no sign of French withdrawal and no evident alternative to the massive aid it gave these states.

In Asia, French relations remained much as they had been. A Chinese trade delegation visited France from September 29 to October 9. Foreign Minister Schumann agreed to go to Peking in 1972 and described Sino-French relations as having made "a great leap forward." Supporting the expulsion of Taiwan, France welcomed China's entry into the UN as an act of realism and a healthy sign that the old Soviet-American world hegemony was broken forever. Japanese Emperor Hirohito, during his European tour, paid a private visit to France in October, lunching with President Pompidou but not otherwise engaging in talks with a country against whose atmospheric nuclear tests his government continued to protest.

JOHN C. CAIRNS
University of Toronto

FRANKLIN, Aretha. See BIOGRAPHY.
FRENCH LITERATURE. See LITERATURE.

300

GABON

The year 1971 was a quiet one in Gabon. The major event was the visit in February of French President Georges Pompidou, the first visit of a French head of state since Gabonese independence.

Political Affairs. President Albert-Bernard Bongo's regime remained secure. In January he announced the conditional release of some of the less important participants in the 1964 abortive coup against his predecessor, Léon Mba.

Economic Development. Gabon is one of the most richly endowed countries in Subsaharan Africa. Mineral production continued to grow in 1971, and, for the first time, oil surpassed timber as the country's most important export. Private capital has helped support the development of Gabon's resources. One of the most recent examples is SOGAPAR, a joint development corporation with an initial capital of 100 million Gabonese francs, 70% of which will be supplied by the French Banque de Paris et des Pays Bas. The Gabon government provides what it calls a "favorable investment climate," and the only sign of economic nationalism has been a gentle pressure for increased "Gabonization" of middle management levels.

The 5-year plan adopted in 1971 provided for an investment of 150 billion francs, of which only 1.8 billion was earmarked for rural development. High on the country's list of priorities is the construction of a trans-Gabon railroad. It will start in Owendo, a new port site that has been surveyed near Libreville, and in a first stage will reach Booué, in the center of Gabon's rich forest district. A second stage will extend the rail line to the iron-mining region of Mekambo. Financing for the first section of the line will be provided by Gabon, France, and the European Development Fund in equal amounts, but also from the World Bank, which has been insisting, however, that private French interests that will benefit mostly from the railroad should be made to contribute more heavily.

EDOUARD BUSTIN, *Boston University*

─────────── GABON • Information Highlights ───────────

Official Name: Gabonese Republic.
Area: 103,346 square miles (267,667 sq km).
Population (1970 est.): 500,000. *Density,* 5 per square mile (2 sq km). *Annual rate of increase,* 1.0%.
Chief City (1969 est.): Libreville, the capital, 57,000.
Government: *Head of state,* Albert-Bernard Bongo, president (took office Dec. 4, 1967). *Head of government,* Albert-Bernard Bongo. *Legislature*—National Assembly (unicameral), 47 members. *Major political parties*—Parti Démocratique Gabonais.
Languages: French (official), Fang, Bantu dialects.
Education: *Literacy rate* (1970), 12% of population. *Expenditure on education* (1965), 20.4% of total public expenditure. *School enrollment* (1968)—primary, 89,187; secondary, 7,744; technical/vocational, 1,373; university/higher, 30.
Finances (1967 est.): *Revenues,* $58,900,000; *expenditures,* $58,900,000; *monetary unit,* CFA franc (277.71 francs equal U. S.$1, Sept. 1971).
Gross National Product (1967): $267,000,000.
National Income (1967): $202,000,000; *national income per person,* $427.
Manufacturing (metric tons, 1969): Residual fuel oil, 318,000; distillate fuel oils, 184,000; gasoline, 122,000.
Crop (metric tons, 1969 crop year): Cassava (1968), 130,000.
Minerals (metric tons, 1969): Crude petroleum, 5,027,000; manganese ore, 711,000.
Foreign Trade (1970): *Exports,* $121,000,000 (chief exports—petroleum, $49,548,000; wood, $33,128,000). *Imports,* $80,-000,000 (chief import, 1968—nonelectrical machinery, $10,768,000). *Chief trading partner* (1968)—France.
Transportation: *Roads* (1967), 3,635 miles (5,850 km); *motor vehicles* (1969), 10,000 (automobiles, 5,200); *national airline,* Air Gabon, Transgabon.
Communications: *Telephones* (1970), 6,694; *radios* (1969), 50,000.

─────────── GAMBIA • Information Highlights ───────────

Official Name: The Gambia.
Area: 4,361 square miles (11,295 sq km).
Population (1970 est.): 360,000. *Density,* 89 per square mile (32 per sq km). *Annual rate of increase,* 20%.
Chief City (1967 est.): Bathurst, the capital, 31,800.
Government: *Head of state,* Sir Dauda Jawara, president (took office as president April 24, 1970. *Head of government,* Sir Dauda Jawara. *Legislature*—House of Representatives (unicameral, 32 elected members. *Major political parties*—People's Progressive party, United party, People's Progressive Alliance.
Languages: English (official), Mandinka, Wolof.
Education: *Literacy rate* (1969), 10% of population.
Finances (1967–68 est.): *Revenues,* $5,961,000; *expenditures,* $5,485,000; *monetary unit,* dalasi (2.0833 dalasi equal U. S.$1, Sept. 1971).
Gross National Product (1967): $33,000,000.
Crops (metric tons, 1969 crop year): Groundnuts, 113,000; rice, 66,000.
Foreign Trade (1967): *Exports,* $12,878,000 (chief exports—peanut oil, $5,760,000; groundnuts, $3,782,000; fodder, $1,575,000. *Imports,* $18,048,000 (chief imports—textile yarn and fabrics, $4,025,000; food, $3,007,000; motor vehicles, $1,538,000; chemicals, $1,280,000). *Chief trading partners* (1967)—United Kingdom (took 69% of exports, supplied 40% of imports); Japan; Portugal.
Transportation: *Roads* (1967), 845 miles (1,360 km); *motor vehicles* (1969), 4,500 (automobiles, 2,500).
Communications: *Telephones* (1970), 1,586; *radios* (1968), 60,-000; *newspapers* (1960), 1 (daily circulation, 1,500).

GAMBIA

The 1970 decision to adopt a republican form of government remained popular in The Gambia in 1971. The ruling People's Progressive party encountered no effective opposition, and President Sir Dauda Jawara discussed creating a one-party state.

Foreign Relations. Senegal's campaign against smuggling from Gambia led to a number of incidents. The major one occurred on January 31, when several Senegalese crossed into Gambia and kidnapped some Gambian citizens. President Jawara protested vigorously to Senegal and notified the UN secretary-general. Tensions eased after an apology by Senegal, but some strain remained. Senegal objected to the Bathurst commercial radio and the meager improvements in trans-Gambian transportation, but a comprehensive trade agreement between the two countries went into effect in June.

Gambia's detente with Guinea, while Guinean-Senegalese relations worsened, was a cause for potential difficulty with Senegal. Gambia agreed to return Guinean refugees, while Senegal refused a similar request. In February, Gen. Yakubu Gowon of Nigeria attended the sixth anniversary celebration of Gambian independence and signed a treaty of friendship. Later in the year, President Jawara aligned Gambia with most of Africa in rejecting a proposal for discussions with South Africa.

Economic Development. The harvest of peanuts, Gambia's major product, amounted to 114,791 tons, an improvement over the previous year, giving the produce marketing board a surplus of over $3.5 million. The board continued to support rice production and initiated a pilot plan for meat production. In June the British Overseas Development Administration granted $4.8 million in interest-free, 25-year loans for the period 1971–74, and a large sum was immediately made available. Further indications of economic growth were the opening of a central bank, new radio studios in Bathurst, and the start on construction of a luxury hotel at Cape St. Mary.

HARRY A. GAILEY
San Jose State College

GANDHI, Indira. See BIOGRAPHY.

GARDENING AND HORTICULTURE

One of the most critical problems facing the commercial horticulturist in the United States in 1971 was the diminishing supply of qualified labor. In other developments, roadside marketing of fresh produce was on the increase throughout the United States and Canada, and an amateur was honored with an All-America Rose Selections award for the first time in the award's history.

Labor Problems. The paucity of a good labor supply in the United States forced many producers of fruits, vegetables, and ornamentals out of business in 1971. Others invested in foreign operations, where good labor was available at extremely low rates. Farm labor in Mexico, for example, was commanding a daily rate equivalent to the hourly rate in the United States. Because of this situation, producers of horticultural crops that require a high labor input, such as the Florida fresh market tomato growers, found themselves in an essentially untenable position.

The diminution in labor supply resulted in much effort being directed toward the development of machines that will mechanically harvest crops that heretofore have been harvested by hand. Prototype machines were developed for harvesting fresh market tomatoes (essentially all tomatoes grown for processing were already being machine-harvested), strawberries, cucumbers, okra, apples, muskmelons, sweet potatoes, lima beans, and peppers. Plant breeders, horticulturists, and agricultural engineers worked together to develop varieties of these crops that are adapted to mechanical harvesting, to find chemicals and other methods that will facilitate mechanical harvesting, and to develop machines that will harvest fruits and vegetables without damaging these commodities that are highly susceptible to bruising. By the end of the year, there appeared to be good prospects of developing machines to harvest these crops satisfactorily.

Roadside Marketing. The scarcity of labor and other economic problems were also major reasons why growers began looking to roadside marketing and pick-your-own programs for outlets for their products. These policies became widespread during 1971 and attracted a great deal of attention. North Carolina held its first Roadside Marketing and Pick-Your-Own Conference during the year, and Pennsylvania adopted a roadside marketing program that was certified by the state department of agriculture.

Even aside from economic considerations, growers and consumers were apparently beginning to recognize the importance and value of on-farm retailing of fresh produce. This increased interest came about partly because of the attitudes of supermarket managers, who prefer processed packaged commodities to fresh fruits and vegetables, and because of the poor quality of the items displayed in many stores. Generally, roadside markets offer better quality produce that is fresh and in season.

Winning Roses. Two magnificent hybrid tea roses, Apollo and Portrait, were chosen as winners of the All-America Rose Selections Awards for 1972, after pre-introductory testing and comparative rating.

Portrait was the result of the hybridizing work of Carl Mayer, an amateur from Cincinnati, Ohio. This was the first time that an amateur had won the honor in the 32 years that the awards have been given. Portrait is a distinctive, colorful, warm, radiant pink hybrid tea rose. Its urn-shaped, deep pink buds open to a soft, almost creamy, white bloom, edged with a deep satiny, blush pink. Occasionally gold tones wash the open bloom and add to its glowing warmth, set off by a clear pink reverse. Fifty or more petals roll back to create a fully double high-centered bloom 4 inches or more across that produces an old rose perfume fragrance. The many flowers are borne on sturdy stems, and the plants grow tall with vigorous upright canes, branching freely and loaded with pink blossoms.

Apollo produces flowers of soft, sunrise yellow, delicately tinted with shadowy infiltrations of crimson. The color lasts throughout the life of the flower, gradually deepening to a canary tone, clear and soft. Apollo possesses the sweet fragrance of an old-fashioned tea rose, which intensifies as the long, slender buds open more fully into mature blossoms. The flowers are usually borne on long stems that are relatively free of thorns. The bushes are vigorous with a fine branching habit, and bloom profusely throughout the spring, summer, and fall. The open blooms, usually of 30 to 35 petals, are large, often attaining a diameter of from 5 to 6 inches (12.7–15.24 cm). The foliage of this rose is a dark, rich green. It is disease resistant and covers the plant well, thus producing a fine background to set off the gorgeous blooms.

Other All-America Winners. Four other flowers and three vegetables were selected as All-America winners for 1972. Ruby Ball, an F_1 (first generation) hybrid red cabbage, won a gold medal, and Carved Ivory, an F_1 hybrid giant cactus-flowered zinnia, was awarded a silver medal. Bronze medals went to Circus, an F_1 hybrid double grandiflora, bicolored salmon and white petunia; Summer Carnival, a hollyhock of mixed colors which can be grown as an annual or a biennial; Gold Galore, an F_1 hybrid American hedge-type marigold; Victory, an F_1 hybrid dark-green slicing cucumber; and Red Head, an F_1 hybrid red cabbage.

New Books. A number of interesting and useful books on flowers and on gardening were published in 1971. Volume IV of *Wild Flowers of the United States* by Harold W. Rickett is an authoritative volume that should be in every public and institutional library that can afford the not-too-modest cost. *Creative Ways with Flowers* by Rachel E. Carr is refreshing in that the author has incorporated an oriental touch in flower arranging for Western living. Josan Hirota's *Bonsai* and Michael Jefferson's *Small Garden Design* should be particularly interesting to those with limited space for gardening.

DONALD W. NEWSOM, *Louisiana State University*

GAS

The U. S. gas industry set records in sales, revenues, and number of customers in 1971 despite a gas supply shortage that held back the rate of increase of overall sales to the lowest level since 1945. Gas consumption continued to outpace the discovery of new deposits, posing a nationwide threat of cutbacks in long periods of subnormal cold.

Business Volume. Preliminary year-end estimates by the American Gas Association (AGA) showed that total sales reached 163 billion therms, up 1.6% from the final figure of 160.4 billion therms for 1970. Revenues from gas sales climbed to $10.9 billion, a 6.4% increase over the $10.3

SELECTED DATA ON U. S. GAS UTILITY INDUSTRY

Customers[1]	1971[2]	1970	Change
Residential	39,194,000	38,461,000	+1.9%
Commercial	3,259,000	3,183,000	+2.4%
Industrial	206,000	201,000	+2.5%
Other	59,000	58,000	.....
Total	42,718,000	41,903,000	+1.9%
Sales (thousands of therms)			
Residential	50,321,000	49,238,000	+2.2%
Commercial	20,807,000	20,065,000	+3.7%
Industrial	85,067,000	84,392.000	+0.8%
Other	6,807,000	6,740,000	.....
Total	163,002,000	160,435,000	+1.6%
Revenues (thousands)			
Residential	$ 5,538,078	$ 5,207,335	+6.4%
Commercial	1,752,116	1,620,446	+8.1%
Industrial	3,360,997	3,181,206	+5.7%
Other	285,826	273,624	.....
Total	$10,937,017	$10,282,611	+6.4%

[1] On December 31. [2] Preliminary.   Source: American Gas Association.

billion revenues in 1970. More than 800,000 customers were added during 1971, bringing the year-end total to 43 million.

Business Outlook. Projections by the AGA show sales reaching 25,075 trillion Btu by 1980, assuming a 4.6% annual growth rate during the 1970's. By 1955, sales are expected to increase to 45,083 trillion Btu—nearly triple the figure for 1971. AGA projections also indicate that about 9 million new customers will be added during the 1970's and that the total number of customers will be more than 67 million by 1995.

Gas Supply. According to the AGA, proved reserves of gas totaled 290.7 trillion cubic feet at the end of 1970. This total—including 26 trillion cubic feet of new Alaskan reserves for the first time—still fell short of the record reserve figure set in 1967. At 1970 consumption rates, the proved reserves of gas amount to about 13 years' supply, and potential reserves amount to an additional 50 years' supply. Meanwhile, wildcat drilling has declined steadily, dropping 40% between 1956 and 1970.

Steps to bring new supplies of gas to market include government-approved price rises for gas sold in interstate commerce, an accelerated program of leasing federally controlled offshore fields, a joint government-industry effort to speed development of new processes to produce gas from coal, and large-scale importation of liquefied natural gas from overseas. One promising alternative is the use of nuclear explosives to stimulate production from natural gas fields. (See also NUCLEAR ENERGY.)

Gas Distribution Network. The vast underground network of pipelines and distribution mains for transporting gas from wells to customers was increased by about 26,000 miles in 1971, raising the total to 941,000 miles. The AGA expects a growth to nearly 2 million miles by 1995.

GENETICS

Advances in genetics during 1971 included the development of a new staining technique that distinguishes all 23 pairs of human chromosomes from one another and the correction of some genetic defects in mammalian cells by the introduction of normal genes.

Chromosome Identification. The identification of chromosomal abnormalities, many of which cause mental and physical defects in man, depends on methods for reliably distinguishing each human chromosome. Normal human somatic, or body, cells (as opposed to germ, or sex, cells) contain 23 pairs of chromosomes. The chromosomes are most readily observed at the metaphase stage of cell division when they are arranged in a nearly two-dimensional array and stain deeply with chemical stains. The chromosome pairs differ from one another to some extent in size and shape, but until recently only five pairs could be distinguished with certainty by observation and measurement and another nine by more sophisticated techniques.

During the past few years, T. Caspersson and his colleagues at the Karolinska Institute in Stockholm have developed a new type of fluorescent chromosome stain. Called quinacrine dyes, they stain different parts of each chromosome with differing intensities. The resulting pattern of fluorescent bands is highly characteristic of each chromosome.

Using this technique in 1971, M. L. O'Riordan, J. A. Robinson, K. E. Buckton, and H. J. Evans, all of the Medical Research Council in Edinburgh, Scotland, succeeded in distinguishing all 23 human chromosome pairs. They were also able to identify the chromosomes involved in several human chromosomal anomalies, including those responsible for some forms of mongolism and for chronic myeloid leukemia. The fluorescent staining technique will be of great value to many aspects of human genetics, particularly in the mapping of human genes. This last process will be facilitated by the use of human-mouse somatic cell hybrids, since mouse chromosomes stained with quinacrine dyes can readily be distinguished from human ones.

Correction of Genetic Cell Defects. Two research groups have succeeded in introducing normal genes into mutant mammalian cells growing in cultures, thereby correcting the effects of the mutations. At the University of Oxford, A. G. Schwartz, P. R. Cook, and Henry Harris corrected a mutation in mouse cells with a gene from chick cells. Since the presence of certain other chick genes might have been detrimental, Harris and his colleagues designed an experiment in which mouse cells containing only a small portion of the chick genetic material, including the desired gene, would be selected. They fused red blood cells from a normal chick with mutant mouse cells that lacked the gene for synthesis of an enzyme called IMP pyrophosphorylase. Red blood cells were chosen as the gene donor because when hybrid cells containing chromosomes from red blood cells divide, the chromosomes break up into small pieces. Most of the fragments are lost during subsequent growth of the hybrid cells, but some random fragments become stably established.

In order to select those cells in which the fragment containing the gene for IMP pyrophosphorylase synthesis had become established, the cells were grown in a special medium that required the presence of this enzyme for cell growth. Those cells that did grow were biochemically and genetically analyzed, and the results confirmed that they contained the chick-type IMP pyrophosphorylase and were like mouse cells in all other respects. Thus, they were the desired cells in which the mouse mutation had been corrected by the incorporation of the needed gene from a chick.

Three scientists of the National Institutes of Health in Bethesda, Md.—Carl R. Merril, Mark R. Grier, and John C. Petricianni—achieved the same goal using a different approach. They used a small bacterial virus as the source of the normal gene. The mutant cells used were human cells from a patient with galactosemia, a disease caused by a mutation in the gene specifying an enzyme called GPU transferase. When the mutant human cells were infected with the bacterial virus or with the virus' hereditary material—that is, its deoxyribonucleic acid (DNA)—they began synthesizing GPU transferase, thus indicating that the virus gene was functioning in the human cells.

These two experiments constitute one of the many steps necessary for the eventual control and therapy of some genetically caused disease through alteration of a cell's genetic makeup.

FRANK G. ROTHMAN, *Brown University*

GENTELE, Goeran. See BIOGRAPHY.

GEOGRAPHY

The importance of geography in the areas of teaching, research, and practical applications continued to grow during 1971. New educational materials and teaching methods were introduced to an increasing number of students in elementary schools and high schools. At universities, geographers used computer technology and other research techniques to pose problems and infer solutions relating to a wide variety of environmental conditions. Geographers continued to work in a broad range of occupations, despite some lessening of opportunities in teaching, government, and industry.

Geographers at Work. The skills of geographers in helping to solve a wide variety of problems were increasingly recognized by many organizations. In several federal agencies, for instance, geographers worked in such diverse fields as intelligence and cartography, made use of such techniques as remote sensing and photo interpretation, and dealt with geographic place-names and foreign political borders.

One of the more significant programs directed by geographers is the Geographic Applications Program of the U. S. Geological Survey. Its goal is to develop scientific tcehniques that measure, record, and analyze environmental changes. This is to be done through the use of earth satellites and high-altitude aircraft equipped with cameras and other remote sensors. Elsewhere, private firms and research organizations continued to employ geographers in jobs dealing with regional planning, environmental quality, management, regional economy, cartography, and map editing.

Geography in Education. Geographers have been deeply involved in the widespread national concern for environmental quality. As a result, they have continued to build teaching programs to enlarge the role of the science and the teaching of geography in solving environmental problems. Moreover, professional associations sponsored several publications and meetings in 1971 that dealt with the proper application of geography to environmental education. During the year emphasis was also placed on the study of U. S. geographic patterns of poverty, racial discrimination, and migration.

One significant result of geographers' activities was the success of the High School Geography Program—a new set of books, maps, and teaching materials—sponsored by the Association of American Geographers and recently completed for 10th grade students. Its popularity was evident from the fact that school districts in nearly every state were using these materials to teach geography to more than 45,000 pupils. Education continued to be the main area of employment for geographers.

Activities of Organizations. The Association of American Geographers (AAG) and the National Council for Geographic Education (NCGE) participated in research projects, publications, conventions, task forces, and other activities in 1971. The AAG had completed or begun work on several publications for acquainting college teachers with new research findings and new techniques of instruction. The NCGE underscored its primary concern for elementary and secondary education by pursuing an active publication program that included issuing a variety of printed material. Discussions between the NCGE and the AAG continued to explore the merits of merging the two organizations.

The American Geographical Society carried on several long-term research programs during 1971, including studies in perception of landscape, marine environment, and Antarctic mapping. Also, work went forward on several important cartographic projects, among them a historical atlas of South Asia. The society published a book about Americans in the Antarctic between 1775 and 1948.

The National Geographic Society continued to support various research projects in such fields as glaciology, oceanography, and astronomy.

J. WARREN NYSTROM
Association of American Geographers

GEOLOGY

Gathering and preliminary analysis of geological data in two major fields of geology continued in 1971. Two manned missions brought back specimens, photographs, and tapes from the moon; while on earth, a series of important ocean explorations was completed. Full evaluation of the deluge of information will take many years.

Lunar Studies. Fra Mauro, where Apollo 14 landed on February 5, is a lunar highland with an extensive blanket of material ejected from Mare Imbrium, a large nearby crater apparently produced by one of the last major meteorite impacts to occur before great lava floods spread over the dark areas of the moon's near side. The Apollo 14 astronauts returned 96 pounds (43.2 kg) of lunar material, most of it either coarsely or finely grained. Several basaltic specimens were dated as having solidified 3.77 billion years ago. Geologists concluded that the Imbrium impact and the crystallization of inflowing lava took place very nearly at the same time, so that the impact must have occurred 100 to 150 million years later than previously thought.

On July 30 the Apollo 15 lunar module landed near Hadley Rill at the base of the Appenines, one of the moon's highest mountain ranges. The astronauts secured 175 pounds (78.7 kg) of lunar rock and soil, including an 8-foot (244-cm) core of loose, near-surface material. Preliminary analysis of the core's upper half showed 24 distinct layers. It is expected that these and the other layers contain a record of local lunar events dating back several billion years.

The unexpected evidences of stratification observed in Hadley Rill and on the slopes of the Appenines also indicate the existence of a record of events that will be amenable to geological interpretation. In addition the Apollo 15 astronauts returned a piece of anorthosite, a plagioclase-rich rock formed at depth. It had been hoped that the sample would prove to be a "Genesis rock" as old as the moon itself—about 4.6 billion years—but this

NASA

APOLLO 15 commander David R. Scott inspects "Genesis rock," the most ancient large moon fragment yet found. Discovered on August 1, it is more than 4 billion years old.

hope was not realized: the rock was dated as 4.15 billion years old.

The photographs taken from the Apollo 15 as it orbited the moon were also of great value. Many of the features observed can only be interpreted as volcanic. This would indicate that the volcanic action has been more important and of longer duration on the moon than had been generally thought.

JOIDES. The project of the Joint Oceanographic Institutions for Deep Earth Sampling, begun in 1965 under a $12.6 million grant from the National Science Foundation, continued its busy schedule by completing seven more "legs."

Leg 13 took place from Aug. 13 to Oct. 6, 1970, in the Mediterranean Sea, where the *Glomar Challenger* drilled 28 core holes at 15 sites. Results were puzzling and in part amazing. There is evidence that the Mediterranean basin was cut off entirely from the Atlantic Ocean a number of times, and that it shrank, dried up, and was converted into a veritable desert. The last such separation from the Atlantic was apparently about 5.5 million years ago. In addition, the findings proved that intensive compression and even mountain building are taking place in the eastern Mediterranean basin. The African plate, or block, of the earth's crust seems to be pushing north against the European block, with unmistakable submarine effects. One drill hole passed through Lower Cretaceous sediments into beds of middle Pliocene ooze, giving firsthand proof of the thrusting of older over younger rocks—a classic feature of Alpine geology.

Leg 14 was spent on the continental margins of northwestern Africa and northern Brazil. From Oct. 9 to Dec. 1, 1970, the drill ship obtained 17 cores from 10 sites. A good succession of fossil-bearing sediments was recovered, ranging from the early Cretaceous into the Oligocene. As suspected, at least one of a number of salt domes proved to be of igneous origin.

Leg 15 was conducted in the Caribbean Sea from Dec. 5, 1970, to Feb. 2, 1971, with drilling at 9 sites. Fossils suitable for correlating the entire Cenozoic Era and part of the Cretaceous Period were recovered, and the middle Tertiary history of the sea basin was found to be intensely volcanic. A second, non-JOIDES expedition by Lamont-Doherty Geological Observatory obtained samples of granite from Caribbean sites as deep as 6,033 feet (1,839 meters). Since granite is essentially a continental rock, the discovery suggests that the area may be a sunken continental fragment.

On Leg 16, 9 sites were drilled between the Panama Canal and Hawaii from February 6 to March 30. In this complex area of ocean floor a number of high-standing crustal blocks have been split by sea-floor spreading and moved from a near-equatorial position to one hundreds of miles away, carrying with they a record of sediments from the original site. The origin of the Isthmus of Panama is seen as a late result of plate movements in this area.

During Leg 17, spent from April 4 to May 25 in the central Pacific Ocean, 8 sites were drilled. It was found that the crust in this area has moved northward as much as 1,800 miles (2,900 km) in the past 100 million years, and a period of great volcanic activity lasting from 110 to 80 million years ago was indicated. Drillings on a submerged, flat-topped mountain called Horizon Guyot proved that the mountain had originated near sea level and later submerged to its present depth of 5,000 feet (1,500 meters).

Leg 18, from May 28 to July 19, took the *Glomar Challenger* from Honolulu to Kodiak, Alaska, with 11 sites drilled. The aim was to explore the continental margin northward in order to sample conditions where oceanic crust actively encounters continental crust. Samples of offshore marine life from over the past 26 million years were recovered, and new information on vegetation—and hence climate

304

—of adjacent lands during this period came from spores and pollen in collected sediments.

Leg 19 was spent in the Bering Sea and western Pacific Ocean from July 22 to September 14. The objective was to learn more about the Aleutian Islands and the deep marginal Bering Sea, trapped between the Aleutian Ridge and the continental mass of Siberia and Alaska.

Red Sea Studies. The deeper waters of the Red Sea continued to be studied in 1971. The water there is hot—138° F (59° C)—and about 10 times as salty as the open ocean. Bottom sediments in the Red Sea are rich in numerous heavy minerals, particularly those containing iron and manganese. The area seems to be one in which ore formation is currently going on, and further study is expected to reveal information vital to prospecting for ore deposits now locked in continental rocks.

(See also OCEANOGRAPHY.)

WILLIAM LEE STOKES, *University of Utah*

GEORGIA

The nation hailed Georgia's new governor, Jimmy Carter, as a symbol of the "New South" after the south Georgia peanut farmer, in his inaugural address, declared: "I say to you quite frankly that the time for racial discrimination is over."

Politics. In his home state, however, the new governor had problems in 1971—the main one being his predecessor, segregationist Lester Maddox.

Maddox, thwarted by a state law prohibiting a governor from succeeding himself, won election as the lieutenant governor, the presiding officer of the Georgia Senate. The power struggle between Carter and Maddox began even before Carter's inauguration, and, as the year ended, it appeared that Maddox had clear control of the Senate and was in position to defeat, or at least delay, any Carter proposal he did not like.

The showdown between the two powerful politicians should come in 1972, when Carter is scheduled to present his plan for reorganization of state government. The governor will ask the legislature to cut the number of state agencies from over 300 to about 20, combining some and abolishing others.

The last man to accomplish such a massive reorganization in Georgia's government was Richard B. Russell. A former governor and a U. S. senator for three decades, Russell died on January 21. Carter chose Atlanta attorney David I. Gambrell to replace Russell.

In October, Georgia's legislators met to reapportion the U. S. House of Representatives and the state Senate and House districts. In the reapportionment the Georgia House voted to cut its membership from 195 to 190, but dissidents challenged the remapping in federal court.

Other Events. Money was another major problem for the state as revenue collections fell drastically. Carter had to declare an across-the-board 3.8% cutback in state spending.

Some private companies also experienced financial difficulties. The Georgia division of Lockheed Aircraft Corporation probably suffered most as the parent company had to ask the federal government to guarantee a $250 million loan needed to avoid bankruptcy. Lockheed employment in Georgia was down from a peak of 33,000 to less than 16,000 at year's end. In February a blast rocked a munitions plant near Brunswick, killing 24 persons.

--- GEORGIA • Information Highlights ---

Area: 58,876 square miles (152,489 sq km).
Population (1970 census): 4,589,575. *Density:* 80 per sq mi.
Chief Cities (1970 census): Atlanta, the capital, 497,421; Columbus, 155,028; Macon, 122,423; Savannah, 118,349; Albany, 72,623; Augusta, 59,862; Athens, 44,342.
Government (1971): *Chief Officers*—governor, Jimmy Carter (D); lt. gov., Lester G. Maddox (D); secy. of state, Ben W. Fortson, Jr. (D); atty. gen., Arthur K. Bolton (D); treas., William H. Burson (D); supt. of schools, Jack P. Nix (D); chief justice, Bond Almand. *General Assembly*—Senate, 56 members (50 Democrats, 6 Republicans); House of Representatives, 195 members (173 D, 22 R).
Education (1970–71): *Enrollment*—public elementary schools, 722,000 pupils; 28,489 teachers; public secondary, 400,000 pupils; 18,930 teachers; nonpublic schools, 28,000 pupils; 1,570 teachers; college and university (fall 1968), 108,816 students. *Public school expenditures* (1970–71), $656,241,000 ($589 per pupil). *Average teacher's salary,* $7,778.
State Finances (fiscal year 1970): *Revenues,* $1,631,621,000 (3% general sales tax and gross receipts taxes, $335,807,000; motor fuel tax, $154,699,000; federal funds, $408,746,000). *Expenditures,* $1,576,441,000 (education, $725,588,000; health, welfare, and safety, $252,751,000; highways, $189,907,000). *State debt,* $870,190,000 (June 30, 1970).
Personal Income (1970): $15,121,000,000; per capita, $3,277.
Public Assistance (1970): $267,131,000. *Average monthly payments* (Dec. 1970)—old-age assistance, $52.55; aid to families with dependent children, $101.25.
Labor Force: *Nonagriculture wage and salary earners* (June 1971), 1,562,300. *Average annual employment* (1969)—manufacturing, 477,000; trade, 320,000; government, 285,000; services, 177,000. *Insured unemployed* (Oct. 1971)—15,700 (1.4%).
Manufacturing (1967): *Value added by manufacture,* $4,683,600,000 (Textiles, $990,600,000; transportation equipment, $741,800,000; food and kindred products, $557,400,000; paper and allied products, $436,700,000).
Agriculture (1970): *Cash farm income,* $1,228,225,000 (livestock, $710,612,000; crops, $433,992,000; government payments, $83,621,000). *Chief crops* (1970)—Peanuts, 1,133,145,000 pounds (ranks 1st among the states); tobacco, 133,305,000 pounds (ranks 4th); corn, 44,206,000 bushels; cotton lint, 290,000 bales.
Mining (1969): *Production value,* $201,000,000 (ranks 27th among the states). *Chief minerals* (tons)—Stone, 27,690,000; clays, 5,557,000; sand and gravel, 3,708,000; iron ore, 184,000.
Fisheries (1970): *Commercial catch,* 14,400,000 pounds ($4,200,000). *Leading species by value* (1970)—Shrimps, $3,371,048; shad, $131,908; oysters, $100,347.
Transportation: *Roads* (1969), 98,901 miles (159,161 km); *motor vehicles* (1969), 2,487,000; *railroads* (1968), 5,449 miles (8,769 km); *airports* (1969), 104.
Communications: *Telephones* (1971), 2,413,000; *television stations* (1969), 13; *radio stations* (1969), 219; *newspapers* (1969), 31 (daily circulation, 973,000).

Racial unrest erupted in Georgia in late summer, with violence and death in Macon and with economic boycotts and alleged beatings in Milledgeville and other cities. School openings caused more problems as demonstrations hit cities with massive, court-ordered busing of students.

Citizen groups sprang up during 1971 to join ecologists in a fight to save the Chattahoochee River from developers in the metropolitan Atlanta area. Ecologists hoped that the U. S. Bureau of Outdoor Recreation would turn a 40-mile stretch of the scenic, free-flowing river into a park. Governor Carter gave a boost to antidevelopment groups by stopping bridge and industrial construction along the river. Conservationists hailed the announcement that Cumberland Island would be developed by the National Park Service as a national seashore.

Concern over drug abuse swept the state as authorities estimated that as many as 10,000 heroin addicts live in Atlanta, with more scattered around the state. Governor Carter established the Georgia Narcotics Treatment Program, and methadone-maintenance centers began springing up. The state braced for another 1,500 addicts the Pentagon said would soon return to Georgia from military service.

GENE STEPHENS
The Atlanta "Constitution"

GERMAN LITERATURE. See LITERATURE.

FRED IHRT/STERN FROM BLACK STAR

West Germany's Chancellor Willy Brandt (*right*) and Soviet Communist party chief Leonid Brezhnev appear in jovial mood as they leave conference in Crimea in September. Three-day talks covered many topics, including German-Soviet relations and arms reductions.

GERMANY

Germany is divided into two separate states. The Federal Republic of Germany (West Germany) is a democratic, parliamentary republic and a member of such Western organizations as the North Atlantic Treaty Organization (NATO), the European Coal and Steel Community, and the European Economic Community (Common Market). The German Democratic Republic (East Germany, also known as DDR from the initials of its name in German) is, in effect, a Communist one-party state. It is affiliated with the Warsaw Pact and the Council for Mutual Economic Assistance (COMECON), the Eastern counterparts of NATO and the Common Market, respectively.

Between these two states, West Berlin, a Western outpost within East Germany, maintains its precarious existence. Economically, it is fully integrated into the Federal Republic, but politically and militarily it has a separate status.

EAST-WEST GERMAN RELATIONS

The most significant inter-German development in 1971 was the signing of the Berlin agreement by the United States, the Soviet Union, Britain, and France on August 23. The accord ended 17 months of complex negotiations. The two German states did not take part in the discussions, since these were based on the agreements of 1944–45 that established Berlin's special status under Big-Four supervision. However, both East and West Germany sought to bring pressure to bear on the talks—the

West Germans, by holding parliamentary committee meetings and party conferences in West Berlin in order to underscore their claim to the city as part of West Germany; the East Germans, by interfering with *Autobahn* traffic between West Berlin and West Germany to stress their rejection of this claim.

The accord, signed by the three Western ambassadors to the Federal Republic and the Soviet ambassador to the German Democratic Republic, provides for unhindered traffic between West Berlin and West Germany, with checks reduced to the presentation of identity papers, simplified baggage and cargo inspections, and the elimination of individual toll payments (in return for an annual lump sum to be paid by the Bonn government). Other provisions grant West Berliners access to East Berlin, and the DDR, which they have not had since 1966 and 1952, respectively, and call for improved telephone, telegraph, and transport services between West Berlin and East Germany. They also permit the retention of existing Federal agencies in West Berlin; safeguard economic, financial, legal, and cultural ties between West Berlin and West Germany; and authorize Bonn to represent West Berlin diplomatically.

On the other hand, the accord states expressly that West Berlin is not a constituent part of the Bonn republic and not governed by it. While the federal president and chancellor may visit the city, they may not perform official acts there. The West German parliament may not meet there at all, but its committees may do so if dealing with problems affecting West Berlin. As a concession to the Soviet Union, Moscow is given the right to open a consulate general in the city, but the agreement also acknowledges the right of the Western powers to be in Berlin—a right repeatedly challenged before by the USSR.

It was agreed that the accord would go into effect as soon as the two German governments implemented the provisions concerning surface traffic and communications. Negotiations on these matters proceeded slowly, since East Berlin insisted on special safeguards lest the eased regulations open up new escape routes to the East Germans. However, on December 17 the East German and West German negotiators signed an agreement on surface transit, and on December 20, West Berlin and East German representatives signed one on visits of West Berliners to the East.

West Berlin. West Berlin's precarious condition was reflected in the population statistics of the 1970 census. Its German-born population dropped from 2.2 million in 1960 to 1.98 million in 1970. People aged 65 and over form 21.3% of the population, while children under 15 account for a mere 15.2%. Its annual death rate exceeded its birth rate by 20,000, and 3,000 more people left the city in 1970 than moved to it. This imbalance would have been even greater had it not been for the influx of foreign workers.

The city's isolation was slightly relieved in January when direct telephone service between East and West Berlin was restored on a very limited basis (20 lines were reopened as against 5,000 in 1952). The city seemed satisfied with Chancellor Willy Brandt's efforts to improve its status and achieve a rapprochement with the DDR. In elections held in March, Brandt's party, the Social Democrats, retained their majority, though it was somewhat reduced. The reaction of West Berlin to the Berlin settlement was restrained. It was too early to tell to what extent the agreement would improve West Berlin's economic prospects. As a first gesture by the East Germans, postal and telegraph services to and from West Berlin were speeded up in October.

FEDERAL REPUBLIC OF GERMANY
(West Germany)

The negotiations over Berlin were a direct result of Chancellor Brandt's *Ostpolitik* ("Eastern policy")—a strategy aimed at a rapprochement with the USSR and Eastern Europe. The Berlin accord could be concluded only because the Kremlin had been reassured about Bonn's peaceful intentions by the latter's nonaggression pacts with Moscow and Warsaw. Pursuing this policy, Federal President Gustav Heinemann paid an official visit to Rumania in May; feelers were put out to Hungary concerning the establishment of diplomatic relations; and talks were initiated with Yugoslavia about the indemnification of victims of Nazi abuses during World War II. A meeting of Brandt and Leonid I. Brezhnev, the secretary-general of the Soviet Communist party, at the latter's Crimean vacation resort in September, was also to further Bonn's *Ostpolitik*. It explored the conclusion of new trade and cultural exchange agreements and the possibility of a mutually balanced reduction of armed forces.

Relations with the West. A mutual reduction of forces is of special concern to Bonn because a withdrawal of part of the U. S. forces in western Europe, especially from West Germany, where most are stationed, may take place after June 1972. To avert such a withdrawal, Bonn agreed in December to increase its contribution toward the upkeep of the U. S. forces by more than $400 million. Efforts by the United States to shore up the economy created further difficulties between the two countries and indirectly also caused a deterioration of Franco-West German relations (see below).

Domestic Politics. The West German government rests on a coalition of Social Democrats (SPD) and Free Democrats (FDP), the former a social reform party, the latter a small party of staunch conservatives and old-line liberals. The coalition has a majority of only six votes in the Bundestag.

As several state and local elections showed, popular support for the government kept declining during the greater part of 1971. One reason was the lack of progress of Brandt's *Ostpolitik* and the slow-moving negotiations over Berlin. More detrimental, however, was the government's inability to check the spreading inflation. Because of the inflation, moreover, Brandt was forced to postpone long-promised reforms.

The opposition parties, the Christian Democratic Union (CDU), and its Bavarian offshoot, the Christian Social Union (CSU), benefited from the electoral losses of SPD and FDP. But while they could assail inflation without impunity, attacks on Brandt's *Ostpolitik* presented problems. A rejection of the treaties with Moscow and Warsaw, submitted for ratification in December, would cause relations with the USSR and eastern Europe to deteriorate. It would also annul the Berlin agreement, whose formal ratification depends on the ratification of the two nonaggression pacts, just as the ratification of those pacts depends on that of the Berlin agreement.

Public opinion polls, moreover, show that a majority of the electorate support Bonn's *Ostpolitik*. This was also indicated by the results of the state elections in Bremen, held in October after the conclusion of the accord on Berlin: the Social Democrats won an absolute majority, as against their previous plurality. It was the first victory the SPD has scored in West German state elections since Brandt became chancellor in October 1969.

Economic Policy. With inflation unchecked, prices rose at an annual rate of 6%. Wage increases, expensive government programs, and a government pledge not to raise taxes kept up this momentum. Moreover, in order to ward off the continuous influx of dollars, which speculators preferred to invest in West Germany rather than in the United States, interest rates were kept low, encouraging a further heating up of the economy.

To halt inflation, the government decided in the spring on a policy of retrenchment. Finance Minister Alex Möller (SPD) was unable, however, to secure the necessary cuts in some of the ministerial budgets, and he resigned in May. His successor, Economics Minister Karl Schiller, also a Social Democrat, combined the two portfolios of economics and finance in a "superministry." His difficult task was rendered still harder by the de facto devaluation of the dollar, which was getting under way just when he assumed his new duties. (See International Finance.)

In August the United States imposed a 10% surcharge on imports and called for a 7% "Buy American" investment tax credit; this quickly affected

—— **WEST GERMANY** • Information Highlights ——

Official Name: Federal Republic of Germany.
Area: 95,743 square miles (247,973 sq km). West Berlin, 86 square miles (481 sq km).
Population (1970 est.): 59,550,000. West Berlin, 2,130,000. *Density*, 627 per square mile (240 per sq km). *Annual rate of increase*, 1.0%.
Chief Cities (1968 est.): Bonn, the capital, 138,090; Hamburg, 1,826,411; Munich, 1,260,553; Cologne, 853,864.
Government: *Head of state*, Gustav Heinemann, president (took office July 1, 1969). *Head of government*, Willy Brandt, federal chancellor (took office Oct. 21, 1969). *Legislature*—Parliament; Bundestag, 496 members; Bundesrat, 45 members. *Major political parties*—Christian Democratic Union; Social Democratic party; Free Democratic party.
Language: German (official).
Education: *Literacy rate* (1970), 99% of population. *Expenditure on education* (1968), 10.9% of total public expenditure. *School enrollment* (1968)—primary, 5,877,384; secondary, 4,224,737; technical/vocational, 2,185,789; university/higher, 430,904.
Finances (1970 est.): *Revenues*, $24,800,000,000; *expenditures*, $24,500,000,000; *monetary unit*, Deutsche mark (3.225 marks equal U.S.$1, Dec. 30, 1971).
Gross National Product (1970 est.): $185,000,000,000.
National Income (1969): $116,231,000,000; *national income per person*, $1,910.
Economic Indexes: *Industrial production* (1970), 153 (1963=100); *agricultural production* (1969), 111 (1963=100); *consumer price index* (1970), 120 (1963=100).
Manufacturing (metric tons, 1969): Crude steel, 45,316,000; coke oven coke, 39,010,000; pig-iron and ferro-alloys, 34,015,000; distillate fuel oils, 33,902,000; beer, 78,795,000 hectoliters.
Crops (metric tons, 1969 crop year): Potatoes, 15,985,000 (ranks 3d among world producers); sugar beets (1968–69), 14,081,000; wheat, 6,000,000; rye, 3,186,000 (ranks 3d in world production); oats, 2,976,000.
Minerals (metric tons, 1969): Coal, 111,780,000; lignite, 107,424,000; crude petroleum, 7,876,000; potash, 2,626,000; iron ore, 1,959,000.
Foreign Trade (1968): *Exports* (1970), $24,757,000,000 (chief exports—nonelectrical machinery, $5,497,700,000; motor vehicles, $3,347,100,000; chemicals, $3,113,900,000; electrical machinery and appliances, $1,947,300,000; iron and steel, $1,829,000,000). *Imports* (1970), $29,814,000,000 (chief imports—petroleum, crude and partly refined, $1,400,500,000; nonelectrical machinery, $1,333,700,000; nonferrous metals, $1,320,300,000; chemicals, $1,191,700,000). *Chief trading partners* (1968)—France (took 12% of exports, supplied 12% of imports); United States (11%—11%); Netherlands (10%—11%); Italy (8%—10%).
Tourism: *Receipts* (1970), $1,021,300,000.
Transportation: *Roads* (1966), 209,495 miles (337,140 km); *motor vehicles* (1969), 13,139,000 (automobiles, 12,194,300); *railroads* (1970), 29,845 miles (48,030 km); *merchant fleet* (1971), 8,679,000 gross registered tons; *national airline*, Deutsche Lufthansa AG; *principal airport*, Cologne.
Communications: *Telephones* (1970), 12,456,268; *television stations* (1968), 63; *television sets* (1969), 15,970,000; *radios* (1969), 28,500,000; *newspapers* (1969), 1,098 (daily circulation, 20,125,000).

German exports to the United States, adding to Schiller's problems. Exports to France also suffered, because Paris did not allow the price of the franc to rise in relation to the decline of the dollar. Thus West German exports to France, too, became more expensive, while French exports to the Federal Republic, especially food, became cheaper.

These developments, moreover, occurred at a time when inflation was turning into "stagflation." In October steel production was reduced 10%, and the chemical and automobile industries were planning similar cutbacks.

Schiller's budget for 1972 called for increased taxes and reduced public investments, despite earlier promises to the contrary, in order to halt inflation. However, by year-end it had become doubtful whether the policy of retrenchment could be maintained if unemployment, as expected, rose. There was also growing discontent among the younger Social Democrats about the distribution of the tax burden. At a special SPD congress in November a majority of the delegates asked the government to subject the highest income brackets to heavier taxation and to reduce taxes of low-income groups.

Social Conditions. One out of every 10 workers in West Germany is a foreigner. It is therefore assumed that these "guest laborers" would be the first ones to lose their jobs if there were large-scale dismissals. However, according to Common Market stipulations, close to half a million of these workers enjoy the same rights as German citizens, and they and their families, even if unemployed, cannot be expelled. A considerable number have married Germans, and even without such ties, a large majority plan to stay permanently in the Federal Republic, despite the fact that many live in unsanitary, overcrowded dwellings, pay excessive rents, and lack the most elementary comforts. Thus the dismissal and expulsion of foreign workers would create great difficulties with their countries of origin and might also cause serious internal problems.

Pollution, urban deterioration, and traffic congestion are other problems of increasing concern. A lack of adequate highways and the absence of speed limits are mainly responsible for the steady increase of highway casualties, which, proportionately, are one third higher than in the United States. A proposed highway building program that was to add 17,000 miles (27,350 km) of major highways by 1985 is being cut back as part of the government's new economy program. A bill providing for a speed limit of 63 miles (100 km) per hour on all highways except *Autobahnen* has also run into difficulties on the grounds that reduced speeds would worsen traffic congestion. Other measures such as raising the standard of drivers' tests and granting drivers' licenses for limited periods of time are also under consideration, as is the adoption of a traffic education program. Such a program, introduced by the state of North Rhine-Westphalia some years ago, may have been at least partly responsible for a decrease in traffic casualties there.

One of the few reform programs that has not been affected by the government's policy of retrenchment, since it involves no significant new expenditures, is one proposing a series of comprehensive legal reforms. It seeks to deal with such problems as divorce, abortion, homosexuality, and the equality of the sexes. One of its proposals lets bride and bridegroom decide whose last name to adopt as their family name and permits the use of both names, hyphenated, if that is preferred.

With illegal abortions estimated at over 500,000 a year, the reform of the abortion laws has become one of the major issues of the reform legislation. Both the Roman Catholic and the Lutheran churches are opposed to a liberalization of the present laws, but the demand for an unrestricted legalization of abortion is increasing. To underscore this demand, 374 women active in public life issued a statement admitting that they had had illegal abortions. Significantly, the courts ignored the confessions, and there were no indictments.

Education. Despite the opening of several new institutions, West German universities were still unable to accommodate all who wanted to study in 1971. The lack of facilities was especially marked in the sciences. Some universities were again troubled by clashes between students and faculty. The former accused the latter of a lack of responsiveness to the students' intellectual and professional needs; the faculties protested against student interference, often Marxist-inspired, with university operations. Controversies also arose over the appointment of Marxists or alleged Marxists to faculties. This issue led to the breakup of the governing SPD-FDP coalition in Bremen, where the FDP charged that the newly founded university was

MASSIVE construction was underway in Munich in preparation for 1972 summer Olympics. At left is television tower. Olympic Village (*top*) will house athletes; sports hall (*above*) will be for indoor events.

being turned into a hotbed of radicalism under SPD auspices. However, in the October elections the bulk of Bremen's electorate ignored these charges and gave increased support to the SPD.

West German high schools took advantage of the growing number of unemployed scientists in the United States to relieve their own shortage of science teachers. Hamburg was the first city to invite jobless American physicists, chemists, and biologists to accept teaching posts in its schools. Other West German cities have since followed Hamburg's example and have also appointed American teachers in English. However, linguistic and disciplinary problems appear to be affecting the success of the program.

GERMAN DEMOCRATIC REPUBLIC
(East Germany)

On May 3, Walter Ulbricht, for reasons of age (77) and health, resigned as first secretary of East Germany's Socialist Unity (Communist) party (SED). His place was taken by Erich Honecker, 58, who had been a Communist party member since 1931, had spent most of the Nazi period in prison, and after the war had built up the Communist youth organization, Free German Youth. Since 1958, Honecker has been a member of the politburo of the SED, in charge of military and security matters, and for the past several years he had been regarded as Ulbricht's heir apparent. A colorless, quiet man, Honecker evidently owed his position to his organizational and technical expertise rather than to any charismatic qualifications.

Ulbricht retains his post as chairman of the council of state, the supreme policy-making body of the government, and has also been made honorary party chairman. How active he still is, is unclear. Willi Stoph remains chairman (minister-president) of the council of ministers, the top executive organ of the government apparatus, and also deputy chairman of the council of state.

Economic Conditions. Owing to an unusually severe winter, power output was seriously reduced in the early part of the year. East Germany's power is produced mainly from lignite, which is hard to mine and transport in freezing temperatures because of its high water content. The lack of any reserve capacity and an increase in private consumption for such appliances as television sets, washing machines, and refrigerators greatly aggravated the situation. Stepped-up night shifts and emergency help rendered by soldiers, farmers, and students, as well as reduced allocations of power for private consumption, could not avert major cutbacks in industrial production.

Other difficulties arose when a prolonged drought in July and August hurt food production and caused serious shortages in potatoes, other vegetables, and fruit. To limit the damage, the harvesting of the cereal crops continued through the nights. Daily progress reports in the newspapers described local arrangements between agricultural cooperatives to dig irrigation ditches, improvised pumping systems that brought in water from rivers some 10 miles (16 km) away, and special contests to encourage further speedups. Daily production quotas were front-page news; on August 6, as *Neues Deutschland* reported, cereal was harvested from 215,000 acres (87,000 hectares), or 3.9% of the DDR's total cropland.

Thus, while productivity kept increasing during 1971, especially in the chemical and electrical industries, and living conditions on the whole were also improving, there was still little margin for error or unexpected developments. A new 5-year plan, inaugurated at the 8th congress of the SED in June, again placed the main emphasis on capital goods production, including the establishment of nuclear power stations. At the same time it promised to meet consumer needs more effectively than had been done in the past. To relieve the continuing housing shortage, the new plan provided specifically for 500,000 new apartments (as against 365,000 built during the preceding five years). However, since no additional manpower would be available, it was stressed that the plan's goals could be met only by a one-third increase in productivity.

Social Conditions. The manpower shortage was in fact one of the major causes of the existing difficulties. It was slightly received by a limited influx of Hungarian and Polish workers—limited primarily by the lack of housing facilities. In consequence, 51% of the population of the DDR is working, while only 44% work in the Federal Republic. The difference results mainly from the greater percentage of married women and elderly people who keep working in the DDR. Married women find continued employment helpful, since prices are high except for necessities such as rent and food; and the elderly find remaining on the job almost obligatory, as pensions are very low.

Cultural Life. As always, a great deal of attention was paid to cultural activities. Most industrial plants and many agricultural cooperatives drew up not only an economic plan but a cultural one as well. In 1970 the cultural units in plants and cooperatives were also urged to organize theater festivals. According to Minister of Culture Klaus Gysi, the proposal met with a warm reception, although more so in the industrial districts than in the rural ones. Book production continued to expand, and the well-appointed, spacious, and bright bookstores—a marked contrast to most other stores in East Germany—indicate the importance that is attributed to them.

Realizing the need for entertainment, Honecker, in his maiden speech as first secretary at the SED congress, complained that TV programs were often boring and called for livelier offerings. In the same vein Minister of Culture Gysi pointed out, at an art festival in Rostock, that more DDR citizens were visiting art galleries and museums than zoos. In consideration of this, he asked artists not to indulge in snobbism, but to produce works that could be readily understood.

Foreign Affairs. Outwardly the international standing of the DDR remained almost unchanged. It was recognized diplomatically by a few more states, among them Chile, the first South American country to do so. Yet there were signs that the East German claim to independent, sovereign status was receiving more serious attention in the West. In Britain, several Labour members of Parliament called for recognition of the DDR; in France, President Georges Pompidou suggested that diplomatic recognition was only a question of time, with the initiative in this matter, however, best left to the Federal Republic. Meanwhile, East German and French parliamentary delegations arranged to meet regularly every six months. Franco-East German

CHANCELLOR BRANDT chats with British Prime Minister Heath (left) in London in May. Brandt gave his full backing to Britain's insistence on a speedy entrance into Common Market during meetings held in the spring.

KEYSTONE

------ **EAST GERMANY • Information Highlights** ------

Official Name: German Democratic Republic.
Area: 41,610 square miles (108,174 sq km).
Population (1970 est.): 17,250,000. *Density,* 411 per square mile (148 per sq km). *Annual rate of increase,* 1.6%.
Chief Cities (1968 est.): East Berlin (1970 est.), the capital, 1,070,000; Leipzig, 590,291; Dresden, 449,848; Karl-Marx-Stadt, 295,443.
Government: *Head of state,* Walter Ulbricht, chairman of the council of state (took office Sept. 24, 1960). *Head of government,* Willi Stoph, minister president (took office Sept. 24, 1964); *First Secretary of the Socialist Unity party,* Erich Honecker (took office May 3, 1971). *Legislature*—Volkskammer (People's Chamber), 500 members. *Major political party*—Socialist Unity party.
Language: German (official).
Education: *Literacy rate* (1971), more than 90% of population. *Expenditure on education* (1968), 8.3% of total public expenditure. *School enrollment* (1968)—primary, 2,378,-257; secondary, 714,518; technical/vocational, 580,580; university/higher, 78,308.
Finances (1969 est.): *Revenues,* $29,622,000,000; *expenditures,* $29,281,000,000; *monetary unit,* Ostmark (2.22 Ostmarks equal U. S.$1, 1971).
Gross National Product (1970 est.): $34,000,000,000.
Economic Indexes: *Industrial production* (1970), 153 (1963 = 100); *consumer price index* (1969), 116 (1963 = 100).
Manufacturing (metric tons, 1969): Cement, 7,410,000; crude steel, 4,824,000; residual fuel oil, 3,880,000; coke oven coke, 2,391,000; pig-iron and ferro-alloys, 2,098,000.
Crops (metric tons, 1969 crop year): Potatoes, 8,832,000; sugar beets (1968–69), 6,998,000; wheat, 1,987,000; rye, 1,936,000 (ranks 4th in world production); oats, 841,000.
Minerals (metric tons, 1969): Lignite, 254,553,000 (ranks 1st among world producers); potash, 2,300,000; salt, 1,-972,000; coal, 1,334,000.
Foreign Trade: *Exports* (1970), $4,581,000,000 (chief exports, 1967—nonelectrical machinery, $950,472,000; transport equipment, $404,603,000; electrical machinery, $302,911,-000). *Imports* (1970), $4,847,000,000 (chief imports, 1968—passenger automobiles, footwear, crude petroleum. *Chief trading partners* (1968)—USSR (took 41% of exports, supplied 44% of imports); Czechoslovakia (11%—10%); Poland (8%—7%); West Germany (7%—7%).
Transportation: *Classified roads* (1968), 28,385 miles (45,679 km); *motor vehicles* (1969), 1,411,800 (automobiles, 1,039,-200); *railroads* (1968), 9,468 miles (15,237 km); *merchant fleet* (1971), 1,016,000 gross registered tons; *national airline,* Interflug; *principal airport,* East Berlin.
Communications: *Telephones* (1970), 1,986,190; *television stations* (1968), 25; *television sets* (1969), 4,337,000; *radios* (1969), 5,983,000; *newspapers* (1968) daily circulation, 7,608,000).

trade kept increasing. Finland, in turn, which has only commercial relations with the two German states, offered to exchange ambassadors with both countries. Most important, despite all declarations to the contrary, the Bonn government kept up its negotiations with East Berlin, as if with another sovereign power.

At the same time, East German relations with the Soviet Union and the East European countries were further strengthened. A COMECON meeting held in Bucharest in July agreed on new areas of economic and technical cooperation among its members. A detailed plan signed at the meeting provides for the coordination of the 5-year plans of the countries concerned and for specified collaboration in the chemical, metallurgical, machine, and electrical industries. Production methods and transportation facilities are to be standardized, and prices and currencies more closely integrated.

As part of this plan, East Germany is thinking of discontinuing its production of trucks and buses in order to concentrate on industrial fields in which other COMECON members are less proficient. In that case trucks and buses would be imported from Czechoslovakia and Hungary, the proposed specialists in this area. The entire plan is to be implemented fully within 15 to 20 years.

ANDREAS DORPALEN, *The Ohio State University*

GHANA

Ghana's 2-year-old civilian government, headed by Prime Minister Kofi A. Busia, continued to consolidate its power in 1971. But on Jan. 13, 1972, while Busia was in London for medical treatment, the government was overthrown in a bloodless military coup led by Col. Ignatius Kutu Acheampong. Ghana's constitution was suspended, Parliament was dissolved, and all political parties were banned. The coup leaders established a National Redemption Council, with Colonel Acheampong as chairman. He charged the Busia government with mismanagement of the economy and with corruption.

Prime Minister Busia had met increasing opposition in 1971, primarily as a result of his program of drastic economic austerity, undertaken to pay the enormous debt inherited from the regime of President Kwame Nkrumah, overthrown in 1966. In December 1971, two weeks before his government was toppled, Busia had ordered a 55% devaluation of Ghana's currency; the value of the new cedi was cut from U. S. $0.98 to U. S. $0.55. At the same time the austerity program was intensified with a reduction in army officer perquisites, including allowances for housing and gasoline.

Domestic Affairs. On April 5, 1971, the annual congress of the National Union of Ghanaian Students urged the government to grant amnesty to all political prisoners, including former President Nkrumah. The congress also called for normalizing relations with Guinea, where Nkrumah has been living in exile since his overthrow. Ghana's minister of youth, social welfare, and rural development replied that any student movement seeking to undermine the government would be banned. On August 24, Parliament, after heated debate, passed a bill banning the restoration of either Nkrumah or his disbanded Convention People's party.

A new political party, the Ghana People's party, was formed in September. Its proclaimed ideology was socialism.

On September 9, Parliament, over opposition protests, passed a bill dissolving the Trades Union Congress (TUC). Minister of Labor William Bruce Konuah had claimed that the TUC was an integral wing of the proscribed Convention People's party. Under the new law existing trade unions were allowed to operate, but were required to register within six months. They were to be free to remain independent or to form new federations.

Essential services were brought to a standstill in Sekondi-Takoradi in mid-September, when industrial workers went on strike to back their demand for abolition of the national development levy.

Economy. Ghana's economy, burdened with the huge debt incurred by Nkrumah, was further hurt by a fall in the price of cacao, the country's chief export. As a result Ghana's trade balance showed a sharp deficit in 1971. The government had been trying to win a moratorium on its foreign debts.

Foreign Affairs. On March 22, Ghana's Parliament accepted the Busia government's policy favoring a dialogue with South Africa as "one of the weapons in the struggle to eliminate apartheid." Foreign Minister William Ofori-Atta announced that he would be prepared to go to South Africa with other African ministers to negotiate with the Vorster government on its policy of apartheid.

Israeli Foreign Minister Abba Eban visited Ghana, as well as several other African nations, in June to discuss his views on the Middle East conflict.

An agreement establishing a Ghana–Ivory Coast Joint Commission on Cooperation was signed in Accra on May 28. Prime Minister Busia paid an official visit to Upper Volta in August, and the two countries agreed to cooperate on a number of economic and health projects.

JUDITH A. GLICKMAN

GHANA • Information Highlights

Official Name: Republic of Ghana.
Area: 92,099 square miles (238,537 sq km).
Population (1970 est.): 9,030,000. *Density,* 93 per square mile (36 per sq km). *Annual rate of increase,* 2.8%.
Chief Cities (1968 est.): Accra, the capital, 615,800; Kumasi, 281,600; Sekondi-Takoradi, 128,200.
Government: *Head of state,* Lt. Col. I. K. Acheampong, chairman of National Redemption Council (led military junta that ousted government of Prime Minister Kofi A. Busia on Jan. 13, 1972). *Organ of government,* 10-member National Redemption Council (established Jan. 13, 1972). *Legislature*—National Assembly (dissolved Jan. 13, 1972). *Major political parties*—Justice party, All People's Republican party (political parties banned Jan. 13, 1972).
Languages: English (official), 50 tribal languages and dialects.
Education: *Literacy rate* (1970), 25% of population. *Expenditure on education* (1968), 18.7% of total public expenditure. *School enrollment* (1967)—primary, 1,288,383; secondary, 213,435; technical/vocational (1966), 17,587; university/higher, 4,768.
Finances (1970 est.): *Revenues,* $428,000,000; *expenditures,* $458,000,000; *monetary unit,* new cedi (1.8182 new cedis equal U. S.$1, Dec. 30, 1971).
Gross National Product (1970): $2,320,000,000.
National Income (1968): $1,661,000,000; *per person,* $198.
Manufacturing (metric tons, 1969): Residual fuel oil, 432,000; cement, 408,000; sawnwood, 365,000 cubic meters.
Crops (metric tons, 1969 crop year): Cassava (1968), 1,446,-000; cacao beans, 415,500 (ranks 1st among world producers); maize, 305,000; sorghum (1968), 83,000.
Minerals (metric tons, 1969): Bauxite, 246,000; manganese ore, 160,000; diamonds, 2,391,000 metric carats.
Foreign Trade (1970): *Exports,* $433,000,000 (chief export—cacao, $294,392,000). *Imports,* $411,000,000. *Chief trading partners* (1968)—United Kingdom (took 20% of exports, supplied 28% of imports); United States (19%—19%).
Transportation: *Roads* (1970), 20,629 miles (33,198 km); *motor vehicles* (1968), 46,800; *railroads* (1970), 805 miles (1,295 km); *merchant fleet* (1970), 166,000 gross registered tons; *national airline,* Ghana Airways Corporation; *principal airports,* Accra, Kumasi, Takoradi, Tamale.
Communications: *Telephones* (1970), 53,934; *television stations* (1968), 3; *television sets* (1969), 12,000; *radios* (1969), 700,000; *newspapers* (1969), 6 (daily circulation, 295,000).

Newspapers trumpeted House of Commons' approval on October 28 of Britain's entry into the Common Market. Unexpectedly large margin of approval was victory for Conservative government.

GREAT BRITAIN

The Conservative government of Prime Minister Edward Heath suffered widespread unpopularity throughout 1971, largely because it found no speedy solution to the variety of economic ills besetting Britain. Inflation, unemployment, and the resulting dislocations were no more palatable for being shared with other nations. And the government's efforts to get business to "stand on its own feet" did not find favor with the general public.

Nevertheless, Heath scored a remarkable victory in the House of Commons, steering an accord on terms of entry into the European Economic Community (EEC, or Common Market) through acrimonious debate to passage. Successful negotiations with the EEC during 1971 marked the culmination of a decade of efforts to attain membership on acceptable terms. With three other new members—Denmark, Ireland, and Norway—Britain signed the EEC treaty in Brussels on Jan. 22, 1972. There remained the matter of passing enabling legislation.

Another Heath triumph in 1971 was an agreement reached with Britain's former African colony of Rhodesia, which paves the way for Britain's acceptance of Rhodesia's independence after constitutional changes in Rhodesia provide for political advancement of the black majority.

GOVERNMENT AND POLITICS

The Heath government, which had been elected much to everyone's surprise in 1970, had appealed to the voters on the basis of its ability to control rising prices and to invigorate the British economy with the spirit of competition. Although the prime minister denied that control of inflation had been promised with dispatch, his Labour opponents represented the 1971 inflationary situation as a clear failure of the Conservative government. The unhealthy combination of rapid inflation with rising unemployment caused a steady and steep decline in the popularity of Heath and the Conservative party.

Although the success of the government's Common Market negotiations in June did something to arrest this decline, the respite proved temporary. Late in the year opinion polls predicted that in any election held in the immediate future, the Labour opposition would lead the government by an average of 8%.

Elections. By-election results confirmed the unpopularity of the Heath government. The ten by-elections during the year revealed anti-Conservative swings of between 1.7% and 11.4%, and the Conservatives lost one parliamentary seat. In the local elections in May, Labour candidates were returned in massive numbers, gaining more than 2,000 seats and wiping out the Conservative dominance built up in previous years.

Government Confidence. Although the degree of unpopularity suffered by the government was unusually great for an administration so recently elected, Conservative spokesmen claimed that it was not unexpected. In the government's view, unpopularity was merely the short-run price to be paid by a determined government whose policies would pay off in the long run. The year was remarkable for the lack of government reshuffles; all senior ministers kept their places. This was interpreted as a sign of Prime Minister Heath's public determination to present his government and his policies as long-term propositions.

Structural Changes. In January 1971 the amalgamation of the traditional civil service grades into a single administrative group took place in line with the recommendations of a 1968 report. In February 1971 the government published its proposed reforms of local government. It recommended replacing some 12,000 varied local bodies with about 370 district councils supervised by a small number of regional councils.

Royal Family. The peripatetic royal family was much on the move in 1971. Queen Elizabeth, Prince Philip, and Princess Anne journeyed to British Columbia, Canada, in May. Princess Anne visited Norway in June, and in October accompanied Prince Philip to Iran to attend the 2,500th anniversary celebrations there. In February and March, Philip had toured Australia and the Pacific Islands.

Prince Charles took a Royal Air Force flying course, and Princess Anne won the European horse trials, thus becoming a possible contender for the British Olympic team. After some controversy, a select committee of Commons approved the Queen's request for more funds.

ECONOMY

Since World War II most British governments have been faced with the dilemma of combining economic growth with stable prices. Inflation on the one hand or stagnation and unemployment on the other seemed the only long-term choices. In 1971 a dramatically new problem arose in the shape of a combination of unemployment, stagnation, and inflation—all at the same time. The failure to limit the pace of price increases and the growth of unemployment to levels not experienced since the war led the government to have second thoughts about its economic strategy.

Conservative Economic Philosophy. During the 1970 election campaign, the Conservatives had advocated a return to some of the precepts of traditional capitalism: reducing government aid to private industry, letting market forces hold more sway, and injecting a spirit of competition and self-sufficiency into the economy.

In some instances the Conservative government was unyielding in its determination to implement these policies. In December 1970 the nationalized airlines, BEA and BOAC, were required to share some of the routes on which they had hitherto had a monopoly, with private airlines. And in November 1971 the government announced its intention of introducing local commercial radio stations, a policy hotly opposed by Labour. By such means the government hoped to limit the alleged ill-effects of publicly owned monopolies.

Rolls Royce Issue. In February 1971, when Rolls Royce, Ltd., announced its inability to continue operations without further injections of financial help, the government refused to underwrite the company as a whole. The government did agree to nationalize the aero-engine and gas-turbine sections of the company on the grounds that they were vital to the British defense program and were more economically viable than the other divisions. The Con-

servatives thus earned the criticism of some of their own supporters for this apparent inconsistency in economic philosophy.

The government then manifested further firmness by refusing to lend its authority to the continuation of a joint project with a U. S. firm, Lockheed Aircraft Corp., by which Rolls Royce would provide the RB-211 engine for the Lockheed L-1011 Tristar airbus. Government insistence that the contract would have to be renegotiated led to a new agreement with Lockheed signed in May, which was more favorable to Rolls Royce.

Other Government Stands. Apart from the Rolls Royce issue, the most controversial manifestation of the government's determination to "make industry stand on its own feet" was its refusal, in June, to put any more public money into Upper Clyde Shipbuilders, a cooperative enterprise underwritten by the previous Labour government. The Conservatives liquidated UCS, but promised to support a new, more viable group that could be reorganized from its remains. In July shipyard workers occupied the UCS yards in protest.

In February a number of previously nationalized inns and breweries were returned to private ownership. In May the government announced its intention of charging admission fees to hitherto-free public museums and galleries. And in June the Transport Holding Company, which administered a

——— **GREAT BRITAIN · Information Highlights** ———

Official Name: United Kingdom of Great Britain and Northern Ireland.
Area: 94,220 square miles (244,030 sq km).
Population (1971 census): 55,346,551. *Density,* 585 per square mile (228 per sq km). *Annual rate of increase,* 1.3%.
Chief Cities (1968 est.): London, the capital (metropolitan area), 7,763,800; Manchester, 2,451,660; Birmingham, 2,446,400; Leeds, 1,730,210; Liverpool, 1,368,630; Glasgow, 960,527.
Government: *Head of state,* Elizabeth II, queen (acceded Feb. 6, 1952). *Head of government,* Edward Heath, prime minister (took office June 19, 1970). *Legislature—Parliament:* House of Commons, 630 members; House of Lords, 975 members. *Major political parties*—Conservative, Labour.
Languages: English (official), Welsh (official).
Education: *Literacy rate* (1971), 99% of population. *School enrollment* (1967–68)—primary, 5,745,454; secondary, 3,786,141; technical/vocational, 166,345; university/higher, 149,994.
Finances (1970–71): *Revenues,* $37,860,000,000; *expenditures,* $33,660,000,000; *monetary unit,* pound (0.4024 pound equal U. S.$1, Sept. 1971).
Gross National Product (1970 est.): $121,000,000,000.
National Income (1970): $92,469,000,000; *national income per person,* $1,660.
Economic Indexes: *Industrial production* (1971), 126 (1963= 100); *agricultural production* (1969), 112 (1963=100); *consumer price index* (June 1971), 135 (1962=100).
Manufacturing (metric tons, 1969): Residual fuel oil, 43,901,-000; crude steel, 26,846,000; pig-iron and ferro-alloys, 16,653,000; gasoline, 10,263,000; wheat flour, 3,747,000.
Crops (metric tons, 1969 crop year): Barley, 8,664,000 (ranks 4th among world producers); sugar beets (1968–69), 7,118,-000; potatoes, 6,215,000; wheat, 3,364,000; oats, 1,308,000.
Minerals (metric tons, 1969): Coal, 152,790,000; salt, 8,605,-000; iron ore, 3,443,000; sulphur, 43,000; tin concentrates, 1,648.
Foreign Trade (1968): *Exports* (1970), $19,351,000,000 (chief exports—nonelectrical machinery, $3,045,168,000; motor vehicles, $1,582,968,000; chemicals, $1,437,984,000; electrical machinery and appliances, $985,992,000). *Imports* (1970), $21,724,000,000 (chief imports—nonelectrical machinery, $1,517,185,000; crude petroleum, $1,429,656,000; non-ferrous metals, $1,362,384,000; chemicals, $997,272,-000). *Chief trading partners*—United States (took 14% of exports, supplied 13% of imports); West Germany (5%—6%); Canada (4%—7%).
Tourism: *Receipts* (1970), $1,038,000,000.
Transportation: *Roads* (1970), 204,000 miles (328,297 km); *motor vehicles* (1969), 13,407,900 (automobiles, 11,643,-200); *railroads* (1970), 15,319 miles (24,648 km); *merchant fleet* (1971), 27,335,000 gross registered tons; *national airline,* BOAC, BEA; *principal airport,* London.
Communications: *Telephones* (1970), 13,947,000; *television stations* (1968), 68; *television sets* (1969), 15,792,000; *radios* (1969), 18,008,000; *newspapers* (1966), 106 (daily circulation, 26,700,000).

variety of publicly owned services, such as docks, road haulage, and travel agencies, was dissolved and its assets sold to private enterprise. In August the government announced the termination of public subsidies for milk for schoolchildren.

Although none of these withdrawals from government intervention in industry radically affected the balance between private and public ownership, both the government and its opponents claimed that a significant change had been made in the government's role in economic and social life. The government claimed that the efficiency (especially in labor utilization) that was supposed to follow from a reduction in government subsidies and intervention would limit price increases by stimulating competition, and would facilitate economic growth. Opponents accused the government of indifference to the human costs of its policies and of exaggerating the extent to which economic growth was a matter for private enterprise rather than governmental stimulation.

Performance of the Economy. Unemployment, the most politically sensitive economic indicator, rose throughout 1971. From a December 1970 figure of 589,000 (2.6% of the work force) it rose to 703,000 (3.1%) in April and 819,000 (3.6%) in

PRIME MINISTER Edward Heath chats with members of London Symphony Orchestra before October concert. Heath conducted *Cockaigne Overture* during benefit performance. His appearance marked the first time that he had conducted a professional orchestra.

WIDE WORLD

September. Already in April the figure represented the highest level of unemployment since May 1940, and the possibility of there being a million workers unemployed by early 1972 was not ruled out.

Nor was unemployment an antidote to inflation. The price index rose from its December 1970 level of 145 (1962 = 100) to 154 by June 1971 and was 10% higher than it had been in June 1970. Neither did unemployment appear to be keeping wages down. The basic hourly rate for manual workers rose 7% between December 1970 and August 1971.

The index of industrial production confirmed the picture of general economic difficulty. From its position at 124 in late 1970 (1963 = 100), it was only at 126 a year later.

On the other hand, the external economic position was more heartening. The large payments surplus that the previous government had built up after devaluation was maintained. A positive balance of payments of £191 million in December 1970 fell to £79 million in March, but had risen to £237 million a few months later. More important, the surplus on visible trade also was maintained.

Budget. The government budget, presented in March 1971, was constructed against a gloomy economic projection. Chancellor of the Exchequer Anthony Barber spoke of the combination of inflation and unemployment as "a new, and in many ways, a baffling combination of evils." Consequently, the budget was cautious: The standard rate of income tax was lowered by just over 2%; child allowances and pensions were increased; and the tax on distributed profits, the selective employment tax, and the surtax all were reduced. The budget released some £500 million into the economy.

Remedial Measures. By July the government was seriously concerned over the combination of rising inflation and falling employment. Chancellor Barber announced cuts in the purchase tax and relaxations in the restrictions on hire-purchase (installment-plan buying). Whereas the budget had estimated an increase in output of 3% between mid-1971 and mid-1972, the July measures were designed to expand the economy in this period by 4% to 4.5%. This prospect of expansion enabled Barber to persuade the Confederation of British Industries to ask its members to hold price increases down to 5% for a year. In December 1971 further expansionary measures were announced, including an early repayment of postwar credits and the moving-up of several of the investment programs of the nationalized industries.

The government's apparent retreat from its earlier confidence in the efficacy of its long-term policies was further manifest in its decision, in November, to increase the subsidies to British shipyards by £3 million. The political consequences of heavy unemployment had begun to undermine the government's ability to keep its sights on the long-run advantages of "slimming-down" the economy.

Labor Relations. The government's comprehensive industrial relations bill was enacted on Aug. 5, 1971, after eight months of debate and protest strikes, and despite official opposition from the Trade Union Congress and the Labour party. Among its controversial provisions were bans on wildcat strikes and on the closed shop and the adoption of a 60-day cooling-off period in strikes involving areas of national interest. In January many workers in the Midlands had stayed away from their jobs in protest against the bill, and the

TUC had called a national demonstration on January 12. In September, following passage of the bill, the TUC instructed its members to refuse to register under the act.

The nation's longest major strike since 1926 ended early in March, when 200,000 postal workers agreed to accept arbitration and returned to their jobs. An estimated $75 million in revenue was lost by the post office and a like amount in wages by the workers during the 47-day strike.

Decimal Currency. On Feb. 15, 1971, decimal currency was officially introduced with few problems. The transition to decimal currency is expected to be completed in 1972. Henceforth, each pound will be worth 100 new pence instead of 240 old.

OTHER DOMESTIC ISSUES

Social Welfare. The government's decision to cease subsidizing school milk revealed the connection between Conservative ideas about the state and the economy, on the one hand, and attitudes toward the scope of welfare services, on the other. During the 1960's the Conservatives had fashioned a philosophy of limited government that concentrated welfare services on those most in need. This point of view, consistent with general Conservative economic policy, was intermittently implemented during 1971.

In March the government created a committee to examine the extent of false claims to the welfare services. Also in March the government announced that welfare benefits to families of men on strike would thereafter be considerably reduced.

Applying the principle of greater selectivity in the distribution of welfare benefits to the field of housing, the government proposed to subsidize tenants according to their incomes, rather than artificially fixing the rents of publicly owned houses. Applied to pensions, this principle brought proposals for grading benefits more strictly according to income. Although the "means test" implications of these trends provoked accusations of harshness from the Labour opposition, the government actually was attempting to redirect welfare expenditures rather than decrease them. Nor was there a portent of significant change in the present balance between state and private roles in welfare, the responsibility still resting overwhelmingly with the former.

Immigration Policy. The government's immigration bill, introduced in February 1971, gave rise to inter-party divisions. The bill proposed to treat immigrants from the Commonwealth on the same footing as aliens. The Labour opposition claimed that this was unjust, and further was likely to damage domestic relations between the races. The government saw it as a logical step in the long-standing policy of attempting to remove the grievances of existing immigrants while reassuring the nonimmigrant population that future immigration would be more strictly controlled.

Education Policy. Government policy in secondary education was attacked as ambivalent, but a 1971 program for improving primary education was highly regarded. The Conservatives surprised many by their decision to continue to support the Open University, which provides subsidized, mainly correspondence-course higher education for those not attending traditional institutions.

Vital Statistics. The decennial census was held in April and an interim report in August revealed a population of 55,346,551, a rise of 2,600,000 in

NORMAN PARKINSON, CAMERA PRESS

PRINCESS ANNE posed in evening dress for official portrait for her 21st birthday, August 15. In a film released the same day for a children's charity, she admitted that life in Buckingham Palace can be lonely.

10 years. In January, the Divorce Reform Act of 1969, which facilitates divorce on the ground of "irretrievable breakdown," came into force.

Environmental pollution was a major topic of public debate throughout the year. On Jan. 13, 1972, 33 leading scientists warned that to avoid environmental catastrophe Britain would have to abandon industrial growth and concentrate on achieving a stable society with a population eventually reduced by half.

FOREIGN AFFAIRS

The main focus of British foreign policy during 1971 was on the last-stage negotiations for entry into the Common Market. After 10 years, two failing bids for membership, and 12 months of negotiation on the third bid, success was achieved. (*Continued on page 318*)

British soldiers patroling through Londonderry stare impassively as Catholic school children jeer.

A Background Report

THE TRAGEDY OF NORTHERN IRELAND

The year 1971 was the 50th anniversary of Northern Ireland's establishment as a federal state within the United Kingdom. Special events had been arranged in order to honor that auspicious day in June 1921, when King George V opened the Northern Irish Parliament at Stormont. However, the reality of 1971 was starkly different, and Northern Irishmen had little cause for celebration. Not since 1922, when 232 persons died in sectarian strife, has the province endured so much violence, fear, and hatred. By Christmas, the death toll for the year was 165, including 40 British soldiers and 11 policemen. Hundreds more had suffered injuries from bombs, bullets, stones, and other missiles. The cost of Ulster's turmoil could also be measured in millions of pounds in damage to property and revenue lost by investors, as well as income from tourists who were scared away.

The Roots of the Problem. The people of Northern Ireland are still imprisoned by their past. In its essentials, their ordeal arises out of a sectarian conflict within a colonial setting. The residents of the area, which was carved out of the ancient province of Ulster to form the substate of Northern Ireland under the Government of Ireland Act of 1920, are torn apart by political, religious, and social forces whose origins are centuries old. While enjoying the financial benefits of the British welfare state, many aroused Roman Catholics in the north wish to end partition of the island and join their coreligionists in the Republic of Ireland. However, the Protestants, who form 65% of Ulster's population, tend to regard a united and republican Ireland as anathema, and many of them have

pledged to fight rather than accept rule from Dublin.

What makes the so-called Ulster question so intractable is that the province, once the most Gaelic and rebellious in Ireland, became by the 1690's the most Anglo-Scottish and Presbyterian as the result of the settlement of Protestants there during the reign of King James I. Ironically, the Protestants of Ulster were staunch champions of Irish independence from Britain in the late 18th century. But a century later, in the 1880's, they were organizing resistance to inclusion in a modest Home Rule settlement sponsored by Irish Nationalists and British Liberals. By 1914, Ulster Unionism was not only sworn to uphold a Protestant ascendancy but also ready to rebel against Home Rule.

Since the creation of Northern Ireland, the Catholic minority there has been subjected to systematic social and economic discrimination and political manipulation. The blatant discrepancy between their condition and that of Catholics south of the border led to the civil rights movement of 1968–69, which was aided and, to a certain extent, led by liberal and socialist activists from the universities. The fierce reaction of extremist Ulster Protestants to freedom marches, in particular the savage beating of demonstrators at Burntollet on Jan. 4, 1969, exposed to the media of the world the bigotry that had kept Ulster Unionism in power for almost 50 years.

The Burntollet incident marked the beginning of a steady escalation of violence in Northern Ireland. In August 1969 the British government finally sent in troops to act as a buffer between the warring Protestants and Catholics. Though welcomed at first by the Catholics, the British soldiers gradually began to alienate this community by arms searches, carried out in Catholic but not Protestant areas, and by indiscriminate arrests. It was amid this growing Catholic disaffection that the illegal Irish Republican Army (I. R. A) began to take direct action. Determined to free Irish soil from the last remnants of British sovereignty, the more militant "Provisional" wing of the I. R. A. started in late 1970 a systematic campaign of guerrilla warfare against the British Army.

1971: The I. R. A. Versus the Army. Rioting broke out again in Belfast in January 1971, when British soldiers fought a series of street battles with Catholic dissidents, causing many injuries. As more and more people became embroiled in the fighting, the hit-and-run tactics of the I. R. A. kept the army constantly on the defensive. As the locus of I. R. A. activism shifted from the old Catholic slum along the Falls Road to the newer Belfast suburbs of Anderstown, Ardoyne, Ballymurphy, and Clonard, more and more people became embroiled in the fighting. Arms searches by British soldiers provoked many Catholics who knew that well-armed Protestants were not similarly harassed.

Sporadic gunfights in Belfast accounted for 13 deaths during February. On March 10 the I. R. A. murdered three young Scottish soldiers. Scores of bombed buildings and endless sniping at soldiers on patrol showed that the I. R. A. could carry on its war with relative impunity.

Appalled by the mounting casualties, Unionist politicians demanded tougher security measures. On March 20 they forced the resignation of their prime minister, Maj. James Chichester-Clark, and replaced him with Brian Faulkner, who assured British officials that he could keep the house of Ulster in order. In ensuing months, however, the I. R. A. stepped up its activities, and British soldiers began to fire on suspects, many of whom had no known ties with the I. R. A.

Tighter security measures and an increase in troop strength to over 12,000 in August failed to intimidate the I. R. A. The killing of more soldiers finally moved Faulkner to invoke Northern Ireland's Special Powers Act, which enabled the army on August 9 to round up some 337 political suspects for interrogation and detention. The internment order was carried out harshly, and reports of brutality by the military and police exasperated moderates on both sides of the border. (Later, a British commission of inquiry found that there had been "physical ill-treatment" but denied "brutality.") Internment succeeded only in polarizing further an already divided community.

On July 18 the 13 members of the opposition in Northern Ireland's Parliament announced their intention to withdraw from that assembly, and, shortly after internment, they decided to support a civil disobedience campaign against payment of rent and property taxes by republicans. In his search for ways to cope with the disorder, Faulkner joined British Prime Minister Edward Heath and Irish Premier Jack Lynch for tripartite talks on September 27–28. However, this historic meeting produced no plans for political settlement.

Although there were a few signs of movement toward constitutional change by the end of the year, following on the proposal of British Labour leader Harold Wilson for the eventual unification of Ireland, Ulster's appetite for self-destruction still seemed insatiable. An explosion in a Belfast bar on December 3 killed 15 people, and on December 12 a hard-line Unionist senator was murdered, apparently by the I. R. A. Martyrdom has become a way of political life in Ulster.

L. PERRY CURTIS, JR.
University of California, Berkeley

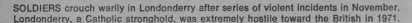

SOLDIERS crouch warily in Londonderry after series of violent incidents in November. Londonderry, a Catholic stronghold, was extremely hostile toward the British in 1971.

GAMMA-PHOTOREPORTERS

318

(Continued from page 315)

Common Market Agreement. Britain's chief market negotiator, Geoffrey Rippon, and the EEC Council of Ministers reached final agreement on the major obstacles in Luxembourg on June 23, following the Paris talks in May between Prime Minister Heath and French Premier Georges Pompidou. Not all outstanding questions were resolved, however. The British were unable to accept the EEC fisheries policy, and the sugar and agricultural policies remained sources of friction. Rippon extracted only a promise that the EEC would consider the interests of the Commonwealth sugar producers when it reviewed its policies in 1974. Britain agreed to a 5-year, 6-step transitional stage leading to the acceptance of the EEC agricultural policy. Fisheries policy was ironed out in December.

Debate in Commons. The terms agreed on were published as a White Paper on July 7, 1971, and accepted by a vote of 356 to 244 in the House of Commons on October 28. After an often bitter debate, the Conservatives allowed their members to vote according to their personal convictions, while Labour invoked strict party discipline. Earlier, the Labour party and the Trade Union Congress had officially taken stands against EEC membership on the Heath terms. Nevertheless, 69 Labour members, including Labour Deputy Leader Roy Jenkins, voted for entry, and 20 abstained. On the other hand, 39 Conservatives voted against the government.

The Labour party announced that it would oppose the enabling legislature wholeheartedly. At the end of 1971 only a minority of the electorate supported entry to the EEC. Heath's success in negotiation had boosted his popularity, but not sufficiently to counteract doubts about Europe.

Rhodesia Accord. The second most important element of British foreign policy was the negotiation of a settlement with the government of Rhodesia. At the Commonwealth Conference in Singapore in January 1971, Prime Minister Heath was chided by African leaders for his alleged failure to discourage Rhodesian independence. Nevertheless, he persisted in his attempts to resolve the Rhodesia deadlock. After an exploratory mission to Rhodesia by Lord Goodman in September, Foreign Secretary Sir Alec Douglas-Home opened negotiations there in November. Rhodesian Prime Minister Ian D. Smith accepted the British proposal to go back to an amended version of the 1969 constitution, which, by linking African educational and social advances with political ones, would make possible the rule of the black majority at some future date. A commission under Lord Pearce will assess the degree to which this is approved by Rhodesian blacks.

The accord signed November 24 was immediately presented to Commons, where it was met with caution by Labour and enthusiasm by the Conservatives. Debate centered on the difficulty of estimating how long it would take before black and white Rhodesians had equal political rights and whether the Rhodesian government would enforce the agreement. Commons approved the plan.

South African Policy. British willingness to consider selling arms to the Republic of South Africa was also attacked at the Singapore conference. Heath defended Britain's right to pursue its own policies and pointed out the threat of the Soviet naval presence in the Indian Ocean. In February the Heath government announced that it could not support a ban on arms to South Africa,

KEYSTONE

BRITAIN expelled 90 Soviet diplomats and officials and denied reentry to 15 others in September after a defector outlined Soviet intelligence network in Britain. Police guarded Soviet commercial offices in London.

such as had been imposed by its Labour predecessors since December 1964. On the other hand, the Heath government denied any "general and continuing legal obligation" to supply arms.

Defense of Malaysia and Singapore. In February a Defence White Paper confirmed the government's intention of participating in defense arrangements East of Suez. In April the Far East Defence Conference, with delegates from Australia, Malaysia, New Zealand, Singapore, and the United Kingdom, met to discuss the external defense of Malaysia and Singapore. Agreement was reached to replace Britain's sole responsibility for defense by a cooperative force, which took over in September.

Malta. In July, Maltese Prime Minister Dom Mintoff demanded that rent for the British and NATO naval bases there be doubled. Britain's refusal was followed in August by Mintoff's demand that NATO forces be withdrawn. NATO agreed to close its Malta base, and Naples became its new naval headquarters. Late in December, Britain announced that it would withdraw its forces from Malta rather than yield to Mintoff's demands.

India and Pakistan. In June internal conflict in Pakistan created a flood of Bengali refugees into India. Britain extended aid, but refused to recognize the self-proclaimed state of Bangladesh in East Pakistan. During the December war between India and Pakistan, two Commonwealth members, Britain maintained an attitude of neutrality.

(See also COMMONWEALTH OF NATIONS; EUROPE. For events in Northern Ireland, see special report accompanying this article.)

A. J. BEATTIE
London School of Economics

GREECE

In 1971, King Constantine II did not appear on Greek soil, and Premier George Papadopoulos seemed to be in firm control of the country.

Internal Affairs. During the year, Premier Papadopoulos moved to consolidate his power, a process in which he had been engaged since April 21, 1967, when a military revolt of which he was a leader overthrew parliamentary government and established a dictatorship. His strength was shown by a cabinet reorganization in August 1971 that brought into office a number of technocrats and reduced the political influence of some colonels who had been instrumental in the 1967 coup. He continued to affirm the ultimate goals of restoration of democracy and full implementation of the constitution of 1968. Essential parts of that constitution, particularly those dealing with civil rights and election of a parliament, remained suspended. The fourth anniversary of the coup was celebrated in April.

On Dec. 12, 1971, a selected group of 10,670 Greeks voted, electing 60 members to a consultative committee to debate draft legislation, which is passed by the cabinet. Papadopoulos subsequently appointed 15 more members. The government presented this as an approach to eventual parliamentary elections. In an address to the nation on December 18, Papadopoulos stated that the consultative committee could by majority vote reject draft legislation but that the cabinet could then overrule the rejection with a public explanation. At the same time he announced that martial law, in effect since April 1967, would be lifted on Jan. 1, 1972, throughout Greece, except in the areas of Athens, the Piraeus,

and Thessaloniki. He also pledged the release of 69 political prisoners. Government sources described most of them as Communists, though 12 were termed royalist officers. Announcement of the release of all 69 was made within a few days of the premier's address.

Lady Fleming, the Greek-born widow of the discoverer of penicillin, Sir Alexander Fleming, with others, for trying to engineer the escape from prison of Alexander Panagoulis, who had been convicted of trying to assassinate Papadopoulos in 1968. She was jailed, later released for health reasons, and then deported to Britain on November 14.

The King's Position. King Constantine II remained a resident of Rome, where he had lived since December 1967, when he failed to oust the military government by force. He continued, however, to be acknowledged within Greece as the rightful king of the Hellenes; and as such his name day on May 21 was celebrated throughout the country.

Relations between the king and the Papadopoulos government were unclear. Because neither side issued any clarification, speculation and rumors were widespread. For example, it was said that elements around Papadopoulos were increasingly opposed to the king's eventual return.

In October, King Constantine and his wife, Queen Anne-Marie, attended the 2,500th anniversary of the Persian Empire at Persepolis. There the king conferred with U. S. Vice President Agnew.

The Agnew Visit. After meeting with Constantine, Agnew made his first visit to Greece, the birthplace of his father. Papadopoulos met him at the airport, setting the tone for an extremely cordial reception. Although over 150 members of the

---

GREECE • Information Highlights

Official Name: Kingdom of Greece.
Area: 50,944 square miles (131,944 sq km).
Population (1970 est.): 8,890,000. *Density*, 172 per square mile (67 per sq km). *Annual rate of increase*, 0.7%.
Chief Cities (1970 est.): Athens (metropolitan area), the capital, with its port Piraeus, 2,000,000; Salonika (and environs), 450,000; Patras, 102,000.
Government: *Head of state*, Constantine II, king (acceded March 6, 1964; in self-exile since December 1967)—Gen. George Zoitakis, regent. *Head of government*, George Papadopoulos, premier (took office Dec. 13, 1967). *Parliament*—dissolved in February 1967.
Languages: Greek (official), English, French.
Education: *Literacy rate* (1970), 82% of population. *Expenditure on education* (1968), 11.1% of total public expenditure. *School enrollment* (1967)—primary, 973,912; secondary, 500,942; vocational, 94,995; higher, 73,438.
Finances (1970 est.): *Revenues*, $1,917,000,000; *expenditures*, $1,793,000,000; *monetary unit*, drachma (30 drachmas equal U. S.$1, Sept. 1971).
Gross National Product (1969): $8,400,100,000.
National Income (1969): $6,630,000,000; *national income per person*, $750.
Economic Indexes: *Industrial production* (1970), 195 (1963= 100); *agricultural production* (1969), 119 (1963=100); *consumer price index* (1970), 118 (1963=100).
Manufacturing (metric tons, 1969): Wheat flour, 539,000; residual fuel oil, 266,000; distillate fuel oils, 219,000; meat, 210,000; wine, 5,160,000 hectoliters.
Crops (metric tons, 1968 crop year): Wheat, 1,701,000; grapes, 1,400,000; olives, 832,000; sugar beets, 676,000; citrus fruits, 470,000; barley, 447,000.
Minerals (metric tons, 1969): Lignite, 6,700,000; bauxite, 1,899,000; magnesite, 580,000; iron ore, 200,000.
Foreign Trade (1970): *Exports*, $643,000,000 (chief exports—tobacco, $90,467,000; currants, raisins, and grapes, $40,-434,000). *Imports*, $1,958,000,000 (chief imports, 1968—transport equipment, $293,403,000; nonelectrical machinery, $205,483,000. *Chief trading partners* (1968)—West Germany (took 20% of exports, supplied 18% of imports); United States, France.
Tourism: *Receipts* (1970), $193,600,000.
Transportation: *Roads* (1968), 27,440 miles (44,151 km); *motor vehicles* (1969), 301,900 (automobiles, 194,900); *railroads* (1970), 1,616 miles (2,601 km); *merchant fleet* (1971), 13,066,000 gross registered tons; *national airline*, Olympic Airways; *principal airport*, Athens.
Communications: *Telephones* (1970), 881,003; *television stations* (1968), 1; *television sets* (1969), 86,000; *radios* (1968), 985,000; *newspapers* (1969), 110.

LADY FLEMING and a co-defendant, Constantine Androutsopoulos (*center*), talk with counsel before the start of trial. She was convicted but released.

U. S. VICE PRESIDENT AGNEW lays wreath on grave of his grandfather during visit to Greece in October. Ceremony took place at Gargalianoi, the home town of Agnew's father.

defunct Greek parliament issued a statement that Agnew's visit would strengthen the government and retard the reestablishment of democracy, Agnew apparently privately urged Papadopoulos to liberalize the regime. Publicly Agnew supported the continuance of U. S. military aid to Greece as a means of countering Soviet strength in the Mediterranean. This aid, however, was drawing heavy criticism in the U. S. Congress. Agnew was obviously moved when he visited his father's home town, Gargalianoi, and placed a wreath at the grave of his grandfather.

Foreign Affairs. President Demetrios Lakas-Bahas of Panama visited Athens in July. Like Agnew, he is of Greek descent. To cement friendships, Deputy Premier Patakos visited Egypt and Ethiopia in February; in March he went to Libya; and in May he went to the Democratic Republic of Congo (now Zaïre) and the Central African Republic. Further evidence of a drawing together of Greece and Egypt was the visit of the Egyptian foreign minister, Mahmoud Riad, to Athens in April. A trip to Athens by President Bokassa of the Central African Republic in April seemed in line with Greek attempts to build its prestige in Africa.

Greek-Turkish relations were colored by the Cyprus problem. Papadopoulos and his ministers were careful to emphasize their pacific sentiments to the Turkish government. Persistent rumors abounded that the Greek government and Archbishop Makarios, president of Cyprus, were quarreling in private.

Greece and Albania finally ended the state of war that had existed between them since World War II. They exchanged diplomatic representatives for the first time since 1939.

Although strong criticism of Greece was heard among some NATO members, the Greek government emphasized its pledge to honor its commitments to the alliance. NATO's secretary-general, Joseph M. A. H. Luns, visited Athens in November.

After Henry J. Tasca, the U. S. ambassador, was criticized by members of Congress for not adequately investigating the attitudes of Papadopoulos' opponents, he began meeting with Greeks who had been politically important before the 1967 coup, and he consulted at Paris with Constantine Caramanlis, premier of Greece from 1955 to 1963. This caused the Greek government in early October to issue a stern warning that it would take measures to prevent diplomats from holding such meetings.

Queen Frederika's Memoirs. Queen Frederika, the widow of King Paul I and mother of King Constantine II, published a volume of memoirs in England. This work revealed that under the direction of her husband she had carried on a political correspondence with U. S. Gen. George C. Marshall during the Greek civil war in the late 1940's.

The Economy. Government spokesmen continued to emphasize the nation's economic advances, claiming that tourism had increased 60% since the 1967 coup, and 50.4% in the first five months of 1971 over those months of 1970, and merchant marine tonnage had almost doubled since 1967.

GEORGE J. MARCOPOULOS
Tufts University

GUATEMALA

Internal disorder overshadowed all other events in Guatemala in 1971. Despite the unrest, however, the economy continued its moderate expansion.

Terrorism. President Carlos Arana Osorio found it increasingly difficult to follow the moderate course for Guatemala that he had plotted at his 1970 inauguration. He admitted that Guatemalans were caught in a "virtual civil war," and that he was able to control neither the left nor the right.

Because of persistent violence, a state of siege, imposed in November 1970, continued into November 1971. Under the suspension of constitutional guarantees, the army had authority to search without warrant, and all political activities were prohibited. Strict press censorship was imposed in March. By April, some 4,000 persons had been arrested, and perhaps 20 to 25 were being killed each week.

The leftist groups kidnapped right-wing businessmen and bankers, assaulted army and police officers, and eliminated political informers. Victor Kaire, the director of one of the nation's largest private financial institutions, was rescued from the guerrillas in August, but another banker, Roberto Alejos Arzu, who had once been a candidate for president, was being held for a $500,000 ransom. In mid-August, the second-ranking official in the secret police was murdered by urban terrorists.

The special targets of the rightists included opposition members of the national legislature and the San Carlos University community. Deputy Adolfo Mijangos López, a paralytic, was gunned down in his wheelchair in January. As spokesman for a centrist opposition bloc, he was the most vocal critic of the regime in the Chamber of Deputies.

--------- **GUATEMALA · Information Highlights** ---------

Official Name: Republic of Guatemala.
Area: 42,042 square miles (108,889 sq km).
Population (1970 est.): 5,200,000. *Density,* 119 per square mile (46 per sq km). *Annual rate of increase,* 3.1%.
Chief City (1970 est.): Guatemala City, the capital, 700,000.
Government: *Head of state,* Carlos Arana Osorio, president (took office July 1, 1970). *Head of government,* Carlos Arana Osorio. *Legislature*—National Congress (unicameral), 55 members. *Major political parties*—Institutional Democratic party, National Liberation Movement, Revolutionary party.
Languages: Spanish (official), Indian dialects.
Education: *Literacy rate* (1970), 30% of population. *Expenditure on education* (1968), 17.2% of total public expenditure. *School enrollment* (1968)—primary, 493,241; secondary, 57,845; vocational, 12,994; higher, 11,935.
Finances (1969): *Revenues,* $151,900,000; *expenditures,* $165,400,000; *monetary unit,* quetzal (1 quetzal equals U.S.$1, Sept. 1971).
Gross National Product (1969): $1,645,000,000.
National Income (1968): $1,343,000,000; *national income per person,* $276.
Economic Indexes: *Industrial production* (1970), 145 (1963=100); *agricultural production* (1969), 103 (1963=100); *consumer price index* (1970), 107 (1963=100).
Manufacturing (metric tons, 1969): Residual fuel oil, 266,000; cement, 224,000; distillate fuel oils, 219,000; sugar, 178,000; wheat flour, 75,000; meat, 58,000.
Crops (metric tons, 1969 crop year): Maize, 736,000; coffee, 105,000; bananas (1968), 100,000; cottonseed, 51,000.
Foreign Trade (1970): *Exports,* $298,000,000 (chief exports—coffee, $102,600,000; cotton, $27,200,000; bananas, $19,600,000; sugar, $9,200,000). *Imports,* $284,000,000 (chief imports, 1967—chemicals, $44,279,000; nonelectrical machinery, $29,206,000; textile yarn and fabrics, $26,226,000; transport equipment, $22,232,000). *Chief trading partners* (1968)—United States (took 28% of exports, supplied 41% of imports); El Salvador (15%—11%); Japan.
Transportation: *Roads* (1964), 7,575 miles (12,190 km); *motor vehicles* (1969), 62,500 (automobiles, 39,900); *railroads* (1970), 510 miles (821 km); *national airline,* Aviateca; *principal airport,* Guatemala City.
Communications: *Telephones* (1970), 38,489; *television stations* (1968), 2; *television sets* (1969), 72,000; *radios* (1968), 559,000; *newspapers* (1967), 9.

University Strike. After an economics professor at the University of San Carlos had been machine-gunned to death on September 30, other university professors left their classrooms to demand a restoration of constitutional guarantees and the freeing of political prisoners. By October 8, the strike had spread to 12,000 university students, whose leaders promised to step up active opposition to the army-backed Arana regime. The government's response was a threat to abandon the principle of university autonomy, and the far right produced a statement blaming the university for the nation's problems.

The Spread of Criticism. Two clerics, including the highest-ranking Episcopalian ecclesiastic in Guatemala, were deported for having violated a ban against political activity by foreigners after they had joined eight other clergymen in issuing a moderately worded declaration calling for a cease-fire in the undeclared "civil war." Meanwhile, in Belgium, the International Association of Democratic Jurists denounced rightist terrorism in Guatemala. In the United States, a subcommittee of the House of Representatives held hearings to determine the degree to which U.S. aid to Guatemala might be contributing to political repression.

Economic Affairs. A growth of 6% in Guatemala's gross national product was forecast in 1971. Trade with the other nations of the Central American Common Market (CACM) expanded until mid-year, when Guatemala stopped importing goods from Costa Rica in reprisal for Costa Rica's imposition of barriers against various Guatemalan products. CACM's uncertain future caused a shift of investment from manufacturing to agriculture and private construction.

Foreign Aid. In June the U.S. government authorized a $7 million rural electrification loan as well as a $2.5 million loan for rural health services. Guatemala also secured a loan of $4 million from the World Bank for livestock development. In July the Nixon administration asked the U.S. Congress to provide $5 million in military aid.

International Affairs. In September, President Fidel Sánchez Hernández of El Salvador and President Arana met in Antigua, Guatemala, to consider ways of accelerating Central American integration. In the same month, West Germany initiated steps to restore normal diplomatic relations with Guatemala. The West Germans had withdrawn virtually all of their diplomatic officials from Guatemala after the murder in 1970 of their ambassador, Karl von Spreti.

Death of Arbenz. Jacobo Arbenz Guzmán, leftist former president of Guatemala, died of a heart attack in Mexico in January 1971. Arbenz had lived in exile since his overthrow in 1954.

LARRY L. PIPPIN
Elbert Covell College, University of the Pacific

GUINEA

The abortive invasion of the Conakry area on Nov. 22, 1970, by a combination of Portuguese officers, Guinean exiles, and mercenaries created repercussions affecting every facet of life in Guinea in 1971. The UN commission sent to investigate Guinea's charges that various nations were involved in the incident reached no conclusion, and in October simply reported the allegations.

Internal Affairs. Details of the invasion and the subsequent trials remain blurred because foreign journalists were barred, and the official accounts

─────── GUINEA • Information Highlights ───────

Official Name: Republic of Guinea.
Area: 94,926 square miles (245,857 sq km).
Population (1970 est.): 3,920,000. *Density*, 41 per square mile (16 per sq km). *Annual rate of increase*, 2.7%.
Chief City (1967 est.): Conakry, the capital, 197,267.
Government: *Head of state*, Sékou Touré, president (took office for 2d term 1968). *Head of government*, Sékou Touré, premier. *Legislature*—National Assembly (unicameral), 75 members. *Major political parties*—Democratic Party of Guinea.
Languages: French (official), local languages, English.
Education: Literacy rate (1969), 10% of population. *Expenditure on education* (1965), 19.4% of total public expenditure. *School enrollment* (1968)—primary, 167,340; secondary, 41,736; vocational, 5,334; higher, 942.
Finances (1967 est.): *Budget* (1967 est.): $167,600,000; *monetary unit*, Guinea franc (277.71 francs equal U. S.$1, Sept. 1971).
Gross National Product (1967 est.): $310,000,000; *per capita GNP*, $83.
Manufacturing (cubic meters, 1967): Sawnwood, 67,000.
Crops (metric tons, 1969 crop year): Cassava (1968), 420,000; bananas (1968), 80,000; groundnuts, 18,000; palm kernels, 15,000; coffee, 15,000.
Minerals (metric tons, 1969): Bauxite, 2,459,000; iron ore (1966), 800,000; diamonds (1966), 51,000 metric carats.
Foreign Trade (1967): *Exports*, $51,000,000 (chief exports—alumina, $26,800,000; bananas, $4,500,000; palm nuts and kernels, $3,000,000; coffee, $2,900,000). *Imports*, $44,-000,000 (chief imports, 1962—cotton fabrics, $7,200,000; rice, $6,300,000; nonelectrical machinery, $4,800,000). *Chief trading partners* (1966)—Communist bloc (took 17% of exports, supplied 39% of imports); United States.
Transportation: *Roads* (1969), 4,725 miles (7,604 km); *motor vehicles* (1969), 20,000 (automobiles, 8,000); *railroads* (1967), 511 miles (822 km); *national airline*, Air Guinée; *principal airports*, Conakry, Kankan.
Communications: *Telephones* (1968), 6,600; *radios* (1969), 90,000; *newspapers* (1969), 1.

were contradictory. A government White Paper issued in April 1971 reported that the invaders had been tried before the National Council of the Revolution and that 92 persons had been sentenced to death and 72 to life imprisonment. At least four were hanged soon after the verdicts were announced.

In January the political bureau of the Parti Démocratique de Guinée reorganized all groups responsible for the "defense of the Revolution." Public holidays for the year were canceled, and Guinea was put on a war footing. In March, President Sékou Touré announced that by mid-year almost 500,000 persons would be trained for the militia.

Purges continued throughout 1971. Officials arrested included the former ambassador to the United States, the army chief of staff, and the governors of Kankan and Labe districts. The Roman Catholic archbishop of Conakry was sentenced to life imprisonment.

Foreign Affairs. Guinea's move to end its self-imposed isolation was almost frustrated by the hysteria that followed the invasion. Various states were charged with aiding the Portuguese in neighboring Guinea-Bissau (Portuguese Guinea) in plots to invade Guinea. Touré stated that France was the "number one organizer of subversion" in West Africa, and that Portugal was making continuous border attacks. Charges against West Germany led to a severing of relations.

Senegal and Ivory Coast were accused of allowing their territory to be used as staging grounds for armed guerrillas, and of harboring Guinean exiles plotting Touré's overthrow. Senegal refused to turn over any exiles to Guinea and retaliated by arresting Guineans who, it alleged, were agents. In September two Guinean MIG aircraft crashed in Ivory Coast, which lent some credence to charges that Guinea was involved in spying there. Guinea and Sierra Leone signed a defense pact in March, and within a week Touré sent 200 troops to Sierra Leone to help restore order after an abortive coup.

Economic Development. With relations broken, West Germany canceled its technical aid to Guinea.

However, the rich Guinean bauxite deposits continued to draw foreign investors. The consortium that operates the Fria plant planned to increase its production by over 30%, and work progressed on the new complex of Boké. Yugoslavia's Minel Enterprises announced plans to finance an $8 million plant, and a Swiss group agreed to work the deposits at Tougué.

HARRY A. GAILEY, *San Jose State College*

GUYANA

The most significant development in Guyana in 1971 was the nationalization of most of the properties producing bauxite, the nation's major export.

Nationalization of the Bauxite Industry. Late in 1970, Prime Minister Forbes Burnham had begun negotiations with the Aluminum Corporation of Canada (ALCAN), owner of Guyana's principal bauxite firm, the Demerara Bauxite Company, for the establishment of a mixed-ownership company in which the Guyana government would have majority control. These talks broke down on Feb. 20, 1971, and it was then announced that the government would expropriate the firm in its entirety.

A bill to nationalize and give "reasonable compensation" for the Demerara Bauxite Company was passed by the National Assembly on March 1, with the date of transfer set for July 15. On the eve of Guyana's assumption of ownership, an agreement was reached with ALCAN that compensation would total $53.3 million, to be paid over a period of not more than 20 years. The Demerara concern was reorganized as the Guyana Bauxite Company, with a Guyanese, Haslyn Harris, as its chief executive officer.

Domestic Affairs. The Burnham government continued to push its program of economic development through self-help, officially named the "Advance Guyana Campaign." In September, the prime minister launched a "Keep Guyana Clean" effort, seeking to involve the populace in cleaning up and beautifying the towns, and a "Grow More Food

─────── GUYANA • Information Highlights ───────

Official Name: Republic of Guyana.
Area: 83,000 square miles (214,969 sq km).
Population (1970 est.): 760,000. *Density*, 8 per square mile (3 per sq km). *Annual rate of increase*, 2.8%.
Chief City (1969 est.): Georgetown, the capital, 97,190.
Government: *Head of state*, President Arthur Chung, president (took office March 17, 1970). *Head of government*, Linden Forbes Burnham, prime minister (took office Dec. 15, 1964). *Legislature*—National Assembly (unicameral), 53 members. *Major political parties*—People's National Congress, People's Progressive party.
Languages: English (official); various East Indian dialects.
Education: *Literacy rate* (1970), 86% of population. *Expenditure on education* (1968), 14.7% of total public expenditure. *School enrollment* (1967)—primary, 138,672; secondary, 51,441; vocational, 1,717; higher, 597.
Finances (1968): *Revenues*, $49,650,000; *expenditures*, $59,-700,000; *monetary unit*, Guyana dollar (2 G. dollars equal U. S.$1, Sept. 1971).
Gross National Product (1969): $234,650,000.
National Income (1969): $189,000,000; *national income per person*, $255.
Manufacturing (metric tons, 1969): Sugar, 389,100; margarine, 1,000; beer, 70,000 hectoliters.
Crops (metric tons, 1969 crop year): Sugarcane (1968–69), 4,000,000; rice, 171,000.
Minerals (metric tons, 1969): Bauxite, 4,306,000 (ranks 5th among world producers); gold, 127 kilograms.
Foreign Trade (1970): *Exports*, $130,250,000 (chief exports—Bauxite, $46,100,000; sugar, $38,100,000; alumina, $23,-200,000). *Imports* (1969) $118,000,000 (chief imports, 1968)—food, $17,769,000; nonelectrical machinery, $15,-930,000; chemicals, $10,620,000). *Chief trading partner* (1968)—United States.
Transportation: *Roads* (1971), 1,685 miles (2,712 km); *motor vehicles* (1969), 23,800 (automobiles, 16,300).
Communications: *Telephones* (1970), 13,560; *radios* (1968), 90,000; *newspapers* (1969), 3 (daily circulation, 40,000).

Campaign," designed to make the country self-suffi-cient in foodstuffs.

International Relations. Guyana took steps in 1971 to improve its relations with neighboring coun-tries. In June, the Guyana-Surinam Border Com-mission met for the first time and agreed to estab-lish a telecommunications link between the two nations. After Guyanese-Brazilian commissions had met in Georgetown in August and October, Brazil agreed to aid Guyanese economic development.

Contacts with more distant countries also ex-panded with the arrival of a high commissioner from Zambia in February and a Soviet ambassador in April.

ROBERT J. ALEXANDER, *Rutgers University*

HAITI

After a long illness, President-for-Life François Duvalier died on April 21, 1971. His only son, Jean-Claude, whom he had named as his political heir, succeeded immediately to the presidency, sur-rounded by advisers selected by his father.

Despite some attempts to improve the image of the regime, no significant changes occurred in the Haitian political system in the early months of the new administration. The economy continued to im-prove slowly, but with the annual per capita income remaining at about $80, the enormity of Haiti's needs offered little room for optimism. Relations with other states remained chilly, although the United States appeared to be reconsidering its ban on major economic aid.

The Succession. Following congressional au-thorization, François Duvalier on Jan. 22, 1971, named his 19-year-old son to succeed him to the life-presidency. The heir apparent was feted with a round of parties and a propaganda barrage extol-ling his virtues. In mid-March the ailing dictator, known to his subjects as "Papa Doc," suffered a severe stroke and was apparently incapacitated. On the night of April 21, he died.

─────── HAITI · Information Highlights ───────

Official Name: Republic of Haiti.
Area: 10,714 square miles (27,750 sq km).
Population (1970 est.): 4,870,000. *Annual rate of increase,* 2.4%.
Chief Cities (1970 est.): Port-au-Prince, the capital, 300,000; Cap Haïtien, 30,000.
Government: *Head of state,* Jean-Claude Duvalier, president for life (took office April 21, 1971). *Head of government,* Jean-Claude Duvalier. *Legislature* (unicameral)—National Assembly, 67 members. *Major political parties*—Parti Unique de l'Action Révolutionnaire et Gouvernementale.
Languages: French (official), Creole patois.
Education: *Literacy rate* (1970), 10.5% of population. *Ex-penditure on education* (1965), 17.4% of total public ex-penditure. *School enrollment* (1966)—primary, 286,187; secondary, 27,431; technical, 6,211; higher, 1,527.
Finances (1968): *Revenues,* $28,040,000; *expenditures,* $28,-040,000; *monetary unit,* gourde (5 gourdes equal U. S.$1, Aug. 1971).
Gross National Product (1969 est.): $353,600,000.
National Income (1968): $379,000,000; *national income per person,* $81.
Manufacturing (metric tons, 1969): Sugar, 65,000; cement, 55,000; meat, 20,000; wheat flour, 11,000.
Crops (metric tons, 1968 crop year): Sugarcane, 4,000,000; maize, 240,000; bananas, 220,000; sisal, 200,000.
Minerals (metric tons, 1969): Bauxite, 748,000; copper ore, 1,800.
Foreign Trade (1969 est.): *Exports,* $38,700,000 (chief exports—coffee, $14,200,000; bauxite, $6,140,000; sisal, $2,900,-000; sugar, $2,700,000). *Imports,* $40,700,000 (chief im-ports—foodstuffs, textiles, petroleum, and machinery). *Chief trading partner* (1968)—United States.
Transportation: *Roads* (1969), 2,024 miles (3,257 km); *motor vehicles* (1969), 16,000 (automobiles, 14,700); *railroads* (1965), 187 miles (301 km); *national airline,* Cohata; *principal airport,* Port-au-Prince.
Communications: *Television stations* (1968), 1; *television sets* (1969), 11,000; *radios* (1969), 81,000; *newspapers* (1969), 6.

The transition of power was accomplished smoothly. Jean-Claude promptly named a new 11-man cabinet, all of whose members had served the elder Duvalier in some capacity. Perhaps the most powerful figure was Luckner Cambronne, the minis-ter of interior, who controlled the security appara-tus. In May, Cambronne organized a new armed group, the "Leopards," reportedly to counter dissi-dent rural militia elements and the powerful se-curity-police organization, the *Tontons Macoutes.*

Jean-Claude was also believed to depend heavily on his own family, seeking especially the advice of

HAITI'S new president, Jean-Claude Du-valier, pays last respects to his father and holds first news conference (*right*).

UPI

FRANÇOIS DUVALIER (1907–1971)

UPI

François Duvalier, dictator of Haiti for almost 14 years, died in Port-au-Prince on April 21, 1971. In failing health for some years, he had named his only son, Jean-Claude, as successor to the life-presidency three months before his death. Known familiarly as "Papa Doc," because of his early medical work among the poor, Duvalier saw himself as the champion of the blacks against the mulatto elite. With the support of the armed forces and his personal following, he ruthlessly suppressed all opposition, whether from students, the old families, or the Catholic Church.

Duvalier was born in Port-au-Prince on April 14, 1907, of a lower-middle-class black family. Despite his origins, he gained a good local education and received a medical degree in 1934. He joined a U.S.-sponsored anti-yaws project in 1943, and in 1944, undertook advanced study in public health at the University of Michigan.

Coming to manhood during the occupation of Haiti by the U.S. Marines (1915–34), Duvalier first demonstrated a strong nationalist streak through literary criticism. Then, in the early 1940's, he joined the Bureau of Ethnology, where he immersed himself in the study of folk culture and vodun (or voodoo). In 1946 he joined a black nationalist party and became director of public health in the government of President Dumarsais Estimé. By 1949, he was secretary of public health and labor. When Estimé was overthrown by a coup in 1950, Duvalier returned to medical practice.

In 1957, Duvalier campaigned for the presidency and was elected as a moderate reformer, a nationalist, and a champion of the blacks. In 1958 he organized the *Tontons Macoutes,* a terrorist force of armed thugs and informers personally devoted to him. Reelected for a second term, he had his handpicked Congress draft a new constitution in 1964, making him president for life.

The Duvalier regime became thoroughly corrupt. As a result, the United States finally suspended all direct economic assistance to Haiti in 1962, and tourism and foreign investments dried up. Only in his last few years did Duvalier try to mitigate somewhat the severity of his rule.

KARL M. SCHMITT

definition of the term "trouble makers," most exiles remained abroad. Although repressive acts decreased, open opposition seemed impossible.

The Economy. Haiti continued its slow recovery from the economic doldrums of the mid-1960's. The decline in the per capita gross national product had been reversed. Tourism, foreign investment in light industries, and agricultural output continued to make modest gains in 1971. Production of sugar and industrial molasses increased, and that of cocoa beans remained level. A continuing decline in coffee production was offset by higher coffee prices.

Most importantly, perhaps, the first hydroelectric units at Peligre Dam were inaugurated in July, substantially increasing national power output. New power lines were being installed and the telephone system restored after almost total collapse. Yet it remained clear that if Haiti were to develop economically it must have external financing.

United States Aid. Cabinet ministers talked of "new development efforts" and openly sought foreign aid, especially that of the United States. These requests met with a favorable response from U.S. Ambassador Clinton Knox. Washington itself remained more cautious, but in the spring aid guarantees again became available for U. S. private investors. U.S. assistance channeled through private relief agencies and international organizations continued at a rate of about $4 million a year.

KARL M. SCHMITT, *University of Texas*

HARRIS, Patricia Roberts. See BIOGRAPHY.

HAWAII

Concern over the economy and threats to the environment preoccupied Hawaiians in 1971.

Economy. The island economy felt the effects of the national recession, largely though a leveling off of tourism. Only a continued rise in the volume of visitors from Japan kept a rather bad year for the hotels from being a disastrous one.

The shipping strike that tied up West Coast ports from July through September depleted supplies of many commodities, despite an unprecedented use of air freight, and hurt business seriously. Construction was depressed. The level of unemployment reached 6% in September, the highest since 1954. The price level reached a new high, rising even after the freeze ordered by President Nixon in August.

Ecology. Anxiety over the fouling of Hawaii's magnificent environment became widespread in 1971. Consumer advocate Ralph Nader's organization and national magazines publicized the fact that Honolulu's raw sewage is pumped out to an ocean outfall near Honolulu harbor and that some of the beaches along Oahu's south shore, all the way to Waikiki, are occasionally polluted by the discharge. Plans were drawn up for a treatment plant, but means of financing its construction were not yet certain.

The federal government directed the state to enforce compliance with standards for water purity. The sugar mills are the chief offenders, discharging in adjacent ocean areas the mud and rocks grabbed by the mechanical cane harvesters. Enforcement creates a dilemma, because the sugar industry is already shrinking and the state government wants to sustain it, not only as a major employer but also as a preserver of the green belt that checks the westward sprawl of Honolulu.

his mother and that of his eldest sister, Marie-Denise Dominique, and her husband, Max. In August, the Dominiques were rumored to be at odds with Cambronne. Max Dominique was subsequently reappointed ambassador to France, and the couple departed for Paris, possibly into temporary exile.

The New Image. The new regime attempted to play up two themes, promising both continuity in the pursuit of old policies, such as black nationalism, and a change in style, such as a decrease in repression. On April 29, the new president declared an amnesty for all exiles except "Communists and trouble makers," and his advisers appeared to be trying to curb some of the more flagrant abuses of power. Most strikingly, cabinet members became accessible to foreign newsmen.

Opponents of the regime insisted that little or nothing had changed. In the absence of any clear

Hawaii's famed landmark, Diamond Head, provides familiar background for Honolulu's modern, changing skyline.

In an effort to hold and utilize the open space that still exists on densely populated Oahu, the state consulted with Stewart Udall, former secretary of the interior and prominent conservationist. Also under study was a plan for mass transit on Oahu, where highway congestion is rapidly approaching the levels experienced in mainland urban areas. Smog, mostly from cars, is no novelty along the traffic corridor between downtown Honolulu and Pearl Harbor.

The degree of concern over the environment was evidenced by a marked expansion in the activities of citizen-interest groups in the state, including Life of the Land, Citizens for Hawaii, Hawaii Conservation Council, ZPG, and others.

Population. Apprehension about overcrowding in the city and county of Honolulu (1970 population, 629,000) was heightened by city planning department projections showing that the total number of people on Oahu by the year 2000 would be between 1,225,000 and 2,000,000—a doubling or tripling in 30 years. The Hawaiian Legislature in 1971 created a commission to draft a population policy for the state, which in 1970 had pioneered in legalizing abortions. The 1971 Legislature sought to discourage some unwanted immigration from the mainland by establishing a one year's residence requirement for general public assistance. A study showed that the major source of population increase, however, was Hawaii's own birthrate.

Robert M. Kamins, *University of Hawaii*

HEALTH CARE. See Social Welfare.
HEART DISEASE. See Medicine.
HEATH, Edward. See Biography.
HIGHWAYS. See Transportation.
HIROHITO. See Biography.

────── **HAWAII • Information Highlights** ──────

Area: 6,450 square miles (16,706 sq km).
Population (1970 census): 769,913. *Density,* 124 per sq mi.
Chief Cities (1970 census): Honolulu, the capital, 324,871; Kailua, 33,783; Kaneohe, 29,903; Hilo, 26,353.
Government (1971): *Chief Officers*—governor, John A. Burns (D); lt. gov., George R. Ariyoshi (D); atty. gen., Bertram T. Kambara (D); supt., Dept. of Education, Shiro Amioka; chief justice, William S. Richardson. *Legislature*—Senate, 25 members (16 Democrats, 8 Republicans, 1 vac.); House of Representatives, 51 members (34D, 17R).
Education (1970–71): *Enrollment*—public elementary schools, 105,000 pupils, 2,349 teachers; public secondary, 79,000 pupils, 1,472 teachers; nonpublic schools (1968–69), 28,-800 pupils, 1,420 teachers; college and university (fall 1970), 37,000 students. *Public school expenditures* (1970–71), $180,155,000 ($1,050 per pupil). *Average teacher's salary,* $10,140.
State Finances (fiscal year 1970): *Revenues,* $608,494,000 (4% general sales tax and gross receipts taxes, $162,689,000; motor fuel tax, $17,723,000; federal funds, $138,585,000). *Expenditures,* $684,595,000 (education, $263,009,000; health, welfare, and safety, $52,937,000; highways, $60,283,000). *State debt,* $528,175,000 (June 30, 1970).
Personal Income (1970): $3,559,000,000; *per capita,* $4,530.
Public Assistance (1970): $50,700,000. *Average monthly payments* (Dec. 1970)—old-age assistance, $95.95; aid to families with dependent children, $250.15.
Labor Force: *Nonagricultural wage and salary earners* (June 1971), 302,300. *Average annual employment* (1969)—manufacturing, 25,000; trade, 63,000; government, 71,000; services, 53,000. *Insured unemployed* (Oct. 1971)—12,700 (4.8%).
Manufacturing (1967): *Value added by manufacture,* $326,200,-000: Food and kindred products, $185,400,000; printing and publishing, $27,000,000; stone, clay, and glass products, $18,400,000; apparel, $16,300,000.
Agriculture (1970): *Cash farm income,* $222,577,000 (livestock, $41,097,000; crops, $170,365,000; government payments, $11,115,000). *Chief crops* (1969)—Sugarcane for sugar and seed (1970), 11,305,000 tons (ranks 1st among the states); papayas, 11,828 tons; macadamia nuts, 4,400; pineapple, 29,714,443 cases canned fruit.
Mining (1969): *Production value,* $29,100,000 (ranks 44th among the states). *Chief minerals* (tons)—Stone, 6,292,-000; sand and gravel, 540,000; pumice, 428,000.
Fisheries (1970): *Commercial catch,* 11,000,000 pounds ($4,000,000). *Leading species by value* (1969), Skipjack tuna, $1,264,094; bigeye and bluefin tuna, $475,506.
Transportation: *Roads* (1969), 3,512 miles (5,650 km); *motor vehicles* (1969), 375,000; *airports* (1969), 25.
Communications: *Telephones* (1970), 424,000; *television stations* (1969), 10; *radio stations* (1969), 29; *newspapers* (1969), 5 (daily circulation, 228,000).

HONDURAS

Two moves of great importance in the political and economic affairs of Honduras were made by the administration of Oswaldo López Arellano early in 1971. President López agreed not to succeed himself, opening the way to the election of a new president in March; and duty-free entry of products from the Central American Common Market (CACM) was suspended indefinitely in January.

New Chief Executive. President Ramón Ernesto Cruz began a 6-year term on June 6, 1971, following a presidential election on March 28. As the ruling Nationalist party's candidate, Cruz, a 68-year-old banker and international lawyer, defeated Jorge Bueso Arias of the opposition Liberal party. Minority parties refused to take part in the election, and almost half of the 900,000 eligible voters stayed away from the polls. A major campaign issue was Honduran participation in the Central American Common Market. The Nationalists favored continuing a boycott of CACM instituted at the beginning of the year.

The elections were held under a "national unity" plan favored by outgoing President López Arellano. According to the unity arrangement, the 64-seat legislature was divided equally between the two major parties, with a Nationalist presiding. However, the Liberals gained a majority in the Supreme Court.

Withdrawal from CACM. On Jan. 1, 1971, Honduras in effect withdrew from the Central American Common Market by discontinuing duty-free imports from other market members. The action was motivated by a rapidly deteriorating fiscal and balance-of-payments situation that Honduras attributed to its disadvantageous position in the market. Although the more industrialized members of CACM agreed to certain structural changes in the organization in June, Honduras gave no immediate sign of altering its policy of nonparticipation.

––––––––– HONDURAS • Information Highlights –––––––––

Official Name: Republic of Honduras.
Area: 43,277 square miles (112,088 sq km).
Population (1970 est.): 2,580,000. *Density,* 57 per square mile (22 per sq km). *Annual rate of increase,* 3.4%.
Chief City (1969 est.): Tegucigalpa, the capital, 253,283.
Government: *Head of state,* Ramón Ernesto Cruz, president (took office June 6, 1971). *Head of government,* Ramón Ernesto Cruz. *Legislature*—National Congress (unicameral), 64 members. *Major political parties*—National party, Liberal party.
Languages: Spanish (official), English.
Education: *Literacy rate* (1970), 48% of population. *Expenditure on education* (1968), 2.9% of gross national product. *School enrollment* (1967)—primary, 366,907; secondary, 31,145; vocational, 3,828; higher, 3,459.
Finances (1970): *Revenues,* $88,900,000; *expenditures,* $104,-400,000; *monetary unit,* lempira (2 lempiras equal U. S.$1, Dec. 1971).
Gross National Product (1969): $646,500,000.
National Income (1969): $564,000,000; *national income per person,* $226.
Economic Indexes: *Manufacturing production* (1966), 151 (1963=100); *agricultural production* (1969), 128 (1969=100); *consumer price index* (1970), 121 (1963=100).
Manufacturing (metric tons, 1969): Cement, 132,000; sugar, 52,000; wheat flour, 28,000.
Crops (metric tons, 1969 crop year): Bananas (1968), 1,509,000 (ranks 6th among world producers).
Minerals (metric tons, 1969): Zinc ore, 8,400; lead ore, 6,700; silver, 113.4; gold, 118 kilograms.
Foreign Trade (1970): *Exports,* $171,000,000 (chief exports—bananas, $71,300,000; coffee, $25,850,000). *Imports,* $222,000,000 (chief imports, 1968—chemicals, $26,178,000; nonelectrical machinery, $21,008,000). *Chief trading partner* (1968)—United States.
Transportation: *Roads* (1970), 3,222 miles (5,185 km); *motor vehicles* (1969), 30,200 (automobiles, 13,500); *railroads* (1970), 752 miles (1,210 km).
Communications: *Telephones* (1970), 12,511; *radios* (1968), 140,000; *newspapers* (1967), 7.

Border Problems. A rash of border incidents broke out in April, two days after Honduras and El Salvador had agreed to resume negotiating final settlement of the disputes that had caused their 1969 border war. The incidents did not prevent a resumption of talks in San José, Costa Rica, on May 20.

Honduras insisted on a demarcation of the disputed border, and President-elect Cruz had asked in March that observers from the Organization of American States be kept in the disputed territory, where most of the sporadic shooting incidents had occurred. However, the OAS announced the withdrawal of half of the 20-man team at the same time that the peace talks were resumed. Cruz returned to the border question in his inaugural address, pledging continued appeals to international organizations until the conflict was settled in favor of Honduras. On November 22, the United States recognized Honduran authority over the Swan Islands.

The Economy. Emergency measures were necessary to shore up the nation's weakened economy. An alarming trade imbalance was checked through restrictions on commercial bank credit. Because foreign exchange reserves were depleted, Honduras obtained a $15 million standby credit from the International Monetary Fund in May. Banana exports rose to about 56 million boxes.

Additional private foreign capital was invested in the country, including $4.5 million in a new shrimp-farming venture near La Ceiba. A loan of $11 million to expand power facilities was obtained from the World Bank and the International Development Agency. The agency also extended a loan of $2.6 million for livestock development, and the Central American Bank for Economic Integration approved a multiplicity of smaller industrial and industry-supporting loans to the amount of about $17 million. More than $2 million was made available by the National Development Bank for promoting investment in industry and tourism. President Cruz discussed other investment possibilities in Mexico while on a state visit in September.

Death of Villeda. On Oct. 8, 1971, Ramón Villeda Morales, head of the Honduran delegation to the United Nations, died of a heart attack in New York. He was president of Honduras in 1957–63.

LARRY L. PIPPIN
Elbert Covell College
University of the Pacific

HONECKER, Erich. See BIOGRAPHY.

HONG KONG

Hong Kong continued to sustain its steady economic growth in 1971. New labor laws were introduced to improve working conditions, and large construction projects were progressing.

Economy. In face of the international monetary crisis the Hong Kong dollar remained a strong and secure currency, backed by its substantial sterling reserve assets. Hong Kong was concerned more about the effects of the 10% surcharge placed on imports into the United States. Hong Kong's cotton textiles were exempted from the surcharge, but the United States wanted it to limit the export of textiles other than cotton. In October, agreement was reached on a plan limiting the growth of such exports to 5% annually for the next three years.

Figures for the first eight months in 1971 showed an increase of 14.9% in domestic exports,

Hong Kong–Macao ferry *Fatshan* capsized with loss of 88 lives, August 17, as Typhoon Rose battered Hong Kong.

19% in imports, and 19% in reexports over the same period in 1970. Domestic exports have been growing at an average rate of nearly 16% annually since 1961. In terms of exports per capita, Hong Kong was among the world's top 10 trading states.

Foreign investments in Hong Kong industries were increasing rapidly. In 1971 the 230 foreign-owned or partially foreign-financed factories had a total capital investment of about U.S.$152 million, of which half was U.S. capital. Hong Kong's 17,200 industrial undertakings employed nearly 590,000 workers in 1971.

The standard of living index, based on that of 1964 as 100, for workers rose to 132 in 1970, an increase of 32%. A law that became effective in April 1970 required that all workers whose monthly wage is U.S.$248 or less must be given four days off each month. An 8-hour working day and a 48-hour working week for women and young factory workers went into effect in December 1971.

Hong Kong is expected to be a focal point in Asia in container shipping. To effect advanced container-handling services, the Kwai Chung Container Terminal Port is being developed at a cost of about U.S.$75 million. By mid-1972, Hong Kong's container facilities will be handling 2,500-3,000 containers a week—80% to 90% of the cargo shipped between Hong Kong and its major trading partners.

Hong Kong's airport is being modernized and expanded. The 8,350-foot (2,545-meter) runway was extended by 2,500 feet (660 meters) to handle 747 jumbo jets and supersonic aircraft. In 1970 air cargo accounted for 21% of domestic exports, 12% of imports, and 24% of reexports. A new air cargo terminal is being built to cope with the rapid expansion of air freight.

A 1-mile (1.6-km) cross-harbor tunnel is under construction from Hung Hom to Kellet Island, and is expected to be finished in August 1972.

Water Supply. The 1964 water supply agreement between Hong Kong and the People's Republic of China expired on June 30, 1970, but its terms continued effective, enabling Hong Kong to receive 15 billion gallons of water annually without further notification. In 1971, China supplied about 30% of Hong Kong's water.

Typhoon. Typhoon Rose, the worst to hit Hong Kong since 1962, struck on Aug. 17, 1971, causing much damage. More than 100 persons died, houses collapsed, farms were devastated, and over 50 vessels were sunk or swept ashore.

DAVID CHUEN-YAN LAI
University of Victoria

——— **HONG KONG • Information Highlights** ———

Official Name: Hong Kong.
Area: 398 square miles (1,034 sq km), including ocean area 1,126 square miles (2,916 sq km).
Population (1970): 4,090,000. *Density,* 9,995 per square mile (3,859 per sq km). *Annual rate of increase,* 1.5%.
Chief City (1961 census): Victoria, the capital, 633,138.
Government: *Head of state,* Elizabeth II, queen. *Head of government,* Sir David Trench, governor (took office 1965). *Major political parties*—Democratic Self-Government party; Labour party of Hong Kong, Socialist Democratic party.
Languages: English (official), Cantonese Chinese.
Education: *Literacy rate* (1970), 85% of population. *Expenditure on education* (1968), 20.7% of total public expenditure.
Finances (1970–71): *Revenues,* $426,436,000; *expenditures,* $395,000,000; *monetary unit,* Hong Kong dollar (5.58 H.K. dollars equal U.S.$1, Dec. 30, 1971).
Manufacturing (metric tons, 1969): Cement, 378,000; cotton yarn, 144,000; beer, 232,000 hectoliters.
Foreign Trade (1968): *Exports* (1970), $2,514,000,000 (chief exports—clothing, $488,800,000; textile yarn and fabrics, $240,000,000). *Imports* (1970), $2,905,000,000 (chief imports—food and live animals, $404,000,000; textile yarn and fabrics, $347,900,000). *Chief trading partners* (1968)—United States (took 34% of exports, supplied 14% of imports); United Kingdom.
Communications: *Telephones* (1970), 502,374; *television sets* (1969), 675,000; *newspapers* (1969), 74.

HOOVER, J. Edgar. See BIOGRAPHY.

HORTICULTURE. See GARDENING AND HORTICULTURE.

HOSPITALS. See MEDICINE.

HOTELS AND MOTELS. See TOURISM.

HOUPHOUËT-BOIGNY, Félix. See BIOGRAPHY.

United States had dramatic upsurge in housing starts in 1971. Many new homes were in developments, like this one in Staten Island, N.Y.

HOUSING

Housing starts climbed to record levels in 1971. Runaway inflation in housing costs caused grave concern, and President Nixon established a wage-price review board for the construction industry. Major legislative proposals were made by the administration and by congressional committees.

Residential Construction. Reacting to an increase in the supply of mortgage funds in the last half of 1970 and the first half of 1971, housing starts moved up to an all-time high of 2,215,000 units (seasonally adjusted rate) in July 1971. The climb was swift: from 1,059,000 units (seasonally adjusted) in January 1970, to 1,400,000 units in June 1970, to 2,000,000 in December 1970.

As has happened many times in the past, housing production was showing a countercyclical tendency. When the general economy is booming and credit is scarce, housing starts tend to go down; when, as in 1971, general economic conditions are lagging and credit is plentiful, the volume of housing production increases.

From 1963 through 1969 conventionally financed housing starts amounted to about 80% of total starts, and Federal Housing Administration and Veterans Administration starts made up the remaining 20%. This situation changed dramatically in 1970 when FHA starts jumped to nearly 30% of the total. The same trend continued in the first seven months of 1971, although the FHA share dropped somewhat.

Construction Costs. The average cost of building a single-family dwelling unit in the United States has been climbing sharply for years. In 1964 the average was $15,550, but by 1967 it had risen to $17,475, and by June 1971 it was $19,600. The E. H. Boeckh residential construction cost index (1957–59 = 100) stood at 136.7 in 1968, 148.0 in 1969, 155.9 in 1970, and 172.8 in July 1971. The construction cost index of the Department of Commerce showed a similar increase—from 142 in 1969 to 163 in June 1971. These increases reflect, to some extent, the fact that houses are larger, better constructed, and contain more amenities. But the recent inflation in housing costs added serious problems in rapidly increasing costs of land, labor, materials, and mortgage funds.

Housing and Urban Development Secretary George Romney has called runaway inflation the most difficult problem facing his department. Housing-cost inflation is proceeding at a faster rate than the cost of living generally. These developments caused President Nixon on March 29, 1971, to establish a wage-price review board for the construction industry in an attempt to dampen inflationary pressures in that industry.

Legislative Proposals. The Nixon administration proposed two major pieces of housing legislation to Congress in 1971. They were:

(1) The Housing Consolidation and Simplification Act of 1971, which was similar to a bill introduced but not passed in 1970. This legislation

would consolidate the confusing array of FHA mortgage insurance programs into eight basic authorities, with relatively simple and flexible terms.

(2) A call for a new system of special revenue sharing for urban community development. It would combine four categorical programs—urban renewal, Model Cities, water and sewer grants, and rehabilitation loans—into a single, more flexible program. Major objectives would be to reduce the fragmentation of federal aid programs, to reduce federal control and red tape, and to give states and localities more freedom in use of federal funds.

The Senate Committee on Banking, Housing, and Urban Affairs developed its own legislative proposals in the Community Development Assistance Act of 1971. This legislation also combined various existing programs into one comprehensive program, but it differed from the administration proposal in a number of ways.

At the same time, legislative initiative was also being taken by the House Committee on Banking and Currency. After commissioning studies by experts, this House committee developed the Housing and Urban Development Act of 1971. It called for an extension and redefinition of national housing goals, new tools for preserving and revitalizing declining neighborhoods, improved management of publicly assisted rental housing, consolidation of community development programs, an urban development bank, block grants for housing to state and metropolitan housing agencies, and extended experimentation in housing allowances in which subsidies for housing are given directly to lower-income families, not attached to specific housing projects.

Mortgage Interest Rates. Sharp fluctuations in mortgage interest rates occurred during 1971. In September 1970 the average interest rate on home mortgages not insured by FHA or VA had reached 8.6%, but during the first half of 1971 the mortgage interest rate dropped steadily. The maximum interest rate permitted on FHA-insured loans was reduced to 7%. Beginning in June 1971, however, mortgage interest rates began another climb. This rise was not the result of a real shortage of mortgage funds, since savings flows into mortgage-lending institutions continued at high levels. Instead, the upward pressures on mortgage interest rates were more the result of inflationary expectations.

Faced with these conditions, President Nixon took drastic steps to peg the interest rate on FHA and VA mortgages at 7%. This was accomplished by a presidential authorization for the Government National Mortgage Association (GNMA) to purchase $2 billion of FHA and VA mortgages at interest rates below those prevailing in the market. GNMA then sells the mortgages to the Federal National Mortgage Association (FNMA) at prevailing prices, absorbing the difference between the purchase and sales price. It was estimated that the $2 billion authorized by the President for this purpose would finance about 1 million housing units. This action was also designed to exert a downward pressure on mortgage interest rates in general.

A Freeze on Rents. The President's announcement on Aug. 16, 1971, of a temporary freeze on prices and wages also covered rents. Thus, for the first time since the Korean War rents were subjected to federal control.

Desegregation. One of the most alarming social developments is the growing polarization of the urban population, with poor blacks and other minorities concentrated in the central cities and surrounded by white, middle-class suburbanites. On June 11, 1971, President Nixon issued a policy statement defining federal policies on equal opportunity in housing. While stating that the administration would not force housing desegregation on suburban jurisdictions, the President said, "We will carry out our programs in such a way that will be helpful as possible to communities which are receptive to the expansion of housing opportunities for all of our people."

Following this presidential statement, the Department of Housing and Urban Development issued drafts of project selection criteria to be used in choosing housing projects to receive federal subsidy assistance. The criteria made it clear that housing projects would receive favorable consideration for subsidy assistance if they were located outside of present areas of minority concentration. The leverage of federal housing subsidy funds would thus be used to encourage the desegregation of housing.

Federal Financing. Federally assisted urban renewal activity continued at a high level in late

HOUSING PLANT in Connecticut opened in April to manufacture prestressed concrete floors and walls for apartments. Operator (*below*) sets mixing controls, while gantry cranes (*bottom*) move out finished panels.

WESTINGHOUSE ELECTRIC CORPORATION

LEVITT BUILDING SYSTEMS

HOUSES ON RAILS cross Illinois en route to Seattle, where they will be assembled into 2-story homes. The modules were built for government's Operation Breakthrough, a program for modernizing housing production.

1970 and early 1971. Federal urban renewal funds obligated or spent amounted to slightly over $1 billion in 1970 and $76 million in the first quarter of 1971. By the end of March 1971, total federal grants made since the beginning of the urban renewal program amounted to nearly $9.5 billion, and 2,927 urban renewal projects and related undertakings had received federal financial support.

By June 1971, nearly $171 million in grants had been approved for 537 neighborhood facilities. At that time, grants of over $63 million had gone for 529 urban beautification projects, and over $53 million in grants had been made to create 262 urban parks.

Over 20,000 direct loans at 3% interest—an outlay of over $30 million—had been approved by April 1971 for rehabilitation in urban renewal and code enforcement areas. Nearly 29,000 grants, totaling nearly $73 million, had been made to low-income homeowners in urban renewal and code enforcement areas.

A total of 1,119,618 low-rent public housing units were completed, under construction, or planned at the end of 1970. During the first half of 1971 federal financing was approved for an additional 155,000 units of public housing. By June 1971, private groups seeking to build rent-supplement projects to house low-income families had received fund reservations for over $132 million. The reservations covered over 132,000 living units. By June 30, 1971, an additional 167,000 units of privately built rental housing for moderate-income families had received federal subsidy assistance. Also, by the end of June 1971, federal interest rate subsidies had been reserved to assist 204,060 low- and moderate-income families to purchase homes.

Government-Assisted Housing. The volume of housing produced with some form of government subsidy reached an all-time high in 1970, and in 1971 it headed even higher. In 1960 the number of housing units built with direct government subsidies (to bring rents or sales prices within the means of low- and moderate-income families) did not exceed 50,000 a year. In 1965 the number was well under 100,000 units. But in 1970 government-subsidized housing starts reached 400,000 units, and in 1971 the number was expected to approach 600,000 units.

M. CARTER MCFARLAND
Federal Housing Administration

THE HOUSING BOOM GETS UNDER WAY

PRIVATE HOUSING STARTS
(Seasonally adjusted at annual rates)

Million

2.5

2.0

1.5

1.0

1968   1969   1970   1971

DATA: U.S. DEPT. OF COMMERCE

HOUSTON

In a hotly contested runoff election on Dec. 7, 1971, Louie Welch was returned to office as mayor for an unprecedented fifth term. The year was also marked by the advancement, both elective and appointive, of a number of blacks and Mexican-Americans to the highest administrative and, in one case, judicial positions they have ever held in Houston.

Politics. Mayor Louie Welch, seeking an unprecedented fifth term, received the strongest opposition of his career from rival candidate Fred Hofheinz. Welch contended that the main issue was law and order, and he claimed that Hofheinz would fire Houston's chief of police, Herman Short, a self-styled "tough cop" who is unpopular with blacks. Hofheinz refused to commit himself to retain Short and attacked Welch for his association with Houston financier, Frank Sharp, the central figure in the Sharptown Bank Scandal. In the first election, Hofheinz garnered enough votes to force Welch into a runoff. Welch won the runoff on December 7 in a race in which over 70% of the whites supported Welch and over 95% of the blacks, Hofheinz.

Offices for Minority Group Members. In January, Andrew Jefferson, appointed district judge for domestic relations, became the first black to hold a district judgeship in Texas. Later in 1971, the school board appointed a black educator, Dr. J. Don Boney, to be chief instructional officer. Two other black educators as well as a Mexican-American educator were named area superintendents. In November, a black candidate, Herman A. Barnett, and a Mexican-American, David T. Lopez, were elected to the school board. In the city elections, Judson Robinson, Jr., became the first black elected to the city council, and Leonel Castillo, the new city comptroller, became the first Mexican-American to win a city-wide election in Houston.

Economic Boom. In the first 10 months of 1971, the value of building permits awarded in Houston totaled $539,142,225, compared with $381,995,026 during the same period in 1970—an increase of 38.5%. Raymond International and three affiliates of Standard Oil of New Jersey announced plans to move their corporate headquarters to Houston. This brought the total number of corporate headquarters located in Houston to over 360. Also in 1971, construction was begun at Barbour's Cut on a $100 million expansion of the city's port.

Education. The year 1971 saw the opening of the University of Texas Medical School, the Houston Community College, and the Houston High School for the Performing Arts. The Houston school board adopted board president George Oser's proposal to begin classes for 4½-year-olds in the fall of 1972.

In August, the school board voted by 4 to 3, to dismiss the superintendent of schools, George Garver. The deciding vote was cast by the only black member of the board. Garver's dismissal provoked strong protests from civic groups, the Houston Teachers Association, and many leaders of the black community. Three of the board members who voted to dismiss Garver chose not to seek reelection in November. Citizens for Good Schools (CGS), a reform group, endorsed three candidates pledged to reinstate Garver. All three were elected by large margins.

VICTOR L. EMANUEL
Institute for Urban Studies, University of Houston

HUNGARY

The most important domestic events in Hungary in 1971 were the animated election campaign, in which nominees opposed to the official candidates were permitted to run, and the beginning of the fourth 5-year plan. The country continued its efforts to increase foreign trade, and it remained subservient to Soviet policy in foreign affairs.

Elections. The Communist-led People's Patriotic Front sponsored its candidates in all 352 electoral districts, in 303 of which its candidates were unopposed. In a cautious liberalization move, the government allowed the nomination of opposition candidates for the first time. Although all nominees had to support the Communist program, differences on local issues led to spirited campaigning in the 49 districts in which elections were contested.

Of the more than 7.3 million eligible voters, 98.7% went to the polls. Slightly more than 1% of those voting invalidated their ballots. All top Communist leaders were unopposed and won new 4-year parliamentary terms. These included János Kádár, the Communist party first secretary; President Pál Lasonczi; and Prime Minister Jenö Fock.

Economy. The 5-year plan for 1971–75 put special emphasis on the chemical industry. There will be particular stress on petrochemical production in an attempt to alleviate further Hungary's dependence on imported oil products. In the past six years oil consumption had doubled to 4,350,000 tons. The 5-year plan provided for further increases, a

---

——— HUNGARY · Information Highlights ———

Official Name: Hungarian People's Republic.
Area: 35,919 square miles (93,030 sq km).
Population (1970 est.): 10,310,000. *Density,* 286 per square mile (111 per sq km). *Annual rate of increase,* 0.3%.
Chief Cities (1968 est.): Budapest, the capital, 2,000,000; Miskolc, 180,000; Debrecen, 160,000.
Government: *Head of state,* Pál Losonczi, chairman of the Presidential Council (took office April 14, 1967). *Head of government,* Jenö Fock, premier (took office April 14, 1967). *Head of Communist party,* János Kádár, First Secretary (took office Oct. 25, 1956). *Legislature*—National Assembly, 352 members.
Language: Hungarian (official).
Education: *Literacy rate* (1970), 98% of population. *Expenditure on education* (1968), 7.4% of total public expenditure. *School enrollment* (1968)—primary, 1,254,745; secondary, 228,229; technical/vocational, 102,613; higher, 52,061.
Finances (1971 est.): *Revenues,* $16,445,000,000; *expenditures,* $16,629,000,000; *monetary unit,* forint (11.74 forints equal U.S.$1, 1971).
Gross National Product (1970 est.): $14,400,000,000.
National Income (1969): $21,550,000,000; *national income per person,* $2,098.
Economic Indexes: *Industrial production* (1970), 146 (1963=100); *consumer price index* (1970), 110 (1963=100).
Manufacturing (metric tons, 1969): Crude oil, 3,032,000; cement, 2,565,000; residual fuel oil, 2,076,000; distillate fuel oils, 1,670,000; wheat flour, 1,278,000; sugar, 443,000; meat, 440,000.
Crops (metric tons, 1969 crop year): Maize, 4,820,000; sugar beets (1968–69), 3,471,000; potatoes, 2,013,000.
Minerals (metric tons, 1969): Lignite, 22,365,000; coal, 4,133,-000; bauxite, 1,935,000; crude petroleum, 1,754,000; iron ore, 168,000; manganese ore, 32,900; natural gas, 3,235,-000,000 cubic meters.
Foreign Trade (1968): *Exports,* $2,317,000,000 (chief exports—nonelectrical machinery, $237,317,000; transport equipment, $214,600,000; electrical machinery, $148,586,-000; fruits and vegetables, $109,727,000). *Imports* (1970), $2,506,000,000 (chief imports—nonelectrical machinery, $287,973,000; chemicals, $186,491,000; transport equipment, $161,508,000; iron and steel, $124,140,000). *Chief trading partners* (1968)—USSR (took 38% of exports, supplied 36% of imports); East Germany (10%—11%); Czechoslovakia (10%—9%); Poland (6%—6%).
Tourism: *Receipts* (1970), $72,400,000.
Transportation: *Roads* (1969), 18,169 miles (29,240 km); *automobiles* (1969), 192,300; *railroads* (1968), 5,454 miles (8,777 km); *national airline,* Hungarian Airlines (Malev); *principal airports,* Budapest, Debrecen.
Communications: *Telephones* (1970), 777,739; *television stations* (1968), 8; *television sets* (1969), 1,596,000; *radios* (1969), 2,531,000; *newspapers* (1969), 27 (daily circulation, 2,181,000).

difficult task since the country's own oil resources are practically nonexistent.

Productivity of the collectivized and nationalized farms is scheduled to increase under the new plan. Some 80% of all arable land has been socialized, and the private lots, to which socialized farmers are entitled, cover only a fraction of the arable land. These lots, however, still account for the disproportionate amount of 20% of agricultural production.

In April the government decreed a new wage system. All workers will now be classified on the basis of the work they perform, and their professional training, educational level, experience, and working conditions. According to official sources, the old system, which was based on decentralized "branch guides," proved both ineffective and unfair to many, particularly those at the lower end of the wage spectrum. The decree was followed by detailed regulations concerning conditions for obtaining a second job. Numerous abuses of the old system by both employers and employees prompted the government's reform action.

In September new regulations aimed at stopping "speculation" and "unearned profits" in real estate were issued. No family will be allowed to own more than one apartment or house, plus a lot destined for recreational purposes or construction of a holiday home. Any family possessing property exceeding these limits will have to dispose of it by the end of 1973.

Foreign Policy. Throughout the year the leading role of the Soviet Union was emphasized in the press, together with comments indicating that both Yugoslavia and Rumania did not fully understand that role—to the detriment of the "Socialist camp."

U. S. contacts with Communist China were interpreted in Hungary as motivated by President Nixon's desire for reelection as well as by China's "imprudent" and "disruptive" foreign policy. Nixon's announced trip to Moscow was taken as new evidence of the Soviet Union's power and decisive importance in international affairs.

Although both the press and radio continued to condemn the "bourgeois theories of convergence," the government approached the International Monetary Fund (IMF). Responding to Budapest's initiative, the IMF sent a mission to Hungary to explore the possibilities of Hungarian membership. If an agreement is reached, Hungary would become the second Communist state—Yugoslavia is already a member—to join the organization.

Foreign Trade. Efforts to stimulate foreign trade, international economic cooperation, and tourism continued.

The exchange of goods with Yugoslavia in 1971 rose by 25% over the 1965–70 average. Joint Yugoslav-Hungarian construction of a pipeline from the Adriatic Sea to Hungary, which will expedite the importation of Middle Eastern oil, was agreed upon in principle. The new pipeline will obviate Hungary's complete dependence on Soviet oil.

In July an agreement with West Germany set the terms for the purchase of $37 million worth of machinery, equipment, plans, gear, and instruments for a chemical factory. It was the largest contract for the purchase of an industrial unit ever made by Budapest. Deliveries are scheduled for 1972. In previous years, the main supplier of comparable items was the Soviet Union.

In September a Hungarian economic delegation headed by Deputy Prime Minister Mátyás Timar visited several South American countries. Hungary has constantly had an unfavorable balance of trade with South America, deficit of $100 million having been reached during 1965–70. Following the visits,

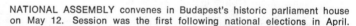

NATIONAL ASSEMBLY convenes in Budapest's historic parliament house on May 12. Session was the first following national elections in April.

UPI

agreements with Chile and Peru were concluded, providing for the export of $15 million worth of Hungarian machinery, buses, and hospital equipment for each country.

In August, after five years of preparations, the World Hunting Exhibition opened its gates in Budapest. Twenty-five countries took an active part, publicizing their main hunting, natural, and cultural attractions. Over 2 million people, including some 200,000 foreigners, visited the exhibition.

JAN KARSKI
Georgetown University

ICELAND

On June 13, 1971, Iceland's voters put an end to a 12-year coalition government controlled by the Independence and Social Democratic parties by wiping out its slim majority in the Althing, or Parliament. In mid-July a cabinet with a considerably more leftist complexion was installed. Noteworthy among its policies was a move to secure the withdrawal of American forces from the U. S. base at Keflavik. On the domestic front, the government increased capital investment and taxes, while also imposing more stringent controls over private corporations.

New Government. On the day after the election, Premier Johann Hafstein announced his resignation. On July 13, Olafur Johannesson, leader of the agrarian Progressive party, formed a new cabinet supported by the Communist-led Labor Alliance, and a splinter party called the Liberal and Leftist Union. The three-party coalition commanded a four-vote majority in the Althing.

On July 14, the government announced that it would extend the offshore fishing boundary from 12

miles (19 km) to 50 miles (80 km). The Althing approved a new and complex corporation law, with increased taxes and stricter controls of banking and other private operations. It also began debate over a government proposal to merge landholdings, with the aim of eliminating small, nonprofitable farm units, signaling a sharp reversal in national agricultural policy. The Althing instituted a major reform in education, merging the elementary school system into a unified 9-year program. Under discussion were proposals to liberalize Iceland's strict laws on marriage and divorce.

Economy. A year of generally favorable economic developments was highlighted by an increase in farm production, after several years of serious crop failures. The fish catch, a major item in the Icelandic economy, was down by one third in 1971, but prices and markets in Spain and Portugal provided greater earnings. Foreign reserves were at a new high despite a decline in dollar holdings due to the U. S. government's radical economic moves in mid-August.

International Affairs. Negotiations toward the elimination of the U. S. Atlantic-alliance base at Keflavik continued through the summer and fall, but the government decided to continue its membership in NATO. Negotiations at Brussels for Icelandic membership in the Common Market foundered on the issue of special treatment for fisheries.

RAYMOND E. LINDGREN
California State College, Long Beach

IDAHO

Cecil D. Andrus, who took office in January 1971 as Idaho's first Democratic governor in 25 years, met opposition during the year from the Republican-controlled Legislature. Agriculture was hurt by unfavorable weather, including an early freeze in the potato fields. Controversy persisted over dams, mining, and logging in the state, and the native Indians made their voices heard. A surprise announcement by Sen. Len B. Jordan, 72-year-old Republican, that he will not seek reelection to the U. S. Senate, enlivened the 1972 political races.

Legislation. Governor Andrus vetoed appropriation bills for education and public health and asked a special session of the Legislature for more money, but the original bills were passed over his veto, thereby forcing a serious cutback in existing programs. Although the budget was balanced without higher taxes, the methods used led the governor to suggest that taxes must be raised next year.

The Legislature adopted a consumer protection act, increased water- and air-pollution controls, provided for contract negotiations between teachers and school boards, and gave 18-year-olds the right to vote. A 1970 initiative, which was passed by a heavy margin, reduced legislators' pay, but members of the 1971 session gave themselves increases, causing a spate of recall petitions.

Bonds. The Idaho Supreme Court ruled as valid the two-thirds vote required for bond issues, which was passed in 1970. The ruling, combined with legislation giving residents who do not pay property taxes the right to vote in bond elections, has made Idaho bonds salable once again. Prospective purchasers had refused to buy Idaho bonds when the 1970 Legislature restricted voting in such elections to payers of property taxes—a restriction contrary

---

——— ICELAND • Information Highlights ———

Official Name: Republic of Iceland.
Area: 39,768 square miles (103,000 sq km).
Population: (1970 est.): 210,000. *Density*, 5 per square mile (2 per sq km). *Annual rate of increase,* 1.5%.
Chief City (1968 est.): Reykjavik, the capital, 81,026.
Government: *Head of state,* Kristján Eldjárn, president (took office June 1968). *Head of government,* Olafur Johannesson, prime minister (took office July 14, 1971). *Legislature*—Althing: Upper House, 20 members; Lower House, 40 members. *Major political parties*—Independence party, Progressive party, Labor Alliance, Social Democratic party.
Language: Icelandic (official).
Education: *Literacy rate* (1969), 99.9% of population. *Expenditure on education* (1966), 14.1% of total public expenditure. *School enrollment* (1968)—primary, 27,356; secondary, 21,584; vocational, 5,000; higher, 1,302.
Finances (1969): *Revenues,* $84,687,000; *expenditures,* $84,-687,000; *monetary unit,* krona (88 kronur equal U. S.$1, Aug. 1971).
Gross National Product (1969): $384,000,000.
National Income (1967): $393,000,000; *national income per person,* $1,972.
Consumer Price Index (1969): 207 (1963=100).
Manufacturing (metric tons, 1969): Fish meal, 60,900; salted fish, 15,500.
Crops (metric tons, 1969 crop year): Milk, 112,000; livestock, 917,000 heads.
Minerals: Shell sand, liparite, perlite, pumice, peat.
Foreign Trade (1969): *Exports,* $108,000,000 (chief exports, 1968, dried and smoked fish, $26,202,000; frozen fish, $24,-945,000; fish meal, $7,064,000). *Imports,* $123,000,000 (chief imports, 1968, machinery and transport equipment, $40,038,000; petroleum products, $15,041,000; chemicals, $11,139,000). *Chief trading partners*—United States (took 27.6% of exports, supplied 8.6% of imports); United Kingdom (14%—12.7%); Fed. Rep. of Germany (8.6%—16.8%); USSR (8.9%—8.0%).
Transportation: *Roads* (1970). 6,000 miles (9,656 km); *motor vehicles* (1969), 43,600 (automobiles, 37,300); *merchant fleet* (1970), 119,000 gross registered tons; *national airline,* Iceland Air, Icelandic Airlines; *principal airports,* Keflavik, Reykjavik.
Communications: *Telephones* (1969), 67,973; *television stations* (1968), 7; *television sets* (1969), 31,000; *radios* (1969), 62,000; *newspapers* (1969), 5 (daily circulation, 77,000).

——————— IDAHO • Information Highlights ———————

Area: 83,557 square miles (216,413 sq km).
Population (1970 census): 713,008. *Density,* 9 per sq mi.
Chief Cities (1970 census): Boise, the capital, 74,990; Pocatello, 40,036; Idaho Falls, 35,776; Lewiston, 26,068; Twin Falls, 21,914; Nampa, 20,768; Coeur d'Alene, 16,228.
Government (1971): *Chief Officers*—governor, Cecil D. Andrus (D); lt. gov., Jack M. Murphy (R); secy. of state, Pete T. Cenarrusa (R); atty. gen., W. Anthony Park (D); treas., Marjorie Ruth Moon (D); supt. of public instruction, Delmer F. Engelking (D); chief justice, Henry F. McQuade. *Legislature*—Senate, 35 members (19 Republicans, 16 Democrats); House of Representatives, 70 members (41 R, 29 D).
Education (1970–71)—*Enrollment*—public elementary schools, 92,841 pupils; 3,695 teachers; public secondary, 89,492 pupils; 4,006 teachers; nonpublic schools (1968–69), 8,800 pupils; 340 teachers; college and university (fall 1968), 27,789 students. *Public school expenditures* (1970–71), $103,595,000 ($595 per pupil). *Average teacher's salary,* $7,059.
State Finances (fiscal year 1970): *Revenues,* $315,434,000 (3% general sales tax and gross receipts taxes, $41,679,-000; motor fuel tax, $25,330,000; federal funds, $78,261,-000). *Expenditures,* $316,366,000 (education, $106,694,000; health, welfare, and safety, $29,410,000; highways, $60,-364,000). *State debt,* $33,102,000 (June 30, 1970).
Personal Income (1970): $2,329,000,000; per capita, $3,206.
Public Assistance (1970): $25,738,000. *Average monthly payments* (Dec. 1970)—old-age assistance, $62.80; aid to families with dependent children, $179.65.
Labor Force: *Nonagricultural wage and salary earners* (June 1971), 216,500. *Average annual employment* (1969)—manufacturing, 40,000; trade, 47,000; government, 47,000; services, 31,000. *Insured unemployed* (Oct. 1971)—3,500 (2.3%).
Manufacturing (1968): *Value added by manufacture,* $610,000,-000. Food and kindred products, $129,441,000; lumber and wood products, $101,698,000; chemicals, $95,046,000.
Agriculture (1970): *Cash farm income,* $711,947,000 (livestock, $304,337,000; crops, $359,658,000; government payments, $47,952,000). *Chief crops* (1970)—Potatoes, 73,-195,000 cwt. (ranks 1st among the states); wheat, 42,-734,000 bushels; hay, 3,957,000 tons; sugar beets, 3,087,000 tons (ranks 2d).
Mining (1969): *Production value,* $126,100,000 (ranks 32d among the states). *Chief minerals* (tons)—Sand, gravel, and stone, 13,000,000; lead, 69,942; zinc, 58,157; silver, 18,655,000 troy ounces.
Transportation: *Roads* (1969), 55,065 miles (88,616 km); *motor vehicles* (1969), 477,000; *railroads* (1968), 2,668 miles (4,294 km); *airports* (1969), 121.
Communications: *Telephones* (1971), 357,800; *television stations* (1969), 7; *radio stations* (1969), 48.

to a U. S. Supreme Court ruling made later in the year.

Conservation. After a five-year delay, a Federal Power Commission examiner recommended construction of hydroelectric dams at two sites—Mountain Sheep and Pleasant Valley—in the Hells Canyon section of the Snake River on the Idaho-Oregon border. A letter to the commission, signed jointly by the governors of Idaho, Oregon, and Washington, protested the recommendation. Sportsmen were trying by court action to block further construction of the Lower Granite Dam, on the Snake River about 30 miles downstream from Lewiston. Controversy also grew over a projected dam on the Teton River, a tributary of the Snake in eastern Idaho.

The American Smelting and Refining Company delayed development of its molybdenum mines in the White Cloud area of the Sawtooth Range until a decision is reached on whether mining will be allowed in high country. Controversy over "clear cutting" in logging operations caused the U. S. Forest Service to restrict the practice severely.

Other Events. Idaho's native Indians are insisting that whites live up to treaty obligations, and their children are demanding that Indian culture be a part of their school curriculum. The Nez Percé tribe received a $3.5 million award for lands taken in the 1880's but not covered by treaty.

Temperatures in prison cells reported to be as high as 118 degrees during an August hot spell sparked a riot in the state penitentiary at Boise.

CLIFFORD DOBLER, *University of Idaho*

ILLINOIS

A budgetary and fiscal crisis, a racetrack scandal, congressional and legislative reapportionment, and political jockeying for the 1972 elections were major developments in Illinois in 1971.

State Financing. Illinois, like most states, was confronted in 1971 with the need to balance increased demands for state aid for welfare, education, conservation, mental health, and other state services against the hostility of taxpayers toward the increased taxes that would be necessary to provide for those services.

Despite increased revenues brought in by the first income-tax law in the state's history, which was passed in 1969, the slowdown in the economy and demands for more money for services from every major interest group in the state confronted Illinois with a fiscal crisis.

Gov. Richard B. Ogilvie, who helped put through the state income tax, and who used the item-by-item veto power granted by Illinois' new constitution to try to bring expenditures into line with revenue, publicly proclaimed his determination to hold the line on what he termed the insatiable demands of those interest groups.

Welfare. Governor Ogilvie tried to put through a major slash in Illinois welfare payments, arguing that many of the recipients in Cook county, which has half the population of the state, should be shifted to federal welfare rolls. A court order blocked the governor's program, and at the end of 1971 the state of Illinois was still subsidizing welfare rolls, which had increased approximately 30%.

Education. The increased demands of a burgeoning school population forced the governor to try to cut back subsidy of elementary and secondary schools and the expanding state university and junior college systems. The universities fought back by trying to get the legislature to override the governor's item veto of their salary increases, but failed. The board of higher education took under consideration a recommendation that was designed to revise the governing structure of the state university system.

Reapportionment. The legislature failed to redistrict the state for Congress, and a federal court adopted a plan that had passed one house. Two districts were taken from Chicago, and the lines were drawn in the state so that the 12-12 division between Republicans and Democrats in 1971 will probably be changed to a 15-man Republican, 9-man Democratic congressional delegation in the 1972 elections. Legislative districts were drawn by the legislature to put a number of Chicago's suburbs in districts with the city so that some of the greatly increased suburban population could be overridden by the city vote.

Ethics Legislation. A scandal broke in 1971, exposing a number of Republican and Democratic political figures who had made huge profits on their purchase of stock in race tracks governed by the state racing board. Ethics legislation demanded by reform groups failed to pass the Legislature for most of the year.

On Dec. 15, 1971, Judge Otto Kerner of the U. S. Court of Appeals in Chicago was indicted by a federal grand jury for conspiracy, bribery, perjury, mail fraud, and income tax evasion, in connection with alleged purchases of racetrack stock during

LAST ROUNDUP in Chicago came on July 30, when the vast, 106-year-old Union Stock Yards closed. An industrial park will be built on the 120-acre site.

1962–68 while he was governor of Illinois. The grand jury called this a bribe, in return for which prime racing dates were awarded to tracks.

Politics. Both parties chose slates for the 1972 elections designed to appeal to newly enfranchised young persons. Governor Ogilvie (48) chose a 30-year-old legislator, James Nowlan, as his running mate for lieutenant governor. The Democratic organization chose Lt. Gov. Paul Simon (42) as its gubernatorial candidate and Neil Hartigan (33) as his running mate. Independent Dan Walker mounted a serious challenge to the Democratic organization in the gubernatorial primary, beginning his campaign with a walk across the length of the state. Incumbent Republican U. S. Sen. Charles Percy announced he would run for reelection. The Democrats chose U. S. Rep. Roman Pucinsky to oppose him.

At the national level, President Nixon came to Illinois three times and sent Vice President Agnew into the state repeatedly in preparation for the 1972 election. Every major Democratic presidential aspirant visited Mayor Richard J. Daley of Chicago. It was clear that Illinois would be a critical state in the 1972 presidential election.

For the Democrats, who have changed their rules for primaries, Illinois became the crucial primary to win. The changes permit presidential candidates to list their names on primary ballots adjacent to names of delegates running for election to the convention. Formerly, would-be delegates were uncommitted, and the result over many years was that Mayor Daley controlled the votes of the entire 170-member delegation—the fourth-largest delegation at the convention. Daley's usual practice was to remain uncommitted until very late and then throw his votes in for the candidate who would help him carry Chicago. Illinois holds its primary on March 21, 1972—third in the nation, after New Hampshire and Florida—another reason that it is important to presidential candidates.

MILTON RAKOVE
University of Illinois at Chicago Circle

ILLINOIS • Information Highlights

Area: 56,400 square miles (146,076 sq km).

Population (1970 census): 11,113,976. *Density,* 198 per sq mi.

Chief Cities (1970 census): Springfield, the capital, 91,753; Chicago, 3,369,359; Rockford, 147,370; Peoria, 126,963; Decatur, 90,397; Joliet, 80,378; Evanston, 79,808; Aurora, 74,182; East St. Louis, 69,996; Skokie, 68,627; Cicero, 67,058; Waukegan, 65,269; Arlington Heights, 64,884.

Government (1971): *Chief Officers*—governor, Richard B. Ogilvie (R); lt. gov., Paul Simon (D); secy. of state, John W. Lewis (R); atty. gen., William J. Scott (R); treas., Alan J. Dixon (D); supt. of public instruction, Michael J. Bakalis (D); chief justice, Robert C. Underwood. *General Assembly*—Senate, 58 members (29 Democrats, 29 Republicans); House of Representatives, 177 members (90 Republicans, 87 Democrats).

Education (1970–71): *Enrollment*—public elementary schools, 1,500,510 pupils, 64,845 teachers; public secondary, 851,303 pupils; 42,940 teachers; nonpublic schools (1968–69), 525,000 pupils; 18,600 teachers; college and university (fall 1968), 390,831 students. *Public school expenditures* (1970–71), $1,967,583,000 ($937 per pupil). *Average teacher's salary,* $10,233.

State Finances (fiscal year 1970): *Revenues,* $4,347,716,000 (4% general sales tax and gross receipts taxes, $1,008,182,000; motor fuel tax, $311,313,000; federal funds, $863,758,000). *Expenditures,* $4,069,153,000 (education, $1,564,302,000; health, welfare, and safety, $578,737,000; highways, $411,598,000). *State debt,* $1,305,942,000 (June 30, 1970).

Personal Income (1970): $51,075,000,000; per capita, $4,516.

Public Assistance (1970): $701,180,000. *Average monthly payments* (Dec. 1970)—old-age assistance, $64.20; aid to families with dependent children, $240.95.

Labor Force: *Nonagricultural wage and salary earners* (June 1971), 4,329,600. *Average annual employment* (1969)—manufacturing, 1,404,000; trade, 945,000; government, 612,000; services, 671,000. *Insured unemployed* (Oct. 1971)—74,000 (2.3%).

Manufacturing (1967): *Value added by manufacture,* $20,016,500,000. Nonelectrical machinery, $3,415,900,000; food and kindred products, $2,512,600,000; electrical equipment, $2,445,300,000; fabricated metals, $1,971,100,000; printing and publishing, $1,600,900,000; chemicals and allied products, $1,565,800,000; paper and allied products, $528,800,000; rubber and plastics, $474,300,000.

Agriculture (1970): *Cash farm income,* $2,866,225,000 (livestock, $1,298,782,000; crops, $1,400,799,000; government payments, $166,644,000). *Chief crops* (1970)—Corn, 744,884,000 bushels (ranks 2d among the states); soybeans, 212,815,000 bushels (ranks 1st); wheat, 35,748,000 bushels.

Mining (1969): *Production value,* $659,815,000 (ranks 8th among the states). *Chief minerals* (tons)—Coal, 64,722,000; stone, 54,857,000; sand and gravel, 44,138,000; zinc, 13,765; cement, 8,720,000 barrels.

Transportation: *Roads* (1969). 129,388 miles (208,224 km); *motor vehicles* (1969). 5,162,000; *railroads* (1968), 10,917 miles (17,569 km); *airports* (1969), 78.

Communications: *Telephones* (1971). 7,110,000; *television stations* (1969). 22; *radio stations* (1969), 209; *newspapers* (1969), 93 (daily circulation, 3,959,000).

Prime Minister Indira Gandhi campaigned widely in successful bid for reelection in March. She enhanced her prestige during 1971 with firm stand against Pakistan.

INDIA

In 1971, India was profoundly affected by the general elections and by the spill-over effects of the civil war in Pakistan, which in December led to war between the two South Asian neighbors.

The elections gave the Ruling Congress party, or Congress (R), the wing of the Congress party led by Prime Minister Indira Gandhi, a surprisingly decisive majority. The results seemed to assure a greater degree of political stability than had existed since the Congress party split in 1969.

The crisis in East Pakistan affected India adversely in many ways. In particular, the mass influx of refugees, which totaled about 10 million at the end of 1971, imposed almost intolerable burdens on India's economic and political system. This was one of several factors that caused heightened tensions with Pakistan and eventual war.

In foreign affairs, aside from the crisis in Indo-Pakistani relations, the highlights were the Indo-Soviet treaty of August and Mrs. Gandhi's visit to several European countries and the United States in October and November.

DOMESTIC AFFAIRS

General Elections. On Dec. 27, 1970, at the request of Mrs. Gandhi, President V. V. Giri had suddenly dissolved the Lok Sabha, the lower house of Parliament, and issued a call for new elections.

India's fifth nationwide general elections were held from March 1 to 10, 1971. The campaign, limited to only a few weeks, was marked by frantic activity by the candidates and parties, and by a high incidence of violence in the volatile state of West Bengal. The main opposition parties—the Old Congress, or Congress (O), the Jana Sangh, the Swatantra party, and the Samyukta Socialist party (SSP)—formed a "grand alliance," which proved to be anything but grand, and campaigned mainly on the slogan, "Remove Indira."

Mrs. Gandhi was, in fact, the main issue in the campaign. She moved about the country indefatigably, appealing for support in her efforts to imple-

ment her socialist program and to remove poverty. Her appeals met with an amazing response. The March elections increased the number of her supporters in the 521-member Lok Sabha from 228 to 350, giving her a commanding two-thirds majority. The strength of the Congress (O) fell from 65 to 16, of the Jana Sangh from 33 to 22, of the Swatantra from 35 to 8, and of the SSP from 17 to 3. The two Communist parties represented in the Lok Sabha fared better: the Communist party of India (CPI) lost one seat, and the Marxist Communist party of India, or CPI (M), gained 6 seats, 20 of its 25 members coming from West Bengal.

Government Changes. Having obtained the "clear mandate" she had sought, Mrs. Gandhi moved promptly to reconstitute her cabinet, dropping five former members, and to reorganize her party. Defense Minister Jagjivan Ram was replaced as president of the Congress (R) by D. Sanjivayya. In April, C. Subramaniam was appointed minister for planning.

In several key states the regular Pradesh Congress Committees (PCC's) were replaced by ad hoc committees. Mrs. Gandhi forced the resignation of two prominent chief ministers, namely Mohanlal Sukhadia in Rajasthan (who had held office for 17 years) and Brahmananda Reddy in Andhra Pradesh, several PCC chiefs, and other Congress leaders.

State Elections. Elections for the state legislative assemblies were held concurrently with the national elections in Orissa, Tamil Nadu, and West Bengal. In Orissa the Congress (R) replaced the Swatantra party as the largest single party in the assembly, but it fell far short of a majority, and an opposition government assumed office. In Tamil Nadu, the ruling Dravida Munnetra Kazhagam, an exclusively local party, was returned to office with a greatly increased majority.

In West Bengal, which had been under President's Rule (direct rule by the central government) since March 1970, the election was a complicated five-sided contest. It resulted in the emergence of the CPI (M) with 112 seats, an increase of 32, and the Congress (R) with 105 seats, an increase of 50, as by far the largest parties. The Congress (R) entered into an alliance with the moderate left-wing parties to form a government. But President's Rule was again imposed in June because of the continuing political instability and disorder and the growing problem of refugees from East Pakistan.

Political changes in several states, mostly favorable to the Congress (R), followed the elections. By mid-June the Congress (R) held office, alone or in coalition, in 10 states; it supported the governments of Kerala, Nagaland, and Tamil Nadu; only one state—Orissa—had a government opposed to it; and four states—Gujarat, Mysore, the Punjab, and West Bengal—were under President's Rule.

New States. Himachal Pradesh, a former union territory, was given full statehood status in January. In late October the government announced a decision to reorganize the political set-up in the northeastern part of the country into five states—Assam, Nagaland, Meghalaya (previously an autonomous state within Assam), and Manipur and Tripura (previously union territories—and two new union territories—the Mizo Hills area, renamed Mizoram, and the North East Frontier Agency, renamed Arunachal Pradesh.

Constitutional Changes. Three amendments to the constitution were adopted in 1971. The 24th amendment restored to Parliament the right to amend any part of the constitution, including the chapter on fundamental rights, a power that had been taken away by the supreme court in a highly controversial decision. The 25th amendment made drastic changes in article 31, relating to property rights, and the 26th abolished the privy purses and other privileges of the former ruling princes. Preventive detention was restored in 1971; it had previously been in force from 1950 to 1969.

Economy. The preliminary results of the decennial census, taken in April, indicated that India's population was about 547 million, instead of the estimated figure of around 550 million.

Largely as a result of good monsoon rains and the "green revolution," food-grain production reached at least 105 million tons, and the need for grain imports was greatly reduced. But industrial production, which had been growing as much as 9% per year, fell alarmingly. The industrial growth rate was as low as 1.8% in the first five months of 1971. Recorded unemployment exceeded 16 million, representing about one half of the urban labor force.

The national budget for 1971–72 was presented to Parliament on May 28. It envisioned capital and revenue expenditures of around $4.5 billion, increased expenditures for defense and civil administration, a rise in taxes of $350 million, and an overall budget deficit of about $585 million. The budget made only a token appropriation of about $80 million for refugee relief, but by the end of 1971 refugee relief expenditures were running between $2 and $3 million a day. Although the government insisted that the fourth 5-year plan would proceed as scheduled, it was considerably curtailed, especially in the rate of investment.

In January, the Aid-India Consortium approved a recommendation of the World Bank that aid to India in 1971–72 should be $1.25 billion. But considerably less than this amount was actually provided. In October the Consortium agreed that an additional $700 million, preferably in the form of

grants, would be required to enable India to meet the costs of refugee relief. But little of this amount had been made available by the end of 1971, and the Indian economy was in a near-desperate state. The budget deficit had risen to about $800 million, even though in November a number of special taxes were imposed on a wide range of services and commodities. The war with Pakistan and the curtailment of U. S. aid imposed new burdens on the economy.

FOREIGN AFFAIRS

War with Pakistan. Civil war erupted in East Pakistan (East Bengal) on March 25, when the Pakistan armed forces, composed almost entirely of West Pakistanis, moved to crush the Bengali autonomy movement. That crisis resulted in one of the largest refugee problems of the 20th century and had a number of serious consequences for India. Thousands of refugees, mostly Hindus, streamed across the borders of East Pakistan into Assam, Tripura, and especially West Bengal, where economic conditions and political unrest were already critical.

From the outset Indian sympathies were almost wholly on the side of the East Pakistanis. A resolution introduced by Mrs. Gandhi and adopted unanimously by both houses of Parliament on March 31 expressed "whole-hearted sympathy and support" for the people of East Pakistan, and called on the government of Pakistan to "put an end immediately to the systematic decimation of the people, which amounts to genocide." Mrs. Gandhi told the Lok Sabha on May 24 that there could be no military solution to the problem of East Pakistan, only a political one acceptable to its people, for which the international community had a special responsibility.

In May a severe cholera epidemic broke out among the Bengali refugees. It was brought under control in a few weeks, but only after several thousand had died. According to Indian figures, the number of refugees had grown to about 5.5 million by mid-June, and to about 10 million by December.

REFUGEE children in India huddle fearfully in November as they wait for food to be distributed. Civil war in East Pakistan created about 10 million refugees.

──────INDIA • Information Highlights──────

Official Name: Republic of India.
Area: 1,261,813 square miles (3,268,090 sq km).
Population (1971 census): 547,000,000. *Density,* 425 per square mile (164 per sq km). *Annual rate of increase,* 25%.
Chief Cities (1969 est.): New Delhi (1967 est.), the capital, 324,283; Bombay, 5,534,358; Delhi, 3,621,101; Calcutta, 3,134,161.
Government: *Head of state,* V. V. Giri, president (took office Aug. 24, 1969). *Head of government,* Mrs. Indira Gandhi, prime minister (took office Jan. 24, 1966). *Legislature*—Parliament; Rajya Sabha (Council of the States), 240 members; Lok Sabha (House of the People), 520 members. *Major political parties*—Congress (R), Jana Sangh, Congress (O), Communist party, Swatantra party.
Languages: Hindi (official), English, 14 national languages.
Education: *Literacy rate* (1970), 29% of population aged 10 and over. *Expenditure on education* (1965), 2.6% of gross national product. *School enrollment* (1965)—primary, 44,-499,000; secondary, 7,650,102; technical/vocational, 450,-101; university/higher, 1,054,273.
Finances (1970): *Revenues,* $4,364,000,000; *expenditures,* $5,189,000,000; *monetary unit,* rupee (7.499 rupees equal U. S.$1, Sept. 1971).
Gross National Product (1970 est.): $49,000,000,000.
National Income (1969): $41,275,000,000; *national income per person,* $77.
Economic Indexes: *Industrial production* (1970), 139 (1963= 100); *agricultural production* (1969), 111 (1963=100); *consumer price index* (1970), 184 (1960=100).
Manufacturing (metric tons, 1969): Cement, 13,624,000; steel, 6,464,000; distillate fuel oils, 4,719,000; residual fuel oil, 4,261,000; sugar, 4,190,000; wheat flour, 1,850,000.
Crops (metric tons, 1969 crop year): Rice, 60,645,000 (ranks 2d among world producers); sorghum (1968), 9,804,000 (world rank 2d); millet (1968), 7,254,000 (world rank 1st); ground nuts, 5,143,000 (world rank 1st); rapeseed (1968), 1,568,000; cotton lint, 1,084,000; tea, 396,000.
Minerals (metric tons, 1969): Coal, 74,736,000; iron ore, 18,-039,000; lignite, 4,188,000; manganese ore, 575,000; gold, 3,405 kilograms.
Foreign Trade (1970): *Exports,* $2,026,000,000 (chief exports —jute fabrics, $225,317,000; black tea, $191,000,000). *Imports,* $2,095,000,000 (chief imports, 1968—nonelectrical machinery $493,310,000; cereals and preparations, $448,-815,000; chemicals, $375,150,000; textile fibers and waste, $162,462,000). *Chief trading partners* (1968)—United States (took 17% of exports, supplied 31% of imports); United Kingdom (15%—7%); Japan (12%—6%); USSR (11%—10%).
Tourism: *Receipts* (1970), $50,800,000.
Transportation: *Roads* (1966), 513,000 miles (825,571 km); *motor vehicles* (1969), 1,047,600 (automobiles, 556,800); *railroads* (1970), 36,126 miles (58,138 km); *merchant fleet* (1971), 2,478,000 gross registered tons; *national airlines,* Air India, Indian Airlines Corporation; *principal airports,* Bombay, Calcutta, Delhi, Madras.
Communications: *Telephones* (1970), 1,159,519; *television stations* (1968), 1; *television sets* (1969), 12,000; *radios* (1969), 10,035,000; *newspapers* (1968), 636 (daily circulation, 6,-982,000).

Mrs. Gandhi and other Indian spokesmen insisted that the refugees must return to their homes, but only after a political solution acceptable to the people of East Pakistan had been reached. Most Indians seemed to accept the contention of the Mukti Bahini, the spearhead of the resistance movement in East Pakistan, that the only acceptable solution was an independent Bangladesh, or Bengal Nation.

Supporters of Bangladesh, including defecting East Pakistani diplomats, were allowed to remain and to operate in India, and many were given guerrilla training and other assistance on Indian soil. As the strains on India mounted, the demand for military action to force a solution in East Pakistan and to enable the refugees to return was heard with increasing frequency and vigor.

At the same time, Pakistan's President Yahya Khan warned that his country would not tolerate continued Indian interference in its affairs. The Pakistan government repeatedly charged India with sustained efforts to "undermine the solidarity and national integrity of Pakistan."

Indian and Pakistani forces were massed along the frontiers between the two countries. In late November, Indian troops crossed the border of East Pakistan and engaged Pakistani forces in a series of clashes. On December 3, according to reports, Pakistani aircraft struck simultaneously at several airfields in western India, an action that, according to Mrs. Gandhi, led to "full-scale war."

Indian forces quickly gained the upper hand in East Pakistan, and on December 6, India recognized Bangladesh as an independent nation. On the western front a strong Pakistani drive in the Jammu section of Kashmir was countered by Indian penetration in several parts of West Pakistan. On December 16, Pakistan's army commander in East Pakistan surrendered unconditionally to India. Mrs. Gandhi then ordered a complete cease-fire with Pakistan, which was accepted by President Yahya Khan on December 17. (See also INDIA-PAKISTAN WAR.)

Relations with Other Countries. India's attitude toward the United Nations and international aid-giving agencies and its relations with many countries were affected by what it regarded as a lack of understanding and support of its policies and by the problems created by the East Pakistan crisis. This was particularly true of India's relations with the United States, whose policies toward the refugee problem and the Indo-Pakistan war seemed to India to be based on hostility toward it and to reflect a pro-Pakistan bias. Relations between India and the United States, in fact, reached one of their lowest points in 1971.

Relations with China remained distant, and were further complicated by China's support for Pakistan. India, however, responded favorably to several friendly gestures by Chinese representatives, and it welcomed the admission of the People's Republic of China into the United Nations in the fall. India also had strained relations with the Arab countries, notably Egypt, which generally supported Pakistan's position in the crisis.

Relations with Britain continued to be marred by misunderstandings and disagreements. At the Commonwealth prime ministers' conference in Singapore, which Mrs. Gandhi did not attend, India's representatives joined in the attacks on Britain's decision to send arms aid to South Africa, and supported the appeal of Prime Minister Bandaranaike of Ceylon to make the Indian Ocean a "zone of peace." India was disturbed by the possible adverse effects of Britain's long-delayed entrance into the European Common Market, and it was not happy with the British policy regarding the Pakistan crisis, at least until the outbreak of the Indo-Pakistan hostilities.

Relations remained warm with the Soviet Union, which had supplied India with most of its foreign military aid since 1965. The increasing closeness of the two states was dramatized by the signing, on August 9, of an Indo-Soviet treaty of peace, friendship, and cooperation. The Indian foreign minister described it as a "treaty of nonaggression," and Mrs. Gandhi insisted that it did not represent a reversal of India's policy of nonalignment. The treaty was widely welcomed in India. Soviet Foreign Minister Andrei Gromyko was in India for the signing of the treaty, and President Nikolai Podgorny visited in October. India appreciated the support of the Soviet Union in its crisis with Pakistan.

In October and November, at a time of increasing tensions with Pakistan, Mrs. Gandhi visited Belgium, Austria, Britain, the United States, France, and West Germany. During her visits she sought to explain India's position regarding the crisis with Pakistan and to seek support.

NORMAN D. PALMER
University of Pennsylvania

India's superior armaments and isolation of Pakistanis permitted rapid Indian advance into East Pakistan, now Bangladesh, during December offensive. (*Above*) Indian tanks roll toward Jessore. (*Right*) Lt. Gen. Jagjit Aurora (*left*), commander of India's eastern forces, and Lt. Gen. A. A. K. Niazi, Pakistani commander in the east, sign the surrender agreement in Dacca.

INDIA-PAKISTAN WAR

For the third time since they became independent in 1947, India and Pakistan plunged into war in 1971. The basic issue was the fate of East Pakistan, which had been pressing for autonomy from the central government in West Pakistan. India championed the demands of the east. The 75 million people in the east had been suppressed by West Pakistani forces since March. After war broke out on December 3, the West Pakistanis in the east were quickly overcome by Indian and rebel troops. The east emerged as Bangladesh (Bengal Nation) when East Pakistan surrendered on December 16.

Background. The current crisis was sparked by the December 1970 elections that brought Sheikh Mujibur Rahman, called Sheikh Mujib, to the fore in East Pakistan. His Awami League, which demanded East Pakistani autonomy, won a majority in Pakistan's National Assembly, but President Yahya Khan postponed its opening. Resulting disorders were followed by the sheikh's imprisonment.

On March 25, West Pakistani troops began an offensive in the east, trying to restore West Pakistani control and later to suppress the Mukti Bahini,

guerrillas who called for independence. The action caused about 1 million deaths and created as many as 10 million refugees, who fled to India, which borders East Pakistan on three sides. The neighboring Bengalis of India are Hindu rather than Muslim but are culturally similar to the Bengalis of East Pakistan. India, backed by the USSR, became increasingly forceful in its support of the east.

Beginning of War. Serious fighting broke out in late November as Mukti Bahini and Indian troops stepped up operations. While denying Indian engagement in East Pakistan, India massed soldiers along East Pakistan's borders. War erupted on December 3, with both sides reporting incursions in the west, the scene of fighting in 1947–48 and 1965. Pakistan charged that India had launched ground attacks, and India accused Pakistan of air raids.

As expected, India's strategy was to concentrate on East Pakistan, while attempting to contain Pakistani forces in the west. Outnumbered, underequipped, and hated by the natives, Pakistani troops in the east also had supply problems. The government in the west seemed hesitant about committing

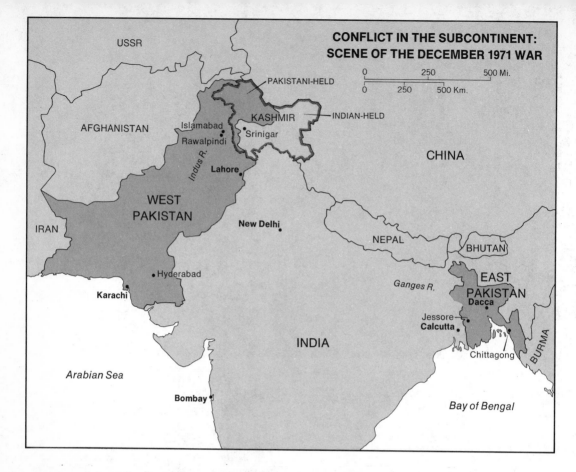

more resources to the east and was prevented from doing so after war began by Indian blockades.

When war erupted, India had over 125,000 troops poised on East Pakistan's borders. They were opposed by 70,000–80,000 Pakistani soldiers. India could also count on the aid of the Mukti Bahini. Indian air power, armor, and artillery were superior to Pakistan's. Pakistan had only 23 jet fighters in the east, and on December 9 the last was destroyed, allowing India to protect its own forces and to harass the Pakistanis at will. Indian forces advanced steadily in the east from December 3.

The UN Security Council began debate on the crisis on December 4, but decision proved impossible. The USSR, supporting India, vetoed cease-fire resolutions, and other nations rejected Soviet resolutions calling for Pakistan to reach a political settlement in the east. Both the United States and newly seated Communist China sided with Pakistan. The issue was then transferred to the General Assembly, which has no enforcement powers. On December 7, the General Assembly approved, 104 to 11, a resolution calling for India and Pakistan to stop fighting. Pakistan indicated its willingness to abide by the resolution, but India rejected its terms.

While attention focused on the east, Pakistan and India battled along their border in the west, particularly in disputed Kashmir. Fighting, including a tank battle near Chhamb, was inconclusive.

Indian Victory. Diplomatic relations between India and Pakistan were broken on December 6, following India's recognition of the new nation of Bangladesh, whose leaders had set up their government in Calcutta. Jessore, a key military headquarters, fell on December 7, assuring Indian control of half of East Pakistan.

As Indian troops pushed steadily toward the regional capital, Dacca, the Pakistanis withdrew into the city's environs. Although India expressed hope that the Pakistanis would surrender, it prepared for a final assault on Dacca. By December 12 the Pakistanis held only a few major towns besides Dacca, and on December 13 the Indians were within artillery range of the capital.

As Indian planes bombed Dacca on December 14, Dr. A. M. Malik, governor of East Pakistan, and his government resigned, dissociating itself from the actions of the West Pakistan government and leaving responsibility for the war to the military. At the same time, Indian forces reached outposts six miles from the capital.

The disclosure on December 15 that the United States was moving naval vessels to the Bay of Bengal greatly increased Indian resentment toward the United States. Ostensibly, the ships were sent to stand by to rescue U.S. civilians and to counter Soviet warships in the area, but India interpreted the naval movement as a thinly veiled threat.

On December 15, Lt. Gen. A. A. K. Niazi, Pakistani commander in Dacca, asked for a cease-fire, but when India refused to consider anything less than surrender, he capitulated. Niazi and Lt. Gen. Jagjit Aurora, commander of India's eastern forces, signed the surrender agreement in Dacca on December 16. Pakistan's Yahya Khan at first pledged to continue the war, but on December 17 he accepted a cease-fire that ended hostilities in the west.

Results of the War. The war produced several definite changes but left some issues unresolved. On December 20, after mounting domestic criticism of his part in Pakistan's defeat, Yahya Khan resigned as president and was succeeded by Zulfikar

Ali Bhutto, deputy prime minister and foreign minister. Although Bangladesh had been established, Bhutto stated his determination to settle differences with the east.

The role and influence of the world's superpowers in the subcontinent appeared to have shifted. The Soviet Union's prestige was greatly enhanced by its support of India, while the U. S. and Communist Chinese images were tarnished. Although the United States proclaimed neutrality, it condemned India's "aggression." The chill in U. S.–Indian relations followed more than two decades of close ties.

The fate of Bangladesh appeared cloudy. It is one of the world's most populous countries, facing devastating problems, especially the refugees. Many of its leaders were killed during the war and the internal strife preceding it. Highly important to the future of Bangladesh is Sheikh Mujib, who returned after his release by Bhutto on Jan. 8, 1972. Finally, basic Indian-Pakistani hostility remained, and until it is resolved there will be little stability on the subcontinent.

STEPHEN P. ELLIOTT

INDIANA

The reelection of two mayors—Richard G. Lugar of Indianapolis and Richard D. Hatcher of Gary, who head Indiana's first and second largest cities—thrust both into the national spotlight in 1971.

Lugar, a 39-year-old Republican closely identified with President Nixon, won the mayoralty post in the state capital in a landslide on November 2. His political prestige had risen earlier in the year when the state Supreme Court held Uni-Gov, his modified approach to metropolitan government for Indianapolis, constitutional. Lugar also received widespread attention while serving as host to an international conference on city government, held in Indianapolis in May.

Hatcher, 38, a Democrat who became Indiana's first black mayor in 1967, easily won return to his office. Gary is now the largest U. S. city to have a second-term black mayor.

Republicans had controlled most of the mayoralty posts in Indiana, but the Democrats gained a modest majority in the 1971 elections. The Democrats thus won most of the cities, but the Republicans retained a majority of towns lacking mayors.

Economy. The state's economy remained sluggish, but it showed improvement over 1970 in total output and average personal income. Unemployment was a bit higher than for 1970, but it roughly approximated the national average. Particularly hard hit was the steel industry in the Calumet region, where production dropped and joblessness increased.

With corn blight reduced and rainfall coming at needed times, farm production was higher. Farm prices, however, were lower than for 1970.

State revenues were tight throughout the year, and some obligations had to be postponed to avoid a fiscal crisis.

Education. Controversies flared during efforts toward integration of blacks in public schools. Tense situations developed in such scattered places as Richmond, Fort Wayne, Kokomo, and Indianapolis, but for the most part violence was limited.

General Assembly. The 1971 session of the Indiana General Assembly marked an important milestone when it formally established the frequency and length of future sessions. It will hold yearly sessions, limited to 61 legislature days in odd-numbered years and to 30 such days, excluding days off, in even-numbered years.

From statehood in 1816 to the adoption of a new constitution in 1851, the assembly met annually for as long as it desired. From 1851 on, however, it met biennially for a maximum of 61 days unless called into special session by the governor.

The 1971 General Assembly also made—or failed to make—other important decisions. One was the adoption of a biennial budget of $3,140,000,000 for fiscal 1971–73, compared with $2,680,000,000 for the two preceding years.

A substantial but unsuccessful effort was made to remodel the tax structure by reducing levies on property while increasing other levies.

In a break with precedent, all legislative seats were redistricted in such a way that each district has only a single legislator.

Enactment of what was called "superbill" resulted in the compilation into one act of the mass of laws approved since 1851.

The General Assembly also prohibited discrimination against women, placed stringent restrictions on the use of phosphate detergents, and reduced the number of patronage appointments in the highway department and other departments of the state government.

DONALD F. CARMONY, *Indiana University*
Editor, "Indiana Magazine of History"

───── **INDIANA • Information Highlights** ─────

Area: 36,291 square miles (93,994 sq km).
Population (1970 census): 5,193,669. *Density:* 141 per sq mi.
Chief Cities (1970 census): Indianapolis, the capital, 745,739; Fort Wayne, 178,021; Gary, 175,415; Evansville, 138,764; South Bend, 125,580; Hammond, 107,790; Anderson, 70,787.
Government (1971): *Chief Officers*—governor, Edgar D. Whitcomb (R); lt. gov., Richard E. Folz (R); secy. of state, Larry A. Conrad (D); atty. gen., Theodore L. Sendak (R); treas., Jack L. New (D); supt., board of education, John J. Loughlin (D); chief justice, Norman F. Arterburn. *General Assembly*—Senate, 50 members (29 Republicans, 21 Democrats); House of Representatives, 100 members (53 R, 46 D, 1 vac.).
Education (1970–71): *Enrollment*—public elementary schools, 683,832 pupils; 26,000 teachers; public secondary, 547,668 pupils, 25,204 teachers; nonpublic schools (1968–69), 134,500 pupils; 4,990 teachers; college and university (fall 1968), 175,904 students. *Public school expenditures* (1970–71), $851,000,000 ($741 per pupil). *Average teacher's salary*, $9,272.
State Finances (fiscal year 1970): *Revenues*, $1,714,889,000 (2% general sales tax and gross receipts taxes, $380,739,000; motor fuel tax, $192,795,000; federal funds, $316,974,000). *Expenditures*, $1,600,681,000 (education, $809,576,000; health, welfare, and safety, $46,974,000; highways, $203,241,000). *State debt*, $583,823,000 (June 30, 1970).
Personal Income (1970): $19,802,000,000; *per capita*, $3,773.
Public Assistance (1970): $127,736,000. *Average monthly payments* (Dec. 1970)—old-age assistance, $55.45; aid to families with dependent children, $138.40.
Labor Force: *Nonagricultural wage and salary earners* (June 1971), 1,845,000. *Average annual employment* (1969)—manufacturing, 747,000; trade, 363,000; government, 288,000; services, 203,000. *Insured unemployed* (Oct. 1971)—33,300 (2.4%).
Manufacturing (1967): *Value added by manufacture*, $10,308,000,000. Primary metal industries, $1,817,900,000; electrical equipment and supplies, $1,601,600,000; transportation equipment, $1,361,000,000.
Agriculture (1970): *Cash farm income*, $1,663,678,000 (livestock, $838,149,000; crops, $714,488,000; government payments, $111,046,000). *Chief crops* (1970)—Corn, 371,998,000 bushels (ranks 4th among the states); soybeans, 104,297,000 bushels (ranks 3d); wheat, 29,799,000 bushels.
Mining (1969): *Production value*, $241,871,000 (ranks 23d among the states). *Chief minerals* (tons)—Stone, 25,559,000; coal, 20,086,000; cement, 14,497,000 barrels.
Transportation: *Roads* (1969), 90,957 miles (146,377 km); *motor vehicles* (1969), 2,806,000; *railroads* (1968), 6,488 miles (10,441 km); *airports* (1969), 61.
Communications: *Telephones* (1971), 2,905,300; *television stations* (1969), 17; *radio stations* (1969), 153; *newspapers* (1969), 83 (daily circulation, 1,703,000).

TAOS-PUEBLO Indians gather on New Mexico reservation in August to celebrate government's return of Blue Lake. The lake has a sacred role in their religion.

INDIANS, AMERICAN

The year 1971 was marked by the continuation of executive and legislative support for Indian aspirations. Personnel shifts within the Bureau of Indian Affairs (BIA) consolidated the aggressively pro-Indian orientation of Bureau policies. Indian efforts to achieve economic and educational independence made significant progress during 1971.

Alaska Native Claims Bill. Government support for the Alaska native land settlement was given unstintingly during the year. Not only was the bill, which in 1970 had been approved by the Senate but ignored by the House of Representatives, brought to life, but the amount of land offered to the natives was increased from 10 million to 40 million acres. The monetary portion of the package, nearly $1 billion, remained at the 1970 figure. House and Senate quickly resolved their differences on the bill for fear that newly aroused conservationists might open up a Pandora's box of amendments that might destroy the delicate compromise laboriously worked out. The President, after verifying the acceptability of the bill to those directly concerned, signed it in December.

The act, with its provision for a native-owned corporation to support the growth of a balanced economy for Alaska's natives, ended one of the most successful negotiations by natives with the U.S. government. The settlement was not a judicial determination, nor was it based on violations of treaties or agreements, the basis of most recent Indian claims in the "lower 48" states. Rather, it represented payment for the "aboriginal title" possessed by the Alaskan natives and recognized by the United States when the territory was purchased from Russia in 1867.

Alcatraz. The symbolic Indian occupation of Alcatraz Island in San Francisco Bay ended on June 11 after a surprise raid by 35 armed U.S. marshals. Fifteen Indian holdouts of the invasion, which began on Nov. 20, 1969, were removed without resistance. The occupation of the island by Indian militants, extensively covered by the media, succumbed to overexposure and indecision. The government avoided a quick and dramatic response to the occupation, a response that might have heightened sympathy for the Indian cause. Instead, the government allowed the occupation to drag on, observed Indian disagreement over what to do with the island, and profited from the Indian inability to establish and gain support for a coherent program of permanent occupation.

Indian Leadership. The character of Indian organizations took a decided change with the establishment of a National Tribal Chairmen's Association. Hitherto, the Indian point of view had tended to be represented by organizations such as the National Congress of American Indians (NCAI). Its representation was weakened, however, by the absence of some of the largest tribes, such as the Navajo, and by the resentment of some chiefs at being represented by an executive not himself a tribal leader. During the year the board of directors of the group called for the removal of the BIA from the Department of the Interior, claiming its bureaucracy was hindering reform. They asked that the BIA be placed under White House authority.

Another challenge to the traditional leadership of the NCAI was the formation of a coalition of urban Indian groups in October, during the first national convention of the American Indian Movement (AIM). The many urban Indian groups have tended to take a more militant stand than other Indian organizations and have accused the NCAI of failing to function as a "grass roots, national impact organization," which organizers of the new coalition hope AIM will become. AIM's militant tactics included an unauthorized intrusion into the offices of the BIA in September and other disruptive demonstrations.

Bureau of Indian Affairs. Although the BIA continued a newly adopted policy reserving all top-level positions for Indians, a series of personnel shifts during the year revealed dissatisfaction with the slow pace of reform on the part of some of the younger militants who had assumed high positions in the bureau. There was also dissatisfaction on the part of Interior Secretary Rogers Morton with the loose manner in which some of the bureau's policies were being carried out. As a result, some of the young radicals resigned, and on July 23 a long-time bureau official, John O. Crow, a one-quarter Cherokee, was appointed deputy commissioner to Commissioner Louis R. Bruce.

After a confused period in which Crow's role, which at first seemed to rival or overshadow Bruce's, was protested by young reformers and organizations such as the NCAI, Commissioner Bruce reasserted himself and made further shifts of personnel that favored the reform-minded group and reduced the influence of some old-time careerists. Bills to raise and strengthen the status of the bureau within the department were introduced during the year but faced an uncertain fate in Congress.

Decisions Affecting the Indian. The Court of Claims, in *Confederate Salish and Kootenai Tribes of the Flathead Reservation, Montana* v. *the United States* (decided Jan. 22, 1971), ruled that the government, by an act of 1904 forcing the allotment of, and sale of surplus lands within, the Flathead Reservation against the will of the Indians residing there and in violation of a treaty of 1855, had not engaged in an exercise of guardianship or management but in an act of confiscation constitutionally requiring that it pay just compensation. Because adequate compensation had not been paid at the time, the court ordered the government to pay the difference between the fair market value of the surplus land taken from the Indians and the compensation *plus* interest.

While the Court of Claims was thus liberally interpreting the government's responsibility to the Indian, the Indian Claims Commission was following a more conservative line. The commission rejected the claim of representatives of the Joseph Band of the Nez Perce Tribe, which was seeking compensation for injuries suffered by the band in a legendary 1,500-mile retreat across the northwest toward Canada in 1877 and, after their capture, during subsequent confinement in the Indian Territory (now Oklahoma). Despite what Commissioner John Vance, in a dissent from the majority opinion, called "blatant wrongs of commission" by the government in violation of its treaty and other obligations leading to the destruction of Joseph's band as an entity, the commission majority denied on March 26 that the claim was compensable under the Indian Claims Commission Act.

A suit brought against the government by the Ft. Sill Apache Tribe of Oklahoma and others, claiming damages for injuries inflicted upon their ancestral bands, was decided on September 24. The Indians asked for compensation for injuries incurred as a result of wrongful acts of U. S. officials and troops in arresting and imprisoning the bands and in evicting the bands from their homelands in violation of treaty pledges. As a result of these actions, the suit charged, the bands were thwarted in their advancement.

The commission rejected the first claim as not within its jurisdiction. The second claim was rejected on the grounds that the general supervision of an Indian tribe by the United States does not suffice to put the United States in the capacity of guardian, trustee, or fiduciary. In a stinging dissent, Commissioners Vance and Brantley Blue asserted that words have lost their meaning if the Apache claim cannot be considered under the broad mandate of the Indian Claims Commission.

Economy and Education. Indians made several notable advances toward economic and educational independence. The Mescalero Apaches began construction of a $12 million resort complex on their New Mexico reservation, while the Utes moved ahead with a hunting and recreation development in Utah. In April, Navajo Community College, which has been in operation since 1968, dedicated the site of its new campus on the Navajo Reservation. The Southwestern Indian Polytechnic Institute, offering training in numerous fields, opened in Albuquerque, N. Mex., in September. In May plans were announced in Davis, Calif., for Deganawidah-Quetzalcoatl University, which will educate Indians and Mexican-Americans.

WILCOMB E. WASHBURN
Smithsonian Institution

PETER MACDONALD delivers inaugural speech as head of Navajo Tribal Council on January 5. He spoke at Window Rock, Ariz., capital of nation's largest tribe.

UPI

INDOCHINA WAR

South Vietnamese President Nguyen Van Thieu called 1971 a transitional year between war and peace. Whether peace was close at hand was problematical, but a transitional year it was in terms of a shift from major to marginal U. S. combat participation in the fighting.

When South Vietnamese forces moved into Laos in early February to disrupt the flow of military traffic down the Ho Chi Minh Trail, there were 41 U. S. ground combat battalions in Vietnam—sufficient to significantly aid the Saigon government's troops in initiating their first major thrust against the Communists on Laotian soil. By November there were only 19 such battalions left in Vietnam, comprising less than 20,000 combat soldiers.

In all, only 152,000 American servicemen remained in the country at year-end. This figure represented a drop of more than 391,000 from the April 1969 peak of 543,400 early in the administration of President Richard M. Nixon.

Whether peace at long last had been achieved in Vietnam, let alone the other Indochinese states of Laos and Cambodia, was open to serious question, however. The joint U. S.-South Vietnamese military intervention in eastern Cambodia in May–June 1970 ostensibly was designed to drive the Vietnamese Communists from this area. Nevertheless, Saigon's troops mounted several campaigns in this region again in 1971, including a major thrust in December, and serious fighting was taking place at year-end between the Cambodians and the North Vietnamese outside Cambodia's capital, Phnom Penh. Continued American bombing of the Ho Chi Minh Trail in Laos and heavy strikes against North Vietnam itself in December indicated that U. S. participation in the air war in Indochina was by no means ended.

THE FIGHTING

President Nixon stated in November that the U. S. offensive role in Vietnam was "already concluded." In the President's words, U. S. troops in South Vietnam were wholly "in a defensive position" by the end of the year.

The U. S. role in the air war, however, declined only moderately during the year—about 15% less than in 1970 in terms of the tonnage of bombs dropped in the three-front Indochinese war. Indeed, a Cornell University study claimed that a greater bomb tonnage (2,916,000 tons) had been dropped in Indochina during the three years of the Nixon administration than in the previous five-year period under President Lyndon B. Johnson (2,865,000 tons). President Nixon warned in November, moreover, that "air strikes on the infiltration routes" would continue "in support of the South Vietnamese until there is a negotiated settlement."

There were 78 air strikes by U. S. fighter-bombers against North Vietnam through November, and North Vietnamese MIG aircraft crossed over the border with Laos ten times during U. S. bombing raids on the Ho Chi Minh Trail. In late November one such MIG fired a missile at a B-52 bomber—the first such incident of the war.

U. S. combat involvement on the main front of the war in Vietnam was largely limited to air support of South Vietnamese ground operations. Battlefield activity in general in South Vietnam was at a record low for the war, as U. S. forces pulled back to defensive positions and sought to avoid combat contact with the enemy. The South Vietnamese thrusts into Laos in February and March and Cambodia throughout the year, coupled with U. S. bombing of the Ho Chi Minh Trail (and the beginning of bombing of the same arteries by planes of the Saigon government), seriously restricted the Communists' capability for mounting a sustained offensive.

The Vietnamese Communists' main elements largely were concentrated near the border regions throughout the year. Like the U. S. troops, they also seemed to be seeking to avoid contact. In August, for example, Communist attacks, all minor, numbered 825 (in contrast with 1,246 such actions in the same month of the previous year). Such assaults as did take place were against South Vietnamese units. In the first three weeks in November, for example, the South Vietnamese suffered 1,080 deaths, as compared with 22 for the Americans.

The Laos Campaign. The six-week campaign by 20,000 South Vietnamese troops to interdict the Ho Chi Minh Trail in Laos, which began February 8, ended earlier than planned and suffered fairly critical evaluation in the U. S. and world press. But it probably halved, though temporarily, the flow of Communist supplies southward and bought valuable time for the Saigon government's pacification efforts inside South Vietnam.

Upward of 30,000 Vietnamese Communist soldiers and more than 1,200 supply vehicles moved down the Ho Chi Minh Trail the first month of the year—a major increase over the average monthly flow for 1970. The South Vietnamese ground forces and supporting U. S. air action reportedly killed more than 6,000 Communists (as compared with 700 South Vietnamese dead and 2,100 wounded). Two out of three North Vietnamese casualties were attributed to U. S. air action, however.

U. S. air support of the South Vietnamese ground thrust was massive, involving saturation bombing and troop-carrying helicopters—the full impact of which, however, was probably severely limited by unexpectedly bad weather. On a November visit to Saigon, Defense Secretary Melvin R. Laird declared that the South Vietnamese could count on comparable U. S. air support if they struck again into Laos in the future.

Cambodian Campaign. The war in Cambodia, which worsened despite heavy U. S. air support and renewed South Vietnamese thrusts across the border, threatened U. S. efforts to disengage from the major Vietnamese front of the Indochinese conflict. U. S. fighter-bombers flew about 1,000 combat missions a month into Cambodia. This was probably the major factor in preventing the Vietnamese Communists from extending their domination of the eastern half of that country and scattered parts of the south and the west.

(Opposite) *Giant peace symbol, bulldozed out of South Vietnamese jungle, was noted in May outside 101st Airborne Division headquarters. The peace sign is popular among U. S. soldiers.*

North Vietnamese military personnel in Cambodia increased from 45,000 to 60,000 in 1971, but probably no more than 10,000 Vietnamese Communists took part in combat at any time. Cambodia's army, which numbered 35,000 men at the time of the coup against Prince Norodom Sihanouk in March 1970, had about 190,000 by the end of 1971. Some 40,000–50,000 of these were U. S.-equipped and trained in South Vietnam. About 2,000 additional soldiers a month were receiving such training by late 1971.

South Vietnamese forces numbering perhaps 25,000 launched a major drive into eastern Cambodia in early December. This was partly a diversionary effort to relieve the pressure on Cambodian troops fighting the North Vietnamese near Phnom Penh. The United States stepped up its air action at year-end for the same reason. The cause of the Cambodian difficulties was twofold: the ineffectiveness of 270 of Cambodia's 300 combat battalions and the fact that the Cambodians were growing bolder in going out to meet the Communists. The latter factor was perhaps encouraging, but it created more problems than in an earlier period when the Cambodians were less active.

Despite the setbacks in Cambodia, the fact that the Vietnamese Communists were fighting there was a main contributing factor to the decline in the struggle in Vietnam itself to probably half the level of intensity of the previous year.

The Vietnamese Home Front. U. S. spokesmen termed security in the Mekong delta in 1971 the best in 10 years, and a larger number of open bridges and roads seemed to support this judgment. Interrupted enemy supply and communications lines weakened the Communists' capacity for sustained activity. It also appeared that the North Vietnamese

U. S. TROOPS erect warning sign near Laos in February. Americans supported South Vietnam's drive against North Vietnamese in Laos but did not cross border.

were consciously pursuing a "protracted" low-level warfare strategy, partly designed not to dissuade the United States from disengaging.

Many observers felt that the security situation in South Vietnam was somewhat better during the first months of 1971 than at year-end. However, there was evidence of stepped-up enemy activity in areas of the country evacuated by U. S. forces, particularly in the north, and increased Vietcong terrorism and political infiltration in the delta.

The year ended quietly enough on the South Vietnamese battlefront, but an uneasiness was evident on the part of both U. S. and Saigon officials. The reasons were varied but related: the ever-widening geographic dispersion of South Vietnam's forces, the imminent termination of a U. S. combat presence in the country, and a fear that the Communists were holding back militarily, as well as politically, pending the departure of U. S. forces.

Casualties. The fact that the war in Vietnam was far from ended for the South Vietnamese was evidenced by the persisting high level of casualties sustained by Saigon's troops. South Vietnamese battle deaths approached or exceeded 20,000 in 1971 for the fourth straight year—more than 15 times the U. S. total in the same year. U. S. deaths in combat, which reached a peak of 14,592 in 1968, dropped to 4,221 in 1970 and 1,302 in 1971. U. S. losses of life on the battlefield averaged 108 a month during the year, compared with 352 a month in 1970. South Vietnamese combat deaths, on the other hand, dropped only from 1,700 to 1,600 a month. The Communists reportedly suffered 6,000 deaths per month in battle during the year.

Only two U. S. soldiers were killed in action during the last week in October, and only one in a week in December—the lowest for a single week since U. S. ground combat forces began fighting in the war in 1965. Fewer than eight battle deaths a week were suffered by U. S. forces during a six-week period ending in mid-November.

U. S. deaths in battle during the Indochina War were more than twice those sustained during the Korean War, greater than the sum of such losses in World War I, and more than one third those suffered in World War II.

THE POLITICS OF DISENGAGEMENT

The Vietnamese Communists offered to release U. S. prisoners of war simultaneously with the departure of U. S. fighting men—if Washington would agree to quit Vietnam by the end of 1971. President Nixon avoided a direct response, but he nonetheless accelerated the U. S. military evacuation timetable.

Negotiations. In the Paris talks on July 1 the Communist Vietnamese advanced a new seven-point plan that seemed to meet many U. S. objections to previous proposals by the other side in the Indochina war. For the first time in the 119 meetings that had taken place between the Paris negotiators, the Communists offered to release all prisoners of war simultaneously with the evacuation from Vietnam of all U. S. forces within the upcoming six-month period. The proposal also stipulated a cease-fire to cover the withdrawal, an end to U. S. support of the Thieu government in Saigon, a coalition regime to succeed Thieu, elections in South Vietnam, neutralization of the country, and ultimate reunification of the two Vietnams. The Communists made it clear that the simultaneous evacuation of U. S. forces and release of the POW's could be separated from the other points—and could take place without Washington's acquiescence in the other matters.

President Nixon's press secretary said that the Communist proposal contained "positive as well as unacceptable elements." The press reported a strongly negative reaction to the plan on the part of the White House. Asked his reaction, Senate Democratic Leader Mike Mansfield termed the offer "a new point of departure" and added "I know the President has been making probes in various parts of the world."

Within the week, Henry A. Kissinger, presidential adviser on national security, was en route to Peking, and in mid-July the President announced that he would visit China. In October, President Nixon stated that by the time he returned from a planned visit to the Soviet Union in May 1972, the United States "will have ended its involvement in Vietnam . . . or at least have made significant progress toward accomplishing that goal."

These diplomatic moves and the stepped-up U. S. withdrawal rate from Vietnam seemed to be the President's reply to the Communist Vietnamese July proposal. Defense Secretary Laird also stated at year-end that South Vietnam now had a "reasonable chance" of survival on its own.

Withdrawal of U. S. Forces. Only 177,000 U. S. servicemen remained in South Vietnam by Dec. 1, 1971. This was 7,000 fewer than President Nixon's proclaimed target of 184,000 by that date. However, there were also 43,200 military personnel outside of Vietnam directly involved in the fighting in that country—the 13,000 officers and men of the Seventh Fleet in the adjacent South China Sea and the 32,200 U. S. military personnel in Thailand to the west of Laos and Cambodia, most of them airmen engaged in supporting ground activity against the Communists.

There were 543,400 U. S. servicemen in Vietnam in April 1969, the peak of U. S. involvement in the fighting, before President Nixon began the U. S. military disengagement from the country. The average monthly withdrawal rate after May 1969 was 13,000. This rate increased to an average of 15,000 for the months preceding December 1971. In November the President announced that an additional 25,000 men would leave the country in December and another 20,000 in January 1972—leaving a total of 132,000 U. S. military personnel in the country by Feb. 1, 1972.

Although he increased sharply the monthly rate of withdrawal for December and January, President Nixon limited this new pullback schedule to two months—in contrast with the seven- or eight-month periods of previous departure announcements. His implied message to Hanoi was twofold: He could decrease as well as increase the disengagement rate for February and subsequent months, and he would get out of Vietnam militarily at his own, not the Communists', rate. The only way to hasten the process—and assure its completion—was through a negotiated settlement, he clearly indicated.

Nevertheless, the U. S. disengagement actually was proceeding on the basis of a de facto, not a negotiated agreement—quite contrary to the President's words. This was probably designed to minimize the loss of U. S. prestige abroad and placate hard-line policy advocates at home.

Expectations in Washington at year-end were that no more than 40,000 U. S. advisory and support personnel would remain in Vietnam by the fall

DIETER LUDWIG, UPI

SURVIVORS of May 21 rocket attack on U. S. fire base sit dejectedly among helmets of their 30 dead buddies.

of 1972. Even these could be greatly reduced in number if Hanoi were to release the 399 or more U. S. POW's it held. President Nixon apparently intended to use this residual contingent to force the release of the prisoners, but Hanoi's tactic was obviously to use the POW's to force a complete U. S. military withdrawal.

Vietnamization. South Vietnam's armed forces took over increased responsibility in 1971 for air combat, helicopter, artillery, and logistical activity in the continuing war against the 240,000 North Vietnamese and Vietcong troops south of the 17th parallel. They also expanded their combat participation in the satellite wars in adjacent Laos and Cambodia.

Some 1.1 million men served under arms for the Saigon government—525,000 in the regular armed forces, 300,000 in the regional forces, and 285,000 in the popular (village and hamlet) forces.

The persisting U. S. air role in Vietnam received much attention in 1971, but 80% of the 3,500 air strikes being flown monthly within South Vietnam were South Vietnamese flights. By November, U. S. in-country air strength was limited to three tactical air squadrons at Danang and one small jet squadron at Bienhoa.

The South Vietnamese gave a good, if not outstanding, account of themselves in fighting in Vietnam and neighboring Cambodia—and even in Laos, considering that they were doing battle on ground much more familiar to the Communists. The Communist Vietnamese, however, had not yet really mounted a major offensive against them.

U. S. Politics. Senatorial critics of the Indochina War were not able to force the President to announce a timetable for complete withdrawal of U. S. forces from Vietnam, but their efforts were a constant pressure on him. The results of major popular polls were clearly antiwar. The Harris survey in mid-October, for example, showed 65% of the American people against the war.

RICHARD BUTWELL
State University of New York at Brockport

PRESIDENT SUHARTO escorts Queen Juliana of Netherlands as she reviews troops in Djakarta in August. Her visit was first by a Dutch monarch to the former colony.

INDONESIA

The most important event in Indonesia in 1971 was the election for the House of Representatives on July 3. Provincial and local councils were chosen at the same time. This was Indonesia's first national election in 16 years and the second in the country's 21 years of independence. The House is the core of the larger People's Consultative Congress, which will elect a new president in 1973.

Elections. Although conducted in an atmosphere of some tension, the voting for the 360 elective seats of the 460-seat House of Representatives was peaceful. Sekber Golkar, the semigovernmental party composed of over 200 occupational groups, was organized to compete in the election with nine other established parties. It won a sweeping victory by capturing 236 seats. Its nearest rival was the Muslim Scholars party, with 60 seats. A surprise in the results of the election was the poor showing of the Indonesian Nationalist party, founded by former President Sukarno, which won only 20 seats. Minor parties took the remaining seats. The 100 nonelective seats were filled by presidential appointment, and they represented the 500,000 members of the armed forces, who were not permitted to vote or stand for election, and other functional groups.

The campaign slogan of the Golkars, "Politics, No! Development, Yes!" emphasized the overriding issue in the campaign—that Indonesia urgently needed the continuance of the government's economic reforms and development programs. The government apparently feared the outcome of the election. Not only did it spend millions on the campaign, but it pressed the army and government servants into supporting Sekber Golkar.

Election Restrictions. The election was hedged in by restrictions. The Communist party was outlawed, and all those involved in the abortive coup of 1965 were barred from voting or standing for election. Maj. Gen. Amir Machmud, the minister of interior affairs and chairman of the electoral commission, laid down "12 commandments" for the conduct of the campaign. Candidates were forbidden to criticize the government, the constitution, or the *Pantjasila,* the five basic principles upon which the republic was founded. They also could not raise the question of religion, refer to the philosophy of Sukarno, or eulogize him in any way.

There seemed to have been considerable dissatisfaction with the elections, for Interior Minister Machmud repeated President Suharto's statement that they had been legitimate. He also appealed to the people not to criticize the elections again.

Cabinet Changes. On September 9, President Suharto announced changes in his cabinet. Four members were relieved of their posts, one ministry was abolished and two new ones created, and six new ministers were appointed. The former ministers were made members of the supreme advisory council. The new cabinet, called the development cabinet, was composed of 25 members including President Suharto.

Foreign Relations. Queen Juliana of the Netherlands made a 10-day state visit to Indonesia in August-September. Although the Netherlands had ruled Indonesia as a colony for over three centuries, Queen Juliana was the first head of the Dutch state to visit the archipelago, and only after it had been independent for two decades.

Indonesia has been leaning strongly toward the non-Communist West during the past several years.

Foreign Minister Adam Malik was concerned about this, and he worked toward bringing Indonesia's nonalignment policies into balance in 1971. He moved to "normalize" Indonesia's relations with Peking, which became a matter of some urgency after Communist China was admitted to the United Nations in October.

Indonesia and the Soviet Union have been cool toward each other, but they have maintained diplomatic relations, and trade between the two countries has been increasing. When the military took control of Indonesia in 1965, several industrial projects sponsored by the Soviet Union were abandoned. Among them were a superphosphate plant in central Java and a steel mill not far from Djakarta, on which $45 million had already been spent and which were three-fourths completed. In July 1971, Indonesia and the Soviet Union signed an agreement to study the feasibility of completing the projects. A Soviet technical team arrived in Djakarta in August to conduct the study.

The United States has become the exclusive supplier of military equipment to Indonesia. It planned to give Indonesia $24.9 million in military assistance for the fiscal year beginning July 1. By comparison, Communist countries had given Indonesia more than a billion dollars of military equipment and supplies during the 1960–65 period, when Sukarno ruled.

Foreign Minister Malik served as president of the 26th General Assembly of the United Nations in 1971. Lobbying at the General Assembly in support of their campaign for independence was the representative of the South Moluccans, 30,000 of whom live in exile in the Netherlands.

Political Prisoners. Indonesia's improved political stability in 1971 encouraged the government to speed the release of the numerous persons who had been imprisoned without trial after the attempted Communist coup in 1965. Most political prisoners are held on the island of Buru in eastern Indonesia.

Amnesty International, an independent organization with headquarters in London, appealed to the Indonesian government in February for the release of 5,000 of the prisoners and the improvement of prison conditions. In August, Foreign Minister Malik announced that 22,000 would be released by the end of the year. In November, the figure was increased to 50,000, leaving some 35,000 still imprisoned.

The Economy. The Indonesian economy has been improving gradually. During the past three years, per capita annual income has increased from U.S.$70 to U.S.$90. Prices have become relatively stable and increased by only 8% during the 12 months ending in March. Abundant rice crops have reduced the need for food imports and aid.

Indonesia's oil production, steadily increasing, approached a million barrels a day in 1971. U.S. companies are the major producers. Indonesia began pumping its first offshore crude oil in September 1971, and this was considered a significant event in the Southeast Asian offshore oil boom.

In the wake of the measures taken by the United States to curb its inflation in early August and the international monetary crisis that followed, the Indonesian government devalued its currency by 10% on August 23. The rate of exchange for the rupiah went from 378 to 414 to U.S.$1. The government also reduced taxes on export items in the hopes of ameliorating its balance-of-payments problem.

There were indications in 1971 that the Indonesian government was reassessing its policy of granting favorable concessions, such as exemptions from taxes for a number of years, to foreign investors. In August, a contract was signed with two U.S. oil companies granting a larger share of profits and other benefits to Indonesia.

The Intergovernmental Group on Indonesia met in Rotterdam in December 1970 and in Amsterdam in April 1971 to consider Indonesia's credit needs for the 1971–72 financial year. Its requirements were estimated at $640 million: $270 million for project aid commitments and $370 million for program aid disbursements. Some creditor nations also made commitments to provide long-term assistance. It was agreed that the easiest possible conditions for repayment would be granted Indonesia. The Group noted that while there had been considerable progress in several areas of the Indonesian economy, the levels of resource mobilization and investment were too low in comparison with other developing countries and with Indonesia's requirements and potential.

The budget for the fiscal year 1971–72 calls for a routine expenditure of Rp 364.1 billion, and Rp 154.9 billion for development. The increase in the routine budget will be used for the promotion of public welfare and for raising the salaries of civil servants and members of the armed forces.

AMRY VANDENBOSCH
University of Kentucky

------ **INDONESIA · Information Highlights** ------

Official Name: Republic of Indonesia.
Area: 735,269 square miles (1,904,347 sq km).
Population (1971 est.): 124,250,000. *Density* (excluding West Irian), 202 per square mile (78 per sq km). *Annual rate of increase*, 2.5%.
Chief Cities (1961 census): Djakarta, the capital, 2,906,533; Surabaja, 1,007,945; Bandung, 972,566.
Government: *Head of state*, Suharto, president (took office March 27, 1968). *Head of government*, Suharto. *Legislature*—People's Consultative Congress, about 650 members; House of Representatives, 460 members. *Major political parties*—Sekber Golkar, Muslim Scholars party, Parmusi, Indonesian Nationalist party.
Languages: Bohasa Indonesia (official), Javanese, Sudanese, Madurese, other Malayo-Polynesian languages, English.
Education: *Literacy rate* (1970), 60% of population. *Expenditure on education* (1960), 0.7% of net domestic product. *School enrollment* (1968)—primary, 12,234,824; secondary, 1,580,312; vocational, 325,235; higher, 192,416.
Finances (1970–71 est.): *Revenues*, $1,177,000,000; *expenditures*, $1,177,000,000; *monetary unit*, rupiah (415 rupiahs equal U.S.$1, July 1971).
Gross National Product (1970 est.): $11,600,000,000.
National Income (1968): $9,659,000,000; *national income per person*, $86.
Economic Indexes: *Agricultural production* (1969), 118 (1963 =100); *consumer price index* (1970), 68,807 (1963=100).
Manufacturing (metric tons, 1969): Kerosene, 1,824,000; gasoline, 1,285,000; distillate fuel oils, 1,158,000.
Crops (metric tons, 1968 crop year): Rice, 16,197,000; natural rubber, 7,520,000 (ranks 2d among world producers); sweet potatoes and yams, 2,300,000 (world rank 2d); cassava, 1,180,000 (world rank 2d); coffee, 157,000.
Minerals (metric tons, 1969): Crude petroleum, 36,620,000; bauxite, 765,000; coal, 192,000; tin concentrates, 16,542.
Foreign Trade (1970): *Exports*, $810,000,000 (chief exports—crude petroleum and products, $282,500,000; rubber, $213,500,000; coffee, $64,700,000). *Imports*, $883,000,000 (chief imports, 1967—machinery and transport equipment, $176,990,000; chemicals, $84,080,000; wheat meal and flour, $16,850,000). *Chief trading partners* (1967)—Japan; United States; West Germany.
Transportation: *Roads* (1964), 6,146 miles (9,891 km); *motor vehicles* (1969), 328,300 (automobiles, 212,100); *railroads* (1967), 3,788 miles (6,100 km); *merchant fleet* (1970), 643,000 gross registered tons; *national airline*, Garuda Indonesian Airways; *principal airport*, Djakarta.
Communications: *Telephones* (1970), 182,319; *television stations* (1968), 4; *television sets* (1969), 75,000; *radios* (1968), 1,500,000; *newspapers* (1965), 85.

INDUSTRIAL PRODUCTION. See ECONOMY OF THE U.S.

INSURANCE

The insurance business in the United States continued in 1971 to grow and to adjust to developments in the social and economic environment. Proposals for change in the existing automobile insurance system gained momentum. In another development, the U. S. Supreme Court held that an uninsured motorist does not have to post security for the damages claimed against him before he is found liable for the accident. In the national health insurance discussion, the industry advanced its own "health care" plan.

PROPERTY AND LIABILITY INSURANCE

Upon completion of a two-year study of automobile insurance, the U. S. Department of Transportation recommended on March 17, 1971, that the states be called on to "begin promptly to shift to a first-party, no-fault compensation system for automobile accident victims." Reform legislation was introduced in Congress late in 1970 and in 25 or more states through 1971. On Jan. 1, 1971, Massachusetts became the first state to adopt a modified no-fault law, in which benefits of up to $2,000 are paid to the insured person by his own insurer. Beyond the $2,000 mark in losses, the liability concept is retained in the Massachusetts law.

Financial Responsibility. In a 9–0 vote, the U. S. Supreme Court held on May 24, 1971, that Georgia's financial responsibility law is unconstitutional. Georgia's Motor Vehicle Responsibility Act had provided that the vehicle registration and driver's license of an uninsured motorist be suspended unless he posts security for damages claimed. The law excluded any consideration of fault or responsibility for the accident at a pre-suspension hearing, but this was held to violate the 14th Amendment guarantee of procedural due process. The decision could affect laws in 37 states that do not require drivers to buy insurance or do not require proof of fault before cancelling licenses.

Self-Insurance. Some large New York banks are considering the creation of a self-insurance system, perhaps a pooling arrangement or even a bank-owned insurer. The self-insurance approach was made known at Federal Reserve Board hearings as the banks sought expansion of the proposed rule to allow a bank holding company to act as an insurer for holding companies and financial institutions.

Crime Insurance. Crimes against property have been rising in recent years, and insurers have been beset by heavy losses in areas prone to criminal activity and civil disorder. Recognizing the social implications of the problem, Congress passed a bill authorizing the Department of Housing and Urban Development to write crime insurance after Aug. 1, 1971, in states in which such insurance is not readily available at "affordable rates."

Breaking Even. The premium volume for property and liability insurance rose to an estimated $33 billion in 1970, a 13% increase over 1969. The property and liability companies recorded statutory underwriting results at about the break-even point. The Insurance Information Institute attributed the improved results mainly to intensive efforts by insurance management to improve operation efficiency, as well as to a slight reduction (an estimated 1.8%) in traffic deaths and injuries. The average amount of paid auto-liability insurance claims continued to rise during 1970.

Catastrophes. There were 21 catastrophes—events involving insured damage of more than $1 million each—in 1970. The most costly was Hurricane Celia, which caused $310 million damage along the Texas Gulf Coast.

LIFE INSURANCE

The average insured U. S. family had $24,600 worth of life insurance at the start of 1971. This amounted to only slightly more than two years of that family's disposable personal income.

Purchases and Payments. New life insurance purchases amounted to $194 billion in 1970. Of this sum, $130 billion represented individually purchased ordinary and industrial life insurance; new purchases of group life insurance totaled $64 billion. During 1970, life insurance companies paid more than $16 billion in benefits to policyholders and in death payments to beneficiaries.

Investments. Assets of the 1,800 legal reserve life insurance companies totaled $207 billion in 1970. Corporate securities accounted for 42.7% and mortgages for 35.9% of these investment holdings. In a time when lenders were charging high interest rates, loans to policyholders reached 7.8% of assets of insurance companies. The net pretax earning rate on life insurance company investments in 1970 was 5.3%, the highest in 50 years.

Urban Program. Life insurance companies committed $333 million more to the industry's Urban Investment Program in 1970. This brought the total commitment to almost $1.6 billion. Started in 1967 with a pledge of $1 billion in loans, the program seeks to improve housing, create jobs, and promote services in the core areas of cities.

Stock vs. Mutual Companies. A study of long-range changes shows a substantial shift in the relationship of stock and mutual life insurance companies, in terms of assets and life insurance in force. Between 1942 and 1969, a study shows, the number of mutual companies increased by 61 to reach 155 companies, while stock companies increased by 1,292 to a total of 1,633. In 1942, U. S. mutual companies had about 80% of life insurance assets, while in 1969 their share measured 68%. Meanwhile, stock companies grew in the amount of life insurance in force, from just over 25% in 1942 to more than 50% in 1969.

HEALTH INSURANCE

Life insurance companies provide a substantial proportion of the nation's health insurance, both on a group basis and to individual purchasers, and consequently they were deeply involved as national health care proposals came into the spotlight in 1970 and 1971. The private health-insuring companies' proposal, known as "health care," called for a series of steps in which public and private efforts would be joined to make use of what it called the best elements to both sectors.

A record 181 million persons had health insurance through private organizations in the United States at the start of 1971. Private health insurance policyholders received $17 billion in benefit payments in 1970. The coverage was provided by insurance companies, Blue Cross-Blue Shield organizations and plans approved by medical societies, and independent plans.

(See also SOCIAL WELFARE—*Health Care*.)

KENNETH BLACK, JR.
Georgia State University

Open-space planning characterizes the new offices of McDonald Corporation in Chicago. Movable partitions and dividers give flexibility to office plan.

Interior Design

Although traditional concepts of architectural design still appealed to some, a contemporary concept, the open-space plan, gained increasing popularity in the early 1970's. By dispensing with walls as rigid space dividers, contemporary designers of homes, offices, or schools made striking design statements that exploited to the full sunlight, trees, and view and efficiently accommodated the needs of the building's occupants.

Residences. In town houses and country houses, in high-rise city apartments and retirement condominiums, contemporary designers were tearing down walls to create large open areas—interior environments. Space was no longer divided into rooms but into activity centers for such purposes as conversation, eating, music, or study. Areas were separated from one another by visual rather than physical barriers—by plants or furniture groupings.

One of the most distinguished New York City apartments was created by the architect Paul Rudolph for the Gardner Cowleses. Small rooms, even though well proportioned, could not adequately dis-

play the enormous contemporary American paintings that the Cowleses collect. Consequently, Rudolph tore down walls and inserted wide corridors, each of which provided a vista focusing on a particularly striking canvas. Open areas were variously arranged for conversing or dining.

In Ohio, I. W. Colburn & Associates designed for the Jesse Philipses a house with two-story-high, angulated glass "gables" to frame a beautiful view of rolling lawns and dense woods. To suit the owner's preference for an impressive, serene atmosphere, the firm allowed a flexible, open-space plan with high ceilings for the public areas of the house. In Palm Beach, Fla., designer Jay Spector opened up the entire front section of a three-room apartment facing the sea. The exterior space, rimmed with a balcony, flowed into and enlarged the undivided interior space, making a single area for indoor and outdoor living.

For his own country house on Fire Island, N. Y., architect Earl Burns Combs built a structure with a cross-shaped floor plan and a center section two stories high. From this huge, airy central court on the main floor flowed areas for dining, cooking, and study. The only space dividers were four large columns supporting second-floor sleeping balconies, which also opened on the central court.

Offices. The concept of open-space planning is pervasive in modern office design. It provides a flexibility in the arrangement of work stations and a possibility of instant change that have proved more economical on expensive land than the traditional fixed division of office space into individual offices or cubicles. The concept of open-space planning for offices (*Bürolandschaft,* or "office landscape") was developed in Germany in the early 1960's. In the United States it was applied in a more free-wheeling manner that could be tailored to fit the client's requirements. Large American design firms creating the "open office-landscape" included Interior Space Design; Trapnell Associates; Luss, Kaplan; and Saphier, Lerner, Schindler.

Open office-landscapes require new kinds of furniture, which can be moved and variously combined. For example, fixed walls have become movable dividers—screens; free-standing, high-rise storage units or shells for office machines; two-sided bulletin boards; or even plants. To the storage units or shells may be attached table desks or other work surfaces, shelves, drawers, files, and doors. Small secretarial storage units and those for computer retrieval are on wheels.

Systems of office furniture successfully adapted to the open office-landscape have been designed by many firms, for example, "Action Office 11" by Herman Miller and "Open Privacy 5" by Jens Risom. Knoll International made the Stephens landscape system (originally designed by William Stephens for

AIRY, two-story central court anchors square house built for architect Earl Burns Combs. Sleeping balconies on second floor look out over the central court.

the Weyerhaeuser building in Tacoma, Wash.) and the Christen landscape system by Andreas Christen. The "Reveal" system, designed by John Nance for the J. G. Furniture Company, encases all power lines to prevent the "black spaghetti" effect on the floor. There are also the metal "Airea" system by All Steel and a Canadian-made oak "Solve" system imported into the United States by Lehigh-Leopold.

William Pulgram designed "Task Force Response Modules" specifically for the offices of the McDonald Corporation in Chicago. Pulgram's designs are probably the most spectacular of all those recently completed on the open office-landscape plan. The upright dividers between work stations—the backs of storage units, bulletin boards, and free-standing, mobile screens—are padded and handsomely upholstered in heavy, textured fabric of neutral color to match the rug. The monochrome fabrics, spread over a large area, greatly reduce sound and give an overall effect of serenity and dignity. For executives who demand even more quiet and isolation from time to time, Pulgram designed a centrally located, circular "meditation room" consisting of a water bed surrounded by ceiling-high, padded and upholstered screens and furnished, if desired, with audio-visual equipment.

Schools. The tumbling down of interior walls in recently built schools represented a new attitude not just toward school facilities but also toward school programs. New educational environments were springing up throughout the country. For example, in New Rochelle, N. Y., one of a chain of Multi-Media learning centers (operated by Multi-Media Education, Inc.) opened on a shopping mall. The children of shopping mothers "play" in a large open room edged with 24 carrels. The carrels are equipped with plug-in technical devices designed by Donald Gillespie of Boston to teach a variety of verbal and numerical concepts.

The New Canaan, Conn., Country School might be described as an open-space plan, child's play village. No walls delineate the various activity areas. The only privacy is that of a storage cubicle for each child in which he can keep his well-loved stones or dead frogs. Pre-packaged "discovery centers," designed by Gertman & Meyers for Universal Education Corp., are actually learning environments. They include a learning room with movable surrounding walls instead of doors, mechanical and electronic equipment, and learning spaces.

Romaldo Giurgola of Mitchell, Giurgola, who is also chairman of the department of architecture at Columbia, has recently built two schools on the open-space plan. The first, the United Nations International School in New York, was built within a city loft. Industrial carpeting, white perimeter walls, and suspended industrial fluorescent lights were fixed in place, but little else was. Books, TV screens, maps, and chalkboards were set in open space. Such an arrangement suited the pupils, who seldom progressed through the day in the same groups but worked individually on programs planned for and by each child.

Giurgola's second school, however, the Penn School in Philadelphia, provides for groups of similar orientation, such as science. The school is organized into five major activity areas, including two for classes. The class areas are flexible enough to accommodate groups of 50 to 500.

JEANNE G. WEEKS
"Interiors" Magazine

international finance

President Nixon, flanked by international monetary experts, announces historic decision to devalue the dollar on December 18. Agreement was made at Group of Ten meeting in Washington, D. C.

WIDE WORLD

Following the deceptive calm of 1970, international finance in the first half of 1971 saw a revival of the crisis conditions characteristic of most of the previous dozen years. The ultimate crisis broke on August 15 when President Nixon suspended the U. S. policy of converting into gold at $35 an ounce all dollars presented to the U. S. Treasury by foreign governments. This action cut loose the international exchange-rate system from the peg to which it had been attached for 37 years.

On December 18 the Group of Ten, the leading Western industrial countries, reached an agreement establishing a new pattern of exchange rates. The U. S. contribution to the package was to raise the official price of gold to $38 an ounce. The United States did not promise to resume the conversion of dollars held by foreign governments into gold.

At the end of 1971 the future outlines of the international monetary system were uncertain, but it appeared unlikely that the world could successfully choose to return to the old system.

PRELUDE TO THE AUGUST CRISIS

Most of the major countries were fighting persistent inflation as 1971 began. Many of them experienced some success, but in many cases success was accompanied by rising unemployment.

Britain. Britain's balance of payments continued to improve. Although many of the international debts incurred in the middle 1960's in defense of the pound were paid off, British reserves at the end of October 1971 stood at $5.2 billion—the highest level since the end of World War II and an increase of $2.5 billion over 1970. Nevertheless, unemployment was running at a record level of more than 3%, and prices were rising at almost 10% a year.

France. The balance of payments of France also continued to improve in 1971. This progress was achieved while keeping the domestic economy under control through a tight monetary policy that generated a record level of unemployment by the end of September.

Canada. The inflow of foreign funds that led Canada in 1970 to abandon its previous par value of 92.5 U. S. cents per Canadian dollar continued in 1971. Despite the appreciation of the Canadian dollar to almost equal value with the U. S. dollar, Canada ran a balance-of-payments surplus of more than $1 billion in the first half of 1971. At the same time unemployment hovered around 7%, and action was taken to stimulate the domestic economy.

West Germany. Faced with accelerating domestic inflation, the Germans followed a relatively tight monetary policy early in 1971. This was necessitated by the nature of the country's federal system, which makes fiscal policy a relatively ineffective policy instrument. Reflecting the somewhat easier monetary policies in the rest of Europe and especially in the United States, West Germany experienced a $3.1 billion increase in its international reserves in the first four months of 1971. Part of this increase in reserves resulted from the activity of the Eurodollar system, which returned dollars to German reserves after they had been first deposited by the German central bank with the Bank of International Settlements (BIS). When this process of reserve credit creation was discovered, the Bundesbank stopped making deposits with the BIS.

May Exchange-Rate Changes. During the last days of April and the first days of May, dollars flowed into West Germany sometimes at a rate of more than $1 billion a day. Confronted by these huge speculative capital inflows, the German central bank on May 5 suspended its support of the dollar and closed the country's foreign-exchange markets. The central banks of Austria, Belgium, the Netherlands, and Switzerland almost immediately took similar action.

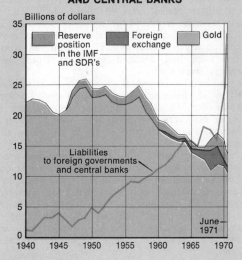

U.S. MONETARY RESERVES AND LIABILITIES TO FOREIGN GOVERNMENTS AND CENTRAL BANKS

Billions of dollars

Reserve position in the IMF and SDR's — Foreign exchange — Gold

Liabilities to foreign governments and central banks

June—1971

PAR VALUES OF CURRENCIES OF MEMBER COUNTRIES OF THE INTERNATIONAL MONETARY FUND

Member	Currency unit	U. S. cents per unit Dec. 20, 1971	Member	Currency unit	U. S. cents per unit Dec. 20, 1971
Australia	Dollar	121.6	Libyan Arab Republic	Dinar	304.
Austria	Schilling	4.2918	Luxembourg	Franc	2.2313
Barbados	E. Caribbean Dollar	54.2	Malawi	Kwacha	130.286
Belgium	Franc	2.2313	Malaysia	Dollar	35.4666
Botswana	S. African Rand	133.3333	Malta	Pound	267.086
Burma	Kyat	18.6961	Mexico	Peso	8.
Canada	Dollar	99.95	Morocco	Dirham	21.4547
Cyprus	Pound	260.571	Netherlands	Guilder	30.8195
Denmark	Krone	14.3266	New Zealand	Dollar	121.6
Dominican Republic	Peso	100.	Nicaragua	Cordoba	14.2857
Ethiopia	Dollar	43.4285	Nigeria	Pound	304.
Finland	Markka	31.0318	Norway	Krone	15.048
France	Franc	19.5477	Panama	Balboa	100.
Gambia	Dalasi	48.	Portugal	Escudo	3.6697
Germany, West	Deutsche Mark	31.0318	Rwanda	Franc	1.0857
Ghana	New Cedi	55.	Saudi Arabia	Riyal	24.1269
Greece	Drachma	3.3333	Sierra Leone	Leone	130.286
Guyana	Dollar	50.	Singapore	Dollar	35.4666
Haiti	Gourde	20.	Somalia	Shilling	15.2
Honduras	Lempira	50.	South Africa	Rand	133.3333
Iceland	Króna	1.1363	Spain	Peseta	1.5510
India	Rupee	13.7376	Swaziland	S. African Rand	133.3333
Iraq	Dinar	304.	Sweden	Krona	270.7775
Ireland	Pound	260.571	Tanzania	Shilling	14.
Israel	Pound	23.8095	Tunisia	Dinar	206.803
Italy	Lira	.1720	Turkey	Lira	7.1429
Jamaica	Dollar	130.286	Uganda	Shilling	14.
Japan	Yen	.3247	United Kingdom	Pound	260.571
Jordan	Dinar	280.	United States	Dollar	100.
Kenya	Shilling	14.	Yugoslavia	Dinar	5.8823
Kuwait	Dinar	304.	Zaïre	Zaïre	200.
Lesotho	S. African Rand	133.3333	Zambia	Kwacha	140.

Countries for which a par value has not been established with the IMF: Algeria, Cameroon, Central African Republic, Chad, People's Republic of the Congo, Dahomey, Equatorial Guinea, Fiji, Gabon, Guinea, Indonesia, Ivory Coast, Khmer Republic (formerly Cambodia), Korea, Laos, Malagasy Republic, Mali, Mauritania, Mauritius, Niger, Senegal, Togo, Upper Volta, Vietnam, Yemen Arab Republic; Yemen, People's Democratic Republic of (formerly Southern Yemen).

The exchange markets remained closed until May 10. When they reopened the Austrian schilling was revalued by 4.9%, and the Swiss franc was revalued by 7%. The German mark and the Dutch guilder were allowed to float, with their value determined by market forces under guidance of monetary authorities. Belgium did not alter its official par value, but it expanded the list of transactions that had to be cleared on the free market for its franc.

United States. In the second quarter of 1971 the United States ran a deficit on its trade account at a seasonally adjusted annual rate of $4.2 billion, while the deficit in the balance of payments on the official reserve transactions basis was at an annual rate of $22.8 billion. With the unfavorable balance of trade persisting, the United States was threatened with its first annual trade deficit since 1893.

The huge deficit in the overall balance of payments reflected primarily capital outflows associated with higher interest rates in Europe. U. S. interest rates were lower due to the continued slowdown in U. S. economic activity and the switch to a more expansionary monetary policy. By midyear, European rates had declined somewhat from their January level.

In the first six months of 1971, U. S. reserves fell by $2 billion and the U. S. gold stock declined to just over $10 billion. Many governments and informed observers believed that the U. S. government would not allow its gold supply to dip below this figure.

The deterioration in the U. S. international financial position took place in the face of continuing domestic economic stagnation and rising unemployment. Democratic politicians called on President Nixon to do something about the domestic economy, to restore the strength of the U. S. dollar, and to prevent the flooding of the U. S. market with imports at a time of rising unemployment in the United States.

U. S. ACTIONS IN AUGUST

The actions announced by President Nixon on August 15 promised to exert a strong influence on the U. S. international financial position.

(1) The President suspended the automatic conversion into gold of dollars accumulated by foreign governments. His objective was to signal to the major countries that they should permit the dollar price of their currencies to increase.

(2) To encourage major countries to respond to this signal, a temporary 10% surcharge was imposed on all dutiable imports. The surcharge applied to about 60% ($25 billion) of U. S. imports.

(3) The President called for countries to take other actions to assist the U. S. balance-of-payments position. For example, they could assume more of the financial burden of mutual defense.

(4) He proposed a "job-development" tax credit for investment. This device was similar to the investment tax credit used by the United States off and on during the 1960's except that imported investment goods were not eligible.

(5) In an effort to reduce domestic inflation, Nixon declared a 90-day wage-and-price freeze, to be followed by a less-drastic "Phase II." If successful, this would further improve the competitive position of U. S. goods in world markets.

The initial stated objective of the Nixon initiatives was a $13 billion turnaround in the U. S. balance of payments on current account. The aim was to convert the $5 billion deficit (figured at an annual rate on a full-employment basis) into an $8 billion surplus: $6 billion to finance public and private long-term capital outflows and $2 billion as a safety margin. It was argued that achieving this goal would require a 16% depreciation of the dollar versus foreign currencies, weighting each country's exchange rate change by its importance in U. S. trade.

(Continued on page 357)

Why and How The Dollar Was Devalued

"Then it's agreed. Until the dollar firms up, we let the clamshell float."

DRAWING BY ED FISHER:
© 1971 THE NEW YORKER MAGAZINE, INC.

In President Nixon's address to the nation announcing his New Economic Policy on Aug. 15, 1971, he said he wanted to "set to rest the bugaboo of what is called devaluation." What does it mean to devalue the dollar? Why did it take place? How was it accomplished? How will it change the international monetary system?

In simplest terms a devaluation or depreciation of the dollar means lowering the price of the dollar in terms of foreign currency. Put the other way around, a devaluation raises the dollar price of foreign currency.

A currency is normally devalued by the same percentage amount with respect to all currencies, by changing its gold value. In the U. S. case it was recognized that the value of the dollar in terms of the stronger currencies, such as the German mark and the Japanese yen, should decline by more than its value in terms of the historically weaker currencies, such as the British pound sterling. The stated initial objective of the Nixon administration's policy was to achieve on average a 16% devaluation of the dollar.

U. S. Policy Choices. There are three balance-of-payments adjustment policies that are alternatives to devaluation. (1) A country can finance its deficit by running down its reserves as long as it has sufficient reserves or, in the case of a reserve currency such as the U. S. dollar, as long as other countries are willing to accumulate dollars. (2) It can use monetary or fiscal policy to curtail aggregate demand in order to reduce imports and restrain the rate of domestic price increase. (3) It can impose controls or restrictions on trade and international capital transactions.

The United States employed all of these policy instruments during the 1960's. Nevertheless, U. S. reserves on June 30, 1971, stood at $13.5 billion, a $5.25 billion decrease since the end of 1961. U. S. dollar liabilities to foreign official holders increased over the period by $21.35 billion to $34.32 billion. Between 1961 and 1970, U. S. imports of goods and services increased by 156%, while exports increased by only 118%. Thus, the United States declared that its objective in seeking a devaluation of the dollar was to achieve a $13 billion turnaround of its current account balance from a deficit of $5 billion to a surplus of $8 billion.

Impact. When a country devalues its currency, the major balance-of-payments impact of the devaluation is on the trade account. The domestic prices of imports rise, and this causes a reduction in imports. At the same time the foreign-currency prices of exports fall, producing an increase in the foreign demand for the exports.

The *unfavorable* rise in the domestic price of imports as a result of a devaluation is one of the reasons why governments are reluctant to devalue their currencies. When there is not full employment in the country, a devaluation can have a *favorable* impact on the gross national product as demand is shifted from foreign to domestic goods.

Both the price and income effects of a devaluation will be small, however, when the foreign sector is a small part of the economy. The impact of a devaluation on the United States, where imports are less than 6% of GNP, will be smaller than would an equal devaluation in Britain, where imports are more than 20% of GNP. Thus, President Nixon was right when he argued that devaluing the dollar would have only a small impact on the United States, but the adjustment forced on smaller foreign economies may be large.

Technical Steps. Because of its special role in the international exchange-rate system, the U. S. dollar was technically difficult to devalue. Before August 15, countries declared par values for their currencies in terms of the U. S. dollar and, under the International Monetary Fund (IMF) agreement, agreed to maintain the value of their currencies within 1% of par by intervening, usually with dollars, in their national foreign-exchange markets.

Under this system the U. S. authorities played a passive role except that in theory the United States stood ready for 37 years to buy and sell gold at $35 an ounce in transactions with foreign central bankers. Thus, the dollar's link to gold provided the link for every national currency through the dollar to gold. In practice, in the 1960's the U. S. discouraged purchases of its gold.

When President Nixon announced on August 15 the suspension of the automatic conversion of dollars into gold for foreign monetary authorities, he set the whole exchange-rate system adrift. There was, moreover, no assurance that foreign countries would permit the dollar price of their currencies to rise—Japan tried to resist the appreciation of the yen for a week and France continued to buy and sell dollars at the old rate.

To demonstrate to foreign governments the seriousness of the United States in seeking a devaluation of the dollar, the President also announced on August 15 the imposition of a 10% import surcharge on dutiable imports. This action had the immediate effect of devaluing all dollars by 10% when used in purchasing such imports.

The problem with the continued imposition of the U. S. import surcharge was that, once most of the other trading nations indicated their willingness to let their currencies appreciate versus the dollar, the existence of the surcharge and the objective of achieving a permanent devaluation of the dollar came into conflict. As the surcharge began to bite and reduce U. S. imports, foreign countries could refuse to let their currencies appreciate further. The longer the surcharge were to stay on, the more accustomed U. S. producers would become to the protection it afforded.

In mid-December 1971, a new set of exchange rates was agreed upon by the Group of Ten, the leading Western industrial nations, and the import surcharge was removed. The United States agreed to raise the official price of gold by 8.57% to $38 an ounce. Subject to congressional approval, the United States could have taken this step on August 15, but other countries would have had to maintain the gold values of their currencies in order to accomplish an effective depreciation of the dollar. Moreover, under the December agreement half a

dozen currencies were appreciated by more than 8.57%.

Changing the System. The system for adjusting exchange rates agreed upon at the 1944 international monetary conference at Bretton Woods, N. H., was designed to ensure that countries would not return after World War II to the chaos of competitive devaluation and trade restrictions that characterized much of the history of the 1920's and 1930's. Exchange rates were to be fixed, and when they needed to be altered the changes were to be cleared with the IMF. To help countries finance short-term balance-of-payments deficits, members of the IMF were allowed to draw upon a pool of currencies contributed by other members.

The IMF, however, provided no device for the regular expansion of international reserves. Increases in the owned reserves of countries had to come from purchases of gold or the accumulation of the currencies of the reserve countries, primarily the U. S. dollar but also the British pound. Because the growth of the world gold supply was inadequate, increases in reserves came primarily from dollar accumulations reflecting U. S. deficits. The system was destined to collapse when the dollars outstanding exceeded the U. S. stock of gold and when other countries lost confidence in the dollar being "as good as gold."

Most countries agreed that there was a problem, but they could not agree on a solution. They reached a tacit agreement during the 1960's, however, to curtail conversions of dollars into gold. During this period, considerable cooperation developed among the major countries as they kept the system limping along from crisis to crisis. In 1967 an agreement was reached to create Special Drawing Rights (SDR's) to supplement countries' gold, foreign exchange, and IMF gold tranche reserves. The first $3.5 billion in SDR's was created in 1970 and $3 billion more in 1971.

Following President Nixon's move to devalue the dollar, the focus of international negotiations was on short-term questions, such as the establishment of new exchange-rate parities (accomplished on December 18) and the removal of the import surcharge (ordered by President Nixon on December 20). Most of the long-term questions were pushed aside.

In the long run the international monetary system will be one in which the monetary role of gold will be eliminated. SDR's or an equivalent manmade asset will form the basis of international reserves, and the expansion in these reserves will be governed by international agreement.

Considerably more flexibility in par value exchange-rate changes was permitted under the December 1971 agreement reached by the Group of Ten. Currencies were to be allowed to fluctuate by 2¼% on either side of their par values. The automatic adjustment thus could amount to as much as 4½%. But the agreement did not allow for the needed greater flexibility in the central exchange rates.

Although the crisis that broke over the international monetary system after Aug. 15, 1971, was not inevitable, the system was headed for collapse. It appeared probable that a crisis would be necessary to bring on a drastic change in the system, although it was not certain that the crisis would produce sensible long-run reform.

EDWIN M. TRUMAN

(Continued from page 354)

AFTERMATH OF THE CRISIS

Following President Nixon's address, the major stock and foreign-exchange markets in western Europe remained closed for a week. When exchange markets reopened on August 23, the governments of most of the major U. S. trading partners permitted their currencies' values to appreciate vis-à-vis the dollar.

Resistance. Japan resisted the pressure for appreciation until August 28, and France established a dual market for the franc. "Commercial francs" used in trade transactions were exchanged at the old parity of 18 U. S. cents per franc, and all other transactions were directed toward the free market.

The reluctance of the French to allow the franc to float created strains within the European Community. The establishment of a common EEC response to the U. S. actions was complicated by the prospect that the Common Market would be enlarged in 1973 through the membership of Denmark, Ireland, Norway, and Britain—Britain having approved in principle entry into the EEC on October 28. Some countries wanted the currencies of the bloc to float together, but the coordination of national macro-economic policies and objectives that would be required for a successful joint float had not yet been developed.

U. S. Difficulties. The third quarter balance-of-payments figures for the United States, including the six weeks before the Nixon announcements, showed a deficit on the official settlements basis of more than $12 billion—more than double the level in the previous quarter. For the first nine months of the year the deficit was estimated at $24 billion.

By November, the average depreciation of the dollar from its May value was about 5%, considerably short of the Nixon administration's 16% goal. This reflected, in part, a concern with how the cross-rates were evolving. For example, if the German mark appreciated by 10% versus the dollar and the French franc did not appreciate at all, the mark would appreciate by 10% versus both currencies.

International discussion after August 15 focused on the removal of the U. S. import surcharge and the reestablishment of stable exchange rates. There was concern that if the U. S. surcharge were left in force too long it would become permanent and invite foreign retaliation.

The way was paved toward a partial resolution of the monetary crisis when President Nixon met with President Pompidou of France in mid-December, and finally agreed to the demand for a modest devaluation of the dollar in terms of gold.

The Group of Ten met on December 17–18 in the Smithsonian Institution in Washington, D. C. The United States agreed, subject to approval by Congress, to raise the official price of gold by 8.57% to $38 an ounce. France and Britain agreed to maintain the gold parities of their currencies, allowing an 8.57% appreciation versus the dollar. The new central rates adopted by Japan, West Germany, Switzerland, Belgium, and the Netherlands involved larger appreciations. Sweden and Italy reduced slightly the gold values of their currencies, producing 7.48% appreciations. The Canadian dollar continued to float.

HOW THE CURRENCIES OF THE UNITED STATES' MAJOR TRADING PARTNERS WERE REVALUED

Currency	Old par (May 1, 1971)	New par (Dec. 20, 1971)	% of increase in value
Japan (yen)	0.2777¢	0.3247¢	16.88
West Germany (mark)	27.32	31.03	13.57
Britain (pound)	240.0	260.57	8.57
France (franc)	18.0	19.55	8.57
Canada (dollar)	92.5	99.95[1]	8.05
Italy (lira)	0.16	0.1720	7.48

[1] Free rate

The weighted average depreciation of the dollar from its May value achieved with respect to these 10 currencies was about 11%. This was expected to produce an eventual $9 billion improvement in the U. S. balance of payments. The Smithsonian agreement, which was later approved by the International Monetary Fund, also provided for the widening—from 1% to 2¼% of par values—of the band within which exchange rates were permitted to fluctuate without requiring government intervention.

On December 20, President Nixon lifted the import surcharge and the discriminatory provisions of the investment tax credit. But the United States did not drop its demand for further trade and defense burden-sharing concessions by other countries.

The December agreements, while removing some of the short-term features of the August crisis, did not deal with the underlying issues which precipitated it. Since the gold inconvertibility of the U. S. dollar was continued, the world was still on a dollar standard. The reform of the international monetary system remained on the agenda.

EDWIN M. TRUMAN
Yale University

INTERNATIONAL LAW. See LAW.

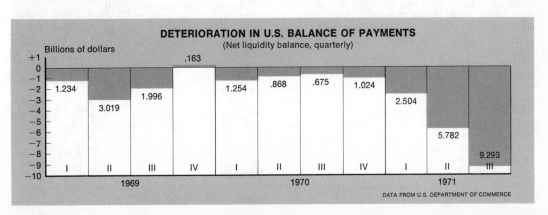

DETERIORATION IN U.S. BALANCE OF PAYMENTS
(Net liquidity balance, quarterly)

Billions of dollars

1969: I 1.234, II 3.019, III 1.996, IV .163
1970: I 1.254, II .868, III .675, IV 1.024
1971: I 2.504, II 5.782, III 9.293

DATA FROM U.S. DEPARTMENT OF COMMERCE

THE NEW YORK TIMES

Toyotas, destined for U. S. market, jam waterfront in Nagoya, Japan. Imported cars continued to sell well in 1971, despite new compact lines offered by U. S. manufacturers.

international trade

The trade of the non-Communist world moderated in 1971 from the boom conditions of the preceding two years as the major developed countries experienced economic setbacks. Repercussions were felt in most of the developing countries.

U. S. exports slowed abruptly while imports surged, throwing the nation's trade into deficit for the first time in the century and helping to bring about a serious deterioration in the balance of payments. That growing deficit and the international monetary crisis of the spring and summer were factors leading to President Nixon's announcement of a new economic policy that, among other purposes, was designed to help improve the U. S. position in world trade.

Developments for the year are discussed in sections titled (1) Trade Trends and (2) Tariffs and Trade Restrictions.

TRADE TRENDS

The foreign trade of the non-Communist world passed the $300 billion mark at an annual rate in the second quarter and was expected to total about $310 billion for the full year 1971. The exceptional expansion seen in 1969 and 1970 had slowed somewhat, however, as the economies of major trading countries were plagued by rising prices and wages, greater unemployment, and leveling or declining production.

There were contrary price movements in key foods and raw materials in 1971. Reflecting the slowing in demand and excess production, coffee, cacao, rubber, wool, and copper prices were substantially lower, limiting the ability of certain countries dependent on these products to finance needed foreign purchases. Prices strengthened for cotton, burlaps, hides, and tea, and for petroleum where sharp monetary gains to producing areas followed new negotiations with the international oil companies. The trend in prices for manufactured products continued strongly upward, too.

Unusual monetary developments during the year —the floating of the deutsche mark in May, the suspension of the U. S. commitment to exchange dollars for gold, and the subsequent revaluation or floating of nearly all the world's major currencies— were expected to have long-range effects on world trade. These developments were too recent, however, for shifts in trading patterns to be discernible in 1971.

United States. The foreign trade of the United States took a dramatic turn for the worse in 1971. As imports exceeded exports for the first time since 1893, trade was in deficit in the first nine months by $894 million expressed as an annual rate. This compared with a surplus of $2.7 billion in 1970.

U. S. exports, at $45.2 billion, rose by only 6% through September as economic activity abroad slowed, adversely affecting demand for American products. In contrast, the pickup in the U. S. economy, as well as actual and threatened strikes that encouraged extensive accumulation of inventories, caused imports to grow to $46.1 billion at an annual rate, 15% over their 1970 level.

The movement of trade in the year was strongly influenced by a series of dock strikes at most U. S. ports. Exports and imports were held up for months on the West Coast, where ports were immobilized from July 1 to October 6. At Gulf and East Coast ports, the possibility of a strike was known well in advance so that imports, and particularly exports, were accelerated before most ports closed at the end of September.

U. S. Exports. The export rise in 1971 was concentrated almost entirely in transport equipment and agricultural products. Aircraft sales, both military and civilian, were especially buoyant. Deliveries of wide-body jets, primarily to western European airlines, were large for the second year in a row. Automotive deliveries to Canada were 25% higher than in the preceding year, as exports surged following the 67-day strike against General Motors in late 1970. Demand improved for American-type cars, strengthening the movement of parts to plants in Canada where they are incorporated into cars for delivery to the United States.

Farm products moved from the country at a record annual rate of $8.2 billion. Export gains were widespread, led by cotton, soybeans, tobacco, wheat, and oils.

U. S. Imports. The strong $4.8 billion import rise in the first nine months was paced by consumer goods, particularly automobiles. Cars brought into the United States from Europe and Japan were 49% greater in value than in 1970. Despite booming sales of their small U. S. competitors, these cars captured almost 17% of the U. S. market through September. Arrivals of U. S.-type cars from subsidiaries in Canada also were up strongly. Several other types of foreign consumer goods arrived in greater quantities than ever before, notably footwear, clothing, motorcycles, and TV sets.

Also rising sharply in value were imports of industrial supplies, induced by recovery in the economy and by the possibility of a strike in the steel industry when labor contracts expired. Although no strike was called, a $700 million increase was recorded in imports of steel.

U. S. Balance of Payments. The balance of international payments showed a drastic deterioration in the first nine months of 1971 as compared with the same period in the previous year. On the net liquidity basis, which is a broad indicator of potential pressures on the dollar resulting from changes in the U. S. liquidity position, the deficit increased to $17.5 billion from $3.8 billion in the full year 1970. The balance on the official reserve transactions basis showed a deficit of $23.4 billion, considerably more than double that in the preceding year. The official balance indicates the current exchange market pressures on the dollar.

Principal factors contributing to the increased deficit were an adverse shift in the merchandise trade balance, a sharp deterioration in the outflow of liquid private capital, and enormous unrecorded outflows associated with speculative activity in foreign exchange markets in the spring and summer.

Export-Import Bank. Once again the Eximbank's business grew strongly in the fiscal year ended June 30, 1971. The Export Expansion Financing Act of 1971 was passed, granting the bank wider use of credit to expand export financing and removing its transactions from the unified federal budget. The latter action allows the bank to extend support to medium-term exports and to begin financing short-term export loans.

U. S. exports supported by Eximbank authorizations in fiscal 1971 rose by 26% to $6.9 billion. Loan authorizations were only slightly above those in the preceding year, but guarantee and insurance authorizations advanced 73%. Of the long-term loans authorized, $1.5 billion was for purchases of U. S. capital equipment and related services by purchasers in 64 countries, while a quarter billion dollars financed defense supplies and services. Policies authorized under the insurance program rose by more than 40% to $1.6 billion.

It is estimated that the bank's contribution to the credit side of the balance of payments totaled more than $3.3 billion from inflows on credits extended to foreigners, sales of loans and notes in the European money market, and amounts paid by foreigners to suppliers.

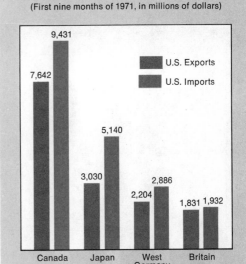

PRINCIPAL U.S. TRADING PARTNERS
(First nine months of 1971, in millions of dollars)

■ U.S. Exports
■ U.S. Imports

Canada: 7,642 / 9,431
Japan: 3,030 / 5,140
West Germany: 2,204 / 2,886
Britain: 1,831 / 1,932

U. S. TRADING PARTNERS, 1970–1971
(Millions of dollars)

Country	Exports and reexports		General imports	
	1970	Jan.-Sept. 1971	1970	Jan.-Sept. 1971
Total.............	$43,226	$33,894	$39,963	$34,353
Argentina............	442	317	172	135
Australia............	985	754	611	466
Belgium-Luxembourg..	1,195	841	696	684
Brazil..............	841	769	669	640
Canada..............	9,084	7,642	11,091	9,431
Chile...............	300	179	154	87
Colombia............	395	300	269	197
France..............	1,484	1,093	942	875
Germany, West.......	2,740	2,204	3,130	2,866
Hong Kong...........	406	329	945	723
India[1].............	573	514	298	260
Italy...............	1,353	1,016	1,316	1,103
Japan..............	4,652	3,030	5,875	5,140
Korea, South........	637	523	370	344
Mexico.............	1,704	1,204	1,222	941
Netherlands.........	1,651	1,361	528	408
Netherlands Antilles...	126	92	416	287
Philippines.........	373	267	476	353
South Africa........	563	464	288	216
Spain..............	712	506	353	355
Switzerland.........	700	512	459	367
Taiwan.............	527	398	549	588
United Kingdom......	2,537	1,831	2,196	1,932
Venezuela..........	759	635	1,082	926
Other countries and undisclosed special category shipments......	8,487	7,113	5,856	5,029

[1] Exports exclude special category shipments for which information is withheld for security reasons. Source: U.S. Department of Commerce.

Canada. Following a year of exceptional growth, Canada saw its exports moderate considerably in the first nine months of 1971. They totaled $13.1 billion (Canadian), or 4.5% above the same period of 1970. Two thirds of the net $600 million increase in sales stemmed from automotive products, most of which moved to the United States from Canadian subsidiaries of U. S. firms.

Wheat shipments increased as large deliveries were made to the People's Republic of China and as exports began under a huge new sale to the USSR. Crude petroleum and lumber deliveries, spurred by signs of recovery in the U. S. economy, advanced by about $100 million each in the January–September period. Canadian products feeling the pinch of re-

U.S. EXPORTS AND IMPORTS: TRADING AT A DEFICIT
(Data seasonally adjusted)

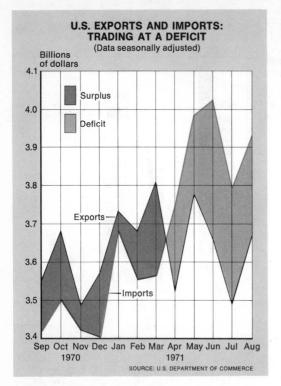

Billions of dollars

- ■ Surplus
- ▨ Deficit

Exports

Imports

Sep Oct Nov Dec Jan Feb Mar Apr May Jun Jul Aug
1970   1971

SOURCE: U.S. DEPARTMENT OF COMMERCE

duced foreign demand were copper, aluminum, iron ore, newsprint, and aircraft.

After a marginal drop in 1970 when Canadian growth was quite slack, imports rose by nearly 7% in the first nine months of 1971. A sizable share of the increase was automotive parts to be incorporated in U. S. compact cars made in Canada for sale in the United States. There were also advances in imports of petroleum, coal, and steel. Aircraft purchases, in contrast, declined by more than $100 million in those months. Arrivals from the United States were almost $400 million greater, and Britain and Japan also provided much larger volumes of goods.

The $220 million surplus on current account of the balance of international payments in the first six months was slightly higher than in the same period of the preceding year. It was, however, far less than the $936 million surplus in the immediately preceding half year. Although the trade balance was unchanged from 1970, the usual deficit on non-merchandise transactions was somewhat lower in 1971. The net movement of capital shifted from an inflow of almost $1 billion in January–June 1970 to a net outflow of $165 million in the same half of 1971. Long-term inflows were cut in half; short-term capital movements turned around from an inflow of $375 million to an outflow of the same amount.

Western Europe. The trade of western Europe, which accounts for about half of the total for the non-Communist world, continued to expand in 1971, and West Germany as usual provided the greatest gains. The first-half total of $75 billion was 11% above the value in the same period of 1970, a somewhat slower rate of increase than in 1969-70. Inflationary tendencies persisted, however, and it was likely that as much as half of that rise was due to price increases. With the general disappearance of excess demand in Europe and with production

running level for many months, imports would normally have slowed considerably. But they appeared to be increasing about as fast as exports.

British trade showed a surplus in the first half of £24 million, with both exports and imports 6% higher than in the final half of 1970. Only about one third of the rise in exports resulted from a larger volume of goods sold; the other two thirds stemmed from advances in price. Import price increases, in contrast, accounted for only one third of the rise in the value of foreign purchases.

After a decade of on-and-off negotiations, agreement was reached on June 23 on terms for Britain's entry into the European Community (Common Market) on Jan. 1, 1973. In late October the British Parliament voted overwhelmingly to join that group. At the same time, Denmark, Norway, and Ireland are also to become full members.

Britain subsequently announced that it would withdraw from the European Free Trade Association on Dec. 31, 1972. EFTA had originally been established as a temporary organization to bridge the gap until entry into the European Community was arranged. After accession was settled for the four applicants, the community made an agreement in principle for the formation of a widened industrial free trade area that would include 16 European countries—the new 10-member European Community, Europe's four neutrals (Sweden, Switzerland, Austria, and Finland), and Portugal and Iceland.

The deutsche mark float in May, which had resulted by November in an appreciation of the German currency of about 10% in relation to the U. S. dollar, apparently had little effect through the summer on Germany's trade. Despite rising prices—in the early part of the year because of rapid wage increases and later because of appreciation of the mark—German exports grew at a faster pace than in the preceding year. The long upswing in the domestic economy lost momentum in 1971, and imports, particularly from non-European Community member countries, slowed somewhat. The German trade surplus, which totaled nearly $4.5 billion in 1970, was running at an even higher rate in the first half of 1971.

The Italian economy, shaken by industrial unrest late in 1969, continued to be in trouble in 1970 and 1971. Export orders provided one of the few stabilizing influences. Foreign sales remained at a high—though not expanding—level for four quarters through March 1971, and then advanced sharply in the second quarter. Imports climbed in value, in large part as a result of higher prices for oil. Since Germany is the leading source of Italian imports, the upward float of the deutsche mark also raised the cost of imports from that country.

Through the middle of 1971, France appeared to have one of the strongest economies in Europe, although some signs of weakness were beginning to appear. Export sales were extremely buoyant at midyear as France benefited from the upward floats of the currencies of competitors. The rate of advance in imports was only half that recorded in 1970.

Latin America. A slackening pace of industrialization, economic instability, growing deficits, and some softening in the region's export earnings caused the trade of Latin American countries through the first half of 1971 to falter somewhat.

The Mexican government, alarmed by a 65% rise in its 1970 trade deficit, limited imports in

1971. Through July, the advance was held to only 1%. At the same time exports grew by just 3%, despite a large gain in sales of manufactures that account for two fifths of the total. Agricultural shipments proved to be sluggish because of poor weather and lower prices.

A boom of several years' duration continued in Brazil, making control of inflation difficult and causing rising demands for imports. Brazilian trade in the first half nevertheless proved less strong than had been expected. Imports rose 4%, while exports were held down by lower coffee receipts and barely advanced. Thus the trade surplus was reduced to $75 million from $105 million in 1970.

As Argentine trade moved into a deficit position for the first time in a decade and reserves dropped alarmingly, the government suspended all imports for six weeks in the early autumn. Argentine exports through July were lower than in 1970 because of a sharp decline in meat and wheat availabilities.

TARIFFS AND TRADE RESTRICTIONS

By far the most significant new action relating to tariffs and restrictions on trade in 1971 was the application by President Richard Nixon on August 15 of a 10% temporary surcharge on U. S. imports and his proposals for related programs to aid U. S. exports—proposals that other nations considered discriminatory. On December 20, two days after the world's exchange rates were realigned by the leading non-Communist industrial nations, Nixon removed the surcharge.

The surcharge, applied under the authority of the Trade Expansion Act of 1962, was levied on all dutiable imports not subject to quantitative limitations imposed under statute. It applied to about half of U. S. purchases from foreign countries. Excluded were nondutiable products and imports already limited by quotas.

To make U. S. exports more competitive with those of other countries, Nixon proposed that Congress pass a job-development tax credit that would give U. S. companies a credit of 10% on the cost of new machinery produced in the United States and in service before Aug. 16, 1972, and 5% thereafter. No credit would be allowed on foreign-made machinery until the import surcharge was removed. After that occurred, a 5% credit would be permitted.

The President also proposed that Congress authorize a Domestic International Sales Corporation export tax incentive, providing tax deferrals for earnings from export sales. All these programs came under strong attack from other countries in the General Agreement on Tariffs and Trade (GATT) and in direct representations to the United States.

Secretary of the Treasury John Connally stated after President Nixon's announcement that the surtax and other actions were necessary to effect a $13 billion turnaround in the U. S. international payments to reach a balance in 1972. According to official explanations, most of this shift would have to come by transforming the current trade deficit into a large surplus.

Textile Agreements. After several years of negotiation and under the threat of mandatory U. S. controls to be imposed October 15, the governments of Taiwan, South Korea, Hong Kong, and Japan signed new agreements limiting the sale of synthetic and wool textiles to the United States. They provided for a reduction in the rate of growth of exports to the United States from the first three

NON-COMMUNIST WORLD TRADE, BY REGIONS, 1970–1971

(Billions of dollars; quarterly figures expressed at annual rates[1])

Area	1970				1971	
	1st Quarter	2d Quarter	3rd Quarter	4th Quarter	1st Quarter	2d Quarter
Total exports, f.o.b.[2]	260.9	284.6	271.4	302.6	293.4	314.3
Developed areas						
U. S. and Canada.....	56.7	63.2	57.6	62.8	61.9	65.3
Western Europe.....	128.2	140.4	132.5	152.6	144.5	154.7
Japan..............	16.5	18.6	20.2	22.0	20.3	23.5
Australia, New Zealand, and South Africa.......	8.2	8.4	8.1	8.1	7.8	8.8
Developing areas						
Latin America.......	13.1	14.7	13.6	13.8	14.6	16.4
Other Western Hemisphere.......	2.2	2.4	2.4	2.3	2.3	2.4
Middle East.........	10.9	10.4	10.8	11.4	12.9	11.5
Other Asia..........	12.9	14.0	14.4	15.3	14.5	16.0
Africa..............	11.7	12.0	11.3	13.4	13.6	15.0
Other countries.....	0.5	0.5	0.5	0.9	1.0	0.7
Total imports, c.i.f.[3]	273.0	299.5	289.0	317.7	309.0	333.0
Developed areas						
U. S. and Canada.....	53.7	58.8	56.2	59.3	59.6	68.7
Western Europe.....	140.9	155.5	146.3	165.1	160.1	169.3
Japan..............	17.6	18.7	19.3	19.9	19.5	20.0
Australia, New Zealand, and South Africa.......	9.2	10.2	10.8	10.8	10.7	10.9
Developing areas						
Latin America.......	12.1	13.7	14.9	15.5	13.8	15.5
Other Western Hemisphere.......	3.5	3.7	3.7	3.8	4.5	4.8
Middle East.........	8.1	8.4	8.0	8.0	8.6	8.9
Other Asia..........	17.6	19.9	19.0	20.4	19.8	22.0
Africa..............	9.4	9.8	10.0	13.8	11.6	11.8
Other countries.....	0.9	0.8	0.8	1.1	0.8	1.1

[1] Figures do not add exactly because of rounding. [2] Free on board. [3] Cost, insurance, and freight. Source: U.S. Department of Commerce.

nations to 7.5% per year for five years (based on April 1970–March 1971), and of 5% for man-made textiles and 1% for wool textiles from Japan for three years. That rate of growth, although far below recent levels, exceeds the current rate of expansion in the domestic textile industry. It thus allows some further increase in the share of the total U. S. textile market attributable to imports.

Preferences. Following international discussions of many years, the European Community became, on July 1, 1971, the first major trading area to put into effect a plan for generalized tariff preferences for imports from developing countries. The beneficiaries were 91 countries belonging to the UN Conference on Trade and Development. Similar plans were to be implemented in 1972 by Britain and Japan.

These plans depart from the century-old principle of nondiscrimination in trade, which is embodied in the "most-favored-nation" clause of the GATT and provides that trade concessions granted one signatory must be automatically extended to all.

The community plan allows duty-free imports of all manufactured goods based on individual commodity ceilings, which would grow each year as total trade of the market expands. No one developing country would be allowed to supply more than 50% of the ceiling for most products. The plan also grants partial reductions in duties and levies, and it sets no limits on quantity for 150 processed agricultural goods. These preferential arrangements will apply to more than $1 billion of goods imported into the community in the first year.

(See also INTERNATIONAL FINANCE.)

FRANCES L. HALL
Director, International Trade Analysis Division
U. S. Department of Commerce

IOWA

Iowa harvested a record corn crop in 1971 as total production exceeded the 1 billion bushel mark for the first time. The 1.2 billion bushel total was the largest ever recorded by any state. Average per-acre yield exceeded 103 bushels. Soybean production in Iowa also appeared to have surpassed all previous records.

Elections. Municipal elections were held in every Iowa city and town in November. For the first time, a woman was elected mayor of Davenport. Mrs. Elizabeth Kirschbaum, a Democrat, assumed the post on Jan. 1, 1972. (Davenport is the only city in Iowa that conducts its municipal election on a partisan basis.) A 19-year-old college student, Jody Smith, was elected mayor of Ayrshire (population 227), and an 18-year-old was elected to the Comanche City Council. It appeared that the under-21-year-old vote was a factor in determining the elections in at least three college communities: Iowa City, Ames, and Indianola.

Government Structure. Iowa's congressional district lines were redrawn, six districts replacing seven. The loss of one seat in the U. S. House of Representatives was due to the fact that the state's population increase during the decade of the 1960's was below the national average.

The number of state judicial districts was reduced from 18 to 8, under a plan proposed by the Iowa district court judges associations. The new districts are designed to equalize case loads per judge and thus reduce the time required for disposing of both civil and criminal cases.

Two major changes in the structure of the state government were approved by the 1971 session of the 64th Iowa General Assembly. The 3-member, full-time Iowa liquor commission was replaced by a single director and a 5-member advisory board to hear appeals. The legislature also created a department of general services, which is charged with centralized purchasing.

Finance. At the end of the fiscal year 1971 the state treasury had a deficit of approximately $3.5 million, according to estimates of the state budget director, Marvin Selden. Democrats claimed that true indebtedness approached $25 million.

Several tax increases were imposed by the 1971 legislature. The largest was a 33% rise in the income tax, retroactive to Jan. 1, 1971. Corporation taxes were increased from 4% to 6% on the first $25,000 of taxable income, from 6% to 8% on $25,000 to $100,000, and from 8% to 10% on income over $100,000. These rates went into effect on July 1, 1971. The cigarette tax was boosted from 10 cents to 13 cents a pack, and the beer tax was increased by one sixth. The legislature also recommended higher prices in the state-owned liquor shops.

All tax increases were aimed at funding a new foundation plan for paying the state school aid for elementary and secondary schools. This plan seeks to assure each school district 70% of the average state cost of educating each pupil in the 1972–73 school year.

People and Jobs. Iowa's population density increased from 49.2 persons per square mile in 1960 to 50.5 in 1970; the national average increase was from 50.6 to 57.5 persons per square mile. Unemployment in Iowa during 1971 hit a 10-year high in June at 5% of the total work force, then declined. This figure was well under the national average. In September there were 1,204,700 Iowans employed and 40,000 looking for jobs.

RUSSELL M. ROSS, *University of Iowa*

IOWA • Information Highlights

Area: 56,290 square miles (145,791 sq km).
Population (1970 census): 2,825,041. *Density:* 50 per sq mi.
Chief Cities (1970 census): Des Moines, the capital, 201,404; Cedar Rapids, 110,642; Davenport, 98,469; Sioux City, 85,925; Waterloo, 75,533; Dubuque, 62,309; Council Bluffs, 60,348.
Government (1971): *Chief Officers*—governor, Robert D. Ray (R); lt. gov., Roger W. Jepson (R); secy. of state, Melvin D. Synhorst (R); atty. gen., Richard C. Turner (R); treas., Maurice E. Baringer (R); supt. of public instruction, vacancy; chief justice, C. Edwin Moore. *General Assembly*—Senate, 50 members (38 Republicans, 12 Democrats); House of Representatives, 100 members (63 R, 37 D).
Education (1970–71): *Enrollment*—public elementary schools, 470,318 pupils; 17,039 teachers; public secondary, 192,-951 pupils; 14,804 teachers; nonpublic schools (1968–69) 95,400 pupils; 4,130 teachers; college and university (fall 1968), 103,516 students. *Public school expenditures* (1970–71), $630,000,000 ($1,004 per pupil). *Average teacher's salary,* $9,129.
State Finances (fiscal year 1970): *Revenues*, $1,173,618,000 (3% general sales tax and gross receipts taxes, $223,-464,000; motor fuel tax, $100,831,000; federal funds, $234,109,000). *Expenditures*, $1,173,652,000 (education, $475,722,000; health, welfare, and safety, $131,368,000; highways, $189,486,000). *State debt,* $97,999,000 (June 30, 1970).
Personal Income (1970): $10,328,000,000; per capita, $3,714.
Public Assistance (1970): $108,290,000. *Average monthly payments* (Dec. 1970)—old-age assistance, $123.40; aid to families with dependent children, $188.75.
Labor Force: *Nonagricultural wage and salary earners* (June 1971), 890,800. *Average annual employment* (1969)—manufacturing, 225,000; trade, 205,000; government, 173,000; services, 142,000. *Insured unemployed* (Oct. 1971)—9,300 (1.6%).
Manufacturing (1967): *Value added by manufacture,* $3,250,-900,000. Food and kindred products, $816,800,000; non-electrical machinery, $753,100,000; electrical equipment and supplies, $373,500,000; chemicals and allied products, $243,600,000.
Agriculture (1970): *Cash farm income,* $4,165,516,000 (livestock, $2,856,412,000; crops, $1,073,289,000; government payments, $235,815,000). *Chief crops* (1970)—Corn, 859,-140,000 bushels (ranks 1st among the states); soybeans, 186,624,000 bushels (ranks 2d); oats, 92,394,000 bushels; hay, 6,910,000 tons (ranks 4th).
Mining (1969): *Production value,* $119,400,000 (ranks 31st among the states). *Chief minerals* (tons)—Stone, 26,500,-000; sand and gravel, 17,500,000; gypsum, 1,225,000.
Transportation: *Roads* (1969), 112,320 miles (180,757 km); *motor vehicles* (1969), 1,754,000; *railroads* (1968), 8,225 miles (13,264 km); *airports* (1969), 97.
Communications: *Telephones* (1971), 1,624,800; *television stations* (1969), 12; *radio stations* (1969), 105; *newspapers* (1969), 43 (daily circulation, 1,004,000).

IRAN

Under the modified autocracy of Shah Mohammed Reza Pahlavi, Iran continued to enjoy stability, order, and economic improvement in 1971. The country was disturbed by a number of terrorist acts by dissident groups, but though spectacular these were not numerous. Iran's visibility to the world increased both because of the great jubilee at Isfahan in October and because current circumstances were forcing the country to assume a more significant role of regional leadership.

Isfahan Celebration. The ancient city of Persepolis was the scene, October 12–15, of a lavish gathering recalling such events as the Diamond Jubilee of Queen Victoria, but really without any close parallel in history. This was the "Feast of the Last Twenty-Five Centuries," the official celebration of the 2,500th anniversary of the founding of the Persian Empire by Cyrus the Great. Technically eight years late, the occasion also commemorated the 30th anniversary of the shah's accession.

Well planned to enhance the prestige of Iran and of the present dynasty, the festival brought to Persepolis the leaders and rulers of 69 states. Despite some absentees such as U. S. President

GAMMA-PHOTOREPORTERS

COLOSSAL and colorful extravaganza marked celebration in Iran in October of 2,500th anniversary of Persian Empire. (Above) Musicians are costumed in dress of various stages of Persian history. (Right) Emperor Haile Selassie of Ethiopia, the shah of Iran and Empress Farah, and President Podgorny of USSR (from left to right) form center of official party. Visiting dignitaries were lodged in sumptuous tents amid the imposing ruins of Persepolis.

GAMMA-PHOTOREPORTERS

Richard Nixon and French President Georges Pompidou, the guests constituted a formidable group including one emperor, eight kings, a cardinal, and grand dukes, crown princes, and statesmen by the score. Of the enormous cost, estimated at $100 million, much was spent on permanent improvements such as new roads and hotels.

Domestic Events. The premier, Amir Abbas Hoveida, who had held office since January 1965, was confirmed in power by the results of the general election of July 11. The ruling Iran Novin (New Iran) party met only token opposition and scored a sweeping victory, which assured it of control of parliament for the next four years. The election was boycotted by the extreme right-wing Pan-Iranist party, but the Mardom (People's) party, the principal opposition group, scored small gains. In the 268-seat Majlis (National Assembly) the Iran Novin party won 230 seats and the Mardom party, which had held 32 seats, took 37. In the Senate, 30 of whose 60 members are appointed by the shah, Iran Novin won 28 of the elective seats and Mardom two.

In the worst terrorist crime of the year, Gen. Ziaddin Farsiou, chief of the Iranian military court, was shot on April 4 as he left his home in Teheran to take his son to school. He died in April 11. The crime was believed to have been committed by members of a nine-man Maoist group who had attacked a police post in Gilan province in March. After police and security forces surrounded the brigands' hideout in Teheran on May 24, a gun battle resulted in the death of three of the gang and capture of others.

Economic Developments. Among the most important large-scale new plans announced in 1971 were the following. On January 5, the government gave its formal approval to an open pit development, costing $33 million, of the Sar Cheshmeh low grade copper deposit by the Selection Trust group of London. In July the state-owned National Iranian Oil Company (NIOC) and a Japanese group agreed to build a $350 million petrochemical complex near Bandar Maashar on the Persian Gulf. NIOC also signed three agreements with two U. S. oil companies and one Japanese group to explore for and develop oil. The proposed development, in cooperation with a Glasgow firm, of Bandar Abbas in the southeast as a naval base was announced on August 13. In March it was disclosed that out of a total budget of 481 billion rials, 182 billion would be spent on development projects.

Foreign Relations. The British withdrawal from the Persian Gulf area, known for several years to be imminent, was actually carried out in 1971, leaving Iran, with its large area and population of 28 million, as the strongest power in the region. The shah announced February 16 that when the British withdrew Iran would take the islands of Abu Musa and the Tunbs at the entrance to the Persian Gulf. He claimed that the islands, in the hands of two minor sheikdoms (Ras al-Khaimah and Sharjam), belonged to Iran, and said "We shall take them back by force if necessary" In May there were complaints by Iran of RAF planes buzzing Iranian ships and the Iranian-claimed islands. However, relations with Britain have in general been good since Iran gave up its claim to Bahrain.

Britain terminated its protecting treaty with the seven Trucial sheikdoms at the end of November, and on November 30 Iran occupied Greater and Lesser Tunbs and Abu Musa. On Greater Tunb

three marines and four policemen of the Ras al-Khaimah garrison were killed. Iraq severed its relations with Iran and Britain on December 1, accusing them of collusion in the Iranian occupation of the islands. Iraq continued its expulsion of Iranians in Iraq.

The shah announced on July 14 that he intended to resume diplomatic relations with Lebanon, broken since April 1969. In a more important diplomatic move, the Teheran government on August 17 recognized Peking as "the sole legal government of China," and Taiwan broke off relations.

Iran, an Islamic but not an Arab nation, is only marginally interested in the chronic Arab hostility to Israel, and continues to supply Israel with oil. A reminder of this was the bazooka attack made by an unmarked launch on June 12 on a tanker sailing from Iran to the Israeli port of Eilat (Elat).

Growing Role of Iran. The shah has stated his intention of building up the most powerful military machine in the Middle East, and in the achievement of this aim he is being actively assisted by both the United States and Britain. Britain has sold Iran 300 Chieftain tanks and plans to sell 500 more by 1975, while refusing them to both Arabs and Israelis. Britain is also supplying Hovercraft and ground-to-air missiles. The United States is selling Iran a total of 140 F-4 Phantom jets and other equipment. Iran is thus strengthening its hand to carry out the policy defined by the shah in October as being "to uphold stability and discourage any aggressive designs in the region."

ARTHUR CAMPBELL TURNER
University of California, Riverside

--------- IRAN • Information Highlights ---------

Official Name: Empire of Iran.
Area: 636,294 square miles (1,648,000 sq km).
Population (1970 est.): 28,660,000. *Density,* 45 per square mile (17 per sq km). *Annual rate of increase,* 3.2%.
Chief Cities (1966 census): Teheran, the capital, 2,719,730; Isfahan, 424,045; Meshed, 409,616; Tabriz, 403,413.
Government: *Head of state,* Mohammed Reza Pahlavi, shah (acceded Sept. 16, 1941; crowned Oct. 6, 1967). *Chief minister,* Amir Abbas Hoveida, premier (took office Jan. 27, 1965). *Legislature*—Parliament; Senate, 60 members, Majlis (lower house), 268 members. *Major political parties* —Iran Novin party, Mardom party.
Languages: Persian (official), Turki.
Education: *Literacy rate* (1970), 25% of population. *Expenditure on education* (1968), 3.3% of gross national product. *School enrollment* (1968)—primary, 2,753,132; secondary, 806,625; technical/vocational, 19,059; university/higher, 58,194.
Finances (1969–70): *Revenues,* $4,400,000,000; *expenditures,* $4,400,000,000; *monetary unit,* rial (75.75 rials equal U. S. $1. Sept. 1971).
Gross National Product (1970 est.): $10,900,000,000.
National Income (1968): $6,812,000,000; *national income per person,* $252.
Economic Indexes: *Industrial production* (1970), 249 (1963= 100); *agricultural production* (1969), 122 (1963=100); *consumer price index* (1970), 114 (1963=100).
Manufacturing (metric tons, 1969): Cement, 2,341,000; wheat flour (1968), 2,300,000; meat, 257,000; residual fuel oil, 11,606; distillate fuel oils, 4,126.
Crops (metric tons, 1969 crop year): Wheat, 4,000,000; rice, 1,100,000; barley, 864,000; cottonseed (1968), 352,000; grapes (1968), 270,000; citrus fruit (1968), 115,000.
Minerals (metric tons, 1969): Crude petroleum, 166,030,000; salt, 352,000; coal (1968), 295,000; chromium ore (1968), 113,200; zinc ore, 22,500; natural gas, 2,781,000,000 cubic meters.
Foreign Trade (1970): *Exports,* $2,355,000,000 (chief exports —petroleum, $2,089,000,000; cotton, $52,938,000). *Imports,* $1,658,000,000 (chief imports, 1967—iron and steel, $159,- 337,000; nonelectrical machinery, $134,825,000; chemicals, $112,692,000; motor vehicles, $77,580,000). *Chief trading partners* (1968)—Japan (took 28% of exports, supplied 7% of imports); United Kingdom (22%—12%); United States (4%—19%); West Germany (3%—22%).
Tourism: *Receipts* (1970), $42,200,000.
Transportation: *Roads* (1970), 24,000 miles (38,623 km); *motor vehicles* (1968), 238,300 (automobiles, 180,400).
Communications: *Telephones* (1970), 286,220; *television stations* (1968), 10; *television sets* (1969), 250,000; *radios* (1968), 2,500,000; *newspapers* (1969), 26.

IRAQ

The Baath party regime in Iraq, most radical of Middle East governments, celebrated on July 17 the third anniversary of the coup that brought it to power, with a review of Soviet-built weapons.

Domestic Affairs. President Ahmad Hassan al-Bakr continued to head an administration whose methods were uncompromisingly authoritarian. Despite the absence of any event in 1971 like the attempted coup of 1970, the atmosphere remained one of suspicion of enemies, foreign and domestic.

Kurdish Problem. The Kurdish minority of 1 million (with others in Iran, Turkey, and Syria) remained Iraq's great unsolved political problem. Successive policies to conciliate the Kurds, almost constantly in revolt since the late 1950's, have proved inadequate or illusory—including the agreement of March 1970. On May 11, 1971, the Iraqi government established a special committee to try to align the Baath and Kurdish Democratic parties.

Economic Developments. The second 5-year plan of 1970–71 was under way. It included an effort to reduce dependence on foreign capital. Although Iraq's major trading partners were in the West, its main source of foreign aid and technical advice was the Soviet Union. By an agreement signed in Baghdad on March 2, the USSR was to supply spare parts for agricultural machinery.

On May 17 a Soviet delegation began discussion of the planned Baghdad-Basra and Mosul-Baghdad pipelines. The ambitious Al-Thartar project, a canal to link the Tigris and Euphrates rivers, was agreed upon in October. The USSR will give equipment and expert help valued at $20 million. The canal, about 25 miles (40 km) long, will channel surplus Tigris water to the Euphrates, using an enlarged Al-Thartar lake to irrigate central Iraq. On Dec. 19, 1971, an agreement was signed for Iraqi-Soviet cooperation on peaceful uses of atomic energy.

In February a French concern began work on the pipeline from the North Rumaila oilfield to Fao on the Persian Gulf. Talks were also resumed on the projected pipeline from Kirkuk to Turkey. A contract was signed on March 4 between the Iraq National Oil Company and the Hungarian Chemokomplex for drilling three wells in Kirkuk province.

Oil. Many of the projects mentioned above are concerned with facilitating or enlarging operations of the nationally owned Iraq National Oil Company (INOC). INOC is the government's chief hope of lessening its economic dependence on the Western-owned Iraq Petroleum Company, chief Iraqi oil producer and chief earner of foreign exchange. By the end of 1971, 10 wells had been drilled at INOC's new North Rumaila field, and it was hoped that in 1972 production there would be running at 5 million tons per year, with triple that to come soon after.

Iraq, with other oil-producing countries, participated in negotiations with the oil companies resulting in the general agreement of February 14. These negotiations were reopened near the end of the year as a result of dollar devaluation. (See MIDDLE EAST.) Iraq also made a favorable contract with the Iraq Petroleum Company on June 7, gaining some $990 million in oil revenue in 1971 as against $549 million in 1970.

Foreign Relations. Hardan Takriti, former vice president of Iraq ousted on Oct. 15, 1970, was assassinated in Kuwait by two gunmen on March 30.

Iraq was on bad terms with all its neighbors. Typical were the pronouncements of President al-Bakr on June 30. He offered to resume cooperation with Egypt—provided President Sadat gave up all attempts at a political settlement with Israel. He warned Iran against "expansionist ambitions" in the Gulf. He excoriated Britain as the "mastermind" behind all recent difficulties in Iraq. On July 5–6, three British diplomats, accused of espionage, were ordered to leave. Iraq, exasperated by the Jordanian monarchy's firm handling of the guerrilla threat to its existence, broke off relations with Amman on July 19, closed its border with Jordan, and demanded Jordan's expulsion from the Arab League.

Iraq eagerly endorsed the leftist coup in the Sudan on July 19, recognized the new regime, and dispatched senior Baath officials to Khartoum. However, they were killed when their plane crashed at Jiddah. President Numeiry regained control in Khartoum, and the Iraqi mission there was expelled.

Iraq was disappointed in its failure, by the end of 1971, to enhance its power in the Persian Gulf, a result anticipated from the British withdrawal in 1971. Instead, all advantage seemed to have accrued to conservative Iran, Iraq's larger and more powerful rival in the area. On December 1, following Iranian occupation of the islands of Abu Musa and the Tunbs, Iraq denounced both Iran and Britain and broke off relations with them. In the last week of 1971, thousands of Iranians permanently domiciled in Iraq were rounded up, driven in buses to the Iranian border, and expelled.

Babylon Revived? An ambitious $26 million plan was being considered for the excavation and restoration of ancient Babylon, historic capital of the Sumerians, Chaldeans, and Alexander the Great. It would include a new Tower of Babel and possibly the Hanging Gardens, as a tourist attraction.

ARTHUR CAMPBELL TURNER
University of California, Riverside

--- **IRAQ • Information Highlights** ---

Official Name: Republic of Iraq.
Area: 167,925 square miles (434,924 sq km).
Population (1970 est.): 9,440,000. *Density,* 55 per square mile (21 per sq km). *Annual rate of increase,* 2.3%.
Chief City (1965 census): Baghdad, the capital, 1,745,328.
Government: *Head of state,* Ahmad Hassan al-Bakr, president (took office July 1968). *Head of government,* Ahmad Hassan al-Bakr. *Legislature*—Legislative power is exercised by the Revolutionary Command Council. *Major political party*—Baath party.
Language: Arabic (official).
Education: *Literacy rate* (1971), 20% to 40% of population. *School enrollment* (1968)—primary, 1,017,050; secondary, 307,178; technical/vocational, 10,596; university, 41,189.
Finances (1967–70 est.): *Revenues,* $1,061,200,000; *expenditures,* $1,061,200,000; *monetary unit,* dinar (.3571 dinar equals U.S.$1, September 1971).
Gross National Product (1970 est.): $3,120,000,000.
National Income (1969): $2,316,000,000; *national income per person,* $248.
Economic Indexes: *Agricultural production* (1969), 153 (1963=100): *consumer price index* (1970), 117 (1963=100).
Manufacturing (metric tons, 1969): Residual fuel oil, 1,451,-000; cement, 1,399,000; distillate fuel oils, 764,000; cigarettes, 5,770,000,000 units.
Crops (metric tons, 1969 crop year): Barley, 1,250,000; wheat, 1,189,000; dates (1968), 333,000; rice, 284,000.
Minerals (metric tons, 1969): Crude petroleum, 73,775,000; salt, 50,000.
Foreign Trade (1970): *Exports,* $1,093,000,000 (chief exports—petroleum, $1,030,000,000. *Imports,* $509,000,000 (chief imports, 1968—iron and steel shapes, $21,448,000; sugar, $17,556,000: tea and maté, $17,080,000; motor vehicles, $16,912,000). *Chief trading partners* (1968)—Italy (took 24% of exports, supplied 5% of imports); France (21%—5%).
Transportation: *Roads* (1970), 12,950 miles (20,840 km); *motor vehicles* (1969), 105,900 (automobiles, 64,200); *railroads* (1970), 1,050 miles (1,690 km); *national airline,* Iraqi Airways; *principal airports,* Baghdad, Basra.
Communications: *Telephones* (1970), 119,650; *television stations* (1968), 2; *television sets* (1969), 220,000; *radios* (1965), 2,500,000; *newspapers* (1968), 5.

PRIME MINISTER Jack Lynch leaves London embassy to meet with British Prime Minister Heath in September. The talks were part of Ireland's effort to reduce Catholic-Protestant conflicts in Northern Ireland.

IRELAND

The intensified sectarian conflict in Northern Ireland cast long shadows over the Republic during 1971. Although shootings and explosions were largely confined to the major urban areas of the six northern counties, the Irish media carried vivid reports of the strife. Several minor bombings, bank raids carried out by "illegal organizations," and serious border "incidents" between British and Irish soldiers served to remind Irishmen forcibly that the troubles in the North were contagious, not to say lethal. (For an account of the disorders in Northern Ireland, see GREAT BRITAIN.)

Political Developments. Faced with a growing rift within the ruling Fianna Fáil party and under pressure from all sides, Prime Minister Jack Lynch worked hard to rally support for his policy of concerned restraint. He continued to advocate peaceful reform in the North, while denouncing the violent politics attractive to younger militants. By year-end his position was being undermined by more extreme republicans, who urged intervention on behalf of the North's Catholic minority.

At the annual conference of Fianna Fáil on February 20, Lynch called again for a reunited Ireland and also held out "an olive branch to the North." On March 9 the Dáil unanimously supported a motion repudiating the use of force in ending partition. If his moderation appealed to most Irishmen, it only angered immoderates, including both the pro-

visional and official factions of the illegal Irish Republican Army, as well as the various branches of the Sinn Fein party.

On August 19, Lynch issued a strong statement protesting the internment of several hundred political suspects in the North, and he gave his support to the "passive resistance" campaign launched by opposition leaders in the northern Parliament. Lynch's search for peace in the North took him first to a meeting with U. S. President Nixon on March 16 and then, on September 27, to talks with British Prime Minister Edward Heath and Northern Ireland's Prime Minister Brian Faulkner. No such tripartite conference had taken place since Ireland's partition in 1922. The three leaders issued a joint statement after the 2-day meeting, condemning violence "as an instrument of political pressure," but no real change of policy ensued.

Economy. Economic activity during the year was sluggish, as the economy slowly recovered from the effects of strikes and deflationary measures in 1970. Rising prices and a growing trade deficit moved some economists to warn that price controls would be necessary if Irish goods were to compete effectively on the world market.

Ireland moved closer to membership in the European Economic Community (EEC, or Common Market) once Britain agreed in June to the EEC's terms for entry. On June 15, Ireland was invited to join the Western European Union, which is tied to the EEC. Following Britain, Ireland adopted a decimal currency on February 15.

Seán Lemass, prime minister from 1959 to 1966, died on May 11. A disciple of President Éamon de Valéra and a veteran of the war of independence, Lemass did much to promote industrial growth in the 1960's.

L. PERRY CURTIS, JR.
University of California, Berkeley

———— IRELAND • Information Highlights ————

Official Name: Republic of Ireland (Éire).
Area: 27,136 square miles (70,283 sq km).
Population (1970 est.): 2,940,000. *Density*, 107 per square mile (42 per sq km). *Annual rate of increase,* 0.4%.
Chief Cities (1966 census): Dublin, the capital, 568,772.
Government: *Head of state,* Éamon de Valéra, president (took office for 2d 7-year term, June 25, 1966). *Head of government,* John (Jack) Lynch, Prime Minister (Taoiseach) (took office Nov. 10, 1966). *Legislature*—Parliament: House of Representatives (Dáil Éireann), 144 members, Senate (Seanad Éireann), 60 members. *Major political parties*—Fianna Fáil, Fine Gael, Labour.
Languages: Irish (official), English (major).
Education: *Literacy rate* (1971), 99% of population. *Expenditure on education* (1968), 11.2% of total expenditure.
Finances (1970): *Revenues,* $1,157,500,000; *expenditures,* $1,358,800,000; *monetary unit,* pound (.3838 pound equals U. S.$1, Dec. 30, 1971).
Gross National Product (1970): $4,092,200,000.
National Income (1970): $3,063,200,000; *national income per person,* $1,042.
Manufacturing (metric tons, 1969): Cement, 1,237,000; gasoline, 511,000; meat 365,000; beer, 3,692,000 hectoliters.
Crops (metric tons, 1969 crop year): Potatoes, 1,430,000; sugar beets (1968), 1,092,000; barley, 776,000.
Minerals (metric tons, 1969): Peat (1968), 4,671,000 (ranks 2d among world producers); limestone (1968), 4,359,000.
Foreign Trade (1968): *Exports* (1970), $1,040,000,000 (chief exports—live animals, $130,114,000; meat, $111,782,000; dairy products, $52,337,000). *Imports* (1970), $1,573,000.-000 (chief imports—nonelectrical machinery, $144,334,000; chemicals, $115,097,000; motor vehicles, $71,930,000).
Transportation: *Roads* (1970), 52,067 miles (83,791 km); *motor vehicles* (1969), 407,700 (automobiles, 358,000); *railroads* (1970), 1,334 miles (2,147 km); *national airline,* Aer Lingus-Irish International Airlines; *principal airport,* Dublin.
Communications: *Telephones* (1970), 287,108; *television stations* (1968), 7; *television sets* (1969), 446,000; *radios* (1968), 860,000; *newspapers* (1969), 7.

ISLAM. See RELIGION.

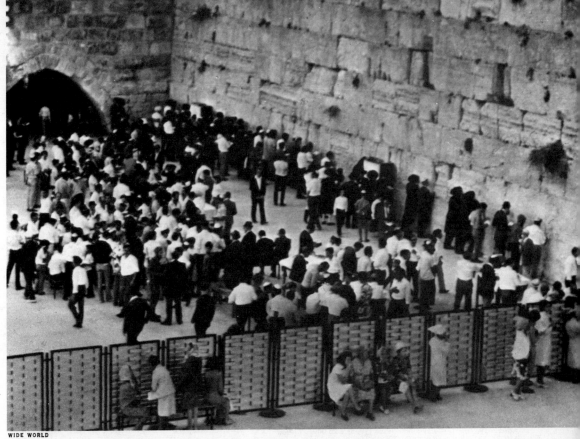

JERUSALEM'S WAILING WALL is visited by praying Jews on the eve of Rosh Hashanah. Low screen separates men and women, in accordance with tradition.

ISRAEL

The government of Prime Minister Golda Meir, a coalition in which her Israel Labour party is the main element, entered its third year in March 1971. On the whole the year was one of growing stability and economic advance. If Israel were simply a country like other countries, one could say without much qualification that it was a successful year.

The position of Israel, however, is unique. The nation is entirely surrounded by hostile neighbors who outnumber it. Farther afield Israel faces the overt hostility of one great power, the neutrality of others, and from one only—the United States—can it expect a hesitant and qualified support.

Thus for Israel the customary division between foreign and domestic affairs hardly exists. It is typical that the withdrawal from the government in August 1970 of the right-wing Gahal party arose out of a foreign policy decision—acceptance of the cease-fire. All domestic questions—immigration, economics, treatment of minorities—are more or less directly related to the basic question of foreign relations, which is survival.

Domestic Affairs. Perhaps the most serious of Israel's domestic problems is a chronic balance-of-payment deficit, which is related to its heavy defense needs. It was noted early in the year by Finance Minister Pinhas Sapir that the trade deficit had almost doubled in 1970, despite a substantial increase in exports. In the budget for the fiscal year beginning April 1, 1971, which was submitted to the Knesset on January 4, defense expenditures were to account for 40% of a total of $3.8 billion.

The proposed budget for 1972–73 was striking in its austerity and included severe restrictions on officials' expenses and a one-year halt on most new official buildings. The budget also envisaged the freezing of dividends, a continuation of most price controls, some restrictions on the financial advantages according to new immigrants, and the holding down of defense expenditures to $1.4 billion.

Immigration continued to run at a rate of over 100,000 per year, with a surprisingly large number of Jews being permitted to emigrate from the Soviet Union. Some immigrants dislike conditions in Israel and leave again, but official statistics are reticent on this point.

Israel was plagued by a wave of strikes, especially in June through September. Sporadic walkouts involved hospitals, electric plants, port facilities, and other public services. Some doctors went on strike in August. Large numbers of civil servants and other public employees were involved. On September 12 the cabinet approved legislation barring strikes by government employees during the life of a contract, on pain of fines and dismissal.

The pressures of life in Israel—including austerity, unusually high taxes, and the constant threat of war—lead to frequent irritation with acts of government. To deal with such grievances, an office equivalent to the Scandinavian ombudsman was created in the Public Complaints Office, inaugurated on September 22 under the direction of Dr. Isaac Nebenzahl, who is also state controller. In the months since the office began operations, several thousand complaints have been dealt with, and the director found about 20% of them justified.

Official Name: State of Israel.
Area: 7,992 square miles (20,700 sq km).
Population (1971 census): 3,000,000. *Density,* 375 per square mile (145 per sq km). *Annual rate of increase,* 23%.
Chief Cities (1970 est.): Jerusalem, the capital, 283,100; Tel Aviv-Jaffa, 382,900; Haifa, 214,500.
Government: *Head of state,* Zalman Shazar, president (took office May 21, 1963; reelected March 17, 1969). *Head of government,* Golda Meir, premier (took office March 17, 1969). *Legislature*—Knesset (unicameral), 120 members. *Major political parties*—Labour-Mapam Alignment, Gahal, National Religious.
Languages: Hebrew (official), Arabic (official), English.
Education: *Literacy rate* (1970), 90% of population. *Expenditure on education* (1967), 7.6% of gross national product. *School enrollment* (1968)—primary, 452,942; secondary, 129,408; technical/vocational, 52,438; higher, 44,758.
Finances (1970): *Revenues,* $1,888,200,000; *expenditures,* $2,-878,570,000; *monetary unit,* pound (4.20 pounds equal U. S.$1, Dec. 30, 1971).
Gross National Product (1970 est.): $5,400,000,000.
National Income (1969): $3,672,000,000; *national income per person,* $1,301.
Economic Indexes: *Industrial production* (1970), 203 (1963 = 100); *agricultural production* (1969), 152 (1963 = 100); *consumer price index* (1970), 138 (1963 = 100).
Manufacturing (metric tons, 1969): Residual fuel oil, 2,327,-000; cement, 1,312,000; distillate fuel oils, 1,144,000.
Crops (metric tons, 1969 crop year): Citrus fruits (1968), 1,223,000; milk, 470,000; wheat, 156,000.
Minerals (metric tons, 1969): Crude petroleum, 2,599,000; phosphate rock, 986,000; potash, 334,000.
Foreign Trade (1970): *Exports,* $731,000,000 (chief exports—polished diamonds, $245,715,000; citrus fruits, $123,600,-000). *Imports,* $1,410,000,000 (chief imports, 1968—diamonds, $180,528,000; nonelectrical machinery, $115,994,-000). *Chief trading partners* (1968)—United States (took 19% of exports; supplied 23% of imports); United Kingdom (12%—20%); West Germany (9%—11%).
Tourism: *Receipts* (1970), $113,500,000.
Transportation: *Roads* (1970), 4,900 miles (7,886 km); *motor vehicles* (1969), 195,900 (automobiles, 134,300); *railroads* (1970), 450 miles (724 km); *merchant fleet* (1970), 714,000 gross registered tons; *national airline,* El Al; *principal airport,* Tel Aviv.
Communications: *Telephones* (1970), 457,721; *television stations* (1967), 1; *television sets* (1968), 26,000; *radios* (1968), 627,000; *newspapers* (1969), 24.

The usually adroit and verbally skilled foreign minister, Abba Eban, was involved in a noisy controversy during October and November, which momentarily seemed to endanger his political future. The storm centered on remarks made by Eban during an interview in October on the David Frost television show, in which he expressed indifference to the possibility of bringing more Nazi war criminals to trial in Israel. Eban had declared: "After the Eichmann thing I ceased to be interested. . . . What can vengeance do? . . . Whether some wretched man in Paraguay or Brazil is brought to justice hardly interests me." Large numbers of Israelis took offense at what they regarded as indifference to the most appalling persecution of Jews in history. Though the ruling Labour party backed Eban and deplored the "unrestrained attacks" on him, there was a bitter and acrimonious debate in the Knesset (November 17), in which one of the judges who had presided at the Eichmann trial took issue with Eban.

Policy Toward the Arabs. Despite fairly frequent acts of violence, it seemed that Israeli policy in administering the lands captured in the 1967 war and largely inhabited by Arabs was meeting with a degree of success. The ministry of justice in June introduced an Arab compensation bill. By its terms, compensation payable over 20 years would go to property owners in annexed East Jerusalem.

The resettlement in new housing of Arabs from the squalid camps of the Gaza Strip was begun. This led to protests from Egypt—which had done nothing for the refugees when it controlled the area. The protest was supported by the UN.

The economic condition of the Arabs under Israeli rule has been improving. Participation in the booming Israeli economy offered them previously nonexistent opportunities. From the Gaza Strip, despite terrorist efforts, over 10,000 Arab workers traveled daily to work. Improvement was particularly noticeable in the West Bank territory, where new seeds, crops, equipment, and methods have been introduced. The right of free movement was granted to inhabitants of the administered areas on July 2. On November 27 it was announced by Israel that in four Arab West Bank towns municipal elections would be held before next May. Abdul Aziz el-Zuabi, a Mapam party member who has sat in the Knesset since 1965, was appointed on May 16 deputy health minister, the highest office so far held by an Israeli Arab.

Economic Matters. The Eilat-Ashquelon pipeline, which had an annual capacity of 24 million tons, was being enlarged to a capacity of 32.5 million tons per year. It is already operating at a profit. The attack on June 12 on an Eilat-bound tanker suggested that this oil-supply route from Iran, vital to Israel, might be in jeopardy; but the unsuccessful attack was not repeated.

The Israeli pound was devalued by 20% on August 22, from a previous value of 3.50 per U.S. dollar to 4.20. The step was accompanied by heavy penalties for unauthorized price increases.

Foreign Relations. There were some actions against guerrilla bases in Lebanon in January, February, and August. The Israeli consul general in Istanbul, Ephraim Elrom, was kidnapped and murdered in May by leftist terrorists.

In a broad sense, very little changed in the basic elements of Israel's international relations in 1971. There was an atmosphere of waiting, accentuated by Egyptian President Sadat's ominous repetition of the theme that 1971 had to be the year of decision —although in fact nothing was decided in 1971. Arab-Israeli confrontation still existed in a chronic limbo of neither war nor peace. Israel continued to occupy the lands won in the 1967 war, at least some of which it regards as essential to its security. Early in the year Mrs. Meir spelled out what she regarded as Israel's "minimum terms": a "united Jerusalem, the capital of Israel," a "security border" on the Jordan River, and an "Israeli presence" at Sharm el-Sheikh.

On March 19, Eban met U. S. Secretary of State Rogers. Eban complained about attempts to force Israel to negotiate with "international organs" rather than with the Egyptian government. Israel, he added, had been "deeply influenced" by its experience with the UN peace-keeping force in 1967.

In the late summer and fall the United States continued to pressure Israel to give up conquered territory and permit the canal to open. The Israeli response was that Egypt was free to open the canal any time, provided free passage was allowed to Israeli ships and cargoes. The question for Israel was whether the United States would be prepared to let Israel have more jet aircraft to balance the large-scale Soviet buildup of arms in Egypt. Mrs. Meir's talk with President Nixon on December 1 apparently did not secure the planes, but it did produce a pledge that the United States would back the "long-term modernization" of Israel's armed forces.

(See also MIDDLE EAST.)

ARTHUR CAMPBELL TURNER
University of California, Riverside

ITALIAN LITERATURE. See LITERATURE.

Milling deputies crowd Parliament chamber during voting for a new president in December. After numerous deadlocks, Giovanni Leone won on the 23d ballot.

ITALY

Italy observed the 25th anniversary of the republic in 1971 amid grave economic depression, the disintegration of the center-left governing coalition, and a resurgence of Fascist strength. In the bitterly fought presidential election in December, some of the centrist forces regrouped long enough—with help from the right—to elect Giovanni Leone, a pro-Western Christian Democrat, to succeed the outgoing Social Democrat, Giuseppe Saragat.

GOVERNMENT

The year began with many Italians expressing deep concern over the country's political apathy and "democratic fatigue." The government headed by Emilio Colombo, a Christian Democrat, consisted of an unstable coalition of Socialists, Social Democrats, and Republicans. Its survival was threatened by political unrest and the pervasive effects of Italy's worst depression since World War II.

Divorce Bill. The government, moreover, was bedeviled by conservative opposition to the divorce bill enacted in 1970. Early in 1971 foes of the bill obtained 1,370,134 signatures to a petition calling for a referendum. At year-end many Christian Democrats and Communists sought to stave off a "religious war" by amending the existing law. Meanwhile, both Communist and Socialist parties filed motions in Parliament calling on the government to open talks with the Vatican with a view to revising the Lateran Concordat of 1929, which makes Roman Catholicism dominant in Italy's legal system.

In another aspect of church-state relations, the constitutional court published a landmark decision on March 17, 1971, declaring unconstitutional a 1926 law prohibiting dissemination of information on birth control. Ironically, the manufacture, sale, and use of contraceptive devices have never been banned in Italy.

Local Government. Another cause of unrest was the introduction of partial self-government in all 20 regions. Fascist-instigated violence erupted in Reggio di Calabria in February, when that city was bypassed in favor of Catanzaro as the regional capital. A compromise was worked out whereby the regional executive offices would be located in Catanzaro and the regional assembly would meet in Reggio di Calabria, but demonstrations persisted for weeks. A similar dispute broke out in L'Aquila, in the region of Abruzzi. In this case the assembly voted to establish seven of its ten executive departments in the rival city of Pescara, while confirming L'Aquila as the regional capital.

Factionalism and Violence. Adding to the chronic political crisis were the bitter factionalism within the Christian Democratic party and the growing desire of Socialist leaders to permit the Communists to share government responsibility. Because of this and in the hope of increasing its bargaining power, the small and somewhat conservative Republican party withdrew from the government coalition on February 26. The Social Democrats also resisted Socialist efforts to bring the Communists into the government. Making it clear that he had no intention of asking the Communists to share power, Premier Colombo called for a vote of confidence in his government. On March 4–5 he received such endorsement—346 to 235 in the Chamber of Deputies and 167 to 111 in the Senate.

Another source of constant tension was the political violence fomented by extremists on the right and the left. The neo-Fascist Italian Social Movement (MSI)—headed by Giorgio Almirante, a newspaper editor during the Mussolini era—encouraged its younger members to wear crash helmets and engage in street fighting. It claimed credit for influencing the cancellation of Yugoslavian President Tito's visit to Rome in December 1970. In March 1971 the government arrested several extreme right-wing plotters but could not find Prince Junio Valerio Borghese, a 64-year-old Fascist war hero who was alleged to have planned the December disorders.

On the extreme left the Communist party was badgered by a radical pro-Chinese minority, who scorned the traditional party organization as "bourgeois" and "pragmatic." These Maoist groups often engaged in open conflict with the old-liners. Late in April a pro-Peking secessionist group launched a daily newspaper, *Il Manifesto,* edited by a member of Parliament.

Elections. On June 14 nearly 8 million voters went to the polls in Rome, Genoa, Bari, and 150 other towns to elect municipal councils; in Sicily they also elected a regional assembly. These elections provided the first major test for Colombo's left-center coalition. In Sicily, where the role of the Mafia was a prime issue, the situation was explosive. A few days before the elections the chief prosecutor of Palermo was murdered, presumably by the Mafia.

--------- **ITALY • Information Highlights** ---------

Official Name: Italian Republic.
Area: 116,303 square miles (301,225 sq km).
Population (1970 est.): 53,670,000. *Density,* 462 per square mile (177 per sq km). *Annual rate of increase,* 0.8%.
Chief Cities (1968 est.): Rome, the capital, 2,656,104; Milan, 1,687,264; Naples, 1,267,073.
Government: *Head of state,* Giovanni Leone, president (took office Dec. 29, 1971). *Head of government,* Emilio Colombo, premier (took office Aug. 6, 1970). *Legislature* —Parliament: Senate, 315 members; Chamber of Deputies, 630 members. *Major political parties*—Christian Democrats, Communists, Socialists, Liberals.
Language: Italian (official).
Education: *Literacy rate* (1970), 93% of population. *Expenditure on education* (1968), 19.8% of total public expenditure. *School enrollment* (1968)—primary, 4,706,180; secondary, 3,489,615; technical/vocational, 874,401; university/higher, 420,417.
Finances (1970 est.): *Revenues,* $17,670,000,000; *expenditures,* $21,000,000,000; *monetary unit,* lira (581.5 liras equal U.S.$1, Dec. 31, 1971).
Gross National Product (1969): $82,330,000,000.
National Income (1969): $66,699,000,000; *national income per person,* $1,254.
Economic Indexes: *Industrial production* (1970), 150 (1963= 100); *agricultural production* (1969), 121 (1963=100); *consumer price index* (1970), 128 (1963=100).
Manufacturing (metric tons, 1969): Residual fuel oil, 49,307,-000; cement, 31,310,000; crude steel, 16,428,000; gasoline, 12,530,000; wine, 71,470,000 hectoliters.
Crops (metric tons, 1968 crop year): Grapes, 10,298,000 (ranks 1st among world producers); tomatoes, 3,258,000 (world rank 2d); olives, 1,933,000 (world rank 2d).
Minerals (metric tons, 1969): Salt, 3,942,000; lignite, 1,933,-000; crude petroleum, 1,522,000; mercury, 1,847 (ranks 2d among world producers).
Foreign Trade (1970): *Exports,* $13,210,000,000 (chief exports, 1968—nonelectrical machinery, $1,730,770,000; transport equipment, $1,078,630,000; textile yarn and fabrics, $785,-050,000; chemicals, $780,170,000). *Imports,* $14,939,000,-000 (chief imports, 1968—petroleum, crude and partly refined, $1,423,330,000; nonelectrical machinery, $970,-210,000; chemicals, $770,330,000; cereals and preparations, $502,850,000). *Chief trading partners* (1968)—West Germany (took 19% of exports, supplied 18% of imports); France (13%—11%); United States (11%—12%).
Tourism: *Receipts* (1970), $1,638,600,000.
Transportation: *Roads* (1969), 176,227 miles (238,596 km); *motor vehicles* (1969), 9,854,200 (automobiles, 9,028,400); *railroads* (1970), 12,750 miles (20,519 km); *merchant fleet* (1971), 8,139,000 gross registered tons; *national airline,* Alitalia.
Communications: *Telephones* (1970), 8,528,354; *television stations* (1968), 72; *television sets* (1969), 9,016,000; *radios* (1969), 11,333,000; *newspapers* (1969), 70 (daily circulation, 6,768,000).

The elections generally showed striking gains for the Fascist MSI at the expense of the Christian Democrats. Although the Communists held their own in the northern cities and in Rome province, they lost strength in Bari and other southern cities. The Socialists and Social Democrats made small gains. In the province of Rome the Fascists increased their share of the vote from 10.7% in 1970 to 15.6% in 1971, while the Christian Democrats dropped from 30.9% to 27.2%. In Sicily the Fascists polled 16.3%; in 1970 they had won 7.2%. The upsurge caused jubilation for the MSI and impelled the center and left parties to issue serious warnings against the "dangerous lure of the right."

No one could claim that Italy's democratic center was giving a good account of itself. But there was hope that Italy's Fascist movement might appear ridiculous and its Communist party anachronistic as soon as the European Economic Community (EEC) was strengthened by the expected participation of Britain, Denmark, Ireland, and Norway.

A second round of local elections, primarily in the northern and central parts of Italy, had originally been scheduled for November 28, but were postponed until March 1972. This enabled politicians to devote all their attention to the election in December 1971 of a new president of the republic. The Social Democrats advocated the reelection of Giuseppe Saragat, who had held the post for seven years. The Christian Democrats were anxious to reclaim this prize, but were faction-ridden and unable to agree on a candidate. Amintore Fanfani, president of the Senate, and Aldo Moro, a former premier, were its front-runners. The Socialists broke ranks with their Christian Democratic and Social Democratic partners to align themselves with the Communist party. The initial candidate of the left-wing bloc was Francesco De Martino, a Socialist deputy premier; later he bowed out in favor of the venerable Socialist Pietro Nenni. The defection of the Socialists threw into question the very future of the center government itself.

The electoral college consisted of 1,008 members (both houses of Parliament plus 58 delegates from the 20 regions). The Christian Democrats held 423 votes, the Communists 259. Twenty-three ballots were cast over a 16-day period before Giovanni Leone, a center-rightist Christian Democrat, squeaked through on Christmas Eve with 518 votes. Nenni, backed by the Socialists and Communists, was the runner-up. Leone's election required the support of the Republican party, which had boycotted the government since February, and the Liberal party, a rightist group outside the government. The Fascists claimed that their ballots helped.

New President. Aged 63, the jovial Leone is the youngest president in Italian history and the second Neapolitan to hold the post. He is a firm supporter of the Atlantic alliance and the European Common Market. In his inaugural address, the new president struck a conciliatory note after the bitterly contested election. He urged labor and management to display a spirit of responsibility and he warned against a "religious war." Most people interpreted this to mean that he favored amendment of the present divorce law (which Leone himself had steered through Parliament), rather than risk an open fight in a referendum on repeal.

President Leone's first official act was to request the moribund Colombo government to remain in office long enough to facilitate a possible visit by

ERUPTIONS of Mt. Etna threatened villages on the slopes of the Sicilian volcano. In May the people of Sant' Alfio marched to the edge of the lava flow (*right*) to pray for divine help. The people credited similar prayers with saving the village in 1928. This time the lava flow again stopped before reaching the town.

the premier with U. S. President Richard Nixon before the latter's journey to Peking and Moscow. This meant temporarily postponing the urgent tasks confronting the nation: reconstructing the disintegrating center-left coalition and tackling the grave economic, social, and educational problems.

ECONOMY

Italy was in the grip of a deep recession in 1971. It fared somewhat worse than the other Western industrial nations in a year of general economic stress. For the first time since World War II, Italy's gross national product did not increase at all. This was in sharp contrast to the 5.8% growth rate of 1969 and the 5.2% increase in 1970.

The industrial slump was especially severe in the building trades. Italy's appliance industry, which in 1969 supplied two thirds of all refrigerators sold in the EEC, also was in trouble. The automobile industry, relatively strong, produced 1.8 million cars in 1971, down only 2% from 1970.

Unemployment. For the first time in a quarter century the official number of unemployed persons exceeded one million, or more than 5% of the labor force. The actual employment picture is gloomier than the figures indicate. Many of the 34 million Italians who, in the statistics, are counted as economically inactive—including youths looking for their first jobs, 10 million housewives, and 7 million pensioners—are actually unused labor reserves or jobless workers in disguise. Moreover, recessions in West Germany, France, and Switzerland are forcing Italian migrant workers to return home, where they have a hard time finding jobs. Only 75% of Italy's industrial plants were utilized in 1971, and many concerns were operating on short hours.

For the first time in many years, 1971 also saw a "return migration" from the cities into the countryside. This is unique among EEC countries. It may please some environmentalists, but for work-

ers who went to Milan in search of a better life, to go back to forlorn southern villages provokes utter despair. There were no new farm jobs. Agriculture was no better off in Italy than in other western European countries, though farming output in 1971 was slightly above that of the preceding year because of favorable weather.

Labor. In a series of strikes throughout 1971, Italy lost more working hours than did any other country in western Europe. Militant workers struck for higher wages (and received significant increases), low-cost housing, and better social services. Radical splinter groups at the plant level often forced the hands of the big unions. On April 7 the nation was gripped by a one-day general strike.

The three major labor unions (Communist, Socialist, and Catholic) agreed on November 21 to merge into one confederation by February 1973. The timetable calls for each of them to dissolve on Sept. 21, 1972, and for a congress representing the new labor organization to convene the following February. The consolidation of organized labor, whose numbers exceed 5 million, will certainly increase labor's political power.

Government Action. During the summer and early autumn of 1971, Italy's government concentrated its attention on the economic recession and sought to accelerate parliamentary action on long-delayed social and fiscal reforms. On August 7 the Senate approved two major bills, dealing with housing and tax reform respectively. The former au-

NEW SUPERHIGHWAY winds through Apennines near Avezzano. Scheduled for completion by 1974, the highway will link Rome with L'Aquila, capital of the Abruzzi region.

thorized municipalities to expropriate private property for low-rent housing and public utilities. To reduce land speculation, compensation will be calculated on the value of farmland rather than on the real estate market price. The tax measure provides for Italy's first general income tax. There are also a levy on corporate revenue and a "value-added" tax. The reforms will go into effect on Jan. 1, 1973.

As the private sector of the economy has been reluctant to make new investments in the face of mounting labor costs unaccompanied by increased productivity, the government decided to take action in July 1971. Acting through the Bank of Italy, it allocated $1 billion to stimulate national production and increase investment in industry and agriculture.

The cost of living having soared by about 6% during 1971, the government felt compelled to introduce price controls on September 22.

During the international monetary talks at year-end Italy sat among the ten leading industrial nations of the non-Communist world. Italy maneuvered to keep to a minimum the revaluation of the lira with respect to the dollar. The lira was devalued only 1% against gold. (See INTERNATIONAL FINANCE.)

INTERNATIONAL RELATIONS

Italy was involved in issues affecting the EEC and NATO in 1971. There was some strain in relations with the United States because of burdens arising from President Nixon's economic policy.

China Policy. Implementing a decision announced in November 1970, the People's Republic of China opened its first embassy in Italy in January 1971. Italy reciprocated in February, expressing the hope that this action would help to lead Peking out of its isolation.

Relations with the United States. On February 18–19, Premier Colombo visited President Nixon in Washington. He explained that Peking had been recognized because of the "reality that Communist China exists." It was speculated that Colombo also gave Nixon assurances he would not bring Communists into the Italian government.

Italian-American trade relations were another topic for discussion during the year. Acting in response to considerable pressure from the United States, the ministry of foreign trade in July unilaterally restricted the value of exports of shoes and textiles during 1971 to $280 million.

Yugoslavia and the Soviet Union. Late in March, President Tito of Yugoslavia made an official visit to Italy. Originally scheduled for December 1970, it had had to be postponed because of Fascist demonstrations in Rome. Tito's visit offered further evidence that the Italian government accepts the permanence of the boundary line with Yugoslavia established in 1954.

From July 5 to 12, Foreign Minister Aldo Moro was in the Soviet Union on an official visit. He and Soviet Foreign Minister Gromyko agreed to regular bilateral consultations. They also reaffirmed their support for an early convocation of a European security conference and for a reduction of troops and arms in Europe.

Treaty with Austria. On July 17 the foreign ministers of Italy and Austria signed a treaty in Rome whereby future disagreements over the predominantly German-speaking region of Alto Adige (South Tyrol) will be referred to the Permanent Court of International Justice. They also signed two other pacts on minor border issues and agreed to closer economic ties. Italy pledged to support Austria's bid for a special association with the EEC that would leave Austrian neutrality intact. In October the Italian Senate gave final approval to a constitutional amendment that broadens the autonomy of Alto Adige and thereby fulfills the treaty obligation.

Role at Malta. At year-end, when the government of Malta put pressure on Britain to evacuate its military bases on the island, Italy, concerned about expanding Soviet naval power in the Mediterranean, sought to mediate the dispute. Earlier, the North Atlantic Treaty Organization had decided to withdraw from Malta and maintain its naval headquarters in Naples.

CHARLES F. DELZELL, *Vanderbilt University*

─────── **IVORY COAST · Information Highlights** ───────

Official Name: Republic of Ivory Coast.
Area: 124,503 square miles (322,463 sq km).
Population (1970 est.): 4,310,000. *Density,* 34 per square mile (13 per sq km). *Annual rate of increase,* 2.3%.
Chief City (1969 est.): Abidjan, the capital, 400,000.
Government: *Head of state,* Félix Houphouët-Boigny, president (reelected to 3d 5-year term, Nov. 29, 1970). *Head of government,* Félix Houphouët-Boigny. *Legislature*— National Assembly (unicameral), 100 members. *Major political party*—Democratic party of the Ivory Coast.
Languages: French (official), tribal languages.
Education: *Literacy rate* (1970), 20% of population. *Expenditure on education* (1968), 27.7% of total public expenditure. *School enrollment* (1968)—primary, 427,029; secondary, 50,088; technical/vocational, 4,020; higher, 2,943.
Finances (1969 est.): *Revenues,* $188,000,000; *expenditures,* $188,000,000; *monetary unit,* CFA franc (277.71 francs equal U. S.$1, Sept. 1971).
Gross National Product (1970 est.): $1,440,000,000.
National Income (1967): $851,000,000; *average annual income per person* (1970), $300.
Manufacturing (metric tons, 1969): Sawnwood (1968), 271,000; residual fuel oil, 267,000; distillate fuel oils, 218,000.
Crops (metric tons, 1968 crop year): Sweet potatoes and yams, 1,400,000; cassava, 530,000.
Minerals (metric tons, 1969): Manganese ore, 57,700; diamonds, 141,000 carats.
Foreign Trade (1970): *Exports,* $469,000,000 (chief exports— coffee, $155,450,000; cacao, $96,287,000). *Imports,* $334,- 000,000 (chief imports, 1968—textile yarn and fabrics, $41,114,000). *Chief trading partners* (1968)—France (took 35% of exports, supplied 51% of imports); United States (15%—6%); Netherlands (10%—5%).
Transportation: *Roads* (1970), 20,701 miles (33,122 km); *motor vehicles* (1969), 80,000 (automobiles, 47,000); *railroads* (1970), 375 miles (603 km); *national airline,* Air Afrique; *principal airport,* Abidjan–Port-Buet.
Communications: *Telephones* (1969), 27,220; *television stations* (1968), 4; *television sets* (1969), 10,000; *radios* (1969), 70,000; *newspapers* (1969), 3.

IVORY COAST

The year 1971 was one of peace and prosperity in the Ivory Coast. Events continued to be dominated by President Félix Houphouët-Boigny, who has headed the country since it became independent. The Ivory Coast remained in the forefront of the African states advocating a dialogue with South Africa.

Domestic Affairs. The minister of education announced on April 13 that in the future all students enrolling in the university would have to sign a pledge to refrain from any political activities except those of the governing Democratic party of the Ivory Coast. The University of Abidjan was closed during the month because of student disturbances. On June 8, President Houphouët-Boigny reshuffled his cabinet and took over the ministry of national education.

Foreign Affairs. At a news conference on April 28, Houphouët-Boigny reaffirmed his policy of a dialogue with South Africa. He said that the Ivory Coast condemned apartheid, but believed that the practice would not be eliminated by force. A 3-man delegation from the Ivory Coast visited South Africa in October and met with Prime Minister Vorster.

French President Georges Pompidou and Israeli Foreign Minister Abba Eban were among the government leaders who visited the Ivory Coast in 1971. On May 28 a pact was signed establishing a Ghana–Ivory Coast Joint Commission on Cooperation.

In October, the Ivory Coast was one of 15 African states to vote against the admission of the People's Republic of China to the United Nations.

Economy. The Ivory Coast remained one of the most prosperous countries in Africa in 1971. It began a new 5-year plan estimated to cost U. S.$900 million, of which 90% will be public, or government-financed investments. The plan stressed regional projects, continued expansion of agriculture and industry, and an acceleration of "Ivorianization."

The new port city of San Pedro began operating in 1971 and is expected to open up the southwestern part of the country for agricultural development. Work also advanced on the first stage of the long-term "African Riviera" project, which has been designed to accommodate some 500,000 tourists a year.

(See BIOGRAPHY—*Houphouët-Boigny, Félix.*)

JUDITH A. GLICKMAN

JACKSON, Jesse. See BIOGRAPHY.

JAMAICA

The approach of general elections in 1972 gave a heavily political coloration to most of the events that preoccupied Jamaicans in 1971.

Budget Controversy. Partisan politics were especially evident in the response of the opposition People's National party to the 1971–72 budget, presented in June by Prime Minister Hugh Shearer and his ruling Jamaica Labour party. The new budget exceded that of the preceding fiscal year by about 15%, and was about three times that of 1962, the year of independence. The opposition denounced the proposed budget as blatantly political, reserving special criticism for its tax-reduction provisions, which included a cut in the land tax.

Economy. Jamaica continued to suffer a variety of economic ills. Although development was rapid, it was not great enough to overcome heavy unemployment, a decline in certain segments of agriculture, and excessive dependence on a few exports.

In April a 3-year program of "radical reorganization" in the deficit-ridden banana industry was announced. It provided for the modernizing of processing and transport facilities and for some price increases to the growers.

Aid from abroad included loans of $13.5 million for education from the World Bank, and $6 million, from the Inter-American Bank, for developing tourism and small manufacturing industries.

Visitors. Distinguished visitors to Jamaica in 1971 included West German Chancellor Willy Brandt and Costa Rican President José Figueres Ferrer.

ROBERT J. ALEXANDER, *Rutgers University*

─────── **JAMAICA · Information Highlights** ───────

Official Name: Jamaica.
Area: 4,232 square miles (10,962 sq km).
Population (1970 est.): 2,000,000. *Density,* 450 per square mile (178 per sq km). *Annual rate of increase,* 1.8%.
Chief City (1960 census): Kingston, the capital, 123,403.
Government: *Head of state,* Elizabeth II, queen (acceded Feb. 6, 1952; represented by Sir Clifford Campbell, governor-general). *Head of government,* Hugh Shearer, prime minister (took office April 11, 1967). *Legislature*—Parliament: Senate, 21 members; House of Representatives, 53 members. *Major political parties*—Jamaica Labour party, People's National party.
Language: English (official).
Education: *Literacy rate* (1970), 85% of population. *Expenditure on education* (1968), 15.1% of total public expenditure. *School enrollment* (1970)—primary, 361,830; secondary, 44,768; technical/vocational, 3,308; higher, 4,564.
Finances (1970 est.): *Revenues,* $263,300,000; *expenditures,* $254,400,000; *monetary unit,* Jamaican dollar (.8333 J. dollar equals U. S.$1. Sept. 1971).
Gross National Product (1969): $1,064,000,000.
National Income (1969): $866,000,000; *per person,* $444.
Manufacturing (metric tons, 1969): Residual fuel oil, 683,000.
Crops (metric tons, 1968 crop year): Bananas, 280,000.
Minerals (metric tons, 1969): Bauxite, 10,319,000 (ranks 1st among world producers).
Foreign Trade (1970): *Exports,* $343,000,000 (chief exports— Alumina, $133,332,000; bauxite, $91,788,000). *Imports,* $522,000,000. *Chief trading partners* (1968)—United States, United Kingdom, Canada.
Transportation: *Roads* (1970), 9,580 miles (15,417 km); *motor vehicles* (1968), 88,900.
Communications: *Telephones* (1970), 66,643; *television stations* (1971), 1; *television sets* (1968), 56,000; *radios* (1969), 450,000; *newspapers* (1967), 2.

Emperor Hirohito of Japan delivers a speech on arrival at Anchorage, Alaska, on September 27. Empress Nagako is at far left, the Nixons at right.

JAPAN

During the first half of 1971, the Japanese modestly deprecated, but nonetheless took great pride in, foreign businessmen's predictions that Japan's gross national product (GNP), which is already the second in the non-Communist world, would soon surpass that of the Soviet Union and might indeed exceed that of the United States by the century's end. In apparent recognition of Japan's "super-power" status, the United States moved to fulfill its promise to return Okinawa to Japanese jurisdiction in 1972.

In the second half of the year, Japan began to feel the attendant stresses of being a great power. What Japanese called the "Nixon shock" hit the nation in three waves: the first was the abrupt shift in U. S. policy toward China; next was U. S. President Richard Nixon's dollar defense plan; and third was what amounted to a U. S. ultimatum on Japanese textile exports to the United States. In a courageous but futile gesture, Japan agreed not only to support but also to co-sponsor the "two Chinas" resolutions of the United States in the UN General Assembly. Although Japan's media criticized this move, calmer observers tried to view events in perspective. Speaking at the dedication of the handsome new Japan House in New York, on September 17, critic Jun Eto remarked that the immediate crises, in fact, obscured a historic shift in the entire international system.

INTERNATIONAL AFFAIRS

To Premier Eisaku Sato and to his majority Liberal Democratic party (LDP), the long-awaited reversion of Okinawa represented a political triumph. Later, however, uncertainties in Japan's China policy and increasing monetary and trade frictions threatened not only the Okinawa treaty but also Japan's entire postwar policy of dependence on the United States.

Reversion of Okinawa. By May, after two years' intensive U. S.-Japanese negotiations, official releases indicated that the reversion of Okinawa would be effected in 1972, in compliance with the Sato-Nixon communiqué of Nov. 21, 1969. On June 17, Foreign Minister Kiichi Aichi in Tokyo and Secretary of State William Rogers in Washington simultaneously signed the Okinawa reversion treaty. Chobyo Yara, the elected chief executive of the Ryukyus, was deliberately absent from the ceremony to express the ambivalence of Okinawans. Yara said that they were happy to return to Japan but uneasy over the terms of the accord.

The 9-article treaty provided that the U. S.-Japan security treaty would be extended to Okinawa without change after reversion. It permits the United States to continue using military bases on Okinawa, but subject to restrictions and the requirement of "prior consultation." In Article VII, the United

JAPAN • Information Highlights

Official Name: Japan.
Area: 142,811 square miles (369,881 sq km).
Population (1970 est.): 103,540,000. *Density,* 720 per square mile (277 per sq km). *Annual rate of increase,* 1.1%.
Chief Cities (1968 est.): Tokyo, the capital, 9,012,000; Osaka, 3,078,000; Yokahama, 2,047,000; Nagoya, 2,000,000; Kyoto, 1,400,000; Kobe, 1,200,000; Kitakyushu, 1,100,000.
Government: *Head of state,* Hirohito, emperor (acceded Dec. 25, 1926). *Head of government,* Eisaku Sato, prime minister (took office Nov. 9, 1964). *Legislature*—Diet: House of Representatives, 486 members; House of Councillors, 250 members. *Major political parties*—Liberal Democratic party, Japan Socialist party, Komeito, Japan Democratic Socialist party, Japan Communist party.
Languages: Japanese (official).
Education: *Literacy rate* (1970), 98% of population. *Expenditure on education* (1968), 20.8% of total public expenditure. *School enrollment* (1968)—primary, 9,383,182; secondary, 9,593,103; technical/vocational, 1,892,481; university/higher, 1,526,764.
Finances (1970): *Revenues,* $22,520,000,000; *expenditures,* $23,442,000,000; *monetary unit,* yen (308.0 yen equal U. S. $1, Dec. 30, 1971).
Gross National Product (1970 est.): $202,000,000,000.
National Income (1969): $131,831,000,000; *national income per person,* $1,518.
Economic Indexes: *Industrial production* (1970), 258 (1963=100); *agricultural production* (1969), 125 (1963=100); *consumer price index* (1970), 144 (1963=100).
Manufacturing (metric tons, 1969): Crude steel, 82,166,000; pig iron and ferroalloys, 59,444,000; cement, 51,387,000.
Crops (metric tons, 1969 crop year): Rice, 18,186,000 (ranks 4th among world producers); sweet potatoes and yams (1968), 3,594,000 (world rank 1st).
Minerals (metric tons, 1969): Coal, 44,690,000; iron ore, 1,068,000; salt, 1,029,000.
Foreign Trade (1968): *Exports* (1970), $19,318,000,000 (chief exports—transport equipment, $2,235,770,000; iron or steel $1,712,610,000; electrical machinery and appliances, $1,-521,610,000; textile yarn and fabrics, $1,435,490,000). *Imports* (1970), $18,811,000,000 (chief imports—petroleum, crude and partly refined, $1,685,410,000; wood, rough or roughly squared, $1,035,940,000; textile fibers and waste, $951,620,000; iron ore and concentrates, $833,910,000). *Chief trading partners* (1968)—United States (took 32% of exports, supplied 27% of imports); Australia (3%—7%); Canada.
Tourism: *Receipts* (1970), $232,000,000.
Transportation: *Roads* (1970), 613,500 miles (987,306 km); *motor vehicles* (1969), 15,145,800 (automobiles, 6,933,-600); *railroads* (1970), 29,300 miles (47,152 km); *merchant fleet* (1971), 30,509,000 gross registered tons; *national airlines,* Japan Airlines, All Nippon Airways; *principal airport,* Tokyo.
Communications: *Telephones* (1970), 23,131,688; *television stations* (1969), 216; *television sets* (1969), 21,879,000; *radios* (1968), 25,742,000; *newspapers* (1969), 169 (daily circulation, 51,498,000).

States promised that reversion would be carried out "in a manner consistent with the policy of the Government of Japan," an indirect way of honoring Japan's nonnuclear policy. The signatories reiterated the principle that peace in the areas of Korea and Taiwan was vital to the security of Japan. In return for certain U. S. assets in Okinawa, Japan agreed to pay the United States $320 million.

For ratification, the treaty must be approved by the U. S. Senate and the Japanese Diet and signed by the President of the United States. During the summer the severe economic strains between the two countries led to fears that opposition might be encountered in the Senate. On November 10, however, that body approved the treaty by a vote of 84–6. On November 24, the lower house of the Diet voted 285–73 in favor of the treaty. It also passed two resolutions, one forbidding the United States to place nuclear arms on Okinawa, and the other calling for a reduction in the number and size of the U. S. bases there.

The "Two Chinas" Issue. Whatever stock of Japanese goodwill the United States gained out of the Okinawa agreement was depleted by the first tremors from what in Japan was called the "Nixon shock." Without prior consultation or forewarning, Tokyo heard on July 16 that the U. S. President planned to visit Peking early in 1972. Japan's entire postwar foreign policy, which had emphasized close

relations with the United States and the neglect of Communist China, was suddenly subjected to severe criticism. Even Premier Sato had occasionally voiced the vain hope that, while Japan continued to recognize the Republic of China (Taiwan), economic and cultural ties with the People's Republic of China (mainland China) might be expanded. Peking had repeatedly denounced the "two Chinas" policy quietly pushed by Japan. This same policy was suddenly openly adopted by the United States.

Throughout July and August, the Sato government's U. S. and China policies were sharply criticized both at home and abroad. It endeavored unsuccessfully to leave the impression that Tokyo and Washington had a fully coordinated policy on China. One week after President Nixon's announcement, Japanese diplomats began consulting with various countries in an effort to determine what the U. S. position on the China representation issue would be, before the 26th UN General Assembly convened on September 21. In mid-August, U. S. Ambassador to the UN George Bush asked Secretary General U Thant to place two resolutions on the UN agenda. One supported the representation of both Chinas in the United Nations, and the other stated that the expulsion of Nationalist China from the United Nations should be designated an "important question," requiring a two-thirds vote in the Assembly.

Early in September the Japanese foreign ministry informed the U. S. embassy in Tokyo that, although Japan would vote for the two resolutions, the Sato government could not yet promise to co-sponsor them because of division within the LDP. Premier Sato and his faction of the party represented the many Japanese sympathetic to the Nationalist Chinese because in 1945 they had treated Japanese prisoners kindly. Also, Japan had signed a peace treaty with Taiwan in 1952. Yet Japanese leaders correctly feared that the resolutions might fail, in which case the Communist Chinese would be even more hostile to Japan. Therefore, major LDP factions, leaders, and even cabinet members opposed the two-Chinas policy.

On September 22, Premier Sato broke the deadlock in his cabinet by announcing that Japan would

AGREEMENT returning Okinawa to Japan is signed in Washington in June by U. S. Secretary of State Rogers (*right*). Japan's ambassador, Nobuhiko Ushiba, smiles because Rogers cannot read copy, which is in Japanese.

THE NEW YORK TIMES

On "International Antiwar Day," October 21, students in Tokyo demonstrate against the Okinawa reversion treaty.

cosponsor the resolutions. This bold—some Japanese called it stubborn—decision was motivated by the need to sustain cooperation with the United States in order to guarantee the reversion of Okinawa.

An Albanian resolution before the UN General Assembly on October 25 seated the People's Republic and expelled the Nationalists by a vote of 76 favoring, 35 opposed, and 17 abstentions. Premier Sato told the Diet that the action constituted "international recognition" of the Peking government, and he predicted that this would eventually lead Japan to recognize mainland China.

U. S.-Japanese Trade Problems. Meanwhile, U. S.-Japanese relations were further complicated by another major tremor from the "Nixon shock." The President's announcement on August 16 of a new economic policy included a plan to defend the international status of the dollar. The United States, having suffered a deficit of almost $1.5 billion in trade with Japan during the first six months of 1971, imposed a 10% surcharge on imports, aimed mainly at Japan. Japan's ministry of international trade and industry forecast that Japan would incur an annual loss of $1.2 billion in exports to the United States under the surcharge.

The basic causes of Japan's international economic problems were to be found not only in uneven U. S.-Japanese trade, but also in Japan's enormous and growing economic strength. On March 31, 1971 (the end of Japan's fiscal year 1970–71), Japan's balance of payments showed a record $2 billion surplus. By September the surplus was $3.3 billion. Gold and foreign exchange reserves had climbed from $3.9 billion to $5.5 billion. Then, through the first seven months of 1971, Japan's reserves tripled. In the single month of August they had increased by over $4.5 billion to reach a total of $12.5 billion. The prediction by Tokyo's financial leaders that Japan would soon feel domestic and international pressure for revaluation of the yen had come true. The financiers charged the Sato administration with delay in adopting a needed new international economic policy for Japan.

The warning was sounded again at a U. S.-Japanese economic conference held in Washington in July. The Sato government replied with a promise to create a new program that would include liberalizing imports and capital investments, applying preferential tariffs, reducing imports tariffs, lowering nontariff trade barriers, reducing aggressive export promotion, increasing international economic cooperation, and adopting appropriate financial policies.

Indeed, a somewhat reluctant movement toward capital liberalization by Japan had been reflected in the government's permission to U. S. and Japanese firms to engage in joint ventures. In June, the Chrysler Corp. had entered into an agreement with Mitsubishi Motors; in July, General Motors signed with Isuzu Motors; and the Ford Motor Co. was expected to complete a pact with Tokyo Kogyo.

It was not as easy to arrive at agreement in the 3-year dispute over textile exports to the United States. This issue, too, threatened the approval of Okinawa reversion in the U. S. Senate; the quarrel triggered the third tremor of the "Nixon shock." In July, after months of futile negotiations, the Japan Textile Federation announced a 3-year plan for voluntary controls on textile shipments, but Washington and U. S. textile interests remained adamant in favoring a negotiated settlement. On September 30, at the height of the U. S.-Japanese economic crisis, Washington presented Tokyo with what the Japanese regarded as an ultimatum. If Japan would not replace the voluntary restraints with a government agreement, then the United States would impose strict import quotas on October 15. At the deadline, in a pact initialed in Tokyo by Minister of International Trade and Industry Kakuei Tanaka and special envoy David M. Kennedy, Japan agreed to limit exports of synthetic and woolen textiles over three years. The United States, in turn, agreed to lift the import surcharge on textiles retroactive to October 1. Textile workers unions in Japan predicted that the settlement would cost them some 300,000 jobs, and they filed a lawsuit in Tokyo to stop the agreement. Japan's textile industry finally promised to cooperate.

Meanwhile, sharp declines in stock prices on the Tokyo exchange were followed by a record $1.2 billion purchase of dollars by the Bank of Japan in one day, August 27, in a desperate attempt to maintain parity of the yen at 360 to the dollar. On August 28, Japan floated the yen temporarily, and its value immediately rose 6.44% to reach 338.20 yen to the dollar on the Tokyo foreign exchange market (as against 360 to the dollar the day before).

Pressure on the yen had subsided early in October, after meetings in Washington of the Group of Ten and the annual conference of the International Monetary Fund. Finance Minister Mikio Mizuta returned from Washington expressing hopes that yen revaluation might be held to a margin of 11%, that bilateral adjustment with the United States would stabilize the yen-dollar rate, and that a multilateral solution of the monetary problem would be forthcoming. On November 10, Mizuta told visiting U. S. Secretary of the Treasury John B. Connally that Japan would not unilaterally revalue the yen unless the U. S. import surcharge was removed and a multilateral currency adjustment with the European Economic Community was made. Finally, as part of a broad agreement on currency rates reached in Washington on December 18, the yen was effectively revalued 16.9% to 308 yen to the dollar as compared with the parity existing in August. (See INTERNATIONAL FINANCE.)

Relations with Peking. One day after President Nixon's announcement, on July 17, of his proposed visit to Peking, Premier Sato welcomed the trip since it might ease tensions in East Asia. Later, in the House of Councillors, he made an indirect appeal to the Chinese Communist leaders to let him, also, visit Peking to normalize relations. He added, however, that Japan had to abide by "international commitments" to the Republic of China (Taiwan). In Peking, Premier Chou En-lai bluntly replied that his government would welcome the visit of a different Japanese premier.

Relations with the USSR. On October 19 the foreign ministers of Japan and the Soviet Union exchanged cables of congratulations on the 15th anniversary of the signing of a joint declaration normalizing their relations. However, a peace treaty still has not been concluded, and the problem of the "northern territories" remains a pending issue between the nations. Upon his return from Moscow, Japan's Communist party chairman, Kenji Miyamoto, claimed that the Soviet leaders would consider the return of Habomai and Shikotan islands in the Kuriles after the conclusion of a peace treaty.

Relations with Korea. As in the case of China, Japan since 1950 has been faced with two opposed Korean governments: the Republic of Korea in the south, which Japan recognizes, and the Democratic People's Republic of Korea in the north. On October 25 the popular Socialist governor of Tokyo, Ryokichi Minobe, left for a visit to Pyongyang in North Korea before going on to Kwangchow and Peking in China. On his trip, Governor Minobe stressed "people-to-people diplomacy," but he was told by North Korea's premier that normalization of relations between the two countries was impossible so long as Japan maintained relations with South Korea.

Imperial Trip. On October 14, Emperor Hirohito and Empress Nagako returned to Tokyo from an 18-day tour of western Europe and meeting with U. S. President Nixon in Anchorage, Alaska, on September 27. It was the first time a reigning Japanese emperor had visited a foreign country. The couple visited Denmark, Belgium, France,

MILITARY REVIEW, held to commemorate Tokyo's Self-Defense Forces Day, featured rockets and missiles for the first time in Japan.

UPI

NEW INTERNATIONAL AIRPORT under construction at Narita, about 35 miles (55 km) east of Tokyo, was bitterly fought by residents of expropriated sites. Here a crane and workmen demolish the last house in the area.

Britain, the Netherlands, Switzerland, and West Germany.

In his statement reviewing the trip, the emperor admitted that Japan would have to make greater efforts to achieve international goodwill. Despite an often indifferent and occasionally hostile reception, particularly in the Netherlands, the foreign minister seemed to look to Europe for a partial solution of U. S.-Japanese trade problems.

DOMESTIC AFFAIRS

The effects of the complex international economic problems on Japan were made worse by the possible onset of a recession. The Economic Planning Agency (EPA) said that exuberant investment during the 1966–70 growth period was the main cause of the slowdown, and that problems such as pollution, housing shortages, and the plight of the aged were characteristics of urban society.

Parties and Politics. When the 65th session of the Diet reconvened on January 22, the Liberal Democratic party (LDP) held a comfortable majority: 303 seats in the (lower) House of Representatives and 137 in the (upper) House of Councillors. The Japan Socialist party (JSP) ranked second with 91 seats in the lower and 63 in the upper house, followed by the Komeito (KMT), the Democratic Socialist party (DSP), and the Japan Communist party (JCP).

In municipal elections held on April 12, however, the issues of inflation and pollution mobilized housewives and dissident voters behind opposition candidates in Japan's two largest cities, Tokyo and Osaka. Backed by the JSP, JCP, and independents, incumbent Tokyo Gov. Ryokichi Minobe received 3,615,299 votes, winning by a record percentage for any candidate in Japan's history. In Osaka, anti-pollution groups helped Ryoichi Kuroda defeat the incumbent LDP governor. LDP candidates, however, won 13 of the 18 governorships up for election in other prefectures.

The campaign for half the seats in the upper house revolved around national issues, such as revaluation of the yen, inflation, and the Okinawa reversion agreement. In the election of June 27 the LDP lost one seat, while the opposition JSP gained. Party seating in the upper house after the election was as follows: LDP, 136; JSP, 66; KMT, 23; DSP, 13; JCP, 10; and independents, 4.

After Premier Sato formed a new cabinet in July, the LDP found that the government's economic and foreign policies were increasingly opposed. On October 27 in the lower house, the LDP turned back a no-confidence motion against Foreign Minister Fukuda and the China policy, by a vote of 274–169. A similar motion against Minister Tanaka, due to opposition to the textile agreement, was rejected by 280–171. On October 28, the LDP rode out another resolution against Fukuda in the upper house.

Economic Developments. In fiscal 1970, Japan's gross national product reached $202 billion (72.7 trillion yen). Although the per capita national income was $1,518, Japan ranked only 15th in the world. Moreover, in the first two quarters of 1971 the estimated annual real growth rate fell to 4%–5%, a sharp drop from the 1970 rate of 9.8%.

In September, the consumer price index in Tokyo soared over 10% above that of the same month in 1970, from 133 to 143.3 (1965 = 100).

On the eve of the new fiscal year, March 29, the Diet passed a general accounts budget of 9.4 trillion yen. On October 30, however, the lower house had to adopt a 244,684 million yen supplementary budget for fiscal 1971. It was designed to encourage business recovery, and it gave priority to public works, including housing and roads.

Other Developments. At the height of the Expo 70 rush in the summer of 1970, All-Nippon Airways carried a record 30,000 passengers in a single day. One inevitable result of such overcrowding was a midair collision between an All-Nippon Boeing 727 and a Self-Defense fighter over northern Japan on July 30, 1971. The loss of 155 passengers and 7 crewmen was the worst air accident in history.

To ease air traffic congestion in the Tokyo area, the government was trying to build a new international airport on the Chiba peninsula east of Tokyo Bay. It was planned to be three times the size of the present, overcrowded Haneda International Airport. Most owners of property at the site sold their land to the government. A few held out, however, and throughout the summer, bands of farmers, union members, and radical students fought the expropriation of necessary land at each step of construction—on the surface, in towers over the site, and in a network of tunnels underground. Hundreds of protesters were arrested by thousands of riot police. Three policemen were killed on September 16, as the last areas were seized to make way for the main 1,312-foot (4,000-meter) runway.

Throughout the year, Japan was preparing for the 1972 Winter Olympic Games. Scheduled for Sapporo, on Hokkaido, the 11-day meeting was expected to welcome more than one million visitors.

ARDATH W. BURKS, *Rutgers University*

JAPANESE LITERATURE. See LITERATURE.

JORDAN

Authorities in Jordan in 1971 were primarily concerned with restoring order and political stability disrupted by the September 1970 civil war. Sporadic clashes continued between the Palestinian commandos and the Jordanian army until July 1971, when the army succeeded in eliminating the guerrilla strongholds in the northern hills.

The assassination of Premier Wasfi al-Tal in Cairo, Egypt, on Nov. 28, 1971, was linked to the commandos. The three captured gunmen were members of an organization known as "Black September," apparently in commemoration of the Jordanian civil war. Premier al-Tal had been attending a meeting of the joint defense council of the Arab League. King Hussein appointed Finance Minister Ahmed al-Lawzi premier on November 29.

Commando Activities. Defeated in September 1970, the commandos had entrenched themselves around the hills of Jerash and Ajlun. On March 25, 1971, a Jordanian spokesman accused them of engaging in sabotage to undermine Jordan's economy and to provoke the army. Clashes occurred again on March 26 in the north, and there was sporadic fighting in Amman. On April 2 the commandos blew up the Trans-Arabian Pipe Line supplying oil to Jordan's refinery at Zarqa. Three days later they damaged two jet fighters at the Mafraq air base. Violence continued through April 6, each side accusing the other of violating previously signed agreements. These events also precipitated a crisis in relations with Libya when, on March 28, President al-Qaddafi called for the Jordanian army to revolt against King Hussein. However, the tension slackened when Syria undertook to mediate the dispute. Although isolated incidents were reported, Jordan returned to its uneasy peace.

Showdown. From July 13 to 19, the Jordanian army launched an offensive against the commandos to reassert the regime's full authority. In a news conference on July 19, Premier al-Tal explained that this action had been taken because of the commandos' harassment of the Ajlun-Jerash highway, a main commercial and military route. At that time the total commando strength in Jordan had dropped to about 3,000 men from a high of nearly 12,000 in September 1970. In the new offensive, between 250 and 350 commandos were killed, some 2,500 were taken prisoner, and 72 crossed into Israel and asked for amnesty. On July 20, 1971, the Jordanian government announced that there were no longer any guerrilla bases in Jordan and that the Cairo and Amman agreements, which had ended the civil war in 1970, had been officially set aside. Most of the prisoners were released.

Arab Response. The responses of Algeria, Iraq, and Syria were quick and critical. On July 19, Iraq made a dramatic gesture in support of the commandos by closing the border with Jordan and asking that the Jordanian ambassador be withdrawn from Baghdad. Algeria suspended diplomatic relations with Jordan on July 29 and promised financial and military aid to the commandos. After heavy border fighting on August 12 between Syria and Jordanian forces, Syria severed diplomatic relations with Jordan, closed the border, and denied Jordan the use of Syrian airspace. Libya had severed ties with Amman in September 1970.

Tripoli and Jedda Conferences. On July 31 the presidents of Egypt, Syria, Yemen, and South Ye-

——— JORDAN • Information Highlights ———

Official Name: Hashemite Kingdom of Jordan.
Area: 37,738 square miles (97,740 sq km).
Population (1970 est.): 2,320,000. *Density,* 60 per square mile (23 per sq km). *Annual rate of increase,* 3.0%.
Chief City (1967 census): Amman, the capital, 330,220.
Government: *Head of state,* Hussein ibn Talal, king (acceded Aug. 11, 1952). *Head of government,* Ahmed al-Lawzi, premier (took office Nov. 29, 1971). *Legislature*—National Assembly; House of Deputies, 60 members; Senate, 30 members.
Language: Arabic (official).
Education: *Literacy rate* (1970), 30% of population. *Expenditure on education* (1968), 11.1% of total public expenditure. *School enrollment* (1968)—primary, 229,691; secondary, 77,630; technical/vocational, 2,491; university/higher, 4,077.
Finances (1970 est.): *Revenues,* $236,900,000; *expenditures,* $247,200,000; *monetary unit,* dinar (.3571 dinar equal U.S.$1, Sept. 1971).
Gross National Product (1968): $552,440,000.
National Income (1968): $478,857,460; *national income per person,* $221.
Consumer Price Index (1970), 115 (1967=100).
Manufacturing (metric tons, 1969): Cement, 511,000; wheat flour, 149,000; distillate fuel oils, 130,000; residual fuel oil, 118,000; beer, 15,000 hectoliters.
Crops (metric tons, 1968 crop year): Wheat (1969), 159,000; tomatoes, 127,000; olives, 13,000; lentils, 11,000.
Minerals (metric tons, 1969): Phosphate rock, 1,089,000; salt, 18,000.
Foreign Trade (1970): *Exports,* $34,000,000 (chief exports, 1970—phosphates, $6,270,000; tomatoes, $4,032,000. *Imports,* $184,000,000 (chief imports, 1967—textile yarns and fabrics, $14,406,000; motor vehicles, $11,903,000; cereals and preparations, $11,472,000). *Chief trading partners* (1968)—United Kingdom (supplied 12% of imports); United States.
Tourism: *Receipts* (1970), $11,840,000.
Transportation: *Roads* (1970), 3,480 miles (5,599 km); *motor vehicles* (1969), 20,500 (automobiles, 15,000); *railroads* (1965), 227 miles (365 km); *national airline,* Jordanian Airlines (ALIA); *principal airport,* Amman.
Communications: *Telephones* (1969), 29,864; *television stations* (1968), 2; *television sets* (1969), 25,000; *radios* (1965), 269,000; *newspapers* (1968), 2.

men met in a summit conference at Tripoli, called by Libyan President al-Qaddafi. The conference strongly condemned the Jordanian government and threatened to take more stringent measures if Jordan continued to reject the Cairo and Amman agreements. On August 4, Saudi Arabia and Egypt proposed that they should mediate a settlement between the Jordanian government and the commandos, but a conference held in Jedda on September 14 failed to bring about a reconciliation.

U.S. Aid. On May 2, U.S. Secretary of State William Rogers arrived in Amman on his Middle East tour. He announced that the United States would continue aid to Jordan. The United States had previously agreed to supply Jordan with $60 million in aid for the 1971 fiscal year—$30 million in grants and $30 million in arms credit. President Nixon announced that Jordan must be stable and viable if it is to make a positive contribution toward working out an enduring peace in the Middle East.

Economic Situation. The Jordanian economy was seriously affected by the events of September 1970, which almost paralyzed the country for two months. The losses to the economy were roughly estimated at 25 million dinars. To make up for those losses, Jordan relied heavily on foreign assistance. In addition to U.S. aid, Jordan received $40 million from Saudi Arabia, $10 million from Britain, and $6 million from the World Bank. The Tapline Company agreed to increase royalties to $9 million a year for the transit of pipelines across Jordanian territory. Recent drilling indicates the possibility of commercial quantities of oil in Jordan.

AMIN A. MAHMOUD
Georgetown University

JORDAN, Vernon E., Jr. See BIOGRAPHY.
JUDAISM. See RELIGION.

KANSAS

Bountiful crops, a cutback on state agency programs by a bickering governor and Legislature, and the activities of an attorney general who vows to enforce all laws "with equal vigor" were 1971 highlights in Kansas.

Agriculture. Record-breaking harvests of 312 million bushels of high-quality wheat and 227 million bushels of sorghum grain made 1971 a banner year for Kansas agriculture. In addition, the 115-million-bushel corn crop was the state's largest since 1932, with the yield per acre of 88 bushels far ahead of the previous record.

Legislation. Gov. Robert B. Docking's "austere but adequate" budget of $945 million was trimmed $32 million by a "go-him-one-better" Legislature. Mainly affected by the cuts were aid to higher education, welfare, and waste treatment facilities. Thus the painful task of instituting major tax increases was avoided for another year, although there were tax adjustments upward on stronger-than-3.2% beer and certain other alcoholic beverages.

Of the 1,064 bills introduced during the 3-month session, 338 became law, but there was a lack of substantive major legislation. A proposal for submission of a constitutional amendment lowering the voting age to 18 in all elections was passed, and

---

KANSAS · Information Highlights

Area: 82,264 square miles (213,064 sq km).
Population (1970 census): 2,249,071. *Density,* 28 per sq mi.
Chief Cities (1970 census): Topeka, the capital, 125,011; Wichita, 276,554; Kansas City, 168,213; Overland Park, 79,034; Lawrence, 45,698; Salina, 37,714; Hutchinson, 36,885.
Government (1971): *Chief Officers*—governor, Robert Docking (D); lt. gov., Reynolds Shultz (R); secy. of state, Mrs. Elwill M. Shanahan (R); atty. gen., Vern Miller (D); treas., Walter H. Peery (R); commissioner, Dept. of Ed., C. Taylor Whittier; chief justice, Harold R. Fatzer. *Legislature*—Senate, 40 members (32 Republicans, 8 Democrats); House of Representatives, 125 members (84 R, 41 D).
Education (1970–71): *Enrollment*—public elementary schools, 303,540 pupils; 13,066 teachers; public secondary, 210,198 pupils; 12,818 teachers; nonpublic schools (1968–69), 48,800 pupils; 2,010 teachers; college and university (fall 1968). 92,486 students. *Public school expenditures* (1970–71), $360,164,000 ($771 per pupil). *Average teacher's salary,* $8,034.
State Finances (fiscal year 1970): *Revenues,* $794,678,000 (3% general sales tax and gross receipts taxes, $145,371,000; motor fuel tax, $81,402,000; federal funds, $197,046,000). *Expenditures,* $792,242,000 (education, $330,545,000; health, welfare, and safety, $22,324,000; highways, $121,531,000). *State debt* $223,590,000 (June 30, 1970).
Personal Income (1970): $8,821,000; per capita, $3,804.
Public Assistance (1970): $114,925,000. *Average monthly payments* (Dec. 1970)—old-age assistance, $65.85; aid to families with dependent children, $201.20.
Labor Force: Nonagricultural wage and salary earners (June 1971), 674,800. *Average annual employment* (1969)—manufacturing, 146,000; trade, 157,000; government, 151,000; services, 101,000. *Insured unemployed* (Oct. 1971)—9,700 (2.3%).
Manufacturing (1967): *Value added by manufacture,* $2,112,400,000. Transportation equipment, $625,800,000; food and kindred products. $277,800,000; chemicals and allied products, $276,300,000; petroleum and coal products, $179,700,000; nonelectrical machinery, $174,000,000.
Agriculture (1970): *Cash farm income,* $2,001,526,000 (livestock, $1,223,200,000; crops. $550,687,000; government payments, $227,639,000). *Chief crops* (1971)—Wheat, 312,000,000 bushels (ranks 1st among the states); sorghum grain, 227,000,000 bushels (ranks 2d); corn, 115,000,000 bushels; hay (1970). 4,102,000 tons.
Mining (1970): *Production value,* $601,454,000 (ranks 12th among the states). *Chief minerals*—Crude helium. 2,603,800,000 cubic feet; natural gas, 917,313,000,000 cubic feet; petroleum, 84,300,000 barrels; natural gas liquids, 30,460,000 barrels.
Transportation: *Roads* (1969). 134,117 miles (215,834 km); *motor vehicles* (1969), 1,515,000; *railroads* (1968), 7,864 miles (12,656 km); *airports* (1969), 109.
Communications: *Telephones* (1971), 1,303,700; *television stations* (1969), 12; *radio stations* (1969), 79; *newspapers* (1969), 50 (daily circulation, 650,000).

---

the amendment was overwhelmingly approved in the follow-up statewide vote on April 6.

The legislators reapportioned the state's congressional districts and passed a law requiring statewide registration of voters. A new program for rehabilitation of juvenile offenders was instituted, and state penal officials were authorized to permit certain prisoners, who have been imprisoned for at least two years and who have good behavior records, to make family visits up to three times a year for a total of not more than 10 days. The possession of marihuana with the intent to sell was made a felony, as opposed to mere possession, which is a misdemeanor. Other new laws legalized charity bingo lotteries by the elimination of criminal penalties, empowered county social welfare boards to appoint one or more investigators to check for possible fraud, and authorized American Indians residing in Kansas to fish and hunt without licenses.

In March the state supreme court nullified on legal technicalities a constitutional amendment, adopted in the November 1970 election, that included provisions for a 4-year gubernatorial term and the streamlining of state government. Consequently, the proposed electorate overhaul of Kansas state government must await another vote of the people.

Caught in the high-level government stalemate over expenditures and additional taxes are development plans for the Kansas Capitol Plaza area, south of the capitol in Topeka. At year's end political togetherness was still not the order of the day.

Law Enforcement. Vern Miller, former sheriff of Sedgwick county who was elected as the first Democratic attorney general in Kansas since the 1890's, took office in January. His campaign slogan, "I will be there, in the courts or in the streets," was soon transmitted into action. Leading drug and gambling raids over the state, he popped out of the trunk of a car in Wichita on July 21, engaged one suspect in a two-block chase, downed him, and sat on him until reinforcements arrived.

"I look at it this way," said Miller. "If a law is on the books, the simplest thing to do is to enforce it. . . . I figure the people want the laws enforced or they wouldn't have them on the books. On the other hand, I don't think any law enforcement officer has the right to get rough and tough just because he is wearing a badge."

NYLE H. MILLER
Kansas State Historical Society

KENTUCKY

Politics, culminating in the November election to fill state offices, demanded a large share of Kentuckians' attention during 1971.

Redistricting. In January, federal Judge Bernard T. Moynahan ruled in a test case that the provision of Kentucky's constitution prohibiting the division of counties in forming legislative districts conflicts with the 14th Amendment to the U. S. Constitution. The General Assembly, called into special session to redraw the district lines, adopted a measure that was criticized on constitutional grounds but became law without the governor's signature. Challenged in federal court, the new law was declared unconstitutional by Judge Mac Swinford, who, however, stated that the November elections could be held under its provisions. At the same time he ordered the next legislature to consider the matter further.

Elections. In November, Kentucky voters followed precedent in refusing to elect two Republican governors in succession. Democrat Wendell H. Ford, lieutenant governor during Republican Gov. Louie B. Nunn's administration, won the gubernatorial election over three opponents, while his party rallied behind him to win all the other state executive offices and to increase its dominance of the General Assembly. The losers in the race for governor were Republican Thomas D. Emberton; independent (Commonwealth party) A. B. "Happy" Chandler, who had filled the office twice; and American party candidate William E. Smith.

Homestead Exemption. In November the voters also approved a constitutional amendment exempting from taxation a home up to the assessed valuation of $6,500, if it is occupied by an owner who has reached age 65.

Political Changes. Two prominent names will be missing from future political calculations. Both Democrat John C. Watts, congressman for 20 years, and Republican William O. Cowger, former mayor of Louisville and twice U. S. representative, died in 1971. In a special election, held Dec. 4, 1971, Democrat William P. Curlin, Jr., was chosen over three opponents to fill the remainder of Watts' term as congressman from the 6th Kentucky District.

Death of a Negro Leader. In March, Whitney M. Young, Jr., a native of Shelby county, died abroad. His body was taken to Lexington, where, following a graveside eulogy by President Nixon, he was buried beside his mother. Three months later his widow removed the body from segregated Greenwood Cemetery to New Rochelle, N. Y., where she resides. Meanwhile, Governor Nunn carried out a plan, made possible by funds allocated by President Nixon, to convert Lincoln School, in Shelby county, to a vocational skills center named for Young.

Education. Kentucky teachers showed less militancy than in 1970, when their effort to strike proved ineffectual. In May the National Education Association issued a report highly critical of the state's support of education but did not call for sanctions. After the November election, Governor-elect Ford was quoted as stating that he would ask for a 12% increase in teachers' pay over the next two years—half the amount requested by the Kentucky Education Association.

The Economy. Growers of Burley tobacco, faced with the end of government subsidies, voted in May in favor of price supports based on poundage controls. Near the end of the year, with Burley production down about 3%, expectations of satisfactory prices were widely held. High yields were forecast for other major crops. Personal income showed a marked gain in 1971.

JAMES F. HOPKINS, *University of Kentucky*

KENYA

The chief event in Kenya in 1971 was the arrest and conviction of 13 persons for planning a coup against the government of President Jomo Kenyatta. The planned coup broke the political calm that had existed in the country since the general elections in December 1969.

Abortive Coup. On June 8, 12 men were sentenced to prison terms ranging from seven to nine and a half years after pleading guilty to charges of conspiring to overthrow the government. The convicted plotters, whose plans were only in a tentative stage of development, included a former cadet in the Kenyan Army, a Nairobi city councillor, a geography professor, and the deputy director general of the Kenya lint and seed marketing board. Later in the month, Gideon Mutiso, a member of the National Assembly, confessed to being involved in the conspiracy and was also jailed.

Following testimony at the trials, in which he was implicated in the plot, Maj. Gen. J. M. L. Ndolo was dismissed as chief of the defense staff. In another major change, Kitili Mwendwa, who had become the first African chief justice of Kenya's supreme court in July 1968, resigned his post in July 1971. He was succeeded by James Wicks, a European.

The political turmoil reflected to some extent the tribal tension that has plagued Kenya. The persons implicated in the coup were primarily members of the Kamba, Luo, and Kalenjin tribal groups. All of these groups had previously given some evidence of disaffection with the dominant position in the government of the Kikuyu, the country's largest group.

Political Affairs. Despite the threat of a coup and other more fundamental problems, Kenya has retained one of the most active parliamentary systems of government in Africa. All members of the unicameral parliament, the National Assembly, belong to the ruling party, the Kenya African National Union

PRESIDENT Jomo Kenyatta (*right*) shows U. S. Vice President Spiro Agnew through rose garden near Nairobi in July. Agnew's stopover was part of his around-the-world diplomatic tour during the summer.

(KANU), but there is much parliamentary discussion of major issues and criticism of the government.

On March 27, Oginga Odinga, formerly leader of the opposition Kenya People's Union (KPU) and before that Kenya's first vice president, was released after 18 months' detention. Odinga and some of his supporters had been detained and the KPU banned after rioting in his home area of Nyanza during a visit by President Kenyatta in October 1969. In September 1971, Odinga rejoined KANU, in which he may again become a major figure.

Economic Development. The second phase of the Seven Forks hydroelectric project on the Tana River began in 1971 with economic assistance totaling $29 million from Sweden and the World Bank.

────────── **KENYA • Information Highlights** ──────────

Official Name: Republic of Kenya.
Area: 224,959 square miles (582,644 sq km).
Population (1970 est.): 10,900,000. *Density,* 47 per square mile (18 per sq km). *Annual rate of increase,* 3.2%.
Chief Cities (1969 est.): Nairobi, the capital, 478,000; Mombasa, 246,000.
Government: *Head of state,* Jomo Kenyatta, president (took office June 1, 1963). *Head of government,* Jomo Kenyatta. *Legislature*—National Assembly, 158 elected members and 12 appointed members. *Major political party*—Kenya African Union.
Languages: English (official), Swahili (unofficial).
Education: *Literacy rate* (1970), 25% of population. *Expenditure on education* (1967), 4.5% of gross national product. *School enrollment* (1968)—primary, 1,209,680; secondary, 109,867; vocational, 1,872; university/higher, 4,967.
Finances (1969 est.): *Revenues,* $215,000,000; *expenditures,* $264,000,000; *monetary unit,* Kenya shilling (7.143 shillings equal U. S.$1, Sept. 1971).
Gross National Product (1970 est.): $1,580,000.
National Income (1969): $1,219,000,000; *national income per person,* $116.
Economic Indexes: *Manufacturing production* (1968), 143 (1963=100); *consumer price index* (1970), 111 (1963=100).
Manufacturing (metric tons, 1969): Residual fuel oil, 985,000; cement, 642,000; distillate fuel oils, 447,000.
Crops (metric tons, 1969 crop year): Agave (1968), 483,000; wheat, 210,000; coffee, 50,000; tea, 36,100.
Minerals (metric tons, 1969): Salt, 42,000; magnesite, 500; gold, 557 kilograms.
Foreign Trade (1970): *Exports,* $217,000,000 (chief exports—coffee, $62,300,000; tea, $35,560,000; sisal, $4,480,000). *Imports,* $397,000,000 (chief imports—chemicals, $31,-490,000; road motor vehicles, $29,350,000; crude and partly refined petroleum, $27,000,000; iron and steel, $17,-200,000). *Chief trading partners* (1968)—United Kingdom (took 25% of exports, supplied 31% of imports); West Germany (10%—8%); United States (7%—7%).
Tourism: *Receipts* (1970), $51,710,000.
Transportation: *Roads* (1970), 26,354 miles (42,411 km); *motor vehicles* (1969), 103,900 (automobiles, 87,900); *railroads* (1969), 3,670 miles (5,906 km).
Communications: *Telephones* (1970), 72,277; *television stations* (1968), 3; *television sets* (1969), 16,000; *radios* (1969), 500,000; *newspapers* (1969), 4.

Unemployment continued to be a major cause of economic stress. A select committee of the National Assembly issued a report on unemployment in December 1970 that stated: "It is now widely acknowledged that unemployment is currently one of the most serious social and economic problems in Kenya." According to the committee, the number of those employed in the modern wage economy rose only from 622,000 to 627,000 during the 1960's, and in 1969 there were still some 1.6 million males outside of wage employment. It is reasonable to assume that people seeking employment will continue to outnumber the jobs available for some time to come.

Foreign Affairs. The principal issue in Kenya's foreign relations in 1971 was the maintenance of the East African Community (EAC). The community provides shared services in areas such as transportation and telecommunications and facilitates trade between the member states, Kenya, Tanzania, and Uganda. As in all such arrangements, some aspects of cooperation have been threatened by national interests. For example, 1971 was the first year in which the national universities of the three states operated as autonomous institutions. Until December 1970 all had been part of the University of East Africa.

The problems of the East African Community became increasingly severe in 1971 because of deteriorating relations between Uganda and Tanzania, which threatened to halt the functioning of several EAC organs. Kenya attempted to steer a neutral course and to avoid backing either Uganda or Tanzania against the other. On October 29, Robert Ouko, EAC minister for economic affairs and a Kenyan, announced that a stalled appropriations bill had been passed and that problems affecting shared services had been solved.

On May 12, Kenya came out strongly against the dialogue with South Africa being proposed by some African states. Such moves were condemned in a joint communiqué issued by President Kenyatta and Nigerian President Yakubu Gowon, who was completing a state visit to Kenya. In July, U. S. Vice President Agnew paid a 3-day visit to Kenya.

An agreement providing for the training of officers of the Kenya Armed Forces in Canada was signed on April 29.

JAY E. HAKES
Louisiana State University in New Orleans

KHRUSHCHEV and wife (*left*) are greeted by President Eisenhower on U. S. visit in 1959, during which premier inspected Iowa corn. Also in 1959, he engaged then-Vice President Nixon in Moscow "kitchen debate."

KHRUSHCHEV, Nikita Sergeyevich

Soviet premier and first secretary of the Communist party: b. Kalinovka, Russia, April 17, 1894; d. Moscow, Sept. 11, 1971.

Nikita Sergeyevich Khrushchev, supreme Soviet leader from 1957 to 1964, was a bold innovator who ended mass purges, reduced police terror, decentralized industrial administration, greatly expanded cropland, made students perform manual labor, and ended official worship of Stalin. In Soviet foreign affairs Khrushchev inaugurated personal diplomacy and cultural exchange, expanded Soviet aid and trade, reopened Russia to tourists, and preached peaceful coexistence, though often creating or aggravating international crises. Witty, talkative, and approachable, he won many friends.

But in his last years of power, many of Khrushchev's major undertakings misfired. Soviet harvests slumped, and industrial growth slowed. China changed from friend to enemy, and the Kremlin lost control over the world Communist movement. When his Cuban policies nearly caused nuclear war with the United States, the USSR had to make a humiliating retreat. Frightened by his failures, Khrushchev's top assistants forced him to retire in 1964. Many of his innovations were soon discontinued.

Early Years. Khrushchev was born and raised in a farm village of the Kursk region—an area of mixed Russian and Ukrainian population south of Moscow and north of the eastern Ukraine. As a child he worked as a shepherd, had a rudimentary education at a parish school, and was taught to repair machinery by his father, the village blacksmith. When 15 years old, Khrushchev left home to work as a machinist at factories and mines of the Donets coal basin in the eastern Ukraine. He avoided military service in World War I by working in locomotive repair plants.

Khrushchev took no part in the Bolshevik Revolution of 1917, but he joined the Communist party in 1918, and fought for three years in the Russian Civil War—first as the leader of a police troop unit and later as the political commissar for a group of Red guerrillas. Remaining in the Donets Basin after the war, he was Communist party secretary—first in a coal mine, then in an industrial institute (where he also studied), in a district, and finally in a region. Having left the Donets Basin in 1928, he held party secretaryships in the Kiev region, in a Moscow industrial institute (where he again studied), in two city wards, and then was party secretary for all Moscow. By 1935 he was first secretary of both Moscow city and region, distinguishing himself by supervising subway construction and ruthlessly purging anti-Stalinists.

In 1938, Khrushchev was promoted to first party secretary of the entire Ukraine, where he spent the next 11 years, sometimes also serving as Ukrainian premier. He was made a full member of the USSR Politburo in 1939. During World War II he became a top-ranking army political commissar on various fronts in and around the Ukraine, achieving the rank of lieutenant general. After the war he sent 2 million Ukrainians to prison camps for alleged wartime collaboration with the Nazis. In 1949 he returned to Moscow to be one of the party secretaries directly assisting Stalin. When Stalin died in 1953, Khrushchev became first secretary of the USSR Communist party. He purged his Politburo rivals in 1957, and became premier in 1958.

Khrushchev's Leadership. Khrushchev ruled the USSR for only eight years, made many mistakes, and died in disgrace. Yet his endless innovations awakened Soviet society from Stalinist lethargy and aroused desire for further changes. These innovations were complex and often contradictory. Thus he was a statist, converting thousands of collective farms into state farms and changing thousands of handicraft collectives into government enterprises. Yet he delegated a little state power to the public by creating a 5-million-man volunteer auxiliary police and 200,000 informal "comrades' courts" to try cases of misdemeanor and misconduct.

Khrushchev abolished taxes in kind on peasant private gardens to encourage gardening, then tried to reduce garden acreage. He ordered 100 million acres (40.5 million hectares) of marginal land—the "new lands"—to be sown with grain, but later converted part of the new lands back into pasture. Under his rule millions of acres were planted with corn (maize) where the climate was unsuitable, but later were replanted with other crops.

Twice Khrushchev started to modernize Soviet manufacturing by rapidly expanding the inadequate chemical industry, and twice lost interest. He decentralized industrial administration by abolishing most Soviet industrial ministries and replacing them with over 100 regional councils, but then recentralized by creating Soviet industrial committees with ministerial rank.

For a brief time, Khrushchev permitted Soviet writers to criticize Soviet faults, but then began sending critical writers to prison camps or insane asylums. He released many minor offenders from prison camps, and altered the law codes to reduce the severity of criminal punishment. Yet he discriminated against Jews, harassed Christian churches, and instituted the death penalty for large-scale embezzling, speculation, and bribe-taking.

In foreign affairs Khrushchev ended the Soviet state of war with Japan, allowed Communist Poland to liberalize its government, withdrew the Soviet army of occupation from Rumania, reduced Austrian reparations, and concluded treaties with the United States creating cultural exchange programs, establishing direct radio-telephone communication between the Kremlin and the White House, and banning aboveground nuclear tests. But Khrushchev also supplied huge quantities of munitions to the Arab countries and North Vietnam, crushed the Hungarian revolution, created four Berlin crises, and sabotaged a 4-power summit meeting in Paris. He risked war with the United States by placing Soviet nuclear missiles in Cuba, but withdrew them when the U. S. Navy blockaded the Cuban coast.

After condemning Stalin's "cult of personality," Khrushchev ordered all Soviet places and enterprises named after Stalin to be given other titles. Then a Soviet mountain peak was renamed Mt. Khrushchev.

On Oct. 14, 1964, Khrushchev was dismissed from the party secretariat and Politburo, and on the following day lost his premiership. He was given a pension and lived his last years on a small estate near Moscow. When he died the Soviet press barely mentioned his death, and there was no state funeral.

Family. Khrushchev was survived by his second wife, Nina Petrovna. His first wife had died in the 1920's, and his two children by that marriage died in World War II. By his second wife he had a son, Sergei, and two daughters, Rada and Yelena. Rada's husband, Aleksei Adzhubei, was editor of the government newspaper *Izvestia* until Khrushchev's ouster.

ELLSWORTH RAYMOND
New York University

KISSINGER, Henry. See BIOGRAPHY.

KOREA

After two decades of unremitting hostility toward each other, the two halves of Korea initiated a north-south dialogue in 1971. In South Korea, Park Chung Hee was reelected to his third 4-year term as president, but he faced a host of economic and political problems. In North Korea, Kim Il Sung, who has held the reins of power since 1949, continued his efforts to mobilize his people in the twin programs of "economic and defense construction."

North-South Dialogue. On August 12, Choi Doo Sun, president of the South Korean Red Cross, proposed that its North Korean counterpart meet with it to help solve the problem of the 10 million Koreans separated from their relatives by the partition of Korea. Two days later, the North Korean Red Cross accepted the proposal. Preliminary talks began on September 20 at Panmunjon. By early November, agreement had been reached on the conference site—Pyongyang and Seoul alternately.

SOUTH KOREA

In the presidential election of April 27, President Park Chung Hee won his third 4-year term over Assemblyman Kim Dae Jung, the candidate of the opposition New Democratic party (NDP). Kim had surprised observers by waging an unusually vigorous campaign, during which he denounced Park's "one-man rule" and "corruption in high places," and by polling 5.4 million votes—45.3% of the total.

A statistical analysis of the election returns showed that two factors—the regional loyalty of voters and the tendency of urbanites to vote for the opposition, while rural areas support the government—influenced the election outcome to a striking degree. Thus Park received his decisive support from the Yongnam region in southeastern Korea and from rural areas, while Kim was strongly endorsed in the Honam region in the southwest and in urban areas.

National Assembly. The opposition of South Korea's urbanites to the government was graphically shown in the National Assembly election of May 25. In the three most populous cities—Seoul, Pusan, and Taegu—the ruling Democratic Republican party (DRP) lost all but 4 of the 32 seats contested. Nationwide, the DRP polled 52% of the total valid votes, and the NDP polled 48%. The enlarged 204-seat National Assembly was divided as follows: DRP, 113; NDP, 89; and minor parties, 2. By nearly doubling its strength, the NDP succeeded in narrowing the gap between the ruling and opposition parties in the assembly to the smallest ever.

However, on December 27, in a pre-dawn session, members of the DRP rammed through the National Assembly a bill giving President Park broad emergency powers. No opposition legislators were on hand. The bill was intended to give legal backing for actions taken under a state of national emergency declared by Park on December 6. Park signed the bill into law on the same day it was passed.

Rise of Kim. In March, President Park appointed as vice president of the party Kim Jong Pil, the architect both of the 1961 coup that brought Park to power and of the DRP. In June he became premier in the new post-election cabinet. Kim had "retired" from politics after a series of factional struggles in the DRP in 1964 and 1968.

Judicial Crisis. In July and August, South Korea experienced the most serious judicial crisis in its history. Enraged by the Seoul District Procurators Office's unprecedented attempt to arrest two judges of the Seoul criminal district court on charges of bribery, judges throughout the nation

─── **SOUTH KOREA** • Information Highlights ───

Official Name: Republic of Korea.
Area: 38,022 square miles (98,477 sq km).
Population (1970 census): 31,461,000. *Density,* 820 per square mile (316 per sq km). *Annual rate of increase,* 2.4%.
Chief Cities (1966 census): Seoul (1970 census), the capital, 5,509,993; Pusan, 1,425,703; Taegu, 845,073; Inchon, 525,072.
Government: *Head of state,* Park Chung Hee, president (took office Dec. 17, 1963). *Premier,* Kim Jong Pil (took office June 3, 1971). *Legislature*—National Assembly, 175 members. *Major political parties*—Democratic Republican party, New Democratic party.
Languages: Korean (official).
Education: *Literacy rate* (1970), 90% of population. *Expenditure on education* (1968), 21.2% of total public expenditure. *School enrollment* (1968)—primary, 5,548,577; secondary, 1,519,343; technical/vocational, 232,237; university/higher, 172,410.
Finances (1970): *Revenues,* $1,455, 950,000; *expenditures,* $1,523,500,000; *monetary unit,* won (370 wons equal U. S.$1, Sept. 1971).
Gross Domestic Product (1970): $8,051,600,000.
National Income (1969): $5,671,000,000; *national income per person,* $182.
Economic Indexes: *Industrial production* (1970), 365 (1963=100); *agricultural production* (1969), 140 (1963=100); *consumer price index* (1970), 178 (1965=100).
Manufacturing (metric tons, 1969): Cement, 4,871,000; wheat flour, 690,000; crude steel, 416,000.
Crops (metric tons, 1969 crop year): Rice, 5,528,000; sweet potatoes and yams (1968), 2,049,000.
Minerals (metric tons, 1969): Coal, 10,272,000; salt, 289,000; asbestos, 5,900; gold, 1,445 kilograms.
Foreign Trade (1968): Exports (1970), $834,000,000 (chief exports—plywood, $65,592,000; textile yarn and fabrics, $61,233,000; metalliferous ores and metal scrap, $25,757,000; textile fibers and waste, $20,023,000). *Imports* (1970), $1,984,000,000 (chief imports—nonelectrical machinery, $283,047,000). *Chief trading partners* (1968)—United States (took 52% of exports, supplied 31% of imports); Japan (22%—42%).
Transportation: *Highways* (1970), 334 miles (537 km); *motor vehicles* (1969), 90,100 (automobiles, 50,300); *railroads* (1971), 3,417 miles (5,499 km); *merchant fleet* (1970), 849,000 gross registered tons.
Communications: *Telephones* (1970), 562,111; *television stations* (1968), 3; *newspapers* (1969), 42.

─── **NORTH KOREA** • Information Highlights ───

Official Name: Democratic People's Republic of Korea.
Area: 46,540 square miles (120,538 sq km).
Population (1969 est.): 14,000,000. *Density,* 295 per square mile (110 per sq km). *Annual rate of increase,* 2.4%.
Chief City (1968 est.): Pyongyang, the capital, 653,100; Chongjin, 184,500.
Government: *Head of state,* Choi Yong Kun, chairman of the Presidium of the Supreme People's Assembly (took office 1957). *Head of government,* Kim Il Sung, premier (took office 1948). *Legislature*—Supreme People's Assembly; 383 members.
Languages: Korean (official).
Finances (1967 est.): *Revenues,* $3,300,000,000; *expenditures,* $3,300,000,000; *monetary unit,* won (1.20 won equal U. S.$1, 1971).
Industrial Production Index: (1968) 267 (1963=100).
Manufacturing (metric tons, 1969): Cement, 2,798,000; metallurgical coke, 2,000,000; pig iron and ferroalloys 1968), 2,000,100.
Crops (metric tons, 1968 crop year): Rice (1965), 2,500,000; potatoes, 930,000; sweet potatoes and yams, 250,000.
Minerals (metric tons, 1969): Coal, 20,100,000; lignite, 4,900,000; iron ore (1968), 3,500,000; salt, 550,000.
Foreign Trade (1962): Chief exports—metals, 48.5% of total export value; farm products, 12%. Chief imports—machines. 34.1% of total import value. *Chief trading partners* (1962)—USSR 60%; Communist China, 3%.
Transportation: *railroads* (1964), 6,500 miles (10,460 km); *principal airports,* Pyongyang, Hamheung, Chunglin.

tendered their resignations en masse. The central issue was not the guilt or innocence of the two judges involved, whose alleged crime was having been entertained by a lawyer representing a party in a pending case. Rather it was the intimidation of all judges by the executive branch. Eventually, the charges were dropped.

Crisis on Campuses. College students demonstrated against the government almost continuously in 1971. Chief complaints were electoral dishonesty and corruption in government. They also opposed compulsory military training. In October, President Park ordered troops to restore order on campuses. Nearly 1,900 students were arrested, eight universities were closed, 125 students were expelled, and hundreds more were drafted into the army.

Economy. In 1971, South Korea began the second year of its policy of stabilization. Nevertheless, difficulties, of which the most serious was inflation, persisted. By the end of October 1971, the wholesale price index had risen 10.9%, an increase of 3.5% over the comparable period in 1970.

Other economic problems included the gap between industrial and nonindustrial sectors, the skyrocketing foreign debt, the increase of declarations of bankruptcy by enterprises financed by foreign loans, growing unemployment, and the adverse effects of U. S. trade policies on Seoul's exports. The government sought to improve its unfavorable trade balance in June by devaluing its currency 13%. In September it began trading with East Europe.

Foreign Affairs. South Korea abandoned its policy of not having relations with Communist nations and began to woo "nonhostile" Communist countries. On December 6, President Park said that the admission of Communist China to the United Nations and the warlike posture of North Korea made it necessary to strengthen national security, and he declared a state of emergency.

Seoul's major diplomatic achievment was its successful lobbying for the shelving of three resolutions on Korea in the UN General Assembly.

NORTH KOREA

North Korea's domestic political scene changed very little in 1971. There was no letup in the glorification of Premier Kim Il Sung, who has been portrayed in North Korea's mass media as the source of all wisdom and the savior of all the Korean people.

In April the Fourth Supreme People's Assembly held its 5th session and adopted an "eight-point program of national salvation." The program, while reiterating Pyongyang's earlier proposals for unification, contained one new element: North Korea jettisoned its earlier insistence on the withdrawal of U. S. troops as a precondition for negotiation.

Economy. North Korea's continuing reluctance to release comprehensive statistics in 1971 seemed to indicate that it had made no real breakthrough in its economic programs. Among the problems plaguing the economy, as revealed by Premier Kim and First Vice Premier Kim Il, were (1) the inability of energy and extractive industries to "supply energy, fuel, and raw material in sufficient quantities," (2) a severe shortage of manpower, (3) scarcity of technical expertise, (4) managerial inefficiency, and (5) the persistence among workers and peasants of "bourgeois" attitudes, such as individualism, egoism, and love of material comfort.

In the new 6-year plan that began in 1971, a major emphasis was placed on resolving these problems. To cope with the labor shortage, for example, the plan called for increased technical innovations and mechanization. Also, in the first three months of 1971, a "100-day battle" was waged by workers and peasants, and reportedly they overfulfilled the "first quarter-year plan."

Foreign Affairs. The most impressive aspect of North Korea's foreign relations in 1971 was its deepening alliance with the People's Republic of China. Aside from the constant exchange of visitors, the two countries concluded a military aid agreement in September under which Peking would provide Pyongyang with "military aid gratis."

Meanwhile, Pyongyang and Moscow continued to exchange visitors, and agreements on trade and aid were renewed. In March, First Vice Premier Kim Il represented North Korea at the 24th Congress of the Communist party of the Soviet Union. In July, Kim's Soviet counterpart, Kiril T. Mazurov, visited Pyongyang to commemorate the 10th anniversary of the North Korean-Soviet Treaty of Friendship, Cooperation, and Mutual Assistance.

While North Korea maintained relations with all East European countries, including Yugoslavia in 1971, those with Rumania appeared to be particularly warm, as manifested by the state visit of Rumanian President Nicolae Ceauşescu in June.

With the start of the Red Cross talks, Japan increased its interest in North Korea. In October, North Korea agreed to the permanent stationing of Japanese reporters in Pyongyang, and it hinted that it was willing to establish normal ties with Japan.

In the first half of the year, North Korean exports to Japan totaled $13.6 million, while its imports from the same country totaled $19.7 million.

BYUNG CHUL KOH
University of Illinois at Chicago Circle

KOSYGIN, Aleksei N. See BIOGRAPHY.

KUWAIT

In early 1971, Kuwait held elections for its 50-seat National Assembly. During the year it also promoted the formation of the Arab Gulf federation, resumed its subsidy to Jordan, and increased its development of oil resources.

Elections. Kuwait elected its National Assembly on Jan. 23, 1971, with about 80% of the eligible

---

KUWAIT · Information Highlights

Official Name: State of Kuwait.
Area: 6,178 square miles (16,000 sq km).
Population (1970 census); 733,196, including 345,898 Kuwaiti citizens. *Density,* 113 per square mile (44 per sq km).
Chief City (1965 census): Kuwait, the capital, 99,609.
Government: *Head of state,* Sabah al-Salim al-Sabal, amir (acceded Nov. 27, 1965). *Prime minister,* Jabir al-Ahmad al-Jabir (took office Nov. 30, 1965). *Legislature*—National Assembly, 50 members. *Major political parties*—Bedouin party; Merchants party, Arab Nationalist Movement (ANM), ANM supporters, independents.
Languages: Arabic (official), English.
Education: *Literacy rate* (1970), 50% of population.
Finances (1970–71): *Revenues,* $894,320,000; *expenditures,* $894,320,000; *monetary unit,* dinar.
Gross National Product (1969): $2,763,600,000.
National Income (1969): $2,202,000,000; *national income per person,* $3,863.
Manufacturing (metric tons, 1969): Residual fuel oil, 7,855,000; distillate fuel oils, 6,491,000; liquefied petroleum gas, 1,473,000.
Minerals (metric tons, 1969): Crude petroleum, 129,548,000; salt, 4,000; natural gas, 3,660,000,000 cubic meters.
Foreign Trade (1968): *Exports,* 1970, $1,581,000,000; *Imports* (1970), $625,000,000. *Chief trading partner* (1968)—United States.
Transportation: *motor vehicles* (1969), 157,300 (automobiles, 120,700); *merchant fleet* (1970), 592,000 gross registered tons; *national airline,* Kuwait Airways.
Communications: *Telephones* (1970), 57,973; *television stations* (1968), 2; *newspapers* (1968), 5.

---

voters going to the polls. The Bedouin party won 17 seats; the conservative Merchants party, 17; the leftist Arab Nationalist Movement (ANM), 5; close supporters of the ANM, 5; and independents, 6.

A new cabinet under Crown Prince Jabir al-Ahmad al-Sabah was formed in February. It included one member of the ANM, Abd al-Aziz Husayn, the new minister of state for cabinet affairs.

Persian Gulf Amirates. Concerted and continued Kuwaiti-Saudi Arabian efforts throughout the spring and summer of 1971 led to an agreement among six small sheikhdoms of the former Trucial States to form the United Arab Amirates, proclaimed Dec. 2, 1971.

Foreign Affairs. The Second Symposium on Palestine was held in Kuwait City on February 13–17. Over 300 delegates attended.

Kuwait's annual $45 million subsidy to Jordan, a result of the 1967 Arab-Israeli war, was resumed in March 1971. It had been suspended and resumed in late 1970 and suspended again in January 1971. The reason for the suspension was the Jordanian army's actions against Palestine nationalists.

A former Iraqi vice president, Hardan Takriti, was assassinated in Kuwait on March 30 during a visit to the country.

Economy. Kuwait's oil production increased in 1970–71. Total production in 1970 reached an average of 2,723,547 barrels per day for the Kuwait Oil Company. Other companies produced over 200,000 barrels a day. The 1971–72 budget showed an expected oil revenue of $932,120,000 of the total budget.

Kuwait made development loans to South Yemen, Iraq, Sudan, Bahrain, and Syria in 1971. Kuwait's second tanker firm, the Kuwait Global Tanker Company, was organized in 1971 with a capital outlay of $1 million. Plans were also made for a new aluminum plant, flour mills, a chlorine and caustic soda plant, and chemical fertilizer plants. On February 17, Kuwait and the British Petroleum and Gulf Oil companies agreed to construct a natural gas processing plant that was to begin to produce propane, butane, and gasoline in early 1972.

SYDNEY NETTLETON FISHER
The Ohio State University

KUZNETS, Simon. See BIOGRAPHY.

President Nixon gestures toward dour AFL-CIO President Meany during November 19 speech to AFL-CIO convention in Miami, Fla. Nixon said he would continue efforts to halt inflation even if labor leaders and unions refused to cooperate.

LABOR

The Nixon administration tried for almost three years to stay out of labor relations and the economy. In 1971, however, it found itself drawn progressively into the vortex by the centripetal forces of inflation and unemployment. In a remarkable turnabout on August 15, President Nixon adopted interventionist policies "to stop the rise in prices, to create new jobs, and to protect the American dollar ..." He imposed a 90-day freeze on wages, prices, and rents, cut the dollar loose from gold, placed a 10% tax on imports, and sought congressional approval of tax relief to spur business investment.

The new policy was not entirely a bolt from the blue: some signals had been given. The Construction Industry Stabilization Committee, created in March to dampen that industry's upward spiral of prices and wages was a distant early warning. Meetings with steel and longshore negotiators, "inflation alerts," and special studies on the economic situation of steel and other industries all evidenced a growing willingness on the part of the administration to play a more active economic role.

Displeasure. Labor leaders expressed displeasure with the policy because dividends, interest, and profits were not included in the freeze. The government, they felt, regarded wages under a few thousand labor contracts as easier to control than millions of prices. Labor was particularly apprehensive about the Pay Board created in Phase II under the Economic Stabilization Act of 1970. The 15 members of the board were divided evenly, representing the public sector, employers, and labor. Labor could be outvoted and would have to rely on persuasion on a panel that would set standards for pay and benefit increases under Phase II.

In view of the dispensation, labor demanded that the board be entirely independent of the Cost of Living Council, which was the government's principal arm in the anti-inflation war. After receiving assurances of the board's autonomy, AFL-CIO President George Meany, the Steelworkers' I. W. Abel, the Machinists' Floyd Smith, the Automobile Workers' Leonard Woodcock, and the Teamsters' Frank Fitzsimmons took up positions as board members. They sought full implementation of signed contracts and retroactive payment of raises withheld during the freeze.

Sweeping aside labor arguments, the Pay Board, by 10 to 5, decreed a 5.5% standard for increases in wages and benefits. It characterized the standard as an average rather than a ceiling. (Later the 7-man Price Commission set a 2.5% standard for price increases.) The Pay Board also ruled out retroactive payment of wage increases except in rare situations. Signed contracts were allowed to go into effect unless complaints were received from either party or from five members of the board.

Dilemma. The Pay Board's actions posed a dilemma for the labor members. If they withdrew, they might be blamed for any failure of the program. If they remained, the union rank and file might charge them with selling out.

SHIPS ride at anchor in San Francisco Bay in September, unable to discharge cargo because of dock strike. Lengthy labor dispute shut down ports from Seattle to San Diego.

In this situation, the labor members took a wait-and-see attitude. A special United Automobile Workers (UAW) convention in early November, called because of the union's poststrike financial woes, supported their president's intent to remain on the board for the present. Later that month, the AFL-CIO's regular biennial convention also supported the preference of the federation's three board members to act very deliberately. Neither the Teamsters' president nor its executive council gave a sign that they disagreed with the other labor members.

Despite the initial rebuff on retroactive pay, labor members continued to lobby for it. Congress provided for most retroactive pay hikes in its extension of the Stabilization Act.

STRIKES AND SETTLEMENTS

As the wage-price freeze set in, levels of overall labor compensation were falling. Some key settlements, however, continued to run to about 10% a year. Over the life of the average major contract (those affecting 5,000 workers or more), wages and benefits went up 8.7% in 1971 (preliminary data) compared with 9.1% in 1970. First-year increases, which best express workers' fears of inflation, remained the same in 1971 as in 1970—13.1%. New data showed that settlements were lower—7.8%— in contracts with escalator clauses than in those without—10.2%. Wages in 1971 rose 8%, down from almost 9% in 1970.

Strikes and other stoppages in negotiations for new contracts also subsided in 1971, although the number of workers bargained for under major contracts was about the same—4.8 million in 1971, compared with 5 million in 1970. About 4,900 stoppages began in 1971. They involved 3.2 million workers and cost 45 million man-days, compared with 3.3 million workers and 66.4 million man-days in 1970.

The 1971 bargaining opened with the unsettled business of the one-day rail strike of Dec. 10, 1970. Other storms threatened, but by midyear settlements

were reached in telephone, the Postal Service, copper, and steel, and the stubborn rail dispute that had clouded labor relations since December 1970 finally yielded to intense ministrations.

Railroads. Three of the four operating unions that struck in December 1970 agreed to terms with the carriers. However, the United Transportation Union (UTU) opposed work-rule changes that it felt threatened members' jobs. The stage was ripe for strike and lockout because the administration had expended its Taft-Hartley weapons and Congress had balked at further intervention.

A federal court upheld the right of a rail union to strike individual carriers so long as it was applying pressure for a national agreement. With that approval, the UTU struck the Southern Railroad and the Union Pacific Railroad in June. A week later, it added the Southern Pacific and the Norfolk & Western. The union announced a schedule of strikes to be imposed each week until settlement was reached. Employers suspended work rules and in July laid off 20,000 workers, three fourths of them firemen.

With 10 carriers struck, the parties achieved agreement on August 2. The pact embodied the pattern of a 42% wage increase over 42 months. Work rules were altered to permit crews to work runs longer than 100 miles. The manning dispute was settled by agreeing that manpower reductions would occur only through normal attrition. Firemen and others laid off because of rule changes would receive extra jobless pay.

Elsewhere on the railroads, the Signalmen's Union threatened to emulate the UTU after a congressional prohibition on strikes and lockouts expired in October. However, as the year ended, continued negotiations prevented any stoppage.

Metal Industries. Bargaining in the can manufacturing, aluminum, copper, and steel industries was linked by the presence of the United Steelworkers. As a settlement was reached with the National Can Co., 36,000 unionists walked out at three other companies. The struck companies soon settled, following the lines of the National Can agreement. The pattern emerging from the can pacts called for 31% increases in wages and benefits over three years, cost-of-living protection, and other improvements.

The four major aluminum manufacturers accepted this pattern with some adjustments. The May pacts covered about 34,000 workers. Alcoa, Kaiser Aluminum, Reynolds Metals, and Ormet Corp. accepted pacts providing at least $1.10 an hour in wage increases over the 3-year life of the agreements. The escalator dealt a minimum adjustment of 25 cents over the final two years.

Copper's Big Four—Kennecott, Phelps Dodge, American Smelting, and Anaconda—resisted the pattern. They were struck by several unions on July 1. First agreements were achieved with two independents—Miami Copper and Magma Copper —calling for a 3-year wage increase of 92 cents an hour and an unlimited cost-of-living escalator. By the end of July, agreement was reached with Kennecott. In addition to the pay increase and cost-of-living protection, pay spreads between jobs and shifts were widened. The other companies came to similar terms.

As July negotiations in steel drew near, the economy grew apprehensive, battening down against the expected buffeting of a prolonged strike. The union indicated it could not accept less than the "metal" pattern, and the steel companies vowed they could not meet the pattern. President Nixon met with the negotiators on July 6 to urge a "constructive" settlement in the public interest. He also released a study by the Cabinet Committee on Economic Policy that showed the steel industry's international posture to be poor. To almost universal surprise, a settlement was achieved on August 1 during a one-day contract extension. The pact matched the "metal" pattern in monetary terms.

Telephone Industry. Supervisors had to keep the nation's communication system open for a week in July when about 500,000 Communication Workers staged a nationwide walkout. Their eventual agreement on pay and benefit increases equaled the roughly 10%-per-year pattern emerging in several industries. In an innovation, workers in large cities got additional pay increases of $5 to $9 a week to defray higher living costs. The terms were shielded from inflation by a new escalator provision. The contract, which the companies estimated would cost $4 billion, was ratified.

Postal Service. The new U.S. Postal Service completed its first round of bargaining with representatives of about 650,000 workers. The negotiations were successful despite an atmosphere of thunder and lightning. The agreement mandated a pay raise of $1,250 a year over two years. Workers with at least six months service received a one-time bonus of $300; others, scaled-down bonuses. A cost-of-living escalator guaranteed a minimum increase of $160 a year.

The Dockworkers. The Nixon administration refrained from moving into the West Coast dock strike—the first in 23 years—from its July inception to early October, although the President did meet briefly with the principals in the negotiations in late September. When Gulf and East Coast longshoremen struck on September 30 and cargoes were stranded in all major ports, the administration secured a T-H injunction—its first—sending West Coast longshoremen back to work until early 1972.

On the West Coast the union sought a guaranteed workweek, a $1.60-an-hour wage boost over two years, and other improvements. On the East Coast the union expressed determination to retain the contractual guarantee of work or pay for a year. Employers expressed equal determination to alter it. A T-H injunction sent the East and Gulf Coast longshoremen back to work in November, and on Jan. 6, 1972, their union, the International Longshoremen's Association, accepted a package involving a wage increase of $1.50 per hour over a three-year period, with the issue of guaranteed wages to be settled on a local basis. At year-end the West Coast dispute remained unresolved.

Soft Coal. Determined to halt frequent wildcat strikes by the United Mine Workers (UMW), mine operators sought contractual rights to withhold pay from miners who walked out in violation of the pact. The operators contended that wildcat strikes had cost more than 1.9 million man-days during the previous contract. Refusal of labor negotiators to accede resulted in a strike by 100,000 miners when the contract expired at midnight on September 30.

Deadlocked negotiations recessed on October 20 but resumed on October 25 when Gov. Arch Moore of West Virginia acted as intermediary. In a little more than two weeks, an agreement was reached. Under it, the miners would get roughly 10% a year in wage increases and benefit improvements. Employer payments to the pension and welfare fund were doubled over the three years. The union's 125-man national scale and policy committee approved the agreement minutes before the wage-price freeze expired on November 13, thus technically beating the implementation of the 5.5% standard imposed in Phase II.

Other Settlements. The 1970 round of bargaining in the automobile industry neared an end when Chrysler Corp. agreed in January 1971 to terms corresponding to those granted earlier by General Motors and Ford. The main issue had been the degree of retroactivity of the first-year "new money."

TELEPHONE STRIKE in July forced executive and supervisory personnel to man the switchboards at Pacific Telephone and Telegraph offices in San Francisco. The entire U.S. telephone system was hard hit as about 500,000 workers walked off jobs in contract dispute.

UPI

After the Chrysler agreement, American Motors and the United Automobile Workers settled on a 47-month contract providing terms similar to those granted by the Big Three automobile makers but delaying the dates of the monetary provisions.

New York City patrolmen placed parity in pay above law and order for one week in January. The dispute involved restoration of parity between patrolmen's and sergeants' pay, the latter having been granted a pay increase. When a court ruling postponed action on the patrolmen's suit, they stayed off duty briefly. In February a state supreme court justice ruled in the patrolmen's favor.

A bitter teachers' strike in Newark, N. J., ended in mid-April after 2½ stormy months that included jailing of union leaders, fining of the union, and beatings of picketing teachers. The teachers received a $500-a-year pay raise beginning July 1, 1972, and other contract improvements. As part of the accord, all suspended teachers were reinstated.

TRADE UNIONS

Faced with relatively high unemployment and other economic tribulations, trade unions closed ranks. Their response to the administration's economic initiatives was closely coordinated by AFL-CIO President George Meany, the AFL-CIO executive council, and the heads of the nation's two largest unions, both of which were outside the federation: Leonard Woodcock of the United Automobile Workers (UAW) and Frank Fitzsimmons of the Teamsters.

Other signs of a dying down of squalls between unions abounded. The activities of the Alliance for Labor Action, made up of the UAW, the Teamsters, and the Chemical Workers—all ousted by the federation for different reasons—were very quiet indeed. In fact, the Chemical Workers withdrew

NONFARM PAYROLL EMPLOYMENT IN THE UNITED STATES

Industry	Annual average 1970	October 1971
Total	70,664,000	71,432,000
Mining	622,000	522,000
Contract construction	3,347,000	3,445,000
Manufacturing	19,393,000	18,782,000
Durable goods	11,203,000	10,667,000
Ordnance and accessories	248,700	188,700
Lumber and wood products	580,300	598,100
Furniture and fixtures	459,900	476,100
Stone, clay, and glass products	637,700	641,400
Primary metal industries	1,306,300	1,171,100
Fabricated metal products	1,386,100	1,345,600
Machinery, except electrical	1,964,100	1,780,000
Electrical equipment	1,913,400	1,794,900
Transportation equipment	1,823,800	1,803,700
Instruments and related products	459,000	434,200
Miscellaneous manufacturing	423,800	432,700
Nondurable goods	8,190,000	8,115,000
Food and kindred products	1,795,900	1,823,700
Tobacco manufactures	79,000	80,500
Textile mill products	964,800	963,400
Apparel and other textile products	1,385,300	1,375,500
Paper and allied products	710,000	687,500
Printing and publishing	1,106,300	1,085,800
Chemicals and allied products	1,056,800	1,002,300
Petroleum and coal products	192,000	190,300
Rubber and plastics products	571,100	598,400
Leather and leather products	328,700	307,500
Transportation and public utilities	4,498,000	4,444,000
Wholesale and retail trade	14,950,000	15,328,000
Wholesale trade	3,849,000	3,906,000
Retail trade	11,102,000	11,422,000
Finance, insurance, and real estate	3,679,000	3,818,000
Services	11,577,000	12,042,000
Government	12,597,000	13,051,000
Federal government	2,705,000	2,661,000
State and local government	9,891,000	10,390,000

Source: Bureau of Labor Statistics, U. S. Department of Labor.

from the alliance and returned to the federation. In yet another show of cooperation, the UAW and the Machinists reestablished their no-raiding pact in the aerospace industry.

A number of mergers took place, marking a show of increased fraternity in the face of economic adversity. In the biggest of all, five postal unions with a membership of over 300,000 merged into the American Postal Workers' Union (AFL-CIO). Other important meldings merged District 50 (severed by its former parent union, the United Mine Workers, in 1970) into the United Steelworkers; the Masters, Mates, and Pilots into the East and Gulf Coast Longshoremen; and the Los Angeles County Employees' Association, a large independent, into the Service Employees International Union.

Teamsters. The leadership of the nation's biggest union changed hands formally at midyear when the imprisoned James R. Hoffa relinquished his Teamsters' presidency and his positions at the head of Local 299 in Detroit and the Central Conference of Teamsters. The union's executive council elevated Frank Fitzsimmons from general vice president to president, acting on Hoffa's recommendation through his son. The Teamsters' convention in July then elected Fitzsimmons to a full term over token opposition. President Nixon visited the convention, the first U. S. president to do so since Franklin D. Roosevelt. In December, Hoffa was released from prison after the President granted him a parole.

Mine Workers. Legal difficulties continued to assail the leadership of the United Mine Workers (UMW). Acting on a suit filed on behalf of a group of miners, a federal district judge ruled in May that the union and a union-owned bank were liable for millions of dollars in damages in their handling of the union's welfare fund. Millions of dollars of the fund had been deposited in noninterest-bearing accounts of the bank over a period of 20 years, depriving the fund of substantial earnings. The judge ordered that all union fund deposits be removed by midyear and that President Boyle of the UMW step down as a trustee of the fund. Boyle's ouster was protested by some 84,000 miners in a 5-day strike.

COURT DECISIONS

By refusing to review a lower court's decision in *Delaware and Hudson Railway Co.*, the U. S. Supreme Court upheld the right of rail unions to strike selected railroads in certain circumstances. To meet tests set up in earlier high court decisions, the appellate court cautioned that such strikes could not be used to whipsaw the carriers into separate agreements. For the present, the ruling freed rail unions from an unwritten but very real ban on strikes. In the past, most strikes were ended by presidential action under the Railway Labor Act or by congressional action.

The employment of black and other minority workers may be vastly affected by the Supreme Court's landmark decision in *Griggs* v. *Duke Power Co.* The court ruled that use of employment tests was forbidden under section 703(h) of the Civil Rights Act of 1964 unless the tests measured mental and mechanical aptitudes required by a specific job. In overruling both lower courts, the high court accepted the Equal Employment Opportunity Com-

(*Continued on page 392*)

The 4-Day Workweek On Trial

More Americans would have more time for leisure and recreation if the concept of the short workweek catches on.

THE NEW YORK TIMES

To both the worker and his boss, the idea of a shortened workweek holds the glowing promise of a more flexible life-style: The boss hopes, in addition, that the change to a shorter week will increase productivity and lower unit costs. So the concept was being applied experimentally across the United States in 1971, even though not as extensively as the volume of publicity would indicate. In all, about 600 manufacturing, service, and governmental units employing more than 75,000 workers were trying a wide variety of workweeks composed of less than five days.

Some units were on the 4-day week, others operated for 4½ days. Most retained 40 hours as the overall work schedule, but some were moving to 36-hour or even 32-hour weeks.

Labor's historical commitment to the 8-hour day regardless of the number of days worked was being re-examined. Management was considering the advantages and disadvantages of changing the work schedule radically. The U. S. Department of Labor held hearings and conducted studies as to the advisability of waiving the daily overtime requirements built into the Walsh-Healey Act and the Contract Work Hours and Safety Standards Act, which regulate federally financed contract work.

Benefits and Drawbacks. Arguments for or against the shortened workweek are numerous and apply differently in each situation. Variable elements include the nature of the industry, size of the company, and type of employee.

In general, management sees the shortened week as a method for developing greater efficiency and maximizing profits though reduction of startup time, decreased absenteeism and tardiness, limiting of downtime for coffee breaks and lunch periods, and the building of higher morale, which reduces costly turnover. Employees like the reductions of commuting time and commuting fares, and the limiting of the costs of meals eaten outside the home and of child-care costs.

Unions are much less likely at the present time to take definitive, all-encompassing stands. Those that are considering long-range explorations into collective bargaining on the issue see advantages based on shortening the number of hours worked per week at straight time. In addition, with the recent emphasis on use of leisure time, the movement of many skilled and semiskilled members of organized labor out of the core city, the increased use of the car for family travel, and the development of new types of continuing education, unions are exploring ways to take advantage of different methods of work scheduling.

Some companies that experimented with the shorter workweek had discovered that possible profits were mostly illusory, that the psychological advantages disappeared after a few weeks or months, and that unanticipated problems had arisen. Unions were cautious in moving ahead, since the changes were not just economically experimental but also were politically dangerous in a trade-union movement that can be callous in overturning labor leaders who are too far ahead of their constituency. Conservative economists enamored of classical theories attacked the approach.

Health, both physical and mental, has not been shown to be necessarily improved by the 10-hour workday or even by four 8-hour work days with a decrease in breaktime. Legislation limiting the number of hours that women can work in any one day is still on the statute books in many states. Because of the lack of long-term study, productivity gains reported by some companies are at least suspect.

The Outlook. The chances of the 4-day workweek becoming a major element in economic arrangements are still distant. It appears likely that in the near future, without major changes in total economic activity, the rate of experimentation with 4-day weeks would continue at the 1971 level. As pragmatic analysis indicates strengths and weaknesses, as the economy changes from production to service, as computer techniques test series of simulated situations, the economic crucible will produce answers. Since it took more than 100 years to establish the 5-day workweek, it is logical that this standard will not be changed soon.

HARVEY L. FRIEDMAN
University of Massachusetts

(*Continued from page 390*)
mission's interpretation of section 703(h) based on a reading of congressional intent. Under the ruling, even unbiased tests administered in a fair and equitable manner were banned if they were not job-related and if they functioned to hold back minority employees or applicants.

FEDERAL LEGISLATION

Federal economic actions in the labor field were dominated by those taken under a 1970 law, the Economic Stabilization Act. However, in 1971 an important bill was passed directed at high unemployment. On July 12, President Nixon signed the Emergency Employment Act authorizing subsidies of $2.25 billion to state and local governments over two years to create 150,000 jobs in environmental protection, health care, education, police and fire work, and other fields. Funding was geared to the level of unemployment. Funding would cease if the jobless rate dipped to 4.5% or below.

The federal minimum wage for 1.6 million workers first covered by the act in 1966 rose to $1.60 an hour from $1.45. The benefited workers included many in small retail and service stores, and in laundries, hotels, restaurants, schools, and hospitals.

President Nixon again asked for new legislation —the Emergency Public Interest Protection Act— to deal more effectively with work stoppages in the railroad, airline, maritime, longshore, and trucking industries. The bill would eliminate the emergency procedures in the Railway Labor Act, transferring all activity to Taft-Hartley provisions. The President would have several options in dealing with national emergency stoppages. As in 1970, the bill did not pass either house.

THE LABOR FORCE

In an economy in which there were not enough jobs for those who wanted them, the number of people entering the labor force slowed from about 2 million in 1970 to about half that number in 1971. Unemployment leveled off at 6% in 1971 after having risen steadily throughout 1970. Roughly 5 million people out of a civilian labor force of about 85 million were out of work at any one time.

Average unemployment rates for selected groups in 1971 were: men, 4.4%; married men, 3.2%; women, 5.7%; teenagers, 16.9%; white workers, 5.4%; black workers, 9.9%; white-collar workers, 3.5%; blue-collar workers, 7.4%; service workers, 6.3%; and farm workers, 2.6%. Joblessness was worse for all groups except farm workers, for whom it was unchanged.

Another index of higher joblessness was the growing number of metropolitan areas with what the government calls "substantial"—6% or higher— unemployment. The U. S. Department of Labor reported that 65 major labor areas had substantial joblessness in October 1971, the highest number in 10 years.

Earnings. Gross average weekly earnings of all workers in the private sector averaged $130.55 in December 1971, up $8.12 from a year earlier. Take-home pay (gross average weekly earnings less federal payroll taxes) was $114.99, up $8.03 from a year ago. Weekly earnings in December 1971 (December 1970 pay in parentheses) were: construction, $215.12 ($204.20); transportation and public utili-

EMPLOYMENT STATUS OF THE U. S. POPULATION

	Annual average 1970	October 1971
Total labor force	85,903,000	87,352,000
Civilian labor force	82,715,000	84,635,000
Employed persons	78,627,000	80,065,000
Agricultural employment	3,462,000	3,470,000
Nonagricultural employment	75,165,000	76,595,000
Unemployed persons	4,088,000	4,570,000

ties, $177.86 ($161.20); mining, $187.90 ($170.28); manufacturing, $150.18 ($138.45); finance, insurance, and real estate, $123.54 ($115.61); services, $103.66 ($99.81); and wholesale and retail trade, $102.95 ($97.08).

A worker with take-home pay of $114.99 in December 1971 could purchase no more with it than he could with $93.41 in 1967. However, his real earnings were up $3.60 over his real earnings in December 1970. The slowing of inflation was evident in this slight advance of real earnings after more than five years of retrogression. But part of the cost of the improvement lay in the unfavorable job market.

Construction Plans. The administration's initial efforts at economic stabilization affected the construction industry. It sought voluntary cooperation of labor and management in stabilizing compensation and prices.. When labor demurred, President Nixon suspended provisions of the Davis-Bacon Act requiring union wage scales on federal projects.

After labor agreed in April to participate, the President reinstated Davis-Bacon and issued an executive order establishing the Construction Industry Stabilization Committee. The committee's principal task was to drive the average settlement down to the average of 1961–68—that is, about 6%. Some 16 to 18 special boards reviewed agreements by craft and referred questionable settlements to the committee. While most pacts were passed, some were rejected as too large. At first the committee could not enforce its will by fiat, but under Phase II it could.

On another front, the administration continued to press its program for expanding minority employment in federally assisted construction projects. To close a loophole, the Philadelphia Plan—the first of its kind—was expanded to cover work on both public and private projects of contractors bidding on government-aided projects valued at $500,-000 or more. Thus minority workers could not be shifted from private to public projects to meet government quotas.

Veterans. As U. S. ground combat in the Vietnam War subsided and more troops were withdrawn and mustered out, the problem of jobs for veterans grew progressively more acute in an economy short on jobs. In June the President directed Labor Secretary James D. Hodgson to head a program to find jobs for veterans. Unemployment rates for veterans were higher than those for nonveterans in the same age groups. Part of the government program required contractors and federal agencies to list all "suitable" job vacancies with the U. S. Training and Employment Service. The agency was to increase its placement efforts on behalf of veterans.

ROBERT W. FISHER
Bureau of Labor Statistics
U. S. Department of Labor

LAIRD, Melvin R. See BIOGRAPHY.

WAR against Communists in Laos intensified in 1971. South Vietnamese (*above*) went into Laos, but Americans (*right*) stopped at border.

LAOS

In 1971 the war in Laos continued in the same seesaw pattern that it has followed for the past 10 years. The Communists took the offensive during the dry months, beginning around October and lasting through the winter, and the government forces regained the initiative with the coming of the rainy season (May–September). For Premier Souvanna Phouma's government, however, there were three ominous developments. First, a South Vietnamese thrust into Laos in February drove the North Vietnamese even deeper into the country. Also, the government's wet-season offensive was the weakest in over five years. Lastly, the fall of the Plain of Jars and most of the Bolovens Plateau in December indicated a worsening of the government's position.

The War. The first six months of 1971 were the worst such half-year period Laos has had in a decade. The government's 70,000 regular troops and Meo tribal forces, supported by the U.S. Central Intelligence Agency (CIA), suffered several major defeats. The Communist North Vietnamese and Pathet Lao local insurgents pushed farther west in the southern panhandle of the country, seizing control of the strategic Bolovens Plateau. This push by the enemy followed the South Vietnamese drive into Laos in February to cut the Ho Chi Minh Trail. It probably was an attempt by North Vietnam to expand its supply routes in the event of any new moves by government forces.

The South Vietnamese thrust relieved pressure on the Meo base at Long Thieng, which appeared on the verge of abandonment early in 1971. The Communists also exerted pressure on the royal capital, Luang Prabang, but then abandoned the siege.

Government forces were so weakened by the dry-season operations of the enemy, who were seemingly able to move almost at will, that for the second year in a row they mounted only a minimal offensive during the monsoon season. The CIA-advised Meo tribesmen resumed their seasonal occupation of the Plain of Jars, but their diminished numbers, and U. S. fears of provoking Communist Vietnamese counteraction in the next dry season's fighting, stopped their eastward thrust fairly early. The strategic town of Pakson in the Bolovens Plateau was also retaken, but government troops suffered their heaviest casualties in three years.

U. S. Involvement. According to U. S. Secretary of State William P. Rogers, U. S. aid and the cost of its operations in Laos totaled $350 million in fiscal year 1971. This was a per capita outlay of $175, nearly three times Laos' per capita gross national product. The actual cost to the United States of its bombing operations in Laos was classified but was estimated to be an additional $1.4 billion. The U. S. Senate in October voted to limit spending in Laos to $350 million for fiscal 1972.

U. S. involvement in Laos was not limited to financial aid. The United States not only financed the 7,500 Thai soldiers fighting in Laos, but also lent its own manpower. In July, Americans employed by the CIA directed and participated in operations on the Plain of Jars. During the action aircraft flown by U. S. pilots landed on the plain. At other times, U. S. personnel crossed over from South Vietnam to take part in strikes against the Ho Chi Minh Trail. U. S. bombing raids were mainly against the trail, but they were also carried out to provide air cover for Laotian government and Meo forces.

Politics. The Communist siege of Luang Prabang and Long Thieng in February led Premier Souvanna Phouma to declare a state of emergency. Although it gave increased powers to the military, the move fell short of martial law, and it left supreme authority in civilian hands—those of Souvanna Phouma.

Tension between civilian and military authorities continued throughout the year. In April, eight persons, including former high-ranking officers, were arrested for planning to overthrow the government. Military leaders were critical of Souvanna's persistent lip service to a neutralist political position despite increasing North Vietnamese intervention in the country. The South Vietnamese thrust into Laos in February emboldened some members of the military to conspire against the premier, but the premier postponed the retirement of army chief Gen. Ouan Ratthikoun, thus preventing a younger, more ambitious officer from assuming this key position—which could be used to establish military rule in the country.

Souvanna's most likely civilian successor, 45-year-old acting Defense Minister Sisouk na Champassak, strengthened the premier's hand in midyear. By changing key regional commanders, he considerably strengthened the government's control over the local military.

"Peace Talks." Negotiations with the Pathet Lao, which had seemed to show some promise in late 1970, broke down early in 1971. The breakdown was largely attributed to the battlefield gains of the Communists.

The Pathet Lao took the initiative in seeking to reopen talks in April. However, they maintained their hard-line stand that an overall U. S. bombing halt was a precondition for a cease-fire between the two sides in the Laotian war. Communist propaganda emphasized that this was the only possible means by which the government could survive. Souvanna's position also was the same—that the North Vietnamese must leave the country before any such bombing halt.

One possible reason why the Pathet Lao sought to reopen the talks was that their position within the coalition of Indochinese Communists may have weakened as the Ho Chi Minh Trail has increased in importance to North Vietnam. Pathet Lao defections rose sharply during the year, as the Vietnamese Communists apparently abandoned their strategy of deferring to local Communist leadership and of not criticizing the Laotians' lack of initiative or their excessive dependence on Hanoi.

Economy. The Laotian economy continued to be heavily dependent on U. S. financial support. Half of Laos' $38 million budget came from U. S. aid funds.

Imports again exceeded exports in 1971, although the exact dimensions of the imbalance were not known because of the high level of smuggling between Laos and neighboring Thailand. The devaluation by 20% of the kip in November lowered its value from 500 to 600 to the U. S. dollar.

Foreign Relations. Souvanna Phouma overtly welcomed the thaw in U. S.-mainland Chinese relations symbolized by the announcement of President Richard Nixon's planned trip to Peking in early 1972. Despite continued Chinese road-building in northern Laos and the use of this means to supply North Vietnamese combat troops, the Laotian premier expressed the hope that Peking would act to ensure the survival of an independent Laos. In the light of the outspoken criticism in the U. S. Senate of the level of U. S. foreign aid in general and of assistance to Laos in particular, Premier Souvanna Phouma feared an early reduction of aid to Laos.

RICHARD BUTWELL
State University of New York at Brockport

Rioting in Córdoba, Argentina, in March led to the ouster of the Levingston regime. It was the second time in two years that the city helped topple the national government.

LATIN AMERICA

The year 1971 brought a slackening of the intense ideological competition of earlier years between the various Latin American governments. Anticipating a détente in East-West relations after the prospective Nixon trips to Peking and Moscow in 1972, Latin leaders engaged in their own summitry. Riding a strong wave of economic nationalism, they seemed to be in the process of establishing a common front vis-à-vis the world powers.

Latin Americans regarded the Nixon administration's New Economic Policy, with its 10% surcharge on processed imports, as onerous and gratuitous in view of the overwhelmingly favorable balance of trade that the United States enjoyed within the hemisphere. But Chile's new Marxist government was not treated by Washington as Castro's Cuba had been treated a decade earlier, and the reasonably measured U. S. reaction to such Latin moves as the expropriation of U. S. companies and the capture and fining of U. S. tuna-fishing boats had at least the negative virtue of not adding fuel to the Latin American's resentment of Uncle Sam's economic and political muscle.

POLITICAL DEVELOPMENTS

The year-old Marxist regime of Salvador Allende in Chile captured the imagination of the hemisphere in 1971, without, however, producing similar phenomena in other nations, as was demonstrated by the failure at the polls of a leftist coalition in Uruguay. Brazil's new social programs and Argentina's effort to bring the Peronists into the political structure seemed to reflect a new sensitivity to political and social imperatives on the part of Latin America's conservative military dictatorships.

Marxist Chile. President Salvador Allende Gossen's left-wing government in Chile, despite its minority popular support (it had received only 36%

of the popular vote in 1970 and controlled neither house of the Congress) was surprisingly successful in accomplishing its limited initial goals in 1971. Most importantly, it acquired controlling interests in the nation's major banks and private industrial concerns. An amendment to the Constitution authorizing the nationalization of the U. S. copper mines was endorsed unanimously by the Congress in July. Within the year, U. S. investment in Chile dwindled from $750 million to $50 million. The government also expropriated 5 million acres for agrarian reform, increased wages by 40%, and claimed to have cut the rate of inflation from 37% to 18% through price controls.

However, these radical changes provoked increased violence and a deep polarization of political opinion. The Christian Democratic party ended its working compact with the government on September 25. The Revolutionary Left Movement (MIR) also broke its truce with the government and organized illegal seizures of farms in southern Chile. Dollar reserves dropped by one third, agriculture declined, food imports rose, and receipts from copper exports were down 25% (although this was largely due to a sharp drop in copper prices on world markets). By December the scarcity of food encouraged the Christian Democrats to organize an unprecedented demonstration by 5,000 housewives.

Leftist Failure in Uruguay. A leftist coalition in Uruguay lost a contest for the presidency, capturing only 18% of the vote in national elections on Nov. 28, 1971. The coalition ,was strongly supported by the Tupamaro urban guerrillas, who suspended their kidnapping and other terrorist activities during the election campaign.

Law and Order in Brazil. With over half of South America's population and land area, Brazil's annual economic growth rate since 1969 had been

395

an extraordinary 9%, although the wealth was being poorly distributed. General Emílio Garrastazú Médici was considered the least tyrannical of the three army generals who had ruled Brazil with practically unlimited powers since 1964. His emphasis on national security, however, stifled virtually all political opposition except that emanating from the hierarchy of the Roman Catholic Church. But the general was understood to have ordered his police to temper the practice of torturing prisoners. In July, he finally ordered a crackdown on the vigilante "Death Squad" groups, which had been murdering supposed criminals and subversives.

To reduce social tensions and raise economic standards, new schemes were undertaken to increase employee profit sharing, extend social security to rural areas, reform education, and reduce adult illiteracy. Work continued on the 3,100-mile (4,900-km) Trans-Amazon Highway, which was to open over a million square miles of land to settlement.

New Directions in Argentina. In Argentina, Gen. Alejandro Augustín Lanusse, the leader of the nation's military junta, removed Gen. Roberto M. Levingston from the presidency on March 23 and assumed the post himself. It remained to be seen whether the new and apparently more benign president would stem the growth and proliferation of guerrilla groups, many of which had ties with Peronist leaders. Soon after his assumption of the presidency, Lanusse launched a campaign to bring the Peronists (representing perhaps a third of the Argentine electorate) back into the open by offering them a chance to participate in future elections.

Bolivian Coup. Bolivia experienced its 184th change of government in its 146 years of independence on August 22, 1971, as a bloody three-day revolt left over 100 dead and 600 wounded. Replacing the leftist president, Juan José Torres, was the more conservative Col. Hugo Banzer Suárez. The politically inexperienced Banzer government faced serious problems—sagging prices and soaring costs in the tin industry, the flight of capital, and debts inherited from the Torres government.

Accommodations in the North. The incidence of violence decreased somewhat in the nations of the Caribbean and Central America. On Hispaniola, the death on April 21 of President François Duvalier, Haiti's dictator for 13 years, provided his 20-year-old son and successor, Jean-Claude, an opportunity to partially dismantle the hated civil militia known as the Tonton Macoutes. In the neighboring Dominican Republic, on June 30, the conservative president, Joaquín Balaguer, was able to foil a right-wing plot to quickly overthrow him.

Consensus politics seemed to be gaining in Central America. On March 28, Honduras held its first direct election of a president since 1932. The National Party leader, Ramón Ernesto Cruz, was elected to the office for a 6-year term. Under a National Unity Plan, the National and Liberal parties divided the 64 National Assembly seats.

In Nicaragua, President Anastasio Somoza, forbidden by the Constitution from succeeding himself at the expiration of his term in May 1972, agreed with the opposition Conservative party that the country would be ruled in 1972–74 by an interim junta, composed of two members of his own Liberal party and one Conservative. A new Constitution, to be adopted during these years, was to permit consecutive presidential terms and open the way for Somoza's possible return to office in 1974.

The Communist Presence. Soviet policy in Latin America continued to promote the collaboration of local Communist parties with united nationalist fronts, with the Marxist government of Chile often cited as the model for other countries. However, the Soviet image of moderation was sullied in Mexico, where alleged Soviet complicity in the training of 50 Mexicans in guerrilla tactics promoted the expulsion of five top-level Soviet diplomats and the withdrawal of the Mexican ambassador from Moscow in March. Ecuador ousted three Soviet officials charged with interference in domestic labor problems and advocacy of a general strike, while in Costa Rica adverse public opinion caused President José Figueres to postpone the reopening of the Soviet Embassy.

Beset by economic problems, Cuba had lost its luster as a Communist showcase. Nevertheless, Premier Fidel Castro received a visit from Soviet Premier Aleksei Kosygin and was apparently assured that Soviet loyalty to Cuba would survive President Nixon's forthcoming visit to Moscow.

The U. S. President's prospective Peking trip lent new respectability to the People's Republic of China, which was tempering its advocacy of guerrilla warfare and emphasizing "nationalism" and "growing unity in the anti-imperialist struggle." On November 2, Peru recognized the mainland Chinese government, a step already taken by Chile and Cuba.

LATIN AMERICAN SUMMITRY

A Latin American diplomat compared the hemispheric diplomacy of the old Cold War era to the meeting of an Indian tribal war council: "The United States was the big chief and everyone got together periodically for a powwow. Squabbles between the chieftains were settled by the big chief." Latin American governments appeared to be well aware that this era had ended, and 1971 brought with it a sudden spurt of diplomatic activity within the region, including numerous meetings between Latin heads of state. A by-product of the new regional diplomacy was the beginning of Cuba's reentry into hemispheric affairs as something other than a fomenter of guerrilla movements.

Presidential Summit Meetings. The presidents of Brazil, Chile, and Mexico were the most active of the conferees. In his first year as president of Mexico, Luis Echeverría Álvarez met with all six Central American chiefs of state. Brazilian President Médici, eager to expand hemispheric trade, met with Colombia's President Misael Pastrana Borrero in July, and the two leaders subsequently issued a statement criticizing U. S. coffee policy. Earlier, Médici had met with President Alfredo Stroessner of Paraguay.

Chile's President Allende set out for Ecuador, Colombia, and Peru at the end of August, seeking support for Chile's expropriation policy should there be a confrontation with the United States. In July he had met with Argentine President Lanusse.

An underlying theme in all of these meetings was a common desire to coordinate policy relating to trade negotiations with the economically powerful developed nations outside of Latin America.

The Reemergence of Cuba. Cuba had been virtually isolated in the Western Hemisphere since the Organization of American States had excluded the Castro government from its councils in 1964. In 1971, Allende broke the ice, inviting Castro to visit Chile. The invitation was a symbolically im-

UPI

CASTRO IN CHILE

WIDE WORLD

UPI

Cuban Premier Fidel Castro toured Chile in November. He addressed a rally of university students in Antofagasta (top), where he drew the rapt attention of some young admirers at right. In the desert town of Maria Elena, Castro accepted a bottle of Coca-Cola (above).

portant turning point for Cuba. The visit (November 10 to December 4) was Castro's first to another Latin nation in 12 years. During his stay in Chile, the Cuban premier indicated that he would cooperate diplomatically with any other "progressive" government that had an "anti-imperialist" foreign policy.

LATIN AMERICA AND THE UNITED STATES

In 1969 the Nixon administration had formulated what was described as a "low profile" policy toward Latin America. Implicit in this policy was the promise of a more balanced relationship in the hemisphere and greater U. S. respect for the sovereign rights of the Latin states. By 1971, however, the U. S. public's growing disenchantment with foreign aid, reflected in congressional reluctance to grant funds, had given the new policy a lower profile than the administration may have intended and had led many Latin Americans to accuse the United States of reneging on its earlier commitments. The President's failure to exclude all Latin American products from the 10% import surcharge, imposed in August 1971, added to the irritation of the Latins, while such manifestations of Latin economic nationalism as the expropriation of privately owned industrial facilities and the fining of U. S. fishermen strained the patience of Washington.

The Finch Mission. To dramatize the continuing interest of his administration in Latin America at the end of a rocky year in hemispheric relationships, President Nixon sent a goodwill mission to six Latin countries in late November 1971. The group was headed by presidential adviser Robert H. Finch and included White House Director of Communications Herbert H. Klein. They visited Ecuador, Peru, Argentina, Brazil, Honduras, and Mexico.

The mission was not generally regarded as a resounding success. Finch began his journey by denigrating the two U. S. presidents most universally esteemed in Latin America: Franklin D. Roosevelt and John F. Kennedy. The mission's first stop in Ecuador was marred by the seizure of four U. S. tuna boats by Ecuador's navy. And Klein, on his return to Washington, reported that he had gained a feeling that the Marxist government of Chile "wouldn't last long," a remark turned to political advantage by Chile's president.

The Tuna War. As early as 1952, Ecuador, Peru, and Chile had asserted that their sovereignty (including exclusive fishing rights) extended 200 miles (360 km) offshore. Since that time, six other nations—El Salvador, Nicaragua, Panama, Argentina, Brazil, and Uruguay—had made similar claims. The United States rejected these claims, maintaining that a nation's territorial waters extend no more than 12 miles (19 km) to sea.

Over the years, the most dramatic confrontation on this issue had been that between the United States and Ecuador, whose 21-boat navy was responsible for the interception of 74 of the 90 U. S. tuna boats seized in 1966–71 by the west coast Latin countries and fined for fishing without licenses. In 1971 alone, Ecuador seized 51 boats, levying $2.5 million in fines.

The U. S. tuna fleet of some 140 vessels depended on South America's west coast for about 13% of its $90-million total annual catch. The U. S. State Department advised the tuna fishermen not to buy licenses lest the action imply recognition of Ecuador's claim.

The United States was constrained in its pressure against Ecuador by the support that country was receiving from Peru and Chile, and by the Texaco-Gulf consortium, which had discovered a huge reservoir of oil in Ecuador's Oriente Province. By mid-1972, when a 333-mile (536-km) pipeline to the Pacific was to be completed, Ecuador was expected to be exporting perhaps 400,000 barrels per day of sweet, low-sulfur oil, with daily shipment of as much as 5 million barrels considered possible by 1975. The U. S. owners of petroleum properties in Ecuador could see themselves becoming valuable hostages in the hands of an Ecuadorian government.

There had been 11 unsuccessful efforts to negotiate a fishing agreement in the years 1961–1970. On Jan. 17, 1971, the United States suspended delivery of some $28 million in military hardware earmarked for Ecuador. Within a week, Ecuador had brought charges before an OAS Meeting of Foreign Ministers that the United States was applying "coercive measures of an economic or political character" in violation of Article 19 of the OAS Charter. After considering the matter, the ministers urged the disputants to refrain from provocative actions and to seek negotiation.

In mid-December, Assistant Secretary Meyer and other U. S. officials flew to Ecuador to propose a compromise, suggesting that they would seek Congressional approval for the purchase of fishing licenses from Ecuador, if Ecuador would agree to stop seizing tuna boats and permit U. S. warships, submarines, and aircraft to pass freely outside of the 12-mile limit. Ecuadorian President José María Velasco Ibarra refused the offer, insisting that national honor required that the United States first lift its ban on the sale of arms.

Nationalization of U. S. Properties. On Sept. 28, 1971, after President Allende had nationalized three mines and other properties of the Anaconda and Kennecott copper companies, the Chilean government announced that $775 million, a sum representing past "excess profits," was being deducted from the $628-million book value of the properties. Thus the Allende administration, far from granting compensation to the two mining concerns, decreed that the companies were in debt to Chile. Compensation assigned for nationalized property of the International Telephone and Telegraph Corporation was only 15% of the $153 million value claimed.

Nationalization was also a dominant goal of the Venezuelan government. President Rafaél Caldera signed a bill nationalizing natural gas in August. Earlier, a measure had been enacted that would force all oil wells, pipelines, and refineries owned by U. S. companies to revert to the government without compensation at the expiration of their current concessions—in most cases, in 1983.

On September, U. S. Treasury Secretary John B. Connally ordered the Export-Import Bank to refuse a $21 million loan to Chile for the purchase of three Boeing jetliners and instructed the U. S. representatives at the World Bank and the Inter-American Development Bank to oppose all loans to Chile, Peru, Ecuador, and Bolivia, pending satisfactory settlements for nationalized properties. An administration statement in January 1972 suggested that these mild retaliatory steps might be followed by sterner U. S. measures.

Trade and Aid. The 10% surcharge applied by the Nixon administration to all processed imports as of Aug. 15, 1971, affected only 20% of Latin exports to the United States, since the bulk of Latin exports consisted of non-processed raw materials and agricultural goods. But Latin Americans remembered the earlier Nixon promise to assist in the diversification of the Latin economies by promoting the production of semi-manufactured goods, and it was precisely these that were affected until the surcharge was lifted in December. The Latin countries felt especially aggrieved about the surcharge because theirs was a deficit trade with the United States in which the Latin nations bought $790 million more than they sold in 1970.

Military Assistance. When Washington imposed a $75 million annual ceiling on hemispheric arms aid in 1967, Latin nations began to turn to Europe for their military supplies. The budget for U. S. military training programs for Latin America had been slashed from a high of $84 million in 1966 to $11.2 million in fiscal 1971. In April 1971, the United States decided to close its Southern Command in Panama, the symbol of the U. S. military presence in Latin America.

It was evident, however, that Washington was not entirely happy about the sharp decline in U. S. military influence, especially in South America, 5 of whose 11 independent nations had military governments. In May, President Nixon proposed that the military aid ceiling be waived in fiscal 1971 and doubled to $150 million in 1972.

Residual Pan Americanism. On the homeward-bound lap of his November mission, Robert Finch announced that the United States was ceding to Honduras the Swan Islands, two Caribbean islets lying far off the Honduran coast. Washington had claimed the islands since 1863 and had used them for guano mining and as sites of weather and communications stations.

The United States also agreed to contribute at least two thirds of the cost of closing the final 250-mile (400-km) gap in the Pan American Highway. Work on this new road through the jungles and swamps of Panama and northern Colombia began in January 1972, with completion planned by 1976.

INTERNATIONAL BODIES

Apart from the fruitful bilateral negotiations, international meetings in 1971 yielded meager results. The Organization of American States, in a year of transition, found it especially difficult to fulfill its role as a harmonizer of divergent views, especially when U. S.-Latin differences were involved. Under the circumstances, the Latin nations welcomed the chance to participate in such meetings as that of the Group of 77, where a congenial bloc of developing countries found a more ready consensus.

Special Meeting of Foreign Ministers. The foreign ministers of the Western Hemisphere convened in Washington, D. C., on January 25 to devise effective action against political kidnapping in the Americas. When a majority refused to accept the demands of six of the foreign ministers (including those of Argentina, Brazil, and Guatemala, where the problem was most serious), these ministers walked out of the conference. A diluted resolution, in which the remaining members agreed to deny asylum to the kidnappers of diplomats and to provide for their extradition, was finally adopted.

General Assembly of the OAS. Under the amended charter of the Organization of American States, which went into effect in 1970, an annual General Assembly at the foreign ministers' level was required. The first such assembly convened in San José, Costa Rica, in April 1971.

The only immediate and practical gain was achieved outside of the agenda and off the floor, when Honduras and El Salvador consented to resume talks looking to a definite settlement of issues involved in their so-called "Soccer War" of 1969.

Group of 77. The Latin republics eagerly participated in the meeting of the Group of 77 (named for the number of its original members) at Lima, Peru, on Oct. 25–Nov. 8, 1971. There, representatives of 95 UN member nations sought to formulate a joint strategy with which to confront the more powerful and industrialized countries in a forthcoming UN General Assembly session. The Latin members were successful in soliciting the support of the Asian and African delegates for their nationalistic "Agreement of Lima," which called for generalized preferential tariff treatment, for a greater voice in decisions by the World Bank and the International Monetary Fund, and other goals.

SOCIAL AND ECONOMIC DEVELOPMENT

Modest advances were registered in the social and economic fields during the first decade of the Alliance for Progress (1961–70). The most important inhibitor of rapid development was the Latin American population explosion and the great migration from farm to city.

A Decade of Economic Progress. Economic growth fell just short of the Alliance's goal of 2.5% per capita per year, although rates were higher in the second half of the decade than in the first. In 1970, the per capita growth rate reached 3.8%.

To sustain this development, Latin America itself raised 94% of the total investment (14% more than was originally planned). Although external financing fell short of its goal of 20%, it had an important catalytic effect in helping to generate national investment. However, loan amortization and interest were proving a serious financial drain.

International trade assumed steadily increasing importance during the decade. Latin America's export earnings improved, especially toward the end of the period, reaching $14 billion in 1970.

Social Progress under the Alliance. While annual growth of agricultural output during the decade (2.6%) compared favorably with that in other regions of the world, it represented a decline from the 1950's. Food production increased 3.6% annually, exceeding the rate of population growth. Agrarian reform lagged, however.

An OAS analysis showed that a tremendous effort had been made in public housing construction, the number of units rising from 88,000 a year during the first half of the decade to 254,000 a year during the second half. But rapid population growth, urbanization, and construction costs prevented the region from narrowing its housing gap.

Though problems of unemployment increased, most countries made substantial gains in education and health. Child mortality and endemic diseases were significantly reduced. Some 18 countries achieved the goal of providing pure water supplies to 70% of their urban inhabitants, although none could furnish it to half its rural population.

MARTIN B. TRAVIS
State University of New York at Stony Brook

LATIN AMERICAN LITERATURE. See LITERATURE.

U. S. Supreme Court Chief Justice Warren Burger sits among bewigged British colleagues at American Bar Association convention in London.

Law

"There is probably no more important legacy that a President of the United States can leave in these times than his appointments to the Supreme Court. . . ."

—*President Nixon, Oct. 21, 1971*

The most important areas of law in the United States and in the law among nations are surveyed for major developments during 1971 under the headings (1) Supreme Court; (2) U. S. Legislation and Case Law; and (3) International Law.

Other legal developments are reviewed in CENSORSHIP; CIVIL LIBERTIES AND CIVIL RIGHTS; CRIME; POLICE; UNITED NATIONS; UNITED STATES; and the special report on Prisons beginning on page 38.

Supreme Court

The 1970–71 term of the Supreme Court, the second under Chief Justice Warren Burger, came to a climax on June 30 with a historic 6-to-3 ruling that voided the injunction the government had secured against publication by the New York *Times* and the Washington *Post* of the secret Pentagon Papers. Moving with such speed that there was no time to prepare a majority opinion, each justice issued his own views while the court handed down a short *per curiam* opinion merely stating the majority's consensus: the government had not met the heavy burden of demonstrating a danger to national security that would justify a prior restraint on freedom of the press.

During the summer recess, the court suffered a major blow with the retirement for reasons of health of Justices Hugo Black and John M. Harlan, intellectual leaders of its liberal and conservative wings, respectively. On September 25, Justice Black died, and Justice Harlan died on December 29.

In filling these two vacancies, the third and

fourth to occur during his first term in office, President Nixon generated controversy reminiscent of the Haynsworth-Carswell rejections by the Senate when he sought to make his second appointment to the court. His two leading choices, submitted to the American Bar Association Judiciary Committee for approval, were rejected by the committee as unqualified for the Supreme Court. He then made two surprise nominations, Lewis F. Powell, Jr., a Richmond lawyer, and Assistant Attorney General William H. Rehnquist, both of whom shared Nixon's view that the court had gone too far in protecting the rights of criminal suspects and defendants. Both appointments were confirmed by the Senate.

Three other decisions attracted national attention. One was the 5-to-4 vote in *United States* v. *Arizona* upholding the vote for 18-year-olds in national elections, as provided for by the 1970 Voting Rights Act. The court went on to rule that Congress lacked constitutional power to enfranchise 18-year-olds in state elections. But this result was promptly achieved as Congress adopted the 26th Amendment enfranchising 18-year-olds in all elections.

Second, the court unanimously rejected the advice of the Department of Justice to move more slowly toward racial integration in the public schools and upheld judicially designed desegregation plans for Charlotte, N. C., including school busing and the assignment of teachers on a racial quota basis. Third, the court held unconstitutional state efforts to relieve financial strain on parochial schools by making state funds available to supplement the salaries of parochial school teachers.

During the term the court continued to be sharply divided. In the 126 cases disposed of by full opinion, the justices wrote 291 majority, concurring, or dissenting opinions. They cast 240 dissenting votes, and only 44 of the decisions were unanimous. The court split 5 to 4 in no less than 28 cases.

In his first full term, Justice Blackmun aligned himself with Chief Justice Burger on the ideological right of the court; they disagreed in only 5 cases. Justices Douglas, Brennan, Marshall, and Black constituted the left wing, with Harlan, White, and Stewart near the center. However, Black was, predictably, in the liberal ranks only on First Amendment issues; he joined Burger and Blackmun in several important decisions. The growing weakness of the left on the Burger Court was shown by the fact that the four liberals cast 137 dissenting votes, to 103 for the other five justices.

CRIMINAL PROSECUTIONS

The modification of Warren Court holdings on the constitutional rights of criminal defendants that President Nixon desired was well under way during the term. For example, in *Miranda* v. *Arizona* (1966) the Warren Court, 5 to 4, held confessions inadmissible in court where the suspect had not been advised of his right to counsel. In *Harris* v. *New York* the Burger Court ruled, 5 to 4, that such a statement could be used to attack the credibility of a defendant who took the stand to testify in his own defense. *Dutton* v. *Evans,* also 5 to 4, admitted an incriminating out-of-court statement by an alleged accomplice to a murder under a state hearsay rule that would have been unconstitutional in a federal court.

Where the Warren Court in *Katz* v. *United States* (1967) had taken a strong stand against electronic bugging, *United States* v. *White* ruled that Katz had not voided the 1952 *On Lee* decision permitting the use of a concealed transmitter, over which a suspect's incriminating statements were broadcast to a third party. The Warren Court several times extended to juvenile courts the same procedural requirements enforced in regular courts, but this process was halted by a 1971 ruling that juveniles do not have a constitutional right to jury trial.

In *Dombrowski* v. *Pfister* (1965) the Warren Court had held that federal courts could enjoin state court proceedings that endangered constitutional freedoms. But in a series of 1971 decisions headed by *Younger* v. *Harris,* the Burger Court ruled that injunctions or declaratory judgments would be granted by federal courts against state prosecutions only where "great and immediate" irreparable injury was threatened.

Constitutionality of the death sentence continued to be troubling. No execution had been carried out in the United States since 1967, leaving about 650 convicts on death rows in 32 states awaiting Supreme Court action. In the 1970–71 term the court again failed to decide whether the death penalty amounts to cruel and unusual punishment, but in two cases it upheld existing procedures in capital cases. *McGautha* v. *California* ruled (6–3) that the absence of any standards to guide juries in deciding whether to impose the death penalty is not unconstitutional, and *Crampton* v. *Ohio* held (6–3) that the practice in some states of furnishing two trials in capital cases, the first to determine guilt, the second to fix the penalty, is not constitutionally required. The court did reverse the death sentences, though not the convictions, of 39 persons on the ground that in selecting the juries all persons opposed to the death penalty had been excluded, contrary to the ruling in the 1968 *Witherspoon* case.

The problem of disruptive court conduct continued. In *Mayberry* v. *Pennsylvania* the trial judge, vilified by the defendant, sentenced him at the end of the trial to 11 to 22 years for contempt. The Supreme Court suggested that summary removal of the defendant from the courtroom, approved the preceding term in *Illinois* v. *Allen,* was preferable, and ruled that the defendant was entitled to trial on the contempt charge before a different judge.

Other cases decided in favor of the defendants were *Palmer* v. *City of Euclid,* unanimously declaring unconstitutional a city ordinance authorizing police to arrest "suspicious persons," and *Bivens* v. *Six Unknown Agents of the Federal Bureau of Narcotics,* which held (6–3) that a private citizen illegally arrested by federal agents can sue them for damages.

FREEDOM OF EXPRESSION AND ASSOCIATION

Where First Amendment freedoms were involved the Burger Court did not depart substantially from the Warren Court policies of vigorous protection. The prime example was *New York Times Co.* v. *United States,* upholding publication of the Pentagon Papers. However, the actual court opinion was only a limited defense of press freedom; three dissenters, Burger, Blackmun, and Harlan, would have legalized the first prior restraint on the press in American history. (See CENSORSHIP.)

In dealing with libel cases the court continued to give the communications media almost complete protection against successful prosecution by enforcing and extending the principle of *New York Times Co.* v. *Sullivan* (1964) that only malicious and knowing falsehoods are actionable. Thus in *Rosenbloom* v. *Metromedia* the court held (5–3) that a radio station acting without malice was not liable in damages to a magazine distributor who was erroneously called a "smut peddler" in a news broadcast.

Organization for a Better Austin v. *Keefe* became famous when it was one of only three precedents cited by the court in the Pentagon Papers case. An injunction had been granted against a Chicago suburban civic group that was protesting the "blockbusting" activities of a realtor in its area by distributing literature against him in the distant suburb where he lived. The injunction was based on the ground that these tactics were an invasion of the realtor's privacy, but the Supreme Court held that an injunction can never be granted against the peaceful distribution of informational literature.

The court reversed (5–4) on First Amendment grounds the conviction of a young man for wearing a jacket inscribed with a four-letter word denouncing the draft. A city ordinance making it a criminal offense for three or more persons to assemble on sidewalks and conduct themselves in an annoying manner was held unconstitutionally vague in *Coates* v. *Cincinnati* (5–4).

In 1961 the Warren Court had upheld the right of bar associations in two states to question applicants about their possible membership in subversive organizations. Surprisingly, the Burger Court in 1971 in effect reversed these holdings, also by a 5-to-4 vote. In two cases Justice Black ruled that no legitimate state interest was served by questions that infringed so directly on First Amendment areas of belief and association. However, a switch by Justice Stewart in a third case yielded a 5-to-4 holding that the New York system of screening bar applicants as to character and fitness was not invalid.

Chief Justice Burger's attacks on the Warren Court's leniency toward obscenity began to have some effect. With Douglas not participating, the court (4–4) deadlocked over Maryland's ruling that the film *I Am Curious Yellow* was obscene. In *United States* v. *Reidel* the federal statute against sending obscene materials through the mail was upheld (7–2) even though the materials were requested by persons who stated they were adults. *United States* v. *Thirty-Seven Photographs* involved a seizure of pictures being brought into the country for publication, and the court upheld (6–3) the power of Congress to exclude "noxious" articles from commerce. The ruling seemed broad enough to cover obscene matter intended only for private use, thus bringing into question a 1969 decision that upheld the right of persons to have obscenity in their own homes.

EQUAL PROTECTION

Besides the Charlotte school desegregation case, the court was unanimous in striking down job discrimination. *Griggs* v. *Duke Power Co.* held that the Civil Rights Act of 1964 prohibited requiring high school education or the passing of standardized general intelligence tests as a condition of employment, where these were not significantly related to successful job performance. Such requirements had disqualified blacks at a higher rate than whites.

In *Palmer* v. *Jackson* the court ruled (5–4) that Jackson, Miss., had not violated the 14th Amendment by closing its municipal swimming pools rather than comply with court orders to desegregate them. Since the pools were closed for both blacks and whites, Justice Black held there was no discrimination involved, but he warned that the same reasoning would not justify closing of public schools. A civil rights law of 1871 was revived in *Griffin* v. *Breckenridge* which unanimously held that blacks may sue in federal courts for damages against whites who use assault and intimidation to violate their civil rights.

Discrimination against blacks in voting was at issue in several cases. In two confusing decisions, the court first in *Connor* v. *Johnson* held that a county in Mississippi must be divided into single-member legislative districts to give black communities a chance to elect members of their own race to the state legislature. But then in an Indiana case, *Whitcomb* v. *Chavis,* a protest by blacks that their voting power was diluted by multimember districts, with all candidates at large, was rejected.

The "one-man, one-vote" principle was limited in *Gordon* v. *Lance,* which upheld a West Virginia Law requiring approval of 60 percent of a district's voters to incur bonded indebtedness or increase tax rates; the reasoning was that no discrimination against any identifiable class was involved.

The ban on sex-based discrimination in the Civil Rights Act of 1964 was applied in *Phillips* v. *Martin Marietta Corp.* The court unanimously refused enforcement of a requirement that female job applicants not have preschool age children, unless this was demonstrated to be an occupational qualification necessary to the operation of the business.

The court had ruled in *Levy* v. *Louisiana* (1968) that state law cannot bar an illegitimate child from suing for his mother's wrongful death when legitimate children can do so. *Labine* v. *Vincent* refused (5–4) to follow that precedent and upheld a Louisiana law on intestate succession that barred illegitimate children, though acknowledged by the father, from claiming the rights of legitimate children.

OTHER DECISIONS

Law of the Poor. The court continued its policy of ensuring that the poor should not be disadvantaged in court proceedings. *Tate* v. *Short* unanimously held it a denial of equal protection to limit punishment to payment of a fine for those able to pay, but to convert this into a prison sentence for those who cannot. *Boddie* v. *Connecticut* ruled (8–1) that due process bars a state from denying the right to file for divorce to persons unable to pay court costs.

However, the court was less disposed than formerly to protect the claims of welfare recipients. *Wyman* v. *James* ruled (6–3) that persons on welfare must admit caseworkers to their homes as a condition of receiving assistance, and that such visits are not unreasonable searches. *James* v. *Valtierra* upheld (5–3) a California constitutional provision requiring that low-rent housing projects be approved by local referendum, on the theory that no racial discrimination was involved. The dissenters thought that a classification explicitly based on poverty was just as invalid under the 14th Amendment as one based on race.

Selective Service. After avoiding the issue of "selective conscientious objection" (objection to particular wars) in the 1970 case *United States* v. *Sisson,* the court in *Gillette* v. *United States,* with only Douglas dissenting, concluded that Congress had intended to grant exemption from military service only to those who by reason of religious training and belief are conscientiously opposed to all wars. In the widely noted case of *Clay* v. *United States,* the court unanimously held that former boxing champion Muhammad Ali had been improperly drafted, because the Justice Department had misled draft officials by advising them that Ali's claim as a conscientious objector was neither sincere nor based on religious tenets.

Citizenship. One of the major holdings of the Warren Court, that U. S. citizenship is a basic right that cannot be withdrawn by Congress, was challenged in *Rogers* v. *Bellei,* which upheld (5–4) a statute providing that persons born abroad who acquire citizenship because one of their parents is a citizen shall lose their citizenship unless they reside in the U. S. continuously for five years between the ages of 14 and 28.

Ecology. Conservationists failed to win any outstanding victories during the term. In *Ohio* v. *Wyandotte Chemicals Corp.* a bold effort by Ohio to act against out-of-state polluters by suing in the original jurisdiction of the Supreme Court failed. The court thought that with such complex, novel, and technical factors as were involved, the case should go through the regular trial court procedures. *Citizens to Preserve Overton Park, Inc.* v. *Volpe* held up federal approval of a highway through a Memphis park and required a new court hearing, but Black and Brennan, dissenting, would have sent the case all the way back to the secretary of transportation, of whom they were very critical.

C. Herman Pritchett
University of California, Santa Barbara

U. S. Legislation and Case Law

Legislation and case law during 1971 again reflected a plethora of subjects characteristic of the emerging social, economic, and legal problems that face the United States.

Federal Legislation. On March 23, 1971, Congress passed the 26th Amendment to the U. S. Constitution, extending the right to vote to citizens 18 years of age or older, and submitted it to the legislatures of the states for ratification. Under Article 5 of the constitution, three fourths (38) of the legislatures of the 50 states were required to ratify it. When Ohio ratified it on June 30, 1971, the requisite number was achieved.

During World War II, President Franklin D. Roosevelt ordered the detention of Americans of Japanese ancestry. During the Korean War, the Emergency Detention Act of 1950 was enacted, with procedures for the apprehension and detention of individuals deemed likely to engage in espionage or sabotage. Although no President has ever used or attempted to use this power, the continued existence of the act aroused public concern lest it be exercised for apprehending and detaining citizens who hold unpopular beliefs and views. A law approved Sept. 25, 1971, repealed this provision by amending the 1950 law to read that "no citizen shall be imprisoned or otherwise detained by the United States except pursuant to an Act of Congress."

The critical area of juvenile crime in the United States saw an increase of 148% during the past decade in violent crime by children under 18. Property crimes, such as burglary, larceny, and auto theft, have increased by 85%. The recidivism rate for offenders under the age of 20, over a four-year period, was 74%. Although children from the ages of 10 to 17 make up only 16% of the national population, they account for more than 32% of all arrests for major serious crimes.

In response to this growing crisis, Congress enacted the Juvenile Delinquency Prevention and Control Act in 1968. On the whole, the program has been a failure owing to inadequate administration. However, a law was approved July 1, 1971, extending the act for one year in order to review its operation, to make necessary changes, and to ensure its effectiveness. The act also creates an interdepartmental Council on Juvenile Delinquency to coordinate federal activities in the field.

Boating has become a major form of recreation for Americans, but the boom in the sport's popularity has brought with it accidents, deaths, and injuries. In the last five years, nearly 7,000 Americans have died in boating mishaps. In light of these statistics, Congress enacted a Federal Boat Safety Act of 1971, approved in August 1971, which establishes a new national program to promote safety in the construction and operation of pleasure boats. (See also BOATING.)

State Legislation. Because only 45% of automobile victims seriously injured are compensated, and court calendars are so congested with these cases that the administration of justice is being adversely affected, the U. S. Congress and more than half the states are considering the feasibility of enacting "no-fault" legislation. Under "no-fault" plans, accident victims can recover from insurance companies, even though they are at fault.

In 1971 the Supreme Judicial Court of Massachusetts upheld the constitutionality of the law on the theory that it does not violate the due process and equal protection clauses of the U. S. Constitution. In the interest of uniformity and for the guidance of state legislators, the national Conference of Commissioners on Uniform State Laws announced that it will draft model state legislation on "no-fault" insurance. (See also INSURANCE.)

Case Law. Indigents have basic rights, and the courts in 1971 had occasion to distinguish them. Thus, the U. S. District courts for Eastern New York (*In re Kras*) and for Colorado (*In re Smith*) ruled that it is a denial of due process and equal protection to refuse a bankruptcy discharge to an indigent merely because he cannot afford the $50 filing fee required by statute. Yet the U. S. District Court for the District of Columbia denied an indigent's petition to compel the commission of patents to examine his patent application without payment of the statutory filing fee, ruling that "no person has a vested right to a patent" (*Boyden* v. *Commissioner of Patents*). But the right to a divorce is "fundamental," declared the U. S. Supreme Court, and as state divorce courts have the jurisdictional monopoly to dissolve marriages legally, to bar an indigent access to these courts solely because of his inability to pay court fees and costs would be a denial of due process (*Boddie* v. *Connecticut*).

By reason of the 6th and 14th Amendments to the U. S. Constitution, courts have granted an accused the right to be represented by counsel at proceedings that can result in his imprisonment. The granting of parole, however, said a California court, is a matter of grace, and hence counsel need not be present at a parole revocation hearing (*In re Tucker*). This appears to be the majority rule. To date, the right to counsel in such proceedings has been granted by New York, Pennsylvania, and Michigan, and by the 2d Federal Circuit. The 4th Federal Circuit considered this issue in another light. It decreed that when the circumstances are such that the hearing would be unjust without counsel present, it would permit such representation (*Bearden* v. *South Carolina*).

Strict products liability of manufacturers and suppliers for injuries to person or damage to property is being extended by the courts. The test has been whether the product is inherently dangerous and can foreseeably result in injury or damage. The U. S. Court of Appeals for the 4th Circuit held in *Gardner* v. *Q. H. S.* that a manufacturer of paraffin-filled hair rollers (who had warned consumers to heat them only in boiling water) was liable to an apartment house owner whose building was burned when the rollers caught fire because the tenant fell asleep and allowed the water to boil away. The court maintained that the manufacturer must anticipate the normal environment in which the product will be used.

The U. S. District Court for Northern Mississippi ruled that a year's residence requirement before a bar applicant would be approved (similar to requirements in other states) violates the equal protection clause of the U. S. Constitution. A reasonable residency requirement, such as 90 days, will be permitted to allow the state to review an applicant's fitness and capacity for the practice of law.

Jury Size. The Judicial Conference of the United States recommended that the size of juries in civil trials in federal district courts be reduced. Several district courts have reduced them to 6 members.

JULIUS J. MARKE, *New York University*

International Law

The major developments in international law in 1971 occurred at the United Nations in four important areas: Chinese representation, World Court, arms control, and the building of world law.

Chinese Representation. Twenty-six years of representation of China in the United Nations by Chiang Kai-shek's Nationalist government came to an end on Oct. 25, 1971, with the General Assembly's adoption of a resolution seating the Peking government of the People's Republic of China as "the only lawful representatives of China." The vote was 76 in favor to 35 opposed, with 17 abstentions. The Assembly action was followed on November 23 by recognition of the Peking government as the representative of China in the Security Council.

Although the United States favored the seating of the Peking government in the Security Council and General Assembly, a change in position coincident with President Nixon's announced 1972 visit to Peking, the United States proposed that the Nationalist government be permitted to remain in the Assembly as a second representative of China. Under the U. S. proposal "China" would be regarded as a single state and an original member of the United Nations; its representation would be split in two to reflect the "long-prevailing de facto situation" without prejudice to the future settlement of internal Chinese problems between two Chinese governments. Considering that each of the two Chinese governments purports to represent the whole of China to the exclusion of the other, the U. S. proposal had no precedent in UN history.

In an atmosphere of intense pressure generated by repeated "warnings" from the U. S. delegation that a refusal to accept Washington's proposal might result in backlash from the Congress at appropriation time, the Assembly voted to seat the Peking government to the total exclusion of the Nationalist government. Among major countries, only Australia, Brazil, and Japan voted with the United States. Every other major state—including Belgium, Canada, Denmark, France, India, Italy, Mexico, the Netherlands, Norway, Pakistan, the Soviet Union, Sweden, the United Kingdom, and Yugoslavia—voted in favor of seating Peking as the sole representative of China.

The seating of Peking marks the start of a new era for the UN in which the organization will have new relevance in dealing with both East-West and North-South world problems. Much will depend upon the reaction of governments to the reality of daily diplomatic contact with Peking, especially that of the U. S. government and the American people to participation in a UN whose actions on world problems cannot be dominated by the United States.

World Court. The International Court of Justice has not had more than one case on its docket at a time since February 1969. On July 29, 1970, the court was asked by the Security Council for an advisory opinion on the continued presence of South Africa in Namibia (South West Africa), which it delivered on June 21, 1971. In its opinion, the court held that the Security Council's action in Resolution 276 (1970) was founded on Article 24 of the UN Charter and was binding on member states under Article 25 of the charter. The court concluded that "South Africa is under obligation to withdraw its administration from Namibia immediately and thus put an end to its occupation of the Territory," and that UN members are obliged "to recognize the illegality of South Africa's presence. . . ."

By year's end, one new case appeared: an application by India for a court ruling that the Council of the International Civil Aviation Organization had no jurisdiction to deal with a complaint by Pakistan challenging India's decision to bar overflights across India by Pakistani aircraft.

The unwillingness of governments to submit disputes to the International Court of Justice was explored in the General Assembly's Legal Committee in 1970 and 1971, in an effort to find means of enhancing the effectiveness of the court in settling disputes and developing international law.

Arms Control. Agreement at the bilateral United States-Soviet Strategic Arms Limitation Talks (SALT) continued to be elusive during 1971 on the crucial questions of the antiballistic missile (ABM) and the multiple independently targeted reentry vehicle (MIRV). But substantial progress was achieved during the year in three other areas, dealing with the use of weapons on the sea-bed; biological weapons; and accidental outbreak of war. (See DISARMAMENT.)

Building of World Law. The International Law Commission is engaged in a basic review of its long-term work program on the basis of a survey of international law prepared by the secretary general. The UN Commission on International Trade Law continues its work on legal aspects of the international sale of goods, payments, commercial arbitration, and shipping legislation. The UN Institute for Training and Research is studying questions of international law in connection with such topics as the transfer of technology to developing countries, international regulation of environmental pollution, and the development of the safeguards system of the International Atomic Energy Agency.

In 1971, UN officials and working groups prepared intensively for the UN Conference on the Human Environment, to be held at Stockholm in June 1972, and the UN Conference on the Law of the Sea, scheduled for 1973. The Stockholm conference will consider questions of the "planning and management of human settlements for environmental quality," with specific proposals relating to housing, construction, industry, transportation, water supply, and waste disposal; questions of the "environmental aspects of natural resources management," soil conservation legislation, and measures to conserve a wide diversity of animal and plant species despite environmental change caused by man-made pollutants; and "identification and control of pollutants and nuisances of broad international significance" relating to worldwide data collection, ocean dumping, and marine pollution. (See ENVIRONMENT.)

The 1973 UN Conference on the Law of the Sea will consider the establishment of an international regime for regulation of the exploitation of the resources of the sea-bed and the ocean floor beyond the limits of national jurisdiction and the establishment of a precise definition of those limits. Other agenda matters include fishing rights, conservation of the living resources of the high seas, preservation of the marine environment, and questions relating to the continental shelf and the territorial sea and international straits.

ARTHUR LARSON, *Duke University*

LEBANON

The first year of President Suleiman Franjieh's administration was turbulent, although relatively successful. Lebanon's first really popular president achieved great success during 1971 as he reestablished internal security, abolished government censorship, and stimulated the economy so that it flourished after many years of stagnation. He also worked to improve relations with all other Arab countries, actively involved Lebanon in Arab politics, and avoided conflicts with Palestinian guerrillas in Lebanon.

At the same time, however, his campaign to reduce corruption in the government barely scratched the surface, and the country was plagued by strikes, demonstrations, armed political clashes, and a devastating April flood. There were also Israeli reprisal attacks for guerrilla raids originating in Lebanon. The cabinet was the object of continuous political attacks and rigid opposition.

Domestic Developments. The 12-member cabinet, headed by Premier Saeb Salam, was composed of young technocrats and advocated a "revolution from the top." Despite many excellent ideas and good intentions, the cabinet was subjected to vicious parliamentary attacks and was firmly opposed. Some of its moves were ill advised, and no less than three decrees had to be repealed when faced with adamant opposition. Rocked by the resignation of two of its members, torn by internal dissensions, continuously pressured to resign, and plagued by daily rumors that it was on its way out, the cabinet was appropriately called "a head without a body."

Still, its successes were numerous and far overshadowed those of most previous governments. Among other accomplishments, it abolished censorship of the news media, put a comprehensive national health insurance plan into effect, and adopted an Arabicizing policy for school curriculums. In the economic sphere the government was very active. An agreement with Saudi Arabia providing for the establishment of a jointly owned oil refinery in Lebanon was initialed, and very favorable agreements with Tapline (Trans-Arabian Pipe Line) and with the Iraq Petroleum Company were negotiated. The government approved a 5-year, 4,000-unit housing development plan and agreed to establish a Lebanese development bank. Tourism increased by more than 30%, wages of government employees were raised by 5%, and pharmaceutical prices were reduced by 25%.

Numerous elements of the population, for various reasons, went on strike. Among them were elementary and secondary school teachers, secondary school pupils, and university students. Taxi drivers, bakers of Arabic bread (a local staple food), telephone operators, bank employees, and some government employees walked off their jobs. A decree raising the customs on 450 "luxury" items resulted in a paralyzing strike by Lebanese merchants, which ended with the repeal of the decree.

The student strikes were Lebanon's most perplexing problem. Although the government bent and offered concessions to the Lebanese University dissidents, they were only partially placated and conducted several strikes. The rigid position of the American University of Beirut student strikers and the inflexible attitude of the university administration resulted in the suspension of the 1970–71 school year on May 25.

Guerrillas and Israel. The Lebanese government "reconciled" the problems arising from guerrilla activities largely by ignoring them. Minor violations by the guerrillas of the 1969 Cairo agreement, which regulated guerrilla-government relations, were continuous, but the guerrillas adhered to the central condition, which confined their main bases to the foothills of Mt. Hermon.

The guerrilla presence in Lebanon during 1971 led to intensified Israeli reprisal attacks over the southern Lebanese border, aimed at villages from which guerrillas were infiltrating Israeli territory. The Israeli raids destroyed many houses and forced hundreds of border villagers to flee from the area. Lebanon lost effective control over a 22-mile-wide (35-km) strip along its southern border. The guerrilla-Jordanian conflict resulted in an influx of guerrillas into southern Lebanon, widespread pro-guerrilla demonstrations, and sympathetic strikes throughout Lebanon. The closing of the Jordanian-Syrian border was a severe blow to Lebanese trade with Jordan and the peninsular states.

International Relations. The government emphasized its strong ties with Arab states and markedly improved relations with Saudi Arabia, Egypt, Iraq, and Syria. Relations with Syria became especially cordial, as many disputes were satisfactorily eliminated and amicable negotiations were conducted on other problems. There was an increase in trade to the point where Lebanon became Syria's second most important commercial partner.

Lebanon attempted to counter past accusations of being completely "pro-Western" by unconditionally recognizing the Peking government as the sole representative of China and by signing an arms pact with the USSR in November. Nevertheless, Lebanon also made arms deals with France and Britain.

JACK L. SCHRIER, *Georgetown University*

--------- LEBANON · Information Highlights ---------

Official Name: Republic of Lebanon.
Area: 4,015 square miles (10,400 sq km).
Population (1970 est.): 2,790,000. *Density,* 658 per square mile (254 per sq km). *Annual rate of increase,* 2.6%.
Chief City: Beirut (1970 est.), the capital, 800,000.
Government: *Head of state,* Suleiman Franjieh, president (took office Sept. 23, 1970). *Head of government,* Suleiman Franjieh. *Legislature*—Chamber of Deputies (unicameral), 99 members. *Major political groups*—Maronite Christians, Sunnite Muslims, Shiite Muslims, Greek Orthodox.
Languages: Arabic (official), French, English.
Education: *Literacy rate* (1970), 86% of population. *Expenditure on education* (1968), 16.9% of total public expenditure. *School enrollment* (1968)—primary, 425,840; secondary, 137,724; vocational, 2,103; higher, 33,587.
Finances (1969 est.): *Revenues,* $179,510,700; *expenditures,* $202,018,300; *monetary unit,* Lebanese pound (3.17 pounds equal U. S.$1, Sept. 1971).
Gross National Product (1968): $1,392,500,000.
National Income (1968): $1,215,000,000; *national income per person,* $471.
Manufacturing (metric tons, 1969): Cement, 1,253,000; residual fuel oil, 884,000; distillate fuel oils, 318,000; kerosene, 207,000; meat, 47,000.
Crops (metric tons, 1968 crop year): Citrus fruits, 238,000; apples, 163,000; grapes, 84,000; pears, 16,000.
Minerals (metric tons, 1969): Salt, 28,000.
Foreign Trade (1968): *Exports* (1970), $198,000,000 (chief exports—apples, pears, and quinces, $13,480,000; eggs in the shell, $7,880,000; aircraft, including parts, $6,851,000; iron and steel manufactures, $5,977,000). *Imports* (1970), $591,000,000 (chief imports—live animals, $36,763,000; automobiles, $22,886,000; wheat and meslin, $15,795,000; paper and cardboard, $14,838,000). *Chief trading partners* (1968)—Saudi Arabia (took 26% of exports, supplied 21% of imports); Syria (7%—9%); United Kingdom.
Tourism: *Receipts* (1970), $131,500,000.
Transportation: *Roads* (1966), 4,660 miles (7,498 km); *motor vehicles* (1969), 145,900 (automobiles, 129,700); *railroads* (1968), 250 miles (402 km).
Communications: *Telephones* (1968), 150,370; *television stations* (1968), 3; *television sets* (1968), 375,000; *radios* (1969), 590,000; *newspapers* (1965), 37.

——————— LESOTHO · Information Highlights ———————

Official Name: Kingdom of Lesotho.
Area: 11,720 square miles (30,355 sq km).
Population (1970 est.): 1,040,000. *Density,* 81 per square mile (32 per sq km). *Annual rate of increase,* 2.9%.
Chief City (1966 census): Maseru, the capital, 14,000.
Government: *Head of state,* Moshoeshoe II, king (acceded March 12, 1960). *Head of government,* Chief Leabua Jonathan, prime minister (took office April 1965): suspended the constitution on Jan. 30, 1970.
Languages: English (official), Sesotho (official).
Education: *Literacy rate* (1969), 40% of population. *Expenditure on education* (1967), 21.6% of public expenditure.
Finances (1970–71 est.): *Revenues,* $16,705,000; *expenditures,* $15,346,000; *monetary unit,* rand (0.7143 rand equals U. S. $1, July 1971).
Gross National Product (1967): $80,000,000.
Crop (metric tons, 1969 crop year): Maize, 112,000.
Foreign Trade (1966): *Exports* (1967), $5,835,000 (chief exports—wool, mohair, diamonds. *Imports* (1967), $33,-320,000 (chief imports—food, drink and tobacco, chemicals, consumer goods). *Chief trading partner* (1966)—South Africa.
Transportation: *Roads* (1969), 1,240 miles (1,996 km); *motor vehicles* (1964), 2,100 (automobiles, 1,800).

LESOTHO

The start of a 5-year development plan and the establishment of a U. S. embassy were the main events in Lesotho in 1971.

Economy. To increase its average per capita income, which was $70, Lesotho launched a 5-year development plan in April; it provided for an expenditure of $38.4 million between 1971 and 1975. One fourth of this amount will be spent on agriculture, which employs 48% of the male labor force. Of the rest of the male labor force, 7% work for pay in Lesotho, while 45% work in South Africa.

A 1969 customs agreement with South Africa increased Lesotho's proportion of the revenue from customs duties so that in 1971 it received $8.5 million, or over half its total revenue.

British aid has met Lesotho's deficits since independence. In 1971, Britain provided about $2 million, and another $1.5 million was promised for 1972. Lesotho's finance minister, Chief Peete, stated that income can equal expenses in five years.

To attract tourists to its mountains—Lesotho is called the Switzerland of Africa—a new Holiday Inn was opened in 1970, and a number of mountain chalets are planned. A $17 million ski resort is planned near the proposed Oxbow Dam.

Political Affairs. Lesotho's 1971 economic drive supplanted the previous year's political agitation. King Alfred Moshoeshoe II returned from exile in December 1970, and political prisoners were released. Effective control continued to be held by Prime Minister Leabua Jonathan.

U. S. Embassy. In May the United States raised its diplomatic relations with Lesotho, Botswana, and Swaziland to embassy level. Charles J. Nelson was named U. S. ambassador to the three nations.

FRANKLIN PARKER, *West Virginia University*

LIBERIA

Liberia's President William V. S. Tubman died on July 23, 1971, and was succeeded by Vice President William R. Tolbert. Tubman's death in London, from complications following a prostate operation, brought to an end one of the longest and most colorful political careers in contemporary Africa. President Tubman was 75 years old at his death, and had been president of Liberia since 1944. He had been elected to his seventh consecutive term in May 1971.

Domestic Affairs. Within five hours of President Tubman's death, Vice President Tolbert, aged 58, was sworn in as Liberia's 19th president. The transition was both quiet and smooth, ending speculation that President Tubman's death might result in a struggle for power among Liberia's leading politicians. Tolbert was formally inaugurated in January 1972 to fill Tubman's full 4-year term.

Gen. George Washington, a former military advisor to President Tubman, was released from jail in April. He and a former university student had been arrested in 1970 on charges of plotting to kill the defense secretary and the army chief of staff.

Foreign Relations. In April, President Tubman denied the charges of Sierra Leone's President Siaka Stevens that Liberia was harboring mercenaries planning to invade neighboring Sierra Leone on behalf of that country's dissident politicians. President Stevens later apologized to President Tubman for having failed to utilize normal diplomatic channels in the matter.

In October, Liberia was one of 15 African states that voted against the admission of the People's Republic of China to the United Nations. Liberia will continue to maintain diplomatic relations with Nationalist China.

Economy. Liberia continued to enjoy favorable economic prospects in 1971, and the government continued geological explorations of the rich Mt. Nimba iron ore reserves. A private Belgian bank announced a $15 million loan for development of a harbor at Harper, and the World Bank announced a $4.7 million loan for expansion of Liberia's hydroelectric power capacity.

The country's favorable economic climate was not affected by the death of President Tubman. President Tolbert announced that the late chief executive's "open door" policy, which encouraged foreign investment on excellent terms, would continue.

VICTOR T. LE VINE
Washington University, St. Louis

——————— LIBERIA · Information Highlights ———————

Official Name: Republic of Liberia.
Area: 43,000 square miles (111,369 sq km).
Population (1970 est.): 1,170,000. *Density,* 27 per square mile (10 per sq km). *Annual rate of increase,* 1.7%.
Chief City (1962 census): Monrovia, the capital, 80,992.
Government: *Head of state,* William Tolbert, president (took office July 23, 1971). *Head of government,* William Tolbert. *Legislature—Congress:* Senate, 18 members; House of Representatives, 52 members. *Political Party—True Whig party.*
Languages: English (official), 28 tribal dialects.
Education: *Literacy rate* (1970), 9% of population. *Expenditure on education* (1968), 2% of gross domestic product. *School enrollment* (1968)—primary, 120,101; secondary, 14,127; technical/vocational, 913; higher, 1,282.
Finances (1969): *Revenues,* $58,000,000; *expenditures,* $60,-100,000; *monetary unit,* Liberian dollar (1L.dollar equals U. S.$1, Sept. 1971).
Gross National Product (1968): $254,000,000.
National Income (1968): $184,000,000.
Manufacturing (metric tons, 1968): Coffee, 3,500; beer, 3,000 hectoliters.
Crops (metric tons, 1968 crop year): Cassava, 430,000; rubber, 66,900; palm kernels, 41,200.
Minerals (metric tons, 1969): Iron ore, 14,786,000; diamonds, 836,000 metric carats; gold, 100 kilograms.
Foreign Trade (1968): *Exports,* $160,772,000 (chief exports—iron ore and concentrates, $118,028,000; natural rubber and gums, $25,582,000; industrial diamonds, $9,073,000). *Imports,* $106,864,000 (chief imports—nonelectrical machinery, $15,146,000; cereals and preparations, $10,482,-000; transport equipment, $9,399,000).
Transportation: *Roads* (1970), 3,400 miles (5,472 km); *motor vehicles* (1970), 23,400 (automobiles, 14,700).
Communications: *Telephones* (1970), 6,051; *television stations* (1968), 1; *television sets* (1969), 6,000; *radios* (1969), 152,000; *newspapers* (1969), 1.

Lyndon Baines Johnson Library opened in Austin, Texas, on May 22. Its 31 million documents make it the largest presidential library.

libraries

Libraries made both good and bad news during 1971. In the United States, would-be censors continued to threaten the intellectual freedom of library users. President Richard M. Nixon nominated members to the National Commission on Libraries and Information Sciences, and recommended a library budget for fiscal 1972 that was significantly lower than that for 1971. The Library of Congress was accused of racial discrimination in employment practices, and new presidential libraries were dedicated in Texas and Massachusetts. International events included preparations for an International Book Year in 1972 and a meeting held in Paris to revise the International Copyright Convention.

Censorship. Two significant instances of censorship occurred in the United States during the year. One involved the sensitivities of policemen and a prize-winning children's book, and the other a public library in Connecticut.

The book *Sylvester and the Magic Pebble* was attacked by the board of directors of the International Conference of Police Associations. The board objected 'to an illustration in the book depicting two pigs in police uniforms. Although the book's general excellence merited the Caldecott Medal for 1969, the police group interpreted the drawing as a visual polemic against law enforcement. Moreover, the International Conference asked members of local police associations to seek removal of the book from libraries in their communities. Before representatives of the Intellectual Freedom Committee of the American Library Association and of the International Conference met in Los Angeles in January 1971, public school libraries in Lincoln, Nebr., Palo Alto, Calif., and Toledo, Ohio, had complied with the request of the police associations, and had either refused to acquire the book or had removed it from their shelves. Police pressure caused similar incidents in Maryland, Ohio, Pennsylvania, and Wyoming.

At the Groton (Conn.) Public Library there was a great deal of tension over "The Fine Art of Lovemaking," an article in the February 1971 issue of *Evergreen Review.* Because the article was accompanied by sketches of human sexual activity, the chief prosecutor for the tenth circuit court contended that it was obscene and asked the court for a temporary injunction requiring the library board to show cause why it should not be enjoined from making that issue of the magazine available to the public. Before the March 16 show-cause hearing could be held, however, the library board voted, 6–3, to eliminate the February *Evergreen Review.* In addition, it decided to restrict access to the other issues of the magazine contained in the library. Thus, under the threat of prosecution, the library board removed the issue before legal proceedings had determined whether it was indeed obscene as several members of the Groton town council had contended. As a result of the controversy, the town council decided, in May, to transfer control over the hiring and firing of the librarian from the library board to the town manager.

National Planning and Legislation. In mid-May, President Nixon announced his nomination for membership on the National Commission on Libraries and Information Sciences. Included on the 15-member commission are information scientists, publishers, research administrators, academic executives, businessmen, and librarians. The chairman of the panel, on which the Librarian of Congress serves ex officio, is Frederick Burkhardt, president of the American Council of Learned Societies. The commission will consult with federal, state, and local governments, as well as with private agencies, in seeking to improve the "provision of informational services to the American people."

The federal budget for the 1972 fiscal year, which President Nixon sent to Congress in late January 1971, recommended the appropriation of $108 million for library construction, services, resources, training, and research, in addition to $6.8 million for the central cataloging program operated by the Library of Congress, which is covered by a different appropriations act. This request was $37.6 million, or 25%, below the $152.4 million appropriated for 1971. The heaviest cuts in the administration's budget were in funds for library services and construction and for academic library resources. Because the budget recommendation fell well below congressional authorizations, Congress voted to appropriate $164.5 million for library programs, $56.5 million more than the $108 million requested by the President. The bill was signed into law on July 9, 1971.

In March, Sen. Frank Church of Idaho reported that very few manuscripts and private papers had been given to libraries since the passage of the 1969 Tax Reform Act, which permits donors to gain income tax benefits only on the original cost of production or purchase of materials rather than on their current market value. A famous composer, for example, could claim tax exemption as a donor only for the cost of the paper and writing materials involved in producing his compositions. Senator Church testified in support of the proposed Gifts to Libraries Incentive Act of 1971, which would permit individuals to deduct the actual market value of materials donated to libraries unless such materials were produced while one was employed by the federal government.

Library of Congress. Between April and June, a series of protests by black staff members occurred at the Library of Congress. The protesters maintained that the library's employment, promotion, and training policies were racially discriminatory. Because the library is part of the legislative branch of the federal government, its employees cannot present grievances to the Civil Service Commission, as do employees of the executive branch. The demonstrations resulted in the firing of 13 black staff members.

It was announced during 1971 that the Library of Congress would create an Office for Preservation Research. Although the library currently spends over $500,000 a year on restoration and deterioration control, it proposed to undertake more basic research on the preservation of library materials. The projected laboratory will investigate the preservation of microfilm, magnetic tape, and motion picture film as well as of books, manuscripts, newspapers, and other printed materials. It is expected that the testing and evaluation services of the office will benefit libraries and archives throughout the country.

A final development at the Library of Congress was the Cataloging-in-Publication Program. Nonfederal funding was being sought for the first three years of this program, during which bibliographic, or catalog-card, information would be printed near the title page of approximately 90,000 individual books. This activity succeeds the Cataloging-in-Source Program which had a one-year trial at the library during 1958–59.

Presidential Libraries. A new presidential library was dedicated on the campus of the University of Texas in Austin during the spring of 1971. The Lyndon Baines Johnson Library—an $18 million building designed by Skidmore, Owings and Merrill and paid for by the university—will be operated by the federal government under the Presidential Libraries Act of 1955. The monumental library, which is virtually windowless, will include the Johnson memorabilia and archives and will be one unit of a complex containing the Lyndon B. Johnson School of Public Affairs and the Sid W. Richardson Hall, a rare book library.

Finnish architect Alvar Aalto designed striking modern library in forest setting for abbey in St. Benedict, Oreg.

MORLEY BAER

In August, the John F. Kennedy Presidential Library in Waltham, Mass., was opened. The library houses most of the official White House files of the Kennedy administration, as well as memorabilia of the late president.

Other U. S. Library News. Merger discussions between the American Society for Information Science (ASIS) and the Special Libraries Association (SLA) ended without action in mid-1971. After polling its membership on the idea of a union with ASIS, the SLA concluded that there was no clear mandate for such a decision. ASIS includes mainly documentalists, computer specialists, and information scientists, while SLA's members are mostly librarians who are also subject specialists. The merger talks had been initiated in 1968.

An issue of mounting concern to public librarians during 1971 involved place of residence. In January, Mildred E. Hutto, a professional librarian in the Hamtramck (Mich.) Public Library since 1949, was discharged because she was not a resident of the city. Mrs. Hutto, a resident of Detroit, had originally been appointed by the Hamtramck civil service commission in the absence of a qualified resident of the city. Although it is an established policy that the residency requirement in the Hamtramck city charter can be waived for certain kinds of professional employees, Mrs. Hutto's employment was terminated without her being warned and given a chance to comply with the residency requirement and before it had been determined whether in fact she had been granted a waiver of the residency rule at the time of her initial employment in 1949. In her suit against the dismissal action by the Hamtramck civil service commission, Mrs. Hutto was supported by both the Michigan Library Association and the American Library Association.

National Library Week. National Library Week, April 18–24, 1971, had as its theme: "You've Got a Right to Read." The 14th annual event was again sponsored by the National Book Committee in collaboration with the American Library Association. The 1971 program concentrated its promotional efforts on the social and economic importance of eliminating illiteracy on all levels. Attention was directed to motivational and environmental factors in the reading competence of children and adults. In a message to the sponsors of National Library Week, President Nixon stressed the importance of "a sturdy system of public and institutional libraries" as a means of improving the reading skills of U. S. citizens.

Library Education. The number of graduate library schools accredited by the American Library Association increased to 55 in 1971 with the approval of the master's degree programs offered by the Palmer Graduate Library School of Long Island University, the School of Library Science of the University of Iowa, and the Graduate Library School of the University of Rhode Island.

A report released in June revealed that the average beginning salary paid to the graduates of accredited library schools outpaced the increase in the cost of living for the period 1967–70. With 1957–58 assigned an index number of 100 and used as a base year, by 1970 the cost-of-living had reached an index of 137 while the index for beginning library salaries had increased to 185. The average annual starting salary for 1970 graduates was $8,611, but the graduates of 1971 had an average estimated at between $8,800 and $9,000.

There were fewer openings for new librarians in 1971 than there had been in 1970, but there was a continuing demand for media specialists and for librarians qualified to work primarily with minority groups. A 1971 survey by the Library Administration Division of the American Library Association indicated that the average salary of an ALA member with a master's degree is $11,103; with a doctorate, $16,090; and with a bachelor's degree, $9,534.

Awards. The 1971 Beta Phi Mu Award for distinguished service to education for librarianship went to Leon Carnovsky, a professor in the Graduate Library School of the University of Chicago. The Melvil Dewey Award for recent creative professional achievement—particularly in the fields of library management, library training, cataloging and classification, and the tools and techniques of librarianship—was given to William J. Welsh, director of the Processing Department of the Library of Congress. The Joseph W. Lippincott Award for distinguished service in the library profession was given to William S. Dix, university librarian of Princeton University and former president of the American Library Association.

Henriette D. Avram, chief of the MARC Development Office at the Library of Congress, was awarded the Margaret Mann Citation for outstanding professional contribution in cataloging and classification. John Phillip Imroth, assistant professor of library and information science in the Graduate School of Library and Information Science of the University of Pittsburgh, received the Esther J. Piercy Award for contributions to librarianship in the field of technical services by younger members of the profession. The Isadore Gilbert Mudge Citation for distinguished contributions to the field of reference librarianship was given to James B. Childs, honorary consultant to the Library of Congress in government document bibliography. Finally, the Scarecrow Press Award for an outstanding contribution to library literature was given to Irene Braden Headley, librarian at Ohio State University, author of *The Undergraduate Library*. (See also below, *American Library Association*.)

International Library Activities. Officers of the International Federation of Library Associations and of the International Federation for Documentation, along with the director of UNESCO's Department of Documentation, Libraries, and Archives, met at the Royal Library of Belgium in Brussels during February to consider coordination and cooperative effort on matters of joint concern. Some of the joint activities being considered are common meetings; the exchange of documents; an international list and guide to education for librarianship and documentation; manuals for teachers and students of classification, cataloging, and bibliography; a committee on standardization; and the organization of symposiums on the problems of librarianship in the developing countries. During 1971 the two associations shared a secretariat building in the Hague. Dialogue between them was expected to be intensified when both meet in Budapest in 1972.

Using as its theme, "The International Organization of the Library Profession," the International Federation of Library Associations held its 37th annual session, in Liverpool, England, Aug. 30–Sept. 4, 1971. A special grant from UNESCO allowed more librarians from developing countries to attend that conference than is ordinarily the case. In 1971 the American Library Association agreed to become

JOHN F. KENNEDY Presidential Library in Waltham, Mass., which will be completed in 1975, opened many new archives in August. Kennedy memorabilia is being stored until it can be arranged in the new library.

UPI

a depository for all documents issuing from the International Federation of Library Associations.

Member nations of UNESCO were involved in preparations for 1972 as the International Book Year (IBY). A meeting of the International Federation of Library Associations was planned to take place in Budapest and to focus on the role of libraries during the IBY, and several governments told UNESCO that they proposed to declare national book and reading years in connection with the worldwide event. An American Committee for the IBY was to be chaired by Emerson Greenaway, past president of the American Library Association, and Theodore Waller, president of the Grolier Educational Corporation of New York.

A conference to revise the Universal Copyright Convention was held at UNESCO headquarters in Paris July 5–24, 1971. UNESCO will continue to provide a secretariat for the Intergovernmental Copyright Committee. Studies involving copyright protection for new kinds of beneficiaries and in view of new communications techniques—especially radio and television transmission by satellite, photographic reproduction, and phonograms—were also conducted during 1971 by UNESCO researchers.

DAN BERGEN
University of Rhode Island

AMERICAN LIBRARY ASSOCIATION

In 1971 the American Library Association (ALA) continued its work of improving and expanding library service in the United States.

Conference and Projects. The 90th annual conference of the ALA was held in Dallas, Texas, on June 20–26. Keith Doms, director of the Free Library of Philadelphia, took office as president;

Katherine Laich, lecturer and coordinator of programs at the University of Southern California's School of Library Science, became vice president and president-elect; and A. P. Marshall, director of the library at Eastern Michigan University, took office as second vice president.

At the conference, the final report of the Activities Committee on New Directions for ALA was made to the ALA Council, the association's governing body. The most far-reaching of the committee's recommendations was to reorganize the Council. In a mail vote, ALA members later approved ratifying the amendments for reorganization by 6,917 to 981.

In another mail ballot, members of the ALA's Adult Services Division and Reference Service Division voted to merge.

The ALA Council approved the Program of Action for Mediation, Arbitration, and Inquiry, involving the establishment of a Committee on Policy and Implementation. The Council also approved a new statement of responsibility for the ALA's American Association of State Libraries, in line with the increasing importance of state library agencies in library development, and approved changing the association's name to the Association of State Library Agencies.

A draft of the revised *Standards for Accreditation* was approved by the Committee on Accreditation. Procedures were established for securing reactions to the draft and for preparing it for presentation to the ALA Council for consideration.

Six institutions of higher learning were named to receive 2-year grants from the School Library Manpower Project, financed by the Knapp Foundation of North Carolina, Inc., and administered by the American Association of School Librarians. They were Arizona State University, Auburn (Ala.) University, Mankato (Minn.) State College, Millersville (Pa.) State College, the University of Denver, and the University of Michigan.

Allie Beth Martin, director of the Tulsa City-County Library, was named coordinator of the Goals of Public Library Service Project sponsored by the Public Library Association and financed jointly by the Council on Library Resources and the National Endowment for the Humanities. The project, a preliminary feasibility study, will prepare for a major inquiry into the goals of public libraries and their relevance to economic and social factors.

Publications. In 1971, ALA publications of special interest included *Latin American Research in the United States and Canada: A Guide and Directory; Champion of a Cause: Essays and Addresses on Librarianship,* by Archibald MacLeish; *American Library Laws; Guides to Educational Media; Services of Secondary School Media Centers; Future of General Adult Books and Reading in America; Educational Media Selection Centers; Books for Children, Preschool Through Junior High School, 1969–70; Melcher on Acquisition; Science Fiction Story Index; Fundamental Reference Sources; Evaluation of Micropublications;* and *Non Book Materials.*

Awards. A number of awards were made in 1971, in addition to those cited above under *Awards.*

The J. Morris Jones–World Book Encyclopedia–ALA Goals Award was divided in 1971. The principal winner was the project "Total Community Library Service: A Conference and Follow-up Activities," whose aims were to define the concept of total community library service and to suggest ways for libraries in a community to work together to achieve this goal. The project's conference—planned for May 1972 in the Washington, D. C. area—was designed to bring together leaders in education, librarianship, government, and higher education. The remainder of the award went to the Freedom to Read Foundation.

The John Newbery Medal for the most distinguished children's book went to Betsy Byars for her *Summer of the Swans;* the Randolph J. Caldecott Medal for the most distinguished picture book was given to Gail E. Haley for *A Story, A Story;* and the Mildred L. Batchelder Award for the most outstanding book published in a foreign country in a foreign language and subsequently published in the United States went to Pantheon Books for its 1969 publication of Hans Baumann's *In the Land of Ur,* translated by Stella Humphreys, with line drawings by Hans Peter Renner.

The Francis Joseph Campbell award was given to Mrs. Ronald H. Macdonald, founder of Recording for the Blind. Sara L. Siebert of the Enoch Pratt Free Library in Baltimore received the Grolier Award for contributions to library service for the young.

The Armed Forces Librarians Achievement Citation was presented to Dorothy Fayne, district director of libraries in the 3d Naval District. Janice Elizabeth Sims, assistant librarian at West Virginia State College, won the ALA Scholarship Award, and trustee citations were given to Jean Smith of the Burbank (Calif.) Public Library and to Jacqueline Enochs of the Pike County (Miss.) Library System.

CURTIS E. SWANSON
American Library Association

LIBYA

Libya's main preoccupation in 1971 was to promote Arab unity against Israel. Economic affairs were marked by a significant increase in crude oil prices.

Arab Federation. On April 17, Libya, Egypt, and Syria agreed on plans for a loose Federation of Arab Republics, pledged against any compromise with Israel. An amendment later required unanimity for federal executive decisions and for the selection of a president. The federation was formally approved by nearly unanimous plebiscites in the three countries on September 1. On October 4, President Anwar el-Sadat of Egypt was elected president of the federation. Sudan was expected to join later.

The union was to be open to any Arab state favoring "democratic socialism." It would have a council of presidents, a federal assembly and court, and a unified military command. The union could intervene in any member country "seriously threatened by internal or external disturbances."

Libya's president, the impulsive and unpredictable Col. Muammar al-Qaddafi, began to alienate other Arab leaders. He called for a summit meeting in Tripoli on July 29 to discuss "armed intervention" against Jordan to prevent the "extermination" of the guerrilla movement there. Only four of the eight Arab leaders invited attended; these were the presidents of Egypt, Syria, Yemen, and South Yemen. They decided to make one more attempt to reconcile Jordan's King Hussein and the Palestine guerrillas. On August 19, the presidents of Libya, Egypt, and Syria held secret talks in Damascus with the Palestinian guerrilla leader Yasir Arafat, apparently to try to settle his differences with King Hussein.

On October 16 an agreement to promote unity between Egypt's Arab Socialist Union and Syria's radical Baath party was announced, with no mention of Libya. Neither was Libya mentioned on October 17, when it was revealed that the Egyptian war minister was being placed in command of Syrian forces facing Israel. However, on November 5, the three countries were reported to have reached an accord on the creation of an economic and social council. On November 25 a meeting of Arab chiefs of staff in Cairo agreed on a plan for military and financial cooperation against Israel. At this meeting, the Libyan delegate threatened to leave unless an understanding was reached on a Libyan proposal for "pan-Arabization of the battle."

In July, Libya expressed strong support for the abortive mutiny against King Hassan of Morocco and withdrew its embassy staff from Morocco. Also in July, Libya opposed a pro-Communist coup against Sudanese President al-Numeiry and seized an airliner with two rebel leaders, subsequently executed in Sudan, en route to replace the president.

According to reports, Colonel Qaddafi tried unsuccessfully in the fall to persuade his inexperienced fellow officers in the Revolutionary Command Council to yield their ministerial positions to competent civilians. Meanwhile, the country's one-party political organization, the Libyan Arab Socialist Union, was being formed.

Economic Affairs. Reports indicated that Libya, in an effort to forestall increased Soviet influence in the Middle East, urged Malta to refuse a proffered Soviet loan. In return, Libya granted Malta an emergency loan of $12 million in August.

Libya signed a 5-year agreement with Western oil companies on April 2, raising the posted price of crude oil about 35% and calling for local investment concessions from the oil firms. Effective Sept. 2, 1971, the dinar became the unit of Libyan currency. In October the nationalization of the insurance industry was completed; in December, the British Petroleum Company in Libya was nationalized.

JOHN NORMAN, *Pace College Westchester*

LIBYA • Information Highlights

Official Name: Libyan Arab Republic.
Area: 679,360 square miles (1,759,540 sq km).
Population (1970 est.): 1,900,000. *Density,* 3 per square mile (1 per sq km). *Annual rate of increase,* 3.7%.
Chief Cities (1968 est.), joint capital, 247,365; Benghazi, joint capital (1964 census), 137,295.
Government: *Chief Organ,* Revolutionary Command Council (RCC). *Head of government,* Col. Muammar al-Qaddafi, premier and president of the RCC (took office Sept. 1, 1969, became premier Jan. 17, 1970).
Languages: Arabic (official).
Education: *Literacy rate* (1970), 30–35% of population. *Expenditure on education* (1967), 11.6% of total public expenditure. *School enrollment* (1966)—primary, 215,841; secondary, 32,591; vocational, 1,064; higher, 2,215.
Finances (1969–70 est.): *Revenues,* $1,193,640,000; *expenditures,* $1,193,640,000; *monetary unit,* Libyan pound (.3289 pound equals U. S.$1, Dec. 30, 1971).
Gross National Product (1970 est.): $4,000,000,000.
National Income (1968): $2,235,000,000; *national income per person,* $1,239.
Manufacturing (metric tons, 1969): Residual fuel oil, 198,-000; distillate fuel oils, 118,000; tobacco, 200.
Crops (metric tons, 1968 crop year): Olives, 140,000; barley, 113,000; dates, 57,000; groundnuts, 13,000.
Minerals (metric tons, 1969): Crude petroleum, 149,702,000 (ranks 5th among world producers); salt, 9,000.
Foreign Trade (1968): *Exports* (1970), $2,366,000,000 (chief export—crude petroleum, $1,868,340,000). *Imports* (1970), $554,000,000. *Chief trading partner*—West Germany.
Tourism: *Receipts* (1970), $11,240,000.
Transportation: *Roads* (1964), 11,577 miles (18,631 km); *motor vehicles* (1969), 131,400 (automobiles, 90,700); *railroads* (1965), 220 miles (354 km); *principal airports,* Benghazi, Tripoli, Sebha.
Communications: *Telephones* (1970), 34,790; *radios* (1969), 77,000; *newspapers* (1967), 7 (daily circulation, 35,000).

CARL LATRAY

Literature

Upstate, recollections by Edmund Wilson (*below*) of tradition passing in northern New York, won wide acclaim. Family's Old Stone House in Talcottville (*above*) was featured prominently.

JAMES A. SUGAR

Developments in world literature during 1971 are reviewed in this article under the following headings: (1) American Literature; (2) Children's Literature; (3) Canadian Literature; (4) English Literature; (5) French Literature; (6) German Literature; (7) Italian Literature; (8) Japanese Literature; (9) Latin American Literature; (10) Soviet Literature; (11) Spanish Literature.

Pablo Neruda, the Chilean poet, was awarded the 1971 Nobel Prize for literature. (See also BIOGRAPHY; PRIZES AND AWARDS—*Nobel Prizes.*)

American Literature

The year 1971 was a curious one in American literature. No recent year has seen the publication of so many significant novels by writers of established reputation. Robert Penn Warren, Wallace Stegner, Bernard Malamud, John Updike, Wright Morris, Joyce Carol Oates, Walker Percy, Shirley Ann Grau, and John Hawkes all contributed new novels, and there were important works by such newer novelists as Irvin Faust, Thomas McGuane, Sandra Hochman, D. Keith Mano, John Gardner, Patricia Dizenzo, and David Slavitt. At the same time, no recent year has seen so few significant collections of short stories. A combination of economic factors, including the failure of a number of magazines that had traditionally provided markets for short fiction, the reluctance of the few remaining journals to take risks on new fiction, and the reluctance of book publishers to accept the expected losses on short story collections in a time of tight money and reduced publishing schedules, all contributed to the dearth of short fiction. The short story will survive, no doubt, but it is not flourishing.

The major literary awards brought few real surprises. In the National Book Awards, the poetry prize went to Mona Van Duyn's *To See, To Take.*

Saul Bellow's *Mr. Sammler's Planet* won the fiction award, James McGregor Burns took the history and biography award for *Roosevelt: The Soldier of Freedom,* and Francis Steegmuller's *Cocteau* won the Arts and Letters prize.

Winners of Pulitzer Prizes for literature included W. S. Merwin for *The Carrier of Ladders* in poetry, James MacGregor Burns for *Roosevelt: The Soldier of Freedom* in history, Lawrance Thompson for *Robert Frost: The Years of Triumph, 1915–1938* in biography, and John Toland for *The Rising Sun* in general nonfiction.

Novels. *Fire Sermon* by Wright Morris is one of that distinguished author's best books, a beautifully written, simple but suggestive story of the encounter between generations. Centering on a cross-country automobile trip taken by an old man and his grandson, the novel is sympathetic to both, and to the two hippies they pick up on the way. However, it points the lesson that there is always some failure of understanding between the old and the young, and that wisdom for the old may mean withdrawing to let the young make their own way.

Wallace Stegner's *Angle of Repose* is about another kind of attempted understanding between generations. A modern man, trying to understand his heritage, reconstructs the lives of his pioneering grandparents, discovering in them a combination of eastern gentility and western crudeness, as well as an uneasy truce between culture and the desire for money. The book suggests a number of reasons for the problems of an American still torn by a divided heritage.

Robert Penn Warren published *Meet Me in the Green Glen,* one of his best works. Like much of his earlier fiction, it has as its central situation murder in a Southern setting. His real concern in the novel, however, is not with the violent events and courtroom dramatics which form its surface but with the struggle of its characters to find ways of sustaining values in conflict with the pressure of modern life. He remains one of the few major novelists whose work holds out hope for the possibility that men may be able to find, if not save, themselves.

The Tenants by Bernard Malamud deals with racial conflict. Two writers, a Negro and a Jew, share quarters in a condemned building and try to bridge the gap between them as each works out his problems as a writer. There are comic aspects to the struggle, but Malamud's grim conclusion is that not even art can bring about genuine communication between the races in our society. Racial conflict is one element in a general social breakdown in Walker Percy's *Love in the Ruins.* The work depicts a future stage in the disintegration of society as we have known it, but suggests that men of faith may still be able to work out personal kinds of salvation.

John Hawkes is a relentlessly experimental novelist whose surrealistic writings have attracted critical but not public admiration. *The Blood Oranges* places two couples in a Mediterranean setting and investigates, in a dreamlike way, the possibilities of sexual relationships. Hawkes handles his material with skill as well as originality. John Updike brought the hero of his 1960 novel *Rabbit, Run,* through the 1960's in a brilliant sequel, *Rabbit Redux,* regarded by some critics as his finest work.

Joyce Carol Oates published *Wonderland,* another of her explorations of madness, horror, and violence. The horrible is emphasized so much that the novel is too close to parodying its own Gothic elements. Shirley Ann Grau's *The Condor Passes* is lower-keyed, an intelligent and well-written reworking of a favorite subject, the rise and decay of a wealthy Southern family. Mary McCarthy's *Birds of America* attempts to delineate the problems of the modern world through its description of the relationship between a famous pianist and her student son, but it is a cranky and uneven work. Hortense Calisher's *Queenie* is another of her witty, stylish dissections of life in urban America.

Patricia Dizenzo and Sandra Hochman contributed to our knowledge of the problems of modern women. Miss Dizenzo's *An American Girl,* despite its seemingly innocuous title, is uncompromising in its condemnation of the lonely and desperate life to which our society drives some women. Miss Hochman's *Walking Papers* is a tough but moving account of the difficulties that accompany divorce.

Other young writers continued to turn to comedy, even if much of it was grim. Tom McHale's *Farragan's Retreat* is an improbable but funny tale of murder and revenge. Irvin Faust's *Willy Remembers* contains the reminiscences of a Spanish-American War veteran who cannot keep historical events or personages straight and who is himself a comic figure of hypocrisy. Jack Matthews' *The Tale of Asa Bean* is a serious comedy about the search for love in urban America. John Gardner's *Grendel,* an inventive retelling of the Beowulf story from the monster's point of view, manages, along the way, to say a good deal about the human condition. J. P. Donleavy's *The Onion Eaters* is a disappointing farce, far below the standard of *The Ginger Man.*

Black writers continued to make an important contribution. In *The Autobiography of Miss Jane Pittman,* Ernest Gaines skillfully and sympathetically described the long life of a black woman whose struggles reflected those of her people. John Oliver Killens aimed satiric barbs at the social climbing of some of the black middle-class and at some aspects of the black power movement in *The Cotillion.* George Cain's *Blueschild Baby* is an affecting picture of black life in U. S. inner cities.

A number of other 1971 novels would have attracted more attention had the competition been less severe. David R. Slavitt's *Anagrams,* Luke Rhinehart's *The Diceman,* Joseph Wambaugh's *The Centurions,* Thomas McGuane's *The Bushwhacked Piano,* Jonathan Strong's *Ourselves,* and D. Keith Mano's *The Death and Life of Harry Goth* were all works of promising younger writers. James Jones' *The Merry Month of May,* Jerzy Kosinski's *Being There,* Daniel Fuchs' *West of the Rockies,* James Leo Herlihy's *The Season of the Witch,* and John Knowles' *The Paragon* were by established writers.

Short Fiction. There were few distinguished works of short fiction in 1971. The fine Southern writer Reynolds Price contributed the most interesting collection, *Permanent Errors,* acute, often touching depictions of people overwhelmed by their problems. Jesse Stuart's *Come Back to the Farm* contains stories of the Kentucky land and people.

Howard Nemerov's *Stories, Fables and Other Diversions* is an uneven collection, leaning too heavily on fantasy. Herbert Gold's *The Magic Will: Stories and Essays of a Decade* uses both fiction and nonfiction to chart his own course through the hazardous 1960's. It is an interesting experiment, and Gold's style is as lively as ever. Cynthia Ozick's *The Pagan Rabbi and Other Stories* was perhaps the best collection from a new writer.

Three: 1971 is a collection of various authors' novellas, that in-between form which is neither short story nor novel. Calvin Kentfield's *The Last One* is the most successful entry in the book, which also includes Arthur Gould's *The Good Professor Who Murdered the Bad Little Girl* and Edith Templeton's *Coffeehouse Acquaintance.*

Poetry. Perhaps the most noteworthy volume of poems published in 1971 was John Berryman's *Love and Fame.* Like much of Berryman's other work, these poems are autobiographical. Often difficult, they show with wit and perception the trials of a man of letters who finds it difficult to reconcile the demands of his public and private lives. Berryman committed suicide on Jan. 7, 1972.

A. R. Ammons, who deserves far more attention than he has so far received, published two fine volumes, *Uplands* and *Briefings: Poems Small and Easy.* No other contemporary poet deals so sympathetically, movingly, and unsentimentally with the relationships between man and nature, and few have Ammons' skill with words, rhythms, and forms.

An older neglected poet, Ramon Guthrie, manifested fine craftsmanship and deep feeling in *Maximum Security Ward: 1964–1970,* the record of a long and painful hospital experience. The publication of the late Charles Olson's collected poems, *Archaeologist of Morning,* made available the work of a man who has had a powerful influence on the theory and practice of modern poetry.

Stanley Kunitz added luster to a distinguished reputation with *The Testing Tree.* These poems are clearer and technically more conventional than his earlier work, but they are the work of a master of his craft, able to convey subtle meanings and acute insights through memorable language. Another fine craftsman, Adrienne Rich, published *The Will to Change: Poems 1968–1970.*

Robert Hayden is a black poet whose work has been neglected for too long. *Words in the Mourning Time* shows his real poetic gifts and his rejection of popular militant views in his attitude toward the problems of race. Clarence Major's *Swallow the Lake* is more intense, more bitter, and less polished than Hayden's work.

Several other notable volumes appeared in 1971. May Swenson's *Iconographs* is interesting both for her experiments with typography and for her linguistic skill. William Dickey's *More Under Saturn* contains a number of striking poems, as does James Wright's *Collected Poems.* Harvey Shapiro's *This World,* Gary Snyder's *Expanding Wave,* and Robert Mezey's *The Door Standing Open* were other important collections.

Literary History and Criticism. Critical attention shifted somewhat from its heavy emphasis on modern literature to a greater concern with the American past. Johanna Johnston's *The Heart That Would Not Hold: A Biography of Washington Irving* is a full study of a writer whose life and art reflected his own times.

Emily Dickinson was the subject of two books. John Cody's *After Great Pain: The Inner Life of Emily Dickinson* is a psychologist's attempt to show a close relationship between the life and work of the poet, and especially the influence of her stunted relationship with her mother. In *The Hidden Life of Emily Dickinson,* John Evangelist Walsh went to great lengths to try to show that the major influence on Miss Dickinson's verse was an obscure poem by Elizabeth Barrett Browning.

Two figures prominent in the rise of American realism were subjected to new study. Kenneth S. Lynn's *William Dean Howells: an American Life* may well be the definitive biography of the 19th century novelist, publisher, editor, and literary arbiter. The book shows how conflicting impulses and influences in Howells' own life made it possible for him to write genteel fiction and criticism and still to encourage such bold and innovative writers as Stephen Crane and Mark Twain. Howells' great friend, Twain, is the subject of Maxwell Geismar's *Mark Twain: An American Prophet,* which emphasizes Twain's role as a social critic.

Important 20th century literary figures also came in for attention. William M. Curtin edited *The World and the Parish: Willa Cather's Articles and Reviews, 1893–1902,* while James Woodress studied the career of the same author in *Willa Cather: Her Life and Art.* Robert Penn Warren paid belated tribute to a giant of early literary naturalism in *Homage to Theodore Dreiser: August 27, 1871– December 28, 1945.* F. Scott Fitzgerald was the subject of a critical study, *The Golden Moment: The Novels of F. Scott Fitzgerald,* by Milton R. Stern, while Gerald and Sara Murphy, Fitzgerald's friends and literary models, were the subject of Calvin Tompkins' *Living Well is the Best Revenge.* Richard Bridgman dealt perceptively with another influential figure in *Gertrude Stein in Pieces.*

There were also several books dealing with broader critical problems. Richard Poirier's *The Performing Self: Compositions and Decompositions in the Languages of Contemporary Life* is, despite its awkward title, an interesting inquiry into the problems of art and language that fascinate so many modern novelists. Quentin Anderson's *The Imperial Self: An Essay in American Literary and Cultural History* is an attempt to lay the blame for the erosion of modern society on an excessive emphasis on self in the work of such influential writers of the American past as Whitman, Emerson, and Henry James. Allen Guttmann wrote *The Jewish Writer in America: Assimilation and the Crisis of Identity.* William H. Gass, himself a novelist, defended modern experiments in fiction in *Fiction and the Figures of Life.* Bruce Cook studied a phenomenon of the 1950's in *The Beat Generation.*

A number of distinguished collections of essays appeared in 1971. Granville Hicks looked at the recent past in *Literary Horizons: A Quarter Century of American Fiction.* Henry Dan Piper edited the work of one of our most perceptive critics, Malcolm Cowley, in *A Many-Windowed House: Collected Essays on American Writers and American Writing.* Donald A. Dike and David H. Zucker were the editors of *Selected Essays of Delmore Schwartz,* with an Appreciation by Dwight Macdonald.

History and Biography. Early American thought and attitudes were strongly influenced by the Puritan theocracy of Massachusetts. The most famous family associated with this influence is the subject of Robert Middlekauff's *The Mathers: Three Generations of Puritan Intellectuals, 1596–1728,* tracing the involvement of Increase, Cotton, and Richard Mather in the development of American ideas. Samuel Eliot Morison went even farther back in history in *The European Discovery of America: The Northern Voyages, A. D. 500–1600.*

Two early presidents were subjects of new biographies, Ralph Ketcham's *James Madison* and Harry Ammon's *James Monroe: The Quest for Na-*

tional Identity. Gerald T. Dunne wrote *Justice Joseph Story and the Rise of the Supreme Court,* which claims for Story a share of the credit usually given to John Marshall for establishing the power of the high court. David Donald's *Charles Sumner and the Rights of Man* deals with the U. S. senator from Massachusetts, who was a staunch opponent of the slave system. In *The American Quest, 1790–1860: An Emerging Nation in Search of Identity, Unity and Modernity,* Clinton Rossiter studied the period from the founding of the Republic to the Civil War.

The American Indian has received increasing attention in recent years. Angie Debo's *A History of The Indians in the United States* and Earl Shorris' *The Death of the Great Spirit: An Elegy for the American Indian* are evidence of this trend, as are *I Have Spoken: American History Through the Voices of the Indians,* compiled by Virginia Irving Armstrong and *Red Power: The American Indians' Fight for Freedom* by Alvin M. Josephy, Jr. However, in 1971, the most widely read book on this subject was Dee Brown's *Bury My Heart at Wounded Knee: An Indian History of the American West.* Brown's book explodes most American myths about the winning of the West by showing the reality of those myths through Indian eyes.

The years between the Civil War and World War I received some attention. One of the most colorful political figures of the period was the subject of two books: Louis W. Koenig's *A Political Biography of William Jennings Bryan* and Charles Morrow Wilson's *The Commoner: William Jennings Bryan.* Allen W. Trelease studied the American South during these years in *White Terror: The Ku Klux Klan Conspiracy and Southern Reconstruction.* Business innovations during this time are of central interest in Sudhir Kakar's *Frederick Taylor: A Study in Personality and Innovation,* about the man who pioneered the principles of "scientific method," and Anne Jardin's *The First Henry Ford: A Study in Personality and Business Leadership.* Ben B. Seligman covered a broad field in *The Potentates: Business and Business Men in American History.*

The background of U. S. difficulties with China in the first half of the 20th century is the subject of Barbara Tuchman's excellent *Stilwell and the American Experience in China, 1911–1945.* In it she shows the frustrations encountered by Gen. Joseph W. Stilwell when he tried to help China move into the modern world. The distinguished Supreme Court justice, Louis D. Brandeis, is the subject of Melvin I. Urofsky's *A Mind of One Piece: Brandeis and American Reform.* Urofsky, with David W. Levy, edited the *Letters of Louis D. Brandeis, Vol. I (1870–1907): Urban Reformer.* Ronald W. Clark attempted, not always successfully, to deal with a complex figure in *Einstein: The Life and Times.* William M. Tuttle, Jr., studied a precursor of a too-common modern phenomenon in *Race Riot,* dealing with a bloody encounter in Chicago in 1919.

Henry A. Wallace was the subject of a two-volume biography by Edward L. and Frederick H. Schapsmeier, *Henry A. Wallace of Iowa: The Agrarian Years, 1910–1940* and *Prophet in Politics: Henry A. Wallace and the War Years, 1940–1945.* Another liberal politician from the same era, Chester A. Bowles, wrote his autobiography, *Promises to Keep: My Years in Public Life 1941–1969.* In *From Trust to Terror: The Onset of the Cold War, 1945–1950,* Herbert Feis studied the problems of the United States and the Soviet Union.

American involvement in Vietnam was the subject of numerous books. *365 Days* by Dr. Ronald J. Glasser is a compassionate, searing account of the suffering of soldiers and civilians in Vietnam from an army doctor's point of view. Ronald Steel, in *Imperialists and Other Heroes: A Chronicle of the American Empire,* lays the blame for most of our troubles in that area on the Kennedys and their intellectual advisers. The most widely discussed book dealing with the history of U. S. involvement in Asia was the work of two television newsmen, *Roots of Involvement: The U. S. in Asia 1784–1971,* by Marvin Kalb and Elie Abel.

Other Nonfiction. The book that excited the most violent controversy in 1971 was B. F. Skinner's *Beyond Freedom and Dignity.* In it, the Harvard psychologist, a leading theoretician of behaviorist psychology, attempted to show that our traditional ideas about individual rights to freedom are not only outmoded but destructive. It is his thesis that man cannot survive unless he can learn to submerge his own interest for the good of the human race, and that this can be done only if belief in the worth of the individual is abandoned. Skinner is not a totalitarian, but it is easy to see how his ideas could be used for totalitarian purposes.

The passing of old ways is also the subject of Edmund Wilson's *Upstate: Records and Recollections of Northern New York,* but he sees that passing as tragic. Acknowledging that his viewpoint is aristocratic, Wilson accepts the rights of others to the products of modern technology but regrets that some of these products help to destroy traditions and man's relationship with the natural world.

The novelist William Maxwell also viewed the past with nostalgia. In *Ancestors* he describes the origins of his pioneering family, the kinds of qualities required by life on the frontier, and the ways in which those qualities have been diluted by the passage of time. Another novelist, Philip Roth, wrote *Our Gang,* a barbed and witty political satire about "Trick E. Dixon" and "His Friends."

The racial problem received vitriolic treatment from the activist poet Imamu Amiri Baraka (Leroi Jones) in *Raise Race Rays Raze: Essays Since 1965.* In *Yazoo: Integration in a Deep-Southern Town,* Willie Morris finds hope in what he saw as the acceptance of integration in his home town. Norman Mailer dealt with very different concerns in two books he published in 1971. *Of a Fire on the Moon* is the story of Apollo 11 and man's first landing on the moon; *The Prisoner of Sex* was his response to attacks from women's liberationists. Neither showed Mailer at the top of his form.

JOHN M. MUSTE, *The Ohio State University*

Children's Literature

Despite rising production costs and shrinking profit margins in 1971, there was a sizeable increase in the number of juvenile titles published. Early estimates placed the figure at 2,000 titles, up some 400 from 1970. While some publishers abandoned their children's lists altogether, others, such as Harper & Row, Prentice-Hall, Lippincott, and Holt, Rinehart & Winston, countered the rise both of production costs and of buyers' resistance by inaugurating paperback lines. Still other houses either expanded their existing programs or announced plans to institute paperback publishing. Among long-established paperback houses, bidding was spirited

DRAMATIC woodcuts of *A Story—A Story* won 1970 Caldecott Medal for illustrator Gail Haley (*above right*). Betsy Byars (*left*) was awarded Newbery Medal for her contribution to literature for children for *The Summer of the Swans.*

for the acquisition of new titles and there was generally a discernible improvement in the quantity and quality of relatively low-priced reading.

Overall, the quality of content in hardcover books in 1971 was not very impressive. Hundreds of picture books, lacking both literary and artistic merit, glutted the market. There were also numerous volumes on ecology and many books for and about minority groups. The caliber of short stories improved and there were several commendable volumes. The category of novels for readers 10 years old and up continued to be assailed both by traditionalists, who sought to protect the young from concerns thought unsuitable for their age, and by progressives, who looked for more realism and relevance in the reading material of teenagers.

Awards. The major awards presented in 1971, for children's books published in 1970, were as follows: The American Library Association's John Newbery Medal for the most distinguished contribution to literature for American children went to Betsy Byars for *The Summer of the Swans,* about a teen-aged girl and her younger, retarded brother. The ALA's Caldecott Medal for the most distinguished picture book went to Gail E. Haley for her illustration in *A Story—A Story,* an African folktale.

The National Book Award for children's books was won by Lloyd Alexander for *The Marvelous Misadventures of Sebastian,* an extravaganza about a young fiddler in the 18th century. The Child Study Association of America presented a dual award. One went to James Lincoln Collier for *Rock Star* for showing "the personal problems of young people today striving to grow up in their own way in a confused . . . world"; the other went to Carli Laklan for *Migrant Girl* for dealing with "the social tragedy of rootless migrant workers and their children."

Fiction. Among picture books for readers 4–7 years old the most noteworthy were William Pène du Bois' *Bear Circus,* presenting a circus performance put on by koala bears for kangaroos; William Steig's *Amos and Boris,* about a mouse and a whale who save each other's lives; Tomi Ungerer's *The Beast of Monsieur Racine,* a sly, richly inventive comedy; Pat Hutchins' *Changes, Changes,* a wordless tale of two wooden dolls who make constructions out of building blocks; Tasha Tudor's *Corgiville Fair,* a charming fantasy about corgis, rabbits, and boggarts, or goblins; and John Burningham's *Mr. Gumpy's Outing,* about an expedition involving animals and humans in an ever more crowded boat.

The outstanding title in the 6–9-year-old grouping was *Father Fox's Pennyrhymes,* nonsense rhymes, jingles, and lullabies by Clyde Watson and calico-bright illustrations by Wendy Watson. Also noteworthy were Nikki Giovanni's poems, *Spin a Soft Black Song;* John Steptoe's *Train Ride,* with its Rouault-like paintings; and Kevin Crossley-Holland's *The Pedlar of Swaffham,* a retelling of an old folktale, with illustrations evocative of Chaucer's world.

For readers 9–12 years old, the best books were Marilyn Sachs' *The Bears' House,* a poignant tale of a 10-year-old girl living in two worlds—in her imagination at times in a miniature house made for Goldilocks and the three bears, and in reality in a fatherless, nearly motherless apartment where she tries to keep the rest of the family together; Sulamith Ish-Kishor's *The Master of Miracle,* a powerful story, set in 16th century Prague, about a rabbi, a boy, and a golem; Reiner Zimnik's *The Bear and the People,* about the travels of a juggler and his two companions, a dancing bear and "Dear God"; and Elizabeth Shub's translation of 12 tales from Grimm, *About Wise Men and Simpletons.*

Among teen-age novels the best—and most controversial—was John Donovan's *Wild in the World,* about loneliness and death on a remote New Hampshire farm (some critics felt there was too much about death). Other noteworthy books were June Jordan's *His Own Where,* a tough yet touching story of a love affair between two young black teen-agers, told in the "Black English" idiom; Nathaniel Benchley's *Gone and Back,* a historical novel of one family's bad luck traveling from Nantucket to Oklahoma at the time of the great land rush; Eleanor Cameron's *A Room Made of Windows,* an elegantly written work that examines the personalities of an 11-year-old would-be writer, her family, and her friends; and Florence Engel Randall's *The Almost Year,* describing a black girl's hostility as she lives with an affluent, white suburban family.

Nonfiction. The most distinguished nonfiction books of 1971 were Edward Rice's *Mother India's Children,* interviews with 20 young Indians, who reveal a surprising diversity of outlooks; Theodore Taylor's *Air Raid—Pearl Harbor!,* a vivid account of the attack on Dec. 7, 1941; Evelyn Sibley Lampman's *Once Upon the Little Big Horn,* a scholarly and highly readable study of the four days leading to the Custer "massacre"; Edwin Tunis' *Chipmunks on the Doorstep,* a fine nature book; and Selma Lanes' *Down the Rabbit Hole,* a pertinent adult critique of young children's literature.

GEORGE A. WOODS
Editor, Children's Books, "The New York Times"

Canadian Literature

Following the crisis of October 1970, when Quebec Labor Minister Pierre Laporte was kidnapped and murdered by French Canadian separatists, Canadian publishers seemed to emphasize public affairs, which included history and biography to some extent. There was also much fiction and scholarship in 1971, though less poetry than usual.

Public Affairs. An earnest look at the Front de Libération du Québec (FLQ) and the War Measures Act is found in *Rumors of War,* a skeptical journal of the October 1970 crisis by Ron Haggart and Aubrey Golden. *Quebec in Question* by Marcel Rioux, a thoughtful, radical separatist sociologist, and *White Niggers of America* by Pierre Vallières, both originally written in French, are now available in English. John J. Barr and Owen Anderson presented some sensational, though questionable, views on western separatism in *The Unfinished Revolt.* Ramsay Cook's *The Maple Leaf Forever* affirms Canadian "non-nationalism" and condemns anything else as dangerous. Glen Frankfurter's *Baneful Domination* contends that Canadians must free themselves from symbols and dreams imposed on them by others.

Apex of Power, edited by Thomas A. Hockin, shows the role of the prime minister in relation to the cabinet, Parliament, the caucus, and the party. *The Party's Over* by James Johnston examines the ousting of John Diefenbaker by the Conservatives. Walter Stewart's *Shrug: Trudeau in Power* attacks Prime Minister Pierre Trudeau. The New Democratic party also had its innings with *Essays on the Left* (edited by Laurier La Pierre), which illustrates social attitudes held by Canadian left-wing intellectuals. In *Welfare: Hidden Disaster,* Morris Shumiatcher challenges the welfare state as being overprotective and stifling and a return to feudalism.

Biography and Autobiography. Ron Poulton's biography of John Ross Robertson, *The Paper Tyrant,* is a fine study of Toronto newspapers at the beginning of the 20th century. In contrast, Marty Dunn's super-slick *Red on White* never manages to touch the real-world struggles of Duke Redbird, the Indian mystic, painter, and leader. Marion MacRae's *MacNab of Dundurn* is an interesting biography of Dundurn, Sir Allan Napier MacNab's magnificent home in Hamilton, Ontario. Mildred Claire Pratt described the family background of her poet father, E. J. Pratt, in *The Silent Ancestors.* Larry Solway's unhappy experiences when he gave too much advice on phone-in radio are outlined in *The Day I Invented Sex.*

History. Among the interesting historical works published in 1971 were James Blower's *Gold Rush,* about the fiasco of Klondikers using the Edmonton route to the Yukon, and Christie Harris' *Figleafing Through History,* a pleasant and informative history of clothing. However, the book that the reading public was eagerly awaiting was Pierre Berton's *The Last Spike,* the sequel to his 1970 book, *The National Dream.* Together the two volumes tell the story of the building of the Canadian Pacific Railroad—in effect, the story of the building of Canada. The work is epic, colorful, and filled with the excitement of western life.

Poetry. The poetry published in 1971 was not nearly so voluminous as usual. Al Purdy selected the work of 30 poets under 30 years of age and presented it as *Storm Warning,* but the book lacks any startling flash. John Newlove's *Click* is not up to Newlove, but it does illustrate his characteristic sarcasm and imagery by use of shock tactics.

Margaret Atwood's technically contrived *Power Politics* displays her verbal fireworks and her cold, cruel diction. Her people erode love in the process of ravaging each other to gain power. George Bowering's *Touch,* selected poems from 1960 to 1970, shows his continuing search for a true poetic form. Louis Dudek's *Collected Verse* illuminates his civilized, rational, and varied approach to poetry.

Fiction. James R. Stevens preserved ancient myths of the Objibwa Indian tribe in *Sacred Legends of the Sandy Lake Crees. Copperhead,* by James Henderson, a fast-paced, slick, germ warfare suspense novel, involving a Canadian secret service man, is filled with sex and sadism. However, it is particularly interesting for its use of detail. Spencer Dunmore was also convincing through the use of detail in *Bomb Run,* which concludes that war is futile. David Knight's *Farquharson's Physique* is warmed-over Blakean innocence and experience, but Farquharson himself is a memorable character. Less memorable are "Groin" and "Ironstem" in George Payerle's plotless *The Afterpeople.* Irene Baird's *Climate of Power* is an unpleasant picture of a civil servant surviving an Ottawa scandal.

James McNamee wrote *Them Damned Canadians Hanged Louis Riel!,* an exceptionally good work, full of fun and fantasy. And Scott Young wrote a credible novel about hockey in *Face Off.* But all these books, regardless of quality, pale before Mordecai Richler's *St. Urbain's Horseman.* The story, revolving around the chief character, Jake Hersh, is episodic, picaresque almost to the point of being digressive, and it has too many subjects, people, and ideas. But it is professional, vital, comic, virtuous, earthy, satirical. It is all Richler in one Richler—satirist, journalist, essayist, and novelist.

MORDECAI RICHLER'S picaresque novel *St. Urbain's Horseman* revolves around an expatriate Canadian Jew in London. Richler, a Canadian, now lives in London.

DEREK BAYES

Scholarship. Architect Peter John Stokes' selection of restored pre-20th century buildings in *Old Niagara-on-the-Lake,* sets a model for further restorations. J. Russell Harper's *Paul Kane's Frontier,* a study of the Canadian artist, shows why Kane was such an important figure in 19th-century Canada. W. Kaye Lamb, former dominion archivist and librarian, who edited *The Journals and Letters of Sir Alexander Mackenzie,* also provided the work with a long, erudite, and informative introduction. The book reveals that Mackenzie was a strong-willed explorer who both pushed and inspired his men.

Ronald Sutherland's *Second Image,* a study of Canadian literature in both French and English, finds similarities that suggest that many of the long-accepted cultural differences do not exist. In *Creation,* Robert Kroetsch, James Bracque, and Pierre Gravel published interviews with three writers as well as some of their writings. The idea of pulling together both the works and comments of these writers was good. However, though the book does show something of Canadian writing in both English and French, the attempt was not thought through well enough before it was published.

Miscellaneous. Master interviewer Adrienne Clarkson captured 13 monologues on the infidelities of 13 married males in *True to You in My Fashion.* In *The Time Gatherers,* Gertrude Katz collected prison writing that not only reveals life behind bars but also shows that penitentiaries fail in their function of rehabilitation. *The Man from Margaree,* edited by Alexander F. Laidlaw, brings together the writings of the volatile Moses M. Coady, the Maritimes' advocate of power and learning for the common man. Cyril Robinson published *Men Against the Sea,* dramatic first-person accounts of terror and heroism, death and rescue.

In his absurd and witty way, Eric Nicol was again funny about the ordinary. His *Don't Move* warns that renovating a house is cheaper than moving but also can be very exasperating. *The Night We Stole the Mountie's Car,* by Max Braithwaite, con-

sists of reminiscences of life on the prairies. Robert Thomas Allen defended the older generation in *We Give You the Electric Toothbrush!* Nature writing and conservation, with an eye to pollution, were William Hillen's concerns in *Blackwater River. Takashima,* by Shizue Takashima, is about a Canadian-born Japanese child in a west-coast prison camp after 1942.

GORDON R. ELLIOTT, *Simon Fraser University*

French Canadian Literature

French works published by the Canadian university press became so numerous—and so specialized—during 1971 that it was almost impossible to keep track of them. It was also difficult to keep up with the French Canadian novelists and essayists, and the poets, as always in Quebec, were prominent.

Poetry. The number of poetry collections had no doubt diminished since the bountiful years of 1960–65, but there were a number of poets who went far in search of a way to speak to their times. The most important poetical work of 1971 was Pierre Perrault's *En Désespoir de cause,* a work of exemplary precision despite a political inspiration—usually disastrous to poetry. *La Salle des rêves,* by Rina Lasnier—probably one of the three greatest French-American poets—was more reserved and came closer to the great mysteries of the soul, bringing together mystical fervor and simplicity of language. Raoul Duguay, an advocate of a global language, published *Apocalypso,* which threatened to become the leading work of partisans of the counter culture.

Fiction. An astonishing amount of fiction was published in 1971, including a number of works deserving of international attention that will probably be denied them because of the problems of translation and distribution. Jacques Benoit published *Patience et Pirlipon,* a love story involving a policeman, that attempts to return to everyday language. *D'un Mur à l'autre,* a more-than-promising novel by the young André Bibeau, describes simply the ambiguous relationship between two men, who are prototypes of the contemporary Québécois.

The publishing house l'Actuelle established an annual award, which went to Gilbert Langlois in 1971 for *Le Domaine Cassaubon,* a novel in the traditional style. This seemed to indicate a resistance to the new novel, which was represented by Gérard Bessette's *Le Cycle.* After a long silence, Jean-Jules Richard published *Faites-leur boire le fleuve,* a long novel about life in Montreal's harbor. Jacques Ferron, another established novelist, produced two new works, *Le Salut de l'Irlande,* in which historic symbolism probes deeply into the problem of national identity, and *Les Roses sauvages,* a plea on behalf of the mentally ill.

Nonfiction. The political events of October 1970 inspired three contradictory works—the official version by Gérard Pelletier in *La Crise d'octobre,* sociologist Fernand Dumont's *La Vigile du Québec,* and *Québec occupé* by J.-M. Piotte and others. *Histoire des Canadas* by Rosario Bilodeau and others is the most imposing book on Canadian history since the work of Mason Wade. A new Marxist-inspired interpretation of history is found in Léandre Bergeron's *Petit Manuel d'histoire du Québec,* which was a best seller in 1971.

ANDRÉ MAJOR
Literary Critic, Montreal

English Literature

The year 1971 was a lackluster one for literature in Britain. With a few notable exceptions the works published were lifeless exercises on well-established themes; however well wrought, most lacked creative vitality. Generally, the dominant mood in 1971 was, as it had been in previous years, one of conservatism and nostalgia. Thom Gunn was the only poet to achieve what might be described as a new level of development in his verse. Memoirs were highly popular, and several 1971 novels were set in the 1930's.

Fiction. In recent years the English novel has been increasingly a female preserve, and in 1971 women novelists virtually preempted the field. Penelope Mortimer's semiautobiographical novel *The Home* was the most talked about of these works. Its publicity grew from the directness and often painful honesty with which the author attempted to come to terms with the crisis of her own marriage. The book's newly divorced heroine battles loneliness, struggles to make some real place for herself in the affections of her children, and learns to face her new existence with courage instead of succumbing to self-pity.

Maureen Duffy's *Love Child* was more controversial. It is narrated by an unidentified child who tells of the exploits of his father, an intellectual titan consulted on major government decisions, and of his mother, a brilliant, beautiful counselor to unnamed but, by implication, vital "committees." Following the adventures across the world of this nameless family of no fixed address or native tongue has something of the appeal of solving crossword puzzles, but there is little behind the glitter and cleverness of the novel's surface.

Many of the novels by other women authors paled beside the verbal wit and intellectual coolness of *The Last and the First*, a posthumous work by Ivy Compton-Burnett, accompanied in its publication by the reissuing of her first novel, *Dolores*. Moira Burgess' *Story of a Sex Murder*, about the lives of Glasgow slum dwellers, was too fragmentary in technique; Caroline Hillier's *The Flood* was severely limited by the contrived metaphor of the title; Maryann Forrest's *Us Lot,* often distinguished by its bizarre humor, was labored; and Caroline Glyn's *The Tower and the Rising Tide* was swamped by its own rhetoric. Isabel Colegate's *Orlando at the Brazen Threshold*, the sequel to *Orlando King,* is an adroit exercise on the Oedipus myth, but ultimately superficial; and Sarah Gainham's *Private Worlds* is the obviously padded conclusion of her otherwise distinguished novel-sequence about Austria during and after World War II.

Margaret Forster's *Mr. Bone's Retreat,* the story of a fussy bachelor whose life is invaded by a hip young couple, was one of the most entertaining novels of 1971. Doris Lessing's imaginative tour-de-force, *Briefing for a Descent into Hell,* describes a classics professor who loses his memory, spends three months in a psychiatric hospital on hallucinogenic drugs, and emerges "cured" to take his place in the acceptable world of middle-class, conformist behavior. Also worthy of special attention are Gillian Tindall's *Fly Away Home,* Angela Carter's *Love,* Gerda Charles' *The Destiny Waltz,* Shena Mackay's *An Advent Calendar,* and Janice Elliott's *A State of Peace.* Iris Murdoch published *An Accidental Man* as well as *The Sovereignty of Good,*

PICTORIAL PARADE

GRAHAM GREENE published *A Sort of Life,* a volume of memoirs, in 1971. Widely acclaimed for its sensitivity, it traces his life until 1931, when he was 27.

another of her brilliant, elegant excursions into philosophy. The latter's theme, like that of so much of her fiction, is man's need to cultivate a greater awareness of the world around him, to submerge "the flat relentless ego" through an enlargement of humanistic sensibilities.

Overall, the ladies had a better batting average than the men. E. M. Forster's long-awaited homosexual novel, *Maurice,* written 1913–14 and posthumously published in 1971, scarcely seemed worth such extravagant publicity, despite its gently ironic vision of Edwardian life. P. G. Wodehouse's *Much Obliged, Jeeves* was well received, and there was high praise for Colin Wilson's spy-thriller, *The Black Room.*

Other works did not fare as well. Alan Sillitoe's *Travels in Nihilon* was described by Auberon Waugh as "a mess." L. P. Hartley's *Mrs. Carteret Receives* was spoiled by the snobbery and ignorance of its inflated characters. Kingsley Amis' *Girl, 20* exposes some of the less publicized ethical dilemmas of the generation gap. However, the author failed to develop his anger at the superficiality of contemporary culture into a well-rounded novel. John Le Carré published *The Naive and the Sentimental Lover* but most critics felt that he was more at home with the crime novel than with such ventures into the metaphysics of love.

On the other hand, Mordecai Richler's *St. Urbain's Horseman* saw the emergence of a major novelist from a long period of experimentation and satirical by-play. The monstrous central character of Peter Ustinov's *Krumnagel* is beautifully described and sympathetic, though the novel itself is poorly organized. *MF* by Anthony Burgess brilliantly describes the fantastic and bizarre adventures of a young American orphan, heir to a large fortune.

The Dice Man, purportedly written by one Luke Rhinehart, but no doubt the work of anonymous "divers hands," was noteworthy for its graphic sex and manic humor. Other interesting novels included Jack Trevor Story's *Little Dog's Day,* an amusing anti-utopian novel; Eric Geen's *Tolstoy Lives in 12N B9,* a witty, engaging work; David Benedictus' *A World of Windows,* a touching study of madness; David Pryce-Jones' *Running Away,* memorable for its intricacy of description despite its ponderous themes; Thomas Keneally's *A Dutiful Daughter,* a disquieting work of black comedy; and B. S. Johnson's *House Mother Normal,* a noteworthy experiment with interior monologue.

Brian Moore's *Fergus* is his most unusual novel. It portrays a successful novelist, but unsuccessful husband, living in a California beach house with a young girl while he completes a film script to finance his divorce, and awaits the favor of a motion picture studio. As he waits, ghosts appear out of his past and come to seem more real than the actual persons in his life. While it is certainly not his most important work, *Fergus* reinforces Moore's very distinguished reputation. Reviewers also praised J. G. Farrell's *Troubles,* a sad, richly textured study of violence; William Cooper's accomplished sardonic entertainment, *You Want the Right Frame of Reference;* Richard Jones' *The Tower is Everywhere;* John Maurice's first novel, *The Divider;* John Jones' *The Same God;* and T. C. Worsley's *Fellow Travellers,* a fictionalized memoir of life in the 1930's.

Numerous novel sequences brought forth new volumes: Anthony Powell's *Books Do Furnish a Room,* the latest in his *Music of Time* chronicle, is more self-contained than his other recent volumes; volume three of Philip Callow's trilogy *Flesh of Morning* is densely structured and obsessive in its use of flashbacks; and Paul Scott's *The Towers of Silence,* the third of four projected volumes on the closing years of the British *raj* in India, is skillfully presented but ultimately inconsequential.

The greatest creative vitality was often to be found in the work of citizens or former residents of former British colonies. Sasthi Brata's *Confessions of an Indian Woman Eater* is a hauntingly vivid work, and V. S. Naipaul's *In a Free State,* an engrossing study of modern India. Other "colonial" work of especial interest includes Jack Cope's *The Rain-Maker,* Paul Theroux' *Jungle Lovers,* and Nadine Gordimer's *A Guest of Honour,* a work of great imaginative resourcefulness.

Nonfiction. Roy Fuller's Oxford Poetry Lectures, reprinted in the *Times Literary Supplement,* while giving further evidence of his wide-ranging ethical concern and his gentle wit, also showed his almost pathetic lack of touch with the generation to whom he was speaking. The *Times Literary Supplement* was also the forum for a running debate on just how much Henry James knew about prison life in 19th century England. *Public Affairs,* a collection of essays and lectures by C. P. Snow, contained few surprises for anyone familiar with his earlier work.

Memoirs were an extremely popular form of nonfiction in 1971. The most important autobiography published during the year were Graham Greene's *A Sort of Life.* As its self-deprecating title indicates it is only a fragment of the whole, ending in 1931 when Greene was 27 years old. The major focus of this beautifully written work is on Greene as a lonely, sensitive, rather depressed child, lacking self-confidence and prone to self-pity. A work of such perception and sensitivity from Greene is now expected by readers. Most reviewers, however, were pleasantly surprised to find the same qualities, combined with the expected wit and elegance in Cecil Beaton's *My Bolivian Aunt,* a fearful, funny, and moving story of the author's amiable and deluded aunt. Another work guaranteed to surprise was Spike Milligan's *Adolf Hitler: My Part in His Downfall,* the first hilarious installment in a projected trilogy dealing with the comedian's career as a gunner. It was greeted as one of the best available accounts of what the war was like for the men who actually fought it.

The zestfully amusing 10th volume of Compton Mackenzie's *My Life and Times* further enhanced one of the most entertaining autobiographies of the century. The work is particularly rich in insights into the workings of the literary world. Also of interest was *Katherine Mansfield: The Memories of LM,* a reminiscence by the author's closest friend. Peter Daubeny's *My World of Theatre* illuminates the world of a great theatrical impresario, and Barbara Caitland's *We Danced all Night* is a delightfully nostalgic glimpse of life in the 1920's. Reviewers also took particular note of autobiographical works by Nicholas Stacey, H. E. Bates, Anne Fremantle, George Ewart Evans, and Vernon Scannel.

Poetry. *British Poetry Since 1945,* edited by Edward Lucie-Smith, abundantly documents the increasingly introspective nature of poetry in Great Britain. Despite its frequent display of technical adroitness and verbal wit, the volume contains little work of real interest. There is scarcely more to recommend *The Young British Poets,* edited by Jeremy Robson. It is characterized by an odd unity —a general gloom that Peter Porter described as the natural tone of "the laureate of low spirits."

The major event in British poetry in 1971 was the publication of Ted Hughes' *Crow.* Like most of his recent work, it uses a bestiary motif—in this case a monstrous black bird that symbolizes all that remains after recognizable values and consolations have disappeared. The world that Crow moves in is drenched in blood and agony, and in it he stands for anything and nothing. Hughes' own technique is equally permissive and fluid. Many reviewers found fault with his metaphor and with individual poems, but none were able to ignore the work of a writer whose verse is increasingly charged with moral concern and rhetorical conviction.

Thom Gunn's *Moly* parallels *Crow* in its concern with "universal flux" and the poet's efforts to contain the flux within the formal shape of the individual poem. Gunn is more clearly the intellectual poet than Hughes, shaping his work toward the understanding and evaluation of experience through the language of discourse.

The *Times Literary Supplement* praised George Macbeth's scrupulous care for language in his *Collected Poems,* but also noted that his verbal sense was often overly fastidious, resulting in "futile and tedious verbal acrobatics." The same reviewer admired the "spare, elegant lucidity" which Geoffrey Grigson displayed in *Discoveries of Bones and Stones,* but found Harold Massingham's *Frost-Gods* overwritten and self-consciously imitative of Gerard Manley Hopkins.

DAVID D. GALLOWAY
Case Western Reserve University

EUGÈNE IONESCO makes his inaugural address to the French Academy. The playwright, a major force in the theater of the absurd, became one of the 40 "Immortals" in February.

French Literature

The year 1971 was a prolific one in French literature. It was particularly rich in the novel.

Poetry. Many collections of poems appeared but there were few outstanding names. One interesting collection was *Loger la Source* by Guy Levis Mano. Another work worthy of mention was *Ce qui sera est* by Albert Marchais. A 1971 issue of *Europe* magazine, devoted to Marie-Jeanne Durry, contained several excellent pieces by her, extracted from the yet unpublished collection *Ligne de vie*.

The death of the fine poet and critic René Lacote (1913–1971), was a great loss to French letters. For over 30 years he served on the editorial board of *Lettres Nouvelles,* where he directed the poetry section with great distinction.

Novels. The 1971 season saw the rebirth and success of the popular novel. Among the best were *Furioso* by Woldemar Lestienne, *Les Pue-la-Mort* by Renzo Bianchini, and *Regarde voir fiston qui est tombé dans l'Hispano* by Roger Boussinot, all set against a background of events that occurred 25 to 30 years ago. The best of these, *Furioso,* tells of four young Frenchmen recruited in London during the Occupation, who enter Nazi Germany in order to recover compromising papers. Other 1971 best sellers were *Une Certaine Dame* by Guy de Cars, the story of a gentleman who turns into a lady, and *La Coloquinte* by Roger Peyrefitte. A more serious work, which like *Furioso* deals with contemporary history, is *Elle, Adrienne* by Madame Edmonde Charles-Roux. It is the story of a love affair between a German aristocrat and a French seamstress in a topsy-turvy Europe. Albert Camus' *La Mort Heureuse,* an interesting preliminary draft of *l'Étranger,* written more than 30 years ago, was published by Gallimard in 1971. Despite its qualities, it is very inferior to the final work.

A number of recognized authors published novels in 1971. *Un Assassin est mon Maître* by Henry de Montherlant, is mostly the psychoanalysis of a librarian suffering from paranoia. It is an interesting novel but not one of Montherlant's best. *L'Autre* by Julien Green, elected to the Académie Française in 1971, is set in Copenhagen just before World War II and after the Liberation. *Le Roseau Pensant* by Jean-Louis Curtis is about an ordinary middle-class citizen, 40 years old, who suddenly realizes his own mortal state as he attends a friend's funeral. It is quite a lovely satire of certain aspects of French society and contemporary life. Marguerite Yourcenar's *Le Denier du Rêve* is an intelligent, sensitive, and marvelously written narrative. Special recognition must be given to *À propos de Clémence* by Claire Etcherelli, a touching story about a salesgirl and a Spanish refugee.

The anti-novel was represented by Alain Robbe-Grillet's *Projet de Révolution à New-York* and by Claude Simon's *Les Corps conducteurs.* In the latter work, the author continues to experiment with a kind of synthesis of surrealist lyricism and the coldness of the Nouveau Roman.

Essays. A considerable number of historical or semi-historical works appeared in 1971. Several deal with the life and work of Gen. Charles de Gaulle or with Gaullism. Among these are *Et de Gaulle vint* by Pierre Louis Guertin; *De Gaulle et l'Alsace* by Jacques Granier; *De Gaulle Vivant* by Louis Terrenoire; *Au Service du Général de Gaulle* by Christian Fouchet; and *De Gaulle Contestataire* by Jacques Debu-Bridel. Also included in this group is *Les Chênes qu'on abat* by André Malraux, a fragment taken from Volume II of his *Anti-Mémoires.* This section describes Malraux's last visit to the aging hero. Malraux also published an important collection of public addresses and speeches entitled *Oraisons Funèbres* in 1971.

Criticism. By far the most important work of criticism to come out in 1971 was Jean-Paul Sartre's book on Gustave Flaubert, *L'Idiot de la famille.* In it, Sartre dissects Flaubert from the moment of his birth until his 26th year. Two other volumes, slated to follow, will take Flaubert from age 26 to his death. The central theme of this extraordinary dissection is that Flaubert was traumatized even before his birth by his "proto-history," then by the lack of loving "aura" in the care of a disappointed mother, and finally by the presence of a brighter older brother, Achille, who had learned to read more quickly than young Gustave. Sartre's work is brilliant, but it is obviously the paradoxical thesis of an exegitist bearing the stamps both of Marxist philosophy and of psychoanalytic theory.

Theater. Jean Anouilh was responsible for the best play of the season. His *Ne Réveillez pas Madame* is an amusing and well-constructed play that repeats the author's constant obsessions, such as man struggling with the lies and rationalizations of society and the lack of communication between human beings. The work also employs his usual techniques, among them the play within a play, motion back and forth in time, and the use of a classical tragic chorus—here represented by a prompter. Another good play was Jean Cau's *Pauvre France,* a bittersweet comedy about parents confronted with the new values of their children.

PIERRE BRODIN
Lycée Français de New York

German Literature

In 1971 as in recent years, German literary life was dominated by political and historical concerns. Although there has been increasing evidence of the cultural self-sufficiency of East Germany, writers in both Germanys have continued to be preoccupied with a common heritage. While German literature, generally, was strong in many areas, it was unusually weak in poetry.

Nonfiction. One of the most significant works published in West Germany was a collection of letters from East Germany, *Briefe aus einem anderen Land.* The book was enthusiastically greeted by writers, critics, and a large reading public as a source of new insight into conditions of life in the East.

Several works of nonfiction dealt with important aspects of German literary history. Peter de Mendelssohn's monumental history of the publishing firm, S. Fischer Verlag, illuminated many facets of literary life from the late 19th century to the present. Renate Matthaei considered the recent past in *Grenzverschiebung,* a study of the literature of the 1960's.

Fiction. The year 1971 saw the publication of several important novels. This fact contradicted the judgment of pessimistic critics and suggested that in present-day Germany the novel continues to be an extremely vital and flexible form of literature. One 1971 novel belongs, in a sense, to a past generation: the posthumously published *Schatten im Paradies* by Erich Maria Remarque (1898–1970). This work portrays with a mixture of irony and sentiment the life of a German immigrant in the United States during World War II.

In the novel, *Gruppenbild mit Dame,* a story about the life of a simple woman, Heinrich Böll, as in his earlier works, again takes a critical attitude toward the materialism of the post–World War II period, extolling the enduring qualities of compassion and love. Love is also the primary concern of Ingeborg Bachmann in her extraordinarily successful first novel, *Malina,* which combines high artistic standards and seriousness with the themes of anxiety, love, and death.

The response to other major novels of 1971 suggests that the less conventional attitudes of younger writers also appeal to a large public. These novels reflect a critical attitude toward both the past and the present. In *Tadellöser & Wolff,* Walter Kempowski portrays, with gentle irony, the frighteningly cheerful world of his parents in the years before and during World War II. Gerhard Zwerenz, however, who formerly lived in East Germany, is passionately aggressive in his novel *Kopf und Bauch,* the largely autobiographical story of an East German worker who goes to the West and there opposes all forms of injustice, repression, and militarism, with which he is confronted.

In short fiction, Alfred Andersch excelled with his collection of stories, *Mein Verschwinden in Providence.* In it he describes various aspects of middle-class life as it was before the beginning of World War II.

Miscellaneous Prose. Several established authors wrote prose sketches and essays based on their own lives and experiences. Jean Amery wrote *Unmeisterliche Wanderjahre,* a self-portrait as well as a portrait of the modern search for meaning in history and human experience. In his sketches, *Zeiten in Cornwall,* Wolfgang Hildesheimer describes a journey into his own past and his quest for identity in an uncertain world. In a collection of prose studies, *Der Jongleur im Kino,* the East German, Franz Fühmann also returns to his past and gives a critical representation of middle-class existence in the years preceding World War II.

A highly ambitious publication was the anthology, *Leporello fällt aus der Rolle,* a collection of sequels to various works of world literature, edited by Peter Härtling. Although the best of these are worthy of their authors' fine reputations, the collection as a whole seemed, to many, to reflect a serious lack of literary tradition in postwar Germany.

Theater. Theatrical life in West Germany was disrupted by violent controversy. In many cities, authors, directors, and actors demanded a greater part in the administration of the state theaters. The ideal of a theater administered collectively was realized in the *Schaubühne* in West Berlin.

There were several noteworthy premieres. Martin Walser's *Kinderspiel* deals with generation conflicts in a middle-class setting. Other important new plays were by less established and younger authors. *Grosse Drachentöterschau* by the East German Wolf Biermann, is a satire directed against all forms of tyranny and repression. Two of the season's plays were written by dramatists still in their twenties. Peter Handke's *Ritt über den Bodensee* is a satirical depiction of modern social conventions and *Rozznjogd* by the Austrian writer Peter Turrini, gives a sharp and pointed picture of the waste and brutality of industrial society. Dieter Forte's *Martin Luther und Thomas Münzer* combines satire and historical analysis in a political drama about the relationship between the Reformation and the growth of capitalism.

JAMES A. QUITSLUND
Williams College

Italian Literature

Italian publishers complained that in 1971 readers shifted from fiction to history, psychology, politics, and science. Nevertheless, literature succeeded in holding a prominent place, and newspapers and magazines devoted the usual long reviews to winners of the major prizes for prose and poetry.

Fiction Awards. To celebrate its 25th anniversary, the important Strega prize was given to two novelists in 1971. The regular Strega was conferred upon Raffaello Brignetti—journalist, mathematician, and author of five novels—for his *La spiaggia d'oro;* and the special jubilee award went to Carlo Cassola for his complete works, but in particular for his most recent novel, *Paura e tristezza.*

La spiaggia d'oro does not fit the customary concept of a best seller—it lacks an exciting plot and its hero is the sea. The novel describes a voyage on a yacht made by a middle-aged professor and a little girl, who are in search of a golden island—a symbol of childhood, purity, and innocence. The poetic qualities of this parable and the mixture of fantasy and half-realism make for pleasant reading. *Paura e tristezza* is typical of Cassola's previous novels of Tuscany with their common folk heroes and heroines. In his straight narrative, which is sober, down to earth, and almost arid, Cassola tells of the tragic destiny of Anne, an ordinary girl crushed by an obscure and dull existence. The novel provoked lively polemics among the critics but appealed to readers, selling 150,000 copies even before it won the Strega Prize.

The Campiello Prize, a highly coveted Venetian award, was given for *Ritratto in piedi* by Gianna Manzini, a fine and sensitive writer who is often compared to Katherine Mansfield. This excellent novel is about the author's childhood and her father, a "knight of the ideal" and an anarchist. It was also unanimously praised by the critics.

Other Fiction. Alberto Moravia's *Io e lui,* his first novel in five years, stirred up a great deal of curiosity and controversy, some critics accusing the author of pornography. In reality, the book is a moral and political fable in the style of the philosophical tales of Diderot and Voltaire. The story revolves around the eternal struggle between the spirit and the flesh, and the protagonist—a movie scenarist with a creative urge—holds funny dialogues with his own sex organ, which he treats as an autonomous and impudent entity. Humor and irony abound in this satirical and highly amusing extravaganza. Another symbolic and sarcastic novel is *Storia di un amicizia* by the octogenarian Aldo Pallazzeschi, considered by his colleagues "the youngest of Italian writers." The plot of the novel is built around the clash between two friends—an exuberant lover of life and an inveterate pessimist. Pallazzeschi draws pointed comic effects from the diversity of their temperaments and opinions.

A place apart should be assigned to Anna Banti's *Je vous écris d'un pays lointain* (the title is a quotation from the French poet Henri Michaux). In this collection of four historical novelettes, evocations of Romans, Goths, and the early Middle Ages serve as a background to a poetic and psychological exploration of the characters, who assume a symbolic meaning. Banti has an acute sense of the flow of time and of the stability of human dreams and passions. On a different level is the imaginative reconstruction of the lives of great artists by Rolando Cristofanelli, an art historian and author of a mythical diary of Michelangelo. In Cristofanelli's new novel, *Il ragazzo Raffaello,* the Renaissance master Raphael, speaking in the first person, tells stories about his adventures and work. The fictional confessions are based on serious documentation.

Two notable novels use modern history as a backdrop. In his *Il ritorno,* Manlio Cancogni reports on an Italian military unit retreating from Bosnia in 1943, but models his tale on Xenophon's *Anabasis* and even bestows Greek names on the Italian protagonists. Alessandro Spina's *Il giovane maronita* presents the Libyan war of 1911 as a collision between two different cultures.

Other novels worthy of mention are Arturo Vivante's *Dottore Giovanni,* about a shy young man falling in love with an American girl who, because he nurses her sinusitis, treats him as a physician; the strange, allegoric, and metaphoric *Adios* by Renato Ghiotto; the best sellers *I cieli della sera* by Michele Prisco and *Una città d'amore* by Alberto Bevilacqua; Armando Meoni's *Le virtù imaginarie,* which presents a subtle analysis of the Florentine middle class; and *Sposa mia,* a surprising study of the joys and pains of chastity, by Enrico Ruffi.

Nonfiction and Poetry. Giacomo Debenedetti, who died in 1967, was posthumously awarded a special Viareggio Prize for *Il romanzo di novecento.* Outstanding among the numerous historical works published in 1971 was Nino Valeri's *Giolitti,* a brilliant biography of the statesman who dominated the Italian political scene in the first two decades of the 20th century. Other books of interest were *Carteggio d'Annunzio-Mussolini, 1919–1938,* and *Storia del partito communista* by Paolo Spriano.

The poetic highlights of 1971 included *Satura* by Eugenio Montale, the dean of Italian poets, and the collections *Su fondamenti spirituali* by Mario Luzi, *Di brace in brace* by Libero de Libero, and *Viaggio d'inverno* by Attilio Bertolucci.

MARC SLONIM
Sarah Lawrence College Foreign Studies

Japanese Literature

Japanese literature in 1971 seemed to reflect a feeling of emptiness and fatigue among numerous writers. Although many published, only a few had anything worthwhile to say.

Essays. *Gekiteki-naru-Nihonjin* (*The Dramatic Japanese*) by Masakazu Yamazaki expresses the idea that the concept of the integrated whole has long been gone. Man now lives in a world of fragments. As a result he must search for a new non-dismembered self through what Yamazaki calls "I-literature." The author claims that the Japanese have traditionally lived their lives knowing that both reality and self are uncertain. In *Ningen metsuboteki Jinsei-annai* (*Destructive Guidance for Life*), Shichiro Fukazawa states that human beings should return to their basic nature, which is doing nothing. Society is artificial; being human is fundamentally a lonely condition.

In the essay *Ningen-ni totte* (*As for Human Beings*) the late Kazumi Takahashi discusses the meaning of religion, revolution, peace, a nation, and death. *Hyogen-no Busshitsuka to Hyogensareta Ningen-no Jiritsu* (*The Materialization of Expression and the Independence of the Expressed Human Being*), by Kenzoe Ooe, is about the search for the self through material existence.

Fiction. The problem of the fragmentation of life is also dealt with in fiction. Mitsuharu Inoue in *Koya* (*The Hut*) attempts to bring life and reality to these fragments and to the piecemeal events of daily existence. *Tsuki-wa Higashini* (*Moon in the East*) by Shotaro Yasuoka, *Shimette Sora Kawaita Sora* (*Damp Skies, Dry Skies*) by Junnosuke Yoshiyuki, and *Yureru Ie* (*Shaking House*) by Senji Kuroi share a common Japanese attitude toward modern life. The first two reject the changing flow of the outer world and retreat into the self; the third symbolizes the uncertainty of modern life.

In *Gunzo-no Hitori* (*One of the Masses*), Shusaku Endo showed himself to be a rare and fine writer as he dealt with some basic questions concerning the nature of man. Other noteworthy novels of 1971 included: *Kogen* (*Plateau*) by Fusao Hayashi; *Esoragoto* (*Fabrication*) by Kenichi Yoshida; *Kaiho-sareta Sekai* (*Liberated World*) by Tatsuzo Ishikawa; *Shi-no Shima* (*Death Island*) by Takehiko Fukunaga; and *Seinen-no Wa* (*The Ring of Youth*) by Hiroshi Noma.

Biography. *Uno Koji Den* (*Biography of Koji Uno*) by Tsutomu Minakami was one of the best biographies of 1971. *Endo Shusaku-no Sekai* (*The World of Shusaku Endo*) by Tomohisa Takeda goes deeply into the world of Endo's literature. *Soseki to Sono Jidai* (*Soseki Natsume and His Age*) by Jun Eto, and *Rai Sanyo to Sono Jidai* (*Rai Sanyo and His Age*) by Shinichiro Nakamura deserved close attention.

Poetry. In the field of *tanka*, a Japanese verse form, there was much controversy about nature, such as nature's place in poetry. Some poets wanted to eliminate nature images entirely. Others dealt with the relationship between man and nature and man's destructive power over nature. Among the notable works in the field of *tanka* were: *Tanka—Kawa Kari* (*River Hunting*) by Masa Ono; *Hana Afureiki* (*Overabundant Flowers*) by Tamiko Oonishi; and *Inorino Kisetsu* (*Seasons for Prayer*) by Yoshinobu Tabayashi.

Outstanding haiku collections included *Haiku—Hana-bie* (*Flower-Chill*) by Kyoichi Takagi; *Chushi-Kan* (*Arrested Thoughts*) by Koji Yasui; *Haru-no Michi* (*Road of Spring*) by Ryuta Iida; and *Nomiyama Shucho Zenkushu* (*Entire Collection of Haiku*) by Shucho Nomiyama.

There were also fine collections in the field of modern poetry—*Koenaki Kinezumi-no Uta* (*Song of the Scroll without Voice*) by Yasuo Irisawa; *Kuroda Saburo Shishu* (*Collection of Saburo Kuroda's Poetry*); *Sho* (*Eulogy*) by Mutsuo Takahashi; and *Nihon Shijin-Sen* (*Selected Poets of Japan*) in 20 volumes.

Drama. A new drama series was started by the Shincho Publishing Company in 1971, possibly indicating the growth in Japan of a reading audience for drama as a form of literature. Among the main plays published in 1971 were: *Mihitsu-no Koi* (*Unnecessary Intention*) and *Seifuku* (*Uniforms*), both by Kimitusa Abe; *Sasori-o Kau Onna* (*The Woman Who Keeps a Scorpion*), *Daisan-no Shogen* (*The Third Testimony*), and *Tengoku-eno Ensei* (*An Expedition to Heaven*) by Rinzo Shiina in the Shincho series; and *Miyamoto Ken Gikyoku-shu: Kakumei-densetsu Yonburaku* (*Collection of Drama by Ken Miyamoto: Four Works on the Legends of Revolution*).

KASHIHI T. TANAKA
University of California, Santa Barbara

HENRI CARTIER-BRESSON FROM MAGNUM

PABLO NERUDA, Chilean poet and diplomat, received the 1971 Nobel Prize for literature. He was cited for "bringing alive a continent's destiny and dreams."

Latin American Literature

The 1971 Nobel Prize for Literature went to the Chilean poet Pablo Neruda. After being told of the award, Neruda commented, "I belong to all the peoples of Latin America, a little of whose soul I have tried to interpret." (See also BIOGRAPHY.)

The Nobel award was only one indication of the continued ascendancy of Latin American letters, a subject discussed by the Instituto Latinoamericano of Columbia University at an April 1971 meeting that was attended by leading South American writers, artists, and sociologists. The first Congreso Continental de la Nueva Narrativa Hispanoamericana, held at the State University of New York at Stony Brook, was established to discuss the high quality of Latin American fiction.

The continuing increase of high-quality Latin American literature was also acknowledged in Spain, where some of the major literary prizes went to Spanish American authors. The Premio Planeta was given to Marcos Aguinis of Argentina for his novel *La cruz invertida*, an analysis of Latin America's typical social ills; the Premio Biblioteca Breve was won by novelist Nevaria Tejera of Cuba; and the Premio Leopoldo Panero of the Instituto de Cultura Hispánica went to the Chilean poet Fernando Gonzáles Urizar for his work *Los siglos del cielo*.

Fiction. Novelist Alvaro Menen Desleal of El Salvador was the recipient of the Miguel Angel Asturias prize, which was founded by the universities of Central America to honor the Guatemalan Nobel Prize laureate. After a silence of several years, the Argentinian author Jorge Luis Borges returned to the narrative form with *Los papeles de Brodie*, in which he goes back to a more realistic and traditional approach to literature. Also in Argentina, Silvana Bullrich published *Entre mis veinte y treinta años,* a collection of her early novels and an autobiographical essay.

José Donoso of Chile published *Cuentos,* a collection of his early short stories, and *El obsceno pájaro de la noche,* a long novel that was hailed by the critics. Mario Benedetti, the Uruguayan novelist who lives in Cuba, also gave two books to the press —*La tregua,* a revitalization of the traditional "diary," and *El cumpleaños de Juan Angel.*

In Mexico, a collection of formerly unpublished short stories by the late Alfonso Reyes was edited by Ernesto Mejía Sánchez under the title *Vida y ficción,* and Rosario Castellanos came out with a new book of short stories, *Album de familia.* Mexico's Premio Nacional de Letras went to Juan Rulfo. In Brazil, Erico Verissimo published a new novel, *Incidentes em Antares.*

Poetry. A highlight of 1971 was the appearance of Pablo Neruda's *Más Piedras del cielo,* which includes a poem of 30 cantos to the lunar rocks, and of the Cuban poet Nicolás Guillén's *El gran zoo,* a collection of poems full of irony. *El Himalaya o la moral de los pájaros,* a collection by Miguel Angel Bustos of Argentina, presents a search for unity and the absolute through the power of the word.

Theater. Mexico was the scene of great activity in the theater during 1971. The novelist Carlos Fuentes presented his symbolic play *El tuerto es rey,* dealing with Cortés and Montezuma. Vicente Leñero added two new plays to his works, *Compañero* and *La Carpa.* The first one deals with Che Guevara and the second is based on the playwright's own novel *Estudio Q.* Mexico also saw the production of *Los prójimos,* a play by the Argentinian author Carlos Gorostiza, which deals with pertinent social problems.

The Guatemalan-Mexican playwright Carlos Solórzano had a great success at the Greenwich Mews Theater in New York City with his *Cruce de vías.* In Argentina the well-known critic Carlos Izcovich presented his first original play, *Amo,* a love story which utilizes the format of the ceremonial theater.

Nonfiction. The major Latin American novelists continued in their role as critics of their own work. The Argentine novelist Julio Cortázar explained his literary and political position in *Viaje alrededor de una mesa;* José Lezama Lima of Cuba published a series of aesthetic essays under the title *Tratados en La Habana;* and Mario Benedetti contributed to *Nueve asedios a García Márquez.* José Miguel Oviedo's *Mario Vargas Llosa, la invención de la realidad* is an excellent critical and biographical study of the Peruvian novelist. Important contributions to the study of the contemporary novel were Cedonio Goic's *La novela chilena,* Andrés Amorós' *Introducción a la novela hispanoamericana actual,* and Zunilda Gertel's *La nueva novela hispanoamericana.*

Obituaries. The Latin American literary world saw the deaths of three important figures during 1971. Argentina lost Armando Discípolo, the creator of the tragic-grotesque theater. Brazil lost Alvaro Lins, noted literary historian and short-fiction writer, and Augusto Meyer, poet and essayist who was one of the leaders of the Modernist movement in Rio Grande do Sul.

MARÍA A. SALGADO
University of North Carolina

Soviet Literature

The fifth congress of the Union of Soviet Writers opened in the Kremlin on June 29, 1971, but failed to fulfill even the most limited expectations. Its resolutions, reaffirming the congress' loyalty to the party spirit and to socialist realism, reflected the present apathetic state of literature in the USSR.

Continuing Censorship. The continuing ideological and artistic restrictions are best illustrated by the fact that Alexsandr Solzhenitsyn's novel *August 1914,* the most important work of the year, was not allowed to appear in the USSR. The ostracized 1970 Nobel laureate was obliged to have it printed abroad. Since the novel is devoted to the early battles between Russia and Germany in World War I and lacks any reference to contemporary life, the arbitrariness of its being censored seems both shocking and inane.

The work, the first of a projected trilogy, depicts the beginning of the hostilities when the Russian invasion of East Prussia turned, after initial success, into a rout. With vigor, imagination, and strong moral indignation, Solzhenitsyn reveals the high command's inefficiency and exposes the fatal errors of the czarist generals and courtiers. One fourth of the book describes civilian life, the rest is packed with military scenes, and although most of them are artistically and psychologically excellent, many readers found the "war part" too heavy.

Vladimir Maksimov is another writer whose work was censored. He succeeded in publishing in the USSR only portions of his novel *Seven Days of Creation,* a vast, dramatic, crude chronicle of the misfortunes endured by the proletarian Lashkov family during the Revolution, the Stalinist terror, and World War II. The complete novel, issued in the West in the fall of 1971, was critically acclaimed. Moscow authorities found particularly subversive the chapters on purges and on the detention for political reasons of a perfectly sane young dissenter in a lunatic asylum (taken from the author's similar personal experience).

War Novels. Among the many works on World War II, the best were *The Last Summer,* which concludes the trilogy by Konstantin Simonov, and *The Troop Train* by Oleg Smirnov, a newcomer, who depicts a military detachment sent, in 1945, from conquered Germany to the Manchurian border to fight the Japanese. In contrast to the direct and uninhibited style of Smirnov's work is the stilted prose of *The Striking Forces* by Nikolai Gorbachev about the growing importance of missiles in the Soviet army.

Soviet Thrillers. Many 1971 best sellers were patriotic spy and detective novels. Among these were Vadim Kozhevnikov's *Special Section,* exalting workers who had kept military assembly lines moving in dangerous circumstances; Yulian Semenov's *Diamonds for the Proletarian Dictatorship,* about white terrorists and security agents in 1918–19; and Arkadi Perventsev's *The Secret Front,* about the nationalist and pro-German movement in the Ukraine in 1946.

Other Fiction. In general, only a few novels diverged from the monotonous, official pattern of socialist realism. Veniamin Kaverin displayed independence of spirit and used modernistic techniques in *In Front of the Mirror,* a story in the form of the correspondence between a scholar and a woman painter who emigrates to Paris and meets Russian expatriates and French artists as she searches for self-expression and love. A more traditional book was Vasili Aksenov's documentary novel *Love of Electricity,* about one of the leading Bolsheviks, Leonid Krassin. Aleksandr Andreyev's *Yesenin,* a mixture of fact and fiction about the great Soviet poet Sergei Esenin, was less successful.

A place apart should be reserved for Yuri Trifonov, author of two interesting novelettes. The protagonist of his *Preliminary Accounts,* an egotistical, cowardly intellectual who reviews his life with disgust, and the actress heroine of *A Long Farewell* are not typical of the so-called "optimistic and positive" figures of average Soviet literature. These unhappy, sloppy, middle-class characters are reminiscent of Chekhov and they are handled with Chekhovian nuance and understatement.

Nonfiction. The 150th anniversary of Fyodor Dostoyevsky's birth (Nov. 11, 1821) was marked by the issuing of numerous reprints of his work and by many new books about him. *Personality of Dostoyevsky* by Boris Bursov, who united scholarship with imaginative, original exposition, provoked lively discussion in the Soviet press.

Obituaries. Three important Soviet authors died in 1971. They were the poet Aleksandr Prokofiev, the literary scholar Viktor Zhirmunsky, and the novelist and short-story writer Leonid Sobolev.

MARC SLONIM
Sarah Lawrence College Foreign Studies

Spanish Literature

The year 1971 afforded new evidence of the liberalizing trend characteristic of the recent Spanish literary scene. Noteworthy was the election of Spain's outstanding playwright, Antonio Buero Vallejo, to the Spanish Royal Academy. Buero Vallejo, who was a political prisoner after the Spanish Civil War, is the first major figure with such credentials to achieve this honor. Also remarkable in this respect is the large amount of published fiction dealing with religion and politics, subjects that were rarely encountered in Spanish literature in past years.

Fiction. Prose narrative, with its wide potential audience, is the last literary form to be released from censorship, the last to recover its plenitude of expression. In this sense, some prize-winning works of 1971 are significant. The Blasco-Ibáñez Prize went to Emilio Granero Sancho's *Barras y estrellas,* a novel set in the Republican sector of warring Spain. The Nadal Prize was awarded to Jesus Fernández Santos' *Libro de las memorias de las cosas,* a novel dealing—for the first time in recent history —with the life and difficulties of dissident Christian sects within staunchly Catholic Spain.

Other important prizes were granted as follows: the Biblioteca Breve Prize was given to Nivaria Tejera's *Sonámbula del sol;* the Alfaguara Prize went to Carlos Droguett's *Todas esas muertes,* the eerie expression of a character's obsession with death; and the Crítica Prize was awarded to Alfonso Grosso's *En guarnición de silla.* Again, as in 1970, a major prize, the Aguilas, was left unawarded for lack of quality in the competing manuscripts.

The appearance of several other important novels seemed to confirm the gradual trend toward an extension of literary freedom. José Luis Castillo-Puche published *Como ovejas al matadero,* the first part of a trilogy that—by focusing on a group of seminarians in 1936—deals directly with Spanish Catholicism since the end of the Civil War. Manuel Ferrand's *La sotana colgada* deals specifically with the frustrations of a modern priest.

Some impressive collections of short stories were published in 1971. These included Juan Antonio Gayo Nuño's *Los monstruos prestigiosos;* Manuel Andujar's *Los lugares vacíos;* Angel Palomino's *Detrás de un aligustre . . . o de un evónimo,* which won the Felguera Prize; and the anthology *Jonas, el mar y 23 cuentos más.*

Nonfiction. Some of the more important scholarly works published in 1971 were José María Castellet's *Iniciación a la lectura de la obra poética de Salvador Espriú,* awarded the Taurus Prize; Ricardo Gullón's *Técnicas de Galdós;* Rubén Benítez' *Bécquer tradicionalista;* José F. Montesino's *Ensayos y estudios de literatura española;* Pierre Ullman's *Larra and Spanish Political Rhetoric,* a major contribution to the understanding of Mariano José de Larra, Spain's first modern writer; and Gonzalo Sobejano's *La novela española de nuestro tiempo.* Other significant publications were Alberto del Monte's *Itinerario de la novela picaresca española;* Manuel Seco's *Arniches y el habla de Madrid;* José Monleón's *Treinta años de teatro de la derecha;* and Paul Descouzis' *Cervantes y la generación del '98.*

The rich contemporary field of the essay included Pedro Laín Entralgo's *A qué llamamos España;* Emilio Lafuente Ferrari's *Ortega y las artes visuales;* José María Rodríguez Méndez' *Ensayo sobre el machismo español;* Joan de Sagarra's *Los rumbos;* and the impressive *Homenaje a Xavier Zubiri,* in honor of the contemporary Spanish philosopher. Two other important nonfiction items, both diaries of creative writers, were Miguel de Unamuno's *Diario íntimo* and Pedro de Lorenzo's *Los cuadernos de un joven creador.*

Poetry. The major prizes for poetry were awarded as follows: the Adonais Prize to Pureza Canelo for her *Lugar común,* and the Crítica Prize to Eladio Cabañero for *Poesía, 1956–1970.*

Important publications by established poets included Claudio Rodríguez' *Poesía, 1953–1966,* containing all his mature work; Justo Jorge Padrón's *Los oscuros fuegos,* an almost perfect fusion of emotion and reflection; and the late Adriano del Valle's *Obra póstuma.*

Hontonar, a new publishing house for poetry, made a strong debut with the appearance of César Simón's *Erosión,* poetry of existential desolation, and Pedro J. de la Peña's *Fabulación del tiempo,* long poems with a focus on time.

Theater. The Lope de Vega Prize was awarded to Rodolfo Hernández' comedy *Tal vez un prodigio.* The Carlos Arniches Prize, specifically for comedy, went to Evaristo Acevedo's *Celtíberos sin esposas.* Other plays that received special attention from the critics were Juan Alonso Gil Albor's *El totem en la arena;* Luis Emilio Calvo Sotelo's *Proceso de un régimen,* a dramatization of the Italian fascist leader Benito Mussolini's political troubles; and Concha Llopis' *Nana para una noche.*

Translations. Important translations into English during 1971 included that of Calderón's *Life is a Dream,* by Edwin Honig; that of Julian Marías' *Circumstance and Vocation,* by Frances M. Lopez-Morillas; and that of Arturo Serrano Plaja's *Magic Realism in Cervantes,* by Robert S. Rudder.

ALFRED RODRIGUEZ
University of Wisconsin—Milwaukee

HEAVY air traffic at Los Angeles International Airport has subjected nearby residents to increasing noise. In response to complaints, the city continued to buy and raze nearly 2,000 homes in adjacent 400-acre area. The total cost was $200 million.

LOS ANGELES

The most dramatic event in Los Angeles, Calif., in 1971 was the earthquake that struck at 6 A.M. on February 9, killing probably 64 persons and injuring more than 1,000. The city also experienced a long and costly dock strike, high unemployment resulting from cutbacks in the aerospace industry, and a continuation of the murder trials of Charles Manson and his "family." (See CALIFORNIA.)

Earthquake. The epicenter of the February 9 earthquake was near Sylmar, in the northern portion of the San Fernando Valley. The magnitude of the quake measured 6.6 on the Richter scale, far below the 8.25 of the great San Francisco quake of 1906, but the strongest since the 1952 quake near Bakersfield. In actual movement of the earth, the 1971 earthquake was the strongest ever recorded in California. (The Richter scale measures only the amount of energy released; the actual motion of the surface depends on a variety of other factors.)

By far the greatest human toll, 45 persons, was taken when an old Veterans' Administration hospital, located near the epicenter, collapsed. A second hospital, the Los Angeles City Hall, office buildings, schools, hundreds of homes, freeway overpasses, and the Lower Von Norman Lake Dam were also damaged or destroyed. The total loss in property damage probably exceeded $500 million. As engineers and seismologists had predicted, the city's newer high-rise buildings survived intact. They swayed and some minor damage occurred, but no important structural damage resulted. Experts pointed out, however, that the hour of the quake worked in favor of mankind: schools and streets were nearly empty at the time, and traffic was light on the freeways.

President Nixon immediately declared the earthquake zone a major disaster area. Weeks after the quake, Sylmar remained a shambles, without gas, heat, water, electricity, or telephone service, and with many houses destroyed or condemned.

Water Supply. A major portion of the California Aqueduct was opened on October 7. For the first time, Feather River water from northern California flowed over the Tehachapi Mountains into the Los Angeles area. Two days later a major rupture occurred in the line, but whether from design error, earthquake damage, or other cause was not known. Repairs were begun immediately. The Aqueduct will not be finished until 1974; a major branch toward the southeast is still under construction. When completed, at a cost of $3 billion, the project will provide Los Angeles and its environs with an improved quality and quantity of water and will reduce reliance on Colorado River water.

Government and Politics. Less of the dramatic happened in Los Angeles city government than had been the case in recent years. The city budget reached another all-time high. And the tax rate increased. But these matters were not really news. In November, Mayor Samuel Yorty announced that he was a candidate for president of the United States and that he would enter a number of presidential primaries. Few took his candidacy seriously. Some believed that he would run for mayor again in 1973 and that he might well be opposed by the former Assembly speaker Jesse Unruh.

In an October referendum voters rejected the appropriation of special construction funds to permit the Los Angeles Unified School District to replace or bring up to earthquake safety standards 177 schools, including one large high school that was so badly damaged in the February earthquake that it had to be dismantled. Apparently the resistance to increased property taxes, obvious for several years, continued to dominate voter attitudes.

Sports. The traditional collegiate powers, University of Southern California (USC) and University of California at Los Angeles (UCLA), each had a mediocre year in football. The Los Angeles Dodgers chased the San Francisco Giants in an exciting baseball race, but lost out at the very end. The great UCLA basketball dynasty continued on its ways, winning another NCAA championship. And the Los Angeles Lakers of the National Basketball Association racked up the longest winning streak in professional sports history—33 games, extending from late October to January 1972.

CHARLES R. ADRIAN
University of California, Riverside

LOUISIANA

A surging demand for political change in Louisiana was translated into action in 1971 as voters put new faces into political office from the state capitol down to the smallest village boards of aldermen. The perjury conviction of the state's attorney general also created a stir.

Elections. Winds of political change reached gale force as the fall elections approached. The record number of political turnovers was caused by

LOUISIANA STADIUM & EXPOSITION DISTRICT

SUPERDOME, seen in artist's rendition, will rise in downtown New Orleans and will host commercial and sports events. Stadium interior (*left*) will feature giant television screens.

a groundswell of public demand for reform at all levels of government. In the closest governor's race in Louisiana's history, U. S. Rep. Edwin W. Edwards won a slim 4,500-vote majority over state Sen. Bennett Johnston out of almost 1,200,000 ballots cast in a runoff Democratic primary on December 18. Edwards was expected to defeat Republican David Treen in a February 1972 general election.

Both Edwards and Johnston, who came in first and second, respectively, in the first gubernatorial primary on Nov. 6, 1971, were reform candidates and newcomers to statewide politics. They ran far ahead of former Gov. Jimmie H. Davis and incumbent Lt. Gov. C. C. Aycock.

Surprise winners in the two-stage Democratic primary included Jimmy Fitzmorris, a twice-defeated New Orleans mayoralty candidate, for lieutenant governor; and state Sen. William Guste, a New Orleans lawyer, for attorney general. This was the first time in recent political history that New Orleanians apparently captured statewide offices.

The winds of change also swept the state's insurance commissioner out of a post he had held for almost a quarter of a century. His successor was a house-moving contractor with no experience in the insurance field.

----- LOUISIANA • Information Highlights -----

Area: 48,523 square miles (125,675 sq km).
Population (1970 census): 3,643,180. *Density:* 83 per sq mi.
Chief Cities (1970 census): Baton Rouge, the capital, 165,963; New Orleans, 593,471; Shreveport, 182,064.
Government (1971): *Chief Officers*—governor, John J. Mc-Keithen (D); lt. gov., C. C. Aycock (D); secy. of state, Wade O. Martin, Jr. (D); atty. gen., Jack P. F. Gremillion (D); treas., Mrs. Mary Evelyn Parker (D); supt. of ed., William J. Dodd (D); chief justice, E. Howard McCaleb (D). *Legislature*—Senate, 39 members (38 D, 1 R); House of Representatives, 105 members (103 D, 1 R, 1 vac.).
Education (1970–71): *Enrollment*—public elementary schools, 508,881 pupils; 21,500 teachers; public secondary, 333,484 pupils; 17,000 teachers; nonpublic (1968–69), 135,800 pupils; 5,580 teachers; college/university (fall 1968), 115,-332 students. *Public school expenditures* (1970–71), $622,-229,000. *Average teacher's salary,* $8,340.
State Finances (fiscal year 1970): *Revenues,* $1,660,273,000 (3% general sales tax and gross receipts taxes, $166,-485,000; motor fuel tax, $119,841,000; federal funds, $410,-793,000). *Expenditures,* $1,593,669,000 (education, $587,-273,000; health, welfare, and safety, $259,781,000; highways, $250,447,000). *State debt,* $864,987,000 (June 30, 1970).
Personal Income (1970): $11,660,000,000; *per capita,* $3,065.
Public Assistance (1970): $237,471,000. *Average monthly payments* (Dec. 1970)—old-age assistance, $77.95; aid to families with dependent children, $82.50.
Labor Force: *Nonagricultural wage and salary earners* (June 1971), 1,049,500. *Average annual employment* (1969)—manufacturing, 181,000; trade, 228,000; government, 207,000; services, 151,000. *Insured unemployed* (Oct. 1971)—22,200.
Manufacturing (1967): *Value added by manufacture,* $2,790,-300,000. Chemicals and allied products, $679,500,000; food and kindred products, $455,000,000; petroleum and coal products, $345,500,000.
Agriculture (1970): *Cash farm income,* $703,705,000 (livestock, $275,667,000; crops, $372,933,000; government payments, $55,105,000). *Chief crops* (tons)—Soybeans, 37,980,000 bushels; rice, 20,397,000 cwt. (ranks 2d among the states); sugarcane, 7,749,000 tons.
Mining (1970): *Production value,* $5,117,365,000 (ranks 2d among the states). *Chief minerals* (tons)—Sulfur, 3,734,-000; natural gas, 7,864,972,000,000 cubic feet; petroleum, 909,590,000 bbls; natural gas liquids, 131,210,000 bbls.
Fisheries (1970): *Commercial catch,* 1,109,600,000 pounds ($62,000,000). *Leading species by value* (1967): Saltwater shrimps, $23,496,179; menhaden, $6,134,338.
Transportation: *Roads* (1969), 52,512 miles (84,508 km); *motor vehicles* (1969), 1,747,000; *railroads* (1968), 3,803 miles (6,120 km); *airports* (1969), 66.
Communications: *Telephones* (1971), 1,780,600; *television stations* (1969), 15; *radio stations* (1969), 125; *newspapers* (1969), 23 (daily circulation, 764,000).

Single-member district reapportionment, combined with the electorate's penchant for change, put new people in about half the seats of the 144-member state Legislature. The defeated incumbents—41 in all—included veteran House Speaker John Garrett. Another 30 declined to run for reelection. Forty-five of the Democratic nominees face Republican, American, or Independent party opposition in February. The reapportionment plan was prepared by a court-appointed special master, the legislature having failed to reapportion itself equitably.

Perjury Conviction. In addition to the "sweep-the-rascals-out" mood of the voters, Attorney General Jack P. F. Gremillion faced another obstacle in his unsuccessful bid for reelection to a fifth consecutive term. He had to campaign concurrently with his trial and conviction by a New Orleans federal court on perjury charges. He was accused of lying to a federal grand jury about his connections with a personal loan company, organized under questionable circumstances, which went bankrupt at the expense of thousands of investors. Gremillion is appealing a 3-year prison sentence.

Other News. New Orleans District Attorney Jim Garrison was indicted by a federal grand jury for allegedly taking kickbacks from illegal pinball machine operators. Ground was broken for a $130 million domed stadium in New Orleans after court fights because state voters approved only a $30 million facility. At mid-year a legislative investigative committee announced that it had found no evidence of organized crime controlling state government.

An international incident flared briefly in New Orleans in late October, when 22 Cuban sugar technicians arrived by air, without visas, to attend a conference. In Baton Rouge, the year 1972 opened on a violent note when two white policemen and two black militants were killed in a street shoot-out on January 10. (See also NEW ORLEANS.)

EDWIN W. PRICE, JR., *Managing Editor
"The Morning Advocate," Baton Rouge*

LUMBER. See FORESTRY AND LUMBERING.

LUXEMBOURG

The most important events in Luxembourg in 1971 were economic, but political dissension among the Socialists was also significant.

Economy. Luxembourg's economic affairs—and its foreign policy—are closely integrated with those of its two larger neighbors, Belgium and the Netherlands, with whom it is united economically in Benelux. To defend its currencies, Benelux agreed on August 21 to form a provisional monetary bloc within the Common Market to enable their currencies to float in common against the dollar.

Like its Benelux partners, Luxembourg is troubled with inflation. The consumer price index rose from 125.5 in December 1970 to 129.7 in July 1971.

Politics. On January 21, five Socialist deputies, joined by a sixth the next day, broke off from the party's group in the Chamber of Deputies to protest a decision to cooperate with the Communists in municipal councils. On March 31 the splinter group formed the Social Democratic party, led by Henry Cravatte, former Socialist party president. Since the Socialists are not in power, the split did not threaten the government, but it may have an effect on the next elections, due not later than 1973.

AMRY VANDENBOSCH, *University of Kentucky*

McMAHON, William. See BIOGRAPHY.
MAGAZINES. See PUBLISHING.

MAINE

The most significant development in Maine in 1971 was the refusal of voters to repeal the state's 2-year-old corporate and individual income tax. In a referendum on November 2, which was forced through the efforts of Scott Lamb of Ellsworth, the electorate voted by a 3-to-1 margin to continue the taxes. It was the first time in the history of the United States that the citizens of a state have been given an opportunity to vote for or against the retention of a tax measure.

Legislature. The possibility of income tax repeal led to extreme restraint by the 1971 Legislature. Few new programs were authorized and some existing services were cut back slightly, arresting an expansionary policy in state expenditures that had existed since the late 1950's.

The Legislature did enact several significant measures including a revenue-sharing plan, tax relief for the elderly, a wild lands zoning law, and an executive reorganization plan. In March the Legislature killed a proposal that would have required every bottle of liquor sold in Maine to carry a health hazard warning. The law authorizing the commissioner of inland fisheries and game to shorten the deer hunting season was invoked in November, reducing the length of the hunting season for the first time in many years.

Environment. Concern with maintaining the quality of Maine's environment continued in 1971. The Environmental Improvement Commission (EIC) rejected on July 21 an application by the Maine Clean Fuels Corporation to construct an oil refinery on Sears Island in Penobscot Bay. The EIC ruled that the company could not demonstrate that its plans would meet the site-selection criteria established by the Legislature to protect the natural environment of the area. The staff of the EIC was significantly expanded to handle future cases.

─────── **LUXEMBOURG · Information Highlights** ───────

Official Name: Grand Duchy of Luxembourg.
Area: 999 square miles (2,586 sq km).
Population (1970 census): 339,848. *Density,* 329 per square mile (131 per sq km). *Annual rate of increase,* 0.8%.
Chief City (1970 census): Luxembourg, the capital, 76,000.
Government: *Head of state,* Jean, grand duke (acceded Nov. 12, 1964). *Head of government,* Pierre Werner, premier (took office Feb. 26, 1959). *Legislature*—Chamber of Deputies (unicameral). 56 members. *Major political parties*—Christian Social, Socialist, Democratic, Communist, Social Democratic.
Languages: French (official), German, Letzeburgesch (indigenous dialect).
Education: *Literacy rate* (1970), 98% of population. *Expenditure on education* (1967), 14.9% of total public expenditure. *School enrollment* (1968)—primary, 35,361; secondary, 17,125; technical/vocational, 7,179; higher, 667.
Monetary Unit: Franc (44.81 francs equal U. S.$1, Dec. 1971).
Gross National Product (1970 est.): $910,000,000.
National Income (1969): $664,000,000; *per person,* $1,965.
Manufacturing (metric tons, 1969): Crude steel, 5,521,000; cement, 207,000; beer, 532,000 hectoliters.
Crops (metric tons, 1969 crop year): Barley, 56,000; wheat, 47,000; oats, 47,000; grapes (1968), 16,000.
Minerals (metric tons, 1969): Iron ore, 1,751,000.
Foreign Trade including Belgium (1968): *Exports* (1970), $11,-609,000,000 (chief exports—iron and steel, $1,311,300,000). *Imports* (1970). $11,344,000,000. *Chief trading partners* (1968)—Netherlands (took 21% of exports, supplied 15% of imports); West Germany (21%—21%); France.
Tourism: *Receipts* (including Belgium, 1970), $348,000,000.
Transportation: *Roads* (1966), 2,759 miles (4,440 km); *motor vehicles* (1969), 96,700 (automobiles, 84,800); *railroads* (1968), 210 miles (338 km); *national airline,* Luxair.
Communications: *Telephones* (1970), 105,531; *television stations* (1968), 1; *TV sets* (1969), 62,000; *radios* (1969), 149,-000; *newspapers* (1969), 7 (daily circulation, 124,000).

--------- **MAINE** • Information Highlights ---------

Area: 33,215 square miles (86,027 sq km).
Population (1970 census): 993,663. *Density:* 32 per sq mi.
Chief Cities (1970 census): Augusta, the capital, 21,945; Portland, 65,116; Lewiston, 41,779; Bangor, 33,168.
Government (1971): *Chief Officers*—governor, Kenneth M. Curtis (D); secy. of state, Joseph D. Edgar (R); atty. gen., James S. Erwin (R); treas., Norman K. Ferguson; commissioner, dept. of educ., Carroll R. McGary; chief justice, Armand A. Dufresne, Jr. *Legislature*—Senate, 32 members (18 Republicans, 14 Democrats); House of Representatives, 151 members (79 R, 71 D, 1 vac.).
Education (1970–71): *Enrollment*—public elementary schools, 175,000 pupils; 7,380 teachers; public secondary, 66,290 pupils; 3,790 teachers; nonpublic schools (1968–69), 30,-100 pupils; 1,510 teachers; college and university (fall 1968), 27,336 students. *Public school expenditures* (1970–71), $175,000,000 ($763 per pupil). *Average teacher's salary,* $8,127.
State Finances (fiscal 1970): *Revenues,* $420,181,000 (5% general sales and gross receipts taxes, $83,240,000; motor fuel tax, $36,557,000; federal funds, $90,708,000). *Expenditures,* $433,326,000 (education, $142,458,000; health, welfare, and safety, $67,803,000; highways, $67,326,000). *State debt,* $232,322,000 (June 30, 1970).
Personal Income (1970): $3,281,000,000; *per capita,* $3,243.
Public Assistance (1970): $61,961,000. *Average monthly payments* (Dec. 1970)—old-age assistance, $60.80; aid to families with dependent children, $146.95.
Labor Force: *Nonagricultural wage and salary earners* (June 1971), 336,100. *Average annual employment* (1969)—manufacturing, 116,000; trade, 64,000; government, 65,000; services, 41,000. *Insured unemployed* (Oct. 1971)—12,500 (5.6%).
Manufacturing (1967): *Value added by manufacture,* $1,069,-500,000. Paper and allied products, $276,800,000; leather and leather products, $197,900,000.
Agriculture (1970): *Cash farm income,* $256,086,000 (livestock, $162,128,000; crops, $92,291,000; government payments, $1,667,000). *Chief crops* (1970)—Apples, 62,000,000 pounds; potatoes, 35,700,000 cwt (ranks 3d among the states); hay, 408,000 tons.
Mining (1970): *Production value,* $22,858,000 (ranks 47th among the states). *Chief minerals* (tons)—Sand and gravel, 11,470,000; stone, 1,051,000; clays, 41,000.
Fisheries (1970): *Commercial catch,* $158,800,000 pounds ($30,700,000). *Leading species by value* (1969), Lobster, $13,597,869; ocean perch, $2,408,184; herring, $1,537,697.
Transportation: *Roads* (1969), 21,341 miles (34,344 km); *motor vehicles* (1969), 496,000; *railroads* (1968), 1,679 miles (2,702 km); *airports* (1969), 43.
Communications: *Telephones* (1971), 490,100; *television stations* (1969), 7; *radio stations* (1969), 48; *newspapers* (1969), 9 (daily circulation, 269,000).

Education. Trustees of the University of Maine voted in November to admit free any "qualified and eligible" North American Indian who has lived in Maine for at least one year.

Carroll McGary was named commissioner of education. Richard Spath, Arthur Buswell, and Louis Calisti were appointed presidents of the Fort Kent, Machias, and Portland-Gorham campuses, respectively, of the University of Maine.

Several appointments were made to the university board of trustees, including the first black man ever to serve, Stanley Evans of Orono.

Indian Affairs. John Stevens, the governor of the Passamaquoddy tribe, became the first Indian to be appointed Maine's commissioner of Indian affairs.

Prison Disturbances. Thomaston state prison was the scene of several disturbances in 1971. Warden Allan Robbins reported that some property damage but no personal injuries resulted. The disturbances were attributed by some to discontent over the alleged lack of prison reforms and by others to the general breakdown in prison discipline throughout the country.

RONALD F. BANKS, *University of Maine*

MALAGASY REPUBLIC

A cabinet reshuffle, violent disorder in the Tuléar region, and the allegation that the United States had fomented a conspiracy against the government were among the events that troubled the Malagasy Republic in 1971.

Cabinet Changes. The cabinet was reorganized after the legislative elections of September 1970 and again in February 1971. Several reasons for the cabinet shifts were reported, including a power struggle occasioned by President Philibert Tsiranana's poor health, personal differences among cabinet ministers, internal opposition to the Malagasy Republic's recent economic agreements with South Africa and to control of the country's trade by European companies, and unrest because of shortages and high prices of essential foodstuffs.

In the cabinet shifts, Second Vice President André Resampa, long considered likely to succeed Tsiranana, suffered a series of demotions. Then, on June 1, he was dismissed from the vice presidency, arrested, and imprisoned on charges of plotting with a foreign power to overthrow President Tsiranana.

Tuléar Disorders. Violence and revolt erupted in the Tuléar region in the southern part of the country. President Tsiranana, staunchly anti-Communist, blamed the pro-Chinese opposition party, Monima, and its leader, Monja Jaona, who, he alleged, had sparked the revolt by convincing his followers that a Communist Chinese ship would shortly deliver weapons and military experts. Rebel casualties were given as 45 dead and 9 injured, and 847 persons arrested. Security forces were said to have suffered 1 dead and 11 injured. Another report estimated that up to 1,000 lives were lost in the revolt. The rebel leader Jaona was arrested, and it was reported that 500 suspects were placed under surveillance on the island of Nosy-Lava.

Relations with the U. S. On June 27, Tsiranana accused the United States of involvement in a plot to overthrow his government. He expelled U. S. Ambassador Anthony D. Marshall and his top aides. Observers suggest that Marshall and the United States were scapegoats, and that by downgrading U. S. influence Tsiranana hoped to assuage pro-Communist factions while he consolidated his power.

FRANKLIN PARKER, *West Virginia University*

--------- **MALAGASY** • Information Highlights ---------

Official Name: Malagasy Republic.
Area: 226,657 square miles (587,041 sq km).
Population (1970 est.): 6,750,000. *Density,* 31 per square mile (11 per sq km). *Annual rate of increase,* 2.5%.
Chief City: Tananarive (1970 est.), the capital, 335,000.
Government: *Head of state,* Philibert Tsiranana, president (elected for 2d term, March 30, 1965). *Vice president,* Calvin Tsiebo. *Legislature*—Parliament; National Assembly, 107 members. Senate, 54. *Major political parties*—Parti Social Démocrate, Parti du Congrès de l'Indépendance.
Languages: Malagasy (official), French (official).
Education: *Literacy rate* (1970), 30% of population. *Expenditure on education* (1967), 20% of total public expenditure. *School enrollment* (1968)—primary, 815,307; secondary, 103,107; technical/vocational, 6,376; higher, 3,429.
Finances (1971 budget est.): *Revenues,* $155,880,000; *expenditures,* $155,880,000; *monetary unit,* Malagasy franc (277.71 francs equal U. S.$1, Sept. 1971).
Gross National Product (1970 est.): $820,000,000.
National Income (1968): $651,000,000; *per person,* $106.
Consumer Price Index (1970), 117 (1963=100).
Manufacturing (metric tons, 1969): Residual fuel oil, 270,000; distillate fuel oils, 101,000; sugar, 99,000.
Crops (metric tons, 1968 crop year): Rice, 1,785,000; cassava, 910,000; sweet potatoes and yams, 254,000.
Minerals (metric tons, 1969): Salt, 7,000; gold, 15 kilograms.
Foreign Trade (1970): *Exports,* $145,000,000 (chief exports—coffee, $39,400,000; vanilla, $13,000,000; rice, $11,055,000; sugar, $5,581,000). *Imports,* $170,000,000 (chief imports, 1967—transport equipment, $19,372,000; textile yarn and fabrics, $16,488,000; chemicals, $15,523,000). *Chief trading partners* (1968)—France (took 33% of exports, supplied 63% of imports); United States (22%—5%).
Transportation: *Roads* (1969), 24,855 miles (40,000 km); *motor vehicles* (1969), 82,200 (automobiles, 43,100); *railroads* (1969), 532 miles (856 km); *national airline,* Air Madagascar; *principal airports,* Tananarive, Majunga.
Communications: *Telephones* (1970), 25,258; *radios* (1969), 105,000; *newspapers* (1969), 10 (daily circulation, 62,000).

MALAWI

The most significant development in Malawi in 1971 was the visit to South Africa by President Hastings Kamuzu Banda, the first African head of state to visit that country.

Foreign Relations. Several events preceded and set the stage for the precedent-setting visit of President Banda to South Africa in August. In July the legations of the two countries were raised to embassies: South Africa's chargé d'affaires in Malawi, J. E. Wentzel, was named ambassador on July 25, and Ambassador Joe Kachingwe of Malawi, the first black ambassador accredited to South Africa, arrived there on July 29. Malawi made this move despite the Organization of African Unity's resolution on June 23 that no African state should have diplomatic dialogue with South Africa.

President Banda and 10 Malawian officials and their wives received a warm reception on their state visit to South Africa on August 16–21. They were welcomed by South African President Jacobus Johannes Fouché and were cheered by both whites and blacks. Banda told 8,000 Africans in Soweto township near Johannesburg, "I do not like this system of apartheid. But I prefer to talk. If I boycott South Africa, I isolate you, my people, my children."

President Banda's talks with South African Prime Minister Balthazar J. Vorster on August 19 were reported to deal with development loans for Malawi, including a $17 million loan for an international airport. Banda also talked with South African black, Asian, and Colored leaders. He paid a nostalgic visit to the railway station at Delmore, near the gold mine in western Witwatersrand, Transvaal, where he had once worked as a clerk and interpreter.

Banda's visit was seen as a major success for South Africa's new policy of friendly diplomatic and trade relations with independent African states. Pondering its effects, observers wondered if it presaged further rapprochement with black Africa and the lessening of threats of guerrilla incursions, a possible increase in black South Africa demands for an end of apartheid, or even a possible backlash among white extremists in South Africa against the Vorster government's new policy of accommodation. The Durban *Sunday Tribune* of August 22 reported that Banda was secretly organizing a summit meeting in Blantyre, provisionally scheduled for February 1972, of white and black leaders in Africa favoring a dialogue with South Africa.

Continuing his policy of improving Malawi's relations with white-ruled African states, President Banda visited Mozambique on September 24–26. While there he visited the site of the projected Cabora Bassa dam, which has been denounced by a number of Africans as a colonialist enterprise.

Political Affairs. Legislative elections scheduled for April were not held. Instead, candidates nominated by the ruling Malawi Congress party were returned unopposed to the National Assembly. President Banda, who has ruled Malawi since it became independent in 1964, was sworn in as life president on July 6.

FRANKLIN PARKER
West Virginia University

MALAYSIA

The resumption of parliamentary democracy, the adoption of a second 5-year development plan, and fresh initiatives in foreign policy marked 1971 in Malaysia, the first full year of Prime Minister Tun Abdul Razak's Alliance government. Constitutional amendments and a strict sedition law virtually prohibited discussion of potentially explosive racial issues. Concurrent with Parliament's opening, on February 20, the sultan of Kedah, Tunku Abdul Halim Muadzam, was formally installed for a 5-year term as Malaysia's new monarch.

Constitutional and Government Changes. Parliament was convened after a 2-year suspension that had followed severe racial riots in May 1969. As a precondition for its recall, the Malay-dominated government had insisted on the passage of constitutional amendments that would remove certain "sensitive" issues from future parliamentary and public discussion. This proscription applied to (1) the special constitutional privileges of the Malays, (2) the fact that Malay is the official national language, (3) the "sovereign" position of the Malay sultans in member states of the Federation, and (4) citizenship rights of non-Malays, especially the Chinese, whose greater economic power was feared by economically disadvantaged Malays.

It was felt that such restrictions would moderate communal tensions and deter future disturbances. To gain the two-thirds vote required, the Alliance relied on support from some opposition parties. The final vote, on March 3, was 125 to 17. Only the Democratic Action party and the People's Progressive party, representing mainly Chinese electorates, cast negative votes.

The government then employed a strict anti-sedition law to enforce the new provisions. In May, four leaders of the Democratic Action party were tried on charges of seditious utterance against the government. Later the editor of the leading Malay-language newspaper, *Utusan Melayu,* was similarly accused, which partially allayed fears in some quarters that anti-sedition laws would be directed mainly against the Chinese.

The National Operations Council, which had been serving as the ruling executive body since early 1970, during the national emergency, was replaced by a National Security Council, set up as a watchdog agency over government efforts to relieve communal tensions. The government also appointed a broadly representative, 50-man National Unity Council to "formulate practical guidelines" for improving national solidarity. Both new agencies were defined as subordinate to the regular cabinet.

Development Plan. The second Malaysia plan, covering 1971–75, was announced in May. It embodied the government's "new economic policy," which was designed to eradicate poverty and correct the existing economic imbalance in favor of the Chinese by the gradual creation of a new Malay commercial and industrial class. Although the primary goal was to lift the income level of the relatively impoverished rural population, mostly Malay, it was apparent that as consumption standards were improved, the mostly non-Malay manufacturing and distributing sector also would benefit.

Development expenditures under the new plan were estimated at $4,780 million, an increase of more than $1,280 million over the first 5-year plan, and were almost evenly divided between the public and private sectors of the economy. Expenditures would favor more heavily populated West Malaysia over the Borneo states of Sarawak and Sabah. A consortium of 15 banks in the United States agreed to provide a $50 million loan to help finance the plan.

The government envisaged an annual 6.5% rise in the gross national product and an average of 120,000 new jobs each year, with unemployment below 7.3% of the labor force. A major innovation was a plan to construct industrial plants in widely dispersed rural areas in order to stimulate their urbanization and modernization. The government itself would be a direct participant in a number of new enterprises, which would gradually be transferred to Malay private entrepreneurs as they completed government-sponsored managerial training programs. Land-development projects would be doubled, to a total of 1 million acres (405,000 hectares) and would create 100,000 new jobs over the five years. Enlarged credit and marketing facilities would be set up for agricultural producers, and a smallholder rubber replanting scheme would be expanded.

In the 1971 budget, total expenditures were fixed at $1,120 million, an increase of $41 million over 1970. Import duties were imposed on a broad range of 39 items.

Foreign Relations. Following Tun Razak's proposal in 1970 for a neutralized Southeast Asia under great-power guarantees, relations with the People's Republic of China improved. Peking made a substantial contribution in relief supplies for victims of the Malaysian floods in January 1971, the worst in the country's history. A Malaysian trade mission visited Peking in May, and a Chinese trade delegation was sent to Kuala Lumpur in August. Malaysia's rubber exports to China were considerably increased. In October, Malaysia supported Peking's admission to the United Nations. However, continued terrorist activity by local Communists made an early exchange of diplomatic representatives between Malaysia and China unlikely.

A new 5-power defense agreement was concluded in London in April with Singapore, Britain, Australia, and New Zealand. It provided for "immediate consultation" among the signatories in case of external attack against Malaysia or Singapore. A joint consultative council is to meet alternately in Kuala Lumpur and Singapore, small defense forces contributed by the other three partners are to be stationed in the defense area, and an integrated air defense system was established.

Consistent with its emphasis on nonalignment, the Razak government stressed the interim character of this defense arrangement. To win outside support for his neutralization proposals, Razak paid formal visits to Indonesia and Thailand in February. In April he met with the premier of France and the chancellor of West Germany.

C. PAUL BRADLEY
Flint College, University of Michigan

——— **MALAYSIA · Information Highlights** ———

Official Name: Federation of Malaysia.
Area: 128,430 square miles (332,633 sq km).
Population (1970 est.): 10,800,000.
Chief Cities (1960 census): Kuala Lumpur (1957 census), the capital, 316,230; Kuching, 50,579; Jesselton, 21,719.
Government: *Head of state,* Sultan Tunku Abdul Halim Mu'adzam, supreme sovereign (took office Feb. 20, 1971). *Head of government,* Tun Abdul Razak, prime minister (took office Sept. 22, 1970). *Legislature*—Parliament: Dewan Ra'ayat (House of Representatives), 144 members; Dewan Negara (Senate), 58 members.
Languages: Malay (official), English, Chinese.
Education: *Literacy rate* (1970), 47% of population in West Malaysia; 23% in East Malaysia.
Total school enrollment (1968–69): 2,153,878.
Finances (1970): *Revenues,* $783,000,000; *expenditures,* $893,-000,000; *monetary unit,* Malaysian dollar (2.82 M. dollars equal U. S.$1, Dec. 30, 1971).
Gross National Product (1969): $3,672,500,000.
Average Annual Income Per Person (1969): $350.
Manufacturing (metric tons, 1969): Distillate fuel oils, 1,463,-000; cement, 973,000; residual fuel oil, 903,000.
Crops (metric tons, 1969 crop year): Natural rubber, 1,210,-700,000 (ranks 1st among world producers).
Minerals (metric tons, 1969): Iron ore, 2,931,000; tin concentrates, 73,325 (ranks 1st among world producers).
Foreign Trade (1970): *Exports,* $1,751,000,000 (chief exports—rubber, $557,930,000; tin, $327,800,000). *Imports,* 1968, $1,468,000,000 (chief imports—crude petroleum, nonelectrical machinery, transport equipment). *Chief trading partners* (1968, West Malaysia)—United States (took 19% of exports, supplied 6% of imports); Singapore (19%–7%).
Transportation: *Roads* (1965), 11,027 miles (17,746 km); *motor vehicles* (1969), 320,800 (automobiles, 254,600).
Communications: *Telephones* (1970), 168,826; *television stations* (1968), 7; *television sets* (1969), 130,000; *radios* (1969), 423,000; *newspapers* (1969), 37.

MALDIVES

The people of the Republic of Maldives maintained their usual leisurely pace during 1971. The tiny nation did not see fit to intrude itself into world affairs, and, in fact, was absent from its seat in the United Nations on October 25 when that body decided the crucial question of seating China. This was in contrast to the diplomatic activity in the previous few years when the nation had been busily establishing relations with foreign countries.

Background. The Maldives, which consist of some 2,000 low-lying coral islands, occupy an area of 115 sq miles (298 sq km) about 400 miles (645 km) southwest of Ceylon. They are covered with coconut palms. The Maldives' chief export is dried bonito, a type of tuna. The population, estimated (July 1, 1970) to be 108,000, mostly Muslim, occupies only 200 or so of the islands. The capital is Malé, with a population of about 12,000.

The islands were a British protected state from 1887 until 1965, when they attained independence as an elective sultanate. On Nov. 11, 1968, they became a republic as the result of a referendum. Amir Ibrahim Nasir, who had been prime minister of the sultanate, was elected to a 4-year term as the republic's first president. The legislature consists of a 54-member body called the Majlis.

MALI • Information Highlights

Official Name: Republic of Mali.
Area: 478,765 square miles (1,240,000 sq km).
Population (1970 est.): 5,020,000. *Density,* 10 per square mile (4 per sq km). *Annual rate of increase,* 1.9%.
Chief Cities (1968 est.): Bamako (city and suburbs), the capital, 182,000; Keyes, 32,000; Segou, 32,000.
Government: *Head of state,* Col. Moussa Traoré, president (assumed office Sept. 19, 1969). *Head of government,* Col. Moussa Traoré.
Languages: French (official).
Education: *Literacy rate* (1970), 5%–10% of population. *Expenditure on education* (1968), 24.2% of total public expenditure. *School enrollment* (1968)—primary, 196,078; secondary, 6,730; technical/vocational, 2,809; university/higher, 420.
Finances (1967–68): *Revenues,* $42,940,000; *expenditures,* $50,000,000; *monetary unit,* Mali franc (555.42 francs equal U. S.$1, Sept. 1971).
Gross National Product (1966): $405,000,000.
National Income (1965): $328,000,000; *national income per person,* $72.
Crops (metric tons, 1968 crop year): Millet and sorghum, 757,000; rice (1969), 190,000; groundnuts, 100,000; cottonseed, 25,000.
Foreign Trade (1970): *Exports,* $24,414,000 (chief exports—cotton, $2,647,000; groundnuts, $2,647,000; fish, $2,503,-000). *Imports,* $39,000,000 (chief imports, 1967—textile yarn and fabrics, $4,825,000; transport equipment, $4,-004,000; nonelectrical machinery, $2,349,000). *Chief trading partners* (1968)—Ivory Coast (took 25% of exports, supplied 9% of imports); France (16%—32%); Senegal (15%—7%); USSR (18%).
Transportation: *Roads* (1970), 7,507 miles (12,081 km); *motor vehicles* (1970), 416 miles (669 km); *principal airport,* Bamako.
Communications: *Telephones* (1968), 7,800; *radios* (1969), 60,000; *newspapers* (1968), 3 (daily circulation, 3,000).

MALI

Tensions among the members of Mali's ruling Military Committee on National Liberation (MCNL) surfaced repeatedly in 1971. The tensions suggested a division into three factions: a group inclined toward improved relations with the Soviet Union, led by Moussa Traoré, the head of state and president of the MCNL; those favoring closer cooperation with France; and those favoring more cooperation with the People's Republic of China. By the end of the year Traoré had gained the upper hand among the military officers and was able to cement relations with the Soviet Union.

Domestic Affairs. In April, Traoré announced that two members of the MCNL—Capt. Yoro Diakité, the first vice president, and Capt. Malik Diallo, the commissioner for information—had been arrested on charges of plotting to overthrow the regime. They were subsequently expelled from both the MCNL and the army. In October, Traoré, previously a lieutenant in the army, was promoted to colonel.

Mali's trade unions continued their bid for power in the absence of national political structures. Late in 1970 the National Union of Malian Workers had called for a return to civilian rule, for the release of political prisoners, and for untrammeled freedom of expression. The MCNL responded by dissolving the union and arresting nearly all union leaders. Sympathetic teachers and students called for a strike, but it was prevented by police and security forces. Union leaders and imprisoned teachers were released by the government in March in an effort to seek an accommodation. In August the MCNL created a new national trade union.

Economy. Mali's economy remained chaotic, although recovery continued to be the MCNL's first priority. The country remained troubled by a trade imbalance, high taxes, smuggling, and limited private foreign investment. Attempts at economic reform were opposed by civil servants and the state corporations that had been established during the

regime of Modibo Keita. The government increased the prices of major consumer goods in an effort to save the state-owned corporations from bankruptcy.

Foreign Affairs. In addition to the rapprochement with the Soviet Union, Mali increased its cooperation with neighboring African states and Western Europe. It participated in laying the groundwork for developing the Liptako-Gourma area with Upper Volta and Niger. Mali also continued to cooperate with Senegal, Guinea, and Mauritania in development of the Senegal River valley.

W. A. E. SKURNIK, *University of Colorado*

MALTA

The formation of a new government following general elections on June 13–14 and changes in relations with Britain and NATO highlighted developments in Malta in 1971.

New Government. The election resulted in a victory for the Malta Labour party over the Nationalist party. Dom Mintoff, Labour's leader, was asked to form a government on June 17, replacing Borg Oliver. The new government took office on June 21, and on June 22 it was announced that the British governor-general, Sir Maurice Dorman, had resigned at Mintoff's request. Dorman was replaced by a Maltese, Sir Anthony Mamo, the chief justice.

Relations with Britain and NATO. On June 25, in a joint Maltese-British statement, Britain acknowledged having received a proposal from Malta, which wanted more funds, to revise the 1964 defense and financial agreements. Mintoff also demanded the withdrawal of NATO forces from the island or payment for their use of Maltese facilities.

Following a series of British-Maltese negotiations, including a meeting between Mintoff and British Prime Minister Heath on September 18–19 during which an agreement was thought to have been reached, Mintoff on Christmas Eve demanded an additional $21 million and gave Britain until New Year's Eve to pay up or get out. He later extended the deadline, but Heath began withdrawing the British troops. The situation remained unresolved in early 1972.

RICHARD E. WEBB
*Former Director, Reference and Library Division
British Information Services, New York*

MALTA • Information Highlights

Official Name: Malta.
Area: 122 square miles (316 sq km).
Population (1970 est.): 330,000. *Density,* 270 per square mile (104 per sq km). *Annual rate of increase,* 0.3%.
Chief City: Valletta (1968 est.), the capital, 15,432.
Government: *Head of state,* Elizabeth II, queen; represented by Sir Anthony Mamo, governor general (took office June 17, 1971). *Head of government,* Dom Mintoff, prime minister (took office June 21, 1971). *Legislature*—House of Representatives (unicameral), 55 members. *Major political parties*—Labour party, Nationalist party.
Languages: Maltese (official), English (official), Italian.
Education: *Literacy rate* (1960), 22% of population aged 15 and over. *Expenditure on education* (1968), 18.6% of total public expenditure.
Finances (1970–71 est.): *Revenues,* $100,543,000; *expenditures,* $104,023,000; *monetary unit,* pound (0.4167 pound equals U. S.$1, Sept. 1971).
National Income (1969): $198,960,000; *national income per person,* $622.
Crops (metric tons, 1968 crop year): Potatoes, 19,000; onions, 6,000; grapes, 4,000; barley, 2,000.
Foreign Trade (1968): *Exports,* $24,737,000 (chief export—clothing, $5,539,000). *Imports,* $122,851,000 (chief import—food and live animals, $31,464,000).
Communications: *Telephones* (1970), 32,839; *television stations* (1968), 1; *television sets* (1969), 44,000; *radios* (1968), 89,000; *newspapers* (1969), 6.

FINANCIAL problems have dimmed hopes that lumber complex in The Pas will help develop Manitoba's vast northern forests. Province took over mill operations in 1971.

MANITOBA

Events of 1971 in Manitoba included controversy over the financial failure of a forest project and the reorganization of metropolitan Winnipeg.

Churchill Forest Industries. On January 8, Premier E. R. Schreyer announced that the provincial government had obtained court orders putting into receivership the companies building the $100 million Churchill Forest Industries complex at The Pas, in northern Manitoba, and had taken physical charge of the plants. He explained that four foreign companies building the complex with large government subsidies were in financial arrears and had not lived up to their contracts. Controversy had surrounded the project since it was announced in 1966 by the Progressive Conservative government.

On January 29, Chief Justice C. Rhodes Smith was named chairman of a three-man board of inquiry into the forest complex at The Pas. Public hearings began in July and continued periodically throughout the year. The many witnesses testifying included former Premier Duff Roblin, directors of the Manitoba Development Fund, and officials of the seized companies. Apparently nobody knew the identity of the European principals behind the Swiss-based corporation, Monaco AG, that was constructing the lumber and pulp mills with more than 80% government financing.

Politics. By winning two by-elections the New Democratic party government secured an outright majority of seats in the Legislative Assembly. In April, St. Rose, a rural constituency, was won from the Liberal party, and suburban St. Vital was won from the Progressive Conservatives. However, the

--------- MANITOBA • Information Highlights ---------

Area: 251,000 square miles (650,091 sq km).
Population: 985,000 (April 1971 est.).
Chief Cities (1966 census): Winnipeg, the capital (257,005); St. Boniface (43,214); St. James (35,685).
Government: Chief Officers—lt. gov., William J. McKeag; premier, Edward R. Schreyer (New Democratic Party); atty. gen., Alvin H. Mackling (NDP); min. of finance, Saul M. Cherniack (NDP); min. of youth and educ., Saul A. Miller (NDP); chief justice, Charles R. Smith. Legislature—Legislative Assembly (convened Aug. 14, 1969); 57 members (28 New Democratic Party, 22 Progressive Conservative, 4 Liberal, 1 Social Credit, 1 Liberal Democrat, 1 Independent).
Education: School enrollment (1968–69 est.)—public elementary and secondary, 231,650 pupils (9,926 teachers); private schools, 9,708 pupils (583 teachers); Indian (federal) schools, 6,225 pupils (254 teachers); college and university, 13,426 students. Public school expenditures (1971 est.)—$86,600,000; average teacher's salary (1968–69 est.) $7,125.
Public Finance (fiscal year 1971 est.): Revenues, $561,110,-000 (sales tax, $126,170,000; income tax, $140,878,000; federal funds, $180,082,000). Expenditures, $556,480,000 (education, $161,360,000; health and social welfare, $227,-580,000; transport and communications, $49,610,000).
Personal Income (1969 est.): $2,785,000,000.
Social Welfare: $44,070,000 (aged and blind, $5,220,000; dependents and unemployed, $28,180,000).
Manufacturing (1968): Value added by manufacture, $443,-002,000 (food and products, $111,649,000; printing and publishing, $39,694,000; clothing, $33,659,000; primary metals, $29,333,000; transportation equipment, $27,520,-000; nonelectrical machinery, $25,172,000).
Agriculture (1969 est.): Cash farm income (excluding supplementary payments), $352,525,000 (livestock, $230,299,000; crops (1968 est.), $186,971,000. Chief crops (cash receipts)—Wheat, $77,540,000 (ranks 3d among the provinces); flaxseed, $15,399,000 (ranks 1st); barley, $12,403,-000 (ranks 3d).
Mining (1969 est.): Production value, $245,595,700. Chief minerals (tons)—Nickel, 64,350 (ranks 2d among the provinces); copper, 37,042 (ranks 4th); zinc, 48,909 (ranks 6th); crude petroleum, 6,189,640 bbl. (ranks 4th).
Transportation: Roads (1968) 44,770 miles (72,400 km); motor vehicles (1969), 394,975; railroads (1969), 4,750 track miles (7,640 km); licensed airports (1970), 19.
Communications: Telephones (1969), 417,575; television stations (1970), 4; radio stations (1967), 13; newspapers (1970), 7 (daily circulation, 239,550).

Progressive Conservatives retained Minnedosa in a November 16 by-election, giving the legislature 31 New Democrats, 21 Progressive Conservatives, 3 Liberals, 1 Independent, and 1 Social Credit member. Former Premier Walter Weir resigned the Progressive Conservative leadership, and 42-year-old Sidney Spivak was elected his successor.

Winnipeg. Rejecting the recommendations of the Boundaries Commission for the reform and reorganization of metropolitan Winnipeg, the provincial government passed legislation creating one large unified city, the third largest in Canada, to replace the Metropolitan Corporation and its 12 component cities and municipalities. Elections for mayor and 50 council seats took place on October 6. Stephen Juba, the mayor of Winnipeg for 11 years, won a landslide victory. The new "unicity" came into being on Jan. 1, 1972.

JOHN A. BOVEY
Provincial Archivist of Manitoba

MANUFACTURING. See ECONOMY OF THE U. S.

MARINE BIOLOGY

The use of systems analysis and mathematical modeling in marine biology increased during 1971. These techniques enable marine biologists to approach specific problems in a highly quantitative manner and to make more accurate predictions. For example, systems analysis helped establish the possibility of a relationship between long-range atmospheric and meteorological phenomena and cycles of fish productivity. Biologists in Yugoslavia reported that primary production by phytoplankton in the middle Adriatic Sea increased with certain atmospheric conditions. This was followed three years later by increased catches of small pelagic fish. This phenomenon may make it possible to predict peak years for finfish productivity and to manage effectively the declining fisheries industry.

The movements and fate of the eggs and larvae of invertebrates and finfishes are important to the renewal of fish stocks and the recruitment of many invertebrate species that serve as food for adult fish. Scientists at the Woods Hole (Mass.) Oceanographic Institution found that the larvae of certain mollusks can cross the Atlantic in either direction by following the major east-west current systems. This has permitted certain species to maintain a genetic continuity between populations on both sides of the Atlantic. The same research team also reported on the reproduction of bivalve mollusks that inhabit abyssal regions of the ocean.

Mercury Contamination. During 1971 a tremendous controversy developed as to whether the presence of mercury in marine fishes used for food by man was a health hazard. However, there is very little information on how much mercury and other heavy metals were present in finfishes and shellfish prior to marine pollution from industry.

Many marine laboratories have been studying this and related problems. Scientists at the Plymouth (England) Marine Laboratory reported that certain marine polychaete worms become acclimated to normally toxic levels of copper and other heavy metals introduced into estuaries by mining operations. Although these worms have become immune to the effects of heavy metals, they may represent a pathway by which heavy metals could enter food chains culminating in the higher forms of life.

WIDE WORLD

DEAD FISH, killed by "red tide," littered beaches near Tampa, Fla., in July. Infusions of fresh water into salt water carry elements that cause the microorganism to proliferate, often reaching levels that destroy the fish.

Sulfide Systems. Marine biologists at the University of North Carolina reported on the importance of sulfide systems, which occur in many marine bottoms throughout the world. Sulfide systems are characterized by black sediments that smell of hydrogen sulfide and are anaerobic. Organic matter, and hence energy, often becomes entrapped in sulfide systems and cannot be recycled to animal communities in the overlying sediments and water columns. Sulfide systems often appear devoid of life, but recent research indicates that they may be inhabited by unique flora and fauna highly adapted to the unusual conditions of the sulfide systems. To what extent these forms enter into the more familiar food chains and what effects could result are not known. Perhaps even more important is the question of how much energy is lost to the sulfide systems, since many estuaries have become increasingly polluted, with concomitant development or extension of sulfide systems.

Red Tides. Numerous "red tides" were reported throughout the world in 1971. They were particularly disastrous off the Gulf Coast of Florida but were also noted off the middle Atlantic coasts of North America, the southern shores of France, the British Isles, and Australia. Scientists have long

435

known that these outbreaks were caused by a super-abundance of single-celled organisms called dino-flagellates. It is not known whether these occurrences are more pronounced or more frequent today or why they occur when they do. When red tides do occur, they frequently result in the death of millions of finfishes. This may be due to a reduction in the available oxygen caused by the large numbers of dinoflagellates but may also result from a toxin produced by the red-tide organisms.

Marine Productivity. The year 1971 saw a marked increase in the efforts of marine biologists to improve the productivity of the world's oceans. Marine scientists in the Philippines reported on progress in rearing kelps and other marine algae to supplement human diets. Biologists of the National Marine Fisheries Service (NMFS), U.S. National Oceanic and Atmospheric Administration, demonstrated the effectiveness of artificial reefs in increasing recreational fishing in areas normally characterized by low yields of fish.

JOHN B. PEARCE, *Laboratory for Environmental Relations of Fishes, Sandy Hook, N.J.*

MARINE CORPS. See DEFENSE FORCES.

MARYLAND

Controversy over the financing of education and the election of a new mayor of Baltimore were significant news events in Maryland in 1971.

Baltimore Mayoral Race. The major election of 1971 in the state was the race for mayor of Baltimore, a contest that brought out 11 candidates. Important campaign issues included the city's growing crime and narcotics problems. The racial issue—blacks make up at least 46% of the city's nearly one million population—was evident but not emphasized. Efforts to make Baltimore the nation's largest city having a black mayor failed in the primaries when Democrats gave a decisive victory to William Donald Shaefer, president of the city council, over five other candidates, including two blacks. In the November elections, voters approved Schaefer over Republican Ross Z. Pierpont. The incumbent, Thomas J. D'Alesandro III, did not seek reelection.

Education. Major innovations and problems marked Maryland's efforts to improve educational financing. At the initiative of Gov. Marvin Mandel, the state assumed $150 million of the cost of school construction in all 24 school districts. The plan had been viewed as a more economical way of bond financing. However, the great gulf between the funds allotted and the local requests of $445 million, as well as the inequities caused by the formula for fund distribution, led to criticism.

In a related issue, Baltimore filed suit in U.S. district court charging that the state's system of financing educational programs is unconstitutional. Alleging that the state formula gives children in wealthy districts greater opportunity than those in poor districts, the case cites the 1969–70 disparity between the city's $425 per-pupil expenditure and Montgomery county's $556 per-pupil cost. Differences result from the local district's ability to supplement state funds from local tax revenues. At year-end the state was considering a measure by which it would assume 55% of the basic total cost of education, thereby equalizing local tax burdens for educational purposes.

A second innovation was Maryland's unique proposal to provide state aid to private and parochial schools. The $12.1 million program would provide scholarships to pupils in nonpublic elementary and secondary schools, with funds to be paid directly to the schools involved. Opponents have petitioned the bill to referendum. The issue will go to the voters in 1972.

Reapportionment. Under proposed reapportionment plans, members of the lower house of the Maryland legislature may represent more than one county, for the first time in the state's history. Based on a system of 10 master districts, the plan would break the state's traditional reliance on county boundaries for delegate selection. If adopted, the plan will go into effect for the 1974 general elections.

Courts. Created by constitutional amendment in 1970, a revised judicial system went into effect in July 1971. The new system of district courts, presided over by appointed attorneys, replaces the much-criticized system of local people's courts, presided over largely by justices of the peace, many with little or no legal training. Two months earlier, the Maryland court of appeals had adopted an official code of judicial ethics, giving such a code the force of law for the first time in the state's history.

(See also BALTIMORE.)

JEAN E. SPENCER, *University of Maryland*

MARYLAND • Information Highlights

Area: 10,577 square miles (27,394 sq km).
Population (1970 census): 3,922,399. *Density:* 381 per sq mi.
Chief Cities (1970 census): Annapolis, the capital, 29,592; Baltimore, 905,759; Dundalk, 85,377; Towson, 77,799; Silver Spring, 77,496; Bethesda, 71,621; Wheaton, 66,247.
Government (1971): *Chief Officers*—governor, Marvin Mandel (D); lt. gov., Blair Lee III (D); secy. of state, Fred L. Wineland (D); atty. gen., Francis B. Burch (D); treas., John A. Luetkemeyer; supt., dept. of education, James A. Sensenbaugh; chief justice, Hall Hammond. *General Assembly*—Senate, 43 members (33 Democrats, 10 Republicans); House of Delegates, 142 members (121 D, 21 R).
Education (1970–71): *Enrollment*—public elementary schools, 519,969 pupils; 21,021 teachers; public secondary, 390,525 pupils; 19,610 teachers; nonpublic schools (1968–69), 131,800 pupils, 5,670 teachers; college and university (fall 1968) 124,993 students. *Public school expenditures* (1970–71), $807,827,000 ($974 per pupil). *Average teacher's salary,* $10,091.
State Finances (fiscal year 1970): *Revenues,* $1,670,011,000 (4% general sales tax and gross receipts taxes, $236,843,-000; motor fuel tax, $111,326,000; federal funds, $283,-931,000). *Expenditures,* $1,541,010,000 (education, $511,-778,000; health, welfare, and safety, $128,250,000; highways, $143,677,000). *State debt,* $1,145,879,000 (June 30, 1970).
Personal Income (1970): $17,117,000,000; per capita, $4,247.
Public Assistance (1970): $209,283,000. *Average monthly payments* (Dec. 1970)—old-age assistance, $62.95; aid to families with dependent children, $162.60.
Labor Force: *Nonagricultural wage and salary earners* (June 1971), 1,335,200. *Average annual employment* (1969)—manufacturing, 281,000; trade, 293,000; government, 245,-000; services, 227,000. *Insured unemployed* (Oct. 1971)—29,000 (3.1%).
Manufacturing (1967): *Value added by manufacture,* $3,781,-300,000. Primary metals, $524,600,000; transportation equipment, $460,500,000; chemicals and allied products, $422,500,000; electrical equipment, $367,200,000.
Agriculture (1970): *Cash farm income,* $401,565,000 (livestock, $267,853,000; crops, $125,726,000; government payments, $7,986,000). *Chief crops* (1970)—Corn, 40,172,000 bushels; soybeans, 5,112,000 bushels; tobacco, 27,040,000 pounds; hay, 735,000 tons.
Mining (1970): *Production value,* $88,589,000 (ranks 38th among the states). *Chief minerals* (tons)—Stone, 15,026,-000; sand and gravel, 13,121,000; bituminous coal, 1,755,-000; clays, 1,183,000.
Fisheries (1970): *Commercial catch,* 77,900,000 pounds ($18,-000,000). *Leading species by value* (1967), Hard blue crabs, $895,694; menhaden, $57,655; shellfish, $53,694; alewives, $35,026.
Transportation: *Roads* (1969), 26,114 miles (42,025 km); *motor vehicles* (1969), 1,795,000; *railroads* (1968) 1,122 miles (1,806 km); *airports* (1969), 15.
Communications: *Telephones* (1971), 2,482,200; *television stations* (1969), 5; *radio stations* (1969), 84; *newspapers* (1969), 12 (daily circulation, 752,000).

Vietnam veterans check computers listing all jobs in Massachusetts during state's employment drive in October.

MASSACHUSETTS

For government and business, as well as for many individual citizens, 1971 was a year of belt-tightening in the Commonwealth of Massachusetts. At a time of high unemployment and general economic austerity, the mood in the state seemed to favor consolidation of gains made in the past and a "hold-the-line" policy on new programs, whether in the public or private sector.

Economic Concerns. Unemployment in the state reached new high levels early in 1971. The rate had slackened by mid-year, but "pockets" of severe unemployment remained, and the state's technological industries—largely research and development firms specializing in space and defense work—remained in the doldrums.

State Government Reorganization. Republican Gov. Francis W. Sargent's plan to restructure the state's executive agencies along the lines of the federal "cabinet" system led to a series of clashes with the Democratic-controlled legislature over the funding of several new departments of state government. The governor finally received only a part of the funds that he had requested for launching the operations of new departments of transportation, community affairs, commerce and development, as well as several other departments organized to replace a multitude of poorly coordinated offices and agencies. A continuing effort, supported by the governor, to cut the size of the state House of Representatives failed to make much progress during the year.

Car Insurance Plan Savings. Massachusetts put the nation's first "no-fault" auto insurance plan into full operation in 1971. By the summer it had become clear that the savings predicted by the plan's proponents were becoming a reality. A proposal to rebate to car owners a part of the monies already collected by the insurance companies was strongly resisted by the insurance industry. The dispute had not been settled as the year ended. Late in the year, however, coverage under the "no-fault" plan was extended by a new law which includes coverage of property damage as well as bodily injuries resulting from car accidents.

Local Election Upsets. Municipal elections in November produced a number of upsets in some of the state's larger cities. In New Bedford and Lynn, incumbent mayors were defeated in their bids for reelection. In both Lynn and Cambridge, several

─── **MASSACHUSETTS • Information Highlights** ───

Area: 8,257 square miles (21,386 sq km).
Population (1970 census): 5,689,170. *Density:* 695 per sq mi.
Chief Cities (1970 census): Boston, the capital, 641,071; Worcester, 176,572; Springfield, 163,905; New Bedford, 101,777; Cambridge, 100,361.
Government (1971): *Chief Officers*—governor, Francis W. Sargent (R); lt. gov., Donald Dwight (R); secy. of the Commonwealth, John F. X. Davoren (D); atty. gen., Robert H. Quinn (D); treas., Robert Q. Crane (D); commissioner, dept. of educ., Neil Sullivan; chief justice, G. Joseph Tauro. *General Court*—Senate, 40 members (30 Democrats, 10 Republicans); House of Representatives, 240 members (178 D, 62 R).
Education (1970–71): *Enrollment*—public elementary schools, 663,000 pupils; 26,948 teachers; public secondary, 515,000 pupils; 24,493 teachers; nonpublic schools (1968–69), 245,500 pupils; 10,570 teachers; college and university (fall 1968), 269,785 students. *Public school expenditures* (1970–71), $805,800,000 ($735 per pupil). *Average teacher's salary,* $9,613.
State Finances (fiscal year 1970): *Revenues,* $2,369,416,000 (3% general sales tax and gross receipts taxes, $168,443,-000; motor fuel tax, $135,816,000; federal funds, $512,-904,000). Expenditures, $2,448,437,000 (education, $527,-286,000; health, welfare, safety, $713,407,000; highways, $239,768,000). *State debt,* $1,861,766,000 (June 1970).
Personal Income (1970): $24,418,000,000; per capita, $4,294.
Public Assistance (1970): $669,680,000. *Average monthly payments* (Dec. 1970)—old-age assistance, $98.25; aid to families with dependent children, $256.70.
Labor Force: *Nonagricultural wage and salary earners* (June 1971), 2,239,200. *Average annual employment* (1969)—manufacturing, 682,000; trade, 474,000; government, 296,-000; services, 453,000. *Insured unemployed* (Oct. 1971)—73,900 (4.3%).
Manufacturing (1967): *Value added by manufacture,* $8,715,-000,000; Electrical equipment and supplies, $1,337,000,-000; nonelectrical machinery, $1,237,800,000; instruments and related products, $612,800,000; printing and publishing, $589,200,000; food and kindred products, $564,400,000.
Agriculture (1970): *Cash farm income,* $169,216,000 (livestock, $86,693,000; crops, $81,904,000; government payments, $619,000). *Chief crops* (1970)—Apples, 107,800,-000 pounds; tobacco, 3,230,000 pounds; cranberries, 957,000 barrels.
Mining (1971): *Production value,* $49,638,000 (ranks 43d among the states). *Chief minerals* (tons)—Sand and gravel, 18,589,000; stone, 7,648,000; clays, 270,000.
Fisheries (1970): *Commercial catch,* 286,200,000 pounds ($45,800,000). *Leading species by value* (1967), Haddock, $10,855,318; sea scallops, $5,271,474; lobster, $2,869,177.
Transportation: *Roads* (1969), 28,897 miles (46,504 km); *motor vehicles* (1969), 2,426,000; *railroads* (1968), 1,495 miles (2,406 km); *airports* (1969), 26.
Communications: *Telephones* (1971), 3,522,900; *television stations* (1969), 11; *radio stations* (1969), 99; *newspapers* (1969), 46 (daily circulation, 2,345,000).

437

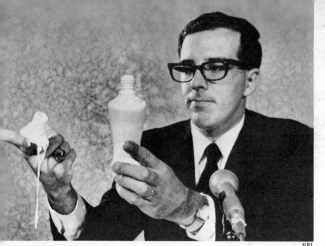

EDIBLE, water-soluble plastic container was demonstrated in August. Developers hope that material will help solve plastic disposal and recycling problems.

UPI

city council seats were won by candidates representing disadvantaged elements in those cities, leading to speculation about a possible trend toward greater political insurgency at the local level in Massachusetts. In Boston, the state's capital and largest city, incumbent mayor Kevin H. White easily won re-election to a second term. (See BOSTON.)

Prison Unrest. Disturbances at New York's Attica State Prison triggered protests by the inmates of several prisons in Massachusetts and threw the spotlight on plans for prison reform, which had been a dormant issue in the state in recent years. Many of the prisoners' protests were centered on the state's so-called "two thirds law," which required that persons convicted of certain felonies serve two thirds of their sentences before becoming eligible for parole. Attempts to repeal or greatly modify this law failed in the legislature in 1971. Although the demonstrations by the prisoners attracted widespread public attention, in no case was a major use of force required to bring the situation under control.

Developments in Higher Education. Four of the largest universities in the state installed new presidents in 1971. At the Massachusetts Institute of Technology, Jerome B. Wiesner, already a member of the institute's administrative staff and a former science adviser to Presidents John F. Kennedy and Lyndon B. Johnson, was chosen as president. Harvard, too, chose one of its own, as Derek C. Bok succeeded retiring Nathan Pusey. At Boston University, John R. Silbur became that university's 7th president. Robert Wood was chosen president of the University of Massachusetts, which was in the process of building a Boston campus to complement its facilities at Amherst in the western part of the state.

The new presidents of the three private universities (M.I.T., Harvard, and B.U.), all made strong statements warning about the plight of higher education. Each stressed the increasing need for state and federal support to solve the financial crises of private colleges.

National Politics. As the year ended, various aspirants to the U. S. presidency began opening up campaign offices in Massachusetts. It appeared that several figures would campaign in the state prior to the presidential primary election, scheduled for March 1972.

HARVEY BOULAY, *Boston University*

MATERIALS

Few outstanding new materials were developed in 1971. New uses were found for old materials, however, and many improvements were made in them.

Glass. Windshields on the 1971 model cars were better than those on older cars. They were thinner, lighter, stronger under impact, and less likely to cause laceration injuries when broken.

A significant development during the year was the willingness of glass bottle manufacturers to buy back used bottles for use as a raw material in the manufacture of new bottles. This policy may lessen the nation's litter problem.

One newly developed window is a double-glazed unit that warms itself, muffles unwanted sound, insulates against cold or heat, and screens out solar glare. In this window, a transparent metallic coating reflects the sun's heat and light and also conducts electricity to warm the glass area when desired. A wide air space between panes helps to reduce sound transmission.

A new lightweight glass bottle with a wraparound plastic sleeve is to be tested in a number of markets in cooperation with major soft drink companies. The new container, called Plastic-Shield, consists of a flat-bottom, teardrop-shaped glass envelope wrapped in a resilient sleeve of polystyrene. The plastic sleeve will be preprinted. The new containers will be lighter in weight than any nonreturnable glass container in use in 1971.

Metals. Titanium continues to replace aluminum for military aircraft components that are subject to high temperatures. The use of titanium in the production of airframe components has grown from a few parts in the early 1950's to 7.5% to 9.4% of the structural weight of currently produced military aircraft, such as the F-4. Most of the titanium is used in the form of sheet metal for surfaces.

One prominent engineer predicted that within five years all motor vehicles will be using disk brakes with steel disks in place of cast iron. Steel dissipates heat more effectively than the cast iron in use in 1971.

Molybdenum, a fairly rare high-temperature-resistant metal often used in alloys, is increasingly being used for various applications. Its use is expected to grow at a rate of at least 7% annually during the 1971–80 period. This growth is coming from a number of sources; for example, alloys containing molybdenum are replacing unalloyed steel in such structural applications as buildings, bridges, and freight cars.

Plastics. One automobile manufacturer predicted that the amount of plastics used in a car will increase from 100 pounds in 1971 to 200 pounds by 1980.

Researchers in Japan, Britain, Sweden, and the United States have been working on the development of plastics that rot away after use. One Japanese company already has test-marketed a plastic containing additives sensitive to ultraviolet light. This plastic decays after being exposed to sunlight for six months. It is hoped that such materials will reduce the plastics disposal problem. (See also CHEMISTRY.)

Ceramics. When California ranchers turned to the University of California, Los Angeles, to find a way to dispose of cow dung, no one expected that the investigation would also result in a way to dispose of used glass bottles. The university researchers combined 5% to 10% of dried cow dung with powdered glass to produce a new kind of insulating brick.

Composites. High interest continued in boron-fiber and graphite-fiber reinforced composites containing metals, phenolics, epoxys, carbon, or graphite as the matrix material. Helicopter tail-rotor drive shafts made of boron (fiber)-epoxy and carbon (fiber)-epoxy composite materials are said to provide a weight reduction of 30% and twice the stiffness of comparable aluminum structures.

A process was developed for fusing Teflon to aluminum, copper, steel, stainless steel, nickel, nylon, paper, glass fibers, or foil. The product is available in rolls up to 36 inches wide and 15 mils thick. It can be used for applications where temperatures up to 600° F are encountered.

JAMES R. TINKLEPAUGH
Alfred University

MAURITANIA

Developments in Mauritania in 1971 continued to be dominated by President Mokhtar Ould Daddah and the ruling Parti du Peuple Mauritanien (PPM).

Domestic Affairs. President Daddah, running unopposed, was elected to his third 5-year term on August 8. The PPM candidates for the 50-member (increased from 40) National Assembly were also elected without opposition. Daddah announced the formation of a new cabinet on August 18 with himself as premier. Seven new ministers, younger and technically educated men, were brought into the government.

Student unrest and strikes early in the year led to the closing of several secondary schools. The education minister, Mohamed Abdellahi Ould Kharchi, was dismissed in March. He was replaced on April 5 by Ba Mamadou Alassane as minister of secondary education, youth, and sports, and by Abdallah Ould Boye as minister of primary education and religious affairs.

Trade unions served as another outlet for discontent. Late in 1970 the government had created a national commission of trade union reconciliation, and unions were warned not to express political opinions contrary to party dogma. But union demonstrations continued. In September some 3,500 workers struck the Miferma iron works at Zouerate.

Foreign Affairs. French President Georges Pompidou visited Mauritania in February. In June, President Daddah was elected chairman of the Organization of African Unity (OAU). He represented the OAU at the United Nations and on visits to many countries to seek diplomatic support for the liberation of southern Africa.

Economy. Mauritania has become one of the largest recipients in Africa of aid from the People's Republic of China. Peking agreed to provide a $25 million loan for a deepwater port at Nouakchott and is also helping to develop rice cultivation.

W. A. E. SKURNIK, *University of Colorado*

MAURITIUS

The gravest problem facing Mauritius in 1971 was Britain's proposed entry into the Common Market. Nearly 85% of Mauritius' export earnings derive from sugar sold to Britain under the Commonwealth Sugar Agreement. The loss of this guaranteed market would be a serious blow to the island. Protracted negotiations in London finally led to an agreement, in June, by which the Common Market countries promised that special care would be taken to see that Mauritius and the other less developed parties to the agreement will be able to sell sugar to Britain at present levels, at least.

Foreign Affairs. Foreign Minister Gaetan Duval maintained that, despite an agreement to allow Soviet trawlers to refit at Port-Louis, Mauritius would remain linked to the West. He also offered a naval base to Britain to replace Simonstown, South Africa. Mauritius was one of the six members of the Organization of African Unity that supported the opening of a "dialogue" with South Africa.

Domestic Affairs. The state of emergency that had been in effect since the Muslim-Creole clashes preceding independence in March 1968 was ended on Dec. 31, 1970. It was replaced by a public order act that provided for preventive detention and banned public meetings during the Legislative Assembly.

The government launched a family planning program to try to check overpopulation, the most serious threat to Mauritian development.

BURTON BENEDICT
University of California, Berkeley

MEANY, George. See BIOGRAPHY.
MEDICARE. See SOCIAL WELFARE.

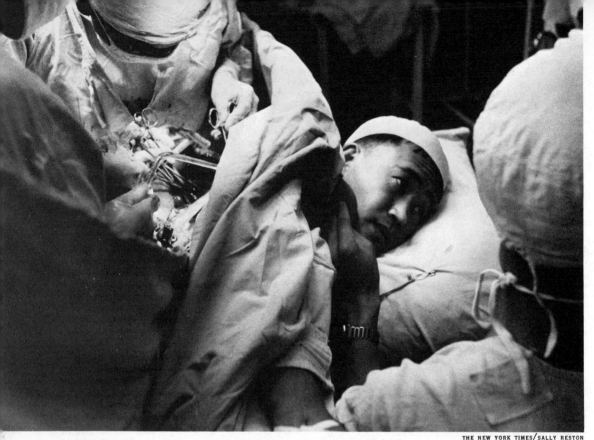

Acupuncture, an ancient Chinese medical technique, attracted wide attention in 1971. Here, nurse (*right*) holds needle in conscious patient's shoulder while doctor performs major lung surgery.

medicine

Developments in the field of medicine during 1971 are reviewed in this article under the following headings: (1) General Survey; (2) Allergies; (3) Cancer; (4) Eye Diseases; (5) Heart and Vascular Disease; (6) Hospitals; (7) Mental Health; (8) Neurology; (9) Nursing; (10) Pediatrics; (11) Pharmacology; (12) Public Health; (13) Respiratory Diseases; (14) Surgery; and (15) Venereal Disease.

General Survey

Physicians and scientists working in the field of medicine continued the struggle during 1971 to find cures, eradicate disease, and improve public health. Generally both successes and setbacks were relatively minor, although there was much promising research. In the United States, President Richard M. Nixon made the fight against cancer a top priority of his administration. His January State of the Union message urged a concerted effort to that end similar to that which "split the atom and took man to the moon." It took the rest of the year for Congress to thrash out a bill for administering the cancer crusade.

The hottest medical news of the year was the astonishing reports out of mainland China of the successful use of acupuncture needles probing the nerves to relieve pain, replace anesthesia in surgery, and even effect cures. Interest in Western medical circles was tempered by skepticism.

The Fight Over Fighting Cancer. Controversy raged throughout 1971 in U. S. government circles over how to marshal forces for an all-out campaign to conquer cancer. One faction argued that the fight should be continued within the National Institutes of Health (NIH)—as it has since the National Cancer Institute was formed in 1937; others maintained that efforts should be consolidated in a new super agency organized along the lines of the National Aeronautics and Space Administration's successful "man-on-the-moon" Apollo program.

Partly as a result of lobbying by the American Cancer Society and private philanthropists, the Senate passed a bill favoring the latter course. A House bill, however, kept the anticancer agency within NIH. At the end of the year a compromise was reached between the two proposals. The expanded fight against cancer will be retained within the National Cancer Institute—and thus remain administratively within NIH—but a panel of experts, reporting directly to the President, will oversee its work. The director of the Institute will be appointed by the President, who will also review all Institute budget requests. The new legislation appropriates $1.6 billion, primarily for research, over the next three years. It also provides for the establishment of 15 cancer centers, where patients will be treated in conjunction with research.

Cyclic AMP. The 1971 Nobel Prize in medicine went to an American, Dr. Earl Sutherland, professor of physiology at Vanderbilt School of Medicine in Nashville, Tenn., for the discovery of a biological molecule called 3′,5′-adenosine monophosphate, or cyclic AMP. This molecule has been found to play an important role in the regulation of the activity of many different hormones.

It was in 1956, while Dr. Sutherland was at Western Reserve University in Cleveland, that he and an associate, Dr. Theodore W. Rall, discovered cyclic AMP. They were trying to learn how the hormone epinephrine, which is released into the bloodstream in response to anger or fear, causes an immediate increase in the amount of the sugar glucose present in the blood. An obvious possibility was that epinephrine breaks down the molecules of animal fat stored in the liver into glucose. On close study, however, the actual sequence of events turned out to be considerably more complex.

Dr. Sutherland found that it was cyclic AMP that did the actual breaking down of the animal fat to glucose, not epinephrine itself. He discovered that AMP did this in response to the presence of epinephrine. If epinephrine was not present, glucose did not appear. In other words, cyclic AMP was a "second messenger," which acted within the cells to release glucose after the arrival of the "first messenger," epinephrine.

Dr. Sutherland and others have shown since that at least a dozen hormones in humans and animals function with the aid of cyclic AMP. These include glucagon and insulin, two hormones involved in blood-sugar control mechanisms, and a variety of pituitary hormones, as well as hormones that regulate nerve cell activity. These hormones travel from their cells of origin to their targets. Inside the target cell, they alter the level of cyclic AMP, which then goes on to do the biochemical work that has previously been known to be associated with these hormones.

Practical applications from the new Nobelist's pioneering work with cyclic AMP for the better management of disease are not yet in the offing. However, the fact that these studies have thrown light on how certain hormones work lends hope to the possibility that new or improved therapeutic measures may become available.

Acupuncture. The hesitant political contact between the United States and mainland China in 1971 sparked a remarkable interest in Chinese medicine among Western observers. Several prominent U. S. physicians—including Dr. Paul Dudley White, the heart specialist, and Dr. Samuel Rosen, the ear surgeon—visited China and brought back favorable reports of the way physicians there have bridged the gap between their traditional Chinese medicine and modern Western practice.

One ancient procedure of Chinese medicine that attracted wide and renewed attention in Western countries was acupuncture. James Reston of the New York *Times* reported that he was treated by acupuncture while he was recovering from an emergency appendectomy he underwent in Peking in the summer. Acupuncture involves probing certain nerve points with long needles. It is said to have originated 3,600 years ago when Emperor Huang-Ti noticed that arrows causing wounds in battle occasionally relieved ailments in other parts of the body. Over the centuries, Chinese doctors worked out an elaborate theory involving the use of needles inserted along a series of invisible pathways called meridians to alter the "vital energy" flowing along the meridians and restore the balance of the body

upset by the disease process. Many acupuncturists do not accept this theory but have no alternative explanation of how acupuncture works.

Most Western physicians faced with successful results with acupuncture attribute it to the well-known "placebo effect," in which the treatment or drug is in itself of little or no value, but a real or apparent improvement results from the patient's own belief that the treatment is therapeutic.

A British physician, Dr. Felix Mann, a Western authority on acupuncture, reported results of a survey of acupuncture treatment of 1,000 British patients suffering from a variety of generally non-serious conditions—such as headaches, constipation, and bronchitis. Some 44% of the group were said to be cured or considerably improved; 29% were moderately improved; and 27% unimproved. In general, Dr. Mann stressed, acupuncture is successful only in diseases that are physiologically reversible—that is where there has been little tissue damage. He noted that he would not use acupuncture as a treatment for infections or such major destructive diseases as cancer.

The use of acupuncture by the Chinese as an anesthetic in surgery astonished medical professionals in the West. Observers reported seeing major procedures such as open heart surgery and removal of tumors performed with acupuncture as the sole anesthetic. The acupuncture needles were inserted, and the patient told the surgeon when numbness had set in. During the operation, acupuncturists continually twisted the needles inserted into the nerve centers that controlled the area being operated on.

III Effects of Hormone Treatment. The keystone to medical treatment is that whatever a physician does to his patient, he must do no harm. However, with the use of modern potent drugs, apparently rational therapy has been known to yield unexpected and undesirable results. A sobering example of this dilemma of modern medicine appeared in the medical literature in 1971, when three Boston physicians linked a synthetic estrogenic hormone used to prevent miscarriages in pregnant women with cases of vaginal cancer occurring two decades later in the daughters of the women concerned.

The hormone, diethylstilbestrol, was relatively widely employed from the mid-1940's to the late 1950's, when questions about its efficacy to prevent miscarriages led most physicians to abandon it. It seems now that its use in pregnant women 25 years ago has planted a hormonal time bomb in the female offspring that may trigger a rare cancer.

Vaginal cancer being unusual in the young, its appearance in eight young women prompted Drs. Arthur Herbst, Howard Ulfelder, and David Proskanzer of the Massachusetts General Hospital to undertake medical detective work to seek the cause. In reviewing the medical backgrounds of the patients and the pregnancy histories of their mothers, they found a common element: all the mothers had been given diethylstilbestrol during their pregnancy to prevent miscarriage. The Boston physicians reported their findings in the *New England Journal of Medicine* in April. Later five more cases turned up in New York and two more in Boston.

The physicians emphasize that their finding does not prove that diethylstilbestrol was the cause of the cancer. They also point out that even if it is the cause, it is extremely rare. Nevertheless, physicians are being alerted not to prescribe synthetic estrogenic hormones during pregnancy and are

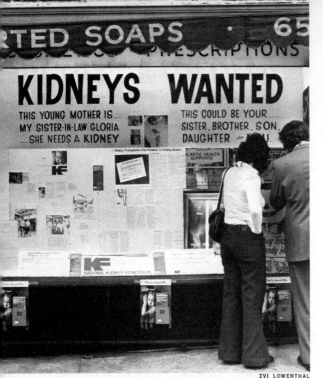

SIGN in New York City pharmacy window calls attention to shortage of kidneys for transplants. Many treatable patients die for lack of suitable transplant.

ZVI LOWENTHAL

being urged to check on young women with unusual menstrual problems or vaginal bleeding for the possibility of vaginal cancer.

The mechanism by which the stilbestrol exercises this delayed reaction—if in fact this substance is the carcinogen—is as yet unknown. It is possible that such cancers may develop more frequently in a woman's later years. Because all the women who are potentially involved are still under 25 years of age, only time can tell how large a group may ultimately be affected.

Heartening News on Hepatitis. In 1971 a significant step was taken toward the possible development of a vaccine against the liver-destroying disease hepatitis. Dr. Saul Krugman and associates at New York University reported that they had succeeded in immunizing a small group of children against serum hepatitis. The children were given doses of specially treated blood obtained from persons known to have hepatitis. This treatment apparently prevented them from developing the abnormalities in blood chemistry associated with hepatitis when they were later exposed to the disease. Dr. Krugman also was successful in protecting individuals from hepatitis by giving them doses of the blood fraction gamma globulin, containing very high amounts of antibodies to hepatitis virus. Neither method is yet ready for widespread use, even for extensive testing.

During the year the U. S. government licensed a test for hepatitis to be used for screening blood intended for transfusions. A large number of severe cases of hepatitis—perhaps 30,000 annually in the United States—are known to have been caused by individuals being transfused with hepatitis-contaminated blood. This can occur even though the donor himself shows no signs of the disease. Use of the test will eventually become mandatory for all donor blood.

Immunization. In September the U. S. Public Health Service announced that it would no longer recommend routine immunization of children against smallpox. The decision reflected the declining risk of exposure to the disease. There was no change in the recommendations to travelers to smallpox endemic areas and for military and hospital personnel or others likely to be exposed to the disease.

Additional encouraging news came from the annual immunization survey conducted by the Center for Disease Control in Atlanta. This showed that significantly more children had been immunized in 1971 against common childhood illnesses such as measles, polio, diphtheria, and pertussis than had been immunized in 1970. For the first time since 1966 the number of those immunized against polio increased. The findings indicate that the chance of outbreaks of these diseases is lessened to some extent.

Infant Mortality. Encouraging figures on the U. S. infant mortality rate were released in 1971. In 1970 the death rate among children under one year of age fell to a record low—19.8 deaths for each 1,000 live births in 1969. However, the United States still ranks only 14th among the world's nations in terms of lowest infant mortality.

Equine Sleeping Sickness. During the summer of 1971 an epidemic of equine encephalomyelitis crossed the border from Mexico into Texas. For the past two years the disease, caused by a new type of virus, had been steadily moving northward from Ecuador through Central America. Humans affected develop symptoms like those of a severe case of flu, and there have been no deaths attributed to the disease. Infected horses, however, die at the rate of 50%. An epidemic threatened, but fortunately, as a spin-off from the much-debated biological warfare program, a vaccine had been developed against the new viral strain. This vaccine, along with extensive spraying of breeding grounds of mosquitoes believed to be carriers, confined the disease to Texas and neighboring states. (See also VETERINARY MEDICINE.)

Hodgkin's Disease. Evidence that Hodgkin's disease, a rare malignancy of the lymph glands, occurs in clusters of people suggested a contagion factor. A report published in 1971 uncovered a group of 11 victims in Albany, N. Y., all of whom had been associated with at least one of the others or with a mutual acquaintance. This is a far greater incidence of Hodgin's disease than would have been expected. Extending their studies, the investigators by the end of the year had uncovered well over 30 cases in different clusters, one group in Mount Kisco, N. Y., and one at the University of Buffalo.

The implication was that Hodgkin's disease is contagious to some degree. The fact that the cases did not appear for several years until after exposure suggests that the infectious agent had a long incubation period. Also, the fact that some of the victims were linked only by unaffected third parties suggests that some people carry the disease without being affected themselves.

Epidemiologists were characteristically cautious in drawing conclusions. They noted the lack of suitable control groups to compare with the diseased group. There remained the possibility that the clusters were chance occurrences, as had proved to be the case in previous similar instances.

CHARLES S. MARWICK
Senior Writer, "Medical World News"

Allergies

In 1971 several substances were recognized as possible causes of allergy symptoms, and several advances were made in allergy treatment.

Allergens. An allergy to enzymes found in household detergents was investigated. The enzymes are produced from bacteria or extracted from plants. In many cases, workers in detergent factories who were exposed to the enzymes developed shortness of breath, wheezing, and fatigue and showed positive skin tests for the enzymes. Although no cases of such respiratory allergies have been reported from household contact with detergents, some scientists think that such sensitivity to the enzymes of household detergents might occur.

Mold growing in home air-conditioning units and humidifiers was found to cause asthma. Cigarette smoke and injectable insulin were also recognized as possible causes of allergic reactions, and ampicillin, a synthetic penicillin, was found more likely than original penicillin to cause rash.

Role of Allergy Reactions in Certain Diseases. The role of an allergy in causing seborrheic dermatitis of the head, a skin disease that causes scaly, red skin eruptions, especially in infants and young children, was investigated during the year. One scientist attributed the disease to a food allergy. Another scientist also suggested that color-blindness may be an allergy-caused disease. On the other hand, studies have revealed that some disorders, such as overactivity of the thyroid gland, can produce symptoms readily confused with those of allergy. Similarly, a newly recognized disease, antitrypsin deficiency, was described as a cause of obstructive lung disease and emphysema, which may appear to be allergic asthma.

Nature of Allergic Reactions. Recent studies of antibodies associated with allergies indicate that they are generated by or localized in tissues at the point where the allergen enters the body. However, tests with radioactively tagged grass pollen show that even in patients with pollen-asthma the offending pollen never reaches the bronchi of the lungs, since they are too large and are filtered out earlier. It was also demonstrated that ragweed pollen asthma is not initiated through reaction with the mucous membranes of the nasal passages or by neurologic reflex from the nose. The possibility remains that asthma is caused by pollen that is swallowed and absorbed by the bloodstream where it causes the production of antibodies that in turn circulate to the nose to cause hay fever or to the chest to produce asthma.

Treatment Advances. The drug disodium chromoglycate was further proved to be helpful in the management of asthma, particularly in children whose asthma is caused by substances outside the body. The drug inhibits the release of histamine, an important mediator substance in asthma. An older drug, isoproterenol, was found to be safe and effective when used intravenously and drew increasing attention as a treatment for acute asthma in children. The use of immunotherapy injections to treat allergies continued to come under scrutiny. It was demonstrated that such injections lead to increased immunoglobulin E production and an associated lessening of allergy symptoms even at intervals as long as six weeks between injections.

IRWIN J. POLK, M.D.
St. Luke's Hospital, New York City

Cancer

Cancer research in 1971 was concerned with the role of hormones in cancer of the breast and vagina, on the likelihood of a viral-cause for cancer in man, and on the protective function of host-defenses. The U.S. Congress enacted a major program of cancer research and authorized spending $1.6 billion over the next three years for this purpose.

Hormones. Certain amounts of estrogen can produce breast cancer in humans, mice, and rats. Dr. Olof Pearson of Case Western Reserve University reported that the pituitary hormone, prolactin, rather than estrogen, is the stimulant to breast cancer in female rats. His studies indicate that estrogen produces cancer in rats only by stimulating the pituitary gland's secretion of prolactin. The pertinence of these observations to human breast cancer remains to be established.

Dr. Arthur L. Herbst and coworkers at the Massachusetts General Hospital reported the occurrence of adenocarcinoma of the vagina in eight girls, aged 15 to 22 years, between 1966 and 1969. This tumor had heretofore been a rarity, and its occurrence in even these numbers provoked much interest. It was discovered that each of these patients had been born of a "high risk" pregnancy occurring in a woman with a prior history of spontaneous abortion and that seven of the eight mothers had had their pregnancy sustained through the use of oral synthetic estrogens. It has not yet been established whether this indicates that the synthetic estrogens have a carcinogenic effect or whether these patients possessed a defective genetic makeup expressed both before and after their birth.

Cancer Viruses. During 1971 virus particles were observed in cultured cell lines from the following human cancers: breast, cervix, Hodgkin's disease, and African, or Burkitt's, lymphosarcoma. In related work, Dr. Dan Moore and co-workers at the Institute of Medical Research, Camden, N.J., demonstrated viral particles in the breast milk of nursing women selected from populations prone to breast cancer. Particles were found in 6 of 10 American women with a family history of breast cancer, but only in 7 of 156 women with a negative family history. The human milk particles are physically identical to the mouse mammary tumor virus that the U.S. physician John J. Bittner found to be transmitted through maternal milk and known to cause breast cancer in mice. While these reports are indicative of the emphasis being given to the search for a virus cause of human cancer, the presence of a virus does not prove causation.

Similar reservations may also apply to the proposed linking between cancer viruses and an RNA-dependent DNA polymerase enzyme reported earlier by Dr. Howard Temin of the University of Wisconsin and Dr. David Baltimore of the Massachusetts Institute of Technology. Discovery of this "reverse transcriptase" activity demonstrates that genetic information can flow from RNA to DNA as well as in the reverse direction. Such activity has been found to be consistently present in purified mammal tumor viruses, but now also has been demonstrated in rapidly dividing cells from noncancerous sources.

Host-Defenses. With the demonstration in the 1950's and 1960's that host rejection of transplanted tissue is mediated by the lymphocytes (one type of white blood cell), a physiological mechanism for cancer surveillance seemed possible. Cancer occurs at an increased frequency in populations having defective cellular immunity; the converse is also true. Dr. Donald Morton, formerly of the National Cancer Institute and now at the University of California at Los Angeles, indicates that lymphocyte-mediated inflammatory response to skin testing with the chemical DNCB is commonly defective in patients with advanced cancer. Work by Karl and Ingegerd Hellstrom of the Washington University Medical School demonstrates an anti-cancer effect of human lymphocytes in culture, but also shows that in some instances serum antibodies can block this effect, thus permitting the cancer to grow. By implication, the total host response to cancer depends on complex interaction of both cellular and humoral factors. Manipulation of the immune system with therapeutic intent continues in an exploratory phase.

Funding and Organization of Cancer Research. In December 1971 a Senate-House conference committee agreed on legislation providing $1.6 billion over the next three years for an expanded research effort on cancer. The legislation focuses on research rather than patient care but does establish some cancer detection and control units. The agreement also keeps cancer research under National Institute of Health (NIH) auspices, thus resolving a controversy that arose earlier in the year when the Senate, in passing legislation identifying the "conquest of cancer" as a national goal, proposed making the National Cancer Institute (NCI) semiautonomous. This proposal was subsequently opposed by a House bill that left the NCI within NIH.

CHARLES W. YOUNG, M. D.
Sloan-Kettering Institute for Cancer Research

Eye Diseases

In 1971 there were many advances in ophthalmologic techniques and intensive study of dyslexia and other problems involving the eyes.

Diagnostic Techniques. An instrument that may soon allow more rapid measurement of visual refraction errors than is now possible has been developed, as has a quick method for testing individuals for red-green blindness. The technique of fluorescein angiography that allows the observation of blood flow through ocular vessels was improved.

Treatment Advances. Cryotherapy, used in the past for the local treatment of herpes corneal ulcers, is now also being applied to the sclera when an inflammation of the iris and ciliary body accompanies the herpes infection of the cornea. Methods of using radioisotopes and the rate of success in such treatment in cases of exophthalmic goiter (an abnormal protrusion of the eyeball caused by a malfunction of the thyroid gland), malignant orbital tumors, and conjunctival neoplasms improved during the year. Other advances included a modified impression method of artificial eye fitting that is expected to improve the appearance of plastic eyes.

New methods of administering topical drugs into the eye promised a reduction in the frequency of needed applications. Ocular toxoplasmosis is now being treated with several drugs, including pyrimethamine, sulfadiazine, folinic acid, prednisone, and aureomycin. Although the treatment still involves risks, the rate of success has been rising. But ophthalmologists increasingly warned of possible effects on the eye of drugs, such as the contraceptive pill, the antimalarial agent chloroquine, and the anti-inflammatory agent indomethacin.

Dyslexia. Dr. Arthur Keeney, chief of Willis Eye Hospital in Philadelphia, and other ophthalmologists suggest that all children suspected of having dyslexia, a marked difficulty in learning to read, be treated by a team consisting of a pediatrician, an ophthalmologist, a psychiatrist, and possibly also a psychologist, a neurologist, an audiologist, and an occupational therapist. Remedial reading was recommended as the therapy of choice. Orthoptic, or visual, training, may be indicated to treat concurrent conditions, but that type of visual training that includes "patterning" and eye muscle exercises was discouraged.

Other Findings. Intensive studies of the geographic and ethnic distribution and patterns of heredity of several hereditary eye diseases, such as Tay-Sachs disease, congenital alacrimia, mallatia leventinese, and a rare form of hereditary epithelial dystrophy of the cornea, were studied in an attempt to understand better and perhaps prevent the birth of afflicted children or find a means of correcting the genetic defect responsible for the condition. Basic research on the retina and its connections with the brain continued, and the possibility of eye damage resulting from occupational exposure to carbon dioxide, microwaves, lasers, and x-rays was studied. Other work revealed that correcting strabismus (squint) frequently improved the vision of children also afflicted with nystagmus (rapid involuntary eyeball movements).

ROLAND I. PRITIKIN, M. D.
Author of "Essentials of Ophthalmology"
M. L. DUCHON, M. D.
Consultant in Ophthalmology

Heart and Vascular Disease

In 1971 there was progress in the medical and surgical treatment of heart and vascular disease.

Medical Progress. An increase in the concentration of fats in blood plasma is associated with a high incidence of premature hardening of the arteries, including the coronary arteries that supply the heart with blood. Dr. Donald S. Fredrickson classified five types of hyperlipoproteinemia, an excess of circulating fatty substances bound to proteins, and determined that cholesterol and triglycerides are the most important to consider. Treatment to reduce the level of these substances in the blood includes weight reduction and dietary changes and new drugs such as clofibrate and cholestyramine.

Advances in the immediate treatment of acute myocardial infarctions have also been reported. West German physicians report that Streptokinase, isolated from the streptococci bacteria and used to dissolve clots in the coronary arteries in patients with acute myocardial infarction, reduces the mortality from 22% to 14% in the first 40 days after hospital admission with no increase in bleeding complications; Belgian physicians report similar findings. Large-scale studies of Streptokinase and Urokinase, a similar drug isolated from human urine, were to be initiated under the auspices of the National Heart and Lung Institute in late 1971.

A report from Framingham, Mass., where over 5,000 residents have been examined repeatedly since 1948, stresses that two thirds of the 120 deaths in persons under 65 in this group occurred suddenly and unexpectedly within one hour of the onset of the terminal event. Over half of the deaths were sudden and unexpected, and half of all persons with sudden deaths had no prior symptoms of heart disease. This report again stresses the need for very quick treatment in cardiac cases, and in a few cities mobile coronary units are continuously available to provide immediate treatment for sudden heart attacks. The best way to control the plague of coronary disease is, however, by prevention. This includes controlling factors considered to increase the occurrence of coronary heart disease, such as a diet high in saturated fats and cholesterol, high blood pressure, excessive intake of sugar, and cigarette smoking. Other potential risk factors are obesity, sedentary living, psychosocial tensions, and a family history of premature arteriosclerotic disease.

Investigators from the Mayo Clinic found that patients who had had a previous heart attack were in greater danger of a second attack in the first few days after surgical operations under anesthesia, particularly if the heart attack had been recent, and suggested that elective surgery be postponed for six months after the heart attack if possible.

New radio-immune assay techniques are now able to determine the concentration of digitalis in the serum, an important advance since in many patients it is difficult to decide whether a disorder of heart rate is caused by too much or too little digitalis.

Cardiovascular Surgery. Cardiologists began treating cardiac shock (mortality with medical treatment averages 86%) associated with heart attacks with intra-aortic counter pulsations produced by timed inflation and deflation of balloons inserted into the aorta. In a few instances life has been prolonged and an occasional patient has survived.

Many patients have received relief from angina pain due to coronary obstruction by grafting one or more veins from the aorta to the branches of the coronary arteries. With increased blood supply to the heart muscle the pain of angina is usually immediately relieved. In the hands of experienced cardiac surgeons the mortality from this procedure is low (4%–6%). Further observation will be needed to evaluate the operation.

Heart Transplants. The great majority of cardiovascular surgeons have discontinued heart transplantations since few patients survive for more than a few months, although there are rare instances of survival for over two years. It is hoped that further research may solve the problem of rejection of the donor heart by the recipient. Much research continues on the development of a satisfactory artificial heart, with encouraging results in animals.

Hypertension. Dr. Frank A. Finnerty, Jr., of Georgetown University has stressed that high blood pressure in black people develops earlier in life and is frequently more severe than in whites. He points out that early diagnosis is desirable because many forms of hypertension can be controlled or occasionally cured.

Pacemakers. A cardiac pacemaker is a battery-powered instrument placed under the skin with wires passing to the interior or exterior of the heart. A small current of electricity stimulates contraction of the heart at a predetermined rate. Battery failure or other complications may occur. Dr. Seymour Furman of New York found that with special equipment for patient and physician, he could check the rate of implanted pacemakers by telephone, and could detect early battery failure.

JOHNSON MCGUIRE, M. D., and
ARNOLD IGLAUER, M. D., *University of Cincinnati*

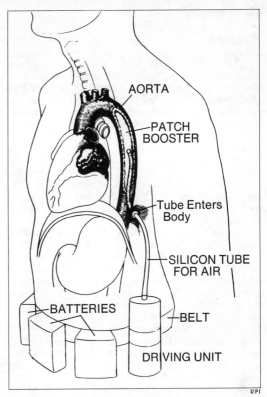

PATCH BOOSTER, a partial mechanical heart driven by an air pump outside the body, supplements the work of a natural heart. Device is sewn into the wall of the aorta, the main artery leaving the heart.

DETROIT surgeons, led by Dr. Adrian Kantrowitz (*right*), implanted a patch booster (*below*), in Haskel Shanks on August 11. The white plastic "balloon," attached in a 5-hour operation, helped pump blood through the body. The patient died in November, but from kidney failure, not a heart malfunction.

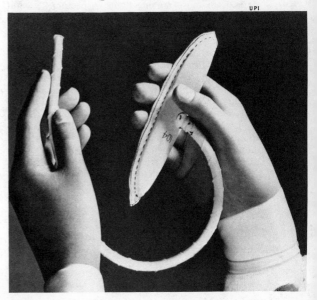

Hospitals

The most significant developments involving hospitals during 1971 were related to hospital economics. The Nixon administration singled out hospital costs, which had been rising sharply for several years, for particular emphasis in the attempt to stabilize the cost of living.

At the same time, American Hospital Association (AHA) statistics showed for the first time in nearly a decade a decline in the rate of hospital bed occupancy. Empty beds are alarming to hospital administrators because a hospital must rely on "income" from patients in order to buy supplies and pay salaries and maintenance costs as well as pay for capital expenditures.

An average of nearly one fourth of all hospital beds in the United States were empty at any given time during 1971. Massachusetts General Hospital in Boston, considered one of the nation's largest and best hospitals, estimated a decline in its bed occupancy of nearly 5% during the year. The situation caught hospitals between a trend of declining income and federal pressure to halt the spiral of continuing room rate increases. Elliot Richardson, secretary of Health, Education, and Welfare (HEW), said in an August speech to the AHA that hospitals are going to have to find a way to adjust to the decline in average bed occupancy. One alternative he put forward was "mothballing" sections of affected hospitals until the population growth could catch up with available space.

The decline in hospital use was more marked in suburban areas than in inner-city institutions. Experts in hospital economics believe that the decline resulted partly from the 1971 economic slump, which caused many persons to postpone elective, or nonemergency, surgery, and from federal pressure on Medicaid and Medicare administrators to use less expensive forms of treatment whenever possible.

Nursing Homes. Several fatal nursing home fires and complaints by congressmen about the conditions in many of the nation's long-term care institutions produced a renewed national interest in nursing homes. President Nixon promised to do something about substandard nursing homes, and outlined a plan to provide federal funds to help states train more nursing home inspectors. Several homes found to be below acceptable standards were notified by the HEW Department that they could no longer receive funds from Medicare or Medicaid unless they corrected deficiencies. Nursing homes were also discussed at the White House Conference on Aging in late November and early December.

Staff Organization. A bill of rights for hospital patients and a model contract for hospital house staff were developed in a March meeting in St. Louis, Mo., the first National House Staff Conference. The model contract would provide for minimum on-the-job benefits and fringe benefits.

Planning. In an attempt to prevent unnecessary construction of hospitals, the administration proposed to Congress that steps be taken to require permission from local and area-wide health planning agencies before hospitals could construct or remodel buildings or add major new equipment. The proposal would be enforced by withholding payments for services financed by federal programs.

JEROME F. BRAZDA
Editor, "Washington Report on Medicine and Health"

Mental Health

Significant developments marked the attack on mental illness and the promotion of mental health in 1971. New activities were launched for the prevention and treatment of alcoholism and drug abuse, and priority concern was aimed at child mental health. (Minority mental health programs) also received new attention. Mental hospitals sought to improve their programs, and the nationwide network of community mental health centers was strengthened. The number of resident patients in mental hospitals continued to decline, and the rate of decline accelerated. Research in the treatment and prevention of mental illness continued, as did new programs of training personnel to care for the mentally ill. The cost of mental illness, estimated at $21 billion for 1968, and the extent of mental illness, afflicting many millions, showed, however, that the problem is still a serious one.

The stage of progress in mental health care was pointed up by a national conference on mental health—the Silver Anniversary Commemoration of the National Mental Health Act of 1946. This conference, held in Washington, D.C., in June, was sponsored by 17 national mental health and allied organizations. They shared new knowledge, summarized accomplishments, and identified priorities.

Alcoholism and Alcohol Abuse. As a result of federal legislation enacted late in 1970, the National Institute of Alcohol Abuse and Alcoholism was established within the National Institute of Mental Health. The newly created institute is responsible for the development of national policies, goals, and programs for the prevention, control, and treatment of alcohol abuse and alcoholism. Alcoholism and problem drinking afflict an estimated 9 million Americans and are the cause of more than 83,000 deaths each year, including half of the more than 50,000 persons killed in highway accidents. Alcoholism has long been considered a social, moral, or criminal problem, and only fairly recently has it become more widely recognized as an illness —one that poses a massive public health problem.

Narcotic Addiction and Drug Abuse. The attack on drug abuse was stepped up during 1971. The extent of illicit drug use, abuse, and addiction in the United States is difficult to determine. The number of "hard narcotic" (mainly heroin) users has been estimated as high as 400,000. The abusers of other drugs, such as the amphetamines and barbiturates, is thought to number millions, as is the number of marihuana users. During the year educational and rehabilitative efforts were increased, as were research and training of personnel to deal with drug users. In June 1971, President Nixon, stating that narcotic addiction is the nation's number one health problem, established a special office to coordinate and intensify federal efforts in drug abuse treatment and prevention, including those in the armed forces. (See also DRUG ADDICTION AND ABUSE.)

Child Mental Health. Serious gaps in mental health services for children came to light as the National Institute of Mental Health made child mental health a top priority concern. Intensified action developed in research, training of personnel to deal with the mental health problems of children, and services. Statistics only hint at the gravity of the problem: in 1968 about 437,000 children were in psychiatric clinics; 33,000 were patients in mental hospitals; 26,000 were in residential treatment centers; 13,000 in day/night services; and 52,000 in community mental health services.

Mental Hospitals. The decline in resident mental hospital patients continued its sharp drop. As of June 1970 there were 338,592 patients in state and county mental hospitals, a drop of 35,392, or 9.5%, from the preceding year. Many factors were responsible for this decline, including new approaches to treatment, psychoactive drugs, and a variety of community mental health services. Mental hospitals themselves sought to progress from serving only as custodial fortresses to providing programs for treatment, rehabilitation, and prevention.

Community Mental Health Services and Centers. A survey of mental health resources in the United States revealed that there are 3,000 facilities providing 17 types of services. Prominent are community mental health services, which, in turn, are marked by a growing network of comprehensive community mental health centers supported by federal, state, and local funds. Some 450 of these centers are providing or gearing for services to 60 million persons. Each center, serving a defined "catchment area," must have at least five essential services: partial hospitalization, 24-hour emergency care, in-patient service, out-patient care, and consultation and education. Many centers are developing other programs, such as children's services, drug-abuse prevention, and alcoholism services.

Minorities' Mental Health. The Department of Health, Education, and Welfare established a new center for minority group mental health problems in the National Institute of Mental Health. Its activities include research, demonstration projects, services, and training, such as projects for training indigenous social workers among Mexican-Americans and Indians.

Crime and Antisocial Behavior. Endeavors to bring the resources of the behavioral sciences to the problem of crime and antisocial behavior were begun in 1971. The mental health aspects of "law and order" received increased attention through the cooperation of many agencies in the mental health field and the criminal justice system. Studies were encouraged in such fields as the treatment of offenders in institutions, an analysis of the juvenile court system, training of personnel, innovative programs for mentally ill offenders, and various issues relating to law and mental health.

Treatment, Research, and Training. Psychotherapy in many forms, from family therapy to encounter groups, was a major technique employed for the 4 million victims of mental illness estimated to have been treated. In addition to still-used psychoanalysis, biochemical approaches, including the use of psychoactive drugs, continued. Partial hospitalization as an alternative to full-time patient care progressed, and innovative uses of this concept were featured by community mental health centers.

Clinical studies of lithium to test its value in treating depression continued. Research also focused on schizophrenia and the depressive illnesses. Hope for the cure of some kinds of mental disorders caused by genetic defect was brought closer to reality through the work of Dr. Carl R. Merril, a National Institute of Mental Health physician, and his associates, who demonstrated that bacterial genes (viruses) can be biologically active in mammalian cells, supplying missing genetic information.

BERTRAM S. BROWN, M. D.
Director, National Institute of Mental Health

Neurology

In 1971 significant advances were made in the understanding and management of Parkinson's disease, the lipid storage diseases, and the leukodystrophies. Attention has been drawn to a number of serious complications of chronic Dilantin administration for the treatment of epilepsy, and the definition of cerebral death has been controversial.

Parkinson's Disease. Recent clinical experience has established that the drug L-dopa is the most effective means of treating Parkinson's disease. Unfortunately, L-dopa has not proved useful in treating other diseases that, like Parkinson's, are due to lesions of the basal ganglia of the brain, and in fact, certain symptoms of basal ganglia disease, such as involuntary movements and dystonia, may be produced in patients with Parkinson's disease if L-dopa is given in excessive amounts.

Lipid Storage Diseases. The lipid storage diseases are rare, genetically determined disorders of infancy and childhood. They are characterized clinically by progressive mental and motor deterioration and pathologically by an abnormal accumulation of specific lipids in the nerve cells and in some instances in other internal organs. It is now known that the abnormal substances that accumulate in the cells are really normal tissue constituents that accumulate because the activity of the specific enzyme necessary for their degradation is deficient. Many of the enzymes that distinguish the various lipid storage diseases have now been identified, and, although these discoveries have not provided a specific treatment for lipid storage diseases or leukodystrophy, they do have important therapeutic applications. Assays of the enzyme levels, for example, make it possible to identify the specific hereditary lipid storage disease and hence to provide intelligent genetic counselling. Further, examination of the amniotic fluid surrounding a fetus can identify the disease before birth, and at the choice of the parents perhaps prevent the birth of children affected with one of these diseases.

Dilantin Toxicity. Diphenylhydantoin, or Dilantin, is by far the most commonly used drug in the treatment of epilepsy, at least in the United States. In recent years it has been recognized that (chronic Dilantin administration) may give rise to folic acid deficiency and anemia and more rarely to peripheral neuropathy. The drug has also been implicated in the causation of disseminated lupus erythematous or a disease very much like it, and even malignant lymphoma. These complications, though rare, are serious and difficult to manage. They point out again that even drugs that are seemingly safe may, after years of administration, have serious and damaging effects.

Definition of Cerebral Death. The question of when cerebral or brain death actually occurs has become an increasingly important and controversial problem, since the time that elapses between death of the brain and the removal of other organs governs the suitability of these organs for transplantation. Now, the generally accepted criteria for brain death are (1) absence of spontaneous respiration and cardiac activity, (2) absence of all spontaneous motor and reflex activity, and (3) no electrical activity occurring in the brain.

MAURICE VICTOR, M. D.
Case Western Reserve University
Cleveland Metropolitan General Hospital

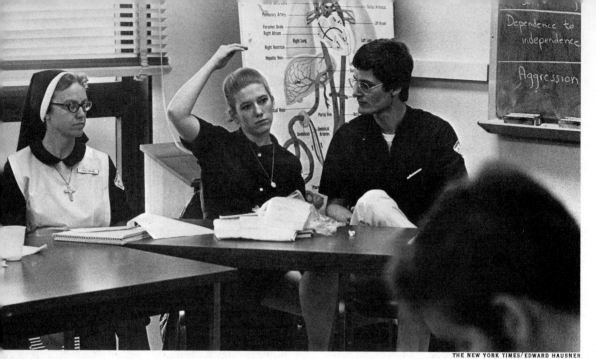

NURSING SCHOOLS are concerned because so few men are attracted to the profession. In New York City's Downstate Medical Center (*above*), 90 percent of students are women.

Nursing

In 1971 the role of the registered nurse was expanded in several areas of health care. The pediatric nurse associate, the nurse midwife, the psychiatric nurse specialist, the nurse specialist in obstetrics and gynecology, and other clinical nurse specialists were seen with greater frequency by patients in a variety of settings.

Specialty Areas. Organized nursing and medicine worked together during the year to redefine their roles in the specialty areas. The American Nurses' Association (ANA) and the American Academy of Pediatrics jointly developed guidelines for training pediatric nurse associates. National conferences were held to implement these guidelines. The ANA also met with the American College of Obstetrics and Gynecology to draw up guidelines for training clinical nurse specialists in obstetrics and gynecology. Joint meetings were held, too, between representatives of the ANA and the American Medical Association to clarify the roles and functions of nurses and physicians.

Places of Employment. Although more than half of the nurses in the United States were still employed in hospitals, more nurses were working in various community jobs, meeting the many different needs of patients. Many nurses were in outpatient clinics in ghettos, in nursing homes, in drug abuse centers, and in family health centers.

The new pediatric nurse associate usually worked in private practice with a pediatrician. In addition to health maintenance, this nurse specialist is responsible for managing common childhood conditions and carrying out predetermined immunization plans. In some cases, the nurse is responsible for initial screening, treatment, parent counseling, and follow-up, including house calls.

Nurse Population. The number of practicing registered nurses increased from 700,000 in 1970 to 723,000 in 1971. Some 515,000 were employed full-time and 208,000 part-time. During the year the ratio of nurses to population increased slightly over that of 1970—from 345 to 353 per 100,000. However, the need for registered nurses continues, and the U. S. Public Health Service estimates that one million nurses will be needed by 1975.

Education. During the 1969–70 academic year, graduations from schools of nursing rose to 43,639, up 3.4% over 1968–69. Enrollments totaled 164,545, a gain of 9.1%. These increases were due primarily to the large number of 2-year, associate degree programs in community colleges. These programs, numbering 444, provide basic education for registered nurses and, along with an increasing number of 4-year baccalaureate programs, are helping to alleviate the nursing shortage. The number of hospital-based diploma programs continues to decrease as nursing education moves into the general system of education.

Registered nurses are obtaining advanced degrees in greater numbers than ever. There are 19,000 RN's with at least a master's degree, and 700 hold doctorates. Advanced preparation is essential for educators, administrators, researchers, and clinical nurse specialists. The U. S. Public Health Service, Division of Nursing, awarded the ANA a 1-year, $42,000 grant to survey the programs and resources for the continuing education of RN's.

ANNE R. WARNER
American Nurses' Association, Inc.

Pediatrics

During 1971 pediatricians became increasingly aware of the problem of infants born addicted to narcotics or with congenital syphilis. They also continued to search for antiviral drugs, since most infectious diseases experienced by children are viral, and to evaluate a variety of health programs designed to improve the health of children.

Infant Narcotic Addiction. The increased use of narcotics, particularly heroin, in the younger population has resulted in an increase in the number of infants born to addicted mothers and themselves addicted. These infants show many of the withdrawal symptoms seen in older addicts and may present difficult diagnostic and therapeutic problems. Symptoms begin shortly after birth and consist of hyperactivity, irritability, tremors, vomiting, diarrhea, rapid and difficult breathing, and occasionally, nasal congestion and sneezing. Babies of mothers maintained on methadone show similar symptoms. Although such infants remain ill for up to ten days, the mortality rate is not excessive and the incidence of serious birth defects does not appear to be greatly increased.

Congenital Syphilis. Pediatricians are again becoming familiar with the symptoms of congenital syphilis. This disease, which had virtually disappeared in the United States, has increased over 30% in the last year. It occurs in infants born of mothers with untreated syphilis. Since treatment of the mother during pregnancy prevents the disease in infants, congenital syphilis occurs mostly in infants of young, often unmarried, mothers who have received no prenatal care. If the infant with congenital syphilis is promptly treated no permanent harm ensues, but without treatment, damage to the eyes and brain of the infant is likely.

Antiviral Drugs. Several new drugs that can attack the replicating cycle of an infecting virus without damaging the host cell of the patient are now in the experimental stage, and it seems certain that these or similar agents will prove useful in treating at least some viral illnesses. Among the most promising of these new drugs are amantadine hydrochloride, which can prevent influenza A-2 infections; idoxuridine, which prevents the growth of the herpes simplex virus, the cause of "fever blisters"; and methisazone, which has proven effective in preventing smallpox in those who have been in close contact with an infected person. Because of the efficacy of methisazone and the rarity of smallpox in the United States, many of the requirements for smallpox vaccination of infants are now being dropped.

Since many of the new antiviral agents are active against only a single specific virus, rapid and accurate laboratory identification of the infecting virus is necessary. A new technique using fluorescent antibodies should permit rapid and accurate identification of the infecting virus. The white blood cells from the infected host contain the virus. These white blood cells are smeared on a slide and layered with fluorescent antibodies. Each antibody is specific, adhering only to a single virus. When examined microscopically using fluorescent light, the intercellular fluorescence identifies the viral agent.

Health Programs for Children. Since 1964 a variety of health programs that affect the health care of children have been funded by the federal government, but it has been difficult to evaluate their impact on the health status of a community. The Denver Department of Health and Hospitals has succeeded in consolidating these funds and in developing a comprehensive family-centered program for 130,000 low-income people—40% of whom are children. Twenty-one pediatricians and from 10 to 12 pediatric nurse practitioners provide the child care. The infant mortality rate in Denver dropped considerably, particularly among those living in low-income homes and among nonwhite children. Significantly, the drop in nonwhite infant mortality was greater in Denver than any other U. S. city of comparable size, providing evidence that intelligent use of federal funds can significantly improve health care in low-income areas.

WILLIAM E. SEGAR, M. D.
University of Wisconsin

Pharmacology

The most significant developments in pharmacology in 1971 involved the evaluation and regulation of drugs already in general use by physicians.

Drug Efficacy Study Evaluation. In 1971 the U. S. Food and Drug Administration (FDA) published a series of reports classifying drugs as "effective," "probably effective," "possibly effective," or lacking proof of efficacy. The evaluations were based on a 6-year FDA-sponsored National Academy of Sciences-National Research Council (NAS-NRC) massive review of drugs marketed between 1938 and 1962 to determine whether the drugs met the efficacy requirements of the 1962 Kefauver-Harris Drug Amendments. After publication of the report, drug companies were given varying periods of time to submit satisfactory data, to take products off the market, or to change the labeling of a drug to reflect the NAS-NRC rating.

Combination Drug Guidelines. Working on a combination drug policy, the FDA published an initial proposal that would have forced manufacturers to prove that there are overwhelmingly sound reasons for using a combined dosage form of a drug. Publication of the proposal precipitated a strong reaction from the drug industry and organized medicine

SCIENTISTS working for private pharmaceutical companies help develop new drugs. This biochemist is carefully observing complicated chemical reactions.

PHOTO COURTESY PFIZER INC.

and in turn, from some administration and congressional circles. The guidelines were subsequently changed, the biggest change being to exempt over-the-counter drugs. The FDA also modified the requirement for adequate and well-controlled clinical investigations in cases where the components of a combination drug are considered safe and effective and not incompatible with one another.

Over-the-Counter Drug Products. As an outgrowth of its decision to exempt over-the-counter products from the combination drug guidelines, the FDA decided to consider over-the-counter drugs separately from prescription products. Dr. Charles C. Edwards, FDA commissioner, formed an outside advisory committee to consider what efficacy standards should be applied to over-the-counter products.

Clinical Guidelines Project. The FDA and representatives of the Pharmaceutical Manufacturers Association worked on the formulation of clinical guidelines to determine the kind of data that the government will require to prove the safety and efficacy of a given class of drugs.

Tolbutamide Relabeling. The FDA decided to require all manufacturers of tolbutamide and some similar agents used to treat diabetes mellitus to indicate on the drug label that diet and insulin therapy are preferable in treating the mild onset of diabetes mellitus. This action was based on the controversial University Group Diabetes Program Study.

Drug Registration Act. In 1971 the House of Representatives passed a drug bill that would require all drug firms to file with the FDA a list of all drugs they manufacture, together with copies of the drug labels. Information on products already registered or on new or discontinued drugs would be filed every six months. The measure is significant because the FDA now has no complete listing of drug products manufactured in the United States.

Drug Abuse Law Implementation. In 1971 the Justice Department's Bureau of Narcotics and Dangerous Drugs and pharmaceuticals manufacturers disagreed on the categories in which drugs should be placed under existing drug abuse control legislation. Amphetamines and two major non-amphetamine products used as stimulants—Ritalin and Preludin—were shifted to a tighter drug control classification.

Nelson Procurement Hearings. Sen. Gaylord Nelson's (D-Wis.) Small Business Subcommittee continued hearings on government drug purchasing policies. The sessions resulted in significantly shifting government purchases away from drugs on the FDA's "possibly effective" and "ineffective" lists and in some cases from brand-name products to their chemical equivalents, which are generally cheaper.

JEANNE F. ANDERSON
Editor, "Washington Drug & Device Letter"

Public Health

In the field of public health, several steps were taken during 1971 toward solving the problems of manpower shortage, rising costs, and getting health care services to the people.

Health Services. The federal government awarded $6.5 million to 66 health care groups throughout the United States for planning and development of Health Maintenance Organizations (HMO's). An HMO is an organized system that accepts the responsibility of providing comprehensive health care to a voluntarily enrolled group for a prepaid fee. Although no panacea for all health care troubles, the HMO concept promises dramatic improvements in getting health services to the people and offers hope for a check in skyrocketing costs. HMO's also provide preventive services and place the incentive on early diagnosis and treatment.

The Emergency Health Personnel Act—signed into law by President Nixon on Dec. 31, 1970—created the National Health Service Corps, enabling the secretary of health, education and welfare to assign Public Health Service workers to areas where personnel and services are inadequate. Although not designed to solve the entire shortage, the act provides an opportunity to demonstrate a viable method for alleviating some of the more acute problems of inner cities and rural areas.

Disease Control. The Center for Disease Control (CDC), charged with controlling communicable and vector-borne diseases, assisted in controlling some 300 epidemics or outbreaks in the United States alone during 1971. Among these were diphtheria in San Antonio, Texas; malaria (associated with illicit drug use) in California; staphylococcus food poisoning in Alabama; Venezuelan equine encephalitis in Texas; hepatitis in several states; hospital infections from contaminated intravenous fluid; rabies in skunks in Washington and Oregon; salmonellosis in Illinois; typhoid on a tourist ship; venereal disease among truck drivers in several states; and tuberculosis in Washington, D. C.

For a second year, CDC continued a nationwide drive to vaccinate children against rubella (German measles). From July 1, 1969, to June 30, 1971, about 30 million children between the ages of 1 and 13 were immunized throughout the United States.

Occupational Safety and Health. The National Institute for Occupational Safety and Health was established in 1971. The institute's activities are directed toward protecting and improving the health of the 80 million workers in the United States. Its scientists study the effects of dusts, chemicals, noise, and other occupational hazards, and develop and recommend standards for prevention and control of hazardous substances in places of work.

National Institute of Mental Health. In 1971 intensified federal action was taken to prevent and control alcoholism by creating the National Institute of Alcohol and Alcoholism as part of the National Institute of Mental Health (NIMH). The NIMH drug-abuse information campaign shifted its emphasis in 1971. Instead of merely giving out factual information about drug abuse, it attempted to give the public a more in-depth education on the subject in hopes of promoting understanding.

The NIMH support of community mental health centers continued, with particular emphasis on the possibility of the center's collaborating with the newly forming Health Maintenance Organizations. Other major NIMH concerns in 1971 were child mental health, mental health problems related to crime, delinquency, and law enforcement, and mental health problems associated with minority groups.

Family Planning. Late in 1970 the first federal legislation dealing exclusively with family planning services was passed. At the close of 1971, funds distributed through the National Center for Family Planning Services supported family planning projects with a capacity for serving 700,000 patients.

VERNON E. WILSON, M. D.
*Administrator, Health Services
and Mental Health Administration*

Respiratory Diseases

The year 1971 was marked by the relative absence of worldwide concern over epidemic respiratory disease. During 1969 and 1970 the appearance of Hong Kong influenza throughout the world had held the attention of all those interested in acute respiratory disease and increased the ever-present human misery exacted by these diseases.

Respiratory diseases, especially the acute viral ones, rank as the most common of the infectious diseases occurring throughout the entire world. When one translates this into lives and money, the toll is even more dramatic. During the 12-month period ending on June 30, 1967, over 201 million episodes of acute respiratory disease were reported in the United States. During the same period, over 57 million work days were lost, and 590 million days of restricted activity were also reported.

During 1971 influenza did occur throughout the world as well as in the United States, but the outbreaks were sporadic and self-limited. Of particular interest was the fact that type B influenza appeared to account for as many outbreaks as the new Hong Kong type.

Respiratory Disease and Air Pollution. It is worthy of repetition that individuals with chronic obstructive pulmonary diseases, such as emphysema, chronic bronchitis, and asthma, experience exacerbations when air pollution increases. Further, it is also known that in cities such as Los Angeles, where smog and air pollution are often critical problems, the number of deaths associated with emphysema has increased more than 1200% during the past decade. Although a direct cause-and-effect relationship between air pollution and the increase in emphysema deaths cannot be definitely proved, recent studies increasingly substantiate the relationship. All that remains to be done is to develop more sensitive techniques for establishing a direct relationship between irritants known to be present in the air and the effect of those irritants on the normal or partially compensated respiratory epithelium, or tissue.

Prevention of Respiratory Disease. Because of the literally hundreds of viral and bacterial agents known to produce respiratory diseases, the only rational approach to their control is to develop preventive measures. A dramatic case in point is the knowledge that even a partial reduction in air pollution would cause a dramatic decrease in the number of individuals who experience exacerbations of their chronic lung diseases.

However, the most common respiratory diseases are those caused by viruses. Studies published in 1971 provide some optimism for those concerned with the control of respiratory disease. Interferon is a substance naturally produced by the body in response to infection by a virus. The body can now be induced to produce interferon when specific man-made substances are injected. Although one particular man-made interferon-inducing substance has been shown to be toxic in laboratory animals, preliminary studies of this substance in human volunteers have produced some promising results. Because the number of volunteers was small, no final conclusions as to the efficacy of this interferon-producing substance can be made at this time. However, this research is important and could possibly lead to an effective method of producing interferon and thus treating at least some viral diseases.

The use of vaccines continues to be the only proven means of preventing respiratory diseases. In 1970 influenza vaccine was the only one known to be of any value in preventing viral respiratory disease in a civilian population. More recently, reports have been published that indicate that other respiratory viruses can be made to mutate in the laboratory. Some preliminary work in human volunteers has indicated that there is a possibility that these mutated viruses might serve as vaccine strains, thus opening the possibility of developing vaccines against other respiratory diseases.

In addition, work is also in progress to improve the present influenza vaccine by artificially combining "free living" influenza viruses so that the single resulting influenza virus may contain the protective properties of its two parents, laboratory and "free living." Although these reports are exciting, mankind is still left with a single respirovirus vaccine-influenza vaccine.

BERNARD PORTNOY, M. D.
University of Southern California

Surgery

Although there were no outstanding breakthroughs in surgery during 1971, important advances were made in a number of areas. Also noteworthy was the decrease in heart transplantation.

Organ Transplantation. Only six heart transplants were performed in the United States during the first six months of 1971. The original enthusiasm for heart transplants has waned, although several teams—notably those of Dr. Norman Shumway of Pasadena, Calif., and Dr. Richard Lower of Richmond, Va.—have persisted and have recorded a few outstanding long-term successes. One of Dr. Lower's patients was thriving more than three years after his heart transplant. The major kidney transplantation teams have continued to report ever-increasing long-term success rates. Presently, a patient receiving a transplanted kidney has a 50% chance of surviving more than three years.

Coronary Artery Surgery. Probably the greatest interest and effort in surgery in 1971 were focused on the surgical treatment of coronary artery disease. This problem, whether manifested by heart attacks, heart failure, or angina pectoris, is still the major cause of death in the United States.

In 1971 the overwhelming majority of operations to correct occluded, or blocked, coronary arteries were of the bypass type. The bypass operation consists of interposing a short length of vein (taken from the patient's leg) between the aorta and the coronary artery beyond the point where it is occluded. One, two, or even three such segments may be used in a single patient. The teams of Dr. Donald Effler at the Cleveland Clinic, Dr. W. Dudley Johnson and Dr. Derward Lepley in Milwaukee, and Dr. Frank Spencer at New York University have been the most active in this operation. Their reported results are remarkably similar: the operative mortality varies from 8% to 14%—a remarkable achievement considering that all of the patients have extremely serious heart disease.

The early follow-up results are also good, with about 75% of the patients totally free of symptoms after the operation. In one remarkable series, Dr. Rogue Pifarre and his colleagues in Maywood, Ill., performed the operation in eight patients during or

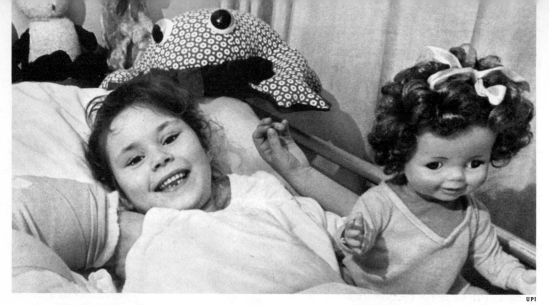

SURGEONS in Detroit saved 6-year-old Marcia Grimm's right arm when they reattached it during an operation in January. The child's arm had been severed in a snowblower accident.

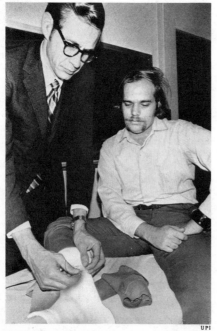

CARL BRIGHTON, Philadelphia orthopedic surgeon, achieved the first successful use of electric current to heal a non-union fracture.

immediately following a severe heart attack (myocardial infarction). Seven of the eight patients survived and were declared free of symptoms.

Gallstones. Gallstones have been a major medical problem of Western man for centuries, and there has been no recourse for patients with symptoms except removal of the gallbladder. Some 500,000 cholecystectomies are performed in the United States each year. The ongoing study of the health of a typical American community—that of Framingham, Mass.—has revealed that 10% of the men and 20% of the women between 55 and 64 years of age had gallstones. Dr. Franz Ingelfinger of Boston, in discussing this study, extrapolated from the data to conclude that there are about 15 million people with gallstones in the United States— a startling statistic, revealing a major national medical problem.

Most gallstones are cholesterol stones resulting from the precipitation of cholesterol microcrystals in the bile that has become concentrated and supersaturated in the gallbladder. The critical elements of the bile in stone formation are cholesterol, bile acids, and the phospholipid lecithin. Bile acids and lecithin help keep cholesterol in solution, not allowing it to precipitate.

Recent research has revealed that bile produced in the livers of patients with gallstones has a slight excess of cholesterol and that the other bile elements are not able to keep this cholesterol in solution. This is particularly true among the American Indians of the Southwest—the Apaches, Hopis, and Navajos—who have an extremely high incidence of gallstones. On the other hand, among Negroes, Japanese, and Chinese, in whom the incidence of gallstones is low, the ratio of bile acids to cholesterol is higher, and the cholesterol is prevented from precipitating. With these leads, researchers are at work to reduce the cholesterol level or to increase the bile acid level of patients with gallstones.

Operating Room Environment. Contrary to the general belief that operations are performed in virtually sterile immediate surroundings, recent bacteriological studies have recovered viable bacteria from nearly all "clean" wounds at the end of an operation. In the best surgical centers, the wound infection rate has been at least 1% and more often considerably higher.

Engineers have found that convection currents throughout the operating room circulate contaminated dust particles, which may carry bacteria swept up from the floor, walls, anesthetic machine or other pieces of equipment, or from the hair of auxiliary personnel who are not scrubbed and gowned. Efforts are being made to reduce convection currents and air turbulence within an operating room, and a number of groups have tried changing the air non-turbulently by means of the aerodynamic principle of laminar flow.

Because sterile conditions are required in the manufacture of certain space hardware, NASA engineers, notably Willis Whitfield, have perfected techniques for achieving true laminar airflow and virtually sterile working conditions. These techniques are being employed in operating rooms and some other critical hospital areas, such as delivery rooms, infant nurseries, and cardiac care units. Preliminary studies reveal that the laminar airflow principle is effective in providing greater air purity.

In an attempt to create even greater operating room sterility, British orthopedic surgeon John Charnley has created a separate small enclosure within the center of a standard operating room. This enclosure—the "Charnley greenhouse"—is provided with highly filtered air by a laminar-flow system, and only the patient and members of the operating team are allowed within it. Although it is small and uncomfortable for the operating team, the "Charnley greenhouse" has resulted in a reduction of wound infection from 10% to 1% in its year of use in that operating room.

Hyperalimentation. Providing adequate nutrition for certain surgical patients with serious complications, particularly those who are unable to take any calories by mouth because of severe gastrointestinal disturbance, is a major problem. Intravenous infusion of liquids to provide enough water, key elements, and vitamins to prevent dehydration and chemical imbalances can be used. But until recently clinicians have been unable to provide their patients with the necessary calories, and consequently the patients often have been unable to withstand stress or to heal properly and sometimes have developed cachexia and died.

In daily surgical practice, dextrose solutions of 5% and occasionally 10% are administered intravenously to provide minimal calories and to prevent chemical imbalance in the body. The administration of 10% dextrose and more concentrated solutions is very irritating to the veins in which they are given and often results in occlusion of the vein by inflammation and thrombosis. A solution to this problem is the insertion of a small-bore plastic catheter into a vein under the skin of the arm and threading it into one of the very large major veins within the thorax. In these large veins, the concentrated dextrose solution exiting from the small plastic catheter is rapidly diluted by the large volume of blood in the vein, and no inflammation or thrombosis occurs. The idea and its practice are not entirely new. Dr. Clarence Dennis of Brooklyn, N. Y., has been using this method for 25 years with good results for patients seriously ill with chronic ulcerative colitis, but until recently the method was not readily adopted by other surgeons.

An impetus to this method—hyperalimentation—was provided by the work of Dr. Stanley Dudrick and his colleagues at the University of Pennsylvania. In their technique, the intravenous catheter is placed via a large vein just under the clavicle (collarbone) into the larger superior vena cava within the thorax, and a sterile solution of 20% dextrose, 5% hydrolyzed protein, and essential vitamins and minerals is administered over a 24-hour period. This procedure provides 3,000 to 4,000 calories a day, as compared with 600 to 800 provided by usual intravenous infusions. The efficacy of this treatment in the management of certain patients has been proved, and the technique is also being used in newborns and other infants with certain congenital abnormalities.

IRVING F. ENQUIST, M. D.
Director of Surgery, Methodist Hospital of Brooklyn

Venereal Disease

Reported cases of primary and secondary syphilis in the United States increased greatly during the year ending June 30, 1971. There were 23,336 cases reported, representing an increase of 15.6% over the number reported the previous year. When the factor of underreporting is considered, it is estimated that 75,000 cases of syphilis occurred during fiscal 1971. Reported cases of congenital syphilis among infants under 1 year of age also increased—from 300 in fiscal 1970 to 397 in fiscal 1971, an increase of 32.3%. Reported total syphilis in all stages numbered 94,255 cases in fiscal 1971, compared with 87,934 cases during 1970.

Gonorrhea, which has been increasing steadily since 1962 and ranks first in incidence among all nationally reported communicable diseases, increased again in fiscal 1971, but at a slower rate than in previous years. There were 624,371 cases reported in fiscal 1971, an 8% increase over the number reported in 1970. Increases were reported in all races and age groups in both urban and rural areas. It is estimated that the actual incidence of gonorrhea is about 2 million cases per year.

Control Programs. Syphilis control activities included a broad surveillance program involving extensive blood testing among diverse groups. During the year ending June 30, 1971, there were 38 million blood specimens examined, of which positive blood tests and subsequent follow-up investigations resulted in approximately 10,000 case reports of infectious syphilis and 62,000 reports of syphilis in other stages. Early syphilis epidemiology during the year included the interviewing of all infectious cases and the field investigation of their sex contacts and other persons suspected of having syphilis. The contact-tracing activities resulted in an additional 4,500 cases of primary and secondary syphilis under diagnosis and treatment. In addition, approximately 18,300 sex contacts exposed to infectious syphilis but who showed no clinical signs of syphilis and whose blood tests were syphilis negative were administered preventive treatment to destroy any possible incubating syphilis.

Efforts to control gonorrhea were also intensified during the year. In addition to patient interviewing and contact investigation activities, gonorrhea culture screening programs were conducted. More than 300,000 women were tested, with the average positivity rate being 7.8%.

Education and Research. An intensified program of venereal disease education aimed at the general public and using all forms of mass media was being conducted throughout the United States, and programmed instruction books were developed for teachers and students in elementary and high school.

Research efforts centered on a continuing search for an immunizing agent for syphilis and for improvement in blood tests for syphilis. In gonorrhea research, "Transgrow," a new medium for the transportation of culture specimens from doctors' offices to laboratories, was developed, and the search for an effective blood test continued.

WILLIAM J. BROWN, M. D.
Chief, Venereal Disease Branch
U. S. Public Health Service

MEIR, Golda. See BIOGRAPHY.
MERCHANT MARINE. See TRANSPORTATION.

Ice grotto formed along Chicago's Lake Michigan shore-line in February when winds sprayed waves over trees.

meteorology

Monitoring of adverse weather and attempts to modify it continued to occupy the attention of meteorologists in 1971. Activities ranged from attempts to reduce the strength of hurricanes to the use of satellites in flood prediction. The World Meteorological Organization of the United Nations met in Geneva in April. It arranged for speedier communications in the World Weather Watch network, and approved plans for the Global Atmospheric Research Program to be initiated in 1974. By the end of 1971, 22 nations had pledged participation in the program.

Hurricane Study. In observing the elusive behavior of tropical storms, theoretical considerations led scientists to conclude that hurricane winds can be maintained only if the ocean surface is warmer than 82° F (28° C). The warmer the water, the stronger are the winds, their energy being derived from the latent heat of condensation. Two hypotheses have been advanced concerning formation of the initial hurricane vortex, one suggesting that eddies are formed by airflow over islands and peninsulas, and the other that such eddies are produced by outbreaks of polar air reaching low latitudes. Hurricanes appear to interact with other vortices present in the atmosphere at the same time, the combined action determining the storm's direction.

Weather Modification and Cloud Physics. Improved theoretical models of hurricanes led to new suggestions as to the sites at which modification attempts would be most effective. In the late summer, attempts were made to modify Hurricane Ginger while it was far offshore, and clouds in the storm's spiral bands were seeded for two days. Some weakening of the hurricane seemed to result, but analyses of the data are not yet complete. Cloud seeding was also used by the state of Florida and the National Oceanographic and Atmospheric Agency in an attempt to break a long drought in Florida, but although some success was recorded the drought actually ended by natural means.

Lack of understanding of most cloud systems has thus far kept rain-making efforts from regular success. One of the world's leading cloud physicists, J. B. Mason, who is director general of the British Meteorological Office, stated at the 15th General Assembly of the International Union of Geodesy and Geophysics in Moscow that vertical motions in the atmosphere are far more important in rain processes than are the microphysical conditions that man can influence in clouds. This is corroborated by studies showing that warm clouds produce rain only if their liquid water content is high enough to sustain the coalescence of small drops, the appropriate level of liquid water content being maintained by dynamic processes in the atmosphere.

Because of the difficulty of observing small-scale processes in actual clouds, much effort has been devoted to the duplication of these processes in the laboratory. Thus it was found that after two droplets several millimeters in diameter collided, the drops remained separate rather than coalescing. Instead a temporary bridge formed between the drops, and two to ten very small droplets were ejected from this bridge. Similarly, when moderate-sized drops froze, they ejected a small cloud of microdroplets about 1/100 to 1/1000 the diameter of the original drop. If the same phenomenon occurs inside a thundercloud, it might contribute to the separation of charges in the cloud. In turn, charges of several hundred volts per centimeter, as observed in mature thunderstorms, will speed the growth rates of cloud drops and hailstones by a factor of ten.

Man's Influence on Climate. Debate continued on the effect of man-made pollutants on the earth's climate. Evidence had been cited that atmospheric turbidity increased markedly in the 1960's, but a reevaluation of solar radiation records showed that the disturbances in fact were produced by volcanic eruptions and that by 1971 solar radiation values had returned to their earlier level. The long-range cooling or heating effects of atmospheric particles have also been questioned, since the length of time that the particles remain is limited to days, because of rather efficient atmospheric self-cleaning. Above 25 miles (40 km), most of the dust in the atmosphere is actually cosmic debris.

However, Soviet scientist M. I. Budyko deduced from his calculations of atmospheric heat balance that present meteorological conditions constitute a very unstable equilibrium and could be upset by relatively small changes in energy reception or reflection. Heat produced by industrial processes and air conditioning could become substantial factors in the earth's heat balance, if it continues to be accelerated at the present rate.

(Continued on page 456)

THE WEATHER IN 1971

An unusual number of tropical storms lashed populated areas in 1971, causing many deaths and much destruction. A summary of the year's weather highlights is given below.

Winter. The most violent storm in 25 years hit western and southwestern Europe at the end of December 1970, and many thousands of motorists were trapped in France by the snow. Cold waves that were detrimental to crops hit Spain, Portugal, and Israel, while 140 persons were killed by cold in India. However, the greatest scourge around the world during the winter season was flooding. Australia, Colombia, Indonesia, the Philippines, and Thailand were all struck by floods that caused fatalities. In Rio de Janeiro alone, the worst storm in that city's history occurred in late February, producing a rainfall of 14 inches (35.6 cm) and causing about 100 deaths. About 90% of western Malaysia suffered from flooding in early January, and the Zambézia subprovince in Mozambique was ravaged by a tropical storm in late January and early February that claimed an estimated 1,000 victims.

In the United States, blizzards and ice storms plagued areas from the Great Plains to the Great Lakes, and record amounts of snow fell in the northeastern states. Precipitation was also heavy in a belt from Missouri to Washington and Oregon, with an accumulation of more than 200 inches (500 cm) of snow in the Cascade Range. The entire area northeast of a line extending from South Carolina to Idaho was colder than average for that time of year. In mid-March the winter season ended violently with a rash of tornadoes in southern states. The storms claimed nearly 100 lives, injured more than 580 persons, and caused property damage in excess of $10 million in Louisiana and Mississippi.

Spring. A record snowfall of 8 inches (20 cm) blanketed Rome, Italy, in March—the greatest amount of snow on the ground there so late in the season in 175 years. Heavy precipitation caused avalanches in northern Italy, while on March 19 an avalanche in the Peruvian Andes Mountains—possibly touched off by an earthquake—caused between 400 and 600 deaths near Chungar. Floods hit Rio de Janeiro again, as well as affecting areas in Angola, Argentina, Iran, Iraq, Israel, Jordan, southern Rumania, El Salvador, and Turkey. Major tropical storms caused casualties in the Philippines and in East Pakistan, which had not yet recovered from the devastating floods of November 1970. In contrast, the village of Cherrapunji, India—traditionally one of the rainiest places in the world—had the driest May since 1854, with only 11 inches (27 cm) instead of the average 67 inches (170 cm) of rainfall. In northeastern Brazil, drought drove starving peasants into towns in search of food, and the Brazilian government placed half a million people on relief work rolls.

In the United States, the Sierra Nevada Range and Wyoming were particularly wet in the spring, but the southwestern states and Florida suffered from drought. In Texas, drought cut the wheat crop by 50%, and the worst dry spell in 15 years caused several dust storms reminiscent of the 1930's. In Florida, the Everglades were hard hit by drought, and 650,000 acres (263,000 hectares) were scorched by fires. Cloud seeding was attempted to relieve the situation, but despite some successes it failed to stem the worst drought in 60 years. By the end of the spring, tornadoes had claimed twice as many lives in the United States as in all of 1970.

Summer. In India, the monsoon season broke out early, with copious rain in the western and northern parts of the peninsula. As the season progressed, rainfall caused many difficulties. Bombay had its heaviest rain of the century, with 15.5 inches (39.4 cm) in 13 hours. In Nepal, monsoon-induced floods killed hundreds of people. In the Indian state of Bihar, 13 million people were affected by floods, and in western Bengal, 45,000 people had to take to their roofs. The Indian government estimated damages at around $300 million. In neighboring East Pakistan, 13,000 villages and 4,000 square miles (over 10,000 sq km) were flooded in August. Thailand and Laos also suffered heavily.

Typhoons also plagued the Far East. North Vietnam was struck by typhoons Harriet and Kim, which caused heavy damages, and later floods were the worst since 1945. Typhoons Rose and Trix caused havoc and death in Hong Kong and Japan, respectively.

In the meantime, heavy rains produced devastating floods in the Putumayo and Caqueta River basins of southwestern Colombia; in the state of Apure, Venezuela; in Siberia; and in the Gamtoos River Valley of South Africa. Rains in Navarre, Spain, caused heavy crop losses, and hailstorms hit the vineyards of the Dordogne, France. The summer also saw severe dry spells in other parts of the world. Iraq had its worst drought in 25 years, and a drought in Kenya materially reduced that country's important tea crops. A drought in Italy caused a rash of brush fires, while the Tiber River in Rome ran dry.

Summer in the United States was very close to average—a bit warmer than average west of the Rocky Mountains, and slightly cooler in the east. Rainfall was very spotty and resulted mostly from thunderstorms. In Texas, the drought continued into July, but in the last part of the summer season it was broken by rain from tropical disturbances.

Autumn. On balance, the fall was warmer than average in the United States. Except in the Western and mountain states, Indian summer lingered on far into December, with many daily temperatures approaching or breaking previous record values. Precipitation was heavy on the Great Plains, and snow was abundant in the Cascade Range and the higher elevations of the Rocky Mountains. Salt Lake City, Utah, had 17 inches of snowfall in October—the snowiest October on record. A severe snowstorm in Utah and Wyoming at the end of October caused fatalities and stranded thousands of motorists on impassable roads.

On a worldwide basis, the autumn season was characterized by an unusual number of tropical storms. In North Atlantic and Caribbean waters as many as three storms roamed around simultaneously. Tropical storm Laura, the last of the lot of 12, occurred in the middle of November. Laura hit Cuba and Honduras hard, and its high winds and excessive rains flooded farms and left thousands homeless.

Elsewhere, typhoon Faye hit Luzon in the Philippines in October, killing scores and causing damage amounting to more than $30 million. Typhoon Hester struck Quang Ngai province of South Vietnam, halting war action, causing casualties among U. S. troops and Vietnamese citizens, and leaving many of them homeless. At the end of October and early in November, a double cyclonic strike across the Bay of Bengal devastated the Indian state of Orissa, which has a flat, low coast. Millions of homes were destroyed, and damage may have reached $400 million. Fatalities were estimated to be in excess of 10,000; most of the victims were in refugee camps for East Pakistanis.

Severe floods also occurred in the Indian state of Uttar Pradesh and in Spain, Venice, and East Java. Drought plagued Kenya, where wildlife was endangered. The Rhine River was at its lowest level in 150 years because of lack of rain. In the southwestern United States, air stagnation on November 3 led to severe smog in Birmingham, Ala. The air pollution measurements reached a record value of 800 micrograms per cubic meter, and a sharp reduction in industrial activities was required to help abate the danger.

H. E. LANDSBERG

WIDE WORLD

RESIDENT of Inverness, Miss., examines wreckage of car after tornado leveled most of town on February 22. Tornadoes pose a perennial threat in southeastern states.

(*Continued from page 454*)

Remote Sensing Techniques. Satellites and airborne instruments have made possible a variety of observations of great potential practical value. For example, the U. S. Applications Technology Satellite 1 launched in 1966 has collected river and rainfall measurements from automated stations for analysis, and weather satellites regularly yield information on the extent of snow covers. In flood-prone areas such as the upper Mississippi River valley, this information has been supplemented by low-flying aircraft, which are instrumented to sense the gamma radiation emanating from the earth's surface. The intensity of the radiation can be interpreted in terms of the water equivalent of the snow—the more snow there is, the less gamma radiation is recorded. Thus the flood potential of a rivershed can be estimated at an early stage in spring. In the case of air pollution, concentrations in the atmosphere may come under continuous satellite surveillance in the future. Spectrometers carried by balloon have already measured such concentrations by measuring the intensity of the spectrum of a particular gas.

Basic meteorological research also benefits from remote sensing techniques. Accumulated data from satellite-borne infrared sensors have enabled Soviet scientists to estimate the distribution and total mass of water vapor in the atmosphere—a staggering 23 trillion gallons. In another development, a research team at the University of Wisconsin summarized five years of satellite data to arrive at a new energy "budget" for the earth as a whole. Such information is of fundamental importance for understanding atmospheric circulation. According to the study, the earth reflects about 30% of incoming radiation back into space, and the earth's own dark radiation causes a heat loss of 1.25 British Thermal Units per square foot (0.34 calorie per square centimeter) per minute. The south polar region annually loses the most heat—about 50% more than the northern polar area—while the greatest heat gains are in the tropics.

Lightning. Satellite observations show that lightning is much more common over land than sea. Of 7,000 nighttime lightning strokes observed between latitudes 35° N and 35° S, where most thunderstorms occur, ten times as many strokes took place on land. Interesting advances were also made in the artificial triggering of lightning. Strokes occur when electrical fields build up to about 500,000 volts in a cloud, but it was found that firing a small rocket carrying steel balls into a thundercloud causes discharges at a field intensity of less than 50,000 volts. Laboratory experiments have shown that lasers can also produce ionized channels that can be used to guide discharges in a strong electrical field.

Clear Air Turbulence (CAT). CAT, discovered when aircraft began operating at high altitudes, has been shown to form along lines separating warm and cold air masses. Winds moving at different speeds in the masses cause breaking waves to form at the interface—hence the turbulent motion. CAT plays a more important role than hitherto assumed in energy dissipation in the atmosphere, accounting for about 20% of the energy. Sensitive radar systems are now capable of detecting CAT at distances of up to 10 miles (16 km).

H. E. LANDSBERG
University of Maryland

MEXICAN AMERICANS

Many Mexican Americans hoped that 1971 would indeed be the year of the Chicano (a name derived from Nahuatl pronunciation of *Mexicano* and used to designate a Mexican American—a U. S. citizen of Mexican heritage or a Mexican living in the United States). But the overall situation for Chicanos remained relatively unchanged, despite such gains as the appointments of Henry Ramirez as chairman of the beleaguered Cabinet Committee on Opportunities for Spanish Speaking People, Raymond Tellez as a member of the Commission on Equal Employment Opportunity, and Romana Bañuelos as treasurer of the United States. Another gain came in the appointment of Frank Angel, Jr., as president of New Mexico Highlands University.

Political and Economic Status. Although Chicano leaders spoke optimistically about 1971, they knew that the gains they envisioned would be achieved only at great cost and sacrifice. The electoral process had disillusioned them in 1970, for the November elections of that year resulted in no appreciable political gains for Chicanos, save a few local offices here and there in predominantly Mexican American communities. In California, the Chicano gubernatorial candidate, Ricardo Romo, polled little better than 1% of the total California vote, thus dashing the hope of a viable Raza Unida party that would unite Chicano voters throughout the Chicano Southwest, Midwest, and Northwest. Chicanos, variously estimated to number between 5 and 10 million, are still represented by only five members in the U. S. Congress—Sen. Joseph M. Montoya and Rep. Manuel Lujan, Jr. (N. Mex.); Rep. Edward R. Roybal (Calif.); and Reps. Eligio de la Garza and Henry B. Gonzalez (Texas).

During the year Chicano unemployment rose to 12%, more than twice the national average, aggravating U. S.–Mexico border problems over the "twin plant" program—a plan under which U. S.-subsidized plants in Mexico produce goods for U. S. consumption. The program is under fire from the AFL-CIO, which maintains that the resulting "Hong Kong" economy is detrimental to Anglo (a term generally implying "English-speaking") and Chicano labor alike.

Activism. Young Chicanos, aware of the effectiveness of confrontation tactics in publicizing *la raza* ("the race"; fully interpreted as "the race of Montezuma's children"), have taken to the streets. Regrettably, the August 1970 antiwar rally organized in East Los Angeles by the National Chicano Moratorium Committee resulted in the death of a Mexican-American newspaperman, Ruben Salazar, who was killed by a tear-gas projectile fired by sheriff's deputies. Consequently, the leaders of the Chicano Moratorium rally in East Los Angeles on Jan. 31, 1971, were cautious in their plans, but violence erupted when a young Chicano was felled by a deputy's bullet.

The tragedy created a mood that was to pervade most Chicano activities throughout the year. At every turn, Chicanos seemed thwarted in their efforts to improve the quality of their lives. Attempts to desegregate public schools in Dallas, Houston, and Corpus Christi resulted in Anglo administrators reclassifying Chicanos as "white" and using them to integrate black schools. In December, 34 Chicano students were arrested at the University of Texas at El Paso as a result of a demonstration protesting the university's handling of Chicano problems.

Chicanos view the Nixon administration as unresponsive, and Chicano elected officials are discouraged by the prospects for Chicanos. Most ultramilitant Chicanos are ready to shun the U. S. two-party system in favor of the Raza Unida party or the Chicano Revolutionary party. But few Chicano leaders are optimistic about a third-party movement, since Chicanos by and large vote traditionally and overwhelmingly Democratic. Nevertheless, in Texas' Rio Grande Valley the Raza Unida party has made significant inroads in places such as Crystal City, where José Angel Gutiérrez, leader of the party in Texas, was elected president of the school board. At a conference held in Washington, D. C., in the fall, Chicano leaders organized a Spanish Speaking Coalition in an attempt to make their voices heard in the 1972 elections.

PHILIP D. ORTEGO
University of Texas at El Paso

MILITANT Chicanos angrily denounced Governor Reagan at rally in Sacramento on August 7. Demonstrators marched 600 miles from southern California to state capital to protest bias against Mexican Americans.

UPI

MEXICO

The year 1971 was one of consolidation and planning by the new administration of President Luís Echeverría, who had taken office Dec. 1, 1970. As a result, a general air of uncertainty prevailed, which was reflected in a slight slowdown in the Mexican economy. There were instances of political subversion and student violence, although nothing on the scale of the university strikes and bloodshed of 1968. There also was talk of new political alignments, but no action was taken to indicate any early threat to Mexico's entrenched majority party.

Capture of Guerrillas. The most spectacular event of the year was the seizure by the government in March of 19 members of an organization known as the Revolutionary Action Movement (MAR). The prisoners, all Mexicans, confessed to having received military-political training in North Korea. Further investigation revealed a connection between the MAR and the Patrice Lumumba University in Moscow. The Mexican government charged that the MAR intended to use force to set up a Communist regime in Mexico. The USSR was informed that five Soviet diplomats in Mexico were personae non gratae, and they quickly left the country.

Many important groups and individuals rallied to the support of Mexican nationalism in this rebuke to the USSR. On the other hand, opposition groups in Mexico tended to find in the affair signs of conservative leanings in the new administration.

Outbreaks of Violence. Intermittently simmering disputes and physical clashes between rightist and leftist students and their allies precipitated a political crisis. On June 10, as several thousand university students demonstrated in the streets of

Mexico City against the government and in favor of leftist goals, they were attacked by an antileftist group known as the Falcons. At least eight students were killed, although there were rumors that the death toll was larger and that many bodies had been hidden. Journalists claimed to have been beaten by the Falcons while the police stood by, refusing to interfere with the attack. The most serious charge, widely aired in the press, was that the Falcons were trained and supported by conservative elements in the government and in the ruling Institutional Revolutionary party (PRI) and that they were directed from police headquarters in the Federal District.

President Echeverría ordered an investigation and forced the resignations of the chief executive of the Federal District, Mayor Alfonso Martínez Domínguez, and the district's police chief. The ouster of the mayor was especially noteworthy in that he was a former secretary-general of the PRI.

From March through June, a series of disturbances occurred in Monterrey in connection with the demand of the rector of the University of Nuevo León that the state government provide it with greater financial support. The dispute soon escalated into student violence. Federal education authorities finally helped force a compromise.

In June about a dozen persons were killed during street clashes in Durango, an underdeveloped state that had long been a center of disturbances. In October, while visiting Durango, Echeverría denounced the June demonstration there as aimed at damaging the prestige of the government.

Incidents of violence also continued in Mexico City's secondary schools, reportedly as part of a

The Economy. There was much talk of an economic slowdown, or "mini-recession," a rather common phenomenon at the beginning of a new administration in Mexico, and hardly surprising in view of the fact that the government had cut 1971 expenditures, partly to reduce the foreign debt and partly to help control inflation. Many economic indicators showed a slowing in the rate of growth. It was hoped, however, that the gross national product would climb by year's end to a level about 6% higher than that of 1970, a rate of growth not much lower than the average annual increase since 1950, although considerably below the boom years of 1968 and 1969.

Business complained frequently that sluggish sales of consumer goods were due largely to a luxury tax imposed at the end of 1970. Late in 1971 the government modified this tax and took other steps to stimulate the economy. In October it announced a 20% increase in public expenditures for 1972. It also removed a 29% export tax on silver and ordered that year-end bonuses be paid to government workers in November rather than December.

On the foreign-trade front, exports in the first 10 months of 1971 were 3.1% higher than in the same period in 1970, with increases reported in sales of alcoholic drinks and tobacco (26%), chemical products (5%), manufactured articles (35.8%), and machinery, machine tools, and electrical materials

WIDE WORLD

Fire and an explosion ripped through famed Caliente race track in Tijuana on August 5. Grandstand and clubhouse were destroyed, but there were no injuries.

struggle between competing elements of the PRI. In September a sensation was created by the kidnapping of the director of airports, Julio Hirschfeld, an act interpreted as political. In November the rector of the University of Guerrero was kidnapped by guerrillas, giving rise to more rumors of a conspiracy to disrupt Mexican institutions.

At the massive annual celebration of the Revolution of 1910, on November 20, the minister of government condemned terrorism as counterrevolutionary. Throughout the year members of the MAR and other ostensibly revolutionary organizations were sentenced for acts of robbery and violence.

New Political Moves. President Echeverría took a number of actions in 1971 that seemed to betoken a possible opening up of the political system, although there was disagreement as to his true intentions. He traveled widely and seemed to welcome critical comment. In the fall he sent to the Congress a bill to reduce the qualifying age for members of the Chamber of Deputies from 25 to 21, and for senators, from 35 to 30. The bill also provided for an increase in minority-party representation. Government supporters hailed these proposals as an advance for democracy.

Meanwhile, some members of the nonviolent left met in November to discuss the possibility of creating a new political party. Present at the meetings were the well-known writers Octavio Paz and Carlos Fuentes, the engineer Heberto Castillo, and Demetrio Vallejo, a radical union leader who had once been jailed for several years as a danger to the state. Some official harassment of Vallejo in 1971 bolstered his image as a martyr to repressive policies.

--------- **MEXICO · Information Highlights** ---------

Official Name: United Mexican States.
Area: 761,602 square miles (1,972,546 sq km).
Population (1970 est.): 50,670,000. *Density,* 65 per square mile (25 per sq km). *Annual rate of increase,* 3.4%.
Chief Cities (1969 est.): Mexico City, the capital, 3,483,649; Guadalajara, 1,352,109; Monterrey, 1,011,887; Ciudad Juarez, 522,032.
Government: *Head of state,* Luís Echeverría Álvarez, president (took office Dec. 1, 1970). *Head of government,* Luís Echeverría Alvarez. *Legislature*—Congress: Senate, 60 members; Chamber of Deputies, 213 members. *Major political parties*—Institutional Revolutionary party (PRI); National Action party (PAN).
Languages: Spanish (official).
Education: *Literacy rate* (1971), 70% of population. *Expenditure on education* (1968), 2.5% of gross national product. *School enrollment* (1968)—primary, 8,539,462; secondary, 1,315,348; technical/vocational, 170,768; university/higher, 192,472.
Finances (1970 est.): *Revenues,* $2,300,000,000; *expenditures,* $2,300,000,000; *monetary unit,* peso (12.50 pesos equal U. S.$1, Dec. 30, 1971).
Gross National Product (1969): $29,400,000,000.
National Income (1968): $24,160,000; *national income per person,* $511.
Economic Indexes: *Industrial production* (1969), 167 (1963= 100); *agricultural production* (1969), 127 (1963=100); *consumer price index* (1970), 126 (1963=100).
Manufacturing (metric tons, 1969): Cement, 6,787,000; residual fuel oil, 6,515,000; crude steel, 3,470,000; sugar, 2,564,000; pig iron and ferroalloys, 2,104,000; beer, 13,-650,000 hectoliters.
Crops (metric tons, 1969 crop year): Sugarcane (1968–69), 30,000,000; wheat, 2,300,000; sorghum (1968), 1,700,000; oranges and tangerines (1968), 892,000; cotton lint, 529,-000.
Minerals (metric tons, 1969): Crude petroleum, 21,415,000; salt, 3,307,000; iron ore, 2,097,000; silver, 1,334.5 (ranks 1st among world producers).
Foreign Trade (1970): *Exports,* $1,373,000,000 (chief exports —cotton, $123,860,000; sugar, $97,598,000; coffee, $86,-149,000; shrimps, $63,014,000). *Imports,* $ 2,461,000,000 (chief imports (1968)—nonelectrical machinery, $504,164,-000; transport equipment, $325,704,000; chemicals, $279,-948,000; electric machinery and appliances, $224,483,000). *Chief trading partners* (1968)—United States (took 58% of exports, supplied 63% of imports); Japan (6%—4%).
Tourism: *Receipts* (1970), $575,000,000.
Transportation: *Roads* (1970), 42,845 miles (68,950 km); *motor vehicles* (1969), 1,670,500 (automobiles, 1,133,100); *railroads* (1970), 14,280 miles (22,981 km); *merchant fleet* (1970), 381,000 gross registered tons; *national airline,* Aeronaves de México, Mexicana Airlines; *principal airport,* Mexico City.
Communications: *Telephones* (1970), 1,372,702; *television stations* (1968), 60; *television sets* (1969), 2,553,000; *radios* (1969), 12,990,000; *newspapers* (1965), 220 (daily circulation, 4,763,000).

(27.8%). Agricultural exports continued to provide the bulk of the nation's export earnings. Imports during this period were 3.5% below those of the first 10 months of 1970.

As usual, the trade deficit in commodity accounts was made up by profits to Mexico from border and tourist transactions. It was expected that the nation would earn some $1.7 billion from about 2.8 million foreign visitors in 1971. Echeverría pointed out in a message of September 1 that tourism and border transactions in 1970 had provided Mexico with 10% more in foreign exchange than it derived from all of its commodity exports.

Efforts to slow inflation provoked much economic and political debate. The Bank of Mexico reported a 4.2% rise in prices in the first 7 months of 1971, compared with a 6.5% rise during the comparable period in 1970.

Government Planning. The Echeverría administration took several steps to increase the effectiveness of government. A National Tripartite Commission was created to coordinate the views of government, labor, and business while studying problems of national development. In October the government introduced legislation to modernize the government's administrative structures. A new Mexican Institute of Foreign Trade was attempting to stimulate exports, and an Industrial Promotion Law to aid industry and tighten quality standards was being studied.

The national budget for 1971 was originally set at 79.7 billion pesos, up 10.3% over 1970. It included 30.8 billion for the executive branch for direct expenditures, and 48.9 billion for the decentralized agencies. Of the direct expenditures, al-most 40% was for economic development, with a similar amount allocated for education, health, and welfare.

A variety of moves was made in the continuing effort to "Mexicanize" enterprises—that is, to establish Mexican control of them through majority ownership. In August the government bought 51% of the famous Cananea mining company from a U. S. corporation, announcing that this was the last important mining company in Mexico that had not been controlled by Mexican capital.

International Relations. Aside from the ouster of the Russian diplomats in March, the most dramatic development in the sphere of Mexican foreign relations in 1971 was the nation's reaction to President Nixon's economic measures of August, and especially to the 10% surtax imposed upon Mexican exports to the United States. Mexican spokesmen made strong statements disagreeing with the U. S. moves but did not threaten retaliation. They quickly announced that the U. S. President's aim of altering exchange relations between the dollar and foreign currencies would not be achieved in Mexico. In fact, the peso maintained a firm relationship with the dollar through the rest of 1971.

Other developments included the signing of a new bilateral air treaty with Cuba that allowed Cubana Airlines to continue its flights to Mexico. The United States and Mexico established a bilateral commission to try to solve the problem of the salinity of Colorado River water flowing into Mexico. In pursuance of its drive for exports, Mexico sent trade missions to many other countries.

ROBERT JONES SHAFER, *Syracuse University*

WORKERS in Puebla parade through city's streets during May Day celebrations. Banner in foreground commemorates 85th anniversary of Haymarket Square riots in Chicago, in which police and workers clashed violently.

KEYSTONE

TUNNEL DISASTER near Port Huron, Mich., took the lives of 21 construction workers in December. An underground natural gas explosion occurred while the men were working on a section of the new water tunnel under Lake Huron between Port Huron and Detroit.

UPI

MICHIGAN

School desegregation and problems of state finance claimed major attention in Michigan during 1971, with a school busing program leading to violence in Pontiac. The state granted 18-year-olds most of the rights of adulthood and adopted a liberalized divorce law.

Legislation. To meet the money crisis, the Legislature approved tax increases, effective August 1. The state income tax rates became 3.9% for individuals (up from 2.6%), 7.8% for corporations (up from 5.6%), and 9.7% for financial institutions (up from 7%). The $250 million gained by the higher rates was allocated to increased welfare case loads, higher medicaid payments, public education, and pay increases for state employees.

Legislation lowering the age of majority from 21 to 18 became effective on Jan. 1, 1972. The new law allows 18-year-olds to make legal contracts and take action in the courts, marry without parental consent, buy and drink alcoholic beverages, draw up wills, and exercise most of the other prerogatives of adulthood. The age of 21 was set as the minimum for admission to the bar and for running for the Legislature.

On August 27 the state supreme court ruled that students of voting age can register and vote in college towns in Michigan rather than in their hometowns. The ruling was made in a suit filed against the Ann Arbor city clerk by eight University of Michigan students. However, the effect of the student vote in local elections in November was inconclusive, despite heavy registration.

The new state divorce law, also effective on Jan. 1, 1972, established only one ground for divorce—that the marriage relationship had broken down beyond repair. The so-called "no fault" law—requiring only that one partner file a complaint in court alleging, without explanation, that the marriage is destroyed—was both hailed and opposed as one of the most liberal in the nation. Lawyers warned that the new law, although simple on its face, has a multitude of implications to be worked out over a period of years in court actions.

A newly adopted prisoner furlough program allows inmates to apply, within four months of parole or release, for leaves of two to five days to visit their homes. About one third of the state's 9,100 prisoners were eligible for such visits.

School Busing Program. Ten school buses were destroyed by explosives in Pontiac, 25 miles northwest of Detroit, on August 30—eight days before classes were to open under a busing program ordered by a federal court. Six persons were accused on September 10 of conspiracy to bomb the buses. The program, involving 8,300 of the district's 24,000 children, was ordered after a federal judge found evidence of school practices designed to "perpetu-

---
MICHIGAN • Information Highlights

Area: 58,216 square miles (150,779 sq km).

Population (1970 census): 8,875,083. *Density:* 154 per sq mi.

Chief Cities (1970 census): Lansing, the capital, 131,546; Detroit, 1,512,893; Grand Rapids, 197,649; Flint, 193,317; Warren, 179,260; Dearborn, 104,199; Livonia, 110,109.

Government (1971): *Chief Officers*—governor, William G. Milliken (R); lt. gov., James H. Brickley (R); secy. of state, Richard H. Austin (D); atty. gen., Frank J. Kelley (D); supt. of public instruction, John W. Porter; chief justice, Thomas M. Kavanagh. *Legislature*—Senate, 38 members (19 Democrats, 19 Republicans); House of Representatives, 110 members (57 D, 52 R., 1 vac.).

Education (1970–71): *Enrollment*—public elementary schools, 1,228,916 pupils; 41,744 teachers; public secondary, 951,-783 pupils; 51,543 teachers; nonpublic schools (1968–69), 342,995 students. *Public school expenditures* (1970–71), $1,715,900,000 ($858 per pupil). *Average teacher's salary,* $10,647.

State Finances (fiscal year 1970): *Revenues,* $4,131,546,000 (4% general sales tax and gross receipts taxes, $828,491,-000; motor fuel tax, $273,735,000; federal funds, $718,-611,000). *Expenditures,* $3,932,246,000 (education, $1,-592,488,000; health, welfare, and safety, $549,370,000; highways, $261,225,000). *State debt,* $958,461,000 (June 30, 1970).

Personal Income (1970): $35,705,000,000; per capita, $4,043.

Public Assistance (1970): $583,844,000. *Average monthly payments* (Dec. 1970)—old-age assistance, $77.30; aid to families with dependent children, $211.60.

Labor Force: *Nonagricultural wage and salary earners* (June 1971), 3,003,200. *Average annual employment* (1969)—manufacturing, 1,170,000; trade, 583,000; government, 520,000; services, 400,000. *Insured unemployed* (Oct. 1971)—84,500 (3.6%).

Manufacturing (1967): *Value added by manufacture,* $17,241,-600,000; Transportation equipment, $5,805,800,000; nonelectrical machinery, $2,750,400,000; fabricated metal products, $1,987,700,000; primary metal industries, $1,-481,700,000; chemicals and allied products, $1,039,600,-000; food and kindred products, $926,000,000.

Agriculture (1970): *Cash farm income,* $961,100,000 (livestock, $482,568,000; crops, $412,834,000; government payments, $65,698,000). *Chief crops* (1970)—Corn, 114,076,000 bushels; wheat, 22,035,000 bushels; dry beans; 6,269,000 cwt. (ranks 1st among the states); hay, 3,260,000 tons.

Mining (1969): *Production value,* $668,247,000 (ranks 9th among the states). *Chief minerals* (tons)—Sand and gravel, 58,092,000; iron ore, 14,058,000; copper, 75,226.

Fisheries (1970): *Commercial catch,* 18,900,000 pounds ($2,-600,000). *Leading species by value* (1967), Chubs, $823,-271; lake herring, $317,200; alewives, $160,440.

Transportation: *Roads* (1969), 114,562 miles (184,365 km); *motor vehicles* (1969), 4,488,000; *railroads* (1968), 6,303 miles (10,143 km); *airports* (1969), 126.

Communications: *Telephones* (1971), 5,134,700; *television stations* (1969). 19; *radio stations* (1969), 196 *newspapers,* (1969), 55 (daily circulation, 2,415,000).

461

ate segregation." The decision was upheld by a federal court of appeals, and the U. S. Supreme Court declined to consider further appeal. Resistance to the busing program was organized by the new National Action Group, which staged demonstrations including a successful effort to force closing for one day of General Motors plants in Pontiac.

The National Action Group, which originated in Pontiac, gained support as a result of a decision by a federal judge in a case that had statewide implications, although directly concerning Detroit. The decision found both the state education department and the Detroit school board guilty of practices calculated to foster segregation and required that both act to correct the condition. The decision did not mention means of remedy but left open the possibility of busing across district lines, a policy advocated by some Detroit residents.

The possibility of cross-busing between Detroit and suburban school districts aroused controversy throughout the metropolitan area. The Legislature reacted by adopting a resolution calling for a national constitutional convention to ban such busing. The state moved to appeal the decision.

School Tax Suits. Gov. William G. Milliken and state Atty. Gen. Frank J. Kelley joined in filing suit against three affluent Michigan school districts, challenging the state's traditional means of supporting education largely through local property taxes. The suit was modeled after a California action that resulted in the property tax being declared unconstitutional in that state.

Discrimination in Hamtramck. On November 23 a federal judge ruled that Hamtramck, a city entirely surrounded by Detroit, has used federal urban renewal and state highway programs to drive Negroes from the city by razing their homes for public improvements. He ordered a construction program to make housing available for low-income families.

CHARLES W. THEISEN, *The Detroit "News"*

MICROBIOLOGY

In 1971 microbiologists studied the microorganisms that cause disease in man, animals, and plants with the hope of bringing them under control and also investigated the beneficial roles of microorganisms in the environment and industry.

Medical Bacteriology and Virology. Although progress has been made in the control and treatment of many microbial-caused human diseases, some, such as cholera and venereal disease, increased in 1971. In the first six months of 1971, 27 countries reported to the World Health Organization over 65,000 cases of cholera with 10,600 deaths. Most of the cases occurred in Pakistan.

Gonorrhea and syphilis, the two major venereal diseases, have reached "epidemic proportions" in many parts of the world. In some countries, reported cases of gonorrhea increased in 1970 from 8% to 20%. In the United States where the rate of venereal disease is increasing, scientists at the Center for Disease Control (CDC) in Atlanta, Ga., have made some progress in experimental research on gonorrhea by succeeding in infecting male chimpanzees. In Poland scientists have tested in rabbits a new experimental vaccine against syphilis. (See also MEDICINE—*Venereal Disease.*)

Venezuelan equine encephalomyelitis (VEE) killed several thousand horses in South and Central America, Mexico, and the southern United States in 1971. Fortunately, an effective vaccine is available and was administered to over one million horses in the southern United States, thus preventing further outbreaks. The disease also affected 30 human beings.

A highly fatal virus-caused disease of hogs—African swine fever—reached the Western Hemisphere in 1971. Confined to Cuba, where over 25,000 diseased hogs were slaughtered, African swine fever is a very serious swine disease for which there is no known cure. (See also VETERINARY MEDICINE.)

Food Microbiology. In July 1971 after the death of a New York man who ate Bon Vivant canned vichysoisse soup contaminated with the botulism-producing bacteria *Clostridum botulinum*, the U. S. Food and Drug Administration ordered all Bon Vivant products withdrawn from the markets. Later in the year, there were several other reports of the possible contamination of some canned food products and these also were recalled.

Microbiological requirements for dehydrated space foods for astronauts stipulate a total plate count of less than 10,000 aerobic organisms (oxygen-living microorganisms) per gram and lower or zero figures for specific bacteria such as fecal coliforms, streptococci, staphylococci, and salmonellae. A 2-year report, published in 1971, showed that of the space foods tested, from 93% to 99% complied with the established requirements. Not meeting the standards were soup and gravy bases, spaghetti and meat sauce, ice cream cubes, and candy.

During the year microbiologists also discovered that the microorganisms responsible for sour dough French-type bread are not the usual bakers' yeast types, but rather different yeasts and bacteria that prefer an acidic environment.

Industrial Microbiology. Several industries use microorganisms to produce large quantities of chemicals, such as amino acids, citric acid, and vitamins for commerce. During 1971 progress was made in producing microbial enzymes for a variety of uses. Likewise, several companies built plants to produce proteins from microorganisms. Many single-cell proteins—SCP—have high nutritional value and are being used to enrich animal food.

Microbial Ecology. The significance of the activities of microorganisms in the ecological balances that exist in nature was increasingly recognized during 1971. Although it has long been thought that only a few specific bacteria (thiobacilli and certain other forms that can use light) oxidize elemental sulfur in the environment, recent studies have shown that many other microorganisms may also exhibit this ability. Some 30 species of the bacteria *Streptomyces,* which are widely distributed in the soil, were shown to oxidize sulfur.

It was also recognized that substances transformed in nature by microorganisms may become toxic or poisonous to other forms of life. Metallic mercury, a discarded byproduct of certain industries, does not remain inactive in the bottom deposits of rivers as once thought, but rather is converted by microorganisms into methyl (or dimethyl) mercury, a substance highly toxic to many higher forms of life.

Bacteriological Warfare Treaty. On Sept. 28, 1971, a far reaching treaty on the renunciation of biological warfare was voted by an international Committee on Disarmament in Geneva and passed by the UN General Assembly on December 16.

J. R. PORTER, *University of Iowa*

Leaders of new Federation of Arab Republics met at Damascus airport on August 18. From left, Anwar Sadat of Egypt, Col. Muammar al-Qaddafi of Libya, and Hafez el-Assad of Syria.

MIDDLE EAST

The year 1971 was a rather indeterminate one in the Middle East, at least in regard to the major problem that has caused all the dangerous crises in the region over the last quarter century—that is, the Arab states' chronic hostility to the existence of Israel. In 1971 there was, at any rate, a pause in the conflict. There were fewer belligerent acts between Egypt and Israel than there had been for at least five years.

Yet there was violence in the Middle East. In Jordan, the Jordanian army and guerrilla groups confronted each other. There was considerable terrorist activity, especially in Turkey. A coup d'etat was foiled in Egypt, but one in Sudan was temporarily successful. There were three political assassinations: a former vice president of Iraq was murdered in Kuwait; the Israeli consul-general in Istanbul was kidnapped and murdered; and the prime minister of Jordan was murdered in Cairo.

In a large region such as the Middle East, comprising about a dozen states, it is misleading to speak as though one issue so dominates the political scene as to exclude all others. There are in fact other problems, other issues, than the chronic Arab-Israeli confrontation. On a number of these other questions, events of some significance and, even, of a fairly decisive nature took place in 1971. Thus,

Egyptian President Sadat emerged as a good deal more than merely Nasser's successor; he proved capable of giving Egypt's policies coherence and proportion. Sadat's position was strengthened by the creation of a 3-state bloc comprising Egypt, Libya, and Syria. In Turkey, on the other hand, events seemed to be moving in an opposite direction as forces tending to disintegration grew stronger. In the Middle East as a whole, guerrilla movements against the existing state structures were seriously, perhaps irremediably, weakened by events in Jordan.

The British decision in 1971 to terminate its military presence in the Persian Gulf area constituted another topic of significance, not so much because it ended the era of regional preponderance and of spheres of interest, but rather because it raised questions about the succession to the vacated role. Finally, the collision between the oil-producing states and the international oil companies reached a more open stage in 1971, as the pressure on the companies steadily increased.

Israel and the Arabs: Neither War nor Peace. In Israeli-Arab relations, 1971 was to a large extent a period of marking time. In a military sense not a great deal occurred: there were a few Israeli actions against guerrilla bases in Lebanon, but there were no incidents on the scale of previous years. On the Egyptian-Israeli front, the most striking of several incidents was that which occurred on September 17, when an Israeli air force transport plane was shot down, 14 miles (22 km) east of the Suez Canal, by missiles fired from Egyptian territory.

Diplomatic Maneuvers. On the diplomatic front, there was a great deal of activity but few significant results. Gunnar Jarring, the UN mediator, visited Jerusalem for talks in January, his first visit since April 1969. He received written proposals from Israel and Egypt. President Sadat agreed to the extension of the cease-fire, first to February 5 and then to March 7. Even after the March date it remained substantially, if not formally, in effect. There was no resumption during 1971 of the "war of attrition" that had prevailed along the canal prior to the beginning of the cease-fire in August 1970. Sadat secretly went to Moscow on March 1 for a 2-day visit.

Much of the diplomatic activity in the first half of the year was concerned with a U. S. push for an "interim solution" that would bring about the reopening of the Suez Canal, an indefinite ceasefire, some troop reductions in the Canal zone, and possibly a partial Israeli withdrawal. This was essentially an elaboration of the plan proposed in 1970 by Israel's General Dayan. It had been dropped because most of Dayan's cabinet colleagues disliked it. The idea continued to be discussed for the rest of the year, and was still widely regarded as a possible approach as 1972 began. Those commentators who saw the opening of the Suez Canal as chiefly benefiting the Soviet Union found U. S. enthusiasm for this goal difficult to understand.

U. S. Secretary of State William Rogers urged this plan during his tour of five Mideast countries at the beginning of May—the first visit by a U. S. secretary of state to the area since Secretary Dulles' visit in 1953. Rogers' visit was immediately followed by USSR President Podgorny's visit to Cairo and the conclusion of the 15-year Soviet-Egyptian treaty, which tied Cairo more tightly to Moscow. Assistant Secretary Joseph Sisco also visited Israel (July 26-August 6), but his visit did not appear to produce any results. Sadat, in an address on July 23 to the Arab Socialist Union, said that he would "not allow 1971 to pass without the battle being resolved, either by war or peace," a theme he repeated later; but in fact the second half of the year also passed inconclusively.

Addressing the UN General Assembly on September 30, Israeli Foreign Minister Abba Eban offered to meet his Egyptian opposite number, Mahmoud Riad, for talks in October. Eban told the Assembly that these talks could be conducted under UN auspices or under the chairmanship of Gunnar Jarring, and might deal with the reopening of the Suez Canal and the establishment of peace on the basis of the memoranda submitted by Israel and Egypt the previous February. He said that direct negotiation was the best way of obtaining an international settlement. He labeled the procedures used by the Jarring mission "ridiculous." Nothing, however, came of this proposal.

On November 20, Sadat, addressing troops at the Canal, said that there was no longer hope of a peaceful solution; and on December 16 the Soviet Ambassador to Cairo said that Moscow would back any Egyptian move to win back territory from Israel. This was the first public endorsement by a Soviet official of any Egyptian decision to resume the war. At the beginning of December, after the

NEW FLAG of Federation of Arab Republics—Egypt, Libya, and Syria—flies for first time in Cairo on Jan. 1, 1972. Hawk in center represents tribe of the prophet Mohammed, whose religion unifies the countries.

UPI

visit to the United States of Israel's Premier Golda Meir, President Nixon pledged U. S. aid in modernizing the Israeli armed forces.

Despite Sadat's belligerent postures, there remained much in his attitude that was ambiguous. He appeared to be subjected to conflicting pressures: on the one hand there were domestic demands for military action, but on the other there was the impressive fact of Israel's military competence. It was typical that a joint meeting on December 28 of Egypt's two most important assemblies, the People's Council (parliament) and the Central Committee of the Arab Socialist Union, issued an inconclusive, indeed inconsistent, statement that "battle" to liberate Sinai was "inevitable," but that efforts at a peaceful settlement must continue.

On the Israeli side, there was a desperate reluctance to give up the territorial military advantage gained in the 1967 war, particularly if the only substitute was to be UN or U. S. assurances. Israel felt that both of those had proved meaningless in 1967. Also, Israel had had very recent experience of the meaning of such assurances, when in August 1970 the Egyptians immediately broke the specific terms of the U. S.-arranged cease-fire by moving up Soviet missiles into the Canal zone after the cease-fire had begun. It might have been supposed that this would lead to widespread condemnation of Egypt and pressure on it; but on the contrary, all the pressure was put on Israel to countenance the transgression without awkward complaints. In 1971 the Israelis remained ready to defend their country's existence against any odds. The weakness in their position was that they did not know how far the United States would support them in a hypothetical war against the divided Arab world, possibly backed by the Soviet Union.

Enhanced Status of Sadat. Two events of the year improved Sadat's position and demonstrated that he might well prove to be not merely an inferior copy of Nasser, but a successful leader on his own account. The first and more important was the triumph of Sadat in crushing a conspiracy against him early in May. It had been led by Vice President Ali Sabry and General Fawzi. The defeat of the plot led not only to the dismissal and trial of important officials but also to a widespread purge of government and party office holders to the number of at least 300. These events left Sadat undisputed master in his own house.

Among the Sadat policies which Sabry had opposed was the creation of the Federation of Arab Republics, which had been in the planning stage in 1970 and was actually announced on April 17, 1971. The bloc comprises Egypt, Syria, and Libya, with the possibility of Sudan's joining later. The plan was reminiscent of the abortive Egyptian-Syrian union of 1958–61, but in fact the new federation was scarcely a union. The announced plan envisages little more to begin with than an attempt to coordinate foreign policies, especially anti-Israeli policies. However, the new organization did raise the interesting question whether 100 jet fighters that France had sold to Libya with the specific condition (obviously unenforceable) that they should not be used in hostilities against Israel would now be available for that purpose.

Internal Problems in Turkey and Jordan. The situation in Turkey—a NATO member and long a model of stability—tended more and more toward anarchy, or toward authoritarianism as the only

UPI

UPI

TENSION along the Suez Canal remained high in 1971, despite efforts to reopen it to shipping. Israelis (*left*) have occupied east bank since 1967. Egypt's Sadat (*right*) peered across canal during June tour of the west bank.

alternative. Violence, which had already disrupted higher education, spilled out into the cities and led to the armed forces' taking over the government from Suleyman Demirel on March 12. The new government of Nihat Erim, faced with continuing violence, introduced martial law on a selective basis by provinces and amended the constitution to give the executive stronger powers.

The intermittent year-long battle between King Hussein of Jordan and the radical guerrilla forces, which in 1970 had seemed a real threat to Hussein's throne and the very existence of the state of Jordan, was ended by July 18 with the ruthless and virtually complete crushing of the guerrilla movement, at least as a military force. The price, which presumably King Hussein thought well worth paying, was the isolation of Jordan (by an embargo that stopped all air and surface traffic) from its pro-guerrilla Arab neighbors, Iraq and Syria.

Jordan also had to put up with the general disapproval of the Arab world for demolishing a favorite myth. For several years the general belief had been gaining ground among observers of the Middle East that the guerrilla bands were a serious "third force," rivaling both Israel and all established Arab governments. This idea—never given more than lip service by Egypt, which would not tolerate the activities of the guerrillas on its territory—was now seen to be ill founded. Replying to mediation attempts by Saudi Arabia, King Hussein said unequivocally on September 22 that there would be "no return to anarchy."

Future of the Gulf Emirates. After some hesitation the British Conservative government decided early in 1971 to proceed with the previous Labour government's plans to pull out from the Persian Gulf, thus ending Britain's century-old protection of the small Trucial States of the area. Six of the seven Trucial States (Abu Dhabi, Dubai, Umm al-Qaiwain, Ajman, Fujairah, and Sharjah) decided on July 18 that they would, as Britain had hoped, form a federation; Ras al-Khaiman stayed out. Kuwait promised support for the federation. Bahrain and Qatar also stayed outside the federation, and both became UN members in September.

It seemed likely that the power vacuum in the Gulf would be filled by Iran, which moved on November 30 to occupy three Persian Gulf islands it had long claimed. More remote but more ominous, however, was the likelihood that the Soviet Union, perhaps using Iraq as a pawn, would attempt to move into this region, which is incredibly rich in oil. With some 20,000 men stationed in Egypt and a fleet in the Indian Ocean, the USSR was already in large part filling Britain's former role in the Middle East.

Oil: the Producing States versus the Oil Companies. The oil-producing states and the great international oil companies remained in a curious relation of mutual dependence and dislike. The companies must have the oil, at any price. The oil-producing states, which produce little else, must sell it. More and more, however, these states are successfully turning the screw to gain higher prices and are securing deals they would have hardly dared to imagine a few years ago. The Organization of Petroleum Exporting Countries met with representatives of 17 Western oil companies in Teheran, Iran, on January 12 and 21. On February 14 an agreement was signed to pay the six Persian Gulf states an additional $10 billion in revenue in the next five years. However, a fresh round of negotiations was called for at the end of November, since the Gulf states said that devaluation had effectively reduced the amount they would be receiving. For the long term, the oil states are beginning to envisage taking over the oil industries of their countries from the oil companies.

OLIPHANT IN THE DENVER POST

"The answer is 'No'—now, let's hear the suggestion!"

CENTO. The Central Treaty Organization held its annual foreign ministers' meeting, which was attended by U.S. Secretary of State Rogers, in Ankara, Turkey, April 30-May 1. The CENTO meeting was dominated by the subject of the current Middle East situation, but little that was helpful emerged from the deliberations.

(See also separate articles on the countries of the Middle East.)

ARTHUR CAMPBELL TURNER
University of California, Riverside

MILWAUKEE

A start on a $15 million convention hall and victory in the city's long fight for state tax reform highlighted the news in 1971 in Milwaukee.

Taxes. After a long campaign led by Milwaukee officials, the state legislature revised the antiquated tax distribution system to provide Milwaukee and other high-tax communities with more state revenues. Milwaukee will get $11.5 million in tax relief from the bill in 1972.

Convention Center. Ground was broken for a 140,000-square-foot (12,880-sq-meter) exposition hall that will be attached to the nearby auditorium and arena by an enclosed skywalk over Kilbourn Avenue, one of the city's main thoroughfares. The new hall plus the auditorium and arena will be operated as a convention center, which officials hope will put Milwaukee in competition for major conventions. Eventually, officials hope to connect the center with downtown stores and hotels via additional elevated walkways. Studies also are being made to determine whether the seating capacity of the arena should be increased by about 5,000 seats. The Milwaukee Bucks and Marquette University basketball teams have been playing to capacity crowds in the 10,200-seat arena.

Renewal. Because of a new agreement between the city and the federal Department of Housing and Urban Development (HUD), federal funds for some Milwaukee renewal projects will be forthcoming after a 14-month delay. HUD agreed to release the money after Milwaukee promised to build more public housing and change its restrictive building codes.

The city's renewal and housing agency, the Department of City Development, was leaderless for a short time when the City Council, in a bitter fight, blocked Mayor Henry W. Maier's appointment of a former staff aide as commissioner of city development. The dispute was one of several that split the council into warring pro-Maier and anti-Maier factions. Another council dispute arose when aldermen picked a convicted rapist to fill a vacancy on the council. The council removed him after the city attorney declared that his right to hold office had not been restored.

Police. The Milwaukee policemen's union declared a "blue flu" strike—actually a work slowdown—in February to emphasize their wage demands. The stoppage ended when a fact-finder was appointed to weigh the demands against the city's offer. The union declared a victory in November when the fact-finder recommended that rules and regulations heretofore set by the police chief be negotiable and that a grievance procedure be set up.

Economy. Unemployment in the Milwaukee area reached a high of 6% of the work force in February. Near the end of the year it was 5%, or slightly more than 26,000 workers. Factory employment declined and the average factory wage fell as industry scheduled less overtime. Budgets for 1972 reached record highs of $257 million for the city and $324 million for the county.

Indian Seizure. On August 14, 25 Indians of the militant American Indian Movement (AIM) took over an abandoned Coast Guard lifeboat station in Milwaukee. By late October they had set up a free clinic and a halfway house for alcoholics.

LAWRENCE C. LOHMANN, *The Milwaukee "Journal"*

MINDSZENTY, József Cardinal. See BIOGRAPHY.

MINING

Activities and trends in mining are reviewed in this article under the headings of World Mineral Production and U. S. Mining Technology. See also the separate article, PETROLEUM.

WORLD MINERAL PRODUCTION

The worldwide economic slowdown that began in 1970 and continued through 1971 affected world mineral production adversely, although, characteristically, only after a fairly long time lag.

In 1970, the latest year for which complete statistics are available, world production increased for 53 minerals and decreased for only 17. However, most of the increases were smaller than the annual rate of production growth experienced in recent years. Moreover, labor contracts and the rigid technical characteristics of mining systems make mine-production rates very resistant to downward pressures. Thus the continuing decline in world mineral consumption (demand) that began in 1970 was reflected first in mineral prices, particularly in 1971, and then in mine output in the middle and end of 1971.

Exploration and Development. Despite the unfavorable economic climate, industry continued to find and develop the new mineral resources required to satisfy the endlessly growing long-term needs of the world. Australia and Canada continued as the major focal points of attention in exploration and development, but significant activity took place in Brazil, Mozambique, Indonesia, and other areas.

There was a resurgence of mining in areas long believed exhausted or lacking in minerals, as well as in areas deemed too remote or too difficult to prospect. This resurgence resulted from advances in the techniques and technology of mineral exploration and new developments in mining and processing minerals, especially from low-grade deposits.

In Europe, a wave of exploration brought about new production from old, long-abandoned mining districts as well as from areas being mined for the first time. Among the many European activities were vast reserves of gas found under the North Sea, new tin mines in England, giant base-metal developments in Ireland, sulfur and copper in Poland, fluorspar and other minerals in France, Spain, and Italy, and bauxite in Greece.

Nationalism. The expanding forces of nationalism reached new intensities in 1970 and 1971, and they accounted for a noticeable lag in mineral development in several parts of the world long known for diversified mineral potential.

Chile has nationalized its nitrate industry, a large foreign-owned iron mine, and several large foreign-owned copper mines (including the expropriation of the remaining U. S. interests in two mines). Chile also was initiating actions for nationalizing still other sectors of its mining industry, including a small, French-owned copper mine.

Peru has revoked a number of foreign-held mineral concessions in various stages of development. The government announced that it intends to develop them itself, and new mineral laws were enacted permitting nationalization and state control of mineral marketing. Predominantly leftist labor unions struck the mines with growing frequency—Cerro Corp. alone was shut down 17 times in the first quarter of 1971—and the unions pressed for complete expropriation of all mines.

Elsewhere, Bolivia nationalized the U. S.-operated Matilda lead and zinc mine and a tin-dredging operation near Catavi. Guyana, fifth among world bauxite producers, nationalized its foreign-owned bauxite mines. Ceylon nationalized its graphite mines and was preparing legislation aimed at taking over all mineral production. Turkey is planning or implementing nationalization of more of its minerals.

Many nations have been altering their laws governing mineral activities in a fashion that seeks to extend and exercise national control over them. The various control mechanisms employed are frequently not in accord with the realities of the increasingly international markets in which mineral products are traded. The overall result has been for countries and firms seeking minerals to concentrate on those few areas of stability such as Australia or Canada and to endeavor to develop alternative sources for vital materials.

Production and Prices. Expressed as a fall in demand for minerals, the general world economic weakness began depressing mineral prices in 1970 and curtailing output in 1971. Other factors also tended to lower output in 1971. The wave of nationalism resulted in innumerable strikes, the loss of skilled foreign technicians and managers (without whom the mines cannot operate efficiently and for whom there are no local replacements), the replacement of experienced management with politicians, and the loss of markets.

Growing popular concern with environmental quality, often expressed in hasty legislation that producers regarded as ill-considered, impeded production and adversely affected the organization of mineral industries and mineral markets. Several large Japanese contracts for the purchase of Peruvian iron ores and Canadian copper ores were canceled or postponed because the sulfur content of the ore does not permit processing in existing Japanese plants under recently enacted antipollution laws. Moreover, the capital investment in various legally required antipollution devices in many countries compelled mineral producers to increase their prices at a time when weakening demand was exerting strong downward pressure on them. Mines and plants closed in some countries.

Precious Metals and Minerals. World output of gold, silver, and platinum rose in 1970. Gold and silver output grew largely as a result of increased by-products recoveries, but platinum, the biggest gainer, advanced as the result of planned mine expansions spurred by a shortage that saw dealer prices rise to $300 per troy ounce in 1969. Steady price erosion to a late 1971 level of $120 to $130 per ounce brought production cutbacks amounting to as much as 50% of capacity among large producers. Gold output continued relatively stable, but late in 1971 free-market prices rose to a 2-year high of $43.22. Silver prices did not respond and remained depressed throughout 1971, falling below $1.29 per ounce in November. Output increased for gem diamonds and fell for industrial diamonds.

Ferrous Metals and Alloys. As world output of iron ore, pig iron, and steel increased in 1970, signs of possible overcapacity began to appear in the iron ore industry. Consumer demand for steel, hence output, began to fall in 1971, and clear signs appeared that several large pending iron ore developments were being reevaluated.

(Continued on page 470)

WORLD PRODUCTION OF MAJOR MINERALS[1]

Aluminum (Thousands of metric tons)

	1969	1970
United States....	3,440.6	3,607.0
USSR[6]....	r1,052.3	1,097.7
Canada....	996.2	964.3
Japan....	568.8	733.0
Norway....	r508.0	529.8
France....	371.7	380.1
West Germany....	262.7	308.4
Australia....	126.4	204.1
India....	131.2	161.5
Italy....	r141.5	147.0
China[6]....	r117.9	127.0
Spain....	103.4	115.2
Ghana....	113.4	113.4
Rumania....	89.7	101.6
Poland....	r97.1	98.9
Switzerland....	77.1	91.6
Austria....	89.8	89.8
Greece....	r81.6	87.1
Netherlands....	72.6	74.4
Sweden....	r67.1	66.2
Hungary....	64.4	66.2
Czechoslovakia[6]....	65.0	65.0
Surinam....	53.5	52.6
Total (est.)....	r9,010.2	9,666.1

Antimony (Metric tons)

	1969	1970
South Africa....	18,213	17,092
China[6]....	r11,800	11,800
Bolivia....	r13,137	11,543
USSR[6]....	6,600	6,700
Mexico....	r3,227	4,468
Turkey....	r3,171	2,770
Thailand....	750	2,357
Yugoslavia....	2,067	r1,996
Morocco....	1,407	1,973
Italy....	1,154	1,253
United States....	851	1,025
Australia....	846	756
Austria....	623	610
Peru....	r613	600
Czechoslovakia[6]....	600	600
Total (est.)....	r66,021	66,930

Asbestos (Thousands of metric tons)

	1969	1970
Canada....	r1,430.5	1,509.0
USSR[6]....	1,000.0	1,043.0
South Africa....	258.2	287.4
China[6]....	160.0	170.0
Italy....	112.5	118.6
United States....	114.2	113.7
Rhodesia[6]....	80.0	80.0
Total (est.)....	r3,302.2	3,471.1

Barite (Thousands of metric tons)

	1969	1970
United States....	977.2	774.9
West Germany....	r437.5	412.6
Mexico....	176.9	319.1
USSR[6]....	280.0	300.0
Italy....	241.9	243.3
Canada....	r129.9	214.1
Ireland....	r160.5	6160.6
China[6]....	140.0	150.0
Peru....	148.8	130.0
North Korea[6]....	120.0	120.0
Rumania....	r99.8	116.5
France....	r95.0	695.0
Morocco....	86.9	84.8
Yugoslavia....	r81.5	r79.7
India....	51.8	71.9
Japan....	62.1	66.2
Spain....	r63.6	r63.5
Iran....	r58.6	60.2
Greece....	r83.1	54.2
Poland[6]....	50.0	50.0
Total (est.)....	r3,842.0	3,829.1

Bauxite (Thousands of metric tons)

	1969	1970
Jamaica....	10,498.8	12,009.7
Australia....	r7,924.2	9,389.3
Surinam....	r5,450.1	5,341.4
USSR[6]....	r4,980.0	4,980.0
Guyana....	r4,306.0	64,562.1
France....	2,773.0	2,992.3
Guinea....	2,459.0	62,641.7
Greece....	r1,916.3	2,278.0
United States....	1,872.6	2,115.4
Yugoslavia....	2,128.0	2,099.2
Hungary....	1,934.6	2,021.9
India....	992.0	1,359.5
Indonesia....	r765.1	1,229.4
Malaysia....	1,073.0	1,139.0
Dominican Rep....	1,093.3	1,066.9
Haiti....	664.5	631.0
China[6]....	450.0	500.0
Brazil[6]....	348.5	497.9
Sierra Leone....	r454.2	439.9
Ghana....	269.3	296.7
Total (est.)....	r52,634.4	57,988.0

Cement (Millions of metric tons)

	1969	1970
USSR[6]....	r89.74	95.20
United States....	r71.06	69.37
Japan....	51.39	57.19
West Germany....	r35.09	38.33
Italy....	r31.50	33.13
France....	27.54	28.90
United Kingdom....	17.42	17.05
Spain....	r15.77	16.54
India....	13.26	13.54
Poland....	11.83	12.18
China[6]....	10.00	10.00
Brazil....	r7.82	9.00
Rumania....	7.51	8.13
East Germany....	r7.41	67.50
Czechoslovakia....	6.73	7.40
Canada....	r7.48	7.32
Mexico....	6.79	7.13
Belgium....	6.27	6.73
Turkey....	5.80	6.37
South Korea....	4.86	5.81
South Africa....	4.99	5.75
Total (est.)....	r542.33	571.37

Chromite (Thousands of metric tons)

	1969	1970
USSR[6]....	1,700.0	1,750.0
South Africa....	1,197.7	1,427.3
Philippines....	469.7	575.8
Turkey....	r453.9	6477.4
Albania....	429.0	6453.6
Rhodesia[6]....	r362.9	362.9
India....	r226.1	265.8
Malagasy Rep....	79.8	140.6
Finland....	71.3	120.5
Iran[6]....	140.0	119.7
Greece....	r60.6	53.3
Yugoslavia....	39.4	40.6
Pakistan....	r22.6	635.8
Sudan....	26.2	26.7
Total (est.)....	r5,348.6	5,921.1

Coal (Millions of metric tons)

	1969	1970
USSR....	608.0	6624.1
United States....	518.0	555.8
China[6]....	r326.6	362.9
East Germany....	r255.9	6261.9
West Germany....	219.5	221.1
Poland....	165.9	172.9
United Kingdom....	153.0	144.6
Czechoslovakia....	106.4	109.4
India....	r79.6	76.0
Australia....	69.4	73.7
South Africa....	52.8	54.6
France....	43.5	44.2
Japan....	44.9	40.1
Bulgaria....	29.0	629.2
Yugoslavia....	26.5	28.4
Hungary....	26.5	27.8
North Korea[6]....	r25.4	26.3
Total (est.)....	r2,877.0	2,981.8

Copper (mine) (Thousands of metric tons)

	1969	1970
United States....	1,401.2	1,560.0
Chile....	r699.1	700.2
Zambia....	748.2	10619.9
Canada....	r520.0	613.3
USSR[6]....	r550.0	570.0
Congo (Zaïre)....	r356.9	349.9
Peru....	r198.8	212.1
Australia....	r131.3	145.6
Philippines....	131.4	145.4
South Africa....	r117.1	127.3
Japan....	r121.1	124.1
China[6]....	100.0	100.0
Yugoslavia....	r81.7	90.8
Poland[6]....	48.3	71.7
Mexico....	66.2	62.0
Bulgaria....	r39.3	639.9
Finland....	r33.1	31.1
Turkey....	26.4	27.2
S. West Africa....	27.6	26.7
Sweden....	25.2	23.1
Rhodesia[6]....	r19.0	20.0
East Germany[6]....	r19.0	20.0
Norway....	r21.1	19.9
Uganda....	19.4	19.2
Total (est.)....	r5,627.3	5,850.0

Diamonds (Thousands of carats)

	1969	1970
Congo (Zaïre)....	14,116	14,086
South Africa....	7,863	8,112
USSR[6]....	7,500	7,850
Ghana....	r2,391	2,523
Angola....	2,021	2,396
S. West Africa....	2,024	62,200
Sierra Leone....	1,989	1,955
Tanzania....	777	708
Liberia[2]....	746	...
Central African Republic....	r535	482
Brazil[6]....	320	320
Total (est.)....	r40,863	42,355

Fluorspar (Thousands of metric tons)

	1969	1970
Mexico....	988.3	978.5
USSR[6]....	400.0	408.2
Spain....	r305.5	338.8
Thailand....	297.6	318.2
France....	r274.9	290.3
Italy....	r257.8	289.3
China[6]....	250.0	272.0
United States....	165.6	244.2
United Kingdom....	r190.3	6213.2
South Africa....	150.3	173.0
Canada....	r119.4	124.1
Total (est.)....	r3,836.1	4,203.3

Gas (natural) (Billions of cubic feet)

	1969	1970
United States....	22,698.2	23,786.5
USSR[6]....	r6,860.0	7,520.0
Canada....	r2,288.0	62,656.0
Venezuela....	r1,673.0	1,710.2
Netherlands....	773.2	1,118.4
Iran....	892.6	1,094.2
Rumania....	r843.1	875.4
Libya....	666.5	6710.0
Mexico....	r609.1	665.0
Total (est.)....	r42,610.7	46,334.9

Gold (Millions of troy ounces)

	1969	1970
South Africa....	31.28	32.16
USSR[6]....	6.25	6.50
Canada....	r2.55	2.34
United States....	1.73	1.74
Ghana....	0.71	0.70
Australia....	0.70	0.62
Philippines....	0.57	0.60
Rhodesia[6]....	60.48	0.50
Japan....	0.25	0.26
Colombia....	0.22	0.20
Brazil....	0.18	0.18
Congo (Zaïre)....	0.18	0.18
Mexico....	0.18	0.18
Total (est.)....	r46.53	47.36

Graphite (Thousands of metric tons)

	1969	1970
Korea, North[6]....	75.3	75.3
USSR[6]....	70.0	75.3
Korea, South....	r74.3	59.5
Mexico....	42.9	55.6
China[6]....	630.0	30.0
Austria....	25.8	27.7
Malagasy....	r16.9	18.2
West Germany....	r17.6	613.2
Ceylon[2]....	11.4	9.8
Total (est.)....	r384.9	378.3

Gypsum (Thousands of metric tons)

	1969	1970
United States....	r8,985.7	8,560.2
France....	r5,959.2	6,088.2
Canada....	r5,782.1	5,844.1
USSR....	r4,565.0	64,700.0
United Kingdom....	4,595.6	4,275.5
Spain....	r3,943.2	64,000.0
Italy[6]....	3,000.0	3,100.0
Iran....	r1,596.5	1,676.3
West Germany....	r1,826.2	1,473.0
Mexico....	1,219.1	1,290.9
India....	r1,389.5	882.7
Australia....	r868.6	6829.3
Poland....	810.0	6825.0
Austria....	676.0	627.8
Japan....	r620.0	581.2
China[6]....	550.0	500.0
Total....	r51,239.1	50,421.9

Iron Ore (Millions of metric tons)

	1969	1970
USSR....	186.0	194.2
United States....	r89.8	91.2
France....	55.4	56.8
Australia....	39.1	51.1
Canada....	r36.3	48.3
China[6]....	r39.6	43.7
Brazil[6]....	33.0	40.2
Sweden....	33.2	31.8
India....	r29.6	30.8
Total (est.)....	r718.5	766.4

Iron (pig) including blast furnace ferroalloys (Millions of metric tons)

	1969	1970
USSR....	681.63	85.90
United States....	r86.19	83.65
Japan....	r58.15	68.05
West Germany....	33.76	33.63
China....	620.00	22.04
France....	18.21	19.22
United Kingdom....	16.65	17.67
Belgium....	11.31	10.85
Canada....	6.95	8.43
Italy....	7.80	8.35
Czechoslovakia....	7.01	7.55
India....	7.36	7.03
Poland....	r6.73	6.98
Australia....	6.19	6.19
Luxembourg....	4.87	4.81
South Africa....	4.36	4.35

WORLD PRODUCTION OF MAJOR MINERALS[1] (Continued)

Iron (pig) (cont'd)
(Millions of metric tons)

	1969	1970
Rumania	3.49	4.21
Brazil	3.90	4.20
Spain	r3.33	4.16
Netherlands	3.46	3.59
Austria	2.82	2.96
Sweden	2.68	2.79
North Korea	62.27	2.36
Mexico	2.16	2.34
East Germany	2.10	2.00
Total (est.)	r414.20	434.68

Lead (smelter) (Thousands of metric tons)

	1969	1970
United States	579.4	604.8
USSR6	440.0	440.0
Australia	343.1	352.6
Japan	186.6	208.7
Canada	169.8	185.6
Mexico	169.0	150.3
France	108.0	6119.7
West Germany	125.8	112.4
China6	100.0	100.0
Bulgaria	95.2	98.0
Yugoslavia	r107.0	97.4
Belgium	r97.2	93.4
S. West Africa	60.9	77.3
Peru	77.5	72.0
Spain	81.2	68.7
Poland	50.7	54.5
North Korea6	54.4	54.4
Italy	62.3	54.3
United Kingdom	39.1	43.8
Sweden	42.1	40.6
Rumania	39.0	39.9
Argentina	r22.0	638.1
Zambia	23.0	26.8
Morocco	26.8	24.9
East Germany6	r24.5	23.6
Total (est.)	r3,235.0	3,299.9

Magnesium (Thousands of metric tons)

	1969	1970
United States	90.62	101.61
USSR6	45.00	49.90
Norway	r31.15	635.38
Japan	9.38	10.34
Canada	r9.65	8.69
Italy	r6.70	6.50
France	4.40	64.54
Total (est.)	r201.17	220.67

Manganese Ore
(Thousands of metric tons)

	1969	1970
USSR6	r6,550.8	6,985.3
South Africa	2,204.1	2,679.5
Brazil	r1,965.0	1,928.7
India	r1,485.1	1,651.1
Gabon	1,363.0	1,453.0
China6	1,000.0	1,000.0
Australia	921.9	803.8
Ghana	r332.8	405.4
Congo (Zaïre)	311.4	346.9
Mexico	r143.6	273.9
Japan	r300.8	271.0
Hungary	156.0	168.8
Rumania6	r127.0	127.0
Morocco	130.6	112.4
Italy	53.0	50.1
Total (est.)	r17,414.3	18,497.5

Mercury (Thousands of flasks)

	1969	1970
USSR6	47.00	48.00
Spain	r64.86	47.69
Italy	48.73	44.38
Mexico	r22.54	30.27
United States	r29.64	27.30
Canada	r21.20	24.40
China6	20.00	20.00
Yugoslavia	14.33	15.46
Turkey	r6.56	8.59
Japan	r6.54	5.91
Philippines	3.48	4.65
Peru	r3.59	3.13
Total (est.)	r290.04	284.50

Molybdenum (Thousands of metric tons)

	1969	1970
United States	r45.3	50.5
Canada	13.4	16.0
USSR6	7.3	7.7
Chile	4.8	6.1
China6	1.5	1.5
Total (est.)	r73.5	82.7

Nickel (Thousands of metric tons)

	1969	1970
Canada	r193.8	277.0
USSR6	105.0	110.0
New Caledonia	90.5	105.4
Cuba6	35.5	35.5

Nickel (cont'd) (Thousands of metric tons)

	1969	1970
Australia	10.8	628.1
Indonesia	7.6	18.0
United States	14.2	13.9
South Africa	r9.1	11.6
Total (est.)	r483.1	621.6

Petroleum, Crude (Millions of barrels)

	1969	1970
United States	3,371.8	3,517.5
USSR	r2,412.9	2,594.6
Iran	r1,232.2	1,397.5
Saudi Arabia	r1,173.9	1,387.3
Venezuela	1,311.8	1,353.4
Libya	1,134.8	1,209.3
Kuwait	r1,021.6	1,090.0
Iraq	r555.2	569.7
Canada	r410.8	461.2
Nigeria	197.2	395.8
Algeria	r345.4	371.8
Indonesia	271.0	311.6
Trucial States	r222.6	283.5
Mexico	149.7	156.5
China6	106.0	146.0
Argentina	130.1	143.4
Qatar	129.8	132.5
Oman	119.7	121.2
Total (est.)	15,214.0	16,689.6

Phosphate (Thousands of metric tons)

	1969	1970
United States	r34,248	35,143
USSR (all forms)	r19,278	20,384
Morocco	10,662	11,399
Tunisia	r2,685	3,016
Nauru Island[2]	2,198	62,200
South Africa	1,679	1,685
Togo	1,473	1,508
China6	1,100	1,200
Jordan	1,087	1,200
Christmas Is.[2]	1,177	61,179
Senegal	r1,199	1,129
North Vietnam (all forms)6	1,229	1,048
Israel	987	1,000
Egypt	660	6700
Total (est.)	r81,703	85,147

Potash[4] (Thousands of metric tons)

	1969	1970
USSR	3,180	4,450
Canada	r3,168	3,106
West Germany	2,626	2,645
United States	2,544	2,476
East Germany	2,346	62,360
France	1,938	61,914
Total (est.)	r17,064	18,546

Pyrite[9] (Thousands of metric tons)

	1969	1970
USSR6	3,500	4,000
Japan	r2,966	2,750
Spain	2,475	2,736
China6	1,800	2,000
Italy	1,475	1,518
Finland	854	963
Cyprus	r927	871
South Africa	837	868
Rumania6	360	807
Norway	r766	747
Sweden	495	575
West Germany	641	554
North Korea6	500	500
Total (est.)	20,930	22,160

Salt (Millions of metric tons)

	1969	1970
United States	40.14	41.55
China6	15.00	15.97
USSR6	r12.00	12.97
West Germany	8.36	9.93
United Kingdom	r8.01	8.44
India	6.38	5.59
France	4.88	65.08
Italy	3.95	4.82
Canada	r4.22	4.58
Mexico	3.89	4.15
Poland	2.82	2.90
Netherlands	2.67	2.87
Rumania	62.36	2.86
East Germany	2.17	62.09
Total (est.)	134.98	141.85

Silver (Millions of troy ounces)

	1969	1970
United States	41.91	45.01
Canada	r43.53	44.62
Mexico	42.90	42.89
Peru	34.15	38.08
USSR6	37.00	38.00
Australia	r24.46	26.13
Japan	10.80	10.80
Bolivia	6.01	6.82
Sweden	3.68	6.11
France	r4.14	4.82

Silver (cont'd) (Millions of troy ounces)

	1969	1970
East Germany6	4.80	4.80
Honduras	3.91	3.82
South Africa	3.34	3.53
Yugoslavia	r3.82	3.42
Chile	3.13	2.39
Ireland	r1.87	2.17
Argentina	r3.11	2.05
West Germany	1.68	1.77
Congo (Zaïre)	61.90	1.71
Philippines	1.56	1.70
Spain	r1.82	61.64
Italy	1.83	1.06
Total (est.)	r292.5	304.5

Sulfur
(elemental) (Millions of metric tons)

	1969	1970
United States (all forms)	r8.70	8.67
Canada (recovered)	r3.86	4.44
Poland (Frasch, ore)	r1.98	62.71
France (recovered)	1.73	1.73
USSR (all forms)6	1.60	1.60
Mexico (all forms)	1.72	1.38
Total (all forms) (est.)	21.10	22.10

Tin (mine) (Thousands of long tons)

	1969	1970
Malaysia	72.2	72.6
Bolivia	29.5	29.6
USSR6	27.0	27.0
Thailand	20.8	21.1
China6	20.0	20.0
Indonesia	17.1	18.8
Australia	8.0	8.7
Nigeria	8.6	7.8
Congo (Zaïre)	6.5	6.3
Total (est.)	224.2	227.3

Titanium
(ilmenite) (Thousands of metric tons)

	1969	1970
Australia	r720.6	886.7
United States	844.8	787.4
Canada	679.7	766.3
Norway	490.7	579.0
Malaysia[2]	132.6	192.5
Finland	138.2	151.0
Total (est.)	3,213.0	3,575.7
(rutile)		
Australia	r362.1	368.1
Sierra Leone	r28.5	44.1
Total (est.)	r396.3	417.4

Tungsten[5] (Metric tons)

	1969	1970
China6	8,000	8,000
USSR6	6,500	6,700
United States	r3,132	3,676
North Korea6	2,140	2,140
South Korea	1,971	2,070
Bolivia	1,841	1,845
Portugal	r1,331	1,785
Canada	r1,462	1,341
Australia	1,250	1,244
Brazil	1,008	1,160
Peru	r689	827
Thailand	r654	711
Japan	r609	677
Total (est.)	r32,091	33,574

Uranium Oxide
(U3O8) (Metric tons)

	1969	1970
United States	r11,141	11,583
South Africa	3,610	4,000
Canada	3,497	3,639
France	r1,533	1,476
Gabon6	540	420
Australia6	300	300
Total (est.)[7]	r20,916	21,770

Zinc (smelter) (Thousands of metric tons)

	1969	1970
United States	944.0	796.3
Japan	712.2	676.2
USSR6	610.0	610.0
Canada	423.1	417.9
Australia	246.3	260.6
Belgium	260.6	241.2
France	253.5	227.3
Poland	207.5	209.0
United Kingdom	151.0	151.0
West Germany	r147.1	150.2
Italy	130.3	142.1
China (refined)6	r90.7	99.8
North Korea6	59.9	89.8
Spain	80.3	89.2
Mexico	80.3	80.7
Bulgaria	r75.8	678.0
Total (est.)	r4,964.5	4,909.7

r Revised. [1] Output of countries not individually listed and estimates are included in world totals. [2] Exports. [3] Smelter. [4] Marketable in equivalent K2O. [5] Contained tungsten (W basis). [6] Estimated. [7] Excludes all socialist bloc countries. [8] Excludes all ferroalloys. [9] Gross weight. [10] Smelter production. Source: U. S. Bureau of Mines.

(Continued from page 467)

Chromite prices remained high as a result of the curtailment of supplies arising from the boycott of Rhodesia. However, reduced steel output eased demand somewhat. The fact that the United States has become almost wholly dependent upon the USSR for chromite led to the passage of legislation permitting resumption of imports from Rhodesia.

The 1970 recession appeared to have brought supply and demand for molybdenum into balance, easing an earlier shortage; but since 1971 brought no improvement in demand, several large producers reduced output. Prices nevertheless remained stable or suffered only minor apparent discounting. Tungsten, on the other hand, remained in the doldrums throughout 1971. Consistently weak prices, declining from $68.50 per short ton unit in December 1970 to around $36 to $41 in August 1971, curtailed production. The large Tungsten Queen mine in North Carolina, for example, closed in September 1971; it had reopened only a year earlier after a 7-year shutdown.

Nonferrous Metals. The aluminum industry developed serious overcapacity as large new facilities initiated several years earlier continued to come into service in the face of continuing poor demand. Actual aluminum prices, compared to the listed 29 cents per pound, fell from 26 cents in May 1970 to a late 1971 low of 22 to 23 cents. Reductions in output were common during the latter half of 1971 when U. S. and Canadian plants were operating at 75% to 80% of capacity and other producers such as Japan and Norway were cutting back. Nevertheless, 1971 aluminum output outside the Communist world probably exceeded demand.

Copper miners, faced with surplus capacity for the first time in a decade, were saved from a wholly bad year by involuntary reduction of output. The U. S. copper strike was followed by rail and dock strikes, Chile had management problems and strikes, and Peru also had strikes. Prices were weak, and a number of mines suspended operations.

Lead and zinc held surprisingly steady in price and, apparently, in output, even though a number of zinc smelters closed, most of them permanently.

Tin output and price remained comparatively stable and showed some improvement by year-end.

Nickel consumption fell markedly during 1971, causing International Nickel to reduce its Canadian output nearly 25% by the end of the year and cut back elsewhere.

Other Metals and Minerals. Production controls instituted in January 1971 on potash producers by the Saskatchewan provincial government began to show results in the form of stronger prices in 1971.

The rising flood of cheap recovered sulfur ($5 to $7 f.o.b. plant) pouring out of Canada and elsewhere made a mockery of the posted Frasch producers' price of $25 to $30 per ton, forced the closing of a number of mines. An Alberta provincial government proposal to control sulfur was quashed by the federal government, but major producers indicated they may initiate a voluntary program. Long-term prospects for sulfur producers continued grim in light of the potential several million tons of elemental sulfur that may be produced annually from thermal power plant, smelter, and other stack gases under antipollution legislation.

FRANK H. SKELDING
President, AMDEC Corporation
Mineral Consultants

U. S. MINING TECHNOLOGY

The directions taken by mining research and technological advances in the United States in 1971 were dictated by three major stimuli:

(1) Legal requirements for improving mine working conditions to meet government standards. Changes in surface and subsurface mining practices thus continued under the 1969 and 1966 U. S. mine safety acts. Unforeseen difficulties have arisen and, although the intent was to decrease accidents, no improvement has been observed.

(2) The psychological effect of pending federal environmental legislation, together with state laws that had recently been enacted. Mining companies were forced to search for new methods of mineral removal, handling, and processing that would not degrade the environment.

(3) Rising costs. To counter inflation, rising costs, manpower requirements, and lower productivity associated with the safety laws, companies demanded more efficient mining techniques.

Working Conditions. Air-filtration systems and refrigerated air ventilation systems were installed and tested underground at many mines. These additions removed or diluted air contaminants to lawful limits and helped to cool working spaces. Dust levels at rock faces were also controlled through mist systems, through water infusion of coal to be mined, and through improved cutting tools and procedures such as liquid jet drilling.

Studies designed to advance air quality in underground environments began at the Bureau of Mining Research at the University of Idaho. A wind tunnel was installed for model analyses of different mine layouts, tunnels, and airway systems.

Predicting Rock Bursts. A joint ASARCO-U. S. Bureau of Mines rock-burst monitor system was tested underground in the Coeur d'Alene mining district of Idaho. Rock strain was continually monitored with geophones; from this imput, the locations of strain concentrations and probable rock bursts were predicted by computer analyses. These sites were "softened" with explosive charges so that natural stresses were absorbed, greatly reducing the danger of brittle rock exploding.

Environmental Impact. The new ASARCO-Phelps Dodge plant at El Paso, Texas, which went on stream in September, demonstrated the practicality of making elemental sulfur from sulfur dioxide contamination in smelter gases. Sulfur dioxide removal sharply reduces atmospheric pollution associated with sulfide ore processing.

Leaching processes for in-place mining and for secondary recovery from tailing piles received further study as to their environmental desirability and economic considerations. Solution mining of potash began in Utah. The Duval Corp. started chemical extraction of copper by leaching with chloride solutions, and Kennecott began a copper-leaching project in its Nevada Kimberly pit.

Liquid Jet Drilling. Significant advances were made in liquid jet technology. This drilling method not only appears to reduce mining costs but also contains built-in safety features. In liquid jet drilling, pulsed water jets, developing pressures from 50,000 to 1 million pounds per square inch, are directed at coal seams or rock faces. The pulsed water breaks apart this rock. This technique minimizes the risk of gas explosions and prevents dust from becoming airborne.

Bigger Machines. In underground mines, larger continuous machines were put into operation during the year. In open-pit mines a new generation of larger ore trucks and ore-handling equipment went into common use. Increased capacities improve overall handling efficiency and also reduce the work force needed to produce a ton of coal or ore. This in turn reduces the costs of maintaining the desired mine safety.

Coking Plant. A major advance in coal-processing technology was made by FMC Corp. at its Kemmerer, Wyo., coke pilot plant. A process for converting low-grade noncoking bituminous coal into metallurgical grade coke became operational. Many areas of the world that have only low-grade coals now may be able to make coke and then develop their own domestic iron-ore deposits.

Undersea Mining. The Dravo Corp., after three years' study, demonstrated that its articulated floating platform could mine the sea to water depths of 1,200 feet. The platform contains underwater storage tanks and ore slurry-handling systems. As another approach to sea-floor mining, a 35,000-ton prototype deep-sea mining ship is being designed by Global Marine for the Hughes Tool Co.

JOHN G. BOND, *Senior Geologist*
Idaho Bureau of Mines and Geology

MINNESOTA

A housing boom, sweeping changes in the court system, an impasse on legislative reapportionment, and a tax crisis helped make news in Minnesota in 1971. Resolution of the tax crisis, which centered on demands for relief from ever-increasing local property taxes in support of schools, required a second special session of the Legislature.

Legislation. Ultimately, Gov. Wendell R. Anderson, a member of the Democratic-Farmer-Labor (DFL) party who had run his gubernatorial campaign mainly on the issue of property tax relief, was able to persuade the Republican-controlled Legislature to meet increased school costs through an increase in state income and sales taxes. The governor and the Legislature failed to agree on a plan for reapportionment, and at year-end a federal court panel was at work on a plan.

Otherwise, the 1971 sessions produced a quantity of significant legislation. Under one judicial reform measure all the probate courts were turned into "county courts" with expanded duties and jurisdictions; some sparsely populated counties were combined into a single court district sharing a full-time judge. Another important measure reduced from 12 to 6 the number of jurors that will hear all contested civil cases and all misdemeanor cases.

Concern for environmental protection was expressed in legislation that included a $35 million money and bonding bill to help municipalities meet the cost of sewage treatment facilities and an "environmental rights act," under which citizens may sue violators of pollution control regulations. Other major bills created a state housing finance agency, provided new watercraft and snowmobile safety laws, and reformed existing laws on alcohol and drug use.

In answer to the demand for annual rather than biennial legislative sessions, the lawmakers proposed a constitutional amendment providing for "flexible sessions." The present limit of 120 meeting days in regular sessions would be retained, but the 120 days could be spread over a 2-year period by a series of recesses. The voters will decide the fate of this amendment in 1972.

Minneapolis Mayoral Election. In an election on June 8, Charles S. Stenvig won a second 2-year term as mayor of Minneapolis, defeating his black opponent, W. Harry Davis, by a margin of 2½ to 1. Davis, the president of the Urban Coalition of Minneapolis, had DFL support. Stenvig was backed by labor unions and a taxpayers' group formed to support him when he first ran for the office as an independent "law and order" candidate.

Economy. The fact that 1971 was an erratic year economically was attributed mainly to recessive conditions of the national economy. The unemployment rate in Minnesota hovered slightly below the national average. Food processing, usually the state's leading industry, showed only slight gains, and farmers suffered substantial loss of income because of low corn prices. But the demand for housing boomed, making the housing and construction industry the strongest sector of the economy and bringing marked increases in sales of lumber and wood products.

New National Park. The Voyageurs National Park, covering some 200,000 acres of Minnesota's lake country near the Canadian border, came into being under congressional legislation signed on January 8. Besides lakes and forests, the park includes areas of historic and geologic interest.

SUE R. BRANDT

MINNESOTA • Information Highlights

Area: 84,068 square miles (217,736 sq km).
Population (1970 census): 3,805,069. *Density:* 46 per sq mi.
Chief Cities (1970 census): St. Paul, the capital, 309,828; Minneapolis, 434,400; Duluth, 100,578; Bloomington, 81,-970; Rochester, 53,766.
Government (1971): *Chief Officers*—governor, Wendell R. Anderson (Democratic-Farmer-Labor); lt. gov., Rudy Perpich (DFL); secy. of state, Arlen I. Erdahl (R); atty. gen., Warren R. Spannaus (DFL); treas., Val Bjornson (R); commissioner, dept. of educ., Howard B. Casmey; chief justice, Oscar R. Knutson. *Legislature*—Senate, 67 members (nonpartisan); House of Representatives, 135 members (nonpartisan).
Education (1970–71): *Enrollment*—public elementary schools, 493,100 pupils; 21,500 teachers; public secondary, 437,-400 pupils; 23,440 teachers; nonpublic schools (1968–69), 154,900 pupils; 6,390 teachers; college and university (fall 1968), 148,621 students. *Public school expenditures* (1970–71), $761,000,000 ($864 per pupil). *Average teacher's salary,* $9,271.
State Finances (fiscal year 1970): *Revenues,* $1,795,668,000 (3% general sales tax and gross receipts taxes, $195,-620,000; motor fuel tax, $122,880,000; federal funds, $381,670,000). *Expenditures,* $1,735,574,000 (education, $676,232,000; health, welfare, and safety, $27,920,000; highways, $230,178,000). *State debt,* $462,512,000 (June 30, 1970).
Personal Income (1970): $14,664,000,000; per capita, $3,793.
Public Assistance (1970): $243,075,000. *Average monthly payments* (Dec. 1970)—old-age assistance, $76.85; aid to families with dependent children, $237.00.
Labor Force: *Nonagricultural wage and salary earners* (June 1971), 1,313,000. *Average annual employment* (1969)—manufacturing, 330,000; trade, 307,000; government, 222,-000; services, 206,000. *Insured unemployed* (Oct. 1971)—17,800 (1.8%).
Manufacturing (1967): *Value added by manufacture,* $4,080,-200,000. Nonelectrical machinery, $912,100,000; food and kindred products, $754,100,000; paper and allied products, $358,500,000; electrical equipment and supplies, $328,-600,000.
Agriculture (1970): *Cash farm income,* $2,167,621,000 (livestock, $1,373,087,000; crops, $642,761,000; government payments, $151,773,000). *Chief crops* (1970)—Corn, 390,-490,000 bushels (ranks 3d among the states); oats, 167,-700,000 bushels (ranks 1st); soybeans, 82,919,000 bushels; hay, 8,155,000 tons (ranks 1st).
Mining (1971): *Production value,* $576,956,000 (ranks 13th among the states). *Chief minerals* (tons)—Iron ore, 49,-500,000; sand and gravel, 48,543,000; stone, 4,304,000.
Transportation: *Roads* (1969), 127,578 miles (205,311 km); *motor vehicles* (1969), 2,144,000; *railroads* (1968), 7,973 miles (12,831 km); *airports* (1969), 127.
Communications: *Telephones* (1971), 2,247,900; *television stations* (1969), 12; *radio stations* (1969), 117; *newspapers* (1969), 31 (daily circulation, 1,136,000).

MISSISSIPPI

The year 1971 was one of unusual political interest, since it marked the first time in the history of Mississippi that a Negro had sought election to the state's highest office. In that contest, William L. Waller, a 46-year-old white Jackson attorney and surprise nominee of the Democratic party, scored a one-sided victory over Charles Evers, the black mayor of Fayette and Loyalist Democrat, who chose to run as an independent.

Elections. In the 1971 quadrennial state and local elections, the leading gubernatorial aspirants adopted a moderate stance on the subject of race. Black candidates generally avoided the Democratic primaries, running instead as independents in the general election. The Republican party offered no candidates for statewide offices and relatively few for lesser posts. The election year was marked by confusion over reapportionment, voter registration, and the lowering of the voting age to 18. Also complicating matters was the April ruling of a three-judge federal panel that elections must be held under 1964 laws rather than under the 1970 "open primary" law.

In the gubernatorial contest, Lt. Gov. Charles L. Sullivan emerged from a 7-man Democratic primary race with a 60,000 vote lead over William Waller. In the runoff primary, however, Waller shocked the

---

MISSISSIPPI • Information Highlights

Area: 47,716 square miles (123,584 sq km).
Population (1970 census): 2,216,912. *Density:* 50 per sq mi.
Chief Cities (1970 census): Jackson, the capital, 153,968; Biloxi, 48,486; Meridian, 45,083; Gulfport, 40,791; Greenville, 39,648; Hattiesburg, 38,277; Pascagoula, 27,264.
Government (1971): *Chief Officers*—governor, John Bell Williams (D); lt. gov., Charles L. Sullivan (D); secy. of state, Heber A. Ladner (D); atty. gen., A. F. Summer (D); supt. of public education, Garvin Johnston (D); chief justice, William N. Ethridge, Jr. *Legislature*—Senate, 52 members (49 Democrats, 3 Republicans); House of Representatives, 122 members (120 D, 1 R, 1 Ind).
Education (1970–71): *Enrollment*—public elementary schools, 312,093 pupils; 12,270 teachers; public secondary, 222,302 pupils; 10,263 teachers; nonpublic schools (1968–69), 20,600 pupils; 1,070 teachers; college and university (fall 1968), 68,667 students. *Public school expenditures* (1970–71), 262,500,000 ($521 per pupil). *Average teacher's salary,* $6,008.
State Finances (fiscal year 1970): *Revenues,* $935,458,000 (5% general sales tax and gross receipts taxes, $227,930,-000; motor fuel tax, $88,502,000; federal funds, $265,995,-000). *Expenditures,* $928,083,000 (education, $345,217,000; health, welfare, and safety, $110,427,000; highways, $125,-643,000). *State debt,* $455,186,000 (June 30, 1970).
Personal Income (1970): $5,772,000,000; per capita, $2,561.
Public Assistance (1970): $101,414,000. *Average monthly payments* (Dec. 1970)—old-age assistance, $49.65; aid to families with dependent children, $46.40.
Labor Force: *Nonagricultural wage and salary earners* (June 1971), 583,900. *Average annual employment* (1969)—manufacturing, 182,000; trade, 104,000; government, 129,-000; services, 66,000. *Insured unemployed* (Oct. 1971)—6,000 (1.5%).
Manufacturing (1967): *Value added by manufacture,* $1,635,-300,000. Apparel and other textiles, $174,700,000; lumber and wood products, $165,800,000; chemicals and allied products, $157,500,000; food and kindred products, $156,-600,000.
Agriculture (1970): *Cash farm income,* $1,058,311,000 (livestock, $513,168,000; crops, $398,643,000; government payments, $146,500,000). *Chief crops* (1970)—Soybeans, 56,064,000 bushels; cotton lint, 1,635,000 bales (ranks 2d among the states); hay, 1,061,000 tons.
Mining (1970): *Production value,* $247,598,000 (ranks 26th among the states). *Chief minerals* (tons)—Sand and gravel, 10,610,000; clays, 1,589,000; natural gas, 125,753,-000,000 cubic feet; petroleum, 64,900,000 barrels.
Fisheries (1970): *Commercial catch,* 301,300,000 pounds ($11,900,000). *Leading species by value* (1969), Menhaden, $3,887,760; red snapper, $929,644; swordfish, $223,056; spotted sea trout, $63,247.
Transportation: *Roads* (1969), 66,655 miles (107,268 km); *motor vehicles* (1969), 1,085,000; *railroads* (1968), 3,653 miles (5,879 km); airports (1969), 67.
Communications: *Telephones* (1971), 891,400; television stations (1969), 9; radio stations (1969), 124; newspapers (1969), 20 (daily circulation, 315,000).

---

political establishment with an easy victory. He then captured 77% of the vote in the general election on November 2, while Charles Evers received 22%. The remaining 1% went to state Supreme Court Justice Thomas P. Brady, who had qualified as an independent only to give white voters a choice if Evers should succeed in having Waller disqualified for excessive campaign expenditures. The record vote of 780,000 represented 71% of an estimated 1,100,000 registrants, of whom 300,000 were black.

Black candidates lost 28 of 29 legislative races, as well as the 3 statewide contests they entered. Even at the county and county district level, where they frequently held a registration edge, blacks won only 49 of the 280 offices they sought.

Legislation. Meeting in regular session in a general election year for the first time this century, the Legislature increased welfare and unemployment benefits, raised salaries for public school teachers, and upped appropriations for higher education. Other actions included passage of sweeping prison reforms and a water pollution abatement program and approval of an ill-fated reapportionment plan for both houses of the Legislature. A major state government reorganization plan, prepared by a select group of business leaders and submitted to the Legislature by Gov. John Bell Williams, failed to gain approval.

Reapportionment. A legislative seating plan, devised in May by a three-judge federal district court and substituted for the one adopted by the 1971 Legislature, was challenged by civil rights lawyers because the plan contained multi-member districts for the 1971 elections. On June 3 the U. S. Supreme Court instructed the district court to suspend the qualifying date for legislative candidates in populous Hinds county (which includes the capital city of Jackson) and, "absent insurmountable difficulties," to prepare a single-member district plan by June 14. The lower court ruled on June 16 that it was impossible to fashion such a plan and thus ordered at-large elections. The order was upheld by the U. S. Supreme Court on June 21.

Public Schools. Enrollment in public schools during September 1971 was down slightly (less than 1%) from September 1970. A federal district judge issued a permanent injunction on October 19 prohibiting the state from withholding funds to the Jackson Municipal Separate School System, which was busing pupils under a court-approved desegregation plan, but contrary to a 1953 state law. An appeal by the state was pending at year's end.

Racial Incidents. An 18-year-old black girl was shot to death a few hours after her graduation on May 25 from the high school in Drew. The first of three white men charged in the slaying was convicted of manslaughter on October 29 and sentenced to 20 years in prison. An exchange of gunfire in Jackson on August 18 resulted in the death of a white policeman and the arrest of 11 members of a black separatist group called the Republic of New Africa.

Other Events. Construction of the federally funded Tennessee-Tombigbee Waterway (involving Tennessee, Alabama, and Mississippi) was halted in July pending the outcome of a lawsuit filed by environmentalists. Violent storms swept across a large area of west central Mississippi on February 21, killing 93 persons and injuring hundreds of others.

DANA B. BRAMMER
University of Mississippi

MISSOURI

Missouri in 1971 solved a financial crisis, approved a bond issue that would raise $150 million to clean up polluted waters, and rejected parimutuel betting.

Legislature. An income tax increase pushed through for a one-year period in the last days of 1970 was made permanent despite efforts by antitax senators to make the increase subject to a referendum. The increase was not sufficient to finance long-delayed state building projects, but it did allow an additional $70 million for public schools and helped finance a record state budget of $750 million. A 2-cent increase in the gasoline tax was approved by the General Assembly but was vetoed by Gov. Warren E. Hearnes. The veto set the stage for a lengthy debate over highway needs and rapid transit. The governor, who had favored tying the tax increase to a bond issue for highway construction, later announced plans for a $730 million bond issue for rapid transit and airports as well as highways. Rare accord by all the top political leaders from the two metropolitan areas had persuaded the governor to include the rapid-transit funds. A vote was delayed until 1972.

The legislature approved the serving of liquor by the drink in restaurants on Sunday but rejected attempts to provide state aid for parochial schools. A debate over airports began when both St. Louis and Illinois announced plans to construct a new airport for the St. Louis area in Illinois. Democrats

---

MISSOURI • Information Highlights

Area: 69,686 square miles (180,487 sq km).
Population (1970 census): 4,677,399. *Density:* 67 per sq mi.
Chief Cities (1970 census): Jefferson City, the capital, 32,-407; St. Louis, 622,236; Kansas City, 507,087; Springfield, 120,096; Independence, 111,662.
Government (1971): *Chief Officers*—governor, Warren E. Hearnes (D); lt. gov., William S. Morris (D); secy. of state, James C. Kirkpatrick (D); atty. gen., John C. Danforth (R); treas., William E. Robinson (D); Commissioner, Bd. of Educ., Arthur L. Mallory; chief justice, James A. Finch, Jr. *General Assembly*—Senate, 34 members (25 Democrats, 9 Republicans); House of Representatives, 163 members (112 D, 51 R).
Education (1970–71): *Enrollment*—public elementary schools, 769,000 pupils; 29,941 teachers; public secondary, 271,000 pupils; 13,411 teachers; nonpublic schools (1968–69), 167,600 pupils; 6,870 teachers; college and university (fall 1968), 68,667 students. *Public school expenditures* (1970–71), $698,568,000 ($761 per pupil). *Average teacher's salary,* $8,373.
State Finances (fiscal year 1970): *Revenues,* $1,480,279,000 (3% general sales tax and gross receipts taxes, $344,799,-000; motor fuel tax, $115,359,000; federal funds, $407,-292,000). *Expenditures,* $1,502,620,000 (education, $573,-467,000; health, welfare, and safety, $267,239,000; highways, $288,746,000). *State debt,* $141,922,000 (June 30, 1970).
Personal Income (1970): $17,252,000,000; per capita, $3,659.
Public Assistance (1970): $237,537,000. *Average monthly payments* (Dec. 1970)—old-age assistance, $76.15; aid to families with dependent children, $112.45.
Labor Force: *Nonagricultural wage and salary earners* (June 1971), 1,636,000. *Average annual employment* (1969)—manufacturing, 459,000; trade, 373,000; government, 282,-000; services, 257,000. *Insured unemployed* (Oct. 1971)—33,700 (2.9%).
Manufacturing (1967): *Value added by manufacture,* $5,895,-000,000. Transportation equipment, $1,258,900,000; food and kindred products, $799,800,000; chemicals and allied products, $545,800,000.
Agriculture (1970): *Cash farm income,* $1,714,145,000 (livestock, $1,128,560,000; crops, $431,666,000; government payments, $153,919,000). *Chief crops* (1970)—Corn, 173,-057,000 bushels; soybeans, 90,896,000 bushels.
Mining (1970): *Production value,* $395,387,000 (ranks 21st among the states). *Chief minerals* (tons)—Stone, 36,618,-000; iron ore, 2,654,000; lead, 435,648; cement, 20,796,-000 barrels.
Transportation: *Roads* (1969), 114,816 miles (184,774 km); *motor vehicles* (1969), 2,313,000; *railroads* (1968), 6,414 miles (10,322 km); *airports* (1969), 95.
Communications: *Telephones* (1971), 2,753,400; *television stations* (1969), 19; *radio stations,* 141; *newspapers* (1969), 54 (daily circulation, 1,782,000).

---

and Republicans cooperated in trying to have the airport built in Missouri. The federal government had yet to make a decision.

Proposed Constitutional Amendments. Constitutional amendments put to the voters dealt with sewage treatment and pari-mutuel betting. The water pollution issue was approved by a large margin and will assure $150 million in state funds to match federal grants for sewage treatment. A scandal over track ownership in Illinois and a large "no" vote in rural areas overcame urban support to defeat pari-mutuel betting on horse racing.

Politics. Christopher (Kit) Bond was inaugurated state auditor in January, giving the state its second Republican officeholder. In association with his former boss, Atty. Gen. John C. Danforth, Bond made headlines frequently by criticizing the Democratic administration.

A Democratic officeholder, State Treas. William E. Robinson, was accused by a grand jury of "profiting in office" by taking a gift of $2,500 from a banker whose bank was made a depository of state funds. Robinson was acquitted in a jury trial.

Reapportionment. With the figures from the 1970 census available, reapportionment of congressional districts and the two state legislative bodies was required. Commissions established to draw new lines for the state Senate and House had mixed results. Political bickering stalemated the House commission, and the job was turned over to the commissioners of the state supreme court, which apparently did the job without regard to the desires of incumbents or politicians. The Senate commission approved a plan in accordance with the one-man, one-vote principle, but the new map was challenged in court on the grounds that the districts were not compact. The legislature itself kept the job of congressional redistricting, but a fight between the two houses brought defeat to all plans. A federal court gave the legislature another try at reapportionment in early 1972.

RONALD D. WILLNOW
The St. Louis "Post-Dispatch"

MITCHELL, John N. See BIOGRAPHY.

MONGOLIA

Continued educational, social, and economic development marked events in Mongolia in 1971. Foreign Affairs remained under the influence of Mongolia's pro-Soviet orientation, and Soviet army units and missiles continued to be stationed in the country. Mongolia's low-profile relations with Communist China were punctuated by belligerent accusations.

Domestic Affairs. The 16th congress of the Mongolian People's Revolutionary party, meeting in June, reelected all members of the Politburo and adopted a new 5-year plan (1971–75). There was a meeting in December of the far less important Great People's Khural, or People's Assembly.

In July, Mongolia celebrated the 50th anniversary of the Communist victory. Soviet Premier Aleksei Kosygin attended the celebration.

During 1971, Mongolia's urban population continued to grow, the birthrate increased, and the life-expectancy was raised to 64 years. Education continued to follow the Soviet pattern, with a change from a four-year to a three-year first elementary stage.

──────── MONGOLIA · Information Highlights ────────

Official Name: Mongolian People's Republic.
Area: 604,248 square miles (1,565,000 sq km).
Population (1970 census): 1,247,000. *Density,* 2 per square mile (1 per sq km). *Annual rate of increase,* 3.1%.
Chief Cities (1970 census): Ulan Bator, the capital, 270,000; Darkhan, 35,000; Nalaikha, 15,000.
Government: *Head of state,* Zhamsarangin Sambu, chief of state (took office July 1954). *Head of government,* Yumzhagiyn Tsedenbal, premier and Communist party first secretary (took office January 1952). *Legislature*—Great Khural (unicameral), 287 members. *Political party*—Mongolian People's Revolutionary party (Communist party).
Language: Khalka Mongolian (official).
Education: *Literacy rate* (1970), 80% of population. *School enrollment* (1970–71)—primary, 239,000; special trade schools, 11,000; university/higher, 8,400.
Finances (1970 est.): *Revenues,* $480,000,000; *expenditures,* $478,200,000; *monetary unit,* tugrik (4 tugriks equal U.S.$1, 1971).
Manufacturing (metric tons, 1968): Gasoline, 16,000; distillate fuel oils, 8,000.
Crops (metric tons, 1968 crop year): Wheat, 188,000; barley, 6,000.
Minerals (metric tons, 1970): Coal, 1,999,300.
Foreign Trade (1965): *Exports,* $75,000,000. *Imports,* $150,000,000. *Chief trading partner*—USSR.
Transportation: *Roads* (1961), 46,700 miles (75,154 km); *railroads* (1966), 887 miles (1,427 km); *national airline,* Mongolair; *principal airport,* Ulan Bator.
Communications: *Telephones* (1970), 17,830; *television stations* (1967), 1; *television sets* (1969), 700; *radios* (1969), 108,000; *newspapers* (1967), 3 (daily circulation, 19,000).

Foreign Affairs. A mysterious crash of a Communist Chinese aircraft in Mongolia in September remained unexplained. All nine persons aboard were killed. There were several high-level visits of leading Mongols to Moscow and of Russians to Ulan Bator. In 1971, Mongolia maintained diplomatic relations with 54 countries.

Economy. Production of petroleum ceased completely in 1971, but more coal was extracted than in any preceding year. The total number of livestock was reported at just under 22 million head, practically the same as in 1950, but the new 5-year plan called for 25 million head by 1975.

ROBERT A. RUPEN
University of North Carolina

MONTANA

The 42d Legislative Assembly of Montana met on Jan. 4, 1971, with a membership of 80 Republicans and 79 Democrats, the Democrats controlling the Senate and the Republicans the House. There was a Democratic governor.

Legislation. In the 60-day legislative session the houses worked in harmony to create an environmental council and to enact statutes aimed at decreasing water pollution and cleaning up strip mining.

In other legislation, cities and counties were given more power in planning and zoning, and the governor was empowered to reorganize some 160 executive agencies into 20 or fewer cabinet-type departments. The minimum wage was raised to $1.60 per hour, and 19 was made the age of adult responsibility. A new law declared that tacit consent for alcohol tests was assumed for auto drivers involved in accidents. When an apportionment law based on the 1970 census and reducing the number of seats in the Assembly was declared invalid, a second law was passed that also reduced the number of seats in the House from 104 to 100 and in the Senate from 55 to 50.

Financial Solutions. After a 27-day special session ended in deadlock on April 3, the governor promised a second special session beginning June 7. Ultimately, total appropriations of $185,874,098 for the 1971–72 biennium were made, an increase of

11%. In a referendum in November the voters were given the choice between a 2% sales tax, long favored by the Republicans, and continuance of a 40% income tax surcharge, supported by the Democrats. The sales tax measure was rejected.

Constitutional Convention. The legislature authorized a constitutional convention to begin in January 1972 to revise the present constitution, which was formulated in 1889. Candidates for the convention were required to list their party preference. The result was the election of 58 Democrats, 36 Republicans, and 6 independents.

Politics. The October 14 announcement by Gov. Forrest Anderson that, because of his health, he would not seek reelection in 1972 led to an increase in political activity. This was balanced somewhat by the decision of U.S. Sen. Lee Metcalf that, contrary to rumor, he would seek a third term in 1972.

Economics. Next to the sales tax, the most controversial issue of the year was the Montana Power Company's request that the Public Service Commission allow the utility to increase its rates for electric power by 17% and for gas by 34%. The commission scheduled extensive hearings throughout the state, and at year-end a decision was pending.

Although there was a generally favorable agricultural situation, Montana's economy was adversely influenced by a high unemployment rate in industry. There was also an 85-day strike—from July 1 to September 22—in the Anaconda Copper Company, idling some 6,100 workers.

MERRILL G. BURLINGAME
Montana State University

──────── MONTANA · Information Highlights ────────

Area: 147,138 square miles (381,087 sq km).
Population (1970 census): 694,409. *Density:* 5 per sq mi.
Chief Cities (1970 census): Helena, the capital, 22,730; Billings, 61,581; Great Falls, 60,091; Missoula, 29,497; Butte, 23,368; Bozeman, 18,670; Havre, 10,558.
Government (1971): *Chief Officers*—governor, Forrest H. Anderson (D); lt. gov., Thomas L. Judge (D); secy. of state, Frank Murray (D); atty. gen., Robert L. Woodahl (R); treas., Alex B. Stephenson (R); supt. of public instruction, Dolores Colburg (D); chief justice, James T. Harrison. *Legislative Assembly*—Senate, 55 members (30 Democrats, 25 Republicans); House of Representatives, 104 members (55 R, 49 D).
Education (1970–71): *Enrollment*—public elementary schools, 107,336 pupils; 5,400 teachers; public secondary, 67,653 pupils; 3,500 teachers; nonpublic schools (1968–69), 18,200 pupils; 770 teachers; college and university (fall 1968), 25,560 students. *Public school expenditures* (1970–71), $138,800,000 ($858 per pupil). *Average teacher's salary,* $8,173.
State Finances (fiscal year 1970): *Revenues,* $350,354,000 (total sales and gross receipts taxes, $48,211,000; motor fuel tax, $28,766,000; federal funds, $115,711,000). *Expenditures,* $343,105,000 (education, $101,892,000; health, welfare, and safety, $32,204,000; highways, $98,665,000). *State debt,* $81,786,000 (June 30, 1970).
Personal Income (1970): $2,418,000,000; per capita, $3,381.
Public Assistance (1970): $27,869,000. *Average monthly payments* (Dec. 1970)—old-age assistance, $67.25; aid to families with dependent children, $157.50.
Labor Force: *Nonagricultural wage and salary earners* (June 1971), 210,400. *Average annual employment* (1969)—manufacturing, 24,000; trade, 47,000; government, 52,000; services, 32,000. *Insured unemployed* (Oct. 1971)—4,000 (3.2%).
Manufacturing (1967): *Value added by manufacture,* $311,600,000; Lumber and wood products, $85,300,000; food and kindred products, $55,200,000; petroleum and coal products, $43,500,000.
Agriculture (1970): *Cash farm income,* $644,407,000 (livestock, $365,990,000; crops, $193,056,000; government payments, $85,361,000). *Chief crops* (1970)—Wheat, 85,167,000 bushels; barley, 65,132,000 bushels (ranks 2d among the states); hay, 4,112,000 tons; sugar beets, 922,000 tons.
Mining (1969): *Production value,* $285,700,000 (ranks 24th among the states). *Chief minerals* (tons)—Copper, 112,766; zinc, 4,897; silver, 3,303,000 troy ounces.
Transportation: *Roads* (1969), 78,253 miles (125,933 km); *motor vehicles* (1969), 478,000; *railroads* (1968), 4,926 miles (7,927 km); *airports* (1969), 116.
Communications: *Telephones* (1971), 357,000; *television stations* (1969), 9; *radio stations* (1969), 45; *newspapers* (1969), 15 (daily circulation, 189,000).

MONTREAL

Montreal, Canada's largest city, passed a relatively quiet year in 1971. The formation of a metropolitan government proceeded, and preparations continued for the 1976 Summer Olympic Games. But there was controversy over educational policy, and social and political conflicts erupted, particularly on June 24, French-Canadian National Day, and on October 29, after the closing of *La Presse*, a French-language newspaper.

The 1971 municipal budget climbed to some $500 million—about 13% higher than in 1970.

Social and Political Turmoil. Two members of the Quebec Liberation Front were found guilty of the 1970 murder of Quebec Labor Minister Pierre Laporte and were sentenced to life imprisonment. On April 30 the antiterrorist Public Order Act of 1970 expired on schedule.

The celebration of National Day by French-Canadians on June 24 ended in a riot, in which about 100,000 Montrealers were opposed by a few hundred policemen. Many arrests followed.

La Presse, Quebec's largest newspaper and the largest French-language daily in North America, ceased publication indefinitely on October 27 after a long labor dispute. Two days later a riot erupted at the end of a union-led demonstration by 15,000 persons protesting the closing of the paper. One woman died, 200 persons were injured, and 60 were arrested as a result of the violence. The union members founded a new daily, *Le Quotidien populaire,* on November 2, but it ended publication after 13 issues.

Long-standing ethnic conflicts were responsible for strife over education policies. The provincial government had tried for many years to reorganize the school system in the Montreal region, but opposition from many groups made changes impossible. However, the government proposed a new law in 1971 to assure school board unification. Conflict immediately arose between French- and English-speaking groups, and tension grew so fierce that after many months of discussion the provincial government decided to withdraw the bill, leaving the school question unsettled.

The University of Montreal was closed on October 22 after numerous acts of violence were committed during a strike by nonteaching employees. University professors voted to respect the union picket lines. Classes were resumed on November 1 following settlement of the dispute.

Metropolitan Government. The Communauté Urbaine de Montréal (CUM), or Montreal Urban Community, entered its first complete year in 1971. It is composed of 29 cities, including Montreal, with a combined population of 2 million. The CUM had a rather difficult beginning, because its component cities were not accustomed to working together. The 1971 budget was $160 million, an increase of $140 million over the 1970 budget, but opposition arose to the important tax increases needed to cover the increased spending.

The CUM produced several interesting results in 1971. Its structures were more solid and efficient, and it was the first time in the history of Montreal that there was an authentic metropolitan government. The most important achievement involved the police forces, of which there had formerly been 29 units in the metropolitan area. Henceforth they will be unified under one command, thereby im-

MONTREAL'S Trans-Canada highway extension, a bare crater in 1971, is due to be completed in 1972.

proving the quality of the police service. The unification of the police forces is the first major step in the organization of a new pattern of administration for Montreal. The formation of the CUM has been expected for almost 20 years.

Other Events. In 1971, Montreal continued the great progress that had started with Expo 67. For example, preparation for the 1976 Summer Olympic Games continued, surely but without a great deal of publicity. Expansion of the metro, Montreal's new subway system, began at the end of 1971 and when work is completed in 1974 its length will have been doubled. Construction was also started on the much-debated new superhighway, which will run through the heart of the city.

The international exhibition "Man and His World" remained popular in its fourth year. The number of visitors seems to have stabilized at about 6 million annually, 40% of them coming from the United States. The exhibition has been a financial and popular success, and it will be continued in the years to come.

Montreal's baseball team, the Montreal Expos, finished the 1971 season in fifth place in the Eastern Division of the National League. The team has been in the National League since the 1969 season. The city's hockey team, the Montreal Canadiens, made an extraordinary comeback in 1971. After an ordinary season, the team surprised everyone by winning the Stanley Cup in May, its fifth championship in seven years.

GUY BOURASSA
Université de Montréal

MOROCCO

The major event in Morocco in 1971 was an unsuccessful military coup against King Hassan II on July 10. The rebellion was quickly suppressed, but discontent remained.

Domestic Affairs. On July 10, armed troops broke into the Skhirat summer palace, where King Hassan was giving a party to celebrate his 42d birthday. Nearly 200 persons were killed, including important diplomatic guests, and the King was held prisoner for two hours. But troops restored the royal authority within 24 hours.

The coup was apparently headed by Gen. Mohamed Medbouh, head of the royal military household, who was killed during the rebellion, and by Colonel Ababou, director of the noncommissioned officers' school at Ahermoumou. Many of the rebels were cadets at the Ahermoumou school, and it was believed that many had been duped into participating in the coup. Ten high-ranking officers—including four generals, five colonels, and a major—were executed in Rabat on July 12 without a trial.

King Hassan dismissed his cabinet on August 4 and promised to rid Morocco of corruption. Two days later he announced the formation of a new cabinet headed by Karim Lamrani as prime minister, and including General Oufkir as minister of defense and Abdellatif Filali as minister of foreign affairs. The King conceded that certain reforms were in order.

Hassan's concession was widely viewed as an overture to the country's political parties. But the political leaders, observing many familiar faces in the new cabinet, maintained that cabinet reshuffling was not an adequate substitute for basic institutional reform. They continued to demand open negotia-

tions between the parties and the government as well as unfettered election of a new parliament authorized to draft a new constitution.

In January and February a strike of secondary school students, motivated mainly by academic questions, spread to the university, where the protest movement became increasingly politicized. The president of the national student union asserted that any basic solution to the defects in the educational system would require the democratization of Morocco's political, economic, and social structures.

On June 14, 193 persons went to trial (some in absentia) in Marrakesh on charges of having plotted against the government. The accused had been in prison since early 1969. Several legal and scholarly groups abroad protested in the wake of claims that the prisoners had been the victims of improper police methods and torture during their incarceration. The defendants eventually refused to plead. On September 17 the court sentenced 5 persons to death, 6 to life imprisonment, and 123 to terms ranging from 18 months to 30 years; 59 were acquitted.

The opponents of King Hassan's regime chiefly complained of the nonrepresentative nature of the government; its close ties with the United States, which was thought to be supporting Israeli occupation of Arab territories; and the slow rate of economic development. They also charged the government with widespread corruption. In April, rumors spread of enormous irregularities involving investments in the tourism sector. The King postponed a trip to the United States and reshuffled several bureaus dealing with economic questions.

Economic Development. The 5-year plan (1968–72) continued to give highest priority to the development of the agricultural sector, which accounted for about one third of the gross national product. The country's 21 dams, including four planned to begin operating in 1971, will permit irrigation of about 2.5 million acres (1 million hectares) of cropland. In August, King Hassan announced plans to distribute 346,000 acres (140,000 hectares) of land to peasants as part of a land reform program that had made 740,000 acres (300,000 hectares) available to small farmers since 1963.

In March the government announced detailed plans for the gradual "Moroccanization" of foreign firms holding exclusive control of the importation of specific brands of products. Many economists, noting a continuing population increase of 3.3% annually, held that only a greater emphasis on industrial development could cause real national income to rise at rates much faster than the population. During the year there was renewed talk of a steel complex at Nador, and efforts were stepped up to find new sources of oil to replace the diminishing stocks of the Gharb region.

Foreign Affairs. Morocco recalled its ambassador from Libya as a result of that government's open support for the abortive July coup. Morocco's territorial differences with Spain were deemphasized as the governments signed an economic, technical, scientific, and cultural cooperation agreement.

U. S. Vice President Spiro Agnew visited Morocco on July 24, and Soviet Premier Alexei Kosygin paid a 3-day visit in October.

JOHN D. RUEDY
Georgetown University

MORTON, Rogers C. B. See BIOGRAPHY.

MOROCCO · Information Highlights

Official Name: Kingdom of Morocco.
Area: 172,413 square miles (446,550 sq km).
Population (1970 est.): 15,530,000. *Density*, 88 per square mile (34 per sq km). *Annual rate of increase*, 2.9%.
Chief Cities (1969 est.): Rabat, the capital-Salé, 435,000; Casablanca, 1,320,000; Marrakesh, 295,000; Fez, 280,000.
Government: *Head of state*, Hassan II, king (acceded Feb. 26, 1961). *Head of government*, Karim Lamrani, prime minister (took office Aug. 6, 1971). *Parliament* (unicameral)—Chamber of Representatives, 240 members. *Major political parties*—Istiqlal, Union Nationale des Forces Populaires.
Languages: Arabic (official), Berber, French.
Education: *Literacy rate* (1969), 15% of population. *Expenditure on education* (1968), 17.1% of total public expenditure. *School enrollment* (1968)—primary, 1,124,333; secondary, 287,438; technical, 13,772; higher, 10,908.
Finances (1970): *Revenues*, $662,800,000; *expenditures*, $789,-600,000; *monetary unit*, dirham (5.06 dirhams equal U. S.$1, April 1971).
Gross National Product (1969): $3,184,000,000.
National Income (1969): $2,798,000,000; *national income per person*, $186.
Economic Indexes: *Industrial production* (1969), 124 (1963 = 100); *agricultural production* (1969), 116 (1963 = 100); *consumer price index* (1970), 111 (1963 = 100).
Manufacturing (metric tons, 1969): Cement, 1,165,000; distillate fuel oils, 451,000; sugar, 117,000.
Crops (metric tons, 1969 crop year): Barley, 2,206,000; wheat, 1,469,000; oranges and tangerines (1968), 775,000.
Minerals (metric tons, 1969): Phosphate rock, 10,662,000 (ranks 2d among world producers); iron ore, 412,000.
Foreign Trade (1969): *Exports* (1970), $488,000,000 (chief exports—phosphates, $108,700,000; citrus fruits, $76,710,000). *Imports*, $684,000,000 (chief import, 1967—nonelectrical machinery, $75,730,000). *Chief trading partners* (1967)—France, West Germany.
Tourism: *Receipts* (1970), $136,400,000.
Transportation: *Roads* (1969), 32,180 miles (51,787 km); *motor vehicles* (1969), 286,300 (automobiles, 207,000); *railroads* (1965), 1,110 miles (1,786 km); *merchant fleet* (1970), 55,000 gross registered tons; *national airline*, Royal Air Maroc; *principal airport*, Casablanca.
Communications: *Telephones* (1970), 153,662; *television stations* (1967), 6; *television sets* (1968), 100,000; *radios* (1969), 826,000; *newspapers* (1971), 7.

1971 20TH CENTURY FOX

Action-packed intrigues of *The French Connection* end with a dramatic chase through New York City. Gene Hackman, portraying a detective, shoots Marcel Bozuffi at conclusion.

Motion Pictures

In 1971, motion pictures were seen by fewer spectators than ever before. Attendance was down in all categories, and there were no convenient morals to be drawn. People's moviegoing habits had simply changed irrevocably from reflex to reflection. The huge reflex audience had been gobbled up by television, and there was nothing left for the motion picture theater but the hit-seekers. Unfortunately, the motion picture industry has always thrived on the premise that even its bad movies could be profitable. In 1971 not even good movies seemed to be a good commercial risk. Motion pictures seemed to be going the way of the theater as a high-risk, selective entertainment.

The Ratings Controversy. The controversy over film classification continued to provide some comedy relief against the grim background of declining grosses. Church and community groups complained that the ratings were being juggled by the major distributors in an effort to obtain wider audiences

for more daring material. The notion that community standards themselves had altered appreciably in the last decade seemed not to be accepted by many of these groups. More sophisticated observers of the ratings controversy noted that the Motion Picture Association of America had scuttled its own system by regarding X-rated movies as moral untouchables. Thus, essentially serious movies, such as *Carnal Knowledge* and *A Clockwork Orange*, were treated as if they were samples of cheap, hard-core pornography in many parts of the United States.

Foreign Films. The vogue for foreign films continued to diminish now that sexual frankness did not have to be imported from abroad. Still, foreign films continued to provide much of the artistic stimulation in 1971. Among the best were the late Kenji Mizoguchi's *The Taira Clan;* Eric Rohmer's *Claire's Knee;* Jerzy Skolimowski's *Deep End;* Claude Chabrol's *Le Boucher;* Jacques Rivette's *The Nun;* Roberto Rossellini's *Socrates;* Federico Fellini's

477

The Clowns; Milos Forman's *Black Peter;* Carlos Saura's *The Garden of Delights;* Bernardo Bertolucci's *The Conformist;* François Truffaut's *Bed and Board;* Vittorio De Sica's *The Garden of the Finzi Continis;* Louis Malle's *Murmur of the Heart;* Dusan Makaveyev's *Innocence Unprotected* and *W. R. Mysteries of the Organism;* Robert Bresson's *Une Femme douce;* Luchino Visconti's *Death in Venice;* Jan Kadar's *Adrift;* Pier Paolo Pasolini's *The Decameron;* Alexandro Jodorowsky's *El Topo;* and Fernando Arrabal's *Viva la Muerte.*

Less successful was Nadine Trintingnant's *It Only Happens to Others,* based on her own real-life tragedy. Raoul Coutard, best known as Jean-Luc Godard's cameraman, directed his own film, *Hoa Binh,* a disconcertingly romantic treatment of the Vietnam War.

Social and Political Commentary. An interesting genre of films focused on the individual caught in a corrosive society. Notable among these were Barbara Loden's *Wanda;* Mike Nichols' *Carnal Knowledge;* Frank D. Gilroy's *Desperate Characters;* Otto Preminger's *Such Good Friends;* Arthur Hiller's *The Hospital;* Hal Ashby's *Harold and Maude;* Jerry Schatzberg's *Puzzle of a Downfall Child;* Jack Nicholson's *Drive, He Said;* Monte Hellman's *Two-Lane Blacktop;* Herbert B. Leonard's *Going Home;* Henry Jaglom's *A Safe Place;* Richard C. Sarafian's *Vanishing Point;* and Ulu Grosbard's *Who Is Harry Kellerman and Why Is He Saying Those Terrible Things About Me?*

The popularity of films on drug addiction declined considerably. Among the commercially unsuccessful pictures on the subject were Jerry Schatzberg's *The Panic in Needle Park;* Ivan Passer's *Born to Win;* and Noel Black's *Jennifer on My Mind.*

A modishly apocalyptic note was struck in such strained exercises in futurism as Stanley Kubrick's *A Clockwork Orange;* Jim McBride's *Glen and Randa;* George Lucas' *THX-1138;* and Dennis Hopper's *The Last Movie.* On a more conventional level of political propaganda were such films as Caspar Wrede's *One Day in the Life of Ivan Denisovich* from the novel by Aleksandr I. Solzhenitsyn; Bo Widerberg's *Joe Hill;* Giuliano Montaldo's *Sacco and Vanzetti;* Stanley Kramer's *Bless the Beasts and Children;* Dalton Trumbo's *Johnny Got His Gun;* and T. C. Frank's *Billy Jack.*

Westerns. The tradition of the classical Western was upheld in 1971 by Howard Hawks' *Rio Lobo,* George Sherman's *Big Jake,* and Henry Hathaway's *Shoot Out.* Robert Altman's *McCabe and Mrs. Miller* provided a more disenchanted vision, but its characters were heroic nonetheless. A consciously homoerotic treatment of the genre was offered in Black Edwards' *Wild Rovers,* Peter Fonda's *The Hired Hand,* and Frank Perry's *Doc,* while liberal allegory carried the day in Paul Bogart's *Skin Game* and Richard C. Sarafian's *Man in the Wilderness.*

Melodramas. The "sleeper" of the year was clearly William Friedkin's *The French Connection,* one of the few movies in recent years to be discovered by audiences without much help from the critics. Other melodramas of 1971 included Clint Eastwood's *Play Misty for Me;* Don Siegel's *Dirty Harry;* Robert Aldrich's *The Grissom Gang;* Richard Brooks' *$;* Alan J. Pakula's *Klute;* Sidney Lumet's *The Anderson Tapes;* Alastair Reed's *The Night Digger;* Mike Hodges' *Get Carter;* Jack Gold's *The Reckoning;* Michael Tuchner's *The Villain;* Gerd Oswald's *Bunny O'Hare;* and Daniel Mann's *Willard.*

Perhaps the most reassuring sign that all was not yet lost for the film industry was the rousing business done by Guy Hamilton's *Diamonds Are Forever,* the latest of the James Bond movies, with an older and more charming Sean Connery as 007. But the enormous response to the return of James Bond was seen by some as an alarming sociological indication that 1970's audiences were actually nostalgic for the hitherto unlamented 1960's.

Documentaries. The documentary showed signs of rejuvenation. Among the notable contributions were Robert Kaylor's *Derby;* Emile De Antonio's *Millhouse;* Louis Malle's *Calcutta;* Peter Gimbel and James Lipscomb's *Blue Water, White Death;* and Walon Green's *The Hellstrom Chronicle.* Bruce Brown's *On Any Sunday,* about motorcycle racing, and Lee H. Katzin's semi-documentary *Le Mans,* about auto racing, both featured Steve McQueen in racing action. Marcel Ophuls' extraordinarily evocative *Le Chagrin et la pitié* was seen at a one-shot showing at the New York Film Festival.

Comedies and Musicals. Comedies in 1971 were as often black as light, and the humor was thus often squashed by horror. However, audience laughter was heard at John Cassavetes' *Minnie and Moskowitz;* Robert B. Bean's *Made for Each Other;* John Korty's *Funnyman;* Woody Allen's *Bananas;* Norman Lear's *Cold Turkey;* Milos Forman's *Taking Off;* Elaine May's *A New Leaf;* Alan Arkin's *Little Murders;* Mark Robson's *Happy Birthday, Wanda June;* and Richard Clement's *A Severed Head.*

Movie musicals have virtually disappeared as a genre. Among the few musicals to open in 1971 were Ken Russell's *The Boy Friend,* Norman Jewison's *Fiddler on the Roof,* and Frank Zappa's *200 Motels.* The commercial failure of *Raga,* a filmed concert of Ravi Shankar's music, suggested that the easy market for rock attractions on the screen had hardened considerably.

Black Films. The black cinema consolidated its commercial position without enhancing its artistic prestige. The year 1971 saw such black films as Gordon Park's *Shaft,* Melvin van Peebles' *Sweet Sweetback's Baadasssss Song,* Don Medford's *The Organization,* and Denis Sanders' *Soul to Soul.*

Nostalgia Craze. Peter Bogdanovich's *The Last Picture Show* led the parade of movies consciously exploiting the audience's craze for nostalgia. Robert Mulligan's *Summer of '42,* Ken Russell's *The Boy Friend,* and James Goldstone's *Red Sky at Morning* all contributed to the trend.

Classics and Costume Films. A number of classics were revamped in 1971. The more interesting of these included Roman Polanski's *Macbeth,* Peter Brook's *King Lear,* Pier Paolo Pasolini's *Medea;* and Michael Cacoyannis' *The Trojan Women.* Otherwise, costume films tended to be the exception rather than the rule with such relics of old-time studio opulence as Abraham Polonsky's *Romance of a Horsethief,* Don Siegel's *The Beguiled,* John Frankenheimer's *The Horsemen,* and Franklin J. Schaffner's *Nicholas and Alexandra.*

Other Films. Ken Russell was one of the more controversial directors of 1971 with *The Music Lovers,* a deliriously decadent vision of Tchaikovsky and the taste he represented, and *The Devils,* about a group of hysterical and repressed 17th century French nuns. Peter Finch and Murray Head executed the most talked-about homosexual kiss in the history of the cinema for John Schlesinger's

(Continued on page 483)

© 1971 COLUMBIA PICTURES

Human sensitivity and cross-currents of emotion received detailed attention in 1971 films. (Above) *In* The Last Picture Show, *Timothy Bottoms has an affair with Cloris Leachman.* (Right) *Peter Finch (center) and Glenda Jackson compete for the affection of Murray Head in* Sunday, Bloody Sunday. *(Below)* Fiddler on the Roof, *Broadway's longest-running musical, finally reached the screen.* (Below right) *Aristocratic Julie Christie used Dominic Guard to further her affair with a tenant farmer, Alan Bates, in* The Go-Between.

© 1971 UNITED ARTISTS

© 1971 UNITED ARTISTS

© 1971 COLUMBIA PICTURES

NOTABLE MOTION PICTURES OF 1971

The following list of films released in 1971 presents a cross-section of the most popular, most typical, or most widely discussed motion pictures of the year.

Adrift. Director, Jan Kadar; screenplay, Imre Gyongyossy with Kadar and Elmar Klos from novel by Lalos Zilahy. With Rade Markovic, Milena Dravic, Paula Pritchett, Josef Kroner.

The Andromeda Strain. Director, Robert Wise; screenplay, Nelson Gidding from novel by Michael Crichton. With Arthur Hill, David Wayne, James Olson, Kate Reid, Paula Kelly, George Mitchell.

Bananas. Director, Woody Allen; screenplay, Allen and Mickey Rose. With Allen, Louise Lasser, Carlos Montalban, Howard Cosell, Roger Grimsby.

Bed and Board. Director, François Truffaut; screenplay, Truffaut, Claude de Givray, and Bernard Revon. With Jean-Pierre Leaud, Claude Jade, Hiroko Berghauer, Barbara Laage.

The Beguiled. Director, Don Siegel; screenplay, John B. Sherry and Grimes Grice from novel by Thomas Cullinan. With Clint Eastwood, Geraldine Page, Elizabeth Hartman, Jo Ann Harris, Darleen Carr.

Big Jake. Director, George Sherman; screenplay, Harry Julian Fink and R. M. Fink. With John Wayne, Richard Boone, Maureen O'Hara.

Billy Jack. Director, T. C. Frank; screenplay, Frank and Teresa Christina. With Tom Laughlin, Delores Taylor, Clark Howat, Bert Freed, Ken Tobey.

Black Beauty. Director, James Hill; screenplay, Wolf Mankowitz from novel by Anna Sewell. With Mark Lester, Walter Slezak, Peter Lee Lawrence, Ursula Glas.

Black Peter. Director, Milos Forman; screenplay, Forman, Jaroslav Papousek, and Ivan Passer. With Ladislav Jakim, Pavla Martinkova, Pavel Sedlacek, Jan Ostroli, Bozena Matuskova.

Blue Water, White Death. Directors, Peter Gimbel and James Lipscomb.

Born to Win. Director, Ivan Passer; screenplay, David Scott Milton. With George Segal, Paula Prentiss, Karen Black, Jay Fletcher, Hector Elizondo.

The Boy Friend. Director, Ken Russell; screenplay, Russell from musical by Sandy Wilson. With Twiggy, Christopher Gable, Max Adrian, Bryan Pringle, Tommy Tune, Antonia Ellis, Vladek Sheybal.

Bunny O'Hare. Director, Gerd Oswald; screenplay, Stanley Z. Cherry and Coslough Johnson from story by Cherry. With Bette Davis, Ernest Borgnine, Jack Cassidy, Joan Delaney, Jay Robinson.

Calcutta. Director, Louis Malle.

Carnal Knowledge. Director, Mike Nichols; screenplay, Jules Feiffer. With Jack Nicholson, Candice Bergen, Arthur Garfunkel, Ann-Margret, Rita Moreno, Cynthia O'Neal, Carol Kane.

Chikamatzu Monogatari. Director, Kenji Mizoguchi; screenplay, Yoshitkata Yoda and Matsutaro Kwaguchi from Kabuki drama, *Chikamatzu Monzemon.* With Kazuo Hasegawa, Kyoko Kagawa, Yoko Minamida, Eitaro Shindo.

Claire's Knee. Director-scenarist, Eric Rohmer. With Jean-Claude Brialy, Aurora Cornu, Beatrice Romand, Laurence De Monaghan.

A Clockwork Orange. Director-scenarist, Stanley Kubrick from novel by Anthony Burgess. With Malcolm McDowell, Patrick Magee, Adrienne Corri, Aubrey Morris, Godfrey Quigley.

The Clowns. Director, Federico Fellini; screenplay, Fellini and Bernardino Zapponi. With Pierre Etaix, Anita Ekberg, and many clowns.

Cold Turkey. Director-scenarist, Norman Lear; story by Lear and William Price Fox, Jr., from unpublished material by Margaret and Neil Rau. With Dick Van Dyke, Pippa Scott, Tom Poston, Edward Everett Horton, Bob (Elliott) and Ray (Goulding), Bob Newhart, Vincent Gardenia.

The Conformist. Director-scenarist, Bernardo Bertolucci from novel by Alberto Moravia. With Jean-Louis Trintignant, Stefania Sandrelli, Dominique Sanda, Pierre Clementi.

The Cop. Director, Yves Boisset; screenplay, Boisset and Claude Veillot. With Michel Bouquet, Françoise Fabian, Bernard Fresson.

The Crook. Director, Claude Lelouch; screenplay, Lelouch, Pierre Uyterhoeven, and Claude Pinoteau. With Jean-Louis Trintignant, Daniele Delorme, Charles Denner, Christine Lelouch, Amidou.

Dead of Summer. Director, Nelo Risi; screenplay, Risi, Anna Gobbi, and Roger Mauge from novel by Dana Moseley. With Jean Seberg, Lugi Pistilli.

Death in Venice. Director, Luchino Visconti; screenplay, Visconti and Nicola Badalucco from novel by Thomas Mann. With Dirk Bogarde, Bjorn Andresen, Silvana Mangano.

The Decameron. Director-scenarist, Pier Paolo Pasolini from Boccaccio. With Franco Citti, Ninetto Davoli, Angela Luce, Pier Paolo Pasolini.

Deep End. Director, Jerry Skolimowski; screenplay, Skolimowski, J. Gruza, and B. Sulik. With Jane Asher, John Moulder-Brown, Diana Dors, Karl Michael Vogler, Christopher Sandford, Louise Martini.

Derby. Director, Robert Kaylor. With Charlie O'Connell, Mike Snell, Christina Snell, Butch Snell.

Desperate Characters. Director-scenarist, Frank D. Gilroy from novel by Paula Fox. With Shirley MacLaine, Kenneth Mars, Gerald O'Loughlin, Sada Thompson.

The Devils. Director-scenarist, Ken Russell from play by John Whiting and book by Aldous Huxley. With Oliver Reed, Vanessa Redgrave, Dudley Sutton, Max Adrian, Gemma Jones, Murray Melvin.

Diamonds Are Forever. Director, Guy Hamilton; screenplay, Richard Maibaum and Tom Mankiewicz from novel by Ian Fleming. With Sean Connery, Jill St. John, Charles Gray, Lana Wood, Jimmy Dean, Bruce Cabot, Bruce Glover, Putter Smith, Bernard Lee.

Dirty Harry. Director, Don Siegel; screenplay, Harry Julian Fink, R. M. Fink, and Dean Riesner. With Clint Eastwood, Harry Guardino, Reni Santoni, Andy Robinson, John Larch, John Mitchum, John Vernon.

Drive, He Said. Director, Jack Nicholson; screenplay, Jeremy Larner and Nicholson. With William Tepper, Karen Black, Michael Margotta, Bruce Dern, Robert Towne, Henry Jaglom.

El Topo. Director-scenarist, Alexandro Jodorowsky. With Jodorowsky, Mara Lorenzio, Paula Romo, Jacqueline Luis, David Silva.

Fiddler on the Roof. Director, Norman Jewison; screenplay, Joseph Stein from play based on stories of Sholem Aleichem. With Topol, Norma Crane, Leonard Frey, Molly Picon.

The French Connection. Director, William Friedkin; screenplay, Ernest Tidyman from book by Robin Moore. With Gene Hackman, Fernando Rey, Roy Scheider, Tony LoBianco, Marcel Bozzuffi.

Funnyman. Director, John Korty; screenplay, Korty and Peter Bonerz. With Bonerz, Sandra Archer, Carol Androsky, Nancy Fish.

The Garden of Delights. Director, Carlos Saura; screenplay, Ragael Azcona and Saura. With Jose Luis Lopez Vasquez, Luchy Soto, Francisco Pierra.

The Garden of the Finzi Continis. Director, Vittorio De Sica; screenplay, Cesare Zavattini, Vittorio Bonicelli, and Ugo Pirro from novel by Giorgio Bassani. With Dominique Sanda, Lino Capolicchio, Helmut Berger, Fabio Testi, Romolo Valli.

The Go-Between. Director, Joseph Losey; screenplay, Harold Pinter from novel by L. P. Hartley. With Julie Christie, Alan Bates, Dominic Guard, Margaret Leighton, Michael Redgrave, Michael Gough.

Going Home. Director, Herbert B. Leonard; screenplay, Lawrence B. Marcus. With Robert Mitchum, Brenda Vaccaro, Jan-Michael Vincent.

Happy Birthday, Wanda June. Director, Mark Robson; screenplay by Kurt Vonnegut, Jr., from his play. With Rod Steiger, Susannah York, George Grizzard, Don Murray, William Hickey, Steven Paul.

Harold and Maude. Director, Hal Ashby; screenplay, Colin Higgins. With Ruth Gordon, Bud Cort, Vivian Pickles, Cyril Cusack.

The Hellstrom Chronicle. Director, Walon Green; screenplay, David Seltzer. With Lawrence Pressman.

The Hired Hand. Director, Peter Fonda; screenplay, Alan Sharp. With Fonda, Warren Oates, Verna Bloom, Robert Pratt, Severn Darden.

Hoa-Binh. Director, Raoul Coutard; screenplay, Coutard, from novel by Françoise Lorrain. With Phi Lan, Huynh Cazenas, Xuan, Ha, Le Quynh, Lan Phuong.

The Horsemen. Director, John Frankenheimer; screenplay, Dalton Trumbo from novel by Joseph Kessel. With Omar Sharif, Leigh Taylor-Young, Jack Palance.

The Hospital. Director, Arthur Hiller; screenplay, Paddy Chayevsky. With George C. Scott, Diana Rigg, Barnard Hughes, Richard Dysart.

Innocence Unprotected. Director-scenarist, Dusan Makaveyev. With Dragoljub Aleksic, Ana Milosavljevic.

Is There Sex After Death? Directors-scenarists, Jeanne and Alan Abel. With Buck Henry, Rubin Carson, Jim Moran, Larry Wolf, Robert Downey.

Joe Hill. Director-scenarist, Bo Widerberg. With Thommy Berggren, Anja Schmidt, Kelvin Malave, Everl Anderson.

King Lear. Director-scenarist, Peter Brook from play by William Shakespeare. With Paul Scofield, Irene Worth, Jack MacGowran, Alan Webb, Cyril Cusack, Patrick Magee.

Klute. Director, Alan J. Pakula; screenplay, Andy K. and Dave Lewis. With Jane Fonda, Donald Sutherland, Charles Cioffi, Roy Scheider.

La Collectioneuse. Director-scenarist, Eric Rohmer. With Patrick Bauchau, Haydee Politoff, Daniel Pommereulle, Mijanou Bardot, Seymour Hertzberg.

The Last Movie. Director, Dennis Hopper; screenplay, Stewart Stern from story by Hopper and Stern. With Hopper, Julie Adams, Sam Fuller, Peter Fonda, Severn Darden, Stella Garcia.

The Last Picture Show. Director, Peter Bogdanovich; screenplay, Larry McMurtry and Bogdanovich from novel by McMurtry. With Timothy Bottoms, Jeff Bridges, Cybill Shepherd, Ben Johnson, Cloris Leachman, Ellen Burstyn, Eileen Brennan.

Le Boucher. Director-scenarist, Claude Chabrol. With Stephane Audran, Jean Yanne.

Le Chagrin et la pitie. Director, Marcel Ophuls; script and interviews, Ophuls and André Harris.

Le Mans. Director, Lee H. Katzin; screenplay, Harry Kleiner. With Steve McQueen, Elga Andersen.

Little Murders. Director, Alan Arkin; screenplay, Jules Feiffer from his play. With Elliott Gould, Marcia Rodd, Vincent Gardenia, Elizabeth Wilson, Jon Korkes, Donald Sutherland, Arkin.

Long Ago Tomorrow. Director-scenarist, Bryan Forbes from novel by Peter Marshall. With Malcolm McDowell, Nanette Newman, Georgia Brown, Bernard Lee.

Macbeth. Director, Roman Polanski; screenplay, Polanski and Kenneth Tynan from play by William Shakespeare. With Jon Finch, Francesca Annis, Martin Shaw, Nicholas Selby, John Stride.

Made for Each Other. Director, Robert B. Bean; screenplay, Renee Taylor and Joseph Bologna. With Renee Taylor, Bologna, Paul Sorvino, Olympia Dukakis, Helen Verbit, Louis Zorich.

Maidstone. Director-scenarist, Norman Mailer. With Mailer, Rip Torn, Joy Bang, Buzz Farbar, Lenny Green, Harris Yulin, Beverly Bently.

McCabe and Mrs. Miller. Director, Robert Altman; screenplay, Altman and Brian McKay from novel by Edward Naughton. With Warren Beatty, Julie Christie, René Auberjonois, Shelley Duvall.

Medea. Director-scenarist, Pier Paolo Pasolini from play by Euripides. With Maria Callas, Giuseppi Gentile, Laurent Terzieff, Margareth Clementi.

Millhouse. Director, Emile De Antonio.

Minnie and Moskowitz. Director-scenarist, John Cassavetes. With Gena Rowlands, Seymour Cassell, Val Avery, Katherine Cassavetes, Lady Rowlands.

Murmur of the Heart. Director-scenarist, Louis Malle. With Lea Massari, Benoit Fereux, Daniel Gelin, Michel Lonsdale.

A New Leaf. Director-scenarist, Elaine May from short story by Jack Ritchie. With Walter Matthau, Elaine May, Jack Weston, George Rose, William Redfield, James Coco, Renee Taylor.

Nicolas and Alexandra. Director, Franklin J. Schaffner; screenplay, James Goldman from book by Robert K. Massie. With Michael Jayston, Janet Suzman, Harry Andrews, Irene Worth, Tom Baker, Laurence Olivier, Michael Redgrave, John McEnery.

The Nun. Director, Jacques Rivette; screenplay, Jean Grualt and Rivette from novel by Denis Diderot. With Anna Karina, Liselotte Pulver, Micheline Presle, Francine Berge, Francisco Rabal.

On Any Sunday. Director-scenarist, Bruce Brown. With Mert Lawwill, Malcolm Smith, Steve McQueen.

One Day in the Life of Ivan Denisovich. Director, Caspar Wrede; screenplay, Ronald Harwood from novel by Aleksandr I. Solzhenitsyn. With Tom Courtenay, Alfred Burke, James Maxwell, Eric Thompson.

Panic in Needle Park. Director, Jerry Schatzberg; screenplay, Joan Didion and John Gregory Dunne from book by James Mills. With Al Pacino, Kitty Winn.

Ramparts of Clay. Director, Jean-Louis Bertucelli; screenplay, Jean Duvignaud. With Leila Schenna and inhabitants of Tehouda, Algeria.

Red Sky at Morning. Director, James Goldstone; screenplay, Marguerite Roberts from novel by Richard Bradford. With Richard Thomas, Catherine Burns, Desi Arnaz, Jr., Richard Crenna, Claire Bloom.

Rio Lobo. Director, Howard Hawks; screenplay, Leigh Brackett and Burton Wohl. With John Wayne, Jorge Rivero, Jennifer O'Neill, Jack Elam.

Romance of a Horsethief. Director, Abraham Polonsky; screenplay, David Opatoshu. With Yul Brynner, Eli Wallach, Jane Birkin, Lainie Kazan, Opatoshu.

Sacco and Vanzetti. Director, Giuliano Montaldo; screenplay, Fabrizio Onofri and Montaldo. With Gian Maria Volonte, Riccardo Cucciolla, Milo O'Shea.

A Safe Place. Director-scenarist, Henry Jaglom. With Tuesday Weld, Orson Welles, Jack Nicholson.

A Severed Head. Director, Richard Clement; screenplay, Frederic Raphael from novel and play by Iris Murdoch. With Ian Holm, Lee Remick, Richard Attenborough, Claire Bloom, Jennie Linden, Olive Revill.

Shaft. Director, Gordon Parks; screenplay, Ernest Tidyman and John D. F. Black. With Richard Rountree, Moses Gunn, Gwen Mitchell, Charles Cioffi.

Shoot Out. Director, Henry Hathaway; screenplay, Marguerite Roberts from novel by Will James. With Gregory Peck, Dawn Lyn, Pat Quinn, Robert F. Lyons.

Skin Game. Director, Paul Bogart; screenplay, Pierre Morton from story by Richard A. Simmons. With James Garner, Lou Gossett, Susan Clark, Brenda Sykes.

Socrates. Director, Roberto Rossellini; screenplay, Rosselini and Marcella Mariana. With Jean Sylvere, Ricardo Palaclos, Beppi Mannaiulo, Anne Caprile.

Such Good Friends. Director, Otto Preminger; screenplay, Esther Dale from David Shaber's adaptation of novel by Lois Gould. With Dyan Cannon, James Coco, Jennifer O'Neill, Ken Howard, Nina Foch, Laurence Luckinbill, Sam Levine.

Summer of '42. Director, Robert Mulligan; screenplay, Herman Raucher from his novel. With Jennifer O'Neill, Gary Grimes, Jerry Houser, Oliver Conant.

Sunday Bloody Sunday. Director, John Schlesinger; screenplay, Penelope Gilliatt. With Peter Finch, Glenda Jackson, Murray Head, Peggy Ashcroft, Tony Britton, Maurice Denham, Bessie Love.

The Taira Clan. Director, Kenji Mizoguchi; screenplay, Yoda Yoshikata and Kyoto Masashige from novel by Eiji Yoshikawa. With Raizo Ichikawa, Michiyo Kogure, Yoshiko Kuga.

Taking Off. Director, Milos Forman; screenplay, Forman, John Guare, Jean-Claude Carriere, and John Klein. With Lynn Carlin, Buck Henry, Linnea Heacock, Georgia Engel, Tony Harvey, Audrey Lindley, Paul Benedict.

THX 1138. Director, George Lucas; screenplay, Lucas and Walter Murch. With Robert Duvall, Donald Pleasence, Magie McOmie, Don Pedro Colley.

The Touch. Director-scenarist, Ingmar Bergman. With Bibi Andersson, Elliott Gould, Max von Sydow.

The Trojan Woman. Director-scenarist, Michael Cacoyannis from Edith Hamilton's translation of play by Euripides. With Katharine Hepburn, Vanessa Redgrave, Genevieve Bujold, Irene Papas.

Two-Lane Blacktop. Director, Monte Hellman; screenplay, Rudolph Wurlitzer and Will Corry. With James Taylor, Warren Oates, Laurie Bird, Dennis Wilson.

Une Femme Douce. Director-scenarist, Robert Bresson from story by Dostoevsky. With Guy Frangin, Dominique Sanda, Jane Lobre.

Viva la Muerte. Director-scenarist, Fernando Arrabal. With Anouk Ferjac, Nuria Espert, Ivan Henriques, Mahdi Chaouch, Jazia Klibi.

Walkabout. Director, Nicholas Roeg; screenplay, Edward Roeg from novel by James Vance Marshall. With Jenny Agutter, Lucien John, David Gumpilil.

Wanda. Director-scenarist, Barbara Loden. With Barbara Loden, Michael Higgins, Frank Jourdano.

Who Is Harry Kellerman and Why Is He Saying Those Terrible Things About Me? Director, Ulu Grosbard; screenplay, Herb Gardner. With Dustin Hoffman, Barbara Harris, Jack Warden, David Burns.

Wild Rovers. Director-scenarist, Blake Edwards. With William Holden, Ryan O'Neal, Karl Malden, Lynn Carlin, Tom Skerritt, Leora Dana, Moses Gunn.

W. R. Mysteries of the Organism. Director-scenarist, Dusan Makaveyev.

Three of the world's foremost directors were associated with three of the year's most acclaimed films. Mike Nichols' Carnal Knowledge (above) *stars Jack Nicholson and Ann-Margret. (Right) Jean-Claude Brialy is attracted to a young girl, Laurence de Monaghan, in Eric Rohmer's* Claire's Knee. *(Below) Claude Jade and Jean-Pierre Leaud begin a rocky marriage in François Truffaut's* Bed and Board.

(Continued from page 478)

Sunday Bloody Sunday, and the consensus was that they brought it off tastefully. Similarly, the incestuous relationship between mother and son in Louis Malle's *Murmur of the Heart* constituted another "tasteful" breakthrough into taboo material.

Joseph Losey's *The Go-Between* was one of the most impeccable entertainments of 1971. Losey was less fortunate with the excessively schematic allegory of *Figures in a Landscape.* Norman Mailer made another effort to transport his literary sensibility to the screen in *Maidstone,* with mixed results. Ingmar Bergman failed to convince American audiences that Elliott Gould belonged in the same Nordic heaven with Bibi Andersson and Max von Sydow. Nonetheless, Bergman's *The Touch* was one of his most compelling films, and Miss Andersson's performance one of the richest of the year.

The gimmicky movie was still very much in demand in 1971 as the success of Robert Wise's *The Andromeda Strain,* Boris Sagal's *The Omega Man,* and Don Taylor's *Escape from the Planet of the Apes* demonstrated. Bryan Forbes' *Long Ago Tomorrow,* treating the problems of emotionally involved paraplegics, suggested that the most half-baked humanism still had a future. Amid the clamor for entertainment suitable for children, such a tasteful effort as James Hill's *Black Beauty* was so completely overlooked that one might be justified in thinking that children had less to do with the clamor than did childish adults with a vain desire to censor other adults.

The Film Industry. At the end of 1971, the Hollywood studio system was tottering but still nominally intact. Production was down, but there were over 100 films on the shelf waiting to be distributed. There also seemed to be a great many companies hitherto unconnected with the film industry anxious to become involved with what remained the most glamorous business of all. Interest in film on the campus continued to increase, but the motion picture field seemed to be only the most conspicuous victim of the current economic recession.

Awards. The National Society of Film Critics selected Eric Rohmer's *Claire's Knee* as the best film of 1971. Its other choices: best actor, Peter Finch, for his performance in *Sunday Bloody Sunday;* best actress, Jane Fonda, for her performance in *Klute;* best supporting actor, Bruce Dern, for *Drive, He Said;* best supporting actress, Ellen Burstyn, for *The Last Picture Show;* best director, Bernardo Bertolucci for *The Conformist;* and best screenplay, Penelope Gilliatt for *Sunday Bloody Sunday.* A special award went to Marcel Ophuls' *Le Chagrin et la pitié* as "a film of extraordinary public interest and distinction."

The New York Film Critics voted *A Clockwork Orange* the best motion picture of 1971, and its director Stanley Kubrick, best director. Other awards went to Gene Hackman as best actor for *The French Connection,* and to Jane Fonda as best actress for *Klute.* Ellen Burstyn and Ben Johnson were named for their supporting performances in *The Last Picture Show.* The honors for best screenplay were tied between Penelope Gilliatt for *Sunday Bloody Sunday* and Larry McMurtry and Peter Bogdanovich for *The Last Picture Show.* (See also PRIZES AND AWARDS.)

ANDREW SARRIS
Columbia University

MOZAMBIQUE

The war between Portuguese forces and Mozambique nationalists continued to dominate events in Mozambique in 1971. In June, the Portuguese National Assembly approved a government bill authorizing greater autonomy for Portugal's overseas territories, particularly Angola and Mozambique. The bill authorized the local legislature to organize the provincial administration, prepare the territory's budget, and raise revenue. The Portuguese government retained control of territorial defense and foreign policy.

The War. Portugal continued in its determination to maintain control of its overseas territories. By the middle of 1971 it had 40,000 soldiers, half of whom were local black recruits, in Mozambique.

Official army sources reported that between June and December 1970 the rebels had casualties of 1,804 dead and 651 wounded, while 132 Portuguese troops had been killed.

On Feb. 1, 1971, the guerrillas were reported to have opened two offensives, one south of the Messalo River and another in the Tete district. On March 14, the Portuguese military commander, Gen. Kaulza de Arriaga, declared that his forces had sealed off the principal infiltration routes along the Tanzanian border and captured the chief insurgent bases in northern Mozambique. But the rebels continued to harass traffic along the road connecting Rhodesia and Malawi. It was reported on August 17 that Malawi had turned two gunboats over to the Portuguese authorities to be used to patrol Lake Malawi against attacks by the Mozambique Liberation Front (FRELIMO).

The Portuguese government was concerned over the deteriorating situation on the home front, where antiwar sentiment and violence appeared to be growing. On April 26, an explosion on a ship off the coast of Mozambique caused the death of 23 crew members. On July 25, three Portuguese suspected of being members of the Lisbon-based Armed Revolutionary Action group were placed under arrest in Nacala, Mozambique, in connection with the explosion.

On May 25 the Portuguese government expelled from Mozambique all members of the White Fathers, a Catholic missionary order. Two members of the order were accused of recruiting terrorists for FRELIMO.

RHEA MARSH SMITH
Rollins College

Leonard Bernstein's *Mass* was a major musical event of 1971. The *Mass* was commissioned for the opening in September of the John F. Kennedy Center for the Performing Arts.

Music

One of the major cultural events of 1971 was the opening, in September, of the John F. Kennedy Center for the Performing Arts in Washington, D. C. For lovers of the arts everywhere, this event seemed to augur a brighter future for the performing arts in the United States. However, the world of music was also darkened in 1971 by the deaths of two distinguished musical figures of the first half of the 20th century, Igor Stravinsky (see STRAVINSKY, IGOR) and Louis Armstrong (see ARMSTRONG, LOUIS).

CLASSICAL MUSIC

The Kennedy Center. The Kennedy Center, the "national cultural center of the United States," was designed by Edward Durell Stone and built at a reported cost of $70 million on a 17-acre site on the east bank of the Potomac River. The ground floor of the structure, which is 630 feet long and 300 feet wide, comprises an opera house, a concert hall, and a theater, the Eisenhower Theater. A film theater is located on the roof-terrace level directly above the Eisenhower Theater.

The Center was officially inaugurated on September 8 with the world premiere, in the opera house, of Leonard Bernstein's *Mass,* a work calling for about 200 participants. The performing forces included a symphony orchestra, a mixed chorus, a boys' choir, several rock and jazz combos, a baritone soloist (Alan Titus), some taped material, and the Alvin Ailey Dance Company. The Latin text of the Roman Catholic Mass was supplemented with texts by Bernstein and Stephen Schwartz. Choreography was by Ailey, and the production was directed by Gordon Davidson; Maurice Peress

conducted. The audience in the 2,200-seat opera house included the composer, members of the Kennedy family, government officials, and well-known figures of the U. S. musical world.

On September 9 the National Symphony Orchestra, under its permanent conductor Antal Dorati, inaugurated the 2,750-seat concert hall with a program of Beethoven, Stravinsky, Mozart, and William Schuman. Among the soloists heard were violinist Isaac Stern and baritone Simon Estes. President and Mrs. Nixon and Mrs. Dwight D. Eisenhower attended. On September 10 the opera house saw the world premiere of Ginastera's opera *Beatrix Cenci,* conducted by Julius Rudel, musical director of the Kennedy Center. Arlene Saunders and Justino Díaz sang leading roles. The work was commissioned by the Opera Society of Washington.

The rest of the Kennedy Center's fall season included, in the opera house, a presentation of Handel's *Ariodante* with Beverly Sills (Julius Rudel conducting) and a revival of Leonard Bernstein's musical *Candide;* and in the concert hall, a Founding Artists series which ranged from the Istomin-Stern-Rose Trio, Gina Bachauer, and the New York Pro Musica to the 5th Dimension, Peggy Lee, and Pearl Bailey. Also in the concert hall, Pierre Boulez and the New York Philharmonic launched a planned series of performances by 12 of the world's leading symphony orchestras. A three-day series called the "1971 House of Sounds" brought jazz luminaries Count Basie and Gerry Mulligan to the Center.

In the summer of 1971, George London, who had been the Kennedy Center's artistic administrator for three years, resigned to become general director of the Los Angeles Music Center Opera Association and executive director of the National Opera Institute. In November, Martin Feinstein became executive director of the Kennedy Center, with responsibilities more general than London's had been.

Other New Facilities. The Pittsburgh Symphony's new home, Heinz Hall for the Performing Arts, was also inaugurated in September with a program including Samuel Barber's *Fadograph of a Yestern Scene,* commissioned by the Alcoa Foundation. William Steinberg, the orchestra's music director, conducted. Converted from a cinema in the city's downtown Golden Triangle area, the 2,700-seat hall cost a reported $7 million to renovate and was unanimously declared an acoustical success. In October the University of Michigan opened its $3.5 million Power Center for the Performing Arts with the world premiere of a musical version of Truman Capote's play *The Grass Harp.*

Perhaps the most distinctive U. S. summer home for the arts is the new Wolf Trap Farm Park for the Performing Arts, which opened in Vienna, Va., on July 1. The 117-acre grounds were the gift of Mrs. Jouett Shouse to the U. S. Department of the Interior. With her additional gift of $2 million, the 3,500-seat open-air Filene Center auditorium was built at the bottom of a natural amphitheater. The Center has facilities for opera, ballet, concerts, and theater. Also part of the Wolf Trap complex is a music school operated by American University.

Abroad, Helsinki saw the opening of Finlandia House, a concert hall and conference center, in December. An 1,800-seat auditorium and a 350-seat chamber-music hall are among its facilities.

Orchestras. Pierre Boulez succeeded Leonard Bernstein as music director of the New York Philharmonic in September. In October, Lorin Maazel, who was named associate principal conductor of London's New Philharmonic Orchestra earlier in the year, was tapped for music director of the Cleveland Orchestra, effective with the 1972–73 season. Lucas Foss was named conductor and music adviser of the Brooklyn Philharmonic for the 1971–72 season.

Abroad, the Hallé Orchestra invited James Loughran to fill the post of principal conductor left vacant by the death in August 1970 of Sir John Barbirolli. Kazuyoshi Akiyama, music director of the Tokyo Symphony and principal conductor of the Osaka Philharmonic, will become music director of the Vancouver Symphony effective with the 1972–73 season.

Concert Life. The dominant figure in New York's concert life in 1971 was Pierre Boulez. In the spring he conducted the New York Philharmonic in an evening of Schoenberg, Berg, and Webern and in an all-Stravinsky memorial concert. He also conducted the Juilliard Ensemble in a program that included his own *Marteau sans Maître* in the "New and Newer Music" series at Alice Tully Hall. As music director of the New York Philharmonic, his influence was felt in the programming of much seldom-heard repertoire, with special concentration on Liszt and Berg. Also new were the "preconcert" recitals given by soloists or orchestra members for subscription holders, and the "Prospective Encounters" series, held in the Martinson Hall of the Shakespeare Festival Public Theater, in which Boulez and his composing and performing colleagues played contemporary music and discussed it with the audi-

ence. One of the pieces on these programs was Mario Davidovsky's *Synchronisms No. 6,* for piano and taped sounds, winner of the 1971 Pulitzer Prize for Music.

The spring saw two programs of the works of Karlheinz Stockhausen: one, of his *Hymnen,* with Stockhausen leading the New York Philharmonic and the Group Stockhausen, supplemented by electronic tape; and another consisting of four works played by the Group Stockhausen in the "New and Newer Music" series. Luciano Berio led the American Symphony Orchestra in the New York premieres of his *Chemins I* for harp and orchestra, and *Epifanie* for voice and orchestra. In March, Alexander Schneider's New School Concerts celebrated their 15th anniversary with an evening of chamber music in the college auditorium; participants included violinist Pinchas Zukerman and pianist Peter Serkin. A four-day Tully Hall festival of the choral music of Josquin des Prés on the 450th anniversary of his death brought in succession four first-class aggregations—the New York Pro Musica, the Prague Madrigal Singers, the Schola Cantorum Stuttgart, and the Capella Antiqua of Munich.

In the fall of 1971, both Virgil Thomson and Roger Sessions became 75 years old, and the Juilliard String Quartet marked its 25th birthday. Thomson was honored by the Philadelphia Orchestra, which played his *Three Pictures for Orchestra;* by Newell Jenkins' Clarion Concerts, which gave the New York premiere of Thomson's *Nativity;* and by an operatic group which presented his 1947 opera *The Mother of Us All* (libretto by Gertrude Stein) in St. Peter's Church, Manhattan. The Juilliard School

PABLO CASALS (*right foreground*), world-renowned cellist, plays at United Nations Day concert on October 24. Casals conducted premiere of his *Hymn to the United Nations* during tribute to peace and the UN.

SPONTANEOUS OVATION greets Sir Rudolf Bing, general manager of New York's Metropolitan Opera, at Lincoln Center in September. Bing will retire at end of 1971–72 season.

toasted Sessions, a faculty member, with a concert including his Concerto for Violin, Cello, and Orchestra. The Juilliard Quartet celebrated its birthday with a concert in Tully Hall.

Other notable events were the first joint appearance anywhere of soprano Victoria de los Angeles and her compatriot the pianist Alicia de Larrocha, in a program of Spanish works at Hunter College Assembly Hall; and an all-Brahms lieder recital in Carnegie Hall by Christa Ludwig in which Leonard Bernstein made one of his rare appearances as piano accompanist. In December, Bernstein, conductor-laureate of the New York Philharmonic, led his 1,000th concert with the orchestra.

At the United Nations in October, 94-year-old Pablo Casals led the UN singers, the Manhattan School of Music Chorus, and the Orchestra of the Festival Casals in his own *Hymn to the United Nations,* set to a poem by W. H. Auden. Both music and text were commissioned by Secretary-General U Thant for the UN anniversary concert.

In August the Chicago Symphony, with music director Georg Solti and principal guest conductor Carlo Maria Giulini, went on the first European tour of its 80-year history and had great success. In the United States, Solti led the orchestra, first in Chicago and later in New York, in two outstanding concert versions of operas, Wagner's *Das Rheingold* and Schoenberg's *Moses und Aron.*

In Los Angeles in May, the Los Angeles Philharmonic Contempo '71 series gave the U. S. premieres of Hans Werner Henze's *Essay on Pigs* and Henri Lazarof's Concerto for Cello and Orchestra. In November, Zubin Mehta initiated his 10th season with the Los Angeles Philharmonic with Mahler's Second Symphony. The beginning of Eugene Ormandy's 36th season as music director of the Philadelphia Orchestra was marked, in September, by a commissioned piece by Samuel Barber, *The Lovers.*

Opera. Sir Rudolf Bing, who was knighted by Queen Elizabeth II of England in 1971, started his final season as general manager of the Metropolitan Opera with Verdi's *Don Carlo* in the 1950 production with which he began his career there. One new production in the fall was the first mounting of Weber's *Der Freischütz* in more than 40 years. Another was a highly acclaimed presentation of Wagner's *Tristan und Isolde,* staged by August Everding, with sets and costumes by Gunther Schneider-Siemssen, and featuring Birgit Nilsson and Jess Thomas with Erich Leinsdorf conducting. In May it was announced that Goeran Gentele, who succeeds Bing next season, had appointed the first music director in the Met's history: Rafael Kubelik, music director of the Bavarian Radio Orchestra. Kubelik's 3-year appointment will begin in 1973.

The New York City Opera's spring season saw the world premiere of *The Most Important Man,* with music and libretto by Gian Carlo Menotti, who was stage director as well. The Chicago Lyric Opera began its fall season with Rossini's *Semiramide,* with Joan Sutherland and Marilyn Horne. The San Francisco Opera's season had standout performances of Strauss' *Der Rosenkavalier,* with Sena Jurinac and Christa Ludwig, and Massenet's *Manon,* with Beverly Sills and Nicolai Gedda. The Western Opera Theater, an offshoot of the San Francisco Opera, offered the first performance anywhere in its original form of the one-act opera *Le Testament de Villon* (1921–22), with music by Ezra Pound. The work was presented at the new Zellerbach Hall, University of California, Berkeley.

In August, John Crosby's Santa Fe Opera offered *Der fliegende Holländer,* led by the Dutch conductor, Edo de Waart, and the world premiere of Heitor Villa-Lobos' *Yerma,* with a libretto based on Lorca's play. Christopher Keene, a young American, won high praise for his conducting of *Yerma.*

The Center Opera of Minneapolis toured the East Coast with its much-praised production of Thomson's *The Mother of Us All* and with the mixed-media "lyric-theater ritual" *Faust Counter*

Faust, staged by W. Wesley Balk and with music by John Gessner. In Minnesota, the St. Paul Opera opened a summer festival with the world premiere of Lee Hoiby's *Summer and Smoke,* with a libretto derived from Tennessee Williams' play. Frank Corsaro staged the work, and Igor Buketoff conducted.

In Europe the refurbished Paris Opéra, closed since early 1970, reopened on September 30 with *Die Walküre,* featuring Régine Crespin, Berit Lindholm, and Jean Cox. Other presentations of the season included an evening of one-act works: Ravel's *L'Heure espagnole* and Puccini's *Gianni Schicchi* and *Il Tabarro.* In June it was announced that Rolf Liebermann, *Intendant* of the Hamburg Opera since 1959, had been appointed administrator of the Théâtres Lyriques Nationaux, which includes both the Opéra and the Opéra-Comique. Liebermann will assume the post in 1973. Georg Solti will be musical adviser for both houses. Bernard Lefort is to be director of the Opéra and Louis Erlo director of the Opéra-Comique.

The Soviet Union and Austria agreed to trade opera companies for a few weeks in the fall. The Bolshoi Theater Ensemble in Vienna performed Mussorgsky's *Boris Godunov,* Tchaikovsky's *Queen of Spades,* and Prokofiev's *War and Peace.* In the last, Mstislav Rostropovich won raves as conductor, and his wife, soprano Galina Vishnyevskaya, was acclaimed for her interpretation of the leading female role. The Vienna State Opera in Moscow offered *Der Rosenkavalier, The Marriage of Figaro,* and *Tristan und Isolde.*

A number of new works had premieres in 1971. Hans Werner Henze's *The Tedious Journey to the Flat of Natasha Ungeheuer* was performed first at the Teatro Olimpico in Rome in May and later at the Berlin Festival by the Deutsche Oper of Berlin. The work, which is for baritone, percussion, jazz quartet, and other instruments, is set to verse by the Chilean Marxist poet Gaston Salvatore. More conventional and immediately successful with its audience was Gottfried von Einem's opera *The Visit of an Old Lady,* with a libretto by Friedrich Dürrenmatt, adapted from his play *The Visit.* The opera was given its first performance by the Vienna Staatsoper during the Vienna Festival in June. Christa Ludwig won lavish praise in the title role.

Festivals. Festival fare was routine throughout the world. Such festivals as Tanglewood, Bayreuth, Edinburgh, and Aldeburgh ran smoothly and professionally, but few generated excitement. The annual festival of the International Society for Contemporary Music was held in London in June; works by György Ligeti, Richard Meale, and Peter Maxwell Davies were hailed. The Salzburg Festival offered its first staging of Berg's *Wozzeck* in the Grosses Festspielhaus. Karl Böhm conducted. Anja Silja and Geraint Evans were acclaimed in the leading roles.

Two festivals remote from one another—the 21st Vienna Festival and Dartmouth College's "Crossroads" Festival of the Arts—shared a musical theme: Franz Schubert. During Vienna's *Schubertfest,* Schubert's complete symphonic works were given, his Masses were heard in 10 Vienna churches, and his string quartets were played by the Amadeus Quartet. During the festival in Hanover, N. H., soprano Elly Ameling and baritone Gérard Souzay sang Schubert lieder, and the West End Chamber Ensemble and the Composers String Quartet played his chamber music.

POPULAR MUSIC

In 1971 rock turned for salvation to Christian themes. The way had been pointed in 1970 by the "rock opera" *Tommy,* about the martyrdom of a Christ-like figure, and was paved in 1971 by the presentation of Galt MacDermot's rock Mass in F at the Episcopal Cathedral Church of St. John the Divine, New York, and by the off-Broadway hit musical *Godspell.* The trend reached its height with the success of the New York production of *Jesus Christ Superstar* by Tim Rice and Andrew Lloyd Webber. At year-end this retelling of Christ's Passion in rock patois was well established.

Elsewhere the rock scene was in disarray. Bill Graham closed his two popular rock emporiums, the Fillmore West in San Francisco and the Fillmore East in New York. A "Celebration of Life" and rock in McCrea, La., in June, succumbed to bad planning and drugs. "Hard" rock was being displaced on the record charts by music closer in spirit to the folk revival of the early 1960's and to rhythm-and-blues roots. In spite of the attempt to avoid disorder by inviting nonjazz performers, the Newport Jazz Festival was cancelled on its second evening, July 3, when swarms of young people poured onto the stage and refused to yield it to the performers or to George Wein, the Festival's producer.

Meanwhile, other kinds of American music were delighting performers and listeners in the United States and abroad. In Upper Salford Township, Pa., the 10th annual Philadelphia Folk Festival presented three days of tranquil music making, ranging from bluegrass and gospel to jazz and traditional English, Irish, and American ballads and chanteys. The National Folk Festival at Wolf Trap Farm Park in Vienna, Va., offered similar fare. At the New Orleans Jazz and Heritage Festival in April, the climactic program, a tribute to Louis Armstrong, was marred because the great jazz trumpeter was in the hospital suffering from what proved to be his final illness. However, such performers as Kid Ory, the Preservation Hall Jazz Band, the New Orleans Ragtime Orchestra, Bobby Hackett, and the Black Eagle Jazz Band provided a vital panorama of New Orleans music. Jazz was also an important part of

LORIN MAAZEL, shown conducting Cleveland Orchestra, was appointed its musical director in October, succeeding the late George Szell. The 41-year-old American has been a conductor since he was a child prodigy of eight.

UPI

BEATLES Ringo Starr (*left*) and George Harrison (*right*) perform at August benefit for East Pakistani refugees. Surprise appearance by Bob Dylan (*center*) marked concert at New York's Madison Square Garden.

the Temple University Festival in Ambler, Pa., and at the Concord Summer Festival in Concord, Calif.

Abroad, Duke Ellington and his 17-piece band were wildly acclaimed on a 5-week tour of Russian cities, including Moscow, Leningrad, and Kiev. And it was certainly an affection more permanent than mere nostalgia that accounted for the fact that one of London's fall-season hits was Jerome Kern's 1927 musical, *Showboat*.

ROBERT S. CLARK
Associate Editor, "Stereo Review"

NADER, Ralph. See BIOGRAPHY.
NARCOTICS. See DRUG ADDICTION.

NATIONAL GUARD

Some state governors found it necessary to call upon National Guard units in 1971 to cope with domestic disturbances, but call-ups were much fewer than in 1970. The tragic killing of four students by Guardsmen in 1970 at Kent State University remained festering in the news media in 1971. Performance of National Guard units in other civil disorders reflected higher standards achieved through increased riot training and improved equipment.

There was a change of command, a major change in policy as to use of Reserves and Guard, and new problems of recruiting, especially among minorities.

Command. Maj. Gen. Francis S. Greenlief was appointed by President Nixon in September 1971 to be the new chief of the National Guard Bureau. He had been in the bureau in several capacities for 10 years. He replaced Maj. Gen. Winston P. Wilson, who had been chief since 1963.

Policy Shift. In his fiscal year 1972 budget message to Congress, Secretary of Defense Melvin Laird said that the National Guard and Reserves, "instead of draftees, will be the initial and primary source for augmentation of the active forces in any future emergency requiring a rapid and substantial expansion of the Armed Forces." This policy was "a new approach to U. S. military manpower, based on a goal of zero draft, and an all-volunteer active force, with increased reliance on National Guard and Reserve forces."

General Greenlief stated the effects of the new policy on the Guard in 1971: (1) important contingency missions were reassigned from active Army to Army Guard units; (2) many Guard units were given deployment schedules identical with or earlier than those of the active forces; (3) the Air Guard was rapidly converting to new aircraft and being "tasked" with missions previously assigned to active units; (4) new late-model equipment was going to the Army and Air National Guard so rapidly that assimilation was a major problem.

Because of a new dependence on the National Guard and a closer relationship of the Guard to national security, new studies and analyses were initiated by the Joint Chiefs of Staff in 1971. It became obvious that the Guard was not ready to meet deployment schedules.

Strength. The effect of a projected no-draft environment and the reduction of U. S. forces in Vietnam was the reduction or elimination of recruitment waiting lists among Guard units. In the Army National Guard waiting lists declined more than 40% in 90 days, and from June to September 1971 the strength of the Army Guard declined by 7,500 men. There was a danger that the National Guard might fall seriously under strength. As 1971 drew to an end, the Army Guard had no waiting list in eight states, and the Air Guard had none in two.

As a result, additional money was provided for recruiting during the year beginning July 1, 1971. The Army Guard assigned recruiters in each state. A special effort to enlist recently discharged veterans at Fort Lewis, Wash., and Fort Knox, Ky., had some success.

Minority Groups. The National Guard continued to have trouble attracting minority groups, particularly Negroes. In 1971 the number of minority participants actually decreased. Special efforts were made to attract more blacks.

Other Developments. Brig. Gen. Cunningham C. Bryant, adjutant general of the District of Columbia National Guard, was the first Negro to be promoted to star rank in the Army or Air National Guard.

A U. S. court in Montgomery, Ala., ruled that Maj. Gen. G. R. Doster, head of the Alabama National Guard, and five other officers of the Guard violated federal law when they tried to force Guard officers to contribute to political campaign funds during 1970. Maj. J. B. Calhoun said that after he refused to make a $100 donation, a campaign of intimidation was mounted against him.

A new service medal for National Guardsmen and Reservists was authorized by Army Secretary Robert F. Froehlke. Details of the criteria for eligibility were awaiting publication.

The National Guard Association held its 93d convention in Honolulu, Sept. 19–25, 1971.

WILLIAM J. McCONNELL, *Colonel, USA, Ret.*
Colorado State University

——————— NAURU • Information Highlights ———————
Official Name: Republic of Nauru.
Area: 8 square miles (21 sq km).
Population (1969 census): 7,000.
Government: Head of state, Hammer DeRoburt, president
(took office May 17, 1968). Head of government, Hammer
DeRoburt. Legislature—Legislative Assembly, 18 mem-
bers.
Languages: Nauruan, English.
Education: Literacy rate (1971), almost 100% of population.
School enrollment (1968)—primary, 1,396.
Finances: Monetary unit, Australian dollar (0.8644 dollar
equals U. S.$1, Sept. 1971).
Gross National Product (1969 est.): $24,000,000.
Minerals (metric tons, 1968): Phosphate rock, 2,198,000
(ranks 5th among world producers).

NAURU

An election, the economy, and air travel were the main concerns in 1971 of the Republic of Nauru, located in the Southwestern Pacific.

Election. President Hammer DeRoburt was returned for a second 3-year term in January, following parliamentary elections. DeRoburt, who had become the first president of the newly independent republic in 1968, was unopposed for reelection.

The Economy. In an independence day address on January 31, the president reminded Nauruans of the limited future of the phosphate industry and called for a reexamination of the welfare state economy. The government announced that it will informally exchange representatives with Japan to improve business contacts and phosphate sales.

Air Travel. A new air terminal was under construction in Nauru in 1971, and plans were under way for extending the island's airstrip to enable it to handle larger jet aircraft. In January, Air Micronesia discontinued its twice-monthly flights from Majuro Atoll in the Marshall Islands as a result of a U. S. ban on refueling at Johnston Island, 700 miles (1,125 km) southwest of Hawaii, to which nerve and mustard gases had been transferred from Okinawa. Air Nauru began flights to Majuro under a 5-year permit from the United States.

HOWARD J. CRITCHFIELD
Western Washington State College

NAVY. See DEFENSE FORCES.

NEBRASKA

A heated legislative session, changes in higher education, good crops, extremes of weather, and football fever characterized Nebraska in 1971.

Legislature and Government. The Legislature enacted 556 of 1,077 bills and held over 119. Four of the governor's 12 vetoes were overridden. Important legislation included reapportioning, establishing a statewide community college system, authorizing a department of environmental control, and providing aid to cities for sewage disposal plants. Eighteen state constitutional amendments were referred to the 1972 primary election ballot.

Since newly elected Gov. J. James Exon had promised in his campaign to hold the line on sales and income taxes, the most controversial legislative issues concerned finances and taxes. The governor's austerity budget cut deeply into the state university's request for funds. He also successfully vetoed the controversial personal property exemption bills and a state school-aid plan. However, his vetoes of a cigarette tax bill and a measure returning additional state funds to cities and counties were overridden, and he failed to remove the sales tax on food because of legislative opposition.

The Nebraska supreme court declared the state's self-defense act unconstitutional. The much-criticized act, passed by the Legislature in 1969, authorized a citizen to "use any means necessary" to defend himself or his property from attack. The long argument over Omaha's annexation of the city of Millard was settled by a mandate from the U. S. Supreme Court upholding annexation.

Education. The University of Nebraska's budget request for a 50% increase for the current fiscal year to $94.7 million was reduced $16.6 million by the governor and the Legislature. A more moderate increase of the present $78.1 million budget by 11.1% has been requested for fiscal year 1972–73.

Administrative changes in the state university system included new chancellors for the Omaha and Lincoln campuses. Two of the state's recently established four-year private colleges, John J. Pershing and Hiram Scott, closed during the year. A third, John F. Kennedy, lost two buildings by fire.

Agriculture and Industry. Total crop production in 1971 exceeded the previous record set in 1969. A July-to-October drought reduced yields of sorghum grain, soybeans, hay, and dry-land corn. Wheat's record per-acre yield of 43 bushels resulted in the second-largest crop in history, while increased acreage and irrigation produced the largest corn crop ever. Construction continued on the nuclear power plants at Fort Calhoun, scheduled to be operational by June 1, 1973, and at Brownville.

Natural Disasters. An early January blizzard paralyzed eastern Nebraska. Unseasonably warm weather then caused flooding, particularly in the

——————— NEBRASKA • Information Highlights ———————
Area: 77,227 square miles (200,018 sq km).
Population (1970 census): 1,483,791. Density: 19 per sq mi.
Chief Cities (1970 census): Lincoln, the capital, 149,518;
Omaha, 346,929; Grand Island, 31,269; Hastings, 23,580;
Fremont, 22,962; Bellevue, 19,449; North Platte, 19,447.
Government (1971): Chief Officers—governor, J. James Exon
(D); lt. gov., Frank Marsh (R); secy. of state, Alan J.
Beermann (R); atty. gen., Clarence A. H. Meyer (R); com-
missioner of education, Cecil E. Stanley; treas., Wayne R.
Swanson (R); chief justice, Paul W. White. Legislature—
(unicameral), 49 members (nonpartisan).
Education (1970–71): Enrollment—public elementary schools,
191,000 pupils; 8,961 teachers; public secondary, 138,000
pupils; 8,200 teachers; nonpublic schools (1968–69), 56,400
pupils; 2,430 teachers; college and university (fall 1968),
60,950 students. Public school expenditures (1970–71),
$213,500,000 ($683 per pupil). Average teacher's salary,
$8,120.
State Finances (fiscal year 1970): Revenues, $486,473,000
(2.5% general sales tax and gross receipts taxes, $74,-
883,000; motor fuel tax, $67,781,000; federal funds, $113,-
629,000). Expenditures, $452,301,000 (education, $174,-
054,000; health, welfare, and safety, $9,970,000; highways,
$79,407,000). State debt, $73,535,000 (June 30, 1970).
Personal Income (1970): $5,513,000,000; per capita, $3,700.
Public Assistance (1970): $58,769,000. Average monthly pay-
ments (Dec. 1970)—old-age assistance, $59.75; aid to
families with dependent children, $152.40.
Labor Force: Nonagricultural wage and salary earners (June
1971), 489,700. Average annual employment (1969)—manufacturing, 86,000; trade, 118,000; government, 97,000; services, 79,000. Insured unemployed (Oct. 1971)—3,200
(1.0%).
Manufacturing (1967): Value added by manufacture, $1,150,-
000,000. Food and kindred products, $428,700,000; non-
electrical machinery, $102,100,000; chemicals and allied
products, $91,700,000.
Agriculture (1970): Cash farm income, $2,218,913,000 (live-
stock, $1,445,488,000; crops, $570,418,000; government
payments, $203,007,000). Chief crops (tons)—Corn, 367,-
275,000 bushels; wheat, 97,204,000 bushels; sorghum grain,
76,449,000 bushels (ranks 3d among the states).
Mining (1970): Production value, $74,641,000 (ranks 37th
among the states). Chief minerals (tons)—Sand and
gravel, 12,000,000; stone, 4,840,000; natural gas, 6,708,-
000,000 cubic feet; petroleum, 11,550,000 barrels.
Transportation: Roads (1969), 101,749 miles (163,745 km);
motor vehicles (1969), 929,000; railroads (1968), 5,499
miles (8,850 km); airports (1969), 80.
Communications: Telephones (1971), 883,700; television stations (1969), 14; radio stations (1969), 61; newspapers
(1969), 19 (daily circulation, 481,000).

Elkhorn Valley, and President Nixon declared 17 counties a disaster area. The flood emergency was compounded by a second heavy snow shutting down businesses and schools and curtailing travel.

Football. Early in January, President Nixon went to Lincoln to honor the University of Nebraska's 1970 football team for its Big Eight championship, its Orange Bowl win over Louisiana State University, and its Number 1 rating by the Associated Press. The team remained undefeated and retained its Number 1 rating through the 1971 season.

ORVILLE H. ZABEL, *Creighton University*

NECROLOGY

NECROLOGY. For a list of prominent persons who died in 1971, see the NECROLOGY on pages 761–772.

NEPAL

In 1971, Nepal reconciled some of its major differences with India, which allowed the two countries to sign a new trade and transit treaty.

Indo-Nepal Treaty. Between October 1970 and August 1971, Nepalese government officials were mainly concerned with renegotiating the 1960 Indo-Nepalese trade and transit treaty. The issues involved in the treaty were vital to Nepal, a landlocked nation whose only present access to world transport lanes is through the Indian port of Calcutta. For India, Nepal's main importance is its position on India's defense perimeter against China.

After concessions from both governments, the treaty was signed on August 13. The Indians agreed to allow increased port facilities in Calcutta for Nepalese goods and to permit the goods to be transported through India by road as well as by rail. The Nepalese gave up their demand for a rail route to East Pakistan across a 12-mile (19-km) neck of Indian territory. They also agreed to close the Nepalese stainless steel and synthetic textile factories that exported to India because India sought to protect its own related industries.

Nepal and Bangladesh. Because of Nepal's close ties with both India and Pakistan, it sought to remain neutral regarding the Pakistani civil war that erupted in March and the immense refugee problem that occurred in India as a result.

──────── **NEPAL • Information Highlights** ────────

Official Name: Kingdom of Nepal.
Area: 54,362 square miles (140,797 sq km).
Population (1971 est.): 11,100,000. *Density*, 200 per square mile (77 per sq km). *Annual rate of increase*, 1.8%.
Chief City (1971 est.): Katmandu, the capital, 195,000.
Government: *Head of state*, Mahendra Bir Bikram Shah Deva, king (acceded 1955). *Chief minister*, Kirtinidhi Bista, prime minister (took office April 14, 1971). *Legislature*—National Panchayat; 125 members.
Language: Nepali (official).
Education: *Literacy rate* (1971), 6% of population. *Expenditure on education* (1967), 6.5% of total public expenditure. *School enrollment* (1966)—primary, 394,700; secondary, 69,317; university/higher, 10,235.
Finances (1970 est.): *Revenues*, $76,200,000; *expenditures*, $83,100,000; *monetary unit*, rupee (10.125 rupees equal U. S.$1, Sept. 1971).
Gross National Product (1969 est.): $895,000,000.
National Income (1968): $701,000,000; *per person*, $66.
Consumer Price Index (1969), 127 (1964=100).
Manufacturing (metric tons, 1969): Sugar, 10,000; cigarettes, 1,125,000,000 units.
Crops (metric tons, 1969 crop year): Rice, 2,410,000; jute.
Foreign Trade (1967): *Exports*, $82,000,000 (chief exports—clarified butter, herbs, jute). *Imports*, $107,000,000. *Chief trading partner* (1971)—India.
Transportation: *Roads* (1970), 1,050 miles (1,689 km); *motor vehicles* (1968), 7,000 (automobiles, 4,000); *railroads* (1970), 53 miles (85 km); *national airline*, Royal Nepal Airlines Corp.; *principal airport*, Katmandu.
Communications: *Telephones* (1970), 3,640; *radios* (1969), 50,000; *newspapers* (1969), 16 (daily circulation, 27,000).

On October 3, East Pakistani diplomats in Pakistan's embassy in Katmandu requested the Nepalese government for asylum and for permission to establish a Bangladesh mission in the capital. The Nepalese government attempted to steer a middle course by granting the diplomats asylum but refusing them permission to open a mission, despite strong pro-Bangladesh sentiment in Katmandu.

The Economy. In his annual message before the National Assembly on June 28, King Mahendra called for the 1970's to be Nepal's development decade. Economic development has been slow, and economic stagnation is likely to undermine the king's power. The national planning commission's first annual progress report for the fourth 5-year plan (1970–75) indicated failure to achieve most targets. The government hopes to achieve a modest 2% increase in per capita income during the plan period.

Internal Politics. In 1971, King Mahendra began the 16th year of his reign in firm control of the government, despite sporadic student demonstrations and rumblings of underground political opposition. He continued to appoint and dismiss ministers in rapid succession. He had served as his own prime minister for about a year when he appointed Kirtinidhi Bista to that position on April 14.

FREDERICK H. GAIGE, *Davidson College*

NERUDA, Pablo. See BIOGRAPHY.

NETHERLANDS

The most important political events in the Netherlands in 1971 were the election of a new Second Chamber on April 28 and the swearing-in of a new ministry on July 6. In economics, inflation was a primary concern.

The Election. There were 28 parties offering candidates for membership in the Second Chamber, the lower house of the Staten-Generaal, or parliament. Half of the parties succeeded in winning one or more seats. The ruling coalition ministry, composed of the Catholic People's party, the Peoples' party for Freedom and Democracy (Liberal), the Anti-Revolutionary party, and the Christian Historical Union, received a setback in the election. Their combined strength in the 150-member Second Chamber fell from 83 to 74.

The Labor party, by increasing its seats from 34 to 39, replaced the Catholic party, whose representation declined from 39 to 35, as the largest group in the Second Chamber. Labor made this gain in spite of the defection from the party of a conservative group, the Democratic Socialists-70, which won 8 seats. The movement to the left might have been greater but for warnings that both individuals and the government were overspending and that the Dutch economy was heading for a recession. The Democratic Socialists-70 denounced Labor's "new left" tendencies and advocated retrenchment.

New Ministry. Since no party won a majority in the Chamber, a coalition had to be formed again. On June 22, after protracted efforts to find a coalition that could command a majority, the queen asked Barend W. Bisheuvel to form a ministry. As the leader of the relatively small Anti-Revolutionary party, Bisheuvel did not command any great political strength, but there was a substantial demand for his appointment. By adding the Democratic Socialists-70 to the parties of the old coalition, a ministry that commanded a majority was formed.

——— **NETHERLANDS • Information Highlights** ———

Official Name: Kingdom of the Netherlands.
Area: 15,770 square miles (40,844 sq km).
Population (1970 est.): 13,020,00. *Density,* 830 per square mile (320 per sq km). *Annual rate of increase,* 1.2%.
Chief Cities (1968 est.): Amsterdam, the capital, 852,479; Rotterdam, 704,858; The Hague, 570,765.
Government: *Head of state,* Juliana, queen (acceded Sept. 4, 1948). *Head of government,* Barend W. Bisheuvel, premier (took office July 6, 1971). *Legislature*—Staten-Generaal; First Chamber, 75 members; Second Chamber, 150 members. *Major political parties*—Catholic People's, Labor, Democratic Socialists-70, Christian Historical Union, Freedom and Democracy, Anti-Revolutionary.
Language: Dutch (official).
Education: *Literacy rate* (1970), 98% of population. *School enrollment* (1967)—primary, 1,427,966; secondary, 1,124,-551; technical/vocational, 559,343; higher, 182,044.
Finances (1970): *Revenues,* $7,912,000,000; *expenditures,* $8,263,000,000; *monetary unit,* guilder (3.245 guilders equal U. S.$1, Dec. 30, 1971).
Gross National Product (1970 est.): $31,500,000,000.
National Income (1969): $23,138,000,000; *national income per person,* $1,797.
Economic Indexes: *Industrial production* (1970), 175 (1963 = 100); *agricultural production* (1969), 123 (1969 = 100); *consumer price index* (1970), 141 (1963 = 100).
Manufacturing (metric tons, 1969): Residual fuel oil, 24,224,-000; crude steel, 4,713,000; cement, 3,296,000.
Crops (metric tons, 1969 crop year): Sugar beets (1968–69), 5,128,000; potatoes, 4,704,000; wheat, 677,000.
Minerals (metric tons, 1969): Coal, 5,564,000; salt, 2,668,000; crude petroleum, 2,020,000.
Foreign Trade (1968): *Exports,* 1970, $11,766,000,000 (chief exports—food, $1,895,000,000; chemicals, $1,108,000,000). *Imports,* 1970, $13,393,000,000 (chief imports—food, $1,110,800,000; nonelectrical machinery, $877,400,000; chemicals, $754,200,000). *Chief trading partners* (1968)—West Germany (took 28% of exports, supplied 26% of imports); Belgium-Luxembourg (14%—18%); France (11%—6%).
Tourism: *Receipts* (1970), $421,000,000.
Transportation: *Roads* (1970), 59,824 miles (96,275 km); *motor vehicles* (1969), 2,585,000 (automobiles, 2,280,000); *railroads* (1968), 2,023 miles (3,256 km); *merchant fleet* (1971), 5,269,000 gross registered tons; *national airline,* Royal Dutch Airlines (KLM); *principal airports,* Amsterdam (Schiphol), Rotterdam.
Communications: *Telephones* (1970), 3,120,766; *television stations* (1968), 13; *television sets* (1969), 2,869,000; *radios* (1968), 3,174,000; *newspapers* (1968), 94 (daily circulation, 3,907,000).

The new ministry was sworn in on July 6. Bisheuvel, who had been minister of agriculture from 1963 to 1967 and leader of his party in the Second Chamber since then, succeeded Petrus S. De Jong as premier. Only three of Bisheuvel's ministers had served in the previous government. W. K. Norbert Schmelzer, leader of the Catholic People's party in the Second Chamber, succeeded Joseph M. A. H. Luns, who had served as foreign minister for 19 years. Luns became secretary general of NATO. The 16 cabinet posts were distributed among the Catholic People's (6), Anti-Revolutionary (3), Freedom and Democracy (3), Christian Historical Union (2), and Democratic Socialists-70 (2) parties.

The new ministry announced a 23-point program, assigning priority to economic austerity, to reducing government expenditures, and to constructing 550,-000 housing units over four years.

Suffrage Qualifications. In January the Staten-Generaal lowered the voting age from 21 to 18 and the age for holding public office from 25 to 21. These will become effective in 1974.

Foreign Relations. Queen Juliana made a 10-day state visit to Indonesia, a former Dutch colony, in August and September. She was given a warm reception by the Indonesians, who had fought the Dutch bitterly when the Netherlands sought to reestablish its rule after World War II. In late October the queen and Prince Bernhard made their first trip to West Germany, a final symbolic step in post-World War II reconciliation.

Emperor Hirohito of Japan was given a cool government reception on his private visit in early October and was greeted with hostility by the press and the people, who remembered Japanese prisons and concentration camps in the Dutch East Indies.

Economy. Inflationary tensions characterized the economy during 1971. The terms of foreign trade deteriorated, and the trade deficit increased. The U. S. dollar crisis in the spring had severe repercussions on the guilder, whose value was allowed to float. Sizable inflows of capital continued.

On August 4 the new government suspended price and wage controls, relying on the cooperation of employers and trade unions to slow inflationary tendencies. The government also relied on a sound fiscal policy to help the economy regain its balance. It pledged to keep public expenditures within the present margin of 6% of the national income. Some previously free public services will be subject to a fee, and the price of others will be increased.

Religion. Tension between the Vatican and the Roman Catholic Church in the Netherlands was intensified by Pope Paul's appointment of Adrian Simonis, a conservative, as bishop of Rotterdam. This action was against the expressed wishes of Rotterdam's liberally inclined priests and laity. Bishop Simonis adheres to the Vatican's position on celibacy of priests and family planning.

AMRY VANDENBOSCH, *University of Kentucky*

NEVADA

Despite the sluggishness of Las Vegas gaming operations, total tax revenues continued to increase in Nevada during 1971 as the Reno and Lake Tahoe casino areas showed substantial growth.

Legislation. Democratic Gov. D. N. "Mike" O'Callaghan's programs fared very well in the 56th Nevada Legislature, despite the fact that the Republicans had a majority in the Assembly. Some Republican legislators were upset by the governor's personal lobbying efforts in the new legislative building, but the direct approach was generally successful. The legislators were happy to go along with the governor's campaign pledge of no new taxes for the 1971–73 biennium.

Among the important measures enacted by the Legislature were the state's first fair-housing act, some anti-pollution and environmental protection laws, the establishment of two new community colleges, and a public employees arbitration act. A liberalized abortion bill was passed by the Assembly but was defeated once again in the more conservative Senate. The Legislature generally followed the governor's budget proposals and made a substantial increase in state support for public schools.

One of the major problems faced by the 1971 Legislature was reapportionment. The legislators agreed to keep the sizes of the two houses the same, with Clark county gaining an additional 6 seats (for a total of 22) in the Assembly and 3 seats (for a total of 11) in the Senate. The two houses split over the question of single- and multi-member districts. All 40 Assembly members will be elected from single-member districts, whereas 13 of the 20 Senators will run in multi-member districts. Court challenges were filed in both Reno and Las Vegas contesting the constitutionality of the multi-member districts and the population disparities among some of the districts.

University of Nevada. The administrators of the new 2-year medical school at the University of Nevada, Reno, had some anxious weeks before

——————— NEVADA • Information Highlights ———————

Area: 110,540 square miles (286,299 sq km).
Population (1970 census): 488,738. *Density:* 4 per sq mi.
Chief Cities (1970 census): Carson City, the capital, 15,468; Las Vegas, 125,787; Reno, 72,863; North Las Vegas, 36,-216; Sparks, 24,187; Henderson, 16,395.
Government (1971): *Chief Officers*—governor, ·Mike O'Calla-ghan (D); lt. gov., Harry M. Reid (D); secy. of state, John Koontz (D); atty. gen., Robert List (R); treas., Michael Mirabelli (D); supt. of public instruction, Burnell Larson; chief justice, David Zenoff. *Legislature*—Senate, 20 members (13 Democrats, 7 Republicans); House of Representatives, 40 members (22 R, 18 D).
Education (1970–71): *Enrollment*—public elementary schools, 73,768 pupils; 2,782 teachers; public secondary, 53,798 pupils; 2,304 teachers; nonpublic schools (1968–69), 4,500 pupils; 200 teachers; college and university (fall 1968), 10,109 students. *Public school expenditures* (1970–71), $94,100,000 ($804 per pupil). *Average teacher's salary,* $9,551.
State Finances (fiscal year 1970): *Revenues,* $287,822,000 (3% general sales tax and gross receipts taxes, $54,710,-000; motor fuel tax, $24,054,000; federal funds, $66,233,-000). *Expenditures,* $266,500,000 (education, $90,279,000; health, welfare, and safety, $24,096,000; highways, $50,-932,000). *State debt,* $34,111,000 (June 30, 1970).
Personal Income (1970): $2,340,000,000; per capita, $4,544.
Public Assistance (1970): $16,652,000. *Average monthly payments* (Dec. 1970)—old-age assistance, $73.20; aid to families with dependent children, $97.95.
Labor Force: *Nonagricultural wage and salary earners* (June 1971), 211,200. *Average annual employment* (1969)—manufacturing, 8,000; trade, 36,000; government, 36,000; services, 75,000. *Insured unemployed* (Oct. 1971)—7,400 (4.6%).
Manufacturing (1967): *Value added by manufacture,* $133,800,-000: chemicals and allied products, $24,300,000; printing and publishing, $16,300,000.
Agriculture (1970): *Cash farm income,* $82,626,000 (livestock, $65,975,000; crops, $14,571,000; government payments, $2,080,000). *Chief crops* (1970)—Barley, 930,000 bushels; wheat, 810,000 bushels; oats, 156,000 bushels.
Mining (1971): *Production value,* $160,743,000 (ranks 30th among the states). *Chief minerals* (tons)—Sand and gravel, 8,873,000; stone, 1,749,000; copper, 94,970; gold, 398,530 troy ounces.
Transportation: *Roads* (1969), 48,829 miles (78,581 km); *motor vehicles* (1969), 329,000; *railroads* (1968), 1,635 miles (2,631 km); *airports* (1969), 52.
Communications: *Telephones* (1933), 333,000; *television stations* (1969), 7; *radio stations* (1969), 27; *newspapers* (1969), 7 (daily circulation, 143,000).

Howard Hughes' representatives assured Atty. Gen. Robert List in October that the billionaire, who had left the state for the Bahamas, would make good on his pledge of a $300,000 annual donation to the school. Some officials were worried that the earlier refusal to grant a gambling license to one of the officers of the Hughes Tool Company might cause Hughes to renege on his promise.

The two university campuses were free of disruption, except for a sit-in by members of the Black Student Union on the Reno campus.

DON W. DRIGGS, *University of Nevada*

NEW BRUNSWICK

The year 1971 was marked by the continued expansion of social welfare programs and by a worsening economic recession that seriously reduced the provinces' capacity to finance them. Politically, the Conservatives continued to be successful.

Although his Conservative government had been elected in 1970 on a retrenchment platform, Premier Richard Hatfield continued the public policies initiated by the previous Liberal administration. Chief of these was the medicare program launched on January 1, which provided free medical care to all residents. Under this plan, which over 90% of the doctors accepted by February, doctors received 87% of their medical fees from the province. The other major development was a social development report in September that advocated a number of revolutionary administrative changes, designed to make poverty programs more humane and efficient. In early fall a Department of Welfare report revealed

that over 50% of some communities in northern New Brunswick were wholly or partially dependent on provincial welfare services.

Economy. Rapidly spreading unemployment in the province's major lumber and paper industries, which depend on the U. S. market, was partly responsible for the increased dependence on welfare. The U. S. recession reduced demand for New Brunswick products. Unemployment rose to more than 10% by late January, and the province's principal paper firm called upon the provincial government to subsidize the forest products industries. This recession was compounded in the summer by the U. S. surcharge on imports. By December several major paper producers were threatening to close down.

Many employers attempted to hold down costs by restricting increases in wages and benefits. This action precipitated a number of industrial disputes. The most serious occurred when 80% of the public school teachers voted to strike unless their demand for a 26% salary increase over two years was met. The teachers finally accepted a 16% increase.

Politics. Louis J. Robichaud, Liberal party leader and former premier, triggered the year's most important political events. He resigned from the Legislature in the spring to accept the Canadian chairmanship of the International Joint Commission. Robert Higgins, a young St. John lawyer, succeeded him as party leader. Robichaud's resignation provided the Conservative government with its first electoral test since the 1970 general election. In the by-election held to fill Robichaud's seat in Kent county, the Conservatives achieved their first victory there in more than 50 years.

WILLIAM ACHESON, *University of New Brunswick*

——————— NEW BRUNSWICK • Information Highlights ———————

Area: 28,354 square miles (73,437 sq km).
Population: 629,000 (April 1971 est.).
Chief Cities (1966 census): Fredericton, the capital (22,460); St. John (51,567); Moncton (45,847).
Government: *Chief Officers*—lt. gov., Hedard J. Robichaud; premier, Richard B. Hatfield (Progressive Conservative); prov. sec., Rodman E. Logan (PC); min. of justice, John B. M. Baxter (PC); min. of finance, Jean-Maurice Simard (PC); min. of educ., J. Lorne McGuigan (PC); chief justice, G. F. G. Bridges. *Legislature*—Legislative Assembly (convened March 1971); 58 members (32 Progressive Conservatives, 26 Liberal).
Education: *School enrollment* (1968–69 est.)—public elementary and secondary, 169,703 pupils (7,252 teachers); private schools, 468 pupils (60 teachers); Indian (federal) schools, 682 pupils (28 teachers); college and university, 7,927 students. *Public school expenditures* (1971 est.)—$107,830,000. *Average teacher's salary* (1968–69 est.), $5,520.
Public Finance (fiscal year 1971 est.): *Revenues,* $418,900,000 (sales tax, $94,770,000; income tax, $49,896,000; federal funds, $198,242,000). *Expenditures,* $438,990,000 (education, $144,270,000; health and social welfare, $111,050,-000; transport and communications, $68,830,000).
Personal Income (1969 est.): $1,302,000,000.
Social Welfare (fiscal year 1971 est.): $29,460,000 (aged and blind, $8,160,000; dependents and unemployed, $14,380,-000).
Manufacturing (1968): *Value added by manufacture,* $240,753,-000 (food and products, $76,097,000; paper and allied industries, $57,433,000; wood industries, $19,737,000.
Agriculture (1969 est.): *Cash farm income* (excluding supplementary payments, $51,758,000 (livestock, $23,322,000). *Chief crops* (1968 est.): (cash receipts)—Potatoes, $12,-543,000 (ranks 2d among the provinces).
Mining (1969 est.): *Production value,* $98,393,595. *Chief minerals* (tons)—Zinc, 158,200 (ranks 4th among the provinces); lead, 56,140 (ranks 3d); coal, 713,646 (ranks 4th); copper, 7,060 (ranks 8th).
Fisheries (1968): *Commercial catch,* 534,801,000 pounds ($14,-624,000). *Leading species*—Herring, 425,371,000 pounds ($4,899,000); lobster, 5,965,000 pounds.
Transportation: *Roads* (1968), 13,330 miles (21,450 km); *motor vehicles* (1969), 199,980; *railroads* (1969), 1,665 track miles (2,680 km); *licensed airports* (1970), 13.
Communications: *Telephones* (1969), 215,533; *television stations* (1970), 3; *radio stations* (1967), 13; *newspapers* (1970), 6 (daily circulation, 110,700).
All figures given in Canadian dollars.

NEW HAMPSHIRE

Tax reform was a dominant issue in New Hampshire in 1971. Other highlights during the year were the passage of a tight state budget and the growing concern about preserving the rugged natural beauty of New Hampshire.

Taxes. In a dramatic move in February, Gov. Walter Peterson urged the legislature to enact a 3% state income tax with extra exemptions for the elderly and a provision for property tax relief for low-income families. However, anti-tax conservatives in both parties decisively defeated the bill, along with a variety of other proposals for the enactment of broad-base taxes. New Hampshire is now the only state without a sales or income tax.

Legislature. The state legislature passed a bare-bones operating budget of about $161 million for the biennium, approximately $100 million less than the amount Governor Peterson had requested. In the absence of new revenue sources, the legislature adopted a policy of selective retrenchment, drastically cutting state aid to local school districts and reducing appropriation requests for the state university system. As a result, university trustees were forced to raise in-state tuition fees to $1,000—the highest of any state university in the country—and to postpone faculty salary increases for the coming biennium. The legislature rejected a modest request for funds to help restore the Derry homestead of the late poet Robert Frost, but it did provide money for restoring the home of Franklin Pierce, the only President born in New Hampshire.

Unapproved proposals in the session included abortion reform, modification of capital punishment, an environmental bill of rights, state participation in the federal food stamp program, and the creation of a state department of environmental control. The legislature also turned down efforts to ban the use of public funds for sex education and to kill the recently enacted business profits tax.

The legislature did authorize the creation of study groups to explore the feasibility of no-fault automobile insurance and open-space taxation. Also approved were new laws allowing absentee voting in primary elections and admitting "irreconcilable conflict" as a ground for divorce.

Environmental Issues. Environmentalists scored a notable victory in 1971 when state agencies rejected a request by private operators to mine earth deposits under Lake Umbagog, a process that would have ruined the lake. There was continuing concern, however, about the adequacy of state controls over the accelerating private development of New Hampshire's land resources. Also, there was some public opposition to tentative plans to construct a major east-west highway across the northern sections of the state.

Politics. In the November municipal elections, Democratic mayoralty candidates ousted Republican administrations in the cities of Manchester, Rochester, and Somersworth.

At year-end, attention was increasingly focused on national politics as a parade of political hopefuls visited the state in anticipation of the 1972 presidential primary. New Hampshire kept its role as the state with the first presidential primary by changing the date for it from March 14 to March 7, thereby beating back Florida's challenge.

JOSEPH P. FORD
University of New Hampshire

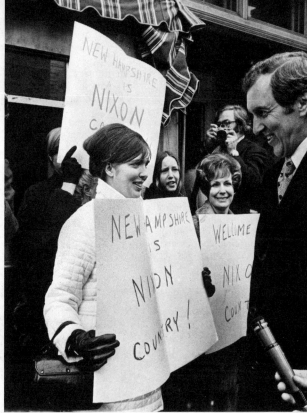

WIDE WORLD

SENATOR Muskie, front-running Democratic presidential candidate, trades quips with Nixon supporters in Manchester during April speaking tour. Presidential hopefuls meet in New Hampshire primary in early 1972.

——— **NEW HAMPSHIRE • Information Highlights** ———

Area: 9,304 square miles (24,097 sq km).
Population (1970 census): 737,681. *Density:* 80 per sq mi.
Chief Cities (1970 census): Concord, the capital, 30,022; Manchester, 87,754; Nashua, 55,820; Portsmouth, 25,717.
Government (1971): *Chief Officers*—governor, Walter Peterson (R); secy. of state, Robert L. Stark (R); atty. gen., Warren B. Rudman (R); treas., Robert W. Flanders; commissioner of education, Newell J. Paire; chief justice, Frank R. Kenison. *General Court*—Senate, 24 members (15 R, 9 D); House of Representatives, 400 members (251 R, 146 D, 3 vac.).
Education (1970–71): *Enrollment*—public elementary schools, 94,624 pupils; 3,935 teachers; public secondary, 64,132 pupils; 3,190 teachers; nonpublic schools (1968–69), 34,-100 pupils; 1,670 teachers; higher (fall 1968), 27,061 students. *Public school expenditures* (1970–71), $105,595,000 ($729 per pupil). *Average teacher's salary,* $8,297.
State Finances (fiscal year 1970): *Revenues,* $281,268,000 (total sales and gross receipts taxes, $62,778,000; motor fuel tax, $23,865,000; federal funds, $56,114,000). *Expenditures,* $273,445,000 (education, $71,583,000; health, welfare, and safety, $24,195,000; highways, $56,620,000).
Personal Income (1970): $2,732,000,000; per capita, $3,608.
Public Assistance (1970): $23,573,000. *Average monthly payments* (Dec. 1970)—old-age assistance, $169.25; aid to families with dependent children, $227.15.
Labor Force: *Nonagricultural wage and salary earners* (June 1971), 264,200. *Average annual employment* (1969)—manufacturing, 98,000; trade, 49,000; government, 35,000; services, 41,000.
Manufacturing (1967): *Value added by manufacture,* $931,900,-000 (electrical equipment, $183,200,000; leather and leather products, $132,500,000; nonelectrical machinery, $129,100,000; paper and allied products, $92,100,000).
Agriculture (1970): *Cash farm income,* $54,975,000 (livestock, $41,496,000; crops, $12,931,000; government payments, $548,000). *Chief crops* (1970)—Apples, 38,000,000 pounds; corn for silage, 256,000 tons; hay, 204,000 tons.
Mining (1971): *Production value,* $8,759,000 (ranks 48th among the states). *Chief minerals* (tons)—Sand and gravel, 6,762,000; stone, 373,000; clays, 39,000.
Fisheries (1970): *Commercial catch,* 1,500,000 pounds ($1,-000,000). *Leading species by value* (1967)—Northern lobsters, $610,300; haddock, $6,000; alewives, $1,650.
Transportation: *Roads* (1969), 14,785 miles; *motor vehicles* (1969), 377,000; *railroads* (1968), 816 miles.
Communications: *Telephones* (1971), 425,300; *television stations* (1969), 2; *radio stations* (1969), 35.

NEW JERSEY

Evidence of corruption at all levels of government again dominated the year in New Jersey. Budget problems and legislative elections complicated the operation of government.

Several leading Hudson county and Jersey City officials went to trial in May on charges of conspiracy and extortion. Mayor Thomas J. Whelan of Jersey City and seven associates were convicted in July. John V. Kenny, Hudson county Democratic leader, succeeded in delaying his trial because of illness. David J. Friedland, Democratic minority leader in the General Assembly, pleaded guilty in a disciplinary hearing before the state supreme court to improperly attempting to have a loan-sharking charge quashed and was suspended from legal practice for six months. Robert J. Burkhardt,

former state Democratic chairman, and William B. Knowlton, a Republican state senator, were indicted for bribery and extortion. Walter H. Jones, a former Republican gubernatorial candidate, was indicted for conspiring to conceal fraud.

Other scandals involved bribery and extortion in connection with cable television franchises in Mercer county and the illegal granting of zoning variances in Camden county. In May, the Bergen county prosecutor was suspended by Gov. William T. Cahill, and in June he was indicted for conspiracy, bribery, and obstruction of justice.

Government and Politics. Problems of governmental finance also plagued New Jersey during the year. Although a committee had been appointed by the governor in 1970 to propose a major revision of the state's tax structure, it was assumed that no report could be expected prior to the November 1971

GOVERNOR William Cahill of New Jersey points out highlights of stadium that will rise in the Hackensack meadows. Primary attraction of sports complex will be football's New York Giants, who announced in August that they would move to New Jersey, but provisions have also been made for baseball and other sports. With Cahill are Giants' owner Wellington Mara and Sonny Werblin, head of authority that will develop the now desolate and swampy meadows (*below*).

——— NEW JERSEY • Information Highlights ———

Area: 7,836 square miles (20,295 sq km).
Population (1970 census): 7,168,164. *Density:* 950 per sq mi.
Chief Cities (1970 census): Trenton, the capital, 104,638; Newark, 382,417; Jersey City, 260,545; Paterson, 144,824; Elizabeth, 112,654; Camden, 102,551.
Government (1971): *Chief Officers*—governor, William T. Cahill (R); secy. of state, Paul J. Sherwin (R); atty. gen., George F. Kugler, Jr. (R); treas., Joseph M. McCrane, Jr.; commissioner, Dept. of Educ., Carl L. Marburger; chief justice, Joseph Weintraub. *Legislature*—Senate, 40 members (28 Republicans, 9 Democrats, 3 vac.); General Assembly, 80 members (59 R, 21 D).
Education (1970–71): *Enrollment*—public elementary schools, 978,120 pupils; 41,831 teachers; public secondary, 503,-880 pupils; 29,069 teachers; nonpublic schools (1968–69), 860,200 pupils; 11,530 teachers; college and university (fall 1968), 170,072 students. *Public school expenditures* (1970–71), $1,530,000,000 ($1,088 per pupil). *Average teacher's salary,* $10,050.
State Finances (fiscal year 1970): *Revenues,* $2,624,852,000 (5% general sales tax and gross receipts taxes, $355,-613,000; motor fuel tax, $200,318,000; federal funds, $458,-611,000). *Expenditures,* $2,539,755,000 (education, $705,-264,000; health, welfare, and safety, $136,778,000; highways, $225,871,000). *State debt,* $1,762,768,000 (June 30, 1970).
Personal Income (1970): $33,674,000,000; per capita, $4,539.
Public Assistance (1970): $416,019,000. *Average monthly payments* (Dec. 1970)—old-age assistance, $77.70; aid to families with dependent children, $252.75.
Labor Force: *Nonagricultural wage and salary earners* (June 1971), 2,633,100. *Average annual employment* (1969)—manufacturing, 897,000; trade, 517,000; government, 356,-000; services, 400,000. *Insured unemployed* (Oct. 1971)—94,000 (4.6%).
Manufacturing (1967): *Value added by manufacture,* $12,738,-200,000; Chemicals and allied products, $2,822,100,000; electrical equipment and supplies, $1,685,000,000; food and kindred products, $1,256,500,000; nonelectrical machinery, $1,041,200,000; fabricated metal products, $899,-700,000; primary metal industries, $578,000,000.
Agriculture (1970): *Cash farm income,* $254,050,000 (livestock, $96,920,000; crops, $152,838,000; government payments, $4,292,000). *Chief crops* (tons)—Peaches, 90,000,-000 pounds (ranks 4th among the states); corn, 5,070,000 bushels; cranberries, 177,000 barrels (ranks 4th); hay, 331,000 tons.
Mining (1970): *Production value,* $89,323,000 (ranks 36th among the states). *Chief minerals* (tons)—Sand and gravel, 17,402,000; stone, 14,251,000; clays, 254,000; zinc, 28,460.
Fisheries (1970): *Commercial catch,* 95,500,000 pounds ($12,-600,000). *Leading species by value* (1969), Surf clams, $4,059,610; menhaden, $643,631; scup or porgy, $631,694; whiting, $285,745.
Transportation: *Roads* (1969) 31,579 miles (50,820 km); *motor vehicles* (1969) 3,490,000; *railroads* (1968), 1,790 miles (2,806 km); *airports* (1969), 21.
Communications: *Telephones* (1971), 4,785,900; *television stations* (1969), 4; *radio stations* (1969), 57; *newspapers* (1969), 31 (daily circulation, 1,753,000).

legislative elections, and the report did not appear until 1972. The tax problem was complicated in January 1972 by a superior court decision ruling unconstitutional the state's system of financing education largely through local property taxes.

In February, Governor Cahill introduced a $1.78 billion budget characterized by him as the product of "a year of agonizing introspection." Disapproving Democrats charged that the budget had been balanced only by drawing upon anticipated 1972 revenue and ignoring 1971 needs, in order to insure the reelection of a Republican Legislature. However, the Democrats were unable to effect any significant changes, and the budget was adopted substantially as presented. Under the new budget, the state's urban-aid program was to receive $24 million, double the 1970 figure.

The November elections resulted in a split Legislature; the Republicans retained control of the Senate by a 24 to 16 margin, but the General Assembly was divided among 40 Democrats, 39 Republicans, and 1 independent—white militant leader Anthony Imperiale of Newark. Governor Cahill declared that he would make no deals with Imperiale in return for his vote. Maneuvering continued through December, as legislative factions attempted to line up the 41 votes needed to organize the General Assembly and elect a speaker.

Other Events. On November 24, only a few weeks after a revolt at New York's Attica prison had led to many deaths, inmates of the Rahway State Prison in New Jersey rioted, took the warden and several guards hostage and gained control of a portion of the prison. Negotiations finally resulted in the release of the hostages and a promise by state authorities to investigate conditions in the prison. By the end of the year, the governor had proposed a comprehensive program of penal reform, although there was still dispute over whether a full amnesty had been promised to the Rahway rioters.

Newark teachers, who had walked off their jobs in 1970, struck again on February 1. The strike became the longest by teachers in a major U. S. city before it was settled on April 18. It was marked by sporadic violence and increased racial tensions in the city. Late in the year there were bitter arguments in Newark over flying the black liberation flag in the schools.

New Jersey became a prospective arena for big league sports with the announcement in August that the New York Giants football team had agreed to shift to a new stadium to be built in the Hackensack Meadowlands. In May the legislature had created a sports and exposition authority to construct the stadium and related facilities.

ERNEST C. ROECK, JR.
Rutgers University

NEW MEXICO

In 1971, New Mexico took major strides in education and in control of alcoholism and drug abuse.

Legislation. The state Legislature unanimously passed a bill, signed by Democratic Gov. Bruce King, giving full adult status to 18-year-olds. They were, however, still forbidden to drink alcoholic beverages until age 21.

Education. King appointed a new Board of Finance, which will sell about 1,400 student loan bonds for college education totaling $1,254,600 at an interest of 6.72%. Future plans call for similar bond issues preceding each semester. This is the first such action by any state.

New Mexico Highlands University in Las Vegas, with a student body that is 54% Mexican-American, received its first Mexican-American president, Frank Angel, Jr., formerly an assistant dean of the University of New Mexico. Students had demonstrated against an earlier appointee from Wisconsin.

Alcoholism and Drug Abuse. Fred Kotzen, director of the Alcoholism Treatment Program, pointed to the success of the out-patient project. It involves the administration of the drug Antabus, which, if the patient also consumes alcohol, makes him violently ill. Of the 225 participants in the project, only 10% have dropped out. Kotzen also announced plans to expand the overall program by adding a 48-bed rehabilitation unit and by producing films and tapes to train staff, analyze patient behavior, provide therapy, and inform the public.

A Drug Abuse Task Force, with an appropriation of $100,000 in state funds, was appointed by the governor to coordinate a statewide treatment and prevention program in local communities. The Department of Hospitals and Institutions will administer the program.

Urban Events. Albuquerque was the scene of riots on June 13 and 14, alleged to be of racial origin, when young Mexican-Americans and others

———— NEW MEXICO · Information Highlights ————

Area: 121,666 square miles (315,115 sq km).

Population (1970 census): 1,016,000. *Density:* 8 per sq mi.

Chief Cities (1970 census): Santa Fe, the capital, 41,167; Albuquerque, 243,751; Las Cruces, 37,857; Roswell, 33,908; Clovis, 28,495; Hobbs, 26,025.

Government (1971): *Chief Officers*—governor, Bruce King (D); lt. gov., Robert A. Mondragon (D); secy. of state, Mrs. Betty Fiorina (D); atty. gen., David L. Norvell (D); treas., Jesse D. Kornegay (D); supt. of public instruction, Leonard Delayo; chief justice, J. C. Compton. *Legislature*—Senate, 42 members (28 Democrats, 14 Republicans); House of Representatives, 70 members (48 D, 22 R).

Education (1970–71): *Enrollment*—public elementary schools, 154,519 pupils; 6,090 teachers; public secondary, 130,637 pupils; 5,530 teachers; nonpublic schools (1968–69), 23,400 pupils; 1,120 teachers; college and university (fall 1968), 38,326 students. *Public school expenditures* (1970–71), $191,919,000 ($713 per pupil). *Average teacher's salary,* $8,214.

State Finances (fiscal year 1970): *Revenues,* $604,901,000 (4% general sales tax and gross receipts taxes, $85,709,000; motor fuel tax, $42,516,000; federal funds, $178,066,000). *Expenditures,* $544,301,000 (education, $266,805,000; health, welfare, and safety, $66,373,000; highways, $89,065,000). *State debt,* $120,694,000 (June 1970).

Personal Income (1970): $3,104,000,000; per capita, $3,044.

Public Assistance (1970): $53,278,000. *Average monthly payments* (Dec. 1970)—old-age assistance, $56.45; aid to families with dependent children, $105.05.

Labor Force: *Nonagricultural wage and salary earners* (June 1971), 302,800. *Average annual employment* (1969)—manufacturing, 20,000; trade, 60,000; government, 86,000; services, 54,000. *Insured unemployed* (Oct. 1971)—6,300 (3.4%).

Manufacturing (1967): *Value added by manufacture,* $204,500,000; Food and kindred products, $40,500,000; ordnance and accessories, $37,300,000; printing and publishing, $16,800,000; stone, clay, and glass products, $16,400,000.

Agriculture (1970): *Cash farm income,* $503,691,000 (livestock, $369,937,000; crops, $90,663,000; government payments, $43,091,000). *Chief crops* (1970)—Sorghum grain, 17,499,000 bushels; wheat, 5,520,000 bushels; hay, 1,044,000 tons; cotton lint, 135,000 bales.

Mining (1970): *Production value,* $1,073,589,000 (ranks 7th among the states). *Chief minerals* (tons)—Copper, 165,260; natural gas, 1,116,729,000,000 cubic feet; petroleum, 130,300,000 barrels; uranium, 11,844,000 pounds.

Transportation: *Roads* (1969), 67,574 miles (108,747 km); *motor vehicles* (1969), 611,000; *railroads* (1968), 2,219 miles (3,571 km); *airports* (1969), 64.

Communications: *Telephones* (1971), 494,400; *television stations* (1969), 7; *radio stations* (1969), 70; *newspapers* (1969), 19 (daily circulation, 208,000).

assembled for a rock concert clashed with police who were checking for the consumption of marihuana and beer. Forty-one persons were injured and $3 million damage was done before the National Guard restored order. Possible underlying causes were long-term resentments by Mexican-Americans, no longer the majority of the city's population, and widespread unemployment among the young.

Albuquerque is the site of the new Albuquerque International Airport and port of entry, which opened in October.

Environment. A coal-fueled power plant at Farmington, built in 1963 as part of a projected 6-plant complex in four states, spread a pall of smog over the once clear Rio Grande Valley. The Senate Interior Committee began hearings on the project in May, and state legislators and citizens formed the New Mexico Committee for Clear Air and Water to work on antipollution measures to be considered during a special legislative session in January 1972.

NORMA S. GILBERT
Texas Woman's University

NEW ORLEANS

In 1971, New Orleans maintained its position as one of the South's leading cities. The year was marked by record-breaking construction, a war on crime, and enhanced national political prestige.

Construction. On the drawing boards in 1971 were at least $380 million worth of office buildings, hotels, and retail outlets within the central business district, which civic officials said needed rejuvenation. The city also adopted a bold policy of turning famous Bourbon and Royal streets into pedestrian malls during peak traffic hours. In supporting the traffic ban, Mayor Moon Landrieu said vehicular traffic was "killing" the French Quarter, the historic old section of the city, which is a major attraction for tourists.

The biggest building boom in the city's 253-year history was marked by the construction of the world's largest indoor arena, the 36-story, $150 million Louisiana Superdome, seating 84,777. After the stadium is completed in 1973, New Orleans expects to become a major-league-baseball city and a potential site of the annual Super Bowl football game. Office building construction was led by work on One Shell Square, a $50 million, 51-story office building, which will be the highest in the city. Several new hotels were under way to bolster the city's tourist industry.

The port, the city's largest industry, continued its $400 million expansion program, begun in 1970, with the leasing of a completely containerized cargo terminal, the first of nine. Tonnage in 1971 increased, to maintain the city's rating behind New York as the second port in the nation in value of foreign commerce and in tonnage of total waterborne commerce. Container handling showed a 94% increase in fiscal 1971 over 1970.

In March the health education authority of Louisiana announced that $100 million would be invested in a new downtown medical complex.

War on Crime. Alarmed by increasing crime during the first three months of 1971, the police department and newspapers launched a successful battle against criminals. By April, decreases in major categories of crime were registered. The police department in 1971 more than doubled the number of its raids on drug peddlers, and a burglary-deterrence program in which citizens were urged to engrave their driver's license number on property in their homes was started. The *Times-Picayune* sponsored a Secret Witness program offering cash rewards to anonymous tipsters who aided police in the arrest of criminals.

A federal strike force cracked down on pinball-machine gambling. On December 5, New Orleans District Attorney Jim Garrison and nine others were indicted on charges of taking money in return for protecting pinball gambling. The case was pending at the end of 1971.

Garrison, who in 1969 had unsuccessfully prosecuted Clay L. Shaw on charges of plotting to kill President John F. Kennedy, remained in the news. A federal judge ruled in May that Garrison could not prosecute Shaw for perjury in the Kennedy case.

Political Activity. New Orleans—and Louisiana—gained prestige in 1971 through positions in the U. S. Congress. Rep. Hale Boggs of New Orleans was elected House majority leader, and F. Edward Hébert of New Orleans became chairman of the House Armed Services Committee. Sen. Allen J. Ellender was named president pro tempore of the U. S. Senate, and Sen. Russell B. Long held the chairmanship of the Senate Finance Committee. Mrs. Dorothy Mae Taylor of New Orleans became the first Negro woman ever to be elected to the state Legislature.

VINCENT P. RANDAZZO, JR.
"The Times-Picayune," New Orleans

NEW YORK

Urban crisis and problems of education, welfare, and crime remained major concerns of New Yorkers in 1971. The state's ever-growing fiscal imbalance, rising taxes, unemployment, and growing costs of government made solutions increasingly difficult.

Budget and Legislation. Gov. Nelson Rockefeller in his annual state of the state message to the Legislature on January 6 did not disclose his budget plans for the fiscal year beginning April 1, 1971, noting that he awaited President Nixon's message on revenue sharing. On February 1 the governor sent his "bare-bones" $8.45-billion budget to the Legislature together with proposed tax increases of $1.1 billion. Although this provided for no new local assistance or services, the Republican-dominated Legislature refused to pass any budget until extensive cuts were made. After many days of debate, it passed, on April 2, a $7.7 billion budget and a reduced tax-increase package of $475 million.

Among the tax measures enacted were those increasing the general state sales tax one cent to a total of four cents, as well as business taxes including a 15% raise in corporate taxes. The sales tax was extended to restaurant meals of less than $1.00—the "hot-dog tax." Defeated were a 10% rise in state income taxes and "nuisance" taxes on beer and liquor licenses.

Major budget trimming came in the areas of welfare, mental health, and public education. A 10% reduction in aid for many of the state's 1.6 million welfare recipients was enacted, along with the elimination of thousands from the Medicaid rolls, by cutting the maximum income for eligibility for a family of four from $5,000 to $4,500. Also signed into law were requirements of one year's residency for welfare assistance and that an employable adult on welfare must accept public welfare jobs.

Eliminated were 10,000 state jobs, either through dismissal or not filling vacancies. By April 1971, 8,250 persons were dismissed, including 2,800 from the department of mental hygiene, 500 from the narcotics addiction control commission, and 500 from the state university.

In June, after an acrimonious political dispute between the governor and Mayor John V. Lindsay of New York City over further state aid to the city, a compromise was worked out providing for a $525 million tax authorization package consisting mostly of an increase in the city's income tax and $300 million in city-issued bonds. The state also guaranteed the payment of $100 million to the city, if that much in new federal aid to the city was not forthcoming. Partially as a result of the dispute and because of the increase in the cost of public services, the Legislature created a commission to investigate the city's structure, management, and fiscal controls.

Despite much belt-tightening, there were a few increases. Legislators' expense allowances, popularly called "lulus," were increased from $3,000 to $5,000. State aid to nonpublic schools for nonreligious education was increased by $33 million. Public school education received an increase of $156 million, which many claimed was inadequate. The South Mall project in Albany received an additional $51 million over the original agreed-upon amount. Comptroller Arthur Levitt predicted that the project would cost in excess of $1.5 billion.

FINANCIAL problems forced New York's cities to seek more state aid in February. Mayors of state's six largest cities headed delegation to meet with Governor Rockefeller in Albany.

THE NEW YORK TIMES

Area: 49,576 square miles (128,402 sq km).
Population (1970 census): 18,190,740. *Density,* 382 per sq mi.
Chief Cities (1970 census): Albany, the capital, 115,781; New York, 7,895,563; Buffalo, 462,768; Rochester, 296,233; Yonkers, 204,297; Syracuse, 197,208.
Government (1971): *Chief Officers*—governor, Nelson A. Rockefeller (R); lt. gov., Malcolm Wilson (R); secy. of state, John P. Lomenzo (R); atty. gen., Louis J. Lefkowitz (R); treas., Edward F. Moylan; commissioner of education, Ewald B. Nyquist; chief judge, Stanley H. Fold. *Legislature*—Senate, 57 members (32 Republicans, 24 Democrats); Assembly, 150 members (79 R, 71 D, 1 vacancy).
Education (1970–71): *Enrollment*—public elementary schools, 1,922,174 pupils; 91,918 teachers; public secondary, 1,554,-842 pupils; 86,217 teachers; nonpublic schools (1968–69), 860,200 pupils; 33,880 teachers; college and university (fall 1968), 704,009 students. *Public school expenditures* (1970–71), $4,336,000,000 ($1,370 per pupil). *Average teacher's salary,* $11,100.
State Finances (fiscal year 1970): *Revenues,* $10,350,729,000 (4% general sales tax and gross receipts taxes, $1,012,-036,000; motor fuel tax, $374,821,000; federal funds, $1,977,504,000). *Expenditures,* $9,894,498,000 (education, $3,362,209,000; health, welfare, and safety, $259,201,000; highways, $649,193,000). *State debt,* $7,387,836,000 (June 30, 1970).
Personal Income (1970): $89,473,000,000; per capita, $4,797.
Public Assistance (1970): $2,673,257,000. *Average monthly payments* (Dec. 1970)—old-age assistance, $104.90; aid to families with dependent children, $292.20.
Labor Force: *Nonagricultural wage and salary earners* (June 1971), 7,155,900. *Average annual employment* (1969)—manufacturing, 1,874,000; trade, 1,438,000; government, 1,175,000; services, 1,330,000. *Insured unemployed* (Oct. 1971)—244,300 (4.3%).
Manufacturing (1967): *Value added by manufacture,* $25,246,-700,000. Printing and publishing, $3,349,400,000; apparel and other textile products, $2,878,700,000; electrical equipment and supplies, $2,683,200,000; nonelectrical machinery, $2,286,000,000; instruments and related products, $2,164,300,000.
Agriculture (1970): *Cash farm income,* $1,139,272,000 (livestock, $815,015,000; crops, $302,248,000; government payments, $22,009,000). *Chief crops* (1970)—Apples, 955,000,-000 pounds (ranks 2d among the states); corn, 22,041,000 bushels; potatoes, 16,861,000 cwt.; hay, 4,396,000 tons.
Mining (1970): *Production value,* $305,381,000 (ranks 19th among the states). *Chief minerals* (tons)—Sand and gravel, 38,886,000; stone, 37,937,000; salt, 5,800,000.
Fisheries (1970): *Commercial catch,* 32,900,000 pounds ($16,-200,000). *Leading species by value* (1967): Sculp or porgy, $639,776; yellowtail flounder, $463,927.
Transportation: *Roads* (1969), 104,716 miles (168,519 km); *motor vehicles* (1969), 6,505,000; *railroads* (1968), 5,670 miles (9,125 km); *airports* (1969), 62.
Communications: *Telephones* (1971), 12,415,600; *television stations* (1969), 26; *radio stations* (1969), 243; *newspapers* (1969), 80 (daily circulation, 7,625,000).

On Dec. 20, 1971, Governor Rockefeller proposed new tax laws, to be considered by a special session of the legislature convening at year-end, to raise an additional $427 million. This was necessitated largely by the defeat of the transportation bond issue and local-spending amendments mentioned below under *Elections.* Rockefeller proposed a 5% surcharge on 1972 state income taxes, elimination of the $12.50 individual and $25 family tax credits, and increased alcohol, cigarette, and gasoline taxes.

Unemployment. The state was hit hard by a 6.1% unemployment rate in July—the highest since December 1962. In some areas the rate was even higher. Buffalo reported 9% unemployment and Long Island over 7%. Part of the nationwide recession, this unemployment aggravated social and economic difficulties facing the state.

Prison Revolt. On Sept. 9–13, 1971, the state was shocked by a revolt in the maximum-security Attica Correctional Facility near Buffalo. For four days there were negotiations among inmates, prison officials including the state commissioner of corrections, Russell G. Oswald, and Black Panthers and their lawyers. These proved unsuccessful, and then Commissioner Oswald, with the consent of Governor Rockefeller, ordered an assault on the prison by state police and correction officers. The riot and the assault that ended it resulted in the death of 43 men—32 prisoners and 11 hostages.

For refusing to take part in the negotiations or come to Attica, Rockefeller was strongly criticized, especially when autopsies revealed that all assault deaths came from shots fired by official personnel. Others argued that there was no other course to take, except that the attack should have occurred immediately and that no negotiations should have taken place. Causes and circumstances of the revolt were still being debated at year-end. (See special report on PRISONS, beginning on page 38.)

Elections. No statewide elections were held in 1971, but voters were presented with a proposed $2.5 billion transportation bond issue and two constitutional amendments augmenting the spending power of local communities, all of which were defeated. The bond issue, which was to provide $1.15 billion for highways and $1.35 billion for mass transit, was defeated despite support from Governor Rockefeller and Mayor Lindsay. The defeat of all the measures was attributed to the antitax, antispending mood of the voters.

LEO HERSHKOWITZ
Queens College, City University of New York

NEW YORK CITY

Budgetary problems, crime, and charges of corruption and mismanagement in various city departments left New Yorkers bewildered in 1971, as did Mayor John V. Lindsay's switch to the Democratic Party.

Budget and Financing. Faced with growing costs and declining revenues, Mayor Lindsay in January proposed a conservative "non-austerity" capital budget of $1.55 billion, for the fiscal year 1971-72. School construction and improvement and expansion of mass transportation received top priority. The environmental protection administration received a $680 million allotment, compared with $386-million a year earlier, mostly to complete facilities for the water pollution control program. The mayor's budget was adopted unanimously by the board of estimate and the City Council.

In May the mayor disclosed plans for a "survival" $9.13 billion expense budget, twice the budget when he took office in 1965. Lindsay asked for increased state aid and permission to increase taxes to meet this record sum, which he said was necessary to prevent "massive cuts in vital city services." Mayor Lindsay asked that the city borrow $360 million, although he had earlier termed the borrowing of $255 million in 1965 by Mayor Robert Wagner a "dangerous practice."

After much debate and recrimination, especially between the mayor and controller Abraham D. Beame, an $8.56 billion budget was adopted. Massive layoffs of city employees were avoided, although there were cutbacks in new hiring and the filling of vacancies. Increases in the city income and commuter tax went into effect, as did taxes on the transfer of real property.

Labor. At the beginning of 1971, the 30,000-member Patrolmen's Benevolent Association, 11,300 Uniformed Firefighters Association, 11,000 Uniformed Sanitationmen's Association, and 45,000 other city employees were negotiating for salary and pension increases. Threats took a more serious turn when firemen used slowdown tactics in an effort to win concessions. The slowdown ended during the summer, and resumed briefly at the end of the year before a final settlement was reached.

In January, an effective 6-day wildcat police strike was triggered by a New York state court of appeals decision that dashed hopes for a retroactive pay increase. In February, however, a ruling by state supreme court Justice Irving Saypol granted retroactive pay to patrolmen.

In June, hundreds of thousands of motorists were trapped in massive traffic jams when 27 of 29 movable bridges in the city were left open by city workers angered over the failure of the state Legislature to approve a pension agreement negotiated with the city in 1970. The 2-day strike ended with an agreement to settle through arbitration.

Police Matters. The 4-member Knapp Commission appointed by Mayor Lindsay in 1970 began its probe of police corruption. Hearings disclosed the extent of police bribery and corruption in matters relating especially to organized crime, prostitution, and narcotics. Contractors asserted that police bribery added 5% to building costs. The investigation, which continued at year's end, cast suspicion on the entire department. Police spokesmen, including Commissioner Patrick V. Murphy, attested to the honesty of most of the men in the department, and Murphy denounced the "renegades and traitors" who, he said, cast unproved aspersions on the force. The fatal shooting of nine policemen and fatal stabbing of a tenth in 1971 deeply angered police.

Welfare. Spiraling welfare costs (about $1.1 billion a year paid by federal, state, and city governments), as well as problems of housing and jobs for the more than one million persons on welfare, again caused grave concern. Housing facilities are restricted with many welfare recipients housed in run-down hotels at great cost to the city. Few decent job opportunities were available to end a vicious cycle of poverty and welfare. A state law passed in the spring made employable welfare recipients subject to assignment on public works projects, for which they would receive pay in lieu of welfare checks. It was expected that as many as 50,000 persons in the city would be assigned to such jobs.

Housing. Housing continued to deteriorate and grow more scarce, even as the white middle class continued to exit from New York City. New legislation signed by Gov. Nelson Rockefeller provided for decontrol of apartments "voluntarily vacated." At year's end rents in controlled apartments were subject to decisions being made in Washington under Phase II of the President's new economic program. Opposition by some Forest Hills, Queens, residents to low-income public housing planned in that area was keyed to white–poor black animosity. The project was backed by Mayor Lindsay and attracted national interest.

Education. In February the board of education announced a $40 million deficit that seemed to require a sharp reduction in the full-time teaching staff, the end of substitute hiring, and the layoff of 10,000 part-time teachers and assistants. But the plans were not implemented, as $25 million of next year's budget was shifted to the current one.

To forestall controversy attendant with the election of a new school board, the Legislature extended the life of the interim board for a year. In May, Isaiah Robinson was named board president, the first black so chosen. Continuing the trend of recent years, the number of whites in the public school population dropped to 42.8%, compared with 61.1% ten years earlier. In Manhattan, whites constituted only 15.1% of the school population.

UPI

TWIN TOWERS of World Trade Center soar above Hudson River in lower Manhattan. Built by the Port of New York Authority, the 110-story skyscrapers have superseded the Empire State as New York City's tallest building. Although the first tenants moved into one tower in 1971, construction of the entire Trade Center is not scheduled to be completed until 1973.

Albert H. Bowker resigned suddenly as chancellor of the City University. He was succeeded by Robert J. Kibbee, president of the Pittsburgh board of education.

Population. New York's population was put at 7,867,760 persons, a 1% increase over 1960. Manhattan's population declined 10% over the same period, the largest population loss of any county in the state. Movement of whites out of the inner city continued as a major trend, with a net loss of 55,519, while 435,840 blacks and other minorities entered.

Politics. The long-rumored switch of Mayor Lindsay to the Democratic party took place in August. Lindsay and his aides then toured the country to test the political climate in his bid for the 1972 Democratic presidential nomination.

In the off-year elections held November 2, voters in the city contributed to the defeat of a $2.5 billion state transportation bond issue, which had been supported by both Mayor Lindsay and Governor Rockefeller.

LEO HERSHKOWITZ
Queens College, City University of New York

NEW ZEALAND

During the year, as New Zealand struggled with inflation, it also intensified its efforts to lessen the economic impact of Britain's impending admittance to the European Economic Community (EEC, or Common Market), which will reduce New Zealand's export markets. Prime Minister Sir Keith Holyoake made a world tour as part of the effort.

——— NEW ZEALAND · Information Highlights ———

Official Name: New Zealand.
Area: 103,736 square miles (268,675 sq km).
Population (1971 census): 2,862,631. *Density,* 26 per square mile (10 per sq km). *Annual rate of increase,* 1.4%.
Chief Cities (metropolitan areas, 1969 est.): Wellington, the capital, 175,500; Auckland, 588,400.
Government: *Head of state,* Elizabeth II, queen (acceded Feb. 6, 1952), represented by Sir Arthur Porritt, governor general (appointed Dec. 17, 1966). *Head of government,* Keith J. Holyoake, prime minister (took office for 3d term Dec. 12, 1966). *Legislature*—House of Representatives (unicameral), 84 members. *Major political parties*—National party, Labour party.
Language: English (official).
Education: *Literacy rate* (1970), 98% of population. *Expenditure on education* (1968), 12.4% of total public expenditure. *School enrollment* (1968)—primary, 509,841; secondary, 179,922; university/higher, 50,433.
Finances (1969–70): *Revenues,* $1,417,000,000; *expenditures,* $1,428,000,000; *monetary unit,* New Zealand dollar (0.8627 N. Z. dollar equal U. S.$1, Sept. 1971).
Gross National Product (1970 est.): $5,770,000,000.
National Income (1969): $4,518,000,000; *national income per person,* $1,627.
Economic Indexes: *Industrial production* (1969), 142 (1963= 100); *agricultural production* (1969), 122 (1963=100); *consumer price index* (1970), 136 (1963=100).
Manufacturing (metric tons, 1969): Gasoline, 1,111,000; meat, 977,000; residual fuel oil, 863,000; cement, 803,000; distillate fuel oils, 598,000.
Crops (metric tons, 1969 crop year): Wheat, 457,000; wool, 328,000; potatoes, 258,000; barley, 233,000.
Minerals (metric tons, 1969): Lignite, 1,876,000; coal, 488,000; gold, 323 kilograms.
Foreign Trade (1970): *Exports,* $1,225,000,000 (chief exports —Wool, $213,472,000; lamb and mutton, $185,920,000; butter, $114,015,000). *Imports,* $1,245,000,000 (chief imports, 1968—chemicals, $110,746,000; nonelectrical machinery, $110,547,000; transport equipment, $94,484,000; textile yarn and fabrics, $87,135,000). *Chief trading partners* (1968)—United Kingdom (took 40% of exports, supplied 31% of imports); United States (18%—12%); Australia.
Transportation: *Roads* (1970), 57,439 miles (92,437 km); *motor vehicles* (1969), 1,031,900 (automobiles, 858,400); *railroads* (1970), 3,300 miles (5,311 km); *merchant fleet* (1970), 186,000 gross registered tons; *principal airports,* Auckland, Wellington.
Communications: *Telephones* (1970), 1,202,590; *television stations* (1968), 4; *television sets* (1969), 617,000; *radios* (1969), 665,000; *newspapers* (1969), 41.

Economy. Although inflation continued, high employment was maintained, government revenue remained high, and dairy exports set new records. In October, however, drastically reduced lamb prices required government action, as half of New Zealand's imports are paid for by overseas earnings on sheep. It appeared that it would be necessary to subsidize some livestock raisers directly for the first time in New Zealand's history.

A series of measures were taken to restrain rampant inflation, which was running at about 10% annually. In February, 70 new items were brought under the price justification scheme. The stabilization of remuneration act set up a five-man authority charged with trying to keep wage increases within the 7% guideline set by the government.

The June budget was generally described as a "wait and see" one, due to the uncertainty of the economic climate. Expenditures for education rose by 28% and for defense by 22%. Despite these increases, government revenues were up sufficiently to make it possible to increase pensions and give modest indirect aid to certain types of farmers. Price increases continued to be frequent, but late in the year began to taper off.

New Zealand's future prosperity depends heavily on the final terms under which Britain enters the EEC. New Zealand, with Deputy Prime Minister John Marshall as chief negotiator, lobbied within the EEC and Britain to have its export levels to Britain guaranteed by the EEC. Not without some misgivings, the government accepted the British-EEC agreement signed in June. It provides that in 1977, after five years of transition, New Zealand will be guaranteed exports of butter and cheese to Britain of not less than 71% of current levels.

Domestic Issues. In the nationwide triennial local elections held in October, the Labour party registered gains in some of the larger cities, especially Wellington and Christchurch. Widespread use was made of such devices to encourage voting as postal voting and extending the balloting period over a number of days.

The report of the royal commission on housing was fairly predictable. It urged the establishment of a national housing authority, fixed a target of 300,000 new houses by 1980, and warned against further large concentration of Maoris and Polynesians in housing areas.

Provisional returns from the census taken in March showed a modest growth of 6.9% in the preceding five years. Marked population increases were registered in cities and among the Maoris, while the decline in rural areas and small towns continued.

In June, Sir Denis Blundell was named to succeed Sir Arthur Porritt as governor-general. Blundell, who will take office in September 1972, will be the first New Zealand resident to hold the post.

Foreign Affairs. Prime Minister Holyoake undertook an extensive world tour in April. He consulted with President Nixon about access for meat exports to the U. S. market and conferred with European leaders about economic safeguards for New Zealand when Britain joins the EEC.

New Zealand's 130-man artillery battery in Vietnam was withdrawn in May. In August it was announced that all New Zealand combat troops would be out of South Vietnam by the end of 1971, leaving only a surgical unit and an army-training team.

GRAHAM BUSH
University of Auckland

NEWFOUNDLAND

As an economic slump continued in 1971, New-foundlanders went to the polls in their first provincial election in five years. The Progressive Conservative party emerged with half of the seats in the House of Assembly, which the Liberals had previously controlled by a large majority.

Election. The campaign leading up to the voting on Oct. 28, 1971, was a quiet one, probably out of consideration for an electorate that had been heavily bombarded by political events since the federal election of 1968. Voter turnout was extremely high, with 88% of those enrolled at the polls.

The result was a staggering blow to the Liberals, who had won all but 3 seats in 1966 and still enjoyed a 25 to 7 majority over the Progressive Conservative (PC) members on election day of 1971. The PC's garnered 52% of the popular vote and elected 21 members to the new house, while the Liberals, polling 44%, elected 20 members. The remaining seat was won by a member of the New Labrador party (NLP), who announced that he would remain independent. The Liberals lost 19 seats, and 7 of their ministers were defeated.

The election signaled the end of the regime of Premier Joseph R. Smallwood and the advance to center stage of a new style of leadership, that of Frank Moores, the 38-year-old leader of the Progressive Conservatives.

However, the immediate future was full of uncertainties. With the House of Assembly so narrowly divided that the defection of a single member could wipe out the PC majority, it seemed unlikely

------ **NEWFOUNDLAND · Information Highlights** ------

Area: 156,185 square miles (404,520 sq km).
Population: 523,000 (April 1971 est.).
Chief Cities (1966 census): St. John's, the capital (79,884); Corner Brook (27;116).
Government: (Elected Sept. 8, 1966; election Oct. 28, 1971 has been contested.) *Chief Officers*—lt. gov., Ewart John Arlington Harnium; premier, Joseph R. Smallwood (Liberal); prov. secy., J. A. Frecker (L); min. of justice, L. R. Curtis (L); prov. treas., E. S. Jones (L); min. of educ., Frederick W. Rowe (L); chief justice, Robert Stafford Furlong. *Legislature*—Legislative Assembly (convened February 1970); 42 members (31 Liberal, 5 Progressive Conservative, 4 Independent-Liberal, 1 Independent, 1 vacant).
Education: *School enrollment* (1968–69 est.)—public elementary and secondary, 151,976 pupils (5,855 teachers); private schools, 230 pupils (26 teachers); college and university, 4,473 students. *Public school expenditures* (1971 est.)—$56,199,000; average teacher's salary (1968–69 est.), $5,600.
Public Finance (fiscal year 1971 est.): *Revenues,* $348,790,-000 (sales tax, $64,390,000; income tax, $33,338,000; federal funds, $216,967,000). *Expenditures,* $411,000,000 (education, $93,570,000; health and social welfare, $121,-630,000; transport and communications, $52,430,000).
Personal Income (1969 est.): $829,000,000.
Social Welfare (fiscal year 1971 est.): $42,260,000 (aged and blind, $3,950,000; dependents and unemployed, $32,060,-000).
Manufacturing (1968): *Value added by manufacture,* $88,386,-000 (food and beverages, $34,606,000; nonmetallic mineral products industries, $4,509,000; printing and publishing industries, $3,692,000; fabricated metals, $3,638,000).
Mining (1969 est.): *Production value,* $239,093,700. *Chief minerals* (tons)—iron ore, 14,733,410 (ranks 1st among the provinces); copper, 19,390 (ranks 4th); zinc, 3,390 (ranks 7th); lead, 21,100 (ranks 4th).
Fisheries (1969 est.): *Commercial catch,* 1,000,000,000 pounds ($30,735,000). *Leading species* (1968)—cod, 366,-169,000 pounds ($14,258,000); flounder and sole, 127,567,-000 pounds ($4,113,000); herring, 321,144,000 pounds ($3,-284,000); lobster, 4,009,000 pounds ($2,500,000).
Transportation: *Roads* (1968), 6,234 miles (10,018 km); *motor vehicles* (1969), 112,027; *railroads* (1969), 943 track miles (1,517 km); *licensed airports* (1970), 8.
Communications: *Telephones* (1969), 127,190; *television stations* (1970), 2; *radio stations* (1967), 7; *newspapers* (1970), 3 (daily circulation, 41,685).
All figures given in Canadian dollars.

that any government formed by Moores could be a stable one. There was speculation that the province might see another election within six months. A new leader of the Liberal party will be elected at a convention in February 1972.

Economic Affairs. There was little doubt that concern over the economy played a part in the election defeat of the Liberals in 1971. Unemployment in Newfoundland was higher than in any other province, averaging nearly 11% while the national rate stood at about 6%. As a part of its continuing policy of industrialization, the provincial government reported in March the signing of agreements with a private firm to build a $130 million petroleum refinery. In April the federal department of regional economic expansion announced a spending program of $40 million on infrastructure projects in Newfoundland.

The budget, released in April, forecast expenditures of $507.6 million in 1971, as against $395.2 million in the preceding year. Transfers from the federal government amounted to nearly 45% of total current expenditures by the provincial government.

SUSAN McCORQUODALE
Memorial University of Newfoundland

NEWSPAPERS. See PUBLISHING.

NICARAGUA

Overshadowing other events in Nicaragua in 1971 was the formulation of plans for a constitutional convention to draft a document under which the nation's powerful president, Anastasio Somoza Debayle, would be eligible for another term in office.

Constitutional Agreement. Under the existing constitution, President Somoza, elected in 1967, was barred from reelection in the balloting scheduled for May 1972. Since he would have no serious rivals if he could legally run, Somoza and his supporters in the dominant National Liberal party began searching for a constitutional device that might enable him to return to office.

Early in 1971, Somoza reached an agreement with Sen. Fernando Aguero, leader of the Conservatives, the nation's second-ranking party. Under the announced formula, the Congress was to summon a convention to rewrite the constitution. The Congress would then dissolve itself, allowing Somoza to rule by decree until the convening of the constitutional convention in the spring of 1972. At that time, Somoza was to relinquish the presidency to a three-man junta consisting of two Liberals and one Conservative. The junta was to rule for two years, while the new constitution was being drawn up. In the subsequent election, to be held in 1974, Somoza would again be eligible for the presidency.

In return for its support, the Conservative party was guaranteed 40% of the seats at the constitutional convention, control of 6 of the nation's 16 departments, and some ministerial positions in any future Somoza administration. Leading the weak opposition to this agreement were four minor political parties which concluded a pact opposing any formula that would allow the continuation of Somoza in the presidency. A chief figure in this opposition was Somoza's former minister of education, Ramiro Sacasa Guerrero.

Political Protest. Actual political disturbances in 1971 were minimal. On January 20, disorders

──────── **NICARAGUA** • Information Highlights ────────

Official Name: Republic of Nicaragua.
Area: 50,193 square miles (130,000 sq km).
Population (1970 est.): 1,980,000. *Density*, 38 per square mile (15 per sq km). *Annual rate of increase*, 3.0%.
Chief Cities (1965 est.): Managua, the capital, 262,047; León, 44,053; Grenada, 28,507.
Government: *Head of state*, Anastasio Somoza Debayle, president (took office May 1, 1967). *Head of government*, Anastasio Somoza Debayle. *Legislature*—Congress; Senate, 16 members; Chamber of Deputies, 42 members. *Major political parties*—National Liberal party, Conservative party.
Languages: Spanish (official).
Education: *Literacy rate* (1969), over 50% of population. *Expenditure on education* (1968), 19% of total public expenditure. *School enrollment* (1967)—primary, 247,065; secondary, 34,221; vocational, 2,851; higher, 5,144.
Finances (1969): *Revenues*, $68,400,000; *expenditures*, $78,-900,000; *monetary unit*, córdoba (7.000 córdobas equal U. S.$1, Dec. 30, 1971).
Gross National Product (1969): $831,000,000.
National Income (1970): $740,000,000; *national income per person*, $370.
Economic Indexes: *Manufacturing production* (1965), 119 (1963=100); *consumer price index* (1969), 117 (1963=100).
Manufacturing (metric tons, 1969): Sugar, 110,000; cement, 109,000; gasoline, 78,000; meat, 57,000.
Crops (metric tons, 1969 crop year): Cottonseed (1968), 155,-000; cotton (lint), 67,000; coffee, 67,000; rice, 60,000.
Minerals (metric tons, 1969): Salt (1967), 11,000; copper ore, 4,200; silver, 12.9; gold (exports), 3,328 kilograms.
Foreign Trade (1969): *Exports*, $155,000,000 (chief exports, 1970—cotton, $34,200,000; coffee, $32,000,000). *Imports*, $176,000,000 (chief imports, 1968—chemicals; nonelectrical machinery; transport equipment). *Chief trading partners* (1968)—United States (took 28% of exports, supplied 38% of imports); Japan (27%—8%).
Transportation: *Roads* (1970), 3,813 miles (6,136 km); *motor vehicles* (1969), 33,100 (automobiles, 24,400).
Communications: *Telephones* (1969), 25,634; *television stations* (1968), 2; *television sets* (1969), 45,000; *radios* (1969), 107,000; *newspapers* (1967), 7.

broke out among students in Managua and León, resulting in the military occupation of two universities. The government charged a Spanish Jesuit priest, José Antonio Salines, with incitement and ordered him out of the country. In late April, 10 schools in Managua and León were occupied after students had mounted another series of protests.

Economic Affairs. The Nicaraguan economy remained virtually unchanged in 1971, with the only significant gain being a moderately higher rate of production of raw materials. A major economic concern was the deterioration of the Central American Common Market (CACM).

As one of the three weaker members of the five-nation common market, Nicaragua had incurred a deficit of nearly $100 million by the end of 1970 and was demanding market reforms. On June 18, Costa Rica announced the closing of its borders to products coming from Nicaragua, El Salvador, and Guatemala, thereby threatening CACM's very existence. The crisis was averted by a meeting in Managua in June of the finance ministers of four of the five original member states (Honduras having suspended its membership). They agreed on reforms in the CACM to assist the deficit nations.

Treaty Termination. On Feb. 17, 1971, the U. S. Senate ratified President Nixon's termination of the ·1916 Bryan-Chamarro Treaty with Nicaragua. The treaty had given the United States perpetual rights to construct a canal across Nicaragua, a 99-year lease on the Corn Islands, and the right to build a naval base on the Gulf of Fonseca. Although never implemented, the treaty was extremely unpopular with Nicaraguans, who viewed it as an infringement of national sovereignty.

ROBERT L. PETERSON
University of Texas, El Paso

NICHOLSON, Jack. See BIOGRAPHY.

NIEBUHR, Reinhold

American Protestant leader, b. Wright City, Mo., June 21, 1892; d. Stockbridge, Mass., June 1, 1971.

Reinhold Niebuhr was the most notable American-born Protestant theologian of the 20th century. With his brother, the late H. Richard Niebuhr, and German-born Paul J. Tillich, he formed a triumvirate that shaped and dominated Protestant thought in North America for several decades around mid-century. Unlike the stereotype of the theologian—an aloof, bookish intellectual hidden away in the corners of a university—Reinhold Niebuhr was often pictured as an American-style activist involved in the causes about which he wrote.

Life. Niebuhr grew up in a small Missouri farming community where his father was pastor of the Evangelical Synod Church. He studied at Yale University, receiving his bachelor of divinity in 1914 and his M. A. in 1915. He then embarked on a pastoral career in Detroit at Bethel Evangelical Church, where he served faithfully from 1915 to 1928.

Effective as he was, Niebuhr also became controversial. During the 1920's he came to see the injustices of the automobile industry's treatment of workers and largely sided with labor in the years of heightening tension between labor and management. His intervention led to his rejection by Detroit elites, but set a pattern for social activists in the churches for some time to come.

After leaving Detroit, Niebuhr taught at New York City's famed Union Theological Seminary, which was then in a position to provide the best platform for a hearing in American liberal Protestantism. Niebuhr profited from and helped propagate some views of Continental thinking, especially those often called neo-orthodox because of their return to biblical thought patterns and the influences of 16th-century reformers. But he drew on this thought to fashion his own personal and dynamic synthesis and cannot easily be typed as neo-orthodox.

Seminary life did not mean cloistered life. Niebuhr fused biblical study with inquiry into the writings of modern thinkers, among them Freud and Marx. While he rejected most modern political forms of Marxism, he did see in Marxist thought some clues concerning collective men and their pretenses and possibilities.

Significantly, Niebuhr's field of teaching was called Applied Christianity, and he tried to apply his own version by direct action. Long a participant in partisan politics, he was a spokesman for liberal positions in both the Liberal and Democratic parties. As labor began to win its way, he faced the issues of war. During most of the 1930's Niebuhr had been a qualified kind of pacifist, but before World War II began he was propagating a Christian realism that asked men to face the injustices posed by nazism, even at the expense of war.

After the war, Niebuhr's realism influenced cold war leaders such as Dean Acheson and George Kennan—a fact that led some members of a later generation during the Vietnam War to grow distant from their mentor, even though he was a consistent opponent of U. S. policies and intervention in Vietnam.

In religious circles, Niebuhr made an impact through his preaching. While not concerned with the committee work details of ecumenical life, he had interests in interreligious contact. He particularly acknowledged his debt to Judaism, an attitude

REINHOLD NIEBUHR (1892–1971)
"He reflected on the grand themes. . . ."

that came to fulfillment in his request that Rabbi Abraham Joshua Heschel be the speaker at his funeral. Likewise, on a more selective basis, he was influenced by and made contributions to Catholic thought and action. His later years were spent as a semi-invalid at Stockbridge, Mass., where he was aided in continuing work and sustained in spirit by his wife, Ursula, herself a gifted religious thinker.

Thought. While Niebuhr busied himself as an organizer and commented as a columnist on the urgent issues of his time, he also reflected on the grand themes of Christian thought and left a body of work that will be consulted by serious people for a long time to come. Preoccupied with themes summarized in the title of his monumental Gifford Lectures, *The Nature and Destiny of Man* (2 vols., 1942–43), he is best remembered, even by conservative Protestants, for the way in which he restored to modern thinking the biblical view of man's fallibility. Regretting later the "pedagogical error" of having employed a discredited term, original sin, to describe this, Niebuhr never wavered from his realistic view of man's finitude and failings. But he also witnessed to a biblical impetus that described the grandeur of man, and he used biblical categories to speak of God's grace and man's destiny.

Devoted as he was to American life, he was critical of views that allowed for a "manifest destiny," through which Americans would subtly dominate others. He dealt with American history through the category of irony, seeing in its record the dangers of national pride. Yet national leaders repeatedly turned to him for counsel.

He published many books during his lifetime. Notable among them are *Moral Man and Immoral Society* (1932), *Beyond Tragedy* (1937), *Faith and History* (1949), and *Man's Nature and His Communities* (1965).

MARTIN E. MARTY, *University of Chicago*

NIGER

Niger celebrated the 11th anniversary of its independence in 1971 amid general calm, as the ruling Progressive party of President Hamani Diori remained unchallenged. To mark the anniversary, Diori pardoned 75 political prisoners and commuted the sentences of 91 others. The Niamey *lycée,* whose students had gone on strike in December 1970, reopened in February.

Relations with Libya. In February, President Diori paid an official visit to Libya and signed a friendship and cooperation agreement with President Muammar al-Qaddafi. In April the grand mufti of Libya paid an official visit to Niger, bringing with him 28,000 Arabic books and $1 million for Islamic charities. The two states established a joint development bank in August, funded by Libya to "avert any foreign pressure that may be exerted on Niger." A friendship association was established, and a joint chamber of commerce was proposed.

Economic Developments. The country as a whole remained hampered by its low level of economic and educational development. However, the uranium processing plant at Arlit went into production, shipping concentrate worth nearly $4 million in its first six months of operation.

Niger, Mali, and Upper Volta agreed to establish a joint authority for development of the Liptako-Gourma region. Among the region's resources are manganese, phosphorus, and bauxite.

Niger received $2.5 million from the United Nations for mineral prospecting, millet production, and a school of administration. The European Development Fund allotted Niger $8.66 million to combat cholera, and the African Development Bank provided $1 million for telephones. France made available $1.5 million for textbooks, university construction, and budget deficits.

Two U. S. companies, Texaco and Bishop Oil, received prospecting concessions in Niger of 98,000 and 15,000 square miles (254,000 and 39,000 sq km), respectively.

CLAUDE E. WELCH, JR.,
State University of New York at Buffalo

--- **NIGER • Information Highlights** ---

Official Name: Republic of the Niger.
Area: 489,190 square miles (1,267,000 sq km).
Population (1970 est.): 4,020,000. *Density,* 8 per square mile (3 per sq km). *Annual rate of increase,* 2.7%.
Chief City (1968 est.): Niamey, the capital, 78,991.
Government: *Head of state,* Hamani Diori, president (reelected to 3d 5-year term Oct. 2, 1970). *Head of government,* Hamani Diori. *Legislature* (unicameral)—National Assembly, 50 members. *Political party*—Parti Progressiste Nigérien.
Languages: French (official), Hausa and other African languages.
Education: *Literacy rate* (1969), 5% of population. *Expenditure on education* (1968), 11.3% of total public expenditure. *School enrollment* (1968)—primary, 81,954; secondary, 4,979; technical/vocational, 145.
Finances (1969–70): *Revenues,* $39,000,000; *expenditures,* $39,000,000; *monetary unit,* CFA franc (277.71 francs equal U. S.$1, Sept. 1971).
Gross National Product (1967 est.): $320,000,000.
National Income (1966): $282,000,000; *national income per person,* $78.
Crops (metric tons, 1968 crop year): Millet, 800,000.
Minerals (metric tons, 1969): Tin concentrates, 60,000; uranium (1971 est.), 750.
Foreign Trade (1968): *Exports,* $37,800,000 (chief export—peanuts, $27,295,000). *Imports,* $41,470,000 (chief import, 1967—textile yarn and fabric, $13,137,000).
Transportation: *Roads* (1969), 4,482 miles (7,213 km); *motor vehicles* (1969), 5,000; *principal airport,* Niamey.
Communications: *Telephones* (1970), 3,298; *radios* (1969), 100,000; *newspapers* (1969), 1 (daily circulation, 2,000).

UNICEF PHOTO BY JACQUES DANOIS

SCARS of war are gradually fading in Nigeria's Biafra region. International relief efforts in 1971 helped rebuild schools (*top*) and maintain reception centers for displaced children (*center*). Schools often have to use crude construction materials as furniture (*below*).

NIGERIA

Economic problems dominated Nigerian affairs in 1971. The military government of Gen. Yakubu Gowon, having defeated Biafra and so ended the civil war in January 1970, continued its attempts to return the country to peacetime operations.

Inflation and Labor Unrest. Finance Commissioner Obafemi Awolowo pointed to inflation and unemployment as Nigeria's two most threatening internal problems. Unemployment remained at a high level in 1971 and was the major reason for the increase in crime in all the states despite several public executions for robbery. As a result of the civil war there was more unemployment among the Ibo of the East-Central state than elsewhere. Ibo have been denied entry into areas where they were heavily employed before the war.

The rise in the cost of living was indicated by the increase in the Lagos price index from 141.5 in December 1969 to 164.5 in 1971. The cost of a small tin of rice was more than double that in 1969.

A report on wages published in September illustrated the economic hopelessness of low-paid city workers, and there were many labor disturbances during the year despite federal decrees prohibiting strikes. Particularly threatening were the riots at Kaduna in January and the Lagos dock workers' strike in early February. Teachers, doctors, postal workers, and ground technicians for Nigerian Airways all engaged in rulebook slowdowns in 1971. Promises by the government to change working conditions ended the go-slow work of most of the middle income dissidents. The award of an extra £N 2 a week blocked more serious difficulties with lower-income workers.

Student Unrest. The activities of university and secondary school students were localized, but potentially very serious. The worst confrontation occurred at the University of Ibadan in February. One student was killed when police and army units occupied the campus following demonstrations against the university administration, foreign instructors, and poor food. The university was closed for two weeks. Students in Lagos demonstrated in sympathy with those in Ibadan.

At the Abeokuta Grammar School, 70 students were arrested in April after they burned examination papers and threw stones at police. The student union at the University of Lagos was suspended in April, and the following month a student riot in Ibadan closed Ibadan Technical College.

Economic Development. Nigeria's economy became increasingly tied to petroleum revenues in 1971. Petroleum production reached 1.5 million barrels a day by February and continued to increase. The country was the world's 10th largest oil producer. In April the government reached an agreement with the major oil companies on new posted prices. This price, which is used to calculate the tax on royalty payments, was increased from $2.36 a barrel to $3.21 a barrel. The tax rate was also increased to 55%. The adjustments will increase Nigeria's revenue by over £N 100 million annually.

The value of Nigeria's agricultural exports declined during 1971. The peanut crop was less than 700,000 tons, a decline of 20% from 1970, and the low price for cacao offset a bountiful harvest. Other export items such as cotton and tin, although reaching record highs, did not make up the deficit resulting from the losses from major crops.

Major capital development in Nigeria during 1971 included the continued expansion of refining and transport facilities along the southeast coast. The ports of Warri, Burutu, Koko, Sapele, Calabar, and Port Harcourt have all been improved. Three times as much tonnage was unloaded at Port Harcourt in 1971 as in 1970. The government was also financing the improvement of major road links such as that connecting Ibadan and Lagos.

The 1971–72 budget was a record £N 475 million, and was made possible by petroleum production. The recurrent budget was £N 219 million, while £N 126 million was transferred to the states. Educational development took much of the recurrent revenue in all areas, but particularly in the Muslim areas in the north, where there has been a continuing demand for trained personnel.

Reconstruction. The East-Central state, which had been the largest part of Biafra, had suffered the most damage in the civil war. Because of the great demands for reconstruction and rehabilitation it was the only state unable to balance its budget in 1971. Its planned total expenditure was £N 25.8 million, although revenue generated in the state amounted to only £N 9 million. Even with a federal grant of £N 11.7 million, the state's budget deficit was over £N 5 million.

In January, General Gowon paid a 6-day visit to the East-Central state, his first since the end of the war. During the year the cities of Enugu, Aba, and Owerri were operating at almost prewar levels. Onitsha's population has returned, but its industry and trade remained poor. The University of Nigeria in Nsukka was reopened. Food production, although adequate, has not reached prewar levels. The oil palm industry lagged, and unemployment was the highest in Nigeria. Ibo fears and the actions of other states in excluding Ibos from jobs made administrator Ukpabi Asika's task almost impossible.

Kwashiorkor, a protein-deficiency disease, was eliminated as a major health problem, and starvation was almost ended. But cholera in the East-Central, Rivers, and South-East states caused hundreds of deaths.

The Military. Nigeria's government continued to be controlled by the military, with almost all major executive posts held by army officers. There was little discussion of an early return to civilian rule. Nigeria's military establishment has been extremely expensive for a developing state. The 200,000-man army cost £N 102.9 million to maintain during the last nine months of 1970, overrunning its budget by £N 64 million. The £N 87.2 million defense budget for 1971-72 was over one third of the country's recurrent budget.

Foreign Affairs. Nigeria attempted to improve its relations with other nations by personal visits by General Gowon and by opening more diplomatic missions. In February, Gowon visited Gambia, Mauritania, and Niger. He traveled to Senegal in March and to Cameroon in April. In May, he was in Ethiopia and Kenya.

During the year diplomatic relations were restored with Tanzania, Zambia, and the Ivory Coast, three of the four African states that had recognized Biafra. But relations with Gabon remained cool. On February 10, Nigeria and the People's Republic of China agreed to exchange ambassadors.

Nigeria continued to support the Organization of African Unity and maintained a hard line against South Africa and Rhodesia. General Gowon reiterated Nigeria's support for African liberation movements, and he rejected the proposal made by President Houphouët-Boigny of the Ivory Coast for a dialogue with South Africa.

HARRY A. GAILEY, *San Jose State College*

NIGERIA · Information Highlights

Official Name: Federal Republic of Nigeria.
Area: 356,668 square miles (923,768 sq km).
Population (1970 est.): 55,070,000. *Density*, 156 per square mile (60 per sq km). *Annual rate of Increase*, 2.6%.
Chief Cities (1969 est.): Lagos, the capital, 841,749; Ibadan, 727,565; Ogbomosho, 370,963; Kano, 342,610.
Government: *Head of state*, Gen. Yakubu Gowon, president (assumed power Aug. 1, 1966). *Head of government*, Gen. Yakubu Gowon.
Languages: English (official), Hausa (official in the north), Ibo, Yoruba, other tribal languages.
Education: *Literacy rate* (1971), 25% of population. *Expenditure on education* (1965), 2.3% of gross national product. *School enrollment* (1968)—primary, 1,791,309; secondary, 200,378; technical/vocational, 19,428; higher, 9,775.
Finances (1968–69 est.): *Revenues*, $425,600,000; *expenditures*, $420,000,000; *monetary unit*, Nigerian pound (0.3571 pound equals U. S.$1, Sept. 1971).
Gross National Product (1970 est.): $9,100,000,000.
National Income (1966): $4,060,000,000; *national income per person*, $68.
Consumer Price Index (1970), 140 (1963=100).
Manufacturing (metric tons, 1969): Cement, 566,000; meat, 270,000; wheat flour, 127,000; beer, 878,000 hectoliters.
Crops (metric tons, 1969 crop year): Sweet potatoes and yams (1968), 125,000,000 (ranks 1st among world producers); cassava (1968), 6,700,000; groundnuts, 1,361,000 (world rank 3d); cocoa beans, 210,700 (world rank 3d).
Minerals (metric tons, 1969): Crude petroleum, 27,000,000; tin concentrates, 8,741.
Foreign Trade (1970): *Exports*, $1,240,000,000 (chief exports—crude petroleum, $713,160,000; cacao, $186,200,000). *Imports*, $1,059,000,000 (chief imports, 1968—nonelectrical machinery, $77,285,000; chemicals, $62,854,000; textile yarn and fabrics, $56,084,000. *Chief trading partners* (1968)—United Kingdom (took 30% of exports, supplied 31% of imports); Netherlands (13%—4%).
Transportation: *Roads* (1970), 56,000 miles (90,120 km); *motor vehicles* (1968), 93,000 (automobiles, 63,000); *railroads* (1970), 2,356 miles (3,769 km); *merchant fleet* (1970), 99,000 gross registered tons; *national airline*, Nigerian Airways.
Communications: *Telephones* (1970), 81,440; *television stations* (1968), 1; *television sets* (1969), 53,000; *radios* (1969), 1,265,000; *newspapers* (1966), 24 (daily circulation, 417,000).

NIXON, Richard M. See BIOGRAPHY.
NOBEL PRIZES. See PRIZES AND AWARDS.

—— **NORTH CAROLINA** • **Information Highlights** ——

Area: 52,586 square miles (136,198 sq km).
Population (1970 census): 5,082,059. *Density:* 106 per sq mi.
Chief Cities (1970 census): Raleigh, the capital, 123,793; Charlotte, 241,178; Greensboro, 144,076; Winston-Salem, 132,913; Durham, 95,438; High Point, 63,259; Asheville, 57,681.
Government (1971): *Chief Officers*—governor, Robert W. Scott (D); lt. gov., H. Pat Taylor, Jr. (D); secy. of state, Thad Eure (D); atty. gen., Robert B. Morgan (D); treas., Edwin Gill (D); supt. of public instruction, Craig Phillips (D); chief justice, William H. Bobbitt. *General Assembly*—Senate, 50 members (43 Democrats, 7 Republicans); House of Representatives, 120 members (96 D, 24 R).
Education (1970–71): *Enrollment*—public elementary schools, 835,739 pupils; 33,322 teachers; public secondary, 356,-448 pupils; 16,243 teachers; nonpublic schools (1968–69), 21,500 pupils; 1,280 teachers; college and university (fall 1968), 148,370 students. *Public school expenditures* (1970–71), $713,486,000 ($642 per pupil). *Average teacher's salary,* $8,168.
State Finances (fiscal year 1970): *Revenues,* $1,944,505,000 (3% general sales tax and gross receipts taxes, $264,-461,000; motor fuel tax, $213,709,000; federal funds, $372,-638,000). *Expenditures,* $1,829,648,000 (education, $899,-550,000; health, welfare, and safety, $81,283,000; highways, $285,495,000). *State debt,* $541,551,000 (June 30, 1970).
Personal Income (1970): $16,246,000,000; per capita, $3,188.
Public Assistance (1970): $178,445,000. *Average monthly payments* (Dec. 1970)—old-age assistance, $63.90; aid to families with dependent children, $116.55.
Labor Force: *Nonagricultural wage and salary earners* (June 1971), 1,779,700. *Average annual employment* (1969)—manufacturing, 713,000; trade, 309,000; government, 254,-000; services, 201,000. *Insured unemployed* (Oct. 1971)—19,400 (1.4%).
Manufacturing (1967): *Value added by manufacture,* $6,606,-500,000. Textile mill products, $2,022,500,000; tobacco manufactures, $975,900,000.
Agriculture (1970): *Cash farm income,* $1,603,577,000 (livestock, $625,072,000; crops, $918,823,000; government payments, $59,682,000). *Chief crops* (1970)—Tobacco, 814,-603,000 pounds (ranks 1st among the states); peanuts, 442,800,000 pounds (ranks 2d); corn, 67,250,000 bushels.
Mining (1969): *Production value,* $85,300,000 (ranks 33d among the states). *Chief minerals* (tons)—Stone, 24,468,-000; sand and gravel, 10,873,000; clays, 3,188,000.
Fisheries (1970): *Commercial catch,* 173,400,000 pounds $9,400,000). *Leading species by value* (1970), Shrimps, $2,479,998; menhaden, $1,614,644.
Transportation: *Roads* (1969), 85,460 miles (137,531 km); *motor vehicles* (1969), 2,717,000; *railroads* (1968), 4,164 miles (6,701 km); airports (1969), 54.
Communications: *Telephones* (1971), 2,384,500; *television stations* (1969), 19; *radio stations* (1969), 259; *newspapers* (1969), 48 (daily circulation, 1,261,000).

NORTH CAROLINA

The 1971 session of the North Carolina General Assembly was the longest on record, introduced the largest number of bills (over 2,500), passed the biggest biennial budget (over $4.3 billion), and was the most expensive to operate (over $2.2 million). An equal opportunity law applying to employment by all units of government—state and local—was the first such law to pass in a Southern state.

Legislation. Among the measures enacted were provisions for (1) increased aid to local governments, (2) a minimum wage of $1.60, (3) an enlarged state kindergarten program, (4) a 10% salary increase for teachers and state employees and increases in retirement benefits, (5) environmental controls, and (6) improvements in the correctional system.

The Assembly implemented the reorganization of state government into 25 departments as required by a constitutional amendment of 1970 and realigned the state's congressional districts. A Police Information Network also was implemented. A North Carolina Drug Authority was established in the Department of Administration to coordinate state efforts related to drug abuse prevention, education, control, treatment, and rehabilitation. Appropriations included $3.3 million for the highway patrol and $1.2 million for the State Bureau of Investigation.

Race Relations. A week of racial tension in Wilmington in early February 1971 left two men dead and others wounded. The trouble was rooted in dissatisfaction among black students, who boycotted a public high school. Governor Scott called in the National Guard and imposed a citywide curfew.

In December, Sammie Chess, Jr., was sworn in as a judge of the Superior Court. Appointed by Governor Scott, he is the first black to hold such a position.

Education and Cultural Activities. A study made in 1971 revealed that North Carolina has the fourth-highest rate of net "immigration" of college students in the United States. For every student leaving to study elsewhere, approximately three students arrive. The 1971 legislature increased out-of-state tuition on a graduated basis.

An adjourned session of the Assembly in October reorganized the system of state-supported higher education. The Consolidated University of North Carolina was abolished, and, effective July 1, 1972, all 16 public higher education institutions will be administered by a 32-member governing board.

In Greensboro a building was dedicated to provide teaching and research facilities for the Center for Creative Leadership, an educational institution funded by the Smith Richardson Foundation. By raising over $850,000 the North Carolina Symphony qualified for a $1 million Ford Foundation matching grant.

Social Services. The North Carolina Human Relations Commission reported that there were 75 official human relations organizations working in the 437 cities and towns and 100 counties. A Commission of Indian Affairs was created by the 1971 legislature to "deal fairly and effectively" with a broad range of Indian affairs.

Fire. Practice bombing operations by the U. S. Air Force in Dare County in March caused a 26,000-acre fire. Stands of young pine were heavily damaged, as were the experimental plantations of a pulp and paper company.

WILLIAM S. POWELL
University of North Carolina

NORTH DAKOTA

Citizen delegates met throughout 1971 to debate a new constitution replacing North Dakota's Constitution of 1889. Highlights of the legislative session included streamlining of the court system and the legislators' refusal to levy new taxes while increasing aid to education. Farmers harvested a bumper crop, with wheat yields averaging more than 75% over 1970. Bad feelings between North Dakota and Canadian farmers, which surfaced during a spring flood, were soothed in October by a compromise, preventing an international incident.

Constitutional Convention. At committee meetings, 98 delegates discussed such questions as adopting a unicameral legislature, eliminating most elective officers, and abolishing tax exemption for church and institutional property. These questions will be resolved when a plenary session in January 1972 draws a proposed new constitution, for submission to the voters later in the year.

Legislation. The Legislative Assembly held the line on new taxes, except for an income surtax to finance a Vietnam veterans' bonus. Funds for higher education were increased by $7 million and

Area: 70,665 square miles (183,022 sq km).
Population (1970 census): 617,761. *Density,* 9 per sq mi.
Chief Cities (1970 census): Bismarck, the capital, 34,703; Fargo, 53,365; Grand Forks, 39,008; Minot, 32,290; Jamestown, 15,385; Dickinson, 12,405.
Government (1971): *Chief Officers*—governor, William L. Guy (D); lt. gov., Richard F. Larsen (R); secy. of state, Ben Meier (R); atty. gen., Helgi Johanneson (R); treas., Bernice Asbridge (R); supt. of public instruction, M. F. Peterson; chief justice, Alvin C. Strutz. *Legislative Assembly*—Senate, 49 members (38 Republicans, 11 Democrats); House of Representatives, 98 members (58 R, 40 D).
Education (1970–71): *Enrollment*—public elementary schools, 100,441 pupils; 4,480 teachers; public secondary, 46,572 pupils; 2,529 teachers; nonpublic schools (1968–69), 18,-500 pupils; 910 teachers; college and university (fall 1968), 27,676 students. *Public school expenditures* (1970–71), $97,500,000 ($689 per pupil). *Average teacher's salary,* $7,060.
State Finances (fiscal year 1970): *Revenues,* $288,536,000 (4% general sales tax and gross receipts taxes, $42,926,-000; motor fuel tax, $19,819,000; federal funds, $71,058,-000). *Expenditures,* $280,977,000 (education, $110,494,000; health, welfare, and safety, $27,056,000; highways, $46,-247,000). *State debt,* $37,324,000 (June 30, 1970).
Personal Income (1970): $1,850,000,000; *per capita,* $2,937.
Public Assistance (1970): $26,145,000. *Average monthly payments* (Dec. 1970)—old-age assistance, $89.55; aid to families with dependent children, $220.55.
Labor Force: *Nonagricultural wage and salary earners* (June 1971), 171,900. *Average annual employment* (1969)—manufacturing, 9,000; trade, 43,000; government, 49,000; services, 29,000. *Insured unemployed* (Oct. 1971)—900 (1.1%).
Manufacturing (1967): *Value added by manufacture,* $112,-800,000. Food and kindred products, $39,900,000; printing and publishing, $14,600,000; nonelectrical machinery, $11,-800,000.
Agriculture (1970): *Cash farm income,* $848,527,000 (livestock, $263,914,000; crops, $417,374,000; government payments, $167,239,000). *Chief crops* (1970)—Wheat, 152,826,000 bushels (ranks 2d among the states); oats, 115,541,000 bushels (ranks 2d); barley, 68,705,000 bushels (ranks 1st); hay, 4,414,000 tons.
Mining (1970): *Production value,* $95,213,000 (ranks 33d among the states). *Chief minerals* (tons)—Sand and gravel, 8,600,000; coal, 4,900,000; natural gas, 35,592,000,-000 cubic feet; petroleum, 22,000,000 barrels.
Transportation: *Roads* (1969), 106,671 miles (171,665 km); *motor vehicles* (1969), 420,000; *railroads* (1968), 5,164 miles (8,310 km); *airports* (1969), 77.
Communications: *Telephones* (1971), 321,000; *television stations* (1969), 11; *radio stations* (1969), 36; *newspapers* (1969), 10 (daily circulation, 185,000).

for elementary and secondary education, by $5 million. The session implemented the state supreme court's constitutional right to exercise supervisory power over the entire state judicial system and appointed a court administrator to assist the supreme court. A small claims court, which may determine cases in which claims do not exceed $200, was created, and a uniform jury selection and service act was ratified. The legislators voted themselves a pay raise and also increased the salaries of supreme court and district judges. Bills to liberalize the state abortion laws were defeated.

Economy. Although cash receipts from farm products and government payments continue to decline, the bumper wheat harvest will gross in excess of $100 million over 1970. Production of flax, oats, barley, and potatoes increased, but sugar beet production was down. Although livestock production decreased, prices in 1971 were up.

North Dakota noted in 1971 the 20th anniversary of the discovery of oil in the state. Its 1,700 producing wells continue to make the crude oil industry the major nonagricultural factor in the state's economy. Tourism enjoyed a 25% increase over 1970.

Farmers' Controversy. In April about 36 square miles of cropland near the Canadian border were flooded when the Pembina River overflowed. North Dakota farmers accused their Manitoba neighbors of diverting water onto the U. S. side by diking a road. The controversy continued into October,

when an agreement was reached banning dikes until an international commission can arbitrate the matter.

STAN CANN, *The Fargo "Forum"*

NORTHERN IRELAND. See GREAT BRITAIN.

NORTHWEST TERRITORIES

At the end of 1971, the government of the Northwest Territories administered most provincial-type services across its entire 1.3 million square miles (3.4 million sq km). Its headquarters are located in Yellowknife, the capital city, and there are also four regional offices. The federal government retains responsibility for the development of natural resources.

Of major significance in 1971 was the all-time-high rate of oil and gas exploration and seismic operations. Three major research groups undertook environmental studies related to pipeline construction in the Arctic in anticipation of a possible pipeline down the Mackenzie Valley.

Council Affairs. In 1971 the Council of the Northwest Territories passed a record budget of $92 million. Legislation passed included a bill lowering the minimum legal age of an adult from 21 years to 18 years, and a securities ordinance to control trading of stocks, bonds and other securities.

Local Government. Development of government at the local level continued to rapidly advance in the Northwest Territories. In 1971, Frobisher Bay in the eastern Arctic and the Dogrib Indian settlement of Rae-Edzo became hamlets. The Arctic communities of Coral Harbour, Pangnirtung, and Pelly Bay, and the Mackenzie settlements of Fort Franklin and Norman Wells, will be incorporated as hamlets on April 1, 1972.

Education. Two large new school-hostel complexes were opened in 1971. At Rae-Edzo a modern "open area" 15-classroom primary school began operating, while in Frobisher Bay a new secondary school with 16 classrooms and 10 vocational shops opened. Over 90% of school-age children are now attending classes in the Northwest Territories, compared with about 15% in 1955.

STUART M. HODGSON
Commissioner, Northwest Territories

Area: 1,304,903 square miles (3,379,703 sq km).
Population: 34,500 (1971 est.).
Chief City (1971 est.): Yellowknife, the capital (7,000).
Government: *Chief Officers*—commissioner, Stuart M. Hodgson; deputy commissioner, John H. Parker; assistant commissioner, C. W. Gilchrist; judge of the Territorial Court, W. G. Morrow. *Legislature*—Territorial Council, 14 members (10 elected·locally, 4 appointed).
Education: *School enrollment* (1971–72 est.): Elementary and secondary, 11,048 pupils, including 4,375 Eskimos, 1,845 Indians, 4,828 others (611 teachers). *Public school expenditures* (1971–72)—$28,031,700.
Public Finance (fiscal year 1970–71): *Revenues,* $61,848,970; (liquor profits, $2,400,792). *Expenditures,* $72,237,464 (education, $13,363,609; social development, $4,848,947; local government, $4,760,908; industrial development, $3,598,124; health, $3,891,588; capital projects, $13,939,101).
Mining (1971 est.): *Production value,* $124,004,060. *Chief minerals* (tons)—Zinc, 225,000; lead, 110,000; gold, 319,-560 (troy ounces); silver, 2,525,000 (troy ounces).
Fur Production (1970–71 est.): $1,112,576 value.
Forest Products (1970): 3,873,000 board feet.
Fisheries (1971): Commercial catch, 3,791,171 pounds ($1,003,881).
Transportation (1971 est.): *Roads,* 916 miles; *motor vehicles,* 8,474; *railroads,* 339 track miles (546 km); *licensed airports,* 15.
Communications (1971): *Telephones,* 7,200; *television stations,* 4; *radio stations,* 4; *newspapers,* 5.

OIL is being produced by this drilling rig in Norway's sector of the North Sea. Although the offshore deposits are large, delivery of the oil has proved very difficult.

PHILLIPS PETROLEUM COMPANY

NORWAY

During 1971 interest in Norway centered on a change in government and on controversy over membership in the European Economic Community (EEC). Norway was little affected by the economic problems of other countries, and it proceeded with test production from North Sea oil fields.

Political Events. Norway's coalition government of four non-Socialist parties resigned in March, after five and one-half years in office, and was followed by a minority Labor government headed by Trygve Bratteli. For months before that, the coalition had been torn by disagreement over the application for membership in the EEC that the Storting (parliament) had made in June 1970. The prime minister, Per Borten, and his Center party, which mainly represents Norway's farmers, had been increasingly opposed to the idea of Norwegian membership. Then, when it was revealed that Borten had shown a confidential document about Norwegian EEC negotiations to the leader of Norway's anti-EEC movement, the three other parties in the coalition insisted that he resign, and the Center party refused to continue in the coalition.

After the crisis, the EEC issue became more and more important in domestic politics. The new Labor government favored continuing the negotiations for full membership; the opposition was split between supporters and opponents of Norwegian entry. Also,

many Labor party supporters in the electorate were in the anti-EEC camp, and the party lost favor with these voters after its return to office. In the autumn local elections, voters showed their feelings by staying away from the polls or by switching their votes to one of the anti-EEC parties. In a low poll, the Labor party won only 41.7% of the vote—2.1% less than in the previous local elections four years earlier. The anti-EEC Center party increased its share of the poll from 9.3% to 11.5%.

The changeover to a socialist government was noticeable in the autumn budget. The upper income groups were the hardest hit by the proposed new taxes or tax increases, including a state wealth tax on companies and on individuals, a new tax on capital gains from share transactions, and the ending of rules that allowed tax deductions for business entertaining.

Economy. With the exception of a few industries, Norway was little affected by the economic stagnation prevailing in many other countries of the world. Exports of aluminum and paper pulp were hit by the decrease in international demand, and production in these industries had to be cut. But most other sectors of industry continued to operate with full employment, and the labor market continued tight.

The rapidly growing offshore oil industry provided a stimulus to the economy in 1971. Foreign oil companies set up bases in Norway for operations in Norwegian waters, new shipping companies were formed to supply and service the drilling platforms, and Norwegian shipyards won orders to build new platforms. Two Norwegian contracting companies started work on a storage tank that the Phillips consortium planned to put on the seabed near its

─────── **NORWAY · Information Highlights** ───────

Official Name: Kingdom of Norway.
Area: 125,181 square miles (324,219 sq km).
Population (1970 est.): 3,880,000. *Density,* 31 per square mile (12 per sq km). *Annual rate of increase,* 0.8%.
Chief Cities (1970 est.): Oslo, the capital, 486,972; Trondheim, 126,170; Bergen, 115,590.
Government: *Head of state,* Olav V, king (acceded Sept. 21, 1957). *Head of government,* Trygve Bratteli, prime minister (took office March 17, 1971). *Legislature*—Storting; Lagting, 38 members. Odelsting, 112 members. *Major political parties*—Conservatives, Liberals, Christian People's party, Center party.
Languages: Norwegian (official).
Education: *Literacy rate* (1971), 99% of population. *Expenditure on education* (1968), 6.1% of gross national product. *School enrollment* (1968)—primary, 387,042; secondary, 296,759; vocational, 64,436; university/higher, 41,790.
Finances (1970 est.): *Revenues,* $2,323,500,000; *expenditures,* $2,512,600,000; *monetary unit,* krone (6.65 kroner equal U. S.$1, Dec. 30, 1971).
Gross National Product (1970): $10,100,000,000.
National Income (1969): $7,443,000,000; *national income per person,* $1,933.
Manufacturing (metric tons, 1969): Cement, 2,480,000; crude steel, 854,000; aluminum (primary), 511,700; newsprint, 511,000; canned fish (1968), 26,100.
Crops (metric tons, 1969 crop year): Potatoes, 721,000; barley, 486,000; oats, 140,000; apples (1968), 65,000.
Minerals (metric tons, 1969): Iron ore, 2,520,000; coal, 392,000; sulfur, 352,000; copper ore, 20,800.
Foreign Trade (1970): *Exports,* $2,457,000,000 (chief exports—ships, $305,200,000; aluminum, $259,245,000; fish, $190,475,000). *Imports,* $3,702,000,000 (chief imports, 1968—ships and boats, $384,000,000; nonelectrical machinery, $291,630,000; chemicals, $237,534,000). *Chief trading partners* (1968)—United Kingdom (took 19% of exports, supplied 12% of imports); Sweden (15%—19%); West Germany.
Tourism: *Receipts* (1970), $156,200,000.
Transportation: *Roads* (1970), 31,825 miles (51,216 km); *motor vehicles* (1969), 845,900 (automobiles, 699,700); *railroads* (1970), 2,756 miles (4,435 km); *merchant fleet* (1971), 21,720,000 gross registered tons; *national airline* (with Denmark and Sweden), Scandinavian Airlines System; *principal airports,* Oslo, Stavanger, Bergen.
Communications: *Telephones* (1970), 1,090,662; *television stations* (1968), 36; *television sets* (1969), 796,000; *radios* (1969), 1,171,000; *newspapers* (1969), 82.

Ekofisk oil field in the autumn of 1972. The cement tank will be 305 feet (90 meters) high and 328 feet (100 meters) in diameter and will have a capacity of 5.7 million cubic feet (160,000 cu meters).

Norsk Hydro, a state-controlled industrial concern, planned to build an oil refinery that could produce 88,000 barrels per day at Mongstad, in west Norway. It was scheduled for completion sometime in 1974 or 1975. Norsk Hydro has a stake in the Ekofisk find, and could refine its share of the oil from the field at the new refinery. Its partner at Mongstad will be Norsk Braendselolje A/S, a close associate of British Petroleum.

Test production from the Ekofisk field started during the summer of 1971 after many delays caused by bad weather and technical difficulties. Initially, four wells were each producing about 10,000 barrels per day. The oil was being refined at various plants around the North Sea. The Phillips consortium planned to improve its facilities and increase its output to about 300,000 barrels per day by 1973. Pipeline routes to deliver the oil to the refineries will be submitted for approval to the Norwegian government.

There were reports that test drilling had shown substantial amounts of oil or gas in two other fields —Petronord consortium's Frigg field and the Tor field, which extends over the concession areas of the Amoco/Noco and Phillips groups. To curb market speculation, the ministry of industry warned in September against drawing "hasty conclusions" about the extent of the deposits. It pointed out that 60 wells had been sunk in Norway's continental shelf, but of the 8 strikes of oil or gas, only Ekofisk had so far been declared commercially acceptable.

Royal Birth. On Sept. 22, 1971, a daughter was born to Crown Princess Sonja and Crown Prince Harald. She was christened Märtha Louise.

THOR GJESTER
"Norwegian Journal of Commerce and Shipping,"
Oslo

NOVA SCOTIA

Crude oil and natural gas began flowing in 1971 from an exploratory well owned by Mobil Oil Canada Ltd. on Sable Island, in the Atlantic 95 miles (153 km) southeast of Cape Canso. Premier Gerald A. Regan announced the strike on October 4. The economic value of this first discovery of oil and natural gas off the East Coast of North America could not be known immediately, but the find stepped up a debate between the provincial and federal governments over ownership of offshore mineral rights.

Politics and Legislation. A Liberal and a Progressive Conservative were elected to the legislature in the November by-elections. This gave the Liberals—who had held only half of the seats after the 1970 general election—a 2-seat majority.

John Buchanan, a lawyer, was elected leader of the province's Progressive Conservative party on March 6. He had served as fisheries and public works minister under the Conservatives.

Legislation passed in the regular session of the legislature abolished the poll tax, lowered the age of majority to 19, and established an ombudsman.

Michelin Dispute. A special session of the legislature convened on June 28 to deal with labor problems plaguing the construction of Michelin Tire Co. plants. The session resulted in an act "to provide for the stabilization of labor relations affecting certain construction projects"—those costing more than $5 million. The act provided that, after a strike has lasted 30 days, the items in dispute must be submitted to an arbitration board whose decision is final and binding on both parties. Eventually, Michelin began operations in two plants, which will provide about 1,800 jobs. Michelin's total investment was $100 million, of which $50 million was provided through a loan by the province's Industrial Estates Ltd.

Industrial Development. Premier Regan announced on February 3 that his government had authorized a $94 million expansion and modernization program for the provincially owned Sydney Steel Corp. mill at Sydney. The program, consisting of five projects, will take 3½ years to complete.

On October 29 it was announced that $95 million would be spent in three years to rehabilitate the Deuterium of Canada Ltd. heavy-water plant at Glace Bay. More than $120 million has been invested, but production had not started by year-end.

Other major undertakings commencing operations were the Canadian General Electric heavy-water plant at Point Tupper, a $75 million investment employing 200 workers; an $80 million Gulf Oil refinery at Point Tupper; and the newsprint phase of Nova Scotia Pulp Ltd.'s $87 million expansion at Point Tupper.

The Nova Scotia unemployment rate rose to its highest level in a decade as the increase in the labor force outstripped the gain in employment.

ANDREW S. HARVEY
Dalhousie University

NOVA SCOTIA • Information Highlights

Area: 21,425 square miles (55,491 sq km).
Population: 770,000 (April 1971 est.).
Chief Cities (1966 census): Halifax, the capital (86,792); Dartmouth (58,745); Sydney (32,767).
Government: *Chief Officers*—lt. gov., Victor de B. Oland; premier, Gerald A. Regan (Liberal); prov. secy., Dr. Maurice E. Delory (L); atty. gen., Leonard L. Pace (L); min. of finance and min. of educ., Peter M. Nicholson (L); chief justice, Alexander Hugh McKinnon. *Legislature*—Legislative Assembly (convened February 1971); 46 members (23 Liberal, 20 Progressive Conservatives, 2 New Democratic, one vac.).
Education: School enrollment (1968–69 est.)—public elementary and secondary, 204,607 pupils (8,487 teachers); private schools, 3,255 pupils (199 teachers); higher, 10,501 students. *Public school expenditures* (1971 est.)—$58,520,000; average teacher's salary (1968–69 est.), $6,296.
Public Finance (fiscal year 1971 est.): *Revenues*, $451,150,-000 (sales tax, $105,370,000; income tax, $55,419,000; federal funds, $212,785,000). *Expenditures*, $571,380,000 (education, $131,800,000; health and social welfare, $230,-230,000; transport and communications, $75,060,000).
Personal Income (1969 est.): $1,760,000,000.
Social Welfare (fiscal year 1971 est.): $48,230,000 (aged and blind, $2,250,000; dependents and unemployed, $23,-010,000).
Manufacturing (1968): *Value added by manufacture*, $261,-044,000 (food and products, $73,004,000; transportation equipment, $35,313,000; paper and allied industries, $34,-233,000; wood industries, $14,057,000).
Agriculture (1969 est.): *Cash farm income* (excluding supplementary payments): $63,014,000 (livestock, $27,452,800; crops (1968 est.), $8,856,000. *Chief crops* (cash receipts) —Fruits, $4,170,000 (ranks 4th among the provinces).
Mining (1969 est.): *Production value*, $54,175,233. *Chief minerals* (tons)—Coal, 2,627,870 (ranks 1st among the provinces); gypsum, 5,211,550 (ranks 1st); sand and gravel, 8,520,000 (ranks 5th); salt, 424,650 (ranks 2d).
Fisheries (1968): *Commercial catch*, 795,188,000 pounds ($54,-600,000). *Leading species*—Scallops, 13,413,000 pounds ($11,861,000); lobster, 15,810,000 pounds ($10,944,000); cod, 143,231,000 pounds ($7,364,000); herring, 351,801,000 pounds ($3,545,000).
Transportation: *Roads* (1968), 15,638 miles (25,162 km); *motor vehicles* (1969), 314,550; *railroads* (1969), 1,301 track miles (2,093 km); *licensed airports* (1970), 7.
Communications: *Telephones* (1969), 272,735; *television stations* (1970), 4; *radio stations* (1967), 16.

All figures given in Canadian dollars.

Technicians in Los Alamos assemble Scyllac, a nuclear power research device. Myriad cables run to capacitor banks, which will store electrical energy created by fusion of atoms.

LOS ALAMOS SCIENTIFIC LABORATORY

nuclear energy

The rate of ordering and constructing nuclear power stations in the United States continued to grow in 1971, showing large increases over the previous two years. In other developments, the U. S. Atomic Energy Commission (AEC) formulated a broad new policy of attempting to evaluate the total environmental impact of any new nuclear power plants. Also radiation limits for nuclear plants were made more stringent in response to public pressure. Solid but unspectacular progress was made in basic and applied research in nuclear energy, and President Nixon expressed his belief that the power needs of the United States in the last decades of the 20th century would be met by breeder reactors.

Nuclear weapons testing and development continued in 1971, although there was strong public opposition to the test at Amchitka Island, Alaska.

NUCLEAR ENERGY AND THE ENVIRONMENT

New Environmental Responsibilities of the AEC. On July 23, 1971, the U. S. court of appeals in Washington, D. C., made a historic decision in a case concerning a projected nuclear power plant at Calvert Cliffs, Md. The court ruled that the AEC must modify its implementation of the National Environmental Policy Act of 1969. In particular, the decision made the AEC responsible for evaluating the total environmental impact of nuclear power plants, not just their radiation effects.

To the surprise of many, the AEC did not attempt to appeal the court of appeals ruling. Instead, newly named AEC Chairman James R. Schlesinger moved quickly to revise AEC regulations to conform to the court decision. Schlesinger said that "the AEC will be directly responsible for evaluating the total environmental impact, including thermal effects, of nuclear plants and for assessing this impact in terms of available alternatives and the need for electric power."

The AEC agreed to assess effects such as thermal pollution—the release of heat from a nuclear power plant into a nearby body of water—in considering the licensing of new and existing nuclear plants. The AEC will review licensing applications involving 91 new nuclear reactors. The licenses for five reactors already in operation will also be reviewed. Their licenses were issued after the effective date of the National Environmental Policy Act.

Radiation Safety Standards. In response to widespread public concern about radioactive emissions from nuclear power plants, the AEC proposed considerably stricter standards on the release of radioactive substances from light-water-cooled reactors. (Light water is ordinary water, H_2O, in contrast to heavy water, D_2O.) The new guidelines, set forth in June 1971, are designed to limit additional radiation exposures of persons living near nuclear power plants to less than 5% of natural background. Natural radiation levels are in the range of 100-125 millirems per year. The proposed levels of exposure due to power-plant effluents are so low that they would not be measurable by existing techniques and must be estimated by calculation. The new guidelines are not expected to be difficult to meet, however, even for older nuclear plants.

Radioactive Waste Disposal. The AEC announced the establishment of a new Division of Waste Management and Transport to meet the radioactive waste disposal challenge posed by the nation's fast-growing nuclear power industry. The division will be in charge of waste disposal programs, research, and the construction and operation of disposal sites for solid radioactive wastes. One site is an abandoned salt mine near Lyons, Kans.

Thermal Pollution Research. In line with its broadened environmental concern, the AEC will construct a $400,000 aquatic ecology facility at Oak Ridge National Laboratory. This facility, scheduled for completion early in 1972, will chiefly be used to study the ways that discharges of heated water from nuclear power plants may affect fish and other aquatic life.

PEACEFUL USES OF NUCLEAR ENERGY

Breeder Reactors. President Nixon continued his strong support of the AEC's program for developing the liquid-metal-cooled fast-breeder reactor (LMFBR) by announcing plans to build a second demonstration plant. Private industry had already pledged $200 million for the first LMFBR project. In the LMFBR, the normally nonfissile uranium-238 is converted to the nuclear fuel plutonium-239, which is used to sustain the chain reaction. This "breeding" of fuel is expected to provide an adequate supply of electrical power for many years to come.

The AEC has made the development of the LMFBR the primary goal of its reactor program, partly because the high operating temperatures of the LMFBR lead to more thermally efficient designs and less thermal pollution. The wide-ranging approach to LMFBR development by the AEC includes: (1) efforts to find a safe and reliable fuel element; (2) programs to collect the data required for LMFBR design and operation; (3) construction of reactor-core mock-ups; and (4) design and development of the plant and its equipment. These efforts will culminate in the building of demonstration plants that operate as part of electric utility systems. The AEC will act in partnership with private industry to construct demonstration units with an electric power capacity in the range from 300 to 500 megawatts.

Nuclear-Electric Power Capacity. The pace of nuclear power plant construction quickened during 1971. By the fourth quarter of the year, U. S. utilities had announced plans for constructing 24 nuclear power plants with a total electric power capacity of 24.56 million kilowatts; 13 plants had been announced for the first nine months of 1970. In 1971 there were 22 nuclear power plants in operation in the United States, and they had a total capacity of 9.13 million kilowatts. The nation's total generating capacity from all sources was 355.26 million kilowatts as of July 31, 1971.

In a revised forecast, the AEC predicted that the United States would have an installed capacity of 150 million kilowatts of nuclear power by 1980 and 300 million kilowatts by the end of 1985. The rest of the world was predicted to have an installed capacity of 127 million kilowatts of nuclear power by 1980 and 270 million kilowatts by 1985.

Peaceful Uses of Nuclear Explosives. In July 1971, the AEC inaugurated a new test series in the Plowshare program for peaceful uses of nuclear explosives by staging the 80-kiloton Miniata test 1,735 feet (530 meters) below the Nevada desert floor.

Miniata is the first of the "Diamond" series of nuclear explosives, which are designed specifically for stimulating production from natural gas fields. The key aims of the series are low cost, small explosive size, simplicity of operation, and low production of residual tritium, a gaseous by-product of an explosion. According to the U. S. Bureau of Mines, the use of nuclear explosives could more than double the known natural gas reserves in the United States.

Miniata is the third AEC test of nuclear explosives for releasing natural gas trapped in underground rocks. The first, Project Gasbuggy, was conducted near Farmington, N. Mex., on Dec. 10, 1967. Project Rulison was conducted near Grand Valley, Colo., on Sept. 10, 1969. The Miniata test explosion produced only one tenth the amount of residual tritium that was produced in Project Rulison.

Californium-252. Uses for Californium-252 (Cf-252), an artificially produced neutron-emitting isotope, continued to be explored under the guidance of the AEC. The powerful neutron-emitting isotopes have been used for analyzing proteins in grains, measuring mercury in foods, certifying documents such as stocks and bonds, and studying electronic components in radiation environments.

NEW U. S. Atomic Energy Commission chairman, James R. Schlesinger, succeeded Glenn T. Seaborg in July.

ATOMIC ENERGY COMMISSION

Needles bearing small amounts of Cf-252 have been donated by the AEC to the International Atomic Energy Agency (IAEA) for use in foreign universities in member states of the IAEA. The needles were first lent to foreign medical institutions for cancer studies. After the neutron sources have decayed to a point where they are no longer useful in medical studies, they will be donated to universities for such uses as neutron radiography, reactor experiments, and mineral exploration. Cf-252 is sold at a cost of $10 per one millionth of a gram.

Nuclear-Powered Heart Pacemaker. The first request in the United States for the implantation of a nuclear-powered heart pacemaker has been filed with the AEC. Plans call for implanting pacemakers in 10 patients, using units powered by plutonium-238. The first known implantation of a heart pacemaker powered by nuclear energy was announced in France in 1970.

Ferret. Putting animals to work went out with the horse-and-buggy era—until 1971, when scientists at the AEC's National Accelerator Laboratory at Batavia, Ill., found they needed to swab out stray steel particles from long pipes used in elementary particle studies. A ferret named Felicia, outfitted with a special collar, was put to the task of pulling a cleaning swab through the 300-foot-long (90-meter) vacuum pipes, each only 12 inches (30.5 cm) in diameter. Felicia saved the AEC the expense of designing a special cleaning machine.

FLOATING nuclear power plants, shown here in drawing, are planned for offshore installation. Westinghouse and Tenneco announced plans for the platform-mounted facilities in August.

MILITARY AND SPACE APPLICATIONS

Nuclear Tests. Nuclear weapons testing by the major powers continued in 1971. Since the 1963 treaty banning tests in the atmosphere or under water, the United States and the USSR have staged only underground explosions—a total of 230 by the United States and about 50 by the USSR, with the explosions ranging up to 6 megatons (TNT equivalent) in size. Atmospheric tests are still conducted by France and mainland China, which are not signatories to the nuclear test-ban treaty.

In the face of strong opposition from environmental groups, President Nixon authorized an underground test explosion, code-named Cannikin, which took place at a depth of 5,875 feet (1,790 meters) on Nov. 6, 1971. A test of the 5-megaton explosive, a prototype of the warhead for the Spartan antimissile missile, had been banned unless specifically authorized by the President on the grounds of national defense. The Cannikin test site, on Amchitka Island in the Aleutian Islands, had originally been selected as an ideal remote location for testing. However, opposition groups had feared the nuclear test might trigger seismic disturbances in the geologically active region. A dramatic affirmation of the safety of the test blast was provided by AEC Chairman James Schlesinger, who brought his family to Amchitka Island to observe the explosion.

U. S. Nuclear Naval Fleet. The U. S. nuclear naval fleet comprises 91 nuclear-powered submarines, 1 deep-submergence research vehicle, 1 nuclear aircraft carrier, 1 guided-missile cruiser, and 2 guided-missile frigates. The research ship NR-1, the world's first nuclear-powered deep-submergence vehicle, is capable of oceanographic and military missions.

Two nuclear-powered aircraft carriers—the *Nimitz* and the *Dwight D. Eisenhower*—were under construction in 1971. These ships will have the most powerful reactors ever used by the U. S. Navy, with about four times the power of the reactors on the aircraft carrier *Enterprise*. The two new aircraft carriers will be able to operate for 13 years without refueling. (See also DEFENSE FORCES.)

Auxiliary Power Systems. Thirteen SNAP (systems for nuclear auxiliary power) nuclear generators using radioisotopes as fuel, and one nuclear reactor system, were launched during the 1961–71 period. The Navy satellite Transit 4A, powered by the SNAP-3A, celebrated its 10th anniversary in space in 1971. The satellite, which is still sending signals to earth, has circled the earth more than 50,000 times. Two nuclear generators placed on the moon in November 1969 already have exceeded their design lifetime. The radioisotope-powered SNAP-27, deployed on the moon in November 1969, was producing 73 watts of power in 1971, allowing the Apollo lunar surface experiment package to function without interruption.

Development Programs. A plutonium-fueled water recovery and waste management system for crew members on space flights is under development by the AEC. The system, which converts wastes into sterile drinking water, can meet the needs of four astronauts for a period of up to 180 days. The system also disposes of nonmetallic cabin wastes, such as paper and food residues, by means of high-temperature incineration.

Other devices under development by the AEC include nuclear-fueled heaters for space voyages, isotopic systems for aircraft guidance, radioisotope-powered heart devices, and nuclear probes for underwater mineral exploration.

BASIC AND APPLIED RESEARCH

Superheavy Elements. Recent advances in nuclear theory have made it seem likely that scientists will soon create a whole new family of superheavy elements. These elements would have atomic numbers far greater than 105, which is the atomic number of hahnium, the element that had the highest known atomic number in 1971. Although evidence for superheavy elements has been sought in moon rocks, mine ores, and cosmic rays, no definite traces have as yet been found. It is likely that the synthesis of such elements will be performed in the laboratory by using accelerators and heavy ion projectiles.

Both the United States and the USSR have made encouraging progress toward the creation of superheavy elements. In the USSR the acceleration of xenon ions to 850 MeV (million electron volts) was reported in October 1971. These ions of xenon gas are the heaviest nuclei ever to be accelerated. This feat is an important first step toward the synthesis of superheavy elements with atomic numbers from 110 to 114.

Progress in heavy ion research was also made at the AEC's Berkeley laboratory, where scientists accelerated nitrogen nuclei to an energy of 36 GeV (billion electron volts). For many years scientists have attempted to provide highly energetic heavy nuclei not only as a step toward superheavy elements but also for cancer studies involving bombardment of human cells. Heavy ion beams will also allow new studies of reactions in complex nuclei.

Particle Accelerators. New AEC accelerator facilities at Los Alamos, N. Mex., and Batavia, Ill., neared completion at the end of 1971. At Los Alamos, an 800-MeV proton linear accelerator is expected to contribute to knowledge of meson interactions. The 200-GeV accelerator at Batavia will be the world's largest proton synchrotron. (See also Physics.)

Air Pollution Research. Putting radiation to work in identifying air pollutants became the subject of research sponsored by the AEC and the National Aeronautics and Space Administration (NASA) in 1971. Two groups in Texas will use X-ray fluorescence techniques and neutron activation techniques to study the composition of the 180 million tons of particulate matter added to the nation's air each year. Trace elements, such as arsenic and mercury, can be assayed by such methods.

Bullet-Hole Test. Testing for bullet holes is one novel use for the radioisotope cadmium-109. A detector containing the isotope has a probe that can be inserted into a small hole. Any trace of lead around the hole produces an X-ray fluorescence that is registered by the detector. Developed by the AEC, the detector is light and portable and is expected to be useful in police work.

U. S. ATOMIC ENERGY COMMISSION

In July 1971, President Nixon nominated James R. Schlesinger to fill the vacancy caused by the resignation of AEC Chairman Glenn T. Seaborg, who had served as chairman since 1961. Nixon also nominated William O. Doub to fill the vacancy on the AEC caused by the death of Theos J. Thompson. Both men were confirmed by the Senate in August 1971.

AEC Reorganizes. The first major reorganization of the AEC in 10 years was announced in December. New will be the Division of Controlled Thermonuclear Research, the position of assistant general manager for environment and safety, the Division of International Security Affairs, and the Division of Applied Technology. Schlesinger said the realignment will provide a coherent management structure and improve program effectiveness. The changes were announced a few months after the AEC had observed its 25th anniversary. The act creating the commission was signed into law by President Truman on Aug. 1, 1946.

INTERNATIONAL CONFERENCE

Nuclear Power. Representatives from 75 countries attended the 4th United Nations International Conference on the Peaceful Uses of Atomic Energy, held at Geneva in September 1971. Glenn T. Seaborg, who served as conference president, pointed out that the worldwide nuclear power capacity was more than 150 million kilowatts in 1971, representing a breakthrough in the use of nuclear power since the 3d Geneva conference in 1964.

At the conference, a good picture was obtained of the worldwide efforts to produce an advanced fast breeder reactor. In the United Kingdom and France, 250-megawatt prototype breeder reactors are expected to be completed in 1972. Both countries envision a rapid follow-up with full-scale 1,000-megawatt plants. In the USSR a 350-megawatt breeder reactor, located at Shevchenko on the Caspian Sea, is scheduled for operation in 1972. A larger, 600-megawatt reactor is planned for 1975.

Desalting Technology. Representatives at the conference also proposed a concerted worldwide effort to refine nuclear desalting technology in the next 20 years. As envisioned by the AEC, a desalting unit with a capacity of 100 million gallons per day could be operational by 1980.

ROBERT E. CHRIEN
Brookhaven National Laboratory

NUMISMATICS. See COIN COLLECTING.
NURSING. See MEDICINE.
OBITUARIES. For a list of prominent persons who died in 1971, see the NECROLOGY on pages 761–772.

FRENCH atomic bomb hangs from giant blimp during tests in June near Mururoa atoll in southern Pacific.

UPI

U.S.S. HAYES, the U.S. Navy's newest and most advanced oceanographic research vessel, began cruising in July. Double hull design utilizes catamaran principles of early Polynesian sailors.

TODD SHIPYARDS CORPORATION

OCEANOGRAPHY

Oceanographers were deeply involved in large-scale international oceanographic experiments as the International Decade of Ocean Exploration (IDOE) completed its second year in 1971. During the year, work done in this program included preliminary studies of large-scale ocean currents and work on methods for measuring the concentration of various materials in the oceans.

Deep-Sea Drilling Project. The material recovered from deep-sea drilling stations all over the globe has substantiated the hypothesis of sea-floor spreading. According to this hypothesis, the material of the earth's crust spreads horizontally from major mid-ocean ridges. The deep-sea drilling project also has made it possible to reconstruct the geologic events that led to the present configuration of oceans and continents.

Fossils recovered from sediments above the equatorial crust off the west coast of Africa indicate that the sediment there is about 45 million years younger than sediments previously recovered from the continental margins of the eastern United States. This evidence conflicts with the simple hypothesis of uniform sea-floor spreading away from both sides of the mid-Atlantic ridges because this hypothesis would make the ages of oceanic crust, and hence the ages of the oldest sediments, identical at the African and American coasts. One possible revision of the hypothesis is that an ancient proto-Atlantic Ocean existed between the continental margins of the United States and Africa before spreading from the mid-Atlantic ridge began.

Drilling in the sea floor between Hawaii and the Marshall-Gilbert Islands showed that the Pacific sea floor has moved northward 1,800 miles (3,000 km) across the equator in the last 100 million years. Volcanic activity was intense in the Central Pacific 70 to 130 million years ago, and many submarine volcanos built themselves close enough to sea level for reefs to form.

Mid-Ocean Dynamics Experiment (MODE-1). British and American oceanographers engaged in theoretical and field work in 1971 in preparation for MODE-1, an extensive investigation of low-fre-

quency motions in the deep sea. These motions are believed to be very important in determining the large-scale circulation of the oceans. The motions are most simply thought of as an irregular superposition of eddies of varying sizes, each having a width of about 120 miles (200 km), and each requiring about one month to complete a revolution. The processes by which the low-frequency motions grow, interact with one another, and then finally decay must be understood before workable predictive models of ocean circulation can be constructed.

Preliminary fieldwork at the experiment site, a 2-degree square southeast of Bermuda, began in October 1971. The major field program is planned for five months in 1973. One British and three U.S. research vessels will participate in launching both free-floating instruments and instruments attached to moored buoys.

The principal goal of the fieldwork will be to obtain a synoptic picture of ocean currents at great depths over the experimental site. The main tools in this effort will be current meters mounted on moored buoys, shipboard tracking of neutrally buoyant floats (ballasted to remain at a preset depth and move with the water there, thus acting as flow tracers), and concurrent measurements of temperature and salinity.

A number of new instruments also will be tested and compared. One of these, already tried out, consists of a free-falling instrument case containing a sensitive voltmeter attached to external seawater contacts. As the instrument falls, it moves horizontally with the water through which it is falling. The voltmeter measures the electric field produced by the motion of the water through the earth's magnetic field. The voltmeter reading can be interpreted as a water-flow speed. Very detailed profiles of the flow from top to bottom can thus be obtained.

With its emphasis on deep circulation, MODE-1 complements the recently completed Soviet Polygon experiment, in which primary emphasis was on the circulation in the upper 4,500 feet (1,400 meters) of the equatorial Atlantic Ocean.

Geochemical Ocean Sections (GEOSECS). Much of our knowledge about how the waters of the sea move about has been obtained by studying the global distributions of the temperature and salinity of seawater and the dissolved oxygen in seawater. Although many substances are carried along with moving water, they have not been used previously as tracers of water movement because standardized measurements of their concentrations have been difficult.

The basic GEOSECS program is a detailed measurement of a number of substances at 120 stations along north-south sections in all three major oceans. Such water properties as dissolved chemical constituents (inorganic carbon, oxygen, nitrogen, nutrients, trace metals and gases, organic matter), natural and man-made radionuclides, and alkalinity will be measured. Because procedures for measuring very small concentrations of materials are difficult, one of the preliminary goals of the work is the intercomparison, in test cruises at sea, of methods developed in various laboratories.

Storm Surge Forecasting. On Nov. 12, 1970, a cyclone devastated parts of East Pakistan. The total number of deaths may have reached 500,000. The storm surge in the Bay of Bengal associated with the high winds and low atmospheric pressures of the cyclone was responsible for many of the fatalities. Work aimed at early-warning forecasting of such surges got under way in 1971.

Undersea Habitats. The last scheduled mission in the undersea habitat Tektite II was successfully completed in late 1970. This ended a program in which nearly 900 man-days of underwater work were carried out by teams of engineers and scientists (including one all-woman group) who remained beneath the sea surface for as long as 30 days.

Soviet oceanographers have developed and operated similar habitats, Chernomore-1 and Chernomore-2, capable of supporting a four-man team at depths of more than 30 meters (100 feet) in the Black Sea for periods up to two or three weeks.

Freshwater Plants in Seawater. Scientists at the Scripps Institution of Oceanography have grown beets in full-strength seawater, which contains 3.5% salt. The plants are first raised in fresh water and then transferred to salt water when several inches tall. An important part of the procedure is abundant aeration of the plant roots.

The plants were grown hydroponically—that is, in liquid solution. This technique is not economically feasible for large-scale cultivation. However, experiments are under way on plants planted in sand and watered periodically with seawater. Sand is preferable to clay soils because it is almost chemically inert. Thus the level of salt around the plant roots never greatly exceeds that of the irrigating fluid.

Successful growth of freshwater plants with saltwater irrigation would make possible the use of seawater or brackish well water to irrigate land that is now dry and barren, and obviate the need for desalinization of irrigation water for such regions.

Sea Pollution. In 1971, mercury concentrations in some samples of deep-sea fish such as tuna and swordfish were found to be sufficiently above U. S. governmental safety limits that certain catches were banned from sale for human consumption. Cases of mercury poisoning from locally taken shellfish and fish had been well documented in Japan before 1960, and mercury levels in some fish taken from certain North American lakes were found to have several times the permissable level in 1970. How-

ever, subsequent and as yet not fully reported studies of freshwater fish preserved as biological specimens suggested that, except in the vicinity of known sources of industrial mercury pollution, the mercury content has not increased greatly over the past several decades. Comparable studies using preserved and recently caught deep-sea fish are now being conducted. During 1971, a study of the Greenland ice sheet showed that the atmospheric content of mercury has doubled over the past 2,000 years and may be accelerating.

This evidence suggests that the globally averaged natural mercury content of the environment may have been about half its present value before human intervention, with only localized exceptions. But it also points out certain aspects of a rational pollution evaluation program *beyond* simple documentation of the presence of a suspected pollutant that should be common to studies of all forms of pollution. Monitoring of pollutant levels must be frequent, varied, and continuously maintained. Simultaneously, research to establish the actual damage to health or environment produced by a given level of pollutant must be carried forward to provide a basis for setting acceptable pollutant levels. The path of the pollutant from its source through the environment to the point of damage must be documented. Finally, legislative action with effective enforcement must be applied to eliminate unacceptable discharges of pollutants. Clearly, the acceptable level of a pollutant will vary as our understanding of its effects evolves.

(See also GEOLOGY.)

MYRL C. HERDERSHOTT
Scripps Institution of Oceanography

OHIO

The conflict between Ohio Democrats and Republicans surfaced frequently in 1971 as Democratic Gov. John J. Gilligan clashed repeatedly with the Republican-controlled legislature. The courts made several significant rulings involving Ohio laws. Campus unrest declined from 1970 levels.

Legislature. In the November 1970 elections in Ohio, evidences of questionable loan procedures by leading Republican administrators had contributed to the election of Gilligan. However, the legislature that convened in January had a Republican majority: the House by 54 to 45; the Senate by 21 to 13. In his inaugural address Gilligan indicated that he would seek greatly increased taxes to support aid for the urban poor, pollution control, the schools, and the cities. His proposed 2-year budget, submitted in March, called for $9.1 billion. On December 10 the legislature finally approved a budget that included the state's first personal income tax.

To meet these expenditures the governor sought a graduated personal income tax and new corporation taxes, together with reductions in real estate taxes. Some labor leaders who had supported Gilligan wanted an emphasis on business taxes and opposed individual income taxes. Many Republicans strongly opposed business taxes and advocated a sales tax increase to 5½%, with its extension to additional services. To lessen the burden of higher education expenses Gilligan proposed deferred tuition payments for students in the four-year Ohio state colleges. Almost all Ohio educators opposed this measure.

The struggle over proposed taxes resulted in a

──────── OHIO • Information Highlights ────────

Area: 41,222 square miles (106,765 sq km).
Population (1970): 10,652,017. *Density:* 262 per sq mi.
Chief Cities (1970 census): Columbus, the capital, 540,025; Cleveland, 750,879; Cincinnati, 452,524; Toledo, 383,818; Akron, 275,425; Dayton, 243,601.
Government (1971): *Chief Officers*—governor, John J. Gilligan (D); lt. gov., John W. Brown (R); secy. of state, Ted W. Brown (R); atty. gen., William J. Brown (D); treas., Gertrude W. Donahey (D); supt., Dept. of Education, Martin W. Essex; chief justice, C. William O'Neill. *General Assembly*—Senate, 33 members (20 Republicans, 13 Democrats); House of Representatives, 99 members (54 R, 45 D).
Education (1970–71): *Enrollment*—public elementary schools, 1,730,900 pupils, 56,559 teachers; public secondary, 951,783 pupils; 48,121 teachers; nonpublic schools (1968–69), 363,200 pupils; 12,990 teachers; college and university (fall 1968), 336,921 students. *Public school expenditures* (1970–71), $1,750,000 ($778 per pupil). *Average teacher's salary,* $8,798.
State Finances (fiscal year 1970): *Revenues,* $3,876,193,000 (4% general sales tax and gross receipts taxes, $658,759,000; motor fuel tax, $320,166,000; federal funds, $657,672,000). *Expenditures,* $3,477,696,000 (education, $1,044,111,000; health, welfare, and safety, $391,107,000; highways, $517,242,000). *State debt,* $1,631,898,000 (June 30, 1970).
Personal Income (1970): $42,610,000,000; per capita, $3,983.
Public Assistance (1970): $422,104,000. *Average monthly payments* (Dec. 1970)—old-age assistance, $60.75; aid to families with dependent children, $164.35.
Labor Force: *Nonagricultural wage and salary earners* (June 1971), 3,871,400. *Average annual employment* (1969)—manufacturing, 1,468,000; trade, 761,000; government, 545,000; services, 544,000. *Insured unemployed* (Oct. 1971)—74,900 (2.6%).
Manufacturing (1967): *Value added by manufacture,* $20,435,400,000. Nonelectrical machinery, $3,253,800,000; primary metal industries, $2,702,500,000; transportation equipment, $2,593,800,000; fabricated metal products, $2,212,200,000.
Agriculture (1970): *Cash farm income,* $1,413,106,000 (livestock, $768,127,000; crops, $555,366,000; government payments, $89,613,000). *Chief crops* (1970)—Corn, 232,078,000 bushels; soybeans, 69,483,000 bushels.
Mining (1970): *Production value,* $590,780,000 (ranks 14th among the states). *Chief minerals* (tons)—Coal, 51,585,000; stone, 46,848,000; sand and gravel, 44,242,000; cement, 12,181,000 barrels.
Fisheries (1970): *Commercial catch,* 8,400,000 pounds ($1,000,000). *Leading species by value* (1969), Yellow perch, $268,815; white bass, $258,776; carp, $140,562.
Transportation: *Roads* (1969), 108,644 miles (174,841 km); *motor vehicles* (1969), 5,740,000; *railroads* (1968), 7,954 miles (12,800 km); *airports* (1969), 99.
Communications: *Telephones* (1971), 6,200,500; *television stations* (1969), 29; *radio stations* (1969), 219; *newspaper* (1969), 96 (daily circulation, 3,522,000).

bitter deadlock, necessitating interim budgets to meet basic expenses and leading to an austerity program. This continued through the summer and fall. By the fall, taxpayer resistance seemed to have passed its peak, for all six bond issues on the November ballot in Columbus won by wide margins.

In addition to taxes, a projected legislative gerrymandering of the state caused bitter political reactions. An apportionment board, controlled by Democrats, recommended a redistricting that was to the disadvantage of many incumbent Republicans and even some Democrats.

Legal Issues. Ohio laws figured in a number of landmark legal decisions during 1971. In February the U. S. Supreme Court in *In Re Stolar* reversed by a 5 to 4 decision the Ohio Supreme Court's approval of an Ohio Bar applicant's rejection. The applicant had refused to answer questions about his membership in alleged subversive organizations. In March the U. S. District Court in Dayton held invalid a law barring women from certain types of strenuous work and limiting working hours. The court ruled that the law was contrary to the Civil Rights Act of 1964.

The U. S. Supreme Court ˙reversed in May the conviction of James Palmer of Euclid for violating a "suspicious persons" ordinance that was too vague. In June the high court overturned a Cincinnati assembly ordinance, holding the law to be so vague as to deny freedom of assembly.

Youth Voting. On June 30, Ohio became the 38th, and decisive, state to ratify the 26th Amendment to the U. S. Constitution, granting 18-year-olds the vote. A court in Cincinnati later ruled that college students could vote in their college communities, much to the dismay of conservative residents in such towns as Athens and Oxford, where relatively transient students far outnumber the townspeople.

Campus Unrest. In contrast with the campus unrest in the spring of 1970, activities at colleges and universities were generally restrained. Repercussions of the Kent State University killings continued, but in July the U. S. District Court in Cleveland dismissed a $4 million suit brought by the parents of a dead student against the state. In August, U. S. Attorney General Mitchell announced that there would be no federal grand jury investigation of the Kent State deaths, as there was no evidence of conspiracy by National Guardsmen.

Race Relations. Efforts at racial integration in the public schools met with little success. Statistics showed that between 1968 and 1970 percentages of blacks in predominantly white schools had slightly increased in Toledo and Dayton but had decreased in Cleveland, Cincinnati, and Akron.

In the November elections Arnold R. Pinkney, a black protégé of Carl B. Stokes, Cleveland's first black mayor, was defeated by a conservative white republican, Ralph J. Perk. Perk was to be Cleveland's first Republican mayor in 30 years.

FRANCIS P. WEISENBURGER
The Ohio State University

OKLAHOMA

Political interest in Oklahoma during the first half of 1971 centered on the attempt of Gov. David Hall, the first Democrat to hold the office in eight years, to push reform legislation through the Democratic-controlled 33d Legislature. A woman became mayor of Oklahoma City. The economic event of the year was the opening of the Oklahoma arm of the Verdigris-Arkansas River Waterway.

Legislation. Marking the first change in 35 years, the gross production tax on oil and gas was increased from 5% to 7%. The state income tax was revised to eliminate many former exclusions, mainly affecting incomes over $15,000. The liquor tax was increased. Most of the additional revenue was for education and health benefits, and $5 million was earmarked to eliminate death traps on state highways.

Collective bargaining became legal for police and firemen, and a modern drug code was enacted. The 18-year-old-voter amendment to the U. S. Constitution was ratified. The governor abolished the office of interagency coordination, established to collect data on civil-disorder suspects.

Woman Mayor. Mrs. Patience Latting of the Oklahoma City council overwhelmingly defeated a fellow councilman, Bill Bishop, in the runoff election on April 6 to become the first woman mayor of Oklahoma City, the state's largest city.

Waterway. Governor Hall was the principal speaker at Muskogee on Jan. 22, 1971, when the Oklahoma link in the Arkansas-Verdigris Waterway was opened for navigation. Muskogee and Catoosa, near Tulsa, are the two Oklahoma ports along the navigation system.

President Nixon officially dedicated the $1.2

OKLAHOMA · Information Highlights

Area: 69,919 square miles (181,090 sq km).

Population (1970 census): 2,559,253. *Density:* 37 per sq mi.

Chief Cities (1970 census): Oklahoma City, the capital, 368,-856; Tulsa, 330,350; Lawton, 74,470; Norman, 52,117.

Government (1971): *Chief Officers*—governor, David Hall (D); lt. gov., George Nigh (D); secy. of state, John Rogers (D); atty. gen., Larry D. Derryberry (D); treas., Leo Winters (D); supt. of public instruction, Leslie R. Risher (D); chief justice, Supreme Court, William A. Berry; presiding judge, Court of Criminal Appeals, Hez J. Bussey. *Legislature*—Senate, 48 members (39 D, 9 R); House of Representatives, 99 members (78 D, 21 R).

Education (1970–71): *Enrollment*—public elementary schools, 350,000 pupils; 14,810 teachers; public secondary, 290,000 pupils; 13,374 teachers; nonpublic schools (1968–69), 17,600 pupils; 890 teachers; college and university (fall 1968), 106,130 students. *Public school expenditures* (1970–71), $345,000,000 ($605 per pupil). *Average teacher's salary,* $7,360.

State Finances (fiscal year 1970): *Revenues,* $1,078,285,000 (2% general sales tax and gross receipts taxes, $93,821,-000; motor fuel tax, $90,867,000; federal funds, $335,474,-000). *Expenditures,* $1,081,600,000 (education, $390,213,-000; health, welfare, and safety, $248,229,000; highways, $129,880,000). *State debt,* $739,612,000 (June 30, 1970).

Personal Income (1970): $8,560,000,000; per capita, $3,269.

Public Assistance (1970): $229,507,000. *Average monthly payments* (Dec. 1970)—old-age assistance, $68.95; aid to families with dependent children, $134.50.

Labor Force: *Nonagricultural wage and salary earners* (June 1971), 778,100. *Average annual employment* (1969)—manufacturing, 130,000; trade, 165,000; government, 185,000.

Manufacturing (1967): *Value added by manufacture,* $1,346,-200,000. Nonelectrical machinery, $184,300,000; food and kindred products, 176,300,000.

Agriculture (1970): *Cash farm income,* $1,176,368,000 (livestock, $824,051,000; crops, $234,366,000; government payments, $117,951,000). *Chief crops* (1970)—Wheat, 98,202,-000 bushels (ranks 4th among the states); sorghum grain, 23,206,000 bushels (ranks 4th); hay, 2,806,000 tons.

Mining (1970): *Production value,* $1,131,114,000 (ranks 4th among the states). *Chief minerals* (tons)—Stone, 18,423,-000; natural gas, 1,579,061,000,000 cubic feet; petroleum, 224,500,000 barrels.

Transportation: *Roads* (1969) 107,809 miles (173,497 km); *motor vehicles* (1969), 1,650,000; *railroads* (1968) 5,451 miles (8,772 km); *airports* (1969), 106.

Communications: *Telephones* (1971) 1,469,200; *television stations* (1969), 9; *radio stations* (1969), 95; *newspapers* (1969), 52 (daily circulation, 846,000).

billion waterway on June 5 with ceremonies at Catoosa, at the head of navigation, 440 miles (708 km) from the mouth of the Arkansas River. Seventeen locks lift vessels en route to Catoosa a total of 420 feet (128 meters).

Toll Road. A Chicago syndicate in November agreed to handle a $74 million bond issue for the construction of the Cimarron Turnpike. This will extend 60.8 miles (97.8 km) west from the Tulsa port of Catoosa to intersect Interstate Highway 35 east of Enid, with links to Ponca City and Stillwater. To be completed in 1974, it will afford highway access to the port for bulk commodities.

Other Events. Tulsa was host on May 15–23 to the International Oil Exposition. Since 1923, Tulsa has been the site of this fair, which attracts exhibitors and visitors from all oil-producing countries. It is held at 5-year intervals.

Rock festivals were prohibited in Oklahoma during 1970, but on July 11, 1971, at Norman, a music festival was held honoring the late Woodie Guthrie, the famed folk singer who emerged from Okemah, Okla., during the dust-bowl days of the Depression.

The No. 1 U. S. college football team—Nebraska—met the No. 2 team—Oklahoma—at Norman on November 25 to decide the Big 8 Conference and mythical national championships. Nebraska won, 35–31.

J. STANLEY CLARK
Oklahoma City University

Chouteau Lock on Verdigris River is part of Arkansas River Waterway, linking Oklahoma with Mississippi River.

U. S. ARMY CORPS OF ENGINEERS

OLDER POPULATION

For older U. S. citizens, a major event of 1971 was the series of White House conferences on aging that began at the community level and culminated at a national meeting of 3,400 delegates in Washington, D. C., from November 28 to December 2. President Richard Nixon addressed the final session.

Among the results of the conference were proposals to increase social security benefits and promises to increase the income of older people in other ways, an administrative decision to develop a positive posture relative to meeting older people's needs, increased efforts to raise the quality of long-term care for the chronically ill elderly, and greater involvement of older people and minority groups in advocacy on behalf of the older population.

The White House Conference Year. Several hundred community White House conferences were held from January through April 1971 to initiate recommendations for national action and policy. Suggestions from these meetings were refined in White House conferences held in 55 states and territories. The formulations from these conferences were forwarded to Washington to be synthesized with recommendations developed by task forces representing 347 national organizations. The consolidated suggestions and ideas provided the basis for the deliberations of the national conference delegates.

The recommendations formulated in the conference were transmitted to appropriate federal agencies for immediate consideration and possible action. They are also being organized for presentation to the President and Congress as guides for the creation of a comprehensive national policy for the older population.

In April, President Nixon requested former Secretary of Health, Education, and Welfare Arthur S. Flemming to take charge of all conference activity, and named him chairman. Flemming met with heads of federal agencies and with dozens of groups across the United States to urge immediate expansion of existing programs and initiation of new ones. He also recommended increased representation of minorities in the conference and set up 17 special concerns sessions to accommodate groups who felt that their special interests might not receive proper attention within the conference structure. The heavy representation of older people (the average age of delegates was just over 60), youth, blacks, Indians, Spanish-speaking groups, and Asian-Americans was one of the conference innovations.

Improving Retirement Income. The Congress increased social security benefits by 10%, effective in May but retroactive to January 1. Beginning January 1972, the social security tax will be paid on the first $9,000 instead of the present $7,800. At the closing White House conference session, President Nixon urged passage of the administration's proposal providing a guaranteed minimum income to all older people and promised to seek elimination of the monthly fee now charged for Part B Medicare. In the week following the conference, the President asked Congress to enact legislation permitting income tax deductions of money set aside for retirement, for universal vesting of pension fund contributions, and for stronger control over pension funds.

Government Action. House and Senate committees held hearings delving into the downgrading of the Administration on Aging (AoA) including a reduced budget request for it, and problems of the White House Conference. These hearings resulted in a 52% increase in the AoA appropriation for fiscal 1972 over the request originally submitted.

In October the Domestic Council of the Executive Office created a Committee on Aging, including the director of the Office of Management and Budget and the chairman of the White House conference. The committee initiated a series of analyses of federal programs and needs relating to aging, to be conducted with the aid of White House conference recommendations. At the White House conference in December, President Nixon reported that he was requesting that the budget for the Administration on Aging be doubled. He also announced that he had invited conference chairman Flemming to become his special consultant on aging.

Focus on Long-Term Care. Widespread criticism of many facilities offering care for long-term chronically ill older people also received attention from the President. He promised to raise the level of care for such patients and stated that federal funds, through Medicaid or Medicare, should not go into substandard institutions. HEW Secretary Elliot Richardson announced an improvement program, the principal elements of which were to add 2,000 inspectors who would work under the direction of state licensing agencies and provide training for personnel of long-term care facilities. The administration promised to expand home care services and sought to enlist national organizations in launching a large supplementary effort.

Health and Medical Care. Limitations on services covered and costs of care for the elderly under Medicaid and Medicare continued to irritate older people and to plague federal and state governments. In 1971, 13 bills for expanded health insurance were introduced in Congress. The most comprehensive and most widely supported by organized labor and senior-citizen organizations was the Kennedy-Griffith proposal for a federally administered program to cover the entire population. Most of the other bills called for partial coverage through combinations of government and private insurance, without change in Medicare. In November, Secretary Richardson announced a 13% increase (from $60 to $68) in the patient's share of the cost of the first day in a hospital (effective January 1972). He also stated that the law would require him to increase the Part B Medicare premium (now $5.60 per month) to $5.80 per month on July 1, 1972.

White House conference delegates recommended extension of coverage to include costs of prescription drugs, mental health services, reduced deductibles, and elimination of the Part B premium as interim measures pending enactment of a total health insurance program.

International Developments. Fifty representatives of other nations shared their knowledge with delegates to the White House conference and participated with U. S. gerontologists in a research symposium in Washington, D. C., from November 28 to December 9. Plans were completed for the 9th International Congress on Gerontology scheduled for Kiev, USSR, July 2–7, 1972. The International Center for Social Gerontology, based in Paris, sponsored a symposium on Work and Aging, which was held in Florence, Italy.

CLARK TIBBITTS
Administration on Aging
U. S. Department of Health, Education, and Welfare

OMAN

Under the leadership of Sultan Qabus Ibn Said, Oman emerged from its old isolation in 1971 to become a member of international organizations.

Foreign Affairs. Oman was admitted to the United Nations on September 1 and to the Arab League at the end of September. The Arab League, in admitting the sultanate, modified its former policy of sympathy with the sultan's rival, the imam of Oman, who has been living in exile.

With the withdrawal of most British garrisons from the Persian Gulf region, Oman remained the principal bastion of British military power in the area. Oman and the United States agreed to establish diplomatic relations on the ambassadorial level.

Internal Affairs. Rebel groups maintained their grip on much of the southern part of the sultanate outside the larger towns. British officers in the sultan's service openly directed the fighting against the dissident groups, who have been supported by Southern Yemen and the People's Republic of China.

Sultan Qabus and his prime minister, Tariq Ibn Taymur, were hampered in their efforts to carry out internal reforms and development by the heavy drain on the treasury caused by the struggle against the rebel forces and by a modest decline in oil production in 1971.

GEORGE RENTZ
Hoover Institution, Stanford University

--- OMAN • Information Highlights ---

Official Name: Sultanate of Oman.
Area: 82,000 square miles (212,379 sq km).
Population (1971 est.): 750,000.
Chief Cities: Muscat, the capital (1968 est.), 7,000; Matrah; Salalah.
Government: *Head of state:* Qabus Ibn Said, sultan (acceded July 20, 1970). *Chief minister,* Tariq Ibn Taymur, prime minister (took office Aug. 9, 1970).
Finance (1971 est.): *Revenues,* $100,000,000; *monetary unit,* saidi riyal.
Crops: Dates, bananas, pomegranates.
Foreign Trade (1971): *Exports* (petroleum), $100,000,000. *Chief trading partners:* India, Britain.

ONTARIO

John Robarts' resignation as premier of Ontario and leader of the Progressive Conservative party and his succession by William Davis dominated the political news in 1971. Ontario is the wealthiest and most populous province in Canada, and its deteriorating economic situation was also an important news factor during the year.

At the Conservative convention held in February to choose a new premier, Davis, the minister of education, won a slim fourth-ballot victory over Allen Lawrence, minister of mines and northern affairs. High expenditures for education and health care and the deteriorating condition of the environment were major campaign issues.

Davis was sworn in as premier on March 1. In the new cabinet, Allen Lawrence became attorney general; Darcy McKeough, treasurer; Robert Welch, minister of education; and A. B. R. Lawrence, minister of health.

Provincial Budget. A record budget proposing expenditures of $4.2 billion, with a deficit of $415 million, was introduced on April 16. Major items were $1.8 billion for education and $904.5 million for health, welfare, and social services—increases of $230 million and $47 million respectively. To stimulate the economy, corporate taxes were cut. In

--- ONTARIO • Information Highlights ---

Area: 412,582 square miles (1,068,589 sq km).
Population: 7,795,000 (April 1971 est.).
Chief Cities (1966 census): Toronto, the provincial capital (1968 est., 299,466); Hamilton (298,121); Ottawa, federal capital (1968 est., 299,466); London (194,416); Windsor (192,544).
Government: *Chief Officers*—lt. gov., W. Ross MacDonald; premier, William G. Davis (Progressive Conservative); prov. secy., John Yaremko (PC); atty. gen., Allen Lawrence (PC); prov. treas., Darcy McKeough (PC); min. of educ., Robert S. Welch (PC); chief justice, George A. Gale. *Legislature*—Legislative Assembly, 117 members (78 Progressive Conservative; 20 Liberal; 19 New Democratic party).
Education: School enrollment (1968–69 est.)—public elementary and secondary, 1,868,788 pupils (79,300 teachers); private schools, 42,986 pupils (3,365 teachers); Indian (federal) schools, 6,752 pupils (278 teachers); college and university, 79,089 students. *Public school expenditures* (1971 est.)—$845,321,000; median teacher's salary (1967–68 est.), $6,900.
Public Finance (fiscal year 1971 est.): *Revenues,* $4,996,250,-000 (sales tax, $1,204,820,000; income tax, $1,355,019,000; federal funds, $860,729,000). *Expenditures,* $5,104,820,000 (education, $1,584,500,000; health and social welfare, $1,817,060,000.
Social Welfare (fiscal year 1971 est.): $281,110,000 (aged and blind, $23,900,000; dependents and unemployed, $177,-860,000).
Manufacturing (1968): *Value added by manufacture,* $9,714,-889,000 (transportation equipment, $1,489,821,000; food and products, $1,165,291,000; primary metals, $937,076,-000; fabricated metals, $892,972,000; electrical products, $775,268,000; chemical and chemical products industries, $766,087,000; nonelectrical machinery, $549,190,000).
Agriculture (1969 est.): *Cash farm income* (excluding supplementary payments), $1,365,938,000 (livestock, $787,458,000; crops (1968 est.), $370,042,000. *Chief crops* (cash receipts)—Tobacco, $136,365,000 (ranks 1st among the provinces); vegetables, $63,078,000 (ranks 1st); fruits, $35,330,000 (ranks 1st); corn, $26,158,000 (ranks 1st); wheat, $22,710,000 (ranks 4th); soybeans, $22,363,000 (ranks 1st).
Mining (1969 est.): *Production value,* $1,214,456,935. *Chief minerals* (tons)—Nickel, 146,837 (ranks 1st among the provinces); copper, 228,944 (ranks 1st); zinc, 349,408 (ranks 1st); cement, 3,269,284 (ranks 1st); sand and gravel, 85,000,000 (ranks 1st); stone, 25,749,000 (ranks 2d).
Transportation: *Roads* (1968), 80,076 miles (128,842 km); *motor vehicles* (1969), 2,953,790; *railroads* (1969), 10,-045 track miles (16,162 km); *licensed airports* (1970), 93.
Communications: *Telephones* (1969), 3,668,630; *television stations* (1970), 19; *radio stations* (1967), 78; *newspapers* (1970), 49 (daily circulation, 1,963,202).
All figures given in Canadian dollars.

November an income tax reduction of 3% was announced.

Health. A major objective of the government has been to extend medical care while trying to restrain costs. Amalgamation of the provincial hospital insurance scheme and the medicare plan (OHSIP) will result in a general reduction of premiums. The maximum payable by a family will be $114 a year. Employed persons will pay only 40% of the premium, the employer the remaining 60%.

Premiums for the aged and poor (about 1.5 million persons) are to be eliminated, and those with low incomes will pay reduced rates. Also effective in April 1972, provincial hospital insurance will extend to nursing home care.

Friction between the government and spokesmen for the medical profession increased when Health Minister Lawrence announced on April 23 a plan to end "double billing." Under this plan, doctors will either have to accept 90% of the fee given on the Ontario Medical Association's fee schedule or bill the patient for the full fee and accept the attendant risks. Currently, doctors may bill OHSIP for the 90% and the patient for the balance, or bill the patient and let him claim the 90% from OHSIP. Investigations into many doctors' claims are also indicated in this new proposal.

Education. In 1971, 42% of the provincial budget was earmarked for education—$1.3 billion on lower education plus nearly $444 million for the universities. In 1970 school boards were restricted on a per capita basis; in 1971 the universities' expenditures were under restraint. On March 10 the amount for Ontario graduate fellowships was cut $1.5 million to $3.5 million and a limit of $1,800 placed on the amount paid graduate assistants. University enrollment was 5% less than forecast, and grants calculated on enrollments were consequently reduced. Despite strong pressure, Premier Davis reaffirmed his government's decision not to extend aid to Roman Catholic schools beyond the 10th grade.

Environment. On March 15, Premier Davis announced his intention to create a department of the environment and also promised stronger antipollution legislation. The cabinet vetoed completion of the Spadina Expressway in Toronto, although it had been approved by the city authorities and the Ontario municipal board.

Provincial Election. The premier was not required to call an election until 1972, but he went to the polls on October 21 and scored a personal triumph. The Progressive Conservative (PC) party, in power for 18 years, was returned with an increased majority—countering a national trend against incumbent government.

The New Democrat party, under their new leader Stephen Lewis, failed to replace the Liberals as the official opposition as had been widely expected. The new legislature will be PC, 78; Liberals, 20; and NDP, 19. The popular vote was PC, 44%; Liberal, 28%; and NDP, 27%.

For the first time, 18-year-olds became eligible to vote in a provincial election. The age of majority was reduced in 1971 so that 18-year-olds were allowed to vote, drink alcoholic beverages, and sign contracts.

PETER J. KING
Carleton University

OREGON

Despite party differences, the 1971 Oregon Legislative Assembly revised the criminal code and passed significant laws protecting the environment.

Legislature. The opening of the legislature was delayed by conflict over the choice of Senate president. A 12-day deadlock between 15 regular Democrats and 14 Republicans allied with the last conservative "coalition Democrat," E. D. Potts, was broken when the latter group finally nominated Democrat John Burns and, on the 54th ballot, persuaded him to break the tie by voting for himself. Bitter partisanship also marked the approval of the 26th Amendment, lowering the voting age to 18.

There was no agreement on a plan for legislative reapportionment, which was left to Secretary of State Clay Myers. The legislature's new "nofault" divorce law simplified divorce procedure.

Criminal Code. One of the most far-reaching actions of the legislature was the adoption of a new criminal code, which attempted to make conviction more certain and the laws more just. The code, which clarified definitions and penalties, reduced the number of crimes by consolidating some and eliminating others, such as most of the illegality of sexual acts between consenting adults.

Ecology. The legislature passed two bills protecting the environment that were the first of their kind in the nation. The "bottle bill" required a deposit after Oct. 1, 1972, on all beer and soft-drink cans and bottles and banned entirely cans with pull-tab openers. The second bill allocated 1% of all state and local highway funds for bicycle paths and foot trails.

Other bills strengthened the powers of state agencies over the disposal of solid wastes, pesticides, fungicides, and nuclear wastes. State control was also increased in regard to nuclear plant siting

Ontario Place, a complex of restaurants, exhibitions, and theater in Lake Ontario near Toronto, opened in May.

ONTARIO DEPT. OF TRADE AND DEVELOPMENT

and safety; air pollution, including automobile emissions and field burning; noise levels; and the filling of estuaries.

Farm Labor. A farm labor bill designed to prevent strikes during harvest season was passed after rancorous dispute. Farm labor leaders, calling it grossly unfair because it prevented workers from organizing, threatened a boycott of Oregon products. Gov. Tom McCall vetoed the bill. At a special legislative session in November, Democrats blocked attempts to pass a new farm labor bill.

Tax Relief. Tax reform, badly needed, was restricted to the introduction of a new principle of property-tax relief. It limited relief to homesteads and based the amount on household income.

Fiscal Crisis. After the legislative session ended, a 5-cent increase in the cigarette tax and a local-option increase in motor vehicle fees were referred to voters by petition, to be decided on at the November 1972 elections. This deferment of taxation, together with other factors, produced a state deficit of $33 million, forcing the governor to call a special session on November 16. This 7-day session quickly agreed to divorce state and federal income-tax regulations, which were automatically reducing state revenues, and to schedule special referendums for approving the increases in the cigarette tax (January 18) and vehicle fee (May 23).

SAMUEL K. ANDERSON
Oregon College of Education

--------- OREGON • Information Highlights ---------

Area: 96,981 square miles (251,181 sq km).
Population (1970 census): 2,091,385. *Density:* 21 per sq mi.
Chief Cities (1970 census): Salem, the capital, 68,296; Portland, 380,620; Eugene, 76,346; Corvallis, 35,153; Springfield, 27,047; Medford, 28,454.
Government (1971): *Chief Officers*—governor, Tom McCall (R); secy. of state, Clay Myers (R); atty. gen., Lee Johnson (R); treas., Robert W. Straub (D); supt. of public instruction, Dale Parnell; chief justice, Kenneth J. O'Connell. *Legislative Assembly*—Senate, 30 members (16 Democrats, 14 Republicans); House of Representatives, 60 members (34 R, 26 D).
Education (1970–71): *Enrollment*—public elementary schools, 280,000 pupils, 12,000 teachers; public secondary, 201,700 pupils; 9,700 teachers; nonpublic schools (1968–69), 33,600 pupils; 1,520 teachers; college and university (fall 1968), 96,333 students. *Public school expenditures* (1970–71), $410,500,000 ($935 per pupil). *Average teacher's salary,* $9,298.
State Finances (fiscal year 1970): *Revenues,* $1,035,308,000 (total taxes and gross receipts taxes, $90,089,000; motor fuel tax, $64,485,000; federal funds, $242,561,000). *Expenditures,* $1,018,526,000 (education, $338,867,000; health, welfare, and safety, $225,975,000; highways, $120,367,000). *State debt,* $689,680,000 (June 30, 1970).
Personal Income (1970): $7,956,000,000; per capita, $3,700.
Public Assistance (1970): $99,869,000. *Average monthly payments* (Dec. 1970)—old-age assistance, $57.85; aid to families with dependent children, $168.20.
Labor Force: *Nonagricultural wage and salary earners* (June 1971), 739,000. *Average annual employment* (1969)—manufacturing, 179,000; trade, 159,000; government, 141,000; services, 108,000. *Insured unemployed* (Oct. 1971)—19,100 (3.5%).
Manufacturing (1967): *Value added by manufacture,* $2,060,500,000. Lumber and wood products, $770,600,000; food and kindred products, $299,500,000; paper and allied products, $154,800,000.
Agriculture (1970): *Cash farm income,* $585,030,000 (livestock, $268,127,000; crops, $293,791,000; government payments, $23,112,000). *Chief crops* (tons)—Wheat, 30,216,000 bushels; potatoes, 16,056,000 cwt.; hay, 2,369,000 tons; pears, 95,000 tons (ranks 3d among the states).
Mining (1971): *Production value,* $68,454,000 (ranks 40th among the states). *Chief minerals* (tons)—Sand and gravel, 18,127,000; stone, 12,633,000; lime, 88,000.
Fisheries (1970): *Commercial catch,* 98,300,000 pounds ($22,800,000). *Leading species by value* (1967), Albacore tuna, $5,859,302; silver or coho, $3,954,240; shell fish, $2,807,622; sole, $848,558.
Transportation: *Roads* (1969), 93,139 miles (149,889 km); *motor vehicles* (1969), 1,335,000; *railroads* (1968), 3,081 miles (4,958 km); *airports* (1969), 94.
Communications: *Telephones* (1971), 1,189,700; *television stations* (1969), 12; *radio stations* (1969), 96; *newspapers* (1969), 21 (daily circulation, 654,000).

OTTAWA

Issues dealing with the environment marked the year 1971 in the Ottawa region. Pollution and transportation were the major environmental concerns in Canada's capital and fourth largest metropolitan area (1971 census: metropolitan area, 596,000). Ottawa was embarrassed in October when Soviet Premier Aleksei Kosygin was attacked, but not injured, while visiting the city.

Government. Denis Coolican continued as chairman of the Regional Council and Kenneth Fogarty as mayor of Ottawa. The City Council, which has had diminished responsibilities since the city has been under regional government, voted to reduce its membership by half. After controversy over the proposed location, the city refused to contribute to the new Portage Bridge to be built across the Ottawa River to Hull by the National Capital Commission.

Environment. Pollution of the Rideau River became a major issue when most of the city's beaches had to remain closed all summer because of dangerously high bacteria levels. To reduce congestion and discourage automobile use in the downtown area, many off-street parking spaces were eliminated and meter rates for the remainder increased by 150%. The Ottawa Transportation Commission is to be placed under regional authority and hopes to extend services more widely within the region.

The proposal to route Highway 417 (the Ottawa-Montreal freeway) into the city encountered great opposition. The highway was to enter the city, through a suburban residential area, to serve as an urban expressway. After a public ballot organized by the press and television, the route was moved eastward, and a special sunken road for express buses was proposed to replace the expressway.

Municipal Finance. Total expenditures estimated by the city of Ottawa for 1971 are $89,540,453, including $36,332,351 for education and a $11,816,275 regional levy. City revenues will include $62,280,382 to be raised by taxes on residential, farm, commercial, and industrial properties, and $16,012,000 received in federal and provincial grants.

The regional municipality estimated expenditures of $45,766,000 for 1971, an increase of approximately 28%. Over half of this increase went to the heavy social welfare expenditures, which in 1970 had exceeded estimates by more than 20%. Some $14 million of the budget was raised by levies on the regional municipalities, and $19.6 million came from provincial grants.

Education. Enrollment figures for area schools indicated a drop in numbers in the primary grades within the city but an increase at all levels in suburban areas. Enrollment in Ottawa in September 1971 was: public primary schools, 25,119; public secondary, 26,624; and Catholic primary, 27,274. Under the Carleton boards of education there were 22,288 public primary students, 10,349 public secondary, and 11,562 in separate schools.

Federal Government. The offices of the federal Department of the Environment were moved across the Ottawa River to Hull, Quebec. Other departments, including Consumer Affairs, are to follow. This is in keeping with the new federal policy of regarding the whole metropolitan area, not just the city of Ottawa, as the national capital.

PETER J. KING
Carleton University

PACIFIC ISLANDS

The year 1971 was marked by increased coordination of economic, social, and political affairs among the islands of the South Pacific. The desire for independence, or at least self-government, intensified.

Producers Association. At the sixth meeting of the Pacific Islands Producers Association, held in Tonga in April, delegates discussed trade and shipping and proposed a regional political forum.

South Pacific Forum. The government leaders of five Pacific island states met at Wellington, New Zealand, in August to found the South Pacific Forum. The agenda emphasized promotion of trade, tourism, education, transportation, and communications. The Forum also conceived of itself as a diplomatic agency for international affairs of mutual interest, and invited new countries to join as they achieve independence. The countries represented were Nauru, Fiji, Tonga, Western Samoa, and the Cook Islands. New Zealand and Australia were also represented.

South Pacific Conference. Representatives of 16 Pacific island nations and territories reviewed the aid projects of the South Pacific Commission at the annual South Pacific Conference at Noumea, New Caledonia, in September. The delegates expressed their growing concern over pollution and other threats to the islands' environments.

The newly elected secretary general of the South Pacific Commission was G. D. F. Betham of Western Samoa, who filled the vacancy resulting from the death of Afioga Afoafouvale Misimoa in February.

Papua New Guinea. The territorial House of Assembly adopted "Papua New Guinea" as the new official name for the Territory of Papua and New Guinea. Australia accepted a tentative timetable for progress during 1972–76 toward self-government. The proposal provides for an increase in the proportion of elected members in the assembly and the retention of central government. Economic and political ties with Australia would be developed during the transition to autonomy.

Gilbert and Ellice Islands. The United Kingdom granted almost complete self-government and a new constitution to the Gilbert and Ellice Islands on April 14. Security and defense are still controlled from London, but a new resident commissioner at Tarawa must obtain approval from an elected legislature for most action. The High Commission for the Western Pacific remains responsible only for the British Solomons and the British share of the New Hebrides British-French Condominium.

German ships manned by Gilbert and Ellice Islands crews increased to over 30 during 1971. The Merchant Marine Training School at Betio, Tarawa, was unable to meet the demand for seamen and stewards.

American Samoa. The legislature of American Samoa will have powers of preliminary budget review and be authorized to meet in two sessions annually as the result of agreements by the U. S. territorial administration.

French Polynesia. France resumed nuclear testing at Mururoa Atoll in 1971 in spite of continued protests from several nations and island territories. Five tests from June to August included explosions of devices suspended from balloons. A sixth test was canceled after a threat by the government of Peru to break diplomatic relations with France.

A French prospecting ship, the *Coquille,* discovered large quantities of mineral nodules on the ocean floor in the vicinity of the Tuamotu Archipelago. The nodules contain manganese, iron, aluminum, nickel, cobalt, and titanium. Studies have been proposed to develop means of economically recovering the minerals, which occur at depths of 3,300 to 19,700 feet (1,000 to 6,000 meters).

Guam. Carlos Garcia Camacho was installed as governor of Guam in January. He had been the last appointed governor, serving since 1968, and became the first governor elected by popular vote.

The rapidly expanding tourist industry was a major cause of labor shortages in Guam, especially in service categories. In 1970 more than 75,000 tourists and businessmen visited the island.

Trust Territory of the Pacific Islands. Franklin Haydn Williams of San Francisco was appointed in March as President Nixon's ambassador for negotiations over the future political status of the Trust Territory. A new political party, the Independence Coalition, was established to press for self-government and claimed 11 of the 33 seats in the Congress of Micronesia. Micronesian students in Hawaii were agitating for independence.

Typhoon Amy severely damaged more than 1,300 homes in the Truk District of Micronesia in May. President Nixon declared the district a major disaster area, and work began immediately on transporting materials for new homes and repairs.

Ryukyu Islands. In formal ceremonies televised by satellite on June 17, Secretary of State William P. Rogers in Washington and Foreign Minister Kiichi Aichi in Tokyo signed a treaty providing for the transfer of Okinawa and 72 smaller islands in the Ryukyu chain to Japan. Japan now controls the major civilian facilities, but the United States will continue to have military bases.

During 1971 the United States moved all mustard and nerve gases on Okinawa to Johnston Island, 700 miles west-southwest of Honolulu. (See also JAPAN.)

Pitcairn Island. The British administration of Pitcairn Island was transferred from Suva, Fiji, to Auckland, New Zealand, as a result of Fijian independence in October 1970. Sir Arthur Galsworthy, British high commissioner in New Zealand, became the new governor of Pitcairn.

HOWARD J. CRITCHFIELD
Western Washington State College

PACIFIC ISLANDS OF THE UNITED STATES

Island or Group	Area (sq mi)	(km)	Population (1970 Census)	Capital (1970 Census)
American Samoa[1]..	76	197	27,159	Pago Pago (2,491)
Baker[2]...........	1	2.6	...	...
Canton and Enderbury[3]	27	70	...	...
Guam[1]..........	212	549	84,996	Agana (2,131)
Howland[2]........	0.6	1.6	...	...
Jarvis[2]...........	2.2	5.7	...	...
Johnston and Sand Islands[5].......	...[5]	...	1,007	...
Kingman Reef[4]...	...[5]	...	...	...
Midway[4].........	2	5	2,220	...
Palmyra[2]........	4	10	...	...
Ryukyu Islands[6]...	848	2,196	982,000[7]	Naha (284,000)[8]
Trust Territory of the Pacific Islands (including Carolines, Marianas, Marshalls)[2]	687	1,779	90,940[8]	Saipan (9,590)[7]
Wake[2]...........	3	8	1,647	...

[1] Unincorporated U. S. territory. [2] Administered by U. S. Department of the Interior. [3] Jointly administered by United Kingdom and United States. [4] Under U. S. Navy control. [5] Less than ½ square mile. [6] Under U. S. military government: to revert to Japan in 1972. [7] 1969 est. [8] 1968 est.

PAINTING AND SCULPTURE. See ART.

Leaders in the Pakistani civil war: Sheikh Mujibur Rahman (*left*) of East Pakistan (Bangladesh); President Mohammad Yahya Khan (*right*); and Ali Bhutto, who was foreign minister until he replaced Yahya Khan as president after the India-Pakistan war.

UPI

UPI

RADIO PAK

THE NEW YORK TIMES

PAKISTAN

Civil war, which broke out in the eastern province of Pakistan in March 1971, brought mounting tensions with India and eventually, on December 3, all-out war between the two nations. After about two weeks of intensive fighting, the national army of Pakistan was defeated and surrendered in East Pakistan. This part of Pakistan (also known as East Bengal) was declared independent under the name Bangladesh (Bengal Nation) and was recognized as such by India.

The president of Pakistan, Gen. Agha Mohammed Yahya Khan, resigned, turning the government over to Zulfikar Ali Bhutto, Pakistan's foreign minister and the leader of West Pakistan's majority party. At year-end, West Pakistan, its constitutional and political structure in chaos, was all that remained of the nation that had included two provinces separated by approximately 1,000 miles of India's landmass.

Internal Politics and Strife. Although hostility between East and West Pakistan had simmered for years, the events leading to civil war began with elections held in December 1970. At that time a constituent assembly, with a total of 313 seats, was elected in Pakistan's first direct national elections in its 23-year history. Of the 169 seats assigned to East Pakistan, 167 were won by the Awami League, an East Pakistani party that had campaigned on a platform of regional autonomy under a central government with limited powers. Encouraged by the electoral victory, the party leader, Sheikh Mujibur Rahman, known as Sheikh Mujib, demanded virtual autonomy for the eastern province, which is distinguished by language and culture from the western province.

President Yahya Khan offered some concessions but generally resisted Sheikh Mujib's demands. By March the situation had deteriorated badly. Appointees of the president were rejected in East Pakistan, and he postponed the convening of the newly elected National Assembly, originally scheduled for March 3. Evacuation of foreigners began in Dacca, the capital of East Pakistan. In spite of a hurried flight to Dacca to confer with Sheikh Mujib, Yahya lost control of the situation and on March 25 ordered the national army to restore order. The Awami League was outlawed, Sheikh Mujib and a number of his followers were arrested, and civil war began.

An immediate result of the military intervention in East Pakistan was an uncertain but large number of deaths of civilians. Refugees, reported ultimately to number 10 million, fled into India. Soon after the intervention, leaders of the autonomy movement (without Sheikh Mujib, who was imprisoned in West Pakistan after his arrest) sought to set up the independent state of Bangladesh, and a liberation army was formed.

Many of Pakistan's Bengali diplomats, including 14 in the United States, resigned their missions abroad and sought political asylum. The regular army forces in East Pakistan, which numbered about 70,000 in late March and were later to be increased, not only had to deal with guerrilla forces, called Mukti Bahini, in East Pakistan but also had to guard against Indian incursions along the border. Reports of the number of people killed in the fighting varied widely.

President Yahya Khan made last-minute but futile efforts to salvage a viable system. In August he replaced the military governor of East Pakistan with a civilian, Dr. A. M. Malik. Although Yahya Khan disqualified large numbers of Awami League members from holding office, he offered an amnesty for most persons in September. He also attempted to convene a national assembly and produce a new constitution, as well as to appoint a new central government headed by a Bengali.

MUKTI BAHINI, or Liberation Force, guerrillas of East Pakistan battled regular Pakistani Army. During December fighting, Mukti Bahini worked with Indian units.

Conflict and War with India. Since the partitioning in 1947 of the former British Indian Empire into the nations of India and Pakistan, relations between the two countries had often been precarious and occasionally had broken into warfare. This longstanding animosity was aggravated by the events of March in East Pakistan, which adjoins the Indian state of West Bengal (the region known as Bengal having been divided in 1947, with the eastern part becoming East Pakistan and the western part a state of India). Many of the refugees who fled across the Indian border were Hindu, and some of them might not choose to return even if conditions of stability were restored in East Pakistan. In the meantime, they competed economically with West Bengalis, they brought disease and famine to India, and their very presence disrupted the internal stability of the Indian state.

In March and April, relations between India and Pakistan virtually collapsed. In April, Pakistan accused India of armed attack, and India officially protested "unprovoked firing on Indian territory." Sporadic fighting and airspace violations continued, and in May the Pakistani chief of military intelligence suggested that there was a strong possibility of war. Fighting of sorts continued all summer with threats and counterthreats from both India and Pakistan.

In October, India began mobilizing its state militias. Pakistan, already under martial law, declared a national emergency. India supported the autonomy of Bangladesh, and although Prime Minister Indira Gandhi warned in June that a solution seemed remote, she disclaimed in November any Indian territorial ambitions in Pakistan or any intention of provoking Pakistan into war. Yet, in October, Pakistan had charged in the United Nations that India was already waging war in East Pakistan.

By November, intense fighting had broken out between regular army and air units of both countries, involving tank battles and air strikes. By December 3 the war was on in earnest. It found Pakistani troops in the East greatly outnumbered by their Indian foe, harassed by East Bengali insurgents, and unable to obtain supplies. Efforts in the United Nations to obtain a quick cease-fire were unavailing. Foreign Minister Bhutto, who had joined the Pakistan delegation at the UN, denounced the Security Council on December 15 for "legalizing aggression" and walked out of that body. After seizing Dacca and accepting the surrender of the Pakistani forces in the East, India ordered a complete cease-fire on December 16. It was accepted in the west the next day. (See INDIA-PAKISTAN WAR.)

Political Aftermath. In the wreckage of the war President Yahya Khan and the military officers who had supported him were discredited, and Yahya resigned. Foreign Minister Bhutto, the most popular West Pakistani leader, was sworn in as president on December 20. He quickly produced a cabinet, promised a complete return to civilian government, and pledged to continue to work for the reunification of Pakistan. He also transferred Sheikh Mujib from prison to house arrest. In January 1972, the sheikh was released, and he returned to Dacca to assume leadership in the new state of Bangladesh.

Foreign Affairs. Virtually all of Pakistan's foreign affairs were affected by the civil war and the struggle with India. The Soviet Union supplied some arms to India and asked both adversaries to refrain from hostilities. The United States, while repeatedly admonishing Pakistan and India to avoid

——— PAKISTAN • Information Highlights ———

Official Name: Islamic Republic of Pakistan.
Area (1970): 365,542 square miles (946,716 sq km).
Population (1969 est.): 126,740,000. *Density,* 335 per square mile (130 per sq km). *Annual rate of increase,* 2.8%
Chief Cities (1969 est.): Islamabad (1967 est.), the capital, 70,000; Karachi, 3,060,000; Lahore, 1,823,000; Dacca, 829,000.
Government: *Head of state,* Zulfikar Ali Bhutto, president (took office Dec. 20, 1971). *Head of government,* Zulfikar Ali Bhutto. *Legislature*—National Assembly, 313 members. *Major political party*—Pakistan People's party.
Languages: Urdu (official), Bengali (official), English.
Education: *Literacy rate* (1970), 20% of population. *Expenditure on education* (1968), 5.6% of total public expenditure. *School enrollment* (1967)—primary, 7,862,973; secondary, 3,034,463; technical/vocational, 23,644; university/higher, 321,203.
Finances (1970–71 est.): *Revenues,* $1,772,700,000; *expenditures,* $1,441,000,000; *monetary unit,* rupee (4.627 rupees equal U. S.$1, Aug. 1971).
Gross National Product (1970 est.): $16,000,000,000.
National Income (1969): $14,679,000,000; *national income per person,* $131.
Economic Indexes: *Industrial production* (1969), 167 (1963= 100); *agricultural production* (1969), 123 (1969=100); *consumer price index* (1970), 128 (1963=100).
Manufacturing (metric tons, 1969): Cement, 2,678,000; residual fuel oil, 1,964,000; distillate fuel oils, 1,036,000; sugar, 541,000.
Crops (metric tons, 1969 crop year): Rice, 21,267,000; jute (1968), 1,036,000 (ranks 1st among world producers); cotton, 542,000; chick peas (1968), 528,000 (world rank 2d).
Foreign Trade (1970): *Exports,* $723,000,000 (chief exports—jute manufactures, $167,400,000; jute, $131,600,000; cotton, $49,761,000). *Imports,* $1,151,000,000 (chief imports, 1968—nonelectrical machinery, $221,277,000; chemicals, $122,304,000; cereals and preparations, $102,795,000; iron and steel, $95,802,000). *Chief trading partners* (1968)—United States (took 12% of exports, supplied 32% of imports); United Kingdom (12%—13%); Japan (7%—12%).
Transportation: *Roads* (1970), 33.600 miles (54,062 km); *motor vehicles* (1969), 213,700 (automobiles, 144,200); *railroads* (1965), 7,039 miles (11,328 km); *merchant fleet* (1970), 566,000 gross registered tons; *national airline,* Pakistan International Airlines; *principal airports,* Karachi, Dacca.
Communications: *Telephones* (1970), 193,493; *television stations* (1968), 5; *television sets* (1969), 80,000; *radios* (1968), 1,203,000; *newspapers* (1968), 139 (daily circulation, 643,000).

open war, continued supplying Pakistan with modest military aid into the summer and was strongly criticized for this action both in the United States

and abroad. Other kinds of aid from the United States also continued—emergency aid for the still suffering victims of the 1970 tidal wave disaster in East Pakistan, as well as economic developmental aid. In January 1972, anticipating that some Commonwealth countries would recognize Bangladesh, Pakistan withdrew from the Commonwealth of Nations.

Economy. One of Sheikh Mujib's demands was for greater economic independence for East Pakistan, which supports a population of some 75 million, compared with West Pakistan's 55 million, in an area less than one fifth that of the west. The densely populated east has only a fractional share of the nation's transportation, communication, and educational facilities, and the average annual income per person there is less than half the average in the west. Yet the east's jute exports account for a large share of Pakistan's badly needed foreign earnings.

The civil war threw the eastern province's largely agricultural economy into complete disarray. Many farmers did not plant their crops, and many who did plant could not tend them. Supply roads and bridges were cut by guerrilla action, making it impossible to market crops already harvested. Food stocks continued low. Business activity of all kinds suffered from absenteeism, managerial disruption, damaged transport, and shortages of goods and currency. The dispatch of a World Bank fact-finding mission to East Pakistan in June underlined the perilous state of the economy. The mission's report was critical of the central government.

West Pakistan was hurt as well. Many of its manufactured products—cheap textiles, for example—have no markets other than those in the east. Altogether, the political crisis had severe repercussions on the nation's economy. At year-end, the economy of Bangladesh was devastated. The economy of the more industrialized west, although less severely affected, was in confusion.

CARL LEIDEN
University of Texas at Austin

THE FLAG OF BANGLADESH is raised at the Awami League headquarters in Chudanga, East Pakistan, as independence is proclaimed, April 11.

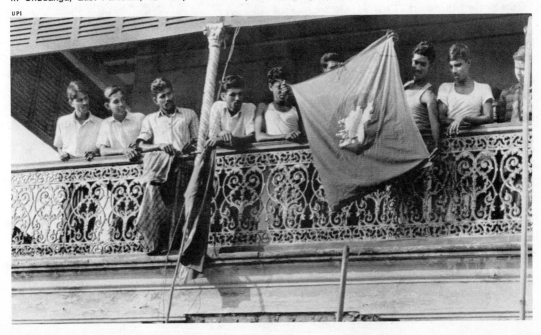

PALEONTOLOGY

Important publications appeared in 1971 on ancient life such as fishes, amphibians, and gliding reptiles. Fossils were discovered of new dinosaur species and a new kind of chordate ancestor.

Carboniferous Ocean Life. The remarkable fauna associated with the bottom-dwelling invertebrates of the Pennsylvania period, about 300 million years ago, were described by William G. Melton, Jr., of the University of Montana. Among the fish fauna were the shark *Ctenacanthus* and the skate *Deltodus;* the ray-finned platysomids and palaeoniscids, a new dorypterid, and a tarrasiid; and a coelacanth. Also found were bilaterally symmetrical, soft-bodied, free-swimming forms with toothlike structures. These conodonts belong to a new phylum related and perhaps ancestral to the chordates.

Triassic Amphibians and Reptiles. Fossils discovered in Antarctica and dating from Triassic time, about 200 million years ago, were dealt with by Edwin Colbert of the American Museum of Natural History. Labyrinthodont amphibians and, perhaps, reptiles such as the thecodonts and mammallike therapsids were generally distinguished, and the primitive reptile *Lystrosaurus* has been identified. The occurrence of these essentially land-living animals in Antarctica strongly supports continental drift theories. (See also ANTARCTICA.)

Colbert also discussed the osteology and aerodynamic adaptations of *Icarosaurus siefkeri,* whose fossil was discovered in Bergen county, N. J., in 1966. This insectivorous or carnivorous lacertilian (lizardlike reptile) was adapted to gliding flight. Seldom on the ground, it glided from tree to tree by means of its patagium, a fold of skin extending from forelimb to hind limb.

Eggs of Cretaceous Age. James A. Jensen of Utah University made a valuable study in Utah of eggshells more than 100 million years old, or Lower Cretaceous age—the oldest egg remains in North America. They may belong to either birds or dinosaurs. Jensen devoted his study to the paleophysiological aspects of observed structures, which were more characteristic of reptilian than bird eggs.

Cretaceous Dinosaurs. Peter M. Galton of the University of Bridgeport, Conn., described a skullcap of a Stegosaurus-like dinosaur on the Isle of Wight as being a new genus and species of Pachycephalosaurid dinosaur, *Yaverlandia bitholus,* of Lower Cretaceous age. He concluded that the domed head was used as a battering ram.

Late Cretaceous rocks of western Canada, about 70 million years old, have yielded remains of large dinosaurs of the family Tyrannosauridae. A reassessment of their relationships was made by Ottawa paleontologist Dale A. Russell, including comparisons between immature and adult individuals. One was a new genus and species, *Daspletosaurus torosus.*

Mammal Studies. One important 1971 mammal study was the American Museum monograph on a horned artiodactyl group, Synthetocertinae, by Thomas H. Patton of Florida State Museum and Beryl E. Taylor of the American Museum. The University of Michigan's Claude W. Hibbard and Philip Bjork dealt with insectivores of the Upper Pliocene in Idaho. In Canada, C. S. Churcher and A. M. Stalker described a postglacial horse, *Equus conversidens.*

WILLIAM E. SWINTON
Massey College, University of Toronto

PANAMA

A government dominated by Omar Torrijos Herrera, a general of the National Guard, imposed increasingly strict controls over political activity and the press in Panama in 1971, while church-state relations worsened. The year also saw a reopening of negotiations with the United States over a new Panama Canal treaty.

Panama Canal Talks. Bilateral negotiations on the canal were resumed in Washington on June 29, after a 4-year lapse. Panamanian representatives demanded complete sovereignty in the Canal Zone, including jurisdiction over the courts, police, and postal system. They asked that the post of governor of the Canal Zone be eliminated and that commercial activities be turned over to Panamanian merchants. Panama also insisted on a larger share of canal tolls. In a public address on October 11, General Torrijos threatened to invade the zone if Panamanian demands were not met.

It was reported that the U. S. negotiators were ready to offer Panama "gradual sovereignty" in the zone, but were not willing to turn over defense responsibilities or operation of the waterway to the Panamanians. The secret talks were expected to extend into 1972.

Political Developments. General Torrijos sought to strengthen the popular base of his 3-year-old de facto government by moves designed to appeal to nationalist and socialist sentiments. Two leftist ministers who had been dismissed a year earlier were rehabilitated: Materno Vásquez became minister of interior and justice, and Rómulo Escobar Bethancourt was named president of the national university. In October, Torrijos called for the formation of a constituent assembly.

Local officials who might have contemplated independent political action were given an object lesson in October, when Paulino Salazar, the mayor of the poverty-stricken city of San Miguelito, was removed from office after requesting greater autonomy. Salazar had been designated mayor by the government and approved by a democratically elected assembly. After his ouster, a substitute mayor was named and the assembly replaced by an appointed council.

The regime was also instrumental in a move that deprived the Arias family of control of its powerful press empire. The action was possible under a unique Panamanian law that allows a minority stockholder to cause the liquidation of a company to protect shareholder interests. A new firm was formed to operate the dailies with assistance from government subsidies. This, in effect, removed an independent and often critical voice from the Panamanian scene.

Church-State Relations. From the beginning of 1971, all requests for visas by priests going to Panama had to be approved by Foreign Minister Juan Antonio Tack. On June 9, Rev. Hector Gallegos, a Colombian, was abducted and apparently assassinated. He had been organizing cooperatives among poor farmers in rural Panama.

Archbishop Marcos McGrath accused the government of discrimination and acts of intimidation against both clerics and laymen. In October the regime notified church officials that five priests, three of them foreigners, were being investigated and faced possible expulsion for antigovernment activities.

Highway Project. On January 13 the United States agreed to supply $100 million toward the construction of a 250-mile (400-km) highway from the city of Panama into northwestern Colombia. Of this sum, $25 million was to be made available before the end of fiscal 1972. Panama was to provide $30 million of the total cost of the project.

LARRY L. PIPPIN
Elbert Covell College
University of the Pacific

PARAGUAY

Friction between church and state and a sluggish economy continued to be areas of concern during 1971. President Alfredo Stroessner met with Brazil's President Médici at the border in July to inaugurate an international bridge over the Apa River. They used the occasion to issue a declaration condemning "violence against human beings" and economic pressures on nations. They repudiated the "division of the world into spheres of influence" and pledged to cooperate for common development.

Domestic Affairs. Despite these desirable goals, Paraguay under Stroessner has had no freedom of the press and little individual liberty. A Chilean investigating team reported that there were at least 180 political prisoners in Paraguayan jails, some of whom had been there for as long as 12 years without trial. The team also charged the government with maintaining two concentration camps. Government actions during the year seemed to confirm the policy enunciated by Sen. Juan Ramón Chaves, president of the Colorado party, that "internal peace will be maintained at all costs."

The weak Paraguayan Communist party secretly held its third congress in Asunción in April. The 26 delegates pledged to intensify the ideological struggle against the present government.

Church-State Relations. The Roman Catholic Church continued its battle with the regime. The Paraguayan episcopal conference denounced the government for violence toward prisoners, corruption,

———— **PARAGUAY · Information Highlights** ————

Official Name: Republic of Paraguay.
Area: 157,047 square miles (406,752 sq km).
Population (June 1970 est.): 2,386,000. *Density,* 15 per square mile (6 per sq km). *Annual rate of increase,* 3.1%.
Chief City (1969 est.): Asunción, the capital, 424,300.
Government: *Head of state,* Gen. Alfredo Stroesner, president (took office Aug. 15, 1954). *Head of government,* Alfredo Stroesner. *Legislature*—Congress: Chamber of Deputies, 60 members; Senate, 30 members. *Major political parties*—Colorado party.
Languages: Spanish (official), Guarani.
Education: *Literacy rate* (1970), 30% of population. *School enrollment* (1969)—primary, 415,791; secondary, 48,629; technical/vocational, 2,779; university/higher, 7,593.
Finances (1969): *Revenues,* $79,320,000; *expenditures,* $82,865,000; *monetary unit,* guarani (126 guaranis equal U. S. $1, Sept. 1971).
Gross National Product (1969): $543,000,000.
National Income (1969): $466,000,000; *national income per person,* $202.
Economic Indexes: *Industrial production* (1969), 137 (1963=100); *agricultural production* (1969), 124 (1963=100); *consumer price index* (1970), 111 (1963=100).
Manufacturing (metric tons, 1969): Tobacco, 152,000; sugar, 46,000; wheat flour (1968), 67,000; cement, 37,000.
Crops (metric tons, 1968 crop year): Cassava, 1,504,000; bananas, 250,000; citrus fruits, 250,000; maize, 153,000.
Foreign Trade (1970): *Exports,* $64,000,000 (chief exports—meat, $15,250,000; timber, $12,640,000; oilseeds, $6,450,000; tobacco, $5,770,000. *Imports,* $64,000,000 (chief imports, 1968—machinery, $11,460,000; wheat and preparations, $5,940,000; mineral fuels and lubricants, $4,850,000; iron and steel products, $4,400,000).
Transportation: *Roads* (1964), 7,786 miles (12,530 km); *motor vehicles* (1968), 13,500 (automobiles, 6,900); *railroads* (1969), 808 miles (1,300 km); *principal airport,* Asunción.
Communications: *Telephones* (1970), 21,225; *television stations* (1968), 1; *television sets* (1969), 17,000; *radios* (1964), 160,000; *newspapers* (1969), 9 (daily circulation, 93,000).

press restrictions, discrimination in government jobs, and inefficient land reform. The archbishop of Asunción refused to take his seat in the council of state, and in March he excommunicated the interior minister and the police chief of Asunción, holding them responsible for the detention of a Uruguayan priest alleged to belong to the terrorist Tupamaros.

Economic Developments. In May the government granted a 10% general wage increase, the first since 1964. By July prices had risen more than 8%, thus cancelling the effect of most of the raise. Government revenues were less than expected, and the administration found itself hard pressed to find counterpart funds for foreign assistance loans. The implementation of the income tax, authorized in late 1970, was postponed until Dec. 31, 1971, to allow for "further study."

Paraguay, which depends heavily on agriculture, attempted to solve widespread production and marketing problems in 1971. The meat industry is moving from canned to refrigerated and frozen meat products. The cotton and tobacco crops suffered severe rain damage in early 1971, but wheat production continued to increase. The National Development Bank, however, placed limits on new loans for harvesting and planting.

Hotel and motel construction flourished despite sluggish tourism. A trade deficit for the year appeared likely, as the value of imports exceeded that of exports by $7.1 million for the first quarter alone. Projects in the planning stage include rural electrification, a bridge over the Paraguay River to Argentina, drilling for oil in the hitherto unproductive Chaco region, and construction of new facilities at the international airport.

LEO B. LOTT
University of Montana

PAUL VI, Pope. See BIOGRAPHY.
PEDIATRICS. See MEDICINE.

PENNSYLVANIA

As 1971 began, Milton Shapp was sworn in as Pennsylvania's 40th constitutional governor and the state's first Jewish chief executive. With the state facing enormous deficits, Shapp immediately proposed enactment of a state income tax.

Taxes. The issue of a proposed state income tax occupied the attention of Pennsylvanians for a substantial portion of the year. The state's first personal income tax, a 3.5% levy, was enacted in March at the behest of Governor Shapp. In June, the state supreme court ruled that this tax violated the state constitutional requirement that "all taxes shall be uniform on the same class of subjects." The levy had been based on federal taxable income, and therefore had allowed exemptions and deductions not permitted by the state constitution. In August, a new personal income tax was passed by the legislature to replace the one declared unconstitutional. The 2.3% rate allowed no exemptions.

Major Legislation. A state lottery was approved by the legislature, and a lottery commission was created to administer its operation. Lottery tickets were scheduled to go on sale in early 1972. The proceeds from the lottery are to go for tax relief of senior citizens.

In other action, the General Assembly became the 21st state legislature to ratify a federal constitutional amendment giving the 18-to-20 age group the right to vote in state and local elections. The

---

PENNSYLVANIA • Information Highlights

Area: 45,333 square miles (117,412 sq km).
Population (1970 census): 11,793,909. *Density,* 262 per sq mi.
Chief Cities (1970 census): Harrisburg, the capital, 68,061; Philadelphia, 1,950,098; Pittsburgh, 520,117; Erie, 129,231; Allentown, 109,527; Scranton, 103,564.
Government (1971): *Chief Officers*—governor, Milton J. Shapp (D); lt. gov., Ernest P. Kline (D); secy. of state, Mrs. C. DeLores Tucker (D); atty. gen., J. Shane Creamer (D); treas., Grace M. Sloan (D); secy., dept. of educ., David H. Kurtzman; chief justice, John C. Bell, Jr. *General Assembly*—Senate, 50 members (27 Democrats, 23 Republicans); House of Representatives, 203 members (113 D, 90 R).
Education (1970–71): *Enrollment*—public elementary schools, 1,260,000 pupils; 55,900 teachers; public secondary, 1,098,100 pupils; 52,900 teachers; nonpublic schools (1968–69), 572,700 pupils; 19,970 teachers; college and university (fall 1968) 372,259 students. *Public school expenditures* (1970–71): $2,088,932,000 ($948 per pupil). *Average teacher's salary,* $9,300.
State Finances (fiscal year 1970): *Revenues,* $4,914,691,000 (6% general sales tax and gross receipts taxes, $948,- 357,000; motor fuel tax, $344,966,000; federal funds, $883,- 059,000). *Expenditures,* $5,113,744,000 (education, $1,777,- 542,000; health, welfare, and safety, $752,011,000; highways, $789,649,000). *State debt,* $3,220,438,000 (June 30, 1970).
Personal Income (1970): $46,649,000,000; per capita, $3,893.
Public Assistance (1970): $889,527,000. *Average monthly payments* (Dec. 1970)—old-age assistance, $102.30; aid to families with dependent children, $246.00.
Labor Force: *Nonagricultural wage and salary earners* (June 1971). 4,291,800. *Average annual employment* (1969)— manufacturing, 1,581.000; trade, 816,000; government, 609,- 000; services 670,000. *Insured unemployed* (Oct. 1971)— 124,800 (3.7%).
Manufacturing (1967): *Value added by manufacture,* $19,276,- 800,000. Primary metal industries, $3,540,700,000; nonelectrical machinery, $1,946,500,000; electrical equipment and supplies, $1,884,300,000; food and kindred products, $1,638,300,000.
Agriculture (1970): *Cash farm income,* $1,065,236,000 (livestock, $777,152,000; crops. $262,925,000; government payments, $25,159,000). *Chief crops* (1970)—Corn, 80,155,000 bushels; oats, 24,795,000 bushels; potatoes, 8,280,000 cwt.; hay, 5,798,000 tons.
Mining (1970): *Production value,* $1,082,241,000 (ranks 6th among the states). *Chief minerals* (tons)—Coal, 90,870,- 000; stone, 66,942,000; sand and gravel, 18,287,000; cement, 43,285,000 barrels.
Transportation: *Roads* (1969) 114,683 miles (184,559 km); *motor vehicles* (1969), 5,760,000; *railroads* (1969), 8,456 miles (13.608 km); *airports* (1969), 64.
Communications: *Telephones* (1971), 7,475,900; *television stations* (1969), 22; *radio stations* (1969), 273; *newspapers* (1969), 109 (daily circulation, 4,037,000).

---

state Planning Board estimated that almost 1 million young Pennsylvanians were enfranchised by the new legislation.

Governor Shapp signed into law a bill granting legislators a $3,000 increase in their nonaccountable expense allowances. The raise boosts a legislator's expense accounts to $8,400. The increase placed members of the legislature in the unusual position of collecting more for expenses than for salary, which is $7,200 annually.

The governor also signed legislation that allows restaurants and taverns in Pennsylvania to sell liquor on Sunday for the first time in 177 years. Any restaurant or tavern whose gross sales include at least 40% food and nonalcoholic beverages can qualify for the Sunday license.

At year-end, the legislature enacted a bill authorizing 51 new judgeships in Pennsylvania, including 25 judicial seats for Philadelphia. With the adjournment of the legislature for 1971, the way was cleared for Governor Shapp to make interim appointments without Senate confirmation, which he promised to do. Interim appointments are those made when the legislature is not in session and the normal requirements of a two-thirds Senate confirmation vote is waived. The state House GOP leader, Rep. Kenneth B. Lee, said his party would file suit to nullify the interim appointments on the ground the appointments are not proper after the first of a 2-year continuing session, which is the present situation.

Administrative Actions. On another front, state Insurance Commissioner Herbert S. Denenberg ordered the Blue Cross hospital insurance system to initiate radical new cost-cutting measures and to pass the savings on to consumers. Among other measures, Denenberg ordered Blue Cross to reorganize its board of directors to better represent the premium payers; to cancel its contracts with all 80 hospitals in Philadelphia and to negotiate new ones; and to provide a published list of room and board costs at each hospital so that policyholders could compare prices when seeking hospitalization. In another action, Denenberg ordered mandatory deductive clauses for comprehensive and collision automobile insurance beginning Jan. 1, 1972. Denenberg's actions heralded a major effort in Pennsylvania on behalf of consumers.

Elections. In the May primary, Pennsylvania voters approved three amendments proposed for the state constitution. The first provides for a change in civil jury verdicts, permitting 10 of 12 jurors to determine the outcome of a civil suit. The second prohibits any denial or abridgment of an individual's right because of sex. The third guarantees Pennsylvanians the right to clean air and pure water and protects the scenic, historic, and aesthetic values of the environment.

In statewide elections, Louis L. Manderino and Robert N. C. Nix, Jr., won seats on the Pennsylvania supreme court. Nix, a former Philadelphia judge, became the first black in the history of the state to sit on the high court.

Employment. A loss of 17,700 jobs from mid-September to mid-October sent the Pennsylvania employment total down to 4,729,900. October unemployment reached 237,000—4.7% of the labor force.

HARRY A. BAILEY, JR., *Temple University*

PENTAGON PAPERS. See CENSORSHIP.

PERSIAN GULF STATES

The withdrawal of British garrisons from the Persian Gulf in 1971 created an entirely new political situation in the region. On the Arabian side of the gulf the amirates of Bahrain and Qatar became independent, as did the United Arab Amirates, a federation formed in 1971 by the former Trucial amirates of Abu Dhabi, Dubai, Sharja, Ajman, Umm al-Qaiwain, and Fujaira. The former Trucial amirate of Ras al-Khaima declined to join the federation.

British Withdrawal. Britain completed the evacuation of its military forces from the bases of Bahrain and Sharja, and key treaties with the Persian Gulf states were abrogated. These treaties had given Britain control over the states' foreign affairs and priority rights in the exploitation of their mineral resources in return for protecting the states from aggression by sea. Thus ended a period of well over a century during which Britain had been the dominant military and political power in the gulf. Britain, however, retained a small military presence in the sultanate of Oman, the northern tip of which has a coastline on the Persian Gulf, and the presence of numerous British advisers in the Persian Gulf states assured a continuing indirect British influence there. Britain negotiated treaties with the new political entities on a basis of full reciprocity.

The other states on the Persian Gulf—Iran, Iraq, Kuwait, and Saudi Arabia—all opposed the introduction of any power from outside the gulf in place of Britain. Iran, which had made clear that its military forces would henceforth be the strongest in the gulf area, pressed its claim to the strategic islands of Abu Musa and the two Tunbs, just inside the mouth of the gulf—islands the British had recognized as belonging to Ras al-Khaima and Sharja. Iran's generally good relations with Saudi Arabia and Kuwait made it unlikely that either would offer military resistance to an Iranian occupation, and Iraq, the one Arab state in the gulf on bad terms with Iran, lacked the means to keep the islands in Arab hands. On November 30, Iran seized the islands amid strong Arab protests.

Bahrain and Qatar, after declaring their independence in the summer, secured membership in the Arab League and the United Nations. These two states and the new federation took steps to strengthen their government structures in order to operate without British protection.

Economy. Abu Dhabi and Qatar continued to rank first and second among the amirates in oil production. Dubai registered a substantial increase in its production and announced plans for further large-scale development of its oil resources. Although the modest production of Bahrain fell off slightly, that country had a considerably more diversified economy than any of the other amirates. The oil-producing amirates benefited by the Teheran agreement in February. In this agreement the concessionaire companies in the Persian Gulf undertook to give the host governments a larger share of the proceeds in return for a guarantee of security of supplies and stable financial arrangements over a 5-year period.

A highway linking Sharja, Ajman, Umm al-Qaiwain, and Ras al-Khaima, built with Saudi Arabian aid, was completed in October.

GEORGE RENTZ
Hoover Institution, Stanford University

INDEPENDENCE came to Bahrain as the British military departed in 1971. Here, Sheik Isa Ibn Salman Al Khalifah sits at head of banquet table as Britain's Sir Stewart Crawford takes place on ruler's right.

PERU

In 1971 the "nationalistic revolution" led by the military continued its efforts to reorganize Peru. Much energy went into reconstruction in the area devastated during the 1970 earthquake. Relations with the Communist countries improved, and Peru became the headquarters of the Andean Pact Nations.

The Continuing National Revolution. Throughout the year, Juan Velasco Alvarado and his military junta issued new laws to further the revolution that they hoped to achieve. In his annual state of the union message on July 28, General Velasco promised to make Peru a "participatory democracy," but he also announced that for the foreseeable future the military would continue to supervise "all activity." The revolution was to be "within the most illustrious tradition of libertarian, socialist, and humanitarian thinking." It was to be neither capitalistic nor communistic.

To develop a mass base, the government announced that it would organize a "Social Mobilization Movement." Most observers reported that the three centers of activity in all Peruvian towns continued to be the military headquarters, the Catholic church, and the Aprista party's *Casa del Pueblo,* or "town hall" the focus of organized opposition to the government.

During the year the administration continued to "nationalize" various economic enterprises. Some concerns sold their Peruvian interests at a loss. The Royal Bank of Canada ceased operations in Peru. Mining concessions held by the Anaconda Copper Co., the Cerro de Pasco Corp., and the American Smelting and Refining Co., reverted to the state because the companies could not meet the government's rigid requirements for financing and developing their operations by fixed dates. In November, W. R. Grace and Co. agreed to sell its chemical and paper industry holdings in Peru, valued at about $44

PERU · Information Highlights

Official Name: Republic of Peru.
Area: 496,223 square miles (1,285,216 sq km).
Population (1970 est.): 13,590,000. *Density,* 26 per square mile (10 per sq km). *Annual rate of increase,* 3.1%.
Chief Cities (1969 est.): Lima, the capital (city and suburbs), 2,415,700; Callao, 321,700; Arequipa, 187,400.
Government: *Head of state,* Gen. Juan Velasco Alvarado, president (took office Oct. 3, 1968). *Head of government,* Juan Velasco Alvarado. *Legislature*—National Congress (suspended Oct. 3, 1968).
Languages: Spanish (official), Quechua, Aymara.
Education: *Literacy rate* (1970), 55% of population. *Expenditure on education* (1968), 26.2% of total public expenditure. *School enrollment* (1968)—primary, 2,334,982; secondary, 563,698; technical/vocational, 93,034; university/higher, 101,099.
Finances (1970 est.): *Revenues,* $952,000,000; *expenditures,* $1,120,000,000; *monetary unit,* sol (38.70 sols equal U. S. $1, Sept. 1971).
Gross National Product (1970 est.): $5,400,000,000.
National Income (1968): $3,145,000,000; *national income per person,* $246.
Consumer Price Index (1970): 146 (1966=100).
Manufacturing (metric tons, 1969): Fish meals, 1,610,000; gasoline, 1,149,000; cement, 1,132,000; sugar, 633,000.
Crops (metric tons, 1969 crop year): Sugarcane (1968–69), 7,000,000; potatoes, 1,722,000; maize, 602,000; cassava (1968), 500,000; rice, 417,000.
Minerals (metric tons, 1969): Iron ore, 5,477,000; crude petroleum, 3,555,000; copper ore, 206,100; silver, 1,073.9; gold, 2,865 kilograms.
Foreign Trade (1970): *Exports,* $1,039,000,000 (chief exports—fish meal, $288,475,000; copper, $261,447,000; sugar, $66,253,000; iron ore, $65,607,000). *Imports,* $619,000,000 (chief imports, 1967—nonelectrical machinery, $131,306,000; motor cars, $53,636,000; iron and steel and products, $43,543,000). *Chief trading partners* (1967)—United States (took 39% of exports, supplied 34% of imports); Japan (15%—6%); West Germany (11%—11%).
Transportation: *Roads* (1966), 28,300 miles (45,543 km); *motor vehicles* (1968), 324,000 (automobiles, 201,500); *railroads* (1969), 1,509 miles (2,428 km); *merchant fleet* (1970), 378,000 gross registered tons.
Communications: *Telephones* (1970), 192,604; *television stations* (1968), 9; *television sets* (1969), 390,000; *radios* (1969), 1,815,000; *newspapers* (1959), 53.

million, to the government. Land reform continued, with the government taking over more large farms to create "cooperatives" run by military officers.

At the same time the government made agreements with a number of international petroleum companies, granting them rights to explore and develop new oil fields. Under these agreements, all oil produced was to be divided at the wellheads, the companies and the government each receiving half. The prospects for an eventual bonanza in oil wealth improved greatly when the state oil company brought in a rich gusher in the northeastern jungle in November.

A new mining law was issued to give workers 10% of the profits in mining companies, as well as participation in their management. The law reaffirmed the Peruvian state's ownership of all mineral deposits, soil and subsoil rights, and the wealth of the sea to a distance of 200 miles (320 km) from the Peruvian coast.

The Economy. As a result of a 1970 ban against holding foreign exchange, a surge of spending within Peru stimulated economic activity from July 1970 to July 1971. Later the economy slumped owing to a decline in the price of copper and fish meal on the world market. Strikes were a disruptive factor throughout 1971.

The gross domestic product had risen by 7.3% in 1970, whereas the rise in 1969 had been 1.3%. Peru was very active in pushing the development of the Andean Group, a free trade association that made significant progress during 1971 toward the economic integration of its five members (Bolivia, Chile, Colombia, Ecuador, and Peru). Construction began on a building in Lima that was to be the headquarters of the Andean common market.

International Relations. During 1971, Peru drew closer to the world's Communist nations. Diplomatic and trade relations were established with the People's Republic of China. Yugoslavia agreed to help finance and build an $80 million irrigation system on the north coast, and the Soviet Union agreed to construct a fishing port at Paita.

On July 29, the Peruvian government, grateful for U. S. help for earthquake relief, conferred on Mrs. Richard M. Nixon the Grand Cross of the Order of the Sun, its highest decoration.

From October 25 to November 6, Peru played host to representatives of 77 of the underdeveloped nations of the world ("The Group of the 77"), who met to define their position at the 1972 conference of the UN Commission on Trade and Development.

HARRY KANTOR, *Marquette University*

PETROLEUM

During 1971 the oil industry started production of oil from Norway's sector of the North Sea, and increased exploration in the Far East, in Arctic regions, and in South America, thus demonstrating its growing concern about overdependence on Middle East sources. Rapidly spreading public concern over air pollution, beach pollution, wildlife losses, and other ecological problems led to higher industry operating and capital costs—as much as 10% higher in some large companies. The emphasis on bigness to reduce costs continued, as exemplified by larger tankers and pipelines and bigger process plants and storage facilities. As 1971 came to an end, profits began to show an upturn.

Production. The world produced crude oil at a rate of 47,661,200 barrels per day (b/d) in 1971, a 4.1% increase over 1970. The output of the United States was about the same as the 1970 level. The Middle East output rose by 14%, and the Far East and Oceania output increased about 11.5%. However, these gains were offset by a 9.2% drop in Africa and big decreases in Europe and Latin America. The best available estimates show an overall gain of 5.9% in the Communist nations.

Exploration. Drilling showed a decrease for the second straight year in 1971. Wells drilled in the non-Communist world totaled 34,200 in 1971, about 2.7% below the 1970 total. The main reason was a 4.3% decline in the United States, where the 1971 total of 26,238 new wells accounted for 77% of the world total. Central and southern Africa showed a healthy 18% gain, western Europe showed a gain of almost 10%, and Latin American countries recorded substantial rises. Well drilling in the Middle East was down 13%, despite strong increases in Iran, Saudi Arabia, and Oman.

Reserves. Improved measuring techniques again led to upward adjustments in estimates of proved crude oil reserves in the world. At year's end, estimated reserves totaled 546 billion barrels, 5.7% above the adjusted end-1969 total.

The world total natural-gas reserves rose 9.9% in 1970, reaching 1,482 trillion cubic feet (tcf) by year-end. The United States has 291 tcf of natural-gas reserves, the USSR has 423 tcf, and the Middle East countries have 276 tcf.

Consumption. The demand for crude oil and liquid hydrocarbons derived from natural gas showed a strong gain in 1971, reflecting the world's rapidly rising energy requirements. The world consumed crude oil and liquid hydrocarbons derived from

WORLD CRUDE OIL PRODUCTION
(Thousands of barrels daily)

	1968[1]	1969[1]	1970[2]	1971[2]
North America				
Canada	1,039.2	1,124.0	1,296.0	1,336.2
Mexico	387.7	410.6	430.0	426.9
United States	9,110.0	9,238.0	9,632.0	9,650.4
Total	10,536.9	10,772.6	10,358.0	11,413.5
South America and West Indies				
Argentina	340.6	356.4	393.0	411.0
Bolivia	37.0	40.4	24.0	30.0
Brazil	160.5	156.2	164.0	168.0
Chile	37.6	36.7	34.0	34.4
Colombia	180.0	211.3	222.0	228.1
Ecuador	5.4	4.4	4.0	3.9
Peru	76.0	73.0	72.0	62.3
Trinidad & Tobago	182.9	157.3	140.0	138.4
Venezuela	3,604.8	3,594.1	3,708.0	3,578.8
Total[3]	4,625.5	4,629.8	4,761.0	4,654.9
Total, Western Hemisphere	15,162.4	15,402.4	16,119.0	16,068.4
Europe (excluding USSR and other Communist countries)				
Austria	51.5	51.3	52.0	50.8
France	54.7	50.2	47.0	38.3
Germany, West	157.5	158.2	151.0	145.8
Italy	29.1	29.0	27.0	24.6
Netherlands	40.9	37.8	36.0	32.7
Norway	0	0	0	4.3
Spain	4.7	8.5	3.0	2.5
United Kingdom	2.0	1.6	2.0	1.6
Yugoslavia	51.7	52.9	55.0	60.9
Total	392.1	389.5	373.0	361.5
USSR and other Communist countries				
Albania	20.7	26.0	28.0	28.0
Bulgaria	9.4	7.2	7.0	7.0
Czechoslovakia	3.7	3.7	4.0	4.0
Germany, East	5.3	5.8	6.0	6.0
Hungary	37.7	36.7	39.0	38.0
Poland	9.6	11.2	12.0	12.0
Rumania	268.8	268.7	270.0	270.0
USSR	6,134.4	6,545.4	7,060.0	7,300.0
Total[4]	6,489.6	6,904.7	7,426.0	7,665.0
Africa				
Algeria	901.7	959.1	1,022.0	602.6
Angola	10.7	10.1	14.0	14.2
Cabinda	8.4	37.3	89.0	94.3
Gabon[5]	90.1	99.9	106.0	113.5
Libya	2,600.0	3,109.1	3,334.0	2,803.6
Morocco	2.0	1.2	1.0	0.9
Nigeria	137.8	541.7	1,085.0	1,498.1
Tunisia	61.6	77.0	87.0	86.8
Total	3,812.3	4,835.4	5,738.0	5,214.0
Middle East				
Abu Dhabi[6]	498.5	611.5	694.0	356.8
Bahrain	75.3	76.1	77.0	75.3
Dubai[6]	0	0	84.0	125.5
Iran	2,841.1	3,374.9	3,829.0	4,513.6
Iraq	1,505.9	1,512.3	1,536.0	1,691.7
Israel	53.0	52.5	70.0	130.7
Kuwait	2,421.1	2,575.5	2,735.0	2,894.5
Murban[6]	0	0	0	542.5
Neutral Zone	428.0	452.0	503.0	550.3
Oman	240.0	327.0	332.0	290.4
Qatar	338.5	355.5	363.0	428.5
Saudi Arabia	2,830.1	3,216.6	3,799.0	4,455.6
Syria	27.2	62.0	83.0	110.0
Turkey	58.4	70.2	69.0	65.0
United Arab Republic	183.2	242.0	331.0	304.0
Total	11,500.2	12,928.1	14,505.0	16,534.4
Far East and Oceania				
Australia	36.6	43.3	178.0	318.9
Brunei and Sarawak	122.3	136.4	160.0	192.4
Burma	15.6	18.0	18.0	19.0
Communist China	196.0	220.0	235.0	240.0
India	133.4	134.0	135.0	143.9
Indonesia	600.4	742.4	880.0	875.3
Japan	15.9	15.1	16.0	16.4
Pakistan	9.8	7.6	7.0	10.0
Taiwan	0	0	1.8	2.0
Total	1,130.0	1,316.7	1,630.8	1,817.9
Total, Eastern Hemisphere	23,324.2	26,374.4	29,672.8	31,592.8
World total	38,486.6	41,776.8	45,791.8	47,661.2

[1] Final. [2] Preliminary (sources: U.S. Bureau of Mines and World Petroleum). [3] Cuba omitted from totals, as current reports indicate production is almost nil. [4] Because of the several sources of data for the USSR and its satellites, figures given for individual countries do not always add up to total shown for the group. [5] Congo (Brazzaville) is included with Gabon. [6] Abu Dhabi includes Dubai until 1970 and Murban until 1971.

UPI

OFFSHORE OIL PLATFORM with five wells, owned by the Amoco Production Co., blazes fiercely in October. Scene of the fire is 40 miles off Louisiana Gulf Coast.

natural gas at a rate of 50,639,000 b/d in 1971, an increase of 8.1% over 1970. There now are seven countries where demand exceeds 2 million b/d. In descending rank, they are the United States, Soviet Union, Japan, West Germany, United Kingdom, France, and Italy. They account for 72% of the world total.

Transportation. By mid-1971, there were 3,154 oil tankers of 10,000 deadweight tons (dwt) or greater, 31 less than in mid-1970. Their tonnage totaled 158,317,747 dwt, 12.8% above the mid-1970 tonnage level. There are 479 new tankers being built; their tonnage will total 77,374,900 dwt.

Refining. World total capacity for fractional distillation of crude oil reached 51,856,400 b/d in 1971, a 7.7% rise over 1970. The United States has 24.4% of the total distillation capacity. The United States, Japan, West Germany, United Kingdom, France, and Italy, which account for 61% of the non-Communist country total, and each has a distillation capacity greater than 2 million b/d.

Of the three conversion processes that are used to manufacture final-sales products such as gasoline, fuel oil, lubricants, and the like, hydrogenation is the fastest growing because it has a significant role in reducing atmospheric pollution. The 1971 gain in hydrogenation was 13.5%, reaching a worldwide rate of 12,379,000 b/d. Catalytic reforming rose 8.5% to 6,299,500 b/d, and catalytic cracking increased by 5.7% to 6,952,100 b/d.

Petrochemical Industry. There were 1,452 petrochemical plants in operation in non-Communist countries in 1971, an increase of 6.4% over 1970. Petrochemicals are used in making synthetic textiles, plastics, synthetic fertilizers, and other products. Synthetic textiles and plastic materials continued to show strong growth in 1971.

WILLIAM C. UHL
Editorial Director, "World Petroleum"

PHARMACOLOGY. See MEDICINE.

GALA dedication ceremonies at Philadelphia's Veterans Stadium on April 4 attracted crowd of 35,000. The $45 million structure, with over 56,000 seats, is the new home of the Phillies and Eagles.

UPI

PHILADELPHIA

The big news in Philadelphia in 1971 was the mayoralty campaign and election. In the Democratic primary, tough law-and-order candidate Frank Rizzo, who resigned as police commissioner to run, easily won nomination in a three-way race with U. S. Congressman William J. Green and state Representative Hardy Williams. Williams was the first black to be a serious candidate for the mayor of Philadelphia. In the general election, Rizzo defeated Republican Thatcher Longstreth, former head of the Philadelphia Chamber of Commerce.

In the general election of 1971, as in 1970, Philadelphia voters approved municipal bond issues. They were four in number: $23.7 million for such public improvements as new playgrounds and libraries; $17.7 million for the water supply and sewage systems; $17 million for the Philadelphia Gas Works; and $50 million for developing the Philadelphia International Airport.

Some 54,000 new voters among the 18- to 20-year-olds registered to vote in November's election: more than 35,000 as Democrats, 14,000 as Republicans, and 4,000 as independents.

Budget and Taxes. The operating budget for the city for fiscal year 1971–72 was listed at $701 million. Although the City Council had cut $82 million from the original request, there was considerable question as to how the city would raise $60 million to balance the current budget. Early in the year, to underwrite a pay raise for the city's 10,000 uniformed employees, incumbent Mayor James H. J. Tate signed a bill increasing the city's 3% wage tax by .31%. No provision was made, however, for the city's nonuniformed employees. In addition, the state supreme court approved a city occupancy tax of $1.25 per $100 of assessed value of that portion of properties used for commercial purposes. This levy on commercial real estate was designed to raise $13.3 million for schools.

Education. Public school education in Philadelphia was a major issue in the city's mayoralty race. In March, as a result of continuing criticism of permissiveness in the schools, the Board of Education approved an eight-point disciplinary code. Reaffirmed or new provisions of the code included: corporal punishment in the first eight grades, a stringent antitrespass law against outside militants who go on campus, immediate suspension of any student involved in violent or criminal acts on school property, and mandatory suspensions for students charged with felonious crimes.

Despite the new code, Superintendent of Schools Mark Shedd, as well as several members of the board, came under heavy criticism from the Democratic mayoralty candidate. Rizzo promised to replace the superintendent as soon as he took office, and by the end of the year he had been successful in having his candidates appointed to the Board of Education. On December 9, Shedd resigned, though he was retained as a "special assistant" for nine months.

In the midst of controversy, the school board pared its proposed budget of $395 million in March to $365 million in June, to $360 million in July, and to $300 million in September. The board conceded that the reduced budget figure fell short of the $359,676,000 needed to operate the schools for fiscal year 1971-72, but there seemed little chance of obtaining additional revenues.

Public school enrollment in Philadelphia dropped to 284,931 in September 1971, several thousand under the 1970 enrollment figure. The end of the post-World War II baby boom was the explanation given for the enrollment decrease.

Employment. In June 1971, 7% of Philadelphia's work force was jobless. This represented a 2.4% increase in unemployment over June 1970. In addition, Philadelphia lost 42,000 jobs to the suburbs between June 1969 and June 1971, when the number of wage and salary workers stood at 920,000.

Population. Philadelphia's population continues to hold at slightly under 2 million. However, the black population has been increasing while the white population has been decreasing. The number of blacks in the city rose from about 528,240 in 1968 to about 656,246 in 1971.

HARRY A. BAILEY, JR.
Temple University

532

PHILANTHROPY

Federal and state support for higher education, scientific research, and public welfare declined in 1971. Budgetary crises developed in many states, forcing retreats from the rapid growth rates of recent years. Private philanthropic support in these fields has shown similar retardation in growth. The basis for private giving in personal incomes, corporate profits, and foundation receipts and assets all reflected the slowdown in the economy.

Personal Giving. Gifts from families and individuals account for four fifths of private philanthropy. While disposable incomes rose 8% from 1969 to 1970, 5.3% of the gain was absorbed by inflation, leaving only 2.7% actual gain. The American Association of Fund-Raising Counsel estimated personal giving in 1970 at $14.3 billion, up 5.2% from 1969. This expansion kept up with inflation, but did little to increase charitable activities.

Foundation Giving. A $1 billion legacy to the Johnson Foundation from the late Robert Wood Johnson, former president of Johnson & Johnson (surgical dressings), made this the world's second-largest foundation, being exceeded only by the $3 billion Ford Foundation. In its first year it is required to disburse about $45 million, and plans to focus on the field of health care, particularly as related to delivery of health services in urban and other areas.

The 4th edition of *The Foundation Directory*, published in late 1971 by The Foundation Center, lists 5,436 foundations holding assets valued at $25.2 billion. These foundations made grants totaling $1.5 billion in 1969, reflecting an annual growth rate of about 7% in recent years. Tabulations covering $793 million in grants in 1970 report the pattern of foundation support as: education, 32%; international activities, 15%; health, 14%; welfare, 13%; sciences, 12%; humanities, 9%; religion, 5%.

Recipients. Reports from agencies receiving philanthropic support present a varied picture. Giving to 24 national health agencies rose from $299 million in 1969 to $321 million in 1970, up 7%. The United Way of America Inc., formerly United Community Funds and Councils, reported that $834 million was raised in 1970 in 2,260 local campaigns, up only 2% from 1969. Voluntary support for colleges and universities for the academic year 1969-70 was estimated at $1,750 million, down $50 million or 2.8% from 1968-69, according to the Council on Financial Aid to Education. Religious giving in 1970 was estimated by the American Association of Fund-Raising Counsel to have risen to $8.2 billion, up 3.5%.

Recent Trends. Noteworthy among recent philanthropic trends has been an increasing number of gifts of large tracts of land for nature preserves, parks, and recreation. Such gifts have been recorded in all sections of the United States, many near large metropolitan areas.

The late Robert Lehman bequeathed his art collection, valued at $100 million, to the Metropolitan Museum of Art in New York City. Most of the $100 million estate of the late Mrs. Alfred I. duPont was left to the Jessie Ball duPont Religious Charitable and Educational Fund.

RALPH L. NELSON
Queens College, City University of New York

PHILATELY. See STAMP COLLECTING.

PHILIPPINES

Major developments in the Philippines in 1971 included the opening of a constitutional convention in June and the holding of general elections in November.

Constitutional Convention. President Ferdinand Marcos was the keynote speaker at the inaugural session of the constitutional convention in Manila on June 1. In his address to the 312 delegates, the president stressed the need for unity and good will.

Former president of the Philippines Carlos P. Garcia, a delegate from Bohol province, was elected president of the convention, but he died three days later. Another former president, Diosdado P. Macapagal of Pampanga province, was subsequently elected as his successor.

By late 1971 two substantive provisions had been approved by the convention. The first was that the new constitution would be promulgated in English, with translations in Spanish, Arabic, and Tagalog and other native languages spoken by more than 50,000 people. The convention also lowered the minimum voting age from 21 to 18 years.

Elections. General elections were held on November 8. At stake were 8 of 24 senatorial seats and several provincial and local government posts. The Liberal party won 6 of the senatorial seats, and the ruling Nationalist party, 2. Voting for gubernatorial posts was two to one in favor of the Nationalist party.

The elections were conducted under an election-reform law enacted by Congress on September 4. The new law gave the commission on elections broad powers and greater independence to enable it to safeguard the electoral process against abuses, frauds, terrorism, and overspending.

Economy. The year 1971 saw a tremendous rise in the prices of commodities, due principally to the floating rate of the peso. A price-control council fixed maximum prices of essential commodities. The council's approval of price increases for many oil products caused transport strikes accompanied by violence in January, February, and June.

There were indications of substantial economic recovery. The level of the country's international reserves rose from $126 million at the start of 1970 to $236.6 million at the beginning of 1971. The gross national product (GNP) for the 1971 fiscal year reached 51,473 million pesos; in fiscal 1970 the GNP had been 48,937 million pesos. Per capita GNP in fiscal 1971 rose to 136 pesos.

Government Projects. The inauguration of the plans of the national housing corporation in Novaliches, Rizal, on February 20 was a significant step in the government's effort to meet the country's desperate need for economical housing.

Construction of the Pantabangan River dam in Nueva Ecija began on June 11. The dam will be the main feature of the Upper Pampanga River Project, designed to improve the economy of a large area of central Luzon. When completed, the dam will irrigate 197,600 acres (80,000 hectares) and generate 100,000 kilowatts of electricity.

Law and Order. At a Liberal party rally at Plaza Miranda, Manila, on August 21, unidentified persons hurled two hand grenades at the speakers' platform. Several persons were killed, and many others were wounded. Liberal party candidates for the Senate and for posts in the Manila city government were among those seriously wounded.

The incident prompted President Marcos to suspend the right of habeas corpus. He declared that lawless elements, guided and directed by a ruthless group of men, had entered into a conspiracy to seize political power in the Philippines. A number of individuals whom government agents knew to be engaged in subversive activities were taken into custody and held for questioning. The legality of the president's actions, however, was questioned in many quarters. Public demonstrations were held, and various organizations demanded the restoration of the right of habeas corpus and of civil liberties. The rights were soon restored in most areas.

Foreign Affairs. On March 12 the foreign ministers of the countries in the Association of Southeast Asian Nations (Indonesia, Malaysia, the Philippines, Singapore, and Thailand) held a conference in Manila. A highlight of the conference was a multilateral agreement on the rights of member countries to make unscheduled commercial flights.

The sudden stationing of troops of Nationalist China (Taiwan) on Itu Aba of the Sprately Island group, midway between the Philippines and South Vietnam, prompted President Marcos on July 11 to make a formal request that the troops be removed. He pointed out that by virtue of the peace treaty with Japan, ratified in San Francisco in 1951, the islands were under the trusteeship of the Allied powers, which included the Philippines.

In November, President Marcos stated that Philippine diplomatic and other relations with Nationalist China would continue despite the admission of the People's Republic of China to the United Nations.

NICOLAS ZAFRA
Emeritus Professor of History
University of the Philippines

--------- PHILIPPINES • Information Highlights ---------

Official Name: Republic of the Philippines.
Area: 115,830 square miles (300,000 sq km).
Population (1970 est.): 38,490,000. *Density,* 330 per square mile (128 per sq km). *Annual rate of increase,* 3.5%.
Chief Cities (1968 est.): Quezon City, the capital, 545,500; Manila, 1,499,000; Cebu, 332,100; Iloilo, 201,000.
Government: *Head of state,* Ferdinand E. Marcos, president (took office for 2d term Dec. 30, 1969). *Head of government,* Ferdinand E. Marcos. *Legislature*—Congress: House of Representatives, 104 members; Senate, 24 members. *Major political parties*—Nationalist party, Liberal party.
Languages: Pilipino (official), English, Spanish.
Education: *Literacy rate* (1970), 80% of population. *Expenditure on education* (1967), 2.8% of gross national product. *School enrollment* (1965)—primary (1967), 6,404,068; secondary, 1,183,307; technical/vocational, 141,961; university/higher, 519,221.
Finances (1971 est.): *Revenues,* $940,000,000; *expenditures,* $890,000,000; *monetary unit,* peso (6.43 pesos equal U. S. $1, Sept. 1971).
Gross National Product (fiscal 1971): $8,371,000,000.
National Income (1969): $4,109,000,000.
Manufacturing (metric tons, 1969): Residual fuel oil, 3,251,000; cement, 2,950,000; sugar, 1,813,000; distillate fuel oils, 1,755,000; gasoline, 1,642,000.
Crops (metric tons, 1968 crop year): Coconut, 7,200,000; rice, 5,227,000; abaca fibers, 670,000 (ranks 1st among world producers).
Minerals (metric tons, 1969): Iron ore, 991,000; salt, 231,000; chromium ore, 161,000; copper, 131,400.
Foreign Trade (1970): *Exports,* $1,067,000,000 (chief exports —wood, $249,800,000; coconut products, $215,000,000; sugar, $187,700,000; copper, $185,200,000). *Imports,* $1,210,000,000 (chief imports, 1968—nonelectrical machinery, $243,030,000; transport equipment, $129,780,000; chemicals, $111,230,000; petroleum, crude and partly refined, $90,400,000). *Chief trading partner* (1968)—United States (took 45% of exports, supplied 34% of imports).
Tourism: *Receipts* (1970), $32,080,000.
Transportation: *Roads* (1970), 36,000 miles (57,935 km); *motor vehicles* (1969), 479,800 (automobiles, 272,200); *railroads* (1970), 1,200 miles (1,931 km); *merchant fleet* (1970), 946,000 gross registered tons; *national airline,* Philippine Airlines; *principal airport,* Manila.
Communications: *Telephones* (1970), 293,543; *television stations* (1968), 14; *television sets* (1969), 350,000; *radios* (1968), 1,633,000; *newspapers* (1966), 23.

PHILOSOPHY

An analysis of the articles in philosophy journals for the year 1971 suggests that most of the established trends in philosophy have continued. There were, however, some new developments during the year.

Ethics and Social Philosophy. In keeping with the public's growing concern about the social and political problems confronting society, philosophers continued to show increased interest in ethics and in social and political philosophy. The recent establishment of such periodicals as *Philosophy & Public Affairs, Social Theory and Practice,* and the *Journal of Social Philosophy* is an indication of this trend.

On the theoretical level, philosophers considered justice, freedom, and law. In regard to law, philosophers discussed H. L. A. Hart's contrast between crimes of strict liability and those for which excuses might be offered. In ethics, they examined in detail R. M. Hare's contention that a moral position must be universalizable, backed by good reasons, and prescriptive. Marx and Marxism continued to receive the most attention in political philosophy; however, interest in both dropped significantly in 1971.

On the practical level, such pressing topics as abortion law reform, drugs, blacks, and ecology received scant attention. However, the American Philosophical Association showed its concern with the concrete issues of man's social experience by passing a resolution favoring immediate withdrawal of U. S. troops from Southeast Asia. It also recommended the training of more black philosophers and opposed discrimination against women and against Jews in the Soviet Union.

Epistemology and Related Fields. Interest in epistemology increased. Less attention was given to the problems of perception and more was given to the concepts of meaning, action, and knowledge. R. M. Chisholm's works dealing with events, actions, intentions, and beliefs were considered. A. J. Ayer's views on perception, verification, and especially personal identity were discussed.

In philosophy of mind, attention continued to focus on the concept of mind and its relation to the brain. Gilbert Ryle's contention that talk about the mind is talk about observable behavior of the body continued to be investigated.

There was little growth in the fields of logic, philosophy of language, and philosophy of science. In philosophy of language, however, increased attention was given to the problem of referring, to speech-acts, and to semantics.

Metaphysics and Philosophy of Religion. Interest in metaphysics generally remained moderate. In the specific area of existentialism, however, the works of Sartre increased sharply in popularity. At the same time, those of Nietzsche showed little change and those of Kierkegaard declined slightly. In phenomenology, Heidegger and Husserl became even more dominant. A new journal, *Analecta Husserliana,* was established to give Husserl scholars more opportunity to express their views.

In philosophy of religion, scholars continued to consider the traditional problem of the validity of proofs of God's existence. However, there was increased concern about the meaning of religious language.

RICHARD H. LINEBACK
Bowling Green State University

photography

The photographic industry passed through a year of consolidation in 1971, with refinements of existing technology being more significant than any new breakthroughs in the design of equipment and imaging systems. By the end of the year, systems hitherto limited to the high-price professional or semiprofessional level were made available to the amateur, while equipment formerly used only by amateurs was upgraded.

Since the end of World War II, Japan has become the largest producer of high-grade photographic equipment in the world. The United States has reacted to Japanese competition not only by developing new photographic products that are easily mass-produced by automated assembly lines but also by largely abandoning the production of high-cost precision equipment.

Germany, long the world leader in the production of precision photographic equipment, was slow to respond to postwar competition, and numerous small German photographic firms were forced to cease operations. Several German firms, however, have adjusted well to the changed economic situation. For instance, Franke & Heidecke, manufacturers of the renowned Rollei line of equipment, opened a plant for producing photographic components in Singapore in 1971. By the end of 1972 the firm expects to be making complete cameras for the world market. Ernst Leitz, Inc., of Wetzlar, Germany, began marketing a very specialized multi-format copying camera in 1971. The camera and optical system are made entirely in Japan, yet they bear the venerable German name of E. Leitz. This is a particularly significant example of the internationalization of the photographic industry.

Over the next 10 years, an increasing degree of international decentralization of the photographic industry can be expected. The same type of economic pressures that changed the photographic industry in the United States and Germany eventually will affect Japan. Costs there already are rising, and manufacturers may be forced to tap even lower-cost portions of the Asian labor pool.

Still Cameras. A few important new still cameras were introduced in 1971. E. Leitz announced the Leica M-5 for the professional and advanced amateur. The most significant innovation in this model is through-the-lens light metering, the first time this feature has ever been offered in a range-finder camera. A substantial number of photographers prefer range-finder focusing to the ground-glass screen found in the now dominant single-lens reflex cameras. A range finder is faster and more reliable in low light conditions, and persons with certain visual defects usually find it easier to use. According to E. Leitz, the new Leica M-5 will not replace any existing models.

Instant-Load Camera with Electronic Shutter. The Eastman Kodak Company introduced a new Instamatic camera, the X-30, which is one of the lowest-priced cameras offering an electronic shutter. The electronic exposure control circuit automatically measures the light level and holds the shutter open for times up to 10 seconds. A signal visible in the viewfinder warns the user if the exposure is too long for a hand-held shot. The new model comes equipped with tripod and cable-release sockets, which are necessary for accurate time exposures. The X-30 exemplifies the trend toward electronic microcircuit controls in cameras for amateurs, following a similar trend toward such controls in high-priced instruments.

35mm Cameras. When Franke & Heidecke introduced the extremely compact Rollei 35 in 1969, it was an instant success. By the end of 1971, nearly two dozen cameras of this type were being offered by German and Japanese manufacturers. They all share certain features—notably, compactness and short focal length lenses. The use of short focal length lenses minimizes focusing problems posed by models that are not equipped with a range finder.

Instant-Picture Cameras. The Polaroid Corporation of Cambridge, Mass., added several new models to its line of instant-picture cameras in 1971, the most interesting being the Polaroid Big Shot. This camera, which costs about $20, has a fixed shutter speed and lens opening and uses a Magicube flashbulb for each exposure. The Big Shot is designed only for making head-and-shoulder portraits in color. Such a single-purpose instrument rarely is made for the mass amateur market.

Movie Cameras. When the Super-8mm film format was introduced in 1965, it was designed primarily for the amateur market. Since then, this film format has found a remarkable degree of acceptance and made significant penetrations into the semiprofessional and professional motion-picture field. The Bauer C Royal-10 Zoom is a completely new movie camera designed for the Super-8 format. It is equipped with devices for obtaining automatic dissolves and time-lapse filming, sophisticated features that previously had been limited to professional equipment. The Rollei SL84, almost identical to the Bauer C Royal-10 Zoom, also was marketed in 1971.

Movie Camera and Tape Recorder Synchronization. It customarily has been difficult to synchronize taped sound with movies because of slight irregularities in the relative speeds of the drive motors of the camera and the tape recorder. The new Bauer Synchron 25 uses advanced electronic circuitry to achieve highly precise regulation. The system depends on an electronic interlock that adjusts the relative speeds of the motors in the movie camera and the tape recorder.

Home Movie Cameras for Normal Lighting Conditions. Still black-and-white and color photography in good natural light or normal room light long has been an accepted fact. However, home movie makers have had to use strong artificial lights (floodlights) to make movies when the natural light level was too low. The strong artificial lighting, needed because only very slow speed films were available, tends to be harsh and unflattering unless handled professionally. The simultaneous introduction in 1971 of a new line of Instamatic Super-8 movie cameras and

(Continued on page 538)

Margaret Bourke–White
(1904-1971)

Man's capacity to endure adversity with simple dignity is captured in pictures by Margaret Bourke-White, longtime Life magazine photographer and one of the great stars of photojournalism, who died on Aug. 27, 1971. Left: *Sweat-drenched black miners in a South African gold mine (1950).* Top: *Survivors of Buchenwald, a major German concentration camp (1945).* Bottom: *Indian political and spiritual leader Mohandas K. Gandhi (1946).*

(Continued from page 535)

a new Ektachrome high-speed (ASA 160) movie film has made it possible to shoot movies even under normal room illumination. The new series of cameras—designated XL—includes the XL33 and the XL55. The XL cameras differ from previous models in that they not only have faster lenses but also have a new shutter and aperture design, enabling 40% more light to reach the film. Since movies made under normal light are very pleasing, the XL cameras are expected to become popular.

Pocket Movie Camera. The new Bolex 233 is a well-made pocket movie camera. It is simple to operate yet capable of high-quality results on Super-8 film. In certain respects, this movie camera parallels the trend to compact 35mm still cameras.

Lenses. A Belgian optical firm, Seven Seas Optics of Brussels, has marketed an extremely wide-angle lens that is designed exclusively for underwater photography. The lens is intended for use with the Nikonos underwater camera, which is unique in that it does not have a separate waterproof housing. The new lens has a 98° angle of view, and the image on the film covers the full 24- by 36-mm image frame. According to the manufacturer, the lens is virtually free of distortion.

Automatic Focusing System. Completely automatic focusing from 3.3 feet to infinity is claimed by Nikon Inc., manufacturers of a new 80mm f/4.5 lens called AF-Nikkor. The new lens, designed for use with Nikon and Nikkormat cameras, is part of a very complex and compact electro-optical system. This system is based on the principle that an in-focus image is more contrasty than an out-of-focus image. A photocell reads contrast differences in a 3mm image circle in the center of a 35mm frame and "hunts" for the area of greatest contrast. A miniature electric motor drives the lens back and forth in response to the contrast-difference signals from the photocell's electronic circuit. Because of its cost, this electro-optical system is not likely to find wide application immediately. However, it is an important indicator of a major trend in camera design—the increasing degree of automation of the important operating functions of the camera.

Telephoto Lens. Ernst Leitz, Inc., began marketing a new telephoto lens for use with its Leicaflex single-lens reflex camera. This lens has a focal length of 560mm, making it the most powerful telephoto lens offered by E. Leitz. An auxiliary shoulder brace allows the Leicaflex to be hand-held, although a tripod normally is recommended for use when any lens having a focal length greater than 135mm is used in a 35mm camera. The use of a sturdy shoulder brace as a substitute for a tripod is intended to make the 560mm lens particularly useful for sport or wildlife photography, where fast action is necessary.

Color Film. Eastman Kodak announced a new Ektachrome color film that is intended primarily for photomicrographic purposes but is also useful in many applications where enhanced contrast or high resolution is desirable. The new film is capable of resolving 200 line pairs per millimeter, which is double that of Kodachrome II, a film noted for its high resolution.

Color Enlargers. Acetate filters traditionally have been used to obtain the necessary additive color filtration when making enlargements from multi-layer color film. However, acetate filters fade with use. The faded filters will create serious problems in color balance, and must be replaced. In 1971 both Simmon Omega Inc. of New York and the Beseler Photo Marketing Company of New Jersey introduced new color enlargers that use dichroic interference filters.

Unlike acetate filters, dichroic filters are not subject to fading when exposed to high-intensity light sources. There is no practical limitation on their usefulness so long as they are not damaged physically. The use of dichroic filters not only eliminates one of the variables that has tended to make color printing tedious but also simplifies the entire process for both professionals and amateurs.

Light Meters. For years, the selenium photovoltaic cell was the standard light-sensitive element in photoelectric exposure meters. The spectral response of selenium is excellent, but it is relatively insensitive to light. More recently, when very high speed lenses and emulsions became commonplace, accurate measuring of very low illumination levels became necessary. The answer was a cadmium sulfide (CdS) photoconductive cell. This cell is very sensitive to light, but its response is not entirely uniform throughout the spectrum. Although the CdS light meter has largely replaced the selenium-cell meter, still better performance has been sought. In 1971 the Sharp Electric Company of Japan developed a light-sensitive silicon cell, called "Silicon Blue," for use in light meters. The company claims this cell has better spectral sensitivity, a wider measuring range, and greater speed of response than that of a CdS cell.

Magicube Burglar Alarm. The Sylvania Corporation began marketing its mechanically fired flashbulb, the Magicube, in 1970. Soon thereafter Defensive Instruments, Inc., of Pennsylvania found a unique security application for the Magicube. Since the flashcube requires no outside power source, a would-be burglar cannot deactivate the system by cutting off the power supply. When the Magicube is mechanically triggered by the intruder, it activates a light-sensitive device, which in turn sets off an alarm.

Microfilm Information Storage and Retrieval Systems. The proliferation of printed material has led to the development of various high-density information storage and retrieval systems. Commonly, some kind of microphotographic data storage system is used. In the past, one of the drawbacks to microfilm systems was the expense and nuisance of sending out the material to be photographed or bringing in a special machine to record the data. At the 1971 National Microfilm Association Convention, Eastman Kodak introduced a complete and simplified microfilm system about the size of an office desk. The Recordak Reliant 700 Microfilmer is a completely self-contained filmer and processor, requiring no outside plumbing connections. The company claims great simplicity of operation in a highly sophisticated technological application. The relatively low cost of the complete system makes it particularly attractive for small business operations.

Literature. *The Space Age Photographic Atlas* (Crown), edited by Ken Fitzgerald, is a fascinating pictorial atlas of the entire earth from pole to pole. Most of the pictures were made on Gemini and Apollo flights. The pictures are accompanied by a descriptive text.

PHILIP L. CONDAX
*Curator, Equipment Archives,
George Eastman House*

PHYSICS

The year 1971 was an eventful one in the world of physics. Highlights of the year included completion of the world's largest particle accelerator. The controversy over quarks continued, while evidence accumulated that elementary particles actually have a substructure. Exotic atoms were created by substituting an antiproton for an electron in an atom. Meanwhile, the manpower surplus in the field of physics continued.

New Accelerators. A giant proton accelerator near Batavia, Ill., was essentially completed in the summer of 1971—one year ahead of schedule and at a cost $100 million less than estimated. This accelerator is the largest instrument for basic research in the world. Its main accelerator ring has a diameter of about 1.25 miles (2 km). In a trial run, a proton beam was accelerated to an energy of 7 GeV (billion electron volts) by the injector accelerators and then allowed to coast through the main accelerator ring. Experiments in which protons will be directed onto target materials should begin shortly. As originally planned, the machine would accelerate protons to an energy of 200 GeV —far surpassing the USSR's 76-GeV machine, which had been the most powerful accelerator in the world. However, the Batavia project has progressed so well that the new accelerator will be able to operate on a limited basis at an energy of 500 GeV.

Several ultrahigh-intensity accelerators are being built, including one at the Los Alamos Meson Physics Facility (LAMPF). These accelerators are known as "meson factories" because they are designed to produce very large numbers of mesons. The LAMPF accelerator will provide one milliampere of protons at energies up to 800 MeV (million electron volts). This accelerator is designed to explore in detail an energy region called medium energy. In addition to permitting measurements of low-yield reactions of basic importance in nuclear physics, the LAMPF linear accelerator will be used for a number of applications. One of the most exciting is cancer therapy using π mesons. Tests with pions (π mesons) indicate that pions are more effective than other radiation in treating cancers. This is because the pions essentially destroy a tumor without destroying normal tissue between the skin and the tumor.

Although the LAMPF accelerator will be excellent for studies with pions, it clearly is not too practical for actual patient treatment. However, scientists at Stanford University have built a linear accelerator that uses superconducting niobium at 2°K to keep the accelerator walls cool. This design eliminates many problems associated with overheating, and it reduces the size and the cost of the accelerator enormously. Plans are under way to establish a major cancer therapy program at Stanford. Some scientists envision 50 such laboratories for cancer therapy, located throughout the country.

Elementary Particles. One of the basic problems in physics is just how elementary are the "elementary" particles. Originally, the atom was considered to be indivisible. Later, Ernest Rutherford demonstrated the existence of a central core—the nucleus—with electrons moving in orbits around the nucleus. Still later the nucleus was discovered to have a substructure—namely, protons and neutrons.

The key to each of these discoveries was the use of higher and still higher energy particles that could

NEW EXPERIMENTS in linear proton acceleration are scheduled for Meson Physics Facility in Los Alamos, N. Mex. Two of accelerator's three stages were successfully tested in June.

probe deeper and deeper into the atom or the nucleus. The question now is whether "elementary" particles such as protons have a substructure—that is, subparticles of some kind. A number of theories consider the proton to consist of pointlike subparticles, with each subparticle having a charge less than a unit negative charge (the charge of an electron) or a unit positive charge. These subparticles are called partons, quarks, or stratons.

In recent experiments at the Stanford Linear Accelerator Center, 21-GeV electrons were scattered from proton and neutrons. It was thought that the scattering from a "solid" proton should be quite different from the scattering from a proton consisting of point subparticles. The unexpected experimental results show too much large-angle scattering and they are tentatively explained by assuming that the proton consists of point subparticles. These subparticles share some of the properties of the hypothetical particles called quarks.

Quarks. The controversy over quarks continued in 1971. In 1969, Charles McCusker of the University of Sydney, Australia, claimed to have observed quarks. Since then, many physicists have challenged McCusker's claims.

In the mid-1960's, theorists Murray Gell-Mann and George Zweig independently proposed the existence of a strange new kind of particle, which Gell-Mann named the "quark." Quarks were considered to be the elementary particles out of which all the others could be constructed. For instance, the proton was considered to consist of three very tightly bound quarks. Many physicists did not take quarks seriously because a quark supposedly had a fractional charge of $\frac{1}{3}$ or $\frac{2}{3}$. This was inconsistent with the concept of the indivisibility of charge, which has been basic since about 1910, when Robert Millikan established that there was a basic unit of electrical charge—the negative charge of an electron.

Nevertheless, experimentalists began searching for quarks. Since quarks are presumed to be very massive, a great deal of energy is needed to create them or to release them. Particles of extremely high energy are present in cosmic rays, so McCusker hunted for quarks that might be produced when cosmic rays struck the atmosphere. Some of the tracks observed in his cloud chamber were attributed to particles with a charge of $\frac{2}{3}$.

In the early 1970's, physicists have taken another approach—simply looking very hard for quarks with the most precise methods available. In Millikan's classic experiment, he balanced the electric and gravitational forces on a small charged drop of oil and determined the value of the charge. Several research groups have tried this approach in searching for quarks, but no quarks were found. Two Stanford physicists, William M. Fairbank and Arthur F. Hebard, have used a similar approach. However, in their experiments, the oil drop is replaced by a superconducting niobium ball kept at very low temperatures. The first preliminary results indicate the presence of a charge of $\frac{1}{3}$. However, no definitive results are yet available, and the preliminary findings may be spurious. If the existence of the quark is confirmed, it will be one of the major discoveries of the century.

Exotic Atoms. One exciting way to study nuclear structure is to replace one of the electrons in an atom with some other negatively charged subnuclear particle. In this way, an "exotic" atom is formed. In the late 1960's such atoms were created by replacing electrons with pions (π mesons), muons (μ mesons), or kaons (K mesons). This is not only a very impressive technical feat but also a useful one because the decay of the resulting atoms can give very important information on the structure of the nucleus. In particular, the study of X rays emitted from μ-mesic atoms (atoms with muons) has been very productive in the past few years.

Late in 1970, new kinds of exotic atoms were formed. A team of German physicists from Karlsruhe and Heidelberg made the new discoveries using the proton synchrotron at the European Organization for Nuclear Research (CERN). They succeeded in substituting antiprotons and negatively charged sigma hyperons for electrons. The antiproton is the antimatter equivalent of the proton. A sigma hyperon is an "elementary" particle. Preliminary measurements indicated that the magnetic moment of the antiproton is about equal to that of the proton. Measurements of the magnetic moment of the sigma hyperon are planned. A determination of this value would be very important for comparison with theoretical predictions.

Manpower. The job crisis for scientists in general and physicists in particular continued in 1971. It was estimated that about 4% of the physicists with new Ph. D.'s in physics were unemployed. Older physicists who found themselves out of jobs, although fewer in number, were hit even harder. So-called underemployment—where scientists occupy positions for which their high degree of training is unnecessary—was perhaps almost as pressing a problem.

The reasons for the shift to a situation in which the supply of physicists exceeds the demand are complex. Basically, the rate of Ph. D. production has exceeded the rate at which new jobs have been created over the years, and this gradually reduced the gap between supply and demand. In the last few years, the problem became acute because a number of adverse factors all occurred at once. Principal among these were reductions in federal research spending, the general economic recession, and cutbacks in areas such as the aerospace industry. One long-term adverse factor is that demographic trends indicate a gradual leveling of the college and university student population and a concomitant leveling of new faculty positions.

While the immediate outcry is that the number of physics students should be reduced, critics of this view fear that such a hasty and drastic solution may create a major shortage of physicists a few years from now. In fact, the number of first-year graduate students in physics in the academic year 1970–71 was 17% less than that in 1969–70.

There is an increased willingness on the part of young physicists in particular to apply their training to a variety of social problems—for instance, medical physics, the environment, and such urban needs as rapid-transit systems. Academic physicists are correspondingly reexamining their curriculums in the light of these changing demands. The long-range results of these new attitudes may be extremely important for the whole field of physics.

GARY MITCHELL
North Carolina State University

PICASSO, Pablo. See BIOGRAPHY.

PITTSBURGH

Strikes, the opening of a new symphony hall, a World Series victory and its celebration, a mayor's battle against his own party, and a battle over mass transit dominated the headlines in Pittsburgh (1970 census: 520,117) in 1971.

Strikes. Teachers, newspaper employees, and about 1,500 of 6,100 municipal employees were out on strike in January. Pressmen employed by the afternoon and Sunday *Pittsburgh Press* struck from January 4 through January 17 in a pay dispute involving a new contract. The morning *Post-Gazette,* printed under contract by the *Press,* was also prevented from publishing. On May 14, printers struck the *Press* in a pay dispute that led to a 129-day newspaper blackout. Before it was over, Teamster drivers and service employees also struck. In both strikes, union members received contracts calling for pay increases.

A Pittsburgh Federation of Teachers strike kept 73,000 city children out of their classrooms for five

HEINZ HALL FOR THE PERFORMING ARTS, PITTSBURGH SYMPHONY ORCHESTRA

PITTSBURGH'S Heinz Hall for the Performing Arts (*above*) opened with concert by Pittsburgh Symphony Orchestra on September 10. Rococo interior (*right*) of former movie theater, built in 1927, features Austrian crystal chandeliers and Italian marble. The hall is in the city's revitalized Golden Triangle section.

school days up to January 11. The teachers won an average yearly pay increase of $1,700.

Fifteen hundred Pittsburgh city employees, including garbagemen, struck or honored picket lines around City Hall on January 5. The walkout—which prompted Mayor Peter F. Flaherty and his staff to collect garbage personally—involved a jurisdictional dispute. Flaherty ordered plumbers to drive trucks previously driven by Teamsters. A court order ended the strike on January 14.

For much of the year, through August 1, the threat of a steel strike hung over Pittsburgh. Although the strike was avoided at the last minute, August was recorded as the steel industry's worst nonstrike month since the 1930's as steel buyers worked off inventories built up in anticipation of the strike. District mills laid off about 12,000 workers because of poor demand for steel.

New Home for Symphony. The Heinz Hall for the Performing Arts opened on September 10 in a former downtown movie theater. The theater had received a face-lift outside and a complete renovation inside at a cost of $6.5 million, thanks largely to the H. J. Heinz family. The hall will be the home of the Pittsburgh Symphony, the Civic Light Opera, the Pittsburgh Ballet Theater, the Pittsburgh Opera, and the Pittsburgh Youth Symphony.

Triumph and Turmoil. Culture took a vacation on October 17, the day the city went wild celebrat-ing a World Series victory by the Pittsburgh Pirates. After defeating the Baltimore Orioles, the Pirates came home to 20,000 fans at the Greater Pittsburgh International Airport. Some 100,000 persons awaited the team in the Golden Triangle, Pittsburgh's glittering downtown. There were 98 arrests, a taxi was overturned and three other cars were damaged, and two fires broke out; but Mayor Flaherty said that reports of a near riot were "greatly exaggerated."

Politics and Mass Transit. Mayor Flaherty continued to war with his own party in 1971 as he declined to back fellow Democrats in the Allegheny county commissioner contest on November 2. The county, which includes Pittsburgh, is governed by three commissioners, and the main campaign issue was a proposed mass-transit plan that would cost an estimated $228.5 million. The Democratic majority commissioners, Leonard Staisey and Thomas Foerster, supported the plan. The Republican minority commissioner, Dr. William Hunt, opposed it—and Mayor Flaherty opposed it, too. Hunt led the race, but he failed to carry running-mate Robert Stokes with him, so Staisey and Foerster retained control of the 3-man board.

DAVID Y. WARNER
The Pittsburgh "Press"

PLASTICS. See MATERIALS.

POLAND

Economic reform and party reorganization dominated the news in Poland during 1971. This was the first full year of Edward Gierek's cautiously liberal leadership of the ruling PZPR (Communist) party. Gierek and the new premier, Piotr Jaroszewicz, spent much of their time in the first half of 1971 traveling around the country to calm and appease the industrial workers still aggrieved after the December 1970 riots and strikes.

Prices and Wages. In January 1971 the regime publicized a so-called consumers' charter, pledging to (1) link output increases in industrial goods with price cuts; (2) devote more effort to consumer research; (3) make consumer products cheaper and more plentiful; and (4) maintain a 2-year freeze on the prices of nonseasonal goods, particularly foodstuffs. By early February food shortages were eased. In March the regime revoked the food price increases that had been made in 1970. Loans from the Soviet Union were credited with making the price cuts possible.

Gierek placated industrial workers by abandoning the incentive plan of his predecessor, Władysław Gomułka, which had geared earnings to productivity increases and caused widespread fear of wage cuts and unemployment. General wage increases, however, were declared insupportable.

A new 5-year plan for 1971-75, emphasizing consumer priorities, housing, and light industry, was approved by the party's sixth national Congress in December. The regime promised to improve health care and other social services by increasing taxes

--- **POLAND · Information Highlights** ---

Official Name: Polish People's Republic.
Area: 120,724 square miles (312,677 sq km).
Population (1970 est.): 32,810,000. *Density*, 270 per square mile (104 per sq km). *Annual rate of increase*, 10%.
Chief Cities (1970 est.): Warsaw, the capital, 1,273,600; Lódz, 747,000; Kraków, 560,300; Wrocław, 509,400; Poznań, 455,500.
Government: *President of the Council of State*—Jozef Cyrankiewicz (took office Dec. 23, 1970); *Premier*—Piotr Jaroszewicz (took office Dec. 23, 1970); *First Secretary, United Workers' party*—Edward Gierek (took office Dec. 20, 1970). *Legislature* (unicameral)—Sejm, 460 members. *Major political parties*—United Workers' party, United Peasants' party, Democratic party.
Languages: Polish (official).
Education: *Literacy rate* (1970), 98% of population. *Expenditure on education* (1968), 5.1% of total public expenditure. *School enrollment* (1968)—primary, 5,603,955; secondary, 1,208,585; technical/vocational, 846,802; university/higher, 305,561.
Finances (1969 est.): *Revenues*, $86,900,000; *expenditures*, $87,200,000; *monetary unit*, zloty (4 zlotys equal U. S.$1, 1971).
Gross National Product (1969 est.): $40,500,000,000.
Average Annual Income Per Person (1969 est.): $700–$900.
Manufacturing (metric tons, 1969): Cement, 11,830,000; crude steel, 11,291,000; pig-iron and ferro alloys, 6,855,000; meat, 1,882,000; sugar, 1,723,000.
Crops (metric tons, 1969 crop year): Potatoes, 44,925,000 (ranks 2d among world producers); sugar beets (1968), 14,800,000; rye (1968), 8,520,000 (world rank, 2d).
Minerals (metric tons, 1969): Coal, 135,010,000 (ranks 6th among world producers); lignite, 30,865,000 (world rank, 6th); salt, 2,817,000; iron ore, 774,000.
Foreign Trade: *Exports* (1970), $3,548,000,000 (chief exports, 1969—Coal, $276,950,000; meat and products, $154,000,-000; ships and boats, $132,000,000; freight wagons, $47,-000,000). *Imports* (1970), $3,608,000,000 (chief imports, 1968—rolled products including pipes, $149,500,000; cotton, $110,700,000; copper concentrates, $101,625,000; crude petroleum, $89,875,000). *Chief trading partners* (1968)—USSR (took 36% of exports, supplied 35% of imports); East Germany (8%—10%).
Transportation: *Roads* (1964), 196,520 miles (316,260 km); *motor vehicles* (1969), 667,900 (automobiles, 423,000); *railroads* (1968), 16,728 miles (26,915 km); *merchant fleet* (1971), 1,760,000 gross registered tons.
Communications: *Telephones* (1970), 1,756,248; *television stations* (1968), 19; *television sets* (1969), 3,828,000; *radios* (1969), 5,649,000; *newspapers* (1969), 43.

on the private sector of Poland's economy—on merchants, retailers, artisans, and private workshops.

Politics. The party Congress brought to a climax Gierek's purge of remnants of the Gomułka regime. By the end of 1971, party leaders in areas of unrest—including Gdańsk, Szczecin, Warsaw, Łódź, and Lublin—had been or were being replaced. Several top officials of the ministry of internal security and the trade union apparatus were fired. About 70% of the delegates to the December Congress had not participated in previous congresses, and the new, 115-member Central Committee of the party retained only 24 incumbents. At the top policy-making level of the Politburo, all those closely identified with Gomułka were ousted.

Most significant, perhaps, was the downfall of Gen. Mieczysław Moczar, who had been considered a rival of both Gomułka and Gierek. When Gierek became party leader in December 1970, Moczar had been promoted to full Politburo membership. However, in June 1971 he was transferred to a less sensitive post as chairman of the supreme control chamber, a government audit commission.

In late June a commission appointed by Gierek to investigate the December 1970 upheaval issued a report blaming Gomułka's autocratic style of government and his confusion and "overreaction" to popular expressions of grievances for the outbreaks. Suspended from membership in the party's Central Committee, Gomułka dropped from public view.

In August, Gierek emphasized the need for a more open party Congress, responsive to rank-and-file demands. The sixth Congress was called a year ahead of schedule.

Religion. In church-state relations the Gierek regime achieved greater mutual cooperation than perhaps had existed at any time since 1956. In March 1971 a conference was held in Warsaw between Stefan Cardinal Wyszyński, the primate of Poland, and Premier Jaroszewicz, the first such state-church meeting in 10 years. In late June the regime announced the transfer to the Polish episcopate of title of some 7,000 church buildings in the formerly German Oder-Neisse territories.

Cultural Affairs. Censorship and cultural policies appeared to ease. The regime permitted publications by authors such as Stefan Kisielewski and Ryszard Gontarz, who had been banned during the 1968 anti-Zionist campaign. The appointment of Wincenty Kraśko as vice premier in charge of cultural affairs was looked upon as a victory for "liberalism," though it was offset by the assignment of a "hard-liner," Stefan Olszowski, to the management of cultural affairs in the Politburo.

Foreign Affairs. The regime followed Soviet leadership on most international issues during 1971. Gierek and Jaroszewicz consulted with Soviet leaders in Moscow in January and June. Liberalization at home won U. S. approval of the sale of $68 million worth of American oil refinery equipment to Poland and generally improved U. S.-Polish relations. Improving Polish-West German relations, however, were strained by Polish charges that the Munich-based Radio Free Europe had been instrumental in provoking the December 1970 riots. The Polish press warned that Poland would refuse to ratify the Polish-West German Treaty of Dec. 7, 1970, unless West Germany revoked the Radio Free Europe license, which, however, was renewed.

ALEXANDER J. GROTH
University of California, Davis

Assaults on policemen increased in 1971, and line-of-duty deaths rose. Here, New York's Mayor Lindsay (*left*) and Police Commissioner Murphy attend funeral for slain patrolman.

POLICE

The personal danger of police work in the United States was underlined in 1971 by a sharp increase in the number of law enforcement officers killed or wounded during encounters with citizens. In November, 10 officers were slain in the line of duty, raising the total of police deaths for the first 11 months of the year to 112, or 18 more than for the same period in 1970. The growing perils of American law enforcement work have been causing recruitment problems, as officers feel compelled to change to safer jobs. In addition, blacks remain cool to taking employment with the "pigs" (still the major term of invective against the police), and college graduates continue to find that restrictions against entry into police service except at the lowest ranks make law enforcement a relatively unattractive career choice.

The 112 police killings were concentrated primarily in the Southern states. The 43 killings that occurred there largely involved firearms, mostly handguns. Seventeen of the officer deaths resulted from ambush-type attacks, 25 occurred while policemen were responding to robbery or burglary calls, 15 resulted from stopping motor vehicles, while the remainder involved other forms of police work.

That the United States is not alone in regard to the growing seriousness of assaults on police personnel was shown in August when five men robbed a jewelry store in Blackpool, England, and opened fire on the unarmed police who were pursuing them. The Blackpool superintendent of police was killed and two constables wounded.

Protecting the Police. The 10,000 officers from all over Britain who attended funeral rites for the police superintendent in Blackpool evidenced the intense feeling among law enforcement personnel about the citizen assaults they are sustaining. In the United States, the most immediate response to the mounting police toll was a call for more stringent control of weapons, particularly handguns. There were also proposals that police slaying be made a federal crime that would be investigated by the Federal Bureau of Investigation.

In Britain, the response to the Blackpool police murder took the form of demands for harsher penalties against criminals. In what was for the English an unprecedented police appeal to the public, some officials asked for a return to older ways, when offenders were flogged and were made to break stones and sew mailbags in prisons. "Prison then was a real deterrent," a police superintendent insisted. Now, he felt, such features as television sets in recreation rooms, transistor radios in cells, and weekend leaves make prison less fearsome and thereby fail to discourage criminal activity.

A further tactic for increasing public support of the police was suggested in a study by Paul R. Wilson and Duncan Chappell, who compared attitudes toward the police in Australia where, as in America, traffic enforcement is a police matter, and in New Zealand, where a special force handles traffic. This latter approach seemed to produce friendlier attitudes to police authority. In New Zealand, 72% of the motorists and 73% of the non-motorists indicated "great respect" for the police, while such respect was reported by 69% of the Australian non-motorists but only 63% of the motorists.

FBI Under Attack. Criticism of the Federal Bureau of Investigation, and particularly of director J. Edgar Hoover, escalated during the year, indicating, perhaps, that the continuing tenure of the bureau's 76-year-old chief was becoming a political liability to the Nixon administration. Most striking was the result of a telephone survey developed jointly by *Newsweek* and the Gallup Organization Inc. showing that 51% of a national sample favored Hoover's retirement, while only 41% thought that Hoover ought to remain in his job.

A number of issues hurt the image of the FBI. There were reports of high-handed personnel practices, with agents out of favor with Hoover being transferred to remote, unattractive sites. Personal feuds between Hoover and other government officials were handicapping cooperation among agencies involved in the exchange of confidential information. In March the theft of records from the two-man FBI office in Media, Pa., was particularly embarrassing to the bureau, which has prided itself on the security of its investigative files. The stolen Media papers, sent anonymously to newspapers and to public figures, also indicated that the FBI had under close surveillance dissenters of the political left and blacks to a far greater extent than most persons had believed. At a November conference in Princeton, N. J., on the work of the FBI, there was strong endorsement of the principle that in the future the work of the bureau ought to be much more closely controlled by persons outside the agency.

Police Corruption. Police officers in general tend to be regarded as notably susceptible to graft and corruption. For one thing, they have the power to make basic decisions about the freedom or imprisonment of persons they encounter. For another, they frequently find themselves in situations considerably more tempting than anything encountered by the average citizen.

The allegation that numerous officers sometimes succumb to such temptations was the theme of an investigation in 1971 that focused attention on lawbreaking by law officers in New York City. The investigative body, headed by Whitman Knapp, a well-known attorney, heard testimony that one policeman had held out $80,000 worth of heroin when he seized several kilos and $127,000 in currency, then shared the loot with two cohorts. William Phillips, a policeman who had been caught taking bribes and trying to fix court cases, was pressed into the service of the Knapp Commission, and put before it tape recordings that, he said, indicated that officers in New York accept bribes amounting to at least $4 million a year. Phillips said that he did not know of a single plainclothesman who was not "on the take." His testimony added several new words to the vocabulary of corruption, such as a "flute," or soda bottle actually filled with whiskey by bartenders for police officers to drink, and a "flake," or false arrest made in order to extort money.

Reactions to the work of the Knapp Commission were not all laudatory. Civil libertarians felt that much of the testimony had been derived by methods that violated the privacy and the rights of the persons involved. New York's Police Commissioner Patrick V. Murphy, who himself earlier had been critical of police corruption, felt that the Knapp Commission was taking the matter too far and was damaging the reputation of a department with 30,300 officers, most of whom were honest and conscientious. Murphy called Phillips a "rogue cop" who, having been caught in criminal acts himself, was now "squirming to get off the hook."

GILBERT GEIS
University of California, Irvine

"POLICE car of tomorrow" features modified body and engine to improve efficiency. Officer displays special enforcement and rescue devices with which car is equipped.

FEDERAL SIGN & SIGNAL CORPORATION

President Nixon addresses crowd gathered at opening of Dwight D. Eisenhower Center in Washington, D.C. New national Republican head-quarters was formally dedicated to memory of the late President on Jan. 15, 1971.

political parties

Competition between the two major United States political parties for the independent vote was lively during 1971, with forces gearing up for the 1972 presidential election. The independent vote was crucial, for Democrats claimed formal allegiance of slightly less than half of American voters and Republicans only slightly over one fourth. President Richard M. Nixon predicted, on March 22, 1971, that "we will never have a time again . . . when you are going to have a polarization of Democrats versus Republicans. I think you are going to have the independents controlling basically the balance of power." Moreover both parties risked losing votes to splinter groups threatening to form new parties or to sit out the election.

The Candidates. President Nixon's renomination by the Republicans was considered a political certainty. Despite criticism of his program of gradual withdrawal from Vietnam, the Indochina War diminished as a domestic political issue. The President's efforts to strengthen the economy through wage-and-price controls drew a mixed reaction. Overtures to mainland China lost him some conservative support but sat well with the general public. Polls confirmed that he would be a formidable candidate against any Democratic nominee.

On July 9, Rep. Paul N. McCloskey of California announced his candidacy for the Republican nomination. Calling his chances "fairly remote," he declared that he would run in the New Hampshire and California presidential primaries to bring pressure to end the war in Vietnam, to register new voters, and to encourage new party leadership. On the Republican Right, Rep. John M. Ashbrook of

Ohio entered the race in late December, hoping to steer the President toward a more conservative line.

Uncertainty was greater over the Republican re-nomination of Vice President Spiro T. Agnew. Speculation arose about the possible candidacy of Secretary of the Treasury John B. Connally, Jr., the only Democrat in the cabinet, with frequent mention of Republican Governors Nelson Rockefeller of New York and Ronald Reagan of California. A November poll in California showed that Agnew would run best and Connally last among Republican voters there, but that all California voters would rank Rockefeller first, Connally second, Agnew third, and Reagan last. President Nixon later expressed his intention to retain the "winning team."

Sen. Edmund S. Muskie of Maine, the Democratic nominee for vice president in 1968, appeared to be his party's front-runner for the presidential nomination. While polls showed Sen. Edward M. Kennedy (Mass.) strong among Democratic voters, he insisted that he was not a candidate. Sen. Hubert H. Humphrey (Minn.), presidential nominee in 1968, also showed strength in the polls. Other Democratic prospects included George McGovern (S. Dak.), an antiwar liberal; Sen. Henry M. Jackson (Wash.), a strong supporter of national defense with a liberal domestic record; Sen. Vance Hartke of Indiana; former Sen. Eugene J. McCarthy (Minn.), who hinted also at third-party activity; and mayors John V. Lindsay of New York and Samuel W. Yorty of Los Angeles. Lindsay left the Republican party to become a Democrat on Aug. 11, 1971, and announced his candidacy for the Democratic presidential nomination on December 28. After preliminary campaigning, Senators Birch Bayh (Ind.), Fred R. Harris (Okla.), and Harold E. Hughes (Iowa) withdrew from consideration.

Gov. George C. Wallace of Alabama, who had run as a third-party candidate in 1968, planned to enter Democratic primaries but gave indications that he might again head a third party. Black leaders discussed circumstances in which a black condition candidacy should be furthered, and Rep. Shirley Chisholm (D., N. Y.) pressed her claims for it. On Nov. 27, 1971, in Dallas, a newly created dissident People's party nominated Dr. Benjamin Spock for president as a stand-in for a "bigger national figure."

Both the Democratic nomination and the possibility of splinter candidacies will reflect, in part, the outcome of presidential primaries in 23 states, beginning in New Hampshire on March 7, 1972.

Congress. At the opening of the 92d Congress on Jan. 21, 1971, Democrats in the House numbered 254 and Republicans 180 (1 vacancy). In the Senate, Democrats numbered 54, Republicans 44, Conservative-Republican 1, and Independent 1. The House elected Carl Albert (D., Okla.) as speaker, to succeed the retiring John W. McCormack. Hale Boggs (D., La.) became majority leader, and Gerald R. Ford (R., Mich.) continued as minority leader. The Senate elected Allen J. Ellender (D., La.) president pro tempore. Mike Mansfield (D., Mont.) and Hugh Scott (R., Pa.) continued as party leaders. Robert C. Byrd (D., W. Va.) became majority whip, narrowly defeating incumbent Edward Kennedy.

Party Organization. The 1972 Democratic nominating convention was set for July 10 at Miami Beach, Fla., and the Republican convention, for August 21 at San Diego, Calif.

The Democratic party, in the wake of internal criticism of the 1968 convention and after study by two commissions, adopted reform procedures at a meeting of its national committee on Feb. 19, 1971. The changes prohibit the unit rule—under which state delegates vote as a block after a majority vote in caucus—and require selection of delegates within the convention year. The meeting also voted to assign delegate seats to states on the dual basis of about 47% for Democratic votes for president and 53% for electoral college strength, which gives the 9 most populous states a majority of the convention, in contrast with a majority held by 13 states in 1968. This controversial apportionment system was upheld by the U. S. Court of Appeals, Washington, D. C.

The Republican National Committee, under the chairmanship of Sen. Robert J. Dole (Kans.) continued to find it easier to raise campaign funds than did the Democratic committee. In December, Congress passed and President Nixon reluctantly signed a bill to finance presidential elections with tax funds. After 1972, a taxpayer will be able to designate $1 of his taxes as a contribution to a political party.

FRANKLIN L. BURDETTE, *University of Maryland*

POLLUTION. See CHEMISTRY; ENVIRONMENT.
POMPIDOU, Georges. See BIOGRAPHY.

THE 1972 PRESIDENTIAL SWEEPSTAKES

The following are biographical sketches of candidates for the Democratic and Republican presidential nominations who had announced their candidacies as of January 1972. Also included is Sen. Edward Kennedy, who declared his intention not to seek the Democratic nomination but who continued to enjoy widespread popular support. A biography of President Nixon, considered the likely Republican candidate, appears in the article BIOGRAPHY.

Ashbrook, John Milan, U. S. congressman from Ohio. Chosen in a national poll in 1970 as one of the five most respected conservatives in the United States, Representative Ashbrook announced his candidacy for the Republican nomination on Dec. 29, 1971. Accusing the Nixon administration of a "leftward drift," he indicated that he might withdraw if the President increased defense spending, dropped his support of a family assistance program, and retained Spiro Agnew as his vice presidential running mate. Ashbrook was born in Johnstown, Ohio, on Sept. 21, 1928. He attended

JOHN
ASHBROOK

Harvard and the Ohio State University law school, and practiced law in the town of his birth, where, from 1953, he also published the weekly *Johnstown Independent.* He entered Congress in 1961.

Chisholm, Shirley (Anita St. Hill), U. S. representative from New York. Mrs. Chisholm announced in 1971 that she would enter several Democratic primaries to ensure that the party's selection of a presidential nominee would not be an exclusively "white, male decision." Born in Brooklyn, N. Y., on Nov. 30, 1924, Shirley Chisholm studied at Brooklyn College and Columbia University and became director of child-care centers in New York City. She was elected to the New York State Assembly in 1964 and in 1968 defeated Republican James Farmer for the congressional seat representing Brooklyn's Bedford-Stuyvesant district. The first black woman elected to the House of Representatives, she campaigned for minority groups, women's rights, peace, and the alleviation of poverty.

Hartke, Vance, U. S. senator from Indiana. Late in December 1971, Senator Hartke, chairman of the Senate's Veterans' Affairs Committee, paid a flying visit to New Hampshire, where the first popular presidential primary of 1972 was to be held on March 7. On January 3, his New Hampshire supporters entered him in the race for the Democratic nomination. An ardent opponent of the war, he began his campaign with a call for an immediate U. S. withdrawal from Indochina. Hartke was born in Stendal, Ind., on May 31, 1919. A graduate of Evansville College, he earned a law degree at the University of Indiana in 1948 and established a law practice in Evansville. He was the city's mayor in 1956–58 and entered the U. S. Senate in 1959, winning reelection in 1964 and 1970.

Humphrey, Hubert Horatio, Jr., U. S. senator from Minnesota. Humphrey, who had been narrowly defeated by Richard Nixon in his 1968 presidential bid, declared

SHIRLEY
CHISHOLM

himself a candidate for renomination on Jan. 10, 1972.
Despite his identification with the Johnson administration's Vietnam War policy during his term as vice president (1965–69), he retained substantial support among middle-of-the-road Democrats and organized labor. Born in Wallace, S. D., on May 27, 1911, Humphrey attended the University of Minnesota (B. A., 1939) and worked as a pharmacist, teacher, and civil servant before being elected mayor of Minneapolis (1945). As a U. S. senator from 1949 to 1964, he compiled a solidly liberal record and was a champion of civil rights and disarmament. He was reelected to the Senate in 1970.

Jackson, Henry Martin, U. S. senator from the state of Washington. Henry ("Scoop") Jackson announced his candidacy for the Democratic presidential nomination on Nov. 11, 1971. A liberal on domestic issues, he remained a steadfast advocate of military preparedness, though he had moderated his earlier staunch support of U. S. involvement in Vietnam. His strong criticism of President Nixon's economic policies was expected to bring him some support from top labor leaders. Jackson was born in Everett, Wash., on May 31, 1912, and earned a law degree at the University of Washington in 1935. After serving as a county prosecutor (1938–40), he won six consecutive terms in the U. S. House of Representatives. He became a U. S. senator in 1952. In 1960–61 he was chairman of the Democratic National Committee.

Kennedy, Edward Moore, U. S. senator from Massachusetts. Heir to the political tradition of his late brothers, President John F. Kennedy and Sen. Robert F. Kennedy, "Ted" Kennedy was considered a leading contender for the 1972 presidential nomination despite his steadfast denials of any intention to enter the race. Though deposed as Senate majority whip in 1971 and still suffering the onus of his involvement in the Chappaquiddick tragedy in 1969, he remained a leading choice of rank-and-file Democrats in all polls. Born in Brookline, Mass., on Feb. 22, 1932, Kennedy studied at Harvard and the University of Virginia. After service as an assistant county district attorney (1961–62), he was elected to fill an unexpired U. S. Senate term in 1962. He was elected in 1964 and 1970 to full Senate terms.

Lindsay, John Vliet, mayor of New York City. Mayor Lindsay announced on Aug. 11, 1971, that he was changing his party affiliation from Republican to Democratic and strongly criticized the Nixon administration for its economic policies, its alleged neglect of the cities, and its failure to end the Vietnam War. On December 28 he declared himself a candidate for the Democratic presidential nomination. Born in New York City on Nov. 21, 1921, Lindsay earned a law degree at Yale (1948), practiced law in New York, and became an executive assistant in the U. S. Department of Justice (1955). He was elected to the U. S. House of Representatives in 1958 and to the New York mayoralty in 1965 as a Republican. He was reelected mayor in 1969 as a Liberal-Independent in a three-way race.

McCarthy, Eugene Joseph, former U. S. senator from Minnesota. McCarthy informally declared his candidacy for the Democratic presidential nomination on Dec. 17, 1971, but indicated that unless the Democratic platform and candidate presented a clear alternative to Nixon administration policies he might launch a new party. Born in Watkins, Minn., on March 29, 1916, he graduated from St. John's University in that state in 1935, earned an M. A. at the University of Minnesota in 1939, and taught at St. Thomas College in St. Paul before entering the U. S. House of Representatives in 1948. He served in the U. S. Senate from 1959 to 1970. In 1968, as an antiwar candidate, he stunned the Johnson administration by winning 42% of the votes in the New Hampshire Democratic presidential primary.

VANCE
HARTKE

HUBERT H.
HUMPHREY

HENRY
JACKSON

EDWARD (TED)
KENNEDY

JOHN V.
LINDSAY

EUGENE
McCARTHY

PAUL
McCLOSKEY, JR.

GEORGE
McGOVERN

EDMUND S.
MUSKIE

GEORGE C.
WALLACE

SAMUEL (SAM)
YORTY

McCloskey, Paul Norton, Jr., U. S. representative from California. "Pete" McCloskey became President Nixon's first Republican challenger when he declared on July 9, 1971, that he would enter presidential primaries in several states on a platform pledged to ending the Indochina hostilities and returning the Republican party to its traditional "moral commitment on social issues." Born in San Bernardino, Calif., on Sept. 29, 1927, McCloskey studied at Stanford University and was a Marine Corps commander in Korea. He later practiced law in California. In 1967 he was elected to Congress after scoring an upset primary victory over former actress Shirley Temple Black. As a congressman he championed conservation and attacked the administration for prolonging the war.

McGovern, George Stanley, U. S. senator from South Dakota. By announcing his candidacy on Jan. 18, 1971, McGovern became the first to officially enter the race. Although polls showed him to have barely increased his small following by the end of 1971, he retained a solid base on college campuses and among grass-roots liberals. Born at Avon, S. D., on July 19, 1922, he served in the Army Air Forces and studied at Dakota Wesleyan and Northwestern universities. As a congressman (1957–62) he was the author and first director of President John F. Kennedy's Food for Peace program. Elected to the Senate in 1962, he was an early opponent of U. S. military involvement in Vietnam and cosponsored the McGovern-Hatfield amendment that sought to establish a deadline for U. S. withdrawal.

Muskie, Edmund Sixtus, U. S. senator from Maine. Muskie continued in 1971 as the front-runner among prospective Democratic challengers, conveying an image of pragmatic liberalism and capitalizing on the favorable impression that he had created in 1968 as Hubert Humphrey's vice-presidential running mate. Although he did not announce his candidacy until Jan. 4, 1972, he embarked in September 1971 on a 4-month, 32-state tour, having earlier visited several foreign countries, including the USSR. Of Polish Roman Catholic parentage, Muskie was born in Rumford, Me., on March 28, 1914. He studied at Bates College and Cornell University. Elected to the Maine Legislature in 1946, he won the governorship in 1954 and, in 1958, became Maine's first popularly elected Democratic U. S. senator.

Wallace, George Corley, governor of Alabama. Wallace, who received 13% of the popular vote in the 1968 presidential election as the candidate of the American Independent party, indicated that he planned to reenter the presidential race in 1972, and, on Jan. 5, 1972, announced that he would be a candidate in the Florida Democratic primary. Born in Clio, Ala., on Aug. 25, 1919, Wallace attended the University of Alabama's law school and later served as an assistant attorney general, a state legislator, and a circuit judge. As governor of Alabama from 1963, Wallace, a Democrat, became a national symbol of Southern resistance to racial integration. Succeeded in 1967 by his wife, Lurleen B. Wallace, who died in 1968, he was elected to a second term as governor in 1970.

Yorty, Samuel William, mayor of Los Angeles, who declared his candidacy in November 1971. A "hawk" on the Vietnam War issue and a champion of "law and order," he was considered to represent the right wing in the Democratic party spectrum. Born in Lincoln, Nebr., on Oct. 1, 1909, Yorty worked his way through Southwestern University and the University of California law school. Beginning his political career as liberal Democrat, he served in the California state Legislature (1936–40 and 1949–50) and in the U. S. House of Representatives (1950–54). In the 1960 presidential race, he endorsed Richard Nixon. He was elected mayor of Los Angeles in 1961, despite lack of support from Democratic leaders, and was reelected to the office in 1965 and 1969.

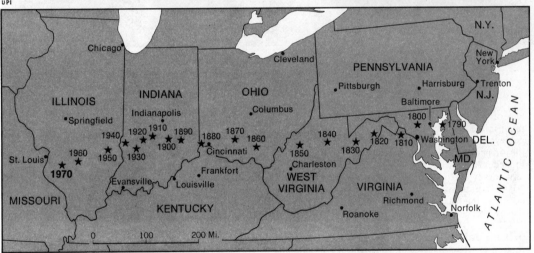

Center of U. S. population moved westward again, 1970 census showed. Farmer Lawrence Friederich poses in his field near Mascoutan, Ill., in April as his family examines new population marker.

population

The population of the world, which reached an estimated 3.7 billion in mid-1971, continued to increase at about 2% per year. At that rate world population will double in some 35 years. The rates of increase, however, ranged from 3.4% in Central America down to 0.6% in northwestern Europe. If the current trend continues, not only will the overall size become more and more unmanageable, but the underdeveloped countries will account for ever-larger proportions of the world's total.

U. S. POST-CENSUS DEVELOPMENTS

The sharp and sometimes irresponsible criticism of the 1970 U. S. census, which may have hampered the enumeration, continued after the count was in.

The Census Bureau itself estimated that there had been an underenumeration of less than 3%, a better record than in any previous count. This error would not be very important if it were equally distributed among all the sectors of the population. But, in fact, it is concentrated among certain subgroups, particularly young Negro males.

The National Research Council issued a report, *America's Uncounted People,* calling attention to the broad consequences of the error. "Failure to count some people in a census," the report stated, "may be viewed as a symptom of some social problem that cannot be adequately understood until the missing individuals are found and their life circumstances are fully described." But neither the council nor

BALDER, TRANSWORLD FEATURES

INDIA promotes voluntary sterilization as part of the attempt to curb its overpopulation. Men who agree to vasectomies are given money and goods by the government. Here, men are entertained by dancers and musicians while waiting to be sterilized.

any of the other critics could suggest any improvement in the Census Bureau's own strenuous efforts to achieve a full count. Persons on the move, with no job or permanent home, are most likely to be overlooked. Also, they often have reasons for evading any survey by a public authority.

1971 Estimate. According to the Census Bureau estimate, the total U. S. population (including armed forces overseas) was about 207.6 million on Oct. 1, 1971. This represented an increase of about 1.0% over the estimate for October 1970, or slightly less than the 1.1% increase during the 1970 calendar year. Most experts were surprised by this fact, for they had expected U. S. fertility to continue its recent rise.

TRENDS IN U. S. FERTILITY

The crude birthrate (the number of births per 1,000 population) depends not only on how many children parents have, but on how many persons there are who have children. As the number of women in the prime child-bearing ages, 20 to 29 years, was increasing by about 4% per year, the number of births (and thus the birthrate) should have risen even if the average family size remained the same. Indeed, this expectation was realized up to 1970, when the birthrate of 18.3 per 1,000 population was the highest in almost 20 years. But in the following year there was an unanticipated drop.

	12 Months Ending in August			
	1968	1969	1970	1971
Birthrate	17.4	17.6	18.0	17.7
Death rate	9.6	9.6	9.4	9.3
Natural increase	7.8	8.0	8.6	8.4

The reasons for this lower birthrate can be divided into two classes—those related to desired family size and those related to improved means of realizing this size.

Desired Family Size. For the past 35 years the Gallup organization has asked a sample of the U. S. population how many children they would like. In the 1971 survey only 23% of the respondents said that the ideal number of children was four or more. This was the lowest ever reported by a Gallup poll. Only four years earlier, in 1967, 40% gave this response, and in 1945 the figure was 49%. Moreover, among those aged 21 to 29 years—the sector of the population that would be expected to contribute most to a rising fertility—only 15% said they considered four or more children to constitute an ideal family.

One can only guess at why the average parent wanted fewer children. It may be that the widespread publicity given to ecological issues was reflected at a personal level. More specific economic trends may have been relevant. For example, such solid middle-class types as engineers and other technicians, who suffered most from economic dislocations during 1970 and 1971, may have decided to reduce the size of their families.

Wider Birth Control. Such contraceptive means as "the pill" (oral contraceptive) or the intrauterine device are, on a mass base, slightly more effective than the pessary, spermicidal jelly, or condom that they in part replaced. But a more important factor in birth control, probably, was the wider dissemination of birth-control means. These means became available through public clinics and hospitals in

(*Continued on page 552*)

─────────── VITAL STATISTICS OF SELECTED COUNTRIES ───────────

	Estimated population mid-1971[1]	Birthrate per 1,000 population[2]	Death rate per 1,000 population[2]	Current population growth (percent)	Number of years to double population[3]	Population under 15 years (percent)[4]	Population projections to 1985 (millions)[1]	Per capita gross national product (U. S. $)[5]
World................	3,706,000,000	34	14	2.0	35	37	4,933	...
North America								
Canada.............	21,800,000	17.6	7.3	1.7	41	33	27.3	2,460
Cuba................	8,600,000	27	8	1.9	37	37	11.0	310
Dominican Republic.....	4,400,000	48	15	3.4	21	47	7.3	290
El Salvador.........	3,600,000	47	13	3.4	21	45	5.9	280
Guatemala..........	5,300,000	42	13	2.9	24	46	7.9	320
Haiti...............	5,400,000	44	20	2.5	28	42	7.9	70
Honduras...........	2,800,000	49	16	3.4	21	51	4.6	260
Mexico.............	52,500,000	42	9	3.4	21	46	84.4	530
Nicaragua..........	2,100,000	46	16	3.0	24	48	3.3	370
Puerto Rico.........	2,900,000	24	6	1.4	50	39	3.4	1,340
United States.........	207,100,000	18.2	9.3	1.1	63	30	241.7	3,980
South America								
Argentina...........	24,700,000	22	9	1.5	47	29	29.6	820
Bolivia.............	4,800,000	44	19	2.4	29	44	6.8	150
Brazil..............	95,700,000	38	10	2.8	25	43	142.6	250
Chile...............	10,000,000	34	11	2.3	31	40	13.6	480
Colombia...........	22,100,000	44	11	3.4	21	47	35.6	310
Ecuador............	6,300,000	45	11	3.4	21	48	10.1	220
Paraguay...........	2,500,000	45	11	3.4	21	45	4.1	230
Peru...............	14,000,000	43	11	3.1	23	45	21.6	380
Uruguay............	2,900,000	21	9	1.2	58	28	3.4	520
Venezuela..........	11,100,000	41	8	3.4	21	46	17.4	950
Europe								
Austria.............	7,500,000	16.5	13.4	0.4	175	24	8.0	1,320
Belgium............	9,700,000	14.6	12.4	0.4	175	24	10.4	1,810
Bulgaria............	8,600,000	17.0	9.5	0.7	100	24	9.4	770
Czechoslovakia......	14,800,000	15.5	11.2	0.5	140	25	16.2	1,240
Denmark............	5,000,000	14.6	9.8	0.5	140	24	5.5	2,070
Finland.............	4,700,000	14.5	9.8	0.4	175	27	5.0	1,720
France.............	51,500,000	16.7	11.3	0.7	100	25	57.6	2,130
Germany, East.......	16,200,000	14.0	14.3	0.1	700	22	16.9	1,430
Germany, West.......	58,900,000	15.0	12.0	0.4	175	23	62.3	1,970
Greece.............	9,000,000	17.4	8.2	0.8	88	25	9.7	740
Hungary............	10,300,000	15.0	11.3	0.4	175	23	11.0	980
Ireland.............	3,000,000	21.5	11.5	0.7	100	31	3.5	980
Italy...............	54,100,000	17.6	10.1	0.8	88	24	60.0	1,230
Netherlands.........	13,100,000	19.2	8.4	1.1	63	28	15.3	1,620
Norway.............	3,900,000	17.6	9.9	0.9	78	25	4.5	2,000
Poland.............	33,300,000	16.3	8.1	0.9	78	30	38.2	880
Portugal............	9,600,000	19.8	10.6	0.7	100	29	10.7	460
Rumania............	20,600,000	23.3	10.1	1.3	54	26	23.3	780
Spain..............	33,600,000	20.2	9.2	1.0	70	27	38.1	730
Sweden............	8,100,000	13.5	10.4	0.5	140	21	8.8	2,620
Switzerland.........	6,400,000	16.5	9.3	1.1	63	23	7.4	2,490
United Kingdom........	56,300,000	16.6	11.9	0.5	140	23	61.8	1,790
USSR..............	245,000,000	17.0	8.1	1.0	70	28	286.9	1,110
Yugoslavia..........	20,800,000	18.8	9.2	1.0	70	30	23.8	510
Africa								
Algeria.............	14,500,000	50	17	3.3	21	47	23.9	220
Congo (Zaïre)........	17,800,000	44	21	2.3	31	42	25.8	90
Ethiopia............	25,600,000	46	25	2.1	33	..	35.7	70
Kenya..............	11,200,000	50	20	3.1	23	46	17.9	130
Morocco............	16,300,000	50	15	3.3	21	46	26.2	190
Nigeria.............	56,500,000	50	25	2.6	27	43	84.7	70
South Africa...........	20,600,000	40	16	2.4	29	40	29.7	650
Sudan..............	16,300,000	49	18	3.2	22	47	26.0	100
Tanzania............	13,600,000	47	22	2.6	27	42	20.3	80
United Arab Republic....	34,900,000	44	15	2.8	25	43	52.3	170
Asia								
Afghanistan..........	17,400,000	50	26	2.5	28	..	25.0	80
Burma..............	28,400,000	40	17	2.3	31	40	39.2	70
Ceylon.............	12,900,000	32	8	2.4	29	41	17.7	180
China (Mainland)......	772,900,000	33	15	1.8	39	..	964.6	90
China (Taiwan)........	14,300,000	26	5	2.3	31	44	19.4	270
India................	569,500,000	42	17	2.6	27	41	807.6	100
Indonesia...........	124,900,000	47	19	2.9	24	42	183.8	100
Iran................	29,200,000	48	18	3.0	24	46	45.0	310
Japan..............	104,700,000	18	7	1.1	63	25	121.3	1,190
Korea, North..........	14,300,000	39	11	2.8	25	..	20.7	250
Korea, South..........	32,900,000	36	11	2.5	28	42	45.9	180
Malaysia............	11,100,000	37	8	2.8	25	44	16.4	330
Nepal..............	11,500,000	45	23	2.2	32	40	15.8	80
Pakistan............	141,600,000	50	18	3.3	21	45	224.2	100
Philippines..........	39,400,000	46	12	3.4	21	47	64.0	180
Thailand............	37,400,000	42	10	3.3	21	43	57.7	150
Turkey.............	36,500,000	43	16	2.7	26	44	52.8	310
Vietnam, North........	21,600,000	...	...	2.1	33	..	28.2	90
Vietnam, South........	18,300,000	...	...	2.1	33	..	23.9	130
Oceania								
Australia.............	12,800,000	20.0	9.1	1.9	37	29	17.0	2,070
New Zealand..........	2,900,000	22.5	8.7	1.7	41	33	3.8	2,000

[1] Estimates from United Nations. [2] Latest available year. North American rates computed by Population Reference Bureau; others from United Nations, adjusted for deficient registration in some countries. [3] Assuming continued growth at current annual rate. [4] Latest available year. Derived from United Nations. [5] 1968 data from International Bank for Reconstruction and Development. Source: Population Reference Bureau, Washington, D. C.

(*Continued from page 550*)
many jurisdictions throughout the country, and this implicit official approval undoubtedly helped dissipate the residual hostility to contraception.

Birth Control Among Catholics. According to a survey of Roman Catholic priests conducted in 1971 by Dr. Thomas K. Burch of the Population Council, only 13% believed that most Catholic couples control their family size exclusively by "rhythm," the only church-sanctioned method. Of all the priests surveyed, 42% said that they advised parishioners to follow their own consciences rather than the church's teaching with respect to birth control. And among priests aged 20 to 29 years this proportion was 78%, falling through successive age categories to only 17% among those 70 and over. Furthermore, 77% believed that the use of "the pill" is morally licit or neutral, so long as it is used ostensibly to regularize the menstrual cycle.

Also during 1971, a reportedly more effective control of fertility by means of periodic abstinence —that is by using the rhythm method—was described at a meeting of the American Chemical Society. According to the paper presented, a woman could easily check her menstrual cycle each day by placing in her mouth a paper strip treated with a particular chemical. When she begins to ovulate, her saliva will acquire an enzyme called alkaline phosphatase, which turns the paper blue. The test is supposed to be accurate in 8 out of 10 cases, which makes it a better indicator than any presently in use.

In short, one important group that for various reasons used to have relatively large families, the Roman Catholics, seem to be moving closer to the norm set by their class position or urban residence.

Abortion. More important to family planning than contraceptive innovations has been the extraordinarily rapid legalization of abortion. This was brought about mainly through the courts, which in a series of cases declared laws prohibiting the operation to be unconstitutional. In almost half of the states, abortions were legal under varying conditions by 1971. In effect, with only the minor inconvenience of a trip to another jurisdiction, they were therefore legal throughout the United States. Once again, this implicit public approval probably loosened the controls that still formally remained. For instance, if one indication of the need for abortion was that of a threat to the woman's health, physicians often seemed to interpret this to mean her psychological health, which could be damaged by giving birth to an unwanted child.

In the 14 states (plus the District of Columbia) that reported on the matter to the vital statistics office in Washington, a total of over 175,000 legal abortions were performed in 1970. This was equivalent to 178 per 1,000 live births, ranging from 894 in New York City (the highest rate) down to quite low rates in some of the reporting areas. Overall, about 60% of the women were under 25, and about 66% were unmarried.

What effect legal abortion has had, and will have, on the birthrate is almost impossible to determine, for one would have to compare the numbers of legal and illegal abortions. The latter figure was certainly much larger, but many women would not undergo an illegal operation because of the high cost, a lack of trust in the abortionist, or an inability to find one. Undoubtedly some of these women are taking advantage of the opportunity to have a legal abortion, and will do so in the future.

PROJECTION OF THE U. S. POPULATION

Based on the results of the 1970 count, a new projection of the U. S. population was prepared by the Census Bureau (*Current Population Reports,* Series P-25, No. 470, November 1971). Mortality and net migration into the country could be predicted with relative certainty, but the trend in fertility— as in all forecasts during the past decades—remained a problem. The Census Bureau prepared projections based on four postulates, that the number of children born to the average woman after completion of her childbearing would be as follows: Series B (unchanged from 1970), 3.10; Series C, 2.78; Series D, 2.45; and Series E, 2.11. The extrapolations are shown in the accompanying table.

Total Population of the United States, 1970–2000

	Series B	Series C	Series D	Series E
1960		180,667,000		
1970		204,800,000		
1980	236,725,000	233,798,000	230,855,000	227,765,000
1990	278,570,000	269,673,000	260,762,000	251,431,000
2000	322,277,000	305,111,000	288,293,000	271,082,000

The results are somewhat startling. If the average woman has only 3.1 children—hardly a large family by current norms—the population at the end of the century would be more than 59% larger. And even if the average falls to barely more than two children, the lowest projection included, the increase would still be by almost a third—because of the growth potential in the current age structure. It is hardly likely that the country will realize the announced aim of some groups, to fall to a rate of zero population growth by the year 2000.

TRENDS IN MORTALITY

May 14, 1941, marked the 175th anniversary of the first vaccination against smallpox, and during this period this disease was transformed from one of the most dreaded killers to a declining remnant. The worldwide eradication program that the World Health Organization launched in 1967 seems to have been successful. The number of countries reporting smallpox cases fell from 91 in 1945 to 23 in 1970 and an estimated 6 in 1971. And the worldwide totals of 30,000 cases in 1970 and an estimated 25,000 in 1971 were the lowest ever recorded by WHO.

Such successes, however, should not be projected into the diseaseless world that some overoptimistic persons seem to expect. Plague, the scourge of the Middle Ages, is still extant and recently spread with the speed of air travel into areas never before infected. The 10 million East Pakistani refugees, living under conditions of extreme poverty, are close to the traditional source of plague epidemics.

In the United States the 19,997 cases of infectious syphilis reported for January–October 1971 was a sizable increase over the 18,428 cases in the comparable period of 1970. The record of some other preventable diseases is even more discouraging. In the epidemiological year (which runs from the 41st week of one calendar year through the 40th week of the next one) 1970–71 there were 77,682 reported cases of measles, an increase of 74% over 1969–70 and of 225% over 1967–68. Most of these patients were unvaccinated children. As in other instances, the breakthrough in clinical medicine could not be sustained in public health.

WILLIAM PETERSEN, *Ohio State University*

PORTUGAL

Confronted with guerrilla warfare in the African territories and dissent at home, Premier Marcello Caetano of Portugal appeared to be growing more conservative in 1971. Previously steering a cautious balance between stability and change, he showed more confidence in his third full year of office and pursued stronger policies. He also had to appease members of the extreme right, who objected to his proposals for constitutional reforms, especially those involving a measure of political and administrative autonomy for the overseas provinces. Caetano's stronger policies met widespread protest from students and labor. There were also instances of sabotage and subversion during the year.

The Portuguese National Assembly, meeting in special session from June through August, approved constitutional reforms relating to the autonomy of the overseas territories, greater religious freedom, and the abolition of press censorship. Premier Caetano, in calling the session, stressed his determination to combat sabotage in Portugal. In November the government announced that it would invoke a provision of the newly revised constitution authorizing the government to adopt "such restrictions on individual liberties and guarantees as are seen to be indispensable" to repress subversion at times when declaration of a state of siege is not justified.

Subversion and Unrest. Militant activists, including Communists, formed a clandestine organization, known as Armed Revolutionary Action (ARA), to sabotage the colonial war effort. In March it claimed credit for an attack on the Tancos air base. It was also blamed for an attack on NATO headquarters near Lisbon in November.

Early in January 1971 the police were called upon twice to restrain student agitation in Lisbon. Students protesting the government's threat to end draft deferments were officially warned that if subversion should continue they would be conscripted at age 21. The Advanced Technical Institute, site of a protest meeting, was closed indefinitely. Four students were imprisoned for membership in the outlawed Communist party and for subversive activities. On February 16–17, 9,000 students of the University of Coimbra struck in protest against an earlier arrest of eight students in Lisbon.

On March 15 the police, armed and with dogs, dispersed a peaceful demonstration of 3,000 saleswomen in Lisbon, who were demanding a 44-hour work week. The government charged the Lisbon Syndicate of Store Employees with "inciting disturbances of public order." Representatives of 15 unions, meeting in Oporto in April, denounced police brutality and demanded adherence to the principles of the International Labor Organization.

On July 26, Lisbon police clashed with some 1,500 bank clerks protesting the arrest of their union secretary. The interior ministry charged that Communists had infiltrated the union and ordered the termination of its activities in Lisbon and Oporto. The secretary of the journalists' union and his wife, a member of the store clerks' union, were both arrested in August, charged with subversion.

Between January and August 1971 the number of persons detained on political charges more than doubled. According to the National Commission for Aid to Political Prisoners, the arrests involved "indiscriminate jailing, torture and beating, and the systematic refusal of legal aid."

In February a former chancellor of the archdiocese of Luanda, Angola, the Rev. Joaquim Pinto de Andrade, was charged with involvement in the nationalist movement in Angola and tried in Lisbon. The defendant, a mulatto, denied the charges, claiming that he was a victim of racial persecution. He was convicted along with nine others. On April 26 a military court in Lisbon convicted Capt. Pedro Rodriguez Peralta of the Cuban army of having served as a training instructor and adviser to the African party for the Independence of Guinea and Cape Verde. The prosecution was unable to prove that Rodriguez had taken up arms against the Portuguese, but he was sentenced to 26 months in prison.

Shipyard. In June plans were approved for construction of what will be Europe's largest shipyard, in the Sado River estuary near Setubal. A $70 million project, the shipyard is expected to be capable of building 700,000-ton supertankers by 1973.

Census. On January 25, Portugal concluded its decennial national census. Many Portuguese were intimidated by the complicated forms and the threat of heavy fines for failure to comply. Some feared the forms would be turned over to the secret police or prove to be a tax trap. The returns revealed that the population of metropolitan Portugal, including Madeira and the Azores Islands, had declined 2% since 1960, to 8,668,000. The shortage in manpower threatens economic development.

International Relations. It was reported on January 5 that the United States had approved the sale of two Boeing 707 jets to the Portuguese government for service to Africa. U. S. Vice President Spiro Agnew concluded an international diplomatic tour with conferences with Premier Caetano and President Américo Thomaz in Lisbon on July 26. In May, Portugal withdrew from participation in UNESCO.

RHEA MARSH SMITH, *Rollins College*

--------- **PORTUGAL · Information Highlights** ---------

Official Name: Portuguese Republic.
Area: 35,553 square miles (92,082 sq km).
Population (1970 census): 8,668,000. *Density*, 253 per square mile (104 per sq km). *Annual rate of increase*, 0.9%.
Chief City (1968 est.): Lisbon, the capital, 828,000.
Government: *Head of state*, Américo Thomaz, president (took office June 9, 1958). *Head of government*, Marcello Caetano, premier (took office Sept. 27, 1968). *Legislature* —National Assembly (unicameral), 130 members.
Language: Portuguese (official).
Education: *Literacy rate* (1970), 65% of population. *Expenditure on education* (1967), 7.9% of total public expenditure. *School enrollment* (1967)—primary, 904,120; secondary, 339,146; vocational, 169,666; university/higher, 39,209.
Finances (1970 est.): *Revenues*, $1,000,000,000; *expenditures*, $1,000,000,000; *monetary unit*, escudo (27.25 escudos equal U. S.$1, Dec. 30, 1971).
Gross National Product (1969): $5,662,000,000.
National Income (1969): $4,851,700,000; *national income per person*, $508.
Manufacturing (metric tons, 1969): Cement, 2,035,000; wheat flour, 441,000; crude steel, 402,000; canned fish, 29,800.
Crops (metric tons, 1969 crop year): Grapes (1968), 1,600,-000; potatoes, 1,126,000; wheat, 452,000; figs (1968), 219,-000 (ranks 2d among world producers).
Minerals (metric tons, 1969): Coal, 416,000; salt, 308,000; iron ore, 80,000; lignite, 8,000.
Foreign Trade (1970): *Exports*, $949,000,000 (chief exports (1970—wine, $63,757,000; cork, $58,120,000; fish, $34,-539,000. *Imports*, $1,582,000,000 (chief imports—nonelectrical machinery, $156,080,000; transport equipment, $122,-972,000; chemicals, $111,738,000; textile fibers and waste, $103,425,000). *Chief trading partners* (1968)—United Kingdom (took 21% of exports, supplied 13% of imports); Angola (13%—9%); United States (11%—7%).
Transportation: *Roads* (1968), 18,571 miles (29,886 km); *motor vehicles* (1969), 599,100 (automobiles, 492,800); *railroads* (1968), 2,248 miles (3,617 km); *merchant fleet* (1970), 870,-000 gross registered tons; *national airline*, Transportes Aereos Portugueses; *principal airport*, Lisbon.
Communications: *Telephones* (1970), 698,075; *television stations* (1968), 6; *television sets* (1969), 352,000; *radios* (1969), 1,406,000; *newspapers* (1967), 29.

U. S. Postal Service contract is signed by Postmaster General Blount as union chiefs look on. Free cover (*below*) marked service's first day of operation, July 1.

POSTAL SERVICE

On July 1, 1971, the establishment of the United States Postal Service as an independent agency of the federal government was completed. The last cabinet-level postmaster-general, Winton M. Blount, became the first postmaster-general in the new Postal Service. He resigned in October, and Elmer T. Klassen was appointed to the post, effective Jan. 1, 1972.

In fiscal 1971, the Postal Service spent $8,864,-712,000 and had revenues of $6,622,524,000. It had 728,911 employees, 31,957 post offices, and handled 87.1 billion pieces of mail.

Rates. Based on procedures that are set out in the Postal Reorganization Act of 1970 and utilizing the new Postal Rates Commission, the rates of mail delivery were raised from 6 to 8 cents per ounce for first class mail and from 10 to 11 cents for air mail, effective May 16. Proportionate increases in second and third class rates, which were to be phased over 5 years, were compressed in the first year to wipe out the $430 million deficit in these classes of mail. Although technically the increases were to be temporary, it is anticipated that the final decision of the Postal Rate Commission will be to adopt these rates.

Labor Relations. One of the major reasons for the passage of the Reorganization Act, and one of the areas where most changes were expected, was in the area of labor relations. Based on private sector collective bargaining patterns, negotiations between a combination of postal unions allied in a coalition known as CAPE—Council of American Postal Employees—and the new Postal Service commenced in January 1971. When an impasse developed, a neutral fact-finding committee issued a 20-page report with no recommendations, and unfair labor practice charges were filed by CAPE. With management's first money offer in late June, the logjam was broken. The desire of the parties to reach a bilateral agreement and the assistance of Assistant Secretary of Labor W. J. Usery produced on July 20, 1971, a 2-year contract covering more than 650,000 workers employed in seven postal crafts.

The Contract. The new contract or "working agreement" bypassed most issues other than those that dealt with wages and job security. It provided for an immediate $300 bonus payment, five $250 wage increases paid periodically through Jan. 20, 1973, and a possible cost-of-living increase of up to $160 per year effective in the second year of the contract. (Because of the wage-price freeze, the Oct. 20, 1971, payment was not made, nor were step increases paid to the personnel from August 15 to November 13.) The unions went to court to enforce payment, contending that the Postal Reorganization Act takes precedence over the Economic Stabilization Act of 1970, on which the wage-price freeze is premised.

Other major provisions of the agreement included the prohibition of any layoffs for any reason during the term of the contract, protection for employees whose jobs are eliminated by technological changes, the limiting of the use of "casual" or "substitute" noncareer employees, and a management rights clause. Issues were sent to joint labor-management study committees for investigation and recommendations. Fourteen major issues were referred to further negotiations, which started on August 16, with a provision for binding arbitration of those issues not resolved after 90 days. By November 13, the parties had agreed on 10 of these, including provisions for local negotiations, promotion procedures, and union-management cooperation; the other 4 went to binding arbitration at the end of 1971. Effective July 1, 1971, five of the seven negotiating unions merged into the American Postal Workers Union, and negotiations leading to a merger of the APWU and the letter-carriers' union were continuing at year-end.

New Programs and Developments. The Postal Service initiated many new programs. In order to free post offices of congestion and allow them to handle letters and other "preferential" mail more efficiently, the Service planned over 30 highly mechanized bulk-mail centers, with operating costs savings of $300,000,000 per year anticipated.

Expedited mail delivery took many forms. In large metropolitan areas, local first class zip-coded mail deposited by 5 P. M. on one day was delivered within the same metropolitan area the next day. A new guaranteed overnight service with premium rates linked 33 major city areas.

In order to make post offices more attractive places in which to work and visit, $40 million will be spent in the next few years to modernize 800 postal facilities in the United States. The number of self-service postal units was increased. Much time was given to product planning and development. A welcome innovation also was the naming of a consumers advocate, a type of ombudsman, to the top level of postal management.

New methods of delivery were tried out. Electronic facsimile transmission between Washington, D. C., and New York City, with premium charges for transmission and delivery, started on October 1. The Transcontinental Gas Pipe Line Corporation proposed the movement of bulk mail through low-pressure pipelines.

Other aspects of the Postal Service also produced important statistics. Complaints about obscene mail dropped 41% from 1970. Charged with responsibility under the Comprehensive Drug Abuse Prevention and Control Act, postal inspectors investigated 3,848 postal-related cases of crimes involving drugs. In all, a record number of 14,496 persons were convicted of breaking a wide variety of postal laws in fiscal 1971.

Problems. All was not rosy for the new operation, however. Many complaints were received about the decline of the quality of service between nonmetropolitan areas. The U. S. Congress had not, as yet, completely adjusted to its more limited role; most personnel decisions were made by bilateral collective bargaining, and operating decisions were made by the new independent system. With the anticipated rise of second and third class rates, some mail is now being handled by a growing number of private delivery systems.

Outlook. Although the record was far from clear and the testing process had only just started, the promise of the Postal Reorganization Act was being met, with minor exceptions, in the operating and personnel areas. The long-range prospects in the fiscal area were still a matter of question. If they are favorably resolved, the act will have been judged to be a most productive piece of legislation.

HARVEY L. FRIEDMAN
University of Massachusetts

POVERTY. See SOCIAL WELFARE.
POWELL, Lewis F., Jr. See BIOGRAPHY.

PRINCE EDWARD ISLAND

During 1971, Prince Edward Island's economy remained strong despite a decline in agriculture. Tourism was up, and unemployment was low relative to the other maritime provinces. Total investment was also up, but primary industries, trade, finance, and commercial services declined.

Industrial Development. Industrial Enterprises, Inc. (IE), a crown corporation to promote industrial development, made loans to industry totaling more than $2 million. The bankruptcy of Seabrook Frozen Foods led IE to assume direction of it and seek ways to return it to private interests.

Major Legislation. The environmental control commission act provided for the establishment of a commission to preserve all aspects of the physical environment and to provide funds for municipal and industrial pollution abatement. The Prince Edward Island labor act consolidated legislation in five statutes, resulting in a comprehensive labor code based on a 2-year review of labor laws. Legislation introduced in the fall session of the Legislature included an education act that will consolidate school districts and establish a foundation program.

Farmers' Protest. Through the National Farmers Union, island farmers have been demanding legislation to abolish corporate farms, establish low-interest loans, discontinue the gasoline tax for farm trucks, and lower vehicle registration fees. On August 21–22, farmers blocked the main access route to the island, and union president Roy Atkinson was charged with conspiracy to intimidate.

ANDREW S. HARVEY, *Dalhousie University*

– PRINCE EDWARD ISLAND • Information Highlights –

Area: 2,184 square miles (5,656 sq km).
Population: 111,000 (April 1971 est.).
Chief Cities (1966 census): Charlottetown, the capital (18,-427); Summerside (10,042).
Government: *Chief Officers*—lt. gov., V. George McKay; premier, Alexander B. Campbell (Liberal); prov. secy. and min. of finance, T. Earle Hickey (L); atty. gen., and min. of education, Gordon L. Bennett (L); chief justice, C. St. Clair Trainor. *Legislature*—Legislative Assembly (convened June 2, 1970); 32 members (27 Liberal, 5 Progressive-Conservative).
Education: *School enrollment* (1968–69 est.)—public elementary and secondary, 29,217 pupils (1,397 teachers); private schools, 140 pupils (11 teachers); Indian (federal) schools, 53 pupils (2 teachers); college and university, 1,369 students. *Public school expenditures* (1971 est.)—$8,282,000; *average teacher's salary* (1968–69 est.), $5,000.
Public Finance (fiscal year 1971 est.): *Revenues*, $81,830,000 (sales tax, $14,750,000; income tax, $4,932,000; federal funds, $50,291,000). *Expenditures*, $79,660,000 (education, $20,250,000; health and social welfare, $23,460,000).
Personal Income (1969 est.): $200,000,000.
Social Welfare (fiscal year 1971 est.): $7,830,000 (aged and blind, $3,160,000; dependents and unemployed, $3,790,-000).
Manufacturing (1968): *Value added by manufacture*, $16,569,-000 (food and beverages, $11,370,000).
Agriculture (1969 est.): *Cash farm income* (exclusive of govt. payments), $37,875,000 (livestock, $23,132,000; crops, 1968 est., $11,366,000). *Chief crops* (cash receipts)—Potatoes, $9,127,000 (ranks 4th among the provinces); vegetables, 1967 est., $841,000; fruits, $404,000.
Fisheries (1969 est.): *Commercial catch*, 49,000,000 pounds ($9,000,000). *Leading species* (1968)—Lobster, 8,731,000 pounds ($5,329,000); mackerel, 7,111,000 pounds ($209,-000); cod, 6,207,000 pounds ($286,000).
Transportation: *Roads* (1968), 3,280 miles (5,278 km); *motor vehicles* (1969), 38,812; *railroads* (1969), 254 track miles (409 km); *licensed airports* (1970), 2.
Communications: *Telephones* (1969), 32,357; *television stations* (1970), 1; *radio stations* (1967), 2.

All figures given in Canadian dollars.

PRISONS. See special feature beginning on page 38.

NOBEL PRIZE winners for 1971 received their awards from King Gustav VI in Stockholm on December 13. From left are Simon Kuznets, economics; Earl Sutherland, medicine; Pablo Neruda, literature; Gerhard Herzberg, chemistry; and Dennis Gabor, physics. Not shown is Willy Brandt, West German chancellor, who received peace prize, which is presented in Norway.

PICTORIAL PARADE

PRIZES AND AWARDS

Prize committees honored individual and group achievement in many fields of endeavor in 1971. Two new awards in journalism focused special attention on the publication of the so-called Pentagon Papers, the U. S. Defense Department's secret study of the Vietnam War. The Drew Pearson Foundation awarded its first annual Drew Pearson Prize to Neil Sheehan of the New York *Times* for his reporting of the Pentagon study. The first Freedom of Information Citation of the Associated Press Managing Editors Association was won by the New York *Times* for its publication of the historic documents.

A selected list of the most important and newsworthy prizes and awards announced in 1971 follows.

NOBEL PRIZES

On Dec. 10, 1971, the 75th anniversary of the death of Swedish manufacturer Alfred B. Nobel, the annual Nobel prizes were presented to winners in the five classifications established in his will—peace, literature, chemistry, physics, and physiology or medicine. On the same day the Alfred Nobel Memorial Prize in Economic Science, established in 1969 by the Bank of Sweden, was presented for the third successive year. The 1971 awards were each worth the equivalent of 450,000 Swedish crowns, or about $90,000.

Pablo Neruda, Chilean poet and diplomat, was awarded the prize for literature; Willy Brandt, the West German chancellor, for peace; and Simon Kuznets, retired Harvard professor, for economics. (For separate articles on these three winners, see BIOGRAPHY.)

Chemistry. The 1971 Nobel Prize for chemistry was won by Gerhard Herzberg, a 66-year-old scientist at the National Research Council in Ottawa, Canada. He was born in Germany, fled from the Nazi regime to Canada in 1935, and became a Canadian citizen. Herzberg was honored in 1971 for his pioneering work in molecular spectroscopy. Using this technique, he determined the structures of many diatomic and polyatomic molecules, including the structures of many free radicals—short-lived molecular fragments whose activities are crucial to many chemical reactions. He also identified certain molecules in planetary atmospheres, comets, and interstellar space.

Physics. The 1971 Nobel Prize for physics was won by Dennis Gabor, a 71-year-old professor emeritus at the Imperial College of Science and Technology, London, England, and a staff scientist at the CBS Laboratories in Stamford, Conn. Gabor was born in Hungary, fled Nazi Germany, and became a naturalized Briton. He was honored in 1971 for his invention of holography. It is a method in which light waves scattered by an object are recorded as an interference pattern on a photographic plate. When this record is placed in a light beam, the original wave pattern is regenerated, and the observer sees in space an extremely realistic three-dimensional image of the object. Although Gabor invented holography in 1948, it became a practical technique only after the invention of the laser in 1960.

Physiology or Medicine. The 1971 Nobel Prize in physiology or medicine was awarded to Dr. Earl Wilbur Sutherland, Jr., "for his discoveries concerning the mechanisms of the action of hormones." The 55-year-old, Kansas-born professor of physiology at the Vanderbilt University School of Medicine in Nashville, Tenn., began his hormone research some 25 years ago. Working on the role of adrenalin in carbohydrate metabolism, Sutherland found that the process occurs by means of an intermediary substance subsequently identified as cyclic adenosine monophosphate, or cyclic AMP. Later he showed that cyclic AMP acts as an intermediary substance in the mechanisms by which various hormones control the metabolic processes of the body and that cyclic AMP is present in bacteria. His basic research has opened up new avenues of medical investigation into hormones.

PULITZER PRIZES

Winners of the Pulitzer Prizes were announced by the president of Columbia University on May 3, 1971. Each prize was worth $1,000 except the public service gold medal. For the first time in seven years, no award for fiction was given.

Journalism. Local general reporting—the staff of the Akron, Ohio, *Beacon Journal,* for its coverage of the disorders at Kent State University in May 1970. Local special reporting—William Hugh Jones of the Chicago *Tribune,* for exposing the bribing of policemen to refer poor sick people to private ambulance companies. Editorial writing—Horance G. Davis, Jr., of the Gainesville, Fla., *Sun,* for editorials in support of peaceful desegregation of Gainesville schools. Editorial cartooning—Paul Conrad of the Los Angeles *Times.* International reporting—Jimmie Lee Hoagland of the Washington *Post,* for his articles on apartheid in South Africa. National reporting—Lucinda Franks and Thomas Powers of United Press International, for their series of articles on Diana Oughton, a radical student killed in a Greenwich Village bomb factory. Spot news photography—John Paul Filo, a photography student, for his photograph of a girl kneeling over a slain student at Kent State University in May 1970. Feature photography—Jack Dykinga of the Chicago *Sun-Times,* for photographs of children in state schools for the retarded. Commentary—William A. Caldwell of the Hackensack, N. J., *Record,* for his daily column on local affairs. Criticism—Harold C. Schonberg, music critic of the New York *Times.* Meritorious public service—the Winston-Salem, N. C., *Journal* and *Sentinel,* for coverage of environmental problems.

Letters. History—James MacGregor Burns, for *Roosevelt: The Soldier of Freedom.* Biography—Lawrance Thompson, for *Robert Frost: The Years of Triumph, 1915–1938.* Poetry—William S. Merwin, for *The Carrier of Ladders.* Drama—Paul Zindel, for *The Effect of Gamma Rays on Man-in-the-Moon Marigolds.* General nonfiction—John Toland, for *The Rising Sun,* an account of Japan during World War II.

Music. Mario Davidovsky, for *Synchronisms No. 6 for Piano and Electronic Sound.*

ARTS

American Composers Alliance, Laurel Leaf Award for "distinguished service to contemporary music"—the Alice M. Ditson Fund of Columbia University.

American Institute of Architects Gold Medal—Louis I. Kahn.

American Institute of Graphic Arts Gold Medal—Will Burtin.

Bard Awards of the City Club of New York for excellence in architecture and urban design—Carl J. Petrilli, Marcel Breuer, and Hamilton Smith.

Brandeis University, Creative Arts Awards ($1,000 each): film—Charles Chaplin, Bruce Baillie; poetry—Richard Wilbur, James Wright; music—Earl Kim, John Harbison; sculpture—Louise Nevelson, Claes Oldenburg; special award for creative achievement in the dance—George Balanchine.

Capezio Dance Award ($1,000)—Arthur Mitchell, dancer and founder-director of the Harlem Dance Theater.

James P. Johnson Award of the Rutgers Institute of Jazz Studies—Earl Hines, jazz pianist.

Edward MacDowell Medal of the MacDowell Colony for "exceptional contributions to the arts"—William Schuman, composer and former president of the Lincoln Center for the Performing Arts.

Metropolitan Opera National Council Awards ($2,000 each) —Barbara Pearson, soprano; Thomas McKinney, baritone.

Dmitri Mitropoulos International Music Competition Awards —Jacques Delacote ($5,000), Wolfgang Balzer ($3,000), and Timothy Reynish ($2,000), conductors.

National Academy of Recording Arts and Sciences, Grammy Awards for excellence in phonograph records: album —Bridge Over Troubled Water, sung by Simon and Garfunkel; classical album—Berlioz: Les Troyens, by the Royal Opera House Orchestra and Chorus, conducted by Colin Davis; classical performance, orchestra—Le Sacre du printemps, conducted by Pierre Boulez; song of the year—Bridge Over Troubled Water by Simon and Garfunkel; new artist—the Carpenters; contemporary female vocal performance—Dionne Warwick for I'll Never Fall in Love Again; contemporary male vocal performance—Ray Stevens for Everything is Beautiful; contemporary vocal performance by a group—the Carpenters for Close to You; female rhythm and blues performance—Aretha Franklin for Don't Play That Song; male rhythm and blues performance—B. B. King for The Thrill is Gone; rhythm and blues performance by a group—the Delfonics for Didn't I; female country performance—Lynn Anderson for Rose Garden; male country performance—Ray Price for For the Good Times; country performance by a group—Johnny Cash and June Carter for If I Were a Carpenter; opera recording—Berlioz: Les Troyens; spoken word recording—Martin Luther King, Jr., for Why I Oppose the War in Vietnam; record of the year—Bridge Over Troubled Water by Simon and Garfunkel.

National Academy of Design, Benjamin Altman Awards—Ann Poor and Sidney Laufman.

National Institute of Arts and Letters awards: art ($3,000) —Ilya Bolotowsky, Robert Goodnough, Alfred Leslie, Norman Lewis, Ludwig Sander, Hedda Sterne, and Harold Tovish; music ($3,000)—Sydney P. Hodkinson, Fred Lerdahl, Roger Reynolds, and Loren Rush; gold medal for sculpture—Alexander Calder; gold medal for music—Elliott C. Carter; Arnold W. Brunner Memorial Prize in Architecture ($1,000)—John Andrews; Marjorie Peabody Waite Award ($1,500)—Ben Behn; Richard and Hinda Rosenthal Foundation Award ($2,000)—Christopher Brookhouse and Donald Perlis; Charles E. Ives Award—Vivian Perlis.

Naumburg Foundation, Naumburg Award ($5,000)—Zola Shaulis and Kun-Woo Paik, pianists.

JOURNALISM

American Medical Association, Medical Journalism Award ($1,000)—Frank Carey of the Associated Press.

American Newspaper Guild, Heywood Broun Memorial Award ($1,000)—Donald Singleton of the New York Daily News.

Maria Moors Cabot Gold Medals for "distinguished journalistic contributions to the advancement of inter-American understanding" ($1,000)—Georgie Anne Geyer of the Chicago Daily News; Julio S. García, director general of Excelsior of Mexico City; Juan Carlos Colombres of Buenos Aires, whose editorial cartoons appear in numerous Argentine publications.

Raymond Clapper Memorial Award for "exceptionally meritorious Washington correspondence" ($1,000)—Jared D. Stout of Newhouse News Service, Max Frankel of the New York Times.

Sidney Hillman Foundation Awards for achievement in the communications field ($500)—John Kifner, Ramsey Clark, Christopher H. Pyle, and the Columbia Broadcasting System.

Freedom of Information Citation of the Associated Press Managing Editors Association—the New York Times, for its publication of the Pentagon Papers.

Long Island University, George Polk Memorial Awards: foreign reporting—Gloria Emerson of the New York Times; national reporting—the Knight newspapers; metropolitan reporting—Richard Oliver of the New York Daily News; community service—Karl Grossman of the Long Island Press; editorials—James F. Clayton of the Washington Post; magazine reporting—the Washington Monthly; television reporting—Alan Levin of National Educational Television; news photography—John Darnell, John Filo, and Howard Ruffner; criticism—Pauline Kael of the New Yorker magazine; book—Otto Fried-

rich for Decline and Fall; freedom of the press award—Walter Cronkite of CBS; special award—I. F. Stone, political writer and editor.

National Magazine Awards, sponsored by Columbia University's Graduate School of Journalism—The Nation, Rolling Stone, Vogue, Esquire, and the Atlantic Monthly.

Overseas Press Club awards: George Polk Memorial Award for the best reporting requiring exceptional courage and enterprise abroad ($500)—John Laurence, Keith Kay, James Clevenger, and Russ Bensley of CBS for The World of Charlie Company; Robert Capa Gold Medal for photography—Kyoichi Sawada of United Press International; Asia Magazine Award—Harvey Meyerson for his book Vinh Long; Vision Magazine Ed Stout Award for reporting on Latin America—David Belnap of the Los Angeles Times; book on foreign affairs—John Toland for The Rising Sun; magazine reporting from abroad—Robert Shaplen of the New Yorker magazine; television reporting from abroad—Kenley Jones of NBC; television interpretation of foreign affairs—Ted Koppel of ABC; radio reporting from abroad—Lou Cioffi of ABC and the team coverage of CBS radio reporters; radio interpretation of foreign affairs—NBC Radio News; cartoon on foreign affairs—Tom Darcy of Long Island's Newsday; photographic reporting from abroad in a magazine or book—Larry Burrows of Life magazine; daily newspaper or wire service photographic reporting from abroad—Dennis Cook of United Press International; daily newspaper or wire service reporting on foreign affairs—John Hughes of the Christian Science Monitor.

Drew Pearson Prize for excellence in investigative reporting ($5,000)—Neil Sheehan of the New York Times, for his reporting on the Pentagon Papers, the U. S. Defense Department's secret study of the Vietnam War.

Thomas L. Stokes Award for journalistic contributions to the protection of the environment ($1,000)—Gladwin Hill of the New York Times.

LITERATURE

Academy of American Poets Fellowship Award ($10,000)—Howard Nemerov.

American Library Association Awards: Newbery Medal—Betsy Byars for Summer of the Swans; Caldecott Medal—Gail E. Haley, illustrator, for A Story, A Story; Beta Phi Mu Award ($50)—Leon Carnovsky, professor at the Graduate Library School of the University of Chicago; Joseph W. Lippincott Award ($1,000)—William S. Dix, librarian at Princeton University; Francis Joseph Campbell Medal—Mrs. Ranald H. MacDonald, founder of Recording for the Blind; Melvil Dewey Award—William J. Welsh, director of the Processing Department of the Library of Congress; Margaret Mann Citation—Henriette D. Avram, chief of the MARC Development Office of the Library of Congress; Clarence Day Award—Dee Alexander Brown, agriculture librarian at the University of Illinois, Urbana; Grolier Award—Sara L. Diebert, coordinator of Work with Young Adults, Enoch Pratt Free Library.

Bancroft Prize of Columbia University for distinguished writing in U. S. history and international relations ($1,000 each)—Erik Barnouw for The Image Empire; David M. Kennedy for Birth Control in America: The Career of Margaret Sanger; Joseph Frazier Wall for Andrew Carnegie.

Black Academy of Arts and Letters Awards ($500 each): nonfiction—George Jackson for Soledad Brother: The Prison Letters of George Jackson; fiction—William Melvin Kelley for Dunsford Travels Everywhere; poetry—Mari Evans for I Am a Black Woman; scholarly work—Franklin W. Knight for Slave Society in Cuba During the Nineteenth Century.

Bollingen Foundation, Bollingen Prize in Poetry ($5,000)—Richard P. Wilbur for Walking to Sleep and Mona Van Duyn for To See, To Take.

Booker Prize, sponsored by the British Publishers Association ($12,000)—V. S. Naipaul for In a Free State.

Carey-Thomas Award for a distinguished project of creative book publishing—Random House, Chanticleer Press, and Maecenas Press of Paris, joint publishers of Picasso 347, a 2-volume edition of Pablo Picasso's erotic drawings.

Goncourt Prize in literature—Jacques Laurent for Les Bêtises.

Governor General's Awards (Canadian): French fiction—Monique Bosco; French nonfiction—Fernand Ouellette; French drama—Jacques Brault; French poetry—Michael Ondaatje; English fiction—Dave Godfrey; English poetry—bpNichol.

Mystery Writers of America, Edgar Allan Poe ("Edgar") Awards for 1970: mystery novel—Maj Sjowall and Per Wahloo for The Laughing Policeman; first mystery novel—Lawrence Sanders for The Anderson Tapes; mystery short story—Margery Finn Brown for In the Forest of Riga the Beasts are Very Wild Indeed; true-crime book—Mildred Savage for A Great Fall.

National Book Awards ($1,000 each): fiction—Saul Bellow for Mr. Sammler's Planet; arts and letters—Francis Steegmuller for Cocteau; science, philosophy, and religion—Raymond Phineas Stearns for *Science in the British Colonies of America,* posthumously; biography—James MacGregor Burns for *Roosevelt: The Soldier of Freedom;* poetry—Mona Van Duyn for *To See, To Take;* translation—Frank Jones for his translation of *Saint Joan of the Stockyards* by Bertold Brecht, and Edward G. Seidensticker for his translation of *The Sound of the Mountain* by Yasunari Kawabata; children's literature—Lloyd Alexander for *The Marvelous Misadventures of Sebastian.*

National Book Committee, National Medal for Literature ($5,000)—E. B. White.

National Institute of Arts and Letters awards in literature ($5,000): Wendell Berry, Stanley Burnshaw, Martin Duberman, Ronald L. Fair, Charles Gordone, Barbara Howes, Arthur Kopit, Leonard Michaels, Leonard Nathan, Reynolds Price, and Wilfrid Sheed.

P. E. N. American Center, Translation Award ($1,000)—Max Hayward for his translation into English of *Hope Against Hope* by Nadezhda Mandelshtam.

Poetry Society of America Awards: Gold Medal—Melville Cane for *Eloquent April;* Alice Fay di Castagnola Award for a work in progress ($3,500)—Marcia Lee Masters and Cornel Lengyel; Shelley Award ($1,800)—Adrienne Rich and Louise Townsend Rich; Melville Cane Award ($500)—Harold Bloom.

Nebula Awards of the Science Fiction Writers of America: novel—Larry Niven for *Ringworld;* novella—Fritz Leiber for *Ill Met at Lankhmar;* novelette—Theodore Sturgeon for *Slow Sculpture.*

PUBLIC SERVICE

Anisfield-Wolf Awards for the best scholarly work concerned with the problem of intergroup understanding ($750 each)—Carlton Mabee for *Black Freedom;* Robert W. July for *A History of the African People;* Anthony F. C. Wallace for *The Death and Rebirth of the Seneca: The History and Culture of the Great Iroquois Nation;* and Stan Steiner for *La Raza: The Mexican Americans.*

Max Berg Award for a "major achievement in prolonging or improving the quality of human life" ($10,000)—Ralph Nader.

Albert Einstein Commemorative Awards for outstanding contributions to man's betterment: Julius Axelrod, Gov. Luis Alberto Ferré of Puerto Rico, David Frost, Danny Kaye, and Paul A. Samuelson.

Family of Man Award of the New York Council of Churches —Whitney M. Young, Jr., posthumously.

Four Freedoms Foundation Award—Sen. Edmund S. Muskie.

Freedoms Foundation awards: George Washington Award ($5,000)—William Pierson; Defender of Freedom Award— Capt. Tibor Bierbaum.

Jerusalem Book Prize for a "contribution to the freedom of the individual in society"—Jorge Luis Borges.

National Conference of Christians and Jews, Charles Evans Hughes Awards for "courageous leadership"—Lucius D. Clay, Tom C. Clark, and Walter E. Washington.

New York Civil Liberties Union, Florina Lasker Civil Liberties Award ($1,000)—Fannie Lou Hamer and Rev. William McKinley Branch.

United Nations Commemorative Medal for "progress toward international good will and brotherhood"—Gov. Nelson Rockefeller.

SCIENCE AND TECHNOLOGY

American Academy of Arts and Sciences, Rumford Award —research teams from Massachusetts Institute of Technology, Cornell University, and the National Radio Astronomy Observatory, for their "pioneer work in interferometry."

American Cancer Society, Alfred P. Sloan Memorial Award for dedication to the cause of cancer control—Mrs. Alfred D. Lasker.

American Chemical Society, Priestley Medal—George B. Kistiakowsky.

American Geographical Society, Charles P. Daly Medal— Gilbert F. White.

American Heart Association, Research Achievement Award —Earl W. Sutherland, Jr., of the Vanderbilt University School of •Medicine.

American Institute of Aeronautics and Astronautics awards: Haley Astronautics Award ($500)—the Apollo 13 astronauts, James Lovell, John Swigert, and Fred Haise; Sylvanus Albert Reed Award ($500)—Ira G. Hedrick; Space Science Award ($500)—William Ian Axford; G. Edward Pendray Award ($500)—Nicholas J. Hoff; special presidential citation—Charles Stark Draper.

American Institute of Physics awards: Karl Taylor Compton Gold Medal ($1,000)—Ralph A. Sawyer, former president of the Optical Society of America; U. S. Steel Foundation Science Writing Award in physics and astronomy ($1,500)—Kenneth F. Weaver, assistant editor of the *National Geographic* magazine.

American Physical Society awards: Tom W. Bonner Prize in nuclear physics ($1,000)—Maurice Goldhaber; Oliver E. Buckley Solid-State Physics Prize ($1,000)—Erwin Hahn; High Polymer Physics Prize ($1,000)—John D. Hoffman and John I. Lauritzen; Irving Langmuir Prize in chemical physics ($5,000)—Michael E. Fisher; Dannie Heinemann Prize in mathematical physics—Roger Penrose.

Atomic Energy Commission (AEC) awards: Ernest Orlando Lawrence Memorial Awards for contributions to the development, use, or control of atomic energy ($5,000 each)— Robert L. Fleischer, P. Buford Price, Robert M. Walker, Thomas B. Cook, and Robert L. Hellens; citations for outstanding contributions to U. S. atomic energy programs— Milton Burton, William E. Ogle, and Duane C. Sewell.

Franklin Institute, Franklin Awards: Paul J. Flory, John H. Van Vleck, Harold G. Mead, William D. McElroy, Felix Wankel, Henry Lee Willet, Zhores Ivanovich Alferov, Martin Ryle, and Hannes Alfven.

History of Science Society, Pfizer Award for a scientific work by an American scholar ($500)—David Joravsky for *The Lysenko Affair.*

Kalinga Prize for the popularization of science, sponsored by UNESCO ($2,400)—Margaret Mead, anthropologist.

Albert Lasker Medical Research Awards ($10,000 each): clinical research—Edward D. Freis of the Veterans Administration Hospital in Washington, D. C.; basic research— Seymour Benzer of the California Institute of Technology, Sydney Brenner of the University of Cambridge, and Charles Yanofsky of Stanford University.

René Leriche Prize for research in heart transplantation —Norman Shumway of Stanford University.

National Academy of Sciences awards: U. S. Steel Foundation Award for research in molecular biology ($5,000)— Masayasu Nomura of the Institute of Enzyme Research at the University of Wisconsin; Daniel Giraud Elliot Medal—Richard Alexander; John H. Carty Medal ($3,000)—James D. Watson; Henry Draper Gold Medal ($1,000)—S. Chandrasekhar.

National Aeronautics Association, Wright Brothers Award —C. R. Smith.

National Medals of Science for 1970—Richard D. Brauer, professor of mathematics, Harvard; Robert H. Dicke, professor of physics, Princeton; Barbara McClintock of the Carnegie Institution of Washington; George E. Mueller, former director of NASA's Apollo program; Albert Sabin, president of the Weizmann Institute of Science in Israel; Allan R. Sandage of the Carnegie Institution of Washington; Hale Observatories, and the California Institute of Technology; John C. Slater, professor of physics and chemistry, University of Florida; John A. Wheeler, professor of physics, Princeton; Saul Winstein, former professor of chemistry, University of California at Los Angeles, posthumously.

National Recreation and Parks Association awards: Distinguished Service Award—Reynold E. Carlson; Humanitarian Award—William F. Laman; Literary Award—John B. Oakes.

Perkin Medal of the Society of Chemical Industry— James Franklin Hyde, for his pioneering role in developing the silicones.

Smithsonian Institution, Langley Medal—Lieut. Gen. Samuel C. Phillips, former director of NASA's Apollo program.

Vetleson Prize for geophysics ($25,000)—S. Keith Runcorn, Allan V. Cox, and Richard R. Doell.

TELEVISION AND RADIO

Academy of Television Arts and Sciences ("Emmy") Awards: best program—*The Andersonville Trial* (PBS); best musical program—*Another Evening with Burt Bacharach* (NBC); comedy series—*All in the Family* (CBS); variety program—*The Flip Wilson Show* (NBC); variety series-talk—*The David Frost Show* (Westinghouse Broadcasting Company); dramatic series—*The Bold Ones* (NBC); single performance in a drama—George C. Scott in *The Price* (NBC), and Lee Grant in *The Neon Ceiling* (NBC); leading actor in a dramatic series—Hal Holbrook in *The Bold Ones* (NBC); leading actress in a dramatic series—Susan Hampshire in *The First Churchills* (PBS); leading actor in a comedy series—Jack Klugman in *The Odd Couple* (ABC); leading actress in a comedy series—Jean Stapleton in *All in the Family* (CBS); supporting dramatic actor—David Burns in *The Price* (NBC); supporting dramatic actress—Margaret Leighton in *Hamlet* (NBC); supporting actor in a comedy series—Edward Asner in *The Mary Tyler Moore Show* (CBS); supporting actress in a comedy series—Valerie Harper in *The Mary Tyler Moore Show* (CBS); writing achievement in dramatic adaptation— Saul Levitt for *The Andersonville Trial* (PBS); writing achievement in comedy, variety, or music—Marty Farrell and Bob Ellison for *The Burt Bacharach Special* (CBS); writing achievement in drama—Tracy Keenan Wynn and Marvin Schwartz for *Tribes* (ABC); directorial achievement in drama—Fielder Cook for *The Price* (NBC); directorial achievement in comedy, variety, or music—Sterling Johnson for *Peggy Fleming at Sun Valley* (NBC); news documentaries—*The Selling of the*

Pentagon (CBS), *The World of Charlie Company* (CBS), and *Pollution is a Matter of Choice* (NBC); magazine-type programing—*The Great American Dream Machine* (PBS) and Mike Wallace and Joseph Wershba of *60 Minutes* (CBS); daytime programing—*Today* (NBC); children's programing—*Sesame Street* (PBS) and Burr Tillstrom of *Kukla, Fran, and Ollie* (PBS).

George Foster Peabody Awards for distinguished achievement in television and radio: special award—*The Selling of the Pentagon* (CBS); television drama—*The Andersonville Trial* (PBS); special series—*Civilisation* (British Broadcasting Corporation); television documentaries—*The Eye of the Storm* (ABC), *Migrant* (NBC), *Hot Dog* (NBC), and *Violence in America* (Westinghouse Broadcasting Company); television magazine-type program—*60 Minutes* (CBS); television special—*Dr. Seuss* (CBS); radio news—Douglas Kiker of WNBC Radio and *The Danger from Within* (WNBC); special awards—Flip Wilson for his shows for NBC; WQXR, the radio station of the New York *Times*, and WWLT-TV, New Orleans.

THEATER AND MOTION PICTURES

Academy of Motion Picture Arts and Sciences ("Oscar") Awards for 1971: best film—*Patton;* best foreign-language film—*Investigation of a Citizen above Suspicion* (Italian); best actor—George C. Scott for *Patton;* best actress—Glenda Jackson for *Women in Love;* supporting actor—John Mills for *Ryan's Daughter;* supporting actress—Helen Hayes for *Airport;* director—Franklin J. Schaffner for *Patton;* screenplay based on material from another medium—Ring Lardner, Jr., for *M*A*S*H;* original screenplay—Francis Ford Coppola and Edmund North for *Patton;* musical score (original or adaptation)—the Beatles for *Let It Be;* nonmusical score—Francis Lai for *Love Story;* original song—*For All We Know* from *Lovers and Other Strangers* by Robb Wilson and Arthur James; art direction—Terry Marsh and Bob Cartwright for *Scrooge;* editing—Hugh S. Fowler for *Patton;* cinematography—Fred A. Young for *Ryan's Daughter;* special visual effects—A. D. Flowers and L. B. Abbott for *Tora! Tora! Tora!;* costume design—Nino Novarese for *Cromwell;* sound—Douglas Williams and Don Bassman for *Patton;* short subject (live action)—John Longenecker, producer, for *The Resurrection of Broncho Billy;* short subject (cartoon)—Lester A. Schoenfeld, producer, for *Is It Always Right to be Right?;* documentary feature film—Bob Maurice, producer, for *Woodstock;* short subject documentary film—Joseph Strick, producer, for *Interviews with My Lai Veterans;* special awards—Orson Welles, for his contributions to the film industry, and Frank Sinatra, for his charitable activities.

American Theater Wing, Antoinette Perry ("Tony") Awards: best drama—*Sleuth* by Anthony Shaffer; best musical—*Company* by George Furth and Stephen Sondheim; best actor (musical)—Hal Linden for *The Rothschilds;* best actor (drama)—Brian Bedford for *The School for Wives;* best actress (musical)—Helen Gallagher for *No, No, Nanette;* best actress (drama)—Maureen Stapleton for *The Gingerbread Lady;* dramatic supporting actor—Paul Sand for *Story Theater;* dramatic supporting actress—Rae Allen for *And Miss Reardon Drinks a Little;* musical supporting actor—Keene Curtis for *The Rothschilds;* musical supporting actress—Patsy Kelly for *No, No, Nanette;* director (drama)—Peter Brook for *A Midsummer Night's Dream;* director (musical)—Hal Prince for *Company;* scenic design—Boris Aronson for *Company;* costume design—Raoul Pene du Bois for *No, No, Nanette;* lighting—R. H. Poindexter for *Story Theater;* choreography—Donald Saddler for *No, No, Nanette.*

Cannes International Film Festival Awards: Gold Palm Grand Prix—*The Go-Between* (British); special jury prizes—*Taking Off* (American) and *Johnny Got His Gun* (American); actor—Ricardo Cucciolla for *Sacco and Vanzetti* (Italian); actress—Kitty Winn for *Panic in Needle Park* (American); director—Joseph Losey for *The Go-Between;* directorial debut—Nino Manfredi for *Per grazia recevuta* (Italian); special prize—Luchino Visconti for *Death in Venice* (Italian).

Drama Desk–Vernon Rice Awards for outstanding achievements in the on- and off-Broadway theater: performance—Sir Ralph Richardson for *Home;* director—Peter Brook for *A Midsummer Night's Dream;* set design—Boris Aronson for *Follies;* costume design—Florence Klotz for *Follies;* composer—Stephen Sondheim for *Follies;* musical book writer—Burt Shevelove for *No, No, Nanette;* writer—Kurt Vonnegut, Jr., for *Happy Birthday, Wanda June.*

New York Drama Critics' Circle Theater Awards: drama—*Home;* American drama—*The House of Blue Leaves;* musical—*Follies.*

New York Film Critics' Awards: best film—*A Clockwork Orange;* actor—Gene Hackman in *The French Connection;* actress—Jane Fonda in *Klute;* director—Stanley Kubrick for *A Clockwork Orange.*

PROTESTANTISM. See RELIGION.

PSYCHOLOGY

In 1971 the psychologist who received the most public attention was B. F. Skinner of Harvard University, whose latest book, *Beyond Freedom and Dignity,* evoked widespread controversy. In this book Skinner argues that "behavior is shaped and maintained by its consequences." He follows this theme to claim that man is controlled from without, not from within, and that the way to build a better society is to arrange for effective rewards for desired behavior.

Skinner's special area of research has long been operant or instrumental conditioning in which behavior is shaped by means of reinforcement (reward) of preselected or desired responses. Thus a pigeon may be trained to turn circles to the left by rewarding responses that orient the head or body to the left and by not rewarding movements to the right. Skinner's learning techniques are used in such diverse operations as behavior-modification therapy, teaching machines, special classroom training programs, and animal training.

In 1971, Skinner received the Gold Medal Award from the American Psychological Association (APA) for his role as a "pioneer in psychological research, leader in theory, master in technology, who has revolutionized the study of behavior."

Teaching Chimpanzees Sign Language. During 1970 and 1971 several articles called attention to the provocative studies of a husband-wife research team, A. R. Gardner and B. T. Gardner, who have taught sign language to a chimpanzee. The Gardners reasoned that earlier attempts to teach chimpanzees to talk had failed because the monkey's vocal equipment is different from man's. They have been able to teach Washoe, a chimpanzee, to make

PSYCHOLOGIST B. F. Skinner, shown in Harvard laboratory, published new book, *Beyond Freedom and Dignity,* in 1971. Book supports his controversial view that man can no longer afford freedom and must be controlled.

KEN HEYMAN

more than 80 different signs and gestures. He can, for example, signal that a door should be opened and can give the signal "dog" when he hears a distant bark. Washoe, however, has not shown any ability to ask questions, and this is of great interest because questioning occurs so prominently among children.

APA Awards and Offices. In 1971 the Distinguished Scientific Achievement Awards of the American Psychological Association were presented to Dr. Roger W. Brown of Harvard University for research on the development of thinking and its relationship to language; Dr. Roger W. Sperry of the California Institute of Technology for work with split brain preparations and research on sensory and motor integrations; and to Dr. Harold H. Kelley of the University of California at Los Angeles for his theory of interpersonal processes.

The APA also installed Dr. Anne Anastasi of Fordham University as president, succeeding Dr. Kenneth Clark. Dr. Clark generated controversy in his presidential address when he suggested that scientists should try to develop a drug that could prevent the world's leaders from feeling hostile, and he expressed the belief that society, to survive, must develop chemical means to prevent people in power from abusing that power. The APA also chose Dr. Leona E. Tyler, a leading authority on individual differences and counseling, as president-elect. Dr. Anastasi and Dr. Tyler are the third and fourth women so honored by U. S. psychologists.

AUSTIN E. GRIGG
University of Richmond

PUBLIC HEALTH. See MEDICINE.

PUBLIC OPINION RESEARCH

In 1971 national surveys continued to measure public opinion on politics, current events, and basic public issues.

Decline in Optimism. A comprehensive survey commissioned by the nonprofit Potomac Associates and conducted by the Gallup Poll in April, reported a significant decline in the public's confidence in the future of American institutions. Almost half the people interviewed believed that current unrest and ill feeling among groups may lead to "a real breakdown in this country." Only 38% were optimistic enough to believe that these problems can be solved, and 15% were undecided. Those taking part in the survey also rated the nation's progress in 1971 somewhat lower than that of a similar study in 1968. The authors of the survey stated that in many such studies conducted in different countries in the past, only once has a country's self-rating failed to improve over previous self-ratings. They concluded that "the American people clearly feel their nation is in trouble."

Political Surveys. In a December report, the Gallup Poll noted a sharp decline in public concern over the war in Vietnam. Considered "the most important problem facing the country" for most of the last six years, the war was mentioned in June by only 33% of those interviewed and in December by only 15%. Economic problems were mentioned more often, and in December, 41% of those polled picked the economy as the nation's primary problem.

President Nixon's performance in office continued to hold the approval of 50% to 55% of opin-

ions sampled. "Trial heat" election polls conducted by the Gallup Poll showed the President holding slight pluralities over Senators Muskie and Kennedy and somewhat larger leads over Senators Humphrey and McGovern, in three-way races with George Wallace. A Gallup Poll of Wallace supporters indicated they would divide quite evenly between President Nixon and Senator Muskie if their man did not make the race.

Survey of Racial Attitudes. In a series of reports on racial attitudes, the Harris Survey showed wide differences between blacks and whites. Roughly equal proportions of both races agreed that there is racial discrimination in the United States. But, in regard to discrimination in 14 specific areas, blacks said they met discrimination in 13, while a majority of whites saw discrimination only in the area of housing. The survey also reported that while stereotyped beliefs about blacks are gradually declining among whites, the negative attitudes that blacks hold concerning whites are actually hardening.

On the other hand, a new report by the National Opinion Research Center on long-term trends in white attitudes found continued progress in white acceptance of integration. The authors noted that the right of blacks to sit anywhere in public vehicles, a highly controversial matter in the first poll in 1942, is no longer a major issue, and they report that the same is now almost true of the right of blacks to use parks, restaurants, and hotels with whites. Assuming these trends continue, they conclude that school integration may no longer be a significant issue six years hence.

WAPOR, AAPOR, and an Anniversary. A joint meeting of the World Association for Public Opinion Research (WAPOR) and the European Society for Opinion and Marketing Research was held at Helsinki, Finland, in August.

The American Association for Public Opinion Research (AAPOR), at its annual meeting in Pasadena, Calif., in May, presented the AAPOR award for "exceptionally distinguished achievement" to Walter Lippmann, whose book *Public Opinion* (1922) is still regarded as a classic in the field.

The Institute for Social Research at the University of Michigan celebrated its 25th anniversary. It has become well known for its studies of psychological factors affecting the economy, its analyses of American voting behavior, and, more recently, its research in racial attitudes.

Elmo Roper. Elmo Roper, who established his first market research firm in 1933, died on April 30, 1971. Along with George Gallup and Archibald Crossley, he achieved fame in 1936 when he used the new techniques of national sampling and personal interviews to forecast Franklin D. Roosevelt's landslide election victory over Alfred Landon, at a time when the prestigious *Literary Digest* mail survey was predicting Landon's election. From 1933 to 1950, Roper produced the *Fortune* magazine survey; more recently he wrote for *Saturday Review*. He is memorialized by the Roper Public Opinion Research Center, which he founded in 1946. The center, which is located at Williams College, includes data from about 9,000 surveys supplied by more than 100 academic and commercial research organizations in 68 countries.

PAUL B. SHEATSLEY
National Opinion Research Center
University of Chicago

A prepared page of the Pentagon Papers, publishing coup of 1971, goes to the New York *Times* composing room.

PUBLISHING

The publishing world and its 1971 activities are reviewed in this article under three headings—Books, Magazines, and Newspapers.

Books

In spite of the uncertainties that beset all business enterprises in the United States in 1971, book publishers did well and retail booksellers fared even better. There was a continued expansion of book sales, up 10% from the 1970 level and nearing the $3.5 billion mark. The number of new titles and new editions issued during the year was estimated at between 30,000 and 40,000—textbooks, subscription sets and general books, fiction, nonfiction, and children's books.

Best Sellers. An examination of the best-seller lists reveals a wide range of public interest. The following lists, arranged alphabetically, represent a composite chosen from the five leaders at 6-month intervals throughout the year.

FICTION

The Day of the Jackal, Frederick Forsyth
The Drifters, James Michener
The Exorcist, William Blatty
Islands in the Stream, Ernest Hemingway
Love Story, Erich Segal
The New Centurions, Joseph Wambaugh
Passions of the Mind, Irving Stone
QB VII, Leon Uris
The Underground Man, Ross MacDonald
Wheels, Arthur Hailey

NONFICTION

Bury My Heart at Wounded Knee, Dee Brown
Civilisation, Kenneth Clark
Eleanor and Franklin, Joseph Lash
Everything You Always Wanted to Know About Sex, David Reuben
Future Shock, Alvin Toffler
The Gift Horse, Hildegard Knef
The Grandees, Stephen Birmingham
The Greening of America, Charles Reich
The Sensuous Man, ''M''
Without Marx or Jesus, Jean-François Revel

Paperback Market. The market for hard-cover editions is being rapidly followed by a paperback market for the same titles. For example, both *Love Story* and *Everything You Always Wanted to Know About Sex* were among the leading sellers in both hard- and soft-cover editions during the year.

Meanwhile, the demand by libraries, schools, and the public for both quality and mass-market paperbacks continued to grow extremely fast. An estimate of 350 million paperbacks sold during the year is considered conservative.

Copyright System. As the result of a summer meeting in Paris, new hope was created for U. S. participation in a workable international copyright system. But at year-end the U. S. Senate had not ratified revisions of existing commitments.

International Sales. The overseas sales of U. S. books in 1971 rose to $230 million, a 10% increase over the previous year. U. S. publishers continued to open new sales offices and warehousing facilities in all parts of the world. Their joint exhibit of American books at the Frankfurt Book Fair, in West Germany, was expanded by 50% over the 1970 exhibit.

Time-Life Book Company acquired substantial holdings in the British firm of Andre Deutsch. But the established practice of copublication—especially of elaborate "picture books"—by publishers from various countries began to wane because of the tightening economic conditions.

Industry Developments. Shortly after the New York *Times* won a U. S. Supreme Court case that enabled it to continue publication of the Pentagon Papers, Bantam Books, Inc., rushed through a paperback book containing these documents as released by the government. The book established a record for instant mass circulation. (See also the *Newspapers* section of this article and the separate article on CENSORSHIP.)

Former President Lyndon B. Johnson wrote a 636-page volume, *The Vantage Point: Perspectives of the Presidency 1963–1969*, published by Holt, Rinehart and Winston.

The outstanding art book of the year was a 9-pound, $50 appraisal of Edward Hopper's contribution to American art. The book, entitled *Edward Hopper*, was published by Harry N. Abrams.

Children's books were highlighted by several volumes recreating in book form the magic of *Sesame Street*, the phenomenally popular television show for children. Several other signs appear to indicate a strengthening of the bond between television and books: Robert Cromie continued to expand the audience for his *Book Beat* program on public broadcasting stations, and David Frost's talk show on the Metromedia network welcomed many authors.

JOSEPH A. DUFFY
American Booksellers Association, Inc.

Magazines

Two years after the death of the *Saturday Evening Post,* another giant magazine quietly ceased publication in 1971. Shunning the financial acrobatics that had failed to save the *Post,* Cowles Communications, Inc., announced without warning on September 16 that the October 19 issue would be the last for *Look.*

The handsomely illustrated biweekly had been founded in 1937, a year after its chief rival, *Life.* It had been profitable for 32 of its 34 years. But the seeds of trouble had been planted with its decision to compete with television's numbers by initiating mass cut-rate subscription sales. Circulation reached a peak of 7,750,000 in 1969, but advertising failed to keep pace, falling off 25% between 1966 and 1971. When Gardner Cowles, the founder and chairman of the board of Cowles Communications, announced the end, he blamed the condition of the national economy, the competition of television, and prospective postal-rate increases.

Look's closing climaxed a period of severe readjustment in the Cowles empire. In May, Cowles had closed *Venture,* a travel magazine. The company also completed a deal with the New York Times Company, transferring *Family Circle,* the *Modern Medicine* group, and other properties to the newspaper for Times stock worth $70 million and

THE LAST ISSUE of *Look* appeared on October 19. The picture magazine, which began publication in 1937, was the victim of diminishing advertising revenues.

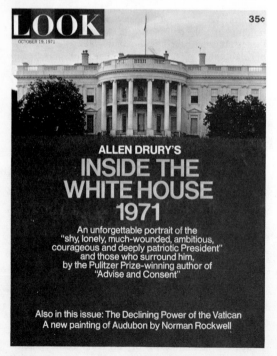

LOOK   35¢
OCTOBER 19, 1971

ALLEN DRURY'S
INSIDE THE
WHITE HOUSE
1971
An unforgettable portrait of the
"shy, lonely, much-wounded, ambitious,
courageous and deeply patriotic President"
and those who surround him,
by the Pulitzer Prize-winning author of
"Advise and Consent"

Also in this issue: The Declining Power of the Vatican
A new painting of Audubon by Norman Rockwell

assumption of $15 million in Cowles debts. At *Look*'s closing, Cowles sold a distribution to Time Inc. for $2,850,000. By year-end, the corporation retained one small magazine production contract.

Advertising. *Look*'s advertising losses stood in contrast to the trend elsewhere in the industry. Magazines reversed the downward swing of 1970, with general and farm magazines up 4% at the end of nine months, to $884.8 million, according to Magazine Publishers Association figures. Similarly, American Business Publications statistics showed a projected 4% advertising increase in 1971—to an estimated total of $869.5 million. Magazine advertising revenues were buoyed during the year by expanded cigarette advertising, which followed the Jan. 1, 1971, ban on broadcast cigarette commercials.

Government. Postal-rate increases caused great concern. Second-class mailing rates, traditionally low to encourage distribution of printed matter, were set to rise 150% in five years under the new Postal Service. Magazine and newspaper publishers tried to block immediate increases in court, but failed. Industry representatives contended that the increases would further unbalance magazines' competition with TV's purportedly free distribution.

In the continuing government effort to police door-to-door subscription sales, five Cowles subsidiaries were fined and subjected to a permanent injunction barring fraud and deceptive practices. The Federal Trade Commission issued an order requiring Time Inc. and a subsidiary to give magazine subscription purchasers a 3-day option to cancel.

Editorial-Publishing. Two major editorships shifted: Grace Mirabella replaced Diana Vreeland at *Vogue,* and Willie Morris resigned as editor of *Harper's* in a dispute with management. He was replaced by Robert Shnayerson. On *New York* magazine, George A. Hirsch quit as publisher, and the founding editor, Clay S. Felker, took over the title.

In the annual National Magazine Awards, *The Nation* won the top public-service prize for special presentations on cable television and on the police. Others honored were *Rolling Stone, Vogue, Esquire,* and *The Atlantic Monthly.*

Saturday Review was sold by Norton Simon, Inc., a conglomerate, to a group of individuals from Boise Cascade Corporation, led by Nicholas Charney and John J. Veronis. The group also acquired the McCall book division. Their plans to change *Saturday Review* caused the resignation in November of its long-time editor, Norman Cousins.

New Ventures. The following publications were started or announced:

Saturday Evening Post, an old title revived as a $1 quarterly by the Curtis Publishing Company.

Liberty, another old title revived, in April, as "the Nostalgia Magazine."

New Woman, which "positions itself between . . . the traditional woman and the radical feminist." It started in June with a nude male centerfold.

Ms., named for the new form of feminine address (pronounced "Miz"). It was to begin in January 1972 under the editorship of Gloria Steinem.

Performance and *Scripts,* two new theater magazines founded by Joseph Papp of the New Shakespeare Festival Theater.

Ecology Today and *Environmental Quality Magazine,* new titles edited in Noank, Conn., and Los Angeles.

JAMES BOYLAN, *Columbia University*

Newspapers

Hostility between press and government continued on all levels during 1971. News embargoes, the subpoenaing of newsmen, police searches, and, for the first time in U. S. history, the use of the courts to censor the news provided evidence of governmental efforts to hamstring newspapers and other media. On their side, newspapers were equally vigorous in exposing the shortcomings in government.

For six days beginning in late January, the U. S. command in Vietnam enforced an embargo on all news of an incursion toward Laos, but the world knew about it anyway.

Subpoenas mounted as courts and prosecutors sought information from newsmen. The subpoena-contempt cases of Earl Caldwell (the New York *Times*), Paul Branzburg (Louisville *Courier-Journal*), and Paul Pappas (WTEV-TV in New Bedford, Mass.) were before the Supreme Court as it entered its fall term. A police search of the premises of the Stanford University daily led to another court confrontation. Later in the year a New York judge closed his courtroom to the press.

Pentagon Papers. The big crisis in government-press relations broke when the New York *Times*, in its issue of Sunday, June 13, began the publication of a five-part series on the history of U. S. involvement in Indochina. The series was based on three months of study, in utmost secrecy, of 47 volumes of documents prepared by the Pentagon to record the decisions of those years. They were classified documents, and the *Times* was clearly breaking the classification. Articles appeared again on Monday and Tuesday. Attorney General John N. Mitchell asked the *Times* on Monday evening to stop the series; the *Times* refused. Meanwhile, the Justice Department had gone to court seeking to force the *Times* to stop the series. A hearing was held on Tuesday before Judge Murray I. Gurfein in U. S. District Court, New York, and he issued a temporary restraining order against the further publication of the series.

There were no Pentagon Papers in the newspaper the next day. The *Times* spoke of an "unprecedented example of censorship" and this "unconstitutional restraint imposed by the attorney general." It was a historic first—the use of court authority to place a prior restraint on publication. Arguments were heard throughout Friday—until 10:30 P.M.—and at Saturday noon Judge Gurfein announced: "I am not going to grant an injunction."

Whitney North Seymour, U. S. attorney, immediately appealed the decision, and Judge Irving R. Kaufman of the Court of Appeals continued the temporary restraining order until the following Monday. By that time Kaufman had assembled a three-judge court, but he told the lawyers that the case was so important that he wished to summon all eight members of the court. Arguments were heard by the entire court the next day, and on Wednesday the ruling came down. The case was returned to Gurfein, and the *Times* was permitted to resume publication provided the government found the material not dangerous to national security.

The ambiguity of the decision meant more anguish at the *Times*. Should the paper resume the series, or should it appeal to the Supreme Court? Before the deadline on Wednesday, June 23, the *Times* had decided to appeal. On Friday the court sent word that the *Times*' petition was granted and that it would hear arguments on Saturday. On the following Wednesday, June 30, the Supreme Court ruled against the government, 6 to 3, and gave the *Times* and the Washington *Post* permission to publish the secret Pentagon study. (See also CENSORSHIP).

Economic Conditions. Although the newspaper business was fundamentally sound, it was clear that it had come through a considerable slump throughout 1970 and part of 1971. Many corporations showed increased earnings, but costs also increased, with the result that net income dropped. Advertising linage was down as 1971 began. The pinch was especially noted among personnel. The New York *Times* reported in March that 300 persons had been dropped from its staff, largely through attrition and early retirements. The June graduates from journalism schools found jobs scarcer than in any year since the Great Depression.

Nevertheless, there was solid evidence in 1971 that the corner had been turned. Papers were thicker. Classified ads, a rich source of newspaper revenue, picked up noticeably. Half-year statements from the Los Angeles *Times*, the Knight newspapers, Southam Press Ltd. of Canada, the Ridder papers, and others showed strong gains, in some cases records. Circulation of U. S. dailies was up slightly for the year, reassuring the industry in the face of sharply increased prices for its product, particularly of Sunday editions. Audited circulation amounted to 62,107,527.

The number of U. S. dailies was down to 1,748, compared with 1,758 in the previous year. Most of the casualties were young papers. Two newcomers were the New York *Mirror*, a struggling infant, and *Today's Post*, a suburban Philadelphia daily. The Newhouse interests bought the Bayonne (N. J.) *Times* and closed it to enlarge the circulation area of their *Jersey Journal* in Jersey City.

Another loss was the *Toronto Telegram*, an evening daily for 95 years, whose 226,000 subscribers were not enough to overcome heavy deficits. The Gannett papers in Rockford, Ill., reopened on January 20 after a 70-day strike. Both Pittsburgh dailies were struck on May 14, and the news blackout lasted for 129 days. The Newark *News* was struck on May 26, and, while the strike was on, management (Media General) sold its building and moved its printing and physical presence to the building of the competing *Star-Ledger*. In the process the *Sunday News* was closed.

Exchanges. A continuing trend of the year was the buying and selling of newspaper properties and the marked growth of chains. Over half of the U. S. dailies are now owned by groups.

The Gannett Co., of Rochester, N. Y., increased its holdings to more than 50 dailies when, in 1971, it acquired the McClure papers of Burlington, Vt., and Chambersburg, Pa.; the Federated Publications, a group of seven based in Battle Creek, Mich.; its morning competition in Binghamton, N. Y.; the properties of the Honolulu *Star-Bulletin;* and the Fort Myers (Fla.) *News-Press.*

The Pulitzer Company of St. Louis bought the *Arizona Daily Star* in Tucson; the *Amsterdam News* in New York was sold to new owners; Howard Publications of Oceanside, Calif., bought both the morning and evening papers in Glens Falls, N. Y.; and the Harte-Hanks chain of San Antonio bought the Framingham (Mass.) *News.*

RICHARD T. BAKER, *Columbia University*

PUERTO RICO

Increasing agitation for independence, financial distress in the tourism and sugar industries, serious unemployment, and social unrest marked 1971 in Puerto Rico. The 450th anniversary of the founding of San Juan, oldest city under the U. S. flag, was observed.

Politics. Fires and bombings increased in San Juan, many attributable to political dissatisfaction. The movement for independence grew steadily, partly because the ruling New Progressive party advocates statehood, which, if attained, would make eventual independence impossible. Two new political parties were established—the Authentic Sovereignty party and the Puerto Rican Union party—both advocating independence. In the 1972 election, three of the six parties will be for independence, one for statehood, and two for improved commonwealth status.

San Juan was host to the 63d annual governors' conference, attended by Vice President Agnew and all but four U. S. governors, September 12–15. On September 12, independence advocates staged a massive but peaceful demonstration-parade, ending at the governors' heavily guarded hotels.

University. March 11 saw the worst riot in the history of the University of Puerto Rico, sparked by the fact that the ROTC, which was to move, was still on campus. Two police officers and one ROTC cadet were killed by gunfire, and 66 other persons were wounded. The ROTC was subsequently moved off campus. Jaime Benítez, who had headed the university for 29 years, was dismissed on October 8.

------- **PUERTO RICO** • **Information Highlights** -------

Area: 3,421 square miles (8,860 sq km).
Population (1970 census): 2,712,033. *Density:* 793 per sq mi.
Chief Cities (1970): San Juan, the capital, 452,749; Bayamón, 147,552; Ponce, 128,233; Carolina, 94,271; Caguas, 63,215; Mayagüez, 68,872; Guaynabo, 55,310; Arecibo, 35,484.
Government (1971): *Chief Officers*—governor, Luis A. Ferré (New Progressive party, took office Jan. 2, 1969); secy. of state, Fernando Chardón (NPP); treas., Wallace González Oliver (NPP); supt. of public instruction, Ramón Mellado; chief justice (vacant). *Legislature*—Senate, 27 members (12 New Progressive party, 15 Popular Democratic party); House of Representatives, 51 members (27 NPP; 24 PDP).
Education (1970–71): *Enrollment*—public elementary schools, 464,199 pupils; public intermediate, 167,494 pupils; public high schools, 104,292 students; 21,750 teachers; nonpublic schools, 88,609 pupils; college and university (fall 1970), 56,070 students. *Public school expenditures* (1970–71), $290,898,057 ($432 per pupil).
Commonwealth Finance (fiscal year 1969–70): *Revenues,* $823,327,000 (excise taxes, $213,000,000; motor fuel tax, $19,719,000; federal funds, $306,000,000). *Expenditures,* $1,081,200,000 (education, $339,100,000; health, welfare, and safety, $231,900,000; highways, $115,700,000).
Personal Income (1969–70): $3,817,100,000; per capita, $1,427.
Public Assistance (1971): $90,494,000. *Average monthly payments* (July 1971)—old-age assistance, $18.35; aid to families with dependent children, $47.58.
Labor Force: *Nonagricultural wage and salary earners* (1970), 827,000. *Average annual employment* (1970)—manufacturing, 738,000; trade, 138,000; government, 113,000; services, 123,000. *Insured unemployed* (Feb. 1971)—104,000 (12%).
Manufacturing (1970): *Value added by manufacture,* $952,700,000; machinery and metal products, $175,000,000; clothing, $169,000,000; foods, $162,500,000; chemicals, $108,400,000; stone and glass products, $48,600,000.
Agriculture (1970): *Cash farm income,* $271,098,000 (livestock, $135,070,000; crops, $114,540,000; government payments, $21,488,000). *Chief crops* (tons)—sugarcane, 5,900,000; coffee, 22,500; tobacco, 6,500.
Tourism (1970): *Revenues,* $223,100,000.
External Trade (fiscal 1970): *Exports,* $1,729,000,000 (chiefly manufactured goods). *Imports,* $2,556,000,000 (raw materials, $47,000,000; consumer goods, $35,000,000; capital goods, $18,000,000).
Transportation: *Highways under maintenance* (1970), 3,684 miles (5,940 km); *motor vehicles* (1970), 614,000; *airports* (1970), 1.
Communications: *Telephones* (1970), 319,301; *television stations* (1971), 11; *radio stations* (1971), 43; *newspapers* (1971), 4 (daily circulation, 277,871).

Squatters. Thousands of landless poor people, said to be aided by the Independence party, built settlements on government and private lands in many parts of the island. On 14 sites, homes were bulldozed or burned by the government or landowners, always at about 5 A. M., and without permitting the squatters to save their possessions.

Economy. Because of the slump in tourism and the rise in costs, the bankrupt Condado Beach Hotel dismissed 350 employees, and closed without notice, stranding its guests. The large Palace Hotel also closed. The luxurious Jerónimo Hilton, still open, was bankrupt and for sale. The government bought the bankrupt Racquet Club hotel, planning to operate it in part as a school to train hotel employees.

In fiscal 1970–71 contracts were signed to establish 50 new industries in Puerto Rico, but in February there were 104,000 unemployed—12% of the labor force—as against 10.8% a year earlier.

Despite the government's 5-year, $100 million rehabilitation program, the sugar industry sagged. The government, which already owned four large sugar mills, leased seven more, leaving only three in private operation.

EARL PARKER HANSON
Former Consultant, Department of State
Commonwealth of Puerto Rico

PULITZER PRIZES. See PRIZES AND AWARDS.

QUEBEC

Economic problems, especially an unemployment rate that rose at times to almost 10% of the population, and constitutional questions were of greater concern in Quebec in 1971 than were strictly political problems. Politically, the year was calm in comparison with 1970, when Premier Robert Bourassa and his newly elected Liberal government were obliged to deal with terrorist activities of the separatist Front for the Liberation of Quebec (FLQ). The major crisis came in October 1970, with the kidnapping of a British diplomat, James R. Cross (who was rescued unharmed in December), and the kidnapping and slaying of Quebec Labor Minister Pierre Laporte.

In January 1971, four FLQ members—Paul Rose and his brother Jacques Rose, Francis Simard, and Bernard Lortie—were charged with kidnapping and murder in the Laporte case. Paul Rose and Simard were convicted on the murder charge and sentenced to life imprisonment on March 13 and May 20, respectively. Lortie was convicted on the kidnapping charge and sentenced in November to 20 years in prison. The trial of Jacques Rose was in progress at year-end.

Legislation. Because of the political crises of the preceding year, it was only during the first few months of 1971 that Premier Bourassa was able to propose a comprehensive legislative program. Measures aimed at expanding the economy and reducing the high unemployment rate received greatest emphasis. These included short-term measures, such as providing development grants for industries where jobs were most likely to be created, and long-term plans, which culminated in passage of a bill setting up a gigantic hydroelectric and industrial project for development of the James Bay area of northwestern Quebec. A decision not to increase taxes was taken in the hope that relief from added tax burdens would make it possible for both consumers and businesses to contribute to economic recovery. The fact that the economic measures brought only moderate gains was attributed in part to the refusal of the federal government to grant the provinces an adequately increased share of federally collected income taxes.

The Assembly passed a variety of important legislation in other areas. The voting age was lowered to 18, and the legal drinking age from 20 to 18. Women were given the right to sit on juries, and the salaries of the premier, cabinet ministers, and legislators were increased. Social welfare, education, and health care were the subject of other major enactments.

James Bay Development Corp. Legislation adopted in July set up a public corporation, the James Bay Development Corp., for development of the rich natural resources of the area surrounding James Bay, a southern arm of Hudson Bay lying between Quebec and Ontario. The project includes plans for a multibillion-dollar hydroelectric development to harness the rivers flowing into the bay. The Quebec Hydro-Electric Commission was given 51% control of the project and the right to name three of the corporation's directors. Planners forecast the creation of some 3,000 jobs by the end of the year and a future expansion to more than 100,000.

Constitutional Questions. The year brought two federal-provincial conferences in regard to major changes in the Canadian constitution. At issue mainly was a formula for future amendment of the constitution. The other provinces gave evidence that they would approve the formula, but Premier

UPI

GIGANTIC MUDSLIDE occurred on May 5 at St. Jean Vianney, a town some 115 miles (185 km) north of Quebec City. Tons of clay collapsed into an underground stream, killing 31 persons.

────── **QUEBEC • Information Highlights** ──────

Area: 594,860 square miles (1,540,669 sq km).
Population (April 1971 est.): 6,030,000.
Chief Cities (1967 est.): Quebec, the capital (164,190); Montreal (1,435,000); Laval (206,000); Verdun (88,928).
Government: *Chief Officers*—lt. gov., Hugues Lapointe; premier, Robert Bourassa (Liberal); min. of justice, Jérôme Choquette (Lib.); min. of finance, Raymond Garneau (Lib.); min. of educ., Guy St. Pierre (Lib.). *Legislature*—National Assembly (convened June 1970); 108 members (72 Liberal, 16 Unité-Québec, 12 Créditistes, 7 Parti Québécois, 1 Independent).
Education: School enrollment (1968–69 est.)—public elementary and secondary, 1,460,000 pupils (73,000 teachers); private schools, 95,375 pupils (6,350 teachers); Indian (federal) schools, 3,625 pupils (155 teachers); college and university, 82,610 students. *Public school expenditures* (1971 est.)—$786,110,000.
Public Finance (fiscal year 1971 est.): *Revenues,* $3,785,150,000 (sales tax, $1,006,580,000; income tax, $1,115,000,000; federal funds, $1,104,264,000). *Expenditures,* $4,019,720,000 (education, $1,191,770,000; health and social welfare, $1,467,260,000; transport and communications, $345,100,000).
Personal Income (1969 est.): $15,718,000,000.
Social Welfare (fiscal year 1971 est.): $506,760,000 (aged and blind, $41,040,000; dependents and unemployed, $200,870,000).
Manufacturing (1968): *Value added by manufacture,* $5,215,464,000 (food and products, $731,478,000; paper and allied industries, $512,531,000; transportation equipment, $405,829,000; fabricated metals, $371,900,000; primary metals, $351,450,000; electrical machinery, $324,317,000).
Agriculture (1969 est.): *Cash farm income* (exclusive of govt. payments), $678,094,000 (livestock, $414,948,000; crops, 1968 est., $56,723,000). *Chief crops* (cash receipts)—Vegetables, $17,632,000 (ranks 2d among the provinces); potatoes, $13,243,000 (ranks 1st); fruits, $9,170,000 (ranks 3d); tobacco, $6,018,000 (ranks 2d).
Mining (1969 est.): *Production value,* $720,067,100. *Chief minerals* (tons)—copper, 157,959 (ranks 2d among the provinces); asbestos, 1,336,000 (ranks 1st); iron ore, 12,875,400 (ranks 3d); zinc, 195,923 (ranks 3d).
Fisheries (1968 est.): *Commercial catch,* 204,522,000 pounds ($8,600,000). *Leading species*—cod, 50,700,000 pounds ($2,100,000); redfish, 70,500,000 pounds ($1,900,000); lobster, 2,800,000 pounds ($1,700,000).
Transportation: *Roads* (1968), 56,548 miles (90,986 km); *motor vehicles* (1969), 1,998,001; *railroads* (1969), 5,329 track miles (8,570 km); *licensed airports* (1970), 73.
Communications: *Telephones* (1969), 2,510,229; *television stations* (1970), 16; *radio stations* (1967), 55; *newspapers* (1970), 14 (daily circulation, 1,026,062).
(All monetary figures given in Canadian dollars.)

Bourassa cast a negative vote because of uncertainty about whether its provisions would guarantee Quebec the right to legislate, independently of the federal government, on matters pertaining to social security. (See also CANADA.)

Economic Mission. Premier Bourassa made a 16-day visit to Europe in April, chiefly to meet businessmen and hold discussions in regard to possible new investments in Quebec. He went successively to Belgium, Britain, Germany, Italy, and France. In France especially he held talks that gave promise of assistance to Quebec's automotive industry and some aspects of the James Bay project.

Changes in Union Nationale Party. The Union Nationale party, which had dominated Quebec politics for more than 20 years before its defeat by the Liberal party in 1970, chose a new leader and a new name in 1971. At a convention in June, Gabriel Loubier was elected as successor to the former leader and premier of Quebec, Jean-Jacques Bertrand. Loubier's narrow victory over Marcel Masse reflected a weak and divided party, and in October, Loubier announced that the need for a new party image had led to a change in name—the Unité-Québec party. On November 1, Masse left the party to sit in the National Assembly as an independent. At year-end observers were expressing doubt that the party could survive as a viable political force.

GUY BOURASSA, *Université de Montréal*

Black Caucus members, all Democratic representatives in Congress, met with President Nixon (*left*) and administration staff on March 25. Nixon appointed a panel to study problems of blacks and other minorities after discussion with caucus.

race relations

Race relations in the United States during 1971 were highlighted by several developments that may have a profound impact on the country in the next few years. These developments were not of the kind typically associated with visible, traumatic action in this field. That is, they did not involve mass demonstrations or violent confrontations precipitated by blacks. Indeed, in a kind of reversion to events of the early 1960's in the South, the mass demonstrations—to the extent that they occurred—were led by white citizens in the North, objecting, sometimes violently, to busing as a means of achieving desegregation when the public schools opened in the fall.

Congressional Black Caucus. In 1971 the 13 black members of the U. S. House of Representatives formed an organization called the Congressional Black Caucus. On March 25 they met with President Richard Nixon and presented him with 61 recommendations covering a wide variety of subjects, from welfare reform to foreign policy. The President responded on May 18 in a 115-page report.

The caucus expressed disappointment with the response and promised to continue to push for "equality of results." The black representatives stated: "Let us say at the outset that we were initially heartened by the evidence offered by the report itself, that the President had taken our March 25th meeting with him sufficiently seriously to respond to our concerns. But in reality the document constitutes less a response than a reply, couched predominantly in the form of bureaucratic reports intent on justifying the status quo. The challenge we tried to catalyze—fresh thinking, the matching of implementation with need, the degree of courage and commitment national leadership has brought to other efforts in the past—appears for the most part to have been ignored."

Throughout the year, the caucus met with black elected officials in various sections of the country, visited several military installations to investigate charges of racial discrimination, and concentrated on developing legislative and executive programs as well as laying plans for the presidential election in 1972.

In June the caucus held its first Congressional Black Caucus Dinner, in Washington, D. C. The dinner, which attracted 2,800 persons at $100 per person, was seen by many as a historic step toward consolidating black political power in the country.

Court Decisions. On January 29, a three-judge federal appeals court ruled that the municipality of Shaw, Miss., must spend its money so as to equalize municipal services to all sections of the city.

Historically in many cities, both Southern and Northern, neighborhoods in which black residents predominate receive inferior municipal services—street lighting, street paving, garbage collection, and the like. This court decision, if upheld and enforced, could make a substantial impact on day-to-day living conditions of black residents throughout the country.

On August 30 the California Supreme Court issued a decision regarding the financing of public school systems. The court declared the state's system of relying on the local property tax as a base of educational financing to be unconstitutional, inasmuch as that system favors children living in wealthy communities. The plaintiffs in the suit cited the $840 per pupil expenditure in their community (Baldwin Park, in Los Angeles county) as compared with $1,231 per pupil in the Beverly Hills community. This decision, likewise, will have major ramifications for poor, especially black, families within a given state.

The Rehnquist Nomination. Because these and possibly other decisions are likely to be appealed to the U.S. Supreme Court, many civil rights advocates strongly opposed President Nixon's nomination of William H. Rehnquist as an associate justice of the court. Bayard Rustin, director of the A. Philip Randolph Institute in New York City, stated: "If Mr. Rehnquist is approved, the bleakest chapter in what has been an unremittingly sorry Nixon administration race relations record will have been written." Clarence Mitchell, director of the Washington bureau of the National Association for the Advancement of Colored People (NAACP), asserted that Rehnquist, as a lawyer practicing in Arizona, had opposed a 1964 open accommodations ordinance in Phoenix and had also opposed efforts to end de facto school segregation there in 1967. The U.S. Senate approved the nomination in December, and many black citizens felt that this appointment would have the major effect of making the Supreme Court more conservative and less favorable to civil rights suits in the future.

U.S. Supreme Court Decisions. In April the U.S. Supreme Court rendered two important decisions that would have an impact on education and public housing. In the education case the court upheld a busing decree governing the joint school system in Charlotte-Mecklenburg county, N.C., and thereby invalidated a North Carolina antibusing law that forbade assignment of any student on account of race or for the purpose of creating a racial balance or ratio in the schools and that prohibited busing for such purposes. The court held the law to be invalid as preventing implementation of desegregation plans required by the 14th Amendment.

Chief Justice Warren Burger wrote: "... as a matter of educational policy, school authorities may well conclude that some kind of racial balance in the schools is desirable quite apart from any constitutional requirements. However, if a state-imposed limitation on a school authority's discretion operates to inhibit or obstruct the operation of a unitary school system or impede the disestablishing of a dual school system, it must fall. ..." He also noted that "just as the race of students must be considered in determining whether a constitutional violation has occurred, so also must race be considered in formulating a remedy." The court did not say that busing is necessary or required in all instances in order to achieve desegregated schools, but it held that there could be no absolute prohibition of the use of busing.

In the public housing case, the Supreme Court upheld California referendum laws providing that no low-rent housing project should be developed, constructed, or acquired in any manner by a state public body until the project is approved by a majority of those voting in a community election. The plaintiffs in the case, who were eligible for low-cost public housing, contended that the state law was unconstitutional because it violated their constitutional rights under the 14th Amendment. The court held that the law did not apply to any particular race: "The Article requires referendum approval for any low-rent public housing project, not only for projects which will be occupied by a racial minority. ... California's entire history demonstrates the repeated use of referendums to give citizens a voice on questions of public policy."

The decision, unlike the North Carolina decision, was not unanimous. Justices Marshall, Brennan, and Blackmun dissented. Justice Marshall wrote: "The article explicitly singles out low-income persons to bear its burden. Publicly assisted housing developments designed to accommodate the aged, veterans, state employees, persons of moderate income, or any class of citizens other than the poor, need not be approved by prior referenda." He

JOE FRAZIER, heavyweight boxing champion, spoke to legislature of his native South Carolina on April 7. Frazier, first black man to address assembly since Reconstruction, called for harmony between the races.
WIDE WORLD

called this "individious discrimination," which the 14th Amendment prohibits. Some civil rights spokesmen condemned the majority opinion because they felt that blacks, who constitute a large proportion of public housing residents, would especially suffer from this decision.

White Resistance to Busing. When the public schools opened in September, there were several violent incidents in Northern cities. White parents in Pontiac, Mich., and other places protested against school board busing policies that were aimed at desegregating the schools. Several buses were burned, and boycotts of schools were called. In no instances were the protests successful in defeating the busing plans. Few observers doubted that busing would be a major issue in future years.

Vice President Agnew and Black Leadership. Tension mounted during the year between some black leaders and Vice President Spiro T. Agnew. On July 17, during a news conference aboard the plane carrying him to Madrid from a 7-day African tour, the vice president denounced unspecified black American leaders for "criticizing ... carping ... complaining" and said that they could "learn much" from Emperor Haile Selassie of Ethiopia, President Jomo Kenyatta of Kenya, and President Joseph Mobutu of the Congo. He was quoted as telling newsmen, "All I see in most of those who are reported in the media at home, who describe themselves as black leaders, is a constant stream of criticism and complaint and no recognition of any efforts that are made on their behalf. ... I don't have to identify them. If you read your newspapers over the past years and see how many of these leaders have been complaining and carping, you will find out that they comprise a very substantial cross section of what describes itself as the black leadership."

These comments drew a number of responses from black leaders around the country. U. S. Rep. Parren J. Mitchell, of Maryland, stated: "Agnew failed to carry his home state of Maryland in the last presidential election primarily because black Marylanders, in unprecedented numbers, had to vote against him because they recognized that this man was not worthy to be the vice president of the United States." Mitchell vowed to work against Agnew again in 1972 if the vice president should be on the Republican ticket. Many other black leaders agreed with Representative Mitchell.

New Organizations. The year witnessed the formation of several new organizations that intended to work in the political arena on local, state, and federal levels. One such group was the National Tenants Organization (NTO). Jesse Gray of Harlem, who became the executive director of NTO in June, stated that his primary goal would be to work on a "national bill of rights" for tenants. NTO would work with local tenant groups in preparing housing bills to be introduced into state legislatures across the country. The organization, interracial in its composition, has approximately 300 local affiliates in 40 states.

In July more than 500 women met in Washington, D. C., at the first national conference of household workers. The meeting was sponsored by the National Committee on Household Employment, which has local affiliates in about 30 cities. The participants discussed ways of organizing to demand a minimum wage and workmen's compensation, including accident and unemployment insur-

ance. Two thirds of U. S. household workers are black, and 98% are women. The average full-time household worker earned $1,523 in 1968. Three states now have minimum wage laws for such workers—Massachusetts, New York, and Wisconsin.

During the year new organizations of black policemen were formed in more than a dozen cities. Their programs range from hiring more black policemen to fighting alleged discrimination within the police departments and to ensuring better protection of persons in minority communities. In Dayton, Ohio, the Black Police Association, consisting of all the city's 23 black officers, submitted a plan calling for "all black officers to donate their off-duty time to combat the dual system of law enforcement in West Dayton."

The NAACP formed a chapter of its organization in West Germany, consisting of black servicemen. This action came after a three-week investigation of complaints from black GI's of racism in the military services, especially in West Germany.

New Leadership for the National Urban League. The civil rights movement suffered a major tragedy in the death on March 11 of Whitney M. Young, Jr., executive director of the National Urban League. Young was attending a meeting in Lagos, Nigeria, of Africans and Americans sponsored by the African-American Institute when he drowned while swimming at a beach resort there (see YOUNG, WHITNEY). In June, Vernon E. Jordan, Jr., the head of the United Negro College Fund, was chosen to succeed Young as executive director, effective Jan. 1, 1972. Later, Jordan announced that the National Urban League would conduct a massive voter-registration drive in Northern and Western cities as part of the organization's new program (see BIOGRAPHY—*Jordan, Vernon*).

Summary and Outlook. Ultimately, 1971 may be viewed as a year of several events in race relations that will have major repercussions in the next few years. The new political organizations will attempt to play an important role in the presidential election and with the administration, Republican or Democratic, that assumes office in 1973. These new organizations will be operating at all levels of government, in both electoral and pressure-group politics.

Significant decisions of lower courts will probably be appealed to the U. S. Supreme Court, and that body will continue to play a crucial role, as well as to increase its influence in expanded fields such as equalizing financial support of public services. These decisions will have important implications for race relations. Increasing efforts will be made to pursue busing, and these events will sharpen issues in the area of school desegregation. The question of where to locate low-cost public housing also will become an increasingly dynamic issue in the years ahead.

In a sense, events of 1971 laid the foundation for a new, vitalized thrust in race relations. The era ahead is likely to be less violent and more political, at least on the part of black and other minorities. But it might be that some white groups, in an attempt to counter the minorities' demands and policies, will become more prone to violence and massive resistance.

CHARLES V. HAMILTON, *Columbia University*

RADIO. See TELEVISION AND RADIO.
RAILROADS. See TRANSPORTATION.

Carlo Maria Giulini (*top*) conducted Royal Opera House and Ambrosian Opera Chorus in powerful recording of Verdi's *Don Carlo*. Cast was featured on album cover.

recordings

In 1971, to boost lagging sales of classical discs, some U. S. record companies utilized established material from older recordings and reissued it in new and attractive formats. This "repackaging" principle met with some success. In popular music, interest in country, folk, and spiritual recordings continued to challenge the once preeminent area of hard rock.

The death of Louis Armstrong was a great loss to the world of jazz. Two fine retrospective collections of his early work were issued.

CLASSICAL RECORDS

Fewer new classical records were released in 1971 than in past years—partly due, no doubt, to economic pressures on the industry and the consumer. What did gain unprecedented momentum was the "repackaging" principle of marketing the classical product. While most companies have always found profitable a certain amount of catalog reshuffling among its older recordings in order to assemble an attractively saleable "new" disc, Columbia and RCA went at repackaging with a vengeance.

Repackaging Best Sellers. Columbia began with its "Greatest Hits" series, devoting one record to a composer and his most popular tunes played by leading artists. The discs were a great success with casual collectors and RCA soon followed suit, using its large roster of prestigious names, such as Van Cliburn and Leontyne Price, as selling points. It makes good commercial sense to get as much mileage as possible from a product, but without a concurrent, vital program of new recording projects this sort of vampirism can only lead to a dead end as the old material is exhausted.

European Firms. Meanwhile, European firms continued to supply the United States with most of the new classical releases: Deutsche Grammophon, London, EMI (Angel), and Philips showed undiminished enterprise, especially in the area of opera recording and expensive boxed sets. Wagner was particularly well treated in 1971, with new versions of *Tannhäuser* (London), *Lohengrin* (DGG), *Die Meistersinger* (Angel), and *Parsifal* (DGG). Three complete sets of Mahler's nine symphonies were recorded by Solti (London), Haitink (Philips), and

RICHARD WAGNER
LOHENGRIN
James King Gundula Janowitz Gwyneth Jones
Thomas Stewart Karl Ridderbusch
Chor und Symphonie-Orchester des Bayerischen Rundfunks
RAFAEL KUBELIK

POLYDOR INC.

RAFAEL KUBELIK led Bavarian Radio Chorus and Symphony Orchestra in 1971 release of Wagner's *Lohengrin*.

Kubelik (DGG). Bernstein also recorded the cycle for Columbia.

Pirated Discs. Another phenomenon of 1971 was the emergence of so-called pirated records—performances, generally operatic, taped privately off the air or in live concert and offered for commercial sale. Although illegal, there seemed to be no convenient method of preventing the pirates from selling their wares. Several artists, in fact, encouraged such activity as a method of circulating their interpretations of roles in operas that the legitimate companies are unwilling to record. Many of these productions were openly displayed in record stores all over the United States: the sound was often remarkably good and the packaging occasionally lavish, with complete librettos, historical notes, and rare reproductions. However dubious this practice may be, collectors were only too glad to pay premium prices for Callas, Caballé, Gedda, and Horne singing some of their most celebrated (and otherwise unavailable) vehicles not to mention a wealth of unusual repertory items that will probably never be recorded.

Outstanding Releases. Following is a selected list of notable classical releases in 1971.

BACH, *Concertos for Harpsichord* (complete): Igor Kipnis, harpsichord; London Strings, Neville Marriner, conductor (Columbia, 4 discs)

BERIO, *Epifanie; Folksongs:* Cathy Berberian, soprano; BBC Symphony Orchestra, Luciano Berio, conductor (RCA)

BERLIOZ, *Requiem, Op. 5:* Ronald Dowd, tenor; London Symphony Chorus and Orchestra, Colin Davis, conductor (Philips, 2 discs)

CRUMB, *Ancient Voices of Children:* Jan DeGaetani, mezzo; Contemporary Chamber Ensemble, Arthur Weisberg, conductor (Nonesuch)

DEBUSSY, *Nocturnes; Rhapsody No. 1 for Clarinet and Orchestra; Printemps:* New Philharmonia Orchestra, Pierre Boulez, conductor (Columbia)

DONIZETTI, *Lucia di Lammermoor:* Beverly Sills, Carlo Bergonzi, and other singers; London Symphony Orchestra, Thomas Schippers, conductor (ABC)

HENZE, *El Cimarron:* William Pearson, baritone; Karlheinz Zöller, flute; Leo Brouwer, guitar; Stomu Yamash'ta, percussion (Deutsche Grammophon)

JANÁČEK, *Sinfonietta; Taras Bulba:* Orchestra of the Bavarian Radio, Rafael Kubelik, conductor (Deutsche Grammophon)

MAHLER, *Symphonies (complete):* Orchestra of the Bavarian Radio, Rafael Kubelik, conductor (Deutsche Grammophon, 14 discs)

MASSENET, *Manon:* Beverly Sills, Nicolai Gedda, and other singers; New Philharmonia Orchestra, Julius Rudel, conductor (ABC, 4 discs)

MOZART, *The Magic Flute:* Pilar Lorengar, Hermann Prey, and other singers; Vienna Philharmonic Orchestra, Georg Solti, conductor (London, 3 discs)

MUSSORGSKY, *Boris Godunov:* Nicolai Ghiaurov and other singers; Vienna Philharmonic Orchestra, Herbert von Karajan, conductor (London, 4 discs)

PROKOFIEV, *Piano Sonata No. 6;* BARBER, *Piano Sonata:* Van Cliburn, piano (RCA)

RACHMANINOFF, *Piano Sonata No. 2:* Vladimir Horowitz, piano (Columbia)

SCHOENBERG, *Pierrot Lunaire:* Jan DeGaetani, speaker; Contemporary Chamber Ensemble, Arthur Weisberg, conductor (Nonesuch)

SCRIABIN, *Piano Sonatas (complete):* Ruth Laredo, piano (Connoisseur Society, 3 discs)

SIBELIUS, *Kullervo:* Bournemouth Symphony Orchestra, Paavo Berglund, conductor (Angel, 2 discs)

STRAUSS, RICHARD, *Der Rosenkavalier:* Christa Ludwig, Gwyneth Jones, and other singers; Vienna Philharmonic Orchestra, Leonard Bernstein, conductor (Columbia, 4 discs)

TIPPETT, *The Midsummer Marriage:* Joan Carlyle, Alberto Remedios, and other singers; Covent Garden Chorus and Orchestra, Colin Davis, conductor (Philips, 3 discs)

VERDI, *Don Carlo:* Montserrat Caballé, Placido Domingo, and other singers; Covent Garden Orchestra, Carlo Maria Giulini, conductor (Angel, 4 discs)

WAGNER, *Die Meistersinger:* Helen Donath, René Kollo, and other singers; Chorus and Orchestra of the Dresden State Opera, Herbert von Karajan, conductor (Angel, 5 discs)

WAGNER, *Tannhäuser:* Helga Dernesch, René Kollo, and other singers; Vienna Philharmonic Orchestra, Georg Solti, conductor (London, 4 discs)

PETER G. DAVIS
Music Editor, "High Fidelity" Magazine

POPULAR RECORDS

Popular music in 1971 was marked by sophistication and naiveté, subtlety and bombast, simplicity and complexity. It was a year of decentralization, in which the fragmentation of the popular-music audience was intensified.

Religious Revival. The enormous popularity of both *Jesus Christ Superstar*, the rock "opera" by Tim Rice and Andrew Lloyd Webber, and of *All Things Must Pass*, the poor man's mysticism of ex-Beatle George Harrison, attested to the continuing strength of the "revival" of fundamentalist religion. The albums sold three million copies each. *Jesus Christ Superstar* was adapted for the Broadway stage and presented in New York in the fall of 1971.

Rock and Roll Revival. In England, audiences hardly noticed *Superstar*, and listeners were not very avid about "Jesus music" generally. Early rock and roll and related types of music held sway there. Enthusiasm for Reggae, or Jamaican "outlaw" music something like early rock, diminished but continued. British groups that faithfully imitated the American rock and roll ensembles of the 1950's were quite popular. In the United States, interest in a rock and roll revival was part of a general craze for nostalgia. Groups imitated Fifties ensembles satirically and were abetted by sock hops, or dances executed in stocking feet, and interest in such things as the old Howdy Doody television show.

Hard Rock. The popular Grand Funk Railroad continued to offer its idea of hard rock—dismally, according to most critics, but the fans were fanatic. The Rolling Stones and the Beach Boys also played rock but in varied contexts and with increasing sophistication. The Stones' *Sticky Fingers* and the Beach Boys' *Surf's Up* were among the best albums of 1971. The rejuvenated Bee Gees, artistically a shadow of their former selves, some critics felt, nevertheless had two fast-selling songs in their album *Trafalgar.* Gravel-voiced Rod Stewart's song *Maggie May* was a major hit even though its theme—the problem of feeling "owned" that can come with feeling loved—would seem too subtle for a year that so easily accommodated the unpolished Grand Funk Railroad.

Folk and Country Music. Many Americans favored folklike music. Cat Stevens, an Englishman, had great success with his albums *Tea for the Tillerman* and *Teaser and the Firecat.* He wrote songs of fragile beauty and sang with a tough-delicate baritone. The popular Kris Kristofferson produced a fine new album, *The Silver-Tongued Devil and I,* and his songs continued to be recorded by many pop and country performers.

It was a good year for several established folk-oriented performers. Judy Collins' *Whales and Nightingales* and Joni Mitchell's *Blue* albums won critical praise. James Taylor's *Mud Slide Slim* did not, but sold well. Rock composer Carole King blossomed as a singer, and her *Tapestry* album was particularly well received. Unclassifiable Jimmy Webb also came out singing on his extraordinary *Words and Music* album.

Country music became increasingly influential—at its own expense, some felt. John Denver's *Take Me Home Country Roads* was the best, artistically and commercially, of countless country-influenced popular songs. Many rock groups moved closer to a country sound. However, some country singers, notably Lynn Anderson, Ray Price, and Jerry Reed, with strings and choruses cooing behind them,

NONESUCH RECORDS

RECORDING of Scott Joplin's piano rags, composed around 1900, stimulated new interest in ragtime music.

sounded more like pop singers. Miss Anderson's version of *Rose Garden,* written by pop singer-songwriter Joe South and featuring lavish orchestration, was a top seller in both the country and pop fields.

NOEL COPPAGE
Contributing Editor, "Stereo Review"

JAZZ RECORDS

Jazz passed an inevitable milestone in 1971 when Louis Armstrong died on July 6. His significance lay not only in the influence he had on jazz, lifting it to an art of universal appeal, but also in the fact that his lifetime paralleled the beginning and possibly the end of jazz as an identifiably separate musical idiom. Both Armstrong and jazz were born in New Orleans—Armstrong on July 4, 1900, and jazz at approximately the same time. When he died, jazz as he knew it seemed about to be absorbed in a broader, all-inclusive style of music dominated, at the moment, by rock. (See ARMSTRONG, LOUIS.)

Retrospective Armstrong Discs. On records, Armstrong's death was marked by the appearance of two collections of his recordings. *The Genius of Louis Armstrong, Volume 1: 1923–1933* (Columbia G 30416, 2 discs) covers the peak of his creativity and includes recordings by his Hot Five and Hot Seven which are foundation stones of jazz improvisation. *Louis Armstrong, July 4, 1900/July 6, 1971* (RCA Victor VPM 6044) carries through Armstrong's big-band period to his return to a small group in the late 1940's.

Renewed Interest in Ragtime. At the same time that currently exploratory jazz musicians tended to become part of a broader, rock-focused music, there was a renewed interest, particularly on records, in the historical aspects of jazz. In 1971 much attention was given to ragtime, one of the early contributory elements to jazz. Biograph Records began issuing a series of recordings of ragtime piano rolls played by Scott Joplin, James P. Johnson, Fats Waller, and Jelly Roll Morton (Biograph Records 1000 Q-1008Q). Two collections of piano rags were recorded by classically trained pianists—*Scott Joplin Piano Rags* played by Joshua Rifkin (Nonesuch 71248) and *Heliotrope Bouquet* played by William

DEEP-VOICED Kris Kristofferson had a successful new album, *The Silver-Tongued Devil and I,* in 1971. He is also noted as a composer and had many songs recorded by pop and country performers during the year.

CBS RECORDS

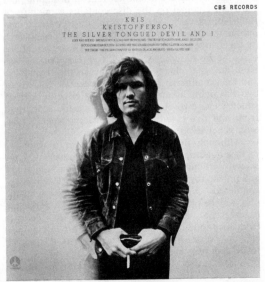

Bolcom (Nonesuch 71257). Ragtime songs in arrangements that were used by orchestras during the Ragtime Era (1897–1917) were recorded by two orchestras, in New Orleans and Los Angeles, respectively—the *New Orleans Ragtime Orchestra* (Pearl 7) and the *Dawn of the Century Ragtime Orchestra* (Arcane 601).

Reissues. RCA revived its Vintage series of reissues, starting with three sets of small group jazz from the late 1930's and early 1940's (Lionel Hampton, RCA Victor LPV 575; Hot Lips Page, RCA Victor LPV 576; Swing, Vol. 1, RCA Victor LPV 578) and three sets by blues singers of the 1940's (Lil Green, RCA Victor LPV 574; Arthur "Big Boy" Crudup, RCA Victor LPV 573; Washboard Sam, RCA Victor LPV 577). Stan Kenton bought back the rights to his old records and began reissuing them on his own Creative World label, sold exclusively by mail.

Other important Releases. Mainstream Records, once a valuable source of jazz and blues recordings, returned to jazz with discs by several contemporary musicians recording for the first time with groups of their own. They included *Hal Galper* (Mainstream 337), *Charles Williams* (Mainstream 312), *Mike Longo* (Mainstream 334), and *Buddy Terry* (Mainstream 336).

Another important release was *Fenix* (Flying Dutchman 10144), by Gato Barbieri, an Argentinian saxophonist, known earlier as part of the avant-garde jazz school. After reabsorbing his native music, he mixed it with his jazz background and found his own individuality.

Other jazz releases of special interest include Count Basie, *Afrique* (Flying Dutchman 10138); Duke Ellington, *New Orleans Suite* (Atlantic 1580); Maynard Ferguson, *M. F. Horn* (Columbia C 30466); Earl Hines, *At Home* (Delmark 212); Billy Taylor, *OK, Billy!* (Bell 6049); and Original Salty Dogs, *Free Wheeling* (GHB 58).

JOHN S. WILSON, *"The New York Times"*
and "High Fidelity" Magazine

AUDIO EQUIPMENT AND TECHNIQUES

In 1971 the community of audio manufacturers and enthusiasts restively waited for the evolution of firm standards for four-channel stereo reproduction. In turn, the evolution of such standards seemed to wait on the development of a four-channel phonograph disc system that would be satisfactory to all.

"Compatibility" has been one of the key concepts in four-channel developments. If a four-channel recording is "compatible," it will reproduce all of its musical information without unacceptable loss on conventional two-channel stereophonic equipment and even on monophonic equipment. Lack of this compatibility has probably slowed the sales of four-channel open-reel and eight-track cartridge tapes. In contrast, all of the present four-channel disc systems are reasonably compatible. Thus the consumer can buy and play the disc recordings no matter what equipment he owns.

Dynaco, Electro-Voice, and Sansui Systems. At the beginning of 1971, Dynaco, Electro-Voice, and Sansui were the leading producers of four-channel disc systems. Each of the systems is based on the use of a matrix for recording sound from four sources on just two channels on the disc. As a matrix recording of this type is made, the four original channels are mixed into two channels with careful manipulation of their relative strengths. For playback, a decoder is used to spread the stereo image over the four encompassing speakers in a manner dictated by the previous manipulations of the original four channels.

Since this matrix technique does not provide any more total channel separation than does conventional stereophony, the integrity of all four channels is not completely preserved. There is some leakage of information into channels where it should not be, and this leakage tends to mar the definition and localization of the stereo image. Within limits, the system designers have been free to adjust channel separation for the best aural effect, maximizing it for one speaker pair and skimping on the other. But the result still is a compromise, and this has impeded the general acceptance of any of the systems.

CBS System. CBS (Columbia) unveiled its four-channel phonograph disc system, called the SQ system, in mid-1971. Like the Dynaco, Electro-Voice, and Sansui systems, it is a matrix technique, but it differs from the other three systems in that it uses phase as well as amplitude manipulations for the recording and recovery of four channels from the two channels recorded on a disc.

By altering the phase angles of the left and right rear channels before they are mixed with the left and right front channels in the recording studio, the SQ system is able to cancel electrically some of the unwanted cross-channel leakage during playback, thereby significantly increasing the total separation provided by the system. Given its options in apportioning channel separation among the four speakers, CBS decided to maximize the left-to-right separation in both the front and the rear and to skimp on the front-to-back separation. However, CBS has designed two playback decoders, and one of them contains logic circuitry to detect and attenuate cross-channel leakage. According to CBS, about 50 SQ-processed LP recordings would be released by the end of 1971.

RCA-JVC System. In October 1971, RCA announced that it will attempt to perfect a four-channel disc system developed by the Japan Victor Corporation (JVC). The JVC system, which is not based on the matrix recording technique, very much resembles the stereo FM multiplex system of radio broadcasting. The left channel on the disc contains a mixture of left-front and left-rear information, and the right channel on the disc contains a mixture of right-front and right-rear information. A frequency-modulated ultrasonic carrier also is recorded in each of the two channels on the disc. The modulations embody the difference information between the left front and rear channels and between the right front and rear channels. The playback decoder consists of two FM demodulator and multiplex circuits, each of which yields two channels (left front and rear, right front and rear), with no audible impairment of interchannel separation.

Although RCA has set no date for introducing its first quadraphonic discs, JVC and Panasonic have shown production-ready decoders and ancillary equipment for the RCA-JVC system. RCA has encountered some difficulties with the JVC system, the knottiest being record wear. Typical mass-produced phonograph pickups would obliterate the delicate frequency modulations on the disc in a few playings, leaving no means for the decoder to distinguish front and rear channels.

RALPH W. HODGES
Associate Technical Editor, "Stereo Review"

GAUNT and still terror-stricken, a Bengali refugee mother in India clutches her child. Strife in East Pakistan (Bangladesh) in 1971 created about 10 million refugees, most of whom fled to India, greatly straining Indian resources.

REFUGEES

At the end of October 1971 the world refugee population was estimated to be 23,857,405, an increase within the year of 6.2 million. Most of these people had fled their homes and found asylum in 67 different countries on every continent. Some, including the South Vietnamese, were refugees in their own countries.

Asia. The two areas accounting for most of the increase were South Vietnam and India. By Oct. 1, 1971, the Indian government said, more than 10 million refugees had arrived there from East Pakistan—the largest and most terrible movement of people in this century. India reacted to the 1971 influx with characteristic generosity, but called upon the international community, through the United Nations, for assistance. The needs of the refugees, added to the poverty of India's own people, formed an overwhelming burden and a threat to India's economic development and the peace of the region.

At the end of September 1971 the UN high commissioner for refugees, the focal individual for refugee assistance from the international community, reported that he had received almost $114 million in contributions. The estimate of funds needed to March 1972 for basic relief such as shelter, clothing, medicine, and food exceeded $600 million. There was little hope for early repatriation of the Pakistani refugees. In December 1971, war between India and Pakistan worsened the refugees' problems.

Another major source of refugees in Asia was the area of Cambodia and Laos into which the Vietnam War had expanded. Estimates differed widely as to the number of refugees in South Vietnam, believed to be 3.5 million, not including 200,000 persons of Vietnamese ethnic origin who had been driven out of Cambodia.

Middle East. Palestinian refugees, numbering 1.5 million, represent one of the world's oldest and most difficult refugee problems. Hope rose for political settlement in the Middle East in 1971, but it faded by year-end. The UN Relief and Works Agency (UNRWA) continued its progress in education, health, and welfare, but it faced a budget deficit of $600 million and the threat of curtailment of some of its most important activities.

Africa. The rural resettlement and development schemes sponsored by the UN High Commission for Refugees and the governments of asylum countries continued to bring many thousands of refugees to self-support and represented a major contribution to the stability of the African continent.

The most serious problem was the continuing flight of refugees from southern Sudan to surrounding countries. There was no apparent progress in efforts by the Sudanese government at Khartoum to persuade the refugees to return.

Europe. There were no major changes in the refugee problem in Europe, although 1971 saw a marked increase in the migration of Jewish people from the USSR to Israel and the West.

Western Hemisphere. Cuba unaccountably interrupted the flow of refugees to the United States, permitting flights only on a reduced and irregular basis. There were estimated to be some 450,000 Cuban refugees in the United States, most of whom had become permanent residents.

R. NORRIS WILSON
United States Committee for Refugees

REHNQUIST, William H. See BIOGRAPHY.

WORLD SYNOD of bishops of the Roman Catholic Church is addressed by Pope Paul VI at its first meeting, September 30, in the Sistine Chapel, Rome.

UPI

RELIGION

Developments in the major religions of the world in 1971, including trends, meetings, and principal events, are covered under the following headings: (1) General Survey; (2) Protestantism; (3) Roman Catholicism; (4) Judaism; (5) Orthodox Eastern Church; (6) Islam; and (7) Oriental Religions. A statistical table giving the membership of U. S. denominations is also included.

General Survey

In 1971 world religious bodies continued to work for ecumenism and greater awareness of social change. Some considered or planned restructuring, partly with these ends in view.

Ecumenism. Leaders of the World Council of Churches, meeting in Addis Ababa, Ethiopia, emphasized the importance of dialogue between Christianity and other faiths. A commission of Roman Catholic and Anglican theologians issued an officially approved statement of their common beliefs about the Eucharist. The Roman Catholic and Orthodox churches each improved relations with other Eastern Churches. In the United States, the National Council of Churches considered plans to admit the Roman Catholic and conservative Protestant churches. Many Protestant denominations in Canada, England, New Zealand, and the United States planned or considered mergers.

Social Awareness. The Synod of Bishops of the Roman Catholic Church, meeting in Rome, called for more vigorous action for social change, including changes in organization to render the church more credible to the poor and oppressed. Pope Paul VI issued an apostolic letter stressing the need for more decisive and creative social action.

In the United States, the Consultation on Church Union urged its nine member-churches to work more actively for racial and economic justice and to give a larger church role to youth, women, and ethnic minorities. Many churches began to reexamine the social implications of their stock holdings and called for representation of the public interest on corporate boards. Jewish groups planned programs to deal with social problems.

In renewed efforts to maintain separation of church and state, the U. S. Supreme Court severely restricted the use of tax funds for parochial schools. A proposed constitutional amendment to permit prayer in public schools was defeated in Congress. Some religious leaders objected to the holding of religious services in the White House.

Restructuring. Roman Catholic bishops agreed on the need for a church constitution but thought that the conservative draft presented to them required much further work. Theologians discussed the validity of the concept of papal infallibility. The Vatican abandoned the term "heresy," meaning theological error, and instituted more liberal procedures for dealing with variant opinions. The Synod of Bishops upheld the popularly much-questioned requirement of celibacy for priests, but many bishops wanted to allow the possibility of ordaining married men in exceptional circumstances.

Anglican leaders, convening in Kenya, narrowly approved the ordination of women as priests, and the first two were ordained in Hong Kong. The Methodist World Conference, meeting in Denver, Colo., reorganized so as better to represent Third World churches, although power remained in the hands of U. S. and British Methodists.

Young People in the United States. The fundamentalist, emotionally oriented "Jesus Revolution" attracted many young people, and "Gospel" music and theater flourished on Broadway (see THEATER). A study revealed that religion courses draw many undergraduates and religion is the fastest-growing field of graduate study in secular universities.

Missions. Missions have taken on new styles and goals. In Roman Catholic countries, the affirmation of new rights for Protestants since Vatican Council II has resulted in dramatic increases in the numbers of Protestants, especially in South America, and in new ecumenical ventures. Social service was increasingly separated from evangelistic work. Indigenous leadership was emphasized, and new forms of interfaith dialogues often supplanted traditional proselytizing. In Africa and South America, the church endorsed revolutionary social movements.

Renewed American contacts with mainland

Religious Body	Members	Religious Body	Members
Adventists, Seventh-day	407,766	Friends United Meeting	69,149
American Carpatho-Russian Orthodox Greek Catholic Church	104,600	Greek Orthodox Archdiocese of North and South America	1,875,000
Apostolic Overcoming Holy Church of God	75,000[1]	Independent Fundamental Churches of America	122,388
Armenian Apostolic Church of America	125,000	Int'l Church of the Foursquare Gospel	89,215[11]
Armenian Church of North America, Diocese of the	300,000	Jehovah's Witnesses	359,146
Assemblies of God	625,027	Jewish Congregations	5,780,000[12]
Baptist Association, American	786,536	Latter-Day Saints, Church of Jesus Christ of	1,930,811[8]
Baptist Association of America, Conservative	300,000	Latter-Day Saints, Reorganized Church of Jesus Christ of	200,113
Baptist Church, United Free Will	100,000[2]	Lutheran Church, The American	2,559,588
Baptist Churches, General Association of Regular	192,495	Lutheran Church in America	3,135,684
Baptist Convention, American	1,454,965[3]	Lutheran Church—Missouri Synod	2,786,102
Baptist Convention, Inc., National Primitive	1,523,000	Lutheran Synod, Wisconsin Evangelical	376,319
Baptist Convention, Inc., Progressive National	521,692[3]	Mennonite Church	85,343
Baptist Convention of America, National	2,668,799[1]	Methodist Church, The United	10,824,010
Baptist Convention, Southern	11,487,708	Methodist Church of North America, Free	64,394
Baptist Convention, U.S.A., Inc., National	5,500,000[4]	Methodist Episcopal Church, African	1,166,301[5]
Baptist Evangelical Life and Soul Saving Assembly of U.S.A., National	57,674[5]	Methodist Episcopal Church, Christian	466,718[13]
Baptist General Conference	101,226	Methodist Episcopal Zion Church, African	940,000
Baptist General Conference, North American	55,080	Moravian Church in America, Northern Province, The	37,058
Baptist Missionary Association of America	183,342	Moravian Church in America, Southern Province, The	22,357
Baptists, Free Will	200,000	North American Old Roman Catholic Church	59,422
Baptists, General Ass'n of General	65,000	Orthodox Church in America (Russian Orthodox Greek Catholic Church of America)	1,000,000
Baptists, Primitive	72,000[6]	Pentecostal Church, Inc., United	200,000
Baptists, United	63,641[7]	Pentecostal Church of God of America, Inc.	115,000[3]
Brethren, Church of the	185,198	Pentecostal Holiness Church, Inc.	66,790
Buddhist Churches of America	100,000[8]	Polish National Catholic Church of America	282,411[14]
Bulgarian Eastern Orthodox Church	86,000[9]	Presbyterian Church, Cumberland	92,368
Christian and Missionary Alliance, The	120,330	Presbyterian Church in the U.S.A., The United	3,165,490
Christian Church (Disciples of Christ)	1,444,465	Reformed Church, Christian	284,737
Christian Reformed Church	284,737	Reformed Church in America	380,133
Church of Christ, Scientist	268,915[10]	Roman Catholic Church, The	47,872,089
Church of God, The	75,290	Romanian Orthodox Episcopate of America	50,000
Church of God (Anderson, Ind.)	147,752	Russian Orthodox Church Outside Russia	55,000[7]
Church of God (Cleveland, Tenn.)	257,995	Serbian Eastern Orthodox Diocese for the U.S.A. and Canada	65,000[3]
Church of the Nazarene	372,943	Spiritualists, International General Assembly of	164,072[1]
Churches of Christ	2,400,000[8]	Unitarian Universalist Association	265,408
Congregational Christian Churches, National Association of	110,000	United Church of Christ	1,997,898
Episcopal Church, The	3,330,272	Wesleyan Church, The	82,358[3]
Evangelical Covenant Church of America	67,522		
Evangelical Free Church of America, The	63,735		

Figures are mainly for the years 1969 and 1970. [1] 1956. [2] 1952. [3] 1967. [4] 1958. [5] 1951. [6] 1950. [7] 1955. [8] 1968. [9] 1962. [10] Data not reported; figure given here from U.S. Census of Religious Bodies, 1936. [11] 1963. [12] 1966. [13] 1965. [14] 1960. (Source: National Council of Churches of Christ in the U.S.A., Yearbook of American Churches for 1971.)

China, however, indicate that most religions there appear to have been eclipsed by the Communist cultural revolution. Observers noted the quasi-religious devotion to the thought of Mao Tse-tung.

Strife. In many places religious, political, and ethnic differences, mutually aggravating, produced conflict. Violence between Protestants and Catholics raged in Northern Ireland. The Jewish Defense League agitated with new militancy in behalf of Soviet Jews, and increased political tensions in the Middle East further strained Jewish-Muslim relations. Longstanding Muslim-Hindu tensions contributed to the war in East Pakistan.

J. A. MARTIN, JR., *Columbia University*

Protestantism

A religion editor characterized 1971 as a "year of indecision" for Protestant churches.

Ecumenism. The Central Committee of the World Council of Churches (WCC) met in Addis Ababa, Ethiopia, in January. The chief topics were dialogue between Christianity and other faiths, nonviolent approaches to social change, and restructuring the council. The WCC's Commission on Faith and Order, meeting at a Jesuit seminary in Louvain, Belgium, dealt with the theme "The Unity of the Church and the Unity of Mankind," signaling the council's commitment to healing rifts in society.

Two important consensus statements on the Eucharist were released: one by a commission of Protestant, Orthodox, and Roman Catholic theologians, and the other by the Anglican–Roman Catholic International Commission with the approval of Pope Paul VI and of Michael Ramsey, the Archbishop of Canterbury.

The documents represented major progress in overcoming historic divisions and moving toward joint participation in the sacraments. Theological agreements were also reached by representatives from Lutheran, Reformed, and United (Protestant) churches meeting at Leuenberg, Switzerland.

In England, Presbyterian and Congregational assemblies voted to unite. The Canadian General Commission on Church Union at Windsor, Ont., considered a draft plan to unite Anglicans, the United Church of Canada, and the Disciples of Christ. In New Zealand a final plan to unite five churches was sent to them for approval in 1972 and 1973. Mission churches in India related to the British Disciples entered the year-old Church of North India. However, the United Methodist Church left the year-old Church of Christ in the Congo (Kinshasa), because, it was said, of a legal dispute.

In the United States the General Board of the National Council of Churches sent a plan for reorganization to its members for approval. The Consultation on Church Union (USA), meeting in September in Denver, Colo., called upon its nine member-churches to work harder to overcome the sociological as well as theological barriers that divide them.

ORDINATION of Carol Anderson as a deacon by the Right Rev. Horace W. B. Donegan, Episcopal Bishop of the New York Diocese. She was one of the first two women to be ordained deacon in the New York diocese.

Polarization and Conservatism. Conflicts and polarities were accentuated in 1971. In Northern Ireland civil war between Protestants and Roman Catholics savagely intensified the traditional political and religious conflict and encouraged future strife. The government of South Africa sentenced Gonville A. ffrench-Beytagh, the Anglican dean of Johannesburg, to five years imprisonment for his long-time protest against the country's policy of racial segregation, and it cancelled the visit of a WCC-sponsored team of church leaders. In the United States controversy centered on the United Presbyterian Church's $10,000 grant to ensure fair treatment for black militant Communist Angela Davis in her trial. Although the church did not endorse Miss Davis' position, hundreds of congregations objected and withheld funds from the national church budget.

Conservatism was active in several churches. The Southern Baptist Convention forced its Sunday School Board to withdraw a quarterly containing photographs of black and white young people conversing. Four dissident conservative groups decided to withdraw from the Presbyterian Church in the United States if it carries out its proposed union with the United Presbyterian Church. In the Lutheran Church–Missouri Synod, however, conservatives led by president Jacob A. O. Preus, who initiated an investigation of the theology of the faculty of Concordia Seminary in 1970, were narrowly defeated. Moderates elected their own candidates to the board of the seminary and refused to regard doctrinal statements by the synod as binding.

Evangelism, Pentecostalism, and Popular Religion. Protestants showed renewed concern for evangelism. Several denominations convened evangelistic "celebrations." The 12th World Methodist Conference, meeting in Denver, initiated a 4-year period emphasizing evangelism. In Amsterdam the first European Congress on Evangelism brought together leaders from different nations and denominations.

Pentecostalism, a movement emphasizing the gift of speaking in tongues, surged forth in numerous places. Charismatic groups manifested themselves in Quebec and Saskatchewan and in the southwestern United States. A new survey revealed that they also constitute two thirds of Latin American Protestants. In a new dimension of ecumenism, theologians from the Pentecostal Fellowship of North America and the Roman Catholic Church held their first dialogue, in Rome.

Religion was an important theme in the entertainment world, as evidenced by the popular success of Leonard Bernstein's *Mass,* the rock-musicals, *Jesus Christ Superstar* and *Godspell,* and folk-singer Judy Collins' rendition of *Amazing Grace.*

Youth. Young people became increasingly active in religious matters. The 8th General Synod of the United Church of Christ included 140 young people among its 700 voting delegates and changed its bylaws to require that 20% of delegates to future synods be young people. In evangelist Billy Graham's northern California crusade, 70% of the "decisions for Christ" were made by students. Young people at the White House Conference on Youth at Estes Park, Colo., spoke of "the hypocrisy of organized religion" and urged churches to become more involved in social and political issues.

The "Jesus Movement," a Jesus-centered youth movement founded in the 1960's, attracted wide attention. The life style of the Jesus people—involving long hair, beads, and opposition to drugs—and their liturgical and theological focus—marked by Gospel-rock music, confrontation evangelism, and Bible study—shaped a new religious approach.

Minorities. Women became leaders in several churches. Mrs Ralph H. Stair was elected the first woman moderator of the United Presbyterian Church. Mrs. Marcus Rohlfs became fifth woman president of the American Baptist Convention. The Anglican Consultative Council, meeting in Kenya, narrowly approved the principle of the ordination of women as priests. Two women were ordained deacons in Hong Kong in November.

Negroes were also prominent in church affairs. The Christian Church (Disciples of Christ) elected its first black moderator, Walter D. Bingham. The National Committee of Black Churchmen sponsored a consultation in Dar es Salaam, Tanzania, between American blacks and African religious and government leaders. The Rev. Jesse Jackson resigned from the Southern Christian Leadership Conference to form a new organization for economic aid to blacks (see BIOGRAPHY). Some churches evaluated their common-stock portfolios with the idea of urging reforms on certain companies, such as Gulf Oil, which operates in Portuguese-controlled Angola.

Deaths. Prominent Protestants who died in 1971 included Angus Dun, Episcopal bishop of Washington, D. C., and Faith and Order leader; George C. Pidgeon, first moderator of the United Church of

Canada; and Reinhold Niebuhr, outstanding American theologian (see NIEBUHR, REINHOLD).

PAUL A. CROW, JR.
General Secretary, Consultation on Church Union

Roman Catholicism

The main event in the Roman Catholic world in 1971 was the Synod of Bishops, beginning on September 30.

Synod. The Synod, representing bishops from all over the world assembled in Rome to advise Pope Paul VI, was the third such body since Vatican Council II. It considered two principal issues—the priesthood, involving the shortage of priests and the concept of celibacy, and social justice. The press, focussing chiefly on celibacy, reported that a number of priests, including many Americans, surveyed either by organization or individually, strongly favored optional celibacy. The bishops upheld the Pope's repeatedly urged position that the ancient requirement of celibacy for priests of the Latin rite not be relaxed. However, in regard to ordaining married men in particular cases, the vote was 87 in favor to 107 against.

On the topic of social justice, the Synod sided with poorer nations, who suffer at the hands of international trade and monetary institutions in which they have no voice. Two American cardinals, John Dearden of Detroit and John Krol of Philadelphia, ex-president and new president, respectively, of the National Conference of Catholic Bishops, spoke urgently in support of peace in Vietnam and of conscientious objection. Other bishops favored a greater role for women in the Church. Indeed, the Synod had two nuns as consultants, and it also broke precedent in hearing an address from a woman, the economist Barbara Ward.

Church in Eastern Europe. The presence at the Synod of two bishops from eastern Europe reflected improved relations between the Church and some Communist governments. One bishop was the Polish primate, Stefan Cardinal Wysynski. The other was József Cardinal Mindszenty, who, to escape a sentence of life imprisonment by the Communist regime of Hungary, had spent 15 years in self-imposed exile in the U. S. Embassy in Budapest. It was believed that Pope Paul had long urged him to relieve political tensions by agreeing to quit Hungary. Mindszenty arrived in Rome on September 28.

Dramatic but less encouraging was the withdrawal from the Synod of 16 Eastern-rite bishops of the Ukrainian Catholic Church led by Josyf Cardinal Slipyj. Although they formed their own synod against the pope's wishes, they disclaimed any intention of leaving the Roman Catholic Church. They wanted more self-government and they objected to Vatican efforts to improve relations with the Soviet government and the Russian Orthodox Church at the expense of millions of Ukrainian Catholics. These believers, who have long been officially merged by the Soviet government with the Russian Orthodox Church, consider themselves "inconvenient witnesses of past evils."

Ecumenism. Ecumenism between Roman Catholic and other churches made quiet but steady progress. Early in the year the Anglican-Roman Catholic International Commission published documents that indicated wide areas of agreement in concepts of authority and ministry. A significant document on the Eucharist appeared in December, with the approval of the pope and the archbishop of Canterbury. It demonstrated deep agreement on the Real Presence of Christ in the Sacrament together with recognition of various emphases in the different Christian traditions. The statement, worded with great theological accuracy, was recognized as an unprecedented step toward church unity.

Peace. World peace was a major concern of the Church in 1971. American bishops stated their views not only at the Synod but also at home. In May, bishops of the Boston area urged a speedy end to the war in Indochina. In September, Lawrence Cardinal Shehan of Baltimore spoke out no less insistently. The National Conference of Catholic Bishops, meeting in Washington in November, stated their conviction that the destruction caused by the Vietnam War outweighed any possible good and declared their

CARDINAL MINDSZENTY (*left*) is greeted by Pope Paul VI at the Vatican, September 28, shortly after the cardinal's arrival from Budapest. The cardinal had acceded to the papal request that he end his 15 years of self-imposed exile in the U. S. embassy in Budapest, where he had sought refuge from a 1949 sentence of life imprisonment imposed by the Hungarian authorities.

consequent "moral obligation to appeal urgently to ... the leaders of all the nations involved ... to bring the war to an end with no further delay." In December, Bishop Carroll T. Dozier of Memphis published a pastoral letter condemning the war and asking for immediate American withdrawal. In what was interpreted by some as a reprisal, his priest superintendent of education was immediately reclassified 1-A by the local draft board.

Other Social Questions. In Latin American society, the thrust toward greater social awareness and reform (*concientización*) continued to meet both welcome and resistance from Roman Catholics. In Brazil, tension increased between the reforming Archbishop Helder Camara and his more conservative confrères. In Panama, the socially minded Father Hector Gallego mysteriously disappeared after a conflict with the government, which denied being implicated but refused permission for an independent investigation.

Minority groups in the United States continued to press for greater recognition of their needs. Both Mexican-Americans and Negroes insisted that at least one priest from each minority be appointed bishop of a diocese. Especially dramatic was the Negro Catholic request of the Vatican that a Negro bishop be appointed to predominantly black Washington, D. C.; a special Negro rite be instituted; and American Negroes be represented in the Curia.

The number of American parochial schools declined further in 1971 as fewer nuns were available to teach, and a U. S. Supreme Court decision made government grants almost impossible. However, the high court ruled favorably on government funds to a Catholic college as educational rather than religious aid.

American Catholics, in what appears to be a minority, intensified their objection to the growing abortion movement. "Birthright," an originally Canadian program that now involves many American Roman Catholics and others, helps people who might be inclined to use abortion and condemns the killing of the "living fetus in the womb."

Liturgy and the Diaconate. The revised Roman breviary (priests' prayer book) appeared in Rome, as did a definitive missal (book for Masses) and a text for new funeral rites. The pope promulgated a new order for the sacrament of Confirmation, which uses the words of the Byzantine tradition.

American bishops requested a report on the office of deacon as a lifetime state as distinct from a step toward priesthood, an office which was restored by the pope in 1967. In various dioceses there were 28 such ordained deacons and 430 candidates, the majority of whom were married.

Christian Revival Movements. Two broadly Christian movements continued to affect many Roman Catholics. The Pentecostal renewal, which emphasizes spontaneous, emotional prayer meetings, attracted large numbers of both young and old people and was supported by individual bishops and theologians. The "Jesus Revolution," stressing a vibrant attachment to the person of Jesus without institutional commitment, appealed to many of the young. Whatever the criticism of the theatrical productions *Godspell, Jesus Christ Superstar,* and Leonard Bernstein's *Mass,* their popular success seemed to reflect the strength of this movement. (See also MUSIC; THEATER.)

C. J. McNaspy, S. J.
Loyola University, New Orleans

Judaism

The year 1971 in the Jewish community was marked by increased awareness of the problems facing Jews. There were also changes in the academic and scholarly worlds.

Soviet Jews. There was a significant rise in Jewish consciousness among the more than 3 million Jews in the Soviet Union. The trials of Jewish dissidents did not deter Jews from demanding their right to religious life and to emigration. A world conference of Jews, which met in Brussels in February, appealed to world public opinion to urge the Soviet Union to comply. The death of the chief rabbi of Moscow, one of the few Jewish religious leaders left in the USSR, was a serious loss, since more than 50 years of Soviet rule have made it almost impossible to train religious authorities.

Judaism in Israel. In Israel, where Orthodox Jewish religious law is the law of the land in some areas of life, the need to modify ancient law in the light of modern situations was increasingly apparent. Storms of protest arose against the Orthodox prohibition of marriage between a Jew and a *mamzer* (child born in adultery) when that prohibition was invoked to forbid the marriage of the offspring of a woman who had remarried without a religious divorce. Women agitated to remove some of the disabilities against them sanctioned by ancient law. In the Reform and Reconstructionist movements, they were training for the rabbinate.

Jews in the United States—*Social Awareness.* In the United States, heightened Jewish awareness of the urban crisis led to a noticeable turning inward to concentrate on problems of the Jewish community rather than of the world at large. Jewish leaders meeting in Pittsburgh established an Institute for Jewish Life to strengthen the Jewish family and improve Jewish education in relation to contemporary life. B'nai B'rith planned programs to deal with the family, drugs, and Jewish urban poor. Day schools, offering Jewish and secular subjects, gained in importance. Many Jews viewed with alarm the rise in Jewish militancy evidenced by the wide publicity accorded the Jewish Defense League.

Academic World. Two great Jewish educational institutions experienced a changing of the guard. Hebrew Union College—Jewish Institute of Religion (Reform) lost its distinguished president Nelson Glueck, who died on February 12. He was replaced by Alfred Gottschalk.

At the Jewish Theological Seminary of America (Conservative), the head for 30 years, the eminent scholar Louis Finkelstein, will resign in 1972. He will be succeeded by historian Gershon Cohen. Rabbi Bernard Mandelbaum will be chancellor.

Scholarly World. The Jewish community mourned the deaths of two Protestant scholars. They were the theologian Reinhold Niebuhr, long-time friend of the Jewish community and one of the first Christian leaders to call for a halt to Christian missionizing among Jews, and the archaeologist William F. Albright, a close ally of Jewish scholars in probing the biblical period of the Jewish faith.

Important works of Jewish scholarship appeared in 1971. One was *Star of Redemption,* the excellent English translation, by William Hallo, of *Der Stern der Erlösung* (1921) by the German-Jewish theologian Franz Rosenzweig. This existentialist presentation of the Jewish faith influenced generations of German-speaking rabbis and teachers.

Another work, long in preparation, was the *Encyclopaedia Judaica,* the first such comprehensive treatment of Jewish culture and faith since 1904. The monumental 16-volume work covering Jewish concepts and experience was compiled by Jewish scholars around the world. Among them were Gershon Scholem of the Hebrew University in Jerusalem, a world authority on Jewish mysticism, and the eminent U.S. biblical scholar H. L. Ginsberg.

SEYMOUR SIEGEL
Jewish Theological Seminary of America

Orthodox Eastern Church

In 1971, Orthodox churches were concerned with preparation for a Pan-Orthodox Council and with ecumenism.

Orthodox Community. The Arrangements Committee for the forthcoming Pan-Orthodox Council unanimously asked Ecumenical Patriarch Athenagoras to convene a pre-synod Pan-Orthodox Conference in July 1972 to revise the agenda of the council. One subject of discussion will be the proposed common Christian observance of Easter on the second Sunday in April.

Representative Orthodox leaders, meeting in Alexandria, Egypt, in October, underscored the unity of the Orthodox faith and of the churches of the Orthodox communion. Orthodox churches generally protested three significant developments: the closing of the Orthodox Theological school in Halki by the Turkish government; the increase of public housing in Old Jerusalem, which they wish to preserve as a historic site; and even the limited intercommunion between Russian Orthodox and Roman Catholics agreed on in 1970. The Orthodox consider the "Common Cup" not a means toward but the result of the unification of Christian churches.

Ecumenism. Closer ties developed between Orthodox churches and non-Chalcedonian churches (Eastern churches outside the Orthodox communion). Theophilos, elected patriarch of the Church of Ethiopia in April, announced formally that his church has "a common Faith with the Orthodox Churches." Two other newly elected church leaders, the Coptic patriarch of Alexandria and the katholikos of the Syrian Orthodox (Malabar Jacobite) Church of India, said the same of their churches. The Armenian Patriarchate of Jerusalem has begun to make its liturgical life more like that of the Orthodox churches.

Relations improved among Orthodox, Roman Catholic, Anglican, Protestant, and Armenian, and other non-Chalcedonian churches in conferences at Geneva, Athens, and Helsinki. Pope Paul and Patriarch Athenagoras exchanged greetings and expressed their joint satisfaction in the strengthening of relations between their churches.

New Saints and Leaders. Patriarch Athenagoras canonized four saints: Raphael, Nicholas, and Irene, all of whom died in 1465, and Pelagia, who died in 1931. He also established the Patriarchal Institute for Patristic Studies in Salonika, Greece.

Prominent among new church leaders was Maximos, elected patriarch of Bulgaria on July 7, and Metropolitan Pimen of Krutitsy and Kolomna, elected patriarch of Moscow on June 2. Pimen's election by voice rather than secret ballot alienated other Orthodox churches. The Russian Orthodox Archdiocese of France and western Europe returned to the jurisdiction of the Ecumenical Patriarchate.

Archbishop Iakovos of the Greek Orthodox Archdiocese of North and South America was named patriarchal exarch by the Ecumenical Patriarch and received the "Man of Conscience" award from the Appeal for Conscience Foundation. He is chairman of the Standing Conference of Canonical Orthodox Bishops in America, which may eventually develop into an autonomous Orthodox Church in America including Orthodox of all national backgrounds. Hoping for such an event, the majority of Orthodox jurisdictions do not recognize Moscow's uncanonical 1970 proclamation of the Metropolia, one of three Russian Orthodox churches in the United States, as the Orthodox Church in America.

BASIL G. VASILIADIS
*Greek Orthodox Archdiocese
of North and South America*

NEW PATRIARCH of the Russian Orthodox Church, Metropolitan Pimen, was chosen by acclamation on June 2.

UPI

Islam

The most significant event in the Islamic world in 1971 was the tragic civil war that broke out in Pakistan in March. Claiming that they were acting to forestall a secessionist movement in East Pakistan, armies from West Pakistan ravaged the eastern province. The "secessionist" Muslims suffered greatly and the sizeable Hindu minority even more.

As a result, a tide of starving, diseased refugees, chiefly Hindu, sought shelter in India. By November the number was estimated to total about 10 million, and the exodus still continued. Pakistan accused the Indian government of actively conspiring against it. Finally, open warfare broke out between the two countries in December, ending two weeks later with the surrender of East Pakistan to Indian troops and the setting up of a new nation, Bangladesh. (See INDIA-PAKISTAN WAR.)

Background to the Tragedy. Underlying the civil war in Pakistan was the long-standing antagonism between Hindus and Muslims that had led to the creation of Pakistan in 1947. As the end of British rule in India had approached, many Indian Muslims feared that unless the Muslim community secured

"SPIRITUAL FESTIVAL" at the University of California at Davis offers sessions in yoga, a discipline that is gaining popularity along with interest in Oriental religions.

political autonomy, it would ultimately be submerged in the vast Hindu majority of the subcontinent. In more positive terms, Muslim leaders argued that Islam, by its very nature as a divinely ordained way of life, could be fully realized only in a state produced by Islamic values and devoted to them. Thus two geographically separated but predominantly Muslim areas of India were politically joined in the new Muslim state of Pakistan. Temporarily the power of a common faith and the vision of its political application unified the Pakistanis. Their patriotism was strengthened in disputes with Hindu India over water rights and Kashmir.

But the veneer of Muslim solidarity hid deep antagonisms within the Muslim community, based on geographical, physical, and cultural differences. Since West Pakistanis had played a more important role in government than their numbers warranted, East Pakistanis had felt excluded and exploited. After the horrors occurring in 1971 the gulf separating them appears to have become unbridgeable.

Future Possibilities. Although the crisis of Pakistan is painfully ironic in the light of the nation's religious vision, it does not mean that the concept of a modern Islamic state is unworkable or that Pakistan must inevitably disintegrate. Rather the

Pakistani ordeal emphasizes that the formation of Pakistan was only the beginning of a quest to define and implement a viable Islamic polity. The horror of Muslims' killing Muslims adds new urgency to that quest.

W. PAUL MCLEAN
Southern Methodist University

Oriental Religions

The religious world of Asia in 1971 was marked by tension and strife.

Hinduism and Islam. In India the comity between Hindus and Muslims during the era of Mohandas Gandhi seemed far in the past as their traditional hostility flared up again. Prime Minister Indira Gandhi's election campaign, a year ahead of schedule, in which she promised to use the wealth of Hindu princes to aid the poor, resulted in a big victory for the Congress party in March but was marred by riots between Hindus and Muslims.

Mutual hostility assumed a new form when, in the same month, Muslim West Pakistan decided to crush the independence movement in East Pakistan. An estimated 200,000 East Pakistani Hindus and Muslims were slaughtered, and an awesome 10 million refugees, two thirds of them Hindu, crossed into the Indian state of West Bengal. Pakistani authorities were reluctant to take the refugees back. India, hard pressed to feed its own population, found itself facing staggering costs to feed and shelter the refugees. Its burden was not eased by the influx of 200,000 Hindus forced out of Buddhist Burma by a nationalization program.

Increasing conflict between India and Pakistan led to open war in December. Within two weeks East Pakistan became independent of West Pakistan as Bangladesh. But the refugee problem remained.

Buddhism. In Buddhist Ceylon some 15,000 "Maoist" rebels staged an insurrection in May, allegedly because the government of Sirimavo Bandaranaike was slow in instituting socialist reforms. Mrs. Bandaranaike criticized the rebels for violating Buddhist traditions of compassion and nonviolence and called for a return to humane conduct, noting that no rebel had come from the Christian, Muslim, or Hindu minorities.

In Kashmir, the Muslim archivist Mohammed Amir reported finding a long-sought Buddhist pillar 50 miles south of Srinagar. Under it were reputedly buried the engraved copper plates recording the conference of Buddhist monks called by the Kushan King Kanishka in the 2d century A. D.

In Japan Soka Gakkai, a religious movement based on Nichiren Buddhism, severed its public ties with its powerful political arm, the Komeito party. It was concerned over charges that it was seeking to impose a fascist political regime on Japan.

Shinto. Church-state relations were also at issue in a case in Japan involving a Communist protest against a Shinto groundbreaking ceremony's being sponsored and paid for by a municipality. An appeals court ruled that the sponsorship of Shinto ceremonies—once part of the state religion—by public bodies was a violation of the constitution.

JOHN B. NOSS
Author of "Man's Religions"

REPUBLICAN PARTY. See ELECTIONS; POLITICAL PARTIES.

RESPIRATORY DISEASES. See MEDICINE.

RHODE ISLAND

Money—or the lack of it—dominated the Rhode Island scene in 1971.

State Income Tax. Although Democratic Gov. Frank Licht had pledged, in his closely contested 1970 election campaign, not to advocate a state personal income tax, once in office he proposed such a tax on the grounds that existing government programs could not be financed without it. A six-month tax was passed by the General Assembly in February, and it was proposed in July to make it permanent. These actions raised a public furor, gave political ammunition to the Republican opposition, and divided the Democratic majority. The reluctant session dragged on to record length before the Democratic leaders were finally able to mobilize the votes needed to pass the bill.

Although the public began grudgingly to recognize the inevitability of the income tax, Licht's policy had political repercussions. Public opinion polls showed a sharp drop in his standing, yet he clearly intended to run for reelection in 1972. Many Democratic legislators uneasily speculated on the possible loss of their seats. On the national level, Democratic Sen. Claiborne Pell looked toward a formidable challenge from the expected candidacy of Republican Secretary of the Navy John Chafee.

At year's end the financial dilemma loomed up again as projected public expenditures threatened to outpace revenue. The administration had to face two unpalatable alternatives—increasing taxes or drastically cutting back programs.

Environment. Taking significant steps in the area of environment, the legislature gave the governor the authority to shut down any polluting activity. It also provided for state regulation of fresh water bogs and other wetlands and established a council on shoreline development.

The Economy. Rhode Island, like most states, was hurt by recession, inflation, unemployment, rising costs, and laggard tax returns, a situation that encouraged state officials to favor federal revenue sharing and a phased national take-over of welfare costs. However, there was some comfort in the fact that although employment in manufacturing fell, employment in non-manufacturing rose to an all-time high. Also, in contrast to earlier recessions, the unemployment rate was not above the national figure. These comparisons testified to the greater diversification of industry achieved by the state in the last 10 years.

Education. Racial conflict broke out in Providence's Central High School in November, as it had a year before, forcing the suspension of classes. A combination of parent and student groups and school and city officials restored stability.

Unrelated to that disturbance but touching off a sharp debate was a plan offered by the new superintendent of Providence schools for the complete administrative reorganization of the school system. The plan, supported by the school committee, was opposed by many administrators.

DAVID D. WARREN
University of Rhode Island

RHODE ISLAND • Information Highlights

Area: 1,214 square miles (3,144 sq km).
Population (1970 census): 949,723. *Density:* 861 per sq mi.
Chief Cities (1970 census): Providence, the capital, 179,116; Warwick, 83,694; Pawtucket, 76,984; Cranston, 74,287; East Providence, 48,207; North Kingstown, 29,793.
Government (1971): *Chief Officers*—governor, Frank Licht (D); lt. gov., J. Joseph Garrahy (D); secy. of state, August P. LaFrance (D); atty. gen., Richard J. Israel (R); treas., Raymond H. Hawksley (D); commissioner, dept. of ed., Fred G. Burke; chief justice, Thomas H. Roberts. *General Assembly*—Senate, 50 members (41 Democrats, 9 Republicans); House of Representatives, 100 members (75 D, 24 R, 1 Independent).
Education (1970–71): *Enrollment*—public elementary schools, 111,157 pupils; 4,538 teachers; public secondary, 76,933 pupils; 4,450 teachers; nonpublic schools (1968–69); 48,400 pupils; 2,000 teachers; college and university (fall 1968), 44,740 students. *Public school expenditures* (1970–71), $159,061,000 ($951 per pupil). *Average teacher's salary,* $9,442.
State Finances (fiscal year 1970): *Revenues,* $438,738,000 (5% general sales tax and gross receipts taxes, $78,324,-000; motor fuel tax, $27,699,000; federal funds, $100,-679,000). *Expenditures,* $444,604,000 (education, $135,-223,000; health, welfare, and safety, $86,788,000; highways, $40,459,000). *State debt,* $373,200,000 (June 30, 1970).
Personal Income (1970): $3,808,000,000; per capita, $3,920.
Public Assistance (1970): $82,190,000. *Average monthly payments* (Dec. 1970)—old-age assistance, $56.80; aid to families with dependent children, $230.00.
Labor Force: *Nonagricultural wage and salary earners* (June 1971), 339,700. *Average annual employment* (1969)—manufacturing, 127,000; trade, 66,000; government, 53,000; services, 53,000. *Insured unemployed* (Oct. 1971)—12,100 (4.4%).
Manufacturing (1967): *Value added by manufacture,* $1,350,-900,000 (textile mill products, $188,200,000; primary metal industries, $162,000,000; nonelectrical machinery, $138,-600,000; fabricated metal products, $96,100,000).
Agriculture (1970): *Cash farm income,* $20,925,000 (livestock, $10,659,000; crops, $10,194,000; government payments, $72,000). *Chief crops* (1970)—Apples, 6,800,000 pounds; potatoes, 1,323,000 cwt.; corn silage, 65,000 tons.
Mining (1971): *Production value,* $4,442,000 (ranks 49th among the states). *Chief minerals*—Sand, stone, and gravel.
Fisheries (1970): *Commercial catch,* 78,400,000 pounds ($9,-700,000). *Leading species by value* (1967)—Scup or porgy, $1,303,624; yellowtail flounder, $487,313.
Transportation: *Roads* (1969), 5,397 miles (8,685 km); *motor vehicles* (1969), 470,000; *railroads* (1968), 146 miles (235 km); *airports* (1969), 7.
Communications: *Telephones* (1971), 530,700; *television stations* (1969), 2; *radio stations* (1969), 22; *newspapers* (1969), 7 (daily circulation, 319,000).

RHODESIA

The main developments in Rhodesia in 1971 were new talks with Britain over the question of Rhodesian independence, economic problems, and the possibility that the United States would purchase Rhodesian chrome ore and thus break the economic sanctions imposed on Rhodesia by the United Nations.

British-Rhodesian Talks. In 1971, British Prime Minister Edward Heath fulfilled his campaign promise to seek a "sensible and just solution" to Rhodesia's unilateral declaration of independence (UDI) in 1965 by initiating talks with Rhodesia. He sent a four-man team headed by Lord Goodman, a legal expert, to Salisbury for exploratory talks on June 23–July 7. The talks set the stage for a top-level meeting between Rhodesian Prime Minister Ian D. Smith and British Foreign Secretary Sir Alec Douglas-Home in Salisbury beginning November 15.

Although details remained secret, Britain's new, more gradual formula for settling the 6-year independence dispute was believed to include several points. Among them were: "unimpeded progress" toward majority rule over a period of 30 years; a ban on any new segregation laws; the elimination of racial discrimination; the raising of the political status of Africans, with British aid for African education and economic development; and the acceptance of the formula for independence by Rhodesia's Africans.

Economic Survey. An economic survey of Rhodesia in 1970 showed that only in tourism was there a notable gain. A record 320,290 tourists brought in almost $28 million. On the minus side was the decline in the economic growth rate from 10% in 1969 to 4.6%. Agricultural output remained static,

——————— RHODESIA • Information Highlights ———————

Official Name (unilateral declaration): Republic of Rhodesia.
Area: 150,333 square miles (389,361 sq km).
Population (1970 est.): 5,270,000. *Density,* 35 per square
  mile (13 per sq km). *Annual rate of increase,* 3.4%.
Chief Cities (1970 est.): Salisbury, the capital (city and
  suburbs), 400,000; Bolawayo, 250,000.
Government: *Head of state,* Clifford Dupont, president (took
  office April 17, 1970). *Head of government,* Ian D. Smith,
  prime minister (took office April 1964). *Parliament—*
  Senate, 23 members; House of Assembly, 66 members.
  *Major political parties—*Rhodesian Front, Centre party.
Languages: English (official), Bantu languages.
Education: *Literacy rate* (1970), 100% of Europeans, Asians,
  and Coloreds. Less than 30% of Africans. *Expenditure
  on education* (1967), 16.9% of total public expenditure.
  School enrollment (1965)—primary, 627,806; secondary,
  15,146; technical/vocational, 832; higher, 1,064.
Finances (1969 est.): *Revenues,* $268,200,000; *expenditures,*
  $272,200,000; *monetary unit,* Rhodesian dollar (0.7142 R.
  dollar equals U. S.$1, 1971).
Gross National Product (1970 est.): $1,440,000,000.
National Income (1969): $1,125,000,000; *per person,* $221.
Economic Indexes: *Industrial production* (1969), 151 (1963=
  100); *consumer price index* (1970), 118 (1963=100).
Manufacturing (metric tons, 1969): Cement, 382,000; sugar,
  120,000; wheat flour, 120,000; meat, 78,000.
Crops (metric tons, 1969 crop year): Maize (1968), 1,020,000;
  tobacco, 61,200; cotton lint, 43,000.
Minerals (metric tons, 1969): Coal, 3,332,000; iron ore
  (1966), 830,000; asbestos (1968), 86,000; copper ore,
  24,000; gold (1967), 15,532 kilograms.
Foreign Trade (1965): *Exports* (1970), $367,000,000 (chief
  exports—tobacco, unmanufactured, $131,510,000; crude
  fertilizers and minerals, $32,091,000. *Imports* (1970),
  $329,000,000 (chief imports—transport equipment, $45,-
  388,000; nonelectrical machinery, $44,612,000; chemicals,
  $37,660,000). *Chief trading partner* (1967)—South Africa.
Tourism: *Receipts* (1971), $28,000,000.
Transportation: *Roads* (1969), 47,754 miles (76,851 km);
  motor vehicles (1969), 178,600 (automobiles, 126,600);
  railroads (1969), 2,655 miles (4,272 km); *national airline,*
  Central African Airways Corp.; *principal airports,* Salisbury, Bolawayo.
Communications: *Telephones* (1970), 122,129; *television stations* (1968), 2; *television sets* (1969), 48,000; *radios*
  (1969), 135,000; *newspapers* (1969), 3 (daily circulation,
  72,000).

while tobacco production dropped from 275 million
pounds before UDI to about 132 million pounds.
Imports and exports increased, but they were below
pre-UDI levels.

Although African employment rose over 4%,
the African population grew at 3.6% a year. At
that rate, Rhodesia's 5.1 million Africans will double
within 18 years. While white immigration was
6,340, the highest in a decade, there was also an
exodus of the economically most active people—
those between 25 and 44 years of age.

UN Sanctions. Rhodesia is said to have a need
for spare parts for industrial equipment and aircraft.
Although the UN sanctions have been evaded by
some countries, the cumulative effect has forced
Rhodesia, in Prime Minister Smith's words, "to sell
at a discount and buy at a premium." Rhodesia's
main economic problem was its inability to attract
foreign development capital. These factors, plus
pressure from the Republic of South Africa, which
has been striving to improve relations with black
African countries, suggested that the Smith government try to reach an agreement with Britain.

U. S. Chrome Imports. Following the UN sanctions against Rhodesia in 1966, the United States increased its imports of more expensive chrome ore
from the Soviet Union, and the price of the ore rose
from $30 to $72 a ton.

In 1971, U. S. companies with chrome-producing
affiliates in Rhodesia continued to lobby for resumption of U. S. purchase of Rhodesian chrome
ore. Championing their cause, Sen. Harry Byrd of
Virginia, a member of the Armed Services Committee, inserted an amendment to the military procurement bill that would permit the imports. On
September 23 the amendment passed in the U. S.
Senate by a vote of 46 to 36. The House approved

it by 252 to 101 on November 10. The enactment
of the bill would join the United States with South
Africa and Portugal as the only nations publicly
breaking the UN sanctions. The UN General Assembly voted to censure the U. S. congressional
action on November 16.

Deaths. Two former prime ministers of Rhodesia died in 1971. Lord Malvern (Godfrey M.
Huggins), prime minister in 1933–1956, died on
May 8 at the age of 87. Sir Edgar Whitehead, prime
minister in 1958–1962, died on September 23 at the
age of 66.

FRANKLIN PARKER, *West Virginia University*

ROGERS, William P. See BIOGRAPHY.
ROMAN CATHOLIC CHURCH. See RELIGION.
RUCKELSHAUS, William. See BIOGRAPHY.

RUMANIA

During 1971, Rumania's leader Nicolae Ceauşescu
maintained a policy of national independence within
the Communist bloc despite the Soviet Union's displeasure with his tactics.

Relations with the USSR. An improvement in
relations with the USSR was marked by Rumania's
admission to the Soviet-sponsored International Investment Bank of Comecon, the bloc's counterpart
to the European Economic Community (EEC, or
Common Market), after years of hesitation. Rumania nevertheless secured a veto of investments
inimical to its self-interest. Ceauşescu also secured
admission to GATT (General Agreement on Tariffs
and Trade), an international body, and even sought
EEC economic preference.

In April, Ceauşescu participated in the 24th
Congress of the Soviet Communist party, where he
reiterated the familiar policy of independence and
respect for each state's right to pursue socialism in
its own way. He also assailed the Moscow-Peking
rift. Moscow then initiated a "war of nerves" by
summoning all East European leaders except
Ceauşescu to a conference in Prague in May.
Ceauşescu did send a minor representative. In July,
Soviet Premier Kosygin presided over a Comecon
meeting in Bucharest, where complex plans were
drafted to integrate bloc economies and to create a
convertible currency system. Rumania was then unsuccessfully pressed to permit Soviet troops to cross
the country for Warsaw Pact maneuvers.

Soviet pressure increased at the time of
Ceauşescu's visit to Communist China in June. Reaction to that much-publicized visit came at a
summit meeting of bloc leaders in the Crimea in
August. Rumania's policies toward the USSR, the
United States, and China were criticized. Moscow's
anger was also aroused by rumors of a Chinese
project to create an "anti-Soviet axis" of Rumania,
Albania, Yugoslavia, and China. Rumania bolstered
these fears by lauding U. S. President Nixon's plans
to visit Peking. When Ceauşescu tightened his
domestic policies, Moscow relaxed its psychological
warfare. Soviet Communist party chief Brezhnev's
visit to President Tito of Yugoslavia in September
concluded with a joint statement in which the Soviet
leader recognized Yugoslavia's—and hence Rumania's—right to proceed toward communism according to its own plans.

Ceauşescu in the Far East. Peking accorded
Ceauşescu the most lavish welcome ever given a
foreign dignitary. Nearly 500,000 people lined the

route from the airport on June 1. Communist party Chairman Mao Tse-tung made a rare public appearance to greet him, and Premier Chou En-lai escorted Ceauşescu on visits to Shanghai and Nanking. China agreed to grant Rumania $244 million in credits, and both nations issued statements criticizing "big power imperialism" and lauding independence for all states.

Ceauşescu next visited North Korea, Mongolia, and North Vietnam. Hungary obediently attacked his tour to indicate Moscow's displeasure over its success. Added anxieties were created in Moscow when a Chinese military delegation visited Rumania in August and promised aid in the case of an "imperialist threat" to Rumania's independence. Intimations that Ceauşescu was acting as an intermediary between Peking and Washington increased the Soviet annoyance.

Internal Reforms. While pursuing a precariously free line in foreign affairs, Ceauşescu sought to forestall a Soviet invasion by tightening controls at home. His actions followed an erratic course. In February he called for more freedom for labor unions and intellectuals. But in July he cracked down on "bourgeois influences" and conducted a "minipurge" among party officials. The head of the United Communist Youth was removed, and educational reforms introduced more vocational training. An emergency meeting of party leaders in August, after Ceauşescu met with the Soviet envoy, marked his espousal of ideological fundamentalism and even a possible return to Stalinism. This was followed in November by the establishment of tighter controls over intellectuals.

U. S. Relations. Talks with U. S. companies were held to increase trade. Foreign firms' interest in Rumania had been heightened by the passage late in 1970 of legislation permitting joint operations between the government and foreign companies. This was followed by U. S.–Rumanian negotiations on joint explorations for oil in the Black Sea. Ceauşescu, interviewed on U. S. television on May 7, expressed hopes for greater trade and cultural exchanges with the United States. Rumania will sponsor a visiting professor at Columbia University in 1972. The visits of President Nixon to Peking and Moscow will have great influence upon Rumania's future actions.

SHERMAN D. SPECTOR, *Russell Sage College*

--------- RWANDA • Information Highlights ---------

Official Name: Republic of Rwanda.
Area: 10,169 square miles (26,338 sq km).
Population (1970 est.): 3,590,000. *Density,* 350 per square mile (133 per sq km). *Annual rate of increase,* 3.0%.
Chief City (1970 est.): Kigali, the capital, 17,000.
Government: *Head of state,* Grégoire Kayibanda, president (took office for a 3d term Sept. 1969). *Head of government,* Grégoire Kayibanda. *Legislature*—National Assembly (unicameral), 47 members. *Major political parties*—Democratic Republican Movement.
Languages: French (official), Kinyarwanda (official).
Education: *Literacy rate* (1971), 10% of population. *Expenditure on education* (1968), 27.3% of total public expenditure. *School enrollment* (1967)—primary, 327,184; secondary, 8,842; technical/vocational, 912; university/higher, 233.
Finances (1970 est.): *Revenues,* $16,600,000; *expenditures,* $16,900,000; *monetary unit,* franc (92.053 francs equal U. S. $1, Dec. 30, 1971).
Gross National Product (1968 est.): $153,000,000.
Average annual income per person (1968 est.): $47.
Manufacturing (1969): Beer, 129,000 hectoliters.
Crops (metric tons, 1968 crop year): Sweet potatoes and yams, 300,000; cassava, 190,000; coffee (1969), 8,700.
Minerals (metric tons, 1969): Tin concentrates, 1,340.
Foreign Trade (1970): *Exports,* $24,708,000 (chief exports—coffee, tin). *Imports,* $29,099,000 (chief imports, 1968—textile yarn and fabrics, transport equipment). *Chief trading partners* (1968)—Belgium-Luxembourg; Uganda.
Transportation: *Roads* (1969), 3,534 miles (5,686 km); *motor vehicles* (1969), 5,300 (automobiles, 3,400).
Communications: *Telephones* (1970), 1,433; *radios* (1968), 30,000.

RWANDA

Under the leadership of President Grégoire Kayibanda, Rwanda continued to show remarkable internal stability in 1971.

As the Tutsis who had fled Rwanda in the 1960's resigned themselves to resettlement in surrounding countries, Rwanda's relations with its neighbors improved.

Development Projects. In 1971, Congo (Zaïre), Rwanda, and Burundi joined in studying potential development of lakes Tanganyika and Kivu, the latter of which has methane deposits. Rwanda also cooperated with Burundi and Tanzania in the Kagera River Project, partially financed by the United Nations Development Program. The first stage of the project, begun in June, involves a survey of hydroelectric resources.

Relations with Uganda. In 1971, Rwanda's relations with Uganda were strained by the growing tension between Tanzania and Uganda. The Ugandan government under Maj. Gen. Idi Amin accused Rwanda of conspiring with Tanzania, Burundi, and Zambia to restore former Ugandan President Milton Obote to power. On July 8, Uganda closed its border with Rwanda. This hurt Rwanda, which exports its coffee through Uganda. After four weeks Uganda opened the border but demanded that Rwanda stop conspiring with its neighbors against Uganda.

EDOUARD BUSTIN, *Boston University*

--------- RUMANIA • Information Highlights ---------

Official Name: Socialist Republic of Rumania.
Area: 91,700 square miles (237,500 sq km).
Population (1970 est.): 20,250,000. *Density,* 218 per square mile (84 per sq km). *Annual rate of increase,* 1.5%.
Chief Cities (1968 est.): Bucharest, the capital, 1,432,000; Cluj, 193,375; Timisoara, 184,797; Brasov, 175,264.
Government: *Head of state,* Nicolae Ceauşescu, president of the State Council and secretary-general of the Communist party (took office July 25, 1965). *Head of government,* Nicolae Ceauşescu. *Legislature*—Grand National Assembly, 465 members. *Major political party*—Communist party.
Languages: Rumanian (official), Hungarian.
Education: *Literacy rate* (1970), 95–98% of population. *School enrollment* (1968)—primary, 2,871,816; secondary, 636,491; technical/vocational, 357,763; higher, 147,637.
Finances (1969 est.): *Revenues,* $24,493,000,000; *expenditures,* $23,800,000,000; *monetary unit,* leu (6 lei equal U. S.$1, 1971).
Gross National Product (1970 est.): $21,400,000,000.
Average annual income per person (1969 est.): $600–700.
Economic Indexes: *Industrial production* (1970), 229 (1963= 100); *consumer price index* (1969), 102 (1966=100).
Manufacturing (metric tons, 1969): Cement, 7,515,000; crude steel, 5,540,000; distillate fuel oils, 4,593,000; residual fuel oil, 3,915,000; gasoline, 2,470,000.
Crops (metric tons, 1969 crop year): Maize, 7,676,000; sugar beets (1968–69), 3,936,000; potatoes, 2,165,000.
Minerals (metric tons, 1969): Crude petroleum, 13,246,000; lignite, 11,113,000; coal, 5,863,000; iron ore, 834,000.
Foreign Trade (1968): *Exports* (1970), $1,851,000,000 (chief exports—machinery and equipment, $313,334,000; fuels, minerals, and metals, $311,623,000; foodstuffs, $207,171,-000). *Imports* (1970), $1,960,000,000 (chief imports—machinery and equipment, $751,900,000; fuels, minerals, and metals, $438,609,000). *Chief trading partners* (1968)—USSR (took 31% of exports, supplied 27% of imports).
Tourism: *Receipts* (1970), $59,800,000.
Transportation: *Roads* (1968), 7,155 miles (11,515 km); *commercial motor vehicles* (1969), 43,900; *railroads* (1967), 6,838 miles (11,004 km); *merchant fleet* (1970), 341,000 gross registered tons; *national airline,* Tarom (Rumanian Air Transport); *principal airport,* Bucharest.
Communications: *Telephones* (1969), 605,983; *television stations* (1968), 16; *television sets* (1969), 1,288,000; *radios* (1969), 3,050,000; *newspapers* (1969), 51 (daily circulation, 3,330,000).

SADAT, Anwar el-. See BIOGRAPHY.
SAMOA. See PACIFIC ISLANDS; WESTERN SAMOA.

SAINT LOUIS

The defeat of a proposed convention center for the downtown area, a brief strike by city employees, and the approval of a new cultural district made news headlines during 1971.

City Government. In April's municipal election, Republican Joseph Badaracco showed that his 1969 election was no accident as he won reelection as president of the Board of Aldermen. He was not strong enough to help into office other Republicans, whose representation on the 28-member board fell from five to three. No other city office was up for election, and Democrats remained in firm control.

The city met its annual fiscal crisis in April by raising taxes on utilities and merchants' gross receipts and by increasing fees for various city services. Threatened widespread cutbacks of city services were held to a minimum, and a pledge of no pay increases for city employees was dropped when four unions went on strike in April. The aldermen quickly acceded to union demands, and the strike ended in three days. Mayor Alfonso J. Cervantes spent considerable time campaigning for state revenue sharing, but without success.

A $12 million libel suit filed by Mayor Cervantes against *Life* magazine for an article alleging links between the mayor and the underworld was dismissed in federal court in August. The 1970 article failed to show malice, the judge ruled.

A taxpayers' rebellion was in evidence as the voters convincingly turned down a city proposal for a $20 million convention center, twice disapproved a tax increase for public schools, and defeated a tax hike for the junior college district. The proposed convention center, a pet project of the mayor, drew support from downtown interests, the newspapers, and the tourist bureau, but the voters saw it as a tax increase and refused support.

One issue the voters did approve in April was the creation of a cultural district to take over the operation of the city's zoo and Art Museum and the Museum of Science and Natural History in St. Louis county. Although this meant a tax increase for voters in suburban St. Louis county, they joined with voters in the city in approving the district, which will now be financed by an area-wide tax.

Labor. A lengthy fight ensued among the city's contractors and labor unions over implementation of a hiring plan for minority groups. The unions drew up a plan, which was approved by one federal agency but rejected by another. In May the U. S. Department of Labor imposed a plan with specific quotas for each union. A crisis developed, however, when some unions refused to accept the plan, and contractors were unable to bid on federally financed projects because of the refusal. At the end of the year federal courts were imposing their own plans, which were agreed to by contractors and unions. Bidding on federal projects was then resumed.

One of the longest strikes in recent years occurred when operating engineers struck the Union Electric Company for four months. Supervisory personnel averted any power problems.

Arson. A major scandal developed when both city newspapers published articles exposing the potentialities of arson-for-profit, which appeared responsible for a 140% increase in fires during the last decade. Profits were made when a building was insured for more than the purchase price and then was burned in order to collect the insurance.

Culture and Recreation. The rock musical *Hair* opened in St. Louis in November despite efforts by the city to keep it out. Circuit Judge Lackland Bloom ruled that the musical was not obscene and did not violate an ordinance passed specifically to bar it. Rock concerts continued to outdraw symphony productions, with The Who attracting nearly 35,000 people.

RONALD D. WILLNOW
The St. Louis "Post-Dispatch"

SAN FRANCISCO

In 1971, San Francisco elected Joseph L. Alioto, its controversial mayor, to a second four-year term. The city also experienced a crippling waterfront strike that closed the port for more than three months, and it remained sharply divided on methods of school integration and the desirability of high-rise buildings.

Election. In the hotly contested mayoral election of November 2, Mayor Alioto led the field of 10 candidates, receiving 97,477 votes, about 38% of the total. His two closest rivals, Harold Dobbs, lawyer and restaurant owner, and Dianne Feinstein, president of the Board of Supervisors, received 69,740 and 55,204 votes, respectively. During the mayoral race Alioto, a lawyer, was under the shadow of an indictment returned in March. He was charged with fee-splitting with Washington State officials during a period before he became mayor.

There were 33 candidates vying for six places on the Board of Supervisors, but four of the incumbents won reelection. Three major bond issues were on the lengthy ballot. Proposition A, authorizing $56 million for building schools, failed to pass, while B ($34 million for harbor improvement) and C

MAYOR Alioto gestures triumphantly as wife smiles after decisive reelection in November. Charge against him of fee-splitting while a lawyer was campaign issue.

WIDE WORLD

($8.5 million for added fire protection) received the two-thirds vote necessary for approval. Proposition T, which was sponsored by opponents of high-rise buildings and which would have fixed a 72-foot height limit on new construction throughout the city, was decisively defeated.

Budget. The tax rate on real and personal property for the 1971–72 fiscal year was reduced slightly. Property taxes were expected to yield $270 million, about 38% of the total budget of $711 million. Of the remaining $441 million, 24% was to come from the state and federal governments, 23% from licenses, fines, and so on, and 15% from public service enterprises.

Construction and Transportation. The construction of lofty buildings in the downtown area continued at a rapid pace and in some quarters caused concern at what was termed the "Manhattanizing" of the city. Hotel building was particularly active. At year's end no less than six major hotels, with a total of more than 6,000 rooms, were under way. Chief among these were the Hilton Tower, the St. Francis Tower, and the unconventionally designed Embarcadero Center Hotel, which is part of the $200 million Embarcadero Center development. Adding an unusual note to the downtown skyline is the Transamerica Building, a pyramid-shaped, 48-story structure.

During the year the Bay Area Rapid Transit (BART) system, being built at a cost of more than $1.3 billion to provide modern high-speed transportation between San Francisco and the communities on the eastern side of the bay, moved nearer to completion. Service over part of the route was scheduled to begin in March 1972. Meanwhile, work on the trans-bay tube and the Market Street subway was far advanced.

Other Events. Although the outbreaks of violence that plagued the city in the past were happily absent during 1971, other events generated much controversy. One was a strike of longshoremen and dock workers that for more than 100 days all but completely tied up the port. In January a tanker collision in the bay resulted in an oil spill of more than 800,000 gallons. At the beginning of the fall term the busing of school children to achieve racial balance was strongly opposed by many parents. However, the threatened large-scale boycott of the buses failed to materialize, and opposition to the plan gradually subsided.

OSCAR LEWIS
Author, "San Francisco: Mission to Metropolis"

SASKATCHEWAN

The New Democratic party (NDP), led by Allan Blakeney, a lawyer from Regina, overthrew Ross Thatcher's Liberal government in the June provincial elections. Other noteworthy events in 1971 included a year-long tourist promotion project called Homecoming '71, in which former Saskatchewan residents were invited to visit the province. Communities, aided by government grants, undertook projects that added to recreational facilities.

New Government. The June 23 elections returned 45 NDP members and 15 Liberals to the Legislative Assembly. Campaign issues included policies toward agriculture, labor, resources and economic development, and educational and medical services. A special legislative session opened on July 28 to deal with some NDP campaign promises.

———— SASKATCHEWAN · Information Highlights ————

Area: 251,700 square miles (651,904 sq km).
Population: 927,000 (April 1971 est.).
Chief Cities (1969 est.): Regina, the capital (140,000); Saskatoon (124,950); Moose Jaw (33,500); Prince Albert (28,000).
Government: *Chief Officers*—lt. gov., Stephen Worobetz; premier, Allan Blakeney (New Democratic Party); atty. gen., Roy Romanow (NDP); min. of educ., Gordon Macmurchy (NDP); chief justice, E. M. Culliton. *Legislature*—Legislative Assembly (special session convened July 8, 1971), 60 members (45 New Democratic party, 15 Liberal).
Education: *School enrollment* (1968–69 est.)—public elementary and secondary, 245,526 pupils (11,109 teachers); private schools, 1,987 pupils (159 teachers); Indian (federal) schools, 5,025 pupils (225 teachers); college and university, 12,697 students. *Public school expenditures* (1971 est.)—$98,660,000. *Average teacher's salary* (1968–69 est.), $6,848.
Public Finance (fiscal year 1971 est.): *Revenues*, $571,030,000 (sales tax, $126,720,000; income tax, $92,583,000; federal funds, $162,701,000). *Expenditures*, $560,900,000 (education, $144,480,000; health and social welfare, $198,710,000; transport and communications, $80,320,000).
Personal Income (1969 est.): $2,413,000,000.
Social Welfare (fiscal year 1971 est.): $41,190,000 (aged and blind, $2,290,000; dependents and unemployed, $27,970,-000).
Manufacturing (1968): *Value added by manufacture*, $170,002,-000 (food and products, $62,568,000; petroleum and coal products, $20,213,000; non-metallic mineral products, $16,-666,000; printing and publishing, $15,028,000; fabricated metals, $12,765,000).
Agriculture (1969 est.): *Cash farm income* (exclusive of government payments), $716,112,000 (livestock, $470,791,000; crops (1968 est.), $660,197,000). *Chief crops* (cash receipts)—Wheat, $349,175,000 (ranks 1st among the provinces); barley, $18,776,000 (ranks 2d).
Mining (1969 est.): *Production value*, $347,652,480. *Chief minerals* (tons)—Potash, 3,146,160 (ranks 1st among the provinces); copper, 18,000 (ranks 6th); uranium, 780 (ranks 2d); crude petroleum, 89,492,800 bbl. (ranks 2d).
Transportation: *Roads* (1968), 127,490 miles (205,186 km); motor vehicles (1969), 472,360; railroads (1969), 8,570 track miles (13.790 km); licensed airports (1970), 34.
Communications: *Telephones* (1969), 358,881; television stations (1970), 6; radio stations (1969), 20; newspapers (1970), 4 (daily circulation, 132,574).
All monetary figures given in Canadian dollars.

As expected, the new government repealed the controversial Essential Services Act. Amendments put through by the Liberals in April had placed virtually all employees and employers under compulsory binding arbitration in labor disputes judged "emergency." Premier Blakeney also announced the cancellation of an agreement that the Liberal government had made in February with Parsons and Whittemore, Inc. of New York City to develop a multi-million dollar pulp mill in northern Saskatchewan.

The legislative session was a somber one as a result of the sudden death on July 23 of Ross Thatcher. Thatcher had assumed leadership of the Liberal party in 1959 and had led it to victory over the NDP in 1964. Dave Steuart, former deputy premier, was unanimously elected interim party leader.

Agriculture. Good crops, combined with increased grain exports, gave cause for cautious optimism in 1971. Crop production increased because the federal government ended LIFT, its crop reduction plan. A federal government bill designed to stabilize fluctuations in the grain income of farmers was shelved in October. Prolonged opposition to the plan in Parliament and the threat of legal action by four Saskatchewan farmers affected the decision. An estimated one third of the province's rapeseed crop was threatened by worms.

Canada Winter Games. Saskatoon was the site of the second Canada Winter Games in February. A unique feature was Mount Blackstrap, a man-made, 300-foot (91-meter) mountain south of the city. More than 2,100 athletes competed in 16 sports.

BRUCE EVANS
Regina Public Library

SATO, Eisaku. See BIOGRAPHY.

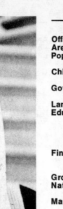

UPI

KING FAISAL confers with President Nixon at White House on May 27. King suggested that U. S. maintain pressure on Israel to withdraw from areas taken in 1967.

SAUDI ARABIA

In 1971, Saudi Arabia retained its role as the most influential of the conservative Arab states in both the political and economic fields.

The Arab World. Saudi Arabia continued its large annual grants to Egypt and Jordan as compensation for their losses in the 1967 war against Israel. Egypt, in particular, is still hurt economically by the closing of the Suez Canal. Egyptian President Sadat's strong attachment to Islam helped contribute to a new cordiality in relations with the devout regime in Saudi Arabia. King Faisal publicly praised Libya's chief of state Col. Muammar al-Qaddafi for establishing Islamic law as the basis for the Libyan judicial code.

Faisal remained firmly convinced that Israel posed a serious threat to the Arab world, and he was less ready than Egypt to reach a settlement with Israel on the basis of the UN Security Council resolution of November 1967. Faisal used his good standing in Washington to try to persuade the United States to modify what he regarded as its too pronounced support of Israel. U. S. Secretary of State William Rogers conferred with Faisal in Saudi Arabia early in May. At the end of May, Faisal met President Nixon at the White House. Later, Vice President Spiro Agnew also visited Saudi Arabia, but Faisal's views did not seem to produce any substantial change in U. S. policy.

Saudi Arabia and Egypt arranged a series of meetings in Jidda between representatives of the Jordanian government and the Palestinian resistance movement in an effort to compose their differences, but no agreement was reached.

Despite the indignation voiced by many Arabs, Saudi Arabia remained silent when Iran, in November, took possession of three islands formerly held by two small states on the Arabian side of the Persian Gulf. Saudi Arabia negotiated with Abu Dhabi and Oman toward a resolution of old boundary disputes. However, tension with Southern Yemen on Saudi Arabia's borders to the south remained high.

The Islamic World. Faisal and the shah of Iran worked together to foster closer cooperation among

──────── SAUDI ARABIA • Information Highlights ────────

Official Name: Kingdom of Saudi Arabia.
Area: 829,997 square miles (2,149,690 sq km).
Population (1969 est.): 7,200,000. *Density,* 7 per square mile (3 per sq km).
Chief Cities (1965 est.): Riyadh, the capital, 225,000; Jidda, 194,000; Mecca, 185,000.
Government: *Head of state,* Faisal Ibn Abd al-Aziz, king (acceded 1964). *Head of government,* Faisal Ibn Abd al-Aziz.
Language: Arabic (official).
Education: *Literacy rate* (1971), 15% of population. *Expenditure on education* (1967), 11.2% of total public expenditure. *School enrollment* (1968)—primary, 363,426; secondary, 67,207; technical/vocational, 855; university/higher, 5,352.
Finances (1970–71 est.): *Revenues,* $1,420,000,000; *expenditures,* $1,420,000,000; *monetary unit,* riyal (4.50 riyals equal U. S.$1, Sept. 1971).
Gross National Product (1970 est.): $4,000,000,000.
National Income (1967): $2,176,000,000; *national income per person,* $311.
Manufacturing (metric tons, 1969): Residual fuel oil, 12,184,000; gasoline, 3,009,000; distillate fuel oils, 2,526,000; jet fuel, 1,798,000; cement, 550,000.
Crops (metric tons, 1968 crop year): Dates, 380,000.
Minerals (metric tons, 1969): Crude petroleum, 148,846,000 (ranks 5th among world producers).
Foreign Trade (1968): *Exports* (1970), $2,424,000,000 (chief exports—crude petroleum, $1,409,010,000; petroleum products, $231,000,000). *Imports* (1970), $710,000,000 (chief imports—rice, $26,689,000; passenger cars, $16,022,000; live animals, $13,111,000; buses, $10,822,000). *Chief trading partners* (1968)—Japan (took 21% of exports, supplied 8% of imports); Italy (10%—6%); United States (2%—23%); United Kingdom (6%—7%).
Transportation: *Roads* (1969), 11,000 miles (17,702 km); *motor vehicles* (1969), 144,800 (automobiles, 78,300); *railroads* (1970), 356 miles (573 km); *national airline,* Saudi Arabian Airlines; *principal airports,* Dhahran, Jidda, Riyadh.
Communications: *Telephones* (1968), 44,250; *television stations* (1968), 3; *television sets* (1967), 40,000; *radios* (1964), 1,000,000; *newspapers* (1969), 6 (daily circulation, 58,000).

Islamic countries, but the machinery established for this purpose had yet to demonstrate any great degree of effectiveness. The Islamic world as a whole was powerless to help Pakistan when its eastern wing was sliced off in the war with India.

Economy. In the first 10 months of 1971, Saudi Arabia's oil production averaged more than 4,700,000 barrels a day, an increase of 27% over the average for the same period in 1970. By the end of 1971, production had climbed above 5,000,000 barrels a day, about double the figure for 1967. When the Persian Gulf petroleum exporting countries concluded a historic agreement with the concessionaire companies at Teheran, Iran, in February 1971, Saudi Arabia, like the rest, secured a considerably larger share of the proceeds from each barrel. Late in 1971, Saudi Arabia joined other petroleum exporting countries in pressing for new arrangements with the concessionaire companies in view of the decline in the value of the dollar.

With oil furnishing about nine tenths of the government's revenue, the budget for the 1971–72 fiscal year rose to $2,396,000,000, some 60% above the budget for the previous fiscal year. Much greater sums were allocated to education, public health, communications, and economic development.

In November, Saudi Arabia agreed to invest $20 million in the oil pipeline Egypt plans to build from the Gulf of Suez to the Mediterranean with the help of an international consortium. Saudi Arabia also undertook to ship 5 million tons of oil a year through the line once it is built.

Scarcity of fresh water has always been a serious problem in Saudi Arabia. In 1971, the Wadi Jaizan dam, the Hasa irrigation and drainage project, and the Jidda desalting plant were completed.

GEORGE RENTZ
Hoover Institution, Stanford University

SEISMOLOGY. See EARTHQUAKES.

WIDE WORLD

SELECTIVE SERVICE

The year 1971 was another one of crisis for Selective Service despite such changes in 1970 as the installation of a new director and the initiation of a draft lottery. The physical harassment of Selective Service headquarters that had been common in 1970 continued to a lesser degree, but 1971 proved to be a time of crisis for different reasons. The very existence of the Selective Service system was challenged.

The draft became the focal point of several interrelated political struggles that included attempts by Congress to reassert its role in foreign policy, the controversy over the desirability and feasibility of an all-volunteer force, and efforts to end the Vietnam War. Consequently, during 1971, Congress carried out its most extensive review of the draft since World War II. Before a new draft law was passed in September the Senate took the extraordinary step of invoking cloture on a filibuster against the draft, the country went without a draft law for several months, and the Nixon administration had to work desperately to win a two-year continuation of the draft.

Draft Lottery. As the year began, the system's new director, Curtis Tarr, reviewed the operation of the draft lottery and declared that "without qualification" it was "effective and much more equitable than the system it replaced." The lottery had probably eased some of the dissent, since those with high numbers, who were unlikely to be called, had little interest in continuing protest. But protests did not disappear. A coalition of civil rights and anti-

RICK DELANEY/BUFFALO COURIER-EXPRESS

Young people seized in August raids on Selective Service offices in Camden, N. J. (*top photo*) and Buffalo, N. Y. (*above*) leave courts under guard.

war groups planned and staged antidraft demonstrations during the year, and in August the FBI allegedly foiled an extensive plot to raid the system's offices. Nonetheless, the lottery itself was accepted, and the period of uncertainty for young men was reduced from seven years to one.

Selective Conscientious Objection. In March, the Supreme Court handed down a decision that halted the recent trend in broadening the definition of conscientious objector. In *Gillette* v. *U. S.,* the court denied the right of conscientious objection to serving in a particular war, saying that such a denial was not unconstitutionally favorable toward organized religion and that a selective basis for objection would confront local boards with too difficult a task. In a strong dissent, Justice William Douglas held that all beliefs growing out of religious training, faith, or individual conscience should be protected. Critics of the decision also insisted that a selective conscientious objection might not be mere expediency but instead reflect more thought, understanding, and sensitivity.

Draft Controversy. A bitter congressional fight developed over the question of an all-volunteer force. Four major factions emerged: (1) Sen. Edward Kennedy and others who wanted further reforms of the Selective Service system, but opposed a volunteer military force as one that would result in "poor people fighting rich men's wars"; (2) senators of such diverse ideological persuasion as Barry Goldwater and Mark Hatfield, who wanted to increase military pay, end the draft, and establish a voluntary force; (3) President Nixon and his supporters who wished to make some reforms in the system and extend it for two years while increasing military pay as a step toward establishing a volunteer force in 1973; (4) lawmakers such as Sen. John Stennis and Rep. F. Edward Hebert who opposed any changes in the system, wanted a four-year extension of the draft, and felt a volunteer force was infeasible.

The debate over ending the draft and beginning a volunteer force centered on the amount of increase in pay or benefits necessary to attract volunteers and the amount that could be spent without detracting from other areas of defense, unbalancing the budget, or inflating the economy. Cost estimates for an all-volunteer force of 2.5 million men varied widely. The 1970 presidential commission on an all-volunteer force had recommended a $3.2 billion increase in military pay. Senators Hatfield and Goldwater called for a $4.3 billion increase, and the President asked Congress for an increase of only $1.5 billion.

Closely related was the see-saw battle over how long the draft should be extended. The Congress came within two votes in the House of Representatives and six in the Senate of extending it for only one year instead of two.

A large faction in the Senate, led by Sen. Mike Mansfield, sought to change the balance of power between the President and Congress in making foreign policy. Their efforts included attempts to place a ceiling on the number of troops that could be drafted, to prohibit assigning draftees to Indochina (65% of the men killed in action in 1970 were conscripts), and to require the withdrawal of troops from Indochina within nine months. Most of these efforts failed, although the struggle was close.

The House and Senate eventually passed draft bills in different versions. A conference committee appointed to resolve differences became deadlocked, and remained that way while the July 1 expiration of the old draft law approached. The committee reached agreement on June 30, but the conference version of the bill stalled in the Senate. All induction ceased as attempts continued to modify or table the bill, and a filibuster, led by Sen. Mike Gravel, developed.

As the stalemate dragged on, the administration became increasingly concerned. It was announced that even though the power to induct had expired, the expiration did not apply to previously deferred registrants who were returning to 1-A status, such as graduating college students. Secretary of Defense Melvin Laird said on July 24 that the government would have to draft such men, but it did not.

In September the Nixon administration mounted a concerted campaign to dislodge the bill. Secretary Laird warned that the U. S. manpower situation would "become chaotic" unless the bill was passed promptly. The President stated that failure to approve the bill would be "one of the most irresponsible acts on the part of the U. S. Senate that I could possibly think of and would make the United States the second strongest nation in the world." The Department of Defense, the Joint Chiefs of Staff, and the various service branches lobbied individual congressmen and senators.

Under this barrage, the antidraft coalition began to weaken. On September 22, senators favoring the bill mustered one vote over the two thirds necessary to close debate and end the filibuster. The final Senate vote was 55 to 30 in favor of the bill.

New Draft Law. After seven months before Congress, and after assuming over half the Senate's time in 1971, the new draft law was virtually what the administration had asked for, although the various factions involved could also claim some satisfaction. The administration got a two-year extension of the draft, a pay increase for military personnel including a reenlistment bonus in combat branches, the power to end undergraduate student deferments, the establishment of a uniform national manpower pool and calls, and the defeat of a variety of moves aimed at weakening the President's hand in foreign policy.

The advocates of an all-volunteer force saw the military pay increased more than $9 million beyond what the President had requested, although he temporarily froze the increase. Those seeking to reassert congressional power in foreign policy succeeded in passing a provision calling on the President to withdraw all troops from Vietnam by a "certain date," to be contingent only on the release of U. S. prisoners of war. They also placed a ceiling on the number of persons who could be inducted without a presidential declaration of a national emergency (130,000 in fiscal year 1972 and 140,000 in fiscal year 1973).

Those seeking a more thorough reform of the draft machinery were pleased with such provisions as the requirement that a local board quorum be present for decisions, the right of registrants to personal appearances before appeal boards, a proviso that a registrant may have witnesses appear on his behalf, the reduction of permissible service on a board from 25 to 20 years, the reduction of the minimum age of board members to 18, and provision for consolidation of smaller boards.

Prospects. Draft officials were slow to issue induction calls under the new laws because of confusion. But only low draft calls were foreseen, and Secretary Laird predicted zero calls for the first three months of 1972. Officials announced that no one with a lottery number over 125 would be called in 1971, compared with 195 in 1970.

The year proved to be the most crucial ever faced by the Selective Service system. Reforms advocated as far back as 1966 were finally brought to pass. But the most important one remained undone: replacing local boards as the supposed decision-makers with trained administrators, and making boards a point of first appeal. Still, the changes, together with low calls and steps toward a volunteer force, offered some hope that the system's future would be calmer.

GARY L. WAMSLEY, *Vanderbilt University*

——————— SENEGAL • Information Highlights ———————

Official Name: Republic of Senegal.
Area: 75,750 square miles (196,192 sq km).
Population (1970 est.): 3,930,000. *Density,* 50 per square mile (19 per sq km). *Annual rate of increase,* 2.2%.
Chief City (1969 est.): Dakar, the capital, 581,000.
Government: *Head of state,* Léopold Sédar Senghor, president (took office September 1960). *Chief minister,* Abdou Diouf, premier (took office Feb. 26, 1970). *Legislature*—National Assembly (unicameral), 80 members. *Major political party*—Senegalese Progressive Union.
Languages: French (official), Wolof, Fulani, Madingo.
Education: *Literacy rate* (1970), 10% of population. *Expenditure on education* (1965), 14.7% of total public expenditure. *School enrollment* (1966)—primary, 231,146; secondary, 42,361; technical/vocational, 11,270; higher, 3,338.
Finances (1970–71 est.): *Revenues,* $169,000,000; *expenditures,* $169,000,000; *monetary unit,* CFA franc (277.71 francs equal U.S.$1, Sept. 1971).
Gross National Product (1970 est.): $720,000,000.
National Income (1968): $676,000,000; *per person,* $183.
Manufacturing (metric tons, 1969): Residual fuel oil, 303,000; cement, 207,000; wheat flour (1968), 79,000.
Crops (metric tons, 1969 crop year): Groundnuts, 885,000; millet and sorghum (1968), 434,000; coffee, 135,000.
Minerals (metric tons, 1969): Phosphate rock, 1,035,000.
Foreign Trade (1970): *Exports,* $152,000,000 (chief exports—groundnuts and oil, $72,953,000). *Imports,* $193,000,000 (chief imports, 1968—cereals and preparations, $36,435,-000). *Chief trading partner* (1968)—France (took 66% of exports, supplied 44% of imports).
Transportation: *Roads* (1969), 9,107 miles (14,653 km); *motor vehicles* (1969), 57,500 (automobiles, 36,500); *railroads* (1970), 645 miles (1,032 km); *national airline,* Air Senegal; *principal airport,* Dakar.
Communications: *Telephones* (1970), 29,264; *television stations* (1968), 1; *television sets* (1969), 1,000; *radios* (1969), 267,000; *newspapers* (1969), 1 (daily circulation, 20,000).

SENEGAL

Senegal was troubled by student and worker unrest in 1971. The unrest reflected the worsening conditions of the country's peanut farmers and the unemployed urban workers, and was also attributed to radical opponents of the government of President Léopold Senghor.

Internal Affairs. Radicals in Senegal's trade unions staged a number of protest strikes in January and February. Attempts were made to fire-bomb the French cultural center to protest the visit of French President Georges Pompidou on February 5. Later in the year, 16 men were convicted of the crime, and two were given life sentences.

Student and teacher dissatisfaction with the Francophile policies of Dakar University led once more to a confrontation with the government. Following the refusal of students to take examinations on February 26, the government closed the university. It was reopened one month later, and new regulations required that students sign a statement promising to respect university rules. Forty-nine students were denied readmission.

Foreign Affairs. French President Pompidou's visit in February demonstrated continued French support for Senghor's government. The visit triggered serious demonstrations in Dakar.

Senegal was involved in conflicts with three neighboring states in 1971. In late January, Senegalese officials invaded Gambia in their attempts to restrict smuggling. Good relations between the countries were not completely restored even after President Senghor met with Gambian President Dauda Jawara at Ziguinchor in March.

More serious was the breakdown of Senegal's relations with Guinea. Guinea's President Sékou Touré had reacted to the 1970 abortive mercenary raid on Conakry by accusing a number of European and African states, including Senegal, of supporting the invasion. Senegal denied any complicity, withdrew its ambassador, and later refused to turn over Guinean exiles to Touré's government. Guinea's appointment of a Senegalese citizen as its chief representative in Dakar was not honored by President Senghor, and in October police in Senegal arrested four members of the Guinean embassy.

The protracted revolt in Portuguese Guinea spilled over into southern Senegal (the Casamance) early in 1971 when the Portuguese shelled towns and sent patrols across the border. Senegal protested Portuguese actions to the UN Security Council, and a UN fact-finding commission in July and August corroborated Senegal's charges.

Economic Development. Senegal's economy was dominated by two problems. The first was the burden of the 37,000-man civil service, which absorbed 50% of the recurrent budget. The second problem was the country's dependence on peanut exports. Despite increasing exports of phosphates and manufactured products, peanuts continued to account for three fifths of all farm revenue and 78% of all exports. Three drought years in a row and decreasing government subsidies resulted in the lowest peanut harvest in 15 years in 1970–71 and accounted for Senegal's $36 million trade deficit in 1971. The Development Fund of the European Common Market made an emergency loan of $7.2 million to help restore Senegal's faltering agriculture.

HARRY A. GAILEY, *San Jose State College*

SHIPPING. See TRANSPORTATION.

SIERRA LEONE

The year 1971 was a turbulent one in Sierra Leone. The government of Prime Minister (later President) Siaka Stevens survived an attempted coup on March 23. The country became a republic on April 19, and two days later Stevens was sworn in as executive president.

Attempted Coup. On March 23 soldiers led by the army commander, Brigadier John Bangura, attempted to assassinate Prime Minister Stevens and overthrow his government. Most of the armed forces remained loyal to the regime, and the coup collapsed on the same day. However, Stevens remained unsure of the army's loyalty and concluded

——————— SIERRA LEONE • Information Highlights ———————

Official Name: The Republic of Sierra Leone.
Area: 27,700 square miles (71,740 sq km).
Population (1969 est.): 2,510,000. *Density,* 90 per square mile (35 per sq km). *Annual rate of increase,* 1.5%.
Chief City (1969 est.): Freetown, the capital, 170,600.
Government: *Head of state,* Siaka P. Stevens, president (took office April 21, 1971). *Head of government,* Siaka P. Stevens. *Legislature*—House of Representatives (unicameral), 78 members. *Major political parties*—All People's Congress, Sierra Leone People's party.
Languages: English (official), Creole.
Education: *Literacy rate* (1969), 10% of population. *Expenditure on education* (1967), 18.8% of total public expenditure. *School enrollment* (1968)—primary, 139,413; secondary, 27,840; technical/vocational (1967), 1,732; university/higher, 837.
Finances (1969): *Revenues,* $60,950,000; *expenditures,* $51,870,000; *monetary unit,* leone (0.7675 leone equals U.S. $1, Dec. 30, 1971).
Gross National Product (1968 est.): $340,000,000.
National Income (1967): $317,000,000; *per person,* $130.
Manufacturing (metric tons, 1969): Residual fuel oil, 143,000; cigarettes, 515,000,000 units.
Crops (metric tons, 1969 crop year): Rice, 407,000.
Minerals (metric tons, 1969): Iron ore, 1,800,000; bauxite, 445,000; diamonds, 1,937,000 carats.
Foreign Trade (1970): *Exports,* $100,000,000 (chief export—diamonds, $63,360,000). *Imports,* $116,000,000 (chief import, 1968—textile yarn and fabrics, $13,658,000). *Chief trading partner* (1968)—United Kingdom.
Transportation: *Roads* (1970), 4,550 miles (7,232 km); *motor vehicles* (1969), 28,900; *railroads* (1970), 371 miles (597 km); *national airline,* Sierra Leone Airways.
Communications: *Telephones* (1970), 6,193; *television stations* (1968), 1; *television sets* (1969), 3,500; *radios* (1969), 140,000; *newspapers* (1969), 5.

a mutual-defense treaty with President Sékou Touré of Guinea, which provided for coordination of their armed forces. On March 28, Guinean armed forces entered Sierra Leone at Stevens' request; the first troops were stationed around his residence.

On June 29, Brigadier Bangura and three other officers were convicted of mutiny and executed. Two other officers had their death sentences commuted to life imprisonment. In September, Minister of Information Kanji Daramy and Minister of Health Cyril Patrick Foray were dismissed because of alleged complicity in the attempted coup.

Establishment of a Republic. Sierra Leone's parliament passed an act on April 16 giving it the power to amend the constitution without the approval of the governor-general. Three days later parliament passed a bill transforming the country into a republic. Acting Governor-General Christopher Okoro Cole was sworn in as the first president, and Stevens remained as prime minister.

On April 21, parliament adopted an amendment that transferred to the office of president the powers previously executed by the prime minister. Stevens was then sworn in as president. Sonie Ibrahim Koroma assumed the office of vice president and prime minister on April 24.

Newspaper Seizure. On August 9 the government took over the *Unity Independent,* a daily newspaper published in Freetown. No explanation was given, but observers suggested that the government had been displeased with the paper's comments on local and international issues. A new, government-owned daily, *The Nation,* began publication on August 12.

Foreign Affairs. In April, Stevens claimed that mercenaries were gathering in Liberia to invade Sierra Leone on behalf of dissident politicians in Freetown. The charge was denied by Liberian President William Tubman.

Israeli Foreign Minister Abba Eban visited Sierra Leone in June to discuss the Middle East crisis. During Eban's stay President Stevens agreed to establish an embassy in Israel, and Eban announced an increase in aid to Sierra Leone.

In August, Sierra Leone became one of the growing number of African states to establish diplomatic relations with the People's Republic of China.

JUDITH A. GLICKMAN

SINGAPORE

Prime Minister Lee Kuan Yew of Singapore battled the press in 1971 in an effort to ensure internal security. He faced opposition from a new leftist political party.

Lee and the Press. The government's abrupt decision in May to force the closure of two English-language newspapers and its arrest of four officials of a leading Chinese-language newspaper created a furor. The proprietor of the *Eastern Sun* was accused of accepting subsidies from Communist Chinese agents in Hong Kong; when he refused to answer the charge, seven editors walked out and the newspaper was closed. Under government pressure, the local branch of the Chase Manhattan Bank foreclosed on the *Singapore Herald,* a critic of the government that was in serious financial difficulty. The four staff members of *Nanyang Siang Pau* were detailed without formal trial under the internal security law, accused of "glamorizing" Communist China and stirring up local Chinese communal emotions.

——————— SINGAPORE • Information Highlights ———————

Official Name: Republic of Singapore.
Area: 224 square miles (581 sq km).
Population (1970 census): 2,074,507. *Density,* 9,100 per square mile (3,550 per sq km).
Chief City (1968 est.): Singapore, the capital, 1,987,000.
Government: *Head of state,* Benjamin Henry Sheares, president (took office Dec. 30, 1970). *Head of government,* Lee Kuan Yew, prime minister (took office May 1959). *Legislature*—Legislative Assembly (unicameral), 58 members. *Major political party*—People's Action party.
Languages: Malay (official), English, Chinese, Tamil.
Education: *Literacy rate* (1971), 75% of population. *Expenditure on education* (1968), 16.8% of total public expenditure. *School enrollment* (1968)—primary, 371,970; secondary, 152,840; technical/vocational, 24,913; university/higher, 12,447.
Finances (1970): *Revenues,* $431,000,000; *expenditures,* $329,000,000; *monetary unit,* Singapore dollar (2.82 S. dollars equal U.S.$1, Dec. 30, 1971).
Gross National Product (1970 est.): $1,820,000,000.
National Income (1968): $1,525,000,000; *per person,* $756.
Manufacturing (metric tons, 1969): Meat, 21,000; fish meal and products, 10,900; beer, 379,000 hectoliters.
Foreign Trade (1968): *Exports* (1970), $1,554,000,000 (chief exports—crude rubber, $286,454,000; petroleum products, $263,529,000. *Imports* (1970), $2,461,000,000 (chief imports—textile yarn and fabrics, $193,384,000; petroleum products, $162,500,000; crude rubber, $129,164,000). *Chief trading partners* (1968)—West Malaysia (took 19% of exports, supplied 16% of imports); United States; Japan.
Transportation: *Roads* (1970), 1,188 miles (1,912 km); *motor vehicles* (1969), 168,000 (automobiles, 135,600); *railroads* (1970), 16 miles (26 km).
Communications: *Telephones* (1970), 136,267; *television stations* (1967), 8; *television sets* (1969), 131,000; *radios* (1969), 102,000; *newspapers* (1969), 11 (daily circulation, 20,000).

Defending these actions before the International Press Institute in Helsinki, Finland, Prime Minister Lee argued that freedom of the press had to be subordinated to Singapore's special security needs arising from the city-state's delicately balanced multiracial population. To some observers the Lee government appeared fearful that Communist China's overtures in Southeast Asia might undermine the loyalty of Singapore's Chinese population.

Political Challenge. A leftist political party, the People's Front, was established early in the year to challenge the People's Action party, which holds all 58 seats in Singapore's parliament. Led by Lui Boon Poh, a lawyer with a labor union background, the new party attacked what it considered the government's overemphasis on foreign investments, its reluctance to sanction wage increases, and its policy of detention without trial. The Front called for reunification with Malaysia.

Economy. The gross domestic product increased 15% in 1970; the previous year's increase had been 14.5%. To a large extent this was due to expansion in manufacturing. Some concern was expressed over the doubling of the national trade deficit, to a record figure of nearly $1,000 million. Contributory factors were the decline in rubber prices, reduced exports to South Vietnam and West Malaysia, and heavy costs incurred in importing new industrial equipment. Singapore's overall financial position remained strong, however; since 1969 external assets had risen from $770 million to $1,170 million.

Foreign Relations. The joint decision with Malaysia, in January, to dissolve the Malaysian-Singapore Airlines and set up separate national airlines reflected continued friction between the two states. Both states, however, joined a new defense grouping with their Commonwealth partners, Britain, Australia, and New Zealand, in April. In January, Singapore hosted for the first time the conference of the Commonwealth heads of government.

C. PAUL BRADLEY
Flint College, University of Michigan

SOCIAL SECURITY. See SOCIAL WELFARE.

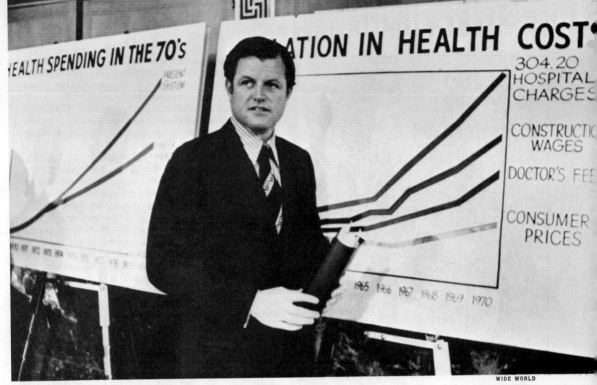

Urging a federal health insurance program, Sen. Edward Kennedy testifies before Senate committee in April. Sharply rising hospital costs sparked interest in a public insurance plan.

social welfare

Legislative activity, new or revised programs, and other news developments in the field of social welfare during 1971 are reviewed in this article under the following headings: (1) General Survey; (2) Health Care; (3) Social Security; and (4) Child Welfare.

General Survey

After two years, U. S. President Richard Nixon's Family Assistance Plan (FAP) for welfare reform was still caught in the quagmire of congressional indecision at the end of 1971. Meantime, the crisis that had provoked it continued. From January through June, 500,000 persons were added to Aid to Families with Dependent Children (AFDC) rolls in the United States. Twenty or more states, which were experiencing increasing financial pressure due to heavy unemployment and rising welfare costs, reduced assistance payment levels, and only about eight states raised levels.

While carefully designed experiments to test the response of low-paid workers to supplemental benefits similar to FAP were still going on, President Nixon agreed with the Republican governors of New York, Illinois, and California to institute "demonstration" projects in selected areas utilizing other forms of incentives—or disincentives—to try to reduce the welfare loads. One New York demonstration, authorized by the U. S. Department of Health, Education, and Welfare (HEW) to start in 1972 in two welfare districts, would require members of families to perform assigned tasks or suffer prescribed reductions in their assistance grants. All such local thrusts were peripheral to the major contest going on in the Congress.

Proposals. FAP was blocked by a Senate filibuster late in 1970. Reintroduced as HR 1, it passed the House of Representatives in June 1971 in a version that offered several important and politically attractive features. The major proposals included:

(1) An additional 5% increase in Social Security benefits (a 10% increase had been voted in March 1971) with provision for automatic cost-of-living adjustments.

(2) National minimum grants in the adult public assistance programs (aged, blind, and disabled) and transfer of their administration to the federal government, thereby effecting a different form of revenue-sharing than advocated by President Nixon.

(3) Modifications of Medicare and extension to groups not now covered.

(4) FAP, to be administered by HEW, limited to families without employable members.

(5) An Opportunities for Families Program (OFP), administered by the U. S. Department of Labor, for families with employable or employed members.

Under either FAP or OFP, a family of four without an employed member could receive $2,400 a year, but a family of eight or more could not receive more than $3,600. (The federally established poverty level, widely challenged as too low, is $3,965 for a family of four.) Under OFP, after the first $720, as earnings increased benefits would decrease, stopping when earnings reached $4,140 for a family of four or $5,940 for a family of eight or more—plus allowances for work expenses and children's earnings. A person refusing job training or employment would forfeit his benefits.

Controversy. Some of the controversial features of HR 1 are:

"The product we advertised is not available at this time. However, we are sending you instead this handsome bumper sticker for the big new car you will want to purchase . . ."

Inequitable benefits. Adult assistance recipients would be treated better than children. The $130 per month for a single aged person is equal to that for a mother and one child under FAP. A blind, disabled, or elderly couple would be assured $195 per month, only $5 less than a family of four. Opposition centers on the inadequacy of FAP.

Inclusion of the working poor. Anything approaching adequate assistance for children raises family income above the earnings of marginal workers, thus presumably creating a disincentive to work. OFP encourages the worker to earn as much as he can but reduces his benefits by nearly two thirds of what he earns. Some feel that this opens the door too wide, while others feel that the incentive offered is not enough.

Work requirements. The bill not only offers inducements to work but requires capable adults, except mothers with children under age 6 (3 after 1974), to accept job training or retraining when offered and to accept jobs that pay 75% or more of the legal minimum wage. It is contended that such requirements lower established minimum wages, establish a form of peonage for low-paid workers, and deprive mothers of choosing whether they can contribute most to the child in the home or in the marketplace. Probable unavailability of jobs after training is countered in the bill with 200,000 public service jobs, a provision more than matched in July by the Emergency Employment Act that set up 300,000 jobs.

Child care. The necessity for suitable arrangements was recognized by a proposal to authorize care for 875,000 children. A national system of child development and day care was proposed in Office of Economic Opportunity legislation that passed Congress—but President Nixon vetoed it on Dec. 9, 1971. The President's veto message contended that the proposal was characterized by "fiscal irresponsibility, administrative unworkability, and family-weakening implications." (For details, see the *Child Welfare* section of this article.)

Childless couples and single persons. The omission of such persons leaves an opening for criticism to those who wish to see the bill remove all low-income people from poverty.

Federalization. The bill proposes to transfer much responsibility and cost from the states to the federal government, thereby reducing inequalities in the public assistance programs. Opposition comes both from those who fear this as an extension of "big government" and those in the wealthier states who fear that inadequate levels of benefits under FAP will leave them with continuing major burdens.

The Senate Finance Committee, which was extremely critical in 1970, showed little enthusiasm over the 1971 bill. Sen. Russell B. Long of Louisiana, committee chairman, said that the guaranteed minimum income aspects of the bill guarantee everyone the opportunity to "loaf" and receive income while doing it. Efforts to get action on the less controversial sections—insurance benefits, Medicare, and adult assistance—were unsuccessful.

Divergence. There were obvious efforts on all sides to gain partisan advantage. Beyond this, controversy over the bill turned on divergent approaches to meeting the needs of people in two population age groups particularly vulnerable to economic insufficiency: the aged and children. In both cases, the trend in social policy seems to be toward increasing public responsibility for providing care. For the aged and for the disabled, HR 1 goes along with this trend and makes more adequate provision. In the case of children, the authors of HR 1 put the needs of children behind the traditional social value of the "work ethic" and attempt to stop the trend by forcing responsibility back upon the family. In both cases, the proposals in this complex bill take the form of amendments to the comprehensive Social Security Act. That act includes both insurance-type protections and needs-determined assistance for children as well as aged persons. When combined with unemployment insurance, it is supposed to provide a floor of support for nearly everybody against most economic contingencies.

In July 1971, more than 17.8 million persons over age 65 were receiving cash benefits under the retirement-insurance provisions of the Social Security Act. They represented about 87% of their age group, an increase from 78% in 1965. Payments were also being made to 9 million under 65 —1.3 million retired, 1.6 million disabled, and 6.1 million survivors or dependents of beneficiaries. The program thus closely approaches the goal of universality with regard to the aged and provides protection for substantial numbers of persons below 65.

Major shortcomings are in the low level of benefits for low-wage earners and the regressive nature of the taxation that finances it. Its weakness in meeting the needs of older persons in the lower income levels is seen in the 2 million recipients of old age assistance, many of whom are in need in spite of their Social Security payments. The financing is regressive because the tax is a flat rate and low-earning persons have to pay on all their earnings, while those with high earnings have to pay only on the first $9,000 ($7,800 through 1971). Thus, those least able to pay carry the heaviest burden proportionally.

One of the sharpest and most politically potent demands coming from the White House Conference on Aging in December was a call for an increase in Social Security benefits. Such demands may lend strength to proposals that would put Social Security on a "pay-as-you-go" basis with the principal financing coming from general tax revenues. Senators Edmund Muskie and Walter F. Mondale are among the "pay-as-you-go" advocates.

Government Role. Traditionally, in the United States, responsibility for the support and upbringing of children, like care of the aged, has rested on the family. Indications are that the government is having to assume an increasing portion of this responsibility. In June 1971, some 4.2 million children of deceased or disabled workers were receiving insurance benefits. An additional 7.4 million, mostly from broken homes, received AFDC. Thus, 11.6 million children, nearly one in six in the country, were receiving some form of governmental support. In 1965, this number was only 6.4 million, or less than one in 10. Children under the disability program increased by 67%, but in AFDC the increase was 125% in the 6-year period.

The reasons for these increases in all dependent groups are many and varied. They include unemployment, which held at 5% to 6% for two years and began affecting high-income workers; a more difficult job market for the handicapped and marginally employable; changing social standards accompanied by increasing prevalence of divorce, separation, and desertion at all economic levels; and an increasing awareness, heightened by the civil rights movement, of the inequalities that have pervaded U. S. economic and social life.

Successful legal aid challenges in the courts have broken down time-honored legal and administrative barriers to eligibility, particularly in AFDC, and have blocked legislative and administrative attempts to reduce expenses arbitrarily. Since a disproportionate number of new AFDC recipients are blacks or other minority-group members, attempts to deal with the problem are often perceived as having racial overtones.

Allowances? HR 1 seeks to reduce the burden on general revenues by forcing greater family support of children. The complex government and bureaucratic structure that it calls for pleases almost nobody. The realities of the situation raise questions whether the idea is workable. In the search for a way out, there are increasing references to a quite different approach: family or children's allowances. The United States is the only major country without some form of such a plan.

An automatic payment of $50 per month to every child would, it is held, raise most families with children out of poverty and, combined with adequate Social Security benefits, minimize the need for a welfare bureaucracy; ease wage setting by removing size of family from consideration; create a vast new reservoir of purchasing power; and promote the healthy development of children.

The cost to the federal government would be great, but proponents contend it would not be impossible because of the many offsetting expenses that could be reduced or eliminated in federal, state, and local budgets. The numbers to be covered would be legion, but already one in six are receiving direct benefits or grants while the other five sixths are receiving direct benefits through the income-tax deductions allowed their parents.

In answer to the argument that family allowances would be "something for nothing," proponents can point to the plan's value as a social utility, not unlike free roads, free police protection, and free education. If HR 1 should again be caught in irreconcilable controversy, family allowances will be waiting in the wings for consideration.

Immediate efforts to liberalize HR 1 will probably proceed along lines of a proposal by Sen. Abraham Ribicoff. He would emphasize career opportunities in the work requirements, greatly expand child care and public-service employment, assure a family of four a $2,800 minimum income in 1973, and provide for increasing benefits to an undated poverty level by 1977.

RALPH E. PUMPHREY
Washington University, St. Louis

Health Care

Public hearings began in 1971 on the subject of National Health Insurance, one of the most sweeping and most expensive domestic legislation issues to face Congress in modern history. It became apparent during the year that a bill would not be passed for at least another year, but by the end of 1971 the issues had become clear.

The emergence of National Health Insurance as major domestic legislation before Congress was significantly different from the manner in which Medicare had been debated in the 1960's. With Medicare the argument centered on whether a federal program of health insurance for the aged was necessary, but during 1971 the debate was not whether there should be National Health Insurance but rather how comprehensive a program should be enacted. The American Medical Association (AMA), which had bitterly but unsuccessfully opposed Medicare in the 1960's, took a markedly different stance with regard to National Health Insurance and even offered its own plan.

Hearings on proposals for National Health Insurance were held by two key congressional committees: the Senate Finance Committee and the House Ways and Means Committee. Early in the year, Sen. Russell Long (Dem., La.), chairman of the Finance Committee, called three days of hearings on National Health Insurance to get an overall look at pending proposals. Then, in October 1971, Rep. Wilbur Mills (Dem., Ark.), chairman of the House Ways and Means Committee, called five weeks of hearings on National Health Insurance, although he did not plan for the committee to write the final bill for consideration until at least 1972.

Throughout the year, different programs for national health insurance were proposed by the Nixon administration; by Sen. Edward M. Kennedy, representing organized labor; by the AMA; and by groups representing the health insurance companies and hospital associations.

Nixon Administration Plan. Witnesses representing the Nixon administration opened testimony before Mills' committee with an outline of the National Health Insurance proposal that President Nixon had made earlier in his health message to Congress. Called the National Health Insurance Partnership Act, the President's plan is based on a National Health Insurance Standards Act (NHISA), which would require employers to see that their workers are covered by health insurance with the employer paying the larger share of the premium.

Low-income families and the families of unemployed persons would be covered by a federal Family Health Insurance Plan (FHIP). Families with no income would pay nothing, but low-income families would pay part of their medical bills according to income through a system of deductibles and coinsurance. Employers and employees would pay for NHISA, but the federal government would pay for FHIP except for the deductibles.

Health Security Act. Senator Edward Kennedy (Dem.-Mass.), the principal sponsor of organized labor's Health Security Act, testified for the proposed measure in both House and Senate hearings, as did labor leaders. Principal House sponsor of the bill was Rep. Martha Griffiths (Dem.-Mich.), a member of the Ways and Means Committee. The Health Security Act was written by the Committee for National Health Insurance, formed by the late Walter Reuther who was then president of the United Auto Workers. The most comprehensive proposal before the 92d Congress, the Health Security bill was quite different from other plans. It proposed a National Health Insurance plan that would be operated and financed entirely by the federal government, offering total health care for all Americans with no payments, deductibles, or coinsurance. It would be financed by a tax on employer-employee payrolls similar to the Social Security program. The bill also proposed the elimination of all existing commercial and nonprofit health insurance companies in favor of a totally federal plan.

Medicredit. Drafted by the AMA, Medicredit proposed coverage of the entire U.S. population through a system of income tax credits, which would help families buy health insurance from existing commercial and nonprofit companies. A system of deductibles and coinsurance would be included in both the basic coverage plan and in a catastrophic illness plan, which would take effect after a family had spent a specified portion of its income on medical bills.

Healthcare. Drafted by the Health Insurance Association of America, the Healthcare plan would rely entirely on the insurance industry. Employers and employees would be encouraged to purchase health insurance for employees. Federal aid to the states would be used to provide health insurance coverage for the poor through insurance pools set up with insurance companies at state levels.

Catastrophic Illness Plans. Most of the plans that were submitted to Congress in 1971 included catastrophic illness protection plans. Such coverage would take effect after a family's basic coverage had been exhausted by abnormally high health care costs. But several bills, notably one by Senator Long, proposed catastrophic health insurance coverage as a separate plan.

Ameriplan. The American Hospital Association testified in favor of its Ameriplan proposal, which would set up a series of Healthcare corporations that would provide a range of health care services to subscribers, including a basic plan and a catastrophic illness plan. The AHA bill was never introduced to Congress, however, because of disagreement among members of the association on the legislative draft of the proposal. However, AHA officials did appear at Ways and Means hearings to testify on the general outlines of the plan, which had been developed by an AHA committee.

JEROME F. BRAZDA
Editor, "Washington Report on Medicine and Health"

Social Security

During 1971, Congress considered legislation calling for major social security changes that included provisions for automatically adjusting monthly benefits to rising prices; higher benefits for widows and widowers; a shift to an age-62 computation point for men; increased benefit amounts currently; and other benefit liberalizations. For Medicare, the proposed legislation would provide automatic enrollment under medical insurance for those entitled to hospital benefits (with opting-out allowed); coverage for the disabled; and limitation on raising the amount of premiums.

Public Law 92-5—an act to increase the public debt, signed in March 1971—also amended the Social Security Act. It raised monthly cash benefits by 10%, retroactive to January 1971 (special age-72 beneficiaries had received a 5% increase); lifted the maximum amount of earnings countable toward benefits and subject to contributions from $7,800 to $9,000, beginning in 1972; and set contribution rates for monthly benefits at 5% for 1973–75 and at 5.15% for 1976 and thereafter.

Financing. During 1971 employers and employees paid contributions of 5.2% each on the first $7,800 of the workers' earnings; the rate was 7.5% for the self-employed. For all alike, 0.6% of the contribution was earmarked for hospital insurance and the rest was for old-age, survivors, and disability insurance. The rates are the same for 1972 but are applied to earnings up to $9,000.

The monthly premium paid by those enrolled in the medical insurance part of Medicare (and matched by the federal government) was $5.30 for the first six months of 1971. In July 1971 it was raised to $5.60, the rate fixed through June 1972; from July 1, 1972, to June 30, 1973, the rate is to be $5.80 a month.

Old-Age, Survivors, and Disability Insurance Operations. In the 12 months ending June 30, 1971, monthly cash benefits totaled $28,757,000,000. Lump-sum death payments amounted to $288,100,-000. In August 1971 about 26,946,000 persons were receiving monthly benefits. All but 9,030,000 were 65 or older. The average benefit for a retired worker in that month was $131, and benefits to disabled workers averaged $145 a month.

Medicare Operations. In the program's fifth year, approved hospital claims totaled 6,400,000, and the average amount reimbursed was $755 per hospital claim, $84 per home health claim, and $376 per extended-care claim. About 43,600,000 medical insurance claims were recorded from July 1970 to June 1971. Allowed charges totaled $2,600,-000,000, and $1,900,000,000 of that amount was reimbursed.

In October 1971, the secretary of health, education, and welfare announced new amounts, effective Jan. 1, 1972, for the deductible and coinsurance payments under the hospital insurance part of Medicare. Under the law, the new amounts are based on the ratio between costs in the preceding year and those in Medicare's first year. The deductible went from $60 to $68. The coinsurance payment—expenses above the deductible in which the patient shares—became $17 (instead of $15) for the 61st to 90th day. For each covered day after the 90th, the patient pays $34 (instead of $30).

ROBERT M. BALL
Commissioner of Social Security

Child Welfare

Child welfare was the subject of considerable controversy in 1971, as a result of legislation sponsored by Minnesota Sen. Walter Mondale and Indiana Rep. John Brademas to provide comprehensive child development and day care programs throughout the United States. This legislation, passed by both houses of Congress, was part of a bill extending the Office of Economic Opportunity. On December 9, however, President Nixon vetoed the measure, denouncing the plan as marked by "fiscal irresponsibility, administrative unworkability, and family-weakening implications."

The controversy over the measure resulted from the belief of conservative leaders that the provisions of the amendment would lead to excessive government influence over young children. A number of professionals in the field of child welfare said the program would be inadequate if the level of funding were not raised. Others saw it as an important breakthrough for children.

Child Advocacy. The concept of child advocacy has continued to receive strong support from the administration. When the Office of Child Development was established in the Office of the Secretary of Health, Education, and Welfare in July 1969, one of the three major missions assigned to it was to act as an advocate by bringing the needs of children to the attention of government and the public, and to serve as an innovator by planning new programs for children and their parents. Child advocacy, according to the Office of Child Development, can be family, community, state, regionally, or nationally directed. The essentials are a child advocacy council, representative of all interests, and a service team or staff to develop and implement programs approved by the council. Research and training of personnel are also encouraged.

The Joint Commission on the Mental Health of Children, following three years of study (1966–69), recommended the establishment of a child advocacy system at every level of society. At the 1970 White House Conference on Children, an "overriding concern" voted by the delegates was the "establishment of a child advocacy agency financed by the federal government and other sources with full ethnic, cultural, racial, and sexual representation." In June 1971 it was announced that two agencies of the Department of Health, Education, and Welfare—the Bureau of Education for the Handicapped (of the Office of Education) and the National Institute of Mental Health (of the Health Services and Mental Health Administration)—had jointly awarded funds totaling $656,000 to "six innovative child advocacy demonstration projects."

Funding of Child Welfare Services. The problem of financing voluntary child welfare organizations and programs was faced by many groups in the private sector. These organizations are dependent on a healthy economy for adequate support from voluntary contributions. Many private organizations prefer not to rely too heavily on federal grants and contracts. However, it was becoming increasingly difficult for such groups to survive any other way. The Office of Child Development felt strongly that not all services to children should derive from the government.

UNICEF. On September 28 at an observance of the 25th anniversary of UNICEF at the State Department, Samuel DePalma, assistant secretary of state for international affairs, said "UNICEF is the best example of international cooperation." In recognition of the outstanding success of UNICEF's programs during the past 25 years, both houses of Congress voted a $15 million authorization for the U. S. contribution to the Children's Fund for fiscal 1972. The United States has traditionally made 40%, and the other countries together 60%, of the total contributions to UNICEF, which is dependent on voluntary contributions rather than assessments. In 1970, 124 countries contributed to UNICEF.

UNICEF was on the front line in 1971 with relief for pregnant mothers and children under nine among the East Pakistani refugees, providing, among other things, food and equipment for 1,000 newly opened food centers.

ISABELLA J. JONES
Executive Director
National Committee for Children and Youth

Demonstrators block traffic on Las Vegas' glittering "Strip" in March as they protest reductions in welfare aid.

UPI

SOCIETIES AND ORGANIZATIONS

This article lists a selection of some of the most noteworthy associations, societies, foundations, and trusts of the United States and Canada. The information for each listing has been furnished by the organization concerned, and includes membership figures, dates of annual meetings, officers, and headquarters location or address.

Alcoholics Anonymous (The General Service Board of A. A., Inc.). Membership: approximately 500,000 in more than 17,000 affiliated groups. Annual conference: New York, N. Y., April 17–22, 1972. Chairman, John L. Norris, M. D. Headquarters: 468 Park Ave. S., New York, N. Y. Mailing Address: Box 459, Grand Central Station, New York, N. Y. 10017.

American Academy of Arts and Letters. Membership: 50. Annual meeting: New York, N. Y., December 1971. President, Aaron Copland; secretary, John Hersey. Headquarters: 633 West 155th St., New York, N. Y. 10032.

American Academy of Arts and Sciences. Membership: approx. 2,600. Annual meeting: Boston, Mass., May 10, 1972. President, Harvey Brooks; secretary, Denis Robinson. Headquarters: 280 Newton St., Brookline Station, Boston, Mass. 02146.

American Academy of Political and Social Science. Membership: 23,500, including 7,000 libraries. Annual meeting: Philadelphia, Pa., April 14–15, 1972. President, Richard D. Lambert; business mgr., Ingeborg Hessler. Headquarters: 3937 Chestnut St., Philadelphia, Pa. 19104.

American Anthropological Association. Membership: 7,900. Annual meeting: Toronto, Canada, Nov. 29–Dec. 3, 1972. President, Anthony F. C. Wallace; exec. director, Edward J. Lehman. Headquarters: 1703 New Hampshire Ave. NW, Washington, D. C. 20009.

American Association for the Advancement of Science. Membership: 129,000 and 293 affiliated groups. Annual meeting: Washington, D. C., Dec. 26–31, 1972. President, Glenn T. Seaborg; exec. officer, William Bevan. Headquarters: 1515 Massachusetts Ave. NW, Washington, D. C. 20005.

American Association of University Professors. Membership: 95,000. Annual meeting: New Orleans, La., May 5–6, 1972. President, Sanford H. Kadish; general secretary, Bertram H. Davis. Headquarters: One Dupont Circle, NW, Washington, D. C. 20036.

American Association of University Women. Membership: 170,000. President, Anne Campbell; general director, Alice L. Beeman. Headquarters: 2401 Virginia Ave. NW, Washington, D. C. 20037.

American Astronomical Society. Membership: 2,800. Meetings: Seattle, Wash., April 8–12, 1972; East Lansing, Mich., Aug. 15–18, 1972. President, Martin Schwarzschild; secretary, L. W. Fredrick; exec. officer, H. M. Gurin. Address: 211 FitzRandolph Rd., Princeton, N. J. 08540.

American Automobile Association. Membership: 14 million in 868 affiliated groups. Annual meeting: Detroit, Mich., Sept. 11–13, 1972. President, William B. Bachman; secretary, William B. Spencer. Headquarters: 1712 G St. NW, Washington, D. C. 20006.

American Bankers Association. Membership: 18.452 banks and branches. Annual meeting: Dallas, Texas, Oct. 7–11, 1972. President, Allen P. Stults; secretary, George H. Gustasson. Headquarters: 1120 Connecticut Ave. NW, Washington, D. C. 20036.

American Bar Association. Membership: 154,508. Meeting: San Francisco, Calif., Aug. 14–17, 1972. President, Leon Jaworski; secretary, Kenneth J. Burns, Jr.; exec. director, Bert H. Early. Headquarters: 1155 East 60th St., Chicago, Ill. 60637.

American Bible Society. 1970 Scripture distribution: 134,801,896 copies. Annual meeting: New York, N. Y., May 11, 1972. President, Edmund F. Wagner; general secretary, Laton E. Holmgren; treas., Charles W. Baas. Headquarters: 1865 Broadway, New York, N. Y. 10023.

American Booksellers Association, Inc. Membership: 3,800. National convention: Washington, D. C., June 4–7, 1972. President, Howard B. Klein; exec. director, Joseph A. Duffy. Headquarters: 175 Fifth Ave., New York, N. Y. 10010.

American Cancer Society, Inc. Membership: 192 voting members; 58 chartered divisions. Annual meeting: New York, N. Y., Oct. 23–25, 1972. President, A. Hamblin Letton, M. D.; secretary, Samuel M. Seegal. Headquarters: 219 East 42d St., New York, N. Y. 10017.

American Chemical Society. Membership: 112,000. National meetings, 1972: Boston, Mass., April 9–14; New York, N. Y., Aug. 27–Sept. 1. President, Max Tishler; exec. director, F. T. Wall. Headquarters: 1155 16th St. NW, Washington, D. C. 20036.

American Civil Liberties Union. Membership: 170,000. Exec. director, Aryeh Neier; board chairman, Edward J. Ennis. Headquarters: 156 Fifth Ave., New York, N. Y. 10010.

American College of Physicians. Membership: 18,600. Annual meeting: Atlantic City, N. J., April 17–21, 1972. President, Hugh R. Butt, M. D.; exec. vice pres., Edward C. Rosenow, Jr., M. D. Headquarters: 4200 Pine Street, Philadelphia, Pa. 19104.

American College of Surgeons. Membership: 32,000. Annual meeting: San Francisco, Calif., Oct. 2–6, 1972. President, J. E. Rhoads, M. D.; director, C. Rollins Hanlon, M. D. Headquarters: 55 E. Erie St., Chicago, Ill. 60611.

American Council of Learned Societies. Membership: 35 professional societies concerned with the humanities and the humanistic aspects of the social sciences. Annual meeting: Tarrytown, N. Y., Jan. 20–22, 1972. President, Frederick Burkhardt; admin. secy., Charlotte Bowman. Headquarters: 345 East 46th St., New York, N. Y. 10017.

American Council on Education. Membership: 1,380 colleges and universities, 135 associated organizations, 74 affiliates, and 71 constituent organizations. Annual meeting: Miami Beach, Fla., Oct. 4–6, 1972. President, Roger W. Heyns; exec. secretary, Charles G. Dobbins. Headquarters: One Dupont Circle, NW, Washington, D. C. 20036.

American Dental Association. Membership: 114,000. Annual session: San Francisco, Calif., Oct. 29–Nov. 2, 1972. President, Carl A. Laughlin, D. D. S.; exec. director, C. Gordon Watson, D. D. S. Headquarters: 211 E. Chicago Ave., Chicago, Ill. 60611.

American Economic Association. Membership: 17,500 and 7,650 subscribers. Annual meeting: Toronto, Ont., Dec. 28–30, 1972. President, John Kenneth Galbraith; secy.-treas., Rendigs Fels. Headquarters: 1313 21st Ave. S., Nashville, Tenn. 37212.

American Farm Bureau Federation. Membership: 2,057,665 families. Annual meeting: December of each year. President, William J. Kuhfuss; secretary-treasurer, Roger Fleming. Headquarters: 225 Touhy Avenue, Park Ridge, Ill. 60068.

American Geographical Society. Membership: 3,500. Annual dinner: New York, N. Y., Nov. 17, 1972. President, Serge A. Korff; director, Burton W. Adkinson. Headquarters: Broadway at 156th St., New York, N. Y. 10032.

American Geophysical Union. Membership: 10,397 and 41 organizations. National Fall meeting: San Francisco, Calif., Dec. 4–8, 1972. President, Homer E. Newell; gen. secy., Charles A. Whitten; exec. director, A. F. Spilhaus, Jr. Headquarters: 1707 L St. NW, Washington, D. C. 20036.

American Heart Association. Membership: 88.764 in 55 affiliates, 139 chapters and 1,000 local subdivisions. Annual meeting: Dallas, Texas, Nov. 16–21, 1972. President, J. Willis Hurst. M. D.; secretary. Elwood Ennis. Headquarters: 44 East 23d St., New York, N. Y. 10010.

American Historical Association. Membership: 18,500. Annual meeting: New Orleans, La., Dec. 28–30, 1972. President, Thomas C. Cochran; exec. secretary. Paul L. Ward. Headquarters: 400 A St. SE, Washington, D. C. 20003.

American Home Economics Association. Membership: 35,000 professionals, 15,000 students in 52 affiliated state organizations. Annual meeting: Detroit. Mich., June 26–30, 1972. President. Dr. Naomi G. Albanese; exec. director, Dr. Doris E. Hanson. Headquarters: 2010 Massachusetts Ave. NW, Washington, D. C. 20036.

American Horticultural Society. Membership: 6,000 individual; 250 organizational, institutional, and commercial. National congress: Seattle, Wash., Sept. 6–9, 1972. President, Dr. David G. Leach; exec. director, O. Keister Evans. Headquarters: 901 N. Washington St., Alexandria, Va. 22314.

American Hospital Association. Membership: 16,000 personal; 7,500 institutional. Annual meeting: Washington, D. C., Feb. 7–10, 1972; Annual convention: Chicago, Ill., Aug. 7–10, 1972. President, Stephen M. Morris; exec. vice pres., Edwin L. Crosby, M. D.; secretary, James E. Hague. Headquarters: 840 N. Lake Shore Dr., Chicago, Ill. 60611.

American Institute of Aeronautics and Astronautics. Membership: 23,031. Exec. secretary, James J. Harford. Headquarters: 1290 Avenue of the Americas, New York, N. Y. 10019.

American Institute of Architects. Membership: 23,150. National convention: Houston, Texas, May 7–11, 1972. President, Max O. Urbahn; first vice pres., S. Scott Ferebee, Jr.; secretary, Preston M. Bolton. Headquarters: 1785 Massachusetts Ave. NW, Washington, D. C. 20036.

American Institute of Biological Sciences. Membership: 14,500, with 44 adherent societies and 16 industrial member groups. Annual meeting: Minneapolis, Minn., Aug. 27–Sept. 1, 1972. President, W. Frank Blair; vice pres., Robert W. Krauss; secy.-treas., Dr. Richard Cowan; director, Dr. John R. Olive. Headquarters: 3900 Wisconsin Avenue, NW, Washington, D. C. 20016.

American Institute of Certified Public Accountants. Membership: 82,000. Annual meeting: Denver, Colo., Oct. 1–4, 1972. President, Walter J. Olipant; exec. vice pres., Leonard M. Savoie; admin. vice pres. and secy., John Lawler. Headquarters: 666 Fifth Ave., New York, N. Y. 10019.

American Institute of Chemical Engineers. Membership: 38,700. Annual meeting: New York, N. Y., Nov. 26–30, 1972. President, T. W. Tomkowit; secy., F. J. Van Antwerpen. Headquarters: 345 East 47th St., New York, N. Y. 10017.

American Institute of Graphic Arts. Membership: 1,900. Annual meeting: New York, N. Y., May, 1972. President, Henry Wolf; exec. director, Edward Gottschall. Headquarters: 1059 Third Ave., New York, N. Y. 10021.

American Institute of Mining, Metallurgical, and Petroleum Engineers, Inc. Membership: 50,143. Annual meeting: San Francisco, Calif., Feb. 20–24, 1972. President, Dennis L. McElroy; exec. director, Joe B. Alford. Headquarters: 345 East 47th St., New York, N. Y. 10017.

American Legion, The. Membership: 2,700,000. National convention: Houston, Texas, Aug. 27–Sept. 2, 1971. National Commander, John H. Geiger; national adjutant, William F. Hauck. Headquarters: 700 N. Pennsylvania St., Indianapolis, Ind. 46206.

American Management Association. Membership: 55,000. Annual meeting: New York, N. Y., Sept. 20, 1972. Chairman of the Board, Don G. Mitchell; president and chief exec. officer, James L. Hayes; secretary, Robert G. Butler. Headquarters: 135 West 50th St., New York, N. Y. 10020.

American Mathematical Society. Membership: 14,200. Annual meeting: Las Vegas, Nevada, Jan. 17–21, 1972. President, Nathan Jacobson; secretary, E. Pitcher. Headquarters: P. O. Box 6248, Providence, R. I. 02904.

American Medical Association. Membership: 214,000. Annual meeting: San Francisco, Calif., June 18–22, 1972. President, Wesley W. Hall, M. D.; secy.-treas., John M. Chenault, M. D. Headquarters: 535 N. Dearborn St., Chicago, Ill. 60610.

American Meteorological Society. Membership: 9,000, including 130 corporate members. President, Prof. Richard J. Reed; exec. director, Dr. Kenneth C. Spengler; secy.-treas., David F. Landrigan. Headquarters: 45 Beacon St., Boston, Mass. 02108.

American National Red Cross. Adult membership: 35,-833,166 in 3,200 chapters. National convention: San Francisco, Calif., May 1–3, 1972. Chairman, E. Roland Harriman; president, George M. Elsey. Headquarters: 17th and D Sts. NW, Washington, D. C. 20006.

American Newspaper Publishers Association. Membership: 1,056. Annual convention: New York, N. Y., April 24–27, 1972. Chairman, Richard H. Blacklidge; president and gen. manager, Stanford Smith. Headquarters: 750 Third Ave., New York, N. Y. 10017.

American Nurses Association. Membership: 200,000 in 54 states and territorial associations. National convention: Detroit, Mich., May 1–5, 1972. President, Hildegard E. Peplau; exec. dir., Eileen M. Jacobi. Headquarters: 10 Columbus Circle, New York, N. Y. 10019.

American Personnel and Guidance Association. Membership: 27,000. National convention: Chicago, Ill., March 26–30, 1972. President, Dr. Garry Walz; acting exec. director, Dr. Joseph McDonough. Headquarters: 1607 New Hampshire Ave. NW, Washington, D. C. 20009.

American Philological Association. Membership: 2,600. Annual meeting: Philadelphia, Pa., Dec. 28–30, 1972. President, Agnes K. L. Michels; secretary-treas., John J. Bateman. Headquarters: University of Illinois, Foreign Languages Building, Urbana, Ill. 61801.

American Physical Society. Membership: 29,000 American and foreign. Annual meeting: San Francisco, Calif., Jan. 31–Feb. 3, 1972. President, Dr. P. M. Morse; exec. secretary, Dr. W. W. Havens, Jr. Headquarters: 335 East 45th Street, New York, N. Y. 10017.

American Psychiatric Association. Membership: 19,071; 65 district branches. Annual meeting: Dallas, Texas, May 1–5, 1972. President Ewald W. Busse. M. D.; secretary, George Tarjan, M. D.; medical dir., Walter E. Barton, M. D. Headquarters: 1700 18th St. NW, Washington, D. C. 20009.

American Psychological Association. Membership: 32,000. Annual meeting: Honolulu, Hawaii, Sept. 1–8, 1972. President, Anne Anastasi; exec. officer, Kenneth B. Little. Headquarters: 1200 17th St. NW, Washington, D. C. 20036.

American Society of Civil Engineers. Membership: 65,000. Annual meeting: Houston, Texas, Oct. 16–20, 1972. President, Oscar S. Bray; exec. director, William H. Wisely. Headquarters: 345 East 47th St., New York, N. Y. 10017.

American Society of Composers, Authors, and Publishers. Membership: 14,000 composers and authors; 4,800 publishers. Annual meeting: New York, N. Y., March, 1972. President, Stanley Adams; secretary, Morton Gould. Headquarters: One Lincoln Plaza, New York, N. Y. 10023.

American Society of International Law. Membership: 5,250. Annual meeting: Washington, D. C., April 27–29, 1972. President, Harold D. Lasswell; exec. director, Stephen M. Schwebel. Headquarters: 2223 Massachusetts Ave. NW, Washington, D. C. 20008.

American Society of Mechanical Engineers. Membership: 63,886. President, Kenneth A. Roe; exec. director and secretary, Rogers B. Finch. Headquarters: 345 East 47th St., New York, N. Y. 10017.

American Society of Newspaper Editors. Membership: 750. National convention: Washington, D. C., April 18–21, 1972. President, C. A. McKnight; secretary, Arthur C. Deck. Headquarters: 750 Third Ave., New York, N. Y. 10017.

American Sociological Association. Membership: 13,500. Annual meeting: New Orleans, La., Aug. 28–31, 1972. President, William J. Goode; secretary, J. Milton Yinger. Headquarters: 1722 N St. NW, Washington, D. C. 20036.

American Statistical Association. Membership: 10,500. Annual meeting: Montreal, Canada, Aug. 14–17, 1972. President, William H. Shaw; secretary, John W. Lehman. Headquarters: 806 15th St. NW, Washington, D. C. 20005.

American Youth Hostels, Inc. Membership: 70,000; 26 councils in the United States. Annual meeting: Phoenix, Ariz., Dec. 9–10, 1972. President, Lyman Moore; exec. director, Frank D. Cosgrove. Headquarters: 20 West 17th St., New York, N. Y. 10011.

Archaeological Institute of America. Membership: 6,000; subscribers, 12,000. President, Rodney S. Young; general secretary, Elizabeth Whitehead. Headquarters: 260 W. Broadway, New York, N. Y. 10013.

Arthritis Foundation, The. Membership: 76 chapters. Annual meeting: Dallas, Texas, June 10, 1972. Chairman of the Board, Charles B. Harding; secretary, Robert H. French. Headquarters: 1212 Ave. of the Americas, New York, N. Y. 10036.

Association of American Publishers. Membership: approx. 250. Annual meeting: Bermuda, May 1972. Chairman of the Board, W. Bradford Wiley; president, Sanford Cobb; vice-presidents, Robert W. Frase, Austin J. McCaffrey. Headquarters: One Park Ave., New York, N. Y. 10016.

Association of Junior Leagues, Inc. Membership: 219 member Leagues in U. S., Canada, and Mexico. Annual conference: Boca Raton, Fla., May 21–25, 1972. President, Mrs. William H. Osler. Headquarters: 825 Third Ave., New York, N. Y. 10022.

Benevolent and Protective Order of Elks. Membership: 1,520,731 in 2,164 Lodges. National convention: Atlantic City, N. J., July 9–13, 1972. Grand Exalted Ruler, E. Gene Fournace; grand secretary, Homer Huhn, Jr. Headquarters: 2750 Lake View Ave., Chicago, Ill. 60614.

B'nai B'rith. Membership: 510,000 in 4,000 local men's, women's, and youth units. President, David M. Blumberg; exec. vice president, Rabbi Benjamin M. Kahn. Headquarters: 1640 Rhode Island Ave. NW, Washington, D. C. 20036.

Boy Scouts of America. Membership: 6,287,284 boys and leaders in 485 Boy Scout councils. Annual meeting: Los Angeles, Calif., May 17–19, 1972. President, Norton Clapp; Chief Scout Executive, Alden G. Barber. Headquarters: North Brunswick, N. J. 08902.

Boys' Clubs of America. Membership: 950,000 in 950 clubs. National convention: Washington, D. C., June 4–8, 1972. President, John L. Burns; national director, A. Boyd Hinds. Headquarters: 771 First Ave., New York, N. Y. 10017.

Camp Fire Girls, Inc. Membership: 700,000 in over 9,000 communities. National council meeting: New Orleans, La., Nov. 9–12, 1972. President, Mrs. Albert E. Bollengier; national exec. dir., Dr. Hester Turner. Headquarters: 1740 Broadway, New York, N. Y. 10019.

Canadian Library Association. Membership: 3,100 persons and 900 organizations. Annual conference: Regina, Saskatchewan, June 10–16, 1972. President, Dean Halliwell. Headquarters: 151 Sparks St., Ottawa, Ont. K1P 5E3.

Canadian Medical Association. Membership: 22,918. Annual meeting: Montreal, Que., June 11–17, 1972. President, H. D. Roberts, M. D.; gen. secy., J. D. Wallace, M. D. Headquarters: 1867 Alta Vista Drive, Ottawa, Ont. K1G 0G8.

Catholic Library Association. Membership: 3,431. National convention: Chicago, Ill., April 3–6, 1972. President, Reverend Joseph P. Browne, C. S. C.; exec. dir., Matthew R. Wilt. Headquarters: 461 W. Lancaster Ave., Haverford, Pa. 19041.

Chamber of Commerce of the United States of America. Membership: about 4,000 trade associations and local chambers, more than 39,000 business members, and nearly 5,000,-000 underlying membership. Annual meeting: Washington, D. C., April 30–May 2, 1972. President, Archie K. Davis; exec. vice president, Arch N. Booth. Headquarters: 1615 H St. NW, Washington, D. C. 20006.

Council on Foreign Relations, Inc. Membership: 1,500. Annual meeting: New York, N. Y., Oct. 13, 1971. President, Bayless Manning. Headquarters: 58 East 68th St., New York, N. Y. 10021.

Daughters of the American Revolution (National Society). Membership: 193,345 in 2,929 chapters. Continental congress: Washington, D. C., April 17–21, 1972. President General, Mrs. Donald Spicer. Headquarters: 1776 D St. NW, Washington, D. C. 20006.

Freemasonry, Ancient Accepted Scottish Rite of (Northern Masonic Jurisdiction): Supreme Council, 33°. Membership: 510,844 in 389 affiliated groups. Annual meeting: Boston, Mass., Sept. 26–28, 1972. Sovereign grand commander, George A. Newbury; grand secy. gen., Laurence E. Eaton; exec. secy., Stanley F. Maxwell. Headquarters: 39 Marrett Road, Lexington, Mass. 02173.

Freemasonry, Ancient and Accepted Scottish Rite of (Southern Jurisdiction): Supreme Council, 33°. Membership: 580,000 in 211 affiliated groups. National convention, Washington, D. C., Oct. 18–21, 1971. Sovereign Grand Commander, Henry C. Clausen; grand secty. gen., C. Fred Kleinknecht. Headquarters: 1733 16th St. NW, Washington, D. C. 20009.

Future Farmers of America. Membership: 427,888 in 50 state associations. National convention: Kansas City, Mo., Oct. 11–13, 1972. National advisor, H. N. Hunsicker; exec. secretary, W. P. Gray. Headquarters: Box 15160 Alexandria, Va. 22309.

Garden Club of America, The. Membership: approx. 12,700 in 178 member clubs. Annual meeting: Memphis, Tenn., April 18–20, 1972. President, Mrs. Frederick C. Tanner; secretary, Mrs. Peter Van S. Rice. Headquarters: 598 Madison Ave., New York, N. Y. 10022.

General Federation of Women's Clubs. Membership: 10,000,000 in 14,000 U.S. organizations and 54 abroad. National convention: Denver, Colo., June 5–9, 1972. President, Mrs. Earle A. Brown; exec. secretary, Mrs. Wilson Y. Christian. Headquarters: 1734 N St. NW, Washington, D. C. 20036.

Geological Society of America. Membership: 8,000. Annual meeting: Minneapolis, Minn., Nov. 13–15, 1972. President, Luna Leopold; exec. secretary, Edwin B. Eckel. Headquarters: P. O. Box 1719, Colorado Bldg., Boulder, Colo. 80302.

Girl Scouts of the U. S. A. Membership: 3,920,000. National president, Mrs. Douglas H. MacNeil; exec. director, Mrs. Henry M. Selby. Headquarters: 830 Third Ave., New York, N. Y. 10022.

Holy Name, Confraternity of the. Membership: 5,000,000 in 19,000 affiliated groups. National director, Brendan Larnen. Headquarters: 141 E. 65th St., New York, N. Y. 10021.

Institute of Electrical and Electronics Engineers, Inc. Membership: 160,000. International convention: New York, N. Y., March 20–23, 1972. President, Robert H. Tanner; general manager, Donald G. Fink. Headquarters: 345 East 47th St., New York, N. Y. 10017.

International Council of Scientific Unions (Conseil International des Unions Scientifiques). Membership: 16 international scientific unions and 62 national societies. General assembly: 1972. President, V. A. Ambartsumian; secretary-general, F. A. Stafleu. Headquarters: 7 Via C. Celso, Rome, Italy 00161.

Jewish War Veterans of the U. S. A. Membership: 100,000 in 750 units. National Commander, Bernard B. Direnfeld; national exec. director, Feliv M. Putterman. Headquarters: 1712 New Hampshire Ave. NW, Washington, D. C. 20009.

Kiwanis International. Membership: 270,000 in 5,800 clubs in U.S. and abroad. Annual convention: Atlantic City, N. J., June 18–21, 1972. President, Wes H. Bartlett; secretary, R. P. Merridew. Headquarters: 101 E. Erie St., Chicago, Ill. 60611.

Knights of Columbus. Membership: 1,200,000. Annual meeting: Toronto, Ont., Aug. 15–17, 1972. Supreme knight, John W. McDevitt; supreme secretary, Virgil C. Dechant. Headquarters: Columbus Plaza, New Haven, Conn. 06507.

Knights of Pythias, Supreme Lodge. Membership: 180,790 in 1,741 subordinate lodges. Biennial meeting: St. Louis, Mo., Aug. 14–17, 1971. Supreme chancellor, Eric D. Fitzpatrick; supreme secretary, Jule O. Pritchard. Office: 47 N. Grant St., Stockton, Calif. 95202.

League of Women Voters of the United States. Membership: 160,000. National convention: Atlanta, Ga., May 1–5, 1972. President, Mrs. Bruce B. Benson; first vice pres., Mrs. David G. Bradley. Headquarters: 1730 M St. NW, Washington, D. C. 20036.

Lions International. Membership: 970,000 in 25,600 clubs in 147 countries and geographic areas. President (1972–73), Georges Friedrichs. Headquarters: York and Cermak Roads, Oak Brook, Ill. 60521.

Loyal Order of Moose. Membership: 1,175,898 in 4,053 units. National convention: Jacksonville, Fla., June 24–29, 1972. Director general, Paul P. Schmitz; supreme secy., Carl A. Weis. Headquarters: Mooseheart, Ill. 60539.

Modern Language Association of America. Membership: 29,000. Annual convention: New York, N. Y., Dec. 27–30, 1972. President, Stuart P. Atkins; exec. secretary, William D. Schaefer. Headquarters: 62 Fifth Ave., New York, N. Y. 10011.

National Academy of Sciences. Membership: approx. 900. Annual meeting: Washington, D. C., April 24–26, 1972. President, Philip Handler; exec. officer, John S. Coleman. Headquarters: 2101 Constitution Ave. NW, Washington, D. C. 20418.

National Association for Mental Health, Inc. Membership: 1,000 state and local organizations. Annual meeting: Detroit, Mich., Nov. 15–17, 1971. President, Irving H. Chase; exec. director, Brian O'Connell. Headquarters: 1800 North Kent St., Rosslyn Station, Arlington, Va. 22209.

National Association for the Advancement of Colored People. Membership: 400,000 in 1,500 units. National convention: Detroit, Mich., July 3–7, 1972. President, Kivie Kaplan; exec. director, Roy Wilkins. Headquarters: 1790 Broadway, New York, N. Y. 10019.

National Association of Manufacturers. Membership: 13,000. Annual meeting: New York, N. Y., Dec. 7–8, 1972. President, W. P. Gullander; secretary, John McGraw. Headquarters: 277 Park Ave., New York, N. Y. 10017.

National Audubon Society. Membership: over 190,000. Annual convention: Milwaukee, Wis., May 20–24, 1971. President, Dr. Elvis J. Stahr; exec. vice pres., Charles H. Callison. Headquarters: 950 Third Ave., New York, N. Y. 10022.

National Conference of Christians and Jews, Inc. Membership: 72 regional offices. Annual meeting: New York, N. Y., Nov. 19–20, 1972. President, Dr. Sterling W. Brown; exec. vice president, Dr. David Hyatt; secretary, Oscar M Lazrus. Headquarters: 43 West 57th St., New York, N. Y. 10019.

National Congress of Parents and Teachers. Membership: 9,210,911 in 40,194 PTA's. National convention: New York, N. Y., May 21–24, 1972. President, Mrs. John M. Mallory; secretary, Mrs. Robert E. Anderson. Headquarters: 700 North Rush St., Chicago, Ill. 60611.

National Council of the Churches of Christ in the U. S. A. Membership: 33 Protestant, Anglican, and Orthodox denominations. Triennial general assembly: Dallas, Texas, Dec. 3–9, 1972. President, Dr. Cynthia Wedel; general secretary, Dr. R. H. Edwin Espy. Headquarters: 475 Riverside Dr., New York, N. Y. 10027.

National Council of the Young Men's Christian Associations. Membership: 5,379,712 in 1,815 organizations. National board chairman, Richard C. Kautz; exec. director, Robert W. Harlan. Headquarters: 291 Broadway, New York, N. Y. 10007.

National Easter Seal Society for Crippled Children and Adults. Membership: 52 state and territorial societies. National convention: Portland, Ore., Nov. 10–13, 1971. President, Thomas C. Teas; exec. director, Jayne Shover. Headquarters: 2023 W. Ogden Ave., Chicago, Ill. 60612.

National Education Association of the U. S. Membership: 1,187,305, with units in every state, and 8,948 local affiliates. Annual meeting: Atlantic City, N. J., June 25–30, 1972. President, Donald E. Morrison; exec. secy., Sam M. Lambert. Headquarters: 1201 16th St. NW, Washington, D. C. 20036.

National Federation of Business and Professional Women's Clubs, Inc. Membership: 175,000 in 3,900 clubs. National convention: Atlantic City, N. J., July 23–27, 1972. President, Miss Osta Underwood; fed. director, Mrs. Lucille H. Shriver. Headquarters: 2012 Massachusetts Ave. NW, Washington, D. C. 20036.

National Federation of Music Clubs. Membership: 600,000 in 4,300 clubs and 13 national affiliates. Annual meeting: Hot Springs, Ark., Aug. 11–14, 1972; biennial convention, Atlantic City, N. J., April 5–9, 1973. President, Dr. Merle Montgomery; office manager, Mrs. John McDonald. Headquarters: 600 S. Michigan Ave., Chicago, Ill. 60605.

National Foundation—March of Dimes, The. Membership: 3,000 chapters. President, Basil O'Connor; senior vice president, Joseph F. Nee. Headquarters: 1275 Mamaroneck Ave., White Plains, N. Y. 10605.

National Recreation and Park Association. Membership includes professional park and recreation administrators and citizens concerned with conservation of human and natural resources. Annual congress: Anaheim, Calif., Oct. 3–6, 1972. Executive director, Dwight F. Rettie. Headquarters: 1601 North Kent St., Arlington, Va. 22209.

National Research Council of Canada. Membership: council, 21; laboratory staff, 3,375. Annual meeting: Ottawa, Ont., March 1972. President, Dr. W. G. Schneider; secretary, A. W. Tickner. Headquarters: Montreal Rd., Ottawa, Ont. K1A 0R6.

National Safety Council. Membership: 11,500. National Safety Congress and Exposition: Chicago, Ill., Oct. 30–Nov. 2, 1972. President, Howard Pyle; secy.-treas., H. W. Champlin. Headquarters: 425 N. Michigan Ave., Chicago, Ill. 60611.

National Tuberculosis and Respiratory Disease Association. Membership: 700 affiliated groups. Annual meeting: Kansas City, Mo., May 21–24, 1972. President, John H. Biddle; managing dir., Robert J. Anderson, M. D. Headquarters: 1740 Broadway, New York, N. Y. 10019.

National Urban League, Inc. President, James A. Linen; secretary, Mrs. Helen Mervis; exec. director, Vernon E. Jordan, Jr. Headquarters: 55 East 52nd St., New York, N. Y. 10022.

National Woman's Christian Temperance Union. Membership: 250,000 in 6,000 local unions. National convention: Miami Beach, Fla., Sept. 6–13, 1972. President, Mrs. Fred J. Tooze; secretary, Mrs. Herman Stanley. Headquarters: 1730 Chicago Ave., Evanston, Ill. 60201.

Planned Parenthood–World Population (Planned Parenthood Federation of America, Inc.). Membership: 188 affiliates throughout U. S. Annual meeting: San Antonio, Texas, Oct. 22–26, 1972. President, Alan F. Guttmacher, M. D.; chairman of the board, Joseph D. Beasley, M. D.; secretary, Mrs. William D. Gregory, II. Headquarters: 810 Seventh Ave., New York, N. Y. 10019.

Rotary International. Membership: 707,500 in 15,025 clubs functioning in 149 countries. International convention: Houston, Texas, June 11–15, 1972. President, Ernst G. Breitholtz; gen. secretary, Harry A. Stewart. Headquarters: 1600 Ridge Ave., Evanston, Ill. 60201.

Special Libraries Association. Membership: 7,000. Annual conference: Boston, Mass., June 4–8, 1972. President, Efren W. Gonzalez; president-elect, Edward G. Strable; exec. director, F. E. McKenna. Headquarters: 235 Park Ave. S, New York, N. Y. 10003.

United States Jaycees, The. Membership: 325,000 in 6,400 affiliated groups. Annual meeting: Atlanta, Ga., June 19–22, 1972. President, Ronald G. S. Au; exec. vice pres., Robert S. Dunbar. Headquarters: Box 7, Tulsa, Okla. 74102.

United Way of America (formerly United Community Funds and Councils of America, Inc.). Membership: United Funds, Community Chests, and Community Health and Welfare Councils in 2,240 North American communities. President, Bayard Ewing; national executive, William Aramony. Headquarters: 801 North Fairfax St., Alexandria, Va. 22313.

Veterans of Foreign Wars of the United States. Membership, V. F. W. and Auxiliary: 2,267,000. National convention: Minneapolis, Minn., Aug. 18–25, 1972. Commander-in-Chief, Joseph L. Vicites; Adj. General, Julian Dickenson. Headquarters: V. F. W. Building, Broadway at 34th St., Kansas City, Mo. 64111.

World Council of Churches (United States Conference). Membership: 27 churches or denominations in U. S. Annual meeting: Toledo, Ohio, April 17–18, 1972. Chairman, John Coventry Smith; exec. secretary, Eugene L. Smith. Headquarters: 475 Riverside Dr., New York, N. Y. 10027.

Young Women's Christian Association of the U. S. A. Membership: approx. 2,600,000. President, Mrs. Robert W. Claytor; exec. director, Edith M. Lerrigo. Headquarters: 600 Lexington Ave., New York, N. Y. 10022.

Zionist Organization of America. Membership: 110,000 in 600 districts. 75th National convention: Jerusalem–Tel Aviv, Israel, July 12–19, 1972. President, Herman L. Weisman; national secy. and exec. director, Leon Ilutovich. Headquarters: 145 East 32d St., New York, N. Y. 10016.

SOCIOLOGY

In 1971 sociologists studied such current social issues as student unrest, changing race attitudes, and a new national loyalty.

Causes of College Student Unrest. Currents of social influence affecting attitudes of college students were described by William H. Sewell in *The American Sociologist* of May 1971. Sewell felt that the enormous expansion and increasing complexity of universities hindered the growth of student loyalty to these institutions. He also found that the growing interest of faculty members in research projects shifts the activities of many professors away from improving their teaching methods and from primary attention to students. Lastly he pointed out an awareness by the students of an expanding distance between themselves and the faculty, the administration, and the trustees, as well as an increasing resentment against the growing mechanization of instruction and the impersonal means of processing students.

In *Sociological Experience* (1971), Scott G. McNall stressed that there was a lack of recognition by university officers of the earlier maturation of college students today. He also pointed out that many regulations are viewed by students as "surplus repression."

Conflicting Perspectives in Race Relations. In an article, "American Sociology and Black Assimilation: Conflicting Perspectives," published in the *American Journal of Sociology* of January 1971, L. Paul Metzer described a shift in the attitude of blacks in the United States. From considering the assimilation of their people into the prevailing white culture, blacks have shifted to a black "ethnicity," or the sense of a distinct black entity of their own in the United States. A major question is raised but not answered: What are the main factors tending today toward a biracial society in a nation that has hitherto emphasized racial assimilation, particularly with reference to immigrant races from Europe, Mexico, and Asia? The unique status of black people in the United States today may now be studied as "a dynamic force with the potential for transforming the black community and black personality in the direction of becoming a major-change agency in American society."

Toward a Unified United States. According to the findings of a macrosociological study by J. C. McKinney of Duke University and Linda B. Bourque of California State College, Los Angeles, the South, "the Confederate South of Twelve States," is becoming "increasingly indistinguishable" from the rest of the United States. This conclusion was reached on the basis of five criteria—urbanization, industrialization, occupational redistribution, income, and education. The results of the study were read at the annual meeting of the Pacific Sociological Association in Honolulu in April and published in the *American Sociological Review* of June 1971.

American Sociological Association. "Social Inequality" was the major theme of the 66th annual meeting of the American Sociological Association in Denver, August 30 to September 2. William H. Sewell of the University of Wisconsin was the association's president for 1971. Special sessions considered such subjects as violence in American society, protest movements, and population control.

EMORY S. BOGARDUS
University of Southern California

SOMALIA

The major political developments in Somalia in 1971 concerned the military government's efforts to maintain stability and implement the goals of the 1969 "socialist" revolution.

The Domestic Scene. The political order was threatened by an attempt in May 1971 to overthrow the Supreme Revolutionary Council (SRC), which had governed Somalia since October 1969. Spearheaded by Generals Salad Gabeyreh and Mohamed Ainashe, the abortive coup attracted some support within political and ethnic factions. Although immediately quashed without violence, it resulted in some dismissals and a reshuffling in government personnel. The coup was seen by the SRC as forming part of an "international colonialist movement."

During 1971 the SRC took steps to restructure Somali society. New self-help schemes were devised to expand agricultural production, health and educational facilities, and the road network. Government salaries were reduced as an economy measure. Plans for decentralizing the machinery of government were inaugurated to obtain popular participation in national development. These objectives were linked with the SRC's program of restoring the sense of national dignity and self-reliance. Most of the Council's material and ideological efforts were aimed at reducing Somalia's dependence on external aid.

Foreign Affairs. Relations with the United States continued to deteriorate as Somalia drew closer to the Soviet Union and as U.S. aid was drastically reduced. With the exception of Italy, the Western nations in general withdrew much of their economic support. The strengthening of ties with the Eastern bloc seemed to be related to Somalia's efforts in building "scientific socialism." For the first time, Mongolia and Poland established embassies in Mogadishu. Improved relations with Kenya continued, and there were no frontier disputes between Somalia and Kenya in 1971.

Somalia took the initiative in bringing the Pakistan-India conflict before the UN General Assembly in December. Somali delegates vigorously condemned Portuguese and South African racial policies. The seventh East and Central African summit conference took place in Mogadishu, and the Organization of African Unity's defense commission met in the city.

A. A. CASTAGNO, *Boston University*

SOUTH AFRICA

South Africa celebrated its 10th anniversary as a republic in 1971. The festivities reached their climax on May 31—Republic Day—at Cape Town when Prime Minister Vorster addressed the nation.

Two events during the year tended to overshadow others. The International Court of Justice found in June that South Africa had no legal position in South West Africa (Namibia). The advisory opinion added more fuel to the long-standing disputes between South Africa and the United Nations, which had requested the court's opinion. In August, President Hastings Banda of Malawi made a 5-day state visit, the first by a black head of state.

The year as a whole was marked by the continuing concern with such issues as the "outward-looking" African policy, the implementation of apartheid, the industrial color bar and the shortage of skilled labor, inflation, tensions arising from the application of the internal security laws, the future of the Coloured people, and apartheid in sports. After years of delay, the government decided in April to permit television in South Africa.

UN Relations. In 1970 the United Nations had asked the International Court of Justice for an advisory opinion on the legality of South Africa's presence in South West Africa. On June 21, 1971, the court found that the presence was illegal, reaffirming an earlier resolution by the UN Security Council, and that the republic was, therefore, under an obligation to withdraw immediately.

Vorster and the opposition leader, Sir De Villiers Graaff, both rejected the court's opinion and reiterated South Africa's determination to continue its administration. Vorster charged that the opinion was legally unsound and politically motivated. He cited the court's refusal to entertain his proposals for an inspection of the territory and for a plebiscite to determine the wishes of the peoples as evidence that South Africa's enemies were not interested in the territory's welfare.

The UN Security Council, at the request of 35 African states, took up "the situation in Namibia" in September. It resolved on October 20 to call on all states to refrain from any dealings with South Africa that included references to South West Africa. The resolution agreed with the court, called for immediate withdrawal, called upon all states to promote the inhabitants' rights, and requested the UN secretary-general to report periodically on the implementation of the resolution.

On October 12 the Security Council censured South Africa for violation of Zambia's frontiers and air space along the Caprivi Strip border. South Africa admitted that such violations had occurred on both sides in the past but denied this latest charge. It also noted that four South African policemen had been injured and a fifth killed by land mines on October 4–5. South Africa charged Zambia with harboring and supporting armed bands making incursions into South West Africa.

International Relations. South Africa continued to explore the possibility of more friendly relations with independent African states while encouraging the already close-working relations with more immediate neighbors such as Lesotho, Swaziland, Botswana, and Malawi. Political leaders from these countries, as well as Malagasy and Mauritius, visited South Africa for discussions, and South Africa's foreign minister visited Malagasy.

The visit of Malawi's President Banda was the first by a black head of state and the first by any head of state since 1947. It was a crucial step in South Africa's declared policy of seeking friendly relations with independent African states, particularly in the light of the Organization of African Unity's July resolution against dialogue with South Africa. Prior to Banda's visit, South Africa and Malawi agreed to raise the status of their diplomatic missions from legation to embassy.

In 1971, South Africa and Lesotho agreed in principle on the Oxbow scheme to supply water to South Africa, and power as well as revenues to Lesotho. The South African Wool Board will establish a Merino stud farm in Lesotho as part of a 5-year technical assistance plan for the Lesotho sheep and wool program. South Africa's De Beers Consolidated Mines Ltd. announced that the Orapa diamond mine in Botswana, the largest single investment in Botswana, began operations in July. South Africa continued to supply vaccines to African countries.

The South African government and people continued to debate their isolation from the world of sport. Once again, the government refused U. S. tennis star Arthur Ashe a visa to play in the national tennis championships. The South African Cricket Association's proposal that the team to visit Australia should include two Africans was denied, and Australia later canceled the tour. However, the government did permit black U. S. golfer Lee Elder to enter South Africa's championship and to play before integrated galleries.

SOUTH AFRICA'S apartheid rules were temporarily relaxed when President Hastings Kamuzu Banda of Malawi became the first black African head of government to pay a state visit. He was welcomed by both races.

─────── **SOUTH AFRICA • Information Highlights** ───────

Official Name: Republic of South Africa.
Area: 471,444 square miles (1,221,037 sq km).
Population (1970 est.): 21,300,000. *Density,* 40 per square mile (16 per sq km). *Annual rate of increase,* 2.4%.
Chief Cities (1970 est.): Pretoria, the administrative capital, 448,000; Cape Town, legislative capital, 817,000; Johannesburg, 1,305,000; Durban, 690,000.
Government: *Head of state,* Jacobus Johannes Fouche, president (took office April 10, 1968). *Head of government,* Balthazar J. Vorster, prime minister (took office Sept. 13, 1966). *Legislature*—Parliament: House of Assembly, 170 members; Senate, 54 members. *Major political parties*—Nationalist, United.
Languages: English (official), Afrikaans (official).
Education: *Literacy rate* (1971), practically 100% of white population. *Expenditure on education* (1961), 4% of national income. *School enrollment* (1963)—primary, 2,546,-824; secondary, 532,299; technical/vocational, 76,724; university/higher, 67,363.
Finances (1970 est.): *Revenues,* $2,300,000,000; *expenditures,* $2,300,000,000; *monetary unit,* rand (0.7500 rand equals U. S.$1, Dec. 30, 1971).
Gross National Product (1970 est.): $17,600,000,000.
National Income (1969): $13,249,000,000; *national income per person,* $598.
Economic Indexes: *Manufacturing production* (1970), 159 (1963=100); *agricultural production* (1969), 117 (1963=100); *consumer price index* (1970), 125 (1963=100).
Manufacturing (metric tons, 1969): Cement, 5,105,000; crude steel, 4,628,000; wheat flour, 671,000; meat, 645,000.
Crops (metric tons, 1969 crop year): Maize, 5,339,000; wheat, 1,279,000.
Minerals (metric tons, 1969): Manganese ore, 1,044,200 (ranks 2d among world producers); chromium ore, 538,800 (world rank 1st); diamonds, 7,863,000 metric carats (world rank 2d); gold, 969,341 kilograms (world rank 1st).
Foreign Trade (1970): *Exports,* $2,148,000 (chief exports—diamonds, $244,084,000; wool, $103,277,000). *Imports,* $3,556,000,000 (chief imports, 1968—nonelectrical machinery, $794,122,000; transport equipment, $429,968,000; chemicals, $217,924,000; electrical machinery and appliances, $197,596,000). *Chief trading partners* (1968)—United Kingdom (took 32% of exports, supplied 24% of imports); Japan (14%—7%); United States (7%—18%); West Germany (7%—13%).
Transportation: *Roads* (1969), 220,000 miles (354,000 km); *motor vehicles* (1969), 1,928,000; *railroads* (1969), 13,621 miles (21,916 km); *merchant fleet* (1970), 511,000 gross registered tons; *national airline,* South African Airways; *principal airports,* Pretoria, Cape Town.
Communications: *Telephones* (1970), 1,482,299; *radios* (1968), 2,700,000; *newspapers* (1967), 23 (daily circulation, 783,000).

A U. S. corporation, Polaroid, decided to use part of its South African profits during an experimental 12-month period to improve the wages of its African workers and to provide them with advanced training and education. The South African Institute of Race Relations expressed the hope that other business firms would follow this example.

Domestic Affairs. In January the Anglican dean of Johannesburg, the Very Rev. Gonville ffrench-Beytagh, was arrested on charges under the suppression of Communism act. He was accused of distributing money to banned organizations and of incitement to violence. He was convicted and in November was sentenced to five years in jail.

The prime minister, speaking in a different context at a press conference, denied that there was any confrontation between church and state. Vorster also announced that the South African police would continue to cooperate with the Rhodesians in anti-terrorist campaigns. Vorster indicated that independence for the Bantu homelands depended on circumstances and on when the homeland felt ready to ask for its independence.

In August the government announced the formation of a provisional administrative body for the Damaras in South West Africa, as the first step toward their attainment of self-government. The government declared that it had spent $464.8 million on development works in the Bantu homelands between 1959 and 1969.

RONALD B. BALLINGER, *Rhode Island College*

SOUTH CAROLINA

The year 1971 in South Carolina saw progress in school integration, opportunities for blacks, and constitutional and government reform.

Governor. From his inauguration in January 1971, Gov. John C. West stressed programs to upgrade the underprivileged and to promote the dignity of all citizens within the state. There was emphasis on greater opportunity for blacks, including the creation of a human relations council, special employment and manpower development programs, expansion of kindergartens, the use of blacks in responsible government positions, improved health services, revision of the food-stamp program, the establishment of a state housing corporation, and planning for fuller use of federal funds. The new governor revived the state reorganization commission to help meet these goals.

Legislature. The General Assembly, in the longest session in its history, was plagued by budgetary and reapportionment questions and pressure by school teachers. Only small raises were given to teachers and state employees, and a balanced budget was enacted without a tax increase. There was a major fight on reapportioning the state Senate. Agreement was reached only through adoption of two plans; if the courts disapprove the first, the second will be tried. Both have shortcomings.

Significant legislation was enacted in such areas as pollution control, traffic safety, insurance reform, grievance procedures for state and local employees, regional-government councils, and county-government reorganization. Five articles of the constitution were revised, and the remaining 12 were being prepared for the 1972 election.

Education. Despite delays and frustrations, all schools opened peacefully in the fall of 1971. Busing and integration increased significantly, but so did the number of private schools. Teachers, demanding more pay and support for education, held 1-day strikes, intensified their lobbying, and strove for local property tax reform. The National Education Association was asked to examine state educational needs, over politicians' strenuous protests.

Major arguments developed over the control of technical education and branches of the university. Leaders debated the necessity of a second medical school and ways of financing higher education. A test case was pending, on tuition grants for students at private colleges. The state department of education stressed plans to improve public schools. Benedict College, a black denominational institution, received a $5 million "seed" grant from the Ford Foundation and started a major fund drive.

Economy. The state government reduced spending by 6% and ended 1971 with a small surplus. Localities and schools raised property taxes. Unemployment was below the national average, but Charleston suffered. Some industries reduced their work week, but industrial expansion exceeded that of 1970. Strong opposition developed over the building of nuclear-related plants and cutting of swampland timber. The state achieved significant reductions in pollution. Agriculture had a bountiful year.

Mendel Rivers. L. Mendel Rivers, who had served in the U. S. House of Representatives since 1940, died on Dec. 28, 1970. As chairman of the powerful House Armed Services Committee he had dotted the Charleston area with defense plants and bases. In a special election on April 27 his godson and aide, Mendel J. Davis, won the House seat.

ROBERT H. STOUDEMIRE
University of South Carolina

─────── SOUTH CAROLINA • Information Highlights ───────

Area: 31,055 square miles (80,432 sq km).
Population (1970 census): 2,590,516. *Density:* 89 per sq mi.
Chief Cities (1970 census): Columbia, the capital, 113,542; Charleston, 66,945; Greenville, 61,208.
Government (1971): *Chief Officers*—governor, John C. West (D); lt. gov., Earle E. Morris, Jr. (D); secy. of state, O. Frank Thornton (D); atty. gen., Daniel R. McLeod (D); treas., Grady L. Patterson, Jr. (D); supt. of dept. of educ., Cyril B. Busbee (D); chief justice, Joseph R. Moss. *General Assembly*—Senate, 46 members (42 Democrats, 2 Republicans, 2 vac.); House of Representatives, 124 members (113 D, 11 R).
Education (1970–71): *Enrollment*—public elementary schools, 382,800 pupils; 15,300 teachers; secondary public, 263,-300 pupils; 12,700 teachers; nonpublic schools (1968–69), 15,700 pupils; 900 teachers; higher (fall 1968), 56,139 students. *Public school expenditures* (1970–71), $392,485,000 ($656 per pupil). *Average teacher's salary,* $7,000.
State Finances (fiscal year 1970): *Revenues,* $926,335,000 (4% general sales tax and gross receipts taxes, $192,552,-000; motor fuel tax, $87,238,000; federal funds, $193,273,-000). *Expenditures,* $892,372,000 (education, $416,899,000; health, welfare, safety, $79,557,000; highways, $122,917,-000). *State debt,* $350,452,000 (June 30, 1970).
Personal Income (1970): $7,681,000,000; per capita, $2,908.
Public Assistance (1970): $64,741,000. *Average monthly payments* (Dec. 1970)—old-age assistance, $48.50; aid to families with dependent children, $77.55.
Labor Force: *Nonagricultural wage and salary earners* (June 1971), 852,300. *Av. annual employment* (1960)—manufacturing, 339,000; trade, 135,000; government, 140,000; services, 83,000. *Insured unemployed* (Oct. '71)—13,300 (2.1%).
Manufacturing (1967): *Value added by manufacture,* $3,030,-300,000. Textile mill products, $1,236,600,000; chemicals and allied products, $474,600,000; apparel, $232,100,000; paper and allied products, $193,200,000).
Agriculture (1970): *Cash farm income,* $496,471,000 (livestock, $180,337,000; crops, $261,700,000; government payments, $54,434,000). *Chief crops* (1970)—Tobacco, 141,075,000 pounds (ranks 3d among the states); soybeans, 20,439,-000 bushels; corn, 10,854,000 bushels.
Mining (1971): *Production value,* $60,380,000 (ranks 42d among the states). *Chief minerals* (tons)—Stone, 9,127,-000; sand and gravel, 6,099,000; clays, 1,977,000.
Fisheries (1970): *Commercial catch,* 16,000,000 pounds ($4,200,000). *Leading species by value* (1967)—Shrimp, $1,679,000; hard, blue crabs, $290,000; alewives, $56,000.
Transportation: *Roads* (1969) 59,825 miles (96,276 km); *motor vehicles* (1969) 1,311,000; *railroads* (1968) 3,131 miles (5,039 km); *airports* (1969), 57.
Communications: *Telephones* (1971) 1,167,500; *television stations* (1969), 11; *radio stations* (1969) 133; *newspapers* (1969), 17 (daily circulation, 557,000).

SOUTH DAKOTA

Indian affairs and fiscal restraint in view of generally disappointing economic conditions dominated South Dakota news in 1971. In June, a group of American Indians occupied the Mount Rushmore National Memorial to dramatize Sioux land claims. Spending curbs were especially evident in higher education.

Legislation. The legislature refused to enact Gov. Richard Kneip's plan to replace property taxes with personal and corporation taxes and turned down petitions for substantial increases in educational appropriations. Meanwhile, the governor exercised his veto power in striking down bills to increase salaries of county officials, provide retirement pay for local judges, and advance spending through state agencies. The only significant advance went to the welfare department, which will receive a $2 million increase in 1972.

Economy. From midyear trends the state budget officer projected that sales tax and cigarette tax receipts would fall below expectations. The recession was given as the reason. Reductions in support of such vital programs as water pollution control, drug control, and veterans' bonuses were expected to result.

—— SOUTH DAKOTA • Information Highlights ——

Area: 77,047 square miles (199,552 sq km).
Population (1970 census): 666,257. *Density:* 9 per sq mi.
Chief Cities (1970 census): Pierre, the capital, 9,699; Sioux Falls, 72,488; Rapid City, 43,836; Aberdeen, 26,476; Huron, 14,299; Brookings, 13,717; Mitchell, 13,425.
Government (1971): *Chief Officers*—governor, Richard F. Kneip (D); lt. gov., William J. Dougherty (D); secy. of state, Alam Larsen (R); atty. gen., Gordon Mydland (R); treas., Neal A. Strand (R); supt. of public instruction, Donald P. Barnhart (NP); presiding judge, Alex Rentto. *Legislature*—Senate, 35 members (24 Republicans, 11 Democrats); House of Representatives, 75 members (46 R, 29 D).
Education (1970–71): *Enrollment*—public elementary schools, 115,000 pupils; 5,950 teachers; public secondary, 51,300 pupils; 2,913 teachers; nonpublic schools (1968–69), 17,-561 pupils; 984 teachers; college and university (fall 1968), 28,909 students. *Public school expenditures* (1970–71), $110,000,000 ($688 per pupil). *Average teacher's salary,* $6,793.
State Finances (fiscal year 1970): *Revenues,* $254,075,000 (4% general sales tax and gross receipts taxes, $47,736,000; motor fuel tax, $24,012,000; federal funds, $86,480,000). Expenditures, $239,644,000 (education, $86,205,000; health, welfare, and safety, $29,353,000; highways, $66,176,000). *State debt,* $29,923,000 (June 30, 1970).
Personal Income (1970): $2,118,000,000; per capita, $3,182.
Public Assistance (1970): $29,348,000. *Average monthly payments* (Dec. 1970)—old-age assistance, $66.85; aid to families with dependent children, $190.20.
Labor Force: *Nonagricultural wage and salary earners* (June 1971), 183,400. *Average annual employment* (1969)—manufacturing, 16,000; trade, 45,000; government, 53,000; services, 30,000. *Insured unemployed* (Oct. 1971)—1,100 (1.1%).
Manufacturing (1967): *Value added by manufacture,* $171,300,-000. Food and allied products, $95,000,000; printing and publishing, $15,800,000.
Agriculture (1970): *Cash farm income,* $1,103,646,000 (livestock, $811,484,000; crops, $200,464,000; government payments, $91,698,000). *Chief crops* (1970)—Oats, 105,329,-000 bushels (ranks 3d among the states); corn, 102,336,-000 bushels; wheat, 39,282,000 bushels; hay, 5,795,000 tons.
Mining (1970): *Production value,* $53,290,000 (ranks 41st among the states). *Chief minerals* (tons)—Sand and gravel, 11,300,000; stone, 2,026,000; cement, 1,567,000 barrels; gold, 582,700 troy ounces.
Transportation: *Roads* (1969), 84,355 miles (135,753 km); *motor vehicles* (1969), 418,000; *railroads* (1968), 3,805 miles (6,123 km); *airports* (1969), 66.
Communications: *Telephones* (1971), 334,500; *television stations* (1969), 10; *radio stations* (1969), 33; *newspapers* (1969), 12 (daily circulation, 171,000).

Farmers had a mediocre year. The advantage gained from a wet spring was offset by drought late in the growing season. Prices at harvest were low.

Indian Affairs. The demonstration at Mount Rushmore was staged by out-of-state Indians, led by members of the American Indian Movement (AIM). The protesters, five of whom were jailed, failed to receive the support of the United Sioux Tribes of South Dakota (an organization of state tribal leaders). Instead, spokesmen criticized them for jeopardizing long-standing endeavors to achieve the same ends through regular processes.

However, the protest added impetus to a movement begun in recent years to dramatize the desires of the state's Indians, and some important programs have resulted. The University of South Dakota has operated a major Indian oral history project, offered a liberal arts program on reservations, and established a program to qualify Indian students for master's degrees and certification in librarianship. The university also has sponsored an Indian language workshop, Indian dances, and training in arts and crafts, which were largely responsible for an increased Indian enrollment.

Higher Education. Under austerity measures, administrators struck out programs and merged departments. The university annexed a former state college at Springfield. Professors accepted greater responsibilities with little additional pay. But there were no moves to limit enrollments or steps that might impair the quality of education.

HERBERT T. HOOVER, *University of South Dakota*

SOUTHERN YEMEN

The People's Democratic Republic of Yemen (Southern Yemen) in 1971 held on its course as the most radical of all the Arab states. Its policies helped prolong conflicts with its Arab neighbors.

Foreign Affairs. Southern Yemen, maintaining that the Yemen Arab Republic (YAR or Northern Yemen) was supporting opponents of its regime, attacked the YAR with army and air force units in October. Soviet advisers in Southern Yemen were reported to have been involved in planning the operation. The YAR threatened to break off diplomatic relations. Southern Yemen also accused Saudi Arabia of seeking to undermine its government, and there was no diminishing of friction between these two countries. Abetted by the People's Republic of China, Southern Yemen continued to provide a sanctuary and a source of military supplies for the guerrillas striving to overthrow the new sultan of Oman to the east.

Southern Yemen relied heavily on military and economic aid from Communist countries. China's economic support, said to amount to $55 million, was concentrated largely on a new highway linking the western and eastern parts of the country. Communist China also established a military mission in Aden. The prime minister of Southern Yemen visited Moscow in 1971, and the Soviet Union furnished MIG-17 fighter planes, helicopters, tanks, and artillery.

Internal Affairs. The great interest shown in Southern Yemen by Communist China and the Soviet Union, due to the country's strategic position, heightened the struggle for power between the pro-Chinese and the pro-Soviet factions in the National Liberation Front (NLF), the governing party. The chief of state, Salim Rubai, was believed to be pro-Chinese and lukewarm toward a policy of subverting the government of the YAR. The secretary of the NLF, Abd al-Fattah Ismail, leaned toward the Soviet Union and a policy of subversion in the north. Neither faction seemed to be gaining a clearcut upper hand. In August, a new prime minister and defense minister, Ali Nasir Muhammad, was appointed.

GEORGE RENTZ
Hoover Institution, Stanford University

—— SOUTHERN YEMEN • Information Highlights ——

Official Name: People's Democratic Republic of Yemen.
Area: 111,075 square miles (287,683 sq km).
Population (1970 est.): 1,280,000. *Density,* 11 per square mile (4 per sq km). *Annual rate of increase,* 2.2%.
Chief City (1970 est.): Aden, the capital, 225,000.
Government: *Head of state,* Salim Rukai, chairman of Presidential Council (took office June 1969). *Head of government,* Ali Nasir Muhammed, prime minister (took office August 1971). *Major political party*—National Liberation Front.
Languages: Arabic, English.
Education: *Literacy rate* (1970), 10% of population, but 35% in Aden. *School enrollment* (1967)—primary, 66,830.
Finances (1969 est.): *Revenues,* $21,500,000; *expenditures,* $38,000,000; *monetary unit,* dinar (0.4167 dinar equal U. S. $1, 1970).
Gross National Product (1968 est.): $127,200,000.
Average annual income per person (1968 est.): $106.
Manufacturing (metric tons, 1969): Residual fuel oil, 3,620,-000; distillate fuel oil, 1,099,000; kerosene, 610,000.
Crop (metric tons, 1969 crop year): Cotton lint, 7,000.
Foreign Trade (1970): *Exports,* $146,000,000 (chief exports—petroleum products, $108,000,000). *Imports,* $201,000,000 (chief import—Crude petroleum, $79,440,000. *Chief trading partners* (1968)—Britain; Japan; Kuwait; Iran.
Transportation: *Roads* (1969), 140 miles (224 km); *motor vehicles* (1969), 11,700 (automobiles, 9,600).

SOVIET LITERATURE. See LITERATURE.

NASA

space exploration

Man's exploration of the solar system continued in 1971 with two highly successful manned missions to the surface of the moon and three flights of unmanned spacecraft to the vicinity of Mars, for important photographic and instrumental studies of that planet. The effort to establish functional manned space stations in orbit around the earth was also advanced during the year, although this activity unfortunately involved the tragic deaths of three cosmonauts. The United States and the Soviet Union discussed the possibilities of combining efforts on some manned space exploration programs. Meanwhile, several significant unmanned satellites were launched in 1971, including a highly complex solar observatory.

MANNED SPACE FLIGHT

Manned space flight in 1971 was marked by both triumph and tragedy. The United States' Apollo 14 and 15 missions vastly increased man's knowledge of the moon, while the Soviet Union's Soyuz 10 and 11 missions were important precursors to the establishment of an earth orbital space station. However, the deaths of the Soyuz 11 cosmonauts demonstrated once again the hazards inherent in the exploration of new frontiers.

Apollo 14. The Apollo 14 mission was launched from Kennedy Space Center, Fla., on Jan. 31, 1971, and was successfully completed on February 9 with the recovery of crew and spacecraft in the mid-

Pacific Ocean. The Apollo 14 crew included veteran astronaut Alan B. Shepard, Jr., and rookies Stuart A. Roosa and Edgar D. Mitchell. Shepard and Mitchell made the descent to the moon in the lunar module *Antares,* while Roosa remained aboard the command module *Kitty Hawk.*

Shepard and Mitchell landed in a valley of the Fra Mauro uplands on February 5, within 30 to 60 feet (9 to 18 meters) of the planned landing point. During their first venture outside *Antares,* the two astronauts deployed several scientific instruments, collected lunar surface material, and took panoramic television pictures of the moon's surface. One of the instruments they used was a laser-reflecting device that enabled scientists back on earth to determine the distance between earth and moon with great precision.

During their second extravehicular period, the astronauts used a wheeled cart to assist them in carrying further instruments to a nearby crater. Shepard and Mitchell collected a total of 108 pounds (49 kg) of moon rocks and fine-grained soils—about as much as the combined total of the samples returned by the Apollo 11 and 12 missions. The rocks were the first to be gathered from a lunar upland. Scientists believe that the Fra Mauro site was formed by debris that showered down when the huge Sea of Rains was created by a planetoid impact on the moon's surface some four billion or more years ago.

(*Opposite*) Apollo 15 astronaut David Scott poses beside flag near the *Falcon*. Apennine Mountains rise in the background. (*Above*) Near the rim of Hadley Rill, James Irwin loads samples onto the lunar rover.

After spending 33 hours and 31 minutes on the moon, Shepard and Mitchell left in the ascent stage of the *Antares* to rendezvous with *Kitty Hawk* and begin the journey back to earth. Taking advantage of weightless conditions during the long trip home, the astronauts conducted experiments to explore the possibilities that a zero-gravity environment offers to various manufacturing processes. For example, weightlessness might facilitate production of new metal alloys, glass, and a whole family of materials that are difficult to manufacture on earth because of gravity. One experiment investigated the electrically induced movement of biological compounds such as protein through a liquid medium—a process, called electrophoresis, that is used in the manufacture of some vaccines. The astronauts also studied the effects of weightlessness on convection and heat flow by heating samples of water, sugar solutions, and carbon dioxide, since several proposed manufacturing processes in space would involve these effects. Another experiment was related to the manufacture of metals and other materials that are strengthened by impregnation with fibers. On earth, gravity often interferes with the production of such composites by making it difficult to keep the fibers uniformly distributed while the metal solidifies.

Apollo 15. The next lunar flight, Apollo 15, was launched on July 26. Again there was one veteran pilot, David R. Scott, and two new astronauts,

James B. Irwin and Alfred M. Worden. The first two made the descent to the moon in the *Falcon* while Worden remained in orbit in the *Endeavour*. Apollo 15 represented the longest and most ambitious exploration of the moon's surface to that time, with Scott and Irwin leaving the *Falcon* three times and spending twice as long on the moon as in any previous mission. They were greatly aided by a new, battery-driven, four-wheel vehicle that enabled them to rove several miles over the lunar surface.

After a journey of nearly 3½ days, Apollo 15 entered orbit around the moon and began to prepare for the landing in the mountainous, previously unexplored Hadley-Apennine region of the moon. On July 30 the *Falcon* flew over the Apennines—the tallest lunar mountain range—and landed close to Hadley Rill. When he stepped out on the moon for the first time, Scott said, "As I stand out here in the wonders of the unknown at Hadley, I sort of realize there is a fundamental truth to our nature: man must explore and this is exploration at its greatest."

The astronauts began their scientific work on the moon by collecting a small contingency sample of lunar rocks. Afterward they assembled their roving vehicle and loaded it with equipment, preparing for a 5-mile (8-km) drive to Hadley Rill and on to the base of the Apennine Mountains. They stopped along the way to collect samples, take photographs, and report on their findings. At each stop an on-board television camera was activated and then controlled from earth, providing spectators with spectacular views of the canyonlike rill and the neighboring mountain slopes. Returning to the landing site after their excursion, the astronauts set up a scientific station. These instruments, together with those set up at the Apollo 12 and 14 landing sites, completed a triangle of stations for transmitting data back to earth, thus enabling the locations of moon tremors to be determined with an accuracy previously impossible.

After spending 6½ hours exploring the moon and collecting more than 50 pounds (22 kg) of rocks, the astronauts reentered the *Falcon* and settled down to 7½ hours of sleep. Scott and Irwin then traveled again in their moon car and gathered more than 100 pounds (45 kg) of samples from an area on the 4-billion-year-old Apennine foothills and from a cluster of younger craters in the moon's so-called Marsh of Decay. They dug a trench 14 to 16 inches (35 to 40 cm) deep and scooped up subsurface soil materials into bags, successfully planting special thermometers to measure heat flow from the moon's interior. They also attempted to collect a core sample, with some difficulty. After more than 7 hours on the surface, the men again entered the lunar module.

During the last extravehicular period, additional rock and soil samples were obtained and photographs were taken of various features as Scott and Irwin explored an area near the rim of Hadley Rill. Back at the landing site, the core sample was finally obtained, and the astronauts reentered the *Falcon* and prepared to lift off and join Worden in the command module. A television camera beamed back a picture of the ascent stage as it rapidly soared into the lunar sky. Packed in with the explorers was a treasure chest of 230 pounds (103 kg) of rocks and soil and photographic film. After rendezvousing, the Apollo spacecraft spent two more days in lunar orbit performing additional scientific experiments. The craft also released a satellite to measure magnetic field intensities in the environment of the moon.

On August 4, Apollo 15 fired its rocket and entered a trajectory back to earth, and three days

later the astronauts splashed down safely in the mid-Pacific Ocean 285 miles (459 km) north of Honolulu, despite the fact that one of the craft's three parachutes failed to deploy. What was perhaps the most rewarding mission of the space age had been concluded. However, the second phase of Apollo 15 is still going on—the attempt to wring fundamental secrets of the moon and the solar system from the materials returned by the astronauts. Approximately 700 scientists are taking part in this effort. Preliminary examination showed that the materials are of three general kinds: dark-colored, iron-rich basalts; a few basalts enriched in feldspar; and light-colored, fragmented rocks consisting of soil-like substances that have been cemented together, or rock fragments that have been welded together by partial remelting. There are also several unique and unusual samples.

Through study of the Apollo 15 materials, scientists hope to be able to characterize lunar rocks that formed prior to the filling of the mare basin. Other studies may provide a better understanding of the formation of rills, the canyonlike depressions that sometimes extend for hundreds of miles across the lunar surface. From all of these studies, new knowledge will be gained of the origin and evolution of the moon and of the solar system as a whole. (See also GEOLOGY.)

Salyut 1 and Soyuz 10. On April 19, the Soviet Union placed the scientific station Salyut 1 in orbit. The station had four sections: a forward compartment that contained an airlock passage and a docking collar for manned Soyuz spacecraft, a biological laboratory, a compartment filled with numerous scientific instruments, and a rear compartment that housed a propulsion system for maneuvering the station and transferring it from orbit to orbit. The function of Salyut 1 was to determine the ability of cosmonauts to endure a period of 30 to 60 days in space and to function there, as well as to test the capabilities of the space station itself.

Shortly before dawn on April 23, Soyuz 10 was launched to demonstrate the first manned earth orbital base by docking with Salyut 1. Cosmonauts Vladimir Shatalov, Alexei Yeliseyev, and Nikolai

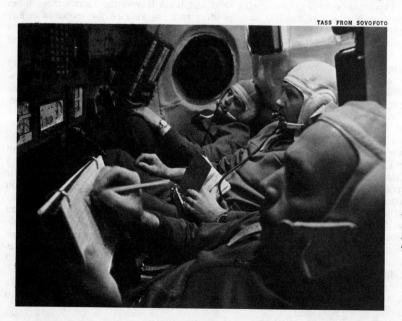

SOYUZ 11's ill-fated crew of (*left to right*) Vladislav Volkov, Georgi Dobrovolsky, and Viktor Patsayev work in the ship's cabin prior to their record-breaking test flight of a prototype space station. A faulty cabin seal led to the deaths of the three cosmonauts as they descended to earth.

Rukavishnikov piloted their spacecraft through maneuvers that tested approach and docking techniques. The tests did not involve any transfer of cosmonauts to Salyut 1. After the two spacecraft orbited in tandem unit it was time for Soyuz 10 to fire its retro-rockets for the return to earth. The manned spacecraft landed 75 miles (120 km) northwest of Karaganda, Kazakhstan, on April 25, after only about 30 orbits. Salyut 1, left alone in space, was moved to a new orbit about 50 miles (80 km) higher, in preparation for the arrival of Soyuz 11—the next phase of the orbital station development program.

Soyuz 11. On June 6, Soyuz 11 was launched into orbit with cosmonauts Viktor Patsayev, Vladislav Volkov, and Georgi Dobrovolsky aboard. The spacecraft achieved rendezvous with Salyut 1 and was soon docked with the station. While Dobrovolsky remained in Soyuz 11 to supervise the operation, Patsayev and Volkov entered Salyut through the new docking-airlock passage. The vehicles were then rigidly coupled together and their electrical and hydraulic systems connected, since the cosmonauts were going to continue to use the cabin system of the Soyuz during their stay in space.

The crew alternated their work cycle with periods of physical exercise and with medical and biological tests. These tests were aided by special medical equipment in the laboratory, and included investigations of the fundamental state of the cosmonauts' vesicular and circulatory systems and measurements of their arterial pressure. The experiments that took advantage of the zero-gravity environment included a study of its effects on higher vegetation, such as cabbage, flax, and bulb onions that were being cultivated hydroponically in the space station.

In addition to being a preliminary test of man's adaptability to space in a long-duration orbital station, the Soyuz 11 mission made observations of geological features on the earth's surface, studied cloud formations, and observed the earth's snow and cloud cover. During the mission the cosmonauts also made surveys of the earth's resources, working with scientific aircraft to obtain spectrographs of the planet's surface in order to determine water reserves and conditions for growing plants. The cosmonauts monitored the weather, as well, the experiments being coordinated with the flights of the Soviet Union's Meteor program of meteorological satellites. Whenever the Salyut was out of radio range of the Soviet Union, communications were maintained by means of Molniya communications satellites and a space-tracking ship stationed in the northern Atlantic Ocean.

On June 29, Soviet scientists ordered the Soyuz 11 mission to be concluded. The three cosmonauts transferred scientific research materials and flight logs back to their spacecraft, then orbited in tandem with Salyut 1 for the next 3 hours until their craft's rocket was fired. At the end of this operation, ground communications with the crew ceased. The reentry and landing of the spacecraft was normal, and a recovery helicopter was hovering at the landing site as the Soyuz dropped slowly through the skies beneath its parachutes. Just as the ship was about to touch down on the earth's surface, landing rockets fired to soften the impact. The automatically controlled landing seemed, in fact, to be a perfect one, but the craft was still silent.

APOLLO 14 MISSION SAVER Donald Eyles points to a duplicate of the faulty switch that threatened to abort the February 5 moon landing. Eyles and his fellow engineers devised an electronic bypass of the switch in two hours.

The recovery team raced to the ship and tore open the hatch. There were the three cosmonauts still strapped in their seats. They were all dead.

News of the tragedy soon spread around the world, and there was a period of intense speculation as to its cause. Since Apollo 15 was soon to be launched, speculation included concern about the possible harmful biological effects of long-duration space flights. However, the fate of the three men was eventually attributed to a faulty seal in Soyuz 11 that resulted in rapid decompression of the landing module and almost instant death thereafter for Patsayev, Volkov, and Dobrovolsky.

U. S. and USSR Cooperation in Space. Plans were being developed in 1971 for cooperative space efforts by the United States and the Soviet Union in such areas as meteorology, study of the moon and the planets, biology and medicine, and cooperative manned spaceflight efforts. Late in the year, joint working groups were attempting to resolve the remaining technical problems associated with developing a rendezvous and docking program compatible with the manned systems of both nations. The effort had come close to defining the first joint manned missions that will be orbited for the testing of the compatible systems. Under consideration is the docking of an Apollo spacecraft with an orbital Soviet station of the Salyut type, and the docking of a Soyuz spacecraft with the U. S. Skylab orbiting laboratory that is being developed by modifying the Saturn 5 rocket.

EARTH SATELLITES AND SPACE PROBES

The United States launched 10 successful nonmilitary earth satellites and space probes in 1971, while the Soviet Union launched more than 24 satellites and space probes that are believed to be of a nonmilitary nature. Japan, Britain, and France each placed two automated spacecraft in orbit, mainland China launched its second earth satellite, and Canada and Italy each launched one satellite.

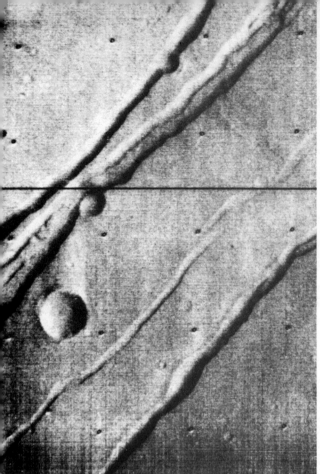

After the Martian dust storm began to abate at the end of 1971, U. S. Mariner 9 at last was able to photograph the surface. The photos revealed rills (left) that sometimes extended for more than 1,000 miles (1,600 km) across the surface, and showed a vast chasm (right) from which extended canyons resembling a network of dry riverbeds. The main canyon in photo is at least 300 miles (480 km) long. (Above) Phobos, the larger of the two Martian moons, is 16 miles long.

After the Dust Settled...

MARS UP CLOSE

U. S. Mars Probe. On May 30, the United States sent Mariner 9 on a trajectory toward Mars, following the unsuccessful launch of Mariner 8. The mission of the probe was to map 70% of the surface of Mars in 90 days, study its features and atmospheric characteristics in detail, and obtain the first photographs of Phobos and Deimos, the two Martian moons. On November 13, Mariner 9 reached the vicinity of Mars and was placed in an orbital path that took it to within nearly 870 miles (1,400 km) of the surface. However, as the probe began its reconnaissance, the first pictures transmitted to earth revealed that a gigantic dust storm was sweeping across the Martian surface and almost totally obscuring it. Instruments aboard the spacecraft indicated that the storm's dust particles were coarse-grained silicates, perhaps something like sand. The instrumental data also confirmed earlier observations that carbon dioxide is the major constituent of the Martian atmosphere.

After about a week in orbit, the spacecraft detected that dust was settling to the surface at the south polar cap. Thereupon it began to take useful pictures and make other measurements of this region. Despite the fact that it was summer in the southern hemisphere of Mars, the temperature at the surface was measured by Mariner's instruments as being in the neighborhood of $-80°$ F ($-27°$ C). On the other hand, the temperature at 60,000 to 100,000 feet (18,000 to 30,000 meters) was found to be warmer, a phenomenon probably related to the effects of the dust in the atmosphere. Other measurements indicated that the Martian at-

mosphere is indeed very thin—as low as 4.2 millibars, or 200 times thinner than the atmosphere on earth. Mariner's photographs of the Martian moons revealed Phobos and Deimos to be irregular and oblong in shape, and scarred by many craters.

Soviet Mars Probes. Following behind Mariner 9 were two Soviet spacecraft, Mars 2 and 3, which had been launched on May 19 and May 28. Just before entering Mars' orbit on November 27, Mars 2 ejected a capsule that entered the atmosphere and delivered to the planet's surface a pennant with a Soviet insignia. This marked the first time that a man-made object touched the surface of Mars. On December 2, Mars 3 also went into orbit around the planet after releasing a capsule that soft-landed in the southern hemisphere by means of parachute. Signals from the capsule were received and recorded by instruments aboard Mars 3, which later transmitted the data to earth during communications sessions. However, the signals received from the capsule were brief and suddenly discontinued.

Soviet Lunar Probes. The Soviet Union's highly successful lunar roving vehicle, Lunokhod 1, which had been ejected by Luna 17 and landed on the moon on Nov. 17, 1970, ceased to operate on Oct. 4, 1971, after its radioisotope heat source lost power and its temperature dropped. During its life of 10½ months, Lunokhod ran up an impressive list of statistics. It drove across 6.5 miles (10.5 km) and mapped 95,000 square yards (79,400 square meters) of the lunar surface; took 200 full-circle, panoramic photographs; snapped 20,000 other pictures; tested the density of the soil at 500

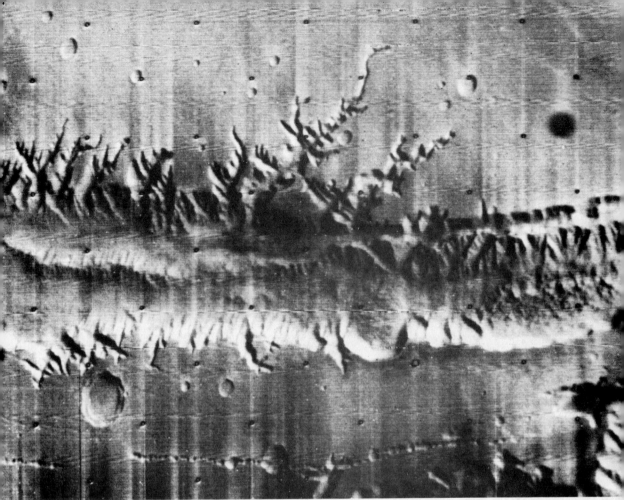

JET PROPULSION LABORATORY, CALIFORNIA INSTITUTE OF TECHNOLOGY, NASA

points, and did chemical analyses of lunar surface materials at 25 points.

On September 2, the Soviet Union launched Luna 18 toward the moon and, after a five-day flight, placed it in lunar orbit. Once the probe had made 54 orbits of the moon, its braking apparatus was fired and the spacecraft descended, reaching the surface in a mountainous area near the Sea of Fertility on September 11. However, it is believed that Luna 18 was unable to touch down successfully in the rugged terrain and instead crash-landed, although this was not confirmed by the Russians.

Luna 19 was launched on September 28 to continue the Soviet Union's exploration of the moon. Luna 19 entered a lunar orbit of 79 to 84 miles (127 to 135 km) on October 2, to photograph and map the moon's surface.

Engineering Test Satellites. The first test satellite of 1971 was Japan's Tansei, launched on February 16 from the Uchinoura Space Center to make measurements of spacecraft temperatures, vibration levels, and flight attitudes. This was followed on March 3 by the second satellite of the People's Republic of China. While the specific purpose of the satellite is unknown, it is believed to be a test satellite similar to the one launched by China on April 24, 1970.

A U. S. test satellite, TETR-4, was ejected into orbit on September 29 as a piggyback satellite of the OSO 7 launch discussed below. TETR-4 transmits simulated Apollo communications signals, to be used in evaluating and developing methods for training ground crews for manned missions.

On October 28, Britain orbited its first technology satellite, Prospero, from the Woomera Test Range in Australia. The small satellite was used to test aspects of satellite technology, and it also carried a micrometeoroid counter.

Atmospheric Research. The first satellite to be launched for atmospheric studies in 1971 was ISIS 2, sent into space on April 1 as part of a joint Canadian-United States program to observe the earth's ionosphere from space. ISIS 2 carries 12 experiments for measuring daily and seasonal fluctuations in the upper atmosphere's electron density, and studying radio and cosmic noise emissions. It was followed on April 24 by Italy's San Marco 3, which investigated the earth's equatorial atmosphere.

On August 7, the United States placed a total of nine satellites in polar orbits, including the Cannon Ball II and the Musket Ball. The satellites measured atmospheric conditions, recorded geophysical data, provided radio calibration targets, and obtained reentry vehicle data. One of the vehicles launched a satellite at a low altitude and then continued into orbit for its own measurement program. The second orbital craft ejected two satellites at a low altitude and then four more satellites at a higher altitude.

Under a cooperative agreement between France and the United States, an EOLE satellite was orbited on August 16. The primary mission of EOLE is to collect information on winds, temperature, and pressure from as many as 500 instrumented balloons that are flying at an altitude of about 39,000

(Continued on page 611)

UNMANNED NONMILITARY EARTH SATELLITES AND SPACE PROBES, 1971

Name	Launch site and date[1]	Launch vehicle[2]	Spacecraft weight at lift-off (pounds)[3]	Initial apsides of orbit (miles)[4]	Initial period (minutes)	Initial inclination (degrees)	Remarks[5]
Cosmos 390	B, 12 Jan	N.A.[6]	N.A.	129/184	89.3	65.0	Unannounced payload
Cosmos 391	P, 14 Jan	N.A.	N.A.	172/514	95.4	71.0	Unannounced payload
Meteor 7	P, 20 Jan	N.A.	N.A.	391/421	97.6	81.2	Meteorological satellite
Cosmos 392	B, 21 Jan	N.A.	N.A.	129/186	89.4	65.0	Unannounced payload
Intelsat 4F-2	K, 26 Jan	A–C	2,450	22,200/22,620	1,450.2	0.6	Communications satellite
Cosmos 393	P, 26 Jan	N.A.	N.A.	176/318	95.2	70.9	Unannounced payload
Cosmos 394	B, 9 Feb	N.A.	N.A.	355/381	96.5	65.9	Unannounced payload
Tansei (MST-1)	U, 16 Feb	Mu-4S	139	615/684	106.0	29.6	Test satellite
Cosmos 395	P, 17 Feb	N.A.	N.A.	329/339	95.4	74.0	Navigation and geodetic satellite
Cosmos 396	P, 18 Feb	N.A.	N.A.	132/193	89.4	65.4	Unannounced payload
Cosmos 397	B, 25 Feb	N.A.	N.A.	367/1,430	114.7	65.8	Maneuverable satellite test
Cosmos 398	B, 26 Feb	N.A.	N.A.	121/171	88.9	51.6	Maneuverable satellite test
Cosmos 399	B, 3 Mar	N.A.	N.A.	129/193	89.5	65.0	Unannounced payload
China 2	S, 3 Mar	N.A.	483	167/1,120	105.9	69.9	Unannounced payload
Explorer 43	K, 13 Mar	Delta M-6	628	152/12,800	5,656.1	28.8	Particle and field studies
Cosmos 400	B, 18 Mar	N.A.	N.A.	615/640	105.0	65.8	Unannounced payload
Cosmos 401	P, 27 Mar	N.A.	N.A.	116/181	89.6	72.8	Unannounced payload
ISIS 2	V, 1 Apr	T-D	578	845/888	113.6	88.1	Ionospheric monitoring
Cosmos 402	B, 1 Apr	N.A.	N.A.	162/173	89.7	65.0	Maneuverable satellite test
Cosmos 403	P, 2 Apr	N.A.	N.A.	134/156	89.0	81.4	Unannounced payload
Cosmos 404	B, 4 Apr	N.A.	N.A.	497/627	103.0	65.9	Maneuverable satellite test
Cosmos 405	P, 7 Apr	N.A.	N.A.	420/438	98.3	81.3	Navigation and geodetic satellite
Cosmos 406	P, 14 Apr	N.A.	N.A.	138/164	89.2	81.3	Unannounced payload
Tournesol (D-2A)	Ko, 15 Apr	D-B	198	284/432	96.2	46.3	Solar radiation monitor
Meteor 8	P, 17 Apr	N.A.	N.A.	379/393	97.4	81.2	Meteorological satellite
Salyut 1	B, 19 Apr	N.A.	N.A.	124/144	88.5	51.6	Orbital scientific station
Cosmos 407	P, 23 Apr	N.A.	N.A.	496/524	101.0	74.0	Navigation and geodetic satellite
San Marco 3	SM, 24 Apr	S	355	138/449	94.1	3.2	Atmospheric studies
Cosmos 408	P, 24 Apr	N.A.	N.A.	131/957	102.1	82.0	Unannounced payload
Cosmos 409	P, 28 Apr	N.A.	N.A.	733/758	109.4	74.0	Unannounced payload
Cosmos 410	B, 6 May	N.A.	N.A.	129/186	89.4	65.0	Unannounced payload
Cosmos 411-418	P, 7 May	N.A.	N.A.	876/951	115.0	74.5	Unannounced payload
Cosmos 419	B, 10 May	N.A.	N.A.	126/211	87.5	51.5	Unannounced payload
Cosmos 420	B, 18 May	N.A.	N.A.	124/150	88.8	51.8	Unannounced payload
Cosmos 421	P, 19 May	N.A.	N.A.	176/306	92.0	71.0	Unannounced payload
Mars 2	B, 19 May	N.A.	10,250	Trajectory to Mars			Arrived Mars November 27
Cosmos 422	P, 22 May	N.A.	N.A.	615/634	105.1	74.0	Unannounced payload
Cosmos 423	P, 27 May	N.A.	N.A.	173/304	91.9	71.0	Unannounced payload
Cosmos 424	P, 28 May	N.A.	N.A.	133/192	89.4	65.4	Unannounced payload
Mars 3	B, 28 May	N.A.	10,250	Trajectory to Mars			Arrived Mars December 2
Cosmos 425	P, 29 May	N.A.	N.A.	317/346	95.3	74.0	Unannounced payload
Mariner 9	K, 30 May	A–C	2,200	Trajectory to Mars			Arrived Mars November 13
Cosmos 426	P, 5 Jun	N.A.	N.A.	245/1,250	109.3	74.0	Unannounced payload
Cosmos 427	P, 11 Jun	N.A.	N.A.	129/187	89.7	72.9	Unannounced payload
Cosmos 428	B, 24 Jun	N.A.	N.A.	129/168	89.1	51.8	Unannounced payload
Explorer 44	W, 8 Jul	S	260	271/391	95.3	51.0	Solar monitor
Meteor 9	P, 16 Jul	N.A.	N.A.	384/404	97.3	81.2	Meteorological satellite
Cosmos 429	P, 20 Jul	N.A.	N.A.	127/161	89.0	51.8	Unannounced payload
Cosmos 430	P, 23 Jul	N.A.	N.A.	128/200	89.6	65.4	Unannounced payload
Molniya 18	B, 28 Jul	N.A.	N.A.	292/24,420	705.0	65.4	Communications satellite
Cosmos 431	B, 30 Jul	N.A.	N.A.	102/176	89.0	51.7	Unannounced payload
Cosmos 432	B, 5 Aug	N.A.	N.A.	130/163	89.0	51.8	Unannounced payload
Cannon Ball II } Musket Ball }	V, 7 Aug	Atlas	794 134	485/570	101.9	87.6	Total of 9 satellites for atmospheric studies
Cosmos 433	B, 8 Aug	N.A.	N.A.	99/162	88.6	49.5	Unannounced payload
Cosmos 434	B, 12 Aug	N.A.	N.A.	122/177	89.0	51.6	Maneuverable satellite test
EOLE 1	W, 16 Aug	S	185	421/563	100.7	50.0	Atmospheric studies
Cosmos 435	P, 27 Aug	N.A.	N.A.	175/314	92.1	71.0	Unannounced payload
Luna 18	B, 2 Sept	N.A.	N.A.	Trajectory to moon			Crashed on moon September 11
Cosmos 436	P, 7 Sept	N.A.	N.A.	319/342	95.2	74.0	Navigation and geodetic satellite
Cosmos 437	P, 10 Sept	N.A.	N.A.	322/340	95.3	74.0	Navigation and geodetic satellite
Cosmos 438	P, 14 Sept	N.A.	N.A.	132/199	89.5	65.4	Unannounced payload
Cosmos 439	P, 21 Sept	N.A.	N.A.	136/191	89.4	65.4	Unannounced payload
Cosmos 440	P, 24 Sept	N.A.	N.A.	175/506	95.3	71.0	Unannounced payload
Shinsei	U, 28 Sept	Mu-4S	137.8	547/1,150	111.8	32.0	Solar and cosmic ray studies
Luna 19	B, 28 Sept	N.A.	N.A.	Trajectory to moon			Arrived moon October 2
OSO 7	K, 29 Sept	Delta N	1,389	204/358	93.6	33.1	Solar monitor
TETR 4	K, 29 Sept	Delta N	44.5	247/354	94.6	33.0	Communications test satellite
Cosmos 442	P, 29 Sept	N.A.	N.A.	131/199	89.5	72.9	Unannounced payload
Cosmos 443	P, 7 Oct	N.A.	N.A.	131/202	89.6	65.4	Unannounced payload
Cosmos 444-451	P, 13 Oct	N.A.	N.A.	879/963	115.0	74.0	Unannounced payload
Cosmos 452	B, 14 Oct	N.A.	N.A.	125/168	89.1	65.0	Unannounced payload
Prospero	Wo, 28 Oct	B.A.	143	343/957	106.4	82.0	Technology satellite
Cosmos 454	P, 2 Nov	N.A.	N.A.	130/176	89.2	65.4	Unannounced payload
Explorer 45	SM, 15 Nov	S	107	137/16,790	469.0	3.6	Particle and field studies
Cosmos 455	P, 17 Nov	N.A.	N.A.	175/321	92.2	71.0	Unannounced payload
Cosmos 456	P, 19 Nov	N.A.	N.A.	135/204	89.7	72.9	Unannounced payload
Cosmos 457	P, 20 Nov	N.A.	N.A.	740/764	109.5	74.0	Unannounced payload
Molniya 2	P, 24 Nov	N.A.	N.A.	286/24,450	706.0	65.4	Communications satellite
Cosmos 459	B, 29 Nov	N.A.	N.A.	140/172	89.4	65.8	Unannounced payload
Cosmos 460	P, 30 Nov	N.A.	N.A.	323/347	95.2	74.0	Unannounced payload
Cosmos 461	P, 2 Dec	N.A.	N.A.	304/326	94.6	69.2	Unannounced payload
Intercosmos 5	KY, 2 Dec	N.A.	N.A.	127/745	98.5	48.4	Upper atmosphere
Cosmos 462	B, 3 Dec	N.A.	N.A.	147/1,143	105.7	65.8	Unannounced payload
Cosmos 463	B, 6 Dec	N.A.	N.A.	133/191	89.4	65.0	Unannounced payload
Cosmos 464	P, 10 Dec	N.A.	N.A.	128/252	90.3	72.9	Unannounced payload
Ariel 4	V, 11 Dec	S	218	303/365	95.4	83.0	Particle and field studies
Cosmos 465	P, 15 Dec	N.A.	N.A.	611/636	105.0	74.0	Unannounced payload
Cosmos 466	B, 16 Dec	N.A.	N.A.	129/188	89.4	65.0	Unannounced payload
Cosmos 467	P, 17 Dec	N.A.	N.A.	173/312	92.0	71.0	Unannounced payload
Intelsat 4F-3	K, 19 Dec	A–C	3,090	22,250/22,400	1,442.0	0.47	Communications satellite
Molniya I (19)	P, 20 Dec	N.A.	N.A.	305/24,400	703.0	65.5	Communications satellite
Cosmos 469	B, 25 Dec	N.A.	N.A.	161/172	89.7	65.0	Maneuverable satellite test
Cosmos 470	P, 27 Dec	N.A.	N.A.	121/169	89.1	65.4	Unannounced payload
Oreol I	P, 27 Dec	N.A.	N.A.	255/1,555	74.0	74.0	Particle and field studies
Meteor 10	P, 29 Dec	N.A.	N.A.	546/562	102.7	81.2	Meteorological satellite

[1] Code for launch sites: B, Baikonur, USSR; K, Cape Kennedy, Fla.; Ko, Kourou, French Guiana; KY, Kapustin Yar, USSR; P, Plesetsk, USSR; S, Shuang Cheng-Tzu, China; SM, San Marco; U, Uchinoura Space Center, Japan; V, Vandenberg AFB (Western Test Range), Calif.; W, Wallops Island, Va.; Wo, Woomera, Australia. [2] Launch Vehicles: A–C, Atlas–Centaur; B–A, Black Arrow; D–B, Diamant–B; S, Scout; T–D, Thrust Augmented Thor–Delta. [3] 1 pound equals 0.45 kg. [4] 1 mile equals 1.61 km. [5] Purposes of USSR spacecraft in many cases are unknown. [6] Not available.

(*Continued from page 609*)

feet (11,900 meters) in the Southern Hemisphere. The specific meteorological objectives of EOLE are to reveal more about the circulation of the atmosphere from the tracks of balloons, provide a basis for a standard reference system of pressure and temperature to be used in the World Weather Program, and learn more about local wind patterns.

The U. S. Explorer 45, the fourth scientific satellite to be launched from Kenya's coast, was orbited on November 15. It carried seven scientific and eight engineering experiments, and it is exploring the earth's inner magnetosphere and the dynamic processes that are occurring there. These processes are basically interactions between electromagnetic waves, static electric and magnetic fields, and charged particles.

On December 2, the Soviet Union launched Intercosmos 5 to study the earth's upper atmosphere and radiation belts. The satellite contains instruments designed by Czechoslovak and Soviet scientists, and the mission was planned by a group representing Bulgaria, Cuba, Czechoslovakia, East Germany, Hungary, Mongolia, Poland, Rumania, and the Soviet Union.

Ariel 4, the fourth in a series of joint satellite projects of the United States and Britain, was launched on December 12. The scientific objective of Ariel 4 is to investigate the interaction between plasma, charged particles, and electromagnetic waves in the upper ionosphere. In recent years a number of observations have been made of intense bands of radio noise in this region, but the observations have usually been by-products of experiments designed to measure cosmic radio emissions or to measure electron densities from vehicles above the top of the ionosphere. Ariel 4 permits the detailed study of these phenomena. On December 27 a cooperative Franco-Soviet satellite, OREOL 1, was launched to study the polar aurora.

Solar Research. The first solar research vehicle launched in 1971 was Explorer 43, sent into orbit by the United States on March 13. Its mission is to obtain adequate particle and field data to allow continuation and extension of studies of the space environment between moon and earth during a period of decreasing solar activity. The scientific payload consists of 12 experiments for measuring energetic particles, plasmas, magnetic and electric fields, and low-frequency radio emissions in space.

On April 15, France launched Tournesol to make solar radiation studies, and on July 8 the United States launched Explorer 44 to monitor the sun's X-ray and ultraviolet radiation. The latter satellite carries 14 experiments to monitor solar electromagnetic emissions on a continuous basis, and to measure stellar radiation from other celestial sources. The information it gathers is being applied to learning more about the physical processes involved in solar flares and other solar phenomena, and the potential effects of these phenomena on short-wave communications as well as on future manned space missions.

Japan launched its third satellite, Shinsei, on September 28, in order to measure microwave bands of solar radio waves as well as to study cosmic rays and ionospheric plasma phenomena. Shinsei weighs seven times more than Japan's first satellite, Osumi, which was orbited in 1970.

The day after Shinsei was launched, the United States orbited the world's most advanced spacecraft for monitoring the sun: the seventh Orbiting Solar Observatory, or OSO 7. The spacecraft has the primary objective of studying the sun's corona, obtaining high-resolution data from the corona in particular spectral bands in the extreme ultraviolet and visible regions of the spectrum during one solar rotation. OSO 7 is also investigating the intensity and spectrum of solar and cosmic X rays over longer time periods. Preliminary results indicate that X-ray observations were made of the beginning of a solar flare for the first time, and that another first was achieved in the photographing of solar streamers. Data returned from OSO 7 also indicate that there are solar "polar caps" that are significantly cooler than the rest of the sun—approximately 1,000,000° as compared with the 2,000,000° over the rest of the surface.

Applications Satellites. On behalf of the 79 member nations of the International Telecommunications Satellite Corporation, the U. S. corporation Comsat launched two communications satellites, each of which is capable of providing up to 9,000 two-way voice channels or up to 12 television channels. Intelsats 4 F-2 and 4 F-3 were launched on January 26 and December 19, respectively.

The Soviet Union successfully launched two more communications satellites during 1971. The 18th and 19th Molniya 1 were put into orbit on July 28 and December 20, and Molniya 2, a new class of satellite, was orbited on November 24 as part of Russia's orbital communications network. Four Soviet meteorological satellites, Meteor 7, 8, 9, and 10, were launched on January 20, April 17, July 16, and December 29, respectively, to observe global weather conditions. The Soviet Union also launched what are believed to be a number of navigational geodetic satellites.

PITT G. THOME
National Aeronautics and Space Administration

ADVANCES IN SPACE TECHNOLOGY

The success of the Apollo 15 lunar landing mission in the summer of 1971 marked another milestone in space technology. Work continued on the development of an orbital shuttle vehicle.

U. S. Apollo Program. The lunar roving vehicle (LRV) used by the Apollo 15 astronauts represented a dramatic improvement in manned operations on the moon. The LRV is an electric car of a sort that might not be practical on the earth's surface, but which performed to perfection the function of transporting two astronauts and their gear around the lunar surface. In particular, the silver-zinc electric batteries of the LRV demonstrated their ability to function in the vacuum of space and over a wide temperature range.

The LRV seems deceptively crude. There is no body or fairings, none being needed for performing in a vacuum. Steering is done with a form of tiller, or "joy stick," and speed control is achieved by varying the frequency of the electric current feeding the separate motors in each wheel. However, the vehicle cost about $30 million to develop. The reasons for this high figure lie in the endless, rigorous reliability tests; the use of new materials; and the development of an electric speed control, minicomputers, and electronic/inertial-guidance systems. Such guidance systems are necessary on the moon, since there is no magnetic field that would enable the astronauts to use a compass, and there are no adequate visual references.

The sensational success of the LRV means that the vehicle will be used in at least one and perhaps two of the three possible remaining Apollo missions in 1972 and 1973. Following the conclusion of the program, U. S. space efforts will concentrate —at least for a while—on earth-orbiting workshops and laboratories. There will be attempts to place greater payloads on the moon, but not with an improved launch vehicle. For the time being it seems that such Saturn propellant improvements as the use of fluorine instead of oxygen to burn the kerosine have been abandoned. Similarly, plans for developing a solid-propellant rocket to replace the liquid-fueled Saturn have been suspended.

Other U. S. Nonmilitary Programs. The National Aeronautics and Space Administration (NASA) is continuing to develop its plans for an orbital shuttle vehicle. Mockups and prototypes have been constructed, but financial and policy considerations have prevented NASA from moving ahead swiftly on the program. While President Nixon has called for the development of a shuttle system, Congress may not yet feel that it is an urgent national priority.

Thus NASA has found that the original concept of a long-life booster, which could have flown every 10 days and been serviced simply as an airplane and landed in the same way, may not be practical within the projected budget plans for the next decade. Another delay has been in the space shuttle main engine, which was to have been used interchangeably by both the orbiter—that is, the spacecraft— and the reusable launching booster. Instead NASA has proposed that the booster be either a manned rocket stage that can be flown back to its base, or an unmanned booster powered by pressure-fed rather than turbine engines. The latter booster would parachute into the ocean after a flight and be towed back to land for refurbishing.

The problem with using a manned booster is the considerable cost of fitting wings and a pilot cabin somewhere into the structure. If a modified Saturn 1-C launch vehicle were so used, it would also have to be redesigned to fly with some grace, since it was not originally intended as an aircraft. The more likely vehicle is the recoverable unmanned booster. It would be about 30 feet (9 meters) in diameter and 100 feet (30 meters) long, and it would be powered by as many as seven engines— yet to be developed—with propellants supplied at pressures of 300 pounds per square inch (21,000 grams per sq cm). The engines would use liquid oxygen and kerosine, although NASA is also looking at a liquid oxygen/propane combination that has certain advantages in final rocket velocity, relatively clean exhaust, and excellent combustion characteristics, with very little of the instability so common to other rocket fuel systems.

U. S. Military Programs. Military rocket and space activities picked up again in 1971 after a relative calm of about two years. Most of the rocket programs were concerned with the development or improvement of smaller rockets.

One such rocket is the Navy's Harpoon, a ship-to-ship missile that uses a solid rocket booster motor. The Harpoon is a powerful weapon in the Navy's arsenal. The solid rockets can be stored on a ship for years, under controlled conditions. They are precisely aimed either by onboard guidance systems that can track a distant target ship, or by a combination of onboard guidance and ship-borne radio commands. The missiles can even be sent to their targets by radio commands from aircraft.

Such solid rockets—which do not exceed about 15 feet (4.5 meters) in length—have totally replaced naval guns on battleships. The last U. S. military engagement using battleship guns was in Indochina, when the *New Jersey* was sent near the coast to fire its cannons at North Vietnam. In future military engagements, ship-to-ship, air-to-ship, and submarine-to-ship solid missiles would reduce naval battles to engagements between adversaries invisible to each other and directed by high-flying aircraft or spacecraft, or radar.

The Air Force also has a large arsenal of air-to-air or air-to-ground solid propellant rockets. The most important is the folding-fin aircraft rocket (FAR), with a diameter of 2.75 inches (7 cm). The rockets, mounted in clusters, are released by the aircraft pilot or by ground command if the target is invisible to him. An FAR can be guided to its target by the pilot through radio command, or it may be heat-seeking—that is, homing in on the infrared energy of a jet aircraft's exhaust. The Army ordered 17,000 such rockets in 1971, and after inspecting them will turn them over to the Air Force. In all, the Air Force has a requirement of about 180,000 solid rocket missiles.

The Air Force is interested in obtaining lighter-weight structures for its tactical smaller rockets as well as for its intercontinental launching vehicles such as Minuteman. Even a 1% change in the structural weight means dramatic gains in range for the rockets. Earlier experiments with high-strength boron fiber structures proved disappointing in this respect. However, experiments have continued with carbon fiber casings and with nose cones and certain fairings made of titanium. Now titanium is proving to be very useful for high-velocity military rockets, improved versions of the Polaris and Poseidon submarine-launched missiles, and leading edges of supersonic fighter aircraft. The metal is already being used for the hotter parts of supersonic inlets.

Materials and Advanced Propulsion Techniques. The development of small, nuclear-isotope power supplies that can deliver about 100 watts of electricity has reached the point at which NASA is ready to use such units in various spacecraft.

Studies have been made on the use of electron and laser welding for the joining and fabrication of delicate space vehicle or rocket structures in which no contamination in the weld can be tolerated. Laser techniques are also being used for the assembling of microelectronic modules and components. An intense beam of laser light is focused to a spot no more than one half of one thousandth of an inch wide, the entire operation being done by welders who are protected from the laser radiation by video or optical devices.

Now under development is a family of reliable and inexpensive high-velocity, upper-stage, solid propellant rockets, such as the rockets of the Vanguard program. Thus, steady improvement in the third, solid stage of NASA's Delta rocket has resulted in a velocity increase of several hundred feet per second. This permits spacecraft to weigh more, or to achieve higher escape velocities when their launching rockets have finished firing.

KURT R. STEHLING
Aerospace Advisor
Executive Office of the President

GENERALISSIMO FRANCO escorts Princess Sophia during National Day celebration in July. Prince Juan Carlos, Mrs. Franco, and U.S. Vice President Agnew follow.

UPI

SPAIN

Generalissimo Francisco Franco completed his 35th year as arbiter of the destiny of Spain on Oct. 1, 1971. He declared to an applauding crowd of 300,000 persons that he would prolong his rule "as long as God gives me life and a clear mind." In honor of the occasion, he granted amnesty to over 3,000 prisoners. Otherwise, police powers were, if anything, strengthened, in a year marked by repression and rumblings of opposition.

Elections for the 104 elective seats of the 558-member Cortes (parliament) were held on September 29. The campaign had been apathetic, and the vote was light. On November 18, Franco assured the cheering deputies that those who expected Spanish political institutions to be "fragmented into multiple political parties" were mistaken. The so-called Opus Dei faction continued to dominate the government, and political attacks were ineffectual. Opus Dei is a Catholic lay organization whose members hold some of the key posts in government.

Repression and Dissent. In the first half of 1971 the police detained, then released, some 2,000 persons under special emergency powers. They also had the authority to levy heavy fines against persons considered troublemakers.

On February 5 the government partially terminated martial law in the troubled Basque province of Guipúzcoa, which had been imposed in December 1970. Special police powers of search and banishment were withdrawn, but the power of unlimited arrest remained in effect and was extended to the whole country until mid-June. Suspects could be held indefinitely without charge. In July the Cortes approved a law empowering the government to impose fines of up to $14,000 and up to 3 months in prison for disturbances of public order.

Students protested in Barcelona on February 13, when the government cancelled a concert by the American folk singer Pete Seeger. Police arrested a total of 36 persons participating in that demonstration and in another a week later. In March and April workers, students, intellectuals, and journalists protested the police emergency powers. The International Confederation of Free Trade Unions and the World Federation of Labor jointly condemned "the growing repression of the Franco regime."

Because of his outspoken dissent from government action, Lt. Gen. Fernando Rodrigo Cifuentes, a right-wing extremist and a former military governor of Guipúzcoa, was relieved of command of the 9th military division in January. Denouncing clerical appeals for clemency in the trial of Basque nationalists in December 1970, Rodrigo had also attacked the Opus Dei, which "under the guise of noble aims, seeks to spread and create discord. . . ."

Opposition from the left continued to threaten public order. Some 50 alleged Communists were arrested in Seville in February 1971. On March 15, 40 alleged members of the Basque nationalist organization, ETA, were charged with planning to bomb a government building, rob a bank, and free ETA members imprisoned at Segovia and Burgos.

The most conspicuous opponent of the Franco regime in Seville, Alejandro Rojas Marcos, was arrested late in March on charges of "illegal propaganda" for his critical statements in a lecture at a student residence. "The political problem of Spain is a problem of human rights," he declared. "There are only two factions: those who want them and those who don't. It is a civil war between those who believe that these past 30 years have been a triumph and those of us who believe they have been a failure."

Some 300 Catalonians defied the police and laws against unauthorized political assembly on November 7 to meet secretly to draft a program of resistance to the Franco regime. Representing diverse groups from monarchists to radicals, they were united in opposition to Franco and sought to prevent the succession of Prince Juan Carlos de Borbón.

Liberalizing Trends. The government did take a new step in adopting a law regulating the status of labor organizations. Preserving the principle of combining labor and management in common syndicates, the law provided worker representation through an elective association within each union, which could present grievances and negotiate wage contracts. There was criticism from clerical and other sources that the new law failed to guarantee workers' rights adequately. Political moderates held that while the law did not significantly expand freedom, it did provide the basis for a later relaxation of authoritarianism.

In a verdict rendered on July 2, the Spanish Supreme Court annulled a fine levied on the daily newspaper *Madrid,* ruling that responsible criticism by the press was beneficial and that the press could not become the instrument of an official spokesman.

Matesa Scandal. The political effects of the Matesa scandal were reduced when the Supreme Court decided on February 24 to issue no further indictments. Two former cabinet ministers and the former head of the Bank of Spain had already been indicted for negligence in handling public funds. The owner of Matesa, a textile machinery company,

and many of those involved were members of Opus Dei. Their political opponents, including the Falangists and Syndicalists, had hoped to capitalize on the scandal and regain influence.

Economy. In January 1971 the government announced bold targets for Spanish economic growth by the end of 1972. The goal was to raise per capita income from $818 to $1,000 a year and attain a projected growth rate of 10% a year, up from 6%. In defiance of the 8% ceiling on wage increases the average salary increase in 1970 was an inflationary 14%, with some as high as 30%. The annual budget for 1971 rose to a record $4.8 billion.

Spanish reserves had doubled in 1970, totaling $1.8 billion early in 1971, a result, in part, of tight credit and the 26% increase in tourist revenues. Business had faltered in 1970, with the automobile industry particularly affected. Credit restrictions were eased slightly in 1971 in an effort to increase purchasing power.

A third 4-year development plan unfolded in November 1971 promised $12 billion in public investment, with an expected $24 billion added from the private sector. Social objectives—including education, old age benefits, housing, and environmental concerns—figured prominently, as did efforts to encourage consolidation of small industries to make them competitive in the European economy. There were no provisions for much-needed tax reform.

By September 1971 the industrial growth of Spain and the large national market had created a gross national product of $30 billion, but Spain had few companies large enough to compete with those of the rest of Europe. To stimulate industrial growth, the Instituto Nacional de Industria (INI), a $6 billion holding company, began to merge units within its control. Merger plans have been approved for two major INI-controlled steel factories, with a combined 6.5 million ton capacity, and a new 5-million ton capacity complex may be added to this combine. The most significant merger planned is between ASTANO, Spain's largest private shipyard, and the INI-controlled yard, Astilleros Españoles. The two yards would have combined orders of $1 billion and the capacity to build 1 million-ton tankers. Three other INI companies are involved in an aerospace concentration.

Foreign Relations. During 1971, Spain prepared to sign its first trade agreement with the Soviet Union since the Spanish Civil War. Although designed to increase trade, its primary significance would be political, as a step toward the restoration of diplomatic relations. Political reconciliation is a delicate issue, with inhibitions on both sides.

On January 31, Prince Juan Carlos de Borbón, the designated successor to Franco, and his wife, Princess Sophia, concluded a 6-day official visit to the United States. The prince conferred with President Nixon and other officials and visited Cape Kennedy. U. S. Vice President Agnew arrived in Madrid on July 17 during a diplomatic tour and conferred with Franco and Prince Juan Carlos.

The impasse between Spain and Britain over Gibraltar eased somewhat in late September. Britain's foreign secretary, Sir Alec Douglas-Home, expressed his willingness to accept an invitation to discuss the Spanish demand that sovereignty—though not actual control—over Gibraltar be granted to Spain.

RHEA MARSH SMITH, *Rollins College*

------ **SPAIN • Information Highlights** ------

Official Name: Spanish State.
Area: 194,884 square miles (504,750 sq km).
Population (1970 est.): 34,000,000. *Density,* 162 per square mile (65 per sq km). *Annual rate of increase,* 1.0%
Chief Cities (1968 est.): Madrid, the capital, 2,850,631; Barcelona, 1,794,381; Valencia, 499,131; Seville, 496,035.
Government: *Head of state,* Francisco Franco, president of the Council of Ministers (officially assumed power Aug. 4, 1939). *Head of government,* Francisco Franco. *Legislature*—Las Cortes Españolas (unicameral), 570 members.
Language: Spanish (official).
Education: *Literacy rate* (1970), 92% of population. *Expenditure on education* (1968), 11.7% of total public expenditure. *School enrollment* (1968)—primary, 3,664,823; secondary, 1,513,290; technical/vocational, 326,416; university/higher, 158,290.
Finances (1969): *Revenues,* $3,880,000,000; *expenditures,* $3,880,000,000; *monetary unit,* peseta (69.56 pesetas equal U. S.$1, Aug. 1971).
Gross National Product (1970 est.): $32,300,000,000.
National Income (1969): $24,429,000,000; *national income per person,* $741.
Economic Indexes: *Industrial production* (1970), 205 (1963 = 100); *agricultural production* (1969), 106 (1963 = 100); *consumer price index* (1970), 155 (1963 = 100).
Manufacturing (metric tons, 1969): Cement, 15,973,000; residual fuel oil, 13,413,000; distillate fuel oils, 6,573,000; crude steel, 5,911,000; wheat flour, 2,750,000; wine, 25,-831,000 hectoliters.
Crops (metric tons, 1969 crop year): Potatoes, 4,789,000; wheat, 4,692,000; sugar beets (1968–69), 4,620,000; citrus fruits (1968), 4,092,000 (ranks 3d among world producers); grapes, 4,002,000 (world rank 3d); tomatoes (1968), 1,150,-000.
Minerals (metric tons, 1969): Coal, 11,627,000; iron ore, 3,267,000; lignite, 2,740,000; salt, 1,862,000; magnesite, 229,000.
Foreign Trade (1968): *Exports,* 1970, $2,387,000,000 (chief exports—fresh fruit and nuts, $199,458,000; petroleum products, $121,388,000; nonelectrical machinery, $116,-635,000; transport equipment, $88,271,000). *Imports,* 1970, $4,715,000,000 (chief imports—nonelectrical machinery, $589,130,000; crude petroleum, $458,560,000; chemicals, $368,659,000; electrical equipment and appliances, $161,-831,000). *Chief trading partners* (1968)—United States (took 18% of exports, supplied 17% of imports); West Germany (10%—13%); United Kingdom (10%—8%).
Tourism: *Receipts* (1970), $1,680,700,000.
Transportation: *Roads* (1969), 82,025 miles (132,003 km); *motor vehicles* (1969), 2,681,900 (automobiles, 1,998,800); *railroads* (1966), 11,395 miles (18,335 km); *merchant fleet* (1971), 3,934,000 gross registered tons; *national airline,* Iberia; *principal airports,* Barcelona, Madrid.
Communications: *Telephones* (1970), 4,126,363; *television stations* (1967), 21; *television sets* (1969), 5,500,000; *radios* (1969), 7,042,000; *newspapers* (1969), 116 (daily circulation, 3,451,000).

SPANISH LITERATURE. See LITERATURE.

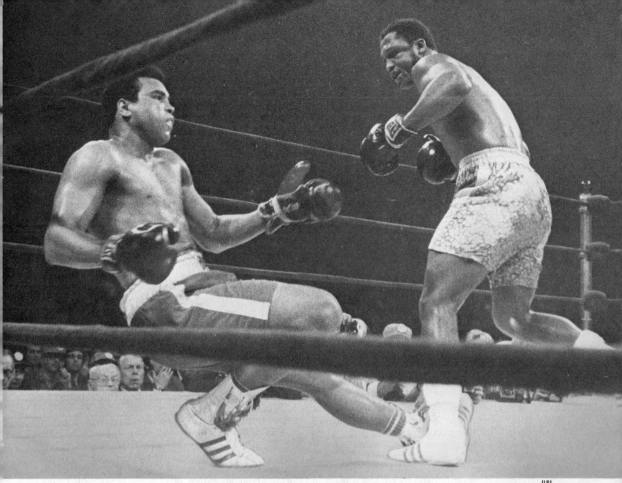

UPI

Champion Joe Frazier, with a stunning left hook, decks Muhammad Ali in final round of heavyweight title bout at Madison Square Garden, March 8. Frazier won unanimous decision over Ali in most lucrative promotion in ring history.

SPORTS

By Bill Braddock
The New York Times

Washington, the nation's capital, wound up the year 1971 without a baseball team but with more men in position to alter the structure of the game than any city with a ball club. The removal of the team to Texas for greater profit irked many congressmen, who began to question again the contention that baseball is a pastime rather than a business engaged in interstate commerce and therefore not subject to antitrust laws.

This concern of the lawmakers came shortly after the Supreme Court, whose justices sit in deliberation just a long home-run drive from the legislative chambers, had decided. to review the decision by which baseball had been declared a pastime. They were to review the case of Curt Flood which was aimed at the reserve clause in baseball contracts. Flood had claimed in his suit that the reserve clause makes him and all other ballplayers, in effect, peons. The lower courts had withheld decisions, declaring that it was up to the Supreme Court to pass on its own ruling.

Congress already had been stirred up over big-time professional sports. The removal of the American League baseball franchise from Seattle to Milwaukee some years ago had certain senators checking on the antitrust provision, and the plan for the merger of the two big basketball leagues had filled hearing rooms with protesting players. The National Basketball Association and the American Basketball Association had decided late in 1970 that a merger such as the two football leagues had achieved would do away with competitive bidding for players demanding huge salaries in their contracts. The football leagues had gotten a sympathetic Congress to pass legislation that gave their merger immunity against antitrust suits. However, the basketball players obtained a federal court injunction against a merger and sent their stars to congressional hearings to protest a proposed law that would give basketball such protection.

The nation's lawmakers, agape at the amount of money involved in sports projects and salaries (a notable example being the $2.5 million guarantee to Joe Frazier and Muhammad Ali for their fight), were becoming more receptive to ideas that sports were more than pastimes. Before the year ended, hockey became involved. The newly formed World Hockey League sued the National Hockey League when it was cut off from a new stadium on Long Island, New York, by the older league's sudden plan to expand and place a team there.

Meanwhile, pro football games were sold out, and tickets were scarce for other major events. Television was picking up more and more of the big attractions. These facts, in turn, disturbed various members of Congress. They demanded that more tickets be available to ordinary fans by limiting season-ticket sales. In addition, they threatened legislation against the practice of blacking out areas around the site of big games and controlling TV programming.

When the major baseball leagues met in December, congressmen were on hand to request a team in Washington. This gave baseball owners more concern about what Congress might do to the antitrust legislation if the Supreme Court upheld the 1922 law as it had done in 1957.

The fans, not too much concerned, poured out in record numbers in support of the pastimes and in adulation of the athletes who performed in them. Many learned, to their delight, that so-called dynasties were of short duration. When the Baltimore Orioles, who had dominated the American League for three years, lost the World Series to Pittsburgh, their predicted long reign as successors to the old New York Yankees came to an abrupt end.

A few months before that, the New York Knicks, proclaimed as the new dynasty to replace the Boston Celtics in pro basketball, were eliminated in the semifinal play-offs, and the Milwaukee Bucks, led by Kareem Abdul-Jabbar (Lew Alcindor), began a new one. Part of the basis for their extended rule was a record 20-game winning streak. The string was obliterated during the 1971–72 season by the Los Angeles Lakers, who won 33 straight before being stopped by the Bucks.

Another short-lived dynasty was the Boston Bruins, who won the National Hockey League championship and the Stanley Cup in the spring of 1970 and blasted all opposition in the 1970–71 season, setting 35 scoring records. But they bowed out ingloriously in the play-offs. Their conquerors were the Montreal Canadiens, whose predecessors had ruled a first-class dynasty.

One dynasty, however, continued its supremacy, and many college basketball coaches doubted that it would ever fall. This was the UCLA team, which won a fifth straight national championship under John Wooden. It was conceded to be the team to beat in 1972, an ominous sign for the Bruins since heavy favorites often come a cropper.

Regardless of the domestic confusion over certain of its aspects, sports led to some exceptional international achievements. Table tennis helped to bring about an easing in U. S. relations with China with the visit of an American team to that once isolated country. Volleyball brought about a series between U. S. and Cuban teams in Havana. American athletes lost in both competitions, but it was felt that the U. S. general public gained, as did those of the host countries.

Dallas defense, led by Bob Lilly (74), is set to dump quarterback Bob Griese in Super Bowl romp over Miami.

UPI

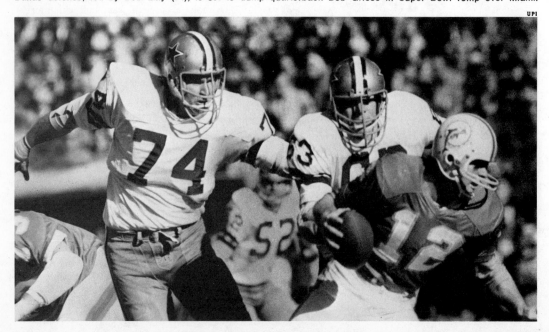

JACKIE STEWART, world Grand Prix titleholder for second time, is kissed by wife after winning British Grand Prix at Silverstone, England, July 17.

AUTO RACING

Shortly after the end of the season, Jackie Stewart, the newly crowned world champion Grand Prix driver, warned the track proprietors that unless measures for greater safety were taken the drivers would boycott certain courses. Two of the best-known Grand Prix drivers, Jo Siffert of Switzerland and Pedro Rodriguez of Mexico, were among those killed during the year. "We are losing too many drivers," the Scotsman said.

One driver who died from crash injuries in America was Danny Caruthers, 21, a few days after he had clinched the Midget Division championship of the United States Auto Club.

Grand Prix racing had an unexciting year. Stewart gained enough points to clinch the title in the Austrian race, August 15, which was won by Siffert. Stewart, who held the title in 1969, won 5 of the 11 events.

The United States Auto Club Championship Trail was won by Joe Leonard, a teammate of Al Unser, the 1970 titleholder. Leonard, driving a P. J. Colt-Ford, captured the Ontario 500, the third of the long races. Al Unser triumphed at Indianapolis for the second straight year. The other 500-mile race, the Schaefer 500 at Pocono Raceway in Pennsylvania, was won by Mark Donohue in a Sunoco McLaren Special. However, Al Unser wound up the year with the most earnings, $356,884, of which $238,454 was gained at Indianapolis. Leonard earned $273,840 and Donohue $169,273 in USAC races.

In the same category was Richard Petty of Randleman, N. C. He earned $333,148, becoming the first stock-car racer to exceed $1 million in winnings. He captured 21 races on the NASCAR circuit and, in winning the Grand National division title, became the third driver to win the title three times. The first was his father, Lee. Petty was pursued mostly by Bobby Allison of Hueytown, Ala., who won a total of $270,000. Tiny Lund won the NASCAR Grand American driving championship.

The Canadian-American series honors again went to the McLaren team, but this time first place

Auto Racing Highlights

World Championship Grand Prix Races

South Africa (Johannesburg, March 6)—Mario Andretti, Nazareth, Pa. (driving a Ferrari; distance: 201.45 miles; time: 1 hour, 47 minutes, 35.5 seconds; average speed: 112.362 miles per hour)

Spain (Barcelona, April 18)—Jackie Stewart, Scotland (Tyrrell-Ford; 172.5 miles; 1:49:03.4; 93.85 mph)

Monaco (Monte Carlo, May 23)—Jackie Stewart (156 miles; 1:52:21.3; 80.6 mph)

Netherlands (Zandvoort, June 20)—Jacky Ickx, Belgium (Ferrari; 208.8 miles; 1:56:20.09; 93.7 mph)

France (Le Castellet, July 4)—Jackie Stewart (198.55 miles; 1:46:41; 111.6 mph)

Britain (Silverstone, July 17)—Jackie Stewart (200 miles; 1:31:31.5; 130.48 mph)

Germany (Adenau, Aug. 1)—Jackie Stewart (170 miles; 1:29:15.7; 114.5 mph)

Austria (Zeltweg, Aug. 15)—Jo Siffert, Switzerland (BRM; 198.5 miles; 1:30:23.91; 134.5 mph)

Italy (Monza, Sept. 5)—Peter Gethin, Britain (BRM; 187.4 miles; 1:18:12.6; 151.31 mph)

Canada (Bowmanville, Sept. 19)—Jackie Stewart (race halted after 64 laps of scheduled 80 because of fog)

United States (Watkins Glen, N. Y., Oct. 3)—François Cevert, France (Tyrrell-Ford; 200 miles; 1:43:51.99; 115.092 mph)

Other Races

Indianapolis 500 (May 29)—Al Unser, Albuquerque, N. Mex. (P. J. Colt-Ford, Johnny Lightning Special; 3:10:11.56; 157.735 mph; purse $238,454)

Schaefer 500 (Pocono International Speedway, Long Pond, Pa., July 3)—Mark Donohue, Media, Pa. (Sunoco McLaren; 3:36:22.3; 138.649 mph; $88,924)

California 500 (Ontario, Calif., Sept. 5)—Joe Leonard, San Jose, Calif. (P. J. Colt-Ford, Samsonite Special; 3:16:54.5; 152.354 mph; $130,039)

Argentina 300 (Rafael, Feb. 28)—Al Unser (won both 150-mile heats; Eagle-Ford; 169.798 mph; $16,000)

Trenton 300—Bobby Unser, Albuquerque, N. Mex. (Olson-ite-Eagle; 2:07:51.65; 140.771 mph; $35,000)

Pennsylvania 500 (Long Pond, Pa., Sept. 25)—Butch Hartman, South Zanesville, Ohio (1969 Dodge; 116.76 mph; $15,300; race, begun on Sept. 19, was stopped after 41 laps (102.5 miles) because of heavy rain and resumed at that point, Sept. 25)

24 Hours of Daytona (Daytona Beach, Fla., Jan. 30-31)—Pedro Rodriguez, Mexico, and Jackie Oliver, England (Gulf-Porsche; 2,261 miles; 109.203 mph)

Sebring 12 Hours of Endurance (Sebring, Fla., March 20)—Vic Elford, England, and Gerard Larousse, France (Porsche; 260 laps; 112.5 mph)

6 Hours of Watkins Glen (Watkins Glen, N. Y., July 24)—Andrea de Adamich, Italy, and Bonnie Peterson, Sweden; Alfa Romeo; 677.4 miles; 112.8 mph; $5,000)

Questor Grand Prix (Ontario, Calif., March 28)—Mario Andretti, Nazareth, Pa. (won both 100-mile heats; 109.69 mph; $38,250)

Nascar Events

Motor Trend 500 (Riverside, Calif., Jan. 10)—Ray Elder, Caruthers, Calif. (Dodge; 4:57:55; 100.783 mph; purse $18,715)

Daytona 500 (Daytona Beach, Fla., Feb. 14)—Richard Petty, Randleman, N. C. (Plymouth; 3:27:40; 144.462 mph; $44,450)

Miller High Life 500 (Ontario, Calif., Feb. 28)—A. J. Foyt, Houston, Texas (Mercury; 3:43:36; 134.168 mph; $51,850)

Carolina 500 (Rockingham, S. C., March 14)—Richard Petty (4:12:55; 118.696 mph; $17,355)

Atlanta 500 (Atlanta, Ga., April 14)—A. J. Foyt (3:42:26; 131.375 mph; $19,625)

Rebel 400 (Darlington, S. C., May 2)—Buddy Baker, Charlotte, N. C. (Dodge; 3:03:46; 130.678 mph; $16,065)

Winston 500 (Talledega, Ala., May 16)—Donnie Allison, Hueytown, Ala. (Mercury; 4:23:32; 147.419 mph; $31,400)

World 600 (Charlotte, N. C., May 30)—Bobby Allison, Hueytown, Ala. (Mercury; 4:16:20; 140.442 mph; $28,400)

Mason Dixon 500 (Dover, Del., June 6)—Bobby Allison (4:03:40; 123.119 mph; $15,720)

Motor State 400 (Irish Hills, Mich., June 3)—Bobby Allison (2:41:13; 149.567 mph; $14,945)

Golden State 400 (Riverside, Calif., June 20)—Bobby Allison (4:17:05; 93.427 mph; $14,395)

Firecracker 400 (Daytona Beach, Fla., July 4)—Bobby Isaac, Catawba, N. C. (Dodge; 2:28:12; 161.947 mph; $16,450)

Northern 300 (Trenton, N. J., July 18)—Richard Petty (2:29:34; 120.347 mph; $6,760)

Dixie 500 (Atlanta, Ga., Aug. 1)—Richard Petty (3:52:05; 129.061 mph; $20,220)

Yankee 400 (Irish Hills, Mich., Aug. 15)—Bobby Allison (2:40:58; 149.799 mph; $15,695)

Southern 500 (Darlington, S. C., Sept. 6)—Bobby Allison (3:48:55; 131.398 mph; $22,450)

Talledega 500 (Talledega, Ala., Aug. 22)—Bobby Allison (3:25:38; 145.945 mph; $19,565)

(Continued on following page)

Auto Racing Highlights (continued)

Delaware 500 (Dover, Del., Oct. 17)—Richard Petty (4:03:
  25; 123.254 mph; $14,570)
American 500 (Rockingham, S. C., Oct. 24)—Richard Petty
  (4:23:24; 113.405 mph; $17,620)
National 500 (Charlotte, N. C., Oct. 10)—Bobby Allison;
  race cut to 357 miles because of rain (2:49:38;
  126.140 mph; $18,450)
American 500 (Rockingham, N. C., Oct. 24)—Richard
  Petty (4:24:43; 113.405 mph; $17,120)
Texas 500 (Bryan, Texas, Dec. 12)—Richard Petty (3:28:20;
  144 mph; $13,315)

Other Countries

BOAC 1,000 (Brands Hatch, England, April 4, 621 miles)
  —Andrea de Adamich, Italy, and Henri Pescarolo,
  France (Alfa Romeo; 6:24:32.2; 97.17 mph)
Monza 1,000 kilometers (Monza, Italy, April 25)—Pedro
  Rodriguez, Mexico, and Jackie Oliver, England
  (Porsche; 4:14:32.6; 147.396 mph)
Francorchamps 1,000 (Belgium, May 9)—Rodriguez and
  Oliver (4:01:09.7; 154.427 mph)
Targa Florio (Palermo, Sicily, May 16, 491 miles)—Nino
  Vaccarella, Italy, and Toine Hezemans, Netherlands
  (Alfa Romeo; 6:35:41; 74.6 mph)
Neurburgring 1,000 (Adenau, West Germany, May 30)—
  Vic Elford, England, and Gerard Larousse, France
  (Porsche; 5:51:49.3; 102.84 mph)
Le Mans 24 Hours (France, June 12–13)—Helmut Marko,
  Austria, and Gys Van Lennen, Netherlands (Alfa
  Romeo; 3,302.6 miles; 137.6 mph)
Francorchamps 24 Hours, Touring (Belgium, July 24–25)
  —Dieter Glemser, West Germany, and Alex Soler-
  Roig, Spain (Ford Capri; 2,724.77 miles; 113.49 mph)
Monte Carlo Rally (Jan. 22–29)—Ove Anderson, Sweden,
  and David Stone, Britain (Renault)

Individual Champions

World Grand Prix—Jackie Stewart, Scotland
U.S. Auto Club—Marlboro Championship Trail: Joe
  Leonard, San Jose, Calif. (3,015 points; $273,840);
  sprint division: Gary Bettenhausen, Tinley Park, Ill.
  (592); midget: Danny Caruthers (398.76; died of
  injuries from crash, 8 days after clinching title);
  dirt track: George Snider, Bakersfield, Calif. (520);
  stock: Butch Hartman, Zanesville, Ohio (3,225.50)
NASCAR—Grand National: Richard Petty, Randleman,
  N. C. (4,435); Grand American: Tiny Lund, Cross,
  S. C. (1,000); late model sportsman: Red Farmer,
  Hueytown, Ala. (9,688); modified: Jerry Cook, Rome,
  N. Y. (5,488); Western Grand National: Ray Elder,
  Caruthers, Calif. (1,456); manufacturers: Grand Na-
  tional: Plymouth; Grand American: Camaro
World Manufacturers Championship—Porsche

Sports Car Club of America

Canadian-American Challenge Cup Series (10 races)—
  Peter Revson, New York (Gulf McLaren Chevrolet;
  142 points; $192,000)
Continental Championship (8 races)—David Hobbs, England (Hot Comb McLaren; 119; $47,350), formula B
  (6 races): Allan Lader, Gresham, Oreg. (Pacifico
  Brabham; 85; $7,700)
Trans-American (11 races)—Javelin; Two-Five Challenge
  (10 races)—Datsun

American Road Race of Champions
(Road Atlanta, Gainesville, Ga., Nov. 26–28;
all races 30 minutes)

A Production—John Greenwood, Pontiac, Mich. (Cor-
  vette; average speed 98.73 mph)
B Production—Allan Barker, Jeffersonville, Ind. (Corvette;
  95.51 mph)
C Production—John Morton, Torrance, Calif. (Datsun;
  94.42 mph)
D Production—Robert McQueen, Tucker, Ga. (Datsun;
  88.61 mph)
E Production—Logan Blackburn, Indianapolis (MGB; 87.93
  mph)
F Production—Larry Campbell, Detroit (Austin-Healey
  Sprite; 85.61 mph)
G Production—Marshall Meyer, Livermore, Calif. (Tri-
  umph; 81.90)
H Production—Randy Canfield, Chevy Chase, Md. (Austin-
  Healey Sprite; 81.90 mph)
A Sedan—Warren Tope, Bloomfield Hills, Mich. (Mustang;
  94.81 mph)
B Sedan—Bob Sharp, Wilton, Conn. (Datsun; 88.18 mph)
C Sedan—Dick Davenport, Wichita, Kans. (Alfa Romeo;
  83.48 mph)
D Sedan—Chris Gross, Ijamsville, Md. (Austin Cooper;
  80.45 mph)
A Sports Racing—Jerry Hansen, Minneapolis (Lola;
  109.43 mph)
B Sports Racing—Pete Harrison, Atlanta, Ga. (Lola;
  100.70 mph)
C Sports Racing—Tom Evans, Santa Barbara, Calif.
  (Alfa; 89.05 mph)
D Sports Racing—Harry Stephenson, Miami, Fla. (Hon-
  da Maru; 84.41 mph)
Formula A—Jerry Hansen, Minneapolis (Lola; 99.59 mph)
Formula B—Robert Lazier, Vail, Colo. (March; 97.66 mph)
Formula C—Harry Reynolds, Pottstown, Pa. (Brabham;
  88.87 mph)
Formula F—Jim Harrell, Tecumseh, Mich. (Titan; 93.93
  mph)

was taken by Peter Revson of New York, with Denis Hulme of New Zealand finishing second. The triumph put Revson second in overall earnings for the year with $335,725.

Bobby Unser posted a closed-course world record of 193.444 mph for open-wheeled race cars at the Michigan Speedway in a Dan Gurney Eagle-Offenhauser.

BASEBALL

It took those traditional antagonists the Giants and Dodgers to evoke some excitement in the 1971 major league pennant races. Play-off berths in three divisions were clinched fairly early in the season—by Baltimore and Oakland in the American League and by Pittsburgh in the National. But San Francisco and Los Angeles became embroiled in a battle for the championship of their division, as happened repeatedly when they represented New York and Brooklyn, respectively. Their business did not end until the last day of the season, when the Giants won the Western Division honors in the National League by one game. The competition stirred up enthusiasm for the exciting World Series that followed and overshadowed the reaction to the removal of the Washington franchise in the American League to Texas.

Actually there seemed no sound reason for the perilous position of the Giants in the closing days. Like the winners in the other divisions, they had built up a good lead at the All-Star break near midseason. The Giants were six games ahead of the second-place Dodgers. In the Eastern Division of the National League, the Pittsburgh Pirates enjoyed a 10-game advantage. In the American League the Baltimore Orioles led the East by 5½ games, and the Oakland Athletics were the best off in the West with an 11½-game edge over the Kansas City Royals.

The attention of many fans at that time was directed to the pitching feats of Vida Blue, Oakland's 22-year-old left-hander who appeared to be on his way toward becoming the second 30-game winner since Dizzy Dean in 1934 and even bettering Denny McLain's 31 in 1968. Blue had 17 victories at All-Star time and was the winning pitcher as the American League beat the National, 6–4, though he gave up three runs.

With 24 games left to play, on September 5, the Giants held a 9-game edge over the Dodgers and apparently just had to play out the schedule. But San Francisco hit a slump, winning only 8 of their next 24 games, while Los Angeles launched an 8-game winning streak and closed in. On September 13 the Dodgers cut the margin to two games, with a 5–4 victory in a game marked by bean-ball pitching and fighting on the field. The next day Los Angeles won, 6–4, with three runs in the ninth and reduced the edge to one game. But that was as close as the Dodgers got. San Diego ended the winning streak, and the Giants managed to keep a step ahead.

The Giants beat Pittsburgh in the first game of the play-offs, and that too was as far as they could go. The Pirates won the next three games and headed for the World Series, an underdog to Baltimore, the world champion. The Orioles had won their division by 12 games over Detroit and swept the play-off series against Oakland, which finished 16 games ahead of Kansas City. The Orioles downed the Athletics in three straight,

WINNING PITCHER Steve Blass and catcher Manny Sanguillen whoop it up as Pittsburgh edges Baltimore, 2–1, in final game of World Series. Title was first for Pirates since 1960. Blass' victory in third game put underdog Pirates on winning track after dropping first two games.

WIDE WORLD

Baseball Highlights

Professional—Major Leagues

AMERICAN LEAGUE
(Final Standings, 1971)

EASTERN DIVISION

	W	L	Pct.
Baltimore	101	57	.639
Detroit	91	71	.667
Boston	85	77	.525
New York	82	80	.506
*Washington	63	96	.396
Cleveland	60	102	.370

* Washington franchise shifted to Dallas-Fort Worth for 1972. Club, to be called Rangers, will play in Western Division.

WESTERN DIVISION

	W	L	Pct.
Oakland	101	60	.627
Kansas City	85	76	.528
Chicago	79	83	.488
California	76	86	.469
Minnesota	74	86	.463
*Milwaukee	69	92	.429

* Will play in Eastern Division in 1972.

NATIONAL LEAGUE
(Final Standings, 1971)

EASTERN DIVISION

	W	L	Pct.
Pittsburgh	97	65	.599
St. Louis	90	72	.556
Chicago	83	79	.512
New York	83	79	.512
Montreal	71	90	.441
Philadelphia	67	95	.414

WESTERN DIVISION

	W	L	Pct.
San Francisco	90	72	.556
Los Angeles	89	73	.549
Atlanta	82	80	.506
Cincinnati	79	83	.488
Houston	79	83	.488
San Diego	61	100	.379

Play-offs—American League: Baltimore Orioles defeated Oakland Athletics, 3 games to 0; National League: Pittsburgh Pirates defeated San Francisco Giants, 3 games to 1

World Series—Won by Pittsburgh Pirates; paid attendance, 7 games, 351,091; total receipts, $3,049,803; commissioner's share, $513,168; players' share, $1,032,257, including full shares of $18,165 for each Pirate and $13,906 for each Oriole; each club's share, $468,739, and each league's share, $468,739

Standings—Pittsburgh (NL) won 4, lost 3, pct. .571; Baltimore Orioles (AL) won 3, lost 4, pct. .429

First Game (Memorial Stadium, Baltimore, Oct. 9): Baltimore 5, Pittsburgh 3; *second game* (Baltimore, Oct. 11): Baltimore 11, Pittsburgh 3; *third game* (Three Rivers Stadium, Pittsburgh, Oct. 12): Pittsburgh 5, Baltimore 1; *fourth game* (Pittsburgh, Oct. 13): Pittsburgh 4, Baltimore 3; *fifth game* (Pittsburgh, Oct. 14): Pittsburgh 4, Baltimore 0; *sixth game* (Baltimore, Oct. 16): Baltimore 3, Pittsburgh 2 in 10 innings; *seventh game* (Baltimore, Oct. 17): Pittsburgh 2, Baltimore 1

All-Star Game (Detroit, July 13)—American 6, National 4

Most Valuable Players—American: Vida Blue, Oakland pitcher; National: Joe Torre, St. Louis 3d baseman

Cy Young Memorial Awards (outstanding pitcher)—American: Vida Blue, Oakland; National: Ferguson Jenkins, Chicago

Rookies of the Year—American: Chris Chambliss, Cleveland 1st baseman; National: Earl Williams, Atlanta catcher

Leading Batters—Percentage: American: Tony Oliva, Minnesota, .337; National: Joe Torre, St. Louis, .363.—Home runs: American: Bill Melton, Chicago, 33; National: Willie Stargell, Pittsburgh, 48.—Runs Batted In: American: Harmon Killebrew, Minnesota, 119; National: Joe Torre, St. Louis, 137

Leading Pitchers—Best Percentage (20 decisions or more): American: Dave McNally, Baltimore, .808 (21–5); National: Don Gullet, Cincinnati, .727 (16–6).—Victories: American: Mickey Lolich, Detroit, 25; National: Ferguson Jenkins, Chicago, 24.—Earned Run Average: American: Vida Blue, Oakland, 1.82; National: Tom Seaver, New York, 1.76

No-Hit Games Pitched—Ken Holtsman, Chicago (NL) vs. Cincinnati, 1–0; Rick Wise, Philadelphia vs. Cincinnati, 4–0; Bob Gibson, St. Louis vs. Pittsburgh, 11–0

Hall of Fame Inductees—David J. (Beauty) Bancroft, Jacob P. Beckley, Charles J. (Chick) Hafey, Harry Hooper, Joseph J. Kelley, Richard W. (Rube) Marquard, Leroy R. (Satchel) Paige, George M. Weiss

Professional—Minor Leagues

(When two teams are named, the first team won the regular season championship and the second won the play-off; otherwise, the team named won both.)

International (AAA)—Rochester

American Association (AAA)—Indianapolis, Eastern Division; Denver, Western Division and play-off

Pacific Coast (AAA)—Tacoma, Northern Division; Salt Lake City, Southern Division and play-off

Mexican League (AAA)—Jalisco, Southern Division and play-off; Saltillo, Northern Division

Eastern (AA)—Elmira, American Division and play-off; Three Rivers, National Division

Dixie (AA)—Amarillo, Western Division; Arkansas, Central Division; Charlotte, Eastern Division and play-off

California (A)—Fresno, first half; Visalia, second half and play-off

Carolina (A)—Kinston, first half; Peninsula, second half and play-off

Florida State (A)—Miami, Eastern and play-off; Daytona Beach, Western

Midwest (A)—Quad Cities, Southern and play-off; Appleton, Northern

New York-Pennsylvania (A)—Oneonta, no play-off

Northern (A)—St. Cloud, no play-off

Northwest (A)—Tri-City, Northern; Bend, Southern; Tri-City declared champion on record against Bend

Western Carolinas (A)—Greenwood won both half seasons

Appalachian (Rookie)—Bluefield

Gulf Coast (Rookie)—Royals

Pioneer (Rookie)—Great Falls

Other Champions

All-American Amateur—New Orleans
American Legion—West Covina, Calif.
Babe Ruth League—Puerto Rico
Babe Ruth Senior—Stamford, Conn.
Bronco League—Bayamon, Puerto Rico
Colt League—Hagerstown, Md.
Connie Mack League—Dallas, Texas
Little League—Taiwan, Nationalist China
Mickey Mantle League—Sweeney Chevrolet, Cincinnati
Pee Wee Reese League—Dallas, Texas
Pony League—Orange, Calif.
National Baseball Congress—Anchorage, Alaska
Sandy Koufax League—Commack, N.Y.
Stan Musial League—Madison, Wis.

Intercollegiate Champions

NCAA—University Division: Southern California (defeated Southern Illinois, 7–2, in final); College Division: Florida Southern (defeated Central Michigan, 4–0, in final)

NAIA—Linfield (defeated David Lipscomb, 9–8, in final, 10 innings)

VIDA BLUE, Oakland's ace left-hander, was voted the American League's most valuable player. Blue, 22, also won the Cy Young award as the league's best pitcher.

beating Blue, who had finished the season with 24 victories and 8 losses, in the first game.

In the World Series the Orioles were 2–1 favorites. They had won 14 straight games. They had four 20-game winning pitchers—Dave McNally (21–5), Pat Dobson (20–8), Jim Palmer (20–9), and Mike Cuellar (20–9). Four Oriole players—Merv Rettenmund, Don Buford, Dave Johnson, and Frank Robinson—were among the top 15 hitters in the league. Their first baseman, John (Boog) Powell, was a slugger of renown, and their third baseman was Brooks Robinson, the outstanding player of the 1970 World Series for his sparkling defensive play and timely hitting. The Pirates boasted of Willie Stargell, who led the majors in homers with 48, and Roberto Clemente, a four-time batting champion who hit .341 in 1971. Their best pitcher was Dock Ellis with a 19–9 record.

TAIWAN'S pitcher carries catcher off the field following victory over Gary, Ind., in Little League World Series.

Baltimore won the first game, 5–3, as expected, routing Ellis after the Pirates had scored three unearned runs off McNally, who pitched a three-hitter. In the second game the Orioles scored 10 runs in the middle three innings and posted an 11–3 triumph behind Palmer. This ran their winning streak to 16 games. But Danny Murtaugh, the Pirates' manager, and Stargell and Clemente were undismayed. "Wait 'til we get them in our ball park in Pittsburgh," they said.

In Pittsburgh the Pirates won the third game, 5–1, with Steve Blass pitching a three-hitter. The next day the Pirates drew even with a 4–3 victory in the first Series night game. The hero was Bruce Kison, a 21-year-old rookie who pitched 6⅓ scoreless innings in relief. Then Nelson Briles hurled a two-hit, 4–0 shutout, beating McNally, and Pittsburgh was ahead, 3 games to 2, as the action shifted back to Baltimore.

The Orioles won the sixth game, 3–2, tying the Series at three games each, as the two Robinsons got a run across in the 10th inning. McNally, in relief of Dobson, was the winning pitcher. In the finale, Blass, the Pirates' starting pitcher, limited the Orioles to four hits, got out of a jam in the eighth inning, and Pittsburgh won, 2–1, becoming world champion for the first time since 1960. The first Pirate run was a homer by Clemente. The deciding run was scored by Stargell in the eighth. He opened with a single and scored, with daring base running, on José Pagan's double to right.

Clemente, the 37-year-old outfielder, was acclaimed the outstanding player in the Series. He hit safely in every game, and his total of 12 hits just missed, by one, tying the Series record.

Three other older players reached new levels of excellence during the season. Willie Mays, 40, scored 82 runs and moved into third place behind Ty Cobb and Babe Ruth in the all-time list with a total of 2,003. His 18 homers gave him 646 as the runner-up to Ruth's 714. Hank Aaron, 37, moved closer to Mays with 47 homers and a total of 639. His 95 runs raised his total to 1,901 for fifth place, only 48 behind Stan Musial. Aaron's 162 hits put him sixth in the all-time list with 3,272. Mays, with 113 hits and a career total of 3,178, moved into eighth place. Jim Bunning struck out 58 batters and passed Cy Young for second place, behind Walter Johnson, with a total of 2,853. Bunning retired at the end of the season.

But the awards, for the most part, went to younger players. Blue was voted the most valuable player and received the American League Cy Young award. Joe Torre, 31, a former catcher and first baseman, playing third base for the St. Louis Cardinals, won the National League batting title and the most valuable player award. Ferguson Jenkins, 27, of the Chicago Cubs, was selected for the National League's Cy Young honor.

The shift of the Washington American League franchise to Dallas-Fort Worth at Arlington, Texas, pulled Robert Short, the owner, out of financial difficulties. The Senators were renamed the Rangers and moved into the Western Division, with Milwaukee shifting to the East.

In November, Baltimore traded Frank Robinson, who had hit his 503d home run during the season, to Los Angeles. At the winter meetings, the Dodgers sent Richie Allen to the White Sox, and the Giants swapped Gaylord Perry, a right-handed pitcher, for southpaw Sam McDowell of Cleveland.

BASKETBALL

Professional

In March, the Milwaukee Bucks gained the full benefit of a coin toss they had won in 1969. The Bucks made a four-game sweep of the play-off series with the Baltimore Bullets and captured the championship of the National Basketball Association. Milwaukee was paced by Lew Alcindor, who went to the Bucks as the result of the coin toss. The flip decided whether Phoenix or Milwaukee, the bottom teams in their respective divisions, would get first pick in the draft in which Alcindor was the No. 1 choice of every team.

After the 7-foot-2-inch star had won the rookie of the year award, the Bucks further strengthened

WIDE WORLD

BRUISING MATCHUP between Milwaukee's Kareem Abdul-Jabbar (*left*) and Wilt Chamberlain of Los Angeles highlighted action in the 1971–72 NBA season.

Professional Basketball Highlights

National Basketball Association
(Final Standings, 1971)
Eastern Conference
Atlantic Division

	W	L	Pct	Scoring Avg For	Agst
New York Knickerbockers	52	30	.634	110.1	105.0
Philadelphia 76ers	47	35	.573	114.8	113.3
Boston Celtics	44	38	.537	117.2	115.1
Buffalo Braves	22	60	.268	105.5	112.1

Central Division

Baltimore Bullets	42	40	.512	112.9	112.3
Atlanta Hawks	36	46	.439	114.0	115.8
Cincinnati Royals	33	49	.402	116.0	119.2
Cleveland Cavaliers	15	67	.183	102.1	113.3

Western Conference
Midwest Division

Milwaukee Bucks	66	16	.805	118.4	106.2
Chicago Bulls	51	31	.622	110.6	105.4
Phoenix Suns	48	34	.585	113.8	111.9
Detroit Pistons	45	37	.549	110.1	110.9

Pacific Division

Los Angeles Lakers	48	34	.585	114.8	111.7
San Francisco Warriors	41	41	.500	107.1	108.5
San Diego Rockets	40	42	.488	113.2	113.4
Seattle SuperSonics	38	44	.463	115.0	117.0
Portland Trail Blazers	29	53	.354	115.5	120.0

Eastern Conference play-offs final: Baltimore defeated New York, 4 games to 3; *Western Conference play-offs final:* Milwaukee defeated Los Angeles, 4 games to 1; *NBA Championship:* Milwaukee defeated Baltimore, 4 games to 0
Most Valuable Player—Lew Alcindor, Milwaukee (name changed to Kareem Abdul-Jabbar, after season's end)
Rookies of the Year—Dave Cowens, Boston, and Geoff Petri, Portland
Leading Scorer—Alcindor, 2,596 points; 31.7 average a game

American Basketball Association
(Final Standings, 1971)
Eastern Division

	W	L	Pct	Scoring Avg For	Agst
Virginia Squires	55	29	.655	123.27	119.74
Kentucky Colonels	44	40	.524	122.19	122.14
New York Nets	40	44	.476	111.04	111.64
Floridians	37	47	.440	114.04	115.56
Pittsburgh Condors	36	48	.429	119.06	121.77
Carolina Cougars	34	50	.405	115.33	119.36

Western Division

Indiana Pacers	58	26	.690	119.07	113.11
Utah Stars	57	27	.679	118.98	111.90
Memphis Pros	41	43	.488	109.23	109.93
*Texas Chaparrals	30	54	.357	121.51	124.50
Denver Rockets	30	54	.357	118.63	122.69

* Won play-off for fourth place, 115–109

Eastern Division play-offs final: Kentucky defeated Virginia, 4 games to 2; *Western Division play-offs final:* Utah defeated Indiana, 4 games to 2; *ABA Championship:* Utah defeated Kentucky, 4 games to 3
Most Valuable Player—Mel Daniels, Indiana
Rookies of the Year—Dan Issel, Kentucky, and Charlie Scott, Virginia
Leading Scorer—Issel, 2,480 points, 29.88 average a game.

their team for the 1970–71 season by acquiring Oscar Robertson, the versatile star from Cincinnati. They won 66 of their 82 games, including a record-breaking streak of 20 in a row. Alcindor (who changed his name to Kareem Abdul-Jabbar after the season) led the league in scoring with a 31.7 average and was voted the most valuable player.

In the play-offs, the Bucks eliminated San Francisco and Los Angeles, each in five games, before routing the Bullets. Baltimore reached the final by pulling through 7-game tussles with Philadelphia and then New York, the defending champions who could not quite find the winning key this time.

In the American Basketball Association, the Utah Stars, newly arrived in Salt Lake City from Los Angeles, surprised the league by beating the Kentucky Colonels for the title in a 7-game series. That triumph came after they had eliminated the Indiana Pacers. Mel Daniels of Indiana was voted the most valuable player. Dan Issel, a rookie with the Colonels, led the scorers with a 29.88 average.

College

The University of California at Los Angeles continued to dominate college basketball. The Bruins captured the National Collegiate (NCAA) title for the fifth straight year and the seventh time in eight years. UCLA's only loss in 30 games was to Notre Dame, 89–82, on the Irish court early in the season.

UCLA's first major test was with its crosstown rival, Southern California, in a conference game on February 6. USC, unbeaten in 16 games, held a 7-point lead with 9 minutes to play. But UCLA switched to slowdown tactics, stole the ball three times, scored 11 straight points, and won, 64–60. The Bruins went on to the Pacific-8 championship with a 14–0 record; disposed of Brigham Young, 91–73, in the NCAA sectional play-off and Long Beach State, 78–65, in the regional. In the semifinal round at the Houston Astrodome, UCLA defeated Kansas, 68–60, and then won the championship by outlasting Villanova, 68–62. The outstanding player for the Bruins was Sidney Wicks.

Amateur Basketball Highlights

Major Tournaments

NCAA (Houston Astrodome)—University of California at Los Angeles (defeated Villanova, 68–62, in final); *College division* (Evansville, Ind.): Evansville (defeated Old Dominion, 97–82, in final)

National Invitation (New York)—North Carolina (defeated Georgia Tech, 84–66, in final)

National Intercollegiate (NAIA)—Kentucky State (defeated Eastern Michigan, 102–82, in final)

Men's AAU—Armed Forces (defeated Marathon Oil, 90–77, in final)

Women's AAU—Hutcherson Flying Queens (defeated Raytown, Mo., Piperettes in final)

College Conference Champions

(Figures in parentheses represent victories and losses in conference games only.)

Atantic Coast—South Carolina (10–4); won championship tournament

Big Eight—Kansas (14–0)

Big Sky—Weber State (12–2)

Big Ten—Ohio State (13–1)

Central Intercollegiate—*North:* Norfolk State (16–0); *South:* tie between North Carolina A&T and Elizabeth City (12–4)

Ivy League—Pennsylvania (14–0)

Mid-American—Miami (9–1)

Middle Atlantic—*University division:* Temple (6–0); *Northern college division:* Philadelphia Textile (9–1); *Southern college division:* Lebanon Valley (12–4)

Missouri Valley—Tie among Drake, Louisville, and St. Louis (9–5); Drake won play-off for berth in NCAA tournament

Ohio Valley—Western Kentucky (12–2)

Pacific-8—University of California at Los Angeles (14–0)

Southeastern—Kentucky (16–2)

Southern—Furman (5–5); won championship tourney

Southwest—Texas Christian (11–3)

Western Athletic—Brigham Young (10–4)

West Coast Athletic—Pacific (12–2)

Leading Major Independents

East—Fordham (26–3); Duquesne (21–4); Villanova (27–7); St. Bonaventure (21–6); Syracuse (19–7); Providence (20–8)

South—Jacksonville (22–4); Georgia Tech (23–4)

Midwest—Marquette (28–1); Notre Dame (20–9)

Southwest—Houston (22–7); New Mexico State (19–8)

Far West—Utah State (20–7); Hawaii (23–5)

Villanova had reached the final by beating Fordham, 85–75; routing previously unbeaten Pennsylvania, 90–47; and edging Western Kentucky, 92–89, in two overtime periods. Villanova, however, was deprived of second-place trophies and $72,347 because Howard Porter, their star and winner of the outstanding player award in the NCAA tourney, had signed a professional contract with an American Basketball League team, making him ineligible.

Evansville defeated Old Dominion, 97–82, in the final of the NCAA College Division championship. Kentucky State downed Eastern Michigan, 102–82, for the NAIA title. In the National Invitation Tourney at Madison Square Garden, North Carolina beat Georgia Tech, 84–66, in the final.

BOXING

In one of boxing's gaudiest spectacles, Joe Frazier, the heavyweight champion, settled an important controversy by defeating Muhammad Ali. Ali, the former titleholder, who won his laurels originally as Cassius Clay, had not lost his title in the ring. It was taken from him when he refused induction into the U.S. Army. Frazier had won the title by whipping those who aspired to replace Ali.

Frazier and Ali, both undefeated, met in Madison Square Garden on March 8 before a crowd of 20,455, which paid a record indoor gate of $1,325,951, and a closed-circuit international television audience. Scalpers got $400 to $600 for $150 ringside tickets.

The battle was bitter and well fought. Ali failed to "sting like a bee and flit like a butterfly," and he took a pounding from the 27-year-old Frazier. Ali was knocked to the canvas in the 15th round and took a mandatory 8-count. The decision went to Frazier unanimously. The referee voted for him 8 rounds to 6, with 1 even, and the judges favored Frazier, 9–6 and 11–4.

Each battler had been guaranteed a purse of $2.5 million, which after a whopping tax bite left them each about $750,000. The promoter, Jack Kent Cook of Los Angeles, reported two months later that the gross income from worldwide film video and other sources totaled over $20 million.

A couple of days after the fight, Frazier entered a hospital to be treated for high blood pressure and exhaustion. On June 28 the Supreme Court ruled that the Justice Department had erred in its presentation of charges against Ali, and his draft-evasion case was dropped. Ali continued with exhibitions and other bouts through the year. Frazier went on the entertainment circuit with his rock group, the Knockouts.

Elsewhere in the boxing world there was much confusion, with the World Boxing Association and the World Boxing Council recognizing different champions in nearly all divisions. Two of the most active fighters were light heavyweights. Bob Foster, the WBC champion, won four bouts, knocking out three of his foes. Vicente Paul Rondon of Venezuela scored knockouts in three defenses of the WBA title, which he won, February 27, by stopping Jimmy Dupree of Jersey City in the sixth round.

Ruben Olivares of Mexico regained the bantam title by outpointing Chucho Castillo of Mexico. Jose Napoles got back the welterweight crown from Billy Backus of Syracuse. Carlos Monzon defeated two former champions, Nino Benvenuto and Emile Griffith, in defending the middleweight title.

Boxing Highlights

World Professional Champions

Flyweight—Masao Oba, Japan, World Boxing Association champion; Erbito Salvarria, Philippines, World Boxing Council

Bantamweight—Ruben Olivares, Mexico

Featherweight—Antonio Gomez, Venezuela, WBA; Kuniaki Shibata, Japan, WBC

Junior Lightweight—Alfredo Marcano, Venezuela, WBA; Ricardo Arrendondo, Mexico, WBC

Lightweight—Ken Buchanan, Scotland, WBA; Pedro Carrasco, Spain, WBC

Junior Welterweight—Nicolino Loche, Argentina, WBA; Bruno Arcari, Italy, WBC

Welterweight—Jose Napoles, Mexico

Junior Middleweight—Koichi Wajima, Japan

Middleweight—Carlos Monzon, Argentina

Light Heavyweight—Vicente Rondon, Venezuela, WBA; Bob Foster, Silver Spring, Md., WBC

Heavyweight—Joe Frazier, Philadelphia

National AAU Championships

(New Orleans, April 30–May 2)

106 Pounds—Gary Griffin, Westwego, La.

112 Pounds—Bobby Hunter, Columbia, S. C.

119 Pounds—Ricardo Carreras, U. S. M. C., New York

125 Pounds—Ricky Boudreaux, Westwego, La.

132 Pounds—James Busceme, Beaumont, Texas

139 Pounds—Ray Seales, Tacoma, Wash.

147 Pounds—Sammy Maul, Dayton, Ohio

156 Pounds—Billy Daniels, Norfolk, Va.

165 Pounds—Joey Hadley, Memphis, Tenn.

178 Pounds—Marvin Johnson, Indianapolis

Heavyweight—Duane Bobick, Bowlus, Minn.

Team—Southern AAU

COACH TOM LANDRY, carried by jubilant Dallas players, breaks out in rare smile following decisive 24–3 win over Miami in Super Bowl.

FOOTBALL

Professional

The Dallas Cowboys, who had failed at the goal line the year before, crossed it three times on Jan. 16, 1972, at New Orleans and won the National Football League championship by beating the Miami Dolphins, 24–3, in the Super Bowl. It was the first time in six tries that the Cowboys had gone all the way in the play-offs, and the victory provided some solace to coach Tom Landry, whose teams previously had been unable to win the big game.

The Dallas attack was paced by Roger Staubach, who had become the regular quarterback in midseason after the Cowboys lost three of their first seven

NATIONAL FOOTBALL LEAGUE
(Final Standings, 1971)

American Conference

Western Division

	Won	Lost	Tied	Pct.	Pts.	Opp.
Kansas City....	10	3	1	.769	302	208
Oakland......	8	4	2	.667	344	278
San Diego.....	6	8	0	.429	311	341
Denver........	4	9	1	.308	203	275

Central Division

	Won	Lost	Tied	Pct.	Pts.	Opp.
Cleveland......	9	5	0	.643	285	273
Pittsburgh.....	6	8	0	.429	246	292
Houston.......	4	9	1	.308	251	330
Cincinnati......	4	10	0	.286	284	265

Eastern Division

	Won	Lost	Tied	Pct.	Pts.	Opp.
Miami.........	10	3	1	.769	315	174
*Baltimore......	10	4	0	.714	313	140
New England...	6	8	0	.429	238	325
N.Y. Jets......	6	8	0	.429	212	299
Buffalo.......	1	13	0	.071	184	394

* Fourth qualifier for play-offs.

Play-offs—Miami defeated Kansas City, 27–24, in second overtime period (22:40 minutes of overtime) at Kansas City, Dec. 25; Baltimore defeated Cleveland, 20–3, at Cleveland, Dec. 26
Conference Championship—Miami (defeated Baltimore, 21–0, at Miami, Jan. 2, 1972)

National Conference

Western Division

	Won	Lost	Tied	Pct.	Pts.	Opp.
San Francisco..	9	5	0	.643	300	216
Los Angeles....	8	5	1	.615	313	260
Atlanta........	7	6	1	.538	274	277
New Orleans...	4	8	2	.333	266	347

Central Division

	Won	Lost	Tied	Pct.	Pts.	Opp.
Minnesota.....	11	3	0	.786	245	139
Detroit........	7	6	1	.538	341	286
Chicago........	6	8	0	.429	185	276
Green Bay.....	4	8	2	.333	274	298

Eastern Division

	Won	Lost	Tied	Pct.	Pts.	Opp.
Dallas.........	11	3	0	.786	406	222
*Washington....	9	4	1	.692	276	190
Philadelphia....	6	7	1	.462	221	302
St. Louis.......	4	9	1	.308	231	279
N.Y. Giants....	4	10	0	.286	228	362

* Fourth qualifier for play-offs.

Play-offs—Dallas defeated Minnesota, 20–12, at Bloomington, Minn., Dec. 25; San Francisco defeated Washington, 24–20, at San Francisco, Dec. 26
Conference Championship—Dallas (defeated San Francisco, 14–3, at Irving, Texas, Jan. 2, 1972)
League Championship (Super Bowl)—Dallas (defeated Miami, 24–3, at New Orleans, Jan. 16, 1972)
Pro Bowl—American Conference 26, National Conference 13, at Los Angeles, Jan. 23, 1972

National Football League Leaders

American Conference

Scoring—Garo Yepremian, Miami (28 FG, 33 extra points, 117 points)
Scoring (nonkickers)—Leroy Kelly, Cleveland (72 pts)
Passing—Bob Griese, Miami (145 of 263 for 2,089 yards, 19 TDs—rating 9½ pts)
Receiving—Fred Biletnikoff, Oakland (61 for 929 yds)
Interceptions—Ken Houston, Houston (9)
Rushing—Floyd Little, Denver (283 for 1,133 yds)
Punting—Dave Lewis, Cincinnati (44.84 yds average)
Punt Returns—Leroy Kelly, Cleveland (average 9.7 yds)
Kickoff Returns—Mercury Morris, Miami (average 28.1 yds)

National Conference

Scoring—Curt Knight, Washington (29 FG, 27 extra points, 114 points)
Scoring (nonkickers)—Duane Thomas, Dallas (78 pts)
Passing—Roger Staubach, Dallas (126 of 211 for 1,882 yards, 15 TDs—rating 8 pts)
Receiving—Bob Tucker, N. Y. Giants (59 for 791 yds)
Interceptions—Bill Bradley, Philadelphia (11)
Rushing—John Brockington, Green Bay (216 for 1,105 yds)
Punting—Tom McNeill, Philadelphia (42 yds average)
Punt Returns—Speedy Duncan, Washington (10.6 yds average)
Kickoff Returns—Tom Williams, Los Angeles (29.7 yds avg)

WALT GARRISON knifes through line and penetrates secondary for good yardage, leading to a score. Dallas Cowboys overpowered Miami in Super Bowl, 24–3.

games. With the 29-year-old former Naval Academy star directing the operations on plays sent in by Landry, the Cowboys won their remaining 7 regular games, 2 play-off contests, and the Super Bowl for 10 straight victories.

Staubach, a fine running quarterback, passed for 2 touchdowns in the Super Bowl as he completed 12 of 19 passes and directed a ground offense that rolled for 252 yards. He was named Player of

COACH BOB DEVANEY gets victory ride following Nebraska's 38–6 romp over Alabama in Orange Bowl. Cornhuskers won No. 1 laurels for second straight season.

the Game, getting the vote over his running backs Duane Thomas, Walt Garrison, and Calvin Hill, and the big men of the strong defensive unit.

The defense, led by Bob Lilly, Lee Roy Jordan, Chuck Howley, Herb Adderley, and Mel Renfro, was outstanding. It held the running of Jim Kiick and Larry Csonka (called Butch Cassidy and the Sundance Kid by Miami fans) to 80 yards. By covering Paul Warfield and Howard Twilley carefully, the Dallas defensive secondary blunted the passing threat of Bob Griese.

The firmness of the Dallas defense had been well established. In winning the National Conference championship, which put them into the Super Bowl, the Cowboys beat the San Francisco 49ers, 14–3. In the division play-offs, they allowed the Minnesota Vikings only one touchdown in a 20–12 triumph. The Cowboys and Vikings had the best league records in regular-season play with 11 victories and 3 losses.

Miami's defense, too, had been outstanding in holding the opposition to 174 points in the 14 regular-season games, although it yielded 34 points to the New England Patriots in a surprise loss that broke an 8-game winning streak. Miami, coached by Don Shula, became the first expansion team to reach the Super Bowl. The Dolphins and the Kansas City Chiefs ended the season with 10–3–1 records, best in the American Conference.

In division play-offs, the Dolphins eliminated the Chiefs, 27–24, in the longest football game on record. Garo Yepremian's 37-yard field goal after 22 minutes and 40 seconds of the second overtime period (the sixth period of the game) won for Miami. The Chiefs had a chance to win with 31 seconds remaining in the fourth quarter, but Jan Stenerud's 31-yard attempted field goal went wide by inches. In the American Conference championship game, Miami trounced the Baltimore Colts, the defending NFL champions, 21–0, for a place in the Super Bowl.

Staubach and Griese were the leading passers in their respective conferences. The top receivers were Bob Tucker of the New York Giants and Fred Biletnikoff of the Oakland Raiders. Duane Thomas of Dallas and Leroy Kelly of Cleveland were the leading nonkicking scorers.

FOOTBALL
College

There were a couple of times during the season when it appeared that Nebraska might not be the No. 1 college football team. Both occasions came during the Thanksgiving Day game against Oklahoma before a stadium crowd of 63,385 at Norman and an international television audience estimated at 13.6 million persons. Oklahoma led at halftime, 17–14, and after losing that advantage was in front, 31–28, with less than 2 minutes to play. But the Cornhuskers, the 1970 national champions, showed why they still deserved the top ranking by marching 74 yards for a touchdown and a 35–31 victory.

The triumph clinched the Big Eight title and sent the Cornhuskers to a New Year's Day meeting with undefeated Alabama in the Orange Bowl. The Crimson Tide had trounced previously unbeaten Auburn, 31–7, for its 11th victory on November 27.

There were two other major undefeated teams. Michigan had won the Big Ten title and all 11 of its games before its match with Stanford in the Rose

Bowl. Toledo, the Mid-American Conference champion, was the winner of 10 games. By beating Richmond in the Tangerine Bowl on December 28. the Spiders concluded their third straight unbeaten season with a string of 35 consecutive victories, second only to Oklahoma's modern record of 47.

The Orange Bowl championship pairing turned out to be "no contest." Nebraska struck for two touchdowns in each of the first two quarters and led, 28–0, before Alabama tallied. The final score, 38–6, showed the fine balance the Cornhuskers had between offense and defense, sparked by Rich Glover, a middle guard. "This is a team without any real weaknesses," said coach Bob Devaney of the team that posted its 23d straight victory. Jerry Tagge, the quarterback, was resourceful and poised, and Jeff Kinney and Johnny Rodgers took care of most of the running.

Oklahoma, with Jack Mildren operating its explosive Wishbone formation, expertly led the nation in rushing with a total of 5,196 yards, an average of 566 a game. In the Sugar Bowl, on New Year's Day, the Sooners crushed Auburn, 40–22. With that triumph Oklahoma gained the No. 2 spot in the Associated Press Poll, as Colorado moved up to No. 3. This gave the Big Eight the three top spots. Colorado had lost only to Oklahoma and Nebraska after upsetting Louisiana State and Ohio State.

In the most exciting game of the New Year's Day classics, Stanford upset Michigan, 13–12, on a 31-yard field goal by Rod Garcia with 12 seconds left. Behind 10–3 in the fourth quarter, Stanford came up with a fake-punt-and-run play which enabled it to keep possession and tie the score. Garcia's second field goal offset a Wolverine safety,

WIDE WORLD

HEISMAN TROPHY winner, Pat Sullivan of Auburn (*right*), is "roughed up" by Cornell's Ed Marinaro, top collegiate rusher, on TV show for 1971 All-America team.

which had given Michigan a 12–10 lead late in the game.

Pat Sullivan, the Auburn quarterback, won the Heisman Trophy as the best player of the year. Second place went to Ed Marinaro of Cornell, who set records for rushing with a three-year total of 4,715 yards and a one-year mark of 1,881.

College Football Highlights

Intercollegiate and Conference Champions

National (AP and UPI polls)—Nebraska
National Football Foundation Award (MacArthur Bowl)—Nebraska
Eastern (Lambert Trophy)—Penn State
Eastern Small College—Lambert Cup: Delaware; Lambert Bowl: Alfred
Atlantic Coast—North Carolina (6–0)
Big Eight—Nebraska (7–0)
Big Sky—Idaho (4–1)
Big Ten—Michigan (8–0)
Ivy League—Tie between Cornell (6–1) and Dartmouth (6–1)
Mid-American—Toledo (5–0)
Missouri Valley—North Texas State (3–1)
Ohio Valley—Western Kentucky (6–1)
Pacific 8—Stanford (5–1)
Southeastern—Alabama (7–0)
Pacific Coast A. A.—Long Beach State (5–1)
Southern—Richmond (5–1)
Southwest—Texas (6–1)
Western Athletic—Arizona State (7–0)

Leading Independents

East—Penn State (10–1); Boston College (9–2)
Midwest—Notre Dame (8–2)
South—Florida State (8–3)
Southwest—Houston (9–2)
Far West—Utah State (8–3)

NCAA Regional Bowls
(All games played Dec. 11)

Boardwalk (East at Atlantic City, N. J.)—Delaware 72, C. W. Post 22
Grantland Rice Bowl (Mideast at Baton Rouge, La.)—Tennessee State 26, McNeese State 23
Pioneer (Midwest at Wichita Falls, Texas)—Louisiana Tech 14, Eastern Michigan 3
Camellia (West at Sacramento, Calif.)—Boise State 32, Chico State 28

NAIA Championship Bowls

Division I (at Birmingham, Ala., Dec. 11)—Livingston U. 14, Arkansas Tech 12
Division II (at Thousand Oaks, Calif., Dec. 4)—California Lutheran 30, Westminster (Pa.) 6

Major Bowl and All-Star Games
(Nov.–Dec. 1971; Jan. 1972)

Alonzo Stagg Bowl (Chicago, Nov. 25)—Samford 20, Ohio Wesleyan 10
Knute Rockne Bowl (Atlantic City, Nov. 26)—Bridgeport 17, Hampden-Sydney 12
Mineral Water Bowl (Excelsior Springs, Mo., Dec. 4)—Bethany (Kans.) 17, Missouri Valley College 14
Azalea Classic (Mobile, Ala., Dec. 4)—Jacksonville State 40, Alabama A & M 21
Share Bowl (Knoxville, Tenn., Dec. 11)—Carson-Newman 54, Fairmount State 3
Orange Blossom Classic (Miami, Fla., Dec. 11)—Florida A & M 27, Kentucky State 9
Sun Bowl (El Paso, Texas, Dec. 18)—Louisiana State 33, Iowa State 15
Pasadena Bowl (Pasadena, Calif., Dec. 18)—Memphis State 28, San Jose State 9
Liberty Bowl (Memphis, Tenn., Dec. 20)—Tennessee 14, Arkansas 13
Fiesta Bowl (Tempe, Ariz., Dec. 27)—Arizona State 45, Florida State 38
North-South Shrine (Miami, Fla., Dec. 27)—South 7, North 6
Tangerine Bowl (Orlando, Fla., Dec. 28)—Toledo 28, Richmond 3
Blue-Gray All-Stars (Montgomery, Ala., Dec. 28)—Gray 9, Blue 0
Peach Bowl (Atlanta, Ga., Dec. 30)—Mississippi 41, Georgia Tech 18
Gator Bowl (Jacksonville, Fla., Dec. 31)—Georgia 7, North Carolina 3
East-West Shrine Classic (San Francisco, Dec. 31)—West 17, East 13
Astro-Bluebonnett Bowl (Houston, Texas, Dec. 31)—Colorado 29, Houston 17
Cotton Bowl (Dallas, Texas, Jan. 1)—Penn State 30, Texas 6
Orange Bowl (Miami, Fla., Jan. 1)—Nebraska 38, Alabama 6
Rose Bowl (Pasadena, Calif., Jan. 1)—Stanford 13, Michigan 12
Sugar Bowl (New Orleans, Jan. 1)—Oklahoma 40, Auburn 22
Senior Bowl (Mobile, Ala., Jan. 8)—South 26, North 21
Hula Bowl (Honolulu, Jan. 8)—North 24, South 7
American Bowl (Tampa, Fla., Jan. 9)—North 27, South 8

LEE TREVINO (*right*), PGA Golfer of the Year,
and Jack Nicklaus, leading money winner,
teamed for U. S. victory in World Cup play.

GOLF

Until the penultimate tournament of the Professional Golfers' Association tour, Lee Trevino had accomplished almost everything he wanted. In those final rounds, however, Jack Nicklaus posted the winning score, won $30,000, and finished the year as the top money winner. Nicklaus, with $244,490, and Trevino, with $231,202, both bettered Jack's previous record for a season ($211,567), and Arnold Palmer was close behind with $209,604.

However, the honors without the dollar-sign belonged to Trevino, who was slowed in the latter part of the year by an emergency appendectomy. In the space of 23 days, the pro from El Paso, Texas, won three national championships—the United States Open, the British Open (the two most prestigious in the world), and the Canadian Open. Only three players before Trevino had won the American and British titles in the same years—the late Bobby Jones in 1930, Gene Sarazen in 1932, and Ben Hogan in 1953.

Trevino took the first of the three by defeating Nicklaus by three strokes in an 18-hole play-off in the U. S. Open at Ardmore, Pa., on June 21. Each had finished the 72 holes with a 280. Two weeks later, Trevino defeated Art Wall in another play-off with a birdie on the first hole for the Canadian title. He avoided a play-off in Britain, July 10, by carding a birdie on the final hole for a 278 total, one better than Lu Liang Huan of Taiwan.

For these and other achievements, Trevino was named Golfer of the Year by the PGA. In another success, he teamed with Nicklaus to capture the World Cup for the United States. Nicklaus led the individual scorers by 7 strokes with 271, and Trevino carded 284 for a U. S. total of 555. The American pros also won the Ryder Cup by beating Britain, 18½–13½.

Palmer had his best season in recent years. He beat Ray Floyd in a sudden-death play-off for the honors in the Hope Desert Classic on February 14, posting his first victory in 14 months. He won the Citrus Open and the Westchester Classic, and the PGA four-ball with Nicklaus. But he complained that he had not won a major tournament since the Masters in 1964.

Gary Cowan of Kitchener, Ont., regained the U. S. Amateur championship, which he had first won in 1966. Steve Melnyk, the 1969 U. S. Amateur titleholder, won the British Amateur, beating Jim Simons of Butler, Pa., in the final. The American amateurs, however, lost to the British in Walker Cup play, 13–11.

Mrs. JoAnne Gunderson Carner of Seekonk, Mass., a five-time winner of the U. S. Amateur title, won the Open as a pro, as Donna Caponi failed in a bid for a third straight championship. Kathy Whitworth took all of the other professional honors. She won the Vare Trophy, was named LPGA Player of the Year, and led in earnings with $43,534.

KATHY WHITWORTH holds cup for winning
Suzuki tourney. She also won Vare Trophy and
was named women's PGA Player of the Year.

CHARLES COODY blasts out of sand trap on way to Masters title at Augusta, Ga., April 11, with a 72-hole score of 279.

UPI

Golf Highlights

Men's Individual Champions

U. S. Open—Lee Trevino, El Paso, Texas
U. S. Amateur—Gary Cowan, Kitchener, Ont.
Masters—Charles Coody, Abilene, Texas
Professional Golfers' Association—Jack Nicklaus, Lost Tree Village, Fla.
British Open—Lee Trevino

American Classic—Jerry Heard
Atlanta Classic—Gardner Dickinson
British Amateur—Steve Melnyk, Jacksonville, Fla.
Byron Nelson Classic—Jack Nicklaus
Campbell-Los Angeles Open—Bob Lunn
Canadian Amateur—Dick Siderowf, Easton, Conn.
Canadian Open—Lee Trevino
Canadian PGA—Wilf Homenuik
Citrus Open—Arnold Palmer
Cleveland Open—Bobby Mitchell
Colonial National—Gene Littler
Crosby Pro-Am—Tom Shaw
Doral-Eastern Open—J. C. Snead
Eastern Amateur—Ben Crenshaw, Austin, Texas
French Amateur—Jean-Charles Desbordes, France
Greensboro Open—Brian Allin
Hartford Open—George Archer
Heritage Classic—Hale Irwin
Hope Desert Classic—Arnold Palmer
Houston Champions—Hubert Green
Jacksonville Open—Gary Player
Kaiser Open—Billy Casper
Kemper Open—Tom Weiskopf
Lefthanders—Bob Dargan, Camden, S. C.
Massachusetts Open—Dave Stockton
Milwaukee Open—Dave Eichelberger
Monsanto Open—Gene Littler
National Airlines Open—Gary Player
National Collegiate (NCAA)—University Division: Ben Crenshaw, Texas; College Division: Stan Stop, Louisiana State Univ., New Orleans
National Intercollegiate (NAIA)—Sammy Rachels, Columbus College, Ga.
New Orleans Open—Frank Beard
North and South Amateur—Eddie Pearce, Temple Terrace, Fla.
PGA Club Professional—Sam Snead
PGA Match Play—DeWitt Weaver
Philadelphia Open—Tom Weiskopf
Phoenix Open—Miller Barber
Robinson Open—Labron Harris
San Diego Open—George Archer
Southern Amateur—Ben Crenshaw, Austin, Texas
Southern Open—John Miller
Thomas-Memphis Open—Lee Trevino
Tournament of Champions—Jack Nicklaus
Tucson Open—J. C. Snead
U. S. Public Links—Fred Haney, Forest Grove, Oreg.
U. S. Senior Pro—Tommy Bolt
U. S. Seniors G. A.—Jim Knowles, Greenwich, Conn.
USGA Junior—Mike Brannan
USGA Senior—Tom Draper
Vardon Trophy—Lee Trevino
Westchester Classic—Arnold Palmer
Western Amateur—Allen Miller, Pensacola, Fla.
Western Open—Bruce Crampton
World Senior Pro—Kel Nagle, Australia
World Series of Golf—Charles Coody

Women's Individual Champions

U. S. Open—JoAnne Carner, Seekonk, Mass.
U. S. Amateur—Laura Baugh, Long Beach, Calif.
Ladies PGA—Kathy Whitworth, Richardson, Texas

Bluegrass Invitation—JoAnne Carner
Burdine's Invitation—Sandra Haynie
Canadian Open—Jocelyn Bourassa, Shawingan, Que.
Dallas Civitan—Sandra Haynie
George Washington Open—Judy Kimball
Heritage Open—Sandra Palmer
Immke Buick Open—Sandra Haynie
North and South Amateur—Barbara McIntire, Colorado Springs, Colo.
Orange Blossom—Jan Ferraris
Raleigh Classic—Kathy Whitworth
Sealy Classic—Sandra Palmer
Sears World Classic—Ruth Jessen
Suzuki—Kathy Whitworth
Trans-Mississippi—Jane Bastanchury, Whittier, Calif.
USGA Junior—Hollis Stacy, Savannah, Ga.
USGA Senior—Carolyn Cudone, Crystal Beach, S. C.
Vare Trophy—Kathy Whitworth
Western Amateur—Beth Barry, Mobile, Ala.

Team Champions

World Cup (professional, at Palm Beach Gardens, Fla., Nov. 11–14)—U. S. (Jack Nicklaus and Lee Trevino) 555; South Africa 567; New Zealand 569; high individual: Nicklaus, 271.
Ryder Cup (professional)—U. S. 18½, Britain 13½
Walker Cup (men's amateur)—Britain 13, U. S. 11
PGA Four-Ball—Arnold Palmer and Jack Nicklaus
NCAA—University Division: Texas; College Division: Louisiana State Univ. at New Orleans
NAIA—St. Bernard (Ala.)

Leading Money Winners in 1971

Men's PGA

Jack Nicklaus	$244,490
Lee Trevino	231,202
Arnold Palmer	209,604
George Archer	147,769
Gary Player	120,917
Miller Barber	117,359
Jerry Heard	112,389
Frank Beard	112,338
Dave Eichelberger	108,312
Billy Casper	107,276
Bruce Crampton	106,736
Tom Weiskopf	106,558

Women's PGA

Kathy Whitworth	$43,534
Sandra Haynie	37,370
Jane Blalock	36,035
Sandra Palmer	35,298
Donna Caponi	24,382
JoAnne Carner	22,883
Jo Ann Prentice	21,035
Judy Rankin	20,222
Pam Barnett	20,000
Marlene Hagge	18,878
Mary Mills	16,550
Marilynn Smith	14,705

12 Top Lifetime

Arnold Palmer	$1,460,013
Jack Nicklaus	1,383,164
Billy Casper	1,236,573
Julius Boros	858,091
Gene Littler	814,848
Gary Player	814,752
Frank Beard	751,431
Bruce Crampton	680,433
Lee Trevino	644,617
Doug Sanders	621,870
George Archer	583,320
Dan Sikes Jr	583,134

12 Top Lifetime

Kathy Whitworth	$342,743
Mickey Wright	283,526
Betsy Rawls	262,597
Sandra Haynie	229,751
Marilynn Smith	227,038
Marlene Hagge	223,755
Carol Mann	216,983
Patty Berg	184,530
Louise Suggs	182,530
JoAnne Prentice	146,172
Shirley Englehorn	145,105
Ruth Jessen	131,440

HERVE FILION of Canada, kissed by wife after victory at Yonkers, December 1. Filion's win was his 500th of the year, a record first for harness drivers.

Harness Racing Highlights

U. S. Trotting Association Champions

Trotters

2-Year-Old—Super Bowl
3-Year-Old—Speedy Crown
4-Year-Old—Marlu Pride
Aged—Fresh Yankee
Trotter of the Year—Speedy Crown

Pacers

2-Year-Old—Strike Out
3-Year-Old—Albatross
4-Year-Old—Steady Star
Aged—Super Wave
Pacer of the Year—Albatross

Harness Horse of the Year

Albatross (141 votes); Steady Star (34); Fresh Yankee (8); Speedy Crown (4)

Major Stakes Winners

Trotting

American Championship (Roosevelt)—Dart Hanover
American Classic (Hollywood)—Fresh Yankee
Colonial (Liberty Bell)—Savoir
Dexter Cup (Roosevelt)—Quick Pride
Hambletonian (DuQuoin, Ill.)—Speedy Crown
Harriman (Yonkers)—Super Bowl
Horseman Futurity (Indianapolis)—Hoot Speed
Kentucky Futurity—Savoir
Lady Suffolk (Roosevelt)—Egyptian Jody
Realization (Roosevelt)—Timothy T.
Roosevelt International—Une de Mai (France)
Roquepine (Roosevelt)—Une de Mai
Volomite (Yonkers)—Fresh Yankee
Westbury Futurity (Roosevelt)—Super Bowl
Yonkers Futurity—Quick Pride

Pacing

Adios Stakes (The Meadows)—Albatross
American Classic (Hollywood)—Albatross
American National Maturity (Sportsman's Park)—Kentucky
Cane (Yonkers)—Albatross
Commodore (Roosevelt)—Albatross
Fox Stakes (Indianapolis)—Strike Out
Good Time (Yonkers)—Laverne Hanover
Horseman Futurity (Indianapolis)—Gamely
Little Brown Jug (Delaware, Ohio)—Nansemond
Martin Tananbaum International (Yonkers)—Laverne Hanover
Messenger Stakes (Roosevelt)—Albatross
Realization (Roosevelt)—Windy Way
Roosevelt Futurity—Strike Out
Sheppard (Yonkers)—Shadow Star

HARNESS RACING

For a period of four days in the autumn, the famed Red Mile at Lexington, Ky., was the fastest racing strip in the world. Five records were set in pacing. One of them—1 minute, 52 seconds—was the fastest time for the mile ever clocked by a harness horse. Steady Star, a 4-year-old driven by Joe O'Brien, posted his amazing mark in a time trial. (Bret Hanover set the previous record of 1:53⅘ in 1967.) The other records, made in races, were 1:56⅘ by Entrepreneur, the best for a 2-year-old pacer; 1:54⅘ in each of two heats by Albatross, a record for 3-year-old pacers for one mile and for two consecutive mile heats; and 1:57⅕ by Decorum, the best for a 2-year-old filly.

The performance of Albatross was not unexpected. The colt—chosen the 2-year-old pacer of 1970—won 25 of 28 races, set a season record by winning $558,000 in purses, and scored a landslide victory in the voting for the Harness Horse of the Year. Albatross, who was purchased early in the year by a syndicate for $1,250,000, was driven by Stanley Dancer. He won the Messenger, the Cane Pace, the Adios Stakes, and American Classic.

Steady Star was the runner-up in the balloting for Horse of the Year.

Speedy Crown, a 3-year-old, was named Trotter of the Year. He had won the Hambletonian. Fresh Yankee, the 1970 Harness Horse of the Year, was the second-place pick and the best of the aged trotters.

Rum Customer, a 6-year-old pacer, by winning the Millionaire Mile at Aurora Downs, Ill., set a lifetime earnings record of $1,001,448.

HOCKEY

During regular-season play, the champion Boston Bruins set 35 individual and team scoring records in winning the East Division honors of the National Hockey League. But in the play-offs, they were bushwhacked by the Montreal Canadiens in the first round. The Canadiens, who had been so inconsistent in midseason that their coach, Claude Ruel, was replaced by Al McNeill, regained a touch of their former greatness. They reached the final by defeating the Minnesota North Stars. Then with Ken Dryden, their rookie goalie, performing spectacularly, the Canadiens twice came from behind in games and outlasted the Chicago Black Hawks, 4 games to 3, to win the Stanley Cup for the 16th time.

The Hawks had been transferred to the West Division at the start of the season in order to place the league's two new teams, Buffalo and Vancouver, in the East.

Dryden's work was so superior that he was voted the Conn Smythe Trophy as the outstanding player in the play-offs. A part-time law student at McGill University, he had been an All-America goalie at Cornell the season before and played on the Canadiens' minor league club at Montreal.

Chief of the record-setters for the Bruins was Phil Esposito, whose 76 goals shattered Bobby Hull's season record of 58. The 6-1 center also had 76 assists for a record point total of 162. The Bruins made history by having the first four leaders in scoring. Trailing right behind Esposito were Bobby Orr (139 points), Johnny Bucyk (116), and Ken Hodge (106). Boston's totals of 399 goals

Hockey Highlights

NATIONAL HOCKEY LEAGUE
(Final Standings, 1971)

East Division

	Won	Lost	Tied	Goals For	Goals Against	Pts
Boston	57	14	7	399	207	121
New York	49	18	11	259	177	109
Montreal	42	23	13	291	216	97
Toronto	37	33	8	248	211	82
Buffalo	24	39	15	217	291	63
Vancouver	24	46	8	229	296	56
Detroit	22	45	11	209	308	55

West Division

	Won	Lost	Tied	Goals For	Goals Against	Pts
Chicago	49	20	9	277	184	107
St. Louis	34	25	19	223	208	87
Philadelphia	28	33	17	207	225	73
Minnesota	28	34	16	191	223	72
Los Angeles	25	40	13	239	303	63
Pittsburgh	21	37	20	221	240	62
California	20	53	5	199	320	45

Stanley Cup Play-offs

Preliminary Series—*East Division:* Montreal defeated Boston, 4 games to 3; New York defeated Toronto, 4 games to 2—*West Division:* Chicago defeated Pittsburgh, 4 games to 0; Minnesota defeated St. Louis, 4 games to 2
Semifinals—Chicago defeated New York, 4 games to 3; Montreal defeated Minnesota, 4 games to 2
Final—Montreal defeated Chicago, 4 games to 3

Individual National Hockey League Awards

Hart Trophy (most valuable player)—Bobby Orr, Boston
Ross Trophy (leading scorer)—Phil Esposito, Boston
Norris Trophy (leading defenseman)—Orr
Lady Byng Trophy (sportsmanship)—Johnny Bucyk, Boston
Calder Trophy (outstanding rookie)—Gilbert Perreault, Buffalo
Vezina Trophy (goalies with fewest goals allowed)—Ed Giacomin and Gilles Villemure, New York
Conn Smythe Trophy (most valuable in play-offs)—Ken Dryden, Montreal goalie

NHL All-Star Teams

(Players are selected by writers and broadcasters in NHL cities. NHL pays $1,000 to each first team member and $500 to each second-team choice.)

Position	First Team	Second Team
Goal	Ed Giacomin, New York	Jacques Plante, Toronto
Defense	Bobby Orr, Boston	Brad Park, New York
Defense	Jean-Claude Tremblay, Montreal	Pat Stapleton, Chicago
Center	Phil Esposito, Boston	Dave Keon, Toronto
Right Wing	Ken Hodge, Boston	Yvon Cournoyer, Montreal
Left Wing	John Bucyk, Boston	Bobby Hull, Chicago

Other Professional Champions

American League—*Eastern Division:* Providence Reds; *Western Division:* Baltimore Clippers; *Calder Cup Play-offs:* Springfield Kings
Central League—*Regular season and play-offs:* Omaha Knights
Western League—*Regular season and play-offs:* Portland Buckaroos

Amateur Champions

Eastern League—*Northern Division:* New Haven Blades; *Southern Division and Play-offs:* Charlotte Checkers
International League—*Regular season:* Muskegon Mohawks; *play-offs:* Port Huron Flags
United States Hockey League—Marquette Iron Rangers
World—Soviet Union
Amateur Hockey Association of the United States—*Pee-wee:* Detroit; *bantam:* Edina, Minn.; *midget:* Detroit; *juvenile:* North Shore, Mass.; *intermediate:* St. Paul; *intermediate open:* Lima, Ohio; *junior:* St. Clair (Mich.) Shore Saints
Canadian—*Senior (Allan Cup):* Galt Hornets; *junior (Memorial Cup):* Quebec Remparts

Intercollegiate

NCAA—Boston University
NAIA—Bemidji
ECAC—*Division I: season:* Boston University; *play-offs:* Harvard; *Division II, season and play-offs:* Bowdoin
WCHA—*Season:* Michigan Tech; *play-offs: Group A:* Minnesota; *Group B:* Denver
Ivy League—Harvard

---

and 1,093 scoring points set team records, as did the total of 121 points in the standings.

Orr, who bettered his own records for scoring by a defenseman, with 37 goals and 102 assists, won the trophies for the most valuable player and the best defenseman and a 5-year contract reported at $1 million. Bucyk was voted the Lady Byng Trophy for sportsmanship. The season's best goaltenders were Ed Giacomin and Gilles Villemure of the New York Rangers. Gilbert Perreault of the Buffalo Sabres was named rookie of the year.

Gordie Howe finally retired after the season. The 43-year-old Detroit forward holds all-time scoring records of 786 goals and 1,809 total points for regular season play, made in a 25-year career. Howe was selected to the league's all-star first team 12 times and to the second team 9 times, for a total of 21. He was voted the most valuable player six times and led the league in scoring in six seasons. He was playing his 117th NHL game the night Bobby Orr was born in 1948. Jean Beliveau, the Montreal star center, also retired after 18 seasons. He was second to Howe in career points with 1,219 and fourth in goals with 507.

In November, the NHL selected Long Island and Atlanta (Ga.) as sites for new franchises for the 1972–73 season. The Long Island team will be based at the new Nassau Coliseum in Hempstead.

UPI

MONTREAL CANADIENS celebrate with champagne after uphill 3–2 win over Chicago Black Hawks in final game of 1971 Stanley Cup play-offs.

CANONERO II, with trainer Juan Arias and jockey Gustavo Avila, after winning Preakness. Horse also won Kentucky Derby but was thwarted in bid for triple crown.

HORSE RACING

When racing interest in the East seemed to have waned following an injury to Hoist the Flag, the leading 3-year-old, Canonero II arrived from Venezuela and gave it a figurative shot in the arm. Canonero, who was purchased with another horse for $12,000, raced to a 3¾-length victory in the Kentucky Derby. The big bay, running in the field from the 12th post, circled the pack in his closing rush and won the $145,500 first prize going away.

The Kentucky-bred colt (whose name in Spanish means "gunner") had been a wedding present to Edgar Caibett from his father-in-law, Pedro Baptista. Canonero II added to his laurels by winning the Preakness (and $137,400) by 1½ lengths in the record time of 1:54 for the 1³⁄₁₆-mile race.

However, Caibett's hope of having a Triple Crown winner ended when Canonero, suffering from a hoof infection, finished fourth to Pass Catcher in the Belmont Stakes. Canonero then was sold to the King Ranch for $1 million and raced no more during the year.

Achieving further honors, Canonero was named best 3-year-old colt of the year. But the award for Horse of the Year went to Ack Ack, a 4-year-old colt who won seven of eight races, all in California, where racing had an exciting year. Chief among the factors that made it so was Willie Shoemaker, the 40-year-old jockey who won 44 stakes, a record for one season. He also increased the number of his world-record victories to 6,280. He guided Ack Ack to triumphs in the Hollywood Gold Cup and the Santa Anita Handicap. Shoemaker's chief opposition was Laffit Pincay, Jr., who set a record for a year with $3,719,694 in earnings and 380 wins.

Offtrack betting entered the picture in New York and seemed so successful that other states were prepared to try it. OTB, which turns over 80% of its net to New York City, also got a shot in the arm from Canonero II. OTB bettors who had the Venezuelan horse in the Derby received $58.20 for a $2 win bet instead of the track price of $19.40. For the Preakness, Canonero paid $12.80 in the OTB and $8.80 at the track. New York tracks were prepared to sue OTB for losses in attendance and handle as the year ended.

Horse Racing Highlights
Champions of the Year
Eclipse Awards

(Consolidation of polls by the Thoroughbred Racing Associations' Board of Selection; editors and writers of the *Morning Telegraph-Daily Racing Form;* and members of the National Turf Writers Association)

Horse of the Year—Mr. and Mrs. Buddy Fogelson's Ack Ack
2-Year-Old Filly—Ogden Phipps' Numbered Account
2-Year-Old Colt—Meadow Stable's Riva Ridge
3-Year-Old Filly—Mrs. H. B. Keck's Turkish Trousers
3-Year-Old Colt—Edgar Caibett's Canonero II
Older Filly or Mare—Mrs. Whitney Stone's Shuvee
Older Colt—Ack Ack
Grass—Rokeby Stable's Run the Gantlet
Steeplechase—Stephen C. Clark's Shadow Brook

Major Stakes Winners

American Derby (Arlington)—Bold Reason
Amory L. Haskell Handicap (Monmouth)—Jontilla
Arlington-Washington Park Futurity—*First Division:* Hold Your Peace; *Second Division:* Governor Max
Belmont Stakes—Pass Catcher
Benjamin F. Lindheimer Handicap (Arlington)—Princess Pout
Brook Steeplechase (Belmont)—Shadow Brook
Brooklyn Handicap (Aqueduct)—Never Bow
California Derby (Golden Gate)—Unconscious
Californian (Hollywood)—Cougar II
Campbell Handicap (Bowie)—Bushido
Century Handicap (Hollywood)—Big Shot II
Champagne Stakes (Belmont)—Riva Ridge
Coaching Club American Oaks (Belmont)—Our Cheri Amour
Colonial Cup Steeplechase (Camden, S. C.)—Inkslinger
Delaware Handicap—Blessing Angelica
Flamingo (Hialeah)—Executioner
Florida Derby (Gulfstream)—Eastern Fleet
Frizette (Belmont)—Numbered Account
Futurity (Belmont)—Riva Ridge
Garden State Stakes—Riva Ridge
Gardenia (Garden State)—Numbered Account
Governor Stakes (Belmont)—Farewell Party
Grand Prix (Arlington)—Son Ange
Gulfstream Park Handicap—Fast Hilarious
Hawthorne Gold Cup—Twice Worthy
Hialeah Turf Cup—Drumtop
Hobson Handicap (Liberty Bell)—Peace Corps
Hollywood Derby—Bold Reason
Hollywood Gold Cup—Ack Ack
Hollywood Turf Handicap—Cougar II
Hopeful (Saratoga)—Rest Your Case
Jersey Derby (Garden State)—Bold Reason
Jockey Club Gold Cup (Aqueduct)—Shuvee
Kentucky Derby (Churchill Downs)—Canonero II
Laurel Futurity—Riva Ridge
Man o' War Handicap (Belmont)—Run the Gantlet
Matchmaker (Atlantic City)—Deceit
Matron (Belmont)—Numbered Account
Meadow Brook Steeplechase (Aqueduct)—Wustenchef
Metropolitan Handicap (Belmont)—Tunex
Michigan Mile (Detroit)—Native Royalty
Monmouth Invitational—West Coast Scout
Mother Goose (Belmont)—Deceit
Oak Leaf Stakes (Santa Anita)—Sporting Lass
Pan American Handicap (Gulfstream)—Chompion
Preakness (Pimlico)—Canonero II
San Juan Capistrano (Santa Anita)—Cougar II
Santa Anita Derby—Jim French
Santa Anita Handicap—Ack Ack
Santa Margarita (Santa Anita)—Manta
Sapling (Monmouth)—Chevron Flight
Selima (Laurel)—Numbered Account
Sorority (Monmouth)—Brenda Beauty
Strub (Santa Anita)—War Heim
Suburban Handicap (Aqueduct)—Twice Worthy
Sunset Handicap (Hollywood)—Over the Counter
Temple Gwathmey Steeplechase (Belmont)—Shadow Brook
Travers (Saratoga)—Bold Reason
United Nations Handicap (Atlantic City)—Run the Gantlet
Washington, D. C. International (Laurel)—Run the Gantlet
Widener (Hialeah)—True North
Wood Memorial (Aqueduct)—Good Behaving
Woodward (Belmont)—West Coast Scout

Other Races

Ascot Gold Cup (England)—Random Shot
Cambridgeshire (England)—King Midas
Canadian Derby (Northlands)—Kims Kid
Epsom Derby (England)—Mill Reef
Epsom Oaks (England)—Altesse Royale
Grand National Steeplechase (England)—Specify
Grand Prix de Paris—Rheffic
Irish Oaks—Altesse Royale
Irish Sweeps Derby—Irish Ball
King George VI and Queen Elizabeth (England)—Mill Reef
Melbourne Derby (Australia)—Silver Knight
1,000 Guineas (England)—Altesse Royale
2,000 Guineas (England)—Brigadier Gerard
Prix de l'Arc de Triomphe (France)—Mill Reef
Queens Plate (Canada)—Kennedy Road
St. Leger (England)—Athens Wood

THE PAN-AMERICAN GAMES opened with flame-lighting ceremony at Cali, Colombia, July 30. Though U. S. athletes won most medals as expected, Cuba's strength proved to be the surprise of the Games.

UPI

PAN-AMERICAN GAMES

Athletes from the United States were expected to dominate the Pan-American Games, as usual, but there were some unexpected results in certain sports that are considered the province of Americans. In basketball, baseball, and volleyball, U. S. teams were defeated by their Latin American neighbors.

The sixth Pan-American Games drew a record number of 4,150 athletes from 30 nations to Cali, Colombia (July 30–August 13) for competition in 19 sports. The U. S. delegation of 382 athletes was the largest, and it came away with the most prizes. The Americans won 105 gold medals for first place, 73 silver medals for second, and 40 bronze medals for third. The total of 218 was more than double that of the second-place country, Cuba, which had 105.

Cuba's strength was the surprise of the Games. The Cubans exceeded Canada's medal total by 25 and won 30 gold medals to Canada's 19. Cuba regained the baseball championship and won titles in men's and women's volleyball and saber. The Cubans also won four individual championships in boxing, three in wrestling, and three in fencing.

The United States men won 20 of the 24 track-and-field events and 16 of 17 titles in swimming; 7 of 10 wrestling championships; 5 of 9 weight-lifting events; 4 of 6 shooting titles; all but four of the gymnastics honors; and the water-polo title.

Frank Heckl, a swimmer from Cerritos, Calif., gathered the most gold medals. He won the 100- and 200-meter freestyle events and the 100-meter butterfly, swam the anchor leg on three winning relay teams, and took a silver medal in the 200-meter individual medley—for a total of seven medals.

Roxanne Pierce, a 16-year-old gymnast from Kensington, Md., won four gold medals, including the all-around championship, and two third-place awards. John Crosby of New Haven, Conn., another gymnast, took eight medals—two gold, five silver, and a bronze.

Leslie Cliff of Canada was the leading medal winner among the women swimmers. She won the 200- and 400-meter medley events and swam on the winning 400-meter relay team, for three gold medals, and took a silver medal in the 100-meter butterfly.

Two world records were set and one tied. Pedro Perez covered 57 feet 1 inch in the triple jump, bettering the mark by one-half inch. In the 200-meter dash, Don Quarrie of Jamaica equaled the record of 19.8 seconds. The U. S. swimming team bettered the world mark for the 800-meter free-style relay with 7:45.82.

Brazil captured the championships in men's and women's basketball. In the men's division, Cuba defeated the United States in the preliminary round robin, 73–69. It was only the second loss by an American five in the Games, the other having been in 1955. The United States failed to qualify for the final round on a point basis, even though it beat Brazil in overtime. Cuba regained the baseball title it had lost to the United States in 1967, beating the Americans, 4–3, in the decisive game.

A surprise triumph was posted for the United States in cycling by John Howard of Springfield, Mo., in the 122.5-mile road race. The gold medal was the first for the United States in this sport. However, the Americans failed to win a first place in either rowing or yachting, which was unusual. Bill Tytus of Seattle finished second to Alberto Demiddi of Argentina, the world champion, in the single sculls for one of two silver medals won by U. S. oarsmen. They also collected three bronze medals.

The Medal Winners

Country	Gold	Silver	Bronze	Total
United States	105	73	40	218
Cuba	30	50	25	105
Canada	19	20	41	80
Brazil	9	7	14	30
Mexico	7	11	23	41
Argentina	6	4	12	22
Colombia	5	9	14	28
Jamaica	4	3	4	11
Puerto Rico	2	4	7	13
Venezuela	2	3	4	9
Netherlands Antilles	1	2	1	4
Trinidad-Tobago	1	1	5	7
Panama	1	1	4	6
Ecuador	1	0	2	3
Guatemala	1	0	0	1
Chile	0	3	4	7
Peru	0	1	4	5
Barbados	0	1	0	1
Uruguay	0	0	3	3
Guyana	0	0	1	1
Total	194	193	208	595

Other participating countries, which failed to win medals: Bahamas, Bermuda, Costa Rica, Dominican Republic, El Salvador, Haiti, Nicaragua, Paraguay, Surinam, Virgin Islands

Swimming Highlights

Men's National AAU Indoor Championships
(Pullman, Wash., April 7–10)

100-Yard Freestyle—Frank Heckl, So. California (0:45.56)
200-Yard Freestyle—Frank Heckl (1:40.55)
500-Yard Freestyle—John Kinsella, Indiana (4:28.85)
1,650-Yard Freestyle—John Kinsella (15:42.38)
100-Yard Backstroke—Mike Stamm, Indiana (0:51.52)
200-Yard Backstroke—Mike Stamm (1:52.26)
100-Yard Breaststroke—Brian Job, Santa Clara (Calif.) S. C. (0:57.75)
200-Yard Breaststroke—Brian Job (2:04.04; equals U. S. record)
100-Yard Butterfly—Frank Heckl (0:49.59)
200-Yard Butterfly—Gary Hall, Indiana (1:48.44; betters U. S. record)
200-Yard Individual Medley—Gunnar Larsson, Phillips 66, Long Beach, Calif. (1:53.38)
400-Yard Individual Medley—Gunnar Larsson (4:01.51)
400-Yard Freestyle Relay—So. California (Kim Tutt, Roger Lyon, Michael Weston, Frank Heckl; 3:02.86)
400-Yard Medley Relay—Indiana (Michael Stamm, Peder Dahlberg, Gary Hall, Mark Spitz; 3:24.56)
800-Yard Freestyle Relay—So. California (Kim Tutt, Andrew Strenk, James McConica, Frank Heckl; 6:42.67)

Diving
(West Point, N. Y., March 31–April 3)

1-Meter—Craig Lincoln, Minnesota (546.72 pts)
3-Meter—Mike Finneran, Santa Clara S. C. (552.78)
Platform—Dick Rydze, Michigan (470.10)

Men's National AAU Outdoor Championships
(Houston, Aug. 25–28)

100-Meter Freestyle—Mark Spitz, Arden Hills S. C., Sacramento, Calif. (0:52.45)
200-Meter Freestyle—Mark Spitz (1:54.74)
400-Meter Freestyle—Tom McBreen, San Mateo, Calif. (4:02.08; betters world record)
1,500-Meter Freestyle—Mike Burton, Arden Hills S. C. (16:09.66)
100-Meter Backstroke—Mel Nash, Greater Pittsburgh S. C. (0:59.28)
200-Meter Backstroke—Charlie Campbell, Pasadena S. C. (2:07.14)
100-Meter Breaststroke—Peder Dahlberg, Gatorade S. C., Bloomington, Ind. (1:06.91)
200-Meter Breaststroke—Rick Colella, Cascade S. C., Seattle (2:25.05)
100-Meter Butterfly—Mark Spitz (0:55.4; Spitz bettered world record in heat, 0:55.01)
200-Meter Butterfly—Mark Spitz (2:03.89; betters world record of 2:03.91 set by Spitz in heat)
200-Meter Medley—Gary Hall, Garden Grove, Calif. (2:10.07)
400-Meter Medley—Gary Hall (4:33.11)
400-Meter Freestyle Relay—Los Angeles A. C. (Frank Heckl, Steve Tyrell, Mike Weston, Don Havens; 3:32.39)
400-Meter Medley Relay—Santa Clara S. C. (Steve Doyle, John Hencken, Reed Slevin, Ed McCleskey; 3:55.26)
800-Meter Freestyle Relay—Phillips 66, Long Beach, Calif. (Andy Strenk, John Halliday, William Furness, Gary Hall; 7:48.58)

Diving (Aug. 19–21)

1-Meter—Mike Brown, Denver (548.49 pts)
3-Meter—Jim Henry, Gatorade S. C., Bloomington, Ind. (569.04)
Platform—Dick Rydze, Pittsburgh (655.53)

Women's National AAU Indoor Championships
(Pullman, Wash., April 7–10)

100-Yard Freestyle—Sandy Neilson, El Monte (Calif.) S. C. (0:53.27)
200-Yard Freestyle—Nancy Spitz, Arden Hills (Calif.) S. C. (1:55.84)
500-Yard Freestyle—Debbie Meyer, Arden Hills (5:02.87)
1,650-Yard Freestyle—Debbie Meyer (17:11.83)
100-Yard Backstroke—Susie Atwood, Lakewood (Calif.) A. C. (0:58.22)
200-Yard Backstroke—Susie Atwood (2:06.08)
100-Yard Breaststroke—Lynn Colella, Cascade S. C., Seattle (1:06.74)
200-Yard Breaststroke—Ann Belikow, Pasadena S. A. (2:29.65)
100-Yard Butterfly—Deena Deardurff, Cincinnati Pepsi Marlins (0:57.06; betters U. S. record)
200-Yard Butterfly—Alice Jones, Pepsi Marlins (2:03.97)
200-Yard Medley—Susie Atwood (2:10.10)
400-Yard Medley—Susie Atwood (4:34.81)
400-Meter Freestyle Relay—Phillips 66, Long Beach, Calif. (Lynn Skrifvars, Cindy Plaisted, Karen Hanssen, Deedee Boone; 3:36.67)
400-Yard Medley Relay—Lakewood A. C. (Susie Atwood, Kim Brecht, Bonnie Adair, Lindy Kiddy; 3:58.61)

800-Meter Freestyle Relay—Arden Hills S. C. (Nancy Spitz, Martha Shillito, Vicki King, Debbie Meyer; 7:50.61)
Team—Santa Clara (Calif.) S. C. (487 pts)

Diving
(West Point, N. Y., March 31–April 3)

1-Meter—Cynthia Potter, Gatorade S. C., Bloomington, Ind. (427.20 pts)
3-Meter—Capt. Micki King, U. S. Air Force, Phillips 66 (393.45 pts)
Platform—Capt. King (362.61)

Women's National AAU Outdoor Championships
(Houston, Aug. 25–28)

100-Meter Freestyle—Linda Johnson, Lakewood (Calif.) A. C. (1:00.35)
200-Meter Freestyle—Linda Johnson (2:08.03)
400-Meter Freestyle—Ann Simmons, Lakewood A. C. (4:24.82)
1,500-Meter Freestyle—Cathy Calhoun, El Monte (Calif.) S. C. (17:19.20; betters world record)
200-Meter Backstroke—Susie Atwood, Lakewood A. C. (1:06.72)
200-Meter Backstroke—Susie Atwood (2:22.91)
100-Meter Breaststroke—Diane Nickloff, Pasadena (1:17.12)
200-Meter Breaststroke—Claudia Clevenger, DeAnza S. C., Cupertino, Calif. (2:45.72)
100-Meter Butterfly—Deena Deardurff, Cincinnati Pepsi Marlins (1:05.03)
200-Meter Butterfly—Ellie Daniel, Elkins Park, Pa. (2:18.40; equals world record Miss Daniel set in heat)
200-Meter Medley—Yoshimi Nishigawa, Japan (2:26)
400-Meter Medley—Jenny Bartz, Santa Clara S. C. (5:08.38)
400-Meter Freestyle Relay—Lakewood A. C. (Linda Johnson, Ann Simmons, Roberta Watt, Bonnie Adair; 4:02.98)
400-Meter Medley Relay—Phillips 66, Long Beach (Lynn Skrifvars, Linda Kurtz, Cindy Plaisted, Shirley Babashoff; 4:32.06)
800-Meter Freestyle Relay—Lakewood A. C. (Linda Johnson, Linda Kiddy, Roberta Watt, Ann Simmons; 8:35.52)

Diving (Aug. 19–21)

1-Meter—Cynthia Potter, Gatorade S. C., Bloomington, Ind. (463.08 pts)
3-Meter—Cynthia Potter (508.05)
Platform—Cynthia Potter (430.56)
Team—Santa Clara S. C. (437)

National Collegiate (NCAA) Championships
(Ames, Iowa, March 25–27)

50-Yard Freestyle—Dave Edgar, Tennessee (0:20.3; NCAA record)
100-Yard Freestyle—Dave Edgar (0:44.69, U. S. record)
200-Yard Freestyle—Jim McConica, So. California (1:39.75)
500-Yard Freestyle—John Kinsella, Indiana (4:27.39; NCAA record)
1,650-Yard Freestyle—John Kinsella (15:26.51; U. S. record)
100-Yard Backstroke—Santiago Esteva, Indiana (0:51.71; NCAA record)
200-Yard Backstroke—Gary Hall, Indiana (1:50.6; U. S. record)
100-Yard Breaststroke—Brian Job, Stanford (0:57.24; NCAA record—Tom Bruce, UCLA, bettered U. S. record with 0:56.86 in trials)
200-Yard Breaststroke—Brian Job (2:03.39; U. S. record)
100-Yard Butterfly—Mark Spitz, Indiana (0:49.42; NCAA record)
200-Yard Butterfly—Mark Spitz (1:50.1)
200-Yard Individual Medley—Gary Hall (1:52.2; U. S. record)
400-Yard Individual Medley—Gary Hall (3:58.25; U. S. record)
400-Yard Freestyle Relay—So. California (Kim Tutt, James McConica, Michael Weston, Frank Heckl; 3:02.38)
400-Yard Medley Relay—Stanford (Fred Haywood, Brian Job, John Ferris, Martin Pedley; 3:22.51; U. S. record)
800-Yard Freestyle Relay—So. California (James McConica, Kim Tutt, Thomas McBreen, Frank Heckl; 6:39.04; U. S. record)
1-Meter Dive—Mike Finneran, Ohio State (520.98 pts)
3-Meter Dive—Phil Boggs, Florida State (552.93)
Team—Indiana University (351)

Synchronized Swimming
AAU Indoor

Solo—Heidi O'Rourke, San Francisco Merionettes
Duet—Heidi O'Rourke and Joan Lang, San Francisco Merionettes
Team—San Francisco Merionettes

AAU Outdoor

Solo—Heidi O'Rourke
Stunts—Gail Johnson, Santa Clara (Calif.) Aquamaids
Duet—Heidi O'Rourke and Joan Lang
Team—San Francisco Merionettes

SWIMMING

Between two near all-winning expeditions to the Pan-American Games and Europe, American swimmers held their private world championships in Houston. Five world marks fell in the AAU title meet, two of which were posted by Mark Spitz of the Arden Hills Swim Club of Carmichael, Calif., and Indiana University.

Only 10 swimmers of the Pan-Am Games team, which won all but 7 of 29 events in men's and women's competition, were included among the 12 men and 12 women who competed in Leipzig and Minsk. Against East Germany in the first meet the Americans won 24 of 28 events, and against the Russians and British at Minsk they won all but 2 of 29 events.

Spitz set two world records at the national championships. In the butterfly, he swam the 100 meter in 55.1 seconds in the trials and the 200 meter in 2:03.89, after breaking the mark in the trial with 2:03.91. Other world marks posted at Houston were 4:02.08 for the 400-meter freestyle by Tom McBreen of San Mateo, Calif.; 17:19.2 in the women's 1,500 meter by Cathy Calhoun of Alhambra, Calif.; and 2:18.4 for the 200-meter butterfly by Ellie Daniel of Elkins Park, Pa.

In Leipzig, Spitz set a world mark of 1:54.2 for the 200-meter freestyle on September 4 and bettered it six days later at Minsk with 1:53.5 on the first leg of the 800-meter relay in which the United States broke the world record with 7:43.33. A double record-breaking performance had also taken place at Leipzig in the 400-meter relay. Roland Mattes, the East German star, bettered the mark for the 100-meter backstroke with a 56.71-second clocking, but the Americans won the event in 3:50.4, taking four seconds off the world mark.

However, the Americans did not have the swimming world to themselves. Shane Gould, a 14-year-old Australian girl, bettered four world marks and tied one. Miss Gould first showed her speed in London, on April 30, by equaling the world mark for 100 meters in 58.9 seconds. The next day she set a world mark of 2:06.5 for 200 meters. In Santa Clara, Calif., on July 9, Miss Gould swam the 400-meter freestyle in 4:21.2 She rested until November, then broke her own mark for 200 meters with 2:05.8 at Sydney and posted one of 4:21.6 for 800 meters. Then, on December 12, she bettered Cathy Calhoun's newly accepted 1,500-meter mark with 17:06, giving her world marks in all the standard metric-distance events.

TENNIS

"Love," one of the terms peculiar to the game of tennis, was not apparent in the dealings between the amateur and professional administrators of the sport in 1971. The International Lawn Tennis Association, firm in its intention to control the tournaments under its sanction, refused to allow World Championship Tennis (the Lamar Hunt group, which directs the contract men pros) or other professional groups to dominate the game by getting more money in guarantees. In July, ILTA said that as of Jan. 1, 1972, the contract pros would be banned from their tournaments (including Wimbledon and Forest Hills). The amateur groups of the various countries, of course, backed the ILTA.

UPI

CHRIS EVERT, 16-year-old tennis sensation, displays winning form in upsetting Britain's Virginia Wade in match that clinched U. S. victory in Wightman Cup play.

On the playing courts, the biggest excitement was provided by two girls, Chris Evert of Fort Lauderdale, Fla., and Evonne Goolagong, a descendant of Australian aborigines. Chris Evert, 16, beat Virginia Wade of Britain in the decisive match of the Wightman Cup tourney, which the United States won, 4 matches to 3. When she continued in the United States Open to defeat higher rated players, she became a sensation and drew crowds to Forest Hills. She was finally stopped, after 46 straight singles match victories, by Billie Jean King, who won the championship.

Miss Goolagong, 19, won the Wimbledon singles title by defeating Margaret Smith Court, 6–4, 6–1, after winning the French title. John Newcombe, a contract pro from Australia, won at Wimbledon, and Stan Smith of Pasadena, Calif., a member of the U. S. Army, took the men's singles at Forest Hills, beating Jan Kodes of Czechoslovakia, the French champion.

With Smith winning two matches and Frank Froehling one, the United States retained the Davis Cup with a 3–2 victory over Rumania in the last Challenge Round competition. Beginning in 1972, the cupholder will play through the zone eliminations as the other nations do.

EVONNE GOOLAGONG of Australia, 19, demonstrates agility and power that brought her singles titles in Wimbledon Open and French Open.

UPI

Mrs. King became the first woman athlete to win over $100,000 in a year with her successes in the women's pro play. Rod Laver, of Australia, did not win any major tourneys, but he earned $292,717 and became the first to go over the $1 million mark in career tennis earnings. He swept all 13 matches in the Tennis Champions Classic and had $160,000 by March 19. Ilie Nastase defeated Smith in the final of the Pepsi Grand Prix in Paris in December.

Tennis Highlights

Major Tournaments

Davis Cup—United States (defeated Rumania, 3-2, at Charlotte, N. C., Oct. 8–10)

Wightman Cup (women)—United States (defeated Britain, 4-3, at Cleveland Heights, Ohio, Aug. 21–23)

Federation Cup (women)—Australia (defeated Britain, 3-0, at Perth)

Stevens Cup (seniors)—United States (defeated Australia in Challenge Round, 3-2, at Forest Hills, N. Y.)

U. S. Open (Forest Hills, N. Y., Sept. 1–15)—men's singles: Stan Smith, Pasadena, Calif.; women's singles: Billie Jean King, Long Beach, Calif.; men's doubles: John Newcombe, Australia, and Roger Taylor, Britain; women's doubles: Rosemary Casals, San Francisco, and Judy Dalton, Australia; mixed doubles: Billie Jean King and Owen Davidson, Australia; men's senior doubles: Straight Clark, Haverford, Pa., and Vic Seixas, Villanova, Pa.

U. S. Clay Court Amateur (Chattanooga, Tenn.)—men's singles: Harold Soloman, Houston; women's singles: Janice Metcalfe, Claremont, Calif.; men's doubles: Roscoe Tanner and Sandy Mayer, Lookout Mountain, Tenn.; women's doubles: Janice Metcalfe and Pamela Farmer, San Diego

U. S. Grass Court Amateur, Men (Southampton, N. Y., Aug. 9–16)—singles: John Gardner, Australia; doubles: Gene Scott, New York, and Vito Geralaitis, New York

U. S. Grass Court Amateur, Women (Wilmington, Del., Aug. 24–29)—singles: Marita Redondo, National City, Calif.; doubles: Pamela Farmer, San Diego, and Janice Metcalfe, Claremont, Calif.

U. S. Senior Grass Court (Baltimore)—singles: Chauncey Steele, Cambridge, Mass.; doubles: Chauncey Steele and Frank Thompson

U. S. Senior, Clay Court (Houston)—singles: Gustavo Palafox, Los Angeles; doubles: Bobby Riggs, Plandome, N. Y., and Tony Vincent, New York

U. S. Senior Women, Grass Court (Narragansett, R. I.)—singles: Betty Rosenquest Pratt, Maitland, Fla., doubles: Betty Pratt and Nancy Neeld, Albuquerque, N. Mex.

U. S. Men's Indoor Open (Salisbury, Md., Feb. 14–21)—singles: Clark Graebner, New York; doubles: Manuel Orantes and Juan Gisbert, Spain

U. S. Men's Indoor (Hampton, Va., March 3–7)—singles: Ilie Nastase, Rumania; doubles: Ilie Nastase and Ion Tiriac, Rumania

U. S. National Amateur Indoor (Salt Lake City, Jan. 28–31) singles: Roscoe Tanner, Lookout Mountain, Tenn.; doubles: Roscoe Tanner and Sandy Mayer, Lookout Mountain, Tenn.

U. S. Women's Indoor (Winchester, Mass., Feb. 24–28)—singles: Billie Jean King, Long Beach, Calif.

U. S. Clay Court (Indianapolis, Aug. 9–15)—men's singles: Zeljko Franulovic, Yugoslavia; women's singles: Billie Jean King, Long Beach, Calif.; men's doubles: Zeljko Franulovic and Jan Kodes, Czechoslovakia; women's doubles: Billie Jean King and July Dalton, Australia

Other U. S. Champions

National Collegiate (NCAA)—singles: Jimmy Connors, University of California, Los Angeles; doubles: Jeff Borowiak and Haroon Rahim, UCLA; team: UCLA (35 pts). College Division: singles: Bob Chappell, University of California, Irvine; doubles: Ron Lague and John Lowman, Rollins; team: University of California, Irvine (25 pts)

National Association of Intercollegiate Athletics—singles: George Amaya, Presbyterian; doubles: George Amaya and Milan Kofol, Presbyterian; team: Redlands (41 pts)

Women's National Collegiate—singles: Pam Richmond, Arizona State; doubles: Pam Richmond and Peggy Michel, Arizona State; team: Arizona State

American Tennis Association—singles: John Wilkerson, Houston; women's singles: Bessie Stockard, Washington, D. C.

USLTA Junior—singles: Raul Ramirez, LaJolla, Calif.; doubles: Chip Fisher, Palo Alto, Calif., and Jim Delaney, Washington

USLTA Girls—singles: Chris Evert, Fort Lauderdale, Fla.; doubles: Janet Newberry, LaJolla, Calif., and Eliza Pande, Palo Alto, Calif.

Interscholastic—singles: John Whitlinger, Shattuck; doubles: Bill Brock and Hunt Harris, Norfolk

Other Countries

Wimbledon Open (England, June 21–July 3)—men's singles: John Newcombe, Australia; women's singles: Evonne Goolagong, Australia; men's doubles: Roy Emerson and Rod Laver, Australia; women's doubles: Billie Jean King, Long Beach, Calif., and Rosemary Casals, San Francisco; mixed doubles: Billie Jean King and Owen Davidson, Australia; senior doubles: Gardner Mulloy, Miami Beach, Fla., and Tony Vincent, New York; junior singles: Bob Kreiss, Berkeley, Calif.; girl's singles: Marina Kroshina, USSR

Australian Open (Sydney, March 7–14)—men's singles: Ken Rosewall, Australia; women's singles: Margaret Smith Court, Australia; men's doubles: John Newcombe and Tony Roche, Australia; women's doubles: Margaret Smith Court and Evonne Goolagong, Australia

French Open (Paris, May 24–June 7)—men's singles: Jan Kodes, Czechoslovakia; women's singles: Evonne Goolagong, Australia; men's doubles: Arthur Ashe, Gun Spring, Va., and Marty Riessen, Evanston, Ill.; women's doubles: Françoise Durr and Gail Chanfreau, France; mixed doubles: Françoise Durr and Jean Claude Barclay, France

Canadian Open (Toronto, Aug. 10–16)—men's singles: John Newcombe, Australia; women's singles: Françoise Durr, France; men's doubles: Tom Okker, Netherlands, and Marty Riessen, Evanston, Ill.; women's doubles: Françoise Durr and Rosemary Casals, San Francisco

Canadian Closed (Winnipeg)—men's singles: Peter Burwash; women's singles: Vicky Berner; men's doubles: Peter Burwash and K. Binns; women's doubles: Vicky Berner and Jane O'Hara

LEADING MONEY WINNERS IN 1971
World Championship Tennis Tour
(Contract Professionals)

Rod Laver	$289,841	Marty Riessen	$76,069
Ken Rosewall	137,687	Cliff Drysdale	69,078
Tom Okker	120,564	Bob Lutz	58,392
Arthur Ashe	99,746	Roy Emerson	46,052
John Newcombe	97,764	Andres Gimeno	34,512

World Championship of Tennis—Ken Rosewall (defeated Rod Laver in final, 6–4, 1–6, 7–6, 7–6, for $50,000)

Pepsi Grand Prix
(Independent Professionals)

Stan Smith	$25,000	Pierre Barthes	$ 9,500
Ilie Nastase	17,000	Clark Graebner	8,500
Zeljko Franulovic	15,000	Tom Gorman	7,500
Jan Kodes	12,000	Frank Froehling	6,500
Cliff Richey	10,500	Roger Taylor	6,000

Masters Tourney (Paris)—Nastase won all six matches and $15,000.

Virginia Slims Tour

Billy Jean King	$95,950	Nancy Gunter	$15,300
Rosemary Casals	53,950	Mary Ann Eisel	10,175
Françoise Durr	44,175	Julie Heldman	9,900
Kerry Melville	29,767	Valerie Ziegenfuss	9,700
Judy Dalton	28,867	Kathy Pigeon	6,367
Ann Jones	25,700	Peaches Bartkowicz	5,650

TRACK AND FIELD

Pat Matzdorf of the University of Wisconsin took care of the one field-event record that had managed to stay on the books the longest. On July 3 at Berkeley, Calif., he cleared 7 feet 6¼ inches in the high jump, bettering the mark of 7′ 5¾″ held by Valery Brumel of the Soviet Union. The feat was achieved in a meet against the Russians and a World All-Star team. Brumel had set his mark in a U. S.-USSR competition in 1963.

The most exciting event of the track year, however, was the "dream mile" race between Jim Ryun and Marty Liquori. Ryun, holder of world records in the mile, half-mile, and 1,500-meter runs, had returned to competition after an 18-month layoff. Liquori was the reigning mile champion, with a string of victories in national and collegiate events. They met in the King Games at Franklin Field, Philadelphia, on May 16. The 21-year-old Liquori, from Cedar Grove, N. J., set the pace in the field of 11 after the half and the 24-year-old Ryun could not quite catch up in the stretch. Liquori's time was 3 minutes 54.6 seconds, and Ryun was a stride back.

One of the astounding stories of the sport was that of Dr. Delano Meriwether, a 27-year-old hematologist who was doing cancer research in Baltimore. He popped up as a contestant in a Maryland indoor 60-yard dash and triumphed. He repeated at Boston, beating some of the nation's leading sprinters. Garbed in a white T-shirt and yellow swim trunks held up by striped suspenders, he captured the 100-yard dash at the National Amateur Athletic Union championships in Eugene, Oreg., in June. When queried about his experience and his instruction, Meriwether revealed that he had never competed in track before and that he did much of his training running up and down the stairs at his home.

His inspiration to become a sprinter had come from television. After watching the running of the 100-yard event the year before, Meriwether remarked to his wife, "I think I can beat those guys." When he did so at Eugene, his wind-assisted (therefore, not recognized) time was 9 seconds, equaling the fastest time recorded for the event.

In track, three world records fell in the standard events. John Smith of UCLA broke the mark for the 440-yard run with a clocking of 44.5 seconds in the AAU meet. The record of 44.7 was held by Curtis Mills. In the same meet, Rod Milburn of Southern University bettered the mark for the 120-yard high hurdles by a fifth of a second, with a 13-second clocking in the semifinals. Six hurdlers had shared the previous record. The mark for the 2-mile run was broken by Emiel Puttemans of Belgium, at Edinburgh in August, with 8:17.8. Ron Clarke had held the record with 8:19.6.

Two other field records held by Soviet stars were broken. Victor Saneyev's mark for the triple jump was exceeded by Pedro Perez of Cuba in the Pan-American Games by one-quarter inch with a 57′ 1″ effort. Antoly Bondarchuk's various official and unofficial marks for the hammer throw (as well as West German Uwe Beyer's 245′ 8½″) were all wiped out by Walter Schmidt of West Germany. The 6-foot 3-inch, 287-pound athlete threw the weight 250 feet 8 inches at Lahr, West Germany, on September 4.

The Atoms Track Club of Brooklyn set a world record for the one-mile relay in the women's National AAU meet. Gale Fitzgerald, Linda Reynolds, Denise Hooten, and Cheryl Toussaint posted a time of 3:38.8 at Bakersfield, Calif., on July 9. But it lasted just over a week. In a U. S.-Africa meet at Durham, N. C., on July 17, Esther Stroy, Mavis Laing, Gwen Norman, and Cheryl Toussaint did 3:38.7.

Track and Field Highlights

Men's AAU Indoor Championships
(Madison Square Garden, N. Y., Feb. 26)

60 Yards—Jean-Louis Ravelomanantsoa, Westmont College (0:06.1)
600 Yards—Andrzej Badenski, Poland (1:10.7)
1,000 Yards—Tom Von Ruden, Pacific Coast Club, Long Beach, Calif. (2:07.3)
Mile—Henryk Szordykowski, Poland (4:06)
3 Miles—Frank Shorter, Florida Track Club, Gainesville (13:10.6)
60-Yard Hurdles—Willie Davenport, unattached (0:07)
Mile Walk—Ron Laird, New York A. C. (6:24.9)
Mile Relay—Villanova (Ken Schappert, Bob Carpenter, Greg Govan, LaMotte Hyman; 3:16.9)
2-Mile Relay—Univ. of Chicago Track Club (Bob O'Connor, Ken Sparks, Ralph Schultz, Lowell Paul; 7:28.6)
Sprint Medley Relay—Pacific Coast Club (Jay Elbel, Bob Frey, Terry Musika, Len Van Hofwegen; 1:53.9)
Pole Vault—Dick Railsback, Southern California Striders, Hollywood (17 ft 6¾ in)
High Jump—Reynaldo Brown, California T. C., Berkeley (7 ft 2 in)
Long Jump—Norman Tate, New York Pioneers (26 ft 4½ in)
Triple Jump—Dave Smith, California T. C. (53 ft. 4¾ in)
Shot Put—Al Feuerbach, Pacific Coast Club (66 ft)
35-Pound Weight—George Frenn, Pacific Coast Club (71 ft 3½ in)

Men's AAU Outdoor Championships
(Eugene, Oreg., June 25–26)

100 Yards—Delano Meriwether, Baltimore Olympic Club (0:09; wind-aided)
220 Yards—Don Quarrie, Southern California Striders, Hollywood (0:20.2; wind-aided)
440 Yards—John Smith, Southern California Striders (0:44.5; betters world record)
880 Yards—Juris Luzins, U. S. Marines (1:47.1)
Mile—Marty Liquori, New York A. C. (3:56.5)
3 Miles—Steve Prefontaine, Oregon T. C., Eugene (12:58.6)
6 Miles—Frank Shorter, Florida T. C., Gainesville (27:27.2)
3,000-Meter Steeplechase—Sid Sink, Bowling Green (8:26.4; U. S. record)
2-Mile Walk—Larry Young, Mid-America T. C., Kansas City (13:49.5)
120-Yard High Hurdles—Rod Milburn, Southern Univ. (0:13.1; wind-aided; in semifinal, Milburn bettered world record with 0:13.0)
440-Yard Intermediate Hurdles—Ralph Mann, Southern California Striders (0:49.3)
Discus—Tim Vollmer, U. S. Army (208 ft 4 in)
Hammer—George Frenn, Pacific Coast Club (230 ft 1 in)
Javelin—Bill Skinner, New York A. C. (267 ft 2 in)
Shot Put—Karl Salb, Mid-America T. C. (67 ft 2¾ in)
Long Jump—Arnie Robinson, San Diego T. C. (26 ft 10¾ in)
Triple Jump—John Craft, Univ. of Chicago T. C. (54 ft 7 in)
High Jump—Reynaldo Brown, California International T. C., Los Angeles (7 ft 3 in)
Pole Vault—Jan Johnson, Univ. of Chicago T. C. (17 ft)

Women's AAU Indoor Championships
(Madison Square Garden, N. Y., Feb. 26)

60 Yards—Pat Hawkins, Atoms T. C., Brooklyn, N. Y. (0:06.9)
220 Yards—Esther Stroy, Sports International, Washington (0:24.6)
440 Yards—Jarvis Scott, Los Angeles Mercurettes (0:55.3)
880 Yards—Abby Hoffman, Canada (2:08.7)
Mile—Doris Brown, Falcons T. C., Seattle (4:47.9)
60-Yard Hurdles—Patty Johnson, Angels T. C., Tacoma, Wash. (0:07.8)
640-Yard Relay—Atoms T. C. (Renee DeSandes, Michelle McMillan, Denise Hooten, Brenda Merritt; 1:14.2)
Medley Relay—Atoms T. C. (Gail Fitzgerald, Carmen Smith Brown, Denise Hooten, Pat Hawkins; 1:46.8)
Mile Relay—Atoms T. C. (Michele McMillan, Shelley Marshall, Gail Fitzgerald, Cheryl Toussaint; 3:54.5)
Shot Put—Lynette Matthews, Falcons T. C. (49 ft 7¾ in)
High Jump—Snezana Hrepevnik, Yugoslavia (6 ft ½ in)
Long Jump—Marilyn King, Millbrae (Calif.) Lions (19 ft 10¾ in)
Team—Atoms Track Club, Brooklyn, N. Y. (30 pts)

(Continued on following page)

Track and Field Highlights (continued)

Women's AAU Outdoor Championships
(Bakersfield, Calif., July 9–10)

100 Meters—Iris Davis, Tennessee State (0:11.2)
200 Meters—Raelene Boyle, Australia (0:23.1)
400 Meters—Mabel Ferguson, West Coast Jets, Pomona, Calif (0:53.3)
800 Meters—Cheryl Toussaint, Atoms T. C., Brooklyn, N. Y. (2:04.3)
1,500 Meters—Kathy Gibbons, Glendale (Ariz.) T. C. (4:19.2)
100-Meter Hurdles—Pat Johnson, Angels T. C., Tacoma, Wash. (0:13.5)
200-Meter Hurdles—Pat Hawkins, Atoms T. C. (0:26.1; U. S. record)
2 Miles—Doris Brown, Falcons T. C., Seattle (10:07)
Mile Walk—Lynn Olson, Wolverine Parkettes, Detroit (7:53.8)
440-Yard Relay—Tennessee State (Diane Hughes, Debra Wentworth, Mattline Render, Iris Davis; 0:48.2; Tiger Belles bettered world record with 0:44.7 in heat)
Mile Relay—Atoms T. C. (Gale Fitzgerald, Linda Reynolds, Denise Hooten, Cheryl Toussaint; 3:38.8; betters world record)
2-Mile Relay—San Jose Cindergals (8:53.6)
880-Yard Medley Relay—Angels T. C. (1:43.5)
Long Jump—Kim Attlesey, Lakewood (Calif.) Spartans (20 ft 8¾ in)
High Jump—Linda Iddings, Angels T. C. (5 ft 8 in)
Javelin—Sherry Calvert, Torrance, Calif. (175 ft 7 in)
Shot Put—Lynn Graham, Fresno (Calif.) Elans (52 ft)
Discus—Josephine de la Bina, Mayor Daley Y. F., Chicago (175 ft 6 in)

U. S. Track and Field Federation Indoor Championships
(Houston Astrodome, Feb. 12–13)
University Division

100 Yards—Cliff Branch, Colorado (0:09.5)
440 Yards—Louis Vicenik, Houston T. C. (0:47)
880 Yards—Mark Wizenreid, Wisconsin (1:49.5)
Mile—Marty Liquori, Villanova (3:57.18)
2 Miles—Sid Sink, Bowling Green (8:34.2)
120-Yard Hurdles—Paul Gibson, Texas-El Paso (0:13.7)
Sprint Medley Relay—Wisconsin (Jim Nichols, Bill Bahnfelth, Mark Kartman, Mark Wizenreid; 3:18)
Distance Medley Relay—Villanova (Wilson Smith, Lamotte Haymon, Chris Mason, Marty Liquori; 9:31.5)
Mile Relay—Oklahoma State (Jim Bolding, Chris Martin, Dennis Schultz, Stan Stolpe; 3:07.84)
2-Mile Relay—Wisconsin (Charles Curtis, Charles Baker, Don Vandrey, Mark Wizenreid; 7:19.8)
Long Jump—Danny Brabham, Baylor (24 ft 8¾ in)
Triple Jump—Pat Onyango, Wisconsin (51 ft 7¾ in)
High Jump—Pat Matzdorf, Wisconsin (7 ft)
Pole Vault—Scott Hurley, Florida (16 ft 6 in)
Shot Put—Karl Salb, Kansas (66 ft ¼ in)

U. S. Track and Field Federation Outdoor Championships
(Wichita, Kans., June 11–12)

100 Yards—George Daniels, Colorado (0:09.2)
220 Yards—George Daniels (0:20.7)
440 Yards—Jay Elbel, Pacific Coast Club (0:46)
880 Yards—Tom Von Ruden, Pacific Coast Club (1:48.2)
Mile—Greg Fredericks, Penn State (4:08.6)
3 Miles—Sid Sink, Bowling Green (13:23.4)
6 Miles—Doug Brown, 2d, Tennessee (28:31.8)
3,000-Meter Steeplechase—Conrad Nightingale, M. A. T. C. (8:46.6)
120-Yard Hurdles—Bill High, Tennessee (0:13.4)
440-Yard Hurdles—Dick Bruggeman, Ohio T. C., Columbus (0:50.2)
440-Yard Relay—Colorado (Cliff Branch, George Daniels, Larry Brunson, Marcus Walker; 0:39.5)
Mile Relay—Tennessee (James Craig, Audry Hardy, Bill James, Darwin Bond; 3:05)
Pole Vault—Jan Johnson, Alabama T. C. (17 ft 3¼ in)
High Jump—Bill Elliott, Pacific Coast Club (7 ft 1 in)
Triple Jump—John Craft, Univ. of Chicago T. C. (54 ft 11½ in)
Long Jump—Preston Carrington, Wichita State (25 ft 11¾ in)
Discus—Rich Fuhs, Univ. of Chicago T. C. (183 ft 7 in)
Shot Put—Randy Matson, Texas Striders, Houston (68 ft 1¾ in)
Javelin—Sam Colson, Kansas (247 ft 7 in)
Hammer—Jacques Accambray, Kent State (213 ft 5 in)
Decathlon—Norm Johnston, unattached (7,298 pts)
Team—Pacific Coast Club, Long Beach, Calif. (72 pts)

National Collegiate (NCAA) Indoor Championships
(Detroit, March 12–13)

60 Yards—Jim Green, Kentucky (0:06)
440 Yards—Tom Ulan, Rutgers (0:48.8)
600 Yards—Tommie Turner, Murray State (1:09.6)
880 Yards—Mark Wizenreid, Wisconsin (1:50.9)
1,000 Yards—Bob Wheeler, Duke (2:07.4)
Mile—Marty Liquori, Villanova (4:04.7)
2 Miles—Marty Liquori (8:37.1)
Invitation Mile—Chuck LaBenz, Long Beach, Calif. (4:00.9)
60-Yard Hurdles—Marcus Walker, Colorado (0:07)

Mile Relay—Adelphi (Ray Lee, Keith Davis, Dennis Walker, Clyde McPherson; 3:15.5)
2-Mile Relay—Texas-El Paso (Peter Romero, Fernando DeLaCerda, Rod Hill, Kerry Ellison; 7:37.4)
Distance Medley Relay—Pittsburgh (Ken Silay, Doral Watley, Mike Schurko, Jerry Richey; 9:45.7)
High Jump—Pat Matzdorf, Wisconsin (7 ft 2 in)
Pole Vault—Scott Wallick, Miami, Ohio (16 ft 8 in)
Long Jump—Henry Hines, So. California (26 ft 1¼ in)
Triple Jump—Mohinder Gill, California Polytechnic at San Luis Obisco (52 ft 9¾ in)
Shot Put—Karl Salb, Kansas (65 ft 9 in)
35-Pound Weight Throw—Al Schoterman, Kent State (68 ft 10¼ in)
Team—Villanova (22 pts)

National Collegiate (NCAA) Outdoor Championships
(Seattle, June 17–19)

100 Yards—Harrington Jackson, Texas-El Paso (0:09.5)
220 Yards—Larry Black, North Carolina Central (0:20.5)
440 Yards—John Smith, UCLA (0:45.3)
880 Yards—Mark Wizenreid, Wisconsin (1:48.8)
Mile—Marty Liquori, Villanova (3:57.6)
3 Miles—Steve Prefontaine, Oregon (13:20)
6 Miles—Garry Bjorklund, Minnesota (27:43)
3,000-Meter Steeplechase—Sid Sink, Bowling Green (8:31)
120-Yard Hurdles—Rod Milburn, Southern Univ. (0:13.6)
400-Yard Hurdles—Ralph Mann, Brigham Young (0:49.6)
Mile Relay—UCLA (Warren Edmonson, Reggie Echols, John Smith, Wayne Collett; 3:04.4)
440-Yard Relay—So. California (Lance Babb, Edesel Garrison, Leon Brown, Willie Deckard; 0:39.5)
Shot Put—Karl Salb, Kansas (66 ft 11½ in)
Discus—Mike Louisiana, Brigham Young (194 ft 10 in)
Javelin—Carl Feldmann, Washington (259 ft)
Hammer—Jacques Accambray, Kent State (227 ft 10 in)
High Jump—Reynaldo Brown, California Polytechnic at San Luis Obisco (7 ft 3 in)
Long Jump—James (Bouncy) Moore, Oregon (25 ft 9¾ in)
Triple Jump—Mohinder Gill, California Polytechnic at St. Luis Obisco (55 ft 1¼ in)
Pole Vault—Dave Roberts, Rice (17 ft 6½ in)
Decathlon—Ray Hipp, Ohio State (7,456 pts)
Team—University of California, Los Angeles (52 pts)

Other AAU Events

440-Yard Relay—New York Pioneer Club (0:40.9)
Mile Relay—United A. A., New York (3:11.5)
Two-Mile Relay—New York Pioneer Club (7:37)
Four-Mile Relay—New York A. C. (17:37)
Distance Medley Relay—New York A. C. (9:59.8)
All-Around—Richard Robinson, New York A. C. (7,279 pts)

Decathlon and Pentathlon Champions

AAU Decathlon—Rick Wanamaker, Des Moines (7,989 pts)
USTFF Decathlon—Rick Wanamaker (7,693 pts)
NCAA Decathlon—Ray Hipp, Ohio State (7,456)
NAIA Decathlon—Bruce Jenner, Graceland (7,407)
AAU Pentathlon—Rick Wanamaker (3,307)

Other Team Championships

NCAA College Division—Kentucky State (42 pts)
NAIA—Eastern Michigan (65)
IC4-A—Indoor: Villanova (42); outdoor: Villanova (32)

International Competitions

At Berkeley, Calif. (July 2–3)—Men's dual meets: U. S. 126; USSR 110; U. S. 138, World All-Stars 91; Triangular: U. S. 178, USSR 163, World All-Stars 111.—Women's dual: USSR 76, U. S. 60; U. S. 80, World All-Stars 53; Triangular: USSR 110½, U. S. 88, World All-Stars 57
At Durham, N. C. (July 16–17)—Men: U. S. 111, Africa 78; Women: U. S. 79, World 53

Marathons

AAU—Ken Moore, Oregon Track Club (2:16:48.6)
Boston—Alvaro Meija, Colombia (2:18:45)
Canadian—John Cliff, Ontario (2:24:57)
USTFF—Bruce Mortenson, Twin Cities T. C. (2:27:46)
Masters—Dennis Coveney, Canada (2:39:00.2); 50–59 Years: Wayne Zook (3:06:33); 60–69: Urban Miller (3:20:47); 70-up: Noel Johnson (4:48:48)

AAU Runs

20 kilometers—Bob Fitts, New York (1:02:55.4)
25 kilometers—Bob Fitts (1:21:39)
30 kilometers—Mike Kimball, Ohio (1:36:26.6, on course run ¼-mile too long because of wrong turn)
One-Hour—Greg Brock (12 miles, 194 yards)
3,000-meter Team Race—New York A. C. (17 pts)

AAU Walks

10 kilometers—Ron Laird, Los Angeles (0:47:09.9)
15 kilometers—Jose Olivares, Mexico (1:06:24)
20 kilometers—Tom Dooley (1:32:18)
25 kilometers—Laird (2:01:48.4)
30 kilometers—Larry Young Independence, Mo. (2:25:40)
35 kilometers—Larry Young (3:02:22)
40 kilometers—Larry Young (3:29:18)
50 kilometers—Larry Young (4:18:29.2)

ARCHERY

World Championships
(York, England, July 29–31)

Men—John Williams, Cranesville, Pa. (2,445 pts); team: United States (7,050)
Women—Emma Gapchenko, USSR (2,380); team: Poland (6,907)

National Field Archery Association Championships
(Cedar City, Utah, July 27–29)

Men—Open bare bow: David Hughes, Irving, Texas (2,106); amateur bare bow: Mike Flier, Pekin, Ill. (1,947); young adult boys bare bow: Scott Mitchell, Bloomington, Ind. (1,960); open freestyle: Victor Leach, Sacramento, Calif. (2,208); amateur freestyle: Gary Lyman, Baywood Park, Calif. (2,213); young adult boys freestyle: Don Rabska, South Lake Tahoe, Calif. (2,087); open bow hunter: Cal Vogt, Canoga Park, Calif. (1,870); over 55 open freestyle: Ed Bain, Vancouver, Wash. (2,082)
Women—Open bare bow: Evvy Briney, Fullerton, Calif. (1,735); young adult girls bare bow: Rulona Rolland, Houston, Texas (1,114); open freestyle: Darlene Collier, Moab, Utah (2,144); amateur freestyle: Phyllis L. Long, La Puente, Calif. (1,935); young adult girls freestyle: Gloria Ward, West Covina, Calif. (942); open bow hunter: Thoma Arnberg, Yreka, Calif. (1,213); over 55 open freestyle: Sandy Elott, Atlanta, Ga. (1,541); over 55 amateur freestyle: Jewel Hamilton, Flagstaff, Ariz. (1,648)

National Archery Association Championships
(Oxford, Ohio, Aug. 9–13)

Men—John Williams, Cranesville, Pa. (2,281); crossbow: George Hall, Somerville, N. J. (2,930); team: Pheasdale Archers, Philadelphia (3,200)
Women—Doreen Wilber, Jefferson City, Iowa (2,766); crossbow: Ann Neill, Cape May Court House, N. J. (2,640); team: York (Pa.) Archers (2,969)

U. S. Open Indoor Championships
(Las Vegas, Nev., Jan. 29–31)

Men—Jack Lancaster, Air Force Academy (600; defeated Bill Mills, Phoenix, in shoot-off); amateur: Gary Lyman, Baywood Park, Calif. (596)
Women—Denise Libby, Rancho Cordova, Calif. (593); amateur: Phyllis Long, La Puente, Calif. (562)

Professional Archers Association Championships
(Grayling, Mich., Sept. 9–12)

Men—Jim Riley, Bellbrook, Ohio (1,177)
Women—Ann Butz, Suffern, N. Y. (1,139)

BADMINTON

All-England Championships (Wembley, England, March 24–27)—Men's singles: Rudy Hartono, Indonesia; women's singles: Eva Twedberg, Sweden; men's doubles: Ng Boon Bee and Punch Gunala, Malaysia; women's doubles: Noriko Takagi and Hiroe Yuki, Japan; mixed doubles: Sven Pri and Ulla Strand, Denmark
United States Open Championships (Las Vegas, Nev., April 12–14)—Men's singles: Muljadi, Indonesia; women's singles: Noriko Takagi, Japan; men's doubles: Ng Boon Bee and Punch Gunala, Malaysia; women's doubles: Noriko Takagi and Hiroe Yuki, Japan; mixed doubles: Jim Poole, Northridge, Calif., and Maryann Breckell, Los Angeles; senior men's singles: Ted Moehlmann, St. Louis; senior men's doubles: Ted Moehlmann and Jim McQuie, Kirkwood, Mo.; senior women's doubles: Lois Alston, Pasadena, Calif., and Beulah Armendariz, Sherman Oaks, Calif.; senior mixed doubles: Ted Moehlmann and Ethel Marshall, Buffalo
United States Closed Championships (Las Vegas, April 8–11)—Men's singles: Stan Hales, Claremont, Calif.; women's singles: Diane Hales, Claremont, Calif.; men's doubles: Don Paup, East Lansing, Mich., and Jim Poole, Northridge, Calif.; women's doubles: Caroline Hein, Seattle, and Clarene Starkey, San Diego; mixed doubles: Don Paup and Helen Tibbetts, Los Angeles
Canadian Open Championships (Montreal, April 2–4)—Men's singles: Rudy Hartono, Indonesia; women's singles: Hiroe Yuki, Japan; men's doubles: Ng Boon Bee and Punch Gunala, Malaysia; women's doubles: Noriko Takagi and Hiroe Yuki, Japan; mixed doubles: Ng Boon Bee and Sylvia Ng, Malaysia

BOBSLEDDING

World Championships (Cervinia, Italy, Jan. 23–31)—2-man: Giafranco Gaspari, driver, and Mario Armano, Italy (2-heat total, 2:22.80); 4-man: Rene Stadler, driver, Max Forster, Eric Schaerer, Peter Schaerer, brake, Switzerland (2-heat total, 2:19.35)
National AAU Championships (Lake Placid, N. Y., Feb. 6–7)—2-man: Paul Lamey, driver, and Robert Huscher, U. S. Navy (4-heat total, 4:45.06); 4-man: James Hickey, driver, Larry Kilburn, James Bridges, Thomas Becker, brake, U. S. Air Force (4-heat total, 4:30.73)
Kennedy Games (Lake Placid, N. Y., Feb. 14–15, 20–21)—2-man: Enzo Vicario, driver, and Corrado del Fabbro, Italy (4-heat total, 4:33.86); 4-man: United States, Jim Hickey, driver (2-heat total, 2:14.04)

BOWLING

American Bowling Congress Tournament (Detroit, March 6–May 23)—Regular Division: singles: Al Cohn, Chicago (738); doubles: Tony Maresca and Bill Haley, Mesa, Ariz. (1,330); all-events: Al Cohn (2,063); team: Carter Tool & Die, Rochester, N. Y. (3,239). Classic Division: singles: Victor Iwlew, Kalamazoo, Mich. (750); doubles: Bill Zuben and Barry Warshafsky, Cranston, R. I. (1,357); all-events: Gary Dickinson, Fort Worth, Texas (2,000); team: Chester Lio Investments, Houston, Texas (3,081; score posted in 3-game roll-off among 6 highest teams). Booster Division: Bay Jewelers, Norfolk, Va. (2,856)
Women's International Bowling Congress (Atlanta, April 8–May 23)—Open Division: singles: Ginny Younginer, Winnsboro, S. C. (667); doubles: Dotty Fothergill North Attleboro, Mass., and Millie Martorella, Rochester, N. Y. (1,263); all-events: Lorrie J. Koch, Carpenterville, Ill. (1,840); team: Koenig and Stray, Wilmette, Ill. (2,891). Division I: singles: Mary Scruggs, Richmond, Va. (698); doubles: Judy Bell, Lithonia, Ga., and Daisy Trout, Marietta, Ga. (1,194); all-events: Joyce Mooney, Pittsburgh (1,721); team: Peeples Beauty Saloon, Detroit (2,659). Division II: singles: Shrlye White, Kansas City, Mo. (583); doubles: Sharon Chambers and June Durham, Jacksonville, Fla. (1,088); all-events: Kathleen Morgan, Devonshire, Bermuda (1,624); team: Lady Bugs, Marietta, Ga. (2,366)
World Championships (Milwaukee, Aug. 21–28)—Men: all-events: Ed Luther, Racine, Wis. (5,968); doubles: Rolando Sebelen and Carlos Diaz, Puerto Rico (2,520); 5-man team: United States (6,194); 8-man team: United States (12,691). Women: all-events: Ashie Gonzalez, San Juan, Puerto Rico (4,535); doubles: Yashimi Fukuda and Michiko Hirooka, Japan (2,302); 4-woman team: United States (4,656); 5-woman team: United States (5,474)
Professional Bowlers Association National Championship (Paramus, N. J., Oct. 10–16)—Mike Limongello, North Babylon, N. Y. (defeated Dave Davis, Miami, Fla., 207–202, in final match)
Bowling Proprietors' Association of America Open Championship (St. Paul, Jan. 9)—Mike Limongello (defeated Teata Semiz, River Edge, N. J., 194–186, in championship game)

Intercollegiate

Association of College Unions–International (Detroit, at ABC tournament)—Singles: Roger Dalkin, Georgia Tech (648); doubles: Dirk Jackson, West Virginia, and Ely Tomines, Colorado State (1,139); all-events: Roger Dalkin (2,020)
National Association of Intercollegiate Athletics (Kansas City, Mo., April 23–24)—Singles: Steve Rumbaugh, West Virginia State (2,894); doubles: Dave Hudson and Glen Hanmer, Harding (804); team: Harding, Ark. (16,294); individual award: John Younger, Claremont-Mudd (defeated Rumbaugh in roll-off, 398–393)
National Duckpin Bowling Congress (Hagerstown, Md., April 3–May 9)—Men: singles: Joe Bitner, Hagerstown (488); doubles: Ed Brown and Paul Sharpe, Washington (871); all-events: Don Meyd, Baltimore (1,336); team: Auto Electric Service, Hagerstown (2,114). Women: singles: Sue Marchone, Washington (460); doubles: Betty Stevens and Allena Roberts, Washington (826); all-events: Peggy Nichols, Baltimore (1,236); team: Overlea Catering, Baltimore (1,861); mixed doubles: Kathy Vail, Glastonbury, Conn., and Alan Hickox, Quinnipiac, Conn. (843)

BRIDGE, CONTRACT

World Team (Taipei, Taiwan, finals, May 15–17)—North America (represented by Dallas Aces—Oswald Jacoby, non-playing captain; Jim Jacoby, Bob Wolff, Mike Lawrence, Bob Goldman, Bill Eisenberg, and Bob Hamman, with Ira Corn, deputy captain) defeated France in final

Spring Nationals
(Atlanta, March 12–22)

Men's Pairs—Georgio Belladonna and Benito Garozzo, Italy
Women's Pairs—Jacqui Mitchell and Amalya Kearse, New York
Men's Team—Alvin Roth, Paul Trent, Alan Sontag, and Bernard Chasen, New York
Women's Team—Tie between team of Katherine Wei, Gail Moss, Judi Friedenberg, all of New York; Marietta Passell, Hartsdale, N. Y., and Helen Utegard, Bethesda, Md.; and team of Barbara Rappaport, East Orange, N. J.; Roberta Epstein, South Orange, N. J., Edith Kemp, Miami Beach, Fla., Gratian Goldstein, Coral Gables, Fla., and Sylvia Stein, Southfield, Mich.
Men's Open Pairs—Tie between Vince and Joan Remey, Southfield, Mich., and Barry Crane, Los Angeles, and Dr. John Fisher, Dallas
Vanderbilt Cup—Bill Eisenberg, Bob Goldman, Bob Hamman, Jim Jacoby, Mike Lawrence, Bob Wolff, and nonplaying captain Ira Corn, all of Dallas

Summer Nationals
(Chicago, July 16–28)

Master Mixed Team—Sue Picus, Parsippany, N. J., Roland Anderson, Wichita, Kans., Marilyn McCrary, Lake City, Iowa, John Anderson, Springfield, Mo.

Life Master Pairs—Alvin Roth, New York, and Barbara Rappaport, East Orange, N. J.
Golden Master Pairs—Chuck Lamprey, White Plains, N. Y., and Sharyn Linkovsky, Montreal
Open Pairs—Brian and Beverly Nelson, Rockport, Ill.
Women's Pairs—Barbara Rappaport, East Orange, N. J., and Roberta Epstein, South Orange, N. J.
Spingold Knockout Team—Joel Stuart, Steve Altman, Peter Weichsel, Gene Neiger, all of New York, and Tom Smith, Greenwich, Conn.

Winter Nationals
(Phoenix, Ariz., Nov. 19–28)

Mixed Pairs—Lew and Eugenie Mathe, Los Angeles
Life Master Men's Pairs—Peter Weichsel and Alan Sontag, New York
Life Master Women's Pairs—Belle Levinson, Skokie, Ill., and Ruth Bloomfield, Chicago
Men's Pairs—Jerry Gaer, San Francisco, and Colby Vernay, Lacon, Ill.
Women's Pairs—Myrna Bergman and Margie Gwozinsky, New York
Open Pairs—Joe Titone, Gardena, Calif., and Irv Kostel, Sherman Oaks, Calif.
Reisinger Board-a-Match Team—George Rapee, William Grieve, Edgar Kaplan, New York; Norman Kaye, Philadelphia; Lew Mathe and Don Krauss, Los Angeles

CANOEING

United States Championships
(Rockford, Ill., Aug. 7–8)

Men's Kayak

Singles, 500 Meters—Henry Krawczyk, Sebago Canoe Club, Brooklyn, N. Y. (1:59.2)
Singles, 1,000 Meters—Tony Ralphs, Newport Beach, Calif. (4:06.1)
Singles, 10,000 Meters—Tony Ralphs (41:53.1)
Tandem, 500 Meters—Tony Ralphs and Bill Leach, Newport Beach, Calif. (1:49.5)
Tandem, 1,000 Meters—Tony Ralphs and Bill Leach (3:46.2)
Tandem, 10,000 Meters—Al Whitney and Jack Brosius, Washington (D. C.) Canoe Club (39:53.1)
Fours, 1,000 Meters—Washington C. C. (Al Whitney, Jack Brosius, Stan Dragon, Jay Goodrow; 3:28.4)
Fours, 10,000 Meters—Sebago C. C. (Mike Johnston, Mike Samokishyn, Gene Krawczyk, Ed Walsh; 39:06.5)

Women's Kayak

Singles, 500 meters—Marcia Smoke, Niles, Mich. (2:06.5)
Singles, 5,000 Meters—Marcia Smoke (22:37.9)
Tandem, 500 Meters—Marcia Smoke and Kathy Mosolino, Niles, Mich. (2:03.2)
Tandem, 5,000 Meters—Virginia Moore and Lorie Smith, Newport Beach, Calif. (21:30.4)
Fours, 500 Meters—Niles, Mich. (Marcia Smoke, Kathy Mosolino, Debbie Jenkins, Marian Flood; 23:19)

Canoe

Singles, 1,000 Meters—Andy Weigand, Newport Beach, Calif. (4:23.2)
Singles, 10,000 Meters—Andy Weigand (47:06.1)
Tandem, 1,000 Meters—Andy Toro, Ann Arbor, Mich., and Andy Weigand (no time)
Tandem, 10,000 Meters—Roland Muhlen and Dave Landonwitch, Cincinnati (42:38.9)
Fours, 1,000 Meters—Washington C. C. (Barry Merritt, Stanley Smith, Mike Ware, Tom Scribner; 3:56.4)

CHESS

World Championship Candidate Matches
Quarterfinals

Bobby Fischer, New York, defeated Mark Taimanov, USSR, at Vancouver, B. C., 6–0
Tigran Petrosian, USSR, defeated Robert Huebner, West Germany, at Seville, Spain (after six draws, Petrosian won a game and Huebner withdrew)
Bent Larsen, Denmark, defeated Wolfgang Uhlmann, East Germany, at Las Palmas, Canary Islands, 5½–3½
Viktor Korchnoi, USSR, defeated Yefim Geller, USSR, at Moscow, 5½–2½

Semifinals

Fischer defeated Larsen, in Denver, 6–0; Petrosian defeated Korchnoi, at Moscow, 5½–4½

Finals

Fischer defeated Petrosian, 6½–2½, at Buenos Aires, and won right to challenge Boris Spassky, of Soviet Union, for world championship in spring of 1972

Women's World Championship Candidate Matches
Semifinals

Alla Kushnir, USSR, defeated Maria Satulovska, USSR, 5½–4½, at Minsk; Nona Alexandria, USSR, defeated Milanka Lazarevic, Yugoslavia, 5½–4½, at Bladel, Netherlands.

United States Champions

Open—Larry Evans, Reno, Nev., and Walter Browne, Australia, co-champions
Amateur—Clarence Kalenan, Philadelphia
Junior—Ken Rogoff, Rochester, N. Y., and Greg Defotis, Chicago, co-champions

CROSS COUNTRY

AAU (San Diego, Calif., Nov. 27, 10,000 meters)—Frank Shorter, Florida Track Club, Gainesville (29 minutes, 19 seconds); team: Florida T. C. (17 pts); masters (Bloomfield Hills, Mich., Nov. 20)—Hal Higdon, Indianapolis (34:21)
NCAA—University Division (Knoxville, Tenn., Nov. 22, 6 miles)—Steve Prefontaine, Oregon (29:14.9); team: Oregon (39 pts). College Division: (Wheaton, Ill., Nov. 13, 5 miles)—Mike Slack, North Dakota State (24:19); team: California State at Fullerton (47 pts)
NAIA (Liberty, Mo., Nov. 20, 5 miles)—Dave Antognoli, Edinboro State (25:40.2); team: Adams State of Colorado (196 pts)
U. S. Track and Field Federation (Stone Mountain, Ga., Nov. 24, 6 miles)—Tie between Ed Leddy and Neil Cusack, East Tennessee State (29.56.8); team: Florida Track Club, Gainesville (23 pts)
IC4-A (New York, Nov. 15, 5 miles)—University Division: Bob Wheeler, Duke (24:27); team: Villanova (45 pts). College Division: Daniel Monihan, Tufts (25:03.7); team: Lehigh (91 pts)
Women's AAU (Wickliffe, Ohio, Nov. 27, 2½ miles)—Doris Brown, Seattle (14:29.4)
Canada (Halifax, N. S., Nov. 21, 12 kilometers)—Richard Munro (38:26.4)

CURLING

World (Mégève, France, March 16–20)—Canada (Don Duguid, skip)
United States (Duluth, Minn., March 1–5)—Edmore, N. Dak. (Dal Dalziel, skip)
Canada (at Quebec)—Manitoba (Dan Duguid, Winnipeg, skip)
Gordon International Medal (at Montreal)—Canada 387, U. S. 318 (Canada 50 matches, 19,566 points to U. S. 26 matches, 17,166 points)
Gordon International Bowl—Montreal Caledonia (R. D. Miller, skip)
Gordon Champion Rink Medal—Schenectady (J. S. Cary, skip)
Dewar Trophy (Utica)—Utica (R. Burchesky, skip)
Douglas Medal (Mount Hope, N. Y.)—New York Caledonian (Joseph Milano, skip)
Dykes Memorial Medal—Brae Burn (J. W. Dacey, skip)
Mitchell Gold Medal—Schenectady (G. P. Link, skip)
United States Women—North Shore Lassies, Glenview, Ill. (Mrs. Alfred Krumholz, Jr., skip)

CYCLING

United States Championships
(Portland, Oreg., Aug. 19–21)

Match Sprint (½-mile)—Gary Campbell, Paramount, Calif.
1,000-Meter Time Trial—Tim Zasadny, Prospect Heights, Ill.
4,000-Meter Pursuit—Michael Neel, Berkeley, Calif.
10 Miles—Hans Nuernberg, Kenosha, Wis.
Road Race (121 miles)—Stephen Dayton, Indianapolis
4,000-Meter Team Pursuit—Southern California (Fred Davis, Westminster; Ron Skarin, Van Nuys; Butch Stinton, Lakewood; Mike Clemens, Goleta)
Women's Sprint (½-mile)—Sheila Young, Detroit
Women's 3,000-Meter Pursuit—Kathy Eckroth, Portland, Oreg.
Women's Road Race—Mary Jan Reoch, Philadelphia
Junior Champion—Ralph Therio, Torrance, Calif.

World Championships
Track Amateur
(Varese, Italy)

1,000-Meter Time Trial—Eduard Rapp, USSR
1,000-Meter Pursuit—Daniel Morelon, France
1,000-Meter Pursuit—Martin Rodriguez, Colombia
1,000-Meter Motor Pace—Horst Gnas, West Germany
Tandem—Werner Otto and Juergen Geschke, East Germany
4-Man Pursuit—Italy
Women's Sprint—Galina Csareva, USSR
Women's Pursuit—Tamra Carbouchina, USSR

Road Amateur
(Mendrisio, Switzerland)

168 Kilometers—Regis Ovion, France
100-Kilometer Time Trial—Belgium
Women—Anna Konkina, USSR

DOG SHOWS

Westminster Kennel Club (New York, Feb. 15–16)—Group winners (3,031 dogs shown)—sporting and best in show: Dr. Milton E. Prickett's English springer spaniel, Ch. Chinoe's Adamant James, of Lexington, Ky.; hound: Mrs. Patricia V. Craige's elkhound, Ch. Vin-Melca's Vagabond, Monterey, Calif.; toy: Mrs. Joyce Graves' Pomeranian, Ch. Duke's Lil Red Baron of O'Kala, of Cypress, Texas; terrier: Florence Coe's Kerry blue, Ch. O'Connell of Kerry Oaks, of Atherton, Calif.; working: Mrs. Margaret S. Smith's standard schnauzer, Ch. Pavo de la Steingasse, of Dallas, Texas; nonsporting: Mr. and Mrs. Frank Dale's miniature poodle, Ch. Tally Ho Tiffany, of Calabasas, Calif.
International Kennel Club (Chicago, April 3–4)—Group winners (3,637 dogs shown): sporting and best in show: Dr. Milton E. Prickett's English springer spaniel, Ch. Chinoe's Adamant James, of Lexington, Ky; nonsporting: Joy S. Tongue's and Joy Ann Sering's standard poodle, Ch. Haus Brau Executive, of Portland, Oreg.; hound: Dr. and Mrs. Lawrence J. Pazourek's bloodhound, Ch. The Rectory's Rabbi, of Glenarm, Md.; working: Sheila and George West's Doberman

pinscher, Ch. Dolph von Tannenwald, of Muttontown, N. Y.; terrier: Mrs. Jane Esther Henderson's West Highland white, Ch. De Go Hubert, of Stockton, N. J.; toy: Mrs. L. S. Gordon Jr.'s and Janet Bennett's Yorkshire terrier, Ch. Continuation of Glenno, of Glenview, Ill.

FENCING

World Championships
(Vienna, July 5–18)

Individual—*Foil:* Vasily Stankovich, USSR; *épée:* Gregory Kriss, USSR; *saber:* Michele Maffei, Italy; *women's foil:* Marie-Chantal Demaille, France
Team—*Foil:* France; *épée:* Hungary; *saber:* USSR; *women's foil:* USSR

United States Championships
(Berkeley, Calif., June 18–25)

Individual—*Foil:* Uriah Jones, Salle Santelle, New York; *épée:* James Melcher, New York Fencers Club; *saber:* Alex Orban, New York A. C.; *women's foil:* Harriet King, Salle Lucia, San Francisco
Team—*Foil:* New York A. C.; *épée:* New York A. C.; *saber:* Salle Cziszar, Philadelphia; *women's foil:* West End, Los Angeles

National Collegiate (NCAA) Championships
(Colorado Springs, Colo., March 18–20)

Individual—*Foil:* Tyronne Simmons, Detroit; *épée:* George Szunyogh, New York University; *saber:* Bruce Soriano, Columbia
Team (3-weapon)—Tie between Columbia and New York University (68 pts)

Women's Collegiate
(Buffalo, N. Y., April 2–3)

Women's Intercollegiate Fencing Association—*Individual:* Ruth White, New York University; *team:* New York University (61 pts)

GYMNASTICS

National AAU Championships
(Cedar Rapids, Iowa, May 6–8)

Men
All-Around—Yoshiaki Takei, Georgia Southern College (110.15 pts)
Side Horse—Ken Liehr, University of Iowa (18.75)
Rings—Yoshiaki Takei (18.95)
Floor Exercises—Yoshiaki Takei (18.275)
Vault—Barry Slotten, University of Iowa (18.15)
Parallel Bars—Brent Simmons, Iowa State Gym Club (18.825)
Team—New York A. C. (305.20)

Women
All-Around—Linda Metheny, McKinley YMCA, Urbana, Ill. (37.20)
Vault—Roxanne Pierce, Kensington, Md. (19.25)
Balance Beam—Tie between Linda Metheny and Theresa Fileccia, McKinley YMCA, Urbana, Ill. (18.90)
Floor Exercises—Linda Metheny (19.20)
Uneven Bars—Roxanne Pierce (18.80)
Team—McKinley YMCA, Urbana, Ill. (109.75)

National Collegiate (NCAA) Championships
(Ann Arbor, Mich., April 1–3)

All-Around—Yoshi Hayasaki, Washington (107.9 pts)
Floor Exercises—Stormy Eaton, New Mexico (9.425)
Side Horse—Russ Hoffman, Iowa State (9.325)
Rings—Charles Ropiequet, Southern Illinois (9.6)
Long Horse—Pat Mahoney, San Fernando Valley (9.225)
Parallel Bars—Tie between Brent Simmons, Iowa State, and Tom Dunn, Penn State (9.3625)
High Bar—Brent Simmons (9.5375)
Team—Iowa State (319.25)

Other Intercollegiate Championships

NCAA College Division—*Individual:* John Crosby (Southern Connecticut, 9.125 pts): *team:* California State College, Fullerton (158.150)
National Association of Intercollegiate Athletics (NAIA)—*Individual:* Paul Tickenoff, Northwestern Louisiana (52.95); *team:* Northwestern Louisiana (154.10)

HANDBALL

AAU Champions
4-Wall (at Shreveport, La., Oct. 6–10)—*Singles:* Pat Kirby, Brooklyn, N. Y.; *doubles:* Simie Fein and Ray Neveau, Milwaukee; *masters singles:* Tom Schoendorf, Greendale, Wis.; *masters doubles:* Cecil Lloyd, Shreveport, La., and Alvis Grant, Dallas
1-Wall (at Brooklyn, N. Y.)—*Singles:* Steve Sandler, New York; *doubles:* Kenny Davidoff and Howie Eisenberg, Brooklyn, N. Y.; *masters doubles:* Lou Caputo and Bill Taub, New York

U. S. Handball Association Champions
4-Wall (at Memphis, March 27–April 3)—*Singles:* Paul Haber, Chicago; *doubles:* Ray Neveau and Simie Fein, Milwaukee; *masters singles:* Rudy Stadlberger, San Francisco; *masters doubles:* Arnold Aguilar and Irv Simon, Los Angeles
3-Wall (Detroit, Sept. 1–6)—*Singles:* Lon Russo, New York; *doubles:* Paul Haber and Andy Upatnieks, Chicago; *masters doubles:* John Scopis and Jim Golden, Detroit

UPI

CH. CHINOE'S ADAMANT JAMES, an English springer spaniel, captured best-in-show honors at Westminster Kennel Club's annual dog show in both 1971 and 1972.

1-Wall (Brooklyn, N. Y., Oct. 16–Nov. 7)—*Singles:* Steve Sandler, New York; *doubles:* Artie Reyer and Wally Ulbrich, Brooklyn; *masters doubles:* Joe Danilczyk and Julie Rothman, New York; *team:* Rockaway Beach Park, New York
Intercollegiate (at Knoxville, Tenn., March 5–7)—*Singles:* Wes Yee, Lake Forest; *doubles:* Joe Hero and Terry Hankins, Texas; *team:* tie between Lake Forest and Texas

HORSE SHOWS

American Horse Shows Association Champions

Working Hunter—Thomas E. Hughes' Castle Hill
Green Working Hunter, first year—Harry Gill's Another March
Green Working Hunter, second year—Mrs. A. C. Randolph's Army Wife
Conformation Hunter—Marvin Van Rapoport's Spindletop Showdown
Green Conformation Hunter—Mr. and Mrs. Kenneth Wheeler's Mark of Success
Amateur-Owner Working Hunter—Jane E. Womble's Perfect Stranger
Small Pony Hunter—Page Estes' Dinkie
Large Pony Hunter—Nancy Baroody's Pride 'N Joy
Junior Working Hunter—Libby MacDonald's You Watch
Three-Gaited Saddle Horse—Julianne Schmutz' Forest Song
Three-Gaited Saddle Horse, Amateur—Mrs. Harry Newman's Foxy Lady
Five-Gaited Saddle Horse—Julianne Schmutz' Chapel Belle
Five-Gaited Saddle Horse, Amateur—Robert F. White's Rob Shriver
Three-Gaited Pleasure Horse, American bred—Mrs. Vernon L. Wise Jr.'s Gentleman Jim
Fine Harness Horse—Mr. and Mrs. A. W. Zelinka's Tashi Ling
Fine Harness Horse, Amateur—Mrs. Alan R. Robson's Starheart Easter Star
Shetland Harness Horse—Fernwood Farm's Fernwood Frisco Kate IV
Shetland Roadsters—Fernwood Farm's Fernwood Frisco Lee
Hackney Ponies—Mr. and Mrs. Kenneth Wheeler's Mr. Orbit
Harness Ponies—Mr. and Mrs. Alan R. Robson's Debbie Fashion
Arabian—Leslie Connor's Kimicias
Half-Arabian—Phil Demery's Stormy Aka
Park Morgan—Mrs. Mary H. DeWitt's Waseeka in Command
Parade Horse—Little Star Farm's Denmark Dollar
Tennessee Walking Horse—Mr. and Mrs. Cebern Lee's Midnight Rebel
Welsh Pleasure Horse—Mrs. J. Austin DuPont's Liseter Twinkle
Stock Horse—Mrs. Katherine H. Haley's Shirley Chex
Trail Horse—Red Cantleberry's Katy O'Grady
Western Pleasure—Jane Gray's Polo Lonnie
Amateur-Owner Jumpers—Michel McEvoy's Advanced Ticket
Junior Jumpers—Anthony D'Ambrosio Jr.'s Samuri

Special Awards

Horseman of the Year—Victor Hugo-Vidal, Stamford, Conn.
Horsewoman of the Year—Mrs. Alan Robson, West Chester, Pa.

Equestrian Championships

Saddle Seat (at Kansas City)—Susie Maccari, Fort Lauderdale, Fla.

Hunter Seat (At Harrisburg, Pa.)—Joy Slater, Far Hills, N. J.
Stock Seat (at Santa Barbara, Calif.)—Lisa Rudnick, Bakersfield, Calif.
Dressage (at Painesville, Ohio)—Jordan Miller, Ossining, N. Y.

National Horse Show Awards

Saddle Seat Trophy (Good Hands)—Judy Maccari, Fort Lauderdale, Fla.
ASPCA Maclay Trophy—Anna Jane White, Atlanta
International Jumping—*Team:* United States (Frank Chapot, Joseph Fargis, Carol Hofmann, Robert Ridland, Neal Shapiro, and William Steinkraus); *individual:* Neal Shapiro; *leading foreign rider:* Barbara Simpson, Canada

U. S. Equestrian Team Championships

Three-Day Championship (Markham Trophy)—James C. Wofford, Milford, Kans., on The Regent
Intermediate (Gladstone Trophy)—Kevin Freeman, Portland, Oreg., on Good Mixture
Open Dressage—Christilot Hanson, Sharon, Ont.

ICE SKATING

Figure Skating

World Championships (Lyons, France, Feb. 23–28)—Men: Ondrej Nepela, Czechoslovakia; women: Beatrix Schuba, Austria; *pairs:* Sergei Ulanov and Irina Rodnina, USSR; dance: Aleksandr Gorshkov and Ludmilla Pachomova, USSR
United States Championships (Buffalo, N. Y., Jan. 28–31)—Men: John Misha Petkevich, Great Falls, Mont.; women: Janet Lynn, Rockford, Ill.; *pairs:* Kenneth Shelley and Jo Jo Starbuck, Downey, Calif.; dance: James Sladky, Syracuse, N. Y., and Judy Schwomeyer, Indianapolis

Speed Skating
World Championships
Men (Goteborg, Sweden, Feb. 13–14)
All-Around—Ard Schenk, Netherlands (171.130 pts)
500 Meters—Dag Fornaess, Norway (0:41.33)
1,500 Meters—Ard Schenk (2:04.8)
5,000 Meters—Ard Schenk (7:18.8)
10,000 Meters—Ard Schenk (15:01.6)

Women (Helsinki, Finland, Feb. 6–7)
All-Around—Nina Statkewich, USSR (191.4 pts)
500 Meters—Anne Henning, Northbrook, Ill. (0:44.6)
1,000 Meters—Diane Holum, Northbrook, Ill. (1:33)
1,500 Meters—Nina Statkewich (2:23.2)
3,000 Meters—Stien Kaiser, Netherlands (4:57.2)

United States National Outdoor
(St. Paul, Minn., Jan. 30–31)
Champion—Jack Walters, Brighton, Mass. (18 pts)
Women's Champion—Sheila Young, Detroit (25 pts)

United States National Indoor
(Flint, Mich., March 6–7)
Champion—Tie between Barth Levy, Brooklyn, N. Y., and Jack Walters, Brighton, Mass. (14 pts)
Women's Champion—Cathy Crowe, St. Louis (15 pts)

North American Outdoor
(Lake Placid, N. Y., Feb. 14)
Champion—Rich Wurster, Ballston Spa, N. Y. (31 pts)
Women's Champion—Ruth Moore, Newton, Mass. (19 pts)

North American Indoor
(Utica, N. Y., March 13–14)
Champion—Pat Maxwell, Rochester, N. Y. (21 pts)
Women's Champion—Carole Moore, New York, N. Y. (13 pts)

LACROSSE

National Collegiate A. A. Champion—Cornell
National Club—Long Island Athletic Club
All-Star College Game—North 9, South 6
Collegiate Division Champions—*Central Atlantic:* tie between Delaware and Lehigh; *Central New York:* Cortland State; *Colonial:* Plymouth State; *Ivy League:* Cornell; *Metropolitan New York:* Hofstra; *Mideastern:* tie between Army and Virginia; *Midwest:* Denison; *New England:* Brown; *Northeast:* Massachusetts; *Northern New York:* tie between Albany State and Ithaca; *Rocky Mountain:* Air Force Academy; *South Atlantic:* tie between Towson State, Washington & Lee

MOTORBOATING

Major Unlimited Class Trophy Winners

Champion Spark Plug Regatta (Miami, May 23)—Miss Budweiser (driver, Dean Chenoweth)
President's Cup (Washington, June 6)—Atlas Van Lines (Bill Muncey)
Kentucky Governor's Cup (Owensboro, June 13)—Atlas Van Lines (Bill Muncey)
Dodge Memorial Cup (Detroit, June 27)—Miss Budweiser (Dean Chenoweth)
Gold Cup (Madison, Ind., July 4)—Miss Madison (Jim McCormick)
Seafair Trophy (Seattle, Aug. 8)—Pride of Pay 'N Pak (Bill Schumacher)
Oregon Emerald Cup (Eugene, Aug. 15)—Pride of Pay 'N Pak (Bill Schumacher)
Atlas Van Lines Trophy (Dallas, Sept. 25)—Pride of Pay 'N Pak
Champion—Miss Budweiser (6,994 pts)

Distance Races

Bahamas 500 (542 miles)—Douglas Silvera, Freeport, Grand Bahamas (7 hours, 23 minutes; average speed 73.4 miles per hour)
Catalina Challenge Trophy (Los Angeles, 188 miles)—Robert Magoon, Miami Beach, Fla. (64.9 mph)
Cowes (England)—Ronnie Bonelli, Italy
Sam Griffith Memorial (Miami, 153 miles)—Bill Wishnick, New York (2:21; 72.87 mph)
Hennessy Grand Prix (Point Pleasant, N. J., 206 miles)—Robert Magoon (70 mph)
Hennessy Key West (180 miles)—Roger Hanks, Midland, Texas
Long Beach (Calif.) Hennessy (188 miles)—Robert Magoon (2:46; 66.9 mph)
Long Beach–Avalon (104 miles, two days)—Gil Gilbert, Beverly Hills, Calif. (1:38; 61.5 mph)
Marathon of Champions (Long Beach, Calif., 225 miles)—Mike Wallace, Venice, Calif. (3:16:07)
Miami–Nassau (184 miles)—Tom Gentry, Honolulu (2:31)
Viareggio–Bastia (Italy)—Bill Wishnick

Champions

World—Bill Wishnick, New York
United States Offshore—Robert Magoon, Miami Beach

Predicted Log Trophies

APBA National Championship—Thomas Chretien, Auburndale, Mass. (6,087 pts)
APBA High Point Award—Chretien (6,087)
George W. Codrington Trophy—Chretien (3,355)
Herbert L. Stone Trophy—Chretien (4,894)
National Martin & Rossi Trophy—Chretien (642)
George K. Mikkelsen Memorial Trophy—Chretien (.061% low for season)

PARACHUTING

United States Championships
(Tahlequah, Okla., June 21–27)

Men—*Overall:* Clayton Schoelpple, Hartwood, Va. (436.3 pts); style: Doug Metcalfe, Chardon, Ohio (7.90); accuracy: Don Strickland, U. S. Army (1.61)
Women—*Overall:* Susie Neuman, Detroit (612.9); style: Susan Rademaekers, Wilbraham, Mass. (10.20); accuracy: Mickey Sleeper, Anchorage, Alaska (5.36)
Team—Security Thunderbow, Oakland, Calif.

POLO

U. S. Polo Association Champions

Open—Oak Brook (Ill.) 8 (Hugo Dalmar Jr., Charles Smith, Allan Scherer, Robert Beveridge), Green Hill Farms (Tulsa) 7
20-Goal—Green Hill Farms 8, Milwaukee 6
16-Goal—Milwaukee 9, Welfare (Texas) 1
12-Goal—Wilson Ranch (Midland, Texas) 7, Norman (Okla.) 5
Intercollegiate—Yale 12, Virginia 11
Interscholastic—Culver Military Institute

International

Coronation Cup (England)—United States 9, Britain 6

RODEO

Rodeo Cowboy Association Champions

All-Around—Phil Lyne, George West, Texas
Saddle Bronco—Bill Smith, Cody, Wyo.
Bareback Bronco—Joe Alexander, Cora, Wyo.
Steer Wrestling—Billy Hale, Checotah, Okla.
Calf Roping—Phil Lyne
Team Roping—John Miller, Oakdale, Calif.
Bull Riding—Bill Nelson, San Francisco

ROLLER SKATING

Roller Skating Rink Operators Association American Champions
(Lincoln, Nebr.)

Men—*Singles:* Michael Jacques, Norwood, Mass.; figures: Ronald Milton, Norwood, Mass.; speed: Pat Bergin, Irving, Texas
Women—*Singles:* April Allen, Houston, Texas; figures: Susie Johnson, Fort Worth, Texas; speed: Shelley Comella, Portland, Oreg.
Pairs—Ron and Gail Robovitsky, Detroit
Dance—Bob and Elayne Leonard, Santa Ana, Calif.
Fours—Dennis Collier, Karen Marshall, Richard Toon, and Judy Jerue, San Leandro, Calif.
Relay—Pat Bergin, Malcolm Williamson, Edward Felter, and Earnest Faries, Irving, Texas
Women's Relay—Stephanie Hemphill, Jill Hemphill, Terry Paine, and Cheryl Johnson, Olympia, Wash.
Mixed Relay—Pat Bergin, Earnest Faries, Patsy Johnson, and Susie Johnson, Irving, Texas

U. S. Amateur Roller Skating Association National Champions
(South Amboy, N. J.)

Men—*Singles:* Randy Dayney, Levittown, N. Y.; figures: Randy Dayney; speed: Charles Gillette, Livonia, Mich.
Women—*Singles:* Colleen Giacomo, South Amboy, N. J.; figures: Colleen Giacomo; speed: Barbara Zawistowski, Elizabeth, N. J.

Pairs—William Boyd and Linda Martin, Seabrook, Md.
Women's Pairs—Robin Dayney and June Frees, Levittown, N. Y.
Dance—Richard Horne and Jane Pankey, Livonia, Mich.
Veteran Dance—Richard and Marion Levesque, Livingston, N. J.
Fours—David Allen, Kathleen Allen, Pasadena, Calif., Susan Austin and Khaled Ali, Pomona, Calif.
Relay—Virgil Dooley and Charles Gillette, Livonia, Mich.
Women's Relay—Peggy Gillette and Sue Maiberger, Livonia, Mich.
Mixed Relay—Virgil Dooley and Sue Maiberger, Livonia, Mich.
Junior Singles and Figures—Keith King, Levittown, N. Y.
Junior Women's Singles and Figures—Barbara Kaffka, Levittown, N. Y.
Junior Speed—Joseph Aidukas, Bayonne, N. J.
Junior Women's Speed—Lillian Baluch, Kendall Park, N. J.

ROWING

United States Championships
(New York, Aug. 6–9)

Single Sculls—James Dietz, New York A. C. (7:14)
Single Sculls (500 meters)—John Van Blom, Long Beach (Calif.) R. A. (1:15)
Doubles—James Dietz and Larry Klecatsky, New York A. C. (7:02)
Pairs—Bob Wetmore and Andy Roberts, Union Boat Club, Boston (7:41.5)
Pairs with Coxswain—Bob Newman, Butch Pope, and Phyne Putnam, Long Beach (Calif.) R. A. (8:50)
Fours—Vesper B. C., Philadelphia (6:44)
Fours with Coxswain—Vesper (6:50.2)
Eights—Union B. C. (5:59.4)
Senior Singles—Jim Castelan, Fairmount R. A., Philadelphia (7:57.5)
Senior Fours—Detroit B. C. (6:54.1)
Veterans Pairs (1,000 meters)—Ed Lynch and Joe Olrich, Cambridge (Mass.) B. C. (3:33)
150-Pound Singles—Larry Klecatsky, New York A. C. (7:26.7)
150-Pound Singles (500 meters)—Robert Belden, Undine Barge Club, Philadelphia (1:19.7)
150-Pound Doubles—Robert Belden and Fred Duling, Undine (6:55.9)
150-Pound Eights—St. Catharines (Ont.) B. C. (6:10)

Intercollegiate Team Champions
(2,000 meters except where noted)

IRA Regatta (Lake Onondaga, Syracuse, N. Y., June 17–19)—Varsity: Cornell (6:06); junior varsity: Navy (6:17.2); freshmen: Pennsylvania (6:16.8); fours with coxswains: Navy (7:00.9); fours without coxswains: California (7:46.2); team—Jim Ten Eyck Trophy awarded to Cornell for varsity race victory after tie in points (13) with Navy
Eastern Sprints (Worcester, Mass., May 7–8)—Heavyweights: varsity: Navy (6:17.2); second varsity: Brown (6:23.2); freshmen: Navy (6:34.1); team (Rowe Cup): Navy, 39 pts; Lightweights: varsity: Harvard (6:39.2); second varsity: Harvard (7:01.5); freshmen: Harvard (7:12.2); team (Jope Cup): Harvard, 38 pts
Dad Vail Trophy (Philadelphia, May 7–8)—Varsity: Georgetown (5:55.2); junior varsity: Marietta (6:04.8); lightweights: Marietta (6:07); freshmen: Marietta (6:05); fours: Manhattan (6:50); team: St. Joseph's (Philadelphia), 13 pts
Mid-America Regatta (Marietta, Ohio, May 1)—Varsity: Virginia (6:29.9); senior varsity: Marietta (6:33.1); lightweights: Marietta (6:47.6); freshmen: Marietta (6:35.9); varsity fours: Virginia (8:11); team: Marietta, 29 pts
Oxford-Cambridge (4½ miles)—Cambridge (17:58)
Western Sprints (Seattle, May 21–22)—Varsity: Washington (6:06.3); junior varsity: Washington (6:14.4); freshmen: Washington (6:10.3); fours with coxswains: Washington (7:07.2)
Yale-Harvard (4 miles)—Harvard (20:06); Yale (20:52)
Cups and Trophies—Adams Cup: Navy (5:57.2); Bill Cup: Rutgers (6:00.5); Blackwell Cup: Penn (5:39.1); Carnegie Cup: Cornell (5:41.2); Childs Cup: Penn (6:27); Cochrane Cup: Wisconsin (6:02.8); Compton Cup: Harvard (6:12.9); Deering Cup: Fordham (6:55.2); Grimaldi Cup: Drexel (7:31, in rerun after first race, won by Marist College, was marred by accident); Holding Cup: Brown (6:31.8); Goes Trophy: Navy (6:09.9); Logg Cup: Princeton (5:41.1); O'Hare Cup: Ithaca (7:03); President's Cup (Marist College): St. Joseph's (8:42.4); Madeira Cup: Penn (5:49); Stein Cup: Harvard (6:11.4); Sulger Trophy: Manhattan (78 pts)
Interscholastic Championships (Syracuse, N. Y., May 21–22)—Single sculls: Tony Haidorfer, Cardinal Dougherty, Philadelphia (7:42.4); double sculls: Angelo Bergamini and Dan Rooney, Blessed Sacrament, New Rochelle, N. Y. (7:35.4); eights: Ridley College School, St. Catharines, Ont. (5:08); quadruple sculls: Washington and Lee, Arlington, Va. (6:07.8); fours: West Park High, St. Catharines, Ont. (6:39)

British Henley
(Henley-on-Thames, June 30–July 3)

Diamond Sculls (singles)—Alberto Demiddi, Argentina (8:08)
Double Sculls—Walton Rowing Club, London (8:21)
Silver Goblets (pairs)—Glyn Locke and Tim Crooks, England (8:07)
Wyfold Challenge Cup (fours)—Harvard (7:37)
Stewards Challenge Cup (fours)—Thames Tradesmen's R. C. (7:12)
Visitors Challenge Cup (fours)—University of London (6:48)
Prince Philip Challenge Cup (fours with coxswain)—London R. C. (7:37)
Britannia Challenge Cup (fours with coxswain)—Hereford R. C., England (7:45)
Ladies Challenge Plate (eights)—University of London (7:00)

Thames Challenge Cup (lightweight eights)—Harvard (6:48)
Princess Elizabeth Cup (schoolboy eights)—Pangbourne College, England (7:04)
Grand Challenge Cup (eights)—Tideway Scullers, England (6:46)

Canadian Henley
(St. Catharines, Ont., Aug. 11–15)

Single Sculls—Richard Stehlik, Malta B. C., Philadelphia (8:14.3)
Single Sculls (500 meters)—Jody Trinsey, Malta (1:45.7)
Association Singles—Jody Trinsey (7:04.1)
Pairs with Coxswain—Ed Kollmer, Sandy Killen, and Joe Maiorano, coxswain, New York A. C. (8:30)
Pairs without Coxswain—Ed Kollmer and Sand Killen (7:57.5)
Fours with Coxswain—New Haven Rowing Club (6:16)
Eights (500 meters)—Argonaut R. C., Toronto (1:22.5)
Doubles—Richard Klecatsky and Pat Klaren, Minnesota B. C., St. Paul (7:43.6)
Eights—New Haven R. C. (6:28.2)
Junior Eights—St. Catharines R. C. (5:56.7)
155-pound Singles—Larry Klecatsky, New York A. C. (7:02.3)
155-pound Eights—Brockville (Ont.) R. C. (6:49.4)

SHOOTING

Trap
Grand American Championships
(Vandalia, Ohio, Aug. 22–28)

Grand American Handicap—Men: Ralph C. Davis, Lorton, Va. (20½ yards, 98, won shoot-off); women: Leona Powers, Mount Sterling, Ohio (18½ yards, 97, won shoot-off); junior: Frank Haynes, Wood River, Ill. (23½ yards, 97); veteran: D. M. Long, Englewood, Ohio (20½ yards, 95); industry: Nick Mack, St. Louis (24½ yards, 95)
Overall—Men: Britt Robinson, Tahoka, Texas (964); women: Dolores Hendersched, White Haven, Pa. (911); junior: Michael Hertlein, Lynchburg, Ohio (941); veteran: John Mardock, Wichita, Kans. (913); industry: Bob Andrews, Little Rock, Ark. (945)
All-Around—Men: Gene Sears, El Reno, Okla. (391); women: Joan Sitler, Newark, Ohio (368); junior: Michael Hertlein, Lynchburg, Ohio (386); veteran: O. B. Stover, Willhar, Minn. (375); industry: Bob Andrews, Little Rock, Ark. (382)
Clay Target—Men: Richard Smith, Newcomerstown, Ohio (200, won shoot-off); women: Ruby Jenner, Waupaca, Wis. (198); junior: Michael Hertlein, Lynchburg, Ohio (199); veteran: Don Engleby, Vermilion, Ohio (196, won shoot-off); industry: Hiram Bradley, South Holland, Ill. (199)
Doubles—Men: Larry Gravestock, Wichita Falls, Texas (99); women: Joan Sitler (88); junior: Michael Hertlein (95); veteran: O. B. Stover (94); industry: Bob Andrews (96)

Skeet
National Skeet Shooting Association Championships
(San Antonio, Texas, July 31–Aug. 7)

All-Around—Open: Robert Paxton, Corpus Christi, Texas (548 x 550); women: Karla Roberts, Bridgeton, Mo. (536 x 550); veteran: R. B. Ross, Brownwood, Texas (527 x 550); senior: J. R. Hiland, Indianapolis (538 x 550); subsenior: John Golla, Fort Lauderdale, Fla. (544 x 550); junior: Tito Killian, San Antonio, Texas (546 x 550); industry: Barney Hartman, St. Lambert, Quebec (547 x 550).
Other Individual Champions—12-gauge: Richard Bienapfl, Plymouth, Minn. (250 x 250); women: Jackie Ramsey, San Antonio, Texas (247 x 250); 20-gauge: Ken Barnes, Bakersfield, Calif. (100 x 100); women: Karla Roberts (100 x 100); 28-gauge: Roger Craemer, Gray, Me. (100 x 100); women: Valerie Johnson, San Antonio, Texas (98 x 100); .410-gauge: Richard Hill, Detroit (100 x 100); women: Valerie Johnson (97 x 100); Champion of Champions: Harry Stilwell, Oreland, Pa. (100 x 100).

SKIING

World Cup

Individual—Men: Gustavo Thoeni, Italy (155 pts); leading American: Tyler Palmer, Kearsarge, N. H. (10th, 60); Women: Annamarie Proell, Austria (210); leading American: Barbara Cochran, Richmond, Vt. (8th, 90)
Team (Nations Cup)—Men: France (505); women: France (828); combined: France (1,333)

United States Championships

Alpine (Aspen, Colo., March 12–14)—Men: downhill: Bob Cochran, Richmond, Vt. (1:34.20); slalom: Otto Tschudi, Norway, Denver Univ. (1:42.39); giant slalom: Bob Cochran (3:25.87); combined (Roch Cup): Bob Cochran (34.87 pts).—Women: downhill: Cheryl Bechdolt, Tahoe City, Calif. (1:23.10); slalom: Barbara Cochran, Richmond, Vt. (1:27.18); giant slalom: Laurie Kreiner, Timmons, Ont. (1:53.66); combined (Bingham Cup): Judy Crawford, Toronto (15.24)
Nordic (Durango, Colo., Feb. 16–21)—Jumping: class A: Jerry Martin, Minneapolis (213.2); veteran: Don Hurst, Marquette, Mich. (136.3); boys: Bill Polanke, Minneapolis (188.2).—Cross-country: Men: 15 kilometers: Mike Elliott, Durango, Colo. (47.40); 30 kilometers: Mike Gallagher, Killington, Vt. (1:40.24); veteran: T. Svenson (28:05); 3 x 10 relay: U. S. Eastern Ski Assn. (Mike Gallagher, Peter Davis, Bob Gray; 1:25.38); 50 kilometers (at Putney, Vt., Feb. 21): Bob Gray (3:15.28); combined (at Brattleboro, Vt., Feb. 21): Robert Kendall, Auburn, Me. (399.8 pts).—Women (at Durango, Colo., Feb. 16–21): 5 kilometers: Sharon Firth, Inuvik, Northwest Territories, Canada (15:46); 10 kilometers: Martha Rockwell, Putney, Vt. (37:07); 3 x 5 relay: Yukon Division, Canada (Shirley Firth, Anita Allen, Sharon Firth; 49:35)

LIN HUI-CHING of China displays aggressive style in winning women's singles title in World Table Tennis Championships at Nagoya, Japan.

UPI

National Collegiate (NCAA) Championships
(Lead, S. Dak., March 4–6)

Downhill: Otto Tschudi, Denver (1:38.94); *slalom:* Otto Tschudi (1:33.40); *Alpine combined:* Otto Tschudi (201.68 pts); *cross-country:* Ole Ivar Hansen, Denver (55:05); *jumping:* Vidar Nilsgard, Colorado (222.5 pts); *Nordic combined:* Bruce Cunningham, New Hampshire (424.9 pts); *skimeister:* John Kendall, New Hampshire (346.8 pts); *team:* Denver (394.7 pts)

Canadian-American Trophy Series

Overall—Men: Lance Poulsen, Olympic Valley, Calif. (105 pts); *women:* Karen Budge, Jackson, Wyo. (173 pts)
Event Leaders—Slalom: Otto Tschudi, Denver (70 pts); *giant slalom:* Lance Poulsen (65); *downhill:* Craig Shanholtzer, Jackson, Wyo. (70). *Women: slalom:* Karen Budge (75); *giant slalom:* Judy Crawford, Toronto (65); *downhill:* Carolyne Oughton, Calgary, Alberta (65)

—————— SOCCER ——————

United States Champions

National Challenge Cup—Hota, New York
Amateur—Kutis, St. Louis
Junior—Seco Junior S. C., St. Louis
NCAA—Howard (defeated St. Louis, 1–0, in final, Dec. 30, at Orange Bowl, Miami; in semifinals, Dec. 28, Howard defeated Harvard, 1–0; St. Louis defeated San Francisco, 3–2)
NAIA—Quincy (Ill.) defeated Davis and Elkins, 1–0, in final
North American Soccer League—Dallas Tornado

Other Countries

English Association Cup—Arsenal
English League Cup—Tottenham Hotspur
Scottish Association Cup—Glasgow Celtic
Scottish League Cup—Partick Thistle
English League, First Division—Arsenal
English League, Second Division—Leicester
English League, Third Division—Preston North End
English League, Fourth Division—Notts County
British Champion—England
European Cup—Ajax of Amsterdam
European Cup of Winners Cup—Chelsea, England
West German, First Division—Borussia Moenchengladbach
West German Federation Cup—Bayern Munich
Spanish League—Valencia

—————— SOFTBALL ——————

American Softball Association Champions

Fast Pitch—Welty Way, Cedar Rapids, Iowa
Women's Fast Pitch—Raybestos Brakettes, Stratford, Conn.
Slow Pitch—Pile Drivers, Virginia Beach, Va.
Women's Slow Pitch—Fort Lauderdale (Fla.) Gators
Industrial Slow Pitch—Pharr Yarn Reds, McAdenville, N. C.
16-inch Slow Pitch—Carlucci Boosters, Chicago

—————— SQUASH RACQUETS ——————

National Champions
Men

Singles—Colin Adair, Montreal
Doubles—Sam Howe, Haverford, Pa., and Ralph Howe, New York
Veterans Singles—Henri Salaun, Boston
Senior Singles—Cal MacCracken, New York
Senior Doubles—William T. Ketchum and Howard Davis, New York
Veterans Doubles—Don Leggat and Chuck Wright, Canada
Team—Toronto
Collegiate—Palmer Page, Pennsylvania
Collegiate Team—Pennsylvania
Lapham Cup (singles)—Canada 9, United States 6
Grant Trophy (doubles)—Canada 4, United States 3

Women

Singles—Mrs. Terry Thesieres, Bala Cynwood, Pa.
Doubles—Mrs. Charles Classen, Haverford, Pa., and Mrs. Francis Vosters, Jr., Wilmington, Del.
Mixed Doubles—Gretchen Vosters, Wilmington, Del., and Kit Spahr, Haverford, Pa.

—————— SURFING ——————

United States Championships
(Huntington Beach, Calif., Sept. 18–19)

Men—David Nuuhiwa, Huntington Beach, Calif.
Women—Joyce Hoffman Lancor, Del Mar, Calif.
Masters—Don Takayama, Encinitas, Calif.
Senior—Les Williams, Dana Point, Calif.
Junior—Barry Amos, Los Angeles
Mixed Tandem—Steve Boehne and Barrie Algaw Boehne, Newport Beach, Calif.
Open Pier Paddle Race—Jack Lincke, Laguna Beach, Calif.
Duke Kahanamoku All-Around Award—Hal Sachs, Capistrano Beach, Calif.

—————— TABLE TENNIS ——————

World Championships
(Nagoya, Japan, March 28–April 7)

Singles—Stellan Bengtsson, Sweden
Women's Singles—Lin Hui-ching, China
Doubles—Istvan Jenyer and Tiber Klampar, Hungary
Women's Doubles—Lin Hui-ching and Cheng Min-chih, China
Mixed Doubles—Chang Shih-lin and Lin Hui-ching, China
Jubilee Cup—Ladislav Stipek, Peru
Swaythling Cup (men's team)—China (Chuang Tse-tung, Li Ching-kuang, and Liang Ko-liang)
Corbillon Cup (women's team)—Japan (Toshiko Kowada, Yukie Ohzeki, and Emiko Ohba)

United States Championships
(Atlanta, Ga., March 19–21)

Singles—Dal Joon Lee, Parma, Ohio
Women's Singles—Connie Sweeris, Grand Rapids, Mich.
Doubles—Dal Joon Lee and Peter Pradit, Chicago
Women's Doubles—Connie Sweeris and Wendy Hicks, Santa Barbara, Calif.
Mixed Doubles—Dell and Connie Sweeris, Grand Rapids, Mich.
Esquire Singles (over 50)—Laszlo Bellak, Miami, Fla.
Esquire Doubles—Sol Schiff, New York, and Jim Verta, Kensington, Md.
Senior Singles (over 40)—Max Marinko, Toronto
Senior Doubles—Bernie Bukiet, New York, and William Meszares, Barrington, Ill.

Canadian International
(Toronto, Sept. 2–5)

Singles—Dell Sweeris, Grand Rapids, Mich.
Women's Singles—Violetta Nesukaitis, Toronto
Doubles—Alan Hydes, England, and Errol Caetano, Toronto
Women's Doubles—Judy Bochenski, Eugene, Oreg., and Patty Cash, San Diego
Mixed Doubles—Alan Hydes and Violetta Nesukaitis
Senior Singles—Tim Boggan, Merrick, N. Y.

—————— VOLLEYBALL ——————

U. S. Volleyball Association
(Binghamton, N. Y.)

Open—Santa Monica (Calif.) YMCA
Women's Open—Los Angeles Renegades
Senior—Balboa Bay Club, Newport Beach, Calif.
College Round-Robin—Santa Monica College

Collegiate

NCAA—UCLA
NAIA—Church College, Hawaii

Olympic Qualifying Play-offs
(Havana, Aug. 17–22)

North American—Cuba (defeated U. S. in final, 8-15, 15-10, 15-6, 15-8)

—————— WATER SKIING ——————

World Championships
(Banolas, Spain, Sept. 15–19)
Men

Overall—George Athanas, Kelowna, British Columbia (2,719.2 pts)
Jumping—Mike Suyderhoud, Petaluma, Calif. (158.9 ft)
Slalom—Mike Suyderhoud (38 buoys)
Tricks—Ricky McCormick, Independence, Mo. (5,567.3 pts)

Women

Overall—Christy Weir, McQueeney, Texas (2,829.4 pts)
Jumping—Christy Weir (99.6 ft)
Slalom—Christie Freeman, Thayer, Mo. (37 buoys)
Tricks—Willy Stahle, Netherlands (4,156 pts)

Team Point Leaders

1. United States (8,553); 2. Australia (7,586); 3. France (6,964); 4. Canada (6,840); 5. Italy (6,427)

United States Championships
(Columbus, Ohio, Aug. 19–22)

Men

Overall—Mike Suyderhoud, Petaluma, Calif. (2,823 pts)
Jumping—Mike Suyderhoud (157 ft)
Slalom—Kris LaPoint, Castro Valley, Calif. (50½ buoys)
Tricks—Ricky McCormick, Independence, Mo. (5,576.9 pts)

Women

Overall—Liz Allan Shetter, Richmond, Va. (2,980 pts)
Jumping—Liz Shetter (106 ft)
Slalom—Christy Weir, McQueeney, Texas (51 buoys)
Tricks—Liz Shetter (3,932.6 pts)

Senior Men

Overall—Harry Price, Mundelein, Ill. (2,630 pts)
Jumping—Mickey McDonald, Webster, N.Y. (102 ft)
Slalom—Tom Wycoff, Connelly Springs, N.C. (39 buoys)
Tricks—Robert Moore, Louisville, Ky. (3,372 pts)

Senior Women

Overall—Barbara Cleveland, Hawthorne, Fla. (3,000 pts)
Jumping—Barbara Cleveland (92 ft.)
Slalom—Barbara Cleveland (49 buoys)
Tricks—Barbara Cleveland (3,448.9 pts)

Masters Tournament
(Callaway Gardens, Ga. July 9–11)

Men

Overall—Ricky McCormick (2,939 pts)
Jumping—Mike Suyderhoud (159 ft)
Slalom—Kris LaPoint (49½ buoys)
Tricks—Wayne Grimditch, Pompano, Fla. (4,620 pts)

Women

Overall—Christy Weir (2,840 pts)
Jumping—Barbara Clack, Miami, Fla. (111 ft)
Slalom—Christy Weir (51 buoys)
Tricks—Christy Weir (3,440 pts)

WEIGHT LIFTING

United States Championships
(York, Pa., June 11–13)

114.5 Pounds—Dave Moyer, Reading, Pa. (584¼ pounds total)
123.5 Pounds—Sal Dominguez, York, Pa. (667)
148.8 Pounds—James Benjamin, Columbus, Ohio (859¾)
165.4 Pounds—Russell Knipp, Fullerton, Calif. (1,008½)
181.9 Pounds—Michael Karchut, River Forest, Ill. (1,008¾)
198.4 Pounds—Rick Holbrook, Park Ridge, Ill. (1,097)
242.5 Pounds—Gary Deal, Seattle (1,157¼)
Super Heavyweight—Ken Patera, Minneapolis (1,306¼)

World Championships
(Lima, Peru, Sept. 18–26)

Flyweight—Z. Smalcerz, Poland (748 pounds)
Bantamweight—G. Chetin, USSR (814)
Featherweight—Yoshinyuri Miake, Japan (852.2)
Lightweight—Zbigniew Kaczmarek, Poland (968)
Middleweight—V. Kanygin, USSR (1,050.5)
Light Heavyweight—B. Pavlov, USSR (1,113)
Middle Heavyweight—D. Rigert, USSR (1,193.5)
Heavyweight—Y. Kazin, USSR (1,215.5)
Super Heavyweight—Vasily Alexeyev, USSR (1,397)

WRESTLING

National AAU Championships
Freestyle
(Tampa, Fla., April 15–17)

105.5 Pounds—Wayne Holmes, Columbus, Ohio
114.5 Pounds—John Morley, New York A.C.
125.5 Pounds—Michi Tanaka, New York A.C.
136.5 Pounds—Rick Sanders, Multnomah A.C., Portland, Oreg.
149.5 Pounds—Gene Davis, Athletes in Action
163 Pounds—Gerry Bell, New York A.C.
180 Pounds—Russ Camilleri, San Francisco Olympic Club
198 Pounds—Wayne Baughman, U.S. Air Force
220 Pounds—Tie between Dominic Carollo, Athletes in Action, and Henk Schenk, Multnomah A.C.
Unlimited—Greg Wojciechowski, Toledo, Ohio
Team—New York A.C. (93 pts)

Greco-Roman
(San Diego, June 10–12)

105.5 Pounds—Alfredo Olvera, Mexico
114.5 Pounds—Enrique Jiminez, Mexico
125.5 Pounds—Dave Hazewinkle, Minnesota W.C., St. Paul
136.5 Pounds—Jim Hazewinkle, Minnesota W.C.
149.5 Pounds—Phil Frey, U.S. Army
163 Pounds—Larry Lyden, Minnesota W.C.
180.5 Pounds—Khosrow Vaziri, Minnesota W.C.
198 Pounds—Wayne Baughman, U.S. Air Force
220 Pounds—Henk Schenk, Multnomah A.C.
Unlimited—Jeff Smith, John Long W.C., Los Angeles
Team—Minnesota Wrestling Club, St. Paul

National Collegiate (NCAA) Championships
(Auburn, Ala., March 25–27)

118 Pounds—Greg Johnson, Michigan State
126 Pounds—Yoshiro Fujita, Oklahoma State
134 Pounds—Roger Weigel, Oregon State
142 Pounds—Darrell Keller, Oklahoma State
150 Pounds—Stan Dziedzic, Slippery Rock
158 Pounds—Carl Adams, Iowa State
167 Pounds—Andy Matter, Penn State
177 Pounds—Geoff Baum, Oklahoma State
190 Pounds—Ben Peterson, Iowa State
Heavyweight—Greg Wojciechowski, Toledo
Team—Oklahoma State (94 pts); *College Division:* California State Polytechnic, San Luis Obispo (118 pts)
National Association of Intercollegiate Athletics (NAIA) team champion—Central Washington State

World Championships
(Sofia, Bulgaria, Aug. 27–30)

Freestyle

105.5 Pounds—Ebrahim Javadi, Iran
114.5 Pounds—Mohammed Ghorbani, Iran
125.5 Pounds—Hideaki Yamagida, Japan
136.5 Pounds—Zagalov Abdulbekov, USSR
149.5 Pounds—Dan Gable, Waterloo, Iowa
163 Pounds—Yuri Gusov, USSR
180.5 Pounds—Tediachvili, USSR
198 Pounds—Rossi Petrov, Bulgaria
220 Pounds—Shota Lomidze, USSR
Heavyweight—Aleksandr Medved, USSR
Team—USSR (42.5 pts)

Greco-Roman

105.5 Pounds—Vladimir Zubkov, USSR
114.5 Pounds—Peter Kirov, Bulgaria
125.5 Pounds—Rustem Kazakov, USSR
136.5 Pounds—Markov, Bulgaria
149 Pounds—Sreten Damjanovic, Yugoslavia
163 Pounds—Viktor Igumenov, USSR
180 Pounds—Hegedus, Hungary
198 Pounds—Naceri Rezanteev, USSR
220 Pounds—Per Svensson, Sweden
Heavyweight—Tomov, Bulgaria
Team—Bulgaria (46 pts)

YACHTING

North American Yacht Racing Union Champions

Men (Mallory Cup)—John Kolius, Houston, Texas
Women (Adams Cup)—Mrs. Romeyn S. Everdell, Duxbury, Mass.
Junior (Sears Cup)—Charlie Scott, Annapolis, Md.
Interclub (Prince of Wales Bowl)—Massachusetts Institute of Technology Nautical Association

Ocean and Long-Distance Racing

Annapolis–Newport (473 miles)—Sorcery, Class A sloop, James F. Baldwin, Locust Valley, N.Y.; also first boat of 91 to finish (elapsed time: 77.8390 hours; corrected time: 68.2607)
Buenos Aires–Rio de Janiero (1,200 miles)—Pluft, Israel Klabin, Brazil (elapsed time: 8 days, 2 hours, 59 minutes, 39 seconds; corrected time: 6:23:02:03). *First to finish:* Ondine, S.A. (Huey) Long, New York (7:09:30)
Chicago–Mackinac (333 miles)—Endurance, Roger DeRusha, Menominee, Mich.
Fastnet (England)—Ragamuffin, Syd Fischer, Australia
Los Angeles–Honolulu (2,225 miles)—Windward Passage, Class A sloop, Robert Johnson, Maui, Hawaii; also first boat to finish (elapsed time: 9:09:06:48, record)
Marblehead–Halifax (360 miles)—Robin, Ted Hood, Marblehead
Miami–Montego Bay (811 miles)—Improbable, David Allen, San Francisco (elapsed time: 3:20:18:52; corrected time: 2:22:48:19. *First to finish:* Windward Passage, Mark Johnson, New York (3:03:40:07)
Miami–Nassau (176 miles)—Running Tide, Jakob Isbrandtson, New York
Port Huron–Mackinac (235 miles)—Charisma, Jesse Philips, Chicago
St. Petersburg–Fort Lauderdale, Fla. (403 miles)—American Eagle, Ted Turner, Atlanta (elapsed time: 51.4705; corrected time, 46.8604). *First to finish:* Windward Passage
St. Petersburg–Isla Mujeres, Mexico (550 miles)—Encore Cheri, Charlie Morgan, owner (Peter Bowker, skipper). *First to finish:* Ondine (3:07:00:54)
Long Beach, Calif.–La Paz, Mexico (970 miles)—Aquarius, John Holiday, Long Beach (corrected time, 8:01:00:14)

Major Trophy Winners

Admiral's Cup (England)—Ragamuffin, Syd Fischer, Australia; *team:* Britain
Congressional Cup—Tom Pickard, Long Beach, Calif.
Intercollegiate Single-Handed—Bill Campbell, U.S. Naval Academy
Kennedy Cup (Intercollegiate Y.R.A.)—John Dane 3d, Tulane
McMillan Cup—Harvard; Charlie Koch, skipper
Morss Trophy (Intercollegiate Y.R.A.)—Southern Cal
One-Ton Cup—Stormy Petrel, Syd Fischer, Australia
Southern Ocean Racing Conference Championship—Running Tide, Jakob Isbrandtson, New York

New-Rate Designs

Variety of new stamps was issued when new postal rates went into effect on May 16. New designs included air mail stamps *(above)* and Paul Revere post cards *(below)*. Indicia on stamped envelopes *(as at bottom)* show they have been revalued for use at the new rates.

STAMP COLLECTING

Stamp collectors had reason to be happy in 1971. The head of the new U. S. Postal Service launched a program of issuing and advertising more collectors' stamps, a show including many great rarities was held in New York City, and plans were announced for a new stamp encyclopedia.

New Postal Service. On July 1, 1971, after having functioned as a department of the federal government for two centuries, the U. S. Post Office became a quasi corporation known as the U. S. Postal Service. The event was accompanied by a nationwide publicity campaign in which a special stamp was issued and millions of specially printed "birthday" envelopes were given out for mailing as first-day souvenirs. Rate increases that followed the changeover resulted in the release of 29 new stamps, postal cards, and stamped envelopes, in addition to the special issues listed in the accompanying table.

Postmaster General William M. Blount announced a program to sell more stamps for collectors' albums instead of postage. He engaged a staff composed of hobbyists, assembled a marketing research team, and commissioned an advertising agency to work on the project. They recommended, among other things, selling full-color posters with enlarged pictures of past and current stamps, preparing packets of commemoratives to be sold as gift packages, and using other sales devices unrelated to mail service. (See also POSTAL SERVICE.)

Anniversary Show. The biggest event of 1971 was the observation of the 75th anniversary of the Collectors Club of New York, the foremost philatelic institution in the United States. The celebrations culminated in ANPHILEX (Anniversary Philatelic Exhibition), easily the most impressive show ever staged. The exhibits, which were by invitation only, included only the world's greatest rarities, such as the "Post Office" Mauritius cover (on which the words "Post Office" appear instead of "Post Paid"), which sold for $380,000; the British Guiana one-cent stamp of 1856 (valued at $280,000); the Baden and Swedish color errors; and innumerable single items worth more than $50,000 each. Never before had all of them been shown at one time.

Publications. The new owner of Scott Publications, Inc., introduced full color to illustrate stamps in both *Scott's Monthly Journal* and the *United States Stamp Catalogue.* He also announced plans for a 3-volume *Scott Encyclopedia of Stamp Design,* which also will employ full color.

ERNEST A. KEHR, *Stamp News Bureau*

U. S. COMMEMORATIVE STAMPS OF 1971

Subject	Denomination	Date of issue
Wool Industry	6¢	Jan. 19
Douglas MacArthur	6¢	Jan. 26
Youth Conference (stamped envelope)	6¢	Feb. 24
Blood Donors	6¢	March 12
Missouri Statehood Sesquicentennial	8¢	May 8
Wildlife Conservation	8¢	June 12
Antarctic Treaty	8¢	June 23
American Revolution	8¢	July 4
Space Accomplishments (2 designs)	8¢	Aug. 2
American Paintings	8¢	Aug. 2
Bowling Industry (stamped envelope)	8¢	Aug. 21
Emily Dickinson	8¢	Aug. 28
San Juan, P.R., 450th Anniversary	8¢	Sept. 12
American Hospitals (postal card)	8¢	Sept. 16
Prevent Drug Abuse	8¢	Oct. 4
CARE's 25th Anniversary	8¢	Oct. 27
Historic Preservation (4 designs)	8¢	Oct. 29
Christmas (2 designs)	8¢	Nov. 10
Conference on Aging (stamped envelope)	8¢	Nov. 15

PAUL CONRAD COURTESY OF THE REGISTER AND TRIBUNE SYNDICATE

"WHAT revenue?"

state government

Under the Constitution of the United States, authority is shared between the federal government and the governments of the 50 states, each with its own executive, legislature, and system of courts. During 1971 the legislatures of 49 states met in regular session (some also in special sessions), and the legislature of the remaining state, Kentucky, met in a special session.

Prominent among state legislative concerns were reapportionment, taxation, and expenditures, especially for public welfare. Others included the environment, revenue-sharing between the federal government and the states, the legal rights of persons age 18 to 21 newly enfranchised by the ratification of the 26th Amendment to the U. S. Constitution, and automobile insurance reform.

Available summaries indicate that the legislatures received more than 100,000 proposals for legislation and passed probably a third of these. For this reason, mention of states that legislated in particular areas must not be considered as all-inclusive; others, not mentioned, may also have acted.

Reapportionment. Apportionment is the distribution of seats in a legislative body. Under U. S. Supreme Court decisions of 1964, U. S. congressional districts and districts in both houses of state legislatures must be substantially equal in population. With a new census in 1970, most legislatures faced the need to reapportion state legislative, as well as congressional, districts.

Legislative. Apportionment is usually considered to be a legislative function, but some states provide for commissions to reapportion. Further, the courts may reject such plans if they do not meet the "one man, one vote" principle enunciated by the U. S. Supreme Court. By the end of 1971,

legislatures in half the states and commissions in another seven had adopted plans. But some of these had been invalidated by courts and redrawn or sent back for redrawing, while suits were pending in several more states. In Minnesota, a federal court undertook to draw a new plan after the governor vetoed the legislature's plan; in West Virginia, the governor vetoed the plan for the Senate but approved the House plan. In Illinois, the state supreme court held the composition of a commission to be invalid but adopted its plan. More than a third of the states put off legislative reapportionment until 1972 or later.

Congressional. Reapportionment acts were adopted in 21 states, and in another state, Illinois, a federal court adopted a plan. Hawaii viewed a 1970 enactment, based on registered voters, as continuing to meet requirements; and Nebraska and New Mexico considered that population shifts shown in the 1970 census were too minor to call for changes. Six states—Alaska, Delaware, Nevada, North Dakota, Vermont, and Wyoming—had only one U. S. representative, elected at large. The remaining 19 states were expected to act in 1972: Alabama, California, Colorado, Connecticut, Florida, Kentucky, Louisiana, Michigan, Mississippi, Missouri, New Jersey, New York, Ohio, Oklahoma, Pennsylvania, Rhode Island, South Carolina, Tennessee, and Washington.

Finance. State governments account for about one fourth of all governmental expenditure in the United States. During the 1971–72 fiscal year the states were expected to collect about $96 billion in general revenue and to spend $102 billion. (Figures are estimates by the U. S. Census Bureau, based on state budgets presented in 1971.) State spending for public welfare was expected to go up considerably and to account for almost one fifth of total state general spending. The other big items in state budgets are education (38% of the total), highways (16%), and health and hospitals (7%).

A tally showed that 35 states increased existing taxes or adopted new ones during 1971 and that at year-end the only states without personal income taxes were Connecticut, Florida, Nevada, South Dakota, Texas, Washington, and Wyoming. Of these 7, Connecticut and Florida had corporate income taxes. In Rhode Island, a temporary income tax adopted in February to cover the first six months of the year was later extended. Pennsylvania adopted a flat-rate tax after a graduated personal income tax measure, enacted in March, had been declared unconstitutional. The Connecticut legislature enacted a personal income tax in July but repealed it in August. Maine voters had a chance at the November election to repeal the state income tax law but rejected this proposition. Florida voters authorized a corporate income tax, and the legislature passed such a tax. Ohio adopted new graduated personal and corporate income taxes.

Personal income tax rates were increased in 13 states, and corporate income tax rates were raised in 13. Sales tax rates were increased, or the tax base broadened, in Alabama, Connecticut, Florida, Minnesota, New York, Tennessee, Texas, and West Virginia. A proposal for a sales tax was turned down by the voters in Montana. North Carolina authorized counties to adopt sales taxes. Cigarette taxes were raised in 19 states, motor fuel taxes in 10 states, and liquor taxes in 10.

Early in 1971, President Richard M. Nixon proposed a federal revenue-sharing plan in two parts:

LUIS FERRÉ (*left*), governor of Puerto Rico, chats with fellow governors at National Governors' Conference in San Juan. Group concentrated on economic problems at September meeting.

an annual general revenue sharing plan, under which $5 billion in new federal funds would go to state and local governments, beginning in fiscal 1973; and an $11 billion grant consolidation, or special revenue sharing, program ($1 billion in new money and $10 billion from 130 existing federal grant-in-aid programs). The "no strings" aspect of the proposal drew opposition from U. S. Rep. Wilbur D. Mills, chairman of the House Ways and Means Committee, as well as others, and the proposal did not become law in 1971.

Welfare. The nation's public welfare program is administered largely by the states or their local governments, under state plans approved by the federal government and with federal funds meeting half or more of the costs. Financing such programs has taken an ever-increasing portion of state funds in recent years, and the Nixon administration proposed a family assistance plan, under which the federal government would take basic responsibility for meeting public welfare needs. Debate on the proposal continued throughout the year. By midyear, a survey by the Council of State Governments indicated that a huge increase in welfare rolls was the major cause of rising welfare spending in 27 states.

Since the level of welfare grants varies from state to state, there is some belief that migration occurs into areas of higher benefits. New York legislated a 1-year residence requirement to discourage migration, but the requirement was held unconstitutional by a federal court, as were similar provisions enacted by Connecticut and Rhode Island. A 1-year residence requirement passed by the Illinois legislature was vetoed by the governor. The U. S. Supreme Court ruled that Montana could not set a residency requirement for eligibility in a welfare program supported entirely by county funds.

Lowered Voting Age. The 26th Amendment to the U. S. Constitution—lowering to 18 the minimum voting age in all federal, state, and local elections—was ratified on June 30. On that date Ohio became the 38th state to approve the amendment and thus provide the number of states (three

fourths of the total) required for ratification. The states approving earlier were Alabama, Alaska, Arizona, Arkansas, California, Colorado, Connecticut, Delaware, Hawaii, Idaho, Illinois, Indiana, Iowa, Kansas, Louisiana, Maine, Maryland, Massachusetts, Michigan, Minnesota, Missouri, Montana, Nebraska, New Hampshire, New Jersey, New York, North Carolina, Oregon, Pennsylvania, Rhode Island, South Carolina, Tennessee, Texas, Vermont, Washington, West Virginia, and Wisconsin.

For the states the new voting age posed two sets of problems. One of these concerned where college students should vote—from their parents' homes or in their college towns. Several courts ruled on questions in this area, with the majority of the decisions favorable to campus-community registration. Among such decisions were those of the Michigan supreme court, the California supreme court, a U. S. district court in Ohio, and a three-judge panel in Pennsylvania. Federal court cases brought by students were pending in several states, and at least a dozen other state court or administrative rulings favored the right of students to register and vote in their college communities.

The other problem posed by lowering the voting age concerned laws on the books that treated those in the 18–21 age bracket as minors. If an 18-year-old was old enough to vote, the reasoning ran, was he not to be treated as an adult in other respects? State actions in this area included the following: Vermont and Michigan granted 18-year-olds full legal rights, including the right to drink alcoholic beverages and to enter into legal contracts. Washington extended all legal rights, except the right to buy liquor, to those 18 and over. North Carolina redefined a "minor" as any person who has not reached age 18 but left the legal age for buying and consumer liquor at 21.

Other legislation affecting minors had nothing to do with the lowering of the voting age. These new state laws authorized physicians to treat minors in certain cases without parental consent; for example, South Dakota (for venereal diseases),

Kansas (for drug abuse), Missouri (for pregnancy, drug abuse, or venereal disease), Rhode Island (drug abuse), Maryland (drug abuse, contraception, venereal disease, and pregnancy), and Idaho (infectious diseases).

Environment. Concern with the health of the environment was expressed in the actions of many legislatures. New laws were so numerous and varied that only a sampling can be given.

Delaware adopted a new coastal zoning act, widely hailed as landmark legislation, that forbids all further industrial development along its coastline and also regulates offshore development. Washington adopted a shoreline protection act and instructed its local governments to review the environmental effects of their action. North Carolina directed that a detailed statement of environmental impact must precede any undertaking financed by the state. Both North Carolina and Washington acted to require industries to report pollutants discharged into air or water. Maryland created a power-plant siting program. Arkansas, Maine, Missouri, and Washington provided for the preservation or protection of natural areas.

Arkansas, Idaho, Illinois, Maine, and South Dakota adopted regulations covering surface mining or strengthened existing laws. Florida, Idaho, Indiana, New York, North Dakota, and Oklahoma legislated against noise pollution. Delaware, Indiana, Iowa, North Carolina, Utah, and Washington provided for pesticide control. Indiana regulated pollution from animal feedlots. Kansas forbade discharge of mercury into state waters, and Florida authorized civil-class actions by private citizens against polluters. Rhode Island authorized its governor to close down on commerce and travel in the event of a hazardous "air pollution episode."

Still other states reorganized their environmental protection agencies. New Hampshire created an air pollution control board, and New Mexico, an environment improvement agency.

Automobile Insurance Reforms. Many states were considering "no fault" motor vehicle accident insurance following the enactment of such a law by Massachusetts in 1970. In 1971, legislation of this kind was enacted in Delaware, Florida, Illinois, and Oregon. The concept is that the insuring company will pay the policyholder for his own loss up to a stipulated amount without the necessity of a lawsuit to determine fault. Proposals for federal "no fault" legislation also were under consideration at year-end.

Gambling and Lotteries. In 1971, Connecticut became the second state to approve offtrack betting (the third, if Nevada is counted) and the fourth to authorize a state lottery. (In Nevada a principal away from the track may lawfully place a bet with a licensed agent if the latter is at the track.) New York had previously authorized off-track betting, and New Hampshire, New Jersey, and New York have state-operated lotteries. Profits go to education. Illinois and Washington authorized bingo for nonprofit organizations. Kansas repealed the penalties for playing bingo but could not fully legalize the game because of a constitutional lottery ban.

State Constitutions and Reorganization. Illinois and Virginia were implementing new constitutions that became effective in 1971. Montana and North Dakota were preparing for constitutional conventions to be held in 1972.

North Carolina moved to reorganize 317 governmental agencies into 19 major departments. Arkansas took similar action, combining some 60 executive agencies, boards, and commissions into 13 cabinet-level departments. Maine created a special committee to draft a master plan to consolidate 250 agencies into 12 new departments.

Other Actions. Consumer protection was the major concern at the meeting of state attorneys general in June. Indiana and Arkansas passed laws creating a consumer protection division under the state attorney general. South Dakota passed a "consumer bill of rights."

Codes of ethics for public officials were a concern in many states. Arkansas adopted a code that requires public officials to file a statement of financial holdings. Connecticut established a legislative committee with responsibility for investigating charges of conflict of interest.

Laws forbidding sex discrimination were passed in Indiana and Delaware, and Pennsylvania voters adopted a similar constitutional amendment. California, Colorado, Florida, Iowa, Michigan, and Oregon enacted "no fault" divorce provisions.

National Governors' Conference. The 63d annual meeting of the National Governors' Conference was held in San Juan, Puerto Rico, on September 12–15. Major topics of discussion included health and welfare, corrections, and "no fault" insurance. The governors also acted on policy statements in six chief areas of interest: executive management and fiscal affairs, human resources, crime reduction and public safety, natural resources, rural and urban development, and transportation.

WILLIAM L. DAY
Illinois Legislative Council

NEW JERSEY'S Governor Cahill (*center*) congratulates winners of state's $1 million lottery. New Jersey's extremely successful revenue-raising lottery has drawn the attention of other states hard-pressed for funds.

WIDE WORLD

STEEL

The international steel industry experienced extraordinary difficulty in 1971 as a cyclical downturn in worldwide steel demand was aggravated by the development of an international monetary crisis.

The International Iron and Steel Institute estimated world raw steel production in 1971 at 632 million net tons, a decrease from the 1970 total of 653 million net tons. The American Iron and Steel Institute estimated U. S. raw steel production for 1971 at 120 million net tons, a drop of 8.7% from the previous year and 14.9% below the 1969 record of 141 million net tons.

World Developments. The USSR became the world leader in raw steel production in 1971. It produced about 130 million net tons and thus took over the world leadership that the United States had held for more than 80 years. The Soviet steel industry is characterized by a highly concentrated production capacity, and half its steel is produced by nine works.

Japan, however, has the world's 10 largest blast furnaces. The largest furnace, situated in Nippon Kokan's Fukuyama Works, was blown in during April 1971. The Fukuyama Works, with an annual capacity exceeding 13 million net tons, is the world's largest steel plant. Japan decreased its steel production to about 94 million net tons in 1971 as the result of a slowdown in domestic growth, compounded by the adverse effects of international economic policies. The major steelmakers announced delays in 1971 in plans to expand facilities.

Steel production of the European Coal and Steel Community (ECSC) dropped 6% in 1971 from the previous year's level. For West German producers, the problem of low steel demand was aggravated by high wage costs, upward revaluation of the mark, and increased steel imports. The ECSC nations scheduled $1.2 billion for capital expenditures in 1971, mostly for making flat-rolled products.

U. S. Developments. Steel production in the United States was seriously distorted in 1971, as steel consumers stockpiled considerable quantities during the first half of the year to guard against the possibility of a strike when a 3-year labor contract covering major producers expired July 30. A strike was averted, but the work-off of excess inventories, combined with lower steel consumption, resulted in a sharp decline in steel production.

The financial performance of the industry in 1971 did not improve over 1970, when its return on net worth ranked it 40th among 41 manufacturing groups. Spokesmen attributed the industry's difficulties to (1) rapid inflation of costs, well beyond gains from improvements in efficiency and increased prices, and (2) a significant erosion of markets, caused primarily by imports.

The U. S. steel industry's capital-investment expenditures for 1971 were estimated at $1.5 billion. This figure was 10% below the 1970 spending, and it reflected both the industry's unsatisfactory financial position and completion of many modernization projects—basic oxygen furnaces, strand (continuous) casting units, high-speed finishing mills, and pollution control equipment.

On Aug. 16, 1971, National Steel Corporation concluded its acquisition of Granite City Steel Company. The merged firm displaced Republic Steel as the third-largest domestic steel producer, after United States Steel and Bethlehem.

GEORGE N. STOUMPAS
American Iron and Steel Institute

STEIN, Herbert. See BIOGRAPHY.

PRODUCTION OF IRON ORE, PIG IRON AND FERROALLOYS, AND RAW STEEL[1]

Country	1970 Iron ore, concentrates and agglomerates (long tons of 2,240 lb)	1970 Pig iron and ferroalloys (short tons of 2,000 lb)	1970 Raw steel[1] (short tons of 2,000 lb)	Country	1970 Iron ore, concentrates and agglomerates (long tons of 2,240 lb)	1970 Pig iron and ferroalloys (short tons of 2,000 lb)	1970 Raw steel[1] (short tons of 2,000 lb)
Algeria	2,953,000	...	...	Liberia	22,637,000	...	...
Angola	6,447,000	...	...	Luxembourg	5,632,000	5,303,000	...[3]
Argentina	295,000	904,000	2,032,000	Malaysia	4,518,000	...	...
Australia	45,175,000	6,834,000	7,539,000	Mauritania	9,301,000	...	...
Austria	3,858,000	3,285,000	4,496,000	Mexico	4,114,000	1,896,000	4,136,000
Belgium	92,000	12,071,000	20,114,000[2]	Morocco	876,000	...	...
Brazil	29,526,000	3,086,000	5,681,000	Netherlands	...	3,961,000	5,194,000
Bulgaria	2,312,000	1,301,000	1,997,000	New Caledonia	177,000	...	...
Burma	2,000	...	...	New Zealand	5,000	...	75,000
Canada	45,372,000	9,296,000	12,346,000	Norway	3,858,000	1,345,000	933,000
Chile	10,876,000	496,000	643,000	Pakistan	5,000	...	180,000
China, Mainland	42,321,000	17,637,000	19,180,000	Peru	9,350,000	198,000	123,000
China, Nationalist	...	72,000	260,000	Philippines	1,575,000	...	95,000
Colombia	1,279,000	231,000	329,000	Poland	2,539,000	7,595,000	12,871,000
Cuba	...	...	60,000	Portugal	138,000	353,000	416,000
Czechoslovakia	1,555,000	8,322,000	12,566,000	Rhodesia	689,000	287,000	140,000
Denmark	30,000	259,000	525,000	Rumania	3,100,000	3,748,000	6,553,000
Egypt	472,000	331,000	250,000	Sierra Leone	2,461,000	...	...
Finland	1,033,000	1,323,000	1,291,000	South Africa	9,153,000	4,552,000	5,225,000
France	56,499,000	21,090,000	26,196,000	Spain	6,869,000	4,497,000	7,981,000
Germany, East	886,000	2,205,000	5,510,000	Sudan	20,000	...	...
Germany, West	6,655,000	37,067,000	49,650,000	Swaziland	2,756,000	...	...
Greece	...	...	549,000	Sweden	30,215,000	2,844,000	6,045,000
Guinea	2,165,000	...	...	Switzerland	...	28,000	499,000
Hong Kong	167,000	...	...	Thailand	25,000	44,000	...
Hungary	581,000	1,962,000	3,414,000	Tunisia	669,000	...	...
India	28,788,000	7,826,000	6,906,000	Turkey	2,313,000	606,000	1,382,000
Iran	2,000	...	...	USSR	191,921,000	94,357,000	127,624,000
Ireland	...	...	62,000	United Kingdom	11,958,000	19,290,000	31,229,000
Israel	...	...	93,000	United States	89,791,000	93,851,000	131,514,000[4]
Italy	1,150,000	9,209,000	19,031,000	Venezuela	21,062,000	573,000	1,022,000
Japan	1,535,000	75,000,000	102,869,000	Yugoslavia	3,474,000	1,378,000	2,441,000
Korea, North	7,874,000	2,425,000	2,200,000	Other Countries	...	...	706,000
Korea, South	551,000	17,000	542,000				
Lebanon	...	...	20,000	Total (estimate)[5]	741,652,000	468,955,000	652,735,000

[1] Steel in the first solid state after melting, suitable for further processing or sale. [2] Figure includes data from Luxembourg. [3] Included under Belgium. [4] United States data exclude 1,723,000 net tons of steel produced by foundries that reported their output to the Bureau of Census but did not report to American Iron and Steel Institute. [5] Detail does not necessarily add to total because figures are rounded. (Sources: Statistical Quarterly Report for Iron and Steel Industry, West Germany Iron and Steel Federation, Düsseldorf; American Iron and Steel Institute, New York.)

UPI

NEW YORK Stock Exchange President Bernard Lasker hands President Richard Nixon a bull, symbolic of buoyant stock market. Presentation of toy leather bull on April 16 recognized Nixon's correct prediction in 1970 that stock prices would rise.

STOCKS AND BONDS

The stock market rode a roller coaster in 1971. Stock prices moved up strongly during the first four months of 1971, extending the advance that began in the middle of 1970. The market then turned downward until August, reflecting a shift in investor sentiment characterized by a general lack of confidence in the economy. President Nixon's mid-August announcement of a New Economic Policy produced a dramatic rally that was followed by another period of weakness. However, investor psychology again shifted to the positive side in late November, and the year ended with a strong upsurge. Major stock market indicators ended the year near their April highs. The bond market also moved higher in the early months of 1971, but then backed off until midyear. Yields started to decline in the final half, and bonds ended 1971 on a favorable note.

Stock Prices. The stock market began 1971 with an impressive show of strength. The list forged ahead almost without interruption until the end of April. There were periods of modest consolidation, but new buying quickly came in to propel stock prices to still higher levels.

The November 1970–April 1971 advance, during which stock market indicators approached their 1968–69 highs, was fueled by a number of elements, not the least of which was the Federal Reserve Board's stimulative monetary policy. In a switch from its previously highly restrictive stance, the Fed was pumping money into the economy at a rate seldom experienced over an extended period. Other factors in the early 1971 rise were the expectation of a solid recovery in the economy and corporate earnings following the 1970 recession, and a decline in interest rates.

STOCKS AND BONDS
(Standard & Poor's Index)

	Date[1]	425 Industrials	20 Rails	55 Utilities	500 Stocks
1970 high	Jan. 5	102.87	38.94	61.71	93.46
1970 low	May 26	75.58	24.65	47.67	69.29
1971 high	Apr. 28	115.84	48.32	64.81	104.77
1971 low	Nov. 23	99.36	35.03	54.48	90.16
1971 close	Dec. 31	112.72	44.61	59.83	102.09

[1] Dates are for industrials. Rail and Utility highs and lows in some instances occurred on other dates.

MOST ACTIVE STOCKS IN 1971— NEW YORK STOCK EXCHANGE

Stock	Sales	Close	Net Change
American Tel & Tel	32,231,900	44¾	− 4⅛
Occidental Petroleum	26,938,800	11⅞	− 6⅝
Federal National Mortgage Assoc.	23,164,100	98¼	+36⅞
Pan American World Airways	21,533,200	15¼	+ 3⅛
Texaco	21,157,900	34⅜	− ½
Gulf Oil	19,852,400	28⅞	− 3½
Chrysler	19,088,700	28⅝	+ ⅝
Greyhound	18,199,800	21	+ 4⅞
Telex Corp.	18,192,300	12	− 4⅝
Eastern Air Lines	17,751,700	22⅝	+ 7½
International Tel & Tel	17,513,800	58⅜	+ 7¾
RCA Corp.	16,769,200	37⅛	+10⅝
Natomas	16,510,000	70	+15⅜
Braniff Airways	15,878,700	15⅞	+ 7⅝
General Motors	15,676,700	80½	Unch.

MOST ACTIVE STOCKS IN 1971— AMERICAN STOCK EXCHANGE

Stock	Sales	Close	Net Change
National General Corp. wts. (new)	12,485,700	6⅜	+ 3¼
Syntex Corp	11,473,600	83	+44¾
Loew's Corp. wts.	9,930,000	22	+ 8
Asamera Oil Corp. Ltd.	9,794,500	17¾	+ 2½
Braniff Airways, Inc. wts.	7,294,600	15⅝	+ 7⅞
Leasco Corp. wts.	6,914,800	7¾	+ 1
Trans World Airlines, Inc. wts.	6,906,500	25	+18⅞
United Brands Co. wts.	6,280,700	3⅜	− ⅞
Beverly Enterprises	6,065,300	10⅜	− 1
Imperial Oil	5,891,500	31¼	+11½
Ling-Temco-Vought wts.	5,725,700	5	+ 2⅜
Instrument Systems	5,665,300	6½	+ ½
Kaiser Industries	5,490,300	8¾	− 3⅞
AMREP Corp.	5,097,000	19½	−18⅜
Nytronics, Inc.	5,091,000	1¾	− ¾

An abrupt change in psychology occurred in late April and, despite minor rallies, stock prices trended downward until August. The steady erosion reflected growing investor realization that the administration's economic game plan was giving little evidence of success. Business recovery was spotty, and as the year progressed it became increasingly apparent that cost-push inflation was not being contained and that unemployment was rising. A sharp rise in interest rates, steel strike threats, and walkouts in the rail and shipping industries added further uncertainties.

During this period, the international monetary situation began to heat up and the dollar weakened in currency markets. The problem was aggravated by a drop in U. S. gold reserves to around $10 billion and a record balance-of-payments deficit.

The critical nature of the situation both at home and abroad prompted the Nixon administration to institute a sweeping series of executive orders and legislative proposals aimed at reversing dangerous trends in the economy. President Nixon's August 15 address, in which a New Economic Policy (NEP) was set forth, sparked a dramatic two-day upsurge in stock prices. It was followed by a more subdued rally that continued into September.

The August–September rally ran out of steam as uncertainties arose over the shape of Phase II of NEP. Stocks dropped sharply in October and November, and broad-based indicators reached new lows for 1971. The decline came to an abrupt halt during the last week of November, after the introduction of Phase II, and the market finished the year with a strong upward move. The change reflected hopes that the international monetary crisis would be resolved. In late December the U. S. dollar was devalued by 8.57%, and other currencies were revalued. With that settled, the market entered the new year on a buoyant note.

Mutual Funds. In May 1971, for the first time since the mutual fund industry began to compile statistics, investors cashed in a larger dollar amount of mutual fund shares than they bought. The funds were in a net redemption position again in June, July, and September, although they managed to end the year with three consecutive months of cash inflow. The temporary plunge into net redemption figures was seen as evidence of growing investor caution.

Earnings and Dividends. An earnings recovery occurred in 1971 for most companies. In terms of Standard & Poor's industrial stock price index, net income (partly estimated) rose to $6.09 a share, from the depressed $5.39 of 1970.

Dividends dipped slightly, and were the equivalent of $3.17 a share on Standard & Poor's 425 index, as against $3.24 for 1970. At year's end, stocks sold at an average price of 18.5 times earnings, with an average dividend return of 2.8%.

Volume. Total trading on the New York Stock Exchange was a record 3,891 million shares in 1971, well above the 2,937 million shares of 1970. American Exchange volume rose from 843 million shares in 1970 to 1,071 million in 1971.

Bond Prices. The bond market rallied sharply in the first two months of 1971, continuing the advance that began in the second half of 1970. In late February, however, yields began to rise and bond prices sagged until midyear, reflecting increasing interest rates and a heavy debt calendar. Another advance in bond prices slowly gathered momentum as the second half of 1971 began, and the bond market ended the year on the upbeat. Yields on highest-grade industrials reached a low of 6.78% on February 13, and then rose to a high of 7.46% on May 19 before ending 1971 at 6.94%. Short-term government yields receded to 4.00% on March 17, then rose to 6.35% on July 28; at year-end, they were 5.30%.

It was possible to describe 1971 as the year investors discovered bonds. In addition to increasing investor attention, the strong bond market of early and late 1971 reflected an increase in the money supply and lower interest rates.

Brokerage House Trends. In marked contrast to 1970, the securities industry survived 1971 without seeing a major house going into liquidation. Despite this increase in stability, the industry was debating matters that could eventually bring great changes in its structure and operations. Proposals under discussion included the reorganization of the New York Stock Exchange into a nationwide market, the possibility of institutional membership on the NYSE, and the question of separation of money management and brokerage functions. Actions taken in 1971 included the adoption of stricter capital requirements for NYSE member firms and approval of a new commission schedule.

One of the major developments of the year was Merrill Lynch, Pierce, Fenner & Smith's announcement that it was going public. Before the year ended, several other Big Board members had followed suit. Merrill Lynch became the first NYSE member firm whose shares were admitted to listing on the Big Board.

CAROLYN J. COLE
Standard & Poor's Corporation

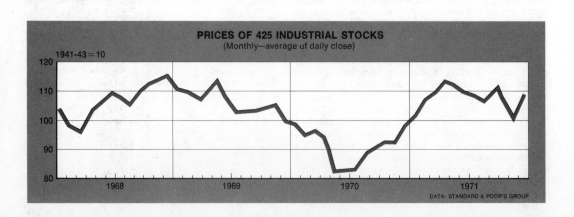

PRICES OF 425 INDUSTRIAL STOCKS
(Monthly—average of daily close)

1941-43 = 10

DATA: STANDARD & POOR'S GROUP

STRAVINSKY, Igor

Russian-American composer; b. Oranienbaum, near St. Petersburg (now Leningrad), Russia, June 17, 1882; d. New York, N.Y., April 6, 1971.

Igor Stravinsky was among the greatest geniuses of modern music. He was one of the most influential of the revolutionary composers who changed the course of music in the early 20th century. In his long composing career, which spanned more than 60 years, he added numerous masterpieces, such as *Firebird, Petrouchka, The Rite of Spring, Symphony of Psalms,* and *Oedipus Rex,* to the repertoire.

Unlike Arnold Schoenberg, the only modern composer who matches him in importance, Stravinsky created no new system to replace traditional harmonic structure. Until he turned to serialism in the mid-1950's, Stravinsky's music was based on tonality, though a tonality so free and varied it would have startled the 19th century masters. However, he was innovative in his use of form, his instrumentation, and his treatment of rhythm and phrase. Unlike Schoenberg's innovations, Stravinsky's contributions were never the focus of a school. Still, Stravinsky's influence was widespread, affecting such composers as Aaron Copland, Samuel Barber, and Darius Milhaud.

Stravinsky led an active professional life, conducting, performing at the piano, and helping prepare his theatrical works for the stage. He also was the author, with the American conductor Robert Craft, of six books, which contain the composer's witty, rambling reflections on music and other subjects. In his long lifetime he was associated with many significant artists in other fields, among them Pablo Picasso, Jean Cocteau, Sergei Diaghilev, W. H. Auden, André Gide, and George Balanchine.

Early Years. Igor Fyodorovich Stravinsky was born at Oranienbaum, near St. Petersburg (now Leningrad), Russia, on June 17, 1882. His father was a leading bass singer at the Imperial Opera in St. Petersburg, and it was there that the boy first heard the music of Mikhail Glinka and Peter Ilich Tchaikovsky, to which he remained devoted all his life. At the age of 9 he began piano lessons, and soon was studying harmony and counterpoint. At his parents' insistence he attended the University of St. Petersburg to read law. In 1902 he met Nikolai Rimsky-Korsakov, for whom he played some of his works. Stravinsky soon became a regular member of Rimsky-Korsakov's circle, and in 1903 began three years of study with the master. He married Catherine Nossenko in 1906.

In February 1909, the impresario Sergei Diaghilev heard some of Stravinsky's works in St. Petersburg and invited the composer to orchestrate some short pieces for his season of Russian ballet and opera in Paris that summer. Thus began an association that continued until Diaghilev's death in 1929.

On June 25, 1910, Diaghilev's Ballets Russes successfully presented the first performance of Stravinsky's *Firebird* in Paris. Next came *Petrouchka,* first given in Paris on June 13, 1911, with Vaslav Nijinsky triumphant in the title role. *The Rite of Spring* was given its premiere in Paris on May 29, 1913. Its bold instrumental colors, insistent and shifting rhythmic patterns, and daring harmonies

CAMERA PRESS-PIX

IGOR STRAVINSKY (1882–1971)
He added masterpieces to the repertoire.

produced an uproar of protest and counterprotest that is unparalleled in musical history. Many critics and scholars date the birth of "modern music" from this moment.

World War I and After. During World War I, Stravinsky lived in Switzerland, working on several vocal and choral scores, which derived their themes from Russian folk sources. Among these works were the short opera *Renard* (1916) and the dance cantata *Les Noces* (1917). The Revolution cut him off from Russia, and he was not to see it again until 1962. In 1920 he took up residence in France.

Meanwhile, Stravinsky was reconsidering his aesthetic stance. *L'Histoire du soldat* (1918), written for narrator, dancers, and a small orchestral ensemble, pointed toward new theatrical combinations and away from the use of the full symphony orchestra. The music is eclectic and reflects Stravinsky's interest in popular forms, including jazz.

Pulcinella (1920), a ballet score commissioned by Diaghilev and based on the music of Giovanni Battista Pergolesi, signaled Stravinsky's new interest in the music of the past, particularly the classical style of the 18th century. This interest was to affect his own music for over 30 years. Stravinsky's neoclassical idiom was dominant in such works as the Piano Sonata (1924), the Concerto for Piano and Winds (1924), the opera-oratorio *Oedipus Rex* (1927), the Violin Concerto (1931), and the ballet *Apollon Musagète* (1928).

Apollon Musagète, choreographed by George Balanchine, was first performed by Diaghilev's Ballets Russes in Paris in 1928. After Balanchine emigrated to the United States in 1933, he and Stravinsky collaborated on other ballets, including *Jeu de cartes* (1936), *Orpheus* (1947), and *Agon* (1957).

In 1930, Stravinsky wrote one of his finest compositions, a work reflecting his own deep religious feeling, the *Symphony of Psalms,* based on biblical texts. It was composed for the 50th anniversary of the Boston Symphony Orchestra.

Early in the 1920's, Stravinsky began to tour widely as a performer, visiting the United States in 1925 and 1935. Though he had become a French citizen in 1934, he left France to settle in the United States in 1939. He became an American citizen in 1945. In 1940, following the death of his first wife the previous year, he married Vera de Bosset.

Later Years. After composing the Symphony in C (1940) and the Symphony in Three Movements (1945), among others, Stravinsky again turned to opera in the late 1940's. W. H. Auden, together with Chester Kallman, provided an English libretto based upon a famous series of engravings by William Hogarth. The result was *The Rake's Progress,* first performed at the Teatro La Fenice in Venice in 1951. Robert Craft, later to be his literary collaborator, helped him with the English versification.

Stimulated, perhaps, by Craft's interest in the music of Anton von Webern, Stravinsky began to incorporate serial elements into his music in the mid-1950's. The choral work *Threni* (1958) was his first totally serial composition. Other works in this style were the opera *The Flood* (1962) and *Requiem Canticles* (1966). He was to remain a serial composer for the rest of his life. Following his death in New York, Stravinsky, in accordance with his wishes, was buried in the Russian corner of San Michele cemetery in Venice, near Diaghilev.

ROBERT S. CLARK
Associate Editor, "Stereo Review"

SUDAN

Sudan was shaken by a coup and countercoup in July 1971. The revolution, led by the Sudanese Communist party and left-wing army officers, appeared to have succeeded on July 19. But it was bloodily suppressed on July 22, by forces loyal to Maj. Gen. Jaafar Mohammad al-Numeiry, president of the Revolutionary Command Council (RCC).

Coup and Countercoup. Late in 1970, President Numeiry had moved to halt the growing influence of the Communist party in the government. The secretary-general of the party, Abdul Khaliq Mahjub, was arrested, and three Communists were dismissed from the RCC. Numeiry had acted after the Communists opposed Sudan's projected federation with Egypt, Libya, and Syria.

Mahjub escaped from prison early in July 1971, and on July 19 his followers captured all the RCC officials in Sudan, including President Numeiry, and some 60 army officers loyal to the president. But neither the Sudanese army nor the people rallied to the Communists and their Sudanese Revolution Council. Iraq recognized the new government, but expected Iraqi aid did not come.

The coup collapsed three days later, on July 22. On that day Libya seized a British airliner en route from London to Sudan and carrying Lt. Col. Babiker al-Nur and Maj. Farouk Osman Hamadallah, who were designated to head the new government. Also on July 22, Egypt assisted in the return of the Sudan Brigade from the Suez Canal. During the day in Sudan, tank and paratroop brigades advanced on the presidential palace in Khartoum and rescued Numeiry after severe fighting.

Most of the persons accused of taking part in the coup were executed soon after Numeiry was restored to power. About 2,000 Communists were believed to have been arrested immediately after the coup collapsed, and 700 more were apprehended by mid-August. It was reported that some of the estimated 1,800 Soviet military advisers in Sudan had also been arrested.

─────── **SUDAN · Information Highlights** ───────

Official Name: Republic of The Sudan.
Area: 967,497 square miles (2,505,813 sq km).
Population (1970 est.): 15,700,000. *Density,* 16 per square mile (6 per sq km). *Annual rate of increase,* 2.8%.
Chief Cities (1968 est.): Khartoum, the capital, 194,000; Omdurman, 206,000.
Government: *Head of state,* Maj. Gen. Jaafar Mohammad al-Numeiry, president (took office Oct. 12, 1971). *Head of government,* Maj. Gen. Jaafar Mohammad al-Numeiry. *Political party*—Sudanese Socialist Union.
Languages: Arabic (official), English, French, and African languages.
Education: *Literacy rate* (1970), 10% of population. *Expenditure on education* (1967), 20.3% of total public expenditure. *School enrollment* (1967)—primary, 496,088; secondary, 144,481; technical/vocational, 4,880; university/higher, 10,404.
Finances (1970 est.): *Revenues,* $453,800,000; *expenditures,* $324,500,000; *monetary unit,* Sudanese pound (0.3482 pound equal U. S.$1, Sept. 1971).
Gross National Product (1970 est.): $1,830,000,000.
Average Annual Income Per Person (1969 est.): $107.
Economic Indexes: *Agricultural production* (1969), 139 (1963= 100); *consumer price index* (1969), 116 (1963=100).
Manufacturing (metric tons, 1969): Cement, 169,000; sugar, 87,000.
Crops (metric tons, 1969 crop year): Sorghum (1968), 710,000; groundnuts, 383,000; cotton lint, 225,000; sesame (1968), 122,000.
Minerals (metric tons, 1969): Salt, 51,000; chromium ore, 12,500; magnesite (1968), 6,500.
Foreign Trade (1970): *Exports,* $293,000,000 (chief exports—cotton, $182,860,000; gum hashab, $24,929,000; groundnuts, $15,825,000). *Imports,* $311,000,000 (chief imports, 1968—textile yarn and fabrics, $56,906,000; chemicals, $25,439,000; transport equipment, $23,541,000; nonelectrical machinery, $17,835,000). *Chief trading partners* (1968)—West Germany (took 15% of exports, supplied 5% of imports); Italy (12%—6%); India (10%—10%); United Kingdom (6%—18%).
Transportation: *Roads* (1970), 6,562 miles (10,560 km); *motor vehicles* (1969), 47,800 (automobiles, 30,100); *railroads* (1970), 2,945 miles (4,739 km); *national airline,* Sudan Airways; *principal airport,* Khartoum.
Communications: *Telephones* (1970), 45,539; *television stations* (1968), 1; *television sets* (1969), 30,000; *radios* (1968), 180,000; *newspapers* (1968), 18.

Sudan severed diplomatic relations with Iraq on July 24. Early in September, Sudan recalled its ambassadors from the Soviet Union and Bulgaria, and ousted the counselor of the Soviet embassy and the Bulgarian ambassador in Khartoum.

Foreign Affairs. In mid-April, Sudan withdrew at the last moment from unity talks with Egypt, Libya, and Syria, largely as a result of Communist opposition. On April 19, Numeiry declared that Sudan must first draft a new constitution and establish a strong internal political organization before joining the Arab federation.

In mid-December, Uganda protested against the incursions of Sudanese forces pursuing southern black separatist guerrillas across the border. Uganda issued a warning that unless Sudanese troops withdrew at once "maximum force" would be used to repel them.

Political Affairs. On August 13 the RCC introduced a provisional constitution, which established the office of president of the Sudanese republic and set up a People's Assembly, which will draft a permanent constitution. In the presidential election beginning on September 15, Numeiry, running unopposed, received 98.7% of the votes cast. He was sworn in on October 12 as the first elected president of Sudan. After the inauguration ceremony the RCC resigned, and Numeiry announced the formation of a new government. He also established a single political party, the Sudanese Socialist Union.

JOHN NORMAN
Pace College Westchester

SUHARTO. See BIOGRAPHY.
SUPREME COURT. See LAW.
SURGERY. See MEDICINE.

SWAZILAND

The main developments in Swaziland in 1971 included a visit by its officials to the Republic of South Africa, plans for national elections in 1972, and educational expansion.

Foreign Relations. Prime Minister Prince Makhosini Dlamini visited the Republic of South Africa in March. His delegation included the minister of works, power, and communications and the minister of state for foreign affairs. They conferred with South African Prime Minister Balthazar J. Vorster on March 26 and, also, it was reported, with the South African minister of transport, Barend Schoeman. The latter talks led to speculation that Swaziland was planning a rail link with South Africa.

The presence of the Swazi foreign minister sparked further speculation that the visit was a bid by Swaziland for closer diplomatic and trade ties with South Africa. Swaziland and South Africa have a common border and a customs agreement, and many Swazis work in South Africa. In April the Swazi government denied it sought closer diplomatic ties.

Domestic Affairs. King Sobhuza II announced in June that Swaziland would hold general elections in 1972, the first since it won independence in 1968.

The cabinet was reshuffled in July, and a new post, the ministry of justice, was created.

Education. In 1971 some 9,000 students—a record number—attended secondary schools in Swaziland. The academic planning mission recommended that proposed 4-year degree courses and polytechnic centers begin operating with 2-year programs by late 1971.

FRANKLIN PARKER, *West Virginia University*

SWEDEN

In 1971, Sweden's economic situation deteriorated further, and the country suffered its most serious labor conflict in 25 years. Other events of the year included the opening of the new Riksdag (parliament) and the decision to withdraw from negotiations for entry into the European Economic Community (EEC).

The Economic Crisis. Several developments in 1971 deepened Sweden's economic difficulties: U. S. policies, inflation, strikes, and unemployment. The brighter side of the picture was a foreign trade surplus of over $300 million for the first 9 months of the year and a slight decline in imports. The U. S. import surtax, imposed in August, cut Swedish ex-ports to the United States, but its effect was counterbalanced by the increase of Swedish exports to members of the European Free Trade Association (EFTA) and the EEC.

Creeping inflation continued, aided by a farm agreement of April 21 that increased agricultural prices and a wage contract concluded with the National Federation of Trades Unions (LO) on June 22, after six months of protracted negotiations. The wage agreement, which spread a 28% increase over a 3-year period, made Swedish labor costs the highest in Europe. Strikes by civil service personnel also resulted in increased salary costs.

The strikes by the civil service and professional workers, including teachers, disrupted Swedish life on a very wide scale and caused considerable controversy. Although civil servants had obtained the right to strike in 1969, the government intervened with both lockouts and legislation to stop the strikes. There was much bitterness after the dispute was settled in June.

The unemployment rate climbed during the spring and summer to the highest point since the 1930's. At the opening of the Riksdag on October 14 the government presented a package of 2 billion kronor that would provide for retraining workers, public investment, release of funds for purchasing equipment, and a tax benefit on depreciation and investment. Another promising reform was the decentralization of government agencies in an effort to lessen the burden on Stockholm and to improve the economy of other urban centers.

Although gains in the gross national product dropped by nearly 2.5% from 1970, Swedish production in such areas as shipbuilding, electronics, forest products, and steel continued to improve. Agriculture experienced a very good season.

CROWN PRINCE Carl Gustav, an avid sailor (*above*), took a more active role in Swedish affairs in 1971. When King Gustav was in Italy in September, the prince (*top, center*) spoke for the monarchy during a cabinet meeting.

Political Developments. On Jan. 12, 1971, the new unicameral Riksdag met in new quarters in the Cultural House in Stockholm. Few of its 350 members looked back with regret to the old bicameral parliament, but they did complain about unexpected pressures of work and lengthy sessions. Some procedural reforms were proposed, but no specific measures were presented to the legislature.

The resignation of Torsten Nilsson as foreign minister in June removed an influential senior cabinet minister, but there was no alteration in policies under his successor Krister Wickman. Gunnar Hedlund, leader of the Conservatives, also resigned, in favor of Thorbjörn Fälldin.

Several times during the spring the government came close to defeat. Two such instances were votes on the Ritsem hydroelectric project and on a proposal to expand the northern railroads, both of which were opposed on grounds of environmental disturbance. Some dissent centered on the "wait and see" economic policy of the government, but this was altered by the October 14 proposals.

In August a parliamentary committee, dominated by the Social Democrats, issued its recommendations for revising the constitution. Its proposals included lowering the voting age to 18 and further restricting the powers of the monarchy. The new constitution must be approved by two sessions of the Riksdag with a general election in between.

Foreign Policy. On March 18, Premier Olof Palme announced Sweden's withdrawal from the EEC negotiations on the grounds that full membership would not be compatible with Swedish neutrality. However, he expressed the hope that Sweden might be able to enter into some form of agreement with the EEC. At the same time, Sweden's effort to strengthen its ties with both EFTA and the Nordic Council showed concern over future isolation when Britain, Denmark, and Norway join the EEC.

The Swedish government issued a formal protest against the USSR's negative policy on Jewish emigration and showed the same displeasure with the widening of the war in Southeast Asia. Sweden agreed to supply 2,000 troops to a new 5,000-man Nordic battalion for the United Nations.

Cultural Events. Changes in the educational system continued with the approval of a new library school at Borås and music programs at Malmö and Göteborg. A new authors' association emerged from the disbandment of four quarreling organizations. One of the group's outstanding members, Lars Forssell, joined the Swedish Academy, replacing the late Sigfrid Siwertz.

RAYMOND E. LINDGREN
California State College, Long Beach

SWITZERLAND • Information Highlights

Official Name: Swiss Confederation.
Area: 15,941 square miles (41,288 sq km).
Population (1970 census): 6,527,000. *Density,* 391 per square mile (151 per sq km). *Annual rate of increase,* 1.3%.
Chief Cities (1969 est.): Bern, the capital, 166,800; Zürich, 432,400; Basel, 213,200; Geneva, 169,500.
Government: *Head of state,* Nello Celio, president of the confederation (took office Jan. 1, 1972). *Head of government,* Nello Celio, president of the Federal Council. *Legislature*—Federal Assembly; Council of States, 44 members; National Council, 200 members. *Major political parties*—Conservative Christian Social party; Social Democratic party; Radical Democratic party.
Official Languages: German, French, Italian.
Education: *Literacy rate* (1971), 100% of population. *Expenditure on education* (1968), 19.3% of total public expenditure. *School enrollment* (1968)—primary, 480,642; secondary, 429,025; technical/vocational, 148,541; university/higher, 38,197.
Finances (1970): *Revenues,* $1,960,200,000; *expenditures,* $1,980,700,000; *monetary unit,* franc (3.950 francs equal U.S.$1, Sept. 1971).
Gross National Product (1970 est.): $20,500,000,000.
National Income (1969): $15,272,000,000; *national income per person,* $2,454.
Manufacturing (metric tons, 1969): Cement, 4,534,000; paper and cardboard, 555,000; crude steel, 500,000.
Crops (metric tons, 1969 crop year): Potatoes, 1,210,000; sugar beets (1968–69), 453,000; wheat, 345,000.
Minerals (metric tons, 1969): Salt, 267,000.
Foreign Trade (1968): *Exports* (1970), $5,128,000,000 (chief exports—chemicals, $814,031,000; watches, clocks, $539,-100,000; electrical machinery, $305,510,000; textile yarn and fabrics, $281,545,000). *Imports* (1970), $6,480,000,000 (chief imports—nonelectrical machinery, $454,880,000; chemicals, $453,975,000; transport equipment, $438,945,-000. *Chief trading partner* (1968)—West Germany (took 14% of exports, supplied 30% of imports).
Transportation: *Roads* (1969), 31,300 miles (50,371 km); *motor vehicles* (1969), 1,385,600 (automobiles, 1,283,700); *railroads* (1970), 3,300 miles (5,311 km); *national airline,* Swissair; *principal airports,* Zürich, Geneva, Basel.
Communications: *Telephones* (1970), 2,846,535; *television stations* (1968), 30; *television sets* (1969), 1,144,000; *radios* (1969), 1,800,000; *newspapers* (1969), 121.

SWITZERLAND

Extension of the franchise to women in federal elections and the first revaluation of the franc in 35 years overshadowed all other events in Switzerland in 1971.

Political Affairs. On February 7, male voters approved, 621,403 to 323,596, a constitutional referendum granting women the vote in federal affairs and eligibility for election to the federal parliament. On the same date the cantons of Aargau, Fribourg, Schaffhausen, and Zug granted similar rights to women in cantonal or municipal matters. Glarus followed suit on May 2, bringing the number of cantons and half-cantons fully enfranchising women to 14 out of 25. Six other cantons have granted limited rights to women in local affairs.

The first nationwide referendum in which women could vote resulted on June 6 in the passage of a constitutional amendment giving the government power to combat air and water pollution. Federal elections, held on October 30–31, brought the election of 11 women to parliament. Extreme right-wing parties gained 10 new seats, reflecting an upsurge of long-existent anti-immigrant sentiment despite a March report showing the first decline in 25 years in the number of foreign workers.

Two "political" trials attracted attention in 1971. The first involved the conviction of members of the Belier movement—a youth organization aimed at achieving separate cantonal status for the Jura region—on charges of trespass and breach of the peace. More serious, though no more emotional, was the conviction of Alfred Frauenknecht, head of the jet engine division of Gebrüder Salzer A. G., for selling blueprints and specifications for the French Mirage 3 jet fighter engine to Israeli agents.

Economic Affairs. Seeking to combat inflation, the Swiss National Bank and the Swiss Bankers Association agreed in February to continue existing restrictions on expansion of credit until July 31, 1972. However, a continued influx of U. S. dollars, plus an unfavorable balance of trade, necessitated further action. On May 9, the government announced a 7% upward revaluation of the franc. Nonetheless, in August large amounts of foreign capital again began to flow into Switzerland. To curb this, interest payments on all foreign-held deposits made after July 31 were banned, and banks were required to maintain 100% reserves on all such deposits, unless compensated by new Swiss investment abroad.

Exports for the first half of 1971 rose 12.8% over 1970 to $2,793.3 million, while imports totaled $3,604.7, an increase of 13.8% over the same period a year before. Along with other European Free Trade Association members not applying for membership in the European Economic Community, Switzerland opened preliminary negotiations with the Common Market in hopes of establishing a series of free-trade agreements.

On January 3, the Swiss Supreme Court ruled that the federal tax officials should provide the U. S. Internal Revenue Service with any information it requested concerning American holdings in Swiss banks, when tax fraud was suspected.

Foreign Affairs. On Dec. 7, 1970, the Swiss ambassador to Brazil, Giovanni Bucher, was kidnapped by Brazilian revolutionaries. He was released on January 16 in return for 70 political prisoners held by the Brazilian government.

In September the government extended diplomatic recognition to the government of North Vietnam. The Swiss continued to handle U. S. affairs in Cuba.

PAUL C. HELMREICH
Wheaton College, Mass.

SWISS MEN voted in February to extend female suffrage. Women, who have local voting rights in many cantons, can now cast their ballots in federal elections.

WIDE WORLD

SYRIA

Under President Hafez al-Assad, Syria's governmental system was altered in 1971 in an apparent move toward decentralization and democratization. Syria's relations with other Arab countries, Jordan excepted, were reestablished where broken and improved greatly as Assad removed Syria from the isolation to which it had been relegated by the previous regime. Its economy, stagnated by the preceding government's policies that had driven out capital investment and thousands of needed workers, technicians, and intellectuals, received a much-needed boost from pragmatic liberalization policies toward people, products, and capital.

Internally, Assad, a general who seized power in November 1970, eased the suffocating and repressive police-state atmosphere that had engulfed Syria, and he emphasized popular participation in Syria's future. With that popular participation and support, Assad led Syria into the Federation of Arab Republics and proposed the formation in Syria of a National Progressive Front. The war with Israel continued to be low key, although the Palestinian guerrillas were actively supported, which almost brought about a war with neighboring Jordan.

Domestic Politics. Constitutional changes made the position of president of the republic the highest office, and a referendum in March confirmed Assad in the position. In February a 173-member People's Council was formed with 85 seats for the Baathists, 40 for "nationalist and progressive" forces, and 48 for workers and peasants unions, medical and bar associations, religious men, and artisans. It was the first Syrian legislative body since 1966 and the first national assembly since 1963, but it is not an elected body. It was appointed and can be dissolved by the president. The form of government duplicates that of Egypt. On April 4 a 28-man "national front" cabinet was announced. President Assad is planning to form a National Progressive Front that will unite the progressive political forces in Syria and that may well replace the Baathist party as the country's ruling instrument.

Other government decrees banned arrest without warrant and replaced a dozen other anti-personal-freedom laws. Also, all Syrians who had smuggled their funds abroad were officially granted an amnesty. The government eased restrictions on the news media, eliminated all aspects of martial law, lightened travel limitations, and increased family allowances, thus expediting travel.

Economy. In 1971 wages were increased while the prices of foodstuffs and other commodities were reduced. No new direct or indirect taxes or duties were levied. Assad lifted restrictions on importing raw materials and machinery and facilitated the importation of previously-banned consumer and luxury goods. A comprehensive 5-year plan, with the great Euphrates Dam project as the keystone, was begun. The government followed a policy of sweeping liberalization in the long-idle private sector. The state encouraged private participation in Syria's economic growth to help make the 5-year plan a success and to make possible the full exploitation of the tripartite federation, both as a market for Syrian products and as a source of cooperation and financial aid.

Syria, the only country outside the Western and Socialist camps that exploits and markets its oil independently, raised its oil prices 6% and initialled very beneficial agreements with Tapline and the Iraq Petroleum Company, two companies whose oil pipelines cross Syria. Syria also increased trade and established several important industrial plants. All of these measures boosted the economy.

Middle East Crisis. Syrian-Israeli conflicts were relatively few and not serious. Although Israel accused Syria of numerous "acts of aggression," these were mainly conducted by Palestinian guerrillas operating from Syria. Because of guerrilla activities in Jordan, Syria's relations with Jordan deteriorated until Syria closed their mutual border on July 25, at the height of the guerrilla-Jordanian clashes. On August 12, Syria severed relations with Jordan, and two days later its planes strafed Jordanian army positions. However, tensions eased, and a shaky peace was established.

Syria's violent anti-Jordanian activities may well have served to hide its own confiscation of heavy arms sent to the guerrillas from Algeria and its extremely restrictive measures toward the guerrillas and their operations. Officially, the government continued to reject a negotiated solution of the Israeli-Arab crisis, but on several occasions Assad declared that he "fully backed" Egypt's diplomatic efforts to reach a peaceful settlement.

Federation. Created on April 17, the union of Syria, Egypt, and Libya in the Federation of Arab Republics became official on September 1. Other, mainly economic, pacts were made, a military union that places their armed forces under a single command was formed, and a constitution was adopted. An important constitutional article permits member states to intervene in any component state in case of an internal or external threat, without a formal request. This provision should provide a strong deterrent to any anti-Assad activities.

JACK L. SCHRIER, *Georgetown University*

SYRIA · Information Highlights

Official Name: Syrian Arab Republic.
Area: 71,498 square miles (185,180 sq km).
Population (1970 est.): 6,300,000. *Density,* 88 per square mile (33 per sq km). *Annual rate of increase,* 2.9%.
Chief Cities (1968 est.): Damascus, the capital, 789,840; Aleppo, 566,770; Homs, 231,877.
Government: *Head of state,* Lt. Gen. Hafez al-Assad, president (took office March 14, 1971). *Chief minister,* Gen. Abdel Rahman Khlefaw, premier (took office May 1971). *Legislature*—People's Council, 173 members. *Major political parties*—Baath party, Syrian Arab Socialist Union, Socialist Union.
Language: Arabic (official).
Education: *Literacy rate* (1971), 40% of population. *School enrollment* (1968)—primary, 813,225; secondary, 257,745; technical/vocational, 4,856; university/higher, 35,005.
Finances (1969 est.): *Revenues,* $313,874,000; *expenditures,* $313,874,000; *monetary unit,* pound (3.82 pounds equal U. S.$1, Sept. 1971).
Gross National Product (1970 est.): $1,460,000,000.
Consumer Price Index (1970): 118 (1963=100).
Manufacturing (metric tons, 1969): Cement, 933,000; residual fuel oil, 602,000; distillate fuel oils, 301,000.
Crops (metric tons, 1969 crop year): Wheat, 1,004,000; barley, 627,000; cottonseed (1968), 270,000; sugar beets (1968–69), 166,000; cotton lint, 147,000.
Minerals (metric tons, 1969): Crude petroleum, 2,889,000.
Foreign Trade (1970): *Exports,* $203,000,000 (chief exports —cotton, $81,100,000; barley, $9,948,000; wool, $2,801,-000). *Imports,* $358,000,000 (chief imports, 1968—nonelectrical machinery, $36,800,000; chemicals, $32,005,000; iron and steel, $28,903,000; cereals and preparations, $26,100,000). *Chief trading partners* (1968)—Lebanon (took 21% of exports, supplied 5% of imports); USSR (11% —9%).
Transportation: *Roads* (1970), 8,118 miles (13,064 km); *motor vehicles* (1969), 47,100 (automobiles, 31,100); *railroads* (1970), 1,030 miles (1,658 km).
Communications: *Telephones* (1970), 103,687; *television stations* (1968), 5; *television sets* (1969), 130,000; *radios* (1965), 1,745,000; *newspapers* (1967), 4 (daily circulation, 85,000).

TANZANIA

Tanzania celebrated the 10th anniversary of the independence of the mainland from British colonial rule on Dec. 9, 1971. Since 1964 the mainland (formerly known as Tanganyika) has been joined politically with the island of Zanzibar.

Political Affairs. Tanzania's first treason trials, in which seven persons were accused of planning to overthrow the government of President Julius K. Nyerere, ended in July. After appeals were exhausted, three persons had been convicted and sentenced to life imprisonment: John Dunstan Chipaka, former secretary-general of the banned African National Congress; Eliya Chipaka, a former army captain; and Bibi Titi Mohamed, a junior minister and president of the National Women's Organization.

On May 9, First Vice President Abeid Karume announced that 19 persons charged with planning to overthrow the government of Zanzibar had been sentenced to death.

Augustine Saida, a Tanzanian citizen, was appointed Tanzania's chief justice in April, replacing Phillip Telfer Georges, a citizen of Trinidad.

Implementation of the Arusha Declaration. Perhaps the most important piece of legislation in 1971 was the acquisition of buildings act passed by the National Assembly on April 23. The act empowered President Nyerere to take control of rented buildings valued at over 100,000 E. A. shillings. Compensation was to be paid for buildings less than 10 years old. By the end of April over 1,000 urban buildings had been acquired by the government.

This nationalization of rental property was part of a broad plan to implement the policies of socialism (*ujamaa*) and self-reliance contained in the 1967 Arusha Declaration. Banks and insurance companies had already been nationalized, and other changes were occurring in commerce, education, and government. In the schools, for example, purely academic instruction was being supplemented by training in practical areas.

Economy. The improvement of transportation facilities is important for a large country such as Tanzania, where the movement of people and goods between the capital and outlying areas has been inhibited by inadequate means of transport. Work continued in 1971 on the Tan-Zam railroad, which will eventually connect the port at Dar es Salaam with the Zambian capital of Lusaka. Construction on the 1,100-mile (1,800-km) rail link began late in 1970 with the help of capital and technicians from the People's Republic of China and was scheduled for completion in 1976. But the rate of construction in 1971 indicated that the railroad may be finished well ahead of the original target date.

To supplement the railroad, a 561-mile (903-km) highway is being built across the country, with capital and technical resources supplied by the United States.

Foreign Affairs. Tanzania's most serious problems in foreign affairs in 1971 stemmed from worsening relations with neighboring Uganda. Tanzania gave asylum to deposed Ugandan President Milton Obote after the successful coup of Maj. Gen. Idi Amin on January 25. Obote was a personal friend of President Nyerere, and his recent "moves to the left" had been widely admired in Tanzania.

Despite attempts by third parties to mediate the dispute, Tanzania and Uganda exchanged verbal blasts throughout the year, and several clashes oc-

------- TANZANIA • Information Highlights -------

Official Name: United Republic of Tanzania.
Area: 363,820 square miles (39,703 sq km).
Population (1970 est.): 13,270,000. *Density,* 36 per square mile (14 per sq km). *Annual rate of increase,* 2.7%.
Chief City (1970 est.): Dar es Salaam, the capital, 300,000.
Government: *Head of state,* Julius K. Nyerere, president (took office April 26, 1964). *Head of government,* Julius K. Nyerere. *Legislature* (unicameral)—National Assembly, 187 members. *Major political parties*—Tanganyika African National Union and its affiliate in Zanzibar, Afro-Shirazi.
Languages: English (official), Swahili (official).
Education: *Literacy rate* (1970), 15–20% of population. *School enrollment* (1967)—primary, 825,000; secondary, 32,276; technical/vocational, 2,077; higher, 1,068.
Finances (1970 est.): *Revenues,* $210,000,000; *expenditures,* $201,000,000; *monetary unit,* shilling (7.143 shillings equal U. S.$1, Dec. 30, 1971).
Gross National Product (1970 est.): $1,100,000,000.
National Income (1968): $761,000,000; *per person,* $62.
Consumer Price Index (1969): 122 (1963=100).
Manufacturing (metric tons, 1969): Residual fuel oil, 368,-000; meat, 161,000; sugar, 92,000; beer, 213,000 hectoliters.
Crops (metric tons, 1969 crop year): Agaves (1968), 1,969,-000; cassava (1968), 1,205,000; cotton lint, 71,000; coffee, 46,000; cloves, about 80% of world's total.
Minerals (metric tons, 1969): salt, 34,000; diamonds, 777,000 metric carats; gold, 498 kilograms.
Foreign Trade (1970): *Exports,* $238,000,000 (chief exports—coffee, $43,680,000; cotton, $34,580,000; sisal, $25,060,000; diamonds, $22,540,000). *Imports,* $272,000,000. *Chief trading partner* (1968)—United Kingdom (took 24% of exports, supplied 28% of imports).
Transportation: *Motor vehicles* (1969), 62,300; *railroads* (1970), 3,670 miles (5,872 km); *national airline,* East African Airways; *principal airport,* Dar es Salaam.
Communications: *Telephones* (1970), 31,587; *radios* (1968), 138,000; *newspapers* (1969), 4 (daily circulation, 61,000).

curred along the border between the two countries. On October, Uganda demanded that Tanzanian troops pull back from the border, and Tanzania accused Uganda of trying to annex part of its territory. On October 29, it was announced that Tanzania and Uganda had agreed to reconcile some of their differences and to maintain the East African Community, of which Kenya was also a member.

Tanzania continued to take a strong stand against white minority governments in Rhodesia and South Africa. President Nyerere opposed British sales of arms to South Africa at the Commonwealth conference in Singapore in January. In February, Moshi was the site of the 18th regular session of the African Liberation Committee of the Organization of African Unity.

JAY E. HAKES
Louisiana State University in New Orleans

TAXATION

Tax changes in the United States in 1971 came in a sweeping revenue act proposed by the Nixon administration as a means of stimulating the U. S. economy through various reductions in business and individual taxes. Congress passed the act, and the President signed it into law on Dec. 10, 1971 (Public Law 92-178).

Key Benefits of the 1971 Revenue Act. For business, the chief attractions of the act are (1) restoration of a 7% investment credit for machinery and equipment; (2) statutory approval, with only one significant modification, of a previous system of liberalized depreciation allowances called the Asset Depreciation Range system (see *U. S. Treasury Rulings*); (3) authorization for the creation of Domestic International Sales Corporations (DISCs), which allow their stockholders to defer tax on 50% of each year's export profits; (4) a new tax credit of 20% of the wages paid to employees who are hired from the Work Incentive welfare program; and (5) termination of the manufacturers' excise tax on automobiles and light trucks.

STATE TAX REVENUE IN THE U. S., BY TYPE OF TAX

(Amounts in millions of dollars)[1]

Tax source	Fiscal year 1971 (prelim.)	Fiscal year 1970	Fiscal year 1969
Total collections.............	**$51,469**	**$47,962**	**$41,931**
General sales and gross receipts..	15,454	14,177	12,443
Motor fuels....................	6,624	6,283	5,644
Alcoholic beverages.............	1,527	1,420	1,246
Tobacco products...............	2,534	2,308	2,056
Insurance......................	1,344	1,182	1,024
Public utilities.................	1,009	918	763
Motor vehicles.................	2,953	2,728	2,475
Motor vehicle operators.........	221	227	210
Corporation in general..........	878	764	625
Alcoholic beverage license.......	123	120	133
Individual income..............	10,196	9,183	7,527
Corporation net income..........	3,420	3,738	3,180
Property.......................	1,126	1,092	981
Death and gift.................	1,104	996	996
Severance.....................	733	686	630
Other.........................	2,294	2,139	1,997

[1] Because of rounding, detail may not add to totals.

For individuals, the key tax benefits include (1) an increase in the personal exemption to $675 for 1971 and to $750 for 1972 and thereafter; (2) liberalization of the low-income allowance for 1971 and an increase in that allowance to a flat $1,300 for 1972 and thereafter; and (3) an increase in the percentage standard deduction to 15% of adjusted gross income, with a limit of $2,000, for 1972 and thereafter. In addition, working parents with children under 15 years of age—and other working taxpayers with disabled spouses or dependents of any age—may be able to deduct up to $400 a month of expenses incurred for caring for the children, dependent, or spouse while the taxpayer works. Taxpayers with adjusted gross income up to $18,000 are entitled to the full amount of the deduction. But for those with incomes above $18,000, the amount deductible is scaled down until no deduction is allowed if income is $27,600 or more.

A number of provisions of the 1971 Revenue Act were designed to reduce or eliminate various tax-saving opportunities. The most widely applicable of these changes covers the interest, dividends, and other "unearned" income of children who may be claimed as dependents by their parents because the children are not over 19 years of age or are still regularly attending school. These children will have their low-income allowance limited to their "earned" income and will compute their percentage standard deduction only on the amount of their "earned income," if any.

Early in 1971, President Nixon signed into law a bill that barred the payment of federal taxes with discounted Treasury bonds redeemed at par (so-called "flower" bonds). This law applied to all Treasury bonds issued after March 3, 1971 (P. L. 92-5, March 17, 1971).

U. S. Court Decisions. The cost of meals and lodging at a hotel was deductible by an individual convalescing there after an operation in a nearby hospital, when the hospital had no room available for that purpose. Three fourths of the cost of household help to care for a semi-invalid's physical needs and to administer required medication three times a day was deductible as a medical expense. But an individual who was advised by his physician not to live alone after having suffered a heart attack could not deduct any of the expense of a live-in worker he hired as a result of the advice.

If an automobile was totally wrecked in a collision, the owner could treat this as a deductible casualty loss, but he could not include in the amount of loss the legal fees and damage payments he incurred in unsuccessfully suing the other party to the collision. A father could not deduct, as his own casualty loss, the damage caused by his minor son to an automobile that the father had previously transferred to the son's ownership.

Food and drinks that a professional man bought in the clubhouse for his fellow golfers at the end of a game did not qualify as a "quiet business meal," which may be deducted without the strict substantiation required for deducting other business entertainment expenses. An individual could deduct the $22.73 he paid for a tax textbook to help him prepare his own income tax return.

The U. S. Supreme Court held that a wife's renunciation of the "community" in a community property state does not excuse her from her liability for federal income taxes on community income, even though it excuses her from taxes and other obligations controlled by state law.

U. S. Treasury Rulings. The daily subsistence allowance that an employer may pay an employee for business travel expenses without requiring the employee to report either the expenses or the allowance on his tax return was raised from $31.25 to $36.00. An employee whose work locations are temporary and subject to frequent change, such as a worker on a construction crew, can deduct as business expenses the cost of traveling from the place of his residence to the various job locations and the expenses of living at these temporary locations.

Businesses were authorized to use a liberalized form of depreciation allowances called the Asset Depreciation Range (ADR) system. This allows a business to spread its depreciation of the cost of machinery and equipment over a period of years that is 20% shorter than the ordinary useful life of the asset, thereby increasing the amount of the annual deduction. The liberalized system was generally approved by Congress in the 1971 Revenue Act, although a special first-year depreciation benefit originally included as part of the ADR rules was retroactively excluded by the new law and the system was renamed the Class Life system.

If an annulment has the same effect on a husband's duty of support under local law as a divorce does, he can deduct as alimony the payments required of him under a decree of annulment or a support agreement incidental to such a decree.

Revenue Collections. Federal internal revenue tax collections for the fiscal year 1971 amounted to $191,647,000,000—down from $195,722,000,000 collected in fiscal 1970.

State tax revenues for the fiscal year 1971 totaled $51,469,000,000—up from $47,962,000,000 in fiscal 1970. On a nationwide basis, per capita state taxes for fiscal 1971 amounted to $250.44. Hawaii had the highest per capita taxes, $472.39, with Delaware the runner-up at $398.17 per capita. New Hampshire had the lowest per capita taxes, $155.47; and Ohio, at $164.46 per capita, the next-lowest. Local government tax collections rose to $38,833,000,000 for fiscal 1970. Property taxes accounted for 85% of the total amount.

OTHER COUNTRIES

Britain overhauled its entire tax structure. It will gradually replace its sales and payroll taxes with a value-added tax. The separate tax and surtax on individual income was replaced by a single graduated schedule of lower rates, with a top rate of 75%. The tax rates on both corporations and capital gains were also reduced. Because of deteriorating economic conditions, special action was taken to cut various purchase taxes by 18% and to increase the first-year tax depreciation deduction to 80% for investments made before August 1973.

Canada made sweeping changes in its tax structure, including a capital gains tax for the first time, a reduction in corporate tax rates, and a change in individual exemptions and tax-rate schedules that will take 1 million persons off the tax rolls and reduce taxes for another 1½ million taxpayers. Toward the end of 1971, emergency reductions were made in both corporate and individual taxes retroactive to July 1, 1971, to counter a 10-year high in the Canadian unemployment rate.

El Salvador offered a 10-year exemption from income, inheritance, and property-transfer taxes as part of an incentive program designed to increase the export of its products outside the Central American Common Market.

Finland imposed a temporary 15% surtax on consumer durables, such as automobiles and television sets, which is added to the basic turnover tax.

India raised its surtax on personal income from 10% to 15% on incomes exceeding $2,000 a year. It also increased the wealth tax on real and personal property from the previous 1%–5% schedule to a 1%–8% schedule and ended or reduced tax concessions previously available to businesses.

Italy adopted a new tax system that (1) replaces a multitude of special taxes with a general personal income tax ranging from 10% to 72% and (2) substitutes a value-added tax on goods and services for its general purchase tax.

Mexico raised its sales tax from 3% to 10% on luxury items, including color television sets, washers and dryers, higher priced automobiles, and wristwatches. It also lowered the annual depreciation deduction permitted for buildings from 5% to 3%, and for machinery from a flat 10% to a series of deductions ranging mostly between 7% and 9%.

The **Netherlands** added a temporary 3% surcharge on its income and corporation taxes and raised its value-added tax from 12% to 14% on many goods and services, but cut the rate to 4% on most foods.

LEON GOLD
Tax Research Institute of America, Inc.

TELECOMMUNICATIONS

Telecommunications is the technology for sending information over a distance. Typically, this information is coded messages sent by telegraph, voice calls or pictures sent by telephone or Picturephone, or sounds or pictures sent by radio or television.

In 1971, telecommunications was a rapidly growing technology. In particular, data communications systems—digital transmission systems designed primarily for communications to or from a computer or between computers—showed promise of a boom.

Data Communications. The potential for competition in the field of telecommunications was vastly increased as a result of hearings held before the Federal Communications Commission (FCC) in 1971. These hearings, which dealt with applications for specialized common carrier services using domestic point-to-point microwave links, opened the

TELEPHONES IN MAJOR COUNTRIES

Country	Telephones Jan. 1, 1970	% increase over 1969	No. per 100 population
Argentina	1,668,426	4.3	6.90
Australia	3,598,692	6.1	29.27
Austria	1,334,339	7.4	18.07
Belgium	1,936,814	4.8	20.05
Brazil	1,787,000	14.5	1.94
Canada	9,302,828	5.5	43.76
Colombia	545,851	1.3	2.63
Czechoslovakia	1,895,229	5.9	13.12
Denmark	1,599,952	5.5	32.45
Finland	1,089,700	8.0	23.13
France	8,114,041	8.1	16.05
Germany, East	1,986,190	4.7	11.61
Germany, West	12,456,268	10.7	20.36
Greece	881,003	15.7	10.00
Hong Kong	502,374	17.8	12.45
Hungary	777,739	13.6	7.54
India	1,159,519	9.7	0.21
Italy	8,528,354	10.0	15.98
Japan	23,131,688	12.7	22.41
Korea, South	562,111	14.7	1.80
Mexico	1,327,702	13.0	2.67
Netherlands	3,120,766	7.0	24.09
New Zealand	1,202,590	4.1	42.63
Norway	1,090,662	5.3	28.20
Poland	1,756,248	6.4	5.38
Portugal	698,075	6.8	7.27
South Africa	1,482,299	6.1	7.34
Spain	4,126,363	10.8	12.46
Sweden	4,306,905	4.8	53.74
Switzerland	2,846,535	6.0	45.38
USSR	unavailable	..	..
United Kingdom	13,947,000	8.1	24.96
United States	115,222,000	5.5	56.38
Yugoslavia	622,939	13.5	3.05

way for competition between small, new specialized companies and large, well-established companies.

In fact, the competition has already begun to appear. For example, one small company established a microwave link between Chicago and St. Louis, and another company said it planned to build a coast-to-coast microwave network. By the end of 1971, specialized common carrier companies had filed applications with the FCC for more than 1,900 new microwave stations. This seemed to be an indication that the hearings could become the most significant in the history of the communications industry.

Typically, a microwave link is established by building a string of towers spaced approximately 25 to 35 miles (40 to 65 km) apart. The towers support antennas for sending information on a microwave beam, which is relayed from one end of the string of towers to the other end. The beam can carry hundreds of voice channels in a telephone network, some channels for relaying television programs, or many channels for sending digital data.

The fastest growing use of microwave links is for digital data communications systems. Such systems are used to collect and distribute business information, to gain quick access to centrally located data banks, and to make computer facilities available to companies that do not have them. So far, the larger established telephone companies have used nationwide average rates in their quotations for data communications services. Given the new competition, however, their rates probably will have to be adjusted downward in many service areas.

Domestic Satellite System. Eight companies sent proposals for building a domestic satellite system to the FCC in 1971. If one of the proposed systems is built, it would include earth stations and two or three communications satellites for handling a combination of telephone, Picturephone, and data services within the United States.

International Satellite Communications. Fifty-four countries signed a permanent charter for the International Telecommunications Satellite Organization (the new Intelsat), which in effect is the first international public utility.

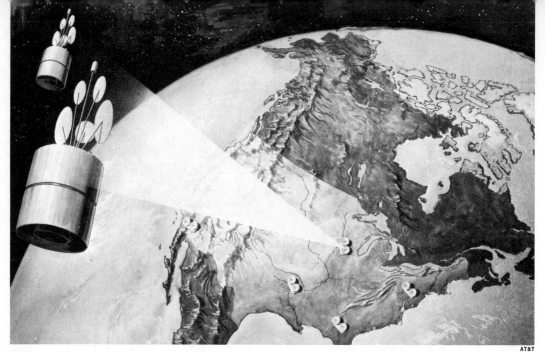

AT&T's proposed multipurpose communications satellite system would consist of 2 satellites and 5 earth stations.

The economies of satellite usage already can be pretty much demonstrated. For example, an Intelsat 4 satellite can handle 9,000 two-way telephone circuits or 12 color television channels, whereas a transatlantic cable can handle 800 two-way voice circuits and has no television capability. The potential benefits from using communications satellites include more efficient operation of airlines, improved maritime communications, long-distance correspondence with a computer, and the opening of international television channels.

U. S.-Mainland China Links. In September 1971, the People's Republic of China agreed to restore direct telephone and telegraph services between mainland China and the United States. Such communications had been broken off since Nov. 15, 1968.

Telephones. The number of telephones in the world increased from 134.6 million on Jan. 1, 1960, to 255.2 million on Jan. 1, 1970, showing a growth of about 90% during the 1960's. As of 1970, the United States had 115.2 million telephones, about 45% of the world total. Japan and the United Kingdom ranked second and third, respectively.

In the United States, the Traffic Service Position System (TSPS) was enlarged in 1971. This system now allows customers to dial person to person, to make a credit-card call, to call collect, to bill a third number, or to dial all calls at a coin telephone. Other advances made by the telephone industry included the introduction of a new speakerphone set, which is smaller, more reliable, and easier to install than earlier models, and the introduction of pocket telephones. Investigations were under way on an experimental device that can dial a telephone when given spoken commands.

Americans place more than six billion toll calls each year. To keep up with this demand, new equipment and new cost-saving techniques are constantly being developed. Although cost savings were emphasized during 1971, the major telephone companies had to seek significant rate increases, primarily because inflationary pressures continued for most of the year.

Picturephones. A transmission system using buried pipe about the size of a person's wrist is being designed to carry 250,000 simultaneous telephone conversations or more than 2,400 Picturephone signals. Also, scientists are working to produce a color version of the black-and-white picture now used in Picturephone service. Picturephone sets were first introduced into commercial service in Pittsburgh, Pa., in July 1970. Since then, the charges for Picturephone service have been reduced from $58 a month to $25.

Submarine Telephone Cables. A 3-minute call from New York to London via transatlantic cable cost $4.05 in 1971, as compared with $12 in 1956. Five transatlantic cables were in use during the year, and a sixth has been requested by the communications industry. Also, a new submarine cable between West Palm Beach, Fla., and the Bahamas has been proposed.

Central Telegram Bureau. The Western Union Telegraph Company announced plans for its first central bureau for handling telegrams originating over the telephone, which account for more than 90% of all telegram traffic. Western Union's new facility will be located in Moorestown, N. J.

Medical Aids. Special portable radios have been developed to broadcast electrocardiograms from inside a moving ambulance or from a house where a person is stricken. Also, tests have been made so that conventional telephone lines to a hospital can be used for monitoring cardiac irregularities in heart patients recovering at home.

Laser Communications. Officials of the United Nations, meeting in buildings two miles apart in Geneva, Switzerland, in 1971, were linked by television signals flashed over a laser beam. However, such optical communications seem more vulnerable to weather conditions than the microwave communications ordinarily used for television transmissions.

PAUL WEINER, *University of Connecticut*

THIEU, Nguyen Van. See BIOGRAPHY.
TITO (Josip Broz). See BIOGRAPHY.

television and radio

In 1971 both television and radio experienced strong government pressure. CBS television, under fire from officials for its controversial special *The Selling of the Pentagon*, emerged victorious when the House of Representatives refused to authorize a contempt citation against the network. The Federal Communications Commission urged that free-form or progressive-rock radio broadcasters be given less control of their programs. Many broadcasters saw this as a threat to freedom of speech.

TELEVISION BROADCASTING

The year 1971 in television was not markedly different from many of those that preceded it. As in recent years, television news did its usual superb job of reporting unusual events, such as the Apollo moon landing missions and the California earthquake. There was continuing uncertainty during 1971 over the formulation of regulations for cable TV. The year also saw increasing pressures on the networks. These came from parents' groups for better children's programs, from blacks for more representation on the air, and from Washington for a change in news reporting from its alleged "liberal" bias to more "objective" reporting. There were many challenges to the renewal of existing television licenses. But with it all, the pollsters reported that the number of viewing hours per home increased during the year, as did the sale of TV sets.

Television News. Of vital concern not only to television but to all of the news media was the angry reaction of Washington to the remarkable CBS documentary *The Selling of the Pentagon*. The program, first presented on February 23, made the claim that the Pentagon was spending millions more of the taxpayers' dollars than it was entitled to on presenting a favorable image of itself to the public. The charge was documented with films of VIP tours of military bases and maneuvers, the cadre of colonels made available for lectures to public groups, the public display at fairs and the like of weaponry, interviews with government officials, and, in general, the Pentagon's efforts to exploit the media for its own purposes.

NOTABLE U.S. TELEVISION PROGRAMS OF 1971

A RENAISSANCE LIFE: A PERSONAL VIEW OF BERNARD BERENSON BY KENNETH CLARK—Special program on the life and work of the great art historian Bernard Berenson, written and narrated by Sir Kenneth Clark. PBS, April 12.

THE AMERICAN WEST OF JOHN FORD—A tribute to the renowned American film director, with clips from Ford motion pictures and narration by Henry Fonda, James Stewart, and John Wayne. CBS, Dec. 5.

BASIC TRAINING (Special of the Week)—An examination by film maker Frederick Wiseman of basic training in the U. S. Army as carried out at Fort Knox, Ky. PBS, Oct. 4.

BEETHOVEN'S BIRTHDAY: A CELEBRATION IN VIENNA WITH LEONARD BERNSTEIN—Special program commemorating the 200th anniversary in 1970 of the birth of Ludwig van Beethoven, with Bernstein conducting the Vienna Philharmonic Orchestra, the Vienna State Opera Chorus, and a group of singers in excerpts from some of the master's works. CBS, Dec. 24.

... BUT WHAT IF THE DREAM COMES TRUE (CBS Reports)—A study of an American family, the Greenawalts of Birmingham, Mich., who reveal that their realization of the American Dream of prosperity and success has not given them the full measure of contentment and satisfaction for which they had striven, narrated by Charles Kuralt. CBS, Nov. 25.

CHICANO (CBS Reports)—Special program focusing on the growing militant movement among Mexican-Americans, notably in Los Angeles, narrated by Hughes Rudd. CBS, Oct. 21.

DECEMBER 6, 1971: A DAY IN THE PRESIDENCY (NBC News Special)—Documentary showing a workday of President Richard Nixon, narrated by John Chancellor. NBC, Dec. 21.

EVENING AT POPS—Special jazz program with Dave Brubeck, Paul Desmond, and Gerry Mulligan, with Arthur Fiedler conducting the Boston Pops Orchestra, PBS, July 25.

THE FIRST CHURCHILLS (Masterpiece Theater)—The story of the colorful life and career of John Churchill, 1st Duke of Marlborough, presented in 12 episodes and starring John Neville and Susan Hampshire. PBS, weekly beginning Jan. 10.

THE GREAT AMERICAN DREAM MACHINE—Program in magazine format, offering serious as well as satiric looks at public and cultural affairs in the United States, and often featuring the resident "consumerist-humorist" Marshall Efron. PBS, weekly from Jan. 6 for 15 weeks; weekly from Oct. 6.

HEIFETZ—Special on the world-famous violin virtuoso Jascha Heifetz, narrated by Francis Robinson. NBC, April 23.

HOME (Special of the Week)—David Storey's poignant play about four patients in what seems to be a mental institution, starring Sir John Gielgud, Sir Ralph Richardson, Dandy Nichols, and Mona Washbourne. PBS, Nov. 29.

JANE EYRE—Television adaptation of Charlotte Brontë's novel, with George C. Scott, Susannah York, Ian Bannen, Jack Hawkins, and others. NBC, March 24.

JULIE AND CAROL AT LINCOLN CENTER—Music and comedy special with Julie Andrews and Carol Burnett. CBS, Dec. 7.

NEW YORK PHILHARMONIC YOUNG PEOPLE'S CONCERT—Violinist Yehudi Menuhin as guest conductor and narrator in an analysis of Béla Bartók's *Concerto for Orchestra*. CBS, Sept. 26.

NEW YORK ILLUSTRATED: THE MELTING POT GROWS OLDER—Documentary contrasting the past and present of New York's Lower East Side, narrated by Ken Alvord. NBC, Oct. 12.

THE PRICE (Hallmark Hall of Fame)—Television adaptation of Arthur Miller's play about the confrontation between two brothers after their father's death, starring George C. Scott, Barry Sullivan, Colleen Dewhurst, and David Burns. NBC, Feb. 3.

THE RECORD MAKERS—A tribute to more than 24 world record-setters, including Willie Mays (baseball), Bing Crosby (recording), and Willie Shoemaker (horse racing), with Flip Wilson as host. NBC, April 2.

THE SELLING OF THE PENTAGON (CBS Reports)—Documentary examining the extensive and often costly efforts of the military to garner public support, narrated by Roger Mudd. CBS, Feb. 23.

THE SIX WIVES OF HENRY VIII—Series of six dramas, one about each of Henry's wives, with Keith Michell as Henry VIII. CBS, weekly beginning Aug. 1.

THE STRUGGLE FOR CHINA (Special of the Week)—Documentary about China's stormy history in the first half of the 20th century and the events leading up to the formation of the People's Republic of China in 1949, narrated by James Mason. PBS, Nov. 1.

UN DAY CONCERT 1971 (Special of the Week)—United Nations birthday concert, with Pablo Casals conducting the Casals Festival Orchestra and featuring such artists as violinist Isaac Stern and pianist Rudolf Serkin. PBS, Oct. 25.

THE UNDERSEA WORLD OF JACQUES COUSTEAU: OCTOPUS, OCTOPUS—Special program with the French undersea explorer. ABC, Dec. 21.

WHEN JOHNNY COMES MARCHING HOME—Documentary discussing the difficulties that returning Vietnam War veterans have in finding employment, narrated by Frank Reynolds. ABC, Sept. 1.

THE ELECTRIC COMPANY, a program from Children's Television Workshop begun in 1971, uses humor and fast-paced delivery to teach basic reading skills to 7- to 10-year-olds. Here, Judge Bill Cosby rules in controversy over punctuation in No Fishing sign.

"Vicious," "disreputable," "distorted," "un-American," and "unprofessional" were some of the words used by some politicians in response to *The Selling of the Pentagon.* CBS News president Richard Salant countered by repeating the program on March 23, with added statements by critics, to whom he himself responded on the air. The original showing had been seen by an estimated 9.6 million viewers, the rerun by an estimated 14.2 million.

In April the Investigations Subcommittee of the House Commerce Committee, both chaired by Rep. Harley O. Staggers (D, W. Va.), issued a subpoena commanding CBS to turn over all the materials used in the making of the documentary— including film that was edited out of the show and not actually broadcast. CBS president Frank Stanton offered the final film and a transcript, but refused all else. He had the support of all the journalistic media. The issue came to a head on July 13, when the House of Representatives refused, by a vote of 226 to 181, to give Staggers a contempt citation against CBS and its president.

While this action seemed to be an affirmation of broadcast journalism's right to full protection under the First Amendment, the question has not wholly been answered. Meanwhile, television broadcasting and the viewing public have suffered. It is noteworthy that all the documentaries announced for the 1971–72 season were of the "non-controversial" variety. It is noteworthy also that in all the contretemps over *The Selling of the Pentagon* not one of the program's critics ever denied its basic charge.

Federal Communications Commission. Of the many pressing problems before the FCC, one of the most important was the fairness doctrine, the long-standing FCC rule that requires the broadcaster to present controversial issues of public concern fully and fairly. Defenders of the doctrine hold that it is needed to guarantee access to the air for persons of differing views. Detractors hold that it tends to make broadcasters avoid controversial subjects. In June the FCC announced a major inquiry into the fairness doctrine and invited comments.

Administration thinking in this area was reflected in a speech by Clay T. Whitehead, director of the White House Office of Telecommunications Policy (OTP) early in October. In the attempt to "redefine the relationships in the Communications Act's triangle of government, private industry, and the public," Whitehead made three startling proposals: (1) eliminate the fairness doctrine and replace it with the statutory right of paid access; (2) change the license-renewal process to get the government out of programming, and at the same time give the broadcaster greater protection against challenges at license-renewal time; and (3) begin to deregulate radio, recognizing that commercial radio is a medium entirely different from television and is akin to magazines.

Problems with governing the activities of cable television continued to plague the FCC. The package of rules and proposed regulations that the commission first offered in 1970 had been met with almost universal distaste, and so study continued. In June, as an "interim" report, FCC chairman

Dean Burch made public the commission's plans to allow real CATV growth in the top 100 U.S. markets. At virtually the same time, President Nixon appointed a high-level committee, with OTP director Whitehead as chairman, "to develop a comprehensive policy with regard to cable television." Despite the resulting confusion about who was in charge, Burch and Whitehead worked out a compromise plan that was approved reluctantly by both the National Association of Broadcasters and the National Cable Television Association.

In terms of membership the FCC played a game of musical chairs. In January the commission regained full strength, for the first time in several months, with recess appointments for Commissioner Robert Wells and Deputy Peace Corps Director Thomas J. Houser. These gave the FCC a Republican majority for the first time in 10 years. Wells' was a full 7-year term, replacing Kenneth Cox, who had resigned the previous September; Houser's was to fill out the rest of Wells' term, until June. In July the President nominated Rep. Charlotte Reid (R, Ill.), replacing Houser, to a full term. Then Wells resigned as of November 1, and FCC general counsel Richard Wiley was named to succeed him.

Children's Programs. The FCC became deeply involved in this area in response to a petition from Action for Children's Television (ACT), and in January it issued a notice of inquiry and proposed rule making. At issue were questions of violence and overcommercialization. ACT, for instance, called for 14 hours a week of children's programs without any commercials. While all concerned groups awaited the surgeon general's study of the effects of television violence on children, the networks made several steps toward upgrading the quality of children's programs. Meanwhile, the results of two studies, both parts of the surgeon general's report, came to light.

Researchers at Harvard found that preschoolers cannot discriminate between the end of a program and the beginning of a commercial, and that teenagers are cynical about commercial messages. At Penn State it was found that preschoolers' behavior changes for the worse when they are shown violent TV programs, and for the better with "socially constructive" ones. In Dean Burch's words, these studies "do tend to confirm our instinctive wisdom."

In the autumn of 1971 the Federal Trade Commission began a series of hearings on the honesty of commercials aimed at children.

Prime-Time Programs. One genuine and refreshing hit show came with the "second season," that is, the new group of shows presented in January. It was *All In The Family,* an Americanized version of the BBC success *Till Death Do Us Part.* The program was sharply attacked by some experts on bigotry for its use of racial slurs. However, its comedy sense, its satirical view of lower middle-class values, and its staging (live-on-tape before an audience in the style of television's "golden age") rapidly propelled it to the top.

Summer, with all its reruns, was marked by the success of the BBC-produced *The Six Wives of Henry VIII.* It was presented not on public TV, as one might expect, but on CBS.

The fall season saw many changes, dictated partly by the FCC's 3-hour-per-night network prime-time limit, and partly by the felt need at CBS and NBC to shake up their schedules in order to

CBS NEWS

CONTROVERSIAL *The Selling of the Pentagon* explored public relations activities of the armed forces. Although editing techniques and point of view were harshly criticized, documentary's charges were not discredited.

reach younger audiences. Ed Sullivan was gone from CBS after 23 years, and 12 series were replaced by 8 new shows. NBC canceled 10 programs, replacing them with 8 others. ABC came up with 5 new programs. Six Hollywood stars made the dip into series TV: Jimmy Stewart, Glenn Ford, Rock Hudson, Anthony Quinn, George Kennedy, and Shirley MacLaine; only three—Stewart, Ford, and Hudson—survived into the "second season."

Public Television. Forward steps were made in improving program quality and in gaining audiences, but the basic questions of structure and long-term financing remained unresolved. In fact, the attempt

NEW COMEDY, *All in the Family,* gained top rating in 1971, with Carroll O'Connor (*seated*) as bigoted Archie Bunker. Jean Stapleton plays his wife, with Sally Struthers and Rob Reiner as daughter and son-in-law.

CBS

SATIRICAL SKETCHES of Marshall Efron enlivened *The Great American Dream Machine.* The PBS program is a combination of interviews, commentaries, satire, and fantasy.

NET

to find answers led to considerable friction among the Corporation for Public Broadcasting (CPB), the White House Office of Telecommunications Policy and its director Clay Whitehead, and, perhaps to a lesser degree, the Congress. At issue was the question of whether public broadcasting should be a centrally controlled network operation, or whether it should be based on the local stations. Whitehead, who had originally collaborated with CPB officials in the preparation of a bill providing for long-term financing, claimed that local control was the intent of the Public Broadcasting Act. He made it clear there would be no long-term financing until understanding had been reached on this point.

There were irritants to the White House and Congress as well, not least of which was the matter of high salaries paid to Sander Vanocur and Robert McNeil, both hired as senior correspondents by the National Public Affairs Center for Television, an offshoot of CPB, and for Bill Moyers, moderator of the Public Broadcasting Service (PBS) program *This Week.* At issue, too, although not in the open, was the question of whether a government-funded enterprise of the nature of PBS could expect to be free of governmental control over its point of view.

People. On December 12, David M. Sarnoff died in his 81st year. A visionary who early foresaw the use of radio as a home center for entertainment and information, the driving force behind the formation and growth of the National Broadcasting Company, and the major figure in the development of American television, Sarnoff was the preeminent pioneer in broadcasting.

At NBC, effective Jan. 1, 1972, David C. Adams, executive vice president, was made chairman of the board, succeeding Walter D. Scott. Julian Goodman continued as president. At CBS, effective Oct. 1, 1971, Frank Stanton was made vice chairman of the board, and Charles Thomas Ireland, Jr., was made president. William Paley, founder of CBS, continued as chairman.

RADIO BROADCASTING

Although there are no statistics available to prove the point, it seems likely that radio made significant gains in revenue and audience in 1971.

On February 20, the Emergency Broadcast System goofed. Instead of the usual test message, it sent out, under the correct code word for the day, an official formal alert. Because the alert came at the usual test time, most radio and television stations, questioned its authenticity. They checked their area key EBS stations to find that all but one, WGN in Chicago, were broadcasting as usual and so did not turn to emergency operations. Within minutes a cancellation message was transmitted. The error had been made by a civilian employee of EBS, who had fed the wrong signal to the transmitter. Investigations followed the incident, and steps were taken to prevent future errors.

Early in March the Federal Communications Commission issued a notice reminding broadcasters that they were responsible for knowing the content of the lyrics that they were broadcasting. The notice was prompted by complaints to the FCC that some lyrics appeared to promote the use of drugs. Broadcasters, especially free-form or progressive-rock broadcasters, felt that the notice was vague and that it raised questions of free speech.

Some three months later it became clear that the FCC took a rather hard view of free-form radio. It issued a statement saying that free-form radio "gives the announcer such control over the records to be played that it is inconsistent with the strict controls that the licensee must exercise to avoid questionable practices." The statement was in response to a petition (eventually dropped) for a stay of transfer of KFMG (FM), Des Moines. Both FCC comments struck a severe blow against free-form broadcasting, which, in its refusal to air commercials it does not believe in and in its conviction that the announcer knows better than management what his audience wants to hear, offers itself as a viable alternative to the impersonal programming subscribed to by most stations.

On April 3, National Public Radio began, interconnecting 90 noncommercial, educational radio stations for *All Things Considered*, a report and commentary on the day's news. NPR was created by the Corporation for Public Broadcasting to assume the functions of the National Educational Radio Network.

FM radio made gains during the year but is still hampered by the lack of receivers. Estimates made by *Broadcasting* magazine reveal that of some 239 million home radios, only 69 million can receive FM; and of some 80 million car radios, only 6 million have FM capability.

JOHN M. GUNN
State University of New York at Albany

TELEVISION AND RADIO ENGINEERING

Commercial television and radio growth in the United States continued to be slow in 1971. Noncommercial educational broadcasting expanded, aided by substantial funding from the Department of Health, Education and Welfare. Federal money was allocated for new stations and for the creation of a noncommercial "fourth network."

Television Broadcasting. During 1971 there was a net increase of only 5 commercial stations in the United States, while educational stations increased by 15. The number of VHF stations (channels 2 to 13) increased by 3, while the number of UHF stations (channels 14 to 69) increased by 17. Several independent UHF stations ceased operation.

Cable Television. Cable television (CATV) growth in the United States during 1971 principally was an expansion of existing systems. The number of homes served by cable television increased from 5.4 to 6.2 million, and the number of CATV systems in operation increased from 2,650 to 2,750.

More cable systems began to originate their own programs. In May 1971, the Eighth Circuit Court of Appeals overturned a Federal Communications Commission (FCC) order requiring larger systems to originate programs. The use of cable systems for purposes other than television distribution remained experimental. One goal is to provide a two-way cable system for subscriber response services.

Television via Satellites. Communications satellites were used increasingly for international relaying of TV programs. Also, the FCC continued to study proposals for building several satellites for relaying TV programs within the United States.

The sixth World Administrative Radio Conference, which convened in Geneva, Switzerland, in June 1971, allocated frequencies for direct television broadcasting from satellites. However, the allocated frequency bands are different from those used for present television broadcasting, so special converters would be required for home receivers.

Color Television Reception. Color television receiver sales hit a new high in 1971 when 7.2 million sets were sold. It is estimated that 50% of the homes in the United States are now equipped with color TV sets. In color receiver design, there were trends toward larger picture-tube sizes and increasing use of modular solid-state circuitry. Tuners were redesigned to provide comparable ease of tuning on all channels. In the more expensive receivers, tuners using variable-capacitance semiconductor diodes were introduced.

Home Video Playback Systems. There was much publicity but little real progress in the development of marketable video playback devices for home use. Most video cassette and playback equipment sold in 1971 was for industrial and educational use, and this equipment was priced out of the reach of most of the public. The production of inexpensive program material with mass appeal continued to be a problem.

SUMMARY OF WORLD TELEVISION, JAN. 1, 1971

Country	Stations	Number of TV Sets	Country	Stations	Number of TV Sets	Country	Stations	Number of TV Sets
Albania	1	2,500	Haiti	1	10,500	Pakistan	5	80,000
Algeria	6	150,000	Honduras	5	45,000	Panama	11	157,500
Argentina	31	3,300,000	Hong Kong	3	429,000	Paraguay	1	25,000
Australia	85	2,950,000	Hungary	11	1,596,000	Peru	18	325,000
Austria	25	1,175,000	Iceland	7	36,000	Philippines	24	421,000
Barbados	1	17,500	India	1	21,000	Poland	24	4,023,000
Belgium	19	2,105,000	Indonesia	4	75,000	Portugal	8	360,000
Bermuda	2	18,000	Iran	8	250,000	Rhodesia	2	45,000
Bolivia	1	8,000	Iraq	4	180,000	Rumania	17	1,289,000
Brazil	50	6,500,000	Ireland	22	522,000	Saudi Arabia	8	300,000
Bulgaria	7	1,030,000	Israel	12	340,000	Senegal	1	1,500
Cambodia	2	18,000	Italy	68	9,100,000	Sierra Leone	1	3,500
Canada	378	7,700,000	Ivory Coast	4	11,000	Singapore	2	149,000
Chile	3	400,000	Jamaica	9	70,000	Southern Yemen	6	22,000
China (Mainland)	30	300,000	Japan	186	24,150,000	Spain	31	4,051,000
Colombia	14	600,000	Jordan	1	50,000	Sudan	2	65,000
Congo (Brazzaville)	1	2,000	Kenya	3	20,000	Sweden	173	3,200,000
Congo (Kinshasha)	1	6,500	Korea	7	300,000	Switzerland	83	1,288,500
Costa Rica	4	120,200	Kuwait	2	90,000	Syria	5	118,000
Cuba	25	555,000	Lebanon	9	250,000	Taiwan	4	420,000
Cyprus	2	42,000	Liberia	1	6,500	Tanzania	1	3,000
Czechoslovakia	28	2,997,000	Libya	2	200,000	Thailand	5	225,000
Denmark	30	1,510,000	Luxembourg	1	71,000	Trinidad and Tobago	2	54,000
Dominican Republic	6	77,000	Malagasy Republic	1	1,000	Tunisia	6	50,000
Ecuador	11	110,000	Malaysia	12	180,000	Turkey	3	100,000
El Salvador	4	100,000	Malta	1	63,000	Uganda	6	12,000
Equatorial Guinea	1	—	Mauritius	1	20,000	United Arab Republic	23	500,000
Ethiopia	1	6,500	Mexico	62	2,675,000	United Kingdom	232	16,750,000
Finland	65	1,061,300	Mongolia	1	600	United States[1]	930	93,347,000
France	106	10,200,000	Morocco	8	145,000	Upper Volta	1	3,000
Gabon	2	2,400	Netherlands	13	3,150,000	Uruguay	12	225,000
Germany (East)	25	5,310,000	Netherlands Antilles	2	32,000	USSR	167	28,000,000
Germany (West)	171	16,800,000	New Zealand	20	625,000	Venezuela	29	700,000
Ghana	4	15,000	Nicaragua	2	55,000	Vietnam (South)	1	14,000
Greece	4	120,000	Niger	1	100	Yugoslavia	35	1,767,000
Guatemala	2	119,000	Nigeria	8	53,000	Zambia	3	18,500
Guyana	—	3,500	Norway	64	853,000			
			Okinawa	2	230,000			

[1] Includes Guam, Puerto Rico, Virgin Islands, and U. S. Military; preliminary estimate. (Source: Television Factbook.)

FM and AM Radio. The number of FM radio stations in the United States increased from 2,624 to 2,775 during 1971. The number of AM radio stations increased from 4,343 to 4,374 as an FCC freeze on new construction continued in effect.

Emergency Broadcast System. The nation's Emergency Broadcast System (EBS), whose purpose is to notify the public of enemy attack or serious local emergencies, had an embarrassing day on Feb. 20, 1971. A false attack alert was transmitted by teletype from the National Emergency Warning Center at Cheyenne Mountain, Colo., to all radio and television broadcast stations. For one reason or another, most of the stations failed to observe the alert. It took 40 minutes to cancel the false message and authenticate its cancellation.

Decision Information Distribution System. The Office of Civil Defense placed the first contract for building a Decision Information Distribution System (DIDS). When completed, the system will include two 200-kw low-frequency transmitters and ten 50-kw low-frequency transmitters at scattered locations in the United States.

HOWARD T. HEAD
A. D. Ring & Associates

TENNESSEE

Passage of some significant legislation and problems associated with achieving racial balance in the schools were in the forefront of the Tennessee scene in 1971.

Legislation and Politics. On March 24, Tennessee became the third state to ratify the 26th Amendment to the U. S. Constitution, lowering the voting age to 18 years. The General Assembly then pioneered in giving persons 18 to 20 years old full legal responsibility as adults.

Other legislation in the 1971 session provided for a presidential preference primary on the first Thursday in May of election years; a new drug-control program; repeal of a "bone dry" liquor law; pollution-control measures; a voluntary program for the sterilization of indigents; measures for judicial reform and revision of taxes on business; and suspension of the compulsory school attendance law for any child required to attend school outside his immediate neighborhood.

Because of internal dissension, the Democratic majority in the legislature failed to cut the number of congressional districts from 9 to 8, an action required by the state's failure to make a sufficient population gain in the 1970 census.

On September 3 a report was released by a committee named by Gov. Winfield Dunn to make a study on cost control. It called for a major restructuring of the state government, which, it was hoped, would save Tennessee taxpayers $217.1 million. Chattanooga and Athens elected Negroes to their city councils for the first time in history. The state Democratic executive committee adopted a formal constitution for the party, and shifted the basis on which county representation is apportioned from performance in the last presidential election to performance in the last gubernatorial one.

Education. When schools opened in the fall, 33 of the state's school systems were under federal court orders to establish racial balance. In the Nashville-Davidson county metropolitan district, school opening was delayed while an appeal was made to the U. S. Supreme Court to stay an order requiring the crosstown busing of more than half the district's school children. When the appeal was denied, the opening was disturbed by picketing parents. In November, Chattanooga reported a 12.3% drop in school enrollment as a result of the busing order.

In accord with a new state law requiring the University of Tennessee to have a woman on its board of trustees, Gov. Dunn appointed Ann Baker Furrow its first woman member.

Other Events. In May, Chattanooga was the scene of rioting that began with a disturbance at a "soul music" concert. In October, street violence and fire-bombing swept Memphis for several days after the revelation that a Negro youth had been beaten to death by police.

On June 1, Tennessee celebrated its 175th anniversary of statehood. Governor Dunn proclaimed October 2 as "Cordell Hull Day," commemorating the 100th anniversary of the birth of former U. S. Secy. of State Cordell Hull, a native Tennessean.

Economic Developments. In November it was reported that Tennessee was leading the Southeastern states in personal income gain, with an increase of more than 9% since January. Through June, the state's economy grew much faster than that of the nation as a whole, especially in home construction. For the first six months of the fiscal year, state tax collections rose 19% over the previous year.

STANLEY J. FOLMSBEE
University of Tennessee

------- **TENNESSEE • Information Highlights** -------

Area: 42,244 square miles (109,412 sq km).
Population (1970 census): 3,924,164. *Density:* 95 per sq mi.
Chief Cities (1970 census): Nashville, the capital, 447,877; Memphis, 623,530; Knoxville, 174,587; Chattanooga, 119,-082; Jackson, 39,996; Johnson City, 33,770; Kingsport, 31,900.
Government (1971): *Chief Officers*—governor, Winfield K. Dunn (R); lt. gov., John S. Wilder (D); secy. of state, Joe C. Carr (D); atty. gen., David M. Pack (D); treas., Thomas A. Wiseman; commissioner, dept. of educ., Elden C. Stimbert; chief justice, Ross W. Dyer. *General Assembly*—Senate, 33 members (19 Democrats, 13 Republicans, 1 other); House of Representatives, 99 members (56 Democrats, 43 Republicans).
Education (1970–71): *Enrollment*—public elementary schools, 685,754 pupils; 21,200 teachers; secondary public, 393,000 pupils; 14,250 teachers; nonpublic schools (1968–69), 33,-800 pupils; 1,960 teachers; college and university (fall 1968), 122,373 students. *Public school expenditures* (1970–71), $500,500,000 ($590 per pupil). *Average teacher's salary,* $7,400.
State Finances (fiscal year 1970): *Revenues,* $1,272,728,000 (3.5% general sales tax and gross receipts taxes, $241,-151,000; motor fuel tax, $130,625,000; federal funds, $358,-231,000). *Expenditures,* $1,271,209,000 (education, $524,-467,000; health, welfare, and safety, $172,601,000; highways, $206,526,000). *State debt,* $416,228,000 (June 30, 1970).
Personal Income (1970): $12,277,000,000; per capita, $3,051.
Public Assistance (1970): $152,330,000. *Average monthly payments* (Dec. 1970)—old-age assistance, $50.65; aid to families with dependent children, $107.70.
Labor Force: *Nonagricultural wage and salary earners* (June 1971). 1,364,600. *Average annual employment* (1969)—manufacturing, 470,000; trade, 255,000; government, 214,-000; services, 176,000. *Insured unemployed* (Oct. 1971)—22,400 (2.3%).
Manufacturing (1967): *Value added by manufacture,* $4,921,-100,000. Chemicals and allied products, $1,155,500,000; electrical equipment, $478,200,000; food and kindred products, $457,600,000; apparel, $412,500,000.
Agriculture (1970): *Cash farm income,* $777,828,000 (livestock, $438,083,000; crops, $268,760,000; government payments, $70,985,000). *Chief crops* (1970)—Tobacco, 117,-864,000 pounds; soybeans, 28,267,000 bushels; hay, 2,036,-000 tons; cotton lint, 390,000 bales.
Mining (1971): *Production value,* $225,917,000 (ranks 27th among the states). *Chief minerals* (tons)—Stone, 33,252,-000; coal, 8,921,000; zinc, 117,600.
Transportation: *Roads* (1969), 77,495 miles (124,713 km); *motor vehicles* (1969), 1,971,000; *railroads* (1968), 3,020 miles (4,860 km); *airports* (1969), 62.
Communications: *Telephones* (1971), 1,947,300; *television stations* (1969), 15; *radio stations* (1969), 198; *newspapers* (1969), 33 (daily circulation, 1,148,000).

TEXAS

Stock scandals that allegedly touched the Texas House leadership and other state officials in 1971 overshadowed a lackluster legislative session and the first stirrings of the 1972 political campaign.

Scandals. Action by the U. S. Securities and Exchange Commission to restrain Frank Sharp, a Houston financier, and a score of other banking and corporation officials from certain illegal stock manipulations revealed a financial relationship between Sharp and several state officials, including the speaker of the House, Gus F. Mutscher, Jr.; several of his top lieutenants; Gov. Preston Smith; and the chairman of the state Democratic executive committee (SDEC), who was also a member of the state banking board. The officials had made quick profits totaling several hundred thousand dollars in stock transactions with Sharp in 1969, about the time when banking legislation that Sharp wanted had been passed by the Legislature. The legislation was eventually vetoed by the governor.

The speaker, one of his aides, and another House leader were indicted in September for bribery, and the chairman of the SDEC was forced to resign.

Legislature. The 140-day regular legislative session and a 4-day special session were not very productive. Legislative redistricting was a problem. No plan for the Senate could be passed, and one passed for the House was invalidated by the Texas courts. This activated a provision of the Texas constitution, never used before, and created ex officio a 5-man legislative redistricting board. The new districts created by the board for both the Texas House and the Texas Senate were promptly challenged in federal court.

Passage of a corporate income tax appeared possible, but conservatives finally won another rise in the state sales tax to help fund a record appropriation of $7.1 billion for the next biennium. In an unprecedented move, Governor Smith vetoed the entire second-year appropriation.

Other significant legislation provided for permanent instead of annual voter registration and allowed registration any time up to 30 days before an election. A broad "ethics" bill was passed to try to prevent improper influence on public officials by requiring financial disclosures. Following up a 1970 constitutional amendment repealing a ban on open saloons, the Legislature legalized on a local option basis the sale of liquor by the drink.

Faced with opposition from some law enforcement officials, the Legislature chose not to act on a needed revision of the penal code, in preparation for several years. It also chose not to pass new laws to improve protection of the environment, to overhaul the regulation of automobile insurance rates, or to shift the high cost of party primaries from candidates to the state or counties or both.

Politics. Governor Smith, Lt. Gov. Ben Barnes, and Dolph Briscoe announced their candidacies for governor in the 1972 elections. Former U. S. Sen. Ralph Yarborough said he would run either for governor or senator. Leaders of La Raza Unida, a militant Mexican-American organization that has had some success in south Texas elections, announced that the party would compete on a statewide basis in 1972.

State Agencies. A better-than-average pay increase (6.8%) was given to state employees. The

PROLONGED drought continued to parch West Texas. In February, Stonewall County ranchers hired Homer F. Berry (*above*), a "rainmaker," in unsuccessful attempt to break dry spell.

parks and wildlife board was torn by a conflict over the purchase of Mustang Island for a state park. The Texas prison system, one of the nation's best, lost its executive director when George Beto voluntarily resigned his post.

Constitution. In May voters passed two constitutional amendments, one of them authorizing the sale of bonds to improve water quality, but rejected a proposal for an ethics commission coupled with one for higher legislative salaries, and a suggested change in the type of ceiling on state welfare spend-

————————— **TEXAS • Information Highlights** —————————

Area: 267,339 square miles (692,408 sq km).
Population (1970 census): 11,196,730. *Density:* 43 per sq mi.
Chief Cities (1970 census): Austin, the capital, 251,808; Houston, 1,232,802; Dallas, 844,401.
Government (1971): *Chief Officers*—governor, Preston Smith (D); lt. gov., Ben Barnes (D); secy. of state, Martin Dies, Jr. (D); atty. gen., Crawford C. Martin (D); treas., Jesse James (D); commissioner of education, J. W. Edgar; chief justice, Supreme Court, Robert W. Calvert; presiding judge, Court of Criminal Appeals, John F. Onion, Jr. *Legislature*—Senate, 31 members (29 Democrats, 2 Republicans); House of Representatives, 150 members (140 D, 10 R).
Education (1970–71): *Enrollment*—public elementary schools, 1,972,800 pupils; 64,600 teachers; secondary public, 729,-700 pupils; 57,300 teachers; nonpublic schools (1968–69), 152,700 pupils; 7,320 teachers; college and university (fall 1968), 379,379 students. *Public school expenditures* (1970–71), $1,600,530,000 ($646 per pupil). *Average teacher's salary*, $8,325.
State Finances (fiscal year 1970): *Revenues*, $3,648,508,000 (4% general sales tax and gross receipts taxes, $552,-561,000; motor fuel tax, $312,349,000; federal funds, $927,-009,000). *Expenditures*, $3,344,948,000 (education, $1,514,-692,000; health, welfare, and safety, $554,057,000; highways, $641,937,000).
Personal Income (1970): $40,181,000,000; per capita, $3,515.
Public Assistance (1970): $532,122,000. *Average monthly payments* (Dec. 1970)—old-age assistance, $62.60; aid to families with dependent children, $118.05.
Labor Force: *Nonagricultural wage and salary earners* (June 1971), 3,646,000. *Average annual employment* (1969)—manufacturing, 749,000; trade, 853,000; government, 651,-000; services, 585,000.
Manufacturing (1967): *Value added by manufacture*, $10,922,-400,000: Chemicals and allied products, $2,076,700,000; petroleum and coal products, $1,800,500,000.
Agriculture (1970): *Cash farm income*, $3,680,017,000 (livestock, $1,945,745,000; crops, $1,191,116,000; government payments, $543,156,000). *Chief crops* (1970)—Sorghum grain, 326,616,000 bushels (ranks 1st among the states).
Mining (1970): *Production value*, $6,341,761,000 (ranks 1st among the states). *Chief minerals*—natural gas, 8,508,-982,000,000 cu ft; petroleum, 1,231,900,000 bbls; natural gas liquids, 299,410,000 bbls; cement, 36,847,000 bbls.
Fisheries (1970): *Commercial catch*, 148,000,000 pounds ($53,-500,000). *Leading species by value* (1967): Shrimp, $46,-355,147; red snapper, $462,473; menhaden, $262,427.
Transportation: *Roads* (1969), 243,450 miles (391,784 km); *motor vehicles* (1969), 6,506,000; *railroads* (1968), 13,951 miles (22,451 km); *airports* (1969), 242.
Communications: *Telephones* (1971), 6,328,600; *television stations* (1969), 54; *radio stations* (1969), 398.

ing. Caught between the existing limitation and rising costs and case loads, the Legislature finally improvised a way to fund the welfare programs.

Education. The state began a program of tuition subsidy for needy students in private colleges and universities, but sharply increased the charges for out-of-state students in state institutions of higher education. The tuition rate for Texas residents remained one of the lowest in the nation. In general, campus turmoil diminished in 1971.

The dedication of the Lyndon B. Johnson Presidential Library at the University of Texas at Austin in late May was attended by President Richard M. Nixon and many nationally prominent persons.

The state program of financial support for local public schools was jolted just before Christmas by a federal court ruling that invalidated the formula (primarily local property taxation) for the distribution of state funds.

Minority Groups. The status of the Negro and Mexican-American minorities continued to improve slowly, but intergroup tensions increased as a result of pressure from the U. S. Department of Health, Education, and Welfare and from the federal courts for faster school desegregation. Some school districts began busing black children into white schools, but efforts to achieve a balance by busing whites into black schools were impeded by boycotts and legal counterattacks.

CLIFTON MCCLESKEY
University of Texas

TEXTILE INDUSTRY

Each U. S. resident consumed an average of 49.2 pounds of fiber in 1971, or 1.7 pounds less than in the preceding year. Consumption was divided among man-made fiber, 27.7 pounds (down 0.2 of a pound); cotton, 19.8 pounds (down 1 pound); and wool, 1.7 pounds (down half a pound).

Fiber Consumption. The annual rate of total mill consumption of fiber in 1971, based on 9-month data, was 10.4 billion pounds, 11% more than a year earlier. The 1971 annual rate of mill consumption included increases of 16% for the man-made fibers and 3% for raw cotton. There were decreases of 20% for raw wool and 50% for silk. At these 1971 rates, man-made fibers maintained their lead in pounds consumed, accounting for 60% of the total of three fibers.

The total value of fibers consumed domestically in 1970 was estimated at $4,640 million. Man-made fibers led at $3,500 million, followed by raw cotton at $850 million, raw wool at $280 million, and silk at $10 million.

Fabric Output. U. S. production of broad woven fabric in 1971, based on first-half actual data, was expected to total about 11.5 billion linear yards, about the same as in 1970.

Prices. The average price of 1-inch middling raw cotton for the first nine months of 1971 was 24.7 cents per pound and raw wool (clean basis, at Boston), was 68.2 cents. List prices remained at 28 cents for rayon staple and 74 cents for 150 denier acetate yard, while 150 denier rayon yarn had increased to $1.03 by August 1971.

Employment and Earnings. Employment in domestic knitting and weaving mills and in finished textile products plants averaged 2,034,000 persons in the first half of 1971. Weekly earnings averaged $102.89 for mill workers and $86.90 for workers in the apparel cutting and related trades.

Foreign Trade. The U. S. textile import balance in 1970 was $1,141 million, a record 7% more than

SELECTED U. S. TEXTILE INDUSTRY DATA

	1968	1969	1970	First half 1971
Fiber Consumption	(Millions of pounds)			
Raw cotton	4,104	3,973	3,774	2,009
Raw wool, total[1]	378	355	273	115
Apparel class	287	261	197	79
Carpet class	91	94	76	36
Raw silk	2	2	1	...
Man-made fibers[2]	5,150	5,413	5,362	3,118
Rayon+acetate yarn	795	744	700	378
Rayon+acetate staple	893	871	714	376
Noncellulosic yarn[3]	1,556	1,649	1,804	1,116
Noncellulosic staple[4]	1,522	1,689	1,740	1,014
Textile glass fiber	384	460	404	234
Total fiber consumption	9,634	9,743	9,410	5,242
Tire cord and tire fabric output[5]				
Total cotton	5	4	2	1
Total man-made	569	637	580	306
Tire cord and cord fabric	555	593	533	281
Rayon	155	119	92	56
Nylon	400	307	294	139
Polyester		167	147	86
Chafer and other	14	44	47	25
Total tire cord and fabric	574	641	582	307
Broad woven fabric output[6]	(Millions of linear yards)			
Cotton	7,477	6,965	6,243	3,200
Man-made fiber	5,185	5,380	5,017	2,454
Woolen and worsted	243	223	179	70
Silk	13	12	8	3
Paper and other fabrics	5	4	3	2
Total broad woven goods	12,923	12,584	11,450	5,729

[1] Clean basis. [2] U.S. producers' domestic shipments plus imports for consumption. [3] Includes nylon, polyester, olefin, saran, spandex, vinyon and TFE–fluorocarbon fiber. [4] Includes acrylic and modacrylic, nylon, olefin, polyester and vinyon. [5] Cotton chafer excluded. [6] Except tire fabrics and carpets, rugs, and felts. (Source: Textile Economics Bureau, Inc.).

the previous high of $1,067 million in 1969. Imports of all textile fibers and products in 1970 were valued at $2,480 million and exports at $1,339 million.

In October 1971, Japan agreed to limit the flow of its man-made and woolen textiles into the United States for three years, and the United States in turn agreed to remove its 10% surcharge on those imports. Other agreements accepted by South Korea, Hong Kong, and Taiwan also called for limiting their textile exports to the U. S. market.

STANLEY B. HUNT
President, Textile Economics Bureau, Inc.

THAILAND

Although the Thais had considerable success in keeping Communist insurgency under control in 1971, the economy continued to deteriorate. The United States, meanwhile, kept up its flow of economic and military aid despite the beginnings of a Thai rapprochement with the Communist Chinese. In November a bloodless coup d'etat led by Field Marshal Thanom Kittikachorn overthrew the constitutional government.

Communist Insurgency. The government continued its containment of the Communist insurgency that had begun in 1965. The discovery of a new Chinese-supplied rebel base in Nakhon Pahnom province, near the border of Laos, was announced in December 1970. Small-scale fighting continued throughout 1971, but it was overshadowed by other developments.

By the end of the year the Thais had shown the effectiveness of social and economic innovations in shoring up outlying villages against Communist infiltration and subversion. The most noteworthy of these was road building. In 1965, at the beginning of the Communist guerrilla movement in northeastern Thailand, only 17% of the villages in the area were within a day's journey of a major road. But by July 1971 the figure had reached nearly 90%. The same tactic was employed along the Burmese border in the spring.

A second development was a gradual thawing of Thai-Chinese relations and, in the words of a Thai official, a "deemphasis on military cooperation with the United States." Although no long-range method of dealing with Communist guerrilla activity had been found by the end of 1971, the Thais largely contained the insurgents during the year.

The Economy. Thailand continued to have difficulty with its balance of payments. Its once great prosperity deteriorated, partly because of U. S. disengagement in Southeast Asia and changing pattern of Thai foreign policy. Considerable effort was made to control the smuggling of narcotics through Thailand to Vietnam, but not much success was achieved.

Politics. For most of the year politics in Bangkok followed their usual uneasy course. Field Marshal Thanom Kittikachorn, Thailand's premier and long-time strongman, turned 60 in 1971 and was under some pressure to retire from the army in accordance with Thai law. In August, however, his position as supreme military commander was extended indefinitely by the cabinet. At the time this action was interpreted as likely to increase the stability of the regime.

In mid-November, however, Thanom, citing Communist insurgency, strikes and student demonstrations, and his dissatisfaction with Thai legislators, seized power in a classic military coup. The takeover was bloodless and produced little reaction. The new government declared that it would continue its predecessor's policies and would honor Thailand's international obligations. Although it abrogated the constitution of 1968, the "revolutionary" government differed little from the one it overthrew, having many of the same leaders as well as retaining old policies. But it governed by decree, without the embarrassment of parliamentary opposition.

Foreign Relations. In May, Thai radio attacks on Communist China were halted, and the government announced that differences between the two countries had narrowed. Thailand abstained from voting in the United Nations when, on October 25, the General Assembly ousted Nationalist China (Taiwan) in favor of Peking.

Reactions with the United States continued as before. At the end of 1971 there were still thousands of U. S. troops in Thailand. American military and economic aid amounted to about $100 million per year. In January, U. S. Secretary of Defense Melvin R. Laird had conferred with Thai leaders in Bangkok. He pledged increased American military aid over the next decade.

It was revealed during the year that U Nu, former prime minister of Burma, was using Thai territory as the base for his National Liberation Front. The group's activities were directed against the Burmese government of General Ne Win.

Nearly 5,000 Thai troops were fighting for the royal government of Laos in 1971. These forces were supported by the United States.

CARL LEIDEN, *University of Texas at Austin*

--- **THAILAND • Information Highlights** ---

Official Name: Kingdom of Thailand.
Area: 198,456 square miles (514,000 sq km).
Population (1970 est.): 35,810,000. *Density,* 180 per square mile (70 per sq km). *Annual rate of increase,* 3.1%.
Chief City (1968 est.): Bangkok, the capital, 2,275,000.
Government: *Head of state,* Bhumibol Adulyadej, king (acceded June 9, 1946). *Head of government,* Thanom Kittikachorn, premier (took office Dec. 8, 1963). *Legislature*—National Assembly (suspended Nov. 17, 1971). *Major political parties*—United Thai People's party; Democratic party.
Language: Thai (official).
Education: *Literacy rate* (1970), over 70% of population, aged 10 and over. *Expenditure on education* (1968), 2.9% of gross domestic product. *School enrollment* (1967)—primary, 4,983,113; secondary, 436,506; technical/vocational, 57,751; university/higher, 38,204.
Finances (1970 est.): *Revenues,* $912,000,000; *expenditures,* $1,300,000,000; *monetary unit,* baht (21 bahts equal U. S. $1, Sept. 1971).
Gross National Product (1970 est.): $7,100,000,000.
National Income (1969): $4,386,000,000; *national income per person,* $126.
Consumer Price Index (1970): 117 (1963=100).
Manufacturing (metric tons, 1969): Cement, 1,826,000; sugar, 325,000; meat, 187,000; tin, 22,402.
Crops (metric tons, 1969 crop year): Rice, 13,410,000; cassava (1968), 2,000,000; maize, 1,568,000; bananas (1968), 1,200,000; natural rubber, 281,800.
Minerals (metric tons, 1969): Lignite, 348,000; iron ore, 289,000; salt, 200,000; tin concentrates, 21,092.
Foreign Trade (1970): *Exports,* $698,000,000 (chief exports—rice, $119,810,000; rubber, $106,286,000; corn, $88,429,000; tin, $77,048,000). *Imports,* $1,252,000,000 (chief imports, 1968—nonelectrical machinery, $180,634,000; transport equipment, $153,095,000; chemicals, $130,990,000; electrical machinery and appliances, $94,837,000). *Chief trading partners* (1968)—Japan (took 22% of exports, supplied 36% of imports); United States (took 12% of exports, supplied 19% of imports).
Transportation: *Roads* (1970), 8,000 miles (12,874 km); *motor vehicles* (1969), 228,000 (automobiles—1969—150,700); *railroads* (1970), 2,235 miles (3,597 km).
Communications: *Telephones* (1970), 134,663; *television stations* (1968), 5; *television sets* (1969), 240,000; *radios* (1969), 2,767,000; *newspapers* (1969), 24.

THANT, U. See BIOGRAPHY.

FRIEDMAN-ABELES

Musical treatments of life of Christ highlighted 1971 season. Rock opera *Jesus Christ Superstar (above)* traced the passion of Christ. *Godspell (left)* followed the Book of Matthew.

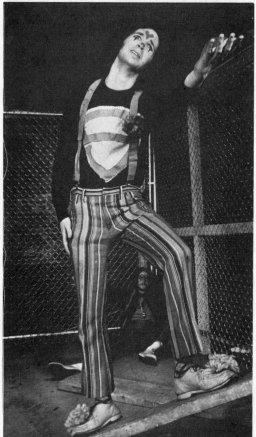

MARTHA SWOPE

theater

Even the most confirmed pessimist among Broadway theatergoers could not have predicted a season duller than that of 1971. During the year the artistic achievement of the legitimate theater in New York reached a new low. Yet despite the absence of a memorable or even a strongly promising new play, more than 40 Broadway shows recorded an overall profit of nearly $2 million. This showing was probably due largely to the fact that curtain time was changed from 8:30 P.M. to 7:30 P.M. The time change was made partly in recognition of the dangers of the city streets late at night and partly as a convenience for a substantial suburban audience.

The Theatre Development Fund expanded its notable effort to restore some slight measure of economic heterogeneity to the Broadway scene, for a long time an unmistakably upper-middle-class preserve. Foundation supported, the Fund buys blocks of tickets and offers them to its subscribers at prices below those of the midtown cinemas. The Fund hopes eventually to create an audience that is truly representative of New York City.

Broadway Plays. With nudity and audience participation taken for granted and the barrage of radical departures from tradition diminished, audiences

(*Continued on page 673*)

BROADWAY OPENINGS IN 1971

PLAYS

Abelard and Heloise, by Ronald Millar; directed by Robin Phillips; with Keith Michell and Diana Rigg; March 10–April 25.

All Over, by Edward Albee; directed by John Gielgud; with Jessica Tandy and Colleen Dewhurst; March 28–May 1.

And Miss Reardon Drinks a Little, by Paul Zindel; directed by Melvin Bernhardt; with Estelle Parson, Julie Harris, and Nancy Marchand; February 25–May 29.

Antigone, by Sophocles; English version by Dudley Fitts and Robert Fitzgerald; directed by John Hirsch; with Martha Henry and Philip Bosco; May 13–June 20.

The Dance of Death, by August Strindberg; directed by Alfred Ryder; with Viveca Lindfors and Rip Torn; April 28–May 2.

A Doll's House, by Henrik Ibsen; directed by Patrick Garland; with Claire Bloom and Donald Madden; January 12–May 1.

An Enemy of the People, by Henrik Ibsen; adapted by Arthur Miller; directed by Jules Irving; with Stephen Elliott, Philip Bosco, and David Birney; March 11–April 25.

Father's Day, by Oliver Hailey; directed by Donald Moffat; with Brenda Vaccaro and Biff McGuire; March 16–March 20.

Four on a Garden, by Abe Burrows; directed by Abe Burrows; with George Irving, Sid Caesar, and Carol Channing; January 30–March 13.

Hedda Gabler, by Henrik Ibsen; directed by Patrick Garland; with Claire Bloom and Donald Madden; February 17–May 8.

How the Other Half Loves, by Alan Ayckbourn; directed by Gene Saks; with Phil Silvers and Sandy Dennis; March 29–June 26.

The Incomparable Max, by Jerome Lawrence and Robert E. Lee; directed by Gerald Freedman; with Clive Revill, Richard Kiley, and Martyn Green; October 19–November 6.

Lenny, by Julian Barry, based on the life and words of Lenny Bruce; directed by Tom O'Horgan; with Cliff Gorman; May 26–

Mary Stuart, by Friedrich Schiller; translated and adapted by Stephen Spender; with Salome Jens and Nancy Marchand; November 12–December 18.

A Midsummer Night's Dream, by William Shakespeare; directed by Peter Brook; with David Waller, John Kane, Alan Howard, and Sara Kestelman; January 20–March 13.

Murderous Angels, by Conor Cruise O'Brien; directed by Gordon Davidson; with Jean-Pierre Aumont and Lou Gosset; December 20–January 9.

Old Times, by Harold Pinter; directed by Peter Hall; with Rosemary Harris, Robert Shaw, and Mary Ure; November 16–

The Philanthropist, by Christopher Hampton; directed by Robert Kidd; with Alec McCowen, Victor Spinetti, and Jane Asher; March 15–May 15.

The Playboy of the Western World, by John M. Synge; directed by John Hirsch; with Martha Henry and David Birney; January 7–February 14.

The Prisoner of Second Avenue, by Neil Simon; directed by Mike Nichols; with Peter Falk and Lee Grant; November 11–

The School for Wives, by Molière; translation by Richard Wilbur; directed by Stephen Porter; with Brian Bedford and Joan van Ark; February 16–May 29.

Scratch, by Archibald MacLeish, based on Stephen Vincent Benét's story *The Devil and Daniel Webster;* directed by Peter H. Hunt; with Patrick Magee and Will Geer; May 6–May 8.

Solitaire, Double Solitaire, by Robert Anderson; directed by Arvin Brown; with Joyce Ebert and Richard Venture; September 30–October 31.

Twigs, by George Furth; directed by Michael Bennett; with Sada Thompson; November 14–

Unlikely Heroes: Three Philip Roth Stories, adapted by Larry Arrick; directed by Larry Arrick; with Lou Jacobi, Tom Rosqui, George Bartenieff, and Michael Tolan; October 26–November 13.

MUSICALS

Ain't Supposed to Die a Natural Death, book, music, and lyrics by Melvin Van Peebles; directed by Gilbert Moses; with Marilyn B. Coleman, Toney Brealond, and Dick Williams; October 20–

Ari, book and lyrics by Leon Uris; music by Walt Smith; directed by Lucia Victor; with David Cryer and Constance Towers; January 15–January 27.

A Day in the Life of Just About Everyone, book, music, and lyrics by Earl Wilson, Jr.; staged by Tom Panko; with June Gable and Earl Wilson, Jr.; March 9–March 14.

Earl of Ruston, book and lyrics by C. C. Courtney and Ragan Courtney; music by Peter Link; directed by C. C. Courtney; with the Courtney Brothers; May 5–May 8.

Follies, book by James Goldman; music and lyrics by Stephen Sondheim; directed by Michael Bennett and Harold Prince; with Alexis Smith, Dorothy Collins, and Yvonne De Carlo; April 4–

Frank Merriwell, book, music, and lyrics by Skip Redwine and Larry Frank; directed by Neal Kenyon; with Larry Ellis and Linda Donovan; April 24 for one performance.

The Grass Harp, book and lyrics by Kenward Elmslie, based on a play by Truman Capote; music by Claibe Richardson; directed by Ellis Rabb; with Barbara Cook, Ruth Ford, and Russ Thacker; November 2–November 6.

Inner City, lyrics by Eve Merriam, based on her book, *The Inner City Mother Goose;* music by Helen Miller; conceived and directed by Tom O'Horgan; with Joy Garrett and Larry Marshall; December 19–

Jesus Christ Superstar, music by Andrew Lloyd Webber; lyrics by Tim Rice; conceived and directed by Tom O'Horgan; with Jeff Fenholt, Ben Vereen, and Yvonne Elliman; October 12–

Johnny Johnson, book and lyrics by Paul Green; music by Kurt Weill; directed by José Quintero; with Ralph Williams and Alice Cannon; April 11 for one performance.

Metamorphoses, based on Ovid and adapted and translated with lyrics by Arnold Weinstein; by The True Brethren; created and directed by Paul Sills; with Paul Sand, Penny White, and Paula Kelly; April 22–July 3.

No, No, Nanette, book by Otto Harbach and Frank Mandel; music by Vincent Youmans; lyrics by Irving Caesar and Harbach; directed by Burt Shevelove; with Ruby Keeler, Patsy Kelly, Helen Gallagher, and Bobby Van; January 19.

On the Town, book and lyrics by Betty Comden and Adolph Green; music by Leonard Bernstein; directed by Ron Field; with Phyllis Newman and Ron Husmann; October 31–

Only Fools Are Sad, by Dan Almagor, based on stories and parables of the Hassidic Jews; directed by Yossi Yzraely; with Galia Ishay; November 22–

70, Girls, 70, book by Fred Ebb and Norman L. Martin; lyrics by Ebb; music by John Kander; directed by Paul Aaron; with Lillian Roth, Mildred Natwick, and Hans Conreid; April 15–May 15.

To Live Another Summer, To Pass Another Winter, a musical from Israel by Hayim Hefer; music by Dov Seltzer; directed by Jonaton Karmon; with Riva Raz, Yona Atari, Aric Lavie, and Ili Girlizki; October 21–

Two Gentlemen of Verona, adapted from William Shakespeare's play by John Guare and Mel Shapiro; music by Galt MacDermot; directed by Shapiro; with Clifton Davis, Jonelle Allen, Raul Julia, and Diana Davila; December 1–

Wild and Wonderful, book by Phil Phillips; music and lyrics by Bob Goodman; directed by Burry Fredrik; with Laura McDuffie and Walter Willison; December 7 for one performance.

You're a Good Man Charlie Brown, based on *Peanuts* by Charles M. Schulz; music and lyrics by Clark Gesner; directed by Joseph Hardy; with Grant Cowan, Dean Stolber, and Liz O'Neal; June 1–June 27.

FRIEDMAN-ABELES

NEW SUCCESSES on Broadway ran gamut from musicals to drama. (Above) Musical adaptation of Shakespeare's Two Gentlemen of Verona won raves as summer production before moving to Broadway. (Right) Neil Simon's new hit, The Prisoner of Second Avenue, starred Peter Falk and Lee Grant. (Below) In Harold Pinter's Old Times, Mary Ure (foreground) and Robert Shaw play a couple whose relationship is shaken by a visit from the wife's former roommate, Rosemary Harris.

FRIEDMAN-ABELES

MARTHA SWOPE

were left with just ordinary plays. To call most of the 1971 crop of American works undistinguished is to understate charitably.

Neil Simon had only one play, *The Prisoner of Second Avenue,* running at the end of 1971. A bittersweet comedy in the new Simon vein of growing seriousness, it was considerably below his usual level. The plot revolves around a middle-aged avertising executive, played with distinction by Peter Falk, who starts to crumble emotionally in the midst of a crumbling New York. Simon tries to dovetail personal chaos with urban blight and comes up, typically, with an upbeat ending as the beset hero finally begins to get his frayed nerves together. The fact that some commentators were tracing Simon's "development" into a psychological and social dramatist is eloquent testimony to the current poverty of American drama.

Paul Zindel, author of the highly successful 1970 play *The Effect of Gamma Rays on Man-in-the-Moon Marigolds,* disappointed with his new offering, *And Miss Reardon Drinks a Little.* As in *Marigolds,* the focus of the new play is on a manless family in great psychological distress. Three sisters, at one time all schoolteachers, reveal their pain and loneliness. The unmasking of their suffering and of the alignments of their interrelationships comprises the play's substance. However, the characterizations are weak and the writing flat. Even the fine performances of Estelle Parsons, Julie Harris, and Nancy Marchand could not give resonance to the play.

Julian Barry's *Lenny,* a play with music, based on the life and words of comedian Lenny Bruce, was one of the most popular offerings of 1971. Imaginatively directed by Tom O'Horgan, it featured a brilliant performance by Cliff Gorman in the title role.

Edward Albee and Robert Anderson were both represented in 1971, with sadly unsatisfying works. Death is the theme of Albee's *All Over,* in which a famous man is dying in the next room as his wife, mistress, and children discuss him. Anderson followed the fashionable trend of linked one-act plays in *Solitaire, Double Solitaire.* Studies in marriage and the family, both are slight works. Another work by a well-known author also fell short of eager expectation. Larry Arrick adapted three stories from Philip Roth's *Goodbye Columbus* under the title *Unlikely Heroes.* The three plays are united by a common concern with their Jewish protagonists' attitudes toward religion. However, Roth's richness of inner conflict and incisive characterization did not translate well onto the stage.

Again, as in the past several seasons, the burden of solid achievement fell upon imports from England. The two most exciting theater events of 1971 were Harold Pinter's *Old Times* and Peter Brook's production of Shakespeare's *A Midsummer Night's Dream.* Pinter's superbly crafted, beautifully written, and marvelously acted play concerns the visit to a married couple of the wife's old roommate after a 20-year interval. Pinter explores memory, regret, and the mystery of identity with exquisite delicacy in this highly individualistic, almost dreamlike play.

Brook's dazzling direction of Shakespeare was a wholly successful attempt to remove the play from the status of a venerated classic and turn it into a vibrant, total theater experience. Under Brook's direction, literary theme and meaning receded and the performance itself, maximum imaginative aliveness on stage, became primary. The result was supremely modern and deeply pleasurable.

Broadway Musicals. Nostalgia was the dominant note of the 1971 season—a longing for the good old days that always seem better in retrospect than when they had to be muddled through. A smash hit production of the 1925 musical *No, No, Nanette* was the most prominent of a number of revivals that also included *On the Town.* There were also such new bottles for old wine as *Follies,* a reminiscence of the Ziegfeld era, and the short-lived *70, Girls, 70,* a reminder that in the midst of the youth explosion there's life in the old girls yet.

The most heralded arrival of the 1971 season was *Jesus Christ Superstar,* directed and staged by Tom O'Horgan. The work, which received mixed notices, enjoyed the largest advance sale in Broadway history. An unexpected hit was Melvin Van Peebles' *Ain't Supposed to Die a Natural Death,* a touching and poetic series of sketches that evoke the complex moods of ghetto life. Another happy event of the season was the arrival on Broadway of the New York Public Theater's sprightly musical production of Shakespeare's *Two Gentlemen of Verona.* A record was set in 1971 by *Fiddler on the Roof,* which, with its 2,845th performance became the longest-running musical in Broadway history.

Off-Broadway. Off-Broadway was as active as ever, providing several interesting plays, though no outstanding ones. As on Broadway, the rage for controversial experiment quieted down. The "tickle-touch" theater shakes no one up any more, and in fact most of it has disappeared. The Living Theater and the Performance Group were gone and the marvelous Open Theater played only some old works for benefits. One group, the Company Theater of Los Angeles, opened at the Guggenheim Museum in New York with an entertainment called *The James*

AGONIES of Vietnam War were explored in *Sticks and Bones.* Davis Rabe drama focused on a blind veteran and the conflicts caused within his family by his injury.

FRIEDMAN-ABELES

FRIEDMAN-ABELES

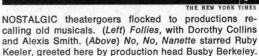

THE NEW YORK TIMES

NOSTALGIC theatergoers flocked to productions recalling old musicals. (*Left*) *Follies,* with Dorothy Collins and Alexis Smith. (*Above*) *No, No, Nanette* starred Ruby Keeler, greeted here by production head Busby Berkeley.

Joyce Liquid Memorial Theater. An audience participation event in which actors and patrons mingled and touched, the Liquid Theater received mixed reviews.

Joseph Papp's Public Theater has become a central outlet for promising new work by young playwrights. Two outstanding works performed there were Robert Montgomery's *Subject to Fits* and David Rabe's *The Basic Training of Pavlo Hummel. Subject to Fits* is a personal and highly original play, full of thought and feeling, a fantasia on the psychological and theological themes of Dostoyevsky's *The Idiot. The Basic Training of Pavlo Hummel* is a vituperative, angry, brutal anti-Vietnam-War play. It opens with the death of its hero so there will be no doubt as to what happens to him in Vietnam. The Army and war are presented as an image of the chaos of American life at the start of the 1970's.

Also in this political mold was a powerful dramatization of the Reverend Philip and the Reverend Daniel Berrigan's draft-file case, *The Trial of the Catonsville Nine.* Presented under the auspices of the Phoenix Theater, it played in the Good Shepherd-Faith Church in New York.

The Chelsea Theater Center of Brooklyn, a fine organization, gave the American premiere of Jean Genet's *The Screens,* a corrosive study of colonialism. The company also offered Heathcote Williams' *AC/DC,* an original condemnation of American dependence on the media, notably television, as a source of experience and as a mirror of reality. The excellent Negro Ensemble Company mounted Derek Walcott's *The Dream on Monkey Mountain,* a lyrical study of an old man imprisoned for drunkenness.

John Guare's *The House of Blue Leaves* is set on the day of Pope Paul's visit to New York. It concerns a zookeeper who dreams of fame as a songwriter and his son who blows up two bystanders in an assassination attempt on the Pope. Guare's bizarre comic imagination runs wild in this savage yet chillingly funny play. The 1971 season also saw the revival of Saul Bellow's amusing satirical comedy *The Last Analysis.*

Outside New York. Supported by grants from the Rockefeller Foundation and helped by the enlarged budget of the National Endowment for the Humanities, regional theater companies in numerous U. S. cities continued to flourish. The excellent Arena Stage in Washington, D. C., has long been an inspiration to theater outside New York. The company, which gave Broadway a big hit, *The Great White Hope,* not long ago, produced in 1971 a musical version of the late Lorraine Hansberry's *The Sign in Sidney Brustein's Window,* slated for a New York run early in 1972. The Arena also continued to encourage new talent and came up with the promising young Michael Weller, whose *Moonchildren,* a sensitive treatment of the despair of modern youth, was also scheduled for Broadway.

Other companies, among them New Haven's Long Wharf and Los Angeles' Mark Taper Forum, were also helping to nourish the New York stage. Under the guidance of its director, Arvin Brown, the Long Wharf repertory group has performed in fine productions of such works as *A Long Day's Journey Into Night.* In 1971 the Long Wharf premiered Robert Anderson's *Solitaire, Double Solitaire,* which later made an ill-fated trip to Broadway. The company also successfully presented the world premiere of Maxim Gorky's *Yegor Bulichev.* The Mark Taper Forum, guided by its director, Gordon Davidson, in past years, gave *Story Theater* its first full-scale production and introduced such works as *The Trial of the Catonsville Nine.* In 1971, the company gave the American premiere of Ronald Miller's *Abelard and Heloise,* which also ran briefly on Broadway.

The reversal of the old trend—from surefire Broadway hits presented in tedious stock versions, to a situation where Broadway is beginning to look more often to regional theater for ideas—is one of the rare encouraging notes of the last few years.

International Theater. In London there were some complaints that the National Theatre was going stale with dull productions of Giraudoux and Pirandello. However, its other two offerings amply compensated. Jonathan Miller directed Georg Büchner's *Danton's Death* and gave it an intelligent and dynamic rendering, utilizing the large range of Christopher Plummer's talent in the title role. Adrian Mitchell's *Tyger,* an experimental play about Blake's visionary world, in which the poet's lyrics are set in various musical styles, such as jazz and rock, proved to be the most controversial new work of 1971.

Elsewhere in London, in *West of Suez,* John Osborne analyzed the decline of the west and showed the importance of trying to salvage a little personal dignity from the myriad humiliations encountered in modern life. Ralph Richardson performed superbly in the play. Simon Gray offered *Butley,* a bitter comedy directed by Harold Pinter.

In Ireland the famous Gate Theater won a new lease on life when it was granted a long overdue government subsidy. The year 1971 marked the centennial of the birth of the great Irish dramatist John Millington Synge, and it was commemorated by productions of most of his plays.

In eastern Europe, notably in Czechoslovakia and Rumania, theater moved in opposite directions—toward censorship in Czechoslovakia and toward greater permissiveness in the use of political themes in Rumania. In Prague, an atmosphere of trigger-quick surveillance prevailed. Shakespeare's *Henry V* and Albee's *A Delicate Balance* were withdrawn when officials took offense at what they considered dangerous political overtones. Otomar Krejac, the director of the fine Theater Behind the Gate, was expelled from the Czech Communist party when he depicted Chekhov's *Three Sisters* as caged birds, presumably a theatrical metaphor for the artist's situation in his country, and seemingly an accurate one. His Theater Behind the Gate was closed indefinitely, and a planned London tour was cancelled.

In Rumania, theater flourished, with new Rumanian plays as well as works from the international repertory being treated with a fair amount of freedom. Many of the plays had political themes. Among the best productions were Liviu Cieliu's version of Büchner's *Leonce and Lena,* which went on to the Edinburgh Festival; D. R. Popescu's *Cat Out of the Bag;* and Horia Levinescu's *Et in Arcadia Ego.*

Awards. Musicals dominated the 1971 Antoinette Perry ("Tony") awards. The George Furth-Stephen Sondheim musical *Company* garnered six Tonies: best musical; best musical director (Harold Prince); best scenic designer (Boris Aronson); best book (George Furth); best lyrics (Stephen Sondheim); and best music (Stephen Sondheim). *No, No, Nanette* won four Tonies: best musical actress (Helen Gallagher); best supporting musical actress (Patsy Kelly); best costume design (Raoul Pene du Bois); and best choreographer (Donald Saddler). Hal Linden of *The Rothschilds* was named best musical actor and Keene Curtis of *The Rothschilds,* best supporting musical actor.

Anthony Shaffer's *Sleuth* was named best dramatic play. Other Tonies were won by Peter Brook (best director, *A Midsummer Night's Dream*); Brian Bedford (best dramatic actor, *The School for Wives*); Maureen Stapleton (best dramatic actress, *The Gingerbread Lady*); Paul Sand (best dramatic actor, supporting role, *Story Theater*); Rae Allen (best dramatic actress, supporting role, *And Miss Reardon Drinks a Little*); and R. H. Poindexter (best lighting design, *Story Theater*).

The New York Drama Critics Circle named the British play *Home* by David Storey as the best play of 1971. Its best-American-play designation went to John Guare's *The House of Blue Leaves. Follies* was voted the best musical.

Paul Zindel's *The Effect of Gamma Rays on Man-in-the-Moon Marigolds,* winner of the Drama Critics Circle award in 1970, won the 1971 Pulitzer Prize.

HAROLD FERRAR, *Columbia University*

TOGO

President Étienne Eyadema continued to consolidate his control of Togo in 1971.

Domestic Affairs. Eyadema, who had seized power in a military coup in 1967, stressed the single political party, the Rassemblement du Peuple Togolais (RPT), as the foundation of his strength. Plans were unveiled for a 3,000-seat "Palace of the People," to serve as the permanent headquarters of the RPT. In September over-enthusiasm by some of his followers led Eyadema to warn that force should not be used to boost RPT membership. The party's national committee called for a referendum to institute a strong presidential regime.

Twenty-one persons were convicted in late 1970 of attempting to overthrow the government. Among those sentenced were two former members of the National Assembly and a former police commissioner. The deputy state prosecutor and five magistrates had walked out during the trial, claiming that some defendants had been brought to trial without sufficient evidence. It was announced in January 1971 that three of the convicted plotters had died; this gave rise to widespread disquiet, especially in southern Togo. Rumors spread that the 10% pay increase given in January was intended to calm political passions aroused by the deaths.

Economy. The national economy remained sluggish, although the 1971 budget of $36 million represented an increase of 25% over that of 1970. The government stressed cooperation with neighboring Ghana through purchase of hydroelectric power from the Volta Dam, telecommunications links financed by the United States, and proposed cooperation in a cement factory. Togo received major financial aid from the European Development Fund ($1.8 million to drill wells), France ($1.27 million for roads, cattle immunization, and telecommunications), West Germany ($500,000 for railroad construction), and the UN Development Program ($400,000 for small-scale industries).

CLAUDE E. WELCH, JR.
State University of New York at Buffalo

------- **TOGO · Information Highlights** -------

Official Name: Togolese Republic.
Area: 21,622 square miles (56,000 sq km).
Population (1970 est.): 1,860,000. *Density,* 81 per square mile (32 per sq km). *Annual rate of increase,* 2.6%.
Chief City (1968 est.): Lomé, the capital, 134,800.
Government: *Head of state,* Étienne Eyadema, president (took office April 14, 1967). *Head of government,* Étienne Eyadema. *Major political party*—Rally of the Togolese People.
Languages: French (official), Ewe, Twi, Hausa.
Education: *Literacy rate* (1970), 10% of population. *Expenditure on education* (1968), 16.6% of total public expenditure. *School enrollment* (1968)—primary, 189,391; secondary, 16,662; technical/vocational, 1,615; higher, 221.
Finances (1971 est.): *Revenues,* $36,000,000; *expenditures,* $36,000,000; *monetary unit,* CFA franc (277.71 francs equal U.S.$1, Sept. 1971).
Gross National Product (1969 est.): $250,000,000.
Average annual income per person (1969 est.): $75.
Manufacturing (1969): Beer, 80,000 hectoliters.
Crops (metric tons, 1969 crop year): Sweet potatoes and yams (1968), 1,160,000; cassava (1968), 1,120,000.
Minerals (metric tons, 1969): Phosphate rock, 1,473,000.
Foreign Trade (1970): *Exports,* $52,000,000 (chief exports—Cacao, $22,815,000; phosphates, $13,395,000; coffee, $9,568,000; palm nuts, $2,362,000). *Imports,* $66,000,000 (chief imports, 1966—cotton woven fabrics, $8,351,000; nonelectrical machinery, $4,842,000; motor vehicles, $2,924,000). *Chief trading partners* (1968)—France (took 39% of exports, supplied 32% of imports); Netherlands (23%—4%); West Germany (10%—7%).
Transportation: *Roads* (1968), 2,933 miles (4,720 km); *motor vehicles* (1969), 10,400 (automobiles, 5,900); *railroads* (1970), 275 miles (443 km); *principal airport,* Lomé.
Communications: *Telephones* (1970), 4,567; *radios* (1969), 40,000; *newspapers* (1967), 2 (daily circulation, 10,000).

TONGA

Tonga was host to the sixth meeting of the Pacific Islands Producers Association in 1971. Delegates from Fiji, Western Samoa, the Gilbert and Ellice Islands, Cook Islands, and Niue, as well as Tonga, met at Nukualofa in April to consider production and trade problems in the banana and copra industries.

Tourism. Tonga began encouraging tourism in 1971. A tourist office was established, and a new hotel was planned for Vavau, an island in northern Tonga. Extension of grassed runways on Tongatapu to accommodate jet aircraft got under way, and airstrips were planned for Vavau and other islands.

Defense Force. New Zealand Prime Minister Keith Holyoake announced in February that his government would establish a 3-year program to help equip and train a Tongan Defense Force. A New Zealand army officer commanding the force will be responsible solely to the Tongan government.

HOWARD J. CRITCHFIELD
Western Washington State College

TORONTO

Situated at the northwestern end of Lake Ontario, Toronto is the capital of Ontario and Canada's second largest city (1971 est. city pop. 688,803; metropolitan area, 2,003,682). In the October 1971 provincial election, Toronto and York elected 17 Progressive Conservatives, 7 New Democrats, and 3 Liberals.

Transportation. A major event in 1971 was the Ontario government's refusal to allow completion of Toronto's Spadina Expressway.

"The city does not belong to the automobile," said Ontario Premier John Davis as he supported the conservationists in their attack on the expressway. He promised a rapid transit system to reduce dependence on automobiles. Ontario's decision may influence transportation patterns in other North American cities.

After halting the Spadina Expressway, Premier Davis, in consultation with American inventor and designer Buckminster Fuller, proposed a residential and commercial complex for part of the semicompleted route.

Meanwhile, plans were continued for the $115 million Spadina Subway. The premier also said that in the future the provincial government would make as large payments for public transit as it did for highways. The federal government began a $13.5 million expansion of Malton Airport.

Government. Albert Campbell, chairman of Metropolitan Toronto (or Metro) expressed irritation at the provincial government and the Ontario municipal board for "eroding" the city's powers. He asked that Pickering, to the east, be added as a seventh borough. The new regional government of York county to the north commenced on January 1.

Education. The University of Toronto was given a new one-chamber government that did not provide student parity. In July the university was forced to call police to evict a tent community from the campus. Seneca Community College, for its third campus, purchased the 696-acre Lady Eaton estate, with its 80-room mansion, for $1.5 million. Ontario Institute for Studies in Education lost its monopoly on educational research funds from the province.

Eaton Centre. Plans proceeded for the $200 million development of 15-acre Eaton Centre, a shopping complex, but there was much opposition to its design and the necessary street closings. The city's request for expropriation powers to help developers was turned down by the Ontario municipal board, which also said Metro needed an adequate land-use plan.

Recreation. Ontario Place, the provincial government's $23 million, 40-acre exhibition on Lake Ontario, adjacent to the Canadian National Exhibition, was opened from May to October. The Art Gallery of Ontario began an $18 million expansion.

Communications. When the 95-year-old *Evening Telegram* ceased publication at the end of October, the *Star* purchased its subscription list, and the *Globe* its building. The *Sun*, a new morning paper, was founded by 60 former *Telegram* employees.

Other Developments. Crime increased from 110,000 incidents in 1968 to 146,000 in 1970. The old city hall, whose fate had been argued for five years, was leased to Ontario for law courts.

FREDERICK H. ARMSTRONG
University of Western Ontario

TOURISM

Each year seems to bring surprises in the field of travel. In 1971 the world's young travelers received a pleasant surprise—drastically lower air fares between the United States and Europe.

For the travel industry all over the globe, 1971 was a banner year. In 1970 a record 167 million tourists had spent a record $15.5 billion during their trips to other countries, the International Union of Official Travel Organizations reported, and travel in 1971 seemed certain to exceed that level. Americans spent $6.2 billion on foreign travel in 1970, the U. S. Department of Commerce said, and first-half figures for 1971 topped the outlay in the comparable 1970 period.

Europe remained the most popular destination for U. S. travelers abroad, with the Caribbean second. So heavy was the crush in Europe that a hotel boom was under way there. Brussels had 10 new hotels under construction, and 62 new hotels were built in Rumania in 1970.

Travel within the United States got a boost and a couple of boots in 1971. The boost was Congress' new law, celebrating certain holidays on the nearest Monday, to give Americans more three-day weekends. The boots were the elimination of more than 150 passenger trains, and sickly airline finances.

Air Travel. The most significant development of the year was the sudden establishment of low youth fares on the transatlantic routes and the frantic fare cutting that followed. It began in June when Sabena, the Belgian-flag carrier, announced a round-trip "youth fare" of $220 between Brussels and New York City. Other carriers quickly followed suit— Pan American alone introduced youth fares to 24 cities in Europe. Hordes of young people took advantage of the fare bonanza, Pan Am counting 5,000 in the first month.

WALT DISNEY WORLD, Florida's counterpart of California's Disneyland, began operations on October 1 near Orlando. Tourists may board a 19th century American horse-drawn streetcar for a visit to a 15th century French castle.

LAURENCE LAURIE & ASSOCIATES

LONDON BRIDGE, moved from the Thames to the resort center of Havasu Lake, Ariz., opened on October 10.

The fare cutting alarmed supplemental airlines, whose chief sales weapon had been their low rates. It also resulted in further reduction of already-low fares by Icelandic Airlines and other nonmembers of the rate-setting International Air Transport Association (IATA). Icelandic's New York–Luxembourg round-trip youth fare dropped to $165, and one British independent, Laker Airways, offered a $78 one-way fare between New York and London.

The low fares were limited to persons under 30 years of age, each carrier defining its own age limits and other standards. But Aeronaves de México introduced a senior-citizen fare as well. Many travelers over 30 became annoyed as they paid $385 to fly to London and back while their youthful seat partners paid only $200. In fact, some of them filed suit against 14 transatlantic airlines, claiming that low youth rates were discriminatory.

In late summer, Lufthansa refused to go along with other IATA carriers seeking to set rates for 1972 and said it would put into effect a $210 fare—regardless of age—between New York and Frankfurt. Because IATA rules stipulate that all member carriers must agree on proposed rates, this meant that a free-for-all transatlantic rate structure was in prospect for 1972.

Late in 1971, however, the IATA carriers reached an agreement setting the lowest New York–Frankfurt fare at $215 and the New York–London fare at $200. First-class rates would remain unchanged, but youth fares on IATA airlines would increase by $100 in summer. A general increase of about 8% for Americans' tickets was also expected, as a result of devaluation of the dollar.

IATA established three seasons for fare determination: *winter* (November–March), *summer* (June–August, eastbound and July–September, westbound); and the *shoulder* seasons (the other months). Excursion rate periods were set at 14–21 days and 21–45 days, with a new 7–8 day $270 winter package trip to Europe.

Another major new passenger airliner was introduced to the traveling public in 1971. The DC-10 made its first commercial passenger flight on August 16 under the insignia of United Airlines. The 3-engine plane, as wide as a Boeing 747 but not as long, has a capacity of 345 passengers, compared with 490 for the 747. Most airlines, however, will fly it in a 250-passenger configuration. Introduction of a similar new airliner, the Lockheed 1011 TriStar, was delayed by Lockheed's financial crisis until 1972. The two supersonics, the French–British Concorde and the Soviet TU-144, were scheduled for delivery in 1974.

In Las Palmas, Mallorca, airport officials claimed a new world record in August for the number of people transported in a single civilian aircraft when 500 persons landed there on a 747 charter flight from Madrid. Ten were in the crew.

U. S. airlines, which had suffered losses of $154 million in 1970, showed same gains in 1971. For the first 9 months of the year, U. S. scheduled airlines reported $25.6 million profit compared with $2.5 million in the same 1970 period. Since final quarters are always losing ones for airlines, a substantial net loss was expected for the year's operations. (See also AIR TRANSPORTATION.)

The Gallup Poll found that 49% of U. S. adults have flown in an airplane, compared with 38% in 1965. Groups with the largest percentage of fliers were Westerners (68%) and professional people (71%); those with the lowest percentage were Southerners (40%) and farmers (18%).

Railroads. Amtrak, the corporation that Congress created to run the remaining U. S. long-distance passenger trains, took over in May and promptly ordered more than 150 trains out of business. Among them were such famous ones as the Twentieth Century Limited, Wabash Cannonball, Pocahontas, Nancy Hanks, Panama Limited, San Francisco Chief, City of Los Angeles, Capitol Limited, and City of Miami. Protests by rail-travel buffs and a last-ditch move by Senate Majority Leader Mike Mansfield proved fruitless.

Six months later, Amtrak went to Capitol Hill seeking $170 million more from an unsympathetic Congress. Amtrak was expected to lose $152.3 million in its first year of operations, and the Interstate Commerce Commission told Congress it might not be possible to breathe new life into the nation's sickly rail passenger system. Indeed, one railroad executive, B. F. Biaggini, president of Southern Pacific, said, "I think Amtrak will preside over the passenger business as it sort of gracefully goes out of business." The National Association of Railroad Passengers charged that the railroads were sabotaging passenger service.

A new concept combining rail and automobile transportation began on Dec. 6, 1971, when Auto-Train—a private corporation—initiated runs between Lorton, Va.—near Washington, D. C.—and Sanford, Fla., near Disney World. The company was transporting a car and four passengers for $190. This included coach seats, meals, and movies on the overnight trip. The first few weeks of service were quickly sold out. (See also TRANSPORTATION.)

Ship Travel. The rapid growth of the cruise business in the late 1960's slowed considerably in 1970 because of the ailing national economy, but business was good in 1971. A survey found that New York's cruise business remained about even in 1970, while in Port Everglades and Miami the growth rate was 17%—small compared with the spectacular increases of the preceding five years. Miami added two new vessels in 1971 to its fleet of ships permanently based there. Another 20 ships were being built or were on the drawing boards in Europe, destined for U. S. markets.

Visitors to the United States. Several innovations were inaugurated to attract more tourists to the hotels in four U. S. gateway cities. New York, Chicago, Washington, and San Francisco offered special summer rates for European visitors. A network of over 180 hotels, through the United States Travel Service (USTS), agreed to provide staffs speaking English and at least three other languages.

Multilingual port receptionists proved a success in New York's Kennedy Airport, so USTS signed contracts to provide such personnel at Seattle–Tacoma and San Juan and was considering them for several other cities. USTS also opened its eighth regional office, in Toronto, making Canada the 41st country in which USTS was actively marketing travel to and in the United States. The agency was showing the Disney-created, 360-degree film *America the Beautiful* in its unique mobile, 6-story-high neoprene balloon theater in various cities around the world—in Tokyo and Leningrad in 1971 and in Mexico City and Paris in 1972.

For the first time, Japan sent the greatest number of overseas visitors to the United States in a 6-month period. In the first half of 1971, total overseas visitors reached 1,084,369, a gain of 7.1%. Japan accounted for 145,569 of these, while the United Kingdom—formerly the leader—sent 125,606 visitors. Canada and Mexico are not included in these figures.

Monetary Changes. Traveling Americans were caught briefly in the monetary uncertainty that gripped other countries when President Nixon announced his new economic policies in August. Some gouging by hotels and shopkeepers was reported, while governments tried to cope with the new situation, but exchange rates then settled down with the dollar usually no more than 5% or 6% lower than before. Devaluation of the dollar at the end of 1971 presaged higher costs for U. S. travelers abroad—about 12%, or an additional $3 per day for the traveler used to spending $25 per day. Devaluation was also expected to bring more visitors from other countries to the United States.

Weekend Travel. The long weekend received official sanction when a new law shifted several holidays to Mondays, giving Americans more three-day weekends and stimulating travel. Holidays changed were Washington's birthday, from February 22 to the third Monday in February; Memorial Day, from May 30 to the last Monday in May; Columbus Day, from October 12 to the second Monday in October; and Veterans Day, from November 11 to the fourth Monday in October.

Attractions. After years of construction, Walt Disney World opened near Orlando, Fla., on Oct. 1, 1971. Similar to, but larger than Disneyland, in California, the $400 million project has several golf courses, hotels, and other tourist facilities as well as a theme park. After a modest start, Disney World attendance soared. On the day after Thanksgiving, so many people turned out that the attraction was forced to close its gates at 1 p. m. after 55,000 persons had entered and traffic on nearby highways was backed up for 15 miles.

JAY CLARKE, *The Miami "Herald"*

Hotels and Motels

As the economic recession deepened, income and occupancy in the U. S. lodging industry slipped to lower levels in 1971 for the second consecutive year. Total sales for the nation's hotels and motels declined to $7.1 billion, from $7.21 billion in 1970. Average guest-room occupancy dropped to 59%—the lowest since before World War II—against 61% in the preceding year.

The recession cut into conventions, business meetings, and pleasure travel. Other causes for the slump were overbuilding in resorts, the decline of urban areas where many older hotels are located, and high prices, due in part to rapidly rising labor costs. Many downtown hotels shut down; even some newer motels went bankrupt.

The number of U. S.-chain hotels and motels was 3.1% higher than in the preceding year and the number of guest rooms rose 4.8% in the same period, according to the 1971 *Directory of Hotel & Motel Systems.* The number of chains increased to 193 from 188 in 1970, even though the total number of U. S. hotels and motels declined.

The Directory also showed that the 25 largest chains accounted for the major part of U. S.-chain growth in 1971. There was a rise of 130 in the number of properties built by the top 25 chains and a gain of 29,558 rooms.

The world's largest hotel/motel system, Holiday Inns, Inc., added 117 inns having 24,275 guest rooms in 1971, giving it a total of 1,407 inns with 206,176 rooms. Holiday had properties in every one of the 50 United States and in Europe, Africa, Canada, the Caribbean, and Latin America. Other major chain additions in 1971: 30 new Sheraton hotels and motor inns with 7,101 rooms; 23 new Howard Johnson's Motor Lodges with 3,392 rooms; and 15 new Royal Inns of America with 2,315 rooms.

The increasing popularity of budget-priced accommodations was underlined by the continued growth of Motel 6, Inc., which had completed 18 motels with a total of 2,125 rooms in 1971.

New Hotels and Motels. The largest new hotel completed in the United States during 1971 was the $62 million, 1,900-room Sheraton-Waikiki in Honolulu, Hawaii. Other major new hotels and motels which opened in the United States during 1971 were the 1,057-room Tempo Bay Resort Hotel in Walt Disney World, near Orlando, Fla.; the 750-room Regency Hyatt O'Hare, in Rosemont, Ill.; and the $30 million, 640-room Park Lane in New York City, the first new hotel in Manhattan since 1965.

Prefabricated steel guest rooms for Tempo Bay Resort Hotel and Polynesian Village at Walt Disney World were produced on an assembly line at the rate of 35 rooms per week by U. S. Steel Corporation's Realty Development Division.

Singapore added 2,620 rooms as three of the largest hotels to be opened outside of the United States were completed in 1971. These hotels were the 1,200-room, 40-story Mandarin Singapore; the 900-room Regency Hyatt Singapore; and the 530-room Shangri-La. Other large new hotels opened in 1971 included the $37.5 million Keio Plaza in Tokyo, the 1,000-room Melia Castilla in Madrid, and the 700-room Regency Hyatt-Acapulco and the 508-room Condesa del Mar, both in Acapulco.

ALBERT E. KUDRLE
American Hotel & Motel Association

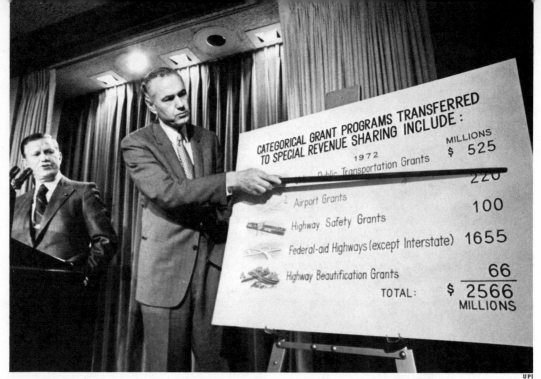

CATEGORICAL GRANT PROGRAMS TRANSFERRED
TO SPECIAL REVENUE SHARING INCLUDE:

	MILLIONS
1972 Public Transportation Grants	$ 525
Airport Grants	220
Highway Safety Grants	100
Federal-aid Highways (except Interstate)	1655
Highway Beautification Grants	66
TOTAL:	$ 2566 MILLIONS

UPI

Secretary of Transportation John Volpe points to details of President Nixon's proposal of March 18 to aid mass transit through federal-state revenue sharing.

transportation

News developments and technological advances in transportation during 1971 are reviewed in this article under the following headings: (1) General Survey; (2) Highways; (3) Motor Transport; (4) Railroads; and (5) Shipping.

Additional transportation news appears in separate entries for AIR TRANSPORTATION; BRIDGES; CANALS; TUNNELS.

General Survey

Progress in the field of transportation was mixed in 1971. In the United States, revenues and investment in transportation generally expanded, but profits did not always keep pace and strikes occurred frequently. Many events, however, pointed the way to better results in the future.

Urban Mass Transit. The obligation concept of the nation's Urban Mass Transportation Assistance Act fared poorly in the fiscal year 1971. The act anticipated a federal obligation of $600 million for the year to improve and extend old bus, rapid transit, and commuter rail systems and to develop new ones—but the administration obligated only $400 million for this purpose. Meanwhile, transit authorities around the nation had placed applications for $2.2 billion with the U. S. Department of Transportation (DOT).

This 1970 act expresses the federal government's intention of spending $10 billion in 12 years to upgrade urban mass transit. The federal government is to provide two thirds of the funds, and local governments are to pay the rest.

Atlanta voted a 1% sales tax in 1971 to help finance a 70-mile (113-km) transit system, and St.

Louis created a Rapid Transit Authority to plan and finance a system.

The Bay Area Rapid Transit System of San Francisco laid the last of its 300 miles (483 km) of steel rails for the system, scheduled to open in March 1972. The system received $40 million from DOT to help finance the purchase of cars.

A $60 million grant—the largest single sum issued by DOT to complete a transit system—went to the Port Authority of Allegheny county, serving Pittsburgh and its suburbs. New buses for Pittsburgh will be financed by a separate grant.

The Metropolitan Transportation Authority of New York received $35.6 million to help buy new rail commuter cars and $7.7 million to make track improvements on the Long Island Rail Road. Also in the New York area, the Port Authority Trans Hudson (PATH) received $16 million toward completion of the Journal Square Transportation Center in Jersey City, N.J., a coordinated rail-bus-auto parking facility. Construction of this $80 million center has been in progress since late 1968.

A grant of $21.4 million was made to help develop a "personal rapid transit" system on the West Virginia University campus at Morgantown. If successful, it will make available a new type of automated rail-transit system, with small cars operating individually or in short trains.

Munich, West Germany, opened its first U-Bahn segment, a 7 mile (11-km) north-south subway line serving 13 stations, in October. Also in October, Montreal began a subway extension project that will double the current 13.7-mile (22-km) subway network. The city had received a $430 million grant from the provincial government.

The Venezuelan cabinet approved credits for about $117 million for construction of the first 5 miles (8 km) of the Caracas subway, and work began in July.

Intercity Trains. Amtrak, a quasipublic corporation, began nationwide passenger service on May 1. Its 184 trains on 16 routes served 85% of the nation's urban population, reaching 114 cities with 100,000 or more population. By fall, Amtrak announced that it would lease 12 more Metroliner cars and buy 1,200 of the best available stainless-steel passenger cars. It asked Congress for $170 million in additional funds and revealed plans for faster and more frequent service in heavily traveled areas. In another rail development, DOT released its "recommendations for Northeast Corridor (Washington, D.C., to Boston) transportation" that call for higher-speed service and increased departure frequencies to meet the needs of passenger travel that is projected to grow at the rate of 10% to 15% a year. Improvements in roadbed, terminal upgrading, and new cars will cost about $460 million. (See also the section on *Railroads.*)

Shares of Expenditures. The Department of Transportation estimated in 1971 that public and private expenditures for transportation goods and services in the United States amounted to more than $161 billion in 1970. Highways accounted for 81% of the spending; air transportation 7.2%; rail transportation, including urban transit, 7%; water 4%; and pipelines 0.8%.

State Departments. Illinois, Maine, and Massachusetts created state departments of transportation during the year, raising the number of such departments to 15.

Pipelines. The Syrian Arab Republic and the Trans Arabian Pipe Line Company reopened a 1,000-mile (1,600-km) pipeline in February 1971, 9 months after it had been damaged. The line annually pumps nearly half a million barrels of oil, approximately 15% of the total Saudi Arabian production, to Zahrani, a port in southern Lebanon. Syria will receive annual transit dues of about $8.5 million, nearly $4 million more than the dues paid under the previous agreement, and it also got a lump-sum payment of $6 million in 1971.

Egypt signed a contract on July 31 for the construction of two 42-inch (107-cm) parallel pipelines that will have a capacity of 80 million tons per year. The lines will connect the Gulf of Suez with the Mediterranean.

The U. S. Interstate Commerce Commission announced that the 92 regulated U. S. pipelines had a 5.8% annual rise in traffic to 8.1 million barrels of oil in 1970. The pipeline companies' $1.16 million in earned revenues was a 7.7% increase over 1969.

Air and Rail Finances. As a group, U. S. scheduled airlines were doing slightly better in 1971, while the nation's railroads were showing generally scant profits. In the first 9 months of the year, the airlines had a net profit of $25.6 million, compared with a profit of only $2.5 million in the same period a year earlier. Profits for the third quarter increased to $160.6 million, compared with $60.5 million in 1970.

In April the Civil Aeronautics Board granted air carriers a domestic coach fare increase of up to 9%, based on its finding that a 12% rate of return should be allowed on a reasonable equipment investment for operations if planes flew with 52.5% of the seats occupied.

Information for the full year of 1970 points up the financial distress of the railroads: the industry's return on net investment was 1.47%, the lowest since 1932 and far below the ICC-recommended level of 6%. Revenues for 1970 reached a record

Construction progressed in 1971 on a 98-mile subway for the Washington (D. C.) Metropolitan Area Transit Authority. It will cost almost $3 billion.

DIAMOND-BLADED CUTTERS create grooves in U. S. Route 22 to reduce skids. A bus crash at this Pennsylvania site had killed seven schoolchildren.

closer to Tokyo on a route of 5,718 miles (9,200 km), compared with the carrier's 7,840-mile (12,550-km), polar route via Anchorage, Alaska.

The USSR began flight tests for its TU-144 supersonic transport. The new SST averaged 995 mph on the 1,180-mile (1,890-km) flight from Moscow to Sofia. The French-British Concorde SST flew at 1,315 mph (2,116 km) in May. The U. S. Senate in March ended funding for further U. S. SST research.

Japan began a 15-year plan to make greater use of its 155-mph trains. In April it started on a $31.4 billion program to construct 5,590 miles (8,930 km) of a new super-express rail mainline linking all major cities.

European Airline Growth. Even though air fares within Europe average 48% higher than in the United States, intra-European revenue passenger miles grew faster than intra-U. S. air travel during 1969 and 1970. The Civil Aeronautics Board said that revenue passenger miles increased 19% in Europe in 1969 (against 9.3% in the United States), and 9.3% in Europe in 1970 (against only 0.5% in the United States).

JAMES R. ROMAN, JR.
The George Washington University

Highways

Preliminary evidence in late 1971 suggested that highway records—in number of registered vehicles and mileage traveled, and in expenditures for new roads—had been set during the year. Highways were also getting safer. The traffic-fatality rate in 1970 had been the lowest in history.

Interstate Roads. On June 30, 1971, there were 32,026 miles open to traffic in the 42,500-mile national system of interstate and defense highways, and construction was in progress on 4,143 more miles, the U. S. Department of Transportation (DOT) reported. Only 4% of the system had not advanced beyond preliminary status.

About 85% of the interstate highways in use can meet the standards of adequacy for future use, DOT said. The rest require additional improvements to meet future standards.

Some $44.76 billion has been expended since acceleration of the federal interstate highway aid program began in 1956. The completed work has cost $32.58 billion—$26.82 billion for construction and $5.76 billion for engineering and right-of-way acquisition. The work under way was estimated to cost $12.18 billion—$8.46 billion for construction and $3.72 billion for engineering and right-of-way acquisition.

Appalachian Regional Development Act. DOT announced that as of June 30, 1971, over $1.4 billion in federal and state funds were obligated for development of highways and local access roads in a 13-state region under the Appalachian Regional Development Act. About 705 miles were completed, and 583 miles were under construction, while engineering work and right-of-way acquisition was under way for an additional 968 miles.

The Appalachian Regional Development Act of 1965 called for appropriations of about $1.1 billion for the development of highways, but in May the General Accounting Office noted that the Regional Commission's latest estimate showed that an additional $2.65 billion would be needed to complete the highway program.

$11,983,000,000, up 5% in a year, but expenses increased 7.7%. Twenty-one of the 72 Class I railroads recorded deficits.

Like the airlines, the railroads were allowed rate increases. The ICC set the boosts at from 3.5% to 12%, varying with the section of country.

Rail and Shipping Strikes. Labor strife beset railroads and ship lines during the year.

Strikes idled the railroads in May until the U. S. Congress enacted a return-to-work order—an order that yielded a 13.5% pay raise for signalmen. In August, after strikes spread to 10 lines, the United Transportation Union received a 42% pay increase to be spread over the succeeding 42 months, but the union agreed to work-rule changes reducing the number of crew changes for each run.

A Taft-Hartley injunction ended the 14-week West Coast dock strike that idled 15,000 members of the International Longshoremen and Warehousemen's Union. Wage differences were of minor importance. Mainly at issue was the union's demand for the rights to stuff and strip containers, a task conducted by members of the Teamsters Union. A failure to agree on a guaranteed annual wage for 2,080 hours led to a strike in Gulf and Atlantic ports by the nearly 50,000 members of the ILA. Employers contended that union members had abused previous agreements, and they proposed employment by individual terminals rather than the traditional hiring-hall system. (See also LABOR.)

Air and Rail Innovations. In April, Scandinavian Airways System instituted service over the trans-Siberian route, putting Copenhagen 4½ hours

Vehicles and Mileage. Motor vehicles registrations climbed to an estimated total of slightly more than 112 million by the end of 1971. DOT said that there were more than 92 million passenger cars and almost 20 million trucks and buses—a gain of 3.6 million vehicles over the 1970 registration.

California led by registering 12.3 million vehicles, followed by New York and Texas, each with about 6.9 million, and Ohio with 6.2 million. The nine states leading in registrations—rounded out by Illinois, Pennsylvania, Florida, Michigan, and New Jersey—accounted for more than half of the national total.

DOT estimated that motor vehicle travel in 1970 increased to 1.125 billion vehicle miles, an increase of 5% over 1969. Passenger cars accounted for 79% of the travel and trucks for 18%. Motorcycles and buses contributed about 1% each.

Fatalities. The 1970 fatality rate on the nation's highways was calculated at 4.9 deaths per 100 million vehicle miles, a record low, down from 5.3 in 1969 and the previous low of 5.1 in 1961. Despite the reduction in the rate of fatalities, 55,300 persons were killed in highway accidents in 1970, and 2 million more were injured. There were an estimated 15.5 million accidents costing at least $16 billion.

Motorcyclists added significantly to the 1970 traffic toll. The National Transportation Safety Board reported that 2,303 of them were killed, an increase of 18.9% in a year, while motorcycle registrations increased by only 8.6%.

Drivers in the 15- to 24-year age range died in traffic in proportionately larger numbers than other groups, the NTSB reported. In 1969, its records show, there were 17,700 fatalities in this group—7,400 more than would have occurred if the fatality rate had been the same as that of drivers 25 and older. The NTSB recommended that initial license examinations be greatly improved and that 2-year probationary licensing be established for drivers under 21.

Fuel Taxes. During 1971, Connecticut increased its motor fuel tax by 2 cents per gallon, and Georgia, Idaho, Maine, and Vermont raised theirs by 1 cent per gallon. In Nebraska, gasoline may now be taxed at 3 cents less per gallon if grain alcohol is used in it as a substitute for lead. This will go into effect Jan. 1, 1973. New York City was authorized to impose an additional 1-cent-per-gallon tax on fuel containing one-half gram or more of lead per gallon.

Financing. States disbursed $9.8 billion in highway-user taxes in 1970, which was an increase of 6% in a year, the U.S. Department of Transportation announced late in 1971. The disbursements were broken down into $6.3 billion for state highways (which included $5 billion for capital outlays, maintenance, and administration, $628 million for safety activities and law enforcement, and $664 million for interest and bond retirement), $2.5 billion for local roads and streets, and $1 billion for nonhighway purposes. Collections had amounted to $10.3 billion, but the high cost of collection and administration greatly reduced the amount available for distribution.

Bus Operations. The National Association of Motor Bus Owners reported that 395 million persons made intercity bus trips in 1970 for a total of about 25 billion bus-passenger miles. For the year, total operating revenues of the 71 Class I bus companies rose 6.6% to $722 million, but expenses rose faster, by 8.2% to $643 million, leaving a net operating revenue of $79 million.

JAMES R. ROMAN, JR.
The George Washington University

THIS BILLBOARD near Freeport, Maine, became the first to be taken down in a federal highway beautification program. Transportation Secretary John Volpe presided over the removal.

UPI

Motor Transport

Truck transportation in the United States increased in 1971 at about the same pace as in 1970. The trucking industry continued efforts to increase efficiency in its operations during 1971 by making greater use of computers for processing billing, tariff, scheduling, and terminal operations data.

New and modified truck designs will continue to be required to meet changing government safety and air-pollution standards. Higher standards for accident-resistant fuel tanks are now effective, while new braking standards and improved lighting systems are anticipated.

Trucking. The U. S. motor truck fleet increased by about one million vehicles during 1971. Registrations, excluding government-owned trucks, reached a record high of about 18.8 million vehicles, compared with 17.8 million in 1970. The industry carried almost 420 billion ton-miles of freight in 1971, compared with about 411 billion ton-miles in 1970.

Total operating revenues for about 15,000 for-hire truck lines engaged in U. S. interstate commerce in 1971 rose to more than $14.5 billion—nearly $3 billion more than the annual freight revenues of all U. S. railroads. Private and for-hire trucking operators not regulated by the Interstate Commerce Commission earned additional billions.

The trucking industry's impact on the economy was felt in several areas. It provided employment for more than 8 million persons and had a payroll of about $64 billion. Record sales were set for all types of trucks, including diesels and truck-trailers, reflecting the greater transport flexibility required by shippers. Trucks used nearly 26 billion gallons of motor fuel in 1971 at a cost of almost $6 billion, exclusive of taxes. Also, motor truck operators paid an estimated $5.7 billion in federal and state highway use taxes in 1971, including taxes levied for construction of the Interstate and Defense Highway System.

The motor carriers continued to seek relief from restrictions imposed on the trucking industry. In particular, they sought changes in the size and weight limitations on trucks operating on the interstate highway system, and they collected data to support the industry's position in the various states.

Containerization. Growth in the containerization of internationally shipped goods continued in 1971. In international trade, the use of containers permits land, sea, and air shipment of goods, with savings in repacking, loading, and unloading as a result of the great flexibility of transfer from one mode of transportation to another. The standardization of container sizes was still unresolved in 1971, but the trucking industry was confident that standards eventually would be worked out by the nations involved in international trade.

WILLIAM A. BRESNAHAN
American Trucking Associations, Inc.

Railroads

A series of events shook the railroad industry to its very foundations in 1971. On May 1, the quasi-governmental National Railroad Passenger Corporation, known as Amtrak, assumed responsibility for the operation of all intercity passenger trains. Sizable freight operations, accounting for 40% of all U. S. intercity ton-miles of transportation services, remained in the hands of private carriers. In the summer, separate studies on the desirability of nationalizing the freight railroads were initiated by the Interstate Commerce Commission, the Senate Interstate and Foreign Commerce Committee, and the Department of Transportation. In the fall, the Philadelphia-based Reading Co., once the bluest of the blue chips, slid over the brink into bankruptcy, the fifth Eastern railroad to go the reorganization route in recent years. (It was preceded by the Penn Central Transportation Co., the Lehigh Valley Railroad, the Boston & Maine Corp., and the Central of New Jersey.)

While the general public tended to view these developments as portents of doom, seasoned observers of the railroad scene were less pessimistic for several reasons. The takeover of passenger trains by a quasi-public corporation undeniably was a potential first step toward a federal railway system; nonetheless, it relieved the railroads of losses on passenger services amounting to about $225 million a year and permitted them to get on with the more profitable job of hauling freight. Moreover, while about 20 carriers operated in the red, including the five in bankruptcy, many of the remaining 50 Class I railroads reported rising earnings. Also, the three nationalization studies turned up evidence that it would be less costly to help the railroads to help themselves, through relaxed regulation and loan guarantees, than to put them under government ownership.

Amtrak. As in the past, the top of the iceberg—the 5% of the railroad business represented by intercity passenger trains—commanded the biggest headlines. Three decades ago about 20,000 passenger trains operated daily between U. S. cities. By May 1, 1971, the day Amtrak took over, the number of trains had shrunk to fewer than 400. Amtrak's first act was to cut the number of trains in half. The surviving routes—involving 16 major city pairs, such as Chicago-Seattle—were selected on the basis of "probable profitability." Pledging to improve service and trim losses, Amtrak came into being on a wave of optimism and public goodwill. But despite the best efforts of a Washington cadre headed by Roger Lewis, the first president of the corporation, Amtrak in its first months seemed able to do little except incur deficits of the same magnitude of those that had burdened the private carriers, with little discernible improvement in service. A $40 million direct grant from the federal government was quickly exhausted, and a $100 million, government-guaranteed loan authorized by the original Amtrak law was inadequate to close the gap. Late in 1971, Amtrak went back to Congress to ask for $170 million to cover its losses until mid-1973.

Auto-Train. The other major railroad passenger development in 1971 was the inauguration on December 6 of an automobile and passenger service between Lorton, Va., and Sanford, Fla. For a flat fee of $190, the privately owned Auto-Train Corporation will ferry one private automobile and up to four passengers between the Washington, D. C., suburb and a site close to Walt Disney World, using the rented tracks of the Richmond, Fredericksburg & Potomac and the Seaboard Coast Line. About 60 customers made the first trip.

Freight. In freight operations, the Penn Central continued to occupy center stage. Freed of its passenger problems, and under an aggressive new management that won the applause of the shipping community for service and equipment improvements,

GRUMMAN AEROSPACE CORP.

UPI

MESSERSCHMITT—BÖLKOW—BLOHM

FASTER GROUND TRAVEL is on the way. Grumman holds a federal contract to build a research model of a 300 mph tracked air cushion vehicle (*top*). A linear induction motor vehicle (*bottom left*) being tested is expected to do 250 mph. And West Germany's MBB electromagnetic train (*bottom right*) may attain 350 mph.

Penn Central in the second year of its bankruptcy nonetheless continued to suffer grievous losses. In the first 10 months of 1971, Penn Central suffered a loss of $220,915,005, compared with a loss of $252,-875,627 in the comparable 1970 period. This was partly due to a recessionary economy and coal and dock strikes, but mostly it was due to a fistful of problems that afflict Eastern railroads even in the best of times. In the East, terminal costs are high and hauls are comparatively short, so the traffic is particularly vulnerable to highway competition. Also, railroads are still paying for the overbuilding of lines that took place in the 19th century. (Penn Central wants to abandon about 8,000 of its 20,000 route miles of line.)

Freight carloadings for the industry were about 25 million cars in 1971, down about 7% from the previous year. But due to a series of rate increases whose full effects were felt during 1971, revenues climbed to a record $12 billion. Labor and operating costs rose less substantially, with the result that such railroads as the Southern, the Norfolk and Western, the Southern Pacific, the Santa Fe, the Seaboard Coast Line, and the Union Pacific were able to remain healthily in the black.

Labor. Outstanding wage cases were settled in 1971 on the formula (42% in 42 months) arrived at in 1970. Of particular importance was final settlement of the long-standing work-rules cases. This came after the United Transportation Union had called selective strikes against 10 railroads in mid-1971. In return for a substantial wage-benefit package and costly employee-protection provisions, the railroads won the right to make important changes in working rules, including rules about interdivisional runs.

Legislation. A surface transportation bill introduced in Congress in 1971 held out the promise of long-sought financial aid and relief from over-regulation. In an unprecedented move, the regulated highway and water carriers joined the railroads in support of this bill. Among other things, it would create an RFC-type corporation to extend loans up to a total of $3 billion to distressed transportation companies; prohibit discriminatory state and local taxation; require the expenditure of 5% of all federal highway money for grade-crossing protection; and speed up procedures for abandonment of unprofitable rail lines.

Regulation. In November the Federal Railroad Administration imposed new standards for the upkeep of railway track. It was estimated that the railroad industry will have to spend an initial $1.629 billion and an additional $116.2 million a year on a continuing basis to meet the new standards, which grew out of a rising public outcry over freight-train derailments.

Equipment. Railroads and private carlines purchased or leased about 55,000 new freight cars and 1,200 new locomotives in 1971. Restoration of the

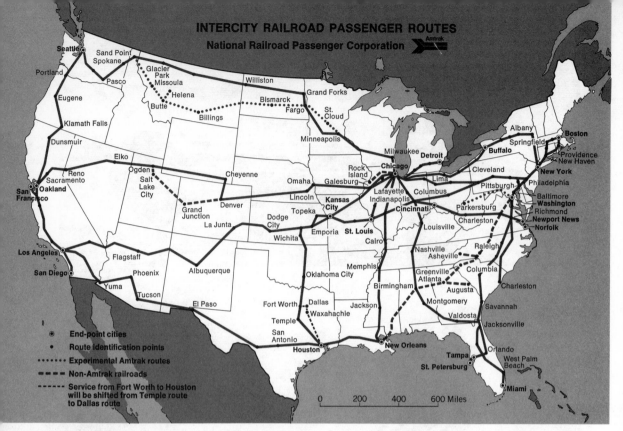

INTERCITY RAILROAD PASSENGER ROUTES

National Railroad Passenger Corporation — Amtrak

◉ **End-point cities**
• **Route identification points**
•••••• **Experimental Amtrak routes**
▬ ▬ ▬ **Non-Amtrak railroads**
▬ ▬ ▬ **Service from Fort Worth to Houston will be shifted from Temple route to Dallas route**

0   200   400   600 Miles

7% investment tax credit was expected to encourage railroads to order an additional 15,000 new cars a year.

Mergers. On August 1 the 541-mile Monon Railroad was merged into the 6,574-mile Louisville & Nashville. Late in 1971, the 10,200-mile Southern Railway announced that it had initiated "exploratory" talks, which could lead to acquisition of the 624-mile Norfolk Southern.

LUTHER S. MILLER
Editor, "Railway Age"

Shipping

World merchant ship tonnage increased again in 1971, chiefly in the fleets of Liberia, Japan, Norway and West Germany. Growth has been primarily in tankers and bulk carriers. Liquid-gas carriers, especially natural gas, and vessels for transporting chemicals have made noted advances in size, design, and number. In the cargo liner trades of western Europe, Australia, Japan and the United States, unit-load vessels such as container- and barge-carrying ships have largely replaced the conventional type of freighter. Elsewhere the latter is still used because extensive capital is needed to construct port facilities that can service unit-load vessels. Even in the areas mentioned above, these large, fast ships are bypassing smaller ports that conventional liners once served.

New flags were joining the list of lesser merchant fleets, notably those of Spain, Brazil, Cyprus, and China.

Tankers make up 38% of the world fleet; dry-bulk carriers 20.5%; conventional freighters 31.4%; unit-load vessels such as container- and barge-carrying-cruise ships and seagoing ferries, 1.3%; liquid gas and chemical carriers 1.0%; fishing and research vessels 3.5%; and miscellaneous, including drilling and service ships for offshore oil wells, 3.3%.

Liberia is a nonmaritime country under whose "flag of convenience" owners of other nationalities register their ships, mainly for low taxes and cheap labor. Other flags of convenience are those of Panama (the oldest) and Cyprus (the newest) whose tonnage reached 1.5 million gross in 1971. These three fleets have a combined tonnage of 45.25 million gross, or over one fifth of the world total. U. S., Greek, and Italian ownership accounts for 70% of flag-of-convenience ships. Almost half of the Liberian fleet is U. S.-owned, primarily by major oil corporations or shipping companies that serve them. Much of the rest is U. S.-financed.

Cyprus in 1971 was fast becoming the new flag of convenience for Greece, possibly replacing Panama. By using the Liberian flag for large bulk ships and the Cypriot flag for their traditional trade, the Greek shipping entrepreneurs are able to retain U. S. financing for the former while escaping U. S. political control, enabling the Cypriot-flag ships to enter Cuban ports.

Of the vessels engaged in ocean trade, 59% are less than 10 years old; only 9% are more than 25 years old. Superships of 100,000 gross tons and over total 162 tankers and 2 dry-bulk carriers.

Shipbuilding. Japan still led in shipbuilding in 1971 but had only 41% of world orders, compared with over half in 1970. Sweden and West Germany

MAJOR MERCHANT FLEETS

	Gross registered tons[1]	
	July 1, 1971	1-year gain or loss
Liberia	38,552,000	+5,256,000
Japan	30,509,000	+3,506,000
Britain	27,335,000	+1,510,000
Norway	21,720,000	+2,373,000
United States	16,266,000	−2,198,000
USSR	16,194,000	+1,363,000
Greece	13,066,000	+2,114,000
World total[2]	247,203,000	+19,713,000

[1] Gross tonnage is volume capacity; deadweight tonnage (dwt.) is lifting capacity. [2] Includes other countries than those listed above.
Source: Lloyd's Register of Shipping, 1971.

remained second and third, each with 6.9%. France and Spain, however, both passed Britain, which stood fourth in 1970. The United States dropped from 12th to 14th, behind Yugoslavia and Poland. A rising newcomer was Brazil, in 18th place between East Germany and Greece. Most of this construction was for Brazil's growing merchant fleet.

Ports. Ports are as essential to world trade and ocean transport as ships. The maritime nations, with the exception of the United States, have either enlarged their old ports or built new ones to accommodate superships. Notable are Bantry Bay in Ireland, Rotterdam, and Marseille. No developed harbor on the East Coast of the United States can accommodate a ship of over 75,000 tons. New Soviet ports include Ilyichovsk, near Odessa on the Black Sea; Nakhodka in the Far East near Vladivostok; and Ventspils in Latvia on the Baltic coast, at the end of the pipeline from the Ural Mountains.

U. S. Shipping. U. S.-flag shipping in 1971 again declined, along with Canada's. Canada, however, had adopted a policy of not fostering a national merchant marine, depending instead on chartered foreign ships.

The U. S. Merchant Marine Act of 1970 was the latest attempt to maintain a U. S.-flag merchant fleet in peacetime by providing building subsidies for 300 ships in 10 years. This effort, through the end of 1971, was still a failure. The U. S. Maritime Administration had unwanted subsidy funds, and few ships were on the ways. Bulk carriers, dry and liquid, were the major U. S. need. The Maritime Administration's standard designs for these types were for vessels of 70,000 tons, the largest that could enter U. S. ports. Operators and unions, however, wanted ships of 225,000 tons, to compete in the world raw-materials trade where U. S.-owned flag-of-convenience ships have been so successful.

The container ship, pioneered by trucking executive Malcolm McLean, and the LASH (Lighter Aboard Ship) barge-carrying ship designed by Jerome L. Goldman of New Orleans gave promise of a U. S. revival in the cargo liner trades. But in 1971 financial troubles plagued American container ship companies, caused by overexpansion and domestic and foreign competition.

In 1971, U. S. ports again had dock strikes, not only on the East Coast where work stoppage had followed every expiration of contract since World War II, but also on the West Coast, which had had dock peace for 20 years.

Inland Waterways. While U. S.-flag ocean shipping lagged, commerce on U. S. rivers and other inland waterways was increasing at a rate of 10% per year. These water routes provide the cheapest transport for bulk materials, thus many new industrial plants were being built along them. As many as 50 barges in one tow are pushed by towboats.

The $1.2 billion Arkansas-Verdigris River Navigation System was completed and President Nixon opened the Port of Catoosa on June 5, 1971, making Tulsa a "seaport."

Ocean Towing. The United States was also pioneering in ocean towing. Bulk trade from U. S. ports to Alaska and the Caribbean was largely moved by tows. A 5,000-ton superbarge, built at Galveston, was in the Hawaiian trade transporting sugar, pineapples, and fertilizer.

JOHN D. HAYES
Rear Admiral, U. S. Navy (Retired)

DOCTOR LYKES, a 51,000-ton vessel built for Lykes Bros. Steamship Co., has a stern elevator. It is the first ship in a new merchant class, the Seabees.

TRINIDAD AND TOBAGO

Political and economic troubles continued to plague Trinidad and Tobago in 1971, although there was no repetition of the black-led rebellion that had nearly toppled the government in 1970.

Political Affairs. The general election in May returned Prime Minister Eric Williams and his Peoples' National Movement (PNM) to power for another five years. Although the PNM captured all 36 parliamentary seats, the election raised many questions. Of 440,000 eligible voters, less than 100,000 participated, of whom 90% voted for the PNM. The Democratic Action Congress, founded by a former PNM leader who had withdrawn from the government during the 1970 rebellion, and the Democratic Labour party, composed mostly of East Indians, boycotted the election.

The absence of any opposition members in the new Parliament raised a fundamental legal question. While the constitution required the participation of opposition members, it also stipulated that Parliament could continue to function without a majority present. To study the problem and possibly revise the constitution, Williams appointed a 9-man constitutional commission of distinguished international legal scholars and professors.

The election reflected growing dissatisfaction with economic and political conditions in Trinidad. Many of the soldiers charged with participating in the 1970 rebellion had been tried, convicted, and sentenced to long prison terms. There were two assassination attempts against government officials. In October, a state of siege was reimposed.

The Economy. Economic conditions continued to deteriorate, with the rate of unemployment rising to close to 20% of the labor force. The government's announced intention of securing a 51% share in any new foreign corporation operating in Trinidad and Tobago slowed industrial development. Tourism, affected by the political disturbances, was not able to contribute to economic growth.

--- TRINIDAD AND TOBAGO • Information Highlights ---

Official Name: Trinidad and Tobago.
Area: 1,980 square miles (5,128 sq km).
Population (1970 est.): 1,070,000. *Density,* 510 per square mile (203 per sq km). *Annual rate of increase,* 2.0%.
Chief City (1970 est.): Port-of-Spain, the capital, 125,000.
Government: *Head of state,* Elizabeth II, queen; represented by Sir Solomon Hochoy, governor-general (took office Aug. 1962). *Head of government,* Eric Williams, prime minister (took office Nov. 1966). *Legislature*—Parliament: Senate, 24 members; House of Representatives, 36 members. *Major political parties*—Peoples' National Movement, Democratic Labour party, Democratic Action Congress.
Languages: English (official), French patois, Spanish.
Education: *Literacy rate* (1970), 80% of population. *Expenditure on education* (1967), 14.1% of total public expenditure. *School enrollment* (1967)—primary, 223,164; secondary, 50,548; technical/vocational, 3,324; higher, 1,267.
Finances (1970 est.): *Revenues,* $147,600,000; *expenditures,* $187,900,000; *monetary unit,* Trinidad and Tobago dollar (2 T. and T. dollars equal U.S.$1, Sept. 1971).
Gross National Product (1968): $748,000,000.
National Income (1968): $646,000,000; *per person,* $633.
Consumer Price Index (1970): 124 (1963=100).
Manufacturing (metric tons, 1969): Residual fuel oil, 13,335,000; gasoline, 2,618,000; sugar, 248,000; cement, 243,000.
Crops (metric tons, 1969 crop year): Sugar cane (1968–69), 2,500,000; grapefruit (1968), 16,000; cocoa beans, 6,000.
Minerals (metric tons, 1969): Crude petroleum, 8,126,000; sulfur, 72,000.
Foreign Trade (1970): *Exports,* $480,000,000 (chief exports, 1969—petroleum, $343,150,000; sugar, $26,200,000). *Imports,* $539,000,000 (chief imports—crude petroleum, $281,550,000). *Chief trading partners* (1968)—United States (took 45% of exports, supplied 15% of imports); United Kingdom (11%—15%); Venezuela (—44%).
Transportation: *Roads* (1970), 4,000 miles (6,400 km); *motor vehicles* (1969), 87,000 (automobiles, 68,500); *railroads* (1970), 109 miles (175 km).

Petroleum continued to be the principle source of government income, but the industry was plagued by "lightning" strikes and the growing militancy of the labor unions. In October 1971, three major oil companies operating in Trinidad formed a consortium to exploit the extensive deposits located off the island's southeastern coast.

THOMAS G. MATHEWS
University of Puerto Rico

TRUDEAU, Pierre Elliott. See BIOGRAPHY.

TUNISIA

The major concerns in Tunisia in 1971 were plans for a smooth transition of power in the event of the death or incapacity of President Bourguiba and plans for economic development.

The Succession. President Habib Bourguiba, whose ailments included a heart condition, hepatitis, and insomnia, visited Walter Reed Army Hospital in the United States in January for medical tests. Concerned about Tunisia's political future after he leaves power, the authoritarian, 68-year-old president instructed Premier Hedi Nouira to propose the following constitutional changes to insure a stable transition in the event of presidential disability or death: (1) the president of the National Assembly would become temporary president until presidential elections took place within one month, the Assembly president himself being ineligible to run; (2) the Assembly would be given authority to censure the government and compel its resignation; and (3) an independent council would be established to pass on the constitutionality of legislation.

Without waiting for these measures to take effect, President Bourguiba began to permit actions consistent with them. Ministers who had formerly served as secretaries devoid of any power began to function as a cabinet and, for the first time, made collective decisions.

Domestic Politics. President Bourguiba demonstrated his real authority on October 26 when he asked Premier Nouira and the cabinet to resign and then to form a new government that same day. At a meeting of the newly created political bureau of the country's only party, the Neo-Destour Socialist party, the president confirmed his support for Premier Nouira by appointing him the party's secretary general.

Bourguiba acted after some political disaffection surfaced at the party's first congress in seven years, which was held at Monastir in late October. At the congress, Ahmed Mestiri, who had been a minister in several governments, led a large faction who favored more democracy within the party and in Tunisian politics in general. Bourguiba and Nouira immediately suspended Mestiri from the party.

Impatience with the regime was reflected in the fact that, in the selection of the 58 members of the central committee of the party, the 1,000 delegates elected first former Premier Bahi Ladgham, whom Bourguiba had ousted in 1970. Mestiri was the second man elected and Premier Nouira was sixth. Mestiri guided a firm resolution through the congress favoring collective direction of political activities, and elections at all levels.

Population Growth and Unrest. Unrest was aggravated by an annual population growth of more than 3% in a country poor in resources and opportunities. Early in January, President Bourguiba

——————— TUNISIA • Information Highlights ———————

Official Name: Republic of Tunisia.
Area: 63,378 square miles (164,150 sq km).
Population (1970 est.): 5,140,000. *Density,* 80 per square mile (31 per sq km).
Chief City (1966 census): Tunis, the capital, 468,997.
Government: *Head of state,* Habib Bourguiba, president (took office July 25, 1957). *Chief minister,* Hedi Nouira, premier (took office Nov. 2, 1970; reappointed Oct. 26, 1971). *Legislature*—National Assembly (unicameral), 90 members. *Major political party*—Destour Socialist party.
Languages: Arabic (official), French.
Education: *Literacy rate* (1970), 25–35% of population. *School enrollment* (1967)—primary, 826,069; secondary, 134,609; technical/vocational, 45,595; university/higher, 7,336.
Finances (1971 est.): *Revenues,* $296,000,000; *expenditures,* $296,000,000; *monetary unit,* dinar (0.484 dinar equal U. S.$1, Dec. 30, 1971).
Gross National Product (1970 est.): $1,240,000,000.
National Income (1969): $910,000,000; *national income per person,* $181.
Economic Indexes: *Industrial production* (1970), 120 (1963= 100); *agricultural production* (1969), 74 (1963=100); *consumer price index* (1970), 128 (1963=100).
Manufacturing (metric tons, 1969): Cement, 603,000; residual fuel oil, 414,000; distillate fuel oils, 304,000; wine, 985,- 000 hectoliters.
Crops (metric tons, 1968 crop year): Wheat (1969), 350,000; olives, 308,000; grapes, 155,000.
Minerals (metric tons, 1969): Crude petroleum, 3,708,000; phosphate rock, 2,599,000 (ranks 4th among world producers); iron ore, 515,000; salt, 283,000.
Foreign Trade (1970): *Exports,* $181,000,000 (chief exports —crude petroleum, $45,000,000; phosphates, $37,000,000; olive oil, $16,000,000; wine, $9,000,000). *Imports,* $305,- 000,000 (chief imports, 1968—nonelectrical machinery, $30,880,000; cereals and preparations, $23,800,000; chemicals, $19,500,000). *Chief trading partners* (1968)—France (took 23% of exports, supplied 33% of imports); Italy (11%—10%); United States (2%—20%).
Tourism: *Receipts* (1970), $58,000,000.
Transportation: *Roads* (1970), 9,662 miles (15,546 km); *motor vehicles* (1969), 97,200 (automobiles, 62,300); *railroads* (1970), 1,488 miles (2,394 km); *national airline,* Tunis Air; *principal airport,* Tunis-Carthage.
Communications: *Telephones* (1970), 68,908; *television stations* (1968), 5; *television sets* (1969), 37,000; *radios* (1968), 450,000; *newspapers* (1969), 4 (daily circulation, 80,000).

cited the rate of population growth as "a veritable calamity," and called for limiting a family to four children as "a maximum." The Department of Material and Child Health Service and Family Planning started a vigorous program in 1971, and there were some 300 family planning centers in Tunisia.

About 50% of the nation's population is under 19 years of age. Many of these young people, who are only partially educated, and largely unemployed, have left the farms, and are swelling the number of malcontents in the cities. Their repeated resort to riots at sport events prompted the government to impose numerous restrictions by mid-1971. President Bourguiba's strictures against the month-long religious observance of Ramadan were so unpopular that by November he had relaxed them.

Economic Development. Premier Nouira's new economic policy of a mixed private-cooperative experiment found its model in the Medjerda Valley farm project. It consists of 125,000 acres (50,000 hectares) of irrigated soil west of Tunis, with some 100,000 persons living on freeholds aided by cooperative service organizations. The project is intended eventually to encompass 300,000 acres (120,000 hectares). The government still maintains the most workable cooperatives consisting of about 1 million acres (400,000 hectares) formerly owned by French settlers. The discovery of oil in the Gulf of Gabes in late 1971 was also expected to boost the economy.

International Relations. In November, Foreign Minister Mohammed Masmoudi warned the Arab nations against "adventurous initiatives." He declared that they should renew efforts to solve the Middle East crisis through the UN Security Council before undertaking new hostilities against Israel.

Early in July, President Bourguiba voiced his support of King Hassan II of Morocco, who had warded off an attempt at a military coup. The Tunisian press assailed the attempt and warned Tunisia's armed forces not to become involved in politics.

JOHN NORMAN, *Pace College Westchester*

TUNNELS

Tunnel driving probably is the most difficult and most risky of all types of construction. On land, tunnel work may be a cut-and-cover operation, a drill-blast-muck sequence, or a boring operation with a mechanical machine called a mole. Despite advanced technology, problems arise and interfere with construction schedules.

Vehicular Tunnels. Straight Creek, highest highway tunnel in the world and longest in North America, continued to be plagued by trouble in 1971. The project consists of twin two-lane tunnels, 1.7 miles (3 km) long, for Interstate 70, a major east-west highway. It pierces the Continental Divide in the Colorado Rocky Mountains at an elevation of 11,000 feet (3,353 meters), about 1,500 feet (457 meters) below Loveland Pass.

Problems arose from shifting rock, soft and unstable formations where solid granite was expected, equipment failures, labor shortages, spiraling costs, and low production at the high elevation. Efficiency of men and machines at the 2-mile-plus (3-km) altitude is no more than 60% of normal.

The first of the twin 47- by 48-foot (14- by 15-meter) horseshoe-shaped tunnels was to have been completed in 1971, but the job already is one year behind schedule. Its original $50 million estimated cost is expected to be boosted by several million, and the completion date is still uncertain.

Mersey Tunnel. At Liverpool, England, a mole is being used to drive an 8,200-foot (2,500-meter) highway tunnel through a sandstone formation under the Mersey River. Work on the 31-foot-diameter (9.5-meter) twin tunnels started in 1968 and is due to be finished in 1973.

Water Tunnels. San Fernando Tunnel is a 5.5-mile (9-km) section of the Metropolitan Water District project to distribute northern California water to the Los Angeles basin. A mechanical mole is driving a 22-foot-diameter (7-meter) bore.

In February 1971 the tunnel crew was working at the heading under San Gabriel Mountain, 3.5 miles (6 km) in from the portal, when the severe Los Angeles earthquake struck right at the tunnel site. While the tunnel took a jolt, its supports remained intact, and the tunnel escaped serious damage. The men emerged unharmed, although the difference in elevation between portal and heading had decreased by 5.7 feet (1.7 meters).

Navajo Tunnel. A boring machine is also working on an $8.7 million project for a new water system in the desert lands of the Navajo Indian Reservation, New Mexico. Two tunnels, totaling 3.5 miles (6 km) in length, are part of a 13-mile (21-km) system to bring water from the Navajo reservoir to the reservation. The tunnel borer, or mole, has 36 cutters, weighs 200 tons, and is designed to cut through sandstone and siltstone at the rate of 20 feet (6 meters) per hour. A laser beam guides the machine through the rock formation.

Lake Mead Tunnels. Lake Mead, extending 115 miles (185 km) behind Hoover Dam, is being tapped to supply water to Las Vegas and other Nevada communities. The project includes an intake tunnel, 1,420 feet (433 meters) long, running from an underground pumping station on the west shore of the lake, out under offshore Saddle Island where the water is 100 feet (34 meters) deep. A flat bench was excavated under water into the sloping lakeward side of the island, and a boring machine was lowered and positioned on the bench directly over the intake tunnel. The machine, weighing 70 tons, drilled a 12-foot-diameter (3.7-meter) vertical shaft through 20 feet (6 meters) of rock to tap the intake tunnel. The complex task of boring a horizontal tunnel and a connecting vertical underwater shaft was done in 1971.

Sewer Tunnels. Work started in 1971 on a 5.6-mile (9-km) sanitary sewer tunnel to serve Rochester, N.Y., and nearby communities. The $37 million interceptor tunnel will have a diameter of 16 feet (5 meters). A boring machine is driving this tunnel at depths ranging from 80 to 200 feet (24 to 61 meters).

New York City hopes to complete an 11.5-mile (18-km) interceptor-collector sewer tunnel in 1972. The new line, which has a 16-foot (5 meter) diameter, will collect waste and storm-water runoff on Manhattan's west side. The line will collect from laterals on crosstown east-west streets and lead the flow to a new sewage treatment plant.

Mining Tunnel. To reach a molybdenum ore deposit 3,000 feet (914 meters) deep, a Colorado mining company is having a contractor drive a 7-mile (11-km) railroad tunnel on a 3% descending grade. The project is due to be completed in 1974.

WILLIAM H. QUIRK
"Contractors & Engineers" Magazine

TURKEY

During 1971, Turkey experienced considerable political unrest, which led to the ousting of the Demirel government and the imposition of martial law by its successor. Despite the political turmoil,

PREMIER NIHAT ERIM took office in March.

UPI

however, the country continued along the path of planned economic development.

Politics. The early part of 1971 was marked by an increase in student rioting and terrorist activities, including bombing, armed robbery, and kidnapping, on the part of the extreme left. Many of these acts were directed against Americans, the avowed aim of the leftists being to pull Turkey out of the Central Treaty Organization (CENTO) and the North Atlantic Treaty Organization (NATO) and thus to expel the large U.S. presence from Turkey.

Despite its seemingly strong position in the Grand National Assembly, the Justice party government of Suleyman Demirel appeared powerless to stem the tide of political unrest. In early March, immediately following the kidnapping of four U.S. airmen, the military chiefs of the country staged a "coup by communiqué," offering Demirel the choice between resignation and a military take-over. Demirel resigned and was replaced on March 19 by a law professor, Nihat Erim, who was charged with forming a "national," non-party government and ending the drift into "anarchy, fratricide, and social unrest."

The Erim government chose to deal with the situation by imposing martial law in 11 of Turkey's 67 provinces, including the three major cities of Istanbul, İzmir, and Ankara. This did not prevent the kidnapping and subsequent murder of the Israeli consul general in mid-May, but by the end of the summer the government appeared to have quelled the disorders at least temporarily.

──────── **TURKEY · Information Highlights** ────────

Official Name: Republic of Turkey.
Area: 301,381 square miles (780,576 sq km).
Population (1970 est.): 35,230,000. *Density,* 116 per square mile (44 per sq km). *Annual rate of increase,* 2.5%.
Chief Cities (1970 census): Ankara, the capital, 1,208,791; Istanbul, 2,247,630; Izmir, 520,686; Adana, 351,655.
Government: *Head of state,* Gen. Cevdet Sunay, president (took office Oct. 27, 1965). *Head of government,* Nihat Erim, premier (took office March 19, 1971). *Legislature*—Grand National Assembly: Senate, 183 members; National Assembly, 450 members. *Major political parties*—Justice party; Republican People's party; Democratic party; Reliance party.
Languages: Turkish (official), Kurdish, Arabic.
Education: *Literacy rate* (1970), 55% of population. *Expenditure on education* (1968), 20.2% of total public expenditure. *School enrollment* (1968)—primary, 4,790,183; secondary, 1,063,546; technical/vocational, 60,576; university/higher, 143,279.
Finances (1971 est.): *Revenues,* $2,165,000,000; *expenditures,* $2,404,000,000; *monetary unit,* lira (14.00 liras equal U.S. $1, Dec. 30, 1971).
Gross National Product (1970 est.): $8,700,000,000.
Economic Indexes: *Industrial production* (1966), 170 (1963 = 100); *agricultural production* (1969), 117 (1963 = 100); *consumer price index* (1970), 156 (1970 = 100).
Manufacturing (metric tons, 1969): Cement, 5,795,000; residual fuel oil, 2,960,000; wheat flour (1968), 1,622,000.
Crops (metric tons, 1969 crop year): Wheat, 10,593,000; sugar beets (1968–69), 4,716,000; grapes (1968), 3,735,000; cotton lint, 400,000; raisins (1968), 300,000 (ranks 1st among world producers); hazelnuts.
Minerals (metric tons, 1969): Coal, 4,684,000; lignite, 4,356,000; crude petroleum, 3,599,000; iron ore, 1,411,000; chromium ore, 259,500 (ranks 3d among world producers).
Foreign Trade (1970): *Exports,* $589,000,000 (chief exports, 1969—cotton, $111,000,000; hazelnuts, $107,700,000; tobacco, $80,700,000; raisins, $23,000,000). *Imports,* $886,000,000 (chief imports, 1968—chemicals, $152,850,000; nonelectrical machinery, $78,610,000; motor vehicles, $64,340,000; electrical machinery and appliances, $54,100,000). *Chief trading partners* (1968)—West Germany (took 17% of exports, supplied 20% of imports); United States (15%—16%); Britain (7%—13%); USSR (6%—4%).
Transportation: *Roads* (1970), 31,700 miles (51,015 km); *motor vehicles* (1969), 294,500 (automobiles, 137,000); *railroads* (1970), 5,700 miles (9,173 km); *merchant fleet* (1971), 697,000 gross registered tons.
Communications: *Telephones* (1970), 513,569; *television sets* (1969), 25,000; *radios* (1969), 3,030,000; *newspapers* (1969), 400 (daily circulation, 1,400,000).

The government's methods, however, came under increasing attack. Some 2,000 persons suspected of subversion were said to have been arrested by June, and many liberals feared that repression might become a permanent aspect of the regime. This fear was increased when, in September, Erim steered through the Grand National Assembly extensive constitutional amendments, which included restrictions on the autonomy of the state universities and the radio and press.

In October the five Justice party members of Erim's cabinet resigned, claiming that the government had lost its non-party character. Erim himself, who saw the move as an expression of non-confidence, resigned on October 27, but his resignation was not accepted by President Cevdet Sunay and the military. He resigned again on December 3 but formed a new cabinet on December 11.

Economy. While Turkey made definite progress under its two 5-year plans (1963–67, 1968–72), it faced serious problems in agriculture, industrial development and production, state economic enterprises, export and import policies, and balance of payments, and a lack of capital, trained managers, and technicians. The gross national product in 1970 stood at some $8,700 million, and there were indications that it would be somewhat lower in 1971. Total revenues in 1971 were estimated at $2,165 million and expenses at $2,404 million, thus the estimated deficit was $239 million, while in 1970 the deficit had been $80 million. The Turkish external debt grew from $1,641 million in 1970 to $1,851 million in 1971.

Turkey's chief trading partners, as in the recent past, continued to be the United States, West Germany, Italy, and Britain, although there was increasing commerce with Communist bloc and Middle Eastern countries. The major Turkish imports were machinery, transport equipment, petroleum products, and iron and steel. The primary exports were tobacco, cotton, and hazelnuts.

Foreign Relations. While continuing its policy of independence, Turkey maintained its position as a member of NATO and CENTO. The Cyprus problem remained unresolved, and Premier Erim indicated that relations with Greece would remain clouded until progress toward a solution was made. On the other hand, relations with other Balkan neighbors (Yugoslavia, Bulgaria, and Rumania) developed somewhat more evenly. Relations with the Soviet Union remained on a basis of cautious realism. Those with Iran, a CENTO ally, and the Arab states were stable during 1971.

Turco-American relations involved complicated problems, but they moved on a more even keel partly because of the decrease of the U. S. military presence in Turkey. One of the major problems between the two countries is the fact that Turkey is the source of about 80% of the heroin that enters the United States. On June 30, however, Turkish and U.S. officials announced an agreement by which the Turkish government agreed to undertake an extensive program to license and control the growth of poppies during the 1971 season, and to stop the cultivation of opium poppies by June 1972. The number of provinces in which poppies can legally be grown has already been reduced to four. President Nixon described this agreement as "by far the most significant breakthrough that has been achieved in stopping the supply of heroin in our worldwide offensive against dangerous drugs."

UPI

Earthquakes ripped eastern Turkey in May, killing over 1,000 and leaving most inhabitants without housing or water. Partially collapsed buildings and hanging balconies were typical in demolished town of Bingöl.

There can be no question, however, that problems lie ahead in implementing this new program. Turkish peasants have been growing poppies for over 400 years, and the difficulty of eradicating the practice is illustrated by the fact that some 300,000 farmers were said to have applied for licenses to raise the crop during the fall season of 1971. Moreover, the legitimate cash crop produces edible seeds and oil, as well as about 116 tons of legal opium annually. It was estimated that some $35 million in aid from the United States would be required over a 3-year period to assist Turkey in shifting from poppies to other cash crops and to compensate for losses.

HARRY N. HOWARD
The American University

UGANDA

On Jan. 25, 1971, a relatively bloodless military coup led by Maj. Gen. Idi Amin, commander of Uganda's armed forces, overthrew the government of President Milton Obote. On February 2 the National Assembly was officially dissolved, and Amin assumed full legislative power.

Domestic Aspects of the Coup. The leaders of the coup charged Obote with tribal favoritism and political repression, with attempting to divide the army, and with pursuing unrealistic economic policies. In fact, Obote's government had failed to hold general elections in more than eight years of independence and had alienated some major ethnic and political groups within the country. At the time of the coup more than one fifth of the seats in the National Assembly were vacant, and a number of prominent politicians, including some former ministers, were being held in detention.

Some of the strongest opposition to Obote had come from the Baganda, Uganda's largest ethnic group. Amin's government quickly moved to attract Bagandan support by permitting the body of Edward Mutesa, the late kabaka of Buganda, to be flown home from London and buried in a state funeral on April 4 at the Kasubi royal tombs. In another attempt to appeal to former opponents of Obote, Amin on January 28 released 55 political detainees, including Benedicto Kiwanuka, the first prime minister of Uganda.

Despite President Amin's popularity in some areas and his frequent tours of the countryside, the new government had difficulty establishing its control in certain places. Fighting erupted several times during the year in rural areas, and at times conflict within the army itself was involved. To deal with opposition, wide powers of detention were announced in a decree of May 11.

The conservatism of the new regime became evident with the announcement of its economic policies during a May Day address by Amin. In 1970, Obote had launched a program to take 60% control of 84 banks, oil companies, and other corporations. Amin stated, however, that in the future the 60–40 formula would be abandoned in favor of a 49–51 ratio, leaving control in the private sector.

Another result of the coup was the tripling of the size of the army, to nearly 20,000 men. The increase caused a sharp rise in the demands of the military on the national budget.

Foreign Reaction to the Coup. Although most foreign governments reacted cautiously to the new regime, in Uganda, several neighbors—Tanzania, Zambia, Sudan, and Somalia—strongly condemned it. The break with Tanzania, the country that had provided asylum for deposed President Obote, was the most serious one because of Uganda and Tan-

--------- UGANDA • Information Highlights ---------

Official Name: Republic of Uganda.
Area: 91,134 square miles (236,036 sq km).
Population (1970 est.): 9,760,000. *Density,* 105 per square mile (40 per sq km).
Chief City (1969 est.): Kampala, the capital, 330,000.
Government: *Head of state,* Maj. Gen. Idi Amin, president (took office Feb. 20, 1971). *Head of government,* Maj. Gen. Idi Amin. *Legislature*—National Assembly (dissolved on Feb. 2, 1971). *Major political parties*—(suspended).
Languages: English (official), Luganda.
Education: *Literacy rate* (1969), 25% of population. *Expenditure on education* (1967), 24.1% of total public expenditure. *School enrollment* (1967)—primary, 641,639; secondary, 42,341; technical/vocational, 3,252; higher, 2,179.
Finances (1969 est.): *Revenues,* $169,720,000; *expenditures,* $207,180,000; *monetary unit,* shilling (7.143 shillings equal U.S.$1, Dec. 30, 1971).
Gross National Product (1969 est.): $1,122,000,000.
National Income (1969): $954,000,000; *per person,* $100.
Consumer Price Index (1970): 152 (1963 = 100).
Manufacturing (metric tons, 1969): Cement, 173,000; meat, 157,000; sugar, 151,000; sawnwood, 59,000 cubic meters; beer, 227,000 hectoliters.
Crops (metric tons, 1969 crop year): Groundnuts (1968), 234,000; cottonseed, 168,000; coffee, 162,000; cotton lint, 86,000; tea, 17,600.
Minerals (metric tons, 1969): Phosphate rock, 368,000; copper ore, 16,500; salt, 5,000.
Foreign Trade (1970): *Exports,* $246,000,000 (chief exports—coffee, $142,000,000; cotton, $49,000,000; copper, $23,-500,000; tea, $13,320,000). *Imports,* $121,000,000 (chief imports, 1968—transport equipment, $19,210,000; non-electrical machinery, $18,410,000; chemicals, $11,410,-000; metal manufactures, $7,347,000). *Chief trading partners* (1968)—United States (took 25% of exports, supplied 41% of imports); United Kingdom (23%—33%); Japan (12%—11%).
Transportation: *Roads* (1964), 31,332 miles (50,423 km); *motor vehicles* (1969), 38,300 (automobiles, 32,300); *railroads* (1970), 3,670 miles (5,906 km).
Communications: *Telephones* (1970), 27,666; *television stations* (1968), 6; *television sets* (1969), 12,000; *radios* (1968), 509,000; *newspapers* (1969), 5.

zania's common membership in the East African Community. Fighting occurred along the Uganda-Tanzania border.

The reaction of some African states to the coup prevented the ministerial and summit meetings of the Organization of African Unity (OAU) from being held in Kampala as planned. The June meetings of the OAU were transferred to Addis Ababa, Ethiopia, despite costly preparations for them by Uganda, but a delegation representing President Amin was seated without protest at the first session.

JAY E. HAKES
Louisiana State University in New Orleans

Maj. Gen. Idi Amin, who took office in January coup, drives jeep in Kampala en route to freeing political prisoners.

UPI

TU-144, the Soviet equivalent of the Anglo-French Concorde, arrives at Le Bourget airport in Paris in May. The supersonic airliner was one of the prime attractions at the Paris Air Show.

USSR

The Soviet Union concluded no less than six major treaties in 1971. Four of these were designed to lessen international tension: a Soviet-British-U. S. pact banning nuclear explosives and other weapons of mass destruction on the bed of all seas and oceans; a Soviet-British-French-U.S. agreement guaranteeing the security of West Berlin; a treaty modernizing direct radiotelegraph communication (the hot line) between the Kremlin and the White House; and another U. S.-USSR pact providing for each of the two countries instantly to warn the other of any missile or nuclear mishap that might be erroneously interpreted as the start of a war. By contrast, a Soviet-Egyptian treaty provided for the USSR to train the Egyptian armed forces for the next 15 years. The USSR also concluded a non-aggression pact with India that was so strongly worded that the Indian government described it as a 20-year military alliance. (India invaded Pakistan four months after this pact was signed.)

Within the USSR, the first Communist party congress in five years brought no change in the Soviet leadership. However, it made the party rules less democratic and increased party control over cultural life and government ministries. The congress adopted a 1971–75 economic program that was the first 5-year plan in USSR history to call for faster expansion of the consumer goods industry than of the heavy, war-potential industry.

Because of official disrespect, no state funeral was held for Nikita Khrushchev, the former Soviet premier, who died of a heart attack on September 11 in a Moscow hospital.

FOREIGN AFFAIRS

United States. Despite many unpleasant incidents, relations between the USSR and United States became more cooperative during 1971. On February 11, the USSR, Britain, and the United States signed the "seabed treaty" banning the emplacement of nuclear explosives and other weapons of mass destruction on the floor of seas and oceans. All nations were invited to sign, and many did, including the Communist countries of Eastern Europe. The USSR ratified this treaty on June 28.

During the year a series of Soviet-U. S. agreements solved various mutual problems. On September 30, the two countries signed a pact for modernizing the Kremlin-White House hot line by utilizing communications satellites. A second treaty of the same date provided that each country immediately notify the other about any nuclear or missile accidents that could be wrongly interpreted as the start of Soviet-U. S. nuclear war.

During the autumn, the United States government issued export licenses to various U. S. firms, authorizing them to sell the USSR $808 million worth of machinery and equipment for a new Soviet truck plant being built on the Kama River, $65 million worth of ore-mining and oil-drilling machinery, and $136 million worth of grain. These shipments should greatly increase annual U. S. exports to the USSR, which stood at a value of $103 million in 1970. Also in the fall of 1971 the Soviet government fishing company paid $89,000 to a U. S. fishing firm for damage done by Soviet trawlers to nets off the New England coast during the spring.

Meanwhile, throughout the year, militant U. S. Jews protested against the mistreatment of Jews in the USSR by harassing Soviet officials and official offices located in the United States. Disturbances occurred in the USSR tourist and airline office in New York City and the Soviet news agency in Washington, D. C. The most serious incidents were a bomb explosion in the offices of Amtorg, a Soviet trading company in New York, and four rifle shots into an apartment of the Soviet mission to the United Nations. No casualties or injuries resulted. The Soviet government officially protested the incidents and received a U. S. government apology. In a brief reprisal, some U. S. diplomats and newsmen were harassed in Moscow. In March, U. S. embassy personnel and Soviet police scuffled in Moscow when the police tried to seize a Soviet surgeon entering the embassy.

SIMPLE headstone in Moscow cemetery marks grave of Nikita Khrushchev, former leader who died September 11. He was not buried in Kremlin wall with Communist heroes, having been in disgrace since his 1964 ouster.

A Soviet ship and a U. S. destroyer collided in May in the Straits of Korea. The USSR government claimed that, during June, U. S. naval ships harassed a cruiser carrying Soviet Defense Minister Andrei Grechko when he was making a tour of the Soviet fleet in the Mediterranean Sea. In October, the USSR and the United States commenced negotiations in Moscow to establish procedures for avoiding such incidents on the sea and in the air in the future.

Throughout much of the year the two countries continued their Strategic Arms Limitation Talks (SALT) alternately in Vienna and Helsinki. Both sides displayed optimism, but there were no concrete results. (See DISARMAMENT.)

Europe. On Soviet initiative, and apparently against the wishes of East Germany, a USSR-U. S.-British-French treaty was signed on September 3 providing for unimpeded civilian traffic between West Germany and West Berlin; visits by West Berliners into East Berlin and East Germany; and the right of West Germany to represent West Berlin in international relations. In exchange for these concessions, the Western powers agreed that West Berlin was not part of the West German state and that the USSR could open consulates and commercial offices in West Berlin. In December the East and West Germans signed the subsidiary agreements necessary to bring the pact into effect.

Other conciliatory gestures toward Western Europe came during the year in the formation of a Soviet-British "joint commission for trade and technology" (January); a long-term trade agreement between the USSR and independent Communist Yugoslavia (February); a West German-Soviet pact providing for the opening of a Soviet consulate in Hamburg and a West German one in Leningrad (April); a Soviet-Finnish treaty of technical and industrial cooperation (April); a long-term trade agreement between the USSR and Norway (June); and the first Soviet trade treaty in history with the Benelux nations (Belgium, the Netherlands, and Luxembourg in July).

These various agreements occurred against a background of anti-Soviet incidents, such as a bomb explosion in April at the doors of the Soviet trade mission in Amsterdam and the harassment of USSR missions in London by militant anti-Soviet Jews. The most dramatic event, however, was the British expulsion on September 24 of 90 employees of the Soviet embassy and commercial missions and denial of reentry to 15 others, on the grounds that all 105 were spies. The USSR retaliated rather mildly by expelling from Moscow four British diplomats and four British businessmen on October 9. A second retaliation came in November, when the Soviet government cancelled the planned British tour of USSR concert artist David Oistrakh because of what it called the "abnormal situation created for Soviet citizens" in Britain.

Asia. During 1971 the Soviet Union gave substantial support to several governments in South Asia. On May 14 the USSR and Ceylon signed an agreement by which the latter was to receive Soviet military planes and arms to help suppress a local rebellion. During the spring the Soviet Union officially appealed to the Pakistani government for less brutal treatment of the East Pakistan rebels. After this appeal failed, it signed, on August 9, a 20-year pact with India providing for mutual nonagression, increased trade, and more technical aid. This treaty contained a clause that both countries would immediately consult each other to eliminate an attack or threat of attack upon either signatory. When India went to war with Pakistan in December, the USSR tried to block UN proposals for a cease-fire.

In the Near East, the USSR signed a pact with Iraq on June 24, providing for Soviet technical aid to Iraqi oil mining and the construction of a major canal. In August the USSR established diplomatic relations with the newly-independent state of Bahrain.

In the Far East, the Soviet Union continued to support North Vietnam in the Vietnam War, concluding agreements in August and October that provided more Soviet economic and arms aid to Hanoi. In February, Soviet Premier Aleksei Kosygin officially denounced the invasion of Laos by South Vietnamese and U.S. troops. Long-term Soviet trade pacts were concluded during the year with both Japan and Mongolia, but only a short-term commercial agreement was signed with Communist China.

As before, Soviet relations with mainland China remained poor, as China rejected Soviet proposals for a world disarmament conference and for a separate disarmament meeting of the five nuclear powers (the USSR, the United States, Britain, France, and China). Negotiations between the USSR and China to determine their common border continued throughout the year with no result. Twice in 1971 the Chinese government refused to let USSR officials inspect the graves of Soviet soldiers who died in China during World War II fighting the Japanese.

Africa. The USSR established even closer relations with Egypt in 1971 by concluding a friendship pact, under whose terms the Soviets would train the Egyptian armed forces for the next 15 years. This treaty was signed on May 27 and ratified by the USSR on June 28. Earlier, in March, the Soviet government had concluded a new agreement to continue economic and technical aid to Egypt.

During the year the USSR concluded a new trade pact with Ghana and a new agreement to provide Soviet technical aid to Morocco. In July the Kremlin expressed official sympathy for King Hassan of Morocco after he suppressed a military-led attempt to dethrone him. By contrast, the Soviet press during the summer strongly condemned the execution of many Communists by the Sudanese government as it suppressed a left-wing revolt. The Sudanese government was so offended that on August 1 it recalled its ambassador from Moscow.

Latin America. Soviet policy toward Latin America in 1971 consisted largely of efforts to befriend legal governments and increase mutual trade. The USSR continued its material aid to Cuba at a rate of about $2 million per day, one third of the shipments being armaments. During the year several Soviet diplomats were expelled from Mexico and Ecuador for alleged espionage.

Canada. When Canadian Prime Minister Pierre Trudeau visited the USSR in May, he concluded a Soviet-Canadian agreement for consultation on matters of mutual interest. The possibility of increasing Soviet-Canadian trade was discussed by USSR Premier Kosygin when he visited Canada in October.

DEFENSE AND SPACE

Armed Forces. The Soviet armed forces in 1971 totaled about 3.3 million men, of whom 2 million were in the army, 480,000 in the air force, 475,000 in the navy, and 350,000 in missile forces. Their armament included some 40,000 tanks, 140 intercontinental bombers, 725 medium bombers, 290 conventional submarines, 80 nuclear submarines, 26 cruisers, 99 destroyers, 2 helicopter carriers, 400 submarine-based missiles, 700 land-based medium missiles, 67 antiballistic missiles (ABM's, all around Moscow), and 1,500 intercontinental missiles (ICBM's). The USSR thus led the United States in number of tanks, submarines, anti-ballistic missiles, and ICBM's.

The location of the Soviet armed forces in 1971 continued to show that the USSR was prepared

TASS FROM SOVFOTO

VALENTINA TERESHKOVA, first woman to fly in space, comforts daughter of Georgi Dobrovolsky at public funeral for Soyuz 11 crew. Three cosmonauts perished when space ship reentered atmosphere on June 30.

more for war in Europe than in either the Far East or the Middle East. Of the total army divisions, 91 were in European Russia and East Europe, 30 in the Soviet East, 28 along the southern frontier, and 8 in western Siberia.

The Soviet armed forces conducted large-scale maneuvers in June along the Black Sea coast, and there were air and air-defense exercises in July in west European Russia. During the summer several million Soviet boys between the ages of 10 and 15 competed in military games, under the supervision of army instructors, throughout the USSR.

Displaying ability to operate far from home

waters, Soviet naval flotillas in 1971 paid official visits to Norway, Denmark, the Netherlands, France, Yugoslavia, and Cuba. All year round the USSR maintained small naval fleets in both the Mediterranean Sea and the Indian Ocean.

Of the approximately 15,000 Soviet military advisers serving abroad during 1971, 10,000 were stationed in Egypt, 1,500 in Algeria, and 1,000 each in Syria, Cuba, and North Vietnam.

On September 22, Marshal Matvei V. Zakharov, who was 73 years old, was dismissed as chief of staff of the USSR armed forces and replaced by 50-year-old Gen. Viktor Georgiyevich Kulikov, who had previously been in command of the Soviet armed forces stationed in East Germany.

Swedish scientists reported that during September a large underground nuclear explosion of several megatons took place on the Soviet Arctic island of Novaya Zemlya.

Space Program. Among the many achievements of the Soviet space program in 1971 were the launching of eight earth satellites from one rocket in May; the landing of an unmanned spacecraft on the moon in September; and the November landing of a capsule on the planet Mars from an unmanned spacecraft launched in May. In April a spaceship with a 3-man crew docked in space with an orbital scientific station. An attempt in June to repeat this feat resulted in a successful docking and in the 3-man crew's boarding and leaving the orbital scientific station, but all crewmen died as they returned to earth because of a leak in the spacecraft. (See SPACE EXPLORATION.)

GOVERNMENT AND POLITICS

The 24th Party Congress. Convening a year behind schedule, the 24th Congress of the Communist party of the USSR met in Moscow from March 30 to April 9. There were 4,963 delegates, representing a total party membership of 14,455,321. The congress elected a new party Central Committee, the largest in Soviet history, consisting of 241 full members and 155 candidate members. Three fourths of the full members were holdovers from the former Central Committee. After the congress the new Central Committee met and reelected the entire 17-man Politburo and the 10 secretaries of the USSR party secretariat. In this reelection, 4 of these 27 leaders received promotions. Rising from candidate membership to full member of the Politburo were Viktor V. Grishin, party chief of Moscow; Dinmukhamed A. Kunayev, party first secretary of the Kazakh republic; and Vladimir V. Shcherbitsky, premier of the Ukrainian republic. Fyodor D. Kulakov, a USSR party secretary supervising agriculture, also attained full Politburo membership.

The congress altered the party statutes to make them less democratic by lengthening the intervals between meetings of the party congresses. In the future the congresses of the party of the USSR and of the parties of the individual Soviet republics will convene every five years instead of the previous four; the regional, city, and district party conferences will meet every two and a half years instead of the previous two; and the committees of the primary party organizations—the lowest units—will assemble every two and a half years instead of the previous one.

Prior to the congress a secretary of a primary party organization in an economic enterprise had the power to veto orders issued by the director of the enterprise, but there was no similar veto in cultural enterprises or the main offices of government ministries. The congress extended the veto power to the primary secretaries in the ministries and noneconomic enterprises. Thus party control over the Soviet government and cultural life increased.

The congress also ordered that all party members be given new membership cards, which will be issued only after a careful check of the member's efficiency and loyalty. In effect this action is a party purge, since "unworthy" members will not receive new cards and will thus be expelled from the party. The checking and card renewal require much time, and should continue for at least a year.

Speeches at the 1971 congress were routine, and largely devoted to describing and approving the new 5-year plan for 1971–75. An exception was the opening address by Soviet President Nikolai Podgorny, who strongly appealed for more "socialist democracy"—a theme not repeated in other speeches.

NOVOSTI FROM SOVFOTO

Increases in consumer goods and rising standard of living are major Soviet objectives. Some workers enjoy such luxuries as a car for vacations. Interest in fashion has brought a reliance on beauty aids and hair-dressing salons. Welder's family (opposite page) has both a modern television and an old-fashioned samovar.

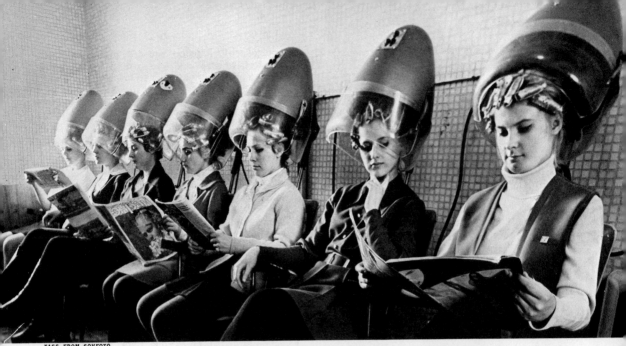

Surburbia, U.S.A.? No, It's the Citadel of Communism

Personnel Changes. After the congress, in July, Politburo member Gennadi I. Voronov lost his position as premier of the Russian republic and was demoted to chairman of the people's control committee—a ministry of the USSR cabinet. He was replaced as premier by Mikhail S. Solomentsev, previously a USSR party secretary, who in November also became a candidate member of the Politburo. Voronov, however, remained a full Politburo member.

Repression. The Soviet regime appeared to become more repressive in 1971. In three separate trials six Ukrainians, three Belorussians, and three Kalmyks (Volga Mongols) were given death sentences for alleged collaboration with the German invaders during World War II. In May a Lithuanian seaman, Simas Kudirka, was sentenced to 10 years' imprisonment for trying to escape to a U. S. ship during a well-publicized but confusing series of events in November 1970.

Though most political prisoners were in prison camps or prisons, the Soviet government was increasingly punishing political offenders by putting them into mental hospitals as patients. According to Amnesty International, 200 political prisoners were in Soviet insane asylums in 1971, whereas in 1969 there had been only 2.

The most illustrious defector from the USSR in 1971 was the 61-year-old physicist Anatoli Pavlovich Fedoseyev, a doctor of technical science and Lenin prize laureate, who in June was given asylum in Britain. He reported that 90% of all Soviet scientific research is for military purposes.

Death of Khrushchev. Nikita Sergeyevich Khrushchev, former USSR premier, died on September 11 from a heart attack while under treatment in a Moscow hospital. He was aged 77. The Soviet press did not announce his death until September 13, when a brief statement of sorrow was issued jointly by the party Central Committee and the USSR council of ministers. There was no state funeral, and police admitted only relatives and close friends to the private burial service. He was not buried with other dead Soviet leaders along the Kremlin wall, but was placed in a monastery cemetery. Obviously the present Soviet leadership, which had removed him from power in 1964, still disliked him. (See Khrushchev, Nikita.)

────── **USSR • Information Highlights** ──────

Official Name: Union of Soviet Socialist Republics.
Area: 8,647,489 square miles (22,402,200 sq km).
Population (1971 est.): 243,900,000.
Chief Cities (1970 census): Moscow, the capital, 7,061,000; Leningrad, 3,950,000; Kiev, 1,632,000; Tashkent, 1,385,000.
Government: *Head of state,* Nikolai V. Podgorny, president (took office 1965); *Premier,* Aleksei N. Kosygin (took office 1964); *Communist party secretary general,* Leonid I. Brezhnev. *Legislature*—Supreme Soviet; Soviet of the Union, 767 members; Soviet of Nationalties, 750 members.
Languages: Russian, Ukrainian, Belorussian, Uzbek, Kazakh, Turkmen, Tadzhik, Kirghiz, Azeri Turkish, Georgian, Armenian, Lithuanian, Lettish, Estonian, and others (official in regions).
Education: *Literacy rate* (1971), 98.5% of adult population. Total school enrollment (1971)—60,800,000 (primary and secondary, 51,800,000; technical/vocational, 4,400,000; university/higher, 4,600,000).
Finances (1971 est.): *Revenues,* $177,100,000,000; *expenditures,* $176,800,000,000; *public debt,* $28,700,000,000; *monetary unit,* ruble (0.9 ruble equals U. S.$1).
National Income (1970): $264,500,000,000; *average annual income per person,* $1,090.
Economic Indexes (1970): Industrial production, 278 (1958=100); agricultural production, 143 (1958=100).
Manufacturing (metric tons, 1970): Crude steel 116,000,000; cement, 95,200,000; chemical fertilizer, 55,400,000.
Crops (metric tons, 1970): Grain, 186,400,000 (ranks 3d among world producers); potatoes, 96,600,000 (world rank, 1st); sugar beets, 78,300,000 (world rank, 1st).
Minerals (metric tons, 1970): Coal, 624,000,000 (ranks 1st among world producers); crude petroleum, 353,000,000 (world rank, 2d); iron ore, 196,000,000 (world rank, 1st); natural gas, 200,000,000,000 cubic meters (world rank, 2d).
Foreign Trade (1970): *Exports,* $12,650,000,000 (chief exports: machinery and equipment, $2,728,000,000; ores and metals, $2,436,500,000; fuels, $1,996,800,000); *imports,* $11,660,000,000 (chief imports: machinery and equipment, $4,076,600,000; consumer goods, $2,120,800,000; foodstuffs, $1,590,000,000). *Chief trading partners* (1970): East Germany (took 15% of exports, supplied 15% of imports); Poland (took 10% of exports, supplied 11% of imports); Czechoslovakia (took 9% of exports, supplied 10% of imports).
Transportation (1970): *Roads,* 300,300 miles (483,200 km); *motor vehicles,* 6,000,000 (automobiles, 1,500,000); *railways,* 83,600 miles (134,600 km); *merchant vessels,* 14,832,000 gross registered tons.
Communications: *Telephones* (1969), 12,000,000; *TV stations* (1971), 167; *TV sets* (1971), 28,000,000; *radios* (1969), 46,700,000; *newspapers* (1971), 9,000.

ECONOMY

The New 5-Year Plan. The new 5-year plan for 1971–75 was published in incomplete outline early in 1971 and approved in the spring by the USSR party congress, which ordered the detailed plan to be ready by August 1. The full plan, however, was not completely drafted until November, when it was adopted by the party Central Committee and the USSR Supreme Soviet (national legislature). No explanation was given for this long delay in compiling the plan, which should have been ready in late 1970.

The 1971–75 plan is the first 5-year plan in Soviet history to provide for faster expansion of light, consumer-goods industry than of heavy, war-potential industry. During the five years, light industrial production is scheduled for an increase of 46%, and heavy industry for one of 43%. Other benefits to the Soviet population will be a rise in the average monthly wage of a state worker or employee from 122 rubles ($134.20) in 1971 to 146 or 149 rubles ($160.60 or $163.90) by 1975. Similarly the average monthly pay of a collective farmer should increase from 73 rubles ($80.30) in 1970 to 98 rubles ($107.80) by 1975. The minimum monthly urban wage would rise from 60 rubles ($66) in 1971 to 70 rubles ($77) by 1974.

Despite this unprecedented concern for the Soviet consumer, the 1971–75 plan allocates only 5% of total capital investments to light industry. Heavy industry, which accounted for 74% of all industrial output during 1971, will still provide 73% of total industrial production in 1975. It is planned that by 1975 the USSR should produce 500 million

metric tons of crude oil and 150 million tons of crude steel, which would exceed the current output of the same items in the United States. (The Soviet output of coal, iron ore, and cement already exceeds the U. S. output.) The most spectacular project in the 1971–75 plan is vast expansion of the new western Siberian oil fields, whose output of petroleum is scheduled to rise from 31 million metric tons in 1971 to 120–125 million by 1975.

The new 5-year plan will allot 26% of all capital investments to agriculture, to which 22% had been allotted in the 1966–70 plan. By 1975 farm output should have increased by 22% over the 1971 level, with the increase resulting from more mechanization and more fertilizer rather than added acreage. Even if this plan is fulfilled, Soviet per capita consumption of meat, eggs, vegetables, and sugar in 1975 will still be below current levels in the United States.

To aid transportation, the new 5-year plan provides for the construction of 3,100 to 3,700 miles (5,000–5,950 km) of new railways and 4,300 to 5,000 miles (6,920–8,050 km) of second track on existing single-track lines, while 3,700 to 4,300 miles (5,950–6,920 km) of existing track is to be electrified. Some 16,800 miles (27,000 km) of new oil pipelines will also be built. The plan calls for a 60% increase in freight haulage by truck transport and only a 22% increase by train transport. The hope is to unburden the overloaded railways, which in 1971 still carried more than 80% of all the freight in the USSR.

Despite the housing shortage, the 1971–75 plan provides for only a 10% increase by 1975 in dwelling construction over the inadequate level of 1970. The foreign trade part of the plan calls for a 50% increase in commerce with the nations of the Council for Mutual Economic Assistance (Comecon, the Communist equivalent of the Common Market; members include the USSR, the East European countries, and Mongolia) but much smaller gains in trade with the rest of the world.

Economic Performances in 1971. The rate of Soviet industrial growth in 1971 was a little under 8%—slightly less than in 1970. In December the world's largest hydroelectric power station, with a capacity of 6 million kilowatts, was completed and went into operation at the town of Divnogorsk on the Yenisei River in central Siberia. During the year the Soviet press revealed that much of the consumer goods produced is defective. For example, half the toys and one third of the television sets put on sale did not operate.

Bad weather in the Volga Valley, the Crimea, northern Central Asia, and other areas caused lower grain, potato, and vegetable crops in 1971 than in 1970. Thus the grain harvest was 180 million metric tons, whereas that of 1970 had totaled 186.4 million. The Soviet press in 1971 revealed that, as a result of insect pests, blight, and weeds, each year 10% to 20% of the grain crop, 20% of the vegetables, and 30% of the fruit are so poor that they are either fed to livestock or left to rot in the fields. It was also disclosed that the productivity of Soviet farm labor was only one fourth that of the United States.

During 1971, pay raises were instituted for both railway workers and farm tractor drivers. On July 1 the minimum monthly pensions of all state workers and employees were raised to 45 rubles ($49.50), and of collective farmers to 20 rubles

($22). Price cuts were made during the year on certain consumer goods such as motorcycles, motorbikes, electric razors, ballpoint pens, raincoats, and household chemicals. However, there were continued store shortages of meat, eggs, vegetables, fruit, clothing, dishes, kitchen utensils, furniture, medicines, eyeglasses, watches, cameras, saws, radios, televisions, washing machines, and textbooks. Only one of every three Soviet households in 1971 possessed a refrigerator.

In 1971, Soviet foreign trade amounted to about 4% of total world commerce. About two thirds of USSR foreign trade was with other Communist countries, one fifth with Western industrial nations, and one sixth with developing nations. At the start of the year, total Soviet foreign aid to non-Communist countries since 1954 amounted to $8 billion in commitments, of which $5 billion had been delivered. The main recipients of foreign aid from the Soviet Union in 1971 were India, Egypt, and Afghanistan.

CULTURE AND SOCIETY

Additional data published in 1971 from the 1970 census revealed that the largest nationalities in the multinational USSR were the Great Russians (129 million, or 53% of the total population), Ukrainians (40,750,000, or 17%), Uzbeks (Central Asian Turks; 9,195,000, or 4%), and Belorussians (9 million, or 4%). The annual growth rate of the entire population of the Soviet Union had slowed from 1.7% in 1960 to only 0.9% in 1970. The 1971 population included 90 million state workers and employees, 41 million retired people living on pensions, and 240,000 scientists and laboratory technicians.

Religion. During 1971 many Soviet Jews sent petitions to the USSR government requesting permission to emigrate to Israel. For the same purpose some Jews conducted group sit-ins in USSR government buildings. The government rejected most of the petitions, and police dispersed the sit-ins. To discourage illegal emigration, four separate trials in Leningrad, Riga (Latvia), and Kishinev (Moldavia) resulted in the sentencing of a total of 23 Jews to prison terms of 1 to 10 years for alleged complicity in an alleged Jewish attempt to hijack a Soviet passenger plane at Leningrad airport in late 1970. Despite such severity, the Soviet government permitted about 12,000 Jews to emigrate during 1971. This was 12 times the number allowed to emigrate the year before.

On June 2, a council of the Russian Orthodox Church elected Metropolitan Pimen the new Moscow Patriarch to replace the former patriarch, who had died. In the past Pimen has been cooperative with the Soviet regime.

During 1971, the Soviet press complained that in Muslim areas of the USSR many villages operated secret mosques and staged religious festivals attended by local Communist officials.

Culture. Despite official attempts at repression, widespread intellectual unrest continued in the USSR during 1971. The police either could not or would not suppress underground literature called "Samizdat." The underground writers represented four distinct groups: Western-style liberals demanding real civil rights; Christian socialists opposing Soviet materialism; humanitarian Marxists objecting to Soviet bureaucratic methods; and Slavophiles desiring a truly Russian regime rather than

UPI

PREMIER KOSYGIN, during October state visit to Canada, talks with hockey star Henri Richard before game in Vancouver. Kosygin's tour, despite anti-Soviet demonstrations, was both a diplomatic and personal success.

the present Communist system. During the summer, Anatoli Levitin-Krasnov, one of the Christian socialist leaders, was sentenced by a Soviet court to three years of imprisonment on charges of writing anti-Soviet propaganda.

Meeting from June 29 to July 2, a congress of the USSR Writers' Union condemned rebellious writers and ordered authors to glorify the Soviet regime. Most of the rebellious writers did not bother to attend the congress, which was dominated by Stalinists subservient to the government.

Education. Data concerning 1971 military manpower indicated that about half of the adult population of the USSR probably has only a grade school education. Other published information showed that one fourth of present grade school graduates do not enter secondary school. Soviet colleges and universities were said to train more engineers but fewer scientists than the U. S. higher education system.

For the first time in Soviet history, the government issued a 5-year plan for improving the Communist indoctrination of college students during 1971–75. Several colleges and universities will conduct research on various aspects of the indoctrination problem. Throughout the USSR all institutions of higher education will mobilize their deans, social science departments, Communist party committees, Communist youth organizations, teachers' unions, sport clubs, and paramilitary societies in a combined effort to imbue students with loyalty to Communism.

ELLSWORTH RAYMOND, *New York University*

UNITED ARAB AMIRATES. See PERSIAN GULF STATES.
UNITED ARAB REPUBLIC. See EGYPT.

ALBANIA
ALGERIA
ARGENTINA
AUSTRALIA
AUSTRIA
BAHRAIN
BARBADOS
BELGIUM
BHUTAN
BOLIVIA
BOTSWANA
BRAZIL
BULGARIA
URMA
URUNDI
ELORUSSIAN SSR

CANADA
CENTR AFRIC REP
CEYLON
CHAD
CHILE
CHINA
COLOMBIA
CONGO
COSTA RICA
CUBA
CYPRUS
CZECHOSLOVAKIA
DAHOMEY
DENMARK
DOMINICAN REP

EL SALVADOR
EQUATORIAL GUINEA
ETHIOPIA
FIJI
FINLAND
FRANCE
GABON
GAMBIA
GHANA
GREECE
GUATEMALA
GUINEA
GUYANA
HAITI
HONDURAS

INDIA
INDONESIA
IRAN
IRAQ
IRELAND
ISRAEL
ITALY
IVORY COAST
JAMAICA
JAPAN
JORDAN
KENYA
KHMER REPUBLIC
KUWAIT

UPI

Newly elected Secretary General Kurt Waldheim of Austria acknowledges UN delegates' applause after his acceptance speech on December 22. He pledged to follow the retiring U Thant (*right*) with "imaginative and realistic" new approaches.

UNITED NATIONS

The most important event to take place in the United Nations in 1971 was the seating of the People's Republic of China, whose representatives replaced those of Nationalist China both in the General Assembly and in the Security Council. The United Nations also selected its fourth secretary general, the Austrian Kurt Waldheim, who began a five-year term on Jan. 1, 1972.

Otherwise, the year was outstanding more for what the United Nations failed to do than for what it accomplished. The most notable failure was summed up on Dec. 22, 1971, by the president of the General Assembly, Indonesia's Adam Malik, who stated that "our inability to prevent the outbreak of war between India and Pakistan, and even more seriously, to put a stop to it once it had broken out, causing death and suffering to millions, stands as a grave setback to our organization."

The seating of mainland China brought into the United Nations the greatest power hitherto excluded from the organization. Its assumption of permanent membership in the Security Council, giving it the right of the veto in that body, made the United Nations a more accurate mirror of the existing balance of power, leading many UN representatives to express the hope that the world body would acquire fresh vitality. It remained to be proved, however, that the addition of another strong voice in UN councils would not, in fact, further hobble the

organization. Soon after the People's Republic of China had been seated, the United Nations' failure to act in the India-Pakistan conflict indicated yet again that the organization was an ineffective instrument for the handling of disputes involving, even indirectly, the interests of the major powers.

When internal conflict erupted in East Pakistan in the spring of 1971, after election results displeasing to the central government had been nullified, UN members were reluctant to involve the organization on grounds that the matter was an "internal question." The outbreak of war between India and Pakistan in early December produced a more acute dilemma. Support for India would have implied approval of the Indian military response, while support of Pakistan's plea for an immediate cease-fire would have allowed the Pakistani government to continue the repressive activity that had led to the Indian intervention. With the major powers divided in their support of the belligerents, the Security Council was deadlocked and unable to act.

Disagreement among the powerful members as to the proper role of the United Nations also manifested itself in other ways in 1971. The financial crisis became more acute as certain powers, disagreeing with some UN programs, withheld portions of their shares of funds obligated in the UN budget, or threatened to reduce their contributions. The fact that the two superpowers, the USSR and the

United States, were among the nations thus threatening the organization was viewed as ominous.

A hopeful sign in the conflict of major UN power interests was the December 21 agreement among the five permanent Security Council members (the United States, the USSR, China, France, and the United Kingdom) on the appointment of Kurt Waldheim as the new secretary general to succeed U Thant, a decision ratified by the General Assembly on the following day. U Thant's impending retirement and the possibility of a deadlock over the appointment of a successor had caused much apprehension during 1971.

The principle activities of the United Nations in its 26th year are discussed below under the headings: (1) General Assembly; (2) Security Council; (3) Economic and Social Council; (4) Trusteeship Council; and (5) International Court of Justice.

GENERAL ASSEMBLY

The 26th regular session of the General Assembly met in New York from Sept. 21 through Dec. 22, 1971. During this session, UN membership was expanded from 127 to 132 states. Bhutan, Bahrain, and Qatar were admitted on the day the Assembly convened, Oman was admitted on October 7, and the United Arab Emirates on December 9.

Political and Security Affairs. The Assembly resolved the question of Chinese representation that had been before it since 1950 and adopted resolutions on arms control and other political questions.

Chinese Representation. The Assembly considered the question of the representation of China from October 18 to October 25. Three main resolutions were considered: (1) a proposal sponsored by Albania and 21 other states calling for the "restoration of the rights" of the People's Republic of China (PRC) and the expulsion of the "representatives of Chiang Kai-shek" (Nationalist China); (2) a proposal by the United States and 21 other states that the issue be considered an "important question" which required a two-thirds majority for adoption of any resolution; and (3) a proposal by the United States and 18 other states affirming the right of the PRC to representation, but also affirming Nationalist China's right of continued representation.

Seventy-three members took part in the extended debate, which focused primarily on the Albanian proposal that argued for the seating of the PRC alone, and the U. S. proposal arguing that both Chinas be represented. During the course of the debate, both the mainland Chinese government, in broadcasts from Peking, and the Nationalist Chinese, in General Assembly debate and in the UN corridors, insisted that there was only one China and that each was its rightful representative. With both Chinese governments arguing their exclusive right to represent one China, the U. S. proposal for seating both became less convincing.

The issue came to a vote on October 25. The U. S. proposal that any vote on the issue require a two-thirds majority was rejected (55 for and 59 against, with 15 abstentions). The Assembly then rejected (51 for, 61 against, 16 abstentions) a U. S. motion for a separate vote on the clause in the Albanian proposal calling for expulsion of "the representatives of Chiang Kai-shek." Following this vote, the Nationalist Chinese foreign minister, Chow Shu-kai, on a point of order, protested the vote and stated that his delegation would no longer participate in the proceedings. Subsequently two Saudi Arabian

amendments to the Albanian proposal were overwhelmingly defeated, as was a proposal to delay the voting. The Albanian resolution seating the PRC and ousting Nationalist China passed by a vote of 76 to 35, with 17 abstentions.

On November 15, a delegation from the People's Republic of China took its place in the Assembly. In welcoming the seating, Ambassador George Bush of the United States stated that "the issues of prin-

---

RALPH J. BUNCHE (1904–1971)

UNITED NATIONS

Ralph Johnson Bunche, Nobel Prize-winning U. S. diplomat, died in New York on Dec. 9, 1971. A key figure in the United Nations from its founding, he served from 1957 as undersecretary for special political affairs and was the highest ranking American in the world body. Dedicated to the cause of world peace and to the UN as the instrument of peace, he sought to create harmony from disorder. He was awarded the Nobel Peace Prize in 1950 for mediating the Palestine conflict in 1949.

By temperament and training, Bunche was the ultimate diplomat, merging political skills with psychological insights. His UN colleagues regarded him as a most effective "international civil servant." Secretary-General U Thant described him as "an international institution in his own right, transcending both nationality and race in a way that is achieved by very few."

An American Negro, who suffered poverty and discrimination in his youth, he was an inspiration to the black community in their civil rights struggle. His personal credo was a broad one: "I have a deep-seated bias against hate and intolerance. I have a bias against racial and religious bigotry. I have a bias against war, a bias for peace. I have a bias which leads me to believe in the essential goodness of my fellow man, which leads me to believe that no problem of human relations is ever insoluble."

Born in Detroit on April 7, 1904, Bunche was orphaned at the age of 13 and brought up by his grandmother in Los Angeles. He worked his way through the University of California at Los Angeles, graduating in 1927, and received M. A. and Ph. D. degrees from Harvard. From 1928 he was intermittently on the faculty of Howard University.

From 1938 to 1940, Bunche assisted Swedish economist and diplomat Gunnar Myrdal on research for his provocative study of the American Negro, *The American Dilemma*. After serving in the Office of Strategic Services during World War II, Bunche joined the State Department in 1944 and participated in the planning and the founding conferences of the United Nations. From 1947 until his retirement in June 1971, he was a permanent member of the UN secretariat. In charge of peacekeeping operations in Suez in 1956, the Congo (Zaïre) in 1960, and Cyprus in 1964, Bunche found particular satisfaction in employing "military men for peace."

The Nobel Prize-winner also held honorary doctorates and awards, including the U. S. presidential Medal of Freedom in 1963. He served on numerous institutional boards, including that of the National Association for the Advancement of Colored People, and was a president of the American Political Science Association.

ciple that divided the General Assembly in recent weeks were deeply felt, and they were indeed hard fought. Those differences should not obscure the proposition on which nearly all of us, including the United States government, agreed: that the moment in history had arrived for the People's Republic of China to be in the United Nations."

East Pakistan. On Dec. 6, 1971, the deadlocked Security Council voted to refer the question of the war in East Pakistan to the General Assembly. (See section on *Security Council* in this article.) On the following day, the Assembly adopted by a margin of 104 to 11, with 10 abstentions, a resolution calling upon India and Pakistan to take all measures forthwith for an immediate cease-fire and withdrawal of their armed forces to their own side of the borders. Within two days, Pakistan had indicated its willingness to accept the cease-fire request.

Arms Control. On December 16 the Assembly adopted 14 resolutions on various aspects of arms control and disarmament. Among these was a request for information on the progress of the International Atomic Energy Agency in the application of safeguards to insure the effectiveness of the Treaty on the Non-Proliferation of Nuclear Weapons, and a proposal to explore the feasibility of holding a World Disarmament Conference in 1972. The Convention on the Prohibition of the Development, Production and Stockpiling of Bacteriological and Toxin Weapons and on Their Destruction was commended to all states for ratification on a vote of 110 to 0, with 1 abstention. By the same margin, the Assembly urged the Geneva Committee on Disarmament to attempt to adopt a similar treaty relating to chemical weapons. Pending such a treaty, the Assembly urged all states to refrain from further production and stockpiling of chemical weapons.

EMERGENCY UN debates failed to halt war between India and Pakistan in 1971. Here, Pakistan's ambassador accuses India of aggression before Security Council on December 4 as Indian ambassador (*left*) listens.

UPI

By a vote of 71 to 2, with 38 abstentions, the nuclear powers were urged to conclude an agreement on the cessation of all nuclear and thermonuclear tests of any kind.

Finally, on a vote of 61 to 0, with 55 abstentions, the Assembly designated the Indian Ocean, together with the air space above it and ocean floor below, as a zone of peace, calling upon all states to halt arms escalation in the area and to dismantle all military bases there.

Other Political Questions. On November 9, the Assembly again requested that all states and organizations do everything possible to promote justice for all people in South Africa. On November 20, it voted by 110 to 1, with 1 abstention, to continue its support of the UN Trust Fund for persons prosecuted in South Africa, Namibia (South West Africa), and Rhodesia, and it adopted seven other resolutions dealing specifically with aspects of the apartheid policies being pursued by South Africa.

On November 29, the Assembly expressed its support of the Working Group on Remote Sensing of the Earth by Satellites, voted to prepare an international treaty concerning the Moon, and adopted and recommended to the member states a Convention on International Liability for Damage Caused by Space Objects.

The Assembly considered, on December 20, the findings of a Special Committee to Investigate Israeli Practices Affecting the Human Rights of the Population of the Occupied Territories—that is, the areas occupied by Israel after the 1967 war. The Assembly subsequently called upon Israel to desist from a variety of activities that were allegedly violating the rights of the people in these territories.

Economic and Financial Affairs. In the sphere of economic affairs and finance, the 26th session of the General Assembly adopted resolutions having to do with development strategy during the Second UN Development Decade, cooperation between the United Nations and the World Tourism Organization, the application of computer technology for development, targets for the World Food Program of 1973–74, the international monetary situation, the increasing burden of debt services, and the UN Volunteers program. It also voted to establish an international university and an intergovernmental sea service.

On December 20, the Assembly voted on a recommendation to amend Article 61 of the UN Charter in order to enlarge the membership of the Economic and Social Council from 27 to 54. The proposal carried by a vote of 105 to 2, with 15 abstentions, but the two negative votes were cast by the United Kingdom and France, permanent Security Council members whose ratifications would be necessary for the amendment itself to be adopted.

Decolonization. The Committee of 24, formed to implement the 1960 Declaration on the Elimination of Colonialization, continued its efforts in 1971. Again, particular stress was placed on Rhodesia, the Portuguese territories, and South Africa's Namibia. The General Assembly adopted several resolutions bearing on the decolonization of these areas and relating to Papua, New Guinea, and the various islands still under colonial rule in the Caribbean Sea and the Indian and Pacific oceans.

Administrative and Budgetary Questions. On Dec. 21, 1971, the Assembly passed a supplementary budget, increasing the UN budget for 1971 by $478,-500 to a total of $194,627,800. On the following

ORGANIZATION OF THE UNITED NATIONS

THE SECRETARIAT

Secretary-General: U Thant (until Dec. 31, 1971), Kurt Waldheim (from Jan. 1, 1972)

THE GENERAL ASSEMBLY (1971)

President: Adam Malik (Indonesia), 26th session. The 132 member-nations were as follows:

Afghanistan	Gambia	Nigeria
Albania	Ghana	Norway
Algeria	Greece	Oman
Argentina	Guatemala	Pakistan
Australia	Guinea	Panama
Austria	Guyana	Paraguay
Bahrain	Haiti	Peru
Barbados	Honduras	Philippines
Belgium	Hungary	Poland
Belorussia	Iceland	Portugal
Bhutan	India	Qatar
Bolivia	Indonesia	Rumania
Botswana	Iran	Rwanda
Brazil	Iraq	Saudi Arabia
Bulgaria	Ireland	Senegal
Burma	Israel	Sierra Leone
Burundi	Italy	Singapore
Cambodia	Ivory Coast	Somalia
Cameroon	Jamaica	South Africa
Canada	Japan	Southern Yemen
Central African	Jordan	Spain
Republic	Kenya	Sudan
Ceylon	Kuwait	Swaziland
Chad	Laos	Sweden
Chile	Lebanon	Syria
China, People's	Lesotho	Tanzania
Republic of	Liberia	Thailand
Colombia	Libya	Togo
Congo (Brazzaville)	Luxembourg	Trinidad and
Costa Rica	Malagasy	Tobago
Cuba	Republic	Tunisia
Cyprus	Malawi	Turkey
Czechoslovakia	Malaysia	Uganda
Dahomey	Maldives	Ukraine
Denmark	Mali	USSR
Dominican	Malta	United Arab
Republic	Mauritania	Emirates
Ecuador	Mauritius	United Kingdom
Egypt[1]	Mexico	United States
El Salvador	Mongolia	Upper Volta
Equatorial Guinea	Morocco	Uruguay
Ethiopia	Nepal	Venezuela
Fiji	Netherlands	Yemen
Finland	New Zealand	Yugoslavia
France	Nicaragua	Zaïre[2]
Gabon	Niger	Zambia

[1] Formerly United Arab Republic. [2] Formerly Congo (Kinshasa).

COMMITTEES

General: Composed of 25 members as follows: The General Assembly president; the 17 General Assembly vice presidents (heads of delegations or their deputies of Belgium, Burundi, China, Costa Rica, France, Greece, Hungary, Japan, People's Democratic Republic of Yemen, Peru, Sierra Leone, Sudan, USSR, United Kingdom, United States, Venezuela, and Zambia), and the chairman of the following 7 main committees, which are composed of all 132 member countries:

First (Political and Security): Milko Tarabanov (Bulgaria)

Special Political: Cornelius C. Cremin (Ireland)

Second (Economic and Financial): Narcisco G. Reyes (Philippines)

Third (Social and Humanitarian): Mrs. Helvi L. Sipila (Finland)

Fourth (Trust and Non-self-governing territories): Keith Johnson (Jamaica)

Fifth (Administrative and Budgetary: E. Olu Sanu (Nigeria)

Sixth (Legal): Zenon Rossides (Cyprus)

THE SECURITY COUNCIL (1972)

(Membership ends on December 31 of the year noted; asterisks indicate permanent membership)

Argentina (1972)	India (1973)	Sudan (1972)
Belgium (1972)	Italy (1972)	USSR*
China (PRC)*	Japan (1972)	United Kingdom*
France*	Panama (1973)	United States*
Guinea (1973)	Somalia (1972)	Yugoslavia (1973)

Military Staff Committee: Representatives of chiefs of staffs of China, France, USSR, United Kingdom, and United States.

Disarmament Commission: Representatives of all 132 members.

THE ECONOMIC AND SOCIAL COUNCIL (1972)

President: Rachid Driss (Tunisia), 50th and 51st sessions (1971). (Membership ends on December 31 of the year noted.)

Bolivia (1974)	Greece (1972)	Niger (1973)
Brazil (1972)	Haiti (1973)	Peru (1972)
Burundi (1974)	Hungary (1973)	Poland (1974)
Ceylon (1972)	Italy (1972)	Tunisia (1972)
Chile (1974)	Japan (1974)	USSR (1974)
China (PRC) (1974)	Kenya (1972)	United Kingdom
Finland (1974)	Lebanon (1973)	(1974)
France (1972)	Madagascar (1973)	United States (1973)
Ghana (1972)	Malaysia (1973)	Zaïre (1973)
	New Zealand (1973)	

THE TRUSTEESHIP COUNCIL (1971–72)

President: David Neil Lane (United Kingdom), 38th session (1971).

Australia[1]	France[2]	United Kingdom[2]
China[2]	USSR[2]	United States[1]

[1] Administers trust territory. [2] Permanent member of Security Council not administering trust territory.

THE INTERNATIONAL COURT OF JUSTICE (1970)

President: Muhammad Zafrullah Khan (Pakistan).
Vice President: Fouad Ammoun (Lebanon).

(Judges listed in order of precedence)

Sir Gerald Fitzmaurice (UK)	Charles D. Onyeama
Luis Padilla Nervo	(Nigeria)
(Mexico)	Federico de Castro (Spain)
Isaac Forster (Senegal)	Hardy C. Dillard (USA)
André Gros (France)	Louis Ignacio-Pinto
César Bengzon (Philippines)	(Dahomey)
Sture Petrén (Sweden)	Eduardo Jiménez de Aréchaga
Manfred Lachs (Poland)	(Uruguay)
	Platon D. Morozov (USSR)

SPECIALIZED AGENCIES

Food and Agriculture Organization of the United Nations (FAO); Intergovernmental Maritime Consultative Organization (IMCO); International Bank for Reconstruction and Development (World Bank; IBRD); International Civil Aviation Organization (ICAO); International Development Association (IDA); International Finance Corporation (IFC); International Labor Organization (ILO); International Monetary Fund (IMF); International Telecommunication Union (ITU); United Nations Educational, Scientific and Cultural Organization (UNESCO); Universal Postal Union (UPU); World Health Organization (WHO); World Meteorological Organization (WMO).

---

day, the Assembly authorized a budget of $213,124,410 for 1972.

The organization's budgetary crisis continued, however, not only because of an increasing backlog of unpaid accounts for peace-keeping forces, but also because of an increasing tendency by some states to withhold contributions from the regular budget for items they disagreed with.

At the beginning of the 1971 Assembly session, Yemen was over two years in arrears in payment of its budget dues. The Assembly nevertheless voted on September 21 to allow Yemen to continue to vote. A week later, the secretary general reported that Yemen had made a sufficient payment of arrears to clear itself of the threat of losing its vote.

SECURITY COUNCIL

The year 1971 was a relatively inactive one for the Security Council. It did, however, consider several aspects of the tense situations existing in the Middle East and Africa, tried unsuccessfully to deal with the crisis in East Pakistan, and managed, with what some considered surprising ease, to agree on the selection of a new UN secretary general.

The Secretary-Generalship. In his 10th year as secretary general, the Burmese statesman U Thant made it clear on many occasions that he would not accept a third successive 5-year term. Toward the end of the year he made it equally evident that he would refuse to serve beyond the end of 1971, even on an interim basis. This confronted the major powers with the necessity of coming to a rapid decision as to his successor.

Balloting in the Security Council commenced on December 17. Earlier conferences had reduced the field to three principal candidates: Kurt Waldheim, Austria's chief UN delegate and former foreign minister, favored by the USSR; Max Jakobson of Finland, an apparent favorite of the United States; and Carlos Ortís de Rozas, the chief delegate from Argentina. On the two initial ballots, Jakobson and Ortíz de Rozas drew negative Soviet votes, which constituted vetoes, while China vetoed Waldheim's candidacy. In the third round of voting on December 22, China abstained, ensuring Waldheim's election. The vote was 11 to 1, with 3 abstentions.

In campaigning for the post, Waldheim and his supporters had stressed his long experience as a diplomat and his potential as an international mediator. After his election, however, there were some indications that he intended to give priority to the task of reorganizing the operations of the 4,000-member UN Secretariat, a project that many UN critics had considered long overdue.

East Pakistan. On July 20, Secretary General U Thant sent a memorandum to the Security Council expressing his concern over developments in East Pakistan and their possible consequences. On August 2 he issued a report on his conversations with representatives of India and Pakistan with respect to organizing UN assistance to refugees fleeing from East Pakistan into India. Finally, in mid-November, he reached agreement with Pakistan over the functioning of a UN relief operation in East Pakistan.

On November 23, as Indian-Pakistani tensions increased, the secretary general made his most urgent statement of concern over the issue. On December 4, the Security Council met at the immediate request of nine states to consider "the recent deteriorating situation which has led to armed clashes between India and Pakistan." A U.S. proposal requesting an immediate cease-fire and withdrawal of forces was defeated. Although 11 members voted in favor of the proposal and only 2 against (with 2 abstentions), one of the negative votes was a Soviet veto.

On the following day, two more draft resolutions were defeated. A Soviet proposal calling for a political settlement in East Pakistan prior to a cease-fire was vetoed by China, and a 7-power draft calling for a cease-fire and withdrawal was again vetoed by the USSR. With the United States and China backing Pakistan and the Soviet Union supporting India, the Council was hopelessly split. On December 6, by a vote of 11–0, with 4 abstentions, it adopted a resolution that referred the matter to the General Assembly under the "Uniting for Peace" formula of 1950.

On December 12, after Pakistan had accepted the Assembly's call for a cease-fire, the Council met again at the request of the United States. On the 13th, a U.S. proposal for a cease-fire and the return of East Pakistan refugees to their homes received the anticipated Soviet veto. Three days later India's foreign minister declared that India had no territorial ambitions and was itself ordering a cease-fire. By this time, however, the Pakistani army in Bangladesh (East Pakistan) had been defeated. (See INDIA-PAKISTAN WAR.)

At last, when it meant little, the Council acted. During its 10th meeting on the problem, on December 21, it adopted by a 13 to 0 vote, with 2 abstentions, a resolution that demanded that a "durable cease-fire and cessation of all hostilities" in the Indian subcontinent be observed and remain in effect until withdrawals of all armed forces took place.

Middle East. Periodically during the year the secretary general reported to the Security Council on his efforts and those of his special representative in the Middle East, Ambassador Gunnar Jarring, to persuade Israel and its Arab neighbors to exercise military restraint and maintain the cease-fire.

On September 13, Jordan complained to the Council about allegedly illegal measures taken by Israel in Jerusalem in defiance of previous Security Council resolutions. On September 25 the Council adopted a resolution calling upon Israel to rescind all such measures and to take no further steps in the occupied section of Jerusalem which might tend to change the status of the city, prejudice the rights of the inhabitants or the interests of the international community, or threaten peace. The resolution passed by 14 to 0, with Syria abstaining.

Cyprus. Upon a recommendation of the secretary general, the Council unanimously decided on May 26 to extend the stationing of the UN Peace-Keeping Force in Cyprus for an additional six-month term ending on December 15. Two days before this deadline, the operation was again extended for six months, "in the expectation" that by June 15, 1972, "sufficient progress toward a final solution will make possible a withdrawal or substantial reduction of the force."

Senegal. On July 6, Senegal requested the Security Council to consider a series of incidents on its border with Guinea (Bissau)—formerly Portuguese Guinea. Senegal claimed these incidents constituted a flagrant violation of its territory by Portuguese military forces. On July 15, the Council condemned Portugal for all acts of violence committed since 1963 and decided (unanimously) to dispatch a special fact-finding mission to the area. The mission returned on August 1. Its report, considered by the Council on September 29, described the situation as one arising largely from the failure of the Portuguese authorities to implement fully the independence of Guinea (Bissau). On November 24, the Council called upon Portugal to take measures to ensure Senegal's territorial integrity.

Republic of Guinea. On August 3 the Republic of Guinea (Conakry) informed the Security Council that its intelligence service had intercepted conversations between Overseas Marine units and two other headquarters units of the Portuguese Colonial Army discussing an imminent military aggression against its frontier with Guinea (Bissau) and against the capital, Conakry. The Council dispatched a three-member mission to report on the situation. The mission completed a brief visit to the area on September 2 and reported to the Council on September 29 that it had gathered evidence supporting the original complaint. On November 30 the Security Council, by consensus, affirmed "that the territorial integrity and independence of the Republic of Guinea must be respected."

Namibia. Responding to a request by 35 African states, the Security Council met four times in September and seven times in October to discuss the situation in Namibia (South West Africa). On October 20, the Council adopted a resolution calling upon all states to abstain from entering into treaty relations with South Africa in all cases in which the

UPI

DELEGATES applaud defeat on October 25 of U. S. resolution that would make a two-thirds vote necessary for UN expulsion of Nationalist China. Expulsion of Taiwan and admittance of Communist China soon followed.

government of South Africa purported to act on behalf of Namibia; to abstain from sending to South Africa diplomatic or special missions that included the territory of Namibia in their jurisdiction; and to abstain from entering into economic dealings with South Africa on behalf of Namibia.

Zambia. On October 6, Zambia accused South African forces of "repeated criminal acts of aggression" along the Zambian border. The Zambian request for Council action was supported by 47 Asian and African states. On October 12, the Council unanimously called upon South Africa to respect territorial integrity of Zambia, warning that it might otherwise meet again to consider further steps.

Arabian Gulf Islands. On November 30, Algeria, Iraq, Libya, and the People's Democratic Republic of Yemen requested a meeting of the Security Council to consider "the dangerous situation in the Arabian Gulf area arising from the occupation by armed forces of Iran of the Islands of Abu Mussa, the Greater Tunb, and the Lesser Tunb." After discussing the matter on December 9, the Council agreed to a proposal by Somalia that further consideration be deferred pending the conclusion of efforts by "states friendly to Iraq and Iran."

ECONOMIC AND SOCIAL COUNCIL

The 50th session of the Economic and Social Council (ECOSOC) met in New York from Jan. 11 to 13, 1971, and from April 26 to May 21. The Council adopted resolutions having to do with capital punishment, social development, narcotics drug control, the "brain drain," the use and conservation of natural resources, methods of assisting Palestine refugees, preparations for a conference on international container traffic, and the use of computers for development. Resolutions were also adopted on apartheid and racial discrimination, equality in the administration of justice, the protection of journalists, and trade union rights in South Africa.

The 51st session of the Council, meeting in Geneva in July, recommended an increase in its own membership from 27 to 54 and passed resolutions on assistance in cases of natural disaster, regional development cooperation, and a forthcoming Conference on Human Environment. The session resumed in New York on October 27 and November 23 and 30.

TRUSTEESHIP COUNCIL

The Trusteeship Council met in New York in its 38th session from May 25 to June 18. It adopted resolutions concerning the political, economic, social, and educational advancement of the two remaining trust territories—New Guinea (administered by Australia) and the Trust Territory of the Pacific Islands (administered by the United States).

INTERNATIONAL COURT OF JUSTICE

The International Court of Justice proceeded in 1972 with various phases of its hearing with respect to the *Request for an Advisory Opinion on the Legal Consequences for States of the Continued Presence of South Africa in Namibia (South West Africa) notwithstanding Security Council Resolution 276 (1970)*.

On August 30 India filed a case against Pakistan. The case had its origin in India's decision in February 1971 to no longer permit overflights of its territory by Pakistani aircraft. Pakistan lodged a complaint against that decision with the Council of the International Civil Aviation Organization. In its case before the International Court, India questioned the jurisdiction of the Council. (See also LAW— *International Law.*)

THOMAS HOVET, JR., *University of Oregon*

Ratification of the 26th Amendment in June granted voting rights to 18-year-olds in state and federal elections. Here, newly enfranchised Indiana University students prepare to vote in Bloomington.

UNITED STATES

Much as the ocean tides are ruled by the phases of the moon, the currents of public affairs in the United States are governed by the quadrennial cycle of presidential elections. In 1971 the Nixon administration moved past the half-way mark of its stewardship and inexorably closer to 1972's judgment day at the polls. So it seemed more than coincidental that in 1971 the dominant fact of national life was the emergence of Richard M. Nixon as a highly visible, activist chief executive.

Abandoning the "low profile" he had hitherto doggedly maintained, the President dealt decisively and dramatically with the two issues traditionally uppermost in the minds of his countrymen—peace and prosperity. In July he astonished the world by announcing plans to visit the People's Republic of China. The following month he achieved equal effect by decreeing a far-reaching system of controls over the deeply troubled economy.

DOMESTIC AFFAIRS

During 1971, President Nixon did not hesitate to inject the prestige of his office into issues outside the ordinary bounds of presidential responsibility. When congressional criticism threatened proposals for expanded cancer research, the President announced

that he himself would take command of the ambitious campaign. When a public uproar followed the conviction of 1st Lt. William L. Calley, Jr., in the murder of South Vietnamese civilians at My Lai, the President announced he would personally review Calley's life sentence. When New York Gov. Nelson Rockefeller authorized armed troopers to put down a prison uprising at great cost in lives, the President made a point of publicly expressing his support of Rockefeller. Whether or not the President's actions and utterances were politically motivated, his opponents inevitably viewed them in that light and reacted accordingly. The result was to heighten anticipation of the forthcoming election campaign, months before the first ballot would be case in the first presidential primary in New Hampshire in March 1972.

To be sure, the year 1971 was marked by tragedies and triumphs unrelated to partisan politics. In February an earthquake rocked the congested Los Angeles area, taking 64 lives and causing some $1 billion worth of property damage. At the other end of the geophysical scale, U. S. astronauts made two more successful journeys to the moon, in February and July, aboard spaceships Apollo 14 and 15. (See SPACE EXPLORATION.)

Social Developments. The nation escaped a repetition of the massive racial disorders that had scarred its cities in the 1960's, but there was further tension and scattered violence. The drive for racial equality scored a major advance when the Supreme Court sanctioned busing as a means of desegregating school systems formerly segregated by law. Government figures showed that the proportion of blacks attending schools with a white majority in the South had increased from 18% in 1968 to 39% in 1970. But the tide seemed to be running in the other direction in the North, where segregated schools were mainly a result of segregated housing patterns. Efforts to introduce busing in the North often met with defiance. In the case of Pontiac, Mich., 10 school buses being prepared for the integration program were bombed.

The chorus of female voices demanding equality swelled, with mixed results. A new National Women's Political Caucus set equal representation of women in government as its goal. But a long-proposed constitutional amendment guaranteeing equal rights for women lingered in a Senate committee. Though women's rights leaders failed to get a woman nominated for the Supreme Court, they could take some satisfaction from the first ruling of the court's history (on November 22) that a state law was unconstitutional because it discriminated against women. The law in question was an Idaho statute that gave preference to men in administering estates.

The younger generation, whose life style had already exerted a significant and sometimes unsettling impact on contemporary mores, won an important political victory. In March, Congress passed, and in June the states completed ratification of the 26th Amendment to the Constitution, granting 18-year-olds the right to vote in state as well as federal elections. Youthful activists pressed further demands. A White House Conference on Youth, convened in Estes Park, Colo., in April, called for an end to the draft, the legalization of marihuana, and permissive abortion laws.

The Nixon Administration. In the midst of this varied agitation, the President sought to run the government on a note of idealism and optimism. To a nation weary of "a long nightmare of war and division, crime and inflation," he offered, in his State of the Union address on January 22, "the lift of a driving dream." The speech sketched a series of proposals intended to lead "to a new American Revolution—a peaceful revolution in which power was turned back to the people—in which government at all levels was refreshed and renewed and made truly responsive to the needs of the people." The cornerstone of the program was a scheme for revenue sharing, under which some $16 billion in federal funds would be turned over to state and local governments, to spend as they saw fit, or with broad discretion in six major areas—urban and rural development, education, job training, law enforcement, and transportation.

As for the federal government itself, the President proposed a structural overhaul. The number of cabinet departments would be reduced from 12 (11 after July 1, 1971, when the Post Office Department became a semi-independent public agency) to 8. Four of the proposed new departments would be super-agencies—absorbing 7 present departments—concerned with human resources, community development, natural resources, and economic development. The Departments of State, Treasury, Defense,

---

UNITED STATES CABINET MEMBERS
(As of Dec. 31, 1971)

Secretary of State—William P. Rogers

Secretary of the Treasury—John B. Connally

Secretary of Defense—Melvin Laird

Attorney General—John N. Mitchell

Secretary of the Interior—Rogers C. B. Morton

Secretary of Agriculture—Earl L. Butz

Secretary of Commerce—Maurice H. Stans

Secretary of Labor—James D. Hodgson

Secretary of Health, Education, and Welfare—Elliot L. Richardson

Secretary of Housing and Urban Development—George W. Romney

Secretary of Transportation—John A. Volpe

---

and Justice would remain substantially unchanged. Finally, Nixon called upon Congress to enact 35 pieces of legislation left over from 1970—principally involving reform of the existing welfare system, which he labeled "a monstrous, consuming outrage."

An implicit requirement for success of the President's blueprint for domestic reform was his design for securing peace abroad. Amid much complaint that he was moving too slowly in "winding down" the Indochina War, Nixon anticipated an end to all war. In a March interview he said that he seriously doubted whether "we will ever have another war. This is probably the very last one."

That remark foreshadowed the announcement on July 15 of his plan to confer with Communist Chinese leaders in Peking "to seek the normalization of relations between the two coutnries." In a televised address the President declared: ". . . there can be no stable peace and enduring peace without the participation of the People's Republic of China and its 750 million people." The groundwork for the conference had been laid during a secret visit to Peking in July by Henry A. Kissinger, the President's national security adviser. Nixon's visit was later scheduled for February 1972.

Though Nixon had stressed that improvement in relations with mainland China would "not be at the expense of our old friends," his overtures to Peking stirred protests from those sympathetic to Chiang

AFL-CIO chief George Meany, foe of administration's new economic policies, glares at Treasury Secretary Connally and President Nixon in this cartoon by Oliphant.

OLIPHANT IN THE DENVER POST

Vietnam War Remained a Major Issue In 1971

UPI

UPI

Controversy over U.S. policies in Vietnam brought both pro- and anti-war demonstrators to Washington, D.C., in the spring. (Above) The Vietnam Veterans Against the War demonstrated in April, with some members hurling their combat medals on the Capitol's steps. (Opposite page) Officials herded arrested protesters onto practice field near RFK Stadium during disruptions of May 3–5. (Left) Carl McIntyre, a fundamentalist minister, led a pro-war rally on May 8, calling for a military victory.

Kai-shek's Nationalist Chinese government in Taiwan. For the most part, however, the President's initiative was applauded.

The Economy. Of immediate concern to President Nixon was the condition of the economy at home. Each month's statistics for the cost of living and unemployment emphasized its dismal state. The jobless rate hovered around 6%, while inflation was running over 4%. In June, Treasury Secretary John Connally insisted that the administration would stick to its "game plan," relying on careful budget management and voluntary cooperation of labor and industry to retard the wage-price spiral and speed the return of prosperity. But the public seemed unpersuaded that this strategy would work.

On August 15 the President suddenly changed the game plan. He decreed a 90-day freeze on wages, rents, and prices, the first such ceilings since the Korean War. Moreover, to meet the nation's balance of payments deficit, he ended the convertibility of the dollar into gold, setting the stage for the devaluation of the dollar by 8.57% on December 18. Also on August 15 the President announced a 10% surcharge on taxable imports (which was lifted on December 20 after the international monetary agreement) and a $4.7 billion cut in federal spending. He called on Congress to terminate the excise tax on autos and to provide tax incentives for industry. (Legislation subsequently passed was retroactive to August 15.)

General approval of the President's actions was mixed with complaints. The sharpest criticism came from organized labor. AFL-CIO President George Meany denounced the proposals as "patently discriminatory" against workers. He contended that while union contracts were "highly visible"—and thus easy to control—the administration had failed to establish effective machinery for regulating prices. Also, the freeze exempted corporate profits and stockholders' dividends.

The controversy continued while the administra-

tion formulated plans for shifting from the temporary 90-day freeze to a more permanent system of controls, dubbed Phase II. Ultimately, however, organized labor agreed to cooperate in the program revealed by the President on October 7. The Phase II machinery subsequently set up included a Price Commission, a Pay Board, and a Committee on Interest and Dividends, along with an extension of the Cost of Living Council, which had been created during the freeze. The Cost of Living Council set as its goal a reduction of the inflationary rate to about 2.5% a year, and the Pay Board established a 5.5% guideline for new wage increases effective with the advent of Phase II on November 14.

The President promised not to make controls "a permanent feature of American life," but proposed no deadline for their termination. The consensus was that he had strengthened both his own position and the economy by these bold economic moves. However, Nixon's New Economic Policy would inevitably cause grievances and complaints. And it remained to be seen whether it would revitalize the economy. (See also ECONOMY OF THE U. S.)

Politics. Nixon's political opponents did not wait for the outcome of his programs to make their own preparations for the 1972 presidential election. In the view of most observers, Sen. Edmund Muskie of Maine, the Democratic vice presidential candidate in 1968, was the favorite contender at year-end. His chief opposition in the primaries seemed likely to come from Sen. George McGovern of South Dakota, Sen. Henry Jackson of Washington, Sen. Hubert Humphrey of Minnesota, the party's 1968 standard bearer, and possibly from Mayor John V. Lindsay of New York. Lindsay, who deserted the Republican party in August, entered the Democratic presidential sweepstakes in December. Others who intended to enter the Democratic primaries included Sen. Vance Hartke of Indiana, former Sen. Eugene McCarthy of Minnesota, Mayor Sam Yorty of Los Angeles, and Rep. Shirley Chisholm of New York City.

WHITE HOUSE WEDDING of Tricia Nixon and Edward Finch Cox on June 12 was a social highlight in Washington. The couple, saying farewell to President and Mrs. Nixon after reception in the White House, were married in a Rose Garden ceremony.

Three Democratic senators—Birch Bayh of Indiana, Harold Hughes of Iowa, and Fred Harris of Oklahoma—who had been considered contenders withdrew from the race. Though he repeatedly disavowed his interest in the nomination, Sen. Edward Kennedy of Massachusetts retained strong popular appeal.

In planning to enter some Democratic primaries, McCarthy, the hero of the antiwar movement in 1968, did not rule out a third party bid. There was speculation that should the Democratic convention not choose a candidate to his liking, he might campaign as the head of a splinter group of liberals. A McCarthy insurgency might mean that four candidates would be in the running. Alabama Gov.

George Wallace, who had received nearly 10 million votes as the candidate of the American Independent party in 1968, asserted that only "a meaningful change in direction" by the two major parties would keep him out of the 1972 campaign. Meanwhile, he prepared to enter select Democratic primaries.

President Nixon also faced opposition within his own Republican party, from both sides of the political spectrum. On the left, Rep. Paul McCloskey of California prepared to enter the New Hampshire primary, pledging he would speed the end of the war in Indochina. On the right, Rep. John M. Ashbrook of Ohio, reflecting conservative resentment at the President's China policy, also announced his candidacy. Neither seemed likely to jeopardize the

President's chances of renomination. There was some question as to whether Nixon would keep Vice President Spiro T. Agnew as his running mate, but the President said he would not break up a "winning team." (See also POLITICAL PARTIES.)

Congress. Nixon went through his third year in office still confronted with Democratic majorities in both houses of Congress, a situation that once again produced frustration and stalemate. The Senate refused to approve further funding for the supersonic transport (SST), a project that had strong administration support. And the legislative mainstays of the "new American Revolution"—welfare reform, revenue sharing, and government reorganization—were bogged down in Congressional committees.

Congress did pass a $5.1 billion school aid bill, and a $2.2 billion measure to provide public service jobs. It first killed the foreign aid program, then agreed to extend it temporarily until modified proposals could be adopted in 1972. After prolonged debate, it also agreed to extensions of the Selective Service System. And more readily, it passed the Economic Stabilization Act, extending the President's authority to carry out his New Economic Policy by controlling wages, prices, and rents. The President managed to win senatorial consent to his nomination of Lewis Powell and William Rehnquist as Supreme Court justices and Earl Butz as secretary of agriculture.

Overall, Nixon was more successful at checking the will of the legislature than in winning support for his own policies. Congress failed to override his vetoes of measures expanding public works programs and setting up day care centers for children of working parents. The threat of a veto persuaded the Democrats to postpone the effective date of a controversial proposal for financing presidential campaigns from federal income tax payments. The tax bill signed by the President on December 10 contained such a provision, but it was not to be effective until 1976.

In the foreign policy field, efforts of Senate doves to end the U. S. involvement in Indochina culminated in an amendment to a military appropriations bill calling for the prompt withdrawal of all U. S. troops. But the President asserted that this policy statement had no legal force.

Impact of the War. Although the President foiled the opposition to the war in the Congress, the fighting in Indochina, past and present, remained a troublesome presence. In June the New York *Times,* the Washington *Post,* and several other newspapers began publishing excerpts from a top secret study of U. S. policy in Vietnam from 1945 through the Johnson administration. Disclosures in the so-called Pentagon Papers stirred charges that the nation had been misled in the past and inferentially called into question the credibility of Nixon's own war policies. The Justice Department, contending that printing these classified documents threatened national security, obtained injunctions against their publication. This was the first time that the federal government had ever used the legal weapon of prior restraint against the press. The newspapers fought back, citing the 1st Amendment, and the Supreme Court ultimately ruled that they might print this material. (See CENSORSHIP.)

The courts-martial of Lt. William L. Calley, Jr., and two other officers, stemming from the My Lai slayings of 1968, also stirred disturbing memories.

——— UNITED STATES • Information Highlights ———

Official Name: United States of America.
Area: 3,615,123 square miles (9,363,169 sq km).
Population (Dec. 31, 1971 est.): 208,554,000. *Density,* 57 per sq mi (22 per sq km). *Annual rate of increase,* 1.2%.
Chief Cities (1970 census): Washington, D. C., the capital, 756,510; New York, 7,895,563; Chicago, 3,369,359; Los Angeles, 2,781,829; Philadelphia, 1,950,098.
Government: *Head of state,* Richard M. Nixon, president (took office Jan. 20, 1969). *Head of government,* Richard M. Nixon. *Legislature*—Congress: Senate, 100 members; House of Representatives, 435 members. *Major political parties*—Democratic, Republican.
Languages: English (official).
Education: *Literacy rate* (1971), 98% of population. *Expenditure on education* (1968), 5.8% of gross national product. *Public school enrollment* (1971)—primary, 28,154,794; secondary, 17,726,156; university/higher, 7,646,300.
Finances (1970–71): *Revenues,* $188,300,000,000; *expenditures,* $211,600,000,000; *monetary unit,* dollar.
Gross National Product (1971 est.): $1,047,000,000,000.
National Income (1971): $876,000,000,000; *national income per person,* $4,200.
Economic Indexes: *Industrial production* (Oct. 1971), 143 (1963=100); *agricultural production* (1969), 104 (1963=100); *consumer price index* (Oct. 1971), 134 (1963=100).
Manufacturing (metric tons, 1969): Gasoline, 237,894,000; crude steel, 128,151,000; pig-iron and ferro alloys, 88,-570,000; cement, 66,627,000.
Crops (metric tons, 1969 crop year): Maize, 116,282,000 (ranks 1st among world producers); wheat, 39,704,000 (world rank 2d); soybeans, 30,397,000 (world rank 1st); sorghum (1968), 18,789,000 (world rank 1st); oranges and tangerines (1968), 7,526,000 (world rank 1st); cotton lint, 2,180,000 (world rank 1st).
Minerals (metric tons, 1969): Coal, 513,436,000 (ranks 1st among world producers); crude petroleum, 455,656,000 (world rank 1st); iron ore, 52,513,000 (world rank 2d); phosphate rock, 34,224,000 (world rank 1st); copper ore, 1,401,200 (world rank 1st).
Foreign Trade (1970): *Exports,* $42,593,000,000 (chief exports, 1968—nonelectrical machinery, $6,313,300,000; transport equipment, $5,850,100,000). *Imports,* $39,768,000,000 (chief imports, 1968—transport equipment, $4,298,500,000; nonelectrical machinery, $2,197,700,000; iron and steel, $2,046,400,000). *Chief trading partners* (1968)—Canada (took 23% of exports, supplied 27% of imports); Japan (9%—12%); United Kingdom; West Germany.
Tourism: *Receipts* (1970), $2,319,000,000.
Transportation: *Roads* (1969), 3,710,299 miles (5,970,984 km); *motor vehicles* (1969), 105,097,000 (automobiles, 86,861,-334); *railroads* (1970), 207,526 miles (333,972 km); *merchant fleet* (1971), 16,266,000 gross registered tons.
Communications: *Telephones* (1971), 119,645,500; *television stations* (1969), 655; *television sets* (1969), 81,000; *radios* (1968), 285,000; *newspapers* (1970), 1,758 (daily circulation, 62,000,000).

On March 29, Calley was convicted of murdering at least 22 South Vietnamese and was sentenced to life imprisonment. In response to widespread protests that Calley was a scapegoat, President Nixon announced that he would review the sentence. This triggered another round of protests from those who felt that the President was improperly interfering in the military legal process.

In August, Calley's sentence was reduced to 20 years by the commanding general of the Third Army. The two other officers tried, Capt. Ernest Medina, Calley's commander, who was charged with murder, and Col. Oran K. Henderson, who was accused of trying to cover up the killings, were acquitted.

Meanwhile, demonstrations and protests against the war were provoked by administration policies. U. S. support of a South Vietnamese incursion into Laos in February seemed to opponents of the war to represent a widening of hostilities. On April 24 hundreds of thousands of demonstrators massed in San Francisco and Washington to demand an immediate end to all fighting in Indochina. Both rallies were marked by an absence of violence and mass arrests. A week later, however, when some 10,000 demonstrators sought to "stop the government" by disrupting traffic in Washington, police made some 7,000 arrests. The police tactics, condemned as unconstitutional by civil libertarians, were defended by the administration as necessary to prevent chaos.

Increasingly, the main confrontation between the administration and the peace movement shifted to the courts, as the Justice Department intensified efforts to meet the threat of violence on the left. In the early morning hours of March 1 a bomb exploded in the deserted Senate wing of the Capitol, following a telephone warning that the blast was intended to protest the Laos invasion. A 19-year-old girl, Leslie Bacon, was arrested as a material witness and subsequently jailed for refusing to answer questions before a federal grand jury probing "national security" matters. Later a U.S. Appeals Court ruled her arrest was illegal.

The most celebrated legal battle between the government and the radicals involved the Rev. Philip Berrigan, a leader of the Catholic war resistance, and a bizarre conspiracy alleged to have as its goal the kidnapping of presidential aide Henry Kissinger and the destruction of the heating system serving federal buildings in Washington. The government released the text of letters discussing the plot, which it said were smuggled in and out of the prison where Father Berrigan was serving a sentence for destroying draft records. Attorneys for Berrigan and his 7 co-defendants charged that publication of the letters prejudiced their clients' rights. The trial, which began in early 1972, promised to turn into a debate over the moral and political issues underlying the war. Among the prominent lawyers representing the accused conspirators was former Attorney General Ramsey Clark.

Black Militants. The other main segment of the radical movement, the black militants, also were engaged in legal battles, and on the local level they could claim some victories. On May 13, 1971, in New York City, 13 Black Panthers were acquitted of plotting to bomb police stations and department stores. The lengthy legal proceedings were estimated

to have cost taxpayers over $2 million. Two weeks later a Connecticut judge dismissed murder and kidnapping charges against Panthers Bobby Seale and Ericka Huggins after a six-month trial ended with a deadlocked jury. The judge claimed that "massive publicity" would make it impossible to retry the defendants fairly.

Prison Unrest. A wave of unrest and violence struck the nation's prisons in 1971. On August 21, George Jackson, one of three black militants known as the Soledad Brothers, was slain while allegedly trying to escape from California's San Quentin prison. Jackson was awaiting trial on charges of murdering a guard at Soledad Prison in January 1970. Two other convicts and three prison guards were killed in the disorder at San Quentin. Doubts about the official version of the incident were raised, when an autopsy report showed that Jackson had been shot in the back, and his friends charged he had been murdered. To stop what he called attempts to "distort the facts," California Gov. Ronald Reagan ordered an inquiry by state prison officials. Reagan himself blamed the violence at California prisons on "self-proclaimed revolutionary forces."

Attica prison in upstate New York was the site of an even bloodier tragedy in September. Some 1,000 inmates took control of the institution, seized hostages, and issued a list of demands for improvements in prison conditions. In four days of negotiations, during which left wing lawyer William H. Kunstler and Black Panther leader Bobby Seale were called in, officials granted all major demands except for amnesty for offenses committed during the uprising. When the prisoners refused to surrender, Corrections Commissioner Russell G. Oswald, backed by Governor Rockefeller, ordered the prison taken

RECREATION WING of sanitarium in Sylmar, Calif., broke away from main building during February 9 earthquake. Disaster killed 64 people, including 3 in the sanitarium.

PIX

UPI

JUBILANT Ernest Medina displays his honorable discharge from the Army shortly after his acquittal in September of involvement in the My Lai massacre. Cartoon symbolizes feeling of Vietnam War critics that the military had made a scapegoat of Lt. William Calley, convicted in March of murders at My Lai.

HAYNIE IN THE
LOUISVILLE COURIER JOURNAL

"...Wipe...wipe... ...wipe...wipe..."

by storm. Nine hostages and 31 prisoners died in the assault; the death toll ultimately reached 43. Rockefeller afterward blamed the "revolutionary tactics of militants" for the uprising and called for state and federal investigations. The Attica riot served to dramatize the appalling inadequacy of the nation's prisons to carry out their assigned task of rehabilitation. (See also special report on prisons beginning on page 38.)

ROBERT SHOGAN
Washington Bureau, "Newsweek" Magazine

FOREIGN AFFAIRS

The gyrations of U. S. foreign policy in 1971 left even the most expert "Nixon-watchers" dizzy. The President's conservative supporters were stunned by his decision, announced on July 15, to accept Peking's "invitation" to visit the People's Republic of China in 1972. (Later he announced that he would also visit the Soviet Union, in May 1972.) His liberal opponents, on the other hand, found themselves outmaneuvered at every turn, whether the question was "Vietnamization," international finance, or executive power in foreign affairs.

A year of "winding down" the Indochina War ended with five days in late December 1971 of the most intensive bombing of North Vietnam since 1968. On Jan. 25, 1972, the President disclosed an 8-point peace plan that had been offered the North Vietnamese through secret channels three months earlier. The proposal provided for total U. S. troop withdrawal and full prisoner exchange within six months of an agreement. The political future of South Vietnam would be determined by free elections, and the future of Indochina would be worked out by the parties concerned in international conferences according to the principles of the 1954 Geneva convention. Although the plan met a hostile reception by North Vietnam, administration critics could no longer argue that Nixon had done nothing toward securing a negotiated settlement. Senate doves, believing that North Vietnam would never accept a settlement that did not positively rule out the Thieu government in South Vietnam, continued to insist on a U. S. withdrawal tied only to

the release of prisoners. Moreover, there was disagreement as to whether the President's plan was really so new as the administration claimed.

Somehow, Nixon managed to stay one turn ahead of both conservatives and liberals throughout 1971. Seven out of ten people responding to a Gallup poll answered that they did not think they were being told the truth about administration policy in Southeast Asia. Paradoxically, Nixon's overall ratings in foreign policy management were on the upswing by year-end. Weary and apathetic from the nation's longest war, Americans failed to get overly excited about the "credibility gap" most felt was still there—and possibly widened. Even the publication of the so-called Pentagon Papers in the New York *Times* and the Washington *Post,* which seemed to confirm the existence of a genuine credibility gap from the beginnings of the Vietnam War—and the substance of the antiwar argument as well—failed to cause more than a momentary uproar in the press. The critical reaction was directed largely against the administration's effort to suppress publication.

Foreign Aid. The many faceted nature of the opposition to administration foreign policy was much in evidence during the debate over the 1971 foreign aid bill. For the first time since massive aid was inaugurated under the Truman Doctrine and the Marshall Plan, Congress refused to authorize funds for administration aid requests, but a stopgap measure continued appropriations at the present level through Feb. 22, 1972. Deputy Defense Secretary David Packard was moved to quip, "I hope we don't go back to a Fortress Arkansas posture," referring to Senate Foreign Relations Committee Chairman J. William Fulbright of Arkansas, a long-time opponent of the Indochina War and of other U. S. "commitments" in the Cold War.

Alone, war critics had been unable to do much to check the President's Indochina policies; they were still unable to block legislation in 1971 calling for new expenditures for advanced weapons systems. Teamed with conservatives, however, they were able to vote down foreign aid, long the least popular of Cold War measures.

WIDE WORLD

VIETNAM VETERAN crosses empty terminal at Oakland, Calif., separation center. Unemployment rates among veterans, particularly blacks, were extremely high in 1971.

China Policy. The defeat of the foreign aid bill came in the wake of the UN General Assembly's October 25 decision to expel Nationalist China and to seat Peking's representative in that body and on the UN Security Council. For the first time since the question had arisen in 1950, the United States had voted to seat the People's Republic of China. But it had used strong leverage to try to prevent Chiang Kai-shek's government from being forced out. U. S. conservatives, like New York Sen. James Buckley, had issued separate warnings—both to the administration and to the United Nations—of their intentions to cut off U. S. funds should the Nationalists be expelled. The conservatives also complained that the presence of presidential aide Henry Kissinger in Peking at the time of the UN vote undercut United States support for Chiang with undecided nations and refuted the President's pledge that his opening wedge to China would not be at the expense of old allies.

The biggest surprise of the year—perhaps of the decade—was Nixon's announcement that he had accepted "with pleasure" Premier Chou En-lai's invitation to visit mainland China. The President expressed his hope of exchanging "views on questions of concern to the two sides." What these questions might be was left to speculators, who found Nixon and his advisers, especially the reticent Kissinger, less than communicative on this point.

China's motives in inviting President Nixon, on the other hand, seemed far less inscrutable. Chou told anyone willing to listen that his country was worried about a resurgent Japan. Caught between the increasingly hostile Soviet Union and a dynamic Japan once again bidding for leadership, at least economically, throughout east Asia, even the Chinese Communists were interested in old-style balance-of-power diplomacy.

To some observers it looked as if U. S. diplomacy had come full circle in Asia; for Washington, too, had a variety of reasons for wanting to plant some doubts in Moscow and Tokyo. Moreover, Kissinger's leading role in the new China policy reflected his personal interest in reducing the ideological components of U. S. foreign policy in favor of traditional balance-of-power politics. Where any Democratic president would have faced strong opposition in initiating a new China policy, Nixon's longstanding Cold War credentials were unchallengeable. Or so it seemed before the conservative revolt.

Indochina Impasse. Few hopes were raised that the President's trip to China, planned for February 1972, would mean a breakthrough for a negotiated settlement in the Indochina War. The "Nixon Doctrine" of a gradual U. S. withdrawal and the "Vietnamization" policy remained unproved at the end of 1971—and still controversial. Troop reductions went ahead at an increased rate, but the air war over Laos and Cambodia was somewhat accelerated. "Mr. Nixon had hushed the sounds of the killing," wrote Garry Wills, author of *Nixon Agonistes,* the most serious political biography of the President, "and changed the color of those killed. The best image he can find for this literally 'absentminded' policy is one of clockwork machinery 'winding down.'"

In February 1971 a U. S.-advised South Vietnamese force invaded Laos to cut the Ho Chi Minh Trail. The raid was pronounced an immediate success by President Nixon and his military advisers. Critics saw it as a rout, with the South Vietnamese troops fleeing for their very lives. Secretary of State William Rogers tried to strike a balanced view: "It made us realize, and it made the South Vietnamese realize, that there's a problem there [Laos]. But they did quite well."

Well enough to realize the President's goal of leaving South Vietnam, and the war, in such a way as to guarantee "a generation of peace"? That was the question of questions. In an attempt to get the right answer, the administration ordered intensive bombing raids against North Vietnam on the final five days of 1971. Once again policymakers pronounced their tactics an unqualified success in destroying an enemy build-up. And once again, critics contradicted these authorities, insisting that nothing permanent could be gained from such "gimmickery," so reminiscent of French tactics in the 1950's.

The controversy over the fate of U. S. prisoners of war held in North Vietnam added an emotional factor to the Indochina debate in 1971. The President insisted that he was doing all he could to secure their release through secret channels. He promised to keep a residual force in South Vietnam until all prisoners were returned. Sen. George McGovern, a contender for the Democratic presidential nomination, charged that he, personally, had been assured by North Vietnamese negotiators at the Paris peace talks that all prisoners would be returned once the United States set a final withdrawal date. McGovern and other opponents of "Vietnamization" also asserted that the President was using the prisoners of war as an excuse to stay in South Vietnam until the regime of President Nguyen Van Thieu was firmly entrenched and the South Vietnamese could *(Continued on page 719)*

92nd CONGRESS OF THE U.S.
(SECOND SESSION)

SENATE

OFFICERS

President of the Senate: Spiro T. Agnew
President Pro Tempore: Allen J. Ellender (D-La.)
Majority Leader: Mike Mansfield (D-Mont.)
Majority Whip: Robert C. Byrd (D-W. Va.)
Minority Leader: Hugh Scott (R-Pa.)
Minority Whip: Robert P. Griffin (R-Mich.)

COMMITTEE CHAIRMEN

Aeronautical and Space Sciences: Clinton P. Anderson (D-N. Mex.)
Agriculture and Forestry: Herman Talmadge (D-Ga.)
Appropriations: Allen J. Ellender (D-La.)
Armed Services: John Stennis (D-Miss.)
Banking, Housing, and Urban Affairs: John J. Sparkman (D-Ala.)
Commerce: Warren G. Magnuson (D-Wash.)
District of Columbia: Thomas Eagleton (D-Mo.)
Finance: Russell B. Long (D-La.)
Foreign Relations: J. William Fulbright (D-Ark.)
Government Operations: John L. McClellan (D-Ark.)
Interior and Insular Affairs: Henry M. Jackson (D-Wash.)
Judiciary: James O. Eastland (D-Miss.)
Labor and Public Welfare: Harrison Williams (D-N. J.)
Post Office and Civil Service: Gale W. McGee (D-Wyo.)
Public Works: Jennings Randolph (D-W. Va.)
Rules and Administration: B. Everett Jordan (D-N. C.)
Veterans' Affairs: Vance Hartke (D-Ind.)

HOUSE

OFFICERS

Speaker of the House: Carl Albert (D-Okla.)
Majority Leader: Hale C. Boggs (D-La.)
Majority Whip: Thomas O'Neill, Jr. (D-Mass.)
Minority Leader: Gerald R. Ford (R-Mich.)
Minority Whip: Leslie C. Arends (R-Ill.)

COMMITTEE CHAIRMEN

Agriculture: W. R. Poage (D-Texas)
Appropriations: George H. Mahon (D-Texas)
Armed Services: F. Edward Hébert (D-La.)
Banking and Currency: Wright Patman (D-Texas)
District of Columbia: John L. McMillan (D-S. C.)
Education and Labor: Carl D. Perkins (D-Ky.)
Foreign Affairs: Thomas E. Morgan (D-Pa.)
Government Operations: Chet Holifield (D-Calif.)
House Administration: Wayne L. Hays (D-Ohio)
Interior and Insular Affairs: Wayne N. Aspinall (D-Colo.)
Internal Security: Richard H. Ichord (D-Mo.)
Interstate and Foreign Commerce: Harley O. Staggers (D-W. Va.)
Judiciary: Emanuel Celler (D-N. Y.)
Merchant Marine and Fisheries: Edward A. Garmatz (D-Md.)
Post Office and Civil Service: Thaddeus J. Dulski (D-N. Y.)
Public Works: John A. Blatnik (D-Minn.)
Rules: William M. Colmer (D-Miss.)
Science and Astronautics: George P. Miller (D-Calif.)
Standards of Official Conduct: Melvin Price (D-Ill.)
Veterans' Affairs: Olin E. Teague (D-Texas)
Ways and Means: Wilbur D. Mills (D-Ark.)

SENATE MEMBERSHIP

(As of December 1971: 55 Democrats, 45 Republicans)

Letters after senators' names refer to party affiliation—D for Democrat, R for Republican. Single asterisk (*) denotes term expiring in January 1973; double asterisk (**), term expiring in January 1975; triple asterisk (***), term expiring in January 1977.

ALABAMA
*J. Sparkman, D
**J. B. Allen, D

ALASKA
**M. Gravel, D
*T. Stevens, R

ARIZONA
**B. Goldwater, R
***P. J. Fannin, R

ARKANSAS
*J. L. McClellan, D
**J. W. Fulbright, D

CALIFORNIA
**A. Cranston, D
***J. V. Tunney, D

COLORADO
*G. Allot, R
**P. H. Dominick, R

CONNECTICUT
**A. A. Ribicoff, D
***L. P. Weicker, Jr., R

DELAWARE
*J. C. Boggs, R
***W. V. Roth, Jr., R

FLORIDA
**E. J. Gurney, R
***L. Chiles, D

GEORGIA
*D. H. Gambrell, D
**H. E. Talmadge, D

HAWAII
**D. K. Inouye, D
***H. L. Fong, R

IDAHO
*L. B. Jordan, R
**F. Church, D

ILLINOIS
*C. H. Percy, R
**A. E. Stevenson III, D

INDIANA
**B. Bayh, D
***V. Hartke, D

IOWA
*J. Miller, R
**H. E. Hughes, D

KANSAS
*J. B. Pearson, R
**R. Dole, R

KENTUCKY
*J. S. Cooper, R
**M. W. Cook, R

LOUISIANA
*A. J. Ellender, D
**R. B. Long, D

MAINE
*M. Chase Smith, R
***E. S. Muskie, D

MARYLAND
**C. McC. Mathias, Jr., R
***J. Glenn Beall, Jr., R

MASSACHUSETTS
*E. W. Brooke, R
***E. M. Kennedy, D

MICHIGAN
*R. P. Griffin, R
***P. A. Hart, D

MINNESOTA
*W. F. Mondale, D
***H. H. Humphrey, D

MISSISSIPPI
*J. O. Eastland, D
***J. C. Stennis, D

MISSOURI
**T. F. Eagleton, D
***S. Symington, D

MONTANA
*L. Metcalf, D
***M. Mansfield, D

NEBRASKA
*C. T. Curtis, R
***R. L. Hruska, R

NEVADA
**A. Bible, D
***H. W. Cannon, D

NEW HAMPSHIRE
*T. J. McIntyre, D
**N. Cotton, R

NEW JERSEY
*C. P. Case, R
***H. A. Williams, Jr., D

NEW MEXICO
*C. P. Anderson, D
***J. M. Montoya, D

NEW YORK
**J. K. Javits, R
***J. L. Buckley, R[1]

NORTH CAROLINA
*B. E. Jordan, D
**S. J. Ervin, Jr., D

NORTH DAKOTA
**M. R. Young, R
***Q. N. Burdick, D

OHIO
**W. B. Saxbe, R
***R. Taft, Jr., R

OKLAHOMA
*F. R. Harris, D
**H. Bellmon, R

OREGON
*M. Hatfield, R
**B. Packwood, R

PENNSYLVANIA
**R. S. Schweiker, R
***H. Scott, R

RHODE ISLAND
*C. Pell, D
***J. O. Pastore, D

SOUTH CAROLINA
*S. Thurmond, R
**E. F. Hollings, D

SOUTH DAKOTA
*K. E. Mundt, R
**G. McGovern, D

TENNESSEE
*H. H. Baker, Jr., R
***W. E. Brock 3d, R

TEXAS
*J. G. Tower, R
***L. M. Bentsen, Jr., D

UTAH
**W. F. Bennett, R
***F. E. Moss, D

VERMONT
**G. D. Aiken, R
***R. T. Stafford, R

VIRGINIA
*W. B. Spong, Jr., D
***H. F. Byrd, Jr., D[2]

WASHINGTON
**W. G. Magnuson, D
***H. M. Jackson, D

WEST VIRGINIA
*J. Randolph, D
***R. C. Byrd, D

WISCONSIN
**G. Nelson, D
***W. Proxmire, D

WYOMING
*C. P. Hansen, R
***G. W. McGee, D

[1] Ran as a Conservative. [2] Ran as an independent.

HOUSE MEMBERSHIP

(As of December 1971: 254 Democrats, 177 Republicans, 4 vacancies)

Letters after representatives' names refer to party affiliation—D for Democrat, R for Republican. The abbreviation "AT-L." in place of congressional district number means "representative at large." Asterisk (*) before member's name indicates incumbent reelected in 1970 (served in the 91st Congress); double asterisk (**) before name indicates nonincumbent elected in 1970; triple asterisk (***) indicates member elected to fill a vacancy after November 1970.

ALABAMA
1. *J. Edwards, R
2. *W. L. Dickinson, R
3. Vacancy
4. *B. Nichols, D
5. *W. Flowers, D
6. *J. Buchanan, R
7. *T. Bevill, D
8. *R. E. Jones, D

ALASKA
At-L. **N. J. Begich, D

ARIZONA
1. *J. J. Rhodes, R
2. *M. K. Udall, D
3. *S. Steiger, R

ARKANSAS
1. *B. Alexander, D
2. *W. D. Mills, D
3. *J. P. Hammerschmidt, R
4. *D. Pryor, D

CALIFORNIA
1. *D. H. Clausen, R
2. *H. T. Johnson, D
3. *J. E. Moss, D
4. *R. L. Leggett, D
5. *P. Burton, D
6. *W. S. Mailliard, R
7. **R. V. Dellums, D
8. *G. P. Miller, D
9. *D. Edwards, D
10. *C. S. Gubser, R
11. *P. N. McCloskey, Jr., R
12. *B. L. Talcott, R
13. *C. M. Teague, R
14. *J. R. Waldie, D
15. *J. J. McFall, D
16. *B. F. Sisk, D
17. *G. M. Anderson, D
18. *R. B. Mathias, R
19. *C. Holifield, D
20. *H. A. Smith, R
21. *A. F. Hawkins, D
22. *J. C. Corman, D
23. *D. Clawson, R
24. *J. H. Rousselot, R
25. *C. E. Wiggins, R
26. *T. M. Rees, D
27. *B. M. Goldwater, Jr., R
28. *A. Bell, R
29. **G. E. Danielson, D
30. *E. R. Roybal, D
31. *C. H. Wilson, D
32. *C. Hosmer, R
33. *J. L. Pettis, R
34. *R. T. Hanna, D
35. *J. G. Schmitz, R
36. *B. Wilson, R
37. *L. Van Deerlin, D
38. **V. V. Veysey, R

COLORADO
1. **J. D. McKevitt, R
2. *D. G. Brotzman, R
3. *F. E. Evans, D
4. *W. N. Aspinall, D

CONNECTICUT
1. **W. R. Cotter, D
2. **R. H. Steele, R[2]
3. *R. N. Giaimo, D
4. **S. B. McKinney, R
5. *J. S. Monagan, D
6. **E. T. Grasso, D

DELAWARE
At-L. **P. S. du Pont 4th, R

FLORIDA
1. *R. L. F. Sikes, D
2. *D. Fuqua, D
3. *C. E. Bennett, D
4. *B. Chappell, Jr., D
5. *L. Frey, Jr., R
6. *S. Gibbons, D
7. *J. A. Haley, D
8. **C. W. B. Young, R
9. *P. G. Rogers, D
10. *J. H. Burke, R
11. *C. Pepper, D
12. *D. B. Fascell, D

GEORGIA
1. *G. E. Hagan, D
2. **M. D. Mathis, D

3. *J. T. Brinkley, D
4. *B. B. Blackburn, R
5. *F. Thompson, R
6. *J. J. Flynt, Jr., D
7. *J. W. Davis, D
8. *W. S. Stuckey, Jr., D
9. *P. M. Landrum, D
10. *R. G. Stephens, Jr., D

HAWAII
1. *S. M. Matsunaga, D
2. *P. T. Mink, D

IDAHO
1. *J. A. McClure, R
2. *O. Hansen, R

ILLINOIS
1. **R. H. Metcalfe, D
2. *A. J. Mikva, D
3. **M. F. Murphy, D
4. *E. J. Derwinski, R
5. *J. C. Kluczynski, D
6. **G. W. Collins, D[2]
7. *F. Annunzio, D
8. *D. Rostenkowski, D
9. *S. R. Yates, D
10. *H. R. Collier, R
11. *R. C. Pucinski, D
12. *R. McClory, R
13. *P. M. Crane, R
14. *J. N. Erlenborn, R
15. Vacancy

16. *J. B. Anderson, R
17. *L. C. Arends, R
18. *R. H. Michel, R
19. *T. F. Railsback, R
20. *P. Findley, R
21. *K. J. Gray, D
22. *W. L. Springer, R
23. *G. E. Shipley, D
24. *C. M. Price, D

INDIANA
1. *R. J. Madden, D
2. *E. F. Landgrebe, R
3. *J. Brademas, D
4. **J. E. Roush, D
5. **E. Hillis, R
6. *W. G. Bray, R
7. *J. T. Myers, R
8. *R. H. Zion, R
9. *L. H. Hamilton, D
10. *D. W. Dennis, R
11. *A. Jacobs, Jr., D

IOWA
1. *F. Schwengel, R
2. *J. C. Culver, D
3. *H. R. Gross, R
4. *J. H. Kyl, R
5. *N. Smith, D
6. *W. Mayne, R
7. *W. J. Scherle, R

KANSAS
1. *K. G. Sebelius, R
2. **W. R. Roy, D
3. *L. Winn, Jr., R
4. *G. E. Shriver, R
5. *J. Skubitz, R

KENTUCKY
1. *F. A. Stubblefield, D
2. *W. H. Natcher, D
3. **R. L. Mazzoli, D
4. *M. G. (Gene) Snyder, R
5. *T. L. Carter, D
6. ***W. P. Curlin, Jr., D
7. *C. D. Perkins, D

LOUISIANA
1. *F. E. Hébert, D
2. *H. Boggs, D
3. *P. T. Caffery, D
4. *J. D. Waggonner. Jr., D
5. *O. E. Passman, D
6. *J. R. Rarick, D
7. *E. W. Edwards, D
8. *S. O. Long, D

MAINE
1. *P. N. Kyros, D
2. *W. D. Hathaway, D

MARYLAND
1. ***W. O. Mills, R
2. *C. D. Long, D
3. *E. A. Garmatz, D
4. **P. S. Sarbanes, D
5. *L. J. Hogan, R
6. **G. E. Byron, D
7. **P. J. Mitchell, D
8. *G. Gude, R

MASSACHUSETTS
1. *S. O. Conte, R
2. *E. P. Boland, D
3. **R. F. Drinan, D
4. *H. D. Donohue, D
5. *F. B. Morse, R
6. *M. J. Harrington, D
7. *T. H. Macdonald, D
8. *T. P. O'Neill, Jr., D
9. **L. D. Hicks, D
10. *M. M. Heckler, R
11. *J. A. Burke, D
12. *H. Keith, R

MICHIGAN
1. *J. Conyers, Jr., D
2. *M. L. Esch, R
3. *G. Brown, R
4. *E. Hutchinson, R
5. *G. R. Ford, R
6. *C. E. Chamberlain, R
7. *D. W. Riegle, Jr., R
8. *J. Harvey, R
9. *G. A. Vander Jagt, R
10. *E. A. Cederberg, R
11. *P. E. Ruppe, R
12. *J. G. O'Hara, D
13. *C. C. Diggs, Jr., D
14. *L. N. Nedzi, D
15. *W. D. Ford, D
16. *J. D. Dingell, D

17. *M. W. Griffiths, D
18. *W. S. Broomfield, R
19. *J. H. McDonald, R

MINNESOTA
1. *A. H. Quie, R
2. *A. Nelsen, R
3. **B. Frenzel, R
4. *J. E. Karth, D
5. *D. M. Fraser, D
6. *J. M. Zwach, R
7. **B. Bergland, D
8. *J. A. Blatnik, D

MISSISSIPPI
1. *T. G. Abernethy, D
2. *J. L. Whitten, D
3. *C. H. Griffin, D
4. *G. V. Montgomery, D
5. *W. M. Colmer, D

MISSOURI
1. *W. L. Clay, D
2. *J. W. Symington, D
3. *L. K. Sullivan, D
4. *W. J. Randall, D
5. *R. Bolling, D
6. *W. R. Hull, Jr., D
7. *D. G. Hall, R
8. *R. H. Ichord, D
9. *W. L. Hungate, D
10. *B. D. Burlison, D

MONTANA
1. **R. G. Shoup, R
2. *J. Melcher, D

NEBRASKA
1. **C. Thone, R
2. **J. Y. McCollister, R
3. *D. T. Martin, R

NEVADA
At-L. *W. S. Baring, D

NEW HAMPSHIRE
1. *L. C. Wyman, R
2. *J. C. Cleveland, R

NEW JERSEY
1. *J. E. Hunt, R
2. *C. W. Sandman, Jr., R
3. *J. J. Howard, D
4. *F. Thompson, D
5. *P. H. B. Frelinghuysen, R
6. **E. B. Forsythe, R[2]
7. *W. B. Widnall, R
8. *R. A. Roe, D
9. *H. Helstoski, D
10. *P. W. Rodino, Jr., D
11. *J. G. Minish, D
12. *F. P. Dwyer, R
13. *C. E. Gallagher, D
14. *D. V. Daniels, D
15. *E. J. Patten, D

NEW MEXICO
1. *M. Lujan, Jr., R
2. **H. L. Runnels, D

NEW YORK
(Districts Redrawn)
1. *O. G. Pike, D
2. *J. R. Grover, Jr., R
3. *L. L. Wolff, D
4. *J. W. Wydler, R
5. **N. F. Lent, R
6. *S. Halpern, R
7. *J. P. Addabbo, D
8. *B. S. Rosenthal, D
9. *J. J. Delaney, D
10. *E. Celler, D
11. *F. J. Brasco, D
12. *S. Chisholm, D
13. *B. L. Podell, D
14. *J. J. Rooney, D
15. *H. L. Carey, D
16. *J. M. Murphy, D
17. *E. I. Koch, D
18. **C. B. Rangel, D
19. **B. S. Abzug, D
20. *W. F. Ryan, D
21. **Herman Badillo, D[1]
22. *J. H. Scheuer, D
23. *J. B. Bingham, D
24. *M. Biaggi, D
25. **P. A. Peyser, R
26. *O. R. Reid, R
27. **J. G. Dow, D
28. *H. Fish, Jr., R
29. **S. S. Stratton, D
30. *C. J. King, R
31. *R. C. McEwen, R
32. *A. Pirnie, R

33. *H. W. Robison, R
34. **J. H. Terry, R[1]
35. *J. M. Hanley, D
36. *F. Horton, R
37. *B. B. Conable, Jr., R
38. *J. F. Hastings, R
39. **J. F. Kemp, R
40. *H. P. Smith III, R
41. *T. J. Dulski, D

NORTH CAROLINA
1. *W. B. Jones, D
2. *L. H. Fountain, D
3. *D. N. Henderson, D
4. *N. Galifianakis, D
5. *W. (Vinegar Bend) Mizell, R
6. *R. Preyer, D
7. *A. Lennon, D
8. *E. B. Ruth, D
9. *C. Raper Jonas, R
10. *J. T. Broyhill, R
11. *R. A. Taylor, D

NORTH DAKOTA
1. *M. Andrews, R
2. **A. A. Link, D

OHIO
1. **W. J. Keating, R
2. *D. D. Clancy, R
3. *C. W. Whalen, Jr., R
4. *W. M. McCulloch, R
5. *D. L. Latta, R
6. *W. H. Harsha, R
7. *C. J. Brown, R
8. *J. E. Betts, R
9. *T. L. Ashley, D
10. *C. E. Miller, R
11. *J. W. Stanton, R
12. *S. L. Devine, R
13. *C. A. Mosher, R
14. **J. F. Seiberling, D
15. *C. P. Wylie, R
16. *F. T. Bow, R
17. *J. M. Ashbrook, R
18. *W. Hays, D
19. **C. J. Carney, D[2]
20. **J. V. Stanton, D
21. *L. Stokes, D
22. *C. A. Vanik, D
23. *W. E. Minshall, R
24. **W. E. Powell, R

OKLAHOMA
1. *P. Belcher, R
2. *Ed Edmondson, D
3. *C. Albert, D
4. *T. Steed, D
5. *J. Jarman, D
6. *J. N. (Happy) Camp, R

OREGON
1. *W. Wyatt, R
2. *Al Ullman, D
3. *E. Green, D
4. *J. Dellenback, R

PENNSYLVANIA
1. *W. A. Barrett, D
2. *R. N. C. Nix, D
3. *J. A. Byrne, D
4. *J. Eilberg, D
5. *W. J. Green, D
6. *G. Yatron, D
7. *L. G. Williams, R
8. *E. G. Biester, Jr., R
9. *J. Ware, R[2]
10. *J. M. McDade, R
11. *D. J. Flood, D
12. *J. I. Whalley, R
13. **L. Coughlin, R
14. *W. S. Moorhead, D
15. *F. B. Rooney, D
16. *E. D. Eshleman, R
17. *H. T. Schneebeli, R
18. ***H. J. Heinz III, R
19. *G. A. Goodling, R
20. *J. M. Gaydos, D
21. *J. H. Dent, D
22. *J. P. Saylor, R
23. *A. W. Johnson, R
24. *J. P. Vigorito. D
25. *F. M. Clark. D
26. *T. E. Morgan, D
27. Vacancy

RHODE ISLAND
1. *F. J. St. Germain, D
2. *R. O. Tiernan, D

SOUTH CAROLINA
1. ***M. J. Davis, D
2. **F. Spence, R

3. *Wm. J. B. Dorn, D
4. *J. R. Mann, D
5. *T. S. Gettys, D
6. *J. L. McMillan, D

SOUTH DAKOTA
1. **F. E. Denholm, D
2. **J. Abourezk, D

TENNESSEE
1. *J. H. Quillen, R
2. *J. J. Duncan, R
3. **L. Baker, R
4. *J. L. Evins, D
5. *R. H. Fulton, D
6. *W. R. Anderson, D
7. *R. Blanton, D
8. *Ed Jones, D
9. *D. Kuykendall, R

TEXAS
1. *W. Patman, D
2. *J. Dowdy, D
3. *J. M. Collins, R
4. *R. Roberts, D
5. *E. Cabell, D
6. *O. E. Teague, D
7. **B. Archer, R
8. *B. Eckhardt, D
9. *J. Brooks, D
10. *J. J. Pickle, D
11. *W. R. Poage, D
12. *J. Wright, D
13. *G. Purcell, D
14. *J. Young, D
15. *E. de la Garza, D
16. *R. C. White, D
17. *O. Burleson, D
18. *R. D. Price, R
19. *G. H. Mahon, D
20. *H. B. Gonzalez, D
21. *O. C. Fisher, D
22. *Bob Casey, D
23. *A. Kazen, Jr., D

UTAH
1. **K. G. McKay, D
2. *S. P. Lloyd, R

VERMONT
At-L. Vacancy

VIRGINIA
1. *T. N. Downing, D
2. *G. W. Whitehurst, R
3. *D. E. Satterfield III, D
4. *W. M. Abbitt, D
5. *W. C. (Dan) Daniel, D
6. *R. H. Poff, R
7. **J. K. Robinson, R
8. *W. L. Scott, R
9. *W. C. Wampler, R
10. *J. T. Broyhill, R

WASHINGTON
1. *T. M. Pelly, R
2. *L. Meeds, D
3. *J. B. Hansen, D
4. **M. McCormack, D
5. *T. S. Foley, D
6. *F. V. Hicks, D
7. *B. Adams, D

WEST VIRGINIA
1. *R. H. Mollohan, D
2. *H. O. Staggers, D
3. *J. M. Slack, D
4. *K. Hechler, D
5. *J. Kee, D

WISCONSIN
1. **L. Aspin, D
2. *R. W. Kastenmeier, D
3. *V. W. Thomson, R
4. *C. J. Zablocki, D
5. *H. S. Reuss, D
6. *W. A. Steiger, R
7. *D. R. Obey, D
8. *J. W. Byrnes, R
9. *G. W. Davis, R
10. *A. E. O'Konski, R

WYOMING
At-L. **T. Roncalio, D

PUERTO RICO
Resident Commissioner
*J. L. Córdova

DISTRICT OF COLUMBIA
Delegate
W. E. Fauntroy, D

[1] New district, no incumbent. [2] Seat vacant when elected. Seated in 91st Congress.

THE NEW YORK TIMES

President Embarks On Round of Talks With World Leaders

UPI

UPI

President Nixon engaged in a busy series of discussions with other world leaders in late 1971, partly in preparation for his planned visits to Peking and Moscow in 1972. (Top) Nixon chats with President Tito of Yugoslavia in White House during Communist leader's visit on October 28. (Above) In December, the President discussed the international monetary crisis with President Pompidou of France in the Azores. Meeting led to an announcement on December 14 that U.S. was willing to devalue the dollar. (Left) A conference in Bermuda on December 20–21 with British Prime Minister Heath focused on international diplomatic issues.

(*Continued from page 714*)

carry on the battle aided only by U. S. airpower. If that was the President's plan, insisted these critics, then Americans would have to prepare for a "Thirty Years' War." (See also INDOCHINA WAR.)

International Economics. The costs of 10 years of war in Indochina had already forced the United States to rethink its economic policy. In remarks in Kansas City on July 5, 1971, President Nixon reviewed U. S. aid to Europe and Asia since the end of World War II, then predicted that in 10 to 15 years five great superpowers—the United States, western Europe, the Soviet Union, mainland China, and Japan—would be competing to dominate the world. "It means," he concluded, "that the United States, as compared with that position we found ourselves in immediately after World War II, has a challenge such as we did not even dream of."

The Department of Commerce, meanwhile, predicted that the trade balance of U. S. exports and imports would fall on the negative side for the first time since 1893. Amid these and other discouraging reports, the administration announced a New Economic Policy, which affected both domestic and foreign affairs.

In explaining why it was necessary for his country to place an additional 10% surtax on foreign goods (imposed August 15 and lifted December 20), Secretary of the Treasury John Connally told an international banking conference in Munich that the United States had an "underlying deficit running at $2 to $3 billion a year." "I find it an impressive fact," the secretary went on, "and a depressing fact, that the persistent underlying balance of payments deficit, which causes such concern, is more than covered, year in and year out, by our net military expenditures abroad."

Putting together President Nixon's prediction that the near future would see increasing economic competition among the five superpowers and Secretary Connally's clear warning that the United States could not afford to keep on spending so much to finance the military shields for Europe and Japan, it was apparent that U. S. officials believed that the "postwar era" had at last come to an end, economically as well as politically.

There were other indications that the effort to reopen communications with mainland China was closely related to a long-term new economic policy. In Kansas City, for example, Nixon had said, "The very success of our policy of ending the isolation of mainland China will mean an immense escalation of their economic challenge, not only to us but to others as well." In another speech before the American Legion, the President said that the economic challenge "is far more serious than the challenge that we confronted even in the dark days of Pearl Harbor." Japanese observers seized on this speech as proof that U. S. policy was directed against their country, but the New Economic Policy was aimed at a condition, not at any one nation.

Finance ministers from the industrial nations of western Europe and from Japan met with Secretary Connally in Washington, December 17–18, and negotiated a new currency exchange agreement, involving devaluation of the U. S. dollar by 8.57% as against gold and the revaluation of other currencies. The President then ended the import surtax, but the outlook was for continued controls on the domestic economy and still more changes in international economic policy. (See also INTERNATIONAL FINANCE.)

Middle East Policy. In the Middle East everyone waited. The uneasy truce negotiated in 1970 continued despite threats from Egyptian President Anwar el-Sadat that 1971 was a "year of decision." U. S. Secretary of State Rogers tried to persuade Cairo and Tel Aviv that it was to their mutual advantage to reopen the Suez Canal as part of an interim agreement, but neither side was convinced.

Both Washington and Moscow publicly recognized their mutual interest in preventing a Middle Eastern blow-up, however, and made serious efforts to keep matters under control and to reassure one another. Secretary Rogers, for example, responded to newsmen who asked if it were not true that the Russians were fishing in troubled waters: "People talk about the Russians wanting to fish in troubled waters, but if the waters are too troubled you can't fish in them; you have a typhoon . . . and if there is a major blowup in the area it doesn't benefit anyone." (See also MIDDLE EAST.)

Cold War Realignments. Soviet-U. S. confrontation in Central Europe was considerably eased by a new four-power agreement on the status of Berlin signed on September 3. Ever since the Berlin Blockade in 1948, that city had been the focal point of European Cold War tensions. By the 1971 agreement, Western access rights were guaranteed in writing for the first time. In turn, the Soviet Union was assured that West Germany would not attempt to incorporate West Berlin into the German Federal Republic. Only a few years earlier any such agreement would have been unthinkable. It was another sign that the quarter-century Cold War, at least as world statesmen have known it, was coming to an end.

If that were so, however, the shape of the new world was still far from clear, with traditional alignments shifting. In southern Asia, for example, the United States found itself allied with Communist China in denouncing India's invasion of East Pakistan in December, while the Soviet Union supported India with words and arms. New Delhi's victory reduced Pakistan's territory by eliminating all of East Pakistan, which declared its independence as the new nation of Bangladesh. What new challenge would emerge in the Asian subcontinent and how the major powers would respond to it was very much a subject of international concern at year-end. The world was, as Secretary Rogers said, in its "most fluid state in memory."

(See also DISARMAMENT; UNITED NATIONS.)

LLOYD C. GARDNER, *Rutgers University*

UNIVERSITIES AND COLLEGES

A selected list of accredited junior colleges, senior colleges, and universities in the United States and Canada appears on the following pages.

The information given for each school comprises the following data: its degree-granting status (if it is a senior college or university); the composition of its student body (by sex); the legal controlling agency; and the total enrollment of students of college grade as reported by the registrar (U. S. figures are for 1970–71; Canadian figures are for 1969–70).

All the U. S. institutions listed are recognized by *Accredited Institutions of Higher Education*, published by the American Council on Education. The Canadian institutions listed are accredited by the provinces in which they are located.

See also EDUCATION.

MAJOR UNIVERSITIES AND COLLEGES, U.S. AND CANADA

Note: Symbols and abbreviations that follow the name of each school listed are as follows: *Level of Instruction*—(1) 2-year junior college; (2) senior college granting bachelor's and/or first professional degree; (3) senior college granting master's and/or second professional degree; (4) college or university offering a doctoral program. *Student Body*—(M) men only; (W) women only; (Coed) coeducational; (Coord) separate colleges for men and women. *Control*—(Public) district, municipal, state, or federal; (Private) proprietary, corporation, or church. *Enrollment*—For the United States, all students of college grade for the academic year 1970–1971 excepting correspondence course students. Canadian figures are for 1969–70.

Name and Location	Level of Instruction	Student Body	Control	Enrollment
Abilene Christian College, Abilene, Texas	3	Coed	Pvt-Church of Christ	3,210
Abraham Baldwin Agricultural College, Tifton, Ga.	1	Coed	Public	1,776
Acadia University, Wolfville, Nova Scotia	3	Coed	Pvt-Baptist	2,040
Adams State College, Alamosa, Colo.	3	Coed	Public	2,995
Adelphi University, Garden City, N.Y.	4	Coed	Private	8,134
Adirondack Community College, Glens Falls, N.Y.	1	Coed	Public	1,285
Adrian College, Adrian, Mich.	2	Coed	Pvt-Methodist	1,526
Aeronautics, Academy of, Flushing, N.Y.	1	Coed	Private	1,439
Agnes Scott College, Decatur, Ga.	2	W	Pvt-Presbyterian	694
Agricultural, Mechanical and Normal College, Pine Bluff, Ark.	2	Coed	Public	3,353
Air Force Institute of Technology, Wright-Patterson AFB, Ohio.	4	Coed	Public	620
Akron, University of, Akron, Ohio.	4	Coed	Public	18,467
Alabama, University of, in Birmingham, Ala.	4	Coed	Public	5,839
Alabama, University of, in Huntsville, Ala.	3	Coed	Public	2,603
Alabama, University of, in Tuscaloosa, Ala.	4	Coed	Public	13,364
Alabama Agricultural and Mechanical College, Normal, Ala.	3	Coed	Public	2,129
Alabama State University, Montgomery, Ala.	3	Coed	Public	2,524
Alamance, Technical Institute of, Burlington, N.C.	1	Coed	Public	830
Alaska, University of, College, Alaska (incl. community colleges at Anchorage, Juneau, Kenai, Ketchikan, Kodiak, Palmer, Sitka).	4	Coed	Public	8,776
Alaska Methodist University, Anchorage, Alaska.	3	Coed	Pvt-Methodist	1,086
Albany Junior College, Albany, Ga.	1	Coed	Public	1,265
Albany State College, Albany, Ga.	2	Coed	Public	1,942
Albemarle, College of the, Elizabeth City, N.C.	1	Coed	Public	849
Alberta, University of, Edmonton, Alberta.	4	Coed	Public	17,342
Albion College, Albion, Mich.	2	Coed	Pvt-Methodist	1,826
Albright College, Reading, Pa.	2	Coed	Pvt-Methodist	1,535
Albuquerque, University of, Albuquerque, N. Mex.	2	Coed	Pvt-Roman Catholic	1,563
Alcorn Agricultural & Mechanical College, Lorman, Miss.	2	Coed	Public	2,520
Alderson-Broaddus College, Philippi, W.Va.	2	Coed	Pvt-Baptist	1,024
Alexander City State Junior College, Alexander City, Ala.	1	Coed	Public	1,113
Alfred University, Alfred, N.Y.	4	Coed	Private	2,773
Allan Hancock College, Santa Maria, Calif.	1	Coed	Public	5,830
Allegany Community College, Cumberland, Md.	1	Coed	Public	1,078
Allegheny College, Meadville, Pa.	3	Coed	Pvt-Methodist	1,811
Alma College, Alma, Mich.	2	Coed	Pvt-Presbyterian	1,282
Alpena Community College, Alpena, Mich.	1	Coed	Public	903
Alverno College, Milwaukee, Wis.	2	Coed	Pvt-Roman Catholic	890
Alvin Junior College, Alvin, Texas.	1	Coed	Public	1,471
Amarillo College, Amarillo, Texas.	1	Coed	Public	4,001
American International College, Springfield, Mass.	3	Coed	Private	3,045
American River College, Sacramento, Calif.	1	Coed	Public	14,023
American University, Washington, D.C.	4	Coed	Pvt-Methodist	15,356
Amherst College, Amherst, Mass.	2	Coed	Private	1,238
Anderson College, Anderson, Ind.	2	Coed	Pvt-Church of God	1,802
Anderson College, Anderson, S.C.	1	Coed	Pvt-Baptist	833
Andrews University, Berrien Springs, Mich.	3	Coed	Pvt-Seventh-day Adventist	2,061
Angelina College, Lufkin, Texas.	2	Coed	Public	862
Angelo State College, San Angelo, Texas	1	Coed	Public	3,821
Anne Arundel Community College, Arnold, Md.	1	Coed	Public	2,933
Antelope Valley College, Lancaster, Calif.	1	Coed	Public	3,630
Antioch College, Yellow Springs, Ohio.	3	Coed	Private	2,575
Appalachian State University, Boone, N.C.	3	Coed	Public	7,087
Aquinas College, Grand Rapids, Mich.	3	Coed	Pvt-Roman Catholic	1,413
Arapahoe Community College, Littleton, Colo.	1	Coed	Public	2,207
Arizona, University of, Tucson, Ariz.	4	Coed	Public	26,123
Arizona State University, Tempe, Ariz.	4	Coed	Public	29,826
Arizona Western College, Yuma, Ariz.	1	Coed	Public	3,000
Arkansas, State College of, Conway, Ark.	3	Coed	Public	4,421
Arkansas, University of, Fayetteville, Ark.	4	Coed	Public	17,053
Arkansas Polytechnic College, Russellville, Ark.	2	Coed	Public	2,497
Arkansas State University, State University, Ark.	4	Coed	Public	6,886
Armstrong State College, Savannah, Ga.	2	Coed	Public	2,406
Aroostook State College, Presque Isle, Me.	2	Coed	Public	556
Art Center College of Design, Los Angeles, Calif.	3	Coed	Private	1,125
Art Institute of Chicago, Schools of the, Chicago, Ill.	3	Coed	Private	1,288
Asbury College, Wilmore, Ky.	2	Coed	Private	1,044
Asheville-Buncombe Technical Institute, Asheville, N.C.	1	Coed	Public	1,024
Ashland College, Ashland, Ohio.	3	Coed	Pvt-Brethren	2,976
Assumption College, Worcester, Mass.	3	Coed	Pvt-Roman Catholic	1,578
Athens College, Athens, Ala.	2	Coed	Pvt-Methodist	1,077
Atlanta University, Atlanta, Ga.	4	Coed	Private	978
Atlantic Christian College, Wilson, N.C.	2	Coed	Pvt-Disciples of Christ	1,747
Atlantic Community College, Mays Landing, N.J.	1	Coed	Public	2,387
Atlantic Union College, South Lancaster, Mass.	3	Coed	Pvt-Seventh-day Adventist	708
Auburn University, Auburn, Ala.	4	Coed	Public	2,914
Auburn Community College, Auburn, N.Y.	1	Coed	Public	15,217
Augsburg College, Minneapolis, Minn.	2	Coed	Pvt-Lutheran	1,697
Augusta College, Augusta, Ga.	3	Coed	Public	2,877
Augustana College, Rock Island, Ill.	2	Coed	Pvt-Lutheran	2,124
Augustana College, Sioux Falls, S.Dak.	3	Coed	Pvt-Lutheran	2,178
Aurora College, Aurora, Ill.	2	Coed	Pvt-Advent Christian	1,261
Austin College, Sherman, Texas.	3	Coed	Pvt-Presbyterian	1,102
Austin Peay State University, Clarksville, Tenn.	3	Coed	Public	3,574
Austin State Junior College, Austin, Minn.	1	Coed	Public	975
Averett College, Danville, Va.	2	Coed	Pvt-Baptist	816
Azusa Pacific College, Azusa, Calif.	3	Coed	Private	970
Babson College, Babson Park, Mass.	3	Coed	Private	1,599
Baker University, Baldwin City, Kans.	2	Coed	Pvt-Methodist	848
Bakersfield College, Bakersfield, Calif.	1	Coed	Public	10,313
Baldwin-Wallace College, Berea, Ohio.	2	Coed	Pvt-Methodist	3,135
Ball State University, Muncie, Ind.	4	Coed	Public	17,837
Baltimore, Community College of, Baltimore, Md.	1	Coed	Public	6,371
Bank Street College of Education, New York, N.Y.	3	Coed	Private	977
Baptist College at Charleston, S.C.	2	Coed	Pvt-Baptist	1,839
Bard College, Annandale-on-Hudson, N.Y.	2	Coed	Private	712
Barry College, Miami, Fla.	2	Coed	Pvt-Roman Catholic	1,260
Barstow College, Barstow, Calif.	1	Coed	Public	1,507

Name and Location	Level of Instruction	Student Body	Control	Enrollment
Bates College, Lewiston, Me.	2	Coed	Private	1,157
Baylor University, Waco, Texas	4	Coed	Pvt-Baptist	6,977
Beaver College, Glenside, Pa.	2	W	Pvt-Presbyterian	768
Bee County College, Beeville, Texas	1	Coed	Public	1,119
Bellarmine-Ursuline College, Louisville, Ky.	2	Coed	Pvt-Roman Catholic	1,612
Belleville Area College, Belleville, Ill.	1	Coed	Public	3,944
Bellevue Community College, Bellevue, Wash.	1	Coed	Public	3,430
Belmont Abbey College, Belmont, N.C.	2	Coed	Pvt-Roman Catholic	679
Belmont College, Nashville, Tenn.	2	Coed	Pvt-Baptist	921
Beloit College, Beloit, Wis.	2	Coed	Private	1,782
Bemidji State College, Bemidji, Minn.	3	Coed	Public	5,100
Benedict College, Columbia, S.C.	2	Coed	Pvt-Baptist	1,340
Benedictine College, The, Atchison, Kans.	2	Coed	Pvt-Roman Catholic	1,399
Bentley College, Waltham, Mass.	2	Coed	Private	3,437
Berea College, Berea, Ky.	2	Coed	Private	1,400
Berkeley-Charleston-Dorchester Technical Education Center, North Charleston, S.C.	1	Coed	Public	1,644
Berkshire Community College, Pittsfield, Mass.	1	Coed	Public	1,935
Berry College, Mount Berry, Ga.	2	Coed	Private	1,044
Bethany College, Lindsborg, Kans.	2	Coed	Pvt-Lutheran	670
Bethany College, Bethany, W.Va.	2	Coed	Pvt-Disciples of Christ	1,089
Bethany Nazarene College, Bethany, Okla.	3	Coed	Pvt-Nazarene	1,720
Bethel College, St. Paul, Minn.	2	Coed	Pvt-Baptist	1,104
Bethune-Cookman College, Daytona Beach, Fla.	2	Coed	Pvt-Methodist	1,065
Big Bend Community College, Moses Lake, Wash.	1	Coed	Public	835
Biola College, La Mirada, Calif.	3	Coed	Private	1,571
Birmingham-Southern College, Birmingham, Ala.	2	Coed	Pvt-Methodist	1,040
Bishop College, Dallas, Texas	2	Coed	Pvt-Baptist	1,623
Bishop's University, Lennoxville, Quebec	3	Coed	Pvt-Anglican	1,025
Bismarck Junior College, Bismarck, N.Dak.	1	Coed	Public	1,270
Black Hawk College, Moline, Ill.	1	Coed	Public	3,762
Black Hills State College, Spearfish, S.Dak.	3	Coed	Public	2,812
Blackburn College, Carlinville, Ill.	2	Coed	Private	589
Blinn College, Brenham, Texas	1	Coed	Public	1,700
Bloomfield College, Bloomfield, N.J.	2	Coed	Pvt-Presbyterian	1,619
Bloomsburg State College, Bloomsburg, Pa.	3	Coed	Public	4,603
Blue Mountain Community College, Pendleton, Oreg	1	Coed	Public	1,013
Blue Ridge Community College, Weyers Cave, Va.	1	Coed	Public	1,315
Bluefield State College, Bluefield, W.Va.	2	Coed	Public	1,316
Bluffton College, Bluffton, Ohio	2	Coed	Pvt-Mennonite	728
Boise State College, Boise, Idaho	3	Coed	Public	7,921
Boston College, Chestnut Hill, Mass.	4	Coed	Pvt-Roman Catholic	10,956
Boston State College, Boston, Mass.	3	Coed	Public	8,500
Boston University, Boston, Mass.	4	Coed	Private	25,124
Bowdoin College, Brunswick, Me.	2	Coed	Private	980
Bowie State College, Bowie, Md.	3	Coed	Public	2,259
Bowling Green State University, Bowling Green, Ohio	4	Coed	Public	16,186
Bradley University, Peoria, Ill.	3	Coed	Private	5,789
Brandeis University, Waltham, Mass.	4	Coed	Private	2,940
Brandon University, Brandon, Manitoba	3	Coed	Public	1,218
Brazosport Junior College, Lake Jackson, Texas	1	Coed	Public	1,290
Brescia College, Owensboro, Ky.	2	Coed	Pvt-Roman Catholic	1,017
Brevard Community College, Cocoa, Fla.	1	Coed	Public	6,141
Briar Cliff College, Sioux City, Iowa	2	Coed	Pvt-Roman Catholic	1,131
Bridgeport, University of, Bridgeport, Conn.	3	Coed	Private	8,944
Bridgewater College, Bridgewater, Va.	2	Coed	Pvt-Brethren	849
Bridgewater State College, Bridgewater, Mass.	3	Coed	Public	5,392
Brigham Young University, Provo, Utah	4	Coed	Pvt-Latter-day Saints	26,626
Bristol Community College, Fall River, Mass.	1	Coed	Public	2,750
British Columbia, University of, Vancouver, B.C.	4	Coed	Public	19,580
Brock University, St. Catharines, Ontario	3	Coed	Public	1,651
Brooklyn, Polytechnic Institute of, Brooklyn, N.Y.	4	Coed	Private	4,504
Brooks Institute, Santa Barbara, Calif.	2	Coed	Private	734
Broome Community College, Binghamton, N.Y.	1	Coed	Public	4,197
Broward Community College, Fort Lauderdale, Fla.	1	Coed	Public	7,077
Brown University, Providence, R.I.	4	Coed	Private	5,733
Brunswick College, Brunswick, Ga.	1	Coed	Public	903
Bryant College, Providence, R.I.	3	Coed	Private	3,429
Bryn Mawr College, Bryn Mawr, Pa.	4	W	Private	1,367
Bucknell University, Lewisburg, Pa.	3	Coed	Private	2,933
Bucks County Community College, Newtown, Pa.	1	Coed	Public	4,552
Buena Vista College, Storm Lake, Iowa	2	Coed	Pvt-Presbyterian	948
Butler County Community College, Butler, Pa.	1	Coed	Public	1,166
Butler County Community Junior College, El Dorado, Kans.	1	Coed	Public	1,721
Butler University, Indianapolis, Ind.	3	Coed	Private	4,403
Cabrillo College, Aptos, Calif.	1	Coed	Public	6,076
Caldwell College, Caldwell, N.J.	2	W	Pvt-Roman Catholic	859
Caldwell Community College & Technical Institute, Lenoir, N.C.	1	Coed	Public	676
Calgary, University of, Calgary, Alberta	4	Coed	Public	7,962
California, University of:				147,279
Berkeley	4	Coed	Public	28,528
Davis	4	Coed	Public	13,319
Irvine (includes California College of Medicine)	4	Coed	Public	6,661
Los Angeles	4	Coed	Public	29,093
Riverside	3	Coed	Public	5,989
San Diego	4	Coed	Public	5,546
San Francisco Art Institute	3	Coed	Public	935
Santa Barbara	3	Coed	Public	13,644
Santa Cruz	3	Coed	Public	3,772
California Baptist College, Riverside, Calif.	2	Coed	Pvt-Baptist	690
California College of Arts & Crafts, Oakland, Calif.	3	Coed	Private	1,559
California Institute of Technology, Pasadena, Calif.	4	Coed	Private	1,504
California Institute of the Arts, Burbank, Calif.	2	Coed	Private	797
California Lutheran College, Thousand Oaks, Calif.	2	Coed	Pvt-Lutheran	1,195
California State College, California, Pa.	3	Coed	Public	6,622
California State College at Bakersfield, Calif.	2	Coed	Public	945
California State College at Dominguez Hills, Calif.	3	Coed	Public	2,600
California State College at Fullerton, Calif.	3	Coed	Public	15,550
California State College at Hayward, Calif.	3	Coed	Public	15,600
California State College at Long Beach, Calif.	3	Coed	Public	25,600
California State College at Los Angeles, Calif.	3	Coed	Public	25,320
California State College at San Bernardino, Calif.	2	Coed	Public	2,800
California State Polytechnic College, Kellogg-Voorhis, Pomona, Calif.	3	Coed	Public	8,572
California State Polytechnic College, San Luis Obispo, Calif.	3	Coed	Public	12,373
Calvin College, Grand Rapids, Mich.	3	Coed	Pvt-Christian Reformed	3,437
Campbell College, Buies Creek, N.C.	2	Coed	Pvt-Baptist	2,207
Campbellsville College, Campbellsville, Ky.	2	Coed	Pvt-Baptist	914
Cañada College, Redwood City, Calif.	1	Coed	Public	6,304
Canal Zone College, Balboa, C.Z.	1	Coed	Public	1,244
Canisius College, Buffalo, N.Y.	2	Coed	Pvt-Roman Catholic	3,912
Cape Cod Community College, West Barnstable, Mass.	1	Coed	Public	1,626
Capital University, Columbus, Ohio	2	Coed	Pvt-Lutheran	2,045
Cardinal Stritch College, Milwaukee, Wis.	2	Coed	Pvt-Roman Catholic	662
Carleton College, Northfield, Minn.	2	Coed	Private	1,521
Carleton University, Ottawa, Ontario	4	Coed	Public	7,139
Carlow College, Pittsburgh, Pa.	2	W	Pvt-Roman Catholic	1,006
Carnegie-Mellon University, Pittsburgh, Pa.	4	Coed	Private	4,963
Carroll College, Helena, Mont.	2	Coed	Pvt-Roman Catholic	1,250
Carroll College, Waukesha, Wis.	2	Coed	Pvt-Presbyterian	1,686
Carson-Newman College, Jefferson City, Tenn.	2	Coed	Pvt-Baptist	1,849
Carthage College, Kenosha, Wis.	2	Coed	Pvt-Lutheran	1,460
Case Western Reserve University, Cleveland, Ohio.	4	Coed	Private	9,371
Casper College, Casper, Wyo.	1	Coed	Public	2,583
Castleton State College, Castleton, Vt.	2	Coed	Public	1,268

Name and Location	Level of Instruction	Student Body	Control	Enrollment
Catawba College, Salisbury, N.C.	2	Coed	Pvt-United Church of Christ	1,099
Catawba Valley Technical Institute, Hickory, N.C.	1	Coed	Public	1,017
Catholic University of America, Washington, D.C.	4	Coed	Pvt-Roman Catholic	6,112
Catholic University of Puerto Rico, Ponce, P.R.	3	Coed	Pvt-Roman Catholic	7,140
Catonsville Community College, Catonsville, Md.	1	Coed	Public	5,550
Cedar Crest College, Allentown, Pa.	2	W	Pvt-Church of Christ	795
Centenary College, Shreveport, La.	2	Coed	Pvt-Methodist	932
Central College, Pella, Iowa	2	Coed	Pvt-Episcopal	1,226
Central Connecticut State College, New Britain, Conn.	3	Coed	Public	12,496
Central Florida Community College, Ocala, Fla.	1	Coed	Public	1,055
Central Methodist College, Fayette, Mo.	2	Coed	Pvt-Methodist	804
Central Michigan University, Mt. Pleasant, Mich.	3	Coed	Public	15,812
Central Missouri State College, Warrensburg, Mo.	3	Coed	Public	12,610
Central Oregon Community College, Bend, Oreg.	1	Coed	Public	911
Central Piedmont Community College, Charlotte, N.C.	1	Coed	Public	8,035
Central State University, Edmond, Okla.	3	Coed	Public	10,608
Central State University, Wilberforce, Ohio	2	Coed	Public	2,554
Central Virginia Community College, Lynchburg, Va.	1	Coed	Public	3,220
Central Washington State College, Ellensburg, Wash.	3	Coed	Public	1,664
Central Y.M.C.A. Community College, Chicago, Ill.	1	Coed	Public	10,962
Centralia College, Centralia, Wash.	1	Coed	Public	3,895
Centre College of Kentucky, Danville, Ky.	2	Coed	Pvt-Presbyterian	2,704
Cerritos College, Norwalk, Calif.	1	Coed	Public	774
Chabot College, Hayward, Calif.	1	Coed	Public	15,583
Chadron State College, Chadron, Nebr.	2	Coed	Public	12,157
Chaffey College, Alta Loma, Calif.	1	Coed	Public	2,469
Chaminade College of Honolulu, Hawaii	2	Coed	Pvt-Roman Catholic	7,565
Chapman College, Orange, Calif.	3	Coed	Pvt-Disciples of Christ	1,480
Charles County Community College, La Plata, Md.	1	Coed	Public	4,501
Charleston, College of, Charleston, S.C.	2	Coed	Public	1,057
Chattanooga State Technical Institute, Chattanooga, Tenn.	1	Coed	Public	878
Chestnut Hill College, Philadelphia, Pa.	2	W	Pvt-Roman Catholic	1,180
Cheyney State College, Cheyney, Pa.	2	Coed	Public	1,120
Chicago, University of, Chicago, Ill.	4	Coed	Private	2,046
Chicago, City Colleges of, Chicago, Ill.:		Coed	Public	39,472
Amundsen-Mayfair College, Chicago	1	Coed	Public	3,593
Kennedy-King College, Chicago	1	Coed	Public	5,295
Loop College, Chicago	1	Coed	Public	8,174
Malcolm X College, Chicago	1	Coed	Public	3,879
Olive-Harvey College, Chicago	1	Coed	Public	5,441
Southwest College, Chicago	1	Coed	Public	4,940
Wright College, Chicago	1	Coed	Public	8,204
Chicago State College, Chicago, Ill.	3	Coed	Public	8,894
Chico State College, Chico, Calif.	3	Coed	Public	6,507
Chipola Junior College, Marianna, Fla.	1	Coed	Public	13,168
Chowan College, Murfreesboro, N.C.	1	Coed	Pvt-Baptist	1,151
Christian Brothers College, Memphis, Tenn.	2	Coed	Pvt-Roman Catholic	1,483
Christopher Newport College, Newport News, Va.	2	Coed	Private	960
Cincinnati, University of, Cincinnati, Ohio	4	Coed	Private	32,454
Raymond Walters General & Technical College, Blue Ash.		Coed	Public	1,768
Cisco Junior College, Cisco, Texas	1	Coed	Public	1,539
Citadel, The, Charleston, S.C.	3	M	Public	1,170
Citrus College, Azusa, Calif.	1	Coed	Public	2,666
Claflin College, Orangeburg, S.C.	2	Coed	Pvt-Methodist	7,408
Claremont Men's College, Claremont, Calif.	2	M	Private	775
Claremont University Center, Claremont, Calif.	4	Coed	Private	833
Clarion State College, Clarion, Pa.	3	Coed	Public	841
Clark College, Atlanta, Ga.	2	Coed	Pvt-Methodist	4,166
Clark College, Vancouver, Wash.	1	Coed	Public	4,649
Clark University, Worcester, Mass.	4	Coed	Private	3,212
Clarke College, Dubuque, Iowa	2	W	Pvt-Roman Catholic	802
Clarkson College of Technology, Potsdam, N.Y.	4	Coed	Private	2,688
Clatsop Community College, Astoria, Oreg.	1	Coed	Public	1,377
Clemson University, Clemson, S.C.	4	Coed	Public	7,888
Cleveland Institute of Art, Cleveland, Ohio	2	Coed	Private	849
Cleveland State Community College, Cleveland, Tenn.	1	Coed	Public	1,922
Cleveland State University, Cleveland, Ohio	3	Coed	Public	14,255
Cochise College, Douglas, Ariz.	1	Coed	Public	1,767
Coe College, Cedar Rapids, Iowa	2	Coed	Pvt-Presbyterian	1,108
Colby College, Waterville, Me.	2	Coed	Private	1,562
Colgate University, Hamilton, N.Y.	3	Coed	Private	2,256
Colorado, University of, Boulder, Colo	4	Coed	Public	21,482
Colorado Springs.	2	Coed	Public	2,312
Denver.	3	Coed	Public	6,987
Colorado College, Colorado Springs, Colo.	2	Coed	Private	1,726
Colorado School of Mines, Golden, Colo.	4	Coed	Public	1,727
Colorado State University, Fort Collins, Colo.	4	Coed	Public	17,045
Columbia Basin College, Pasco, Wash.	1	Coed	Public	3,762
Columbia State Community College, Columbia, S.C.	1	Coed	Public	892
Columbia Union College, Takoma Park, Md.	2	Coed	Pvt-Methodist	1,442
Columbia University, New York, N.Y.	4	Coed	Pvt-Seventh-day Adventist	914
Barnard College, New York.	2	W	Private	15,920
Teachers College, New York.	4	Coed	Private	1,949
Columbus College, Columbus, Ga.	2	Coed	Public	5,280
Community College of Allegheny County, Pittsburgh, Pa.:				3,241
Allegheny Campus	1	Coed	Public	4,602
Boyce Campus	1	Coed	Public	3,697
Community College of Baltimore, Md.	1	Coed	Public	6,371
Community College of Delaware County, Media, Pa.	1	Coed	Public	2,453
Community College of Philadelphia, Pa.	1	Coed	Public	5,652
Compton College, Compton, Calif.	1	Coed	Public	6,045
Concord College, Athens, W. Va.	2	Coed	Public	1,980
Concordia College, Moorhead, Minn.	2	Coed	Pvt-Lutheran	2,360
Concordia College, St. Paul, Minn.	2	Coed	Pvt-Lutheran	810
Concordia Teachers College, River Forest, Ill	3	Coed	Pvt-Lutheran	1,529
Concordia Teachers College, Seward, Nebr.	3	Coed	Pvt-Lutheran	1,670
Connecticut, University of, Storrs, Conn.	4	Coed	Public	20,028
Connecticut College, New London, Conn.	3	Coed	Private	1,767
Connors State College, Warner, Okla.	1	Coed	Public	762
Contra Costa College, San Pablo, Calif.	1	Coed	Public	6,417
Converse College, Spartanburg, S.C.	3	W	Private	774
Cooke County Junior College, Gainesville, Texas.	1	Coed	Public	1,581
Cooper Union, New York, N.Y.	2	Coed	Private	1,123
Copiah-Lincoln Junior College, Wesson, Miss.	1	Coed	Public	900
Coppin State College, Baltimore, Md.	2	Coed	Public	1,811
Cornell College, Mount Vernon, Iowa	2	Coed	Pvt-Methodist	938
Cornell University, Ithaca, N.Y.	4	Coed	Private	19,600
Corning Community College, Corning, N.Y.	1	Coed	Public	2,820
Corpus Christi, University of, Corpus Christi, Texas.	2	Coed	Pvt-Baptist	611
Creighton University, Omaha, Nebr.	4	Coed	Pvt-Roman Catholic	4,128
Cuesta College, San Luis Obispo, Calif.	1	Coed	Public	4,111
Culver-Stockton College, Canton, Mo.	2	Coed	Pvt-Disciples of Christ	782
Cumberland College, Williamsburg, Ky.	2	Coed	Pvt-Baptist	1,857
Cumberland County College, Vineland, N.J.	1	Coed	Public	1,577
Curry College, Milton, Mass.	2	Coed	Private	931
Cuyahoga Community College—Metropolitan Campus, Cleveland, Ohio.	1	Coed	Public	10,446
Cuyahoga Community College—Western Campus, Parma Heights, Ohio.	1	Coed	Public	5,862
Cypress College, Cypress, Calif.	1	Coed	Public	6,765
Dakota State College, Madison, S. Dak.	2	Coed	Public	1,334
Dakota Wesleyan University, Mitchell, S.Dak.	2	Coed	Pvt-Methodist	609
Dalhousie University, Halifax, Nova Scotia.	4	Coed	Private	4,831
Dallas, University of, Dallas, Texas.	3	Coed	Pvt-Roman Catholic	1,359
Dallas Baptist College, Dallas, Texas.	2	Coed	Pvt-Baptist	1,451

Name and Location	Level of Instruction	Student Body	Control	Enrollment
Dalton Junior College, Dalton, Ga.	1	Coed	Public	961
Dana College, Blair, Nebr.	2	Coed	Pvt-Lutheran	962
Danville Community College, Danville, Va.	1	Coed	Public	1,664
Danville Junior College, Danville, Ill.	1	Coed	Public	1,703
Dartmouth College, Hanover, N.H.	4	Coed	Private	3,928
David Lipscomb College, Nashville, Tenn.	2	Coed	Pvt-Church of Christ	2,320
Davidson College, Davidson, N.C.	2	M	Pvt-Presbyterian	1,053
Davidson County Community College, Lexington, N.C.	1	Coed	Public	4,488
Dayton, University of, Dayton, Ohio	4	Coed	Pvt-Roman Catholic	9,120
Daytona Beach Community College, Daytona Beach, Fla.	1	Coed	Public	2,478
Dean Junior College, Franklin, Mass.	1	Coed	Private	947
De Anza College, Cupertino, Calif.	1	Coed	Public	5,171
Defiance College, Defiance, Ohio	2	Coed	Pvt-Church of Christ	1,137
DeKalb College,Clarkston, Ga.	1	Coed	Public	5,357
Delaware, University of, Newark, Del.	4	Coed	Public	15,730
Delaware State College, Dover, Del.	2	Coed	Public	1,393
Delaware Valley College of Science & Agriculture, Doylestown, Pa.	2	Coed	Private	1,278
Del Mar College, Corpus Christi, Texas.	1	Coed	Public	5,523
Delta College, University Center, Mich.	1	Coed	Public	6,004
Delta State College, Cleveland, Miss.	3	Coed	Public	3,482
Denison University, Granville, Ohio.	2	Coed	Private	2,170
Denver, University of, Denver, Colo.	4	Coed	Pvt-Baptist	9,350
DePaul University, Chicago, Ill.	4	Coed	Pvt-Roman Catholic	9,194
DePauw University, Greencastle, Ind.	2	Coed	Pvt-Methodist	2,370
Desert, College of the, Palm Desert, Calif.	1	Coed	Public	3,421
Detroit, University of, Detroit, Mich.	4	Coed	Pvt-Roman Catholic	9,638
Detroit Institute of Technology, Detroit, Mich.	2	Coed	Private	1,154
Diablo Valley College, Pleasant Hill, Calif.	1	Coed	Public	12,160
Dickinson College, Carlisle, Pa.	2	Coed	Pvt-Methodist	1,642
Dickinson State College, Dickinson, N.Dak.	2	Coed	Public	1,676
Dillard University, New Orleans, La.	2	Coed	Private	968
District of Columbia Teachers College, Washington, D.C.	2	Coed	Public	2,782
Dixie College, St. George, Utah.	1	Coed	Public	1,283
Doane College, Crete, Nebr.	2	Coed	Pvt-United Church	721
Dodge City Community Junior College, Dodge City, Kans.	1	Coed	Public	780
Dominican College, Racine, Wis.	2	Coed	Private	828
Dominican College of San Rafael, San Rafael, Calif.	3	Coed	Pvt-Roman Catholic	717
Donnelly College, Kansas City, Kans.	1	Coed	Pvt-Roman Catholic	742
Dordt College, Sioux Center, Iowa.	2	Coed	Pvt-Christian Reformed	932
Dowling College, Oakdale, N.Y.	2	Coed	Private	1,800
Drake University, Des Moines, Iowa.	4	Coed	Private	7,586
Drew University, Madison, N.J.	4	Coed	Pvt-Methodist	1,556
Drexel University, Philadelphia, Pa.	4	Coed	Private	8,894
Drury College, Springfield, Mo.	2	Coed	Pvt-Church of Christ	2,390
Dubuque, University of, Dubuque, Iowa.	3	Coed	Pvt-Presbyterian	1,070
Duke University, Durham, N.C. (incl. Trinity College & Woman's College)	4	Coord	Pvt-Methodist	8,061
DuPage, College of Glen Ellyn, Ill.	1	Coed	Public	8,213
Duquesne University, Pittsburgh, Pa.	4	Coed	Pvt-Roman Catholic	8,080
Dutchess Community College, Poughkeepsie, N.Y.	1	W	Public	4,401
D'Youville College, Buffalo, N.Y.	2	Coed	Pvt-Roman Catholic	1,187
Earlham College, Richmond, Ind.	2	Coed	Pvt-Friends	1,972
East Carolina University, Greenville, N.C.	3	Coed	Public	11,615
East Central Junior College, Decatur, Miss.	1	Coed	Public	662
East Central State College, Ada, Okla.	3	Coed	Public	2,914
East Los Angeles College, Los Angeles, Calif.	1	Coed	Public	13,606
East Mississippi Junior College, Scooba, Miss.	1	Coed	Public	1,032
East Stroudsburg State College, East Stroudsburg, Pa.	3	Coed	Public	3,362
East Tennessee State University, Johnson City, Tenn.	3	Coed	Public	9,776
East Texas Baptist College, Marshall, Texas.	2	Coed	Pvt-Baptist	756
East Texas State University, Commerce, Texas.	3	Coed	Public	9,471
Eastern Arizona College, Thatcher, Ariz.	1	Coed	Public	1,736
Eastern Connecticut State College, Willimantic, Conn.	3	Coed	Public	2,022
Eastern Illinois University, Charleston, Ill.	3	Coed	Public	8,903
Eastern Iowa Community College, Muscatine, Iowa.	1	Coed	Public	744
Eastern Kentucky University, Richmond, Ky.	3	Coed	Public	10,699
Eastern Mennonite College, Harrisonburg, Va.	2	Coed	Pvt-Mennonite	995
Eastern Michigan University, Ypsilanti, Mich.	3	Coed	Public	22,619
Eastern Montana College, Billings, Mont.	3	Coed	Public	4,224
Eastern Nazarene College, Quincy, Mass.	3	Coed	Pvt-Nazarene	851
Eastern New Mexico University, Portales, N.Mex.	3	Coed	Public	6,168
Eastern Oklahoma State College, Wilburton, Okla.	1	Coed	Public	1,336
Eastern Oregon College, La Grande, Oreg.	3	Coed	Public	1,717
Eastern Utah, College of, Price, Utah.	1	Coed	Public	750
Eastern Washington State College, Cheney, Wash.	3	Coed	Public	7,000
Edgecliff College, Edgecliff, Ohio.	2	Coed	Pvt-Roman Catholic	821
Edinboro State College, Edinboro, Pa.	3	Coed	Public	6,851
Edison Junior College, Fort Myers, Fla.	1	Coed	Public	1,427
El Camino College, Torrance, Calif.	1	Coed	Public	19,377
El Centro College, Dallas, Texas.	1	Coed	Public	6,703
Elgin Community College, Elgin, Ill.	1	Coed	Public	2,509
Elizabeth City State University, Elizabeth City, N.C.	2	Coed	Public	1,104
Elizabethtown College, Elizabethtown, Pa.	2	Coed	Pvt-Brethren	1,707
Ellsworth Community College, Iowa Falls, Iowa.	1	Coed	Public	1,133
Elmhurst College, Elmhurst, Ill.	2	Coed	Private	2,896
Elmira College, Elmira, N.Y.	2	Coed	Pvt-Church of Christ	2,903
Elon College, Elon College, N.C.	2	Coed	Pvt-Church of Christ	1,715
Embry-Riddle Aeronautical Institute, Daytona Beach, Fla.	1	Coed	Private	1,889
Emerson College, Boston, Mass.	2	Coed	Private	1,724
Emmanuel College, Boston, Mass.	3	W	Pvt-Roman Catholic	1,449
Emory University, Atlanta, Ga.	4	Coed	Pvt-Methodist	5,126
Emporia, College of, Emporia, Kans	2	Coed	Pvt-Presbyterian	858
Endicott Junior College, Beverly, Mass.	1	W	Private	836
Enterprise State Junior College, Enterprise, Ala.	1	Coed	Public	1,389
Erskine College, Due West, S.C.	2	Coed	Pvt-Presbyterian	772
Essex Community College, Baltimore, Md.	1	Coed	Public	4,142
Evangel College, Springfield, Mo.	2	Coed	Pvt-Assemblies of God	1,120
Evansville, University of, Evansville, Ind.	3	Coed	Pvt-Methodist	5,373
Everett Community College, Everett, Wash.	1	Coed	Public	4,974
Fairfield University, Fairfield, Conn.	3	Coed	Pvt-Roman Catholic	3,612
Fairleigh Dickinson University, Rutherford, Teaneck, Madison, N.J.	4	Coed	Private	19,953
Fairmont State College, Fairmont, W.Va.	3	Coed	Public	3,551
Fashion Institute of Technology, New York, N.Y.	1	Coed	Public	5,207
Fayetteville State College, Fayetteville, N.C.	2	Coed	Public	1,419
Fayetteville Technical Institute, Fayetteville, N.C.	1	Coed	Public	886
Ferris State College, Big Rapids, Mich.	3	Coed	Public	9,057
Ferrum Junior College, Ferrum, Va.	1	Coed	Pvt-Methodist	1,226
Findlay College, Findlay, Ohio.	2	Coed	Pvt-Church of God	1,258
Fisk University, Nashville, Tenn.	3	Coed	Private	1,256
Fitchburg State College, Fitchburg, Mass.	3	Coed	Public	4,548
Flathead Valley Community College, Kalispell, Mont.	1	Coed	Public	1,140
Florence State University, Florence, Ala.	3	Coed	Public	2,844
Florida, University of, Gainesville, Fla.	4	Coed	Public	23,958
Florida Agricultural & Mechanical University, Tallahassee, Fla.	3	Coed	Public	5,024
Florida Atlantic University, Boca Raton, Fla.	3	Coed	Public	7,072
Florida Institute of Technology, Melbourne, Fla.	3	Coed	Private	1,971
Florida Junior College at Jacksonville, Fla.	1	Coed	Public	6,660
Florida Keys Community College, Key West, Fla.	1	Coed	Public	969
Florida Memorial College, Miami, Fla.	2	Coed	Pvt-Baptist	777
Florida Presbyterian College, St. Petersburg, Fla.	2	Coed	Pvt-Presbyterian	1,050
Florida Southern College, Lakeland, Fla.	2	Coed	Pvt-Methodist	1,468
Florida State University, Tallahassee, Fla.	4	Coed	Public	17,252
Florida Technological University, Orlando, Fla.	3	Coed	Public	4,906
Fontbonne College, St. Louis, Mo.	2	Coed	Pvt-Roman Catholic	778

Name and Location	Level of Instruction	Student Body	Control	Enrollment
Foothill College, Los Altos Hills, Calif.	4	Coed	Public	5,459
Fordham University, Bronx, N.Y.	4	Coed	Pvt-Roman Catholic	12,591
Forsyth Technical Institute, Winston-Salem, N.C.	1	Coed	Public	966
Fort Hays Kansas State College, Hays, Kans.	3	Coed	Public	5,442
Fort Lewis College, Durango, Colo.	2	Coed	Public	2,122
Fort Valley State College, Fort Valley, Ga.	3	Coed	Public	2,338
Framingham State College, Framingham, Mass.	3	Coed	Public	4,222
Frank Phillips College, Borger, Texas.	1	Coed	Public	635
Franklin & Marshall College, Lancaster, Pa	3	Coed	Pvt-Church of Christ	2,797
Franklin College of Indiana, Franklin, Ind.	3	Coed	Pvt-Baptist	779
Franklin Institute of Boston, Boston, Mass.	1	Coed	Private	1,363
Franklin Pierce College, Rindge, N.H.	2	Coed	Private	2,706
Freed-Hardeman College, Henderson, Tenn.	2	Coed	Pvt-Church of Christ	742
Fresno City College, Fresno, Calif.	1	Coed	Public	12,658
Fresno State College, Fresno, Calif.	4	Coed	Public	16,700
Friends University, Wichita, Kans.	3	Coed	Pvt-Friends	1,005
Frostburg State College, Frostburg, Md.	3	Coed	Public	2,331
Fullerton Junior College, Fullerton, Calif.	1	Coed	Public	14,327
Fulton-Montgomery Community College, Johnstown, N.Y.	1	Coed	Public	1,391
Furman University, Greenville, S.C.	3	Coed	Pvt-Baptist	2,234
Gadsden State Junior College, Gadsden, Ala.	1	Coed	Public	2,727
Gainesville Junior College, Gainesville, Ga.	1	Coed	Public	953
Gallaudet College, Washington, D.C.	3	Coed	Private	820
Galveston College, Galveston, Texas	1	Coed	Public	1,106
Gannon College, Erie, Pa.	3	Coed	Pvt-Roman Catholic	3,869
Gardner-Webb College, Boiling Springs, N.C.	2	Coed	Pvt-Baptist	1,528
Gaston College, Dallas, N.C.	1	Coed	Public	2,052
Gavilan College, Gilroy, Calif.	1	Coed	Public	1,997
General Motors Institute, Flint, Mich.	3	Coed	Private	3,075
Genesee Community College, Flint, Mich.	1	Coed	Public	8,659
Genesee Community College, Batavia, N.Y.	1	Coed	Public	1,742
Geneva College, Beaver Falls, Pa.	3	Coed	Pvt-Presbyterian	1,636
George C. Wallace State Technical Junior College, Dothan, Ala.	1	Coed	Public	1,027
George Peabody College for Teachers, Nashville, Tenn.	4	Coed	Private	1,980
George Washington University, Washington, D.C.	4	Coed	Private	21,480
George Williams College, Downers Grove, Ill.	3	Coed	Private	798
Georgetown College, Georgetown, Ky.	3	Coed	Pvt-Baptist	1,425
Georgetown University, Washington, D.C.	4	Coed	Pvt-Roman Catholic	8,047
Georgia, University of, Athens, Ga.	4	Coed	Public	21,181
Georgia College at Milledgeville, Milledgeville, Ga.	3	Coed	Public	1,922
Georgia Institute of Technology, Atlanta, Ga.	4	Coed	Public	8,292
Southern Technical Institute, Marietta, Ga.	2	Coed	Public	1,627
Georgia Southern College, Statesboro, Ga.	3	Coed	Public	5,719
Georgia Southwestern College, Americus, Ga.	2	Coed	Public	2,416
Georgia State University, Atlanta, Ga.	4	Coed	Public	14,521
Georgian Court College, Lakewood, N.J.	3	W	Pvt-Roman Catholic	727
Gettysburg College, Gettysburg, Pa.	3	Coed	Pvt-Lutheran	1,916
Glassboro State College, Glassboro, N.J.	3	Coed	Public	9,967
Glendale State College, Glendale, Calif.	1	Coed	Public	5,832
Glendale Community College, Glendale, Ariz.	1	Coed	Public	6,335
Glenville State College, Glenville, W.Va.	3	Coed	Public	1,617
Goddard College, Plainfield, Vt.	3	Coed	Private	1,261
Gogebic Community College, Ironwood, Mich.	1	Coed	Public	645
Golden Gate College, San Francisco, Calif.	3	Coed	Private	3,925
Golden West College, Huntington Beach, Calif.	1	Coed	Public	4,400
Gonzaga University, Spokane, Wash.	4	Coed	Pvt-Roman Catholic	2,668
Gordon College, Wenham, Mass.	3	Coed	Private	724
Goshen College, Goshen, Ind.	2	Coed	Pvt-Mennonite	1,283
Goucher College, Baltimore, Md.	3	W	Private	1,060
Graceland College, Lamoni, Iowa.	2	Coed	Private[1]	1,295
Grambling College, Grambling, La.	3	Coed	Public	3,674
Grand Canyon College, Phoenix, Ariz.	2	Coed	Pvt-Baptist	851
Grand Rapids Junior College, Grand Rapids, Mich.	1	Coed	Public	5,357
Grand Valley State College, Allendale, Mich.	2	Coed	Public	3,301
Grand View College, Des Moines, Iowa.	2	Coed	Pvt-Lutheran	1,463
Grays Harbor College, Aberdeen, Wash.	1	Coed	Public	3,226
Grayson County Junior College, Denison, Texas.	1	Coed	Public	2,662
Great Falls, College of, Great Falls, Mont.	2	Coed	Pvt-Roman Catholic	1,165
Green Mountain College, Poultney, Vt.	1	W	Pvt-Methodist	471
Green River Community College, Auburn, Wash.	1	Coed	Public	4,741
Greenfield Community College, Greenfield, Mass.	1	Coed	Public	1,516
Greenville College, Greenville, Ill.	2	Coed	Pvt-Methodist	819
Greenville Technical Education Center, Greenville, S.C.	1	Coed	Public	1,410
Grinnell College, Grinnell, Iowa.	3	Coed	Private	1,261
Grossmont College, El Cajon, Calif.	1	Coed	Public	9,922
Grove City College, Grove City, Pa.	2	Coed	Pvt-Presbyterian	2,090
Guam, University of, Agana, Guam.	3	Coed	Public	2,348
Guelph, University of, Guelph, Ont.	4	Coed	Public	5,921
Guilford College, Greensboro, N.C.	3	Coed	Pvt-Friends	1,757
Guilford Technical Institute, Jamestown, N.C.	1	Coed	Public	1,375
Gulf Coast Junior College, Panama City, Fla.	1	Coed	Public	2,009
Gustavus Adolphus College, St. Peter, Minn.	2	Coed	Pvt-Lutheran	1,907
Gwynedd-Mercy College, Gwynedd Valley, Pa.	2	W	Pvt-Roman Catholic	1,057
Hagerstown Junior College, Hagerstown, Md.	1	Coed	Public	1,324
Hamilton College, Clinton, N.Y.	3	M	Private	916
Hamline University, St. Paul, Minn.	3	Coed	Pvt-Methodist	1,249
Hampden-Sydney College, Hampden-Sydney, Va.	3	M	Pvt-Presbyterian	682
Hampton Institute, Hampton, Va.	3	Coed	Private	2,768
Hanover College, Hanover, Ind.	3	Coed	Pvt-Presbyterian	1,003
Harcum Junior College, Bryn Mawr, Pa.	1	W	Private	915
Hardin-Simmons University, Abilene, Texas.	3	Coed	Pvt-Baptist	1,741
Harding College, Searcy, Ark.	3	Coed	Pvt-Church of Christ	1,916
Harford Community College, Bel Air, Md.	1	Coed	Public	2,232
Harris Teachers College, St. Louis, Mo.	3	Coed	Public	1,452
Harrisburg Area Community College, Harrisburg, Pa.	1	Coed	Public	3,799
Hartford, University of, West Hartford, Conn.	3	Coed	Private	9,605
Hartford State Technical College, Hartford, Conn.	1	Coed	Public	1,668
Hartnell College, Salinas, Calif.	1	Coed	Public	3,818
Hartwick College, Oneonta, N.Y.	3	Coed	Private	1,682
Harvard University, Cambridge, Mass.	4	M	Private	18,465
Radcliffe College, Cambridge, Mass.	3	W	Private	1,235
Hastings College, Hastings, Nebr.	3	Coed	Pvt-Presbyterian	862
Haverford College, Haverford, Pa.	3	M	Pvt-Friends	726
Hawaii, Church College of, Oahu, Hawaii.	2	Coed	Pvt-Latter-day Saints	1,307
Hawaii, University of, Honolulu, Hawaii.	4	Coed	Public	22,118
Heidelberg College, Tiffin, Ohio.	3	Coed	Pvt-Church of Christ	1,258
Henderson County Junior College, Athens, Texas.	1	Coed	Public	1,340
Henderson State College, Arkadelphia, Ark.	3	Coed	Public	3,224
Hendrix College, Conway, Ark.	3	Coed	Pvt-Methodist	979
Henry Ford Community College, Dearborn, Mich.	1	Coed	Public	11,982
Hibbing State Junior College, Hibbing, Minn.	1	Coed	Public	781
High Point College, High Point, N.C.	3	Coed	Pvt-Methodist	1,090
Highland Park College, Highland Park, Mich.	2	Coed	Public	3,558
Highline Community College, Midway, Wash.	1	Coed	Public	7,094
Hillsdale College, Hillsdale, Mich.	3	Coed	Private	1,119
Hinds Junior College, Raymond, Miss.	1	Coed	Public	2,681
Hiram College, Hiram, Ohio.	3	Coed	Pvt-Disciples of Christ	1,191
Hobart & William Smith Colleges, Geneva, N.Y.	3	Coord	Private	1,597
Hofstra University, Hempstead, L.I., N.Y.	4	Coed	Private	12,760
Hollins College, Hollins College, Va.	3	W	Private	1,116
Holmes Junior College, Goodman, Miss.	1	Coed	Public	897
Holy Cross, College of the, Worcester, Mass.	3	M	Pvt-Roman Catholic	2,478
Holy Family College, Philadelphia, Pa.	3	W	Pvt-Roman Catholic	800
Holy Names, College of the, Oakland, Calif.	3	W	Pvt-Roman Catholic	860
Holyoke Community College, Holyoke, Mass.	1	Coed	Public	3,402
Honolulu Community College, Honolulu, Hawaii.	1	Coed	Public	1,937

[1] Reorganized Church of Jesus Christ of Latter Day Saints.

Name and Location	Level of Instruction	Student Body	Control	Enrollment
Hood College, Frederick, Md.	3	W	Pvt-Church of Christ	627
Hope College, Holland, Mich.	2	Coed	Pvt-Reformed	2,071
Houghton College, Houghton, N.Y.	2	Coed	Pvt-Methodist	1,181
Houston, University of, Houston, Texas	4	Coed	Public	25,582
Houston Baptist College, Houston, Texas	2	Coed	Pvt-Baptist	1,142
Howard County Junior College, Big Spring, Texas	1	Coed	Public	1,194
Howard Payne College, Brownwood, Texas	3	Coed	Pvt-Baptist	1,387
Howard University, Washington, D.C.	4	Coed	Public-Private	8,937
Hudson Valley Community College, Troy, N.Y.	1	Coed	Public	5,767
Humboldt State College, Arcata, Calif.	3	Coed	Public	6,543
Huntingdon College, Montgomery, Ala.	2	Coed	Pvt-Methodist	780
Huron College, Huron, S.Dak.	2	Coed	Pvt-Presbyterian	729
Huston-Tillotson College, Austin, Texas.	2	Coed	Pvt-Church of Christ and Methodist	664
Hutchinson Community Junior College, Hutchinson, Kans.	1	Coed	Public	2,130
Idaho, College of, Caldwell, Idaho	3	Coed	Pvt-Presbyterian	1,119
Idaho, University of, Moscow, Idaho	4	Coed	Public	7,007
Idaho State University, Pocatello, Idaho	4	Coed	Public	7,627
Illinois, University of, Urbana & Chicago, Ill.	4	Coed	Public	54,989
Illinois Benedictine College, Lisle, Ill.	2	Coed	Pvt-Roman Catholic	966
Illinois College, Jacksonville, Ill.	2	Coed	Pvt-Presbyterian and Church of Christ	889
Illinois Institute of Technology, Chicago, Ill.	4	Coed	Private	7,613
Illinois State University, Normal, Ill.	4	Coed	Public	18,585
Illinois Valley Community College, Oglesby, Ill.	1	Coed	Public	2,694
Illinois Wesleyan University, Bloomington, Ill.	3	Coed	Pvt-Methodist	1,693
Immaculata College, Immaculata, Pa.	3	W	Pvt-Roman Catholic	1,506
Immaculate Heart College, Los Angeles, Calif.	3	Coed	Pvt-Roman Catholic	624
Imperial Valley College, Imperial, Calif.	1	Coed	Public	2,651
Incarnate Word College, San Antonio, Texas.	3	Coed	Pvt-Roman Catholic	1,321
Indian River Community College, Fort Pierce, Fla.	1	Coed	Public	1,676
Indiana Central College, Indianapolis, Ind.	3	Coed	Pvt-Methodist	2,455
Indiana Institute of Technology, Fort Wayne, Ind.	3	Coed	Private	773
Indiana State University, Terre Haute, Ind.	4	Coed	Public	17,003
Indiana University, Bloomington, Ind.	4	Coed	Public	30,368
Indiana University Regional Campuses — East at Richmond	1	Coed	Public	829
Fort Wayne	2	Coed	Public	3,990
Kokomo	2	Coed	Public	1,715
Northwest at Gary	2	Coed	Public	4,516
Purdue at Indianapolis	2	Coed	Public	14,605
South Bend	2	Coed	Public	4,803
Southeast at Jeffersonville	2	Coed	Public	2,408
Indiana University of Pennsylvania, Indiana, Pa.	3	Coed	Public	10,347
Insurance, College of, New York, N.Y.	3	Coed	Private	1,569
Inter American University of Puerto Rico, San Germán, P.R.	3	Coed	Private-Presbyterian	8,718
Iona College, New Rochelle, N.Y.	3	Coed	Pvt-Roman Catholic	3,780
Iowa State University, Ames, Iowa.	4	Coed	Public	19,620
Iowa, University of, Iowa City, Iowa.	4	Coed	Public	20,604
Iowa Wesleyan College, Mt. Pleasant, Iowa.	2	Coed	Pvt-Methodist	896
Itawamba Junior College, Fulton, Miss.	1	Coed	Public	901
Ithaca College, Ithaca, N.Y.	3	Coed	Private	4,062
Jackson Community College, Jackson, Mich.	1	Coed	Public	3,635
Jackson State College, Jackson, Miss.	3	Coed	Public	4,665
Jackson State Community College, Jackson, Tenn.	1	Coed	Public	1,400
Jacksonville State University, Jacksonville, Ala.	3	Coed	Public	5,645
Jacksonville University, Jacksonville, Fla.	3	Coed	Private	3,137
James H. Faulkner State Junior College, Bay Minette, Ala.	1	Coed	Public	1,086
Jamestown College, Jamestown, N. Dak.	2	Coed	Pvt-Presbyterian	645
Jamestown Community College, Jamestown, N.Y.	1	Coed	Public	2,265
Jarvis Christian College, Hawkins, Texas.	2	Coed	Pvt-Disciples of Christ	707
Jefferson College, Hillsboro, Mo.	1	Coed	Public	1,106
Jefferson Community College, Watertown, N.Y.	1	Coed	Public	1,470
Jefferson Davis State Junior College, Brewton, Ala.	1	Coed	Public	613
Jefferson State Junior College, Birmingham, Ala.	1	Coed	Public	4,753
Jersey City State College, Jersey City, N.J.	3	Coed	Public	9,264
John Brown University, Siloam Springs, Ark.	2	Coed	Private	757
John C. Calhoun State Technical Junior College, Decatur, Ala.	1	Coed	Public	2,087
John Carroll University, Cleveland, Ohio.	3	Coed	Pvt-Roman Catholic	4,146
John Tyler Community College, Chester, Va.	1	Coed	Public	1,852
Johns Hopkins University, Baltimore, Md.	4	Coed	Private	9,735
Johnson C. Smith University, Charlotte, N.C.	2	Coed	Pvt-Presbyterian	1,136
Johnson State College, Johnson, Vt.	3	Coed	Public	811
Joliet Junior College, Joliet, Ill.	1	Coed	Public	4,130
Jones County Junior College, Ellisville, Miss.	1	Coed	Public	2,119
Juilliard School, The, New York, N.Y.	4	Coed	Private	1,010
Juniata College, Huntingdon, Pa.	2	Coed	Pvt-Brethren	1,210
Kalamazoo College, Kalamazoo, Mich.	3	Coed	Pvt-Baptist	1,365
Kansas, University of, Lawrence, Kans.	4	Coed	Public	19,393
Kansas City Art Institute, Kansas City, Mo.	2	Coed	Private	782
Kansas City Kansas Community Junior College, Kansas City, Kans.	1	Coed	Public	1,520
Kansas State College of Pittsburg, Kans.	3	Coed	Public	6,388
Kansas State University, Manhattan, Kans.	4	Coed	Public	13,847
Kansas State Teachers College, Emporia, Kans.	3	Coed	Public	6,982
Kansas Wesleyan University, Salina, Kans.	2	Coed	Pvt-Methodist	2,205
Kapiolani Community College, Honolulu, Hawaii	1	Coed	Public	1,444
Kaskaskia College, Centralia, Ill.	1	Coed	Public	5,870
Kearney State College, Kearney, Nebr.	3	Coed	Public	2,706
Keene State College, Keene, N.H.	3	Coed	Public	3,203
Kellogg Community College, Battle Creek, Mich.	1	Coed	Public	1,037
Kendall College, Evanston, Ill.	1	Coed	Pvt-Methodist	1,563
Kennesaw Junior College, Marietta, Ga.	1	Coed	Public	2,418
Kenosha Technical Institute, Kenosha, Wis.	1	Coed	Public	1,754
Kent State University, Kent, Ohio.	4	Coed	Public	28,235
Kentucky, University of, Lexington, Ky.	4	Coed	Public	29,011
Kentucky State College, Frankfort, Ky.	2	Coed	Public	1,042
Kentucky Wesleyan College, Owensboro, Ky.	2	Coed	Pvt-Methodist	1,159
Kenyon College, Gambier, Ohio.	2	Coed	Pvt-Episcopal	857
Keuka College, Keuka Park, N.Y.	2	W	Private	1,023
Keystone Junior College, La Plume, Pa.	1	Coed	Public	2,672
Kilgore College, Kilgore, Texas.	1	Coed	Public	787
King's College, The, Briarcliff Manor, N.Y.	2	Coed	Pvt-Roman Catholic	2,381
King's College, Wilkes-Barre, Pa.	2	Coed	Private	2,788
Kirkwood Community College, Cedar Rapids, Iowa.	1	Coed	Public	1,484
Knox College, Galesburg, Ill.	2	Coed	Private	1,301
Knoxville College, Knoxville, Tenn.	3	Coed	Private-Presbyterian	4,961
Kutztown State College, Kutztown, Pa.	3	Coed	Public	2,161
Lafayette College, Easton, Pa.	2	M	Pvt-Presbyterian	1,312
Lake City Community College, Lake City, Fla.	1	Coed	Public	738
Lake Erie College, Painesville, Ohio.	3	Coed	Private	1,365
Lake Forest College, Lake Forest, Ill.	2	Coed	Pvt-Presbyterian	2,533
Lake Michigan College, Benton Harbor, Mich.	1	Coed	Public	1,174
Lake-Sumter Community College, Leesburg, Fla.	1	Coed	Public	1,668
Lake Superior State College, Marie, Mich.	3	Coed	Public	2,364
Lakehead University, Port Arthur, Ontario	4	Coed	Private	10,874
Lamar State College of Technology, Beaumont, Texas.	3	Coed	Public	1,301
Lambuth College, Jackson, Tenn.	3	Coed	Pvt-Methodist	876
Lander College, Greenwood, S.C.	3	Coed	Private	924
Lane College, Jackson, Tenn.	2	Coed	Pvt-Methodist Episcopal	5,442
Lane Community College, Eugene, Oreg.	1	Coed	Public	11,381
Laney College, Oakland, Calif.	1	Coed	Public	1,109
Langston University, Langston, Okla.	2	Coed	Public	7,242
Lansing Community College, Lansing, Mich.	1	Coed	Public	1,790
Laredo Junior College, Laredo, Texas.	1	Coed	Public	

Name and Location	Level of Instruction	Student Body	Control	Enrollment
La Salle College, Philadelphia, Pa.	3	Coed	Pvt-Roman Catholic	6,975
Lasell Junior College, Auburndale, Mass.	1	W	Private	922
Lassen College, Susanville, Calif.	1	Coed	Public	1,425
Laurentian University of Sudbury, Sudbury, Ontario.	4	Coed	Public	1,778
Laval University, Quebec, Quebec.	4	Coed	Pvt-Roman Catholic	10,372
La Verne College, La Verne, Calif.	3	Coed	Pvt-Brethren	1,158
Lawrence Institute of Technology, Southfield, Mich.	3	Coed	Private	4,333
Lawrence University, Appleton, Wis.	2	Coed	Private	1,409
Lebanon Valley College, Annville, Pa.	2	Coed	Pvt-Methodist	1,346
Lee College, Cleveland, Tenn.	2	Coed	Pvt-Church of God	1,110
Lee College, Baytown, Texas	1	Coed	Public	3,365
Lees-McRae College, Banner Elk, N.C.	1	Coed	Pvt-Presbyterian	660
Leeward Community College, Oahu, Hawaii	1	Coed	Public	4,469
Lehigh University, Bethlehem, Pa.	4	Coed	Private	5,127
Le Moyne College, Syracuse, N.Y.	2	Coed	Pvt-Roman Catholic	1,818
LeMoyne-Owen College, Memphis, Tenn.	2	Coed	Pvt-Church of Christ	687
Lenoir Community College, Kingston, N.C.	1	Coed	Public	1,469
Lenoir Rhyne College, Hickory, N.C.	2	Coed	Pvt-Lutheran	1,341
Lesley College, Cambridge, Mass.	3	W	Private	812
Lethbridge, University of, Lethbridge, Alberta	3	Coed	Public	1,261
Le Tourneau College, Longview, Texas.	2	Coed	Private	768
Lewis & Clark College, Portland, Oreg.	3	Coed	Pvt-Presbyterian	2,188
Lewis-Clark State School, Lewiston, Idaho.	2	Coed	Public	1,282
Lewis College, Lockport, Ill.	3	Coed	Pvt-Roman Catholic	2,440
Limestone College, Gaffney, S.C.	2	Coed	Private	626
Lincoln College, Lincoln, Ill.	1	Coed	Private	721
Lincoln Memorial University, Harrogate, Tenn.	2	Coed	Private	947
Lincoln University, Jefferson City, Mo.	3	Coed	Public	2,411
Lincoln University, Lincoln University, Pa.	3	Coed	Public	1,027
Lindenwood College, St. Charles, Mo.	2	Coed	Pvt-Presbyterian	693
Linfield College, McMinnville, Oreg.	2	Coed	Pvt-Baptist	1,058
Livingston College, Salisbury, N.C.	2	Coed	Pvt-Baptist	1,812
Lock Haven State College, Lock Haven, Pa.	2	Coed	Pvt-Methodist Episcopal	720
Logan-Williamson Area Community College, Logan, W.Va.	2	Coed	Public	2,436
Loma Linda University, Loma Linda, Calif.	1	Coed	Public	863
Long Beach City College, Long Beach, Calif.	4	Coed	Pvt-Seventh-day Adventist	3,187
Long Island University, Greenvale, N.Y. (incl. Bklyn. Center; Bklyn. College of Pharmacy; C.W. Post & Southampton campuses, Long Island, N.Y.)	1	Coed	Public	28,000
Longwood College, Farmville, Va.	4	Coed	Private	20,975
Lorain County Community College, Elyria, Ohio	3	W	Public	2,238
Loras College, Dubuque, Iowa.	1	Coed	Public	3,586
Loretto Heights College, Denver, Colo.	3	Coed	Pvt-Roman Catholic	1,586
Los Angeles City College, Los Angeles, Calif.	3	Coed	Pvt-Roman Catholic	805
Los Angeles Harbor College, Wilmington, Calif.	1	Coed	Public	18,069
Los Angeles Pierce College, Woodland Hills, Calif.	1	Coed	Public	16,000
Los Angeles Southwest College, Los Angeles, Calif.	1	Coed	Public	2,940
Los Angeles Trade-Technical College, Los Angeles, Calif.	1	Coed	Public	15,433
Los Angeles Valley College, Van Nuys, Calif.	1	Coed	Public	19,475
Louisburg College, Louisburg, N.C.	1	Coed	Pvt-Methodist	785
Louisiana College, Pineville, La.	2	Coed	Pvt-Baptist	904
Louisiana Tech University, Ruston, La.	4	Coed	Public	7,969
Louisiana State University & Agricultural & Mechanical College System, Baton Rouge and New Orleans, La.	4	Coed	Public	35,031
Louisville, University of, Louisville, Ky.	4	Coed	Public	9,668
Lowell State College, Lowell, Mass.	3	Coed	Public	2,295
Lowell Technological Institute, Lowell, Mass.	4	Coed	Public	6,987
Lower Columbia College, Longview, Wash.	1	Coed	Public	2,262
Loyola College, Baltimore, Md.	3	Coed	Pvt-Roman Catholic	3,029
Loyola University, Chicago, Ill.	4	Coed	Pvt-Roman Catholic	17,271
Loyola University, New Orleans, La.	4	Coed	Pvt-Roman Catholic	4,997
Loyola University of Los Angeles, Los Angeles, Calif.	3	Coed	Pvt-Roman Catholic	3,664
Lubbock Christian College, Lubbock, Texas.	2	Coed	Pvt-Church of Christ	957

Name and Location	Level of Instruction	Student Body	Control	Enrollment
Luther College, Decorah, Iowa.	2	Coed	Pvt-Lutheran	2,083
Lycoming College, Williamsport, Pa.	2	Coed	Pvt-Methodist	1,597
Lynchburg College, Lynchburg, Va.	3	Coed	Pvt-Disciples of Christ	1,915
Lyndon State College, Lyndonville, Vt.	2	Coed	Public	726
Macalester College, St. Paul, Minn.	3	Coed	Pvt-Presbyterian	2,093
Macomb County Community College, South Campus, Warren, Mich.	1	Coed	Public	14,346
Macon Junior College, Macon, Ga.	1	Coed	Public	1,674
McGill University, Montreal, Quebec.	4	Coed	Private	14,754
McLennan Community College, Waco, Texas	1	Coed	Public	2,216
McMaster University, Hamilton, Ontario.	4	Coed	Private	6,924
MacMurray College, Jacksonville, Ill.	2	Coed	Pvt-Methodist	986
McMurry College, Abilene, Texas	2	Coed	Pvt-Methodist	1,546
McNeese State College, Lake Charles, La.	3	Coed	Public	5,594
McPherson College, McPherson, Kans.	2	Coed	Pvt-Brethren	640
Madison Area Technical College, Madison, Wis.	1	Coed	Public	4,033
Madison College, Harrisonburg, Va.	3	Coed	Public	4,432
Maine, University of, Portland, Me.	3	Coed	Public	22,576
University of Maine at Farmington	2	Coed	Public	1,530
University of Maine at Orono.	4	Coed	Public	10,136
University of Maine at Portland-Gorham	3	Coed	Public	7,125
University of Maine at Presque Isle	2	Coed	Public	1,205
Mainland, College of the, Texas City, Texas	1	Coed	Public	1,259
Malone College, Canton, Ohio.	2	Coed	Pvt-Friends	860
Manatee Junior College, Bradenton, Fla.	1	Coed	Public	2,485
Manchester College, North Manchester, Ind.	2	Coed	Pvt-Brethren	1,510
Manhattan College, Bronx, N.Y.	3	Coed	Pvt-Roman Catholic	4,940
Manhattan School of Music, New York, N.Y.	3	Coed	Private	976
Manhattanville College, Purchase, N.Y.	3	W	Pvt-Roman Catholic	1,444
Manitoba, University of, Winnipeg, Man.	4	Coed	Public	12,592
St. Paul's College, Winnipeg, Manitoba	4	Coed	Public	628
Mankato State College, Mankato, Minn.	3	Coed	Public	12,363
Mansfield State College, Mansfield, Pa.	2	Coed	Public	3,178
Marian College, Indianapolis, Ind.	2	Coed	Private	1,008
Marietta College, Marietta, Ohio.	3	Coed	Private	2,328
Marin, College of, Kentfield, Calif.	1	Coed	Public	5,728
Marion College, Marion, Ind.	2	Coed	Pvt-Methodist	869
Marist College, Poughkeepsie, N.Y.	3	Coed	Pvt-Roman Catholic	1,773
Marquette University, Milwaukee, Wis.	4	Coed	Pvt-Roman Catholic	10,678
Mars Hill College, Mars Hill, N.C.	2	Coed	Pvt-Baptist	1,494
Marshall University, Huntington, W.Va.	4	Coed	Public	10,255
Marshalltown Community College, Marshalltown, Iowa	1	Coed	Public	707
Mary Baldwin College, Staunton, Va.	2	W	Pvt-Presbyterian	867
Mary Hardin-Baylor College, Belton, Texas.	2	Coed	Pvt-Baptist	647
Mary Manse College, Toledo, Ohio.	2	Coed	Pvt-Roman Catholic	1,061
Marycrest College, Davenport, Iowa.	2	Coed	Pvt-Roman Catholic	924
Marygrove College, Detroit, Mich.	3	Coed	Pvt-Roman Catholic	52,225
Maryland, University of, College Park & Baltimore, Md.	4	Coed	Public	1,057
Maryland Institute, College of Art, Baltimore, Md.	3	Coed	Private	1,044
Marymount College, Tarrytown, N.Y.	3	W	Pvt-Roman Catholic	
Marymount College of Loyola University, Los Angeles, Calif.	2	W	Pvt-Roman Catholic	899
Marymount College of Virginia, Arlington, Va.	2	W	Pvt-Roman Catholic	668
Marymount Manhattan College, New York, N.Y.	1	Coed	Pvt-Presbyterian	1,085
Maryville College, Maryville, Tenn.	2	Coed	Pvt-Roman Catholic	768
Marywood College, Scranton, Pa.	3	Coed	Pvt-Roman Catholic	1,968
Massachusetts, University of, Amherst, Mass.	4	Coed	Public	24,989
Massachusetts Bay Community College, Watertown, Mass.	1	Coed	Public	2,912
Massachusetts College of Art, Boston, Mass.	3	Coed	Public	901
Massachusetts Institute of Technology, Cambridge, Mass.	4	Coed	Private	7,557
Maui Community College, Kahului, Hawaii.	1	Coed	Public	1,056
Mayville State College, Mayville, N.Dak.	2	Coed	Public	935
Memorial University of Newfoundland, St. John's, Nfd.	4	Coed	Public	5,157

Name and Location	Level of Instruction	Student Body	Control	Enrollment
Memphis State University, Memphis, Tenn.	4	Coed	Public	18,774
Merced College, Merced, Calif.	1	Coed	Public	4,638
Mercer County Community College, Trenton, N.J.	1	Coed	Public	4,672
Mercer University, Macon, Ga.	3	Coed	Pvt-Baptist	1,903
Mercy College, Dobbs Ferry, N.Y.	2	Coed	Pvt-Roman Catholic	1,192
Mercy College of Detroit, Detroit, Mich.	2	Coed	Pvt-Roman Catholic	1,605
Mercyhurst College, Erie, Pa.	2	W	Pvt-Roman Catholic	675
Meredith College, Raleigh, N.C.	2	W	Pvt-Baptist	1,109
Meridian Junior College, Meridian, Miss.	1	Coed	Public	1,571
Merrimack College, North Andover, Mass.	2	Coed	Pvt-Roman Catholic	2,833
Merritt College, Oakland, Calif.	4	Coed	Public	10,284
Mesa College, Grand Junction, Colo.	2	Coed	Public	6,336
Mesabi State Junior College, Virginia, Minn.	2	Coed	Public	2,413
Messiah College, Grantham, Pa.	2	Coed	Pvt-Brethren	781
Methodist College, Fayetteville, N.C.	2	Coed	Pvt-Methodist	661
Metropolitan Junior College, Kansas City, Mo.	2	Coed	Public	810
Metropolitan State College, Denver, Colo.	4	Coed	Public	7,778
Miami, University of, Coral Gables, Fla.	4	Coed	Private	6,853
Miami University, Oxford, Ohio.	4	Coed	Public	16,035
Hamilton Campus.	2	Coed	Public	12,249
Middletown Campus.	1	Coed	Public	1,724
Miami-Dade Junior College, Miami, Fla.	4	Coed	Public	2,242
Michigan, University of, Ann Arbor, Mich.	4	Coed	Public	27,950
Dearborn Campus.	2	Coed	Public	36,967
Flint.	2	Coed	Public	1,819
Michigan State University, East Lansing, Mich.	4	Coed	Public	44,092
Michigan Technological University, Houghton, Mich.	4	Coed	Public	4,903
Middle Georgia College, Cochran, Ga.	1	Coed	Public	2,252
Middle Tennessee State University, Murfreesboro, Tenn.	4	Coed	Public	8,093
Middlebury College, Middlebury, Vt.	3	Coed	Private	1,677
Middlesex County College, Edison, N.J.	1	Coed	Public	6,536
Midland Lutheran College, Fremont, Nebr.	2	Coed	Pvt-Lutheran	927
Midlands Technical Education Center, Columbia, S.C.	1	Coed	Public	926
Midwestern University, Wichita Falls, Texas.	3	Coed	Public	4,308
Miles College, Birmingham, Ala.	3	Coed	Pvt-Methodist	1,139
Millersville State College, Millersville, Pa.	3	Coed	Public	5,387
Milligan College, Milligan College, Tenn.	3	Coed	Private	798
Millikin University, Decatur, Ill.	2	Coed	Pvt-Presbyterian	1,796
Mills College, Oakland, Calif.	3	W	Private	939
Millsaps College, Jackson, Miss.	3	Coed	Pvt-Methodist	952
Milton College, Milton, Wis.	2	Coed	Private	859
Milwaukee Area Technical College, Milwaukee, Wis.	1	Coed	Public	14,273
Milwaukee School of Engineering, Milwaukee, Wis.	3	Coed	Private	2,431
Mineral Area College, Flat River, Mo.	1	Coed	Public	1,058
Minnesota, University of, Minneapolis, Minn.	4	Coed	Public	60,852
Duluth.	3	Coed	Public	5,712
Morris.	2	Coed	Public	1,719
Minot State College, Minot, N.Dak.	3	Coed	Public	3,616
MiraCosta College, Oceanside, Calif.	1	Coed	Public	2,530
Misericordia, College, Dallas, Pa.	2	W	Pvt-Roman Catholic	941
Mississippi, University of, University, Miss.	4	Coed	Public	8,507
Mississippi College, Clinton, Miss.	3	Coed	Pvt-Baptist	2,371
Mississippi Delta Junior College, Moorhead, Miss.	1	Coed	Public	1,049
Mississippi Gulf Coast Junior College, Perkinston, Miss.	1	Coed	Public	3,010
Mississippi State College for Women, Columbus, Miss.	3	W	Public	2,657
Mississippi State University, State College, Miss.	4	Coed	Public	9,605
Mississippi Valley State College, Itta Bena, Miss.	2	Coed	Public	2,005
Missouri, University of: Columbia.	4	Coed	Public	48,896
Kansas City.	4	Coed	Public	22,572
Rolla.	4	Coed	Public	9,592
St. Louis.	4	Coed	Public	6,542
Missouri Baptist College, Hannibal, Mo.	1	Coed	Pvt-Baptist	10,190
Missouri Southern College, Joplin, Mo.	2	Coed	Public	753
				3,185
Missouri Valley College, Marshall, Mo.	2	Coed	Pvt-Presbyterian	912
Missouri Western College, St. Joseph, Mo.	2	Coed	Public	2,884
Mitchell College, New London, Conn.	1	Coed	Private	1,318
Mobile State Junior College, Mobile, Ala.	1	Coed	Public	915
Modesto Junior College, Modesto, Calif.	1	Coed	Public	8,704
Mohawk Valley Community College, Utica, N.Y.	1	Coed	Public	3,992
Molloy Catholic College for Women, Rockville Center, N.Y.	2	W	Pvt-Roman Catholic	1,128
Moncton, University of, Moncton, New Brunswick.	3	Coed	Pvt-Roman Catholic	2,686
Monmouth College, Monmouth, Ill.	3	Coed	Pvt-Presbyterian	1,300
Monmouth College, West Long Branch, N.J.	3	Coed	Private	5,427
Monroe Community College, Rochester, N.Y.	1	Coed	Public	8,410
Montana, University of, Missoula, Mont.	4	Coed	Public	982
Montana College of Mineral Science and Technology, Butte, Mont.	3	Coed	Public	8,230
Montana State University, Bozeman, Mont.	4	Coed	Public	10,453
Montclair State College, Montclair, N.J.	3	Coed	Public	3,269
Monterey Peninsula College, Monterey, Calif.	1	Coed	Public	2,454
Montevallo, University of, Montevallo, Ala.	3	Coed	Public	8,484
Montgomery County Community College, Conshohocken, Pa.	1	Coed	Public	3,057
Montreal, University of, Montreal, Quebec.	4	Coed	Pvt-Roman Catholic	13,062
Jean-de-Brébeuf, College of, Montreal, Quebec.	2	Coed	Pvt-Roman Catholic	1,082
Loyola College, Montreal, Quebec.	2	Coed	Pvt-Roman Catholic	4,281
Moorhead State College, Moorhead, Minn.	3	Coed	Public	5,310
Moorpark College, Moorpark, Calif.	1	Coed	Public	5,655
Moravian College, Bethlehem, Pa.	2	Coed	Pvt-Moravian	1,718
Morehead State University, Morehead, Ky.	3	Coed	Public	6,703
Morehouse College, Atlanta, Ga.	2	M	Private	1,009
Morgan State College, Baltimore, Md.	3	Coed	Public	5,106
Morningside College, Sioux City, Iowa.	2	Coed	Pvt-Methodist	1,645
Morris Brown College, Atlanta, Ga.	2	Coed	Pvt-Methodist Episcopal	1,456
Morris Harvey College, Charleston, W.Va.	3	Coed	Private	3,123
Morton College, Cicero, Ill.	1	Coed	Public	2,714
Mount Allison University, Sackville, New Brunswick.	3	Coed	Pvt-United Church	1,331
Mount Holyoke College, South Hadley, Mass.	3	W	Private	1,921
Mount Mary College, Milwaukee, Wis.	2	W	Pvt-Roman Catholic	860
Mount St. Joseph-on-the-Ohio, College of, Mt. St. Joseph, Ohio.	2	Coed	Pvt-Roman Catholic	906
Mount St. Mary College, Newburgh, N.Y.	2	Coed	Pvt-Roman Catholic	696
Mount St. Mary's College, Los Angeles, Calif.	3	M	Pvt-Roman Catholic	1,127
Mount St. Mary's College, Emmitsburg, Md.	3	W	Pvt-Roman Catholic	1,111
Mount St. Vincent, College of, Riverdale, N.Y.	3	W	Pvt-Roman Catholic	958
Mount St. Vincent University, Halifax, Nova Scotia.	2	Coed	Pvt-Roman Catholic	710
Mount San Antonio College, Walnut, Calif.	1	Coed	Public	14,862
Mount San Jacinto College, Gilman Hot Springs, Calif.	1	Coed	Public	1,445
Mount Union College, Alliance, Ohio.	2	Coed	Pvt-Methodist	1,268
Mount Wachusett Community College, Gardner, Mass.	1	Coed	Public	1,771
Muhlenberg College, Allentown, Pa.	2	Coed	Pvt-Lutheran	1,843
Mundelein College, Chicago, Ill.	3	W	Pvt-Roman Catholic	1,311
Murray State College of Agriculture and Applied Science, Tishomingo, Okla.	1	Coed	Public	705
Murray State University, Murray, Ky.	3	Coed	Public	7,460
Muskegon Community College, Muskegon, Mich.	1	Coed	Public	3,856
Muskingum College, New Concord, Ohio.	2	Coed	Pvt-Presbyterian	1,373
Napa College, Napa, Calif.	1	Coed	Public	3,200
Nassau Community College, Garden City, N.Y.	2	Coed	Public	16,510
Nasson College, Springvale, Me.	2	Coed	Private	799
National College of Education, Evanston, Ill.	3	Coed	Private	2,737
Naval Postgraduate School, Monterey, Calif.	4	Coed	Public	1,882
Navarro Junior College, Corsicana, Texas.	1	Coed	Public	1,084
Nazareth College of Rochester, N.Y.	2	W	Pvt-Roman Catholic	1,462
Nebraska, University of, Lincoln and Omaha, Nebr.	4	Coed	Public	20,810

Name and location	Level of Instruction	Student Body	Control	Enrollment
Nebraska Wesleyan University, Lincoln, Nebr.	2	Coed	Pvt-Methodist	1,224
Nevada, University of, Reno and Las Vegas, Nev	4	Coed	Public	12,473
New Brunswick, University of, Fredericton, New Brunswick.	4	Coed	Public	4,806
New England College, Henniker, N.H.	2	Coed	Private	1,050
New Hampshire, University of, Durham, N.H.	4	Coed	Public	9,989
New Haven, University of, West Haven, Conn.	3	Coed	Private	4,834
New Mexico, University of, Albuquerque, N.Mex.	4	Coed	Public	18,107
New Mexico Highlands University, Las Vegas, N.Mex.	3	Coed	Public	2,479
New Mexico Institute of Mining & Technology, Socorro, N.Mex.	4	Coed	Public	873
New Mexico Junior College, Hobbs, N.Mex.	1	Coed	Public	1,090
New Mexico State University, Las Cruces, N.Mex.	4	Coed	Public	10,065
New Rochelle, College of, New Rochelle, N.Y.	3	W	Pvt-Roman Catholic	1,168
New School for Social Research, New York, N.Y.	4	Coed	Private	3,648
New York, City University of, New York, N.Y.:				
Bernard M. Baruch College, New York.	3	Coed	Public	11,550
Borough of Manhattan Community College, New York	1	Coed	Public	7,600
Bronx Community College, Bronx.	1	Coed	Public	8,700
Brooklyn College, Brooklyn.	3	Coed	Public	27,320
City College, New York.	4	Coed	Public	20,190
Graduate Center, New York.	4	Coed	Public	2,000
Herbert H. Lehman College, Bronx.	3	Coed	Public	11,520
Hunter College, New York.	3	Coed	Public	21,060
John Jay College of Criminal Justice, New York.	3	Coed	Public	4,900
Kingsborough Community College, Brooklyn.	1	Coed	Public	5,900
New York City Community College, Brooklyn.	1	Coed	Public	13,750
Queens College, Flushing.	3	Coed	Public	20,488
Queensborough Community College, Bayside.	1	Coed	Public	11,820
Richmond College, Staten Island.	3	Coed	Public	1,880
Staten Island Community College, Staten Island.	1	Coed	Public	7,070
York College, Flushing.	3	Coed	Public	2,040
New York, State University of, Albany, N.Y.:	4	Coed	Public	313,740
Agricultural & Technical College at Alfred.	1	Coed	Public	3,799
Agricultural & Technical College at Canton.	1	Coed	Public	1,884
Agricultural & Technical College at Cobleskill.	1	Coed	Public	2,004
Agricultural & Technical College at Delhi.	1	Coed	Public	2,236
Agricultural & Technical College at Farmingdale.	1	Coed	Public	10,670
Agricultural & Technical College at Morrisville.	1	Coed	Public	2,476
College of Forestry at Syracuse University, Syracuse.	4	Coed	Public	1,768
Downstate Medical Center, Brooklyn.	4	Coed	Public	1,142
Maritime College, Bronx	2	M	Public	747
State University College at Brockport.	3	Coed	Public	8,302
State University College at Buffalo.	3	Coed	Public	10,182
State University College at Cortland.	3	Coed	Public	5,130
State University College at Fredonia.	3	Coed	Public	4,768
State University College at Geneseo.	3	Coed	Public	5,278
State University College at New Paltz.	3	Coed	Public	8,027
State University College at Oneonta.	3	Coed	Public	5,435
State University College at Oswego.	3	Coed	Public	8,044
State University College at Plattsburgh.	3	Coed	Public	5,220
State University College at Potsdam.	3	Coed	Public	4,568
State University at Albany.	4	Coed	Public	13,288
State University at Binghamton.	4	Coed	Public	7,182
State University at Buffalo.	4	Coed	Public	23,723
State University at Stony Brook.	4	Coed	Public	10,697
Upstate Medical Center, Syracuse.	4	Coed	Public	742
New York Institute of Technology, Old Westbury, L.I., N.Y.	2	Coed	Private	5,207
New York University, New York, N.Y.	4	Coed	Private	32,323
Newark College of Engineering, Newark, N.J.	4	Coed	Public	5,961
Newark State College, Union, N.J.	3	Coed	Public	11,692
Newberry College, Newberry, S.C.	2	Coed	Pvt-Lutheran	805
Newton College of the Sacred Heart, Newton, Mass.	3	W	Pvt-Roman Catholic	862
Newton Junior College, Newton, Mass.	1	Coed	Public	679
Niagara County Community College, Niagara Falls, N.Y.	1	Coed	Public	3,105
Niagara University, Niagara University, N.Y.	3	Coed	Pvt-Roman Catholic	3,562
Nicholls State University, Thibodaux, La.	3	Coed	Public	5,138
Nichols College, Dudley, Mass.	2	M	Private	672
Norfolk State College, Norfolk, Va.	2	Coed	Public	5,195
North Adams State College, North Adams, Mass.	3	Coed	Public	2,034
North Carolina, University of, Chapel Hill, N.C.:		Coed	Public	45,771
Asheville.	2	Coed	Public	1,010
Chapel Hill.	4	Coed	Public	17,567
Charlotte.	4	Coed	Public	4,068
Greensboro.	4	Coed	Public	6,828
Wilmington.	2	Coed	Public	1,890
North Carolina State University at Raleigh	4	Coed	Public	13,340
North Carolina Central University, Durham, N.C.	3	Coed	Public	3,797
North Central College, Naperville, Ill.	2	Coed	Pvt-Methodist	3,538
North Central Technical Institute, Wausau, Wis.	1	Coed	Public	869
North Dakota, University of, Grand Forks, N.Dak.	4	Coed	Public	9,312
North Dakota State School of Science, Wahpeton, N.Dak.	1	Coed	Public	2,884
North Dakota State University, Fargo, N.Dak.	4	Coed	Public	7,136
North Florida Junior College, Madison, Fla.	1	Coed	Public	1,208
North Georgia College, Dahlonega, Ga.	2	Coed	Public	1,151
North Idaho Junior College, Coeur d'Alene, Idaho.	1	Coed	Public	1,185
North Iowa Area Community College, Mason City, Iowa.	1	Coed	Public	1,858
North Park College, Chicago, Ill.	2	Coed	Pvt-Evangelical Covenant	1,422
North Shore Community College, Beverly, Mass.	1	Coed	Public	3,754
North Texas State University, Denton, Texas.	4	Coed	Public	15,307
Northampton County Area Community College, Bethlehem, Pa.	1	Coed	Public	3,030
Northeast Alabama State Junior College, Rainsville, Ala.	1	Coed	Public	695
Northeast Louisiana University, Monroe, La.	4	Coed	Public	8,031
Northeast Mississippi Junior College, Booneville, Miss.	1	Coed	Public	1,563
Northeast Missouri State College, Kirksville, Mo.	3	Coed	Public	7,075
Northeastern Illinois State College, Chicago, Ill.	3	Coed	Public	8,409
Northeastern Junior College, Sterling, Colo.	1	Coed	Public	1,342
Northeastern Oklahoma Agricultural & Mechanical College, Miami, Okla.	1	Coed	Public	2,289
Northeastern State College, Tahlequah, Okla.	3	Coed	Public	5,480
Northeastern University, Boston, Mass.	4	Coed	Private	38,000
Northern Arizona University, Flagstaff, Ariz.	4	Coed	Public	9,100
Northern Colorado, University of, Greeley, Colo.	4	Coed	Public	12,777
Northern Essex Community College, Haverhill, Mass.	1	Coed	Public	2,614
Northern Illinois University, De Kalb, Ill.	4	Coed	Public	25,398
Northern Iowa, University of, Cedar Falls, Iowa.	4	Coed	Public	10,534
Northern Michigan University, Marquette, Mich.	3	Coed	Public	8,180
Northern Montana College, Havre, Mont.	2	Coed	Public	1,575
Northern Oklahoma College, Tonkawa, Okla.	1	Coed	Public	1,325
Northern State College, Aberdeen, S.Dak.	3	Coed	Public	3,679
Northern Virginia Community College, Annandale, Va.	1	Coed	Public	9,779
Northland College, Ashland, Wis.	2	Coed	Pvt-Church of Christ	641
Northrop Institute of Technology, Inglewood, Calif.	2	Coed	Private	1,982
Northwest Community College, Powell, Wyo.	1	Coed	Public	721
Northwest Mississippi Junior College, Senatobia, Miss.	1	Coed	Public	1,563
Northwest Missouri State College, Maryville, Mo.	3	Coed	Public	5,530
Northwest Nazarene College, Nampa, Idaho.	2	Coed	Pvt-Nazarene	1,118
Northwestern College, Orange City, Iowa.	2	Coed	Pvt-Reformed	769
Northwestern Michigan College, Traverse City, Mich.	1	Coed	Public	1,712
Northwestern State College, Alva, Okla.	2	Coed	Public	2,543
Northwestern State University of Louisiana, Natchitoches, La.	3	Coed	Public	5,947

Name and Location	Level of Instruction	Student Body	Control	Enrollment
Northwestern University, Evanston, Ill.	4	Coed	Private	15,571
Norwalk State Technical College, Norwalk, Conn.	1	Coed	Public	2,126
Norwich University, Northfield, Vt.	4	M	Private	1,059
Notre Dame, College of, Belmont, Calif.	4	Coed	Pvt-Roman Catholic	1,486
Notre Dame, University of, Notre Dame, Ind.	4	Coed	Pvt-Roman Catholic	7,967
Notre Dame of Maryland, College of, Baltimore, Md.	2	W	Pvt-Roman Catholic	947
Oakland Community College, Bloomfield Hills, Mich.	1	Coed	Public	7,240
Auburn Hills Campus	1	Coed	Public	1,760
Highland Lakes Campus	1	Coed	Public	6,000
Orchard Ridge Campus	1	Coed	Public	6,975
Oakland University, Rochester, Mich.	4	Coed	Public	2,670
Oberlin College, Oberlin, Ohio.	3	Coed	Private	2,815
Ocean County College, Toms River, N.J.	1	Coed	Public	1,868
Occidental College, Los Angeles, Calif.	3	Coed	Pvt-United Presbyterian	2,774
Odessa College, Odessa, Texas	1	Coed	Public	1,159
Oglethorpe College, Atlanta, Ga.	2	Coed	Private	940
Ohio Dominican College, Columbus, Ohio.	2	Coed	Pvt-Roman Catholic	2,201
Ohio Northern University, Ada, Ohio.	2	Coed	Pvt-Methodist	50,541
Ohio State University, Columbus, Ohio.	4	Coed	Public	23,978
Ohio Wesleyan University, Delaware, Ohio.	3	Coed	Pvt-Methodist	2,597
Ohlone College, Fremont, Calif.	1	Coed	Public	3,884
Okaloosa-Walton Junior College, Niceville, Fla.	1	Coed	Public	2,178
Oklahoma, University of, Norman, Okla.	4	Coed	Public	21,810
Oklahoma Baptist University, Shawnee, Okla.	2	Coed	Pvt-Baptist	1,653
Oklahoma Christian College, Oklahoma City, Okla.	2	Coed	Pvt-Church of Christ	1,106
Oklahoma City University, Oklahoma City, Okla.	3	Coed	Pvt-Methodist	1,946
Oklahoma College of Liberal Arts, Chickasha, Okla.	2	Coed	Public	926
Oklahoma Panhandle State College of Agricultural and Applied Science, Goodwell, Okla.	2	Coed	Public	1,341
Oklahoma State University, Stillwater, Okla.	4	Coed	Public	20,793
Old Dominion University, Norfolk, Va.	3	Coed	Public	10,085
Olivet College, Olivet, Mich.	3	Coed	Public	906
Olivet Nazarene College, Kankakee, Ill.	3	Coed	Pvt-Nazarene	1,835
Olympic College, Bremerton, Wash.	1	Coed	Public	4,650
Oral Roberts University, Tulsa, Okla.	2	Coed	Private	1,020
Orange Coast College, Costa Mesa, Calif.	1	Coed	Public	8,160
Orange County Community College, Middletown, N.Y.	1	Coed	Public	4,105
Orangeburg-Calhoun Technical Education Center, Orangeburg, S.C.	1	Coed	Public	1,593
Oregon, University of, Eugene, Oreg.	4	Coed	Public	16,529
Oregon College of Education, Monmouth, Oreg.	3	Coed	Public	3,091
Oregon State University, Corvallis, Oreg.	4	Coed	Public	15,361
Oregon Technical Institute, Klamath Falls, Oreg.	1	Coed	Public	1,481
Otero Junior College, La Junta, Colo.	1	Coed	Public	756
Ottawa, University of, Ottawa, Ontario.	4	Coed	Pvt-Roman Catholic	7,200
Ottawa University, Ottawa, Kans.	2	Coed	Pvt-Baptist	823
Otterbein College, Westerville, Ohio.	2	Coed	Pvt-Methodist	1,413
Ouachita Baptist University, Arkadelphia, Ark.	3	Coed	Pvt-Baptist	1,393
Our Lady of the Lake College, San Antonio, Texas.	3	Coed	Pvt-Roman Catholic	1,834
Ozarks, School of the, Point Lookout, Mo.	2	Coed	Pvt-Presbyterian	1,004
Pace College, New York, N.Y.	3	Coed	Private	10,056
Pacific, University of the, Stockton, Calif.	4	Coed	Private	5,080
Pacific Lutheran University, Tacoma, Wash.	3	Coed	Pvt-Lutheran	2,999
Pacific Union College, Angwin, Calif.	3	Coed	Pvt-Seventh-day Adventist	1,934
Pacific University, Forest Grove, Oreg.	3	Coed	Pvt-Church of Christ	1,249
Paine College, Augusta, Ga.	2	Coed	Pvt-Methodist Episcopal & Methodist	691
Palm Beach Junior College, Lake Worth, Fla.	1	Coed	Public	5,494
Palomar College, San Marcos, Calif.	1	Coed	Public	5,186
Pan American College, Edinburg, Texas.	2	Coed	Public	5,054
Paris Junior College, Paris, Texas.	1	Coed	Public	799
Park College, Parkville, Mo.	2	Coed	Pvt-Presbyterian	676
Parkersburg Community College, Parkersburg, W.Va.	1	Coed	Public	1,482
Parks College of Aeronautical Technology, Cahokia, Ill.	2	Coed	Pvt-Roman Catholic	742
Parsons College, Fairfield, Iowa.	2	Coed	Private	1,669
Pasadena City College, Pasadena, Calif.	1	Coed	Public	14,796
Pasadena College, Pasadena, Calif.	3	Coed	Pvt-Nazarene	1,260
Pearl River College, Poplarville, Miss.	1	Coed	Public	1,123
Peninsula College, Port Angeles, Wash.	1	Coed	Public	1,926
Pembroke State University, Pembroke, N.C.	2	Coed	Public	1,386
Pennsylvania, University of, Philadelphia, Pa.	4	Coed	Private	19,557
Pennsylvania State University, University Park, Abington, Allentown, Altoona, Chester, Dubois, Erie, Hazelton, Hershey, McKeesport, Middletown, Monaca, Mont Alto, New Kensington, Schuylkill, Scranton, Sharon, Uniontown, Wilkes-Barre, Wyomissing and York, Pa.	4	Coed	Public	55,403
Pensacola Junior College, Pensacola, Fla.	1	Coed	Public	5,412
Pepperdine College, Los Angeles, Calif.	3	Coed	Pvt-Church of Christ	6,730
Peru State College, Peru, Nebr.	2	Coed	Public	1,135
Pfeiffer College, Misenheimer, N.C.	2	Coed	Pvt-Methodist	882
Philadelphia College of Art, Philadelphia, Pa.	2	Coed	Private	1,625
Philadelphia College of Bible, Philadelphia, Pa.	3	Coed	Private	632
Philadelphia College of Pharmacy & Science, Philadelphia, Pa.	4	Coed	Private	946
Philadelphia College of Textiles & Science, Philadelphia, Pa.	2	Coed	Private	2,064
Philander Smith College, Little Rock, Ark.	2	Coed	Pvt-Methodist	639
Phillips University, Enid, Okla.	3	Coed	Pvt-Disciples of Christ	1,392
Phoenix College, Phoenix, Ariz.	1	Coed	Public	9,897
Pikeville College, Pikeville, Ky.	2	Coed	Pvt-Presbyterian	739
Pittsburgh, University of, Pittsburgh, Bradford, Greensburg, Johnstown, and Titusville, Pa.	4	Coed	Private	31,650
Pitzer College, Claremont, Calif.	3	Coed	Private	721
Plymouth State College, Plymouth, N.H.	3	Coed	Public	2,474
PMC Colleges, Chester, Pa.	3	Coed	Private	3,061
Point Park College, Pittsburgh, Pa.	2	Coed	Private	2,821
Polk Community College, Winter Haven, Fla.	1	Coed	Public	3,477
Pomona College, Claremont, Calif.	3	Coed	Private	1,292
Porterville College, Porterville, Calif.	1	Coed	Public	1,561
Portland, University of, Portland, Oreg.	4	Coed	Pvt-Roman Catholic	1,959
Portland Community College, Portland, Oreg.	1	Coed	Public	12,651
Portland State University, Portland, Oreg.	3	Coed	Public	11,059
Potomac State College of West Virginia University, Keyser, W.Va.	1	Coed	Public	745
Prairie State College, Chicago Heights, Ill.	1	Coed	Public	3,696
Prairie View Agricultural & Mechanical College, Prairie View, Texas.	3	Coed	Public	4,575
Pratt Institute, Brooklyn, N.Y.	3	Coed	Private	4,541
Prince Edward Island, University of, Charlottetown, P.E.I.	1	Coed	Public	1,566
Prince George's Community College, Largo, Md.	1	Coed	Public	6,223
Princeton University, Princeton, N.J.	4	Coed	Private	5,160
Principia College, Elsah, Ill.	2	Coed	Pvt-Christian Science	808
Providence College, Providence, R.I.	3	Coed	Pvt-Roman Catholic	2,969
Puerto Rico, University of, Rio Piedras, P.R.	4	Coed	Public	42,516
Puerto Rico Junior College, Rio Piedras, P.R.	1	Coed	Private	4,006
Puget Sound, University of, Tacoma, Wash.	3	Coed	Pvt-Methodist	3,665
Purdue University, Lafayette, Ind.	4	Coed	Public	25,844
Purdue University Regional Campuses:				
Calumet at Hammond.	2	Coed	Public	4,640
Fort Wayne.	2	Coed	Public	2,441
Indianapolis.	2	Coed	Public	14,605
Quebec, University of, Quebec, Que.	2	Coed	Public	7,255
Queens College, Charlotte, N.C.	2	W	Pvt-Presbyterian	657
Queen's University at Kingston, Ontario.	4	Coed	Private	7,519
Quincy College, Quincy, Ill.	2	Coed	Pvt-Roman Catholic	2,166

Name and Location	Level of Instruction	Student Body	Control	Enrollment
Quinnipiac College, Hamden, Conn.	3	Coed	Private	2,931
Quinsigamond Community College, Worcester, Mass.	1	Coed	Public	3,218
Radford College, Radford, Va.	3	Coed	Public	4,159
Randolph-Macon College, Ashland, Va.	2	Coed	Pvt-Methodist	800
Randolph-Macon Woman's College, Lynchburg, Va.	2	W	Pvt-Methodist	778
Redlands, University of, Redlands, Calif.	3	Coed	Pvt-Baptist	1,970
Reed College, Portland, Oreg.	3	Coed	Private	5,659
Reedley College, Reedley, Calif.	1	Coed	Public	1,303
Regis College, Denver, Colo.	3	Coed	Pvt-Roman Catholic	2,229
Regis College, Weston, Mass.	2	W	Pvt-Roman Catholic	1,424
Rend Lake College, Ina, Ill.	2	Coed	Public	898
Rensselaer Polytechnic Institute, Troy, N.Y.	4	Coed	Private	5,070
Rhode Island, University of, Kingston, R.I.	4	Coed	Public	15,066
Rhode Island College, Providence, R.I.	3	Coed	Public	6,414
Rhode Island Junior College, Providence, R.I.	1	Coed	Public	3,581
Rhode Island School of Design, Providence, R.I.	3	Coed	Private	1,161
Rice University, Houston, Texas	4	Coed	Private	3,121
Richmond, University of, Richmond, Va.	3	Coord	Pvt-Baptist	4,789
Ricks College, Rexburg, Idaho	1	Coed	Pvt-Latter-day Saints	5,019
Rider College, Trenton, N.J.	3	Coed	Private	6,123
Rio Grande College, Rio Grande, Ohio	2	Coed	Private	786
Rio Hondo College, Whittier, Calif.	1	Coed	Public	10,130
Ripon College, Ripon, Wis.	2	Coed	Private	1,067
Riverside City College, Riverside, Calif.	1	Coed	Public	9,384
Rivier College, Nashua, N.H.	3	W	Pvt-Roman Catholic	734
Roanoke College, Salem, Va.	2	Coed	Pvt-Lutheran	1,399
Robert Morris College, Pittsburgh, Pa.	2	Coed	Private	4,349
Roberts Wesleyan College, Rochester, N.Y.	2	Coed	Pvt-Methodist	736
Rochester, University of, Rochester, N.Y.	4	Coed	Private	8,587
Rochester Institute of Technology, Rochester, N.Y.	3	Coed	Private	10,887
Rochester State Junior College, Rochester, Minn.	1	Coed	Public	2,320
Rock Valley College, Rockford, Ill.	1	Coed	Public	3,715
Rockford College, Rockford, Ill.	3	Coed	Private	1,417
Rockhurst College, Kansas City, Mo.	3	Coed	Pvt-Roman Catholic	1,200
Rockingham Community College, Wentworth, N.C.	1	Coed	Public	2,469
Rockland Community College, Suffern, N.Y.	1	Coed	Public	5,080
Rollins College, Winter Park, Fla.	3	Coed	Private	3,443
Roosevelt University, Chicago, Ill.	3	Coed	Private	6,844
Rosary College, River Forest, Ill.	3	W	Pvt-Roman Catholic	1,195
Rosary Hill College, Buffalo, N.Y.	2	Coed	Pvt-Roman Catholic	1,292
Rose-Hulman Institute of Technology, Terre Haute, Ind.	3	M	Private	1,077
Rosemont College, Rosemont, Pa.	2	W	Pvt-Roman Catholic	670
Rowan Technical Institute, Salisbury, N.C.	1	Coed	Public	723
Russell Sage College, Troy, N.Y.	3	Coed	Private	4,114
Rust College, Holly Springs, Miss.	2	Coed	Pvt-Methodist	724
Rutgers—The State University of New Jersey, New Brunswick, N.J.	4	Coord	Public	32,600
Sacramento City College, Sacramento, Calif.	1	Coed	Public	10,945
Sacramento State College, Sacramento, Calif.	3	Coed	Public	19,750
Sacred Heart, College of the, Santurce, P.R.	2	W	Pvt-Roman Catholic	797
Sacred Heart College, Wichita, Kans.	2	Coed	Pvt-Roman Catholic	652
Sacred Heart University, Bridgeport, Conn.	2	Coed	Pvt-Roman Catholic	2,074
Saddleback College, Mission Viejo, Calif.	1	Coed	Public	3,170
Saginaw Valley College, University Center, Mich.	3	Coed	Public	1,830
St. Ambrose College, Davenport, Iowa	2	Coed	Pvt-Roman Catholic	1,410
St. Andrews Presbyterian College, Laurinburg, N.C.	2	Coed	Pvt-Presbyterian	840
St. Anselm's College, Manchester, N.H.	2	Coed	Pvt-Roman Catholic	1,615
St. Augustine's College, Raleigh, N.C.	2	Coed	Pvt-Episcopal	1,118
St. Benedict, College of, St. Joseph, Minn.	2	W	Pvt-Roman Catholic	736
St. Bernard College, St. Bernard, Ala.	2	Coed	Pvt-Roman Catholic	651
St. Bonaventure University, St. Bonaventure, N.Y.	4	Coed	Pvt-Roman Catholic	2,621
St. Catherine, College of, St. Paul, Minn.	2	W	Pvt-Roman Catholic	1,339

Name and Location	Level of Instruction	Student Body	Control	Enrollment
St. Clair County Community College, Port Huron, Mich.	3	Coed	Public	2,842
St. Cloud State College, St. Cloud, Minn.	3	Coed	Public	10,131
St. Edward's University, Austin, Texas	2	Coed	Pvt-Roman Catholic	1,052
St. Elizabeth, College of, Convent Station, N.J.	2	W	Pvt-Roman Catholic	755
St. Francis, College of, Joliet, Ill.	3	W	Pvt-Roman Catholic	806
St. Francis College, Fort Wayne, Ind.	3	Coed	Pvt-Roman Catholic	2,226
St. Francis College, Biddeford, Me.	2	Coed	Pvt-Roman Catholic	1,035
St. Francis College, Brooklyn, N.Y.	3	Coed	Pvt-Roman Catholic	2,505
St. Francis College, Loretto, Pa.	3	Coed	Pvt-Roman Catholic	1,639
St. Francis Xavier University, Antigonish, Nova Scotia	3	Coed	Pvt-Roman Catholic	2,954
St. John Fisher College, Rochester, N.Y.	2	Coed	Pvt-Roman Catholic	855
St. John College of Cleveland, Ohio	2	W	Pvt-Roman Catholic	1,347
St. Johns River Community College, Palatka, Fla.	1	Coed	Public	1,181
St. John's University, Collegeville, Minn.	3	M	Pvt-Roman Catholic	1,581
St. John's University, Jamaica, N.Y.	3	Coed	Pvt-Roman Catholic	13,619
St. Joseph College, West Hartford, Conn.	2	W	Pvt-Roman Catholic	750
St. Joseph's College, Rensselaer, Ind.	2	Coed	Pvt-Roman Catholic	1,366
St. Joseph's College, Calumet Campus, East Chicago, Ind.	2	Coed	Pvt-Roman Catholic	1,605
St. Joseph's College, Philadelphia, Pa.	2	Coed	Pvt-Roman Catholic	6,938
St. Lawrence University, Canton, N.Y.	3	Coed	Private	2,354
St. Leo College, St. Leo, Fla.	1	Coed	Pvt-Roman Catholic	1,172
St. Louis, Junior College District of, St. Louis, Mo.	1	Coed	Public	18,216
Florissant Valley Community College, St. Louis, Mo.	1	Coed	Public	5,445
Forest Park Community College, St. Louis, Mo.	1	Coed	Public	5,840
Meramec Community College, Kirkwood, Mo.	1	Coed	Public	6,931
St. Louis University, St. Louis, Mo.	4	Coed	Pvt-Roman Catholic	10,125
St. Martin's College, Olympia, Wash.	2	Coed	Pvt-Roman Catholic	644
St. Mary College, Xavier, Kans.	2	W	Pvt-Roman Catholic	671
St. Mary's College, St. Mary's College, Calif.	3	M	Pvt-Roman Catholic	1,155
St. Mary's College, Notre Dame, Ind.	2	W	Pvt-Roman Catholic	1,719
St. Mary's College, Winona, Minn.	2	Coed	Pvt-Roman Catholic	995
St. Mary's College of Maryland, St. Mary's City, Md.	2	Coed	Public	848
St. Mary's Dominican College, New Orleans, La.	2	W	Pvt-Roman Catholic	780
St. Mary's Junior College, Minneapolis, Minn.	1	W	Pvt-Roman Catholic	643
St. Mary's Seminary & University, Baltimore, Md.	4	M	Pvt-Roman Catholic	681
St. Mary's University, Halifax, N.S.	3	Coed	Pvt-Roman Catholic	2,054
St. Mary's University, San Antonio, Texas	3	Coed	Pvt-Roman Catholic	4,211
St. Michael's College, Winooski Park, Vt.	3	Coed	Pvt-Roman Catholic	1,435
St. Norbert College, West De Pere, Wis.	2	Coed	Pvt-Roman Catholic	1,673
St. Olaf College, Northfield, Minn.	2	Coed	Pvt-Lutheran	2,569
St. Peter's College, Jersey City, N.J.	2	Coed	Pvt-Roman Catholic	4,744
St. Petersburg Junior College, St. Petersburg, Fla.	1	Coed	Public	9,628
St. Philip's College, San Antonio, Texas	1	Coed	Public	2,218
St. Rose, College of, Albany, N.Y.	3	W	Pvt-Roman Catholic	1,446
St. Scholastica, College of, Duluth, Minn.	2	W	Pvt-Roman Catholic	817
St. Teresa, College of, Winona, Minn.	2	W	Pvt-Roman Catholic	1,047
St. Thomas, University of, St. Paul, Minn.	2	Coed	Pvt-Roman Catholic	2,430
St. Thomas, University of, Houston, Texas	2	Coed	Pvt-Roman Catholic	1,250
St. Vincent College, Latrobe, Pa.	2	M	Pvt-Roman Catholic	952
St. Xavier College, Chicago, Ill.	3	Coed	Pvt-Roman Catholic	985
Salem College, Salem, W.Va.	2	Coed	Private	1,502
Salem State College, Salem, Mass.	3	Coed	Public	6,922
Salisbury State College, Salisbury, Md.	3	Coed	Public	1,461
Salve Regina College, Newport, R.I.	3	W	Pvt-Roman Catholic	1,220
Sam Houston State University, Huntsville, Texas	3	Coed	Public	10,787
Samford University, Birmingham, Ala.	3	Coed	Pvt-Baptist	2,663
San Antonio College, San Antonio, Texas	1	Coed	Public	14,524
San Bernardino Valley College, San Bernardino, Calif.	1	Coed	Public	13,647
San Diego, University of, College for Men, San Diego, Calif.	3	M	Pvt-Roman Catholic	815
San Diego City College, San Diego, Calif.	1	Coed	Public	4,250
San Diego Evening College, San Diego, Calif.	1	Coed	Public	10,695
San Diego Mesa College, San Diego, Calif.	1	Coed	Public	7,395
San Diego State College, San Diego, Calif.	4	Coed	Public	34,802

Name and Location	Level of Instruction	Student Body	Control	Enrollment
San Fernando Valley State College, Northridge, Calif.	3	Coed	Public	22,218
San Francisco, City College of, San Francisco, Calif.	1	Coed	Public	17,299
San Francisco, University of, San Francisco, Calif.	3	Coed	Pvt-Roman Catholic	6,801
San Francisco State College, San Francisco, Calif.	4	Coed	Public	18,216
San Jacinto College, Pasadena, Texas	1	Coed	Public	7,139
San Joaquin Delta College, Stockton, Calif.	1	Coed	Public	11,510
San Jose City College, San Jose, Calif.	1	Coed	Public	14,104
San Jose State College, San Jose, Calif.	3	Coed	Public	33,632
San Mateo, College of, San Mateo, Calif.	1	Coed	Public	14,373
Sandhills Community College, Southern Pines, N.C.	1	Coed	Public	1,255
Santa Ana College, Santa Ana, Calif.	1	Coed	Public	8,337
Santa Barbara City College, Santa Barbara, Calif.	1	Coed	Public	5,699
Santa Clara, University of, Santa Clara, Calif.	4	Coed	Pvt-Roman Catholic	5,983
Santa Fe, College of, Santa Fe, N.Mex.	2	Coed	Pvt-Roman Catholic	1,258
Santa Fe Junior College, Gainesville, Fla.	1	Coed	Public	3,295
Santa Monica College, Santa Monica, Calif.	1	Coed	Public	12,573
Santa Rosa Junior College, Santa Rosa, Calif.	1	Coed	Public	9,494
Sarah Lawrence College, Bronxville, N.Y.	3	Coed	Private	840
Saskatchewan, University of, Saskatoon and Regina, Sask.	4	Coed	Public	13,338
Savannah State College, Savannah, Ga.	2	Coed	Public	2,444
Schoolcraft College, Livonia, Mich.	1	Coed	Public	5,296
Scranton, University of, Scranton, Pa.	3	Coed	Pvt-Roman Catholic	2,942
Seattle Central Community College, Seattle, Wash.	1	Coed	Public	10,898
Seattle Pacific College, Seattle, Wash.	3	Coed	Pvt-Methodist	2,014
Seattle University, Seattle, Wash.	3	Coed	Pvt-Roman Catholic	3,368
Seminole Junior College, Sanford, Fla.	1	Coed	Public	2,256
Sequoias, College of the, Visalia, Calif.	1	Coed	Public	4,943
Seton Hall University, South Orange, N.J.	4	Coed	Pvt-Roman Catholic	9,449
Seton Hill College, Greensburg, Pa.	2	W	Pvt-Roman Catholic	790
Shasta College, Redding, Calif.	1	Coed	Public	3,258
Shaw University, Raleigh, N.C.	2	Coed	Pvt-Baptist	1,154
Shepherd College, Shepherdstown, W.Va.	2	Coed	Public	1,876
Sherbrooke, University of, Sherbrooke, Quebec	4	Coed	Pvt-Roman Catholic	4,135
Shippensburg State College, Shippensburg, Pa.	3	Coed	Public	5,004
Shoreline Community College, Seattle, Wash.	1	Coed	Public	4,567
Siena College, Loudonville, N.Y.	3	Coed	Pvt-Roman Catholic	1,853
Siena Heights College, Adrian, Mich.	3	Coed	Pvt-Roman Catholic	695
Sierra College, Rocklin, Calif.	1	Coed	Public	4,000
Simmons College, Boston, Mass.	3	W	Private	2,216
Simon Fraser University, Burnaby, B.C.	4	Coed	Public	4,365
Simpson College, Indianola, Iowa.	3	Coed	Pvt-Methodist	1,001
Sinclair Community College, Dayton, Ohio.	1	Coed	Public	3,745
Sioux Falls College, Sioux Falls, S.Dak.	2	Coed	Pvt-Baptist	979
Sir George Williams University, Montreal, Quebec.	4	Coed	Pvt-YMCA	5,919
Siskiyous, College of the, Weed, Calif.	1	Coed	Public	840
Skagit Valley College, Mount Vernon, Wash.	1	Coed	Public	3,463
Skidmore College, Saratoga Springs, N.Y.	2	Coed	Private	1,868
Skyline College, San Bruno, Calif.	1	Coed	Public	4,631
Slippery Rock State College, Slippery Rock, Pa.	3	Coed	Public	5,446
Smith College, Northampton, Mass.	3	W	Private	2,478
Snead State Junior College, Boaz, Ala	1	Coed	Public	882
Snow College, Ephraim, Utah.	1	Coed	Public	890
Solano College, Vallejo, Calif.	1	Coed	Public	5,175
Sonoma State College, Rohnert Park, Calif.	3	Coed	Public	6,838
South, University of the, Sewanee, Tenn.	3	Coed	Pvt-Episcopal	993
South Alabama, University of, Mobile, Ala.	4	Coed	Public	5,221
South Carolina, University of, Columbia, S.C.	4	Coed	Public	17,044
South Carolina State College, Orangeburg, S.C.	3	Coed	Public	2,148
South Dakota, University of, Vermillion, S.Dak.	4	Coed	Public	6,360
Springfield, S.Dak.	2	Coed	Public	1,189
South Dakota School of Mines & Technology, Rapid City, S.Dak.	4	Coed	Public	1,752
South Dakota State University, Brookings, S.Dak.	4	Coed	Public	6,791
South Florida, University of, Tampa, Fla.	3	Coed	Public	18,011
South Georgia College, Douglas, Ga.	1	Coed	Public	1,073
South Plains College, Levelland, Texas	1	Coed	Public	1,849
South Texas Junior College, Houston, Texas	1	Coed	Private	4,378
Southeast Missouri State College, Cape Girardeau, Mo.	3	Coed	Public	7,299
Southeastern Community College, Whiteville, N.C.	1	Coed	Public	1,156
Southeastern Louisiana University, Hammond, La.	3	Coed	Public	5,452
Southeastern Massachusetts University, North Dartmouth, Mass.	3	Coed	Public	4,537
Southeastern State College, Durant, Okla	3	Coed	Public	3,189
Southern Baptist College, Walnut Ridge, Ark.	1	Coed	Pvt-Baptist	812
Southern Baptist Theological Seminary, Louisville, Ky.	4	Coed	Pvt-Baptist	1,083
Southern California, University of, Los Angeles, Calif.	4	Coed	Public	20,797
Southern Colorado State College, Pueblo, Colo.	2	Coed	Public	7,069
Southern Connecticut State College, New Haven, Conn.	3	Coed	Public	12,513
Southern Idaho, College of, Twin Falls, Idaho.	1	Coed	Public	2,307
Southern Illinois University, Carbondale, Ill.	4	Coed	Public	38,809
Southern Illinois University, Edwardsville,	4	Coed	Public	24,543
Southern Methodist University, Dallas, Texas.	4	Coed	Pvt-Methodist	14,266
Southern Missionary College, Collegedale, Tenn.	3	Coed	Pvt-Seventh-day Adventist	1,332
Southern Mississippi, University of, Hattiesburg, Miss.	4	Coed	Public	10,075
Southern Oregon College, Ashland, Oreg.	3	Coed	Public	4,635
Southern State College, Magnolia, Ark.	2	Coed	Public	2,085
Southern University, Baton Rouge, La.	3	Coed	Public	9,722
Southern Utah State College, Cedar City, Utah.	2	Coed	Public	2,008
Southwest Baptist College, Bolivar, Mo.	1	Coed	Pvt-Baptist	1,219
Southwest Missouri State College, Springfield, Mo.	3	Coed	Public	8,963
Southwest Texas Junior College, Uvalde, Texas.	1	Coed	Public	1,325
Southwest Texas State College, San Marcos, Texas.	3	Coed	Public	10,188
Southwest Virginia Community College, Richlands, Va.	1	Coed	Public	899
Southwestern at Memphis, Tenn.	2	Coed	Pvt-Presbyterian	1,051
Southwestern Baptist Theological Seminary, Fort Worth, Texas.	4	Coed	Pvt-Baptist	1,845
Southwestern College, Chula Vista, Calif.	1	Coed	Public	7,006
Southwestern College, Winfield, Kans.	2	Coed	Pvt-Methodist	675
Southwestern Junior College of the Assemblies of God, Waxahachie, Texas.	1	Coed	Pvt-Assemblies of God	635
Southwestern Louisiana, University of, Lafayette, La.	4	Coed	Public	10,259
Southwestern Michigan College, Dowagiac, Mich.	1	Coed	Public	941
Southwestern Oregon Community College, Coos Bay, Oreg.	1	Coed	Public	1,827
Southwestern University, Georgetown, Texas.	3	Coed	Pvt-Methodist	5,174
Spalding College, Louisville, Ky.	3	Coed	Pvt-Roman Catholic	1,267
Spartanburg County Technical Education Center, Spartanburg, S.C.	1	Coed	Public	886
Spartanburg Junior College, Spartanburg, S.C.	1	Coed	Pvt-Methodist	886
Spelman College, Atlanta, Ga.	2	W	Private	967
Spokane Community College, Spokane, Wash.	1	Coed	Public	5,805
Spring Arbor College, Spring Arbor, Mich.	3	Coed	Pvt-Methodist	730
Spring Hill College, Mobile, Ala.	3	Coed	Pvt-Roman Catholic	970
Springfield College, Springfield, Mass.	4	Coed	Private	2,647
Stanford University, Stanford, Calif.	4	Coed	Private	12,350
Stanislaus State College, Turlock, Calif.	3	Coed	Public	5,700
State Technical Institute at Memphis, Tenn.	1	Coed	Public	1,669
Stephen F. Austin State College, Nacogdoches, Texas.	3	Coed	Public	9,614
Stephens College, Columbia, Mo.	2	W	Private	2,140
Stetson University, De Land, Fla.	3	Coed	Pvt-Baptist	2,586
Steubenville, College of, Steubenville, Ohio.	3	Coed	Pvt-Roman Catholic	1,380
Stevens Institute of Technology, Hoboken, N.J.	4	M	Private	2,650
Stillman College, Tuscaloosa, Ala.	2	Coed	Pvt-Presbyterian	658
Stonehill College, North Easton, Mass.	2	Coed	Pvt-Roman Catholic	1,658
Stout State University, Menomonie, Wis.	3	Coed	Public	6,223
Stratford College, Danville, Va.	2	W	Private	563
Suffolk County Community College, Selden, N.Y.	1	Coed	Public	9,677

Name and Location	Level of Instruction	Student Body	Control	Enrollment
Suffolk University, Boston, Mass.	3	Coed	Private	5,068
Sul Ross State College, Alpine, Texas.	3	Coed	Public	2,600
Sullivan County Community College, South Fallsburg, N.Y.	1	Coed	Public	1,209
Sumter Area Technical Education Center, Sumter, S.C.	1	Coed	Public	1,192
Surry Community College, Dobson, N.C.	1	Coed	Public	824
Susquehanna University, Selinsgrove, Pa.	2	Coed	Pvt-Lutheran	1,309
Swarthmore College, Swarthmore, Pa.	3	Coed	Private	1,164
Sweet Briar College, Sweet Briar, Va.	2	W	Private	715
Syracuse University, Syracuse, N.Y.	4	Coed	Private	15,320
Tacoma Community College, Tacoma, Wash.	1	Coed	Public	3,762
Taft College, Taft, Calif.	1	Coed	Public	656
Talladega College, Talladega, Ala.	2	Coed	Pvt-Church of Christ	533
Tallahassee Community College, Tallahassee, Fla.	1	Coed	Public	2,100
Tampa, University of, Tampa, Fla.	2	Coed	Private	2,417
Tarleton State College, Stephenville, Texas.	2	Coed	Public	2,973
Tarrant County Junior College, Fort Worth, Texas.	1	Coed	Public	10,653
Taylor University, Upland, Ind.	2	Coed	Private	1,425
Temple Buell College, Denver, Colo.	2	W	Private	813
Temple Junior College, Temple, Texas.	1	Coed	Public	1,142
Temple University, Philadelphia, Pa.	4	Coed	Private	31,592
Tennessee, University of, Knoxville, Tenn.	4	Coed	Public	27,723
Tennessee State University, Nashville, Tenn.	4	Coed	Public	4,404
Tennessee Technological University, Cookeville, Tenn.	3	Coed	Public	6,262
Tennessee Wesleyan College, Athens, Tenn.	2	Coed	Pvt-Methodist	761
Texarkana College, Texarkana, Texas.	1	Coed	Public	1,952
Texas, University System of, Austin, Texas.	4	Coed	Public	74,125
Austin, Texas.	3	Coed	Public	45,442
Arlington.	3	Coed	Public	14,115
El Paso.	3	Coed	Public	11,484
Texas Agricultural & Mechanical University, College Station, Texas.	4	Coed	Public	14,316
Texas Arts and Industries University, Kingsville, Texas.	3	Coed	Public	8,468
Texas Christian University, Fort Worth, Texas.	4	Coed	Pvt-Disciples of Christ	6,433
Texas Lutheran College, Seguin, Texas.	2	Coed	Pvt-Lutheran	984
Texas Southern University, Houston, Texas.	4	Coed	Public	5,485
Texas Southmost College, Brownsville, Texas.	1	Coed	Public	1,689
Texas State Technical Institute, Waco, Texas.	1	Coed	Public	1,558
Texas Tech University, Lubbock, Texas.	4	Coed	Public	20,008
Texas Wesleyan College, Fort Worth, Texas.	2	Coed	Pvt-Methodist	1,760
Texas Woman's University, Denton, Texas.	4	W	Public	5,366
Thames Valley State Technical College, Norwich, Conn.	1	Coed	Public	1,077
Theodore Alfred Lawson State Junior College, Birmingham, Ala.	1	Coed	Public	1,205
Thiel College, Greenville, Pa.	2	Coed	Pvt-Lutheran	1,401
Thomas More College, Fort Mitchell, Ky.	2	Coed	Pvt-Roman Catholic	2,227
Thomas Nelson Community College, Hampton, Va.	1	Coed	Public	2,204
Thornton Community College, South Holland, Ill.	1	Coed	Public	4,827
Thunderbird Graduate School of International Management, Thunderbird Campus, Glendale, Ariz.	4	Coed	Private	807
Tift College, Forsyth, Ga.	2	W	Pvt-Baptist	642
Toledo, University of, Toledo, Ohio.	4	Coed	Public	14,894
Toronto, University of, Toronto, Ontario.	4	Coed	Public	21,134
St. Michael's College, University of, Toronto.	4	Coed	Pvt-Roman Catholic	2,198
Trinity College, University of, Toronto.	3	Coed	Public	745
Victoria University, Toronto.	3	Coed	Public	2,554
Tougaloo College, Tougaloo, Miss.	2	Coed	Pvt-Disciples of Christ	736
Towson State College, Towson, Md.	3	Coed	Public	9,911
Transylvania University, Lexington, Ky.	2	Coed	Pvt-Disciples of Christ	859
Treasure Valley Community College, Ontario, Oreg.	1	Coed	Public	1,484
Trent University, Peterborough, Ontario.	3	Coed	Private	1,287
Trenton State College, Trenton, N.J.	3	Coed	Public	9,903
Trevecca Nazarene College, Nashville, Tenn.	2	Coed	Pvt-Church of Nazarene	730
Trinidad State Junior College, Trinidad, Colo.	1	Coed	Public	1,559
Trinity College, Hartford, Conn.	3	Coed	Private	1,967
Trinity College, Washington, D.C.	3	Coed	Pvt-Roman Catholic	857
Trinity College, Deerfield, Ill.	2	Coed	Pvt-Evangelical	785
Trinity University, San Antonio, Texas.	3	Coed	Pvt-Presbyterian	2,894
Tri-State College, Angola, Ind.	2	Coed	Private	1,845
Troy State University, Troy, Ala.	3	Coed	Public	5,736
Tufts University, Medford, Mass.	4	Coed	Private	5,266
Tulane University, New Orleans, La.	4	Coord	Private	8,395
Tulsa, University of, Tulsa, Okla.	4	Coed	Pvt-Presbyterian	6,407
Tusculum College, Greeneville, Tenn.	2	Coed	Pvt-Presbyterian	677
Tuskegee Institute, Tuskegee Institute, Ala.	2	Coed	Private	2,918
Tyler Junior College, Tyler, Texas.	1	Coed	Public	3,897
Ulster County Community College, Stone Ridge, N.Y.	1	Coed	Public	2,230
Umpqua Community College, Roseburg, Oreg.	1	Coed	Public	1,003
Union College, Barbourville, Ky.	3	Coed	Pvt-Methodist	926
Union College, Lincoln, Nebr.	2	Coed	Pvt-Seventh-day Adventist	893
Union College, Cranford, N.J.	1	Coed	Private	2,876
Union College and University, Schenectady, N.Y.	3	Coed	Private	4,656
Union University, Jackson, Tenn.	2	Coed	Pvt-Baptist	806
United States Air Force Academy, Colorado Springs, Colo.	2	M	Public	4,128
United States Coast Guard Academy, New London, Conn.	2	M	Public	969
United States International University (including California Western Campus, Elliott Campus, and School of Performing Arts), San Diego, Calif.	4	Coed	Private	4,108
United States Merchant Marine Academy, Kings Point, N.Y.	2	M	Public	1,026
United States Military Academy, West Point, N.Y.	2	M	Public	4,036
United States Naval Academy, Annapolis, Md.	2	M	Public	4,375
Upper Iowa University, Fayette, Iowa.	2	Coed	Private	1,188
Upsala College, East Orange, N.J.	2	Coed	Pvt-Lutheran	1,843
Ursinus College, Collegeville, Pa.	2	Coed	Pvt-Church of Christ	2,031
Utah, University of, Salt Lake City, Utah.	4	Coed	Public	21,729
Utah State University, Logan, Utah.	4	Coed	Public	9,091
Utah Technical College at Provo, Utah.	1	Coed	Public	2,061
Utah Technical College at Salt Lake City, Utah.	1	Coed	Public	1,661
Valdosta State College, Valdosta, Ga.	3	Coed	Public	3,232
Valencia Junior College, Orlando, Fla.	1	Coed	Public	3,216
Valley City State College, Valley City, N.Dak.	2	Coed	Public	1,369
Valparaiso University, Valparaiso, Ind.	3	Coed	Pvt-Lutheran	4,590
Vanderbilt University, Nashville, Tenn.	4	Coed	Private	6,397
Vassar College, Poughkeepsie, N.Y.	3	Coed	Private	1,900
Ventura College, Ventura, Calif.	1	Coed	Public	8,285
Vermont, University of, Burlington, Vt.	4	Coed	Public	9,214
Victor Valley College, Victorville, Calif.	1	Coed	Public	1,909
Victoria College, Victoria, Texas.	1	Coed	Public	1,632
Victoria, University of, Victoria, B.C.	4	Coed	Public	5,239
Villa Maria College, Erie, Pa.	2	W	Pvt-Roman Catholic	617
Villanova University, Villanova, Pa.	4	Coed	Pvt-Roman Catholic	9,378
Vincennes University, Vincennes, Ind.	1	Coed	Public	3,318
Virgin Islands, College of the, St. Thomas, V.I.	2	Coed	Public	1,446
Virginia, University of, Charlottesville, Va.	4	Coed	Public	8,038
Clinch Valley College, Wise, Va.	2	Coed	Public	812
Mary Washington College, Fredericksburg, Va.	2	W	Public	2,168
Virginia Commonwealth University, Richmond, Va.	4	Coed	Public	14,211
Virginia Military Institute, Lexington, Va.	2	M	Public	1,146
Virginia Polytechnic Institute, Blacksburg, Va.	4	Coed	Public	12,041
Virginia State College, Petersburg, Va.	3	Coed	Public	3,178
Virginia Union University, Richmond, Va.	2	Coed	Pvt-Baptist	1,313
Virginia Wesleyan College, Norfolk, Va.	2	Coed	Pvt-Methodist	634
Virginia Western Community College, Roanoke, Va.	1	Coed	Public	2,754
Voorhees College, Denmark, S.C.	2	Coed	Pvt-Episcopal	624

Name and Location	Level of Instruction	Student Body	Control	Enrollment
W. W. Holding Technical Institute, Raleigh, N.C.	1	Coed	Public	715
Wabash College, Crawfordsville, Ind.	2	M	Private	854
Wagner College, Staten Island, N.Y.	3	Coed	Pvt-Lutheran	3,265
Wake Forest University, Winston-Salem, N.C.	4	Coed	Pvt-Baptist	3,326
Walker College, Jasper, Ala.	1	Coed	Private	732
Walla Walla College, College Place, Wash.	3	Coed	Pvt-Seventh-day Adventist	1,245
Walla Walla Community College, Walla Walla, Wash.	1	Coed	Public	1,564
Walsh College, North Canton, Ohio	2	Coed	Pvt-Roman Catholic	994
Wartburg College, Waverly, Iowa	3	Coed	Pvt-Lutheran	1,404
Washburn University of Topeka, Kans.	4	Coed	Public	4,765
Washington, University of, Seattle, Wash.	4	Coed	Public	33,202
Washington and Jefferson College, Washington, Pa.	2	Coed	Private	976
Washington and Lee University, Lexington, Va.	4	M	Private	1,526
Washington College, Chestertown, Md.	2	Coed	Private	677
Washington State University, Pullman, Wash.	4	Coed	Public	14,667
Washington University, St. Louis, Mo.	4	Coed	Private	11,070
Waterbury State Technical College, Waterbury, Conn.	1	Coed	Public	1,551
Waterloo, University of, Waterloo, Ont.	4	Coed	Public	10,299
Waterloo Lutheran University, Waterloo, Ontario	3	Coed	Pvt-Lutheran	2,758
Wayland Baptist College, Plainview, Texas	3	Coed	Pvt-Baptist	689
Wayne Community College, Goldsboro, N.C.	1	Coed	Public	1,306
Wayne State College, Wayne, Nebr.	3	Coed	Public	2,972
Wayne State University, Detroit, Mich.	4	Coed	Public	35,655
Waynesburg College, Waynesburg, Pa.	2	Coed	Pvt-Presbyterian	1,113
Weatherford College, Weatherford, Texas	1	Coed	Public	1,165
Weber State College, Ogden, Utah	4	Coed	Public	10,157
Webster College, St. Louis, Mo.	3	Coed	Private	1,545
Wellesley College, Wellesley, Mass.	3	W	Private	1,766
Wells College, Aurora, N.Y.	3	W	Private	632
Wenatchee Valley College, Wenatchee, Wash.	1	Coed	Public	1,673
Wentworth Institute, Boston, Mass.	1	M	Private	1,849
Wesley College, Dover, Del.	1	Coed	Pvt-Methodist	1,118
Wesleyan University, Middletown, Conn.	4	Coed	Private	1,869
West Chester State College, West Chester, Pa.	3	Coed	Public	8,251
West Coast University, Los Angeles, Calif.	3	Coed	Private	1,029
West Florida, University of, Pensacola, Fla.	3	Coed	Public	3,652
West Georgia College, Carrollton, Ga.	3	Coed	Public	5,503
West Hills College, Coalinga, Calif.	1	Coed	Public	1,339
West Liberty State College, West Liberty, W.Va.	3	Coed	Public	4,347
West Los Angeles College, Culver City, Calif.	1	Coed	Public	4,239
West Texas State University, Canyon, Texas	4	Coed	Public	7,905
West Valley College, Campbell, Calif.	1	Coed	Public	10,513
West Virginia Inst. of Technology, Montgomery, W.Va.	3	Coed	Public	2,444
West Virginia State College, Institute, W.Va.	3	Coed	Public	3,663
West Virginia University, Morgantown, W.Va.	4	Coed	Public	19,858
West Virginia Wesleyan College, Buckhannon, W.Va.	2	Coed	Pvt-Methodist	1,771
Westchester Community College, Valhalla, N.Y.	1	Coed	Public	5,286
Western Carolina University, Cullowhee, N.C.	3	Coed	Public	5,430
Western Connecticut State College, Danbury, Conn.	3	Coed	Public	4,094
Western Illinois University, Macomb, Ill.	4	Coed	Public	14,307
Western Kentucky University, Bowling Green, Ky.	4	Coed	Public	11,215
Western Maryland College, Westminster, Md.	3	Coed	Pvt-Methodist	
Western Michigan University, Kalamazoo, Mich.	4	Coed	Public	21,713
Western Montana College, Dillon, Mont.	3	Coed	Public	1,106
Western New England College, Springfield, Mass.	3	Coed	Private	3,432
Western New Mexico University, Silver City, N.Mex.	3	Coed	Public	1,425
Western Ontario, University of, London, Ontario	4	Coed	Public	10,698
Western Piedmont Community College, Morganton, N.C.	1	Coed	Public	1,032
Western State College of Colorado, Gunnison, Colo.	3	Coed	Public	3,485
Western Washington State College, Bellingham, Wash.	4	Coed	Public	11,360
Westfield State College, Westfield, Mass.	3	Coed	Public	3,597
Westmar College, Le Mars, Iowa	3	Coed	Pvt-Methodist	1,074
Westminster College, Fulton, Mo.	2	M	Pvt-Presbyterian	703
Westminster College, New Wilmington, Pa.	3	Coed	Pvt-Presbyterian	1,944
Westminster College, Salt Lake City, Utah	2	Coed	Pvt-Methodist	835
Westmont College, Santa Barbara, Calif.	2	Coed	Private	843
Wharton County Junior College, Wharton, Texas	1	Coed	Public	1,974
Wheaton College, Wheaton, Ill.	3	Coed	Private	1,950
Wheaton College, Norton, Mass.	2	Coed	Private	1,152
Wheeling College, Wheeling, W.Va.	2	Coed	Pvt-Roman Catholic	744
Wheelock College, Boston, Mass.	3	Coed	Private	709
Whitman College, Walla Walla, Wash.	3	Coed	Private	1,105
Whittier College, Whittier, Calif.	3	Coed	Private	2,367
Whitworth College, Spokane, Wash.	3	Coed	Pvt-Presbyterian	1,517
Wichita State University, Wichita, Kans.	4	Coed	Public	12,395
Wilberforce University, Wilberforce, Ohio	3	Coed	Pvt-Methodist Episcopal	
Wilkes College, Wilkes-Barre, Pa.	3	Coed	Private	3,577
Wilkes Community College, Wilkesboro, N.C.	1	Coed	Public	759
Willamette University, Salem, Oreg.	4	Coed	Pvt-Methodist	1,713
William and Mary, College of, Williamsburg, Va.	4	Coed	Public	7,332
William Carey College, Hattiesburg, Miss.	2	Coed	Pvt-Baptist	797
William Jewell College, Liberty, Mo.	3	Coed	Pvt-Baptist	849
William Paterson College of New Jersey, Wayne, N.J.	3	Coed	Public	7,139
William Penn College, Oskaloosa, Iowa	3	Coed	Pvt-Friends	842
William Rainey Harper College, Palatine, Ill.	1	Coed	Public	6,420
William Woods College, Fulton, Mo.	2	W	Pvt-Disciples of Christ	854
Williams College, Williamstown, Mass.	3	Coed	Private	1,418
Williamsport Area Community College, Williamsport, Pa.	1	Coed	Public	2,730
Wilmington College, Wilmington, Ohio	2	Coed	Pvt-Friends	945
Windham College, Putney, Vt.	2	Coed	Private	923
Windsor, University of, Windsor, Ont.	4	Coed	Private	5,020
Wingate College, Wingate, N.C.	1	Coed	Pvt-Baptist	1,637
Winnipeg, University of, Winnipeg, Manitoba	4	Coed	Pvt-United Church	2,420
Winona State College, Winona, Minn.	3	Coed	Public	4,260
Winston-Salem State University, Winston-Salem, N.C.	3	Coed	Public	1,401
Winthrop College, Rock Hill, S.C.	3	Coed	Public	3,887
Wisconsin, University of, Madison & Milwaukee, Wis.	4	Coed	Public	70,582
Wisconsin State University—Eau Claire, Wis.	3	Coed	Public	8,288
Wisconsin State University—La Crosse, Wis.	3	Coed	Public	7,317
Wisconsin State University—Oshkosh, Wis.	3	Coed	Public	12,072
Wisconsin State University—Platteville, Wis.	3	Coed	Public	5,404
Wisconsin State University—River Falls, Wis.	3	Coed	Public	4,323
Wisconsin State University—Stevens Point, Wis.	3	Coed	Public	9,297
Wisconsin State University—Superior, Wis.	3	Coed	Public	3,268
Wisconsin State University—Whitewater, Wis.	3	Coed	Public	10,135
Wittenberg University, Springfield, Ohio	3	Coed	Pvt-Lutheran	3,289
Wofford College, Spartanburg, S.C.	3	M	Pvt-Methodist	989
Woodbury College, Los Angeles, Calif.	2	Coed	Private	2,236
Wooster, College of, Wooster, Ohio	2	Coed	Pvt-Presbyterian	1,185
Worcester Junior College, Worcester, Mass.	1	Coed	Private	2,225
Worcester Polytechnic Institute, Worcester, Mass.	4	M	Private	2,225
Worcester State College, Worcester, Mass.	3	Coed	Public	3,819
Wright State University, Dayton, Ohio	3	Coed	Public	11,002
Wyoming, University of, Laramie, Wyo.	4	Coed	Public	8,900
Wytheville Community College, Wytheville, Va.	1	Coed	Public	932
Xavier University, Cincinnati, Ohio	3	Coed	Pvt-Roman Catholic	6,134
Xavier University of Louisiana, New Orleans, La.	3	Coed	Pvt-Roman Catholic	1,422
Yakima Valley College, Yakima, Wash.	1	Coed	Public	2,441
Yale University, New Haven, Conn.	4	Coed	Private	8,927
Yeshiva University, New York, N.Y.	4	Coord	Pvt-Jewish	3,750
York College of Pennsylvania, York, Pa.	1	Coed	Private	2,321
York County Technical Education Center, Rock Hill, S.C.	1	Coed	Public	2,815
York University, Toronto, Ont.	4	Coed	Public	7,734
Youngstown State University, Youngstown, Ohio	3	Coed	Public	15,030
Yuba College, Marysville, Calif.	1	Coed	Public	4,170

UPPER VOLTA

The principal events of 1971 in Upper Volta revolved about the results of the December 1970 general elections and the formation of the first parliamentary government since Gen. Sangoulé Laminzana took power in 1966.

Government. The elections, in which 48% of the registered voters went to the polls, resulted in a clear victory for the Voltaic Democratic Union (UDV), which won 37 of the 57 seats in the new National Assembly. The Party of African Regroupment (PRA) won 12 seats, the National Liberation Movement (MLN) won 6, and 2 went to independents. In February, President Laminzana, who will remain head of state until 1975, appointed Gérard Kango Ouedraogo, leader of the UDV, as prime minister. In the new cabinet, the UDV received 8 of the 15 ministerial posts; the PRA, 2; and the military, 5, the one third required by the constitution.

Foreign Relations. During 1971, Upper Volta appeared to take a more conservative stance in international affairs than many of its African neighbors. Early in the year, it indicated what the president called an "open mind" on the question of opening a dialogue with South Africa—proposed by Ivory Coast President Houphouët-Boigny. In October, it voted against the admission of the People's Republic of China to the United Nations.

Prime Minister Kofi Busia of Ghana visited Upper Volta in August. The two countries agreed to sign conventions dealing with migrant labor, border demarcation, and the development of the Volta River valley.

Economy. Upper Volta's economic situation continued to deteriorate because of the serious drought that affected most of West Africa in 1970–71. The trade deficit increased, and production of cotton and cattle declined by as much as one third from 1970 levels. In September, however, Upper Volta, Mali, and Niger announced that they would jointly undertake the development of their mineral-rich Liptako-Gourma region. Sizable deposits of copper, manganese, limestone, phosphate, and phosphorus may be exploited if financing is adequate.

Upper Volta continued to receive substantial foreign aid, principally from France, the Development Fund of the European Common Market, and the World Bank.

VICTOR T. LE VINE
Washington University, St. Louis

------ **UPPER VOLTA • Information Highlights** ------

Official Name: Republic of Upper Volta.
Area: 105,869 square miles (274,200 sq km).
Population (1970 est.): 5,380,000. *Density,* 49 per square mile (19 per sq km). *Annual rate of increase,* 2.0%.
Chief Cities (1970 est.): Ouagadougou, the capital, 115,000; Bobo Dioulasso, 72,000.
Government: *Head of state,* Gen. Sangoulé Lamizana, president (took office Jan. 3, 1966). *Chief minister,* Gérard Kango Ouedraogo, prime minister (took office Feb. 13, 1971). *Legislature*—National Assembly (unicameral), 57 members. *Major political parties*—Voltaic Democratic Union; National Liberation Movement; Party of African Regroupment.
Languages: French (official), Mossi.
Education: *Literacy rate* (1971), 5%–10% of population. *School enrollment* (1968)—primary, 99,827; secondary, 10,-529; technical/vocational, 1,298; university/higher, 122.
Finances (1969 est.): *Revenues,* $36,860,000; *expenditures,* $36,860,000; *monetary unit,* CFA franc (277.71 francs equal U. S.$1, Sept. 1971).
Gross National Product (1968): $257,000,000.
Average Annual Income Per Person (1968): $50.
Manufacturing (metric tons, 1969): Meat, 9,000; beer, 58,000 hectoliters.
Crops (metric tons, 1968 crop year): Sorghum, 825,000; millet, 361,000; maize, 137,000; groundnuts, 92,000.
Minerals (1966): Gold, 567 kilograms.
Foreign Trade (1968): *Exports,* $21,000,000 (chief exports—live animals, $10,229,000; raw cotton, $3,703,000). *Imports,* $41,000,000 (chief imports—textile yarn and fabrics, $6,263,000; transport equipment, $4,000,000; petroleum products, $2,715,000). *Chief trading partners* (1968)—Ivory Coast (took 53% of exports, supplied 21% of imports); France (14%—44%); Ghana (10%—1%).
Transportation: *Roads* (1970), 9,100 miles (14,645 km); *motor vehicles* (1969), 12,100 (automobiles, 5,800).
Communications: *Telephones* (1970), 1,398; *television stations* (1968), 1; *television sets* (1968), 500; *radios* (1969), 80,000.

URUGUAY

On Nov. 28, 1971, after a year marred by economic crises and terrorist successes against an ineffectual government, general elections were held in Uruguay. The ruling Colorado party, despite its troubles, was returned to power by a slim plurality.

Political Developments. Although Uruguay has been considered Latin America's most successful democracy, there was every reason in 1971 to expect its collapse. Prolonged martial law and press censorship were employed, in violation of both Uruguayan tradition and constitutional provisions. But order could not be maintained against the Tupamaros, an extreme leftist, terrorist group of about 3,500. They kidnapped prominent persons and, when caught, escaped from prison with ease.

President Jorge Pacheco Areco was censured by the Congress, which was openly at odds with him during most of the year, but he did not resign, since that would have precipitated an immediate parliamentary election. Many cabinet crises and resignations occurred. High unemployment and rapid inflation continued, and several general strikes were mounted in protest.

A wide coalition of anti-government forces, including Communists, Socialists, Christian Democrats, and even the Tupamaros, combined to organize the Frente Amplio ("Broad Front"), which selected retired Gen. Líber Seregni Mosquera as its candidate for the presidency. The Colorado and Blanco (or Nation) parties, which had dominated Uruguayan government for many decades, continued to conduct politics as usual, knowing that a complex election law protected their advantage.

In the November election the Colorado party narrowly outpolled the Blancos. Thus, under Uruguayan law, the presidency fell to the leading vote-getter among the seven Colorado party candidates running for the office. The winner was Agriculture Secretary Juan M. Bordaberry, the choice of President Pacheco, and considered the most conservative candidate. Seregni garnered about 18% of the vote—nearly double the combined vote, in previous elections, of the parties backing him.

Some 70 years of growing socialism had led to government control of major sectors of the economy, universal social security, and a public payroll that included one third of all the workers. It had created a large middle class heavily committed to the existing system. Despite that system's recent failures, most voters refused to turn to the Frente, which they regarded as a leap into the unknown.

Economic Affairs. Stabilization measures failed to halt either the depression or the inflation (21% in 1971), and only minor economic gains were being registered. The gross national product rose by 5%, up from 4.5% in 1970. The increase was mainly in agricultural and industrial goods, with consumer goods becoming even more scarce.

─────── URUGUAY • Information Highlights ───────

Official Name: Eastern Republic of Uruguay.
Area: 68,536 square miles (177,508 sq km).
Population (1970 est.): 2,890,000. *Density,* 40 per square mile (16 per sq km). *Annual rate of increase,* 1.3%.
Chief City (1970 est.): Montevideo, the capital, 1,400,000.
Government: *Head of state,* Juan M. Bordaberry, president (took office December 1971). *Head of government,* Juan M. Bordaberry. *Legislature*—National Assembly: Senate, 31 members; Chamber of Deputies, 99 members.
Education: *Literacy rate* (1970), 91% of population. *Expenditure on education* (1965), 3.7% of gross national product. *School enrollment* (1968)—primary, 369,816; secondary, 160,693; technical/vocational, 35,648; higher, 18,650.
Finances (1969): *Revenues,* $182,100,000; *expenditures,* $185,100,000; *monetary unit,* peso (250 pesos equal U. S. $1, Sept. 1971).
Manufacturing (metric tons, 1969): Residual fuel oil, 804,000; cement, 467,000; meat, 430,000; sugar, 63,000.
Crops (metric tons, 1969 crop year): Sugar beets (1968–69), 485,000; wheat, 403,000; maize, 139,000.
Foreign Trade (1970): *Exports,* $233,000,000 (chief exports— Meat, $87,800,000; wool, $73,200,000; hides, $24,300,000). *Imports,* $233,000,000 (chief imports—crude petroleum, $21,310,000; machinery, $13,090,000). *Chief trading partners* (1968)—Britain (took 21% of exports, supplied 5% of imports); U. S. (12%—23%); W. Germany (7%—9%).

Exports rose as wool shipments reached a new high, and severe import restrictions contributed to an improved balance of trade. External debts grew, however, and international reserves fell from $91 million in early 1970 to $31.6 million on March 31, 1971. Bad weather, a recession in Argentina, and fear of terrorists combined to depress the normally lucrative tourist trade.

International Affairs. British Ambassador Geoffrey Jackson was kidnapped by the Tupamaros in January and freed eight months later. Brazilian Consul Aloysio Dias Gomide, kidnapped in July 1970, was released for ransom in February. Relations with Argentina and Brazil improved somewhat.

In August, Uruguay joined various other Latin American nations in claiming that its territorial waters extended 200 miles (320 km) out to sea.

PHILIP B. TAYLOR, JR.
University of Houston

UTAH

The retirement of a political maverick, problems in higher education, the death of an internationally known radio narrator, and the achievements of the Utah Stars professional basketball team were major events in Utah in 1971.

Politics. J. Bracken Lee, mayor of Salt Lake City, announced his retirement from political life at the age of 72. He was famous for his forthright style of independent politics.

Lee was elected mayor of the small city of Price in 1935, winning by two votes on the Progressive party ticket, and held office for 12 years. After failing to win a seat in Congress in 1942 and a close loss as the Republican candidate for governor in 1944, he was elected governor in 1948, the first Republican to hold the office since 1924.

"Brack," as he was called, served two terms as governor, but infuriated his Republican backers by refusing to use his full patronage powers. He alienated what he called "the school lobby" by slashing appropriations. He antagonized organized labor, and frustrated veterans and farmers by his reluctance to grant subsidies. As a newspaper reported, "The combative, irascible chief executive used the veto frequently, culling out appropriations that he believed had been lobbied through." He virtually repudiated the Republican party by saying that it "has become as corrupt as the Democratic party."

In 1959, without major party support, Lee was elected mayor of Salt Lake City. He remained in that office until he retired. Most Utahans expect that he will not keep quiet. They believe he meant it when he said, "They'll never shut me up."

Education. Higher education in Utah appeared to be in a period of major evolution. Severe pressures caused administrators and educators to reexamine traditional concepts. A governor's commission recommended retention of tenure in Utah colleges, but the issue remained unresolved. Constitutional conflict developed between the state board of higher education and the state board of education over jurisdictional responsibilities. Teacher shortages at the elementary and secondary school levels were eliminated, and graduates found it difficult to find teaching positions.

Religion. Apostle Richard L. Evans of the Church of Jesus Christ of Latter-day Saints, who narrated the "Spoken Word" heard on Sundays with the nationwide radio and television programs of the Salt Lake City Tabernacle Choir, died on November 1. His 3-minute "sermonettes," which he wrote and broadcast for over 40 years, were heard by millions.

Sports. The Utah Stars, in their first year as a major league professional team, won the American Basketball Association (ABA) championship on May 18 when they defeated Kentucky by 131 to 121. It was the first national professional team title in Utah's history. The Stars drew 262,342 spectators to 42 home games, an average of 6,246 a game. The figure was an ABA record.

LORENZO K. KIMBALL, *University of Utah*

─────── UTAH • Information Highlights ───────

Area: 84,916 square miles (219,932 sq km).
Population (1970 census): 1,059,273. *Density:* 13 per sq mi.
Chief Cities (1970 census): Salt Lake City, the capital, 175,-885; Ogden, 69,478; Provo, 53,131; Bountiful, 27,853.
Government (1971): *Chief Officers*—governor, Calvin L. Rampton (D); secy. of state, Clyde L. Miller (D); atty. gen., Vernon B. Romney (R); treas., Golden L. Allen (R); supt. of public instruction, Walter D. Talbot; chief justice, E. R. Callister, Jr. *Legislature*—Senate, 28 members (16 Republicans, 12 Democrats); House of Representatives, 69 members (38 D, 30 R, 1 other).
Education (1970–71): *Enrollment*—public elementary schools, 165,486 pupils; 5,850 teachers; secondary public, 138,516 pupils; 5,500 teachers; nonpublic schools (1968–69), 6,000 pupils; 310 teachers; college and university (fall 1968), 69,916 students. *Public school expenditures* (1970–71), $185,361,000 ($643 per pupil). *Average teacher's salary,* $8,073.
State Finances (fiscal year 1970): *Revenues,* $552,785,000 (4% general sales tax and gross receipts taxes, $90,976,-000; motor fuel tax, $37,805,000; federal funds, $161,-883,000). *Expenditures,* $527,938,000 (education, $253,-904,000; health, welfare, safety, $55,513,000; highways, $103,418,000). *State debt,* $103,089,000 (June 1970).
Personal Income (1970): $3,489,000,000; *per capita,* $3,210.
Public Assistance (1970): $47,260,000. *Average monthly payments* (Dec. 1970)—old-age assistance, $54.30; aid to families with dependent children, $155.90.
Labor Force: *Nonagricultural wage and salary earners* (June 1971), 369,200. *Average annual employment* (1969)—manufacturing, 54,000; trade, 78,000; government, 99,000; services, 54,000. *Insured unemployed* (Oct. 1971)—6,400 (2.7%).
Manufacturing (1967): *Value added by manufacture,* $777,900,-000. Food and kindred products, $102,900,000; transportation equipment, $90,200,000; nonelectrical machinery, $53,300,000; petroleum and coal products, $50,800,000.
Agriculture (1970): *Cash farm income,* $236,569,000 (livestock, $182,469,000; crops, $42,956,000; government payments, $11,144,000). *Chief crops* (1970)—Barley, 7,353,-000 bushels; wheat, 5,976,000 bushels; hay, 1,592,000 tons.
Mining (1970): *Production value,* $629,587,000 (ranks 16th among the states). *Chief minerals* (tons)—Coal, 4,852,000; copper, 305,800; petroleum, 23,500,000 barrels; gold, 420,-000 troy ounces.
Transportation: *Roads* (1969) 39,439 miles (63,469 km); *motor vehicles* (1969), 601,000; *railroads* (1968), 1,771 miles (2,850 km); *airports* (1969), 58.
Communications: *Telephones* (1971), 595,600; *television stations* (1969), 3; *radio stations* (1969), 41; *newspapers* (1969), 5 (daily circulation, 256,000).

VANCOUVER

The largest city in British Columbia and the third-largest in Canada, until the "new" Winnipeg came into existence on Jan. 1, 1972, Vancouver in 1971 was concerned with pollution, metropolitan transportation, and shipping. Preliminary census figures put the population of the city at 422,278 and of the metropolitan area at 1,071,081.

Government. The Greater Vancouver Regional District, a loose federation of 14 local councils, worked effectively in 1971. It controlled or prepared to control pollution, public housing, and transportation. In November it began negotiations to take over the province's bus system, as the first step toward an efficient rapid-transit operation within 15 to 20 years. In the same month the way was cleared to finance a tunnel under Burrard Inlet, affording a third Vancouver-North Shore link.

When plans for a hotel-apartment project at the entrance to popular Stanley Park were nearly defeated by a vote of the taxpayers, the Vancouver Council warily rejected plans for a 750-foot (230-meter) Space Needle building and began to express concern about the province's plan for a 700-foot (215-meter) skyscraper in the city's center.

Vancouver's efforts to alleviate its share of Canada's high unemployment included the creation of a unique job project engaging 33 artists, sculptors, musicians, and composers.

Commerce. In November the federal government named a 10-man Port of Vancouver Authority. Improvement of the port's container-handling facilities was given first priority. The port had an unusually active year, due to the U. S. longshoremen's strike and the diversion of ships to Vancouver. A record total of 35 million tons of cargo was handled in 1971, up from 27 million in 1970.

The Canada Development Corporation, a government agency to promote Canadian investment, will move its headquarters from Ottawa to Vancouver within two years it was announced in November.

Events. The top news story of 1971 was the marriage—in a secret ceremony in North Vancouver on March 4—of Prime Minister Pierre Elliott Trudeau, 51, and Margaret Sinclair, 22, daughter of a former Canadian minister of fisheries.

Queen Elizabeth II, Prince Philip, and Princess Anne visited Vancouver in May, and Soviet Premier Aleksei Kosygin visited the city in October.

The Calgary Stampeders defeated the Toronto Argonauts, 14–11, in the Canadian Football League final for the Grey Cup in Vancouver in November.

Education. While enrollment at Simon Fraser University was steady at 5,048, the University of British Columbia had a drop for the first time in 23 years—to 20,183 from 20,940 in 1970. Some 10,000 persons were taking courses at Vancouver City College.

DON MACLACHLAN
"The Province," Vancouver

VENEZUELA

Venezuela celebrated its 150th year of independence in 1971, against a background of student unrest, controversial oil policies, and friction with neighboring Colombia.

Creeping Nationalization. The role of foreign petroleum concerns in the economy became increasingly limited by official policies of economic nationalism. Early in 1971, Congress revealed its mood by passing a banking law requiring that 80% ownership of all banks in Venezuela be in the hands of Venezuelans. Another law raised the income taxes of oil companies from 52% to 60%, a rate expected to add at least $130 million to annual government revenues. The administration expected to balance a $2.3 billion national budget with income derived from this and other new oil taxes, including a 59½-cent-per-gallon increase in the petroleum export tax.

The most controversial new measure was the law of reversion. Under terms of a 1943 law, all oil concessions were to revert to the government, without compensation, at the time of their expiration, although many were not scheduled to expire until 1983. The new law imposed an annual levy amounting to 10% of a company's declared value, and required that the concern deposit this sum in a special guaranty fund each year until its concession expires. The money was to be recoverable if facilities were turned over in good working order.

In addition, between 1971 and 1983, the activities of the oil companies were to be subject to review and revision, and all unexploited concessions were to revert to Venezuela immediately. The affected companies planned to test the constitutionality of the law. Meanwhile, they were deprived of a valuable source of income when President Rafaél Caldera nationalized the natural-gas reserves.

When rich new oil fields were opened in Lake Maracaibo in November, exploitation rights were granted to three foreign companies under a new system of service contracts described as the most severe in the history of Venezuelan petroleum mining.

Student Unrest. Protests and demonstrations occurred frequently in 1971. A major irritant was the

---

————— VENEZUELA • Information Highlights —————

Official Name: Republic of Venezuela.
Area: 352,143 square miles (912,050 sq km).
Population (1970 est.): 10,400,000. *Density,* 27 per square mile (11 per sq km). *Annual rate of increase,* 3.5%.
Chief Cities (1969 est.): Caracas, the capital (metropolitan area), 2,064,033; Maracaibo, 625,100; Barquisimeto, 280,086.
Government: *Head of state,* Rafaél Caldera, president (took office March 11, 1969). *Head of government,* Rafaél Caldera. *Legislature*—National Congress: Senate, 52 members; Chamber of Deputies, 214 members. *Major political parties*—Democratic Action party (AD), Social Christian party (COPEI), People's Electoral Movement (MEP).
Language: Spanish (official).
Education: *Literacy rate* (1970), 90% of population. *Expenditure on education* (1968), 18.4% of total public expenditure. *School enrollment* (1968)—primary, 1,602,443; secondary, 385,622; technical/vocational, 118,618; university/higher, 58,747.
Finances (1970): *Revenues,* $2,100,000,000; *expenditures,* $2,200,000,000; *monetary unit,* bolivar (4.50 bolivares equal U. S.$1, Sept. 1971).
Gross National Product (1968): $9,146,000,000.
National Income (1968): $7,774,000,000; *national income per person,* $803.
Manufacturing (metric tons, 1969): Residual fuel oil, 38,922,000; distillate fuel oils, 7,644,000; gasoline, 2,715,000; cement, 2,140,000.
Crops (metric tons, 1968 crop year): Bananas, 949,000; maize (1969), 670,000; cassava, 341,000.
Minerals (metric tons, 1969): Crude petroleum, 188,128,000 (ranks 3d among world producers); iron ore, 12,416,000; natural gas, 7,980,000,000 cubic meters; gold, 593 kilograms; diamonds, 76,000 metric carats.
Foreign Trade (1970): *Exports,* $2,637,000,000 (chief exports—petroleum, $2,398,410,000; iron ore, $144,643,000. *Imports,* $1,739,000,000 (chief imports, 1968—nonelectrical machinery, $328,886,000; transport equipment, $213,207,000; chemicals, $164,000,000; electrical machinery and appliances, $140,745,000). *Chief trading partners* (1968)—U. S. (took 33% of exports, supplied 50% of imports); Netherlands Antilles; Canada; Britain.
Transportation: *Roads* (1970), 22,506 miles (36,219 km); *motor vehicles* (1968), 679,100 (automobiles, 482,000); *railroads* (1969), 220 miles (354 km); *merchant fleet* (1970), 393,000 gross registered tons.
Communications: *Telephones* (1970), 377,662; *television stations* (1966), 9; *television sets* (1968), 700,000; *radios* (1969), 1,685,000; *newspapers* (1969), 38.

occupation of the Central University by federal troops in October 1970. The troops were withdrawn in April, but classes remained closed until June. By August, the university was paralyzed again, this time by students protesting plans to move several facilities to off-campus locations. About 90% of the faculty members supported the student strikers. In May, secondary schools were closed as a result of rioting that followed the shooting of two teachers.

Political Developments. With presidential primaries scheduled for 1972 in preparation for 1973 elections, at least eight presidential hopefuls were in evidence, including former president and strongman Marcos Pérez Jiménez and perennial candidate Jovito Villalba. The divided center and left parties were seeking a common candidate to oppose those of President Caldera's Social Christian party (COPEI) and the opposition Democratic Action party (AD). In spite of a gain in popularity, Caldera remained weak in Congress, where his party was a minority.

Colombian Disputes. Relations between Colombia and Venezuela were troubled by immigration and territorial controversies in 1971. Colombia accused Venezuela of expelling Colombian nationals, while Venezuela charged that they were in the country illegally. Of secondary importance was a dispute concerning conflicting claims to underwater territory in the Gulf of Venezuela.

In June, Venezuelan planes fired on two U. S. survey helicopters in the belief that they were from Colombia. The presidents of both countries were apparently embarrassed by this incident and shortly dispatched representatives to Rome to hold talks.

Economic Developments. The central planning board estimated the year's rate of economic growth at 6.1%, well above the 5% average annual growth rate of the 1960's. Imports from the United States during the first seven months of 1971 were up by 11% over the preceding year. The state steel company's output was increasing, and a combined Venezuelan-Colombian company announced plans to build a steel plant in Colombia to process Venezuelan ore.

The government planned to invest $45 million in "phase 2" of its plan to become self-sufficient in sugar within 15 years, and $11.7 million in a subway system in Caracas. It also planned to build 500,000 new housing units by 1975.

LEO B. LOTT, *University of Montana*

VERMONT

The convening of the Vermont General Assembly in January 1971 revealed a heavy backlog of work and an accumulation of new problems. An acrimonious session resulted in the creation of an Agency for Administration, whose secretary took his place in the new cabinet of superagency heads directly responsible to the governor. Proposals for other superagencies are still under discussion.

Government. Landmark legislation was enacted granting 18-year-olds full legal rights and responsibilities as citizens. Originally planned merely to lower the voting age, the bill was heavily amended by the conservatives in the hope of killing it. To the surprise of many, the bill passed and became effective July 1. On that day, registered 18-year-olds cast their first ballots in a special election in Westfield. Since then, some of the young people have served on juries.

U. S. Sen. Winston L. Prouty of Vermont died on September 10, and Gov. Deane C. Davis immediately appointed Rep. Robert T. Stafford, a Republican, to the vacancy. Assured that Stafford would vote with the administration on the draft bill then before the Senate, the White House sent an Air Force jet to bring the new senator to Washington in time for the draft bill vote.

In a November primary to choose candidates for Stafford's unexpired congressional term, six Republicans and four Democrats sought the position. After heavy expenditures a conservative from each party was chosen, but extremists in both parties were defeated. Three independent and third-party candidates will also appear on the January 1972 ballots by petition.

Senator Stafford will face a Democrat, Randolph Major, in the January election for the remainder of Senator Prouty's term. Major's chief campaign effort has been a walking tour of the state from the Canadian border to the Massachusetts line.

Governor Davis strongly supported the public utilities in their contest with conservationists over the operation of the Yankee nuclear power plant at Vernon. Scare headlines of winter power failures and utility warnings of brown-outs induced the governor to request of the Atomic Energy Commission that partial operation of the plant be permitted immediately.

Miscellaneous. A propane gas explosion and fire in Chester in November damaged 75 homes and destroyed several commercial buildings. Surprisingly, no one was seriously injured in the disaster.

A record 146 inches of snow fell during the winter in Burlington, with proportionately high amounts in the mountains, and late April found the ski industry exhausted but happy.

ANDREW E. NUQUIST
University of Vermont

─────── **VERMONT · Information Highlights** ───────

Area: 9,609 square miles (24,887 sq km).
Population (1970 census): 444,732. *Density:* 47 per sq mi.
Chief Cities (1970 census): Montpelier, the capital, 8,609; Burlington, 38,633; Rutland, 19,293; Bennington, 14,586.
Government (1971): *Chief Officers*—governor, Deane C. Davis (R); lt. gov., John S. Burgess (R); secy. of state, Richard C. Thomas (R); atty. gen., James M. Jeffords (R); treas., Frank H. Davis (R); commissioner, Dept. of Educ., James Oakey; chief justice, James S. Holden. *General Assembly* —Senate, 30 members (22 Republicans, 8 Democrats); House of Representatives, 150 members (94 R, 48 D, 8 R-D).
Education (1970–71): *Enrollment*—public elementary, 71,412 pupils; 3,027 teachers; secondary public, 41,290 pupils; 2,555 teachers; nonpublic schools (1968–69), 16,300 pupils; 900 teachers; college, university (fall 1968), 17,787 students. *Public school expenditures* (1970–71), $110,063,-000 ($1,088 per pupil). *Average teacher's salary,* $8,420.
State Finances (fiscal year 1970): *Revenues,* $274,624,000 (3% general sales tax and gross receipts taxes, $17,065,-000; motor fuel tax, $16,094,000; federal funds, $71,029,-000). *Expenditures,* $288,767,000 (education, $98,910,000; health, welfare, and safety, $40,309,000; highways, $56,-959,000). *State debt,* $220,603,000 (June 30, 1970).
Personal Income (1970): $1,596,000; per capita, $3,491.
Public Assistance (1970): $31,376,000. *Average monthly payments* (Dec. 1970)—old-age assistance, $75.40; aid to families with dependent children, $220.40.
Labor Force: *Nonagricultural wage and salary earners* (June 1971), 150,300. *Average annual employment* (1969)—manufacturing, 44,000; trade, 27,000; government, 24,000; services, 27,000. *Insured unemployed* (Oct. 1971)—4,000 (3.9%).
Manufacturing (1967): *Value added by manufacture,* $515,000,-000. Nonelectrical machinery, $101,800,000; food and kindred products, $39,900,000.
Agriculture (1970): *Cash farm income,* $164,472,000 (livestock, $147,984,000; crops, $15,108,000; government payments, $1,380,000). *Chief crops* (tons)—Apples, 38,000,000 pounds; hay, 904,000 tons; maple syrup, 305,000 gallons (ranks 2d among the states); potatoes, 240,000 cwt.
Transportation: *Roads* (1969), 14,320 miles (23,045 km); *motor vehicles* (1969), 215,000; *railroads* (1968), 771 miles.
Communications: *Telephones* (1971), 235,600; *television stations* (1969), 2; *radio stations* (1969), 19.

VETERINARIAN in Brownsville, Texas, draws blood sample to test colt suspected of having contracted Venezuelan equine encephalomyelitis. This usually fatal virus struck thousands of U.S. horses in 1971.

VETERINARY MEDICINE

Three exotic animal diseases—Venezuelan equine encephalomyelitis, African swine fever, and Newcastle disease of poultry—threatened the health and safety of animals and man in North America in 1971.

Venezuelan Equine Encephalomyelitis (VEE). The virus of VEE has been known to exist in South America since 1936, but it was not until 1969 that it spread into Central America and Mexico. In Mexico, in 1970 and 1971, between 6,000 and 12,000 horses died from VEE, and thousands were vaccinated with an experimental vaccine (TC-83) developed for the U.S. Department of Defense in a futile attempt to stop VEE's northward spread.

Soon after the disease hit southern Texas late in June, the secretary of agriculture declared a state of emergency. The vaccine was distributed widely and rapidly in Texas and adjoining states, and veterinarians were mobilized to administer it to as many horses as possible. To retard the spread of the mosquito-carried virus, the Air Force was called on to spray vast mosquito-breeding areas with the insecticides malathion and dibrom. It was the largest spraying program ever attempted in the United States, covering some 8.7 million acres. Horses in Texas and neighboring states were quarantined immediately and horses throughout the southern United States somewhat later.

VEE in the United States was finally brought under control after 1.7 million horses in the critical areas had been vaccinated. However, over 1,400 horses died and more than 80 persons became ill with VEE, but fortunately none died. The overall cost of the control program approached $20 million.

There was some criticism of the U.S. Department of Agriculture (USDA) for not employing the vaccine more widely and more quickly. On the other hand, the USDA proved that it could mobilize its forces and the nation's private veterinary practitioners in time to contain a dangerous disease. Before the program was completed, at least one veterinary biologics firm was producing vaccine supplies.

African Swine Fever. African swine fever, which mimics hog cholera, became rampant in Cuba in 1971 and was finally brought under control by the slaughter of 400,000 infected or exposed swine there. Although this very highly contagious and lethal disease never reached the mainland of North America, its presence in Cuba threatened directly the U.S. swine industry and the progress of the successful hog cholera eradication program scheduled for completion in 1972.

Newcastle Disease. A highly virulent strain of Newcastle disease was introduced into the United States through the importation of infected parakeets and other exotic birds from South America. This strain, if not controlled, could devastate the U.S. poultry industry. Fortunately, the infected birds died quickly, and native poultry was not exposed to the disease. The episode pointed up the continuing hazard that importations of possibly diseased animals poses to U.S. poultry and livestock.

Chicken Vaccine. On March 1, 1971, the USDA licensed under public patent a vaccine that will protect chickens from developing lesions of Marek's disease, a leading cause of mortality in chickens. The new vaccine was developed from a strain of herpes virus that was first discovered in turkeys in 1968, and by the end of its first six months of use the vaccine was believed to have increased broiler supplies by 8%.

ARTHUR FREEMAN, D.V.M.
Editor of the Journal of the American Veterinary Medical Association

"One man, one vote ... What's more democratic
than that?"

DON WRIGHT, THE MIAMI NEWS

UPI

UPI

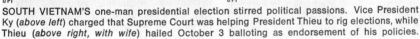
SOUTH VIETNAM'S one-man presidential election stirred political passions. Vice President
Ky (*above left*) charged that Supreme Court was helping President Thieu to rig elections, while
Thieu (*above right, with wife*) hailed October 3 balloting as endorsement of his policies.

VIETNAM

The two Vietnams vied politically as well as
militarily in 1971. Both held elections—neither one
democratic. Both also made economic gains, although natural disaster cancelled much of North
Vietnam's advance.

SOUTH VIETNAM

The winding down of the U.S. role in the
fighting had the predictable result of reducing U.S.
political influence on the Saigon government. The
United States, which has fought in the Vietnam
War on the side of political "self-determination"
south of the 17th parallel, showed displeasure over
South Vietnam's one-man presidential election, but
there was little else the administration could do.

Presidential Politics. President Thieu, a plurality victor at the polls in 1967, along with his
then running-mate Vice President Nguyen Cao Ky,
vowed to win by a bigger margin in 1971. Thieu
initially had two opponents—Ky, with whom he

had broken, and Gen. Duong Van Minh (Big
Minh), leader of the 1963 coup against President
Diem. In response to Thieu's pressure the National
Assembly passed a law that required presidential
candidates to obtain the endorsement of 40 members of the legislature or 100 of the 554 provincial
councillors. Big Minh and Ky agreed that the general should seek the legislators' support and the
vice president the councillors' backing—only to
discover that the provincial politicians had already
signed to support Thieu.

The Thieu-pressured supreme court disqualified
Ky's candidacy. When it subsequently reversed itself, Ky refused to run. Big Minh also bowed out.

Thieu ended up with 94.3% of the vote in an
uncontested election on October 3. Of 7 million registered voters, 87.7% were officially announced as
having gone to the polls, but press observers reported that this was a much-inflated figure.

In November, following the presidential vote,
the government allowed highly publicized memorial
services for the late President Diem. It was an

739

PEB IN THE PHILADELPHIA INQUIRER

"I dreamt we were Vietnamizing the world!"

apparent bid to identify wtih a new assertiveness of independence from U. S. influence.

In August's less controlled, but still far from free, voting for 159 seats in the House of Representatives, pro-Thieu candidates won a large majority. Opposition elements increased their representation, however.

Economy. South Vietnam's dependence on U. S. economic aid was dramatized by the government's frenzied reaction to President Nixon's mid-August 10% cut in U. S. foreign aid and to the difficulties encountered by foreign assistance in the U. S. Congress. Nixon subsequently waived the cut for South Vietnam, for which he sought $565 million in economic aid for 1971–72, an increase of $160 million.

In an effort to relieve this dependence and to prepare for an ultimate end to U. S. aid, Thieu proclaimed in November the most fundamental economic reforms in more than a decade. The piastre was devalued from 270 to 410 to the dollar for most transactions. There were other fiscal reforms.

ALERT and apprehensive, South Vietnamese infantrymen guard encampment. ARVN troops took hill from North Vietnamese on May 27, after three days of fighting.

WILLIE VICOY, UPI

———— SOUTH VIETNAM • Information Highlights ————

Official Name: Republic of South Vietnam.
Area: 67,108 square miles (173,809 sq km).
Population (1970 est.): 18,330,000. *Density,* 265 per square mile (103 per sq km). *Annual rate of increase,* 2.8%.
Chief City (1968 est.): Saigon, the capital, 1,682,000.
Government: *Head of state,* Nguyen Van Thieu, president (took office reelected Oct. 3, 1971). *Head of government,* Nguyen Van Thieu. *Legislature*—National Assembly; Senate, 60 members; House of Representatives, 159 members.
Languages: Vietnamese (official), French, English.
Education: *Literacy rate* (1970), 50% of population. *Expenditure on education* (1968), 4.2% of total public expenditure. *School enrollment* (1968)—primary, 2,083,642; secondary, 574,033; technical/vocational, 13,651; university/higher, 39,515.
Monetary unit: piastre (275.00 piastres equal U. S.$1, Sept. 1971).
Gross National Product (1970 est.): $4,000,000,000.
National Income (1967): $2,563,000,000.
Manufacturing (metric tons, 1969): Cement, 247,000; meat, 139,000; beer, 1,342,000 hectoliters.
Crops (metric tons, 1969 crop year): Rice, 5,115,000; cassava (1968). 260,000; natural rubber, 26,200.
Foreign Trade (1970): *Exports,* $11,000,000 (chief exports—rubber, $8,840,000). *Imports,* $550,360,000 (chief imports, 1968—road motor vehicles, $53,390,000; chemicals, $49,-300,000; nonelectrical machinery, $45,660,000; textile yarn and fabric, $42,600,000). *Chief trading partners*—Japan; United States.
Transportation: *Roads* (1970), 12,850 miles (20,680 km); *motor vehicles* (1969), 97,300 (automobiles, 38,700); *railroads* (1970), 875 miles (1,408 km).

Earlier, in March, the government had enacted other reforms. The price for imported rice, wheat flour, and sugar was increased by 50%, and investors were encouraged to use the country's banking system rather than Chinese middlemen-lenders. Inflation, a chronic problem, was well controlled during the early months of 1971, but the November reforms had the initial impact of sharply driving up the cost of many necessities.

Pacification. The second phase of South Vietnam's pacification program got under way in 1971. Based on the expectations of declining fighting and reduced U. S. economic aid, it aimed to double income by 1975, provide jobs for discharged servicemen, advance industrialization, and encourage foreign investment. Its purpose—to "Vietnamize" the heavily dollar-supported economy—was regarded by the Thieu government as comparable in importance to its increasing military responsibilities. The first phase, meanwhile, continued. Its goal is to root out Communist agents and develop institutions of local government.

Unrest. Despite successes in the war, there were several signs of unrest and potential new troubles. Some students, workers, and particularly disabled veterans demonstrated against the October 3 election. Catholics joined long-dissatisfied Buddhists as opponents of the regime. War weariness seemed to be increasing, and there were growing numbers of anti-American acts, some of them violent. The election split the troops, whose morale was otherwise adversely affected by the difficulties encountered in the military thrust into Laos in February.

Communist terrorism, in contrast with larger war activity, was markedly stepped up during 1971. There were 30 deaths a day at one point, and Nguyen Van Bong, head of a "loyal opposition" group and a potential political leader, was assassinated.

NORTH VIETNAM

North Vietnam seemed to strengthen its political position in 1971, but its economy—recovering impressively from U. S. bombing, particularly in agriculture—was badly hurt by some of the heaviest rains the country has ever experienced.

——— NORTH VIETNAM • Information Highlights———

Official Name: Democratic Republic of Vietnam.
Area: 61,294 square miles (158,750 sq km).
Population (1970 est.): 21,150,000. *Density,* 347 per square mile (134 per sq km). *Annual rate of increase,* 3.5%.
Chief City (1960 census): Hanoi, the capital, 414,620.
Government: *Head of state,* Tong Duc Thang, president (took office September 1969). *Head of government,* Pham Van Dong, premier (took office July 1954). *Communist party first secretary,* Le Duan. *Legislature*—National Assembly, 420 members.
Language: Vietnamese (official).
Education: *Literacy rate* (1960), 65% of population. *Expenditure on education* (1968), 18.4% of total public expenditure.
Monetary Unit: Dong (2.94 dongs equal U. S.$1, 1971).
Gross National Product (1969 est.): $1,600,000,000.
Manufacturing (metric tons, 1969): Cement, 500,000.
Crops (metric tons, 1968 crop year): Rice, 4,920,000; sweet potatoes and yams, 800,000; cassava, 700,000.
Minerals (metric tons, 1969): Coal, 3,200,000; phosphate rock, 1,050,000; salt, 150,000.
Transportation: *Roads* (1963), 4,076 miles (6,560 km); *railroads* (1964), 621 miles (1,000 km).

Politics. North Vietnam's first elections since 1964—the 1968 balloting was postponed because of U. S. bombing—were followed by the new National Assembly's reendorsement of the collective leadership that has ruled since Ho Chi Minh's death in 1969. All but 7 of the 529 candidates seeking 420 seats in the election on April 11 were endorsed by the Vietnam Fatherland Front, controlled by the ruling Workers' (Communist) party.

In June the National Assembly reelected 83-year-old Ton Duc Thang as president, Pham Van Dong as premier, Truong Chinh as chairman of the Assembly's standing committee, Vo Nguyen Giap as defense minister, and Xuan Thuy, chief of the north's Paris negotiating team, as minister without portfolio. Pham Van Dong and Truong Chinh, together with Le Duan, who holds no government office but is party secretary and probably the strongest of the three, comprise the effective governing triumvirate.

The Assembly elections were significant in at least two ways. They suggested that the leadership felt less hard-pressed than at any time in more than five years. Also, for the first time, there were no elections for representatives for Vietnam south of the 17th parallel. This was probably because of the establishment of the self-proclaimed "provisional revolutionary government" of South Vietnam in 1969.

Economy. At mid-year, the economy appeared to be headed for an extraordinary performance, but widespread flooding in September destroyed about 10% of the expected record rice crop. As a result, both China and the USSR sent Hanoi food supplies.

The flooding also caused much damage to industry. In mid-year the government indicated that industrial growth was proceeding at an annual rate of 7.4%, compared with 5% for 1970. But Pham Van Dong's state-of-the-nation address in March was one of several indicators that industry was not recovering from the effects of war as rapidly as the government's figures seemed to suggest.

Relations with China and USSR. Chinese Premier Chou En-lai paid a surprise visit to Hanoi in March and promised greater military aid to North Vietnam, a pledge apparently redeemed in September by a new economic and military assistance agreement. Premier Pham Van Dong returned his visit in November and met with Mao Tse-tung. Extended aid to the North Vietnamese also was vowed by Soviet President Podgorny during an October appearance in Hanoi. Pham Van Dong's call in Peking for the USSR and China to "rebuild their unity" was more an endorsement of the Chinese

than the Soviet side in the dispute. However, North Vietnam also indicated publicly its suspicions of direct Sino-U. S. contacts.

RICHARD BUTWELL
State University of New York at Brockport

VIETNAM WAR. See INDOCHINA WAR.

VIRGIN ISLANDS

For the U. S. Virgin Islands, 1971 marked its first year under an elected governor. Gov. Melvin H. Evans, a black physician, took the oath of office from U. S. Supreme Court Justice Thurgood Marshall on January 4.

Alien Labor. Governor Evans undertook a broad program of action to deal directly with the problem of alien labor from neighboring islands in the Lesser Antilles. The alien laborers, who comprise about 40% of the Virgin Islands' work force, were a key issue in the 1970 election campaign.

One prong of the alien-labor campaign was an effort to improve living conditions and social services provided for legally employed aliens. Secondly, the government moved decisively at the close of the tourist season to deport over 1,000 aliens illegally working. Many others left voluntarily. Very few new aliens were permitted to enter the Virgin Islands to compete for jobs with the growing numbers of native unemployed.

Economy. One of the reasons for increasing unemployment was the decline in the tourist industry, which resulted from the slowing of the U. S. economy, low air fares to Europe, and the rising costs of a Caribbean vacation. Nevertheless, the islands enjoyed a favorable balance of trade with the United States. The shipment of a wide variety of petroleum products to the United States accounted for most of the islands' $70 million increase in exports in 1971 over those of the previous year.

Government. Politically, the government of the Virgin Islands moved ahead through legislative action with plans for a constitutional assembly. The assembly, which met in November, was to draw up the first constitution, which will define the powers of the Legislature and the governor. These powers have been defined through legislation enacted by the U. S. Congress or executive orders transmitted through the Department of the Interior.

In the closing months of 1971, a bill was presented to Congress that would allow the Virgin Islands to have a resident commissioner who would participate in the deliberations of the U. S. House of Representatives. The resident commissioner would have a voice but no vote in the House.

THOMAS G. MATHEWS
University of Puerto Rico

——— VIRGIN ISLANDS • Information Highlights ———

Area: 133 square miles (344 sq km). St. Croix, 82 sq mi; St. Thomas, 32 sq mi; St. John, 19 sq mi.
Population (1970): 62,468.
Chief City (1970): Charlotte Amalie (St. Thomas), the capital, 12,220.
Government: *Governor*—Melvin H. Evans (took office Jan. 4, 1971). *Territorial Legislature,* 15 members.
Education: *School enrollment* (1970–71)—public schools, 17,362. *Average teacher's salary,* $7,700.
Finance (fiscal year 1971): *Revenues,* $138,850,518; *expenditures,* $124,679,386.
Trade with the United States (1970–71): *Exports,* $240,300,-000; *imports,* $168,500,000.
Transportation: *Roads* (1971), about 350 miles (563 km); *motor vehicles* (1971): 27,485.
Communications: *Telephones* (1971), 24,644; *newspapers* (1971), 2 (daily circulation, about 7,000).

VIRGINIA

In 1971 a growing liberalism in Virginia state politics was revealed. The year also produced considerable confusion within the two-party system.

November Elections. The biggest political news of the year was the election in November of state Sen. Henry Howell of Norfolk as lieutenant governor, a position left vacant by the death of J. Sargent Reynolds, a Democrat. Howell ran as an independent and garnered 40% of the vote.

Reynolds' death caused a major political power struggle, significant not because of the office at stake but because of the implications for the gubernatorial race in 1973. Republicans hoped to elect a lieutenant governor and groom him to succeed the popular Republican incumbent, Linwood Holton. In an August convention they nominated George Shafran of Arlington, a freshman member of the House of Delegates, who was a moderate aligned politically with the governor.

Howell, a candidate for the Democratic gubernatorial nomination in the primaries of 1969 and an acknowledged aspirant for the office in 1973, declined to seek the Democratic nomination and announced as an independent. He gave as his reason the party's decision to nominate by convention, rather than primary. With most of the Howell faction absent, the Democratic party convention in

---
VIRGINIA · Information Highlights

Area: 40,817 square miles (105,716 sq km).
Population (1970 census): 4,648,494. *Density:* 117 per sq mi.
Chief Cities (1970 census): Richmond, the capital, 249,430; Norfolk, 307,951; Virginia Beach, 172,106; Newport News, 138,177; Hampton, 120,779.
Government (1971): *Chief Officers*—governor, Linwood Holton (R); lt. gov., J. Sargeant Reynolds (D); secy. of state, Cynthia Newman (R); atty. gen., Andrew P. Miller (D); treas., Walter W. Craigie, Jr.; supt. of public instruction, Woodrow W. Wilkerson; chief justice, Harold F. Snead. *General Assembly*—Senate, 40 members (33 Democrats, 7 Republicans); House of Delegates, 100 members (75 D, 24 R, 1 Ind).
Education (1970–71): *Enrollment*—public elementary schools, 685,754 pupils; 29,500 teachers; secondary public, 393,000 pupils; 21,300 teachers; nonpublic schools (1968–69), 60,200 pupils; 3,370 teachers; college and university (fall 1968), 127,526 students. *Public school expenditures* (1970–71), $809,600,000 ($800 per pupil). *Average teacher's salary,* $8,700.
State Finances (fiscal year 1970): *Revenues,* $1,768,415,000 (3% general sales tax and gross receipts taxes, $210,045,000; motor fuel tax, $146,477,000; federal funds, $327,927,000). *Expenditures,* $1,681,245,000 (education, $673,781,000; health, welfare, and safety, $59,864,000; highways, $335,158,000). *State debt,* $323,194,000 (June 30, 1970).
Personal Income (1970): $17,082,000,000; per capita, $3,586.
Public Assistance (1970): $128,680,000. *Average monthly payments* (Dec. 1970)—old-age assistance, $68.70; aid to families with dependent children, $178.80.
Labor Force: *Nonagricultural wage and salary earners* (June 1971), 1,501,900. *Average annual employment* (1969)—manufacturing, 370,000; trade, 295,000; government, 293,000; services, 208,000. *Insured unemployed* (Oct. 1971)—8,500 (0.8%).
Manufacturing (1967): *Value added by manufacture,* $4,067,700,000. Chemicals and allied products, $762,000,000; tobacco manufactures, $421,800,000; food and kindred products, $392,700,000; textile mill products, $328,300,000.
Agriculture (1970): *Cash farm income,* $616,504,000 (livestock, $334,692,000; crops, $261,801,000; government payments, $20,011,000). *Chief crops* (1970)—Peanuts, 306,000,000 pounds; tobacco, 126,015,000 pounds; corn, 31,144,000 bushels; hay, 1,778,000 tons.
Mining (1970): *Production value,* $405,431,000 (ranks 20th among the states). *Chief minerals* (tons)—Coal, 39,335,000; stone, 36,158,000; sand and gravel, 11,915,000.
Fisheries (1970): *Commercial catch,* 583,200,000 pounds ($26,900,000). *Leading species by value* (1967), Oysters, $5,959,026; menhaden, $2,993,441; hard blue crabs (1970), $2,387,934; alewives (1970), $327,377.
Transportation: *Roads* (1969), 60,705 miles (97,693 km); *motor vehicles* (1969), 2,161,000; *railroads* (1968), 3,951 miles (6,358 km); *airports* (1969), 46.
Communications: *Telephones* (1971), 2,475,900; *television stations* (1969), 12; *radio stations* (1969), 173; *newspapers* (1969), 32 (daily circulation, 1,003,000).

August nominated a moderate, George Kostel of Clifton Forge, a member of the House of Delegates.

In this campaign, as in his 1969 gubernatorial campaign, Howell appealed to consumers, Negroes, and labor. He particularly criticized the State Corporation Commission, which he accused of insensitivity to the needs of the little man. He obtained formal endorsement from union and Negro groups.

Shafran attempted to appeal to the electorate on the basis of his support of Governor Holton's administration. He also emphasized his opposition to massive school busing. Kostel emerged as the most conservative of the three, mainly because of his ability to forge an alliance between moderate and conservative Democrats.

Elections for the newly redistricted General Assembly produced no significant alteration in its partisan complexion. Democrats still outnumbered Republicans in the House of Delegates by a three-to-one margin and in the Senate by four to one. However, many veteran conservative Democratic incumbents chose not to seek reelection, so that the new Assembly will represent a large (31%) turnover in membership.

The race for the lieutenant governship emphasized the growing mood of progressivism in Virginia politics on the state level. No candidate could be labeled a right-wing conservative, and the most liberal of all won the race and 40% of the vote. Yet by forging a third force in the state, Howell may have retarded the development of two-party politics in Virginia. Ironically, his political opposite, conservative Sen. Harry F. Byrd, Jr., had contributed to the same result in 1970 when he also won a victory running as an independent. Within two years, therefore, the Virginia Democratic party had been abandoned by these two antithetical leaders and had embarked on a course that left its identity and future highly uncertain. By contrast, the Republican party had maintained better internal coherence, yet it had demonstrated an inability to capitalize on the divisions among Democrats.

General Assembly. The General Assembly met in special sessions during the first half of the year, mainly to implement the revised state constitution approved in 1970 and to reapportion the state's legislative and congressional districts. The legality of the reapportionment adopted by the Assembly was challenged in the federal courts. The courts ordered the redrawing of various district lines, especially for the House of Delegates, to achieve greater population parity.

In other actions, the Assembly adopted 104 measures designed to implement the revised constitution, approved a $23.6 million revenue bond issue for college dormitories, authorized a study of pari-mutuel betting on horse races, and allowed local governing bodies to grant tax relief to elderly homeowners of limited means.

Supreme Court Appointment. With the resignations of U. S. Supreme Court Justices Harlan and Black, it was speculated that President Nixon would nominate Republican Rep. Richard Poff of Virginia's 6th District. When opposition developed because of Poff's civil rights record, he asked to have his name withdrawn from consideration. Nixon then nominated another Virginian, Lewis Powell of Richmond. The Senate confirmed the nomination.

WILLIAM LARSEN
Radford College

VITAL STATISTICS

Natural increase—the excess of births over deaths—added 1,797,000 persons to the population of the United States in 1970. The rate of natural increase—live births per 1,000 population (birthrate) minus deaths per 1,000 population (death rate)—was 8.8 persons per 1,000 population in 1970, as compared with 8.2 in 1969.

For the first 8 months of 1971, the natural increase in population was 1,072,000, as compared with 1,141,000 for the corresponding period in 1970. The population base was larger in the 1971 period, so the rate of natural increase fell below that for 1970.

The rate of natural increase in 1969, 1970, and 1971 was only about half of the high level of 16 per 1,000 in 1954–57. This decline is almost entirely attributable to the decline in the birthrate since the mid-1950's.

Births. The number of live births in 1970 was 3,718,000, and the birthrate was 18.2 births per 1,000 population. The number of births and the birthrate increased between 1968 and 1970. The fertility rate—the number of births per 1,000 women 15–44 years of age—increased slightly between 1968 and 1970. However, in 1970, the birthrates for women in certain age groups were below those observed in 1968.

A comparison of the first 8 months of 1971 with the corresponding period in 1970 reveals an apparent reversal in trend: the number of births declined by 3% (2,356,000 compared to 2,429,000); the birthrate declined by 4% (17.2 per 1,000 compared to 17.9); the fertility rate declined by 5% (82.1 births per 1,000 women 15–44 years of age compared to 86.3). Because the number of women of childbearing age (15–44) and the number of women 20–29 years of age (where birthrates are highest) have been increasing annually by about 2% and 4%, respectively, the declines in births and in the birthrate during the first 8 months of 1971 were especially notable.

It was too early to ascertain whether the recent decline in the birthrate was a temporary aberration, attributable to the 1970–71 economic recession. The birthrate declined steadily and considerably between 1957 and 1968, from 25.3 to 17.5, and perhaps it is the 1968–70 rise that should be regarded as the departure from the general trend. Two long-term factors partly explain low and declining birthrates: (1) according to the Census Bureau, the percentage of women 20–24 years of age who are single has been rising since 1960; (2) a 1970 national fertility study discovered that married women in their late twenties who were married in their early

ESTIMATED ABRIDGED LIFE TABLE FOR THE TOTAL U.S. POPULATION, 1970

Age interval[1]	Average remaining lifetime[2]	Age interval[1]	Average remaining lifetime[2]
0–1	70.8	45–50	30.1
1–5	71.2	50–55	25.9
5–10	67.4	55–60	22.0
10–15	62.5	60–65	18.3
15–20	57.7	65–70	15.0
20–25	53.0	70–75	12.0
25–30	48.3	75–80	9.5
30–35	43.7	80–85	7.2
35–40	39.0	85 and over	5.3
40–45	34.5		

[1] Period of life between two exact ages stated in years. [2] Average number of years of life remaining at beginning of age interval. Source: Public Health Service, HEW, Monthly Vital Statistics Report: Annual Summary for U.S. 1970.

LEADING CAUSES OF DEATH IN U.S., 1970[1]

Cause of death	Death rate per 100,000 population	Percent of total deaths
All causes	940.4	100.0
Diseases of heart	360.3	38.3
Cancer	162.0	17.2
Strokes	101.7	10.8
Accidents	54.2	5.8
Influenza and pneumonia	30.5	3.2
Certain causes of mortality in early infancy	20.9	2.2
Diabetes mellitus	18.5	2.0
Arteriosclerosis	15.9	1.7
Cirrhosis of liver	15.8	1.7
Bronchitis, emphysema, and asthma	14.9	1.6
All other causes	145.8	15.5

[1] Based on a 10% sample of deaths. Source: Public Health Service, HEW, Monthly Vital Statistics Report: Annual Summary for U.S. 1970.

twenties expected an average of 2.53 children, whereas a corresponding group of women in 1965 expected an average of 3.05 children.

Deaths. An estimated 1,921,000 deaths occurred in the United States in 1970, or about 5,000 more than in 1969. The death rate fell 0.9% from 948.9 deaths per 100,000 population in 1969 to 940.4 in 1970. The estimated expectation of life at birth in 1970 was 70.8 years for the total population. It is the highest life expectancy ever attained and compares with 70.5 in 1969.

During the first 8 months of 1971, there were 1,284,000 deaths, as compared with 1,288,000 for the corresponding period in 1970. The death rate for January–August 1971 was 9.4 per 1,000, as compared with 9.5 for January–August 1970.

The four leading causes of death, in order of rank, are heart disease, cancer, stroke, and accident. In 1970 these causes accounted for 75.3% of all deaths in the United States. A comparison with 1969 reveals that in 1970, there were decreases in the death rates for heart disease (1.0%) and accidents (3.2%), almost no change in the death rate for stroke, and a 1.2% increase in the death rate for cancer—mainly attributable to a rise in the death rate for lung cancer.

Marriages and Divorces. About 2,179,000 marriages took place in the United States in 1970, as compared with the slightly smaller number of 2,146,000 in 1969 and the record 2,291,000 in 1946, the first full year after World War II. The marriage rate—marriages per 1,000 population—increased between 1962 and 1970. It was 10.7 in 1970, 10.6 in 1969, and 8.5 in 1962.

The rise in marriages and the marriage rate during the 1960's is attributable to the increase in the young marriageable population, ages 18–24. In 1970 there were about 25 million persons in this age group, as compared with 16 million in 1960. When age and sex are taken into account, a different picture emerges: for women 20–24 years of age, the percent married dropped from 69.3% to 65.1% between 1960 and 1967. For men in the same age group, the percent married dropped from 45.9% to 45.2% between 1960 and 1967.

Divorces and annulments granted in 1970 were about 715,000, about 77,000 or 12% greater than the total for 1969. The 1970 divorce rate was 3.5 per 1,000 population, as compared with 3.2 for 1969. The divorce total for 1970 was at a record high, and the divorce rate for 1970 was exceeded only by that of 1946 when it reached 4.3.

BERNARD OKUN
*Brooklyn College
of the City University of New York*

WASHINGTON

In 1971 the state of Washington continued to suffer economic troubles and encountered some legal problems as well.

Legislature. The Legislature was under pressure to find relief for the state's sagging economy but was faced with massive resistance to new taxes. It passed an austere budget, which saw most of the new revenue coming from additional taxes on cigarettes and liquor, and it raised the assessment of property but placed a ceiling of 6% on actual increases in property taxes in any one year.

Redistricting, required every 10 years by the state constitution, bogged down in the Legislature. Only under threat of having the U. S. district court take over the task did the Legislature instruct interim committees to produce a plan for approval by a special session of the Legislature in 1972.

But the Legislature cast a cloud over the legality of all these bills by passing them after the legislative clock had been stopped at just before midnight of the last session.

Economy. The problems of the Boeing Company, the state's largest industrial employer, worsened as a result of continued oversupply of planes in the air transport industry. A shortage of jobs in this and related industries was largely responsible for an unemployment rate of about 15% in the Puget Sound region, the highest rate in the nation for a major metropolitan area. A contributing ele-

──────── **WASHINGTON · Information Highlights** ────────

Area: 68,192 square miles (176,617 sq km).
Population (1970 census): 3,409,169. *Density:* 51 per sq mi.
Chief Cities (1970 census): Olympia, the capital, 23,111; Seattle, 530,831; Spokane, 170,516; Tacoma, 154,581.
Government (1971): *Chief Officers*—governor, Daniel J. Evans (R); lt. gov., John A. Cherberg (D); secy. of state, A. Ludlow Kramer (R); atty. gen., Slade Gorton (R); treas., Robert S. O'Brien (D); supt. of public instruction, Louis Bruno; chief justice, Orris L. Hamilton. *Legislature*—Senate, 49 members (29 Democrats, 20 Republicans); House of Representatives, 99 members (51 R, 48 D).
Education (1970–71): *Enrollment*—public elementary schools, 442,618 pupils; 17,480 teachers; secondary public, 375,094 pupils; 15,900 teachers; nonpublic schools (1968–69), 56,-500 pupils; 2,350 teachers; college and university (fall 1968), 153,902 students. *Public school expenditures* (1970–71), $665,000,000 ($873 per pupil). *Average teacher's salary,* $9,520.
State Finances (fiscal year 1970): *Revenues,* $1,956,640,000 (4.5% general sales tax and gross receipts taxes, $546,-236,000; motor fuel tax, $140,878,000; federal funds, $357,930,000). *Expenditures,* $1,972,584,000 (education, $788,420,000; health, welfare, and safety, $264,866,000; highways, $198,945,000). *State debt,* $719,724,000 (June 30, 1970).
Personal Income (1970): $13,883,000,000; per capita, $3,993.
Public Assistance (1970): $234,634,000. *Average monthly payments* (Dec. 1970)—old-age assistance, $67.15; aid to families with dependent children, $210.75.
Labor Force: *Nonagricultural wage and salary earners* (June 1971), 1,049,700. *Average annual employment* (1969)—manufacturing, 279,000; trade, 247,000; government, 238,-000; services, 168,000. *Insured unemployed* (Oct. 1971)—56,800 (7.3%).
Manufacturing (1967): *Value added by manufacture,* $3,764,-200,000: Transport equipment, $972,800,000; food and kindred products, $444,300,000; lumber and wood products. $433,900,000; paper and allied products, $377,700,000.
Agriculture (1970): *Cash farm income,* $850,467,000 (livestock, $291,086,000; crops, $501,493,000; government payments. $57,888,000). *Chief crops* (1970)—Apples, 1,370,-000,000 pounds (ranks 1st among the states); wheat, 100,-731,000 bushels (ranks 3d); potatoes, 35,590,000 cwt (ranks 2d); hay, 2,335,000 tons.
Mining (1969): *Production value,* $80,900,000 (ranks 35th among the states). *Chief minerals* (tons)—Sand, gravel and stone, 46,500,000; clays, 271,000; zinc, 10,212.
Fisheries (1970): *Commercial catch,* 132,600,000 pounds ($31,-100,000). *Leading species by value* (1969), Salmon, $13,-990,338; halibut, $2,377,910; ocean perch, $777,160.
Transportation: *Roads* (1969) 74,570 miles (120,006 km); *motor vehicles* (1969), 2,109,000; *railroads* (1968), 4,932 miles (7,937 km); *airports* (1969), 12.
Communications: *Telephones* (1971), 1,996,300; *television stations* (1969); 13; *radio stations* (1969), 133; *newspapers* (1969), 23 (daily circulation, 1,046,000).

ment was the U. S. Senate's vote on March 24 to end federal funding of two prototype Boeing 2707's —the controversial supersonic transport (SST).

The Courts. After receiving secret testimony for several months, a King county (Seattle) grand jury on July 27 indicted 19 incumbent and former city and county officials for conspiring to perpetuate a policy of tolerance for offenses relating to bribery, gambling, prostitution, extortion, blackmail, and violation of liquor laws. Those accused included the Seattle City Council president, several police officials, a former King county prosecutor, a former sheriff, a retired Seattle police chief, a former assistant police chief, and three former police captains. On October 22, Superior Court Judge W. R. Cole dismissed the indictments on the grounds that between the time the grand jury had been convened and the time it made its indictment, a new state grand-jury law had gone into effect, rendering that grand jury unlawful. At year-end the King county prosecutor was pressing for a supreme court review of the decision.

A federal grand jury on March 23 indicted San Francisco Mayor Joseph Alioto and former Washington state Attorney General John J. O'Connell and Assistant Attorney General George K. Faler for conspiring to split legal fees. The fees had been paid to Alioto for representing a group of 15 cities and public utilities during the mid-1960's in antitrust actions against 29 manufacturers of electrical equipment. It was charged that a contract limit set at $1 million for legal fees had been secretly removed by O'Connell and that Alioto subsequently received a total of $2.3 million. Of this sum O'Connell received $530,000 and Faler received $272,000, at a time when both men were in the employ of the state.

Hijacking. In a bizarre case of air piracy, a Northwest Orient Airlines jet approaching the Seattle-Tacoma International Airport on November 24 was commandeered by a hijacker, who demanded and received $200,000 and four parachutes. He then instructed the pilot to proceed slowly toward Mexico City at a low altitude with the back door open. When the plane landed at Reno, Nev., for refueling, the sky pirate was not aboard.

WARREN W. ETCHESON
University of Washington

WASHINGTON, D. C.

Improving the quality of government in the District of Columbia highlighted efforts in 1971.

Home Rule. For the seventh time since 1952, the Senate in October passed a bill to give the city elected self-government. Like the six earlier bills, it was expected to die in the House.

Government. A "Little Hoover Commission," created by Congress, began hearings in November 1971 to examine the efficiency of the city's operations, primarily the planning and budget-making processes. Further reorganization of city agencies may result. Earlier, the city council had urged combining all agencies with urban-renewal responsibilities.

On Dec. 1, 1971, Mayor Walter E. Washington appointed Joseph P. Yeldell of the city council to succeed Philip J. Rutledge as head of the city's Human Resources Department. Created in 1970, the agency merged health, welfare, vocational rehabilitation, veterans, and narcotics programs.

Watergate, an elegant Potomac complex completed in 1971, features offices, shops, and fashionable apartments.

Budget. Not until Dec. 15, 1971, almost six months after the previous budget had expired, did Congress approve the city's 1971–72 budget. In a compromise decision, the House and Senate agreed to a $932.5 million figure—$225 million over fiscal 1970–71 but $112.7 million less than the city had sought. Congressional leaders had been critical of the city council's refusal to approve the mayor's request for a property-tax increase of 30 cents and its approval of only a 10-cent increase. Of the city's budget, $166 million was a federal payment to supplement local revenues.

Elections. In an intense campaign, Marion Barry defeated Anita F. Allen, president of the city school board, by 10,000 votes for the at-large seat on the board in the November 2 elections. Runoffs in five city wards were held on November 23. Barry's endorsement proved a critical factor in ward elections. Barry headed Pride, Inc., a black self-help group. While only about 16% of the eligible voters went to the polls, the number reportedly exceeded turnouts for off-year school elections elsewhere.

Kennedy Center. The $70 million John F. Kennedy Center for the Performing Arts opened with the premiere of Leonard Bernstein's *Mass* on September 8. Its three theaters were badly needed in the District. (See also ARCHITECTURE; MUSIC.)

Education. A marked decline in the number of children under 5 in the city may improve the quality of education in the future. In 1970, 59,735 in the city were under 5, down 25% from 1960. Elementary school enrollment in 1970 was over 95% black. By federal court action on May 25, equalized pupil-teacher spending was ordered throughout the city.

In October a federal decision was made to cut out funds for the unique community school-control program in Anacostia. The plan, begun in 1968 with $1 million, called for election of local management boards for 11 schools and for an area-wide board. Reasons given for the cut were lack of evidence that the $2.25 million program in 1971 was improving academic achievement, and lack of local interest—only 437 of some 30,000 eligible voters turned out for board elections.

The controversial Clark plan for special tutoring during regular classes may be abandoned in favor of remedial classes for students needing them.

Metro. In a continuation of the struggle to get congressional support for area-wide rapid rail transit in the Washington area, President Nixon issued a statement on November 18 urging resolution of legal problems delaying completion of the federal highway system through the city and calling for congressional approval of funds to complete the transit system. As in previous years, Congress withheld its support for Metro subway funds until assured that the city would complete the North Central Freeway. On December 3, in a rare setback for its leadership, the House voted to release $72 million in Metro funds. Completion of 5 miles (8 km) of the subway was planned for mid-1974 and of the full 98-mile (158-km) system by 1980.

Crime. While serious crimes in the city decreased by 1.1% in 1970, robberies increased over 23% and reported rapes by 80%. In efforts to control a growing drug problem, the city began expanding its Narcotics Treatment Administration. In October the Justice Department sent to Congress a major drug control bill for the city, which would reduce first-offense penalties for drug possession but increase sentences up to life imprisonment for dealers convicted of "continuing criminal enterprise." No existing law provides any penalties for this repetitive type of offense.

JEAN E. SPENCER, *University of Maryland*

WEATHER. See METEOROLOGY.
WEST INDIES. See CARIBBEAN and articles on Caribbean countries.

—— WEST VIRGINIA • Information Highlights ——

Area: 24,181 square miles (62,629 sq km).
Population (1970 census): 1,744,237. *Density:* 76 per sq mi.
Chief Cities (1970 census): Charleston, the capital, 71,505; Huntington, 74,315; Wheeling, 48,188; Parkersburg, 44,- 208; Morgantown, 29,431; Weirton, 27,131.
Government (1971): *Chief Officers*—governor, Arch A. Moore, Jr. (R); secy. of state, John D. Rockefeller IV (D); atty. gen., Chauncey H. Browning, Jr. (D); treas., John H. Kelly (D); supt. of schools, Daniel B. Taylor; President Supreme Court of Appeals, Fred H. Coplan. *Legislature* —Senate, 34 members (23 Democrats, 11 Republicans); House of Delegates, 100 members (68 D, 32 R).
Education (1970–71): *Enrollment*—public elementary schools, 221,779 pupils; 8,760 teachers; secondary public, 177,751 pupils; 7,865 teachers; nonpublic schools, 14,000 pupils; 650 teachers; college and university (fall 1968) 59,264 students. *Public school expenditures* (1970–71), $253,200,000 ($684 per pupil). *Average teacher's salary*, $7,800.
State Finances (fiscal year 1970): *Revenues,* $844,644,000 (3% general sales tax and gross receipts taxes, $181,710,- 000; motor fuel tax, $49,944,000; federal funds, $254,294,- 000). *Expenditures,* $865,437,000 (education, $306,020,000; health, welfare, and safety, $85,895,000; highways, $231,- 841,000). *State debt,* $554,596,000 (June 30, 1970).
Personal Income (1970): $5,269,000,000; per capita, $2,929.
Public Assistance (1970): $75,388,000. *Average monthly payments* (Dec. 1970)—old-age assistance, $68.30; aid to families with dependent children, $111.25.
Labor Force: *Nonagricultural wage and salary earners* (June 1971), 520,300. *Average annual employment* (1969)—manufacturing, 131,000; trade, 93,000; government, 95,000; services, 64,000.
Manufacturing (1967): *Value added by manufacture,* $2,169,- 500,000: Chemicals and allied products, $836,300,000; primary metal industries, $488,200,000; stone, clay, and glass products, $235,300,000.
Agriculture (1970): *Cash farm income,* $114,682,000 (livestock, $84,486,000; crops, $26,608,000; government payments, $3,588,000). *Chief crops* (1970)—Apples, 242,000,000 pounds; tobacco, 3,145,000 pounds; corn, 3,120,000 bushels; hay, 873,000 tons.
Mining (1970): *Production value,* $1,181,693,000 (ranks 5th among the states). *Chief minerals* (tons)—Coal, 140,513,- 000; stone, 9,244,000; natural gas, 230,459,000,000 cubic feet; petroleum, 3,149,000 barrels.
Transportation: *Roads* (1969), 35,820 miles (57,645 km); *motor vehicles* (1969), 836,000; *railroads* (1968), 3,549 miles (5,711 km); *airports* (1969), 21.
Communications: *Telephones* (1971), 762,600; *television stations* (1969), 9; *radio stations* (1969), 78; *newspapers* (1969), 31 (daily circulation, 493,000).

WEST VIRGINIA

Coal mining made headlines in 1971 as a miners' strike adversely affected the economy and a bill restricting surface mining created controversy. A former governor, W. W. Barron, pleaded guilty in a bribery trial.

Economic Affairs. West Virginia's economy continued its third consecutive year of growth through September but dipped sharply when the bituminous-coal miners struck in October. Gov. Arch A. Moore, Jr., entered the stalemated coal talks and directed the arbitration that ended in a settlement in mid-November. Pacing the state's growth was an unprecedented road-building program, one of the nation's most ambitious, which received support in the regular session of the state Legislature in March.

Government. The Democratic-dominated Legislature passed much of its own and the Republican governor's programs, which included approval of additional road bonds. Stricter mine safety and inspection standards were enacted. A bill to enforce stronger surface mining regulations became the session's stormiest issue. It was passed but failed to satisfy either its proponents or opponents.

Other major bills were tax increases for almost all areas of business, from about a 10% base to almost 150% on coal. A statewide kindergarten system was established, teachers and state police received 7.5% pay raises, and 18-year-olds were given state and local voting rights. A congressional redistricting plan was also approved. The House of Delegates was stunned by the sudden death of its popular speaker, Ivor Boiarsky, on March 12, only a few hours before the session ended.

Governor Moore approved virtually the entire legislative package, but he vetoed certain budget items, which made a special session necessary in April. The session provided additional funds for a welfare program that by midyear was cited for its progress in reducing case loads. During this session West Virginia became the 21st state to approve voting by 18-year-olds in national elections.

Another special session was called in October to consider redistricting the state's Senate and House of Delegates. On November 22, Governor Moore approved the plan for the House, which most observers felt was headed for a certain court challenge, and vetoed the plan for the Senate. His action left the entire matter of delegate and senatorial representation unresolved less than three months from the filing deadline for the May 1972 primary elections.

By late 1971 battle lines were already being drawn for the 1972 political campaign. Control over surface mining will be the most emotional issue in the nation's leading coal-producing state.

Bribery Trial. A 2-year series of sensational trials involving members of former Gov. W. W. Barron's administration (1961–65) was climaxed in February with the indictment of the former chief executive on charges of jury tampering, bribery, and conspiracy. In March he pleaded guilty to a charge of bribing a jury foreman in an earlier trial in which he had been acquitted. He paid a $50,000 fine and on November 10 entered a federal prison to begin a 12-year term.

DONOVAN H. BOND
West Virginia University

WESTERN SAMOA

In 1971, Western Samoa expanded its role in South Pacific affairs under its new prime minister, Tupua Tamasese Lealofi IV.

International Relations. During an official visit by Prime Minister Tamasese to New Zealand late in 1970, matters of mutual concern, including migration, were discussed. Western Samoa faces overpopulation and wants New Zealand to adopt more liberal immigration policies for Samoans.

Early in 1971, the prime minister attended the Commonwealth conference of prime ministers in

—— WESTERN SAMOA • Information Highlights ——

Official Name: Independent State of Western Samoa.
Area: 1,097 square miles (2,842 sq km).
Population (1970 est.): 150,000. *Density,* 126 per square mile (49 per sq km). *Annual rate of increase,* 2.6%.
Chief City (1966 census): Apia, the capital, 25,480.
Government: *Head of state,* Malietoa Tanumafili II, king (acceded Jan. 1, 1962). *Head of government,* Tupua Tamasese Lealofi IV, prime minister (took office Feb. 25, 1970). *Legislature*—Legislative Assembly, 47 members.
Languages: Samoan (official), English.
Education: *Literacy rate* (1969), 90% of population. *School enrollment* (1968)—primary, 26,261; secondary, 9,400; technical/vocational, 92.
Finances (1970 est.): *Revenues,* $7,112,000; *expenditures,* $7,635,000; *monetary unit,* tala (.8627 tala equal U. S.$1, Sept. 1971).
Consumer Price Index (1969): 116 (1963=100).
Crops (metric tons): Bananas (1968), 3,000; cocoa beans (1969), 2,700.
Foreign Trade (1968): *Exports,* $5,278,000 (chief exports— copra, $2,613,000; cocoa beans, $1,735,000). *Imports,* $7,630,000 (chief imports—textile yarn and fabrics, $577,- 000; chemicals, $477,000; wheat meal and flour, $470,000; preserved fish, $420,000). *Chief trading partners* (1968)— New Zealand (took 33% of exports, supplied 25% of imports); Australia (—22%).

Singapore, where he charged that Oriental fishermen based in American Samoa had violated Western Samoa's territorial waters.

The U. S. ambassador to New Zealand, Kenneth Franzheim II, was appointed to serve also as U. S. ambassador to Western Samoa. Franzheim will make occasional trips to Apia from Wellington.

Airport Construction. A jet airport was under construction during 1971 at Faleolo, on Upolu island. It was expected to be completed by June 1972.

Obituary. Afioga Afoafouvale Misimoa, the first Western Samoan to serve as secretary general of the South Pacific Commission, died on Feb. 18, 1971. He had held the office since January 1970 and had previously served as a member of the Samoan legislature and as a Western Samoan representative on the South Pacific Commission.

HOWARD J. CRITCHFIELD
Western Washington State College

WHOLESALE SALES. See ECONOMY OF THE UNITED STATES.

WISCONSIN

A major revision of the shared-tax program and approval of the merger of its two state university systems highlighted developments in Wisconsin in 1971.

Legislature. The political forces at work in the Legislature were altered in 1971 as the state's first governor to be elected for a 4-year term took office. Democrat Patrick J. Lucey, elected in November 1970, had time on his side. For the 1971–73 biennium, he requested a record state budget, of $1.98 billion, for a spending level 27% higher than the previous biennium and increased the corporation tax rate for the first time in 51 years. Also included in the budget were two controversial proposals: the merger of the state's two university systems and a revision of the formula by which the state returns taxes to local units of government.

The ensuing battle between the Democratic-controlled Assembly and the Republican-dominated Senate resulted in the longest legislative session on record. The budget was not adopted until October 27, almost four months after the start of the biennium in July. Throughout the session, the Republicans charged the Democrats with being ruthless in their use of power—a charge the Democrats ignored because previously, when a Republican was governor, they had accused the Republicans of the same fault. Few other important pieces of legislation were passed.

Universities Merger. A merger of the University of Wisconsin system and the Wisconsin state university system had been proposed before, but in 1971 Governor Lucey made it a goal of his administration. He maintained that it was wasteful for the state to operate two independent—and sometimes competing—systems of higher education. There was opposition to the governor's view at first: both boards of regents objected to a merger, and forces behind the University of Wisconsin expressed displeasure at being linked with a system that had grown out of teachers colleges.

While the Legislature stopped short of ordering a full merger, it approved a plan combining the two boards of regents, and it set up a committee to work out details of the merger by 1973. Immediately, however, the state universities—at Eau Claire, La Crosse, Menomonie, Oshkosh, Platteville, River Falls, Stevens Point, Superior, and Whitewater—became part of the University of Wisconsin system, whose main campuses are in Madison, Milwaukee, Green Bay, and Parkside. The merged system, with 130,000 students, became the nation's fourth-largest, behind those of New York, California, and New York City. John C. Weaver, president of the University of Wisconsin, was named head of the system.

Shared Taxes. Under Wisconsin's old law, the state returned income and other taxes to local communities on the basis of the amount collected in the localities. In recent years there were increasing objections from big cities, notably Milwaukee, which maintained that the arrangement benefitted high-income suburbs at the expense of the cities. After a prolonged legislative battle, a new formula was devised, which included a community's need. By the new formula an additional $5 million will go to Milwaukee immediately, and there will be lesser gains for hundreds of small communities. High-income suburbs and medium-sized cities will lose.

Economy. Wisconsin was affected by the sluggish economic conditions that prevailed throughout the country. But from the second quarter of 1970 to the second quarter of 1971, personal income in Wisconsin increased by 7%, 0.5% more than the national average increase.

PAUL SALSINI, *The Milwaukee "Journal"*

─────── **WISCONSIN** · Information Highlights ───────

Area: 56,154 square miles (145,439 sq km).
Population (1970 census): 4,417,933. *Density:* 77 per sq mi.
Chief Cities (1970 census): Madison, the capital, 172,007; Milwaukee, 717,372; Racine, 95,162; Green Bay, 87,809; Kenosha, 78,805; West Allis, 71,723; Appleton, 57,143.
Government (1971): *Chief Officers*—governor, Patrick J. Lucey (D); lt. gov., Martin J. Schreiber (D); secy. of state, Robert C. Zimmerman (R); atty. gen., Robert W. Warren (R); treas., Charles P. Smith (D); supt. of public instruction, William C. Kohl (NP); chief justice, E. Harold Hallows. *Legislature*—Senate, 33 members (20 Republicans, 12 Democrats, 1 vac.); Assembly, 100 members (66 D, 33 R, 1 vac.).
Education (1970–71): *Enrollment*—public elementary schools, 584,360 pupils; 25,958 teachers; secondary public, 409,376 pupils; 23,094 teachers; nonpublic schools, 257,900 pupils; 9,630 teachers; college and university (fall 1968), 172,239 students. *Public school expenditures* (1970–71), $883,304,000 ($988 per pupil). *Average teacher's salary,* $9,640.
State Finances (fiscal year 1970): *Revenues,* $2,132,166,000 (4% general sales tax and gross receipts taxes, $272,614,000; motor fuel tax, $130,512,000; federal funds, $344,009,000). *Expenditures,* $2,018,701,000 (education, $725,792,000; health, welfare, and safety, $172,764,000; highways, $135.523,000).
Personal Income (1970): $16,735,000,000; per capita, $3,722.
Public Assistance (1970): $253,746,000. *Average monthly payments* (Dec. 1970)—old-age assistance, $106.70; aid to families with dependent children, $226.40.
Labor Force: *Nonagricultural wage and salary earners* (June 1971), 1,542,700. *Average annual employment* (1969)—manufacturing, 518,000; trade, 323,000; government, 255,000; services, 217,000. Insured unemployed (Oct. 1971)—25,800 (2.3%).
Manufacturing (1967): *Value added by manufacture,* $7,014,100,000: Nonelectrical machinery, $1,590,200,000; food and kindred products, $910,300,000; electrical equipment and supplies, $697,300,000; paper and allied products, 663,500,000.
Agriculture (1970): *Cash farm income,* $1,661,760,000 (livestock, $1,379,087,000; crops, $231,017,000; government payments, $51,656,000). *Chief crops* (1970)—Corn, 143,520,000 bushels; oats, 104,594,000 bushels (ranks 4th among the states); potatoes, 12,768,000 cwt; hay, 10,601,000 tons (ranks 1st).
Mining (1969): *Production value,* $79,793,000 (ranks 39th among the states). *Chief minerals* (tons)—Sand and gravel, 42,815,000; stone, 18,954,000; lime, 244,000.
Fisheries (1970): *Commercial catch,* 48,500,000 pounds ($2,500,000).
Transportation: *Roads* (1969), 102,299 miles (164,630 km); *motor vehicles* (1969), 2,075,000; *railroads* (1968), 6,007 miles (9,667 km); *airports* (1969), 99.
Communications: *Telephones* (1971), 2,370,100; *television stations* (1969), 17; *radio stations* (1969), 163; *newspapers* (1969), 38 (daily circulation, 1,221,000).

Women in traditionally male jobs were in the news in 1971. Female firsts included Jeanne Holm (*top left*) as Air Force general, Gene Sims (*left*) as airport tower chief. Margaret Decker (*above*) is a dynamite blaster for excavation firm.

WOMEN'S LIBERATION MOVEMENT

In 1971, equality for women gained support as a legitimate civil rights movement. Activists shifted from the pioneer work of image-making and consciousness-raising to political action and demands for specific changes in practices newly recognized as sexist. There was a sharp drop in births as well as in marriages, and a growing and significant number of unattached young women were in a position to feel the many different ways in which American society casts women in subordinate roles.

Almost all who gave thought to woman's role moved away from the traditional view. A Harris poll found women equally divided on "efforts to strengthen and change women's status." There was growing use of the form of address, Ms., the maritally ambiguous female equivalent of Mr. There were also more token women on major boards (IBM and Ford Foundation), at the head of professional organizations (American Psychological Association), and in such traditional "male" posts as captain in the New York City police force and a deaconate in the Protestant Episcopal Church. As in 1970, August 26, the anniversary of U. S. woman suffrage, was celebrated with "equality marches."

Organizations. Militant women's organizations grew and multiplied. The change-oriented National Organization for Women (NOW) more than tripled its membership to 15,000 and had 200 chapters all over the United States as well as in Hong Kong, Canada, and elsewhere. Its national conference demanded women's rights planks in political party platforms and a guaranteed annual income. Members announced a task force on the "masculine mystique," on the use of violence as a solution to

problems, and a tax-deductible legal defense and education fund. They also resolved against the oppression of lesbians and in support of only "change-oriented" volunteer work.

Special-purpose organizations, such as the Women's Equity Action League (WEAL) and the Professional Women's Caucus, expanded their membership and programs. Traditional women's organizations, such as the League of Women Voters, were more militant, and hundreds of "women's caucuses" and "women's committees" worked inside universities, government agencies, labor unions, and professional associations. Other groups formed around specific programs, such as NOW's Stockholders Action Program for feminist stockholders, or around demographic ties.

Politics. In July, a broad cross-section of women formed a nonpartisan National Women's Political Caucus to get women to work for feminist issues in legislatures and to support women candidates for public office. Many regional and state caucuses were formed to follow through. Patience Latting was elected mayor of Oklahoma City. A Gallup poll reported that two thirds of the men and women polled would vote for a well-qualified woman for president. Shirley Chisholm, black congresswoman from Brooklyn, announced for the presidency.

The Democratic National Committee considered a plan for seating women delegates to the 1972 convention proportionate to women voters in the constituencies, and named Patricia Harris, a black woman lawyer, to head the influential Credentials Committee. President Nixon leaked the names of two women candidates under consideration for the U. S. Supreme Court and said he was trying to appoint more women to office.

Legislation. The Equal Rights Amendment, providing that "equality of rights under the law shall not be denied or abridged" on account of sex, passed the House. However, the Senate vote was deferred until 1972. Feminist groups lobbied for broadly conceived, publicly funded child care centers.

Employment. In a 1971 case, *Phillips* v. *Martin Marietta Corporation,* the Supreme Court ruled that an employer could not deny a job to a woman because she had children unless they denied jobs to fathers on the same basis. Executive orders set forth government policy forbidding federal contractors to discriminate in employment on the basis of sex as well as of race and religion. Detailed guidelines spelling out the responsibility of contractors for affirmative action programs with specific goals and timetables were under study by major corporations, and similar guidelines were requiring review of pay and promotion practices within the federal establishment. The most dramatic action was taken by women college professors, who by reason of their professional status are exempt from the Fair Labor Standards Act and therefore not covered by the Equal Pay Act of 1963, nor are they covered by Title VII of the Civil Rights Act of 1964. These women endangered the federal funds of hundreds of universities by filing formal charges of sex discrimination against them.

Federal wage and hour compliance authorities received complaints of unequal pay against nearly twice as many establishments in fiscal 1971 as in 1970. At the end of 1971 the wage freeze slowed the promotion of women needed to achieve equality.

Education. Educators and social scientists presented programs for nonsexist child rearing. Benjamin Spock apologized for stating in his standard baby care manual that babies needed the constant attention of mothers and admitted that they needed "sensitive, enthusiastic care" that could be provided by others. The Campfire Girls became coeducational, as did many formerly one-sex preparatory schools. At the college level, experts in psychology, sociology, history, and other disciplines identified the male bias in their areas. Freud's doctrine of penis envy was widely criticized. "Women's studies" appeared on numerous campuses to focus attention on the contributions and sex roles of women. Women law students were active in identifying male bias in the theory and practice of law.

Media. NOW studied the image of women projected on television programs and secured an FCC rule requiring broadcasters to set up affirmative action plans. Advertisers playing on traditional femininity were attacked for portraying women as mindless "sex" objects.

Feminist books were plentiful, with numerous special studies, biographies of underrecognized women, "nonsexist" children's books, and anthologies. Germaine Greer's *The Female Eunuch* was a best seller. *New Woman,* a national monthly magazine for autonomous women, was launched, as were many less ambitious entries. Existing women's magazines devoted increasing space to feminist themes. Newsletters, pamphlets, and specialized liberation publications multiplied. Newspapers continued to break up stereotyped woman's page segregation of women's news, and although the legal right to classify want ads by sex remained in doubt, many papers voluntarily desegregated help wanted columns.

Women's Liberation Abroad. Male voters in Liechtenstein refused women the vote. Swiss women, however, won the right to vote. In Norway, a group known as the New Feminists elected female majorities in 50 city councils, including Oslo. In Britain, Women's Liberation groups urged implementation of the Equal Pay Act of 1970. Canada enacted a law assuring women equal pay for equal work. Egypt's new constitution declared the equal status of men and women. In Japan the shortage of labor has put more women to work. More than 40% of Japanese women now work outside the home, and for the first time they have moved into jobs on ocean-going ships and in the production of sake.

CAROLINE BIRD
Author of "The Invisible Scar" and "Born Female"

WOOL

World wool production in 1971–72 declined moderately for the third consecutive season. It fell to 5,975 million pounds (greasy basis), well below the peak of 6,181 million pounds reached in 1968–69. Declines in non-Communist countries were partly offset by increases in Communist countries. U. S. wool production continued to decline.

Consumption. World wool consumption in 1970 declined to 3,465 million pounds (clean basis), compared with the peak of 3,537 million pounds in 1969. U. S. raw wool consumption for all uses accounted for 7% of the 1970 total.

U. S. Wool Textile Industry. Wool consumption in U. S. textile mills during 1971 declined severely for the third year in a row. Lagging consumer demand for textiles and styling changes that favored competitive fibers each took a toll. Also, there was an expansion of imports of textile products that were priced below domestic goods.

Indicators of demand suggested that in 1971 apparel wool consumption would decline substantially below the 164 million pounds of 1970. In the first eight months of 1971, imports of raw apparel wool were running 48% below corresponding 1970 imports.

Net imports of semiprocessed and manufactured wool textile products also declined as demand shifted to imports of competitive textiles.

Mill consumption of carpet wool in 1971 was expected to approximate the 77 million pounds consumed in 1970. In the first eight months of 1971, imports of carpet wool—which is not produced domestically—were running 24% ahead of the 73 million pounds imported in 1970.

RUTH JACKENDOFF
The Wool Bureau, Inc.

WORLD PRODUCTION OF VIRGIN WOOL
(Million pounds, greasy basis)

Country and types	Average 1956–57 to 1960–61	1970–71	1971–72 Forecast	% of total
Australia	1,582	1,935	1,934	33
USSR	690	915	945	16
New Zealand	539	736	728	12
Argentina	414	427	407	7
South Africa	296	257	257	4
United States	309	187	177	3
Uruguay	181	164	143	2
Other countries	1,333	1,384	1,384	23
Total	5,344	6,005	5,975	100
Of which:				
Merino (fine)	2,177	2,395	2,380	40
Crossbred (medium to coarse)	1,955	2,326	2,308	39
Total apparel type	4,132	4,721	4,688	79
Other (mostly carpet type)	1,212	1,284	1,287	21

Source: Commonwealth Secretariat.

WORLD BANK. See INTERNATIONAL FINANCE.

WYOMING

Environmental problems and passage of the Republican legislative program marked the year 1971 in Wyoming.

Government. The Legislature met in its regular 40-day biennial session in January and February. Gov. Stanley Hathaway, beginning his second 4-year term, obtained approval for most of his program from a Legislature dominated by his own Republican party. Bills passed included those providing for a legislative service agency, a new minor court system, a revised criminal code, and a new narcotics code. A study to determine the best uses for unappropriated Green River water, legislative reapportionment, and increased state aid to school districts were also approved. In a special July session the Legislature ratified the 26th Amendment to the U. S. Constitution, giving 18-year-olds the right to vote.

Among six state constitutional amendments to be submitted for consideration by the electorate in 1972 was one that would institute a new system of selecting judges. Another would establish annual sessions of the Legislature.

Economy. Farm earnings reached a record $250 million, mainly because of increased yields and ample irrigation water. The number of farm and ranch units declined to about 8,200, averaging about 4,500 acres in size.

Mineral production continued at the record level attained in 1970, with petroleum output approaching 150 million barrels. Strip mining of coal increased to satisfy the growing needs of Wyoming and midwestern electric plants. No significant oil or gas discovery occurred. The amount of oil exploration and drilling fell behind that of 1970, particularly in Campbell County, where boom conditions have prevailed since 1967.

Environment. State environmental protection rules, which had been instituted for utilities, took effect in November. Construction applications for large power plants now must be filed two years in advance. Lumberers and surface mine operators adopted new procedures to reduce hazards to the environment, in accordance with laws passed in 1969.

Much discussion centered around Sen. Gale McGee's bill calling for a 2-year moratorium on clear cutting of timber in national forests. The U. S. Forest Service modified its policy for Wyoming, reducing the size limit for new timbering contracts and forbidding rectangular cuts.

Investigations revealed that hundreds of bald and golden eagles had been slain illegally in Wyoming, some by poisoning and others by gunfire from helicopters. Senator McGee presided over hearings on predator-control practices and introduced a bill in Congress providing heavy penalties for destruction of eagles.

T. A. LARSON
University of Wyoming

─────── **WYOMING · Information Highlights** ───────

Area: 97,914 square miles (253,597 sq km).
Population (1970 census): 332,416. *Density:* 3 per sq mi.
Chief Cities (1970 census): Cheyenne, the capital, 40,914; Casper, 39,361; Laramie, 23,143; Rock Springs, 11,657; Sheridan, 10,856.
Government (1971): *Chief Officers*—governor, Stanley K. Hathaway (R); secy. of state, Mrs. Myra Thomson (R); atty. gen., Clarence A. Brimmer (R); treas., James Griffith (R); supt. of public instruction, Robert G. Schrader (R); chief justice, John J. McIntyre. *Legislature*—Senate, 30 members (19 Republicans, 11 Democrats); House of Representatives, 61 members (40 R, 20 D, 1 other).
Education (1970–71): *Enrollment*—public elementary schools, 46,602 pupils; 2,341 teachers; secondary public, 40,284 pupils; 2,280 teachers; nonpublic schools (1968–69), 3,800 pupils; 190 teachers; college and university (fall 1970), 15,000 students. *Public school expenditures* (1970–71), $76,000,000 ($927 per pupil). *Average teacher's salary,* $8,687.
State Finances (fiscal year 1970): *Revenues,* $228,062,000 (3% general sales tax and gross receipts taxes, $30,967,000; motor fuel tax, $16,370,000; federal funds, $81,886,000). *Expenditures,* $214,420,000 (education, $70,701,000; health, welfare, and safety, $5,325,000; highways, $66,522,000). *State debt,* $51,091,000 (June 30, 1970).
Personal Income (1970): $1,162,000,000; per capita, $3,420.
Public Assistance (1970): $8,448,000. *Average monthly payments* (Dec. 1970)—old-age assistance, $59.25; aid to families with dependent children, $145.65.
Labor Force: Nonagricultural wage and salary earners (June 1971), 114,500. *Average annual employment* (1969)—manufacturing, 7,000; trade, 24,000; government, 28,000; services, 15,000. *Insured unemployed* (Oct. 1971)—600 (0.8%).
Manufacturing (1967): *Value added by manufacture,* $86,200,-000. Petroleum and coal products, $36,900,000; food and kindred products, $14,100,000; sawmills and planing mills, general, $6,600,000; stone, clay, and glass products, $6,500,000; printing and publishing, $6,300,000.
Agriculture (1970): *Cash farm income,* $250,315,000 (livestock, $199,940,000; crops, $35,190,000; government payments, $15,185,000). *Chief crops* (1970)—Wheat, 6,259,000 bushels; barley, 5,922,000 bushels; hay, 1,853,000 tons; sugar beets, 956,000 tons.
Mining (1970): *Production value,* $683,324,000 (ranks 11th among the states). *Chief minerals* (tons)—Coal, 6,630,000; natural gas, 324,873,000,000 cubic feet; petroleum, 160,-130,000 barrels; uranium, 5,807,000 pounds.
Transportation: *Roads* (1969), 40,486 miles (65,154 km); *motor vehicles* (1969), 238,000; *railroads* (1968), 1,848 miles (2,974 km); *airports* (1969), 42.
Communications: *Telephones* (1971), 195,900; *television stations* (1969), 3; *radio stations* (1969), 30; *newspapers* (1969), 9 (daily circulation, 73,000).

YEMEN ARAB REPUBLIC

A permanent constitution for the Yemen Arab Republic was presented to the National Assembly on Jan. 2, 1971. It had been signed at Sana on Dec. 28, 1970, and proclaimed the following day. The constitution called for a Consultative Assembly (Majlis al-Shura) of 159 members, of which 127 were to be elected by the people and 32 were to be appointed by the president of the Republican Council. Also provided were a 3-to-5-member Presidential Council elected by the Majlis and a cabinet and prime minister appointed by the Presidential Council. Political parties were outlawed.

New Government. Elections for the Majlis began in February 1971, and its first meeting was held in Sana on April 19. Three members of the Presidential Council were chosen: Abd al-Rahman al-Iryani, Gen. Hassan al-Amri, and Muhammad

─────── **YEMEN · Information Highlights** ───────

Official Name: Yemen Arab Republic.
Area: 75,290 square miles (195,000 sq km).
Population (1970 est.): 5,730,000. *Density,* 66 per square mile (26 per sq km).
Chief Cities (1966 est.): Sana, the capital, 100,000; Taiz, 80,000; Hodeida, 45,000.
Government: *Head of state,* Presidential Council (took office April 1971). *Head of government,* Muhsin al-Ayni, prime minister (took office Sept. 11, 1971). *Legislature*—Majlis al-Shura (Consultative Assembly), 159 members.
Language: Arabic (official).
Education: *Literacy rate* (1970), 15% of population. *Expenditure on education* (1967), 6.8% of total public expenditure. *School enrollment* (1967)—primary, 56,267; secondary, 18,185; technical/vocational, 232.
Finances (1967–68 est.): *Revenues,* $47,600,000; *expenditures,* $47,600,000; *monetary unit,* rial (1.250 rials equal U. S.$1, Sept. 1971).
Average annual income per person (1966 est.), $120.
Crops (metric tons): Wheat (1968), 15,000; coffee (1969), 3,000.
Foreign Trade (1967): chief exports—coffee; hides and skins; salt; kat (a narcotic drug). Chief imports—textiles; sugar; glass.

Osman. On May 3 a cabinet was formed under Prime Minister Ahmad Muhammad Numan, a moderate from the previous Republican Council. Failure to resolve the grave financial crisis forced Numan's resignation on July 20, however, and a new cabinet was formed under General al-Amri on August 24. Early in September, al-Amri was dismissed and exiled after he murdered a photographer in bizarre circumstances. Muhsin al-Ayni, a former prime minister, resumed that role on September 18, and the army was given four seats in his new cabinet.

Development Plans. In the summer of 1971 the UN Development Program approved three projects for Yemen aimed at: (1) improving agricultural output in cereals and introducing soybeans and fruits; (2) irrigating the Tihama plain so as to produce cotton, sesame, peanuts, tomatoes, and forage crops; and (3) modernizing farming methods in the Taiz district. Aid was received from Hungary and from West Germany during the year, and Iraq promised a loan in the near future.

SYDNEY NETTLETON FISHER
The Ohio State University

YEMEN, PEOPLE'S DEMOCRATIC REPUBLIC OF.
See SOUTHERN YEMEN.

YOUNG, Whitney Moore, Jr.

American civil rights leader: b. Lincoln Ridge, Ky., July 31, 1921; d. Lagos, Nigeria, March 11, 1971.

The fairest view of the active career of Whitney Moore Young, Jr., executive director of the National Urban League, who died in Lagos, Nigeria, on March 11, 1971, is contained in his own words: "voice for the voiceless, hope for the hopeless, power for the powerless." This excerpt from a speech mirrors the short life struggle (49 years) of Whitney Young, and defines the purpose which he fashioned for his organization.

Early Career. Young began his schooling in Lincoln Ridge, Ky., his birthplace, where his father was principal of Lincoln Institute. He graduated from Kentucky State College and secured an M. A. in social work from the University of Minnesota. Young served in the Army during World War II, and after the war he was dean of the Atlanta University School of Social Work. He joined the Urban League in 1961.

The Urban League. Throughout its life, the National Urban League, founded in 1910, had addressed itself, in a difficult and at times almost impossible public opinion, to the task of being a voice for the voiceless. While its spotty success was dictated by the powerlessness of the Negro minority, it was Whitney Young, arriving on the national scene in the years of massive change in the civil rights movement, who gave the phrase meaning.

Dynamic is a weak word to describe his 10 years as director of the Urban League. It was almost as if he knew that his time was not to be long, for he hurried his tasks, piling trip upon trip and continent upon continent, with structural and financial expansion topping all past concepts. Off he was on the earliest planes, home on the latest ones. Public ground transportation was too slow or its frequencies too orthodox; he often drove his own car to fill his demanding schedules.

WHITNEY YOUNG, JR. (1921–1971)

". . . voice for the voiceless, hope for the hopeless, power for the powerless."

Young brought to his new position an intimate knowledge of the disabilities of black people in America. He brought, too, the sure knowledge of what the white citadels of economic and political power could contribute to what was inadequately known as "the race problem." Young's goal was to get from the powerful more power for the powerless. Jobs were all-important. For blacks, he compressed their problem into one sentence, "Pride and dignity come when you reach in your pocket and find money, not a hole." For the industrial whites and their financiers who had the means to plan and the political machinery to execute, Young hammered at employment for blacks, and at education and at training programs for minorities.

For him, Black Power was Green Power, or the power of the dollar. His definition was "pride and community solidarity," without violence. He did not bite his tongue when talking to white businessmen. He did not skip phrases when talking with his own people. He won reluctant cooperation from thoughtful black radicals when he turned his face against emotionally beguiling separatism, declaring, "Our enemies would like nothing better than to have us separated."

Perhaps Young was a bridge between the two races at a most abrasive period in their lives together. The old whites, and those younger ones who wanted to keep the old ways, could not abide the angry young Negroes who were through, forever, with the old ways, crass or subtle. And the old blacks, timidly aware of their shortchanging at every turn, but aware, too, of the powerlessness of the group, shuddered at the truth of the basic complaints of their young, but shuddered more at the wild rhetoric and the predictable violence among the undisciplined.

Young was busy in this time of turmoil with building his National Urban League to minister to the needs of his people and of the nation. While he was pleading with corporation heads, stating his case to the media, and extending scholarship aid and training to young blacks, he was conferring with Presidents Kennedy, Johnson, and Nixon in behalf of policies that would open up opportunities for all minorities. He was not to get his pet idea, "a domestic Marshall plan," as such, but many of its components were included in the projects he launched.

Death. It was characteristic of Young's energy that death came to him far from home, in a black nation making its way to stability and progress in a world of independent states. It was fitting that it should be Nigeria, whose people are restless and talented and adventuresome as was Whitney Young. And it was altogether in character that he should be attending a conference on the development of a dialogue between the West and Black Africa. A measure of his success in the ceaseless quest for racial justice is found in the attendance of 6,000 persons at his funeral—the largest in the 40-year history of the Riverside Church in New York City. None present could quarrel with the minister's description of him: "tenacious in his beliefs and winsome in their presentation."

ROY WILKINS
*Executive Director, National Association
for the Advancement of Colored People*

YUGOSLAVIA

The year 1971 in Yugoslavia witnessed internal political conflicts, the adoption of a major constitutional reform, a continuation of contradictory economic trends, and the personal diplomacy of President Tito.

Political Conflicts. Many conflicts stirred up the country during the year, especially within the League of Communists of Yugoslavia (LCY). Regional nationalist rivalries with economic undertones, militant opposition by students, and nonconformism by intellectuals (leading to the temporary banning of newspapers, magazines, books, and phonograph records) had assumed such proportions that in a speech in Priština on April 14, Tito complained that "our very existence is in question, our socialist state, our community."

Mass disturbances erupted in Croatia in December. Following a general strike of Croatian students protesting the federal government's economic policies, Tito assailed Croatian Communist leaders for "rotten liberalism" and toleration of nationalist activities. On December 12 the president of LC in Croatia, Savka Dabčević-Kučar, and Mika Tripalo, one of the most prominent younger LC leaders, resigned their posts. As a consequence,

violent demonstrations mainly by students took place in Zagreb, followed by mass arrests and a widespread purge of LC functionaries.

Constitutional Reform. On June 30, at a joint session of the chambers of the Federal Assembly, the final and hotly debated text of the constitutional amendments, numbered 20 to 40, was adopted by acclamation. The aim of the reform is to increase the prerogatives of Yugoslavia's six constituent republics and two autonomous provinces, especially in foreign trade earnings and the distribution of investment funds. Proponents of the reform hailed it as a means of strengthening the sovereignty of the republics, while lending support to the spirit of decentralized workers' self-management. Opponents of the reform assailed it as a weakening of Yugoslav federalism that could lead to national disintegration.

Implementing the reform, a collective State Presidency was established. It has 23 members (3 from each republic and 2 from each province) including Tito, who on July 29 was reelected president of the republic for the next five years. On July 30 the Federal Assembly elected a new prime minister—Džemal Bijedić, a 54-year-old Muslim from Bosnia. He had initial difficulties in completing the new 22-member Federal Executive Council, composed of 3 representatives from each republic and 2 from each province.

Economy. To combat economic instability, the dinar was devalued on January 23 (its rate changing from 12.5 to 15 for one U. S. dollar). The government put new limits on imports, investments, consumer credit, and foreign travel. Despite these measures, inflation continued unabated: imports were running far ahead of exports; prices and the cost of living (on the average, 20% above 1970) were soaring; and almost one million workers were still employed abroad.

On the other hand, industrial production expanded rapidly in 1971, increasing 11% over the previous year. Overall agricultural production was also higher than in 1970, with a record wheat harvest of 5.6 million tons (48% more than in 1970), and with a maize (corn) production of 7.3 million (5% above 1970). Likewise, invisible trade earnings increased from such sources as tourism, the

PRESIDENT TITO of Yugoslavia is greeted warmly on his arrival at Andrews Air Force Base, near Washington, D. C., on October 27 to begin visit to the United States.

——— YUGOSLAVIA • Information Highlights ———

Official Name: Socialist Federal Republic of Yugoslavia.
Area: 98,766 square miles (255,804 sq km).
Population (1970 est.): 20,530,000. *Density*, 205 per square mile (80 per sq km). *Annual rate of increase*, 1.1%.
Chief Cities (1961 census): Belgrade, the capital (1966 est.), 698,000; Zagreb, 430,802; Skopje, 165,529.
Government: *Head of state*, Tito (Josip Broz), president (first elected Jan. 14, 1953). *Prime minister*, Džemal Bijedić (took office July 30, 1971). *Legislature*—Federal Assembly (5 chambers), 670 members. *Major political parties*—League of Communists of Yugoslavia (LCY).
Languages: Serbo-Croatian, Slovenian, Macedonian (all official).
Education: *Literacy rate* (1970), 80% of population. *Expenditure on education* (1968), 5% of gross material product. *School enrollment* (1968)—primary, 2,875,075; secondary, 688,822; technical/vocational, 481,396; university/higher, 231,444.
Finance: Budget (1970 est.), $1,095,000,000; monetary unit, dinar (17.0 dinars equal U. S.$1, Dec. 30, 1971).
Gross National Product (1969 est.): $11,900,000,000.
Economic Indexes: *Industrial production* (1970), 168 (1963= 100); *agricultural production* (1969), 131 (1963=100); *consumer price index* (1970), 248 (1963=100).
Manufacturing (metric tons, 1969): Cement, 3,964,000; crude steel, 2,220,000; wheat flour, 2,076,000; pig-iron and ferroalloys, 1,288,000; wine, 7,060,000 hectoliters.
Crops (metric tons, 1969 crop year): Maize, 7,821,000; wheat, 4,882,000; potatoes, 3,144,000; sugar beets (1968), 2,910,000; grapes (1968), 1,270,000.
Minerals (metric tons, 1969): Lignite, 25,815,000; crude petroleum, 2,699,000; bauxite, 2,128,000; iron ore, 1,051,000; gold, 2,819 kilograms.
Foreign Trade (1968): *Exports* (1970), $1,679,000,000 (chief exports—transport equipment, $127,704,000; non-ferrous metals, $110,056,000; electrical machinery and appliances, $86,368,000). *Imports* (1970), $2,874,000,000 (chief imports—nonelectrical machinery, $351,500,000; chemicals, $188,280,000; transport equipment, $181,432,000; iron and steel, $115,024,000). *Chief trading partners* (1968)—USSR (took 16% of exports, supplied 10% of imports); Italy (14%—15%); West Germany (10%—18%); United States (7%—5%).
Tourism: Receipts (1970), $274,600,000.
Transportation: *Roads* (1970), 49,048 miles (78,933 km); *motor vehicles* (1969), 671,100 (automobiles, 562,500); *railroads* (1970), 7,366 miles (11,852 km); *merchant fleet* (1971), 1,543,000 gross registered tons.
Communications: *Telephones* (1970), 622,939; *television stations* (1968), 38; *television sets* (1969), 1,546,000; *radios* (1969), 3,320,000; *newspapers* (1969), 23 (daily circulation, 1,612,000).

savings of Yugoslav workers employed abroad, and emigrants' remittances. Unemployment decreased slightly, and the balance of trade improved.

Foreign Relations. Summit contacts with both East and West marked Yugoslavia's foreign policy in 1971. On March 25–27, Tito visited Italy. On March 29 he met with Pope Paul VI, the first Communist chief of state to do so. Later in the year Tito traveled to Iran (October 13–17), India (October 17–20), and Egypt (October 20–21; he had already visited Egypt in February). A few days later he made an official visit to the United States (October 28–November 2), and then toured Canada (November 2–7) and Britain (November 7–8). A joint statement on the U. S.-Yugoslav talks stressed "U. S. interest in Yugoslavia's independent and nonaligned position and policy."

The USSR's Leonid I. Brezhnev paid an unofficial visit to Yugoslavia on September 22–25. The joint Soviet-Yugoslav statement emphasized willingness "for deepening cooperation" between the two states and their ruling parties, which should be based on the principles set forth in the Belgrade Declaration of 1955.

Sino-Yugoslav relations were markedly improved by the visit of Yugoslavia's foreign minister, Mirko Tepavac, to mainland China (June 8–15) where he met Chinese Premier Chou En-lai. Yugoslav-Albanian relations improved when on February 5 the two governments decided to raise their diplomatic posts to the rank of embassy.

MILORAD M. DRACHKOVITCH
Stanford University

YUKON TERRITORY

The continued expansion of its economy highlighted 1971 in the Yukon Territory. Value of mineral production, primarily lead, zinc, and asbestos, reached $100 million. This represented a sevenfold increase since the 1961 total of $13 million. Zinc led the list with 247 million pounds; followed by lead, 212 million pounds; asbestos, 118,000 tons; and silver, 3.5 million ounces. Other minerals produced include copper, gold, cadmium, and nickel.

Tourism. Tourism, the Yukon's second-largest industry, also showed considerable gains during the year. About 180,000 persons visited the territory in 1971, an increase of 15% over 1970. The estimated value of the industry in 1971 was $12 million.

By far the largest number of visitors to the Yukon were from the United States, according to the records of the Yukon Territory's tourism and information service. California led the states in number of tourists; Alaska was second.

Transportation. The development of transportation in the territory was significant in 1971. Construction went ahead at a rapid pace on the Dempster Highway. This highway, when completed in 1974, will stretch from Dawson, on the Yukon River, to Inuvik, near the East Channel of the Mackenzie River in the Northwest Territories and, it is hoped, to Tuktoyaktuk on the Beaufort Sea. Open to the public for approximately 150 miles (240 km) in 1971, the Dempster Highway is now within 100 miles (160 km) of the Arctic Circle. The territorial government had more than 2,400 road miles (3,800 km) under its administration at year-end.

The portion of the Alaska Highway within Yukon Territory—from eastern British Columbia to Alaska—is expected to be turned over to the territory in 1972. It is now maintained by the federal department of public works.

Government. The year 1971 was the first in which two elected members of the seven-member territorial council served in administrative posts. Also, in 1971 the federal government turned over the administration of justice to the territorial government.

BRIAN R. MARTIN
Yukon Department of Travel and Information

——— YUKON TERRITORY • Information Highlights ———

Area: 207,076 square miles (536,327 sq km).
Population: 17,000 (June 1, 1971 est.).
Chief City (1971 census): Whitehorse, the capital (11,084).
Government: *Chief Officers*—Commissioner, James Smith; Executive Committee Members: R. A. Hodgkinson (appointed), K. Fleming (appointed); Mrs. H. Watson (elected); N. S. Chamberlist (elected). *Territorial Council*—Elected members (speaker, Ron Rivet; K. McKinnon, D. Taylor, Mrs. H. Watson, N. S. Chamberlist, F. Tanner, M. Stutter.
Education: *School enrollment* (March 1971)—Elementary and secondary, 4,521 pupils; vocational training center, 488 pupils (17 full-time teachers).
Public Finance (fiscal year 1968 est.): *Revenues*, $10,270,000 (liquor profits, $142,000; motor vehicle licenses and fuel tax, $1,044,000; property tax, $330,000; federal funds, $6,306,000. *Expenditures*, $12,136,000 (education, $4,310,000; health and social welfare, $1,710,000; transport and communications, $2,336,000).
Social Welfare (fiscal year 1968 est.): $635,000 (aged and blind, $50,000; dependents and unemployed, $93,000).
Mining (1971 est.): *Production value*, $100,000,000. *Chief minerals* (tons)—Zinc, 123,500; asbestos, 118,000; lead, 106,000; silver, 3,500,000 oz.
Transportation: *Roads* (1971 est.), 2,461 miles (3,960 km); *motor vehicles* (1971), 13,876; *railroads* (1971), 58 track miles (93 km); *licensed airports* (1970), 8.
All monetary figures given in Canadian dollars.

ZAÏRE REPUBLIC. See CONGO, DEMOCRATIC REPUBLIC OF (KINSHASA).

ZAMBIA

Zambia's major concerns in 1971 included friction with Portuguese Mozambique over guerrilla activities and with South Africa over its charge that Zambia's President Kenneth D. Kaunda had secretly sought South African aid against an alleged threat of invasion by Rhodesian and Portuguese troops.

Zambia-Mozambique Friction. There were border incidents between Zambia and Portuguese Mozambique in March. Portugal charged Zambia with complicity in the detention of five Portuguese agricultural experts by Mozambique guerrillas at their base in eastern Zambia. Zambia denied the allegation and charged that Portugal was blockading Zambian imports, including essential maize, at Mozambique ports. The alleged blockade, later reported lifted, and the decline in Zambia's maize production forced Zambia to purchase 1.5 million bags of maize from Rhodesia and 2.7 million bags from other sources.

Relations with South Africa. South Africa's Prime Minister Balthazar J. Vorster reported on April 21 that Zambian President Kaunda—though publicly a leading critic of South Africa—had in the past three years made several secret requests to Vorster for South African aid in the event of an invasion of Zambia by Rhodesian forces and forces from Portuguese Mozambique. The Zambian foreign minister called Vorster's charge an utter fabrication.

On October 5, Prime Minister Vorster reported that terrorists who had caused South African casualties in the Caprivi Strip (South West Africa) had been pursued into the territory to which they had fled. The press interpreted this to mean they had been pursued into Zambia, but Vorster denied it.

Political Affairs. Tribal unrest and political discord were accentuated in 1971 by declining copper prices (Zambia is the world's third-largest copper producer), food shortages, and the high cost of transporting goods across black-ruled Tanzania.

On January 1, President Kaunda reinstated all but one of the cabinet ministers and other officials suspended in November 1970 on charges of embezzling public funds. In April 1971 he dismissed two cabinet officers who had been critical of government policy.

Mulungushi Conference. In May, the United National Independence party (UNIP) met in Mulungushi and adopted a new party constitution. The position of deputy party leader was eliminated in the hope of removing a cause of political infighting. Other changes were aimed at stemming the growing opposition from the Bemba, Zambia's largest tribe.

New Opposition Party. On August 22, Vice President Simon M. Kapwepwe, a Bemba, resigned from the cabinet to form a new opposition party, the United Progressive party (UPP). Kapwepwe's long association with Kaunda ended over the rejection of Kapwepwe's plea that younger, better-educated Africans replace the older politicians, whom he considered inept. In alliance with the African National Congress party (ANC), the socialist UPP began to attract a large following.

The government arrested some 90 political opponents, 75 of them UPP officials, on September 20 on charges of gunrunning and preparing for guerrilla activities. Kapwepwe was not arrested.

FRANKLIN PARKER
West Virginia University

ZAMBIA • Information Highlights

Official Name: Republic of Zambia.
Area: 290,585 square miles (752,614 sq km).
Population (1970 est.): 4,300,000. *Density,* 14 per square mile (6 per sq km). *Annual rate of increase,* 2.5%.
Chief City (1969 census): Lusaka, the capital, 238,200.
Government: *Head of state,* Kenneth David Kaunda, president (reelected Dec. 19, 1968). *Head of government,* Kenneth David Kaunda. *Legislature*—National Assembly, 105 elected members. *Major political parties*—United National Independence party, African National Congress, United Progressive party.
Languages: English (official), Bemba, Lozi, Luvale, Tonga, Nyanja.
Education: *Literacy rate* (1970), 15%–20% of population. *Expenditure on education* (1966), 6.2% of gross national product. *School enrollment* (1968)—primary, 609,490; secondary, 46,742; technical/vocational, 2,174; university/higher, 871.
Finances (1970): *Revenues,* $640,360,000; *expenditures,* $504,420,000; *monetary unit,* kwacha (0.7143 kwacha equals U.S.$1, Sept. 1971).
Gross National Product (1969 est.): $1,400,000,000.
National Income (1968): $961,000,000; *national income per person,* $236.
Manufacturing (metric tons, 1969): Cement, 208,000; sugar, 34,000; meat, 16,000.
Crops (metric tons, 1969 crop year): Maize (1968), 590,000; groundnuts, 74,000; tobacco, 5,300.
Minerals (metric tons, 1969): Copper ore, 719,500 (ranks 3d among world producers); coal, 397,000; zinc ore, 68,200.
Foreign Trade (1970): *Exports,* $1,001,000,000 (chief export—copper, $953,540,000). *Imports,* $502,000,000 (chief imports, 1968—nonelectrical machinery, $81,620,000; transport equipment, $80,900,000). *Chief trading partners* (1968)—United Kingdom (took 29% of exports, supplied 23% of imports); Japan.
Transportation: *Motor vehicles* (1968), 74,000 (automobiles, 48,200); *railroads* (1970), 655 miles (1,054 km).
Communications: *Telephones* (1970), 51,598; *television stations* (1967), 2; *television sets* (1969), 20,000; *radios* (1969), 55,000; *newspapers* (1969), 1.

ZOOLOGY

Perhaps the most significant development in 1971 was the increasing awareness of the effects of man's activities on the animal world. Various techniques to reduce this conflict are being investigated, especially biological controls to reduce the use of large amounts of pesticides.

Pesticides. Zoologists continued to investigate the impact of pesticides on animal populations. Thomas J. Cade of Syracuse University and associates reported on DDT residues and eggshell changes in Alaskan falcons and hawks. They found that Alaskan tundra peregrines were highly contaminated and that taiga peregrines, Aleutian peregrines, and rough-legged hawks were progressively less contaminated. No contamination was found in gyrfalcons. The degree of contamination was correlated with differences in exposure to DDT. The gyrfalcons and rough-legged hawks reside in Alaska throughout the year in areas where pesticides are little used. In contrast, the highly contaminated peregrines make extensive annual migrations and contact some of the world's most polluted areas.

The peregrines have lost many young from thin-shelled eggs that break before hatching, and the production of new individuals does not equal the adult mortality rate. Thus the peregrines are rapidly decreasing in number, while gyrfalcons and rough-legged hawks show no such decrease.

Pheromones. Just as the well-known hormones are chemicals secreted within an animal that influence many different processes, pheromones are chemicals secreted externally that influence other individuals of the same species. One group of pheromones are sex attractants.

Since the continued public outcry against pesticides has caused increased interest in "natural" biological controls, one approach has been to isolate and identify pheromones that attract males to females.

Ideally, once identified, they can be synthetically produced and used to bait traps. Reduction in males would then decrease the reproductive success of the pest insect, hopefully to the point that pesticides would not be necessary.

Two Cornell University entomologists, Wendell L. Roelofs and Ring T. Carde, identified the pheromone of nine related species of small moths. A team of Japanese entomologists at Kyoto University isolated and chemically identified the sex pheromone of the almond moth and the Indian meal moth. The Japanese team also discovered that the sex pheromone of the southern army worm is identical to that of the almond moth. Almost simultaneously a team from the University of Georgia and Syracuse University reported their results from studies of the same species. This team emphasized the fact that pheromones have two distinct functions that are not necessarily triggered by the same organic compound. One function is the "attracting" response, and the other is the "sexual stimulatory" response.

Genetics. One of the problems faced in the control of insects by pesticides is that resistance to insecticides evolves in natural populations in a relatively short time. As a result, new insecticides, often with many undesirable side effects, are constantly being produced. Unfortunately, once a given insecticide is discarded, the frequency of resistance genes in natural populations rarely is reduced, even though the insecticide is no longer used.

M. J. Whitten, an Australian entomologist, is exploring the possibility of developing laboratory-raised insects with known gene and chromosomal rearrangements for producing sensitivity to insecticides and cold weather. Theoretically, the introduction of such genetically engineered insects into natural populations would produce two results favorable to the control of the pest species. First, interbreeding between the genetically engineered insects or their progeny would result in sterile offspring, thus directly reducing the total population. Second, the treated insects would easily be eliminated as a result of their cold sensitivity or their susceptibility to a known insecticide.

For years geneticists have known that in vertebrates (and many other animals), the sex of an offspring is controlled by a pair of chromosomes—one in the egg and the second in the sperm. These chromosomes exist in two forms, a large X chromosome and a smaller Y chromosome. Female mammals have two X chromosomes (XX); male mammals have one X and one Y chromosome (XY). In contrast, female birds are XY and male birds are XX. Just how this chromosomal difference controls sex determination is not clearly understood. Ursula Mittwoch of University College London has presented evidence that the Y chromosome may affect the growth rate of the rudimentary gonadal structures that develop in an embryo. According to this view, the faster growing rudiments develop into testes in mammals and ovaries in birds.

Behavior. The importance of olfaction, or sense of smell, in animals continues to be investigated. Dietland and Christine Muller-Schwarze, working at Utah State University, reported that the types of olfactory stimulation received by newborn precocial mammals, such as deer and pronghorned antelope, influence their social behavior throughout life. For example, they exposed newborn deer to pronghorn odor only and found that these deer preferred to associate with pronghorns in later life.

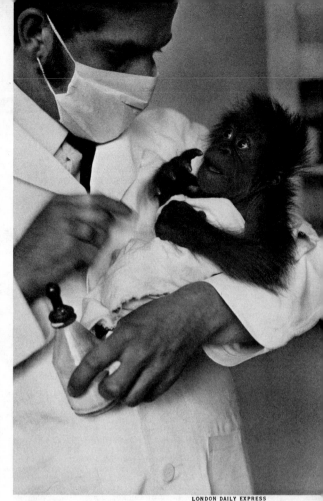

LONDON DAILY EXPRESS

KEEPER Mike Colebourne of the Bristol Zoo, England, cuddles Ginger, three-week-old Sumatran orangutan. Ginger was the first orangutan to be born in England.

Gordon M. Burghardt of the University of Tennessee reported on his studies of the possible influence of maternal diet on the food preferences of newborn garter snakes. He found that feeding pregnant females on a diet of only earthworms or only fish had no effect on the food preferences of newborn young—both preferred worms.

Evolution of Defense Mechanisms. The evolution of mechanisms on the surface of plants to discourage herbivores has long been assumed. The spines of cacti are typically given as examples.

Lawrence E. Gilbert of Stanford University has discovered one species of passion flower, *Passiflora adenopoda,* that has evolved a previously unreported mechanism for defense against the caterpillars of a *Heliconius* butterfly. In an insectary at Stanford, a number of species of passion flowers were growing. All but members of the *P. adenopoda* groups suffered heavy damage from the butterfly larvae. Gilbert placed some larvae on leaves of this species. The following day he discovered that none of the larvae had moved more than a few millimeters and that all were dead or partially dehydrated. Close examination of the leaf surface revealed that the passion flower had tiny plant hairs with hooklike ends that anchored the caterpillars' feet in place. The immobilized larvae then starved.

E. LENDELL COCKRUM
University of Arizona

contributors

Following is a list of the distinguished authorities who contributed articles to this edition of THE AMERICANA ANNUAL. Their professional affiliations are shown, together with the titles of their articles.

ACHESON, WILLIAM, Assistant Professor of History, The University of New Brunswick: NEW BRUNSWICK

ADAMS, GEORGE, Legislative Reference Librarian, Connecticut State Library: CONNECTICUT

ADRIAN, CHARLES R., Professor of Political Science, University of California, Riverside: CALIFORNIA; LOS ANGELES

ALEXANDER, ROBERT J., Professor of Economics and Political Science, Rutgers University: COSTA RICA; DOMINICAN REPUBLIC; GUYANA; JAMAICA

ALVEY, EDWARD, JR., Professor Emeritus of Education, Mary Washington College, University of Virginia: EDUCATION

AMBRE, AGO, Economist, Current Business Analysis Division, Office of Business Economics, U. S. Department of Commerce: ECONOMY OF THE U. S.—Industrial Production

ANDERSON, JEANNE F., Editor, Washington Drug & Device Letter: MEDICINE—Pharmacology

ANDERSON, SAMUEL K., Associate Professor of History, Oregon College of Education: OREGON

ARMSTRONG, FREDERICK H., Associate Professor of History, Talbot College, University of Western Ontario: TORONTO

BAILEY, HARRY A., JR., Chairman, Department of Political Science, Temple University: PENNSYLVANIA; PHILADELPHIA

BAKER, RICHARD T., Professor of Journalism, Columbia University: PUBLISHING—Newspapers

BALL, ROBERT M., Commissioner, Social Security Administration: SOCIAL WELFARE—Social Security

BALLINGER, RONALD B., Professor and Chairman, Department of History, Rhode Island College: SOUTH AFRICA

BANKS, RONALD F., Assistant to the President, University of Maine: MAINE

BARR, LOIS F., Reporter, The Denver Post: COLORADO

BARRETT, RUSSELL H., Professor of Political Science, University of Mississippi: AUSTRALIA

BEATTIE, A. J., Senior Lecturer in Political Science, London School of Economics and Political Science: GREAT BRITAIN; HEATH, EDWARD

BENDER, CHESTER R., Admiral, USCG; Commandant, U. S. Coast Guard: COAST GUARD

BENEDICT, BURTON, Professor of Anthropology, University of California, Berkeley: MAURITIUS

BERGEN, DANIEL P., Associate Professor, Graduate Library School, University of Rhode Island: LIBRARIES

BIRD, CAROLINE, Author, The Invisible Scar and Born Female; Consulting Editor, New Woman: WOMEN'S LIBERATION MOVEMENT

BLACK, KENNETH, JR., Regents Professor of Insurance, Georgia State University; Coauthor, Life Insurance and Cases in Life Insurance: INSURANCE

BOGARDUS, EMORY S., Professor Emeritus of Sociology, University of Southern California; Editor Emeritus, Sociology and Social Research: SOCIOLOGY

BOK, BART J., Professor of Astronomy, University of Arizona: ASTRONOMY

BOND, DONOVAN H., Executive Director of Development and Professor of Journalism, West Virginia University: WEST VIRGINIA

BOND, JOHN G., Senior Geologist, Idaho Bureau of Mines and Geology: MINING—U. S. Mining Technology

BOULAY, HARVEY, Assistant Professor of Political Science, Boston University: BOSTON; MASSACHUSETTS

BOURASSA, GUY, Département de Science Politique, Université de Montréal: MONTREAL; QUEBEC

BOVEY, JOHN A., Provincial Archivist of Manitoba: MANITOBA

BOWERS, Q. DAVID, Columnist, Coin World; Author, Coins and Collectors: COIN COLLECTING

BOYLAN, JAMES R., Graduate School of Journalism, Columbia University: PUBLISHING—Magazines

BRADDOCK, BILL, Sports Department, The New York Times: SPORTS

BRADLEY, C. PAUL, Professor of Political Science, Flint College, University of Michigan: MALAYSIA; SINGAPORE

BRAEMAN, JOHN, Professor of History, University of Nebraska: DEWEY, THOMAS E.

BRAMMER, DANA B., Assistant Director, Bureau of Governmental Research, University of Mississippi: MISSISSIPPI

BRAZDA, JEROME F., Editor, Washington Report on Medicine & Health: MEDICINE—Hospital; SOCIAL WELFARE—Health Care

BRESNAHAN, WILLIAM A., Managing Director, American Trucking Associations, Inc.: TRANSPORTATION—Motor Transport

BRIDGE, LAWRENCE, Chief, Business Outlook Division, Office of Business Economics, U. S. Department of Commerce: ECONOMY OF THE U. S.—Retail Sales; Wholesale Sales

BRODIN, PIERRE, Director of Studies, Lycée Français de New York: FRENCH LITERATURE

BROWN, BERTRAM S., Director, National Institute of Mental Health: MEDICINE—Mental Health

BROWN, WILLIAM J., Chief, Venereal Disease Branch, U. S. Public Health Service, Atlanta, Ga.: MEDICINE—Venereal Diseases

BURDETTE, FRANKLIN L., Professor and Director, Bureau of Governmental Research, University of Maryland: ELECTIONS; POLITICAL PARTIES

BURKS, ARDATH W., Professor of Political Science and Director of International Programs, Rutgers University: JAPAN; SATO, EISAKU

BURLINGAME, MERRILL G., Professor of History, Montana State University: MONTANA

BUSH, GRAHAM, Senior Lecturer in Political Studies, The University of Auckland: NEW ZEALAND

BUSTIN, EDOUARD, Associate Professor of Political Science, Boston University: BURUNDI; CONGO (BRAZZAVILLE); CONGO (KINSHASA); GABON; RWANDA

BUTWELL, RICHARD, Chairman, Department of Political Science, State University of New York at Brockport; Author, Southeast Asia Today—and Tomorrow: BURMA; CAMBODIA; INDOCHINA WAR; LAOS; VIETNAM

CAIRNS, JOHN C., Professor of History, University of Toronto: FRANCE; POMPIDOU, GEORGES

CANN, STAN, State Editor, The Forum, Fargo, N. Dak.: NORTH DAKOTA

CARMONY, DONALD F., Professor of History, Indiana University; Editor, Indiana Magazine of History: INDIANA

CASTAGNO, A. A., Director, African Studies Program, Boston University: SOMALIA

CHALMERS, J. W., Faculty of Education, University of Alberta: ALBERTA

CHINN, RONALD E., Associate Professor and Head, Department of Political Science, University of Alaska: ALASKA

CHRIEN, ROBERT E., Physicist, Brookhaven National Laboratory: NUCLEAR ENERGY

CLARK, J. STANLEY, Department of History, Oklahoma City University; Author, The Oil Century, from the Drake Well to the Conservation Era: OKLAHOMA

CLARK, ROBERT S., Associate Editor, Stereo Review: MUSIC; STRAVINSKY, IGOR

CLARKE, JAY, Sunday Editor, The Miami Herald: TOURISM

COCKRUM, E. LENDELL, Professor, Department of Biological Sciences, University of Arizona: ZOOLOGY

COHEN, SIDNEY, Consultant, National Institute of Mental Health: DRUG ADDICTION AND ABUSE

COLE, CAROLYN J., Editor, *Facts and Forecasts,* Standard & Poor's Corp.: STOCKS AND BONDS

CONDAX, PHILIP L., Equipment Archives Curator, George Eastman House: PHOTOGRAPHY

COPPAGE, NOEL, Contributing Editor, *Stereo Review:* RECORDINGS—*Popular Records*

CRITCHFIELD, HOWARD J., Professor and Chairman, Department of Geography, Western Washington State College: FIJI; NAURU; PACIFIC ISLANDS; TONGA; WESTERN SAMOA

CROW, PAUL A., JR., General Secretary, Consultation on Church Union: RELIGION—*Protestantism*

CURTIS, L. PERRY, JR., Associate Professor of History, University of California, Berkeley: GREAT BRITAIN—*Northern Ireland;* IRELAND

DAVIS, PETER G., Music Editor, *High Fidelity* Magazine: RECORDINGS—*Classical Records*

DAWSON, RICHARD E., Associate Professor of Political Science, Washington University: MISSOURI

DAY, WILLIAM L., Director of Research, Illinois Legislative Council: STATE GOVERNMENT

DELZELL, CHARLES F., Professor and Chairman, Department of History, Vanderbilt University: ITALY

DOBLER, CLIFFORD, Professor of Business Law, University of Idaho: IDAHO

DOLAN, PAUL, Professor of Political Science, University of Delaware: DELAWARE

DORPALEN, ANDREAS, Professor of History, The Ohio State University: GERMANY; BRANDT, WILLY

DORSEN, NORMAN, Professor of Law, New York University: CIVIL LIBERTIES AND CIVIL RIGHTS

DRACHKOVITCH, MILORAD M., Senior Fellow, The Hoover Institution, Stanford University: YUGOSLAVIA

DRIGGS, DON W., Chairman, Department of Political Science, University of Nevada, Reno: NEVADA

DuBOIS, RUTH MARY (PACKARD), Freelance Writer and Guest Lecturer, Fashion Institute of Technology, New York City: CHANEL, GABRIELLE (COCO); FASHION

DUCHON, M. L., Consultant in Ophthalmology: MEDICINE—*Eye Diseases*

DUFF, ERNEST A., Professor of Political Science, Randolph-Macon Woman's College: COLOMBIA

DUFFY, JOSEPH A., Executive Director, American Booksellers Association, Inc.: PUBLISHING—*Books*

DUNNE, JOHN R., New York State Senator: PRISONS (part)

DUPREE, LOUIS, American Universities Field Staff: AFGHANISTAN

DUPREE, NANCY HATCH, American Universities Field Staff: AFGHANISTAN

DURRENCE, J. LARRY, Department of History, Florida Southern College: FLORIDA

ELLIOTT, GORDON R., Assistant Professor of English, Simon Fraser University: CANADIAN LITERATURE

EMANUEL, VICTOR L., Research Associate, Institute for Urban Studies, University of Houston: HOUSTON

ENQUIST, IRVING F., M. D., Director of Surgery, Methodist Hospital of Brooklyn: MEDICINE—*Surgery*

ETCHESON, WARREN W., Professor of Business Administration, University of Washington: WASHINGTON

EVANS, BRUCE, Coordinator of Information Services, Regina Public Library: SASKATCHEWAN

FAIRBROTHERS, DAVID E., Professor of Botany, Rutgers University: BOTANY

FEINBERG, SAMUEL, Columnist, *Women's Wear Daily:* CLOTHING INDUSTRY

FERRAR, HAROLD, Assistant Professor of English and Comparative Literature, Columbia University: THEATER

FISHER, PAUL, Director, Freedom of Information Center, University of Missouri: CENSORSHIP

FISHER, ROBERT W., Economist, Bureau of Labor Statistics, U. S. Department of Labor: LABOR

FISHER, SIDNEY NETTLETON, Professor of History, The Ohio State University; KUWAIT; YEMEN ARAB REPUBLIC

FOGELSON, RAYMOND D., Associate Professor of Anthropology, University of Chicago: ANTHROPOLOGY

FOLMSBEE, STANLEY J., Professor Emeritus of History, University of Tennessee: TENNESSEE

FORD, JOSEPH P., Assistant Professor of Political Science, University of New Hampshire: NEW HAMPSHIRE

FOWLER, JOHN, Architect: ARCHITECTURE

FREEMAN, ARTHUR, Editor, Journal of the American Veterinary Medical Association: VETERINARY MEDICINE

FRIEDMAN, HARVEY L., Assistant Professor of Political Science, and Director, Labor Relations and Research Center, University of Massachusetts: LABOR (part); POSTAL SERVICE

GAIGE, FREDERICK H., Director, South Asian Studies Program, Davidson College: BHUTAN; NEPAL

GAILEY, HARRY A., Professor of History, San Jose State College: GAMBIA; GUINEA; NIGERIA; SENEGAL

GALLOWAY, DAVID D., Associate Professor of English, Case Western Reserve University: ENGLISH LITERATURE

GARDNER, LLOYD C., Professor of History, Rutgers University: UNITED STATES—*Foreign Affairs*

GEIS, GILBERT, Visiting Professor, Program in Social Ecology, University of California, Irvine; Author, *Man, Crime, and Society:* CRIME; POLICE

GIBBONS, CHARLES A., Statistician, Foreign Regional Analysis Division, Economic Research Service, U. S. Department of Agriculture: FOOD—*World Food Supply*

GILBERT, NORMA S., Department of History and Government, Texas Woman's University: NEW MEXICO

GJESTER, THOR, City Editor, *Norwegian Journal of Commerce and Shipping,* Oslo: NORWAY

GOLD, LEON, Vice President–Directing Editor, Tax Research Institute of America: TAXATION

GORDON, MAYNARD M., Editor, *Motor News Analysis* and *The Imported Car Reports:* AUTOMOBILES

GORMAN, JOHN A., Associate Chief, National Income and Wealth Division, Bureau of Economic Analysis, U. S. Department of Commerce: ECOLOGY OF THE U. S.—*National Income and Product*

GRIGG, AUSTIN E., Dean, Richmond College, University of Richmond, Va.: PSYCHOLOGY

GROTH, ALEXANDER J., Professor of Political Science, University of California, Davis: POLAND

GULICK, LEWIS, Diplomatic Affairs Reporter, The Associated Press: FOREIGN AID

GUNN, JOHN M., Professor of Radio-TV-Film, State University of New York at Albany: TELEVISION AND RADIO—*Television Broadcasting; Radio Broadcasting*

HAKES, JAY E., Assistant Professor of Political Science, Louisiana State University in New Orleans: KENYA; TANZANIA; UGANDA

HALL, FRANCES L., Director, International Trade Analysis Division, Bureau of International Commerce, U. S. Department of Commerce: INTERNATIONAL TRADE

HAMILTON, CHARLES V., Professor of Political Science, Columbia University: RACE RELATIONS

HANSON, EARL PARKER, Geographer; Former Consultant to the Puerto Rico Department of State: PUERTO RICO

HARTLING, SALLY C., Instructor in Sociology, University of Texas, Arlington: DALLAS

HARTZOG, GEORGE B., JR., Director, National Park Service: CAMPING (part)

HARVEY, ANDREW S., Economic Research Associate, Institute of Public Affairs, Dalhousie University: NOVA SCOTIA; PRINCE EDWARD ISLAND

HAYES, JOHN D., Rear Admiral, USN (Ret.); U. S. Naval Academy Alumni Association: TRANSPORTATION—*Shipping*

HEAD, HOWARD T., Partner, A. D. Ring & Associates, Consulting Radio Engineers: TELEVISION AND RADIO—*Television and Radio Engineering*

HELMREICH, E. C., Thomas B. Reed Professor of History and Political Science, Bowdoin College: AUSTRIA

HELMREICH, PAUL C., Associate Professor of History, Wheaton College, Norton, Mass.: SWITZERLAND

HENDERSHOT, LELAND C., Editor-in-Chief, American Dental Association: DENTISTRY

HENDERSHOTT, MYRL C., Assistant Professor of Oceanography, Scripps Institution of Oceanography: OCEANOGRAPHY

HERSHKOWITZ, LEO, Professor of History, Queens College, City University of New York: NEW YORK CITY; NEW YORK STATE

HINTON, HAROLD C., Professor of Political Science, The George Washington University: CHINA (part)

HODGES, RALPH W., Associate Technical Editor, *Stereo Review:* RECORDINGS—*Audio Equipment and Techniques*

HODGSON, STUART M., Commissioner, Northwest Territories: NORTHWEST TERRITORIES

HOOVER, HERBERT T., Associate Professor of History, The University of South Dakota: SOUTH DAKOTA

HOPKINS, JAMES F., Professor of History, University of Kentucky: KENTUCKY

HOVET, THOMAS, JR., Professor of Political Science, University of Oregon: THANT, U; UNITED NATIONS; WALDHEIM, KURT

HOWARD, HARRY N., Adjunct Professor of Middle East Studies, School of International Service, The American University: TURKEY

HUCKSHORN, ROBERT J., Professor and Chairman, Department of Political Science, Florida Atlantic University: NIXON, RICHARD M.

HUNKINS, KENNETH L., Senior Research Associate, Lamont-Doherty Geological Observatory of Columbia University: ARCTIC REGIONS

HUNT, STANLEY B., President, Textile Economics Bureau, Inc.: TEXTILE INDUSTRY

HUTH, JOHN F., JR., Reporter-Columnist, *The Plain Dealer,* Cleveland, Ohio: CLEVELAND

IGLAUER, ARNOLD, Associate Clinical Professor of Medicine, College of Medicine, University of Cincinnati: HEART AND VASCULAR DISEASE

JACKENDOFF, RUTH, Director, Department of Economics and Statistics, The Wool Bureau, Inc.: WOOL

JACOBS, WALTER DARNELL, Professor of Government and Politics, University of Maryland: BLOUNT, WINTON M.; BURNS, ARTHUR F.; CONNALLY, JOHN B.; LAIRD, MELVIN R.; MITCHELL, JOHN N.; ROGERS, WILLIAM P.

JENSEN, J. GRANVILLE, Professor of Geography, Oregon State University: CONSERVATION

JONES, ISABELLA J., Executive Director, National Committee for Children and Youth: SOCIAL WELFARE— *Child Welfare*

KAMINS, ROBERT M., Professor of Economics, University of Hawaii: HAWAII

KANTOR, HARRY, Professor of Political Science, Marquette University: CHILE; PERU

KARSKI, JAN, Department of Government, Georgetown University: BULGARIA; HUNGARY

KEHR, ERNEST A., Director, Stamp News Bureau; Executive Chairman, Philatelic Press Club; Stamp News Editor, The Chicago *Daily News:* STAMP COLLECTING

KELLER, EUGENIA, Managing Editor, *Chemistry:* CHEMISTRY

KIMBALL, LORENZO K., Assistant Professor of Political Science, University of Utah: UTAH

KING, PETER J., Associate Professor of History, Carleton University: ONTARIO; OTTAWA

KLEIN, STANLEY, Science Editor, WEVD Radio, New York: COMPUTERS

KOH, BYUNG CHUL, Associate Professor of Political Science, University of Illinois at Chicago Circle: KOREA

KOLEHMAINEN, JOHN I., Chairman, Department of Political Science, Heidelberg College, Tiffin, Ohio: FINLAND

KOMINUS, NICHOLAS, Kominus Agri-Info Associates: AGRICULTURE—*Fruits; Grains; Vegetables*

KREITZMAN, STEPHEN, Professor of Biochemistry, Emory University School of Dentistry: BIOCHEMISTRY

KREPS, CLIFTON H., JR., Wachovia Professor of Banking, University of North Carolina: BANKING

KUDRLE, ALBERT E., Director of Information, American Hotel & Motel Association: TOURISM—*Hotels and Motels*

LAI, DAVID CHUEN-YAN, Assistant Professor of Geography, University of Victoria, B. C.: HONG KONG

LANDSBERG, H. E., Research Professor, Institute for Fluid Dynamics and Applied Mathematics, University of Maryland: METEOROLOGY

LARSEN, WILLIAM, Professor of History, Radford College: VIRGINIA

LARSON, ARTHUR, Director, Rule of Law Research Center, Duke University: LAW—*International Law*

LARSON, T. A., Professor of History, University of Wyoming; Author, *History of Wyoming:* WYOMING

LAWRENCE, ROBERT M., Department of Political Science, Colorado State University: DEFENSE FORCES (part)

LEFEVER, ERNEST W., Senior Fellow, Foreign Policy Studies Program, The Brookings Institution: DISARMAMENT AND ARMS CONTROL

LEIDEN, CARL, Professor of Government, University of Texas: EGYPT; PAKISTAN; SADAT, ANWAR EL-; THAILAND

LEONARD, OLEN E., Department of Sociology, University of Arizona: BOLIVIA

LE VINE, VICTOR T., Associate Professor of Political Science, Washington University, St. Louis: CAMEROON; CENTRAL AFRICAN REPUBLIC; CHAD; LIBERIA; UPPER VOLTA

LEVY, JAMES R., Assistant Professor of History, Pomona College: ARGENTINA

LEWIS, OSCAR, Author, *San Francisco: Mission to Metropolis, The Big Four,* and other books: SAN FRANCISCO

LINDGREN, RAYMOND E., Professor of History, California State College, Long Beach: DENMARK; ICELAND; SWEDEN

LINDSEY, ROBERT H., Aviation Reporter, *The New York Times:* AEROSPACE INDUSTRY; AIR TRANSPORTATION

LINEBACK, RICHARD H., Chairman, Department of Philosophy, Bowling Green State University, Ohio: PHILOSOPHY

LIVINGSTONE, WILLIAM, Reviewer, *Ballet Review;* Managing Editor, *Stereo Review:* DANCE

LOHMANN, LAWRENCE C., City Hall Reporter, The Milwaukee *Journal:* MILWAUKEE

LOTT, LEO B., Professor and Chairman, Department of Political Science, University of Montana: PARAGUAY; VENEZUELA

LYNCH, J. JOSEPH, S. J., Director, Fordham Seismic Observatory: EARTHQUAKES

McCLESKEY, CLIFTON, Professor of Government, University of Texas at Austin: TEXAS

McCONNELL, WILLIAM J., Assistant Professor of Political Science, Colorado State University; Colonel, USA (Ret.): DEFENSE FORCES—*U. S. Army; U. S. Marine Corps;* NATIONAL GUARD

McCORQUODALE, SUSAN, Assistant Professor of Political Science, Memorial University of Newfoundland: NEWFOUNDLAND

McFARLAND, M. CARTER, Special Assistant to the Assistant Secretary, Department of Housing and Urban Development: HOUSING

McGUIRE, JOHNSON, Clinical Professor of Medicine, College of Medicine, University of Cincinnati; Director, Cardiac Laboratory, Cincinnati General Hospital: HEART AND VASCULAR DISEASE

MacLACHLAN, DONALD, Assistant City Editor, *The Province,* Vancouver: VANCOUVER

McLEAN, W. PAUL, Assistant Professor of Religion, Southern Methodist University: RELIGION—*Islam*

McNASPY, C. J., S. J., University Professor in Religious Studies, Loyola University, New Orleans: PAUL VI, POPE; RELIGION—*Roman Catholicism*

MACAULAY, NEILL, Associate Professor of History, University of Florida: CUBA

MAHMOUD, AMIN A., Instructor in Middle East History, Georgetown University: JORDAN

MAJOR, ANDRÉ, Literary Critic, Montreal: FRENCH CANADIAN LITERATURE

MARCOPOULOS, GEORGE J., Associate Professor of History, Tufts University: CYPRUS; GREECE

MARKE, JULIUS J., Law Librarian and Professor of Law, New York University: LAW—*U. S. Legislation and Case Law*

MARTIN, BRIAN R., Information Officer, Yukon Department of Travel and Information: YUKON TERRITORY

MARTIN, J. A., JR., Professor of Religion, Columbia University: RELIGION—*General Survey*

MARTY, MARTIN E., Professor of Modern Church History, University of Chicago; Author, *Righteous Empire: The Protestant Experience in America:* NIEBUHR, REINHOLD

MARWICK, CHARLES S., Senior Writer, *Medical World News:* MEDICINE—*General Survey*

MATHEWS, THOMAS G., Research Professor, Institute of Caribbean Studies, University of Puerto Rico: BARBADOS; CARIBBEAN; TRINIDAD AND TOBAGO; VIRGIN ISLANDS

MATTICK, HANS W., Director, Center for Studies in Criminal Justice, University of Chicago Law School: PRISONS (part)

MECHAM, J. LLOYD, Professor Emeritus of Government, University of Texas at Austin: BRAZIL

MEREDITH, J. R., Director, Bureau of Economics and Statistics, British Columbia: BRITISH COLUMBIA

MEYER, EDWARD H., President and Chief Executive Officer, Grey Advertising, Inc.: ADVERTISING

MICKELSEN, OLAF, Department of Food Science and Human Nutrition, Michigan State University; Secretary, American Institute of Nutrition: FOOD—*Nutrition*

MIESEL, VICTOR H., Associate Professor, Department of the History of Art, University of Michigan: ART

MILLER, ARTHUR R., Professor of Law, University of Michigan; Author, *The Assault on Privacy:* CIVIL LIBERTIES AND CIVIL RIGHTS—*Surveillance*

MILLER, LUTHER S., Editor, *Railway Age:* TRANSPORTATION —*Railroads*

MILLER, NYLE H., Secretary, Kansas State Historical Society: KANSAS

MILLEVILLE, HOWARD P., Extension Food Technologist, Oregon State University: FOOD—*U. S. Food Industry*

MITCHELL, GARY, Associate Professor of Physics, North Carolina State University at Raleigh: PHYSICS

MORGAN, CHARLES S., General Manager, National Fire Protection Association: FIRES

MUSTE, JOHN M., Professor of English, The Ohio State University: AMERICAN LITERATURE

NELSON, RALPH L., Professor of Economics, Queens College, City University of New York: PHILANTHROPY

NEWELL, RICHARD S., Associate Professor of History, University of Northern Iowa: ASIA

NEWSOM, DONALD W., Professor and Head, Department of Horticulture, Louisiana State University: GARDENING AND HORTICULTURE

NIEDERHOFFER, ARTHUR, Professor of Sociology, John Jay College of Criminal Justice, City University of New York: PRISONS (part)

NOLAN, WILLIAM C., Associate Professor of Political Science, Southern State College: ARKANSAS

NORMAN, JOHN, Professor of History and Government, Pace College Westchester: LIBYA; SUDAN; TUNISIA

NOSS, JOHN B., Emeritus Professor of Philosophy, Franklin and Marshall College; Author, *Man's Religions:* RELIGION—*Oriental Religions*

NUQUIST, ANDREW E., Professor Emeritus of Political Science, University of Vermont: VERMONT

NYSTROM, J. WARREN, Executive Director, Association of American Geographers: GEOGRAPHY

OJHA, ISHWER C., Chairman, Department of Political Science, Boston University: CHINA (part)

OKUN, BERNARD, Professor of Economics, Brooklyn College, City University of New York: VITAL STATISTICS

O'MARA, RICHARD, The Baltimore *Evening Sun:* BALTIMORE

ORTEGO, PHILIP D., Executive Director, Chicano Affairs Program, and Professor of English, University of Texas at El Paso: MEXICAN AMERICANS

PALMER, NORMAN D., Professor of Political Science and South Asian Studies, University of Pennsylvania: CEYLON; INDIA

PANO, NICHOLAS C., Assistant Professor of History, Western Illinois University: ALBANIA

PARKER, FRANKLIN, Benedum Professor of Education and Research Associate, Human Resources Institute, West Virginia University: BOTSWANA; EQUATORIAL GUINEA; LESOTHO; MALAGASY REPUBLIC; MALAWI; RHODESIA; SWAZILAND; ZAMBIA

PEARCE, JOHN B., Acting Laboratory Director, Laboratory for Environmental Relations of Fishes, Sandy Hook, N. J.: MARINE BIOLOGY

PETERSEN, WILLIAM, Robert Lazarus Professor of Social Demography, The Ohio State University; Author, *Population* (2d ed.): POPULATION

PETERSON, ROBERT L., Associate Professor of Political Science, University of Texas at El Paso: EL SALVADOR; NICARAGUA

PHEBUS, GEORGE E., JR., Supervisor, Processing Laboratory, Department of Anthropology, National Museum of Natural History, Smithsonian Institution; ARCHAEOLOGY—*Western Hemisphere*

PHILLIPS, JACKSON, Vice President, Moody's Investors Service: ECONOMY OF THE U. S.—*Economic Review*

PIPPIN, LARRY L., Professor of Political Science, Elbert Covell College, University of the Pacific: GUATEMALA; HONDURAS; PANAMA

POINTER, W. DONALD, Associate General Secretary, American Correctional Association: PRISONS (part)

POLK, IRWIN J., Director of Children's Allergy Service, St. Luke's Hospital, New York City: MEDICINE—*Allergies*

PORTER, J. R., Professor and Chairman, Department of Microbiology, College of Medicine, University of Iowa: MEDICINE—*Microbiology*

PORTNOY, BERNARD, Associate Professor of Community Medicine, Public Health, and Pediatrics, University of Southern California: MEDICINE—*Respiratory Diseases*

POWELL, WILLIAM S., Curator, North Carolina Collection, University of North Carolina: NORTH CAROLINA

PRICE, EDWIN W., JR., Managing Editor, *The Morning Advocate,* Baton Rouge, La.: LOUISIANA

PRITCHETT, C. HERMAN, Professor of Political Science, University of California, Santa Barbara: BLACK, HUGO L.; LAW—*Supreme Court*

PRITIKIN, ROLAND I., Eye Surgeon and Consulting Ophthalmologist; Author, *Essentials of Ophthalmology:* MEDICINE—*Eye Diseases*

PUMPHREY, RALPH E., Professor of Social Work, Washington University, St. Louis: SOCIAL WELFARE

PYLE, HOWARD, President, National Safety Council: ACCIDENTS AND DISASTERS

QUIRK, WILLIAM H., Editorial Director, *Contractors & Engineers:* BRIDGES; DAMS; TUNNELS

QUITSLUND, JAMES A., Assistant Professor of German, Williams College: GERMAN LITERATURE

RAKOVE, MILTON, Professor of Political Science, University of Illinois at Chicago Circle: CHICAGO; ILLINOIS

RANDALL, CHARLES E., Staff, *Journal of Forestry:* FORESTRY AND LUMBERING

RANDAZZO, VINCENT P., JR., Assistant City Editor, *The Times-Picayune,* New Orleans, La.: NEW ORLEANS

RATHBONE, ROBERT B., Director, Information Division, Agricultural Research Service: AGRICULTURE—*U. S. Agricultural Research*

RAYMOND, ELLSWORTH, Associate Professor of Politics, New York University; Author, *The Soviet State* and *A Picture History of Eastern Europe:* BREZHNEV, LEONID; COMMUNISM; KOSYGIN, ALEKSEI; KHRUSHCHEV, NIKITA; UNION OF SOVIET SOCIALIST REPUBLICS

RAYMOND, JACK, President and Chief Executive Officer, International Institute for Environmental Affairs; Author, *Power at the Pentagon:* ENVIRONMENT

RENTZ, GEORGE, Curator of the Middle East Collection, The Hoover Institution, Stanford University: OMAN; PERSIAN GULF STATES; SAUDI ARABIA; SOUTHERN YEMEN

REOCK, ERNEST C., JR., Director, Bureau of Government Research, Rutgers University: NEW JERSEY

RODRIGUEZ, ALFRED, Professor of Spanish and Portuguese, University of Wisconsin, Milwaukee: SPANISH LITERATURE

ROMAN, JAMES R., JR., Associate Professor of Business Administration, The George Washington University: TRANSPORTATION—*General Survey; Highways*

RONNE, EDITH M., Antarctic Specialist: ANTARCTICA

ROSS, RUSSELL M., Professor and Chairman, Department of Political Science, University of Iowa: IOWA

ROTHMAN, FRANK G., Professor of Biology, Brown University: GENETICS

ROWLETT, RALPH M., Associate Professor of Anthropology, University of Missouri: ARCHAEOLOGY—*Eastern Hemisphere*

RUEDY, JOHN D., Associate Professor of History, Georgetown University: ALGERIA; MOROCCO

RUPEN, ROBERT A., Professor of Political Science, University of North Carolina: MONGOLIA

SALGADO, MARÍA A., Assistant Professor of Spanish, University of North Carolina at Chapel Hill: LATIN AMERICAN LITERATURE

SALSINI, PAUL, State Editor, The Milwaukee *Journal:* WISCONSIN

SARRIS, ANDREW, Associate Professor of Cinema, Columbia University: MOTION PICTURES

SCHMITT, KARL M., Professor of Government, University of Texas at Austin: DUVALIER, FRANÇOIS; HAITI

SCHNEIDERMAN, RONALD A., Senior Editor—Government Electronics and Features, *Electronic News:* ELECTRONICS

SCHRATZ, PAUL R., Director, Office of International Studies, University of Missouri; Captain, USN (Ret.): DEFENSE FORCES—*U. S. Navy*

SCHRIER, JACK L., Instructor in Middle East History, Georgetown University: LEBANON; SYRIA

SCHWAB, PETER, Assistant Professor of Political Science, State University of New York at Purchase: ETHIOPIA

SEGAR, WILLIAM E., Professor of Pediatrics, University of Wisconsin: MEDICINE—*Pediatrics*

SHAFER, ROBERT JONES, Professor of History, Syracuse University: MEXICO

SHARP, E. PRESTON, General Secretary, American Correctional Association: PRISONS (part)

SHEATSLEY, PAUL B., Director, Survey Research Service, National Opinion Research Center, University of Chicago: PUBLIC OPINION RESEARCH

SHOGAN, ROBERT, Washington Bureau, *Newsweek:* UNITED STATES—*Domestic Affairs*

SIEGEL, SEYMOUR, Professor of Theology, Jewish Theological Seminary: RELIGION—*Judaism*

SKELDING, FRANK H., President, AMDEC Corp., Mineral Consultants: MINING—*World Mineral Production*

SKURNIK, W. A. E., Associate Professor of Political Science, University of Colorado: MALI; MAURITANIA

SLOAN, HENRY S., Associate Editor, *Current Biography:* BIOGRAPHY (in part); NECROLOGY (in part)

SLONIM, MARC, Director, Sarah Lawrence College Foreign Studies: ITALIAN LITERATURE; SOVIET LITERATURE

SMITH, RHEA MARSH, Professor of History, Rollins College: ANGOLA; MOZAMBIQUE; PORTUGAL; SPAIN

SPECTOR, SHERMAN D., Professor of History, Russell Sage College; Author, *A History of the Balkan Peoples:* RUMANIA

SPENCER, JEAN E., Assistant Professor of Government, University of Maryland: MARYLAND; WASHINGTON, D. C.

STEHLING, KURT R., Aerospace Adviser, Executive Office of the President: SPACE EXPLORATION—*Advances in Space Technology*

STEPHENS, GENE, Staff Writer, The Atlanta *Constitution:* ATLANTA; GEORGIA

STOKES, W. LEE, Professor of Geology, University of Utah: GEOLOGY

STOUDEMIRE, ROBERT H., Associate Director, Bureau of Governmental Research and Associate Professor of Political Science, University of South Carolina: SOUTH CAROLINA

STOUMPAS, GEORGE N., Metallurgical Engineer, American Iron and Steel Institute: STEEL

STRUNG, NORMAN, Author, *Camping in Comfort:* CAMPING (part)

SWANKIN, DAVID A., Director of Washington Office, Consumers Union: CONSUMER AFFAIRS

SWANSON, CURTIS E., Manager, Public Relations Division, American Library Association: LIBRARIES—*American Library Association*

SWINTON, WILLIAM E., University Professor, University of Toronto; Fellow of Massey College, Toronto: PALEONTOLOGY

TABORSKY, EDWARD, Professor of Government, University of Texas at Austin: CZECHOSLOVAKIA

TAN, CHESTER C., Professor of History, New York University; Author, *The Boxer Catastrophe* and *Chinese Political Thought in the Twentieth Century:* CHINA (part)

TANAKA, KASHIHI, Assistant Professor of Japanese, University of California, Santa Barbara: JAPANESE LITERATURE

TAYLOR, PHILIP B., JR., Professor of Political Science; Director of Latin American Studies, University of Houston: ECUADOR; URUGUAY

TAYLOR, ZACK, Boats Editor, *Sports Afield;* Regional Editor, *Waterway Guide:* BOATING

THEISEN, CHARLES W., Staff Writer, The Detroit *News:* DETROIT; MICHIGAN

THOMAS, JAMES D., Associate Professor of Political Science, University of Alabama: ALABAMA

THOME, PITT G., Deputy Director for Earth Observations, National Aeronautics and Space Administration: SPACE EXPLORATION—*Manned Space Flight; Earth Satellites and Space Probes*

THOMPSON, RICHARD E., Legislative Counsel, National League of Cities and United States Conference of Mayors: CITIES AND URBAN AFFAIRS

TIBBITTS, CLARK, Associate Coordinator for Technical Committees, Administration on Aging, Department of Health, Education, and Welfare: OLDER POPULATION

TINKLEPAUGH, JAMES R., Associate Professor and Director of Technical Services, College of Ceramics at Alfred University, State University of New York: MATERIALS

TRAVIS, MARTIN B., Chairman, Department of Political Science, State University of New York, Stony Brook: LATIN AMERICA

TROMBLEY, KENNETH E., Editor, *Professional Engineer:* CANALS

TRUMAN, EDWIN M., Assistant Professor of Economics, Yale University: INTERNATIONAL FINANCE

TURNER, ARTHUR C., Professor of Political Science, University of California, Riverside: ACHESON, DEAN; AFRICA; EUROPE; IRAN; IRAQ; ISRAEL; MIDDLE EAST

UHL, WILLIAM, Editorial Director, *World Petroleum:* PETROLEUM

VANDENBOSCH, AMRY, Professor Emeritus of Political Science, University of Kentucky: BELGIUM; INDONESIA; LUXEMBOURG; NETHERLANDS; SUHARTO

VASILIADIS, BASIL G., Chief Secretary, Greek Orthodox Archdiocese of North and South America: RELIGION—*Orthodox Eastern Church*

VICTOR, MAURICE, Professor of Neurology, Case Western Reserve University; Chief, Neurology Service, Cleveland Metropolitan General Hospital: MEDICINE—*Neurology*

WAMSLEY, GARY L., Assistant Professor of Political Science, Vanderbilt University: SELECTIVE SERVICE

WARD, NORMAN, Britnell Professor of Political Science, University of Saskatchewan, Saskatoon: CANADA; TRUDEAU, PIERRE E.

WARNER, ANNE R., Director, Public Relations Department, American Nurses' Association, Inc.: MEDICINE—*Nursing*

WARNER, DAVID Y., City Hall Reporter, The Pittsburgh *Press:* PITTSBURGH

WARREN, DAVID D., Professor of Political Science, University of Rhode Island: RHODE ISLAND

WASHBURN, WILCOMB E., Chairman, Department of American Studies, Smithsonian Institution; Adjunct Professor, The American University: INDIANS, AMERICAN

WEBB, RICHARD E., Former Director, Reference and Library Division, British Information Services: BERMUDA; COMMONWEALTH OF NATIONS; MALTA

WEEKS, JEANNE, Managing Editor, *Interiors;* Associate, Association of Interior Designers: INTERIOR DESIGN

WEINER, PAUL, Associate Professor of Economics, University of Connecticut: TELECOMMUNICATIONS

WEISENBURGER, FRANCIS P., Professor of History, The Ohio State University: OHIO

WELCH, CLAUDE E., JR., Associate Professor of Political Science, State University of New York at Buffalo: DAHOMEY; NIGER; TOGO

WESTERN, JOE, Kominus Agri-Info Associates: AGRICULTURE—*World Agriculture; U. S. Agriculture; Dairy Products; Livestock and Poultry*

WHITAKER, DONALD R., Chief, Current Economic Analysis Division, National Marine Fisheries Service: FISHERIES

WHITE, JOHN P., Chairman, Department of Political Science, Arizona State University: ARIZONA

WILKINS, ROY, Executive Director, National Association for the Advancement of Colored People: YOUNG, WHITNEY

WILLNOW, RONALD D., City Editor, The St. Louis *Post-Dispatch:* MISSOURI; SAINT LOUIS

WILSON, JOHN S., Reviewer of Jazz Records, *The New York Times* and *High Fidelity* Magazine; Author, *Jazz: The Transition Years—1940–1960:* ARMSTRONG, LOUIS; RECORDINGS—*Jazz Records*

WILSON, R. NORRIS, Executive Vice President, United States Committee for Refugees: REFUGEES

WILSON, VERNON E., Administrator, Health Services and Mental Health Administration, U. S. Public Health Service: MEDICINE—*Public Health*

WOODS, GEORGE A., Children's Books Editor, *The New York Times:* CHILDREN'S LITERATURE

YANG, M. G., Assistant Professor, Department of Food Science and Human Nutrition, Michigan State University: MEDICINE—*Nutrition*

YOUNG, CHARLES W., Sloan-Kettering Institute for Cancer Research: MEDICINE—*Cancer*

ZABEL, ORVILLE H., Professor of History, Creighton University: NEBRASKA

ZAFRA, NICOLAS, Professor Emeritus of History, University of the Philippines: PHILIPPINES

ZUBKOFF, HARRY M., Writer-Editor, Office of the Secretary of the Air Force: DEFENSE FORCES—*U. S. Air Force*

necrology · 1971

The following is a selected list of over 350 prominent persons who died during 1971. Separate articles on those persons whose names are preceded by an asterisk (*) may be found in the text under their own heading. Cross references in this list are to articles in the text where biographical sketches of the subject will be found.

Abel, Rudolf (68), former secret agent of the USSR: b. St. Petersburg (now Leningrad), Russia, 1903; d. USSR, Nov. 15, 1971. Colonel Abel conducted a clandestine Soviet intelligence network from a base in New York City from 1948 until his arrest in 1957. He is believed to have joined the Soviet intelligence service in 1927 and to have penetrated the German intelligence apparatus during World War II. He entered the United States illegally in 1948 and trafficked in stolen defense secrets while posing as an artist. Exposed after the defection of one of his subordinates, he was tried in 1957 and sentenced to a 30-year prison term. In 1962 he was exchanged for Francis Gary Powers, the pilot of a U-2 surveillance plane that had been brought down in the USSR in 1960.

Acheson, Dean (78), U. S. diplomat: d. Sandy Spring, Md., Oct. 12.

Adams, Sir Grantley (73), West Indian political leader; founded the Barbados Labour party in 1942; was Barbados' first prime minister (1954–58) and prime minister of the West Indies Federation (1954–58): d. Bridgetown, Barbados, Nov. 29.

Adams, Dr. Roger (82), U. S. scientist; awarded the National Medal of Science (1965) for his researches in organic chemistry; headed the University of Illinois department of chemistry (1926–54): d. Champaign, Ill., July 6.

Adelsberger, Lucie (76), German-American research scientist; was one of the first to demonstrate a possible link between virus and certain human cancers; she worked mainly in immunology and allergy until being imprisoned at Auschwitz by the Nazis; was on the staff of New York City's Montefiore Hospital (1947–71): d. New York, N. Y., Nov. 2.

Adonis, Joe (Giuseppe Antonio Doto) (69), Italian-born U. S. gambler; a leader of the U. S. underworld, he was convicted of violating New Jersey's gambling laws in 1951 and returned to Italy: d. Ancona, Italy, Nov. 26.

Aebi, Rudolf (73), U. S. ophthalmologist; performed one of the first cornea transplants (1951); developed ophthalmic techniques and instruments: d. New York, N. Y., Jan. 2.

Agagianian, Gregory (Peter XV) **Cardinal** (75), Roman Catholic prelate: b. Akhaltizikhe, Russian Georgia, Sept. 15, 1895; d. Rome, Italy, May 16, 1971. A member of the Sacred College of Cardinals since 1946, he was considered the leading non-Italian candidate for the papacy. Educated at Propaganda Fide College in Rome, he was ordained a priest in 1917. He was appointed vice-rector of the Armenian College in Rome in 1921 and rector in 1932. Ordained a titular bishop in 1935, he was named patriarch of Cilicia of the Armenians two years later. In 1946 he was made a cardinal, becoming the youngest member of the Sacred College. As head of the Congregation for Propagation of the Faith, in 1964 he issued 12 principles outlining the missionary role, with special emphasis on the needs of emerging nations of the third world. Although exiled from Russia, he was recognized as the spiritual leader of Roman Catholic Armenians in the Soviet Union.

Albright, William F. (80), U. S. biblical archaeologist and linguist; especially noted for deciphering dead languages; was professor of Semitic languages at Johns Hopkins (1929–58): d. Baltimore, Sept. 19.

Alfaro, Ricardo J. (88), Panamanian statesman; was president (1931–32) following the country's first revolution; served on the International Court of Justice (1959–64), and as UN delegate: d. Panama City, Feb. 23.

Allen, James E., Jr. (60), former U. S. commissioner of education: b. Elkins, W. Va., April 25, 1911; d. near Peach Springs, Ariz., Oct. 16, 1971. He spent much of his career in the New York state department of education, serving as commissioner from 1955 to 1968. He joined the department in 1947 after several years in West Virginia's department of education and as a research fellow at Harvard. As New York state commissioner, he was instrumental in advancing racial desegregation in New York's schools in the 1960's. Appointed U. S. commissioner of education by President Nixon in 1969, he re-

signed in June 1970 after criticizing the administration's stance on school desegregation and U. S. military activities in Southeast Asia.

Amer, Ali Ali (64), Egyptian military leader; was chief of the Egyptian forces in Sinai during war with Israel in 1956; was named chief of staff of the armed forces in 1959; in 1964 became head of the Arab Unified Military Command: d. Alexandria, Egypt, Feb. 10.

Anderson, Gilbert ("Bronco Billy") (88), U. S. film actor; made his debut in *The Great Train Robbery* (1903), the first movie with a story; went on to become the first star of motion-picture Westerns: d. Hollywood, Calif., Jan. 20.

Andrews, George W. (65), U. S. congressman; served as U. S. Democratic representative from Alabama since 1944; was chairman of Legislative Subcommittee and member of Appropriations Subcommittee on Public Works: d. Birmingham, Ala., Dec. 25.

Andreyev, Andrei A. (76), Soviet statesman; was the only close associate of Stalin to remain in favor when Nikita Khrushchev came to power; played key role in restoration of collective farming: d. Moscow, USSR, Dec. 5.

Angeli, Pier (39), Italian-born U. S. actress; appeared in films, notably *Teresa* (1951), and on television: d. Beverly Hills, Calif., Sept. 10.

Arbenz, Jacobo Guzman (57), Guatemalan statesman, called the "Red Colonel"; was president from 1951 until 1954, when he was accused of leading country toward communism and overthrown by a right-wing military coup: d. Mexico City, Mexico, Jan. 27.

Armand, Louis (66), French engineer; after World War II he oversaw the rebuilding of the French railroads; was president (1958–59) of Euratom, the Western European atomic energy organization: d. Viler-sur-Mer, France, Aug. 31.

Astor of Hever, 1st Baron (Col. John Jacob Astor 5th) (85), U. S.-born English newspaper publisher; was chief proprietor (1922–66) of *The Times* of London and a Conservative member of the House of Commons (1922–45): d. Cannes, France, July 19.

Azcarate, Pablo de (81), Spanish lawyer and statesman; served as deputy secretary-general of the League of Nations (1932–36) and Spain's ambassador to Britain (1936–39): d. Geneva, Switzerland, Dec. 13.

Bacci, Antonio Cardinal (85), Italian Roman Catholic prelate; was ranking church Latinist, and wrote the Latin versions of encyclicals for four popes: d. Rome, Italy, Jan. 20.

Ballantine, Edward (84), U. S. composer and pianist; taught music at Harvard University (1912–47); composed orchestral pieces, musical plays, and the popular piano variations on *Mary Had A Little Lamb:* d. Martha's Vineyard, Mass., July 2.

Basch, Antonin (74), Czechoslovak-U. S. economist; held several posts in Prague; in the United States he was chief economist of the International Bank for Reconstruction and Development (1942–57); he taught at several universities and wrote many books: d. Washington, D. C., March 18.

Bashev, Ivan H. (55), Bulgarian statesman; as foreign minister of Bulgaria (1962–71), visited Rumania, Turkey, and Yugoslavia in attempt to improve relations with Communist and non-Communist neighbors: d. Sofia, Bulgaria, Dec. 13.

Beall, J. Glenn (76), U. S. congressman; served as Republican representative (1942–52) and senator (1952–64) from Maryland: d. Frostburg, Md., Jan. 14.

Beberman, Max (45), U. S. mathematician; was professor of education at the University of Illinois (1958–71); helped develop the New Math: d. London, England, Jan. 24.

Beinecke, Frederick (84), U. S. businessman and bibliophile; was chairman of the executive committee of Sperry and Hutchinson Company, a trading stamp concern, from 1953 to 1966; he had one of the largest private collections of western Americana in existence; with his brothers he gave a rare book and manuscript library to Yale University: d. Great Barrington, Mass., July 30.

Ben-Meir, Israel S. (60), U. S.-born Israeli lawyer and religious leader; was an ordained rabbi; he settled in Israel (1950) and served in the Knesset and as deputy minister of the interior (1963–69); leader of the National Religious party: d. Jerusalem, April 4.

Berle, Adolf A(ugustus), **Jr.** (76), U. S. lawyer, diplomat, and economist: b. Boston, Mass., Jan. 29, 1895; d. New York, N. Y., Feb. 17, 1971. A member of the original "brain trust" of President Franklin D. Roosevelt's New Deal administration, and an authority on Latin America, he served the federal government in various capacities over the years. He graduated from Harvard Law school in 1916, and from 1919 until his death he was a partner in the New York law firm of Berle & Berle. He served as a professor of corporation law at Columbia University from 1927 to 1964. As counsel to the Reconstruction Finance Corporation under the New Deal he helped formulate legislation. He was assistant secretary of state for Latin American affairs from 1938 to 1944 and ambassador to Brazil in 1945–46. During the early 1960's he went on diplomatic missions to Latin America for President John F. Kennedy. A founder of the Liberal party of New York state, he served as its chairman from 1952 to 1955. His published works include *The Modern Corporation and Private Property* (1932).

Bernal, John Desmond (70), Irish physicist; his discoveries in crystallography helped create the foundations of molecular biology; was an expert on explosives and on sea waves; wrote *Science in History* (4 vols., 1971), which has a Marxist viewpoint: d. London, Sept. 15.

Berryman, James (69), U. S. political cartoonist; worked for the Washington *Evening Star* (1923–64); won Pulitzer Prize in 1950: d. Venice, Fla., Aug. 11.

Billy, André (88), French literary critic and author; wrote novels and biographies of such writers as Balzac and Stendhal; he was dean of the Prix Goncourt jury: d. Fountainbleau, France, April 10.

*Black, Hugo (85), U. S. Supreme Court justice: d. Bethesda, Md., Sept. 25.

Blanchfield, Florence A. (87), U. S. nurse; the first woman to receive a commission in the regular Army (1947), she had served as superintendent of the Army Nurse Corps during World War II: d. Washington, D. C., May 12.

Blegen, Carl (84), U. S. archaeologist; in 1939 he found the palace of Nestor, king of Pylos that is described by Homer in the *Odyssey*: d. Athens, Greece, Aug. 25.

Blessing, Karl (71), German banker; was president of West Germany's Bundesbank (1958–69) and used it to stabilize the mark—especially during Germany's 1966–67 recession—and, in 1969, to effect a 9% upward revaluation of the mark: d. Rasteau, France, April 25.

Bourke-White, Margaret (67), U. S. photojournalist: b. New York, N. Y., June 14, 1904; d. Darien, Conn., Aug. 27, 1971. A venturesome and accomplished photographer with a passion for gritty realism, she was a pioneer in the art of telling stories by means of pictures. Taking up photography in the mid-1920's, she produced notable picture portfolios on various industries and their workers, the U. S. dust bowl, and life in the Soviet Union. In 1936 she collaborated with the author Erskine Caldwell, to whom she was later briefly married, on a study of Southern tenant farmers and sharecroppers entitled *You Have Seen Their Faces*. A staff member of *Life* magazine from its founding in 1936 until 1969, she produced some of her most impressive work while covering battlefield action during World War II.

Boyd Orr, Lord (John) (90), British nutritionist: b. Kilmaurs, Ayrshire, Scotland, Sept. 23, 1880; d. Brechin, Angus, Scotland, June 25, 1971. A leading international authority on nutrition, he was the first director of the Food and Agricultural Organization of the United Nations (1945–49) and received the 1949 Nobel Peace Prize for his role in helping to avert famine in post-World War II Europe. After studying medicine at Glasgow University he became interested in nutrition and founded the Rowett Research Institute on Animal Nutrition. His survey *Food, Health and Income* (1936), which dealt with the relationship between hunger and poverty, helped inspire the creation of the Mixed Commission of the League of Nations. He was knighted in 1935 and created a baron in 1949.

Bragg, Sir William Lawrence (81), British physicist; with his father, Sir William Henry Bragg, he shared the 1915 Nobel Prize for physics for discovering crystal structure by means of X-ray diffraction: d. London, England, July 1.

Bronfman, Samuel (80), Canadian businessman; was founder and president of Distillers Corporation–Seagrams, Ltd., of Montreal and New York, the world's largest distiller: d. Montreal, Quebec, July 11.

Bronson, Betty (64), U. S. actress; played the title role in the silent film *Peter Pan* (1924) and in other early movies;

came out of retirement in 1961 to play character roles in movies and on television: d. Pasadena, Calif., Oct. 19.

Budgen, Frank (89), British author; his close friendship, from 1918, with James Joyce, resulted in many studies of the author and his works, including *James Joyce and the Making of "Ulysses"* (1934): d. London, England, April 26.

Bunche, Ralph (67), U. S. diplomat: d. New York, N. Y., Dec. 9. (See UNITED NATIONS.)

Burke, Thomas A. (73), U. S. political figure; was Democratic mayor of Cleveland (1945–53) and U. S. senator from Ohio (1953–54): d. Cleveland, Ohio, Dec. 5.

Burnett, Leo (79), U. S. advertising executive; founded the Chicago-based Leo Burnett Co. in 1935; his agency created the Jolly Green Giant and the Marlboro Man; was director (1941–62) and chairman (1962–63) of the Advertising Council: d. Lake Zurich, Ill., June 7.

Burt, Sir Cyril Lodowic (88), British educational psychologist; in the early 1900's he helped set up England's first child guidance clinic; was one of the first educational psychologists to stress the importance of the social backgrounds of children investigated: d. London, England, Oct. 10.

Byington, Spring (77), U. S. character actress; made her Broadway debut in *Beggar on Horseback* (1924); her later vehicles included *Once in a Lifetime* (1930); she began her busy film career in *Little Women* (1934) and soon became known for her roles of loveable, motherly women; perhaps her greatest popularity came from her portrayal of the mother-in-law in the televison series *June Bride* (1954–59): d. Hollywood, Calif., Sept. 7.

Callori di Vignale, Federico Cardinal (81), Italian Roman Catholic prelate; held various posts in the papal household; named cardinal in 1965; d. Vatican City, Aug. 10.

Campbell, E. Sims (65), U. S. illustrator; as cartoonist for *Esquire*, he created "Eski," a pop-eyed, mustachioed figure who became the magazine's trademark and appears on its covers: d. White Plains, N. Y., Jan. 27.

Campbell, John W. (61), U. S. science fiction editor and author; was editor (1937–71) of *Analog* (formerly *Astounding Science Fiction*), raising it from an adventure pulp to a leading science fiction and fact magazine that promoted some of the best writers in the field; his own books include the novelette *Who Goes There?* (1938), filmed in 1951 as *The Thing*: d. Mountainside, N. J., July 11.

Carpenter, George (81), Canadian journalist; with the Montreal *Gazette* from 1912 to 1970, and became its managing editor in 1939; wrote column *Rod and Gun* under the name of Izaak Hunter: d. Montreal, Quebec, Feb. 1.

Carr, Albert (69), U. S. economist and author; was economic adviser to President Franklin Roosevelt and special consultant to President Harry Truman; his books include *How To Attract Good Luck* (1952): d. New York, N. Y., Oct. 28.

Castellani, Aldo (95), Italian authority on tropical diseases; traced the parasitic causes of sleeping sickness and developed vaccines against it; in 1926 he helped establish the School of Tropical Medicine at Tulane University in New Orleans: d. Lisbon, Portugal, Oct. 3.

Cerf, Bennett (73), U. S. book publisher: b. New York, N. Y., May 25, 1898; d. Mount Kisco, N. Y., Aug. 27, 1971. Renowned in the publishing trade as the developer of the Modern Library and founder of Random House, he was also known to millions as a panelist on the *What's My Line?* television program in the 1950's and 1960's. A Phi Beta Kappa graduate of Columbia University, Cerf joined the firm of Simon & Schuster at its formation in 1923. Two years later he bought the Modern Library, a line of reprinted classics, which he redesigned, expanded, and promoted into the most successful series of its kind. In 1930 he founded Random House, serving as its president until 1965 and as chairman until 1970. The firm published Eugene O'Neill, William Faulkner, and many other outstanding contemporary authors. Cerf's most famous coup was his publication of an unabridged version of James Joyce's *Ulysses* in 1934, after leading a campaign that secured a U. S. court reversal of a ban against its publication on grounds of obscenity.

Cerny, Josef (86), Czech patriot; served as member of Parliament and minister of interior during 20-year existence of prewar democratic Czechoslovakia; jailed by Nazis and exiled after 1948: d. New York, N. Y., Dec. 7.

Chabou, Abdel Kader (46), Algerian military leader; led the military security services and was de facto commander in chief of the army; he was considered his country's second in command: d. near Algiers, Algeria, April 2.

Chanel, Gabrielle (Coco) (87), French fashion designer: d. Paris, France, Jan. 11. (See FASHION.)

Chernick, Jack (59), U. S. physicist; pioneered in developing water-moderated nuclear power reactors, including the high-flux beam reactor at the Brookhaven National Laboratory (N. Y.): d. Upton, N. Y., April 8.

Chrisholm, Brock (74), Canadian psychiatrist; was Toronto's first practicing psychiatrist; he was director general of the World Health Organization (1948–53): d. Victoria, B. C., Feb. 2.

Clark, Walter Van Tilburg (62), U. S. author; wrote *The Ox-Bow Incident* (1940), a novel about the lynching of three innocent men, which was made into a highly praised film in 1943: d. Reno, Nev., Nov. 10.

Clark Flores, José de Jesus (62), Mexican sports executive; was a vice president of the International Olympic Committee and president of the Pan-American Sports Committee: d. Mexico City, Mexico, April 18.

Clarke, Richard W. (74), U. S. newspaper editor; succeeded his father in 1939 as managing editor of the New York *Daily News;* became its first executive editor in 1946, and was its editor from 1951 to 1968: d. New York, N. Y., Feb. 26.

Cleland, Ralph E. (78), U. S. botanist; was professor and chairman of the botany department of Indiana University (1938–63); his work on the gene changes in the evening primrose (1930's) contributed to the theory of evolution: d. Bloomington, Ind., June 11.

Collier, Marie (44), Australian soprano; sang in opera houses throughout the world; achieved stardom as Tosca at Covent Garden in 1965; made her Metropolitan Opera debut as Christine Mannon in the world premier of Martin David Levy's *Mourning Becomes Elektra* (1967): d. (accident) London, England, Dec. 7.

Colombo, Joe Cesare (41), Italian designer of furniture and interiors; his rolling kitchen is displayed at New York City's Museum of Modern Art: d. Milan, Italy, July 30.

Confrey, Zez (76), U. S. jazz pianist and composer; wrote *Kitten on the Keys* (1924): d. Lakewood, N. J., Nov. 22.

Constantine, Lord (Learie Constantine) (69), Trinidad-born British athlete and lawyer; was all-round cricket star (1920's–30's); served as high commissioner for Trinidad and Tobago to London (1962–64) and was the first black peer (1969) in the House of Lords: d. London, England, July 1.

Cooper, Dame Gladys (82), British actress; from 1905 to 1971 she appeared in London and New York in every type of play, notably in *The Chalk Garden* (1955); she was also in many films, such as *My Fair Lady* (1964), and on television, including *The Rogues,* a series: d. London, England, Nov. 17.

Coryell, Charles DuBois (58), U. S. nuclear chemist; worked on the first atom bomb during World War II; was professor of chemistry at the Massachusetts Institute of Technology (1946–71): d. Boston, Mass., Jan. 7.

Covey, James H., Jr. (47), U. S. publisher; was president of the Tampa (Fla.) *Tribune* Company (1966–68); served (1968–71) as executive editor and then publisher of the Honolulu *Star-Bulletin:* d. Rome, Italy, June 22.

Crommelin, Henry (66), U. S. vice admiral; before his retirement (1959) he was a much-decorated naval hero of World War II, and was assistant chief of naval operations in Washington, D. C.: d. Elmore county, Ala., March 2.

Culbertson, William (65), U. S. clergyman; was bishop of the New York and Philadelphia area of the Reformed Episcopal Church (1937–42) and president of the Moody Bible Institute (1948–71): d. Chicago, Ill., Nov. 16.

Curtis, King (36), U. S. bandleader, composer, and saxophonist; led the Kingpins, a blues and "soul" band; he wrote many songs, including *Soul Serenade* and *Instant Groove;* fatally stabbed in a fight: d. New York, N. Y., Aug. 14.

Dale, Charlie (90), U. S. comedian; was the deadpan partner in the vaudeville team Smith and Dale, which headlined at the Palace theater for years and performed at the opening of Radio City Music Hall: d. Teaneck, N. J., Nov. 16.

Dall, John (50), U. S. stage and screen actor; played opposite Bette Davis in motion picture *The Corn Is Green* (1945); starred on Broadway in *Red Gloves* (1948): d. Hollywood, Calif., Jan. 15.

Damon, S. Foster (78), U. S. author and scholar; wrote extensively on poetry; was noted for many books on William Blake: d. Smithfield, R. I., Dec. 27.

Darvi, Bella (42), Polish-born U. S. film and television actress; appeared in *Hell and High Water* (1954), *The Egyptian* (1954), and *The Racers* (1955); thereafter her career went badly: d. (suicide) Monte Carlo, Monaco, about Sept. 11.

Davidson, Gustav (75), Polish-born U. S. poet; was an authority on angels in literature; wrote award-winning *A Dictionary of Angels* (1967): d. New York, N. Y., Feb. 6.

De Kruif, Paul (Henry) (80), U. S. author and bacteriologist: b. Zeeland, Mich., March 2, 1890; d. Holland, Mich.,

UPI   JOHN LOENGARD, LIFE
                 MAGAZINE © TIME INC.

Bennett Cerf   John M. Harlan

Feb. 28, 1971. The author of such popular best sellers as *The Microbe Hunters* (1926), *The Hunger Fighters* (1928), and *Men Against Death* (1932), he translated the achievements of medical science into the language of the layman. After obtaining his Ph. D. degree in microbiology from the University of Michigan in 1916 he joined its faculty as an assistant professor. In 1920 he became an associate at the Rockefeller Institute for Medical Research. He collaborated with Sinclair Lewis on the novel *Arrowsmith* (1925) and was coauthor, with Sidney Howard, of the successful play *Yellow Jack* (1934). His books include *Our Medicine Men* (1922), *Seven Iron Men* (1929), *Why Keep Them Alive?* (1936), *The Fight for Life* (1938), *Health is Wealth* (1940), *Kaiser Wakes the Doctors* (1943), *Male Hormone* (1945), *Life Among the Doctors* (1949), *Man Against Insanity* (1957), and the autobiography *The Sweeping Wind* (1962).

D'Erlanger, Theodore (81), Russian-born French choreographer and ballet teacher; worked with many great dancers, including Pavlova: d. Paris, France, July 16.

*Dewey, Thomas E. (68), former governor, New York state: d. Bal Harbour, Fla., March 16.

Dobrovolsky, Lt. Col. Georgi Timofeyevich (43), Soviet cosmonaut; was commander of the space vehicle *Soyuz 11;* after remaining in space for 24 days, he and his crewmen were killed when a sudden drop in air pressure occurred within the space capsule as it was reentering earth's atmosphere on June 30.

Dodd, Thomas J(oseph) (64), U. S. senator: b. Norwich, Conn., May 15, 1907; d. Old Lyme, Conn., May 24, 1971. A Democrat from Connecticut, he served in the U. S. Senate from 1959 to 1971 and attained considerable influence as a member and vice-chairman of the Senate Internal Security Subcommittee. He was also a member of the Foreign Relations Committee. After graduating from Yale Law School in 1933 he served two years as an agent for the FBI. From 1938 to 1954 he was a special assistant in the Justice Department. In 1945–46 he was executive trial counsel at the Nuremberg war crimes trials. He served in the U. S. House of Representatives from 1953 to 1957. Despite his vigorous anticommunism stance, in the Senate he supported civil rights, welfare legislation, and increased social security. He also advocated strong gun controls, opposed television violence, and cosponsored the Drug Abuse Prevention Act (1970). In 1967 he was censured by a Senate vote of 92–5 for having diverted political campaign funds to his own use. In 1970 he made an unsuccessful bid for a third term.

Dufhues, Josef Hermann (68), German politician; a moderate conservative, he cofounded the Christian Democratic party after World War II, and served as party manager (1962–66): d. Rheinhausen, West Germany, March 26.

Dun, Angus (79), U. S. prelate; was Episcopal bishop of Washington, D. C. (1944–62); officiated at many national ceremonies and was active in ecumenical affairs: d. Washington, D. C., Aug. 12.

Dupré, Marcel (85), French organist and composer, noted as a brilliant improviser; he won the Grand Prix de Rome in 1914 for his cantata *Psyché;* in 1920 he played the entire organ works of Bach from memory; he toured Europe, America, and Australia: d. Meudon, France, May 30.

Duvalier, François (65), Haitian president: d. Port-au-Prince, Haiti, April 21. (See HAITI.)

Eckert, Wallace J. (69), U. S. astronomer; was professor of celestial mechanics at Columbia University (1926–67);

largely responsible for introduction of the computer into astronomy: d. Englewood, N. J., Aug. 24.

Eckert, William D(ole) (62), U. S. retired military officer and baseball commissioner: b. Freeport, Ill., Jan. 20, 1908; d. Freeport, Bahamas, April 16, 1971. Appointed commissioner of major league baseball in 1965, he was replaced three years later by baseball officials who felt that he lacked the required flamboyant image. A West Point graduate, he became an Army pilot, later studied at the Harvard Graduate School of Business Administration, and served the Army as an expert in supply and logistics during World War II. After his retirement as a lieutenant general in the Air Force in 1961, he served as an executive of real estate and electronics firms.

Edelman, John W. (78), U. S. trade unionist and consumer advocate; an early promoter of labor-sponsored, low-cost housing; served as chairman of the board of the National Consumers Union (1961–69): d. Arlington, Va., Dec. 27.

Eder, Phanor J. (90), Colombian-born U. S. lawyer; specialized in inter-American law; helped establish the Inter-American Law Center and founded the *American Journal of Comparative Law*: d. New York, N. Y., March 5.

Edmondson, J. Howard (46), U. S. political figure; was governor of Oklahoma (1958–63); filled unexpired term (1963–64) of the late U. S. Sen. Robert Kerr: d. Edmond, Okla., Nov. 17.

Edwards, Phil (63), Canadian physician and athlete, the first black recipient of a medical degree from McGill University; was consultant to the Canadian government in tropical and chest diseases; won five bronze medals in Olympic track events (1928, 1932, 1936): d. Montreal, Quebec, Sept. 6.

Ehrlich, Jacob W. (Jake) (71), U. S. criminal lawyer; known for flamboyant courtroom skills and success in saving the lives of clients in capital cases; author of *Ehrlich's Blackstone*, a law commentary: d. San Francisco, Calif., Dec. 24.

Eisenhower, Edgar (82), U. S. lawyer; was the older brother of Dwight D. Eisenhower, and their friendly rivalry often made national news: d. Tacoma, Wash., July 12.

Engelhard, Charles W(illiam) (54), U. S. industrialist and racehorse owner: b. New York, N. Y., Feb. 15, 1917; d. Boca Grande, Fla., March 2, 1971. The head of a multi-million-dollar precious-metals empire, he was also noted as the owner and breeder of champion racehorses. He graduated from Princeton University in 1939 and succeeded his father in 1950 as president of Engelhard Minerals and Chemicals Corporation. The Engelhard empire, with its core in Engelhard Hanovia, Inc., controls properties in some 50 countries and has extensive holdings in South Africa. Originally dealing primarily in gold, Engelhard expanded his operations to include platinum and diamonds, as well as copper, timber, and oil resources. At the time of his death he owned some 300 horses, including Nijinsky II, a winner of England's Triple Crown.

Ephron, Phoebe (57), U. S. playwright; with her husband, Henry Ephron, wrote situation comedies, notably *Take Her, She's Mine* (1961): d. New York, N. Y., Oct. 13.

Ervine, St. John (87), Irish playwright and critic; wrote stage plays, including *The First Mrs. Fraser* (1928) and *Anthony and Emma* (1925); was a drama critic for *The Sunday Observer* (1930's); wrote for and managed (1915) Dublin's Abbey Theatre: d. London, Jan. 24.

Ettinger, Richard P. (77), U. S. publisher; was a cofounder (1913) and chairman of the board (1949–71) of the publishing house Prentice-Hall, Inc.; author of reference books on corporate law: d. Miami, Fla., Feb. 24.

Evans, Joseph E. (52), U. S. newspaper editor; served as editorial page editor of the *Wall Street Journal* since 1969; author of *Through Soviet Windows* (1957): d. Pelham Manor, N. Y., Dec. 27.

Fairchild, Sherman M(ills) (74), U. S. inventor and industrialist: b. Oneonta, N. Y., April 7, 1896; d. New York, N. Y., March 28, 1971. A prolific inventor in such areas as aviation and photography, he used his financial resources to put his ideas into practice. A student at Arizona, Harvard, and Columbia universities, he ended his education without graduating. During the early 1920's he started a mapmaking business and an aerial survey company. Later, as head of Fairchild Aviation Corporation, he introduced such innovations as folding wings and hydraulic brakes in the manufacture of aircraft. After Fairchild Aviation went out of business in 1931 he founded Fairchild Recording Equipment Corporation. At the time of his death he was chairman of Fairchild Camera and Equipment Company and of Fairchild Hiller Corporation.

Farrell, Glenda (66), U. S. actress; was featured in many Broadway shows, notably *Life Begins* (1932) and *Life of Riley* (1942); she began her movie career in *Little Caesar* (1930), and became typecast as the dizzy, wisecracking, tough blonde: d. New York, N. Y., May 1.

Ferm, Alexis C. (101), Swedish-born U. S. educator; developed schools (1898–1920) based on the theory of "freedom of education," and served as coprincipal, with his wife, of the famed Ferrer Modern School (N. J., 1920–50): d. Fairhope, Ala., June 16.

Fernandel (Fernand Contandin) (67), French comedian: b. Marseille, France, May 8, 1903; d. Paris, France, Feb. 26, 1971. One of France's most beloved motion-picture personalities, he was known for his expressive, mobile face, and his flair for pantomime. He appeared in some 150 films. He was perhaps best known internationally for his role as the pugnacious Italian village priest in *Little World of Don Camillo* (1951). He began his career as a café singer at the age of 10 and had attained some popularity in Paris music halls by the time he entered motion pictures in 1930. His films include *The Well-Digger's Daughter, Topaz, The Cupboard Was Bare, The Sheep Has Five Legs, Paris Holiday, My Wife's Husband,* and *The Return of Don Camillo.* He also wrote and recorded songs, appeared in plays, staged operettas, and headed a motion-picture production company.

Fleming, Peter (64), British author, traveller, and adventurer; after an unsuccessful venture into the Brazilian jungles, he wrote *Brazilian Adventure* (1933), a parody of boastful adventure stories; later wrote about his extensive travels and about current world events; was the brother of Ian Fleming, creator of the James Bond spy stories: d. Black Mount, Argyllshire, Scotland, Aug. 19.

Flick, Elmer (94), U. S. athlete, who is in the Baseball Hall of Fame; was a leading hitter for both the National and American Leagues (1898–1910): d. Bedford, Ohio, Jan. 9.

Flippen, Jay C. (70), U. S. character actor; known for his raspy voice and rough features, he starred on Broadway in *The Great Temptations* (1926), and later appeared in more than 50 motion pictures—including *Cat Ballou* (1953)—and on television: d. Los Angeles, Calif., Feb. 3.

Ford, Arthur A. (75), U. S. clergyman; ordained a Disciples of Christ clergyman; he became involved with extrasensory perception in 1924, and was the psychic medium working with Rev. James A. Pike: d. Miami, Fla., Jan. 4.

Foster, Joseph C. (67), U. S. businessman; built up the Foster Grant Company of Leominster, Mass., from a small novelties manufacturer to a major producer of plastics, resins, and sunglasses: d. New York, N. Y., Nov. 10.

Fox, Sam (89), U. S. music publisher; pioneered in publishing music written for motion pictures; was musical producer of many scores for Fox Films and Movietone News: d. San Francisco, Calif., Nov. 31.

Friedman, Mordche (80), Austrian-born religious leader; was president of the Union of Hassidic Rabbis, and Hassidic leader of the Rizhiner dynasty: d. New York, N. Y., March 2.

Gallop, Sammy (55), U. S. lyricist; wrote the lyrics for many Broadway musicals, including *Star and Garter* (1942), and for such songs as *There Must be a Way* and *Autumn Serenade*: d. (suicide) Van Nuys, Calif., Feb. 24.

Garcia, Carlos P. (74), Philippine statesman: b. Talibon, Bohol province, Philippines, Nov. 4, 1896; d. Quezon City, Philippines, June 14, 1971. As president of the Philippines in 1957–61 he promoted industrial development and land reform and introduced the strongly nationalistic "Filipino First" policy. A lawyer and teacher, he served in the House of Representatives and as governor of Bohol before World War II and led guerrilla forces against the Japanese during the war. After the war he served in the Senate as minority floor leader. He was vice president in 1953–57, serving concurrently, in 1954–57, as minister of foreign affairs. In 1954 he presided over the Manila conference at which the Southeast Asia Treaty Organization was established. Shortly before his death he was elected president of the country's constitutional convention.

Gilbert, Billy (77), U. S. character actor; played in vaudeville, burlesque, and the legitimate theater; produced Broadway plays and wrote and directed movies; appeared in about 300 films, mostly comedies; was known for his funny sneeze: d. Hollywood, Calif., Sept. 23.

Gilden, Bert (56), U. S. author; with his wife, formed the writing team "K. B. Gilden," authors of the best-selling novel *Hurry Sundown* (1965): d. Bridgeport, Conn., April 4.

Gipson, Lawrence Henry (90), U. S. historian; was professor of history at Lehigh University (1924–54); won Pulitzer Prize in 1962 for *The Triumphant Empire*; his major work was the 15-volume *The British Empire Before the American Revolution* (1938–70): d. Bethlehem, Pa., Sept. 26.

Giron, César (38), Venezuelan matador; a full matador at 18, he starred in bullrings in Spain and Latin America for over 15 years: d. Maracay, Venezuela, Oct. 19.

Glatstein, Jacob (75), Polish-born U. S. Yiddish author; was a columnist for the *Day-Jewish Journal* and wrote novels, essays, and poems in Yiddish; his work has been widely translated and anthologized: d. New York, N. Y., Nov. 19.

Glueck, Nelson (70), U. S. rabbi, educator, and biblical archaeologist; in 1934 he identified the sites of King Solomon's mines; a leader in American Reform Judaism and president of Hebrew Union College–Jewish Institute of Religion (1947–71): d. Cincinnati, Ohio, Feb. 12.

Goddard, Lord (94), British judge; was lord chief justice from 1946 to 1958; he initiated changes that helped courts in coping with tremendous increases in numbers of cases, but opposed abolition of the death penalty: d. London, England, May 29.

Goetze, Albrecht (74), German-born U. S. Assyriologist; in 1948 he translated the Akkadian Eshnunna Code (early 18th century B. C.), one of the earliest known law systems; he taught Assyriology and Babylonian literature at Yale University (1934–65): d. Garmisch, West Germany, Aug. 15.

Goode, Jack (63), U. S. comedy actor, best known for his roles in musical comedies; made his Broadway debut in *Of Thee I Sing* (1933); played in *The Pajama Game* (1954) and *The Bells Are Ringing* (1956); he also made movies and appeared on television: d. Frenchtown, N. J., June 24.

Goodrich, Carter (73), U. S. educator; was professor of history and economics at the University of Pittsburgh (1963–71); served as chairman (1939–45) of the International Labor Organization: d. Mexico City, Mexico, April 7.

Goshal, Kumar (71), Indian-born U. S. journalist; lectured and wrote on Asian and African affairs; was foreign affairs editor of the *National Guardian* (1950–63); wrote *The People of India* (1944): d. South Norwalk, Conn., May 29.

Goslin, Leon Allen (Goose) (70), U. S. baseball player: b. Salem, N. J., Oct. 16, 1900; d. Bridgeton, N. J., May 15, 1971. Elected to baseball's Hall of Fame in 1968, he won the American League batting championship in 1928 with an average of .379, barely defeating Heinie Manush for the title. His lifetime batting average was .316. Between 1921 and 1938 he played left field with the Washington Senators, the St. Louis Browns, and the Detroit Tigers. In five World Series he had an average of .287 and hit seven home runs. He led the league in triples in 1923 and 1925, and batted in 129 runs in 1924, leading the league in that category. After leaving the major leagues in 1938 he became a manager in the minor leagues.

Gregory, Noble J. (74), U. S. political figure; was a congressman from Kentucky for 22 years (1936–58) and served on the House Ways and Means Committee for 15 years: d. Mayfield, Ky., Sept. 26.

Griemsmann, John W. E. (55), U. S. scientist; was a pioneer in microwave technology and a founder of the Microwave Research Institute at Polytechnic Institute of Brooklyn: d. New York, N. Y., Dec. 16.

Griswold, S. Smith (62), U. S. pioneer in fight against air pollution; fought for development of a less polluting auto engine; headed the Los Angeles County Air Pollution Control District: d. Bethesda, Md., April 20.

Gromaire, Marcel (78), French artist; his style, between expressionism and cubism, was perhaps best represented in his painting *La Guerre* (1925); also made engravings and designed tapestries: d. Paris, France, April 11.

Gross, Clara Regina (72), U. S. physician; a pioneer in aviation medicine, served since 1934 as a medical examiner for the Federal Aviation Administration: d. New York, N. Y., Dec. 6.

Guthrie, Sir (William) Tyrone (70), British theatrical director and producer: b. Tunbridge Wells, England, July 2, 1900; d. Newbliss, County Monaghan, Ireland, May 15, 1971. A great-grandson of the Irish actor Tyrone Power, he graduated from Oxford University in 1923 and became an actor with the Oxford Playhouse. Later he was director of the Scottish National Theatre and the Cambridge Festival Theatre, directed and wrote plays for the British Broadcasting Corporation, and staged Broadway productions. In 1933 he began to direct Shakespearean repertory for the Old Vic in London, which he headed for about 12 years. He was director of the Stratford (Ontario) Shakespeare festival in 1953–55, and in 1963 he founded the Tyrone Guthrie repertory theatre in Minneapolis. His published works include the play *Top of the Ladder* (1950) and the autobiography *A Life in the Theatre* (1960). He was knighted in 1961.

Haggerty, Cornelius J. (77), U. S. labor leader; was president of the Building and Construction Trades Department of the AFL–CIO (1960–71); helped increase job opportunities for blacks: d. Palm Springs, Calif., Oct. 10.

Hardin, Lil (68), U. S. jazz pianist; was the second wife (1924–38) of the late Louis Armstrong and helped him in his career: d. Chicago, Ill., Aug. 27.

Harlan, John Marshall (72), U. S. jurist: b. Chicago, Ill., May 20, 1899; d. Washington, D. C., Dec. 29. As the 89th justice of the U. S. Supreme Court (1955–71), he was noted for the conservative nature of his decisions. He often ruled in favor of private business in antitrust actions by the government. However, on several occasions he sided with civil libertarians, voting to proceed "with all deliberate speed" in carrying out previous school desegregation orders (1955) and supporting free counsel to indigent defendants charged with major crimes (1963). The grandson of a supreme court justice, he was educated at Princeton University and Balliol College, Oxford. Admitted to the New York bar in 1925, he soon became the protégé of Emory R. Buckner, a senior partner at the New York firm of Root, Clark, Buckner & Howland. He was appointed by President Eisenhower to the U. S. Court of Appeals for the Second Circuit in early 1954 and to the Supreme Court later that year. A "lawyer's judge" and a nonactivist, he was respected by his colleagues for the scholarly and literary style of his written opinions.

Harridge, Will (86), U. S. baseball executive: b. Chicago, Ill., Oct. 16, 1886; d. Evanston, Ill., April 9, 1971. One of organized baseball's most respected figures, he was president of the American League of Professional Baseball Clubs from 1931 to 1959. In 1911, while working as a railroad clerk, he was hired to serve as secretary to American League president Byron Bancroft Johnson. He remained in that post until 1927, when he became league secretary. His 27-year tenure as American League president was the longest in the league's history.

Hart, Teddy (74), U. S. actor; spent six years in vaudeville then acted in many Broadway plays, notably as Frankie in *Three Men on a Horse* (1937) and in the popular musicals *The Boys from Syracuse* (1938) and *One Touch of Venus* (1943); also made films: d. Los Angeles, Calif., Feb. 17.

Hart, Thomas C. (94), U. S. naval officer; served in the Navy from 1893 to 1945, and was commander in chief of the Asiatic Fleet at the time of Pearl Harbor (1941); was appointed Republican senator from Conn. (1945–46): d. Sharon, Conn., July 4.

Hawkes, Albert W. (92), U. S. political figure; was Republican senator from New Jersey (1943–49): d. Palm Desert, Calif., May 9.

Haynes, Henry (51), U. S. singer, guitarist, and comedian; was "Homer" of "Homer and Jethro," a country music and comedy team organized in 1936: d. Hammond, Ind., Aug. 7.

Hayton, Leonard G. (63), U. S. composer; was music director for Metro-Goldwyn-Mayer (1940–53), for his wife—the singer Lena Horne—and for 20th Century Film Corporation (1954–1971); he received Academy Awards for the scoring of *On the Town* (1949) and *Star* (1968): d. Palm Springs, Calif., April 24.

Hayward, Leland (68), U. S. theatrical producer and impresario: b. Nebraska City, Nebr., Sept. 13, 1902; d. Yorktown Heights, N. Y., March 18, 1971. A versatile, flamboyant entrepreneur, he produced or coproduced such Broadway hits as *A Bell for Adano*, *South Pacific*, *Mister Roberts*, *Gypsy*, and *The Sound of Music* and helped guide the careers of such bright lights of the entertainment world as James Stewart, Clark Gable, Judy Garland, and Katharine Hepburn. As a literary agent, he represented Ernest Hemingway and Edna Ferber. After studying briefly at Princeton University and working as a Hollywood press agent, he became a theatrical agent in 1926. He merged his operations with the Music Corporation of America in 1945 and was for a time one of its vice presidents. As an aviation entrepreneur he founded a flying school at Thunderbird Field, Arizona, that trained Army pilots during World War II, and he cofounded Southwest Airways in 1946. His most recent enterprise was the off-Broadway production *The Catonsville Nine* (1971), which he coproduced.

Heflin, Van (60), U. S. actor: b. Walters, Okla., Dec. 10, 1910; d. Hollywood, Calif., July 23, 1971. A versatile performer, he appeared in over 50 films. In 1942 he won an Academy Award as best supporting actor for his portrayal of an alcoholic newspaperman in *Johnny Eager*. A graduate of the University of Oklahoma, he attended Yale Drama School and worked as a seaman on cargo ships before beginning his acting career. On Broadway he appeared as the cynical reporter in *Philadelphia Story* (1939) and as a longshoreman in *A View From the*

Bridge (1955). Films in which he has appeared include *The Outcasts of Poker Flat, Saturday's Heroes, H. M. Pulham Esq., Tennessee Johnson, Green Dolphin Street, Possessed,* and *Shane.* His last screen appearance was in the role of a mad bomber in *Airport* (1970).

Heller, James G. (79), U. S. rabbi; a leader in Reform Judaism, the Zionist movement, and the United Jewish Appeal; wrote biography of Isaac M. Wise, founder of American Reform Judaism: d. Cincinnati, Ohio, Dec. 19.

Herbert, Sir Alan Patrick (81), English writer, humorist, and social reformer: b. London, England, Sept. 24, 1890; d. London, Nov. 11, 1971. A. P. Herbert was equally known as an author of humorous verse and essays in the magazine *Punch,* as a novelist and playwright, and as a crusader for conservation and the reform of outworn laws. Educated at Oxford, he began contributing to *Punch* in 1918 and joined the staff in 1924. A member of Parliament from 1935 to 1950, he was responsible in 1937 for the passage of the Matrimonial Causes Act, liberalizing Britain's divorce laws. He produced more than 60 books, including an autobiography, *APH: His Life and Times,* written at the age of 79.

Hickenlooper, Bourke B. (75), former U. S. senator from Iowa: b. Blocktón, Iowa, July 21, 1896: d. Shelter Island, New York, Sept. 4, 1971. A Republican, Senator Hickenlooper was a cosponsor of the Atomic Energy Act of 1954, under which private development of atomic energy resources for peaceful uses was launched. A graduate of Iowa State College, he entered the state legislature in 1934 and was elected governor of Iowa in 1942. He served in the U. S. Senate from 1945 to 1968. He became chairman of the Joint Congressional Committee on Atomic Energy in 1949. In 1962, he sponsored the Hickenlooper Amendment, which added to that year's foreign-aid bill the provision that aid be discontinued to any nation that seized the property of U. S. citizens without granting adequate compensation. Though his record was generally conservative, his support made possible the conclusion of a consular treaty with the USSR in 1967.

Hilliard, Bob (53), U. S. lyricist; wrote the lyrics for many well-known songs—including *Dear Hearts and Gentle People* and *Our Day Will Come*—and two Broadway musicals: d. Hollywood, Calif., Feb. 1.

Hitt, Parker (93), U. S. cryptologist; pioneered in modern code-breaking procedures and wrote the first textbook on the subject, *Manual for the Solution of Military Ciphers:* d. Front Royal, Va., Mar. 2.

Hodges, Russ (61), U. S. sportscaster; was regular announcer for the New York (later San Francisco) Giants baseball team (1948–70): d. San Francisco, Calif., April 19.

Hodgins, Eric (71), U. S. author; worked in advertising, then wrote light satirical novels, such as the popular *Mr. Blandings Builds His Dream House* (1946); also wrote *Episode* (1964), describing his struggle against the effects of a crippling stroke: d. New York, N. Y., Jan. 7.

Holland, Spessard L. (79), U. S. political figure; was governor of Florida (1941–45) and U. S. senator (1946–70); a Democrat, his politics were conservative: d. Bartow, Fla., Nov. 7.

Holman, Libby (65), U. S. torch singer of the 1920's and 1930's; was best known for her rendition of such songs as *Body and Soul,* and for the personal tragedies that plagued her life: d. Stamford, Conn., June 18.

Horsfall, Dr. Frank L., Jr. (64), U. S. virologist; was president and director of the Sloan-Kettering Institute for Cancer Research (1960–71); noted researcher into cancer-causing viruses and the role of heredity and cancer: d. New York, N. Y., Feb. 19.

Hoth, Hermann (85), German military officer; was a Nazi general and led unsuccessful army campaign in Russia (1941–43); convicted at Nuremberg in 1948; he was released in 1954: d. Goslar, West Germany, Jan. 25.

Hough, Lynn H. (93), U. S. Methodist clergyman, and a noted preacher and scholar in the field of Christian humanism; was dean of Drew Theological Seminary (1934–47): d. New York, N. Y., July 14.

Houssay, Bernardo Alberto (84), Argentinian physiologist; received the 1947 Nobel Prize in physiology or medicine (shared with Carl F. and Gerty T. Cori) for pointing out the role of the pituitary gland in carbohydrate metabolism: d. Buenos Aires, Argentina, Sept. 21.

Hughes, Charles F. ("Chuck") (28), U. S. football player; was a wide receiver (offensive end) for the Detroit Lions; collapsed during a game: d. Detroit, Mich., Oct. 24.

Jackson, Adm. R(ichard) **H**(arrison) (105), U. S. naval leader; commanded gunboats of the Yangtse River Patrol during the revolution in China (early 1900's); commanded all battleship divisions (1920's): d. San Diego, Calif., Oct. 2.

Jones, Robert Tyre, Jr. (69), U. S. golfer: b. Atlanta, Ga., March 17, 1902; d. Atlanta, Dec. 18, 1971. Often called the greatest golfer of the century, Bobby Jones capped a brief but brilliant career in 1930 when he captured golf's four major crowns, the U. S. and British amateur and open titles. The record had not been equaled at the time of his death. Mastering ill health and a violent temper while in his teens, Jones became one of the most precise drivers and putters in the game. A lawyer by profession, he competed only as an amateur, winning the U. S. open championship four times between 1923 and 1930, the U. S. amateur title five times, and the British open three times. After completing his "grand slam" in 1930, at the age of 28, he retired from competition.

Johnson, Alvin (Saunders) (96), U. S. educator and economist: b. Homer, Nebr., Dec. 18, 1874; d. Upper Nyack, N. Y., June 7, 1971. Honored as a "scholar, teacher, humanitarian, and citizen of the world," he cofounded the New School for Social Research in New York City in 1919, and was its president from 1928 to 1945. Its graduate faculty of political and social science, which he organized in 1933, served as a "university in exile" for refugee scholars from Nazi-occupied Europe. He studied at the University of Nebraska, served in the Spanish-American War, and obtained his Ph. D. from Columbia University in 1902. He taught at Columbia, Yale, Stanford, and Cornell universities and served in 1917–23 as an editor of the *New Republic.* He wrote nearly 1,000 articles on economics, education, and other topics. His autobiography, *Pioneer's Progress,* was published in 1960.

Kchessinska, Mathilde (99), Russian dancer; the first Russian ballerina to become known throughout Europe, was noted for spectacular technique; became prima ballerina assoluta in Russian Imperial Ballet of St. Petersburg (1895): d. Paris, France, Dec. 7.

Kelly, Harry F. (75), U. S. public official; served as Republican governor of Michigan (1943–47), and as a member of the Michigan supreme court (1953–70): d. West Palm Beach, Fla., Feb. 8.

Kelly, Mervin J. (77), U. S. physicist and executive; was president of the Bell Laboratories (1951–59) and won numerous awards for his work on both communications devices and military research and development: d. Port Saint Lucie, Fla., March 18.

Kemper, John M. (59), U. S. educator; as headmaster of Phillips Academy (Andover) for 23 years, directed the private school through its greatest period of growth: d. Andover, Mass., Dec. 4.

Kent, Rockwell (88), U. S. artist: b. Tarrytown Heights, N. Y., June 21, 1882; d. Plattsburgh, N. Y., March 13, 1971. A nonconformist in his life-style and political views, he was noted for his romantic-realist oil paintings, watercolors, drawings, lithographs, and woodcuts, many of them depicting stark and rugged natural landscapes. After studying at the Columbia School of Architecture he worked several years as an architect. Later, as an artist, his love of adventure took him to Maine, Newfoundland, Alaska, Greenland, and Tierra del Fuego. His works include murals for public buildings as well as illustrations for books. Active in leftist causes since the late 1920's, he frequently clashed with congressional investigators, including Sen. Joseph R. McCarthy. In 1960 he donated a number of his paintings and drawings to the Soviet Union, which awarded him the Lenin Prize in 1967. His work is represented in the Metropolitan Museum of Art, the Corcoran Gallery in Washington, and the Pushkin Museum in Moscow. Among his books is the autobiography, *It's Me O Lord* (1955).

*Khrushchev, Nikita (78), former Soviet premier: d. Moscow, USSR, Sept. 11.

King, Dennis (73), British-born U. S. actor, best known for his portrayal of François Villon in *The Vagabond King* both on stage (1925) and in the film (1930); he costarred with most of the leading actresses of his day, and played both romantic roles and in the classics; his last appearance was in John Osborne's *A Patriot for Me* (1969): d. New York, N. Y., May 21.

Knox, E. V. (89), British humorist; was editor of *Punch* (1932–49) and credited with modernizing the magazine; wrote under pen name "Evoe": d. London, England, Jan. 2.

Koch, Adrienne (58), U. S. historian; she held professorships in philosophy, history and economics at several universities; her books include *The Philosophy of Thomas Jefferson* (1943) and *Jefferson and Madison: The Great Collaboration* (1950): d. New York, N. Y., Aug. 28.

Konenkov, Sergei Timofeyevich (97), Soviet sculptor; worked in a monumental style, using exaggerated forms; lived and worked in the United States from 1924 to 1945; executed portraits of prominent figures, including

Robert (Bobby) Jones, Jr.

Allan Nevins

Pushkin, Tolstoy, Dostoyevsky, and Oliver Wendell Holmes: d. Moscow, USSR, Oct. 9.

Krenkel, Ernest T. (68), Soviet polar explorer; a pioneer in Soviet exploration of the Arctic, was radio operator for mission that spent nine months in 1937–38 on first ice floe manned for scientific research: d. Moscow, USSR, Dec. 8.

Lacassagne, Antoine (87), French physician; noted for his pioneering study of radiation as a cancer-creating agent and as a means of fighting cancer: d. Paris, France, Dec. 15.

Lander, Harald (66), Danish choreographer and ballet master; joined the Royal Danish Ballet as a dancer in 1923; as its ballet master (1932–51) he led the company to international fame; was ballet master of the Paris Opera (1952–71); he choreographed many ballets, notably the widely performed *Études:* d. Copenhagen, Denmark, Sept. 14.

Lawless, Theodore K. (78), U. S. dermatologist; he won the 1954 Spingarn Medal of the National Association for the Advancement of Colored People for "distinguished merit and achievement among American Negroes"; he organized the medical laboratories and taught at Northwestern Medical School (1924–1941); he pioneered in the use of radium as a treatment for cancer; he also served on Cook County (Ill.) Prison Welfare Commission, the Chicago Board of Health, and the advisory board of the Chicago Civil Liberties Committee: d. Chicago, Ill., May 1.

Lee, Manfred B. (66), U. S. author; along with his cousin Frederic Dannay, created the "Ellery Queen" mystery series, which start with *The Roman Hat Mystery* (1929), and went on to include 33 novels, numerous short-story anthologies, and an Ellery Queen magazine: d. Waterbury, Conn., April 3.

Lemass, Sean (71), Irish political figure; was prime minister of the Irish Republic (1959–66); a freedom fighter in the Easter Rising of 1916; he served in successive de Valera cabinets until assuming the prime ministry: d. Dublin, Ireland, May 11.

Lennart, Isobel (55), U. S. writer; was award-winning author of motion picture screenplays, including *Anchors Aweigh* and *Funny Girl:* d. Hemet, Calif., Jan. 25.

Leopold, Nathan F. (66), one of the defendants in the Leopold and Loeb murder case of 1924: b. Chicago, Ill., 1905; d. San Juan, Puerto Rico, Aug. 29, 1971. With his friend Richard Loeb, Leopold, a wealthy and highly intelligent 19-year-old graduate of the University of Chicago, kidnapped and murdered 14-year-old Bobby Franks in an attempt to commit a perfect crime. Quickly apprehended, the two were represented by Clarence Darrow at a five-week court hearing in Chicago in the summer of 1924, during which the "Great Defender" broke precedent by citing psychiatric testimony short of a claim of insanity to save them from death sentences. Condemned to life imprisonment, Loeb died in jail in 1936. Leopold was paroled in 1958 and spent the last 13 years of his life in Puerto Rico as an assistant in a medical mission and a mathematics teacher.

Levin, Rabbi Yehuda Leib (76), Soviet religious leader; was chief rabbi of Moscow's Central Synagogue; opposed militant U. S. Zionist groups in their demonstrations against Soviet anti-Semitism, insisting that Soviet Jews have all their rights: d. Moscow, USSR, Nov. 17.

Lewis, Joe E. (69), U. S. nightclub comedian; started in burlesque and vaudeville; his low-comedy material and delivery were based on his personal experiences with drink, gambling, and cronies: d. New York, N. Y., June 4.

Lewis, Ted (80), U. S. entertainer; was a jazz clarinetist,

bandleader, and song and dance man; his trademark was a cane and top hat and the motto "Is everybody happy?"; he popularized *Me and My Shadow, On the Sunny Side of the Street,* and many other songs: d. New York, N. Y., Aug. 25.

Lindbeck, John M. H. (55), U. S. historian; directed the East Asian Institute at Columbia University (1967–71) and was considered the foremost contributor to Chinese studies in the U. S.: d. Danbury, Conn., Jan. 9.

List, Siegmund Wilhelm (91), German field marshal; an expert on the Blitzkrieg; led forces that cracked the French Maginot Line in May 1940; sentenced to life imprisonment in 1948, but released on a medical parole in 1952: d. Garmisch-Partenkirchen, West Germany, Aug. 17.

Lloyd, Harold (Clayton) (77), U. S. motion-picture comedian: d. Burchard, Nebr., April 20, 1893; d. Hollywood, Calif., March 8, 1971. Known to millions of fans during Hollywood's golden age of comedy as a fumbling, bewildered, bespectacled young man, who often found himself in impossible situations, he appeared in some 500 films and became the industry's highest-paid performer during the 1920's. He began his career as a movie extra and was hired by Hal Roach in 1914 to appear in one-reel slapstick comedies, portraying characters called "Willie Work" and "Lonesome Luke." Never without his trademark, a pair of dime-store horn-rimmed spectacle frames, he was seen during the 1920's in such five-reel silent comedies as *Grandma's Boy, Why Worry, Girl Shy, The Freshman,* and *The Kid Brother.* One of his most memorable scenes, in *Safety Last* (1923), found him dangling from the hands of a clock atop a 14-story building. His talking films, between 1929 and 1945, included *Movie Crazy, The Milky Way, Professor Beware,* and *Mad Wednesday.* Excerpts from his films were compiled in *Harold Lloyd's World of Comedy,* released in 1962.

Lowe, Edmund (79), U. S. film actor; in *What Price Glory* (1926) he created the tough, fearless hero who was to become a movie stereotype; the last of his many films was *Heller in Pink Tights* (1960): d. Hollywood, Calif., April 21.

Lowery, Robert (57), U. S. screen actor; appeared in many films in the 1930's and 1940's, including *The Mark of Zorro, Drums Along the Mohawk,* and *The Rise and Fall of Legs Diamond:* d. Hollywood, Calif., Dec. 26.

Luboshutz, Pierre (76), Russian-born pianist; with his wife, Genia Nemenoff, formed a successful duo-piano team (1937–68); both later headed the piano department at Michigan State University (1962–68): d. Rockport, Me., April 17.

Lucas, Dione (62), English culinary authority and restauranteur: b. Venice, Italy, Oct. 10, 1909; d. London, England, Dec. 18, 1971. A specialist in French haute cuisine, she taught the virtues of taking great pains and ample time while preparing gourmet dishes. In the early 1930's, after studying at the École du Cordon Bleu in Paris, she opened the Petit Cordon Bleu Restaurant in London. In 1942 she founded the Cordon Bleu restaurant and school in New York. She later opened several more restaurants and cooking schools in the United States, became one of the first to demonstrate cooking on television, and published several cook books, including the *Cordon Bleu Cook Book* (1947), a perennial best seller.

Luce, Claire McGill (47), U. S. publishing executive; wife of *Time* magazine publisher Henry Luce III, she was investment analyst for Time, Inc.; was a director of the China Institute in America (1964–71): d. Fishers Island, N. Y., June 22.

Lukács, György (86), Hungarian Marxist philosopher: b. Budapest, Hungary, April 13, 1885; d. Budapest, June 4, 1971. One of Europe's leading Marxist theorists, he had a major influence on Communist thought in Europe during the first four decades of the 20th century. Combining Marxism with liberal humanism, he elaborated on Marx's early theory of alienation of man by modern industrial society and formulated a Marxist system of aesthetics that rejected political control of artists in socialist society. He studied at Heidelberg and Berlin. In 1918 he joined the Communist party, and in 1919 he was minister of education in Bela Kun's short-lived Hungarian Communist regime. During the Nazi period and World War II he lived in the USSR. An anti-Stalinist, he took part in the abortive Hungarian revolt of 1956. He wrote more than 30 books, including *History and Class Consciousness* (1923), *The Attack on Reason* (1945), *Goethe and His Time* (1947), *The Historical Novel* (1955), *Realism in Our Time* (1956), and *Aesthetics* (1963).

Lukas, Paul (76), Hungarian-born U. S. actor; played many roles on stage, in films, and on radio and television; won the Academy Award for the best actor of 1943 in *Watch on the Rhine:* d. Tangiers, Morocco, Aug. 15,

Lynn, Diana (45), U. S. actress; played in many light stage and screen comedies in 1940's, including *Our Hearts Were Young and Gay* and *Meet Me at the Fair:* d. Los Angeles, Calif., Dec. 18.

McCann, William Sharp (81), U. S. physician and educator; was first chairman of the department of medicine at the University of Rochester Medical School, where he taught from 1924 to 1957: d. Rochester, N. Y., June 10.

McDonald, James E. (51), U. S. physicist; specialized in cloud studies at University of Arizona's Institute of Atmospheric Physics (1954–71); outspoken proponent of the existence of UFO (unidentified flying objects): d. Tucson, Ariz., June 13.

McDonald, Maurice J. (68), U. S. businessman; cofounded (1948) McDonald's Hamburgers, a giant chain of roadside restaurants featuring low-cost hamburgers: d. Palm Springs, Calif., Dec. 11.

McFarland, Gary (38), U. S. jazz composer and vibraharpist; appeared with many noted jazz musicians; composed the jazz ballet *Reflections in the Park* (1964): d. New York, N. Y., Nov. 2.

McGregor, Gordon Roy (69), Canadian aviator; was head of Air Canada (formerly Trans-Canada Air Lines) and built it into a model airline: d. Montreal, Quebec, March 8.

McMahon, Horace (64), U. S. character actor; he portrayed many gangsters and policemen in films and plays; played the gravel-voiced detective, Lt. Mike Parker, on the television series *Naked City:* d. Norwalk, Conn., Aug. 17.

McNamara, Reggie ("Iron Man") (83), Australian-born U. S. bicycle racer; competed in many six-day bicycle races and broke several world records: d. Belleville, N. Y., Oct. 9.

Maier, Reinhold (81), West German liberal political figure; in 1945 he became prime minister of the newly formed state which, in 1951, became Baden-Württemberg; retired in 1953: d. Stuttgart, West Germany, Aug. 18.

Malone, Kemp (82), U. S. linguist and philologist; taught English literature at Johns Hopkins (1924–56); edited Old English works and wrote many books, principally on medieval literature: d. Eastport, Me., Oct. 13.

Malvern, Lord (Godfrey Martin Huggins) (87), Rhodesian government official; was prime minister of Rhodesia (1933–53) and first prime minister of the Central African Federation (1953–56): d. Salisbury, Rhodesia, May 8.

Manna, Charlie (51), U. S. comedian; was best known for his comedy routine about an astronaut who can do nothing without his crayons: d. New York, N. Y., Nov. 9.

Manush, Heinie (69), U. S. baseball player: b. Tuscumbia, Ala., July 20, 1901; d. Sarasota, Fla., May 12, 1971. One of major league baseball's leading hitters, he had a lifetime batting average of .330 and a career total of 2,524 hits. He was elected to baseball's Hall of Fame in 1964. Manush, an outfielder, began his 17-year major league career with the Detroit Tigers in 1923 and later played with the Washington Senators, the St. Louis Browns, the Boston Red Sox, the Brooklyn Dodgers, and the Pittsburgh Pirates. In 1926, while with the Tigers, he led both leagues in hitting when he batted .378. His batting average exceeded .300 during 11 seasons.

Martin, Thomas E. (78), U. S. legislator; was Republican congressman (1939–54) and senator (1954–61) from Iowa: d. Seattle, Wash., June 27.

Mays, David J. (74), U. S. lawyer and historian; won the Pulitzer Prize (1953) for biography *Edward Pendleton 1721–1803;* was former president of the Richmond and Virginia bar associations: d. Richmond, Va., Feb. 17.

Melo, Francisco de Assis (67), Brazilian military officer; was a leader in 1964 Brazilian revolution; served as chief justice of the Supreme Military Court: d. Rio de Janeiro, Brazil, Jan. 21.

Mikkelsen, Ejnar (90), Danish explorer; he led the 1906–08 Anglo-American polar expedition and a 1909–12 expedition to Greenland; wrote many books on his adventures: d. Copenhagen, Denmark, May 3.

Miller, Dr. Benjamin F. (63), U. S. physician, known for his medical books for the layman—including *Complete Medical Guide;* was editor in chief of *The Modern Medical Encyclopedia:* d. Philadelphia, Pa., June 28.

Mindlin, Henrique (60), Brazilian architect; president of the Brazilian Institute of Architects; he designed many of Brazil's prominent buildings, including the Jornal do Brazil Building: d. Rio de Janeiro, Brazil, July 6.

Moholy-Nagy, Sibyl (67), German-born architectural writer; the widow of painter Laszlo Moholy-Nagy, she was a noted critic and teacher; named "critic of the year" in 1970 by the American Institute of Architects: d. New York, N. Y., Jan. 8.

Mondadori, Arnoldo (81), Italian publisher; founded Arnoldo Mondadori Editore—which published Italy's leading magazines and popular books; as well as the first Italian translations of such writers as Thomas Mann and John Steinbeck: d. Milan, Italy, June 9.

Mowrer, Paul Scott (84), U. S. journalist, author, and poet; was chief foreign correspondent (1920's–30's) and editor (1935–44) of *The Chicago Daily News;* awarded Pulitzer Prize for foreign correspondence (1928): d. Beaufort, N. C., April 4.

Mulzac, Hugh N. (84), U. S. mariner; in 1942 he became captain of the Liberty ship *Booker T. Washington,* making him the first Negro to command a U. S. merchant ship: d. East Meadow, N. Y., Jan. 31.

Murphy, Audie (46), U. S. war hero and actor: b. near Kingston, Texas, June 20, 1924; d. (air crash) near Roanoke, Va., May 28, 1971. The most decorated U. S. soldier of World War II, he was awarded the Congressional Medal of Honor for killing 240 Germans singlehandedly in January 1945. After the war he embarked on a moderately successful career as an actor, appearing in some 40 motion pictures. A sharecropper's son, he joined the Army in 1942, served in Europe and North Africa, and earned a battlefield commission as a first lieutenant. He suffered three serious wounds and received 28 U. S. and foreign decorations, including the French Croix de Guerre. After making his motion-picture debut in a small role in *Beyond Glory* (1948), he played in such films as *The Kid From Texas* (1950), *The Red Badge of Courage* (1951), *Destry* (1955), *Night Passage* (1957), *The Quiet American* (1958), and the screen version of his autobiography, *To Hell and Back* (1955). He also appeared in the television series *Whispering Smith.*

Myers, Debs (59), U. S. political press aid; was a newspaperman and was managing editor of *Newsweek;* he was adviser to many prominent U. S. political figures, including Robert F. Kennedy and Adlai E. Stevenson: d. New Haven, Conn., Feb. 2.

Nash, (Frederick) **Ogden** (68), U. S. poet: b. Rye, N. Y., Aug. 19, 1902; d. Baltimore, Md., May 19, 1971. With his good-natured, witty, often outrageous verse, pinpointing the foibles and absurdities of the modern age, he sought to liberate poetry from the conventions of grammar, prosody, and spelling. He studied briefly at Harvard and worked as a bond salesman, teacher, and writer of advertising copy before turning to the writing of humorous verse in 1930. His rhymes appeared regularly in the *New Yorker* and in other magazines, and he published some 20 books of verse, including *Hard Lines* (1931), *Happy Days* (1933), *I'm a Stranger Here Myself* (1938), *Many Long Years Ago* (1945), *Parents Keep Out* (1951), *You Can't Get There From Here* (1957), *Everyone But Thee and Me* (1962), and *Bedriddance* (1970). He collaborated with Kurt Weil and S. J. Perelman on the 1943 Broadway musical hit *One Touch of Venus,* for which he wrote the lyrics.

Nevins, Allan (80), U. S. historian: b. Camp Point, Ill., May 20, 1890; d. Menlo Park, Calif., March 5, 1971. A leading authority on U. S. history, he was the author of over 50 books and hundreds of articles and reviews. His work was distinguished by its profound humanism and meticulous research. He won Pulitzer prizes, for a biography of Grover Cleveland, in 1933, and a study of Hamilton Fish, in 1937. Nevins was DeWitt Clinton professor of history at Columbia University from 1931 to 1958. A graduate of the University of Illinois, he began his career as a journalist in New York in 1913 and joined the Columbia faculty in 1928. His works include *The Emergence of Modern America* (1927), *Frémont: Pathmarker of the West* (1939), and the eight-volume *Ordeal of the Union* (1947–71). In his studies of such industrial giants as John D. Rockefeller and Henry Ford he challenged James A. Beard's thesis that American thought was determined by economic self-interest. After retirement from Columbia he was senior research associate of the Huntington Library in California (1958–69), professor at Oxford University (1964), chairman of the Civil War Centennial Commission (1961–66), and president of the American Academy of Arts and Letters (1966–68).

*Niebuhr, Reinhold (79), U. S. Protestant leader: d. Stockbridge, Mass., June 1.

Niehans, Paul (89), Swiss surgeon; developed a treatment (injections from fetus of unborn animals) to arrest the aging process; was physician of Pope Pius XII; in later years, he did cancer research: d. Montreux, Switzerland, Sept. 1.

Noshimura, Ejichi (67), Japanese political figure; helped found (1959) and was chairman of (1967–71) the antiCommunist Democratic Socialist party: d. Tokyo, Japan, April 27.

Nye, Gerald P. (78), U. S. legislator; was Republican senator from North Dakota (1925–44) and leading isolationist before World War II; he helped expose the Teapot Dome oil lease scandal, and was one of the drafters of the 1936 Neutrality Act: d. Washington, D. C., July 17.

O'Donnell, Emmett (Rosy) (65), U. S. general: b. Brooklyn, N. Y., Sept. 15, 1906; d. McLean, Va., Dec. 26. In 1941, as a major in the Army Air Corps, he commanded a squadron of B-17's in a successful attack on Japanese naval vessels in the Philippines. Promoted to brigadier general in 1944, he led the first major raid of Superfortresses against Tokyo. During the Korean War he was assigned to Japan to lead the Far East Bomber Command. From 1959 until his retirement in 1964 he was commander of the Pacific Air Forces.

Padilla, Ezequiel (80), Mexican public official; was foreign minister of Mexico during World War II and signed the UN charter in 1945; was credited with keeping Mexico out of the war; served as senator (1934-40 and 1964-71): d. Mexico City, Sept. 6.

Palmer, Dewey H. (72), U. S. medical engineer; founded the Consumers Union, publishers of *Consumer Reports* (1936): d. Oradell, N. J., May 14.

Parker, Cecil (73), British actor; appeared as the "typical British gentleman" in many stage and screen productions, including the play *Blithe Spirit* (1941) and the film *The Court Jester* (1956): d. Brighton, England, April 20.

Parry, Adam M. (43) and **Anne** (39), professors of the classics; Adam Parry, a specialist on Thucydides, was chairman of the classics department at Yale University; Mrs. Parry (the former Anne Reinberg), a Latinist, was a lecturer in the classics at Yale and associate professor at the University of Massachusetts: d. (traffic accident) near Colmar, France, June 11.

Patsayev, Viktor Ivanovich (38), Soviet cosmonaut; worked as design engineer in the field of precision instruments; became a cosmonaut in 1968, and was the test engineer aboard the space vehicle *Soyuz 11*: d. reentering earth's atmosphere, June 30.

Penney, J(ames) **C**(ash) (95), U. S. business executive: b. Hamilton, Mo., Sept. 16, 1875; d. New York, N. Y., Feb. 12, 1971. Combining the precepts of the Golden Rule with pragmatism, he built the J. C. Penney Co., which he had founded, into the fifth-largest U. S. retail merchandising chain, with 1,660 department stores and sales totaling $4.1 billion. Starting with a one-third interest in a dry-goods store in Wyoming in 1902, he acquired additional stores. By 1913, when the J. C. Penney Co. was incorporated, it comprised 48 stores, with headquarters in New York. In 1907, Penney introduced a profit-sharing plan for employees as an incentive measure. He served as president of the company in 1913-17 and as honorary chairman and chairman of the board from 1917 to 1958. He also engaged in banking and farming and was noted for his philanthropic and religious activities. His writings include the autobiographical *Fifty Years With the Golden Rule* and *View From the Ninth Decade*.

Pennington, Anne (76), U. S. dancing star of the 1920's; popularized *The Black Bottom*, a lively song and dance, in George White's *Scandals of 1926*: d. New York, N. Y., Nov. 4.

Perl, Arnold (58), U. S. writer and producer; wrote Broadway play *The World of Sholom Aleichem* (1957); was executive producer and writer of TV series *East Side, West Side* (1960's): d. New York, N. Y., Dec. 11.

Petersham, Maud (82), U. S. author; with her husband, Miska Petersham, she wrote many children's books, notably *A Rooster Crows*, which won the 1946 Caldecott Award, and the series *This Is America*: d. Ravenna, Ohio, Nov. 29.

Pillsbury, Eleanor Bellows (58), U. S. leader in national health activities and wife of Philip W. Pillsbury, former head of the Pillsbury Co.; worked with Red Cross and various health organizations; was president of the Planned Parenthood Federation of America: d. Wayzata, Minn., Aug. 27.

Pollack, Ben (65), U. S. bandleader and drummer, known as the "father of swing"; organized many bands (1930's-40's) and helped start careers of such musicians as Glenn Miller and Harry James: d. Palm Springs, Calif., June 7.

Popović, Milentije (57), Yugoslavian Communist official; was president of the Yugoslav Parliament (1967-71) after serving as minister of finance and in various other posts: d. Belgrade, Yugoslavia, May 8.

Porterfield, Robert H. (66), U. S. actor; during the Depression he founded and directed the Barter Theater, which accepted food or other goods in place of cash for admission; he also acted on Broadway and in the films *Sergeant York* (1941) and *The Yearling* (1946): d. Abingdon, Va., Oct. 28.

Potter, David (60), U. S. historian; he was professor at Stanford University (1961-71) and president of the American Historical Association (1970-71); wrote on Civil War history, including *The South and the Sectional Conflict* (1968): d. Stanford, Conn., Feb. 18.

Prochazka, Jan (42), Czechoslovak film writer; served as vice president of the Czechoslovak Union of Writers; his advocacy of the liberal reforms of 1968 led to his expulsion from the Communist party: d. Prague, Czechoslovakia, Feb. 20.

Prokovief, Aleksandr Andreyevich (70), Soviet poet; often wrote on patriotic themes; his 1961 collection *Invitation to a Journey* won a Lenin Prize: d. Leningrad, USSR, Sept. 18.

Proskauer, Joseph M. (94), U. S. judge; was political adviser to presidential candidate Alfred E. Smith in the 1920's, served on the New York state supreme court (1923-30), and worked to get a declaration of human rights into UN charter in 1945: d. New York, N. Y., Sept. 10.

Prouty, Winston L. (65), U. S. politician; served in U. S. House of Representatives (1951-58) and was junior senator from Vermont (1959-71); urged a cease-fire in Vietnam under international supervision; advocated a guaranteed annual income: d. Boston, Sept. 10.

Puller, Lt. Gen. Lewis B. (73), U. S. Marine; enlisted as a private at the outbreak of World War I; was the most decorated Marine: d. Hampton, Va., Oct. 11.

Rafferty, Chips (62), Australian film star; created the character of the lanky, drawling Dinkum; his films included *Massacre Hill* (1950); he also appeared in Australian and U. S. television series: d. Sydney, Australia, May 27.

Rákosi, Mátyás (78), Hungarian-born Communist leader; while living in the USSR, he accompanied the Soviet Army to Hungary (1944) and later served as deputy premier until his exile to USSR (1956): d. Gorky, USSR, Feb. 5.

Reading, Marchioness (Stella Charnaud Isaacs) (77), British social worker; when her husband, the first Marquess of Reading, died in 1935, she traveled incognito across the U. S. in order to get to know the American people; she organized the Women's Voluntary Service for Civil Defense; in 1958 she was created a life peeress and became the first woman to take a seat in the House of Lords: d. London, England, May 22.

Reams, Frazier (74), U. S. political figure; was the only Independent in the U. S. House of Representatives, when he served as congressman from Ohio (1951-54): d. Oakland, Calif., Sept. 15.

Reeves, Alec (69), British electronics scientist and inventor; is credited with the development in 1938 of pulse-code modulation, a method of sending many telephone conversations over one wire: d. London, England, Oct. 13.

Reinhardt, G. Frederick (59), U. S. diplomat; served in various diplomatic posts (1937-68), including those of ambassador to Vietnam (1955-57) and to Italy (1961-68): d. Geneva, Switzerland, Feb. 22.

Reith, Lord (John Charles Walsham Reith) (81), British business executive, called the "father of the BBC"; he joined the British Broadcasting Company in 1922 and guided its rise to a national institution: d. Edinburgh, Scotland, June 16.

Rennie, Michael (62), British-born U. S. actor; portrayed a wide variety of characters, but usually appeared suave and polished; was in plays in London and New York, notably in *Mary, Mary* (1961) on Broadway; made British films and more than four dozen U. S. movies; played Harry Lime in the U. S. television series *The Third Man*: d. London, England, June 10.

Robertson, A. Willis (84), U. S. legislator; a Democrat from Virginia, he served in the U. S. House of Representatives (1933-46) and the U. S. Senate (1946-66); was an expert in foreign trade, banking, currency, and taxation: d. Lexington, Va., Nov. 1.

Rodale, J. I. (72), U. S. nutritionist and publisher; was concerned with the chemicals and additives used in food production; he founded the magazine *Organic Farming and Gardening* (1942); popularized the organic food movement: d. New York, N. Y., June 7.

Rogers, James G. (88), U. S. lawyer and public official; was assistant secretary of state under Herbert Hoover (1931-33), and handled negotiations with Canada for the St. Lawrence Seaway; wrote books of verse and songs, including *Dolores*: d. Denver, Colo., April 23.

Rogoff, Harry (88), U. S. editor; was editor in chief (1951-64) of the *Jewish Daily Forward*, the leading U. S. Yiddish-language newspaper; an active columnist with the paper until his death: d. New York, N. Y., Nov. 30.

Roper, Elmo (Burns, Jr.) (70), U. S. public opinion analyst: b. Hebron, Nebr., July 31, 1900; d. Norwalk, Conn., April 30, 1971. A pioneer in the development of political polls, he was among the first to predict election results with considerable accuracy by using scientific sampling techniques. Educated at the universities of Minnesota and Edinburgh, he came to New York in 1933 and became a partner in a market research firm that was later known as Roper Research Associates, Inc. Applying market research techniques, he used small, representative cross sections of the public to predict the presidential votes of 1936, 1940, and 1944 within a 1% margin of accuracy but erred in his predictions of the 1948 and 1960 contests. From 1935 to 1950 he conducted public opinion surveys for *Fortune* magazine. He also served as an editor at large of *Saturday Review* and wrote a syndicated column. During World War II he was a deputy director of the Office of Strategic Services. He retired from his firm in 1966, retaining the title of senior consultant.

Rose, Carl (68), U. S. cartoonist; his illustrations, blending genial satire and detailed craftsmanship, appeared in numerous magazines and books (1928–71) including *The New Yorker* and *The Atlantic Monthly* magazines: d. Rowayton, Conn., June 21.

Ruggles, Carl (95), U. S. composer; his music was praised by musicians but was unpopular in concert halls because of its uncompromising dissonance; the best known of his few compositions is *Sun-Treader*: d. Bennington, Vt., Oct. 24.

Russell, Richard B(revard, Jr.) (73), U. S. senator: b. Winder, Ga., Nov. 2, 1897; d. Washington, D. C., Jan. 21, 1971. One of the most influential men in the U. S. Senate, he represented the patrician paternalism of the Old South. A Democrat from Georgia, he served in the Senate from 1933 until his death and was its senior member and leader of its Southern bloc. The son of a chief justice of the Georgia supreme court, he graduated from the University of Georgia law school in 1918 and was elected to the Georgia House of Representatives in 1921. He served as governor of Georgia in 1931–33. As a senator, he supported much of President Franklin D. Roosevelt's early New Deal legislation but grew increasingly conservative in his later years. He was chairman of the Senate Armed Services Committee from 1951 to 1969 and president pro tempore of the Senate in 1969–71. In 1952 he made an unsuccessful bid for the Democratic presidential nomination.

Ryba, Dominic ("Mike") (68), U. S. baseball player; was pitcher for the St. Louis Cardinals (1935–38) and the Boston Red Sox (1941–46): d. Springfield, Mo., Dec. 13.

Sadiq, Ghulam Mohammed (59), Indian statesman; associated with Prime Minister Indira Gandhi's New Congress party; was chief minister of Indian part of Kashmir since 1964: d. Chandigarh, India, Dec. 12.

Saerchinger, César (86), French-born U. S. broadcasting executive and musicologist; as European director of the Columbia Broadcasting System (1930–37) he systematized transatlantic radio broadcasting; he also wrote many books and articles on music: d. Washington, D. C., Oct. 10.

Saint-Denis, Michel (73), French-born British actor, director, playwright, and theater consultant; headed two acting schools in London; was artistic adviser to the Comédie Française and consultant director of the drama division of New York City's Juilliard School of Music; was co-director (1961–66) and consulting director (1966–71) of England's Royal Shakespeare Company: d. London, England, July 31.

Sánchez Cantón, Francisco Javier (80), Spanish art expert; director of Madrid's Prado Museum (retired 1968) and dean of the faculty of philosophy and letters at the University of Madrid for 20 years: d. Pontevedra, Spain, Nov. 23.

Sarabhai, Vikram A. (52), Indian atomic scientist; did important work in cosmic ray and space research; chairman of India's Atomic Energy Commission since 1966: d. Kerala state, India, Dec. 30.

Sarnoff, David (80), U. S. broadcasting pioneer and chairman of the RCA Corporation: b. Uzlian, Minsk province, Russia, Feb. 27, 1891; d. New York, N. Y., Dec. 12, 1971. A giant of the electronics communications industry for over 50 years, he introduced both radio and television to mass audiences in the United States. Brought to America at the age of 10, he started his career as a $5.50-a-week office boy at the Commercial Cable Company in New York. While manning an experimental rooftop wireless station on April 14, 1912, he was the first on the U. S. mainland to receive signals from the sinking *S. S. Titanic*. After World War I, he persuaded his superiors in the newly created Radio Corporation of America to produce inexpensive radio receivers for home use. In 1926 he presided over the establishment of the National Broadcasting Company, an RCA subsidiary which became the first radio broadcasting network. Sarnoff became president of RCA in 1930 and board chairman in 1947. Having forecast the future growth of a television industry as early as 1923, he supervised much of the necessary research in the 1930's. Later, his RCA engineers produced the color television system adopted for general use in the United States in 1953.

Sato, Naotake (89), Japanese statesman; a career diplomat, was considered Japan's greatest conference expert; served as Japanese representative to the USSR (1942–45): d. Tokyo, Japan, Dec. 18.

Schine, J. Myer (78), U. S. businessman; a real estate and hotel man, his move in 1965 to sell his holdings—valued at more than $150 million—set off a 3-year legal conflict: d. New York, N. Y., May 8.

Schlanger, Ben (66), U. S. architect; in the 1960's he introduced the idea of small movie houses; he designed New York City's Cinema I and Cinema II—two small theaters in a single building: d. New York, N. Y., May 3.

Schlossberg, Joseph (95), Russian-born U. S. labor leader; was a founder (1914) and secretary-treasurer of the Amalgamated Clothing Workers of America; was an activist in American-Jewish affairs: d. New York, N. Y., Jan. 15.

Seferis, George (pen name of *Georgios Seferiades*) (71), Greek diplomat and poet, who won the Nobel Prize for literature in 1963: b. Smyrna (now Izmir), Turkey, Feb. 29, 1900; d. Athens, Greece, Sept. 20, 1971. He was educated in Athens, Paris, and London, and from 1925 to 1962 served in the Greek foreign service, notably as ambassador to the United Nations (1956–57) and ambassador to Britain (1957–62). His verse captures the classical character of modern Greece and the tragic experience of its people in the 20th century. Seferis was also a distinguished critic and translator, and helped introduce American poetry to Greece.

Serlin, Oscar (70), Polish-born U. S. producer; produced such stage hits as *Life With Father* (1939), and *The Moon Is Down* (1942): d. New York, N. Y., Feb. 27.

Siroky, Viliam (69), Czechoslovak premier (1953–63); adhered strictly to policies of USSR: d. Prague, Czechoslovakia, Oct. 6.

Skouras, Spyros P. (78), Greek-born U. S. motion-picture executive; president and operating head of 20th Century Fox (1942–62) and chairman of its board (1962–69); chairman of Prudential-Grace Shipping Lines (1969–71): d. Mamaroneck, N. Y., Aug. 16.

Smith, Carl H. (75), U. S. pediatrician; he directed the division of pediatric hematology at the New York University–Cornell Medical Center and in 1952 helped organize the Children's Blood Foundation; wrote *Blood Diseases in Infancy and Childhood*: d. New York, N. Y., April 23.

Soong, T. V. (77), Chinese financier and government official: b. Shanghai, China, 1894; d. San Francisco, Calif., April 25, 1971. The oldest son of a Shanghai banking family that includes Mme. Chiang Kai-shek and Mme. Sun Yat-sen, he served the Chinese Nationalist government during the 1930's and 1940's as finance minister, foreign minister, and premier. Educated at Harvard University, he came under the influence of Sun Yat-sen, the founder of the Chinese Republic, and supported Generalissimo Chiang Kai-shek in his struggles against Communist forces. As finance minister he introduced financial re-

William V. S. Tubman   David Sarnoff

KEYSTONE   UPI

forms, standardized the currency, and centralized the banking system. He founded the Bank of China in 1936. During World War II he was China's negotiator for support from the United States and other Western countries. In 1945 he served as chairman of the UN Conference at San Francisco. Appointed acting president of the legislative Yuan, the equivalent of premier, in 1945, he resigned in 1947, after attempts at coalition with the Communists failed.

Spingarn, Arthur B. (93), U. S. attorney and former president of the National Association for the Advancement of Colored People: b. New York, N. Y., March 28, 1878; d. New York, Dec. 1, 1971. As the NAACP's vice president (1911–40) and president (1940–66), Spingarn spanned the era of the organization's early growth and its greatest achievements. A white man, he joined the NAACP as a young lawyer at its formation in 1909 and replaced his brother, Joel E. Spingarn, as its president more than 30 years later. Under his stewardship after 1940, the NAACP's black legal team, led by Thurgood Marshall, won the 1954 U. S. Supreme Court decision outlawing segregation in public schools, and the organization's membership grew from 85,000 to more than 400,000 members.

Stangl, Franz Paul (63), German prison commandant; in 1942–43, he headed the Treblinka, Poland, concentration camp; in 1970 he was sentenced to life imprisonment for his part in the Nazi extermination of more than 400,000 Jews: d. Düsseldorf, West Germany, June 28.

Stanley, W(endell) M(eredith) (66), U. S. biochemist: b. Ridgeville, Ind., Aug. 16, 1904; d. Salamanca, Spain, June 15, 1971. For his pioneering work on the nature of viruses he shared the 1946 Nobel Prize in chemistry with two other scientists. Educated at Earlham College and the University of Illinois, he began his study of the nature of viruses in 1932. After successfully isolating the tobacco mosaic virus he concluded that viruses belong to the twilight zone between living organisms and lifeless chemicals. During World War II he developed a partly effective influenza vaccine. Appointed professor of molecular biology and biochemistry at the University of California in 1946, he founded the University of California Virus Laboratory in 1948 and served as its director until his retirement in 1969. He also devoted much of his effort to the promotion of cancer research.

Steiner, Max R. (83), U. S. film composer; wrote many prize-winning scores for motion pictures, including *Gone with the Wind, The Informer, Now, Voyager,* and *Since You Went Away*: d. Hollywood, Calif., Dec. 28.

Stern, Bill (64), U. S. sportscaster; began broadcasting for NBC radio in 1935 and became immensely popular for his breezy style and colorful anecdotes: d. Rye, N. Y., Nov. 19.

Stevens, James F. (79), U. S. author; wrote first of his popular versions of Paul Bunyan and Babe the Blue Ox in 1925 while working in an Oregon logging camp: d. Seattle, Wash., Dec. 30.

Storke, Thomas More (94), U. S. newspaperman; owned and published newspapers in Santa Barbara, Calif., almost uninterruptedly from 1900 to 1964; won a Pulitzer Prize in 1962 for his editorials against tactics used by the John Birch Society: d. Santa Barbara, Oct. 12.

*Stravinsky, Igor (88), Russian-American composer: d. New York, N. Y., April 6.

Strickland, Cowles (68), U. S. theater director; in 1928 he founded the Berkshire Playhouse at Stockbridge, Mass.; taught drama at American University (1962–71); wrote *The Technique of Acting* (1962): d. Washington, D. C., Oct. 20.

Svedberg, Theodor H. E. (86), Swedish nuclear chemist; received Nobel Prize (1926) for his work with colloids and for his development of the ultracentrifuge: d. Stockholm, Sweden, Feb. 26.

Switzer, Mary Elizabeth (71), U. S. civil servant; as commissioner of vocational rehabilitation in the U. S. Department of Health, Education and Welfare (1967–70), she was the highest ranking woman in the federal government: d. Washington, D. C., Oct. 16.

Symonds, Gardiner (67), U. S. industrialist; was president (1943–66) and chairman of the board (1966–71) of Tenneco, Inc., and was credited with building it from a natural gas company into a giant comglomerate: d. Houston, Texas, June 2.

Tal, Wasfi Mustafa (51), premier of Jordan: b. Irbid district, Jordan, 1920; d. Cairo, Egypt, Nov. 28, 1971. Jordanian Premier Wasfi Tal, known as King Hussein's "crisis man," was assassinated by gunmen of a Palestinian guerrilla organization while entering a Cairo hotel after a meeting of the Arab League's Joint Defense Council. A graduate of the American University in Beirut, Lebanon, he served in the British Army in World War II and was later with the Palestine Liberation Army in its operations against Zionist forces. Entering the Jordanian civil service in 1949, he served four times as premier (1961–67). His fifth appointment, in October 1970, followed the civil war between Hussein's army and the Palestine guerrilla groups. Tal vigorously suppressed the guerrillas during his final term in office.

Tamm, Igor (Evgenyevich) (75), Soviet physicist: b. Vladivostok, Russia, July 8, 1895; d. Moscow, USSR, April 12, 1971. One of the Soviet Union's leading scientists, he was noted for his work in combining quantum mechanics with Einstein's theory of relativity in the 1930's and 1940's, when both theories were condemned by Communist authorities. He shared the 1958 Nobel Prize in physics with two other scientists for his role in explaining the Cherenkov effect. His work, with Andrei D. Sakharov, in controlled thermonuclear fusion is credited with having contributed to the development of the Soviet hydrogen bomb in the early 1950's. He graduated in 1918 from Moscow University, where he later taught, and joined the Lebedev Physics Institute in 1934. Designated a Hero of Socialist Labor in 1950, he was awarded the Stalin Prize twice and the Order of Lenin three times. He was an outspoken champion of greater freedom for scientists in the USSR.

Teeters, Negley K. (74), U. S. criminologist; was an early advocate of humanizing prisons and attempting to rehabilitate inmates: d. Oneonta, N. Y., Oct. 30.

Terry, Paul H. (84), U. S. pioneer in animated cartoons; began creating animated cartoons in the 1920's and built up Terrytoons, Inc.; created many characters including Mighty Mouse and Gandy Goose: d. New York, N. Y., Oct. 25.

Thatcher, W. Ross (54), Canadian public official, who was premier of Saskatchewan for seven years (1964–71); as head of Saskatchewan's Liberal party, he advocated free enterprise and fought against socialism; he lost a bid for reelection in June 1971: d. Regina, Sask., July 23.

Tiger, Dick (42), Nigerian boxer: b. near Aba, Nigeria, Aug. 14, 1929; d. Aba, Dec. 13, 1971. Tiger was middleweight boxing champion of the world twice and light-heavyweight champion once. Born Richard Ihetu, he was the son of an Ibo farmer. He began his boxing career in 1952, having received his training from British army officers. His determined, aggressive style carried him to the middleweight title in 1962, when he defeated Gene Fullmer in San Francisco. He lost the crown in 1963 to Joey Giardello and regained it from him two years later, only to lose it to Emile Griffith in 1966. In that year he won the light-heavyweight title from José Torres, but in 1968 lost it to Bob Foster, suffering his first knockout in 81 professional fights. A contributor to the Biafran cause during the Nigerian civil war (1967–70), he died penniless.

Tiselius, Arne Wilhelm Kaurin (69), Swedish biochemist; won the 1948 Nobel Prize in chemistry for work including the development of a system for making large molecules move through a solution under the influence of electricity to facilitate study: d. Uppsala, Sweden, Oct. 29.

Tovey, Sir John (85), British naval commander; led the Home Fleet during World War II, and was responsible for the sinking of the German battleship *Bismarck* (1941): d. Madeira, Jan. 12.

Trittipo, James (43), U. S. television art director; won Emmy awards for *Hollywood Palace* (1965), *An Evening with Fred Astaire* (1968), and *Robert Young and the Family* (1970): d. Los Angeles, Calif., Sept. 15.

Tubman, William V. S. (75), president of Liberia: b. Harper, Liberia, Nov. 29, 1895; d. London, England, July 23, 1971. He was serving his sixth consecutive term as the 18th president of the oldest independent republic in Africa. A member of his country's ruling elite, made up of descendants of black immigrants from the United States, he was educated in Liberia and served in that nation's Senate before winning the presidency in 1943. His policies featured the extension of full rights to native tribesmen, whose rivalries he did much to suppress, and maximum economic development of Liberia through the encouragement of foreign capital investment.

Tukey, Harold (75), U. S. horticulturist; was concerned with plant growth regulators and the use of radioisotopes in plant research; headed Michigan State University's horticulture department (1945–63): d. Boca Raton, Fla., Nov. 9.

Turnage, Allen H. (80), Lt. Gen., U. S. Marines; was commanding general of the Third Marine Division during World War II: d. Bethesda, Md., Oct. 22.

Turner, Malcolm (82), Scottish journalist, radio sports commentator, and authority on the history of the prize ring; was sports editor of the *Scottish Daily Express* (1933–63): d. Glasgow, Scotland, Dec. 14.

Turnesa, Jim (57), U. S. golfer, who won the Professional

Golfers Association championship in 1950; one of seven brothers who were noted golfers: d. Elmsford, N. Y., Aug. 27.

Tvardovsky, Aleksandr T. (61), Soviet poet and editor; author of *Tyorkin in the Other World*, a poetical satire of the Stalinist era; as controversial editor of *Novy Mir*, a literary monthly, published Aleksandr Solzhenitsyn's *One Day in the Life of Ivan Denisovich*: d. Moscow, USSR, Dec. 17.

Ullman, James Ramsey (63), U. S. author and mountain climber; wrote several novels, notably *The White Tower* (1945) and *River of the Sun* (1951), and other books, including *Americans on Everest* (1964): d. Boston, Mass., June 20.

Uris, Percy (72), U. S. builder; was chairman of the board of Uris Buildings Corporation, which he built up with his brother, Harold D. Uris; donated large sums to Cornell and Columbia universities: d. Palm Beach, Fla., Nov. 20.

Val, Joseph P. (68), U. S. journalist; was sports editor of *The New York World-Telegram and The Sun* (1931–57): d. Queens, N. Y., Jan. 16.

Valachi, Joseph Michael (66), U. S. underworld figure: b. New York, N. Y., Sept. 22, 1903; d. La Tuna Federal Correctional Institution, Texas, April 3, 1971. A member of the Mafia, or Cosa Nostra, for 32 years, he gained national attention in 1963, when he revealed the inner workings of organized crime in the United States in televised hearings before the Senate Permanent Investigations Subcommittee. His criminal record included arrests for robbery, assault, gambling, and narcotics offenses. In 1962, while serving a sentence at Atlanta federal penitentiary, he was given the "kiss of death" by a Mafia leader who suspected him of being an informer. Later he killed a fellow inmate, whom he believed to be his intended executioner, and he was serving a life sentence for the murder at the time of his death. His memoirs, *The Valachi Papers*, were published in 1969.

Valencia, Guillermo (62), Colombian president (1962–66); initiated many social and economic reforms, greatly decreasing inflation in Colombia: d. New York, N. Y., Nov. 4.

Van Deventer, Fred (67), U. S. radio and television personality; originated the radio and TV quiz show *Twenty Questions;* served as newscaster for WOR Radio in 1940's: d. Colonial Heights, Va., Dec. 2.

Van Slyke, Donald D. (88), U. S. biochemist; his main contribution was bringing chemistry into medicine through his studies of proteins, fats, and blood; revolutionized the treatment of diabetes: d. Garden City, N. Y., May 4.

Vargas Badillo, Pablo (63), Puerto Rican newspaper editor; was city editor (1926–46) and editor (1946–68) of San Juan's *El Mundo;* in his editorials he favored statehood for Puerto Rico: d. San Juan, P. R., Sept. 2.

Vaux, O. P., The Rev. Rolando de (67), French archaeologist and Roman Catholic priest; headed the École Biblique, Jerusalem French biblical and archaeological school; helped edit the Dead Sea Scrolls: d. Jerusalem, Israel, Sept. 10.

Vickers, Martha (46), U. S. actress; starred in films in the 1940's, notably *The Big Sleep* (1944); was married to actor Mickey Rooney (1949–51): d. Hollywood, Calif., Nov. 4.

Viguers, Ruth Hill (67), U. S. author and editor; an international expert on children's books, she coauthored *A Critical History of Children's Literature*: d. Boston, Mass., Feb. 3.

Vilar, Jean (59), French actor and director; started the Théâtre National Populaire (1951–63), which brought low-price theater to people throughout France; founded the Avignon Festival (1947): d. Séte, France, May 28.

Villeda Morales, Ramón (62), president of Honduras (1957–63); he was overthrown by a military coup d'etat to prevent a feared Communist take-over; he was Honduras' chief UN delegate in 1971: d. New York, N. Y., Oct. 8.

Volkov, Vladislav Nikolayevich (35), Soviet cosmonaut; first went into space in 1969 aboard the *Soyuz 7* for a week-long mission; was flight engineer aboard the *Soyuz 11:* d. reentering earth's atmosphere, June 30.

Voloshen, Nathan M. (73), U. S. lawyer; he was found guilty in 1970 of using the office of Speaker of the U. S. House of Representatives John W. McCormack to defraud agencies of the federal government: d. New York, N. Y., Aug. 23.

Waniolka, Franciszek (58), Polish political figure; became deputy premier in 1962 and a member of the Communist party's Politburo in 1964: d. Warsaw, Poland, April 15.

Warnecke, Carl I. (80), Canadian-born U. S. architect; worked on many major projects, including Oakland (Calif.),

airport, buildings at the University of California, Berkeley, and the John F. Kennedy grave site at Arlington, Va.: d. San Francisco, Calif., March 27.

Washington, Kenny (52), U. S. athlete; star collegiate and professional football halfback at the University of California, Los Angeles (1937–39) and for the Los Angeles Rams (1946–49), where he was one of the first blacks in pro football: d. Los Angeles, Calif., June 24.

Webster, Sir David (67), British business executive; was general administrator of the Royal Opera House in Covent Garden and played a leading role in the creation of the Royal Opera Company and the Royal Ballet: d. London, England, May 11.

Weigel, Helene (70), Austrian actress and director; the wife of German playwright Bertolt Brecht, she starred in many of his works, including *Mother Courage;* after his death (1956), she took over direction of his repertory company, the Berliner Ensemble: d. East Berlin, Germany, May 6.

Weinstock, Herbert (65), U. S. music critic, author, translator, and editor; wrote many books and articles on music, especially opera, including the biographies *Tchaikovsky* (1943), *Handel* (1946), and *Vincenzo Bellini, His Life and His Operas* (1971): d. New York, N. Y., Oct. 21.

Whitehead, Sir Edgar (66), British politicial figure; was the last prime minister of Rhodesia before the colony attained independence in 1965; had favored accommodation between the races there, but used force against African Nationalists: d. Newbury, Berkshire, England, Sept. 22.

Widener, George D. (82), U. S. horse breeder; raised thoroughbred horses in Lexington, Ky. (1916–62); his horse Jaipur won Belmont and Travers stakes (1962): d. Philadelphia, Pa., Dec. 8.

Wilson, John C. (61), U. S. businessman and civic leader; became president of the Haloid Corporation in 1946, acquired rights to a xerography machine, and built his company into the Xerox Corporation; was chairman of the Presidential Committee on Health Education: d. New York, N. Y., Nov. 22.

Wilson, May (80), U. S. pediatrician; authority on rheumatic fever and heart diseases, she established a relation between genetic factors and susceptibility to rheumatic fever; was professor of clinical pediatrics at Cornell University (1959–64): d. Woods Hole, Mass., June 14.

Wind, Edgar (71), German-born British art historian; was professor of art history at Oxford (1955–67); his books include *Bellini's Feasts of the Gods* (1948) and *Giorgione's Tempesta* (1969): d. London, England, Sept. 12.

Wintersteiner, Oskar Paul (72), Austrian-born U. S. biochemist; he isolated penicillin-G and streptomycin in chrystalline form; he taught at Columbia University (1929–41) and was director of the division of organic chemistry at the Squibb Institute of Medical Research (1941–59): d. Graz, Austria, Aug. 15.

Wood, Garfield ("Gar") (90), U. S. businessman and boatsman; invented the hydraulic lift for motor trucks and helped develop many types of launches, including the naval PT boat (1930's); known as the "Gray Fox" for his motorboat racing triumphs (1930's): d. Miami, Fla., June 19.

Wylie, Philip (69), U. S. writer and social critic: b. Beverly, Mass., May 12, 1902; d. Miami, Fla., Oct. 25, 1971. Though the author of over 30 books and countless magazine articles, he was best known for his *Generation of Vipers* (1942), in which he castigated Americans for indulging in uncritical "mother worship" and coined the term "momism" to define the phenomenon. After some years as a magazine editor and Hollywood scriptwriter, he scored a success with the novel *Finnley Wren* (1934), which struck many of the iconoclastic themes that he was to develop in *Generation of Vipers, An Essay on Morals* (1947), *Opus 21* (1949), and other books. His targets included Hollywood, the clergy, sexual hyprocrisy, advertising, and American youth. He received the Freedom Foundation's gold medal in 1953.

Wynn, Nan (55), U. S. actress and singer; appeared in many Broadway and film musicals, notably *The Seven Lively Arts* (1944) on the stage and *Million Dollar Baby* (1941) on the screen: d. Santa Monica, Calif., March 21.

Yangel, Mikhail K. (60), Soviet rocket designer and space technician; believed to have been the chief designer of the USSR's space program (1966–71): d. Moscow, USSR, Oct. 25.

*Young, Whitney (49), U. S. civil rights leader: d. Lagos, Nigeria, March 11.

Zhdanov, Dmitri Arkadievich (63), Soviet anatomist; was president of the World Association of Anatomists; wrote more than 100 works, notably *Functional Anatomy of the Lymphatic System* (1942): d. Moscow, Sept. 26.

A

index

Main article headings appear in this Index as bold-faced capitals; subjects within articles appear as lower-case entries. Main article page numbers and general references are listed first under each entry; the sub-entries which follow them on separate lines direct the reader to related topics appearing elsewhere. Both the general references and the subentries should be consulted for maximum usefulness of this Index. Illustrations are indexed herein. Cross references are to the entries in this Index.

F